The Good Pub
Guide 2010

The Good Pub Guide 2010

Edited by
Alisdair Aird and Fiona Stapley

Managing Editor: Karen Fick
Associate Editors: Tim Locke, Patrick Stapley
Editorial Assistance: Fiona Wright

EBURY PRESS
LONDON

Please send reports on pubs to

The Good Pub Guide
FREEPOST TN1569
WADHURST
East Sussex
TN5 7BR

or feedback@goodguides.com

or visit our website:
www.thegoodpubguide.co.uk

Good Guide publications are available at special discounts for bulk purchases
or for sales promotions or premiums. Special editions, including personalised
covers, excerpts of existing Guides and corporate imprints, can be created in
large quantities for special needs. Enquiries should be sent to the Sales
Development Department, Random House, 20 Vauxhall Bridge Road, London
SW1V 2SA (020 7840 8400).

Published in 2009 by Ebury Press, an imprint of Ebury Publishing

A Random House Group Company

The Random House Group Limited Reg. No. 954009

Addresses for companies within the Random House Group can be found at
www.randomhouse.co.uk

A CIP catalogue record for this book is available from the British Library

Typeset from authors' files by Clive Dorman
Edited by Jacqueline Krendel and Nicky Thompson
Project managed by Nicky Thompson

Printed in the UK by CPI Cox & Wyman, Reading, RG1 8EX

ISBN 9780091928902

To buy books by your favourite authors and register for offers visit www.rbooks.co.uk

Contents

Introduction

Around 4% to 5% of pubs have closed in this last year. Though this is grim news, it isn't in fact far out of line with the 3% rate of job losses in the private sector as a whole – bearing in mind that a failing pub is likely to have had fewer staff than a thriving one. And the closure rate certainly doesn't compare badly with the 6% closure rate of urban shops, or the 5-6% contraction in the national economy. Indeed, faced with the recent smoking ban, with above-inflation increases in beer duty, with high fuel prices stopping people driving far for a pub meal, and with the credit crunch bringing heavily indebted pub companies to their knees, it's remarkable that so many pubs are thriving.

This edition of the *Guide* has 132 new Main Entries, and nearly 1,500 new small-print Lucky Dip entries, all showing that there's plenty of life yet in the British Pub. Particular highlights are the Queens Arms at East Garston (Berkshire), Victoria at Perranuthnoe (Cornwall), Yew Tree at Clifford's Mesne and Fossebridge Inn (Gloucestershire), Eagle at Barrow and Clog & Billycock at Pleasington (Lancashire), Crown at East Rudham and Dabbling Duck at Great Massingham (Norfolk), Plough at Kingham (Oxfordshire), Red Barn at Blindley Heath (Surrey), Holly Bush in Alcester (Warwickshire) and Potting Shed at Crudwell and Outside Chance at Manton (Wiltshire). Several of these are pubs which had previously closed and have now been reopened after careful transformation by new owners. Among them, the Potting Shed at Crudwell is **New Pub of the Year 2010.**

Three or four years ago a young couple took over a near-derelict pub, closed for some time, in a remote village on the Hampshire/Wiltshire border – the sort of place which is at the heart of these statistics. They have put in the single magic ingredient that makes the difference between a failing local and a thriving and profitable pub – the enthusiastic, energetic and imaginative commitment with which thousands of other landlords and landladies across the country are ensuring the survival of their pubs. George and Sonia Humphrey have made their pub a welcoming and relaxing proper country pub, with well liked unpretentious food, good drinks and a fine log fire. Their Cross Keys at Upper Chute (Wiltshire) is **Country Pub of the Year 2010.**

In Scotland, a higher proportion of pubs have been closing than in the South. Here again, good landlords and landladies make all the difference. As in the countryside, good publicans can transform many town and city pubs. However handsome the building, however ornate the décor, the pub will fail unless it's well run. It's the publican who makes the difference between a tired and doomed mausoleum and a bustling success. An extreme case in point is the Café Royal in Edinburgh, a splendid building owned by Punch, the UK's biggest pubco. Its welcoming manageress Valerie Graham ensures good food and drink, helpful staff and a thriving atmosphere. The Café Royal in Edinburgh (Scotland) is **Town Pub of the Year 2010.**

SURREY BREAKS THE £3 A PINT BARRIER

In the country as a whole, the average pub price of a pint of beer is £2.68. This marks a 10p increase since last year. The pub and beer industry blames tax increases (conveniently forgetting about the 2.5% VAT reduction – which should have allowed a 5p price *cut*). Many pubs hiked their prices by 5p or 10p this last April, blaming the Budget's 2% beer duty increase. But this duty is levied on the price at the brewery, making the increase equivalent to only around 1p a pint. At a time of very low retail price inflation, and given people's increasing tendency to drink much cheaper supermarket beer at home instead of paying high pub prices, the 10p increase in pub prices strikes us as foolhardy.

Surrey is now Britain's costliest area for pub-goers. The price of a pint there averages £3.01 – substantially more even than London's average of around £2.90 a pint. Bad news, too, for drinkers in Berkshire, Buckinghamshire and Sussex, who now have to pay around £2.85. Averaging around £2.80 a pint, Hertfordshire, the Isle of Wight, Kent, Scotland and Suffolk are little better.

The West Midlands, Nottinghamshire and Staffordshire are best value for beer, averaging around £2.40 a pint. Cheshire, Cumbria, Derbyshire, Lancashire, Shropshire and Worcestershire are also reasonable, at around £2.50 a pint.

Pubs brewing their own beer offer big savings – over 40 of the Main Entries do so, averaging 33p a pint cheaper than comparable pubs selling branded beers. Price champion among them is the Church Inn at Uppermill near Oldham in Lancashire, selling good pints for £1.50 – for that, you'd get only half a pint in Surrey. If the spring they use for brewing water is flowing well, you may find nearly a dozen of its own good beers to choose from at the Church House. You might not get so many in a dry summer, though, for instance at the lively August bank holiday Rush Cart Festival when they hold their annual face-pulling competition. For its fine range at such exemplary bargain prices, the Church Inn at Uppermill (Lancashire) is **Own-Brew Pub of the Year 2010.**

Some individual breweries actually beat the bargain prices of the own-brew pubs. Beers which we found at such low prices in several of our Main Entries are (starting with the cheapest) Sam Smiths, Hydes, Castle Rock, Lees and Donnington. Special praise to Donnington which operates in Gloucestershire, not a particularly cheap area, and which has some delightful pubs (no fewer than ten of them in this edition, including two splendid Main Entries). Donnington, based at a picturesque ancient watermill, is **Brewery of the Year 2010.**

In Norwich, Colin Keatley runs the Fat Cat with tremendous enthusiasm and energy, bringing happy streams of customers from far and wide to this town pub. For £2 a pint (the lowest price of any of the Norfolk Main Entries) he sells his own good beer brewed in a nearby sister pub, the Cidershed, stocks a remarkable range of quickly changing real ales from around the country, has a row of pumps dispensing exotic beers from the continent, and has dozens of interesting bottled beers on sale. The Fat Cat in Norwich (Norfolk) is **Beer Pub of the Year 2010.**

NEW TRENDS IN PUB WINE

After over 20 years of working towards higher standards in pub wine, we can now say that quality is at least reasonable in almost all good pubs, and that many now take a serious and rewarding interest in it. Some pub-owning firms such as Adnams, Wadworths and, on a much smaller scale, Brunning & Price can be relied on to supply all their pubs with enjoyable wines. Many individual pubs have a great range, by the glass and/or bottle – more than one third of our Main Entries now qualify for a Wine Award.

A small but increasing number of pubs now go beyond simply serving a good choice. Several such as the Red Lion at Sibbertoft (Northamptonshire) and Vine Tree at Norton (Wiltshire) run tutored tastings. Some like the Culm Valley at Culmstock (Devon) import wine direct from small vineyards; others such as the Rose at Peldon (Essex) and Inn at West End (Surrey) are run by wine merchants. The Harris Arms at Portgate (Devon) and Anchor at Nayland (Suffolk) are the first we know of to grow their own vines. Quite a few now have their own wine shop: good examples are the Old Bridge in Huntingdon (Cambridgeshire), Yew Tree at Clifford's Mesne and White Hart at Winchcombe (Gloucestershire), Inn at Whitewell (Lancashire) and Vine Tree at Norton (Wiltshire). The Yew Tree and White Hart both have an excellent scheme where you can have a bottle with your meal for just its shop price plus £5. This is much lower than the usual mark-up, and as mark-ups are normally a straight multiple (say, three times the cost price) the saving increases greatly as the price of the wine increases. The Yew Tree, with its charmingly informal 'shop', is **Wine Pub of the Year 2010.**

BURY IN LANCASHIRE – WHISKY CAPITAL OF THE WORLD?
We were surprised this year to find a pub selling over 500 whiskies – not some tavern in Scotland, but tucked away on the edge of Bury in Lancashire. The pub is the Fishermans Retreat in Ramsbottom, owned by Hervey Magnall. It was his father who started the collection, for fun, adding a new one each week. The Fishermans Retreat in Ramsbottom (Lancashire) is **Whisky Pub of the Year 2010.**

MANY PUBS NOW CUTTING FOOD PRICES
In this recession, we are all cutting down on eating out. The silver lining is that well run pubs are holding food prices steady, in spite of rising costs. In a detailed comparison of the prices that each of our Main Entries charges for snacks and starters, main corses and puddings, compared with what they were charging last year, we found that prices have on average stayed virtually unchanged. Even more encouragingly, we found that 30% of pubs now sell some food more cheaply than last year. Sometimes this is by adding more economical dishes to the menu. Sometimes this is simply by cutting costs – finding more economical suppliers or ingredients, often locally. And there are now significantly more special offers and bargains, with enterprising publicans coming up with appealing variations on two-course and three-course lunches, early-evening specials, theme nights, a meal with a free drink and two-for-one bargains.

All this has meant that more pubs now qualify for our Bargain Award than ever before – one in 11 Main Entries, up from one in 12 last year. What works brilliantly for both pub and customers is when a pub succeeds not only in keeping prices down, but also in offering good food that's interesting as well as good value. Using organic local produce, the Lewes Arms in Lewes might typically serve grilled goats cheese salad with beetroot, watercress and shallots, a good steak and kidney pie, fresh local-landed fish, a proper paella and aloo gobi curry with all the works, all around the £6 or £7 mark – that's to say, around £5 less than other good pubs in that part of the country typically charge for their most popular dishes. The Lewes Arms in Lewes (Sussex) is **Bargain Pub of the Year 2010.**

FADDY TRENDS OR HONEST CHARACTER?
In our nearly 30 years of producing this *Guide*, we have seen all sorts of passing fads in pub décor come and go, from the acres of red plush banquettes, leatherette stools and wall-to-wall turkey carpeting of the early 1980s to today's influx of high-backed dining chairs in brown or black leather on blond woodstrip flooring. What the pub designers can't buy in, though, is the deep-down appeal of genuine character, as in hundreds of our listed pubs. From three dozen or so favourite unspoilt pubs, our choice as **Unspoilt Pub of the Year 2010** is the White Lion in Barthomley (Cheshire). This ancient thatched tavern, delightfully unchanging, and with good value bar lunches, is run really well by its welcoming landlady Laura Condliffe.

PUB WEEKENDS AWAY – NOW BETTER VALUE THAN GOING ABROAD
Among the 214 Main Entries which have earned our Place to Stay Award, you can pay as little as £55 for bed and breakfast for two, or – in a couple of places – right up to £200 or more. By and large you get what you pay for – all the hi-tech mod cons at the top end, just simple comfort, decent food and a warm welcome at the cheapest. A typical price, in a comfortably smart inn, is around £90. Recent changes in the £/€ exchange rate make that compare more favourably than ever before with places to stay in continental Europe. It represents great value – especially if you are prepared to bargain and hold out for their best possible rate.

The very best inns give you the comfort of a decent hotel, but add the friendly informality of a thriving bar, and often a big dose of real character, making for a memorable stay. Currently top among them, backed by warm endorsements from many happy readers, the Bear in Crickhowell (Wales) is **Inn of the Year 2010.**

FIRST CATCH YOUR PIG...

The big recent move to using local produce in pub food has developed a very enterprising new twist. A small but significant and rapidly growing number of good pubs are now growing more than just small back-yard quantities of salads, vegetables and fruit for their own kitchens, and/or raising their own free-range chickens, ducks, pigs and even cattle and sheep. Prime examples are the George & Dragon at Clifton (Cumbria), on the Lowther Estate which owns and supplies it; Brown Horse, Winster (Cumbria), with meat, poultry and produce from their own estate; European at Piddletrenthide (Dorset), lamb from the family farm – and, like several other pubs, it swaps drinks or meals for customers' produce and catches; Wheatsheaf at Braishfield (Hampshire), their own rare-breed pigs, poultry, fruit and veg; Stagg at Titley (Herefordshire), their own pigs, chickens and vegetables; Mill Race at Walford (Herefordshire), produce from their own farm; Fishermans Retreat in Ramsbottom (Lancashire), their own beef, venison and trout; Cook & Barker Arms at Newton on the Moor (Northumbria), their own farm produce; Half Moon at Cuxham (Oxfordshire), their own pigs and chickens; White Hart, Fyfield (Oxfordshire), their own veg, fruit and herbs; Nut Tree, Murcott (Oxfordshire), their own pigs and veg; Lamb, Satwell (Oxfordshire), their own chickens; Anchor at Nayland (Suffolk), produce from their adjacent farm, traditionally worked by heavy horses; Golden Key at Snape (Suffolk), their own bees, chickens, pigs, sheep and beef; Jolly Farmers at Buckland (Surrey), their own farm shop and Saturday market; Parrot at Forest Green (Surrey), their own farm; Potting Shed at Crudwell (Wiltshire), their own fruit and veg plus more from allotments they loan to villagers; Butchers Arms at Eldersfield (Worcestershire), their own cattle; Star at Harome (Yorkshire), splendid kitchen garden.

These are all extreme examples of the great care which good pub chefs now put into getting superb ingredients for their cooking. Hundreds of pubs which don't have their own farms or kitchen gardens are now bringing the same sharp focus to bear on the quality of their ingredients. This often pays off in raising the standard of their food to a memorable level.

The pubs and inns which stand out nationally as favourites for a special meal out are the Hinds Head in Bray (Berkshire), Cock at Hemingford Grey (Cambridgeshire), Bell at Sapperton (Gloucestershire), Stagg at Titley (Herefordshire), Olive Branch at Clipsham (Leicestershire and Rutland), Woods in Dulverton (Somerset), Compasses at Chicksgrove (Wiltshire), Bell & Cross at Holy Cross (Worcestershire), Star at Harome (Yorkshire), Hardwick near Abergavenny (Wales) and – a newcomer to the *Guide* – Gun in East London. All these are civilised dining pubs specialising in imaginative meals, ideal for a memorable treat. But all except the Bell are also perfectly happy to do just a sandwich – and the Bell will do you a good ploughman's instead.

With the recession breathing down our necks, the appealing pricing of their imaginative set lunches makes the Cock at Hemingford Grey **Dining Pub of the Year 2010**.

THE TOP PUBS AND PUBLICANS

Hours: 15 daily, half an hour less on Sunday. *Duties* including but certainly not limited to: staff admin and training (must be able to deal with difficult and unreliable employees), catering and cellar management, supplies procurement, ad hoc emergency relief work (could be anything from broken lavatories to fist fights), customer relations (facing extremes of rude and unreasonable behaviour), endless paperwork and bureaucratic red tape. *Rewards:* usually under £15,000 a year. Tempted by that job description? It's a fair account of a publican's working life; and earlier this year a survey commissioned by the House of Commons Business and Enterprise Committee showed that 67% of pub lessees earn under £15,000 a year.

This makes clear what a very special breed good publicans are: they seem to thrive on all of that, with smiles on their faces, and with enough good spirits left over to make all their customers happy, too.

From among the thousands of good landlords and landladies who run pubs in this *Guide*, a handful stand out as exemplary. They are Suzy Turner of the Red Lion at Litton (Derbyshire), André and Adrian Large of the Cross House at Doynton and Jo and Jon Carrier of the Five Mile House at Duntisbourne Abbots (Gloucestershire), Tim Gray of the Yew Tree at Lower Wield and Hassan Matini of the Trooper near Petersfield (Hampshire), Peter and Assumpta Golding of the Chequers at Churchill (Oxfordshire), Simon and Catherine Davy of the Jackston Stops at Stretton (Leicestershire and Rutland), Maggie Chandler of the George in Kilsby (Northamptonshire) and Peter and Veryan Graham of the George at Croscombe (Somerset).

Tim Gray has made the Yew Tree a warm-hearted proper country pub. He has held down the price of his good local beer so that you save nearly 60p a pint compared with what the average pub in his county charges. His interesting wines are great value and his food is most enjoyable. Above all, he's the sort of landlord you remember as rather special. Tim Gray of the Yew Tree at Lower Wield is **Landlord of the Year 2010**.

Eight interesting and appealing pubs on top form this year are the Bell at Aldworth (Berkshire), Five Mile House at Duntisbourne Abbots (Gloucestershire), Highwayman at Nether Burrow (Lancashire), Woods in Dulverton (Somerset), Bell & Cross at Holy Cross and Nags Head in Malvern (Worcestershire), Blue Lion at East Witton and Crown at Roecliffe (Yorkshire). With its charming small rooms, helpful welcoming staff, good food and drinks, strong sense of individuality and must-come-again appeal, the Bell & Cross at Holy Cross is **Pub of the Year 2010**.

What is a Good Pub?

The Main Entries in this *Guide* have been through a two-stage sifting process. First of all, some 2,000 regular correspondents keep in touch with us about the pubs they visit, and double that number report occasionally. We also get a flow of reports sent to us at **feedback@goodguides.com**. This keeps us up to date about pubs included in previous editions – it's their alarm signals that warn us when a pub's standards have dropped (after a change of management, say), and it's their continuing approval that reassures us about keeping a pub as a Main Entry for another year. Very important, though, are the reports they send us on pubs we don't know at all. It's from these new discoveries that we make up a shortlist, to be considered for possible inclusion as new Main Entries. The more people who report favourably on a new pub, the more likely it is to win a place on this shortlist – especially if some of the reporters belong to our hard core of about 600 trusted correspondents whose judgement we have learned to rely on. These are people who have each given us detailed comments on dozens of pubs, and shown that (when we ourselves know some of those pubs, too) their judgement is closely in line with our own.

This brings us to the acid test. Each pub, before inclusion as a Main Entry, is inspected anonymously by one of the editorial team. They have to find some special quality that would make strangers enjoy visiting it. What often marks the pub out for special attention is good value food (and that might mean anything from a well made sandwich, with good fresh ingredients at a low price, to imaginative cooking outclassing most restaurants in the area). The drinks may be out of the ordinary – maybe several hundred whiskies, remarkable wine lists, interesting ciders or a wide range of well kept real ales possibly with some home-brewed or bottled beers from all over the world. Perhaps there's a special appeal about it as a place to stay, with good bedrooms and obliging service. Maybe it's the building itself (from centuries-old parts of monasteries to extravagant Victorian gin-palaces), or its surroundings (lovely countryside, attractive waterside, extensive well kept garden), or what's in it (charming furnishings, extraordinary collections of bric-a-brac).

Above all, though, what makes the good pub is its atmosphere – you should be able to feel at home there, and feel not just that *you're* glad you've come but that *they're* glad you've come. A good landlord or landlady makes a huge difference here – they can make or break a pub.

It follows from this that a great many ordinary locals, perfectly good in their own right, don't earn a place in the *Guide*. What makes them attractive to their regular customers (an almost clubby chumminess) may even make strangers feel rather out-of-place.

Another important point is that there's not necessarily any link between charm and luxury. A basic unspoilt village tavern, with hard seats and a flagstone floor, may be worth travelling miles to find, while a deluxe pub-restaurant may not be worth crossing the street for. Landlords can't buy the Good Pub accolade by spending thousands on refits, soft music and elaborate menus – they can only win it, by having a genuinely personal concern for both their customers and their pub.

Using the *Guide*

THE COUNTIES

England has been split alphabetically into counties. Each chapter starts by picking out the pubs that are currently doing best in the area, or are specially attractive for one reason or another.

The county boundaries we use are those for the administrative counties (not the old traditional counties, which were changed back in 1976). We have left the new unitary authorities within the counties that they formed part of until their creation in the most recent local government reorganisation. Metropolitan areas have been included in the counties around them – for example, Merseyside in Lancashire. And occasionally we have grouped counties together – for example, Rutland with Leicestershire, and Durham with Northumberland to make Northumbria. If in doubt, check the Contents.

Scotland, Wales and London have each been covered in single chapters. Pubs are listed alphabetically (except in London which is split into Central, East, North, South and West), under the name of the town or village where they are. If the village is so small that you probably wouldn't find it on a road map, we've listed it under the name of the nearest sizeable village or town. The maps use the same town and village names, and additionally include a few big cities that don't have any listed pubs – for orientation.

We list pubs in their true county, not their postal county. Just once or twice, when the village itself is in one county but the pub is just over the border in the next-door county, we have used the village county, not the pub one.

STARS ★

Really outstanding pubs are awarded a star, and in a few cases two: these are the aristocrats among pubs. The stars do NOT signify extra luxury or specially good food – in fact some of the pubs which appeal most distinctively and strongly of all are decidedly basic in terms of food and surroundings. The detailed description of each pub shows what its particular appeal is, and this is what the stars refer to.

FOOD AWARD 🍴

Pubs where food is quite outstanding.

STAY AWARD 🛏

Pubs that are good as places to stay at (obviously you can't expect the same level of luxury at £60 a head as you'd get for £100 a head). Pubs with bedrooms are marked on the maps as a dot within a square.

WINE AWARD ♀

Pubs with particularly enjoyable wines by the glass – often a good choice.

BEER AWARD 🍺

Pubs where the quality of the beer is quite exceptional, or pubs which keep a particularly interesting range of beers in good condition.

BARGAIN AWARD £

Pubs with decent snacks at £3.75 or less, or worthwhile main dishes at under £7.

RECOMMENDERS

At the end of each Main Entry we include the names of readers who have recently recommended that pub (unless they've asked us not to).

Important note: the description of the pub and the comments on it are our own and not the recommenders'; they are based on our own personal inspections and on later verification of facts with each pub. A good pub which has no reader recommenders, or one that we judge deserves to stay in the Main Entries despite a very recent management change includes the acronym BOB (buyer's own brand) as a recommender.

LUCKY DIPS

The Lucky Dip section at the end of each county chapter includes brief descriptions of pubs that have been recommended by readers in the year before the *Guide* goes to print and that we feel are worthy of inclusion. We do not include a pub unless readers' descriptions make the nature of the pub quite clear, and give us good grounds for trusting that other readers would be glad to know of the pub. A bare mention that food is served shouldn't be taken to imply a recommendation of the food. The same is true of accommodation and so forth. At the end of the entry we print the recommenders' names. BB means we have inspected a pub and found nothing against it and LYM means the pub was a Main Entry in a previous edition of the *Guide*. In both these cases, the description is our own; in others, it's based on the readers' reports. This year, we have deleted many previously highly rated pubs from the *Guide* simply because we have no very recent reports on them. This may well mean that we have left out some favourites – please tell us if we have!

LUCKY DIPS WITH ☆

Roughly speaking these pubs are as much worth considering as some of the Main Entries themselves.

The Lucky Dips, particularly the starred ones, are under consideration for inspection for a future edition so please let us have any comments you can make on them using the report forms in this *Guide*, by writing to us at The Good Pub Guide, FREEPOST TN1569, WADHURST, East Sussex TN5 7BR or by emailing us at **feedback@goodguides.com**.

LOCATING PUBS

To help readers who use digital mapping systems we include a **postcode** for every pub.

Pubs outside London are given a British Grid four-figure **map reference**. Where a pub is exceptionally difficult to find, we include a six-figure reference in the directions. The Map number (Main Entries only) refers to the map in our *Guide*.

MOTORWAY PUBS

If a pub is within four or five miles of a motorway junction, we give special directions for finding it from the motorway. The Special Interest Lists at the end of the book include a list of these pubs, motorway by motorway.

PRICES AND OTHER FACTUAL DETAILS

The *Guide* went to press during the summer of 2009, after each pub was sent a checking sheet to get up-to-date food, drink and bedroom prices and other factual information. By the summer of 2010 prices are bound to have increased, but if you find a significantly different price please let us know.

Breweries or independent chains to which pubs are 'tied' are named at the beginning of the italic-print rubric after each Main Entry. That generally means the pub has to get most if not all of its drinks from that brewery or chain. If the brewery is not an independent one but just part of a combine, we name the combine in brackets. When the pub is tied, we have spelled out whether the landlord is a tenant, has the pub on a lease or is a manager. Tenants and leaseholders of breweries generally have considerably greater freedom to do things their own way, and in particular are allowed to buy drinks including a beer from sources other than their tied brewery.

Free houses are pubs not tied to a brewery. In theory they can shop around but in practice many free houses have loans from the big brewers, on terms that bind them to sell those breweries' beers. So don't be too surprised to find that so-called free houses may be stocking a range of beers restricted to those from a single brewery.

Real ale is used by us to mean beer that has been maturing naturally in its cask. We do not count as real ale beer which has been pasteurised or filtered to remove its natural yeasts. If it is kept under a blanket of carbon dioxide to preserve it, we still generally mention it – as long as the pressure is too light for you to notice any extra fizz, it's hard to tell the difference. (For brevity, we use the expression 'under light blanket pressure' to cover such pubs; we do not include among them pubs where the blanket pressure is high enough to force the beer up from the cellar, as this does make it unnaturally fizzy.)

Other drinks: we've also looked out particularly for pubs doing enterprising non-alcoholic drinks (including good tea or coffee), interesting spirits (especially malt whiskies), country wines, freshly squeezed juices and good farm ciders.

Bar food usually refers to what is sold in the bar; we do not describe menus that are restricted to a separate restaurant. If we know that a pub serves sandwiches we say so – if you don't see them mentioned, assume you can't get them. Food listed is an example of the sort of thing you'd find served in the bar on a normal day and we try to indicate any difference we know of between lunchtime and evening.

Children If we don't mention children at all, assume that they are not welcome. All but one or two pubs allow children in their garden if they have one. 'Children welcome' means the pub has told us that it lets them in with no special restrictions. In other cases we report exactly what arrangements pubs say they make for children. However, we have to note that in readers' experience some pubs make restrictions that they haven't told us about (children only if eating, for example). If you come across this, please let us know, so that we can clarify with the pub concerned for the next edition. The absence of any reference to children in a Dip entry means we don't know either way. Children's Certificates exist, but in practice children are allowed into some part of most pubs in this *Guide* (there is no legal restriction on the movement of children over 14 in any pub). Children under 16 cannot have alcoholic drinks. Children aged 16 and 17 can drink beer, wine or cider with a meal if it is bought by an adult and they are accompanied by an adult.

Dogs If Main Entry licensees have told us they allow dogs in their pub or bedrooms we say so. Absence of reference to dogs means dogs are not welcome. If you take a dog into a pub you should have it on a lead. We also mention in the text any pub dogs or cats (or indeed other animals) that we've come across ourselves, or heard about from readers.

Parking If we know there is a problem with parking we say so, otherwise assume there is a car park.

Credit cards We say if a pub does **not** accept them; some which do may put a surcharge on credit card bills, to cover charges made by the card company. We also say if we know that a pub tries to retain customers' credit cards while they are eating. This is a reprehensible practice, and if a pub tries it on you, please tell them that all banks and card companies frown on it – and please let us know the pub's name, so that we can warn readers in future editions.

Telephone numbers are given for all Main Entries that are not ex-directory.

Opening hours are for summer; we say if we know of differences in winter, or on particular days of the week. In the country, many pubs may open rather later and close earlier than their details show (if you come across this, please let us know – with details). Pubs are allowed to stay open all day if licensed to do so. However, outside cities many english and welsh pubs close during the afternoon. We'd be grateful to hear of any differences from the hours we quote.

Bedroom prices normally include full english breakfasts (if available), VAT and any automatic service charge. If we give just one price, it is the total price for two people sharing a double or twin-bedded room for one night. Otherwise, prices before the / are for single occupancy, prices after it for double. A capital B against the price means that it includes a private bathroom, a capital S a private shower. As all this coding packs in quite a lot of information, some examples may help to explain it:

£60	on its own means that's the total bill for two people sharing a twin or double room without private bath; the pub has no rooms with private bath, and a single person might have to pay that full price.
£60B	means exactly the same – but all the rooms have private bath
£60(£90B)	means rooms with private baths cost £30 extra
£35/£60(£90B)	means the same as the last example, but also shows that there are single rooms for £35, none of which has a private bathroom

If there's a choice of rooms at different prices, we normally give the cheapest. If there are seasonal price variations, we give the summer price (the highest), but during the winter there may be all sorts of cheaper rates and bargain breaks.

Meal times Bar food is commonly served from 12-2 and 7-9, at least from Monday to Saturday. If we don't give a time against the *Bar food* note at the bottom of a Main Entry, you should be able to get bar food at those times. However, we do spell out the times if they are significantly different. To be sure of a table it's best to book before you go. Sunday hours vary considerably from pub to pub, so it's best to ring before you leave.

Disabled access Deliberately, we do not ask pubs about this, as their answers would not give a reliable picture of how easy access is. Instead, we depend on readers' direct experience. If you are able to give us help about this, we would be particularly grateful for your reports.

SAT NAV AND ELECTRONIC ROUTE PLANNING

In conjunction with Garmin, *The Good Pub Guide* is now available for your Sat Nav. Available as an SD card or download, it integrates quickly and easily into your Garmin Sat Nav and gives you access to all recommended pubs in the *Guide*. The Sat-Nav guide will tell you the nearest pubs to your current location, or you can get it to track down a particular pub. For more details on this, and how you can buy it, go to www.garmin.co.uk. Microsoft® AutoRoute™, a route-finding software package, shows the location of *Good Pub Guide* pubs on detailed maps and shows our text entries for those pubs on screen.

OUR WEBSITE (www.thegoodpubguide.co.uk)

Our website includes every pub in this *Guide* plus many more. It has sophisticated search tools and shows the location of every pub on detailed maps.

CHANGES DURING THE YEAR – PLEASE TELL US

Changes are inevitable during the course of the year. Landlords change, and so do their policies. We hope that you will find everything just as we say but if not please let us know, using the tear-out card in the middle of the book, the report forms at the back of the book, or just a letter. You don't need a stamp: the address is The Good Pub Guide, FREEPOST TN1569, WADHURST, East Sussex TN5 7BR. You can also send us reports at **feedback@goodguides.com**.

Authors' Acknowledgements

This *Guide* would be impossible to produce without the huge help we have from the many thousands of readers who report to us on the pubs they visit, often in great detail. Particular thanks to these indefatigable and greatly valued correspondents: LM, Chris and Angela Buckell, Tracey and Stephen Groves, the Didler, George Atkinson, Guy Vowles, Phil and Jane Hodson, Michael and Jenny Back, Jeremy King, Gerry and Rosemary Dobson, N R White, Michael Dandy, Phil Bryant, Martin and Karen Wake, Michael Doswell, Paul Humphreys, Alan Thwaite, Alan and Eve Harding, Tony and Wendy Hobden, Dr and Mrs M E Wilson, David and Sue Smith, Ian Phillips, Brian and Anna Marsden, Phyl and Jack Street, Susan and John Douglas, Gordon and Margaret Ormondroyd, Steve Whalley, Pete Baker, Peter Meister, Joan and Michel Hooper-Immins, Dennis Jenkin, JJW, CMW, Barry and Anne, Reg Fowle, Helen Rickwood, Dave Irving, Jenny Huggins, Ewan and Moira McCall, Tom McLean, Donna and Roger, Michael and Alison Sandy, Terry Buckland, Mike and Eleanor Anderson, Ann and Colin Hunt, Andy and Jill Kassube, Richard Fendick, Ross Balaam, R T and J C Moggridge, Edward Mirzoeff, Sara Fulton, Roger Baker, Keith and Chris O'Neill, Pat and Tony Martin, Martin and Pauline Jennings, Martin Grosberg, Chris Evans, Dr and Mrs J Temporal, Dennis Jones, Tina and David Woods-Taylor, Mr and Mrs W W Burke, John Wooll, Joe Green, John Saville, Bob and Margaret Holder, WW, Dave Braisted, Michael Butler, Phil and Sally Gorton, John Beeken, Rob and Catherine Dunster, MLR, Simon and Mandy King, Brian and Janet Ainscough, Margaret Dickinson, Dr Kevan Tucker, Dr and Mrs A K Clarke, Mike and Mary Carter, Chris Flynn, Wendy Jones, Louise English, Peter F Marshall, Tom and Jill Jones, Val and Alan Green, Derek and Sylvia Stephenson, D R England, Julian and Jill Tasker, Andy and Claire Barker, Neil and Anita Christopher, Terry and Nickie Williams, Bruce Bird, Gareth Lewis, Sheila Topham, Charles and Pauline Stride, Jamie May, Mike Gorton, Keith and Sue Ward, Comus and Sarah Elliott, Jörg Kasprowski, Mrs Margo Finlay, Jenny and Brian Seller, Colin Moore, Mark, Amanda, Luke and Jake Sheard, M G Hart, Roger and Lesley Everett, MP, R L Borthwick, Henry Pursehouse-Tranter, David Lamb, Giles and Annie Francis, Mark Flynn, GSB, Stephen Corfield, Ryta Lyndley, Bruce and Sharon Eden, KC, Denys Gueroult, B and M Kendall, Mike and Sue Loseby, Ian Malone, MDN, Jerry Brown, Eithne Dandy, C and R Bromage, Dr D J and Mrs S C Walker, John Branston, Tom Evans, Dr J Barrie Jones, Marlene and Jim Godfrey, Paul and Ursula Randall, Clive and Fran Dutson, Adrian and Dawn Collinge, Claire Archer, Simon and Sally Small, David Jackson, Jeff and Wendy Williams, Michael B Griffith, Susan and Nigel Brookes, John R Ringrose, Tim Maddison, Sue and Mike Todd, Roy Hoing, R C Vincent, Michael and Deborah Ethier, Mr and Mrs Maurice Thompson, Karen Eliot, Colin Gooch, Gwyn and Anne Wake, Sally and Tom Matson, Richard and Jean Green, Kevin Thorpe, Simon Collett-Jones and John and Joan Nash. We are also most grateful for the help and guidance we have had from the late Nick Holding.

Warm thanks, too, to John Holliday of Trade Wind Technology, who built and looks after our database.

Alisdair Aird and Fiona Stapley

England

Bedfordshire

Not long ago we were hard pushed to find decent pub food here, but we've seen great improvements recently. Of particular note are the Plough at Bolnhurst, Black Horse at Ireland, Red Lion at Milton Bryan, Horse & Jockey at Ravensden (an interesting new entry), and, best of all, the comfortably elegant Hare & Hounds in Old Warden – our Bedfordshire Dining Pub of the Year. For bargain food, head to the charmingly unchanging Cock at Broom, or Engineers Arms in Henlow, where you'll also find an impressive beer range, especially at their several annual beer festivals. Another appealing new entry is the pubbily traditional Bedford Arms in Souldrop, and in the Lucky Dips we'd pick out the Black Horse in Woburn. Wells & Youngs is the area's main brewery, and the much smaller Potton is well worth trying.

AMPTHILL
TL0338 MAP 5

Prince of Wales
Bedford Street (B540 N from central crossroads); MK45 2NB

Civilised lunch pub with contemporary décor and menu; bedrooms

The neatly modernised interior of this open-plan L-shaped bar-brasserie is on two levels, with big leather deco-style armchairs and sofas at low tables on wood strip flooring as you come in. It then angles around past a slightly sunken flagstoned bit, with an exposed brick fireplace, to a partly ply-panelled dining area with comfortable dark leather dining chairs set around a mixed set of sturdy tables. Modern prints decorate the mainly cream walls (dark green and maroon accents at either end), it's all nicely lit and the piped music is quite well reproduced. They have Wells & Youngs Bombardier and Eagle on handpump, good coffee, and service is brisk and helpful. There are picnic-sets out on a nicely planted two-level lawn, and a terrace by the car park. We have not yet had reports on the five newish bedrooms.

🍴 As well as lunchtime snacks such as tortilla wraps, baked potatoes and filled baguettes, bar food might include duck terrine, lamb samosa with crème fraîche, goats cheese rarebit, butternut squash and mushroom risotto, baked pollack filled with crab on wilted spinach and pork tenderloin medallions with sherry and mushroom cream sauce, and they've an english-style menu with dishes such as spam fritters with tomato chutney, battered cod and steak and ale pudding. Puddings include wild berry eton mess and apple crumble and custard. *Starters/Snacks: £5.50 to £6.50. Main Courses: £7.00 to £22.00. Puddings: £5.00*

Charles Wells ~ Lease Richard and Neia Heathorn ~ Real ale ~ Bar food (12-2.30, 7-9.30) ~ Restaurant ~ (01525) 840504 ~ Children welcome ~ Dogs allowed in bar ~ Open 12-3, 6-11; 12-midnight Sat; 12-4 Sun; closed Sun evening ~ Bedrooms: £55S/£70S

Recommended by Michael Butler, Michael Dandy, Ross Balaam

For those of you who use Sat-Nav devices, we include a postcode for every entry in the *Guide*.

BIDDENHAM   TL0249   MAP 5

Three Tuns

Village signposted from A428 just W of Bedford; MK40 4BD

Straightforward extended village pub with fairly priced food and good children's play area in big garden

New licensees have just settled in at this pleasant thatched pub. The traditional low-beamed lounge has wheelback chairs round dark wood tables, window seats and pews on a red turkey carpet, and country paintings. The green-carpeted oak-panelled public bar has photographs of the local football, rugby and cricket teams, a TV, skittles and darts; piped music. On handpump, Greene King Abbot is well kept alongside one or two guests such as Batemans XXXB. There are seats in the attractively sheltered spacious garden, lots of picnic-sets on a big decked terrace, and swings and a climbing frame; quiz night alternate Thursdays; more reports on the new regime please.

🍴 **Bar food now includes sandwiches, ploughman's, sausage and mash, steak, mushroom and Guinness pie, mushroom and red pepper stroganoff and scampi, with specials such as rabbit pie and fried plaice with white wine and mushroom sauce.** *Starters/Snacks: £4.00 to £5.50. Main Courses: £7.00 to £15.00. Puddings: £3.95*

Greene King ~ Lease Paul and Jan Clark ~ Real ale ~ Bar food (12-2, 6-9; not Sun evening) ~ Restaurant ~ (01234) 354847 ~ Children in dining area ~ Dogs welcome ~ Open 12-3, 6-11; 12-4, 7-10.30 Sun
Recommended by John Saville, Paul Dunne, Stuart Turner, Revd R P Tickle

BOLNHURST   TL0858   MAP 5

Plough 🍴 ♀

Kimbolton Road; MK44 2EX

Stylish conversion of ancient building with thriving atmosphere, charming staff, top-notch food and drinks, and lovely garden

This is a well run ship, with views into the busy kitchen, and helpful staff coping happily with the chatty crowd. It's a strikingly beautiful old building, with impressive timbers set off nicely by light and airy contemporary décor. Sourced with care, the range of drinks here includes local Potton Village Bike and a couple of guests such as Adnams and Buntingford on handpump, a very good carefully annotated wine list (inluding organic vintages), with well over a dozen by the glass, home-made lemonade (in summer) and tomato juice, and local apple juice; board games. The attractive tree-shaded garden overlooks a pond, where you can still see the remains of the moat that used to surround the pub.

🍴 **Beautifully presented food, from a well balanced changing menu, is prepared using carefully sourced ingredients, some from named producers. Served with complimentary home-made bread, dishes work their way up from a few simple dishes such as bangers and mash and steak sandwich to tasty canapés such as devils on horseback, starters such as seared scallops with roast fennel, chilli and green olive tapenade, carpaccio of local venison and home-made tagliatelle rabbit ragoût, with main courses such as baked salsify and morel mushrooms in pastry with creamed spinach, braised brill with tomato and coriander chowder and 28-day-hung aberdeenshire steaks. Puddings might be sticky toffee pudding and marinated pineapple with five spice ice-cream, and they've a very good cheese platter; reasonably priced set lunch menu.** *Starters/Snacks: £5.25 to £6.95. Main Courses: £11.50 to £24.95. Puddings: £5.95 to £6.50*

Free house ~ Licensees Martin and Jayne Lee and Michael Moscrop ~ Real ale ~ Bar food (12-2, 6.30-9.30) ~ (01234) 376274 ~ Children welcome ~ Dogs allowed in bar ~ Open 12-3, 6.30-11; closed Sun evening, Mon, first two weeks in Jan
Recommended by Ryta Lyndley, Michael Sargent, Carol Beeby, Susan and Jeremy Arthern, J Woodgate

BROOM   TL1743 MAP 5

Cock ★ £

High Street; from A1 opposite northernmost Biggleswade turn-off follow Old Warden 3,
Aerodrome 2 signpost, and take first left signposted Broom; SG18 9NA

**Friendly village green pub with straightforward tasty food, beers tapped from the cask and
caravanning and camping facilities**

Happily, little changes from year to year at this much-loved traditional little house.
There's no bar counter, so the Greene King IPA, Abbot and Ruddles County are tapped
straight from casks by the cellar steps off the central corridor. Original latch doors lead
from one quietly cosy little room to the next (four in all), with warming winter fires, low
ochre ceilings, stripped panelling, and farmhouse tables and chairs on antique tiles;
piped (perhaps classical) music, darts, bar billiards and board games. There are picnic-
sets and flower tubs on the terrace by the back lawn.

⊞ **Food is down-to-earth but reasonably priced and tasty; sandwiches, soup, ploughman's,
scampi, vegetarian curry and filled yorkshire puddings.** *Starters/Snacks: £3.85.*
Main Courses: £6.45 to £7.25. Puddings: £2.25 to £3.95

Greene King ~ Tenants Gerry and Jean Lant ~ Real ale ~ Bar food ~ Restaurant ~
(01767) 314411 ~ Children welcome ~ Dogs welcome ~ Open 12-3(4 Sat, Sun), 6-11;
closed Sun evening

Recommended by Andy Lickfold, Pete Baker, the Didler, Michael Dandy, Michael B Griffith, Laurence Milligan

HENLOW   TL1738 MAP 5

Engineers Arms 🍺 £

A6001 S of Biggleswade; High Street; SG16 6AA

**Fabulous range of beautifully kept beers and other drinks and snacks (all day) at
charmingly spick and span village pub; no smoking garden**

One reader describes this traditional local as a real beer lover's pub, and it's an apt
description, given the ten handpumps. Besides their house beers (Caledonian Deuchars
IPA, Everards Tiger and Fullers London Pride), guests come from a tremendous range of
smaller, often far-flung brewers such as Buntingford, Iceni, Northumberland, Tower and
Southport. They also stock four ciders, a perry, and many belgian bottled beers. Helpful
staff are very knowledgeable about the range, and the pub holds quarterly bank holiday
beer festivals, and a bigger one in mid-October. They also keep decent wines by the
glass, Tyrrells crisps and serve good coffee. The comfortable green-carpeted front room
has lots of old local photographs on its green fleur-de-lys wallpaper, tidily kept and
interesting bric-a-brac collections, traditional green-cushioned wall seats, settles and
other dark seats, armchair-style bar stools, daily papers and a good log fire. A small tiled
inner area has wide-screen TV, and beyond is a step up to another comfortable carpeted
area, with a second TV, juke box, silenced fruit machine and board games; the good-
natured spaniel is called Chico. The back terrace has picnic-sets and heaters and the
garden is no smoking; more reports please.

⊞ **A limited range of good value snacks, including sausage rolls, pies and pizzas, are
served most of the time they are open.** *Starters/Snacks: £1.10 to £6.00*

Free house ~ Licensees Kevin Machin and Claire Sturgeon ~ Real ale ~ Bar food (snacks when
open) ~ (01462) 812284 ~ Children welcome in back room ~ Dogs allowed in bar ~ Live blues
monthly Fri or Sat; 1970s disco last Fri of month ~ Open 12-midnight (1 Fri, Sat)

Recommended by Michael Dandy, Michael and Deborah Ethier, R T and J C Moggridge

IRELAND   TL1341   MAP 5

Black Horse

off A600 Shefford—Bedford; SG17 5QL

Contemporary décor, imaginative food, good wine list, and lovely garden with attractive terraces and play area; bedrooms

The airy interior of this picturesque dining pub (in a nice peaceful rural setting) has recently been stylishly refurbished. Though the interior is cottagey with low ceilings and little cottage windows, the new strip wood or stone flooring, ceiling spotlights, comfortable mix of modern banquettes, bucket chairs and low tables, simple ornaments and lamps give a pleasing feel of spreading spaciousness. Attentive staff serve Fullers London Pride, Greene King IPA and a local guest such as Allendale Golden Plover, over a dozen wines by the glass and good coffee from the long black bar counter. Outside, the various terraces give a clever sense of garden rooms, with their individual furnishings and mature topiary. One terrace is prettily surrounded by white wicket fencing and gives on to a neatly kept garden with a play area. We'd love to hear from readers about the bedrooms here.

🍴 **Food is very good and attractively presented. As well as filled ciabattas, the changing menu might include smoked ham and parsley terrine with home-made mustard chutney, fillet of smoked mackerel on toast with a poached egg and hollandaise sauce, burger, onion and brie filo tart, battered fish of the day, marinated shoulder of lamb with sweet pepper kebabs and 31-day-hung rib-eye steak.** *Starters/Snacks: £4.95 to £9.95. Main Courses: £8.95 to £10.95. Puddings: £5.95*

Free house ~ Licensee Jim Campbell ~ Real ale ~ Bar food (12-3(5 Sun), 6.15-10; not Sun evening) ~ Restaurant ~ (01462) 811398 ~ Children welcome ~ Open 11.30-3, 6-11; 12-5 Sun ~ Bedrooms: /£55S

Recommended by Michael Dandy, Eleanor Dandy, Giles Barr, Peter and Margaret Glenister, Geoff and Carol Thorp, Giles Barr, Eleanor Dandy, Michael Sargent, Eithne Dandy, Malcolm Clydesdale

MILTON BRYAN   SP9730   MAP 4

Red Lion ♀

Toddington Road, off B528 S of Woburn; MK17 9HS

Beamed pub quite near Woburn Abbey and Safari Park with good food, chatty obliging staff and pretty views from garden

The interior of this homely old pub has been kept fairly traditional. The immaculately kept beamed bar has dark pub furniture on polished wood, flagstones and red carpets, cream-coloured and exposed brick walls, and cheery fresh flowers. Greene King IPA, Abbot and Old Speckled Hen are kept under light blanket pressure, and ten wines and a local apple juice are sold by the glass. In summer, a plethora of carefully tended hanging baskets makes a spectacular show, and there are plenty of tables, chairs and picnic-sets out on the terrace and lawn, which look across to a delightful row of thatched black and white timbered cottages.

🍴 **Using some thoughtfully sourced ingredients, very enjoyable bar food includes sandwiches, changing dishes such as prawn cocktail, thai fishcakes, pork terrine with apple and date chutney, lasagne, sausage and mash, battered cod, roast salmon on warm asparagus and broad bean salad with tomato and saffron dressing, roast mediterranean vegetable tart and aberdeen angus steak, and very tasty puddings such as toffee peach meringue, lemon tart with raspberry coulis and sticky toffee pudding.** *Starters/Snacks: £3.95 to £7.95. Main Courses: £8.50 to £13.50. Puddings: £4.50 to £5.50*

Greene King ~ Lease Paul Ockleford ~ Real ale ~ Bar food (12-2.30(3 Sun), 7-9.30) ~ Restaurant ~ (01525) 210044 ~ Children welcome lunchtimes if eating ~ Open 11.30-3, 6-11; 12-4 Sun; closed Mon in winter, Sun evening

Recommended by Peter Serlin, John Saville, Mike and Jennifer Marsh, B R and M F Arnold, Gerry and Rosemary Dobson, Rob and Catherine Dunster, Malcolm and Sue Scott

NORTHILL   TL1446   MAP 5

Crown

Ickwell Road; village signposted from B658 W of Biggleswade; SG18 9AA

Prettily situated village pub with nice old interior, inviting atmosphere, enjoyable food and big child-friendly garden

This attractive old building is situated just across from the church, in a green and peaceful village. Big tables under cocktail parasols out in front look over the village pond. Inside, you can choose between the cosy bar (snugly traditional with a big open fire, flagstones, heavy low beams and comfortable bay window seats) and the more formal light walled main dining room with elegantly laid tables on bare boards. The atmosphere throughout is warm and relaxed with friendly service and fairly unobtrusive piped music. Greene King IPA and Abbot and a couple of guests from brewers such as Bath and Hydes on handpump, nine wines by the glass and over 30 malt whiskies are served from the copper-topped counter. A sheltered side terrace (with picnic-sets) opens up into a very large back garden with well spaced canopied tables, plenty of trees and shrubs, a good play area, and masses of room for children to run around.

🍽 **All home made, and where possible prepared with locally sourced ingredients such as free-range meat from a nearby farm, the nicely pubby bar menu includes a good range of lunchtime sandwiches, tortillas and ciabattas, as well as sausage and mash, chilli, burger, scampi, omelettes, and daily specials such as roast pork belly stuffed with orange and sausage-meat, rice and vegetable cake with tomato sauce and beef wellington. There's also a more elaborate restaurant menu.** *Starters/Snacks: £4.75 to £9.95. Main Courses: £8.95 to £10.95. Puddings: £4.50*

Greene King ~ Tenant Kevin Blois ~ Real ale ~ Bar food (12-2.30, 7-9; 12-8 Sun; 12-9 Sat in summer) ~ Restaurant ~ (01767) 627337 ~ Children welcome ~ Dogs allowed in bar ~ Open 11.30-3, 6-11; 11.30-11 Sat; 12-11 Sun; 11.30-3.30, 6-11 Sat in winter

Recommended by Malcolm and Sue Scott, Michael Dandy, D C Poulton, Pete Baker

OLD WARDEN   TL1343   MAP 5

Hare & Hounds 🍽 ♀

Village signposted off A600 S of Bedford and B658 W of Biggleswade; SG18 9HQ

BEDFORDSHIRE DINING PUB OF THE YEAR

Popular but comfortably elegant dining pub with emphasis on good food served by welcoming well turned out staff; lovely gardens

Thoughtful care and attention to detail go into the running of this jolly nice place. Four beautifully kept beamed rooms, with dark standing timbers, work their way around the central servery. Cleverly blending contemporary styling with the attractive old structure, décor is in cosy reds and creams, with upholstered armchairs and sofas on stripped flooring, light wood tables and coffee tables, a woodburning stove in an inglenook fireplace and fresh flowers on the bar. Prints and photographs depict historic aircraft in the famous Shuttleworth Collection just up the road. Wells & Youngs Eagle IPA and Youngs are on handpump, with eight or so wines by the glass including some from a local vineyard; piped music. The pub is part of the 200-year-old swiss-styled Shuttleworth Estate, and the glorious sloping garden (with tables on a terrace) which stretches up to pine woods behind the pub dates back to the same period, and was designed in the same style. Though there's an ample car park, you may need to use the village hall parking as an overflow. There are some substantial walks nearby.

🍽 **Food here is beautifully prepared and presented. They make an effort to use local and organic ingredients (such as pork from the Shuttleworth Estate), the breads and ice-cream are home made, and they sell a small range of home-made larder goods. The changing menus might include whitebait, ploughman's, battered haddock, pie of the day, mussels, prawns and scallops in thai sauce, 28-day-hung rump steak, and puddings such as warm strawberry bakewell tart or caramelised lemon tart, and british cheeses.** *Starters/Snacks: £4.95 to £10.95. Main Courses: £10.95 to £12.95. Puddings: £6.00*

Charles Wells ~ Lease Jane Hurt ~ Real ale ~ Bar food (till 2.30 Sun) ~ Restaurant ~
(01767) 627225 ~ Children welcome ~ Dogs allowed in bar ~ Open 11.30-3, 6-11;
12-10.30 Sun; closed Mon except bank hols

Recommended by Peter and Margaret Glenister, Michael Dandy, P Waterman, Nick Turner, Eithne Dandy, Roger and Lesley Everett, David and Ruth Shillitoe

RAVENSDEN   TL0754   MAP 5

Horse & Jockey ♀

Village signed off B660 N of Bedford; pub at Church End, off village road; MK44 2RR

Contemporary comfort, with old-fashioned virtues on the food and drinks side

Careful lighting, hardwood venetian blinds, modern leather easy chairs in the bar, the
quiet colour scheme of olive greys and dark red, the meticulous layout of one wall of old
local photographs, and the pleasing chunky tables and high-backed seats in the bright
dining room with its well lit prints and contemporary etched glass screen all tell you that
this is a place where trouble is taken to get things just so (the modern lavatories are
exemplary). Service is charming, they have a good choice of wines by the glass, guest
ales from brewers such as Adnams, Black Sheep and Cottage as well as Wells & Youngs on
handpump, nicely served coffee, and a rack of recent *Country Life* issues as well as daily
papers. The dining room overlooks a sheltered terrace with smart modern tables and
chairs under cocktail parasols, with a few picnic-sets on the grass beside, and the
handsome medieval church in its churchyard just beyond; there is a heated smokers'
shelter.

⑪ **Enjoyable food includes sensibly priced two- and three-course lunches, and (not
Sunday) evening takeaways, as well as starters such as devilled whitebait and crispy duck
salad with duck dumplings and chilli plum sauce, main courses such as salmon and cod
fishcakes with pea and parsley sauce, steak and kidney pudding, king prawn and seafood
linguine with cream and white wine sauce, chicken caesar salad and sirloin steak, with
puddings such as warm pear, fig and pecan frangipane tart and a traditional hot pudding.**
Starters/Snacks: £4.00 to £8.50. Main Courses: £8.95 to £18.50. Puddings: £4.95 to £6.95

Free house ~ Licensees Darron and Sarah Smith ~ Real ale ~ (01234) 772319 ~ Children
welcome ~ Dogs welcome ~ Open 12-3, 5-12; 12-midnight; 12-11 Sun

Recommended by Michael Sargent, Michael Dandy, Eithne Dandy, Sarah Flynn, D C Poulton

RISELEY   TL0462   MAP 5

Fox & Hounds

High Street; village signposted off A6 and B660 N of Bedford; MK44 1DT

Relaxing old pub with emphasis on good steaks; pleasant garden

This cheery establishment has been in the same welcoming hands for over 20 years now.
It's generally quite traditional with timber uprights under heavy low beams and
unobtrusive piped classical or big band music. A clubby lounge area has comfortable
leather chesterfields, low tables and wing chairs. A decent range of drinks takes in Wells
& Youngs Eagle and Bombardier with a guest such as Youngs on handpump, bin-end
wines and a range of malts and cognacs. They don't take bookings on Saturday night so
you may have to wait for a table. An attractively decked terrace with wooden tables and
chairs has outside heating, and the pleasant garden has shrubs and a pergola.

⑪ **The speciality here is steaks. You choose your piece, you pay by weight, and you can
watch it being cooked on an open grill. Other good food might include stilton and
broccoli soup, whitebait, ploughman's, mushroom and aubergine lasagne, grilled dover
sole, steak and mushroom pie and roast chump of lamb with rosemary sauce, and
puddings such as spotted dick and jam roly-poly. Even if you don't see anything you
fancy, it's worth asking as they're very obliging and will try to cope with particular food
requests.** *Starters/Snacks: £2.95 to £6.75. Main Courses: £7.95 to £14.25. Puddings: £3.95*

Charles Wells ~ Lease Jan and Lynne Zielinski ~ Real ale ~ Bar food (11.30-1.45, 6.30-9.30(10 Sat); 12-2, 7-9 Sun) ~ Restaurant ~ (01234) 708240 ~ Children welcome ~ Dogs allowed in bar ~ Open 11.30-2.30, 6.30-11; 12-3, 7-10.30 Sun

Recommended by John Cook, Michael Dandy, Michael Sargent, Tim and Mark Allen

SOULDROP   SP9861   MAP 4

Bedford Arms ◧

Village signposted off A6 Rushden—Bedford; High Street; MK44 1EY

Cosy and friendly proper country tavern with good value food in cottagey dining area

There's no doubting that this is a true pub (the games room was even a brew house once), and not some eatery masquerading as one. It's given real heart by its lively welcoming licensees, and is relaxed and chatty at lunchtime, with a few regulars settled into the bar chairs by the counter, which has Adnams, Black Sheep, Greene King IPA, a guest such as Potbelly Ambrosia on handpump and several wines by the glass. There are just a few more seats in this small low-beamed area, including a couple of tables in one very low-ceilinged snug hutch of an alcove. The cottagey dining area has more low beams (one way through is a real head-cracker if you're careless), and a central fireplace – and, like the rest of the pub, broad floorboards, shelves of china, and country prints. In the evenings and at weekends the roomy mansard-ceilinged public area perks into life, with well placed hood skittles as well as darts and board games; it has a big inglenook fireplace, and opens on to a neat garden with pretty flower borders. The landlady is fond of her pets – look out for Gin and Tonic, the rabbits in the garden and if you're sitting in the dining room you will probably hear the cats, Crackers, Hobnob and Rum, thundering about upstairs.

🍴 **Bar food includes sandwiches, baguettes and ciabattas, prawn cocktail, garlic mushrooms, battered cod, cottage pie, chilli, leek and stilton bread and butter pudding, curries, mixed grill and steaks; Sunday roasts.** *Starters/Snacks: £3.00 to £6.00. Main Courses: £7.25 to £15.50. Puddings: £3.95*

Free house ~ Licensees Sally and Don Rushworth ~ Real ale ~ Bar food (12-2, 6.30-9; 12-4 Sun) ~ (01234) 781384 ~ Children welcome ~ Dogs welcome ~ Open 12-3, 6-11; 12-midnight(12.30 Sun) Fri, Sat; closed Mon except bank hols when open all day

Recommended by D C Poulton, Richard Tingle

WOBURN   SP9433   MAP 4

Birch ♀

3.5 miles from M1 junction 13; follow Woburn signs via A507 and A4012, then in village turn right and head out on A5130 (Newport Road); MK17 9HX

Well run dining establishment with focus on good imaginative food, good wines and attentive service

Busy eclectic décor, a little old here and a little new, and friendly service all make for a nice relaxing atmosphere. White liming on the servery, rough wall planking and some white-painted chairs contrast effectively with good dark hardwood flooring, soft brown leather sofas, bar stools and deep armchairs with white cushions, and there are splashes of bright blue dotted around. Modern prints on cream walls, deeply coloured ceilings and handsome flower arrangements add to the feel of the place. The carefully lit back part consists of an extensive but well divided and comfortable dining area, the central part of which is given an airy conservatory feel by its ceramic tile floor, light panelling and glazed pitched roof, with a step up either side to carpeted or bare-boards sections with attractive artwork on their soft canary walls; unobtrusive piped music and daily papers. They keep a good range of interesting wines by the glass, and the Adnams and Fullers London Pride on handpump are particularly enjoyed by readers. There are tables out on a sheltered deck.

⑪ Food is well prepared and nicely presented. The changing menu might include lunchtime dishes such as ciabattas, battered fish, caesar salad and steaks, with evening dishes such as potted crab and prawns, pork belly, fried salmon wrapped in parma ham and sage, and puddings such as berry meringue soufflé and raspberry and pine nut tart. *Starters/Snacks: £4.95 to £7.95. Main Courses: £8.95 to £16.95. Puddings: £5.95*

Free house ~ Licensee Mark Campbell ~ Real ale ~ Bar food (12-2.30, 6-10; 12-5 Sun) ~ Restaurant ~ (01525) 290295 ~ Children welcome ~ Open 11.30-3, 6-12; 12-6 Sun; closed Sun evening

Recommended by John Saville, Mrs Jane Kingsbury, Michael Sargent, Geoff and Carol Thorp, Howard Dell, Gerry and Rosemary Dobson, Michael Dandy, Ross Balaam

LUCKY DIP

Besides the fully inspected pubs, you might like to try these Lucky Dips recommended to us and described by readers (if you do, please send us reports: feedback@goodguides.com).

ARLESEY [TL1937]
Vicar's Inn SG15 6UX [Church Lane]: Small cosy two-bar local with two real ales, often unusual; garden with Easter Island theme *(Michael and Deborah Ethier)*
BEDFORD [TL0550]
Park MK40 2PF [Park Ave/Kimbolton Rd]: Large modernised pub with mix of furnishings inc leather sofas in partly flagstoned linked areas, enjoyable food from pubby favourites and pizzas up, well kept Wells & Youngs Bombardier and Eagle, decent wines by the glass, good coffee, daily papers, conservatory eating area (best to book Sun lunch); piped music; garden with tables on decking, open all day *(Bruce and Sharon Eden, Eithne Dandy)*
BLETSOE [TL0157]
☆ *Falcon* MK44 1QN [Rushden Rd (A6 N of Bedford)]: Good value food (all day Sun) with imaginative touches, cheerful attentive staff, Wells & Youngs and a guest ale, good choice of wines by the glass, good coffees, open fires each end of comfortably traditional low-beamed bar, side snug, dining room, daily papers; unobtrusive piped music; children welcome, big riverside garden with sheltered terrace, open all day wknds *(Meg and Colin Hamilton, Peter Martin, David Handforth, D C Poulton, Ryta Lyndley, LYM, Lucy Rhodes, G Jennings, Michael Dandy)*
CARDINGTON [TL0847]
Kings Arms MK44 3SP [The Green; off A603 E of Bedford]: Comfortably refurbished village dining pub with contemporary rustic feel, well cooked reasonably priced food inc standard and more enterprising dishes, Sun roasts, good choice of wines by the glass, well kept Greene King IPA, Timothy Taylors Landlord and Wells & Youngs Bombardier; helpful friendly staff, attractive linked areas with nice mix of varying-sized tables on bare boards and coir matting, log fire, interesting local airship photographs; well behaved children and dogs welcome, disabled facilities, good tables and chairs out on peaceful front terrace, open all day *(Michael Dandy, Eithne Dandy, D C Poulton, Peter Martin)*

CLOPHILL [TL0838]
Stone Jug MK45 4BY [N on A6 from A507 roundabout, after 200 yds 2nd turn on right into Back St]: Secluded stone-built local, cosy and welcoming, with enjoyable bargain pubby lunchtime food from sandwiches up, well kept ales such as Everards Beacon, Fullers London Pride, Oldershaws Ahtanum Gold and Shepherd Neame Spitfire, pleasantly unpretentious comfortable bar with family area and darts in small games extension; piped music; small pretty back terrace, roadside picnic-sets *(Michael Dandy, Ross Balaam)*
FLITTON [TL0535]
White Hart MK45 5EJ [Brook Lane]: Two-roomed village pub with newish young chef/landlord doing interesting changing local food, well kept beers, decent wines, friendly staff and atmosphere; nice views of nearby church from garden *(Peter Martin)*
GREAT BARFORD [TL1351]
Anchor MK44 3LF [High St; off A421]: Open-plan bar with ales such as Adnams, St Austell, Theakstons and Wells & Youngs, friendly staff, usual food from sandwiches up, back restaurant; piped music; picnic-sets overlooking River Ouse by medieval bridge and church, bedrooms *(Michael Dandy, Mrs Hazel Rainer)*
HARROLD [SP9456]
Oakley Arms MK43 7BH [between A6 and A428, E of Northampton; High St]: Cosy and comfortable refurbished beamed pub with several linked areas around central bar, good value locally sourced interesting food from monthly changing menu, well kept Wells & Youngs Eagle and guests; quiet garden tables, bedrooms *(Revd R P Tickle, D C Poulton, Michael Dandy)*
HENLOW [TL1738]
Crown SG16 6BS [High St]: Small inviting pub with good choice of all-day food and of wines by the glass, well kept Adnams Broadside and Greene King IPA, good coffee, nice log fire, daily papers; piped music, games machine; terrace and small garden, open all day *(Michael and Deborah Ethier, Michael Dandy)*

HOUGHTON CONQUEST [TL0441]
☆ *Knife & Cleaver* MK45 3LA [Between B530 (old A418) and A6, S of Bedford]: 17th-c dining pub under newish management; cosy dark-panelled bar with maps, drawings and old documents, comfortable seating and a blazing fire, airy conservatory restaurant with hanging plants, family room, carefully sourced seasonal food inc separate seafood menu, Potton Village Bike and a guest ale, Stowford Press cider, good choice of wines by the glass and of well aged malt whiskies; unobtrusive piped music; neatly kept garden with terrace, nine bedrooms *(LYM, Robert Turnham, R T and J C Moggridge)*

KEYSOE [TL0763]
☆ *Chequers* MK44 2HR [Pertenhall Rd, Brook End (B660)]: Good value tasty home-made food in down-to-earth village local with long-serving licensees, two homely comfortably worn-in beamed rooms divided by stone-pillared fireplace, real ales such as Boddingtons and Thwaites, reasonably priced wines; piped music, no credit cards; garden with play area, cl Mon evening, Tues *(Michael and Jenny Back, D C Poulton, LYM)*

LANGFORD [TL1840]
Plough SG18 9QA [Church St]: Changed hands in July 2008 and again in Nov 2008: Simple comfortable two-bar pub, Greene King IPA and good choice of wines by the glass from central servery, pubby food; piped music, TV; children and dogs welcome, good-sized garden with play area, open all day *(Michael Dandy, Nic Sharp)*

LINSLADE [SP9126]
Globe LU7 2TA [off A4146 nr bridge on outskirts]: Newly refurbished 19th-c pub very popular for nice setting below Grand Union Canal, lots of rooms, beams and flagstones, log and coal fires, several well kept Greene King ales and a guest, good winter hot drinks, enjoyable usual food (all day wknds), friendly efficient service; piped music; children welcome in eating areas, disabled facilities, tables up on embankment and in garden, open all day *(Ross Balaam, Charles and Pauline Stride, Mike and Jennifer Marsh, LYM)*

MAULDEN [TL0538]
☆ *Dog & Badger* MK45 2AD [Clophill Rd]: Attractive family pub smartly redecorated by welcoming new licensees, good home-made pubby food from snacks up inc good value set menu, Wells & Youngs ales, friendly staff, bare-boards bar with log fire, beams and exposed brickwork, steps down to two carpeted areas and restaurant; piped music; tables out at front (nice open country views) and in back garden, play area, open all day Fri-Sun *(D C Poulton, B R and M F Arnold, Michael Dandy, Dudley and Moira Cockroft, Paul Goldman)*

POTTON [TL2249]
Royal Oak SG19 2LU [Biggleswade Rd]: Neatly kept part-thatched traditional pub with large bar and spacious dining areas, oak beams and log fire, food from

sandwiches and pubby favourites to restaurant dishes, interesting british cheese selection, Greene King and a guest ale, decent wines by the glass; tables in small garden, boules, open all day (from 3 Mon) *(Jay Nicholl)*

SLIP END [TL0818]
Frog & Rhubarb LU1 4BJ [Church Rd (B4540), not far from M1 junction 10]: Smart and cosy locals' bar with some leather sofas, steps down to roomy contemporary dining area with conservatory-style windows overlooking terrace, wide choice of reasonably priced interesting food, friendly helpful young staff, Greene King ales *(Michael and Alison Sandy)*

SOUTHILL [TL1441]
White Horse SG18 9LD [off B658 SW of Biggleswade]: Well run and comfortable country pub with extensive eating area, wide range of good value generous pubby food from baguettes up, welcoming staff, changing well kept ales such as Adnams and Potton, good wine choice; piped music; lots of tables in large pleasant neatly kept garden with play area *(LYM, Michael Dandy, D C Poulton)*

STEPPINGLEY [TL0135]
French Horn MK45 5AU [off A507 just N of Flitwick; Church End]: This dining pub, a previous Main Entry, closed Jan 2009; there was no news of its future as we went to press *(LYM)*

SUTTON [TL2247]
☆ *John o' Gaunt* SG19 2NE [off B1040 Biggleswade—Potton]: Traditional country local in pretty village with 14th-c packhorse bridge, easy chairs in cosy low-beamed lounge bar with bird of prey pictures, public bar with traditional games inc hood skittles (dogs welcome here), warmly welcoming long-serving licensees, well kept changing ales, good value food using local ingredients (perhaps inc the finnish landlady's meat and fish buffet), log fires; picnic-sets in well sheltered garden with play area, open all day Sun *(LYM, Julia Mackay)*

TEMPSFORD [TL1652]
Wheatsheaf SG19 2AN [Church St]: 18th-c village pub with open fire in cosy lounge, Special Operations Executive memorabilia (nearby World War II base), friendly service, wide choice of generous bargain pub food from sandwiches up, small helpings available, well kept Adnams Broadside and Theakstons, pleasant restaurant; may be piped music; tables on decking and in big garden (some traffic noise) *(Jerry Brown, Michael Dandy)*

THURLEIGH [TL0558]
Jackal MK44 2DB [High St]: Friendly quiet village pub with easy chairs and good fire in tiled-floor bar (where dogs allowed), another in comfortable carpeted dining lounge, good home-made food and service, well kept Wells & Youngs ales; piped music; roadside seats out in front, more in nice rambling back garden *(D C Poulton)*

TODDINGTON [TL0028]

☆ **Sow & Pigs** LU5 6AA [Church Sq]: Quaint 19th-c pub named after carving on church opposite, lots of pig decorations, also old books and knick-knacks, mixed bag of furnishings inc pews, two armchairs and a retired chesterfield, friendly chatty landlady, well kept Greene King and guest ales, good coffee, home-made lunchtime food (not Sun) from good cheap rolls to local rare-breed meats inc good pork chops, restaurant, two log fires, games; children allowed, picnic-sets in small garden, bedrooms, open all day (Andy and Jill Kassube, Mel Smith, Conor McGaughey)

WOBURN [SP9433]

Bell MK17 9QJ [Bedford St]: Small beamed bar area, longer bare-boards dining lounge up steps, pleasant décor and furnishings, decent all-day good value food from sandwiches to some interesting dishes, friendly helpful service, Greene King ales, good choice of wines by the glass, good coffee; piped music, games; children welcome at lunchtime, back terrace, hotel part across busy road, handy for Woburn Park (Michael Dandy)

☆ **Black Horse** MK17 9QB [Bedford St]: Long and narrow stylishly updated 18th-c dining pub with warm friendly atmosphere, all-day food inc deli board and wide choice of other dishes, Greene King ales, good choice of wines by the glass, several bare-boards areas ranging from bar with old leather settles and coal fire through more contemporary furnishings, steps down to pleasant back restaurant; piped music; children in eating areas, summer barbecues in attractive sheltered back courtyard, open all day (LYM, John and Joyce Snell, Michael Dandy, Eleanor Dandy, Giles Barr, Martyn and Sue Smith, Mr and Mrs John Taylor)

Inn at Woburn MK17 9PX [George St]: Attractive Georgian hotel with sofas and high-backed leather seats in beamed bar, Wells & Youngs Bombardier and Eagle, good service, up-to-date all-day bar food and good reasonably priced set lunches, good choice of wines by the glass; 50 bedrooms, open all day (Michael Dandy, Mike and Jennifer Marsh)

Post Office address codings confusingly give the impression that some pubs are in Bedfordshire, when they're really in Buckinghamshire or Cambridgeshire (which is where we list them).

Berkshire

A smashing choice of pubs here, from quite unspoilt to very food-minded – something for everyone and every mood. On top form this year are the unspoilt Bell at Aldworth, the Sun in the Wood at Ashmore Green, the Hinds Head in Bray (owned by Heston Blumenthal of the nearby Fat Duck restaurant and our choice as Berkshire Dining Pub of the Year), the Chequers in Cookham Dean (a smashing choice of drinks), the Queens Arms at East Garston (new to the *Guide* this year, a charming find), the Plume of Feathers in Hungerford (another new entry, with carefully cooked pubby food), the Crown & Garter at Inkpen (a proper particularly welcoming little local), the Royal Oak at Paley Street (also a new entry, run by Sir Michael Parkinson's son, with a growing reputation for good british food), and the Winterbourne Arms at Winterbourne (a popular stop from the busy nearby M4). And check out these top Lucky Dips inspected and approved by us: Olde Red Lion in Chieveley, Jolly Farmer in Cookham Dean, Bunk at Curridge, Swan at Inkpen and Bird in Hand at Knowl Hill. The favourite local beer is West Berkshire, with Butts much enjoyed too.

ALDWORTH   SU5579   MAP 2

Bell ★ ♀ 🍺 £

A329 Reading—Wallingford; left on to B4009 at Streatley; RG8 9SE

Exceptional unspoilt pub, super value snacks, very well kept beers, good quality house wines, lovely friendly atmosphere and nice garden; can be busy

---

Quite unspoilt and unchanging, this 14th-c country pub is held dear in the hearts of its many loyal customers. It's a special place and has been run by the same family for over 250 years – they continue to ban mobile phones, piped music and games machines. The rooms have benches around the panelled walls, an ancient one-handed clock, beams in the shiny ochre ceiling, and a woodburning stove. Rather than a bar counter for service, there's a glass-panelled hatch from which they serve the very well kept Arkells BBB and Kingsdown, local West Berkshire Old Tyler and Mild and a monthly guest from West Berkshire; also Upton farm cider, good house wines and mulled wine at Christmas; no draught lager. As you might expect, the pub games here are traditional: darts, shove-ha'penny and dominoes. The quiet, old-fashioned cottagey garden is by the village cricket ground, and behind the pub there's a paddock with farm animals. In summer there may be occasional morris dancers, while at Christmas local mummers perform in the road by the ancient well-head (the shaft is sunk 365 feet through the chalk). It tends to get very busy at weekends; dogs must be kept on leads.

🍴 **Excellent value bar food is limited to filled hot crusty rolls and a variety of ploughman's; in winter they also do home-made soup.** *Main Courses: £2.60. Puddings: £3.00*

Free house ~ Licensee H E Macaulay ~ Real ale ~ Bar food (11-2.45, 6-9; 12-2.45, 7-9 Sun) ~ No credit cards ~ (01635) 578272 ~ Children welcome if well behaved ~ Dogs welcome ~ Open 11-3, 6-11; 12-3, 7-10.30 Sun; closed Mon and Mon bank hol evenings

---

We say if we know a pub allows dogs.

Recommended by Pam and John Smith, Mr Ray J Carter, Phil and Sally Gorton, Michael B Griffith, Samantha McGahan, Michael and Deborah Ethier, the Didler, Rob Winstanley, Mr and Mrs H J Langley, Dick and Madeleine Brown, Edward Bainton, Fred and Kate Portnell, Catherine Pitt, Pete Baker, Martin and Marion Vincent, Roger Wain-Heapy

ASHMORE GREEN   SU4969 MAP 2

Sun in the Wood ♀

B4009 (Shaw Road) off A339, then right on to Kiln Road, then left on to Stoney Lane. Pub 1 mile on left; RG18 9HF

Cheery family pub with a genuine mix of customers, plenty of room, tasty food, beer and wine, and friendly licensees

Now into their 13th year, the hard-working licensees at this well run country pub – along with their attentive staff – are as enthusiastic as ever. There's a loyal following from regular customers, and plenty of visitors, too, of all ages. The high-beamed front bar is comfortable and unimposing and has bare boards on the left, carpet on the right, and a mix of nice old chairs, padded dining chairs and stripped pews around sturdy tables. It opens into a big back dining area which has the same informal feel, candles on tables, and some interesting touches like the big stripped bank of apothecary's drawers. There's a small conservatory sitting area by the side entrance. Wadworths IPA, 6X and Bishops Tipple are well kept on handpump, and they offer a fine choice of wines by the glass. Outside, the attractive decked terrace has seats under green parasols, heaters, plenty of flowering tubs, and old-fashioned street lights, and there's a big woodside garden with lots of picnic-sets, a small child-free area, and a popular nine-hole woodland crazy golf pitch. It's hard to believe the pub is only a few minutes away from the centre of Newbury. More reports please.

🍴 **As well as freshly baked baguettes, the enjoyable food includes soup, ploughman's, chicken liver pâté with caramelised onion chutney, seafood bake topped with fresh herb and cheese crust, ratatouille and goats cheese tart on bean cassoulet, steak and kidney pie, beer-battered haddock, gammon and egg, chicken, root vegetable and potato casserole with sage and onion dumplings, crispy pork belly on bubble and squeak cake with apple fritters and onion gravy, and puddings like raspberry and vanilla pod crème brûlée with fresh berries and chocolate, coffee and Cointreau mousse. Thursday is steak night, they offer good value two-course meals, and Sunday roasts.** *Starters/Snacks: £5.00 to £6.00. Main Courses: £8.50 to £10.50. Puddings: £4.95*

Wadworths ~ Tenant Philip Davison ~ Real ale ~ Bar food (12-2(2.30 Sat), 6-9.30; 12-4 Sun; not Mon) ~ Restaurant ~ (01635) 42377 ~ Children welcome ~ Open 12-2.30, 6-11; 12-4, 6-11 Sat; 12-5 Sun; closed Mon, Sun evening; 25-26 Dec, 1 Jan
Recommended by Mary Dyke, Evelyn and Derek Walter, Stephen Moss, Dr and Mrs A K Clarke

BRAY   SU9079 MAP 2

Crown

1.75 miles from M4 junction 9; A308 towards Windsor, then left at Bray signpost on to B3028; High Street; SL6 2AH

Low-beamed, busy pub with roaring log fires in knocked-through rooms, enjoyable food

To be sure of a table in this 14th-c dining pub, it's best to arrive early or book in advance. Some of its heavy old beams are so low you may have to mind your head, and there are plenty of timbers handily left at elbow height where walls have been knocked through. The three roaring winter log fires are extremely cosy. The partly panelled main bar has oak tables and leather-backed armchairs, and one dining area has photographs of World War II aeroplanes. Courage Best and Directors on handpump are served alongside a guest such as Wadworths 6X and a decent choice of wines. There are tables and benches out in a sheltered flagstoned front courtyard (which has a flourishing grape vine), and in the large back garden.

🍴 **Enjoyable bar food at lunchtime includes soup, deep-fried brie with home-made onion marmalade, wild boar sausages, home-made chicken and tarragon pie or lasagne, coriander** and chilli crab cakes with lime and mango dressing, and tagliatelle carbonara, with evening choices like moules marinière, rack of english lamb with rosemary and garlic jus, confit of duck leg with wild mushroom sauce, roast fillet of scottish salmon on roasted mixed pepper salad with a sweet dill vinaigrette dressing, and scottish sirloin steak with a green peppercorn sauce. *Starters/Snacks: £5.50 to £8.95. Main Courses: £10.20 to £19.95. Puddings: £4.00 to £4.50*

Scottish Courage ~ Lease John and Carole Noble ~ Real ale ~ Bar food (not Sun or Mon evenings) ~ Restaurant ~ (01628) 621936 ~ Children in restaurant ~ Open 11-3, 6-11; 12-3, 7-10.30 Sun; closed 25 and 26 Dec

Recommended by Tom and Ruth Rees, Stephen Moss, Dr and Mrs A K Clarke

Hinds Head 🍽 ♀

High Street; car park opposite (exit rather tricky); SL6 2AB
BERKSHIRE DINING PUB OF THE YEAR

Top-notch gastropub with outstanding classic british food in traditional surroundings, a fine choice of drinks, and efficient service

For obvious reasons (the renowned Fat Duck restaurant nearby is under the same ownership), most customers come to this handsome old pub to enjoy the excellent food which is prepared in a simpler style than at the Fat Duck and served in a friendly and informal atmosphere. You're made just as welcome if all you want is a drink and a chat. The thoroughly traditional L-shaped bar has dark beams and panelling, polished oak parquet, blazing log fires, red-cushioned built-in wall seats and studded leather carving chairs around small round tables, and latticed windows. They keep Greene King IPA, Elgoods Mad Dog, Rebellion IPA, and Timothy Taylors Landlord on handpump, a dozen interesting wines by the glass (including two champagnes) from an extensive list, 24 malt whiskies, a fine choice of teas and coffees, and an excellent bloody mary. They may ask to retain your credit card.

🍽 **Consistently excellent food includes snacks like devils on horseback or scotch quail eggs, sandwiches, soup, pheasant and bacon terrine with spiced pear chutney, raw scotch beef with caper and shallot dressing, superb mussels, chicken, ham and leek pie with mustard sauce, pork sausages with caramelised onion gravy, oak-smoked pollack, duck egg and cockles, barnsley chop with minted peas, whole lemon sole with crab and pickled lemon salad, blade of highland beef with irish black and white pudding, Aberdeen beef steaks, and puddings.** *Starters/Snacks: £5.95 to £10.95. Main Courses: £12.95 to £29.50. Puddings: £5.85 to £7.80*

Free house ~ Licensee Clive Dixon ~ Real ale ~ Bar food (12-2.30, 6.30-9.30; 12-4 Sun; not Sun evening) ~ Restaurant ~ (01628) 626151 ~ Children welcome ~ Dogs allowed in bar ~ Open 11-11; 12-10.30 Sun; closed 25 and 26 Dec

Recommended by Mr Ray J Carter, Andy and Claire Barker, Simon Rodway, Dr and Mrs A K Clarke, Minda and Stanley Alexander, Mandy and Simon King, Simon Collett-Jones, Humphry and Angela Crum Ewing

COOKHAM DEAN   SU8785   MAP 2

Chequers 🍽 ♀

Dean Lane; from Cookham follow signpost Cookham Dean, Marlow (unsuitable for heavy vehicles); SL6 9BQ

Restauranty dining pub with good food, friendly staff and cosy bar

There's an interesting choice of drinks in this friendly dining pub – though many customers are here to enjoy the well presented food. As well as Marlow Rebellion Smuggler and IPA and St Austells Tribute on handpump, there are quite a few wines by the glass, a smashing bloody mary with ten infused vodkas to choose from, all sorts of cocktails, ten single malt whiskies, and good coffees and teas. The compact bar has beams and flagstones and comfortable old sofas, and on the mixed dining tables on either side of the bar, there are fresh flowers and crisp white linen; welcoming service, a relaxed atmosphere, and maybe piped music. The area on the left, with an open stove in its big brick fireplace, leads back into a conservatory that looks on to the neat slope of the lawn. There are picnic-sets outside, some on a front terrace.

🍴 **Imaginative bar food includes soup, sautéed chicken livers with a herb blini and pepper sauce, baked figs wrapped in pancetta and glazed with cashel blue cheese, fish stew with clams, home-made mascarpone and spinach dumplings with roasted peppers, aubergine, courgettes and a smoked garlic cream sauce, fillet of bass with a dill cream sauce, smoked haddock fillet with a poached egg, crème fraîche potato cake and grain mustard sauce, breast of guinea fowl with dauphinoise potatoes, braised savoy cabbage and red wine jus, and puddings like lemon cheesecake with raspberry compote and chocolate brownie with chocolate sauce; side orders are extra. There's a two-course lunch (not Sunday) for £9.95, and popular Sunday roasts.** *Starters/Snacks: £4.95 to £9.95. Main Courses: £10.95 to £17.95. Puddings: £3.95 to £4.95*

Free house ~ Licensee Peter Roehrig ~ Real ale ~ Bar food (12-2.30, 6.30-9.30; 12-9.30 Sun) ~ Restaurant ~ (01628) 481232 ~ Children welcome ~ Open 11-3, 5.30-11; 11-12 Fri and Sat; 11-11 Sun

Recommended by Paul Humphreys, Chris Sale, Fred and Kate Portnell, P Waterman, Hunter and Christine Wright, P Farrar, David A Hammond

EAST GARSTON
SU3676   MAP 2

Queens Arms ♀

3.5 miles from M4 junction 14; A338 N then village signposted at Great Shefford; Newbury Road; RG17 7ET

Smart new dining pub with good food and exemplary country bar

In the same small successful group as the Anchor at Lower Froyle and Peat Spade at Longstock, this opened in autumn 2008, on a quiet country lane away from the village. The roomy opened-up bare-boards bar seems almost instantly restful, perhaps because of its soft lighting and dark blue ceiling and walls – they nicely set off the many smallish mainly antique prints. Many feature jockeys (this is after all racehorse-training country), and prominent among the daily papers on a corner table by one old leather armchair is the day's *Racing Post*. There's an interesting mix of chairs around the well spaced tables, which even in daytime have lit candles in ornamental sticks. The long counter serves Loddon Ferrymans Gold and Wells & Youngs Bitter from handpump, a fine choice of wines by the glass and of brandies and whiskies, good coffee and appetising bar nibbles, and the staff are friendly and interested; well reproduced piped music such as blues and jazz. Opening off on the right is a lighter dining area with bigger horse and country prints on its puce walls, and again a pleasing mix of furniture including one elaborately carved settle and a pair of chairs with entertainingly assertive high backs. On our inspection visit in early summer 2009 it looked as though they were about to open a sheltered terrace by the dining room. We haven't yet heard from readers who have spent a night here, but would expect it to be a nice place to stay in; there are plenty of downland walks nearby.

🍴 **Good bar food includes soup, duck eggs benedict with black pudding, chicken liver and foie gras pâté with onion marmalade, a meat platter with pickles, sausage and mash with red onion gravy, mushroom and leek nut crumble, skate wing with capers and basil, beef in ale pie, steaks with béarnaise or café de paris butter, and puddings like baked alaska with strawberry sauce and chocolate tart with rhubarb fool; they also have home-made fudge.** *Starters/Snacks: £4.90 to £7.50. Main Courses: £10.50 to £17.90. Puddings: £5.50 to £6.95*

Free house ~ Licensee Matt Green-Armytage ~ Real ale ~ Bar food (12-3(4 Sun), 7-9.45(9 Sun)) ~ (01488) 648757 ~ Children welcome but must be over 12 in bedrooms ~ Dogs allowed in bar ~ Open 11-1am(midnight Sun) ~ Bedrooms: /£95S

Recommended by BOB

Post Office address codings confusingly give the impression that some pubs are in Berkshire, when they're really in Buckinghamshire, Oxfordshire or Hampshire (which is where we list them).

FRILSHAM   SU5573   MAP 2

Pot Kiln 🍴 🍺

From Yattendon take turning S, opposite church, follow first Frilsham signpost, but just after crossing motorway go straight on towards Bucklebury ignoring Frilsham signposted right; pub on right after about half a mile; RG18 0XX

Country dining pub, bustling little bar, local beers, and traditional pub dishes up to imaginative modern cooking; suntrap garden and nearby walks

In lovely walking country and surprisingly isolated, this is a popular dining pub where it's essential to book to be sure of a table. And although the emphasis is very much on the imaginative restaurant food, friendly locals do still gather in the little bar where they offer West Berkshire Brick Kiln Bitter, Mr Chubbs Lunchtime Bitter and Maggs Magnificent Mild, and a weekly changing guest beer on handpump. The main bar area has dark wooden tables and chairs on bare boards, and a good winter log fire, and the extended lounge is open plan at the back and leads into a large, pretty dining room with a nice jumble of old tables and chairs, and an old-looking stone fireplace; darts and board games. This is a charming rural spot, and seats in the big suntrap garden have good views of the nearby forests and meadows.

🍽 Using home-made bread, some home-grown vegetables, and venison shot by the landlord, the good choice of imaginative bar food includes soup, filled rolls, ploughman's, devilled chicken livers on toast, warm pigeon salad with smoked bacon and black pudding, sausage and mash, roe deer burger, cornish cod with saffron beans, cockles and clams, fallow deer stew with rosemary dumplings, slow-roast belly of pork with root vegetable purée, beef faggots with celeriac and horseradish mash, and puddings like pear and apple crumble and crème brûlée with poached rhubarb. *Starters/Snacks: £5.50 to £6.95. Main Courses: £7.00 to £9.95. Puddings: £5.75*

Free house ~ Licensees Mr and Mrs Michael Robinson ~ Real ale ~ Bar food (12-2, 7-9; 12-3 Sun; not Sun pm, not Tues) ~ Restaurant ~ (01635) 201366 ~ Children welcome ~ Dogs allowed in bar ~ Open 12-3, 6-11; 12-11 Sat; 12-10.30 Sun; closed Tues; 25 Dec

Recommended by Robert Watt, Graham and Toni Sanders, the Didler, Ben Andrews, Dr and Mrs A K Clarke, Samantha McGahan, A J Bowen, N R White, Paul Humphreys

HENLEY   SU7682   MAP 2

Little Angel 🍴 🍷

A4130, just over bridge E of Henley; RG9 2LS

Relaxed linked contemporary areas plus attractive conservatory, good modern bar food, helpful service, and several wines by the glass

Civilised and rather smart, this attractive pub is more or less open-plan but with several clearly distinct seating areas. There's a mix of well spaced dining and wooden chairs and tables on the bare, light boards, comfortable bar chairs, tub chairs and sofas, and quite a bit of artwork on the creamy yellow walls. In one corner a case of art books and the like helps to set the tone. There's a winter woodburning stove and an airy conservatory. The attractive curved bar counter has a good choice of wines by the glass (plus champagne), smoothies and cocktails, and Brakspears Bitter and Oxford Gold on handpump; board games, unobtrusive piped music, TV, and friendly and efficient young staff. A sheltered floodlit back terrace has tables under cocktail parasols, looking over to the local cricket ground.

🍽 Using local organic produce and game from the Hambleden Estate, the modern bar food includes lunchtime sandwiches and burgers, as well as eggs benedict, duck liver and foie gras parfait with mango and ginger chutney, white crab tian with pressed tomato consommé, brochettes from the chargrill like harissa lamb with yoghurt, garlic and coriander or tiger prawns with chorizo and scallops, aubergine baked with sweet potato and courgette ratatouille with gruyère glaze, beef and mushroom suet pudding, teriyaki tuna loin with chilli and ginger noodles, interesting salads, roast black leg chicken with caramelised shallot risotto, steaks, and puddings like chocolate brownie with vanilla clotted cream ice-cream or fresh strawberry shortbread with lemon mascarpone. *Starters/Snacks: £4.50 to £8.95. Main Courses: £8.95 to £23.00. Puddings: £4.50 to £5.50*

Brakspears ~ Lease Douglas Green ~ Real ale ~ Bar food (12-3, 6.30-10; 12-10 Sat (till 9.30 Sun); not bank hol pm) ~ Restaurant ~ (01491) 411008 ~ Children lunchtimes; must be well behaved ~ Dogs allowed in bar ~ Live jazz most Weds ~ Open 11-11.30; 11-12 Sat; 12-11 Sun

Recommended by Chris Glasson, Tom and Ruth Rees, Roy Hoing, Michael Dandy, Peter and Judy Frost, Ian Phillips

HOLYPORT
SU8977 MAP 2

Belgian Arms
Handy for M4 junction 8/9, via A308(M) and A330; SL6 2JR

Popular dining pub with friendly staff, interesting food and waterside garden terrace

In a pretty spot by the village green, this bustling place has good quality wooden seats and tables on a terrace overlooking the pond – just the place for a drink in sunny weather. Inside, the low-ceilinged bar has well spaced tables and chairs on a stripped wooden floor, interesting cricketing memorabilia on the walls, a china cupboard in one corner, a winter log fire and a discreetly placed TV. The old cellar room is a dining area; piped music. Brakspears Bitter and Oxford Gold on handpump, and there are quite a few wines by the glass.

🍴 **Interesting bar food includes soup, chicken liver pâté with cumberland sauce, chargrilled squid with tomato, garlic, chilli and mint, button mushroom pie with parsnip mash, bangers with honey mash, smoked haddock and leek fishcake with creamed spinach, cheddar and lemon, lambs liver and bacon with parsley onion sauce, chicken breast with smoked bacon, pumpkin purée and tarragon sauce, beef, onion and red wine pie, and puddings like white chocolate and Baileys cheesecake with raspberry coulis and apple crumble and custard.** *Starters/Snacks: £4.50 to £6.00. Main Courses: £6.00 to £22.00. Puddings: £4.00 to £5.95*

Brakspears ~ Tenant Jamie Sears ~ Real ale ~ Bar food (12-2.30(3.30 Sun), 6.30-9) ~ Restaurant ~ (01628) 634468 ~ Children welcome ~ Dogs allowed in bar ~ Open 11-3, 5.30-11 (all day Fri-Sun)

Recommended by Ian Wilson, David and Sue Smith, Simon Collett-Jones, Peter Barton, June and Robin Savage

HUNGERFORD
SU3368 MAP 2

Plume of Feathers
High Street; street parking opposite; RG17 0NB

An oasis in this appealing small town, with good home cooking and a relaxed family atmosphere

From its smallish bow-windowed façade, this stretches a long way back around its island bar, open-plan, from black leather sofa and armchairs around low tables under lowish beams on the left at the front, through mixed tables with padded chairs or cushioned small pews on the bare boards, to an open fire in the stripped fireplace at the back. They have a good choice of wines by the glass alongside Greene King IPA and Ruddles Best on handpump and good coffee, and the scottish landlord and staff are friendly and helpful. The sheltered back courtyard isn't large but is well worth knowing on a warm day: prettily planted, and with a swing seat as well as green-painted metal tables and chairs.

🍴 **It's nothing elaborate about the menu here which gains our Food Award, but the care that the landlady puts into lifting even pubby standards out of the ordinary. As well as filled lunchtime panini and a sandwich of the day, filled baked potatoes and ploughman's, bar food includes soup, baked camembert with red onion chutney, a home-made burger with cheese, chicken breast stuffed with ricotta, sage and leek, smoked haddock omelette, steak and stilton in Guinness pie, liver and bacon, marinated lamb rump, and puddings such as chocolate fudge cake and sticky toffee pudding with toffee sauce; Sunday roasts.** *Starters/Snacks: £4.25 to £5.25. Main Courses: £7.95 to £12.95. Puddings: £5.25*

Greene King ~ Lease Hayley and Jimmy Weir ~ Real ale ~ Bar food ~ (01488) 682154 ~ Children welcome ~ Dogs welcome ~ Open 11-3, 5.30(6 Sat)-11; 12-4 Sun; closed Sun evening

Recommended by JCW, Anne Morton

HURST   SU8074   MAP 2

Green Man

Hinton Road, off A321 just outside village; RG10 0BP

An interesting mix of bars in bustling pub with decent food, and plenty of space outside on terrace and in big garden

The dining area in this partly 17th-c pub has been newly refurbished with modern sturdy wooden tables and high-backed chairs on the solid oak floor, and the rest of the pub has been redecorated. But the old-fashioned bar still has black standing timbers and dark oak beams around cosy alcoves, cushioned wall seats and built-in settles around copper-topped and other pub tables, and attractive prints, Edwardian enamels and decorative plates on cream or terracotta walls; it's warmed by a hot little fire in one fireplace and a nice old iron stove in another. Brakspears Bitter, Wychwood Hobgoblin, and a guest such as Brakspears Pride of the River on handpump, and half a dozen wines by the glass. No piped music, games machines or TVs. The sheltered, heated terrace has tables under giant umbrellas, there are picnic-sets under big oak trees in the large garden, and there's a good sturdy children's play area.

Ⓜ **Using carefully chosen produce and ingredients (and some vegetables and fruit grown by locals in exchange for vouchers that can be used in the pub), the good, popular bar food includes lunchtime sandwiches, baked potatoes and lighter dishes, plus spicy cajun chicken, mushroom and red pepper stroganoff, toulouse sausages, steak in ale pie, moroccan lamb tagine, chicken in a creamy parmesan sauce, and daily specials such as cornish cod fillet topped with basil, onion and tomato on couscous, slow-roasted lamb shank with local honey and mint, and venison strips with brandy and wild mushrooms in a creamy sauce.** *Starters/Snacks: £2.90 to £4.85. Main Courses: £7.80 to £9.75. Puddings: £1.95 to £4.25*

Brakspears ~ Tenants Simon and Gordon Guile ~ Real ale ~ Bar food (12-2.30, 6-9.30; 12-9 Sun) ~ Restaurant ~ (0118) 934 2599 ~ Children welcome ~ Open 11-3, 5.30-11; 12-10.30 Sun

Recommended by Guy Vowles, Priscilla Sandford, D J and P M Taylor, John Coatsworth, Fred and Kate Portnell, I A Herdman, Dr and Mrs A K Clarke, June and Robin Savage, Donna and Roger

INKPEN   SU3764   MAP 2

Crown & Garter 🍺 🛏

Inkpen Common: Inkpen signposted with Kintbury off A4; in Kintbury turn left into Inkpen Road, then keep on into Inkpen Common; RG17 9QR

Remote-feeling pub with appealing layout, lovely garden and nearby walks, local ales and tasty food in nicely lit bars, and especially friendly landlady

The particularly friendly landlady of this attractive old 16th-c brick pub sets a very high standard which is reflected in all the pub's traditional activities. The appealing low-ceilinged and relaxed panelled bar has West Berkshire Mr Chubbs Lunchtime Bitter and Good Old Boy and a guest such as Arkells Moonlight on handpump, decent wines by the glass and several malt whiskies. Three areas radiate from here; our pick is the parquet-floored part by the raised log fire which has a couple of substantial old tables and a huge old-fashioned slightly curved settle. Other parts are slate and wood with a good mix of well spaced tables and chairs, and nice lighting. There's a front terrace for outside eating, a lovely long side garden with picnic-sets, and plenty of good downland walks nearby. In a separate single-storey building, the bedrooms form an L around a pretty garden. James II is reputed to have used the pub on his way to visit his mistress locally.

Ⓜ **Changing daily, the well liked bar food includes filled baguettes, soup, squid in tempura batter with thai jelly, antipasti of italian meats, chicken tikka with onion bhaji, escalope of beef with fried egg and capers, fish and chips, pot roast lamb shank with piquant mint gravy, leeks and goats cheese tart, ribeye steak with peppercorn sauce, and puddings such as tipsy bread and butter pudding and dark and white chocolate pots with orange sherbert.** *Starters/Snacks: £4.95 to £7.95. Main Courses: £9.95 to £19.95. Puddings: £4.95 to £7.95*

Free house ~ Licensee Gill Hern ~ Real ale ~ Bar food (not Sun evening or Mon/Tues lunchtimes) ~ Restaurant ~ (01488) 668325 ~ Children allowed in bar only and must be over 7 in evenings and in bedrooms ~ Dogs allowed in bar ~ Open 12-3, 5.30-11; 12-5, 7-10.30 Sun; closed Mon and Tues lunchtimes ~ Bedrooms: £69.50B/£99B

Recommended by Alun Jones, Michael and Deborah Ethier, Paul Boot, Mr and Mrs H J Langley, Mr and Mrs P D Titcomb, Paul A Moore

PALEY STREET
SU8676   MAP 2
Royal Oak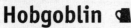
B3024 W; SL6 3JN

Friendly little pub with informal bar, good choice of wines, excellent british cooking in smarter dining room, and helpful service

Owned by Sir Michael Parkinson and his son Nick, this 17th-c pub is a stylish place with a relaxed, friendly atmosphere. The smallish bar is informal with beams, an open fire, leather sofas, Fullers London Pride on handpump and a good, wide choice of wines (and champagne) by the glass; helpful service. The dining area stretches back with bare boards, flagstones and some stripped brick, a mix of well spaced wooden tables and chairs, and cricketing prints and photographs of celebrity friends on the walls; piped jazz. The pub dog is called Boris.

🍴 Excellent british cooking using seasonal produce includes fish soup with rouille and croutons, sea kale with blood orange hollandaise, cornish sprats with mayonnaise, pigeon, chicken liver and pistachio terrine, pasty with buttered leeks and pumpkin seed salad, slow-cooked gloucester old spot belly pork with scotch broth, halibut with samphire, mussels and beurre blanc, peppered haunch of venison with creamed spinach, and puddings like cambridge burnt cream with shortbread or baked alaska. They also offer a good value two- and three-course set menu. *Starters/Snacks: £2.50 to £9.00. Main Courses: £10.00 to £24.00. Puddings: £6.50 to £8.50*

Fullers ~ Lease N D Parkinson ~ Real ale ~ Bar food (12-2.30, 6.30-9.30 (10 Fri and Sat); 12-3.30 Sun; not Sun evening) ~ Restaurant ~ (01628) 620541 ~ Children welcome but no pushchairs in restaurant ~ Open 12-3, 6-12; 12-4 Sun; closed Sun evening; 25 Dec, 1 Jan

Recommended by David Tindal, Peter Sampson

READING
SU7173   MAP 2
Hobgoblin 🍺
2 Broad Street; RG1 2BH

No-frills pub with small panelled rooms, cheerful atmosphere and eight quickly changing real ales

There's a new landlady running this cheerfully basic pub who is sticking to its tradition of no food and a fine range of real ales. There are eight kept well on handpump which include three from the West Berkshire Brewery alongside five guests from interesting smaller brewers such as Arkells, Bridge of Allen, Dark Star, Downton and Marble. Pump clips cover practically every inch of the walls and ceiling of the simple bare-boards bar – a testament to the enormous number of brews that have passed through the pumps over the past few years (now over 6,000). They've also lots of different bottled beers, czech lager on tap, Weston's farm cider and perry and country wines. Up a step is a small seating area, but the best places to sit are the three or four tiny panelled rooms reached by a narrow corridor leading from the bar; cosy and intimate, each has barely enough space for one table and a few chairs or wall seats, but they're very appealing if you're able to bag one; the biggest also manages to squeeze in a fireplace. It does get very busy, especially at weekends; piped music and TV.

🍴 **No food.**

Community Taverns ~ Manager Katrina Fletcher ~ Real ale ~ No credit cards ~ (0118) 950 8119 ~ Open 11-11; 12-10.30 Sun; closed 25-26 Dec, 1 Jan

Recommended by Martin and Marion Vincent, the Didler, Dr and Mrs A K Clarke

RUSCOMBE   SU7976   MAP 2

Royal Oak

Ruscombe Lane (B3024 just E of Twyford); RG10 9JN

Wide choice of popular food at welcoming pub with interesting furnishings and paintings and adjoining antiques and collectables shop

Bustling and homely, the open-plan carpeted interior of this village pub is well laid out so that each bit is fairly snug, but still manages to keep the overall feel of a lot of people enjoying themselves. A good variety of furniture runs from dark oak tables to big chunky pine ones, with mixed seating to match – the two sofas facing one another are popular. Contrasting with the old exposed ceiling joists, mostly unframed modern paintings and prints decorate the walls – mainly dark terracotta over a panelled dado. Brakspears Bitter, Fullers London Pride and a guest such as Skinners Betty Stogs on handpump, and a dozen nicely chosen wines (including champagne) by the glass. Picnic-sets are ranged around a venerable central hawthorn in the garden behind (where there are ducks and chickens); summer barbecues. The landlady's antiques and collectables shop is open during pub hours. The pub is on the Henley Arts Trail.

🍴 Using their own eggs, the good, varied bar food includes sandwiches, soup, ploughman's, sausages and mash with caramelised onion gravy, ham and egg, and beer-battered fish with more elaborate choices such as black pudding stack with a wholegrain mustard mash and peppercorn sauce, red thai chicken and prawns on noodles, tomato and spinach risotto, salmon fillet with prawn cream sauce, confit of duck with mash and green peppercorns with sausages in red wine sauce, and lamb shank with rosemary jus. *Starters/Snacks: £4.25 to £8.95. Main Courses: £6.25 to £10.95. Puddings: £3.50 to £5.50*

Enterprise ~ Lease Jenny and Stefano Buratta ~ Real ale ~ Bar food (12-2.30, 7-9.30; 12-3 Sun; not Sun or Mon evenings) ~ Restaurant ~ (0118) 934 5190 ~ Children welcome ~ Dogs welcome ~ Open 12-3, 6-11; 12-4 Sun; closed Sun and Mon evenings

Recommended by Miss A Hawkes, Paul Humphreys

SHINFIELD   SU7367   MAP 2

Magpie & Parrot 🍺

2.6 miles from M4 junction 11, via B3270; A327 just SE of Shinfield – heading out on Arborfield Road, keep eyes skinned for small hand-painted green Nursery sign on left, and Fullers 'bar open' blackboard; RG2 9EA

Unusual homely little roadside cottage with warm fire, lots of bric-a-brac in cosy small bars; hospitable landlady

They now offer some lunchtime food in this homely little cottage – and Friday night fish and chips. The bar has been extended this year into what had been a private sitting room but you still go in through the lobby with its antiquated telephone equipment. A cosy and inviting high-raftered room has a handful of small polished tables and a comfortable mix of individualistic seats from Georgian oak thrones to a red velveteen sofa, not to mention the armchair with the paw-printed cushion reserved for Aitch the pub dog. Everything is spick and span, from the brightly patterned carpet to the plethora of interesting bric-a-brac covering the walls: miniature and historic bottles, dozens of model cars, veteran AA badges and automotive instruments, and mementoes of a pranged Spitfire (do ask about its story – they love to chat here). Fullers London Pride, Timothy Taylors Landlord and a weekly guest beer on handpump at the small corner counter. There are teak tables on the back terrace and an immaculate lawn beyond; they may have hog roasts and morris men at various summer events and two beer festivals in June and December with 22 real ales; aunt sally. Note the unusual opening hours.

🍴 **Lunchtime bar food includes toasties, pies, ham and egg, and so forth, and on Friday evenings they offer fish and chips.** *Starters/Snacks: £3.95 to £6.95*

Free house ~ Licensee Mrs Carole Headland ~ Real ale ~ Bar food (12-2; not evenings except Fri 6-8) ~ No credit cards ~ (0118) 988 4130 ~ Dogs allowed in bar ~ Open 12-7; 12-4 Sun; closed evenings

Recommended by Dr and Mrs A K Clarke, Phil and Sally Gorton, Susan and John Douglas

STANFORD DINGLEY   SU5771   MAP 2

Old Boot

Off A340 via Bradfield, coming from A4 just W of M4 junction 12; RG7 6LT

Neat pub with emphasis on imaginative food; country furnishings and rural garden views

Most tables in this stylish 18th-c pub are laid for dining and to be sure of a place you must book in advance, especially at weekends. The beamed bar has two welcoming fires (one in an inglenook), fine old pews, settles, old country chairs and polished tables. There are some striking pictures and hunting prints, boot ornaments in various sizes and fresh flowers. Three real ales might include West Berkshire Good Old Boy, Fullers London Pride and a changing guest on handpump; eight wines by the glass. There are seats in the quiet sloping back garden or on the terrace and pleasant rural views; more tables out in front. More reports please.

🍴 **Popular bar food includes filled baguettes, goats cheese and onion tart, crab and smoked salmon salad, vegetable risotto, fresh cod and chips, sausage and mash, beef in Guinness pie, lamb shank with tomatoes and rosemary, a duo of brill and john dory in paprika sauce, and puddings like red fruit crumble and chocolate brownie with toffee ice-cream.** *Starters/Snacks: £5.50 to £7.50. Main Courses: £8.50 to £12.50. Puddings: £5.95*

Free house ~ Licensee John Haley ~ Real ale ~ Bar food ~ Restaurant ~ (0118) 974 4292 ~ Children welcome ~ Dogs allowed in bar ~ Open 11(12 Sun)-3, 6-11

Recommended by A J Bowen, T R and B C Jenkins

WHITE WALTHAM   SU8477   MAP 2

Beehive 🍺

Waltham Road (B3024 W of Maidenhead); SL6 3SH

Honest bar food and welcoming staff at traditional village pub

Opposite the village cricket field, this solidly run country local is run by a friendly landlord. To the right, several comfortably carpeted spacious areas have country kitchen chairs around sturdy tables, and there's a conservatory. The neat bar to the left is brightened up by cheerful scatter cushions on its comfortable seats – built-in wall seats, captain's chairs and a leather wing armchair. Brakspears Bitter, Fullers London Pride, Greene King Abbot and a changing guest from Loddon or Rebellion on handpump, with a good choice of soft drinks; piped music and board games. Picnic-sets and teak seats out in front on the terrace take in the pub's rather fine topiary, and there's more seating on a good-sized sheltered back lawn; good disabled access and facilities.

🍴 **Well liked honest bar food includes sandwiches, filled baked potatoes, chicken liver pâté, home-cooked ham and egg, steak and kidney pie, home-made thai-style salmon fishcakes with sweet chilli dip, tagliatelle with artichoke hearts, tomatoes, spinach and pesto, lamb loin with red wine jus, slow-roast belly of pork with bubble and squeak, cider and grain mustard sauce, steaks, and puddings like fruit crumble and treacle tart.** *Starters/Snacks: £4.50 to £8.95. Main Courses: £8.95 to £10.95. Puddings: £4.95*

Enterprise ~ Lease Guy Martin ~ Real ale ~ Bar food (12-3, 5.30-9.30; 12-9.30(8.30 Sun) Sat) ~ Restaurant ~ (01628) 822877 ~ Children welcome ~ Dogs allowed in bar ~ Open 11-3, 5.30-11; 11-12 Sat; 12-10.30 Sun; closed 26 Dec

Recommended by Stan Edwards, Dr and Mrs A K Clarke, June and Robin Savage, Paul Humphreys, Tracey and Stephen Groves, D and M T Ayres-Regan

WINTERBOURNE

Winterbourne Arms ♀

3.7 miles from M4 junction 13; at A34 turn into Chievley Services and follow Donnington signs to Arlington Lane, then follow Winterbourne signs; RG20 8BB

Relaxing, friendly country pub with popular bar food, real ales, lots of wines by the glass and large landscaped garden

Enjoyed by many of our readers as a relaxing and friendly break from the M4, this is a pretty black and white village house. The traditional bars have stools along the counter, a collection of old irons around the big fireplace with its warming log fire, and early prints and old photographs of the village on the pale washed or exposed stone walls; piped music. Big windows take in peaceful views over rolling fields. Fullers London Pride, Ramsbury Gold and Winterbourne Whistle Wetter on handpump and 20 wines by the glass including sparkling and sweet wines. There are seats outside in the large landscaped side garden and pretty flowering tubs and hanging baskets. The surrounding countryside here is lovely, with nearby walks to Snelsmore Common and Donnington Castle.

🍽 Popular bar food includes filled baguettes, ploughman's, soup, wild mushrooms with garlic and herbs on toast, home-made burger with cheese and bacon, gammon and eggs, fish pie, duck breast with rosemary and orange sauce, calves liver with bacon and onion gravy and blue cheese mash, scottish rib-eye steak with green peppercorn sauce, daily specials, and puddings like raspberry crème brûlée and sticky toffee pudding. *Starters/Snacks: £4.50 to £7.95. Main Courses: £7.95 to £16.95. Puddings: £4.25 to £5.95*

Free house ~ Licensee Frank Adams ~ Real ale ~ Bar food (12-2.30, 6-9.30; 12-3.30, 6-10.30 Sun) ~ Restaurant ~ (01635) 248200 ~ Children welcome ~ Dogs allowed in bar ~ Open 12-3, 6-11; 12-10.30 Sun

Recommended by Martin and Pauline Jennings, Peter Sampson, Bill Fillery, Dr and Mrs J D Abell, Samantha McGahan, Mike and Sue Loseby, John Saville, Andy and Claire Barker, Mike and Heather Watson, John Robertson, Brian and Rosalie Laverick, Annette Tress, Gary Smith, Paul A Moore

LUCKY DIP

Besides the fully inspected pubs, you might like to try these Lucky Dips recommended to us and described by readers (if you do, please send us reports: feedback@goodguides.com).

ALDERMASTON [SU6067]
Butt RG7 4LA [Station Rd, Aldermaston Wharf; off A4/A340 E]: Big pub nr lock on Kennet & Avon Canal, friendly attentive service, wide food range from sandwiches up, several areas inc two-level eating part, unusual prints, new world wines; piped radio; plenty of tables outside, attractive countryside (Miss A Hawkes)
☆ *Hinds Head* RG7 4LX [Wasing Lane]: Creeper-clad red brick 17th-c inn at heart of attractive old village, spacious but homely bar, red patterned carpet, wooden pews, old tables, big red sofa, brasses over fireplace, Fullers and a guest beer, decent choice of wines, quite a collection of malt whiskies, enjoyable food, neat staff, board games; piped music; children welcome if eating, seats in garden, bedrooms (David and Sue Smith, LYM, Sara Fulton, Roger Baker)
ARBORFIELD CROSS [SU7667]
Bull RG2 9QD: Refurbished not long ago, reasonably priced food from good baps up, central bar, log fire, attractive pictures and bric-a-brac; no under-12s inside, and they may try to keep your credit card while you

eat; pleasant garden (Roy Hoing, Paul Humphreys)
ASTON [SU7884]
☆ *Flower Pot* RG9 3DG [small signpost off A4130 Henley—Maidenhead at top of Remenham Hill]: Roomy popular country pub with nice local feel, roaring log fire, array of stuffed fish and fishing prints on dark green walls of attractively done airy country dining area, food from banquettes to fish and game, Brakspears, Hook Norton and Wychwood ales, quick friendly service, snug traditional bar with more fishing memorabilia; very busy with walkers and families wknds; lots of picnic-sets giving quiet country views from nice big dog-friendly orchard garden, side field with chickens, ducks and guinea fowl, crocodile on roof, bedrooms (Roy Hoing, Michael Dandy, BB, DHV, Susan and John Douglas, Paul Humphreys, David and Sue Smith)
BEECH HILL [SU6964]
Elm Tree RG7 2AZ [3.3 miles from M4 junction 11: A33 towards Basingstoke, turning off into Beech Hill Rd after about 2 miles]: Five carefully furnished and

decorated rooms, one with dozens of clocks, Hollywood photographs and blazing fire, nice views especially from simply furnished more modern barn-style restaurant and conservatory, quick friendly staff, enjoyable if not cheap food (all day wknds) from hearty baguettes up inc some unusual dishes, well kept Fullers London Pride, Greene King IPA and Old Speckled Hen and a guest beer, amazing ladies'; children welcome away from bar, benches and tables on front decking in nice setting, open all day *(LYM, David and Sue Smith, Stan Edwards)*

BRACKNELL [SU8566]

Golden Retriever RG12 7PB [Nine Mile Ride (junction A3095/B3430)]: Popular Vintage Inn pastiche of olde-worlde beamed, tiled and thatched pub, comfortable farmhouse-style décor in maze of linked rooms, decent food all day, Caledonian Deuchars IPA, Fullers London Pride and Sharps Doom Bar, plenty of wines by the glass, young attentive staff, log fires, daily papers; ample seating outside, open all day *(Ian Phillips)*

BURGHFIELD [SU6870]

Cunning Man RG30 3RB [Burghfield Bridge]: Comfortable thatched Vintage Inn by Theale—Reading Canal, usual good value food choice, ales from Fullers, Hancocks, Hogs Back and Wadworths, efficient staff; plenty of tables outside, good moorings, open all day *(DHV, Reg Fowle, Helen Rickwood, Peter and Audrey Dowsett, Bob and Laura Brock)*

CHEAPSIDE [SU9469]

☆ *Thatched Tavern* SL5 7QG [off A332/A329, then off B383 at Village Hall sign]: Civilised dining pub with a good deal of character, interesting up-to-date food, friendly service, good choice of wines by the glass and farm cider as well as a couple of well kept ales, daily papers, big inglenook log fire, low beams and polished flagstones in cottagey core, three smart carpeted dining rooms off; children in restaurant, rustic tables on attractive sheltered back lawn, open all day wknds, handy for Virginia Water *(Chris Sale, LYM)*

CHIEVELEY [SU4773]

☆ *Olde Red Lion* RG20 8XB [handy for M4 junction 13 via A34 N-bound; Green Lane]: Attractive village pub with welcoming log fire, friendly landlord and staff, buoyant local atmosphere, well kept Arkells ales, good choice of unpretentious yet imaginative food, low-beamed L-shaped bar with lots of brassware, back restaurant with paintings for sale; piped music, games machine, TV; small garden, bedrooms *(BB, J V Dadswell)*

COOKHAM [SU8985]

☆ *Bel & the Dragon* SL6 9SQ [High St (B4447)]: Smart old dining pub with panelling and heavy Tudor beams, log fires, bare boards and simple country furnishings in two-room front bar and dining area, more formal back restaurant, helpful friendly staff

(but service can slow when busy), enjoyable food at prices you might expect for the area, real ales such as Brakspears and Rebellion good choice of wines; children welcome, garden with terrace tables, Stanley Spencer Gallery almost opposite, open all day *(N R White, LYM, Phil Bryant)*

Ferry SL6 9SN [Sutton Rd]: Splendidly placed riverside pub with relaxing contemporary décor, Rebellion IPA and Timothy Taylors Landlord, some interesting lagers and good wine range, decent food (popular Sun lunchtime), light and airy Thames-view dining areas upstairs and down, sofas and coffee tables by fireplace, small servery in beamed core; piped music; children welcome, extensive decking overlooking river *(Susan and John Douglas, BB, Mrs June Wilmers, David Tindal)*

Kings Arms SL6 9SJ [High St]: Extensively updated linked areas behind old façade, good cheerful service, good range of pubby and more elaborate food at fair prices, good beer choice; pleasant garden behind *(LYM, Robert Gomme)*

COOKHAM DEAN [SU8785]

☆ *Jolly Farmer* SL6 9PD [Church Rd, off Hills Lane]: Traditional pub owned by village consortium, old-fashioned unspoilt bars with open fires, prompt friendly service, well kept ales, farm cider, decent wines and coffee, good choice of sensibly priced food from nice baguettes up, good-sized more modern eating area and small dining room, old and new local photographs, pub games, no music or machines, friendly black lab called Czar; well behaved children welcome, tables out in front and in good garden with play area *(Chris Sale, Paul Humphreys, R K Phillips, LYM, David and Sue Smith)*

CURRIDGE [SU4871]

☆ *Bunk* RG18 9DS [handy for M4 junction 13, off A34 S]: Pub/restaurant with good interesting food from baguettes up, well kept ales inc West Berkshire, good choice of wines by the glass, courteous efficient staff, smart recently extended stripped-wood bar with log fire, spacious dining conservatory overlooking meadows and woods; tables in neat garden and on terrace, fine woodland walks nearby, seven bedrooms *(BB, Mr Ray J Carter)*

EAST ILSLEY [SU4981]

Swan RG20 7LF [just off A34 Newbury—Abingdon; High St]: Recently refurbished Greene King pub with their beers and enjoyable well priced food from sandwiches up, good Sun carvery, cheerful staff, comfortable seating by log fire; well behaved children and dogs welcome, tables in courtyard and walled garden, good bedrooms *(LYM, Edward and Ava Williams, Val and Alan Green)*

ETON [SU9677]

Watermans Arms SL4 6BW [Brocas St]: Low-ceilinged, part-panelled pub facing Eton College boat house, horseshoe servery with well kept Brakspears, Fullers London Pride,

Hogs Back TEA and Wychwood Hobgoblin, friendly staff, food (all day Fri, Sat, not Sun evening) from sandwiches to fish, roomy back dining area, overhead Thames map and lots of old river photographs; soft piped music; children welcome, covered tables outside *(LYM, Phil Bryant, Bruce Bird, Andy and Jill Kassube)*

FINCHAMPSTEAD [SU7963]

Queens Oak RG40 4LS [Church Lane, off B3016]: Relaxed well worn-in country local, largely open-plan, with mix of simple seats and tables, some in airy parquet-floored area on right, well kept Brakspears ales and a guest, friendly attentive staff, good value home-made food, separate dining room where children allowed; picnic-sets, some sheltered, in good-sized garden with aunt sally, play area and Sun lunchtime barbecues; open all day at least in summer *(Gwyn and Anne Wake, BB, David and Sue Smith)*

HAMPSTEAD NORREYS [SU5376]

White Hart RG18 0TB [Church St]: Friendly low-beamed village pub improved by new management, fireside seating and good-sized dining area, decent sensibly priced bar food, well kept Greene King ales; children welcome, back terrace and garden *(Stan Edwards)*

HUNGERFORD [SU3368]

Bear RG17 0EL [3 miles from M4 junction 14; town signed at junction]: Minimalist neo-scandinavian décor, a useful stop for all-day bistro food inc good range of sandwiches, restaurant; bedrooms comfortable and attractive *(Samantha McGahan, Roger Wain-Heapy, LYM)*

HUNGERFORD NEWTOWN [SU3571]

☆ *Tally Ho* RG17 0PP [A338 just S of M4 junction 14]: Good cooking from home-baked bread to interesting dishes in pleasantly traditional beamed pub, well kept Wadworths (full range) and decent house wines, friendly licensees and pub dog, open fire; piped pop music; children welcome, picnic-sets outside *(John and Penelope Massey Stewart, BB, John and Jill Perkins)*

HURLEY [SU8281]

☆ *Dew Drop* SL6 6RB [small yellow sign to pub off A4130 just W]: Nice rustic setting, popular food from good baguettes up, Brakspears ales, enjoyable house wine, good service (free wknd transport for local customers), traditional games; children and dogs welcome, french windows to terrace, new landscaped back garden with nice views, boules, barbecue, good walks, open all day Sat, cl Sun evening *(Paul Humphreys, David Tindal, LYM, David and Sue Smith)*

☆ *Olde Bell* SL6 5LX [High St]: Handsome upmarket – though fairly priced – timbered inn with some remarkable ancient features inc Norman doorway and window, bar recently carefully restored to charming semblance of a rustic tavern, simple rugs on tiled floor, well worn wall hangings and armchairs, rocking chair by log fire, good

staff, interesting food choice using local produce, Rebellion IPA and Mutiny, stylish contemporary restaurant; children and dogs welcome, fine gardens, open all day *(Susan and John Douglas, LYM)*

INKPEN [SU3564]

☆ *Swan* RG17 9DX [Lower Inkpen; coming from A338 in Hungerford, take Park St (first left after railway bridge, coming from A4)]: Rambling beamed country pub with strong organic leanings in its wines, beers and home-made food from sandwiches and pubby things to more upscale dishes (farming owners have interesting organic shop next door), cosy corners, eclectic bric-a-brac, three log fires, friendly helpful staff, good Butts and West Berkshire ales, local farm cider, pleasant restaurant, flagstoned games area; piped music; well behaved children welcome in eating areas, picnic-sets out in front tiered garden, good bedrooms, open all day in summer *(N R White, D Nightingale, Pete Baker, LYM, M J Daly, Michael and Deborah Ethier)*

KINTBURY [SU3866]

☆ *Dundas Arms* RG17 9UT [Station Rd]: Fine summer pub, with tables out on deck above Kennet & Avon Canal and pleasant walks; well kept Adnams, Ramsbury, West Berkshire and a guest ale, good coffee and wines by the glass, good reasonably priced home-made pub food (not Sun), evening restaurant; they may try to keep your credit card while you eat outside; comfortable bedrooms with own secluded waterside terrace, good breakfast, cl Sun evening *(Brian and Janet Ainscough, Jeff and Wendy Williams, LYM, T R and B C Jenkins, Julia and Richard Tredgett)*

KNOWL HILL [SU8178]

☆ *Bird in Hand* RG10 9UP [A4, quite handy for M4 junction 8/9]: Relaxed, civilised and roomy, with cosy alcoves, heavy beams, panelling and splendid log fire in tartan-carpeted main area with leather chairs, wide choice of enjoyable home-made food even Sun evening inc occasional good value set menus, well kept Brakspears and local guests such as Ascot and West Berkshire, good choice of other drinks, attentive prompt service, much older side bar, smart restaurant; soft piped music; tables out on front terrace, Sun summer barbecues, 15 tidy modern bedrooms *(DHV, Andy and LYM, Jill Kassube, Simon Collett-Jones, Paul Humphreys, June and Robin Savage)*

☆ *Old Devil* RG10 9UU [Bath Rd (A4)]: Roomy and popular refurbished roadhouse, leather sofas and chairs in bar, well spaced tables with fresh flowers in dining areas each side, chintzy feel, friendly efficient service, wide choice of decent food, Fullers London Pride, good range of wines by the glass; pleasant verandah above attractive lawn *(David and Sue Smith, Paul Humphreys)*

Royal Oak RG10 9YE [pub signed off A4]: Under new ownership and returned to a traditional pub (was restauranty), carpeted

L-shaped room with central bar and log fire, Brakspears and Rebellion, good value pubby food; piped music, TV, quiz nights; children and dogs welcome, good-sized informal garden overlooking fields, nearby walks, open all day wknds *(Susan and John Douglas, LYM)*

LAMBOURN [SU3180]

Malt Shovel RG17 8QN [Upper Lambourn]: décor and customers reflecting race-stables surroundings, traditional locals' bar, enjoyable home-made food in smart modern dining extension inc good Sun carvery, good choice of wines by the glass, real ales, helpful staff; racing TV *(Michael Sargent, Mrs Jane Kingsbury)*

LITTLEWICK GREEN [SU8379]

Cricketers SL6 3RA [not far from M4 junction 9; A404(M) then left on to A4 – village signed on left; Coronation Rd]: Proper old-fashioned country pub with new enthusiastic landlord, Badger and Wells & Youngs ales, good choice of wines by the glass, reasonably priced food from lunchtime baguettes up; piped music; charming spot opp cricket green, bedrooms, open all day wknds *(Paul Humphreys, Andy and Jill Kassube, LYM)*

Shire Horse SL6 3QA [Bath Rd (A4)]: Chef & Brewer taking its name from Courage's former adjoining shire horse centre, comfortable and attractive linked areas with old beams, tiled floors and cosy corners, Adnams, Fullers London Pride and Wells & Youngs Bombardier, good choice of sensibly priced wines by the glass, cafetière coffee, decent food all day inc good value baguettes served promptly by young staff; nice garden with good quality furniture and heaters *(Susan and John Douglas, LYM)*

LONGLANE [SU4971]

Lamb RG18 9LY [B4009]: Under newish management, with unusual food choice from lots of enjoyable tapas to pheasant etc *(Stan Edwards)*

MAIDENHEAD [SU8683]

Lemon Tree SL6 6NW [Golden Ball Lane, Pinkneys Green, off A308 N]: Low-beamed linked rooms and good-sized smart airy dining area, good value enjoyable pubby food inc some interesting dishes, friendly service (can be slow when busy), Hogs Back and Thwaites ales, good coffee and choice of wines by the glass; picnic-sets out on grass behind, open all day *(Michael Dandy, DHV, D and M T Ayres-Regan)*

☆ *Robin Hood* SL6 6PR [Furze Platt Rd, Pinkneys Green (A308N)]: Well run Greene King dining pub with their ales and good choice of wines by the glass, extensive series of well divided and varied eating areas off oak-boarded bar, enjoyable food inc popular kangaroo burgers, friendly helpful service, feature fireplace; piped music; broad picnic-sets on big front terrace and lawn, sheltered bower with awning, open all day *(Eithne Dandy, BB, Paul Humphreys)*

NEWBURY [SU4766]

King Charles RG14 5BX [Cheap St]:

Enjoyable food inc good Sun roast, friendly landlord and staff, real ale, imaginative décor; children welcome *(Samantha McGahan, Simon and Philippa Hughes)*

Lock Stock & Barrel RG14 1AA [Northbrook St]: Popular modern pub standing out for canalside setting, with partly flagstoned bar, suntrap balcony and terrace looking over a series of locks towards handsome church, low ceiling and panelling, lots of windows, good choice of food all day, quick efficient service even when busy, well kept Fullers beers; canal walks *(BB, Phil Bryant)*

PANGBOURNE [SU6376]

Cross Keys RG8 7AR [Church Rd, opp church]: Good bar and restaurant food (not Sun evening) from baguettes to steaks inc good value set lunches, own-baked bread, Greene King ales, good wine choice, linked beamed rooms with simple bar on right, neat dining area on left; service can be slow, piped pop music may obtrude, paid parking some way off; nice back streamside terrace with sizeable heated marquee, open all day *(BB, David Rule)*

Swan RG8 7DU [Shooters Hill]: Attractive Thames-side pub dating from 17th c, good choice of wines by the glass, Greene King ales, friendly staff, lounge with open fire, river-view dining balcony and conservatory (food all day); piped music, sports TV; picnic-sets on terrace overlooking weir and moorings, open all day *(John and Elisabeth Cox, June and Robin Savage)*

READING [SU7273]

Eldon Arms RG1 4DX [Eldon Terr]: Two-room backstreet pub well run by long-serving licensees, well kept Wadworths, cosy lounge, lots of bric-a-brac *(the Didler)*

☆ *Fishermans Cottage* RG1 3DW [Kennet Side – easiest to walk from Orts Rd, off Kings Rd]: Nice spot by canal lock and towpath, good value lunches esp sandwiches (very busy then but service quick), full Fullers beer range, small choice of wines, modern furnishings, pleasant stone snug behind woodburning range, light and airy conservatory, small darts room; influx of regulars evenings, SkyTV; dogs allowed (not in garden), waterside tables, lovely big back garden *(Susan and John Douglas, DM, the Didler)*

Griffin RG4 7AD [Church Rd, Caversham]: Roomy Chef & Brewer in beautiful Thames-side spot overlooking swan sanctuary, separate areas with several log fires, Courage and Wells & Youngs beers, reliable good value food, cafetière coffee, good friendly service; tables in attractive heated courtyard, open all day *(D J and P M Taylor, Tony Hobden, Tony and Wendy Hobden)*

Nags Head RG1 7XD [Russell St]: Friendly local with good mix of customers, friendly landlord, well kept ale inc West Berkshire Dark Mild, good value food, open fire; live music Sun *(John Slade)*

☆ *Retreat* RG1 4EH [St Johns St]: Friendly 1960ish backstreet local with well kept

Loddon Ferrymans Gold, Ringwood Best and changing guest ales, farm ciders, reasonable prices, back bar with darts, pool and juke box; jazz, folk and blues evenings; open all day Fri-Sun *(the Didler)*

Slug & Lettuce RG1 2AG [Riverside Level, Oracle Centre]: Spacious bar and dining areas, good value food inc meze for two, attentive service; attractive setting by Kennet & Avon Canal, handy for abbey gardens and museum *(Peter and Audrey Dowsett)*

☆ *Sweeney & Todd* RG1 7RD [Castle St]: Cross between café and pub with exceptional value home-made pies all day, also ploughman's, casseroles and roasts, in warren of private little period-feel alcoves and other areas on various levels, prompt cheery service, small well stocked bar with several real ales and Weston's cider, children welcome in restaurant area, open all day (cl Sun and bank hols) *(John Branston, Susan and John Douglas, the Didler, JCW, LYM, D J and P M Taylor)*

SHEFFORD WOODLANDS [SU3673]

☆ *Pheasant* RG17 7AA [less than ½ mile from M4 junction 14 – A338 towards Wantage then 1st left on to B4000]: Tucked-away horse-racing inn with large new bedroom extension, welcoming old-school landlord and friendly staff, good regularly changing traditional food, well kept ales, log fires and stone floors, four rooms inc end dining area with burgundy décor and bistro atmosphere, public bar with games inc ring the bull; attractive views from garden, 11 new bedrooms *(LYM, Tony and Tracy Constance)*

SONNING [SU7575]

☆ *Bull* RG4 6UP [off B478, by church; village signed off A4 E of Reading]: Smartened up old-world inn in pretty setting nr Thames, low heavy beams, cosy alcoves, cushioned antique settles and low-slung chairs, inglenook log fires, well kept Fullers, food from grand baguettes to steaks (remember this is a pricey area), friendly waistcoated staff, back dining part (children allowed), small public bar; charming courtyard, five attractive bedrooms, open all day summer wknds *(Susan and John Douglas, John Coatsworth, Paul Humphreys, John Saville, LYM)*

STANFORD DINGLEY [SU5771]

Bull RG7 6LS [off A340 via Bradfield]: 15th-c two-bar character village pub under new ownership, good choice of ales and wines, food from baps up, prompt service; plenty of seating in big side garden, comfortable bedroom block *(Robert Watt, Martin Sagar, LYM)*

STREATLEY [SU5980]

Swan RG8 9HR [High St]: Small upscale riverside bar in welcoming hotel, well kept West Berkshire Old Father Thames, decent food and coffee; children welcome, tables on terrace and in colourful Thames-side grounds, bedrooms, many with river views and own terraces *(LYM, Susan and John*

Douglas, Michael and Deborah Ethier)

SULHAMSTEAD [SU6269]

Spring RG7 5HP [Bath Rd (A4)]: Remarkable barn conversion with giant bellows, huge cushions and craft fabrics over balustraded gallery restaurant, settles in big bar; extensive gardens *(Peter and Audrey Dowsett)*

SUNNINGHILL [SU9367]

Dog & Partridge SL5 7AQ [Upper Village Rd]: Modern feel under newish hard-working owners with emphasis on the enjoyable food, friendly staff, real ales, good range of wines; piped music; children welcome, nice garden *(Chris Sale)*

THEALE [SU6471]

Fox & Hounds RG7 4BE [Station Rd, Sheffield Bottom (out past the station)]: Large neatly kept pub, friendly and relaxed, with chatty landlord, several Wadworths ales, decent wines and coffee, promptly served enjoyable food (all day Fri-Sun) from baguettes up, L-shaped bar with traditional mix of furniture on bare boards and carpet inc area with modern sofas and low tables; children and dogs welcome, outside seating at front and sides, lakeside bird reserve opposite, open all day *(Phil Bryant, David and Sue Smith)*

THREE MILE CROSS [SU7167]

Swan RG7 1AT [A33 just S of M4 junction 11; Basingstoke Rd]: Genuine welcome, reliable home-made pubby food inc good sandwiches, five well kept ales; originally a 17th-c posting house *(Peter Sampson)*

WALTHAM ST LAWRENCE [SU8376]

☆ *Bell* RG10 0JJ [B3024 E of Twyford; The Street]: Heavy-beamed and timbered village local with cheerful landlord and chatty regulars, good log fires, efficient service, good value pubby bar food (not Sun evening) from good sandwich range up inc interesting pizzas, small choice of main dishes (may ask to keep your credit card while you eat), well kept changing local ales such as Loddon and West Berkshire, plenty of malt whiskies, good wine, daily papers, compact panelled lounge; children and dogs welcome, tables in back garden with extended terrace, open all day wknds *(Tracey and Stephen Groves, Fred and Kate Portnell, LYM, Geoff and Teresa Salt, Paul Humphreys)*

Star RG10 0HY [Broadmoor Rd]: Friendly new licensees at this old pub with beams, brasses and open fire, good value standard food, real ales; nice secluded back garden *(Paul Humphreys)*

WARGRAVE [SU7878]

St George & Dragon RG10 8HY [High St]: Large smartly refurbished M&B dining pub with decking overlooking Thames, food from meze to traditional dishes (service can be slow) *(N B Vernon, Hunter and Christine Wright, Paul Humphreys)*

WEST ILSLEY [SU4782]

Harrow RG20 7AR [signed off A34 at E Ilsley slip road]: Appealing country pub in peaceful spot overlooking cricket pitch and pond, Victorian prints in deep-coloured knocked-through bar, some antique furnishings, log fire, Greene King ales, good choice of wines by the glass; children in eating areas, dogs allowed in bar, picnic-sets in big garden, more seats on pleasant terrace, cl Sun evening *(Henry Snell, Samantha McGahan, LYM)*

WICKHAM [SU3971]

Five Bells RG20 8HH [3 miles from M4 junction 14, via A338, B4000; Baydon Rd]: Welcoming thatched pub in racehorse-training country, Adnams and Fullers ales, good choice of reasonably priced wines, friendly licensees and good service, pubby food from nice baguettes up, flagstones and big log fire, stylish décor with some tables tucked into low eaves; children in eating part, informal garden with decking and play area, good value bedrooms, interesting church nearby with overhead elephants *(Paul Humphreys, LYM)*

WINDSOR [SU9676]

☆ *Carpenters Arms* SL4 1PB [Market St]: Town pub ambling around central servery with particularly well kept changing ales such as Everards, Harveys, Pilgrim and Sharps Doom Bar, good value pubby food all day from sandwiches up inc good range of pies, friendly helpful service (can be slow when busy), good choice of wines by the glass (and bargain bottles), sturdy pub furnishings and Victorian-style décor inc two pretty fireplaces, family areas up a few steps, also downstairs beside former tunnel entrance with suits of armour; piped music, no nearby parking; tables out on cobbled pedestrian alley opp castle, handy for Legoland bus stop, open all day *(Andy and Jill Kassube, Michael Dandy, David M Smith, N R White, BB, D J and P M Taylor)*

☆ *Two Brewers* SL4 1LB [Park St]: In the shadow of Windsor Castle with three compact unchanging bare-board rooms, well kept Fullers, Wadworths and Wells & Youngs ales, good choice of wines by the glass, enjoyable food (not wknd evenings), efficient friendly staff, thriving old-fashioned pub atmosphere, open fire, daily papers; piped music, no children inside; tables out by pretty Georgian street next to Windsor Park's Long Walk, open all day *(Michael Dandy, Ron and Sheila Corbett, Simon Collett-Jones, John Saville, Andy and Jill Kassube, Peter Barton, LYM)*

WINNERSH [SU7871]

☆ *Wheelwrights Arms* RG10 0TR [off A329 Reading—Wokingham at Winnersh crossroads by Sainsburys, signed Hurst, Twyford; then right into Davis Way]: Cheerfully bustling beamed local with enjoyable bargain food from huge lunchtime sandwiches up (may ask to keep a credit card while you eat), quick friendly service, Wadworths IPA, 6X and guest beers, good value wines, big woodburner, bare black boards and flagstones, cottagey dining area; children welcome, disabled parking and facilities,

picnic-sets in smallish garden with terrace, open all day wknds *(Paul Humphreys, BB, June and Robin Savage)*

WOKINGHAM [SU8268]

Three Frogs RG40 1SW [London Rd, nr A329]: New management so popular for their enjoyable pub food that you may have to book at busy times, separate eating area, good beers and wines – and they've restored a proper old-style inn sign *(D J and P M Taylor)*

WOODSIDE [SU9271]

Duke of Edinburgh SL4 2DP [Woodside Rd (narrow turn off A332 Windsor—Ascot S of B3034)]: Welcoming local with well kept Arkells beers, good choice of wines by the glass, friendly prompt service, sofas in roomy and civilised middle lounge, usual bar food from good range of proper sandwiches up, separate dining room, solidly furnished main regulars' bar; silent big-screen TVs, quiz night, darts; children welcome, tables out in front and in pleasant garden with summer marquee *(Peter Barton, E McCall, T McLean, D Irving)*

☆ *Rose & Crown* SL4 2DP [Woodside Rd, Winkfield, off A332 Ascot—Windsor]: Welcoming pub with low-beamed bar and extended dining area, good attentive service, enjoyable food (not Sun or Mon evening) using good ingredients from lunchtime sandwiches and baguettes to more elaborate evening restaurant dishes and popular Sun lunch, well kept Greene King ales, interesting affordable wines; piped music, games machine; children in eating areas, tables and swing in side garden backed by woodland, bedrooms, open all day, cl Sun evening *(LYM, Gerry and Rosemary Dobson)*

WOOLHAMPTON [SU5766]

Rowbarge RG7 5SH [Station Rd]: Big canalside pub now in Blubeckers chain, good if rather pricey fresh food all day, helpful friendly service, well kept West Berkshire ales, good log fire in neatly modernised beamed bar, panelled side room, large water-view conservatory; children welcome, tables out by water and in roomy garden *(LYM, N R White, Steve Culshaw, Bob and Laura Brock, Roy and Jean Russell, Charles and Pauline Stride)*

YATTENDON [SU5574]

☆ *Royal Oak* RG18 0UG [The Square; B4009 NE from Newbury; turn right at Hampstead Norreys, village signposted on left]: Appealing civilised old-world inn with panelled and prettily decorated brasserie/bar, good if pricey food (not Sun evening), nice log fire and striking flower arrangements, well kept West Berkshire beers, several wines by the glass, friendly unhurried service; well behaved children welcome, tables in lovely walled garden, more in front by peaceful village square, attractive bedrooms, open all day *(the Didler, Anne Morton, Graham and Toni Sanders, LYM, Dr and Mrs A K Clarke, Roy Hoing)*

Buckinghamshire

Plenty of choice here, from the resolutely traditional up to sophisticated places for fine dining – and with the lovely Chilterns you can be sure of some rewarding walks and country gardens. The fine-looking National Trust-owned Kings Head in Aylesbury is worth a visit for its well kept local Chiltern beers, as is the friendly White Horse at Hedgerley, truly traditional, with a healthy showcase of eight real ales, and well stocked beer festivals. Food worth going the extra mile for is to be found at the Royal Oak at Bovingdon Green, Mole & Chicken at Easington, and, with a new Food Award this year, in the Frog at Skirmett. With its nice country atmosphere and imaginative menu it's our Dining Pub of the Year. The warm and friendly Crown at Cuddington and Queens Head at Little Marlow (rather good food) are new entries this year, and three top Lucky Dips, inspected and approved by us, are the Nags Head in Great Missenden, Stag & Huntsman at Hambleden and Red Lion at Little Missenden. Rebellion is the county's top local brewery, with Vale and Chiltern popular too.

AYLESBURY   SP8113   MAP 4

Kings Head ◖

Kings Head Passage (narrow passage off Bourbon Street), also entrance off Temple Street; no nearby parking except for disabled; HP20 2RW

Handsome town centre pub with civilised atmosphere, good local ales (used in the food too) and friendly service

This rather special 15th-c building is owned by the National Trust, and comes as something of a surprise, tucked away as it is in a modern town centre. Its early Tudor windows are particularly beautiful and the former Great Hall has stunning 15th-c stained glass showing the Royal Arms of Henry VI and Margaret of Anjou. Three truly timeless rooms have been restored with careful and unpretentious simplicity – stripped boards, cream walls with little decoration, gentle lighting, a variety of seating which includes upholstered sofas and armchairs, cushioned high-backed settles and some simple modern pale dining tables and chairs dotted around. Most of the bar tables are of round glass, supported on low cask tops. It's all nicely low-key – not smart, but thoroughly civilised. The neat corner bar has Chiltern Ale, Beechwood Bitter, 300s Old Ale, a guest on handpump and some interesting bottled beers. Service is friendly and there's no piped music or machines; disabled access and facilities. The atmospheric medieval cobbled courtyard has teak seats and tables, some under cover of a pillared roof, and a second-hand bookshop. The pub comprises just one part of the building, with other parts given over to a coffee shop, Tourist Information Office, arts and crafts shop and conference rooms.

🍴 **A nice feature here is the handful of recipes that use beer as an ingredient – they've made sausages made with different ales, bacon and beer suet roll and even roast pineapple with a beer marmalade glaze for pudding. Other dishes (there's a gently historic touch to the entire menu) include sandwiches, ploughman's, roast vegetable pie, toad in the hole and railway lamb curry.** *Starters/Snacks: £4.10 to £7.00. Main Courses: £8.50 to £9.90. Puddings: £3.95*

Chiltern ~ Manager Neil Pickles ~ Real ale ~ Bar food (12-2(3 Sat), 6-9; not Sun-Tues evenings) ~ (01296) 718812 ~ Open 11-11; 12-10.30 Sun

Recommended by Roger Shipperley, Tim and Ann Newell, Tracey and Stephen Groves, Gordon Davico, Mr and Mrs A Hetherington, Ryta Lyndley

BENNETT END   SU7897   MAP 4

Three Horseshoes

Horseshoe Road; from Radnage follow unclassified road towards Princes Risborough and turn left into Bennett End Road, then right into Horseshoe Road; HP14 4EB

In lovely location with quite an emphasis on slightly elaborate meals

You can opt to sit in one of the small traditional rooms or in the more spacious modern restaurant at this nicely converted old country inn. To the left of the entrance (mind your head) is the flagstoned and darkly-lit snug bar with a log fire in the raised stone fireplace with original brickwork and bread oven. To the right of the entrance are two further sitting areas, one with a long wooden winged settle, and the other enclosed by standing timbers with wooden flooring and a woodburning stove. Big windows in the light and airy dining room overlook seats in the garden, a red telephone box endearingly half submerged in the middle of one of the duck ponds, and the valley beyond. Smartly uniformed staff are friendly and attentive, and drinks include Rebellion IPA and a guest beer on handpump, 13 wines by the glass, summer Pimms and winter mulled wine; piped music; more reports on the nice-looking bedrooms please.

Good (if not cheap) bar food at lunchtime might include sandwiches, french onion soup, seasonal game terrine with fig chutney, home-made burger, sausages with potato purée and grilled steak. The pricier evening menu might include thai crab cakes with mango salsa and pea shoots, sautéed rump of veal with lemon sauce and fried bass with chilli, garlic and ginger dressing, with puddings such as créme brûlée with vanilla poached pineapple and hot bitter chocolate fondant with pistachio ice-cream.
Starters/Snacks: £4.50 to £9.00. Main Courses: £9.50 to £17.50. Puddings: £5.75 to £7.00

Free house ~ Licensee Simon Crawshaw ~ Real ale ~ Bar food (12-2.30, 7-9.30; 12-4 Sun) ~ Restaurant ~ (01494) 483273 ~ Children welcome except Sat evening in dining room ~ Dogs welcome ~ Open 12-3, 6-11; 12-6 Sun; closed Sun evening, Mon and Tues after bank hol ~ Bedrooms: £80B/£120S(£110B)

Recommended by Howard Dell, Dick Vardy, Torrens Lyster, Kevin Thomas, Nina Randall, Roy Hoing, John Silverman

BOVINGDON GREEN   SU8386   MAP 2

Royal Oak 🍴 🍷

0.75 miles N of Marlow, on back road to Frieth signposted off West Street (A4155) in centre; SL7 2JF

Fantastic choice of european wines by glass and popular british food in jolly civilised pub

A relaxed but genuine welcome and attention to detail attracts a really good mix of customers to this civilised old pub. Several attractively decorated areas open off the central bar, the half-panelled walls variously painted in pale blue, green or cream: the cosiest part is the low-beamed room closest to the car park, with three small tables, a woodburner in an exposed brick fireplace, and a big pile of logs. Throughout there's a mix of church chairs, stripped wooden tables and chunky wall seats, with rugs on the partly wooden, partly flagstoned floors, co-ordinated cushions and curtains, and a very bright, airy feel; thoughtful extra touches enhance the tone: a big square bowl of olives on the bar, carefully laid out newspapers and fresh flowers or candles on the tables. Drinks include Brakspears Bitter, local Rebellion IPA and a guest such as Timothy Taylors Landlord on handpump, nearly two dozen wines by the glass (all european), nine pudding wines and a good choice of liqueurs; board games and piped music. A terrace with good solid tables leads to an appealing garden, and there's a smaller side garden; pétanque.

As far as cooking goes, the good quality ingredients here are carefully sourced and

served in tempting combinations. The menu may not be cheap but readers feel it's well worth the money. Dishes might include seared soused salmon fillet on horseradish potato salad with beetroot syrup, fried scallops and black pudding with cauliflower purée, coq au vin with sage and onion dumplings, battered pollack and hand-cut chips, ox cheek, red onion, potato and thyme pasty with stout roasting juices, roast pork chop with salt and pepper squid on sautéed chorizo, roast lamb on champ with roast shallot jus, herb-crusted sea trout on spiced tomato with olive couscous and properly hung rib-eye steak with béarnaise sauce, watercress and hand-cut chips. Puddings might be panettone bread and butter pudding with condensed milk ice-cream, rhubarb and rosehip trifle or roast mulled figs with wensleydale and oat biscuits. A good few tables may have reserved signs (it's worth booking ahead, especially on Sundays). *Starters/Snacks: £3.75 to £7.50. Main Courses: £11.25 to £16.75. Puddings: £4.25 to £6.75*

Salisbury Pubs ~ Lease James Penlington ~ Real ale ~ Bar food (12-2.30(3 Sat, 4 Sun), 6.30-9.30(10 Fri, Sat)-10) ~ Restaurant ~ (01628) 488611 ~ Children welcome ~ Dogs allowed in bar ~ Open 11-11; 12-10.30 Sun

Recommended by T R and B C Jenkins, Roger and Anne Newbury, Gary Ingram, Tracey and Stephen Groves, Simon Rodway, Michael Dandy, Lee Fathers, T A R Curran, M E and J R Hart, David Tindal, Andy Ingle

CHENIES   TQ0298   MAP 3

Red Lion ★ ◖

2 miles from M25 junction 18; A404 towards Amersham, then village signposted on right; Chesham Road; WD3 6ED

Delightful pub with long-serving licensees, a bustling atmosphere, and very well liked food; no children

The friendly licensee couple who've run this much loved village pub for over 20 years are delighted with their new dining room extension. With neat and modern décor, it forms quite a contrast with the very traditional, unpretentious L-shaped bar (no games machines or piped music) which has comfortable built-in wall benches by the front windows, other traditional seats and tables, and original photographs of the village and traction engines; there's also a small back snug. Well kept Lion Pride is brewed for the pub by Rebellion and served on handpump alongside Vale Best Bitter, Wadworths 6X and a guest, a dozen wines by the glass and some nice malt whiskies. The hanging baskets and window boxes are pretty in summer, there are picnic-sets on a small side terrace, and good local walks.

🍴 Food includes fish cake with horseradish and beetroot dip, chicken satay, pasta with bolognese, shortcrust lamb or steak and kidney pie, sausage and mash, chilli, roast pork belly with apple sauce and rump steak. *Starters/Snacks: £4.25 to £6.95. Main Courses: £6.50 to £13.95. Puddings: £3.95 to £4.50*

Free house ~ Licensee Mike Norris ~ Real ale ~ Bar food (12-2, 7-10(6.30–9.30 Sun)) ~ Restaurant ~ (01923) 282722 ~ Dogs allowed in bar ~ Open 11-2.30, 5.30-11; 12-3, 6.30-10.30 Sun

Recommended by Danielle and Simon, Roy Hoing, Howard Dell, Tracey and Stephen Groves, N R White, Charles Gysin, Mr and Mrs Paul Ridgeway, Tim Maddison, Sue Demont, Tim Barrow

CUDDINGTON   SP7311   MAP 4

Crown ◖

Village signposted off A418 Thame—Aylesbury; Spurt Street; HP18 0BB

Convivial low-beamed thatched cottage with inglenook bar and good dining area

Friendly staff bring warmth to the two very low-beamed linked rooms of the tiled-floor front bar, even when it's not the time of year to find a log fire burning in the big inglenook on the right. A Fullers pub, it has two Fullers beers and a guest such as Adnams on handpump, decent wines by the glass, and a comfortable mix of pubby furnishings including capacious housekeeper's chairs and cushioned settles. The carpeted back area, with dark red walls above its panelled dado, is also more or less divided into two rooms, with country-kitchen chairs around a nice variety of stripped or polished tables. It opens on to a neat side terrace with contemporary garden furniture and planters, and there are some picnic-sets under cocktail parasols out in front.

⚄ **Bar food includes starters such as tempura king prawns with wasabi butter, penne with meatballs and arrabiata, butternut and gorgonzola risotto with rocket pesto, fish and chips and mushy peas, confit duck leg with beetroot and orange salad, chargrilled mediterranean vegetables, chicken saltimbocca with sweet potato mash and rib-eye steak; Tuesday is fish night and Wednesday is pie and pudding night; Sunday roasts.** *Starters/Snacks: £4.50 to £8.95. Main Courses: £8.50 to £14.94. Puddings: £4.50 to £5.95*

Fullers ~ Tenants David and Heather Berry ~ Real ale ~ Bar food (till 3 Sun) ~ Restaurant ~ (01844) 292222 ~ Children welcome ~ Open 12-3, 6-11; 12-10.30 Sun
Recommended by Roger Edward-Jones

DORNEY   SU9279   MAP 2

Pineapple

2.4 miles from M4 junction 7; turn left on to A4, then left on B3026 (or take first left off A4 at traffic lights, into Huntercombe Lane S, then left at T junction on main road – shorter but slower); Lake End Road; SL4 6QS

Extraordinary choice of sandwiches in popular down-to-earth pub with cheery helpful staff

---

This nicely old-fashioned pub has shiny low Anaglypta ceilings, black-panelled dados and sturdy country tables – one very long and another in a big bow window. There's a woodburning stove at one end, a pretty little fireplace in a second room and china pineapples join other decorations on a set of shelves in one of three cottagey carpeted linked rooms on the left. It's bare boards on the right where the bar counter has Black Sheep Bitter, Fullers London Pride and Wells & Youngs Bombardier on handpump and several wines by the glass; friendly staff and piped music. A roadside verandah has some rustic tables, and there are plenty of round picnic-sets out in the garden, some on fairy-lit decking under an oak tree; the nearby motorway can be heard out here.

⚄ **A remarkable selection of up to 1,000 varieties of sandwiches in five different fresh breads that come with your choice of hearty vegetable soup, salad or chips, and run from cream cheese with beetroot, smoked salmon and cream cheese to chicken, avocado, crispy bacon and lettuce with honey and mustard dressing and spicy 'passage to India'. Their well liked Sunday roasts draw a crowd; they may ask you to leave your credit card behind the bar.** *Starters/Snacks: £6.95*

Punch ~ Lease Stuart Jones ~ Real ale ~ Bar food (12-9) ~ (01628) 662353 ~ Children welcome ~ Dogs welcome ~ Open 11-11; 12-10.30 Sun
Recommended by Priscilla Sandford, Dr and Mrs A K Clarke, Michael Dandy, Paul Humphreys, B J Harding, Piotr Chodzko-Zajko, LM

EASINGTON   SP6810   MAP 4

Mole & Chicken 🍴 🍷 🛏

From B4011 in Long Crendon follow Chearsley, Waddesdon signpost into Carters Lane opposite indian restaurant, then turn left into Chilton Road; HP18 9EY

Lovely views from deck and garden, inviting interior, good professional service and enjoyable food; nice bedrooms

---

The attractive raised terrace at this bustling old pub, with views over fine rolling countryside, is an idyllic place for a summer's lunch or sunset drink. Inside, the opened-up interior is arranged so that its different parts seem quite snug and self-contained without being cut off from the relaxed sociable atmosphere. The beamed bar curves around the serving counter in a sort of S-shape, and there are cream-cushioned chairs at oak and pine tables on flagstones, a couple of dark leather sofas, and fabric swatches stylishly hung as decorations on creamy walls, lit candles and good winter log fires. Drinks run from a thoughtful choice of wines, including a dozen by the glass, over

40 malt whiskies, and Hook Norton Bitter and a guest such as Vale Best beer on handpump; piped music.

🍴 Prepared using carefully sourced ingredients, the menu includes lunchtime snacks such as minute steak and onion bap, dry aged ham, egg and chips, indonesian stir fry and chicken and bacon caesar salad, and specials such as devilled kidneys on toast, fried herring roes with capers and parsley butter, crab and coriander cakes with aioli and sweet chilli, chilli fried squid, green pea risotto with a poached egg, battered fish, chicken and mushroom pie and 28-day dry-aged steak; good value two- and three-course menus at some times. *Starters/Snacks: £4.50 to £8.00. Main Courses: £6.00 to £10.00. Puddings: £5.00 to £5.00*

Free house ~ Licensees Alan Heather and Steve Bush ~ Real ale ~ Bar food (12-2.30(4 Sat), 6-9.30; 12-9 Sun) ~ Restaurant ~ (01844) 208387 ~ Children welcome ~ Dogs allowed in bar ~ Jazz last Sun of month ~ Open 12-3(4 Sat), 6-11; 12-10 Sun ~ Bedrooms: £70B/£95B

Recommended by Karen Eliot, Gordon Davico, M and GR, Rich Read, John Rodgers, Dennis and Doreen Haward, Felicity Davies

FINGEST   SU7791   MAP 2
Chequers
Village signposted off B482 Marlow—Stokenchurch; RG9 6QD

Friendly, spotlessly kept old pub with big garden and good reasonably priced food

The several neatly kept old-fashioned rooms at this convivial 15th-c place are warm, cosy and traditional, with large open fires, horsebrasses, pewter tankards, and pub team photographs on the walls: the friendly unaffected public bar has real rural charm. Brakspears Bitter and Oxford Gold, Wychwood Hobgoblin and a guest are served on handpump alongside a dozen wines by the glass, jugs of Pimms and several malt whiskies; board games. French doors from the smart back dining extension open to a terrace (plenty of picnic-sets), which leads on to the big garden with fine views over the Hambleden valley. Over the road is a unique Norman twin-roofed church tower – probably the nave of the original church. This is good walking country with quiet pastures sloping up to beechwoods and you can make your way on foot from here to other pubs in this chapter.

🍴 Enjoyable, honest bar food includes smoked salmon, ploughman's, chilli, rabbit pie, scampi, baked avocado with mushroom sauce, sweet chicken and pineapple curry and lamb cutlets and traditional puddings. *Starters/Snacks: £4.75 to £6.95. Main Courses: £7.95 to £14.75. Puddings: £4.95 to £5.95*

Brakspears ~ Tenants Ray Connelly and Christian Taubert ~ Real ale ~ Bar food (12-2, 6-9; not Mon evening) ~ Restaurant ~ (01491) 638335 ~ Children in eating area of bar ~ Dogs allowed in bar ~ Open 12-3, 6-11; 12-4 Sun; closed Sun evening

Recommended by Richard Endacott, the Didler, Noel Grundy, Anthony and Marie Lewis, Paul Humphreys, Andy and Jill Kassube, Martin and Karen Wake, Susan and John Douglas, Roy Hoing, Tracey and Stephen Groves, Howard Dell

FORTY GREEN   SU9291   MAP 2
Royal Standard of England 🍺
3.5 miles from M40 junction 2, via A40 to Beaconsfield, then follow sign to Forty Green, off B474 0.75 miles N of New Beaconsfield; keep going through village; HP9 1XT

Ancient place with fascinating antiques in rambling rooms and good choice of drinks

A genuinely historic pub, this old inn evolved from a Saxon dwelling into an alehouse, and has been trading for nearly 900 years – hopefully the welcome was as cheerily friendly in earlier days as it is now. Its rambling rooms have huge black ship's timbers, lovely worn floors, finely carved old oak panelling, roaring winter fires with handsomely decorated iron firebacks and cluttered mantelpieces, and there's a massive settle apparently built to fit the curved transom of an Elizabethan ship. Nooks and crannies are filled with a fascinating collection of antiques, including rifles, powder-flasks and bugles, ancient pewter and pottery tankards, lots of tarnished brass and copper, needlework samplers and richly coloured stained-glass. Bass, Brakspears, Chiltern Ale, Marstons Pedigree and Rebellion IPA and Mild and Theakstons are well kept on handpump, there's a great carefully annotated list of bottled beers and malt whiskies, farm ciders, perry, somerset brandy and around a dozen wines by the glass; shove-ha'penny. Seats outside in a neatly hedged front rose garden or under the shade of a tree; they may ask to hold your credit card.

🍴 **Bar food includes lunchtime sandwiches and ploughman's as well as onion soup, devilled lamb's kidneys on fried toast, charcuterie, moules marinière, mushroom and spinach lasagne, battered fish and chips, steak and kidney pudding, mutton shepherd's pie, pork belly with bubble and squeak, and puddings such as treacle tart or spotted dick; Sunday roasts.** *Starters/Snacks: £3.50 to £8.00. Main Courses: £4.50 to £17.95. Puddings: £4.00 to £5.50*

Free house ~ Licensee Matthew O'Keeffe ~ Real ale ~ Bar food (12-9.45(9 Sun)) ~ (01494) 673382 ~ Children welcome ~ Dogs welcome ~ Open 11-11(10.30 Sun)

Recommended by Anthony Longden, Paul Humphreys, Susan and John Douglas, Richard and Liz Thorne, D and M T Ayres-Regan, Dr and Mrs A K Clarke, the Didler, Roy Hoing, Tracey and Stephen Groves, Peter Martin, Howard Dell, John Silverman

GREAT KINGSHILL   SU8798   MAP 4

Red Lion ♀

A4128 N of High Wycombe; HP15 6EB

Carefully refurbished pub with contemporary décor, fairly priced brasserie-style pub food, local beers and friendly licensees

The cosy little bar at this thriving pub has brown leather sofas and armchairs, low tables and an open log fire. To its left, a spacious dining room has a contemporary brown colour scheme with modern paintings on striped brown wallpaper, candles on tables and some original flagstones. The dedicated licensees generate a good attentive attitude in their staff and the atmosphere is relaxed and comfortable; Rebellion IPA and seasonal Rebellion guest on handpump and a good wine list.

🍴 **As well as filled baguettes, good, brasserie-style food might include roast red pepper and tomato soup, charcuterie, mushroom risotto, oysters, sausage and mash, ploughman's and steak. The evening menu tends to be more elaborate, with dishes such as roast halibut with king scallops and bacon and lemon butter sauce, catalan chicken, squid and chorizo stew and saddle of venison with blackberry jus. Puddings might include bread and butter pudding and hazelnut meringue; two- and three-course lunchtime menu and tapas on Wednesday evening.** *Starters/Snacks: £4.50 to £9.00. Main Courses: £10.00 to £19.00. Puddings: £5.00*

Pubmaster ~ Managers Kim and Chris O'Brien ~ Real ale ~ Bar food (12-2.30, 6-9(9.30 Fri, Sat)) ~ Restaurant ~ (01494) 711262 ~ Well behaved children welcome ~ Open 12-3, 6-11 (may close earlier if quiet); 12-4 Sun; closed Sun evening, Mon

Recommended by Tracey and Stephen Groves

GROVE   SP9122   MAP 4

Grove Lock ♀ 🍺

Pub signed off B488, on left just S of A505 roundabout (S of Leighton Buzzard); LU7 0QU

By Grand Union Canal with plenty of room inside and lots of seats overlooking the water; open all day

The open-plan modern bar here has a lofty high-raftered pitched roof. It's warm and comfortable with terracotta and wallpapered walls, squishy brown leather sofas on diagonal oak floor boarding, an eclectic mix of tables and chairs, a couple of butcher's block tables by the bar, a big open-standing winter log fire and canal themed artwork. Steps take you up to the original lock-keeper's cottage (now a three-room restaurant area) which is partly flagstoned, has more winter log fires and looks down on the narrow canal lock. Friendly staff serve Fullers London Pride and a couple of Fullers seasonal beers from handpumps, and several wines by the glass; piped music and newspapers. There are plenty of seats and picnic-sets in the terraced waterside garden and on the canopied decking area overlooking the Grand Union Canal.

🍴 **Readers enjoy the food here, which includes sandwiches, toasties, breaded chicken caesar salad, chicken satay, burgers, sausage and mash, cod and chips, scampi, braised lamb shank with redcurrant and mint glaze, root vegetable curry, lots of summer salads and daily specials such as pork stroganoff and steak, mushroom and Guinness pie.** *Starters/Snacks: £3.95 to £5.95. Main Courses: £7.95 to £12.95. Puddings: £4.95*

Fullers ~ Managers Gregg and Angela Worrall ~ Real ale ~ Bar food (12-9(8 Sun)) ~ Restaurant ~ (01525) 380940 ~ Open 11-11; 12-10.30 Sun

Recommended by Chris Smith, Ross Balaam, Charles and Pauline Stride, Michael Dandy, Susan and John Douglas, Anthony and Marie Lewis

HADDENHAM   SP7408   MAP 4

Green Dragon ♀
Churchway; HP17 8AA

Neatly updated dining pub with modern pubby menu and pleasant garden

A shuttered cottage frontage with red brick trim and neat little window boxes belies the airy open-plan interior of this neatly modernised dining pub. An interesting mix of old tables and chairs and dark brown leather sofas contrasts with fresh white and cream walls. Areas of exposed flint wall and two log fires give a nod to tradition. Sharps Doom Bar and Timothy Taylors Landlord, a guest such as Courage, and over a dozen wines by the glass are served from a smart new dark wood counter, and lucky dogs may get a dog biscuit. Behind the pub, there's a big sheltered gravel terrace, and picnic-sets under cocktail parasols in an appealing garden. This part of the village is very pretty, with a duck pond unusually close to the church.

🍴 **Bar food includes a good choice of sandwiches and baguettes, chicken liver parfait with fig chutney and toasted brioche, crispy squid rings with chilli, lime and coriander, battered fish of the day with chunky chips, venison and wild mushroom suet pudding, bream fillet with braised fennel and red pepper coulis and 28-day-hung steak. Puddings include sticky toffee pudding with praline ice-cream and apple, raisin and cinnamon crumble.** *Starters/Snacks: £7.00 to £9.00. Main Courses: £8.50 to £16.95. Puddings: £6.00 to £8.00*

Enterprise ~ Lease John Phipps and Andrew Pritchard ~ Real ale ~ Bar food (12-2.30, 6.30-9.30) ~ (01844) 291403 ~ Children welcome ~ Dogs allowed in bar ~ Open 12-11(10.30 Sun)

Recommended by Nina Bell, Mike and Sue Richardson, Gordon Davico, John Branston

HAWRIDGE COMMON   SP9406   MAP 4

Full Moon ◀
Hawridge Common; left fork off A416 N of Chesham, then follow for 3.5 miles towards Cholesbury; HP5 2UH

Attractive country pub with half a dozen real ales and pubby food; plenty of nearby walks

If you arrive at this 18th-c pub on four hooves, you can hitch your horse in the paddock by the car park. The low-beamed little bar at the heart of the pub is very traditional, with ancient flagstones and checkered floor tiles, built-in floor-to-ceiling oak settles, hunting prints and an inglenook fireplace; piped music, cribbage and cards. They keep Adnams, Bass, Fullers London Pride, Timothy Taylors Landlord, and a couple of changing guest such as Brakspears and Hook Norton Old Hooky on handpump, and several wines by the glass. Historically, the pub was the traditional meeting place for the Lord of the Manor of Hawridge to hold court, mainly concerned with the use of the commons, especially grazing rights and enclosures. Today, there are lots of walks across the common, and on fine days there are views over fields and a windmill beyond from the pleasant garden and heated covered terrace.

⊞ **Popular bar food includes sandwiches, smoked fish platter, grilled goats cheese with pesto, sausage and mash, battered haddock, steak and kidney suet pudding and sirloin steak, with puddings such as apple pie and warm chocolate brownies. Daily specials might include seared scallops, seared calves liver with lardon gravy, cajun marinated pork chop with chilli sauce, chicken madras and grilled rib-eye steak.** *Starters/Snacks: £5.00 to £5.50. Main Courses: £9.95 to £15.00. Puddings: £5.00 to £5.25*

Enterprise ~ Lease Peter and Annie Alberto ~ Real ale ~ Bar food (12-2, 6.30-9(6-9 Sun)) ~ Restaurant ~ (01494) 758959 ~ Children welcome ~ Dogs welcome ~ Open 12-11(10.30 Sun)

Recommended by Tracey and Stephen Groves, Richard and Sissel Harris, Roy Hoing, Susan and John Douglas, Malcolm and Sue Scott, D J and P M Taylor

HEDGERLEY

SU9687 MAP 2

White Horse ★ ◀

2.4 miles from M40 junction 2; at exit roundabout take Slough turn-off then take Hedgerley Lane (immediate left) following alongside M40; after 1.5 miles turn right at T junction into Village Lane; SL2 3UY

Old-fashioned drinkers' pub with lots of beers tapped straight from the cask, regular beer festivals and a cheery mix of customers

This traditional gem of a country pub is something of a beer showcase. Greene King IPA, Rebellion IPA and at least five daily changing guests, sourced from all over the country, are tapped straight from casks kept in a room behind the tiny hatch counter, and their Easter, May, Spring and August bank holiday beer festivals (they can get through about 130 beers during the May one) are a highlight of the local calendar. This fine range of drinks extends to three farm ciders, still apple juice, a perry, belgian beers, ten or so wines by the glass and winter mulled wine. It's a happy welcoming place, with warm friendly service from the chatty staff and hardworking licensees. The cottagey main bar has plenty of unspoilt character, with lots of beams, brasses and exposed brickwork, low wooden tables, standing timbers, jugs, ballcocks and other bric-a-brac, a log fire, and a good few leaflets and notices about village events. A little flagstoned public bar on the left has darts and board games. A canopy extension leads out to the garden, which has tables and occasional barbecues. In front are lots of hanging baskets and a couple more tables overlooking the quiet road. There are good walks nearby, the pub is handy for the Church Wood RSPB reserve and is popular with walkers and cyclists, so it can get crowded at weekends.

⊞ **Lunchtime bar food such as sandwiches, ploughman's, cold meats and quiches, and changing straightforward hot dishes.** *Starters/Snacks: £5.00 to £7.00. Main Courses: £5.00 to £8.50. Puddings: £3.50*

Free house ~ Licensees Doris Hobbs and Kevin Brooker ~ Real ale ~ Bar food (lunchtime only) ~ (01753) 643225 ~ Children in canopy extension area ~ Dogs allowed in bar ~ Open 11-2.30, 5-11; 11-11 Sat; 12-10.30 Sun

Recommended by Anthony Longden, N R White, Mike and Eleanor Anderson, LM, the Didler, Susan and John Douglas, Roy Hoing, Stephen Moss, Piotr Chodzko-Zajko, Roger Shipperley

LACEY GREEN

SP8201 MAP 4

Pink & Lily ♀ ◀

From A4010 High Wycombe—Princes Risboro follow Loosley sign, then Gt Hampden, Gt Missenden one; HP27 ORJ

Good all-rounder with several real ales, good choice of wines, seasonal food and big garden

Framed on a wall is a Rupert Brooke poem (there's a room dedicated to him too) that begins with a mention of this now extended and modernised dining pub. The little tap room, however, has been well preserved, with built-in wall benches on the red flooring tiles, an old wooden ham-rack hanging from the ceiling and a broad inglenook with a low mantelpiece (there's always a fire in winter). The airy main bar has typical pub furniture, an open fire and some cosier side areas, and there's a conservatory-style extension with big arches decorated in various shades of brown, beige and cream. There's a relaxed happy atmosphere and staff are polite and friendly. Batemans and three changing guests such as Wells & Youngs Bombardier, Rebellion Smuggler and Vale Gravitas ensure a good variety of real ales, and they've also 27 wines by the glass including organic and Fairtrade ones; piped music, board games, dominoes and cribbage. The big garden has lots of wooden tables and seats.

🍴 **Good food includes sandwiches, filled ciabattas and hot open flat breads, ploughman's, smoked mackerel and beer rarebit on crostini, chorizo, chilli and chicken risotto, sausage and horseradish mash, oxtail casserole with carrot and swede mash, steak and ale pie, baked salmon with a herb crust with red pepper coulis, gruyère, pecan and red pesto bread and butter pudding and sirloin steak, as well as tempting daily specials such as tuna steak with pineapple and chilli salsa.** *Starters/Snacks: £4.50 to £6.25. Main Courses: £7.50 to £10.50. Puddings: £4.50*

Enterprise ~ Lease Shakira Englefield ~ Real ale ~ Bar food (12-2.30, 6.15-9(9.15 Fri, Sat); 12-8(4 winter) Sun) ~ Restaurant ~ (01494) 488308 ~ Children welcome ~ Dogs welcome ~ Open 11-11; 12-8(4 winter) Sun

Recommended by Roy Hoing, the Didler, Tracey and Stephen Groves, Chris Maunder, Mel Smith

LEY HILL   SP9901   MAP 4

Swan 🍺

Village signposted off A416 in Chesham; HP5 1UT

Charming, old-fashioned pub with chatty customers and decent food

It's worth wandering over the common (there's a cricket pitch and a nine-hole golf course here) opposite this little timbered 16th-c pub to turn back and take a look at the very pretty picture it makes with its picnic-sets amongst flower tubs and hanging baskets, (with more in the large back garden). Inside, the friendly licensees keep everything spic and span and the atmosphere is relaxed and chatty. The main bar is cosily old fashioned with black beams (mind your head) and standing timbers, an old range, a log fire, a nice mix of old furniture and a collection of old local photographs. Adnams, Brakspears, Fullers London Pride, Timothy Taylors Landlord and a guest such as St Austell Tribute are on handpump, with several wines by the glass. The dining area is light and airy with a raftered ceiling, cream walls and curtains and a mix old tables and chairs on timber floors.

🍴 **As well as lunchtime ciabatta sandwiches, the changing bar menu might include moules marinière, 21-day-hung sirloin steak sandwich, sausage, bubble and squeak, battered cod and chips, home-made burger and tagliatelle with chicken, chorizo and mushrooms. The pricier à la carte menu might include coq au vin, cod steak with scallop and paprika foam and pork belly with caramelised pear purée and red wine jus, with puddings such as apple and pear crumple, sticky toffee pudding with banana ice-cream and dark and white chocolate fondant and english cheeses.** *Starters/Snacks: £2.95 to £6.95. Main Courses: £8.50 to £10.50. Puddings: £4.95 to £5.95*

Punch ~ Lease Nigel Byatt ~ Real ale ~ Bar food (12-2.30(3 Sun), 7-9; not Sun or Mon evenings) ~ Restaurant ~ (01494) 783075 ~ Children welcome ~ Open 12-3, 5.30-11; 12-10.30 Sun

Recommended by Angela and Ray Seger, C R Cann, Roy Hoing, John and Elisabeth Cox

---

If a service charge is mentioned prominently on a menu or accommodation terms, you must pay it if service was satisfactory. If service is really bad you are legally entitled to refuse to pay some or all of the service charge as compensation for not getting the service you might reasonably have expected.

LITTLE MARLOW
SU8787 MAP 2

Queens Head

Village signposted off A4155 E of Marlow near Kings Head; bear right into Pound Lane cul de sac; SL7 3RZ

Charmingly tucked away, with enjoyable food and appealing garden

This pretty tiled cottage, in a quiet spot and covered with creepers in summer, strikes a nice balance between the style of an unpretentious country pub and the food quality of somewhere rather more ambitious. They have Brakspears and Fullers London Pride on handpump, quite a range of whiskies, good coffee, and the neatly dressed staff are efficient; unobtrusive piped music. The main bar, with a table of magazines by the door, and simple and comfortable pub furniture on its polished boards, leads back to a sizeable squarish carpeted dining extension, with good solid tables. Throughout are old local photographs on the cream or maroon walls, panelled dados painted brown or sage, and lit candles. On the right is a small quite separate low-ceilinged public bar. The garden, though not large, is a decided plus, sheltered and neatly planted, with some teak tables, some quite close-set picnic-sets, and some white-painted metal furniture in a little wickerwork bower.

🍴 Bar food includes snacks such as ploughman's, steak and mozzarella ciabatta, garlic and tarragon mushrooms on toasted brioche, starters such as watercress and spinach soup, fried scallops on honey-glazed pork belly, main courses such as pork chop with apple and onion hash and rib-eye steak, and puddings such as toffee crème brûlée with apple sorbet and rhubarb and vanilla cheesecake. *Starters/Snacks: £4.50 to £8.50. Main Courses: £9.95 to £15.95. Puddings: £4.95 to £5.50*

Punch ~ Licensees Daniel O'Sullivan and Chris Rising ~ Real ale ~ Bar food (12-2.30(4 Sat, Sun), 6.30-9.30) ~ Restaurant ~ (01628) 482927 ~ Children welcome ~ Dogs welcome ~ Open 12-11

Recommended by D J and P M Taylor, D and M T Ayres-Regan, Roger and Lesley Everett, Roy Hoing, Susan and John Douglas, Simon Collett-Jones

LITTLE MISSENDEN
SU9298 MAP 4

Crown 🍺 £

Crown Lane, SE end of village, which is signposted off A413 W of Amersham; HP7 0RD

Long-serving licensees and pubby feel in little brick cottage; attractive garden

With its new sympathetically constructed extension, this small brick cottage now feels a little more spacious. It's been in the same family for over 90 years and the friendly landlord proudly keeps it all spotless. A good mix of customers, including a loyal bunch of regulars, adds to the cheerfully chatty atmosphere. Adnams Bitter, Hook Norton Gold, St Austells Tribute, and a guest or two, such as Woodfordes Wherry on handpump or tapped from the cask, farm cider and several malt whiskies. It's all very traditional, with old red flooring tiles on the left, oak parquet on the right, built-in wall seats, studded red leatherette chairs, and a few small tables; darts and board games. The large attractive sheltered garden behind has picnic-sets and other tables; the interesting church in the pretty village is well worth a visit. We're curious to hear from readers who have stayed in the compact little bedrooms in the newly converted barn (continental breakfasts in your room only).

🍴 Straightforward bar food such as winter soup, good fresh sandwiches, buck's bite (a special home-made pizza-like dish), filled baked potatoes, ploughman's and steak and kidney pie. *Starters/Snacks: £3.50 to £4.75. Main Courses: £7.50 to £8.50*

Free house ~ Licensees Trevor and Carolyn How ~ Real ale ~ Bar food (lunchtime only, not Sun) ~ (01494) 862571 ~ Children over 12 allowed ~ Open 11-3, 6-11; 12-3, 7-11 Sun ~ Bedrooms: /£75S

Recommended by Anthony Longden, Tracey and Stephen Groves, Dr W I C Clark, Dick Vardy, N R White

PENN

SU9093   MAP 4

Old Queens Head ♀

Hammersley Lane/Church Road, off B474 between Penn and Tylers Green; HP10 8EY

Smartly updated pub with flourishing food side

Airy and open-plan, this reworked place is a stylish mix of contemporary and chintz. It has well spaced tables in a variety of linked areas, with a modicum of old prints, and comfortably varied seating on flagstones or broad dark boards. Stairs take you up to an attractive two-level dining room, part carpeted, with stripped rafters. The active bar side has Greene King IPA and Ruddles County on handpump, good fresh juices and nearly two dozen old-world wines by the glass. Once tired of the display behind the counter, the turntable-top bar stools let you swivel to face the log fire in the big nearby fireplace. The young staff are pleasant and efficient; lots of daily papers and well reproduced piped music. The L-shaped lawn, sheltered by shrubs, has picnic-sets, some under cocktail parasols; St Margaret's church is just across the quiet road.

🍴 Enjoyable modern food (not cheap) includes weekday lunchtime sandwiches, crispy squid with harissa and mint raita, bacon, egg, bubble and squeak and hollandaise sauce, pigeon and rabbit terrine with apple relish and toasted soda bread, fried duck breast on chilli and ginger pak choi with duck spring roll and hoisin, chestnut mushroom, brie and tomato tart with watercress and walnut pesto, gruyère and thyme-crusted haddock fillet on cauliflower and clam risotto and rib-eye steak; side orders extra. *Starters/Snacks: £3.75 to £7.00. Main Courses: £10.75 to £16.75. Puddings: £4.25 to £6.75*

Salisbury Pubs ~ Lease Becky and David Salisbury ~ Real ale ~ Bar food (12-2.30(3 Sat, 4 Sun), 6.30-9.30(10 Fri, Sat)) ~ Restaurant ~ (01494) 813371 ~ Children welcome ~ Dogs allowed in bar ~ Open 11-11; 12-10.30 Sun

Recommended by John Faircloth

PRESTWOOD

SP8799   MAP 4

Polecat

170 Wycombe Road (A4128 N of High Wycombe); HP16 0HJ

Enjoyable food and chatty atmosphere in several smallish civilised rooms; attractive sizeable garden

The slightly chintzy rooms at this well maintained place bestow the air of a smarter type of country pub. Several smallish rooms, opening off the low-ceilinged bar, have an assortment of tables and chairs, various stuffed birds, stuffed white polecats in one big cabinet, small country pictures, rugs on bare boards or red tiles, and a couple of antique housekeeper's chairs by a good open fire. Brakspears Bitter, Flowers IPA, Greene King Old Speckled Hen, and Marstons Pedigree on handpump, quite a few wines by the glass, and 20 malt whiskies; piped music. The garden is most attractive with lots of spring bulbs and colourful summer hanging baskets and tubs, and herbaceous plants; quite a few picnic-sets under parasols on neat grass out in front beneath a big fairy-lit pear tree, with more on a big well kept back lawn. They don't take bookings at lunchtime so you do need to arrive promptly at weekends to be sure of a table.

🍴 Tasty food includes lunchtime sandwiches and ploughman's, as well as smoked salmon terrine with lime crème fraîche, half a pint of shell-on prawns, home-made pies, seafood bake, beef bourguignon, chicken madras, bean and vegetable hot pot, sirloin steak, and puddings such as blueberry crème brûlée and profiteroles with chocolate sauce. Daily specials might include warm pigeon salad with raspberry dressing, herb-crusted bass fillets with lemon butter and chicken breast poached in pear and whisky. *Starters/Snacks: £4.10 to £5.40. Main Courses: £9.70 to £12.80. Puddings: £4.60*

Free house ~ Licensee John Gamble ~ Real ale ~ Bar food (12-2, 6.30-9 (not Sun evening)) ~ (01494) 862253 ~ Children welcome ~ Dogs welcome ~ Open 11.30-2.30, 6-11.30; 10-3 Sun; closed Sun evening

Recommended by Peter and Jan Humphreys, Ken Richards, Howard and Margaret Buchanan, Tracey and Stephen Groves, Gordon Davico, Roy Hoing, Howard Dell

SKIRMETT   SU7790   MAP 2

Frog ⊞ ♈ ⇔

From A4155 NE of Henley take Hambleden turn and keep on; or from B482 Stokenchurch—Marlow take Turville turn and keep on; RG9 6TG

BUCKINGHAMSHIRE DINING PUB OF THE YEAR

Bustling pub with popular modern cooking in traditional atmosphere, fine choice of drinks, lovely garden and nearby walks

Still very much retaining its feel as a country pub (once or twice a year they even have a sale of local game), the neatly kept beamed bars at this well run pub have been gently altered since the last edition of this *Guide*. It looks pleasing in its new chalky heritage colours, and emphasising what was already a special feature, the chimney breast around the striking hooded fireplace (with a bench around the edge, sofa and low table in front and a pile of logs sitting beside it) has been papered with newspaper sheets celebrating the year that the current licensees took over. A previously little-used room, with a huge feature pewter-framed mirror, has recently been incorporated into the bar. A mix of comfortable old furnishings on nice old wooden floors keep it all feeling as friendly and relaxing as ever; piped music. Rebellion IPA, Sharps Doom Bar and a guest are on handpump, with a dozen wines by the glass (including champagne), and about two dozen carefully sourced malt whiskies. A side gate leads to a lovely garden with a large tree in the middle, and the unusual five-sided tables are well placed for attractive valley views. There are plenty of nearby hikes (Henley is close by) and just down the road is the delightful Ibstone windmill. There's a purpose-built outdoor heated area for smokers. The breakfasts are very good.

⊞ **Imaginative and reliably enjoyable food includes tasty sausage and onion baguette, warm potato rösti with black pudding, smoked salmon and a poached egg, grilled goats cheese and poached pear bruschetta, fried hake with sweet pepper sauce, roast veal chop with tarragon sauce, steamed guinea fowl breast with calvados and lime with confit leg, mushroom and asparagus lasagne and grilled rump steak, daily specials such as mussels in red thai sauce and battered haddock and chips, and puddings such as chocolate nut brownies, banoffi pie and knickerbocker glory. Coffee is good and comes with delicious shortbread.** *Starters/Snacks: £4.95 to £6.95. Main Courses: £11.50 to £16.50. Puddings: £5.50*

Free house ~ Licensees Jim Crowe and Noelle Greene ~ Real ale ~ Bar food (12-3, 6.30-9.30) ~ Restaurant ~ (01491) 638996 ~ Children welcome ~ Dogs allowed in bar ~ Open 11.30-3, 6-11; 12-10.30 Sun; closed Sun evening Oct-April ~ Bedrooms: £60B/£80B

Recommended by Mike and Sue Richardson, Fred and Kate Portnell, Tracey and Stephen Groves, Richard and Liz Thorne, Andy and Jill Kassube, T R and B C Jenkins, Mark Farrington, Martin and Karen Wake, Noel Grundy, Paul Humphreys, Michael Dandy

TURVILLE   SU7691   MAP 2

Bull & Butcher ♈

off A4155 Henley—Marlow via Hambleden and Skirmett; RG9 6QU

Traditional beamed pub with inglenooks and big garden, lovely Chilterns village

A stone's throw from the Chilterns Way in a particularly pretty village (it's popular with television and film companies), this black-and-white pub can get very full at weekends. Its two traditional low-ceilinged, oak-beamed rooms both have inglenook fireplaces, and the bar, with cushioned wall settles and a tiled floor, has a deep well incorporated into a glass-topped table. On warm summer days, a gentle breeze drifts in through the half-open stable half-door. Brakspears Bitter, Oxford Gold and Hook Norton Hooky Dark and a seasonal Brakspears beer are on handpump, alongside Addlestone's cider and 16 wines by the glass; piped music and TV. There are seats on the lawn by fruit trees in the attractive garden, and plenty of walks from here in the lovely Chilterns valley.

🍴 **Bar food includes soup, chicken liver parfait with onion jam, ploughman's, beer-battered cod with mushy peas, a pie of the day, vegetable hotpot, bangers and mash and pork fillet with mustard crust.** *Starters/Snacks: £5.95 to £7.95. Main Courses: £10.95 to £18.95. Puddings: £4.95*

Brakspears ~ Tenant Lydia Botha ~ Real ale ~ Bar food (12-2.30(4 Sat, Sun and bank hol Mon), 6.30(6 Sat, 7 Sun)-9.30; not bank hol evenings) ~ (01491) 638283 ~ Children welcome but not in bar ~ Dogs welcome ~ Live music monthly ~ Open 11(12 Sun)-11

Recommended by Ross Balaam, Gordon Davico, Tracey and Stephen Groves, Anthony and Pam Stamer, Andy and Jill Kassube, Susan and John Douglas, Mark Farrington, Martin and Karen Wake, Laurence Smith, Tim Maddison

WOOBURN COMMON   SU9187   MAP 2

Chequers

From A4094 N of Maidenhead at junction with A4155 Marlow road keep on A4094 for another 0.75 miles, then at roundabout turn off right towards Wooburn Common, and into Kiln Lane; if you find yourself in Honey Hill, Hedsor, turn left into Kiln Lane at the top of the hill; OS Sheet 175 map reference 910870; HP10 0JQ

Busy hotel with bustling bar and restaurant

The friendly bar at the heart of this busy hotel and restaurant continues to thrive as a welcoming local. It feels nicely pubby, with low beams, standing timbers and alcoves, characterful rickety furniture and comfortably lived-in sofas on bare boards, a bright log-effect gas fire, pictures, plates, a two-man saw and tankards. In contrast, the bar to the left, with its dark brown leather sofas at low tables on new wood floors, feels cool and modern. They have a good sizeable wine list (with a dozen by the glass including a good rioja), a fair range of malt whiskies and brandies, and well kept Greene King IPA, Old Speckled Hen and Rebellion Smuggler on handpump. The piped music can be a bit loud. The spacious garden, set away from the road, has cast-iron tables.

🍴 **As well as an extensive choice of sandwiches and ciabattas, the good pubby bar menu includes grilled pork chop with mash and apple sauce, panzanella salad, pea and prawn risotto, battered haddock and chips, chicken curry, chilli, fish of the day, rib-eye steak, and puddings such as apple and pear crumble, banana eton mess and spotted dick and custard.** *Starters/Snacks: £3.95 to £8.95. Main Courses: £8.95 to £16.95. Puddings: £4.50 to £5.25*

Free house ~ Licensee Peter Roehrig ~ Real ale ~ Bar food (12-2.30, 6.30-9.30(10 Sun); 12-10(9.30 Sun) Sat) ~ Restaurant ~ (01628) 529575 ~ Children welcome ~ Open 11-12.30(midnight Sun) ~ Bedrooms: £99.50B/£107.50B

Recommended by Peter and Giff Bennett, Tracey and Stephen Groves, Roy Hoing, Stewart Bingham

LUCKY DIP

Besides the fully inspected pubs, you might like to try these Lucky Dips recommended to us and described by readers (if you do, please send us reports: feedback@goodguides.com).

ADSTOCK [SP7229]
Folly MK18 2HS [A413 SE of Buckingham]: Dining tables in roomy L-shaped beamed bar, nice light furniture in bright and airy further dining area, wide choice of enjoyable food from baguettes and baked potatoes to tempting puddings, Greene King IPA and Shepherd Neame Spitfire, quick friendly service; good play area in good-sized garden with fruit and other trees, bedrooms in separate back block *(George Atkinson)*
AMERSHAM [SU9597]
Crown HP7 0DH [Market Sq]: Spotless modernised hotel bar, leather, polished wood

and beams, interesting 16th-c features in comfortable lounge, pleasant formal dining area, enjoyable food from sandwiches to some interesting dishes, young helpful staff, Bass, good range of wines by the glass; attractive split-level outside area inc cobbled courtyard, bedrooms *(BB, Phyl and Jack Street, Michael Dandy)*
Eagle HP7 0DY [High St]: Rambling low-beamed pub with enjoyable wholesome food inc good puddings, quick friendly service, Adnams and Fullers London Pride, good choice of wines by the glass, log fire, simple décor with a few old prints, pub games; pleasant streamside walled back garden,

hanging baskets *(Michael Dandy, Peter and Giff Bennett)*

ASKETT [SP8105]

☆ *Three Crowns* HP27 9LT: Reopened under good landlord, wide food choice, beamed and boarded dining rooms either side of small bar, fresh modern décor, comfortable leather chairs *(Peter and Jan Humphreys)*

AYLESBURY [SP8114]

Hop Pole HP19 9AZ [Bicester Rd]: Open-plan pub tied to Vale, their ales and lots of guest beers, good value food; open all day *(Roger Shipperley)*

BEACHAMPTON [SP7736]

Bell MK19 6DX [Main St]: Good choice of ales inc local ones in big beamed pub with pleasant view down attractive streamside village street, log fire dividing bar from lounge and attractive dining area, nice range of home-made pubby food, friendly service, pool in small separate games room; piped music; open all day, terrace and play area in big garden *(George Atkinson)*

BEACONSFIELD [SU9490]

Royal Saracens HP9 2JH [a mile from M40 junction 2; London End (A40)]: Striking timbered façade, well updated open-plan layout, comfortable chairs around light wood tables, massive beams and timbers in one corner, good atmosphere, welcoming helpful young staff, wide choice of enjoyable food inc shared dishes and bargain meals, well kept ales such as Timothy Taylors Landlord, quite a few wines by the glass; attractive sheltered courtyard *(Keith and Ann Arnold, LYM)*

BLEDLOW [SP7702]

Lions of Bledlow HP27 9PE [off B4009 Chinnor—Princes Risboro; Church End]: Great views from bay windows of relaxed take-us-as-you-find-us Chilterns pub with low 16th-c beams, ancient floor tiles, inglenook log fires and a woodburner, real ales such as Marlow Rebellion and Wadworths 6X, bar food from sandwiches up, helpful service, games room; well behaved children allowed, picnic-sets out in peaceful sloping garden with sheltered terrace, nice setting, good walks *(LYM, the Didler, Susan and John Douglas, Paul Humphreys, Mel Smith)*

BRADENHAM [SU8297]

☆ *Red Lion* HP14 4HF [by Walters Ash turn off A4010]: Charming, neatly kept and nicely furnished, with friendly landlord, several well kept ales and enjoyable pubby food from good choice of baguettes up, simple carpeted bar one side, good-sized smarter cheerfully tiled dining room the other, unspoilt NT village; no under-10s; cl Mon lunchtime *(Alan and Anne Driver, Guy Charrison, Ross Balaam)*

BRILL [SP6514]

Pheasant HP18 9TG [off B4011 Bicester—Long Crendon; Windmill St]: Simply furnished beamed pub in marvellous spot looking over to ancient working windmill, nearby view over nine counties, good food,

polite helpful service, well kept local Vale ales, good value house wines, attractive dining room up a step; piped music, no dogs; children welcome, verandah tables, superior picnic-sets in garden with decking, bedrooms, open all day wknds *(Ross Balaam, LYM)*

BURROUGHS GROVE [SU8589]

Three Horseshoes SL7 3RA [Wycombe Rd (back rd Marlow—High Wycombe)]: Long deep former coaching inn doing well under Marlow Brewery, full range of their good ales, wide choice of largely eastern food, smart efficient staff, comfortable traditional furnishings on several levels *(Tracey and Stephen Groves)*

CADMORE END [SU7793]

Blue Flag HP14 3PF [B482 towards Stokenchurch]: Comfortable beamed bar (civilised atmosphere influenced by separate modern hotel wing), well kept ales and decent wines, enjoyable good value food, lots of proper big dining tables, attractive little restaurant; some motorway noise; 14 bedrooms *(BB, Roy Hoing)*

Old Ship HP14 3PN [B482 Stokenchurch—Marlow (Marlow Road)]: Tiny, carefully restored old cottage with newish licensees, two little low-beamed rooms separated by standing timbers, simple furnishings (one chair still has a hole for game called five-farthings), coal fire, Black Sheep, Sharps Doom Bar and Youngs tapped straight from the cask down in cellar, wines by glass, bassett hound and great dane; children and dogs welcome, cl Sun evening and Mon, seats in sheltered garden and on terrace; parking on other side of road *(the Didler, Mark Farrington, Pete Baker, LYM)*

CADSDEN [SP8204]

Plough HP27 0NB [Cadsden Rd]: Welcoming recently extended pub with airy open-plan bar/dining area, well spaced tables on wood floor, very popular with families and Chilterns ramblers, well kept Greene King ales, good attractively presented inexpensive food from sandwiches up, friendly service; lots of tables in delightful quiet front and back garden, pretty spot on Ridgeway Path, bedrooms, open all day wknds *(Paul Humphreys, Torrens Lyster, Roy Hoing)*

CHALFONT ST GILES [SU9893]

Fox & Hounds HP8 4PS [Silver Hill]: Small quietly set 16th-c local with well kept St Austell Tribute, limited choice of good value lunchtime food (not Sun), open fire in simple unspoilt interior, darts and pool; pleasant garden behind with play area *(R K Phillips)*

☆ *Ivy House* HP8 4RS [A413 S]: Open-plan dining pub now tied to Fullers, their ales include Gales, good if not cheap food, friendly young staff, good wines by the glass, espresso coffee, comfortable fireside armchairs in carefully lit and elegantly cosy L-shaped tiled bar, lighter flagstoned dining extension; pleasant terrace and sloping garden (can be traffic noise), five bedrooms

(Roy Hoing, BB)

☆ **White Hart** HP8 4LP [Three Households, Main St]: Bustling place under new management, emphasis on imaginative if pricey food, four Greene King beers, several wines by the glass, modern furnishings in bar and bare-boards dining room; piped music; well behaved children welcome, dogs in bar, picnic-sets on sheltered back terrace and in garden beyond, 11 barn bedrooms, open all day Sun *(Kevin Thomas, Nina Randall, LYM, Roy Hoing, Phyl and Jack Street)*

CHEARSLEY [SP7110]

☆ **Bell** HP18 0DJ [The Green]: Traditional cosy beamed pub on attractive village green, Fullers Chiswick, London Pride and seasonal brews, good wines by the glass, bar food from sandwiches up, fast friendly service, enormous fireplace, cribbage, dominoes; children in eating area, dogs welcome, plenty of tables in spacious back garden, terrace and attractive play area *(David Lamb, LYM)*

CHEDDINGTON [SP9217]

Old Swan LU7 0RQ [off B488 N of Tring; High St]: Pretty low-beamed open-plan thatched pub with friendly landlady and staff, well kept Greene King and Wells & Youngs ales, good home-made food, restaurant; children welcome, garden with enclosed play area *(Ross Balaam, LYM)*

CHESHAM [SP9604]

Black Horse HP5 3NS [Vale Rd, N off A416 in Chesham]: Neatly extended popular black-beamed country pub with good choice of enjoyable food inc OAP lunch Weds, real ales, decent wines, good service; tables on back grass *(LYM, Roy Hoing, Joan Baillie)*

CHICHELEY [SP9045]

☆ **Chester Arms** MK16 9JE [quite handy for M1 junction 14]: Cosy and pretty, with low-beamed rooms off semicircular bar, log fire, comfortable settles and chairs, helpful friendly service, wide choice of good popular home-made meals, children's helpings, Greene King ales, decent wines, good coffee, daily papers, interesting back dining room down steps; picnic-sets in small back garden and out in front *(Michael Dandy, BB)*

CLIFTON REYNES [SP9051]

☆ **Robin Hood** MK46 5DR [off back rd Emberton—Newton Blossomville; no through road]: Unpretentious stone-built 16th-c village pub, dark beams, woodburner in small lounge's inglenook, welcoming licensees, he cooks well doing some interesting dishes and good value Sun roasts, Greene King and rotating guests, Weston's farm ciders, lots of *Robin Hood* film stills, dining conservatory, table skittles in simple public bar; plenty of tables in big garden with heated terrace, riverside walks to Olney, cl Mon *(BB, Colin and Janet Roe)*

COLESHILL [SU9594]

Mulberry Bush HP7 0LU [Magpie Lane/A355]: This modern roadside dining pub has been acquired by the owner of the Royal Standard of England at Forty Green (see Main Entry section); refurbishment is planned and the pub may change its name to the Harte & Magpie; news please *(Michael Dandy)*

☆ **Red Lion** HP7 0LH [Village Rd]: Small well worn-in popular local with helpful welcoming long-serving licensees, wide choice of good value pubby food (not Sun evening) from sandwiches up, Vale Wychert and guest ales, quick service, two open fires, thriving darts and dominoes teams; TV for racing, games machine; front and back gardens, sturdy climbing frames, good walks, open all day wknds *(N R White, BB, Roy Hoing)*

COLNBROOK [TQ0277]

Ostrich SL3 0JZ [1.25 miles from M4 junction 5 via A4/B3378, then 'village only' rd; High St]: Spectacular timbered Elizabethan building (with even longer gruesome history), recently given contemporary makeover with comfortable sofas on stripped wood and a startling red plastic and stainless-steel bar counter, real ales such as Courage Directors, Fullers London Pride and Greene King Old Speckled Hen, efficient friendly service, good upscale food and restaurant – bar serving largely as ante-room for diners; soft piped music, music and comedy nights upstairs *(LYM, A Darroch Harkness)*

DENHAM [TQ0487]

Falcon UB9 5BE [Village Rd]: Cheery open-plan local, several well kept ales, good food, bare boards and quarry tiles, old painted woodwork, coal-effect gas fires with inglenook fireside seats below ancient cupboards, lower back dining area, interesting history of Denham; sports TV; teak tables out on terrace, comfortable new character bedrooms *(Graham and Glenis Watkins, Kevin Thomas, Nina Randall, Simon Rodway)*

☆ **Swan** UB9 5BH [village signed from M25 exit 16]: Civilised dining pub in lovely village, interesting well presented food (not Sun, Mon evenings), Courage Best, Rebellion IPA and Wadworths 6X, good wine choice, stylish mix of old chairs and solid tables, heavily draped curtains, open fires, fresh flowers, daily papers; piped music; children welcome, extensive floodlit garden with sheltered terrace, open all day Sun *(John Silverman, Richard and Sissel Harris, Mrs Margo Finlay, Jörg Kasprowski, Evelyn and Derek Walter, Susan and John Douglas, LYM, Kevin Thomas, Nina Randall)*

DINTON [SP7610]

Seven Stars HP17 8UL [signed off A418 Aylesbury—Thame, nr Gibraltar turn-off; Stars Lane]: Pretty pub with inglenook bar, comfortable beamed lounge and spacious dining room, real ales such as Fullers London Pride, good choice of food inc set deals, friendly service; tables under cocktail parasols in sheltered garden with terrace, pleasant village *(LYM, David Lamb)*

DORNEY [SU9279]
☆ *Palmer Arms* SL4 6QW [2.7 miles from M4 junction 7, via B3026; Village Rd]: New owners at this smartly modernised extended dining pub in attractive conservation village – reports please; all-day fresh food from pub favourites to more elaborate things using local produce, lots of wines by the glass, Greene King ales, open fires, daily papers, civilised front bar, elegant back dining room; soft piped music; children welcome, dogs in certain areas, disabled facilities, stylish terrace overlooking mediterranean-feel garden, enclosed play area, open all day *(Dr and Mrs A K Clarke, LYM, Peter Price, Michael Dandy)*

EVERSHOLT [SP9832]
Green Man MK17 9DU [Church End]: Contemporary refurbishment of early Victorian country pub with emphasis on eating (but keeping local feel), new furniture on wood floors, enjoyable sensibly priced food inc blackboard specials, Fullers ales, good service; dogs welcome, big terrace, picturesque village *(Alexandra Upton, Gill and Keith Croxton)*

FLACKWELL HEATH [SU8889]
Crooked Billet SL7 3SG [off A404; Sheepridge Lane]: Cosily old-fashioned 16th-c pub with lovely views (beyond road) from suntrap front garden, low beams, good choice of reasonably priced food, eating area spread pleasantly through alcoves, prompt friendly service, well kept Brakspears, good open fire *(BB, Roy Hoing)*

FRIETH [SU7990]
Prince Albert RG9 6PY [off B482 SW of High Wycombe]: Friendly cottagey Chilterns local with low black beams and joists, high-backed settles, big black stove in inglenook, log fire in larger area on the right, food (mainly lunchtime) from sandwiches up, well kept Wychwoods Hobgoblin; children and dogs welcome (resident friendly black lab), nicely planted informal side garden with views of woods and fields, open all day *(R K Phillips, Ross Balaam, Paul Humphreys, the Didler, Pete Baker, LYM, Noel Grundy)*

GREAT HAMPDEN [SP8401]
☆ *Hampden Arms* HP16 9RQ [off A4010 N and S of Princes Risborough]: Nicely placed dining pub opp village cricket pitch, reasonably priced food made by landlord from lunchtime sandwiches to substantial main dishes, friendly service, Adnams, a seasonal Vale ale and Addlestone's cider from small corner bar, good choice of wines by the glass, big woodburner in more spacious back room; children and dogs welcome, nice tree-sheltered garden, good walks nearby *(LYM, Mel Smith, John and Eileen Kent, Roy Hoing)*

GREAT MISSENDEN [SP8901]
☆ *Cross Keys* HP16 0AU [High St]: New licensees at this relaxed village pub, unspoilt beamed bar divided by standing timbers, traditional furnishings inc high-backed

settle, log-effect gas fire in huge fireplace, well kept Fullers ales, decent food from sandwiches up inc Sun roasts, spacious beamed restaurant, cheerful helpful staff; children and dogs welcome, back terrace with picnic-sets, smokers' shelter planned, open all day *(Jill Bickerton, N R White, Roy Hoing, LYM)*

☆ *Nags Head* HP16 0DG [old London rd; E – beyond Abbey]: Civilised and neatly revamped by licensees of Bricklayers Arms, Flaunden (see Herts section), similar good if pricey food using local produce and own smoked fish and meat, Black Sheep, Fullers London Pride and Timothy Taylors Landlord, good armagnac range and wines by the glass, unusual bar counter (windows behind face road), carpet throughout, low beams on left, loftier on right, log fire, relaxed atmosphere, Roald Dahl links; garden picnic-sets, seven comfortably redone bedrooms, open all day *(Kevin Thomas, Nina Randall, BB, Mrs Shirley Hughes)*

HAMBLEDEN [SU7886]
☆ *Stag & Huntsman* RG9 6RP [off A4155 Henley—Marlow]: Unchanging handsome brick and flint pub in pretty Chilterns village, congenial old-fashioned front public bar with masses of beer mats, big fireplace in low-ceilinged partly panelled lounge bar, Loddon Hoppit, Rebellion IPA, Wadworths 6X and a guest beer, farm cider and good wines, friendly efficient staff, good reasonably priced pubby food (not Sun evening winter), secluded dining room, traditional games; darts, TV, piped music; children welcome, dogs in bar, good garden with some raised areas and decking, nice walks, bedrooms; refurbishments planned, when there will be a very limited service *(Ross Balaam, LYM, Roy Hoing, Susan and John Douglas, Michael Dandy, John Saul, Anthony Longden, Klaus and Elizabeth Leist)*

HAWRIDGE [SP9505]
☆ *Rose & Crown* HP5 2UG [signed from A416 N of Chesham; The Vale]: Roomy open-plan pub dating from 18th c, good value home-made food from sandwiches up (popular lunchtime with OAPs), well kept Fullers London Pride and guest beers, good cider, big log fire, peaceful country views from upper restaurant area; children welcome, broad terrace with lawn dropping down beyond, play area, open all day wknds *(Roy Hoing, LYM)*

HIGH WYCOMBE []
Turnpike HP12 4RQ [New Rd]: Big modern pub with friendly attentive staff, good value bar food, decent beers *(Stan Edwards)*

HYDE HEATH [SU9300]
Plough HP6 5RW [off B485 Great Missenden—Chesham]: Prettily placed pub overlooking village green, good value food in bar and evening restaurant extension, friendly landlord, real ales such as Adnams, Fullers London Pride and Wells & Youngs, open fires *(LYM, Roy Hoing)*

ICKFORD [SP6407]
Rising Sun HP18 9JD [E of Thame; Worminghall Rd]: Carefully restored pretty thatched local, cosy low-beamed bar, friendly staff and locals, good value food made to order, real ales such as Black Sheep *(David Lamb)*

LACEY GREEN [SP8100]
Whip HP27 0PG [Pink Rd]: Cheery and attractive local welcoming walkers, mix of simple traditional furnishings in smallish front bar and larger downstairs dining area, reliable food from good lunchtime soup and sandwiches to generous Sun lunches, five well kept quickly changing ales inc local Chiltern, Oct beer festival with jazz, copious coffee, friendly service; fruit machine, TV; tables in sheltered garden looking up to windmill *(Tracey and Stephen Groves, BB)*

LAVENDON [SP9153]
Green Man MK46 4HA [A428 Bedford—Northampton]: Handsome 17th-c thatched pub in pretty village, friendly attentive staff, good value food from soup and sandwiches up, Greene King ales, good choice of wines by the glass, good coffee, roomy and relaxed open-plan wood-floored area with two raised sections, beams, lots of stripped stone and open woodburner, big carpeted evening/wknd restaurant; piped music; children welcome, tables and heaters outside, open all day *(George Atkinson, Michael Dandy, Bruce and Sharon Eden)*
☆ *Horseshoe* MK46 4HA [A428 Bedford—Northampton; High St]: Immaculate low-beamed village pub with log fire and plush banquettes, airy dining extension, enjoyable food from baguettes to great range of fish (ex-fisherman landlord), Fullers ESB and Wells & Youngs Eagle, good value small but interesting wine list, quick cheerful service, skittles in public bar, steps between levels; piped music; appealing good-sized garden behind with terrace, decking and play area, cl Sun evening *(Jack Pridding, BB, Colin and Janet Roe, George Atkinson)*

LEDBURN [SP9022]
Hare & Hounds LU7 0QB [off B488 Ivinghoe—Leighton Buzzard, S of Linslade]: Country-style bar and back dining area, wide choice of reasonably priced food, Greene King and guest ales, quick friendly down-to-earth service even when busy, Great Train Robbery memorabilia; pleasant back garden, handy for Ascott (NT) *(David Lamb)*

LITTLE HAMPDEN [SP8503]
☆ *Rising Sun* HP16 9PS [off A4128 or A413 NW of Gt Missenden; OS Sheet 165 map ref 856040]: Comfortable beamed dining pub in delightful out-of-the-way setting, opened-up bar with woodburner and log fire, good honest reliable food inc popular Sun lunch (can be busy wknds), friendly service, Adnams and Shepherd Neame Spitfire, good short wine list, winter mulled wine and spiced cider; piped music; terrace tables, lovely walks (walkers welcome), appealing bedrooms, cl Sun evening and Mon

(John Faircloth, Piotr Chodzko-Zajko, Roy Hoing, LYM)

LITTLE KINGSHILL [SU8999]
Full Moon HP16 0EE [Hare Lane]: Picturesque country pub with friendly staff, enjoyable generous pub food, Adnams, Fullers London Pride and Wells & Youngs, good choice of wines by the glass, pleasantly traditional beamed bar with open fire, bigger carpeted dining room, some Carry On memorabilia, buoyant atmosphere evenings and wknds; neat attractive garden *(Roy Hoing, Mike and Eleanor Anderson)*

LITTLE MARLOW [SU8788]
☆ *Kings Head* SL7 3RZ [A4155 about 2 miles E of Marlow; Church Rd]: Long flower-covered pub with open-plan low-beamed bar, wide blackboard choice of enjoyable food from plenty of sandwiches to popular Sun roasts, smart dining room, Adnams Broadside, Fullers London Pride and Timothy Taylors Landlord, quick cheerful service even though busy, log or coal fires, Sun bar nibbles, cricket memorabilia; children welcome; big attractive walled garden behind popular with families *(D and M T Ayres-Regan, Chris Glasson, Paul Humphreys, BB, Roy Hoing)*

LITTLE MISSENDEN [SU9298]
☆ *Red Lion* HP7 0QZ: Small two-room 15th-c local reopened after restoration of fire damage, still charmingly unpretentious, with coal fires, friendly retriever, well kept Marstons Pedigree, Greene King IPA and Wadworths 6X, decent wines, generous good value standard food inc nice fairly priced proper sandwiches, occasional piano singalongs; tables and busy aviary in sunny side garden by river with ducks, swans and fat trout *(Roy Hoing, Susan and John Douglas, Dr W I C Clark)*

LITTLEWORTH COMMON [SP9386]
☆ *Blackwood Arms* SL1 8PP [3 miles S of M40 junction 2; Common Lane, OS Sheet 165 map ref 937864]: Small brick pub in lovely spot on edge of beechwoods with good walks, sturdy furniture on bare boards, roaring log fire, cream and mulberry décor, dark woodwork and blinds, welcoming service, wide choice of good food inc some indonesian influences and a notable sticky toffee pudding, well kept Brakspears and a guest beer; children and dogs welcome, good garden with paved area and pergola *(LM, Anthony and Marie Lewis, LYM)*
Jolly Woodman SL1 8PF [2 miles from M40 junction 2; off A355]: Multilevel rambling country pub with good range of changing ales inc Cottage Champflower, Hop Back Summer Lightning, St Austell Tribute and Shepherd Neame Spitfire, good fresh food, beamed and timbered areas inc armchair snug, log fire, central woodburner, old bottled beer collection; outside picnic-sets and colourful hanging baskets, good site by Burnham Beeches, open all day *(Michael Dandy, Susan and John Douglas, LYM, Phil Bryant)*

LONG CRENDON [SP6908]
Eight Bells HP18 9AL [High St]: Unassuming old timbered pub doing well under newish landlady, simple wooden furniture on long airy main room's tiled floor, well kept Wadworths and interesting guest beers, short choice of sensible food (pies recommended), darts, open fire; charming garden with aunt sally *(Doug Kennedy)*
Gurkha Tavern HP18 9EE [Bicester Rd (B4011)]: Handsome thatched pub (formerly the Chandos Arms) under new management (landlord is an ex Gurkha), wide choice of enjoyable nepalese and indian food, also Sun carvery, Fullers London Pride and Greene King IPA, pleasant low-beamed linked areas, log fire; big-screen TV *(David Lamb)*
LOUDWATER [SU9090]
Derehams HP10 9RH [off A40 E of High Wycombe, almost opp village turn-off]: Linked low-ceilinged bar areas, friendly old-fashioned local atmosphere, well kept beers inc Brakspears and Greene King, enjoyable pubby food, log fire *(Anthony Longden)*
LUDGERSHALL [SP6617]
☆ *Bull & Butcher* HP18 9NZ [off A41 Aylesbury—Bicester; bear left to The Green]: Nicely old-fashioned low-beamed country pub, tiles, flagstones and inglenook fireplace, good choice of reasonably priced food, Greene King IPA and Vale VPA, back dining room, exemplary ladies'; picnic-sets on pleasant front terrace overlooking green, cl Mon and lunchtimes Tues and Thurs, open all day wknds *(David Lamb, Lucien Perring, BB)*
MAIDS MORETON [SP7035]
Wheatsheaf MK18 1QR [Main St, just off A413 Towcester—Buckingham]: Attractive thatched and low-beamed local, cheery staff and atmosphere, wide choice of good value food from good sandwiches up, Tring ales and a guest like Silverstone Pitstop, farm cider, decent choice of wines, lots of pictures and bric-a-brac in old part, two inglenooks, settles and chairs, conservatory restaurant with woodburner; unobtrusive piped music; seats on front terrace, hatch service for pleasant quiet enclosed garden behind *(George Atkinson, MLR, Helene Grygar)*
MARLOW [SU8586]
Hare & Hounds SL7 2DF [Henley Road (A4155 W)]: This 17th-c much modernised pub with beams and inglenook has recently been taken over by the 2008 winners of Raymond Blanc's BBC TV series *The Restaurant*; news please *(Tracey and Stephen Groves, LYM)*
MARSH GIBBON [SP6423]
Plough OX27 0HQ [Church St]: Old stone-built beamed village pub with plenty of tables, good choice of reasonably priced food, friendly helpful staff *(David Lamb)*
MARSWORTH [SP9114]
☆ *Red Lion* HP23 4LU [village signed off B489 Dunstable—Aylesbury; Vicarage Rd]: Low-beamed partly thatched village pub with real ales such as Batemans, Crouch Vale, Tring

and Vale, cheerful old-fashioned service, good value food from enterprising baguettes up, decent wines, leather sofas and open fires in lounge, steps up to snug parlour and games area, nice variety of seating inc traditional settles; small sheltered garden, not far from impressive flight of canal locks *(LYM, Andrew Scarr, Roy Hoing, Ross Balaam, Tracey and Stephen Groves)*
MILTON KEYNES [SP9137]
Wavendon Arms MK17 8LJ [not far from M1 junctions 13 and 14]: Pleasant front bar with mix of modern furniture, airy contemporary tiled-floor restaurant, Timothy Taylors Landlord, good choice of wines by the glass, popular up-to-date food, good service; tables out in back garden with terrace, more in front *(Michael Dandy, Eithne Dandy)*
NEWTON BLOSSOMVILLE [SP9251]
Old Mill Burnt Down MK43 8AN [4 miles from M1 junction 14; off A428 at Turvey – Clifton Rd]: Smartly refurbished old beamed and stone-built pub, three linked areas on two levels, mixed furnishings on stone floor, three real ales inc Timothy Taylors Landlord, welcoming efficient staff, good food; courtyard seating, three comfortable bedrooms *(Michael Sargent)*
OAKLEY [SP6312]
Chandos Arms HP18 9QB [The Turnpike]: Small peaceful 16th-c village pub, chef/landlord doing enjoyable food inc some unusual choices in bar and end restaurant, friendly service *(David Lamb, Andrew Finn)*
OLNEY [SP8851]
☆ *Swan* MK46 4AA [High St S]: Friendly beamed and timbered linked rooms, wide choice of good value generous food from sandwiches up, well kept Shepherd Neame and guest ales, good value wines by the glass, quick helpful service, daily papers, attractive flowers, rather close-set pine tables, log fires, small back bistro dining room (booking advised for this); back courtyard tables, some cover *(BB, Michael Sargent, Jim Lyon, Michael Dandy)*
OVING [SP7821]
☆ *Black Boy* HP22 4HN [off A413 N of Aylesbury]: Extended 16th-c timbered pub nr church, low heavy beams, enormous inglenook, steps up to snug stripped-stone area, Brakspears Bitter and Rebellion Mutiny, lots of wines by the glass, pubby bar food and more elaborate restaurant menu, modern dining room with good-sized pine tables and picture windows; piped music; children and dogs welcome, tables on spacious sloping lawns and terrace (music here summer Suns), expansive Vale of Aylesbury views, cl Sun evening, Mon *(P and J Shapley, John Faircloth, John Beeken, LYM, Stephen Castle, Gordon Davico, David and Sue Smith, Mel Smith)*
PENN [SU9193]
☆ *Crown* HP10 8NY [B474 Beaconsfield—High Wycombe]: Busy Chef & Brewer opp 14th-c church on high ridge with distant views, interesting décor and attractive furnishings

in linked areas around low-ceilinged medieval core, wide range of generous food all day inc fixed price bargains (Mon-Thurs) and Sun roasts, friendly service, well kept Fullers London Pride and guest ales, good choice of wines by the glass, interesting summer cocktails, two roaring log fires; piped music (outside too), games machine; children very welcome, lots of tables in attractive split-level garden, open all day *(Tracey and Stephen Groves, Roy Hoing, LYM)*

PENN STREET [SU9295]

☆ *Hit or Miss* HP7 0PX [off A404 SW of Amersham, then keep on towards Winchmore Hill]: Well laid out low-beamed pub with own cricket ground, good well presented freshly made food, well kept Badger ales, decent wines, friendly attentive staff, cheerful atmosphere in three clean linked rooms, log fire, candles on tables, comfortable leather sofas and chairs, interesting cricket and chair-making memorabilia; piped music; children and dogs welcome, picnic-sets out in front, pleasant setting, open all day *(D and M T Ayres-Regan, Tracey and Stephen Groves, LYM, J C Upshall, Kevin Thomas, Nina Randall)*

Squirrel HP7 0PX: Family-friendly sister pub to nearby Hit or Miss, open-plan bar with flagstones, log fire, comfortable sofas as well as tables and chairs, good value home-made traditional food from baguettes (not Sun evening), good children's meals, well kept changing ales, good service, free coffee refills, bric-a-brac and cricketing memorabilia, darts; big garden with good play area and village cricket view, lovely walks, open all day wknds *(Roy Hoing, Mel Smith, Tracey and Stephen Groves)*

POUNDON [SP6425]

Sow & Pigs OX27 9BA [Main St]: Small quaint village local under new management, well kept and clean, several real ales *(David Lamb)*

PRESTON BISSETT [SP6529]

White Hart MK18 4LX [off A421 or A4421 SW of Buckingham; Pound Lane]: Thatched, timbered and low-beamed 18th-c village pub now run by a chinese family, three cosy rooms, log fire, home-made traditional pubby food (there is also a monthly chinese evening), real ales; some seats outside *(John Stowe, LYM, E A and D C T Frewer)*

SAUNDERTON [SU8099]

Rose & Crown HP27 9NP [Wycombe Rd]: Comfortably if slightly starkly modernised pub/hotel with contemporary décor and artwork in L-shaped bar, nice log fire, cosy alcove with sofa, Timothy Taylors Landlord, good choice of wines and teas, friendly staff, bar snacks and smart upmarket restaurant with good food inc well presented modern dishes and good value set meals; piped music; tables out in front and in nice garden with decking and play area, good Chilterns walks, 14 comfortable bedrooms *(Martin and Karen Wake, BB)*

SHERINGTON [SP8946]

White Hart MK16 9PE [off A509; Gun Lane]: Good changing ales such as Archers, Greene King, Purity and Rebellion, helpful landlord and friendly staff, good pub food (not Sun evening) from sandwiches and tapas up, bright fire, two-room bar, contemporary flagstoned dining room; children and dogs welcome, picnic-sets in garden with terrace, pretty hanging baskets, bedrooms in adjacent building *(George Atkinson, Peter Martin, Michael B Griffith, Michael Dandy)*

ST LEONARDS [SP9107]

White Lion HP23 6NW [Jenkins Lane, by Buckland Common; off A4011 Wendover—Tring]: Neat open-plan pub, highest in the Chilterns, with old black beams, well kept ales such as Batemans and Greene King, good value pub food, friendly service, log-effect gas fire; children and dogs welcome, attractive sheltered garden, good walks *(BB, Roy Hoing)*

STOKE GOLDINGTON [SP8348]

☆ *Lamb* MK16 8NR [High St (B526 Newport Pagnell—Northampton)]: Chatty village pub with friendly helpful licensees, up to four interesting changing ales, Weston's farm cider, decent wines by the glass, good generous home-made food (all day Sat, not Sun evening) from baguettes to bargain Sun roasts, good public bar with table skittles, two small pleasant dining rooms, quiet lounge with log fire and sheep decorations; may be quiet piped music, TV; dogs welcome, terrace and sheltered garden behind, open all day wknds *(JJW, CMW, BB, Elizabeth Whelan)*

STONE [SP7912]

Bugle Horn HP17 8QP [Oxford Rd, Hartwell (A418 SW of Aylesbury)]: Long low 17th-c stone-built family dining pub, friendly and comfortable linked rooms, good choice of modestly priced home-made food from good daytime sandwiches up, friendly service, Brakspears and Hook Norton Old Hooky, lots of wines by the glass, several log fires, prettily planted well furnished conservatory; tables on attractive terrace, lovely trees in large pretty garden, pastures beyond, open all day *(David Lamb, Mel Smith, Tim and Ann Newell)*

STONY STRATFORD [SP7840]

Old George MK11 1AA [High St]: Attractive and lively beamed and timbered inn, cosily pubby, with good value all-day food inc lunchtime carvery, quick friendly staff, real ales such as Fullers London Pride and Greene King IPA, good coffee, small dining room up at the back; piped music, lavatories up rather awkward stairs; tables in courtyard behind, bedrooms *(George Atkinson, Dr and Mrs A K Clarke)*

TAPLOW [SU9185]

Feathers SL1 8NS [Taplow Common, opp Cliveden entrance (NT)]: Rambling olde-worlde Chef & Brewer family dining pub, good choice of sensibly priced all-day food in roomy beamed eating areas, Fullers

London Pride, Greene King and Wells & Youngs Bombardier, good choice of decent wines, good coffee, friendly efficient service; piped music, games; children welcome, disabled facilities, charming courtyard, large garden (dogs allowed only by front picnic-sets), open all day *(Mr and Mrs G Owens)*

THE LEE [SP8904]

☆ *Cock & Rabbit* HP16 9LZ [back roads 2.5 miles N of Great Missenden, E of A413]: Warmly welcoming italian-run dining pub, stylish and comfortable, with reasonably priced home-made food (not Sun or Mon evenings) inc good fresh fish, pasta, real ales such as Fullers and Greene King, decent wines, good lively staff, panelled locals' bar, charming back dining areas welcoming children; big garden with tables on verandah, terraces and lawn *(Paul Humphreys, Roy Hoing, LYM)*

☆ *Old Swan* HP16 9NU [Swan Bottom, back rd 0.75 miles N of The Lee]: Tucked-away16th-c dining pub under new management, three attractively furnished linked rooms, low beams and flagstones, cooking-range log fire in inglenook, good choice of food, Brakspears; big back garden with play area, good walks *(LYM, Susan and John Douglas, Paul Humphreys, Gordon Davico, Mel Smith, R K Phillips)*

WADDESDON [SP7316]

Bell HP18 0JF [High St]: New licensees doing good value food from sandwiches to steaks and Sun roasts, nice eating area by small bar, friendly service, well kept ales such as Shepherd Neame Spitfire, Vale Castle and Wells & Youngs Bombardier; tables out at front and back *(Gill and Keith Croxton, Mel Smith, Ross Balaam)*

WENDOVER [SP8607]

Firecrest HP22 6QG [London Rd (A413 about 2 miles S)]: Popular roadside Vintage Inn, good value food all day inc smaller dishes, neat efficient staff, Wells & Youngs Bombardier, civilised eating areas, old fireplace, pictures on stripped brickwork; disabled parking *(David Lamb)*

WEST WYCOMBE [SU8394]

George & Dragon HP14 3AB [High St; A40

W of High Wycombe]: In preserved Tudor village, dark rambling hotel bar with massive beams and sloping walls, big log fire, Courage Best, Brakspears, St Austell Tribute and a guest, fairly priced food, friendly staff, small family dining room; children and dogs welcome, garden with fenced play area, character bedrooms (magnificent oak staircase), handy for West Wycombe Park, open all day wknds *(Alan and Anne Driver, LYM, Martin and Karen Wake)*

WESTON TURVILLE [SP8510]

Chequers HP22 5SJ [Church Lane]: Comfortably refurbished gastropub with low 17th-c beams, flagstones and large log fire, up-to-date food in bar and dining rooms, friendly helpful staff, well kept Adnams, Black Sheep and Fullers London Pride, wide choice of wines by the glass, stylish solid wooden furniture; children and dogs welcome, tucked away in attractive part of village, tables on large front terrace, open all day *(John Saville)*

WESTON UNDERWOOD [SP8650]

☆ *Cowpers Oak* MK46 5JS [signed off A509 in Olney; High St]: Wisteria-covered beamed pub in pretty thatched village, warmly welcoming, with generous good value interesting food (all day wknds) using local supplies, even their own pigs, five well kept changing ales, nice medley of old-fashioned furnishings, woodburners, dark red walls, dark panelling and some stripped stone, back restaurant (best to book Sun), good traditional games room, daily papers; piped music, TV; children very welcome, dogs in main bar, small suntrap front terrace, more tables on back decking and in big orchard garden (no dogs) with play area and farm animals, farm shop, bedrooms, open all day wknds *(LYM, JJW, CMW, Peter Martin, George Atkinson)*

WHITCHURCH [SP8020]

White Swan HP22 4JT [High St]: Thatched two-bar Fullers local with quickly served bargain two-course meals, other dishes cooked to order; picnic-sets in big rambling back garden looking over fields to distant Chilterns *(David Lamb, LYM)*

Post Office address codings confusingly give the impression that some pubs are in Buckinghamshire, when they're really in Bedfordshire or Berkshire (which is where we list them).

Cambridgeshire

This is a great area for civilised pubs with good, often restauranty food – worthwhile places for a special meal out. Top examples include the George in Buckden, Crown in Elton (a *Guide* discovery this year), Cock at Hemingford Grey (a lovely pub, just carefully redecorated and our Cambridgeshire Dining Pub of the Year), very smart Old Bridge Hotel in Huntingdon (with a new wine shop), Pheasant at Keyston (super modern cooking), Hole in the Wall at Little Wilbraham, Three Horseshoes at Madingley, Bell in Stilton (just the place for an A1 break), and Anchor at Sutton Gault. While these dining pubs suit special occasions, thank goodness for unspoilt simplicity, too. Some unspoilt pubs doing particularly well here this year include the Cambridge Blue and Free Press in Cambridge, genteel little Fountain in Ely, Queens Head at Newton (in the same family for three generations), and Chequers at Pampisford (another new *Guide* entry). Despite its Rutland-sounding name, Oakham is the county's top beer, with Elgoods, Ufford, Milton and City of Cambridge also favoured.

BUCKDEN
TL1967 MAP 5

George ⊞ ☖ ⇌
High Street; PE19 5XA

Modern stylish refurbishment of handsome coaching inn, friendly staff, first-rate modern cooking, real ales, fine choice of wines and lovely bedrooms

---

Although by no means a traditional pub, the bar in this handsome Georgian-faced hotel is a comfortable and relaxed place for a drink. It's all very stylish with contemporary furnishings throughout, and the bar has some wonderful fan beamwork, leather and chrome bar chairs, a log fire, Adnams Best and a changing guest like Nethergate IPA on handpump from a chrome-topped counter, 20 wines (including champagne) by the glass and a good choice of teas and coffees; hospitable staff. The bustling brasserie has smart cream dining chairs around carefully polished tables set with proper white napkins and pretty foliage arrangements, and this leads out on to the pretty sheltered terrace with box hedging and flowering plants and seats under large parasols. The charming bedrooms are all named after a famous George.

⊞ Imaginative brasserie-style food includes sandwiches, soup, dorset crab salad with chilli, red onion and lemon dressing, foie gras and wild mushroom terrine with tomato and red pepper chutney, duck rillette with toasted pinenuts, raisins and orange dressing, stuffed chicken breast wrapped in pancetta with shitake mushroom sauce, hand-rolled gnocchi with roasted butternut squash and pesto, peppered rare grilled yellow-fin tuna with warm spicy lentil salsa, and puddings such as peanut butter and chocolate cheesecake with strawberry jelly and sticky toffee pudding with caramel sauce and rum and raisin ice-cream. They also serve afternoon tea. *Starters/Snacks: £5.50 to £12.95. Main Courses: £9.95 to £14.95. Puddings: £5.50 to £7.50*

Free house ~ Licensee Cynthia Schaeffer ~ Real ale ~ Bar food (12-2.30, 7-9.30) ~ Restaurant ~ (01480) 812300 ~ Children welcome ~ Dogs welcome ~ Open 12-11(11.30 Sat;10.30 Sun) ~ Bedrooms: £80S/£100B

Recommended by H Bramwell, Michael Sargent, Ryta Lyndley, Michael Dandy, Stuart Turner, Gerry and Rosemary Dobson, R T and J C Moggridge

CAMBRIDGE
TL4658 MAP 5

Cambridge Blue 🍺 £
85 Gwydir Street; CB1 2LG

Friendly backstreet pub, simply decorated with lots to look at, and interesting ales

With around 14 real ales on handpump or tapped from the cask plus a friendly welcome, it's not surprising that this backstreet pub is so busy. As well as nine guests, there might be Abbeydale Absolution, Bartrams Damson Stout, Elgoods Black Dog, Oakham Inferno, Potbelly Beijing Black, and Potton Gold – but the list is endless and they change constantly. Quite a choice of bottled beers and malt whiskies as well. There's an attractive little conservatory and two peaceful rooms that are simply decorated with old-fashioned bare-boards style furnishings, candles on the tables, and a big collection of breweriana; board games, cards and dominoes. The big back garden is surprisingly rural feeling. It does get very busy at weekends.

🍴 **Traditional bar food includes filled ciabattas and baked potatoes, soup, spicy butternut stew, chicken and ham or steak and mushroom pie, a curry of the day, sausage and mash with onion gravy, and puddings like apple and blackberry pie.** *Starters/Snacks: £2.50 to £5.00. Main Courses: £5.00 to £10.00. Puddings: £3.00 to £4.00*

Free house ~ Licensees Jethro and Terri Scotcher-Littlechild ~ Real ale ~ Bar food (12-2(12-4 weekends), 6-9) ~ (01223) 471680 ~ Children and dogs allowed in conservatory ~ Dogs welcome ~ Open 12-2.30, 5-11; 12-11(10.30 Sun) Sat; closed evenings 25 and 26 Dec

Recommended by Ben Guy, the Didler, Chris and Angela Buckell, Jerry Brown, John Saville

Free Press £
Prospect Row; CB1 1DU

Quiet and unspoilt with some interesting local décor, and good value food

In fine or poor weather, this little pub is just the place for a quiet drink. If it's sunny you can sit in the suntrap sheltered and paved garden but in cooler weather there are newspapers to read by the warm log fire; the unspoilt atmosphere is undisturbed by mobile phones, piped music or games machines. In a nod to the building's history as home to a local newspaper, the walls of its characterful bare-board rooms are hung with old newspaper pages and printing memorabilia, as well as old printing trays that local customers are encouraged to top up with little items. Greene King IPA, Abbot and Mild and a guest or two such as Bath Ales Gem or Hydes Jekyll Gold on handpump, several malt whiskies, a dozen wines by the glass, and lots of different fruit juices; assorted board games. There may be summer morris men. Wheelchair access.

🍴 **Home-made pubby food includes lunchtime sandwiches and toasted ciabatta, ploughman's, soup, pasta dishes and salads, with evening meals like sausage and mash, chunky beef chilli, and gammon with bubble and squeak; daily specials and a very good value three-course meal Mon-Weds evenings.** *Starters/Snacks: £1.95 to £5.95. Main Courses: £6.95 to £9.50. Puddings: £2.95 to £3.95*

Greene King ~ Tenant Craig Bickley ~ Real ale ~ Bar food (12-2(2.30 Sat and Sun), 6-9; not Sun evening) ~ (01223) 368337 ~ Children welcome ~ Dogs welcome ~ Open 12-2.30, 6-11; 12-11 Sat; 12-3, 7-10.30 Sun; closed 25 and 26 Dec, 1 Jan

Recommended by the Didler, Virginia Williams, D Miles, Giles and Annie Francis, Chris and Angela Buckell, Michael Dandy

---

Post Office address codings confusingly give the impression that some pubs are in Cambridgeshire, when they're really in Bedfordshire, Lincolnshire, Norfolk or Northamptonshire (which is where we list them).

ELSWORTH   TL3163   MAP 5

George & Dragon

Off A14 NW of Cambridge, via Boxworth, or off A428; CB3 8JQ

Busy dining pub with quite a choice of interesting food served by efficient staff

No matter how busy this brick-built dining pub is, you can be sure of courteous, friendly service from the hard-working staff. It's best to book in advance to be sure of a table. A pleasant panelled main bar, decorated with a fishy theme, opens on the left to a slightly elevated dining area with comfortable tables and a good woodburning stove. From here, steps lead down to a garden room behind with tables overlooking attractive garden terraces. On the right is a more formal restaurant. Greene King IPA and Old Speckled Hen and a guest beer on handpump and decent wines. The Rose at Stapleford (see the Lucky Dip section) is under the same ownership.

🍴 **As well as a good value two- and three-course weekday menu, Friday steak night and first Monday in the month themed evenings, the popular bar food includes lunchtime sandwiches, filled baguettes and ploughman's, smoked salmon and crab fishcake, deep-fried breaded brie with plum and apple chutney, ham and egg, roasted vegetable curry, steak and kidney pie, fresh fillet of haddock mornay, Aberdeen angus steaks, daily specials, and puddings like white chocolate chunk brownies with hot chocolate sauce and bakewell tart with custard.** *Starters/Snacks: £4.00 to £8.50. Main Courses: £10.00 to £18.00. Puddings: £2.75 to £4.75*

Free house ~ Licensees Paul and Karen Beer ~ Real ale ~ Bar food (12-2, 7-9.30; 12-3 Sun; not Sun evening) ~ Restaurant ~ (01954) 267236 ~ Children welcome ~ Dogs allowed in bar ~ Open 11-2.45, 6-11; 12-3, 6-10 Sun; closed Sun evening in Jan and Feb

Recommended by Michael and Jenny Back, Michael Dandy, Gordon and Margaret Ormondroyd, R T and J C Moggridge, Simon Watkins

ELTON   TL0893   MAP 5

Black Horse ♀

B671 off A605 W of Peterborough and A1(M); Overend; PE8 6RU

Well run dining pub with country furnishings and super views from big garden

Even though many of the customers to this handsome honey-stone dining pub are here to enjoy the good food, our readers are keen to tell us that if it's only a drink you want, you will be made just as welcome. There are roaring log fires, hop-strung beams, a homely and comfortable mix of furniture (no two tables and chairs seem the same), antique prints, and lots of ornaments and bric-a-brac including an intriguing ancient radio set. Dining areas at each end of the bar have parquet flooring and tiles, and the stripped stone back lounge towards the restaurant has an interesting fireplace. Digfield Barnwell Bitter, Everards Tiger, Oakham JHB and Woodfordes Wherry on handpump, and quite a few wines by the glass. The big garden has super views across to Elton Hall park and the village church, there are seats on the terrace, and a couple of acres of grass for children to play.

🍴 **They grow their own herbs and much of their own fruit, salad and vegetables (including asparagus) for the wide range of good bar food: sandwiches, soup, home-made duck spring rolls with sweet and sour sauce, crab linguine, smoked pigeon breast with redcurrant sauce, ham and egg, lamb burgers, brie and red onion tart, calves liver with onion gravy, pork chop with black pudding and an apple cider sauce, bass with saffron, fennel and tomato broth, duck breast with sweet roast potatoes and a fruits of the forest sauce, and puddings like their own rhubarb crumble and warm chocolate and marshmallow brownie with chocolate sauce; they also offer a popular two- and three-course menu (not Sunday lunchtime when their roasts are the thing to go for).** *Starters/Snacks: £4.95 to £8.95. Main Courses: £5.95 to £16.95. Puddings: £4.95*

Free house ~ Licensee John Clennell ~ Real ale ~ Bar food (12-2, 6-9; all day in summer) ~ Restaurant ~ (01832) 280240 ~ Children welcome ~ Dogs allowed in bar ~ Open 11-11(midnight Sat); 12-11 Sun

Recommended by R T and J C Moggridge, George Atkinson, Oliver and Sue Rowell, Dave Braisted, Peter Meister, Justin and Emma King, Dr D J and Mrs S C Walker

Crown ⑪ ♀ 🛏

Off B671 S of Wansford (A1/A47), and village signposted off A605 Peterborough—Oundle; Duck Street; PE8 6RQ

Lovely thatched inn in charming village, super food cooked by young chef/landlord, up to six real ales, well chosen wines and friendly atmosphere; bedrooms

Run by a friendly young chef/landlord and his wife, this is a lovely, stylishly refurbished thatched stone inn overlooking the green of a charming village. The layout inside is most attractive. A softly lit beamed bar has an open fire in the stone fireplace, good pictures and pubby ornaments on pastel walls, and cushioned settles and chunky farmhouse furniture on the tartan carpet. The beamed main dining area has fresh flowers and candles, and similar tables and chairs on its stripped boards; a more formal, circular, conservatory-style restaurant is open at weekends. The good mix of locals and visitors appreciate the helpful, efficient service, with Greene King IPA, a beer named for the pub and guests like Black Sheep, Oakham JHB and Woodfordes Wherry on handpump, besides well chosen wines by the glass. There are tables outside on the front terrace. We've no doubt that this would be an enjoyable place to stay, but have yet to hear from readers who have stayed here. Elton Mill and Lock are a short walk away.

🍴 The landlord's cooking is serious and extremely good. It might include soup, chicken liver and brandy parfait with quince and raisin chutney, seared scallops topped with grilled champagne sabayon on braised swiss chard, beef pie, beer-battered haddock, lancashire hotpot, pasta in an interesting spinach and cheese sauce, monkfish done inventively again with a clever sauce, a skewer of marinated beef rump, onion and red pepper with a potato skin stuffed with smooth black pudding topped with crispy bacon and a creamy horseradish sauce, and puddings like warm chocolate, almond and walnut brownie with chocolate sauce and ice-cream and apple and blackberry crumble; they also do two- and three-course lunches (Tuesday-Friday) and Sunday roasts. *Starters/Snacks: £5.80 to £9.50. Main Courses: £10.00 to £17.00. Puddings: £5.95*

Free house ~ Licensees Marcus and Rosalind Lamb ~ Real ale ~ Bar food (12-2(3 Sun), 6.30-9; not Sun evening, not Mon) ~ Restaurant ~ (01832) 280232 ~ Children allowed until 7.30pm; not Sat evening ~ Dogs allowed in bar ~ Open mike night third Mon evening of the month ~ Open 12-11 (Mon 5-11); 12-10.30 Sun; closed Mon lunchtime ~ Bedrooms: £60B/£90B

Recommended by Michael Doswell

ELY   TL5380   MAP 5

Fountain 🍺

Corner of Barton Square and Silver Street; CB7 4JF

Happily escaping tourists but close to cathedral

Somehow, despite being very close to the cathedral, this simple but genteel town corner pub manages to escape the tourists. There are old cartoons, local photographs, regional maps and mementoes of the neighbouring King's School on the elegant dark pink walls, and tied-back curtains hanging from gold colour rails above the big windows. Above one fireplace is a stuffed pike in a case, and there are a few antlers dotted about. An extension at the back provides much-needed additional seating. Adnams Broadside, Fullers London Pride, Woodfordes Wherry and a guest beer on handpump. Note the limited opening times below. More reports please.

🍴 No food.

Free house ~ Licensees John and Judith Borland ~ Real ale ~ No credit cards ~ (01353) 663122 ~ Children welcome away from bar until 8pm ~ Dogs welcome ~ Open 5-11; 12-2, 6-11.30 Sat; 12-2, 7-10.30 Sun; closed weekday lunchtimes

Recommended by Mrs Hazel Rainer, the Didler

If we know a pub does summer barbecues, we say so.

FEN DITTON   TL4860   MAP 5

Ancient Shepherds

Off B1047 at Green End, The River signpost, just NE of Cambridge; CB5 8ST

Beamed and comfortable with coal fires and well liked food

Perhaps the nicest room in this beamed and friendly old pub is the softly lit central lounge where you can't fail to be comfortable on one of the big fat dark red button-back leather settees or armchairs which are grouped round low dark wood tables. The warm coal fire and heavy drapes around the window seat with its big scatter cushions add to the cosiness. Above a black dado, the walls (and ceiling) are dark pink and decorated with comic fox and policeman prints plus little steeplechasing and equestrian ones. On the right the smallish more pubby bar, with its coal fire, serves Adnams Bitter and Greene King IPA and maybe Old Speckled Hen on handpump, while on the left is a pleasant restaurant. The licensee's west highland terrier, Billie, might be around outside food service times.

🍴 **Good, enjoyable bar food includes lunchtime filled baguettes, tasty soup and pubby dishes like ham and egg, lasagne, beef in ale pie and popular smoked haddock and spring onion fishcakes, with more elaborate evening choices such as deep-fried whitebait or brie with gooseberry coulis, chicken liver pâté, plaice stuffed with prawns in parsley sauce, pork loin with a cream and mustard sauce, half a duck with brandy and oranges, peppered fillet steak, and puddings such as lemon and ginger cheesecake and fruit pavlova; Sunday roasts.** *Starters/Snacks: £4.50 to £7.95. Main Courses: £9.50 to £12.95. Puddings: £4.95*

Punch ~ Tenant J M Harrington ~ Real ale ~ Bar food (12-2, 6.30-9; not Sun or Mon evenings) ~ Restaurant ~ (01223) 293280 ~ Children in eating area of bar ~ Dogs allowed in bar ~ Open 12-2.30, 6.30-11; 12-5 Sun; closed Sun and Mon evenings

Recommended by Peter Martin, Mrs M K Matthews, D Miles, John and Elisabeth Cox, Mrs Carolyn Dixon, Paul and Margaret Baker, Alan and Eve Harding, M and GR, John Marsh, Rob and Catherine Dunster, John Saville

HELPSTON   TF1205   MAP 5

Blue Bell 🍺

Woodgate; off B1443; PE6 7ED

Bustling and friendly, fine choice of beers and tasty food including good value lunches

Consistently reliable, this is a bustling, friendly place held dear in the hearts of many of our readers. It's run by a hard-working landlord and his cheerful staff who take great care of both the pub and their customers. The lounge, parlour and snug have comfortable cushioned chairs and settles, plenty of pictures, ornaments, mementoes and cart-wheel displays, and a homely atmosphere. The dining extension is light and airy with a sloping glass roof. Grainstore Ten Fifty and (exclusive to this pub) John Clare, and quickly changing guests such as Fullers Hock and Hook Norton Hooky Bitter on handpump, and summer scrumpy cider. They may have marmalade for sale; piped music, pool and TV. A sheltered and heated terrace has cafe-style chairs and tables and an awning; pretty hanging baskets and wheelchair access. The poet John Clare lived in the newly restored cottage next door which should be open to the public by the time this edition is published.

🍴 **As well as a very good value two-course lunch (not Sunday), the extremely popular, tasty bar food includes sandwiches, soup, duck and port pâté, stilton mushrooms, steak in ale pie, gammon and egg, half-roast chicken, barnwell sausage, stilton and vegetable crumble, and daily specials such as barbecue spare ribs, sweet potato, red pepper and green bean tagine, fish pie, lamb hotpot, liver and bacon and crispy chilli beef.** *Starters/Snacks: £3.95 to £6.95. Main Courses: £6.95 to £14.95. Puddings: £3.95*

Free house ~ Licensee Aubrey Sinclair Ball ~ Real ale ~ Bar food (12-2, 6-9; 12-2 Sun; not Sun or Mon evenings) ~ Restaurant ~ (01733) 252394 ~ Children welcome away from bar; must leave by 9pm ~ Dogs allowed in bar ~ Open 11.30-2.30(3 Sat), 5(6 Sat)-11; 12-6 Sun

Recommended by Michael and Jenny Back, Gordon and Margaret Ormonroyd, Ian and Helen Stafford, Roy Bromell, Carolyn Browse, R T and J C Moggridge, H Paulinski

HEMINGFORD GREY

TL2970 MAP 5

Cock 🍴 ♇ ◗

Village signposted off A14 eastbound, and (via A1096 St Ives road) westbound; High Street; PE28 9BJ

CAMBRIDGESHIRE DINING PUB OF THE YEAR

Imaginative food in pretty pub, extensive wine list plus other drinks including four real ales, bustling atmosphere, and smart restaurant

The inside of this enjoyable pub has been carefully refurbished recently but without changing the character of either the bar or the dining areas. There are dark or white-painted beams, lots of contemporary pale yellow and cream paintwork, artwork here and there, fresh flowers and church candles, and throughout, a really attractive mix of old wooden dining chairs, settles and tables. They've sensibly kept the traditional public bar on the left for drinkers only: an open woodburning stove on the raised hearth, bar stools, wall seats and a carver, steps that lead down to more seating, Buntingford Highwayman IPA, Great Oakley Gobble, Oldershaw Harrowby Pale Ale and Wolf Golden Jackal on handpump, 15 wines by the glass and local farm cider. Service is excellent. In marked contrast, the stylishly simple spotless restaurant on the right – you must book to be sure of a table – is set for dining with flowers on each table, pale stripped wooden floorboards and another woodburning stove. There's a friendly, bustling atmosphere and a good mix of locals and visitors. This is a pretty little pub with lovely hanging baskets and seats and tables among stone troughs and flowers in the neat garden.

🍴 **Excellent modern food includes ciabatta or focaccia sandwiches, soup, chicken liver crostinis, roquefort blue cheese salad with curried apple, walnuts, celery and aioli, purple sprouting broccoli risotto with goats cheese and baby spinach, braised pork with pistachio crust, baked apple, couscous and truffled cheese, guinea fowl with chorizo, potato cake and port sauce, daily specials like various home-made sausages with a choice of mash and sauces and fish dishes such as cured salmon with pickled clams and beetroot, seared scallops, mushroom tart, rocket and truffle oil, lobster and cod fishcakes and bass fillets with cauliflower and saffron puree, escargot and pancetta; puddings like pear and almond tartlet with crème fraîche and candied ginger and orange and white chocolate mousse with Grand Marnier crème anglaise. They also offer a popular two- and three-course lunch menu.** *Starters/Snacks: £4.00 to £7.00. Main Courses: £10.00 to £17.00. Puddings: £5.00 to £6.00*

Free house ~ Licensees Oliver Thain and Richard Bradley ~ Real ale ~ Bar food (12-2.30(3 Sun), 6.30-9(6.15-9.30 Fri and Sat; 8.30 Sun)) ~ Restaurant ~ (01480) 463609 ~ Children in restaurant only but must be over 5 in evening ~ Dogs allowed in bar ~ Open 11.30-3, 6-11; 12-4, 6.30-10.30 Sun; closed 26 Dec

Recommended by Mrs B Barwick, Michael Sargent, Jeff and Wendy Williams, Gordon and Margaret Ormondroyd, Christopher Turner, Barry Collett, Jamie May, Howard and Margaret Buchanan, John Wooll, Alison and Pete, Sally Anne and Peter Goodale

HEYDON

TL4339 MAP 5

King William IV

Off A505 W of M11 junction 10; SG8 8PW

Rambling rooms with fascinating rustic jumble, quite a few vegetarian dishes on sizeable menu; pretty garden

It's worth a visit to this neatly kept dining pub, not just for the wide choice of food, but to look at the amazing collections. The nooks and crannies in the rambling beamed rooms are filled with ploughshares, yokes and iron tools, cowbells, beer steins, samovars, brass or black wrought-iron lamps, copper-bound casks and milk ewers, harness, horsebrasses and smith's bellows – as well as decorative plates, cut-glass and china ornaments. Adnams Bitter, Fullers London Pride, Greene King IPA and Timothy Taylors Landlord on handpump, a dozen wines by the glass, several malt whiskies, and helpful staff; warming log fire and piped music. There are teak seats and tables and outdoor heaters on the terrace as well as more seats in the pretty garden. More reports please.

⑪ From a sizeable – if not cheap – menu, the wide choice of food includes lunchtime wraps, sandwiches and filled baguettes, baked potatoes, soup, smoked chicken and pistachio terrine wrapped in parma ham with a spiced pear chutney, scallops with black pudding, pea purée and citrus dressing, beer, mushroom and stout pie, mediterranean vegetable and goats cheese wellington on truffle mash, sausages with colcannon, mash and red onion gravy, smoked haddock fillet on bubble and squeak with poached egg and hollandaise, thai green chicken curry, wok-fried duck with stir-fried vegetables, noodles, hoisin and plum sauce, and puddings like honey and Malteser cheesecake with dark chocolate sauce and mulled wine and winter berry bread pudding with vanilla custard. *Starters/Snacks: £6.95 to £8.25. Main Courses: £9.95 to £18.95. Puddings: £5.95 to £6.95*

Free house ~ Licensee Elizabeth Nicholls ~ Real ale ~ Bar food (12-2(2.30 Sun), 6.30(7 Sun)-9.30(10 Sat, 9 Sun)) ~ Restaurant ~ (01763) 838773 ~ Children welcome ~ Dogs allowed in bar ~ Open 12-2.30, 6.30-11.30; 12-3, 6-12(7-11 Sun) Sat; closed 25 and 26 Dec

Recommended by Virginia Williams, R T and J C Moggridge, Mrs M K Matthews

HINXTON

TL4945   MAP 5

Red Lion

2 miles off M11 junction 9 northbound; take first exit off A11, A1301 N, then left turn into village – High Street; a little further from junction 10, via A505 E and A1301 S; CB10 1QY

Pink-washed and handy for Duxford and M11, friendly staff and neat, big, newly landscaped garden; new bedrooms

They've now opened eight smart ensuite bedrooms in a separate flint and brick building to the side of this carefully extended pink-washed 16th-c inn. The low-beamed bar is mainly open-plan, with a bustling and convivial atmosphere, leather chesterfields on wooden floors, an old wall clock, a dark green fireplace; Adnams Bitter, Greene King IPA, Woodfordes Wherry and a guest such as Nethergate Augustinian Ale on handpump, 12 wines by the glass and Aspall's cider; there are some unusual foreign insects in glass cases. An informal dining area has high-backed settles and the smart restaurant is decorated with various pictures and assorted clocks. The neatly kept big garden (which was being landscaped as we went to press) has a pleasant terrace with picnic-sets, a dovecote and views of the village church.

⑪ Good interesting bar food includes sandwiches and filled baguettes, soup, chicken and pistachio terrine with sweet peppers and basil jelly, seared scallops with salmon mousse, potato rösti and yellow pepper vinaigrette, wild mushroom tagliatelle, steak in ale or chicken and leek pies, smoked haddock and soft poached egg with a mustard cream sauce, lamb shank with pea and mint risotto and rich veal jus, chicken breast with madeira velouté, daily specials, and puddings like super chocolate marquise with passion-fruit jelly; Sunday roast. They often have a two- and three-course set menu during the week. *Starters/Snacks: £4.50 to £7.00. Main Courses: £9.00 to £15.00. Puddings: £2.00 to £6.00*

Free house ~ Licensee Alex Clarke ~ Real ale ~ Bar food (12-2, 6.45-9; 12-2.30, 6.45-9.30 Fri and Sat; 12-2.30, 7-9 Sun) ~ Restaurant ~ (01799) 530601 ~ Well behaved children welcome ~ Dogs welcome ~ Open 11-3, 6-11; 12-4, 7-10.30 Sun; closed evenings 25 and 26 Dec and 1 Jan ~ Bedrooms: £80B/£110S(£95B)

Recommended by Anthony Barnes, Mrs Margo Finlay, Jörg Kasprowski, M and GR, Edward Mirzoeff, R T and J C Moggridge, Paul Humphreys

HUNTINGDON

TL2471   MAP 5

Old Bridge Hotel ⑪ ♀ 🛏

1 High Street; ring road just off B1044 entering from easternmost A14 slip road; PE29 3TQ

Georgian hotel with smartly pubby bar, splendid range of drinks and excellent food

This is, of course, a civilised Georgian hotel rather than a pub but it does have a quietly chatty bar with a good mix of customers (suited diners and those in jeans and T-shirts rub shoulders quite happily), a log fire, comfortable sofas and low wooden tables on polished floorboards and Adnams Bitter, City of Cambridge Hobsons Choice and Elgoods

Golden Newt on handpump; first class service. They also have an exceptional wine list (a dozen by the glass in the bar) and have opened a wine shop in what had been a private dining room. Most customers are here though to enjoy the imaginative food served by excellent staff which can be eaten in the big airy Terrace (an indoor room, but with beautifully painted verdant murals suggesting the open air) or in the slightly more formal panelled restaurant. This is a very nice place to stay.

🍽 As well as sandwiches and various smart nibbles, the well presented restauranty food might include soup, potato gnocchi with Portland crab, lime, chilli and ginger, confit duck and foie gras terrine with truffled pease pudding and toasted brioche, tagliatelle with carbonara sauce, fillet of pollack with pease pudding and chips, gratin of vegetables with broccoli, jerusalem artichoke and beetroot purée, saddleback sausages with braised pork cheek and onion gravy, gressingham duck breast with braised red cabbage and a duck pie, steaks, and puddings like vanilla panna cotta with spiced apple compote and apple sorbet and bread and butter pudding with apricot compote and vanilla ice-cream; also, a two- and three-course set lunch (not Sunday) and afternoon tea. *Starters/Snacks: £6.95 to £8.95. Main Courses: £10.95 to £24.00. Puddings: £5.95*

Huntsbridge ~ Licensee John Hoskins ~ Real ale ~ Bar food (12-2, 6.30-10) ~ Restaurant ~ (01480) 424300 ~ Children welcome ~ Dogs welcome ~ Open 11-11 ~ Bedrooms: £95B/£135B

Recommended by Michael Sargent, Bruce and Sharon Eden, Martin and Pauline Jennings, Phil Bryant, Jeremy King, R T and J C Moggridge, Mrs B Barwick, Mrs Hazel Rainer, Michael Dandy, John and Helen Rushton

KEYSTON

TL0475   MAP 5

Pheasant 🍽 ♀

Just off A14 SE of Thrapston; village loop road, off B663; PE28 0RE

Relaxed bar in smart dining pub with highly thought-of modern food and fine range of drinks

Most customers come to this attractive long, low thatched dining pub to enjoy the fine modern cooking but they do keep Digfield Barnwell Bitter, Grainstore Ten Fifty, Potbelly Best and a changing guest on handpump. The immaculately kept spacious oak-beamed bar has a comfortably civilised atmosphere, open fires, simple wooden tables and chairs and country paintings on the pale walls; there are three distinct dining areas as well. 16 wines by the glass (plus eight sweet wines and two champagnes), and fine port and sherry; very good service. There are seats out in front of the building and on a back terrace.

🍽 At lunchtime, the modern food might include soup, ploughman's, burger with gruyère, home-made black pudding with celeriac remoulade and a fried egg, tuna niçoise salad, whole grilled rainbow trout with salsa verde, and crispy pork belly braised shallots; evening choices such as oysters with bloody mary shooter and pickled cucumber, moules and frites, vegetable and polenta terrine with beetroot, soft boiled pheasant eggs and goats cheese, chicken leg ravioli with braised fennel, turnip tops and wild mushrooms, steak with café de paris butter, and puddings like chocolate fondant with pear purée and spiced plum ice-cream and floating island with rhubarb and blood orange compote. They also offer a two- and three-course set lunch. *Starters/Snacks: £4.50 to £7.00. Main Courses: £10.50 to £20.00. Puddings: £5.50*

Free house ~ Licensee Taffeta Scrimshaw ~ Real ale ~ Bar food ~ Restaurant ~ (01832) 710241 ~ Children welcome ~ Dogs allowed in bar ~ Open 12-11(till 4 Sun); closed Sun evening and all day Mon

Recommended by Michael Sargent, J F M and M West, Oliver and Sue Rowell, Clive Flynn, J C M Troughton, Ryta Lyndley, Paul and Margaret Baker, Martin and Pauline Jennings

KIMBOLTON

TL0967 MAP 5

New Sun

High Street; PE28 0HA

Interesting bars and rooms, tapas menu plus other good food and pleasant back garden

---

Just the place to drop into and fitting in well with the village's delightfully harmonious high street, this is a pleasant old pub. The cosiest room is perhaps the low-beamed front lounge with a couple of comfortable armchairs and a sofa beside the fireplace, standing timbers and exposed brickwork, and books, pottery and brasses. This leads into a narrower locals' bar with Wells & Youngs Bombardier and Eagle and a weekly changing guest on handpump, and about a dozen wines (including champagne) by the glass; piped music and quiz machine. The dining room opens off here. The conservatory has doors opening on to the terrace where there are smart seats and tables under giant umbrellas. Do note that some of the nearby parking spaces have a 30-minute limit.

🍴 Using local game and meat and seasonal allotment vegetables, popular bar food includes sandwiches, soup, a range of tapas, king prawns in garlic and chilli, popular caesar salad with salmon or chicken, home-cooked ham and egg, steak and kidney pudding, loin and leg of rabbit stuffed with tarragon sauce with mustard mash, spinach tagliatelle with wild mushrooms, pesto cream and truffle oil, beef stroganoff, daily specials such as Friday beer-battered haddock and liver and bacon with onion gravy, and puddings like vanilla and star anise crème brûlée with mulled pear and steamed chocolate pudding with chocolate sauce. *Starters/Snacks: £4.00 to £7.25. Main Courses: £9.95 to £22.00. Puddings: £4.25 to £5.50*

Charles Wells ~ Lease Stephen and Elaine Rogers ~ Real ale ~ Bar food (12-2.15(2.30 Sun), 7-9.30; not Sun or Mon evenings) ~ Restaurant ~ (01480) 860052 ~ Children allowed in front bar and eating areas ~ Dogs allowed in bar ~ Open 11.30-2.30, 6(6.30 Sat)-11; 12-10.30 Sun

Recommended by Peter Dandy, Charles Mear, Fr Robert Marsh, John Picken, Mark Rogers, Nick Temple

LITTLE WILBRAHAM

TL5458 MAP 5

Hole in the Wall

Taking Stow cum Quy turn off A14, turn off A1303 Newmarket Road at The Wilbrahams signpost, then right at Little Wilbraham signpost; High Street; CB1 5JY

Charming tucked-away dining pub – quite a find

Whether you are lucky enough to be a local or maybe a visitor dropping in for a drink or a meal, you will be warmly welcomed by the friendly and thoughtful team running this enjoyable pub. The carpeted ochre-walled bar on the right is a cosy place for a robust no-nonsense pub lunch, with its logs burning in the big brick fireplace, 15th-c beams and timbers, snug little window seats and other mixed seating around scrubbed kitchen tables. For more of an occasion, either the similar middle room (with another fire in its open range) or the rather plusher main dining room (yet another fire here) fill the bill well. Woodfordes Wherry and Nelsons Revenge and a changing guest like Buntingford Golden Plover on handpump, a good choice of wines by the glass, and unusual soft drinks such as pomegranate and elderflower pressé. Service is unfailingly helpful. The neat side garden has good teak furniture and a little verandah. It's a very quiet hamlet, with an interesting walk to nearby unspoilt Little Wilbraham Fen.

🍴 Changing every few weeks, the well prepared, enjoyable food includes soup, free-range chicken livers on toast with walnuts, grapes and brandy, scrambled eggs and smoked salmon, crispy free-range pork belly with celeriac and apple coleslaw and rhubarb cider dressing, green thai vegetable curry, shepherd's pie, cajun-spiced monkfish with saffron mash, crispy spinach and roast tomato sauce, home-made chicken kiev, beef and mushroom in ale stew with horseradish mash, and puddings like pear and butterscotch crumble with vanilla ice-cream and dark chocolate and amaretti torte with chocolate sauce. *Starters/Snacks: £3.50 to £8.00. Main Courses: £10.50 to £12.95. Puddings: £5.75 to £8.50*

Free house ~ Licensees Stephen Bull, Jenny and Chris Leeton ~ Real ale ~ Bar food ~ Restaurant ~ (01223) 812282 ~ Well behaved children welcome ~ Dogs allowed in bar ~

Open 11.30-3, 6.30-11; 12-3 Sun; closed Sun evening, all day Mon; two weeks Jan, two weeks Oct

Recommended by Dr Phil Putwain, K C Watson, David and Sharon Collison, Mark Farrington, Jeff and Wendy Williams, David Gunn, Robert Gomme

MADINGLEY   TL3960   MAP 5

Three Horseshoes 🍴 ♀

Off A1303 W of Cambridge; High Street; CB3 8AB

Civilised dining pub, outstanding wine list, bar food plus sophisticated italian meals and efficient service

If it's a relaxed drink or an enjoyable bar meal you're after in this civilised thatched dining pub, you must head for the pleasantly relaxed little airy bar. This has an open fire, simple wooden tables and chairs on bare floorboards, stools at the bar counter and pictures on green walls; it can be a bit of a crush here at peak times. There's also a pretty conservatory restaurant where they serve sophisticated italian meals. Adnams Bitter and a couple of guests such as Church End Goats Milk and Morrissey Fox Blonde on handpump and an outstanding wine list with 20 by the glass, plus sweet wines and ports. More reports please.

🍴 There's no doubt that the italian food in the restaurant is excellent (at a price) but the better value bar food is extremely good, too and they offer a fair-priced three-course choice: soup, milano salami, pickled red cabbage and toasted hazelnuts, grilled pigs trotter with braised lentils and salsa verde, beer-battered cod with mushy peas, pappardelle with sun-dried tomatoes, crème fraîche and marjoram, slow-braised chicken legs with onion, bacon, red wine and olive oil mash, chargrilled mackerel with caper and parsley salad and warm potatoes, and puddings like pineapple fool and panna cotta with marinated prunes. *Starters/Snacks: £5.00 to £6.00. Main Courses: £8.00 to £12.00. Puddings: £4.00 to £6.00*

Free house ~ Licensee Richard Stokes ~ Real ale ~ Bar food (12-2(2.30 Sat and Sun), 6.30-9.30 (6-8 Sun)) ~ Restaurant ~ (01954) 210221 ~ Children welcome ~ Open 11.30-3, 6-11; 12-3, 6-9 Sun

Recommended by P and D Carpenter, Dr Kevan Tucker

NEWTON   TL4349   MAP 5

Queens Head ★ 🍺 £

2.5 miles from M11 junction 11; A10 towards Royston, then left on to B1368; CB2 5PG

Lovely traditional old pub in the same family for many years, simple popular food and fair choice of drinks

Happily, nothing changes in this unspoilt and staunchly traditional old pub, and it's still run by the third generation of the same genuinely welcoming family. The peaceful main bar has a low ceiling and crooked beams, bare wooden benches and seats built into the cream walls, paintings and bow windows. A curved high-backed settle stands on yellow tiles, a loudly ticking clock (which they sometimes forget to wind so it's not always accurate!) and a lovely big log fire crackles warmly. The little carpeted saloon is similar but even cosier. Adnams Bitter and Broadside and a seasonal guest tapped from the cask, farm cider and several wines by the glass. Darts, shove-ha'penny, table skittles, dominoes, cribbage and nine men's morris. There are seats in front of the pub, with its vine trellis. This is a popular place so you will need to get here early for a seat during peak times, and there may be a queue of people waiting for the doors to open on a Sunday.

🍴 A limited range of basic but well liked food, which comes in hearty and very fairly priced helpings: toast and beef dripping, lunchtime sandwiches (including things like banana with sugar and lemon), a mug of their famous home-made soup and filled Aga-baked potatoes; evening and Sunday lunchtime plates of excellent cold meat, smoked salmon, cheeses and pâté. *Starters/Snacks: £2.90 to £3.80. Main Courses: £4.30 to £5.80*

Free house ~ Licensees David and Robert Short ~ Real ale ~ Bar food (12-2.15, 7-9.30) ~ No credit cards ~ (01223) 870436 ~ Very well behaved children welcome in games room ~ Dogs welcome ~ Open 11.30-2.30, 6-11; 12-2.30, 7-10.30 Sun; closed 25 and 26 Dec

Recommended by Jerry Brown, Tim Maddison, Conor McGaughey, C Galloway, R T and J C Moggridge, Pat and Tony Martin, Tom and Ruth Rees, Mrs J Ekins-Daukes

PAMPISFORD   TL4948   MAP 5

Chequers ◧ £

2.6 miles from M11 junction 10: A505 E, then village and pub signed off; Town Lane; CB2 4ER

Cosy and civilised proper traditional pub with good value food – a nice find so close to the motorway

Cheerful helpful staff make this neatly kept old place a welcome stop. It has comfortably pubby old-fashioned furnishings under the low beams in its ochre ceiling, with some booth seating on the pale ceramic tiles of its cream-walled main area, and a low step down to a floor-boarded part with dark pink walls (and a television). They have Adnams Broadside, Greene King IPA, Sharps Doom Bar and Woodfordes Wherry on handpump, a good choice of wines by the glass, and nicely served coffee. The prettily planted simple garden has picnic-sets and is lit by traditional black streetlamps.

🍽 **The very fairly priced bar food includes a good range of light and main dishes at lunchtime such as filled baguettes and filled baked potatoes, soup, chicken liver pâté with onion jam, a trio of fishcakes with sweet chilli and tartare sauces, local sausages, home-made burger with blue cheese dressing, roast artichoke and red pepper lasagne with mozzarella and mascarpone, and steak in guinness pie, with evening choices like black tiger prawns in a thai curry sauce, wild and button mushrooms in a creamy garlic and wine sauce, spiced slow-roasted lamb shank, stilton chicken with red onion marmalade, and crispy duck in honey and oyster sauce with a spicy plum and stem ginger sauce; they also have a pie and a pint and a seafood evening, and an OAP lunch deal.** *Starters/Snacks: £4.00 to £6.00. Main Courses: £8.90 to £16.75. Puddings: £4.25*

Free house ~ Licensee Maureen Hutton ~ Real ale ~ Bar food (12-2, 6-9 (but some during afternoon also)) ~ (01223) 833220 ~ Children welcome ~ Dogs allowed in bar ~ Open 11-11(10.30 Sun)

Recommended by Christopher Roberts, D and M T Ayres-Regan, Dave Braisted, Charles Gysin

PETERBOROUGH   TL1899   MAP 5

Brewery Tap ◧ £

Opposite Queensgate car park; PE1 2AA

Fantastic range of real ales including own brews and popular thai food in huge conversion of old labour exchange

The fine choice of own-brewed real ales plus changing guests and the tasty thai food continue to draw customers into this striking modern conversion of an old labour exchange. There's an easy-going relaxed feel to the open-plan contemporary interior, with an expanse of light wood and stone floors for drinkers and blue-painted iron pillars holding up a steel-corded mezzanine level. It's stylishly lit by a giant suspended steel ring with bulbs running around the rim and steel-meshed wall lights. A band of chequered floor tiles traces the path of the long sculpted light wood bar counter, which is boldly backed by an impressive display of bottles in a ceiling-high wall of wooden cubes. A sofa seating area downstairs provides a comfortable corner for a surprisingly mixed bunch of customers of all ages; there's a big screen TV for sporting events, piped music and games machines and DJs or live bands at the weekends. A vast two-storey-high glass wall divides the bar and the brewery, giving fascinating views of the massive copper-banded stainless brewing vessels. From here they produce their own Oakham beers (Bishops Farewell, Inferno, JHB and White Dwarf) but they keep up to nine guests from thoughtfully chosen countrywide brewers as well; also, a good number of bottled belgian beers and quite a few wines by the glass. It gets very busy in the evening. The pub is owned by the same people as Charters (see below).

🍴 **The thai food is very good and extremely popular and runs from snacks such as chicken satay or tempura vegetables to soups like aromatic crispy duck noodle or tom yum and to main courses such as curries, noodle and rice dishes, salads and stir fries.** *Starters/Snacks: £2.99 to £3.99. Main Courses: £5.49 to £7.99. Puddings: £2.99 to £3.29*

Own brew ~ Licensee Jessica Loock ~ Real ale ~ Bar food (12-2.30, 6-9.30; 12-10.30 Fri, Sat) ~ Restaurant ~ (01733) 358500 ~ Children welcome during food service times only ~ Dogs allowed in bar ~ Live bands monthly ~ Open 12-11; closed 25 and 26 Dec, 1 Jan
Recommended by Pat and Tony Martin, Mike and Sue Loseby, R T and J C Moggridge, the Didler, Andy and Jill Kassube, Roger Fox, Rona Murdoch, Ian and Helen Stafford

Charters 🍺 £
Town Bridge, S side; PE1 1FP

Remarkable conversion of dutch grain barge with impressive real ales and good value pan-asian food

In fine weather, this unusual place really comes into its own as it has one of the biggest pub gardens in the city. It was once a barge working on the rivers and canals of Holland, Belgium and Germany and is now moored on the River Nene and houses a sizeable timbered bar on the lower deck and an oriental restaurant on the upper deck. Old wooden tables and pews provide plenty of seating, and there's an impressive range of real ales that includes four Oakham beers and around eight quickly changing guests from an interesting variety of brewers. They also keep around 30 foreign bottled beers, and hold regular beer festivals; piped music, games machines and darts. More reports please.

🍴 **As well as lunchtime wraps and panini, the pan-asian food includes lots of good value set-course meals, starters such as mixed tempura, penang chicken skewers and various parcels and rolls, and main courses that include noodle, rice and wok dishes, curries and seafood; they do a takeaway menu, too.** *Starters/Snacks: £2.00. Main Courses: £4.95 to £5.95*

Free house ~ Licensee Paul Hook ~ Real ale ~ Bar food (12-2.30(3.30 Sun), 5.30-10.30) ~ Restaurant ~ (01733) 315700 ~ Children welcome ~ Dogs allowed in bar ~ Live bands occasionally Fri and Sat after 11pm ~ Open 12-11(later Fri, Sat)
Recommended by Rona Murdoch, Barry Collett, the Didler

REACH   TL5666   MAP 5
Dyke's End 🍺
From B1102 E of A14/A1103 junction, follow signpost to Swaffham Prior and Upware – keep on through Swaffham Prior (Reach signposted from there); Fair Green; CB5 0JD

Candlelit rooms in former farmhouse, enjoyable food and own-brewed beer

With its own-brewed beers and enjoyable food, it's not surprising that this 17th-c farmhouse is so popular. A high-backed winged settle screens off the door and the simply decorated ochre-walled bar has stripped heavy pine tables and pale kitchen chairs on dark boards and one or two rugs. In a panelled section on the left are a few smarter dining tables, and on the right there's a step down to a red-carpeted part with the small red-walled servery and sensibly placed darts at the back; board games. All the tables have lit candles in earthenware bottles, and there may be a big bowl of lilies to brighten up the serving counter. As well as their own-brewed Devils Dyke Bitter and No 7 Pale Ale, they keep a couple of guests such as Adnams Bitter and Woodfordes Wherry on handpump alongside a decent wine list and Old Rosie cider. There are picnic-sets under big green canvas parasols out in front on the grass and Banger and Butter, the dachshunds, may have pride of place on a rug spread on the lawn. This is an attractive spot next to the church and the charming village green.

🍴 **Good bar food includes sandwiches, soup, home-cured gravadlax, linguine with duck ragoût, their renowned beer-battered fish and chips, local sausages with onion gravy, rosemary-baked chicken with tuscan potatoes, sage and taleggio risotto, fillet of bream** with caper butter, seasonal game, and puddings like treble chocolate brownie with vanilla pod ice-cream and date pudding with sticky toffee sauce. *Starters/Snacks: £4.50 to £6.50. Main Courses: £9.95 to £16.95. Puddings: £4.50*

Free house ~ Licensee Simon Owers ~ Real ale ~ Bar food (12-2(3 Sun), 7-9; not Sun evening, not Mon all day) ~ Restaurant ~ (01638) 743816 ~ Children allowed but must be well behaved ~ Dogs welcome ~ Quiz last Sun of month ~ Open 12-2.30, 6-11; 12-11(10.30 Sun) Sat; closed Mon lunchtime

Recommended by Sally Anne and Peter Goodale, John and Elisabeth Cox, Ryta Lyndley, John Wooll, Bettye Reynolds, John Saville, P and D Carpenter

STILTON
TL1689 MAP 5

Bell (♨) 𝖸 🛏

High Street; village signposted from A1 S of Peterborough; PE7 3RA

Fine coaching inn with several civilised rooms including a residents' bar, well liked food, and very pretty courtyard; bedrooms

Handy as a stop from the busy A1, this elegant 17th-c coaching inn has a good mix of customers and two neatly kept bars with an informal and relaxed atmosphere. There are bow windows, sturdy upright wooden seats on flagstone floors as well as plush button-back built-in banquettes, and a good big log fire in one handsome stone fireplace; one bar has a large cheese press. The partly stripped walls have big prints of sailing and winter coaching scenes, and there's a giant pair of blacksmith's bellows hanging in the middle of the front bar. Crouch Vale Brewers Gold, Digfield Barnwell Bitter, Fullers London Pride, Greene King IPA and Abbot and Hop Back Crop Circle on handpump or tapped from the cask, a dozen malt whiskies and 20 wines by the glass. Also, a bistro, restaurant and residents' bar. Through the fine coach arch is a very pretty sheltered courtyard with tables and a well which dates back to Roman times.

▥ **A high standard of bistro-style food includes dishes like sandwiches, soup, chicken liver parfait with pear and thyme chutney, cornish crab risotto, ham hock, apple and stilton pie with cumberland jelly, sun blush tomato and spinach cannelloni, roast free-range chicken with a mushroom, thyme and garlic sauce, venison and red wine pasty, steamed fillet of hake in savoy cabbage with poached egg and butter sauce, and puddings such as banana clafoutis with cinnamon ice-cream and warm gingerbread sponge with marmalade ice-cream.** *Starters/Snacks: £3.25 to £7.00. Main Courses: £11.95 to £16.45. Puddings: £4.75 to £6.95*

Free house ~ Licensee Liam McGivern ~ Real ale ~ Bar food (12-2.30(3 Sat and Sun), 6-9.30(9 Sun)) ~ Restaurant ~ (01733) 241066 ~ Children allowed in bistro ~ Open 12-3, 6-11(midnight Fri and Sat) ~ Bedrooms: £73.50B/£100.50B

Recommended by Mrs Hazel Rainer, Mrs P Bishop, John Robertson, Paul Humphreys, Kevin Thomas, Nina Randall, N R White, Ian and Nita Cooper, Paul and Marion Watts, Gordon and Margaret Ormondroyd, R T and J C Moggridge, Pete Coxon, Dr A McCormick, Martin and Karen Wake, Blaise Vyner

SUTTON GAULT
TL4279 MAP 5

Anchor (♨) 𝖸

Village signed off B1381 in Sutton; CB6 2BD

Tucked-away inn with charming candlelit rooms, good modern food, real ale and thoughtful wine list; bedrooms

It's not an easy thing to combine excellent food, lovely bedrooms and good service – all with the informal and relaxed atmosphere of a proper pub – but the licensees here have managed to achieve just that. Our readers this year have again been enthusiastic about all aspects of this charming 17th-c inn. If it's just a drink you want after a walk along the high embankment by the river (good bird-watching), you will be warmly welcomed and they keep a beer from Milton tapped from the cask and a dozen wines by the glass (including champagne); helpful, friendly service. The four heavily timbered rooms are stylishly simple with two log fires, antique settles and well spaced candlelit scrubbed pine tables on gently undulating old floors, and good lithographs and big prints on the walls. There are some seats outside.

🍴 From an interesting menu using local produce, the consistently high standard of food includes soup, grilled dates wrapped in bacon with a mild grain mustard cream sauce, hot smoked eel and smoked salmon on herb blinis with pea shoots and horseradish cream, chicken liver pâté with red onion marmalade, sausage casserole, herb pancake stuffed with ratatouille and ricotta, smoked haddock and salmon fishcakes on minted mushy peas with lemon butter sauce, moroccan-style chicken with citrus couscous, haunch of venison with celeriac and potato dauphinoise and redcurrant gravy, and puddings such as warm chocolate and pecan brownie with vanilla ice-cream and rhubarb crème brûlée; also, a good value two- and three-course weekday lunch menu and Sunday roasts. *Starters/Snacks: £4.95 to £6.50. Main Courses: £12.50 to £19.50. Puddings: £4.95 to £5.50*

Free house ~ Licensees Carlene Bunten and Adam Pickup ~ Real ale ~ Bar food (12-2, 7-9(6.30-9.30 Sat evening; 6.30-8.30 Sun evening)) ~ Restaurant ~ (01353) 778537 ~ Children welcome ~ Open 12-2.30, 7-10(6.30-11 Sat); 12-3, 6.30-10 Sun; closed evenings 25 and 26 Dec ~ Bedrooms: £59.50S/£75(£79.50S)(£115B)

Recommended by Mrs Margo Finlay, Jörg Kasprowski, Mr and Mrs B Murray, Peter J and Avril Hanson, M and GR, B R and M F Arnold, John Redfern, John Saville, John Wooll, Mike and Shelley Woodroffe, Jeff and Wendy Williams, Geoff and Carol Thorp, David Johnson, Michael Jefferson, Malcolm and Kate Dowty, P and D Carpenter

THRIPLOW

TL4346   MAP 5

Green Man

3 miles from M11 junction 10; A505 towards Royston, then first right; Lower Street; SG8 7RJ

Comfortable and cheery with homely food and changing ales

As one of our readers said, it's a bit incongruous for a pub with this name to be painted such a vivid blue, but it does make an excellent backdrop for the floral displays. Inside, it's comfortably laid out with modern tables and attractive high-backed dining chairs and pews, and there are some small pictures on deeply coloured walls; two arches lead through to a restaurant on the left. Four regularly changing real ales are likely to be from brewers such as Batemans, Nethergate, Oakham, Slaters and Woodfordes; darts. There are tables and an outdoor heater outside. The pub is handy for Duxford. More reports please.

🍴 Homely bar food includes filled baguettes, sausages with whole-grain mustard mash and onion gravy, battered cod and chips, chilli con carne, roast butternut squash and pinenut risotto, pork loin with cider gravy, slow-roasted lamb shoulder, and puddings. *Starters/Snacks: £5.00 to £7.00. Main Courses: £8.00 to £13.50. Puddings: £4.50*

Free house ~ Licensee Ian Parr ~ Real ale ~ Bar food (not Sun evening or Mon) ~ (01763) 208855 ~ Children welcome away from the bar ~ Open 12-3, 6-11; closed Sun evening, all day Mon

Recommended by Paul Humphreys, Mr and Mrs John Taylor, Roger and Lesley Everett

LUCKY DIP

Besides the fully inspected pubs, you might like to try these Lucky Dips recommended to us and described by readers (if you do, please send us reports: feedback@goodguides.com).

ABINGTON PIGOTTS [TL3044]
Pig & Abbot SG8 0SD: Popular local with two small bars and restaurant, good choice of food from bar meals up inc ample Sun lunch, friendly attentive staff, Adnams, Fullers London Pride and two guest beers, open woodburner in inglenook; garden, pretty village with good walks, open all day wknds *(Lucien Perring)*

ARRINGTON [TL3250]
☆ *Hardwicke Arms* SG8 0AH [Ermine Way (A1198)]: Handsome 18th-c coaching inn with 13th-c origins and 1792 work by Sir John Soane, enjoyable food from sandwiches and up-to-date snacks to game and fish, Greene King IPA and two interesting guest beers such as Buntingford, good friendly service, dark-panelled dining room, huge central fireplace, daily papers; piped music;

12 bedrooms, handy for Wimpole Hall, open all day *(LYM, Michael Dandy, Marion and Bill Cross)*

BARNACK [TF0704]

☆ *Millstone* PE9 3ET [off B1443 SE of Stamford; Millstone Lane]: Timbered bar in stone-built pub with clean contemporary feel, open fires, cosy corner, paintings by local artists, Adnams, Greene King Old Speckled Hen and Everards Tiger, several well priced wines by the glass, enjoyable pubby food with modern touches (not Sun evening, Mon, Tues); sheltered courtyard, pretty village nr Burghley House *(G Jennings, LYM, Roy Bromell, Ian and Helen Stafford)*

BARRINGTON [TL3849]

Royal Oak CB2 5RZ [turn off A10 about 3.75 miles SW of M11 junction 11, in Foxton; West Green]: Rambling thatched Tudor pub with tables out overlooking classic village green, heavy low beams and timbers, mixed furnishings inc leather sofa, friendly helpful service, enjoyable if not particularly cheap food from ciabattas to steak, children's helpings, Adnams, Greene King and Wells & Youngs ales, several wines by the glass, good coffee, light and airy dining conservatory; piped music; children welcome, open all day Sun *(Michael Dandy, LYM)*

BOXWORTH [TL3464]

☆ *Golden Ball* CB3 8LY [High St]: Attractive partly thatched building, comfortable open-plan contemporary bar with scrubbed pine tables, three-part restaurant in original core, friendly helpful staff, enjoyable generous food from lunchtime snacks to more substantial evening dishes, well kept Wells & Youngs ales; nice garden and heated terrace, pastures behind, 11 good quiet bedrooms in adjacent block, substantial breakfast, open all day *(Geoffrey Hughes, Bruce and Sharon Eden, BB, Michael Dandy, Simon Collett-Jones)*

BRANDON CREEK [TL6091]

☆ *Ship* PE38 0PP [A10 Ely—Downham Market]: Lovely spot on Norfolk border at confluence of Great and Little Ouse, plenty of tables out by the moorings; welcoming helpful staff, good choice of enjoyable pub food inc specials, real ales such as Adnams, St Austell, Shepherd Neame Spitfire and seasonal beers, spacious tastefully modernised bar with massive stone masonry in sunken former forge area, big log fire one end, woodburner the other, interesting old photographs and prints, evening restaurant; bedrooms *(Mrs Hazel Rainer, R C Vincent, LYM)*

BUCKDEN [TL1967]

☆ *Lion* PE19 5XA [High St]: Partly 15th-c coaching inn, black beams and big inglenook log fire in airy and civilised bow-windowed entrance bar with plush bucket seats, wing armchairs and settees, decent bar food inc good value lunchtime sandwiches, good choice of wines, Greene King ales, friendly staff, no music or machines, panelled back restaurant beyond latticed window partition; children welcome, bedrooms *(BB,*

Michael Dandy, Nigel and Sue Foster, Gerry and Rosemary Dobson, Lois Dyer)

CAMBRIDGE [TL4458]

Anchor CB3 9EL [Silver St]: Well laid out if touristy pub in beautiful riverside position by a punting station, fine river views from upper bar and suntrap terrace, well kept beer, good bar lunches from sandwiches up, evening baguettes, popular Sun roast, good service; children in eating areas, wheelchair access, open all day *(John and Gloria Isaacs, Chris and Angela Buckell, LYM, Ian and Jane Haslock)*

Bath CB2 3QN [Bene't St]: Unpretentious panelled pub with Greene King ales, sensibly priced food (as Eagle next door); sports TV, piped music, games machine *(Michael Dandy)*

Burleigh Arms CB5 8EG [Newmarket Rd]: Two well furnished bars, good food choice, prompt service, good wines by the glass; terrace *(John Marsh)*

Castle CB3 0AJ [Castle St]: Full Adnams beer range and several guests in big airy bare-boards bar, several pleasantly simple rooms, wide range of good value quick pubby food from sandwiches up, friendly staff, peaceful upstairs (downstairs can be louder, with piped pop music – live jazz Sun night); picnic-sets in good walled back courtyard *(the Didler, J K Parry, Jerry Brown, Michael Dandy)*

Clarendon Arms CB1 1JX [Clarendon St]: Partly flagstoned, with interesting wall hangings and other collectables, friendly attentive service, bustling local atmosphere, Greene King ales, reasonably priced food, carpeted dining area, books and daily papers, darts, cribbage; piped music, TV, simple good value bedrooms, open all day *(John Marsh)*

☆ *Eagle* CB2 3QN [Bene't Street]: The star is for this rambling and interesting ancient building's striking architectural features (even one ceiling left unpainted since World War II to preserve airmen's signatures worked in with Zippo lighters, candle smoke and lipstick; good choice of well kept ales such as Black Sheep, Fullers London Pride, Greene King IPA, Stonehenge and Wells & Youngs Bombardier, bargain bar food; wheelchair access via side entrance, attractive cobbled and galleried courtyard, can get very busy with tourists and students, open all day *(Giles and Annie Francis, Ian and Jane Haslock, Rob and Catherine Dunster, the Didler, Simon Watkins, Michael Dandy, Michael Sargent, John and Gloria Isaacs, Chris and Angela Buckell, Peter and Giff Bennett, LYM, Ian Phillips, J K Parry, John Saville, Chris Evans)*

Granta CB3 9EX [Newnham Terrace]: Early 19th-c pub with quiet balcony and heated terrace taking full advantage of view over mill pond, ducks and weeping-willow meadow, good value usual food from sandwiches up, Greene King ales with a guest such as Everards, efficient service; punt hire *(Ian Phillips)*

☆ **Kingston Arms** CB1 2NU [Kingston St]: Well kept interesting changing ales from a dozen or so handpumps, enjoyable lunchtime food freshly made from good ingredients, companionably big plain tables and basic seating, thriving chatty largely studenty atmosphere, good choice of wines by the glass, friendly service, no music or children inside, two internet points; disabled access, small pretty back yard, torch-lit, heated and partly covered, open all day Fri-Sun *(Jerry Brown, Chris and Angela Buckell, BB)*

☆ **Live & Let Live** CB1 2EA [Mawson Rd]: Popular old backstreet local, friendly and relaxed, with Everards Tiger, Nethergate Umbel Magna and six changing guests tapped from the cask, lots of bottled belgian beers, local ciders, bargain food, heavily timbered brickwork rooms with sturdy varnished pine tables on bare boards, country bric-a-brac and some steam railway and brewery memorabilia, gas lighting (not always lit), cribbage and dominoes; children and dogs welcome, disabled access *(Revd R P Tickle, Dr David Cockburn, Dave Braisted, Chris and Angela Buckell, LYM, Giles and Annie Francis)*

Mitre CB2 1UF [Bridge St, opp St John's Coll]: Welcoming M&B pub with soft lighting and old-fashioned tavern décor, tasty bargain food, friendly service, well priced wines by the glass, well kept changing beers, farm cider, log-effect fire; disabled access *(Mrs Hazel Rainer, Revd R P Tickle, Chris and Angela Buckell, Michael Dandy, J K Parry)*

☆ **Old Spring** CB4 1HB [Ferry Path; car park on Chesterton Rd]: Extended Victorian pub, roomy and airy, with smartly old-fashioned scrubbed-wood décor, bare boards, lots of old pictures, enjoyable home-made food inc enterprising dishes and Sun roasts, efficient pleasant service, well kept Greene King IPA, Abbot and three guests, good coffee and choice of wines by the glass, two log fires, long back conservatory; piped music, no under-21s evenings, dogs outside only; disabled facilities, large heated well planted terrace, open all day *(Mrs Hazel Rainer, Simon Watkins, LYM)*

CASTOR [TL1298]

Prince of Wales Feathers PE5 7AL [off A47]: Friendly stone-built local with well kept Woodfordes and interesting guest beers, landlady doing limited choice of good value lunchtime food, farm cider and perry, darts, dominoes, pool, setter called Maddy; games machine, Sat live music; children welcome, garden tables, open all day *(Ian and Helen Stafford)*

CATWORTH [TL0873]

Racehorse PE28 0PF [B660, S of A14]: Large friendly rather elegant village pub, well kept ales, good food choice inc Sun carvery, racing memorabilia, restaurant *(Guy and Caroline Howard)*

CLAYHITHE [TL5064]

☆ **Bridge Hotel** CB5 9HZ [Clayhithe Rd]: Popular Chef & Brewer with good choice of enjoyable sensibly priced food, plenty of tables inside and out (even so, get there early as they don't take reservations), friendly attentive staff, small bar area, well kept Courage Directors, beams and timbers; picturesque spot by River Cam with pretty waterside garden *(LYM, M and GR, Dr and Mrs T C Dann, Simon Watkins, Paul Humphreys)*

CROYDON [TL3149]

☆ **Queen Adelaide** SG8 0DN [off A1198 or B1042; High St]: Spreading open-plan carpeted local with wide range of enjoyable food inc Mon-Weds OAP lunches, friendly prompt service, real ales such as Badger and Elgoods, several wines by the glass, lots of spirits, big low-beamed main area with standing timbers dividing off part with settees, banquettes and stools, games area with pool, conservatory extension, daily papers; piped music (even in gents' – a shrine to Marilyn Monroe), TV, machines; heated terrace with smokers' shelter, lawn with play area, new bedrooms, open all day Fri-Sun *(R T and J C Moggridge, P and D Carpenter, BB, Michael Dandy, Simon Watkins)*

DULLINGHAM [TL6357]

Boot CB8 9UW [Brinkley Rd]: Unfussy country pub with up to four well kept changing ales, good value simple food, community-spirited licensees *(Jerry Brown)*

DUXFORD [TL4746]

John Barleycorn CB2 4PP [handy for M11 junction 10; signed off A505 E at Volvo junction]: Thatch, shutters, low beams, charming old-world furnishings, prints and china, gentle lighting, good generous reasonably priced food from open sandwiches up all day, good service even when busy, well kept Greene King IPA and Abbot, decent wines; may be piped music; tables out among flowers, pleasantly simple beamed bedrooms, open all day *(Ross Balaam, Philip Denton, LYM)*

EATON SOCON [TL1658]

Crown PE19 8EN [Gt North Rd (B4128, nr A1/A428 interchange)]: Chef & Brewer with linked low-beamed areas, moderately priced food from sandwiches and baked potatoes up, Courage Directors, Hook Norton, Theakstons and Wells & Youngs Bombardier, wide choice of wines, good coffee, two coal-effect gas fires; can get busy evenings, games machine, piped music; garden, comfortable bedroom block *(Michael Dandy)*

ELTISLEY [TL2759]

☆ **Eltisley** PE19 6TG [signed off A428; The Green]: Flagstoned bar with beams, timbering, some zinc-topped cast-iron tables and big log fire, attractive dining areas inc stylish barn room, good carefully sourced home-made food, friendly service, Wells & Youngs ales, good choice of wines by the glass; children welcome, nice garden, good value bedrooms *(Eithne Dandy, Michael Dandy, Nick Turner, LYM, Maggie Oliver)*

ELY [TL5479]

☆ **Cutter** CB7 4BN [Annesdale, off Station Rd (or walk S along Riverside Walk from Maltings)]: Beautifully placed contemporary riverside pub with reasonably priced generous food from sandwiches up inc good value Sun roasts in carpeted dining bar and smart restaurant, Greene King, Shepherd Neame Spitfire and Woodfordes Wherry, good coffee and wines by the glass; outside tables popular with smokers *(Ryta Lyndley, Michael Dandy, Robert Turnham, LYM, DF, NF, Mrs Hazel Rainer)*

Lamb CB7 4EJ [Brook St (Lynn rd)]: Wide choice of good locally sourced food in panelled lounge bar inc OAP deals (Mon), friendly staff, good choice of wines by the glass, Greene King ales; close to cathedral, bedrooms *(David Greene, Michael Dandy)*

Minster Tavern CB7 4EL [Minster Place]: Victorian/Edwardian décor in older beamed M&B nr cathedral, good pubby bar food from sandwiches up, four real ales inc Greene King and Shepherd Neame Spitfire *(Robert Gomme, John and Helen Rushton)*

West End House CB6 3AY [West End, off Cambridge Rd]: Old corner local with beams, open fires, some stripped brickwork, mixed furniture inc leather armchairs, pews and plush banquettes, assorted pictures and pub bric-a-brac, good choice of well kept ales, sandwiches and light snacks inc good ploughman's (not Sun); courtyard garden with pergola, open all day Fri, Sat *(Chris Evans)*

ETTON [TF1406]

Golden Pheasant PE6 7DA [just off B1443 N of Peterborough, signed from nr N end of A15 bypass]: Refurbished by new landlady with restaurant next to comfortable bar, enjoyable food inc early-evening bargains, good welcoming staff, Greene King IPA, decent wines by the glass; children welcome, good-sized tree-sheltered garden *(Michael and Jenny Back, Ian and Helen Stafford, BB)*

FORDHAM [TL6270]

☆ **White Pheasant** CB7 5LQ [off A142/B1102 N of Newmarket; Market St]: Light and airy open-plan dining pub, well kept beers such as Nethergate and Woodfordes Wherry, good wines by the glass inc champagne, quite a few malt whiskies, log fire, nice mix of mismatched furniture inc big farmhouse tables, rugs on bare boards, some stripped brickwork, cheery log fire; food can be good but is not cheap and service may be slow; well behaved children welcome *(B A Lord, George Cowie, Frances Gosnell, Dave Braisted, BB, LYM)*

FOWLMERE [TL4245]

☆ **Chequers** SG8 7SR [B1368]: Civilised and gently refurbished 16th-c country dining pub, two comfortable downstairs rooms with log fire, room upstairs with beams, timbers and some interesting moulded plasterwork above one fireplace, good if pricey upscale food, Adnams ales and a guest like Sharps

Doom Bar, good choice of wines by the glass and whiskies, conservatory (children allowed here); piped music; terrace with smart dark green furniture, neat floodlit garden *(John Robertson, David and Valerie Mort, Virginia Williams, Roy Hoing, Alan and Eve Harding, LYM, David and Ruth Shillitoe, D E Ball)*

GODMANCHESTER [TL2470]

☆ **Exhibition** PE29 2HZ [London Rd]: Attractive choice of rooms inc main bar with re-created shop-fronts on walls, complete with doors and stock in windows; cosy, with big flagstones, traditional furnishings, fairy lights, enjoyable well priced food, well kept Fullers London Pride, decent choice of wines by the glass; picnic-sets on back lawn (a couple in front, too), open all day *(Derek and Sylvia Stephenson, Elizabeth Lester, Michael Dandy, Virginia Williams, R T and J C Moggridge, LYM, John Saul, Alan and Eve Harding)*

GRANTCHESTER [TL4355]

☆ **Blue Ball** CB3 9NQ [Broadway]: Particularly well kept Adnams and a guest such as Timothy Taylors Landlord in character bare-boards village local, said to be the area's oldest, proper hands-on landlord, good log fire, Aspall's cider, cards and traditional games inc shut the box and ring the bull, lots of books; dogs welcome, tables on small terrace with lovely views to Grantchester meadows, nice village *(Conor McGaughey, Jerry Brown, Pete Baker)*

GREAT CHISHILL [TL4239]

☆ **Pheasant** SG8 8SR [follow Heydon signpost from B1039 in village]: Good freshly made food using local produce in popular split-level flagstoned pub with beams, open fires, timbering and some elaborately carved though modern seats and settles, welcoming landlady and friendly service, real ales such as Adnams, Courage Best and Directors and Theakstons, good choice of wines by the glass, small dining room, darts, cribbage, dominoes; children welcome, charming secluded back garden with small play area *(LYM, Mrs Margo Finlay, Jörg Kasprowski, Marion and Bill Cross)*

GUYHIRN [TF3903]

☆ **Oliver Twist** PE13 4EA [follow signs from A47/A141 junction S of Wisbech]: Comfortable open-plan lounge with buoyant local atmosphere, good generous inexpensive home-made food from sandwiches to steaks, cheerful attentive service, interesting changing real ales, big open fires, neat sturdy furnishings, restaurant; may be piped music; six bedrooms *(BB, Malcolm M Stewart)*

HEMINGFORD ABBOTS [TL2870]

Axe & Compass PE28 9AH [High St]: Appealing 15th-c two-bar thatched pub with flagstones and inglenook, friendly helpful staff, Adnams and Greene King IPA, good choice of wines by the glass, good value fresh pubby lunchtime food from baguettes up inc OAP and children's meals, wider evening menu, contemporary extension dining areas, afternoon tea and coffee; soft piped music, games machine, TV, pool, quiz or live music nights; children and dogs welcome, disabled facilities, garden tables and separate menu, nearby walks, quiet pretty village, open all day *(Michael Dandy, JJW, CMW, Peter and Felicity Brasier)*

HISTON [TL4363]

Red Lion CB4 9JD [High St]: Cheery and friendly, with half a dozen well kept changing ales (spring and early autumn beer festivals), many bottled belgian beers, good value generous pub lunches, proper character landlord, lots of pubby memorabilia, log fire in well used lounge, games in extended public bar; big garden, open all day Sat *(Jerry Brown)*

HOLYWELL [TL3370]

☆ *Old Ferry Boat* PE27 4TG [signed off A1123]: Partly thatched Greene King pub in lovely peaceful setting, low beams, open fires and interesting side areas, window seats overlooking Great Ouse, real ales, decent wines by the glass, good coffee, reasonably priced food (all day in summer – service well organised to cope with crowds); quiet piped music, games; children welcome, plenty of tables and cocktail parasols on front terrace and riverside lawn, moorings, seven good bedrooms, open all day wknds *(Ian Phillips, Lois Dyer, LYM, Mrs Hazel Rainer, Ross Balaam)*

HORSEHEATH [TL6147]

Old Red Lion CB1 6QF [Linton Rd]: Well refurbished and neatly kept Greene King pub, good value food, efficient staff; 12 comfortable bedroom cabins *(Mrs Jane Kingsbury, Simon Watkins)*

HUNTINGDON [TL2371]

☆ *George* PE29 3AB [George St]: Relaxed, friendly and comfortable hotel lounge bar, generous reasonably priced sandwiches and bar and brasserie meals, Greene King IPA and Abbot, good choice of wines by the glass, good coffee (or tea and pastries); piped music; magnificent galleried central courtyard, comfortable bedrooms *(LYM, Ian and Nita Cooper, Michael Dandy)*

LEIGHTON BROMSWOLD [TL1175]

☆ *Green Man* PE28 5AW [signed off A14 Huntingdon—Kettering]: Enjoyable good value food in neatly modernised open-plan village pub, real ales such as Timothy Taylors Landlord, pleasant staff, heavy low beams, inglenook log fire, pool and boules *(Ryta Lyndley, LYM)*

LINTON [TL5546]

Crown CB21 4HS [High St]: Friendly traditional local in nice village, comfortable and well run, good choice of food from chef/landlord (recipes on pub website) from sandwiches up (not Sun evening), well kept beers, decent wines, big log fire, bare boards, brasserie-style restaurant; five refurbished bedrooms, open all day Sun till 8pm *(Mrs Margo Finlay, Jörg Kasprowski)*

MEPAL [TL4481]

Three Pickerels CB6 2AR [Bridge Rd]: Recently modernised old riverside inn;

popular good value pub food, Greene King ales and a guest, interesting old local photographs; garden and decking overlooking New Bedford River and grassland, four bedrooms, open all day Fri-Sun *(Terry Mizen)*

NORTHBOROUGH [TF1407]

Packhorse PE6 9BL [Lincoln Rd]: Newly reworked as smart dining pub, new licensees doing enjoyable reasonably priced food, Adnams and Theakstons, polite helpful staff *(Ian and Helen Stafford)*

PETERBOROUGH [TL1898]

Old Monk PE1 1LZ [Cowgate]: Roomy relaxed open-plan Wetherspoons in sympathetically converted draper's, fine ale range, bargain food all day, lots of stripped pine inc cosy booths on left; can get very busy with young people Fri, Sat evenings *(Roger Fox)*

SPALDWICK [TL1372]

☆ *George* PE28 0TD [just off A14 W of Huntingdon]: Friendly 16th-c pub with good individual up-to-date food, stylish décor, sofas in bar, larger bistro area, lots of wines by the glass, local real ales, good coffee; children welcome *(J Roberts, D Vigers, Charman family, LYM)*

ST IVES [TL3171]

White Hart PE27 5AH [Sheep Market]: Well kept old town-centre pub with enjoyable home cooking, good helpings and sensible prices, warm friendly service and atmosphere; attractive courtyard, bedrooms *(Robert Turnham)*

ST NEOTS [TL1859]

☆ *Chequers* PE19 2TA [St Marys St (B1043 S of centre)]: Friendly 16th-c village pub with small carpeted beamed bar, appealing mix of furniture inc unusual rocking chair, log fire in big inglenook, beers such as Archers, Elgoods and Thwaites, tasty food from sandwiches up inc wkdy OAP two-course lunches, attractive back restaurant with rugs on brick floor; piped music; children allowed in restaurant, tables on terrace and in sheltered garden, cl Sun evening and Mon *(Michael Dandy, John and Elisabeth Cox, LYM)*

STAPLEFORD [TL4751]

Longbow CB2 5DS [Church St]: Welcoming bright local, simple and roomy, with five well kept changing ales, local Cassels' cider, standard food inc bargain Sun lunch, well chosen reasonably priced wines, pleasant staff, darts and pool; some live music; open all day Fri *(Jerry Brown)*

STILTON [TL1689]

Stilton Cheese PE7 3RP [signed off A1; North St]: Former coaching inn with wide range of enjoyable food from sandwiches up inc lots of fish, a couple of real ales, decent wines, welcoming staff, interesting old interior with log fire in unpretentious central bar, good tables in two rooms off, separate two-room restaurant; no dogs; tables out in back garden with sheltered decking, bedrooms *(JJW, CMW, Oliver and Sue Rowell)*

STOW CUM QUY [TL5159]

Quy Mill CB5 9AG [Newmarket Rd]: Best

Western hotel (not a pub) with neat friendly staff in its well appointed bar, good food, three well kept changing ales, wide choice of whiskies and wines; comfortable bedrooms *(Jerry Brown)*

STRETHAM [TL5072]

Lazy Otter CB6 3LU [Elford Closes, off A10 S of Stretham roundabout]: Big rambling family pub on Great Ouse, good views from waterside conservatory and big garden, cheerful staff, good value enjoyable food, good wine choice, interesting guest ales such as Bull Box, clean and nicely furnished, warm fire; piped music can be obtrusive; bedroom annex, open all day *(Ryta Lyndley, Adele Summers, Alan Black, Mrs Hazel Rainer, LYM, Ian and Nita Cooper)*

UFFORD [TF0904]

☆ *White Hart* PE9 3BH [back rd Peterborough—Stamford, just S of B1443; Main St]: 17th-c village pub with good food all day using local organic supplies and their own free-range eggs, nice coffee and wines by the glass, welcoming service, own good Ufford ales (brewed here) and guests, comfortable seating, log fire and railway memorabilia in busy stripped stone and flagstoned bar, rustic back dining area and conservatory; children welcome, big garden with terrace and play area, bedroom block, open all day *(Tom Evans, Roy Bromell, Ray and Winifred Halliday, the Didler, LYM, Jeff and Wendy Williams)*

UPWARE [TL5372]

Five Miles From Anywhere, No Hurry CB7 5ZR: Aptly named spacious modern pub in fine riverside site with elaborate play area, extensive moorings and public slipway (day boats for hire, riverboat stop), picnic-sets on heated waterside terrace and on lawns by weeping willows; friendly prompt service, real ales such as Caledonian Deuchars IPA, Elgoods Mild, Greene King Old Speckled Hen and St Austell Tribute, good choice of pubby food inc Mon bargains, open fire, restaurant, pool room; may be piped music, games machines; children welcome, disabled facilities, open all day in summer *(LYM, Dudley and Moira Cockroft)*

WANSFORD [TL0799]

Haycock PE8 6JA [just off A1 W of Peterborough]: Big hotel and conference centre, useful break for all-day food from sandwiches up, good wine choice, Bass and Black Sheep, variety of seating areas with plenty of character, big log fire, brasserie and airy conservatory; may expect you to pay full price in advance if you book meals on special days; children in eating areas, attractive courtyard and garden near river, dogs allowed in bar and comfortable bedrooms, open all day *(LYM, Roy Bromell, Eithne Dandy, Pete Coxon, Derek Thomas)*

WARESLEY [TL2454]

Duncombe Arms SG19 3BS [Eltisley Rd (B1040, 5 miles S of A428)]: Comfortable welcoming old pub, long main bar, fire one end, good range of good value generous wholesome food from lunchtime sandwiches up, well kept Greene King ales, good choice of wines by the glass, good service, back room and restaurant; occasional live music; picnic-sets in small shrub-sheltered garden *(Denise Edwards, BB)*

WHITTLESFORD [TL4648]

Bees in the Wall CB2 4NZ [North Rd; handy for M11 junction 10]: Comfortably worn-in split-level timbered lounge with flowers on polished tables and country prints, small tiled public bar with old wall settles, darts and local football pictures, decent good value food from sandwiches up (not Sun, Mon evenings), well kept Fullers London Pride, Timothy Taylors Landlord and a guest beer, open fires; may be piped classical music, games machine; no dogs, picnic-sets in big paddock-style garden with terrace, bees' nest visible in wall, handy for Duxford air museum, open all day wknds *(Kevin Thorpe)*

Tickell Arms CB2 4NZ [off B1379 S of Cambridge, handy for M10 junction 10, via A505; North Rd]: Restaurant rather than pub (can go for a drink though) with accomplished chef producing top-end pricey food, extensive wine list, bottled beers, some cheaper lunchtime food from sandwiches up (they add an optional 12½% service charge), afternoon tea; great building and atmosphere, with ornate heavy furnishings, soft lighting, good log fire, attractive flower-filled Victorian-style conservatory overlooking ducks and black swans on pond in formal terraced garden, cheerful staff *(LYM, Kevin Thorpe)*

WISBECH [TF4509]

Hare & Hounds PE13 1JR [North Brink]: Friendly pub well run by pleasant landlady, well kept Elgoods and guest ales, basic lunchtime bar food, may be good free nibbles early Fri evening *(Ian and Debs)*

A few pubs try to make you leave a credit card at the bar, as a sort of deposit if you order food. This is a bad practice, and the banks and credit card firms warn you not to let your card go like this.

Cheshire

Pubs doing particularly well all round this year are the Hanging Gate at Langley, the nicely refurbished Sutton Hall near Macclesfield, the particularly friendly Smoker at Plumley and the Roebuck in Mobberley – which gains our title of Cheshire Dining Pub of the Year. Returning to the Main Entries this year is the Plough at Eaton, scoring on both food and drinks. Others we'd commend especially for drinks are the Bhurtpore at Aston, the Mill and the Old Harkers Arms (both in Chester) and the Grosvenor Arms at Aldford. The White Lion at Barthomley is a perennial favourite for its timeless atmosphere, and many of the county's other good pubs gain from being fine buildings, or in appealing surroundings – the Ship at Wincle is a prime example. A few top Lucky Dips, almost all already inspected and approved by us: the Victoria in Altrincham, Cock o' Barton at Barton, Ring o' Bells in Frodsham, Harrington Arms at Gawsworth, Nags Head at Haughton, Swan at Kettleshulme and Highwayman at Rainow. Much the most successful local beer is Weetwood; Storm, Coach House, Spitting Feathers, Betwixt and Beartown are popular, too.

ALDFORD   SJ4259   MAP 7

Grosvenor Arms ★
B5130 Chester—Wrexham; CH3 6HJ

Spacious place with buoyantly chatty atmosphere, impressive range of drinks, well balanced sensibly imaginative menu, good service; lovely big terrace and gardens

They dispense a very wide array of drinks here from a fine-looking bar counter, including more than 20 wines served by the glass, an impressive range of whiskies, distinctive soft drinks such as peachy and elderflower cordial and Willington Fruit Farm pressed apple juice, as well as seven real ales, with Thwaites Original and Weetwood Eastgate alongside interesting guests such as Northumberland Original, Thwaites Nutty Black and Weetwood Oast House Gold. Cream-painted areas are sectioned by big knocked-through arches and a variety of wood, quarry tile, flagstone and black and white tiled floor finishes – some good richly coloured turkey rugs look well against these natural materials. Good solid pieces of traditional furniture, plenty of interesting pictures and attractive lighting keep it all intimate enough. A big panelled library room has tall bookshelves lining one wall, and lots of substantial tables well spaced on its handsomely boarded floor. Lovely on summer evenings, the airy terracotta-floored conservatory has lots of gigantic low hanging flowering baskets and chunky pale wood garden furniture. This opens out to a large elegant suntrap terrace, and a neat lawn with picnic-sets, young trees and an old tractor. Attentive service is friendly and reliable, and they keep a good selection of board games.

🍴 Food is very good: the well balanced changing menu includes something to please most tastes, and local ingredients include asparagus from a nearby farm. As well as sandwiches, there might be starters such as shropshire blue cheesecake or scallops with pressed ham hock and cauliflower purée, and a choice of light bites like mussels or steak sandwich on ciabatta or main courses including roast pork fillet with chorizo faggots, thai seafood curry, and cambozola and roast butternut squash salad. Their puddings might feature

belgian waffle with ice cream and butterscotch sauce, cherry crumble tart or raspberry and amaretti trifle. They also run special food weeks. *Starters/Snacks: £4.50 to £7.50. Main Courses: £8.50 to £16.00. Puddings: £4.90 to £5.60*

Brunning & Price ~ Manager Tracey Varley ~ Real ale ~ Bar food (12-9.30(9 Sun)) ~ (01244) 620228 ~ Children welcome ~ Dogs allowed in bar ~ Open 11.30-11; 12-10.30 Sun

Recommended by Alex and Claire Pearse, Gerry and Rosemary Dobson, Clive Watkin, Paul Boot, J S Burn, Mr and Mrs J Palmer, David and Katharine Cooke, Revd D Glover, M G Hart, Don Bryan, Bruce and Sharon Eden

ASTBURY
SJ8461   MAP 7

Egerton Arms ⇔
Village signposted off A34 S of Congleton; CW12 4RQ

Cheery village pub with straightforward bar food, large garden and nice bedrooms

Originally a farmhouse, parts of this dates back to the 16th c and it makes a pleasant place to sit outside at well placed tables and enjoy the views of the church. Rambling around the bar, its cream-painted rooms are decorated with the odd piece of armour and shelves of books. Mementoes of the Sandow Brothers who performed as 'the World's Strongest Youths' are particularly interesting as one of them was the landlady's father. In summer, dried flowers replace the fire in the big fireplace. Three Robinsons ales such as Double Hop, Trouble and Strife and Unicorn are on handpump, and they serve Pimms and a range of malt whiskies. Out in front is a play area with a wooden fort. Despite the large car park you might struggle for a place Sunday lunchtime. More reports please.

🍴 **As well as sandwiches, bar food might include herrings in dill marinade, steak and kidney pudding, grilled trout with honey and almonds, lasagne, sweet potato, chickpea and spinach currey, spinach curry, steaks, and pudding such as lemon meringue pie and white and dark chocolate truffle cake.** *Starters/Snacks: £3.95 to £4.95. Main Courses: £8.50 to £14.95. Puddings: £3.75 to £3.95*

Robinsons ~ Tenants Alan and Grace Smith ~ Real ale ~ Bar food (11.30-2, 6-9) ~ Restaurant ~ (01260) 273946 ~ Children welcome ~ Open 11.30-11; 11.30-3, 6.30-11 Sun ~ Bedrooms: £50S/£80S(£70B)

Recommended by Neil Kellett, Paul J Robinshaw, Mike Proctor, Chris Brooks

ASTON
SJ6146   MAP 7

Bhurtpore ★ ♀ ◖
Off A530 SW of Nantwich; in village follow Wrenbury signpost; CW5 8DQ

Fantastic range of drinks (especially real ales) and tasty curries in warm-hearted pub with some unusual artefacts; big garden

It's well worth a special trip here to sample the terrific range of 11 superbly kept real ales, and in summer they hold a beer festival. Salopian Golden Thread tends to be on most of the time, but the rest changes constantly, and they usually get through over 1,000 different brews in a year. These might be from any part of the country though they do try to give preferential treatment to local beers – so you might find on offer the likes of Acorn Old Moor Porter, Brains Dark, Hopback Summer Lightning, Moorhouses Premier and Thornbridge Jaipur IPA. They also stock dozens of unusual bottled beers and fruit beers, a great many bottled ciders and perries, over 100 different whiskies and carefully selected soft drinks; good wine list. The pub takes its unusual name from the town in India where a local landowner, Lord Combermere, won a battle; it also explains why a collection of exotic artefacts in the carpeted lounge bar has an indian influence – look out for the turbaned statue behind the counter, proudly sporting any sunglasses left behind by customers; also good local period photographs, and some attractive furniture. Tables in the comfortable public bar are reserved for people not eating; board games, pool, TV and games machine. At lunchtime and early weekday evenings the atmosphere is cosy and civilised, and on weekends, when it gets packed, the cheery staff cope superbly.

🍴 **The enjoyable menu has sandwiches and panini (not Fri or Sat evenings), starters with a spicy theme, a choice of up to eight tasty curries and baltis, salmon fillet with orange and herb crumb topping and hearty meat dishes such as sausages from outdoor reared local pigs and braised steak in belgian trappist ale. Daily changing specials include lighter meal options, as well as main courses like herdwick mutton pie and braised belly pork. They feature game dishes such as venison and pigeon pie and pheasant breast in season; puddings might include rhubarb and apple oat crumble or chocolate and raspberry brownie.** *Starters/Snacks: £4.50 to £6.95. Main Courses: £5.50 to £15.95. Puddings: £4.50 to £4.75*

Free house ~ Licensee Simon George ~ Real ale ~ Bar food (12-9.30 Sat, Sun) ~ Restaurant ~ (01270) 780917 ~ Children welcome (until 8.30pm Fri, Sat) ~ Dogs allowed in bar ~ Open 12-2.30(3 Sat), 6.30-11.30; 12-midnight Fri, Sat; 12-11.30 Sun

Recommended by Malcolm and Pauline Pellatt, Dave Webster, Sue Holland, Mike Proctor, R T and J C Moggridge, Martin Grosberg, the Didler

BARTHOMLEY
SJ7752   MAP 7

White Lion ★ £

A mile from M6 junction 16; from exit roundabout take B5078 N towards Alsager, then Barthomley signposted on left; CW2 5PG

Charming 17th-c thatched village tavern with classic period interior and good value straightforward tasty lunchtime food

'The epitome of what a pub should be: completely unspoilt and welcoming' was one reader's comment on this friendly, unpretentious place. The main bar is timelessly informal, with a blazing open fire, heavy low oak beams (dating back to Stuart times), attractively moulded black panelling, Cheshire history and prints on the walls, latticed windows and thick wobbly old tables. Up some steps, a second room has another welcoming open fire, more oak panelling, a high-backed winged settle, a paraffin lamp hinged to the wall; shove-ha'penny; local societies make good use of a third room. Five real ales include Mansfield, Marstons Bitter and guests – usually Jennings Cocker Hoop and Snecklifter, and Wychwood Hobgoblin. On a summer's day, it can be quite idyllic here enjoying a drink outside on seats or picnic-sets on the cobbles, and taking in the views of the attractive old village and the early 15th-c red sandstone church of St Bertiline (where you can learn about the Barthomley massacre).

🍴 **The short traditional menu includes enjoyable sandwiches (some made with hot beef, ham or pork), ploughman's, staffordshire oatcakes with bacon, cheese, onions, tomatoes and beans, steak pie and their most popular main course, hotpot with french bread.** *Main Courses: £5.25 to £8.50. Puddings: £2.50*

Marstons ~ Tenant Laura Condliffe ~ Real ale ~ Bar food (lunchtime only) ~ (01270) 882242 ~ Children welcome away from bar until 9pm ~ Dogs welcome ~ Open 11.30-11; 12-10.30 Sun

Recommended by Dave Webster, Sue Holland, Edward Mirzoeff, Pauline and Philip Darley, I A Herdman, Paul J Robinshaw, Piotr Chodzko-Zajko, the Didler, Dr and Mrs A K Clarke, Mike Proctor, John R Ringrose, Joe Green, David Green, Patricia Walker

BICKLEY MOSS
SJ5550   MAP 7

Cholmondeley Arms ♀

Cholmondeley; A49 5.5 miles N of Whitchurch; the owners would like us to list them under Cholmondeley Village, but as this is rarely located on maps we have mentioned the nearest village which appears more often; SY14 8HN

Imaginatively converted high-ceilinged schoolhouse with decent range of real ale and wines, well presented food and sizeable gardens

Handily placed for Cholmondeley Castle Gardens, this clever schoolhouse adaptation is thoroughly good fun and makes a memorable setting for a meal or a drink. The cross-shaped lofty bar, high gothic windows, huge old radiators and old school desks on a gantry above the bar all leave no doubt that that's what it was. Well used chairs in all shapes and forms – some upholstered, some bentwood, some with ladderbacks and some with wheelbacks – are set in groups round an equally eclectic mix of tables, all on comfy carpets. There's a stag's head over one of the side arches, an open fire and lots of Victorian portraits and military pictures on colourwashed walls; TV and piped music. Shropshire Gold and Weetwood Eastgate Pedigree and a couple of guests from brewers such as Wincle Beer Company and Woodlands are served from a pine-clad bar, alongside around eight interesting and reasonably priced wines by the glass, all listed on a blackboard. There are seats outside on the sizeable lawn and more in front overlooking the quiet road.

🍴 **Readers very much enjoy the food here, which runs from lunchtime sandwiches (not Sun), starters such as hot crab pâté or smoked salmon cornet, through devilled kidneys on toast, stuffed pancakes, lasagne and steaks, to daily specials with a seasonal focus – their 'winter warmers' might include beef and winter vegetable casserole, grilled halibut and hot madras beef. There's also wide range of puddings such as bakewell tart, syrup sponge and chocolate banana split, and lots of their own ice-creams and sorbets.** *Starters/Snacks: £4.95 to £7.25. Main Courses: £7.25 to £18.00. Puddings: £3.95 to £4.75*

Free house ~ Licensee Carolyn Ross-Lowe ~ Real ale ~ Bar food (12-2.30, 6-10; all day Sat, Sun) ~ (01829) 720300 ~ Children welcome ~ Dogs welcome ~ Open 10-3.30, 6-11; 10-11 Sat, Sun ~ Bedrooms: £55B/£80B

Recommended by Mr and Mrs James Freund, Guy Vowles, George and Maureen Roby, Ray and Winifred Halliday, Mike Proctor, Paul and Gaynor Heath

BUNBURY
SJ5658   MAP 7

Dysart Arms

Bowes Gate Road; village signposted off A51 NW of Nantwich; and from A49 S of Tarporley – coming this way, coming in on northernmost village access road, bear left in village centre; CW6 9PH

Civilised chatty dining pub attractively filled with good furniture in thoughtfully laid out rooms; very enjoyable food, lovely garden with pretty views

Readers continue to like this very friendly and delightfully comfortable Brunning & Price country pub. Its knocked-through rooms have an amiable, homely and sociable atmosphere: they are immaculately kept and ramble gently around the pleasantly lit central bar. Cream walls keep it light, clean and airy, with deep venetian red ceilings adding cosiness, and each room (some with good winter fires) is cleverly furnished with an appealing variety of well spaced sturdy wooden tables and chairs, a couple of tall filled bookcases and just the right amount of carefully chosen bric-a-brac, properly lit pictures and plants. Flooring ranges from red and black tiles, to stripped boards and some carpet. Service is efficient and friendly. Thwaites and Weetwood Eastgate and a couple of guests such as Crouch Vale Brewers Gold and Titanic Lifeboat are very well kept on handpump, alongside a good selection of 16 wines by the glass and just over 20 malts. Sturdy wooden tables on the terrace and picnic-sets on the lawn in the neatly kept slightly elevated garden are lovely in summer, with views of the splendid church at the end of the pretty village, and the distant Peckforton Hills beyond.

🍴 **From a changing menu, food is tasty, just imaginative enough, attractively presented and fairly priced. As well as sandwiches, there might be cheshire cheese patty or potted salt beef starters, lighter dishes like crab and spinach quiche or 'proper' corned beef hash, and a varied choice of main courses such as slow-roasted belly pork, smoked haddock rarebit, roast parsnip and chestnut crumble, and their popular home-made steakburger. Puddings could include vanilla and gingerbread cheesecake, bakewell tart or chocolate bread.** *Starters/Snacks: £4.40 to £7.95. Main Courses: £7.95 to £17.50. Puddings: £4.45 to £5.25*

Brunning & Price ~ Manager Greg Williams ~ Real ale ~ Bar food (12-9.30(9 Sun)) ~ (01829) 260183 ~ Children welcome ~ Dogs allowed in bar ~ Open 11.30-11; 12-10.30 Sun

Recommended by Maurice and Gill McMahon, R T and J C Moggridge, C R Taylor, Pam and John Smith, Dave Webster, Sue Holland, Mike Proctor, Paul Boot, J S Burn, Mr and Mrs J Palmer, Bruce and Sharon Eden, Dr and Mrs D Scott, Revd D Glover, Richard and Maria Gillespie

BURLEYDAM   SJ6042   MAP 7

Combermere Arms

A525 Whitchurch—Audlem; SY13 4AT

Roomy and attractive beamed pub successfully mixing good drinking side with imaginative all-day food; rear and front garden

Since the last edition of the *Guide* the running of this attractively laid out pub has been taken on by the former deputy manager, and it continues its winning ways. The interior combines light and space with a cosy feel. Trademark Brunning & Price furnishings and décor take in their usual eclectic mix of dark wood furniture and rugs on wooden (some old and some new oak) or stone floors, cream walls filled with prints, deep red ceilings and open fires. Friendly staff extend an equally good welcome to drinkers and diners, with both aspects of the business seeming to do well here. Half a dozen real ales are usually from smaller brewers such as Salopian, Sharps, Thwaites, Weetwood, Wincle and Wychwood. They also stock around 100 whiskies and 17 wines by the glass from an extensive list; a few board games. During summer evenings, they put candles on tables in the pretty, well tended garden.

🍴 **As well as interesting sandwiches and ploughman's, the daily-changing menu of enjoyable food often gives a contemporary twist to a traditional dish and might include starters such as shropshire blue cheese, pear and walnut tart or tempura squid, 'light bites' like salt cod, potato and sweet onion baked omelette, and main courses such as sausage and spring onion mash, beer-battered haddock with mushy peas, roast butternut squash, red pepper, dolcelatte and spinach lasagne and their bestselling home-made Weetwood steak and ale pie; puddings such as rhubarb crumble with rhubarb and ginger ice-cream, white chocolate cheesecake, apricot bakewell tart and local ice-creams; british cheeseboard featuring local smoked cheshire.** *Starters/Snacks: £4.50 to £6.25. Main Courses: £8.95 to £15.95. Puddings: £4.50 to £6.50*

Brunning & Price ~ Manager Lisa Hares ~ Real ale ~ Bar food (12-9.30; 12-10 Fri, Sat; 12-9 Sun) ~ (01948) 871223 ~ Children welcome ~ Dogs allowed in bar ~ Open 11.30-11

Recommended by Paul and Margaret Baker, Tom and Jill Jones

BURWARDSLEY   SJ5256   MAP 7

Pheasant

Higher Burwardsley; signposted from Tattenhall (which itself is signposted off A41 S of Chester) and from Harthill (reached by turning off A534 Nantwich—Holt at the Copper Mine); follow pub's signpost on up hill from Post Office; OS Sheet 117 map reference 523566; CH3 9PF

Fantastic views, local beer and good range of very enjoyable food at heavily beamed and roomily fresh conversion of old inn

A great place to head for if you are walking the scenic Sandstone Trail along the Peckforton Hills, this half-timbered sandstone 17th-c pub is open all day. Its beamed interior has an airy modern feel, with wooden floors and well spaced furniture, including comfy leather armchairs and some nice old chairs. They say the see-through fireplace houses the largest log fire in the county, and there's a pleasant restaurant. Local Weetwood Best and Eastgate beers are served alongside a couple of guests such as Copper Dragon Golden Pippin and Spitting Feathers Special, as well as local farm cider and apple juice; quiet piped music, daily newspapers. On a clear day the telescope on the terrace (with nice hardwood furniture) lets you make out the pier head and cathedrals in Liverpool, while from inside you can see right across the Cheshire plain. A big side lawn has picnic-sets and on summer weekends they sometimes have barbecues.

🍴 **Besides sandwiches (served until 6pm), the changing menu might include starters like grilled sardines or eggs benedict, a choice of 'deli boards' featuring cheeses, pâté, charcuterie items and smoked fish with bread and chutney, main courses such as haddock in beer batter, home-made steakburger, tomato and red onion tart or caesar salad, and puddings such as warm chocolate fudge cake or apple and raspberry crumble.**

Starters/Snacks: £3.50 to £6.00. Main Courses: £8.50 to £18.00. Puddings: £4.50 to £5.00

Free house ~ Lease Andrew Nelson ~ Real ale ~ Bar food (12-9.30 (10 Fri, Sat; 8.30 Sun); 12-3, 6-9.30 Mon) ~ (01829) 770434 ~ Children welcome in bar till 6pm ~ Dogs welcome ~ Open 11-11 ~ Bedrooms: £65B/£85B

Recommended by Noel Woods, Dave Irving, Jenny Huggins, John and Verna Aspinall, Jeremy King, Adrian and Dawn Collinge, Julian and Jill Tasker, Gerry and Rosemary Dobson

CHESTER
SJ4066   MAP 7

Albion ★ ◧

Albion Street; CH1 1RQ

Strongly traditional pub with comfortable Edwardian décor and captivating World War I memorabilia; pubby food and good drinks

You might find the vintage 1928 Steck pianola being played in this atmospheric Victorian haunt. Uniquely in Chester for a pub of this period it has kept its original layout, and its homely interior is entirely dedicated to the Great War of 1914-18; most unusually it's the officially listed site of four war memorials to soldiers from the Cheshire Regiment. Throughout its tranquil rooms (no games machines or children here) you'll find an absorbing collection of World War I memorabilia, from big engravings of men leaving for war, and similarly moving prints of wounded veterans, to flags, advertisements and so on. The post-Edwardian décor is appealingly muted, with dark floral William Morris wallpaper (designed on the first day of World War I), a cast-iron fireplace, appropriate lamps, leatherette and hoop-backed chairs, a period piano and cast-iron-framed tables; there's an attractive side dining room too. Service is friendly, though this is a firmly run place (the landlord has been here nearly 40 years now): groups of race-goers are discouraged (opening times may be limited during meets), and they don't like people rushing in just before closing time. Beers come from Adnams, Batemans and Wells & Youngs, perhaps with a guest such as Hook Norton Gold. They also stock new world wines, fresh orange juice, organic bottled cider and fruit juice, over 25 malt whiskies and a good selection of rums and gins. Dog owners can request a water bowl and cold sausage for their pets. The bedrooms are comfortable and furnished in keeping with the pub's style with modern bathrooms.

◧ **Served in generous helpings, bar food includes doorstep sandwiches, cumberland sausage from Penrith, filled staffordshire oatcakes, cottage pie, creamy coconut chicken from a local organic farm, lambs liver, bacon and onions in cider gravy, curries, stews, casseroles, and puddings such as chocolate torte or bread and butter pudding with marmalade.** *Starters/Snacks: £4.90. Main Courses: £6.00 to £9.75. Puddings: £4.95*

Punch ~ Lease Michael Edward Mercer ~ Real ale ~ Bar food (12-2, 5-8(8.30 Sat); not Sun evening) ~ No credit cards ~ (01244) 340345 ~ Dogs allowed in bar ~ Open 12-3, 5(5.30 Mon, 6 Sat, 7 Sun)-11(10.30 Sun) ~ Bedrooms: £65B/£75B

Recommended by Roger and Anne Newbury, Derek and Sylvia Stephenson, Dave Webster, Sue Holland, Margaret White, Steve Narey, Gwyn and Anne Wake, J S Burn, Joe Green, Colin Moore, Pam and John Smith, Barry Collett, the Didler, Rob and Catherine Dunster, Neil Whitehead, Victoria Anderson

Mill ◧ £

Milton Street; CH1 3NF

Big hotel with huge range of real ales, good value food and cheery service in sizeable bar

A modern conversion of an old mill, this hotel straddles either side of the Shropshire Union Canal, with a glassed-in bridge connecting the two halves. Its very neatly kept bar has stripped light wood flooring throughout, with marble-topped tables, some exposed brickwork and supporting pillars, and local photographs and cigarette cards framed on cream-papered walls. The comfortable cruiser-style bar has an astonishing range of up to 16 real ales. Mill Premium and Cornmill are brewed especially for them by Coach House and Phoenix, respectively, and are well kept alongside Oakham JHB, Weetwood Best and a dozen guests that change on a daily basis; also a dozen wines by the glass and a farm cider. Service here is very friendly and you'll find a real mix of customers; quiet piped music and unobtrusively placed big-screen sports TV. Readers say the bedrooms are comfortable and make a handy base for exploring the city.

🍴 **Very reasonably priced pubby food includes sandwiches, ciabattas and enjoyable hot dishes such as curry and rice, fish and chips and their popular steak and ale pie.** *Starters/Snacks: £0.95 to £6.95. Main Courses: £6.50 to £6.95. Puddings: £3.95*

Free house ~ Licensees Gary and Gordon Vickers ~ Real ale ~ Bar food (11.30(12 Sun)-10) ~ Restaurant ~ (01244) 350035 ~ Children welcome, but not in bar after 9pm ~ Live jazz Mon; dinner dance Fri, Sat ~ Open 10am-1am; 11am-midnight Sun ~ Bedrooms: £73B/£91B

Recommended by Colin Moore, Ben Williams, Alan Johnson, Joe Green

Old Harkers Arms ♀ ◀

Russell Street, down steps off City Road where it crosses canal – under Mike Melody antiques; CH3 5AL

Well run spacious canalside building with great range of drinks (including lots of changing real ales) and good value tasty food

You'll find a very wide range of beers at this airy, high-ceilinged converted early Victorian warehouse, with around nine real ales on handpump, including Flowers Original, Thwaites Original and Weetwood Cheshire Cat, with regularly changing guests from brewers such as Betwixt, Hawkshead, Moorhouses, Spitting Feathers and Titanic; in addition there are also more than 100 malt whiskies, 50 well described wines (with around half of them by the glass), four farmhouse ciders and local apple juice. Through the tall windows you can watch canal and cruise boats chug their way past. Huge brick pillars and cleverly divided-off areas create some intimate places, and cheery staff spread a happy bustle. Mixed dark wood furniture is grouped on stripped wood floors, walls are covered frame-to-frame with old prints, and the usual Brunning & Price wall of bookshelves is to be found above a leather banquette at one end. Attractive lamps add cosiness, and the bar counter is apparently constructed from salvaged doors; there is a selection of board games.

🍴 **As well as a good range of sandwiches, nicely presented bar food might include snacks and starters such as salt beef and black pudding hash cake with poached egg, chilli and coriander king prawns and grilled sardines on toast, alongside main courses like pork loin and bubble and squeak, spiced lentil cakes, ploughman's with local cheeses and braised shoulder of lamb. Eggs and chicken used here are free range: the owners say they visit their local farm suppliers to see the animals for themselves. Puddings could include mango parfait or Baileys crème brûlée as well as hot waffles and a british cheeseboard.** *Starters/Snacks: £4.50 to £7.95. Main Courses: £8.50 to £16.95. Puddings: £4.25 to £5.25*

Brunning & Price ~ Manager Paul Jeffery ~ Real ale ~ Bar food (12-9.30) ~ (01244) 344525 ~ Older children welcome until 5pm if well behaved ~ Dogs allowed in bar ~ Open 11.30-11; 12-10.30 Sun

Recommended by Dave Webster, Sue Holland, Bruce and Sharon Eden, Maurice and Gill McMahon, Joe Green, the Didler, Dr Kevan Tucker, Ian and Nita Cooper, Don Bryan

COTEBROOK
SJ5765   MAP 7

Fox & Barrel

A49 NE of Tarporley; CW6 9DZ

Pretty white cottage rejuvenated with a stylishly airy décor and an enterprising menu

Since reopening in 2008, this pub has shed its cluttered appearance and in its place it has become much lighter and airier. The licensee is well known to us from his days at the helm of the Grosvenor Arms in Aldford – a longstanding and several times award-winning Main Entry. The original bar is dominated by a big log fireplace and a bigger uncluttered dining area has attractive rugs and an eclectic mix of period tables on polished oak floorboards, with extensive panelling on the walls, which are hung with a couple of hundred framed old prints. Outside is plentiful seating on a terrace and in the garden, which contains old fruit trees and a tractor. Real ales include Caledonian Deuchars IPA,

Thwaites and a couple of guests such as Brains Bread of Heaven or Exmoor Hound Dog; good array of wines, with 24 by the glass.

🍴 **The changing menu has imaginative snacks and sandwiches, and might include starters such as cider-soused mackerel, oysters, or goats cheese soufflé, with main courses ranging from pubby standards like steak and ale pie, beer-battered haddock, steakburger and ploughman's to more imaginative dishes like roasted cod loin with curried mussels and dishes served with their café de paris butter – the menu lists its 22 flavourings.** *Starters/Snacks: £4.50 to £8.45. Main Courses: £7.95 to £16.95. Puddings: £3.95 to £5.75*

Punch ~ Lease Gary Kidd ~ Real ale ~ Bar food (12-9.30(9 Sun)) ~ (01829) 760529 ~ Children welcome ~ Dogs allowed in bar ~ Open 12-11(10.30 Sun)

Recommended by Paul Boot, Bruce and Sharon Eden, BOB, Jackie Jones

EATON   SJ8765   MAP 7

Plough 🛏

A536 Congleton—Macclesfield; CW12 2NH

Neat and cosy village pub with four interesting beers, bar food, views from big attractive garden; good bedrooms

Not far from the fringes of the Peak District, this red-brick 17th-c pub has views of nearby hills from the big tree-filled gardens; there are picnic-sets on the lawn, as well as a covered decked terrace with outdoor heaters. The carefully converted bar has plenty of beams and exposed brickwork, a couple of snug little alcoves, comfortable armchairs and cushioned wooden wall seats on red patterned carpets, long red curtains, leaded windows and a big stone fireplace. Moved here piece by piece from its original home in Wales, the heavily raftered barn at the back is a striking restaurant. Beers include Hydes Bitter (very reasonably priced) and three guests from brewers such as Beartown, Greene King and Wells & Youngs. The decent wine list includes 11 by the glass. Service is friendly and attentive; piped music, TV. The appealingly designed bedrooms are in a converted stable block.

🍴 **It's advisable to book if you are eating. Food includes lunchtime sandwiches, as well as soup, prawns in garlic butter, steak and kidney pudding, thai green curry, 10oz rib-eye steak and some interesting daily specials such as fillet steak stroganoff and tuna fillet; three-course Sunday lunch.** *Starters/Snacks: £3.95 to £7.50. Main Courses: £7.95 to £19.95. Puddings: £3.95 to £4.95*

Free house ~ Licensee Mujdat Karatas ~ Real ale ~ Bar food (12-2.30, 6-9.30; 12-8 Sun) ~ Restaurant ~ (01260) 280207 ~ Children welcome ~ Dogs allowed in bedrooms ~ Live music last Fri of month ~ Open 11am-midnight(1am Sat, 11 Sun) ~ Bedrooms: £60B/£75B

Recommended by Paul and Margaret Baker, Pam and John Smith, Phil Merrin, Rob and Catherine Dunster, John Ashford

LACH DENNIS   SJ7072   MAP 7

Duke of Portland 🍴 🍷

Holmes Chapel Road (B5082, off A556 SE of Northwich); CW9 7SY

Good food in stylish upscale dining pub which doesn't neglect the beer side

Run by friendly, young staff, this civilised pub is an inviting place for a relaxed meal but you are equally welcome if you just want to pop in for a drink. A bar area, gently decorated in beige, grey and cream, has comfortable leather armchairs, square pouffes and sofas around chunky low tables, with nicely framed prints above its panelled dado. More importantly, its handsomely carved counter serves four ales from handpump, including Marstons Pedigree and guests from brewers such as Batemans, Brakspear, Jennings and Wychwood. The interesting changing choice of about a dozen wines by the glass is fairly priced. The young staff are attentive and helpful; daily papers. The main dining room, with its lofty ceiling, sturdy balustrades and big pictures, gives quite a sense of occasion, but keeps a fairly relaxed feel – perhaps because of the friendly mixture of styles in the comfortable dining chairs on its floorboards; piped music, TV. Outside, a neat terrace has alloy tables and chairs among modernist planters. The family have recently celebrated 35 years at their locally famous Belle Epoque restaurant in Knutsford.

🍴 They take great care over sourcing really good ingredients from named local suppliers, showing justifiable pride in their meats and cheeses; even the chips come in for admiration and are cooked in beef dripping. Starters typically include black pudding, sautéed cheshire mushrooms or roasted beetroot and delamere goats cheese salad. Mains might feature butternut squash and chestnut pie, haddock and chips, confit of lamb, roasted local wild boar with plums and herb dumplings, and 21-day-hung sirloin steak. Their bestselling puddings are crème brûlée, warm chocolate brownie and sticky toffee pudding. *Starters/Snacks: £3.95 to £8.95. Main Courses: £7.95 to £18.95. Puddings: £4.95*

Marstons ~ Lease David and Matthew Mooney ~ Real ale ~ Bar food (12-2.30, 5.30-10; 12-8 Sun) ~ Restaurant ~ (01606) 46264 ~ Children welcome ~ Dogs allowed in bar ~ Open 12-11; 12-3, 5.30-11 in winter

Recommended by Mr and Mrs John Taylor, Mrs P J Carroll, Tom and Jill Jones, Alan Poole, Malcolm and Pauline Pellatt

LANGLEY   SJ9569   MAP 7

Hanging Gate ♀

Meg Lane, Higher Sutton; follow Langley signpost from A54 beside Fourways Motel, and that road passes the pub; from Macclesfield, heading S from centre on A523 turn left into Byrons Lane at Langley, Wincle signpost; in Sutton (0.5 miles after going under canal bridge, ie before Langley) fork right at Church House Inn, following Wildboarclough signpost, then 2 miles later turning sharp right at steep hairpin bend; OS Sheet 118 map reference 952696; SK11 0NG

Remotely set old place with fires in traditional cosy rooms, lovely views from airy extension and terrace

First licensed nearly 300 years ago, this low-beamed old drovers' pub high up in the Peak District was in fact built much earlier. Still in their original layout, its three cosy little low-beamed rooms are simply furnished. The tiny little snug bar, at its pubbiest at lunchtime, has a welcoming log fire in a big brick fireplace, a single table, plain chairs and cushioned wall seats (though there's barely room in here to sit), and a few old pub pictures and seasonal photographs on its creamy walls. Beers served in here include well kept Hydes Original, Jekylls Gold and Spin Doctor and a guest such as Morland Original on handpump, quite a few malt whiskies and ten wines by the glass. The second room, with a section of bar counter in the corner, has only five tables, and there's a third appealing little oak-beamed blue room. Down some stone steps, an airy dining extension has terrific views over a patchwork of valley pastures to distant moors and the tall Sutton Common transmitter – seats out on the crazy-paved terrace also have great views; piped music, board games, dominoes, books. It does get busy so it's best to book on weekends.

🍴 Bar food from the menu and changing specials board (good but not cheap) could include sandwiches (home-made bread), soup, wild salmon steak with crayfish tails, steak and ale pie, grilled vegetables with goat's cheese, and home-made puddings such as warm bakewell tart or hot chocolate pudding. *Starters/Snacks: £3.95 to £7.95. Main Courses: £9.95 to £19.95. Puddings: £3.25 to £4.95*

Hydes ~ Tenants Ian and Luda Rottenbury ~ Real ale ~ Bar food (12-2.30(4 Sun), 6.30(6 Sun)-9.30) ~ Restaurant ~ (01260) 252238 ~ Children welcome in family room ~ Dogs welcome ~ Open 11-3, 5-11; 11-11 Sat, Sun

Recommended by Rob and Catherine Dunster, David and Katharine Cooke, the Haytons, Pam and John Smith, Mike Proctor, Hilary Forrest, the Didler, Lesley and Peter Barrett

Post Office address codings give the impression that some pubs are in Cheshire, when they're really in Derbyshire (and therefore included in this book under that chapter) or in Greater Manchester (see the Lancashire chapter).

MACCLESFIELD   SJ9271   MAP 7

Sutton Hall

Leaving Macclesfield southwards on A523, turn left into Byrons Lane signposted Langley, Wincle, then just before canal viaduct fork right into Bullocks Lane; OS Sheet 118 map reference 925715; SK11 0HE

Recently refurbished historic building set in attractive grounds; fine range of drinks and good food

Since the last edition of the *Guide* the conversion of this splendid 16th-c baronial hall by new owners Brunning & Price has been completed, and readers have been impressed with the imaginative blend of old and new. The hall that forms the heart of the building is beautifully impressive, particularly in the entrance space. The bar is divided into separate areas by tall oak timbers, and has some antique squared oak panelling, broad flagstones and a raised open fire. Six real ales – Thwaites, Wadworth 6X and Weetwood Cheshire Cat are on offer plus three guests such as Brains SA, St Austell Tribute and Storm Red Mist – plus several wines by the glass. Lovely grounds have tables on a tree-sheltered lawn.

🍴 **Bar food follows the usual Brunning & Price policy (the chef is given guided free rein) and include imaginative sandwiches, interestingly turned-out pub staples like ploughman's and beer-battered haddock, and a few other more creative dishes, all fairly priced to reflect the good quality of the ingredients. Starters might feature japanese vegetable dumplings or hare and ham hock terrine, and there's a 'light bites' section with items like smoked haddock and watercress tart or rump steak sandwich, as well as main courses, such as slow-roast pork with apple fritters and parsnip, chicken, leek and bacon pie or smoked haddock and salmon fishcakes.** *Starters/Snacks: £4.45 to £8.95. Main Courses: £6.95 to £15.50. Puddings: £4.50 to £5.20*

Brunning & Price ~ Manager Neil Gander ~ Real ale ~ Bar food (12-10(9.30 Sun)) ~ (01260) 253211 ~ Children welcome ~ Dogs allowed in bar ~ Open 11.30-11; 12-10.30 Sun

Recommended by Noel Grundy, Beryl and David Sowter, Brian and Anna Marsden, Susan and Nigel Brookes, R T and J C Moggridge, Steve Whalley, BOB

MARBURY   SJ5645   MAP 7

Swan 🍺 £

NNE of Whitchurch; OS Sheet 117 map reference 562457; SY13 4LS

Charmingly set proper country pub with good value food and drinks

In a quietly attractive village with a lakeside church, this is a half-mile's stroll from the Llangollen Canal. Beers on handpump are Caledonian Deuchars IPA and a couple of changing guests from regional breweries such as Weetwood (from nearby Wrenbury); to coincide with the village fête, on the second weekend in May they hold a real ale festival with up to 19 beers served. All 16 of the reasonably priced wines on the list are available by the glass. The roomy partly panelled lounge has upholstered banquette seating and country furniture, a copper-canopied fireplace with a good winter log fire (masses of greenery in summer), daily papers, board games, quiet piped music and discreet lighting. Candlelit at night, the cottagey turkey-carpeted dining room has another inglenook fireplace, and a magnificent sculpture of a swan, carved from a pear tree blown down in the pub's garden in 2007 storms. There are well spaced picnic-sets and big shrubs in the garden itself. The chocolate-brown labrador is called Cally. We heard very late as we went to press that the pub has changed hands – we're keeping our fingers crossed.

🍴 **The Bargain Award is for their very popular two-course lunch deals (Tues-Fri), when they offer a selection of dishes with starters like spinach and ricotta tortellini, home-cured gravadlax, or grilled black pudding and smoked bacon salad, followed by pubby main courses such as scampi and chips, ham hock or three-cheese ploughman's, gammon steak with egg and pineapple, and their bestselling lambs liver and bacon with mustard mash. The more elaborate 'posh nosh' menu (not part of the lunch deal) might include roast breast of duck, chicken suprême, grilled salmon steak or locally shot pheasant; puddings could be winter berry pavlova, double crumble with custard or sticky toffee pudding. The monthly Swan Supper Society (usually second Weds of the month; welcomes**

visitors too) is good value as well as good fun. *Starters/Snacks: £4.20 to £5.30. Main Courses: £7.50 to £8.50. Puddings: £4.70*

Oxford Hotels ~ Lease Penny Edge and John Griffiths ~ Real ale ~ Bar food (12-3, 6.30-9, 12-9 Sat, Sun) ~ Restaurant ~ (01948) 662220 ~ Children welcome ~ Dogs allowed in bar ~ Live music first Tues and last Sun of month ~ Open 12-3, 6.30-11; 12-11 Sat, Sun

Recommended by Charles and Pauline Stride, John and Joyce Farmer

MOBBERLEY
SJ7879   MAP 7

Roebuck 🍴 🍷

Mill Lane; down hill from sharp bend on B5085 at E edge of 30mph limit; WA16 7HX

CHESHIRE DINING PUB OF THE YEAR

Stylish and airy country interior, warm welcome and very helpful service, very good food, good wine list, courtyard and garden

Hung with flower baskets, this attractive place is much liked as an all-rounder for food and drink, and readers find a warm welcome from the attentive staff. Old tiled and boarded floors carry a comfortable mix of relaxed country furnishings, from cushioned long wood pews (rescued from a welsh chapel) to scrubbed pine farmhouse tables and a mix of old chairs. The wine list is short but well chosen and very reasonably priced, with just over a dozen by the glass; also Black Sheep, Tetleys, Timothy Taylors Landlord and a guest such as Jennings Cocker Hoop; piped music. A cobbled courtyard has benches and tables and there are picnic-sets in an enclosed and well manicured beer garden (and more by the car park).

🍴 **The enjoyable food is thoughtfully prepared and features traditional dishes with an appealing twist. As well as upmarket sandwiches (not evenings), dishes might include soup, starters like devilled lambs kidneys on toast, caesar salad made with free-range chicken, or potted goosenargh duck, and main courses such as roast pork fillet with mustard sauce, slow-cooked lamb shank, winter vegetable and barley stew, whole grilled fleetwood plaice, and sweet potato, chickpea and spinach tagine with coriander couscous. Puddings could be warm chocolate fondant with home-made vanilla ice-cream, steamed syrup sponge and custard or toffee cheesecake; british cheeseboard. Side orders are extra so you might want to add a couple of pounds to the prices below, and you will probably need to book.** *Starters/Snacks: £4.25 to £5.95. Main Courses: £9.95 to £15.95. Puddings: £4.25 to £5.30*

Free house ~ Licensee Jane Marsden ~ Real ale ~ Bar food (12-2.30, 5.30-9.30; 12-9.30(8 Sun) weekends) ~ (01565) 873322 ~ Children welcome ~ Open 12-3, 5-11; 12-11 Sat; 12-10.30 Sun

Recommended by Noel Grundy, Gerry and Rosemary Dobson, Mrs P J Carroll, Steve Whalley

PEOVER HEATH
SJ7973   MAP 7

Dog 🍺

Off A50 N of Holmes Chapel at the Whipping Stocks, keep on past Parkgate into Wellbank Lane; OS Sheet 118 map reference 794735; note that this village is called Peover Heath on the OS map and shown under that name on many road maps, but the pub is often listed under Over Peover instead; WA16 8UP

Homely pub with interesting range of beers and straightforward food

You can enjoy a pint of bitter for just £1.85 at this unpretentious pub; the five well kept real ales on handpump are Copper Dragon, Hydes Bitter and Dark Mild, Weetwood and a guest such as Moorhouses. They also have a good range of malt whiskies and wines by the glass. The neatly kept bar here is gently old fashioned with a comfortably cottagey feel. Neat tied-back floral curtains hang in little windows, a curved cushioned banquette is built into a bay window and mixed furnishings, mostly traditional dark wheelbacks, are arranged on a patterned carpet. A coal fire, copper pieces and pot plants dotted around add to the homely feel; games machine, darts, pool, dominoes, board games, TV and piped music. There are picnic-sets beneath colourful hanging baskets on the peaceful lane, and more out in a pretty back garden. It's a pleasant walk from here to the Jodrell Bank Centre and Arboretum; recently refurbished bedrooms. More reports please.

🍴 Bar food includes many pub standards, such as soup and sandwiches, starters like battered mushrooms, smoked salmon salad or manx kippers, and main courses including steak and ale pie, oatcakes stuffed with leeks, mushrooms and cheese, and cod and chips. The pudding choice might feature baked lemon cheesecake, bread and butter pudding and chocolate fudge cake. *Starters/Snacks: £3.50 to £8.50. Main Courses: £9.75 to £16.50. Puddings: £3.95*

Free house ~ Licensee Steven Wrigley ~ Real ale ~ Bar food (12-2.30, 6-9; 12-8.30 Sun) ~ Restaurant ~ (01625) 861421 ~ Children welcome ~ Dogs allowed in bar ~ Live music once or twice monthly Fri ~ Open 11.30-3, 4.30-11.30; 11.30-11.30 Sat; 12-11.30 Sun ~ Bedrooms: £60B/£80B

Recommended by Susan and Nigel Brookes, John Saville, Anne and Steve Thompson, Gerry and Rosemary Dobson, Peter Dowd

PLUMLEY SJ7075 MAP 7

Smoker

2.5 miles from M6 junction 19: A556 towards Northwich and Chester; WA16 0TY

400-year-old pub with spotless comfortable lounges, welcoming staff and good food

A handy escape from the M6, this relaxed partly thatched old pub strikes a happy chord as soon as you walk in. It has dark panelling, open fires in impressive period fireplaces, deep sofas, other comfortable seats and settles in its three connecting rooms, and a sweet collection of copper kettles; piped music. Look out for the Edwardian print of a hunt meeting outside (tucked in among the military prints), which shows how little the pub's appearance has changed over the centuries. Very helpful staff serve a good choice of wines and whiskies, with well kept Robinsons Dizzy Blonde and Unicorn and a guest such as Robinsons Trouble and Strife on handpump. The sizeable garden has roses, flower beds and a children's play area.

🍴 As well as sandwiches, the enjoyable food includes starters such as chicken liver pâté with onion marmalade, scrambled egg and smoked salmon, and crispy duck pancake, while main courses might be a vegetarian special, the bestselling roast beef with yorkshire pudding, or choices from the meat and fish selections like steak, ale and mushroom pie, red thai chicken curry, mussels, poached salmon or grilled plaice. The changing menu of home-made puddings could have chocolate and orange cheesecake, tiramisu and apple crumble and custard, as well as ice-cream and a british cheeseboard. *Starters/Snacks: £3.95 to £6.95. Main Courses: £7.95 to £17.95. Puddings: £4.95*

Robinsons ~ Tenants John and Diana Bailey ~ Real ale ~ Bar food (10-2.15, 6-9.30; 10-9 Sun) ~ Restaurant ~ (01565) 722338 ~ Children welcome outside bar until 9pm ~ Open 10-3, 6-11; 10am-10.30pm Sun

Recommended by Dennis Jones, Paul and Margaret Baker, K C and B Forman, Pam and John Smith

PRESTBURY SJ8976 MAP 7

Legh Arms 🛏

A538, village centre; SK10 4DG

Comfortable and immaculately kept inn with good food, appealingly individual bar, terraced garden and beautiful bedrooms

A relaxing place to stay in a prosperous village, the Legh Arms is distinctly upmarket, with friendly and efficient staff. Its bar areas are smartly traditional, very much smart-hotel-lounge, with plenty of elegant soft furnishings. Though opened up, it is well divided into several intimate areas, with muted tartan fabric over a panelled dado on the right, ladderback dining chairs, good solid dark tables, stylish french steam train prints, italian costume engravings and a glass case of china and books. On the left there are brocaded bucket seats around more solid tables, antique steeplechase prints, and staffordshire dogs on the stone mantelpiece, all warmed by a good coal fire; a snug panelled back part has cosy wing armchairs and a grand piano, and a narrow side offshoot has pairs of art deco leather armchairs around small granite tables, and antique costume prints of french tradesmen. The bar, towards the back on the left, has well kept Robinsons Hatters Mild and Unicorn on handpump and nice house wines (seven by the glass), a good range of malts and cognacs, good coffee, and maybe genial regulars perched on the comfortable leather bar stools; this part looks up to an unusual balustraded internal landing. There are daily papers on a coffee table, and magazines on an antique oak dresser; piped music. A garden behind has a terrace with outdoor heating, tables and chairs.

⑪ **Very tasty bar food might include soup, sandwiches, spicy fishcakes with sweet chilli sauce, thai chicken curry, pea, leek and mint risotto with goats cheese, and the most popular choices of fish and chips, slow-roast pork belly with apple sauce and steak and ale pie; puddings such as chocolate torte and sticky toffee pudding. The pricier menu in the sumptuous restaurant is more elaborate.** *Starters/Snacks: £3.50 to £8.50. Main Courses: £7.95 to £11.95. Puddings: £4.50*

Robinsons ~ Tenant Peter Myers ~ Real ale ~ Bar food (12-10) ~ Restaurant ~ (01625) 829130 ~ Children welcome away from bar ~ Open 12-10 ~ Bedrooms: £70S/£95B

Recommended by Susan and Nigel Brookes, Revd D Glover, Malcolm and Pauline Pellatt, Pam and John Smith, Chris Brooks

TARPORLEY
SJ5562   MAP 7

Rising Sun
High Street; village signposted off A51 Nantwich—Chester; CW6 0DX

Friendly, bustling and quaint, with pubby food

Low-ceilinged and characterful, this brick-fronted family-run pub has happy-to-please staff serving Robinsons Dizzy Blonde, Unicorn and a seasonal ale from handpumps. It's cosily furnished with well chosen tables surrounded by eye-catching old seats (including creaky 19th-c mahogany and oak settles), an attractively blacked iron kitchen range and sporting and other old-fashioned prints on the walls. There are one or two seats in a tiny side bar where they might put on a portable TV for major sporting events; piped music. More reports please.

⑪ **Alongside pub standards such as soup, sandwiches and toasties, the unusually extensive menu lists more than half a dozen tasty pies, wide choices of fish, poultry, casserole and grilled meat dishes (such as seafood pancake, chicken maryland, beef bourguignon, braised rabbit and mixed grill), as well as spicy indian and oriental food and a dozen vegetarian items. Puddings might include home-made sherry trifle, raspberry meringue roulade, ice-creams and sorbets.** *Starters/Snacks: £2.95 to £5.85. Main Courses: £6.50 to £16.25. Puddings: £3.95*

Robinsons ~ Tenant David Robertson ~ Real ale ~ Bar food (11.30-2, 5.30-9.30(9 Mon); 12-9 Sun) ~ Restaurant (evening) ~ (01829) 732423 ~ Children welcome away from bar ~ Open 11.30-3, 5.30-11; 11.30-11 Sat; 12-10.30 Sun

Recommended by Derek and Sylvia Stephenson, the Didler

WILLINGTON
SJ5367   MAP 7

Boot
Boothsdale, off A54 at Kelsall; CW6 0NH

Friendly and attractive dining pub (you may need to book at weekends) with suntrap terrace

Served by attentive staff in a lovely old building adapted from a row of cottages, the four real ales on handpump here change constantly but usually include two or three from the Weetwood brewery, just a mile away, such as Cheshire Cat and Old Dog; there are also some 30 malt whiskies and a decent wine list. The interior has been opened up around the central bar, leaving small unpretentiously furnished room areas, with lots of original features, and there's a woodburning stove. The charming flagstoned restaurant (with a roaring log fire) has wheelback chairs around plenty of tables. An extension with french windows overlooks the garden (the three donkeys, and Sooty and Sweep the cats, are popular with children), and picnic-sets in front on the raised stone terrace are an idyllic suntrap in summer. No pushchairs inside. More reports please.

🍴 Besides regularly changing specials such as spicy crab fishcakes, bass, smoked haddock with rarebit topping or pork belly, other dishes could include soup, olives and bread, sandwiches and baguettes, starters or light dishes like warm rösti or smoked haddock fishcakes, and main courses such as steak and ale or fisherman's pie, 10oz rump or rib-eye steaks, moroccan curried chicken and cumberland sausage, followed by puddings such as sticky toffee pudding or rhubarb crumble. *Starters/Snacks: £3.00 to £7.00. Main Courses: £7.50 to £11.50. Puddings: £4.50 to £5.50*

Punch ~ Licensee Mike Gollings ~ Real ale ~ Bar food (11-9.30) ~ Restaurant ~ (01829) 751375 ~ Well behaved children welcome, no pushchairs ~ Open 10am-midnight

Recommended by Roger and Anne Newbury, Pamela and Alan Neale, Derek and Sylvia Stephenson, Paul Boot

WINCLE   SJ9665   MAP 7

Ship
Village signposted off A54 Congleton—Buxton; SK11 0QE

Popular sandstone 16th-c village pub in good walking country, thoughtful staff, Lees beers, good inventive food and little garden

Ideally placed in super countryside, and handy for walks on to the Roaches ridge and into the unspoilt Dane Valley, this is a warming place to come into if you've been out on the hills. The carpeted and gently lit lounge bar and restaurant provide a comfier alternative, and the sympathetically designed extension into the old stables, with flagstone floors, beams and wood-burning stove, helps ease the weekend bustle. Three or four real ales come from the J W Lees portfolio. A small garden has wooden tables. They sell their own book of local walks. More reports please.

🍴 As well as imaginative and generously served sandwiches, tasty bar food could include starters such as winter vegetable soup, fried lamb kidneys with red onion cream sauce on black pudding, or crab cake with anchovy aioli, and main courses such as their popular steak and ale pie, trout fillets with new potatoes and spring vegetables, home-made beef burger and penne pasta with wild mushrooms. *Starters/Snacks: £3.25 to £6.95. Main Courses: £9.95 to £15.95. Puddings: £4.95 to £5.95*

Lees ~ Tenant Christopher Peter Knights ~ Real ale ~ Bar food (12-2.30(3 Sat, 4 Sun), 6.30-9 (not Sun)) ~ No credit cards ~ (01260) 227217 ~ Children welcome except in bar and dining room ~ Dogs allowed in bar ~ Open 12-3, 6.30-11; 12-11 Sat; 12-10.30 Sun; closed Mon except bank hols

Recommended by BOB, Brian and Anna Marsden, Gwyn and Anne Wake, DC

WRENBURY   SJ5947   MAP 7

Dusty Miller
Village signposted from A530 Nantwich—Whitchurch; Cholmondeley Road; CW5 8HG

Generous food and views of busy canal from bars and terrace of big mill conversion

This well converted 19th-c corn mill makes the perfect spot for watching the comings and goings of craft along the Shropshire Union Canal, which runs immediately outside, and passes beneath a weighted drawbridge. The best vantage points include the gravel terrace with its picnic-sets among rose bushes and indoor tables by a series of tall glazed arches. Inside you can still see the old lift hoist up under the rafters. The atmosphere is low-key restauranty, with some emphasis on the generously served food, though drinkers are welcome, and in summer the balance may even tip. The very spacious modern feeling main bar area is comfortably furnished with a mixture of seats (including tapestried banquettes, oak settles and wheelback chairs) round rustic tables. Further in, a quarry-tiled part by the bar counter has an oak settle and refectory table. Friendly staff serve three well kept Robinsons beers – Old Tom, Unicorn and a seasonal ale – on handpump and from the cask, as well as farm cider; eclectic piped music. More reports please.

🍴 As well as soup and sandwiches, the monthly changing menu might include starters like deep-fried garlic and ginger creel prawns or potted cheese made with cheddar and shropshire blue, and main courses such as their bestselling braised chuck steak with Old Tom winter ale, thai-style mixed bean curry and chargrilled marinated lamb steak with port and redcurrant gravy, alongside specials such as roast hake fillet with shetland mussels; puddings such as sticky toffee pudding and a crumble of the day with custard; british cheeses are featured as cheeseboard or ploughman's. Their free-range pork comes from 1.5 miles away in Wrenbury and seasonal vegetables are supplied by the hobby market gardener next door to the pub. *Starters/Snacks: £4.35 to £7.95. Main Courses: £8.95 to £15.95. Puddings: £4.75 to £4.95*

Robinsons ~ Tenant Mark Sumner ~ Real ale ~ Bar food (12-2(2.30 Sun), 6.30-9.30(7-9 Sun)) ~ Restaurant ~ (01270) 780537 ~ Children welcome until 9.30pm ~ Dogs allowed in bar ~ Folk last Fri of month ~ Open 11.30(12 Sun)-3, 6.30(7 Sun)-11; closed Mon except bank hols

Recommended by Bob and Laura Brock, Paul and Gail Betteley, Meg and Colin Hamilton, A Darroch Harkness

LUCKY DIP

Besides the fully inspected pubs, you might like to try these Lucky Dips recommended to us and described by readers (if you do, please send us reports: feedback@goodguides.com).

ACTON BRIDGE [SJ5974]
Hazel Pear CW8 3RA [Hill Top Rd]: Welcoming country pub with good value home cooking inc bargain OAP lunches, cheerful attentive service, well kept Marstons Pedigree and Timothy Taylors Landlord, good wine choice; children welcome, open all day *(Alan and Eve Harding, Mr and Mrs John Taylor)*
ALDERLEY EDGE [SJ8478]
Drum & Monkey SK9 7LD [Moss Rose; just off Heyes Lane (which is off A34)]: Cheerful friendly service, well kept Robinsons, open fire, wide choice of good value food from sandwiches up; big terrace overlooking pretty bowling green *(Brian and Anna Marsden)*
Merlin SK9 7QN [Harden Park]: Substantial Victorian building with pleasant modern décor in bar and eating areas (emphasis on popular food from snacks up), well kept Timothy Taylors Landlord, interesting continental beers on tap and good choice of wines by the glass; tables on terrace by riverside garden, nice Innkeepers Lodge bedrooms, good breakfast *(Andy and Claire Barker)*
ALPRAHAM [SJ5759]
Travellers Rest CW6 9JA [A51 Nantwich—Chester]: Unspoilt four-room country local in same friendly family for three generations, well kept Caledonian Deuchars IPA, Tetleys Bitter and Mild and wknd guests, low prices, leatherette, wicker and Formica, some flock wallpaper, fine old brewery mirrors, darts and dominoes, back bowling green; no machines, piped music or food (apart from crisps and nuts), cl wkdy lunchtimes *(the Didler, Dave Webster, Sue Holland, Pete Baker)*

ALTRINCHAM [SJ7688]
☆ *Victoria* WA14 1EX [Stamford St]: Civilised and welcoming street-corner dining pub, airy and uncluttered, with panelling and chunky tables, lots of wood, slate and exposed brick, comfortable fireside settees on right, sensibly short choice of good seasonal food (not Sun evening) such as herdwick mutton hotpot and pink veal and mushroom pudding, Sun roasts, two well kept ales such as Greene King Old Speckled Hen and Jennings Cumberland, good wine; no dogs; children welcome, some outside seating at front, open all day *(Dave and Shirley Shaw, Sarah Lucas, Elisabeth Lawrence, Matthew Smithson, Siobhan Pollitt)*
ANDERTON [SJ6475]
Stanley Arms CW9 6AG [just NW of Northwich; Old Rd]: Busy friendly local by Trent & Mersey Canal overlooking amazing restored Anderton boat lift, wide choice of good value well presented pubby food from sandwiches up, well kept ales inc Greene King, John Smiths and Tetleys, nice family dining area; tables on decked terrace, play area, overnight mooring *(Tom and Jill Jones, Mr and Mrs A Curry, Ben Williams)*
AUDLEM [SJ6543]
Lord Combermere CW3 0AQ [The Square (A529/A525)]: Refurbished under hard-working welcoming new licensees, enjoyable home-made food, well kept ales, sofas, stripped pine and Vettriano prints; handy for Shrops Union Canal *(Pete Yearsley)*
Shroppie Fly CW3 0DX [Shropshire St]: Three-room former warehouse by Locks 12/13 of Shrops Union Canal, welcoming staff, five ales, good value pub food, bar made from original barge, canal memorabilia,

mainly modern furnishings, central fire, pool in public bar; piped music, live Sat; children welcome, waterside terrace, open almost all day summer *(David and Sue Smith, LYM, Ben Williams)*

BARTON [SJ4454]

☆ *Cock o' Barton* SY14 7HU [Barton Rd (A534 E of Farndon)]: Handsome beamed sandstone country pub with stylish modern décor and good enterprising up-to-date food, friendly efficient staff; tables outside *(Susan and Nigel Brookes, LYM)*

BEESTON [SJ5559]

Beeston Castle Hotel CW6 9NJ [A49 S of Tarporley]: Comfortable pub below castle, friendly efficient staff, wide choice of good food inc bargain OAP lunches, small wing chairs and nicely placed tables in spacious bar, log fire, well kept Greene King IPA and Wells & Youngs Bombardier, short well chosen wine list, restaurant; children allowed till 8pm, comfortable bedrooms, good walking country, open all day Sun *(Alan and Eve Harding)*

BELL O' TH' HILL [SJ5245]

☆ *Blue Bell* SY13 4QS [just off A41 N of Whitchurch]: Heavily beamed partly 14th-c country local with friendly licensees and chatty locals, Salopian Shropshire Gold, Oakham JHB and guest ales, Thatcher's farm cider, reliable well priced food from sandwiches and baguettes up, two cosy and attractive rooms, well behaved alsatian; children and dogs welcome, pleasant garden, small caravan site next door, cl Mon *(LYM, MLR)*

BOLLINGTON [SJ9377]

Church House SK10 5PY [Church St]: Welcoming village pub doing well under returned licensees, enjoyable food, good service, Greene King IPA, Wells & Youngs Bombardier and a guest such as Beartown Kodiak, roaring fire, separate dining room; children welcome, good local walks *(Dr D J and Mrs S C Walker)*

Holly Bush SK10 5PW [Palmerston St]: Panelling and traditional décor, good value generous food, good service under newish licensees, local ales *(David and Diane Young)*

Spinners Arms SK10 5PW [Palmerston St]: Spotlessly clean under new licensees, well kept Black Sheep, Boddingtons, Caledonian Deuchars IPA and Greene King Ruddles; limited food at least initially *(Tony Goff)*

BOTTOM OF THE OVEN [SJ9872]

Stanley Arms SK11 0AR [A537 Buxton—Macclesfield, 1st left past Cat & Fiddle]: Isolated moorland pub, small, friendly and cosy, lots of shiny black woodwork, plush seats, dimpled copper tables, good coal fires in all rooms inc dining room, generous well cooked traditional food, well kept Marstons and guest beers; piped music; children welcome, picnic-sets on grass behind, bedrooms; may close Mon in winter if weather bad *(LYM, Dr D J and Mrs S C Walker)*

CHELFORD [SJ8175]

Egerton Arms SK11 9BB [A537 Macclesfield—Knutsford]: Rambling village pub dating from 16th c, low beams and big fireplaces, good choice of enjoyable food from pub favourites up, friendly attentive service, well kept ales from old brass pumps, restaurant, some live music; garden picnic-sets, open all day *(Dr D J and Mrs S C Walker)*

CHESTER [SJ4065]

☆ *Bear & Billet* CH1 1RU [Lower Bridge St]: Handsome timbered 17th-c Okells pub with four changing guest ales such as Copper Dragon Best Bill, belgian and US imports, nice range of wines by the glass and of reasonably priced home-cooked pubby food, interesting features and some attractive furnishings in friendly and comfortable open-plan bar with fire, sitting and dining rooms upstairs; sports TV; pleasant courtyard, open all day *(the Didler, Dave Webster, Sue Holland, BB)*

Falcon CH1 1RS [Lower Bridge St]: Striking ancient building with handsome beams and brickwork, good value bar food (not Sun) from sandwiches to enterprising specials, friendly helpful staff, bargain Sam Smiths; piped music, games machine; children allowed lunchtime (not Sat) in airy attractive upstairs room; open all day Sat, interesting vaults tours *(LYM, Colin Moore)*

Olde Boot CH1 1LQ [Eastgate Row N]: Good value in lovely 17th-c Rows building, heavy beams, dark woodwork, oak flooring, flagstones, some exposed Tudor wattle and daub, old kitchen range in lounge beyond, old-fashioned settles and oak panelling in upper area popular with families, enjoyable food, bargain Sam Smiths OB, good service; piped music *(Joe Green, Colin Moore, the Didler, LYM)*

Ship Victory CH1 3EQ [George St]: Friendly old local with chatty landlord, low beams and simple décor, well kept Tetleys and changing guest beers, music nights *(the Didler)*

Telfords Warehouse CH1 4EZ [Tower Wharf, behind Northgate St nr railway]: Well kept interesting ales in large converted canal building, generous fresh up-to-date food, efficient staff, bare brick and boards, high pitched ceiling, big wall of windows overlooking water, massive iron winding gear in bar, some old enamelled advertisements, steps to heavy-beamed area with sofas, artwork and restaurant; late-night live music, bouncers on door; tables out by water, open all day *(BB, the Didler, Colin Moore, Rob and Catherine Dunster)*

☆ *Union Vaults* CH1 3ND [Francis St/Egerton St]: Friendly old-fashioned street-corner local, well kept Caledonian Deuchars IPA and two changing guest ales, three separate dining areas, friendly staff, old local photographs, back games room; piped music, sports TV; good outside seating for smokers, open all day *(Dave Webster, Sue Holland, the Didler, Joe Green)*

CHILDER THORNTON [SJ3678]

☆ *White Lion* CH66 5PU [off A41 S of M53 junction 5; New Rd]: Low two-room whitewashed country pub, keeping old-fashioned unpretentious feel after change of landlord, good value straightforward food, Thwaites ales, open fire, framed matchbooks, no music or machines; children welcome, tables out in covered front area and secluded back garden, play area, open all day *(MLR)*

CHRISTLETON [SJ4565]

Plough CH3 7PT [Plough Lane]: Popular 18th-c country local, three linked areas, up to nine ales inc Spitting Feathers and Theakstons, enjoyable home-made local food (not Sun), garden with play area, nice setting *(the Didler, Alan and Eve Harding)*

CHURCH LAWTON [SJ8255]

Red Bull ST7 3AJ [Congleton Rd S (A34)]: Welcoming pub by Trent & Mersey Canal lock, good value home-made food, well kept Robinsons, several rooms inc upstairs lounge and eating area, open fires; no credit cards *(Ben Williams, Richard and Karen Holt)*

COMBERBACH [SJ6477]

Spinner & Bergamot CW9 6AY [Warrington Rd]: Comfortably plush beamed 18th-c village pub (named after two racehorses) doing well under current licensees, good freshly prepared bar and restaurant food (12-7.30 Sun), four ales inc rarities for the area, good wines, log fires, hunting prints and lots of toby jugs and brasses, daily papers, softly lit back dining room with country-kitchen furniture and big inglenook, tiled family room with TV; piped music; picnic-sets on sloping lawn, lots of flowers, bowling green, open all day *(Quentin Spratt, Dr and Mrs D Scott)*

CONGLETON [SJ8663]

Beartown Tap CW12 1RL [Willow St (A54)]: Friendly tap for small nearby Beartown brewery, their interesting beers well priced and perhaps a guest microbrew, farm cider, belgian beers, bare boards in down-to-earth bar and two light airy rooms off, no food, games or music; upstairs lavatories; open all day Fri-Sun *(the Didler)*

Castle CW12 3LP [Castle Inn Rd (A527 SE)]: Attractive early 19th-c cottage-row conversion, dark beams, enjoyable food in large or small helpings, well kept Adnams Broadside, Greene King Old Speckled Hen and Timothy Taylors Landlord, back restaurant (children welcome here), Tues quiz night; open all day *(Jeremy King)*

CREWE [SJ7055]

Borough Arms CW1 2BG [Earle St]: Own microbrewery and lots of changing ales and belgian beers, friendly enthusiastic landlord, two small rooms off central bar and downstairs lounge, no machines; occasional sports TV, no under-21s; picnic-sets on back terrace and lawn, cl wkdy lunchtimes, open all day wknds from 12 *(Dave Webster, Sue Holland, the Didler)*

Rising Sun CW2 8SB [Middlewich Rd (A530), Wistaston]: Olde-worlde Chef & Brewer with

plenty of individuality, beamery, panelling, prints, two log fires and lots of separate areas, nine particularly well kept real ales inc one brewed for the pub by Titanic, occasional beer festivals, good choice of wines by the glass, cheerful efficient service, wide range of enjoyable well priced food, raised eating area; children's facilities, good disabled access (inc lift), tables and play area outside, quiet countryside, open all day *(Alan and Eve Harding)*

CULCHETH [SJ6595]

Harrow WA3 5DL [Church Lane]: Bright modern pub with good service and choice of good value food inc OAP lunch; keg beer *(Ben Williams)*

DARESBURY [SJ5782]

Ring o' Bells WA4 4AJ [B5356, handy for M56 junction 11]: Reliable Chef & Brewer with wide choice of food all day, several real ales, lots of wines by the glass, comfortable library-style areas and part more suited to walkers (canal is not far), young staff; children in eating areas, good disabled access, tables in long partly terraced garden, pretty village, church with *Alice in Wonderland* window, open all day *(LYM, Roger Noyes, Revd D Glover, Pat and Tony Martin)*

DELAMERE [SJ5769]

Vale Royal Abbey CW8 2HB [Chester Rd, Oakmere]: Greene King pub, well laid out and run, with their beer kept well *(John and Helen Rushton)*

FADDILEY [SJ5852]

☆ *Thatch* CW5 8JE [A534 Wrexham—Nantwich]: Attractive thatched, low-beamed and timbered dining pub carefully extended from medieval core, open fires, raised room to right of bar, back barn-style dining room (children allowed), friendly helpful service, relaxing atmosphere, real ales inc Greene King Old Speckled Hen, Timothy Taylors Landlord and Wells & Youngs Bombardier, enjoyable food inc children's helpings; soft piped music, silent games machine; charming country garden, landlords listed on outside plaque, open all day *(LYM, Jeremy King)*

FARNDON [SJ4154]

Farndon Arms CH3 6PU [High St]: Light contemporary décor in three linked areas, decent food, small bar with real ales such as Greene King Old Speckled Hen, Timothy Taylors Landlord and Theakstons Old Peculier; piped pop music, TV; pretty village *(Jeremy King)*

FRODSHAM [SJ5277]

Bulls Head WA6 6BS [Bellemonte Rd, Overton – off B5152 at Parish Church sign; M56 junction 12 not far]: Cheerful local with good beers, sports, teams etc, enjoyable food inc popular Sun lunch *(anon)*

☆ *Ring o' Bells* WA6 6BS [Bellemonte Rd, Overton – off B5152 at Parish Church sign; M56 junction 12 not far]: Charming early 17th-c pub with bargain unpretentious food, good long-serving landlady and friendly staff, locals and cats, little rambling rooms, beams, dark oak panelling and stained glass, changing ales from central servery, games room; children in eating areas, lovely secluded and interesting back garden with pond *(Ann and Tony Bennett-Hughes, LYM, J S Burn, Eric Eustance)*

GAWSWORTH [SJ8869]

☆ *Harrington Arms* SK11 9RJ [Church Lane]: Rustic 17th-c farm pub all the better now for having a full food operation, Robinsons Hatters Mild, Unicorn and a guest ale, two small gently updated rooms (children allowed in one), bare boards and panelling, fine carved oak bar counter; sunny benches on small front cobbled terrace *(the Didler, LYM, Dr D J and Mrs S C Walker)*

GURNETT [SJ9271]

☆ *Old Kings Head* SK11 0HD [30 Bradley Smithy]: Beamed split-level former coaching house and smithy by Macclesfield Canal aqueduct (moorings), recently refurbished but keeping old-fashioned feel, good straightforward reasonably priced food inc nice pies (all freshly made so be prepared for a wait), Marstons Pedigree, Thwaites and Wells & Youngs Bombardier, good choice of wine, friendly staff, old kitchen range, restaurant; quiet piped music, no credit cards; tables outside *(Richard and Karen Holt, Mr and Mrs Bannister, Dr D J and Mrs S C Walker)*

HASLINGTON [SJ7355]

Fox CW1 5QZ [Crewe Rd]: Recently refurbished under new landlord, bargain all-day bar food wkdys (not Fri evening or Mon), evening restaurant Tues-Thurs *(anon)*

HAUGHTON MOSS [SJ5855]

☆ *Nags Head* CW6 9RN [off A49 S of Tarporley]: Spotless black and white pub, friendly staff, Flowers, Sharps Doom Bar and a guest, food all day inc generous tasty bar food and lunchtime buffet, pews, heavy fireside settle in small quarry-tiled room, button-back wall banquettes in carpeted room with log fire, oak-beamed conservatory; children and dogs welcome, nicely maintained garden with picnic-sets, bowling green, open all day *(LYM)*

HENBURY [SJ8873]

Cock SK10 3LH [Chelford Rd]: Doing well under current licensees, with well kept Robinsons, short choice of enjoyable fairly simple food *(Dr D J and Mrs S C Walker)*

HUXLEY [SJ5061]

Farmers Arms CH3 9BG [off A51 SE of Chester]: Long low white building with bar and separate restaurant, small cosy rooms with bric-a-brac and open fires, good food (not Mon) esp steaks, traditional Sun lunches, well priced wines, friendly service, real ales; tables outside, sumptuous hanging baskets and wisteria-edged doorway, bar cl Mon-Thurs lunchtime, open all day Fri-Sun *(Ann and Tony Bennett-Hughes, J Bittlestone)*

HYDE [SJ9493]

Joshua Bradley SK14 5EZ [Stockport Rd, Gee Cross]: Former mansion handsomely

converted to pub/restaurant keeping panelling, moulded ceilings and imposing fireplaces, good range of pubby food, Hydes ales; heated terrace, play area *(Dennis Jones)*

KELSALL [SJ5268]

Morris Dancer CW6 0RS [Chester Rd (A54)]: Friendly efficient licensees successfully reworking this converted stable block as a thriving traditional village pub, good home-made food in bar and restaurant, well kept local Weetwood ales and guests, good choice of wines by the glass, open fires, plenty of events inc Mon night jazz; children welcome, back terrace with barbecue *(Su Titchner, Dennis Jones)*

KERRIDGE [SJ9276]

Lord Clyde SK10 5AH [Clarke Lane, off A523]: Recently reopened under new hard-working chef/landlord, contemporary feel with good regional and local food, well kept Flowers Original and Greene King Old Speckled Hen *(Des Mannion)*

KETTLESHULME [SJ9879]

☆ *Swan* SK23 7QU [B5470 Macclesfield—Chapel-en-le-Frith]: Smartly renovated little stone-built beamed 16th-c pub, good food from chef/owner inc great fresh fish range and popular Sun lunch, well kept Marstons and two interesting guest beers, farm cider, log fires, old settles and pews, Dickens prints; children and dogs welcome, large garden with stream, good walks, cl Mon lunchtime, open all day wknds *(Dr D J and Mrs S C Walker, Annette and John Derbyshire, Roger Yates, David Heath, Dr Peter Crawshaw, Dennis Jones)*

LANGLEY [SJ9471]

☆ *Leather's Smithy* SK11 0NE [off A523 S of Macclesfield, OS Sheet 118 map ref 952715]: Isolated stone-built pub up in fine walking country next to reservoir, well kept Theakstons, Wells & Youngs and guest ales, lots of whiskies, enjoyable bar food from sandwiches and bloomers up, good cheerful service, pleasant relaxing atmosphere, beams and log fire, flagstoned bar, carpeted dining areas, interesting local prints and photographs; unobtrusive piped music; no dogs, picnic-sets in garden behind and on grass opposite, open all day wknds *(Michael Butler, LYM, Dave Irving, Jenny Huggins)*

LITTLE BOLLINGTON [SJ7286]

Olde No 3 WA14 4TA [A56, under 3 miles from M56 exit 7]: Cosy old beamed pub by Bridgewater Canal, several changing ales such as Marstons Pedigree, Theakstons Old Peculier and Timothy Taylors Landlord, enjoyable food (not Mon), coal fire *(John Watson)*

Swan With Two Nicks WA14 4TJ [2 miles from M56 junction 7 – A56 towards Lymm, then first right at Stamford Arms into Park Lane; use A556 to get back on to M56 westbound]: Extended village pub full of beams, brass, copper and bric-a-brac, some antique settles, log fire, welcoming helpful service, good choice of enjoyable food from filling baguettes up inc popular Sun lunch (best to book), several good local ales inc one brewed for the pub, decent wines, nice coffee; children and dogs welcome, tables outside, attractive hamlet by Dunham Hall deer park, walks by Bridgewater Canal, open all day *(LYM, Norma and Noel Thomas, Gerry and Rosemary Dobson)*

LOWER PEOVER [SJ7474]

Bells of Peover WA16 9PZ [just off B5081; The Cobbles]: Improving Chef & Brewer in charming spot, lovely old building with panelling, beams, open fires and antiques, well kept Timothy Taylors Landlord and Wells & Youngs Bombardier, good value food inc set deals and Sun roasts; piped music; no children unless eating full meal in dining room; disabled facilities, terrace tables, big side lawn with trees, rose pergolas and little stream, on quiet cobbled lane with fine black and white 14th-c church, open all day *(LYM, Tom and Jill Jones, Pam and John Smith)*

Crown WA16 9QB [B5081, off A50]: Comfortable and attractive L-shaped bar with two rooms off, good food (all day Sun), fresh-cooked so can take a while, up to six real ales inc Caledonian Deuchars and Courage Directors, quick friendly service, low beams and flagstones, lots of bric-a-brac inc interesting gooseberry championship memorabilia, darts and dominoes; tables outside, open all day Sun *(Tom and Jill Jones)*

LYMM [SJ7087]

Barn Owl WA13 0SW [Agden Wharf, Warrington Lane (just off B5159 E)]: Comfortably extended building in picturesque setting by Bridgewater Canal, good value fresh food all day inc OAP bargains, Marstons Bitter and Pedigree and guest beers, decent wines by the glass, friendly atmosphere, pleasant service even though busy; disabled facilities, may be canal trips, open all day *(Ben Williams)*

☆ *Spread Eagle* WA13 0AG [not far from M6 junction 20; Eagle Brow (A6144, in centre)]: Big cheerful rambling beamed pub, charming black and white façade, good value home-made food all day from sandwiches and baguettes through two-course bargains to steaks, particularly well kept Lees ales, good choice of wines, good service, comfortable two-level lounge, proper drinking area by central bar, coal fire, lots of brasses, separate games room with pool; piped music; attractive village, open all day *(R T and J C Moggridge, BB, Pete Baker, Ben Williams)*

MACCLESFIELD [SJ9272]

Railway View SK11 7JW [Byrons Lane (off A523)]: Pair of 1700 cottages knocked into roomy pub with attractive snug corners, six or more changing ales such as Storm and Weetwood (beer prices reduced Mon), farm cider, good value simple home-made food, friendly service, remarkably shaped gents';

music nights and beer festivals; back terrace overlooking railway, open all day wknds *(the Didler)*

Waters Green Tavern SK11 6LH [Waters Green, opp station]: Seven quickly changing and interesting largely northern ales in roomy L-shaped open-plan local, good value home-made lunchtime food (not Sun), friendly staff and locals, back pool room *(the Didler)*

MADELEY HEATH [SJ7845]

Old Swan CW3 9LD [Crewe Rd]: Reopened under new owners, clean-cut modern refurbishment, low-priced food (all day Sun) from good baguettes up, reasonably priced wine, friendly staff *(Susan and Nigel Brookes)*

MALPAS [SJ4847]

Red Lion SY14 8NE [Old Hall St]: Partly panelled bar with fine longcase clock, enthusiastic landlord a champion of local real ales *(Paul Boot)*

MARTON [SJ8568]

☆ *Davenport Arms* SK11 9HF [A34 N of Congleton]: Comfortable, roomy and tasteful, good fresh food (not Mon) from baguettes up in bar and refurbished dining room, friendly obliging service, Courage Directors, Theakstons Best and a guest beer, log fire; no dogs; nr ancient half-timbered church (and Europe's widest oak tree), cl Mon lunchtime, open all day wknds *(Dr D J and Mrs S C Walker, Pam and John Smith)*

MOBBERLEY [SJ7980]

Church Inn WA16 7RD [Church Lane]: Welcoming relaxed old village pub, Black Sheep, Jennings Cumberland and a guest ale, friendly service, standard food, armchairs and big log fire; children welcome, disabled facilities, tables on small terrace, play area, own bowling green *(Kate Johnson)*

Frozen Mop WA16 7AL [Faulkners Lane]: Child-friendly former Brewers Fayre, good choice of food inc pizzas and spit grills, lots of reasonably priced wines by the glass inc choice of champagnes; leather armchairs in lounge by bar, light and airy dining area; tables out on decking *(Mrs E E Sanders)*

☆ *Plough & Flail* WA16 7DB [Paddock Hill; small sign off B5085 towards Wilmslow]: Light and airy family pub with consistently good unpretentious home-made food, attentive cheerful service, good wines by the glass, real ales; good garden with play area *(W K Wood, John and Barbara Hirst, Helen Cobb, Mrs P J Carroll)*

MOTTRAM [SJ8878]

Bulls Head SK10 4QH [Wilmslow Rd]: Now upmarket dining pub aka Osteria Mauro, good restauranty food, charming attentive service, well kept Boddingtons as well as continental lagers *(Tom and Jill Jones)*

MOULDSWORTH [SJ5170]

Goshawk CH3 8AJ [Station Rd (B5393)]: Comfortable family dining pub with masses of pictures and nice mix of largely pine furniture in extensive series of rooms inc small 'library' area, large double-sided log fire, attentive cheerful uniformed staff, good food from sandwiches to upscale restauranty dishes (all day; free rail travel from Chester if you eat), enterprising wines by the glass, well kept Black Sheep, Timothy Taylors Landlord and guests; piped music, no dogs; disabled facilities, good spot nr Delamere Forest with big outdoor space inc good play area and bowling green, open all day *(Tom and Jill Jones, Robin and Yvonne Calvert, Gerry and Rosemary Dobson)*

☆ **NANTWICH** [SJ6452]

☆ *Black Lion* CW5 5ED [Welsh Row]: Old black and white building smartened up under newish landlord but keeping beams, timbered brickwork, open fire and some atmosphere, now doing enjoyable reasonably priced food, changing ales inc Phoenix and Weetwood *(Phil Merrin, BB, Alun Jones)*

Boot & Shoe CW5 5RP [Hospital St]: Traditional layout with several rooms off central bar, simple furnishings, old local photographs, good choice of unusual real ales, generous food from speciality baguettes and somewhat oriental tapas to pubby favourites inc Sun roast, occasional live music; TVs throughout; open all day *(Martin Grosberg)*

Vine CW5 5RP [Hospital St]: Dates from 17th c, sympathetically modernised and stretching far back with old prints, books and dimly lit quiet corners, well kept Hydes beers inc seasonal ones and maybe a guest, friendly service and locals, lunchtime sandwiches, baguettes, wraps, baked potatoes and simple hot dishes, raised sitting areas; unobtrusive piped music and TV; children welcome, small outside area at back, open all day *(Martin Grosberg, BB)*

NESTON [SJ2976]

☆ *Harp* CH64 0TB [Quayside, SW of Little Neston; keep on along track at end of Marshlands Rd]: Tucked-away two-room country local, well kept interesting changing ales, good malt whiskies, basic good value home-made lunchtime food, woodburner in pretty fireplace, pale quarry tiles and simple furnishings, hatch servery in one room; children allowed in room on right, new garden behind, picnic-sets up on grassy front sea wall facing Dee marshes and Wales, glorious sunsets with wild calls of wading birds; open all day *(BB, Ann and Tony Bennett-Hughes, MLR)*

NORLEY [SJ5772]

Tigers Head WA6 8NT [Pytchleys Hollow]: Refurbished 17th-c inn nr Delamere Forest, friendly licensees, good value no-nonsense food, well kept Mild and other changing ales *(J S Burn)*

OLLERTON [SJ7776]

☆ *Dun Cow* WA16 8RH [Chelford Rd; outskirts of Knutsford towards Macclesfield]: Attractive country pub recently acquired by Robinsons, modern décor, two fine log fires; good disabled access *(LYM)*

OVER TABLEY [SJ7279]

Windmill WA16 0HW [by M6 junction 19]: Light and airy two-room 18th-c pub

comfortably updated in recent years, decent food for most of the day inc popular Sun carvery, breakfasts too, well kept Robinsons ales, efficient friendly service; children welcome, outside tables under substantial umbrellas, seven comfortable bedrooms, open all day from 8am Mon-Sat *(Pam and John Smith, Gerry and Rosemary Dobson)*

PARKGATE [SJ2778]

Boathouse CH64 6RN [village signed off A540]: Black and white timbered pub with well spaced tables in attractively refurbished linked rooms, enjoyable food from bar food to restaurant meals, cheerful staff, good value wines, Timothy Taylors Landlord, tea and coffee, big conservatory with great views to Wales over silted Dee estuary *(Alan and Eve Harding, Paul Humphreys)*

PLUMLEY [SJ7275]

Golden Pheasant WA16 9RX [Plumley Moor Lane (off A556 by the Smoker)]: Civilised well extended pub under new management, locally sourced food inc Sun carvery, real ales, comfortable lounge areas, roomy restaurant and conservatory; children welcome, spacious gardens inc play area and bowling green, bedrooms *(LYM, Pam and John Smith, H L Roberts)*

RAINOW [SJ9678]

☆ *Highwayman* SK10 5UU [A5002 Whaley Bridge—Macclesfield, NE of village]: Welcoming 17th-c moorside pub with current tenants doing good interesting locally sourced food, cheerful efficient service, Thwaites Lancaster Bomber, cosy low-beamed rooms with lovely log fires, separate restaurant; outside seating, grand views *(the Didler, LYM, Robert and Ann Lees)*

RODE HEATH [SJ8057]

Broughton Arms ST7 3RU [Sandbach Rd (A533)]: Friendly pub by Trent & Mersey Canal, bar food, Burton Bridge and Marstons Pedigree, reasonable prices; picnic-sets on heated terrace and waterside lawn, good moorings opposite *(Charles and Pauline Stride, Ben Williams)*

SHOCKLACH [SJ4349]

Bull SY14 7BL [off B5069 W of Malpas]: Welcoming village pub doing well under current owners, contemporary feel with beams, open fire and unusual furniture on stone and wood floors, good range of interesting fresh food from changing menu, extensive wine list, five ales inc Marstons Pedigree, friendly informal service, conservatory; back terrace and garden *(Noel Woods, Mr and Mrs J Palmer)*

STRETTON [SJ6282]

Stretton Fox WA4 4NU [Spark Hall Close, Tarporley Rd, just off M56 junction 10 exit roundabout]: Good Vintage Inn in spaciously converted farmhouse, surprisingly rural setting, interesting variety of rooms pleasantly done in their usual faux-old style, extensive choice of generous well priced food, cheerful young staff (service can be slow when busy), varying number of ales but good choice of wines *(Simon J Barber)*

SUTTON [SJ9469]

☆ **Ryles Arms** SK11 0NN [Hollin Lane, Higher Sutton]: Popular dining pub in fine countryside, good generous food (all day wknds) from sandwiches and juicy home-made burgers to more elaborate dishes, ales inc Marstons Pedigree and local Storm, decent well priced wines, good choice of whiskies, pleasant décor, hill-view dining room, no music or games; french windows to terrace, good bedrooms in converted barn, open all day wknds *(Rob and Catherine Dunster, LYM)*

SWETTENHAM [SJ7967]

☆ **Swettenham Arms** CW12 2LF [off A54 Congleton—Holmes Chapel or A535 Chelford—Holmes Chapel]: Attractive gently upmarket country pub in pretty setting by lavender plot and scenic Quinta arboretum, imaginative choice of good food from sandwiches up in immaculate line of individually furnished rooms from sofas and easy chairs to dining area (must book Sun) with well spaced tables, fine range of well kept changing real ales, good wine choice, efficient friendly service, log fires; children welcome, picnic-sets on quiet side lawn, open all day Sun *(LYM, Debbie Hiom, Pam and John Smith)*

TATTENHALL [SJ4858]

Letters CH3 9PX [High St]: Thriving traditional village local, beams and big fireplace, Cains and a guest beer, integral chinese restaurant and take-away, pool, games machines; attractive village *(Neil Whitehead, Victoria Anderson)*

THELWALL [SJ6587]

Pickering Arms WA4 2SU [Thelwall New Rd (B5157, nr M6 junction 20)]: Friendly and attractive olde-worlde low-beamed pub with 16th-c roots, decent well priced food from sandwiches up, Theakstons Best and Wells & Youngs Bombardier; tables on cobbled forecourt, pleasant conservation village nr Ship Canal *(Brian and Anna Marsden)*

WILMSLOW [SJ8481]

King William SK9 1BQ [Manchester Rd (A538)]: Old-fashioned two-room Robinsons pub, low ceilings, cosy alcoves off bar, wide choice of food all day from tapas to traditional, good wine range inc spanish, some live music; TV in back bar; children welcome, garden tables, six bedrooms, open all day *(G D K Fraser)*

WRENBURY [SJ5947]

Cotton Arms CW5 8HG [Cholmondeley Rd]: Beamed and timbered village pub in popular spot by canal locks and boatyard, good value pub food in two large comfortable dining areas, friendly staff, well kept ales, lots of brass, open fire, side games room *(Charles and Pauline Stride)*

Cornwall

Pubs new to the *Guide* this year – or back in these pages after a break – include the old-fashioned Cobweb in Boscastle, the remote Trengilly Wartha near Constantine, the Bush at Morwenstow, the carefully refurbished Victoria in Perranuthnoe (good food), the Roseland at Philleigh (a new microbrewery this year) and the Driftwood Spars at Trevaunance Cove (another own-brew pub and a nice place to stay). Others doing especially well these days include the Rising Sun at Altarnun (good food here too), the ancient Crown at Lanlivery, the Plume of Feathers at Mitchell (a good place to stay), the Pandora idyllically placed near Mylor Bridge, the friendly Turks Head in Penzance, the bustling Blue Peter in Polperro, Blue at Porthtowan (very popular beach bar), the Port Gaverne Inn near Port Isaac (informal small bar in seaside hotel) and the Old Ale House in Truro (super value food). Flourishing Lucky Dips are the Queens Arms at Botallack, Smugglers Den at Cubert, Seven Stars in Falmouth, Fountain in Mevagissey, Cornish Arms at Pendoggett and Ship at Portloe. The county's top brewers are Sharps and St Austell, quite closely followed by Skinners, with Blackawton heading a good number of smaller brewers.

ALTARNUN   SX2083   MAP 1

Rising Sun 🍴 🍺

Off A39 just W of A395 junction; pub NW of village; PL15 7SN

Welcoming pub with a good mix of customers, several real ales and imaginative food; camping field

With first-rate food and four real ales, this friendly pub is very popular with both locals and visitors. The low-beamed, L-shaped main bar has plain traditional furnishings, bare boards and polished delabole slate flagstones, some stripped stone and a couple of coal fires. From the nearby Penpont Brewery there might be Cornish Arvor, St Nonnas and Rowghtor as well as Skinners Betty Stogs on handpump, several wines by the glass and local cider; piped music. Outside, there are seats on a terrace with more in the garden opposite and they now have a pétanque pitch. There's a field for camping (and a smart shower block) screened off by high evergreens. The village itself is well worth a look and the church is beautiful. Dogs are allowed in the bar if on a lead.

🍴 Using the best local produce, the first-class bar food might include lunchtime sandwiches using their home-made bread (the crab or their own corned beef are both very good), ploughman's or fisherman's (local fresh, smoked and pickled fish), cornish rarebit, field mushroom on toast with a free-range egg and pesto, a changing vegetarian frittata, sausages with sage and onion gravy, crispy duck leg confit with celeriac and carrot slaw, seared wild sea trout fillet with a horseradish lemon cream, free-range chicken breast with sautéed leek and mushroom and tarragon sauce, 10oz boxeater steak, and puddings like molten centre belgian chocolate cake with raspberry sauce and sticky toffee pudding. *Starters/Snacks: £3.95 to £8.95. Main Courses: £8.50 to £20.00. Puddings: £4.95*

Free house ~ Licensee Andy Mason ~ Real ale ~ Bar food (12-2(2.30 weekends), 6-9) ~ Restaurant ~ (01566) 86636 ~ Well behaved children allowed in bar but not in restaurant ~ Dogs allowed in bar ~ Open 11-2.30, 5.30-11; 11-11 Sat; 12-10.30 Sun

Recommended by David Hoare, the Didler, Reg Fowle, Helen Rickwood, Klaus and Elizabeth Leist, Penny Lang, Jacquie Jones, David Heath, Colin McKerrow, Richard and Patricia Jefferson, John and Bernadette Elliott, Susan Lang

BLISLAND
SX1073 MAP 1

Blisland Inn 🍺
Village signposted off A30 and B3266 NE of Bodmin; PL30 4JF

Super choice of real ales and beer-related memorabilia in welcoming local; home-made food and cheerful service

With a fine choice of real ales and a chatty, friendly atmosphere, this busy little local is a popular place in a pretty village. Every inch of the beams and ceiling is covered with beer badges (or their particularly wide-ranging collection of mugs), and the walls are similarly filled with beer-related posters and memorabilia. Up to eight real ales are kept at any one time, tapped from the cask or on handpump. Two are brewed for the pub by Sharps – Blisland Special and Bulldog – and there might be Bass, Blackawton Westcountry Gold, Greene King Abbot and Flankers Tackle, Sharps Own and Skinners Cornish Blonde. They also have a changing farm cider, fruit wines and real apple juice; good service. The carpeted lounge has a number of barometers on the walls, a rack of daily newspapers for sale and a few standing timbers, and the family room has pool, table skittles, euchre, cribbage and dominoes; piped music. Plenty of picnic-sets outside. The popular Camel Trail cycle path is close by – though the hill up to Blisland is pretty steep. As with many pubs in this area, it's hard to approach without negotiating several single-track roads.

🍴 **Tasty, pubby food includes filled lunchtime baps, soup, burgers, fish or egg and chips and scampi, with daily specials like steak and mushroom pie, stuffed peppers, lasagne and moussaka, and puddings such as spotted dick and sticky toffee pudding.** *Starters/Snacks: £3.95 to £5.95. Main Courses: £5.95 to £13.95. Puddings: £3.95 to £5.65*

Free house ~ Licensees Gary and Margaret Marshall ~ Real ale ~ Bar food ~ (01208) 850739 ~ Children in family room only ~ Dogs welcome ~ Live music most Sat evenings ~ Open 11.30-11; 12-10.30 Sun

Recommended by R J Herd, David Heath, John and Bernadette Elliott, R K Phillips, the Didler, Michael B Griffith, Andrea Rampley, Joe Green, Mrs M K Matthews, Chris Glasson, R T and J C Moggridge, Chris and Sheila Smith, Reg Fowle, Helen Rickwood

BODINNICK
SX1352 MAP 1

Old Ferry
Across the water from Fowey; coming by road, to avoid the ferry queue turn left as you go down the hill – car park on left before pub; PL23 1LX

Bustling local across the water from Fowey, simple little rooms with nautical bits and pieces; lots of summer customers

Our readers have enjoyed their visits to this friendly old pub for many years. It's nicely old fashioned and unchanging and to make the most of the pretty river views you must arrive early to bag a seat on the front terrace or by the window in the homely little restaurant. Three simply furnished small rooms have quite a few bits of nautical memorabilia, a couple of half model ships mounted on the wall and several old photographs, as well as wheelback chairs, built-in plush pink wall seats and an old high-backed settle; there may be several friendly cats and a dog. The family room at the back is actually hewn into the rock; piped music and TV. Sharps Own and in summer, Sharps Coaster, on handpump, several wines by the glass and a farm cider. Mobile phones are banned and a 50p fine goes to the RNLI. The pub is best reached by parking in the public car park in Fowey and taking the small ferry across the water. The lane beside the pub, in front of the ferry slipway, is extremely steep and parking is limited. There are lovely circular walks from here.

🍴 Bar food includes sandwiches, ploughman's, filled baked potatoes, pasties, soup, home-cooked ham and egg, various burgers, steak in ale pie, chicken curry, specials such as breaded garlic mushrooms with garlic dip, vegetable lasagne and beef bourguignon, and puddings like apple pie or spotted dick with custard. *Starters/Snacks: £5.25 to £6.50. Main Courses: £7.95 to £9.50. Puddings: £3.50 to £4.95*

Free house ~ Licensees Royce and Patricia Smith ~ Real ale ~ Bar food (12-3, 6-9; 12-2.30, 6.30-8.30 in winter) ~ Restaurant ~ (01726) 870237 ~ Children welcome ~ Dogs allowed in bar and bedrooms ~ Open 11-10.30; 12-10 in winter ~ Bedrooms: £85S(£90B)/£95B

Recommended by Suzy Miller, Patrick Barber, Chris Glasson, Francis Vernon, Canon Michael Bourdeaux

BOSCASTLE   SX0991   MAP 1

Cobweb

B3263, just E of harbour; PL35 0HE

Heavy beams, flagstones, lots of old jugs and bottles, a cheerful atmosphere, real ales, enjoyable pubby food and friendly staff

---

The heavy beams in the two bars of this bustling village pub are hung with hundreds of bottles and jugs, the walls are covered with lots of pictures of bygone years, and there's a cheerful, chatty atmosphere created by a good mix of customers. As well as a cosy log fire, there are comfortable high-backed winged settles, a couple of venerable carved chairs, flagstones, and St Austell Tribute and Proper Job, Sharps Doom Bar and a local guest on handpump. There's a second winter fire and more conventional seats and tables, too. Darts, pool and juke box. This is a pretty village close to the tiny steeply cut harbour.

🍴 Good value, tasty bar food includes sandwiches, soup, spinach and ricotta cannelloni, thai chicken curry, moroccan lamb, steak in ale pie, liver and bacon, pork and cider casserole, chicken breast wrapped in bacon with stilton sauce, a local fish platter, and puddings like banoffi pie and chocolate pudding. *Starters/Snacks: £3.95. Main Courses: £7.95 to £8.95. Puddings: £3.95*

Free house ~ Licensees Ivor and Adrian Bright ~ Real ale ~ Bar food (11(12 Sun)-2.30, 6(6.30 Sun)-9.30) ~ Restaurant ~ (01840) 250278 ~ Children welcome ~ Dogs allowed in bar ~ Live entertainment Sat evenings ~ Open 10.30am(midday Sun)-11pm(midnight Sat)

Recommended by Irene and Derek Flewin, Ross Balaam, Gerry and Rosemary Dobson, the Didler, Ted George, David Eagles, Barry and Anne, R K Phillips

CADGWITH   SW7214   MAP 1

Cadgwith Cove Inn

Down very narrow lane off A3083 S of Helston; no nearby parking; TR12 7JX

Fine walks in either direction from old-fashioned inn at the bottom of fishing cove; bedrooms

---

In a fishing cove at the bottom of a charming village, this little local has a good bustling atmosphere when the cheerful locals crowd in. The two snugly dark front rooms have plain pub furnishings on their mainly parquet flooring, a log fire in one stripped stone end wall, lots of local photographs including some of gig races, cases of naval hat ribands and of fancy knot-work and a couple of compass binnacles. Some of the dark beams have ships' shields and others have spliced blue rope hand-holds. Otter Bitter, Sharps Doom Bar, Skinners Betty Stogs and a guest beer on handpump and Weston's cider. A back bar has a huge and colourful fish mural; piped music and euchre. There are green-painted picnic-sets on the good-sized front terrace, some under a fairy-lit awning, looking down to the fish sheds by the bay. The bedrooms overlook the sea; fine coastal walks in either direction. Whilst it's best to park at the top of the village and meander down through the thatched cottages, it is quite a steep hike back up again.

🍴 Bar food includes sandwiches, soup, spinach and feta pie, lasagne, daily specials such as local fish casserole or monkfish with pancetta, fish and chips with mushy peas, braised

pheasant, and puddings. *Starters/Snacks: £3.75 to £6.95. Main Courses: £5.95 to £8.95. Puddings: £3.50 to £4.50*

Punch ~ Lease David and Lynda Trivett ~ Real ale ~ Bar food ~ (01326) 290513 ~ Well behaved children welcome away from main bar ~ Dogs welcome ~ Live folk Tues evening, cornish singers Fri evening ~ Open 12-11 (1am Fri; 10.30 Sun); 12-3, 7-11 in winter ~ Bedrooms: £30.25(£47.50S)/£60.50(£82.50S)

Recommended by Adrian Johnson, Dave Webster, Sue Holland, Dr and Mrs M E Wilson, Ewan and Moira McCall

CONSTANTINE   SW7328   MAP 1

Trengilly Wartha

Nancenoy; off A3083 S of Helston, via Gweek then forking right; TR11 5RP

Bustling inn in several acres of gardens, plenty of room inside, too; real ales, lots of wines and whiskies, good food using local produce and friendly atmosphere; bedrooms.

There have been quite a few changes here over the last few years. What was the restaurant is now a cosy bistro, liked by customers who want to book a table with waitress service and the function room – where they serve their award-winning breakfasts – now has a garden area. The long low-beamed main bar with its woodburning stove and mix of tables and chairs, is kept for those just wanting a drink and for less formal dining, and the light conservatory is popular with families; football table. Sharps Cornish Coaster, Skinners Betty Stogs and a beer named for the pub on handpump, 20 wines by the glass and 40 malt whiskies. There are six acres of gardens with tables under large parasols and boules; lots of surrounding walks. Their cricket team keeps busy!

⑪ **Using fish straight from the boats, local shellfish, free-range pork from the farm next door and local vegetables, the enjoyable bar food includes sandwiches, ploughman's, soup, pâté with home-made chutney, proper burgers with chilli mayonnaise, sausages with mustard mash and onion gravy, lasagne, a vegetarian risotto of the day, pork with apricots and a mustard cream sauce, and daily specials such as Falmouth mussels, beef stroganoff, lamb shank with rosemary and garlic jus, king prawns in a wild mushroom and parmesan sauce on pasta and duck breast with plum and chilli sauce.** *Starters/Snacks: £4.00 to £8.50. Main Courses: £7.80 to £19.00. Puddings: £4.50 to £5.50*

Free house ~ Licensees Will and Lisa Lea ~ Real ale ~ Bar food ~ Restaurant ~ (01326) 340332 ~ Children welcome away from bar area ~ Dogs allowed in bar and bedrooms ~ Folk night every other Weds ~ Open 11(12 Sun)-3(3.30 Sat and Sun), 6-midnight ~ Bedrooms: £50B/£80B

Recommended by the Weirs, the Whites, Mrs M S Tadd, Anthony Rogers, John and Bryony Coles, Peter Randell, Brian and Anita Randall, Dr and Mrs M E Wilson, Andy and Claire Barker

HELSTON   SW6522   MAP 1

Halzephron ♀ 🛏

Gunwalloe, village about 4 miles S but not marked on many road maps; look for brown sign on A3083 alongside perimeter fence of RNAS Culdrose; TR12 7QB

Popular inn in lovely spot with well liked food, local beers and bedrooms; good nearby walks

This is a lovely spot and very popular at peak times so you will need to book to be sure of a table. The neatly kept rooms have comfortable seating, copper on the walls and mantelpiece, a warm winter fire in the woodburning stove and St Austell Tribute and Sharps Own and Doom Bar on handpump; also, eight wines by the glass and 40 malt whiskies. The dining Gallery seats up to 30 people; darts and board games. There are lots of fine surrounding unspoilt walks with views of Mount's Bay. Gunwalloe fishing cove is just 300 yards away and Church Cove with its sandy beach is a mile away – as is the church of St Winwaloe (built into the dunes on the seashore).

⑪ **Good bar food includes sandwiches, soup, smoked mackerel pâté, beef in ale ragoût, fresh crab platter, braised pork belly with celeriac and apple purée, potato rösti, and a sage, tarragon and wild mushroom cream, sautéed mediterranean vegetables with fresh** pasta and garlic bread, fillet of beef with horseradish mash and red wine jus, roast cod topped with tapenade on garlic pommes purée with roast plum tomato and red wine reduction, and puddings. *Starters/Snacks: £4.95 to £7.95. Main Courses: £8.50 to £18.50. Puddings: £3.90 to £5.50*

Free house ~ Licensee Angela Thomas ~ Real ale ~ Bar food ~ Restaurant ~ (01326) 240406 ~ Children in family room ~ Dogs welcome ~ Open 11-2.30, 6-11; 12-2.30, 6-10.30 Sun; 6.30 opening time in winter ~ Bedrooms: £50S/£90S

Recommended by Dave Webster, Sue Holland, Nick Lawless, Michael and Ann Cole, Ewan and Moira McCall, Revd R P Tickle, Jacquie Jones, Susie Symes, John and Gloria Isaacs, P J Checksfield, M and L Towers, Marianne and Peter Stevens, R and S Bentley, Dr and Mrs M W A Haward, Steve Kirby, Marianne Welsh, Simon Donan, Edna Jones, Andy and Claire Barker

LANLIVERY   SX0759   MAP 1

Crown 🍺

Signposted off A390 Lostwithiel—St Austell (tricky to find from other directions); PL30 5BT

Chatty atmosphere in nice old pub with old-fashioned rooms and well liked food and drink; the Eden Project is close by; bedrooms

Warmly welcoming and with some real character, this popular place is one of Cornwall's oldest pubs. The main bar has a warming log fire in the huge fireplace, traditional settles on the big flagstones, some cushioned farmhouse chairs, a mix of wooden chairs and tables and Sharps Doom Bar, Skinners Betty Stogs, Cornish Knocker and Spriggan Ale on handpump. A couple of other rooms are similarly furnished and there's another open fire; darts and board games. There is a huge lit-up well with a glass top by the porch, and plenty of picnic-sets in the quiet garden. The Eden Project is only ten minutes away.

🍴 **Well liked bar food includes sandwiches, smoked mackerel pâté, chargrilled chicken caesar salad, a quiche of the day, ham and free-range eggs, apple and cider sausages with wholegrain mustard mash and caramelised onion gravy, braised lamb shoulder with red wine and rosemary gravy, fresh local crab gratin, chicken in white wine, cream and tarragon sauce, cheesy ratatouille, steak in ale pie and steaks.** *Starters/Snacks: £2.95 to £8.50. Main Courses: £7.95 to £14.95. Puddings: £4.00 to £5.95*

Wagtail Inns ~ Licensee Andrew Brotheridge ~ Real ale ~ Bar food (12-2.30, 6.30-9; 12-9 in summer) ~ Restaurant ~ (01208) 872707 ~ Children welcome but must be away from bar ~ Dogs allowed in bar and bedrooms ~ Occasional live music Sun ~ Open 12-11(10.30 Sun) ~ Bedrooms: /£79.95S

Recommended by Andrea Rampley, Dennis Jenkin, Mr and Mrs Gravener, Andy and Claire Barker, Nick Lawless, Dr and Mrs M W A Haward, Brian and Anita Randall, Phil and Jane Hodson, T R and B C Jenkins, Mr and Mrs W D Borthwick, Mrs P Bishop, Jean and Douglas Troup

LOSTWITHIEL   SX1059   MAP 1

Globe 🍷 🍺

North Street (close to medieval bridge); PL22 0EG

Unassuming bar in traditional local, interesting food and drinks and friendly staff; suntrap back courtyard with outside heaters

There's a warm welcome for both visitors and locals in this 13th-c town local. The unassuming bar is long and somewhat narrow with a bustling, relaxed atmosphere, a good mix of pubby tables and seats, customers' photographs on pale green plank panelling at one end, nice more or less local prints (for sale) on canary walls above a coal-effect stove at the snug inner end and a small red-walled front alcove. The ornately carved bar counter, with comfortable chrome and leatherette stools, dispenses Badger Tanglefoot, Sharps Doom Bar, Shepherd Neame Spitfire and Skinners Betty Stogs from handpump, with a dozen reasonably priced wines by the glass and 20 malt whiskies. Piped music, darts and board games. The sheltered back courtyard is not large, but has some attractive, unusual pot plants and is a real suntrap (with an extendable overhead awning and outside heaters). You can park in several of the nearby streets. The 13th-c church is worth a look and the ancient river bridge, a few yards away, is lovely.

🍴 **As well as lunchtime sandwiches, filled baguettes and baked potatoes and ploughman's, the enjoyable bar food might include soup, scallops with bacon, pork and chicken pâté, mushrooms in port and stilton, smoked haddock fishcakes, chilli, chicken curry, brie and redcurrant tart, venison sausages with onion gravy, daily specials like rabbit and bacon pie or slow-roast lamb shoulder in rosemary and mint, and puddings such as ginger and black treacle sponge and cherry pie.** *Starters/Snacks: £4.50 to £7.95. Main Courses: £7.95 to £14.95. Puddings: £3.50 to £4.95*

Free house ~ Licensee William Erwin ~ Real ale ~ Bar food ~ Restaurant ~ (01208) 872501 ~ Children welcome ~ Dogs allowed in bar ~ Live music Weds evening ~ Open 12-11(midnight Fri and Sat); 12-2.30, 6(5 Fri)-11 weekdays in winter ~ Bedrooms: /£70B

Recommended by B and M Kendall, PL, Dave Webster, Sue Holland, Peter Salmon, Dave Braisted, Evelyn and Derek Walter, John and Joan Calvert, Phil and Jane Hodson

MALPAS

SW8442   MAP 1

Heron

Trenhaile Terrace, off A39 S of Truro; TR1 1SL

Lovely creekside spot, attractively decorated pub, friendly service and good food

Friendly new licensees run this idyllically placed creekside pub; there are seats under heaters on the terrace to make the most of the view and a couple of window tables inside, too. The long, narrow bar has several areas leading off and a raised part at one end – it's all very light and airy with blue and white décor and furnishings throughout. There are two gas fires, mainly wooden floors with flagstones by the bar, modern yacht paintings on the wood-planked walls, some brass nautical items, heron pictures, a stuffed heron in a cabinet and a chatty atmosphere. St Austell IPA and Tribute and a guest like Proper Job on handpump. Parking is difficult, especially at peak times.

🍴 **Popular bar food includes lunchtime filled rolls, wraps, crab sandwiches and platters, local sausages and mash, ham and egg, battered fish, mushroom lasagne and steak in ale pie with a herby suet crust, plus evening dishes like a trio of local fish in parsley butter, chicken in a creamy mushroom sauce with crispy pancetta and lamb cutlets with minted mash and red wine and redcurrant sauce; daily specials such as smoked haddock chowder and goujons of monkfish in a lime and chilli batter, and puddings like chocolate trifle and fruit crumbles.** *Starters/Snacks: £4.50 to £5.50. Main Courses: £7.25 to £13.95. Puddings: £4.95*

St Austell ~ Tenants Jonathan and Karen Berg ~ Real ale ~ Bar food ~ (01872) 272773 ~ Children welcome ~ Open 11-11(11.30 Sat and Sun); 11-3, 6-11 winter weekdays

Recommended by Ian Phillips, John Marsh, Andrea Rampley, Comus and Sarah Elliott, W N F Boughey, Mrs Brenda Calver, Mark Flynn, Glenwys and Alan Lawrence

MITCHELL

SW8554   MAP 1

Plume of Feathers 🛏

Just off A30 Bodmin—Redruth, by A3076 junction; take the southwards road then turn first right; TR8 5AX

Contemporary décor in several rooms, friendly welcome, real ales and quite a choice of daily specials; comfortable bedrooms

This is a pleasing place with a warm welcome – and very handy for the A30. As well as a public bar, there are other rooms with appealing and contemporary décor, Farrow & Ball pastel-coloured walls, paintings by local artists, stripped old beams, painted wooden dado and two fireplaces. Greene King IPA, Sharps Doom Bar, a changing ale from Skinners and Wadworths 6X on handpump and several wines by the glass; piped music, games machine and TV. The well planted garden areas have plenty of seats and the bedrooms are comfortable.

🍴 **Good food at fair prices includes lunchtime sandwiches, soup, chicken liver parfait with onion marmalade, fishcake with sweet chilli, pasta with white crab meat, white wine,** garlic and fresh herb butter, confit of duck leg with orange glaze, parsnip mash and parsnip crisps, garlic-marinated chicken breast with chorizo, red onion and sautéed potato salad, and daily specials such as local mussels with cider and cream, steak in ale pie, apple, black pudding and english mustard pork sausages with onion gravy, beer-battered pollack and lamb or chicken curry. *Starters/Snacks: £2.50 to £6.50. Main Courses: £8.50 to £10.50. Puddings: £1.65 to £5.25*

Free house ~ Licensee Joe Musgrove ~ Real ale ~ Bar food (10 (for breakfast)-10) ~ Restaurant ~ (01872) 510387/511125 ~ Children welcome but must be away from bar ~ Dogs allowed in bar and bedrooms ~ Open 9am-midnight(11pm Sun) ~ Bedrooms: £66.25S(£73.75B)/£90S(£100B)

Recommended by Nick and Meriel Cox, Dennis Jenkin, R J Herd, John Marsh, Michelle and Graeme Voss, W N F Boughey, Marcus Mann, Phil and Jane Hodson, Gerry and Rosemary Dobson, Norman and Sarah Keeping, Stephen Moss, Andy and Claire Barker, Lesley and Peter Barrett, Bernard Stradling

MITHIAN   SW7450   MAP 1

Miners Arms

Just off B3285 E of St Agnes; TR5 0QF

Cosy pub with open fires in several smallish rooms and friendly staff

You can be sure of a cheery welcome from the staff and locals in this 400-year-old pub. Several cosy little rooms and passages are warmed by winter open fires, there are pubby furnishings on the patterned carpet and the small back bar has an irregular beam and plank ceiling, a wood block floor and bulging squint walls (one with a fine old wall painting of Elizabeth I). Another small room has a decorative low ceiling and lots of books. Sharps Doom Bar and perhaps Skinners Betty Stogs on handpump; piped music, board games and darts. There are seats outside on the back terrace and in the garden with more on the sheltered front cobbled forecourt. More reports please.

Traditional bar food includes filled baguettes, steak in ale pie, vegetable lasagne, gammon and egg, lamb shank in minted gravy, and puddings like forest fruit meringue and chocolate fudge brownie. *Starters/Snacks: £5.00 to £7.00. Main Courses: £7.00 to £12.00. Puddings: £5.00*

Punch ~ Lease Anouska House ~ Real ale ~ Bar food (12-2.30, 6-9) ~ Restaurant ~ (01872) 552375 ~ Children allowed away from bar ~ Dogs allowed in bar ~ Open 12-midnight(11pm Sun)

Recommended by Dennis Jenkin, John Marsh, David and Sue Smith, Mrs Angela Graham

MORWENSTOW   SS2015   MAP 1

Bush

Signed off A39 N of Kilkhampton; Crosstown; EX23 9SR

Friendly, ancient pub in fine spot, character bar and airy dining rooms, real ales, carefully sourced produce for well liked food and seats outside; bedrooms

Once a haunt for smugglers, this ancient place dates back to the 13th c. It's a ten-minute walk to Vicarage Cliff, one of the grandest parts of the Cornish coast (with 400-ft precipices) and just off the South West Coast Path. The bar has ancient built-in settles, flagstones, a woodburning stove in a big stone fireplace, lots of brass and copper knick-knacks, some horse tack and St Austell HSD and Tribute and Skinners Betty Stogs on handpump. Other rooms are set for dining with pale wooden dining chairs and tables, pictures on creamy yellow walls, beams and fresh flowers; the dining room has big windows overlooking the picnic-sets on the grass outside. As well as bedrooms, they have self-catering, too.

Using meat from their own farm, produce from other local farms, game from local shoots and local fish, the bar food includes filled baguettes, soup, hummus and olives with home-made flatbread, chicken liver parfait with onion jam, ploughman's, mussels, red wine and blue cheese risotto with spiced walnuts, beef-battered pollack, local

sausages with onion gravy, tarragon-stuffed chicken breast wrapped in parma ham with jerusalem artichoke purée and red wine sauce, whole john dory with caper and parsley brown butter, and puddings like rich chocolate cake with crème fraîche and crushed pistachios and apple and cherry crumble; they also offer cream teas and Sunday roasts. *Starters/Snacks: £4.50 to £6.50. Main Courses: £8.00 to £17.00. Puddings: £4.95*

Free house ~ Licensees Rob and Edwina Tape ~ Real ale ~ Bar food (11-9; Sun lunch till 3.30) ~ (01288) 331242 ~ Children welcome ~ Dogs allowed in bar and bedrooms ~ Open 11am-12.30am ~ Bedrooms: £45S/£79S(£79B)

Recommended by John and Fiona Merritt, Quentin and Carol Williamson, Ryta Lyndley, the Didler, Geoffrey and Karen Berrill, Jean and David Lewis, Rona Murdoch

MYLOR BRIDGE SW8137 MAP 1

Pandora ★★ ♀

Restronguet Passage: from A39 in Penryn, take turning signposted Mylor Church, Mylor Bridge, Flushing and go straight through Mylor Bridge following Restronguet Passage signs; or from A39 further N, at or near Perranarworthal, take turning signposted Mylor, Restronguet, then follow Restronguet Weir signs, but turn left down hill at Restronguet Passage sign; TR11 5ST

Beautifully placed waterside inn with seats on long floating pontoon, lots of atmosphere in beamed and flagstoned rooms, and some sort of food all day in summer

The position of this lovely medieval thatched pub is very special, and in fine weather you can sit with your drink on the long floating pontoon and watch children crabbing and visiting dinghies pottering about in the sheltered waterfront. Inside, several rambling, interconnecting rooms have low wooden ceilings (mind your head on some of the beams), beautifully polished big flagstones, cosy alcoves with leatherette benches built into the walls, old race posters, model boats in glass cabinets, and three large log fires in high hearths (to protect them against tidal floods). St Austell HSD, Tinners and Tribute and a guest such as Bass on handpump; a dozen wines by the glass. It does get very crowded and parking is difficult at peak times.

🍴 **Good, popular bar food includes sandwiches, filled baked potatoes, soup, moules marinière, langoustines in garlic butter with sweet chilli mayonnaise, barbecue spare ribs (as a starter or main course), local pork sausages with red onion gravy, beer-battered cod, spinach and mushroom macaroni with garlic bread, rib-eye steak, daily specials, and puddings like earl grey jelly with lemon granita and dark chocolate tart with white chocolate ice-cream and praline shards.** *Starters/Snacks: £4.50 to £8.00. Main Courses: £7.00 to £14.00. Puddings: £4.50 to £8.00*

St Austell ~ Tenant John Milan ~ Real ale ~ Bar food (all day Easter-Sept; 12-3, 6.30-9 winter) ~ Restaurant ~ (01326) 372678 ~ Children welcome away from bar area ~ Dogs allowed in bar ~ Open 11am-midnight (11pm in winter)

Recommended by Adrian Johnson, Kelvin and Carol Butcher, Mrs Mary Woods, John and Bernadette Elliott, Clive Watkin, Andrea Rampley, John Marsh, D R Robinson, M P Mackenzie, the Didler, Mr and Mrs Gravener, John and Fiona McIlwain, Peter Salmon, Jim Lyon, DFL, R T and J C Moggridge, David Rule, Kalman Kafetz, Mrs P Sumner, Stuart Turner, Steve Kirby, Joan York, Andy and Claire Barker, M Bryan Osborne

PENZANCE SW4730 MAP 1

Turks Head

At top of main street, by big domed building (Lloyds TSB), turn left down Chapel Street; TR18 4AF

Cheerfully run pub, the oldest in town, with a good, bustling atmosphere and decent food and beer

Well run by friendly licensees, this bustling old town pub always has a good mix of visitors and locals. The bar has old flat irons, jugs and so forth hanging from the beams, pottery above the wood-effect panelling, wall seats and tables and a couple of elbow-rests around central pillars; piped music. Otter Bitter, Sharps Doom Bar and Skinners

Betty Stogs on handpump and helpful service. The suntrap back garden has big urns of flowers. There has been a Turks Head here for over 700 years – though most of the original building was destroyed by a Spanish raiding party in the 16th century.

🍴 Popular bar food includes lunchtime sandwiches, filled ciabatta and filled baked potatoes, soup, mussels in wine and cream, goats cheese and caramelised red onion tart, cod and chips, a pie of the day, sizzling tandoori monkfish, winter hotpots and casseroles, and puddings like bread and butter pudding and apple pie with custard; there's a very good value OAP lunch menu, a two-course evening menu a couple of times a week and themed evenings. *Starters/Snacks: £1.75 to £5.95. Main Courses: £6.95 to £12.95. Puddings: £3.95 to £4.95*

Punch ~ Lease Jonathan and Helen Gibbard ~ Real ale ~ Bar food (12-2.30, 6-10) ~ Restaurant ~ (01736) 363093 ~ Children welcome ~ Dogs welcome ~ Open 11-11(midnight Sat and Sun)

Recommended by David Crook, Jerry Brown, Michael and Alison Sandy, Neil and Anita Christopher, Alan Johnson, Dave Webster, Sue Holland, Tony and Jill Radnor, Dr and Mrs R E S Tanner, Tim and Ann Newell, R J Herd

---

PERRANUTHNOE   SW5329   MAP 1

Victoria 🍴

Signed off A394 Penzance—Helston; TR20 9NP

Carefully refurbished inn close to Mounts Bay beaches, friendly welcome, local beers, imaginative fresh food and seats in pretty garden; bedrooms

---

Readers have been extremely warm in their praise of this well run old pub recently – for the friendly welcome from the hard-working licensees and their staff, the relaxed atmosphere and the super food. There are exposed joists in the L-shaped bar, various cosy corners, a woodburning stove, an attractive mix of dining chairs around wooden tables on the oak flooring, china plates and all sorts of artwork on the walls and fresh flowers. What had been the family room is now the restaurant. Sharps Doom Bar and St Austell Tribute on handpump and several wines by the glass; piped music. The pub labrador is called Bailey. The pretty tiered garden has white metal furniture under green parasols and the beaches of Mounts Bay are a couple of minutes' stroll away.

🍴 Imaginative and rather delicious, the well presented food includes lunchtime sandwiches, soup, blue cheese and onion tarte tatin with spiced pear, crab with garlic aioli and herb salad, tagliatelle with mushrooms, rosemary cream and walnuts, haddock and chips with minted peas, slow-roasted pork belly with black pudding, champ potato and apple sauce, chicken breast with smoked bacon, bubble and squeak potato cake and roast garlic, local steaks, daily fresh fish dishes, and puddings such as warm chocolate and walnut brownie with seville orange marmalade ice-cream and vanilla and lemon crème brûlée with stewed rhubarb and ginger; they keep interesting west country cheeses. *Starters/Snacks: £4.50 to £7.50. Main Courses: £7.95 to £17.50. Puddings: £5.00 to £7.95*

Pubfolio ~ Lease Anna and Stewart Eddy ~ Real ale ~ Bar food (not Sun evening or winter Mon) ~ Restaurant ~ (01736) 710309 ~ Children welcome ~ Dogs allowed in bar ~ Open 12-2.30, 6.30-11; 12-2.30 Sun; closed Sun evening, winter Mon, one week Jan, 25-26 Dec, 1 Jan ~ Bedrooms: £45S/£70S

Recommended by Nigel Long, Catherine and Richard Preston, James Sturtridge, Bryan and Mary Blaxall, Jan Taplin, Bruce and Sharon Eden, Dave Webster, Sue Holland

---

PERRANWELL   SW7739   MAP 1

Royal Oak 🍷

Village signposted off A393 Redruth—Falmouth and A39 Falmouth—Truro; TR3 7PX

Welcoming and relaxed with an emphasis on well presented food and thoughtful wines

---

Most customers come to this pretty and quietly set village pub to enjoy the popular food but they do keep Skinners Betty Stogs and a changing guest beer on handpump; good wines by the glass, summer sangria and winter mulled wine. The roomy, carpeted bar has a gently upmarket atmosphere, horsebrasses and pewter and china mugs on its black beams and joists, plates and country pictures on the cream-painted stone walls and cosy wall and other seats around candlelit tables. It rambles around beyond a big stone fireplace (with a winter log fire) into a snug little nook of a room behind, with just a couple more tables. They hope to add a back decked area and bedrooms this year.

🍴 Listed on wooden boards in the shape of an oak tree, the good, interesting food includes lunchtime sandwiches and filled baguettes, their much-ordered tapas and meze plates (for sharing), portabella mushrooms in stilton sauce, crab bake, steak and mushroom or fish pie, sausage and mash, crispy beer-battered cod, various curries, seafood tagliatelle, chicken teriyaki, duck confit with a sweet tomato and orange reduction, and puddings such as chocolate fudge brownie and fruit crumbles; Sunday roast. *Starters/Snacks: £5.95 to £8.75. Main Courses: £9.95 to £17.50. Puddings: £3.75 to £5.25*

Free house ~ Licensee Richard Rudland ~ Real ale ~ Bar food (12-2.30, 6.30-9.30) ~ Restaurant ~ (01872) 863175 ~ Children welcome ~ Dogs allowed in bar ~ Open 11-3, 6-11; 11.30-3.30, 6-11 Sun

Recommended by John and Fiona McIlwain, J K and S M Miln, Dr David Smith, John Marsh, Gene and Tony Freemantle, David Crook, Mrs M K Matthews

PHILLEIGH   SW8739   MAP 1

Roseland 🍺

NE of St Mawes just E of King Harry Ferry; TR2 5NB

Friendly licensees in busy pub, new microbrewery plus guests, imaginative food and informal, chatty atmosphere

As we went to press they were just about to open their own microbrewery here with Roseland Cornish Shag on handpump plus Skinners Betty Stogs and maybe Sharps Doom Bar as guests. It's a popular little pub with a good mix of both local and holiday customers and to be sure of a seat, it's best to book in advance. The two bar rooms (one with flagstones and the other carpeted) have wheelback chairs and built-in red-cushioned seats, open fires, old photographs and some giant beetles and butterflies in glass cases. The tiny lower area is liked by regulars and there's a back restaurant, too. There are seats on a pretty paved front courtyard and to the side of this, a new shop selling local produce and locally made gifts; the King Harry ferry and Trelissick Gardens are close by.

🍴 Imaginative bar food includes lunchtime sandwiches, filled baked potatoes and ploughman's, soup, duck pâté with orange and red wine marmalade, braised lambs kidneys and bacon with button mushrooms in a filo basket with potato purée, smoked haddock fishcake with a poached egg and asparagus, sausages and mash, crab risotto, corn-fed chicken with leek and garlic confit, pancetta rösti and a mushroom, brandy and cream sauce, and puddings like rum and raisin bread and butter pudding with glazed bananas and crème anglaise and dark chocolate cheesecake with oriental ginger cream; they also do cod and chips and steak nights. *Starters/Snacks: £5.25 to £6.50. Main Courses: £10.25 to £12.95. Puddings: £5.25*

Free house ~ Licensee Philip Heslip ~ Real ale ~ Bar food ~ Restaurant ~ (01872) 580254 ~ Children welcome ~ Dogs allowed in bar ~ Open 11am-midnight(11.30 Sun); 11-3, 6-midnight winter

Recommended by Mr and Mrs W D Borthwick, Donna and Roger

POLKERRIS   SX0952   MAP 1

Rashleigh

Signposted off A3082 Fowey—St Austell; PL24 2TL

Fine beach-side spot, heaters on sizeable sun terrace, several real ales and bar food

The lovely position by a splendid beach with a restored jetty and far-reaching views continues to draw lots of customers to this village pub in fine weather. There's also a big front terrace with heaters and an awning. Inside, the bar is cosy and the front part has comfortably cushioned seats and four real ales on handpump: Otter Bitter, Sharps Doom Bar, Timothy Taylors Landlord and a guest such as Skinners Betty Stogs. They also have several wines by the glass, farm cider and organic soft drinks. The more basic back area has local photographs on the brown panelling and a winter log fire, and in the restaurant, every table has a sea view. There's plenty of parking either in the pub's own car park or the large village one. The local section of the Cornish Coast Path is renowned for its striking scenery. More reports please.

🍴 Bar food includes sandwiches and filled baguettes, soup, pasties, beer-battered cod, lasagne, steak pie, winter stews, daily specials like grilled goats cheese with figs, seasonal asparagus or strawberries and local fish, and puddings such as lemon meringue pie or chocolate and pear cake. *Starters/Snacks: £4.20 to £6.50. Main Courses: £7.50 to £13.95. Puddings: £2.95 to £3.95*

Free house ~ Licensees Jon and Samantha Spode ~ Real ale ~ Bar food (12-2, 6-9; cream teas and snacks during the afternoon) ~ Restaurant ~ (01726) 813991 ~ Children welcome ~ Piano player Sat evening ~ Open 11-11; 12-10.30 Sun

Recommended by Paul Walmsley, Phil and Jane Hodson, Kelvin and Carol Butcher, Francis Vernon, Peter Martin, Dave Webster, Sue Holland, the Didler, Roy Hoing, B and M Kendall, Mr and Mrs B Hobden, Mrs Angela Graham, Andy and Claire Barker, C Sale, David Crook

POLPERRO
SX2050 MAP 1

Blue Peter
Quay Road; PL13 2QZ

Friendly pub overlooking pretty harbour, with fishing paraphernalia and paintings by local artists

There's always a good mix of customers of all ages in this busy and friendly little pub. Families must use the upstairs room (try to get a window seat overlooking the harbour if you can) whereas locals tend to head for the downstairs bar. This cosy low-beamed room has fishing regalia, photographs and pictures by local artists, traditional furnishings including a small winged settle and a polished pew on the wooden floor, candles everywhere, a solid wood bar counter and a simple old-fashioned atmosphere. One window seat looks down on the harbour, another looks out past rocks to the sea. St Austell Tribute and guests such as Otter Ale, Sharps Doom Bar and a couple of changing beers named for the pub on handpump; maybe local cider, too. There are a few seats outside on the terrace and more in an upstairs amphitheatre-style area. The pub is quite small, so it does get crowded at peak times. They take bookings for fishing and boating trips on behalf of local fishermen and also have a cash machine as there is no bank in the village.

🍴 Well liked bar food includes sandwiches and wraps, ploughman's, soup, chilli con carne, cottage pie, chicken or fish curries, various platters, daily specials such as caribbean crab cakes, vegetable stir fry, a pie of the day, local sardines and mackerel, and puddings. *Starters/Snacks: £3.95 to £6.95. Main Courses: £6.95 to £12.95. Puddings: £3.95 to £4.50*

Free house ~ Licensees Steve and Caroline Steadman ~ Real ale ~ Bar food ~ Restaurant ~ (01503) 272743 ~ Children in upstairs family room only ~ Dogs allowed in bar ~ Live music weekends ~ Open 10.30am(11am Sun)-11.30pm(midnight Sat)

Recommended by the Didler, Steve Kirby, the Brewers, Suzy Miller, Evelyn and Derek Walter, Lawrence Pearse

---

'Children welcome' means the pub says it lets children inside without any special restriction. If it allows them in, but to restricted areas such as an eating area or family room, we specify this. Some pubs may impose an evening time limit. We do not mention limits after 9pm as we assume children are home by then.

PORT ISAAC   SX0080   MAP 1

Port Gaverne Inn ♀ ⇌

Port Gaverne signposted from Port Isaac and from B3314 E of Pendoggett; PL29 3SQ

Lively bar with plenty of chatty locals in popular small hotel near sea and fine cliff walks

Of course, this is not a pub in the true sense but the bustling small bar here is always full of chatty locals (often with their dogs, too) and many of our readers have been happily visiting this little inn for years – either for a just drink before a walk or to stay overnight. The cheerful bar has a relaxed atmosphere, low beams, flagstones as well as carpeting, a big log fire, some exposed stone and helpful staff. In spring, the lounge is usually filled with pictures from the local art society's annual exhibition and at other times there are interesting antique local photographs. You can eat in the bar or the 'Captain's Cabin' – a little room where everything is shrunk to scale (old oak chest, model sailing ship, even the prints on the white stone walls. St Austell Tribute, Sharps Doom Bar and Cornish Coaster and a guest beer on handpump, a good wine list and several whiskies; cribbage and board games. There are seats in the terraced garden and splendid clifftop walks all around.

🍴 Bar food includes sandwiches, ploughman's, soup, smoked mackerel pâté, home-cooked ham and egg, vegetable lasagne, local crab salad and battered fish of the day; evening meals such as bass fillet with garlic, ginger, lemon grass and chilli and pork escalope with a madeira, tomato and mushroom sauce. *Starters/Snacks: £5.00 to £7.00. Main Courses: £7.00 to £14.50. Puddings: £3.50 to £4.95*

Free house ~ Licensee Graham Sylvester ~ Real ale ~ Bar food ~ Restaurant ~ (01208) 880244 ~ Children welcome ~ Dogs allowed in bar and bedrooms ~ Open 11-11; 12-11 Sun ~ Bedrooms: £65B/£110B

Recommended by Barry and Anne, Susan Lang, Dave Lowe, J L Wedel, Adrian Johnson, John and Bernadette Elliott, Bill and Marian de Bass, J K and S M Miln, Sue Demont, Tim Barrow, Gerry and Rosemary Dobson, John and Sharon Hancock, Mr and Mrs Richard Osborne

PORTHLEVEN   SW6225   MAP 1

Ship

Village on B3304 SW of Helston; pub perched on edge of harbour; TR13 9JS

Fisherman's pub built into cliffs, fine views from seats on terrace and tasty bar food

From this friendly old fisherman's pub there's a marvellous view over the pretty working harbour and out to sea, and if you are lucky, you might be able to bag a window seat inside or one of the tables out in the terraced garden; at night, the harbour is interestingly floodlit. The knocked-through bar has a relaxed atmosphere, welcoming log fires in big stone fireplaces and some genuine individuality. The family room is a conversion of an old smithy with logs burning in a huge open fireplace; the candlelit dining room also looks over the sea. Courage Best and Sharps Doom Bar and Own on handpump; piped music and games machine.

🍴 Honest bar food includes sandwiches and toasties, filled baked potatoes, ploughman's, garlic mushrooms, smoked haddock fishcake with lime and chilli salsa, barbecue chicken, chilli con carne, vegetable bake, steak and kidney pudding, lasagne, and puddings like treacle tart or caramel apple pie. *Starters/Snacks: £3.35 to £5.75. Main Courses: £9.95 to £13.95. Puddings: £4.75 to £5.50*

Free house ~ Licensee Colin Oakden ~ Real ale ~ Bar food ~ (01326) 564204 ~ Children in family room ~ Dogs welcome ~ Open 11.30-11; 12-10.30 Sun

Recommended by Peter Salmon, the Didler, Andy and Claire Barker, Michael and Ann Cole, Revd R P Tickle, Comus and Sarah Elliott, Phil and Jane Hodson, Andrea Rampley, John and Gloria Isaacs, Ewan and Moira McCall, Kelvin and Carol Butcher, Mr and Mrs Gravener, Clifford Blakemore, Donna and Roger, Bryan and Mary Blaxall, Susie Symes, John Marsh, M Bryan Osborne

PORTHTOWAN   SW6948   MAP 1

Blue

Beach Road, East Cliff; use the car park (fee in season), not the slippy sand; TR4 8AW

Informal, busy bar – not a traditional pub – right by wonderful beach with modern food and drinks; lively staff and customers

'A tonic in winter' and 'great fun' are just two phrases our readers have used to describe this cheerful bar recently. It's certainly not a traditional pub but it does serve real ale and is right by a fantastic beach which makes it incredibly popular with customers of all ages – and their dogs. The atmosphere is easy and informal and huge picture windows look across the terrace to the huge expanse of sand and sea. The front bays have built-in pine seats and the rest of the large room has chrome and wicker chairs around plain wooden tables on the stripped wood floor, quite a few high-legged chrome and wooden bar stools and plenty of standing space around the bar counter; powder blue-painted walls, ceiling fans, some big ferny plants, two large TVs showing silent surfing videos and fairly quiet piped music; pool table. Several wines by the glass, cocktails, shots and giant cups of coffee all served by perky, helpful young staff.

⏍ Good modern bar food using local, seasonal produce includes lunchtime filled baps, soup, risotto of prawns with asparagus and mint, tasty burgers, nice pizzas, beer-battered pollack, mussels steamed with bacon, leeks, cider and cream, chargrilled mackerel with tomato, black olives and red onion salad and grilled wild bass with crushed new potatoes and lemon oil. *Starters/Snacks: £4.50 to £6.50. Main Courses: £8.00 to £11.50. Puddings: £3.50 to £5.00*

Free house ~ Licensees Tara Roberts and Luke Morris ~ Real ale ~ Bar food (12-9; limited menu in afternoon) ~ (01209) 890329 ~ Children welcome ~ Dogs welcome ~ Live bands Sat evening, comedy last Thurs of month ~ Open 10am-11pm(midnight Sat; 10.30 Sun); 11-6 Mon and Tues and 11-11 Weds-Fri in winter

Recommended by Jonathon Bunt, John Marsh, Tim and Ann Newell, Andy and Claire Barker, David Crook

RUAN LANIHORNE   SW8942   MAP 1

Kings Head

Off A3078; TR2 5NX

Country pub in quiet hamlet, small bar, several dining areas, real ales and seats outside

The little right-hand bar in this neatly kept pub is just the place to sit for a relaxed drink after a walk. There's a winter log fire, comfortable sofas and seats around a low table or two, a few high bar chairs used by locals and Skinners Betty Stogs, Cornish Knocker and a beer named for the pub on handpump; several wines by the glass and farm cider. Further to the right are two connected dining rooms with lots of china cups hanging from ceiling joists, plenty of copper and brass, old cigarette cards in picture frames, a glass cabinet filled with old glass bottles, hunting prints and an aquarium. The restaurant is to the left of the main door; piped music. Across the road is a sunken terrace with seats and tables under trees and outdoor heaters. The nearby church is interesting. More reports please.

⏍ Well liked bar food includes sandwiches, ploughman's, soup, chicken liver pâté, local sausages with red onion marmalade, evening dishes like free-range chicken breast stuffed with cranberry relish, wrapped in parma ham with a sage and balsamic jus and de-boned duckling with pepper sauce, and puddings such as gingerbread and apple pudding with green ginger wine and brandy sauce; daily specials and Sunday roast. *Starters/Snacks: £3.00 to £7.95. Main Courses: £9.50 to £17.95. Puddings: £5.35*

Free house ~ Licensees Andrew and Niki Law ~ Real ale ~ Bar food (12.30-2, 6.30-9; not winter Sun evening or Mon) ~ Restaurant ~ (01872) 501263 ~ Well behaved children welcome in dining areas only ~ Dogs allowed in bar ~ Open 12-2.30, 6-11; closed Sun evening and all day Mon in winter

Recommended by Jennifer Sheridan, M Bryan Osborne, Chris and Angela Buckell, Comus and Sarah Elliott, Donna and Roger, John Marsh, Stephen and Jean Curtis

ST KEW   SX0276   MAP 1

St Kew Inn 🍴

Village signposted from A39 NE of Wadebridge; PL30 3HB

Grand-looking 15th-c pub with neat bar and dining areas, first-rate food and big garden

Although the food is exceptionally good, this substantial stone pub does have the atmosphere of a proper pub and you can be sure of a friendly welcome from the knowledgeable staff. The neatly kept bar has beams, stone walls, winged high-backed settles and wheelback chairs around varnished rustic tables on the tartan carpet, all sorts of jugs here and there, a woodburner in the stone fireplace and St Austell HSD, IPA, Tinners and Tribute tapped from wooden casks behind the counter; several wines by the glass. There are also three dining areas. The flowering tubs and baskets are very pretty in summer.

🍴 First-rate modern bar food at lunchtime includes sandwiches, soup, chicken and duck liver terrine with chutney and pickles, free-range pork and apple sausages with mustard mash and shallot gravy, goats cheese and asparagus tart, free-range ham and eggs and whole grilled lemon sole with café de paris butter; evening dishes such as local mussels in cider, cream and chives, fresh crab on toast, chicken and leek pie with home-made baked beans, john dory with olives, capers, rosemary and sunblush tomatoes, and puddings like crème caramel with agen prunes and steamed chocolate sponge pudding with clotted cream. *Starters/Snacks: £4.50 to £7.50. Main Courses: £7.95 to £16.95. Puddings: £4.95 to £7.50*

St Austell ~ Tenants Paul Ripley and Sarah Allen ~ Real ale ~ Bar food ~ Restaurant ~ (01208) 841259 ~ Children welcome away from main bar ~ Dogs allowed in bar ~ Live local bands monthly ~ Open 11-3, 6-11(midnight Sat); 12-3, 7-10.30 Sun

Recommended by Edna Jones, Paul Smurthwaite, David Eberlin, Christopher Scott, the Didler, Andrea Rampley, W N F Boughey, Anthony Barnes, Bill and Marian de Bass, John and Bernadette Elliott

TREGADILLETT   SX2983   MAP 1

Eliot Arms

Village signposted off A30 at junction with A395, W end of Launceston bypass; PL15 7EU

Interesting collections in several small rooms, real ales and seats outside

This creeper-covered pub has plenty to look at inside. The series of small rooms have interesting collections that include 72 antique clocks (including seven grandfathers), 400 snuffs, hundreds of horsebrasses, old prints, old postcards or cigarette cards grouped in frames on the walls, quite a few barometers and shelves of books and china. Also, a fine old mix of furniture on the delabole slate floors, from high-backed built-in curved settles, through plush Victorian dining chairs, armed seats, chaise longues and mahogany housekeeper's chairs, to more modern seats; open fires. Courage Best, Sharps Doom Bar and Own on handpump; piped music, games machine and darts. The hanging baskets and flowering tubs are quite a sight and there are seats in front of the pub and at the back of the car park.

🍴 Bar food includes filled baguettes, soup, burgers, vegetable curry, ham and egg, a pie of the day, battered cod, steaks, and puddings. *Starters/Snacks: £4.50 to £6.95. Main Courses: £6.95 to £16.95. Puddings: £4.50 to £4.95*

S&N ~ Lease Chris Hume ~ Real ale ~ Bar food (12-2, 6-9) ~ Restaurant ~ (01566) 772051 ~ Children in front two bars ~ Dogs allowed in bar ~ Open 11.30-11(midnight Fri and Sat); 12-10.30 Sun ~ Bedrooms: £45B/£70S(£65B)

Recommended by John and Bernadette Elliott, Joan York, Comus and Sarah Elliott, Mrs Mary Woods, Mr and Mrs H J Stephens, Mick and Moira Brummell, the Didler, Chris Glasson, R T and J C Moggridge, Mr and Mrs Richard Osborne

We say if we know a pub allows dogs.

TRESCO
SV8815 MAP 1

New Inn ♀ ◖ ⊨
New Grimsby; Isles of Scilly; TR24 0QG

Attractive inn close to quay and ferries, with chatty bar and light dining extension, enjoyable food and drinks; sunny terrace

Well run and especially busy during the holiday season, this extended inn – the island's only pub – was once a row of fishermen's cottages. There is a little locals' bar but visitors tend to head for the main bar room or the light, airy dining extension: comfortable old sofas, banquettes, planked partition seating and farmhouse chairs and tables, a few standing timbers, boat pictures, a large model sailing boat, a collection of old telescopes and plates on the delft shelf. The Pavilion extension has cheerful yellow walls and plenty of seats and tables on the blue wooden floors and looks over the flower-filled terrace with its teak furniture, huge umbrellas and views of the sea. Ales of Scilly Scuppered, St Austell Tribute and Skinners Tresco Tipple on handpump, 13 good wines by the glass, quite a choice of spirits and several coffees; piped music, darts, pool and board games.

🍴 As well as lunchtime sandwiches, the popular bar food includes soup, devilled whitebait, salmon fishcakes with chive fish cream and spinach, meaty or vegetarian burgers with garlic mayo and red onion jam, breast of corn-fed chicken with wild mushrooms, liver and crispy pancetta with wholegrain mustard mash and onion gravy, fish and chips, steaks, and puddings like apple and blackberry crumble and chocolate truffle cone with ice-cream. *Starters/Snacks: £4.50 to £8.00. Main Courses: £9.00 to £17.50. Puddings: £5.00 to £8.00*

Free house ~ Licensee Robin Lawson ~ Real ale ~ Bar food (12-2.15, 6-9) ~ Restaurant ~ (01720) 422844 ~ Children welcome ~ Dogs allowed in bar ~ Live music every ten days ~ Open 11-11; 12-10.30 Sun; 11-2.30, 6-11 mid-Nov to mid-Feb winter ~ Bedrooms: £100B/£200B

Recommended by Bernard Stradling, Michael Sargent, R J Herd, Bob Potter, C J Fletcher

TREVAUNANCE COVE
SW7251 MAP 1

Driftwood Spars ◖ ⊨
Off B3285 in St Agnes; Quay Road; TR5 0RT

Friendly old inn, plenty of history, own-brew beers and wide range of other drinks, modern cooking; attractive bedrooms; beach nearby

Originally a marine warehouse and fish cellar, this 17th-c inn is just up the road from the beach and its dramatic cove and is surrounded by plenty of coastal walks. The bustling bars are timbered with massive ships' spars – the masts of great sailing ships, many of which were wrecked along this coast – and there are dark wooden farmhouse chairs, tub chairs and settles around dark wooden tables, padded bar stools by the bar counter, old ship prints, lots of nautical and wreck memorabilia, and a winter log fire; there's said to be an old smugglers' tunnel leading from behind the bar, up through the cliff. They have their own Driftwood brewery and always keep two of their own-brew beers plus St Austell Tinners, Sharps Doom Bar, an ale from Skinners and a couple of guests on handpump; also, 50 malt whiskies, 11 rums, several wines by the glass and sometimes their own alcoholic ginger beer. Service is friendly and helpful. There are seats in the garden and the summer hanging baskets are pretty. Many of their attractive bedrooms overlook the coast.

🍴 Using local produce, the good bar food includes filled ciabattas, soup, chicken liver pâté with red onion marmalade, poached john dory stuffed with shellfish mousse with ceviche dressing, free-range chicken with wild mushroom fricassee, sweet potato and aubergine gratin with watercress and rocket salad, moules marinière, beer-battered pollack and chips, steak in Guinness pie, tapenade roasted salmon with shellfish chowder and parsley oil, and puddings like sticky toffee and banana sponge with honeycomb ice-cream or milk chocolate and Frangelico (hazelnut liqueur) cheesecake with dark hot chocolate and marshmallow foam; Sunday roasts. *Starters/Snacks: £3.25 to £7.50. Main Courses: £8.50 to £17.00. Puddings: £4.50 to £6.95*

Free house ~ Licensee Louise Treseder ~ Real ale ~ Bar food (12-2.30, 6.30-9(9.30 summer)) ~

Restaurant ~ (01872) 552428 ~ Children welcome ~ Dogs allowed in bar and bedrooms ~
Live music Sat evenings and occasional Fri ~ Open 11-11(2am Sat) ~ Bedrooms: £45S/£86S
Recommended by Damon Rutland, Chris Reading, the Didler, Gaye and Simon, Chris Glasson

TRURO

SW8244   MAP 1

Old Ale House 🍺 £
Quay Street; TR1 2HD

Eight real ales and good value, wholesome food in particularly well run, bustling town pub

---

Busy at almost any time of the day, this well run town pub is popular with a really good
mix of customers. They keep eight real ales on handpump or tapped from the cask which
change every day but might include Butcombe, Fullers London Pride, Greene King Abbot,
Otter Ale, St Austell HSD, Sharps Doom Bar, Skinners Kiddlywink and Wooden Hand
Cornish Mutiny; they hold two beer festivals a year with up to 26 ales. Eleven wines by
the glass and quite a few country wines. The dimly lit bar has an engaging diversity of
furnishings, some interesting 1920s bric-a-brac, beer mats pinned everywhere, matchbox
collections and newpapers and magazines to read. There's an upstairs room with pool,
juke box and table football.

🍴 **Tasty wholesome bar food prepared in a spotless kitchen in full view of the bar
includes open sandwiches and half bloomers with toppings such as bacon, onions and
melted cheese or tuna, mayonnaise and melted cheese, soup, sautéed potatoes with
bacon and mushrooms in a creamy garlic sauce, cauliflower and broccoli bake, various
sizzling skillets, a pie of the day, lamb and mint hotpot and beef stew.** *Starters/Snacks:*
£3.25 to £3.95. Main Courses: £3.95 to £5.75. Puddings: £3.45

Enterprise ~ Tenants Mark Jones and Beverley Jones ~ Real ale ~ Bar food ~ (01872) 271122 ~
Children allowed but away from bar ~ Open 11-11(midnight Sat); 12-11 Sun; closed 25 and
26 Dec, 1 Jan

*Recommended by the Didler, Michael and Alison Sandy, Dr and Mrs M W A Haward, Ted George, George and
Beverley Tucker, Ian Phillips, Alan Johnson, B and M Kendall*

WATERGATE BAY

SW8464   MAP 1

Beach Hut
B3276 coast road N of Newquay; TR8 4AA

**Bustling, informal beach bar with cheerful young staff, good mix of customers, decent
drinks and popular food**

The position of this bustling, modern bar couldn't be better as it is right on the beach.
There's a good mix of customers of all ages, the atmosphere is informal and relaxed, and
the young staff are helpful and friendly. To set the scene inside there are surfing
photographs on the planked walls, a large surfboard above a sizeable leatherette wall
seat by one big table and another above the bar counter. Wicker and cane armchairs with
blue or pink cushions around green and orange-painted tables sit on the nicely weathered
stripped wooden floor, there's plenty of mushroom and cream paintwork, orange blinds
and an unusual sloping bleached-board ceiling. Big windows and doors open out on to a
glass-fronted decking area – where there are some picnic-sets – and look across the sand
to the sea. There's also a slightly simpler end room. Decent wines by the glass, lots of
coffees and teas and hot chocolate; piped soft rock music. They also run an extreme
sports academy.

🍴 **As well as usefully serving breakfast and other meals and snacks all day, the generous
helpings of well liked food include cheese fondue, nachos, stir-fried squid with spiced sea
salt, szechuan peppers and oyster sauce, chicken and prawn laksa, local organic pork
steak stuffed with mozzarella and sage, mussels, good proper burgers (meaty or
vegetarian), rib-eye steak, and puddings like warm rhubarb pudding and dark chocolate
fudge cake; home-made cakes, too.** *Starters/Snacks: £4.50 to £7.50. Main Courses: £9.50 to*
£16.50. Puddings: £4.65

Free house ~ Licensee Mark Williams ~ Bar food (all day from 8.30am) ~ (01637) 860877 ~ Children welcome ~ Dogs allowed in bar ~ Open 8.30am-11pm; 10.30-5 in winter

Recommended by Ryta Lyndley, Alec Lewery

WIDEMOUTH

SS1902   MAP 1

Bay View 🛏

Village signposted (with Bude Coastal Route) off A39 N of Pounstock; Marine Drive; EX23 OAW

Sizeable hotel, wonderful views of Widemouth Bay, real ales, bistro food and cheerful atmosphere; bedrooms

With a bustling atmosphere, quite a mix of customers and friendly staff, this family-run hotel makes the most of its smashing setting. Contemporary picnic-sets on the front decking look across the road and dunes to a magnificent stretch of sand and the sunsets can be lovely. To the side, there's an equipped children's play area and good, solid picnic-sets on grass beside it. Inside are several spreading, interestingly decorated areas with some modern seaside paintings and large sea and sunset photographs, rugs on stripped wooden floors, flagstones, comfortably cushioned leather sofas, low chunky tables with lit church candles and several fireplaces with log-effect gas fires or decorative pebbles. A front part has pale wooden tables and chairs and a dresser with little wooden beach huts and china plates. Sharps Doom Bar, Skinners Betty Stogs and a beer named for them on handpump, some unusual bottled beers and several wines by the glass; piped pop music, darts, pool, bar billiards, board games and TV.

🍴 **As well as sandwiches, good bistro-style bar food includes soup, brandied pâté, king scallops with garlic butter and hogs pudding, a pie of the day, beer-battered fish and chips, a proper burger with red onion marmalade, mixed bean chilli, chicken in a creamy bacon and leek sauce, lamb shank with redcurrant and mint gravy, steaks, fresh fish of the day, and puddings.** *Starters/Snacks: £5.00 to £6.50. Main Courses: £10.00 to £19.50. Puddings: £5.00 to £7.00*

Free house ~ Licensees Dave and Cherylyn Keene ~ Real ale ~ Bar food (12-2.30, 6-9; 12-9 Sun) ~ Restaurant ~ (01288) 361273 ~ Children welcome ~ Dogs allowed in bar ~ Open 9am-midnight; closed evening 25 Dec ~ Bedrooms: £38S/£76S

Recommended by John Urquhart, John and Sharon Hancock, the Didler, Paul and Annette Hallett

ZENNOR

SW4538   MAP 1

Tinners Arms

B3306 W of St Ives; TR26 3BY

Good mix of customers, friendly atmosphere, real ales and tasty food; bedrooms

After enjoying one of the fine nearby coastal walks, this well run and popular pub is a friendly place for a drink or a meal. In good weather, you can sit on benches in the sheltered front courtyard or at tables on a bigger side terrace. Inside, there are low wooden-ceilings, cushioned settles, benches and a mix of chairs around wooden tables on the stone floor, antique prints on the stripped plank panelling and a log fire in cool weather. Sharps Own, a beer named for the pub and St Austell Tinners on handpump. The pub was built in 1271 to house the masons who constructed St Senara's church.

🍴 **At lunchtime, the tasty bar food might include sandwiches, ploughman's, home-cooked ham and egg, a proper beef burger and a vegetarian dish of the day, with daily specials like duck soup with noodles, scallops with hand-made black pudding and pea sauce and scampi with home-made tartare sauce, evening dishes such as local crab with apple and herb dressing, wild mushroom risotto, line-caught mackerel with salsa verde, duck breast with crème de cassis and blackcurrant sauce, and puddings like treacle tart with clotted cream and warm chocolate cake.** *Starters/Snacks: £4.95 to £7.50. Main Courses: £7.25 to £15.50. Puddings: £4.50 to £6.00*

Free house ~ Licensees Grahame Edwards and Richard Motley ~ Real ale ~ Bar food (12-2.30, 6.30-9) ~ (01736) 796927 ~ Children welcome away from main bar ~ Dogs welcome ~ Open 11-11; 12-10.30 Sun; 11-3, 6.30-11 in winter ~ Bedrooms: £50/£90S

Recommended by Steve Kirby, the Didler, Dr and Mrs M W A Haward, Alan Johnson, Dr Peter Crawshaw, Mrs Angela Graham, Mr and Mrs Gravener, Andrea Rampley, Donna and Roger, Mrs M K Matthews, Terry and Linda Moseley, Ewan and Moira McCall, David and Sue Smith, Stuart Turner, Joan York, Steve Crick, Helen Preston

---

LUCKY DIP

Besides the fully inspected pubs, you might like to try these Lucky Dips recommended to us and described by readers (if you do, please send us reports: feedback@goodguides.com).

ANGARRACK [SW5838]
Angarrack Inn TR27 5JB [Steamers Hill]: New management at this small village pub below railway viaduct (the amazing bric-a-brac collection has gone) *(LYM, Alan Johnson)*
BOLINGEY [SW7653]
Bolingey Inn TR6 0DH [Penwartha Rd – no inn sign]: Quiet, picturesque and unspoilt local tucked away in small village, cosy atmosphere, well kept local and national beers, small choice of good inexpensive food inc fresh fish, friendly staff; tables outside, handy for Perranporth but away from the tourists *(Ian Phillips)*
BOLVENTOR [SX1876]
☆ *Jamaica Inn* PL15 7TS [signed just off A30 on Bodmin Moor]: Genuinely 18th-c bar with oak beams, stripped stone, massive log fire and well kept Sharps Doom Bar (easy to ignore the big all-day cafeteria, games machines, souvenir shop and tourist coaches), young enthusiastic staff, bar food, plaque commemorating murdered landlord Joss Merlyn, great Daphne du Maurier connection; pretty secluded garden with play area, bedrooms, moorland setting *(Abi Benson, Dr and Mrs M E Wilson, Michael and Alison Sandy, Phil and Jane Hodson, J F M and M West)*
BOSCASTLE [SX0990]
☆ *Napoleon* PL35 0BD [High St, top of village]: Good atmosphere in low-beamed 16th-c pub with good value generous blackboard bar food, St Austell ales tapped from the cask, decent wines, good coffee, friendly service, log fires, interesting Napoleon prints, slate floors and cosy rooms on different levels inc small evening bistro, traditional games; piped music; children welcome, small covered terrace and large sheltered garden, steep climb up from harbour (splendid views on the way), open all day *(LYM, the Didler, Gordon Stevenson)*
BOTALLACK [SW3632]
☆ *Queens Arms* TR19 7QG: Friendly unpretentious pub with good food choice inc local seafood, all meat sourced within 3 miles, well kept Sharps Doom Bar, a Skinners ale brewed for the pub and guest beers, cheerful staff, log fire in unusual granite inglenook, dark wood furniture, tin mining and other old local photographs on stripped stone walls, attractive family extension; tables out in front and pleasant

back garden with chickens, wonderful clifftop walks nearby, open all day *(Brian and Jenny Salmon, Stuart Turner)*
BOTUSFLEMING [SX4061]
Rising Sun PL12 6NJ [off A388 nr Saltash]: Convivial low-ceilinged rural local, lively games bar, smaller quieter stripped stone room with two good coal fires, changing real ales; picnic-sets in garden looking over quiet valley to church, has been cl Mon-Thurs lunchtimes, open all day wknds *(the Didler)*
BREAGE [SW6128]
Queens Arms TR13 9PD [3 miles W of Helston just off A394]: L-shaped local with friendly landlord and staff, half a dozen well kept ales, farm cider, decent wines by the glass, enjoyable good value food from baguettes with cornish brie and ham to seafood and steaks; good coal fires, plush banquettes, brass-topped tables, daily papers, restaurant, back games area with pool; piped music; dogs welcome, some picnic-sets outside, covered smokers' area, bedrooms, medieval wall paintings in church opposite, open all day Sun *(David and Julie Glover, Dennis Jenkin, BB, David and Sue Smith)*
BUDE [SS2006]
Brendon Arms EX23 8SD: Popular (particularly in summer) canalside pub, with two big friendly pubby bars, back family room, well kept ales inc St Austell and Sharps, enjoyable bargain food inc good crab sandwiches and interesting specials, good coffee; juke box, sports TV, pool and darts; children and dogs (public bar) welcome, disabled access, picnic-sets on front grass, heated smokers' shelter, bedrooms and holiday apartments *(Ryta Lyndley)*
CALLINGTON [SX3569]
Bulls Head PL17 7AQ [Fore St]: Ancient unspoilt local with handsome black timbering and stonework, lovely relaxed atmosphere, centenarian landlady, well kept St Austell ales *(Giles and Annie Francis)*
CALSTOCK [SX4368]
Tamar PL18 9QA [Quay]: Dating back to 17th c, lovely setting yards from the river with its imposing viaduct, spotless comfortable bare-boards bars, good generous straightforward food at bargain prices, summer cream teas, well kept changing ales inc St Austell and Sharps, impressive helpful service, modern dining room, darts and pool,

live music; children away from bar and well behaved dogs welcome, shiny tables and chairs on sunny decking, heated smokers' shelter, hilly walk or ferry to Cotehele (NT) *(anon)*

CARGREEN [SX4362]
Crooked Spaniard PL12 6PA [off A388 Callington—Saltash]: Much-altered pub in grand spot by Tamar, with smart river-view dining extension and waterside terrace – always some river activity, esp at high tide; cosy and comfortable panelled bar, huge fireplace in another room, good reasonably priced food inc Sun carvery, well kept ales, friendly service; under same management as Crooked Inn at Trematon
(Prof Michael Patterson)

CAWSAND [SX4350]
Cawsand Bay PL10 1PG [The Bound]: Beach café with enjoyable food esp fish, super harbour views from upstairs bar with well kept ales inc a guest beer; bedrooms
(Peter and Janet Astbury)
☆ ***Cross Keys*** PL10 1PF [The Square]: Pretty pub in picturesque square opp boat club, friendly and simple-smart, with wide range of enjoyable generous food esp seafood (worth booking in season) in small bar and large attractive stripped-pine dining room, reasonable prices, changing ales such as Archers, Dawlish and Skinners, flexible service; pool, may be piped music, no nearby parking; children and dogs welcome, seats outside, pleasant bedrooms *(Jonathon Bunt, Dennis Jenkin)*

COVERACK [SW7818]
Paris TR12 6SX [The Cove]: White and blue-painted seaside hotel above harbour in beautiful fishing village, comfortable carpeted L-shaped bar, large dining room with spectacular bay views, Sharps Doom Bar and Skinners Betty Stogs, standard food inc Sun carvery, large model of namesake ship (wrecked nearby in 1899), no mobile phones; more sea views from garden with picnic-sets, bedrooms *(Dr and Mrs M E Wilson, Michael and Ann Cole)*

CRANTOCK [SW7960]
☆ ***Old Albion*** TR8 5RB [Langurroc Rd]: Picture-postcard thatched village pub, low beams, flagstones and open fires, old-fashioned small bar with brasses and low lighting, larger more open room with local pictures, informal atmosphere, home-made food inc sandwiches and ploughman's, Sharps and Skinners, farm cider, decent house wines, pool and darts at back of lounge; loads of summer visitors, souvenirs sold; dogs welcome, tables out on small terrace, open all day *(W N F Boughey, LYM, Phil and Jane Hodson)*

CREMYLL [SX4553]
☆ ***Edgcumbe Arms*** PL10 1HX: Super setting by Plymouth foot-ferry, good Tamar views, picnic-sets out by water; attractive layout and décor, with slate floors, big settles, comfortably old-fashioned furnishings inc fireside sofas, old pictures and china, well

kept St Austell ales, cheerful staff, food from doorstep sandwiches up, good family room/games area; pay car park some way off; children in eating area, dogs allowed in one bar (most tables here too low to eat from), bedrooms, open all day
(Shirley Mackenzie, Mr and Mrs W W Burke, LYM)

CROWLAS [SW5133]
Star TR20 8DX [A30]: Big open-plan bar with five interesting changing ales inc its own growing range of good Penzance microbrews, sewing-machine tables in raised area, pool, adjacent dining area, no intrusive music; tables outside, open all day
(Alan Bowker)

CROWN TOWN [SW6330]
Crown TR13 0AD [B3303 N of Helston]: Open-plan 18th-c roadside local with particularly well kept Skinners ales tapped from stillroom casks and a guest beer, good choice of reasonably priced evening food, side eating area, fine collection of brassware and jugs hanging from beams, log-effect fire; piped music, pool; children and dogs welcome, picnic-sets in garden with terrace, bedrooms in four lodges, cl lunchtime
(Donna and Roger, Tom McLean)

CROWS NEST [SX2669]
☆ ***Crows Nest*** PL14 5JQ [signed off B3264 N of Liskeard; OS Sheet 201 map ref 263692]: Old-fashioned 17th-c pub back under the family who made it a popular Main Entry some years ago (and now getting busier), enjoyable food from chef/landlord, well kept St Austell ales, decent wines by the glass, big log fire, attractive furnishings under bowed beams; children welcome, picnic-sets on terrace by quiet lane, handy for Bodmin moor walks *(John and Bernadette Elliott, LYM)*

CUBERT [SW7857]
☆ ***Smugglers Den*** TR8 5PY [off A3075 S of Newquay]: Big welcoming open-plan 16th-c thatched pub, fresh generous enjoyable food inc local seafood, well kept Sharps, Skinners and St Austell, good service, neat ranks of tables, dim lighting, stripped stone and heavy beam and plank ceilings, West Country pictures and seafaring memorabilia, steps down to further area with enormous inglenook, another step to big side family dining room, well lit pool area, darts; piped music, games machine; dogs welcome, small courtyard and lawn with climbing frame, has been cl winter Mon-Weds lunchtime
(Dr Peter Crawshaw, the Didler, W N F Boughey, BB, John and Jan Parkinson, Carole Hall)

DEVORAN [SW7938]
☆ ***Old Quay*** TR3 6NE [Devoran from new Carnon Cross roundabout A39 Truro—Falmouth, left on old road, right at mini-roundabout]: Large welcoming pub with two light and fresh rooms off bar, enjoyable good value food, up to six well kept ales (mainly Sharps), interesting wines by the glass, good friendly young staff, big coal fire, daily

papers, boating bric-a-brac, some attractive prints, euchre played Weds and Sun, evening restaurant; they may try to keep your credit card while you eat; imaginatively terraced suntrap garden behind with shrub-formed alcoves, idyllic spot in peaceful creekside village, lovely views, nearby walks, end of coast-to-coast cycle way; dogs welcome, open all day summer *(MA, Betty Rose, BB, John Marsh, Michael and Alison Sandy)*

DOWNDERRY [SX3153]
Inn on the Shore PL11 3JY: Large place nestling in beach cliffs and recently reopened under Singer Inns; copes well with large numbers of diners, enjoyable food inc fresh fish, children's menu, helpful young staff, well kept St Austell and Sharps, restaurant with Whitsand Bay views, conservatory, some live music; lots of seats on decking overlooking beach, enclosed garden with play area, five bedrooms, open all day *(Peter and Janet Astbury, Lawrence Pearse)*

EDMONTON [SW9672]
☆ *Quarryman* PL27 7JA: [off A39 just W of Wadebridge bypass]: Welcoming three-room beamed bar, part of a small holiday courtyard complex; some good individual cooking besides generous pubby lunchtime food inc good baguettes, salads and fish and chips, good curry night (first Tues of month), attentive staff, Sharps (summer only), Skinners and a couple of guest beers, interesting decorations inc old sporting memorabilia, cribbage and dominoes, no machines or mobiles; well behaved dogs and children welcome, disabled facilities being installed, courtyard with picnic-sets, open all day *(Dave Lowe, Kelvin and Carol Butcher, the Didler, Mrs Jill Silversides, Barry Brown, Dr and Mrs M W A Haward, LYM)*

EGLOSHAYLE [SX0071]
☆ *Earl of St Vincent* PL27 6HT [off A389, just outside Wadebridge]: Pretty dining pub with 200 antique clocks, all in working order – also golfing memorabilia, art deco ornaments, rich furnishings, decent food from sandwiches to steaks and St Austell ales; piped music; well behaved children allowed lunchtime, lovely garden *(Mrs Angela Graham, Mr and Mrs Gravener, LYM, the Didler, Andrea Rampley, Ian Phillips, Kelvin and Carol Butcher)*

FALMOUTH [SW8132]
5 Degrees West TR11 4AU [Grove Place, by harbourside car park]: Modern open-plan bar with mixed furnishings inc squashy sofas and low tables on stripped wood floors, lots of steel and etched glass, log fire in driftwood-effect fireplace, local artwork, enjoyable food, St Austell Tribute and good choice of wines by the glass (inc local ones), coffees, teas and hot chocolate, back dining area; piped music may be loud; disabled facilities, attractive sheltered back terrace *(LYM)*
Boslowick TR11 4PZ [Prislow Lane]: Large suburban black and white beamed and panelled Victorian local, lovely curving

staircase, carpeted, roaring fire, comfortable seating, Sharps Doom Bar and Skinners, good value straightforward food, big games room with pool *(Dr and Mrs M E Wilson)*
☆ *Chain Locker* TR11 3HH [Custom House Quay]: Busy place in fine spot by inner harbour with window tables (pub dog prefers the seats here) and lots outside, Sharps and Skinners ales, generous bargain food from sandwiches and baguettes to fresh local fish and interesting vegetarian choices (also cater for smaller appetites), cheery young staff, bare boards and masses of nautical bric-a-brac, darts alley; games machine, piped music; well behaved children and dogs welcome, self-catering accommodation, open all day *(Stephen and Jean Curtis, Michael and Alison Sandy, Dr and Mrs M E Wilson, LYM, George Atkinson, Joe Green)*
Kings Head TR11 3EQ [Church St]: Rambling old pub with reasonably priced food, Sharps and St Austell ales, beams, bare boards and mixed seating inc some sofas, pleasant alcove area overlooking street; piped music may be loud music *(George Atkinson, LYM)*
Seaview TR11 3EP [Wodehouse Terrace]: Convivial maritime local above 111-step Jacob's Ladder, stunning harbour and dockyard view from picture windows and a few tables outside, lots of dark oak and appropriate bric-a-brac, roaring fires each end, affable landlord, Fullers London Pride and Sharps Doom Bar; big-screen sports TV; bedrooms *(Dr and Mrs M E Wilson)*
☆ *Seven Stars* TR11 3QA [The Moor (centre)]: Quirky 17th-c local, unchanging and unsmart, with long-serving and entertaining vicar-landlord, no gimmicks, machines or mobile phones, warm welcome, Bass and Skinners Cornish Knocker tapped from the cask, home-made rolls, chatty regulars, big key-ring collection, quiet back snug; corridor hatch serving roadside courtyard *(the Didler, Gavin Robinson, Joe Green, Dr and Mrs M E Wilson, BB)*
Watermans TR11 3AT [Market St]: Unassuming pub with well priced Sharps Cornish Coaster and Doom Bar and Skinners Betty Stogs, picture window overlooking harbour, bring your own food; side pool table, back TV; tables out on quay *(Michael and Alison Sandy, the Didler)*
Wodehouse Arms TR11 3PN [Killgrew St]: Well kept St Austell local with interesting choice of home-made food using local produce *(Joe Green)*

FLUSHING [SW8033]
Royal Standard TR11 5TP [off A393 at Penryn (or foot ferry from Falmouth); St Peters Hill]: Trim waterfront pub with great views to Falmouth from front terrace, bistro-bar feel with enjoyable interesting food; piped music *(David Rule)*

FOWEY [SX1251]
Galleon PL23 1AQ [Fore St; from centre follow Car Ferry signs]: Superb spot by harbour and estuary, good ale range inc local microbrews, good generous food from

sandwiches to plenty of fish, reasonable prices, nice choice of wines, fast friendly service, fresh modern nautical décor, lots of solid pine, dining areas off; pool, jazz Sun lunchtime, evenings can get loud with young people; children welcome, disabled facilities, attractive extended waterside terrace and sheltered courtyard with covered heated area, estuary-view bedrooms *(Dave Webster, Sue Holland, Mr and Mrs W W Burke, Mick and Moira Brummell, BB)*

☆ *King of Prussia* PL23 1AT [Town Quay]: Handsome quayside building with good welcoming service in roomy neat upstairs bar, bay windows looking over harbour to Polruan, good pubby bar food, St Austell ales kept well, sensibly priced wines, side family restaurant; piped music; seats outside, open all day in summer, six pleasant bedrooms *(B and M Kendall, Alan Johnson, Chris Glasson, LYM, Liz Hryniewicz, Nick Lawless)*

Lugger PL23 1AH [Fore St]: Friendly centrally placed pub, good mix of locals and visitors (can get busy) in unpretentious bar, comfortable small candlelit back dining area, well kept St Austell ales, generous good value food inc nice simply prepared fish specials (crab salad particularly good), big waterfront mural; piped music; children welcome, pavement tables *(BB, the Didler, David Uren, Dave Webster, Sue Holland, Nick Lawless, Mr and Mrs W W Burke)*

Safe Harbour PL23 1BP [Lostwithiel St]: Redecoration ongoing at this 19th-c former coaching inn set away from main tourist area, lounge/dining area and locals bar, good value locally sourced home-made food, well kept St Austell ales, welcoming landlord, old local prints, upstairs overflow dining room; pool, darts, games machine, juke-box; heated side terrace, seven bedrooms, self-catering apartment, open all day *(Nick Lawless, Liz Hryniewicz, Dave Webster, Sue Holland, David Uren)*

☆ *Ship* PL23 1AZ [Trafalgar Sq]: Bustling local with friendly staff, good choice of good value generous food from sandwiches up inc fine local seafood, well kept St Austell ales, coal fire and banquettes in tidy bar with lots of yachting prints and nauticalia, steps up to family dining room with big stained-glass window, pool/darts room; piped music, small sports TV; dogs allowed, comfortably old-fashioned bedrooms, some oak-panelled *(LYM, Nick Lawless, James Morrell, Peter Martin)*

GOLANT [SX1254]

☆ *Fishermans Arms* PL23 1LN [Fore St (B3269)]: Bustling partly flagstoned small waterside local with lovely views across River Fowey from front bar and terrace, good value generous home-made food inc good crab sandwiches and seafood, efficient friendly service, Sharps Doom Bar and Skinners Betty Stogs, good wines by the glass, log fire, interesting pictures, back family room; piano, TV; dogs welcome, pleasant garden,

cl Sun afternoon *(B and M Kendall, Roger and Linda Hargreaves, BB, the Didler)*

GORRAN HAVEN [SX0141]

☆ *Llawnroc* PL26 6NU [Chute Lane]: Comfortable and relaxed family-friendly granite hotel (try reading its name backwards), home-made food inc good fish and big Sun lunch in good-sized dining area, St Austell beers and one brewed for them by Sharps, good wine choice, reasonable prices, friendly dedicated service, some refurbishment; big garden overlooking cove and quiet fishing village, barbecues, good value bedroom block, open all day *(Scott Broughton, Phil and Jane Hodson)*

GULVAL [SW4831]

Coldstreamer TR18 3BB: Welcoming local with comfortable dining atmosphere, attractive restaurant with military prints, enjoyable food, well kept ales and decent wines, unusual high ceilings; quiet pleasant village very handy for Trengwainton Gardens, and for Scillies heliport – turn right opp entrance *(Jonathon Bunt, Kalman Kafetz)*

GURNARDS HEAD [SW4337]

☆ *Gurnards Head Hotel* TR26 3DE [B3306 Zennor—St Just]: 500 yards from Atlantic in outstanding bleak National Trust scenery, plenty of walks inland and along cliffy coast; bar rooms painted in bold, strong colours, interesting mix of furniture, pictures by local artists, open fires, St Austell and Skinners ales, real cider, several wines by glass, darts and board games, candlelit restaurant (food had been through a bumpy patch – we're hoping things are now back on track – reports please); children and dogs welcome, large garden, bedrooms *(Mr and Mrs Richard Osborne, LYM, Tim Sanders, Hannah Barlow, Helen and Brian Edgeley, Susie Symes, John and Verna Aspinall, M Bryan Osborne)*

GWEEK [SW7026]

Gweek Inn TR12 6TU [back roads E of Helston]: Cheerful family chain pub, large comfortable open-plan bar with low beams, brasses, lots of motoring trophies (enthusiast licensees) and woodburner in big stone fireplace, good friendly service, well kept Greene King Old Speckled Hen, Sharps Doom Bar and Skinners Betty Stogs, decent wines, good reasonably priced standard food inc nice puddings choice (may try to keep your credit card while you eat), bright and roomy back restaurant, live music Fri; children welcome, tables on grass (safe for children), summer kiosk with all-day snacks, short walk from seal sanctuary *(Dr and Mrs M E Wilson)*

HELFORD [SW7526]

Shipwrights Arms TR12 6JX [off B3293 SE of Helston, via Mawgan]: Thatched pub of great potential by beautiful wooded creek, at its best at high tide, terraces making the most of the view, plenty of surrounding walks, summer foot ferry from Helford Passage; nautical décor, winter open fire, separate dining area; has had Flowers, Sharps and

Skinners ales, decent wines, friendly staff, bar food inc summer barbecues and lunchtime buffet platters, but up for sale as we go to press, as it's been for two years – news please; quite a walk from nearest car park, has been cl winter Sun and Mon evenings *(LYM, the Didler, Michael and Ann Cole, Ian Phillips, Dr and Mrs M E Wilson)*

HELFORD PASSAGE [SW7626]

☆ *Ferry Boat* TR11 5LB [signed from B3291]: Big family bar in super position, about a mile's walk from gate at bottom of Glendurgan Garden (NT), by sandy beach with swimming, small boat hire, fishing trips and summer ferry to Helford, suntrap waterside terrace with covered area and barbecues; full St Austell range kept well, good range of wines by the glass, friendly cheerful service, restaurant; may be piped music, games area with pool and SkyTV, steep walk down from the overflow car park; usually open all day summer (with cream teas and frequent live entertainment), bedrooms *(John Marsh, LYM)*

HELSTON [SW6527]

☆ *Blue Anchor* TR13 8EL [Coinagehall St]: Many (not all) love this 15th-c no-nonsense, highly individual, thatched local; quaint rooms off corridor, flagstones, stripped stone, low beams and well worn furniture, traditional games, family room, limited bargain lunchtime food (perhaps best time for a visit), ancient back brewhouse still producing their own distinctive and very strong Spingo IPA, Middle and seasonals like Bragget with honey and herbs; seats out behind, bedrooms, open all day *(Donna and Roger, Ian and Nita Cooper, Ian Barker, Joan and Michel Hooper-Immins, David Uren, LYM, the Didler, Tom McLean, Dave Webster, Sue Holland)*

HESSENFORD [SX3057]

Copley Arms PL11 3HJ [A387 Looe—Torpoint]: Village pub with slightly old-fashioned feel, popular with families and passing tourists, reasonably priced food from baguettes to Sun lunch and restaurant dishes in linked areas, well kept St Austell ales, nice wine choice, variety of teas and coffee, log fires, tables in cosy booths, one part with sofas and easy chairs, big family room; piped music, dogs allowed in one small area; sizeable and attractive streamside garden and terrace (but by road), play area, bedrooms *(Mrs Mary Woods, Jean and Douglas Troup, Prof Michael Patterson, Suzy Miller, John and Joan Calvert, Evelyn and Derek Walter)*

LAMORNA [SW4424]

Lamorna Wink TR19 6XH [off B3315 SW of Penzance]: Great collection of warship mementoes, sea photographs, nautical brassware, hats and helmets in proper no-frills country local with well kept Sharps and Skinners ales, lunchtime sandwiches, pasties and baked potatoes from homely kitchen area (perhaps not out of season), swift service, coal fire, pool table, books and perhaps local produce for sale; children in

eating area, picnic-sets outside, short stroll above beautiful cove with good coast walks *(Donna and Roger, LYM, Michael and Ann Cole)*

LANNER [SW7339]

☆ *Fox & Hounds* TR16 6AX [Comford; A393/B3298]: Cosily comfortable rambling low-beamed pub with excellent friendly service, wide choice of good fresh food from sandwiches to massive steaks, St Austell ales tapped from the cask, good house wines, warm fires, high-backed settles and cottagey chairs on flagstones, stripped stone and dark panelling, newspapers and books; pub games, piped music; children welcome in dining room, dogs in bar, disabled facilities, great floral displays in front, picnic-sets in neat back garden with pond and play area, open all day wknds *(John Marsh, Jonathon Bunt, David Crook, LYM)*

LELANT [SW5436]

☆ *Old Quay House* TR27 6JG [Griggs Quay, Lelant Saltings; A3047/B3301 S of village]: Large neatly kept modern pub in marvellous spot by bird sanctuary estuary, good value food inc good salad bar, real ales such as Bass, St Austell Tribute and Sharps Doom Bar, good service, dining area off well divided open-plan bar, children allowed upstairs; garden with views over saltings, decent motel-type bedrooms, open all day summer *(Lesley and Peter Barrett, Alan Johnson)*

LERRYN [SX1356]

☆ *Ship* PL22 0PT [signed off A390 in Lostwithiel; Fore St]: Lovely spot esp when tide's in, Sharps and Skinners ales, local farm cider, good wines, country wines and whiskies, wide food choice, sensible prices, huge woodburner, attractive adults-only dining conservatory (booked quickly evenings and wknds), games room with pool; dogs on leads and children welcome, picnic-sets and pretty play area outside, nr famous stepping-stones and three well signed waterside walks, decent bedrooms in adjoining building *(David Crook, LYM, Nick Lawless, Dave Webster, Sue Holland)*

LIZARD [SW7012]

Top House TR12 7NQ [A3083]: Neat pub with lots of good local sea pictures, fine shipwreck relics and serpentine craftwork (note the handpumps), good log fire, Sharps and Skinners ales, good range of food, friendly staff; sheltered terrace, interesting nearby serpentine shop *(J K and S M Miln, BB, Dave Webster, Sue Holland)*

LOOE [SX2553]

Globe PL13 1HN [Station Rd]: Good welcoming atmosphere with friendly pub golden labrador, good value food from sandwiches up, decent wines by the glass *(Dr J Barrie Jones)*

Jolly Sailors PL13 2EP [Princes Sq, West Looe; just off quayside]: Friendly old inn with neatly kept atmospheric beamed bar, local paraphernalia, two real ales, helpful interested new landlord, weekly sea shanties;

comfortable recently renovated bedrooms, coastal footpath nearby, excellent stroll to nearby Polperro *(Andrew Lake, Alicia Kuczera)*

Olde Salutation PL13 1AE [Fore St, E Looe]: Good welcoming local bustle in big squarish slightly sloping beamed and tiled bar, good value food from notable crab sandwiches to wholesome specials and Sun roasts, fast friendly service, well kept ales inc Sharps Doom Bar, red leatherette seats and neat tables, blazing fire in nice old-fashioned fireplace, lots of local fishing photographs, side snug with olde-worlde harbour mural, step down to simple family room; may be piped music, forget about parking; open all day, handy for coast path *(BB, Christine and Neil Townend, David Uren)*

LOSTWITHIEL [SX1059]

Earl of Chatham PL22 0EP [Grenville Rd]: Traditional pub with open fire, wide choice and generous helpings of tasty real home cooking *(Paul Rudd)*

☆ *Royal Oak* PL22 0AG [Duke St]: Fine choice of bottled beers from around the world in nice town local dating from 13th c, Bass, Fullers London Pride and Sharps Doom Bar, enjoyable food, spacious neat lounge with log-effect gas fire, beamed and flagstoned back public bar, darts and board games, restaurant; may not take credit cards, games machines, TV; children welcome, dogs in bar, picnic-sets on raised terrace by car park, bedrooms, good breakfast, open all day and till late wknds when there may be music *(Andy and Claire Barker, Dave Braisted, LYM)*

LUDGVAN [SW5033]

☆ *White Hart* TR20 8EY [off A30 Penzance—Hayle at Crowlas]: Appealing old-fashioned 19th-c pub under enthusiastic newish licensees (also run the Turks Head in Penzance), friendly and welcoming, with Sharps, Skinners and a changing guest beer tapped from the cask, extensive menu inc good local fish, small unspoilt beamed rooms with wood and stone floors, nooks and crannies, woodburners, newspapers; interesting church next door *(the Didler, Dave Webster, Sue Holland, LYM)*

MARAZION [SW5130]

Cutty Sark TR17 0AP [the Square]: More hotel than pub, not far from beach, public bar with Sharps ales, decent food, open fire, stripped stone and nautical bric-a-brac, pleasant separate hotel bar, restaurant; good bedrooms with lovely view of St Michael's Mount *(Donna and Roger, Dave Webster, Sue Holland)*

Fire Engine TR17 0BB [Higher Fore St]: Open plan, with St Austell ales and cider from central bar, varied reasonably priced food, friendly staff, interesting local maritime photographs, fantastic St Michael's Mount views from back windows; suntrap sloping lawn with lower terrace *(Dave Webster, Sue Holland, Alan Bowker)*

Godolphin Arms TR17 0EN [West End]: Great views across beach and Mounts Bay towards St Michael's Mount, real ales inc Sharps,

informal lower bar with pool table, upper lounge bar and dining room, Sun carvery, family room with play area; decked terrace, ten brightly painted bedrooms, most with sea view, good breakfast *(Ian Phillips, Donna and Roger, Dave Webster, Sue Holland)*

Kings Arms TR12 0AP [The Square]: Old one-bar pub in small square, friendly landlord, good value fresh food, well kept St Austell; picnic-sets out in front *(Dave Webster, Sue Holland, Giles and Annie Francis, David and Sue Smith)*

MAWGAN [SW7025]

Ship TR12 6AD: New licensee at this former 18th-c courthouse; high-ceiling bare-boards bar with woodburner in stone fireplace, end snug, raised eating area, traditional home-made locally sourced food, two well kept local beers; piped music – live some wknds; well behaved children and dogs on leads welcome, garden with picnic-sets, open all day Sun, cl winter Mon lunchtime, *(Peter Holmes, Michael and Ann Cole, Mr Ray J Carter)*

MAWNAN SMITH [SW7728]

☆ *Red Lion* TR11 5EP [W of Falmouth, off former B3291 Penryn—Gweek; The Square]: Homely old thatched pub with cosy series of carpeted and dimly lit linked beamed rooms, open-view kitchen doing wide choice of good food from interesting menu esp seafood (should book summer evening), quick friendly service, lots of wines by the glass, Greene King and Sharps kept well, good coffee, daily papers, fresh flowers, woodburner, dark woodwork, country pictures, plates and bric-a-brac; piped music, TV; children and dogs welcome, picnic-sets outside, handy for Glendurgan and Trebah Gardens, open all day *(LYM, Stephen and Jean Curtis, Comus and Sarah Elliott, Dr and Mrs M E Wilson)*

MEVAGISSEY [SX0144]

☆ *Fountain* PL26 6QH [Cliff St, down alley by Post Office]: Friendly fishermen's pub, low beams, slate floor, some stripped stone, good coal fire, old local pictures, welcoming staff, well kept St Austell, enjoyable food from simple lunchtime menu, back locals' bar with glass-topped cellar (and pool, games machine and sports TV), good value upstairs restaurant; occasional sing-songs; dogs welcome, bedrooms, pretty frontage with picnic-sets, open all day summer *(Andy and Claire Barker, Ted George, the Didler, Joe Green, David Uren, Alan Bulley, David and Sue Smith, BB, Ian Phillips)*

☆ *Ship* PL26 6UQ [Fore St, nr harbour]: 16th-c pub with interesting alcove areas in big open-plan bar, low beams and flagstones, nice nautical décor, open fire, uniformed staff, wide range of generous pubby food inc good fresh fish, small helpings available, full St Austell range kept well, back pool table; games machines, piped music, occasional live; dogs allowed, children welcome in two front rooms, comfortable bedrooms, open all day summer *(Ted George,*

*Joe Green, Phil and Jane Hodson,
Chris Glasson, R K Phillips)*

MINIONS [SX2671]

Cheesewring PL14 5LE: Popular village pub
useful for Bodmin Moor walks, real ales inc
Sharps Doom Bar and Special, reasonably
priced food, lots of brass and ornaments
(Ian Phillips)

MOUSEHOLE [SW4726]

☆ *Old Coastguard* TR19 6PR [The Parade (edge
of village, Newlyn coast road)]: More
hotel/restaurant than pub, though they do
keep real ales and a fair choice of wines by
the glass; lovely position with neat and
attractive sizeable mediterranean garden by
rocky shore with marble-look tables out on
decking, up-to-date food, light and airy
modern bar with potted plants, lower dining
part with glass wall giving great view out
over garden to Mounts Bay; children in
eating areas, sea-view bedrooms, good
breakfast, open all day *(the Brewers, LYM)*

☆ *Ship* TR19 6QX [Harbourside]: Busy
harbourside local in lovely village, opened-
up dimly lit main bar with black beams,
flagstones, open fire, panelling, built-in
wooden wall benches and stools around low
tables, photographs of local events, sailors'
fancy ropework, St Austell ales, darts, pubby
food; piped music – live monthly wknds, TV,
games machine; children and dogs welcome,
bedrooms, open all day *(Alan Johnson, LYM,
Carole Hall, the Brewers, the Weirs,
the Whites, Andrea Rampley, Ewan and
Moira McCall, Marianne and Peter Stevens,
Tony and Jill Radnor)*

MULLION [SW6719]

Old Inn TR12 7HN [Nr church – not down in
the cove]: Extensive thatched and beamed
family food pub with central servery doing
generous good value food (all day July/Aug)
from doorstep sandwiches to pies and
evening steaks, fast service in linked eating
areas with lots of brasses, plates, clocks,
nautical items and old wreck pictures, big
inglenook fireplace, two or more real ales,
lots of wines by the glass; children welcome,
picnic-sets on terrace and in garden, good
bedrooms, open all day wknds and Aug *(LYM,
Comus and Sarah Elliott)*

MYLOR BRIDGE [SW8036]

Lemon Arms TR11 5NA [Lemon Hill]: Popular
and friendly traditional village pub with
helpful staff, good choice of generous
sensibly priced unfussy food, St Austell ales,
decent wine choice; unobtrusive piped
music; children and dogs welcome, disabled
access, back terrace, good coastal walks
*(Alan Bowker, David Elliott, Mick and
Moira Brummell, J D O Carter)*

NEWBRIDGE [SW4231]

Fountain TR20 8QH [A3071 Penzance—
St Just]: Stone-built pub with big pine
tables and cheery inglenook log fire in
attractively old-fashioned beamed and
flagstoned core's rosy dining area, friendly
efficient staff, above-average pubby food inc
good fish, full St Austell range kept well,

modern extension; tables in pretty front
courtyard, bedrooms, camping available
(Jane and Alan Bush)

PADSTOW [SW9175]

☆ *Golden Lion* PL28 8AN [Lanadwell St]:
Cheerful black-beamed locals' bar, high-
raftered back lounge with plush banquettes,
well kept ales inc Sharps Doom Bar,
reasonably priced simple bar lunches inc
good crab sandwiches, evening steaks and
fresh seafood, prompt friendly service, coal
fire; pool in family area, piped music, games
machines, sports TV; terrace tables,
bedrooms, open all day *(Conor McGaughey,
the Didler, Michael B Griffith, John Saville,
Dave Lowe, BB)*

☆ *London* PL28 8AN [Llanadwell St]: Relaxed
proper fishermen's local with lots of pictures
and nautical memorabilia, jolly atmosphere,
good staff, well kept St Austell ales, decent
choice of malt whiskies, good value bar
lunches inc fresh local fish, more elaborate
evening choice (small back dining area –
get there early for a table), great log fire;
can get very busy, games machines but
no piped music – live Sun night; dogs
welcome (if the resident collies approve),
open all day, good value bedrooms
*(Tim and Ann Newell, LYM, Clive Allen,
Conor McGaughey)*

PAUL [SW4627]

☆ *Kings Arms* TR19 6TZ: Appealing beamed
local opp church, cosy bustling atmosphere,
St Austell ales, enjoyable sensibly priced
food from sandwiches up, local artwork for
sale, darts, live bluegrass Tues evenings;
children and dogs welcome, five bedrooms,
open all day summer *(Stuart Turner)*

PELYNT [SX2054]

☆ *Jubilee* PL13 2JZ [B3359 NW of Looe]:
Popular early 17th-c beamed inn with well
kept St Austell Tribute, good wines by the
glass, home-made locally sourced food from
good sandwiches up inc Sun roasts, friendly
staff, interesting Queen Victoria mementoes
(pub renamed 1897 to celebrate her jubilee),
some handsome antique furnishings, log fire
in big stone fireplace, separate bar with
darts, pool and games machine; children and
dogs welcome, disabled facilities, large
terrace, 11 comfortable bedrooms, open all
day wknds *(LYM, Dennis Jenkin, Evelyn and
Derek Walter)*

PENDOGGETT [SX0279]

☆ *Cornish Arms* PL30 3HH [B3314]:
Picturesque friendly old coaching inn with
traditional oak settles on civilised front bar's
handsome polished slate floor, fine prints,
above-average food from good sandwiches
and fresh fish to splendid steaks and Sunday
lunch (best to book), also excellent new thai
menu from two resident thai chefs,
particularly welcoming service, well kept
Bass and Sharps Doom Bar, good wines by
the glass, comfortably spaced tables in small
dining room, proper back locals' bar with
woodburner and games; provision for
children, disabled access (staff helpful),

terrace with distant sea view, bedrooms, open all day (M A Borthwick, Mark Porter, Paul and Jane Meredith, LYM, Mrs Teresa Bateman)

PENELEWEY [SW8140]

☆ **Punch Bowl & Ladle** TR3 6QY [B3289]: Calm thatched dining pub, virtually a restaurant in evenings, in picturesque setting nr Trelissick Gardens, big settees, rustic bric-a-brac, several room areas, generous sensibly priced home-made food from good sandwiches to local steaks (Thurs very popular with elderly lunchers), children's helpings, efficient helpful service, St Austell ales, good wine choice; unobtrusive piped music; children and dogs on leads welcome, small back sun terrace, open all day summer (LYM, Comus and Sarah Elliott, J K and S M Miln, Ian Phillips, Dennis Jenkin, Michael and Alison Sandy, M Bryan Osborne)

PENHALLOW [SW7650]

Plume of Feathers TR4 9LT: Neatly smartened-up 18th-c beamed pub with good value food inc sensibly priced Sun roast, good drinks choice inc two local beers; picnic-sets in nice garden (Mick and Moira Brummell)

PENTEWAN [SX0147]

Ship PL26 6BX [just off B3273 St Austell—Mevagissey; West End]: Big 17th-c beamed pub opp tiny village's harbour, comfortable and clean with bar, snug and lounge/dining area, lots of dark tables and open fire, up to four St Austell ales, good reasonably priced fresh food inc plenty of fish, curries and popular Sun carvery, helpful staff; piped music, occasional live; children and dogs welcome, views from tables outside, nr good sandy beach and big caravan park, open all day summer, all day wknds winter (Hector Speight, Fi Exton, Paul Hobbs, Joe Green)

PENZANCE [SW4730]

Admiral Benbow TR18 4AF [Chapel St]: Well run rambling pub, full of life and atmosphere and packed with interesting nautical gear, friendly thoughtful staff, good value above-average food inc local fish, real ales such as Sharps, Skinners and St Austell, cosy corners, fire, downstairs restaurant, upper floor with pool, pleasant view from back room; children welcome, open all day summer (LYM, Kalman Kafetz, Jerry Brown, Tim and Ann Newell)

☆ **Dolphin** TR18 4EF [Barbican; Newlyn road, opp harbour after swing-bridge]: Part old-fashioned pub and part bistro, good value food esp fresh fish (landlady's husband is a fisherman), St Austell ales, good wines by the glass, helpful service, roomy bar, great fireplace, dining area a few steps down, cosy family room; big pool room with juke box etc, no obvious nearby parking; pavement picnic-sets, open all day (Tony and Jill Radnor, LYM, the Didler, Robert W Buckle)

PERRANARWORTHAL [SW7738]

☆ **Norway** TR3 7NU [A39 Truro—Penryn]: Large pub doing well under enterprising current

licensees, helpful friendly service, wide choice of generous carefully prepared food using local produce inc vegetarian options, all-day Sun carvery, morning coffee and afternoon tea, good selection of St Austell ales and of wines by glass, unusual sherry menu with accompanying nibbles, half a dozen linked areas, beams hung with farm tools, lots of prints and rustic bric-a-brac, old-style wooden seating and big tables on slate flagstones, open fires, Mon night quiz; children well catered for, tables outside, open all day (BB, Michael and Alison Sandy, Jonathon Bunt, David Crook)

PERRANPORTH [SW7554]

Green Parrot TR6 0JP: Fair-sized pub with real ales such as St Austell Tribute, usual food, pool; parking fee refunded at bar (Mick and Moira Brummell)

Watering Hole TR6 0JL: Busy holiday bar right on miles of golden sand, popular food from baguettes and pubby standards to steaks and amazing Sun carvery, enterprising Thurs evening and Sun afternoon summer barbecues, real ales inc Sharps Doom Bar, quick service; lively bank nights, sports TV; great sunset views from picnic-sets outside (David Knowles)

POLGOOTH [SW9950]

Polgooth Inn PL26 7DA [well signed off A390 W of St Austell; Ricketts Lane]: Big welcoming country pub, separate servery for enjoyable generous food from doorstep sandwiches up (only roasts on Sun), children's helpings and reasonable prices, well kept St Austell ales, good wine choice, eating area around sizeable bar with woodburner, good big family room; fills quickly in summer (handy for nearby caravan parks); dogs welcome, steps up to play area, tables out on grass, pretty countryside (Andy and Claire Barker, Russell and Beccy Potton, LYM)

POLPERRO [SX2051]

☆ **Crumplehorn Mill** PL13 2RJ [top of village nr main car park]: Converted mill keeping beams, flagstones and some stripped stone, snug lower beamed bar leading to long attractive main room with cosy end eating area, wide choice of good food from snacks to specials, welcoming friendly service, well kept St Austell and Sharps, log fire; children welcome, outside seating, good value bedrooms, self catering (Allan and Janice Webb, BB, Lawrence Pearse, Peter Salmon)

PONSANOOTH [SW7537]

Stag Hunt TR3 7EE [A393 Penryn—Redruth]: Nicely redecorated, with enjoyable food from pubby favourites to the newish landlady's authentic curries, good choice of beers (Jonathon Bunt, LYM)

PORT ISAAC [SW9980]

☆ **Golden Lion** PL29 3RB [Fore Street]: Bustling local atmosphere in simply furnished old rooms, open fire in back one, window seats and three balcony tables looking down on rocky harbour and lifeboat slipway far below, straightforward food inc good fish range, St Austell ales, darts, dominoes, cribbage; piped music, games machine; children in eating areas, dramatic cliff walks, open all day (LYM, the Didler, Sue Demont, Tim Barrow, the Brewers, Barry and Anne)

Slipway PL29 3RH [Middle St]: Small hotel just across from delightful village's slipway and beach, small unpretentious cellar-like bar with low dark beams, flagstones and some stripped stonework, Sharps ales, decent wines by the glass, nice bar food, good restaurant; leave car at top of village unless you enjoy a challenge; children welcome, crazy-paved heated terrace with awning, bedrooms, open all day in summer (the Brewers, LYM)

PORTHLEVEN [SW6225]

Harbour Inn TR13 9JB [Commercial Rd]: Large neatly kept pub/hotel in outstanding harbourside setting, pleasant well organised service, expansive lounge and bar with impressive dining area off, big public bar, St Austell ales, comprehensive wine list; quiet piped music; picnic-sets on big quayside terrace, decent bedrooms, some with harbour view, good breakfast (Dr and Mrs M E Wilson, John and Gloria Isaacs, Allan G Murray)

PORTLOE [SW9339]

☆ *Ship* TR2 5RA: Another change of landlord at this unspoilt bright L-shaped local, enjoyable generous food inc local fish, well kept St Austell ales, good choice of wines, prompt friendly service, interesting nautical and local memorabilia and photographs; piped music; disabled access to main bar, smokers' gazebo, sheltered and attractive streamside picnic-sets over road, pretty fishing village with lovely cove and coast path above, open all day Fri-Sun summer (Kim Smith, Dr and Mrs M E Wilson, Chris and Angela Buckell, Barry Collett, BB, Comus and Sarah Elliott, David Uren)

PORTSCATHO [SW8735]

Plume of Feathers TR2 5HW [The Square]: Cheerful largely stripped stone pub in pretty fishing village, well kept St Austell and other ales, Healey's cider, pubby food from sandwiches up, bargain fish night Fri, sea-related bric-a-brac in comfortable linked room areas, small side locals' bar (can be very lively evenings), restaurant; very popular with summer visitors, warm local atmosphere out of season; piped music; children and dogs welcome, disabled access, lovely coast walks, open all day summer (and other times if busy) (Chris and Angela Buckell, Comus and Sarah Elliott, David Uren, LYM)

QUINTRELL DOWNS [SW8560]

Two Clomes TR8 4PD [A392 E]: Attractive extended largely unspoilt 18th-c former cottage with well kept beers inc Sharps Doom Bar, reasonably priced food, quiet friendly service, welcoming fire in L-shaped bar, dining room; pretty and sunny garden with terrace, handy for campsites

(Peter Salmon)

ROCHE [SW9861]

Victoria PL26 8LQ: Now a largely extended modern pub with traditional front bar and nicely done eating areas inc big front conservatory, popular food all day from sandwiches up, well kept St Austell ales, helpful service; 42 reasonably priced bedrooms in attached block (Michael and Alison Sandy, LYM)

SCORRIER [SW7244]

Fox & Hounds TR16 5BS [B3298, off A30 just outside Redruth]: Long partly panelled well divided bar, big log or coal fires each end, red plush banquettes, hunting prints, stripped stonework and creaky joists, wide choice of good interesting food from snacks up inc vegetarian options, St Austell Tribute and Sharps Doom Bar, friendly licensees; unobtrusive piped music; picnic-sets out in front, handy for Portreath—Devoran cycle trail (Michael and Alison Sandy, LYM)

SENNEN COVE [SW3526]

☆ *Old Success* TR19 7DG [Off A30 Land's End road]: The star's for the glorious Whitesand Bay view, from the terraced garden or inside this traditional seaside hotel; unpretentious bar with lifeboat memorabilia, ship's lanterns, black and white photographs, big ship's wheel used as coat stand, well kept Sharps and Skinners, local cider, good food (all day in hols), friendly service, darts, restaurant; piped music, TV; children welcome, dogs in bar, basic decent bedrooms, four self-catering flats, open all day (Dr and Mrs M W A Haward, Andy and Claire Barker, Christine and Phil Young, LYM, David and Sue Smith, Alan Johnson, Mr and Mrs Gravener, Joan York, Ewan and Moira McCall, Stuart Turner)

ST BLAZEY [SX0654]

Cornish Arms PL24 2NG [Church St]: Friendly local with immaculate Victorian décor, well kept St Austell ales and guests, popular well priced food from generous sandwiches and snacks up, games area with pool; piped music; bedrooms (DFL)

ST BREWARD [SX0977]

☆ *Old Inn* PL30 4PP [off B3266 S of Camelford; Churchtown]: Broad slate flagstones, low oak beams, stripped stonework, two massive granite fireplaces dating from 11th c, welcoming friendly staff, good pubby food inc carvery Sat (evening) and Sun, well kept Bass and Sharps, lots of wines by the glass, sensibly placed darts, roomy extended restaurant with tables out on deck; piped music, games machine; provision for dogs and children, moorland behind (cattle and sheep wander into the village), open all day Fri-Sun and summer (Kelvin and Carol Butcher, the Didler, LYM)

ST DOMINICK [SX4067]

☆ *Who'd Have Thought It* PL12 6TG [off A388 S of Callington]: Large comfortable country pub doing very well under current management, wide choice of good food from generous sandwiches to blackboard specials, efficient friendly staff, well kept St Austell ales, decent wines, superb Tamar views especially from conservatory, cosily plush lounge areas with open fires; dogs allowed in public bar, garden tables, handy for Cotehele (NT) (Ted George, Jacquie Jones, LYM, Mr and Mrs E L Fortin, Dennis Jenkin)

ST EWE [SW9746]

Crown PL26 6EY [off B3287]: Low-beams and flagstones, traditional furnishings, two nice log fires, St Austell ales kept well, good house wines, helpful attentive licensees, generous if pricey locally sourced food (less choice off season), large back dining room up steps; piped music; children in eating areas, dogs allowed in bar but not garden, disabled facilities, handy for Lost Gardens of Heligan, usually open all day wknds (LYM, David Crook)

ST ISSEY [SW9271]

Ring o' Bells PL27 7QA [A389 Wadebridge—Padstow; Churchtown]: Cheerful 18th-c village pub with open fire at one end of beamed bar, darts and pool the other, well kept Courage Best, John Smiths, Sharps Doom Bar and Skinners Cornish Knocker, good choice of wines and whiskies, friendly service, good fresh local food in long narrow side dining room; can get packed in summer, car park across road; children and dogs welcome, decked courtyard, three bedrooms, open all day wknds (LYM, Mick and Moira Brummell)

ST IVES [SW5140]

Castle TR26 1AB [Fore St]: Cosy and spotless, with good range of well kept ales tapped from the cask (beer festivals), good friendly service, ample fairly priced usual food, good value coffee, comfortable plain seats and lots of dark panelling in one long low-ceilinged room, stained glass, old local photographs, maritime memorabilia; unobtrusive piped music; bustling in summer, relaxing out of season (Donna and Roger)

Lifeboat TR26 1LF [Wharf Rd]: Thriving quayside pub, wide choice of good value all-day food, three St Austell ales, friendly helpful staff, well spaced harbour-view tables and cosier corners, nautical theme; sports TV; dogs welcome, good disabled access and facilities, open all day (Alan Johnson)

☆ *Sloop* TR26 1LP [The Wharf]: Busy low-beamed, panelled and flagstoned harbourside pub with bright St Ives School pictures and attractive portrait drawings in front bar, booth seating in back bar, good value food from sandwiches and interesting baguettes to lots of fresh local fish, quick friendly service even though busy, Greene King and Sharps, good coffee; piped music, TV; children in eating area, a few beach-view seats out on cobbles, open all day (breakfast from 9am), cosy bedrooms, handy for Tate Gallery (LYM, Klaus and Elizabeth Leist, Alan Johnson, the Didler, Donna and Roger)

Union TR26 1AB [Fore St]: Popular and friendly low-beamed pub, roomy but cosy, with good value food from baguettes to local seafood specials and good vegetarian options, well kept ales inc Courage and Sharps, decent wines, coffee, daily papers, small hot fire, leather sofas, dark woodwork and masses of old local photographs; staff can be under pressure at busy times, no tabs, piped radio (Alan Johnson, George Atkinson, Donna and Roger, Tim and Ann Newell)

ST JUST IN PENWITH [SW3731]

Commercial TR19 7HE [Market Sq]: Former coaching inn, in same family for a century, good local atmosphere, good value home cooking; comfortable bedrooms, good breakfast (Michelle Woolcock, Jackie Edwards)

Kings Arms TR19 7HF [Market Sq]: Unpretentious local with well kept St Austell ales, some tapped from the cask, friendly relaxed service, comfortable elderly furniture on stone floors, local photographs, good value freshly made bar food from baguettes up; popular live music nights; dogs welcome, tables out in front, good value bedrooms with big breakfast, open all day (the Didler)

☆ *Star* TR19 7LL [Fore St]: Relaxed and informal dimly lit low-beamed local, friendly landlord, well kept St Austell ales, no food (bring your own lunchtime sandwiches or pasties), coal fire, darts and euchre, nostalgic juke box, live celtic music Mon evening, open mike Thurs; tables in attractive back yard with smokers' shelter, open all day (the Didler, George and Beverley Tucker, LYM)

Wellington TR19 7HD [Market Sq]: Unpretentious, busy and friendly, with good ample food at reasonable prices, well kept St Austell beers, decent wines, polite cheerful service, good local atmosphere, clean and tidy; bedrooms, good breakfast (John and Gloria Isaacs, the Didler, George and Beverley Tucker)

ST MAWES [SW8433]

Idle Rocks TR2 5AN [Tredenham Rd (harbour edge)]: Comfortable, old-fashioned waterfront hotel with lovely sea views, Skinners Betty Stogs and decent wines by the glass (at a price), enjoyable lunchtime food in two-tier restaurant looking on to terrace and harbour (more formal in evening but still relaxed), also nice snacks in pleasant small bar area and separate lounge, daily papers, friendly helpful young staff; well behaved dogs (but no small children) allowed on sun terrace over harbour, smallish bedrooms overlooking the water are the best bet (Dennis Jenkin, BB)

☆ *Rising Sun* TR2 5DJ [The Square]: Light and airy, with relaxed nicely redone bar on right with end woodburner, seaview bow window opposite, rugs on stripped wood, a few dining tables, sizeable carpeted left-hand bar with dark wood furniture, above-average food, well kept St Austell ales, good wines by the glass, friendly staff, wood-floored conservatory; piped music; sunny terrace with picnic-sets just across road from harbour wall, bedrooms *(Michael and Alison Sandy, David Uren, Andy and Claire Barker, Comus and Sarah Elliott, George Atkinson, LYM)*

Victory TR2 5DQ [Victory Hill]: Locals' bare-boards bar on left, carpeted dining area on right with partitions (may be upstairs dining room in season), Otter and Sharps, decent pubby food inc local fish, log fires, welcoming staff, plain wooden seating, board games; piped music; one or two picnic-sets outside, good value bedrooms, open all day *(LYM, Mr and Mrs A H Young, Barry Collett, MA, Julie and James Horsley, Comus and Sarah Elliott, David Uren, Gordon Tong)*

ST MAWGAN [SW8765]
☆ *Falcon* TR8 4EP [NE of Newquay, off B3276 or A3059]: New licensees at this attractive old stone inn, big bar with log fire, large antique coaching prints and falcon pictures, St Austell ales, darts and pool; children welcome, front cobbled courtyard and peaceful back garden with wishing well, pretty village, bedrooms, has been open all day in summer, more reports please *(D W Stokes, W N F Boughey, LYM)*

ST MERRYN [SW8874]
Cornish Arms PL28 8ND [Churchtown (B3276 towards Padstow)]: Now being managed by Rick Stein as a traditional local rather than gastropub; inexpensive food such as mussels and chips, steak and tribute pie and scampi in a basket, friendly staff, well kept St Austell ales, good choice of wines by the glass, log fire, fine slate floor, some 12th-c stonework and RNAS memorabilia; children and dogs welcome, picnic-sets at front and on sunny side terrace under large heated parasols, open all day summer *(LYM)*

Harlyn Bay Inn PL28 8SB [Harlyn Bay; NE on B3276, first left for 1.1 miles, right into Sandy Lane and immediately right again]: Useful seaside pub with good choice of good value food; plenty of tables out under awnings, nice sheltered beach across road *(D W Stokes)*

ST TEATH [SX0680]
White Hart PL30 3JT [B3267]: Welcoming flagstoned village local under same family for 50 years, good value generous food from sandwiches to good steaks and Sun roasts, friendly helpful service, good range of real ales, decent wines, coal fire, neat dining room off; games bar, live music wknds; children very welcome, open all day wknds, comfortably refurbished bedrooms, good breakfast *(LYM, DFL)*

ST TUDY [SX0676]
Cornish Arms PL30 3NN [off A391 nr Wadebridge]: Attractive low-beamed 16th-c village local with well kept Bass, St Austell, Sharps and a possible guest, decent home-made food in flagstoned front bar and

restaurant, pool room; children welcome *(the Didler)*

STITHIANS [SW7640]
Cornish Arms TR4 8RP [Frogpool, which is not shown on many roadmaps but is NE of A393 – ie opp side to Stithians itself]: Welcoming unspoilt 18th-c village pub revitalised by enthusiastic landlady, long beamed bar, fires either end, good value generous food inc OAP bargain lunches, enterprising specials and Sun roast, local ales and ciders, decent wines by the glass; well behaved children and dogs welcome, good bedrooms, may be cl Mon *(BB, John Marsh)*

TREBARWITH [SX0585]
Port William PL34 0HB [Trebarwith Strand]: Lovely seaside setting with glorious views and sunsets, waterside picnic-sets across road and on covered terrace, fishing nets, fish tanks and maritime memorabilia inside, gallery with local artwork, well kept St Austell Tinners and HSD, farm cider, enjoyable food, helpful friendly staff; pool and other games, piped music; children in eating area, well equipped comfortable bedrooms, open all day *(LYM, Colin McKerrow, G K Smale, Mrs A Taylor)*

TREBURLEY [SX3477]
☆ *Springer Spaniel* PL15 9NS [A388 Callington—Launceston]: Friendly well run place with good locally sourced food inc sandwiches with choice of interesting breads, well kept Sharps and Skinners, good wine choice, reasonable prices, clean décor with high-backed settle by woodburner, high-backed farmhouse chairs and other seats, olde-worlde prints, further cosy room with big solid teak tables, attractive restaurant up some steps; dogs very welcome in bar, children in eating areas, covered terrace *(Giles and Annie Francis, Mrs M S Tadd, Drs J and J Parker, Simon J Barber, Dennis Jenkin, LYM)*

TREEN [SW3923]
☆ *Logan Rock* TR19 6LG [just off B3315 Penzance—Lands End]: Low-beamed traditional bar with St Austell HSD and other ales, courteous service, standard food all day in summer from sandwiches up, smaller more enterprising choice out of season, inglenook fire, lots of games in family room, small back snug with excellent cricket memorabilia – landlady eminent in county's cricket association; may be piped music, no children inside; small pretty garden with covered area, good coast walks *(the Didler, John and Gloria Isaacs, Stuart Turner, LYM, Kalman Kafetz, Dr and Mrs M W A Haward)*

TREWARMETT [SX0686]
Trewarmett PL34 0ET [B3263]: Welcoming early 18th-c pub with thick stone walls and plenty of atmosphere, popular with locals, good carvery and landlord rears his own kobe-style beef, local ales, bedrooms *(Andrew Lawrance, Klaus and Elizabeth Leist)*

TRURO [SW8244]
Try Dower TR1 2LW [Lemon Quay]: Bustling

Wetherspoons in former newspaper offices on the quay, up to eight real ales at bargain prices, their usual meal deals, efficient service, pastel décor, sofas, family tables and quiet areas; TV news; good market outside Weds and Sat *(Tim and Ann Newell, Comus and Sarah Elliott)*

TYWARDREATH [SX0854]

New Inn PL24 2QP [off A3082; Fore St]: Relaxed timeless local, Bass tapped from the cask and St Austell ales on handpump, caring friendly landlord, back games/ children's room; large secluded garden behind, nice village setting, bedrooms *(Dave Webster, Sue Holland, the Didler, BB)*

WADEBRIDGE [SW9872]

Swan PL27 7DD [Molesworth St]: Pleasant open-plan bar, enjoyable food, friendly staff, well kept St Austell ales and HSD, restaurant; music may be loud till late; six bedrooms *(Dr J Barrie Jones)*

WATERGATE BAY [SW8464]

Phoenix TR8 4AB: Spectacular coast and sunset views from open balcony, bar/restaurant upstairs with enjoyable food inc interesting fish dishes, downstairs bistro bar and pizzeria, well kept St Austell Tribute, Sharps Doom Bar and Skinners Betty Stogs, decent wines, sensible prices, friendly efficient staff, live folk/blues/jazz Fri, open mike Sat; well behaved children and dogs welcome, disabled facilities, plenty of outside seating, open all day *(Alec Lewery)*

ZELAH [SW8151]

Hawkins Arms TR4 9HU [A30]: 18th-c beamed stone-built local, enjoyable good value food inc freshly cooked pies, well kept real ales such as Skinners, log fire, copper and brass in bar and dining room; children welcome, pleasant back terrace *(Geoff and Marianne Millin)*

ISLES OF SCILLY

ST AGNES [SV8808]

☆ *Turks Head* TR22 0PL [The Quay]: One of the UK's most beautifully placed pubs, idyllic sea and island views from garden terrace, can get very busy on fine days, good food from pasties to popular fresh seafood (best to get there early), friendly licensees and good service, well kept ales and cider; has been cl winter, open all day other times *(Michael Sargent, Nick Hawksley, Mr and Mrs S Wilson, LYM, R J Herd, Dr and Mrs R E S Tanner)*

ST MARTIN'S [SV9116]

Seven Stones TR25 0QW [Lower Town]: Stunning location and sea-and-islands view, 11 steps up to big main bar after 111 paces up the hill to this long single-story stone building; smartened up by newish owners doing good fresh food from baguettes to splendid local seafood and organic veg, summer teas and sandwiches, well kept St Austell, Skinners and perhaps Ales of Scilly as a guest beer, decent wines, bar billiards, local art for sale, nice window seats; lots of terrace tables some on decking, lovely walks, limited winter opening *(Michael Sargent)*

ST MARY'S [SV9010]

☆ *Atlantic Inn* TR21 0HY [The Strand; next to but independent from Atlantic Hotel]: Spreading and hospitable dark bar with well kept St Austell ales, good range of sensibly priced food, sea-view restaurant, low beams, hanging boat and other nauticalia, mix of locals and tourists – busy evenings, quieter on sunny lunchtimes; darts, pool, games machines; nice raised verandah with wide views over harbour, good bedrooms in adjacent hotel *(Michael Sargent, Gwyn and Anne Wake, BB, C J Fletcher)*

'Children welcome' means the pub says it lets children inside without any special restriction. If it allows them in, but to restricted areas such as an eating area or family room, we specify this. Places with separate restaurants often let children use them, hotels usually let them into public areas such as lounges. Some pubs impose an evening time limit – let us know if you find one earlier than 9pm.

Cumbria

This is a very strong county, with a wide variety of pubs doing really well this year. Several are new to the *Guide*: the Cross Keys at Carleton, George & Dragon at Clifton (delicious food using estate produce), Black Bull in Coniston (brewing its own beers) and Brown Horse at Winster (lovely food, also using produce from their own estate). Others on great form are the Punch Bowl at Askham, Masons Arms on Cartmel Fell, Punch Bowl at Crosthwaite, Britannia by Elterwater, Drunken Duck up above Hawkshead, Watermill at Ings, Strickland Arms at Levens, Kirkstile Inn at Loweswater, Black Swan at Ravenstonedale, Langstrath at Stonethwaite, Farmers Arms in Ulverston and the Gate Inn at Yanwath. Quite a few of these serve fantastic food, too: our Cumbrian Dining Pub of the Year is the Gate at Yanwath. Some highlights of the Lucky Dip section: the Kirkstone Pass Inn high above Ambleside, Crown & Mitre at Bampton Grange, Wheatsheaf at Brigsteer, Oddfellows Arms at Caldbeck, Sun at Crook, George & Dragon at Garrigill and the Hawkshead Brewery Bar at Staveley. Hawkshead is Lakeland's top small brewery, closely followed by Coniston, with other local favourites including Tirril, Keswick, Dent, Hesket Newmarket, Barngates, Yates and Ulverston, and quite a few others worth tracking down. The dominant area brewery is Jennings, part of the Marstons combine.

AMBLESIDE
NY3704 MAP 9

Golden Rule

Smithy Brow; follow Kirkstone Pass signpost from A591 on N side of town; LA22 9AS

Simple town local with cosy, relaxed atmosphere and real ales; no food

Locals and walkers with their dogs enjoy this basic little town pub because it never changes at all. It's just the place for a drink and a chat (they offer no food) and the bar area has built-in wall seats around cast iron-framed tables (one with a local map set into its top), horsebrasses on the black beams, assorted pictures on the walls, a welcoming winter fire and a relaxed atmosphere. Robinsons Cumbria Way, Dizzy Blonde, Double Hop, Hartleys XB, Hatters and Unicorn on handpump. A brass measuring rule hangs above the bar. There's also a back room with TV (not much used), a left-hand room with darts and a games machine and a further room down a couple of steps on the right with lots of seating. The back yard has benches and a covered heated area, and the window boxes are especially colourful. There's no car park.

⊞ **No food.**

Robinsons ~ Tenant John Lockley ~ Real ale ~ No credit cards ~ (015394) 32257 ~ Children welcome away from bar ~ Dogs welcome ~ Open 11am-midnight; 12-midnight Sun

Recommended by MP, David and Sue Smith, Andy and Jill Kassube, Chris Sale, Chris Johnson, Mr and Mrs Maurice Thompson, Helen Clarke, Dr and Mrs Jackson

NY5046 MAP 10

Dukes Head 🛏

Off A6 S of Carlisle; CA4 9PB

Friendly welcome, interesting food in comfortable lounge, heated outside area and day fishing tickets; good value bedrooms

You can be sure of a friendly welcome from the knowledgeable landlord in this nicely old-fashioned inn. The comfortable lounge bar has oak settles and little armchairs among more upright seats, oak and mahogany tables, antique hunting and other prints, and some brass and copper powder-flasks above the open fire. Black Sheep Bitter, Jennings Bitter and Caledonian Deuchars IPA on handpump, Weston's cider and sometimes home-made lemonade and ginger beer; the separate public bar has darts, table skittles, board games and TV. There are seats on a heated area outside with more on the lawn behind; boules. Day tickets for fishing are available.

🍴 **Often generous helpings of enjoyable bar food include sandwiches, soup, a salad of black pudding, local sausage and chorizo topped with a poached egg and mustard vinaigrette, hot potted solway shrimps, steak and kidney in ale pie, sweet potato and vegetable red curry, chicken breast in a cream, white wine and tarragon sauce, salmon with dry vermouth, leeks and prawns, popular roast duckling with apple sauce and stuffing, and daily specials like smoked trout mousse, sausage and mash with onion gravy and a slice of haggis and venison steak with mushroom and red wine sauce; they hold popular curry evenings.** *Starters/Snacks: £3.95 to £6.75. Main Courses: £8.95 to £15.95. Puddings: £3.25 to £4.25*

Punch ~ Tenant Henry Lynch ~ Real ale ~ Bar food ~ Restaurant ~ (016974) 72226 ~ Children welcome ~ Dogs allowed in bar and bedrooms ~ Open 11am-midnight(12.30am Sat) ~ Bedrooms: £42.50S/£62.50S

Recommended by Comus and Sarah Elliott, Angus Lyon, Paul Boot, Christine and Neil Townend, Archibald Rankin, J M Renshaw, Michael Lamm, T Walker, Alastair Stevenson

NY5123 MAP 9

Punch Bowl 🛏

4.5 miles from M6 junction 40; village signposted on right from A6 4 miles S of Penrith; CA10 2PF

Well furnished inn in lovely spot with choice of different seating areas, log fires, imaginative food and good service

You can be sure of a friendly welcome from the courteous and helpful licensees of this attractive inn. It's a popular place for an enjoyable meal but being a country local, regulars do pop into the bar for a pint of Copper Dragon Best Bitter and Hawkshead Bitter on handpump; they also have ten wines by the glass and 40 malt whiskies. The spreading main bar has good-sized round and oblong tables with spindleback chairs and comfortable red or black leather tub chairs on its turkey carpet, an antique settle by the log fire in its imposing stone fireplace, local photographs and prints, and coins stuck into the cracks of the dark wooden beams (periodically taken out and sent to charity). The lively locals' area has sturdy wooden stools, wall benches and window seats, pool and TV; piped music. A snug separate lounge has button-back leather settees and easy chairs, and the attractive beamed formal dining room has regency striped wallpaper. There are tables out on a flower-filled terrace and a marquee. Dogs are not allowed in the restaurant. The bedrooms were recently refurbished; country sports can be arranged.

🍴 **Good, well presented bar food includes lunchtime filled baps, soup, sautéed chicken livers, salmon and queenie scallop terrine wrapped in vine leaves with a honey, dill and lemon yogurt dip, wild mushroom, butternut squash, chickpea and spinach balti, cumberland sausage with black pudding and sage mash, steak in ale cobbler with a herb scone and chicken stuffed with apricot and smoked cheese, wrapped in bacon with a white onion cream sauce, with daily specials like mussels in a white wine, spring onion, chilli and ginger sauce, spaghetti bolognese and fillet of bass with seafood risotto.** *Starters/Snacks: £4.50 to £7.00. Main Courses: £8.95 to £16.50. Puddings: £5.50*

Enterprise ~ Lease Louise and Paul Smith ~ Real ale ~ Bar food (12-2(4 Sun), 6-9;
all day June-Sept) ~ Restaurant ~ (01931) 712443 ~ Children welcome ~ Dogs welcome ~
Live music some weekends ~ Open 10am-midnight(1am Sat) ~ Bedrooms: £59.50B/£85B

*Recommended by Tina and David Woods-Taylor, Cedric Robertshaw, Graham and Elizabeth Hargreaves,
M E and J R Hart, Christine and Neil Townend, Michael Doswell*

BAMPTON

NY5118   MAP 10

Mardale 🍺 🛏️

*7.1 miles from M6 junction 39. A6 through Shap, then left at Post Office, signed to
Bampton. After 3.5 miles cross river in Bampton Grange then next right. In Bampton turn
left over bridge by Post Office; CA10 2RQ*

Appealing country dining pub, with relaxed welcoming feel and spotless furnishings

In a quaint village, this is a pretty pub with friendly staff. There are several opened-up
rooms decorated in a clean-cut and contemporary manner, with chunky modern country
tables and chairs on big flagstones, a few rugs here and there, one or two big Lakeland
prints and a modicum of rustic bygones on pastel walls (and in one big brick fireplace), a
few beams in the white ceilings and a log fire in a second stylish raised fireplace.
Coniston Bluebird, Hesket Newmarket High Pike Dark Amber Bitter, Keswick Thirst Rescue
and Tirril Red Barn Ale on handpump, 40 european bottled beers and several wines by
the glass. Dogs will find a water bowl (and maybe even a biscuit) in the nicely lit bar,
which is welcoming to walkers and has comfortable backed stools. There are good walks
straight from the door, for example to the nearby Haweswater nature reserve.

🍽️ **A short choice of good lunchtime food using seasonal local produce includes a fantastic
value two-course Farmers Lunch menu as well as sandwiches, soup, morecambe bay potted
shrimps and an all-day breakfast; in the evening, there might be a local lamb or
vegetarian burger, salmon and dill fishcakes stuffed with brie, cumberland tattie pot,
slow-roasted pork belly with local bacon on a crisp bubble and squeak cake with roasted
butternut squash, black pudding and cumberland sauce, steaks, and puddings like
blueberry crème brûlée and rhubarb crumble and custard.** *Starters/Snacks: £3.25 to £5.95.
Main Courses: £7.50 to £16.50. Puddings: £4.50*

Free house ~ Licensee Sebastian Hindley ~ Real ale ~ Bar food (all day) ~ (01931) 713244 ~
Well behaved children welcome ~ Dogs welcome ~ Open 11-11(10.30 Sun) ~
Bedrooms: £50S/£80S

Recommended by David and Katharine Cooke, Jane Rostron, Michael Doswell, Margaret Dickinson, Sian Morris

BASSENTHWAITE

NY2332   MAP 9

Sun

Off A591 N of Keswick; CA12 4QP

Bustling old pub with tasty, good value food, real ales and cheerful service

With friendly licensees and a relaxed atmosphere, it's not surprising that our readers
enjoy this white-rendered slate house with its lattice windows. The rambling bar has low
17th-c black oak beams, two good stone fireplaces with big winter log fires, built-in wall
seats and plush stools around heavy wooden tables and areas that stretch usefully back
on both sides of the servery. Jennings Bitter, Cumberland Ale, Lakeland Stunner and a
seasonal guest on handpump, with some interesting whiskies. A huddle of white houses
looks up to Skiddaw and other high fells, and you can enjoy the view from the tables in
the front yard by the rose bushes and honeysuckle. The pub is handy for osprey viewing
at Dodd Wood and the village is charming. Dogs are not encouraged between 6-9pm.

🍽️ **Good value, generously served bar food includes sandwiches, lasagne, a fine steak
pudding, mackerel fishcakes, cumberland sausage with egg, half a roast chicken with
gravy and stuffing, lamb shank in a red wine and berry sauce and Sunday roast lunch.**
Starters/Snacks: £3.50 to £4.95. Main Courses: £7.95 to £15.00. Puddings: £3.95

Jennings (Marstons) ~ Lease Ali Tozer ~ Real ale ~ Bar food (12-2, 6-8.45; not Mon lunch) ~ (017687) 76439 ~ Children welcome ~ Dogs allowed in bar ~ Open 12-11.30(11 Sun); closed until 4.30pm Mon

Recommended by W K Wood, Rob and Catherine Dunster, Sylvia and Tony Birbeck

BASSENTHWAITE LAKE   NY1930   MAP 9

Pheasant ★ ⊗ ⊘ ⇋

Follow Pheasant Inn sign at N end of dual carriageway stretch of A66 by Bassenthwaite Lake; CA13 9YE

Charming, old-fashioned bar in smart hotel with enjoyable bar food and fine range of drinks; excellent restaurant and attractive surrounding woodlands; comfortable bedrooms

Of course this is not a pub but a civilised, particularly well run hotel (which many of our readers love staying at) but it does house a surprisingly pubby, unchanging bar – which is charming and old fashioned and just the place to enjoy a quiet pint or informal lunch. There are mellow polished walls, cushioned oak settles, rush-seat chairs and library seats, hunting prints and photographs, and Bass, Coniston Bluebird and Jennings Cumberland on handpump served by friendly, knowledgeable staff; also, 12 good wines by the glass and over 60 malt whiskies. Several comfortable lounges have log fires, beautiful flower arrangements, fine parquet flooring, antiques and plants. Dogs are allowed in the residents' lounge at lunchtime and they do let them into the bar during the day too, unless people are eating. There are seats in the garden, attractive woodland surroundings and plenty of walks in all directions.

⊗ **Enjoyable lunchtime bar food includes open sandwiches, ploughman's, good soup with home-made bread, chicken liver or stilton, walnut and apricot pâté, their own potted silloth shrimps, baked goats cheese tartlet with red onion marmalade, various caesar salads, crab cakes with pickled cucumber and chilli and tomato salsa, shepherd's pie, daily specials, and puddings.** *Starters/Snacks: £5.95 to £9.95. Main Courses: £10.45 to £12.95. Puddings: £5.45 to £5.75*

Free house ~ Licensee Matthew Wylie ~ Real ale ~ Bar food (not in evening – restaurant only then) ~ Restaurant ~ (017687) 76234 ~ Children allowed if over 8 ~ Dogs allowed in bar and bedrooms ~ Open 11.30-2.30, 5-10.30(11 Sat); 12-2.30, 6-10.30 Sun ~ Bedrooms: £85B/£160B

Recommended by John and Sylvia Harrop, Louise Gibbons, Stuart Turner, Noel Grundy, Sylvia and Tony Birbeck, Mike and Sue Loseby, Alison and Pete, Chris Maunder, Tina and David Woods-Taylor, Mr and Mrs J Roberts, W K Wood, G D K Fraser

BEETHAM   SD4979   MAP 7

Wheatsheaf ⊘ ⇋

Village (and inn) signposted just off A6 S of Milnthorpe; LA7 7AL

17th-c inn with handsome timbered cornerpiece, lots of beams, interesting food and quite a choice of drinks

This striking old coaching inn usefully serves food all day – very handy after enjoying one of the many nearby walks. There's an opened-up front lounge bar with lots of exposed beams and joists and the main bar (behind on the right) has an open fire, Thwaites Wainwright and Tirril Queen Jean on handpump, a dozen wines by the glass and quite a few malt whiskies. Two upstairs dining rooms are open only at weekends; piped music. The 14th-c church opposite is pretty. More reports please.

⊗ **Quite a choice of bar snacks and more substantial meals includes hot and cold sandwiches, soup, ploughman's, chicken liver pâté with bramley apple marmalade, potted shrimps with tarragon and citrus butter, steak and mushroom in ale pie, cumberland sausage and mash, minted lamb shank, gammon with honey and orange, wild mushroom, tomato and goats cheese bread and butter pudding with chilli oil, and puddings like sticky toffee pudding with caramel sauce and crème brûlée with boozy berries; they also offer a good value early-bird menu and Sunday roasts.** *Starters/Snacks: £4.25 to £6.50. Main Courses: £6.95 to £16.95. Puddings: £4.25 to £7.25*

Free house ~ Licensees Mr and Mrs Skelton ~ Real ale ~ Bar food ~ Restaurant ~
(015395) 62123 ~ Children welcome ~ Open 12-3, 5-11; 12-11(10.30 Sun) Sat ~
Bedrooms: £65B/£75B

*Recommended by Pam and John Smith, Ray and Winifred Halliday, Jo Lilley, Simon Calvert, Karen Eliot,
Michael Doswell*

BOUTH
SD3285   MAP 9

White Hart 🍺

Village signposted off A590 near Haverthwaite; LA12 8JB

**A fine range of well kept real ales, tasty bar food and plenty of bric-a-brac in cheerful
Lakeland inn; good surrounding walks; bedrooms**

Well run and genuinely friendly, this bustling inn keeps a fine range of six changing real
ales on handpump: Black Sheep Best Bitter, Coniston Bluebird, Jennings Cumberland and
three guests; also 25 malt whiskies. The sloping ceilings and floors show the building's
age, and there are lots of old local photographs and bric-a-brac, farm tools, stuffed
animals, a collection of long-stemmed clay pipes and two woodburning stoves; piped
music. There are some seats outside and fine surrounding walks.

🍴 **Well liked bar food includes sandwiches, soup, steak in guinness pie, halibut steak in
garlic and parsley butter, cumberland sausage with rich onion and cranberry gravy, rare
breed sirloin steak and daily specials.** *Starters/Snacks: £3.95 to £6.25. Main Courses:
£10.75 to £15.75. Puddings: £4.75*

Free house ~ Licensee Nigel Barton ~ Real ale ~ Bar food (12-2, 6-8.45; all day Sun) ~
Restaurant ~ (01229) 861229 ~ Children in bar until 9pm ~ Dogs allowed in bedrooms ~
Live music fortnightly summer Sun and winter Fri ~ Open 12-11(10.30 Sun) ~ Bedrooms:
£52.50S(£42.50B)/£90S(£70B)

*Recommended by Rob and Penny Wakefield, Dr Peter Andrews, Blaise Vyner, Michael Lamm,
Mr and Mrs Maurice Thompson*

BOWNESS-ON-WINDERMERE
SD4096   MAP 9

Hole in t' Wall 🍺

Lowside; LA23 3DH

Bustling old pub with split-level rooms, country knick-knacks, real ales and tasty food

Full of interest, this unchanging place is Bowness's oldest pub. The two split-level rooms
have beams, stripped stone and flagstones, lots of country bric-a-brac and old pictures
and there's a splendid log fire under a vast slate mantelpiece (in summer the logs are
replaced with fresh flowers); the upper room has attractive plasterwork. Robinsons
Double Hop, Hartleys XB and Unicorn on handpump and several wines by the glass;
friendly staff, and juke box. The small flagstoned front courtyard has sheltered picnic-sets
under a large umbrella and outdoor heaters. The pub does get very busy during the
tourist season. More reports please.

🍴 **Decent bar food includes sandwiches, ploughman's, soup, chicken liver pâté with
cumberland sauce, caesar salad, cumberland sausage with onion gravy and apple sauce,
beef in guinness or fish pies, lasagne, a daily changing vegetarian dish, lamb henry, and
puddings like lemon mousse and chocolate sponge.** *Starters/Snacks: £4.25 to £6.50.
Main Courses: £7.95 to £11.75. Puddings: £3.95 to £4.50*

Robinsons ~ Tenant Susan Burnet ~ Real ale ~ Bar food (12-2(2.30 Sun), 6-8; 12-3, 4-7 Fri,
Sat; not Sun evening) ~ (015394) 43488 ~ Children welcome ~ Live entertainment Fri and
Sun in high season ~ Open 11-11; 12-10.30 Sun

Recommended by Michael Butler, Kerry Law

Tipping is not normal for bar meals, and not usually expected.

SD2190 MAP 9

Blacksmiths Arms

Off A593 N of Broughton-in-Furness; LA20 6AX

Good food, local beers and open fires in charming small pub liked by walkers

Readers like to come back to this charming little pub on a regular basis. It's in a fine spot with superb surrounding walks and you can be sure of a warm welcome from the friendly, cheerful licensees. There are warm log fires in the bars and three of the four simply but attractively decorated small rooms have straightforward chairs and tables on ancient slate floors. Clarks Classic Blonde, Moorhouses Premier Bitter and Stringers Best Bitter on handpump, nine wines by the glass and summer farm cider. There are three smallish dining rooms, and darts, board games, dominoes and cribbage. The hanging baskets and tubs of flowers in front of the building are pretty in summer.

🍴 **Good, interesting bar food includes lunchtime sandwiches and ploughman's, soup, goats cheese with toasted pine nuts and sun-dried tomatoes in a balsamic syrup, smoked salmon and caper fishcakes with a sour cream and herb sauce, ham hock and black pudding terrine, cumberland sausages with coarse-grain mustard mash and red wine gravy, mixed bean casserole, chicken stuffed with creamy cheese with garlic mash and a roasted red pepper and tomato sauce, fish pie topped with cheesy mash, roasted herb-crusted lamb rump with sweet potato purée and balsamic and red wine sauce, and puddings like vanilla panna cotta with Cointreau-flamed strawberries and warm chocolate brownie with hot chocolate sauce.** *Starters/Snacks: £3.65 to £5.55. Main Courses: £8.50 to £13.95. Puddings: £2.50 to £4.25*

Free house ~ Licensees Mike and Sophie Lane ~ Real ale ~ Bar food (12-2, 6-9; not Mon lunchtime) ~ Restaurant ~ (01229) 716824 ~ Children welcome ~ Dogs welcome ~ Open 12-11(5-11 Mon); 12-10.30 Sun; 12-2.30, 5-11 Tues-Fri in winter; closed Mon lunchtime

Recommended by Tina and David Woods-Taylor, Maurice and Gill McMahon, Tim Maddison, V and E A Bolton, the Didler

NY5329 MAP 9

Cross Keys

Off A66 roundabout at Penrith on A686 to Alston, on right after a quarter mile, after farmshop; CA11 8TP

Friendly refurbished pub with several connected seating areas, real ales and tasty bar food

Run by the same family that owns another of our Main Entries, the Highland Drove in Great Salkeld, this friendly pub has been refurbished recently. The beamed main bar has pubby tables and chairs on the light wooden floorboards, modern metal wall lights and pictures on the bare stone walls, and Courage Directors, Theakstons Black Bull, Tirril 1823 and Wells & Youngs Bombardier on handpump. Steps lead down to a small area with high bar stools around a high drinking table and then upstairs to the restaurant – a light, airy room with big windows, large wrought-iron candelabras hanging from the vaulted ceiling, pale solid wooden tables and chairs and doors to a verandah. At the far end of the main bar, there's yet another couple of small connected bar rooms with darts, games machine, pool, juke box and dominoes; TV and piped music. And although many customers are here to eat, the friendly staff are just as happy if all you want is a drink.

🍴 **Tasty bar food includes hot or cold sandwiches, soup, chicken liver and orange parfait with spiced plums, various platters to share, beer-battered haddock, chargrilled chicken breast with a creamy tarragon sauce, gammon with egg and pineapple, lamb hotpot, steak in ale pie, roast vegetable and goats cheese tarte tatin with confit of tomatoes, tuna steak with a herby sauce and steaks.** *Starters/Snacks: £3.50 to £7.95. Main Courses: £7.95 to £16.95. Puddings: £4.95*

Free house ~ Licensee Paul Newton ~ Real ale ~ Bar food (12-2.30, 5.30-9(6-8.30 Sun); not 25 Dec, lunch 26 Dec, 1 Jan) ~ Restaurant ~ (01768) 865588 ~ Children welcome ~ Dogs allowed in bar ~ Open 12-2.30, 5-midnight; midday-1am Sat(midnight Sun)

Recommended by Helen Clarke

CARTMEL   SD3778   MAP 7

Kings Arms

The Square, off Causeway; LA11 6QB

Timbered pub in ancient village with seats facing lovely village square

Right in the centre of the village, this timbered pub has prized seats outside overlooking the square; there's a fine medieval stone gatehouse nearby. Inside, the neatly kept, rambling bar has small antique prints on the walls, a mixture of seats including old country chairs, settles and wall banquettes, fresh flowers on the tables and tankards hanging over the bar counter. A friendly atmosphere, quite a mix of customers, Barngates Tag Lag, Bass and Hawkshead Bitter and Red on handpump and several wines by the glass; good service and piped music. More reports please.

🍴 **Traditional bar food includes lunchtime sandwiches, beer-battered cod, cumberland sausage on bubble and squeak with onion gravy, gammon and egg, vegetable curry, local salt marsh lamb chops with minted butter, steak in guinness pie, daily specials, and puddings such as sticky toffee pudding and bread and butter pudding.** *Starters/Snacks: £3.45 to £5.95. Main Courses: £7.95 to £14.95. Puddings: £3.95*

Enterprise ~ Lease Richard Grimmer ~ Real ale ~ Bar food (12-2.30, 5.30-8.30) ~ Restaurant ~ (01539) 536220 ~ Children welcome ~ Dogs allowed in bar ~ Open 11-11(10.30 Sun)

Recommended by Pat and Graham Williamson, Dr John R and Hazel Allen, JDM, KM, Margaret Dickinson, Michael Lamm, Dr Kevan Tucker, N R White

CARTMEL FELL   SD4189   MAP 9

Masons Arms 🍺

Strawberry Bank, a few miles S of Windermere between A592 and A5074; perhaps the simplest way of finding the pub is to go uphill W from Bowland Bridge (which is signposted off A5074) towards Newby Bridge and keep right then left at the staggered crossroads – it's then on your right, below Gummer's How; OS Sheet 97 map reference 413895; LA11 6NW

Plenty of character in beamed bar, good food, real ales plus many foreign bottled beers; fine views from terrace

'A cracking little pub' says one reader about this well run place and plenty of people agree with him. It's in a lovely spot with stunning views down over the Winster Valley to the woods below Whitbarrow Scar – rustic benches and tables on the terrace make the most of this. Inside, the main bar has a friendly atmosphere and plenty of character, with low black beams in the bowed ceiling and country chairs and plain wooden tables on polished flagstones. A small lounge has oak tables and settles to match its fine Jacobean panelling, there's a plain little room beyond the serving counter with pictures and a fire in an open range, a family room with an old-parlourish atmosphere and an upstairs dining room; piped music, TV and board games. Cumbrian Dickie Doodle, Hawkshead Lakeland Gold, Thwaites Wainwright and Ulverston Laughing Gravy on handpump, quite a few foreign bottled beers, several wines by the glass and locally made damson beer and gin. There are comfortable self-catering cottages and apartments behind.

🍴 **Much enjoyed food includes lunchtime sandwiches, ciabattas and wraps, various nibbles, soup, steak in ale pie, pork belly with black pudding fritter and red wine jus, leek, butter bean and gruyère pie, battered fresh haddock with home-made tartare sauce, chicken tikka masala, marinated, slow-cooked minted lamb, good sticky spare ribs, pheasant breast on grilled pineapple with a creamy pepper sauce, and puddings like clotted cream cheesecake with drambuie-soaked fruit and gingerbread and rhubarb crumble.** *Starters/Snacks: £3.95 to £7.25. Main Courses: £9.95 to £14.95. Puddings: £5.25*

Individual Inns ~ Managers John and Diane Taylor ~ Real ale ~ Bar food (12-2.30, 6-9; all day weekends) ~ Restaurant ~ (015395) 68486 ~ Children welcome ~ Open 11.30-11; 12-10.30 Sun

Recommended by Tony and Jill Radnor, Ewan and Moira McCall, Helen and Brian Edgeley, Mary McSweeney, Anthony Green, Jo Lilley, Simon Calvert, Ann and Tony Bennett-Hughes, Nick Lawless, Mr and Mrs P R Thomas

CASTERTON

SD6379 MAP 7

Pheasant ♀

A683 about 1 mile N of junction with A65, by Kirkby Lonsdale; OS Sheet 97 map reference 633796; LA6 2RX

Neat beamed rooms in pleasant inn; seats in attractive garden with fell views; bedrooms

The bedrooms in this traditional 18th-c inn are being updated this year. It's a well run place with neatly kept, modernised beamed bars, wheelback chairs and dark red button-back wall banquettes on the patterned carpets, a nicely arched oak framed fireplace with a gas-effect fire, and Dent Aviator and Theakstons Best Bitter on handpump. Also, six wines by the glass, 21 malt whiskies and helpful staff; piped music and board games. There are some tables under cocktail parasols outside by the road, with more in the pleasant garden. The nearby church (built for the girls' school of Brontë fame here) has some attractive pre-Raphaelite stained-glass and paintings.

As well as some tempting daily specials, the popular bar food at lunchtime includes sandwiches, ploughman's, soup, smoked mackerel mousse, mushrooms and asparagus in a parsley cream sauce with pasta, gammon and egg, chicken cooked in tomato and pepper sauce and crispy battered haddock, with evening choices like poached fresh pears with stilton dressing, spinach, feta cheese and mushroom strudel with salsa sauce, spicy lamb, beef stroganoff, salmon supreme wrapped in smoked salmon and baked in butter, crispy duckling off the bone with sage and onion stuffing and roast beef with yorkshire pudding and gravy. *Starters/Snacks: £3.95 to £7.00. Main Courses: £8.50 to £15.95. Puddings: £4.90 to £5.60*

Free house ~ Licensee the Dixon family ~ Real ale ~ Bar food (12-2, 6-9) ~ Restaurant ~ (015242) 71230 ~ Children welcome ~ Open 12-3.30(3 Sun), 6-11(10.30 Sun); closed two weeks Jan ~ Bedrooms: £39B/£90B

Recommended by Mr and Mrs Ian King, Ewan and Moira McCall, Tom and Jill Jones, Dr and Mrs T E Hothersall, Derek and Sylvia Stephenson

CHAPEL STILE

NY3205 MAP 9

Wainwrights ◪

B5343; LA22 9JH

Fine choice of beers, lovely views and surrounding walks

Happily, little changes in this white-rendered Lakeland house. It remains a friendly place, popular with walkers, and still keeps a good range of seven real ales on handpump: Black Sheep Bitter, Jennings Cumberland and Sneck Lifter, Hawkshead Lakeland Gold, Thwaites Original, Lancaster Bomber and Wainwright and Yates Best Bitter; quick, friendly service. They also have 16 wines by the glass and some malt whiskies. The slate-floored bar has plenty of room, an open fire and it is here that walkers and their dogs are welcomed. Other spreading areas have beams and a few standing timbers, some half-panelling, cushioned settles and a mix of dining chairs around wooden tables on the carpet, an old kitchen range and a relaxed atmosphere; piped music, TV, board games, dominoes and games machine. Picnic-table sets out on the terrace have fine views.

Quickly served, reasonably priced bar food includes sandwiches, filled baked potatoes, soup, steak in ale or fish pie, cumberland sausage, lasagne, venison casserole, their popular lamb shoulder, and puddings such as apple pie and chocolate fudge cake. *Starters/Snacks: £3.75 to £5.95. Main Courses: £8.75 to £10.95. Puddings: £3.75*

Free house ~ Licensee Mrs C Darbyshire ~ Real ale ~ Bar food (12-2, 6-9) ~ (015394) 38088 ~ Children welcome ~ Dogs welcome ~ Open 11.30-11; 12-11 Sun; 11.30-3, 6-11 in winter

Recommended by John Saville, Glenn and Julia Smithers, John and Helen Rushton, Ewan and Moira McCall, Mr and Mrs Maurice Thompson, Martin Smith

Prices of main dishes sometimes now don't include vegetables – if in doubt ask.

CLIFTON NY5326 MAP 9

George & Dragon 🍴 🍷 🛏

A6; near M6 junction 40; CA10 2ER

Carefully restored and friendly old coaching inn, attractive bars and sizeable restaurant, local ales and fine choice of wines, excellent food and seats outside; bedrooms

Owned by the Lowther Estate, this 18th-c former coaching inn has been carefully and sympathetically restored recently. There's a relaxed reception room with leather chairs around a low table in front of an open fire, bright rugs on flagstones, a table in a private nook to one side of the reception desk (just right for a group of six) and a comfortable bed for Porter the patterdale terrier. Through some wrought-iron gates is the main bar area with more cheerful rugs on flagstones, assorted wooden farmhouse chairs and tables, grey panelling topped with yellow-painted walls, photographs of the estate and of the family with hunting dogs, various sheep and fell pictures and some high bar stools by the panelled bar counter. Hawkshead Bitter and Lancaster Blonde on handpump and 15 wines by the glass from a well chosen list; very friendly service. A further room with another open fire and more leather chairs is similarly furnished. The sizeable restaurant to the left of the entrance is made up of four open-plan rooms: plenty of old pews and church chairs around tables set for dining, candles in a disused fireplace, a contemporary open kitchen and similar décor to the bars. Outside, there are tables on the decoratively paved front entrance with more in a high-walled enclosed courtyard, and a herb garden.

🍽 **Using produce from the estate, the delicious honest food from a concise menu includes sandwiches, soup, twice-baked cheese soufflé, crab spring rolls with chilli dipping sauce, organic chicken liver pâté with chutney, blue cheese, celery and walnut risotto, speciality sausage with mash, yorkshire pudding and onion gravy, five-spice chicken drumsticks with asian coleslaw, braised shorthorn beef and oxtail steamed pudding with mushy peas, daily specials like wild boar carpaccio with pear and truffle oil, wild trout with baby fennel, almonds and saffron potatoes, pheasant breast with cider cream, and puddings such as white chocolate bread and butter pudding and rhubarb and cinnamon crumble.** *Starters/Snacks: £4.50 to £6.95. Main Courses: £8.95 to £15.95. Puddings: £4.95 to £5.95*

Free house ~ Licensee Paul McKinnon ~ Real ale ~ Bar food (12-2.30, 6-9.30) ~ Restaurant ~ (01768) 865381 ~ Children welcome ~ Dogs allowed in bar and bedrooms ~ Open 12-11(1am Sat, 11 Sun) ~ Bedrooms: £63.75S/£85S

Recommended by Malcolm and Jo Hart

COCKERMOUTH NY1230 MAP 9

Bitter End 🍺

Kirkgate, by cinema; CA13 9PJ

Own-brewed beers and lots of bottled beers in three interesting bars

With eight real ales – including their own – and three interesting bars, it's not surprising that this charming little pub is so popular. From their own small brewery, the beers include Cockermouth Pride and Gold Pale Ale, and they keep six guests from all over the country: Bitter End Lakeland Pale Ale, Coniston Bluebird, Hawkshead Lakeland Gold, Hesket Newmarket Skiddaw Special Bitter, Jennings Bitter, Nelson Jack Knife, Titanic Iceberg and Ulverston Another Fine Mess. Quite a few bottled beers from around the world and eight wines by the glass. The cosy main rooms have a different atmosphere in each – from quietly chatty to sporty, with the décor reflecting this, such as unusual pictures of a Cockermouth that even Wordsworth might have recognised, to more up-to-date sporting memorabilia, various bottles, jugs and books, and framed beer mats; welcoming log fire and piped music. The public car park round the back is free after 7pm.

🍽 **Good value traditional bar food includes sandwiches, steak in ale pie, cumberland sausage with caramelised onion sauce, goats cheese, tomato, red onion and garlic in puff pastry with home-made tomato sauce, fish in beer batter, lasagne, steaks, and puddings.** *Starters/Snacks: £4.50 to £4.75. Main Courses: £8.95 to £14.95. Puddings: £3.25*

Own brew ~ Licensee Susan Askey ~ Real ale ~ Bar food (12-2, 6-9) ~ (01900) 828993 ~
Children welcome ~ Open 11.30-2.30, 6-11.30(11 Sun); 11.30-midnight Sat; 12-3, 6-11 Sun;
11.30-2.30, 6-midnight Sat in winter

*Recommended by Helen Clarke, Mr and Mrs Maurice Thompson, the Didler, Keith and Rowena Ward,
Edward Mirzoeff*

CONISTON   SD3097   MAP 9

Black Bull

Yewdale Road (A593); LA21 8DU

**Own-brewed beers in bustling inn, Donald Campbell memorabilia, cheerful walkers' bar and
seats outside; bedrooms**

A couple of beers brewed on site here are named after Donald Campbell's *Bluebird*, and
there's quite a lot of memorabilia devoted to the attempting of the water speed records;
they also brew Coniston Blacksmiths, Oatmeal Stout and Oldman which they keep well on
handpump, too. This is a bustling old inn and the cheerful back area has slate flagstones
and is liked by walkers and their dogs, while the beamed and carpeted front part has
cast-iron-framed tables, comfortable banquettes and stools, an open fire and a relaxed,
comfortable feel. There are tables out in the former coachyard; parking may not be easy
at peak times.

🍴 **Generous helpings of tasty bar food includes sandwiches and toasties, filled baked
potatoes, ploughman's, soup, mushrooms in garlic, cream and white wine, morecambe bay
potted shrimps, a changing vegetarian dish, gammon and eggs, chilli, beer-battered fresh
haddock, cumberland sausage, a half-shoulder of slow-roasted lamb in mint gravy, daily
specials, and puddings.** *Starters/Snacks: £3.95 to £7.45. Main Courses: £8.50 to £15.95.
Puddings: £4.50*

Own brew ~ Licensee Ronald Edward Bradley ~ Real ale ~ Bar food (all day) ~ Restaurant ~
(015394) 41335/41668 ~ Children welcome ~ Dogs allowed in bar and bedrooms ~
Open 10am-11pm ~ Bedrooms: £49.50S/£90S

*Recommended by Nick Lawless, David and Sue Smith, Christine and Phil Young, Tony Goff, Maurice and
Gill McMahon, Tony and Maggie Harwood, Angus Lyon*

CROSTHWAITE   SD4491   MAP 9

Punch Bowl 🍽 🍷 🛏

Village signposted off A5074 SE of Windermere; LA8 8HR

**Stylish dining pub, fine choice of drinks, impressive food, good wines and real ales; seats
on terrace overlooking valley; lovely bedrooms**

What makes this stylish hotel stand out for us is not just the fact that it's such a
smashing place to stay in splendid bedrooms or even that the food is so good, it's the
genuine way that walkers and their wet dogs are welcomed into the public bar. This room
is raftered and hop-hung with a couple of eye-catching rugs on flagstones, bar stools by
the slate-topped counter, and Barngates Tag Lag and Westmorland Gold, Coniston
Bluebird Bitter and Hawkshead Lakeland Gold on handpump; lots of wines by the glass
and around a dozen malt whiskies. This opens on the right into two linked carpeted and
beamed rooms with well spaced country pine furnishings of varying sizes, including a big
refectory table. The walls, painted in restrained neutral tones, have an attractive
assortment of prints, and there are some copper objects and a dresser with china and
glass; winter log fire, woodburning stove, lots of fresh flowers and daily papers. On the
left, the wooden-floored restaurant area (also light and airy and attractive) has
comfortable high-backed leather dining chairs. Throughout, the pub feels relaxing and
nicely uncluttered. There are some tables on a terrace stepped into the hillside,
overlooking the lovely Lyth Valley. Breakfasts are super, afternoon tea is thrown in and a
newspaper of your choice is brought to your room with morning tea.

🍴 **Using their own lamb and vegetables, the often contemporary food at lunchtime** includes sandwiches, soup, salmon ballantine with pickled beetroot and horseradish crème fraîche, beer-battered hake with balsamic glaze, wild mushroom risotto, roast chicken with confit garlic and herb jus, and smoked haddock with champ mash and hollandaise; evening dishes such as roasted foie gras with duck egg, crispy potatoes and tartare sauce, scallops with confit pork, celeriac purée, five spiced jus and apple salad, lamb loin with hotpot vegetables and rosemary jus, and rib-eye steak with twice-cooked chips and béarnaise or pepper sauce, wild mushrooms, snails and garlic butter, with puddings like Valrohna chocolate tart with beer ice-cream and glazed rice pudding with orange compote. *Starters/Snacks: £4.00 to £7.00. Main Courses: £9.50 to £22.00. Puddings: £4.50 to £5.95*

Free house ~ Licensee Jenny Sisson ~ Real ale ~ Bar food (all day) ~ Restaurant ~ (015395) 68237 ~ Children welcome ~ Dogs allowed in bar ~ Open 11am-midnight ~ Bedrooms: £93.75B/£125B

Recommended by Margaret and Jeff Graham, Anthony Green, Revd D Glover, Pat and Graham Williamson, Michael Doswell, Glenn and Julia Smithers, David Thornton

ELTERWATER

NY3204   MAP 9

Britannia 🍺

Off B5343; LA22 9HP

Well run and extremely popular inn surrounded by wonderful walks and scenery; six real ales and enjoyable food; bedrooms

'As good as ever' reports one reader – and lots more agree with him. This is a particularly well run and very popular pub in a glorious location, with walks of every gradient right from the front door. There's a friendly and nicely old-fashioned atmosphere, and a small, traditionally furnished back bar plus a front one with a couple of window seats looking across to Elterwater itself through the trees; winter coal fires, oak benches, settles, windsor chairs, a big old rocking chair, and a smashing choice of real ales on handpump: Coniston Bluebird and a beer from Coniston named for the pub, Dent Aviator, Jennings Bitter, Lancaster Blonde and Thwaites Wainwright. Quite a few malt whiskies, too. The lounge is comfortable and there's a hall and dining room. Plenty of seats outside and summer morris and step garland dancers.

🍴 Usefully serving tasty bar food all day, there might be lunchtime cold and hot filled rolls and ploughman's, as well as soup, cumberland pâté with port sauce, brie in a crisp thyme crumb with red onion marmalade, home-battered haddock, steak and mushroom in ale or chicken, ham and leek pies, wild and button mushroom stroganoff, daily specials such as morecambe bay shrimps in chive butter, lamb rump with sweet potato mash and redcurrant jus, game casserole in Guinness gravy with a suet dumpling, and puddings like lemon crème brûlée and sticky toffee pudding with hot toffee sauce. *Starters/Snacks: £4.20 to £5.80. Main Courses: £8.95 to £14.00. Puddings: £3.00 to £5.50*

Free house ~ Licensee Clare Woodhead ~ Real ale ~ Bar food (all day) ~ Restaurant ~ (015394) 37210 ~ Children welcome ~ Dogs allowed in bar and bedrooms ~ Open 10am-11pm ~ Bedrooms: £94S(£84B)/£114S(£104B)

Recommended by Mr and Mrs Maurice Thompson, Peter and Eleanor Kenyon, Tina and David Woods-Taylor, Noel Grundy, Margaret Dickinson, N R White, Ewan and Moira McCall, Chris Johnson, James and Helen Read, John and Helen Rushton, Peter and Liz Holmes, Jo Lilley, Simon Calvert, Dr Kevan Tucker

GREAT SALKELD

NY5536   MAP 10

Highland Drove 🍴

B6412, off A686 NE of Penrith; CA11 9NA

Bustling place with a cheerful mix of customers, good food in several dining areas, fair choice of drinks and fine views from upstairs verandah; bedrooms

Although there's quite an emphasis on the enjoyable food in this well run and neatly kept country pub, it has the relaxed atmosphere of a good, friendly local rather than a gastropub. The chatty main bar has sandstone flooring, stone walls, cushioned wheelback chairs around a mix of tables and an open fire in a raised stone fireplace. The downstairs eating area has cushioned dining chairs around wooden tables on the pale wooden floorboards, stone walls, ceiling joists and a two-way fire in a raised stone fireplace that separates this room from the coffee lounge with its comfortable leather chairs and sofas. There's also an upstairs restaurant. Best to book to be sure of a table. Theakstons Black Bull and a couple of guests such as Keswick Thirst Blossom and John Smiths on handpump, several wines by the glass and around 25 malt whiskies. Piped music, TV, juke box, darts, pool, games machine and dominoes. The lovely views over the Eden Valley and the Pennines are best enjoyed from seats on the upstairs verandah. There are more seats on the back terrace.

🍴 Good food in the downstairs bar might include lunchtime filled baguettes, soup, black pudding and bacon salad topped with toasted pine nuts and honey mustard dressing, barbecued pork spare ribs, a charcuterie plate, beer-battered haddock, home-made burger, mediterranean vegetable pasta, gammon and egg, fruity chicken curry and local venison casserole. *Starters/Snacks: £3.95 to £7.95. Main Courses: £6.95 to £15.95. Puddings: £4.95*

Free house ~ Licensees Donald and Paul Newton ~ Real ale ~ Bar food (not Mon lunchtime except bank hols) ~ Restaurant ~ (01768) 898349 ~ Children welcome ~ Dogs allowed in bar ~ Open 12-3, 6-midnight; 12-1am Sat(midnight Sun); closed Mon lunchtime except bank hols ~ Bedrooms: £35S/£65S

Recommended by Chris Millar, Karen Eliot, Henry Snell, Mike and Lynn Robinson, J Crosby, Richard J Holloway, R Macfarlane, Mr and Mrs Maurice Thompson, Lee and Liz Potter

HAWKSHEAD

NY3501   MAP 9

Drunken Duck

Barngates; the hamlet is signposted from B5286 Hawkshead—Ambleside, opposite the Outgate Inn; or it may be quicker to take the first right from B5286, after the wooded caravan site; OS Sheet 90 map reference 350013; LA22 0NG

Stylish small bar, several restaurant areas, own-brewed beers and bar meals as well as innovative restaurant choices; lovely bedrooms, stunning views

If it's more of a casual, pubby visit you want after a walk, then this civilised inn is best visited at lunchtime – but try to arrive early if you want a seat. The small, smart bar has leather bar stools by the slate-topped bar counter, leather club chairs, beams and oak floorboards, photographs, coaching prints and hunting pictures on the walls, and some kentish hop bines. From their Barngates brewery, there might be Cat Nap, Cracker, Moth Bag, Pride of Westmorland and Westmorland Gold on handpump as well as 18 wines plus three pudding wines by the glass, a fine choice of spirits and belgian and german draught beers. In the evening, the emphasis is definitely on the imaginative (and pricey) modern cooking in the three restaurant areas. The bedrooms are beautifully appointed. Outside, wooden tables and benches on grass opposite the building offer spectacular views across the fells, and there are thousands of spring and summer bulbs.

🍴 From the lunch menu (up until 4pm), the good bar food includes sandwiches (which you can take away as well), ploughman's, soup, smoked mackerel pâté, wild mushrooms on toasted truffle brioche, braised beef cobbler, breast of chicken with mushroom sauce, confit duck leg with bean casserole, sirloin steak with pepper sauce, and puddings like chocolate and brandy torte and warm almond and treacle tart with caramel sauce; the restaurant menu is more elaborate with choices like duck breast with roast sweet potato and confit garlic risotto and fillet of halibut with parmentier potatoes, baby carrots and leeks and red wine reduction. They list all their suppliers. *Starters/Snacks: £4.25 to £7.95. Main Courses: £7.25 to £15.00. Puddings: £5.50*

Own brew ~ Licensee Steph Barton ~ Real ale ~ Bar food (12-4, 6.30-9.30) ~ Restaurant ~ (015394) 36347 ~ Children allowed until 6pm ~ Dogs allowed in bar ~ Open 11.30-11; 12-10.30 Sun ~ Bedrooms: £90B/£120B

Recommended by David Field, John Saville, Martin and Pauline Jennings, Noel Grundy, Simon Rodway, Chris Johnson, Mrs Sheila Stothard, Maurice and Gill McMahon, Mike and Sue Loseby, N R White, Richard Hennessy, Howard Kissack, Tim and Rosemary Wells, Mr and Mrs Maurice Thompson, Dr Kevan Tucker

Queens Head
Main Street; LA22 0NS

Lovely timbered pub with friendly bustling atmosphere; bedrooms

---

In a charming village, this black and white timbered pub is especially pretty in summer with its lovely window boxes – and there are plenty of seats to admire them from, too. The low-ceilinged bar has heavy bowed black beams, red plush wall seats and plush stools around heavy traditional tables, lots of decorative plates on the panelled walls and an open fire; a snug little room leads off. Robinsons Cumbria Way, Double Hop and Unicorn on handpump, quite a choice of whiskies and several wines by the glass; TV. As well as bedrooms in the inn, they have two holiday cottages to rent in the village. Residents can get a parking pass from the inn for the public car park about 100 yards away.

🍴 **Meals can be eaten either in the bar or the more formal restaurant: sandwiches, soup, a changing pâté, leek and blue cheese bake, beer-battered haddock, slow-roasted shoulder of lamb, local pheasant and steaks.** *Starters/Snacks: £4.25 to £6.95. Main Courses: £10.25 to £18.50. Puddings: £5.25*

Robinsons ~ Tenants Mr and Mrs Tony Merrick ~ Real ale ~ Bar food (12-2.30, 6.15-9.30; 12-5, 6.16-9.30 Sun) ~ Restaurant ~ (015394) 36271 ~ Children welcome ~ Open 11am(midday Sun)-midnight ~ Bedrooms: £60B/£90B

Recommended by Martin and Pauline Jennings, Christine and Phil Young, Martin Smith, Tracey and Phil Eagles, Peter and Liz Holmes

HESKET NEWMARKET
NY3438 MAP 10

Old Crown 🍺
Village signposted off B5299 in Caldbeck; CA7 8JG

Straightforward local with own-brewed beers in attractive village

---

A new licensee has taken over this unpretentious local – still owned by a co-operative of 147 local people. The own-brewed real ales are still the main strong draw, which on handpump might include Hesket Newmarket Blencathra Bitter, Doris's 90th Birthday Ale, Great Cockup Porter, Haystacks, Helvellyn Gold, Skiddaw Special Bitter, Old Carrock Strong Ale, Catbells Pale Ale and Sca Fell Blonde. The little bar has a few tables, a log fire, bric-a-brac, mountaineering kit and pictures and a friendly atmosphere; piped music, darts, board games, pool and juke box. There's also a dining room and garden room. The pub is in a pretty setting in a remote, attractive village. You can book tours to look around the brewery: £10 for the tour and a meal.

🍴 **Bar food includes lunchtime sandwiches, filled baguettes and soup, evening choices such as a meaty or vegetarian curry, cumberland sausage, steak in ale pie and beer-battered haddock, and puddings like apple crumble and bakewell tart; Sunday roast.** *Starters/Snacks: £3.50 to £4.75. Main Courses: £6.95 to £12.50. Puddings: £3.95*

Own brew ~ Tenant Keith Graham ~ Real ale ~ Bar food (12-2, 6.30-9; not Mon-Thurs lunchtimes) ~ Restaurant ~ (016974) 78288 ~ Children welcome ~ Dogs allowed in bar ~ Open 12-2.30, 5.30-11; closed Mon-Thurs lunchtimes (open bank hol Mon)

Recommended by Tina and David Woods-Taylor, Dr Kevan Tucker, Mike and Sue Loseby, Comus and Sarah Elliott, V and E A Bolton, Stephen Colling

INGS
SD4498 MAP 9

Watermill 🍺
Just off A591 E of Windermere; LA8 9PY

Busy, cleverly converted pub with fantastic range of real ales including own brew, well liked food; bedrooms

---

Both locals and visitors very much enjoy their visits to this bustling inn. The good food is usefully served all day, it's a popular place for an overnight break and they keep a fantastic range of around 16 real ales on handpump. As well as their own-brewed Watermill A Bit'er Ruff and W'Ruff Night, Collie Wobbles, Blackbeard, Dog'th Vadar and Isle of Dogs and other permanent ales like Coniston Bluebird, Hawkshead Bitter and Theakstons Old Peculier, they have guests such as Barngates Westmorland Gold, Hop Back Summer Lightning, Keswick Thirst Ascent, Loweswater Gold, Moorhouses Black Cat, Oakham JHB and Yates Fever Pitch; they have a beer festival in May. Also, scrumpy cider and a huge choice of foreign bottled beers and malt whiskies. The building has plenty of character and is cleverly converted from a wood mill and joiner's shop and the bars have a friendly, bustling atmosphere, a happy mix of chairs, padded benches and solid oak tables, bar counters made from old church wood, open fires and interesting photographs and amusing cartoons by a local artist. The spacious lounge bar, in much the same traditional style as the other rooms, has rocking chairs and a big open fire. Darts and board games. Seats in the gardens and lots to do nearby. Dogs may get free biscuits and water. Some bedrooms are bigger than others but this is a nice play to stay.

🍴 **Popular bar food served all day includes lunchtime sandwiches, filled baguettes and filled baked potatoes (till 5pm), as well as soup, smoked trout salad, garlic mushrooms, various platters, lasagne, cumberland sausage with beer and onion gravy, vegetable chilli, gammon and free-range egg, beef in ale pie, minted lamb henry, daily specials such as tempura prawns, black bean pork and steamed fillet of salmon, and puddings like sticky toffee pudding with butterscotch sauce and Guinness cake.** *Starters/Snacks: £3.75 to £5.95. Main Courses: £8.95 to £13.25. Puddings: £4.25 to £4.75*

Free house ~ Licensee Brian Coulthwaite ~ Real ale ~ Bar food (12-9) ~ (01539) 821309 ~ Children welcome ~ Dogs allowed in bar and bedrooms ~ Storytelling first Tues of month ~ Open 11.45-11; 12-10.30 Sun ~ Bedrooms: £44S/£80S

Recommended by Adrian Johnson, Dennis Jones, Jo Lilley, Simon Calvert, Mike and Sue Loseby, Michael Tack, Mike Ernest, JDM, KM, Pam and John Smith, Michael Butler, N R White, Pauline and Philip Darley, Paul Boot, J S Burn, Andy and Jill Kassube, the Didler, Kerry Law, Tony and Maggie Harwood, Arthur Pickering, Mr and Mrs Maurice Thompson, Brian and Anita Randall

KESWICK

NY2623   MAP 9

Dog & Gun 🍺

Lake Road; CA12 5BT

Bustling and friendly unpretentious town pub with popular food and drink

After a break of a year, the long-serving landlord is back at the helm here. It's a friendly pub with a good-natured atmosphere and a cheerful mix of customers – and dogs are genuinely welcomed, too. The homely bar has low beams, a partly slate floor (the rest are carpeted or bare boards), some high settles, a fine collection of striking mountain photographs by the local firm G P Abrahams, brass and brewery artefacts and coins (which go to the Mountain Rescue Service) in beams and timbers by the fireplace. Hawkshead Lakeland Gold, Keswick Thirst Ascent, Thirst Fall, Thirst Rescue and Thirst Run and Theakstons Old Peculier on handpump.

🍴 **They serve no fried food but the tasty meals include sandwiches, filled baked potatoes, ploughman's, chicken liver pâté, sausage and mash, vegetable curry, chicken stuffed with cheese and wrapped in bacon, steak in ale or chicken, ham and leek pies, their not-to-be-missed famous goulash, daily specials, and puddings such as sticky toffee pudding or jam roly-poly.** *Starters/Snacks: £3.25 to £5.25. Main Courses: £5.25 to £9.00. Puddings: £3.60*

Orchid ~ Manager Peter Ede ~ Real ale ~ Bar food (all day) ~ (017687) 73463 ~ Children welcome only if dining and before 9pm ~ Dogs welcome ~ Open 12-11

Recommended by Phil Bryant, Helen Clarke, Peter and Mary Burton, Nick Lawless, Chris and Maggie Kent, Mike and Sue Loseby, Mary McSweeney, N R White, Fred and Lorraine Gill, Adrian Johnson, Andrew and Kathleen Bacon, Mr and Mrs Maurice Thompson, Michael Tack, Rob and Catherine Dunster

> People named as recommenders after the Main Entries have told us that the pub should be included. But they have not written the report – we have, after anonymous on-the-spot inspection.

KIRKBY LONSDALE

SD6178   MAP 7

Sun ♀ ⇌

Market Street (B6254); LA6 2AU

Nice contrast between mellow bar and stylish contemporary restaurant, good interesting food and several real ales; comfortable bedrooms

---

They've cleverly managed to preserve the character of this friendly 17th-c inn while making it comfortably modern, too. The attractive rambling bar has two log fires and some interesting seats from pews to armchairs to cosy window seats; also, beams, flagstones and stripped oak boards, nice lighting, and big landscapes and country pictures on the cream walls above its handsome panelled dado. There's also back lounge with a leather sofa and comfortable chairs. Jennings Cumberland Ale, Hawkshead Bitter, Marstons Pedigree and Timothy Taylors Landlord on handpump, several wines by the glass and plenty of malt whiskies; piped music. The back dining room is very up to date: comfortable tall-backed seats and tables on woodstrip flooring, a clean-cut cream and red décor with a modicum of stripped stone and attractive plain modern crockery. It's an unusual-looking building with its upper floors supported by three sturdy pillars above the pavement and a modest front door.

🍴 At lunchtime, the well liked bar food includes sandwiches, soup, chicken livers and mushrooms on toasted brioche, home-cooked honey-roast ham with free-range egg, pork and leek sausages with red onion gravy, cheese pie with ratatouille and braised oxtail in port; evening dishes such as morecambe bay mussels in coconut milk, chilli and coriander, mascarpone and blue cheese risotto with candied beetroot, rabbit terrine with rhubarb jelly, a trio of local lamb, scallops with black pudding and bacon, and puddings like white chocolate and vanilla crème brûlée with crisp honeycomb and poached pear in red wine with greek yoghurt. *Starters/Snacks: £3.95 to £5.95. Main Courses: £5.95 to £7.95. Puddings: £4.95*

Free house ~ Licensee Mark Fuller ~ Real ale ~ Bar food ~ Restaurant ~ (015242) 71965 ~ Children welcome ~ Dogs allowed in bar and bedrooms ~ Open 11-11 ~ Bedrooms: /£90S(£110B)

Recommended by Ray and Winifred Halliday, Pat Crabb, Eilidh Renwick, Mary McSweeney, Ian and Helen Stafford, Dennis Jones

---

LANGDALE

NY2806   MAP 9

Old Dungeon Ghyll 🍺

B5343; LA22 9JY

Straightforward place in lovely position with real ales and fine walks; bedrooms

---

Thankfully, this straightforward and friendly local never changes from year to year. It's the perfect place for damp walkers and climbers as it's at the heart of the Great Langdale Valley and surrounded by fells including the Langdale Pikes flanking the Dungeon Ghyll Force waterfall. The whole feel of the place is basic but cosy and there's no need to remove boots or muddy trousers – you can sit on seats in old cattle stalls by the big warming fire and enjoy Black Sheep Bitter, Jennings Cumberland, Theakstons Old Peculier and Yates Bitter on handpump; up to 30 malt whiskies and farm cider. Darts and board games. It may get lively on a Saturday night (there's a popular National Trust campsite opposite). A couple of readers have felt the accommodation side could do with a bit of a tweak.

🍴 Decent helpings of traditional food include lunchtime sandwiches, filled baked potatoes and ploughman's, soup, pizzas, spicy chilli, battered haddock, a vegetarian dish of the day and cumberland sausage with onion gravy. *Starters/Snacks: £3.45 to £6.75. Main Courses: £8.25 to £10.95. Puddings: £4.25*

Free house ~ Licensee Neil Walmsley ~ Real ale ~ Bar food (12-2, 6-9) ~ Restaurant ~ (015394) 37272 ~ Children welcome ~ Dogs allowed in bar and bedrooms ~ Open 11-11(10.30 Sun); closed Christmas ~ Bedrooms: £50/£100(£110S)

Recommended by Dave Irving, Jenny Huggins, the Didler, Chris Johnson, Mary McSweeney, John and Helen Rushton, Mr and Mrs Maurice Thompson, Simon Daws, Ewan and Moira McCall, Tim Maddison

LEVENS   SD4987   MAP 9

Strickland Arms ♀ ◖

4 miles from M6 junction 36, via A590; just off A590, by Sizergh Castle gates; LA8 8DZ

Friendly, open-plan pub, popular for home-made food and local ales

Particularly well run and handy for the M6, this is an enjoyable place offering a good value and extremely popular two-course lunch menu and local real ales. It's a largely open-plan dining pub with a light and airy modern feel, and the bar on the right has oriental rugs on the flagstones, a log fire, Thwaites Original and Lancaster Bomber and a couple of guests from breweries like Coniston, Dent, Hesket Newmarket and Tirril on handpump, 30 malt whiskies and several wines by the glass; staff are friendly and obliging. On the left are polished boards and another log fire, and throughout there's a nice mix of sturdy country furniture, candles on tables, hunting scenes and other old prints on the walls, heavy fabric for the curtains and some staffordshire china ornaments; there's a further dining room upstairs, piped music and board games, and seats out in front on a flagstone terrace. The Castle, in fact a lovely partly medieval house with beautiful gardens, is open in the afternoon (not Friday or Saturday) from April to October. They have disabled access and facilities. The pub is owned by the National Trust.

🍴 As well as the above-mentioned two-course weekday lunch menu, the good bar food includes lunchtime filled baguettes, a soup and a sandwich option, and various salads and platters, as well as duck liver and orange pâté, home-potted morecambe bay shrimps, courgette and bell pepper lasagne, sausages with red onion and wholegrain mustard sauce, beefburger in a warm ciabatta with sweet chilli sauce, steak in ale pie, lamb hotpot with pickled red cabbage, mixed game casserole, and puddings such as rich chocolate and brandy mousse and sticky toffee pudding with butterscotch sauce. *Starters/Snacks: £4.25 to £5.95. Main Courses: £9.95 to £15.95. Puddings: £5.00*

Free house ~ Licensees Kerry Parsons and Martin Ainscough ~ Real ale ~ Bar food (12-2(2.30 Sat), 6-9; all day Sun) ~ (015395) 61010 ~ Children welcome ~ Dogs welcome ~
Open 11.30-11(midnight Sat); 10.30 Sun); 11.30-3, 5.30-11 weekdays in winter

Recommended by Margaret and Jeff Graham, Dr Kevan Tucker, Andy and Claire Barker, Peter and Josie Fawcett, Mr and Mrs Maurice Thompson, Pam and John Smith, Ray and Winifred Halliday, Andy and Jill Kassube, Jo Lilley, Simon Calvert, V and E A Bolton, Revd D Glover, Dr Peter Andrews, Cedric Robertshaw, Tony and Maggie Harwood, Mr and Mrs P R Thomas, Michael Doswell, Paul Boot

LITTLE LANGDALE   NY3103   MAP 9

Three Shires ◖ 🛏

From A593 3 miles W of Ambleside take small road signposted The Langdales, Wrynose Pass; then bear left at first fork; LA22 9NZ

Friendly inn with valley views from seats on terrace, good lunchtime bar food with more elaborate evening meals and several local real ales; comfortable bedrooms

This is a lovely place to stay in a gorgeous spot and customers tend to return again and again. It's been run by the same friendly people for 27 years and has been a Main Entry in this book for all of that time. There's a good mix of customers and a genuine welcome for walkers. With warm winter fires and lovely views from seats on the terrace over the valley to the partly wooded hills below Tilberthwaite Fells, it's popular all year round; there are more seats on a well kept lawn behind the car park, backed by a small oak wood. Inside, the comfortably extended back bar has a mix of green lakeland stone and homely red patterned wallpaper (which works rather well), stripped timbers and a beam-and-joist stripped ceiling, antique oak carved settles, country kitchen chairs and stools on its big dark slate flagstones, and lakeland photographs. An arch leads through to a small, additional area and there's a front dining room. Coniston Old Man, Hawkshead Red, Jennings Cumberland and a beer new to us, Emmerdale Blonde on handpump, over 50 malt whiskies and a decent wine list; darts and board games. The three shires are the historical counties Cumberland, Westmorland and Lancashire, which meet at the top of the nearby Wrynose Pass. The award-winning summer hanging baskets are very pretty.

🍴 Well liked bar food at lunchtime includes sandwiches and filled baguettes, ploughman's, local sausages with onion rings, beef in ale pie, scampi and daily specials, with evening choices such as baked brie with honey and thyme, grilled fillet of black bream with fennel and orange salad, baked field mushrooms with goats cheese, haddock on herb mash with a poached egg and mustard sauce, confit of pork belly with hoisin sauce and stir-fried pak choi, venison stew, and puddings like baked vanilla cheesecake with lemon curd cream and raspberries and roasted pineapple with Malibu syrup and coconut, lime and white rum ice-cream. *Starters/Snacks: £4.25 to £6.50. Main Courses: £7.75 to £15.95. Puddings: £4.95 to £6.50*

Free house ~ Licensee Ian Stephenson ~ Real ale ~ Bar food (12-2, 6-8.45; not 24 or 25 Dec) ~ Restaurant ~ (015394) 37215 ~ Children welcome until 9pm ~ Dogs allowed in bar ~ Open 11-10.30(11 Fri and Sat); 12-10.30 Sun; 11-3, 6-10.30 in winter; closed 24 and 25 Dec ~ Bedrooms: /£92B

Recommended by John and Helen Rushton, Ewan and Moira McCall, Peter and Eleanor Kenyon, John and Sue Woodward, Tina and David Woods-Taylor, Dr Kevan Tucker, T Walker, Mr and Mrs Maurice Thompson, Stuart Turner, Peter Salmon, JDM, KM, Dave Irving, Jenny Huggins

LOWESWATER   NY1421   MAP 9

Kirkstile Inn 🍺 🛏

From B5289 follow signs to Loweswater Lake; OS Sheet 89 map reference 140210; CA13 0RU

Busy popular inn set in lovely spot with own-brewed beers and tasty food; bedrooms

Surrounded by stunning peaks and fells, this 16th-c inn has a really friendly and relaxed atmosphere and a good mix of both locals and walkers. The bustling main bar is low-beamed and carpeted with a roaring log fire, comfortably cushioned small settles and pews and partly stripped stone walls; there's a slate shove-ha'penny board. As well as their own-brewed Loweswater Grasmoor Dark, Kirkstile Gold and Melbreak Bitter on handpump, they keep up to three guest beers and ten wines by the glass. The fine view can be enjoyed from picnic-sets on the lawn, from the very attractive covered verandah in front of the building and from the bow windows in one of the rooms off the bar.

🍴 Tasty bar food includes filled baguettes and baked potatoes, soup, smoked haddock, salmon and prawn parfait, warm goats cheese with sun-dried tomato, olive and pine nut salad, vegetable risotto, steak in ale pie, pork tenderloin with leek, pancetta and stilton sauce, their popular slow-cooked lamb shoulder with redcurrant, honey and red wine sauce, salmon fillet with chilli syrup and garlic and chive crushed potatoes, daily specials, and puddings such as fruit crumble of the day and chocolate and raspberry brownie. *Starters/Snacks: £3.50 to £7.95. Main Courses: £8.25 to £16.95. Puddings: £4.75*

Own brew ~ Licensee Roger Humphreys ~ Real ale ~ Bar food (12-2, 6-9) ~ Restaurant ~ (01900) 85219 ~ Children welcome ~ Dogs allowed in bar and bedrooms ~ Occasional jazz ~ Open 11-11 ~ Bedrooms: £59.50B/£89B

Recommended by Mr and Mrs Maurice Thompson, Sylvia and Tony Birbeck, Martin Smith, the Didler, Mike and Sue Loseby, Edward Mirzoeff, N R White, Dennis Jones, Angus Lyon

NEAR SAWREY   SD3795   MAP 9

Tower Bank Arms 🍺

B5285 towards the Windermere ferry; LA22 0LF

Backing on to Beatrix Potter's farm with a good range of ales; bedrooms

Our readers tend to enjoy this little country pub most outside the summer holiday period when it can get pretty crowded. It's run by a friendly landlord and the low-beamed main bar has plenty of rustic charm, seats on the rough slate floor, game and fowl pictures, a grandfather clock, a log fire and fresh flowers. Barngates Mothbag and Tag Lag, Hawkshead Bitter, Keswick Thirst Blossom and Ulverston Lonesome Pine on handpump (in winter the choice may be smaller); board games. Many illustrations in the Beatrix Potter books can be traced back to their origins in this village, including this pub which features in *The Tale of Jemima Puddleduck*. There are pleasant views of the wooded Claife Heights from seats in the garden.

🍴 As well as lunchtime sandwiches, the well liked bar food includes soup, chicken liver pâté, mussels with chilli, lime, lemon grass and white wine, beer-battered haddock, beef in ale stew, vegetable pasta in a tomato and basil sauce, barbary duck with a sweet plum and ginger sauce, slow-cooked lamb shoulder with mint and rosemary jus, and puddings such as sticky toffee pudding and meringue with mixed berries. *Starters/Snacks: £3.95 to £6.25. Main Courses: £10.50 to £13.25. Puddings: £4.00 to £4.50*

Free house ~ Licensee Anthony Hutton ~ Real ale ~ Bar food (12-2, 6-9(8 Sun, winter Mon-Thurs and bank hols) ~ Restaurant ~ (015394) 36334 ~ Children welcome until 9pm ~ Dogs allowed in bar and bedrooms ~ Open 11-11; 12-10.30 Sun; 11.30-2.30, 5.30-10.30(11 Fri and Sat) in winter; closed one week Jan ~ Bedrooms: £55S/£83S

Recommended by Ann and Tony Bennett-Hughes, Stuart Turner, Peter Herridge, Martin Smith, Jo Lilley, Simon Calvert, N R White, Noel Grundy

RAVENSTONEDALE   NY7203   MAP 10

Black Swan

Just off A685 SW of Kirkby Stephen; CA17 4NG

Bustling hotel with thriving bar, several real ales, enjoyable food and good surrounding walks; bedrooms

This rather grand looking, family run hotel is in a charming peaceful village. It's attractively refurbished but with original period features throughout; the thriving U-shaped bar has stripped stone walls, plush bar stools by the bar counter, a comfortable green button-back banquette, various dining chairs and little plush stools around a mix of tables and fresh flowers. Black Sheep Ale and Best Bitter; John Smiths and guests like Hawkshead Red and Tirril 1823 on handpump, ten wines by the glass and a dozen malt whiskies; piped music, TV, darts, board games, and books, newspapers and magazines to read. Service is genuinely friendly and helpful. There are picnic-sets in the tree-sheltered streamside garden over the road; this is excellent walking country at the foot of the Howgill Fells and there are leaflets describing the walks, their length and their difficulty (or easiness). They also run the village store with outside café seating.

🍴 Using only local suppliers, the very good bar food includes hot and cold lunchtime sandwiches and panini, filled baked potatoes and beer-battered fish, as well as soup, chicken liver pâté with red onion marmalade, black pudding with apple, bacon and creamy pepper sauce, fishcakes on wilted spinach with home-made tartare sauce, vegetarian puff pastry tart, a pie of the day, smoked haddock with a poached egg and drizzle of cheese sauce, daily specials such as moules marinière, chicken breast stuffed with mushrooms and baked with lime, parsley and crème fraîche and venison in chocolate and red wine, and puddings like creamy cheesecake with cherry compote and mint and lime-infused panna cotta with tequila. *Starters/Snacks: £3.95 to £5.95. Main Courses: £4.95 to £14.95. Puddings: £3.95 to £5.95*

Free house ~ Licensees Louise and Alan Dinnes ~ Real ale ~ Bar food (12-2, 6-9) ~ Restaurant ~ (015396) 23204 ~ Children welcome ~ Dogs allowed in bar and bedrooms ~ Live music last Weds of month ~ Open 8am(8.30am Sun)-midnight(1am Sat) ~ Bedrooms: £47B/£75B

Recommended by David Lowe, Margaret Dickinson, Mrs E Appleby, Stuart Paulley

SANDFORD   NY7316   MAP 10

Sandford Arms 🛏

Village and pub signposted just off A66 W of Brough; CA16 6NR

Neat little former farmhouse in tucked away village with enjoyable food and ale; bedrooms

The friendly landlord is also the chef in this careful conversion of 18th-c farm buildings. The L-shaped carpeted main bar has stripped beams and stonework, a collection of Royal Doulton character jugs and some Dickens ware, and Black Sheep Best Bitter and a beer from Lancaster and Tirril on handpump. The compact and comfortable dining area is on a slightly raised balustraded platform at one end, there's a more formal separate dining room and a second bar area with broad flagstones, charming heavy-horse prints, and an end log fire; piped music. There are seats in the front garden and in the covered courtyard. More reports please.

🍴 Using only local meat and game, the tasty bar food includes sandwiches, soup, local black pudding topped with apple and pepper sauce, salmon fishcakes, steak in ale pie, vegetable lasagne, niçoise salad, chicken in a garlic, mushroom, bacon and cream sauce, gammon and egg, slow-cooked lamb shoulder with minted gravy, and puddings. *Starters/Snacks: £4.95 to £5.95. Main Courses: £8.95 to £19.95. Puddings: £4.50 to £4.75*

Free house ~ Licensee Steven Porter ~ Real ale ~ Bar food (all day weekends April-Oct; not winter Tues) ~ Restaurant ~ (017683) 51121 ~ Children welcome ~ Dogs allowed in bedrooms ~ Open 11-2.30, 6.30-11; 11-11 Sat; closed Tues in winter ~ Bedrooms: £45B/£65B

Recommended by Stephen Bennett, Tim and Liz Sherbourne, Mrs Hazel Rainer

SEATHWAITE
SD2295 MAP 9

Newfield Inn 🍺
Duddon Valley, near Ulpha (ie not Seathwaite in Borrowdale); LA20 6ED

Climbers' and walkers' cottagey inn with genuine local feel and hearty food

In a quieter corner of the Lakes, this friendly 16th-c inn has lots of fine walks from the doorstep. It usefully serves food all day for the walkers and climbers who crowd in but still manages to keep a relaxed and genuinely local atmosphere. The slate-floored bar has wooden tables and chairs, some interesting pictures and Jennings Cumberland Ale and Snecklifter and a couple of guests like Dent Golden Fleece and Hawkshead Bitter on handpump; several malt whiskies. There's a comfortable side room and a games room with board games. Tables outside in the nice garden have good hill views. The pub owns and lets the next-door self-catering flats and there's a large area for children to play.

🍴 Using only local farms and suppliers, the traditional bar food includes filled rolls, lunchtime snacks like beans on toast and ham, egg and chips, soup, garlic mushrooms, lasagne, steak pie, battered cod, spicy bean casserole, steaks, daily specials, and puddings like pineapple upside-down cake and pear and chocolate crumble. *Starters/Snacks: £3.95 to £5.50. Main Courses: £5.95 to £16.95. Puddings: £3.95 to £4.45*

Free house ~ Licensee Paul Batten ~ Real ale ~ Bar food (all day) ~ Restaurant ~ (01229) 716208 ~ Children welcome ~ Dogs allowed in bar ~ Open 11-11; closed evenings 25 and 26 Dec

Recommended by David Field, Paul and Jane Walker, Tim Maddison, Mr and Mrs W W Burke

STAVELEY
SD4797 MAP 9

Eagle & Child 🍺 🛏
Kendal Road; just off A591 Windermere—Kendal; LA8 9LP

Welcoming inn with warming log fires, a good range of local beers and enjoyable food; bedrooms

There's a friendly, bustling atmosphere and a welcoming fire under an impressive mantelbeam in this little inn that will cheer up even the dreariest of days. The roughly L-shaped flagstoned main area has plenty of separate parts to sit in and pews, banquettes, bow window seats and high-backed dining chairs around polished dark tables. Also, police truncheons and walking sticks, some nice photographs and interesting prints, a few farm tools, a delft shelf of bric-a-brac and another log fire. The real ales on handpump come from Cumbrian breweries like Coniston, Dent, Hawkshead, Jennings, Keltek, Keswick and Ulverston, there are several wines by the glass and farm cider. An upstairs barn-theme dining room (with its own bar for functions and so forth) doubles as a breakfast room. There are picnic-sets under cocktail parasols in a sheltered garden by the River Kent, with more on a good-sized back terrace, and a second garden behind.

⊞ As well as their popular lunch for a fiver (not Sundays), the enjoyable bar food includes sandwiches, soup, thai salmon fishcakes with chilli and basil dip, chicken liver pâté, vegetable or steak in ale pies, gammon with egg and pineapple, lamb hotpot, chicken wrapped in bacon in a barbecue sauce topped with cheese, lamb shank with redcurrant, thyme and red wine, and puddings. *Starters/Snacks: £4.95 to £7.95. Main Courses: £8.95 to £17.95. Puddings: £4.75 to £5.95*

Free house ~ Licensees Richard and Denise Coleman ~ Real ale ~ Bar food (12-2.30, 6-9) ~ Restaurant ~ (01539) 821320 ~ Children welcome ~ Dogs allowed in bar ~ Open 11-11 ~ Bedrooms: £45S/£65S

Recommended by Tony and Maggie Harwood, Mr and Mrs Maurice Thompson, Jo Lilley, Simon Calvert, Dennis Jones, N R White, Russell and Alison Hunt, the Didler, MLR, John Andrew, Roger and Carol Maden, Brian and Anita Randall, John and Helen Rushton, Pam and John Smith

STONETHWAITE
NY2513   MAP 9

Langstrath ◧ ⇤

Off B5289 S of Derwent Water; CA12 5XG

Civilised little place in lovely spot with friendly licensees, interesting food and drink; bedrooms

The hard-working and friendly licensees of this civilised little inn are sure to give you a warm welcome – and many of our readers are happy to return again and again. The neat and simple bar (at its pubbiest at lunchtime) has a welcoming coal and log fire in a big stone fireplace, just a handful of cast-iron-framed tables, plain chairs and cushioned wall seats, and on its textured white walls maybe quite a few walking cartoons and attractive Lakeland mountain photographs. Black Sheep, a changing beer from Jennings and a couple of guests such as Hawkshead Bitter and Red on handpump, 25 malt whiskies and several wines by the glass; quite a few customers also drop in for tea and coffee; board games. The little oak-boarded room on the left (actually the original cottage built around 1590) is now a residents' lounge; the restaurant has fine views. Outside, a big sycamore shelters several picnic-sets and there are fine surrounding walks as the pub is in a lovely spot in the heart of Borrowdale and en route for the Cumbrian Way and the Coast to Coast Walk.

⊞ Good bar food includes lunchtime filled baguettes, soup, morecambe bay potted shrimps and welsh rarebit, as well as cheese soufflé, black pudding and dry-cured bacon salad with a honey and mustard dressing, steak and mushroom pudding, salmon and smoked haddock fishcakes with tartare sauce, lentil and sunblush tomato cottage pie topped with cheesy mash, corn-fed chicken with pancetta and a lemon and thyme dressing, slow-cooked lamb with carrot and swede mash and red wine gravy, daily specials, and puddings like vanilla crème brûlée and sticky toffee pudding with butterscotch sauce. *Starters/Snacks: £4.25 to £6.00. Main Courses: £9.50 to £15.50. Puddings: £4.25 to £5.00*

Free house ~ Licensees Sara and Mike Hodgson ~ Real ale ~ Bar food (12-2.15, 6-9; not Mon or mid-Nov to mid-Feb) ~ Restaurant ~ (017687) 77239 ~ no children under 6 in bedrooms ~ Dogs allowed in bedrooms ~ Open 12.30-10.30(10 Sun); closed Mon all year and from mid-Nov to mid-Feb ~ Bedrooms: /£85S(£90B)

Recommended by Dave Wright, Steve Kirby, Simon Daws, Jonathan Lane, Arthur Pickering

TALKIN
NY5457   MAP 10

Blacksmiths Arms ♀ ⇤

Village signposted from B6413 S of Brampton; CA8 1LE

Neatly kept; welcoming and a nice place to stay

There are several neatly kept carpeted rooms in this pleasant village inn – and the bars are a popular place for a drink or meal after enjoying one of the surrounding walks. The warm lounge on the right has a log fire, upholstered banquettes, tables and chairs, and country prints and other pictures on the walls. The restaurant to the left is attractive, there's a long lounge opposite the bar with smaller round tables, and another room up a couple of steps at the back. Black Sheep, Brampton Best, Caledonian Deuchars IPA and Yates Bitter on handpump, 20 wines by the glass and 30 malt whiskies; piped music. There are a couple of picnic-sets outside the front door with more in the back garden.

🍴 As well as lunchtime sandwiches, toasties and filled baked potatoes, the reasonably priced, pubby bar food might include soup, deep-fried mushrooms with garlic dip, mushroom stroganoff, sweet and sour chicken, steak and kidney pie, scampi, salmon in a parsley and lemon sauce, loin of lamb in a creamy mint sauce, daily specials, puddings, and Sunday roast beef. *Starters/Snacks: £3.75 to £4.95. Main Courses: £5.75 to £15.95. Puddings: £2.95 to £4.95*

Free house ~ Licensees Donald and Anne Jackson ~ Real ale ~ Bar food (12-2, 6-9) ~ Restaurant ~ (016977) 3452 ~ Children welcome ~ Open 12-3, 6-midnight ~ Bedrooms: £40S/£65S

Recommended by Dr Kevan Tucker, Alan Thwaite, Alistair and Kay Butler, Mike and Lynn Robinson, Barry and Anne, Michael Sargent

THRELKELD
NY3225 MAP 9

Horse & Farrier 🍺
A66 Penrith—Keswick; CA12 4SQ

Well run 17th-c fell-foot dining pub with good food and drinks; bedrooms

The views from this attractive white-painted inn are smashing – up to Blease and Gategill fells or over to Clough Head behind the houses opposite; there are good walks straight from the village. The neat, mainly carpeted bar has sturdy farmhouse and other nice tables, seats from comfortably padded ones to pubby chairs and from stools to bigger housekeeper's chairs and wall settles, country pictures on its white walls, one or two stripped beams and some flagstones. Jennings Bitter, Cumberland and Sneck Lifter and a couple of seasonal guests on handpump, several wines by the glass and winter open fires; friendly, efficient service. The partly stripped stone restaurant is smart and more formal, with quite close-set tables. They have good disabled access and facilities, and a few picnic-sets outside. If you plan to stay, the rooms in the inn itself are the best bet.

🍴 Decent bar food includes lunchtime sandwiches, soup, a curry of the day, fresh battered cod, mediterranean vegetable lasagne, gammon and pineapple, and steak and kidney pie; more elaborate choices also, such as duck liver pâté, field mushroom filled with ratatouille topped with creamy blue cheese, pork belly on grain mustard mash with apple sage and spring onion sauce, slow-braised lamb shoulder with redcurrant and mint sauce, and seared yellow fin tuna with fennel risotto and salsa, and puddings. *Starters/Snacks: £4.50 to £5.95. Main Courses: £6.95 to £8.95. Puddings: £3.95 to £4.25*

Jennings (Marstons) ~ Lease Ian Court ~ Real ale ~ Bar food (12-2, 5-9 (all day July-Nov); all day Fri-Sun) ~ Restaurant ~ (017687) 79688 ~ Children welcome ~ Dogs allowed in bar and bedrooms ~ Open 7.30am(11 Sun)-midnight ~ Bedrooms: £40B/£80B

Recommended by Tina and David Woods-Taylor, Dr Kevan Tucker, Mary M Grimshaw, Steve Godfrey, Ian and Jane Irving, Peter and Mary Burton

ULVERSTON
SD3177 MAP 7

Bay Horse 🍴🍷 🛏
Canal Foot signposted off A590 and then you wend your way past the huge Glaxo factory; LA12 9EL

Civilised waterside hotel at its most relaxed at lunchtime, with super food, wine and beer; a nice, smart place to stay

They usefully open at 9am for morning coffee and some food is served almost all day in this civilised hotel. It's at its most informal at lunchtime and the bar has a relaxed atmosphere despite its smart furnishings: attractive wooden armchairs, some pale green plush built-in wall banquettes, glossy hardwood traditional tables, blue plates on a delft shelf, a huge stone horse's head and black beams and props with lots of horsebrasses. Magazines are dotted about, there's an open fire in the handsomely marbled grey slate fireplace and decently reproduced piped music; board games. Jennings Cocker Hoop and Cumberland and Wychwood Dirty Tackle on handpump, several wines by the glass (champagne, too) from a carefully chosen and interesting wine list and ten malt whiskies. The conservatory restaurant has fine views over Morecambe Bay (as do the bedrooms) and there are some seats out on the terrace. More reports please.

🍽 Good lunchtime food served in the bar (main meals till 2, snacks till 6) includes hot and cold sandwiches, filled baked potatoes, soup, steak and kidney pie and lamb shank braised with orange and ginger, with evening choices like button mushrooms in a tomato, cream and brandy sauce on a peanut butter croûton, chicken liver pâté with cranberry and ginger purée and a tomato and orange salad, baked courgettes with feta cheese, spinach and macadamia nuts and a gruyère and crème fraîche sauce and smoked haddock, prawn and leek pie; puddings such as dark chocolate praline terrine with Frangelico (hazelnut liqueur) custard and cape brandy pudding, and they also offer two- and three-course set menus.

Free house ~ Licensee Robert Lyons ~ Real ale ~ Bar food (12-6 (2 in conservatory restaurant, 4 Mon), 7-8.30) ~ Restaurant ~ (01229) 583972 ~ Children must be over 9 in evening restaurant and if staying overnight in peak season ~ Dogs allowed in bar and bedrooms ~ Open 9am-11(10.30 Sun) ~ Bedrooms: £80B/£120B

Recommended by BOB, John and Sylvia Harrop

Farmers Arms 🍽 ♀ 🍺
Market Place; LA12 7BA

Attractively modernised town pub with quickly changing real ales, a dozen wines by the glass and good food

The atmosphere in this straightforward-looking but flourishing town pub is always lively and friendly and there's a really good mix of customers of all ages. The front bar is appealingly modernised but the original fireplace and timbers blend in well with the more contemporary furnishings – mostly wicker chairs on one side and comfortable sofas on the other; the overall effect is rather unusual, but somehow it still feels like a proper village pub. A table by the fire has newspapers, glossy magazines and local information, and a second smaller bar counter leads into a big raftered eating area. Coniston Bluebird, Courage Directors, Hawkshead Bitter, Stringers Best and Theakstons Best on handpump, a dozen wines by the glass, and piped music. In front is a very attractive terrace with outdoor heaters, plenty of wooden tables looking on to the market cross, and lots of colourful plants in tubs and hanging baskets. If something's happening in town, the pub is usually a part of it and they can be busy on Thursday market day.

🍽 Reasonably priced enjoyable bar food includes sandwiches, soup, garlic mushrooms on toasted bloomer with stilton, deep-fried whitebait, sharing platters of meats, cheeses and seafood, mushroom and butter bean balti, home-made burger with bacon, stilton and honey, cumberland sausage with onion gravy, cajun chicken with cream, onions and mushrooms, beef and mushroom in ale pie, mexican salmon with nachos, salsa and sour cream, duck breast on black pudding mash with red wine jus, and puddings.
Starters/Snacks: £3.95 to £5.95. Main Courses: £8.95 to £12.95. Puddings: £3.00 to £4.25

Free house ~ Licensee Roger Chattaway ~ Real ale ~ Bar food (11-3, 5-8) ~ Restaurant ~ (01229) 584469 ~ Children allowed during food service ~ Open 9am-midnight; 10am-11pm Sun

Recommended by Jo Lilley, Simon Calvert, Dr Peter Andrews, Karen Eliot, Maurice and Gill McMahon

WINSTER   SD4193 MAP 9

Brown Horse
A5074 S of Windermere; LA23 3NR

Welcoming bar, smarter restaurant and informal atmosphere, super food using own estate produce, real ales, good wines and seats outside; bedrooms

Many of the customers in this bustling dining pub are here to enjoy the exceptional food but there's a proper public bar, too. This has a relaxed atmosphere, beams and some half-panelling, stools and a mix of wooden chairs around pubby tables (each with a lit candle), a woodburning stove in a little stone fireplace, and high bar chairs by the counter where they keep Coniston Bluebird, Lancaster Amber and Moorhouses Bitter or Timothy Taylors Landlord on handpump, a dozen good wines by the glass and damson gin. The restaurant has a relaxed, informal atmosphere, high-backed leather dining chairs around attractive light and dark wood tables, more candles and fresh flowers. Piped music, darts and board games. There's a front terrace with solid tables and chairs. We have not heard from readers who have stayed here but expect this to be a fine place to spend some time. They also have a farm shop selling their own estate produce.

The free-range meat and poultry used in the first-rate cooking comes from their own estate and they grow their own fruit, vegetables and salad: sandwiches, soup, home-cured ham hock and egg terrine with piccalilli and crispy flat bread, serrano ham with a salad of olives, melon and manchego, black pudding with candied apple and home-cured bacon salad, trio of sausages with bubble and squeak, red onions and cider gravy, roasted pepper, red onion and sunblush tomato tart with a brie and pine nut crust, cod, smoked haddock and salmon pie with a tarragon potato cake, chicken breast with a broth of puy lentils, bacon, herbs and new potatoes, and puddings. Starters/Snacks: £3.95 to £6.95. Main Courses: £9.95 to £17.95. Puddings: £3.50 to £5.95

Free house ~ Licensees Karen and Steve Edmondson ~ Real ale ~ Bar food (12-2, 6-9) ~ Restaurant ~ (015394) 43443 ~ Children welcome ~ Dogs allowed in bar ~ Open 11-11(10.30 Sun) ~ Bedrooms: /£80S

Recommended by Tina and David Woods-Taylor, Christopher Mobbs, Jane and Alan Bush, Michael Tack

YANWATH   NY5128   MAP 9

Gate Inn 🍴 🍷

2.25 miles from M6 junction 40; A66 towards Brough, then right on A6, right on B5320, then follow village signpost; CA10 2LF

CUMBRIA DINING PUB OF THE YEAR

Emphasis on imaginative food but with local beers and thoughtful wines, a pubby atmosphere and warm welcome from helpful staff

If you're on the M6 and fancy a civilised break, then you'd be hard pushed to find a better place to take one than this immaculately kept 17th-c inn. Of course many customers are here to enjoy the highly thought-of food but there is a proper bar of charming antiquity and you can be sure of a friendly welcome. The cosy bar has country pine and dark wood furniture, lots of brasses on the beams, church candles on all the tables and a good log fire in the attractive stone inglenook. Hesket Newmarket Doris's 90th Birthday Ale, Keswick Thirst Run and a changing beer from Tirril on handpump, a dozen wines by the glass, quite a few malt whiskies and Weston's Old Rosie cider. Two restaurant areas have oak floors, panelled oak walls and heavy beams; piped music. There are seats on the terrace and in the garden.

At lunchtime, the excellent food includes sandwiches, soup, a platter of fish, cheese and meat with chutney and pickles, queen scallops marinated in citrus juices, vodka, tomatoes and red onion, beer-battered fresh fish, mushroom, pea and broad bean risotto, mutton and black pudding hotpot and venison burger with fig and elderflower relish, with evening dishes like curried crab chowder, steamed scottish mussels, smoked chicken and tiger prawn fricassée with wild mushrooms, chilli hazelnuts and egg noodles, galloway beef fillet in tamari marinade with a warm salad of beetroot, chard and courgette, pork belly with a warm salad of pak choi, beansprouts and sugar snap and spring onion sauce, and puddings like marmalade cheesecake with fresh berry compote and chantilly cream and sticky date pudding with toffee sauce and home-made vanilla ice-cream. Starters/Snacks: £4.50 to £8.95. Main Courses: £7.95 to £15.00. Puddings: £5.95 to £7.95

Free house ~ Licensee Matt Edwards ~ Real ale ~ Bar food (12-2.30, 6-9) ~ Restaurant ~ (01768) 862386 ~ Children welcome ~ Dogs allowed in bar ~ Open 12-11

Recommended by Philip and Jude Simmons, Michael and Maggie Betton, Phil Bryant, Tracey and Stephen Groves, Dave Braisted, J S Burn, Mrs M Cohen, Pauline and Philip Darley, Dr and Mrs A K Clarke, Barry and Anne, Sylvia and Tony Birbeck, Mrs C Farley, Peter and Eleanor Kenyon

LUCKY DIP

Besides the fully inspected pubs, you might like to try these Lucky Dips recommended to us and described by readers (if you do, please send us reports: feedback@goodguides.com).

ALSTON [NY7146]

Alston House CA9 3RN [Townfoot]: Comfortable pub/hotel, friendly and relaxed, with a welcome for walkers, well kept beers inc local Hesket Newmarket, decent wines by the glass, enjoyable fresh local home cooking, fireside easy chairs, pine tables in pubby dining area; children and dogs welcome (friendly pub spaniel), bedrooms *(Marcus Byron)*

Cumberland CA9 3HX [Townfoot]: Bustling local popular with walkers and motorcyclists, three changing ales, three ciders, friendly staff, enjoyable pub food; terrace with great views from picnic-sets, quoits pitch, good value bedrooms *(Mr and Mrs Maurice Thompson, R T and J C Moggridge)*

AMBLESIDE [NY4008]

☆ *Kirkstone Pass Inn* LA22 9LQ [A592 N of Troutbeck]: Lakeland's highest pub, in grand scenery, hiker-friendly décor of flagstones, stripped stone and dark beams and furniture, lots of old photographs and bric-a-brac, open fires, cheap standard food all day from 9.30, changing ales such as Hesket Newmarket Kirkstone Pass and Tirril Old Faithful and Red Screes, hot drinks, daily papers, games and books; soft piped music, they may try to keep your credit card while you eat; well behaved children and dogs welcome, tables outside with incredible views to Windermere, camping field next door, three bedrooms, open all day *(Helen Clarke, Dennis Jones, R Butt, Tim and Rosemary Wells, Mike Wignall, Vicky Sherwood, LYM, N R White)*

Queens LA22 9BU [Market Place]: Roomy hotel bar with dining area, half a dozen mainly local ales such as Hawkshead and Yates all helpfully described, inexpensive generous food, friendly service; bedrooms *(Chris Johnson, Mr and Mrs Maurice Thompson, Dr and Mrs Jackson)*

Royal Oak LA22 9BU [Market Place]: Busy two-room beamed local, three Keswick ales, friendly staff; courtyard tables *(Mr and Mrs Maurice Thompson)*

Unicorn LA22 9DT [North Rd]: Bustling backstreet beamed local with plenty of atmosphere, excellent staff, well kept Robinsons, decent bar food, coal fire; regular live music; dogs welcome in bar, six good value bedrooms (two sharing bath), good breakfast *(Chris Johnson, Dr and Mrs Jackson, V and E A Bolton)*

☆ *Wateredge* LA22 0EP [Borrans Rd]: Lovely spot with sizeable garden running down to the edge of Windermere, lots of tables out here, same splendid view through big windows in much-modernised bar, cheerful staff, ales from Barngates, Theakstons and Tirril, several wines by the glass, wide choice of enjoyable if not cheap food till 9pm, cosy beamed area down steps with fireside sofa;

piped music; children welcome in eating areas, open all day, comfortable bedrooms *(LYM, Margaret and Jeff Graham, John and Sylvia Harrop, Chris Johnson, John Butterfield)*

APPLEBY [NY6819]

☆ *Royal Oak* CA16 6UN [B6542/Bongate]: Attractive old beamed and timbered coaching inn doing well under current licensees, promptly served popular bar food (all day Sun), well kept ales such as Black Sheep, Hawkshead and Jennings, friendly young staff, log fire in panelled bar, armchair lounge with carved settle, traditional snug, nicely refurbished dining room; piped music; children and dogs welcome, terrace tables, good-sized bedrooms, good breakfast, open all day *(LYM, Mr and Mrs Staples, Michael Lamm, Chris Smith, Jane and Martin Bailey)*

ARMATHWAITE [NY5045]

☆ *Fox & Pheasant* CA4 9PY: Friendly newish landlady in spotless and attractive Victorian coaching inn dating from 18th c, River Eden views, Robinsons ales, decent wines by the glass, sensibly short choice of good reasonably priced fresh food, inglenook log fire in main beamed and flagstoned bar, another in second bar, charming small dining room; picnic-sets outside, comfortable bedrooms *(W M Lien)*

ASKHAM [NY5123]

Queens Head CA10 2PF [lower green; off A6 or B5320 S of Penrith]: Two-room lounge with log fires, lots of beams, copper and brass, enjoyable good value food, Black Sheep and Lancaster ales, wide choice of wines, friendly staff, nice local feel; children welcome, pleasant garden; bedrooms comfortable with creaking floorboards, good breakfast *(Margaret Dickinson, LYM)*

BAMPTON GRANGE [NY5218]

☆ *Crown & Mitre* CA10 2QR: Comfortable and welcoming with enjoyable generous local food (steaks particularly good), friendly helpful staff, Black Sheep and local guest beers, fresh modern décor with some leather chairs, sofas and log fire, smaller bar with pool, stripped wood furniture in cheerful red-walled dining room; eight well refurbished bedrooms *(Dr Kevan Tucker, David and Katharine Cooke)*

BARBON [SD6282]

☆ *Barbon Inn* LA6 2LJ [off A683 Kirkby Lonsdale—Sedbergh]: Charmingly set fell-foot village inn, civilised and comfortable, with warmly welcoming landlord and chatty staff, good well priced food from baguettes up inc nice vegetarian options, changing ales such as Barngates Westmorland Gold and Marstons Pedigree, good wine choice, blazing log fire, some sofas, armchairs and antique carved settles, attractive restaurant; children and dogs welcome, sheltered pretty garden, good walks, refurbished bedrooms

(LYM, Dr Kevan Tucker, Chris and Meredith Owen, Tony and Maggie Harwood, Michael Doswell)

BARDSEA [SD3074]

☆ ***Bradylls Arms*** LA12 9QT [Main St]: Enjoyable food inc fresh seafood and some particularly good authentic portuguese specialities (portuguese night Tues), nice sandwiches too, good choice of locally brewed ales and of wines, good coffee, welcoming relaxed atmosphere, plush seating and some stripped stone, popular richly decorated bare conservatory restaurant with lovely Morecambe Bay views; garden with play area, very attractive village near sea *(John and Sylvia Harrop, BB)*

BLENCOW [NY4532]

Crown CA11 0DG: Friendly quietly positioned little local, bright and well furnished, with irish chef/landlord doing wide choice of enjoyable good value food such as slow-roast beef in Guinness, game and Sun roasts, reasonably priced beer and wine, good service; cl wkdy lunchtime *(Chris Clark, Mike and Penny Sutton, Donald F Cameron)*

BOOT [NY1701]

☆ ***Brook House*** CA19 1TG: Converted small Victorian hotel with good views and walks, friendly family service, wide choice of good sensibly priced home-made food inc some interesting dishes, great whisky selection, several well kept mainly cumbrian ales inc Coniston and Yates, decent wines, log fires, small plushly modernised bar, comfortable hunting-theme lounge, peaceful separate restaurant; tables outside, seven good value bedrooms, good breakfast (for nearby campers too), excellent drying room, open all day *(the Didler, David and Katharine Cooke, Derek and Sylvia Stephenson)*

Woolpack CA19 1TH [Bleabeck, midway between Boot and Hardknott Pass]: Last pub before the notorious Hardknott Pass, up to five well kept real ales and by now maybe their own brew, good generous home-made food, woodburner, hunting prints, brasses and fresh flowers; children welcome, nice garden with mountain views, bedrooms and bunkhouse, open all day at least in summer *(B and F A Hannam)*

BOTHEL [NY1839]

Greyhound CA7 2HS: New licensees doing enjoyable proper food, Jennings Cumberland, good wine choice *(Helen Clarke)*

BOWLAND BRIDGE [SD4189]

☆ ***Hare & Hounds*** LA11 6NN [signed from A5074]: Attractive country pub reopened after refurbishment, welcoming young staff, real ales inc one brewed for the pub, enjoyable well executed traditional food, good roaring log fire in small bar, areas off with polished flagstones, some stripped stone; children welcome, picnic-sets at front and in spacious side garden, bedrooms, quiet hamlet in lovely scenery *(Stuart Turner, LYM)*

BOWNESS-ON-WINDERMERE [SD4096]

Angel LA23 3BU [Helm Rd]: More minimalist-style restaurant than pub, but worth knowing for its impressive food and good choice of wines, service is good, too *(Pat and Graham Williamson, Margaret Dickinson)*

Royal Oak LA23 3EG [Brantfell Rd]: Handy for steamer pier, split-level bar with well kept ales such as Coniston Bluebird, Everards Tiger, Greene King Abbot and Jennings Cumberland, reasonably priced food, friendly efficient service, games room; children welcome, tables out in front, bedrooms *(Mr and Mrs Maurice Thompson, Dennis Jones)*

Village Inn LA23 3DE [Lake Rd]: Busy opened-up town pub, good choice of well kept ales inc Black Sheep, enjoyable bar food all day, low beams and red plush banquettes, partitions with some stained-glass, separate restaurant; front terrace tables *(Michael Tack)*

BRAITHWAITE [NY2323]

Coledale Hotel CA12 5TN [signed off A66 W of Keswick, pub then signed left off B5292]: Small old-fashioned Victorian hotel below Whinlatter Pass, two bustling bars, real ales such as Jennings, Keswick and John Smiths, reasonably priced hearty food, friendly efficient staff, good fire, plush banquettes and studded tables, darts and dominoes, big dining room; piped music may be loud; fine Skiddaw views, garden with slate terrace and sheltered lawn, pretty bedrooms, open all day *(LYM, Margaret Dickinson)*

Royal Oak CA12 5SY: Bustling local atmosphere, good choice of enjoyable food (best to book evenings) inc children's helpings, prompt helpful service, four well kept Jennings ales, well worn-in flagstoned bar; piped music, SkyTV; dogs welcome except mealtimes, open all day *(Mike and Eleanor Anderson, Neil Tribe)*

BRANTHWAITE [NY0524]

Wild Duck CA14 4SZ: Family-friendly pub with good value food inc smaller helpings, Theakstons *(Tina and David Woods-Taylor)*

BRIGSTEER [SD4889]

☆ ***Wheatsheaf*** LA8 8AN: Attractive relaxed dining pub with good well priced food from interesting sandwiches (nice breads baked here) to steaks and game, cheerful attentive staff, ales such as Abbeydale, Dent, Hesket Newmarket and Jennings, neat minimalist décor in linked rooms off central bar; pretty village *(Paul Boot, Peter and Josie Fawcett, Margaret Dickinson, Roger Thornington, Tony and Maggie Harwood, Walter and Susan Rinaldi-Butcher)*

BROUGHTON-IN-FURNESS [SD2187]

Old Kings Head LA20 6HJ [Church St]: Smart but relaxed family-run pub with son cooking enjoyable popular food, friendly obliging service, well kept Beckstones and a guest ale, stone fireplace, chintz and knick-knacks, separate games area; big attractive garden behind with covered heated terrace, comfortable bedrooms *(Angus Lyon)*

BUTTERMERE [NY1716]

☆ ***Bridge Hotel*** CA13 9UZ [just off B5289 SW of Keswick]: Popular with walkers (but no dogs), with lakeside and other walks for all levels nearby; although a hotel, has traditional comfortable beamed bar, Black Sheep, Hawkshead, Keswick and Theakstons Old Peculier, straightforward bar food (not Weds and may close if quiet), plush dining room; may debit your card with a steep voidable deposit if you eat outside; children welcome, flagstoned terrace, bedrooms, self-catering, open all day (David and Sue Smith, N R White, the Didler, Paul and Margaret Baker, LYM, Mr and Mrs Maurice Thompson, Clive Watkin)

Fish CA13 9XA: Spacious, light and airy former coaching inn on NT property between Buttermere and Crummock Water, fine views, Jennings ales and guests, wide range of good value food, helpful staff; terrace tables, popular with walkers and anglers, bedrooms (BB, Mr and Mrs Maurice Thompson, the Didler)

CALDBECK [NY3239]

☆ **Oddfellows Arms** CA7 8EA [B5299 SE of Wigton]: Friendly split-level pub with nice spacious feel, particularly well kept Jennings, enjoyable food from lunchtime sandwiches up inc great home-made chips, good choice of wines by the glass, affable landlord, quick pleasant service, fine old photographs and woodburner in bustling comfortable front bar, big back dining room, exemplary lavatories; piped music, games area with darts, pool and TV; children and muddy walkers welcome, open all day Fri-Sun and summer, low-priced bedrooms, nice village (Helen Clarke, Piotr Chodzko-Zajko, Phil Bryant)

CARLISLE [NY4056]

Kings Head CA3 8RF [pedestrianised Fisher St]: Heavy beams, lots of old local prints, drawings and black and white photographs, friendly service, bargain pub lunches, well kept Yates and a recherché guest beer, raised dining area; piped music, TV; interesting historical plaque outside, partly covered courtyard, open all day (the Didler, Jeremy King)

Woodrow Wilson CA1 1QS [Botchergate]: Wetherspoons with fine range of local ales inc two from Geltsdale, their usual bargain food, pleasant raised side booth area; attractive terrace, open all day (the Didler)

CARTMEL [SD3778]

Cavendish Arms LA11 6QA [Cavendish St, off main sq]: Open-plan simply furnished low-ceilinged bar with great log fire (not always lit), Jennings Cumberland and Wells & Youngs Bombardier, helpful staff, extensive range of food, linen napkins, restaurant; children welcome, tables out in front and behind by stream, nice village with notable priory church, good walks, ten bedrooms, open all day (Mr and Mrs W W Burke, LYM)

CONISTON [SD3098]

☆ **Sun** LA21 8HQ: 16th-c pub in terrific setting below dramatic fells, interesting Donald Campbell and other Lakeland photographs in old-fashioned back bar with beams, flagstones, good log fire in 19th-c range,

cask seats and old settles, well kept Coniston Bluebird, Hawkshead and three guest beers, good choice of wines by the glass, good value bar food, darts, cribbage, dominoes, big conservatory restaurant off carpeted lounge, more seating upstairs; children and dogs welcome, great views from pleasant front terrace, big tree-sheltered garden, comfortable bedrooms, good hearty breakfast, open all day (Ewan and Moira McCall, Tim Maddison, Christine and Phil Young, Rob and Catherine Dunster, Maurice and Gill McMahon, LYM)

CROOK [SD4695]

☆ **Sun** LA8 8LA [B5284 Kendal—Bowness]: Good bustling atmosphere in low-beamed bar with two dining areas off, good varied traditional food (all day wknds) from unusual sandwiches to enterprising hot dishes, winter game and lovely puddings, reasonable prices, prompt cheerful helpful service, well kept Coniston Bluebird and Hawkshead, good value wines, roaring log fire, fresh flowers (Sylvia and Tony Birbeck, Mr and Mrs Maurice Thompson, LYM)

CROOKLANDS [SD5383]

Crooklands Hotel LA7 7NW [A65/B6385, nr M6 junction 36]: Best Western hotel much extended from 16th core, pubby bar with good atmosphere, stripped brick and stonework, comfortable chairs and settles, log fires, Theakstons, pleasant staff, snug brick-floored second bar, good value straightforward food at sensible prices in intimate stable-theme carvery, more ambitious evening upstairs bistro, afternoon teas, games area with crafts, shop with local produce and crafts (normal shop hours only); comfortable bedrooms (BB, Michael Doswell)

DEAN [NY0725]

Royal Yew CA14 4TJ [just off A5086 S of Cockermouth]: Busy modernised village local in nice spot, good range of enjoyable food from sandwiches up, well kept Jennings and guest beers, good choice of wines by the glass, cheerful service (Helen Clarke)

DENT [SD7086]

☆ **Sun** LA10 5QL [Main St]: Lively and friendly old-fashioned local with changing range of ales, enjoyable good value walkers' food from sandwiches up, beamed and flagstoned traditional bar with coal fire and darts, lots of local events; children welcome, open all day in summer (LYM, Ann and Tony Bennett-Hughes, David and Sue Smith)

DOCKRAY [NY3921]

Royal CA11 0JY [A5091, off A66 or A592 W of Penrith]: Former coaching inn with bright open-plan bar, Black Sheep, Jennings and a guest beer, straightforward food (can be pricy) from sandwiches up, two dining areas, walkers' part with stripped settles on flagstones; picnic-sets in large peaceful garden, great setting, comfortable bedrooms, open all day (Tina and David Woods-Taylor, LYM, Mr and Mrs Maurice Thompson)

EAMONT BRIDGE [NY5228]

Beehive CA10 2BX [handy for M6 junction

40]: Pleasant roadside pub in attractive village, enjoyable straightforward food inc proper chips, cosy bar, open fire; tables outside *(Helen Clarke)*

ENNERDALE BRIDGE [NY0615]
Shepherds Arms CA23 3AR [off A5086 E of Egremont]: Walkers' inn well placed by car-free dale, weather-forecast blackboard and helpful books, lots of pictures, log fire and woodburner, Coniston Bluebird, Jennings, Timothy Taylors Landlord and guests like Hesket Newmarket, good wine choice, reasonably priced food, panelled dining room and conservatory; may be piped music; children and dogs welcome, bedrooms, open all day (may be winter afternoon break Mon-Thurs) *(LYM, Tina and David Woods-Taylor)*

ESKDALE GREEN [NY1200]
☆ *Bower House* CA19 1TD [0.5 mile W]: Civilised old-fashioned stone-built inn extended around beamed and alcoved core, good fires, efficient friendly staff, well kept Coniston Bluebird, Hesket Newmarket Great Cockup and Theakstons, good choice of interesting food in bar and biggish restaurant; nicely tended sheltered garden by cricket field, charming spot with great walks, bedrooms, open all day *(David and Sue Smith, Tina and David Woods-Taylor, David Jackson, LYM)*

FAR SAWREY [SD3795]
☆ *Sawrey Hotel* LA22 0LQ: Comfortable, warm and welcoming stable bar with tables in wooden stalls, harness on rough white walls, even water troughs and mangers, big helpings of good value simple lunchtime bar food, well kept Black Sheep, Jennings and Theakstons, good coffee, pleasant staff, appealingly relaxed and old-fashioned second bar in main hotel, log fires in both, restaurant; seats on nice lawn, beautiful setting, walkers, children and dogs welcome, good bedrooms *(LYM, Noel Grundy)*

FOXFIELD [SD2085]
☆ *Prince of Wales* LA20 6BX [opp station]: Cheery bare-boards pub with half a dozen good changing ales inc bargain beers brewed here and at their associated Tigertops brewery, bottled imports, farm cider, enjoyable home-made food inc lots of unusual pasties, hot coal fire, pub games inc bar billiards, daily papers and beer-related reading matter; children very welcome, games for them, reasonably priced bedrooms, opens mid-afternoon wkdys, open all day Fri-Sun *(the Didler, BB)*

GARRIGILL [NY7441]
☆ *George & Dragon* CA9 3DS [off B6277 S of Alston]: Small traditional 17th-c inn in attractive quiet village, popular with walkers and mountain-bikers; Black Sheep and guests such as Hop Back Summer Lightning, Jennings Fish King and Tetleys, reasonably priced well chosen wines, good value home-made food inc good local lamb, log fires in flagstoned bar and adjoining stone-and-panelling dining area; pleasant bedrooms, open all day Sat, has been cl winter wkdy lunchtimes *(Neil Kellett, LYM)*

GLENRIDDING [NY3816]
Travellers Rest CA11 0QQ [back of main car park, top of road]: Friendly unpretentious low-beamed and panelled two-bar pub with big helpings of decent food for hungry walkers (all day in summer, from breakfast on), Jennings Cumberland, simple yet comfortable pubby décor; Ullswater views from terrace picnic-sets; open all day Sun and summer *(John and Helen Rushton, Phil Bryant)*

GRASMERE [NY3307]
☆ *Tweedies* LA22 9SW [part of Dale Lodge Hotel]: Lively properly pubby atmosphere in big square hotel bar, warm and cosy, with enjoyable food from pizzas and lunchtime baguettes to some imaginative dishes and Sun roast (which is free for under-8s), four or five changing ales, farm cider, wide choice of wines by the glass, attractively updated traditional décor, sturdy furnishings in adjoining flagstoned family dining room; walkers and dogs welcome, picnic-sets out in large pleasant garden, bedrooms *(Mr and Mrs Maurice Thompson, Malcolm and Lynne Jessop)*

GREAT STRICKLAND [NY5522]
Strickland Arms CA10 3DF: Cosy and civilised old two-bar Eden Valley village pub, good value home-made food inc local specialities, well kept Black Sheep, small attractive dining room, open fires *(anon)*

GREYSTOKE [NY4430]
Boot & Shoe CA11 0TP: Small pub in pretty village by green, newish licensees doing some interesting reasonably priced food inc popular theme nights; on national cycle route, bedrooms *(Mike and Penny Sutton, Angus Lyon)*

HARTSOP [NY4013]
Brothers Water CA11 0NZ [on Kirkstone Pass rd]: Cosy pub with glorious picture-window views across the lake, local real ales, generous food inc breakfast; bedrooms, also bunkhouse, self-catering and campsite, great walks, open all day *(Edward Leetham)*

HAVERTHWAITE [SD3284]
Anglers Arms LA12 8AJ [just off A590]: Busy split-level lived-in pub with good choice of real ales, friendly helpful staff, good fairly priced generous fresh food from sandwiches to steaks, sports memorabilia, separate upstairs dining room, lower area with pool; handy for steam railway *(Mr and Mrs Maurice Thompson, Tony and Maggie Harwood, Dennis Jones)*

HAWKSHEAD [SD3598]
☆ *Kings Arms* LA22 0NZ [The Square]: Busy low-ceilinged bar with traditional pubby furnishings, log fire, Coniston, Hawkshead and Moorhouses ales, summer farm cider, good choice of wines and whiskies, pubby food from lunchtime sandwiches and ploughman's up, side dining area; piped music, live 3rd Thurs of month, games machine; children and dogs welcome, terrace overlooking central square of lovely Elizabethan village, bedrooms, self-catering

cottages, free fishing permits for residents, open all day till midnight *(Peter and Liz Holmes, Mr and Mrs Maurice Thompson, LYM, Ewan and Moira McCall)*

KENDAL [SD5192]

Burgundys Wine Bar LA9 4DH [Lowther St]: Small attractive three-level bistro bar with (despite the name) four ales inc Hawkshead Red, Yates Fever Pitch and two guests, enthusiastic landlord happy to talk about them, bottled imports, ciders and unusual wines, helpful staff, lunchtime choice from sandwiches to light hot dishes; cl Mon evening and Sun-Weds lunchtimes *(Mr and Mrs Maurice Thompson)*

Castle LA9 7AD [Castle St]: Well run bustling local by River Kent and nr castle, well kept Jennings, Tetleys and guests such as Black Sheep and Dent, good value popular bar lunches from sandwiches up, cheerful service; big-screen TV and games in separate public bar; roadside tables *(Mr and Mrs Maurice Thompson, Clive Allen, David and Sue Smith)*

KESWICK [NY2623]

☆ *George* CA12 5AZ [St Johns St]: Handsome old place with attractive traditional black-panelled side room, open-plan main bar, old-fashioned settles and modern banquettes under Elizabethan beams, big log fires, daily papers, four Jennings ales kept well, prompt courteous service, restaurant; piped music; children welcome in eating areas, dogs in bar, bedrooms, open all day *(LYM, Mike and Eleanor Anderson)*

Pack Horse CA12 5JB [Pack Horse Court, off Market Sq]: Extended low-beamed cosy pub in attractive alley courtyard, woodburner, full range of Robinson ales, welcoming staff and locals, enjoyable food in two upper floors, Weds quiz night; open all day *(LYM, Mr and Mrs Maurice Thompson)*

☆ *Swinside Inn* CA12 5UE [Newlands Valley, just SW]: Brilliant peaceful valley setting, long brightly busy bar with Jennings Cumberland, Theakstons Best and a guest beer, friendly staff, quick generous basic food at popular prices, games area beyond central log fire (two more elsewhere – best atmosphere in original south-end core); piped music; children and dogs welcome, tables in garden and on upper and lower terraces giving fine views across to the high crags and fells around Grisedale Pike, bedrooms, open all day *(Tina and David Woods-Taylor, J S Burn, LYM, Sylvia and Tony Birbeck)*

Twa Dogs CA12 4JU [Penrith Rd]: Jennings ales, quick friendly service, enjoyable home-made pubby food; open all day *(Guy and Caroline Howard)*

LAMPLUGH [NY0720]

Lamplugh Tip CA14 4SB [A5086 Cockermouth —Cleator Moor]: Refurbished by new licensees in dark modern minimalist style, Jennings and local microbrews, enjoyable food from pubby standbys to more interesting dishes *(Tina and David Woods-Taylor)*

LANGDALE [NY2906]

Stickle Barn LA22 9JU [by car park for Stickle Ghyll]: Lovely views from roomy and

busy café-style walkers' and climbers' bar (boots welcome), three or four changing ales such as Barngates, decent good value food inc packed lunches, quick friendly service, mountaineering photographs; piped music – live Sat, games machines, TV; big terrace with inner verandah, open all day; bunkhouse accommodation *(Adrian Johnson, Chris Johnson, Mr and Mrs Maurice Thompson)*

LANGWATHBY [NY5633]

Shepherds CA10 1LW [A686 Penrith—Alston]: Welcoming and cosy open-plan beamed village pub, good substantial home-made food at reasonable prices, friendly efficient service, well kept ales such as Tirril, decent wine choice, comfortable banquettes, bar down steps from lounge, games room; tables and chairs on big back terrace, attractive spot on huge green of Pennines village, play area *(Mr and Mrs Maurice Thompson, Phil Bryant)*

LEVENS [SD4885]

Hare & Hounds LA8 8PN [off A590]: Welcoming village pub handy for Sizergh Castle, with partly panelled low-beamed lounge bar, front tap room with coal fire, pool room down steps, well kept ales inc Black Sheep, friendly efficient service, good home-made pub food, restaurant; children welcome, good views from terrace *(LYM, Mr and Mrs Richard Osborne)*

LORTON [NY1526]

☆ *Wheat Sheaf* CA13 9UW [B5289 Buttermere—Cockermouth]: Nice relaxed local atmosphere, four Jennings ales, several good value wines, good generous home-made food (not Mon-Weds lunchtimes) from sandwiches to fresh fish (Thurs, Fri) inc some caught by affable landlord, neatly furnished bar with roaring fire, smallish restaurant; children welcome, tables outside, camp site behind *(Sylvia and Tony Birbeck, BB)*

MUNGRISDALE [NY3630]

☆ *Mill Inn* CA11 0XR [off A66 Penrith—Keswick]: Partly 16th-c bustling inn surrounded by stunning scenery and spectacular walks, traditional dark wood furnishings, hunting pictures, log fire in stone fireplace, well kept Hartleys, Jennings and Robinsons from wooden counter with old millstone built into it, up to 30 malt whiskies, interesting food from irish chef/landlord, friendly helpful staff, active dominoes team, winter pool and darts; piped music; children and dogs welcome, garden with seats by little river, bedrooms, open all day; please note that there's a quite separate Mill Hotel here *(David and Katharine Cooke, Tina and David Woods-Taylor, Mike and Penny Sutton, J Crosby, Dr Kevan Tucker, LYM, Mary M Grimshaw, S Holder, Robert Wivell, Mike and Sue Loseby)*

PATTERDALE [NY3915]

Patterdale Hotel CA11 0NN: Large hotel's bar popular with locals, residents and walking parties for its generous food, Hesket Newmarket Helvellyn Gold and Scafell Blonde, helpful staff; bedrooms *(Abi Benson, Mr and Mrs Maurice Thompson)*

PENRITH [NY5130]

Lowther Arms CA11 7XD [Queen St]:
Comfortable and welcoming local in
handsome 17th-c building, long bar with
beams, bare boards and flagstones, log fire
and mix of traditional furniture in various
alcoves and recesses, reliable reasonably
priced food, several beers inc Caledonian
Deuchars IPA, Jennings and Ringwood
Fortyniner, good value house wine, prompt
friendly service *(Phil Bryant)*

Stoneybeck CA11 8RP: Roadside pub doing
well under newish landlord; good fresh
interesting food in sizeable modern dining
room, more sparsely furnished bar, welcoming
friendly staff *(Stuart and Alison Ballantyne)*

PENRUDDOCK [NY4227]

☆ *Herdwick* CA11 0QU [off A66 Penrith—
Keswick]: Attractively cottagey and
sympathetically renovated 18th-c inn, warm
atmosphere, well kept Jennings and summer
guest beers from unusual curved bar, decent
wines, friendly efficient service, food from
lunchtime sandwiches up, good open fire,
stripped stone and white paintwork, nice
dining room with upper gallery, games room
with pool and darts; children in eating areas,
five good value bedrooms *(LYM, Pauline and
Philip Darley, Angus Lyon)*

POOLEY BRIDGE [NY4724]

Sun CA10 2NN: Friendly panelled pub, well
kept Jennings range and a guest, good wine
choice, good lounge bar, steps past servery
to bigger bar, enjoyable reasonably priced
pub food, restaurant; intermittent piped
music; garden tables, great views, bedrooms
(Tim and Rosemary Wells)

PORTINSCALE [NY2423]

Farmers Arms CA12 5RW [off A66 at
Grane/Newlands Valley sign]: Smart little
village local with enjoyable food, three well
kept ales, friendly staff *(Chris Evans)*

RAVENGLASS [SD0894]

Ratty Arms CA18 1SN: Extended former
waiting room a 200-metre walk over the
footbridge from the Ravenglass & Eskdale
terminus and rail museum (and right on
main-line platform), well kept Jennings and
Theakstons, good value pub food, friendly
service; children welcome, big courtyard,
open all day wknds and summer *(LYM,
Tim and Rosemary Wells)*

RAVENSTONEDALE [NY7401]

☆ *Fat Lamb* CA17 4LL [Crossbank; A683
Sedbergh—Kirkby Stephen]: Isolated in
great scenery (good walks), with pews in
relaxing and cheerfully unsmart bar, coal fire
in traditional black inglenook range, good
local photographs and bird plates, friendly
helpful staff, wide choice of good proper
food from filled baguettes to enjoyable
restaurant meals, well kept Tetleys, decent
wines; facilities for disabled, children and
dogs welcome, tables out by nature-reserve
pastures, bedrooms, open all day *(BB,
Yvonne and Mike Meadley)*

☆ *Kings Head* CA17 4NH [Pub visible from
A685 W of Kirkby Stephen]: Quaint country
inn with friendly helpful staff, well kept

Black Sheep, Dent and two guest ales, farm
cider and perry, enjoyable food using local
produce from good beef sandwiches up,
comfortable carpeted lounge and bar, hot log
fires, sizeable dining room with shelves of
whisky-water jugs, lower games room;
children and dogs welcome, picnic-sets out
in front, by stream across lane and in garden
with red squirrel feeders, three comfortable
bedrooms, open all day *(Dr D J and
Mrs S C Walker, LYM)*

ROSTHWAITE [NY2514]

Scafell CA12 5XB [B5289 S of Keswick]: Big
plain slate-floored back bar useful for
walkers, weather-forecast board, well kept
ales such as Black Sheep, Copper Dragon,
Keswick and Theakstons, blazing log fire,
sandwiches, afternoon teas; piped music,
pool; dogs welcome, tables out overlooking
beck, hotel with appealing cocktail bar/sun-
lounge and dining room, bedrooms not big
but good *(Dr D J and Mrs S C Walker, BB,
Sylvia and Tony Birbeck, Phil Bryant)*

SANTON BRIDGE [NY1101]

☆ *Bridge Inn* CA19 1UX [off A595 at Holmrook
or Gosforth]: Nice place, up for sale as we
went to press, with relaxed beamed bar and
timbered bar, log fire, some booths around
big stripped tables, Jennings and guest ales,
traditional bar food, darts and board games,
italian-style bistro, small reception hall with
daily papers, comfortable more hotelish
lounge; piped music, games machine;
children and dogs welcome, seats outside by
quiet road, charming riverside spot with fell
views and plenty of walks, bedrooms, open
all day *(R N and M I Bailey, LYM)*

SCALES [NY3426]

☆ *White Horse* CA12 4SY [A66 W of Penrith]:
Friendly traditional Lakeland pub, warm fires
in comfortable beamed bar, little snug and
another room with butter churns, kettles,
marmalade slicer and black range; Camerons
Castle Eden and perhaps a beer brewed for
them, well presented straightforward food;
piped music; children welcome, garden
tables, pretty flowering tubs, lovely setting
below Blencathra (leave muddy boots
outside), open all day in summer
(Graham and Elizabeth Hargreaves, LYM)

SEDBERGH [SD6592]

Bull LA10 5BL [Main St]: Friendly unpretentious
bar in rather rambling hotel, well kept ales
such as Black Sheep, bar food, popular with
locals and walkers; children and dogs welcome,
bedrooms *(Dr D J and Mrs S C Walker)*

☆ *Dalesman* LA10 5BN [Main St]: Vibrant
linked rooms with good range of well kept
ales, good value hearty food (all day Sun)
from sandwiches to aberdeen angus steaks,
log fire, modern furnishings alongside the
sporting prints, stripped stone and beams;
piped music; children welcome, picnic-sets
out in front, bedrooms, open all day *(Mr and
Mrs Ian King, LYM, David and Sue Smith,
Dr D J and Mrs S C Walker)*

☆ *Red Lion* LA10 5BZ [Finkle St (A683)]:
Cheerful family-run beamed local, down to
earth and comfortable, with good value

generous comfort food (meat from next door butcher), full Jennings range kept well, friendly staff, splendid coal fire; sports TV, very busy wknds, no dogs (BB, Arthur Pickering, Dr D J and Mrs S C Walker)

SHAP [NY5614]

☆ **Greyhound** CA10 3PW [A6, S end]: Good value former coaching inn, quickly served enjoyable food in open-plan bar from sandwiches up, more choice in two restaurants, well kept Jennings and up to half a dozen guest beers, good reasonably priced house wines, cheerful bustle and friendly helpful young staff; may be unobtrusive piped classical music, dogs welcome; ten comfortable bedrooms, good breakfast, popular with coast-to-coast walkers (Mr and Mrs Maurice Thompson, J S Burn)

STAINTON WITH ADGARLEY [SD2472]

Stagger Inn LA13 0NN [Long Lane]: Enjoyable food with good choice of wines and good service (Colin McKerrow)

STAVELEY [SD4798]

☆ **Hawkshead Brewery Bar** LA8 9LR [Staveley Mill Yard, Back Lane]: Spacious modern span-roof beer hall, tap for good Hawkshead beer range, local farm cider, good wine and soft drinks choice, helpful chatty staff, long nicely made bavarian-style tables, groups of leather sofas, new oak boards, view down into brewery or over River Kent, food from adjoining café and bakery, T-shirts etc for sale; brewery tours available, open 12-6 (may be later) (Mr and Mrs Maurice Thompson, the Didler, Dennis Jones, MLR)

STORTH [SD4780]

Ship LA7 7HW [B5282]: Roomy modernised beamed pub with glorious view over estuary to mountains beyond, wide choice of good value generous standard food from baguettes up, friendly staff, Marstons Pedigree and Theakstons, decent reasonably priced wines; subdued piped music; children, dogs and walkers welcome, barbecues and picnic-sets out on grass by good play area, bedrooms (LYM, Julia and Richard Tredgett)

TEBAY [NY6104]

Cross Keys CA10 3UY: Friendly chatty atmosphere in comfortable beamed former coaching inn handy for M6 junction 38, promptly served usual food inc good local steaks, Black Sheep and Tetleys, decent wine, coal fire, separate eating area, games room with darts and pool; picnic-sets in back garden, good value bedrooms (John and Bryony Coles, Abi Benson)

TIRRIL [NY5026]

☆ **Queens Head** CA10 2JF [B5320, not far from M6 junction 40]: Attractively old-fashioned linked bars with low beams, black panelling, flagstones, bare boards, high-backed settles and four open fireplaces inc a roomy inglenook, well kept Robinsons, good range of enjoyable fairly priced food, restaurant; piped music and pool in back bar; children welcome in eating areas, bedrooms, open

all day Fri-Sun (M E and J R Hart, Peter Herridge, John Roots, Phil Bryant, LYM, Mr and Mrs Ian King)

TROUTBECK [NY4103]

☆ **Mortal Man** LA23 1PL [A592 N of Windermere; Upper Rd]: This previously popular inn was closed as we went to press (LYM)

☆ **Queens Head** LA23 1PW [A592 N of Windermere]: Interestingly furnished and decorated rambling beamed and flagstoned bar, great log fire in raised stone fireplace, another coal fire, Robinsons ales from counter based on finely carved Elizabethan four-poster, hops and fresh flowers, all-day food (can be expensive), newer dining rooms similarly decorated to main bar; piped music; children welcome, dogs in bar, seats outside with fine view over Troutbeck valley to Applethwaite moors, bedrooms, open all day (Michael Doswell, LYM, Dr Kevan Tucker, Margaret Dickinson, Mr and Mrs W W Burke, J Crosby, Helen Clarke, V and E A Bolton)

Sportsman CA11 0SG [B5288, just off A66]: Small bar and large dining area, standard food, well kept Jennings ales and an interesting guest beer, good wine choice; children welcome, pretty back terrace overlooking valley, open all day (Angus Lyon)

WASDALE HEAD [NY1807]

Wasdale Head Inn CA20 1EX [NE of Wast Water]: Mountain hotel worth knowing for its stunning fellside setting and the interesting Great Gable beers it brews, available in taster glasses; roomy walkers' bar with nice fire and side hot food counter serving enjoyable meals all day (may be restricted winter), decent choice of wines and malt whiskies, striking mountain photographs, traditional games, old-fashioned residents' bar, lounge and restaurant; children welcome, dogs allowed in bar, open all day (the Didler, Tim and Rosemary Wells, LYM, David and Sharon Collison, Simon Daws, Tina and David Woods-Taylor, Tim Maddison)

WEST CURTHWAITE [NY3248]

Royal Oak CA7 8BG: Simple and comfortable, with young chef/landlord doing wide choice of good fresh food using local produce, Jennings ales, good choice of wines with strong australian leanings, friendly landlady, efficient service, family dining area; terrace picnic-sets, open all day wknds (Helen Clarke)

WIGTON [NY2548]

Black A Moor CA7 9EX [Market Hill]: Interestingly spartan and old fashioned, selling just beers and spirits – no food or wine (Helen Clarke)

WITHERSLACK [SD4482]

Derby Arms LA11 6RH [just off A590]: Nicely redecorated family pub, heavy curtains, rugs and dark oak, Coniston Bluebird and Thwaites Wainwright, enjoyable food from sandwiches up, evening entertainment (Ray and Winifred Halliday)

Derbyshire

Outstanding for beer and good value for food are Dead Poets at Holbrook and – brewing their own – the Brunswick in Derby and John Thompson near Melbourne. The John Thompson, a *Guide* stalwart since our very first edition, gains a Place to Stay Award this year. The Old Poets Corner in Ashover is a strong all-rounder, and the Cheshire Cheese at Hope, a lovely place to stay in the heart of the Peak District, gains a Beer Award. Other pubs on fine form, all with worthwhile food, include the smartly upgraded Devonshire Arms at Beeley (now our Derbyshire Dining Pub of the Year), Plough in Hathersage, Red Lion at Litton, Lathkil at Over Haddon, mildly upmarket White Horse at Woolley Moor and Cock & Pullet at Sheldon. Lovers of unspoilt pubs should beat a path to the Barley Mow at Kirk Ireton, the Olde Gate at Brassington or the Quiet Woman at Earl Sterndale. We have not tracked down any new Main Entries here this year, but have found nearly 40 new Lucky Dips. Stars in that section include the Church Inn at Chelmorton, Crispin at Great Longstone, Devonshire Arms in Hartington, Ladybower Inn above the Ladybower Reservoir and Derby Tup in Whittington Moor. The county's two top breweries are Whim and Peak Ales, with Thornbridge rapidly gaining admirers, and quite a clutch of other worthwhile microbreweries.

ALDERWASLEY
SK3153   MAP 7

Bear ★ ♀

Village signposted with Breanfield off B5035 E of Wirksworth at Malt Shovel; inn 0.5 miles SW of village, on Ambergate—Wirksworth high back road; DE56 2RD

Country inn with plenty of character in low-beamed cottagey rooms; good range of real ales, peaceful garden and bedrooms

Six real ales are on handpump at this character-laden tavern, with Bass, Greene King Old Speckled Hen, Hartington, Timothy Taylors Landlord, Thornbridge Jaipur and a guest such as St Petersburg, and they do several wines by the glass as well as malt whiskies. With warming open fires in winter, the dark, low-beamed rooms have a cheerful miscellany of antique furniture including high-backed settles and locally made antique oak chairs with derbyshire motifs. Other décor includes Staffordshire china ornaments, old paintings and engravings. One little room is filled right to its built-in wall seats by a single vast table. Well spaced picnic-sets out on the side grass have peaceful country views. There's no obvious front door – you get in through the plain back entrance by the car park. More reports on the newish owners please.

🍴 As well as sandwiches and home-made crusty rolls, the regularly changing menu offers a wide choice of food with some unusual touches: starters might include carpaccio of beef or beer-battered haggis balls with whisky sauce; main courses could feature curry, or chicken breast stuffed with austrian smoked cheese, alongside classic roasts, steak and potato pie and seafood dishes; while vegetarians have several options, such as homity pie or brie and caramelised red onion tartlet. Desserts might feature profiteroles, banana fritters or bread and butter pudding with custard, and the ice-cream is from the Chatsworth Estate. You need to book to be sure of a table. *Starters/Snacks: £3.95 to £5.95. Main Courses: £8.95 to £22.95. Puddings: £4.50*

Free house ~ Licensee Pete Buller ~ Real ale ~ Bar food (12-9.30(9 Sun)) ~ Restaurant ~ (01629) 822585 ~ Children welcome in designated areas ~ Dogs allowed in bar ~ Open 12-midnight(10.30 Sun) ~ Bedrooms: /£75S(£95B)

Recommended by Richard, Dr S J Shepherd, Richard Cole, Cathryn and Richard Hicks, David and Carole Sayliss, P A Rowe, Annette Tress, Gary Smith, Paul and Margaret Baker, Peter F Marshall, Eric Condliffe, the Didler, Jim Farmer, Alex Harper, Ryta Lyndley, Derek and Sylvia Stephenson, Graeme Askham

ASHOVER
SK3462   MAP 7

Old Poets Corner 🍺 £ 🛏

Butts Road (B6036, off A632 Matlock—Chesterfield); S45 0EW

A fine range of interesting real ales and ciders in simple village pub with enthusiastic owners; hearty, reasonably priced food

A major attraction at this delightfully laid-back and deservedly popular pub is its impressive range of ciders, perries and up to nine real ales, with beers from the pub's own microbrewery, which produces Ashover Light Rail, Coffin Lane Stout and Poet's Tipple; also Timothy Taylors Landlord and several guests, as well as fruit wines, malt whiskies and belgian beers, and there are brewery tours as well as regular beer festivals. The enthusiastic landlord is very keen on music and holds acoustic, folk and blues sessions once or twice a week – posters around the walls list the range of what's coming up, including weekly quiz nights, occasional poetry evenings and morris dancers. With a cosy, lived-in feel, the bar has a mix of chairs and pews with well worn cushions, a pile of board games by a piano, a big mirror above the fireplace, plenty of blackboards, and lots of hops around the counter; piped music; there's also a simple dining room. A small room opening off the bar has another fireplace, a stack of newspapers, vintage comics and a french door leading to a tiny balcony with a couple of tables. The bedrooms are attractive, and they also have a holiday cottage for up to eight people.

🍴 **Good honest bar food, very reasonably priced and served in generous helpings, includes sandwiches and hot baguettes, soup, deep-fried whitebait, a choice of sausages made with locally raised meats, haddock in beer batter with chips and mushy peas, vegetable lasagne and chilli con carne, with specials like fish pie or mussels. On Sundays they do a lunchtime carvery and serve curries in the evening.** *Starters/Snacks: £2.00 to £5.00. Main Courses: £6.95 to £10.00. Puddings: £1.50 to £3.95*

Own brew ~ Licensees Kim and Jackie Beresford ~ Real ale ~ Bar food ~ Restaurant ~ (01246) 590888 ~ Children welcome in dining area until 9pm ~ Dogs allowed in bar and bedrooms ~ Live music Sun and Tues evenings ~ Open 12-11 ~ Bedrooms: /£70S

Recommended by the Didler, Pete Coxon, Peter F Marshall, Dr Peter Andrews, Keith and Chris O'Neill, Sam Frankland, B and M Kendall, Ryta Lyndley, Ben Williams

BEELEY
SK2667   MAP 7

Devonshire Arms 🍴 🍷 🍺 🛏

B6012, off A6 Matlock—Bakewell; DE4 2NR
DERBYSHIRE DINING PUB OF THE YEAR

Contemporary twist to lovely old interior; local beers, good wine list, interesting carefully sourced food, attractive comfortable bedrooms

In a lovely setting in an attractive village in the Peak District, this handsome stone-built village inn was converted from cottages back in 1741 and is on the fringes of the great Chatsworth Estate – you can walk to Chatsworth House itself. Contemporary colours nicely set off attractive traditional features: between black beams, flagstones, stripped stone, traditional settles and cheerful log fires you will find light brightly coloured modern furnishings, prints and floral arrangements. Despite the accent on dining, drinkers are made to feel welcome: six changing real ales will most likely include Peak Ales Chatsworth Gold, Theakstons Old Peculier, Whim Hartington and Thornbridge Jaipur, and they've several wines by the glass from a well chosen list and a good range of malt whiskies, as well as local mineral water. Good modish new bedrooms are comfortable.

🍴 All dishes are cooked to order (so there might be a wait at busy times), and the short but very well balanced changing menu might include starters of crispy king scallop or home-cured jellied ham, with main courses like local pigeon, free-range chicken curry, home-cured belly pork, or roasted brie, mushroom and leek tart. Straightforward snacks and bar food like soup, sandwiches, olives, local bangers, fish and chips, local sausage and mash, and very generous ploughman's are also available, as is afternoon tea (3-6pm). For those staying overnight, there's an extensive breakfast buffet, as well as a full-works breakfast with local produce. *Starters/Snacks: £3.95 to £12.95. Main Courses: £9.95 to £23.00. Puddings: £5.95*

Free house ~ Licensee Alan Hill ~ Real ale ~ Bar food (12-9.30) ~ (01629) 733259 ~ Children welcome ~ Dogs allowed in bedrooms ~ Open 12-11 ~ Bedrooms: /£125B

Recommended by James A Waller, Roger Yates, D F Clarke, Stephen Woad, Bruce and Sharon Eden, B and M A Langrish, Keith and Chris O'Neill, Mike and Sue Loseby, Dr D J and Mrs S C Walker, Paul and Margaret Baker, Dr and Mrs A K Clarke, Richard Cole, Dr S J Shepherd

BRASSINGTON

SK2354   MAP 7

Olde Gate ★

Village signposted off B5056 and B5035 NE of Ashbourne; DE4 4HJ

Lovely old interior, candlelit at night, country garden

A few minutes' drive from Carsington Water, this unspoilt building with mullioned windows has a very inviting garden, with a good number of tables looking out to idyllic little silvery-walled pastures; there are also some benches in the small front yard. It's a listed building so we are sure that the recent opening up of an unused Georgian panelled room will be a gentle improvement. It's still full of lovely old furnishings and features, from a fine ancient wall clock to rush-seated old chairs and antique settles, including one ancient black solid oak one. Log fires blaze away, gleaming copper pots sit on a 17th-c kitchen range, pewter mugs hang from a beam, and a side shelf boasts a collection of embossed Doulton stoneware flagons. To the left of a small hatch-served lobby, another cosy beamed room has stripped panelled settles, scrubbed-top tables, and a blazing fire under a huge mantelbeam. Jennings Cumberland, Marstons Pedigree and a guest from a brewer such as Brakspear are on handpump, and they keep a good selection of malt whiskies; board games; maybe Sunday evening boules in summer and Friday evening bell-ringers.

🍴 Lunchtime bar food includes soup and sandwiches, and liver parfait or warm goats cheese tartlet starters, with main courses like gammon and chips, cheese, leek and potato cakes, and breast of chicken in cajun spices, as well as their popular steak and Guinness pie. The evening menu might add more elaborate dishes such as fillet of bass on fresh samphire grass, red pepper risotto cakes or braised blade of beef. *Starters/Snacks: £4.25 to £5.95. Main Courses: £6.50 to £15.95. Puddings: £4.50 to £6.50*

Marstons ~ Lease Peter Scragg ~ Real ale ~ Bar food (12-2(2.30 Sun), 6-8.45 Tues-Sat; not Sun evening or Mon) ~ (01629) 540448 ~ Children welcome except in lounge ~ Dogs welcome ~ Open 12-2.30(3.30 Sat, Sun), 6-11.30(midnight Sat); 12-3.30, 8-11.30 Sun in winter; closed all day Mon, Tues lunchtime

Recommended by the Didler, Brian and Jacky Wilson, Mike Proctor, Tully, David and Sue Atkinson, David Hunt, Richard

DERBY

SK3635   MAP 7

Brunswick 🍺 £

Railway Terrace; close to Derby Midland station; DE1 2RU

One of Britain's oldest railwaymen's pubs, now something of a treasure trove of real ales, with its own microbrewery adjacent

Well worth seeking out for the range of beers, this former railwaymen's hostelry dating from 1842 offers seven or eight beers from their own microbrewery from just £1.70 a pint. They have a total of 16 or so beers on handpump or tapped straight from the cask –

including changing guests from breweries such as Everards, Marstons and Timothy Taylors. You can do a tour for £7.50 (price includes a meal and a pint). The welcoming high-ceilinged bar has heavy well padded leather seats, whisky-water jugs above the dado, and a dark blue ceiling and upper wall with squared dark panelling below. Another room is decorated with little old-fashioned prints and swan's neck lamps, and has a high-backed wall settle and a coal fire; behind a curved glazed partition wall is a chatty family parlour narrowing to the apex of the triangular building. Informative wall displays tell you about the history and restoration of the building, and there are interesting old train photographs; games machines and darts. There are two outdoor seating areas, including a terrace behind. They'll gladly give dogs a bowl of water.

🍴 **Straightforward and very inexpensive lunchtime bar food includes toasties, home-made soup, chilli and chips, and weekly changing specials such as ostrich burgers, wild boar sausages and chilli cheese burgers (on Sunday filled baguettes only).** *Starters/Snacks: £1.50 to £3.00. Main Courses: £3.00 to £6.00.*

Everards ~ Tenant Graham Yates ~ Real ale ~ Bar food (11.30-2.30 Mon-Weds; 11.30-5 Thurs and Sat; 11.30-7 Fri) ~ No credit cards ~ (01332) 290677 ~ Children in family parlour ~ Dogs welcome ~ Open 11-11; 12-10.30 Sun

Recommended by John and Helen Rushton, Pam and John Smith, Bob, John Honnor, Andy Lickfold, Martin Grosberg, the Didler, Rona Murdoch

EARL STERNDALE   SK0966   MAP 7

Quiet Woman
Village signposted off B5053 S of Buxton; SK17 0BU

Unspoilt, friendly and splendidly unpretentious rural local in lovely Peak District countryside

Reassuringly no-frills and old-fashioned this will appeal to those who like unchanged country pubs. The interior is very simple, with hard seats, plain tables (including a sunken one for dominoes or cards), low beams, quarry tiles, lots of china ornaments and a coal fire. There's a pool table in the family room (where you may be joined by a friendly jack russell eager for a place by the fire), darts and dominoes. Jennings Dark Mild and Marstons Best and Pedigree, and a guest such as Black Sheep, are on handpump. They also sell gift packs of their own-label bottled beers which are Quiet Woman Old Ale, Quiet Woman Headless and Nipper Ale – the latter named after one of their previous jack russells (you can also buy Nipper or Quiet Woman woollen sweaters and polo shirts). There are picnic-sets out in front, and the budgies, hens, turkeys, ducks and donkeys are great entertainment for children. It's a popular place with walkers, with some very rewarding hikes across the nearby Dove valley towards Longnor and Hollinsclough. They have a caravan for hire in the garden, and you can arrange to stay at the small campsite next door. You can buy free-range eggs, local poetry books and even silage here, and occasionally local dry-cured bacon and sausages.

🍴 **Bar food is limited to locally made and very tasty pork pies (not always available).**

Free house ~ Licensee Kenneth Mellor ~ Real ale ~ Bar food ~ No credit cards ~ (01298) 83211 ~ Children allowed in pool room ~ Open 12-3(Sat 4, Sun 5), 7-11
Recommended by the Didler, Dennis Jones, B and M Kendall, Barry Collett, M J Winterton

FENNY BENTLEY   SK1750   MAP 7

Coach & Horses
A515 N of Ashbourne; DE6 1LB

Cosy former coaching inn with pretty country furnishings and roaring open fires

Serving food all day and warmed in winter by log fires, this coaching inn lies within a few minutes' walk of the popular Tissington Trail (which follows a former railway line), best joined at the nearby picture-book village of Tissington. The main part of the building is quite traditional, with flagstone floors, black beams hung with horsebrasses and wagon wheels, and pewter mugs and prints, hand-made pine furniture that includes flowery-cushioned wall settles and exposed brick hearths. There's also a conservatory dining room; quiet piped music, and board games. Marstons Pedigree and a couple of guests such as Derby Hop Till You Drop or Ossett Silver King are on handpump, and the landlord is knowledgeable about malt whiskies (he stocks about three dozen). There are views across fields from tables in the side garden by an elder tree, and modern tables and chairs under cocktail parasols on the front terrace. Note they don't take all major credit cards. More up-to-date reports please.

🍴 Bar food might include lunchtime sandwiches, baguettes and ploughman's, soup, starters such as warmed goats cheese and black pudding stack, cajun spiced potato wedges or the continental deli board with cured meats and baked brie, and main courses like baked loin of cod, sage and rabbit pie with herbed shortcrust pastry, lamb rump steak, and oatcake filled with bacon, black pudding and mushrooms. Specials (featuring fish on Fridays) and Sunday roasts; puddings from the blackboard. *Starters/Snacks: £3.75 to £5.25. Main Courses: £8.95 to £13.95. Puddings: £4.25 to £4.95*

Free house ~ Licensees John and Matthew Dawson ~ Real ale ~ Bar food (12-9) ~ Restaurant ~ (01335) 350246 ~ Children welcome ~ Open 11-11; 12-10.30 Sun

Recommended by the Didler, Brian and Rosalie Laverick, M J Winterton, Ken and Barbara Turner, Mike Proctor, Glenwys and Alan Lawrence, Phil and Jane Hodson

FOOLOW
SK1976   MAP 7

Bulls Head 🍺
Village signposted off A623 Baslow—Tideswell; S32 5QR

A nicely located inn by a village green, with well kept ales and decent food

At the heart of a very pretty village in the limestone country of the Peak District, this likeable place was up for sale as we went to press. It has a simply furnished flagstoned bar where the old photographs on display feature a good collection of Edwardian naughties. Adnams, Black Sheep, Peak Ales Swift Nick and a guest beer are well kept on handpump and they've just over two dozen malts; piped music. A step or two takes you down into what may once have been a stables with its high ceiling joists, stripped stone and woodburning stove. On the other side, a sedate partly panelled dining room has more polished tables and plates arranged around on delft shelves. The west highland terriers are called Holly and Jack. Picnic-sets at the side have nice views. It's in an enjoyable area for a good country walk – from here you can follow paths out over rolling pasture enclosed by dry-stone walls, and the plague village of Eyam is not far away, or you can just stroll round the green and duck pond.

🍴 Tasty bar food includes lunchtime snacks such as sandwiches, hot filled baps and soup, thai fishcakes with sweet chilli sauce, stilton-stuffed field mushrooms, minted lamb casserole and steak, ale and mushroom pie. The evening menu is slightly more restauranty, with starters such as smoked haddock rarebit, duck and mango salad or ham hock and pease pudding terrine, and main courses like venison medallions in cumberland sauce or roast bass with fennel. They do a good value OAP two-course lunch menu during the week. *Starters/Snacks: £4.95 to £5.75. Main Courses: £7.95 to £10.95. Puddings: £4.25*

Free house ~ Licensee William Leslie Bond ~ Real ale ~ Bar food (12-2 (3 Sun), 7-9) ~ Restaurant ~ (01433) 630873 ~ Children welcome ~ Dogs allowed in bar and bedrooms ~ Live music Fri evening ~ Open 12-3, 6.30-11; closed Mon except bank hols ~ Bedrooms: £55S/£75S

Recommended by Sam Frankland, David and Carole Sayliss, Peter F Marshall, T R and B C Jenkins

---

Please tell us if the décor, atmosphere, food or drink at a pub is different from our description. We rely on readers' reports to keep us up to date: feedback@goodguides.com, or (no stamp needed) The Good Pub Guide, FREEPOST TN1569, Wadhurst, E Sussex TN5 7BR.

HASSOP

SK2272   MAP 7

Eyre Arms

B6001 N of Bakewell; DE45 1NS

Neatly kept comfortable pub, with pretty views from the garden

From the little garden by this ivy-clad 17th-c place you look straight out into fine Peak District countryside to the accompaniment of a gurgling fountain. Cheery log fires warm the low-ceilinged oak beamed rooms: the dining room is dominated by a painting of the Eyre coat of arms above the stone fireplace. Other traditional furnishings include cushioned oak settles, comfortable plush chairs, a long-case clock, old pictures and lots of brass and copper. The small public bar has an unusual collection of teapots, as well as Black Sheep, Marstons Pedigree and Peak Ales Bakewell Bitter on handpump and several wines by the glass; piped classical music, darts. More reports please.

🍴 **Bar food includes lunchtime sandwiches, ploughman's and baked potatoes, soup, whitebait, and main courses featuring meat, fish and vegetarian dishes such as venison pie, as well as daily changing specials.** *Starters/Snacks: £4.00 to £6.25. Main Courses: £7.70 to £14.75. Puddings: £4.40 to £4.55*

Free house ~ Licensees Nick and Lynne Smith ~ Real ale ~ Bar food (12-2, 6.30-9) ~ (01629) 640390 ~ Children welcome ~ Open 11-3, 6.30-11; closed Mon evenings Nov-Easter

Recommended by Chris Gallagher, B and M Kendall, DC, Chris Brooks

HATHERSAGE

SK2380   MAP 7

Plough 🍴 ♟ 🛏

Leadmill; B6001 towards Bakewell, OS Sheet 110 map reference 235805; S32 1BA

Comfortable dining pub usefully placed for exploring the Peak District, with good food, beer and wine, waterside garden and bedrooms

A family team run this very convivial dining pub in the scenic Derwent valley, and readers have enjoyed staying here. The fairly traditional neatly kept bar has dark wood tables (all laid for dining), a big log fire at one end and a woodburning stove at the other; quiet piped music. They've a good wine list (with a dozen by the glass), 25 malt whiskies, and well kept on handpump are Batemans, Black Sheep, Fullers London Pride and Wells & Youngs Bitter and a guest such as Timothy Taylors Landlord. The pretty suntrap garden goes right down to the Highlow Brook.

🍴 **As well as lunchtime pubby standards such as fish and chips, ploughman's and pie of the day, the changing menu might include starters like rabbit and bacon terrine or steamed scallops with rhubarb, and main courses such as chargrilled rib-eye steak or lamb cutlets, stuffed breast of free-range chicken, fillet of cod and langoustine or twice-baked blue cheese soufflé. Food is not cheap, and you are advised to book a table.** *Starters/Snacks: £4.50 to £10.00. Main Courses: £10.50 to £19.00. Puddings: £4.50 to £6.95*

Free house ~ Licensees Bob, Cynthia and Elliott Emery ~ Real ale ~ Bar food (11.30-9; 12-8 Sun) ~ Restaurant ~ (01433) 650319 ~ Children welcome ~ Open 11.30-11; 12-10 Sun ~ Bedrooms: £90B/£120B

Recommended by Mr and Mrs Roberts, Barry and Anne, Kevin Thomas, Nina Randall, James A Waller, Tom and Ruth Rees, Brian and Jacky Wilson, Kathy and Chris Armes, W K Wood, Richard Marjoram, Richard and Emily Whitworth, David and Cathrine Whiting, Fred and Lorraine Gill, Paul and Gail Betteley, Michael and Maggie Betton, Mrs R A Cartwright, Bruce and Sharon Eden, John Robertson

Scotsmans Pack 🛏

School Lane, off A6187; S32 1BZ

Cosy inn with decent, good value food

Usefully placed for walkers and near the churchyard containing the supposed grave of Little John, this popular place has a pleasant terrace adjoining a trout-filled stream.

Perhaps the nicest area is on the left as you enter, with a fireplace and patterned wallpaper somewhat obscured by a splendid mass of brasses, stuffed animal heads and the like. Elsewhere there's plenty of dark panelling, lots of hanging tankards, plates on delft shelving and other knick-knacks arranged around the bar, and a good few tables, many with reserved signs (it's worth booking ahead, particularly at weekends). Five real ales, kept under light blanket pressure, feature Jennings Cumberland, Marstons Bitter and Pedigree, and two guests from breweries such as Ringwood or Wychwood; piped music, games machine, TV, board games and darts.

🍴 **Reasonably priced food includes sandwiches, ploughman's, soup, deep-fried brie with cranberry sauce, and main courses like sirloin steak, steak pie, mixed grill, salmon steak, and gorgonzola and walnut tortellini.** *Starters/Snacks: £3.25 to £6.95. Main Courses: £8.75 to £16.95. Puddings: £3.50 to £4.50*

Marstons ~ Lease Nick Beagrie, Steve Bramley and Susan Concannon ~ Real ale ~ Bar food (12-2, 6-9; 11-9 Sat, Sun) ~ (01433) 650253 ~ Children welcome ~ Open 11.30-3, 5.30-11; 11am-midnight Fri, Sat; 12-midnight Sun ~ Bedrooms: £45S/£75B

Recommended by Bruce and Sharon Eden, Carole Hall, John Branston, Keith and Chris O'Neill, Malcolm and Pauline Pellatt, Brian and Jacky Wilson, Barry and Anne, Peter F Marshall, K Almond, Richard Marjoram

HAYFIELD

SK0388 MAP 7

Lantern Pike
Glossop Road (A624 N) at Little Hayfield, just N of Hayfield; SK22 2NG

Friendly retreat from the surrounding moors of Kinder Scout, with reasonably priced food and bedrooms

A nice place to come down to if you've been walking up in the windswept moors or up on Lantern Pike itself, this homely place has been an inn since 1851. The traditional red plush bar proudly displays photos of the original *Coronation Street* cast, many of whom were regulars here, along with Terry Warren, one of its earlier script writers, and Arthur Lowe of *Dad's Army* fame. It's quite possible that the interior, with its warm fire, brass platters in numbers, china and toby jugs, fresh flowers on the tables and counter lined with red plush stools (Howard Town Wrens Nest and Timothy Taylors Landlord, a guest such as Caledonian Deuchars on handpump, and several malt whiskies) hasn't changed much since those days; TV and piped music. Tables on a stonewalled terrace look over a big-windowed weaver's house towards Lantern Pike. More up-to-date reports please.

🍴 **As well as sandwiches, the changing blackboard menu might include soup, spicy chicken wings, chilli, vegetarian dish of the day, braised lamb cutlets with mint gravy, steak and ale pie, curries, and puddings such as sherry trifle and fruit crumble. All dishes are made on the premises, and the menus feature fresh fish and seafood such as lemon sole, sea bream, red mullet and whole lobster delivered direct from Grimsby.** *Starters/Snacks: £2.95 to £4.25. Main Courses: £8.00 to £14.00. Puddings: £3.75*

Enterprise ~ Lease Stella and Tom Cunliffe ~ Real ale ~ Bar food (12-2.30(4 Sat), 5-8.30; 12-8.30 Sun) ~ Restaurant ~ (01663) 747590 ~ Children welcome ~ Open 12-11; 12-3, 5-11 in winter ~ Bedrooms: £45B/£64B

Recommended by Dennis Jones, Chris Brooks, John and Helen Rushton

Royal
Market Street, just off A624 Chapel-en-le-Frith—Buxton; SK22 2EP

Bustling old-fashioned hotel with a good range of real ales

Friendly staff at this traditional hotel serve Hydes alongside four guest ales from brewers such as Bollington, Hornbeam, Northumberland and Saltaire on handpump, and they keep around 16 malts as well as special brandies; they hold a beer festival on the first weekend of October. Inside, some nice old dark panelling recalls the building's former life as a vicarage. Separate feeling areas work their way round a counter and have several fireplaces, bookshelves, brasses and house plants, newspapers to read and piped music. There's a sunny terrace in front. More reports please.

🍴 The good value, very traditional bar menu includes sandwiches, soup, garlic mushrooms, spinach and mushroom pancake, cod and chips, chicken curry, sirloin steak, hotpot, and cheese and onion pie, as well as daily changing fish and vegetarian dishes and a hot pudding. On Mondays to Thursdays there are weekday lunchtime and early evening two-course meal deals, with an additional discount for pensioners. *Starters/Snacks: £2.95 to £4.95. Main Courses: £5.25 to £13.95. Puddings: £2.50 to £3.50*

Free house ~ Licensee David Ash ~ Real ale ~ Bar food (12-2.30, 6-9; 12-9(6 Sun and bank hols) Sat) ~ Restaurant ~ (01663) 742721 ~ Children welcome with restrictions ~ Dogs allowed in bar ~ Live soul music last Fri of month ~ Open 11-11(midnight Sat, 10.30 Sun) ~ Bedrooms: £50B/£70B

Recommended by the Didler

HOLBROOK   SK3645   MAP 7

Dead Poets 🍺 £

Village signposted off A6 S of Belper; Chapel Street; DE56 0TQ

Reassuringly pubby and unchanged, with an excellent range of real ales and simple cottagey décor

Places as simple and unaltered as this atmospheric drinkers' local are becoming hard to come by nowadays. Although there's a range of basic snacks, beer is the thing: Greene King Abbot and Marstons Pedigree are served in jugs from the cellar, alongside six guests on handpump from breweries such as Abbeydale, Exmoor, Oakham, Timothy Taylors, Whim, Hop Back and Theakstons. They also serve Old Rosie and Thatcher's farm cider. It's quite a dark interior with low black beams in the ochre ceiling, stripped stone walls and broad flagstones, although there is a lighter conservatory at the back. There are candles on scrubbed tables, a big log fire in the end stone fireplace, high-backed winged settles forming snug cubicles along one wall, and pews and a variety of chairs in other intimate corners and hideaways. The décor makes a few nods to the pub's present name (it used to be the Cross Keys) including a photo of W B Yeats and a poem dedicated to the pub by Les Baynton, and there are old prints of Derby; piped music. Behind is a sort of verandah room with lanterns, heaters, fairy lights and a few plants, and more seats out in the yard.

🍴 Alongside cobs (nothing else on Sundays), bar food is limited to a few good value hearty dishes such as home-made soup and chilli con carne or casserole. *Starters/Snacks: £2.25 to £2.95. Main Courses: £4.25*

Everards ~ Tenant William Holmes ~ Real ale ~ Bar food (12-2 only) ~ No credit cards ~ (01332) 780301 ~ Children welcome in conservatory till 8pm ~ Dogs welcome ~ Open 12-2.30, 5-12; 12-midnight Fri, Sat; 12-11 Sun

Recommended by the Didler, Kerry Law, Richard

HOPE   SK1783   MAP 7

Cheshire Cheese 🍺 🛏

Off A6187, towards Edale; S33 6ZF

Cosy up-and-down old stone pub, with good real ales, in attractive Peak District village; bedrooms

'A welcoming sight after a walk along the ridge from Castleton' wrote one reader about this very popular 16th-c haunt, which can easily fill to capacity with locals as well as tourists. Parking is limited, so it might indeed be worth arriving on foot: there is a glorious range of local walks, taking in the summits of Lose Hill and Win Hill, or the cave district of the Castleton area, and the village of Hope itself is worth strolling around. The three very snug oak-beamed rooms are arranged on different levels, each with its own coal fire. Peak Ales Swift Nick, and three guests such as Bradfield Blonde, Copper Dragon Golden Pippin and Phoenix Old Oak Black are well kept on handpump, and they've a good range of spirits and several wines by the glass.

🍴 As well as lunchtime snacks such as sandwiches and salads, food includes daily changing dishes such as grilled black pudding with mustard sauce, steak and kidney suet pudding, mixed grill, cream cheese and broccoli bake, roast cod with prawn and dill sauce, and lamb shank in minted gravy; puddings such as chocolate pudding in chocolate sauce or spotted dick. *Starters/Snacks: £3.95 to £5.95. Main Courses: £6.95 to £12.95. Puddings: £3.95 to £4.95*

Enterprise ~ Lease Craig Oxley ~ Real ale ~ Bar food (12-2(2.30 Sat, Sun), 6.30-9 (8.30 Sun); not Mon, Tues evening) ~ (01433) 620381 ~ Children welcome 12-9 ~ Dogs allowed in bar ~ Open 12-2, 6.30-11.30, 12-11.30 Weds-Sat; 12-10.30 Sun ~ Bedrooms: £50S/£75S(£85B)

Recommended by Virginia Williams, Dave Irving, Jenny Huggins, Dr and Mrs J Temporal, David and Carole Sayliss, Chris Brooks, the Didler, Alan Sutton, Peter F Marshall, Malcolm and Pauline Pellatt, Pete Baker

KIRK IRETON   SK2650   MAP 7

Barley Mow 🍺 🛏

Village signed off B5023 S of Wirksworth; DE6 3JP

Character-laden old inn that focuses on real ale and conversation rather than food

Marvellously unaltered over the years, this fine Jacobean house has been an inn since around 1800, and evokes how some grander rural pubs might have looked a century or so ago. With a good mix of customers of all ages and a very kindly landlady, it's a place to sit and chat. The small main bar has a relaxed very pubby feel, with antique settles on the tiled floor or built into the panelling, a roaring coal fire, four slate-topped tables and shuttered mullioned windows. Another room has built-in cushioned pews on oak parquet and a small woodburning stove, and a third room has more pews, a tiled floor, low beams and big landscape prints. In casks behind a modest wooden counter are five well kept, often local, changing real ales mostly from smaller brewers such as Abbeydale, Burton Bridge, Leatherbritches, Storm and Whim; farm cider too. There's a good-sized garden, a couple of benches out in front and a shop in what used to be the stable; and the hilltop village is very pretty, and within walking distance of Carsington Water. Bedrooms are comfortable and readers enjoy the good breakfasts served in the stone-flagged kitchen.

🍴 Very inexpensive lunchtime filled rolls are the only food; the decent evening meals are reserved for those staying here.

Free house ~ Licensee Mary Short ~ Real ale ~ No credit cards ~ (01335) 370306 ~ Children welcome at lunchtime ~ Dogs welcome ~ Open 12-2, 7-11(10.30 Sun) ~ Bedrooms: £35S/£55B

Recommended by the Didler, Mavis Devine, Pete Baker

LADYBOWER RESERVOIR   SK2084   MAP 7

Yorkshire Bridge

A6013 N of Bamford; S33 0AZ

Pleasantly genteel hotel close to the Upper Derwent Valley Reservoirs

This nicely refurbished inn makes a useful stopping point in the dramatic Upper Derwent Valley, and takes its name from the huge reservoir that is close by. Inside, one area has a country cottage feel with floral wallpaper, sturdy cushioned wall settles, staffordshire dogs and toby jugs above a big stone fireplace, china on delft shelves, and a panelled dado. Another extensive area, also with a fire, is lighter and more airy with pale wood furniture, good big black and white photographs and lots of polished brass and decorative plates on the walls. The Bridge Room (with yet another fire) has oak tables and chairs, and the Garden Room gives views across a valley to steep larch woods. Copper Dragon Golden Pippin and Scotts 1816, Kelham Island Pale Rider and a guest such as Peak Ales Bakewell Best are on handpump, and there are several wines by the glass and malt whiskies; darts, dominoes, games machine and piped music; disabled lavatories. More up-to-date reports please.

🍴 **Straightforward bar food includes lunchtime rolls and baked potatoes, and soup, salads, quiche, pot-roasted lamb, steak and kidney pie and a daily changing fish dish.** *Starters/Snacks: £3.75 to £5.95. Main Courses: £8.25 to £17.00. Puddings: £4.50 to £5.50*

Free house ~ Licensees Trevelyan and John Illingworth ~ Real ale ~ Bar food (12-2, 6-9(9.30 Fri, Sat)) ~ (01433) 651361 ~ Children welcome until 9.30pm ~ Open 10-11; 11-10.30 Sun ~ Bedrooms: £65B/£96B

Recommended by Bruce and Sharon Eden, Bob, Brian and Jean Hepworth, Mike and Sue Loseby, N R White, Cedric Robertshaw, Brian and Anna Marsden, David and Carole Sayliss

LITTON
SK1675 MAP 7

Red Lion

Village signposted off A623, between B6465 and B6049 junctions; also signposted off B6049; SK17 8QU

Convivial all-rounder with reasonably priced food and unspoilt charm, prettily placed by village green

Nicely traditional and well run by an extremely enthusiastic and ever-cheerful landlady, this pub has received consistent praise from readers, though note it does get very full at times, so do book if you want to eat here. The two homely linked front rooms have low beams and some panelling, and blazing log fires. There's a bigger back room with good-sized tables, and large antique prints on its stripped stone walls. The small bar counter has very well kept Oakwell Barnsley and Abbeydale Absolution plus a couple of guests such as Adnams Broadside and Whim Hartington, a good choice of decent wines, with a dozen by the glass, and several malt whiskies (all spirits are available as doubles for an extra £1); darts, board games and piped music. Outdoor seating is on the pretty village green, which is covered in daffodils in early spring. A particularly interesting time to visit this Peak District village is during the annual well-dressing carnival (usually the last week in June), when locals create a picture from flower petals, moss and other natural materials.

🍴 **Well liked bar food includes sandwiches and filled baguettes, soup, lambs liver and bacon, steak and kidney pie, cumberland or vegetarian sausage and mash, and specials such as garlic and rosemary lamb shank and simply prepared fresh fish, as well as hot puddings like apple and berry crumble and custard. Unusually, there's an entire gluten-free menu too. It can get busy here – it's best to book a table.** *Starters/Snacks: £2.00 to £6.95. Main Courses: £6.95 to £8.95. Puddings: £4.25*

Enterprise ~ Lease Suzy Turner ~ Real ale ~ Bar food (12-8(8.30 Thurs-Sun)) ~ (01298) 871458 ~ Children over 6 welcome until 9pm ~ Dogs allowed in bar ~ Open 12-11(midnight Fri, Sat); 12-10.30 Sun

Recommended by Maurice and Janet Thorpe, Peter F Marshall, Gary Rollings, Debbie Porter, Mrs Jordan, Richard, WAH, Chris Brooks, Paul and Margaret Baker, Hazel Matthews, Susan and John Douglas, Alan Thwaite, Phil Taylor, Sian Watkin, Dr and Mrs J Temporal, the Didler

MELBOURNE
SK3427 MAP 7

John Thompson 🍺 £ 🛏

Ingleby, which is NW of Melbourne; turn off A514 at Swarkestone Bridge or in Stanton by Bridge; can also be reached from Ticknall (or from Repton on B5008); DE73 7HW

Own-brew pub that strikes the right balance between attentive service, roomy comfort and good value lunchtime food

Named after John Thompson who runs this pub and its microbrewery, and continues to get everything right here as he has done during every year this *Guide* has been published: comments such as 'this pub should never be allowed to close' are typical of many. Everything ticks along in a perfectly relaxed way, with plenty of readers enthusing about the quality of the beer brewed out back here, the tasty good value food, and the friendly efficient staff. Simple but comfortable, the big modernised lounge has ceiling joists, some old oak settles, button-back leather seats, sturdy oak tables, antique prints and paintings and a log-effect gas fire; piped music. A couple of smaller cosier rooms open off; piano, games machine, board games, darts, TV, and pool in the conservatory. They usually serve three of their own beers but may supplement a guest such as Black Sheep or Greene King IPA. Surrounded by pretty countryside and near the Trent river, there are lots of tables by flowerbeds on the neat lawns, or you can sit on the partly covered terrace. Six detached chalet lodges have recently been built in the grounds, and readers have enjoyed these too.

🍴 The short lunchtime menu includes sandwiches, soup, baked potatoes, salads, pasta bake and a roast beef carvery, and puddings like fruit crumble and Mrs Thompson's bread and butter pudding – a speciality of the pub for the past 40 years. *Starters/Snacks: £3.00 to £7.00. Main Courses: £6.25 to £7.25. Puddings: £3.00 to £3.75*

Own brew ~ Licensee Nick Thompson ~ Real ale ~ Bar food (lunchtime only, not Mon) ~ (01332) 862469 ~ Children and dogs welcome in conservatory ~ Open 11-2.30, 6-11; 11-11 Sat; 12-10.30 Sun; closed Mon lunchtime ~ Bedrooms: /£60S

Recommended by the Didler, Gwyn and Anne Wake, Mr and Mrs J T Clarke, Theo, Anne and Jane Gaskin, Rona Murdoch, Pete Baker, Margaret Walster, Pam and John Smith, Audrey McKenzie, Paul J Robinshaw, Yvonne Brown, Dr and Mrs T E Hothersall, Dr S J Shepherd, Barbara Parker, P and I Gowan, Ian and Jane Irving

MONYASH   SK1566   MAP 7

Bulls Head

B5055 W of Bakewell; DE45 1JH

Unpretentious local with very tasty home cooking

An inviting place for a meal or a drink this village local also has inexpensive accommodation. Its high-ceilinged rooms are quite simple with a good log fire, straightforward furnishings, horse pictures and a shelf of china. A small back bar room has darts, board games and pool; may be quiet piped music. Burton Ale, John Smiths and a guest such as Bradfield Farmers Blonde or Whim Hartington are on handpump. A gate from the pub's garden leads into a nice village play area and this is fine walking country. More reports please.

🍴 Bar food (very sensibly priced) includes sandwiches, ploughman's, salads, garlic mushrooms, steak and kidney pie, casseroles and breaded fish. *Starters/Snacks: £3.00 to £6.25. Main Courses: £8.95 to £14.50. Puddings: £4.00 to £4.50*

Free house ~ Licensee Sharon Barber ~ Real ale ~ Bar food (12-2.30, 6.30-9(9.30 Sat); 12-9 Sun) ~ Restaurant ~ (01629) 812372 ~ Children welcome ~ Dogs allowed in bar and bedrooms ~ Open 12-3, 6-11; 12-midnight Sat, Sun ~ Bedrooms: £25/£45

Recommended by Ian and Helen Stafford, Mr and Mrs R Shardlow, S P Watkin, P A Taylor, Pam and John Smith

OVER HADDON   SK2066   MAP 7

Lathkil 🍺

Village and inn signposted from B5055 just SW of Bakewell; DE45 1JE

Traditional pub well placed for Lathkill Dale with super views, good range of beers and decent food

In an ideal position for walks along one of the most enchantingly secretive dales in the Peak District, this much liked inn has choice views from its walled garden and from the pub windows too; muddy boots must be left in the lobby. It can get very busy here, though, both with walkers and day trippers. The airy room on the right as you go in has a nice fire in the attractively carved fireplace, old-fashioned settles with upholstered cushions and chairs, black beams, a delft shelf of blue and white plates, original prints and photographs, and big windows. On the left, the sunny spacious dining area doubles as an evening restaurant. They keep Everards Tiger and Whim Hartington, three guests from brewers such as Abbeydale, Peak Ales and Spire on handpump, a reasonable range of wines (including mulled wine) and a decent selection of malt whiskies; piped music and board games.

🍽 The popular buffet-style lunch menu includes simple filled rolls, mediterranean vegetable and pine nut pie, several salads, shepherd's pie, and venison and blackberry casserole. The supper menu has starters like crab cakes or vegetable spring roll, and main courses such as lasagne, battered cod, shepherd's pie and thai vegetable curry; good puddings such as blackberry and apple crumble. On Friday and Saturday evenings they have a more elaborate à la carte menu instead, with main courses like roast honey duck breast with orange and brandy sauce, and butternut squash, spinach and wild mushroom lasagne. *Starters/Snacks: £4.25 to £5.50. Main Courses: £7.50 to £13.00. Puddings: £3.60 to £3.80*

Free house ~ Licensee Robert Grigor-Taylor ~ Real ale ~ Bar food (12-2(2.30 Sat, Sun), 6-8(7-8.30, Fri, Sat)) ~ Restaurant ~ (01629) 812501 ~ Children welcome away from bar, and on Fri and Sat if dining ~ Dogs allowed in bar ~ Open 11.30-11; 12-10.30 Sun; 11.30-3, 6-11 Mon-Fri in winter ~ Bedrooms: £45B/£65S(£80B)

Recommended by Peter F Marshall, Gwyn and Anne Wake, John Beeken, the Didler, Chris Brooks, Guy Vowles, Roger Thornington, Mrs Jordan, Brian and Anna Marsden, Richard

SHELDON   SK1768   MAP 7

Cock & Pullet £

Village signposted off A6 just W of Ashford; DE45 1QS

Well run village pub with an appealingly unfussy atmosphere and good value bar food

This cosily unpretentious, family-run place is very much a village local, and the food and beers are very reasonably priced and served by courteous staff. With its low beams, exposed stonework, flagstones, scrubbed oak tables, pews and open fire, it looks like it's been a pub for hundreds of years, but surprisingly it was only converted some dozen years ago. A collection of 30 clocks, various representations of poultry (including some stuffed) and a cheerful assembly of deliberately mismatched furnishings are dotted around the little rooms. A plainer public bar has pool, darts and a TV; piped music. Black Sheep and Timothy Taylors Landlord are on handpump with one guest such as Whim Hartington. At the back a pleasant little terrace has tables and a water feature, and as this pretty village is just off the Limestone Way it's a popular all year round stop with walkers.

🍽 Inexpensively priced bar food typically includes soup, sandwiches, fish pie, a curry of the day, a vegetarian dish, steak in ale pie and specials; Sunday roast. *Starters/Snacks: £2.75 to £4.50. Main Courses: £5.75 to £9.75. Puddings: £2.75 to £3.50*

Free house ~ Licensees David and Kath Melland ~ Real ale ~ Bar food (12-2.30, 6-9) ~ Restaurant ~ No credit cards ~ (01629) 814292 ~ Children welcome at lunchtime and evenings until 8pm ~ Dogs allowed in bar and bedrooms ~ Open 11(12 Sun)-midnight ~ Bedrooms: /£60B

Recommended by Dr and Mrs A K Clarke, Chris Brooks, Jo Lilley, Simon Calvert, Peter F Marshall, S P Watkin, P A Taylor, Dennis Jones, J and E Dakin, DC

WOOLLEY MOOR   SK3661   MAP 7

White Horse

Badger Lane, off B6014 Matlock—Clay Cross; DE55 6FG

Dining pub run by young licensee couple, with good food in attractive old stone building in pretty countryside

Pleasantly refurbished and in a charming rural spot, this smart old inn is enjoyed for its food. There's a buoyantly chatty feel to the tap room, with Black Sheep and a couple of guests with at least one including a beer from Peak Ales on handpump, and great views of Ogston Reservoir from the conservatory; piped music. The garden has a boules pitch, picnic-sets, and a children's play area with a wooden train, boat, climbing frame and swings.

⑪ Good bar food (not cheap) includes sandwiches and filled baguettes, soup, scallops, caesar salad, sausages and mash, cod in beer batter, and puddings such as dark chocolate tart, with specials featuring fish dishes; generous Sunday roasts. The restaurant offers a more elaborate menu. *Starters/Snacks: £3.95 to £6.00. Main Courses: £9.95 to £14.95. Puddings: £4.95*

Free house ~ Licensees David and Melanie Boulby ~ Real ale ~ Bar food (12-1.45(2.15 Sun), 5.45-8.45; not Sun evening) ~ Restaurant ~ (01246) 590319 ~ Children welcome except in bar after 9pm ~ Open 12-2.30, 5.30-11; 12-3 Sun; closed Sun evening

Recommended by Michael and Margaret Slater, Phil and Jane Hodson, Sam Frankland, Robert F Smith, Peter F Marshall, Michael and Maggie Betton

LUCKY DIP

Besides the fully inspected pubs, you might like to try these Lucky Dips recommended to us and described by readers (if you do, please send us reports: feedback@goodguides.com).

ASHBOURNE [SK1846]

☆ *Smiths Tavern* DE6 1GH [bottom of Market Place]: Neatly kept traditional pub, chatty and relaxed, stretching back from heavily black-beamed bar through lounge to attractive light and airy end dining room, friendly efficient staff, good choice of above-average sensibly priced food using local produce, well kept Marstons-related ales, lots of whiskies and vodkas, daily papers, traditional games; children welcome, open all day summer Sun *(Mr and Mrs W W Burke, LYM)*

ASHFORD IN THE WATER [SK1969]

☆ *Bulls Head* DE45 1QB [Church St]: Comfortable two-bar beamed pub dating from 16th c, well kept Banks's and Robinsons, good proper food from lunchtime sandwiches up inc some unusual dishes, cheery fire, daily papers; may be piped music; overshoes for walkers, tables out behind and in front, lovely village *(Justin and Emma King, David and Carole Sayliss, Richard Farmer)*

ASHOVER [SK3463]

Black Swan S45 0AB [Church St]: Popular village pub with well priced food inc good range of sandwiches, beamed open-plan bar with fire, well kept Black Sheep, Greene King Abbot, Thornbridge Wild Swan and a couple of guests, prompt cheerful service, dining room; popular with younger people wknds, may be live music; terrace, good local walks *(the Didler)*

Crispin S45 0AB [Church St]: Well run carefully extended old building with very welcoming staff, reasonably priced enjoyable food, well kept Marstons-related real ale, good choice of wine; log fires, several attractive areas from beamed original core to back conservatory, dogs welcome in bar *(Jennifer Little, Darryl Wall, Barry Steele-Perkins, Michael and Margaret Slater)*

BARLBOROUGH [SK4777]

Rose & Crown S43 4ET [handy for M1 junction 30; High St]: Extended roadside village pub with rooms arranged around central bar, stone, timber and lots of crimson plush, leather sofas; generous fair-priced

food inc enjoyable Sun roast, Greene King and guest ales, good choice of soft drinks and wine, specialist teas, restaurant; piped music and live acoustic (Fri evening), Weds quiz night, big TV; children and dogs welcome, picnic-sets and play area in side garden, rustic benches facing Norman cross in front, cl Mon, Tues lunchtime *(JJW, CMW)*

BARLOW [SK3474]

☆ *Old Pump* S18 7TD [B6051 (Hackney Lane)]: Villagey dining pub with newish landlord, long narrow beamed bar with fresh flowers and tiny alcove, book-ended by dining room and two comfortably traditional little rooms, two monthly changing real ales, popular food; children welcome, some tables out at front and in sheltered side garden, bedrooms, open all day Sun *(Keith and Chris O'Neill, LYM)*

Tickled Trout S18 7SL [Valley Rd, Common Side; B6051 NW of Chesterfield]: Beamed dining pub with enjoyable food, well kept Marstons ales, decent wines, comfortable banquettes and good-sized tables, old-world prints, dining area; unobtrusive piped music; terrace tables *(Keith and Chris O'Neill, LYM)*

BELPER [SK3547]

Cross Keys DE56 1FZ [Market Pl]: Friendly pub with well kept Bass, Batemans (inc a house beer) and one or two guests, straightforward food, coal fire and bar billiards in lounge, pool and TV in bar; regular beer festivals, open all day *(the Didler)*

Devonshire DE56 1BA [Bridge St]: Recently refurbished and concentrating on food, good well balanced choice inc popular carvery, two real ales *(Stephen Shepherd)*

Fishermans Rest DE56 2JF [Broadholme Lane]: Well kept Marstons ales, good food, great view; garden with play area, pleasant surroundings *(Dr S J Shepherd, John and Carol Shepherd)*

Talbot DE56 2UA [Bridge Foot]: Family-run small 17th-c coaching inn with good choice of beer, enjoyable evening restaurant (not Sun) and Fri lunchtime bar food; seven attractively simple, recently redone bedrooms *(Bruce M Drew)*

Thorntree DE56 1FF [Chesterfield Rd (B6013)]: Comfortable two-bar local with congenial licensees, five changing ales inc Bass and Greene King (Dr S J Shepherd)

BIRCH VALE [SK0286]

Waltzing Weasel SK22 1BT [New Mills Rd (A6015 E of New Mills)]: Civilised nicely furnished wine-bar-style pub with well kept Marstons and other ales, decent wine and food inc bargain OAP lunches; friendly efficient staff, cosy fire, daily papers, live jazz some Thurs; children and dogs welcome, disabled access, bedrooms with nice views (Dennis Jones, David Hoult, LYM, Brian and Anita Randall)

BIRCHOVER [SK2362]

Druid DE4 2BL [off B5056; Main St]: Two-storey dining pub under new ownership; four spacious areas, good food and friendly service, well kept beers such as Marstons Pedigree; children welcome, picnic-sets out in front, good area for walks, open all day Sat, cl Sun evening (LYM, Trevor and Sylvia Millum)

BOLSOVER [SK4770]

Blue Bell S44 6HF [High St, off A632]: 18th-c, pleasant and friendly, with half a dozen real ales, sandwiches all day and (not Sun evening or Mon, Tues) good value pub meals; beams and brass in dining lounge (no dogs here), pool room, conservatory; quiz nights Mon and Weds; piped radio; children welcome, wide views from garden (JJW, CMW)

BONSALL [SK2758]

☆ **Barley Mow** DE4 2AY [off A5012 W of Cromford; The Dale]: Friendly, basic, one-room beamed stone-built pub, colourful atmosphere and character furnishings, decent straightforward food, well kept Greene King Abbot and Whim Hartington; coal fire, pictures and bric-a-brac, live music Fri, Sat inc landlord playing his accordian; short walk out to lavatories; nice little front terrace, walks organised from the pub, open all day wknds, cl Mon (Pete Baker, the Didler, Rona Murdoch)

BRACKENFIELD [SK3658]

Plough DE55 6DD [A615 Matlock—Alfreton, about a mile NW of Wessington]: Much modernised oak-beamed stone-built 18th-c former farmhouse in lovely setting, tidy and welcoming three-level bar, cheerful log-effect gas fire; several well kept ales inc interesting local brews, good value fresh food, appealing stone-built lower-level restaurant extension; big neatly kept gardens with play area (J K and S M Miln)

BUXTON [SK1266]

☆ **Bull i' th' Thorn** SK17 9QQ [Ashbourne Rd (A515) 6 miles S of Buxton, nr Flagg and Hurdlow]: Fascinating medieval hall doubling as straightforward roadside dining pub, handsome panelling, old flagstones and big log fire, armour, longcase clocks and all sorts of antique features; good value straightforward food all day, well kept Robinsons ales, jovial landlord, plain games

room and family room; children and dogs welcome, terrace and big lawn, rare breeds farm behind, good walks, bedrooms, big breakfast, open all day from 9.30am, may be cl Mon (Brian and Jacky Wilson, the Didler, Dennis Jones)

☆ **Old Sun** SK17 6HA [High St]: Charming old building with friendly helpful landlady, well kept Marstons-related ales with a guest such as Wychwood Hobgoblin, good choice of wines by the glass, farm cider, bargain food from good sandwiches and baked potatoes up served till 10pm, several cosy and interesting traditional linked areas, low beams and soft lighting, open fires, bare boards or tiles, stripped wood screens, old local photographs; piped music, TV; children in back bar, open all day (Barry Collett, the Didler, Rob and Catherine Dunster, LYM)

BUXWORTH [SK0282]

Navigation SK23 7NE [S of village towards Silkhill, off B6062]: Another change of management for this popular pub by restored canal basin; well priced Hornbeam, Howard Town, Timothy Taylors Landlord, Theakstons and guest ales, enjoyable pubby food from sandwiches up, cheery young staff, linked rooms with coal and log fires, flagstones and low ceilings, canalia and brassware, games room with pool, darts and Wii console; piped music; children and dogs welcome, disabled access, tables on sunken flagstoned terrace, play area and pets corner, open all day (Charles and Pauline Stride, Ben Williams, LYM)

CASTLETON [SK1582]

☆ **Bulls Head** S33 8WH [Cross St (A6187)]: Roomy and attractively refurbished stone inn, good reasonably priced food from ciabattas up, helpful friendly service, well kept Robinsons, log fires, wood panelling, leather sofas, live jazz; some roadside picnic-sets, five bedrooms (Barry and Anne, Carole Hall)

☆ **Castle Hotel** S33 8WG [High St/Castle St]: Roomy and welcoming Vintage Inn with extensive choice of sensibly priced all-day food, good selection of real ales and of wines by the glass, friendly helpful staff, log fires, stripped-stone walls, beams and some ancient flagstones; piped music; children welcome, heated terrace, comfortable bedrooms, good breakfast, open all day (J and E Dakin, LYM, N R White, Mrs J Ekins-Daukes, Jonathan Evans, R C Vincent)

☆ **George** S33 8WG [Castle St]: Busy but relaxed, good value food from hearty sandwiches to imaginative main dishes, four well kept ales, two good-sized rooms, one mainly for eating, ancient beams and stripped stone, no music; children and dogs welcome, wide forecourt with lots of flower tubs, good walks, may be cl Mon lunchtime (Keith and Chris O'Neill)

Olde Cheshire Cheese S33 8WJ [How Lane]: Two simple linked beamed areas, cosy and spotless, with five well kept real ales, good range of reasonably priced food all day, decent house wine, log fire, lots of photographs, toby jugs and local paintings; sensibly placed darts, back dining room; piped music, and they may try to keep your credit card while you eat; children welcome, dogs in bar, bedrooms *(BB, Fred and Lorraine Gill)*

☆ *Olde Nags Head* S33 8WH [Cross St (A6187)]: Small solidly built and recently refurbished hotel dating from 17th c, interesting antique oak furniture and coal fire in civilised beamed and flagstoned bar with nice pictures, beers such as Black Sheep and Timothy Taylors; good coffee, helpful staff, locally sourced food (inc meat from rare breeds) in bars and bistro, good value Sun carvery (second helpings encouraged); attractive village, comfortable bedrooms, open all day till late *(R C Vincent, Fred and Lorraine Gill, LYM)*

CHELMORTON [SK1170]

☆ *Church Inn* SK17 9SL [between A6 and A515 SW of Buxton]: Old stone-built pub, cosy in winter and cool in summer, convivial flagstoned bar with pine panelled counter and woodburner in two-way fireplace, carpeted dining area with wood-effect fire; simple well cooked tasty food, well kept Marstons, Adnams and two local guest ales, sensible prices, prompt cheerful service, games room with pool and darts; piped music; well behaved children and dogs welcome, tables on split-level partly covered terrace, four annex bedrooms; superb walking country *(Gwyn and Anne Wake, Peter F Marshall, Malcolm and Pauline Pellatt, Barry Collett)*

CHESTERFIELD [SK3871]

Barley Mow S40 1JR [Saltergate]: Recently knocked-through L-shaped bar with wide choice of enjoyable home-made food from sandwiches up, bargains for two early evening and Sat, Mon lunchtime, best to book Sun lunch (12-4); well kept Black Sheep, Fullers London Pride and Wychwood Hob Goblin, good fruit drinks, original Wards brewery stained-glass; hanging baskets and some sunny picnic-sets outside *(Keith and Chris O'Neill)*

Chesterfield Hotel S41 7UA [Malkin St/Corporation St]: Recently reopened after careful restoration, already very popular under its welcoming beer-enthusiast landlord; half a dozen or more changing ales such as Everards, Titanic and its Leatherbritches house beer, home-made food using local ingredients, open fire, oak panelling and stripped wood floors *(the Didler)*

Rutland S40 1XL [Stephenson Pl]: Uncomplicated pub next to crooked-spire church, thriving atmosphere, well kept Badger Best, Timothy Taylors Landlord, local Brampton and several other interesting changing ales, Weston's farm cider, low-priced pub food all day from sandwiches up; friendly polite service even when busy, rugs and assorted wooden furniture on bare

boards, old photographs, darts; piped music; children welcome, open all day *(Tony Hobden, Alan Johnson, Keith and Chris O'Neill)*

CLIFTON [SK1645]

Cock DE6 2GJ [Cross Side, opp church]: Comfortable two-bar family local with friendly staff, jovial landlord, dark beams and period feel, good choice of home-made food from baguettes up, well kept Marstons Pedigree, Timothy Taylors Landlord and Wells & Youngs Bombardier, decent choice of wines by the glass, reasonable prices, darts; children really welcome, garden tables, climber and slide *(Baden and Sandy Waller)*

CODNOR [SK4249]

Poet & Castle DE5 9QY [Alfreton Rd]: Reopened by former owners of Old Poets Corner in Ashover, lots of changing ales inc Ashover, Everards and Titanic, farm ciders, simple wholesome food, comfortable low-ceilinged bar/lounge, music nights; open all day *(the Didler)*

COXBENCH [SK3643]

Fox & Hounds DE21 5BA [off B6179 N of Derby; Alfreton Rd]: Friendly village pub nicely set by Trent & Mersey Canal, wide choice of good interesting fresh food, reasonable prices, well kept Marstons Pedigree, long partly flagstoned, beamed and panelled bar, attractive raised restaurant area, family room; can get very busy; terrace picnic-sets with view of canal, lovely hanging baskets and flower tubs, open all day *(K E and B Billington, John Beeken, John Lowe)*

CRICH [SK3454]

Cliff DE4 5DP [Cromford Rd, Town End]: Cosy and unpretentious two-room local with well kept Black Sheep, Greene King IPA and local ales, reliable straightforward food, friendly staff and regulars, open fire; children welcome, great views and walks, handy for National Tramway Museum *(the Didler)*

CROMFORD [SK2956]

Boat DE4 3QF [Scarthin, off Market Place]: Traditional 18th-c local reopened under new landlord, good range of real ales, relaxed atmosphere, coal fire, long narrow low-beamed bar with stripped stone and bric-a-brac; darts and pool area, some live music, quiz night; children and dogs welcome, back garden, open all day wknds *(Derek and Sylvia Stephenson, BB)*

CUTTHORPE [SK3273]

Gate S42 7BA [Overgreen; B6050 W of village]: Picture-window views from chatty area around bar, neat glass-fronted dining lounge down steps, enjoyable food inc local buffalo (wknd booking advised), well kept Black Sheep, Fullers London Pride and a guest ale, good choice of wines by the glass; terrace tables *(Keith and Chris O'Neill)*

DENBY [SK4047]

Bulls Head DE5 8PW [Denby Common, between A609 and A6007 S of Ripley]: Well restored after a fire and opened up in clean contemporary style with galleried eating area, good, well presented interesting food, smart service by young efficient staff, well kept beers such as Jennings Cumberland, Mon jazz evenings; picnic-sets in garden behind *(Derek and Sylvia Stephenson, Phyl and Jack Street)*

Denby Lodge DE5 8PH [Church St]: Modern pub with new licensees, enjoyable low-priced home cooking, welcoming landlord, a real ale; handy for nearby Denby Pottery *(Sylvia and Tony Birbeck)*

DERBY [SK3538]

☆ **Abbey Inn** DE22 1DX [Darley St, Darley Abbey]: A treasure, former abbey gatehouse opp Derwent-side park (pleasant riverside walk from centre), massive 15th-c or older stonework remnants, brick floor, studded oak doors, coal fire in big stone inglenook, stone spiral stair to upper bar (open Sun afternoon) with oak rafters and tapestries; pleasant service, bargain Sam Smiths and lunchtime bar food; the lavatories with their beams, stonework and tiles are worth a look too; piped music; children welcome, open all day wknds *(the Didler, LYM, Rona Murdoch, Kevin Flack)*

☆ **Alexandra** DE1 2QE [Siddals Rd]: Imposing Victorian pub with two simple rooms, good heavy traditional furnishings on dark-stained floorboards, shelves of bottles, breweriana, and lots of railway prints and memorabilia; Castle Rock and quickly changing guest ales, lots of continental bottled beers and more on tap, tasty filled rolls; piped music, fruit machine; children and dogs welcome, nicely planted yard, open all day, afternoon break Sun *(the Didler, C J Fletcher, Pam and John Smith, LYM, Bob)*

Babington Arms DE1 1TA [Babington Lane]: Large, well run, open-plan Wetherspoons with massive bank of handpumps for great real ale choice, regulars inc Derby, Falstaff, Greene King Abbot and Marstons Pedigree; good welcoming service, well priced food, comfortable seating with steps up to relaxed back area; attractive verandah, open all day *(C J Fletcher, the Didler, David Carr)*

Falstaff DE23 6UJ [Silver Hill Rd, off Normanton Rd]: Basic unsmart local, aka the Folly, brewing its own good value ales, guest beers too, left-hand bar with games, coal fire in quieter lounge; occasional disco; open all day *(the Didler)*

☆ **Flower Pot** DE1 3DZ [King St]: Extended real ale pub with glazed panel showing its own new Headless microbrewery, and great choice of reasonably priced changing beers from small breweries (over 20 at wknds), some cask-tapped; friendly staff, three linked rooms inc comfortable back bar with lots of books, side area with old Derby photographs and brewery memorabilia, good value basic bar food, daily papers, pub games; piped music/juke box, separate concert room – good live bands Thurs-Sat and busy then; disabled access and facilities, tables on small cherry-tree terrace, open all day *(the Didler, Pam and John Smith)*

☆ **Olde Dolphin** DE1 3DL [Queen St]: Quaint 16th-c timber-framed pub just below cathedral; four small dark unpretentious rooms, big bowed black beams, shiny panelling, opaque leaded windows, lantern lights and coal fires; well kept ales such as Adnams, Bass, Black Sheep, Caledonian Deuchars IPA, Greene King Abbot, Marstons Pedigree and Timothy Taylors Landlord (good July beer festival), bargain simple food all day, good value upstairs steak bar (not always open); no children; terrace tables, open all day *(the Didler, LYM, Pam and John Smith)*

Rowditch DE22 3LL [Uttoxeter New Rd (A516)]: Welcoming two-bar local with well kept Marstons Pedigree and guest beers, country wines, Mon cheese night, attractive small snug on right, coal fire, Sat piano-player; small pleasant back garden; may be installing microbrewery *(the Didler)*

☆ **Smithfield** DE1 2BH [Meadow Rd]: Friendly bow-fronted local, well kept changing ales such as Durham, Headless, Oakham, Roosters and Whim, hearty bar lunches, back lounge with traditional settles, old prints, curios and breweriana, coal fires, daily papers; piped music, good games room (children welcome here), quiz and band nights; riverside terrace with wknd barbecues, open all day *(the Didler)*

☆ **Standing Order** DE1 3GL [Irongate]: Spacious Wetherspoons in grand and lofty-domed former bank, central bar, booths down each side, handsome plasterwork, pseudo-classical torsos, high portraits of mainly local notables; usual popular food all day, good range of real ales, reasonable prices, daily papers, quick service even when very busy; good disabled facilities, open all day *(the Didler, Dave Braisted, BB)*

Station Inn DE1 2SN [Midland Rd, below station]: Friendly local, simple and neatly kept, with particularly well kept Bass (in jugs from cellar), Black Sheep and guests; good food lunchtime and early evening in large back lounge and dining area, long panelled and quarry-tiled bar, stained glass, side room with darts, pool and TV; piped music; ornate façade, open all day Fri, cl Sun evening *(the Didler)*

DRONFIELD [SK3479]

Coach & Horses S18 2GD [Sheffield Rd (B6057)]: Well managed and comfortably refurbished tap for Thornbridge microbrewery's interesting beers, friendly staff informative about them; good home-made food, using local produce, such as pigeon risotto, decent wines by the glass, pleasant civilised furnishings inc sofas; next to Sheffield FC ground, open all day Fri-Sun *(the Didler, Andy and Jill Kassube, Mozzer Cooper, Jonny Major)*

DUCKMANTON [SK4371]

Arkwright Arms S44 5JG [Chesterfield Rd (A632)]: Friendly local on outskirts, lots of real ales and ciders, good value food lunch and evening (till 7.30pm); no children in bar; field with picnic-sets, open all day *(JJW, CMW)*

EDALE [SK1285]

Old Nags Head S33 7ZD [off A625 E of Chapel-en-le-Frith; Grindsbrook Booth]: Relaxed well used traditional pub at start of Pennine Way, good friendly staff, well kept local ales, log fire, flagstoned area for booted walkers, airy back family room with board games, pubby food; can get very busy wknds, TV; front terrace and garden, open all day, cl Mon, Tues lunchtimes out of season *(C J Fletcher, LYM, Jonathan Evans, Andrew Whitney, John and Helen Rushton)*

Rambler S33 7ZA: Refurbished stone-built country hotel with extensive bar rambling through linked rooms, flagstones, quarry tiles, bare boards and carpet, good solid furnishings, cosy informal dining room; sensibly priced food all day from sandwiches up, four well kept real ales; children, dogs and walkers welcome, lots of picnic-sets in garden with play area, bedrooms *(Tony Mills)*

ELMTON [SK5073]

Elm Tree S80 4LS [off B6417 S of Clowne]: Softly lit and popular country pub with good value unpretentious bar food all day, children's menu, up to seven ales inc Black Sheep and Wells & Youngs, wide choice of wines; efficient service, stripped stone and panelling, back barn restaurant (Fri, Sat evening and for good Sun lunch); children welcome if eating, garden tables, play area *(JJW, CMW)*

ELTON [SK2260]

☆ *Duke of York* DE4 2BW [village signed off B5056 W of Matlock; Main St]: Unspoilt local kept spotless by very long-serving friendly landlady; bargain Adnams Broadside and Marstons Pedigree, lovely little quarry-tiled back tap room with coal fire in massive fireplace, glazed bar and hatch to flagstoned corridor, nice prints and more fires in the two front ones – one like private parlour with piano and big table, the other with pool, darts, dominoes; outside lavatories; in charming village, open 8.30-midnight, and Sun lunchtime *(Pete Baker, the Didler)*

FENNY BENTLEY [SK1850]

Bentley Brook DE6 1LF [A515 N of Ashbourne]: Sizeable place with two refurbished bars separated by central log fire, real ales inc Leatherbritches from long granite-effect servery, good choice of wines, generous well priced pubby food inc Sun carvery, friendly service, dining room; piped music; terrace picnic-sets, play area, country views, bedrooms, open all day *(LYM, Martin and Alison Stainsby)*

FLAGG [SK1167]

Duke of York SK17 9QG [off A515 Buxton—Ashbourne, five miles from Buxton]: Popular low-ceilinged simple pub with warm welcome from landlord and Captain Jack the parrot; well kept Robinsons ales, low priced enjoyable pub food, open fires, attractive bar, sun lounge and pretty dining room *(Hilary Forrest)*

FOOLOW [SK2078]

☆ *Barrel* S32 5QD [Bretton, N of village]: Outstanding views from stone-roofed turnpike inn's front terrace, old-fashioned low-beamed knocked-through bar with modern extension, well kept Greene King ales, simple choice of good value, well cooked food, friendly young staff, lots of pictures and log fire; piped music, may be live Weds; children and dogs welcome, courtyard garden, good walking, four neat simple bedrooms, decent breakfast, open all day wknds *(Keith and Margaret Kettell, Richard, LYM, Peter F Marshall, Fiona Salvesen, Ross Murrell, Keith and Chris O'Neill, Robin M Corlett, Alan Thwaite)*

FROGGATT EDGE [SK2476]

☆ *Chequers* S32 3ZJ [A625, off A623 N of Bakewell]: Smart dining pub with good, if not cheap, interesting food (all day wknds) from unusual sandwiches up; solid country furnishings in civilised and cosily attractive dining bar with woodburner, antique prints and longcase clock, good choice of wines by the glass, changing ales such as Black Sheep and Wells & Youngs Bombardier; unobtrusive piped music; children welcome, peaceful back garden with Froggatt Edge just up through the woods behind, comfortable bedrooms (quarry lorries use the road from 6am wkdys), very good breakfast, open all day wknds *(LYM, Dr and Mrs J Temporal, Matt Waite, Dr S J Shepherd, James A Waller, J K and S M Miln)*

Grouse S11 7TZ [Longshaw, off B6054 NE of Froggatt]: Plush front bar, log fire and wooden benches in back bar, big dining room, decent home cooking with good value smaller helpings, well kept Caledonian Deuchars IPA, Banks's and Marstons Pedigree, friendly service, handsome views; dogs welcome, verandah and terrace, neat bedrooms, good moorland walking country, open all day *(James A Waller, Michael and Margaret Slater, C J Fletcher)*

GLOSSOP [SK0294]

Globe SK13 8HJ [High St W]: Good changing ales inc its own microbrew and local guest ales, bottled beers and farm cider; nice vegetarian food, friendly licensees, comfortable relaxed atmosphere, old fittings and photographs, frequent live music upstairs, occasional beer festivals; garden, cl lunchtime and Tues, open till early hours *(the Didler)*

Star SK13 7DD [Howard St]: Unpretentious alehouse opp the station with six well priced changing beers such as local Howard Town, Pictish, Shaws and Whim, and farm cider; straightforward food, friendly helpful staff, interesting layout inc flagstoned tap room with hatch service, old local photographs; piped music; bedrooms, cl lunchtime Mon-Thurs, open all day Fri-Sun *(Dennis Jones, the Didler)*

GREAT HUCKLOW [SK1777]

Queen Anne SK17 8RF [Main St]: New landlady doing good, more adventurous food in comfortably refurbished 17th-c low-beamed stone-built pub; real ales such as Copper Dragon, Jennings and Tetleys, big log fire, gleaming brass and copper, walkers' bar, pub games, french windows to small back terrace and charming garden with picnic-sets and lovely views, two quiet bedrooms, good walks, cl Mon, open all day Fri-Sun *(David and Ruth Hollands, the Didler)*

GREAT LONGSTONE [SK1971]

☆ *Crispin* DE45 1TZ [Main St]: Spotless family-run pub increasingly popular for its enjoyable wholesome good value food inc OAP lunches, all freshly made so can be a wait; well kept Robinsons ales, good wine and whisky choice, welcoming and particularly obliging landlord, buoyant atmosphere, log fire; picnic-sets out in front *(Peter F Marshall, James A Waller, David and Carole Sayliss)*

HARDWICK HALL [SK4663]

Hardwick Inn S44 5QJ [quite handy for M1 junction 29; Doe Lea]: Golden stone building dating from 15th c at the south gate of Hardwick Park, several busy well furnished linked rooms, fine range of some 220 malt whiskies and of wines by the glass, well kept Black Sheep, Greene King Old Speckled Hen, Theakstons XB and Old Peculier and Wells & Youngs Bombardier; log fire, bar food all day, carvery restaurant; unobtrusive piped music; they may try to keep your credit card while you eat; children allowed, pleasant back garden, more tables out in front, open all day *(Rosemary K Germaine, D C Leggatt, J Stickland, Peter F Marshall, Joan York, LYM, the Didler, Stephen Wood, Michael Butler, Ellie Weld, Mike Turner)*

HARTINGTON [SK1260]

Charles Cotton SK17 0AL [Market Pl]: Popular four-square stone-built hotel in attractive village centre, large bar, simple dining room off, tearoom too, sensibly short choice of good food from chef; good choice of changing real ales such as Teignworthy Reel and local Whim, bottled beers and real cider, good wines, nice coffee, pleasant well trained young staff; nostalgic piped music; refurbished bedrooms, open all day *(the Didler, Richard and Jean Green)*

☆ *Devonshire Arms* SK17 0AL [Market Pl]: Attractive welcoming old pub, well kept Marstons Pedigree, Jennings Cumberland and Wells & Youngs Bombardier, good generous home-made food (all day wknds) in lounge bar (nice if you can sit away from the doors) and smart daytime teashop/evening restaurant; friendly helpful staff, log fire in flagstoned public bar welcoming walkers and dogs; children welcome, tables out in front facing village duck pond, more in small garden, good walks *(Susan and Nigel Brookes, Dennis Jones, John and Joan Calvert, Brian and Anna Marsden, Alan Johnson, Richard)*

HATHERSAGE [SK2680]

Fox House S11 7TY [A6187/A625 3 miles towards Sheffield – just inside S Yorks]:

Popular, well run, 18th-c stone-built Vintage Inn with several linked rooms on different levels, oak-framed open fireplaces, wide range of good value food from sandwiches up, well kept ales, good wine choice, quick friendly service; nice moorland location, good views from back terrace, bedrooms *(BB, Brian and Jacky Wilson)*

HAYFIELD [SK0387]

☆ *Pack Horse* SK22 2EP [off A624 Glossop—Chapel-en-le-Frith; Market St]: Smartly modernised dining pub with good fresh food all day at reasonable prices, from baguettes to some interesting main dishes and Sun roasts, good choice of real ales and of spirits and wines; friendly efficient service, nice chatty atmosphere, cosier areas near door; piped music; open all day *(C M Ashton, BB)*

Sportsman SK22 2LE [Kinder Rd]: Wide choice of enjoyable food in roomy and neatly kept traditional pub, friendly staff, well kept Thwaites beers, decent wines, lots of malt whiskies, two coal fires; handy for Kinder Scout walks, bedrooms *(Michelle Griffiths)*

HEATH [SK4467]

Elm Tree S44 5SE [just off M1 junction 29; A6175 towards Clay Cross, then first right]: Roadside pub with half-panelled lounge/dining areas, good choice of enjoyable well priced blackboard food (all day wknds) inc generous Sun carvery, three Jennings ales and a guest, wide choice of wines; mix of traditional wooden furniture and leather armchairs on wood and stone floors, woodburner in stone fireplace, darts in smallish bar; soft piped music; children and dogs welcome, some picnic-sets out at front, attractive garden with play area and lovely views to Bolsover and beyond (but traffic noise) *(JJW, CMW, R E and J M Hooper)*

HOGNASTON [SK2350]

☆ *Red Lion* DE6 1PR [off B5035 Ashbourne—Wirksworth]: Traditional 17th-c inn with open-plan beamed bar, three open fires, attractive mix of old tables, old-fashioned settles and other comfortable seats on ancient flagstones; friendly licensees, good home-made food from shortish menu in bar and conservatory restaurant, nice wines by the glass, Marstons Pedigree and three local guests; piped music; boules, handy for Carsington Water, three good bedrooms, big breakfast *(Brian and Anna Marsden, Arthur Pickering, LYM, Jan and Alan Summers)*

HOLYMOORSIDE [SK3369]

Lamb S42 7EU [Loads Rd, just off Holymoor Rd]: Small cheerful village pub kept spotless, up to half a dozen or so particularly well kept ales such as Adnams, Black Sheep, Daleside Blonde, Fullers London Pride and Timothy Taylors Landlord, charming lounge, coal fire in cosy bar, pub games; tables outside, leafy spot, cl wkdy lunchtimes *(the Didler)*

HORSLEY WOODHOUSE [SK3944]

Old Oak DE7 6AW [Main St (A609 Belper—

Ilkeston)]: Busy roadside local linked to nearby Bottle Brook and Leadmill microbreweries, their ales and wknd back bar with another half-dozen well priced guest ales tapped from the cask; linked beamed rooms, blazing coal fires, farm cider, chatty staff, good basic snacks, occasional live music; children and dogs welcome, hatch to covered courtyard tables (nice views), cl wkdy lunchtimes, open all day wknds *(Rona Murdoch, Brian Coleman, the Didler)*

HULLAND WARD [SK2647]

Black Horse DE6 3EE [Hulland Ward; A517 Ashbourne—Belper]: 17th-c pub with good fresh food at sensible prices inc local game in low-beamed quarry-tiled bar or back country-view dining room, popular Sun carvery, well kept Bass, Harviestoun, Peakstones Rock and two changing guests, friendly licensees; children welcome, garden tables, comfortable bedrooms, nr Carsington Water, open all day Fri-Sun *(the Didler)*

ILKESTON [SK4742]

Good Old Days DE7 5LJ [Station Rd]: Welcoming half-timbered, one-room pub formerly the Ilford Club (new owner adding downstairs family room and kitchen); well kept, interesting changing small brewery ales, simple food, darts, dominoes and pool; piped music, TV; children and dogs welcome, tables in canalside garden, pub moorings, open all day Fri-Sun *(Christie, the Didler)*

KELSTEDGE [SK3463]

Kelstedge Inn S45 0DX [Matlock Rd]: Enjoyable well priced food inc three daily roasts and OAP wkdy bargains, warmly welcoming staff; six bedrooms *(Mr and Mrs R Shardlow)*

LADYBOWER RESERVOIR [SK1986]

☆ *Ladybower Inn* S33 0AX [A57 Sheffield—Glossop, junction with A6013]: Fine views of attractive reservoir from open-plan stone-built pub, clean and spacious, with friendly staff, good reasonably priced interesting food using prime local produce, well kept ales such as Bradfield Farmers, Greene King Ruddles County and Wentworth Best, decent wines by the glass, red plush seats; can get crowded in summer, and parking across fast road – take care; children and muddy walkers welcome, low stone seats and tables outside, good value bedrooms in converted annex, good breakfast *(D J and P M Taylor, Mrs J Ekins-Daukes, James A Waller, Derek Stapley)*

LEES [SK2637]

Black Cow DE6 5BE [just off Langley Common—Longford rd, off B5020 W of Derby]: Wholesome old-fashioned village local, well kept beer, well priced traditional pub food, friendly staff and cats, open fires *(TB)*

LITTLE LONGSTONE [SK1971]

Packhorse DE45 1NN [off A6 NW of Bakewell via Monsal Dale]: Three comfortably refurbished linked beamed rooms, pine tables and flagstone floor, welcoming enthusiastic landlord, well kept Thornbridge

ales, good choice of wines by the glass, substantial good value food (Sat breakfast from 8.30), coal fires; hikers welcome (on Monsal Trail), terrace in steep little back garden *(LYM, Dennis Jones)*

LULLINGTON [SK2513]

☆ *Colvile Arms* DE12 8EG [off A444 S of Burton; Main St]: Popular neatly preserved 18th-c village pub with high-backed settles in simple panelled bar, cosy comfortable beamed lounge, pleasant atmosphere, friendly staff; four well kept ales inc Bass, Marstons Pedigree and a Mild, enjoyable good value food; may be piped music; picnic-sets on small sheltered back lawn overlooking bowling green, cl wkdy lunchtimes *(LYM, the Didler)*

MAKENEY [SK3544]

☆ *Holly Bush* DE56 0RX [from A6 heading N after Duffield, take 1st right after crossing River Derwent, then 1st left]: Down-to-earth two-bar village pub (ex farmhouse) with three blazing coal fires (one in old-fashioned range by snug's curved high-backed settle), flagstones, beams, black panelling and tiled floors, lots of brewing advertisements; half a dozen or so well kept changing ales (some brought from cellar in jugs), real cider, cheap food inc rolls and pork pies, may be local cheeses for sale, games lobby with hatch service (children allowed here), regular beer festivals; picnic-sets outside, dogs welcome, open all day Fri-Sun *(the Didler, BB)*

MATLOCK BATH [SK2958]

Temple DE4 3PG [Temple Walk]: 18th-c hotel with wonderful Derwent valley views, comfortable bar, dining area and restaurant, usually three well kept changing ales from more or less local small breweries (regular beer festivals), nice wines, good well priced freshly cooked food; children welcome, tables outside, summer barbecues, bedrooms, open all day wknds *(the Didler)*

MELBOURNE [SK3825]

Blue Bell DE73 8EJ [Church St]: Friendly chatty two-bar pub with full range of good local Shardlow ales, substantial bar food inc wide range of hot rolls, sporting pictures, games in public bar; sports TV in both bars; terrace tables, nice setting nr church *(MP, Pete Baker, JB)*

MILFORD [SK3545]

William IV DE56 0RR [Milford Bridge]: Friendly and relaxing stone-built riverside pub, long room with low beams, bare boards, quarry tiles, old settles and a blazing coal fire; well kept Bass, Marstons Pedigree, Timothy Taylors Landlord and guests, good filled rolls; cl lunchtime wkdys, open all day wknds *(the Didler)*

MILLERS DALE [SK1473]

☆ *Anglers Rest* SK17 8SN [just down Litton Lane; pub is PH on OS Sheet 119 map ref 142734]: Spotless ivy-clad pub in lovely quiet riverside setting on Monsal Trail, two bars and dining room, log fires, enjoyable home-made standard food (not Tues lunchtime, pie night Thurs), couple of well kept real ales; efficient pleasant service, reasonable prices, darts, pool and muddy walkers in public bar; children welcome, wonderful gorge views and riverside walks *(Mr and Mrs R Coleby, Peter F Marshall, the Didler)*

MILLTOWN [SK3561]

☆ *Miners Arms* S45 0HA [off B6036 SE of Ashover; Oakstedge Lane]: Very good home-made food (must book) in appealing L-shaped pub, clean and bright, with friendly staff, Greene King and guest ales, good wine, warm local atmosphere, log fires, quieter eating area further back; may be soft piped classical music; children welcome, attractive country walks from the door, cl Sun evening, Mon, Tues, winter Weds and 10 days Aug *(Mr and Mrs R Shardlow, the Didler, LYM)*

Nettle S45 0ES [Fallgate, Littlemoor]: Interesting old beamed pub with coal fire in small traditional bar, linked busier areas behind, well kept Bradfield Farmers Blonde and guests, good value changing bar food, pub games; open all day Sun *(the Didler)*

MONSAL HEAD [SK1871]

☆ *Monsal Head Hotel* DE45 1NL [B6465]: Popular hilltop inn under newish licensees, cosy stables bar with stripped timber horse-stalls, harnesses and brassware, cushioned oak pews on flagstones, big open fire; Peakstones Rock and guest ales, german bottled beers, several wines by the glass, bar food from lunchtime sandwiches up (they may try to keep your credit card while you eat); children (over 3), dogs and muddy walkers welcome, big garden, stunning Monsal Dale views with its huge viaduct, seven bedrooms, open all day till midnight *(LYM, Ian and Debs, Mike and Sue Loseby, Paul J Robinshaw, Keith and Chris O'Neill, Cathryn and Richard Hicks, Derek and Sylvia Stephenson)*

MORLEY [SK3942]

Rose & Crown DE7 6DG [Woodside]: Well run Vintage Inn with well kept real ales such as Bass and Timothy Taylors Landlord, quick friendly service, good food choice at reasonable prices, lots of wines by the glass, beams and log fire *(Nigel and Sue Foster, Dr S J Shepherd)*

NEW MILLS [SJ9886]

Fox SK22 3AY [Brookbottom; OS Sheet 109 map ref 985864]: Tucked-away unmodernised country local, a nice summer family outing; friendly long-serving landlord, particularly well kept Robinsons, good value basic food (not Tues evening) inc good sandwiches, log fire, darts and pool; children welcome, lots of tables outside, good walking area, open all day wknds *(David Hoult, John Fiander, the Didler)*

OAKERTHORPE [SK3856]

Amber DE55 7LL [Furnace]: Charming old-fashioned village local with friendly landlady, good pubby food, well kept Abbeydale, Fullers London Pride, Timothy

Taylors Landlord and guests, blazing winter fires, lots of antiques inc a piano, well worn seating; good views from the back terrace, walks *(the Didler, Derek and Sylvia Stephenson)*

OCKBROOK [SK4236]

☆ *Royal Oak* DE72 3SE [off B6096 just outside Spondon; Green Lane]: Quiet 18th-c village local run by same friendly family for half a century, bargain honest food (not wknd or Tues evenings) from super lunchtime cobs to steaks, Sun lunch and OAP meals; Bass and interesting guest beers, good soft drinks choice, tiled-floor tap room, turkey-carpeted snug, inner bar with Victorian prints, larger and lighter side room, nice old settle in entrance corridor, open fires, darts and dominoes; sheltered cottage garden and cobbled front courtyard, separate play area *(BB, Pete Baker, the Didler)*

OLD GLOSSOP [SK0494]

Queens SK13 7RZ [Shepley St]: Open-plan dining pub with quick service even when busy, small bar area with well kept Black Sheep, upstairs restaurant; front picnic-sets *(John Fiander)*

PARWICH [SK1854]

Sycamore DE6 1QL [next to church]: Chatty old country pub, well run by cheerful welcoming young landlady, super log fire in neat comfortable main bar, generous wholesome food lunchtimes and most Weds-Sat evenings, Robinsons beers inc seasonal, lots of old local photographs, hatch-served tap room with games; tables out in front and on grass by car park, quiet village, good walks *(Malcolm and Pauline Pellatt, the Didler, Paul J Robinshaw, Pete Baker)*

PENTRICH [SK3852]

☆ *Dog* DE5 3RE [Main Rd (B6016 N of Ripley)]: Extended traditional pub, cosy and smartly fitted out, very popular wknds for its good fresh up-to-date food (best to book); reasonable prices, well kept Bass, Marstons Pedigree and guest beers, lots wines by the glass, friendly efficient staff, beams and panelling; tables in attractive garden behind, quiet village, good walks *(P Dawn, the Didler)*

PILSLEY [SK2371]

Devonshire Arms DE45 1UL [off A619 Bakewell—Baslow; High St]: Promising start from new licensees, simple well presented mostly home-made food, three well kept local Peak ales, cheerful welcoming staff, cosy and appealing lounge bar with open fire, another in walkers'/family bar area; handy for Chatsworth farm and craft shops, lovely village *(Peter F Marshall)*

RIDDINGS [SK4352]

Moulders Arms DE55 4BX [off B6016 S of Alfreton; Church St]: Pretty 17th-c thatched pub with good value straightforward enjoyable food inc Mon-Sat OAP lunches, well kept Marstons Pedigree and a guest ale, two small beamed bars and immaculate cosy candlelit dining room; darts, gleaming brasses, no music or TV; children welcome, no dogs, elaborate heated smokers' shelter, usually open all day (Phil and Jane Hodson)

RIPLEY [SK3950]

Pear Tree DE5 3HR [Derby Rd (B6179)]:
Long open bar with hot coal fires each end,
small lounge, old-fashioned and unspoilt,
well kept and priced Greene King ales inc a
Mild, friendly chatty staff, darts and
dominoes; open all day (the Didler)

ROWARTH [SK0189]

Little Mill SK22 1EB [signed well locally; off
A626 in Marple Bridge at Mellor sign, sharp
left at Rowarth sign]: Beautifully tucked-
away 18th-c family pub, Banks's, Marstons
Pedigree and three guests, good value
generous food all-day (till 7pm Sun) inc
wknd carvery; roomy open-plan bar and
upstairs restaurant, big log fire, unusual
features inc working waterwheel and vintage
Pullman-carriage bedrooms, live music Fri
evenings; children and dogs welcome,
disabled access, verandah with terrace
below, pretty garden dell across stream,
good play area, picnic-sets on decking, open
all day (Brian and Anna Marsden, LYM)

ROWSLEY [SK2565]

Grouse & Claret DE4 2EB [A6 Bakewell—
Matlock]: Attractive family dining pub in old
stone building, spacious, clean and
comfortable, with friendly helpful staff,
enjoyable food (all day wknds) from
sandwiches and pubby things to more
enterprising dishes, decent wines; open
fires, tap room popular with walkers; tables
outside, good value bedrooms
(Stuart Paulley, David Carr)

☆ **Peacock** DE4 2EB [Bakewell Rd]: Civilised
small 17th-c country hotel with comfortable
chairs and sofas and a few antiques in
spacious uncluttered lounge, interesting
stone-floored inner bar, restful colours;
enjoyable if not cheap food from lunchtime
sandwiches to restaurant meals, Greene King
IPA and a local guest beer, good wines,
beautifully served coffee; attractive riverside
gardens, trout fishing, good bedrooms (LYM,
Mr and Mrs W W Burke)

SHARDLOW [SK4430]

☆ **Malt Shovel** DE72 2HG [3.5 miles from M1
junction 24, via A6 towards Derby; The
Wharf]: Busy old-world beamed pub in
18th-c former maltings, interesting odd-
angled layout with cosy corners, Marstons-
related ales, quick friendly service, bargain
food (not Sat evening) from baguettes up,
good central open fire, farm tools and bric-
a-brac; lots of terrace tables by Trent &
Mersey Canal, pretty hanging baskets and
boxes (the Didler, Richard and Jean Green,
Patricia Walker, LYM, Rona Murdoch)

Old Crown DE72 2HL [off A50 just W of M1
junction 24; Cavendish Bridge, E of village]:
Good value pub with half a dozen or more
well kept Marstons and related ales, nice
choice of malt whiskies, pubby food (not Fri,
Sun evenings) from sandwiches and
baguettes up; beams with masses of jugs
and mugs, walls covered with other bric-a-
brac and breweriana, big inglenook fireplace;

children and dogs welcome, simple good
value bedrooms, good breakfast, open all day
(the Didler, LYM)

SPARKLOW [SK1265]

Royal Oak SK17 9QJ [Monyash—Longnor rd,
just off A515 S of Buxton]: Relaxed country
atmosphere in open-plan pub, wide choice of
fairly priced all-day food, friendly helpful
service, three ales inc Whim Hartington,
good wine choice, two bar areas, log fire,
restaurant; children welcome, on Tissington
Trail, barn with bunk bedrooms, campsite
(Ian and Suzy Masser, Mike Proctor)

SPARROWPIT [SK0980]

Wanted Inn SK17 8ET [junction
A623/B6061]: Attractive easy-going 16th-c
stone-built pub, all beams, copper and
brasses one end, and a tidy plainer bar with
local photographs (dogs allowed here);
prompt friendly service, well kept Robinsons
ales, sensibly priced simple home-made food
from toasties to good Sun lunch, tiled floors,
table football; piped music; picnic-sets by
car park, beautiful countryside (John and
Helen Rushton)

SPONDON [SK3935]

☆ **Malt Shovel** DE21 7LH [off A6096 on edge of
Derby, via Church Hill into Potter St]:
Homely traditional pub with several well
kept mainly Marstons-related ales from hatch
in tiled corridor with cosy panelled and
quarry-tiled or small turkey-carpeted rooms
off, helpful staff, inexpensive bar lunches,
old-fashioned décor, huge inglenook, steps
down to big games bar with darts and pool;
lots of picnic-sets, some under cover, in big
well used back garden with good play area,
open all day Fri-Sun (the Didler, Pete Baker,
BB)

STANTON IN PEAK [SK2364]

☆ **Flying Childers** DE4 2LW [off B5056
Bakewell—Ashbourne; Main Rd]: Cosy
beamed right-hand bar with fireside settles
and lots of character, larger comfortable
lounge, well kept Black Sheep, Wells &
Youngs Bombardier and interesting local
guest beers; friendly licensees and chatty
regulars, inexpensive bar lunches, dominoes
and cribbage; in delightful steep stone
village overlooking rich green valley, good
walks, cl Mon, Tues lunchtimes (the Didler,
Pete Baker)

SUTTON CUM DUCKMANTON [SK4371]

Arkwright Arms S44 5JG [A632 Bolsover—
Chesterfield]: Friendly mock-Tudor pub with
bar, pool room and dining room, all with real
fires, good value food (not Sat, Sun
evenings), up to nine changing ales, a dozen
real ciders and two perries (beer/cider
festivals on bank hols); games machine; no
children in bar, dogs in pool room only,
picnic-sets at front and in garden with play
equipment, open all day (JJW, CMW)

TICKNALL [SK3523]

Staff of Life DE73 1JH [High St (Ashby
Rd)]: Spacious main bar with smaller room
off, emphasis on simple pubby food inc
popular Sun lunch, Timothy Taylors Landlord

and a guest beer, friendly staff, open fire; unobtrusive piped music; garden, bedrooms, handy for Calke Abbey *(Paul J Robinshaw, David Barnes)*

TIDESWELL [SK1575]

Star SK17 8LD [High St]: Friendly good value pub with several unspoilt rooms, three real ales, pubby bar food, decent wines, brisk cheerful service, local paintings (most for sale) and old photographs, restaurant; public bar with TV and games machine; bedrooms *(Alan Johnson, Phil Taylor, Sian Watkin)*

TUPTON [SK3966]

Britannia S42 6XP [Ward St, New Tupton]: Tap for Spire brewery (can arrange tours), four of theirs kept well and up to four guest beers, good bottled range, farm cider, chatty licensees, lively bar with sports TV, quieter lounge; open from 4 Mon-Fri, from 3 Sat, all day Sun *(the Didler)*

WARDLOW [SK1875]

☆ *Three Stags Heads* SK17 8RW [Wardlow Mires; A623/B6465]: Basic no-frills farm pub of great individuality, flagstoned floors (often muddied by boots and dogs in winter), old country furniture, heating from cast-iron kitchen ranges, old photographs; plain-talking landlord and locals in favourite corners, Abbeydale ales inc Black Lurcher (brewed for the pub at a hefty 8% ABV), lots of bottled beers, hearty seasonal food on hardy home-made plates, may be free roast chestnuts; no credit cards; children and dogs welcome, hill views from front terrace, cl Mon-Thurs and Fri lunchtimes, open all day wknds *(the Didler, Rona Murdoch, Mike Proctor, LYM, Pete Baker, Dennis Jones)*

WENSLEY [SK2661]

Red Lion DE4 2LH [Main Rd (B5057 NW of Matlock)]: Friendly unspoilt farm pub run by chatty brother and sister, assorted 1950s-ish furniture, piano in main bar (landlord likes sing-songs), unusual tapestry in second room (usually locked, so ask landlady); no games or piped music, just bottled beer, soft or hot drinks, sandwiches or home-baked rolls perhaps using fillings from the garden – may sell their fruit too; outside gents'; open all day (may close if quiet) *(the Didler, Pete Baker)*

WHITTINGTON [SK3875]

Cock & Magpie S41 9QW [Church Street N, Old Whittington, behind museum]: Old stone-built family-run dining pub, enjoyable standard food inc some good value deals, friendly well organised service, well kept Marstons and related ales, good soft drinks choice; conservatory, separate public bar with games room; piped music, quiz nights

Tues, Thurs, no dogs; children welcome in dining areas; next to Revolution House museum *(Keith and Chris O'Neill)*

WHITTINGTON MOOR [SK3873]

☆ *Derby Tup* S41 8LS [Sheffield Rd; B6057 just S of A61 roundabout]: Spotless no-frills Tynemill pub with up to ten well kept interesting changing ales from long line of gleaming handpumps, good choice of other drinks inc farm cider; pleasant service, simple furniture, coal fire and lots of standing room as well as two small side rooms (children allowed here), daily papers, good value basic bar lunches; can get busy wknd evenings; dogs welcome, open all day at least Fri-Sun *(the Didler, LYM, Keith and Chris O'Neill)*

Red Lion S41 8LX [Sheffield Rd (B6057)]: Simple two-room 19th-c stone-built local tied to Old Mill with their real ales, friendly hard-working landlady, thriving atmosphere, old local photographs, dim lighting; live music (can be loud), sports TV; open all day *(the Didler)*

WINSTER [SK2460]

☆ *Bowling Green* DE4 2DS [East Bank, by NT Market House]: Classic traditional pub with good chatty atmosphere, character landlord and welcoming efficient service, enjoyable generous reasonably priced food, changing well kept ales, end log fire, dining area and family conservatory; nice village, good walks, open all day wknds, cl Mon, Tues *(Michael and Margaret Slater)*

Miners Standard DE4 2DR [Bank Top (B5056 above village)]: Simply furnished 17th-c stone local, relaxed at lunchtime and livelier in evenings, with well kept real ales such as Black Sheep, Flowers IPA and Marstons Pedigree, good value generous pubby food inc huge pies, big woodburner, lead-mining photographs and minerals, lots of brass, backwards clock, ancient well, snug and restaurant; children allowed away from bar, attractive view from garden, campsite next door, interesting stone-built village below, open all day wknds *(Reg Fowle, Helen Rickwood, Dennis Jones, Trevor and Sylvia Millum, Malcolm and Pauline Pellatt)*

WIRKSWORTH [SK2854]

Royal Oak DE4 4FG [North End]: Small chatty old-fashioned terraced local with proper friendly licensees, well kept changing ales inc Bass, Timothy Taylors Landlord and Whim Hartington (may let you taste first), dominoes, may be good filled cobs; key fobs, old copper kettles and other bric-a-brac, interesting old photographs; opens 8pm, cl lunchtime exc open Sun (12-3) *(the Didler)*

Post Office address codings confusingly give the impression that a few pubs are in Derbyshire, when they're really in Cheshire (which is where we list them).

Devon

This is one of Britain's best loved (and biggest) areas for pubs – so it's tricky to pick out the very top ones, with such diversity and so many excellent licensees. There are some lovely waterside locations too – just right for sunny summer drinks. Special places this year are the carefully renovated Turtley Corn Mill at Avonwick, unspoilt Fountain Head in Branscombe (good own-brew beers), friendly Merry Harriers in Clayhidon (handy for the M5), Five Bells at Clyst Hydon with its lovely front garden, newly smartened-up Culm Valley at Culmstock (fantastic food and our Devon Dining Pub of the Year), waterside Turf Hotel in Exminster, Church House in Marldon, quayside Ship in Noss Mayo, Harris Arms in Portgate (fantastic wines), foody Jack in the Green in Rockbeare, Start Bay at Torcross (exceptionally popular for its super fresh fish), and smashing little Rugglestone just outside Widecombe. New entries include the Sloop at Bantham, Abbey Inn at Buckfast, Tuckers Arms at Dalwood, Ferry Boat in Dittisham and the Grove in King's Nympton. Particularly strong Lucky Dips include the Royal Castle Hotel in Dartmouth, Hoops at Horns Cross and Queens Arms in Slapton. Otter is, by a long way, Devon's top beer, and among a fine choice of others to try here the most popular are Dartmoor, Branscombe Vale, O'Hanlons and Teignworthy.

AVONWICK   SX6958   MAP 1

Turtley Corn Mill ♀

0.5 miles off A38 roundabout at SW end of South Brent bypass; TQ10 9ES

Careful conversion of tall mill house with interestingly furnished spreading areas, local beers, well liked food, and huge gardens

With its working waterwheel and interesting ducks on a small lake in the extensive gardens, this carefully converted tall mill house is a most attractive sight; there are plenty of well spaced picnic-sets and a giant chess set. Inside, the spreading series of linked areas have big windows looking out over the grounds, a pleasant array of prints, a history of the mill and some other decorations (framed 78rpm discs, elderly wireless sets, house plants) on pastel walls, and a mix of comfortable dining chairs around heavy baluster-leg tables in a variety of sizes. There are bookcases, fat church candles and oriental rugs in one area, dark flagstones by the bar, a strategic woodburning stove dividing one part, a side enclave with a modern pew built in around a really big table, and so on. Dartmoor Jail Ale, St Austell Tribute, Sharps Doom Bar, and Summerskills Tamar on handpump, ten wines by the glass, up to 50 malt whiskies, and decent coffee; board games. They will keep your credit card if you eat outside.

⚑ **Well presented, enjoyable food includes sandwiches, soup, caramelised onion tarte tatin with gruyère, home-cured gravadlax, ham and free-range eggs, smoked haddock and salmon fishcakes, beer-battered haddock, mixed vegetable curry, rabbit and smoked bacon pie, bass fillets on fennel risotto, lemon and thyme-roasted chicken on tagliatelle, and puddings like steamed orange pudding with seville orange marmalade and clotted cream, and lemon and vanilla cheesecake with candied lemon peel.** *Starters/Snacks: £4.50 to £6.75. Main Courses: £9.50 to £16.95. Puddings: £5.95*

Free house ~ Licensees Lesley and Bruce Brunning ~ Real ale ~ Bar food (12-9.30(9 Sun)) ~ (01364) 646100 ~ Children welcome until 7.30pm ~ Dogs allowed in bar ~ Open 11-11; 12-10.30 Sun ~ Bedrooms: /£89S

Recommended by B J Harding, Dr and Mrs A K Clarke, Mr and Mrs C R Little, Henry Pursehouse-Tranter, Lynda and Trevor Smith, Andy and Claire Barker

BANTHAM   SX6643 MAP 1

Sloop ♀ 🛏

Off A379/B3197 NW of Kingsbridge; TQ7 3AJ

Friendly old pub close to fine beach and walks, character bar, real ales and enjoyable food; bedrooms

With only a ten-minute walk to the surfing beach and fine cliff walks, this 14th-c pub is a popular place with holiday visitors – though there are plenty of chatty locals, too. The black-beamed bar has a good bustling atmosphere, country chairs around wooden tables, stripped stone walls and flagstones, a woodburning stove, and easy chairs in a quieter side area. St Austell Dartmoor Best and Tribute on handpump and friendly staff; darts, table skittles and piped music. There are some seats outside at the back.

🍴 **Enjoyable bar food includes lunchtime sandwiches, moules marinière, fresh local crab salad, brie parcels with tomato and red onion chutney, ham, egg and chips, fresh beer-battered cod, beef or wild mushroom stroganoff, smoked haddock and gruyère fishcakes with chilli mayonnaise, daily specials such as sun-dried tomato, basil and parmesan soufflé, chicken stuffed with mozzarella, wrapped in bacon in a rich mushroom sauce, scallops and black pudding with pea purée, steak in ale pie and rustic lamb shanks, and puddings like crème brûlée and sticky toffee pudding.** *Starters/Snacks: £4.25 to £6.95. Main Courses: £7.25 to £14.75. Puddings: £4.75*

Free house ~ Licensee Andrew Turner ~ Real ale ~ Bar food ~ Restaurant ~ (01548) 560489 ~ Children welcome ~ Dogs welcome ~ Open 11-3, 6-11; all day summer Sun and Sat; 11.30-3, 6.30-10.30 Sun ~ Bedrooms: /£82B

Recommended by MP, David Crook, Mike Gorton, Lynda and Trevor Smith, Jo Rees, Peter and Margaret Glenister

BEESANDS   SX8140 MAP 1

Cricket

About 3 miles S of A379, from Chillington; in village turn right along foreshore road; TQ7 2EN

Welcoming small pub by beach, with enjoyable food (especially fish) and beer; bedrooms

Just over the sea wall in front of this friendly little pub is Start Bay beach; there are picnic-sets by the wall and the pub is popular with South Devon Coastal Path walkers. Inside, it's neatly kept and open-plan with dark traditional pubby furniture (carpeted in the dining part and with a stripped wooden floor in the bar area), and some nice, well captioned photographs of local fisherpeople, knots and fishing gear on the walls. Fullers London Pride and Otter Bitter on handpump, several wines by the glass and local cider; piped music. The cheerful black labrador is called Brewster. The bedrooms have fine sea views and the breakfasts are hearty; good wheelchair access.

🍴 **As well as the very popular fresh local fish and shellfish such as mussels, lobsters, scallops, lemon sole, plaice, skate and bass, the well liked bar food includes lunchtime sandwiches and salads, soup, smoked mackerel on toast, steak in ale pie, home-cooked ham with free-range eggs, calves liver and smoked bacon, seafood pancake, daily specials and evening steaks.** *Starters/Snacks: £5.00 to £8.00. Main Courses: £6.00 to £14.00. Puddings: £3.00 to £6.00*

Heavitree ~ Tenant Nigel Heath ~ Real ale ~ Bar food ~ Restaurant ~ (01548) 580215 ~ Children welcome ~ Dogs allowed in bar ~ Open 11-11; 11-3, 6-11 Mon-Fri in winter ~ Bedrooms: £45S/£65S

Recommended by Roger Wain-Heapy, Mark Sykes, Peter and Margaret Glenister, Adrian and Dawn Collinge, Richard Tilbrook, Roy Hoing, David Elliott

BLACKAWTON   SX8050   MAP 1

Normandy Arms

Off A3122 W of Dartmouth; TQ9 7BN

Interesting food cooked by chef/patron in friendly, refurbished pub

You can be sure of an enjoyable meal cooked by the chef/landlord in this friendly pub – though do note the restricted opening times. There's a drinkers' area with tub leather chairs and sofas in front of the woodburning stove, St Austell Dartmoor Best Bitter and Tribute on handpump and several wines by the glass; piped music. The two main dining areas have high-backed leather dining chairs around wooden tables on the grey slate floors and pictures of the village and the pub over the years. There are some benches outside in front of the building and picnic-sets in a small garden across the lane.

🍴 Good bar food includes lunchtime sandwiches, soup, chicken liver and foie gras parfait with tomato chutney and truffle oil, bacon, potato and black pudding with a poached egg and honey and mustard dressing, home-made ravioli filled with spinach and goats cheese with a red pepper coulis, brill fillet with spring onion champ, prawns and creamed leeks, guinea fowl breast with red wine sauce, fillet of local beef with horseradish and parsley butter, and puddings like passion fruit crème brûlée with bitter chocolate sorbet and warm plum tarte tatin with vanilla ice-cream. *Starters/Snacks: £4.50 to £7.95. Main Courses: £7.50 to £14.95. Puddings: £5.75*

Free house ~ Licensees Sharon Murdoch and Peter Alcroft ~ Real ale ~ Bar food (not lunchtimes except Sun, not Sun evening (except Aug)) ~ (01803) 712884 ~ Children welcome ~ Dogs welcome ~ Open 7-11 Tues-Thurs; 12-2.30, 7-11 Fri and Sat; 12-2.30, 7-10.30 summer Sun; closed winter Sun evenings, all day Mon, lunchtimes Tues-Sat; one week spring

Recommended by Mike Ambrose, Roger Wain-Heapy, J S Burn

BRANSCOMBE   SY1888   MAP 1

Fountain Head 🍺

Upper village, above the robust old church; village signposted off A3052 Sidmouth—Seaton, then from Branscombe Square follow road up hill towards Sidmouth, and after about a mile turn left after the church; OS Sheet 192 map reference SY188889; EX12 3BG

Old-fashioned stone pub with own-brewed beers and reasonably priced food

Our readers very much enjoy sitting outside this unspoilt old pub with a pint of their own-brewed beer and the sound of the little stream gurgling under the flagstoned path. Inside there's a welcome for all and an unchanging, old-fashioned feel – no games machines, piped music or TV. The room on the left (formerly a smithy) has forge tools and horseshoes on the high oak beams, a log fire in the original raised firebed with its tall central chimney, and cushioned pews and mate's chairs. On the right, an irregularly shaped, more orthodox snug room has another log fire, white-painted plank ceiling with an unusual carved ceiling-rose, brown-varnished panelled walls, and rugs on its flagstone-and-lime-ash floor. Their own beers include Branscombe Vale Branoc, Jolly Geoff and Summa That and their annual beer festival is held in June; several wines by the glass and local cider. Paintings (and greeting cards) painted by local artists for sale, darts, cards, dominoes, and board games. There are pleasant nearby walks.

🍴 As well as lunchtime sandwiches and ploughman's, the reasonably priced bar food includes soup, pâté of the day, fresh local crab, mussels and fish, lasagne, chicken and gammon with honey and ginger, steaks, and a spit roast, barbecue and live music on summer Sunday evenings. *Starters/Snacks: £4.20 to £6.95. Main Courses: £6.95 to £9.00. Puddings: £4.25*

Free house ~ Licensees Jon Woodley and Teresa Hoare ~ Real ale ~ Bar food ~ Restaurant ~ (01297) 680359 ~ Children welcome away from bar area ~ Dogs welcome ~ Open 11-3, 6-11; 12-3, 6-10.30 Sun

Recommended by the Didler, John and Fiona McIlwain, Revd R P Tickle, Laurence Milligan, John Wymer, Helene Grygar, Richard Stanfield, George Atkinson, Phil and Sally Gorton, Phyl and Jack Street

Masons Arms ♀ 🍺 🛏

Main Street; signed off A3052 Sidmouth—Seaton, then bear left into village; EX12 3DJ

Rambling low-beamed rooms, woodburning stoves, good choice of real ales and wines, popular food and seats in quiet terrace and garden; bedrooms

With a good mix of both locals and visitors, the rambling main bar at the heart of this picturesque 14th-c longhouse has plenty of character and a relaxed, friendly atmosphere. There are ancient ships' beams, a massive central hearth in front of the roaring log fire (where spit roasts are held) and comfortable seats and chairs on slate floors. The Old Worthies bar also has a slate floor, a fireplace with a two-sided woodburning stove and woodwork that has been stripped back to the original pine. There's also the original restaurant (warmed by one side of the woodburning stove) and another beamed restaurant above the main bar. Branscombe Vale Branoc, Otter Bitter, St Austell Tribute, a guest such as Branscombe Vale Best, and a beer named for the pub on handpump, a dozen wines by the glass and quite a few malt whiskies; darts, shove-ha'penny, cribbage, dominoes and board games. Outside, the quiet flower-filled front terrace has tables with little thatched roofs, extending into a side garden. You may have to leave your credit card behind the bar.

🍽 **Good bar food includes lunchtime sandwiches, soup, mussels in garlic, lemon and coriander, goats cheese panna cotta with spicy guacamole, a plate of cured meats with tomato chutney, beer-battered haddock, chicken curry, chilli vegetable ragoût with pasta, sausages with horseradish mash, lamb shank with feta filled peppers, confit of aromatic duck leg with truffle oil mash, steamed venison and mushroom pudding, and puddings like white chocolate crème brûlée and honey, mascarpone and vanilla torte.** *Starters/Snacks: £4.50 to £6.50. Main Courses: £10.50 to £15.50. Puddings: £4.50*

Free house ~ Licensees Colin and Carol Slaney ~ Real ale ~ Bar food ~ Restaurant ~ (01297) 680300 ~ Children in bar with parents but not in restaurant ~ Dogs allowed in bar and bedrooms ~ Open 11-11; 12-10.30 Sun; 11-3, 6-11 weekdays in winter ~ Bedrooms: /£80S(£85B)

Recommended by Dr Ian Mortimer, Barry Steele-Perkins, Andrew Shore, Maria Williams, the Didler, Lee and Liz Potter, Gavin Robinson, Phyl and Jack Street, Dr S J Shepherd, Simon Donan, Andrea Rampley, Richard Stanfield, Mike Gorton, Mr and Mrs P D Titcomb

BRIXHAM

SX9256   MAP 1

Maritime

King Street (up steps from harbour – nearby parking virtually non-existent); TQ5 9TH

Informal little one-bar pub with friendly landlady and lots to look at; bedrooms

As well as a warm welcome from the landlady, you should also get some amusement from the lively terrier and the african grey parrot (but mind your fingers). The only bar is crammed full of interest: hundreds of key fobs and chamber-pots hang from the beams, there's a binnacle by the door, cigarette cards and pre-war ensigns from different countries, toby jugs and horsebrasses, mannequins, pictures of astronomical charts and plenty of mugs and china jugs. There are two warming coal fires, cushioned wheelback chairs and pink-plush cushioned wall benches, flowery swagged curtains, and Bays Best and St Austell Tribute on handpump alongside 78 malt whiskies. The small TV might be on if there's something the landlady wants to watch; darts, piped music and board games. Fine views down over the harbour and almost non-existent nearby parking.

🍽 **No food.**

Free house ~ Licensee Mrs Pat Seddon ~ Real ale ~ No credit cards ~ (01803) 853535 ~ Well behaved children allowed ~ Dogs allowed in bar ~ Open 12-3, 7-1am ~ Bedrooms: £20/£40

Recommended by R T and J C Moggridge, Henry Pursehouse-Tranter, David Carr

---

By law pubs must show a price list of their drinks. Let us know if you are inconvenienced by any breach of this law.

BUCKFAST   SX7467   MAP 1

Abbey Inn ♀
Just off A38 at A384 junction; Buckfast Road; TQ11 OEA

Right by River Dart with tables on terrace, neat rooms, well liked bar food and St Austell beers; bedrooms

Seats on the terrace in front of this former quarry house look over the River Dart – as do all the bedrooms. It's a sizeable, pleasant place and the bar has partly panelled walls, quite a mix of chairs and tables, local paintings, and a woodburning stove in an ornate fireplace. The big dining room has more panelling and river views. St Austell Dartmoor Best, HSD and Tribute on handpump, several wines by the glass and local cider; helpful, obliging staff and piped music. The pub is down a steep little drive from the car park.

🍴 **Well liked bar food at lunchtime includes sandwiches and filled baguettes, ploughman's, soup, honey roast ham and egg, sausages with wholegrain mustard mash and onion gravy, and salmon fishcakes, with evening dishes like a trio of smoked fish with horseradish dressing, tagliatelle with roasted vegetables in a tomato sauce topped with mozzarella, and free-range chicken breast filled with cheddar cheese, wrapped in bacon in a red wine and shallot sauce, and daily specials such as casseroles and pies, cajun chicken salad, mushroom stroganoff and lamb shank.** *Starters/Snacks: £3.95 to £5.95. Main Courses: £6.95 to £13.95. Puddings: £3.95 to £4.25*

St Austell ~ Tenants Rob Bowrin, Tim Whitmee ~ Real ale ~ Bar food (12-3, 6-9; not Sun evening) ~ Restaurant ~ (01364) 642343 ~ Children welcome ~ Dogs welcome ~ Open 11-11 ~ Bedrooms: £55S/£75S

Recommended by Glenda Bennett, Alison Trowell, Norman and Sarah Keeping, Henry Pursehouse-Tranter, Michael Dandy

BUCKLAND BREWER   SS4220   MAP 1

Coach & Horses
Village signposted off A388 S of Monkleigh; OS Sheet 190 map reference 423206; EX39 5LU

Friendly old village pub with a mix of customers, open fires and real ales; good nearby walks

In a pretty village, this ancient thatched pub has been run by the same friendly family for over 20 years. The heavily beamed bar has comfortable seats (including a handsome antique settle) and a woodburning stove in the inglenook – there's also a good log fire in the big stone inglenook of the cosy lounge. A small back room has darts and pool; several cats. Cotleigh Golden Seahawk, Sharps Doom Bar, and a guest such as Fullers London Pride or Shepherd Neame Spitfire on handpump, and around eight wines by the glass; skittle alley (that doubles as a function room), piped music and occasional TV for sports. There are picnic-sets on a front terrace and in the side garden, and the pub is handy after a visit to the RHS garden Rosemoor. Walks on the nearby moorland and along the beaches of Westward Ho!

🍴 **Bar food includes sandwiches, ploughman's, filled baked potatoes, pasties, soup, and daily specials such as butternut squash, leek and parsnip cakes with stilton sauce, beef and mushroom pie, chicken breast stuffed with brie in an apricot and orange sauce, pork tenderloin in a creamy peppercorn sauce and duck breast with a plum and ginger sauce; Sunday roasts.** *Starters/Snacks: £4.75 to £6.25. Main Courses: £7.25 to £14.95. Puddings: £3.75 to £4.50*

Free house ~ Licensees Oliver Wolfe and Nicola Barrass ~ Real ale ~ Bar food ~ Restaurant ~ (01237) 451395 ~ Well behaved children welcome ~ Open 12-3, 5.30(6 Sun)-midnight

Recommended by Bob and Margaret Holder, the Didler, John Marsh, Ryta Lyndley

BUCKLAND MONACHORUM

SX4968 MAP 1

Drake Manor ◀

Off A386 via Crapstone, just S of Yelverton roundabout; PL20 7NA

Nice little village pub with snug rooms, popular food, quite a choice of drinks and pretty back garden; bedrooms

They now offer bed and breakfast accommodation as well as an attractive self-catering apartment in this charming and friendly little pub. And although there's now quite an emphasis on the enjoyable food, the long-serving landlady tells us that it is still very much a local with plenty of regular customers. The heavily beamed public bar on the left has brocade-cushioned wall seats, prints of the village from 1905 onwards, some horse tack and a few ship badges on the wall, and a really big stone fireplace with a woodburning stove; a small door leads to a low-beamed cubbyhole. The snug Drakes Bar has beams hung with tiny cups and big brass keys, a woodburning stove in an old stone fireplace, horsebrasses and stirrups, a fine stripped pine high-backed settle with a hood, and a mix of other seats around just four tables (the oval one is rather nice). On the right is a small, beamed dining room with settles and tables on the flagstoned floor. Shove-ha'penny, darts, euchre and board games. Courage Best, Greene King Abbot, Otter Ale and Sharps Doom Bar on handpump, 20 malt whiskies, ten wines by the glass, and a couple of draught ciders. The sheltered back garden – where there are picnic-sets – is prettily planted and the floral displays in front are very attractive all year round.

⑪ **Using local produce, the enjoyable daily specials might include crab and avocado salad with lime and coriander dressing, garlic mushrooms, braised rabbit with apricots and madeira, scallops on spinach with a light mustard and chive sauce, and roast rack of lamb with a fruity port sauce; also, sandwiches, soup, bass, cod, lime and ginger fishcake with yoghurt dressing, battered haddock, gammon with pineapple and cheese, steak and kidney pie, wild mushroom, red onion and stilton tart, steaks, and puddings like panna cotta with a fruit coulis and treacle and orange tart.** *Starters/Snacks: £3.95 to £5.95. Main Courses: £7.95 to £14.95. Puddings: £3.75 to £3.95*

Punch ~ Lease Mandy Robinson ~ Real ale ~ Bar food (12-2, 7-10(9.30 Sun)) ~ Restaurant ~ (01822) 853892 ~ Children in restaurant and area off main bar ~ Dogs allowed in bar ~ Open 11.30-2.30(3 Sat), 6.30-11(11.30 Fri and Sat); 12-11 Sun ~ Bedrooms: /£80B

Recommended by Joan and Michel Hooper-Immins, Nick and Meriel Cox, Mike Gorton, Richard Tilbrook, Alec and Sheelagh Knight

CADELEIGH

SS9107 MAP 1

Cadeleigh Arms ♀

Village signposted off A3072 just W of junction with A396 Tiverton—Exeter in Bickleigh; EX16 8HP

Attractively refurbished and civilised pub in rolling countryside, carefully chosen wines, well liked bar food and relaxed atmosphere

Attractive and rather civilised, this bustling little pub is run by friendly licensees. They keep Otter Ale and Bitter on handpump but quite a bit of emphasis is placed on the popular food; farm cider and a carefully chosen small wine list. To the left of the door, high-backed farmhouse, church and blond wooden chairs around a mix of tables (one is an old barrel) sit on the grey carpet, and there's a bay window seat, an ornamental stove in the stone fireplace and rather striking hound paintings; darts. This part leads to a flagstoned room with a high-backed settle to one side of the log fire in its big sandstone fireplace, and similar chairs and tables. Down a couple of steps is a light and airy dining room with country landscapes, pale wooden chairs and tables, and views over the valley; unobtrusive piped music. There are some picnic-sets on a gravel terrace with more on a sloping lawn. More reports please.

⑪ **Well liked bar food includes sandwiches, soup, salmon fishcake with creamed leeks, baked fig wrapped in parma ham with mozzarella, bangers and mash with cider gravy, a tian of mediterranean vegetables with goats cheese, fish or chicken and ham pie, and**

daily specials like tenderloin of pork with roasted root vegetables, confit duck leg with redcurrant jus, and local sirloin steak with roasted vine tomatoes and field mushrooms.

Free house ~ Licensee Jane Dreyer ~ Real ale ~ Bar food (12-2.30, 7-9; not Sun evening or Mon) ~ Restaurant ~ (01884) 855238 ~ Children welcome ~ Dogs allowed in bar ~ Open 12-2.30-ish, 6-11; 12-2.30 Sun; closed Sun evening, all day Mon; 25 Dec

Recommended by Martin and Sue Hopper, Pam Dingley, R J Walden

CLAYHIDON

ST1817　MAP 1

Merry Harriers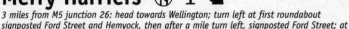

3 miles from M5 junction 26: head towards Wellington; turn left at first roundabout signposted Ford Street and Hemyock, then after a mile turn left, signposted Ford Street; at hilltop T-junction, turn left towards Chard – pub is 1.5 miles on right; EX15 3TR

Bustling dining pub with imaginative food, several real ales and quite a few wines by the glass; sizeable garden

A new garden area with plenty of tables and chairs has been opened up here adding to the sizeable existing garden and small terrace; they've started their own vegetable garden and now keep chickens. It's a friendly place, very popular with both our readers and locals, and handy for the M5. There are several small linked green-carpeted areas with comfortably cushioned pews and farmhouse chairs, candles in bottles, a woodburning stove with a sofa beside it, and plenty of horsey and hunting prints and local wildlife pictures. Two dining areas have a brighter feel with quarry tiles and lightly timbered white walls. Cotleigh Harrier, Otter Head and a guest like Exmoor Hound Dog on handpump, 14 wines by the glass, two local ciders, 20 malt whiskies and a good range of spirits; skittle alley and solitaire. This is a good walking area.

Naming their suppliers and using local produce, the good, interesting food includes lunchtime sandwiches, filled baguettes and ploughman's, as well as soup, pork and bramley apple terrine with home-made chutney, scallops with lemon butter sauce and crispy parma ham salad, thai-style beef salad with noodles and soy and chilli dressing, steak and kidney pie in ale gravy, mixed vegetable tajine with lentils and chickpeas, chicken suprême with chorizo on ratatouille, and slow-roasted lamb shoulder with mint pesto stuffing; also daily specials like mussels with a cider cream and herb sauce, mackerel fillets in light beer batter with horseradish mayonnaise and 12oz gammon steak with pineapple and eggs, and puddings like dark chocolate mousse with pistachio biscuits and vanilla crème brûlée. *Starters/Snacks: £4.00 to £5.50. Main Courses: £8.00 to £13.00. Puddings: £4.00 to £5.00*

Free house ~ Licensees Peter and Angela Gatling ~ Real ale ~ Bar food (not Sun evening or Mon) ~ Restaurant ~ (01823) 421270 ~ Children welcome ~ Dogs allowed in bar ~ Open 12-3, 6.30-11; 12-3 Sun; closed Sun evening, all day Mon; 25 and 26 Dec

Recommended by John and Gloria Isaacs, Piotr Chodzko-Zajko, Bob and Margaret Holder, Sue Ruffhead, John and Verna Aspinall, Gerry and Rosemary Dobson, Mike Gorton, Bruce and Sharon Eden

CLYST HYDON

ST0201　MAP 1

Five Bells

West of the village and just off B3176 not far from M5 junction 28; EX15 2NT

Attractive thatched pub with several distinctive areas, well liked food and drink, and carefully planted cottagey garden

It's worth making a special trip to this attractive thatched pub in either spring or summer when the immaculate cottagey front garden is full of thousands of flowers – the big window boxes and hanging baskets are quite a sight, too. Inside, the bar is divided at one end into different seating areas by brick and timber pillars: china jugs hang from big horsebrass-studded beams, there are many plates lining the shelves, lots of copper and brass, and a nice mix of dining chairs around small tables, with some comfortable pink plush banquettes on a little raised area. Past the inglenook fireplace is another big (but narrower) room they call the Long Barn, with a series of prints on the walls, a pine dresser at one end, and similar furnishings. Cotleigh Tawny, O'Hanlons Royal Oak and Otter Bitter on handpump, local farm cider, a good choice of soft drinks, and several wines by the glass; board games. Up some steps outside is a sizeable flat lawn with picnic-sets, a play frame and pleasant country views.

🍴 Tasty, popular bar food includes soup, scallops in bacon and leeks with garlic mayonnaise, pheasant, chicken and bacon terrine with cranberry and apple chutney, spinach, ratatouille and cream cheese lasagne, steak and kidney suet pudding, chicken suprême stuffed with sun-dried tomatoes, mozzarella and basil in a tomato and basil sauce, smoked haddock, leek and gruyère tart, lamb shank in red wine, orange and rosemary gravy, and puddings like date pudding with toffee sauce and raspberry mousse; they also offer a good value two-course lunch menu. *Starters/Snacks: £4.25 to £6.75. Main Courses: £7.95 to £15.95. Puddings: £4.75 to £5.75*

Free house ~ Licensees Mr and Mrs R Shenton ~ Real ale ~ Bar food (not Mon lunchtime) ~ (01884) 277288 ~ Children welcome ~ Live jazz second Weds of the month and folk duo fourth Fri of month ~ Open 11.30-3, 6.30-11; 12-3, 6.30-10.30 Sun; closed Mon lunchtime

Recommended by Peter Burton, Evelyn and Derek Walter, Mark Sykes, Mr and Mrs Richard Osborne, D F Clarke

COCKWOOD   SX9780   MAP 1

Anchor 🍷 🍺

Off, but visible from, A379 Exeter—Torbay; EX6 8RA

Busy, popular dining pub specialising in seafood (other choices available), with six real ales too

They keep a fine range of six real ales on handpump in this busy pub: Bass, Otter Ale, Bitter, Bright and Head, and Timothy Taylors Landlord. There's a fine wine list of 300 (bin ends and reserves and 12 by the glass), 20 brandies, 20 ports and 130 malt whiskies; lots of liqueur coffees too. As well as an extension made up of mainly reclaimed timber and decorated with over 300 ship emblems, brass and copper lamps and nautical knick-knacks, there are several small, low-ceilinged, rambling rooms with black panelling and good-sized tables in various alcoves, and the snug has a cheerful winter coal fire; piped music and games machine. From the tables on the sheltered verandah you can look across the road to the inlet. There's often a queue to get in, but they do two sittings in the restaurant on winter weekends and every evening in summer to cope with the crowds.

🍴 A huge range of fish dishes include 27 different ways of serving River Exe mussels, nine ways of serving local scallops and five ways of serving oysters, as well as crab and brandy soup, and various platters to share. Non-fishy dishes feature as well such as sandwiches, ploughman's, chicken wrapped in bacon stuffed with garlic and herb cheese, steak and kidney pudding, daily specials and puddings. *Starters/Snacks: £3.75 to £6.95. Main Courses: £5.95 to £9.50. Puddings: £4.25*

Heavitree ~ Tenants Mr Morgan and Miss Sanders ~ Real ale ~ Bar food (all day) ~ Restaurant ~ (01626) 890203 ~ Children welcome if seated and away from bar but no pushchairs ~ Dogs allowed in bar ~ Jazz/blues Weds, folk/light rock Thurs ~ Open 11-11; 12-10.30 Sun

Recommended by Robert Blake, Michael and Lynne Gittins, John and Fiona McIlwain, N R White, Tom Evans, D F Clarke, the Didler, Mr and Mrs P D Titcomb

COLEFORD   SS7701   MAP 1

New Inn 🍷 🛏

Just off A377 Crediton—Barnstaple; EX17 5BZ

Thatched 13th-c inn with interestingly furnished areas, inventive food and real ales

As well as being an enjoyable place to stay (and the breakfasts are good, too), this 600-year-old inn has welcoming licensees who have carefully redecorated most of the interior this year. It's a U-shaped building with interestingly furnished areas: ancient and modern settles, cushioned stone wall seats, some character tables – a pheasant worked into the grain of one – and carved dressers and chests; also, paraffin lamps, antique prints on the white walls and landscape plates on one of the beams, with pewter tankards on another. Captain, the chatty parrot will greet you with a 'hello' or even a 'goodbye'. Brains Rev James, Otter Ale and Sharps Doom Bar on handpump, local cider, a dozen wines by the glass, and several malt whiskies; good, cheerful service, piped music, darts and board games. There are chairs and tables on decking under the willow tree by the babbling stream and more on the flagstoned terrace (under the new awning) and on the lawn.

🍴 Using local produce, the inventive bar food includes filled baguettes, ploughman's, duck, chicken, pork and armagnac pâté, cauliflower, cumin and fresh coriander fritters with lime yoghurt dip, salads such as tuna niçoise or feta, orange and walnut, beer-battered cod, home-baked ham and free-range egg, sausges with red onion marmalade, a stack of roasted mediterranean vegetables on polenta topped with goats cheese, grilled red mullet fillets on pea purée and potato cake with fresh beetroot crisps, chicken breast with a mushroom and cider cream sauce, antiguan-style beef stew with chilli and coconut rice, and puddings like raspberry crème brûlée and a plate of chocolate puddings; they hold special food evenings such as a pie and a pint deal. *Starters/Snacks: £4.50 to £6.95. Main Courses: £6.95 to £10.50. Puddings: £5.00*

Free house ~ Licensees Carole and George Cowie ~ Real ale ~ Bar food ~ Restaurant ~ (01363) 84242 ~ Children welcome ~ Dogs allowed in bar ~ Occasional live jazz in summer ~ Open 12-3, 6-11; 12-3, 7-10.30 Sun; closed 25 and 26 Dec ~ Bedrooms: £65B/£85B

Recommended by Mrs P Sumner, Paul and Gail Betteley, Andrea Rampley, Tom Evans, Dr A McCormick

COMBEINTEIGNHEAD
SX9071   MAP 1

Wild Goose 🍷 🍺

Just off unclassified coast road Newton Abbot—Shaldon, up hill in village; TQ12 4RA

Fine choice of real ales in well run, friendly pub with seats in attractive garden

Run by friendly, helpful licensees, this popular, bustling pub is much enjoyed by our readers. They keep a fine range of seven real ales on handpump such as Otter Bright and Skinners Betty Stogs and five constantly changing guests, and they've two farm ciders and ten wines by the glass. The back beamed spacious lounge has a mix of wheelbacks and red plush dining tables, a decent collection of tables, and french windows to the garden, with nice country views beyond. The front bar has seats in the window embrasures of the thick walls, flagstones in a small area by the door, some beams and standing timbers, and a step down on the right at the end, with dining chairs around the tables and a big old fireplace with an open log fire. There's a small carved oak dresser with a big white goose, piped music and board games, and also a cosy section on the left with an old settee and comfortably well used chairs. The sheltered and walled back garden – beneath the 14th-c church tower – has plenty of seats around outdoor heaters.

🍴 Well liked traditional home-made bar food includes tasty club sandwiches, soup, smoked salmon pâté, steak and kidney pie, local mussels, beer-battered fresh haddock, sausages with mustard mash, bean ragoût, lamb cutlets with redcurrant sauce, whole brixham plaice, and puddings like chocolate and vanilla cheesecake and summer pudding. *Starters/Snacks: £3.95 to £5.95. Main Courses: £5.95 to £14.75. Puddings: £4.50 to £5.45*

Free house ~ Licensees Jerry and Kate English ~ Real ale ~ Bar food ~ Restaurant ~ (01626) 872241 ~ Children in dining room only ~ Dogs allowed in bar ~ Open 11-3, 5.30-11(midnight Sat); 12-3, 7-11 Sun

Recommended by J D O Carter, Mike Gorton, David Heath, Laurence Smith

---

Real ale to us means beer which has matured naturally in its cask – not pressurised or filtered. We name all real ales stocked. We usually name ales preserved under a light blanket of carbon dioxide too, though purists – pointing out that this stops the natural yeasts developing – would disagree (most people, including us, can't tell the difference!)

CULMSTOCK

Culm Valley ⊕ ♀ ◧

B3391, off A38 E of M5 junction 27; EX15 3JJ

DEVON DINING PUB OF THE YEAR

Quirky, friendly dining pub with imaginative food, interesting real ales, lively atmosphere, and outside seats overlooking River Culm

Smartened up this year with some fresh new paintwork, this friendly pub is genuinely appealing to those who like slightly quirky places. It's run by a cheerful and welcoming, slightly off-beat landlord, the atmosphere is lively and informal and there's a healthy mix of both chatty locals and visitors. The bar has a hotch-potch of modern and unrenovated furnishings, horse racing paintings and various knick-knacks to do with racing on the walls, a big fireplace, and a long elm bar counter; further along is a dining room with a chalkboard menu, a small front conservatory, and leading off here, a little oak-floored room with views into the kitchen. A larger back room has paintings by local artists for sale. Board games and a small portable TV for occasional rugby, rowing and racing events; the dogs are called Lady and Spoof. The landlord and his brother import wines from smaller french vineyards, so you can count on a few of those as well as some unusual french fruit liqueurs, somerset cider brandies, vintage rum, good sherries and madeira, local farm ciders, and real ales such as Art Brew Brut, Blackawton Saltash Sunrise, Cotleigh Kookaburra, Cottage Hound Dog and Exeter Lighterman tapped from the cask. Outside, tables are very attractively positioned overlooking the bridge and the River Culm. The gents' is in an outside yard. They don't take credit cards and, as we were going to press, were thinking about accepting debit cards – they do take cheques; best to check beforehand.

⊞ Imaginative food using as much free-range and organic local produce as possible might include lunchtime sandwiches, interesting soups, home-cured bresaola, thai duck salad, a tapas plate (for sharing), home-made brawn, all sorts of sausages (the spicy west indian ones are popular), pancakes filled with spinach, ricotta and parmesan, spring lamb made into meatballs, barnsley chops and so forth, chicken curry, beer-battered fresh fish, line-caught bass roasted in garlic, good steaks, and puddings like chocolate marquise and sticky toffee; popular Sunday roast beef. *Starters/Snacks: £4.00 to £7.00. Main Courses: £8.00 to £18.00. Puddings: £5.00*

Free house ~ Licensee Richard Hartley ~ Real ale ~ Bar food (not Sun evening) ~ Restaurant ~ No credit cards ~ (01884) 840354 ~ Children allowed away from main bar ~ Dogs welcome ~ Irish folk first Weds of month ~ Open 12-3, 6-11; 11-11 Fri and Sat; 12-10.30 Sun ~ Bedrooms: £35B/£65B

Recommended by G K Smale, Evelyn and Derek Walter, John and Fiona Merritt, FJS and DS, Brian and Anita Randall, Adrian Johnson, John and Hilary Penny, Christine and Neil Townend, Michael and Ann Cole, Adrian and Dawn Collinge, Simon Watkins, Tony and Tracy Constance, John Urquhart, Comus and Sarah Elliott, Michael Beale

DALWOOD

Tuckers Arms

Off A35 Axminster—Honiton; EX13 7EG

Pretty, thatched inn with friendly, hard-working young licensees, real ales, well liked bar food, and attractive summer hanging baskets

You can be sure of a genuinely friendly welcome from the young licensees in this thatched and pretty 800-year-old inn. The fine flagstoned bar has a lot of atmosphere, plenty of beams, a mixture of dining chairs, window seats and wall settles, and a log fire in the inglenook fireplace. The back bar has an enormous collection of miniature bottles. Branscombe Vale Branoc, Otter Bitter, Palmers Best and a guest beer on handpump, several wines by the glass and up to 20 malt whiskies. Piped music and double skittle alley. In summer, the hanging baskets are pretty and there are seats in the garden.

⊞ Well liked bar food at lunchtime includes filled cobs and filled baked potatoes, ploughman's, beer-battered fish with pea purée, a proper burger topped with bacon and cheese, and cajun chicken as well as soup, garlic mushrooms en croûte, crab cakes with sweet chilli dip, ham and egg, beef in ale pie, herb-studded lamb rump with rosemary and redcurrant jus, barbary duck with a sticky blueberry glaze, line-caught bass and steaks; the Sunday roast is popular. *Starters/Snacks: £4.25 to £6.45. Main Courses: £6.95 to £10.95. Puddings: £4.05 to £6.00*

Free house ~ Licensee Tracey Pearson ~ Real ale ~ Bar food ~ Restaurant ~ (01404) 881342 ~ Children in restaurant but must be well behaved ~ Dogs allowed in bar ~ Open 11.30-3, 6.30(6 Sat)-11.30; 12-4, 7-10.30 Sun ~ Bedrooms: £42.50S/£69.50S

Recommended by Marcus Mann, Paul Aldred, Bob and Margaret Holder, Neil Kellett

DARTMOUTH

SX8751   MAP 1

Cherub

Higher Street; walk along river front, right into Hauley Road and up steps at end; TQ6 9RB

Handsome old building with plenty of atmosphere; can get busy at peak times

Under a new licensee, this fine old pub was already 300 years old when Francis Drake used it. It looks at its best in the summer, with lots of pretty hanging baskets below the two heavily timbered upper floors which each jut out further than the one below. Inside, the bustling bar has tapestried seats under creaky heavy beams, leaded lights, a big stone fireplace with a woodburning stove, and St Austell Dartmoor Best and Proper Job, Sharps Doom Bar and one or two guest beers on handpump; quite a few malt whiskies and several wines by the glass. Upstairs is the low-ceilinged restaurant; piped music.

🍴 **Good bar food includes sandwiches, soup, chicken liver pâté with redcurrant and caramelised onion marmalade, stilton-stuffed mushrooms, greek-style feta and tomato pie, seasonal game pie, lambs liver and crispy bacon with sage gravy, roast cod loin with chorizo and sunblush tomato risotto, daily specials like steak in ale or fish pie or local bass fillets in citrus butter, and puddings such as Baileys bread and butter pudding and raspberry and rhubarb crumble.** *Starters/Snacks: £4.25 to £6.95. Main Courses: £7.95 to £12.95. Puddings: £4.95*

Free house ~ Licensee Dean Singer ~ Real ale ~ Bar food ~ Restaurant ~ (01803) 832571 ~ Dogs allowed in bar ~ Open 11am-midnight; 11-3, 6-11 Mon-Thurs in winter

Recommended by Terry and Linda Moseley, the Didler, Dr Ian Mortimer, Dick and Madeleine Brown, Donna and Roger, Hazel Morgan, Bernard Patrick, Mike Batchelor, Andrea Rampley, Christine and Neil Townend, Peter and Margaret Glenister, Michael Dandy, Roger Wain-Heapy, Tom and Jill Jones, John Day

DITTISHAM

SX8654   MAP 1

Ferry Boat

Manor Street; best to park in village – steep but attractive walk down; TQ6 0EX

Cheerful riverside pub with shipping knick-knacks, real ales and friendly staff

To make the most of this little pub's fine riverside position, it's best to arrive early and try to bag one of the seats in the big picture window. There's a lively mix of locals, sailors and visitors, beams, open log fires, brass gear and a ship's clock, ship's badges over the serving counter, photographs of boats and ships, and straightforward pubby furniture; they chalk the tide times up on the wall. Friendly staff serve Bass, St Austell Tribute, Sharps Doom Bar and Wells & Youngs on handpump; piped music. If you arrive by boat there are moorings on the adjacent pontoon and there's a bell to summon the ferry across the Greenway Quay. Parking nearby is not easy – best to park by the church.

🍴 **Pubby bar food at lunchtime includes filled baguettes, soup, sausage and egg, a pie of the day and lasagne, with evening meals such as grilled sardines, tiger prawns in garlic butter, beer-battered cod, fillets of bass in white wine and cream, moules, steaks, and puddings like hazelnut pavlova and sticky toffee pudding.** *Starters/Snacks: £6.00 to £7.95. Main Courses: £7.95 to £15.00. Puddings: £3.50 to £4.25*

Punch ~ Lease Ray Benson ~ Real ale ~ Bar food (12-2(4 Sun), 7-9) ~ (01803) 722368 ~ Children welcome ~ Dogs welcome ~ Open 12-11.30(10.30 Sun)

Recommended by Dr Ron Cox, Peter and Margaret Glenister, Henry Pursehouse-Tranter

DREWSTEIGNTON

SX7390 MAP 1

Drewe Arms

Off A30 NW of Moretonhampstead; EX6 6QN

Pretty thatched pub, warmly welcoming, proper basic bar plus dining rooms, well liked food and real ales; bedrooms

In a charming village and handy for Castle Drogo, this thatched pub is a friendly and pretty place. There's an unchanging and unspoilt room on the left which still has a serving hatch and basic wooden wall benches, stools and tables. And three dining areas – Mabel's Kitchen with its original Raeburn and a history of Aunt Mabel (Britain's longest serving and oldest landlady, whom both editors of this *Guide* remember well), the Card Room which has a woodburning stove, and the back Dartmoor Room which is ideal for a private party, with lots of prints and pictures on the walls and an array of copper saucepans. Exmoor Gold, Otter Ale and Druid Ale (brewed by Otter exclusively for the pub) tapped from casks in the original tap room; skittle alley. There are seats under umbrellas along the front terrace surrounded by lovely flowering tubs and hanging baskets, with more in the terraced garden. As well as comfortable bedrooms, they have bunk rooms which are ideal for walkers.

🍴 **Good bar food includes soup, popular lunchtime platters, chicken liver pâté with a sweet chilli onion marmalade, smoked duck and orange salad, sausages with red wine gravy, vegetarian quiche, beer-battered cod, lamb cutlets on garlic-crushed potatoes with a redcurrant sauce, daily specials like cornish sardines, local mussels and beef stroganoff, and puddings like gooseberry cheesecake and chocolate mocha tart; on Wednesday evenings they do takeaway fish and chips.** *Starters/Snacks: £4.95 to £5.95. Main Courses: £9.95 to £12.95. Puddings: £3.50 to £5.25*

Enterprise ~ Lease Fiona Newton ~ Real ale ~ Bar food (all day in summer; 12-2.15, 6-9.30 in winter) ~ Restaurant ~ (01647) 281224 ~ Children welcome ~ Dogs allowed in bar and bedrooms ~ Open 11am-midnight; 11-3, 6-midnight Mon-Fri in winter ~ Bedrooms: /£80B

Recommended by Dr and Mrs A K Clarke, Dr Ian Mortimer, Mrs Angela Graham, Di and Mike Gillam, B J Harding, David Crook, Roy and Lindsey Fentiman

EAST ALLINGTON

SX7648 MAP 1

Fortescue Arms 🍴

Village signposted off A381 Totnes—Kingsbridge, S of A3122 junction; TQ9 7RA

Pretty village pub, good choice of drinks, highly thought-of food cooked by landlord/chef and attractive outside seating; bedrooms

Many customers come to this pretty village pub to enjoy the good, interesting food but drinkers are very welcome and they do keep Butcombe Bitter, Dartmoor IPA and Wyre Piddle Piddle Artist on handpump, several wines by the glass including a local one, austrian wines and spirits (Mr Rott, the chef, is from Austria), and local cider and juices. The main part of the two-room bar has a nice mix of wooden tables and cushioned dining chairs on the black slate floor, an open log fire, a dark green dado under cream walls, church candles and some brewery memorabilia, and attractive tartan curtains. The second room is set for eating with similar furniture, a few old photographs, and red carpeting; darts, board games and unobtrusive piped music; There's also a stylish contemporary restaurant. There are picnic-sets in the sheltered courtyard and teak steamer chairs under a pair of small pointy marquees on the terrace.

🍴 **Cooked by one of the licensees, the very good food includes sandwiches, soup, seared scallops on broad bean purée with saffron sauce, sliced smoked duck breast with waldorf salad and chutney, vegetarian lasagne, chicken wiener schnitzel, local pheasant wrapped in black forest ham with a tangy berry sauce, monkfish on spinach with a roasted red pepper sauce, local deer steak with a wild mushroom sauce, and puddings such as monbazillac poached pears with chocolate sauce and crème anglaise, and malakoff torte (sponge fingers soaked in rum, coffee and cream); enjoyable breakfasts.** *Starters/Snacks: £4.50 to £8.80. Main Courses: £8.20 to £12.95. Puddings: £5.65*

Free house ~ Licensees Tom Kendrick and Werner Rott ~ Real ale ~ Bar food (12-2.30, 6.30-9.30; not Mon lunchtime) ~ Restaurant ~ (01548) 521215 ~ Children in own area; no children under 6 in restaurant ~ Dogs allowed in bar ~ Open 12-2.30, 6-11; 12-2.30, 6-10.30 Sun; closed Mon lunchtime ~ Bedrooms: £40S/£60S

Recommended by Mrs L Aquilina, Pauline and Philip Darley, Lynda and Trevor Smith, Roger Wain-Heapy

EXETER
SX9292   MAP 1

Hour Glass ◖

Melbourne Street, off B3015 Topsham Road (some nearby parking); EX2 4AU

Inventive food in old-fashioned local, friendly service and good choice of real ales and wines by the glass

With a smashing range of wines by the glass and some inventive food, it's not surprising that this small old-fashioned back street pub gets so busy at peak times. There are beams, a mix of pub chairs and tables on the bare boards, dark red walls, an open fire in a small brick fireplace and a relaxed, chatty atmosphere; resident cats, piped music and board games. Branscombe Vale Branoc, Exeter Lighterman, Otter Bitter and a guest such as Exeter Avocet or Yeovil Star Gazer on handpump, served from the central island bar.

◖ **Good, interesting bar food includes sandwiches, soup, smoked eel with potato terrine and rhubarb, pork rillettes with toast and pickles, risotto with pea, mint, vermouth and pecorino, squid stew with chickpeas and preserved lemon, tagliatelle with rabbit and mustard, grilled rib-eye steak with horseradish cream, and puddings like white chocolate parfait with berries and aged balsamic, and rice pudding with kirsch poached pear.** *Starters/Snacks: £2.00 to £6.50. Main Courses: £10.00 to £16.50. Puddings: £4.50 to £6.50*

Enterprise ~ Lease J Slade ~ Real ale ~ Bar food (12.30-2.30(3 weekends), 7-9.30) ~ Restaurant ~ (01392) 258722 ~ Children in dining area ~ Dogs allowed in bar ~ Open 12-3, 5-11; 12-11 Fri and Sat; 12-10.30 Sun; closed Mon lunchtime; 25 and 26 Dec, 1 Jan

Recommended by John and Fiona McIlwain, the Didler, Dr and Mrs M E Wilson, Mike Gorton

Imperial ◖ £

New North Road (St David's Hill on Crediton/Tiverton road, above St David's station); EX4 4AH

19th-c mansion in own grounds with interesting seating areas and cheap food and drink

The setting of this fine mansion is impressive as it stands in its own six-acre hillside park and is reached along a sweeping drive; there are plenty of picnic-sets in the grounds and elegant garden furniture in the attractive cobbled courtyard. Inside, the light and airy former orangery has an unusual lightly mirrored end wall, and there are various different areas including a couple of little clubby side bars, a left-hand bar that looks into the orangery, and a fine ex-ballroom filled with elaborate plasterwork and gilding brought here in the 1920s from Haldon House (a Robert Adam stately home that was falling on hard times). The furnishings give Wetherspoons' usual, solid, well spaced comfort, and the walls are hung with plenty of interesting pictures and other things to look at. Up to 14 real ales on handpump such as Exmoor Gold, Greene King IPA and Abbot, Marstons Pedigree, Otter Bright and nine guests.

◖ **Very reasonably priced bar food includes filled panini, meaty or vegetarian burgers (the price also includes a pint), battered cod, beef in ale or popular cottage pie, pasta with tomato and basil sauce, a decent curry and sausages and mash.** *Starters/Snacks: £2.59. Main Courses: £5.79 to £7.49. Puddings: £1.79 to £3.79*

Wetherspoons ~ Manager Paul Dixey ~ Real ale ~ Bar food (all day) ~ Restaurant ~ (01392) 434050 ~ Children welcome ~ Open 9am-midnight(1am Sat)

Recommended by Henry Snell, the Didler, Dr and Mrs A K Clarke, Mike Gorton, Pat and Tony Martin, Dr and Mrs M E Wilson, Ben Williams

---

Every entry includes a postcode for use in Sat-Nav devices.

EXMINSTER   SX9686 MAP 1

Turf Hotel ★

Follow the signs to the Swan's Nest, signposted from A379 S of village, then continue to end of track, by gates; park and walk right along canal towpath – nearly a mile; there's a fine seaview out to the mudflats at low tide; EX6 8EE

Remote but very popular waterside pub with fine choice of drinks, super summer barbecues and lots of space in big garden

Even after 20 years, the Redferns are still working their magic at this lively and extremely popular pub. You can't get here by car, you must either walk (which takes about 20 minutes along the ship canal) or cycle, or catch a 60-seater boat which brings people down the Exe estuary from Topsham quay (15-minute trip, adult £4.50, child £2); there's also a canal boat from Countess Wear Swing Bridge every lunchtime. Best to phone the pub for all sailing times. For those arriving in their own boat there is a large pontoon as well as several moorings. Inside, the end room has a slate floor, pine walls, built-in seats, lots of photographs of the pub, and a woodburning stove; along a corridor (with an eating room to one side) is a simply furnished room with wood-plank seats around tables on the stripped wooden floor. Exeter Ferryman, Otter Ale and Bitter, and O'Hanlons Yellowhammer on handpump, local Dragon Tears cider, local juices, ten wines by the glass (and local wine too) and jugs of Pimms. There are plenty of picnic-sets spread around the big garden, and the children's play area was built using a lifeboat from a liner that sank off the Scilly Isles around 100 years ago. Although the pub and garden do get packed in fine weather and there are inevitable queues, the staff remain friendly and efficient. The sea and estuary birds are fun to watch at low tide.

🍽 **Good bar food using organic and local produce includes lunchtime sandwiches and toasties, soup, hummus with roasted garlic and sun-dried tomatoes, smoked mackerel pâté with beetroot chutney, mussels in white wine, garlic and cream, beer-battered fish of the day with tartare sauce, hungarian pork goulash, vegetable tart, salmon and dill fishcakes, daily specials, and puddings. The barbecue is much used in good weather.** *Starters/Snacks: £4.50 to £6.50. Main Courses: £7.50 to £9.75. Puddings: £2.00 to £4.50*

Free house ~ Licensees Clive and Ginny Redfern ~ Real ale ~ Bar food (12-2.30(3 Sat), 6.30-9(9.30 Sat); not Sun evening) ~ (01392) 833128 ~ Children welcome ~ Dogs welcome ~ Open 11-11; 12-10.30 Sun; open only weekends in Oct, Nov, Feb; closed Dec and Jan

Recommended by Barry Steele-Perkins, David Carr, Richard Mason, J D O Carter, Mike Gorton, John and Fiona McIlwain, R T and J C Moggridge, the Didler, John and Helen Rushton, FJS and DS, Mr and Mrs P D Titcomb

HAYTOR VALE   SX7777 MAP 1

Rock ★ 🍽 🛏

Haytor signposted off B3387 just W of Bovey Tracey, on good moorland road to Widecombe; TQ13 9XP

Civilised Dartmoor inn at its most informal at lunchtime; super food, comfortable bedrooms, and pretty garden

Civilised and neatly kept, this very well run place is genuinely welcoming and has an easy, relaxed atmosphere. It's at its most informal at lunchtime when there's a nod towards pubbiness as walkers pop in for a pint of Dartmoor Jail Ale, Otter Bright or St Austell Dartmoor Best on handpump and a light meal. In the evening, though, it becomes a restaurant-with-rooms with all space given over to the excellent food. The two communicating, partly panelled bar rooms have lots of dark wood and red plush, polished antique tables with candles and fresh flowers, old-fashioned prints and decorative plates on the walls, and warming winter log fires (the main fireplace has a fine Stuart fireback). There are seats in the large, pretty garden opposite, with tables and chairs on a small terrace next to the pub itself. The bedrooms are comfortable with good facilities (some are up steep stairs), and the breakfasts are smashing. There is a car park at the back.

🍽 **At lunchtime, the enjoyable food includes sandwiches, ploughman's, soup, chicken liver parfait with red onion marmalade, goats cheese and caramelised red onion tart, haddock and bacon fishcakes, steak in ale pie, wild mushroom risotto, and thai chicken curry;**

evening dishes such as mussels in coconut, chilli and lemon grass, scallops with vanilla and celeriac purée and crispy parma ham, roasted lamb rump with parsnip purée and port sauce, and ruby-red beef fillet with wild mushroom jus, and puddings like chocolate brownie and pear and almond bakewell with clotted cream; they also offer a two- and three-course set menu. *Starters/Snacks: £4.95 to £5.95. Main Courses: £14.00 to £15.95. Puddings: £4.00 to £5.95*

Free house ~ Licensee Christopher Graves ~ Real ale ~ Bar food ~ Restaurant ~ (01364) 661305 ~ Children welcome ~ Dogs allowed in bedrooms ~ Open 11(10.30 Sat)-11; 12-11 Sun; closed 25 and 26 Dec ~ Bedrooms: £66.95B/£76.95S(£95.95B)

Recommended by Mrs Mary Woods, Anthony Barnes, Barry Steele-Perkins, Cathryn and Richard Hicks, Barry and Anne, Paul and Gail Betteley, Dr Ian Mortimer, John and Gloria Isaacs, Tom and Ruth Rees

HOLNE

SX7069 MAP 1

Church House

Signed off B3357 W of Ashburton; TQ13 7SJ

Medieval inn on Dartmoor, plenty of surrounding walks, log fires, real ales, and tasty bar food; bedrooms

Run by an attentive landlord, this medieval inn is close to open moorland and therefore popular with walkers – especially at lunchtime. The lower bar has stripped pine panelling and an 18th-c curved elm settle, and is separated from the lounge bar by a 16th-c heavy oak partition; open log fires, lit candles and fresh flowers in both rooms. Otter Bright and Teignworthy Gun Dog on handpump, and several good wines by the glass; piped music. The bedrooms are comfortable and clean. Charles Kingsley (of *Water Babies* fame) was born in the village. The church is well worth a visit.

🍴 Tasty bar food includes lunchtime sandwiches and filled baguettes, soup, local pasties, grilled goats cheese on a herb croûton, whitebait, devilled kidneys, home-cooked ham and eggs, steak in ale pie, fish and chips, liver and bacon casserole, and puddings such as sticky toffee pudding with butterscotch sauce and poached pears in red wine with a hot chocolate sauce. *Starters/Snacks: £4.50 to £6.95. Main Courses: £7.50 to £12.95. Puddings: £3.50 to £4.95*

Free house ~ Licensee Steve Ashworth ~ Real ale ~ Bar food (12-2.30(3 Sun), 7-9) ~ Restaurant ~ (01364) 631208 ~ Children welcome away from bar areas ~ Dogs welcome ~ Open 12-3, 7-11(10.30 Sun evening) ~ Bedrooms: £40S/£80S

Recommended by Mr and Mrs A Scadding, Frances Naldrett, Mrs J Ekins-Daukes

HORNDON

SX5280 MAP 1

Elephants Nest 🍺 🛏

If coming from Okehampton on A386 turn left at Mary Tavy Inn, then left after about 0.5 miles; pub signposted beside Mary Tavy Inn, then Horndon signposted; on the Ordnance Survey Outdoor Leisure Map it's named as the New Inn; PL19 9NQ

Isolated old inn surrounded by Dartmoor walks, some interesting original features, real ales and popular food; bedrooms

There are plenty of walks all around this attractively furnished old inn and both walkers and their dogs are welcome. The main bar has lots of beer pump clips on the beams, high bar chairs by the bar counter, and Dartmoor Jail Ale, Palmers IPA, Sharps Doom Bar, and a guest like O'Hanlons Yellowhammer on handpump, farm cider and several wines by the glass. There are two other rooms with nice modern dark wood dining chairs around a mix of tables, and throughout there are bare stone walls, flagstones, and three woodburning stoves; darts. The spreading, attractive garden has plenty of picnic-sets under parasols (they've also opened a walled garden for adults only), and from here you look over dry-stone walls to the pastures of Dartmoor's lower slopes and the rougher moorland above. The bedrooms are comfortable and well appointed.

🍴 Good, popular bar food includes lunchtime filled baguettes and wraps, soup, ham hock terrine with pickled mushrooms and wasabi mayonnaise, king prawns sizzling in lemon, garlic chilli and parsley butter, fish pie, cumberland sausage with onion gravy, lamb curry, burger with red onion marmalade, steaks, daily specials like wild mushroom and butternut squash risotto, calves liver with madeira sauce, and cornish plaice with lemon butter, capers and prawns; also puddings such as treacle tart with clotted cream and bread and butter pudding with whisky and marmalade. *Starters/Snacks: £5.95 to £8.95. Main Courses: £8.95 to £18.95. Puddings: £4.50*

Free house ~ Licensee Hugh Cook ~ Real ale ~ Bar food ~ (01822) 810273 ~ Children welcome away from bar and not in the adult part of garden ~ Dogs welcome ~ Open 12-3, 6.30-11 ~ Bedrooms: £65B/£80B

Recommended by John and Bernadette Elliott, Mr and Mrs M J Matthews, Andrea Rampley, Dr and Mrs M W A Haward, FJS and DS, Dr and Mrs M E Wilson

KING'S NYMPTON   SS6819   MAP 1

Grove ⑪

Off B3226 SW of South Molton; EX37 9ST

Thatched 17th-c pub in remote village, locals beers, interesting bar food and cheerful licensees

In a lovely village, very much off the tourist route, this thatched 17th-c pub is doing particularly well at the moment, thanks to the way its cheerful licensees run it. The low-beamed bar has a winter open fire, lots of bookmarks hanging from the ceiling, simple pubby furnishings on the flagstoned floor, bare stone walls, and Exmoor Ale, Red Rock (from the Red Rock Brewery) and Teignworthy Spring Tide on handpump, several wines by the glass and 34 malt whiskies; darts and board games. The surrounding countryside is quiet and wooded with twisty valley pastures. They have a self-catering cottage to rent.

⑪ **Imaginative bar food includes sandwiches, ploughman's, interesting soup, chicken liver pâté, grilled goats cheese salad with garlic croutons, ostrich burger with salsa, vegetarian wellington with a tomato and chilli sauce, stew of local rabbit, chicken breast stuffed with mozzarella, asparagus and parma ham, plaice with herb butter, and puddings such as white chocolate cheesecake with rhubarb compote and lemon burnt cream; Sunday roasts.** *Starters/Snacks: £4.00 to £4.50. Main Courses: £6.00 to £19.50. Puddings: £3.75 to £4.50*

Free house ~ Licensees Robert and Deborah Smallbone ~ Real ale ~ Bar food (12-2(3 Sun), 6-9; not Mon lunchtime) ~ Restaurant ~ (01769) 580406 ~ Children welcome but must be seated and supervised ~ Dogs welcome ~ Open 12-3, 6-11; 12-4, 7-10.30 Sun; closed Mon lunchtime except bank hol Mon

Recommended by Robert and Carole Hewitt, Mark Flynn

KINGSBRIDGE   SX7344   MAP 1

Dodbrooke Inn ◀ £

Church Street, Dodbrooke (parking some way off); TQ7 1DB

Chatty, bustling local, genuinely welcoming licensees, good mix of customers and honest food and drink

The friendly licensees have been running this quaint, bustling small local for 20 years now. There's always a happy mix of locals of all ages but you'll be made just as welcome if it's your first visit, and the atmosphere is comfortably traditional. There are bow windows, plush stools and built-in simple cushioned stall seats around straightforward pub tables (and an interesting barrel one), ceiling joists, some horse harness, old local photographs and china jugs, and a log fire. Well kept Bass, Dartmoor IPA and Jail Ale and Sharps Doom Bar on handpump, and local farm cider. There's a simply furnished little dining room as well.

⑪ **Honest and good value, the well liked bar food includes sandwiches, ploughman's, a changing pâté, garlic mushrooms, sausage or scampi basket, home-cooked ham and egg, daily specials such as fresh crab, scallops with bacon, baked bass with red onions, fresh** lemon sole, and rump steak with a cream, pepper and brandy sauce, and puddings like fresh lemon tart or belgian chocolate pudding. *Starters/Snacks: £4.25 to £6.95. Main Courses: £6.95 to £14.95. Puddings: £4.50 to £4.95*

Free house ~ Licensees Michael and Jill Dyson ~ Real ale ~ Bar food (12-1.30, 6-9(7-8.30 Sun) ~ (01548) 852068 ~ Children welcome if over 5 ~ Open 12-2, 5(7 Sun)-11(10.30 Sun); closed Mon and Tues lunchtimes; evenings 25 and 26 Dec

Recommended by Neil Robertson, MP

KINGSTON

SX6347   MAP 1

Dolphin 🛏️

Off B3392 S of Modbury (can also be reached from A379 W of Modbury); TQ7 4QE

Peaceful old pub with walks down to the sea, cheerful atmosphere and decent drinks and food

This is a cosy and traditional country pub with plenty of cheerful locals – though the hospitable landlady offers a warm welcome to visitors, too. There are several knocked-through beamed rooms with cushioned wall settles, wheelback chairs and stools around a mix of wooden tables on the red patterned carpet, amusing drawings and photographs on the stone walls, and an open fire as well as a woodburning stove. Courage Best, Otter Ale and Sharps Doom Bar on handpump, and summer farm cider. There are some seats and tables outside and nice walks down to the sea from here. The gents' is across the road.

🍴 **Well liked bar food includes sandwiches, ploughman's, soup, crispy whitebait, steak in ale or fish pie, various curries, cashew nut paella, belly pork slow-cooked in cider, daily specials such as gammon steak and cod and chips, and puddings like bread and butter pudding.** *Starters/Snacks: £3.95 to £5.95. Main Courses: £8.95 to £16.95. Puddings: £4.95*

Punch ~ Lease Janice Male ~ Real ale ~ Bar food (12-2.30, 6-9; not Sun evening) ~ (01548) 810314 ~ Children welcome ~ Dogs allowed in bar ~ Open 12-3, 6-11(10.30 Sun) ~ Bedrooms: £42.50B/£68B

Recommended by Chris and Libby Allen, Roger Wain-Heapy, Peter and Andrea Jacobs, Jerry Brown, Geoff and Carol Thorp, David Uren, Alan and Anne Driver, Suzy Miller, MB, Peter and Margaret Glenister

MARLDON

SX8663   MAP 1

Church House 🍴 🍷

Just off A380 NW of Paignton; TQ3 1SL

Spreading bar plus several other rooms in this pleasant inn, well liked drinks and bar food, and seats on three terraces

As well as several real ales and imaginative food, this attractively furnished pub has a friendly, bustling atmosphere. The spreading bar has several different areas that radiate off the big semicircular bar counter, with unusual windows, some beams, dark pine chairs around solid tables on the turkey carpet, and yellow leather bar chairs. Leading off here is a cosy little candlelit room with just four tables on the bare-board floor, a dark wood dado and stone fireplace. There's also a restaurant with a large stone fireplace and at the other end of the building, a similarly interesting room is split into two parts with a stone floor in one bit and a wooden floor in another (which has a big woodburning stove). The old barn holds yet another restaurant with art displays by local artists. Bass, Bays Gold, Otter Ale and St Austell Dartmoor Best on handpump, and ten wines by the glass; piped music. There are picnic-sets on three carefully maintained grassy terraces behind the pub.

🍴 **Using their own-grown vegetables, the good bar food might include sandwiches, curried mussel soup with a tomato, fennel and coriander compote, duck and pistachio terrine with spiced plums, baked basil roulade with goats cheese and beetroot dressing, corn-fed chicken suprême filled with caramelised onion and feta cheese with a sage cream velouté, slow-cooked lamb shoulder with a tomato and rosemary sauce, and chargrilled fillet steak with toasted croûte and pâté and madeira sauce.** *Starters/Snacks: £5.50 to £7.00. Main Courses: £9.00 to £19.95. Puddings: £4.95 to £6.50*

Enterprise ~ Lease Julian Cook ~ Real ale ~ Bar food (12-2(2.30 weekends), 6.30-9.30(9 Sun)) ~ Restaurant ~ (01803) 558279 ~ Children welcome but no under-8s Sat evening ~ Dogs allowed in bar ~ Open 11.30-2.30(3 Sat and Sun), 5(5.30 Sat and Sun)-11(11.30 Sat, 10.30 Sun)

Recommended by Dr A McCormick, Michael Dandy, Pat Crabb, Andrea Rampley, Mrs C Farley

MOLLAND   SS8028   MAP 1

London 🍺

Village signposted off B3227 E of South Molton, down narrow lanes; EX36 3NG

A proper Exmoor inn with customers and their dogs to match, a warm welcome, honest food, farm cider and real ales; bedrooms

By the time this *Guide* is published, the friendly licensees hope to have opened their Toby Jug microbrewery here. They also keep Cotleigh Tawny, Exmoor Ale and Jollyboat Freebooter on handpump, several wines by the glass, farm cider and home-made lemonade. This remains very much a traditional Exmoor pub with the local farmers and gamekeepers (and their working dogs) being very much the focal part of things. The two small linked rooms by the old-fashioned central servery have hardly changed in 50 years and have lots of local stag-hunting pictures, tough carpeting or rugs on flagstones, cushioned benches and plain chairs around rough stripped trestle tables, a table of shooting and other country magazines, ancient stag and otter trophies, and darts and board games. On the left an attractive beamed room has accounts of the rescued stag which lived a long life at the pub many years ago, and on the right, a panelled dining room with a great curved settle by its fireplace has particularly good hunting and gamebird prints, including ones by McPhail and Hester Lloyd. A small hall has stuffed birds and animals. The low-ceilinged lavatories are worth a look, with their Victorian mahogany and tiling (and in the gents', a testament to the prodigious thirst of the village cricket team). There are picnic-sets in the cottagey garden. Don't miss the next-door church, with its untouched early 18th-c box pews – and in spring, a carpet of daffodils in the graveyard.

🍴 **Traditional home-made bar food includes sandwiches, ploughman's, potted shrimps, chicken liver pâté, omelettes, venison and mushroom or chicken and bacon pies, ham and egg, vegetable lasagne, changing sausages with onion gravy, various quiches and tarts, battered fish and chips, and puddings like pear crumble or treacle tart.** *Starters/Snacks: £4.00 to £5.00. Main Courses: £6.50 to £10.50. Puddings: £4.10*

Free house ~ Licensees Deborah See and Toby Bennett ~ Real ale ~ Bar food (12-2(3 Sun), 7-9; not winter Sun evening) ~ Restaurant ~ No credit cards ~ (01769) 550269 ~ Children welcome ~ Dogs allowed in bar and bedrooms ~ Open 12-3, 6.30-midnight; 12-5 Sat ~ Bedrooms: /£60B

Recommended by Mr and Mrs P D Titcomb, Tony Winckworth, Keith and Sue Ward, the Didler, Mike Gorton, FJS and DS

NEWTON FERRERS   SX5447   MAP 1

Dolphin

Riverside Road East – follow Harbour dead end signs; PL8 1AE

Terraces looking down over the River Yealm, a simply furnished bar, traditional food and local ales

It's worth carrying your beer across the little lane from this 18th-c pub to seats on the terrace where there's a grandstand view of the boating action on the busy tidal River Yealm. Inside, the L-shaped bar has a few low black beams, slate floors, some white-painted plank panelling, and simple pub furnishings including cushioned wall benches, bar stools and small winged settles. It can get packed in summer. Badger Tanglefoot, First Gold and Phins Ale on handpump and ten wines by the glass; euchre Monday evenings and a quiz on Tuesday evenings. Parking by the pub is very limited, with more chance of a space either below or above. You can walk along the waterfront to the west end of the village. More reports please.

🍴 Bar food includes chunky sandwiches, ploughman's, chicken caesar salad, moules marinière, a proper burger, spaghetti with artichokes and roasted cherry tomatoes, sausages with caramelised onions and red wine gravy, local seafood pie, daily specials like wild mushroom risotto, beer-battered fish and steak and kidney pie, and puddings such as rhubarb crumble and sticky toffee pudding with toffee sauce; they serve breakfast from 10-11.30am and Sunday roasts. *Starters/Snacks: £3.75 to £5.95. Main Courses: £5.95 to £11.95. Puddings: £4.25 to £6.95*

Badger ~ Tenants Jackie Cosens and Adrian Jenkins ~ Real ale ~ Bar food (12-2.30, 6-9.30; all day weekends) ~ (01752) 872007 ~ Children welcome as long as seated and with adults ~ Dogs welcome ~ Open 10am-11pm(10.30pm Sun); 10-2.30, 6-11 Mon-Thurs in winter

Recommended by Roger Wain-Heapy, M G Hart

NOSS MAYO

SX5447 MAP 1

Ship 🍷 🍺

Off A379 via B3186, E of Plymouth; PL8 1EW

Busy pub, seats overlooking inlet and visiting boats, thick-walled bars with log fires, west country beers, popular food and friendly atmosphere

---

Our readers very much enjoy their visits to this well run and popular pub. There's a warm welcome to all from the friendly staff and both the beer and food are good. And of course the front terrace in fine weather is a huge bonus – you can sit at the octagonal wooden tables under parasols and look over the inlet, and visiting boats can tie up alongside; there are outdoor heaters for cooler evenings. Inside, it's attractively furnished and the two thick-walled bars have a happy mix of dining chairs and tables on the wooden floors, log fires, bookcases, dozens of local pictures and charts, newspapers and magazines to read, and a chatty atmosphere; board games, dominoes and cards. Dartmoor Jail Ale, St Austell Tribute and Summerskills Tamar on handpump, 25 malt whiskies and ten wines by the glass. Parking is restricted at high tide.

🍴 Good bar food includes filled baguettes, ploughman's, soup, potted mackerel, seared scallops with bacon, warm marinated chicken, bacon and avocado salad, sausages with onion gravy, steak and kidney pie, gammon and free-range eggs, tagliatelle with tomato, caper and olives, loin of pork with a mustard and cider sauce, duck breast on noodles with plum sauce and oriental vegetables, and puddings like baked vanilla cheesecake with raspberry coulis and warm chocolate brownie with chocolate sauce. *Starters/Snacks: £4.75 to £7.50. Main Courses: £9.00 to £12.00. Puddings: £5.25 to £5.75*

Free house ~ Licensees Charlie and Lisa Bullock ~ Real ale ~ Bar food (all day) ~ Restaurant ~ (01752) 872387 ~ Children welcome ~ Dogs allowed in bar ~ Open 11-11; 12-10.30 Sun

Recommended by Roger Wain-Heapy, Suzy Miller, MB, John and Verna Aspinall, Alain and Rose Foote, Michael and Maggie Betton, Hugh Roberts, Roy Hoing, Di and Mike Gillam, Lynda and Trevor Smith, Gary Rollings, Debbie Porter, June and Robin Savage, David Rule, FJS and DS

PETER TAVY

SX5177 MAP 1

Peter Tavy Inn 🍷

Off A386 near Mary Tavy, N of Tavistock; PL19 9NN

Old stone inn with pretty garden, bustling bar with beams and big log fire, and good choice of food and drink

---

This friendly pub was originally a farm cottage and the village blacksmith's. It's well run by helpful, efficient licensees and there's a nice bustling atmosphere and plenty of chatty customers. The low-beamed bar has high-backed settles on black flagstones, smaller settles in stone-mullioned windows, a fine log fire in the big stone fireplace, and Blackawton Original Bitter, Dartmoor Jail Ale, Otter Bright and Sharps Doom Bar on handpump; local cider, 30 malt whiskies and nine wines by the glass. There's also a snug dining area and restaurant. From the picnic-sets in the pretty garden there are peaceful views of the moor rising above nearby pastures.

🍴 Well liked lunchtime bar food includes filled baguettes and baked potatoes, toasted ciabatta with toppings, soup, chicken liver and mushroom pâté, ham and egg, lamb curry, popular steak and stilton pie, and vegetable crumble with a cheese and walnut topping, with evening dishes like cream cheese, chive, mozzarella and tomato tart, a duo of smoked fish, pork tenderloin in a mango and chilli sauce, game casserole with dumplings, mexican fajitas, and salmon fillet with pancetta and a honey and mustard sauce. *Starters/Snacks: £4.50 to £6.95. Main Courses: £6.95 to £15.95. Puddings: £4.20 to £4.75*

Free house ~ Licensees Chris and Joanne Wordingham ~ Real ale ~ Bar food ~ (01822) 810348 ~ Children welcome ~ Dogs welcome ~ Open 12-3, 6-11(10.30 Sun); closed 25 Dec and evening 26 Dec

Recommended by Helen and Brian Edgeley, Phil and Jane Villiers, Dennis Jenkin, Andrea Rampley, David and Katharine Cooke, Dr Ian Mortimer, Jacquie Jones, Ted George, Irene and Derek Flewin

PORTGATE

SX4185 MAP 1

Harris Arms ♀

Turn off A30 E of Launceston at Broadwoodwidger turn-off (with brown Dingle Steam Village sign), and head S; Launceston Road (old A30 between Lewdown and Lifton); EX20 4PZ

Enthusiastic, well travelled licensees in roadside pub with exceptional wine list and popular food

---

You can be sure of a friendly welcome from the hard-working licensees in this popular roadside pub. It's an enjoyable place with well liked food and fantastic wines – both Mr and Mrs Whiteman are qualified award-winning wine-makers and are more than happy to help you through their eclectic list. With helpful notes and 30 of their favourites by the glass, there are plenty of gems to choose from – and you can buy them to take home, too. The bar has burgundy end walls and cream ones in between, some rather fine photographs, a huge table at one end (brought back from New Zealand), a long red-plush built-in wall banquette and a woodburning stove; afghan saddle-bag cushions are scattered around a mixture of other tables and dining chairs. On the left, steps lead down to the dining room with elegant beech dining chairs (and more afghan cushions) around stripped wooden tables, and some unusual paintings on the walls. Bays Gold and Sharps Doom Bar on handpump, Luscombe organic soft drinks, and summer cider; there may be a pile of country magazines. There are seats under outdoor heaters on a decked area amongst pots of lavender, and plenty of picnic-sets in the sloping back garden looking out over the rolling wooded pasture hills. They are growing 24 vines.

🍴 Honest bar food includes soup, home-cured gravadlax, a changing home-made terrine, deep-fried whitebait, king prawns piri-piri, ham and egg, fishcakes, a pie of the week, battered fish with home-made tartare sauce, roast breast of chicken with wild mushrooms, brandy and cream, pork belly with black pudding croquette and sage and apple jus, daily specials; and puddings like berry brûlée and treacle pudding. *Starters/Snacks: £5.95 to £8.95. Main Courses: £8.95 to £10.95. Puddings: £5.00*

Free house ~ Licensees Andy and Rowena Whiteman ~ Real ale ~ Bar food ~ Restaurant ~ (01566) 783331 ~ Children welcome ~ Dogs welcome ~ Open 12-3, 6.30-11; 12-4 Sun; closed Sun evening, all day Mon

Recommended by Sue Ruffhead, Mary Goodfellow, Mo and David Trudgill

POSTBRIDGE

SX6780 MAP 1

Warren House

B3212 0.75 miles NE of Postbridge; PL20 6TA

Straightforward old pub, relaxing for a drink or snack after a Dartmoor hike

---

Friendly and with plenty of atmosphere, this straightforward place is most welcome after a hike on Dartmoor. One of the fireplaces in the cosy bar is said to have been kept alight almost continuously since 1845, and there are simple furnishings like easy chairs and settles under the beamed ochre ceiling, old pictures of the inn on the partly panelled stone walls, and dim lighting (fuelled by the pub's own generator); a family room also. Otter Ale, Ringwood Old Thumper, St Austell Tribute and a guest beer on handpump, local farm cider and malt whiskies; piped music, darts and pool. The picnic-sets on both sides of the road have moorland views.

🍴 **Decent bar food includes filled baguettes and baked potatoes, ploughman's with cornish yarg, tasty pasties, local jumbo sausage, mushroom stroganoff, rabbit pie, steak in ale pie, breaded plaice, daily specials, and puddings like sticky toffee pudding with toffee sauce.** *Starters/Snacks: £3.95 to £6.25. Main Courses: £6.00 to £11.00. Puddings: £4.95*

Free house ~ Licensee Peter Parsons ~ Real ale ~ Bar food (all day but more restricted winter Mon and Tues) ~ (01822) 880208 ~ Children in family room ~ Dogs allowed in bar ~ Open 11-11; 12-10.30 Sun; 11-5 Mon and Tues during Nov-Feb

Recommended by Paul and Margaret Baker, Steve Derbyshire, Andrea Rampley, Mrs Mary Woods

RATTERY
SX7461   MAP 1

Church House

Village signposted from A385 W of Totnes, and A38 S of Buckfastleigh; TQ10 9LD

One of Britain's oldest pubs with some fine original features and peaceful views

As we went to press we heard that this old pub was up for sale so it might well be that when this *Guide* is published, there will be new people at the helm here. It's one of the country's oldest pubs and is worth a visit to see some of the fine original features – notably the spiral stone steps behind a little stone doorway on your left as you come in that date from about 1030. There are massive oak beams and standing timbers in the homely open-plan bar, large fireplaces (one with a little cosy nook partitioned off around it), traditional pubby chairs and tables on the patterned carpet, some window seats, and prints and horsebrasses on the plain white walls; the dining room is separated from this room by heavy curtains and there's a lounge area too. Butcombe Bitter, Dartmoor IPA and Jail Ale, and Otter Ale on handpump and several malt whiskies and wines by the glass. The garden has picnic-sets on the large hedged-in lawn and peaceful views of the partly wooded surrounding hills. More reports please.

🍴 **Bar food includes sandwiches, toasties, filled baguettes and baked potatoes, ploughman's, soup, devilled whitebait, a fry-up, meaty or vegetable lasagne, steak and kidney pie, sausages with onion gravy, battered cod, pork loin cutlets in apple and sage sauce, and citrus and olive lamb shank.** *Starters/Snacks: £4.50 to £6.95. Main Courses: £7.35 to £14.95. Puddings: £4.75 to £5.25*

Free house ~ Licensee Ray Hardy ~ Real ale ~ Bar food (11.30-2, 6.30-9) ~ Restaurant ~ (01364) 642220 ~ Children welcome ~ Dogs allowed in bar ~ Open 11-2.30, 6-11; 12-3, 6-10.30 Sun

Recommended by Lucien Perring, Paul Goldman, June and Robin Savage, B J Harding, MP

ROCKBEARE
SY0195   MAP 1

Jack in the Green 🍴 ♇

Signposted from new A30 bypass E of Exeter; EX5 2EE

Neat dining pub with traditionally furnished bars, real ales, a dozen wines by the glass and imaginative meals

They do offer three real ales on handpump but most customers come to this sizeable, well run dining pub to enjoy the carefully presented, popular food. It's been run by the same friendly and enthusiastic licensees for 17 years now and the neatly kept, comfortable bar has wheelback chairs, sturdy cushioned wall pews and varying-sized tables on its dark blue carpet, a dark carved oak dresser, sporting prints and nice decorative china; piped music. The larger dining side is similarly traditional in style: some of its many old hunting and shooting photographs are well worth a close look and there are button-back leather chesterfields by the big woodburning stove. Butcombe Bitter, O'Hanlons Yellowhammer and Otter Ale, 12 wines by the glass and local cider. There are plenty of seats outside in the new courtyard.

🍴 Using top-quality local produce, the very good – not particularly cheap – food includes bar snacks like ploughman's, soup, terrine of ham knuckle with spiced pineapple pickle, grilled black pudding with dry-cured bacon and poached duck-egg salad, leek and dolcelatte risotto, bangers and mash with onion gravy, free-range chicken, mushroom and tarragon pie, and beer-battered fresh fish with home-made tartare sauce, with more elaborate choices such as sesame tuna with avocado and lime purée, rack of lamb with honey-roast garlic purée and basil mash, and duck breast with rhubarb chutney; puddings like passion fruit mousse with coconut sorbet and lavender crème brûlée; Sunday roasts. *Starters/Snacks: £4.95 to £7.95. Main Courses: £8.95 to £14.95. Puddings: £5.95*

Free house ~ Licensee Paul Parnell ~ Real ale ~ Bar food (all day Sun) ~ Restaurant ~ (01404) 822240 ~ Well behaved children in one bar only ~ Open 11-3, 5.30(6 Sat)-11; 12-10.30 Sun; closed 25 Dec-6 Jan

Recommended by Cathryn and Richard Hicks, Henry Snell, P Waterman, Robert Blake, Oliver and Sue Rowell, John and Dinah Waters, Dr and Mrs M E Wilson, Mrs C Osgood, Andy and Claire Barker, David and Cathrine Whiting, Barry Steele-Perkins, Ron and Sheila Corbett, Mrs Mary Woods, B and M Kendall

SHEEPWASH   SS4806   MAP 1

Half Moon 🍷 🛏

Off A3072 Holsworthy—Hatherleigh; EX21 5NE

Ancient inn loved by fishermen, with 12 miles of River Torridge and fishing facilities, real ales and enjoyable food; bedrooms

In a tiny Dartmoor village off the beaten track, this 15th-c inn is a friendly place. The main bar is simply furnished with solid old furniture and there's a wealth of beams and a large log fireplace fronted by flagstones. St Austell Dartmoor Best, Black Prince and Tribute, and Wells & Youngs Bombardier on handpump, several wines by the glass, and a decent choice of malt whiskies. There's an attractive separate dining room with black oak woodwork polished to perfection; bar billiards. Some of the bedrooms are in a converted stable and are ideal for guests with dogs. The inn has a rod room, good drying facilities and a small tackle shop; they can issue rod licences, too.

🍴 Very good, often interesting bar food includes panini sandwiches, filled baked potatoes, ploughman's, soup, smoked pigeon breast with warm butternut squash, bacon and pine nut salad, juniper-smoked trout, various pies like steak and stilton, fish, and game, pork, chilli and apricot meatballs, home-cooked ham and eggs, sausage and mash with onion gravy, wild rabbit casserole, wild mushroom stroganoff, smoked fillet of cod, Guinness and beef stew with dumplings, lamb and coconut curry, and puddings like treacle tart and blueberry eton mess. *Starters/Snacks: £3.95 to £4.95. Main Courses: £6.95 to £14.95. Puddings: £4.25*

Free house ~ Licensees Chris and Tony Green ~ Real ale ~ Bar food ~ Restaurant ~ (01409) 231376 ~ Well behaved children welcome ~ Dogs allowed in bar and bedrooms ~ Open 11-3, 6-11; 12-10.30 Sun ~ Bedrooms: £45B/£90B

Recommended by Dr A McCormick, Ryta Lyndley

SIDBURY   SY1496   MAP 1

Hare & Hounds 🍺

3 miles N of Sidbury, at Putts Corner; A375 towards Honiton, crossroads with B3174; EX10 0QQ

Large, well run roadside pub with log fires, beams and attractive layout, popular daily carvery, efficient staff and a big garden

Although this very popular, sizeable roadside pub is now owned by Heartstone Inns, there have thankfully been no changes. There are two good log fires (and rather unusual wood-framed leather sofas complete with pouffes), heavy beams and fresh flowers, plenty of tables with red plush-cushioned dining chairs, windows seats and a long bar with well used bar stools. It's mostly carpeted, with bare boards and stripped stone walls at one end. At the opposite end, on the left, another dining area has french windows leading out to a large marquee, providing extra seating, and on into the garden. Branscombe Vale Best Bitter and Otter Bitter and Ale are tapped from the cask. The big garden, giving marvellous views down the Sid valley to the sea at Sidmouth, has picnic-sets and a children's play area.

🍴 Using only local produce, it's the good, daily carvery with a choice of four meats and enough turnover to keep up a continuous supply of fresh vegetables that is so enjoyable here – every lunchtime and evening and all day Sunday. Also, sandwiches and filled baguettes, soup, platters, mushroom, broccoli and stilton bake, a daily curry, coq au vin, battered haddock with home-made tartare sauce, and steaks. *Starters/Snacks: £3.95 to £5.95. Main Courses: £8.25 to £14.95. Puddings: £4.50*

Heartstone Inns ~ Managers Graham Cole and Lindsey Chun ~ Real ale ~ Bar food (all day) ~ (01404) 41760 ~ Children welcome ~ Dogs allowed in bar ~ Open 10am-11pm; 12-10.30 Sun

Recommended by Dr and Mrs M E Wilson, FJS and DS

SIDFORD   SY1389   MAP 1

Blue Ball 🍺

A3052 just N of Sidmouth; EX10 9QL

Big, popular inn with friendly staff, five real ales, popular food inc breakfasts, and a neat garden; bedrooms

Since 1912, this handsome thatched pub has been run by the same friendly family. It's in a very useful spot being close to both the busy M5 and A303 – and coastal walks are only about ten minutes away – so their breakfasts served from 8-10am should prove very popular. The central bar covers three main areas: light beams, bar stools and a nice mix of wooden dining chairs around circular tables on the patterned carpet, three log fires, prints, horsebrasses and plenty of bric-a-brac on the walls, and Bass, Otter Bitter, St Austell Tribute and a couple of guests like Black Sheep and Exmoor Hound Dog on handpump; attentive service. The public bar has darts, a games machine and board games; skittle alley and piped music. There are seats on a terrace and in the flower-filled garden and a well designed wooden smokers' gazebo.

🍴 Well liked bar food includes hot and cold sandwiches, filled baked potatoes, ploughman's, soup, deep-fried whitebait, nachos with chicken, guacamole, sour cream and salsa, meat or vegetarian lasagne, beer-battered cod, honey-roast ham and eggs, steak and kidney pudding, and daily specials like chicken in white wine and wild mushroom sauce and braised rump of lamb on walnut mash with lentils in a rosemary and garlic sauce. *Starters/Snacks: £4.25 to £5.75. Main Courses: £6.50 to £13.95. Puddings: £3.95 to £4.75*

Punch ~ Lease Roger Newton ~ Real ale ~ Bar food (8-10 for breakfast, 12-3, 6-9; all day Sun) ~ Restaurant ~ (01395) 514062 ~ Children in dining areas only ~ Dogs allowed in bar ~ Open 11-11(midnight Sat); 12-11 Sun ~ Bedrooms: £60B/£95B

Recommended by Mark Flynn, John Wymer, John and Fiona McIlwain, Steve Whalley, John and Fiona Merritt, Dr and Mrs M E Wilson

SPREYTON   SX6996   MAP 1

Tom Cobley 🍺

From A30 Whiddon Down roundabout take former A30 (opposite A382), then first left, turning left at crossroads after 1.1 miles; in village centre turn left; can also be reached from A3124; EX17 5AL

Amazing range of real ales, cheerful licensees and home-made food in busy village pub

The range of real ales kept on handpump or tapped from the cask, in this thriving village pub, is quite extraordinary. Up to 22 are kept in top condition by the particularly cheerful and welcoming landlord: Cotleigh Tawny, Otter Ale and Head, St Austell Proper Job and Tribute, Sharps Doom Bar and quickly changing guests. Farm cider, too. The comfortable little bar has straightforward pubby furnishings, an open fire in the brick fireplace, local photographs, country scenes and some old jokey west country bumpkin prints, and sporting trophies; darts and piped music (in the restaurant). There's a large back restaurant with beamery. Seats in the tree-shaded garden, with more out in front by the quiet street. Big breakfasts. There are plans to build the village shop in the pub's garden.

🍴 If you are thinking of eating, it might be best to book ahead as they do get very busy: sandwiches and toasties, filled baked potatoes, ploughman's, soup, pasties, meat or vegetarian lasagne, omelettes, chicken, ham and leek pie, steak and kidney suet pudding, sausages in onion gravy, home-cooked ham and eggs, and battered cod. The restaurant menu is more elaborate; Sunday roasts. *Starters/Snacks: £3.95 to £6.50. Main Courses: £6.95 to £9.95. Puddings: £3.95*

Free house ~ Licensees Roger and Carol Cudlip ~ Real ale ~ Bar food ~ Restaurant ~ (01647) 231314 ~ Children welcome ~ Dogs allowed in bar ~ Open 12-3(4 Sun), 6-midnight(1am Sat); closed Mon lunchtime ~ Bedrooms: £24.50(£40S)/£50(£80S)

Recommended by Dave Lowe, Mike Gorton

STOCKLAND   ST2404   MAP 1

Kings Arms ♀

Village signposted from A30 Honiton—Chard; and also, at every turning, from N end of Honiton High Street; EX14 9BS

Pleasant old inn with elegant bar, cosy restaurant and local beers and cider

This is a friendly old thatched pub and the dark beamed and elegant Cotley Bar has solid refectory tables and settles, attractive landscapes, a medieval oak screen (which divides the room into two) and a great stone fireplace across almost the whole width of one end. The cosy restaurant has a huge inglenook fireplace and bread oven; piped music. Exmoor Ale, Otter Ale and St Austell Tribute on handpump and 25 malt whiskies. At the back, a flagstoned bar has cushioned benches and stools around heavy wooden tables; there's also a darts area, a room with more tables, a games machine, pool and a neat skittle alley. On the front terrace, there are tables under parasols and a lawn with enclosed trees and shrubs.

🍴 Quite a range of well liked bar food includes sandwiches, ploughman's, soup, home-cured gravadlax, strips of fillet steak with roquefort, steak in ale pie, beer-battered cod, home-made burgers, calves liver and bacon, king scallops flamed in whisky, fillet of lamb in red wine, slow-roasted pork belly, and puddings like crème brûlée and tiramisu. *Starters/Snacks: £4.00 to £6.50. Main Courses: £6.50 to £15.50. Puddings: £5.00*

Free house ~ Licensee Shaun Barnes ~ Real ale ~ Bar food ~ Restaurant ~ (01404) 881361 ~ Children welcome but not in bar areas after 9pm ~ Dogs allowed in bar and bedrooms ~ Some live music Fri and Sat evenings ~ Open 11.30-3, 6-11; 12-3, 6.30-10.30 Sun ~ Bedrooms: £45S/£70S

Recommended by Bob and Margaret Holder, Jeremy and Jane Morrison, John Gould

STOKENHAM   SX8042   MAP 1

Church House ♀

Opposite church, N of A379 towards Torcross; TQ7 2SZ

Refurbished and extended old pub in pretty countryside, well liked food and real ales

A lot of refurbishment has taken place in this attractive old pub over the last year. There's a new conservatory, a new bar counter and flagstone flooring, new carpets and two large new terraced areas with plenty of picnic-sets. But the three rambling, low-beamed, open-plan original areas still have a bustling atmosphere, lots of knick-knacks, quite a mix of seating, Greene King Abbot, Otter Ale and Head and a changing guest on handpump, several bourbons and local cider. There's a children's play area with swings and a slide. The pub was built to cater for the masons building the ancient church next door, and overlooks a common.

🍴 Tasty bar food includes **sandwiches, soup, a cheese platter, ploughman's, various tartlets, spinach and goats cheese ravioli with butternut squash and tomato sauce, home-made sausages with caramelised onions, chicken breast with mushroom sauce, salmon and cod bake with a herb crust, game casserole, and puddings like their famous sundae and chocolate brownies.** *Starters/Snacks: £3.95 to £6.95. Main Courses: £7.50 to £15.95. Puddings: £4.50*

Heavitree ~ Tenants Richard Smith and Simon Cadman ~ Real ale ~ Bar food ~ Restaurant ~ (01548) 580253 ~ Children welcome ~ Dogs allowed in bar ~ Jazz Weds evening ~ Open 11-11

Recommended by Mr and Mrs H J Stephens, Paul Hagan, Dennis Jenkin, Mrs Mary Woods, MP, Roger Wain-Heapy, B J Harding

TIPTON ST JOHN   SY0991   MAP 1
Golden Lion
Signed off B3176 Sidmouth—Ottery St Mary; EX10 0AA

A good mix of diners and drinkers in friendly village pub and plenty of seats in attractive garden

Well run by friendly, competent licensees, this popular and attractive village pub is much enjoyed by our readers. Many customers do come to eat but a few tables are still reserved for those just wanting a chat and a pint, and they keep Bass and Otter Ale and Bitter on handpump; ten wines by the glass and local soft drinks. The main bar – which is split into two – has a comfortable, relaxed atmosphere, as does the back snug, and throughout the building there are paintings from west country artists, art deco prints, tiffany lamps and hops, copper pots and kettles hanging from the beams; maybe piped music and board games. There's a new verandah for dog walkers and smokers, seats on the terracotta-walled terrace with outside heaters and grapevine, and more seats on the grass edged by pretty flowering borders; summer Sunday evening jazz out here.

🍴 Good bar food at lunchtime includes **sandwiches, ploughman's, soup, smoked duck salad with onion marmalade, moules frites with crusty bread, home-cooked ham and egg, and steak and kidney pudding, with evening choices like creamy garlic mushrooms, deep-fried brie, home-cured gravadlax, a vegetarian dish of the day, pork tenderloin in creamy cider and apple, chicken in a light cream and sherry sauce, lamb kebab marinated in garlic and rosemary, and puddings like lime and ginger cheesecake and sticky chocolate pudding; they also offer a good value winter two-course menu.** *Starters/Snacks: £4.50 to £6.20. Main Courses: £9.50 to £17.50. Puddings: £4.75*

Heavitree ~ Tenants François and Michelle Teissier ~ Real ale ~ Bar food ~ (01404) 812881 ~ Children welcome ~ Jazz summer Sun evenings ~ Open 12-2.30(3 Sat), 6-11; 12-3, 7-10.30 Sun; closed Sun evening Sept-May

Recommended by Mike Gorton, J D O Carter, Martin Sagar, Norman and Sarah Keeping, Helene Grygar, Dr and Mrs M E Wilson, Michael and Lynne Gittins

TOPSHAM   SX9688   MAP 1
Bridge Inn ★ 🍺
2.5 miles from M5 junction 30: Topsham signposted from exit roundabout; in Topsham follow signpost (A376) Exmouth on the Elmgrove Road, into Bridge Hill; EX3 0QQ

Wonderful old drinkers' pub with up to eight real ales and in the landlady's family for five generations

Mrs Cheffers-Heard is the fifth generation of her family to run this utterly old-fashioned and unchanging gem. It's held dear in the hearts of many of our readers for its friendly, chatty and relaxed atmosphere and the fact that there are no noisy games machines, piped music or mobile phones to spoil that. There's also a fine range of changing real ales tapped from the cask: Art Brew Brut, Branscombe Vale Branoc, Exe Valley Bitter and a seasonal beer, Exeter Ferryman, O'Hanlons Yellowhammer and Teignworthy Harveys. Organic cider, country wines, non-alcoholic pressés and decent wines by the glass, too. The little lounge partitioned off from the inner corridor by a high-backed settle has some fine old traditional furnishings; log fire; A bigger lower room (the old malthouse) is open at busy times. Outside, picnic-sets overlook the weir.

🍴 Simple, tasty bar food includes well filled meaty and vegetarian pasties, sandwiches, a hearty winter soup and ploughman's. *Starters/Snacks: £4.25 to £4.50. Main Courses: £6.50 to £6.90*

Free house ~ Licensee Mrs C Cheffers-Heard ~ Real ale ~ Bar food (lunchtime only) ~ No credit cards ~ (01392) 873862 ~ Children in two rooms ~ Dogs allowed in bar ~ Live folk first Sun lunchtime of month ~ blues first Mon evening of month ~ Open 12-2, 6-10.30(11 Fri and Sat); 12-2, 7-10.30 Sun

Recommended by Richard and Anne Ansell, John and Fiona McIlwain, Terry and Linda Moseley, Barry Steele-Perkins, Mr and Mrs A H Young, Dr and Mrs M E Wilson, Andrea Rampley, Ian Barker, the Didler, Julian Distin, FJS and DS, Mark and Heather Williamson, Stephen Moss, Adrian and Dawn Collinge, Pete Baker, Mr and Mrs P D Titcomb

TORBRYAN   SX8266   MAP 1

Old Church House

Most easily reached from A381 Newton Abbot—Totnes via Ipplepen; TQ12 5UR

Ancient inn with original features in neat rooms, friendly service, and decent food and beer

The fine original features in this partly thatched 13th-c inn are well worth seeing and the various rooms have bags of atmosphere. The particularly attractive bar on the right of the door is neatly kept and bustling and has benches built into the fine old panelling as well as a cushioned high-backed settle and leather-backed small seats around its big log fire. On the left, there's a series of comfortable and discreetly lit lounges, one with a splendid deep inglenook Tudor fireplace with a side bread oven; piped music and TV. Skinners Betty Stogs and Cornish Knocker on handpump and 30 malt whiskies; friendly service. Plenty of nearby walks. The part Saxon church next door has a battlemented Norman tower.

🍴 Generous helpings of lunchtime bar food includes filled baguettes, soup, garlic mushrooms, pâté with red onion marmalade, vegetable bake, cottage pie, a roast of the day, and haddock mornay, with evening dishes like moules marinière, a field mushroom topped with stilton crumble and bacon lardons, gammon with cider and cheese, and honey-glazed duck with a wild plum sauce; Sunday roasts. *Starters/Snacks: £3.95 to £5.75. Main Courses: £4.95 to £14.95. Puddings: £3.95*

Free house ~ Licensees Kane and Carolynne Clarke ~ Real ale ~ Bar food ~ Restaurant ~ (01803) 812372 ~ Children welcome away from bar ~ Dogs allowed in bar ~ Live music Sun evenings ~ Open 11-11 ~ Bedrooms: £54B/£79B

Recommended by Ronnie Jones, Mike Gorton, Dr and Mrs M E Wilson, J D O Carter

TORCROSS   SX8242   MAP 1

Start Bay

A379 S of Dartmouth; TQ7 2TQ

Fresh local fish dishes in exceptionally popular, straightforward dining pub; seats outside overlooking the beach

It's perhaps best to visit this well run place out of season because it does get packed then and queues often form outside even before the doors open. It's the carefully sourced fresh fish and shellfish at fair prices that draws in the crowds and they dress their own cock crabs and shell their hand-picked scallops, and take delivery of the fish caught off the beach in front of the pub. The whole place is very much set out for eating with wheelback chairs around plenty of dark tables or (round a corner) back-to-back settles forming booths; country pictures and some photographs of storms buffeting the pub on the cream walls and a winter coal fire. A small chatty drinking area by the counter has a brass ship's clock and barometer and there's more booth seating in a family room with sailing boat pictures. Pool and darts in the winter. Bass and Otter Ale and Bitter on handpump, local cider, juices and local wine, too. They do warn of delays in food service at peak times, but the staff remain friendly and efficient. There are seats (highly prized) outside that look over the three-mile pebble beach, and the freshwater wildlife lagoon of Slapton Ley is just behind the pub. Dogs are allowed outside food-serving hours.

Their speciality is fish in light batter: cod or haddock (medium, large or jumbo), plaice, lemon sole and other fish dishes as available; also, sandwiches, filled baked potatoes, burgers, steaks, and puddings like summer pudding or treacle sponge. *Starters/Snacks: £4.20 to £6.95. Main Courses: £5.80 to £14.95. Puddings: £2.80 to £4.00*

Heavitree ~ Tenant Stuart Jacob ~ Real ale ~ Bar food (11.30-2.15, 6-9.30(10 Sat)) ~ (01548) 580553 ~ Children in large family room ~ Open 11.30-11

Recommended by David Heath, Mrs Mary Woods, Mike Gorton, Geoffrey Medcalf, Donna and Roger, Peter and Margaret Glenister, Michael Dandy, Eamonn and Natasha Skyrme, Steve Derbyshire

TOTNES
SX8059 MAP 1

Steam Packet
St Peters Quay, on W bank (ie not on Steam Packet Quay); TQ9 5EW

Seats outside overlooking the quay, interesting layout and décor inside, and popular food and drink; bedrooms

From the seats and tables under parasols on the terrace in front of this busy pub you can look over the River Dart and there are plenty of attractive flowering tubs; outdoor heaters for cooler weather. Inside, it's interestingly laid out with bare stone walls and wooden flooring, and the end part has an open log fire, a squashy leather sofa with lots of cushions against a wall of books, a similar seat built into a small curved brick wall (which breaks up the room), and a TV. The main bar has built-in wall benches and plenty of stools and chairs around traditional pub tables, and a further area has a coal fire and dark wood furniture. Courage Best, Dartmoor Jail Ale and Otter Bright on handpump and Weston's cider. The conservatory restaurant has high-backed brown or black leather dining chairs around wooden tables and smart window blinds. You can walk along the river.

Good bar food includes sandwiches, soup, tuna and spring onion fishcakes with curried peach chutney, mussels with tomato and chorizo, home-made burger with bacon and mozzarella, sunblush tomato and thyme risotto, beer-battered fresh haddock, slow-roasted lamb shank with moroccan-style couscous, and daily specials like poached salmon niçoise, toad in the hole, and steak and kidney suet pudding. *Starters/Snacks: £4.25 to £6.95. Main Courses: £7.95 to £14.95. Puddings: £4.50 to £4.95*

Buccaneer Holdings ~ Manager Richard Cockburn ~ Real ale ~ Bar food (all day in summer; 12-2.30(3 Sat, 4 Sun); 6-9.30(9 Sun) in winter) ~ Restaurant ~ (01803) 863880 ~ Children welcome ~ Dogs allowed in bar ~ Open 11-11; 12-10.30 Sun; closed evenings 25 Dec and 26 Dec and 1 Jan ~ Bedrooms: £59.50B/£79.50B

Recommended by Henry Pursehouse-Tranter, Marianne and Peter Stevens, Dave Braisted, Michael Dandy, Mike Gorton

WIDECOMBE
SX7276 MAP 1

Rugglestone
Village at end of B3387; pub just S – turn left at church and NT church house, OS Sheet 191 map reference 720765; TQ13 7TF

Unspoilt local near busy tourist village, with just a couple of bars, cheerful customers, friendly staff and homely food

Just the place to refuel after a walk, this is a smashing little local with a good mix of regulars and visitors. The unspoilt bar has just four tables, a few window and wall seats, a one-person pew built into the corner by the nice old stone fireplace, and a rudimentary bar counter dispensing Butcombe Bitter, St Austell Dartmoor Best and a couple of guests like O'Hanlons Yellowhammer and Blackawton West Country Gold tapped from the cask; local farm cider and a decent small wine list. The room on the right is a bit bigger and lighter-feeling with another stone fireplace, beamed ceiling, stripped pine tables, and a built-in wall bench. There's also a small room which is used for dining. The pub is in rural surroundings, though just up the road from the bustling tourist village, and there are seats across the little moorland stream in the field and tables and chairs in the garden. They have a holiday cottage to rent out.

🍴 **Well liked bar food includes filled baps and baguettes, soup, meaty or cheese pasties, chicken liver and cranberry pâté, fried whitebait, a burger with cheese and bacon, ham and eggs, cheese and spinach cannelloni in a tomato sauce, steak and kidney pie, beer-battered fresh haddock and spicy meatballs.** *Starters/Snacks: £3.95 to £6.95. Main Courses: £7.95 to £9.95. Puddings: £3.95*

Free house ~ Licensees Richard Palmer and Vicky Moore ~ Real ale ~ Bar food ~ Restaurant ~ (01364) 621327 ~ Children allowed but must be away from bar area ~ Dogs welcome ~ Open 11.30-3, 6-midnight; 11.30am-midnight Sat; 12-11.30 Sun

Recommended by W K Wood, the Didler, JHW, Barry and Anne, Les and Norma Haydon, Hazel Morgan, Bernard Patrick, Dr Ian Mortimer

WINKLEIGH   SS6308   MAP 1

Kings Arms

Village signposted off B3220 Crediton—Torrington; Fore Street; EX19 8HQ

Friendly pub with woodburning stoves in beamed main bar, west country beers and popular food

You can be sure of a friendly welcome in this thatched village pub. It's a cosy place with an attractive beamed main bar with old-fashioned built-in wall settles and benches around scrubbed pine tables on flagstones and a woodburning stove in a cavernous fireplace; another woodburning stove separates the bar from the dining rooms (one has military memorabilia and a mine shaft). Butcombe Bitter, Sharps Doom Bar and Coaster on handpump and local cider; darts, board games, shut the box, dominoes and cribbage. There are seats in the garden.

🍴 **Usefully served all day, the popular bar food includes sandwiches and filled baguettes, filled baked potatoes, ploughman's, omelettes, ham and egg, sausages with mash and onion gravy, vegetable shepherd's pie, steak and kidney parcel, chicken rogan josh, lambs liver with bacon, loin of lamb with redcurrant and rosemary, salmon fillet with a mustard and dill sauce, mixed grill, and puddings like sticky toffee pudding and rich chocolate mousse.** *Starters/Snacks: £2.25 to £5.75. Main Courses: £6.50 to £14.95. Puddings: £1.95 to £4.95*

Enterprise ~ Lease Chris Guy and Julia Franklin ~ Real ale ~ Bar food (all day) ~ Restaurant ~ (01837) 83384 ~ Children welcome ~ Dogs welcome ~ Open 11-11; 12-10.30 Sun

Recommended by R J Walden, Mark Flynn, Mrs P Sumner, Tom Evans, Geoffrey Medcalf, Stephen Moss

WOODBURY SALTERTON   SY0189   MAP 1

Diggers Rest

3.5 miles from M5 junction 30: A3052 towards Sidmouth, village signposted on right about 0.5 miles after Clyst St Mary; also signposted from B3179 SE of Exeter; EX5 1PQ

Bustling village pub with new licensees, real ales, well liked food and lovely views from the terraced garden

Cheerful, friendly licensees run this thatched village pub and there's a warm welcome for all. The main bar has antique furniture, local art on the walls, and a cosy seating area by the open fire with its extra large sofa and armchair. The modern extension is light and airy and opens on to the garden which has contemporary garden furniture under canvas parasols on the terrace and lovely countryside views. Butcombe Blond,Otter Bitter and St Austell Proper Job on handpump, ten wines by the glass and farm cider; piped music. More reports please.

🍴 Bar food includes lunchtime filled baguettes and ciabattas, soup, a cheese platter, local sausages with onion gravy, battered haddock, steak in ale pie, mushroom, spinach and cashew nut stroganoff, with evening extras such as scallops with a sweet chilli dressing, duck liver parfait with chutney, crab linguine, local belly of pork with a wholegrain mustard and apple jus, duckling breast with thyme rösti potatoes, lemon sole, and puddings like pear and cardamon brûlée tart and chocolate and orange cheesecake. *Starters/Snacks: £4.75 to £7.25. Main Courses: £8.95 to £16.95. Puddings: £4.50 to £4.95*

Free house ~ Licensees Philip and Shelley Berryman ~ Real ale ~ Bar food (12-2.15, 6.30-9.15) ~ (01395) 232375 ~ Well behaved children welcome ~ Dogs allowed in bar ~ Open 11-3, 5.30-11; 12-3, 5.30-10.30 Sun

Recommended by Michael and Lynne Gittins, DW T, Dr and Mrs M E Wilson

LUCKY DIP

Besides the fully inspected pubs, you might like to try these Lucky Dips recommended to us and described by readers (if you do, please send us reports: feedback@goodguides.com).

ASHBURTON [SX7569]
Royal Oak TQ13 7AD [East St]: Small friendly local, generous fair-priced home cooking, fresh flowers *(Paul Goldman)*
Victoria TQ13 7QH [North St]: Refurbished street-facing Georgian pub at end of village; carpeted bar with stripped stone, log fire, dark wheelbacks, brasses, bar stools, good Otter and occasional guests; enjoyable food inc local fish and game, restaurant, daily papers; piped music; picnic-sets in riverside garden, smokers' shelter, three bedrooms *(JHW, Phil Merrin)*
ASHPRINGTON [SX8157]
☆ *Durant Arms* TQ9 7UP [off A381 S of Totnes]: Still for sale but open as usual, more small country hotel than pub, very popular, with decent food, St Austell ales and local wines in three comfortable linked and turkey-carpeted areas, one with small corner bar counter; piped music; children welcome in top lounge, flagstoned back courtyard, comfortable bedrooms *(Gerry and Rosemary Dobson, LYM)*
ASHWATER [SX3895]
Village Inn EX21 5EY: Roomy and well decorated slate-floored pub doing well under current welcoming licensees, wide choice of above-average generous food from sandwiches up, fair prices, well kept Dartmoor, Sharps and a guest beer, good wine list; dining room, pool room, no music or machines, venerable grapevine in conservatory; tables on interestingly planted terrace *(John and Bernadette Elliott, Mark Flynn)*
AXMOUTH [SY2591]
☆ *Harbour Inn* EX12 4AF [B3172 Seaton—Axminster]: Prettily set thatched pub doing well under hard-working and popular owners (she's spanish), low beams, bare boards and flagstones, traditional settles and big log fires; traditional settles and big log fires; good proper cooking, adventurous without being too fancy, from plenty of

snacks up, good value Sun roast (food all day then), Badger ales, friendly staff, big simple summer family bar; children very welcome, disabled access and facilities, tables in neat back garden *(LYM, David and Sue Smith, Richard Stanfield, George Atkinson)*
BAMPTON [SS9520]
☆ *Exeter Inn* EX16 9DY [A396 some way S, at B3227 roundabout]: Long, low, stone-built roadside pub reopened after major refurbishment, several updated linked rooms, mainly flagstoned, two log fires and woodburner; large restaurant, traditional food inc plenty of fresh fish, up to four changing ales such as Cotleigh and Exmoor tapped from the cask, decent coffee, daily papers, no piped music; children and dogs welcome, disabled facilities, tables out in front, ten revamped bedrooms, fairly handy for Knightshayes, open all day *(BB)*
☆ *Quarrymans Rest* EX16 9LN [Briton St]: Doing well under current licensees; big beamed and carpeted lounge, friendly and relaxed, with inglenook woodburner and leather sofas, comfortable stripped stone dining room with heavy pine tables and leather chairs, imaginative good value food from entertaining chef/landlord; five well kept beers and two farm ciders, games room, no music; picnic-sets out in front and in pretty secluded back garden, smokers' shelter, three bedrooms *(Peter and Jan Humphreys, Peter Moffat, Michael Cleeve)*
BEER [ST2289]
Anchor EX12 3ET [Fore St]: Refurbished sea-view dining pub with enjoyable food inc good local fish, Greene King and Otter, good value wines, coffee, helpful service (can take a while when busy), rambling open-plan layout with old local photographs, large eating area; sports TV, piped music; reasonably priced bedrooms, lots of tables in attractive clifftop garden over road; delightful seaside village – parking may not

be easy *(Mr and Mrs P D Titcomb, George Atkinson, Howard and Margaret Buchanan, LYM, Neil and Anita Christopher)*

☆ *Barrel o' Beer* EX12 3EQ [Fore St]: Lively and informal family-run pub with good interestingly cooked local fish and seafood (they cure and smoke their own) as well as simpler more straightforward dishes, sandwiches too (the crab's good); Exe Valley Bitter and Devon Glory and a guest beer, good farm ciders, log fire, small back dining area; piped music; dogs welcome, open all day *(David Hunt, BB)*

☆ *Dolphin* EX12 3EQ [Fore St]: Hotel's friendly open-plan local quite near sea, comfortable old-fashioned décor, oak panelling, nautical bric-a-brac and interesting nooks inc marvellous old distorting mirrors and antique boxing prints; huge range of good value food inc fresh local fish, large back restaurant, well kept Cotleigh and Dartmoor ales, decent wine and coffee; piped music; children and dogs welcome, back picnic-sets, bedrooms *(George Atkinson, Joan and Michel Hooper-Immins, Mike Gorton, B and F A Hannam, LYM)*

BERRYNARBOR [SS5546]

Olde Globe EX34 9SG [off A399 E of Ilfracombe]: Rambling dim-lit rooms geared to family visitors (cutlasses, swords, shields and rustic oddments), with reasonably priced straightforward food, real ales, games area – and genuine age behind the trimmings, with ancient walls and flagstones, high-backed oak settles and antique tables, lots of old pictures; piped music; children looked after well, dogs welcome, crazy-paved front terrace, play area, pretty village *(Bob and Margaret Holder, B M Eldridge, Pat and Tony Martin, LYM)*

BICKLEIGH [SS9307]

Fishermans Cot EX16 8RW: Greatly extended thatched riverside Marstons pub, enjoyable food, their real ales, lots of round tables on stone and carpet, pillars, plants and some panelled parts, fishing bric-a-brac, fairy lights in a willow, raised dining area, charming view over shallow rocky race below 1640 Exe bridge; piped music, can get busy at wknds; terrace and waterside lawn, 19 good bedrooms, open all day *(Adrian and Dawn Collinge, BB)*

BIGBURY [SX6647]

Royal Oak TQ7 4AP: Welcoming multi-level village pub with good value food inc local fish, good choice of wines by the glass, beers tapped from the cask, restaurant with round tables and wicker chairs, nicely refurbished outside lavatories; children welcome, garden with views, bedrooms, open all day *(Suzy Miller)*

BISHOP'S TAWTON [SS5629]

☆ *Chichester Arms* EX32 0DQ [signed off A377 outside Barnstaple; East St]: Friendly 15th-c cob and thatch pub, well priced good generous food from home-made soup and sandwiches to fresh local fish and seasonal

game (all meat from named farms); quick obliging service even when crowded, well kept Exmoor ales and Marstons Pedigree, decent wines, heavy low beams, large stone fireplace, restaurant; children welcome, disabled access not good but staff very helpful, picnic-sets on front terrace and in back garden, open all day *(LYM, David Eberlin, E J Sayer)*

BLACK DOG [SS8009]

Black Dog EX17 4QS [off B3042 at Thelbridge]: Popular thatched and beamed village pub with hard-working landlord, enjoyable food inc good Sun carvery *(Mrs P Sumner)*

BLACKMOOR GATE [SS6443]

Old Station House EX31 4NW [A39/A399]: Former station on redundant line interestingly converted into big family dining place, Cotleigh, Exmoor and St Austell beers, welcoming landlord and efficient staff, wide food choice from sandwiches and baguettes up, inc two-for-one wkdy deals and wknd carvery, coffee; carved pews, plush dining chairs, soft red lighting, lots of bric-a-brac; spacious games area with two well lit pool tables, darts, piped music; small room for under-5s, skittle alley, picnic-sets and play area in big garden with good views, open all day *(BB, George Atkinson)*

BOVEY TRACEY [SX8178]

Cromwell Arms TQ13 9AE [Fore St]: Old beamed local with keen pricing, good value bar lunches, St Austell ales, good wine choice, several areas with high-backed settles; small terrace *(Comus and Sarah Elliott)*

BRADWORTHY [SS3213]

Bradworthy Inn EX22 7TD [The Square]: Thatched pub doing well under newish owners, good menu, well kept beer, huge fire in big main bar, smaller bar and eating area, friendly locals; dogs welcome, comfortable bedrooms *(Jean and David Lewis)*

BRAMPFORD SPEKE [SX9298]

☆ *Lazy Toad* EX5 5DP [off A377 N of Exeter]: Former Agricultural Inn doing well after careful restoration by newish licensees, beams and flagstones, settles and log fire, separate eating area, good well priced food from locally sourced ingredients and own smokery, home-grown herbs and soft fruits, may rear own meat in future; good friendly service even when busy, Adnams, St Austell Tribute and Warriors Golden Wolf, friendly resident cocker called Sam; disabled facilities, courtyard and garden *(R P Sawbridge, David Hall)*

BRATTON CLOVELLY [SX4691]

Clovelly EX20 4JZ: Thriving local with big helpings of enjoyable wholesome food, Fullers London Pride and guest beers, good fire, cheerful staff, pool *(David and Katharine Cooke, Comus and Sarah Elliott)*

BRENDON [SS7547]

☆ *Rockford Inn* EX35 6PT [Rockford; Lynton—Simonsbath rd, off B3223]: Welcoming new licensees in unspoilt and interesting 17th-c beamed inn by East Lyn river (pub has fishing permits); low-priced fresh food from lunchtime snacks up inc substantial evening meals and popular Sun roasts, Cotleigh and Exmoor ales, Thatcher's farm cider, interesting wines; small linked rooms with mix of padded settles and chairs around sturdy tables, open fire and three woodburners, fishing books, board games; piped music; children and dogs welcome, good walks, five bedrooms (some sharing bathrooms), open all day but cl Mon lunchtime *(Lora Raffael, Sheila Topham, LYM)*

☆ *Staghunters* EX35 6PS: Welcoming new licensees in idyllically set, recently renovated hotel with gardens by East Lyn river, neat bar with woodburner, good value food, good log fire, Exmoor Ale and Gold, restaurant; can get very busy; walkers and dogs welcome, 12 good value bedrooms *(Mrs Y Quelch)*

BRIXHAM [SX9256]
Quayside TQ5 9TJ [King St]: Enjoyable good value food, friendly efficient service; bedrooms good value too, comfortable and attractively quaint *(Carol Beeby)*

BRIXTON [SX5552]
Foxhound Clipper PL8 2AH: Popular and welcoming two-bar beamed village local; chef/landlord doing good value food from sandwiches up inc good savoury pancakes, five beers inc Skinners and Summerskills, Weston's cider from the barrel, extensive wine list, large collection of toby jugs; live music and other events *(Jerry Brown)*

BROADHEMBURY [ST1004]
Drewe Arms EX14 3NF [off A373 Cullompton—Honiton]: Reopened under licensees previously at the Dartmoor Union in Holbeton, charming old building with oak-boarded bar and carpeted dining area, big stone fireplace, low-beamed snug, food (all day Sun) in bar and separate restaurant (they hope to build on the pub's former high reputation for food – reports please); Otter and two guest ales, farm cider, good choice of wines by the glass; children and dogs welcome, back garden with terrace, open all day wknds *(LYM)*

BUDLEIGH SALTERTON [SY0681]
☆ *Salterton Arms* EX9 6LX [Chapel St]: Light open-plan layout, mixed seating inc some comfortable, stone floors and woodburner; low-priced food, three well kept ales, farm cider, thriving pubby atmosphere, darts, roomy upstairs gallery restaurant; games machine; children welcome, open all day wknds *(Jo Rees, Dr and Mrs M E Wilson, LYM)*

BUTTERLEIGH [SS9708]
Butterleigh Inn EX15 1PN [off A396 in Bickleigh]: Friendly small-roomed heavy-beamed country pub under new licensees, enjoyable food, real ales such as O'Hanlons and Otter, big fireplace, pine dining chairs around country kitchen tables in one room, darts in another; attractive garden, comfortable bedrooms *(Malcolm Smith, LYM, G and P Vago)*

CALIFORNIA CROSS [SX7053]
☆ *California* PL21 0SG [brown sign to pub off A3121 S of A38 junction]: Neatly modernised 18th-c or older pub with beams, panelling, stripped stone and a log fire, wide choice of good sensibly priced food from sandwiches to steaks in dining bar and family area, good restaurant menu, popular Sun lunch (best to book), good friendly service; sofa in small separate snug, Coachmans Best, Fullers London Pride and Greene King Abbot, decent wines, local farm cider; piped music; children and dogs welcome, good tables in attractive garden and back terrace, open all day *(BB, Steve and Miriam Jones, Lucien Perring)*

CHAGFORD [SX7087]
☆ *Ring o' Bells* TQ13 8AH [off A382]: Ancient, black and white pub, Butcombe and Teignworthy ales, good friendly service, enjoyable freshly cooked food, beamed and panelled bar, log fire in big fireplace, pub dogs; dogs and well behaved children welcome, sunny walled garden behind, bedrooms, nearby moorland walks, open all day *(Dr and Mrs A K Clarke, LYM, A B and C A Bailey)*

CHALLACOMBE [SS6941]
Black Venus EX31 4TT [B3358 Blackmoor Gate—Simonsbath]: Low-beamed 16th-c pub with friendly helpful landlady, two well kept changing ales, Thatcher's farm cider, varied food from sandwiches up, pews and comfortable chairs, woodburner and big open fire (not always lit), roomy and attractive dining area; garden tables, grand countryside *(B M Eldridge, BB, Sheila Topham)*

CHERITON BISHOP [SX7792]
Mulberry EX6 6JH: Former Good Knight, good contemporary reworking under new architect landlord, enjoyable generous food from home-baked bread and familiar favourites to good up-to-date dishes, welcoming service, new restaurant; garden tables with water for dogs, six smart bedrooms *(R and M Thomas)*

☆ *Old Thatch Inn* EX6 6JH [off A30]: Old-fashioned thatched pub well geared to the holiday traffic and generally very well liked; traditionally furnished lounge and rambling beamed bar separated by big stone fireplace, O'Hanlons Royal Oak and Yellowhammer, Otter, Sharps Doom Bar and a guest beer, quite a choice of bar food from sandwiches up; children and dogs welcome, sheltered garden, pretty tubs and baskets, bedrooms, cl Sun evening *(Comus and Sarah Elliott, B and M Kendall, David and Sue Smith, Mr and Mrs A H Young, Mr and Mrs Richard Osborne, R T and J C Moggridge, LYM, M Bryan Osborne, Dr and Mrs M E Wilson, Nick Lawless, Ray and Winifred Halliday)*

CHRISTOW [SX8384]
Artichoke EX6 7NF: Pretty thatched local with small comfortable open-plan rooms stepped downhill, low beams, some black panelling and flagstones; reliable food inc fish, game and nice puddings, lovely log fire (another in dining room), Otter tapped from

cask, welcoming helpful service; tables on back terrace, pretty village nr Canonteign Waterfalls and Country Park *(BB, Amanda Goodridge, Peter and Helen Loveland)*

CHUDLEIGH [SX8679]

Bishop Lacey TQ13 0HY [Fore St, just off A38]: Partly 14th-c low-beamed church house with cheerful obliging landlady and staff, real ales inc Dartmoor, O'Hanlons and Sharps, farm cider, enjoyable home cooking inc good curries, two log fires, dark décor, dining room; live bands in next-door offshoot; children welcome, garden tables, good value bedrooms, open all day *(the Didler)*

CHULMLEIGH [SS6814]

Red Lion EX18 7DD [East St]: Old pub well divided into three comfortable and interestingly varied areas, good range of beers and wine, above-average food, friendly licensees; TV in big games room *(C R Cann)*

CHURCHSTOW [SX7145]

Church House TQ7 3QW [A379 NW of Kingsbridge]: Much refurbished pub dating from 13th c, heavy black beams and stripped stone, wide choice of home-made food, friendly efficient staff, well kept local ales, decent wines, back conservatory with floodlit well feature; well behaved children welcome, tables on big terrace *(LYM, Geoff and Marianne Millin, MP, Hugh Stafford)*

CLAYHIDON [ST1615]

Half Moon EX15 3TJ: Attractive old village pub with warm friendly atmosphere, wide choice of good home-made food from high-quality ingredients, well cared for Cotleigh ales and a guest, Skinner's cider, fine wine list, tasteful furniture and inglenook fireplace in the comfortable bar; children and dogs welcome, delightful calming views from picnic-sets in tiered garden over road *(John and Fiona Merritt, Jerry Brown)*

CLYST ST GEORGE [SX9888]

St George & Dragon EX3 0QJ: Spaciously extended open-plan Vintage Inn, fresh and cheerful décor, with careful lighting, low beams and some secluded corners, log fires; welcoming and helpful young staff, real ales, good choice of wines by the glass, good value and usually busy; bedrooms in adjoining Innkeepers Lodge, open all day *(Dr and Mrs M E Wilson)*

CLYST ST MARY [SX9791]

☆ *Half Moon* EX5 1BR [under a mile from M5 junction 30 via A376]: Attractive old pub next to disused multi-arched bridge (Devon's oldest) over Clyst; current management putting more emphasis on the reasonably priced home-made food using local meat and fish, Greene King, Otter and Wells & Youngs ales, good choice of wines by the glass, red plush seating and plenty of dining tables, log fire; nostalgic juke box, live music Sat night; children welcome in lounge (no under-11s in restaurant), disabled access, six bedrooms, open all day wknds *(Dr and Mrs M E Wilson, Alain and Rose Foote)*

COCKWOOD [SX9780]

☆ *Ship* EX6 8RA [off A379 N of Dawlish]: Comfortable traditional 17th-c pub overlooking estuary and harbour; good value generous food inc good fish dishes and puddings (freshly made by landlady so takes time), Butcombe and Sharps Doom Bar, friendly helpful staff, partitioned beamed bar with big log fire and ancient oven, decorative plates and seafaring memorabilia, small restaurant; piped music; children and dogs welcome, nice steep-sided garden *(Roger and Carol Maden, Paul Booth, Dr and Mrs John Fripp)*

COLYFORD [SY2592]

Wheelwright EX24 6QQ [Swan Hill Rd (A3052 Sidmouth—Lyme Regis)]: Attractive 17th-c thatched pub, welcoming and civilised, with low beams, log fire, soft lighting, enjoyable fresh food all day inc good fish and local produce, well kept Badger ales and a guest, good wine choice, new back extension; children and dogs welcome, picnic-sets on front terrace *(John Burgess, Richard Stanfield)*

COLYTON [SY2494]

Gerrard Arms EX24 6JN [St Andrews Sq]: Unpretentious open-plan local with Bass, Branscombe Vale Branoc and a guest beer tapped from the cask, skittle alley, lunchtime food inc Sun roasts; tables in courtyard and informal garden *(the Didler)*

☆ *Kingfisher* EX24 6NA [off A35 and A3052 E of Sidmouth; Dolphin St]: Low-beamed village pub with four well kept changing ales such as Sharps and Ringwood, good wines by the glass, food from baguettes to home-made pub favourites, local crab, Sun roasts and occasional theme nights; stripped stone, plush seats and elm settles, pub games, skittle alley; outside gents', piped music, games machine; dogs and children welcome, terrace tables, garden with water feature, boules, open all day Sun and in summer *(the Didler, LYM, Richard Stanfield, Neil and Anita Christopher)*

COMBEINTEIGNHEAD [SX9072]

☆ *Coombe Cellars* TQ12 4RT [Shaldon rd, off A380 opp main Newton Abbot roundabout]: Big waterside pub recently well reworked by M&B; comfortable modern feel with mix of new and traditional furnishings, wide choice of good value food all day, well kept Butcombe and Timothy Taylors Landlord, lots of wines by the glass, lovely estuary views; good disabled facilities, terrace, open all day *(LYM, David Carr, David Restarick, Ken Thompson)*

CORNWORTHY [SX8255]

☆ *Hunters Lodge* TQ9 7ES [off A381 Totnes—Kingsbridge]: Small low-ceilinged two-roomed bar, welcoming chatty staff, sensibly priced food cooked by landlady, well kept Sharps Doom Bar, traditional seating around heavy elm tables, cottagey dining room, log fire in big 17th-c fireplace; children and dogs welcome, big lawn with terrace and extensive views, cl Mon lunch *(MP, LYM)*

COUNTISBURY [SS7449]
Blue Ball EX35 6NE [A39, E of Lynton]:
Beautifully set, rambling, heavy-beamed
pub, friendly licensees, good range of food
in bar and restaurant, three ales inc one
brewed for the pub, decent wines, farm
ciders, reasonable prices, handsome log
fires; piped music; children, dogs and
walkers welcome (two pub dogs), views from
terrace tables, good nearby cliff walks (pub
provides handouts of four circular routes);
comfortable bedrooms, open all day (Mr and
Mrs D J Nash, LYM, Steve Ryman, Caroline and
Gavin Callow, Judith Coles)

CREDITON [SS8300]
Crediton Inn EX17 1EZ [Mill St (follow
Tiverton sign)]: Small friendly local, well
kept Fullers London Pride, Sharps Doom Bar
and quickly changing guest beers (150 a
year), cheap well prepared food, back games
room; open all day Mon-Sat, free skittle alley
can be booked (the Didler)

CROYDE [SS4439]
Billy Budds EX33 1LZ [B3231 NW of
Braunton; Hobbs Hill]: Speedy cheerful
service for families, bar and restaurant food
inc good burgers, real ales, stripped
brickwork and beams, old local photographs;
sports TV; large gardens shared with
neighbouring Thatched Barn (same
management), good play area (Alex Tucker)
Thatched Barn EX33 1LZ [B3231 NW of
Braunton; Hobbs Hill]: Lively thatched pub
nr great surfing beaches, australian-run with
cheerful efficient young staff, laid-back feel
and customers to match (can get packed in
summer); rambling and roomy, with beams,
settles and good seating, wide choice of
enjoyable generous all-day food from
sandwiches and baguettes up, well kept
changing local ales, morning coffee, teas,
smart restaurant with dressers and lots of
china; piped music; children in eating areas,
tables on flower-filled suntrap terraces, large
gardens shared with neighbouring Billy
Budds, good play area, bedrooms simple but
clean and comfortable, open all day (LYM,
Alex Tucker, Pat and Tony Martin)

DARTINGTON [SX7861]
Cott TQ9 6HE [Cott signed off A385 W of
Totnes, opp A384 turn-off]: Long 14th-c
thatched pub with heavy beams, flagstones
and inglenook log fire, bar with smallish
drinking area one end, close-set dining
tables the other, Greene King ales, enjoyable
food from sandwiches up, restaurant;
children and dogs on leads welcome,
awkward disabled/pushchair access, picnic-
sets in garden and on pretty terrace, seven
bedrooms, open all day at least in summer
(B J Harding, MB, LYM, Henry Pursehouse-
Tranter)

DARTMOUTH [SX8751]
☆ **Floating Bridge** TQ6 9PQ [Coombe Rd]:
Bistro-style quayside pub under same
ownership as nearby Dart Marina Hotel;
warmly welcoming landlady and helpful staff,
three well kept ales inc Otter and St Austell

Tribute, good range of reasonably priced
food from enjoyable lunchtime sandwiches to
fish and seafood, may have bargain evening
deals, sizeable restaurant, good Dart and
ferry-crossing views, newspapers; seats out
front and back, nice hanging baskets
(Ian Malone, Richard and Sissel Harris,
Michael Dandy)
☆ **Royal Castle Hotel** TQ6 9PS [the Quay]:
Rambling 17th-c or older hotel behind
Regency façade overlooking inner harbour,
good well priced lunches in upstairs
restaurant, long traditional downstairs bar
with dining area for all-day food from
sandwiches to good steaks, perhaps winter
lunchtime spit-roasts from their 17th-c
range, more contemporary bar on left (TV,
piped music may be loud, dogs welcome –
no children); friendly efficient staff, well
kept Dartmoor and Sharps ales, good choice
of wines; live music Thurs, Sun; children
allowed lunchtime; 25 comfortable
bedrooms with secure parking,
open all day (Mrs Mary Woods, Gerry and
Rosemary Dobson, Richard Tilbrook, Mr and
Mrs W W Burke, Michael Dandy, LYM, Mike and
Sue Shirley, Susan and Nigel Wilson)

DAWLISH [SX9676]
Marine EX7 9DJ [Marine Parade]: Friendly
seafront family pub with views of Lyme Bay
and Exmouth, good value food especially
ploughman's, Otter ale; bedrooms (Alain and
Rose Foote)
Swan EX7 9AT [Old Town St]: Comfortable
and welcoming 17th-c local (oldest inn
here), varied good value food, well kept
local ale, unobtrusive piped music (mostly
classical); large terrace and pleasant garden
behind (David Carr)

DAWLISH WARREN [SX9778]
Mount Pleasant EX7 0NA [Mount Pleasant
Rd]: Marvellous sea views from family pub
with carpeted heavily beamed lounge and
rooms off, Otter and Wadworths 6X, good
choice of food, darts and pool; terrace tables
(Donna and Roger)

DODDISCOMBSLEIGH [SX8586]
☆ **Nobody Inn** EX6 7PS [off B3193]: Long a
favourite, this 16th-c inn changed hands in
2008, and after a bit of a hiatus seems to be
getting back on track, with well kept ales
such as Exe Valley, local ciders, a great wine
and whisky choice, friendly staff and decent
bar food; good log fire, beamed lounge with
handsomely carved antique settles among
other seats, guns and hunting prints by big
inglenook, redecorated evening restaurant;
children and dogs welcome, new garden
seating, well refurbished bedrooms, open
all day (W K Wood, J D O Carter,
Cass Stainton, J L Wedel, Chris and
Angela Buckell, Anthony Longden, Adrian and
Dawn Collinge, LYM, Gene and Kitty Rankin,
Peter Leather)

DREWSTEIGNTON [SX7489]
☆ **Fingle Bridge Inn** EX6 6PW [E of village;
OS map ref 743899 – may be shown under
its former Anglers Rest name]: Idyllic

wooded Teign valley spot by 16th-c pack-horse bridge, lovely walks and a magnet for summer visitors; much extended former tea pavilion, tourist souvenirs and airy café feel, west country real ales, food from baguettes and good local cheese ploughman's up, Sun carvery, friendly helpful service, log fire; children and dogs welcome, waterside picnic-sets; has been cl winter evenings (Adrian and Dawn Collinge, LYM, Dr and Mrs M E Wilson)

DUNSFORD [SX8189]
☆ *Royal Oak* EX6 7DA [signed from Moretonhampstead]: Comfortably worn-in village inn, good generous food cooked to order, changing ales inc Dartmoor and Sharps, local farm cider, friendly landlord; airy lounge bar with woodburner and view from small sunny dining bay, simple dining room, steps down to games room with pool; quiz nights, piped music; children well looked after, sheltered tiered garden, good value bedrooms in converted barn (the Didler, Robert Gomme, LYM)

EAST BUDLEIGH [SY0684]
Rolle Arms EX9 7DL [Oak Hill, Lower Budleigh (A376)]: Popular and hard-working new young licensees, well kept Otter ales, imaginative food using local supplies, thriving local atmosphere, bare boards and dark woodwork, long dining room on right (David Hunt)
Sir Walter Raleigh EX9 7ED [High St]: Quiet low-beamed village local, Adnams Broadside, Otter and St Austell Tribute, books on shelves, restaurant down step; no children, parking some way off; dogs welcome, wonderful medieval bench carvings in nearby church, handy too for Bicton Park Gardens (FJS and DS, LYM, Mrs Jordan, Dr and Mrs M E Wilson)

EAST PRAWLE [SX7836]
Pigs Nose TQ7 2BY [Prawle Green]: Relaxed, quirky, three-room 16th-c inn with low beams and flagstones, local ales tapped from the cask, farm ciders, enjoyable if limited food, open fire, mix of old furniture, lots of interesting bric-a-brac and pictures, jars of wild flowers and candles on tables; bird log, darts, small family area with unusual toys, nice dogs, laid-back service can be slow; unobtrusive piped music, hall for live bands (friendly landlord was 60s tour manager); tables outside, nice spot on village green (W K Wood, MB, the Didler, Roger Wain-Heapy, Geoff and Carol Thorp, Simon Foster)

EXETER [SX9292]
Chaucers EX4 3LR [basement of Tesco Metro, High St]: Large, dim-lit, modern olde-worlde pub/bistro/wine bar down lots of steps; beamed low ceiling and timber-framed walls, several levels with booths and alcoves, comfortable furnishings, candles in bottles, Jennings, Marstons and guest ales, well priced wines, enjoyable good value food from snacks to specials, quick friendly service; piped music, no children (Adrian and Dawn Collinge, Michael Dandy)

Double Locks EX2 6LT [Canal Banks, Alphington, via Marsh Barton Industrial Estate; OS Sheet 192 map ref 933901]: Unsmart and individual, by ship canal, remote yet busy, Wells & Youngs and guest ales, Gray's farm cider in summer, wide variety of good value plain home-made bar food all day; piped music, live wknds, service can get swamped; children and dogs welcome, seats out on decking with distant view to city and cathedral (nice towpath walk out – or hire a canoe at the Quay); good big play area, camping, open all day (Jackie Givens, the Didler, Mr and Mrs P D Titcomb, Michael Beale, Richard Mason, LYM, Donna Delamain)
Fat Pig EX1 1BL [John St]: Refurbished Victorian pub with Exeter Ferryman, Hop Back Summer Lightning, O'Hanlons Royal Oak and changing guest beers, good wine choice, imaginative blackboard food, welcoming fire in nice fireplace; tables in heated courtyard (Mike Gorton)
Georges Meeting House EX1 1ED [South St]: Comfortable lively Wetherspoons in grand former 18th-c chapel dominated by a tall pulpit at one end; stained-glass, original pews in three-sided gallery, some leather sofas, their usual food and good west country cheese, fish and meat, six ales, good wine choice; children welcome when eating, quality furniture in attractive side garden, open all day (Ryta Lyndley, Mike Gorton, Dr and Mrs M E Wilson, the Didler)
Great Western EX4 4NU [St Davids Hill]: Regulars enjoy up to a dozen or so changing real ales inc some choice rarities in large commercial hotel's comfortably worn-in plush-seated bar; friendly efficient staff, wholesome good value fresh food all day from sandwiches and generous baked potatoes up (kitchen also supplies the hotel's restaurant), daily papers; may be piped music, sports TV, pay parking; children welcome, 35 bedrooms, open all day (Andy and Jill Kassube, Joan and Michel Hooper-Immins, Tony and Wendy Hobden, the Didler, BB)
Old Fire House EX4 4EP [New North Rd]: Compact city-centre pub in Georgian building tucked away behind high arched wrought-iron gates, ten changing ales, good choice of wines, bargain food, friendly staff, simple furniture, hops on beams; popular with young people in evenings; piped music, live folk and jazz; picnic-sets in small front courtyard (the Didler, Dr and Mrs M E Wilson, Mike Gorton, David Gray, Andy and Jill Kassube)
Port Royal EX2 4DR [Weirfield Path, off Weirfield Rd – left-bank path downstream from The Quay]: Low gabled waterside pavilion with sofas and settles in long convivial nautical-theme lounge, good choice of real ales and wines, interesting fresh food from bar snacks up in smart dining area, friendly service; public bar with darts, pool, games machines and piped music; river-view tables (Les and Norma Haydon)

Ship EX1 1EY [Martins Lane, nr cathedral]: Pretty 14th-c heavy-beamed building with olde-worlde, city pub style, thriving friendly atmosphere, well kept Greene King and Otter ales, farm cider, bargain food all day wkdys, comfortable upstairs restaurant; piped music and games machines (Dr and Mrs M E Wilson, Michael Dandy, LYM)

Welcome EX2 8DU [Haven Banks, off Haven Rd (which is first left off A377 heading S after Exe crossing)]: Two-room pub little changed since 60s (ditto the juke box), gas lighting and flagstones, very friendly old-school landlady, changing ales; a few tables out overlooking basin on Exeter Ship Canal, can be reached on foot via footbridges from the Quay (the Didler)

Well House EX1 1HB [Cathedral Yard, attached to Royal Clarence Hotel]: Big windows looking across to cathedral in partly divided open-plan bar, good choice of local ales such as Otter, quick service, wide range of food, daily papers, sofa, lots of Victorian prints, Roman well below (can be viewed when pub not busy); open all day (Andy and Jill Kassube, the Didler, Tony and Wendy Hobden, BB, Dr and Mrs M E Wilson)

White Hart EX1 1EE [South St]: Attractively old-fashioned rambling bar, heavy beams, oak flooring, nice furnishings inc antiques, charming inner cobbled courtyard; now tied to Marstons, with their ales and reasonably priced standard food; bedrooms (Les and Norma Haydon, LYM, Joan and Michel Hooper-Immins, Dr and Mrs M E Wilson)

EXMOUTH [SY9980]

Grove EX8 1BJ [Esplanade]: Roomy, unpretentious old-fashioned family pub set back from the beach, basic traditional furnishings, caricatures and local prints, good value all-day food inc plenty of fish, quick obliging staff, Wells & Youngs and guest beers, decent house wines, good coffee, attractive fireplace at back, sea views from appealing upstairs dining room and balcony; live music Fri; picnic-sets in big garden (no view) with play area (Dr and Mrs M E Wilson, Peter Salmon, Mark Flynn, Alain and Rose Foote, Jo Rees, Michael and Lynne Gittins, David Hunt)

EXTON [SX9886]

Puffing Billy EX3 0PR: Brightly decorated well laid out dining pub with good helpings of inventive modern food using named local organic suppliers, friendly service, local beers and good wine choice in the new bar extension; picnic-sets outside (Dr and Mrs M E Wilson, R P Sawbridge, Ian Malone)

FROGMORE [SX7742]

Globe TQ7 2NR [A379 E of Kingsbridge]: Extended and refurbished, with well kept Otter, Skinners and South Hams, local farm cider in summer, nice wines, well priced food from sandwiches to steak, good friendly service, fine log fire in cosy restaurant, darts; piped music, TV, games machine; terrace tables, creek and coast walks, eight good bedrooms, good breakfast (A C Powell, LYM, Tony and Gill Powell)

GEORGEHAM [SS4639]

☆ **Rock** EX33 1JW [Rock Hill, above village]: Beamed family pub much improved under newish licensees; chef/landlord doing good food from ciabattas to plenty of fish and popular Sun roasts, quick friendly service even when packed, up to five well kept changing ales, farm cider and decent wine choice; open fire, old red quarry tiles, pleasant mix of rustic furniture, smallish dining room, separate vine-adorned back conservatory, skittle alley; piped music; dogs welcome, disabled access, flower-decked front terrace, some seating out behind, open all day (Dr S J Shepherd, Bob and Margaret Holder, BB, David Eberlin)

HARTLAND [SS2524]

Hart EX39 6BL [The Square]: Village pub scoring highly on the food side under current ownership, changing real ales (Roger Chapple)

HARTLAND QUAY [SS2224]

Hartland Quay Hotel EX39 6DU [off B3248 W of Bideford, down toll road (free Oct-Easter); OS Sheet 190 map ref 222248]: Unpretentious old hotel worth knowing for the formidable cliff scenery; stuffed fish and shipwreck pictures, down-to-earth friendly staff, St Austell beer, basic cheap food; dogs welcome, lots of tables outside (can be packed with tourists), good value bedrooms, seawater swimming pool, rugged coast walks; cl mid-winter (Dave Braisted, S P Watkin, P A Taylor)

HATHERLEIGH [SS5404]

☆ **Tally Ho** EX20 3JN [Market St (A386)]: Good generous uncomplicated food (not Sun evening) from lunchtime sandwiches up, inc a rather special curry, good value wines, real ales such as local Clearwater and St Austell, quick friendly service; attractive heavy-beamed and timbered linked rooms, sturdy furnishings, big log fire and woodburner, traditional games, restaurant, busy Tues market day (beer slightly cheaper then); unobtrusive piped music; dogs welcome, tables in nice sheltered garden, three good value pretty bedrooms, open all day (LYM, Rona Murdoch, Dr J Barrie Jones, the Didler)

HAWKCHURCH [ST3400]

Old Inn EX13 5XD [off B3165 E of Axminster, nr Dorset border]: 16th-c pub doing well under new owners, friendly atmosphere, enjoyable home-made food inc good Sun lunch, well kept real ales such as Branscombe Vale, Otter and Palmers, good value local farm cider; log fires in long low-beamed main bar, good-sized dining room; picnic-sets in flower-filled back courtyard (Basil D Nunn)

HEANTON PUNCHARDON [SS5034]

Tarka EX31 4AX: Castle-look Vintage Inn overlooking estuary, staff particularly helpful with children (Pat and Tony Martin)

HEMERDON [SX5657]

Miners Arms PL7 5BU: In the same family

for over 100 years, friendly and attractive, with low beams, log fire, internal well, separate snug, Bass and two guest ales, conservatory restaurant with enjoyable fresh local food; children and dogs welcome, good pastoral views from restaurant and roomy flagstoned terrace, garden with play area, open all day wknds *(Amy Hurn)*

HOLSWORTHY [SS3403]

Old Market EX22 6AY [Chapel St]: Town centre pub with John Smiths and three other well kept ales, bargain food from sandwiches up, Sun carvery, restaurant, function room; dogs welcome in garden, three bedrooms *(Pat Sycamore)*

Rydon Inn EX22 7HU [Rydon (A3072 W)]: Enjoyable food in comfortable dining pub with two dining rooms; disabled access and facilities, dogs welcome by arrangement in part of bar, garden tables *(Jean and David Lewis)*

HONITON [ST1599]

Heathfield EX14 2UG [Walnut Rd]: Ancient pub smartly refurbished by Greene King, their ales, reasonably priced food inc bargain meals, cheerful service; bedrooms *(Bob and Margaret Holder)*

☆ *Holt* EX14 1LA [High St]: Welcoming family-run pub doing good interesting food inc good value tapas, own smoked meat and fish from the open kitchen, four well kept Otter ales, flagstoned bar, old stripped pine and open fire, upstairs dining area, occasional live music *(Tim Thornburn, Sophie Clapp, JHW)*

Red Cow EX14 1PW [High St]: Town-centre pub with scrubbed tables, pleasant alcoves, beams, log fires and subdued lighting, well kept Otter, good simple hearty food, reasonable prices; pavement tables, bedrooms *(BB, David and Sue Smith)*

HOPE COVE [SX6740]

☆ *Hope & Anchor* TQ7 3HQ: Bustling unpretentious inn, friendly and comfortably unfussy, in lovely seaside spot; good open fire, quick helpful service, good value straightforward food inc lots of fish, well kept St Austell Dartmoor and a beer brewed for the pub, reasonably priced wines; flagstones and bare boards, dining room views to Burgh Island, big separate family room; piped music; children and dogs welcome, sea-view tables out on decking, great coast walks, bedrooms, good breakfast, open all day *(LYM, Steve and Miriam Jones, David Barnes, Theocsbrian, David Uren, John Saville, Simon J Barber)*

HORNS CROSS [SS3823]

☆ *Hoops* EX39 5DL [A39 Clovelly—Bideford, W of village]: Welcoming picturesque thatched inn with oak settles, beams and inglenook fires in pleasant bar, good food, generous if not cheap, using local suppliers, efficient friendly service even when busy, well kept ales such as local Country Life and one brewed for the pub, local farm cider, good wine choice, daily papers, darts; piped music, TV; well behaved children in eating

area till 8pm, dogs allowed in bar, tables in small courtyard, comfortable bedrooms, good breakfast, open all day *(John and Jackie Chalcraft, John Urquhart, LYM, Ryta Lyndley, Paul and Annette Hallett, Annette Tress, Gary Smith)*

HORSEBRIDGE [SX4074]

☆ *Royal* PL19 8PJ [off A384 Tavistock—Launceston]: Cheerful ancient local with dark half-panelling, slate floors and interesting bric-a-brac; simple good value food from home-made soup and baked potatoes to fresh scallops, friendly landlord and staff, well kept St Austell and Skinners, Rich's farm cider, log fires, bar billiards, cribbage, dominoes, café-style side room, no music or machines; no children in evening, picnic-sets on terrace and in big garden, quiet rustic spot by lovely old Tamar bridge *(LYM, Giles and Annie Francis, Peter Andrews, Jacquie Jones)*

IDDESLEIGH [SS5608]

☆ *Duke of York* EX19 8BG [B3217 Exbourne—Dolton]: The licensees who made this friendly informal inn such a universal favourite will have left by the time this *Guide* is published; we'd be grateful for news on the inevitable changes; it's been very much a homely unspoilt local – chatty regulars in their wellies, perhaps a dog or two, roaring log fire, Adnams Broadside, Cotleigh Tawny, Sharps Doom Bar; children and dogs welcome, little back garden, quirky bedrooms, open all day *(LYM)*

IDE [SX8990]

☆ *Poachers* EX2 9RW [3 miles from M5 junction 31, via A30; High St]: Busy local, nice non-standard mix of old chairs and sofas, good generous food, both traditional and inventive (worth booking evenings), Bass, Branscombe Vale Branoc, Otter and one brewed locally for the pub, good value house wines, big log fire; picnic-sets in pleasant garden, comfortable attractive bedrooms, small quaint village, cl Mon lunchtime *(the Didler)*

IDEFORD [SX8977]

☆ *Royal Oak* TQ13 0AY [2 miles off A380]: Unpretentious 16th-c thatched and flagstoned village local with friendly helpful service, Greene King, Otter and guest beers, basic pub snacks; navy theme inc interesting Nelson and Churchill memorabilia, big log fireplace; children and dogs welcome, tables out at front and by car park over road *(the Didler)*

ILFRACOMBE [SS5247]

George & Dragon EX34 9ED [Fore St]: Oldest pub here, handy for harbour, clean and comfortable, with local atmosphere, helpful friendly staff, four well kept mainstream real ales, decent wines, low-priced tasty pub food cooked by landlord; attractive olde-worlde décor with stripped stone, beams, open fireplaces, lots of ornaments, china etc; no mobile phones; piped music, cash machine but no credit cards *(JDM, KM, B M Eldridge, Mrs C Osgood)*

ILSINGTON [SX7876]

Carpenters Arms TQ13 9RG: Very pretty unspoilt 18th-c local next to church in quiet village, friendly licensees, well kept ales, wholesome cheap food, log fire, parlour off main public bar; good walks *(John and Gloria Isaacs)*

INSTOW [SS4730]

Wayfarer EX39 4LB [Lane End]: Unpretentious locals' pub tucked away near dunes and beach, welcoming efficient staff, well kept ales tapped from the cask, winter mulled wine, good choice of enjoyable generous home-made food using local fish and meats; children and dogs welcome, enclosed garden behind, six well presented bedrooms (some with sea view), open all day *(Wendda Johnson, D P and M A Miles)*

KENTISBEARE [ST0606]

Keepers Cottage EX15 2EB [not far from M5 junction 28, via A373]: Friendly old thatched cottage with a wide range of decent generous food, real ales tapped from the cask *(M S Lee)*

Wyndham Arms EX15 2AA [3.5 miles from M5 junction 28, via A373]: Village pub now rescued from closure by enthusiastic local volunteers who have helped with its refurbishment; pleasant staff, enjoyable food, well kept beers, big log fire in long beamed main bar, restaurant, games room; sheltered courtyard *(BB, John and Dinah Waters)*

KILMINGTON [SY2798]

☆ *Old Inn* EX13 7RB [A35]: Thatched 16th-c pub with welcoming licensees, enjoyable good value food using local suppliers, Cotleigh and Otter ales, good choice of wines, small polished-floor front bar with traditional games, back lounge with leather armchairs by inglenook log fire, small restaurant; children welcome, skittle alley, two gardens *(Anthony Double, LYM, Richard and Sue Fewkes, Faith Thomas)*

KINGSWEAR [SX8851]

Royal Dart TQ6 0AA [The Square]: Victorian building in fine setting by ferry and Dart Valley Railway terminal; South Hams and Teignworthy ales (may let you sample first), enjoyable food, bargain prices, chatty staff, unpretentious modernised bar, great view of Dartmouth from balcony outside upstairs restaurant; interesting World War II history when used as naval base; riverside tables *(Chris Evans, the Didler, N R White)*

Ship TQ6 0AG [Higher St]: Tall and attractive 15th-c two-bar local, entertaining landlord, well kept ales inc Adnams, Greene King IPA and Otter, farm cider, nice wines; honest straightforward food inc good fresh fish (best views from upstairs restaurant), log fires, interesting décor; a couple of river-view tables outside, open all day Fri-Sun and summer *(the Didler, Richard Tilbrook)*

Steam Packet TQ6 0AD [Fore St]: Small traditional local with friendly staff, well kept Bays and guest beers, pubby food in bar and restaurant; tables out in front, good views across to Dartmouth *(the Didler)*

LAKE [SX5288]

☆ *Bearslake* EX20 4HQ [A386 just S of Sourton]: Rambling low thatched stone pub, leather sofas and high bar chairs on crazy-paved slate floor one end, three more smallish rooms with woodburners, toby jugs, farm tools and traps; Otter and Teignworthy ales, good range of spirits and whiskies, decent wines, beamed restaurant; children allowed, large sheltered streamside garden, Dartmoor walks, six comfortable olde-worlde bedrooms, filling breakfast *(Chris and Angela Buckell, BB)*

LANDSCOVE [SX7766]

Live & Let Live TQ13 7LZ: Open-plan local with friendly landlady, good value home cooking inc bargain winter lunches, Ringwood, Teignworthy and occasional guest ale, farm ciders, log fire; decked terrace, more tables in small orchard across lane, cl Mon *(Mr and Mrs Martin Tomlinson, LYM, J D O Carter)*

LEE [SS4846]

Grampus EX34 8LR [signed off B3343/A361 W of Ilfracombe]: Attractive unpretentious 14th-c beamed pub, real ales such as local Jollyboat, well priced pubby food, friendly landlord, relaxed atmosphere, pool; dogs very welcome, lots of tables in appealing sheltered garden, short stroll from sea – superb coast walks *(BB, Phil Griffiths)*

LIFTON [SX3885]

☆ *Arundell Arms* PL16 0AA [Fore St]: Consistently good interesting lunchtime bar food in substantial country-house fishing hotel, warmly welcoming and individual, with rich décor, nice staff and sophisticated service, good choice of wines by the glass, morning coffee with home-made biscuits, afternoon tea, evening restaurant; can arrange fishing tuition – also shooting, deer-stalking and riding; pleasant bedrooms, useful A30 stop *(MA)*

LITTLEHEMPSTON [SX8162]

Tally Ho! TQ9 6NF [off A381 NE of Totnes]: Low-beamed 14th-c pub, neat and cosy, with interesting mix of chairs and settles, lots of cheerful bric-a-brac on stripped stone walls, some panelling; efficient friendly service even when busy, enjoyable food from sandwiches to steaks, Greene King IPA and perhaps a guest, restaurant; piped music; children welcome, flower-filled terrace, bedrooms (main railway line nearby) *(LYM, Glenda Bennett)*

LUPPITT [ST1606]

☆ *Luppitt Inn* EX14 4RT [back roads N of Honiton]: Unspoilt little basic farmhouse pub, amazing survivor of past times, friendly chatty landlady, tiny room with corner bar and a table, another not much bigger with fireplace, cheap Otter tapped from the cask, intriguing metal puzzles made by neighbour; no food or music, lavatories across the yard; cl lunchtime and Sun evening *(the Didler, John and Fiona McIlwain)*

LUSTLEIGH [SX7881]

☆ *Cleave* TQ13 9TJ [off A382 Bovey Tracey—Moretonhampstead]: Beautifully set country tavern, friendly tactful staff, food from good sandwiches up, real ales such as Otter, relaxed low-ceilinged bars, antique high-backed settles among other seats, log fire; children welcome, sheltered garden, has been open all day in summer *(LYM, Jim Lyon)*

LYDFORD [SX5184]

☆ *Castle Inn* EX20 4BH [off A386 Okehampton—Tavistock]: Tudor inn recently bought by St Austell, home-made food (all day Thurs-Sun), twin bars, big slate flagstones, bowed low beams, granite walls, four inglenook log fires, notable stained-glass door, restaurant; lovely nearby NT river gorge; open all day *(LYM)*

Dartmoor Inn EX20 4AY [Downton, A386]: Attractive restaurant-with-rooms rather than pub, several small civilised and relaxed stylishly decorated contemporary areas, interesting and imaginatively presented expensive food, separate bar menu (not Fri, Sat evenings), good wines by the glass, well kept real ale; children welcome, dogs allowed in small front log-fire bar, terrace tables, three spacious comfortable bedrooms, good breakfast, cl Sun evening, Mon *(Roger Wain-Heapy, John and Dinah Waters, Terry and Linda Moseley, Guy Vowles, Mrs Elizabeth Powell, Dr Ian Mortimer, LYM)*

LYMPSTONE [SX9984]

Redwing EX8 5JT [Church Rd]: This bustling local, long popular with readers for both food and drink, closed in 2008, and was being refurbished under new local ownership in 2009, with plans for reopening in summer 2009, with emphasis on local produce; news please *(BB)*

Swan EX8 5ET [The Strand]: Pleasant olde-worlde décor, split-level dining area with leather sofas by big fire, good value generous food inc good fresh fish and italian specials, real ales inc Marstons, friendly staff; games room with pool; small front garden with smokers' area *(the Didler, Dr and Mrs M E Wilson)*

LYNMOUTH [SS7249]

☆ *Rising Sun* EX35 6EG [Harbourside]: Wonderful position overlooking harbour, bustling beamed and stripped stone bar with Exmoor and St Austell ales, farm cider, imaginative if not cheap blackboard food inc plenty of good fish, nice fire; upmarket hotel side with attractive cosy restaurant; piped music, parking can be a problem – expensive by day, sparse at night; dogs welcome (old-fashioned attitude to children), neat bedrooms in cottagey old thatched building stepped up hills, good breakfast, gardens up behind *(Peter and Giff Bennett, Lynda and Trevor Smith, George Atkinson, LYM, W Dark)*

MAIDENCOMBE [SX9268]

Thatched Tavern TQ1 4TS [Steep Hill]: Much extended three-level thatched building under newish welcoming family management, wide choice of good value enjoyable pubby food in light and airy back eating area, good

service, nice coffee, traditional bar with Badger ales; children allowed, pleasant garden with picnic-sets and fun nooks and crannies, small attractive village above small beach *(Eithne Dandy, Michael Dandy, Jon Hargreaves)*

MALBOROUGH [SX7039]

Royal Oak TQ7 3RL [Higher Town]: Cosy well worn-in local with interesting choice of enjoyable food, good beer and wine, welcoming friendly staff, log fire; some folk nights *(Liane Pilgrim)*

MANATON [SX7578]

☆ *Kestor* TQ13 9UF [Water; 0.75 miles SE]: Modern Dartmoor-edge inn in splendid spot nr Becky Falls, popular with walkers and locals, welcoming homely feel with open stone fires either end of long carpeted bar, faux beams, good range of enjoyable home-made food from good lunchtime sandwiches up; attentive friendly young staff, well kept Otter, farm cider, good wine choice, light conservatory dining room with views; piped music; nice bedrooms *(Mike Parkes, Dr and Mrs M E Wilson)*

MEAVY [SX5467]

☆ *Royal Oak* PL20 6PJ [off B3212 E of Yelverton]: Friendly new licensees in heavy-beamed partly 15th-c pub, pews and plush banquettes, smaller locals' bar with flagstones and big fireplace, Dartmoor Jail and IPA, Sharps Doom Bar and a guest beer; seats outside and on green of pretty Dartmoor-edge village *(Wendda Johnson, David and Sue Smith, John Branston, MB, LYM)*

MODBURY [SX6551]

Modbury Inn PL21 0RQ [Brownston St]: Small traditional bar with well kept Otter, good value restaurant with enterprising country food, unfussy service; tables on attractive terrace, four comfortably refurbished bedrooms, open all day Sat *(A C Powell, MP)*

MORELEIGH [SX7652]

New Inn TQ9 7JH [B3207, off A381 Kingsbridge—Totnes in Stanborough]: Busy old-fashioned country local with attentive landlady (same family for several decades); limited choice of wholesome generous home cooking, reasonable prices, Palmers tapped from the cask, good inglenook log fire, character old furniture, nice pictures, candles in bottles; may be cl Sat lunchtime, race days *(Roger Wain-Heapy, LYM)*

MORETONHAMPSTEAD [SX7586]

White Hart TQ13 8NF [A382 N of Bovey Tracey; The Square]: Smartly refurbished small 17th-c hotel under newish ownership, stripped floor back bar with log fire, helpful friendly service, real ales, good choice of wines by the glass, bar food, elegant relaxing lounge with open fire, attractive brasserie; children and dogs welcome, courtyard tables, 28 well equipped country-style bedrooms, well placed for Dartmoor, open all day *(LYM)*

White Horse TQ13 8NF [George St]: Refurbished pub doing well under

chef/landlord; some live music
(Dr Ian Mortimer, Di and Mike Gillam)

MORTEHOE [SS4545]

Chichester Arms EX34 7DU [off A361
Ilfracombe—Braunton]: Welcoming place
with varied choice of enjoyable food from
newish chef, quick friendly service, real ales
such as local Barum Original, reasonably
priced wine; plush and leatherette panelled
lounge, comfortable dining room, pubby
locals' bar with darts and pool, interesting
old local photographs; skittle alley and
games machines in summer children's room,
tables out in front and in shaded pretty
garden, good coast walk (Mr and Mrs P Bland,
Chris Reading)

Ship Aground EX34 7DT [signed off A361
Ilfracombe—Braunton]: Open-plan beamed
village pub handy for coast walks, ales such
as Cotleigh Tawny and Greene King Abbot,
decent food and wine, upstairs carvery some
days, big log fires, massive rustic
furnishings, interesting nautical brassware,
big back family room with games area;
sheltered sunny terrace with good views, by
interesting church (David Eberlin, LYM,
B M Eldridge, JDM, KM)

MUDDIFORD [SS5638]

Muddiford Inn EX31 4EY [B3230
Barnstaple—Ilfracombe]: Family pub dating
from 16th c, plenty of character, enjoyable
generous reasonably priced food, local real
ale, open fire, fancier menu for pleasant
separate restaurant; big garden, handy for
Marwood Gardens (Julie Morey, Andy Wescott)

NEWTON ABBOT [SX8571]

Dartmouth TQ12 2JP [East St]: Genuine old
place brewing its own beers, interesting
guests and farm ciders too, decent wines,
low ceilings, dark woodwork, roaring log fire;
children welcome till 7, nice outside area,
open all day (the Didler)

Locomotive TQ12 2JP [East St]: Cheerful
traditional town pub with friendly staff,
Adnams and guest ales, linked rooms inc
games room with pool; TV, juke box; open
all day (the Didler, David Carr)

☆ *Olde Cider Bar* TQ12 2LD [East St]: Basic
old-fashioned cider house, casks of
interesting low-priced farm ciders (helpful
long-serving landlord may give you samples),
a couple of perries, more in bottles, good
country wines from the cask too, baguettes
and pasties etc; great atmosphere, dark
stools made from cask staves, barrel seats
and wall benches, flagstones and bare
boards; small back games room with
machines; terrace tables, open all day
(Dr Ian Mortimer, David Carr, the Didler)

Richard Hopkins TQ12 2EH [Queen St]: Big
partly divided open-plan Wetherspoons with
their usual food, Bays, Cottage, Otter and
several changing guest beers; open all day
(the Didler)

Two Mile Oak TQ12 6DF [A381 2 miles S, at
Denbury/Kingskerswell crossroads]:
Appealing beamed coaching inn, log fires,
traditional furnishings, black panelling and
candlelit alcoves, well kept Bass and Otter
tapped from the cask, straightforward bar
food inc wkdy lunchtime bargains; piped
music, TV, games machine; children in
lounge, dogs in bar, terrace and lawn, open
all day (Peter Salmon, LYM, the Didler)

Wolborough TQ12 1JQ [Wolborough St]:
Popular simply modernised local,
Teignworthy Reel and two guest beers
tapped from the cask; open all day
(the Didler)

NEWTON ST CYRES [SX8798]

Beer Engine EX5 5AX [off A377 towards
Thorverton]: Friendly former railway hotel
brewing four good beers for the last
25 years, wide choice of good food inc local
fish and popular Sun lunch; service can be
slow; children welcome, decked verandah,
steps down to garden, open all day
(the Didler, Dr A J and Mrs Tompsett,
Mike Gorton, LYM, John and Bryony Coles,
Roger and Carol Maden)

NEWTON TRACEY [SS5226]

Hunters EX31 3PL [B3232 Barnstaple—
Torrington]: Extended 15th-c pub doing well
under newish owners, massive low beams
and log fire, good reasonably priced
imaginative food, well kept St Austell and
guest ale, decent wines, friendly prompt
service; disabled access, skittle alley popular
with locals, tables on small terrace behind,
open all day (BB, Mark Flynn, Ken and
Margaret Grinstead, Phil and Sally Gorton)

NOMANSLAND [SS8313]

Mount Pleasant EX16 8NN [B3137
Tiverton—South Molton]: Informal country
local, huge fireplaces in long low-beamed
main bar, Cotleigh Tawny and Sharps Doom
Bar, several wines by the glass, Weston's Old
Rosie cider; nice mix of furniture inc cosy
old sofa, candles on tables, country pictures,
daily papers, dining room (former smithy),
darts in public bar; piped music; well
behaved children and dogs welcome, picnic-
sets in back garden, open all day (LYM,
Bob and Margaret Holder)

OTTERTON [SY0885]

Kings Arms EX9 7HB [Fore St]: Big open-
plan pub handy for families from extensive
nearby caravan site, enjoyable pubby food
from doorstep sandwiches up, Sun carvery,
fast friendly service even when busy, Fullers
London Pride and Otter, reasonable prices,
restaurant; TV, darts, pool and good skittle
alley doubling as a family room; dogs
welcome, beautiful evening view from
picnic-sets in good-sized attractive back
garden with play area, bedrooms, charming
village; open all day (J D O Carter)

PAIGNTON [SX8860]

Isaac Merritt TQ3 3AA [Torquay Rd]:
Spacious and well run open-plan
Wetherspoons' conversion of former shopping
arcade, particularly good ale range, food all
day, friendly welcoming service, low prices,
comfortable family dining area; no piped
music, air conditioning; good disabled
access (the Didler, Henry Pursehouse-Tranter)

PARRACOMBE [SS6644]

☆ **Fox & Goose** EX31 4PE [off A39 Blackmoor Gate—Lynton]: Relaxed rambling pub, hunting and farming memorabilia and interesting photographs, real ales such as Bays and Exmoor, good choice of wines by the glass, farm cider, sandwiches and blackboard food inc lots of fish and good west country cheeses, log fire (not always roaring), separate dining room; children and dogs welcome, small front verandah, terraced garden leading to garden room (LYM, Mark Sykes, B M Eldridge, Betsy and Peter Little, George Atkinson, Adrian and Dawn Collinge)

PAYHEMBURY [ST0801]

Six Bells EX14 3HR: Welcoming village local on green, delightful atmosphere, well kept beer, wholesome good value wkdy lunches (Mark Flynn)

PETROCKSTOWE [SS5109]

Laurels EX20 3HJ [signed off A386 N of Hatherleigh]: Refurbished former coaching inn, hospitable, clean and well run, good generous freshly made pubby food, well kept St Austell Tribute and other local beers (Gwyn Thatcher, R J Walden)

PLYMOUTH [SX4854]

☆ **China House** PL4 0DW [Sutton Harbour, via Sutton Rd off Exeter St (A374)]: Attractive conversion of Plymouth's oldest warehouse, lovely boaty views, dimly lit and inviting interior with beams and flagstones, bare slate and stone walls, two good log fires, interesting photographs, enjoyable food, good choice of real ales and wines by the glass, attentive staff; piped music, no dogs; good parking and disabled access/facilities, tables out on waterside balconies, open all day (MB, Dick and Madeleine Brown, LYM)

Dolphin PL1 2LS [Barbican]: Basic unchanging chatty local, good range of beers inc cask-tapped Bass, coal fire (not always lit), Beryl Cook paintings inc one of the friendly landlord; open all day (the Didler, Ian Barker, Dr J Barrie Jones)

Fishermans Arms PL1 2NN [Lambhay St, Barbican]: Ancient pub tastefully modernised, sensibly priced bar lunches from filled rolls up, well kept St Austell ales, farm cider and perry (David and Gill Carrington)

Navy PL1 2LE [Southside St, Barbican]: Daytime recommendation (this area can get yobby in the evening) for no-nonsense waterside local, very generous bargain food inc good steaks and fry-ups, polite efficient service, Wells & Youngs Bombardier, cosy corner seats; sports TV; tables out on balcony, handy for aquarium (Jerry Brown)

PLYMPTON [SX5456]

George PL7 2HJ [Ridgeway]: Pleasantly refurbished former coaching inn, friendly helpful staff, enjoyable food upstairs inc bargains, changing ales such as Courage, Greene King Abbot and Otter; terrace tables (Alain and Rose Foote, David and Teresa Frost)

POSTBRIDGE [SX6578]

East Dart PL20 6TJ [B3212]: Central Dartmoor hotel by pretty river, big comfortable open-plan bar, good value generous food from sandwiches to carvery, St Austell ales, decent wines by the glass, good service, log fire, hunting murals, pool room; can take coaches; dogs welcome, tables out in front and behind, decent bedrooms, some 30 miles of fishing (Dennis Jenkin, Mr and Mrs J B Coles, Robin M Corlett, BB)

POUNDSGATE [SX7072]

☆ **Tavistock Inn** TQ13 7NY [B3357 continuation]: Friendly and picturesque, liked by walkers, plenty of nearby hikes; beams and other original features like narrow-stepped granite spiral staircase, original flagstones, ancient log fireplaces, Courage Best, Otter and Wychwood Hobgoblin, traditional bar food (all day in summer); children and dogs welcome, tables on front terrace and in quiet back garden, pretty summer flower boxes, open all day then (LYM, JHW, Steve Derbyshire, FJS and DS)

PRINCETOWN [SX5973]

☆ **Plume of Feathers** PL20 6QQ [central mini-roundabout]: Bustling extended four-room local with wide choice of good value generous food inc Sun carvery, cheerful attentive service even when busy, real ales inc good Dartmoor Jail, decent choice of wines by the glass, dimly lit interior with two log fires, beams, slate floors and granite walls, solid slate tables, big family room; disabled facilities, garden with play area, good value bedrooms, bunkhouse, good camp site, open all day (J D O Carter, Joyce and Maurice Cottrell)

PUSEHILL [SS4228]

Pig on the Hill EX39 5AH [off B3226 nr Westward Ho!]: Spotless family holiday dining pub on farm, with its own good Country Life and occasional guest ales, good range of fresh generous pub food, small bar; extensive seating in raised gallery and adjacent room through archways, pig decorations, games room with skittle alley; good views, huge playground, small swimming pool, boules, may be cl winter Weds (Richard and Robyn Wain)

RACKENFORD [SS8518]

☆ **Stag** EX16 8DT [pub signed off A361 NW of Tiverton]: Sympathetic renovations at this 12th-c thatched pub with its ancient cobbled 'tunnel' entry passage between massive walls; new chef/landlord doing rather upmarket food using local organic meat and Brixham fish, Cotleigh, Exmoor and occasional guest ales, scrubbed pine tables and country furnishings, huge inglenook fireplace, low beams, Jacobean panelling, flagstones, separate oak-floor white tablecloth restaurant with woodburner; darts, skittle alley, highwayman ghost; children and dogs welcome, disabled facilities, two picnic-sets out in front, decking and enclosed garden behind, open all day, cl Sun evening (Keith and Sue Ward, LYM)

RINGMORE [SX6545]
Journeys End TQ7 4HL [signed off B3392 at Pickwick Inn, St Anns Chapel, nr Bigbury; best to park opp church]: Ancient village inn with friendly chatty licensees, character panelled lounge and other linked rooms, half a dozen changing local ales tapped from the cask, local farm cider, decent wines, pubby food from sandwiches up, log fires; bar billiards (for over-16s), bright back family dining conservatory with board games; pleasant big terraced garden with boules, attractive setting nr thatched cottages not far from sea, bedrooms antique but comfortable and well equipped *(Suzy Miller, Michael and Maggie Betton, LYM, the Didler, David Barnes)*

ROBOROUGH [SS5717]
New Inn EX19 8SY [off B3217 N of Winkleigh]: 16th-c thatched country pub refurbished by friendly new owners, good value bistro-style food, good selection of local beers and ciders, locals' bar, lounge leading to snug dining area, inglenook log fire; small garden *(Nigel and Jenny Wallis, BB)*

SALCOMBE [SX7438]
Ferry Inn TQ8 8JE [off Fore St nr Portlemouth Ferry]: Splendid location, breathtaking estuary views from three floors of stripped-stone bars rising from sheltered and attractive flagstoned waterside terrace, inc top one opening off street (this may be only one open out of season); middle dining bar, classic seaside pub menu, Palmers and farm cider, good house wines, friendly young staff, some refurbishment under way; piped music, can get busy, no nearby parking *(B J Harding, LYM, MP)*
☆ *Fortescue* TQ8 8BZ [Union St, end of Fore St]: Good proper pub with five linked nautical-theme rooms, friendly service, popular promptly served food from hot-filled rolls up, ales such as Bass, Courage Directors and Otter, decent wines, good woodburner, old local black and white shipping pictures, big public bar with games, small dining room; children welcome, courtyard picnic-sets *(Gerry and Rosemary Dobson, Roger Wain-Heapy)*
Kings Arms TQ8 8BU [Fore St]: Imaginative reasonably priced food in tastefully redecorated dining room; good smokers' area outside, separate upper deck with good harbour views *(B J Harding)*
Victoria TQ8 8BU [Fore St]: Neat and attractive 19th-c family pub opp harbour car park, colourful window boxes, nautical décor and comfortable furnishings, enjoyable reasonably priced food inc good fresh fish, well kept St Austell ales, decent wines, friendly efficient service, separate family area; busy wknds, piped music; large sheltered tiered garden behind with good play area, bedrooms *(Roger Wain-Heapy, Tom and Jill Jones, MP, Martin and Marion Vincent, Alan and Anne Driver)*

SAMPFORD PEVERELL [ST0314]
☆ *Globe* EX16 7BJ [a mile from M5 junction 27, village signed from Tiverton turn-off;

Lower Town]: Spacious comfortable village pub backing on to Grand Western Canal, popular with walkers and locals; enjoyable good value home-made food from sandwiches to massive mixed grill and popular carvery (Fri, Sat evenings, all day Sun, Mon lunch), breakfast (8-11am), coffee and cream teas, seven well kept ales inc Cotleigh, Otter and Sharps, good wine choice; friendly efficient staff, cosy beamed lounge with boothed eating area, back restaurant; big-screen sports TV in bar, piped music; children and dogs welcome, disabled facilities, courtyard and enclosed garden with play equipment, six bedrooms, open all day *(John and Bryony Coles, Adrian and Dawn Collinge, Joan and Michel Hooper-Immins, LYM)*

SANDY PARK [SX7189]
☆ *Sandy Park Inn* TQ13 8JW [A382 Whiddon Down—Moretonhampstead]: New owners for friendly little thatched inn (more reports please), snug bars, beams, varnished built-in wall settles around nice tables, high stools by counter; Otter, St Austell Tribute and guest beers, food from good sandwiches up, small dining room on left, inner private room; children and dogs welcome, big garden with fine views and smokers' shelter, open all day; five bedrooms with bathrooms *(LYM, R T and J C Moggridge, Mr and Mrs R A Saunders, Dr Ian Mortimer)*

SHALDON [SX9472]
London Inn TQ14 8AW [Bank St/The Green]: Lively and cheerfully bustling pub, wide choice of good value generous food, good friendly service even when busy, Greene King and Otter, decent wines; pool, juke box; children welcome, good value bedrooms, opp bowling green in pretty waterside village *(Roy and Lindsey Fentiman)*
☆ *Ness House* TQ14 0HP [Ness Drive]: Updated Georgian hotel on Ness headland overlooking Teign estuary, comfortable nautical-theme bar, assorted furniture on bare boards, log fire, Badger ales and decent wines by the glass, young well trained staff, food to suit most pockets in narrow beamed restaurant or small conservatory; no dogs; children welcome, disabled facilities, terrace with lovely views, back garden with picnic-sets, nine bedrooms, open all day *(Mrs C Farley, John and Helen Rushton, Henry Tinny, Mr and Mrs Martin Tomlinson)*

SHEBBEAR [SS4309]
☆ *Devils Stone Inn* EX21 5RU [off A3072 or A388 NE of Holsworthy]: Charming tucked-away 16th-c village pub with big oak-beamed bar, three other rooms, good value home cooking by landlady (takeaways too), cheerful staff and regulars, good range of well kept beers, winter mulled wine, small restaurant area with huge inglenook log fire; family room, darts and pool; garden with play area, simple bedrooms *(Ryta Lyndley, Rob Marsh, LYM)*

SIDMOUTH [SY1287]
Dukes EX10 8AR [Esplanade]: More

restaurant than pub, but long bar on left has Branscombe Vale, Dartmoor and Otter ales, good food all day inc local fish, young eager staff, daily papers, linked areas inc conservatory and flagstoned eating area (once a chapel); big-screen TV, may be summer queues; children welcome, disabled facilities, prom-view terrace tables, bedrooms in adjoining Elizabeth Hotel, open all day *(Steve Whalley, Joan and Michel Hooper-Immins, Mark Flynn)*

☆ **Old Ship** EX10 8LP [Old Fore St]: Friendly traditional pub in pedestrian zone nr sea (local parking limited to 30 mins), partly 14th-c with low beams, mellow black woodwork early 17th-c carved panelling, nautical theme; good value food (not Sun evening) inc local fish and some adventurous dishes, well kept Branscombe Vale Branoc, Fullers London Pride and Otter, decent wine choice, prompt service even when busy; no piped music; close-set tables – raftered upstairs family area is more roomy; dogs allowed *(Mike Gorton, Mark Flynn, BB, Rona Murdoch)*

☆ **Swan** EX10 8BY [York St]: Cheerful old-fashioned town centre local, well kept Wells & Youngs, good value food from splendid sandwiches up, helpful long-serving licensees, lounge bar with interesting pictures and memorabilia, darts and warm coal fire in bigger, light and airy public bar with boarded walls and ceilings, separate dining area; dogs welcome, nice small flower-filled garden *(David and Sue Smith, Steve and Liz Tilley)*

SILVERTON [SS9503]

Lamb EX5 4HZ [Fore St]: Flagstoned local with changing ales inc Exe Valley tapped from the cask, enjoyable pubby food, friendly landlord, separate eating area; handy for Killerton (NT), open all day Thurs-Sun *(the Didler, Nigel and Sue Foster)*

Three Tuns EX5 4HX [Exeter Rd]: 17th-c or older, with comfortable sofas, period furniture and log fire in attractively old-fashioned beamed lounge, food here or in cosy restaurant welcoming children, Exe Valley and guest beers, fair-sized public bar; pretty inner courtyard, handy for Killerton (NT) *(the Didler)*

SLAPTON [SX8245]

☆ **Queens Arms** TQ7 2PN: Neatly modernised one-room village local with welcoming landlady, good inexpensive straightforward food using local suppliers, well kept Dartmoor, Otter and Teignworthy, snug comfortable corners, World War II mementoes, dominoes and draughts; parking needs skill; children and dogs welcome, lots of tables in lovely suntrap stepped back garden *(Donna and Roger, MP, Roger Wain-Heapy, Julian Distin, Tom Evans, Simon Foster)*

Tower TQ7 2PN [off A379 Dartmouth—Kingsbridge]: Well worth knowing for the charm of its low-beamed flagstoned and bare-boards bar, and lovely garden with

chickens pecking around and overlooked by imposing ivy-covered 14th-c tower ruin; some enjoyable if ambitiously priced food, Butcombe, Otter and St Austell Tribute served cool, farm cider, log fires (may not all be lit); three bedrooms, good breakfast, has been cl Sun evening, winter Mon *(Mark Sykes, the Didler, B J Harding, Simon Foster, LYM, Roger Wain-Heapy, Mr and Mrs G Owens)*

SOURTON [SX5390]

☆ **Highwayman** EX20 4HN [A386, S of junction with A30]: A fantasy of dimly lit stonework and flagstone-floored burrows and alcoves, all sorts of things to look at, one room a make-believe sailing galleon; local farm cider (perhaps a real ale in summer), organic wines, good proper sandwiches or pasties, friendly chatty service, nostalgic piped music; outside fairy-tale pumpkin house and an old-lady-who-lived-in-the-shoe house – children allowed to look around pub but can't stay inside; period bedrooms with four-posters and half-testers, bunk rooms for walkers and cyclists *(LYM, the Didler, Tom Evans)*

Prewley Moor Arms EX20 4HT [A30/A386 roundabout]: Handy beamed pub, friendly and neatly kept, with enjoyable fresh food, a fireplace at each end; children really welcome *(Sue Lethbridge)*

SOUTH MOLTON [SS7425]

Mill Inn EX36 3QF [just off A361 at Bish Mill roundabout]: Large dining room, cosy little bar with log fire, beams hung with farm tools, Barum Original, Fullers London Pride and Sharps Doom Bar, decent pub food, good friendly service even when busy; dogs welcome *(George Atkinson)*

SOUTH POOL [SX7740]

Millbrook TQ7 2RW [off A379 E of Kingsbridge]: Charming little creekside pub with current management giving it more of a bistro flavour at night; dining area off cheerful compact bar, good food from generous if not cheap lunchtime crab sandwiches up, well kept ales such as Palmers and South Hams tapped from the cask, local farm cider, log fires; no piped music; children welcome, covered seating and heaters for front courtyard and waterside terrace *(LYM, Alan and Anne Driver, Simon Foster, Roger Wain-Heapy, Mrs Mary Woods)*

SOUTH TAWTON [SX6594]

Seven Stars EX20 2LW [off A30 at Whiddon Down or Okehampton, then signed from Sticklepath]: Unpretentious beamed local in attractive village, decent pubby food, fires in cosy bar and large square restaurant; children welcome, bedrooms *(LYM, Jacquie Jones)*

SOUTH ZEAL [SX6593]

Oxenham Arms EX20 2JT [off A30/A382]: Stately interesting 12th-c building, reopened spring 2009 under new management, elegant mullioned windows and Stuart fireplaces in beamed and partly panelled front bar, small beamed inner room with open fire and remarkable old monolith; real ales tapped from the cask, quite a few wines by the glass, contemporary dining room; imposing garden with lovely views, seven bedrooms *(Michael B Griffith, LYM)*

STAPLE CROSS [ST0320]

Staplecross Inn TA21 0NH [Holcombe Rogus—Hockworthy]: Simply and sensitively renovated Exmoor-edge village pub, short choice of good value honest food, Butcombe, Otter and a guest beer, friendly landlady; three linked rooms with quarry tiles, stripped stone and huge woodburners, pleasant wooded setting *(John and Fiona McIlwain, Anthony Longden)*

STAVERTON [SX7964]

☆ *Sea Trout* TQ9 6PA [off A384 NW of Totnes]: New licensees and some refurbishment at this much extended beamed village inn/hotel; good range of home-made food inc local fish and thai influences, well kept Palmers, Thatcher's farm cider, decent choice of wines by the glass, comfortable hunting/fishing theme lounge, traditional locals' bar, restaurant and conservatory; children and dogs welcome, disabled access, attractive paved back garden, good nearby walks, ten quiet redecorated bedrooms, open all day from 9am for coffee *(LYM, Brian and Janet Ainscough)*

STICKLEPATH [SX6494]

☆ *Devonshire* EX20 2NW [off A30 at Whiddon Down or Okehampton]: Warmly welcoming licensees in old-fashioned 16th-c thatched village local next to foundry museum; low-beamed slate-floored bar with big log fire, longcase clock and easy-going old furnishings, unusual key collection, sofa in small snug, well kept Bass and St Austell ales tapped from the cask, farm cider, good value sandwiches and home-made pasties from the Aga; games room, lively folk night 1st Sun of month; dogs welcome, open all day Fri, Sat, bedrooms, good walks *(the Didler, Edward Leetham, LYM, Neil and Anita Christopher, Ross Balaam)*

STOKE FLEMING [SX8648]

Green Dragon TQ6 0PX [Church St]: Local regulars in friendly village pub with yachtsman landlord, well worn-in with beams and flagstones, boat pictures and cats, snug with sofas and armchairs, grandfather clock, open fire, well kept Otter, good choice of wines by the glass, reasonably priced food inc good fish soup; dogs welcome, tables out on partly covered heated terrace *(John and Fiona Merritt, LYM, Richard Tilbrook, Mr and Mrs G Owens, Dennis Jenkin)*

STOKE GABRIEL [SX8457]

☆ *Church House* TQ9 6SD [off A385 just W of junction with A3022; Church Walk]: Early 14th-c, lounge bar with fine medieval beam-and-plank ceiling, black oak partition wall, window seats cut into thick butter-coloured walls, huge log fireplace, ancient mummified cat; Bass, Hancocks HB and a guest beer, straightforward bar food (steak and kidney

pie a hot tip), little locals' bar; no children, piped music may obtrude, limited parking; dogs welcome in bar, picnic-sets on small front terrace, open all day *(Donna and Roger, R T and J C Moggridge, Dr and Mrs M E Wilson, Richard Tilbrook, LYM)*

STRETE [SX8446]

☆ *Kings Arms* TQ6 0RW [A379 SW of Dartmouth]: Unusual cross between village local and seafood restaurant, same good generous food in terracotta-walled country-kitchen bar and more contemporary blue-green restaurant up steps, Adnams Best and Otter, good wines by the glass; piped music; children and dogs welcome, back terrace and garden with views over Start Bay, open all day, cl Sun evening *(Cathryn and Richard Hicks, Roger Wain-Heapy, LYM, Richard and Sissel Harris)*

TALATON [SY0699]

Talaton Inn EX5 2RQ [former B3176 N of Ottery St Mary]: Simply modernised country pub dating from 16th c, roomy and comfortable timbered lounge bar and restaurant, good food choice and service, well kept Otter and guest ales, fresh flowers and candles; large carpeted public bar/skittle alley, pool; picnic-sets out in front *(Mrs Betty Williams, Revd R P Tickle)*

TAVISTOCK [SX4873]

Market Inn PL19 9BB [Whitchurch Rd]: Two-bar local, popular for bargain hearty food, well kept local ales, quick friendly service; live music Sat night – can be quite loud *(David and Sue Smith)*

Trout & Tipple PL19 0JS [Parkwood Rd, towards Okehampton]: Welcoming pub doing good food inc various trout dishes (nearby trout farm), well kept Dartmoor Jail and three quickly changing guest ales (Feb, Oct beer festivals), farmhouse cider, decent wines; interesting bar décor with fly-fishing theme, lots to look at, nice log fire, ex-stables dining room, upstairs games room; they ask to keep your credit card while you eat; children and dogs welcome, terrace seating, cl Tues lunchtime *(David and Sue Smith)*

TEDBURN ST MARY [SX8194]

Kings Arms EX6 6EG [off A30 W of Exeter]: Picturesque thatched pub, open-plan but comfortable, enjoyable pubby food, Otter and St Austell ales, local farm cider, neat efficient staff; heavy-beamed and panelled L-shaped bar, lantern lighting and snug stable-style alcoves, big log fire, lots of brass and hunting prints, modern restaurant, end games bar; piped music; children in eating area, back terrace tables, garden, bedrooms *(John Marsh, Comus and Sarah Elliott, LYM)*

Red Lion EX6 6EQ: Friendly village pub with good local atmosphere, well kept ales in open-plan bar, end dining areas with enjoyable food inc Sun roasts, fresh décor, light polished woodwork, carpets, blazing fire; skittle alley/function room, tables outside *(Dr and Mrs M E Wilson)*

THORVERTON [SS9202]

Thorverton Arms EX5 5NS: Nicely appointed 16th-c coaching inn with wide range of well prepared bar food from sandwiches up, inc children's menu, charming welcoming service, three well kept ales, good coffee, lots of country magazines, small restaurant; tables in flower-filled garden, pleasant village, six comfortable bedrooms *(Frank and Gill Brown)*

THURLESTONE [SX6743]

Village Inn TQ7 3NN [part of Thurlestone Hotel]: Small much refurbished pub attached to smart family hotel and emphasising wide food choice from sandwiches (particularly good crab) to blackboard hot dishes from open kitchen behind servery; efficient friendly service, well kept Palmers, comfortable country-style furnishings, dividers forming alcoves, may be Tues quiz night, some live music; children and dogs welcome, handy for coast path *(B J Harding, Hugh Stafford, Lucien Perring)*

TOPSHAM [SX9688]

Exeter Inn EX3 0DY [High St]: Well run 17th-c local with friendly chatty landlord, well kept Teignworthy Beachcomber and interesting guest ales, farm cider, long bar and front area with pool table, reasonable prices; big-screen sports TV; bedrooms, open all day *(the Didler)*

☆ **Globe** EX3 0HR [Fore St; 2 miles from M5 junction 30]: Substantial traditional inn dating from 16th c, solid comfort in heavy-beamed bow-windowed bar (popular with locals), good interesting home-cooked food from tasty sandwiches up, reasonable prices, Bass, Sharps Doom Bar and guest beers, good value house wines, prompt service; log-effect gas fire, compact dining lounge, good value restaurant; children in eating area, well priced attractive bedrooms, open all day *(Barry Steele-Perkins, LYM, Les and Norma Haydon, the Didler, Alissa Delbarre)*

☆ **Lighter** EX3 0HZ [Fore St]: Big well run pub looking out over quay, quickly served food from good sandwiches and light dishes to fresh fish, Badger ales, nautical décor, panelling and large central log fire, friendly staff, good children's area; games machines, piped music; handy for antiques centre, lots of waterside tables outside – good bird views at half tide *(Gwyn and Anne Wake, Dr and Mrs M E Wilson, Barry Steele-Perkins, Dr A J and Mrs Tompsett, the Didler, BB)*

TORQUAY [SX9265]

Buccaneer TQ1 3LN [Babbacombe Downs Rd]: Friendly open-plan pub with well kept St Austell ales, popular home-made food, darts and pool in games area, great sea views; open all day *(the Didler)*

Crown & Sceptre TQ1 4QA [Petitor Rd, St Marychurch]: Friendly two-bar local in 18th-c stone-built beamed coaching inn, half a dozen or more mainstream and other changing ales, interesting naval memorabilia and chamber-pot collection, good-humoured long-serving landlord, basic good value

lunchtime food (not Sun), snacks any time; dogs and children welcome, open all day Fri *(the Didler)*

Hole in the Wall TQ1 2AU [Park Lane, opp clock tower]: Ancient two-bar local nr harbour, good value usual food, well kept Sharps Doom Bar and a guest beer, Blackawton cider, proper old-fashioned landlord and friendly service; smooth cobbled floors, low beams and alcoves, lots of nautical brassware, ship models, old local photographs, chamber-pots; restaurant/ function room (band nights); small terrace, open all day *(Les and Norma Haydon, the Didler)*

TORRINGTON [SS4919]

Royal Exchange EX38 8BT [New St]: Small well worn-in local with friendly landlord, bargain home-made food inc Weds curry night, good drinks' choice with some inexpensive real ales (early June beer festival); efficient service, nice fire, darts and pool; children welcome, good-sized garden *(Mark Flynn)*

TOTNES [SX8060]

Albert TQ9 5AD [Bridgetown]: Beams, flagstones and panelling, lots of knick-knacks, good local atmosphere, Bridgetown ales brewed here, friendly landlord; nice garden *(the Didler)*

Bay Horse TQ9 5SP [Cistern St]: Traditional two-bar pub dating from 15th c, friendly landlord, good value home-made food, well kept Dartmoor, Otter, Sharps and interesting guest beers; piped music, some live; nicely redone bedrooms *(John Goom, the Didler, Matt Broadgate)*

Kingsbridge Inn TQ9 5SY [Leechwell St]: Attractive rambling pub reopened under new landlady, enjoyable food, real ales, black beams, timbering and some stripped stone, log fires, plush seats; eating areas inc small upper part (children allowed here) *(LYM, Di and Mike Gillam)*

☆ **Royal Seven Stars** TQ9 5DD [Fore St, The Plains]: Civilised old hotel, warm and friendly under current owners, roomy and cosy bay-windowed bars off flagstoned reception (former coach entry) with imposing staircase and sunny skylight; Courage Best and Greene King Old Speckled Hen, good value food inc winter bargains, pretty restaurant; tables out in front, river across busy main road, bedrooms *(the Didler, Mr and Mrs Martin Tomlinson, Roger Wain-Heapy)*

Rumour TQ9 5RY [High St]: Civilised and up-to-date, well kept ales inc Greene King and Skinners, wide-ranging wines by the glass, local fruit juices, enjoyable food from pizzas to some enterprising dishes using local produce, bare-boards bistro with bentwood chairs and informal contemporary décor; open all day, cl Sun lunchtime *(the Didler, Giles and Annie Francis)*

TRUSHAM [SX8582]

☆ **Cridford Inn** TQ13 0NR [off B3193 NW of Chudleigh, just N of big ARC works]:

Interesting 14th-c pub, Norman in parts, with UK's oldest domestic window, lots of stripped stone, flagstones and stout timbers, inglenook woodburner; smart white leather bar seats, chic low-beamed restaurant, polite staff, enjoyable food, good wine choice, real ales inc Teignworthy; children in eating area, nice sunny terrace, letting cottages *(Mike Gorton, Di and Mike Gillam, LYM, Barry Steele-Perkins)*

TUCKENHAY [SX8156]

Maltsters Arms TQ9 7EQ [Take Ashprington road out of Totnes (signed left off A381 on outskirts), keeping on past Watermans Arms]: Lovely spot by wooded creek, with waterside tables, pleasant layout inside, great range of wines by the glass, good beer choice and farm cider, food from snacks to restaurant dishes; dogs and children allowed, bedrooms, open all day *(Gaye and Simon, MP, John Day, LYM, Alan and Anne Driver, John Chambers, Roger and Diana Morgan)*

UMBERLEIGH [SS6024]

☆ *Rising Sun* EX37 9DU [A377 S of Barnstaple]: Open again after refurbishment under new management, civilised fishing inn with good food from light dishes to fine steaks, friendly staff, real ales such as St Austell, good wines by the glass, farm cider; relaxed partly divided bar with woodburner, flagstones and lots of stuffed fish and fishing memorabilia; over River Taw salmon and sea trout beats; children and dogs welcome, tables outside, nine good bedrooms, open all day summer *(Mark Lange, LYM)*

UPOTTERY [ST2007]

Sidmouth Arms EX14 9PN: Atractive pub in pleasant village setting, roomy and comfortable, with helpful staff, well kept Otter, good value food, cricket photographs *(Edward and Ava Williams)*

WELCOMBE [SS2317]

☆ *Old Smithy* EX39 6HG [signed off A39 S of Hartland]: Cosy thatched pub with good enterprising food using fresh fish and other local produce, Sharps Doom Bar and two changing guests, good coffee; friendly buoyant atmosphere combining local regulars and the surfing contingent in simple open-plan family bar with old dark wood tables and open fires; children and dogs welcome, plenty of seats in pretty terraced garden, lovely setting by lane leading eventually to attractive rocky cove, open all day summer, normally cl wkdy lunchtimes in winter *(LYM, Quentin and Carol Williamson)*

WEMBWORTHY [SS6609]

☆ *Lymington Arms* EX18 7SA [Lama Cross]: Large early 19th-c beamed dining pub, clean and bright, with wide choice of reliably good food (not Sun evening or Mon), friendly helpful service, well kept Dartmoor IPA and Sharps Doom Bar, Winkleigh farm cider, decent wines; comfortably plush seating and red tablecloths in partly stripped stone bar, big back evening restaurant (not Sun, Mon); children welcome, picnic-sets outside,

pleasant country setting, bedrooms *(Mrs P Sumner, Ron and Sheila Corbett, BB)*

WESTON [ST1400]

☆ *Otter* EX14 3NZ [off A373, or A30 at W end of Honiton bypass]: Big busy family pub with heavy low beams, enjoyable food from light dishes to substantial meals and good Sun carvery, OAP specials; cheerful helpful staff, Cotleigh and Otter beers, good value wines, good log fire; piped music; children welcome, disabled access, picnic-sets on big lawn leading to River Otter, play area *(Philip Kingsbury, LYM, Anthony Double)*

WHITCHURCH [SX4972]

Whitchurch Inn PL19 9ED [village signed off A386 just S of Tavistock, then keep on up into Church Hill]: Cheerful beamed local owned by the church, neatly renovated with woodburner at each end, friendly competent service, long sparklingly kept bar for the Dartmoor and other local ales, nice changing choice of wines by the glass, good food (particularly local meats) fairly priced; comfortable furnishings, butter-coloured plaster crisply cut away to show stonework *(Mrs C Sleight, BB)*

WIDECOMBE [SX7176]

Old Inn TQ13 7TA [B3387 W of Bovey Tracey]: Busy comfortably refurbished Badger dining pub with good-humoured landlord, large eating area and roomy side conservatory with central fire – get there before about 12.30 in summer to miss the coach-loads – enjoyable good value food, well kept real ales; children and dogs welcome, nice garden with water features and pleasant terrace, great walks from this pretty moorland village *(Irene and Derek Flewin, LYM, Dr and Mrs M E Wilson, Paul and Margaret Baker, JHW)*

WONSON [SX6789]

☆ *Northmore Arms* EX20 2JA [A30 at Merrymeet roundabout, take first left on old A30, through Whiddon Down; new roundabout and take left on to A382; then right down lane signposted Throwleigh/Gidleigh; continue down lane over hump-back bridge; turn left to Wonson; OS Sheet 191 map ref 674903]: Far from smart and a favourite with those who take to its idiosyncratic style (not everyone does): two simple old-fashioned rooms, log fire and woodburner, low beams and stripped stone, well kept Adnams Broadside, Cotleigh Tawny and Exe Valley Dobs tapped from the cask, good house wines, cheap plain food (all day Mon-Sat), darts and board games; children and dogs welcome, picnic-sets outside, two modest bedrooms, beautiful remote walking country, normally open all day *(the Didler, LYM, Anthony Longden)*

WOODBURY [SY0087]

White Hart EX5 1HN [3.5 miles from M5 junction 30; A376, then B3179; Church St]: Two-bar village local with fine choice of good value straightforward food (not Sun), Bass and Everards Tiger, decent wines, log fire, no piped music; attractive small walled garden with aviary, skittle alley, nice spot by church in peaceful village *(Dr and Mrs M E Wilson, Michael and Lynne Gittins)*

WOODLAND [SX7869]

☆ *Rising Sun* TQ13 7JT [village signed off A38 just NE of Ashburton, then pub usually signed, nr Combe Cross]: Surprisingly plush and expansive, with friendly efficient staff, wide choice of good food from sandwiches to enterprising main dishes and local seafood, well kept Dartmoor Jail Ale and a local guest beer, good choice of wines by the glass, Luscombe farm cider; beams and soft lighting, snug corner by log fire, family area, restaurant; picnic-sets and play area in spacious garden, children and dogs welcome, four comfortable bedrooms *(Donna and Roger, Neil Ingoe, LYM, J Hughes, Richard and Maria Gillespie)*

WOOLACOMBE [SS4543]

Red Barn EX34 7DF: Modern seaside bar and restaurant with good value food all day, well kept St Austell and guest ales (early Dec beer festival), efficient staff coping well when busy, surfing pictures and memorabilia; children and dogs welcome, open all day *(Bob and Margaret Holder, Chris Reading)*

YEALMPTON [SX5851]

☆ *Rose & Crown* PL8 2EB [A379 Kingsbridge—Plymouth]: New owners for civilised place with big central bar counter, all dark wood and heavy brass, good solid leather-seated bar stools, attractive mix of furnishings, good lighting, stripped wooden floor, carpeted dining areas; has had adjacent seafood restaurant, Otter, St Austell Tribute and Sharps Doom Bar, quite a few wines by the glass, modern bar food; children welcome, dogs in bar, has been open all day Sun *(LYM, Michael and Maggie Betton, Di and Mike Gillam)*

If a pub tries to make you leave a credit card behind the bar, be on your guard. The credit card firms and banks which issue them condemn this practice. After all, the publican who asks you to do this is in effect saying: 'I don't trust you'. Have you any more reason to trust his staff? If your card is used fraudulently while you have let it be kept out of your sight, the card company could say you've been negligent yourself – and refuse to make good your losses. So say that they can 'swipe' your card instead, but must hand it back to you. Please let us know if a pub does try to keep your card.

DORSET

New to the Main Entries, or returning after a break, are the Three Horseshoes at Burton Bradstock, Chetnole Inn at Chetnole, Langton Arms at Tarrant Monkton and the Crown at Uploders. Others on top form, all well liked for their food, are the Greyhound at Sydling St Nicholas, European at Piddletrenthide, New Inn at Church Knowle, Museum at Farnham and Marquis of Lorne at Nettlecombe. The Greyhound at Sydling St Nicholas takes our top title of Dorset Dining Pub of the Year. The Square & Compass at Worth Matravers and the Vine at Pamphill stand out for simple rural charm; the Digby Tap in Sherborne is an urban counterpart. Others worth a special mention are the ever-efficient Smugglers at Osmington Mills, stylish Cow in Poole, Cricketers at Shroton, Green Man in Wimborne Minster and Fishermans Haunt at Winkton. Three top Lucky Dips are the Stapleton Arms at Buckhorn Weston, Gaggle of Geese at Buckland Newton and Blue Raddle in Dorchester. Palmers and Badger are the county's main brewers; popular Davids to these local Goliaths are Dorset and (no relation) Dorset Piddle.

BURTON BRADSTOCK   SY4889   MAP 1
Three Horseshoes
Mill Street; DT6 4QZ

Cottagey thatched pub with welcoming staff and a full range of Palmers beers

Just 400 yards away from Chesil Beach and the coastal path, this old thatched place (once the village shop and post office) is a cosy place to come into. Its pleasant low-ceilinged L-shaped bar has a woodburner, with an array of pictures and local photos, and there's a separate restaurant; piped music. Palmers 200, Copper, Gold, IPA and Tally Ho are on handpump (kept under light blanket pressure in winter), and several wines by the glass. The suntrap back garden is nicely sheltered, and has picnic-sets.

🍴 **Generously served and usually enjoyable bar food (booking advised at peak times) features seasonally available local fish and game and includes lunchtime sandwiches, soup, goats cheese and spinach tart, steak and ale pie, and specials like bass on crispy spinach or local wild rabbit; children's menu and restaurant menu.** *Starters/Snacks: £4.50 to £5.95. Main Courses: £7.50 to £10.50. Puddings: £1.50 to £4.50*

Palmers ~ Tenant Paul Middlemast ~ Real ale ~ Bar food (12-2, 6-9) ~ Restaurant ~ (01308) 897259 ~ Children welcome ~ Dogs allowed in bar ~ Open 11-midnight; 12-10.30 Sun

Recommended by Michael Dandy, Norman and Sarah Keeping, Bob and Margaret Holder, M G Hart, Jenny and Peter Lowater, Fred and Lorraine Gill, Rona Markland, L Hawkins

---

'Children welcome' means the pub says it lets children inside without any special restriction. If it allows them in, but to restricted areas such as an eating area or family room, we specify this. Some pubs may impose an evening time limit. We do not mention limits after 9pm as we assume children are home by then.

CHETNOLE
ST6008 MAP 2

Chetnole Inn ◨

Village signposted off A37 a few miles S of Yeovil; DT9 6NU

Attractive, neatly kept country pub, beams and huge flagstones, country décor, real ales, popular food and seats in back garden with ducks; bedrooms

Beside an old church and tucked away in lovely countryside, this is an attractive and neatly kept beamed country inn with friendly licensees. There's a bar with huge flagstones, wheelback chairs and wooden tables, old tools on lemon walls, lots of hops and a woodburning stove, and a snug liked by locals with a couple of leather sofas close to an open fire, darts, juke box, games machine and board games; skittle alley. The attractive dining room has more wheelback chairs around pale wooden tables on stripped floorboards, fresh flowers and linen napkins, and a small open fire. Otter Bitter and Sharps Doom Bar and a couple of guest beers like Dorset Piddle and Greene King Abbot on handpump. There are picnic-sets in the back garden (where they keep ducks) and a few out in front.

🍴 Using their own duck eggs and local produce, the well liked bar food includes lunchtime sandwiches, a good ploughman's, soup, beef carpaccio with a beetroot and red onion salad, tiger prawns with a sweet chilli dip, a tapas plate, ham and eggs, sausages with red onion gravy, blue cheese and tomato tart, slow-roast pork belly with pork and sage jus, chicken breast with pancetta in a creamy leek and thyme sauce, lambs liver with crispy bacon, spring onion mash and a merlot wine jus, skate wing with brown caper butter, and puddings like chocolate brownie with cherry ice-cream and chocolate sauce and panna cotta with summer berries. *Starters/Snacks: £4.70 to £6.70. Main Courses: £8.00 to £15.00. Puddings: £4.30 to £5.75*

Free house ~ Licensee Mike Lewis ~ Real ale ~ Bar food (12-2, 6.30(7 Sun)-9) ~ Restaurant ~ (01935) 872337 ~ Well behaved children welcome ~ Dogs allowed in bar ~ Open 12-2.30, 6.30(7 Sun)-11 ~ Bedrooms: /£85B

Recommended by Paul and Annette Hallett, Eithne Dandy, Michael Dandy, Pat and Roger Davies

CHURCH KNOWLE
SY9381 MAP 2

New Inn ♀

Village signposted off A351 just N of Corfe Castle; BH20 5NQ

An attractive 16th-c pub with pleasantly furnished rooms and an inviting garden; well positioned for walks

Thoroughly enjoyed by many readers, this welcoming rural pub in the Purbecks takes considerable pride in its food and wine. Part of the fun is the entertaining miscellany of bric-a-brac (including a stuffed hoopoe and a glass case with some interesting memorabilia, like ration books and Horlicks tablets). The two main areas, linked by an arch, are attractively furnished with farmhouse chairs and tables, and a log fire at each end. You can choose wines (with help from the staff if you wish) from a tempting display in the walk-in wine cellar and there are several by the glass and a wine of the month; also herefordshire apple juice. Flowers Original, Greene King Old Speckled Hen and Wadworths 6X are on handpump along with a guest like Dorset JD. There are disabled facilities, and there is a function room with its own bar and dance floor; TV. You can camp in two fields behind (you must book); fine surrounding walks and good views from the good-sized garden.

🍴 Bar food includes lunchtime sandwiches and ploughman's, with starters such as blue vinney soup, grilled sardines or cods roe on toast; main courses include casseroles, beer-battered haddock, and steak and stilton pie. The daily changing specials board is dedicated to local produce and fish, such as locally caught torbay sole, and the home-made puddings might feature Guinness and chocolate mousse, lemon posset or strawberry shortbread tower. It's best to book, especially at weekends. *Starters/Snacks: £4.50 to £6.50. Main Courses: £7.50 to £15.00. Puddings: £4.95 to £5.50*

Punch ~ Tenants Maurice and Rosemary Estop ~ Real ale ~ Bar food (12-2.15, 6-9.15) ~

Restaurant ~ (01929) 480357 ~ Children welcome ~ Open 10(12 Sun)-3, 6-11; 11-11 Sat,
Sun in summer hols; closed Mon evening Jan-Mar

*Recommended by Adrian Johnson, Phil and Jane Hodson, Pat and Roger Davies, Joan and Michel Hooper-Immins,
R and S Bentley, Mike and Sue Loseby, John Roots, Dr Phil Putwain, Colin Dorling, Michael Butler, Robert Watt,
James A Waller*

FARNHAM   ST9515   MAP 2

Museum ♀ 🛏

Village signposted off A354 Blandford Forum—Salisbury; DT11 8DE

Stylish and civilised inn with appealing rooms (and a bustling bar) and super bedrooms

This thatched free house has an excellent choice of wines with several by the glass and
Ringwood Best Bitter along with a couple of guests such as Keystone Porter and Palmers
IPA on handpump. The little flagstoned bar remains a real focus for locals of all ages and
has a lively atmosphere, light beams, a big inglenook fireplace, good comfortably
cushioned furnishings and fresh flowers on all the tables. Cheery yellow walls and
plentiful windows give the place a bright, fresh feel. To the right is a dining room with a
fine antique dresser, while off to the left is a cosier room, with a very jolly hunting
model and a seemingly sleeping stuffed fox curled in a corner. Another room feels rather
like a contemporary baronial hall, soaring up to a high glass ceiling, with dozens of
antlers and a stag's head looking down on a long refectory table and church-style pews.
This leads to an outside terrace with more wooden tables. The bedrooms in the main
building are very comfortable.

🍴 **Bar food (no sandwiches) is from the restaurant menu, carefully compiled and
interesting but definitely not cheap: it might include soup or starters such as potted
brown shrimps or peppered beef fillet with truffled rocket salad, followed by their
bestselling slow-roast belly of gloucester old spot pork, grilled panaché of local brixham
seafood, or broad bean and ricotta tortellini; unusual puddings like steamed blood orange
pudding with whisky and orange marmalade ice-cream or roasted pineapple with black
pepper and rum caramel; local cheeses.** *Starters/Snacks: £7.00 to £14.00. Main Courses:
£18.50 to £6.50. Puddings: £6.50*

Free house ~ Licensee David Sax ~ Real ale ~ Bar food (12-2(2.30 Sat), 7-9.30; 12-3, 7-9 Sun)
~ Restaurant (Fri and Sat evening and Sun lunch) ~ (01725) 516261 ~ Children welcome ~
Dogs allowed in bar and bedrooms ~ Open 12-3(4 Sun), 6-11.30(11 Sun) ~
Bedrooms: £85B/£95B

*Recommended by Mrs L Saumarez Smith, JCW, P Waterman, Andrew Hollingshead, Cathryn and Richard Hicks,
Julia and Richard Tredgett, Mr and Mrs W W Burke, John and Enid Morris*

MIDDLEMARSH   ST6607   MAP 2

Hunters Moon

A352 Sherborne—Dorchester; DT9 5QN

Plenty of bric-a-brac in linked areas, reasonably priced food and a good choice of drinks

Drinks at this former coaching inn feature Butcombe Bitter and a couple of guests such
as Adnams Broadside and Sharps Doom Bar on handpump and farm cider, while all their
wines are available by the glass. The comfortably welcoming interior rambles around in
several linked areas, with a great variety of tables and chairs, plenty of bric-a-brac from
decorative teacups, china ornaments and glasses, through horse tack and brassware, to
quite a collection of spirits' miniatures. Beams, some panelling, soft lighting from
converted oil lamps, three log fires (one in a capacious inglenook), and the way that
some attractively cushioned settles form booths, all combine to give a cosy relaxed feel;
children's books and toys, and board games. A neat lawn has circular picnic-sets as well
as the more usual ones, and the ensuite bedrooms are in what was formerly a skittle alley
and stable block. More up-to-date reports please, particularly on the food.

🍴 **Bar food includes lunchtime filled baguettes and bloomers, soup, portland scallops, a
wide choice of steaks, pizza, baked potatoes and pasta, pub classics such as scampi,**

lasagne and slow-roasted lamb shank, battered cod, and daily specials such as pheasant or venison. It's good to see that many main dishes are offered in smaller or larger portion sizes. Among the puddings are a cheesecake of the day, dorset apple cake and lemon tart. *Starters/Snacks: £4.25 to £6.50. Main Courses: £4.95 to £16.45. Puddings: £3.95 to £4.75*

Enterprise ~ Lease Dean and Emma Mortimer ~ Real ale ~ Bar food (12-2, 6-9.30(9 Sun)) ~ (01963) 210966 ~ Children welcome ~ Open 11.30-2.30, 6-11; 11-11 Sat, Sun; 11-2.30, 6-10.30 in winter; closed 25-26 Dec ~ Bedrooms: £55S/£65S

Recommended by M G Hart, R J and G M Townson, Jill Bickerton, Mike and Sue Loseby

MUDEFORD
SZ1792 MAP 2

Ship in Distress ♀
Stanpit; off B3059 at roundabout; BH23 3NA

Wide choice of fish dishes, quirky nautical décor and friendly staff in cheerful cottage

The interior of this former smugglers' pub is thoroughly good fun, stashed as it is with all manner of nautical bits and pieces. There's everything from rope fancywork and brassware through lanterns, oars, ceiling nets and ensigns, to an aquarium, boat models (we particularly like the Mississippi steamboat), and the odd piratical figure; darts, games machine, board games, a couple of TV sets and piped music. Besides a good few boat pictures, the room on the right has masses of snapshots of locals caught up in various waterside japes, under its glass tabletops. Brains Rev James and Ringwood Fortyniner are served on handpump alongside a couple of guests that change about three times a week and might include Moorhouses Blond Witch and Warwickshire Falstaff; several wines by the glass. A spreading two-room restaurant area, as cheerful in its way as the bar, has contemporary works by local artists for sale and a light-hearted mural sketching out the impression of a window open on a sunny boating scene, as well as a lobster tank. There are tables out on the suntrap back terrace and a covered area for smokers.

⦙⦙ **Enjoyable fresh local fish and seafood are the thing here, although there are also meat and vegetarian options: sandwiches and reasonably priced bar food such as moules marinière or fish pie, as well as more expensive à la carte offerings (which you can eat in the bar or in the restaurant) like smoked salmon and halibut roulade, irish rock oysters, lamb cutlets with herb crust, rib-eye steak and whole roasted bream; puddings.** *Starters/Snacks: £4.50 to £8.95. Main Courses: £6.95 to £18.50. Puddings: £4.95*

Punch ~ Lease Colin Pond and Maggie Wheeler ~ Real ale ~ Bar food (12-2.30, 6.30-9.30; 12-2, 7-9 winter) ~ Restaurant ~ (01202) 485123 ~ Children welcome ~ Dogs allowed in bar ~ Open 10am-midnight; 11-11 Sun

Recommended by David Randall, Katharine Cowherd, John and Annabel Hampshire, N R White, JDM, KM, I D Barnett, Graham Oddey

NETTLECOMBE
SY5195 MAP 2

Marquis of Lorne ⬛
Off A3066 Bridport—Beaminster, via West Milton; DT6 3SY

Tasty food and beer in welcoming country pub in beautiful countryside, with a large, mature garden

Homely and traditional, and in a delightful rural spot, this is a good all-rounder. The bars and dining rooms are named after local hills. The comfortable bustling main bar has a log fire, mahogany panelling and old prints and photographs around its neatly matching chairs and tables; two dining areas lead off, the smaller of which has another log fire. The wooden-floored snug (liked by locals) has board games and table skittles; TV and piped music. Three real ales from Palmers are well kept on handpump, with Copper, IPA and 200, and Tally Ho in winter, plus a decent wine list with 12 by the glass. The maturing big garden is full of pretty herbaceous borders, and has a rustic-style play area among the picnic-sets under its apple trees. Eggardon Hill, one of Dorset's most spectacular Iron Age hill forts, is within walking distance.

🍴 In addition to tasty sandwiches and filled baguettes, bar food includes soup, starters such as chicken liver, pork and port pâté, goats cheese tart or local scallops with risotto, parmesan and basil dressing, and main courses like lambs liver and bacon, local fish specials and several vegetarian options like goats cheese, spinach, tomato and courgette filo parcels. Meat and fish are sourced from within three miles of the pub; puddings include a crumble or pie of the day and local luxury ice-creams. They also run popular special functions such as greek, italian, chinese or indian food nights. *Starters/Snacks: £4.50 to £7.50. Main Courses: £8.95 to £16.95. Puddings: £2.95 to £4.50*

Palmers ~ Tenants David and Julie Woodroffe ~ Real ale ~ Bar food ~ Restaurant ~ (01308) 485236 ~ No children under 10 in bedrooms ~ Dogs allowed in bar ~ Open 12-2.30(3 Sun), 5-11; open 6.30 evenings in winter ~ Bedrooms: £50S/£95S

Recommended by Fred and Lorraine Gill, Michael Bayne, Yana Pocklington, Patricia Owlett, Dr Kevan Tucker, Mr P Avery, Ian Malone, Jenny and Peter Lowater, R J and G M Townson, Brian and Jacky Wilson

OSMINGTON MILLS   SY7381 MAP 2

Smugglers
Off A353 NE of Weymouth; DT3 6HF

Centuries-old inn useful for the coastal path; copes well with the peak-time crowds

---

On a very attractive spot near the coast where smuggling was indeed once rife, this bustling family-oriented pub has decent food and cheerfully efficient service. Woodwork divides the spacious bar into cosy, welcoming areas, with logs burning in two open stoves and old local pictures scattered about, and various quotes and words of wisdom painted on the wall ('a day without wine is a day without sunshine'). Some seats are tucked into alcoves and window embrasures. The games machines are kept sensibly out of the way; piped music and board games. Three ales from Badger feature First Gold, Tanglefoot and a seasonal brew like Fursty Ferret on handpump. There are picnic-sets out on crazy paving by a little stream, with a thatched bar (which during some summers offers Pimms and plates of smoked salmon) and a good play area (including a little assault course) beneath a steep lawn. Free dog biscuits are provided on the bar counter.

🍴 Handily served all day, bar food (they will do smaller helpings) includes soup, lunchtime sandwiches, potato wedges, buffalo wings with blue cheese dressing, a larder board for two people, and main courses such as roast butternut squash, steak and ale pie, fish pie or steak, and puddings like chocolate fudge sundae or dorset apple cake; children's menu. *Starters/Snacks: £3.25 to £5.25. Main Courses: £5.99 to £11.99. Puddings: £1.99 to £5.25*

Badger ~ Manager Sonia Henderson ~ Real ale ~ Bar food (12-9.30(9 Sun)) ~ (01305) 833125 ~ Children welcome ~ Dogs allowed in bar ~ Open 11-11; 12-10.30 Sun ~ Bedrooms: £70B/£85B

Recommended by Yana Pocklington, Patricia Owlett, Robert Watt, the Didler, Chris and Jeanne Downing, Ann and Colin Hunt, Pat and Tony Martin, Dr Kevan Tucker, Gerald and Gabrielle Culliford

PAMPHILL   ST9900 MAP 2

Vine 🍺
Off B3082 on NW edge of Wimborne: turn on to Cowgrove Hill at Cowgrove signpost, then turn right up Vine Hill; BH21 4EE

Charming and unchanging, run by the same family for three generations

---

Splendidly old-fashioned and simple, this tiny place is as good as ever. Frequented by locals but also welcoming to visitors, it's been run by the same family for three generations but is actually owned by the National Trust as part of the Kingston Lacy estate. Of its two tiny bars one, with a warm coal-effect gas fire, has only three tables, the other just half a dozen or so seats on its lino floor, some of them huddling under the stairs that lead up via narrow wooden steps to an upstairs games room; darts and board games. Local photographs (look out for the one of the regular with his giant pumpkin) and notices decorate the painted panelling; quiet piped music. Two real ales served on handpump or from the cask usually feature Fullers London Pride and a guest from a brewery such as Goddards, Hidden or Otter; still cider and a selection of foreign bottled beers. There are picnic-sets and benches out on a sheltered gravel terrace and more share a fairy-lit, heated verandah with a grapevine. Round the back a grassy area with tables has a climbing frame; outside lavatories. The National Trust estate includes Kingston Lacy house and the huge Badbury Rings Iron Age hill fort (itself good for wild flowers), and there are many paths. They don't accept credit cards or cheques.

🍴 **Lunchtime bar snacks such as good, fresh sandwiches and ploughman's.** *Starters/Snacks: £3.00 to £5.50*

Free house ~ Licensee Mrs Sweatland ~ Real ale ~ Bar food (11.30(12 Sun)-2; not evenings) ~ No credit cards ~ (01202) 882259 ~ Children welcome away from bar ~ Dogs welcome ~ Open 11(12 Sun)-3, 7-10.30(11 Sat)

Recommended by Pete Baker, the Didler, Richard and Anne Ansell, Martin and Karen Wake, Mr and Mrs P D Titcomb

PIDDLETRENTHIDE
SY7198 MAP 2

European 🍴 🛏️
B3143 N of Dorchester; DT2 7QT

Mellow, civilised and intimate dining pub with a fresh rustic look, caring staff and thoughtfully presented food

With the accent firmly on dining, this imaginatively refurbished and spotless roadside inn has been giving readers great pleasure recently, and the service and welcome are first class. The atmosphere is chatty and relaxed, and its two opened-up linked beamed rooms are attractively furnished with quite a mix of dining chairs, lit church candles on all sorts of wooden tables, little country cushions on the comfortable, mushroom-coloured built-in wall seats, pretty window blinds, and nicely worn rugs on terracotta tiles. Yellow walls are hung with duck and hunting prints, fishy plates and a couple of fox masks, and there are interesting fresh flower arrangements, hand-made walking sticks for sale, newspapers to read and maybe one or more of the pub dogs on a cushion in front of the woodburning stove in the sandstone fireplace; dominoes and cribbage. Palmers Copper and maybe a couple of guests from brewers such as Cottage and Yeovil on handpump, good wines by the glass, home-made elderflower cordial in season, and they have their own damson vodka and sloe gin too. There are a few picnic-sets in front and at the back, with an outdoor heater. The two bedrooms have good views.

🍴 The sound cooking includes starters like portland scallops or home-smoked duck breast with apple and rosemary jelly, and main courses such as fried loin and fillet of lamb, home-made nettle ravioli with sage butter or fillet of bass with hollandaise sauce; super puddings might include lemon posset, hot chocolate fondant or english rhubarb tart with rhubarb ice-cream. Lunchtime sandwiches are also available. All their meat is sourced within Dorset, with lamb from owner Mark's family farm: they invite customers to trade their home-grown and freshly caught produce with them and feature many suppliers on their website.
Starters/Snacks: £4.00 to £8.00. Main Courses: £9.00 to £16.00. Puddings: £4.00 to £5.50

Free house ~ Licensees Mark and Emily Hammick ~ Bar food ((not Sun evening or Mon)) ~ (01300) 348308 ~ Children welcome ~ Dogs welcome ~ Open 11.30-3, 6-11; 11.30-3.30 Sun; closed two weeks end of Jan-early Feb; closed Sun evening and all day Mon ~ Bedrooms: £55B/£80B

Recommended by Mr and Mrs W W Burke, Paul and Annette Hallett, Marianne and Peter Stevens, Gerald and Gabrielle Culliford, Glenwys and Alan Lawrence, Dr R P Ashfield, Mr and Mrs Edward Mason, Joe Meier

PLUSH
ST7102 MAP 2

Brace of Pheasants 🛏️
Off B3143 N of Dorchester; DT2 7RQ

Fairly smart but relaxed 16th-c thatched pub with friendly service and a decent garden; nearby walks

Hidden away on a little-frequented lane and well placed for walks in beautifully folded countryside, this village inn has a decent-sized garden and terrace, including a lawn sloping up towards a rockery. The airy beamed bar has good solid tables, windsor chairs, fresh flowers, a huge heavy-beamed inglenook at one end with cosy seating inside, and a good warming log fire at the other. Ringwood Best along with local guests such as Palmers Copper and Piddle Jimmy Riddle are tapped from the cask and there's a good choice of wines with 18 by the glass; friendly service. From here an attractive bridleway behind goes to the left of the woods and over to Church Hill. The ensuite bedrooms are nicely fitted out and comfortable.

🍴 Enjoyable bar food includes sandwiches, soup, starters like breaded somerset goats cheese or beer-battered pigeon strips with red onion marmalade, and main courses such as the popular local venison pie with horseradish crust or monkfish marinated with lime, ginger and garlic; puddings might feature vanilla and orange bread-and-butter pudding, dorset ice-creams and sorbets or, unusually, warm scandinavian fruit soup. The daily changing menu has special rates for two-course lunches and dinners. *Starters/Snacks: £4.00 to £8.00. Main Courses: £9.00 to £14.00. Puddings: £5.00 to £6.00*

Free house ~ Licensees Phil and Carol Bennett ~ Real ale ~ Bar food ~ Restaurant ~ (01300) 348357 ~ Children welcome ~ Dogs allowed in bar ~ Open 12-3, 7-11; 12-4 Sun; closed Sun evening and all day Mon ~ Bedrooms: £85B/£95B

Recommended by James A Waller, the Didler, Dr and Mrs J Temporal, Gerry and Rosemary Dobson, Peter and Liz Holmes, John Sleigh, Stewart Bingham, Mr and Mrs W W Burke, G Vyse, Mike and Sue Loseby, Lt Col and Mrs Patrick Kaye, Robert Watt, M G Hart, Phyl and Jack Street

POOLE
SZ0391   MAP 2

Cow ♀

Station Road, Ashley Cross, Parkstone; beside Parkstone Station; BH14 8UD

Interesting open-plan pub with contemporary décor, good modern food, and fine wines

Mellow and informal inside, this stylish one-room bar belies its somewhat unpromising location by the railway station. It has a mix of wooden tables and dining chairs, a couple of low tables by some comfortable squashy sofas with huge colourful cushions and high leatherette bar chairs. A coal-effect gas fire in a brick fireplace, with another in the entrance hall, and quite a discreet flat screen TV in one corner; piped music, board games and a good array of newspapers. Ochre ragged walls are hung with a vintage songsheet of *Three Acres and A Cow*, Twickenham Rugby Museum replicas of 1930s and 1940s rugby prints and big modern cow prints in bright pinks, yellows and blues. Fullers London Pride, Ringwood Best and a guest such as Exmoor Hound Dog on handpump, and an extensive wine list with about ten wines by the glass and many remarkable bottles (the most expensive being a Château Pétrus at £650). In the evening you can eat very well in the sizeable bistro where there are more heavy stripped tables on bare boards and plenty of wine bottles lining the window sills. Seats outside on the enclosed and heated terrace.

🍴 From a sensibly short menu, the good modern lunchtime bar food (not cheap) includes filled baguettes, soup, and classic main courses with an upmarket touch: sausages and mash with onion gravy, bacon, bubble-and-squeak and free-range eggs, fishcakes, roast butternut squash gnocchi, cod and chips, pies, and puddings like coffee mousse or coconut crème brûlée; more elaborate evening options from the seasonally changing menu in the bistro might feature venison, bream or rabbit dishes. *Starters/Snacks: £5.50 to £7.95. Main Courses: £11.95 to £19.50. Puddings: £6.50 to £8.00*

Free house ~ Licensee David Sax ~ Real ale ~ Bar food (12-2.30(4 Sun), 7-9.30; not Sun evening) ~ Restaurant ~ (01202) 749569 ~ Children allowed until 7pm ~ Dogs allowed in bar ~ Open 11-11.30(midnight Sat); 12-10.30 Sun

Recommended by JDM, KM, Terry and Linda Moseley, Mr and Mrs W W Burke, Alan Wright

---

Please keep sending us reports. We rely on readers for news of new discoveries, and particularly for news of changes – however slight – at the fully described pubs: feedback@goodguides.com, or (no stamp needed) The Good Pub Guide, FREEPOST TN1569, Wadhurst, E Sussex TN5 7BR.

POWERSTOCK
SY5196   MAP 2

Three Horseshoes ♀
Off A3066 Beaminster—Bridport via West Milton; DT6 3TF

Friendly inn in fine countryside with imaginative food and a fair choice of drinks; walks nearby

Enjoyed by readers for its food and beer, this welcoming village pub is very much in deepest Dorset – a village snuggled within back lanes far from any major town and in fine walking country. Inside, the L-shaped bar has good log fires, magazines and newspapers to read, stripped panelling, country furniture including settles, Palmers Copper and IPA on handpump, and several wines by the glass served by friendly staff. There are local paintings for sale in the dining room; piped music and board games. Smart teak seats and tables under large parasols on the back terrace (steps down to it) have a lovely uninterrupted view and there's a big sloping garden. Two of the bedrooms have fine valley views.

🍴 **Using home-grown vegetables, fruit and herbs, and cooked by the landlord/chef, the enterprising food typically includes lunchtime filled rolls, an interesting soup, starters like thai-style fishcakes or seared scallops, and main courses such as rabbit casserole with chorizo dumplings, roasted red snapper, ostrich sausages with mustard mash, and organic lamb faggots with onion gravy; puddings such as rum and raisin chocolate torte or spiced plum crumble.** *Starters/Snacks: £4.95 to £6.95. Main Courses: £7.95 to £15.85. Puddings: £4.95*

Palmers ~ Tenant Andy Preece ~ Real ale ~ Bar food (12-2.30, 7-9.30; 12-3, 7-8.30 Sun) ~ Restaurant ~ (01308) 485328 ~ Children welcome ~ Dogs welcome ~ Open 11-3, 6.30-11.30(midnight Sat); 12-4, 7-11 Sun ~ Bedrooms: £60S/£85B

Recommended by G Vyse, Iain Jones, Lewis Caplin, George Atkinson, Terry and Linda Moseley

SHAVE CROSS
SY4198   MAP 1

Shave Cross Inn
On back lane Bridport—Marshwood, signposted locally; OS Sheet 193 map reference 415980; DT6 6HW

Caribbean touches to food and drink in a 13th-c pub; carefully tended garden

This delightful former monks' lodging dates back some 800 years, and it also has what is believed to be England's oldest skittles alley, now housing bar billiards and a juke box (both somewhat rarities nowadays); darts and pool too. The original timbered bar is a lovely flagstoned room, surprisingly roomy and full of character, with country antiques, two armchairs either side of a warming fire in an enormous inglenook fireplace and hops round the bar – a scene little altered from the last century. Branscombe Vale Branoc, Dorset Best, their own-label 4Ms and a guest from a brewery, such as Piddle, on handpump, alongside half a dozen wines by the glass, farm cider, several vintage rums and a caribbean beer; piped music (jazz or caribbean). Lovingly tended, the sheltered flower-filled garden with its thatched wishing-well, carp pool and children's play area is very pretty. There are seven ensuite boutique hotel-style rooms.

🍴 **As well as soup and pub classics like ploughman's, beer-battered haddock and local boar or venison sausages and mash, the bar food (good, but not cheap) features dishes influenced by the owners' travels in the Caribbean, such as guyanese goat curry, jerk chicken and cajun chicken, along with a choice of specials; there's also a two- and three-course fixed-price restaurant menu with more elaborate dishes like hot spicy cuban seafood bouillabaisse and roasted créole duck breast.** *Starters/Snacks: £5.00 to £8.50. Main Courses: £12.95 to £25.00. Puddings: £6.50*

Free house ~ Licensee Mel Warburton ~ Real ale ~ Bar food ~ Restaurant (7-9.30) ~ (01308) 868358 ~ Children welcome ~ Dogs allowed in bar and bedrooms ~ Open 11-3, 6-midnight; 12-3, 7-midnight Sun; closed Mon except bank hols ~ Bedrooms: /£160B

Recommended by Adrian Johnson, the Didler, Gene and Kitty Rankin, Richard Stanfield, Terry and Linda Moseley, Pat and Tony Martin, Tim Venn

SHERBORNE
ST6316   MAP 2

Digby Tap ◼ £
Cooks Lane; park in Digby Road and walk round corner; DT9 3NS

Regularly changing ales in simple alehouse, usefully open all day, very inexpensive beer and food

In a back street just moments away from Sherborne Abbey, this chatty tavern is a nicely unchanged place with a constantly interesting range of reasonably priced beers from £2 a pint. Sharps Cornish Coaster or Otter Bitter and three others such as Box Steam Tunnel Vision, Cheddar Goats Leap and Cotleigh Tawny Owl, plus several wines by the glass and malt whiskies. Its simple flagstoned bar is chatty and full of character. A little games room has pool and a quiz machine and there's a TV room. There are some seats outside.

⚄ **Good value, straightforward bar lunchtime food includes sandwiches, filled baguettes and baked potatoes, ham, egg and chips, chilli beef, and maybe liver and bacon, mixed grill or plaice stuffed with prawns; no puddings.** *Starters/Snacks: £1.65 to £3.25. Main Courses: £3.25 to £5.25*

Free house ~ Licensees Oliver Wilson and Nick Whigham ~ Real ale ~ Bar food (12-1.45, not Sun) ~ No credit cards ~ (01935) 813148 ~ Children welcome until 6pm in snug room ~ Dogs welcome ~ Open 11-11; 12-11 Sun

Recommended by Mike and Mary Clark, Michael Dandy, Michael B Griffith, Phil and Sally Gorton, Mike and Sue Loseby

SHROTON
ST8512   MAP 2

Cricketers ♉ ◼ 🛏
Off A350 N of Blandford (village also called Iwerne Courtney); follow signs; DT11 8QD

Well run pub with neatly uniformed and friendly staff, well liked food and lots of wines by the glass; walks and nice views nearby

A useful stop-off for walkers on the Wessex Ridgeway, this pub lies beneath the formidable Iron Age grassy ramparts of Hambledon Hill and they now offer accommodation in the garden annex; we would welcome reports from any readers who stay here. The bright divided bar has a big stone fireplace, alcoves and cricketing memorabilia, and beers from breweries such as Butcombe, Otter, Piddle and St Austell are served from pumps with little cricket bat handles. They've also several wines by the glass and quite a few malt whiskies; good friendly service from the attentive landlord and his uniformed staff. The comfortable back restaurant overlooks the garden and has a fresh neutral décor; piped music. The garden is secluded and pretty with big sturdy tables under cocktail parasols, well tended shrubs and a well stocked (and well used) herb garden by the kitchen door. Walkers are welcome if they leave their walking boots outside.

⚄ **As well as filled baguettes and ploughman's, the well liked bar food might include soup, seared scallops with chive cream glaze, home-cured gravadlax, tagliatelle with mushroom, white wine and cream sauce, medallions of venison with port and wild mushroom jus, breast of chicken on dauphinoise potatoes with bacon and madeira cream, steak and ale pie, mussels from Poole Harbour, and fillet of bass on mussel and saffron cream. Sunday roasts; half portions and a special menu for children.** *Starters/Snacks: £4.95 to £6.95. Main Courses: £4.95 to £12.95. Puddings: £4.95*

Heartstone Inns ~ Managers Andrew and Natasha Edwards ~ Real ale ~ Bar food (12-2.30, 6.30-9.30; not Sun evening) ~ Restaurant ~ (01258) 860421 ~ Children welcome ~ Open 11-3, 6-11.30; 11-10.30 Sun ~ Bedrooms: £45S/£75S

Recommended by Colin and Janet Roe, Edward Mirzoeff, R J Herd, Paul and Annette Hallett, Robert Watt, George Atkinson, Douglas and Ann Hare, Leslie and Barbara Owen, Terry and Linda Moseley

---

Post Office address codings confusingly give the impression that some pubs are in Dorset, when they're really in Somerset (which is where we list them).

Greyhound ⑪ ♀ ⇔

Off A37 N of Dorchester; High Street; DT2 9PD

DORSET DINING PUB OF THE YEAR

Genuinely welcoming staff, attractively presented food, a good range of drinks and country décor in beamed rooms

Hard to fault, this splendid pub in a classic Dorset village seems to get everything right. Sydling Bitter brewed for the pub by St Austell is on handpump along with Wadworths 6X and a guest such as Otter Ale, and 14 wines are sold by the glass; several malt whiskies; fairly unobtrusive piped music and board games. On Thursdays they now have a cocktail hour, with four different cocktails offered each week. The beamed and flagstoned serving area is airy and alluring with a big bowl of lemons and limes, a backdrop of gleaming bottles and copper pans, and plenty of bar stools, with more opposite ranging against a drinking shelf. On one side a turkey-carpeted area with a warm coal fire in a handsome portland stone fireplace has a comfortable mix of straightforward tables and chairs and country decorations such as a stuffed fox eyeing a collection of china chickens and a few farm tools. At the other end, a cosy separate dining room with smart white table linen has some books and a glass-covered well set into its floor, and a garden room with succulents and other plants on its sills has simple modern café furniture. The small front garden has a wooden climber and slide alongside its picnic-sets. The bedrooms are in a separate block.

⑪ **Extremely accomplished, if not cheap, bar food features meat reared in Dorset and a range of fish including shellfish from Lyme Bay; on a short lunchtime snack menu are sandwiches, filled baguettes, ploughman's, and a new range of classic dishes at lower prices, such as warm scallop and bacon salad or pork and smoked bacon burger. The main menu might include mediterranean fish soup, butternut squash and mascarpone risotto, venison wellington with parma ham, or oxtail and blue vinney pudding with a medallion of beef fillet; vegetables are extra. Daily specials; puddings like vanilla and passion-fruit brûlée and chocolate and coffee mousse pot with Amaretto biscuit.** *Starters/Snacks: £3.95 to £9.95. Main Courses: £7.00 to £20.95. Puddings: £4.95*

Free house ~ Licensees John Ford, Karen Trimby, Ron Hobson, Cherry Ball ~ Real ale ~ Bar food (12-2(3 Sun), 6.30-9; not Sun evening) ~ Restaurant ~ (01300) 341303 ~ Children welcome ~ Dogs allowed in bar ~ Open 11-2.30, 6-11; 12-3 Sun; closed Sun evening ~ Bedrooms: /£70S(£80B)

Recommended by John Saville, James A Waller, Tom McLean, Peter Fish, John and Hilda Burns, John Wymer, Bruce Jamieson, Mr and Mrs W W Burke, Ian and Deborah Carrington, Joan and Michel Hooper-Immins, Russell New, Ann and Colin Hunt, M G Hart, Barrie and Anne King, P R Light, Terry and Linda Moseley, P Waterman

Langton Arms ◀ ⇔

Off A354; DT11 8RX

Fresh flowers in light rooms, bistro, good children's play area and comfortable bedrooms

Next to the church in a lovely village, this updated 17th-c thatched dining inn gives a friendly welcome. Hung with old photos of local farming life from past decades, the beamed bar has flagstone floors, a light oak counter with recessed lighting, fresh flowers on the wooden tables, and Ringwood Best and a guest beer such as Piddle Jimmy Riddle on handpump; TV in the public bar. The bistro restaurant is in an attractively reworked barn and the skittle alley doubles as a family room during the day; piped music. They are licensed for weddings. Tarrant Monkton is a charming village (with a ford that can flow quite fast in wet weather) that makes a useful base for walks or pottering around the area. Dogs are allowed only in the Carpenters Bar and in the comfortable ensuite bedrooms (in a modern block at the back). In fine weather, you can sit at picnic-sets outside and there's a wood-chip children's play area in the garden.

⑪ **Served all day at weekends, straightforward bar food has lunchtime filled baguettes, and sharing platters with selections such as charcuterie, greek-style meze or marinated** crispy beef, as well as ploughman's and local sausages; the main menu changes with the produce available and is strong on local meat and seafood, with a carvery/buffet and classic dishes such as beef bourguignon, ocean pie with parmesan mash, local faggots with chive mash, calves liver and chicken suprême. Puddings might include treacle tart, crumble or home-made ice-cream; local cheeses. *Starters/Snacks: £4.95 to £9.95. Main Courses: £8.95 to £18.95. Puddings: £5.50 to £6.95*

Free house ~ Licensees Barbara and James Cossins ~ Real ale ~ Bar food (11.30-2.30, 6-9.30(10 Fri); 12-10 Sat; 12-9 Sun) ~ Restaurant ~ (01258) 830225 ~ Children in family room ~ Dogs allowed in bar and bedrooms ~ Open 11-11; 12-10.30 Sun ~ Bedrooms: £70B/£90B

Recommended by Robert Watt, Noel Grundy, James A Waller, Roy and Jean Russell, Barry and Anne, Mr and Mrs P D Titcomb, Hazel Morgan, Bernard Patrick

UPLODERS   SY5093   MAP 2

Crown

Signed off A35 E of Bridport; DT6 4NU

Homely, low-beamed village pub with log fires and an inviting atmosphere

Not many pubs in Britain boast a harmonium, but in this pleasantly chatty place you are welcome to try playing theirs. Warmed in winter by log fires, the bar is flagstoned and full of polished bric-a-brac, including a shelf of toby jugs. Its few black beams are liberally festooned with pewter and china tankards, copper kettles, horsebrasses and service hats, and there's a bright log fire; piped music. Palmers Copper and IPA are served on handpump, and there's an extensive wine list with several by the glass. Sturdy balustrading with standing timber pillars divides the pub into different parts. You can eat in the bar itself or in another area down a few steps. There are tables out in an attractive two-tier garden, in quiet village surroundings.

🍽 **Tasty food includes sandwiches, soup, seared scallops with pea and mint purée, and main courses such as spring lamb chop with redcurrant and red wine sauce, vegetable lasagne, specials like fillet of bass with hot tartare sauce, and puddings like white chocolate and orange torte.** *Starters/Snacks: £4.20 to £6.50. Main Courses: £6.50 to £19.90. Puddings: £4.50*

Palmers ~ Tenants Ralph and Gail Prince ~ Real ale ~ Bar food (12-2.30(3 Sun), 6-9) ~ Restaurant ~ (01308) 485356 ~ Dogs welcome ~ Open 12-3, 6-11

Recommended by Malcolm and Kate Dowty, Phyl and Jack Street, L Hawkins, David and Ros Hanley, Mrs S Knight, G F Couch

WEST BAY   SY4690   MAP 1

West Bay 🍽 🛏

Station Road; DT6 4EW

RestaurANTY seaside inn with an emphasis on seafood

'The sort of pub where you feel you are somewhere a bit special, but without feeling you have to be on best behaviour' remarked one reader who walked along the coast path from Eype to work up an appetite to come to this dining pub. An island servery separates the fairly simple bare-boards front part, with its coal-effect gas fire and mix of sea and nostalgic prints, from a cosier carpeted dining area with more of a country kitchen feel; piped music. Though its spaciousness means it never feels crowded, booking is virtually essential in season. Palmers 200, Copper Ale and IPA are served on handpump alongside good house wines (with eight by the glass); several malt whiskies. There are tables in the small side garden, with more in a large garden; plenty of parking. Several local teams meet to play in the pub's skittle alley. The bedrooms are quiet and comfortable.

🍽 **Enjoyable food has lunchtime ploughman's, soup, crab and other sandwiches, and a few lighter-bite items like scampi or fish pie. The main menu (not cheap) focuses mostly on fish and shellfish, with local produce; starters might include grilled langoustines or fowey mussels and main courses such as deep fried pollack, skate wing with capers and shrimp,**

surf and turf rib-eye steak with scallops and prawns, and beef, lamb and venison sausages; daily changing puddings. *Starters/Snacks: £4.50 to £10.00. Main Courses: £13.50 to £24.00. Puddings: £4.75 to £6.50*

Palmers ~ Tenants Richard and Lorraine Barnard ~ Real ale ~ Bar food (12-2(2.15 Sun); 6.30-9) ~ Restaurant ~ (01308) 422157 ~ Children welcome ~ Dogs allowed in bar ~ Open 12-4, 6-11; 12-11 Sat; 12-3 Sun; 12-3, 6-11 (closed Mon) in winter ~ Bedrooms: £60B/£90B

Recommended by Peter Meister, David and Julie Glover, Terry and Linda Moseley, Michael Dandy, John and Fiona McIlwain, Robert Watt, Dr Kevan Tucker, George and Beverley Tucker, R J Davies, Pamela and Alan Neale, Bob and Margaret Holder

WEST STOUR   ST7822   MAP 2

Ship 🍷 🛏

A30 W of Shaftesbury; SP8 5RP

Civilised and pleasantly updated roadside dining inn, offering a wide range of food

With welcoming and neatly dressed staff, this well cared-for roadside inn makes a comfortable place for a meal. On the right two carpeted dining rooms, with stripped pine dado and shutters, are furnished in a similar pleasantly informal style, and have some attractive contemporary nautical prints. The bar on the left, with a cool sage-green décor and big sash windows, has a mix of seats around nice stripped tables on the dark boards or flagstones of its two smallish rooms; the gossipy inner one has a good log fire and its bow window looks beyond the road and car park to a soothing view of rolling pastures; TV, darts, board games and piped music. As well as several malt whiskies, elderflower pressé and organic apple juices, they have good wines by the glass, and Otter Bitter, St Austell Tribute and a guest from a regional brewery such as Exmoor on handpump. The bedlington terrier is called Douglas. As there's a sharp nearby bend, keep your fingers crossed that drivers are obeying the 30mph limit when you walk from or to the car park opposite.

🍴 **Served in generous helpings, food includes a wide choice of lunchtime baguettes, ciabattas and panini, as well as soup, starters like mussels or home-made pâté, and main courses such as honey-baked ham, fish pie, sausages and mash, and spinach, mushroom and blue vinney roly-poly. The fresh fish specials board could offer whole bream with green beans, thyme and fennel, roast monkfish wrapped in pancetta with spinach mash or roast cod fillet with a crab and herb crust; puddings like peach parfait with orange sorbet, belgian waffle with chocolate sauce or lime, ginger and coconut cheesecake.** *Starters/Snacks: £4.00 to £7.00. Main Courses: £9.00 to £18.00. Puddings: £4.50 to £6.95*

Free house ~ Licensee Gavin Griggs ~ Real ale ~ Bar food (not Sun evening) ~ Restaurant ~ (01747) 838640 ~ Children welcome ~ Dogs allowed in bar ~ Open 12-3, 6-11(midnight Sat); 12-11 Sun ~ Bedrooms: £55B/£80B

Recommended by George Atkinson, Paul and Annette Hallett, Nick and Sylvia Pascoe, Steve Jackson, G Vyse, Robert Watt, Colin and Janet Roe, Maria Furness

WIMBORNE MINSTER   SZ0199   MAP 2

Green Man £

Victoria Road at junction with West Street (B3082/B3073); BH21 1EN

Cosy and warm-hearted town pub with bargain simple food

Even early in the day quite a few regulars drop in for a chat at this cheery family-run pub, and there are photo montages of several of them in their younger days. Copper and brass ornaments brighten up the muted warm tones – soft lighting, dark red walls, maroon plush banquettes and polished dark pub tables in four small linked areas. One of these has a log fire in a biggish brick fireplace, another has a coal-effect gas fire, and they have two darts boards (the games machine is silenced, but they have piped music), and TV; the Barn houses a pool table and table football in the summer months. Very well kept and served on handpump are Wadworths Henrys, 6X and Bishops Tipple. There's a nice little border terrier called Cooper, and a back terrace has heaters and picnic-sets. The front is lavished in summer with floral displays that have repeatedly won Wimborne in Bloom awards.

🍴 **As well as a very popular breakfast, they offer a wide choice (lunchtimes only) of sandwiches, filled rolls and baked potatoes and simple pubby dishes like fish and chips, burgers or lasagne, with some smaller portion options, as well as new menu additions such as whitebait and deep-fried camembert; good Sunday roasts.** *Starters/Snacks: £2.50 to £4.25. Main Courses: £4.50 to £8.50. Puddings: £2.50*

Wadworths ~ Tenants Kate Kiff and Andrew Kiff ~ Real ale ~ Bar food (10-2) ~ Restaurant ~ (01202) 881021 ~ Children allowed until 7pm ~ Dogs allowed in bar ~ Live music Fri, Sat and Sun evenings ~ Open 10am-11pm (midnight Sat)

Recommended by Graham and Jane Lynch-Watson, Alan Wright

WINKTON   SZ1696   MAP 2
Fishermans Haunt 🛏️
B3347 N of Christchurch; BH23 7AS

Well run, roomy riverside inn, with caring staff, comfortable rooms and thoughtfully prepared food

Near the fringes of the New Forest and to a clutch of fisheries on the River Avon, this inn has been comfortably refurbished and substantially improved under its new owners. The two lounge bars are divided into various pleasant areas, with brocaded chairs around tables and two log fires in winter. At one end, big windows look out on the neat front garden, and there are attractive views of the River Avon from the restaurant. Fullers ESB, HSB and London Pride, and Gales Seafarers on handpump, and a good choice of wines, with several by the glass. The quiet back garden has tables among the shrubs, and heaters in a covered area, and there are 12 comfortable bedrooms, some with disabled access; disabled lavatories.

🍴 **Very well prepared and reasonably priced food includes soup, sandwiches, sharing platters with cheeses or smoked meats, starters such as soft herring roe or crispy bacon rösti, and main courses (some with smaller portion options) like local venison burger, fisherman's skillet of mixed fish with savoury crumble, mussels, local trout salad and London Pride steak pie.** *Starters/Snacks: £4.95 to £6.95. Main Courses: £5.95 to £20.00. Puddings: £3.95 to £6.00*

Gales (Fullers) ~ Manager Keith Perks ~ Real ale ~ Bar food (12-9(9.30 Sat)) ~ Restaurant ~ (01202) 477283 ~ Children welcome ~ Dogs allowed in bar and bedrooms ~ Music quiz night with DJ every Fri ~ Open 11-11(midnight Fri, 10.30 Sun) ~ Bedrooms: £65B/£85B

Recommended by Sara Fulton, Roger Baker, Sue and Mike Todd, B Targett, Baden and Sandy Waller

WORTH MATRAVERS   SY9777   MAP 2
Square & Compass ★ 🍺
At fork of both roads signposted to village from B3069; BH19 3LF

Unchanging country tavern, masses of character, in the same family for many years; lovely sea views and fine nearby walks

Much as it was around 100 years ago when the Newman family first took this on, this is a wonderfully idiosyncratic pub. There's no bar counter; Palmers Copper and three guests like Hopback Crop Circle, Milton Caligula and Sharps Eden Ale as well as up to 13 ciders, including one made on the premises, are tapped from a row of casks and passed to you in a drinking corridor through two serving hatches; several malt whiskies. A couple of basic unspoilt rooms have simple furniture on the flagstones, a woodburning stove and a loyal crowd of friendly locals; darts and shove-ha'penny; a table tennis championship is held here twice a year. From benches out in front there's a fantastic view down over the village rooftops to the sea around St Aldhelm's Head; there may be free-roaming hens, chickens and other birds clucking around your feet. A little museum (free) exhibits local fossils and artefacts, mostly collected by the current friendly landlord and his father; mind your head on the way out. There are wonderful walks from here to some exciting switchback sections of the coast path above St Aldhelm's Head and Chapman's Pool; you will need to park in the public car park 100 yards along the Corfe Castle road (which has a £1 honesty box).

🍴 **Bar food is limited to tasty home-made pasties and pies, served till they run out.** *Starters/Snacks: £2.80*

Free house ~ Licensee Charlie Newman ~ Real ale ~ Bar food (all day) ~ No credit cards ~ (01929) 439229 ~ Children welcome ~ Dogs welcome ~ Live music most Sats ~ Open 12-11; closed weekdays 3-6 in winter

Recommended by Chris Flynn, Wendy Jones, Pete Baker, JDM, KM, Rona Markland, Terry and Linda Moseley, Mr and Mrs P D Titcomb, Mike and Sue Loseby, Michael Butler, Andrea Rampley, I A Herdman, Adrian Johnson, the Didler, John and Enid Morris, Mike and Eleanor Anderson

LUCKY DIP

Besides the fully inspected pubs, you might like to try these Lucky Dips recommended to us and described by readers (if you do, please send us reports: feedback@goodguides.com).

ABBOTSBURY [SY5785]
Ilchester Arms DT3 4JR [Market St (B3157)]: Rambling stone-built inn with old pine tables and settles, beams and log fires, lots of rustic bric-a-brac, prints of the famous swans, real ale, good house wines in three glass sizes, usual food; large games room with pool and darts, conservatory restaurant; quiet piped music, TV, games machine; children in eating areas, picnic-sets out by car park, ten bedrooms, open all day *(LYM, John and Enid Morris, Richard Stanfield)*
Swan DT3 4JL [Rodden Row (B3157)]: Unpretentious stone-built pub in pretty village, something of a 1970s feel, friendly staff, Courage and Theakstons XB, decent wine choice, pubby food, family room; back terrace and small garden with country view *(Michael Dandy)*
ASKERSWELL [SY5393]
☆ *Spyway* DT2 9EP [off A35 Bridport—Dorchester]: Popular prettily set beamed country pub, reasonably priced food from sandwiches to good Sun roasts, charming family service, real ales such as Badger and Otter tapped from the cask; old-fashioned high-backed settles, cushioned wall and window seats, old-world décor, local pictures for sale, dining area with steps down to overflow area; disabled access, children in eating areas, spectacular views from back terrace and large attractive garden, good walks, comfortable bedrooms *(George Atkinson, the Didler, LYM)*
BENVILLE LANE [ST5303]
Talbot Arms DT2 0NN [Benville Lane; off A356 NW of Dorchester]: Village pub reopened under experienced licensees, roomy bar with St Austell and a guest beer *(John Wymer)*
BLANDFORD FORUM [ST8806]
Crown DT11 7AJ [West St]: Best Western hotel's refurbished spacious bar (less pubby now), full Badger range from nearby brewery inc seasonal ales, adjacent eating area,

decent range of bar food from good sandwiches up, genteel restaurant; tables outside, bedrooms *(Joan and Michel Hooper-Immins)*
BOURNEMOUTH [SZ0891]
Goat & Tricycle BH2 5PF [West Hill Rd]: Interesting two-level rambling Edwardian local (two former pubs knocked together) with Wadworths and guest beers kept well from pillared bank's impressive rank of ten or more handpumps, farm cider; bargain pubby food from good baguettes up inc Sun lunch, friendly staff, coal fire, lots of bric-a-brac inc hundreds of hats and helmets; can get rather noisily studenty; children welcome, good disabled access, heated yard with flower tubs, water feature and covered bower *(Joan and Michel Hooper-Immins, Alain and Rose Foote)*
BOURTON [ST7731]
☆ *White Lion* SP8 5AT [High St, off old A303 E of Wincanton]: Lively 18th-c low-beamed and stripped-stone dining pub with welcoming energetic landlord, appealing place with fine inglenook fire in pubby bar, two cosy rooms off and good-sized restaurant; bar snacks and enjoyable good value main meals, good service, beers such as Butcombe and Sharps Doom Bar, Thatcher's cider, nice wines; picnic-sets on new back paved area and raised lawn, two neat bedrooms *(Edward Mirzoeff, LYM, Mike and Cherry Fann)*
BRIDPORT [SY4692]
George DT6 3NQ [South St]: Cheery well worn-in two-bar town local, traditional dark décor, assorted furnishings and floor rugs, bargain home-made chip-free pub lunches (not Sun) cooked in sight, good crab sandwiches; well kept Palmers, good choice of wines by the glass, efficient service, hot coal fire, hatch-served family room; piped radio, upstairs lavatories; dogs welcome, open all day, from 9am for popular wkdy breakfast or coffee *(the Didler, Joan and*

Michel Hooper-Immins, John Wymer,
L Hawkins, LYM)

Woodman DT6 3NZ [South St]: Lively and
friendly local, well kept Branscombe Vale and
guest beers, decent straightforward food
even on Sun, skittle alley; attractive garden,
open all day (John Wymer, the Didler)

BUCKHORN WESTON [ST7524]

☆ **Stapleton Arms** SP8 5HS [Church Hill]:
Attractive and welcoming upmarket bistro
dining pub, scrubbed tables and squashy
sofas in log-fire bar, stylish dining room
with well spaced mahogany tables,
chandeliers and big mirrors; good up-to-date
daily changing fresh food, at a price, from
sandwiches up, friendly attentive staff,
Butcombe, Hidden, Otter and changing guest
ales, huge range of bottled beers, Cheddar
Valley cider, good choice of wines and soft
drinks; tables outside, pleasant countryside,
four comfortable bedrooms, good breakfast,
open all day wknds (Ian Malone, Joan and
Michel Hooper-Immins, Samantha McGahan,
Mark Flynn)

BUCKLAND NEWTON [ST6804]

☆ **Gaggle of Geese** DT2 7BS: Taken over by
owners of the good European at
Piddletrenthide (see Main Entry section);
civilised 19th-c country pub with relaxed
atmosphere and attractive décor, sofas and
armchairs next to large log fire, books and
games, good home-made locally sourced
food inc Sun roasts, friendly efficient staff;
Ringwood, St Austell and two west country
guest ales, good wine choice, nice coffee,
red candlelit dining room with persian rugs
and mix of old and new furniture, darts,
skittle alley; children and dogs welcome,
garden with terrace, orchard and pond,
paddock with chickens and goats, charity
poultry auction May and Sept, bedrooms
planned, open all day wknds (Ann and
Colin Hunt, Pat and Roger Davies, BB)

CATTISTOCK [SY5999]

☆ **Fox & Hounds** DT2 0JH [off A37 N of
Dorchester]: Welcoming and attractive
17th-c or older pub, helpful service,
enjoyable good value food inc OAP meals,
Palmers ales from attractively carved
counter, Taunton cider, good value wine
choice; flagstones and nicely moulded
Jacobean beams, stripped stone, log fire in
huge inglenook, minimal décor, table
skittles, pleasant side dining room, back
public bar with well lit darts and TV,
immaculate skittle alley; piped pop music,
live some Sats; dogs welcome, good local
walks, comfortable bedrooms, cl Mon
lunchtime, open all day wknds (I A Herdman,
Roger Thornington, Nic Soden, Hannah Elder,
BB)

CERNE ABBAS [ST6601]

☆ **New Inn** DT2 7JF [Long St]: Handsome Tudor
inn with mullioned window seats in neatly
kept carpeted beamed bar, open fire, old
photographs and prints, jug collection, good
service, generous enjoyable food from
sandwiches/baguettes up, nice wine choice,

Palmers IPA, comfortable restaurant; children
welcome, lots of tables on coachyard terrace
and attractive sheltered lawn beyond, eight
bedrooms, open all day wknds and summer
(Michael Dandy, LYM, Alan Johnson, Joan and
Michel Hooper-Immins, Ann and Colin Hunt)

CHARMINSTER [SY6793]

Inn For All Seasons DT2 9QZ [North St]: Bar
with easy chairs, sofas and log fire, two well
kept real ales, enjoyable food inc Sun
carvery, attentive service, bright airy back
conservatory-style dining room, fresh
flowers; long sloping garden to stream with
fields beyond, bedrooms (Mr and Mrs Draper,
B and K Hypher)

CHICKERELL [SY6480]

Lugger DT3 4DY [West St]: Bustling and
welcoming stone-built pub, olde-worlde
beamed décor, good wide-ranging reasonably
priced food (opens 8.30am for breakfast and
coffee) inc fresh fish; friendly efficient
service, good choice of local beers, fairly
large two-part dining area; garden, bedrooms
and self-catering cottages
(Roy and Lindsey Fentiman)

CHIDEOCK [SY4191]

☆ **Anchor** DT6 6JU [off A35 from Chideock]:
Simple seaside pub in outstanding spot,
dramatic sea and cliff views and big front
terrace; well kept Palmers ales, good choice
of wines by the glass, local farm cider, good
value home-made food (all day in summer)
inc fresh fish from lunchtime crab
sandwiches to bouillabaisse, quick friendly
service despite crowds, woodburners,
interesting local photographs; can get a bit
untidy outside; children and dogs welcome,
open all day in summer (Richard Stanfield,
David and Sue Smith, Richard Mason,
Joan and Michel Hooper-Immins, LYM,
Pamela and Alan Neale, the Didler, Mr and
Mrs P D Titcomb, Dr S J Shepherd, David and
Julie Glover, David Lamb, Rona Markland)

☆ **George** DT6 6JD [A35 Bridport—Lyme
Regis]: Pleasantly traditional thatched
roadside village pub, friendly new licensees
making a promising start with sensibly
priced imaginative food, well kept Palmers
and helpful service; dark-beamed lounge bar
with good log fire, comfortable wall and
window seats, old tools and local
photographs, high shelves with bottles and
china, brassware; piped music; children and
dogs welcome, terrace, cl Sun evening winter
(LYM, John Burgess, Bob Clucas)

CHILD OKEFORD [ST8213]

☆ **Saxon** DT11 8HD [signed off A350
Blandford—Shaftesbury and A357
Blandford—Sherborne; Gold Hill]: Welcoming
village pub, quietly clubby snug bar with log
fire and more spacious side room (where
children allowed); four well kept changing
ales inc Butcombe, good choice of wines and
country wines, reasonably priced home-made
food inc set deals, traditional games;
attractive back garden, good walks on
neolithic Hambledon Hill, four comfortable
new bedrooms (LYM, Mrs Elaine Lee)

CHRISTCHURCH [SZ1592]

☆ *Olde George* BH23 1DT [Castle St]: Bustling and cheerfully old-fashioned two-bar low-beamed pub dating from 15th c, friendly efficient staff, six well kept changing ales such as Dorset Piddle, Ringwood and Otter, nice wine, good choice of sensibly priced interesting food all day, using local suppliers, Sun carvery and different evening menu; lots of teak seats and tables in heated characterful coach yard, open all day *(Val and Alan Green, BB)*

COLEHILL [SU0302]

☆ *Barley Mow* BH21 7AH [Colehill signed from A31/B3073 roundabout; Long Lane]: Welcoming part-thatched, part-tiled pub with enjoyable food inc good light lunches in low-beamed main bar, friendly service, well kept Badger ales; open fire in brick inglenook, attractive oak panelling, some Hogarth prints, family area; piped music; pleasant enclosed lawn behind with terrace and boules *(LYM, Malcolm and Jane Levitt, Pat and Roger Davies, Robert Watt)*

CORFE CASTLE [SY9681]

Fox BH20 5HD [West St]: Old-fashioned take-us-as-you-find-us stone-built local, real ales such as Greene King Abbot and Wadworths 6X tapped from the cask, good log fire in early medieval stone fireplace, glassed-over well in second bar; dogs but not children allowed, informal castle-view garden *(the Didler, Mike and Sue Loseby, LYM)*

☆ *Greyhound* BH20 5EZ [A351; The Square]: Bustling and picturesque old pub in centre of tourist village, three small low-ceilinged panelled rooms, steps and corridors, well kept changing ales such as Ringwood, local farm cider, food from baguettes to seafood, friendly staff, traditional games inc Purbeck long board shove-ha'penny, family room; piped music, live Fri; garden with fine castle and countryside views, pretty courtyard opening on to castle bridge, open all day wknds and summer *(LYM, the Didler, John Roots, Mike and Sue Loseby, Fred and Lorraine Gill)*

CORFE MULLEN [SY9798]

☆ *Coventry Arms* BH21 3RH [A31 W of Wimborne; Mill St]: 15th-c pub with four dining areas and bar, wide range of good food (best to book) inc some unusual dishes, using local meat and fish and own veg and herbs, may be fixed price deals, good breakfast till 11am, friendly service; Timothy Taylors Landlord and other well kept ales tapped from the cask, good wine choice inc champagne by the glass, large central open fire, low ceilings, flagstones, bare boards, evening candles and fishing décor, mummified cat (to ward off evil spirits); big garden with tables by small river *(Mike and Shelley Woodroffe, Mrs Mary Woods, Peter Salmon, Katharine Cowherd, Mr and Mrs W W Burke)*

CORSCOMBE [ST5205]

☆ *Fox* DT2 0NS [towards Halstock]: Thatched and rose-clad 16th-c country dining pub with plenty of rustic charm, beams and flagstones, built-in settles, sporting prints, inglenook fire; well cooked if fairly pricey food inc very good venison, steaks and fresh fish, Butcombe Bitter and Exmoor, several wines by the glass, conservatory; children in dining areas, streamside lawn across lane, can be tricky to find at night (not well lit), bedrooms *(LYM, J S Burn, Gene and Kitty Rankin, Dr A McCormick, Paul and Annette Hallett)*

DORCHESTER [SY6990]

☆ *Blue Raddle* DT1 1JN [Church St, nr central short stay car park]: Cheery and welcoming, long carpeted and partly panelled bar, well kept Otter and Sharps Doom Bar, decent wines and coffee, Weston's farm cider, good value food from generous sandwiches to good wild boar stew, open fire; piped music; disabled access, but one step, cl Mon lunchtime *(the Didler, Patrick and Daphne Darley, Gene and Kitty Rankin, Joan and Michel Hooper-Immins, Terry and Linda Moseley, BB, Michael Dandy)*

Kings Arms DT1 1HF [High East St]: Georgian hotel's bar with thriving atmosphere, carpeted throughout and comfortably furnished, open fire, interesting photographs; Dorset Piddle and Shepherd Neame ales, decent wines, enjoyable food from sandwiches up, two-for-one deals and Sun carvery, attentive service, restaurant; close associations with Nelson and Hardy's *Mayor of Casterbridge*; bedrooms *(LYM, the Didler, Michael Dandy)*

Tom Browns DT1 1HU [High East St]: Under new management this unpretentious Dorset Brewing Company local plans to reopen its microbrewery; friendly bare-boards L-shaped bar, Dorset ales inc Tom Browns Bitter and guests, limited choice of bar food, Sun roast, traditional games, vintage juke box and regular live music; well behaved children and dogs welcome, disabled access, big garden down to river, open all day *(Stan Edwards, Joan and Michel Hooper-Immins, BB)*

EAST END [SY9998]

Lambs Green BH21 3DN [Lambs Green Lane]: Roomily extended pub with well kept ales such as St Austell Tribute and Wells & Youngs Bombardier, reasonably priced straightforward food, friendly staff; fine Wimborne Minster views from attractive garden *(Alan Wright)*

EAST MORDEN [SY9194]

☆ *Cock & Bottle* BH20 7DL [B3075 W of Poole]: Popular dining pub with interesting vintage car and motorcycle bric-a-brac, wide choice of changing food (not cheap, but can be good and best to book), Badger ales, several wines by the glass, good service, two dining areas with heavy plough beams; children in restaurant area only; garden and adjoining field, pleasant pastoral outlook *(John and Enid Morris, Pamela and Alan Neale, Yana Pocklington, Patricia Owlett,*

William Ruxton, Dr and Mrs J Temporal,
Mr and Mrs P D Titcomb, Peter Veness, LYM,
Andy Lickfold)

EVERSHOT [ST5704]

Acorn DT2 0JW [off A37 S of Yeovil]:
Upmarket inn (Sow & Acorn in *Tess of the
D'Urbevilles*) with two well kept changing
ales, good choice of wines by the glass inc
champagne, real ciders, decent food in
restaurany front part with up-to-date décor
as well as log fires and oak panelling; bar
snacks from interesting open sandwiches to
salads and pubby hot dishes in beamed and
flagstoned back bar with darts and pool,
skittle alley; piped music; children allowed
in eating areas, dogs in bar, terrace with
dark oak furniture, ten bedrooms, pretty
village, good surrounding walks, open all day
(Roger Thornington, Alan Johnson,
Michael Dandy, LYM, John Wymer)

GILLINGHAM [ST7926]

Buffalo SP8 4NJ [off B3081 at Wyke, 1 mile
NW of Gillingham, pub 100 yds on left]:
Busy and welcoming Badger local, their ales
kept well, sensibly priced food from pub
standards up inc Sun carvery, stripped stone
and brick in two linked bars, adjoining
carpeted restaurant; piped music; children
welcome, dogs in smaller bar only, disabled
access, back terrace and garden with picnic-
sets, play area (Lt Col and Mrs Patrick Kaye)

GUSSAGE ALL SAINTS [SU0010]

☆ *Drovers* BH21 5ET [8 miles N of Wimborne]:
Partly thatched pub with friendly staff, good
choice of enterprising well cooked food at
sensible prices, Ringwood ales and guests
kept well, good wines by the glass; log fire
and pleasantly simple country furnishings,
public bar with piano and darts; tables on
pretty front lawn with views across the
Dorset hills, adjoining farm shop, quiet
village (LYM, Stan Edwards, Robert Watt,
John R Ringrose, Julia and Richard Tredgett,
Pat and Roger Davies)

HAZELBURY BRYAN [ST7408]

Antelope DT10 2EB: Appealing and
welcoming village local with inglenook log
fire and traditional wooden furnishings in
main bar, well done straightforward food
using local farm produce, well kept Badger
real ales, decent wine choice; pool in
separate skittle alley; large garden with
pleasant views (Rob Winstanley)

HORTON [SU0407]

Drusillas BH21 7JH [Wigbeth]: Picturesque
17th-c beamed pub/restaurant in nice
countryside looking out to Horton folly,
tablecloths even in the bar, wide choice of
food from snacks up inc lots of fish and
good vegetarian options, good value wines,
Ringwood ales and a guest; pleasant staff,
log fire, thatched extension; children
welcome (Jennifer Banks, Mr and
Mrs W W Burke, Robert Watt)

IBBERTON [ST7807]

Crown DT11 0EN: Nicely updated traditional
village pub, ochre walls, flagstones, toby
jugs and open fire, dining area at the back;

Butcombe, Palmers and Ringwood, above-
average pubby food inc interesting dishes
and good value set deals, friendly helpful
staff; lovely garden, beautiful spot under
Bulbarrow Hill (M and GR, BB)

KING'S STAG [ST7210]

Green Man DT10 2AY [B3143, S of A3030]:
Bright and open local, with good-sized
helpings of enjoyable if pricey food, three
well kept ales, interesting reasonably priced
wine choice, farm cider, friendly informal
staff; restaurant area down on left, Sun
carvery in former skittle alley (Robert Watt,
Laurie Scott)

KINGSTON [SY9579]

Scott Arms BH20 5LH [West St (B3069)]:
New landlord at this extensively modernised
holiday pub rambling through several levels,
some sofas and easy chairs, beams, stripped
stone, bare boards and log fires; well kept
Ringwood, reasonably priced food (can be
slow to come), family dining area; darts,
pool, games machine, piped music; large
attractive garden with outstanding views of
Corfe Castle and the Purbeck Hills, good
walks (Michael Butler, John Roots, Mike and
Sue Loseby, LYM, the Didler)

LANGTON HERRING [SY6182]

☆ *Elm Tree* DT3 4HU [off B3157]: Quietly
placed village pub a walk from Fleet lagoon,
comfortable main beamed and carpeted
rooms with lots of big old kitchen tables,
old-fashioned settles and inglenook,
traditionally furnished dining extension;
enjoyable food inc interesting daily specials,
friendly service (can be slow), Adnams and
several wines by glass; children and dogs
welcome, pretty flower-filled sunken garden
with outdoor heaters, open all day in
summer (Terry and Linda Moseley, Mr and
Mrs W W Burke, Hugh Stafford, JDM, KM, LYM,
Phil and Jane Hodson, Fred and Lorraine Gill,
Yana Pocklington, Patricia Owlett,
Adrian Johnson)

LITTON CHENEY [SY5490]

☆ *White Horse* DT2 9AT: Relaxed and
unpretentious, with good value food from
sandwiches and traditional dishes to
imaginative cooking with good fresh local
ingredients, particularly well kept Palmers
ales, decent reasonably priced wines by the
glass, pleasant service; big woodburner, lots
of pictures, some pine panelling, stripped
stone and flagstones, country kitchen chairs
in dining area, table skittles; may be piped
jazz; children and dogs welcome, disabled
access, good spot on quiet lane into quaint
village, picnic-sets on pleasant streamside
front lawn (George Atkinson, BB, L Hawkins)

LYME REGIS [SY3391]

☆ *Harbour Inn* DT7 3JF [Marine Parade]: More
eating than pubby, with friendly efficient
service even at busy times; food from
lunchtime sandwiches to local fish, good
choice of wines by the glass, Otter and
St Austell, farm cider, clean-cut modern
décor keeping original flagstones and stone
walls (lively acoustics), thriving family

atmosphere; big paintings for sale, sea views from front windows; piped music; disabled access from street, verandah tables *(Gerry and Rosemary Dobson, Alain and Rose Foote, Terry and Linda Moseley, Rosemary Richards)*

☆ *Pilot Boat* DT7 3QA [Bridge St]: Popular modern all-day family food place nr waterfront, neatly cared for by long-serving licensees; friendly service even when busy, good value enjoyable food inc plenty of fish, well kept Palmers ales, good choice of wines by the glass, plenty of tables in cheery nautically themed areas, skittle alley; quiet piped radio; children and dogs welcome, tables out on terrace (watch out for seagulls) *(Joan and Michel Hooper-Immins, Stan Edwards, Neil and Brenda Skidmore, Mrs Jordan, Alain and Rose Foote, Colin Gooch, LYM, Pat and Tony Martin, Richard Mason)*

Royal Lion DT7 3QF [Broad St]: Attractive coaching inn dating from 17th c, comfortably old-fashioned many-roomed bar with log fire and dark panelling, well kept Bass and guest beers, good value pub meals, efficient service; games room, upstairs restaurant; bedrooms *(Peter Rozée, LYM)*

☆ *Royal Standard* DT7 3JF [Marine Parade, The Cobb]: Right on broadest part of beach, properly pubby bar with log fire, fine built-in stripped high settles, local photographs and even old-fashioned ring-up tills, quieter eating area with stripped brick and pine, friendly helpful service; three Palmers ales, good choice of wines by the glass, food from massive crab sandwiches up inc local fish, good cream teas, darts, prominent pool table, some live music; may be piped pop, gets very busy in season - long waits then; children welcome, good-sized sheltered suntrap courtyard with own servery and wendy house *(Derek and Sylvia Stephenson, Pat and Tony Martin, David A Hammond, Peter Salmon, Gene and Kitty Rankin, BB)*

MANSTON [ST8116]

☆ *Plough* DT10 1HB [B3091 Shaftesbury—Sturminster Newton, just N]: Good-sized traditional country pub with well kept Palmers ales, plentiful appetising home-made food from sandwiches up (they will cater for special diets), prompt friendly service; richly decorated plasterwork, ceilings and bar front, conservatory; garden tables *(Steve Jackson, David Lamb)*

MARSHWOOD [SY3799]

☆ *Bottle* DT6 5QJ [B3165 Lyme Regis—Crewkerne]: Simple unchanging 16th-c thatched country local (kept out of the Main Entries only by a lack of recent reports); big inglenook log fire, tasty bar food, Greene King Old Speckled Hen, Otter, Yeovil Star Gazer and a guest ale, farm cider, beer festival and stinging nettle championships mid-Jun; modern extension with skittle alley, pool, TV and piped music, disco last Sat of month; provision for children and dogs, big garden with play area, camping

field, pretty walking country, cl Mon exc school hols *(Terry and Linda Moseley, LYM)*

MELBURY OSMOND [ST58707]

Rest & Welcome DT2 0NF [Yeovil Rd (A37)]: Unassuming two-bar roadside inn under new ownership, enjoyable home-made food inc specials board, real ales, friendly service, cottagey décor, back skittle alley; children and dogs welcome *(A B Farnell)*

MILTON ABBAS [ST8001]

☆ *Hambro Arms* DT11 0BP [signed off A354 SW of Blandford]: Well managed pub in beautiful late 18th-c thatched landscaped village, two beamed bars and restaurant, good log fire, well kept ales such as Dorset Piddle and Ringwood, good interesting food from sandwiches and panini up, popular Sun carvery, gourmet evenings, prompt service even when busy; darts, pool and TV in back public bar; no dogs, children in restaurant, tables on terrace, comfortable bedrooms, open all day wknds *(Mr and Mrs W W Burke, LYM)*

MUDEFORD [SZ1891]

☆ *Haven House* BH23 4AB [beyond huge seaside car park at Mudeford Pier]: Popular much-extended pub in great spot on beach, with superb views and bird watching, good value pubby food and seafood, well kept Ringwood and other ales, cheerful efficient service, popular linked family cafeteria (all day in summer); nice in winter with old-fashioned feel in quaint little part-flagstoned core; tables on sheltered back terrace, lovely seaside walks (dogs banned from beach May-Sept) *(Kevin Flack, David Jackson, LYM)*

Nelson BH23 3NJ [75 Mudeford]: Friendly well run local, four well kept real ales, good service, wide range of food from bar meals to authentic thai dishes (inc Sun buffet) in bright modern back dining area with big palms and white tablecloths; sports TV; pleasant back terrace *(Mr and Mrs W W Burke, Alan Wright)*

PIDDLEHINTON [SY7197]

☆ *Thimble* DT2 7TD [High St (B3143)]: Hospitable neatly kept partly thatched pub with two handsome fireplaces and deep glazed-over well in attractive low-beamed core, well kept Palmers and Ringwood, good wines by the glass, friendly staff, good value straightforward bar food from sandwiches up; interesting bottle collection, darts and cribbage; children and dogs welcome, floodlit garden with summer house, barbecues, stream and little bridge *(Dennis Jenkin, LYM, Sarah and Roger Baynton-Williams, Robert Watt, Michael Butler, P R Light, Mr and Mrs P D Titcomb, Ian and Deborah Carrington)*

PIDDLETRENTHIDE [SY7099]

☆ *Piddle* DT2 7QF [B3143 N of Dorchester]: Most tables set for the good food with an emphasis on fish, but also enjoyable sandwiches and ploughman's, comfortable leatherette sofas in refurbished bar, polite helpful staff, Dorset Piddle and Ringwood ales, well chosen wines; children's room, end pool room with sports TV; dogs welcome in bar, informal streamside garden with picnic-sets and play area, good bedrooms *(Ann and Colin Hunt, Dennis Jenkin, BB)*

Poachers DT2 7QX [B3143 N of Dorchester]: Bright up-to-date décor, comfortable lounge end, Butcombe, Palmers Copper and Ringwood Fortyniner, good wine, generous food from ciabattas up, three linked beamed dining areas; piped music; dogs welcome, garden with tables on decking and stream at bottom, 21 comfortable good value motel-style bedrooms around residents' heated swimming pool, good breakfast, open all day *(Phyl and Jack Street, Dennis Jenkin)*

POOLE [SZ0690]

Inn in the Park BH13 6JS [Pinewood Rd, off A338 towards Branksome Chine, via The Avenue]: Popular open-plan bar in substantial Edwardian villa (now a small hotel), Wadworths and other ales, good value generous standard food (not Sun evening) from good sandwiches to fresh seafood, cheerful young staff; log fire, oak panelling and big mirrors, airy and attractive restaurant (children allowed) and Sun carvery; tables on small sunny terrace, comfortable bedrooms, quiet pine-filled residential area just above sea, open all day *(LYM, Phyl and Jack Street, JDM, KM)*

Nightjar BH13 7HX [Ravine Rd, Canford Cliffs]: Comfortable and well run Ember Inn with leather armchairs, sofas and so forth, several separate areas, good choice of changing ales from long bar (three-glass tasting trays available), occasional beer festivals, good wines by the glass, wide range of good value all-day food; piped music, games machines, two quiz nights; picnic-sets on pleasant shaded lawn, nice quiet spot in upmarket district, open all day *(JDM, KM)*

PORTLAND [SY6872]

George DT5 2AP [Reforne]: Cheery 17th-c stone-built local mentioned by Thomas Hardy, low doorways and beams, flagstones, small rooms, reputed smugglers' tunnels, scrubbed tables carved with names of generations of sailors and quarrymen, interesting prints and mementoes; Courage Directors and Greene King Abbot, Addlestone's cider, basic bargain lunches, children's room, newer end bar, events most nights; pleasant back garden, open all day *(Joan and Michel Hooper-Immins, the Didler)*

Royal Portland Arms DT5 1LZ [Fortuneswell]: Busy local, large and comfortable, with fine range of changing ales (many west country microbrews) tapped from the cask, farm cider, friendly licensees, wknd live bands; open all day, till late Fri, Sat *(the Didler)*

PORTLAND BILL [SY6768]

Pulpit DT5 2JT: Extended touristy pub in great spot nr Pulpit Rock, landlady's steak and kidney pie popular, other quickly served food from good sandwiches to fried fish, well kept Fullers and Ringwood, picture-window

views, dark beams and stripped stone; may be piped music; dogs welcome, disabled access, tiered sea-view terrace, play area, short stroll to lighthouse and cliffs *(Colin Gooch, Philip Vernon, Kim Maidment, Joan and Michel Hooper-Immins, Dennis Jenkin)*

PUDDLETOWN [SY7594]

Blue Vinney DT2 8TE [the Moor]: Friendly welcome from young hard-working newish licensees, new tables and chairs set for dining, wide choice of enjoyable bar food from baguettes up, beers such as Davenports, Gales, Robinsons and York; terrace overlooking garden *(Glenwys and Alan Lawrence, John Butcher)*

PUNCKNOWLE [SY5388]

Crown DT2 9BN [off B3157 Bridport—Abbotsbury]: New landlord and refurbishment at this 16th-c thatched inn; good value pubby food from lunchtime sandwiches and baked potatoes up, inc vegetarian and children meals, full Palmers ale range kept well, a dozen wines by the glass, nice coffee, inglenook log fires each end of low-beamed stripped stone lounge, steps up to public bar with books, magazines and another log fire, snug; dogs welcome, disabled facilities, views from peaceful pretty back garden, good walks, one bedroom *(L Hawkins, LYM, Alan Johnson, Christine and Neil Townend, Mr and Mrs P D Titcomb)*

PYMORE [SY4794]

Pymore Inn DT6 5PN [off A3066 N of Bridport]: Newish licensees in attractive Georgian beamed and stone-built pub with good atmosphere, chef/landlord doing enjoyable food inc good fish choice (most tables laid for eating), friendly prompt service; St Austell ales, good choice of wines by the glass, prints on panelled walls, old settles and woodburner, small pretty dining room; wheelchair access, large pleasant garden *(Bob and Margaret Holder)*

SHAFTESBURY [ST8722]

Half Moon SP7 8BS [Salisbury Rd, Ludwell (A30 E, by roundabout)]: Comfortable and pleasantly extended Badger family dining pub with their usual food inc popular Sun lunch, well kept if not cheap beers, quick helpful service, spotless housekeeping; low ceilings, tiled and wood floors on different levels, mixed tables and chairs, old local photographs; garden with adventure playground *(B and K Hypher, Robert Watt)*

Two Brewers SP7 8HE [St James St]: Nicely tucked away below steep famously photogenic Gold Hill, well divided open-plan plush-seated bar, log fire, lots of decorative plates, friendly staff; Fullers London Pride, Greene King Old Speckled Hen, Ringwood Best and Fortyniner, and one from St Austell or Sharps, reasonably priced wines, Stowford Press cider; food from baguettes up (children's helpings of any dish) inc good value Sun roasts, back dining room, skittle alley; children in eating areas, dogs in bar, picnic-sets in attractive good-sized garden with pretty views (Dr and Mrs M E Wilson, Colin and Janet Roe, LYM, Mr and Mrs Draper)

SHERBORNE [ST6316]

Half Moon DT9 3LN [Half Moon St]: Handy Marstons food pub with their ales from long counter, beams and wood floors, raised dining area, competitively priced usual food from bar snacks up (you may have to have a proper meal to use the bright and airy restaurant), friendly staff; piped music, games; bedrooms (Michael Dandy)

White Hart DT9 3PX [Cheap St]: Nooks and crannies in rambling old pub with enjoyable fresh local food at bargain prices, good service and well kept Badger ales (anon)

STOKE ABBOTT [ST4500]

New Inn DT8 3JW [off B3162 and B3163 2 miles W of Beaminster]: Spotless 17th-c thatched pub with friendly licensees and pleasant efficient service, well kept Palmers ales, traditional bar food at sensible prices from sandwiches up; log fire in big inglenook, beams, brasses and copper, some handsome panelling, paintings for sale, flagstoned dining room; occasional piped music; wheelchair access, children welcome, two lovely gardens, unspoilt quiet thatched village, good walks, bedrooms (LYM, Fred and Lorraine Gill)

STOURPAINE [ST8609]

White Horse DT11 8TA [Shaston Rd; A350 NW of Blandford]: Traditional country local carefully extended from original core; landlord/chef doing good choice of food from lunchtime sandwiches and bar meals to ambitious dishes (particularly evenings), bargain mid-week lunchtime, friendly prompt service, well kept Badger ales, sensible wine list, nice layout and décor, scrubbed tables; pool; bedrooms (Stan Edwards, Robert Watt)

STRATTON [SY6593]

Saxon Arms DT2 9WG [off A37 NW of Dorchester; The Square]: Traditional but recently built flint-and-thatch local, open-plan, bright and spacious, with open fire, part flagstones, part carpet, light oak tables and comfortable settles; prompt helpful service, well kept Greene King Ruddles County, Ringwood Best and Timothy Taylors Landlord, good value wines, wide choice of generous food inc fish and game, lunchtime set deals, large comfortable dining section on right, traditional games; piped music; children and dogs welcome, terrace tables overlooking village green, open all day wknds (Ian and Deborah Carrington, M G Hart, John and Tania Wood, LYM, Michael Dandy)

STURMINSTER MARSHALL [SY9500]

Red Lion BH21 4BU [opp church; off A350 Blandford—Poole]: New licensee at this attractive village pub opp the handsome church; welcoming bustling local atmosphere, wide choice of enjoyable imaginative home-made food inc good value wkdy set lunches and Sun roasts, efficient service, well kept Badger ales, nice wines,

old-fashioned roomy U-shaped bar with nice log fire, good-sized lived-in dining room in former skittle alley; piped music; children and dogs welcome, disabled access, back garden with wicker furniture and picnic-sets, open all day Sun (BB, I A Herdman, Peter Veness, Ann and Colin Hunt)

STURMINSTER NEWTON [ST7814]

Swan DT10 1AR [off A357 Blandford—Sherborne, via B3092; Market Pl]: Civilised beamed market-town bar with fireside sofa, panelling and stripped brick, well kept Badger ales, pleasant all-day dining area with good choice of usual food, friendly service; piped music; terrace and garden, good value bedrooms, open all day (Joan and Michel Hooper-Immins, LYM, Stan Edwards)

SWANAGE [SZ0278]

☆ *Red Lion* BH19 2LY [High St]: Busy low-beamed 17th-c two-bar local with friendly helpful landlord, good value simple food inc nice fish, wonderful choice of ciders, reasonably priced ales such as Caledonian Deuchars IPA, Flowers, Ringwood and Timothy Taylors Landlord; piped music, some live; children's games in large barn, picnic-sets in extended garden with partly covered back terrace, comfortable bedrooms in former back coach house, open all day (Ian and Barbara Rankin, the Didler)

SYMONDSBURY [SY4493]

☆ *Ilchester Arms* DT6 6HD [signed off A35 just W of Bridport]: Welcoming part-thatched old pub with new cheery landlord and attentive staff, good value lunchtime food from sandwiches up, wider evening range inc local fish, well kept Palmers ales, Taunton farm cider, nice wines; cosy rustic open-plan low-beamed bar with high-backed settle built in by inglenook, pretty restaurant with another fire; pub games, skittle alley doubling as family room (no children in bar); level entrance (steps from car park), tables in brookside back garden with play area, peaceful village, good walks (Malcolm and Kate Dowty, David and Julie Glover, LYM, George Atkinson, Joan and Michel Hooper-Immins, L Hawkins)

UPWEY [SY6785]

Old Ship DT3 5QQ [off A354; Ridgeway]: Quiet 16th-c beamed pub with traditional décor, lots of alcoves and log fires each end, new management doing enjoyable sensibly priced food, three real ales, friendly attentive staff; picnic-table sets in garden with terrace, interesting walks nearby (Phil and Jane Hodson, Alan Johnson, LYM)

WAREHAM [SY9287]

Duke of Wellington BH20 4NN [East St]: Small traditional 18th-c beamed pub with friendly service, half a dozen mainly local ales kept well, wide choice of reasonably priced food especially fish, some original features inc panelling, copper ornaments, old local photographs; piped music; back courtyard tables, bedrooms, open all day (the Didler, Mike Gorton)

Kings Arms BH20 4AD [North St (A351, N end of town)]: Traditional thatched town local with very well kept real ales, good value pubby food, friendly staff, back serving counter and two bars off flagstoned central corridor; children welcome, garden behind *(LYM, Matthew Cull)*

WAREHAM FOREST [SY9089]

Silent Woman BH20 7PA [Wareham—Bere Regis]: Deceptively big pub (originally row of cottages), well cared for by friendly hard-working licensees; civilised traditional lounge bar, with old log fire, extended into stripped-masonry dining area with country bygones, enjoyable home-made food, well kept Badger ales; dogs welcome, no children inside, wheelchair access, plenty of garden seating inc a covered area, walks nearby, seasonal opening – may be cl Sun evening, Mon, and open all day Sat *(Fiona Avery, Suzy Miller)*

WAYTOWN [SY4797]

Hare & Hounds DT6 5LQ [between B3162 and A3066 N of Bridport]: Attractive 18th-c country local up and down steps, friendly caring staff, well kept beers inc Palmers tapped from the cask, enjoyable good value food from sandwiches and baguettes up inc popular Sun lunch; coal fire, two small cottagey rooms and pretty dining room, no music; lovely Brit valley views from sizeable and unusual garden with good play area *(John Norton)*

WEST BEXINGTON [SY5386]

☆ *Manor Hotel* DT2 9DF [off B3157 SE of Bridport; Beach Rd]: Relaxing quietly set hotel with long history and fine sea views, comfortable log-fire lounge and bustling black-beamed cellar bar with another fire; helpful friendly staff, enjoyable bar food from sandwiches up, cream teas, Butcombe and Dorset beers, organic cider, quite a few malt whiskies and several wines by the glass, hot drinks, good restaurant with Victorian-style conservatory; piped music; service can be slow at busy times; dogs allowed in bar, charming well kept garden with plenty of picnic-sets, comfortable bedrooms, open all day *(LYM, Irene and Derek Flewin)*

WEST PARLEY [SZ0898]

Curlew BH22 8SQ [Christchurch Rd]: Vintage Inn in style of period house, nicely mixed furnishings in informal beamed areas around central bar, two log fires, enjoyable food, plenty of good value wines, friendly well trained staff; lots of tables outside *(David and Sally Frost)*

WEST STAFFORD [SY7289]

Wise Man DT2 8AG [signed off A352 Dorchester—Wareham]: 16th-c open-plan beamed pub nr Hardy's cottage, fully refurbished after bad thatch fire in 2006; flagstone and wood floors, enjoyable food from sandwiches up, Butcombe Bitter, Dorset Jurassic and Ringwood Best, good choice of wines by the glass; plenty of seats outside, lovely walks nearby *(Glenwys and Alan Lawrence, BB)*

WEYMOUTH [SY6878]

Excise House DT4 8TR [Hope Sq, by Brewers Quay]: Well worn-in pub in former brewery, decent beer, straightforward food; children welcome *(Colin Gooch)*

Ship DT4 8BE [Custom House Quay]: Neatly modern extended waterfront pub with several nautical-theme open-plan levels; three well kept Badger ales from long bar, good choice of wines by the glass, enjoyable good value usual food (only upstairs at night) from sandwiches, baguettes and ciabattas up; unobtrusive piped music; wheelchair access downstairs, some quayside seating and pleasant back terrace *(LYM, Gerry and Rosemary Dobson)*

Wellington Arms DT4 8PY [St Alban St]: Handsome green and gold 19th-c tiled façade, well restored panelled interior, carpets, banquettes, mirrors and lots of old local photographs; well kept Ringwood ales, bargain pubby food from sandwiches up inc a daily roast, friendly landlord; children welcome in back dining room, disabled access, open all day from 10am *(Joan and Michel Hooper-Immins, Phil and Jane Hodson, the Didler)*

WIMBORNE MINSTER [SU0100]

Olive Branch BH21 1PF [Hanham Rd/East Borough]: Opened-up 18th/19th-c town house, airy contemporary décor and coloured vases alongside handsome panelling and ceilings; welcoming service, up-to-date approach to enjoyable bistro food using local ingredients, good selection of west country cheeses, nice wine choice, well kept Badger ales, good coffee, big conservatory dining area; children welcome, picnic-sets on lawn running down to small river *(Dominic Barrington, Joan and Michel Hooper-Immins)*

Willett Arms BH21 1RN [Oakley Hill (B3073, just off A31/A341)]: Big comfortably refurbished chain pub popular for impressive choice of food from nice snacks to some good value inventive main dishes; helpful service, Ringwood Best, Fullers London Pride and Timothy Taylors Landlord, extensive wine list, log fire; large outside seating area *(Sue and Mike Todd, F J Tucker)*

WINFRITH NEWBURGH [SY8085]

Red Lion DT2 8LE [A352 Wareham—Dorchester]: Comfortable Badger family dining pub with their real ales, huge helpings of enjoyable food inc fresh fish, good wine choice, young attentive staff, beamy décor and candlelit tables to give old-fashioned atmosphere; TV room, piped music; children welcome, tables in big sheltered garden (site for caravans), good bedrooms *(David Lamb, Guy and Caroline Howard)*

WINTERBOURNE ABBAS [SY6190]

Coach & Horses DT2 9LU: Big roadside former coaching inn with long side dining area, wide choice of pubby food (all day Sun) from well filled rolls to popular carvery (must buy voucher at bar before queuing) and cook-at-the-table grills using volcanic rock; well kept Archers, Palmers and Ringwood Best, sensibly priced wines by the glass, pleasant service, unusual pictures, games end with darts and pool; piped music, Sun quiz night; children welcome, disabled access, a few picnic-sets outside, colourful hanging baskets, play area and aviary, five bedrooms *(Phil and Jane Hodson, BB)*

WOOL [SY8486]
Ship BH20 6EQ [Dorchester Rd (A352)]:

Roomy open-plan thatched and timbered family pub, enjoyable reasonably priced food all day from baguettes and baked potatoes up, small helpings available; low-ceilinged linked areas and plush back restaurant, friendly prompt service, well kept Badger ales, decent wines, good coffee; quiet piped music; picnic-sets overlooking railway in attractive fenced garden with terrace and play area, handy for Monkey World and Tank Museum, pleasant village *(William Ruxton)*

Essex

Essex has a good batch of traditional pubs that have resisted the urge to steamroller through with a stylish contemporary interior: the charming old Viper at Mill Green (good value), the Mole Trap at Stapleford Tawney, the bustling Hoop at Stock, and for its astonishing collection of horsebrasses and good value food the Green Man at Little Braxted. Half the Main Entries here have a beer award, and several tap a great range straight from the cask – nine at the White Hart at Margaretting Tye. The Chequers at Goldhanger comes in as a new entry for its all-round appeal, enjoyable food and great beers. Inspiring food is to be found at the Cricketers at Clavering (with vegetables from Jamie Oliver's organic garden, lovely bedrooms too), the Bell at Horndon-on-the-Hill, the Rose at Peldon (sensible prices) and the Sun at Dedham – good all round and our Essex Dining Pub of the Year. Notable Lucky Dip pubs are the Axe & Compasses at Arkesden, Crooked Billet in Leigh-on-Sea and Swan at Little Totham. Crouch Vale and Nethergate are the area's top brewers, with Brentwood, Saffron, Farmers and particularly, Mighty Oak also popular.

AYTHORPE RODING   TL5915   MAP 5

Axe & Compasses ◀
B184 S of Dunmow; CM6 1PP

Friendly roadside stop, nice balance of eating and drinking

Although popular with diners, locals also pop in for a pint at this neatly kept pub. Well kept beer is served from temperature-stabilised casks of ale racked behind the bar and broached in rotation as they come to their prime. Along with Nethergate IPA, three or four guests might be from local brewers such as Brentwood Best, Fen Red Fox and Saffron; also Weston's farm cider on handpump. The counter has comfortable bar chairs, with leatherette settles, stools and dark country chairs around a few pub tables on pale boards and turkey carpet; the original part on the left has dark old bent beams and wall timbers, with a two-way fireplace marking off a snug little raftered dining area, which has sentimental prints on dark masonry and a big open-faced clock; piped music. The small garden behind has stylish modern tables and chairs.

🍴 Tasty well presented food includes a range of bar nibbles such as mini yorkshire puddings, roast beef and shell-on prawns, starters such as devilled kidneys, oysters, guinea fowl and ox tongue with waldorf salad, main courses such as steak, stilton and oyster pie, mushroom and bread and butter stilton pudding with artichoke purée, cod and mushy peas, roast tuna wrapped in crispy potato with braised chicory, fennel and orange salad, grilled rib-eye steak, and puddings such as black cherry knickerbocker glory. *Starters/Snacks: £4.50 to £6.50. Main Courses: £9.95 to £15.95. Puddings: £5.50*

Free house ~ Licensee David Hunt ~ Real ale ~ Bar food (12-2.30, 6-9; 12-9(8 Sun) Sat) ~ Restaurant ~ (01279) 876648 ~ Children welcome ~ Dogs allowed in bar ~ Open 11-11 (11.30 Sat); 12-10.30 Sun

Recommended by Paul and Ursula Randall, Mrs Margo Finlay, Jörg Kasprowski

BIRCHANGER   TL5122   MAP 5

Three Willows

Under a mile from M11 junction 8: A120 towards Bishops Stortford, then almost immediately right to Birchanger Village; don't be waylaid earlier by the Birchanger Services signpost; CM23 5QR

Full of cricketing memorabilia, a happy civilised place serving good food

With the friendly landlord very much in evidence, this cricket-themed dining pub is popular with an older lunchtime set and is a reliable place for a good meal. You need to arrive early for a table as it can get very busy. The spacious carpeted main bar is full of cricketing prints, photographs, cartoons and other memorabilia, and there's a small well furnished lounge bar; fruit machine. Friendly attentive staff serve Greene King Abbot and IPA and a guest on handpump, and decent house wines. Though children are not welcome inside, there is plenty for them outside including a sturdy climbing frame, swings and a basketball hoop. There are picnic-sets out on a terrace (with heaters) and on the lawn behind (you can hear the motorway and Stansted Airport out here).

🍴 Besides a wide range of generously served pubby standards such as sandwiches, filled baked potatoes and ploughman's (all lunchtime only), steak and ale pie, steaks and vegetable curry, they serve quite a lot of fresh fish – maybe cod, tuna steak, crab salad and lemon sole. Puddings might include raspberry and hazelnut meringue and jaffa puddle pudding. *Starters/Snacks: £3.50 to £6.00. Main Courses: £8.95 to £14.95. Puddings: £3.90*

Greene King ~ Tenants Paul and David Tucker ~ Real ale ~ Bar food (12-2, 6-9.30) ~ (01279) 815913 ~ Dogs allowed in bar ~ Open 11.30-3, 6-11; 12-3 Sun; closed Sun evening

Recommended by KC, Mrs Margo Finlay, Jörg Kasprowski, John Saville, Roy Hoing, Stephen and Jean Curtis, Justin and Emma King, Mrs M K Matthews, J Marques, David and Valerie Mort, Grahame and Myra Williams

BURNHAM-ON-CROUCH   TQ9495   MAP 5

White Harte

The Quay; CM0 8AS

Lovely waterside position, and with an aptly nautical theme to the décor

You can relax watching yachts on the River Crouch from a handful of tables on a small jetty area just across the road from this comfortably old-fashioned hotel. Inside, the relaxed partly carpeted bars are filled with assorted nautical bric-a-brac and hardware – anything from models of Royal Navy ships to a compass set in the hearth. Other traditionally furnished high-ceilinged rooms have sea pictures on panelled or stripped brick walls, with cushioned seats around oak tables, and an enormous log fire making it cosy in winter. In summer they open the doors and windows, giving the place a nice airy feel. Charming staff serve Adnams and Crouch Vale Best from handpump.

🍴 Bar food includes lunchtime sandwiches, soup, steak and kidney pie, a choice of three local fish (cod, plaice and skate) and specials such as lasagne, curry and cottage pie. *Starters/Snacks: £2.90 to £4.60. Main Courses: £7.60 to £10.80. Puddings: £3.50 to £3.90*

Free house ~ Licensee G John Lewis ~ Real ale ~ Bar food ~ Restaurant ~ (01621) 782106 ~ Children welcome ~ Dogs allowed in bar and bedrooms ~ Open 11-11; 12-10.30 Sun ~ Bedrooms: £28(£62B)/£50(£82B)

Recommended by George Atkinson, LM, Hazel Morgan, Bernard Patrick, Tina and David Woods-Taylor, David Jackson

---

Bedroom prices normally include full english breakfast, VAT and any inclusive service charge that we know of. Prices before the '/' are for single rooms, after for two people in double or twin (B includes a private bath, S a private shower). If there is no '/', the prices are only for twin or double rooms (as far as we know there are no singles).

CLAVERING
TL4832   MAP 5

Cricketers

B1038 Newport—Buntingford, Newport end of village; CB11 4QT

Attractively updated traditional dining pub, very well run; a nice place to stay

There's the genuine feeling throughout this well run place that the longstanding licensees and friendly staff truly care about their customers. Recent years have seen a gentle freshening up of the décor, but it still cleverly keeps all its old-fashioned charm, with just a dash of extra sparkle from some new materials and furnishings. The main area has bays of deep purple button-back banquettes and neat padded leather dining chairs, dark floorboards, very low beams (the padding is a necessity, not a gimmick), and a big open fireplace. Back on the left is more obviously an eating part – two fairly compact carpeted areas, a step between them. The right side is similar but set more formally for dining, and has some big copper and brass pans on its dark beams and timbers. They have well kept Adnams Bitter and a couple of guests such as Woodfordes Wherry and Nelsons Revenge on handpump, Aspall's cider, over a dozen wines by the glass, freshly squeezed orange, pear and apple juices and good coffee; piped music. Signed books by son Jamie are on sale. The attractive front terrace has wicker-look seats around teak tables among colourful flowering shrubs.

As well as sandwiches, seasonal dishes (served with organic vegetables from Jamie's garden) are not cheap but then the ingredients are very good: starters such as ham and leek terrine, bruschetta of wild rocket and home-smoked wood pigeon with artichoke pesto, antipasti platter and smoked haddock and pea risotto, main courses such as bass on warm tomato and olive salad with basil crème fraîche, roast duck with fig and port jus, sautéed king scallops with chorizo, spring onions and saffron potatoes, steak and kidney pie with suet pastry, and puddings such as warm treacle tart with whisky and caramel ice-cream and vanilla and banana crème brûlée with scottish shortbread, and an english cheeseboard. *Starters/Snacks: £4.00 to £9.00. Main Courses: £8.00 to £17.00. Puddings: £6.00*

Free house ~ Licensee Trevor Oliver ~ Real ale ~ Bar food (12-2(2.30 Sun), 6.30-9.30) ~ Restaurant ~ (01799) 550442 ~ Children welcome ~ Open 10-11 ~ Bedrooms: £65B/£90B

Recommended by Philip Vernon, Kim Maidment, David and Ruth Hollands, Mrs Margo Finlay, Jörg Kasprowski, David and Valerie Mort, Evelyn and Derek Walter, J Marques, Mr and Mrs John Taylor, Mr and Mrs B Watt, Paul Humphreys, N R White

DEDHAM
TM0533   MAP 5

Sun

High Street (B2109); CO7 6DF

ESSEX DINING PUB OF THE YEAR

Popular stylish inn in Constable country, with seasonal italian food and an impressive wine selection

Readers are full of praise for this beautifully furnished old coaching inn. The building is lovely, and do look out for the particularly good coaching arch. High carved beams, squared panelling, wall timbers and big log fires in splendid fireplaces are the historic setting for high settles, sofas with sorbet coloured cushions and other good quality wooden tables and chairs. A charming little window seat in the bar looks across to the church, which is at least glimpsed in several of Constable's paintings. Relaxed and friendly but efficient young staff serve Adnams Broadside and Crouch Vale Brewers Gold and a couple of guests from brewers such as Acorn and Spectrum, a very good selection of more than 70 wines (20 by the glass) and some interesting soft drinks; TV, piped music and board games. On the way out to mature trees and picnic-sets on the quiet back lawn, notice the unusual covered back staircase with what used to be a dovecote on top, and if you have time, beautiful walks into the heart of Constable country lead out of the village, over water meadows towards Flatford Mill. The panelled bedrooms are nicely done with abundant character, and an annex houses their fruit and vegetable shop.

🍴 The menu here is now pretty determinedly italian. Food is not cheap but prices reflect the quality of the ingredients used in a menu which places much emphasis on seasonal game, fish, fruit and vegetables. The daily changing choice might include antipasti, spinach and garlic soup, mushroom risotto, meatballs with roast lemon potatoes and spinach, tagliatelle with lamb ragoût, grilled chicken with borlotti beans, and puddings such as panna cotta with rhubarb and orange, lemon and ricotta cheesecake. A few snacks include good sandwiches, a cold seafood platter and ploughman's. *Starters/Snacks: £6.00 to £10.00. Main Courses: £11.00 to £17.00. Puddings: £5.50 to £7.50*

Free house ~ Licensee Piers Baker ~ Real ale ~ Bar food (12-2.30(6 Fri-Sun), 6.30-9.30 (10 Fri, Sat)) ~ Restaurant ~ (01206) 323351 ~ Children welcome ~ Dogs allowed in bar ~ Open 11-11 ~ Bedrooms: /£130B

Recommended by Marion and Bill Cross, Felicity Davies, Terry and Jackie Devine, John and Enid Morris, Jean and Douglas Troup, John Saville, Sally Anne and Peter Goodale, Peter and Heather Elliott, Ryta Lyndley, N R White

GOLDHANGER
TL9008   MAP 5

Chequers 🍺
Just off B1026 E of Heybridge; The Square, Church Street; CM9 8AS

Good range of real ales in cheerful village pub, simple furnishings, friendly staff and popular bar food

This is an unspoilt old village pub looking across the churchyard, with good nearby estuary walks and plenty of bird-watching. There's a beamed central bar with simple pubby furnishings, Batemans XXXB, Caledonian Deuchars IPA and Wells & Youngs Bitter plus three changing guest beers on handpump, and friendly service from the cheerful staff; they hold regular beer festivals. Several rooms open off including the restaurant with plenty of wheelback chairs around tables set for dining; open fires, darts and bar billiards. There are picnic-sets under parasols on the back terrace.

🍴 Popular bar food includes lunchtime sandwiches, winter soup, duck and port pâté with cumberland sauce, thai mussels, ham and free-range eggs, jumbo beer-battered cod, asparagus, broccoli, pea and broad bean risotto, 8oz steakburger with bacon and emmenthal, chicken and bacon in a creamy stilton and leek sauce, jamaican jerk steak with crispy prawns, whole bass with fennel and thyme, and puddings like banana and toffee cheesecake and bread and butter pudding. *Starters/Snacks: £4.50 to £6.90. Main Courses: £8.25 to £13.90. Puddings: £4.65*

Punch ~ Lease Philip Glover ~ Real ale ~ Bar food (12-3, 6.30-9; not Sun evening or bank hol Mon evening) ~ Restaurant ~ (01621) 788203 ~ Children welcome except for one bar ~ Dogs allowed in bar ~ Open 11-11; 12-10.30 Sun

Recommended by Jean and David Lewis, Colin Smith, Susan and Nigel Wilson

GOSFIELD
TL7829   MAP 5

Kings Head
The Street (A1017 Braintree—Halstead); CO9 1TP

Comfortably contemporary dining pub with proper public bar

Bright splashes of colour warm the interior of this old beamed pub. The softly lit beamed main bar, with red panelled dado and ceiling, has neat modern black leather armchairs, bucket chairs and a settee as well as sturdy pale wood dining chairs and tables on its dark boards, and a log fire in a handsome old brick fireplace with big bellows. Black timbers mark off a red carpeted and walled dining area with red furnishings, opening into a carpeted conservatory; piped music. They have Adnams Bitter, Broadside and Timothy Taylors Landlord on handpump, a dozen wines by the glass and 29 single malts; daily papers. The good-sized quite separate public bar, with a purple pool table, darts and TV, has its own partly covered terrace; the main terrace has round picnic-sets.

🍴 Neat black-clad young staff serve dishes that include smoked duck breast with pesto mayonnaise, salmon roulade, chicken and mushroom pie, rib-eye steak with peppercorn sauce, home-made burger with a choice of toppings, grilled pork loin with suffolk cider sauce, venison and red wine sausages with onion and port gravy, grilled cod with coconut, chilli and coriander sauce, and puddings such as plum and almond tart with clotted cream and home-made fruit crumble. *Starters/Snacks: £7.25 to £10.50. Main Courses: £7.95 to £17.50. Puddings: £5.00*

Enterprise ~ Lease Mark Bloorfield ~ Real ale ~ Bar food (12-2.30, 6-9.30; 12-9.30(6 Sun) Sat) ~ Restaurant ~ (01787) 474016 ~ Children welcome ~ Dogs allowed in bar ~ Open 12-3, 6-11; 12-11 Sat; 12-10.30 Sun

Recommended by Patrick Reeve, Mrs Margo Finlay, Jörg Kasprowski

HASTINGWOOD
TL4807   MAP 5

Rainbow & Dove £

0.5 miles from M11 junction 7; Hastingwood signposted after Ongar signs at exit roundabout; CM17 9JX

Pleasantly traditional low-beamed pub with good value food; handy for M11

Freshened up with a coat of paint since last year, this unpretentious 16th-c cottage is not the biggest of pubs and as the very reasonably priced pubby food is popular it's worth getting here early. Of the three little low-beamed rooms opening off the main bar area, the one on the left is particularly beamy, with the lower part of its wall stripped back to bare brick and decorated with brass pistols and plates. Adnams Broadside, Greene King IPA and possibly a guest are on handpump, with ten wines by the glass; piped music, winter darts and occasional jazz nights. Hedged off from the car park, a stretch of grass has picnic-sets; dogs welcome lunchtimes only.

🍽 **Good value traditional meals include lunchtime sandwiches and baked baguettes as well as ploughman's, chicken or vegetable curry, steak, kidney and ale pie and battered cod, with puddings such as apple pie or spotted dick.** *Starters/Snacks: £3.95 to £7.95. Main Courses: £7.50 to £13.65. Puddings: £3.90 to £4.10*

Punch ~ Lease Andrew Keep and Kathryn Chivrall ~ Real ale ~ Bar food (12-2.30(3 Sun), 7-9.30) ~ (01279) 415419 ~ Children welcome ~ Dogs welcome ~ Open 11.30-3, 6-11.30; 12-3.30, 6-midnight Sat; 12-4 Sun; closed Sun evening

Recommended by Colin and Janet Roe, Tim and Claire Woodward, John Saville, Gordon and Margaret Ormondroyd, Jerry Brown, David and Sue Smith, Jeremy King, David Greene

HORNDON-ON-THE-HILL
TQ6783   MAP 3

Bell ♀ 🍺 🛏

M25 junction 30 into A13, then left into B1007 after 7 miles, village signposted from here; SS17 8LD

Very popular historic pub with mostly restauranty food and very good range of drinks

Although imaginative food is the key point at this beautiful Tudor inn, the heavily beamed bar does have an appealing pubby appearance with its lovely high-backed antique settles and benches, and rugs on the flagstones and highly polished oak floorboards. Look out for the curious collection of ossified hot cross buns hanging along a beam in the saloon bar. The first was put there some 90 years ago to mark the day (it was a Good Friday) that Jack Turnell became licensee. During the war, privations demanded that they hang a concrete bun. The hanging tradition continues to this day, but now the oldest person in the village (or available on the day) hangs the bun. An impressive range of drinks includes Bass (tapped straight from the cask), Greene King IPA and Crouch Vale Brewers Gold with three guests, and over a hundred well chosen wines (16 by the glass). You do need to get here early or book as tables are often all taken soon after opening time.

🍽 **As well as two or three pubbier dishes such as sausage and mash and salmon and smoked haddock fishcakes, the changing menu might include parsnip soup with maple crème fraîche, crispy crab ravioli on spinach and chive velouté, carpaccio of pigeon with** rabbit won ton on hazelnut, apple and lettuce salad, veal kidney fricassée with mushroom cappuccino and wilted rocket, ginger and soy marinated duck breast with plum compote and hollandaise sauce, roast wild rabbit and fried beef fillet with mushroom duxelles, and with puddings such as dark chocolate tart with pistachio ice-cream, lemon posset blueberry compote, sesame seed tuile and pear sorbet, and a british cheeseboard with red onion marmalade. *Starters/Snacks: £4.95 to £9.00. Main Courses: £10.50 to £21.95. Puddings: £5.10 to £6.95*

Free house ~ Licensee John Vereker ~ Real ale ~ Bar food (12-1.45, 6.30-9.45; 12-2.15, 7-9.45 Sun; no food bank hol Mons) ~ Restaurant ~ (01375) 642463 ~ Children in eating area of bar and restaurant ~ Dogs allowed in bar and bedrooms ~ Open 11-2.30, 5.30-11; 11-3, 6-11 Sat; 12-4, 7-10.30 Sun ~ Bedrooms: £59B/£68B

Recommended by Sandra Harrold, Gordon and Margaret Ormondroyd, Stephen Mowatt, Mrs Margo Finlay, Jörg Kasprowski, John and Enid Morris, John Silverman, Penny Turko

LITTLE BRAXTED

TL8413   MAP 5

Green Man £

Kelvedon Road; village signposted off B1389 by NE end of A12 Witham bypass – keep on patiently; OS Sheet 168 map reference 848133; CM8 3LB

Prettily traditional brick-built pub with a garden and reasonably priced food

Completely unravaged by the recent trend for modern sofas and refurbishments, this homely place is thoroughly traditional, even boasting a collection of some 200 or more horsebrasses, along with harnesses, mugs hanging from beams, tankards over the bar, a lovely copper urn and plenty of pictures and notices. Patterned carpets, little curtained windows and windsor chairs lend a cottagey atmosphere, and in winter, the traditional little lounge is especially appealing with its warm open fire. The tiled public bar has books, darts, cards, cribbage and dominoes, and friendly staff serve Greene King IPA, Abbot and Ruddles and possibly a guest, and nine wines by the glass. Picnic-sets in the pleasant sheltered garden behind are a good place to while away an hour or two. More reports please.

🍴 **Good sensibly priced food in generous helpings includes lunchtime sandwiches and warm baguettes, soup, ploughman's, baked potatoes, sausage and mash, and specials such as minted lamb shank in redcurrant gravy, thai chicken curry or steak and kidney pudding, and good home-made puddings.** *Starters/Snacks: £2.75 to £3.95. Main Courses: £5.75 to £9.50. Puddings: £3.50*

Greene King ~ Tenant Matthew Ruffle ~ Real ale ~ Bar food (12-2.30, 6-9; 12-6 Sun) ~ Restaurant ~ (01621) 891659 ~ Children until 8pm ~ Dogs allowed in bar ~ Open 11.30-3, 5-11; 12-11 Sun

Recommended by Hazel Morgan, Bernard Patrick, Alvin and Yvonne Andrews, Mr and Mrs John Taylor, Penny Lang

LITTLE WALDEN

TL5441   MAP 5

Crown

B1052 N of Saffron Walden; CB10 1XA

Bustling 18th-c cottage with a warming log fire and hearty food

Décor at this homely low-ceilinged local is traditional, with bookroom-red walls, floral curtains, bare boards and navy carpeting. A higgledy-piggledy mix of chairs ranges from high-backed pews to little cushioned armchairs spaced around a good variety of closely arranged tables, mostly big, some stripped. The small red tiled room on the right has two little tables. They light a fire in one of the three fireplaces, though not in the unusual walk-through one! Four changing beers are tapped straight from casks racked up behind the bar – normally Adnams Best, City of Cambridge Boathouse, Greene King Abbot and Woodfordes Wherry; piped light music; disabled access. Tables out on the terrace take in views of surrounding tranquil countryside; they are planning new bedrooms.

🍴 **The fairly traditional bar food is good value and popular, so you may need to book at**

weekends: sandwiches, including a delicious hot pork baguette (not Sun), whitebait, salmon fishcakes, steak and mushroom pie, four cheese ravioli, lasagne, cod fillet, rib-eye steak, and puddings such as fruit crumble and bread and butter pudding; Sunday roasts *Starters/Snacks: £4.25 to £6.95. Main Courses: £8.25 to £12.95. Puddings: £3.50 to £4.50*

Free house ~ Licensee Colin Hayling ~ Real ale ~ Bar food (not Sun and Mon evenings) ~ Restaurant ~ (01799) 522475 ~ Children welcome ~ Dogs welcome ~ Trad jazz Weds evening ~ Open 11.30-3, 6-11; 12-10 Sun ~ Bedrooms: £55S/£65S

Recommended by the Didler, David Jackson, R T and J C Moggridge

MARGARETTING TYE
TL6801 MAP 5

White Hart ◀

From B1002 (just S of A12/A414 junction) follow Maldon Rd for 1.3 miles, then turn right immediately after river bridge, into Swan Lane, keeping on for 0.7 miles; The Tye; CM4 9JX

Fine choice of ales tapped from the cask in cheery country pub with good family garden

The neatly kept exterior of this cream-painted weatherboarded pub makes a good impression as soon as your arrive here. Inside, the open-plan yet cottagey interior has walls and wainscoting newly painted in chalky pastel colours, a mix of attractive old chairs and a stuffed deer's head mounted on the chimney breast above the woodburning stove. A neat back conservatory on the right has dark tiles, John Ireland brewing cartoons, and the front lobby has a charity paperback table; darts, quiz machine, skittles, board games and piped music. They keep an impressive range of nine well kept real ales, all tapped straight from the cask. Besides well kept Adnams Best and Broadside and Mighty Oak IPA and Oscar Wilde, they bring on a constant stream of nationwide guest beers from brewers such as Archers, Farmers Ales and Nethergate. They do takeaways and have interesting bottled beers, too, and during their popular June and October beer festivals have up to 60 beers a day; winter mulled wine. There are plenty of picnic-sets out on grass and terracing around the pub, with a sturdy play area, a safely fenced duck pond, an aviary with noisy cockatiels (they don't quite drown the larks) and pens of rabbits, guinea-pigs and a pygmy goat. Dogs are very welcome, they even have towels in the porch for a clean-up before pooch goes in. By the time this edition is in the shops, their new bedrooms should be open – do let us know how you find them if you stay here.

🍴 **Bar food includes sandwiches, pâté of the day, fried camembert with fruit coulis, king prawn cocktail, baked bass, steak and ale pie, liver and bacon, seasonal game dishes, battered catch of the day, leek, red onion and feta quiche (the chef is vegetarian so the vegetarian dishes here should be good), and puddings such as mixed berry cheesecake, hot chocolate fudge cake and home-made crumbles and pies.** *Starters/Snacks: £3.75 to £5.95. Main Courses: £7.00 to £19.95. Puddings: £3.00 to £5.50*

Free house ~ Licensee Elizabeth Haines ~ Real ale ~ Bar food (12-2(3 Sat, 4 Sun), 6.30-9(9.30 Sat, 8.30 Sun); not Mon evening) ~ (01277) 840478 ~ Children in conservatory ~ Dogs welcome ~ Open 11.30-3, 6-midnight; 11.30(Sun)-midnight Sat ~ Bedrooms: /£60B

Recommended by Mrs J Slowgrove, Evelyn and Derek Walter, David Jackson, Robert Turnham, Mrs Roxanne Chamberlain, Paul and Ursula Randall

MILL GREEN
TL6401 MAP 5

Viper ◀ £

The Common; from Fryerning (which is signposted off NE bound A12 Ingatestone bypass) follow Writtle signposts; CM4 0PT

Delightfully unpretentious with local ales, simple pub food and no modern intrusions

Tucked quietly away in the woods, this timeless old local is charmingly unspoilt. Its cosy little lounge rooms have spindleback and armed country kitchen chairs and tapestried wall seats around neat little old tables, and there's a log fire. Booted walkers (and dogs) are directed towards the fairly basic parquet-floored tap room, which is more simply furnished with shiny wooden traditional wall seats and a coal fire. Beyond, another room has country kitchen chairs and sensibly placed darts, also dominoes and cribbage; the pub cat is Millie and the white west highland terrier is Jimmy. They stock an interesting range of five well kept beers on handpump: Viper (produced for the pub by Nethergate), local brewery Mighty Oak Jake the Snake and Oscar Wilde and a couple of quickly changing guests from brewers such as JHB and Nethergate; also Wilkins' farm cider, straight from the barrel. Live bands play during their Easter and August beer festivals. Tables on the lawn overlook a beautifully tended cottage garden – a dazzling mass of colour in summer, further enhanced at the front by overflowing hanging baskets and window boxes. Morris men often dance here.

🍴 Simple but tasty bar snacks might include sandwiches, soup, steak and ale pie, curry and lasagne; Sunday roasts. The tasty bread comes from a local baker a mile or so down the road. Starters/Snacks: £3.50 to £4.95. Main Courses: £6.95 to £8.95. Puddings: £3.95 to £4.95

Free house ~ Licensees Peter White and Donna Torris ~ Real ale ~ Bar food (12-2(3 Sat, Sun); not evenings) ~ No credit cards ~ (01277) 352010 ~ Dogs welcome ~ Open 12-2, 6-11; 12-11(10.30 Sun) Sat

Recommended by N R White, Mrs Roxanne Chamberlain, the Didler

PELDON   TM0015   MAP 5

Rose 🍴 � 🛏

B1025 Colchester—Mersea (do not turn left to Peldon village); CO5 7QJ

Friendly dining pub in an appealing building with good food, thoughtful staff and great wine choice

Doing very well under its friendly new landlady, this appealing pastel-coloured old inn has a delightfully traditional interior, with standing timbers supporting the heavy low ceilings with their dark bowed 17th-c oak beams, alcoves that conjure up smugglers plotting over bygone contraband, little leaded-light windows and a gothick-arched brick fireplace. There are creaky close-set tables and some antique mahogany and padded wall banquettes. In contrast, the very spacious airy conservatory dining area (disabled access), with views over the garden, has a modern brightly lit feel. On handpump are Adnams Best and Broadside, Greene King IPA and an interesting guest. As the pub is run by the Essex wine merchant Lay & Wheeler, they have a very good wine list, with about 25 by the glass, listed with helpful descriptions on a blackboard. Friendly efficient table service throughout emphasises the dining aspect and, as it can get very busy, you do need to book. The spacious garden is relaxing, with good teak seats and ducks on a pretty pond; good breakfasts.

🍴 Much enjoyed, changing bar food (prices remain sensible) might include interesting sandwiches, starters such as tiger prawn and cashew nut stir fry on rice noodles, caramelised tomato and balsamic tart, main courses such as chicken curry, duck breast with cranberry jus, creamed leek and asparagus filo tart, fried cod and chips, sword fish with ratatouille and pesto, and puddings such as white chocolate and raspberry mousse, baked vanilla and rhubarb cheesecake and toffee and date crème brûlée. Starters/Snacks: £3.50 to £8.75. Main Courses: £9.25 to £12.95. Puddings: £1.60 to £4.95

Lay & Wheeler ~ Licensee Annie Reidy ~ Real ale ~ Bar food (12-2.15, 6.30-9(9.30 Fri, Sat); 12-9(6 in winter) Sun) ~ Restaurant ~ (01206) 735248 ~ Children welcome away from bar ~ Open 11-11; 12-10.30 Sun; 12-7 Sun in winter ~ Bedrooms: £40S/£60S

Recommended by P and J Shapley, Mrs P Lang, David Jackson, Evelyn and Derek Walter, Gordon Neighbour, Mandy and Simon King, John and Enid Morris, Mike and Mary Carter

---

The letters and figures after the name of each town are its Ordnance Survey map reference. 'Using the *Guide*' at the beginning of the book explains how it helps you find a pub, in road atlases or large-scale maps as well as in our own maps.

PLESHEY   TL6614   MAP 5

White Horse

The Street; CM3 1HA

Ancient inn nicely packed to the gills with knick-knacks and crafts

---

As the good value food is popular, you will need to book if you want to eat at this friendly old village pub. It's crammed with cheerful clutter, sells crafts, locally made preserves, greetings cards and gifts, and even has its own little art gallery. Furnishings take in wheelback chairs and tables with cloths, and a fireplace has an unusual curtain-like fireguard. Glass cabinets in the big, sturdily furnished dining room are filled with lots of miniatures and silverware, and there are flowers on tables. A snug room by the tiny bar counter has brick and beamed walls, a comfortable sofa, some bar stools and a table with magazines to read. Sharps Doom Bar is tapped straight from the cask and they've several wines by the glass; piped music. Doors from here open on to a terrace and a grass area with trees, shrubs and tables. The pub hosts monthly jazz buffets (not in summer) and a midsummer barbecue.

🍴 **Enjoyable fairly priced bar food includes fried brie wedges with mango chutney, prawn cocktail, fried herring roes on toast, steak and kidney pie, rabbit poached in cider with creamy mushroom sauce, chicken breast with spicy coconut sauce, duck casserole with orange sauce and roast rack of lamb, with puddings such as toffee apple fudge cake and dark chocolate truffle cake.** *Starters/Snacks: £5.00 to £7.50. Main Courses: £9.50 to £15.50. Puddings: £3.95*

Free house ~ Licensees Mike and Jan Smail ~ Real ale ~ Bar food (12-3(4.30 Sun), 7-9) ~ Restaurant ~ (01245) 237281 ~ Children welcome ~ Dogs allowed in bar ~ Open 11.30-3, 6.30-11; 12-4.30 Sun; closed Tues, Weds evening, all day Mon

Recommended by Roy and Lindsey Fentiman, Marion and Bill Cross, Philip Denton, David Jackson

STAPLEFORD TAWNEY   TL5001   MAP 5

Mole Trap 🍺

Tawney Common, which is a couple of miles away from Stapleford Tawney and is signposted off A113 just N of M25 overpass – keep on; OS Sheet 167 map reference 500013; CM16 7PU

Tucked away but humming with customers, traditionally run with an interesting selection of guest beers

---

One reader tells us this isolated little country pub (do persevere down the country lane to get here) is 'just as I remember so many pubs in my youth'. It's run with considerable old-fashioned individuality and is the sort of place to fall into easy chat with the locals who prop themselves along the counter. The smallish carpeted bar (mind your head as you go in) has a black dado, beams and joists, brocaded wall seats, library chairs and bentwood elbow chairs around plain pub tables, and steps down through a partly knocked-out timber stud wall to a similar area. There are a few small pictures, 3-D decorative plates, some dried-flower arrangements and (on the sloping ceiling formed by a staircase beyond) some regulars' snapshots, with a few dozen beermats stuck up around the serving bar, and warming fires; quiet piped radio. As well as Fullers London Pride on handpump, they have three constantly changing guests from smaller brewers such as Harviestoun and Nethergate. The pub fills up quickly at lunchtimes, so it's worth getting here early if you want to eat. Outside are some plastic tables and chairs and a picnic-set, and a happy tribe of resident animals, many rescued, including friendly cats, rabbits, a couple of dogs, hens, geese, a sheep, goats and horses. Do make sure children behave well, and note that food service stops promptly, sometimes even before the allotted time.

🍴 **Besides sandwiches and popular Sunday roasts, tasty food includes ploughman's, lasagne, steak and kidney pie, ham, egg and chips and a vegetarian option like quiche, with traditional home-made puddings such as cherry and apple pie and lemon meringue pie.** *Starters/Snacks: £3.95 to £6.50. Main Courses: £8.95 to £10.50. Puddings: £3.95*

Free house ~ Licensees Mr and Mrs Kirtley ~ Real ale ~ Bar food (not Sun, Mon evenings) ~ No credit cards ~ (01992) 522394 ~ Open 11.30-2.30(3 Sat, 4 Sun), 6-11(10.30 Sun)

Recommended by David Jackson, the Didler, R T and J C Moggridge, Evelyn and Derek Walter, P and J Shapley, Mrs Roxanne Chamberlain, David and Valerie Mort

STOCK

TQ6999   MAP 5

Hoop 🍺

B1007; from A12 Chelmsford bypass take Galleywood, Billericay turn-off; CM4 9BD

Happy weatherboarded pub with interesting range of beers and large garden

With all its wood fixtures and fittings, including a bare board floor, wooden tables and brocaded wooden settles, the fairly simple interior of this old weatherboarded pub feels pubbily functional – just the right down-to-earth setting for the cheery locals and visitors enjoying the happy bustle here. Standing timbers and beams in the open-plan bar hint at the building's great age and its original layout as a row of three weavers' cottages. In winter, a warm fire burns in a big brick walled fireplace. Friendly staff serve Adnams and Hoop, Stock and Barrel (brewed for the pub by Brentwood) on handpump, and three guests from brewers such as Crouch Vale, Mighty Oak and Wells & Youngs. The pub opens all day during the eight days of their beer festival around the May summer bank holiday, when you'll have the chance to enjoy over 160 real ales and 60 ciders and perries. A restaurant up in the timbered eaves is light and airy with pale timbers set in white walls and more wood flooring. Prettily bordered with flowers, the large sheltered back garden has picnic-sets and a covered seating area.

🍽 **Very pubby food includes sandwiches, ploughman's, baked potatoes, potted shrimps, battered fish and chips, shepherd's pie, fish pie, toad in the hole, ham, egg and chips, rib-eye steak, and puddings such as bread and butter pudding and mixed berry pavlova.** *Starters/Snacks: £4.00 to £6.00. Main Courses: £6.00 to £10.00. Puddings: £4.00 to £5.00*

Free house ~ Licensee Michelle Corrigan ~ Real ale ~ Bar food (12-2.30(3 Sat, 5 Sun), 6-9(9.30 Fri, Sat); not Sun evening) ~ Restaurant ~ (01277) 841137 ~ Children welcome away from bar ~ Dogs allowed in bar ~ Open 11-11(11.30Sat); 12-10.30 Sun

Recommended by MJVK, John Saville, John and Enid Morris, DFL, Louise English, Mrs Margo Finlay, Jörg Kasprowski, John Prescott, Edward Mirzoeff

STOW MARIES

TQ8399   MAP 5

Prince of Wales 🍺

B1012 between South Woodham Ferrers and Cold Norton Posters; CM3 6SA

Unfussy local with interesting beers

The licensee at this little white weatherboard pub was a co-founder of Crouch Vale Brewery so you can be sure that the half a dozen widely sourced guests here, from brewers such as Dark Star, Hopback, Newby Wyke and Titanic, will be well kept. He also stocks bottled and draught belgian beers and fruit beers. Few of the characterful little low-ceilinged rooms have space for more than one or two tables and wall benches on their tiled or bare-boards floors, though the room in the middle squeezes in quite a jumble of chairs and stools. There are seats and tables in the back garden and a new terrace leading to a new conservatory dining area. Between the picket fence and the pub's weatherboarded frontage is a terrace (with herbs in Victorian chimneypots) sheltered by a huge umbrella. More reports please.

🍽 **Besides filled ciabattas, the bar menu includes burgers, garlic prawns, whitebait and ham, egg and chips, with over a dozen specials such as battered fish and chips, pies, skate, lasagne and rib-eye steak. On winter Thursday evenings they fire up the old bread oven to make pizzas in the room that was once the village bakery, and on some summer Sundays, they barbecue steaks and all sorts of fish such as mahi-mahi and black barracuda.** *Starters/Snacks: £2.50 to £4.95. Main Courses: £5.45 to £13.95. Puddings: £3.95 to £4.95*

Free house ~ Licensee Rob Walster ~ Real ale ~ Bar food (12-2.30, 7(6 Fri, Sat)-9.30, 12-9 Sun) ~ Restaurant ~ (01621) 828971 ~ Children in family room ~ Live music third Thurs of month ~ Open 11(12 Sun)-11(midnight Fri, Sat) ~ Bedrooms: £45B/£68B

Recommended by John Saville, David Jackman, David Jackson, N R White

WENDENS AMBO

TL5136   MAP 5

Bell

B1039 just W of village; CB11 4JY

Cheery local with pubby bar food and entertaining play area in big garden

This deep pink wonky fronted old village inn has found its way back into the *Guide* thanks to its efficient new landlady. The small cottagey low-ceilinged rooms are traditional and pubby with locals gathered for a pint around the little serving counter, brasses on ancient timbers, wheelback chairs around neat tables, comfortably cushioned seats worked into snug alcoves, quite a few pictures on cream walls and an inviting open fire. Adnams and Woodfordes Wherry are well kept on handpump, along with a couple of changing guests from brewers such as Saffron and Timothy Taylors, also Weston's Old Rosie; during the August bank holiday weekend they bring in dozens of real ales for their beer and music festival. The extensive back garden has a suntrap terrace leading to a big tree-sheltered lawn and a great timber play area that should keep kids entertained for a while; board games and piped music.

🍴 Tasty food includes filled baguettes, smoked salmon and capers, curry of the day, sausages and mash, fish and chips, steak, mushroom and ale or fish pie, sirloin steak, goats cheese and red onion marmalade puff pastry tart, and changing specials such as roasted mediterranean vegetables and slow-roasted belly of pork; good Sunday lunches. *Starters/Snacks: £3.50 to £6.50. Main Courses: £7.00 to £12.00. Puddings: £3.50 to £5.00*

Free house ~ Licensee Anne Güney ~ Real ale ~ Bar food (12-3, 6.30-9 (not Sun evening and Mon)) ~ Restaurant ~ (01799) 540382 ~ Children welcome ~ Dogs welcome ~ Open 11.30-3, 5-11.30; 11(12 Sun)-midnight Fri, Sat

Recommended by Mrs Margo Finlay, Jörg Kasprowski, Eddie Edwards, Jerry Brown, Andrew Scarr

LUCKY DIP

Besides the fully inspected pubs, you might like to try these Lucky Dips recommended to us and described by readers (if you do, please send us reports: feedback@goodguides.com).

ARKESDEN [TL4834]
☆ **Axe & Compasses** CB11 4EX [off B1038]: Thatched pub with welcoming greek cypriot licensees doing wide range of good if not cheap food; good choice of wines by the glass, efficient service, Greene King ales, easy chairs, upholstered oak and elm seats, open fire and china trinkets in cosy lounge bar, built-in settles in smaller public bar with darts and board games, restaurant allowing children; pretty hanging baskets, new furniture on side terrace, beautiful village *(Philip and Jan Medcalf, Andrew Scarr, David Jackson, DFL, LYM)*

BELCHAMP ST PAUL [TL7942]
Half Moon CO10 7DP [Cole Green]: Thatched pub with well kept beers, generous good value honest food, friendly attentive service, snug beamed lounge, open fire, cheerful locals' bar, restaurant; children welcome, tables out in front and in back garden *(LYM)*

BLACKMORE [TL6001]
Prince Albert CM4 0RT [The Green]: Friendly local with several linked areas around central servery, wide choice of home-made food inc good fresh fish and Sun lunch, Fullers London Pride and Greene King IPA, pool in outbuilding; children welcome, nice village-green location nr duck pond *(Karen Sloan)*

BOREHAM [TL7509]
Queens Head CM3 3EG [Church Rd, off B1137 Chelmsford—Hatfield Peverel]: Traditional friendly local tucked away by church, homely and spotless, with well kept Adnams, Crouch Vale Brewers Gold, Greene King IPA and Woodfordes Wherry; good service, simple tasty home-cooked food (not Sun evening) inc Sun roast, snug beams-and-brickwork saloon, more tables down one side of long public bar with darts at end; may be piped music; small garden, good walks *(Clare Phillips, J Woodgate)*

BRENTWOOD [TQ5993]
Artichoke CM15 8DZ [Shenfield Common]: Large, friendly and popular Toby Carvery,

enjoyable good value fresh food (expect queues at busy times – particularly Sun lunch), interesting blow-ups of old postcards *(Karen Sloan, Robert Lester)*

BULMER TYE [TL8438]

Fox CO10 7EB [A131 S of Sudbury]: Well refurbished and popular with welcoming bustling staff, wide range of enjoyable food inc good value set meals, vegetarian options and bargain taster-size puddings; Greene King IPA and local beers from small bar on left, pleasant conservatory; terrace tables *(Mrs P Lang, Mrs Anna Glover, Oliver and Sue Rowell, John Prescott)*

BURNHAM-ON-CROUCH [TQ9596]

Ship CM0 8AA [High St]: Welcoming Adnams pub with efficient friendly service, enjoyable generous food inc Sun lunches, reasonable prices, attractive nautical-theme interior; comfortable bedrooms *(Andy Lickfold)*

CHATHAM GREEN [TL7115]

Windmill CM3 3LE: Doing well under friendly newish management, good value pub food in small beamed and flagstoned bar and dining room, well kept Fullers London Pride, Mighty Oak Burntwood and a Greene King beer labelled for the pub, reasonably priced wines by the glass, helpful staff; a few picnic-sets outside, seven bedrooms in remains of former windmill, open all day Sat, till 7pm Sun *(Paul and Ursula Randall, Roy and Lindsey Fentiman, Mark Morgan, Edith Pateman)*

CHELMSFORD [TL7107]

☆ *Alma* CM1 7RG [Arbour Lane, off B1137]: Upscale pub/restaurant under newish management, airy contemporary décor, good food from lunchtime ciabattas, bar dishes and bargain off-season lunches up, friendly polite service, open fires, leather sofas and flagstones in bar with real ales such as Adnams Broadside and Greene King IPA, good choice of wines by the glass, smart dining area; piped music; pleasant tables outside, children welcome in restaurant, open all day *(Mike and Mary Carter, LYM, Mrs Margo Finlay, Jörg Kasprowski)*

☆ *Queens Head* CM2 0AS [Lower Anchor St]: Lively well run Victorian side-street local with well kept Crouch Vale ales and interesting changing guests; summer farm cider, good value wines, friendly staff, winter log fires, bargain lunchtime food from doorstep sandwiches up (not Sun); children welcome, colourful courtyard, open all day *(the Didler, PHB)*

Railway Tavern CM1 1LW [Duke St]: Small welcoming railway-theme local with well kept ales inc Greene King Abbot, bargain freshly made simple lunchtime food, afternoon sandwiches, back seating area done like a railway carriage; pleasant garden behind *(Joe Green, PHB)*

Riverside CM2 6LJ [Victoria Rd]: Open-plan weatherboarded watermill conversion, low heavy beams, dark corners and some mill gearing, well kept Wells & Youngs ales and a guest, food from light dishes up in bar and separate restaurant; attractive waterside

terrace and decking, well thought-out bedrooms *(Joe Green, DFL)*

Rose & Crown CM1 2PD [Rainsford Rd (A1060 W)]: Pleasantly refurbished pub/restaurant with particularly good value food, well kept Greene King IPA, friendly courteous staff, open fires *(Bruce M Drew)*

CHIGNALL SMEALY [TL6711]

Pig & Whistle CM1 4SZ [NW of Chelmsford; Chignall Rd, just S of village]: Popular for its sensibly priced home-made food and well kept Shepherd Neame ales; traditional pub atmosphere with beams, soft lighting and pleasantly compact tables, collection of rag/straw dolls; may not accept credit cards; children welcome, terrace tables with wide views *(Roy and Lindsey Fentiman, Paul and Ursula Randall)*

CHIGWELL [TQ4493]

Blue Bell IG7 6QQ [High Rd]: Enjoyable food in agreeable surroundings, attentive service *(Patti Mickelson)*

CHRISHALL [TL4439]

Red Cow SG8 8RN [High St; off B1039 Wendens Ambo—Gt Chishill]: Recently refurbished 14th-c thatched pub with lots of atmosphere, beams and open fire, good home-made food, well kept beers, imaginative wine list; nice garden *(P and D Carpenter)*

CLACTON ON SEA [TM1716]

Robin Hood CO15 4ED [London Rd]: Traditional dimly lit refurbishment with enjoyable bargain food, good choice of beers, sensibly priced wines and nice coffee, pleasant efficient staff; children welcome, tables in nice garden *(Ryta Lyndley)*

COGGESHALL [TL8224]

☆ *Compasses* CM77 8BG [Pattiswick, signed off A120 W]: Attractively reworked as more country restaurant than pub, good choice of enjoyable food using local produce, also cheaper set menu (Mon-Fri) and children's meals; well kept Woodfordes Wherry, good wine choice, cheerful attentive staff, neatly comfortable spacious beamed bars and barn restaurant with good-sized tables; plenty of lawn and orchard tables, rolling farmland beyond *(LYM, Charles Gysin, R K Phillips, Michael Booth, Mrs P Lang)*

COLCHESTER [TM9824]

Hospital Arms CO3 3HA [Crouch St (opp hospital)]: Friendly pub with several small linked areas, wide range of good condition Adnams ales, enjoyable pubby food from sandwiches and baguettes up, home of Colchester RFC; games machines *(Kevin Flack, Pat and Tony Martin)*

COLNE ENGAINE [TL8530]

Five Bells CO6 2HY [signed off A1124 (was A604) in Earls Colne; Mill Lane]: Welcoming traditional village pub with good home-made food using local produce inc some modern bistro-style dishes, well kept Greene King ales; friendly efficient service, woodburner and old photographs in lounge/dining room, public bar, no music; attractive front terrace with gentle views *(Penny Lang)*

ELMDON [TL4639]

Elmdon Dial CB11 4NH [Heydon Lane]: Well

refurbished and looked after with good home-made food from sandwiches, panini and unpretentious pubby things up, charming staff, well kept ales such as Mighty Oak Oscar Wilde and Timothy Taylors Landlord, bar, snug and restaurant; opp church with unusual 17th-c stained-glass sundial (hence pub's name), cl Mon *(Mrs Jane Kingsbury)*

EPPING FOREST [TL4501]

Forest Gate CM16 4DZ [Bell Common]: Large friendly open-plan pub dating from 17th c, good mix of customers, well kept Adnams, Nethergate and guest beers, enjoyable home-made bar food; tables on front lawn *(the Didler)*

FEERING [TL8720]

☆ *Sun* CO5 9NH [Feering Hill, B1024]: Interesting old pub with 16th-c beams (watch out for the very low one over the inner entrance door), plenty of bric-a-brac, woodburners in huge inglenook fireplaces, nice carved bar counter with half a dozen well kept ales, efficient service, enjoyable food from sandwiches up, daily papers, board games; well behaved children allowed, partly covered paved terrace, attractive garden behind, some wknd barbecues *(LYM, the Didler, the Gray family)*

FINGRINGHOE [TM0220]

Whalebone CO5 7BG [off A134 just S of Colchester centre, or B1025]: Airy country-chic rooms with cream-painted tables on oak floors, well kept Wells & Youngs Bombardier, Woodfordes Wherry and a guest beer, good changing food choice with some interesting cooking (can be a long wait); TV, piped music, no children; charming back garden with peaceful valley view, front terrace, open all day wknds *(LYM, Ryta Lyndley, Janelle Howell)*

FULLER STREET [TL7416]

Square & Compasses CM3 2BB [back rd Great Leighs—Hatfield Peverel]: Small refurbished traditional country pub, welcoming and popular, with fresh local food from sandwiches up, choice of local ales and wines by the glass, big log fire in L-shaped beamed bar, attention to detail such as linen napkins; soft piped music; gentle country views from tables outside *(Paul and Ursula Randall, Barbara Cornell, LYM, Mrs Margo Finlay, Jörg Kasprowski)*

FYFIELD [TL5707]

Black Bull CM5 0NN [Dunmow Rd (B184, N end)]: Traditional 15th-c pub with huge helpings of enjoyable food inc lots of fish and good steaks (ex-Smithfield chef), real ales such as Fullers London Pride and Greene King, friendly staff; heavy low beams and standing timbers in comfortably opened-up pubby bar and country-style dining area, open fire, traditional games; piped music, sports TV, games machine; tables out among flower tubs *(Jeremy King, LYM, Mrs Margo Finlay, Jörg Kasprowski, Marion and Bill Cross)*

☆ *Queens Head* CM5 0RY [corner of B184 and Queen St]: Smart dining pub dating from 15th c, enterprising if not cheap food (not Sun evening) from light dishes up inc

popular set menu; snug low-beamed L-shaped bar with fresh flowers on sturdy elm tables, comfortable seating inc button-back banquettes and high-backed chairs, facing fireplaces, Adnams, Crouch Vale and three guest ales, Weston's Old Rosie cider, good choice of wines by the glass; piped music, no children; small outside covered area at front, prettily planted back garden with picnic-sets down to sleepy River Roding, open all day wknds *(Marion and Bill Cross, Andy and Jill Kassube, Howard Dell, LYM, Anne and Michael Bogod, Tina and David Woods-Taylor)*

GREAT BRAXTED [TL8614]

Du Cane Arms CM8 3EJ [Tiptree Rd, off A12 Witham—Kelvedon]: Neatly refurbished in clean-cut contemporary style, good food inc traditional and more up-to-date dishes from short menu and specials board, well kept Greene King and local ales such as Farmers and Mighty Oak Maldon Gold, decent wines; children welcome, well looked after gardens front and back with picnic-sets, open all day Sat, cl Sun evening and Mon *(Nic and Sandra Ruben)*

GREAT CHESTERFORD [TL5142]

Crown & Thistle CB10 1PL [just off M11 junction 9 (A11 exit roundabout); High St]: Welcoming pub in affluent village, very good home-made food inc cheaper OAP meals, friendly helpful landlord, well kept Greene King ales, several wines by the glass, tea and coffee; log fire, fresh flowers, simple heavy furnishings on bare boards, attractive restaurant; bedrooms *(Mrs Margo Finlay, Jörg Kasprowski, Mark Gamble)*

GREAT HENNY [TL8738]

Henny Swan CO10 7LS [Henny St]: This popular Main Entry dining pub was closed as we went to press – news, please *(LYM)*

GREAT HORKESLEY [TL9732]

Yew Tree CO6 4EG [The Causeway (A134)]: Large and attractive flower-covered thatched pub (rebuilt and extended in the 1970s after a fire), beams and soft lighting, friendly attentive staff, popular well presented food in good helpings, several real ales; tables in pleasant courtyard with fountain, open all day *(N R White)*

GREAT WARLEY STREET [TQ5890]

Thatchers Arms CM13 3HU [Warley Rd]: Pretty beamed pub by village green, Greene King ales, varied decent food; may be piped music; tables on verandah and out behind *(David Rule, Quentin and Carol Williamson)*

GREAT YELDHAM [TL7638]

Waggon & Horses CO9 4EX [High St]: Cheerful 16th-c timbered village inn with attractive L-shaped beamed bar, well kept Greene King IPA and three changing regional ales inc Nethergate, good well priced generous fresh food from baguettes to fish and steaks, friendly service, popular restaurant; games room with pool, darts and shove-ha'penny; piped music, games machines; children and dogs welcome, disabled access, picnic-sets on front terrace and in garden behind, 16 bedrooms, most in

modern back extension, open all day
(Adele Summers, Alan Black)

☆ **White Hart** C09 4HJ [Poole St (A1017 Halstead—Haverhill)]: Striking old black and white timbered dining pub, stone and wood floors, some dark oak panelling, lovely old fireplace, even a cell where prisoners were kept on route to Chelmsford Assizes; an emphasis on the food from light lunches up (can be pricey), Adnams and one or two guest beers; children welcome, attractive garden with well tended lawns and pretty seating, 11 bedrooms, open all day (LYM, Gordon Neighbour)

HARWICH [TM2632]

New Bell CO12 3EN [Outpart Eastward]: Small very friendly traditional local, Greene King IPA and changing guests, simple lunchtime food such as huffers and enterprising soups, back lounge, newspapers and books; tables on small terrace, open all day Sun in summer (Sara Price, Dr A B Clayton, PHB)

HATFIELD HEATH [TL5115]

Thatchers CM22 7DU [Stortford Rd (A1005)]: Olde-worlde beamed and thatched pub with good value fresh pubby food from sandwiches up, well kept Greene King IPA, Wells & Youngs Bombardier and a guest ale from long counter, decent house wines; lovely log fire, copper kettles, jugs, brasses, plates and pictures in L-shaped bar, back dining area; no children in bar, may be piped music; at end of large green, tables out in front under cocktail parasols (Jerry Brown)

HERONGATE [TQ6491]

☆ **Old Dog** CM13 3SD [Billericay Rd, off A128 Brentwood—Grays at big sign for Boars Head]: Carefully refurbished popular country pub dating from 16th c, enjoyable food, real ales, quick friendly service, comfortable back lounge area, long attractive dark-beamed bar, and appealing raftered restaurant upstairs; pleasant front terrace and neat sheltered side garden (LYM, DFL)

HEYBRIDGE BASIN [TL8706]

Old Ship CM9 4RX [Lockhill]: Now more restaurant than pub (friendly waitress service in the bar, drinkers may have to sit outside), pale wood chairs and tables, estuary views upstairs, home-made food inc breakfast all morning; dogs and children welcome, seats outside, some overlooking water by canal lock with lovely views of the saltings and across to Northey Island; open all day 8am-midnight (Jean and David Lewis)

LANGHAM [TM0232]

Shepherd & Dog CO4 5NR [Moor Rd/High St]: Chatty village pub decorated with entertaining miscellany of items, Greene King and Nethergate beers, wide choice of sensibly priced food inc curries (cooked by landlord's father), friendly attentive service; piped music; children and dogs welcome, enclosed side garden, open all day Sun (N R White, LYM)

LAYER DE LA HAYE [TL9720]

Donkey & Buskins CO2 0HU [off B1026 towards Colchester]: Friendly old-fashioned family-run country pub with bar and three dining areas, good range of reasonably priced hearty food inc local fish and Sun roasts, amiable service, local Farmers and Greene King beers, general mix of furnishings and ornaments, Sun quiz night; pleasant garden, handy for Abberton Reservoir's fishermen and birders, two bedrooms, open all day wknds (E A and D C T Frewer, Gordon Neighbour)

LEIGH-ON-SEA [TQ8385]

☆ **Crooked Billet** SS9 2EP [High St]: Homely old pub with waterfront views from big bay windows, packed on busy summer days and service may slow, well kept Adnams, Fullers London Pride and three changing guests inc seasonal ales; enjoyable basic pub food, log fires, beams, panelled dado and bare boards, local fishing pictures and bric-a-brac; piped music, winter jazz Fri nights, no under-21s after 6pm; side garden and terrace, seawall seating over road shared with Osbornes good shellfish stall (plastic glasses for outside), pay-and-display parking by fly-over; open all day (LM, N R White, David Jackson, LYM)

LITTLE BADDOW [TL7807]

Generals Arms CM3 4SX [The Ridge; minor rd Hatfield Peverel—Danbury]: Roomily knocked through and airy, with friendly efficient service, well kept Shepherd Neame, good range of pubby food from sandwiches to specials, reasonably priced wines; attractive terrace and good-sized back lawn with play area, nice walks nearby (LYM, John Saville)

LITTLE DUNMOW [TL6521]

Flitch of Bacon CM6 3HT [off A120 E of Dunmow; The Street]: Informal country local, Fullers London Pride, Greene King IPA and a local Mild, food from baguettes up (not Sun evening, and has been cl Mon lunchtime); simple small timbered bar with cushioned pews, fire (may not be lit), children welcome in back eating area; piped music; a few picnic-sets outside, peaceful views, bedrooms (Paul Lucas, LYM)

LITTLE TOTHAM [TL8811]

☆ **Swan** CM9 8LB [School Rd]: Warmly welcoming country local with good changing range of real ales tapped from the cask such as Adnams, Crouch Vale, Mauldons and Mighty Oak, farm ciders and perry; enjoyable straightforward good value food (not Sun evening, Mon), low 17th-c beams, log fire, tiled games bar with darts, dining extension, Jun beer festival; children and dogs welcome, disabled facilities, small terrace and picnic-sets under cocktail parasols on sizeable front lawn, camping in back field, open all day (the Didler, Mrs M S Forbes, Jerry Brown, David Jackson, Jean and David Lewis)

LITTLEY GREEN [TL6917]

Compasses CM3 1BU [off A130 and B1417 SE of Felsted]: Unpretentiously quaint and old-fashioned country pub, isolated but thriving, with big huffers, local real ales, good range of whiskies, roaring log fire; tables in big back garden, benches out in front, good walks (the Didler, Roy and Lindsey Fentiman)

MALDON [TL8407]

☆ **Blue Boar** CM9 4QE [Silver St; car park round behind]: Quirky cross between coaching inn and antiques or auction showroom, most showy in the main building's lounge and dining room, interesting antique furnishings and pictures also in the separate smallish dark-timbered bar and its spectacular raftered upper room; good Farmers ales brewed at the back, Adnams and Crouch Vale too, enjoyable fresh food, friendly helpful staff; tables outside, bedrooms inc four-poster rooms, good breakfast, open all day *(Pete Baker, LYM, Susan and Nigel Wilson)*

Jolly Sailor CM9 5HP [Church St/The Hythe]: Charming timber-framed quayside pub, three Greene King ales and great choice of wines by the glass, friendly helpful landlady and staff, food from rolls, sandwiches and baked potatoes to plenty of fish; piped music; tables out overlooking Thames barges, play area and parakeet aviary *(John Saville)*

MARGARETTING [TL6701]

Black Bull CM4 9JA [Main Rd]: Friendly neat village local, well kept Greene King IPA and Old Speckled Hen, decent home-made food inc popular themed evenings, bright comfortable dining room *(Paul and Ursula Randall, Mrs P J Pearce)*

Red Lion CM4 0EQ [B1002 towards Mountnessing]: Beamed and timbered dining pub under new management, good value food, Greene King ales; piped music; good disabled access, garden *(P and J Shapley)*

MATCHING GREEN [TL5310]

Chequers CM17 0PZ [Downhall Rd]: Victorian pub comprehensively modernised as contemporary upmarket pub/restaurant, not cheap but enjoyable traditional and mediterranean-style food from ciabattas up; pleasant staff, well kept Greene King IPA, candles on pine tables, lounge with sofas and open fire, american-style central bar, cabaret nights; garden, quiet spot with picnic-sets overlooking pretty cricket green, cl Mon *(Mrs Margo Finlay, Jörg Kasprowski)*

MONK STREET [TL6128]

Farmhouse CM6 2NR [just off B184 S of Thaxted]: Partly 16th-c country pub, good value food in carpeted bar and restaurant, Mighty Oak ales; good-sized attractive garden with terrace and play area, 11 bedrooms *(MLR)*

MORETON [TL5307]

Nags Head CM5 0LF [signed off B184, at S end of Fyfield or opp Chipping Ongar school]: Cosy and friendly country pub with obliging newish landlord, generous well prepared food from tasty lunchtime sandwiches up, Greene King ales; three big log fires, comfortable mix of tables and medley of salvaged rustic beams and timbers, restaurant; children welcome, picnic-sets on side grass *(Gordon Neighbour, Charles and Pauline Stride)*

MOUNT BURES [TL9031]

Thatchers Arms CO8 5AT: Bright extended country pub with good fresh food using local game and meats, mid-week meal deals, well kept Adnams and local guest ales, good

range of other drinks, friendly service; peaceful Stour valley views from dining room; dogs welcome, plenty of picnic-sets out on the grass, cl Mon, open all day wknds *(Sarah Mennell, Colin Smith)*

NEWNEY GREEN [TL6506]

☆ **Duck** CM1 3SF [W of Chelmsford]: Tucked away old pub with attractive rambling dining bar, dark beams, timbering, panelling and interesting bric-a-brac, comfortable furnishings; enjoyable food inc good value Sun lunch, well kept Shepherd Neame ales, decent wines by the glass, friendly attentive service, monthly jazz nights; pleasant terrace *(Paul and Ursula Randall, LYM)*

NEWPORT [TL5234]

Coach & Horses CB11 3TR [Cambridge Rd (B1383)]: Well kept friendly local, big helpings of good food (freshly made so may take a while), pleasant staff, well kept Adnams, Greene King and a guest beer; tables outside *(Patti Mickelson)*

PAGLESHAM [TQ9492]

☆ **Plough & Sail** SS4 2EQ [East End]: Relaxed 17th-c dining pub in pretty spot, generally good food from sandwiches through familiar favourites to interesting specials inc fresh fish, popular Sun lunch, friendly attentive staff but service can be slow when busy; well kept changing ales, decent house wines, low beams and big log fires, pine tables, lots of brasses and pictures, traditional games; unobtrusive piped music; attractive garden, open all day Sun *(Mrs Margo Finlay, Jörg Kasprowski, John Saville, LYM)*

☆ **Punchbowl** SS4 2DP [Church End]: 16th-c former sailmaker's loft with low beams and stripped brickwork, pews, barrel chairs and lots of brass, lower room laid for dining; beers such as Adnams, Cottage and Nethergate, helpful friendly service, straightforward fairly priced food, cribbage and darts; piped music (mostly 1960s and 70s); children usually welcome but check first, lovely rural view from sunny front garden *(Louise English, George Atkinson, LYM, Mrs Margo Finlay, Jörg Kasprowski)*

PELDON [TL9916]

Plough CO5 7QR [Lower Rd]: Enjoyable blackboard food in small traditional tiled and white-boarded village bar, quick friendly service, Greene King and a guest ale, well spaced stripped pine tables and coastal paintings in restaurant, public bar *(BB, David Jackson)*

RICKLING GREEN [TL5129]

Cricketers Arms CB11 3YG [just off B1383 N of Stansted Mountfitchet]: This previous Main Entry dining pub closed in 2008; new management were preparing to reopen it as we went to press – reports please *(LYM)*

RIDGEWELL [TL7340]

White Horse CO9 4SG [Mill Rd (A1017 Haverhill—Halstead)]: Comfortable low-beamed village pub with good range of well kept ales tapped from the cask and three farm ciders, good generous food (changing bar and restaurant menus), friendly service, fireside sofa, no music; no dogs; terrace tables, new bedroom block with good disabled access, open all day *(Jerry Brown, MLR)*

ROMFORD [TQ5189]

Coach House RM1 3DL [Main Rd (A118)]: Hotel with cheerful horse-racing theme bar, conservatory and more formal restaurant, good italian food, good range of beers and wine, friendly efficient staff; terrace tables, comfortable bedrooms, open all day from breakfast on *(Robert Lester)*

SHEERING [TL5013]

Crown CM22 7LZ [The Street]: Neatly kept and comfortable, with friendly efficient service, Greene King IPA, Sharps Doom Bar and a guest such as Brentwood Clockwork Orange, good choice of decent fairly priced pubby food from sandwiches up, easy chairs and fireside sofa as well as more upright seating in open-plan carpeted bar; garden picnic-sets *(BB)*

STANSTED [TL5024]

Cock CM24 8HD [Silver St]: Bar and dining area with half-panelled walls and wood floors, mix of dark wood furniture with some leather sofas and chairs, good choice of enjoyable bargain food served on modern china inc traditional Sun lunch, friendly staff; games machine; tables on decked terrace, garden with play area *(Mrs Margo Finlay, Jörg Kasprowski)*

STISTED [TL7923]

☆ *Dolphin* CM77 8EU [A120 E of Braintree, by village turn]: Cheerful heavily beamed and timbered bar, good value fresh straightforward food (not Tues or Sun evenings); chatty licensees, Greene King and guest ales, log fire, bright eating area on left (children allowed); pretty garden, nice hanging baskets *(Ryta Lyndley, LYM, the Didler)*

STOCK [TQ6897]

Old Kings Head CM4 9PQ [Stock Rd]: Well furnished and neatly kept, locally popular for good choice of reasonably priced food, Greene King ale, prompt pleasant service *(Gordon Neighbour)*

TOLLESBURY [TL9510]

Hope CM9 8RG [High St]: Enjoyable reasonably priced pubby food; games room *(Gordon Neighbour)*

UGLEY [TL5129]

Chequers CM22 6HZ [Cambridge Rd (B1383)]: Welcoming red-brick roadside pub with low-beamed opened-up bar, well kept Greene King IPA and a guest ale, several wines by the glass, wide choice of food from sandwiches up inc popular Sun carvery, good service; windsor chairs and plain tables on carpet and wood laminate, small pictures and plates, coal-effect gas fire, large room behind used as overspill restaurant; piped music; children welcome away from bar, no dogs, disabled access, terrace picnic-sets, open all day *(KC)*

UPSHIRE [TL4100]

Horseshoes EN9 3SN [Horseshoe Hill, E of Waltham Abbey]: Friendly Victorian local, simple and clean, with popular fairly priced food (not Mon) inc lots of fresh fish, well kept McMullens ales; tidy garden overlooking

Lea Valley, more tables out in front, good walks *(Andy Millward)*

WEST BERGHOLT [TL9528]

White Hart CO6 3DD [2 miles from Colchester on Sudbury rd]: Welcoming village pub, former old coaching inn, with good choice of reasonably priced food inc plenty of fish, set lunch deals and children's menu, three ales inc Adnams, comfortable dining area; big garden (wknd barbecues planned), four bedrooms, cl Sun evening *(Marion and Bill Cross, Tony and Shirley Albert)*

WIDDINGTON [TL5331]

☆ *Fleur de Lys* CB11 3SG [signed off B1383 N of Stansted]: Welcoming and caring licensees in unpretentious low-beamed and timbered village pub, well cooked food in bar and restaurant inc good Sun roasts, children's helpings; well kept Adnams, Hook Norton and guest beers, decent wines, inglenook log fire, games in back bar; picnic-sets on pleasant side lawn *(R G McFarland, LYM)*

WIVENHOE [TM0321]

Black Buoy CO7 9BS [off A133]: Attractive open-plan partly timbered bar (16th c behind the more recent façade), good cheerful service, enjoyable home-cooked food at low prices, well kept ales inc Adnams and Greene King, good choice of wines by the glass, open fires, upper dining area glimpsing river over roofs; own parking (useful here), pleasant village *(Charles Gysin, Ryta Lyndley, BB)*

Flag CO7 9HS [Colchester Rd, upper village]: Notable for its wide choice of bargain food, good value coffee, too; good service *(Ryta Lyndley)*

Rose & Crown CO7 9BX [The Quay]: Unpretentious Georgian-faced pub on River Colne barge quay, low beams, lots of ship pictures, scrubbed floors and log fires, well kept Adnams Broadside with several guest beers, good house wines, wide choice of good value straightforward food all day from fresh baguettes up (next-door bakery); friendly young staff, local and nautical books and maps, no piped music; dogs welcome, lots of waterside picnic-sets, no traffic (free car park five mins away), open all day Sun *(Mrs Jordan, Mrs P J Pearce, Ryta Lyndley, BB)*

WRITTLE [TL6706]

Wheatsheaf CM1 3DU [The Green]: Friendly traditional two-room 19th-c local, well kept Greene King, Mighty Oak and guest ales, folk nights 3rd Fri of the month; terrace tables, open all day Fri-Sun *(the Didler)*

YOUNGS END [TL7319]

Green Dragon CM77 8QN [Former A131 Braintree—Chelmsford (off new bypass), just N of Essex Showground]: Low-ceilinged modernised dining pub with contemporary leather furniture and log fire, reasonably priced tasty food (all day Sun), Greene King ales; piped music; children welcome till 8pm, picnic-sets on heated terrace and back lawn *(Russell and Alison Hunt, Justin and Emma King, Marion and Bill Cross, Roy and Lindsey Fentiman, Philip Denton, Mrs Margo Finlay, Jörg Kasprowski)*

Gloucestershire

This county is blessed with splendid pubs – often with delicious food – run by particularly friendly, hard-working licensees. Doing especially well here this year are the Red Lion at Ampney St Peter, Boat at Ashleworth Quay, Red Hart at Blaisdon, Kings Head in Bledington, Seven Tuns in Chedworth, Royal Oak in Cheltenham, Tunnel House at Coates, Green Dragon near Cowley, Kings Arms in Didmarton, Cross House in Doynton, Five Mile House at Duntisbourne Abbots, Lamb in Great Rissington, Inn For All Seasons at Little Barrington, Fox at Lower Oddington, Weighbridge in Nailsworth, Ostrich at Newland, Anchor in Oldbury-on-Severn, Bell at Sapperton, Horse & Groom at Upper Oddington and the Ram in Woodchester. For a special meal out our choice as Gloucestershire Dining Pub of the Year is the Bell at Sapperton. New to this year's *Guide* are the friendly Craven Arms at Brockhampton (lovely views), Yew Tree at Clifford's Mesne (some serious food here, and a wine shop, too), Fossebridge Inn in Fossebridge, Ragged Cot at Hyde and Mount at Stanton (both refreshed in food and in style by new licensees), Gumstool near Tetbury (civilised and relaxed, part of a smart hotel) and White Hart in Winchcombe (enthusiastic young landlord with a go-ahead approach to wine). Top tips in the Dips: Fox at Broadwell, Corinium and Twelve Bells in Cirencester, Bull in Fairford, Hunters Hall at Kingscote, New Inn at Mayshill, Kings Arms at Mickleton, Fox at Old Down, and Swans at Southrop and Swineford. The county's favourite beers are (in rough order) Wickwar, Uley, Stroud, Goffs and Donnington, with quite a few others to look out for, led by Cotswold Spring and Severn Vale.

ALMONDSBURY
ST6084 MAP 2

Bowl

1.5 miles from M5 junction 16 (and therefore quite handy for M4 junction 20); from A38 towards Thornbury, turn left signposted Lower Almondsbury, then first right down Sundays Hill, then at bottom right again into Church Road; BS32 4DT

New licensee for busy pub, handy for M5, with popular food, fine range of real ales and a pretty setting

Brains brewery has taken over this friendly pub and installed a new licensee but readers have been quick to tell us that there's still a warm welcome for both visitors and locals. Being close to the M5 means this is a popular stopping point for a drink or a meal so it's best to arrive early if you want to eat in the main bar – which has the most character. This room is long and beamed with traditional settles, cushioned stools and mate's chairs around elm tables, horsebrasses on stripped bare stone walls and a big winter log fire at one end, with a woodburning stove at the other. There's also a restaurant extension. Bath Ales Barnstormer, Brains Bitter and Rev James, Butcombe Bitter, Fullers London Pride, and St Austell Tribute on handpump, a dozen wines by the glass and farm cider; piped music. There are seats in front of the pub and on the back terrace, and the flowering tubs, hanging baskets and window boxes are lovely in summer. This is a pretty setting next to the church.

🍴 Well liked bar food includes sandwiches, good filled baguettes, hand-made spinach and ricotta ravioli with basil pesto, thai pork rissoles with shallot and chilli jam, beef and mushroom lasagne, cajun chicken fajitas with guacamole and salsa, beer-battered haddock with minted mushy peas, gammon and free-range eggs, steaks, and puddings like date and walnut pudding with toffee sauce and welsh cake and honey cheesecake with strawberry coulis. *Starters/Snacks: £3.95 to £5.95. Main Courses: £6.95 to £15.95. Puddings: £4.95*

Brains ~ Manager Mr N Torrance ~ Real ale ~ Bar food (all day) ~ Restaurant ~ (01454) 612757 ~ Children allowed during food service times ~ Open 12-11(10.30 Sun) ~ Bedrooms: /£69S

Recommended by Gerry and Rosemary Dobson, Bob and Margaret Holder, Barry and Anne, Dr S J Shepherd, Sheila Topham, Andy and Claire Barker, WAH, the Brewers, Donna and Roger, Pat and Tony Martin, Ellie Weld

AMPNEY ST PETER
SP0801 MAP 4

Red Lion 🍺
A417, E of village; GL7 5SL

Friendly landlord in charming unspoilt little pub; note the limited opening hours

The genuinely friendly, long-serving landlord and his chatty local customers are sure to draw you into conversation when you drop into this unspoilt and unchanging little pub – it's that sort of place. A central corridor, served by a hatch, gives on to the small right-hand tiled-floor public bar. This has just one table, a wall seat and one long bench facing an open fire. Behind this bench is an open servery (no counter, just shelves of bottles) and – by the corridor hatch – handpumps for the well kept Hook Norton Bitter plus a weekend guest like Timothy Taylors Landlord or Golden Best; reasonably priced wine. There are old prints on the wall, and on the other side of the corridor, a small saloon with panelled wall seats around its single table, old local photographs, another open fire, and a print of Queen Victoria one could believe hasn't moved for a century – rather like the pub itself. The side garden has some seats. Please note the limited opening hours.

🍴 **No food.**

Free house ~ Licensee John Barnard ~ Real ale ~ No credit cards ~ (01285) 851596 ~ Children and dogs in the tiny games room ~ Open 6-8.30(10.30 Fri and Sat); 12-2.30 Sun; closed lunchtimes except Sun; Sun evening

Recommended by the Didler, Dave Irving, Jenny Huggins, Roger Shipperley, E McCall, T McLean, D Irving, Mr Ray J Carter, Giles and Annie Francis, Donna and Roger, K Turner

ASHLEWORTH
SO8125 MAP 4

Queens Arms 🍴 🍷 🍺
Village signposted off A417 at Hartpury; GL19 4HT

Neatly kept pub with imaginative food, thoughtful wines and sunny courtyard

Neatly kept by south african licensees, this low-beamed dining pub has a civilised main bar with a nice mix of farmhouse and brocaded dining chairs around big oak and mahogany tables on the green carpet, and faintly patterned wallpaper and washed red ochre walls; at night it is softly lit by fringed wall lamps and candles. Brains Rev James and guests like Greene King IPA or Timothy Taylors Landlord on handpump, 14 wines by the glass including south african ones, 22 malt whiskies, winter mulled wine and summer home-made lemonade; piped music, board games and (on request) a skittle alley. The little black cat, Bonnie, does still entertain customers with her ping-pong ball but now that she is 13, she is a bit less active. There are cast-iron chairs and tables in the sunny courtyard; two perfectly clipped mushroom-shaped yews dominate the front of the building.

🍴 **Good and imaginative – if not cheap – bar food might include filled baguettes, baked field mushrooms filled with goats cheese and caramelised onions, scallops with bacon,** mushroom and garlic risotto, moules marinière, crab-stuffed red snapper with a chilli, ginger and garlic dressing, calves liver with bacon and onion mash topped with a rich sage and port sauce, chicken breast stuffed with spinach and cream cheese with a chive and white wine cream sauce, a south african spicy lamb stew, ostrich fillet steaks with a brandy and green peppercorn cream sauce, and puddings like triple chocolate brownie and pecan nut and maple syrup pie. *Starters/Snacks: £4.95 to £8.95. Main Courses: £7.95 to £18.50. Puddings: £4.95 to £6.95*

Free house ~ Licensees Tony and Gill Burreddu ~ Real ale ~ Bar food (not Sun evening) ~ Restaurant ~ (01452) 700395 ~ Well behaved children allowed ~ Open 12-3, 7-11; 12-3 Sun; closed Sun evening; 25 and 26 Dec

Recommended by Theocsbrian, Bernard Stradling, John and Helen Rushton, Dr and Mrs C W Thomas, Kim Merrifield, Edna Jones

ASHLEWORTH QUAY   SO8125   MAP 4

Boat ★ ◪

Ashleworth signposted off A417 N of Gloucester; quay signed from village; GL19 4HZ

Delightful and unchanging Severn-side pub with swiftly changing beers – and in the same family for hundreds of years

A reader describes this quaint and unpretentious old place as 'one of the classical pubs of England' – and he's quite right. It's been in the same family since it was originally granted a licence by Charles II and is really rather special. The little front parlour has a built-in settle by a long scrubbed deal table that faces an old-fashioned open kitchen range with a side bread oven and a couple of elderly fireside chairs; there are rush mats on the scrubbed flagstones, house plants in the window, fresh garden flowers, and old magazines to read; cribbage and dominoes in the front room. Two antique settles face each other in the back room where swiftly changing beers such as Church End Nuns Ale, RCH Pitchfork, Wye Valley Butty Bach and a couple of guest ales are tapped from the cask, along with the full range of Weston's farm ciders. The front suntrap crazy-paved courtyard is bright with plant tubs in summer and there's a couple of picnic-sets under parasols; more seats and tables under cover at the sides.

🍴 **Lunchtime filled rolls and ploughman's as well as cakes and ice-cream.** *Starters/Snacks: £2.10*

Free house ~ Licensees Ron, Elisabeth and Louise Nicholls ~ Real ale ~ Bar food (lunchtime only; not Mon and Weds) ~ No credit cards ~ (01452) 700272 ~ Children welcome ~ Open 11.30-2.30(3 Sat), 6.30-11; 12-3, 7-11 Sun; evening opening 7 in winter; closed all day Mon, Weds lunchtime

Recommended by Keith and Sue Ward, Guy Vowles, the Didler, Pete Baker, Edna Jones, Theocsbrian

BARNSLEY   SP0705   MAP 4

Village Pub 🍴 ☗

B4425 Cirencester—Burford; GL7 5EF

Enjoyable modern food in civilised communicating rooms, candles and open fires, good choice of drinks, and seats in back courtyard; bedrooms

As the contemporary food in this smart, civilised country pub is so very good, most customers are here to enjoy a meal but locals do still pop in for a drink and a chat, and dogs are welcome, too. The low-ceilinged communicating rooms have flagstones and oak floorboards, oil paintings, plush chairs, stools and window settles around polished candlelit tables, three open fireplaces and country magazines and newspapers to read. Butcombe Bitter, Hook Norton Best, and Sharps Doom Bar on handpump, and an extensive wine list with eight by the glass. The sheltered back courtyard has plenty of good solid wooden furniture under umbrellas, outdoor heaters and its own outside servery. The parent company went into administration in May 2009 and the administrators expect to sell the pub as a going concern, and certainly, as we went to press, this was still working as normal with the same staff.

🍴 **Imaginative food includes sandwiches, interesting soup, potted rabbit with celeriac and mustard, veal tartare with watercress salad, smoked duck breast salad with roasted beets and sherry vinegar dressing, twice baked double cheese soufflé, roasted cod niçoise salad, escalope of guinea fowl with rocket and fennel, lambs sweetbreads with broad beans and wild mushroom risotto cake, john dory with braised octopus, chickpeas, tomato and oregano, and puddings such as rum baba with roasted peaches and zabaglione ice-cream and chocolate and espresso tart.** *Starters/Snacks: £5.00 to £7.50. Main Courses: £11.00 to £18.50. Puddings: £5.50 to £6.00*

Free house ~ Licensees Tim Haigh and Rupert Pendered ~ Real ale ~ Bar food (12-2.30, 7-9.30(10 Fri and Sat)) ~ (01285) 740421 ~ Well behaved children welcome ~ Dogs welcome ~ Open 11-3, 6-11.30; 11-11 Sat and Sun ~ Bedrooms: £75S/£95S(£120B)

Recommended by J Crosby, Mrs P Lang, Martin Lee, Guy Vowles, Bernard Stradling, Charles Gysin

BISLEY
SO9006 MAP 4

Bear 🍺

Village signposted off A419 just E of Stroud; GL6 7BD

Friendly 16th-c inn with decent food and beer, and garden across a quiet road

This is an elegantly gothic 16th-c inn in a steep stone-built village, with enthusiastic, friendly licensees. The meandering L-shaped bar has a bustling atmosphere, a long shiny black built-in settle and a smaller but even sturdier oak settle by the front entrance, and brass and copper implements around an enormously wide low stone fireplace (not very high – the ochre ceiling's too low for that); the separate stripped-stone area is used for families. St Austell Tribute, Tetleys and Wells & Young Bombardier on handpump. A small front colonnade supports the upper floor of the pub, and the sheltered little flagstoned courtyard made by this has a traditional bench. The garden is across the quiet road, and there's quite a collection of stone mounting-blocks.

🍴 **Bar food includes filled baguettes, soup, popular prawn and mussel chowder, creamy garlic mushrooms, tuna niçoise, mixed nut and lentil loaf with fresh tomato sauce, home-baked ham with egg, steak and kidney pie, spicy lamb goulash, stilton chicken, fish pie, beef bourguignon, daily specials, and puddings.** *Starters/Snacks: £4.50 to £7.95. Main Courses: £8.95 to £13.95. Puddings: £3.95*

Punch ~ Lease Colin and Jane Pickford ~ Real ale ~ Bar food (12-2(3 weekends), 6-9; not Sun evening) ~ Restaurant ~ (01452) 770265 ~ Children welcome but at busy times in dining room only ~ Dogs allowed in bar ~ Open 12-3, 6-11; 12-12 Sat; 12-10.30 Sun ~ Bedrooms: £50S/£65S

Recommended by Guy Vowles, Dave Irving, Jenny Huggins, Evelyn and Derek Walter

BLAISDON
SO7016 MAP 4

Red Hart 🍺

Village signposted off A4136 just SW of junction with A40 W of Gloucester; OS Sheet 162 map reference 703169; GL17 0AH

Relaxed and friendly, interesting bric-a-brac in attractive rooms and several real ales

There's a fair choice of real ales on handpump in this friendly village inn: Adnams Broadside, Butcombe Bitter, Hook Norton Hooky Bitter, Ludlow Gold and Otter Amber. The flagstoned main bar has cushioned wall and window seats, traditional pub tables, a big sailing-ship painting above the log fire, a relaxing atmosphere and, maybe, Spotty the jack russell (who is 13 now); attentive service and piped music. On the right, there's an attractive beamed restaurant with interesting prints and bric-a-brac, and on the left, you'll find additional dining space for families; board games and table skittles. There are some picnic-sets in the garden and a children's play area, and at the back of the building is a terrace for summer barbecues. The little church above the village is worth a visit.

We say if we know a pub has piped music.

🍴 Bar food includes sandwiches, soup, steak in ale pie, ham and egg, fishcakes, daily specials like pork belly with black pudding and mint mash, rack of ribs in barbecue sauce, baked cod and lamb with red wine and rosemary, and puddings; roast Sunday lunch. *Starters/Snacks: £4.35 to £8.00. Main Courses: £6.55 to £14.40. Puddings: £4.35*

Free house ~ Licensee Guy Wilkins ~ Real ale ~ Bar food ~ Restaurant ~ (01452) 830477 ~ Children allowed but must be well behaved ~ Dogs welcome ~ Open 12-3, 6(7 Sun)-11

Recommended by Paul and Sue Merrick, Neil and Anita Christopher, Mr and Mrs M J Girdler, David and Gilly Wilkins

BLEDINGTON

SP2422 MAP 4

Kings Head 🍴 🍷 🍺 🛏

B4450; OX7 6XQ

Beams and atmospheric furnishings in a rather smart old place, super wines by the glass, interesting food and friendly service; bedrooms

We've had especially warm and enthusiastic reports on this rather smart old place over the last year, with many readers very much enjoying the relaxed and friendly atmosphere and polite service from the young, efficient staff. It's a pretty setting, just back from the village green, with ducks pottering about in the stream and there are seats at the front and in the back courtyard garden. The main bar is full of ancient beams and other atmospheric furnishings (high-backed wooden settles, gateleg or pedestal tables) and there's a warming log fire in the stone inglenook where there are bellows and a big black kettle; sporting memorabilia of rugby, racing, cricket and hunting. To the left of the bar, a drinking space for locals has benches on the wooden floor and a woodburning stove. Hook Norton Best and guests such as Arkells Moonlight, Butts Barbus Barbus and Vale Best Bitter on handpump, an excellent wine list with ten by the glass, 20 malt whiskies and interesting bottled ciders; piped music, board games and darts. This is a smashing place to stay and the breakfasts are very good.

🍴 As well as highly thought-of daily specials, the popular bar food includes lunchtime sandwiches (the croque monsieur is well liked) and ploughman's, curried fresh mussels with ginger and coriander, devilled lambs kidneys and mushrooms on toast, locally smoked guinea fowl caesar salad, sausages with mustard mash and red onion marmalade, beer-battered fresh fish of the day with pea purée, beef in ale stew with fresh herb dumplings, chargrilled venison steak with bubble and squeak and redcurrant jus, and puddings like chocolate caramel brownie with vanilla ice-cream and rhubarb crème brûlée. *Starters/Snacks: £4.50 to £7.50. Main Courses: £10.00 to £18.95. Puddings: £5.00*

Free house ~ Licensees Nicola and Archie Orr-Ewing ~ Real ale ~ Bar food (12-2(2.30 weekends), 7-9(9.30 Fri and Sat)) ~ Restaurant ~ (01608) 658365 ~ Children welcome ~ Dogs allowed in bar ~ Open 11.30-3, 6-11; 11.30-11 Sat; 12-11 Sun; closed 25 and 26 Dec ~ Bedrooms: £60B/£75B

Recommended by Paul and Marion Watts, Fred and Kate Portnell, Ian Malone, Myra Joyce, John and Jackie Chalcraft, Ann and Colin Hunt, Helene Grygar, Richard Greaves, Derek Thomas, Guy Vowles, Bernard Stradling, Jamie May, Anthony and Pam Stamer, Noel Grundy, Paul Humphreys, Lesley Dick

BOURTON-ON-THE-HILL

SP1732 MAP 4

Horse & Groom

A44 W of Moreton-in-Marsh; GL56 9AQ

Handsome Georgian inn, fine range of food and drink, and lovely views from seats outside; stylish bedrooms

There are plenty of original period features in this honey-coloured stone inn and the light and airy bar has a nice mix of wooden chairs and tables on bare boards, stripped stone walls, and a good log fire. Goffs Jouster, North Cotswold Pigbrook Bitter, and Purity Pure Ubu on handpump, 14 wines including fizz by the glass, local lager and home-made summer cordials. Plenty of seats under smart umbrellas in the large back garden for eating and drinking, and lovely views over the surrounding countryside. It's best to get here early to be sure of a space in the smallish car park. More reports please.

🍴 Using local and home-grown produce, the short choice of good – if not cheap – modern food includes soup, seared carpaccio of beef with chilli, ginger, radish and soy, deep-fried whitebait with lemon mayonnaise, griddled burger with red onion marmalade with rosemary aioli, pasta roulade of roasted squash with spinach and ricotta and sage butter, old spot pork chop with apple compote and mustard cream sauce, roast fillet of turbot with sautéed wild mushrooms, and puddings like baked maple syrup custard tart with poached rhubarb and chocolate fudge brownie with chocolate sauce. *Starters/Snacks: £4.00 to £7.00. Main Courses: £10.00 to £18.00. Puddings: £4.50 to £6.50*

Free house ~ Licensee Tom Greenstock ~ Real ale ~ Bar food (not Sun evening) ~ Restaurant ~ (01386) 700413 ~ Children welcome ~ Open 11-2.30, 6-11; 12-3.30 Sun; closed Sun evening; 25 and 31 Dec ~ Bedrooms: £70B/£105B

Recommended by Roger Braithwaite, Michael Doswell, Jane and Alan Bush, Derek Thomas, Paul Boot, Bernard Stradling, Richard Tilbrook, Anthony and Pam Stamer, Bob Butterworth, Keith and Sue Ward, Dennis and Gill Keen, Andrew and Ruth Triggs, Paul Humphreys

BRIMPSFIELD

S09413   MAP 4

Golden Heart 🍺

Nettleton Bottom (not shown on road maps, so we list the pub instead under the name of the nearby village); on A417 N of the Brimpsfield turning northbound; GL4 8LA

Nice old-fashioned furnishings in several cosy areas, big log fire, friendly licensees, and seats on a suntrap terrace; bedrooms

You can be sure of a warm welcome from the friendly licensees in this bustling roadside pub. It's just the place for a pint and a chat, and has some genuine old character. The main low-ceilinged bar is divided into five cosily distinct areas; there's a roaring log fire in the huge stone inglenook fireplace in one, traditional built-in settles and other old-fashioned furnishings throughout, and quite a few brass items, typewriters, exposed stone and wood panelling. Newspapers to read. A comfortable parlour on the right has another decorative fireplace and leads into a further room that opens on to the terrace. Brakspears Bitter, Butcombe IPA, Festival Gold, and Otter Bitter on handpump, some rare ciders, and a dozen wines by the glass. From the tables and chairs under parasols on the suntrap terrace, there are pleasant views down over a valley; nearby walks. The bedrooms are at the back of the pub and so escape any road noise.

🍴 Bar food includes some more ambitious dishes, alongside familiar pubby things such as sandwiches, ploughman's, filled baked potatoes, omelettes and chicken curry. *Starters/Snacks: £5.25 to £6.25. Main Courses: £9.95 to £14.95. Puddings: £4.25*

Free house ~ Licensee Catherine Stevens ~ Real ale ~ Bar food (12-3, 6-10; all day Fri, Sat and Sun) ~ (01242) 870261 ~ Children welcome ~ Dogs welcome ~ Open 12-3, 5.30-11; all day school hols; 12-11 Sat; 12-10.30 Sun ~ Bedrooms: £35S/£55S

Recommended by Colin Moore, Giles and Annie Francis, Tracey and Stephen Groves, E McCall, T McLean, D Irving, Mrs Jane Kingsbury, Adrian and Dawn Collinge, Neil and Anita Christopher, Guy Vowles, Keith and Sue Ward, Eddie Edwards, M G Hart

BROAD CAMPDEN

SP1537   MAP 4

Bakers Arms 🍺

Off B4081; GL55 6UR

Friendly village pub with five real ales, traditional food and good mix of customers

In a peaceful village, this is a traditional pub with a chatty, relaxed atmosphere and six real ales on handpump. The tiny beamed bar has perhaps the most character and it's here that the friendly locals tend to gather. There's a mix of tables and seats around the walls (which are stripped back to bare stone), an inglenook fireplace at one end, and from the attractive oak bar counter; Donningtons BB, Fullers London Pride, Stanway Stanney Bitter, Tetleys and Wells & Youngs Bombardier; darts and board games. The dining room is beamed, with exposed stone walls. There are seats on a terraced area with more by flower tubs on other terraces and in the back garden.

🍴 As well as daily specials such as salmon fishcakes, faggots in gravy, coq au vin and lamb shank in mint gravy, the bar food might include lunchtime sandwiches and filled baguettes, filled giant yorkshire puddings and ploughman's, soup, breaded mushrooms with garlic mayonnaise, macaroni cheese, steak and kidney pudding, chicken curry, fish pie, and puddings like spotted dick and bakewell tart. *Starters/Snacks: £3.50 to £5.50. Main Courses: £6.95 to £9.50. Puddings: £3.95*

Free house ~ Licensees Ray and Sally Mayo ~ Real ale ~ Bar food (12-9 in summer; 12-2(2.30 Sat and Sun), 6-9 in winter) ~ Restaurant ~ No credit cards ~ (01386) 840515 ~ Children welcome away from bar ~ Folk music third Tues evening of month ~ Open 11.30-11; 12-10.30 Sun; 11.30-2.30, 4.45-11 Mon-Thurs in winter; closed 25 Dec, evenings 26 and 31 Dec

Recommended by Noel Grundy, Michael Dandy, Di and Mike Gillam, R T and J C Moggridge

BROCKHAMPTON

SP0322 MAP 4

Craven Arms ♀

Off A436 Andoversford—Naunton; GL54 5XQ

Friendly village pub with well liked traditional food, real ales, seats in a big garden and nice surrounding walks

After enjoying one of the surrounding walks, this attractive 17th-c pub in a gentrified hillside village is just the place for a friendly drink or meal. There are low beams, thick roughly coursed stone walls and some tiled flooring, and though much of it has been opened out to give a sizeable eating area off the smaller bar servery, it's been done well to give a feeling of several communicating rooms. The furniture is mainly pine with some wall settles and tub chairs, there are gin traps and various stuffed animal trophies, and a log fire. Otter Bitter, Stroud Budding, Wye Valley Butty Bach and a guest beer on handpump, and several wines by the glass; darts, pool, juke box and board games. The dog is called Max, the cat Polly and the cockerel Wilbert. There are seats in the large garden and lovely views.

🍴 Well liked traditional bar food includes filled baguettes, goats cheese and beetroot confit salad, steak in ale or fish pie, beer-battered fish, slow-cooked lamb, venison bourguignon, and steaks cooked on hot stones. *Starters/Snacks: £3.95 to £5.50. Main Courses: £7.95 to £14.95. Puddings: £4.50*

Free house ~ Licensees Barbara and Bob Price ~ Real ale ~ Bar food (not Sun evening or Mon) ~ Restaurant ~ (01242) 820410 ~ Children welcome ~ Dogs allowed in bar ~ Open 12-3, 6-11; 12-11 Sat; 12-8.30 Sun; closed Mon

Recommended by Rich and Mo Mills, Helene Grygar, Mrs G Casey, Neil and Anita Christopher, R Ball, Stuart Doughty, Mari Jo Cruise

CHEDWORTH

SP0512 MAP 4

Seven Tuns ♀

Village signposted off A429 NE of Cirencester; then take second signposted right turn and bear left towards church; GL54 4AE

Handy for nearby Roman villa and with several open fires, lots of wines by the glass, good bar food and plenty of seats outside

In a charming village and with a consistently friendly, lively atmosphere, this delightful little 17th-c pub is enjoyed by customers of all ages. The small snug lounge on the right has comfortable seats and decent tables, sizeable antique prints, tankards hanging from the beam over the serving bar, a partly boarded ceiling, and a good winter log fire in a big stone fireplace. Down a couple of steps, the public bar on the left has an open fire and this leads into a dining room with yet another open fire. Wells & Youngs Bombardier and Youngs Special, and a couple of guest beers on handpump, up to 14 wines by the glass and 19 malt whiskies; darts, skittle alley and piped music. One sunny terrace has a boules pitch and across the road there's another little walled raised terrace with a waterwheel and a stream; plenty of tables and seats. There are nice walks through the valley.

🍴 Well liked bar food at lunchtime includes filled ciabatta sandwiches, ploughman's, soup, chicken and bacon caesar salad, gloucester old spot sausages on apple mash with real ale gravy, asparagus and sun-dried tomato risotto, cider-battered fish and chips, home-made burger, and home-cooked ham and eggs, with evening dishes such as king scallops and crispy black pudding on minted crushed peas with a citrus dressing, duck liver pâté with orange and mango marmalade, roasted vegetable filo parcels with plum sauce, rack of lamb with redcurrant gravy, yellow-fin tuna and king prawn fishcakes, and rump steak with a dark rum and shallot sauce. *Starters/Snacks: £5.00 to £9.00. Main Courses: £9.00 to £12.00. Puddings: £4.00 to £5.00*

Youngs ~ Tenant Mr Davenport-Jones ~ Real ale ~ Bar food (12-3, 7-9) ~ Restaurant ~ (01285) 720242 ~ Children welcome ~ Dogs welcome ~ Open 12-midnight; 12-3.30, 6-midnight winter

Recommended by Jeff and Wendy Williams, Neil and Anita Christopher, E McCall, T McLean, D Irving, MBHJ, Susan Lang, Edward Mirzoeff, Richard Tilbrook, Richard and Sheila Fitton

CHELTENHAM   SO9624   MAP 4

Royal Oak ♀ 🍺
Off B4348 just N; The Burgage, Prestbury; GL52 3DL

Bustling and friendly with quite a range of bar food (Sunday lunch all day), good choice of drinks, seats in sheltered garden, and handy for Cheltenham racecourse

Never people to rest on their laurels, the hard-working and enthusiastic licensees of this attractive Cotswold stone pub are busier than ever this year. There are lots of organised events – picnics, walks, a charity cycle ride, annual beer and cider festivals, and a quarterly comedy club; they are also brewing their own ale with Severn Vale to support Cask Ale Week. The congenial low-beamed bar has fresh flowers and polished brasses, a comfortable mix of seating on the parquet flooring from country chairs and a cushioned pew to dark green banquettes built in on either side of its stone fireplace, and there are some interesting pictures on the ochre walls. A changing beer from Dark Star and Wye Valley plus Timothy Taylors Landlord on handpump, nine wines by the glass and local soft drinks. Service is efficient and friendly. Dining room tables are nicely spaced so that you don't feel crowded and the skittle alley can also be used as a function room; piped music. There are seats and tables under canopies on the heated terrace and a sheltered garden. This is the closest pub to Cheltenham racecourse, so it does get busy on race days.

🍴 Often interesting, the bar food at lunchtime includes filled warm ciabatta sandwiches, ginger and sesame chicken goujons with thai green dip, crayfish and salmon fishcakes with salsa verde, szechuan peppercorn roast pork belly with noodles, provençale leg of lamb hotpot, and scottish salmon with watercress pesto, with evening dishes like duck pâté with honey and fig chutney, sautéed pigeon breast with glazed beetroot, blood orange and mizuna leaves, cannelloni of roast red pepper, sunblush tomato and ricotta cheese, seared lamb rump with chives and creamed goats cheese, confit of duck leg with wild venison sausages and red wine reduction, and braised beef with pearl barley and root vegetables. Puddings and Sunday roasts. *Starters/Snacks: £4.75 to £7.50. Main Courses: £7.50 to £14.95. Puddings: £4.95 to £5.50*

Enterprise ~ Lease Simon and Kate Daws ~ Real ale ~ Bar food (all day Sun) ~ Restaurant ~ (01242) 522344 ~ Children welcome until 8pm ~ Open 11(12 Sun)-11; 11-3, 5.30-11 Mon-Thurs in winter

Recommended by Michael Sargent, B M Eldridge, Kerry Law, Stuart Doughty, Andy and Claire Barker, Rob and Catherine Dunster

---

'Children welcome' means the pub says it lets children inside without any special restriction. If it allows them in, but to restricted areas such as an eating area or family room, we specify this. Places with separate restaurants often let children use them, hotels usually let them into public areas such as lounges. Some pubs impose an evening time limit – let us know if you find one earlier than 9pm.

CHIPPING CAMPDEN

SP1539 MAP 4

Eight Bells

Church Street (which is one way – entrance off B4035); GL55 6JG

Handsome inn with massive timbers and beams, log fires, well liked food, and seats in the large terraced garden; handy for Cotswold Way; bedrooms

As well as being an enjoyable place to stay with good breakfasts, this handsome old inn has a proper pubby feel and a friendly welcome for both visitors and locals. The bars have heavy oak beams, massive timber supports and stripped stone walls with cushioned pews, sofas and solid dark wood furniture on the broad flagstones, and log fires in up to three restored stone fireplaces; daily papers to read. Inset into the floor of the dining room is a glass panel showing part of the passage from the church by which Roman Catholic priests could escape from the Roundheads. Hook Norton Best, Goffs Jouster, Purity Pure Ubu and a guest such as Wye Valley HPA on handpump from the fine oak bar counter; quite a few wines by the glass, Old Rosie cider and country wines. Piped music and board games. There's a large terraced garden with plenty of seats, and striking views of the almshouses and church. The pub is handy for the Cotswold Way walk which takes you to Bath.

🍽 Enjoyable food includes lunchtime sandwiches (not Sunday) and a two- and three-course set lunch menu as well as soup, home-smoked trout and horseradish pâté, spicy greek-style lamb koftas with tzatziki, wild mushroom risotto, beer-battered fish and chips, pork and leek sausages with a cider and coarse grain mustard sauce, scottish salmon wrapped in parma ham with a spiced catalan bean cassoulet, lamb shank on garlic mash with thyme gravy, and puddings like lemon and lime cheesecake with raspberry coulis and chocolate crème brûlée with home-made shortbread. *Starters/Snacks: £6.50 to £7.50. Main Courses: £9.50 to £16.00. Puddings: £5.75 to £6.25*

Free house ~ Licensee Neil Hargreaves ~ Real ale ~ Bar food ~ Restaurant ~ (01386) 840371 ~ Well behaved children welcome; must be over 6 in bedrooms ~ Dogs allowed in bar ~ Open 12-11(10.30 Sun) ~ Bedrooms: £60S/£85B

Recommended by Martin and Pauline Jennings, Stuart Doughty, Noel Grundy, Eithne Dandy, Hugh Roberts, Les and Judith Haines, Geoffrey Hughes, Martin Smith, Michael Dandy, Rob and Catherine Dunster, Mr Ray J Carter, Robert Ager, Dr and Mrs A K Clarke

CLIFFORD'S MESNE

SO6922 MAP 4

Yew Tree 🍴 🍷 🍺

From A40 W of Huntley turn off at May Hill 1, Clifford's Mesne 2½ signpost, then pub eventually signed up steep narrow lane on left; Clifford's Mesne also signposted off B4216 S of Newent, pub then signed on right; GL18 1JS

Unusual dining pub nicely tucked away on slopes of May Hill; wine bargains

This is the place for a bottle of good value wine with your pub meal. A back room is laid out as an informal wine shop, with a good range, fairly priced. The point is that if you have a bottle with your meal here, they charge just the shop price plus £5. So you end up paying, say, £11 for a wine which in another pub would typically cost £18, or £16 instead of over £30, or even £25 instead of around £60 – the better the wine, the bigger the bargain. We wish that more pubs used this customer-friendly pricing system. The smallish two-room beamed bar has an attractive mix of small settles, a pew and character chairs around interesting tables including antiques, rugs on an unusual stone floor, and a warm woodburning stove. You can eat more formally up a few steps, in a carpeted dining room beyond a sofa by a big log fire. They have interesting bottled beers as well as quickly changing real ales such as Cotswold Spring Gloucestershire's Glory, Goffs Jouster, and RCH Pitchfork and PG Steam on handpump, local farm cider and good value winter mulled wine; under the charming landlady service is prompt and genial; daily papers. There may be unobtrusive, piped, nostalgic pop music. Teak tables on a side terrace are best placed for the views, with plenty of nearby walks, and there are steps down to a sturdy play area.

🍴 **Some serious cooking here: a hotly tipped fish soup, sun-dried tomato, fennel, feta and anchovy tart, mussels steamed in a choice of cider and saffron or provençale sauce, home-cured gravadlax, lentil and cider loaf, steak and kidney pudding, breast of chicken stuffed with oxford blue cheese in a creamy leek sauce, quite a few fish main courses such as swordfish dusted with cajun spices or haddock fillet stuffed with crayfish mousse, and rare-breed meats such as gloucester old spot loin steak with a pink peppercorn and chive butter; home-made puddings and local cheeses.** *Starters/Snacks: £4.25 to £6.70. Main Courses: £10.00 to £14.50. Puddings: £3.50 to £4.50*

Free house ~ Licensees Mr and Mrs Philip Todd ~ Real ale ~ Bar food (12-2, 6-9; 12-4 Sun) ~ Restaurant ~ (01531) 820719 ~ Children welcome ~ Dogs welcome ~ Live acoustic guitar monthly ~ Open 12-2.30, 6-11; 12-5 Sun; closed all day Mon and Tuesday lunchtime

Recommended by Reg Fowle, Helen Rickwood, TB, K and B Barker, Alastair Stevenson, Bernard Stradling, Neil and Anita Christopher, J E Shackleton, R J Amor

COATES

SO9600 · MAP 4

Tunnel House 🍺

Follow Tarlton signs (right then left) from village, pub up rough track on right after railway bridge; OS Sheet 163 map reference 965005; GL7 6PW

Warm welcome for all at this friendly, interestingly decorated pub, lots of character, popular food and drink, and seats in the sizeable garden; guards derelict canal tunnel

Down a pot-holed track, this is a lively, friendly pub where all are welcome – children and dogs, too. It's popular with students from the Royal Agricultural College (and there are photos of them on the walls) and the atmosphere is very laid back and informal. The rambling rooms have beams, flagstones, a happy mix of furnishings including massive rustic benches and seats built into the sunny windows, lots of enamel advertising signs, race tickets and air travel labels, a stuffed wild boar's head and stuffed owl, plenty of copper and brass and an upside-down card table complete with cards and drinks fixed to the beams; there's a nice log fire with sofas in front of it. The more conventional dining extension and back conservatory fill up quickly at mealtimes. Three changing real ales from breweries such as Hook Norton, Stroud, Uley, Wickwar and Wye Valley on handpump, several wines by the glass, and two draught ciders; quick, friendly service. Piped music, TV and juke box. There are impressive views from tables on the pleasant terrace in front of the eccentric bow-fronted stone house and a big garden sloping down to the derelict entrance tunnel of the old Thames and Severn Canal (which is under slow restoration). Good walks nearby; disabled lavatories.

🍴 **Using local, seasonal produce, the good bar food includes lunchtime sandwiches or filled baguettes and ploughman's, soup, moules marinière, warm salad of pigeon, black pudding and lardons, beer-battered cod, a pie of the day, popular cheese and bacon burger, gloucester old spot sausages with red onion marmalade, marinated pepper, courgette, aubergine and feta lasagne, evening extras such as pork tenderloin with apple and celeriac purée and venison loin with rösti and roasted field mushrooms, and puddings like white chocolate and Baileys crème brûlée with raspberry ripple ice-cream and mango cheesecake with pistachio cream.** *Starters/Snacks: £4.00 to £6.95. Main Courses: £8.50 to £12.95. Puddings: £4.95*

Free house ~ Licensee Rupert Longsdon ~ Real ale ~ Bar food (12-2(2.30 Sat and Sun), 6.30-9.15(9.30 Sat and Sun)) ~ (01285) 770280 ~ Children welcome ~ Dogs welcome ~ Open 11-3, 6-11.30; 11-11.30 Fri and Sat; 12-10.30 Sun

Recommended by Neil and Anita Christopher, Pete Baker, Nick and Meriel Cox, Brian and Anita Randall, Peter Meister, Stuart Doughty, Richard and Sheila Fitton, Chris and Angela Buckell, John Beeken

---

Post Office address codings confusingly give the impression that some pubs are in Gloucestershire, when they're really in Warwickshire (which is where we list them).

COWLEY   SO9714 MAP 4

Green Dragon 🏨

Off A435 S of Cheltenham at Elkstone, Cockleford signpost; OS Sheet 163 map reference 970142; GL53 9NW

Cosy and old-fashioned bars with winter fires, good food, real ales and terraces overlooking Cowley Lake; comfortable bedrooms

Deservedly busy and rather smart, this well run country inn remains extremely popular with our readers. There's a good bit of real character and the two beamed bars have a cosy and genuinely old-fashioned feel with big flagstones and wooden boards, winter log fires in two stone fireplaces, candlelit tables, a woodburning stove and Butcombe Bitter, Courage Directors and Otter Ale on handpump; friendly, efficient service. The furniture and the bar itself in the upper Mouse Bar were made by Robert Thompson, and little mice run over the hand-carved chairs, tables and mantelpiece; there's also a larger Lower Bar and upstairs restaurant; piped music. Terraces outside overlook Cowley Lake and the River Churn, and the pub is a good centre for the local walks. The bedrooms are very comfortable and well equipped and the breakfasts are good.

🍴 **Well presented, interesting bar food includes good lunchtime sandwiches (not Sunday), ploughman's, tian of risotto rice, saffron, crab meat and crème fraîche, warm chicken liver and bacon salad with herby croutons, pork and sage burger with spiced apple chutney, fillet of haddock in lemon batter, mushroom ravioli in a tomato provençale sauce, steak and kidney suet pudding, slow-cooked ham hock with dijon mustard and sage cream reduction, fillet of bass with a misto olive tapenade on a rocket, red onion and parmesan salad, and venison haunch steak with rosemary and garlic sauce.** *Starters/Snacks: £4.50 to £9.95. Main Courses: £9.95 to £16.95. Puddings: £3.95 to £6.25*

Buccaneer Holdings ~ Managers Simon and Nicky Haly ~ Real ale ~ Bar food (12-2.30(3 Sat, 3.30 Sun), 6-10(9 Sun)) ~ Restaurant ~ (01242) 870271 ~ Children welcome ~ Dogs allowed in bar and bedrooms ~ Open 11-11; 12-10.20 Sun ~ Bedrooms: £70B/£95B

Recommended by Nigel and Sue Foster, Giles and Annie Francis, Susan Lang, Mike and Mary Carter, E McCall, T McLean, D Irving, Guy Vowles, M S Lee, J Crosby, Michael and Joan Johnstone, Keith and Sue Ward, H Paulinski, Pete Baker, Dave Irving, Jenny Huggins, Dave Braisted

CRANHAM   SO8912 MAP 4

Black Horse 🍺

Village signposted off A46 and B4070 N of Stroud; look out for small sign up village side turning; GL4 8HP

Friendly, old-fashioned country pub with obliging staff and real ales

Walkers are fond of this down-to-earth country local as the Cotswold Way is only a mile away. It's popular with locals too and the cosy little lounge has just three or four tables. The main bar has window seats and other traditional furniture and a good log fire, and the atmosphere is friendly and convivial; there are a couple of upstairs dining rooms as well. Hancocks HB, Sharps Doom Bar and a couple of guests like Black Sheep and Stroud Tom Long on handpump. Outside, there are tables to the side of the pub and some in front; the labradoodle is called Percy and the jack russell, Baxter. They have a successful pub cricket team and regular morris dancers. More reports please.

🍴 **Well priced pubby food includes sandwiches, soup, ploughman's, various quiches, cumberland sausage and mash, chicken in stilton sauce, hungarian goulash, beef bourguignon, and steak and kidney or fish pie.** *Starters/Snacks: £3.50 to £5.50. Main Courses: £6.50 to £11.95. Puddings: £2.95 to £3.75*

Free house ~ Licensees David and Julie Job ~ Real ale ~ Bar food (not Sun evening or Mon) ~ Restaurant ~ (01452) 812217 ~ Children welcome if well behaved ~ Dogs allowed in bar ~ Open 12-2.30, 6.30-11; closed Mon

Recommended by Dr and Mrs Jackson, Pete Baker, Andrew Shore, Maria Williams, Suzy Miller

DIDMARTON   ST8187   MAP 2

Kings Arms ♀ ⇔
A433 Tetbury road; GL9 1DT

Bustling pub with knocked-through rooms, several local beers, good bar food and pleasant back garden; bedrooms and self-catering cottages

This rather smart 17th-c former coaching inn is carefully restored and spotlessly kept. The several knocked-through beamed bar rooms work their way around a big central counter, with deep terracotta walls above a dark green dado in some rooms, yellow and cream paintwork in others, an attractive mix of wooden tables and chairs on bare boards, quarry tiles and carpet, fresh flowers, and a big stone fireplace. There's also a smart restaurant. Three real ales from breweries such as Severn Vale, Timothy Taylors and Uley on handpump and ten wines by the glass; darts and TV. There are seats out in the pleasant back garden and boules, and as well as comfortable bedrooms, they have self-catering cottages in a converted barn and stable block. Westonbirt Arboretum is close by.

🍴 **Enjoyable bar food at lunchtime includes sandwiches and filled baguettes, port and stilton pâté, plates of charcuterie or antipasti, chicken breast marinated in dijon mustard and tarragon, spicy tomato sauce with pasta, and bass fillet on pepperade (a red pepper and onion sauce), with evening dishes like seared scallops with chorizo and paprika, sautéed pigeon breast with black pudding and home-made pickle, gloucester old spot sausages with onion gravy, venison casserole, gressingham duck breast on sweet potato mash with peppercorn sauce, and puddings such as apple and rhubarb crumble and chocolate fudge brownie with cream and chocolate ice-cream.** *Starters/Snacks: £3.00 to £7.50. Main Courses: £9.95 to £15.95. Puddings: £5.85*

Free house ~ Licensees R A and S A Sadler ~ Real ale ~ Bar food (12-2.15, 6-9; 12-7.45 Sun) ~ Restaurant ~ (01454) 238245 ~ Children welcome ~ Dogs allowed in bar ~ Open 11-11; 12-10.30 Sun ~ Bedrooms: £65S/£95S

Recommended by Rod Stoneman, Andy and Claire Barker, the Brewers, Mark O'Sullivan, J Crosby, Jamie May, Guy Vowles

DOYNTON   ST7174   MAP 2

Cross House ◼
Village signposted with Dyrham off A420 Bristol—Chippenham just E of Wick; High Street; BS30 5TF

Friendly staff and customers, honest food, five real ales and 16 wines by the glass; close to Dyrham Park and walking country

Run by an exceptionally helpful and convivial landlord, this 18th-c village pub is an old-fashioned place with a relaxed, easy-going atmosphere. The softly lit carpeted bar has some beams and stripped stone, simple pub furniture brightened up with cheerful scatter cushions, a woodburning stove in a big stone fireplace, and a happy mix of customers. Two or three steps take you down to a cottagey candlelit dining room. Bass, Bath Ales Gem Bitter, Courage Best, Fullers London Pride and Timothy Taylors Landlord on handpump, promptly served by friendly staff, and 16 decent wines by the glass; darts, games machine and piped music. There are picnic-sets out by the road. This is fine walking country and Dyrham Park is quite close.

🍴 **Honest bar food at reasonable prices includes good sandwiches, ham and egg with bubble and squeak, faggots, lambs liver and bacon, steak and kidney, rabbit or fish pies, salmon and broccoli fishcakes and leg of lamb with barbecue sauce.** *Starters/Snacks: £3.00 to £6.00. Main Courses: £8.95 to £12.95. Puddings: £3.50 to £3.95*

Unique (Enterprise) ~ Lease André and Adrian Large ~ Real ale ~ Bar food (11.30-2(2.30 Sun), 6-9.30(10 Fri and Sat, 9 Sun)) ~ Restaurant ~ (0117) 937 2261 ~ Children welcome ~ Dogs allowed in bar ~ Open 11.30-3, 6-11; 12-4, 7-10.30 Sun

Recommended by Andy and Claire Barker, Dr and Mrs C W Thomas, Chris and Angela Buckell, Mr and Mrs P R Thomas, Colin and Peggy Wilshire, Dr and Mrs A K Clarke, Stan Edwards, Barry and Anne

DUNTISBOURNE ABBOTS

SO9709   MAP 4

Five Mile House ⓘⓎ 🍺

Off A417 at Duntisbourne Abbots exit sign; then, coming from Gloucester, pass filling station and keep on parallel to main road for 200 yards; coming from Cirencester, take Duntisbourne Abbots services sign, then immediate right and take underpass below main road, then turn right at T junction; avoid going into Duntisbourne Abbots village; pub is on the old main road; GL7 7JR

A lively landlord and a favourite with many for its good food, beer and atmosphere; plenty of original character, open fires and newspapers; nice views from the garden

A winning combination of father and son run this genuinely friendly village pub with cheerful good-naturedness, and it's a great favourite with many of our readers who return on a regular basis to enjoy the well kept real ales and popular food. There's plenty of original character and the front room has a companionable bare-boards drinking bar on the right (plenty of convivial banter from the locals), with wall seats around the big table in its bow window and just one other table. On the left is a flagstoned hallway tap room snug formed from two ancient high-backed settles by a stove in a tall carefully exposed old fireplace; newspapers to read. There's a small cellar bar, a back restaurant down steps and a family room on the far side; darts. Cotswold Spring Gloucestershire's Glory, Donningtons BB, Otter Ale and Wye Valley Butty Bach on handpump and an interesting wine list (strong on new world ones); the friendly pub dog is called Sacha, and the gardens have nice country views and a very smart smokers' shelter. The country lane was once Ermine Street, the main Roman road from Wales to London.

🍴 Cooked by the landlord and his team, the very popular bar food includes lunch for a fiver (sandwiches, ploughman's, filled baked potatoes, home-made burger and chicken and chips), as well as other lunchtime dishes such as ham and eggs, various omelettes, beer-battered haddock, salads, and vegetarian lasagne; also, soup, deep-fried whitebait with garlic mayonnaise, home-made pâté or terrine, gloucestershire old spot sausages with onion gravy, chicken breast stuffed with stilton wrapped in bacon on a creamy mushroom and sweet pepper sauce, gammon with egg and pineapple, game pie and lamb shoulder with port jus. *Starters/Snacks: £4.25 to £6.95. Main Courses: £7.95 to £18.95. Puddings: £4.50*

Free house ~ Licensees Jo and Jon Carrier ~ Real ale ~ Bar food (12-2.30(3 Sun), 6-9; not winter Sun evening) ~ Restaurant ~ (01285) 821432 ~ Children welcome if well behaved ~ Dogs allowed in bar ~ Open 12-3, 6-11; 12-3, 7-10.30 Sun

Recommended by Mrs P Sumner, Dr A J and Mrs Tompsett, Giles and Annie Francis, Michael R B Taylor, Bren and Val Speed, Neil and Anita Christopher, the Didler, Mr and Mrs J Brown, Graham and Helen Eastwood, Guy Vowles, Dennis Jenkin, Donna and Roger, Bernard Stradling, Di and Mike Gillam, E McCall, T McLean, D Irving, Dave Irving, Jenny Huggins, Tom and Ruth Rees, George and Maureen Roby, Mike and Jenny Beacon, J Crosby

DURSLEY

ST7598   MAP 4

Old Spot 🍺 £

Hill Road; by bus station; GL11 4JQ

Unassuming and cheery town pub with up to ten real ales and regular beer festivals

The friendly landlord in this smashing town local is always willing to chat about his excellent choice of changing real ales from all over the country. On handpump, these might include Butcombe Blonde and Uley Old Ric, with guests like Cottage Blower Bentley, Dorset Jurassic, Fullers London Pride, Sarah Hughes Dark Ruby Mild, Otter Bitter, St Austell Black Prince and Severn Vale Session; they also hold four annual beer festivals a year and stock quite a few malt whiskies, too. There are always plenty of good-humoured locals and the front door opens into a deep pink little room with stools on shiny pine-boarded bar counter and old enamel beer advertisements on the walls and ceiling; there's a profusion of porcine paraphernalia. A small room on the left leads off from here and the little dark wood floored room to the right has a stone fireplace. A step takes you down to a cosy Victorian tiled snug and (to the right) the meeting room. There are seats in the heated and covered garden.

🍴 Bar food includes toasted filled ciabatta sandwiches, ploughman's, a grazing board of meats, cheeses and fish (good for sharing), haddock and chive fishcakes, cottage pie, home-cooked ham with parsley sauce, tagliatelle topped with roast vegetables and goats cheese, pork and apple burger with bacon and parmesan, and chicken fajitas. *Starters/Snacks: £3.25 to £5.75. Main Courses: £6.45 to £9.85. Puddings: £3.75*

Free house ~ Licensee Steve Herbert ~ Real ale ~ Bar food (12-3; no evening meals) ~ (01453) 542870 ~ Children in family room only ~ Dogs welcome ~ Open 11(12 Sun)-11

Recommended by Chris and Angela Buckell, Mr and Mrs W W Burke, Andy and Claire Barker, Liz Hryniewicz, the Didler, Neil and Anita Christopher, Michael and Joan Johnstone, Ben Guy, PL, Colin and Peggy Wilshire

FORD
SP0829   MAP 4

Plough
B4077 Stow—Alderton; GL54 5RU

16th-c inn opposite racehorse trainer's yard, lots of horse talk, bustling atmosphere and good food and beer; bedrooms

Many of the customers here are to do with racing as a well known racehorse trainer's yard is opposite, and much of the conversation is to do with horses. The licensee is also pretty keen on the sport and in April 2009 was one of ten novice riders selected to take part in the John Smith's People's Race. There's a chatty atmosphere and the beamed and stripped-stone bar has racing prints and photos on the walls, old settles and benches around the big tables on its uneven flagstones, oak tables in a snug alcove, open fires or woodburning stoves (a couple are the real thing); darts, TV (for the races), board games and maybe piped music. Donnington BB and SBA on handpump. There are some picnic-sets under parasols and pretty hanging baskets at the front of the stone building and a large back garden with a play fort for children. The Cotswold Farm Park is nearby. The comfortable bedrooms away from the pub are the quietest and there are views of the gallops. It does get pretty packed on race meeting days.

🍴 Well liked bar food includes lunchtime sandwiches and filled baguettes, ploughman's, soup, thai crab fishcakes with a sweet chilli sauce, pâté of the day, steak and mushroom in ale pie, gloucester old spot sausages with onion gravy, ham and eggs, and daily specials with evening extras like giant chicken kiev, half a crisp roast duckling with a peach and thyme sauce, slow-roast lamb shoulder with mint jelly and steaks. They serve breakfasts on race days and hold seasonal asparagus feasts; Sunday roasts. *Starters/Snacks: £5.00 to £7.00. Main Courses: £7.00 to £17.00. Puddings: £3.00 to £5.00*

Donnington ~ Tenant Craig Brown ~ Real ale ~ Bar food (all day Fri-Sun) ~ (01386) 584215 ~ Children welcome ~ Dogs allowed in bar ~ Open 11-11 ~ Bedrooms: £40S/£70S

Recommended by Mr and Mrs Barrie, Guy Vowles, Clive and Fran Dutson, the Didler, Keith and Ann Arnold, Helene Grygar, R J Herd, Chris Glasson, Giles and Annie Francis, Michael Sargent, DFL, Paul Humphreys, Brian Glozier, Myra Joyce, Jeff and Wendy Williams, Nick and Meriel Cox, Peter Sampson, Peter and Audrey Dowsett, Martin and Pauline Jennings

FOSSEBRIDGE
SP0711   MAP 4

Fossebridge Inn
A429 Cirencester—Stow-on-the-Wold; GL54 3JS

Fine old inn with proper bar, good mix of customers, real ales, fine food and seats in four acres of grounds; lovely bedrooms

'A favourite of ours' say several of our readers about this handsome Georgian inn, and it's an enjoyable place for either a drink or a meal. At its heart is the bustling, friendly bar which has plenty of locals dropping in for a pint and a chat, and the two rooms have beams and arches, stripped stone walls and fine old flagstones, a happy mix of dining chairs, stools and wooden tables, and copper implements, candles, fresh flowers and a good log fire. Festival Amber and St Austell Proper Job and Tribute on handpump and several wines by the glass. The two dining rooms are rather grand. Outside, there are

picnic-sets under parasols and four acres of lawned, streamside gardens with a lake.
Lovely bedrooms. The Roman villa at Chedworth is nearby.

🍴 **First-rate bar food includes sandwiches, ploughman's, soup, goats cheese and honey soufflé, haddock and prawn fishcake with grain mustard sauce, ham and eggs, cumberland sausages with cheddar mash and caramelised onion gravy, a burger with bacon and cheese and tomato relish, chicken with potato and aubergine terrine and a barley and wild garlic broth, best end of lamb with garlic and rosemary jus, and puddings such as dark chocolate truffle torte with strawberry and champagne jelly and baked raspberry cheesecake with eton mess.** *Starters/Snacks: £5.25 to £7.25. Main Courses: £10.50 to £17.00. Puddings: £5.95*

Free house ~ Licensee Lizzie Jenkins ~ Real ale ~ Bar food (12-3, 6.30-10) ~ Restaurant ~ (01285) 720721 ~ Children welcome ~ Dogs welcome ~ Open 12-12(11.20 Sun) ~ Bedrooms: £110B/£120B

Recommended by Dr and Mrs A K Clarke, Keith and Sue Ward, Guy Vowles, Tom and Ruth Rees

GREAT RISSINGTON   SP1917   MAP 4

Lamb ♀ ⇌

Off A40 W of Burford, via Great Barrington; GL54 2LN

Well run, bustling inn, interesting, enjoyable bar food, fair choice of drinks and seats in the sheltered garden; bedrooms and good surrounding walks

You can be sure of a warm welcome from the friendly licensee and his staff in this comfortable partly 17th-c inn. There's always a good mix of customers and most people head for the rather civilised two-roomed bar which has heritage red and stone coloured walls, fixed cushioned seating with fluted backs in a dark faux-aged suede, high-backed leather chairs grouped around polished tables, and a woodburning stove in the Cotswold-stone fireplace. Some interesting things to look out for are parts of a propeller, artefacts in display cases and pictures of the canadian crew from the Wellington bomber that crashed in the garden in October 1943; also, photographs of the guide dogs that the staff, customers and owners have raised money to sponsor. The restaurant has another woodburning stove and various old agricultural tools on the walls. Hook Norton Best and Wye Valley St George on handpump, quite a few wines by the glass from a comprehensive list and several malt whiskies; piped music, darts and TV for sports. You can sit outside on the front terrace or in the sheltered, well kept hillside garden. There's a local circular walk which takes in part of the idyllic village, church, River Windrush and stunning countryside surrounding the pub.

🍴 **Popular bar food includes filled baguettes and baked potatoes, soup, duck liver and orange pâté with cumberland sauce, deep-fried whitebait, cajun chicken strips with red onion, tomato and croûton salad, porcini mushroom ravioli with a tomato, onion and basil sauce, steak and kidney pie, beer-battered fresh haddock, half a shoulder of lamb with a redcurrant and red wine gravy, cod loin with a herb crust in cheese sauce, and gressingham duck breast on puy lentils with a brandy and orange jus. They also offer a good value two-course menu on Tuesdays, Thursdays and Saturday lunchtime and hold a curry evening on the last Thursday of the month.** *Starters/Snacks: £4.50 to £6.95. Main Courses: £5.95 to £16.95. Puddings: £3.50 to £6.50*

Free house ~ Licensees Paul and Jacqueline Gabriel ~ Real ale ~ Bar food (12-2.30, 6.30-9(9.30 Fri and Sat)) ~ Restaurant ~ (01451) 820388 ~ Children welcome ~ Dogs allowed in bar and bedrooms ~ Open 11.30-11.30; 12-11 Sun ~ Bedrooms: £55B/£80B

Recommended by Guy Vowles, Mr and Mrs I and E Bell, Paul Humphreys, Andrew and Judith Hudson, Roger Fox, Helene Grygar, Martin and Pauline Jennings, Betty Laker

---

We mention bottled beers and spirits only if there is something unusual about them – imported belgian real ales, say, or dozens of malt whiskies; so do please let us know about them in your reports.

GUITING POWER   SP0924   MAP 4

Hollow Bottom

Village signposted off B4068 SW of Stow-on-the-Wold (still called A436 on many maps);
GL54 5UX

Popular old inn with lots of racing memorabilia and a good bustling atmosphere

Even when this snug old stone cottage is really busy (which it usually is), the staff
remain prompt and efficient. There's a wide mix of both visitors and locals – in particular
those involved in racing, and lots of racing memorabilia including racing silks, tunics,
photographs, race badges, framed newspaper cuttings and horseshoes. The comfortable
beamed bar has plenty of atmosphere and a winter log fire in an unusual pillar-supported
stone fireplace, and the public bar has flagstones and stripped stone masonry, and racing
on TV; newspapers to read, darts, board games and piped music. Fullers London Pride,
North Cotswold Spring In Your Step and a beer named for the pub (from Badger) on
handpump, ten wines (including champagne) by the glass, and several malt whiskies.
From the pleasant garden behind the pub are views towards the peaceful sloping fields;
decent nearby walks.

🍴 **Bar food includes good filled baguettes and baked potatoes, ploughman's, soup, ham
and eggs, cottage pie, gloucester old spot sausages or pork fillet in cider and cream, wild
mushroom and spinach lasagne, slow-cooked lamb shoulder and daily specials.**
Starters/Snacks: £4.25 to £9.95. Main Courses: £8.45 to £16.95. Puddings: £3.95 to £5.75

Free house ~ Licensees Hugh Kelly and Charles Pettigrew ~ Real ale ~ Bar food (all day) ~
Restaurant ~ (01451) 850392 ~ Children welcome ~ Dogs allowed in bar and bedrooms ~
Live jazz brunch first Sat of month ~ Open 9am-12.30am ~ Bedrooms: £50B/£75B

*Recommended by Susan Lang, Helene Grygar, Michael and Jenny Back, Dennis and Gill Keen, Richard Marjoram,
Bernadette Fitzjohn, Keith and Sue Ward, DFL, Guy Vowles, Mr and Mrs Barrie*

HINTON DYRHAM   ST7376   MAP 2

Bull

2.4 miles from M4 junction 18; A46 towards Bath, then first right (opposite the Crown);
SN14 8HG

**17th-c stone pub in peaceful village, with friendly atmosphere, enjoyable food, real ales
and a sizeable garden with children's play equipment**

There's a friendly, relaxed atmosphere in this pretty pub situated on the edge of an
attractive village. The main bar is chatty with two huge fireplaces, low beams, oak settles
and pews on ancient flagstones, horsebrasses, and a nice window seat; there's also a
stripped stone back area and a simply furnished restaurant. Wadworths IPA and 6X and a
couple of changing guests like Wadworths Bishops Tipple and Summersault on handpump,
and several malt whiskies and wines by the glass; piped music. Plenty of picnic-sets and
play equipment in a sizeable sheltered upper garden with more seats on the sunny front
balcony. The pub is handy for the M4.

🍴 **As well as pork from their own herd of gloucester old spot pigs, the well liked bar food
includes sandwiches and ploughman's (not Friday or Saturday evenings), soup, crispy
whitebait, ham and egg, steak in ale pie with horseradish pastry, cod in soda and lime
batter, lambs liver and bacon with mustard mash and onion gravy, stilton, leek and
mushroom crumble, lancashire hotpot, and puddings like passion fruit crème brûlée and
jaffa chocolate pudding with rich chocolate sauce.** *Starters/Snacks: £5.50 to £8.95.*
Main Courses: £8.95 to £15.95. Puddings: £4.75 to £6.95

Wadworths ~ Tenants David and Elizabeth White ~ Real ale ~ Bar food (12-2, 6-9; 12-3.30,
7-8.30 Sun) ~ Restaurant ~ (0117) 937 2332 ~ Children allowed in restaurant only until 7.15pm
~ Dogs allowed in bar ~ Open 12-3, 6-11.30; 12-11.30 Sat and Sun; closed Mon lunchtime

Recommended by Dr and Mrs A K Clarke, Peter Martin, Lise Chace, David A Hammond, Steve and Liz Tilley

---

If we know a pub has an outdoor play area for children, we mention it.

HYDE   SO8801   MAP 4

Ragged Cot ♀ 🍺 🛏️

Burnt Ash; off A419 E of Stroud, OS Sheet 162 map reference 886012; GL6 8PE

Attractively refurbished 17th-c inn, lots of wood and light paintwork, good choice of drinks, high quality food and newly landscaped garden; bedrooms

---

Reopened after quite a makeover, this 17th-c cotswold stone inn is doing well under its new owners. The rambling bar has three connecting rooms with beams, old school chairs around pale wooden tables on the stripped wood flooring, cushioned window and wall seats, leather bar stools and a couple of large log fires, one with a wooden settle beside it. It's all very light and airy with pale paintwork, fresh flowers and plants; dogs are made very welcome with sheepskin rugs and baskets. Jennings Cumberland, Marstons Pedigree, Ringwood Best and a guest from Brakspears on handpump and several wines by the glass from an interesting, thoughtful list. The newly landscaped garden has plenty of seats under parasols.

🍴 High-quality bar food includes sandwiches, ploughman's, soup, duck liver parfait with shallot marmalade, smoked salmon platter with fennel and lemon dressing, burger with crispy bacon and cheese, gloucester old spot bangers and mash, chicken and ham hock pie, home-baked ham and free-range egg, beer-battered fish, lamb suet pudding with mashed swede, and roast duck with red cabbage. *Starters/Snacks: £5.50 to £7.00. Main Courses: £9.00 to £14.00. Puddings: £5.00*

Brunel Pub Company Ltd ~ Tenant Tom Nunn ~ Real ale ~ Bar food (12-3(4 Sun), 6-11) ~ Restaurant ~ (01453) 884643 ~ Children welcome ~ Dogs welcome ~ Open 10am-11pm ~ Bedrooms: £80S/£95S(£120B)

Recommended by Guy Vowles, Andy and Claire Barker, JJW, CMW

KILKENNY   SP0118   MAP 4

Kilkeney Inn

On A436, 1 mile W of Andoversford, near Cheltenham – OS Sheet 163 map reference 007187; GL54 4LN

Good food in contemporary dining pub with real ales, several wines by the glass, and seats outside with country views; bedrooms

---

New licensees for this neatly kept and spacious dining pub who were planning to open more letting bedrooms as we went to press. It was originally six stone cottages, and the extended, bright beamed bar has neatly alternated stripped cotswold stone and white plasterwork, as well as gleaming dark wheelback chairs around the tables on quarry tiles or carpeting, fresh flowers and candles, and a woodburning stove. There's also a light and airy conservatory; piped music. St Austell Tribute and Wells & Youngs Bitter on handpump, and a good choice of wines by the glass. From the seats and tables out on the terrace and lawn there are attractive Cotswold views.

🍴 Good bar food includes lunchtime filled ciabatta sandwiches, soup, chicken liver and orange pâté, filo-wrapped prawns with sweet chilli mayonnaise, gammon and egg, beef, mushroom and stilton pie, open ravioli of mediterranean vegetables with a cherry tomato dressing, chicken on sweet potato and baby onions with cranberries and red wine sauce, minted lamb steak, bass with leek, pine nut and bacon bubble and squeak and a white wine and crayfish sauce, and puddings like warm dark chocolate and orange brownie with Cointreau and chocolate sauce and rum and raisin cheesecake. *Starters/Snacks: £3.95 to £6.50. Main Courses: £9.95 to £17.00. Puddings: £5.95*

Charles Wells ~ Lease Michele and Kevin Johnston ~ Real ale ~ Bar food ~ Restaurant ~ (01242) 820341 ~ Well behaved children allowed ~ Open 11-3, 5.30-11; 11-11 Sun ~ Bedrooms: /£95S

Recommended by JCW, Neil and Anita Christopher, Dr A J and Mrs Tompsett, KC, Colin Moore, Neil Kellett, Keith and Sue Ward

LITTLE BARRINGTON
SP2012 MAP 4

Inn For All Seasons 🍴 🍷
On A40, 3 miles W of Burford; OX18 4TN

Fish specials as well as other interesting food in creeper-covered old inn; fine wines, big log fire and pleasant garden; very busy during Cheltenham Gold Cup Week

---

There's a lively buzz of conversation as you walk through the door of this handsome old coaching inn and it's all kept spic and span. You'll get a smiling welcome from the smart barman, and the attractively decorated, mellow lounge bar has low beams, stripped stone and flagstones, old prints, leather-upholstered wing armchairs and other comfortable seats; country magazines to read and a big log fire. Wadworths IPA and a guest from Fullers, Sharps or Wye Valley on handpump, lots of wines by the glass from a particularly good list, over 60 malt whiskies, and a dozen brandies; newspapers to read. There's also a conservatory and restaurant. Cribbage, board games and piped music. The pleasant garden has tables, a play area and aunt sally, and there are walks straight from the inn. It gets very busy during Cheltenham Gold Cup Week.

🍴 **Good bar food includes sandwiches, hand-raised pork pie, ploughman's, duck liver and foie gras parfait with sauternes wine jelly, bubble and squeak galette with smoked bacon and a fried egg, field mushroom burger with sautéed spinach, onions and beef tomato, local game casserole with herb dumplings, venison sausages with red wine jus, free-range chicken with caramelised garlic, white bean and wild mushroom ragoût, lots of fish dishes like irish rock oysters, whole cock crabs, sea trout steak on roasted samphire with a vermouth and dill butter sauce, and poached skate wing with a baby caper and shallot butter sauce, and puddings such as coconut and pineapple crème brûlée and plum pudding with brandy butter.** *Starters/Snacks: £4.50 to £8.50. Main Courses: £7.50 to £14.50. Puddings: £4.95 to £7.25*

Free house ~ Licensees Matthew and Heather Sharp ~ Real ale ~ Bar food (12-2.30, 7-9) ~ Restaurant ~ (01451) 844324 ~ Children welcome ~ Dogs allowed in bar and bedrooms ~ Open 10.30-2.30, 6-10.30(11.30 Sat); 12-10.30 Sun ~ Bedrooms: £68B/£115B

Recommended by David Lamb, Edward Mirzoeff, Tom and Ruth Rees, Ann and Colin Hunt, John Holroyd, Richard Wyld, Tracey and Stephen Groves, Andy and Claire Barker, Peter and Audrey Dowsett

LITTLETON-UPON-SEVERN
ST5989 MAP 2

White Hart
3.5 miles from M48 junction 1; B4461 towards Thornbury, then village signposted; BS35 1NR

A good mix of customers and log fires in three main rooms, nice country furnishings, and good beer and food; nearby walks

---

This cosy old former farmhouse has three main rooms with log fires and fine furnishings such as long cushioned wooden settles, high-backed settles, oak and elm tables and a loveseat in the big low inglenook fireplace; as we went to press, there were plans afoot for some refurbishment. There are flagstones in the front, huge tiles at the back, and smaller tiles on the left, plus some old pots and pans, a lovely old White Hart Inn Simonds Ale sign and hops on beams; by the black wooden staircase are some nice little alcove seats. Similarly furnished, a family room has some sentimental engravings, plates on a delft shelf and a couple of high chairs; a back snug has pokerwork seats. Wells & Youngs Bitter and Special and guest beers like Bath Ales Golden Hare and St Austell Tribute on handpump, and several wines by the glass. Outside, there are picnic-sets on the neat front lawn with interesting cottagey flowerbeds, and by the good big back car park are some attractive shrubs and teak furniture on a small brick terrace. Several enjoyable walks from the pub. They may ask to keep your credit card behind the bar.

🍴 **Using some home-grown produce and their own chickens for eggs, the interesting modern food might include lunchtime filled baguettes, soup, fresh crab and crayfish tian with cucumber salsa, speciality sausages with caramelised onions and red wine gravy, steak in ale pie, tomato and ricotta pasta, baked salmon fillet on squash fondant with a mussel and sorrel sauce, best end of lamb with roast butternut squash and caramelised**

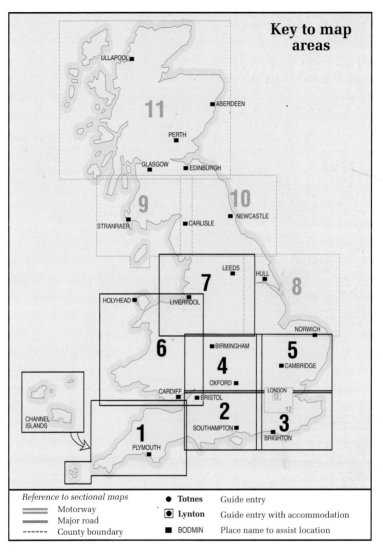

Key to map areas

ULLAPOOL ■

11

■ ABERDEEN

PERTH ■

GLASGOW ■ ■ EDINBURGH

9

10

STRANRAER ■ ■ CARLISLE NEWCASTLE

LEEDS ■ HULL ■

7

8

HOLYHEAD ■ LIVERPOOL

NORWICH ■

6

■ BIRMINGHAM

5

4

■ CAMBRIDGE

OXFORD ■

CARDIFF ■ ■ BRISTOL

LONDON
13
12

CHANNEL
ISLANDS

2

1

SOUTHAMPTON ■

3

PLYMOUTH ■

BRIGHTON

Reference to sectional maps		
▬▬ Motorway	● **Totnes**	Guide entry
▬▬ Major road	◉ **Lynton**	Guide entry with accommodation
----- County boundary	■ BODMIN	Place name to assist location

MAPS IN THIS SECTION

For Maps 8 – 13 see later colour section

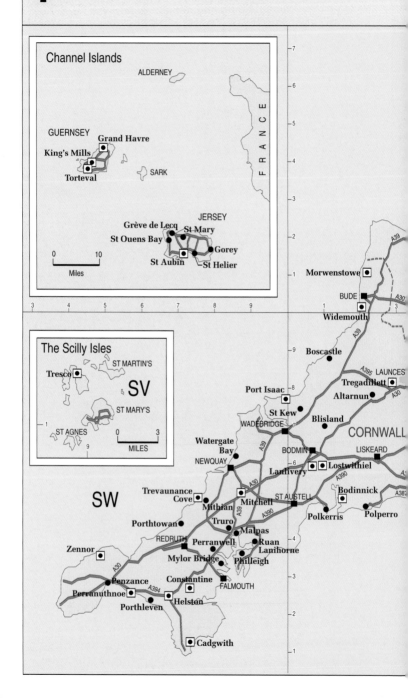

SS

ST

Portishead
Clapton-in-Gordano
M5

WESTON
SUPER MARE

Churchill

A38

A39
MINEHEAD

LYNTON

ILFRACOMBE

A39

WATCHET

A39

Simonsbath

Luxborough

Monksilver

A358

Triscombe

A38

BRIDGWATER

A372

2

Tarr

A396

SOMERSET

Waterrow

Stoke St Gregory

Pitney

BARNSTAPLE

A39

A39

A377

Molland

Dulverton

TAUNTON

A378

Huish
Episcopi

Buckland Brewer

A361

B4322

Appley

A38

North Curry

King's Nympton

DEVON

TIVERTON

A396

Culmstock

Clayhidon

Ashill

Hinton St George

Chiselborough

A303

A3124

Winkleigh

Cadeleigh

A373

Stockland

A30

Sheepwash

A386

Coleford

Clyst Hydon

Dalwood

Shave
Cross

OKEHAMPTON

Spreyton

A377

Rockbeare

A35

HONITON

A35

BRIDPORT

M5

Exeter

Tipton St John

Sidbury

A3052

West Bay

A30

Drewsteignton

A30

Sidford

Branscombe

Portgate

A386

Horndon

Topsham

Exminster

A38

Woodbury
Salterton

ter Tavy

Postbridge

EXMOUTH

Cockwood

Haytor Vale

A379

Combeinteignhead

A382

TAVISTOCK

Widecombe

Buckland
Monachorum

Holne

Buckfast

Torbryan

NEWTON ABBOT

Marldon

TORQUAY

Rattery

Totnes

PLYMYOUTH

A38

Avonwick

PAIGNTON

SY

A379

Dittisham

Brixham

Blackawton

Dartmouth

ewton Ferrers

Kingston

A381

East Allington

Noss Mayo

Kingsbridge

Stokenham

Bantham

A379

Torcross

SALCOMBE

Beesands

SX

0   10   20
MILES

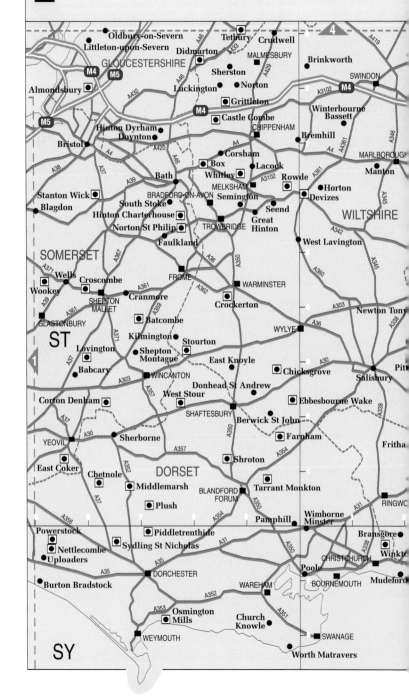

Oldbury-on-Severn
Littleton-upon-Severn
Didmarton
Tetbury
Crudwell
GLOUCESTERSHIRE
MALMESBURY
Brinkworth
Sherston
SWINDON
Almondsbury
Luckington
Norton
Winterbourne Bassett
Grittleton
Castle Combe
CHIPPENHAM
Bremhill
Hinton Dyrham
Doynton
Corsham
MARLBOROUGH
Bristol
Box
Lacock
Manton
Bath
Whitley
MELKSHAM
Rowde
Stanton Wick
BRADFORD-ON-AVON
Semington
Horton
Devizes
Blagdon
South Stoke
Hinton Charterhouse
Seend
WILTSHIRE
Norton St Philip
TROWBRIDGE
Great Hinton
Faulkland
SOMERSET
West Lavington
Wells
Croscombe
FROME
WARMINSTER
Wookey
Cranmore
SHEPTON MALLET
Crockerton
GLASTONBURY
Batcombe
WYLYE
Newton Tony
ST
Kilmington
Stourton
Lovington
Shepton Montague
East Knoyle
Chicksgrove
Babcary
WINCANTON
Salisbury
Pitt
Corton Denham
Donhead St Andrew
West Stour
Ebbesbourne Wake
SHAFTESBURY
Berwick St John
Frith
Sherborne
Farnham
YEOVIL
East Coker
Shroton
Chetnole
DORSET
Middlemarsh
BLANDFORD FORUM
Tarrant Monkton
RINGWO
Plush
Pamphill
Wimborne Minster
Powerstock
Piddletrenthide
Bransgore
Nettlecombe
Sydling St Nicholas
CHRISTCHURCH
Winkt
Uploaders
Poole
Mudeford
Burton Bradstock
DORCHESTER
BOURNEMOUTH
WAREHAM
Osmington Mills
Church Knowle
WEYMOUTH
SWANAGE
SY
Worth Matravers

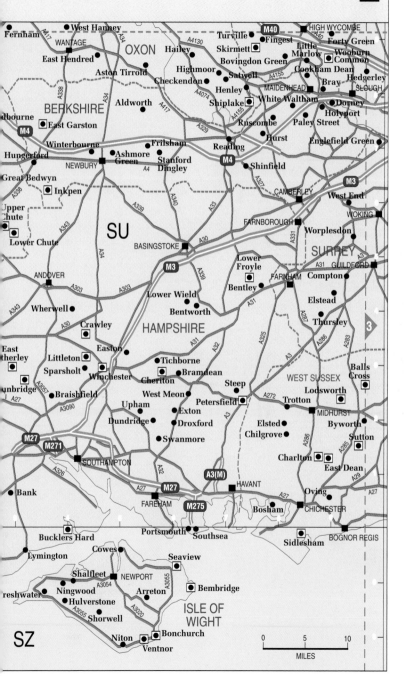

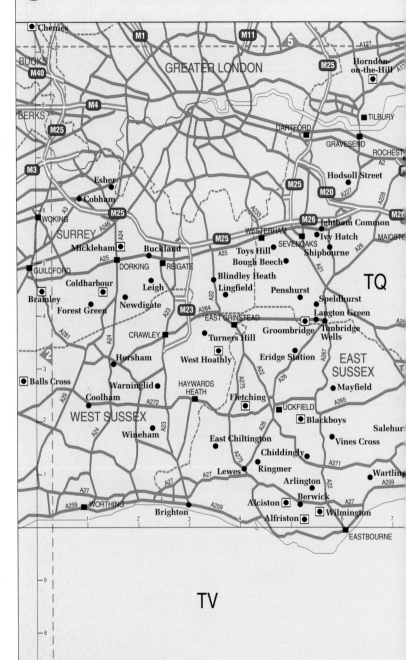

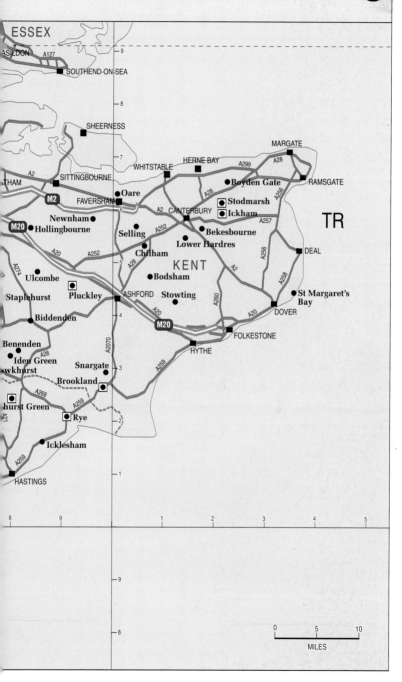

ESSEX

ASILDON · A127
SOUTHEND-ON-SEA

9

8

SHEERNESS

7

WHITSTABLE
HERNE BAY
MARGATE
A299
A28
RAMSGATE

THAM
A2
SITTINGBOURNE
M2
FAVERSHAM
Oare
Boyden Gate
A28
Stodmarsh
CANTERBURY
Ickham
A2
A256
A257
TR

6

M20
Newnham
Hollingbourne
A20
A252
Selling
Chilham
A252
A28
Bekesbourne
Lower Hardres
A256
DEAL

Ulcombe
KENT
Bodsham
A2
A258

5

Staplehurst
Pluckley
ASHFORD
Stowting
A260
St Margaret's
Bay

A274
Biddenden
A20
M20
DOVER
A20
FOLKESTONE

4

Benenden
A2070
HYTHE

Iden Green
A28
wkhurst
Snargate
A259

3

Brookland
A268
A259
hurst Green
A21
Rye

2

Icklesham
A259

1

HASTINGS

8   9   1   2   3   4   5

9

8

0   5   10

MILES

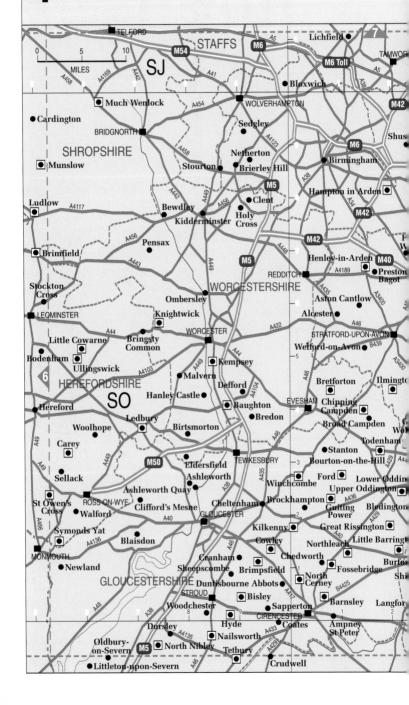

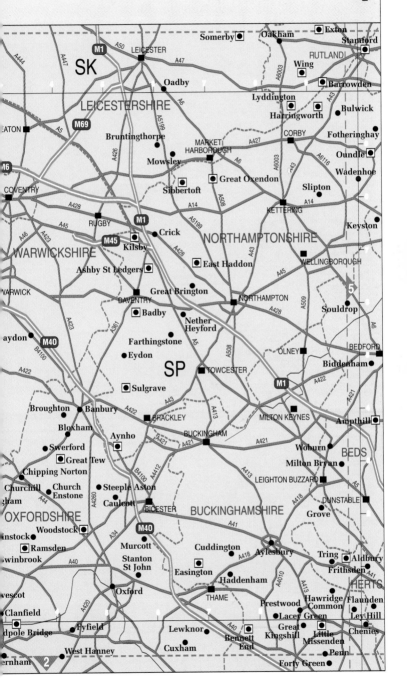

Somerby
Oakham
Exton
Stamford
A444
A447
M1
A50
LEICESTER
A47
SK
A6003
Wing
RUTLAND
Oadby
Barrowden
A6
Lyddington
LEICESTERSHIRE
Harringworth
Bulwick
ATON
M69
A5
Bruntingthorpe
MARKET
HARBOROUGH
CORBY
Fotheringhay
M6
A426
Mowsley
A427
A6003
A6116
Oundle
COVENTRY
A428
Sibbertoft
Great Oxendon
A508
Slipton
Wadenhoe
RUGBY
M1
A14
A14
Keyston
A46
A423
A45
A5199
KETTERING
WARWICKSHIRE
M45
Crick
NORTHAMPTONSHIRE
Kilsby
A428
A43
WELLINGBOROUGH
Ashby St Ledgers
East Haddon
A45
5
WARWICK
Great Brington
NORTHAMPTON
A509
Souldrop
DAVENTRY
Badby
A6
A23
Nether
Heyford
A428
BEDFORD
aydon
M40
Farthingstone
A361
A508
OLNEY
Biddenham
B4100
Eydon
A5
SP
TOWCESTER
A422
Sulgrave
M1
A422
A421
Broughton
Banbury
A422
BRACKLEY
A413
MILTON KEYNES
Ampthill
Bloxham
Aynho
A421
BUCKINGHAM
A421
BEDS
Swerford
A421
Woburn
Great Tew
B4100
A412
Milton Bryan
Chipping Norton
A413
LEIGHTON BUZZARD
A5
Churchill
Church
Steeple Aston
BICESTER
A418
DUNSTABLE
gham
Enstone
Caulcott
BUCKINGHAMSHIRE
Grove
A44
A4260
OXFORDSHIRE
M40
A41
instock
Woodstock
Murcott
Cuddington
A418
Aylesbury
Tring
Aldbury
Ramsden
Stanton
St John
Frithsden
A41
winbrook
A40
Easington
A4010
A413
HERTS
Haddenham
Hawridge
vescot
Oxford
THAME
Prestwood
Common
Flaunden
Clanfield
A420
Lacey Green
Ley Hill
dpole Bridge
Fyfield
Lewknor
A40
Great
Kingshill
Little
Chenies
Bennett
Missenden
West Hanney
Cuxham
End
Penn
ernham
2
Forty Green

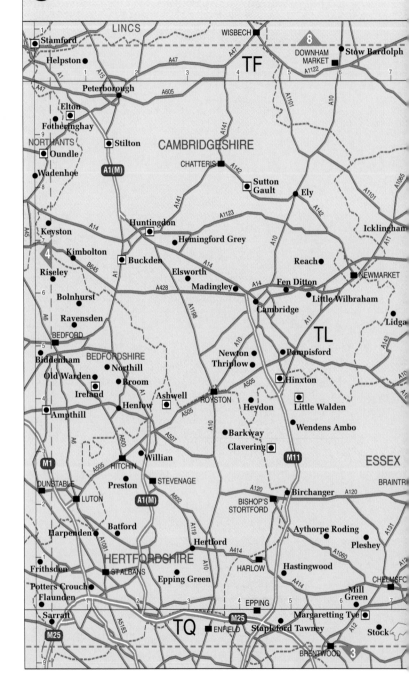

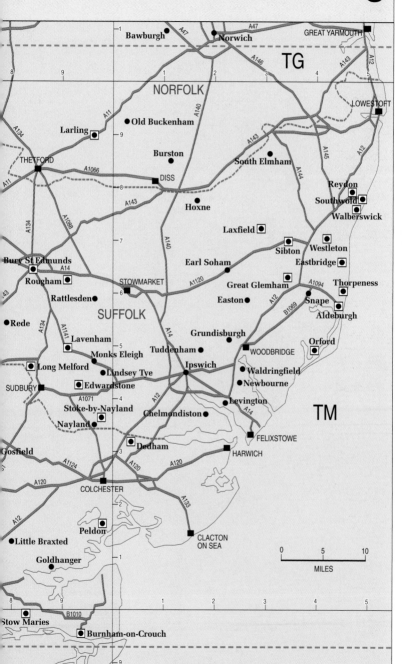

Bawburgh
A47
Norwich
A47
GREAT YARMOUTH
A146
TG
A143
A12
LOWESTOFT
NORFOLK
A11
Old Buckenham
A140
A143
A144
A145
A12
Larling
A134
THETFORD
A11
A1066
DISS
A143
Burston
South Elmham
Reydon
Southwold
Walberswick
A1068
Hoxne
A140
Laxfield
Westleton
Sibton
Bury St Edmunds
A14
Earl Soham
Eastbridge
Rougham
STOWMARKET
A1120
Great Glemham
A1094
Thorpeness
Rattlesden
SUFFOLK
A14
Easton
A12
Snape
Aldeburgh
B1069
Rede
A1141
Lavenham
Grundisburgh
Orford
Monks Eleigh
Tuddenham
WOODBRIDGE
Long Melford
Lindsey Tye
Ipswich
Waldringfield
SUDBURY
Edwardstone
Newbourne
A1071
Levington
Stoke-by-Nayland
Chelmondiston
A12
A14
TM
Nayland
Dedham
FELIXSTOWE
Gosfield
A1124
A120
A120
HARWICH
A120
COLCHESTER
A12
Peldon
A133
Little Braxted
CLACTON
ON SEA
Goldhanger
0   5   10
MILES
Stow Maries
B1010
Burnham-on-Crouch

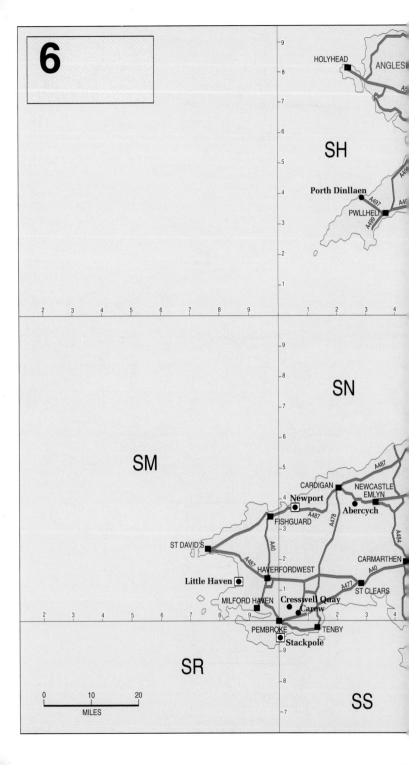

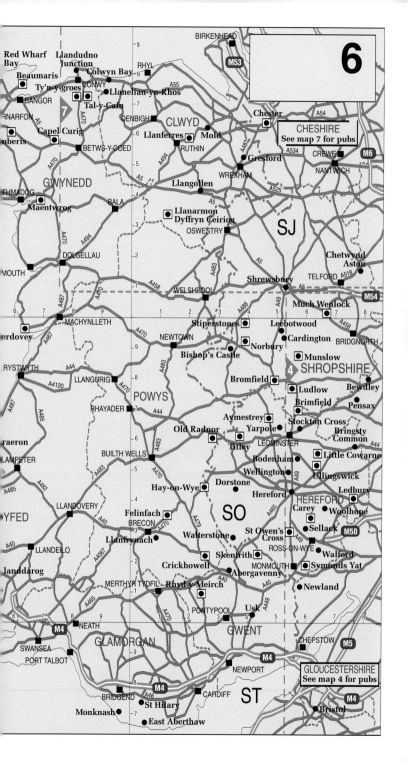

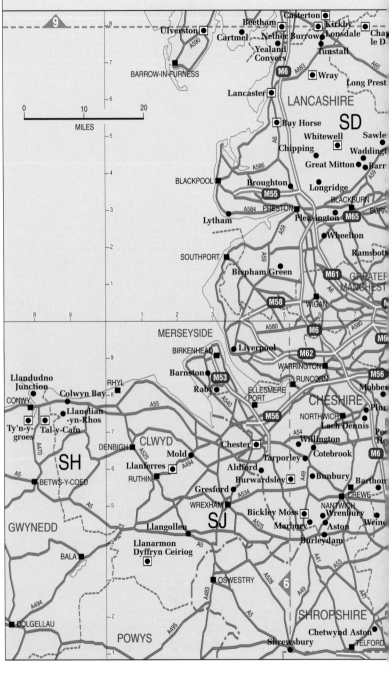

9

Ulverston

Beetham
Casterton
Kirkby
Lonsdale
Cha
le D

Cartmel
Nether Burrow
Tunstall

Yealand
Conyers

BARROW-IN-FURNESS

Wray

Long Prest

Lancaster

LANCASHIRE

SD

0   10   20
MILES

Bay Horse

Whitewell
Sawle

Chipping
Waddingt

Great Mitton
Barr

BLACKPOOL

Broughton
Longridge

BLACKBURN

Broughton

BURN

PRESTON
Pleasington

Lytham

Wheelton

Ramsbot

SOUTHPORT

Bispham Green

GREATER
MANCHEST

WIGAN

MERSEYSIDE

Liverpool

BIRKENHEAD

Barnston

WARRINGTON

RUNCORN

Raby

ELLESMERE
PORT

CHESHIRE

Mobbe

Llandudno
Junction

RHYL

CONWY

Colwyn Bay

NORTHWICH

Plo

Lach Dennis

Pe
He

Llanelian
-yn-Rhos

Ty'n-y-
groes

Tal-y-Cafn

Chester

Willington

DENBIGH

CLWYD

Cotebrook

Tarporley

SH

Mold

Aldford

Bunbury

Llanferres

Burwardsley

Barthon

BETWS-Y-COED

RUTHIN

Gresford

CREWE

WREXHAM

NANTWICH

GWYNEDD

Bickley Moss

Wrenbury

Aston

Wrinc

Llangollen

SJ

Marbury

BALA

Llanarmon
Dyffryn Ceiriog

Burleydam

OSWESTRY

6

DOLGELLAU

POWYS

SHROPSHIRE

Chetwynd Aston

Shrewsbury

TELFORD

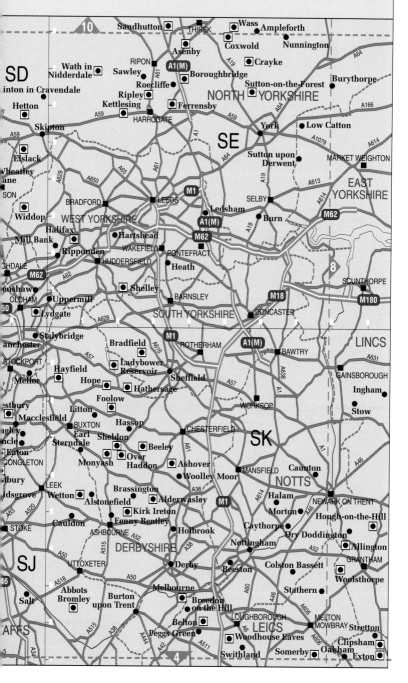

10

Sandhutton THIRSK Wass Ampleforth
Asenby Coxwold Nunnington
A64

SD Wath in Nidderdale RIPON A61 A1(M) Crayke
inton in Cravendale Sawley Boroughbridge A19 Sutton-on-the-Forest Burythorpe
Hetton Roecliffe NORTH YORKSHIRE A64
Ripley A166
Skipton Kettlesing Ferrensby A59
A59 HARROGATE A1 York Low Catton A1079 A614
Elslack A64 SE
heatley A629 A65 A61 A19 Sutton upon Derwent MARKET WEIGHTON
ane A650 EAST
SON A613 YORKSHIRE
Widdop BRADFORD LEEDS M1 SELBY A614
WEST YORKSHIRE Ledsham A1(M) Burn M62
Halifax Hartshead A19
Mill Bank Ripponden WAKEFIELD M62 PONTEFRACT Heath
HDALE HUDDERSFIELD Heath 8
M62 A62 SCUNTHORPE
enshaw OLDHAM Shelley BARNSLEY M18 M180
Lydgate A628 SOUTH YORKSHIRE DONCASTER
60

Stalybridge M1 LINCS
anchester Bradfield A616 ROTHERHAM A1(M) BAWTRY
STOCKPORT Hayfield Ladybower Reservoir A638 A631 GAINSBOROUGH
Mellor Hope Sheffield A57 Ingham
stbury Foolow Hathersage Stow
Macclesfield Litton WORKSOP
gley BUXTON Hassop CHESTERFIELD SK
ncle Earl Sheldon A61
Eaton Sterndale Beeley A46
ONGLETON Over Haddon Ashover Caunton
bury Monyash Woolley Moor MANSFIELD NOTTS
dsgrove LEEK Brassington A38 Halam NEWARK ON TRENT
Wetton Alstonefield Alderwasley M1 Morton Hough-on-the-Hill
Cauldon Kirk Ireton Caythorpe Dry Doddington
STOKE Fenny Bentley Holbrook A614 Allington
ASHBOURNE A52 GRANTHAM
A515 DERBYSHIRE A38 Nottingham A52
SJ UTTOXETER A50 Derby Beeston Colston Bassett Woolsthorpe
6 A50 A60 Stathern
Salt A518 Melbourne Breedon on the Hill MELTON MOWBRAY
Abbots Bromley Burton upon Trent Belton A606 Stretton
AFFS Peggs Green LOUGHBOROUGH A6 LEICS Clipsham
A515 A38 A444 Woodhouse Eaves A606 Oakham Exton
A34 4 Swithland Somerby

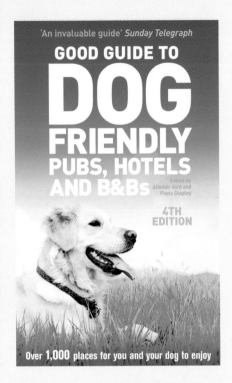

**shallots in a redcurrant and rosemary sauce, and venison and foie gras burger with
gooseberry chutney.** *Starters/Snacks: £3.95 to £6.95. Main Courses: £7.50 to £14.95.
Puddings: £4.95 to £5.95*

Youngs ~ Managers Jamie and Diane Reed ~ Real ale ~ Bar food (12-2(3 Sat), 6-9(10 Sat);
all day Sun) ~ (01454) 412275 ~ Children welcome away from main bar area ~ Dogs welcome ~
Open 12-11

*Recommended by Dr and Mrs A K Clarke, Chris and Angela Buckell, Will Stevens, Mr and Mrs M J Girdler, Donna and
Roger, Mr and Mrs D J Nash, Tom Evans, Philip and Jude Simmons*

LOWER ODDINGTON
SP2326   MAP 4

Fox ⏏ ☶ ☖

Signposted off A436 between Stow and Chipping Norton; GL56 0UR

Popular dining inn with excellent food and wines, several real ales, and helpful staff

There is a small pubby part by the bar counter in this welcoming, creeper-covered old
place and locals do pop in for a pint and a chat, but most customers are here to enjoy
the first-class food. The simply furnished bar rooms have beams and flagstones, a mix of
wooden dining chairs around pine tables, fresh flowers, hunting scene figures above the
mantelpiece and a growing number of hunting pictures, a display cabinet with pewter
mugs and stone bottles, daily newspapers and an inglenook fireplace. Greene King Abbot,
Hook Norton Bitter and Purity Pure Ubu on handpump, and several wines by the glass.The
red-walled, elegant dining room has another open fire, dark wood furniture, and candles.
Outside, the cottagey garden is pretty and there are lots of white tables and chairs under
an awning on the heated terrace. A good eight-mile walk starts from here (though a
stroll around the pretty village might be less taxing).

⏏ **Served by neat, uniformed staff, the interesting modern food might include soup,
seared scallops with ginger dressing, chicken in a mild curry and apricot mayonnaise,
moules marinière, courgette and pesto tagliatelle, steak and kidney pie, pork fillet
stuffed with black pudding with a creamy mustard sauce, bass with lemon and dill butter,
braised lamb shank with roast garlic and red wine, and puddings like sticky gingerbread
pudding and crème brûlée.** *Starters/Snacks: £5.00 to £7.95. Main Courses: £10.95 to £15.75.
Puddings: £5.50*

Free house ~ Licensees James Cathcart and Ian MacKenzie ~ Real ale ~ Bar food (12-2.30,
6.30-10; 12-3.30, 7-9.30 Sun) ~ (01451) 870555 ~ Children welcome ~ Dogs allowed in bar ~
Open 12-3, 6-midnight; 12-4, 6.30-11 Sun ~ Bedrooms: /£68S(£95B)

*Recommended by Noel Grundy, Peter and Josie Fawcett, Chris Glasson, Phil and Helen Holt, Jay Bohmrich,
Jeff and Wendy Williams, Guy Vowles, Anthony and Pam Stamer, Bernard Stradling, Martin Smith, Fred and
Kate Portnell, Keith and Sue Ward, Susan Lang, Alan Thwaite, MDN, Richard Greaves, Rod Stoneman*

NAILSWORTH
ST8499   MAP 4

Egypt Mill ☖

Just off A46; heading N towards Stroud, first right after roundabout, then left; GL6 0AE

Stylishly converted mill with lovely summer terrace and interesting split-level bar

In summer, the floodlit terrace garden overlooking the millpond beside this handsome
16th-c hotel is a lovely place to relax and there's a little bridge over from the car park.
It's a fine conversion of a three-floor stone-built mill still with working waterwheels and
the millstream flowing through, and the brick-and-stone-floored split-level bar gives
good views of the wheels. There are also big pictures and lots of stripped beams in the
comfortable carpeted lounge, along with some hefty yet elegant ironwork from the old
mill machinery. Nailsworth Mayor's Bitter and Stroud Budding on handpump, and several
wines by the glass; piped music and TV. It can get quite crowded on fine weekends, but
it's spacious enough to feel at its best when busy.

⏏ **Popular bar food at lunchtime includes sandwiches, soup, macaroni cheese, local
sausages with onion gravy, omelettes with free-range eggs, a proper burger, and fillet of**

smoked haddock with parsley sauce and poached egg; with evening choices such as smoked ham and foie gras terrine, wild mushrooms and devilled kidneys on toasted home-made brioche, steak and kidney suet pudding, mushroom, tomato and mozzarella parcel with tomato and oregano dressing, beer-battered haddock with mushy peas, confit of duck cassoulet, and puddings like chocolate and orange sponge with orange custard and chocolate and hazelnut tart; Sunday roast. *Starters/Snacks: £5.00 to £9.50. Main Courses: £7.95 to £12.00. Puddings: £5.25*

Free house ~ Licensees Stephen Webb and Rob Aldridge ~ Real ale ~ Bar food (12-2, 6.30-9.30(9.45 Fri and Sat); all day Sun) ~ Restaurant ~ (01453) 833449 ~ Children welcome ~ Open 11-11(midnight Sat); 12-11 Sun ~ Bedrooms: £80S/£90S

Recommended by Tom and Ruth Rees, Andy and Claire Barker, Stan Edwards, Brian and Pat Wardrobe

Weighbridge

B4014 towards Tetbury; GL6 9AL

Super two-in-one pies served in cosy old-fashioned bar rooms, a fine choice of drinks, lots of black ironware hanging from beams, and a sheltered landscaped garden

Extremely well run and consistently enjoyed by our readers, this bustling pub has a really good, welcoming atmosphere and genuinely helpful staff. The relaxed bar has three cosily old-fashioned rooms with stripped stone walls, antique settles and country chairs, window seats and open fires. The black beamed ceiling of the lounge bar is thickly festooned with black ironware – sheepshears, gin traps, lamps, and a large collection of keys, many from the old Longfords Mill opposite the pub. Upstairs is a raftered hayloft with an engaging mix of rustic tables. No noisy games machines or piped music. Uley Old Spot and Wadworths 6X with a guest from Stroud on handpump, 16 wines (and champagne) by the glass, Weston's cider and several malt whiskies. Behind the building is a sheltered landscaped garden with picnic-sets under umbrellas. Good disabled access and facilities.

⦿ **The hugely popular two-in-one pies come in a large bowl, and half the bowl contains the filling of your choice whilst the other is full of home-made cauliflower cheese (or broccoli mornay or root vegetables) and topped with pastry: turkey and trimmings, salmon in a creamy sauce, steak and mushroom, roast root vegetables, pork, bacon and celery in stilton sauce or chicken, ham and leek in a cream and tarragon sauce; you can also have mini versions or straightforward pies. Other dishes include filled baguettes, filled baked potatoes, omelettes, vegetable pasta, slow-cooked lamb rump with bordelaise sauce, roast chicken with a chervil sauce and garlic and rosemary mash, and puddings such as rhubarb crumble and chocolate brownie with chocolate sauce.** *Starters/Snacks: £2.95 to £6.20. Main Courses: £8.40 to £15.85. Puddings: £4.95 to £6.45*

Free house ~ Licensee Howard Parker ~ Real ale ~ Bar food (all day) ~ Restaurant ~ (01453) 832520 ~ Children allowed away from the bars until 9pm ~ Dogs welcome ~ Open 12-11(10.30 Sun)

Recommended by Dave Irving, Jenny Huggins, E McCall, T McLean, D Irving, Stuart Doughty, Neil and Anita Christopher, Ben Guy, James Morrell, Tom and Ruth Rees, JJW, CMW, Julian Saunders, Andrew Shore, Maria Williams, Jem Sweet, Andy and Claire Barker

NEWLAND SO5509   MAP 4

Ostrich

Off B4228 in Coleford; or can be reached from the A466 in Redbrook, by the turning off at the England/Wales border – keep bearing right; GL16 8NP

Liked by walkers and their dogs, with a friendly feel in the spacious bar, super choice of beers, open fire, daily papers and good food

Deservedly popular, this relaxed old pub has a marvellous choice of eight real ales on handpump well kept by the friendly, cheerful landlady: Butcombe Blond, Fullers London Pride, Hook Norton Old Hooky, RCH East Street Cream, Timothy Taylors Landlord, Uley Pigs Ear, Wye Valley Butty Bach, and Wells & Youngs Bitter. The low-ceilinged bar is spacious but cosily traditional with creaky floors, window shutters, candles in bottles on the tables, miners' lamps on the uneven walls, and comfortable furnishings such as cushioned window seats, wall settles and rod-backed country-kitchen chairs. There's a fine big fireplace, newspapers to read, perhaps quiet piped jazz, and board games. The pub lurcher is called Alfie. There are picnic-sets in a walled garden behind and out in front; the church, known as the Cathedral of the Forest, is well worth a visit, and this is a charmingly picturesque village.

🍴 **Good, interesting food includes soup with home-made bread, ploughman's with home-made chutney, duck and orange terrine with seville orange marmalade, three-cheese tart with sun-dried tomatoes and basil, steak in ale pie, sausages with dauphinoise potatoes and onion gravy, salmon and spinach fishcakes with parsley sauce, chicken with apricot and fresh herb stuffing and a leek, white wine and cream sauce, and roast rump of lamb with merguez sausage and rich marsala sauce.** *Starters/Snacks: £5.50 to £6.00. Main Courses: £5.50 to £19.00. Puddings: £4.50*

Free house ~ Licensee Kathryn Horton ~ Real ale ~ Bar food (12-2.30, 6.30(6 Sat)-9.30) ~ Restaurant ~ (01594) 833260 ~ Children welcome ~ Dogs allowed in bar ~ May have live jazz on summer evenings in garden ~ Open 12-3, 6.30-11; 12-3, 6-midnight Sat; 12-4, 6.30-10.30 Sun

Recommended by Richard and Sally Beardsley, LM, Chris and Angela Buckell, Di and Mike Gillam, John and Fiona McIlwain, Mr and Mrs D J Nash, Neil Jones

NORTH CERNEY   SP0208   MAP 4

Bathurst Arms ♀
A435 Cirencester—Cheltenham; GL7 7BZ

Bustling inn with beamed bar, open fires, fine wines, real ales and well liked food; comfortable bedrooms

With plenty of genuine character, this is a handsome old inn where both drinkers and diners feel equally at home. The original beamed and panelled bar has a fireplace at each end (one quite huge and housing an open woodburner), a good mix of old tables and nicely faded chairs, and old-fashioned window seats. There are country tables in an oak-floored room off the bar, as well as winged high-backed settles forming a few booths around other tables; piped music. The restaurant has leather sofas and another woodburning stove. Hidden Pint, Hook Norton First Light, and Wickwar Cotswold Way on handpump; there's a wine room where you can choose your own wines and 30 by the glass, and local soft drinks and juices. The pleasant riverside garden has picnic-sets sheltered by trees and shrubs, and plenty of surrounding walks. Cerney House Gardens are worth a visit.

🍴 **Using local, seasonal produce as well as growing some of their own herbs and vegetables, the interesting bar food includes sandwiches, home-made pork pie, soup, carpaccio of local venison with gremolata and horseradish cream, brixham crab fritter with lime vinegar and micro herb salad, beer-battered fish, a proper burger, root vegetable gratin, rabbit stew, seared chump lamb with rosemary gnocchi, spiced squash purée and red wine reduction, skate wing with cockles and star anise cream, and puddings such as vanilla and thyme panna cotta and apple and cinnamon crumble with crème anglaise; they also offer a good value two-course lunchtime menu that includes a glass of wine (not Sundays).** *Starters/Snacks: £3.50 to £4.95. Main Courses: £10.95 to £16.95. Puddings: £4.95*

Free house ~ Licensee James Walker ~ Real ale ~ Bar food (12-2(2.30 Fri-Sun), 6(7 Sun)-9(9.30 Fri and Sat) ~ Restaurant ~ (01285) 831281 ~ Children welcome ~ Dogs allowed in bar and bedrooms ~ Open 12-3, 6-11; 12-11(10.30 Sun) Sat ~ Bedrooms: £60B/£80B

Recommended by Stuart Doughty, Mr and Mrs J Brown, Cedric Robertshaw, Russell Grimshaw, Kerry Purcell, J Crosby, Michael Doswell, Ken Marshall, Guy Vowles, E McCall, T McLean, D Irving, Melanie Harries, Christopher Pincher, R L Borthwick, Canon Michael Bourdeaux, Peter Hadkins, Mr and Mrs M J Girdler, K Turner, Andrew Geraghty, Howard and Lorna Lambert, Fred and Lorraine Gill, Richard and Sheila Fitton

---

Half pints: by law, a pub should not charge more for half a pint than
half the price of a full pint, unless it shows that half-pint price on its price list.

NORTH NIBLEY   ST7596   MAP 4

New Inn 🍺

E of village itself; Waterley Bottom – OS Sheet 162 map reference 758963; GL11 6EF

Good choice of real ales and draught ciders in a friendly country pub, tasty food and seats in the garden

In a secluded rural setting, this former cider house is popular with walkers and with those interested in real ales. From antique beer pumps there might be Cotleigh 25, Goffs Jouster, Wickwar Brewery Draft and Wye Valley Butty Bach, and they hold two beer festivals a year (best to phone for dates). Also, five draught ciders and an August cider festival. The lounge bar has cushioned windsor chairs and high-backed settles against the partly stripped stone walls, and the simple, cosy public bar has darts and board games. There are lots of tables on the lawn, with more on a covered decked area (where there is an outdoor pool table). More reports please.

🍴 **Well liked bar food includes filled baguettes, ploughman's, traditional bar meals, daily specials, and puddings like apple crumble.** *Starters/Snacks: £3.00 to £7.00. Main Courses: £8.00 to £14.00. Puddings: £4.00 to £6.00*

Free house ~ Licensee Les Smitherman ~ Real ale ~ Bar food (not Mon) ~ Restaurant ~ (01453) 543659 ~ Children welcome ~ Dogs welcome ~ Open 12-2.30, 6-11; 11-11 Sat; 11-10.30 Sun; closed Mon lunchtime ~ Bedrooms: £40S/£60S

Recommended by Mr and Mrs J B Coles, Chris and Angela Buckell, Guy Vowles

NORTHLEACH   SP1114   MAP 4

Wheatsheaf 🍴 🍷 🛏

West End; the inn is on your left as you come in following the sign off the A429, just SW of its junction with the A40; GL54 3EZ

Smart coaching inn under new licensee, with excellent contemporary food, real ales, candles and fresh flowers, and a relaxed atmosphere; good bedrooms

A new licensee has taken over this handsome 17th-c stone coaching inn and made considerable changes. The whole place has been redecorated and refurbished and there's now quite an emphasis on the excellent modern cooking. The big-windowed airy linked rooms have high ceilings, contemporary paintwork, lots of pictures, church candles and fresh flowers, an attractive mix of dining chairs and stools around wooden tables, flagstones in the central bar and wooden floors in the airy dining rooms, and two open fires. Fullers London Pride, Hook Norton Hooky Bitter and St Austell Tribute on handpump and several wines by the glass from a french list. There are seats in the pretty back garden and they have fishing on the River Coln.

🍴 **Excellent bar food using top local ingredients includes soup, oysters, devilled kidneys or brown shrimps on toast, confit duck and foie gras terrine with apple chutney, smoked haddock fishcake with spinach and mustard, pork belly with curried lentils and chutney, breast of free-range chicken with creamed peas and bacon, duck hash with spring greens and fried egg, steak frites with béarnaise sauce, and puddings like chocolate brownie and eton mess; they also offer a good value two- and three-course set menu; Sunday roasts.** *Starters/Snacks: £5.00 to £6.00. Main Courses: £10.00 to £16.00. Puddings: £5.00*

Punch ~ Lease Sam Pearman ~ Real ale ~ Bar food (12-2.30, 6.30-10; 12-3, 6-9.30 Sun) ~ Restaurant ~ (01451) 860244 ~ Children welcome ~ Dogs welcome ~ Open 9am-11(10.30 Sun) ~ Bedrooms: £70S/£100S

Recommended by David and Cathrine Whiting, Dr and Mrs A K Clarke, Mr and Mrs W W Burke, T Harrison, Guy Vowles, Mike and Mary Carter, George Atkinson, Jean and Douglas Troup

---

Bedroom prices normally include full english breakfast, VAT and any inclusive service charge that we know of. Prices before the '/' are for single rooms, after for two people in double or twin (B includes a private bath, S a private shower).

OLDBURY-ON-SEVERN

ST6092   MAP 2

Anchor ♀ ◧

Village signposted from B4061; BS35 1QA

Bustling country pub with well liked food, a fine choice of drinks, a pretty garden and hanging baskets

Our readers tend to come back to this genuinely friendly pub on a regular basis as the staff are welcoming, the locals chatty, and both the real ales and bar food extremely good. The neatly kept lounge has an easy-going atmosphere, modern beams and stone, a mix of tables including an attractive oval oak gateleg, cushioned window seats, winged seats against the wall, oil paintings by a local artist and a big winter log fire. Diners can eat in the lounge or bar area or in the dining room at the back of the building (good for larger groups) and the menu is the same in all rooms. Well priced for the area and kept on handpump in very good condition, the beers might include Bass, Butcombe Bitter, Otter Bitter, and guests such as Bath Ales Wild Hare and Wickwar BOB. They also have a fine range of 83 malt whiskies and 14 wines by the glass. In summer, you can eat in the pretty garden and the hanging baskets and window boxes are lovely then; boules. They have wheelchair access and a disabled lavatory. Plenty of walks to the River Severn and along the many footpaths and bridleways, and St Arilda's church nearby is interesting, on its odd little knoll with wild flowers among the gravestones (the primroses and daffodils in spring are quite a show).

⊞ Enjoyable and reasonably priced, the bar food includes ciabatta sandwiches, ploughman's, soup, mussels with shallots, white wine and cream, confit of duck with a sweet and sour sauce, home-baked ham and eggs, smoked haddock and salmon fish pie, lamb curry, spinach and ricotta ravioli, crisp local pork belly and black pudding with mustard mash, salmon fillet with an orange, chive and cream sauce, and puddings such as raspberry pavlova and chocolate puddle pudding with vanilla ice-cream; they also offer a good value two-course weekday lunchtime menu. *Starters/Snacks: £5.50 to £8.25. Main Courses: £7.35 to £13.75. Puddings: £4.25*

Free house ~ Licensees Michael Dowdeswell and Mark Sorrell ~ Real ale ~ Bar food (12-2(2.30 Sat, 3 Sun), 6-9) ~ Restaurant ~ (01454) 413331 ~ Children in dining room only ~ Dogs allowed in bar ~ Open 11.30-3, 6(6.30 winter weekdays)-midnight; 11.30-1am Sat; 12-11 Sun

Recommended by Colin and Peggy Wilshire, James Morrell, John and Verna Aspinall, Tom and Ruth Rees, Alan and Eve Harding, Andrew Shore, Maria Williams, Dr and Mrs C W Thomas, Tom Evans

SAPPERTON

SO9403   MAP 4

Bell

Village signposted from A419 Stroud—Cirencester; OS Sheet 163 map reference 948033; GL7 6LE

GLOUCESTERSHIRE DINING PUB OF THE YEAR

Super pub with beamed cosy rooms, a really good mix of customers, delicious food, local ales, and a very pretty courtyard

'Near perfection for an english country pub' is how one of our readers describes this charming place. It's run with great care and consistent attention to detail by the hard-working licensees and their friendly staff who welcome both those popping in for a drink and a chat and customers wanting a special meal out. Harry's Bar (named after their sociable springer spaniel) has big cushion-strewn sofas, benches and armchairs where you can read the daily papers with a pint, in front of the woodburning stove – or simply have a pre-dinner drink. The two other cosy rooms have stripped beams, a nice mix of wooden tables and chairs, country prints and modern art on stripped stone walls, one or two attractive rugs on the flagstones, fresh flowers and open fires. The gents' has schoolboy humour cartoons on the walls. Bath Ales Gem, Butcombe Bitter, Otter Bitter and Uley Old Spot on handpump, over 20 wines by the glass and carafe from a large and diverse wine list with very helpful notes, Ashton Press cider, 20 malt whiskies, several armagnacs and cognacs and local soft drinks. There are tables out on a small front lawn and in a partly covered and very pretty courtyard, for eating outside. Horses have their own tethering rail (and bucket of water).

🍴 As well as a lunchtime daily pub classic dish, the particularly good, imaginative bar food (using top-quality meat from local farms) includes ploughman's, portland crab tart with avocado and cucumber, hand-pressed terrine of guinea fowl with apricots and pistachios, hand-made ravioli with wild garlic and oyster mushrooms, home-ground beefburger with bacon and cheese and dill pickles, beer-battered fresh pollack, bacon chop with black pudding and a free-range egg, and local pork belly with sweet potato purée. Evening choices such as warm salad of pigeon breast with fresh fig and bacon, goats cheese with poached pears in brandy and walnuts, fillet of veal with wild mushrooms, salted ox cheek with braised red cabbage and sultana and lime dressing, venison casserole, and puddings like passion-fruit crème brûlée with crystal crackles and baked pumpkin cake with raisins and deep-fried ice-cream; popular Sunday roasts. *Starters/Snacks: £4.95 to £8.50. Main Courses: £9.95 to £20.00. Puddings: £6.75*

Free house ~ Licensees Paul Davidson and Pat LeJeune ~ Real ale ~ Bar food (12-2.15, 7-9.30(9 Sun)) ~ (01285) 760298 ~ Children allowed but must be over 10 in evenings ~ Dogs welcome ~ Open 11-2.30(3 Sat), 6.30-11; 12-10.30 Sun

Recommended by T A R Curran, Richard and Sheila Fitton, Michael Doswell, Henry Midwinter, James Morrell, K Turner, John Holroyd, Stuart Doughty, E McColl, T McLean, D Irving, J Crosby, Bernard Stradling, Helene Grygar, Tom and Ruth Rees, Peter Sampson, Neil Kellett

SHEEPSCOMBE
SO8910 MAP 4

Butchers Arms

Off B4070 NE of Stroud; GL6 7RH

Fine views, real ales and pubby food and friendly young licensees

Reached down narrow lanes, this rural 17th-c stone pub is popular with a good mix of customers including walkers on their way to or from the Slad Valley. The bustling lounge bar has beams, wheelback chairs and cushioned stools around simple wooden tables, built-in cushioned seats in the big bay windows, interesting oddments like assorted blow lamps, irons and plates, and a woodburning stove; friendly service. The restaurant has an open log fire. Butcombe Gold, Otter Bitter and a guest like St Austell Tribute on handpump, several wines by the glass and Weston's cider; darts, chess, dominoes, cribbage and board games. The views over the lovely surrounding steep beechwood valley are terrific and there are seats outside. It is thought that this area was once a royal hunting ground for Henry VIII.

🍴 Using meat raised in the hills, the tasty bar food includes lunchtime sandwiches, soup, salmon, cod, lemon and dill fishcakes, chicken stuffed with apricots and thyme with toasted cashew nuts, salad and a red wine and shallot dressing, popular steak, ham and eggs, stout and stilton pie, beer-battered fish, vegetarian filo parcel with goats cheese, aubergine and roasted red peppers, and daily specials like rabbit with prunes on noodles, pork and black pudding cakes with pear mayonnaise and sauerkraut, and venison with wild mushrooms and home-made cranberry sauce; also, Sunday roasts and a pie and a pint deal (not Saturdays). *Starters/Snacks: £4.25 to £6.75. Main Courses: £7.25 to £13.50. Puddings: £3.75 to £4.25*

Free house ~ Licensee Mark Tallents ~ Real ale ~ Bar food (12-2.30, 6.30-9.30; all day weekends) ~ (01452) 812113 ~ Children welcome ~ Dogs allowed in bar ~ Open 11.30-3, 6.30-11; 11.30-11.30 Sat; 12-10.30 Sun

Recommended by Mr and Mrs P R Thomas, Mr and Mrs I and E Bell, Neil and Anita Christopher, Giles and Annie Francis, Tom and Ruth Rees, Martin and Pauline Jennings, John Holroyd

---

Anyone claiming to arrange or prevent inclusion of a pub in the *Guide* is a fraud. Pubs are included only if recommended by genuine readers and if our own anonymous inspection confirms that they are suitable.

STANTON

SP0634   MAP 4

Mount

Village signposted off B4632 SW of Broadway; keep on past village on no-through road up hill, bear left; WR12 7NE

17th-c pub in a lovely spot with fantastic views; keen, friendly young licensees and good bar food

An enthusiastic and friendly young couple are now running this 17th-c pub. It's in a lovely spot up a steep lane from the golden-stone village, with fantastic views over the Vale of Evesham towards the welsh mountains; seats on the terrace are much prized on fine days. Inside, there's a friendly welcome for both drinkers and diners, and the bars have low ceilings, heavy beams, flagstones and a big log fire in the inglenook fireplace. The roomy extension has big picture windows overlooking the attractive garden. Donnington BB and SBA on handpump and a good choice of wines by the glass; darts but no noisy games machines or piped music. The pub is on the Cotswold Way National Trail.

🍴 Good, popular bar food includes lunchtime filled baguettes, ploughman's, soup, chicken liver and foie gras parfait with red onion marmalade, various tapas, free-range three-egg omelette, tomato and chickpea curry, gloucester old spot sausage on cheddar mash with a rich jus, beer-battered haddock, sirloin steak with café de paris butter, daily specials and puddings; they also serve a three-course set menu and Sunday roasts. *Starters/Snacks: £4.50 to £6.50. Main Courses: £8.50 to £15.00. Puddings: £4.50*

Donnington ~ Tenants Karl and Pip Baston ~ Real ale ~ Bar food (12-2(fish and chips till 2.30), 6-9) ~ Restaurant ~ (01386) 584316 ~ Children welcome ~ Dogs welcome ~ Open 12-3, 6-11; 12-11 summer Sat and Sun
Recommended by Keith and Sue Ward, Alan Jones, A and M Jones, John and Joyce Farmer, P and J Shapley, Martin and Pauline Jennings, Tom Holman

TETBURY

ST8494   MAP 4

Gumstool 🍴 ☐ 🛏

Calcot Manor Hotel, A4135 W; GL8 8YJ

Civilised bar with relaxed atmosphere (part of the very smart Calcot Manor Hotel), super choice of drinks and enjoyable food

Although this bar/brasserie is attached to the very smart Calcot Manor Hotel, it does have an informal and relaxed atmosphere and our readers enjoy their visits very much. Butcombe Bitter and Gold and Sharps Own on handpump, a dozen interesting wines by the glass and lots of malt whiskies. The stylish layout is well divided to give a feeling of intimacy without losing the overall sense of contented bustle: flagstones, elegant wooden dining chairs and tables, well chosen pictures and drawings on mushroom-coloured walls, and leather armchairs in front of the big log fire; piped music. Westonbirt Arboretum is not far away.

🍴 Prices are reasonable for such a civilised setting: chicken liver parfait with onion marmalade, toasted muffin with locally smoked salmon, poached egg and hollandaise sauce, warm cornish crab and leek tart, tagliatelle with butternut squash and Amaretti, seared scallop salad with avocado and crispy pancetta, calves liver with caramelised shallots and smoked bacon, spit-roast free-range chicken with lemon, thyme and roasted root vegetables, free-range pork and herb sausages with onion gravy, beer-battered cod, organic mutton with herb dumpling, and aged scottish steaks. *Starters/Snacks: £6.95 to £9.25. Main Courses: £9.00 to £13.50. Puddings: £5.65*

Free house ~ Licensees Paul Sadler and Richard Ball ~ Real ale ~ Bar food (12-2, 5.30-9.30(9 Sun)) ~ Restaurant ~ (01666) 890391 ~ Children welcome ~ Open 12-10.30 ~ Bedrooms: £207B/£230B
Recommended by Bernard Stradling, Tom and Ruth Rees, Les and Judith Haines, Dr and Mrs C W Thomas, Gordon and Margaret Ormondroyd

Trouble House ⏀ ♀

A433 towards Cirencester, near Cherington turn; GL8 8SG

Smart and friendly bars with customers to match, an ambitious menu, good drinks and attentive service

Run by a talented chef/patron, this rather smart place is popular for its excellent food, though they do still keep Wadworths IPA and 6X on handpump (in the small saggy-beamed middle room) and several wines by the glass including champagne. Furnishings are mainly close-set stripped pine or oak tables with chapel, wheelback and other chairs, and there are attractive mainly modern country prints on the cream or butter-coloured walls. On the left is a parquet-floored room with a big stone fireplace, a hop-girt mantelpiece and some big black beams; piped music and attentive service. You can also sit out at picnic-sets on the gravel courtyard behind.

🍴 Excellent bar food includes sandwiches, soup, cannelloni of suckling pig and field mushroom with butternut squash purée and cep velouté, warm tart of fine beetroot, caramelised onion and goats cheese, lemon sole with beurre noisette, grilled scallop and asparagus, venison, mushroom and cranberry sausages with caramelised onion gravy, risotto of smoked haddock with roasted red peppers, slow-cooked gloucester old spot pork belly, potato purée and chicken jus with mushrooms, tomato, baby onions and tarragon, and puddings like hot chocolate fondant with milk ice-cream and coffee crème brûlée. *Starters/Snacks: £4.50 to £9.50. Main Courses: £13.95 to £16.95. Puddings: £5.50*

Wadworths ~ Tenants Martin and Neringa Caws ~ Real ale ~ Bar food (12-2(2.30 Sun), 7-9.30; not Sun evening or Mon) ~ (01666) 502206 ~ Children in restaurant ~ Dogs welcome ~ Open 11.30-3, 6.30-11; 11.30-3.30 Sun; closed Sun evening, all day Mon; two weeks Jan

Recommended by Richard Wyld, J Crosby, Richard and Sheila Fitton, David and Stella Martin, Bernard Stradling, Jan and Roger Ferris, Geoff and Brigid Smithers

TODENHAM   SP2436   MAP 4

Farriers Arms ♀

Between A3400 and A429 N of Moreton-in-Marsh; GL56 9PF

Friendly country pub with interesting décor, good bar food and fine views

This is an enjoyable and unspoilt old pub with friendly, helpful service from the landlady and her staff and a lovely atmosphere. The bar has nice wonky white plastered walls, hops on the beams, fine old polished flagstones by the stone bar counter and a woodburner in a huge inglenook fireplace. A tiny little room off to the side (full of old books and interesting old photographs) can seat parties of ten people. Black Sheep, Hook Norton Hooky Bitter and Wye Valley Butty Bach on handpump, ten wines by the glass, and locally brewed lager; piped music, darts and board games. The pub has fine views over the surrounding countryside from the back garden and there are a couple of tables on a small terrace by the quiet little road looking over to the church; aunt sally. Good surrounding walks.

🍴 Well liked bar food includes filled baguettes, soup, stilton and apricot tart, breaded goats cheese with red onion marmalade, steak in ale pie, roast chicken on lyonnaise potatoes with a madeira sauce, gammon and egg, roast vegetables and goats cheese cannelloni with pesto and parmesan cream, duck breast on braised cabbage with parsnip crisps and port and redcurrant sauce, and local sirloin steak with a black pepper sauce. *Starters/Snacks: £4.00 to £6.00. Main Courses: £8.00 to £15.00. Puddings: £4.95 to £5.50*

Free house ~ Licensees Nigel and Louise Kirkwood ~ Real ale ~ Bar food (12-2(2.30 Sun), 6(6.30 Sun)-9) ~ Restaurant ~ (01608) 650901 ~ Children welcome ~ Dogs allowed in bar ~ Open 12-3, 6(6.30 Sun)-11

Recommended by B R and M F Arnold, Keith and Sue Ward, John Holroyd, John Robertson, Ian and Nita Cooper, Alun and Jennifer Evans, Rob and Catherine Dunster, Clive and Fran Dutson, Phyl and Jack Street, Ken and Barbara Turner, W M Paton

---

It's very helpful if you let us know up-to-date food prices when you report on pubs.

UPPER ODDINGTON   SP2225   MAP 4

Horse & Groom ⊗ ⚲

Village signposted from A436 E of Stow-on-the-Wold; GL56 0XH

Pretty 16th-c cotswold stone inn with imaginative food, lots of wines by the glass, local beers and other local drinks; bedrooms

There's always a warm welcome from the friendly licensees and their staff in this neatly kept and attractive dining pub. The bar has pale polished flagstones, a handsome antique oak box settle among other more modern seats, some nice armchairs at one end, oak beams in the ochre ceiling, stripped stone walls, and a log fire in the inglenook fireplace. Wickwar BOB, Wye Valley Bitter and Hereford Pale Ale on handpump, 25 wines by the glass (including champagne), local apple juice and pressé, local cider, and a locally brewed lager. There are seats and tables under green parasols on the terrace and in the pretty garden.

🍴 **Enjoyable bar food includes sandwiches, soup, italian cured ham with clementine and parmesan salad, radicchio and red chard, seared sesame tuna with pickled ginger and cucumber salad and teriyaki dressing, gloucester old spot loin steak with black pudding and red onion crust, celeriac purée, olive oil mash and mustard jus, casserole of autumn root vegetables with chestnuts topped with a cheese cobbler and braised leek, local pheasant with thyme and garlic-roasted sweet potatoes and orange-glazed chicory, generous halibut steak on spinach and garlic potato purée, and puddings like orange panna cotta with glazed apricots and cardamon and white chocolate crème brûlée with lime shortbread biscuit. They list their local suppliers on the back of the menu and bake their own daily bread.** *Starters/Snacks: £5.95 to £7.95. Main Courses: £8.95 to £20.95. Puddings: £6.75*

Free house ~ Licensees Simon and Sally Jackson ~ Real ale ~ Bar food ~ Restaurant ~ (01451) 830584 ~ Children welcome ~ Open 12-3, 5.30-11; 12-3, 6-10.30 Sun ~ Bedrooms: £76S/£95S(£105B)

Recommended by Stuart Doughty, Keith and Sue Ward, B R and M F Arnold, T A R Curran, Graham Oddey, Julie and Bill Ryan, Alan Thwaite, Martin and Pauline Jennings, Alun and Jennifer Evans, John and Elisabeth Cox, Julian Saunders

WINCHCOMBE   SP0228   MAP 4

White Hart ⚲ 🛏

High Street (B4632); GL54 5LJ

Village pub with own wine shop, real ales, sausage menu and other good food; bedrooms

The hard-working and enthusiastic young landlord of this 16th-c village pub loves wine and has a 'Try before you buy' policy every night from 6pm to 7.30pm. The wines come from the wine shop next to the bar where you can choose what you want to drink with your meal – and take bottles away with you as well; there are 20 by the glass at the bar, too. The main bar area has a mix of wooden dining chairs, cushioned fabric chairs and small pine settles around pine tables, cream walls, big windows looking on to the village street, and Goffs Jouster and Otter Ale on handpump; several malt whiskies. There's also a smaller restaurant.

🍴 **They specialise in sausages with lots of different ones like gloucester old spot pork, cider and wholegrain mustard, venison and red wine, beef in ale, and lamb, mint and apricot, as well as soup, ploughman's, chicken liver parfait with home-made grape chutney, smoked eel and crispy pancetta salad with piccalilli dressing, corned beef fritters with quail egg and spicy tomato dressing, mushroom and leek pie with carrots and caraway, fish pie with mussels and prawns, chicken with morel and broad bean sauce, turbot with crab sauce and a warm herb, corn and shallot salad, and puddings like roast plum and poppyseed knickerbocker glory and a chocolate plate of brownie, mousse and ice-cream.** *Starters/Snacks: £1.95 to £5.95. Main Courses: £7.95 to £19.95. Puddings: £4.95 to £5.50*

Enterprise ~ Lease Peter Austen ~ Real ale ~ Bar food (all day) ~ Restaurant ~ (01242) 602359 ~ Children welcome ~ Dogs allowed in bar and bedrooms ~ Open 9am-midnight; 10am-10.30 Sun ~ Bedrooms: £65S(£75B)/£75S(£85B)

Recommended by Jack Morley, Ann and John Jordan, Michael Dandy

WOODCHESTER

SO8302 MAP 4

Ram ◗

High Street, South Woodchester; off A46 S of Stroud; GL5 5EL

Interesting ales, a friendly landlord and fair-priced food in attractive country pub

The welcoming and obliging landlord in this very busy country pub keeps six particularly well kept real ales on handpump. They change constantly but include Butcombe Bitter, Stroud Budding and Uley Old Spot, alongside three guests like Butcombe Brunel, Otter Bitter and Stroud Organic. The relaxed L-shaped beamed bar has a nice mix of traditional furnishings (including several cushioned antique panelled settles) on bare boards, stripped stonework and an open fire. There are seats outside on the terrace and spectacular valley views; in summer they hold various events out here – open-air theatre, live music and so forth.

🍴 Good value, enjoyable bar food includes sandwiches, soup, gloucester old spot sausages with mash and onion gravy, steak in ale or chicken, leek and ham pies, chicken breast with mango salsa, and puddings such as treacle sponge with custard or white chocolate and raspberry cheesecake; on Monday-Thursday they offer a £6 main course.
Starters/Snacks: £3.00 to £7.95. Main Courses: £6.00 to £11.50. Puddings: £4.25 to £4.50

Free house ~ Licensee Tim Mullen ~ Real ale ~ Bar food (12-2(2.30 weekends), 6-9; 6.30-8.30 Sun) ~ Restaurant ~ (01453) 873329 ~ Children welcome ~ Dogs welcome ~ Open 11-11(10.30 Sun)

Recommended by Andrew Shore, Maria Williams, Dave Irving, Jenny Huggins, Andy and Claire Barker, Tom and Ruth Rees, Dave Braisted, Mr Rene-Cason, Chris and Angela Buckell

---

LUCKY DIP

Besides the fully inspected pubs, you might like to try these Lucky Dips recommended to us and described by readers (if you do, please send us reports: feedback@goodguides.com).

ALDERTON [SP9933]
Gardeners Arms GL20 8NL [Beckford Rd, off B4077 Tewkesbury—Stow]: Attractive thatched Tudor pub with snug bars and informal restaurant, wide choice of decent home-made food from filled baps and baked potatoes to bistro dishes, fresh fish (inc take-away fish and chips) and good Sun roast; well kept Greene King and guest beers, above-average wines, hospitable landlady and good service, log fire; may be piped music; dogs and children welcome, tables on sheltered terrace, good-sized well kept garden with boules *(LYM, Martin and Pauline Jennings)*
AMBERLEY [SO8401]
Black Horse GL5 5AL [off A46 Stroud—Nailsworth to Amberley; left after Amberley Inn, left at war memorial; Littleworth]: Relaxed local with spectacular valley views from conservatory, good choice of changing ales (mostly local), decent wines by the glass, food from baguettes up, friendly helpful staff; flagstones and high-backed settles, woodburner, cheerful sporting pictures, large family area on left, games room, live music; they keep your card in a locked box if running a tab; big TV; children, walkers and wet dogs welcome, plenty of tables on pleasant back terrace with barbecue, more on secluded lawn; best to park by war memorial and walk down

(Chris and Angela Buckell, LYM, Dave Irving, Jenny Huggins, Karen Eliot, Ann and Colin Hunt, E McCall, T McLean, D Irving, John Coatsworth)
AMPNEY CRUCIS [SP0701]
☆ *Crown of Crucis* GL7 5RS [A417 E of Cirencester]: Bustling food pub, very popular particularly with older people, good value and plenty of choice inc Sun lunchtime carvery; real ales in small comfortable neat bar, good house wines, efficient service, pleasant décor, split-level restaurant; children welcome, disabled facilities, lots of tables out on grass by car park, quiet modern bedrooms around courtyard, good breakfast, open all day *(Peter and Audrey Dowsett, LYM)*
APPERLEY [SO8528]
☆ *Coal House* GL19 4DN [village signed off B4213 S of Tewkesbury; Gabb Lane]: Splendid riverside position, plenty of tables on front terrace and lawn with Severn views, helpful cheerful staff; Hook Norton Best and a guest beer, Stowford Press cider, plenty of blackboards for inexpensive usual food, two light and airy dining areas; no dogs; children welcome, wheelchair access possible, play area, moorings *(Chris and Angela Buckell, BB)*
ARLINGHAM [SO7110]
Red Lion GL2 7JH: Beamed roadside pub with well kept ales inc John Smiths, farm

cider, usual food reasonably priced inc children's menu and Sun roasts, pool room, skittle alley; dogs welcome, picnic-sets out at front and in small courtyard and back garden, petanque, not far from Severn estuary walks; three bedrooms, open all day wknds, cl Tues lunchtime and Mon *(Dr A Y Drummond)*

AUST [ST5788]
Boars Head BS35 4AX [0.5 mile from M48 junction 1, off Avonmouth rd]: Marstons pub handy for the 'old' Severn bridge, their ales and Bath Gem, good house wines, wide food choice from baguettes to steak, dark furniture in linked rooms and alcoves, beams and some stripped stone, huge log fire; piped music; wheelchair access possible, children in eating area away from bar, dogs on leads in bar; pretty sheltered garden *(LYM, Colin Moore, Chris and Angela Buckell, Donna and Roger, Guy Vowles)*

AWRE [SO7008]
☆ **Red Hart** GL14 1EW [off A48 S of Newnham]: Tall village inn with enjoyable home-made local food, real ale (may only be one), farm cider, good wines by the glass; heavy-beamed and flagstoned bar, illuminated well and with other interesting features, board games; piped music; children and dogs welcome, front picnic-sets, comfortable bedrooms, good breakfast, cl Sun evening and Mon, Tues lunchtimes in winter, open all day Sat *(Dr and Mrs C W Thomas, LYM, Abi Benson)*

AYLBURTON [SO6101]
Cross GL15 6DE [High St]: Decent choice of good food, well kept ales such as Flowers IPA, Greene King Abbot, Tetleys and Wadworths 6X, welcoming obliging staff, light and airy open-plan layout with flagstone floors and spruce décor; children welcome, disabled facilities, picnic-sets in pleasant orchard garden *(Eric Thomas Yarwood)*

BIBURY [SP1106]
☆ **Swan** GL7 5NW [B4425]: Hotel in lovely spot facing River Coln, with comfortable and attractive side bar used by locals, blazing fire, well kept Hook Norton, friendly attentive staff; nice modern adjoining brasserie with enjoyable up-to-date food inc good value Sun lunches, smart formal dining room; heated flagstone terrace, pleasant waterside garden, luxurious bedrooms *(George Atkinson, Giles Barr, Eleanor Dandy, Stuart Doughty, Keith and Sue Ward, BB)*

BIRDLIP [SO9316]
Air Balloon GL4 8JY [A417/A436 roundabout]: Loftily placed busy chain dining pub, standard value food all day from sandwiches, baguettes and wraps up, friendly helpful service; changing ales such as Hook Norton Old Hooky, many levels and alcoves inc restaurant and brasserie, pubbier front corner with open fire, beams and stripped stone; unobtrusive piped music; tables, some covered, on heated terrace and in garden with play area, open all day *(Phyl and Jack Street)*

Royal George GL4 8JH: Welcoming two-level beamed bar beyond hotel reception, airy and open, wide range of enjoyable good value food from sandwiches up, good wine choice, Greene King ales; prompt friendly service, soft lighting, part with armchairs and low tables, comfortable restaurant; piped music, busy Thurs quiz night; dogs welcome, heated terrace, fine grounds, 34 bedrooms, good breakfast *(Guy Vowles, Tom McLean, Neil and Anita Christopher, Dave Irving, Jenny Huggins, John Coatsworth)*

BLAKENEY [SO6606]
Cock GL15 4DB [Nibley Hill/A48]: Enjoyable food, welcoming bar with real ales, local ciders and perry; children welcome, lovely view from big garden, six comfortable bedrooms *(Jessica Triggs, Abi Benson)*

BOURTON-ON-THE-WATER [SP1620]
Duke of Wellington GL54 2BY [Sherbourne St]: Large friendly refurbished stone-built inn, good quality generous food all day, well kept real ales, relaxing open-plan carpeted bar with leather sofas, back dining room, log fires, newspapers; darts, Sun quiz night; garden with riverside picnic-sets, five redone bedrooms *(Mr and Mrs W W Burke, Ted George)*

BOX [SO8500]
☆ **Halfway House** GL6 9AE [by Minchinhampton Common]: This smartly renovated, light and airy open-plan dining pub reopened late 2008 under new management; food generally good, real ales such as Hancocks from central bar, friendly staff, downstairs restaurant; piped music; children and dogs welcome, garden tables, open all day; more reports please *(Guy Vowles, E McCall, T McLean, D Irving, Tom and Ruth Rees, LYM, Chris and Angela Buckell, Dave Irving, Jenny Huggins)*

BRIDGEYATE [ST6873]
White Harte BS30 5NA [London Rd (A420/A4175)]: Popular rambling heavy-beamed pub overlooking village green, carpeted throughout; helpful staff, Butcombe, Courage Best and Marstons Pedigree from unusual bar counter, bargain pubby food, some stripped masonry and panelling, pub dog called Maggie; disabled access *(Chris and Angela Buckell)*

BROADWELL [SP2027]
☆ **Fox** GL56 0UF [off A429 2 miles N of Stow-on-the-Wold]: Relaxing pub above broad green in pleasant village, friendly staff, good range of homely pub food (not Sun evening and stops early lunchtime) from sandwiches to popular Sun lunch, well kept low-priced Donnington BB and SBA, decent wines, good summer lemonade, nice coffee; stripped stone and flagstones, beams hung with jugs, log fires, darts, dominoes and chess, plain public bar with pool room, pleasant restaurant; may be piped music; tables out on gravel, good big family-friendly garden with aunt sally, meadow behind for Caravan Club members *(George Atkinson, Noel Grundy, Roger Fox, John and Sue Woodward, BB, K H Frostick)*

BROCKWEIR [SO5301]

Brockweir Inn NP16 7NG [signed just off A466 Chepstow—Monmouth]: Welcoming country local well placed for Wye Valley, beams and stripped stonework, quarry tiles, sturdy settles, woodburner, snug carpeted alcoves, well kept local ales, enjoyable food, upstairs restaurant, conservatory, public bar; no credit cards; children in eating areas, small garden with interesting covered terrace, bedrooms; has been open all day Sat *(LYM, Dave Irving, Jenny Huggins)*

CAMP [SO9111]

☆ *Fostons Ash* GL6 7ES [B4070 Birdlip—Stroud, junction with Calf Way]: Popular open-plan dining pub with good food inc interesting lunchtime sandwiches and imaginative light dishes, lunchtime bargains, real ales such as Goffs Jouster, Greene King Old Speckled Hen and Stroud Organic, decent wines by the glass; neat staff, daily papers, one end with easy chairs and woodburner; piped music; rustic tables in garden with heated terrace and play area, good walks *(BB, Neil and Anita Christopher)*

CERNEY WICK [SU0796]

Crown GL7 5QH: Village inn with newish landlord; roomy modern lounge bar, comfortable conservatory dining extension, enjoyable inexpensive food, well kept ales, coal-effect gas fires, games in public bar; children welcome, good-sized garden with swings, small motel-style bedroom extension *(Giles and Annie Francis, BB, Tim and Rosemary Wells)*

CHACELEY [SO8530]

Yew Tree GL19 4EQ [Stock Lane]: Remote, rambling country pub back to former name after spell as Old Ferry, spacious river-view dining-room, good choice of reasonably priced pubby food, welcoming attentive staff, Wye Valley Butty Bach and two guests; bar in original 16th-c core with log fire, quarry tiles and stripped-stone walls, second bar with pool, juke box and machines, skittle alley; children and dogs welcome, wheelchair access, terrace and attractive waterside lawns, summer barbecues and beer festival, Severn moorings *(Chris and Angela Buckell, BB)*

CHARLTON KINGS [SO9620]

Merry Fellow GL53 8AU [School Rd/Church St]: Family pub improved under new licensees, well kept Caledonian Deuchars, Greene King, Otter and Sharps, Stowford Press farm cider, good bargain food inc Sun roasts; terrace tables, open all day *(Mike and Mary Clark)*

Owl GL53 8EB [Cirencester Rd (A435)]: Friendly open-plan extended family dining pub with modern bright interior, Brakspears, Flowers and Fullers London Pride, low-priced simple food; big garden *(Stuart Doughty, BB)*

Reservoir GL54 4HG [Dowdeswell Reservoir, London Rd (A40)]: Large well reworked roadside pub opp reservoir, charming décor and young staff, wide choice of good reasonably priced straightforward food, well kept beer *(Jo Rees, Mr and Mrs J Brown)*

CHEDWORTH [SP0608]

Hare & Hounds GL54 4NN [Fosse Cross; A429 N of Cirencester, some way from village]: Rambling interestingly furnished stone-built restauranty pub with good if pricey food, well kept Arkells, decent house wines, cheerful helpful service; low beams and wood floors, soft lighting, cosy corners and little side rooms, two big log fires, small conservatory; children welcome away from bar, disabled facilities, bedrooms, open all day Fri-Sun *(Guy Vowles, LYM)*

CHELTENHAM [SO9421]

Bath Tavern GL53 7JT [Bath Rd]: One-room friendly bay-windowed local with well kept Bath Spa and Gem, good choice of wines by the glass, bargain generous pubby food from good crab sandwiches up, nice resident dog *(Joe Green, Prof Kenneth Surin)*

Jolly Brewmaster GL50 2EZ [Painswick Rd]: Open-plan linked areas around big semi-circular serving bar, good range of ales such as Archers, Caledonian Deuchars IPA, Donnington SBA and Hook Norton Best, up to eight farm ciders, perhaps a perry; friendly obliging young staff, log fires; dogs welcome, coachyard tables *(Grant Langdon)*

Kings Arms GL52 3AR [High St, Prestbury]: M&B bargain carvery dining pub in well converted rambling old inn, generous helpings, Wadworths ales; handy for Cheltenham races *(John Wooll)*

☆ *Plough* GL52 3BG [Mill St, Prestbury]: Thatched village local opp church, comfortable front lounge, service from corner corridor hatch in flagstoned back tap room, grandfather clock and big log fire; personable licensees, well kept Adnams Best and Broadside and Wells & Youngs Bombardier tapped from the cask, Stowford Press cider, basic pub food inc ready-filled rolls; outstanding good-sized flower-filled back garden with immaculate boules pitch *(P Dawn, Guy Vowles, B M Eldridge, Rob and Catherine Dunster)*

Retreat GL50 2AB [Suffolk Parade]: Pub/wine bar with well kept beers, good value wines, good choice of whiskies, enjoyable generous pub food, deep red walls, bare floors and dark wood furniture, friendly staff and atmosphere; children welcome, small back terrace *(Kevin Thomas, Nina Randall, Rod Stoneman)*

Swan GL50 1DX [High St]: Friendly modernised and recently redecorated local, leather sofas on bare boards, enjoyable good value food from shortish menu (not Sat, Sun evenings), pleasant staff; three well kept changing ales, Thatcher's cider, conservatory, Mon quiz night, live music some Thurs; sports TV, games machine; tables in heated courtyard, open all day (till 12pm Fri, Sat) *(Louise Perry, P Dawn)*

CHIPPING CAMPDEN [SP1539]

☆ *Kings* GL55 6AW [High St]: Fresh eclectic contemporary décor in bar/brasserie and separate restaurant, cheery helpful service, food from lunchtime sandwiches and baguettes to pubby dishes and more elaborate meals, Hook Norton and a guest, good choice of wines by the glass, good log fire, daily papers; secluded back garden with picnic-sets and terrace tables, 12 comfortable bedrooms, open all day Sat *(Michael Dandy, LYM, Eithne Dandy, Stuart Doughty)*

☆ **Lygon Arms** GL55 6HB [High St]: Appealing low-beamed bar, good value food till late evening from decent sandwiches to interesting more pricey dishes, good wine choice; real ales such as Hook Norton and Sharps, open fires, stripped stone and lots of horse pictures, small back restaurant; children welcome, tables in shady courtyard, comfortable beamed bedrooms, good breakfast, open all day wknds and summer *(Michael Dandy, LYM, Ian and Judi Purches, Gene and Kitty Rankin)*

Noel Arms GL55 6AT [High St]: Handsome old inn with polished oak settles, attractive old tables and chairs, armour, antique prints, tools and traps on stripped stone walls; decent food from sandwiches to some interesting dishes, Hook Norton and Purity ales, coal fire, new austrian coffee lounge (7.30am-6pm), good restaurant; children welcome, courtyard tables, 26 well appointed bedrooms, good breakfast *(Michael Dandy, George Atkinson, LYM)*

☆ **Red Lion** GL55 6AS [Lower High St]: Linked beamed rooms with flagstones, stripped stone and log fires, good value fresh food from sandwiches and baguettes up, friendly efficient service, Greene King ales, decent wine choice, fine range of malt whiskies, roomy eating area and upstairs dining room; may be quiet piped classical music, big-screen sports TV and pool in games bar; sheltered back courtyard, five comfortable character bedrooms *(Michael Dandy)*

CIRENCESTER [SP0202]

☆ **Corinium** GL7 2DG [Dollar St/Gloucester St]: Civilised and comfortable, with big log fire, antique coaching prints, good mix of tables, sofas and small armchairs, well kept Uley Laurie Lee and another local ale, Thatcher's cider, decent wines, enjoyable bar food from sandwiches up, nicely decorated restaurant; piped music; entrance through charming courtyard with tables, attractive back garden, good bedrooms *(Guy Vowles, BB, E McCall, T McLean, D Irving, Rob and Catherine Dunster)*

Drillmans Arms GL7 2JY [Gloucester Rd, Stratton]: Popular old two-room local, friendly and relaxing, with interesting changing real ales, good bar food, usual food, low beams, skittle alley doubling as eating area; tables out by small car park *(E McCall, T McLean, D Irving, Dave Irving, Jenny Huggins)*

Fleece GL7 2NZ [Market Pl]: Civilised comfortable old hotel with good value enterprising food, friendly effective largely hispanic staff, good choice of wines by the glass, well kept Hook Norton and a guest beer; bay window looking up market place to parish church, roomy lounge and restaurant; terrace tables, bedrooms *(BB, George Atkinson, E McCall, T McLean, D Irving, Mr and Mrs W W Burke, Dave Irving, Jenny Huggins, Robert W Buckle)*

Oddfellows Arms GL7 1HF [Chester St]: Unassuming backstreet local with four well kept ales, nice choice of good value simply served food; good-sized terrace *(Guy Vowles)*

Plough GL7 2LB [Stratton]: Arkells pub with good service, their real ales, good value food inc generous ham ploughman's and OAP bargain lunches, rustic pine tables in open-plan bar, separate dining room *(E McCall, T McLean, D Irving)*

☆ **Twelve Bells** GL7 1EA [Lewis Lane]: Cheery backstreet pub with dry-humoured landlord's son cooking good generous local food at reasonable prices inc some unusual dishes lunchtime and early evening (may be goose around Christmas); five or six quickly changing interesting ales all in fine condition, good coal fires in all three small old-fashioned low-ceilinged rooms, sturdy pine tables and rugs on quarry tiles in back dining area, pictures for sale, clay pipe collection; piped music; small sheltered unsmart back terrace *(Stuart Doughty, Guy Vowles, Ian and Nita Cooper, BB, E McCall, T McLean, D Irving, Giles and Annie Francis, K Turner)*

Wheatsheaf GL7 1JF [Cricklade St]: Busy unchanging local with five or so real ales, inexpensive pub food inc OAP bargains Weds and Fri, well used skittle alley; no children in bar, big-screen TV in back room, no credit cards; courtyard and play area out behind, open all day *(Peter and Audrey Dowsett)*

CLEARWELL [SO5708]

Butchers Arms GL16 8JS [High St]: Large and attractive old stone-built pub with well kept real ales, enjoyable reasonably priced food, friendly young staff; subdued red upholstery, dark low beams, big log fire, separate dining room; children welcome, tables in neat sheltered courtyard with pond and flowers *(R T and J C Moggridge)*

CODRINGTON [ST7278]

Codrington Arms BS37 6RY [Wapley Rd; handy for M4 junction 18, via B4465]: Family dining pub dating partly from the 15th c, several comfortable rooms, well spaced tables, wide choice of blackboard food, quick friendly service, well kept real ales, good house wines, big log fire; piped music; big garden with good views and play area *(MRSM)*

COLD ASTON [SP1219]

Plough GL54 3BN [aka Aston Blank; off A436 (B4068) or A429 SW of Stow-on-the-Wold]: Attractive little 17th-c pub with new chef/landlord, well kept Cotswold, Hook Norton and North Cotswold ales, good choice of wines, standing timbers, low black beams and flagstones, inglenook; small side terraces, unspoilt village with plenty of walks; cl Mon *(Anthony and Pam Stamer, LYM, Helene Grygar)*

COLESBOURNE [SO9913]
Colesbourne Inn GL53 9NP [A435 Cirencester—Cheltenham]: Civilised 19th-c grey stone gabled coaching inn, wide changing choice of enjoyable if not cheap food all home-made (can take a while), friendly staff, Wadworths IPA and 6X, lots of wines by the glass; linked partly panelled rooms, log fires, soft lighting, comfortable mix of settles and softly padded seats, candlelit back dining room; TV above fireplace; dogs welcome, views from attractive back garden and terrace, nine nice bedrooms in converted stable block, good breakfast *(LYM, Mike Sandford-West)*

COLN ST ALDWYNS [SP1405]
New Inn GL7 5AN [back road Bibury—Fairford; Main St]: Refurbished 16th-c creeper-covered hotel in peaceful village; dimly lit with low beams, some stripped stonework and a tiled floor, enjoyable bar food from good sandwiches and deli boards up inc set lunches, real ales such as Hook Norton and Wadworths 6X, dining rooms; provision for children and dogs, plenty of seats on split-level terrace, meadow-side garden, 13 stylish bedrooms, open all day *(LYM, Henry Midwinter)*

COOMBE HILL [SO8827]
Swan GL19 4BA [A38/A4019]: Light and airy dining pub popular for big helpings of good value fresh food from generous sandwiches up, several rooms, polished boards and panelling, red leather chesterfields; quick attentive service, Greene King Abbot, Uley Old Spot and a guest beer, decent house wine; piped music *(Dr A J and Mrs Tompsett)*

DYMOCK [SO6931]
Beauchamp Arms GL18 2AQ: Friendly recently extended parish-owned pub with good licensees, well kept beers such as Greene King St Edmunds, good value home-made pubby food (not Sun evening); disabled facilities, small pleasant garden with pond, cl Mon lunchtime *(KN-R, Chris Evans)*

EASTCOMBE [SO8904]
Lamb GL6 7DN: Two-bar pub with peaceful valley views from lovely terrace and garden, three or four real ales, enjoyable food, welcoming efficient staff; flagstoned stripped-stone dining room and sunken conservatory-style area *(Alan Bulley)*

EASTLEACH TURVILLE [SP1905]
☆ *Victoria* GL7 3NQ [off A361 S of Burford]: Spotless open-plan low-ceilinged rooms around central servery, attractive seats built in by log fire, unusual Queen Victoria pictures, Arkells ales, several wines by the glass, good value above-average pub food (not winter Sun evening) from good baguettes up, welcoming friendly staff; piped music; children and dogs welcome, small pleasant front garden with picnic-sets overlooking picturesque village, good walks *(Helene Grygar, Giles and Annie Francis, Michael Cooper, Dr and Mrs M E Wilson, Dennis and Doreen Haward, LYM)*

EBRINGTON [SP1839]
☆ *Ebrington Arms* GL55 6NH [off B4035 E of Chipping Campden or A429 N of Moreton-in-Marsh]: Ancient stone-built pub refurbished in unusual colours and fabrics, good interesting affordable food, cheerful service; usually three well kept small brewery ales such as Cotswold Spring, Thatcher's farm cider, lively low-beamed bar with stripped stone, flagstones and inglenooks, attractive dining room; children welcome, picnic-sets on pleasant sheltered terrace, good play area, bedrooms *(Guy Vowles, Keith and Sue Ward, LYM, Michael and Anne Brown, Stuart Doughty)*

EDGE [SO8409]
☆ *Edgemoor* GL6 6ND [Gloucester Rd (A4173)]: Tidy, modernised and spacious 19th-c dining place with panoramic valley view across to Painswick from picture windows and from tables on the pretty terrace; wide choice of good value food inc fine home-made puddings, efficient service, orderly rows of tables, well kept local real ales, good coffee, restaurant; children welcome, good walks nearby, has been cl Sun evening *(Neil and Anita Christopher, LYM, Martin and Pauline Jennings)*

ELKSTONE [SO9610]
☆ *Highwayman* GL53 9PL [Beechpike; A417 6 miles N of Cirencester]: Interesting rambling 16th-c building, low beams, stripped stone, log fires, cosy alcoves, antique settles, armchairs and sofa among more usual furnishings; good value home-made food, full Arkells range, good house wines, big back eating area; disabled access, good family room, outside play area *(the Didler, LYM)*

EPNEY [SO7611]
Anchor GL2 7LN [not far from M5 junction 12; SW on A38 then turn right into Castle Lane and keep on]: Popular summer pub worth knowing for its good Severn-side lawns (tables along top of levee), lovely sunset views and great riverbank walks; friendly landlord and locals, well kept Adnams, Fullers and Uley, huge helpings of enjoyable pubby food, teas and coffees, two sizeable bars with carpets and flagstones, panelling, sofas in bay windows, lots of sporting prints and photographs, children's room; juke box and fruit machine; dogs allowed on leads *(Dr A Y Drummond, Julian Powell, Chris and Angela Buckell)*

EWEN [SU0097]
☆ *Wild Duck* GL7 6BY [off A429 S of Cirencester]: Fine 16th-century inn with stylishly old-fashioned furnishings and pictures in high-beamed log-fire main bar, lounge with handsome Elizabethan fireplace and antique furnishings, some interesting if not cheap food, six real ales such as Butcombe, Theakstons, Wells & Youngs, Wye Valley and one brewed for the pub, very good choice of wines by the glass; piped music; children welcome, tables in neatly kept heated courtyard (if you eat here they

may ask to keep your credit card behind the bar); garden, 12 individually furnished bedrooms, open all day *(E McCall, T McLean, D Irving, Anne Morris, LYM, Neil and Anita Christopher, Peter and Audrey Dowsett, Tom and Ruth Rees, Helen Hartley, Adrian and Dawn Collinge)*

FAIRFORD [SP1501]

☆ *Bull* GL7 4AA [Market Place]: Sizeable beamed and timbered hotel bar, civilised and popular with locals, comfortably old-fashioned pubby furnishings (nice bow window seats overlooking little market square), aircraft pictures (RAF base nearby) and thespian photographs, coal-effect gas fire, wide choice of good reasonably priced food, Arkells ales, nice little residents' lounge; dogs in bar, children welcome; charming village and church; 22 bedrooms, open all day *(Paul Boot, Stuart Doughty, LYM, Peter and Audrey Dowsett)*

☆ *Railway Inn* GL7 4AR [London Rd (A417)]: Attractively opened-up, light and airy place with stripped coral ragstone, good pubby food from light lunches up; friendly landlady and staff, well kept ales such as Timothy Taylors Landlord, good choice of wines by the glass; terrace tables *(Gary Bloyce, Mo and David Trudgill, Paul A Moore)*

FORTHAMPTON [SO8731]

Lower Lode Inn GL19 4RE: Brick-built 15th-c pub with River Severn moorings and plenty of waterside tables (prone to winter flooding); beams, flagstones, enormous log fire and traditional seating, enjoyable usual pubby food inc Sun roasts, friendly helpful landlady, four well kept interesting ales, restaurant, back pool room and juke box; children and dogs welcome (lots of summer holiday families), disabled facilities, caravan site, good value bedrooms with good breakfast, open all day *(MLR)*

FRAMPTON COTTERELL [ST6681]

Globe BS36 2AB [Church Rd]: Friendly efficient staff, well kept ales such as Box Steam, Butcombe, Cotswold Spring and Sharps, hearty local food; garden with play area *(Donna and Roger, David and Jenny Gabriel)*

FRAMPTON MANSELL [SO9202]

☆ *Crown* GL6 8JG [brown sign to pub off A491 Cirencester—Stroud]: Welcoming newish licensees doing a good range of traditional home-made pub food at reasonable prices; well kept changing local ales inc Stroud and Uley, two log fires and woodburner, heavy beams, stripped stone and rugs on bare boards, restaurant, efficient charming service; children and dogs welcome (there's a friendly pub dog), disabled access, picnic-sets in sunny front garden, pretty outlook, 12 decent bedrooms, open all day from 12 *(Ian and Melanie Henry, Myra Joyce, LYM, Keith Buckingham)*

GLASSHOUSE [SO7121]

☆ *Glasshouse Inn* GL17 0NN [off A40 just W of A4136]: Appealing old-fashioned and antique furnishings, cavernous black hearth, flagstoned conservatory, well kept ales inc Butcombe tapped from the cask, Stowford Press cider, decent straightforward home-made food from sandwiches up; piped music, no under-14s inside, no bookings except Sun lunch, and they may try to keep your credit card while you eat; good disabled access, neat garden with interesting topiary and lovely hanging baskets, nearby paths up wooded May Hill, cl Sun evening *(LYM, the Didler, Mike and Mary Carter, Ian and Nita Cooper)*

GLOUCESTER [SO8318]

Café René GL1 1TP [Southgate St]: Lots of character and life in a friendly place with great choice of real ales and good value wines, enjoyable food inc bargain Sun roast *(Andy and Claire Barker)*

☆ *Dick Whittingtons House* GL1 2PE [Westgate St]: Unusual in being listed Grade I, early Tudor behind its 18th-c façade, probably former guild hall and mansion house; under new management with welcoming staff, straightforward food (not Sun evening), six changing local ales inc Wickwar, wide range of customers from shoppers to rugby supporters; piped music and some live; children and dogs welcome, attractive courtyard, open all day *(the Didler, P Dawn, Theocsbrian)*

Fountain GL1 2NW [Westgate St/Berkeley St]: Popular and civilised, with good range of real ales, farm cider, reasonably priced usual food, attractive prints, handsome stone fireplace (pub dates from the 17th c), plush seats and built-in wall benches, log-effect gas fire; good disabled access, pleasant courtyard; handy for cathedral; open all day *(BB, B M Eldridge, the Didler, Di and Mike Gillam)*

New Inn GL1 1SF [Northgate St]: Actually one of the city's oldest structures, lovely medieval building with galleried courtyard; recently refurbished with three bars (back one busiest), Butcombe, Wychwood and up to eight guests inc smaller local breweries, cheap lunchtime food, coffee shop, restaurant; 35 good value bedrooms, open all day (till 1.30am Thurs-Sat) *(the Didler)*

Queens Head GL2 9EJ [Tewkesbury Rd, Longford (A38)]: Neat and comfortable, with good food (sensible about gluten-free etc), friendly staff, real ale, good choice of wines by the glass *(Dr John Henry Lonie)*

GREAT BARRINGTON [SP2013]

☆ *Fox* OX18 4TB [off A40 Burford—Northleach; pub towards Little Barrington]: 17th-c inn, with stripped stone, simple country furnishings and low ceiling, Donnington BB and SBA, farm cider and good apple juice, wide choice of enjoyable quickly served food (all day Sun and summer Sat, not Mon evening in winter) from sandwiches up; big bare-boards river-view dining room with riverbank mural, traditional games, Aug folk festival ('Foxstock'); can get very busy, games machine, TV; children and dogs welcome, heated terrace by River Windrush (swans and private fishing), informal orchard with pond, four bedrooms, open all day *(LYM, the Didler, George Atkinson, M G Hart, William Goodhart, David Glynne-Jones, David Lamb, Pete Baker, Richard Wyld, Giles and Annie Francis)*

GREET [SP0230]

Harvest Home GL54 5BH [Evesham Rd (B4078 by Winchcombe Station bridge)]: Newish licensees in neatly kept airy country pub with lovely Malvern Hills views, enjoyable sensibly priced food from baguettes to nice fish, good range of real ales inc Timothy Taylors Landlord, Stowford Press cider, good choice of wines; friendly atmosphere, beams, log fires and bay window seats, big raftered barn restaurant; sizeable garden, not far from medieval Sudeley Castle and Winchcombe GWR station *(LYM, Kathryn Birkett, Dr A J and Mrs Tompsett, Richard Hodges)*

GRETTON [SP0130]

Royal Oak GL54 5EP [off B4077 E of Tewkesbury]: Popular country pub with linked bare-boarded or flagstoned rooms, friendly licensees and good service, enjoyable straightforward generous food at reasonable prices, well kept Goffs and a guest ale, decent wines; nice mix of furniture, beams hung with tankards and chamber-pots, interesting old motor-racing pictures, dining conservatory; children and dogs welcome, fine views from flower-filled terrace, big pleasant garden with play area and tennis, GWR private railway runs past, good nearby walks; open all day summer wknds *(MLR, Dr A J and Mrs Tompsett, D J Lindsay, LYM)*

GUITING POWER [SP0924]

☆ *Farmers Arms* GL54 5TZ [Fosseway (A429)]: Stripped stone, flagstones, cheap Donnington BB and SBA, wide blackboard range of unpretentious food from simple sandwiches up, prompt friendly service; good coal or log fire, carpeted back dining area, games area with darts, dominoes, cribbage, pool, skittle alley; piped music, games machine; children welcome, garden with quoits, lovely village, good walks, bedrooms *(LYM, Dr A J and Mrs Tompsett, the Didler, Di and Mike Gillam)*

HAMBROOK [ST6479]

Hambrook BS16 1RY [Bristol Rd, handy for M4 junction 19]: Much rebuilt old pub with wide choice of enjoyable food, dining extension off small friendly bar, long-serving landlord and son *(Stan Edwards)*

White Horse BS16 1RY [Bristol Rd]: Good choice of pubby food, well kept beers, friendly welcome *(Stan Edwards)*

HAWKESBURY UPTON [ST7786]

☆ *Beaufort Arms* GL9 1AU [High St]: Hook Norton, Wickwar BOB and good guest beers, local farm cider, good soft drinks' choice, friendly landlord and staff, good value popular standard food, thriving local atmosphere; extended uncluttered dining lounge on right, darts in more spartan

stripped-brick bare-boards bar, interesting local and brewery memorabilia, lots of pictures (some for sale), skittle alley; well behaved children welcome, disabled access and facilities, picnic-sets in pleasant smallish garden, on Cotswold Way; open all day *(Jim and Frances Gowers)*

HORSLEY [ST8497]

☆ *Tipputs* GL6 0QE [Tiltups End; A46 2 miles S of Nailsworth]: Enjoyable food all day from good value lunches to interesting evening meals, cheerful efficient service, Greene King ale; beams, stripped stone, big log fire and abstract art, comfortable leather seats in anteroom to galleried barn restaurant; nice chairs and tables in pretty garden with raised deck, lovely setting, open all day *(Alan and Eve Harding, Tom and Ruth Rees)*

HUNTLEY [SO7219]

Red Lion GL19 3DU [North Rd (A40 Gloucester—Ross-on-Wye)]: Comfortable beamed bar and restaurant, good choice of beers and wines, fresh largely local food, quick service, friendly helpful staff; log fires *(Lucien Perring)*

IRON ACTON [ST6883]

Lamb BS37 9UZ [B4058/9 Bristol—Chipping Sodbury]: Half a dozen well kept changing ales inc Box Steam and Butcombe, several farm ciders, good wines inc some interesting country ones, pubby food all day from sandwiches up, helpful cheerful staff; huge fireplace in low-ceilinged carpeted bar, panelling and stripped stone, old prints and more modern art, pool upstairs; piped music, games machine, no dogs; wheelchair access, big garden with front terrace, bedrooms, open all day *(Chris and Angela Buckell)*

KEMBLE [ST9899]

☆ *Thames Head* GL7 6NZ [A433 Cirencester—Tetbury]: Stripped stone, timberwork, log fire, intriguing little front alcove, pews in cottagey back area with log-effect gas fire in big fireplace, country-look dining room with another big fire; wide choice of enjoyable food, good value wines, Arkells 2B and 3B, friendly obliging staff, skittle alley; TV; children welcome, tables outside, good value four-poster bedrooms, good breakfast, nice walk to nearby Thames source *(John and Sharon Hancock, Stephen Woad, LYM, Dan Farrall)*

KINETON [SP0926]

Halfway House GL54 5UG [signed from B4068 and B4077 W of Stow-on-the-Wold]: Unpretentiously comfortable pub under new management, traditional food, well kept Donnington BB and SBA from nearby brewery, decent wines, farm cider, pub games, restaurant; children welcome, sheltered back garden, simple comfortable bedrooms, good walks *(LYM)*

KINGSCOTE [ST8196]

☆ *Hunters Hall* GL8 8XZ [A4135 Dursley—Tetbury]: Tudor beams, stripped stone, big log fires and plenty of character in individually furnished spotless linked rooms, some sofas and easy chairs; wide choice of good food from lunchtime sandwiches up, Greene King and Uley ales, friendly prompt service, flagstoned back bar with darts, pool and TV; children and dogs welcome, garden with good play area, bedrooms, open all day *(LYM, Brian Goodson, Tom and Ruth Rees)*

KINGSWOOD [ST7491]

Dinneywicks GL12 8RT [The Chipping]: Smallish done-up village inn, two linked bars with good value home-made food in pleasant eating area, well kept Wadworths tapped from the cask, obliging service; interesting village with some good architecture; open all day Sat *(Jude Fogarty)*

KNOCKDOWN [ST8388]

Holford Arms GL8 8QY [A433]: Popular and comfortable, enjoyable and interesting food from sandwiches up, up to three real ales, cheerful staff; nice mix of furnishings inc sofas and armchairs by huge log fireplace (pub's retrievers like it there), modern prints and local paintings, dark panelling and stripped stone; piped music may obtrude, some folk nights; children and dogs welcome, disabled access, neat side garden, handy for Westonbirt Arboretum *(Chris and Angela Buckell)*

LECHLADE [SU2199]

Riverside GL7 3AQ [Park End Wharf, A361]: Substantial popular riverside inn recently well refurbished by Arkells, roomy and comfortable, with their real ales, sensibly priced food, wood and stripped stone; soft drinks' cabin for children, picnic-sets on attractive sheltered Thames-side terrace, well designed smokers' area, 14 bedrooms *(Peter and Audrey Dowsett, Dr and Mrs M E Wilson)*

Trout GL7 3HA [A417, a mile E]: Refurbished low-beamed dimly lit pub with three linked areas, Courage and Sharps ales, farm cider, good choice of other drinks, good coffee, wide range of enjoyable food, cheery attentive staff; log fire, stuffed fish and fishing prints (pub has fishing rights), board games, dining room, jazz nights Tues, Sun, early Jun steam rally; children welcome, nice big Thames-side garden, boules, aunt sally, play area, camping; open all day summer and Sat *(George Atkinson, JJW, CMW, LYM)*

LITTLE WASHBOURNE [SO9933]

Hobnails GL20 8NQ [B4077 Tewkesbury—Stow-on-the-Wold]: Attractive traditional front core with 15th-c beams and log fire, comfortable and extensive eating areas around this, wide choice of enjoyable food inc popular good value carvery, friendly obliging service, good range of local ales, decent wines; children welcome, disabled facilities, terrace tables, play area, bedroom extension *(Dr A J and Mrs Tompsett, LYM)*

LONGBOROUGH [SP1729]

Coach & Horses GL56 0QU [Larch Hill, Ganborough]: Stone-built Donnington pub under helpful new landlord; ales kept well, farm cider, sympathetic updating keeping the unspoilt rustic flavour inc some stripped flint, log fire, darts, cribbage; children welcome, nice new garden tables looking

down on village *(Tracey and Stephen Groves, Roger Fox)*

LOWER LYDBROOK [SO5916]

Anchor GL17 9SB [B4234]: Welcoming ancient inn with enjoyable food, a real ale, Stowford Press cider, comfortably carpeted two-room beamed bar, big stone fireplace; no piped music, restaurant; pretty garden, lovely setting, bedrooms, cl Tues *(Dave Statham)*

LOWER SWELL [SP1725]

Golden Ball GL54 1LF [B4068 W of Stow-on-the-Wold]: Simple and spotless stone-built beamed local with well kept Donnington BB and SBA from the pretty nearby brewery, good range of ciders and perry, enjoyable straightforward food inc curry nights; friendly landlord, big log fire, games area behind sturdy chimneystack, small evening restaurant, conservatory; no dogs or children; small garden with occasional barbecues, aunt sally and quoits, pretty village, good walks; three decent simple bedrooms *(LYM, Neil and Anita Christopher)*

MAISEMORE [SO8121]

White Hart GL2 8HY [just NW of Gloucester]: Cosy village local, friendly staff, well kept real ales; piped music; roadside tables, plenty of room outside *(Giles and Annie Francis)*

MARSHFIELD [ST7773]

☆ *Catherine Wheel* SN14 8LR [High St; signed off A420 Bristol—Chippenham]: High-ceilinged stripped-stone front part with medley of settles, chairs and stripped tables, cottagey back family bar, charming Georgian dining room with open fire in impressive fireplace; friendly staff, good range of real ales inc Courage and Sharps, farm cider, interesting wines by the glass, good straightforward well priced food inc Sun lunch; darts, dominoes, no music or machines; flower-decked back yard, unspoilt village, bedrooms, open all day Sat *(Lise Chace, Ian Phillips, Dr and Mrs A K Clarke, LYM, Donna and Roger, GSB, Geoff and Brigid Smithers)*

Lord Nelson SN14 8LP [A420 Bristol—Chippenham; High St]: Linked beamed rooms (inc former stables still with runnel down uneven flagstones), Bath and Courage ales, Stowford Press cider, quickly served inexpensive generous food; plain tables and chairs, open fires, bistro restaurant, games bar with pool and machines; charming small courtyard, bedrooms in cottage annex *(Donna and Roger, Guy Vowles, Dr and Mrs A K Clarke)*

MAYSHILL [ST6882]

☆ *New Inn* BS36 2NT [Badminton Rd (A432 Frampton Cotterell—Yate)]: Good food (all day Sun) in popular largely 17th-c coaching inn with two comfortably carpeted bar rooms leading to restaurant; friendly staff, well kept changing ales such as Bristol Beer Factory and Cotswold Spring, Stowford Press cider, log fire; children and dogs welcome, garden with play area *(Donna and Roger, Jim and Frances Gowers)*

MEYSEY HAMPTON [SU1199]

Masons Arms GL7 5JT [just off A417 Cirencester—Lechlade; High St]: Welcoming 17th-c village local, with longish open-plan beamed bar with big inglenook fire at one end, well kept changing ales (have been known to run out), farm cider, friendly staff, straightforward food, restaurant; piped music; children and dogs welcome, tables out on green, pleasant compact bedrooms, good breakfast *(Prof H G Allen, LYM, Ken and Margaret Grinstead, E McCall, T McLean, D Irving, Jeff and Sue Evans)*

MICKLETON [SP1543]

☆ *Kings Arms* GL55 6RT [B4632 (ex A46)]: Civilised open-plan family lounge, good well presented food from well filled sandwiches to unusual specials and good value OAP lunches, courteous well trained staff, beers from Greene King, Hook Norton and Marstons, farm cider, several wines by the glass; nice mix of comfortable chairs, soft lighting, interesting homely décor with lots to look at, log fire, small locals' bar with darts, dominoes and cribbage; piped music; unusual tables in courtyard and sizeable garden, attractive village, handy for Kiftsgate and Hidcote *(Ingrid Anson, Paul Humphreys, Brian and Pat Wardrobe, Michael Dandy, BB, Martin and Pauline Jennings)*

MINCHINHAMPTON [SO8500]

Old Lodge GL6 9AQ [Nailsworth—Brimscombe – on Common fork, left at pub's sign; OS Sheet 162 map ref 853008]: Smartly reworked dining pub recently acquired by the Food Club chain, civilised bistro feel with wood floors, stripped-stone walls and modern décor and furnishings, enjoyable food from pub classics up, real ales, decent wines by the glass; children welcome, tables on neat lawn looking over NT common with grazing cows and horses, refurbished bedrooms *(LYM, Dave Irving, Jenny Huggins)*

MORETON-IN-MARSH [SP2032]

Black Bear GL56 0AX [High St]: Unpretentious beamed and stripped-stone pub, well kept local Donnington, good coffee, good value wholesome pub food, attentive landlord, large airy dining room, public bar with games and sports TV; tables outside, big bedrooms sharing bathrooms *(S Holder, BB)*

Inn on the Marsh GL56 0DW [Stow Rd]: Interesting 19th-c beamed bar with warm layout inc lovely curved sofa, quite a dutch flavour to the bric-a-brac, models, posters etc; dutch chef/landlady doing national specialities alongside pubby favourites (cooked to order, so allow for a wait), friendly service, well kept Marstons-related ales, inglenook woodburner, modern conservatory restaurant; may be piped music, quiz machine; children and dogs welcome, seats at front and in back garden *(JCW, Robert Ager, Ian and Nita Cooper, Rob and Catherine Dunster)*

☆ *Redesdale Arms* GL56 0AW [High St]: Cheerful and relaxed old coaching inn with

prettily lit alcoves, sofas and a big stone fireplace in the solidly furnished comfortable panelled bar on the right, darts in flagstoned public bar, log fires, stripped stone; Hook Norton and Wye Valley, decent wines and coffee, enjoyable generous food, spacious back child-friendly brasserie and dining conservatory; piped music, TVs, games machine; heated floodlit courtyard decking, 24 comfortable bedrooms beyond, open all day from 8am *(Mr and Mrs W W Burke, BB, Michael Sargent, George Atkinson, Michael Dandy, Keith and Sue Ward, Rob and Catherine Dunster)*

NAILSWORTH [ST8499]

Village Inn GL6 0HH [Bath Rd]: Thriving pub brewing its own good value Nailsworth ales, guest beers and bargain take-aways too; appealingly done series of rambling linked areas with steps down to back area for view of the process, woody décor with panelling, dividers and oak floors, log fire, pub food, brewery tours; dogs welcome, open all day *(Dave Irving, Jenny Huggins, the Didler, Mr Rene-Cason)*

NAUNTON [SP1123]

☆ *Black Horse* GL54 3AD [off B4068 W of Stow]: Friendly stripped-stone proper pub with well kept Donnington BB and SBA, good simple fresh food from huge baguettes to Sun roasts (veg may come from local allotments), good service; plain tables, flagstones, black beams and log fire, darts, cribbage, dominoes, dining room; piped music; children and dogs welcome, some nice seating outside, bedrooms, charming village, fine Cotswold walks *(Pete Baker, Noel Grundy, Richard Tilbrook, Roger Fox, LYM, Malcolm Rand)*

NETHER WESTCOTE [SP2220]

Westcote Inn OX7 6SD [off A424 Burford—Stow]: Sadly this good pub, a favourite with the racing fraternity, was closed as we went to press; we have hopes that it will reopen – news, please *(LYM)*

NEWENT [SO7225]

George GL18 1PU [Church St]: Friendly well worn-in former coaching inn, three or four changing well kept ales such as Battledown and Cottage, inexpensive lunchtime food from sandwiches up, log fire, open-plan L-shaped bar, evening restaurant; children welcome, bedrooms, nice location opp The Shambles museum, open all day *(TB, MLR)*

NORTH NIBLEY [ST7495]

Black Horse GL11 6DT [Barrs Lane]: Emphasis on enjoyable somewhat restauranty food, but pub favourites too, well kept ales such as Exmoor, Stroud and Wickwar, decent wines, beamed bar, two dining areas, log fires, live music and events; a few tables in pretty garden, nr Cotswold Way, six bedrooms, good breakfast *(Guy Vowles, LYM)*

NORTHLEACH [SP1114]

Sherborne Arms GL54 3EE [Market Pl]: Comfortably traditional refurbishment, good choice of enjoyable food from baguettes up inc good Sun lunch, children's meals, friendly attentive staff, Greene King Old Speckled Hen, Sharps Doom Bar and Worthington Bitter, good wines and coffee; bar on left (popular with locals) stretching back from smallish front area, cosy lounge on right with wing armchairs and sofas around big stone fireplace, large stripped stone restaurant up a slope beyond; TV and fruit machine; one or two picnic-sets out in front, three bedrooms *(Neil and Anita Christopher, George Atkinson, BB)*

NYMPSFIELD [SO7900]

Rose & Crown GL10 3TU [The Cross; signed off B4066 Stroud—Dursley]: Stone-built 17th-c pub under new management, good choice of reasonably priced home-made food (all day Fri-Sun) inc OAP wkdy lunch deals, Butcombe, Severn Vale, Wye Valley and Uley ales, decent wines, local farm cider, coffees and teas; log fire in bare-boards beamed front bar with pine tables, pews and old settles, large back dining area, regular events; children and dogs welcome, disabled access, picnic-sets in side yard and sheltered lawn with good play area, three bedrooms adjacent, handy for Cotswold walks and Woodchester (NT), open all day *(BB, Neil and Anita Christopher, Alistair Forsyth)*

OLD DOWN [ST6187]

☆ *Fox* BS32 4PR [off A38 Bristol—Thornbury; Inner Down]: Fine range of real ales in popular low-beamed village local, good reasonably priced hearty food with some interesting specials, friendly efficient staff, farm cider and good choice of wines by the glass, log fire, carpeted eating area, high-backed settles in family room; children welcome, disabled access, verandah with grapevine, garden play area *(Chris and Angela Buckell, Andrew Shore, Maria Williams, James Morrell, Charles and Pauline Stride, John and Gloria Isaacs, Donna and Roger)*

OLD SODBURY [ST7581]

☆ *Dog* BS37 6LZ [3 miles from M4 junction 18, via A46 and A432; The Hill (a busy road)]: Welcoming and popular two-level bar with low beams and stripped stone, extensive choice of enjoyable food from sandwiches up inc meal deals, friendly young staff, well kept Wadworths 6X and other changing ales; games machine, juke box; children welcome, big garden with barbecues and good play area, bedrooms, open all day *(Donna and Roger, Tom Evans, Roy Hoing, Meg and Colin Hamilton, the Brewers, Stephen Woad, Dave Irving, Jenny Huggins, LYM)*

PAINSWICK [SO8609]

Falcon GL6 6UN [New St]: Sizeable old open-plan stone-built inn, popular and friendly, with newish family doing enjoyable food inc enterprising dishes, real ale, good choice of wines by the glass; panelling, high ceilings, cheerfully rustic bare-boards front bar, mainly carpeted dining area with lots of prints, high bookshelves and shelves of ornaments by coal-effect fire; dogs welcome, bedrooms, opp churchyard famous for its 99 yews *(Susan Lang, Guy Vowles, BB)*

PARKEND [SO6107]

Woodman GL15 4JF [Folly Rd; Whitecroft]: Roomy and relaxed stripped-stone bar, heavy beams, forestry decorations, artwork for sale, smaller back bar and dining room; good choice of enjoyable fresh food, well kept Wadworths 6X and other ales, decent wines, pleasant service; picnic-sets on front terrace facing green, sheltered back courtyard and garden, bedrooms, good Forest of Dean walks *(Neil and Anita Christopher, BB)*

PAXFORD [SP1837]

☆ *Churchill Arms* GL55 6XH [B4479, SE of Chipping Campden]: New licensees have taken over this unpretentious pub, too recently for us to form a firm view: a former food favourite (so hopes are high), perhaps Arkells Moonlight, Hook Norton and a guest, good log fire, simply furnished flagstoned bar, low ceilings and some timbering, assortment of old tables and chairs, dining extension; children have been welcome, seats outside, bedrooms; news on the new regime please *(LYM)*

QUENINGTON [SP1404]

Keepers Arms GL7 5BL [Church Rd]: Cosy and comfortable village local improved under newish amiable landlord; stripped stone, low beams and log fires, value for money food in bar and restaurant, good range of beers; dogs welcome, picnic-sets outside, bedrooms *(Mo and David Trudgill, David Hill, E McCall, T McLean, D Irving)*

REDBROOK [SO5309]

☆ *Boat* NP25 4AJ [car park signed on A466 Chepstow—Monmouth, then 100-yard footbridge over Wye; or very narrow steep car access from Penallt in Wales]: Beautifully set Wye-side pub with up to five changing well kept ales tapped from casks, several ciders and country wines, good value simple food from baguettes and baked potatoes up (nothing fried), helpful staff; stripped stone walls, flagstone floors and roaring woodburner; dogs and children welcome, rough home-built seats in informal tiered suntrap garden with stream spilling down waterfall cliffs into duckpond, open all day *(LYM, Bob and Margaret Holder, B M Eldridge, LM, Michael and Alison Sandy)*

RODBOROUGH [SO8502]

Bear GL5 5DE [Rodborough Common]: Comfortably cosy and pubby beamed and flagstoned bar in smart hotel, warm welcome, pleasant window seats, good log fire, hops hung around top of golden stone walls, interesting reproductions; good choice of well kept beer inc local Stroud and Nailsworth, bar food that's reasonably priced considering the surroundings, service can be slow, afternoon teas, restaurant; children welcome, lovely walks, bedrooms *(Dave Irving, Jenny Huggins, BB)*

SAPPERTON [SO9303]

Daneway Inn GL7 6LN [Daneway; off A419 Stroud—Cirencester]: Quiet tucked-away local in charming wooded countryside; flagstones and bare boards, amazing floor-to-ceiling carved oak dutch fireplace, sporting prints, Wadworths ales, Weston's farm cider, reasonably priced generous simple food from filled baps up, friendly staff; small family room, traditional games in inglenook public bar; no dogs; camping possible, terrace tables and lovely sloping lawn, good walks by canal under restoration with tunnel to Coates (Stuart Doughty, Martin and Marion Vincent, Guy Vowles, E McCall, T McLean, D Irving, LYM)

SELSLEY [SO8303]

Bell GL5 5JY [Bell Lane]: Neatly kept and comfortable, with warmly welcoming service, good value home cooking, interesting watercolours in dining room
(Mrs Rosemary Reeves)

SHIPTON MOYNE [ST8989]

Cat & Custard Pot GL8 8PN [off B4040 Malmesbury—Bristol; The Street]: Popular welcoming local with well kept Flowers, Timothy Taylors and Wadworths, Thatcher's cider, well priced wines, food from sandwiches to restaurant dishes (booking recommended), friendly hard-pushed staff; several dining areas, beams and bric-a-brac, hunting prints, cosy back snug; dogs welcome, wheelchair access, picturesque village (Chris and Angela Buckell, Richard Stancomb, BB)

SIDDINGTON [SU0399]

☆ *Greyhound* GL7 6HR [Ashton Rd; village signed from A419 roundabout at Tesco]: Two linked rooms each with a big log fire, enjoyable pubby food from sandwiches up, some unusual specials, well kept Wadworths, welcoming service; slate-floored bar with darts and cribbage; piped music; garden tables, open all day (LYM, E McCall, T McLean, D Irving, Neil and Anita Christopher)

SLAD [SO8707]

Woolpack GL6 7QA [B4070 Stroud—Birdlip]: Friendly and unpretentiously old-fashioned hillside village local with lovely valley views; several linked rooms with Laurie Lee and other interesting photographs, some of his books for sale, log fire and nice tables, decent pubby food (not Sun evening) from sandwiches and baguettes up inc generous Sun roast, well kept Uley and guest ales, local farm ciders and perry, decent wines by the glass; good young staff, games and cards; dogs welcome (Dr A J and Mrs Tompsett, Dave Irving, Jenny Huggins, Crispin Pemberton, Pete Baker)

SLIMBRIDGE [SO7204]

Tudor Arms GL2 7BP [Shepherds Patch; off A38 towards Wildfowl & Wetlands Trust]: Welcoming and obliging, with generous food (all day wknds) from baguettes up, half a dozen interesting changing ales, good wines by the glass, farm cider; linked areas with parquet floor, flagstones or carpet, some leather chairs and settles, comfortable dining room, conservatory, darts, pool and skittle alley; children and dogs welcome, disabled facilities, picnic-sets outside, handy for Wildfowl Trust and canal boat trips,

bedrooms in small annex, open all day (Neil and Anita Christopher, Betty Laker, Steve and Liz Tilley)

SNOWSHILL [SP0933]

Snowshill Arms WR12 7JU: Unpretentious country pub in honeypot village (so no shortage of customers), Donnington ales, reasonably priced straightforward food from sandwiches up, log fire, stripped stone, neat array of tables, local photographs; skittle alley, charming village views from bow windows and big back garden with little stream and play area; children welcome if eating, handy for Snowshill Manor and Cotswold Way walks (LYM, Paul Goldman, Robert Ager, Guy Vowles)

SOMERFORD KEYNES [SU0195]

☆ *Bakers Arms* GL7 6DN: Pretty stone-built country pub popular for food from baguettes and ciabattas up, real ales, good house wine, two log fires, lots of pine tables in two linked stripped-stone areas with soft lighting and burgundy walls, young staff; children very welcome, big garden with play area and good barbecues, lovely Cotswold village (Richard and Sheila Fitton, E McCall, T McLean, D Irving)

SOUTH CERNEY [SU0497]

Old George GL7 5UA [Clarks Hay]: Pleasantly decorated cosy bars, good value home-made food inc interesting things and local rare-breed meat; Wadworths 6X and Wells & Youngs Bitter, log fire, roomy simple back dining area; riverside garden, handy for Cotswold Water Park (Mr and Mrs M J Girdler)

Royal Oak GL7 5UP [High St]: Thriving sympathetically extended ancient local, cosy bars and small back dining area, friendly staff, Fullers London Pride and guest beers, food from good value sandwiches up, woodburner; pleasant garden behind with big terrace and summer marquee (E McCall, T McLean, D Irving)

SOUTHROP [SP2003]

☆ *Swan* GL7 3NU [off A361 Lechlade—Burford]: 17th-c creeper-covered upscale dining pub in pretty village, now reopened under new management (from successful London restaurant), very good cooking from bar meals to enterprising restaurant food, set menus and Sun roasts, good wines; appealing décor, light front rooms with flagstones and log fire, snug with another fire; children welcome, two tables out in front, more in sheltered back garden, pretty village especially at daffodil time (LYM, Graham Oddey)

ST BRIAVELS [SO5504]

George GL15 6TA [High St]: Wadworths pub improved under new management, their beers and wide choice of enjoyable food inc good value OAP meals; spotless rambling linked black-beamed rooms with attractive old-fashioned décor and a big stone fireplace, restaurant; can get very busy wknds (booking advised Sun); children and dogs welcome, flagstoned terrace over former moat of neighbouring Norman fortress, four newly refurbished bedrooms *(LYM, Bob and Margaret Holder, Brian and Jacky Wilson, Tom Evans, David A Hammond)*

STAUNTON [SO7829]

Swan GL19 3QA [Ledbury Rd (A417)]: Nice local atmosphere and enjoyable good value home-made food from generous sandwiches to good local steaks and fish, prompt friendly service; well kept Timothy Taylors Landlord, Shepherd Neame Spitfire and a summer guest ale, Stowford Press cider, three interconnecting rooms, beams and wood floors, comfortable sofas, open fire, conservatory; piped music; dogs and children welcome, disabled facilities, sizeable pretty garden, cl Sun, Mon evenings *(Guy Vowles)*

STAVERTON [SO9022]

Pheasant GL51 0SS [Gloucester Rd (B4063 W of Cheltenham)]: Attractively fresh contemporary décor, good bar and restaurant food making use of local produce, friendly efficient staff, well kept real ales such as Fullers London Pride and Sharps Doom Bar, good fire *(Jo Rees)*

STOKE GIFFORD [ST6279]

Beaufort Arms BS34 8PB [North Rd, not far from Bristol Parkway]: Well run Ember Inn, tidy and spacious, with value-conscious food all day, several real ales *(Colin Moore)*

STOW-ON-THE-WOLD [SP1729]

Coach & Horses GL56 0QZ [Ganborough (A424 about 2.5 miles N)]: Beamed and flagstoned country pub, bright and clean, with reasonably priced tasty food, friendly tenants, well kept Donnington ales and farm cider, decent wines by the glass; good fires, steps up to carpeted dining area with high-backed settles; children welcome, popular skittle alley, garden *(K H Frostick, Clive and Fran Dutson, Ken and Margaret Grinstead, LYM)*

Eagle & Child GL54 1BN [attached to Royalist Hotel, Digbeth St]: Smart little bar attached to handsome old hotel, woodburner, flagstones, low beams and dark pink walls, back conservatory, nice mix of tables; up-to-date food from sandwiches up, good if not great wine and malt whisky choice, may have Hook Norton, friendly staff; may be piped music; children and dogs welcome, small back courtyard, good bedrooms, open all day *(Phil Bryant, LYM, Michael Dandy, Myra Joyce, Mrs Brenda Calver)*

Grapevine GL54 1AU [Sheep St]: Substantial hotel with quiet comfortable bar, upscale bar food from sandwiches and hot baguettes up, friendly staff, good coffee and choice of wines by the glass, Hook Norton; attractive brasserie/restaurant with live vine; piped music; pavement tables, bedrooms, open all day *(Michael Dandy)*

Kings Arms GL54 1AF [The Square]: Enjoyable food from good sandwiches to lots of fish, real food for children, helpful staff, good choice of wines by the glass, Greene King IPA and Abbot, good coffee (opens early for this); daily papers, some Mackintosh-style chairs on polished boards, bowed black beams, some panelling and

stripped stone, log fire, charming upstairs dining room; piped music; bedrooms, open all day *(Michael Dandy, BB)*

☆ *Queens Head* GL54 1AB [The Square]: Splendidly unpretentious for this upmarket town, well kept low-priced Donnington BB and SBA, good wines by the glass, good value sandwiches and basic pub meals (not Sun) inc proper steak and kidney pudding, cheerful helpful service; bustling and chatty stripped-stone front lounge, heavily beamed and flagstoned back bar with high-backed settles, big log-effect fire, horse prints, usual games; quiet piped music; dogs and children positively welcome, tables in attractive sunny back courtyard, occasional jazz Sun lunchtime, open all day *(LYM, the Didler, Tom Holman, Terry Miller, Noel Grundy, Mr and Mrs M J Girdler, Mike Buckingham, Neil and Anita Christopher, Tracey and Stephen Groves, Phil Bryant, Michael Dandy, Ann and Colin Hunt)*

☆ *Talbot* GL54 1BQ [The Square]: Light and airy modern décor, relaxed café-bar feel, food from sandwiches and baguettes up from shortish menu, bright friendly service even when busy, Wadworths ales, lots of good value wines by the glass, good coffee; big log fire, plain tables and chairs on wood block floor, modern prints, daily papers; no children inside, may be piped radio, lavatories upstairs; bedrooms nearby; open all day *(Michael Dandy, BB)*

Unicorn GL54 1HQ [Sheep St (A429 edge of centre)]: Handsome hotel with comfortably traditional low-beamed upmarket bar, nice mix of tables, chairs and settles on wood/flagstone floor, big log fire; Hook Norton and Wye Valley ales, good range of food from lunchtime sandwiches up inc set price menu, friendly helpful staff, formal restaurant; car park with barrier across busy road; 20 bedrooms *(Michael Dandy, George Atkinson, Eithne Dandy, Neil and Anita Christopher)*

White Hart GL54 1AF [The Square]: Small former coaching inn with pleasant simple bar and dining area behind, pubby food from baguettes up inc reasonably priced lunches, Arkells ales; back courtyard, bedrooms *(Mr and Mrs W W Burke, Michael Dandy, BB)*

STROUD [SO8505]

Lord John GL5 3AB [Russell St]: Airy split-level Wetherspoons in former PO sorting office, tables in alcoves, their usual good value food and wide choice of sensibly priced ales inc interesting guest beers; disabled facilities, terrace tables *(Dave Irving, Jenny Huggins)*

SWINEFORD [ST6969]

☆ *Swan* BS30 6LN [A431, right on the Somerset border]: Popular and welcoming stone-built pub with full Bath Ales range kept well, good interesting reasonably priced food (not Sun evening), children's menu, enterprising wine choice, prompt friendly service; big open fire, plain furniture on bare boards or tiles, pastel paintwork and panelled dado, occasional beer and cider festivals; wheelchair access, large garden with good play area, open all day (till midnight Fri, Sat) *(Donna and Roger, Martin Sagar, Chris and Angela Buckell)*

TETBURY [ST8893]

☆ *Priory* GL8 8JJ [London Rd]: More civilised eating house than pub, with central log fire in comfortable if somewhat high-raftered stone-built former stables, and a strong emphasis on interesting local produce, even a slant to their wood-fired pizzas; cheerful service, Courage Best and Uley, decent wines by the glass; comfortable coffee lounge, live music Sun; children very welcome, roadside terrace picnic-sets, 14 good bedrooms *(BB, Mrs Arrowsmith, Mr and Mrs A Curry, Eleni Papandoniou)*

☆ *Snooty Fox* GL8 8DD [Market Place]: High-ceilinged stripped-stone hotel lounge, unstuffy, with well kept real ales such as Otter, Nailsworth and Wickwar, good house wines, friendly young staff; medieval-style chairs and cast-iron tables, elegant fireplace, brass ceiling fans and Ronald Searle pony-club cartoons, nice side room and ante-room, restaurant; unobtrusive piped music, bar can get very busy wknd evenings; children and dogs welcome, comfortable bedrooms *(LYM, E McColl, T McLean, D Irving)*

TEWKESBURY [SO8832]

Bell GL20 5SA [Church St]: Hotel bar interesting for its black oak beams and timbers, 17th-c oak panelling and medieval leaf-and-fruit frescoes; big log fire, tapestries and armchairs, well kept Greene King, decent bar food and house wines, good coffee; children and dogs welcome, garden above Severn-side walk, bedrooms *(J F M and M West, Chris Glasson, BB)*

☆ *Gupshill Manor* GL20 5SG [Gloucester Rd (off A38 S edge of town)]: Quaint ancient timbered building with Tardis-like extensive series of varied lounge and dining areas, plenty of easy chairs and sofas, open fires, beams and timbers; well priced food (all day Sun) from pubby dishes up inc two for one lunches, well kept Greene King ales, good choice of wines by the glass, nice coffees, friendly staff; piped music; children welcome, disabled access, teak tables on extensive terrace with heaters, open all day *(BB, Jo Rees, Mrs J Carlill, Robert W Buckle, Brian and Pat Wardrobe)*

☆ *Olde Black Bear* GL20 5BJ [High St]: County's oldest pub, well worth a look for its intricately rambling rooms with ancient tiles, heavy timbering and low beams; reasonably priced wines, up to five real ales, open fires, well worn furnishings, pubby food; piped music, and they may try to keep your credit card while you eat; children welcome, terrace and play area in riverside garden, open all day *(the Didler, Dave Braisted, Dr and Mrs A K Clarke, Jeremy King, Comus and Sarah Elliott, LYM)*

Royal Hop Pole GL20 5RT [Church St]: Well

done Wetherspoons conversion of old inn, keeping original features, their usual value-minded all-day food and drink; lovely garden leading down to river, bedrooms *(John Dwane)*

Tudor House GL20 5BH [High St]: Quiet Tudor hotel, three or four real ales; river-view garden behind, 25 nicely modernised old bedrooms *(John Dwane)*

TODDINGTON [SP0432]

Pheasant GL54 5DT [A46 Broadway—Winchcombe, junction with A438 and B4077]: Attractive extended stone-built roadside pub with emphasis on good choice of reasonably priced food, friendly helpful staff, real ales such as Stanway; lots of railway prints – handy for nearby preserved Gloucestershire Warwickshire railway station; no dogs while food served *(B M Eldridge, Giles and Annie Francis)*

UPPER FRAMILODE [SO7510]

Ship GL2 7LH [Saul Rd; not far from M5 junction 13 via B4071]: Welcoming and relaxed 17th-c former coaching inn, enjoyable sensibly priced food inc plenty of fresh fish and signature steak and kidney pie (handed-down recipe), Sun roasts, summer cream teas; well kept ales such as Sharps Doom Bar, Timothy Taylors Landlord, Wickwar Cotswold Way and Wychwood Hobgoblin, good choice of wines by the glass, efficient friendly service, two bars, beams and nice log fire, restaurant extension; children and dogs welcome, wheelchair access, big garden with large decked area by Severn's Stroudwater Canal offshoot (being restored), good walks, three bedrooms (one catering for disabled guests), open all day summer, all day Fri-Sun winter *(James Skinner, David and Ann Davies, Chris and Angela Buckell)*

UPTON CHENEY [ST6969]

Upton Inn BS30 6LY [signed off A431 at Bitton]: 18th-c stone-built village pub under new management since 2008, refurbished bar with old prints on stone and dark panelled walls, old tables and captain's chairs, step up to carpeted/bare-boards dining area with log fire and carvery; home-made food from sandwiches up, welcoming helpful staff, well kept Badger ales, modern opulent mock-regency restaurant with pictures of Bath; piped jazz or classical music; children and dogs welcome, wheelchair access, picnic-sets on terrace and in back garden, picturesque spot with Avon valley views *(Chris and Angela Buckell, MRSM)*

WHITECROFT [SO6005]

Miners Arms GL15 4PE [B4234 N of Lydney]: Friendly unpretentious local with up to five changing ales, farm ciders and perries, generous pub food, two rooms on either side of bar, slate and parquet floors, pastel walls with old photographs, conservatory, skittle alley; piped music; children and dogs welcome, disabled access, good gardens front and back, one with pleasant little stream, quoits and boules, nice local walks, handy for steam railway, open all day *(Chris and Angela Buckell)*

WHITMINSTER [SO7607]

☆ *Frombridge Mill* GL2 7PD [Frombridge Lane (A38 nr M5 junction 13)]: Comfortable mill-based dining pub, some tables overlooking river, reliable reasonably priced food inc popular lunchtime carvery, efficient friendly staff, well kept Greene King ales; picnic-sets in garden with play area, pretty riverside setting, footbridge from car park *(Dr A J and Mrs Tompsett, Steve Whalley)*

WINCHCOMBE [SP0228]

☆ *Plaisterers Arms* GL54 5LL [Abbey Terrace]: 18th-c, with stripped stonework, beams, Hogarth prints, bric-a-brac and flame-effect fires, well kept Goffs Jouster and Timothy Taylors Landlord, good cider, wines and coffee, enjoyable food from shortish menu, helpful service; two chatty front bars both with steps down to dim-lit lower back dining area with stall tables, darts; dogs welcome, good play area in charming secluded back garden, long and narrow, comfortable, simple bedrooms (tricky stairs) *(BB, Michael Dandy, R C Vincent, Dr A J and Mrs Tompsett, M Greening)*

WINTERBOURNE [ST6678]

Willy Wicket BS36 1DP [Wick Wick Close, handy for M4 junction 19 via M32, A4174 E]: Popular and relaxing Vintage Inn family dining pub with good all-day food, Butcombe and St Austell, two eating areas off big central bar, friendly service, two log fires, stripped stone, picture windows; open all day *(Alexander Ross)*

WITHINGTON [SP0315]

Mill Inn GL54 4BE [off A436 or A40]: Idyllic streamside setting for mossy-roofed old stone inn, beams, flagstones, inglenook log fire, plenty of character with nice nooks and corners; darts and dominoes, bargain pubby food, dining room; piped music, keg beer (but decent wine list); children very welcome, large pretty garden, splendid walks, four old-fashioned bedrooms, good breakfast *(Gene and Kitty Rankin, LYM, E McCall, T McLean, D Irving, Dr and Mrs M E Wilson, Guy Charrison)*

WOODCHESTER [SO8403]

☆ *Old Fleece* GL5 5NB [Rooksmoor; A46 a mile S of Stroud – not to be confused with Fleece at Lightpill, a little closer in]: Part of the small Food Club chain, wide choice of interesting fresh food from unusual lunchtime sandwiches up, children's helpings, friendly helpful staff, well kept Bass and Greene King IPA, good wines by the glass; three unpretentious linked rooms,

big windows and bare boards, large log fire, candles, daily papers, stripped stone or dark salmon-pink walls; children welcome, two roadside terraces, one heated *(Dave Irving, Jenny Huggins, BB, Alan Bulley)*

☆ *Royal Oak* GL5 5PQ [off A46; Church Road, north Woodchester]: Relaxing and comfortable low-beamed bar on right with oak tables, soft seats by big log fire in huge fireplace next to old-fashioned stripped-stone dining area on left; locally sourced home-made food (not Sun evening) from new landlady (she's romanian so may be dishes like sour soup and mici sausages), Sun roasts, welcoming staff, real ales from Hook Norton, St Austell and Sharps, fresh flowers, nice views, live music weekly; children and dogs welcome, some seating out at front, more on back terrace, cl Mon *(Dave Irving, Jenny Huggins, E McCall, T McLean, D Irving, LYM)*

WOODMANCOTE [SO9727]

Apple Tree GL52 9QG [Stockwell Lane]: Interesting choice of good value food in roomy former cider house, now a well run family pub with log fires and comfortable sofas; cheerful courteous staff, Greene King ales, decent wines, restaurant; garden with fine views, idyllic hillside spot *(Jo Rees)*

YATE [ST6983]

Codrington Arms BS37 7LG [Just north of 'the Fox' junction on B4059]: Welcoming and pleasantly refurbished stone-built roadside pub, enjoyable lunchtime food and more elaborate evening menu, efficient service, well kept Greene King ales; wood-burner in bar with old local photographs, leather sofa and chairs in raised section, light and airy part-panelled dining area (children here); piped music, no dogs; some wheelchair access, attractive garden with play area, open all day wknds *(Dr and Mrs C W Thomas, Chris and Angela Buckell, Neil and Anita Christopher)*

Cross Keys BS37 7LQ [signed off B4059 Yate bypass at 'the Fox'; North Rd]: Unpretentious two-bar beamed village local, reasonably priced food (not Sun, Mon) from sandwiches up inc good old-fashioned puddings, Bass, Courage Best and guests such as Box Steam and Bristol Beer Factory; cheerful chatty landlord, warming woodburner, stripped stone and panelling, flagstones and carpet, mixed pubby furniture inc pews and old dining tables, brasses and prints, cards; fruit machine and darts in public bar; disabled access (perhaps a bit tricky for some wheelchairs), open all day Fri-Sun *(Chris and Angela Buckell, Donna and Roger)*

Hampshire

The county has plenty of pubs run with real individual charm by long-serving licensees, making you feel truly welcome, whether it's an unspoilt local or a smart dining pub. On top form this year are the Oak at Bank, Sun in Bentworth, Flower Pots at Cheriton, Bakers Arms in Droxford, Chestnut Horse in Easton, Royal Oak at Fritham, Yew Tree at Lower Wield, Trooper near Petersfield, Plough at Sparsholt, Harrow at Steep, Tichborne Arms in Tichborne, Thomas Lord in West Meon, Mayfly near Wherwell, Black Boy in Winchester, and, gaining new entries in this edition, Master Builders House at Bucklers Hard and Ship in Lymington. Quite a few pubs here now merit one of our Food Awards: for consistent enjoyment and fair prices given the quality, our Hampshire Dining Pub of the Year is the Plough at Sparsholt. This is a good county too for beer lovers, as many of our main entries here keep a fine range of local ales. The dominant local brew is Ringwood, part of the Marstons empire; the top independent is Bowman, followed by fff, and several good if less common beers such as Flowerpots, Itchen Valley, Hampshire and Oakleaf. Gales, formerly local, now comes from Fullers of London. Finally, some hot tips, almost all inspected and approved by us, among the Lucky Dip pubs: Red Lion at Boldre, Greyfriar at Chawton, Robin Hood at Durley, Jolly Farmer in Locks Heath, Castle Inn at Rowland's Castle, Cricketers Arms at Tangley and Bugle in Twyford.

BANK   SU2806   MAP 2

Oak 🍺

Signposted just off A35 SW of Lyndhurst; SO43 7FD

Tucked-away and very busy New Forest pub with well liked food and interesting décor

Even on cold and wet winter lunchtimes, this tucked-away pub is always busy with customers keen to enjoy the roaring log fire, several real ales, well liked food and prompt, friendly service. On either side of the door in the bay windows of the L-shaped bar are built-in red-cushioned seats, and on the right there are two or three little pine-panelled booths with small built-in tables and bench seats. The rest of the bare-boarded bar has some low beams and joists, candles in individual brass holders on a line of stripped old and newer blond tables set against the wall, fishing rods, spears, a boomerang and old ski poles on the ceiling, and brass platters, heavy knives and guns on the walls. There are cushioned milk churns along the bar counter, little red lanterns among hop bines above the bar and Butcombe Bitter, Fullers London Pride, and Gales HSB and maybe Seafarers on handpump; piped music. The pleasant side garden has picnic-sets and long tables and benches by the big yew trees.

🍴 Well liked bar food includes big lunchtime doorstep sandwiches like crayfish and rocket, home-cooked ham and eggs, a pie of the day, venison sausages, salmon fishcakes, lamb casserole with dumplings, beef bourguignon, scallops, king prawns and bacon salad and asparagus and tomato gratin. *Starters/Snacks: £4.95 to £7.50. Main Courses: £8.50 to £16.50. Puddings: £4.50*

Fullers ~ Manager Martin Sliva ~ Real ale ~ Bar food (12-2.30, 6-9.30; 12-2.30, 5-9 Sun) ~
(023) 8028 2350 ~ Children welcome until 6pm ~ Dogs welcome ~ Open 11.30-11;
12-10.30 Sun; 11.30-3, 6-11 weekdays in winter

*Recommended by Pam and John Smith, Michael Dandy, Steve and Liz Tilley, Mrs Margo Finlay, Jörg Kasprowski,
Jennifer Banks, N R White, Jenny and Brian Seller, Terry and Nickie Williams, Patrick Spence, Leslie and
Barbara Owen, Mr and Mrs A Garforth, Mike and Sue Loseby, Mr and Mrs P D Titcomb*

BENTLEY   SU8044   MAP 2

Bull

*A31 Alton—Farnham dual carriageway, E of village itself; accessible from both
carriageways, but tricky if westbound; GU10 5JH*

Cosy old place with tasty food and real ales – an unexpected trunk road respite

'Everything a pub should be' says one of our readers about this bustling 15th-c pub.
You can be sure of a friendly welcome and the attractive main room on the right, restful
despite some traffic noise, has soft lighting, flowers and candles on the tables, witty
sayings chalked on low black beams in its maroon ceiling, lots of local photographs on
partly stripped brick walls, and pub chairs around neat, stripped, pub tables. The back
room on the left has a good log fire in a huge hearth, a cushioned pew by one long oak-
planked table, and in a snug and narrow back alcove, another pew built around a nice
mahogany table. Courage Best, Ringwood Best and Timothy Taylors Landlord on
handpump and several wines by the glass; newspapers to read. There are plenty of pretty
summer flowering tubs and hanging baskets outside, and picnic-sets and a teak table and
chairs on the side terrace.

🍴 **Generous helpings of good bar food includes sandwiches, ploughman's, soup, potted
brown shrimps with melba toast, devilled chicken livers, roasted butternut squash risotto
with blue cheese, chicken fillet stuffed with mozzarella and parma ham on sweet potato
mash with a creamy white wine sauce, pork medallions with a sweet vermouth and coarse
grain mustard sauce, and daily specials like garlic mediterranean prawns, seared king
scallops, duck and mushroom stroganoff, fillet of pork wellington and whole roasted bass.**
Starters/Snacks: £4.95 to £8.95. Main Courses: £9.95 to £20.95. Puddings: £5.00 to £5.25

Enterprise ~ Lease Grant Edmead ~ Real ale ~ Bar food (12-2.30, 6.30-9.30; 12-8.30 Sun) ~
Restaurant ~ (01420) 22156 ~ Children welcome away from bar ~ Dogs allowed in bar ~
Open 10.30am(10am Sat)-11pm; 12-10.30 Sun

Recommended by Janet Whittaker, John and Joyce Snell, Ann and Colin Hunt, Ian Phillips

BENTWORTH   SU6640   MAP 2

Sun ◀

*Sun Hill; from the A339 coming from Alton, the first turning takes you there direct; or in
village follow Shalden 2½, Alton 4½ signpost; GU34 5JT*

Marvellous real ales and welcoming landlady in popular country pub; nearby walks

A favourite with many of our readers, this charming 17th-c country pub is run by a
welcoming landlady who keeps a fine choice of seven real ales on handpump: Brains Rev
James, Fullers London Pride, Gales HSB, Palmers Gold, Ringwood Best, Stonehenge
Pigswill and Timothy Taylors Landlord. The two little traditional communicating rooms
have high-backed antique settles, pews and schoolroom chairs, olde-worlde prints and
blacksmith's tools on the walls, and bare boards and scrubbed deal tables on the left; big
fireplaces (one with an open fire) make it especially snug in winter; an arch leads to a
brick-floored room with another open fire. There are seats out in front and in the back
garden and pleasant nearby walks.

🍴 **Generous helpings of good bar food includes sandwiches, soup (the creamy haddock
chowder is popular), hummus with pitta bread, mushroom, bacon and stilton starter,
goats cheese salad with walnuts and honey, ham and egg, pork and leek sausages, steak
in ale pie, liver and bacon, a thick, home-made burger, fresh tagliatelle with smoked
salmon, lemon and dill cream sauce, daily specials, and puddings such as banoffi pie and**

sticky toffee pudding. *Starters/Snacks: £3.95 to £5.25. Main Courses: £8.95 to £15.95. Puddings: £3.95*

Free house ~ Licensee Mary Holmes ~ Real ale ~ Bar food ~ (01420) 562338 ~ Children welcome ~ Dogs welcome ~ Open 12-3, 6-11; 12-10.30 Sun

Recommended by DGH, Martin and Karen Wake, Stephen Moss, Mr and Mrs H J Langley, Michael Sargent, Laurence Smith, the Didler, Susan and John Douglas, R B Gardiner, Mr and Mrs C Prentis, Rob, Phil and Sally Gorton

BRAISHFIELD
SU3724 MAP 2

Wheatsheaf ♀
Village signposted off A3090 on NW edge of Romsey, pub just S of village on Braishfield Road; S051 0QE

Interesting and unusual décor, real ales, good choice of wines and food using some of their own produce; nearby walks

The eclectic décor in this rambling pub appeals to a lot of our readers and the atmosphere is very friendly and relaxed. There are all sorts of tables from elegant little oak ovals through handsome Regency-style drum tables to sturdy more rustic ones, with a similarly wide variety of chairs, and on the stripped brick or deep pink-painted walls a profusion of things to look at, from Spy caricatures and antique prints through staffordshire dogs and other decorative china to a leg in a fishnet stocking kicking out from the wall and a jokey 'Malteser grader' (a giant copper skimmer). Ringwood Best and guests like Bowman Wallops Wood, Otter Bitter and Triple fff Altons Pride on handpump, and 16 wines by the glass; daily papers, several reference books, piped music, board games, and a quiz on the last Thursday of the month. Disabled access and facilities. Unusually, the chairs, tables and picnic-sets out on the terrace are painted in greek blue; boules. There are woodland walks nearby and the pub is handy for the Sir Harold Hillier Arboretum.

〖¶〗 **Using their own rare breed pigs (they make their own sausages and black puddings), their own chickens and ducks (for eggs and meat), their own fruit and vegetables and seasonal local game, the bar food includes sandwiches, terrine of wild rabbit, duck and pistachio nut, quail egg and smoked salmon on toast, risotto of dolcelatte and wild mushroom, old spot pork chop with apple and black pudding, sausage and mash, chicken stuffed with stilton, wrapped in bacon with mushroom sauce, beer-battered pollack, home-cooked gammon and egg, meaty or fishy mixed grills, and puddings like profiteroles and apple crumble. They hold gourmet burger evenings on Wednesdays, have a two- and three-course set menu, summer hog roasts and winter pie nights.** *Starters/Snacks: £4.25 to £5.95. Main Courses: £8.95 to £14.95. Puddings: £4.95*

Enterprise ~ Lease Peter and Jenny Jones ~ Real ale ~ Bar food (12-2.30, 6-9.30; all day Sun) ~ (01794) 368372 ~ Children welcome away from bar ~ Dogs welcome ~ Open 12-11

Recommended by Phyl and Jack Street, John Chambers, Franklyn Roberts, Gene and Kitty Rankin, Simon and Mandy King, Mrs Margo Finlay, Jörg Kasprowski, Diana Brumfit, Martin and Karen Wake

BRAMDEAN
SU6127 MAP 2

Fox 〖¶〗
A272 Winchester—Petersfield; S024 0LP

Civilised dining pub with popular food and friendly staff; no children inside

This comfortable and deliberately unchanging 17th-c weatherboarded dining pub is known for its reliably good bar food. The carefully modernised black beamed open-plan bar is civilised and grown up (no children inside), with tall stools with proper backrests around the L-shaped counter and comfortably cushioned wall pews and wheelback chairs – the fox motif shows in a big painting over the fireplace and on much of the decorative china. Greene King Morlands Original on handpump, decent wine by the glass, and piped music. At the back of the building there's a walled-in terraced area and a neatly kept spacious lawn spreading among the fruit trees. Good surrounding walks. Dogs may be allowed in the bar if the pub is not too busy.

🍴 **Popular bar food includes lunchtime sandwiches, wild boar pâté, scallops fried with bacon, steak and kidney pie, chicken curry, fresh fillet of battered cod, confit of duck with an orange gravy, pork fillet with stilton and brandy sauce, halibut in lime and chilli butter, and puddings such as apple, blackberry and almond crumble and chocolate st emilion.** *Starters/Snacks: £3.75 to £7.95. Main Courses: £9.95 to £15.95. Puddings: £4.75 to £5.25*

Greene King ~ Tenants Ian and Jane Inder ~ Real ale ~ Bar food (not Sun evening) ~ (01962) 771363 ~ Open 10-3, 6.30-11; 12-3.30 Sun; closed Sun evenings

Recommended by Simon Collett-Jones, R and S Bentley, Janet Whittaker, J A Snell, Phyl and Jack Street, Helen and Brian Edgeley, Betty Laker

BRANSGORE   SZ1997   MAP 2

Three Tuns 🍺

Village signposted off A35 and off B3347 N of Christchurch; Ringwood Road, opposite church; BH23 8JH

Interesting food in pretty thatched pub with proper old-fashioned bar and good beers as well as a civilised main dining area

With its thatched roof and lovely hanging baskets, this little pub is very pretty in summer. The roomy low-ceilinged and carpeted main area has a fireside 'codgers' corner' as well as its good mix of comfortably cushioned low chairs around a variety of dining tables, and opens on to an attractive and extensive shrub-sheltered terrace with picnic-sets on its brick pavers; beyond here are more tables out on the grass, looking out over pony paddocks. On the right is a separate traditional regulars' bar that seems almost taller than it is wide, with an impressive log-effect stove in a stripped brick hearth, some shiny black panelling and individualistic pubby furnishings. Hop Back Summer Lightning, Ringwood Best and Fortyniner, St Austell Tribute, Sharps Doom Bar and Timothy Taylors Landlord on handpump and a good choice of wines by the glass. Service is well organised and polite.

🍴 **As well as lunchtime sandwiches and ploughman's, the often interesting bar food includes soup, tempura soft shell crab with garlic mayo and pickled white cabbage, sushi with hot wasabi and soy sauce, moules marinière, chicken caesar salad, beer-battered cod, aubergine and mushroom parcel with roasted red pepper sauce, chicken rubbed with salt and thyme and finished with mushrooms and a real ale cream sauce, sausages with rich onion gravy, meatballs with tagliatelle, five-spiced pork with oriental sauce and egg noodles, and puddings like apple and rhubarb crumble and sticky toffee pudding with vanilla seed ice-cream. Sunday roasts.** *Starters/Snacks: £4.95 to £7.95. Main Courses: £7.95 to £18.95. Puddings: £4.50*

Enterprise ~ Lease Nigel Glenister ~ Real ale ~ Bar food (12-2.15, 6-9.15; all day Sat and Sun) ~ Restaurant ~ (01425) 672232 ~ Children in restaurant and lounge but not main bar ~ Dogs allowed in bar ~ Open 11.30-11; 12-10.30 Sun; closed evenings 25 and 26 Dec and 1 Jan

Recommended by Andy and Jill Kassube, Mr and Mrs J Mandeville, Phyl and Jack Street, Richard and Anne Ansell, Laurence Smith

BUCKLERS HARD   SU4000   MAP 2

Master Builders House 🛏

From M27 junction 2 follow signs to Beaulieu; turn left on to B3056 and then left to Bucklers Hard – the hotel is 2 miles along on the left; SO42 7XB

Lovely spot overlooking river in a charming village, character bar with open fires and part of hotel; real ales, pubby food, popular outdoor barbecue and seats outside; bedrooms

Part of a sizeable hotel in a charming, carefully preserved waterside village, this dimly lit two-level room is the original yachtsman's bar. It's got a great deal of character and a wide mix of chatty customers of all ages, and the main part has heavy beams, a warm winter log fire in an old brick fireplace (have a look at the list of all the ship builders dating from the 18th c on a wooden plaque to one side of it), benches and cushioned wall seats around long tables, rugs on the wooden floor and mullioned windows. There are some bar stools on quarry tiles by the counter where they serve Marstons Pedigree and Ringwood Best on handpump and decent wines by the glass; friendly young staff. Stairs lead down to a lower room with a fireplace at each end and similar furnishings. There's a front terrace with seating (used by restaurant guests) and plenty of picnic-sets below that on the lawn which overlooks the lovely river and boating activity; the outdoor barbecue is very popular. A small gate at the bottom leads to a walkway beside the water; idyllic in fine weather.

🍴 **Bar food includes lunchtime sandwiches, soup, a bowl of chipolatas with mustard, a fishy smokehouse platter, ham and free-range eggs, tempura-battered fish and chips, a big salmon fishcake with tartare sauce, linguine with mushrooms, 10oz rib-eye steak, and puddings like custard tart with earl grey prunes and nutmeg ice-cream and rhubarb crème brûlée.** *Starters/Snacks: £5.00 to £9.00. Main Courses: £9.00 to £18.00. Puddings: £6.00*

Free house ~ Licensee Christoph Brooke ~ Real ale ~ Bar food (12-2.30, 6.30-9.30) ~ Restaurant ~ (01590) 616253 ~ Children welcome ~ Dogs allowed in bar and bedrooms ~ Open 11-11(10.30 Sun) ~ Bedrooms: £89B/£99B

Recommended by John Saville, Ann and Colin Hunt

CHERITON   SU5828   MAP 2

Flower Pots ★ 🍺 £

Pub just off B3046 (main village road) towards Beauworth and Winchester; OS Sheet 185 map reference 581282; SO24 0QQ

Own-brew beers in rustic pub with simple rooms and simple food; no children inside

The same friendly family have owned this homely and traditional village local for over 40 years. The two straightforward little rooms are rustic and simple, though the one on the left is a favourite, almost like someone's front room, with country pictures on its striped wallpaper, bunches of flowers and some ornaments on the mantelpiece over a small log fire. Behind the servery is disused copper filtering equipment, and lots of hanging gin traps, drag-hooks, scaleyards and other ironwork. The neat extended plain public bar (where there's a covered well) has board games. Their own-brewed ales (you can tour the brewery by arrangement) include Flowerpots Bitter, Goodens Gold and Porridge Pale that are tapped from casks behind the bar counter. The pretty front and back lawns have some old-fashioned seats, and there's a summer marquee; maybe summer morris dancers. The pub is near the site of one of the final battles of the Civil War, and it got its name through once belonging to the retired head gardener of nearby Avington Park. No children inside.

🍴 **Bar food from a fairly short straightforward menu includes sandwiches, toasties and baps, filled baked potatoes, ploughman's, soup and various hotpots (the lamb and apricot is popular); on Wednesday evenings they serve only curries. The menu and serving times may be restricted if they're busy.** *Starters/Snacks: £3.80 to £7.60. Main Courses: £7.20 to £8.20*

Own brew ~ Licensees Jo and Patricia Bartlett ~ Real ale ~ Bar food (not Sun evening or bank hol evenings) ~ No credit cards ~ (01962) 771318 ~ Dogs welcome ~ Open 12-2.30, 6-11; 12-3, 7-10.30 Sun ~ Bedrooms: £45S/£75S

Recommended by Peter and Liz Holmes, the Didler, Phil and Sally Gorton, Barry Steele-Perkins, A D Lealan, Ann and Colin Hunt, Gerald and Gabrielle Culliford, Janet Whittaker, Irene and Derek Flewin, Peter Sampson, Tony and Jill Radnor

---

Stars after the name of a pub show exceptional quality. One star means most people (after reading the report to see just why the star has been won) would think a special trip worth while. Two stars mean that the pub is really outstanding – for its particular qualities it could hardly be bettered.

CRAWLEY   SU4234   MAP 2

Fox & Hounds ♀

Off A272 or B3420 NW of Winchester; SO21 2PR

**Attractive building, three roaring winter log fires, several real ales and reasonably priced
food; bedrooms**

This solidly constructed mock-Tudor building is one of the most striking in a village
of fine old houses. Each timbered upper storey successively juts further out, with lots of
pegged structural timbers in the neat brickwork, and elaborately carved steep gable-ends.
The neat and attractive linked rooms have three log fires, a mix of attractive wooden
tables and chairs on polished floors, lots of bottles along a delft shelf, and a civilised
atmosphere. The traditional little bar has built-in wall seats and Ringwood Best and
Fortyniner, Wadworths 6X and Wells & Youngs Bombardier on handpump, and
14 wines by the glass; friendly licensees and efficient young staff. There are picnic-sets
in the gardens (one of which has some children's play equipment). The bedrooms, in
converted outbuildings, are named after the ducks on the village pond.

🍴 As well as sandwiches and basket meals, the reasonably priced bar food includes soup,
stilton mushrooms, duck and orange pâté, baked camembert with redcurrant jelly, five-
bean chilli, salmon and dill fishcakes, lasagne, a curry of the day, a rack of barbecue pork
ribs, apricot-stuffed chicken wellington, steak and mushroom in ale pie, and home-made
puddings such as fruit crumble and white chocolate mousse with dark chocolate chips.
Starters/Snacks: £4.25 to £4.95. Main Courses: £7.95 to £13.50. Puddings: £4.25 to £5.95

Enterprise ~ Lease Peter and Kathy Airey ~ Real ale ~ Bar food (12-2, 7-9; 12-4 Sun;
not Sun evening) ~ Restaurant ~ (01962) 776006 ~ Children welcome ~ Open 11-3,
6-11(midnight Sat); 12-6 Sun; closed Sun evening ~ Bedrooms: /£60B

Recommended by Phyl and Jack Street, I A Herdman

DROXFORD   SU6018   MAP 2

Bakers Arms

A32 5 miles N of Wickham; High Street; SO32 3PA

**Attractively opened-up and friendly pub with well kept beers, good, interesting cooking
and cosy corners**

With friendly, polite staff making customers feel genuinely welcome, local beers and
imaginative food, it's not surprising that this attractively laid-out pub is doing so well.
Food does play a big part here but the central bar with its warm atmosphere is kept as the
main focus: they have Bowman Swift One and Wallops Wood on handpump, Stowford Press
cider, and a careful short choice of wines by the glass. Well spaced mixed tables on carpet
or neat bare boards spread around the airy L-shaped open-plan bar, with low leather
chesterfields and an assortment of comfortably cushioned chairs down at one end; a dark
panelled dado, dark beams and joists and a modicum of country oddments emphasise the
freshness of the crisp white paintwork. There's a good log fire and board games. To one
side, with a separate entrance, is the village post office. There are picnic-sets outside.

🍴 Depending on what's available locally and using their own, daily-baked bread, the
imaginative food might include lunchtime sandwiches and ploughman's, onion soup with
wild garlic pesto, pressed chicken terrine with onion jam, fried lambs kidneys with crispy
bacon salad, roasted polenta with blue cheese and field mushrooms, local pork sausages
with onion gravy, chicken, ham and creamy leek pie, fillet of gurnard with saffron risotto
and tomato dressing, crispy duck leg with chorizo and thyme gravy, and puddings like
chocolate and fudge brownie with butterscotch ice-cream and sticky toffee pudding with
caramel sauce and vanilla ice-cream. *Starters/Snacks: £4.50 to £7.00. Main Courses: £9.95 to
£16.95. Puddings: £5.50*

Free house ~ Licensees Adam and Anna Cordery ~ Real ale ~ Bar food (not Sun evening or Mon)
~ (01489) 877533 ~ Well behaved children welcome ~ Dogs welcome ~ Open 11.45-3, 6-11;
12-3 Sun; closed Sun evening and Mon

Recommended by Val and Alan Green, Diana Brumfit, Ann and Colin Hunt, Chris Sale

DUNBRIDGE

SU3225 MAP 2

Mill Arms ◀

Barley Hill, just by station on Portsmouth—Cardiff line; SO51 OLF

Extended coaching house with plenty of space, several real ales, bistro-style food and a pretty garden; bedrooms

This much extended 18th-c former coaching inn has plenty of space both inside and out. There's a relaxed, friendly atmosphere in the high-ceilinged rooms with scrubbed pine tables and farmhouse chairs on the oak or flagstone floors, a couple of log fires, several sofas, and Ringwood Best with guests such as Bath Ales Gem Bitter, Greene King Abbot and Wickwar BOB on handpump; several wines by the glass, and prompt service. There's also a dining area, a dining conservatory and a skittle alley; piped music. The large, pretty garden has lots of picnic-sets, and there are plenty of walks in the surrounding Test Valley countryside.The bedrooms are bright and comfortable. Dunbridge railway station is opposite.

🍴 Good bistro-style bar food includes sandwiches, terrine of duck rillette with apricot chutney, six grilled oysters with spinach, pancetta and parmesan glaze, home-made burger with cheese, home-baked ham and free-range eggs, rabbit and prune cannelloni with carrot and ginger purée, popular beer-battered haddock, dolcelatte and semolina gnocchi with fennel and roasted red onion, confit leg of pheasant and pheasant breast stuffed with haggis on sweetcorn, cod with crayfish bubble and squeak and lobster bisque sauce, and puddings like lemon steamed pudding with fresh ginger custard and chocolate brûlée; they also have a two-course set menu (not Sunday). *Starters/Snacks: £4.50 to £6.95. Main Courses: £8.95 to £10.50. Puddings: £4.75 to £6.50*

Enterprise ~ Lease Mr I Bentall ~ Real ale ~ Bar food (12-2.30, 6-9.30; 12-9.30 weekends) ~ Restaurant ~ (01794) 340401 ~ Children welcome ~ Dogs allowed in bar and bedrooms ~ Open 12-2.30, 6-11; 12-11 Sat and Sun ~ Bedrooms: /£70B

Recommended by Phyl and Jack Street, P J Checksfield, Ann and Colin Hunt

DUNDRIDGE

SU5718 MAP 2

Hampshire Bowman ◀

Off B3035 towards Droxford, Swanmore, then right at Bishop's W signpost; SO32 1GD

Friendly country pub with quickly changing real ales, homely food and peaceful garden with children's play equipment

With some genuine character and a friendly relaxed atmosphere, this is a proper country pub with a good mix of customers – and no noisy games machines, piped music or mobile phones to disturb the bustling and chatty feel. There's a good range of real ales tapped from the cask such as Bowman Quiver, Swift One and Wallops Wood, Palmers 200 and Stonehenge Danish Dynamite, farm cider in summer, and six wines by the glass. There's a smart stable bar that sits comfortably alongside the cosy unassuming original bar, some colourful paintings, board games, puzzles and Daisy the pub dog. There are picnic-sets on the attractive lawn, a giant umbrella with lighting and heating on the terrace (where you can enjoy the lovely sunsets), and children's play equipment; peaceful nearby downland walks.

🍴 Well liked homely bar food includes sandwiches, filled baguettes and baked potatoes, ploughman's, soup, vegetable lasagne, home-cooked ham and egg, battered cod, liver and bacon with onion gravy, and daily specials like goats cheese in filo pastry, sausages and mash, chicken breast with bacon, mushrooms and stilton, mixed game casserole and various pies. *Starters/Snacks: £3.95 to £5.95. Main Courses: £7.50 to £12.95. Puddings: £4.95*

Free house ~ Licensee Heather Seymour ~ Real ale ~ Bar food (12-2.30, 6.30-9; all day Fri-Sun) ~ (01489) 892940 ~ Children welcome ~ Dogs welcome ~ Open 12-11(10.30 Sun)

Recommended by the Didler, Val and Alan Green, Ann and Colin Hunt, Jim and Jill Harris

---

Unlike other guides, entry in this *Guide* is free. All our entries depend solely on merit.

EAST TYTHERLEY

SU2927 MAP 2

Star ⟨♉⟩

S edge of village, off B3084 N of Romsey; SO51 OLW

Warm welcome for drinkers and diners in pretty pub; inventive food, real ales and comfortable bedrooms

Whether it's a quiet drink you want or an enjoyable meal, this pretty country pub with its friendly, hard-working licensees will fit the bill. The bar has comfortable sofas and tub armchairs, pubby dining tables and chairs, bar stools and chairs, an overflowing bookcase to one side of the log fire, and rich red walls. The restaurant is attractively set with proper linen napkins and tablecloths. Hepworths Prospect Organic and Hidden Pleasure and Quest on handpump, several wines by the glass, malt whiskies and a range of apple juices; piped music and board games. There are picnic-set sets in front and tables and chairs on the back terrace by a giant chessboard. The bedrooms overlook the cricket pitch and the breakfasts are particularly good; nearby walks.

⟨Ⅲ⟩ Cooked by the licensees' son, the inventive, attractively presented food at lunchtime might include sandwiches and platters, soup, steamed scottish mussels with white wine and cream, goats cheese and red onion tart with beetroot chutney, cumberland sausages with apple mash and thyme jus, carrot and red onion savoury bread and butter pudding, and chicken suprême with vegetable and puy lentil casserole, with evening choices like crab soufflé, pigeon breast with pearl barley risotto, and parsley and hazelnut pesto, salmon, cod and prawn pie with leek mash, wild mushroom and stilton tagliatelle, and braised pork belly with sage polenta, celeriac purée, haricot beans, and a smoked bacon and garlic casserole, and puddings such as white chocolate cheesecake with maple syrup and panettone bread and butter pudding with apricot coulis; good local cheeses and Sunday roasts. *Starters/Snacks: £4.25 to £6.50. Main Courses: £7.25 to £16.50. Puddings: £5.50*

Free house ~ Licensees Alan and Lesley Newitt ~ Real ale ~ Bar food ~ Restaurant ~ (01794) 340225 ~ Children welcome ~ Dogs allowed in bar and bedrooms ~ Live music Fri evenings ~ Open 11-2.30(3 Sat), 6-10.30; 11.30-3 Sun; closed Sun evening, Mon, one week July ~ Bedrooms: £55S/£80S

Recommended by Ann and Colin Hunt, Peter Craske, Glenwys and Alan Lawrence

EASTON

SU5132 MAP 2

Chestnut Horse ⟨♉⟩ ⟨♉⟩

3.6 miles from M3 junction 9: A33 towards Kings Worthy, then B3047 towards Itchen Abbas; Easton then signposted on right – bear left in village; SO21 1EG

Cosy dining pub with log fires, fresh flowers and candles, deservedly popular food and friendly staff; Itchen Valley walks nearby

This is an enjoyable dining pub, and as one reader put it, rather a treat to come to. It's busy and friendly with helpful, well organised staff and very good food. The open-plan interior manages to have a pleasantly rustic and intimate feel with a series of cosily separate areas and the snug décor takes in candles and fresh flowers on the tables, log fires in cottagey fireplaces and comfortable furnishings. The black beams and joists are hung with all sorts of jugs, mugs and chamber-pots, and there are lots of attractive pictures of wildlife and the local area. Badger K&B Sussex Bitter, First Gold and Hopping Hare on handpump, several wines by the glass and 30 malt whiskies. There are seats and tables out on a smallish sheltered decked area with colourful flower tubs and baskets, and plenty of nearby walks in the Itchen Valley.

⟨Ⅲ⟩ As well as lunchtime sandwiches, the good, carefully cooked (if not cheap) food might include soup, tian of crab and crayfish with sakura cress, sautéed kidneys with a wholegrain mustard and whisky cream sauce, generous moules marinière, beer-battered cod with minted pea purée, brioche parcel of wild mushrooms, aubergine and spinach with a velvety onion sauce, confit pork belly with sage and onion dumplings and glazed apple, game pastries (rabbit wellington, venison pie and pigeon with sultana shortbread) with a sweet cider sauce, and puddings like baked alaska and double chocolate and raspberry roulade; there's also a good value two-course set menu (not Saturday evening or

Sunday lunch). *Starters/Snacks: £4.00 to £8.00. Main Courses: £12.00 to £18.00. Puddings: £5.00 to £8.00*

Badger ~ Tenant Karen Wells ~ Real ale ~ Bar food (12-2.30, 6(7 Sat)-9.30; 12-4 Sun; not Sun evening) ~ Restaurant ~ (01962) 779257 ~ Children welcome ~ Dogs allowed in bar ~ Open 12-3, 5.30-11.30; 12-11(10 Sun) Sat; 12-6 Sun in winter; closed evening 25 and 26 Dec and 1 Jan

Recommended by John Robertson, Helen and Brian Edgeley, Martin and Karen Wake, Jenny and Brian Seller, Pam and John Smith, Ann and Colin Hunt, D and J Ashdown, Phyl and Jack Street, Stephen Moss

EXTON   SU6120   MAP 2

Shoe

Village signposted from A32 NE of Bishop's Waltham – brown sign to pub into Beacon Hill Lane; SO32 3NT

Hard-working licensees in country pub by River Meon, with comfortable linked rooms and nice food

On the South Downs Way in the heart of the Meon Valley, this is a pleasant and popular country pub with friendly licensees. The three linked rooms have a relaxed atmosphere, comfortable pub furnishings, cricket and country prints, and in the right-hand room (which is panelled), a log fire. Wadworths 6X, IPA and a seasonal guest on handpump and 14 wines by the glass; helpful, welcoming service. You can sit at one of the many picnic-sets and watch the ducks on the River Meon in the back garden and there are seats under parasols at the front. They have baby-changing facilities, a disabled lavatory and ramp access.

🍽 **Cooked by the landlord using home-grown produce (and they make their own bread, pickles and chutney), the well liked food includes sandwiches and platters, soup, scallops in lemon and herb butter, glazed goats cheese on mediterranean vegetables, home-cured salmon with dill, home-cooked ham with free-range eggs, lambs liver and bacon with onion gravy, thai green chicken curry, wild mushroom risotto, salmon and crab fishcakes with a lemon and basil cream sauce, confit of duck with spring onion potato and raspberry sauce, and puddings like french lemon tart and chocolate brownie.**
Starters/Snacks: £4.50 to £6.95. Main Courses: £7.95 to £15.95. Puddings: £5.50

Wadworths ~ Tenants Mark and Carole Broadbent ~ Real ale ~ Bar food (12-2, 6-9(9.30 Fri and Sat, 8.30 Sun); not Mon evening) ~ Restaurant ~ (01489) 877526 ~ Children welcome ~ Dogs allowed in bar ~ Open 11-3, 6-11(10.30 Sun); closed Mon evening

Recommended by Stephen Moss, Harriet Crisp, Ann and Colin Hunt, Simon Collett-Jones, Tony Hewitt, Tony and Wendy Hobden

FRITHAM   SU2314   MAP 2

Royal Oak 🍺

Village signed from exit roundabout, M27 junction 1; quickest via B3078, then left and straight through village; head for Eyeworth Pond; SO43 7HJ

Rural New Forest spot and part of a working farm; traditional rooms, log fires, seven real ales and simple lunchtime food

As this lovely simple country tavern is a favourite with many and certainly a place customers tend to return to on a regular basis, it's best to arrive early to be sure of a table. Three neatly kept black beamed rooms are straightforward but full of proper traditional character, with prints and pictures involving local characters on the white walls, restored panelling, antique wheelback, spindleback and other old chairs and stools with colourful seats around solid tables on the oak flooring, and two roaring log fires; both the chatty locals and the staff are genuinely friendly. The back bar has quite a few books. Seven real ales are tapped from the cask: Bowman Royal Oak and Wallops Wood, and five changing guests from local breweries. Also, ten wines by the glass (mulled wine in winter) and a September beer festival. Summer barbecues may be put on in the neatly kept big garden which has a marquee for poor weather, and petanque. The pub is part of a working farm so there are ponies and pigs out on the green and plenty of livestock nearby.

🍴 **The much liked simple lunchtime food is limited to winter soups, ploughman's, pies and quiches, sausages and local crab in summer.** *Main Courses: £4.50 to £8.50*

Free house ~ Licensees Neil and Pauline McCulloch ~ Real ale ~ Bar food (12-2.30(2 winter weekdays, 3 weekends); not evenings) ~ No credit cards ~ (023) 8081 2606 ~ Children welcome if well behaved ~ Dogs welcome ~ Open 11-3(2.30 winter weekdays), 6-11 (all day July and August); 11-11 Sat; 12-10.30 Sun

Recommended by Miss J F Reay, Richard and Anne Ansell, Peter Meister, the Didler, Ann and Colin Hunt, Mr and Mrs W W Burke, Pete Baker, Mr and Mrs P D Titcomb, Janet Whittaker, N R White, John Chambers, A D Lealan, John Roots, Kevin Flack, Robin and Tricia Walker

---

LITTLETON   SU4532   MAP 2

Running Horse ♀

Village signposted off B3049 just NW of Winchester; Main Road; SO22 6QS

New licensee in this smart dining pub, newly extended restaurant, well liked food in elegant rooms, decent choice of drinks and nice terraces

---

A new licensee has taken over this smart dining pub and, as we went to press, was extending the back, flagstoned restaurant. The bar has some deep leather chairs as well as ochre-cushioned metal and wicker ones around matching modern tables on its polished boards, good colour photographs of Hampshire landscapes and townscapes, a log fire, and venetian blinds in its bow windows. The neat modern marble and hardwood bar counter (with swish leather, wood and brass bar stools) has Greene King Old Speckled Hen and a changing guest such as Andwell Resolute on handpump, and a dozen wines by the glass. Good disabled access and facilities, and piped music. There are green metal tables and chairs out on terraces front and back and picnic-sets on the back grass by a spreading sycamore. More reports on the new regime, please.

🍴 **At lunchtime, the bar food now includes sandwiches and filled ciabattas, soup, spicy crab and salmon fishcakes with wasabi mayonnaise, chicken curry, beer-battered haddock, creamy wild mushroom tagliatelle and calves liver with port and pancetta jus. Evening dishes may feature chicken breast in a mustard and fennel seed crust with chargrilled aubergines, roast rump of lamb with garlic, red wine and rosemary sauce, silver bream fillet with anchovy and caper butter, and puddings like baked chocolate cheesecake with chocolate sauce and pineapple carpaccio marinated in pistachio syrup with champagne sorbet and a langue de chat biscuit.** *Starters/Snacks: £4.95 to £9.95. Main Courses: £8.95 to £11.95. Puddings: £5.50*

Free house ~ Licensee Charlie Lechowski ~ Real ale ~ Bar food (12-2, 6-9(9.30 Fri and Sat, 8.30 Sun)) ~ Restaurant ~ (01962) 880218 ~ Children welcome if well behaved ~ Dogs allowed in bar ~ Open 11-3, 5.30-11; 12-9.30 Sun ~ Bedrooms: £65B/£85B

Recommended by Dave Braisted, Phyl and Jack Street, Ann and Colin Hunt, Mr and Mrs M Stratton, Richard Abnett, John and Joan Calvert, Michael Doswell, David Jackson

---

LOWER FROYLE   SU7643   MAP 2

Anchor 🛏

Village signposted N of A31 W of Bentley; GU34 4NA

Interestingly refurbished, lots to look at, civilised but informal atmosphere, real ales and good wines, and enjoyable food; comfortable bedrooms

---

Despite there being quite an emphasis on the enjoyable food in this rather civilised tile-hung 14th-c pub, those just wanting a drink are made equally welcome. There's a relaxed, chatty atmosphere, low beams and standing timbers, flagstones in the bar and wood-stripped floors elsewhere, sofas and armchairs dotted here and there, a mix of nice old tables and dining chairs, lit candles in candlesticks, an open fire, and high bar chairs at the counter. Throughout there are all sorts of interesting knick-knacks, books, lots of copper, horsebrasses, photographs (several of Charterhouse School), and all manner of pictures and prints; paint colours are fashionable, values are traditional, and they keep Triple fff and Wells & Youngs Best plus local guests on handpump and good wines by the glass. The bedrooms are stylish.

🍴 **Good lunchtime bar food using local, seasonal produce includes sandwiches, various platters, soup, jellied ham hock with parsley and piccalilli, pea and mint risotto, a burger with bacon, cheese and relish, beer-battered haddock, salt beef hash and eggs, cumberland sausage with champ and onion gravy, and smoked haddock with scrambled egg, spinach and muffin; evening choice such as squid, mussels and chorizo on toast with chilli and garlic, devilled whitebait with garlic mayonnaise, free-range chicken kiev with baked lemon dressing, skate wing with shrimps, capers and brown butter, and pork loin with black pudding potato cake and apple sauce, with puddings like chocolate and caramel mousse and raspberry and cinnamon torte; they charge extra for side orders which can bump up the price.** *Starters/Snacks: £3.50 to £10.00. Main Courses: £10.00 to £17.00. Puddings: £5.50 to £7.50*

Free house ~ Licensee Lucy Townsend ~ Real ale ~ Bar food (12-2.30(3 Sat), 6.30-9.30(10 Sat); 12-4, 7-9 Sun) ~ Restaurant ~ (01420) 23261 ~ Children welcome but must be over 10 to stay overnight ~ Dogs allowed in bar ~ Open 11-11 ~ Bedrooms: /£130S

Recommended by Tony and Jill Radnor, Mark Flynn, Barry Steele-Perkins, Martin and Karen Wake, E Ling

LOWER WIELD   SU6339   MAP 2

Yew Tree 🍴 ♀

Turn off A339 NW of Alton at Medstead, Bentworth 1 signpost, then follow village signposts; or off B3046 S of Basingstoke, signposted from Preston Candover; SO24 9RX

Smashing landlord, relaxed atmosphere, super choice of wines and popular food in popular country pub; sizeable garden and nearby walks

'Love, care and attention' is what Mr Gray says makes a good pub – and he should know. It's his friendly welcome to all his customers and his hard work and enthusiasm that make this tile-hung country pub so special. There's a small flagstoned bar area on the left with pictures above its stripped brick dado, a steadily ticking clock and log fire. Around to the right of the serving counter – which has a couple of stylish wrought-iron bar chairs – it's carpeted, with a few flower pictures; throughout there is a mix of tables, including some quite small ones for two, and miscellaneous chairs. Twelve wines by the glass from a well chosen list which may include Louis Jadot burgundies from a shipper based just along the lane and summer rosé. Bowman Swift One and a beer from Triple fff named after the pub on handpump; winter quiz nights. There are solid tables and chunky seats out on the front terrace, picnic-sets in a sizeable side garden, pleasant views and a cricket field just across the quiet lane. Nearby walks.

🍴 **Good bar food includes sandwiches, soup, thyme and blue cheese creamy mushrooms on herbed toast, salmon and cornish crab cake with home-made tartare sauce, sausages of the week with mustard mash and onion gravy, chicken wrapped in parma ham with a bacon and goats cheese sauce, portabello mushrooms topped with butternut squash, tomato, feta and sesame seed ragoût, whole bass stuffed with a thai herb bundle and drizzled with citrus oil, duck confit on honey-herbed couscous with a rich raisin jus, and puddings like chocolate and orange truffle cake and rhubarb, apple and ginger crumble.** *Starters/Snacks: £3.95 to £6.95. Main Courses: £7.50 to £17.95. Puddings: £4.50*

Free house ~ Licensee Tim Gray ~ Real ale ~ Bar food (not Mon) ~ (01256) 389224 ~ Children welcome ~ Dogs allowed in bar ~ Open 12-3, 6-11; 12-10.30 Sun; closed Mon; first two weeks in Jan

Recommended by Geoff and Molly Betteridge, Peter Barton, John Oates, Denise Walton, Peter and Andrea Jacobs, Tony and Jill Radnor, N B Vernon, Robert Davies, Stephen Moss, R B Gardiner

---

The 🍺 symbol shows pubs which keep their beer unusually well, have a particularly good range or brew their own.

LYMINGTON
SZ3295 MAP 2

Ship

Quay Road; SO41 3AY

Lively, well run pub overlooking harbour with seats outside on quay; fair value, interesting food and good choice of drinks

This lively, well run pub is in a prime spot overlooking the harbour of the civilised little town. It's extremely popular and to bag one of the contemporary chrome-and-wood chairs around wooden tables or one of the cushioned benches on the decked terrace, you must get here early or come outside peak times. It's all very light and modern, with lots of nautical bits and pieces such as big model yachts, ship-printed canvas hangings, ropework, old ships' timbers and various huge flags. On the left, there's a raised log fire, tiled or wooden tables with more chrome-and-wood chairs, and comfortably cushioned wall seats. Plenty of standing room in front of the bar counter; Shepherd Neame Spitfire and Tetleys on handpump, decent house wines (the bottles are stored in an unusual wall rack) and good soft drinks. Past here a raised area has brightly cushioned wall seats, stools and other seats around all sorts of tables (including a nice glass-topped chest one). By the french windows on to the terrace are some unusual high rustic tables and chairs and this part leads into the very attractive restaurant: subtle lighting and church candles, standing timbers, planked walls, mirrors on blue and cream paintwork, driftwood decorations and an attractive mix of furniture; friendly and efficient young staff. There are showers for visiting sailors.

🍴 **Very reasonably priced for the location, the enjoyable bar food includes sandwiches and wraps (until 6pm), ploughman's, soup, tiger prawns in coconut tempura batter with sweet chilli, coriander and coconut dip, pork, apple and cider pâté with apricot chutney, a pie of the day with mustard mash, pasta with spinach and mushrooms in tomato sauce, home-made burger with various toppings, sticky lemon, honey and chilli chicken with coleslaw, baked salmon fishcakes with capers, smoked salmon and lemon chive crème fraîche, medallions of pork fillet with honey roasted pear and thyme jus, and a mixed grill; puddings like chocolate hazelnut brownie and baked vanilla cheesecake with red cherry compote; also Sunday roasts.** *Starters/Snacks: £3.50 to £7.95. Main Courses: £7.95 to £14.95. Puddings: £3.95 to £4.95*

Mitchells & Butlers ~ Manager Chris James ~ Real ale ~ Bar food ~ Restaurant ~ (01590) 676903 ~ Children welcome ~ Dogs welcome ~ Open 11-11(midnight Fri and Sat)
Recommended by Michael Dandy

PETERSFIELD
SU7227 MAP 2

Trooper

From B2070 in Petersfield follow Steep signposts past station, but keep on up past Steep, on old coach road; OS Sheet 186 map reference 726273; GU32 1BD

Charming landlord, popular food, decent drinks, and little persian knick-knacks and local artists' work; comfortable bedrooms

Our readers enjoy their visits here very much and the cordial Mr Matini continues to offer a genuinely friendly welcome to all. The bar has a mix of cushioned dining chairs around dark wooden tables, old film star photos and paintings by local artists for sale, little persian knick-knacks here and there, quite a few ogival mirrors, lit candles all over the place, fresh flowers, and a well tended log fire in the stone fireplace; there's now a sun room with lovely downland views; carefully chosen piped music and newspapers and magazines to read. Bowman Swift One, Ringwood Best and Triple fff Altons Pride on handpump, and several wines by the glass. The attractive raftered restaurant has french windows to a paved terrace with views across the open countryside, and there are lots of picnic-sets on an upper lawn. The horse rail in the car park ('horses and camels only before 8pm') does get used, though probably not often by camels.

🍴 **Good, enjoyable – if not cheap – bar food includes lunchtime sandwiches and filled baguettes, soup, filo wrapped goats cheese with apricot and stem ginger chutney, mussels** in garlic butter and white wine, ham and free-range eggs, beer-battered cod, leek, squash and butterbean stew, pork medallions with wild mushrooms in a cider and sage cream, shoulder of lamb with a rich honey and mint gravy, fresh fish of the day, and puddings such as chocolate and toasted hazelnut tart and pistachio and rosewater meringues with poached plums in rosewater syrup. They have a home-made pie and pudding deal on **Tuesdays.** *Starters/Snacks: £5.50 to £7.00. Main Courses: £10.00 to £21.00. Puddings: £5.50 to £7.50*

Free house ~ Licensee Hassan Matini ~ Real ale ~ Bar food (not Sun evening or Mon lunchtime) ~ (01730) 827293 ~ Children must be seated and supervised by an adult ~ Dogs allowed in bar ~ Open 12-11; 12-5 Sun; closed Sun evening, Mon lunchtime, 25 and 26 Dec, 1 Jan ~ Bedrooms: £69B/£89B

Recommended by Janet Whittaker, David and Sue Atkinson, Alex Harper, Roger and Lesley Everett, Martin and Karen Wake, Ann and Colin Hunt, T A R Curran, Sue Ruffhead

PORTSMOUTH   SZ6399   MAP 2

Old Customs House

Vernon Buildings, Gunwharf Quays; follow brown signs to Gunwharf Quays car park – usually quickest to park on lower level, come up escalator, turn left towards waterside, then left again; PO1 3TY

Handsome historic building well converted in a prime waterfront development

---

Once an 18th-c customs house, this fine brick building then became the administration centre for HMS *Vernon* and the Royal Navy's mine clearance and diving school (it has some memorabilia of those days). It's well laid out inside with several big-windowed high-ceilinged rooms off a long central spine which houses the serving bar and a separate food/coffee ordering counter – they have lots of good coffees and teas, as well as a decent range of wines by the glass, and Fullers Discovery, ESB, HSB, London Pride and Seafarers on handpump. This floor, with good disabled access and facilities, has bare boards, nautical prints and photographs on pastel walls, coal-effect gas fires, nice unobtrusive lighting, and well padded chairs around sturdy tables in varying sizes; the sunny entrance area has leather sofas. Broad stairs take you up to a carpeted more restauranty floor, with similar décor. Staff are efficient, housekeeping is good, the piped music well reproduced, and the games machines silenced. Picnic-sets out in front are just yards from the water. Just around the corner is the graceful Spinnaker Tower (165 metres tall with staggering views from its viewing decks).

🍴 They usefully serve food all day starting with a proper breakfast; also, sandwiches, ploughman's, soup, lancashire cheese on toast with crispy bacon, smoked mackerel and red onion pâté, steak and mushroom in ale pie, tuna niçoise, chargrilled vegetable wellington, sausages with onion and roasted cherry tomato gravy, beer-battered cod, chargrilled pork fillet with mustard mayonnaise, and puddings like sticky apple and caramel pudding and eton mess. *Starters/Snacks: £3.95 to £6.95. Main Courses: £6.95 to £12.95. Puddings: £4.75*

Fullers ~ Manager David Hughes ~ Real ale ~ Bar food (all day from 9am) ~ Restaurant ~ (023) 9283 2333 ~ Children allowed until 8pm but must go to upstairs restaurant after that ~ Open 9am-midnight(12.30 Fri, 1am Sat, 11pm Sun)

Recommended by Andy and Claire Barker, Philip and June Caunt, Ann and Colin Hunt, Alan and Eve Harding, Val and Alan Green

SOUTHSEA   SZ6499   MAP 2

Wine Vaults 🍺

Albert Road, opposite Kings Theatre; PO5 2SF

A fine range of real ales, reasonably priced food and a bustling atmosphere

---

It's the fine range of nine real ales on handpump that draws in the customers here. There are several rooms on different floors – all fairly straightforward and chatty – and the main bar has wood-panelled walls, pubby tables and chairs on the wooden floor, bar stools by the long plain bar counter, and Fullers Chiswick Bitter, ESB, Discovery, HSB, London Pride, and four changing guests on handpump; there's a restaurant area away from the hustle and bustle of the bars. Maybe newspapers to read, piped music and TV for sports events. It does get crowded at the weekend but is quieter during the week. More reports please.

🍴 Some sort of food is offered all day and might include sandwiches (until 5pm), soup, and pubby dishes like filled baked potatoes, burgers, various nachos, steak in ale pie, beer-battered haddock, vegetable lasagne, bangers and mash, and ham and eggs. *Starters/Snacks: £3.95 to £6.95. Main Courses: £6.95 to £17.95. Puddings: £3.95 to £4.75*

Fullers ~ Manager Sean Cochrane ~ Real ale ~ Bar food (all day) ~ Restaurant ~ (023) 9286 4712 ~ Children welcome until 7.30pm ~ Dogs allowed in bar ~ Open 12-11(12 Fri and Sat; 10.30 Sun)

Recommended by Ann and Colin Hunt, the Didler

SPARSHOLT   SU4331   MAP 2

Plough 🍽 ♟

Village signposted off B3049 (Winchester—Stockbridge), a little W of Winchester; SO21 2NW

HAMPSHIRE DINING PUB OF THE YEAR

Neat, well run dining pub with interesting furnishings, an extensive wine list and popular bar food; garden with children's play fort

Always busy, this well run dining pub places firm emphasis on the good, popular bar food, though they do keep Wadworths IPA, 6X, JCB, and seasonal beers on handpump. The main bar has an interesting mix of wooden tables and chairs with farm tools, scythes and pitchforks attached to the ceiling. There's an extensive wine list with a fair selection by the glass, including champagne and pudding wine, and service is friendly and efficient. Disabled access and facilities. Outside there are plenty of seats on the terrace and lawn, and a children's play fort.

🍴 Good bar food includes sandwiches, ciabattas and ploughman's, soup, grilled goats cheese with herb croûton and olive dressing, timbale of salmon and prawns with lemon dressing, sautéed kidneys and smoked bacon with wild mushrooms and port sauce, beef and mushroom in ale pie, ground steak burgers with pepper sauce, pork and chive sausages with red wine gravy, wild mushroom, courgette and asparagus tagliatelle, breast of chicken, black pudding and apple with bacon and bean jus, smoked haddock with welsh rarebit topping, and puddings like banana panna cotta with chocolate sauce and vanilla cheesecake with mixed berries. *Starters/Snacks: £4.95 to £8.95. Main Courses: £11.50 to £16.95. Puddings: £5.75*

Wadworths ~ Tenants Richard and Kathryn Crawford ~ Real ale ~ Bar food (12-2, 6-9) ~ (01962) 776353 ~ Children welcome except in main bar area ~ Dogs welcome ~ Open 11-3, 6-11

Recommended by John and Joan Calvert, Phyl and Jack Street, Keith and Sue Ward, Peter and Liz Holmes, Peter and Andrea Jacobs, Glenwys and Alan Lawrence, Mr and Mrs P D Titcomb, Jeff and Wendy Williams, Fred and Kate Portnell

STEEP   SU7525   MAP 2

Harrow 🍺

Take Midhurst exit from Petersfield bypass, at exit roundabout first left towards Midhurst, then first turning on left opposite garage, and left again at Sheet church; follow over dual carriageway bridge to pub; GU32 2DA

Unchanging, simple place with long-serving landladies, beers tapped from the cask, unfussy food and big free-flowering garden; no children inside

Nothing is contrived here and, thankfully, nothing changes either. This remains a genuinely unspoilt little pub which has been in the same family since 1929. Everything revolves around village chat and the friendly locals who will probably draw you into light-hearted conversation, and there are adverts for logs next to calendars of local views being sold in support of local charities, news of various quirky competitions and no pandering to modern methods – no credit cards, no waitress service, no restaurant, no music; and outside lavatories. The cosy public bar has hops and dried flowers hanging from the beams, built-in wall benches on the tiled floor, stripped pine wallboards, a good log fire in the big inglenook, and wild flowers on the scrubbed deal tables; board games. Real ales are tapped straight from casks behind the counter from breweries such as Bowman, Hop Back, Oakleaf, Ringwood and Suthwyk, and they've local wine, and apple and pear juice; staff are polite and friendly, even when under pressure. The big garden is left free-flowering so that goldfinches can collect thistle seeds from the grass. The Petersfield bypass doesn't intrude on this idyll, though you will need to follow the directions above to find the pub. No children inside and dogs must be on leads.

🍴 **Good helpings of unfussy bar food include sandwiches, home-made scotch eggs, hearty ham, split pea and vegetable soup, ploughman's, cottage pie, flans and quiches, and puddings such as super treacle tart or seasonal fruit pies.** *Starters/Snacks: £4.50. Main Courses: £8.50 to £12.50. Puddings: £4.25*

Free house ~ Licensees Claire and Denise McCutcheon ~ Real ale ~ Bar food (not Sun evening) ~ No credit cards ~ (01730) 262685 ~ Dogs welcome ~ Open 12-2.30, 6-11; 11-3, 6-11 Sat; 12-3, 7-10.30 Sun; closed winter Sun evenings

Recommended by Phil and Sally Gorton, Tony and Jill Radnor, the Didler, Keith and Sue Ward, Mike and Eleanor Anderson, Ann and Colin Hunt, Peter Price, Sue Ruffhead

SWANMORE   SU5815   MAP 2

Rising Sun ♀ ◀

Village signposted off A32 N of Wickham and B2177 S of Bishop's Waltham; pub E of village centre, at Hillpound on the Droxford Road; SO32 2PS

Friendly licensees make this proper country pub a warmly welcoming all-rounder; well kept beers and popular food

There's always a cheerful, welcoming atmosphere in this 17th-c coaching inn and our readers enjoy their visits here very much. The low-beamed carpeted bar has some easy chairs and a sofa by its good log fire, and a few tables with pubby seats. Beyond the fireplace on the right is a pleasant much roomier dining area, with similarly unpretentious furnishings, running back in an L past the bar; one part of this has stripped brick barrel vaulting. Greene King Old Speckled Hen, Marstons Pedigree and Ringwood Best and Fortyniner on handpump, and a dozen wines by the glass; faint piped music. There are picnic-sets out on the side grass with a play area, and the Kings Way long-distance path is close by – some readers tell us it is best to head north where there is lovely downland country, fine views and interesting winding lanes.

🍴 **Well liked bar food at lunchtime includes sandwiches or filled baguettes and baked potatoes, ploughman's, soup, omelettes, fresh beer-battered fish, a pie of the day, creamy cheese, mushroom and tomato pasta, and lambs liver and bacon, with evening dishes such as duck liver pâté with cumberland sauce, locally smoked trout with horseradish, pork fillet with a creamy red pepper sauce, duck breast in a beetroot and sage sauce, local salmon, and puddings.** *Starters/Snacks: £4.75 to £7.90. Main Courses: £7.60 to £12.75. Puddings: £4.75*

Punch ~ Lease Mark and Sue Watts ~ Real ale ~ Bar food (12-2(2.30 Sun), 6-9(8.30 Sun)) ~ Restaurant ~ (01489) 896663 ~ Children allowed but must be well behaved ~ Dogs allowed in bar ~ Open 11.30-3, 5.30-11; 12-3.30, 5.30-10.30 Sun

Recommended by Phyl and Jack Street, Stephen Moss, Val and Alan Green, Ann and Colin Hunt, Gill and Keith Croxton

---

'Children welcome' means the pub says it lets children inside without any special restriction. If it allows them in, but to restricted areas such as an eating area or family room, we specify this. Some pubs may impose an evening time limit. We do not mention limits after 9pm as we assume children are home by then.

TICHBORNE   SU5730   MAP 2

Tichborne Arms

Village signed off B3047; SO24 0NA

Welcoming, traditional pub in rolling countryside, with five real ales and good, seasonal bar food; big garden

---

Liked by walkers – and their dogs – this attractive thatched pub keeps a good choice of real ales tapped from the cask: Bowman Eldorado and Swift One, Hogs Back TEA, Palmers Copper and Sharps Doom. There are also ten wines by the glass and farm cider; friendly licensees and chatty locals. The comfortable square-panelled room on the right has wheelback chairs and settles (one very long), a woodburning stove in the stone fireplace, all sorts of antiques, pictures and stuffed animals, and latticed windows. On the left is a larger, livelier, partly panelled room used for eating. Pictures and documents on the walls recall the bizarre Tichborne Case, in which a mystery man from Australia claimed fraudulently to be the heir to this estate. The big, neat garden has plenty of picnic-sets, and the surrounding countryside is attractively rolling; the Wayfarers Walk and Itchen Way pass close by.

🍴 Enjoyable bar food using seasonal produce includes hearty sandwiches, good ploughman's with their own chutneys, soup, baked brie with redcurrant sauce, chicken liver pâté, scallops with garlic butter, bangers and mash, mackerel with home-grown rhubarb sauce, chicken stuffed with sun-dried tomatoes and watercress, steak and kidney pudding, popular fish pie, lamb stew, winter game dishes, and puddings such as chocolate and cherry mousse and various cheesecakes; Sunday roasts. *Starters/Snacks: £4.95 to £6.95. Main Courses: £7.95 to £12.95. Puddings: £4.50*

Free house ~ Licensee Nicky Roper ~ Real ale ~ Bar food (not Sun evening) ~ (01962) 733760 ~ Children welcome ~ Dogs welcome ~ Open 11.30-3(4 Sat), 6-11(11.30 Sat); 12-4 Sun; evening opening 6.30 in winter; closed Sun evening

Recommended by the Didler, Sandiford Durvin, Stephen and Jean Curtis, Gerald and Gabrielle Culliford, Ann and Colin Hunt, Pete Baker, Pam and John Smith

UPHAM   SU5320   MAP 2

Brushmakers Arms

Off Winchester—Bishop's Waltham downs road; Shoe Lane; SO32 1JJ

Pleasant old place with extensive displays of brushes, local beers and well liked food

---

This is a proper village local with a good mix of customers – and dogs are welcome in the bar as well. Picking up on the pub's name, the walls in the L-shaped bar (divided in two by a central brick chimney with a woodburning stove) are hung with quite a collection of old and new brushes. A few beams in the low ceiling add to the cosiness, and there are comfortably cushioned settles and chairs and a variety of tables including some in country-style stripped wood; there's also a little back snug with fruit machine, dominoes and board games. Fullers London Pride and ESB, Ringwood Best and a changing guest beer on handpump; the pub cats are called Gilbert and Kera and the ghost is known as Mr Chickett (apparently seen as a shadowy figure searching the pub for his lost money and belongings). The big garden is well stocked with mature shrubs and trees and there are picnic-sets on a sheltered back terrace amongst tubs of flowers, with more on the tidy tree-sheltered lawn. It's best to park by the duck pond; good walks nearby. More reports please.

🍴 Well liked bar food includes lunchtime sandwiches, soup, garlic sardines, cheese and bacon skins, mushroom stroganoff, steak in ale pie, chicken with stilton and mushroom sauce, belly of pork in sweet chilli sauce, winter game dishes, tuna loin with a pea and mint risotto, and puddings like raspberry and mango cheesecake and apple and rhubarb crumble. *Starters/Snacks: £4.95 to £5.50. Main Courses: £8.95 to £16.95. Puddings: £4.95*

Free house ~ Licensee Keith Venton ~ Real ale ~ Bar food (12-2, 6(7 Sun)-9(9.30 Fri, Sat)) ~ (01489) 860231 ~ Children welcome ~ Dogs allowed in bar ~ Open 11-3, 5.45-11; 12-3, 7-10.30 Sun

Recommended by Sue Orchard, Ann and Colin Hunt, Val and Alan Green, Bruce and Penny Wilkie

WEST MEON

SU6424   MAP 2

Thomas Lord 🍺

High Street; GU32 1LN

Friendly pub, cheerful licensees; interesting décor and lots of wood in several rooms, imaginative food and fine choice of beers

The formal garden here is most attractive with plenty of seats and tables and an outdoor bar, and there's also a chicken run and a neat area for home-grown produce. Inside, it's friendly and relaxed, and individually decorated in a rustic style. There's an interesting mix of wooden dining and pubby chairs around lots of different wooden tables (each with a candle on it – lit on a dark day), an old brown leather sofa by one of the log fires (there are two), bare boards, some cricketing prints and memorabilia, various pictures and portraits above the wooden dados, and stuffed animals in display cabinets above the bar counter. The back room is lined with books which you can buy for 50p. The welcoming, chatty landlords keep a fine range of real ales tapped from the cask such as Bowman Eldorado and Swift One, Itchen Valley Winchester Ale, Ringwood Best and Triple fff Alton's Pride; also farm ciders, several wines by the glass and decent coffee; board games. Good walks to the west of the village.

🍴 **Enjoyable – if not cheap – food, using carefully sourced local produce, includes sandwiches, soup, potted squirrel and bacon with pumpkin chutney, smoked trout, watercress and vegetable tart, beef burger with garlic and nettle cheese, roasted butternut squash and sprouting lentil bake with goats cheese, pork sausages with greens and cider cream, smoked gammon and egg, chicken breast with honey mustard cream, salmon and lemon verbena fishcake with crab sauce, and puddings like rhubarb custard brûlée and pear crumble.** *Starters/Snacks: £5.00 to £9.00. Main Courses: £11.00 to £17.00. Puddings: £4.00 to £5.50*

Enterprise ~ Lease David Thomas and Richard Taylor ~ Real ale ~ Bar food (12-2(3 weekends), 7-9(9.30 Fri and Sat)) ~ (01730) 829244 ~ Children welcome ~ Dogs welcome ~ Open 11-3, 6-11; 11am-midnight Sat and Sun

Recommended by Simon Collett-Jones, Val and Alan Green, Ann and Colin Hunt, Jennifer Hurst, David M Smith, Mr and Mrs W W Burke, David and Ruth Hollands

WHERWELL

SU3839   MAP 2

Mayfly

Testcombe (over by Fullerton, and not in Wherwell itself); A3057 SE of Andover, between B3420 turn-off and Leckford where road crosses River Test; OS Sheet 185 map reference 382390; SO20 6AX

Extremely popular pub with decking and conservatory seats overlooking the River Test, well kept beers, and wide range of enjoyable bar food usefully served all day

Particularly on a fine day, the setting for this friendly pub is idyllic. It's on an island between the River Test and a smaller river to the back, and there are tables on a decked area that overlook the water – best to get here early if you want to bag one of these. Inside, the spacious, beamed and carpeted bar has fishing pictures and fishing equipment on the cream walls, rustic pub furnishings and a woodburning stove. There's also a conservatory with riverside views; piped music. Palmers Gold, Ringwood Best, Wadworths 6X and Wychwood Hobgoblin on handpump and lots of wines by the glass; good, courteous service.

🍴 **Usefully served all day, the popular bar food includes a daily hot and cold buffet (at its largest in summer), as well as soup, duck and orange pâté, spinach and mascarpone lasagne, sausages with onion gravy, smoked haddock and spring onion fishcakes, gammon with egg or pineapple, lamb and mango curry, chicken stuffed with spinach and goats cheese wrapped in pancetta with a tarragon and tomato cream sauce, venison steak with red wine and chocolate jus, and duck on sweet potato and grain mustard mash with a sweet dark cherry sauce.** *Starters/Snacks: £4.95 to £6.75. Main Courses: £6.75 to £15.95. Puddings: £5.50*

Enterprise ~ Lease Barry Lane ~ Real ale ~ Bar food (11.30-9) ~ (01264) 860283 ~
Children welcome if well behaved ~ Dogs welcome ~ Open 10am-11pm

*Recommended by David A Hammond, Michael and Jenny Back, Phyl and Jack Street, Stephen Allford,
Shirley Mackenzie, Sally and Tom Matson, David Wyatt, Louise Gibbons*

WINCHESTER

SU4828   MAP 2

Black Boy ◖

*A mile from M3 junction 10 northbound; B3403 towards city then left into Wharf Hill;
rather further and less easy from junction 9, and anyway beware no nearby daytime parking
– 220 metres from car park on B3403 N, or nice longer walk from town via College Street
and College Walk, or via towpath; SO23 9NQ*

**Busy town pub with several different areas crammed full of interesting knick-knacks;
straightforward lunchtime bar food and local ales**

If you like real ales, chatty locals and some pretty curious knick-knacks, then this old-
fashioned place is just the pub for you. There's plenty of eccentric character and
fascinating things to look at in the several different areas that run from a bare-boards
barn room with an open hayloft, down to an orange-painted room with big oriental rugs
on red-painted floorboards. There's a stuffed baboon, a stuffed dog, a snake, a pigeon
and other random animals, floor-to-ceiling books in some parts, lots of big clocks,
mobiles made of wine bottles or strings of spectacles, some nice modern nature
photographs in the lavatories and on the brightly stained walls on the way, and plenty of
other things that you'll enjoy tracking down. Furnishings are similarly wide-ranging; two
log fires. The five well kept beers on handpump are more or less local: Flowerpots Bitter,
Hop Back Summer Lightning and Ringwood Best, alongside a couple of guests from
breweries such as Bowman, Hampshire, Itchen Valley and Triple fff; decent wines, piped
music, table football and board games. There are a couple of slate tables out in front
with more seats on an attractive secluded terrace.

⑪ Lunchtime bar food includes sandwiches with chips or soup, a pasta dish, beer-
battered cod, toad in the hole, and chips and caesar salad or shepherd's pie.
Starters/Snacks: £5.50 to £7.50. Main Courses: £7.50 to £10.00. Puddings: £3.50 to £4.50

Free house ~ Licensee David Nicholson ~ Real ale ~ Bar food (not Sun evening, Mon,
or Tues lunchtime) ~ (01962) 861754 ~ Children must be well behaved and supervised ~
Dogs welcome ~ Open 12-11(midnight Fri and Sat); 12-10.30 Sun

*Recommended by John and Annabel Hampshire, Pete Baker, Ann and Colin Hunt, Georgina Campbell, Val and
Alan Green, Chris Sale, Brad W Morley, Michael and Alison Sandy, Phil and Sally Gorton*

Willow Tree

*Durngate Terrace; no adjacent weekday daytime parking, but Durngate car park is around
corner in North Walls; a mile from M3 junction 9, by Easton Lane into city; SO23 8QX*

**Snug pub with landlord/chef using much local produce for enjoyable food; nice riverside
garden**

Just a couple of minutes from the town centre, this Victorian local is run by a cheerful
and friendly landlord. The carpeted lounge bar on the right has a relaxed atmosphere,
wall banquettes, low ceilings and soft lighting; two bays of good sturdy dining tables at
the back have quite a few books around them. There's a separate proper public bar,
Greene King Abbot and Old Speckled Hen and a summer guest like Bath Ales Gem Bitter
on handpump, 15 wines by the glass and several malt whiskies; piped music, TV, games
machine, juke box (a rarity nowadays), chess, backgammon and pool. There's also a more
comfortable dining room. A narrow tree-shaded garden, partly paved and with plenty of
heaters, stretches back between two branches of the River Itchen.

⑪ Cooked by the landlord, well liked bar food includes sandwiches, ploughman's,
omelettes, beer-battered cod, a vegetarian dish, calves liver and bacon with onion gravy,
bangers and mash, scampi, and a half shoulder of lamb; they also do a good value
lunchtime dish and Sunday roasts. *Starters/Snacks: £5.00 to £7.50. Main Courses: £7.50 to
£15.00. Puddings: £4.50 to £6.50*

Greene King ~ Tenant James Yeoman ~ Real ale ~ Bar food (12-2.30(4 Sun), 6-10; not Sun evening) ~ Restaurant ~ (01962) 877255 ~ Children welcome ~ Open 12-11(10.30 Sun)

Recommended by Michael and Alison Sandy

Wykeham Arms ♀

Kingsgate Street (Kingsgate Arch and College Street are now closed to traffic; there is access via Canon Street); SO23 9PE

Tucked-away pub with lots to look at, several real ales and 20 wines by the glass; no children inside

Various bustling rooms, radiating from the central bar in this tucked-away old pub, have 19th-c oak desks retired from nearby Winchester College, a redundant pew from the same source, kitchen chairs and candlelit deal tables, and big windows with swagged curtains; all sorts of interesting collections are dotted around. A snug room at the back, known as the Jameson Room (after the late landlord Graeme Jameson), is decorated with a set of Ronald Searle 'Winespeak' prints, a second one is panelled, and all of them have log fires. Fullers London Pride, Chiswick, Gales HSB and a guest like Hook Norton Old Hooky on handpump, 20 wines by the glass and several malt whiskies. There are tables on a covered back terrace, with more on a small courtyard. More reports please.

🍴 Bar food includes sandwiches, soup, ham hock terrine, grilled sardines with tomato and pepper salsa, artichoke, asparagus and chive risotto, swordfish steak with sun-fried tomatoes, olives and rocket salad, rack of spring lamb with dauphinoise potatoes, pork chop on sage potatoes with calvados jus, sirloin steak on the bone with truffle mash and pepper sauce, and puddings such as white chocolate cheesecake with raspberry coulis and lemon posset with almond shortbread. *Starters/Snacks: £5.25 to £6.95. Main Courses: £6.50 to £12.95. Puddings: £5.25 to £6.95*

Gales (Fullers) ~ Managers Dennis and Ann Evans ~ Real ale ~ Bar food (12-2.30(sandwiches till 3 Sat), 6.30-9) ~ Restaurant ~ (01962) 853834 ~ Dogs allowed in bar and bedrooms ~ Open 11-11; 11.30-10.30 Sun ~ Bedrooms: £65B/£115B

Recommended by Chris and Libby Allen, Ellie Weld, Martin and Karen Wake, R K Phillips, Fred and Kate Portnell, the Didler, Janet Whittaker, Ann and Colin Hunt, John Oates, Denise Walton, Philip and June Caunt, John and Annabel Hampshire, Phil and Sally Gorton, Phyland Jack Street, Chris Sale, Val and Alan Green, Michael and Alison Sandy, Peter and Liz Holmes, David and Sheila Pearcey, Mrs Mary Woods, Mr and Mrs A Curry, Christopher and Elise Way, Pam and John Smith

LUCKY DIP

Besides the fully inspected pubs, you might like to try these Lucky Dips recommended to us and described by readers (if you do, please send us reports: feedback@goodguides.com).

ALRESFORD [SU5832]
☆**Bell** SO24 9AT [West St]: Comfortable Georgian coaching inn with welcoming licensees, interesting good value food from sandwiches and light dishes up, good real ales, fairly priced wines; log fire, daily papers, nice décor, smallish dining room; attractive back courtyard, good bedrooms, open all day *(John Oates, Denise Walton, Ann and Colin Hunt)*
Cricketers SO24 9LW [Jacklyns Lane]: Large comfortable and friendly local with popular low-priced food inc bargain lunches (book ahead Sun); real ales, good service, cottagey eating area down steps; sizeable garden with covered terrace and good play area *(D and J Ashdown)*
ALTON [SU7138]
French Horn GU34 1RT [The Butts (A339 S of centre, by railway bridge)]: Cheery popular catslide-roof local, with six well kept ales

from long counter such as Butcombe, Fullers London Pride, Ringwood and Shepherd Neame Spitfire, good food (all day Sun) from sandwiches to some more upmarket dishes, good coffee; tankards and whisky-water jugs on beams, bowler hats and french horn above inglenook log fire, partly stripped brick dining room, pleasant staff, separate skittle alley; piped pop music; children welcome, covered heated smokers' terrace, picnic-sets in two garden areas, bedrooms in adjacent building, open all day *(BB, Maureen and Keith Gimson, Tony and Wendy Hobden, Phil and Sally Gorton)*
AMPFIELD [SU4023]
White Horse SO51 9BQ [A3090 Winchester—Romsey]: Beams, roaring log fires and comfortable period-style furnishings giving warm-hearted rustic feel, plenty of room for both eaters and drinkers, friendly staff; well kept Ringwood and Wadworths, good choice

of food and of wines by the glass, Victorian prints in dining room; tables outside, pub backs on to village cricket green; handy for Hillier Arboretum, good walks in Ampfield Woods *(Phyl and Jack Street, HPS)*

ARFORD [SU8236]

☆ *Crown* GU35 8BT [off B3002 W of Hindhead]: Low-beamed pub with coal and log fires in several areas from bustling local-feel bar to cosy candlelit upper dining room; enjoyable if not cheap food from sandwiches to game and splendid puddings, friendly efficient staff, Adnams, Fullers London Pride, Greene King Abbot and a guest beer, decent wines by the glass; piped music; children welcome in eating areas, picnic-sets out in peaceful dell by a tiny stream across the road *(LYM, Tony and Jill Radnor, Keith and Margaret Jackson, R B Gardiner)*

AXFORD [SU6043]

Crown RG25 2DZ [B3046 S of Basingstoke]: Country pub with efficient friendly staff, well kept Fullers London Pride, several wines by the glass, home-made food from sandwiches to good fish and chips and Sun roasts; three linked rooms, small log fire; children welcome, suntrap terrace and sloping shrub-sheltered garden, cl Mon *(Graham and Toni Sanders, LYM, Rosemary)*

BALL HILL [SU4263]

Furze Bush RG20 0NQ [leaving Newbury on A343, turn right towards East Woodhay]: Pews and pine tables, clean airy décor, wide choice of quickly served enjoyable bar food, well kept real ales, decent wines; reasonable prices, log fire, restaurant; children welcome, tables on terrace by good-sized sheltered lawn with fenced play area *(Mr and Mrs H J Langley, LYM)*

BARTON STACEY [SU4341]

Swan SO21 3RL [village signed off A30]: Former coaching inn with enjoyable food, interesting mix of menus, pleasant staff, real ales inc Wadworths 6X, good choice of wines; chesterfields in nice little lounge area between beamed front bar and popular dining area, back restaurant (not always open); tables on front lawn and in informal back garden *(Greta and Christopher Wells, B and F A Hannam, Mr and Mrs W Taylor)*

BEAULIEU [SU3902]

Montagu Arms SO42 7ZL [almost opp Palace House]: Civilised hotel's less formal Monty's bar/brasserie, good food using quality local ingredients, polite efficient service, good choice of beers inc Ringwood Best, lots of malt whiskies, sofas and easy chairs, bare boards, books and panelling; may be piped music, live Sun; children and dogs welcome, front courtyard picnic-sets, comfortable bedrooms, attractive surroundings, open all day *(Caroline McArthur, Ann and Colin Hunt, LYM)*

BEAUWORTH [SU5624]

Milbury's SO24 0PB [off A272 Winchester—Petersfield]: Good atmosphere in attractive ancient pub with four Greene King and other

ales, friendly landlord, simple traditional bar food, reasonably priced wines by the glass; log fires in huge fireplaces, beams, panelling and stripped stone, massive 17th-c treadmill for much older incredibly deep well; piped music; children in eating areas, garden with fine downland views, good walks, has been open all day wknds and summer *(Helen and Brian Edgeley, Ann and Colin Hunt, the Didler, LYM)*

BISHOP'S WALTHAM [SU5517]

Barleycorn SO32 1AJ [Lower Basingwell St]: Comfortable two-bar Punch Tavern with new licensees, good value enjoyable food from short menu, Fullers London Pride, Ringwood Best and Shepherd Neame Spitfire, decent wine, log fire, some low ceiling panelling; small back garden *(Val and Alan Green)*

☆ *Bunch of Grapes* SO32 1AD [St Peters St – just along from entrance to central car park]: Neat and civilised little pub in quiet medieval street, smartly furnished keeping individuality and unspoilt feel (run by same family for a century), Courage Best and Greene King IPA tapped from the cask, good chatty landlord and regulars; charming back terrace garden with own bar, opening times may vary *(Stephen and Jean Curtis, the Didler, BB, Val and Alan Green)*

BOLDRE [SZ3198]

☆ *Red Lion* SO41 8NE [off A337 N of Lymington]: Attractive black-beamed rooms with entertaining collection of bygones, pews and other seats, log fires, attentive friendly staff; well kept Ringwood ales and a guest beer, great choice of wines by the glass, decent coffee, generous enjoyable food from sandwiches to plenty of fish; children and dogs allowed, tables outside with nicely spruced-up garden, open all day *(Liz and Brian Barnard, Glenwys and Alan Lawrence, LYM, Jeff and Wendy Williams, Mr and Mrs P D Titcomb, Keith and Margaret Kettell, Phyl and Jack Street, Mayur Shah, Michael and Jenny Back, Janet Whittaker, Ann and Colin Hunt)*

BRAISHFIELD [SU3725]

Newport Inn SO51 0PL [Newport Lane – from centre follow Michelmersh, Timsbury signpost]: Plain old-fashioned two-bar brick local, well kept Fullers/Gales ales, bargain sandwiches or ploughman's, cribbage; piped music, piano sing-songs Sat; informal and relaxing tree-shaded garden *(the Didler, Phil and Sally Gorton, BB)*

BRAMBRIDGE [SU4721]

☆ *Dog & Crook* SO50 6HZ [nr M3 junction 12, via B3335]: Bustling 18th-c pub, traditional home-made food inc plenty of fresh fish, cosy dining room, beamed bar with friendly drinking end, Fullers and Ringwood Best, lots of wines by the glass, neat efficient staff; piped music, TV, regular events and summer music nights; dogs welcome, garden with heated decking and arbour, Itchen Way walks nearby *(Ann and Colin Hunt, Phyl and Jack Street, LYM)*

BROCKENHURST [SU3002]
Rose & Crown SO42 7RH [Lyndhurst Rd
(A337)]: Large main-road pub/hotel with
13th-c origins, sizeable dining area off small
carpeted bar, good choice of food from
sandwiches up inc bargain OAP set lunch,
children's menu and Sun carvery, Marstons
and related ales; covered terrace, good-sized
garden, 14 bedrooms *(Michael Dandy,
Tony and Wendy Hobden)*
BROOK [SU2713]
Bell SO43 7HE [B3079/B3078, handy for
M27 junction 1]: Really a hotel and plush
restaurant (with golf club), in same family
for over 200 years, but has neatly kept bar
with lovely inglenook fire, good choice of
well kept ales inc Ringwood and good bar
food from sandwiches to steaks, helpful
friendly uniformed staff; big garden,
delightful village, 25 comfortable bedrooms
(Marcus Mann)
☆ *Green Dragon* SO43 7HE [B3078 NW of
Cadnam, just off M27 junction 1]:
Immaculate big New Forest dining pub
dating from 15th c, good welcoming service
even when busy, enjoyable fresh food inc
plenty of seasonal game and fish as well as
sensibly priced pubby favourites; Fullers and
Ringwood, daily papers, bright linked areas
with stripped pine and other pubby
furnishings; attractive small terrace and
larger garden, paddocks beyond, picturesque
village *(PL, George and Gill Rowley, Bob and
Angela Brooks, Philippe Victor, BB)*
BROUGHTON [SU3032]
Tally Ho SO20 8AA [High St, opp church;
signed off A30 Stockbridge—Salisbury]:
Relaxed local atmosphere in open-plan
largely tiled square bar, helpful welcoming
landlady, good value home-made food from
sandwiches up, two well kept Ringwood ales,
good house wines; two open fires, hunting
prints and other pictures, darts; no piped
music; children welcome, charming secluded
back garden, good walks; has been cl Tues
(Ann and Colin Hunt, BB)
BURGHCLERE [SU4660]
Carpenters Arms RG20 9JY [Harts Lane, off
A34]: Pleasantly furnished small pub with
cheerful helpful landlord, generous food from
well presented sandwiches to some
ambitious dishes, well kept Arkells, decent
choice of wines by the glass; good country
views from dining extension and terrace
picnic-sets, unobtrusive piped music;
children and dogs welcome (resident
springers), handy for Sandham Memorial
Chapel (NT), six comfortable annex
bedrooms, open all day *(Mr and
Mrs H J Langley)*
BURITON [SU7320]
☆ *Five Bells* GU31 5RX [off A3 S of
Petersfield]: Low-beamed 17th-c pub with
pleasant staff, fresh pubby food from
baguettes up, Badger beers, good wines by
the glass; big log fire, daily papers, flowers
and church candles, some ancient stripped
masonry and woodburner on public side;

games machine, piped music; children and
dogs welcome, nice garden and sheltered
terraces; pretty village, good walks, self-
catering in converted stables, open all day
*(LYM, Barry Steele-Perkins, N R White,
Ann and Colin Hunt)*
BURLEY [SU2103]
Queens Head BH24 4AB [The Cross; back rd
Ringwood—Lymington]: Large pub dating
partly from 17th c and probably earlier,
several rambling rooms, good friendly
atmosphere, some flagstones, beams,
timbering and panelling; wide choice of
food, well kept ales, nice coffee; pub and
New Forest village can get packed in
summer; children welcome, open all day
(LYM, Ann and Colin Hunt)
☆ *White Buck* BH24 4AZ [Bisterne Close;
0.7 miles E, OS Sheet 195 map ref 223028]:
Long comfortably divided bar in 19th-c
mock-Tudor hotel, vast choice of enjoyable
generous food, Fullers/Gales and a guest
beer, good wines by the glass and coffee,
lots of worthwhile pictures, log fires each
end, courteous attentive staff; pleasant end
dining room with tables out on decking
(should book – but no bookings Sun
lunchtime); children and dogs welcome,
heated front terrace and spacious lawn,
lovely New Forest setting, superb walks
towards Burley itself and over Mill Lawn;
good quiet bedrooms, open all day
*(BB, Sara Fulton, Roger Baker, Mr and
Mrs P D Titcomb, Mrs Jordan, N B Vernon,
A and B D Craig, Gill and Keith Croxton)*
BURSLEDON [SU4809]
☆ *Fox & Hounds* SO31 8DE [Hungerford
Bottom; 2 miles from M27 junction 8]:
Popular rambling 16th-c Chef & Brewer of
unusual character, ancient beams,
flagstones and big log fires, linked by
pleasant family conservatory area to ancient
back barn with buoyant rustic atmosphere,
lantern-lit side stalls, lots of interesting
farm equipment; real ales such as Adnams
and Ringwood, lots of wines, good coffee,
enjoyable reasonably priced food from
sandwiches up, cheerful obliging staff,
daily papers; children allowed, tables
outside *(Phyl and Jack Street, Ann and
Colin Hunt, LYM)*
☆ *Jolly Sailor* SO31 8DN [off A27 towards
Bursledon Station, Lands End Rd; handy for
M27 junction 8]: Busy efficiently laid out
Badger dining pub in prime spot overlooking
yachting inlet; good service, reliable food,
their usual ales and good wine choice, log
fires; open all day *(Ann and Colin Hunt,
LYM, the Didler, Gael Pawson, Mr and
Mrs P D Titcomb)*
CADNAM [SU2913]
☆ *Sir John Barleycorn* SO40 2NP [Old Romsey
Rd; by M27 junction 1]: Wide choice of good
up-to-date food in picturesque low-slung
thatched pub extended from low-beamed and
timbered medieval core; attentive prompt
service, Ringwood and a guest such as
Itchen Valley, two good log fires, modern

décor and stripped wood flooring; dogs and children welcome, suntrap benches in front and out in colourful garden, open all day *(Michael Dandy, Mr and Mrs A Garforth, Phyl and Jack Street, Chris and Meredith Owen, LYM, R J Davies)*

White Hart SO40 2NP [Old Romsey Rd, handy for M27 junction 1]: Big rambling Blubeckers family restaurant pub, enjoyable food all day, Greene King ales, cheerful efficient service, spotless simple modern furnishings on parquet floors, stripped brickwork; well reproduced piped music, turned down on request; garden tables, play area *(Mike Gorton, Michael Dandy, LYM)*

CHALTON [SU7316]

☆ **Red Lion** PO8 0BG [off A3 Petersfield—Horndean]: Largely extended thatched all-day dining pub with interesting 16th-c core around ancient inglenook fireplace; wide range of food from good sandwiches up, well kept Fullers/Gales ales and lots of country wines, decent coffee, helpful smart staff, well spaced tables; children and dogs allowed, good disabled access and facilities, nice views from neat rows of picnic-sets on rectangular lawn by large car park; good walks, handy for Queen Elizabeth Country Park; open all day *(Ann and Colin Hunt, Ian Phillips, Phyl and Jack Street, Glen and Nola Armstrong, LYM, Janet Whittaker, N B Vernon)*

CHAWTON [SU7037]

☆ **Greyfriar** GU34 1SB [off A31/A32 S of Alton; Winchester Rd]: Popular flower-decked beamed dining pub opp Jane Austen's house; enjoyable food from good baguettes and sandwiches up, Sun roasts, Fullers ales, decent wines by the glass, good coffees, relaxed atmosphere and quite a few older mid-week lunchers; comfortable seating and sturdy pine tables in neat linked areas, open fire in restaurant end; piped music; tables on terrace in small garden; dogs in bar, children until 9pm, good nearby walks, open all day *(Susan and Nigel Brookes, Patrick Spence, LYM, B M Eldridge, Maureen and Keith Gimson, Roy and Lindsey Fentiman, I A Herdman, Tracey and Stephen Groves, D and J Ashdown)*

CHILWORTH [SU4118]

Chilworth Arms SO16 7JZ [Chilworth Rd (A27 Southampton—Romsey)]: Stylish modern dining pub with enjoyable food from traditional pub dishes and home-made pizzas to more adventurous things, good wine choice, attentive staff; chunky furniture, part divided off with leather sofas, armchairs and log fire; disabled facilities, large garden with terrace, open all day *(Phyl and Jack Street, Roy and J Rutter, C J Pratt)*

CHURCH CROOKHAM [SU8252]

Foresters GU52 9EP [Aldershot Rd]: Restaurant pub with enjoyable food inc Mon-Thurs meal deals 12-7.30pm; pleasant efficient staff, real ales, two beamed areas, high-ceilinged tiled-floor extension; french doors to garden, roadside verandah *(KC)*

COLDEN COMMON [SU4821]

☆ **Fishers Pond** SO50 7HG [Main Rd (B3354)]: Big busy well organised family pub in style of converted mill by pretty woodside lake; log fires and cosy old-world corners (get there early for window seats), Fullers London Pride and Ringwood Best, decent coffee, reliable all-day food, efficient service; tables on big part-covered terrace; handy for Marwell Zoo *(Phyl and Jack Street, Terry and Nickie Williams, Joan and Michel Hooper-Immins, Ann and Colin Hunt)*

COPYTHORNE [SU3115]

Empress of Blandings SO40 2PE [Copythorne Crescent; off A31]: Roomy Badger pub/restaurant with their ales, moderately priced food and some cosy corners; picnic-sets in garden front and back, open all day *(Phyl and Jack Street)*

CRONDALL [SU7948]

Plume of Feathers GU10 5NT [The Borough]: Attractive smallish 15th-c village pub, popular for good range of enjoyable home-made food from standards to more innovative dishes, friendly helpful staff, Greene King and some unusual guest ales, good wines by the glass; beams and dark wood, prints on cream walls, log fire in big brick fireplace; children welcome; picturesque village *(KC, Martin and Karen Wake, Roderick Braithwaite, Simon and Sally Small)*

CURDRIDGE [SU5314]

Cricketers SO32 2BH [Curdridge Lane, off B3035, just under a mile NE of A334 junction]: Open-plan low-ceilinged Victorian village pub, with neat staff, cheerful and efficient; sensibly priced food, Greene King ales, banquettes in lounge area, traditional public area, rather smart dining part; quiet piped music; tables on front lawn, pleasant footpaths *(Ann and Colin Hunt)*

DEANE [SU5449]

Deane Gate RG25 3AX [B3400 W of Basingstoke]: Former posting inn with Jane Austen connections, comfortable lounge, restaurant, good choice of enjoyable food; garden (no smoking signs on seats), bedrooms *(Jennifer Banks)*

DIBDEN PURLIEU [SU4106]

Heath SO45 4PU [Beaulieu Rd; B3054/A326 roundabout]: Spacious dining pub, bright and clean with contemporary linked areas, good choice of enjoyable food, hardworking young friendly staff; beers such as Ringwood, Shepherd Neame Spitfire and Wadworths 6X; children welcome *(Phyl and Jack Street)*

DROXFORD [SU6118]

Hurdles SO32 3QT [Station Rd, Brockbridge]: Smart warmly welcoming dining pub mixing traditional with modern, interesting well presented food from baguettes up inc good value set menu (Mon-Fri), monthly gourmet evenings, several wines by the glass (some quite pricey), Bowman Wallops Wood, Hop Back Summer Lightning and Ringwood Best; chesterfields by log fire; children and dogs welcome, smokers' shelter, open all day wknds (till 8pm Sun) *(Phyl and Jack Street, Sally and Tom Matson, Val and Alan Green)*

White Horse SO32 3PB [A32; South Hill]: Rambling pub with several spick and span areas, low beams, bow windows, sofas, alcoves and log fires; two dining rooms, good wines by the glass, good indian food inc takeaways (some other dishes too inc good value ciabattas); roomy separate public bar with plenty of games, also TV and CD juke box; children and dogs welcome, sheltered flower-filled courtyard, rolling walking country, open all day *(LYM, Ann and Colin Hunt)*

DUMMER [SU5846]

Queen RG25 2AD [under a mile from M3 junction 7; take Dummer slip rd]: Comfortable beamed pub well divided with lots of softly lit alcoves, Courage Best, Fullers London Pride, John Smiths and a guest such as Hogs Back TEA, decent choice of wines by the glass, popular food from lunchtime sandwiches and light dishes up, friendly service (can be slow); big log fire, Queen and steeplechase prints, no mobile phones, restaurant allowing children; games machine, well reproduced piped music; picnic-sets under cocktail parasols on terrace and in extended back garden, attractive village with ancient church *(LYM)*

DURLEY [SU5116]

Farmers Home SO32 2BT [B3354 and B2177; Heathen St/Curdridge Rd]: Helpful long-serving landlord in comfortable beamed pub with two-bay dining area and big restaurant; generous reasonably priced food inc fresh fish and lovely puddings, well kept Fullers/Gales ales and Ringwood Best, decent wine, log fire; children welcome, big garden with good play area, nice walks *(Diana Brumfit, Ann and Colin Hunt)*

☆ *Robin Hood* SO32 2AA [Durley St, just off B2177 Bishop's Waltham—Winchester; brown signs to pub]: Open-plan beamed pub reopened under the same enthusiastic licensees as at the Plough at Sparsholt (see Main Entries), friendly welcoming staff, Greene King ales, good food from varied menu; log fire and leather sofas in bare-boards bar, dining area with stone floor and mix of old pine tables and chairs, bookcase door to lavatories; children and dogs welcome, disabled facilities, decked terrace with barbecue, garden with play area and nice country views, open all day Sun *(Phyl and Jack Street, LYM)*

EAST BOLDRE [SU3700]

☆ *Turf Cutters Arms* SO42 7WL [Main Rd]: Small dimly lit New Forest country local under welcoming young licensees, ponies wandering past, perhaps a regular arriving on horseback; lots of beams and pictures, nicely worn-in furnishings on bare boards and flagstones, log fire, simple local food from sandwiches and basic dishes to quite a lot of game, good choice of well kept ales, several dozen malt whiskies; children

welcome, garden tables, good heathland walks *(BB, Phil and Sally Gorton)*

EAST MEON [SU6822]

☆ *Olde George* GU32 1NH [Church St; signed off A272 W of Petersfield, and off A32 in West Meon]: Relaxing heavy-beamed rustic pub, popular for bar and restaurant food from sandwiches up, good service; inglenook log fires, cosy areas around central bar counter, Badger ales, good choice of wines; children welcome, nice back terrace, five comfortable bedrooms (book well ahead), good breakfast; pretty village with fine church, good walks *(Ann and Colin Hunt, Nigel Thompson, LYM, Prof and Mrs S Barnett)*

EAST STRATTON [SU5339]

Northbrook Arms SO21 3DU [brown sign to pub off A33, 4 miles S of A303 junction]: Substantial big-windowed brick pub recently taken over by the landlord of Yew Tree at Lower Wield (see Main Entries); should be one to watch – news, please *(LYM)*

EASTLEIGH [SU4418]

Cricketers SO53 3HN [Chestnut Ave]: Lively local with lots of Greene King ales and a guest such as Ringwood Best, good value food inc Weds curry and Thurs steak nights; log fire, sofas, tall bar tables and plenty of dining room; no piped music *(HPS)*

EASTON [SU5132]

Cricketers SO21 1EJ [off B3047]: Pleasantly smartened-up traditional local under new management, Marstons-related ales inc Ringwood, good choice of wines by the glass, home-made pubby food in bar and smallish restaurant; dark tables and chairs on carpet, bare-boards area with darts, shove-ha'penny and other games; sports TV, piped music (and some live); children and dogs welcome, front terrace with heated smokers' shelter, handy for Itchen Way walks, three refurbished bedrooms; open all day summer *(BB, Ann and Colin Hunt)*

ELLISFIELD [SU6345]

Fox RG25 2QW [Green Lane, Upper Common]: Friendly tucked-away pub doing good country food using local produce, Wadworths 6X and interesting guest beers, nice range of wines by the glass; open fires, pleasant lounge area on left, main dining area opposite; welcomes children (no under-10s after 7.30pm) and well behaved dogs, attractive garden with decking, good walks *(Phyl and Jack Street, Bob Venus, Stephen Allford)*

EMERY DOWN [SU2808]

☆ *New Forest* SO43 7DY [village signed off A35 just W of Lyndhurst]: In one of the best bits of the New Forest for walking; well run and popular under new licensees, good reasonably priced food (all day wknds) inc local venison, attentive uniformed staff, Ringwood and guest beers, good choice of wines by the glass, coffee and tea all day; attractive softly lit separate areas on varying levels, each with its own character, hunting prints, two log fires; piped music; children and dogs welcome, covered heated terrace, small pleasant three-level garden, bedrooms

planned, open all day *(Brian Collins,
Eithne Dandy, Mr and Mrs P D Titcomb,
N R White, Martin Gough, LYM, Mr and
Mrs Roberts)*

EMSWORTH [SU7405]
Blue Bell PO10 7EG [South St]: Small
timeless quayside pub with memorabilia
everywhere, enjoyable no-nonsense food
using local meat and fish (not Sun evening),
John Smiths; live music; open all day
(Terry and Nickie Williams)
☆ *Coal Exchange* PO10 7EG [Ships Quay, South
St]: Cosy cheerful L-shaped Victorian local,
well kept Fullers range and a guest ale, good
value fresh comfort food inc some unusual
choices, Tues curry night; log fire each end,
low ceilings; dogs welcome, tables outside;
handy for Wayfarers Walk and Solent Walk;
open all day Fri-Sun *(Ann and Colin Hunt,
Tony and Wendy Hobden, Caryn Mackenzie)*

EVERSLEY [SU7861]
☆ *Golden Pot* RG27 0NB [B3272]: Enjoyable
food from baguettes up in neatly refurbished
linked areas with nicely spaced tables,
highly efficient cheerful service, real ales,
good wines by the glass; piped music; dogs
allowed in bar, picnic-sets outside with
masses of colourful flowers, cl winter
Sun evening *(D and J Ashdown, LYM)*

EVERTON [SZ2994]
Crown SO41 0JJ [Old Christchurch Rd; pub
signed just off A337 W of Lymington]:
Quietly set New Forest-edge restaurant/pub
with enjoyable varied food, Ringwood and
guest ales, reliable wine choice; two
attractive dining rooms off tiled-floor bar,
log fires; picnic-sets on front terrace and
back grass *(David Sizer, BB)*

FACCOMBE [SU3958]
☆ *Jack Russell* SP11 0DS [signed from A343
Newbury—Andover]: Light and airy creeper-
covered pub in village-green setting
opposite pond by flint church; good bar food
(not Sun evening) from snacks to Sun roasts,
well kept Greene King IPA and Shepherd
Neame Spitfire, good coffee, darts, decorous
bar and carpeted conservatory restaurant;
disabled facilities, lawn by beech trees,
bedrooms, good walks *(I A Herdman,
Edward Leetham, BB, Mr and Mrs H J Langley)*

FAREHAM [SU5706]
Lord Arthur Lee PO16 0EP [West St]: Large
busy open-plan Wetherspoons, eight
reasonably priced well kept beers from small
brewers, their usual good value food, family
area; named for the local 1900s MP who
presented Chequers to the nation *(Val and
Alan Green)*

FARNBOROUGH [SU8756]
☆ *Prince of Wales* GU14 8AL [Rectory Rd, nr
station]: Half a dozen or more good
changing ales in friendly Edwardian local,
stripped brickwork, open fire and antiquey
touches in its three small linked areas;
popular lunchtime food (not Sun) from
sandwiches to imaginative specials, good
service, decent malt whiskies; open all day
Sun *(Dr Martin Owton, Phil and Sally Gorton)*

FARRINGDON [SU7135]
Rose & Crown GU34 3ED [off A32 S of Alton;
Crows Lane – follow Church, Selborne, Liss
signpost]: New owners at this early 19th-c
pub; attractive L-shaped bar, friendly
service, real ales inc Adnams, log fire, back
dining room, no food Sun evening, live Jazz
nights (third Mon of month); wide views
from big back garden *(BB, Glen and
Nola Armstrong)*

FAWLEY [SU4603]
Jolly Sailor SO45 1DT [Ashlett Creek]:
Cottagey waterside pub nr small boatyard
and sailing club; straightforward bar food,
Marstons Pedigree and Ringwood Best, raised
log fire, mixed pubby furnishings on bare
boards, second bar with darts and pool;
children welcome, tables outside looking
past creek's yachts and boats to busy
shipping channel, handy for Rothschild
rhododendron gardens at Exbury *(LYM)*

FLEET [SU7955]
De Havilland Arms GU51 1HA [The Key]:
Welcoming local on huge new estate,
enjoyable food all day, Badger ales, caring
staff, good attention to detail *(Nick and
Sylvia Pascoe)*
Heron on the Lake GU51 2RY [Old Cove Rd]:
Welcoming Chef & Brewer by Fleet Pond, lots
of beams, nooks and corners, old pictures,
two log fires, Courage Directors, Hogs Back
TEA and two guest ales; decent reasonably
priced food, friendly attentive service, good
coffee; piped music; open all day
(Jennifer Banks)

FORDINGBRIDGE [SU1414]
☆ *George* SP6 1AH [Bridge St]: Lovely spot,
contemporary décor keeping a pleasant
degree of pubby cosiness, wide choice of
modern (if not cheap) food from snacks up
in three comfortable dining areas, Greene
King IPA and Morlands Original, decent
wines; decked terrace (no service here) and
conservatory restaurant overlooking River
Avon with lots of ducks and trout, open
all day *(BB, Roy and Lindsey Fentiman,
Richard and Sue Fewkes)*

FROGHAM [SU1712]
☆ *Foresters Arms* SP6 2JA [Abbotswell Rd]:
Friendly chatty New Forest pub,
chef/landlord doing good value blackboard
food from sandwiches to very popular Sun
lunch (compact dining room fills quickly);
attentive young staff, Wadworths ales, good
wines by the glass, cosy rustic refurbishment
with frog-themed bar; children and dogs
welcome, pleasant garden with pretty front
verandah and good play area, small camp
site adjacent, nearby ponies, deer and good
walks; cl Tues *(John and Joan Calvert, LYM,
N R White, Barrie Cornish)*

GOODWORTH CLATFORD [SU3642]
Royal Oak SP11 7QY: Comfortably modern
L-shaped bar with friendly obliging staff,
good carefully sourced food from pub staples
to uncommon dishes, well kept local ales,
welcoming landlord; sheltered and very
pretty dell-like garden, large and neatly

kept, attractive Test Valley village, good walks by River Anton *(Phyl and Jack Street)*

GOSPORT [SZ5998]

Alverbank House PO12 2QT [Stokes Bay Rd, Alverstoke]: Pleasant partly divided hotel lounge, civilised bar with well kept Ringwood, guest beers and a great choice of malt whiskies; good interesting food inc OAP bargains, plenty for vegetarians, cheerful helpful staff; piped music; in woods at end of Stanley Park, nice big mature garden with Solent and Isle of Wight views, play area, good bedrooms *(Ann and Colin Hunt, Philip and June Caunt)*

☆ *Jolly Roger* PO12 4LQ [Priory Rd, Hardway]: Old beamed harbour-view pub with enjoyable fairly priced food (can take a while), four real ales such as Adnams, Greene King and Shepherd Neame, decent house wines; lots of bric-a-brac, log fire, attractive eating area inc new conservatory; open all day *(Sally and Tom Matson, Ann and Colin Hunt, Stephen Moss)*

Queens PO12 1LG [Queens Rd]: Classic bare-boards local; long-serving landlady keeps Ringwood Fortyniner, Roosters, Wells & Youngs Special and two guests in top condition, quick service, three areas off bar with good log fire in interesting carved fireplace, sensibly placed darts; TV room – children welcome here daytime; cl lunchtimes Mon-Thurs, open all day Sat *(Ann and Colin Hunt)*

HAMBLE [SU4806]

☆ *Bugle* SO31 4HA [3 miles from M27 junction 8]: Roomy refurbished waterside pub, relaxed and sociable, with enjoyable if not cheap food (all day wknds) using local ingredients and fresh fish, good choice of ales and wines; woodburner, sturdy furniture, beams, flagstones and bare beams; river-view terrace, open all day *(Bob and Angela Brooks, LYM, Gael Pawson, Mrs Mary Woods)*

Olde Whyte Harte SO31 4JF [High St; 3 miles from M27 junction 8]: Cheery proper pub with big inglenook log fire, well integrated flagstoned eating area allowing children, generous fresh food all day inc plenty of fish, Fullers/Gales ales, good wines by the glass, decent coffee; cheeky graffiti on low dark 16th-c beams, monkey and yachting memorabilia; piped music; small walled garden, handy for nature reserve, open all day *(LYM, Gael Pawson)*

HAMBLEDON [SU6414]

Vine PO7 4RW [West St]: 400-year-old beamed village pub under new management, well priced food, well kept Marstons, lots of old sporting and country prints, plenty of bric-a-brac, nice mix of furnishings; garden with decking *(LYM, Patrick Spence, Mike Samuels)*

HARTLEY WINTNEY [SU7656]

Cricketers RG27 8QB [Cricket Green]: Leisurely and relaxed, with a couple of easy chairs, cricket memorabilia, Courage Directors, Sharps Doom Bar and Wells & Youngs Bitter, friendly efficient service, good

value linked french restaurant; some tables outside *(Graham and Toni Sanders, LM)*

HAWKLEY [SU7429]

Hawkley Inn GU33 6NE [off B3006 nr A3 junction; Pococks Lane]: Useful easy-going walkers' pub (on Hangers Way), splendid real ale range from central bar, local farm cider, open fires, bar food; piped music; children and dogs welcome, terrace tables and garden, good bedrooms, open all day wknds *(Phil and Sally Gorton, LYM, Tony and Jill Radnor, Philippa Heelis)*

HIGHCLERE [SU4359]

Red House RG20 9PU [Andover Rd (A343)]: Traditional building reopened summer 2008 after striking contemporary refurbishment; extensive bar and separate restaurant, Timothy Taylors Landlord and West Berkshire ales, good range of reasonably priced up-to-date food *(Mr and Mrs W W Burke)*

HILL TOP [SU4003]

Royal Oak SO42 7YR [B3054 Beaulieu—Hythe]: Good-sized neatly kept pub looking out over New Forest, well kept ales inc Adnams Broadside, good range of above-average food; pleasant garden behind, handy for Exbury Gardens *(Dr Martin Owton)*

HOOK [SU7153]

Hogget RG27 9JJ [a mile W, A30/A287]: Nicely refurbished and extended with the emphasis on dining side, reopened 2008 under helpful couple who previously ran the good Vine in Hambledon; good home-made food from local ingredients, well kept Marstons-related ales, wide choice of wines by the glass, friendly relaxed atmosphere; heated outside area *(Peter Mercer)*

HORSEBRIDGE [SU3430]

John o' Gaunt SO20 6PU [off A3057 Romsey—Andover, just SW of King's Somborne]: Nice spot in River Test village, good value food inc some interesting dishes, friendly service, Ringwood and Palmers ales; log fire in simple L-shaped bar, nice prints in small back dining area; picnic-sets out in side arbour *(BB, Ann and Colin Hunt)*

HOUGHTON [SU3432]

☆ *Boot* SO20 6LH [Village signposted off A30 in Stockbridge]: Bustling country local with lots of stuffed creatures in cheery log-fire bar, generous enterprising food, Ringwood ales, nice relaxed service, roomy more decorous lounge/dining room; well behaved children and dogs welcome, long garden with half a dozen picnic-sets down by lovely (unfenced) stretch of River Test, where they have fishing; good walks and opp Test Way cycle path *(LYM, Robert Watt, Martin and Karen Wake, Julia and Richard Tredgett, Edward Mirzoeff)*

HURSLEY [SU4225]

Dolphin SO21 2JY [A3090 Winchester—Romsey]: Big roadside family dining pub, stripped 16th-c beams and brickwork, long-serving licensees and efficient cheery staff; reasonably priced food, well kept real ales; piped music; attractive garden, animals for children to watch *(Terry Buckland)*

KEYHAVEN [SZ3091]

☆ *Gun* SO41 0TP: Busy 17th-c pub looking over boatyard and sea to Isle of Wight, low-beamed bar with nautical bric-a-brac and plenty of character (less in family rooms and conservatory); good choice of generous food using local produce inc crab, beers tapped from the cask such as Flowers Original, Ringwood Best, Shepherd Neame Spitfire and Wychwood Hobgoblin, lots of malt whiskies, efficient good-natured young staff; bar billiards; piped music; back conservatory, tables out in front and in big back garden with swings and fish pond, can stroll down to small harbour and walk to Hurst Castle *(BB, Jenny and Brian Seller)*

KING'S SOMBORNE [SU3531]

Crown SO20 6PW [Romsey Rd (A3057)]: Long, low, thatched pub opp village church, friendly landlord, good, well priced simple home-made food, well kept ales such as Greene King IPA and Ringwood, local cider, good wines and coffee; several linked rooms, fresh flowers; garden behind, Test Way and Clarendon Way footpaths nearby *(Ann and Colin Hunt, Mr and Mrs H J Langley)*

LANGSTONE [SU7104]

☆ *Royal Oak* PO9 1RY [off A3023 just before Hayling Island bridge; Langstone High St]: Charmingly placed waterside dining pub overlooking tidal inlet and ancient wadeway to Hayling Island, boats at high tide, wading birds when it goes out; four real ales inc Greene King, good choice of wines by the glass, good reasonably priced pub food inc all-day sandwiches and snacks, smart friendly staff, spacious flagstoned bar and linked dining areas, log fire; children in eating areas, nice garden, good coastal paths nearby, open all day *(LYM, Ann and Colin Hunt)*

Ship PO9 1RD [A3023]: Busy waterside 18th-c former grain store, lovely views to Hayling Island from roomy, softly lit nautical bar with upper-deck dining room, Fullers ales, good choice of wines by the glass; log fire, wide range of generous reasonably priced food inc local fish and venison; children welcome, plenty of tables on heated terrace by quiet quay, good coast walks, open all day *(Tony and Wendy Hobden, Irene and Derek Flewin)*

LINWOOD [SU1910]

High Corner BH24 3QY [signed from A338 via Moyles Court, and from A31; keep on]: Big rambling pub very popular for its splendid New Forest position up a track, with extensive neatly kept wooded garden and lots for children to do; some character in original upper bar, big back extensions for the summer crowds, nicely partitioned restaurant, verandah lounge, interesting family rooms, wide choice of bar snacks and restaurant-style food, well kept Wadworths; welcomes dogs and horses (stables and paddock available), seven redecorated bedrooms, has been open all day wknds *(Mr and Mrs W W Burke, LYM)*

LISS [SU7826]

Jolly Drover GU33 7QL [London Rd, Hill Brow]: Neatly run comfortable old pub notable for its very friendly service (good with disabled people); pubby carpets and terracotta walls, leather sofas by inglenook, beamed part with dark wood furniture, wide choice of enjoyable pub food using local organic meat, well kept Ringwood Best and Timothy Taylors Landlord, good choice of wines by the glass; tables and chairs on sheltered terrace, six bedrooms in barn conversion, good breakfast; cl Sun evening *(Ross Balaam, Philip and Christine Kenny)*

LOCKS HEATH [SU5006]

☆ *Jolly Farmer* SO31 9JH [Fleet End Rd, not far from M27 junction 9]: Relaxing series of softly lit linked rooms, nice old scrubbed tables and masses of interesting bric-a-brac and prints; wide choice of enjoyable food (all day wknds) inc good value two-sitting Sun lunch, quick friendly service, interesting long-serving landlord, Fullers/Gales ales, decent wines and country wines, coal-effect gas fires; two sheltered terraces (one with play area and children's lavatories), five nice bedrooms, good breakfast, nearby walks; open all day *(Phyl and Jack Street, M G Hart, LYM, Ann and Colin Hunt)*

LONG SUTTON [SU7447]

☆ *Four Horseshoes* RG29 1TA [signed off B3349 S of Hook]: Welcoming open-plan black-beamed country local with two log fires, long-serving landlord cooking bargain pubby food, friendly landlady serving good range of changing ales such as Palmers, decent wines and country wine; no piped music or machines; small glazed-in verandah; disabled access, picnic-sets on grass over road, boules pitch and play area, three good value bedrooms (bunk beds available for cyclist/walkers) *(Tony and Jill Radnor, BB)*

LONGPARISH [SU4244]

☆ *Plough* SP11 6PB [B3048, off A303 just E of Andover]: Comfortably upmarket open-plan country pub under welcoming new ownership, newly extended bar area, oak floors and flagstones, leather chairs and open fires; food from lunchtime sandwiches to bistro-style dishes, good value two-course set menu and very popular Sun lunch, decent choice of wines by the glass, Black Sheep, Ringwood and a guest ale; children and dogs welcome, disabled access and facilities, tables on deck in nice garden, open all day summer *(Phyl and Jack Street, LYM)*

LOWER SWANWICK [SU4909]

Ship SO31 7FN [Bridge Rd]: Quiet and friendly Fullers pub with their beers, reasonably priced pubby food, comfortable panelled lounge, lots of marine artefacts, separate eating area; good River Hamble views and walks *(Val and Alan Green)*

LYMINGTON [SZ3293]

☆ *Chequers* SO41 8AH [Ridgeway Lane, Lower Woodside – dead end just S of A337 roundabout W of Lymington, by White Hart]: Welcoming local atmosphere, friendly landlord and pleasant young staff, generous enjoyable food, real ales such as Ringwood and Wadworths 6X, polished boards and quarry tiles, attractive pictures, plain chairs and wall pews, traditional games; may be piped music; well behaved children allowed, tables and summer marquee in neat walled back family garden, attractive front terrace, handy for bird-watching on Pennington Marshes *(Mr and Mrs P D Titcomb, Pete Coxon, A and B D Craig, Franklyn Roberts, LYM)*

☆ *Fishermans* SO41 8FD [All Saints Rd, Woodside]: Doing well under current management, good choice of traditional and more interesting food inc popular Sun lunch, friendly helpful staff, well kept Fullers/Gales ales, decent wines, pleasant atmosphere *(Graham and Glenis Watkins, Colin Wood, David Sizer)*

☆ *Kings Head* SO41 3AR [Quay Hill]: In steep cobbled lane of smart small shops, friendly dimly lit old local with Adnams, Fullers/Gales, Greene King and Ringwood ales, several wines by the glass, pleasant helpful staff, sensibly priced food; nicely mixed old-fashioned furnishings in rambling beamed and mainly bare-boarded rooms, log fire, good classic yacht photographs, daily papers; may be piped pop music; children and dogs welcome, nice little back sunny courtyard, open all day wknds *(Mr and Mrs A Garforth, M Ross-Thomas, Drs J and J Parker, Mr Ray J Carter, Miss J F Reay, Alan Wright, I A Herdman, LYM, Mayur Shah, Dr S J Shepherd, Stephen Moss, Richard and Sissel Harris, Michael Dandy)*

Wagon & Horses SO41 5SB [Undershore Rd; rd to IOW ferry]: Well run local with Wadworths 6X, friendly staff, reasonably priced food *(Chris Sale)*

LYNDHURST [SU2908]

Crown SO43 7NF [top end of High St opp church]: Best Western hotel with cheerful log fire and comfortable leather seating in pleasant bar (shame the panelling's been overpainted); enjoyable bar food from sandwiches up, good service, Ringwood Best and Fortyniner, good coffee, several wines by the glass, restaurant; piped music; comfortable bedrooms, good breakfast, open all day *(Michael Dandy, Steve and Liz Tilley, Phyl and Jack Street)*

Waterloo Arms SO43 7AS [Pikes Hill, just off A337 N]: Rambling thatched 17th-c New Forest pub with low beams and stripped brick, pleasant furnishings, log fire, good ale range inc Ringwood, pubby food inc Sun roasts, friendly helpful staff, comfortable bar, roomy back dining area; heated terrace and nice big garden with play area *(Neil Hardwick, Phyl and Jack Street, Michael Dandy, Pete Coxon)*

MAPLEDURWELL [SU6851]

Gamekeepers RG25 2LU [off A30, not far from M3 junction 6]: Dark-beamed dining pub with good if not cheap home-made food from baguettes up, welcoming landlord, well kept Badger ales, good coffee; a few sofas by

flagstoned and panelled core, well spaced tables in large dining room; piped music, TV; children welcome, terrace and garden, lovely thatched village with duck pond, good walks, open all day *(LYM, LM)*

MARCHWOOD [SU3809]

Pilgrim SO40 4WU [Hythe Rd, off A326 at Twiggs Lane]: Picturesque thatched pub now owned and extended by Fullers, good choice of enjoyable food inc very popular Sun lunch, friendly service, open fires; new bedroom block in former restaurant across road *(Phyl and Jack Street, LYM, Paula Crompton)*

MEONSTOKE [SU6120]

Bucks Head SO32 3NA [village signed just off A32 N of Droxford]: Partly panelled L-shaped dining lounge looking over road to water meadows; good value food inc popular Sun roasts, well kept Greene King ales, decent wines, log fire, plush banquettes, rugs on bare boards and well spaced tables; friendly public bar (dogs welcome) with leather settee by another log fire, darts and juke box; small garden, lovely village setting with ducks on pretty little River Meon, good walks; open all day wknds *(Ann and Colin Hunt, BB)*

MICHELDEVER [SU5142]

Dove SO21 3AU [Micheldever Station, off A33 or A303]: Large pub under new ownership, interconnecting rooms around central bar, good food and service, log fire; small side terrace *(Phyl and Jack Street)*

MINLEY MANOR [SU8357]

Crown & Cushion GU17 9UA [A327, just N of M3 junction 4A]: Attractive small traditional pub with enjoyable fairly priced food, Adnams Broadside, Bass and Tetleys, coal-effect gas fire; big separate raftered and flagstoned rustic 'meade hall' behind, very popular wknds (evenings more a young people's meeting place), with huge log fire; staff cope well when busy; children in eating area, heated terrace overlooking own cricket pitch *(LYM, Peter Sampson)*

MINSTEAD [SU2810]

Trusty Servant SO43 7FY [just off A31, not far from M27 junction 1]: Attractive 19th-c building in pretty New Forest hamlet with interesting church, wandering cattle and ponies and plenty of easy walks; recently reopened after bright and simple mildly upscale refurbishment, two-room bar and big dining room, welcoming new management, good drinks' choice, enjoyable food from chunky sandwiches up; big sloping garden, open all day *(Caroline McArthur, Ann and Colin Hunt, Kevin Flack, Phyl and Jack Street, LYM)*

NEW CHERITON [SU5827]

☆ *Hinton Arms* SO24 0NH [A272 nr B3046 junction]: Neatly kept popular country pub with cheerful accommodating landlord, four real ales inc Bowman Wallops Wood and one brewed for the pub by Hampshire, nicely served wines by the glass, generous food inc game specials, sporting pictures and memorabilia; TV lounge; terrace, big garden, very handy for Hinton Ampner House (NT) *(Phyl and Jack Street, Val and Alan Green, BB, David and Sheila Pearcey)*

NEW MILTON [SZ2495]

House Martin BH25 6QF [Christchurch Rd (A337)]: Pleasantly refurbished popular dining pub with good value food all day, Badger and Ringwood ales, good service, conservatory *(Alan Wright)*

NEWTOWN [SU4763]

Swan RG20 9BH [A339 2 miles S of Newbury, by junction with old A34]: Attractive old flagstoned pub recently carefully refitted in modern style, good menu, well laid-out tables, management with an eye for detail; children welcome, lovely streamside back garden *(Ian Nesbit)*

NORTH WALTHAM [SU5645]

Fox RG25 2BE [signed off A30 SW of Basingstoke; handy for M3 junction 7]: Good food from sandwiches to venison and popular Sun roasts (best to book), helpful efficient staff, real ales such as Adnams, Ringwood and St Austell, foxy décor, log fire in bright elongated dining area; children welcome, lovely garden with farmland views, pleasant village in nice spot (walk to Jane Austen's church at Steventon) *(Patrick Spence, John R Ringrose)*

ODIHAM [SU7450]

Bell RG29 1LY [The Bury]: Simple unspoilt two-bar local in pretty square opp church, well kept Courage, bargain pubby food, log fire *(Mark Flynn, Ann and Colin Hunt)*

OTTERBOURNE [SU4522]

Otter SO21 2HW [Boyatt Lane off Winchester Rd]: Unpretentious dining pub with enjoyable food, good staff, real ale; garden tables *(M and GR, A and B D Craig)*

OVINGTON [SU5631]

☆ *Bush* SO24 0RE [off A31 W of Alresford]: Charming spot with streamside garden and pergola dining terrace, appealing low-ceilinged bar, high-backed settles, pews and masses of old pictures, blazing fire; Wadworths ales, good if pricey food (not Sun evening, and they may try to keep your credit card while you eat); children (perhaps best to book) and dogs welcome, nice walks, open all day summer hols *(Julia and Richard Tredgett, Peter Sampson, LYM, Pam and John Smith, Ben Andrews)*

PARK GATE [SU5108]

Village Inn SO31 1AZ [Botley Rd]: Pleasantly refurbished Ember Inn with three real ales and usual food, good service, civilised family atmosphere *(Keith and Sue Ward)*

PETERSFIELD [SU7423]

Good Intent GU31 4AF [College St]: Neat and tidy proper pub with well kept Fullers/Gales and a guest ale, enjoyable fresh pubby food strong on sausages, friendly licensees; low oak beams and log fires in 16th-c core, well spaced good-sized pine tables with flowers, camera collection, cosy family area; piped music, live Sun; dogs welcome, front terrace, bedrooms *(Tony and Wendy Hobden)*

Queens GU32 2AH [Village St, Sheet]: Well run traditional pub with well kept ale, roaring fire in old-fashioned bar, good Sun bar nibbles *(Michael B Griffith)*

Square Brewery GU32 3HJ [The Square]: Neatly kept Fullers pub with four of their ales, small choice of above-average sensibly priced pub food, armchairs one end with TV and games machines *(Jeremy David)*

White Horse GU32 1DA [up on old downs rd about halfway between Steep and East Tisted, nr Priors Dean – OS Sheet 186 or 197, map ref 715290]: Charming building high and isolated on the downs, two well worn-in idiosyncratically old-fashioned rustic parlours (candlelit at night), family dining room, open fires throughout, cheerful staff, good range of real ales, beer festivals; tables out by floodlit pond, open all day wknds *(Ann and Colin Hunt, the Didler, LYM)*

PLAITFORD [SU2719]

Shoe SO51 6EE [Salisbury Rd]: Lively, roomy and attractively lit, with young welcoming staff, well kept ales such as Ringwood Best and Wells & Youngs Bombardier, farm cider, good fresh food, live music wknds; children and dogs welcome, garden behind; bedrooms *(Dr S J Shepherd, Stuart Turner)*

PORTSMOUTH [SZ6399]

American Bar PO1 2JA [White Hart Rd]: Spacious colonial-theme bar/restaurant popular for reasonably priced food from all-day sandwiches, baguettes and bar meals to fresh local fish and seafood, Courage Directors and a guest beer, good friendly service; garden behind, handy for IOW ferry *(Colin Moore)*

Fountain PO2 9AA [London Rd, North End]: Tiled pub with large bar and family room off, nicely polished brass, interesting pub pictures, mirrors each end, unusual ceiling lights, well kept Badger Best and Gales HSB; seats outside *(Ann and Colin Hunt)*

Still & West PO1 2JL [Bath Sq, Old Portsmouth]: Great location with super views of narrow harbour mouth and across to Isle of Wight, especially from glazed-in panoramic upper family area and waterfront terrace with lots of picnic-sets; nautical bar with fireside sofas and cosy colour scheme, Fullers ales, good choice of wines by the glass, food all day; piped music may be loud, nearby pay & display; children welcome, handy for historic dockyard, open all day *(LYM, Paul Rampton, Julie Harding, Kevin Flack, Mike and Jennifer Marsh, Susan and John Douglas, Paul and Marion Watts, B M Eldridge)*

ROCKBOURNE [SU1118]

☆ *Rose & Thistle* SP6 3NL [signed off B3078 Fordingbridge–Cranborne]: Attractive 16th-c thatched pub with civilised flagstoned bar, antique settles, old engravings and cricket prints, good coal fire, traditional games; real ales such as Fullers/Gales and Hampshire, good range of wines, log fires in two-room restaurant; may be piped classical music; children and dogs welcome, neat front garden, charming tranquil spot in lovely village, good walks *(Kevin Flack, Mr and Mrs P D Titcomb, Robert Watt, LYM)*

ROMSEY [SU3520]

☆ *Three Tuns* SO51 8HL [Middlebridge St (but car park signed straight off A27 bypass)]: Interesting bistro food inc reasonably priced up-to-date bar lunches, bargain evening fish and chips and all-day Sun roast in attractively furnished bow-windowed pub with flagstones, black beams and panelling; Ringwood, Wychwood Hobgoblin and a guest beer, good amiable service; piped music; children allowed at lunchtime, nice back terrace *(Irene and Derek Flewin, Georgina Campbell, LYM)*

ROTHERWICK [SU7156]

Coach & Horses RG27 9BG [signed from B3349 N of Hook; also quite handy for M3 junction 5]: Individual furnishings and log fires in two beamed front rooms, hard-working young couple doing good value locally sourced home-made food from lunchtime sandwiches up (not Sun evening), well kept Badger ales, daily papers, games; children and dogs welcome, tables out at front and in back garden, pretty flower tubs and baskets, shop selling basic provisions, open all day wknds, cl Mon *(Nigel Lander, LYM)*

Falcon RG27 9BL [off B3349 N of Hook, not far from M3 junction 5]: Jovial portuguese landlord and tapas, as well as more usual pub food (roasts etc only Sun) in big bright simply decorated pub; Fullers London Pride and Sharps Doom Bar, efficient service; piped music; children and dogs welcome, tables out in front, sizeable back garden, open all day Sun *(D P and M A Miles, David and Sheila Pearcey, Philip and June Caunt, LYM, I A Herdman)*

ROWLAND'S CASTLE [SU7310]

☆ *Castle Inn* PO9 6DA [off B2148/B2149 N of Havant; Finchdean Rd]: Only an absence of recent reports keeps this cheerful proper country pub out of the Main Entries: friendly hands-on tenants, comfortable bar with enormous log fire and good choice of of Fullers/Gales ales, nice coffee, neat staff; two appealing little dining rooms on left, attractively priced pubby food with more exotic evening choices; children and dogs welcome, pony paddock by good-sized garden, good disabled facilities, open all day *(Tony and Wendy Hobden, LYM, Ann and Colin Hunt)*

SELBORNE [SU7433]

☆ *Selborne Arms* GU34 3JR [High St]: Character tables, pews and deep settles made from casks on antique boards in an appealing bar, changing largely local real ales, sensible range of promptly served food from baguettes up, good choice of wines by the glass (three glass sizes), nice coffee; big log fire, daily papers, smart carpeted dining room with lots of local photographs; plenty of garden tables, arbour, terrace, orchard and good play area, walks up Hanger, and handy

for Gilbert White museum; open all day wknds *(David and Sue Atkinson, Michael B Griffith, BB)*

SETLEY [SU3000]

Filly SO42 7UF [Lymington Rd (A337 Brockenhurst—Lymington)]: Popular roadside pub with wide choice of generous enjoyable home-made food inc Sun carvery, Ringwood ales, decent wines, helpful cheerful service; interesting if sometimes crowded beamed front bar with inglenook, nice eating area at back; children welcome, sheltered tables outside, New Forest walks, open all day *(Mr and Mrs P D Titcomb, Ann and Colin Hunt, Colin Wood, LYM, Guy and Caroline Howard, Phyl and Jack Street)*

SHAWFORD [SU4724]

Bridge Hotel SO21 2BP: Reliable, beamed riverside Chef & Brewer family dining pub, with promptly served food all day, efficient friendly staff, Hogs Back TEA, Palmers Copper and Ringwood Fortyniner, decent wines; several interesting rooms, smart décor, cosy nooks and corners; pleasant terrace, big garden, play area, downland and Itchen Way walks *(Phyl and Jack Street, Tony Hobden, Ann and Colin Hunt)*

SHEDFIELD [SU5613]

Old Forge SO32 2JA [Winchester Rd (B2177)]: Friendly, with wide choice of enjoyable good value food inc popular Sun carvery, plenty of seating, coloured walls, black beams and dark oak *(Samuel Fancett)*

Samuels Rest SO32 2JB [Upper Church Rd (signed off B2177)]: Unspoilt rural village local, fresh pubby food served by cheerful landlady inc good value Sun roasts, well kept ales inc Ringwood or Wadworths, nice eating area away from bar; piped radio in public bar; garden with terrace *(Ann and Colin Hunt)*

SHERBORNE ST JOHN [SU6255]

Swan RG24 9HS [Kiln Rd]: Comfortably divided 17th-c thatched pub, good choice of good value fresh local food, and of wines and beers, farm cider, good smiling service; large pleasant garden with play area, handy for the Vyne (NT) *(Jennifer Banks, Fran Lane, Mr and Mrs J Alderton)*

SHIRRELL HEATH [SU5714]

Prince of Wales SO32 2JN [High St (B2177)]: Reopened after refurbishment, attentive hospitable service, enjoyable good value home-made pubby food inc OAP deals, good choice of local ales inc one brewed for the pub, front bar with restaurant behind; back garden with terrace *(Samuel Fancett, Peter Salmon)*

SILCHESTER [SU6262]

☆ *Calleva Arms* RG7 2PH [The Common]: Good varied food at sensible prices from sandwiches up, Fullers/Gales and a guest beer, decent wines by the glass, interestingly carved seats in roomy bar, smart dining areas, family conservatory; handy for the Roman site, sizeable attractive garden *(Humphry and Angela Crum Ewing, J V Dadswell)*

SOPLEY [SZ1596]

☆ **Woolpack** BH23 7AX [B3347 N of Christchurch]: Pretty thatched dining pub bouncing back after 2008 fire damage; rambling open-plan low-beamed bar, welcoming helpful staff, standard food lifted out of the ordinary by good preparation, real ales such as Ringwood Best and Fortyniner, good choice of wines by the glass, modern dining conservatory; children in eating areas, terrace and charming garden with weeping willows, duck stream and footbridges; open all day (Sue and Mike Todd, LYM)

SOUTHAMPTON [SU4214]

Crown SO17 1QE [Highcrown St, Highfield]: Well kept ales inc Fullers London Pride, Ringwood Best and Timothy Taylors Landlord in civilised, relaxed local, substantial bargain lunchtime food from baked potatoes up, helpful staff, log fire, beams and brasses, banquettes and round tables; piped music; can be packed with students and academics from nearby university; dogs allowed in main bar, heated covered terrace, popular Sun quiz night, open all day (Tracey and Stephen Groves)

Giddy Bridge SO15 2AF [London Rd]: Massive choice of well priced real ales in pleasant Wetherspoons, partly divided and not too big, upstairs area with balcony terrace, good staff, sensibly priced food (Val and Alan Green)

South Western Arms SO17 2HW [Adelaide Rd, by St Denys station]: Friendly local with ten or so well kept changing ales, good staff, easy-going atmosphere, basic food and décor (bare boards and brickwork, toby jugs and stag's head on beams, lots of woodwork, ceiling beer mats); darts, pool and table football in upper gallery allowing children; terrace picnic-sets (Stephen Moss, Joe Green)

Stile SO17 1TS [University Rd, Highfield]: Friendly open-plan, with several good ales inc Black Sheep and Fullers London Pride, quickly served low-priced college-canteen food (Val and Alan Green, Tracey and Stephen Groves)

White Star SO14 3DJ [Oxford St]: Smart, modern red-walled bar, banquettes and open fire, comfortable sofas and armchairs in secluded alcoves by south-facing windows; good food from interesting baguettes and up-to-date light dishes up, pleasant upper dining area, rather sophisticated friendly aproned staff in black uniforms, Fullers London Pride, good wines by the glass inc ports and sweet wine, lots of cocktails; they may try to keep your credit card while you eat; sunny pavement tables, open all day (Gael Pawson)

SOUTHSEA [SZ6499]

☆ **Hole in the Wall** PO5 3BY [Great Southsea St]: Small friendly unspoilt local in old part of town, up to six good changing ales inc local Oakleaf, Bowman and Irving, Wheal Maiden alcoholic ginger beer, Thatcher's ciders; evening speciality local sausages and substantial pies, old prints, dark panelling, nicely worn boards, over 700 pumpclips on ceiling, daily papers, quiz night Thurs, Oct beer festival; small outside tiled area at front with benches, cl til 4pm but open Fri lunchtime (Mrs Maricar Jagger, Joan and Michel Hooper-Immins, Mike and Eleanor Anderson)

STOCKBRIDGE [SU3535]

Grosvenor SO20 6EU [High St]: Old-fashioned hotel with relaxing high-ceilinged main bar, log fire, Greene King ales, food from well filled sandwiches up, oak-panelled restaurant, back conservatory, helpful staff; piped music, TV; children and dogs welcome, good-sized back garden, 26 bedrooms (Ann and Colin Hunt, Phil and Sally Gorton, Helen and Brian Edgeley, M G Hart, LYM)

☆ **White Hart** SO20 6HF [High St; A272/A3057 roundabout]: Thriving divided beamed bar, attractive décor with antique prints, oak pews and other seats, quick friendly service; reliable generous fresh food from good sandwiches to game, Fullers ales, good coffee and wines by the glass, comfortable restaurant with blazing log fire (children allowed); disabled access and facilities, terrace tables, nice garden, good bedrooms, open all day (Helen and Brian Edgeley, Edward Mirzoeff, Dennis Jenkin, Val and Alan Green, LYM, Phyl and Jack Street)

STRATFIELD TURGIS [SU6960]

Wellington Arms RG27 0AS: Handsome, small country inn with relaxing armchairs and other individual furnishings in restful and surprisingly pubby tall-windowed two-room bar, part with polished flagstones, part carpeted; good staff, Badger ales, food from chunky sandwiches up, open fire; garden, comfortable bedrooms (Jennifer Banks)

STUBBINGTON [SU5402]

Crofton PO14 3QF [Crofton Lane]: Modern two-bar estate local, neat and airy, with friendly efficient staff, four well kept changing ales, good value wines, enjoyable nicely varied food inc popular weekday OAP deals; dogs welcome (Sally and Tom Matson)

SUTTON SCOTNEY [SU4639]

Coach & Horses SO21 3JH [Oxford Rd, just off A30]: Welcoming licensees doing reliable homely food, good service, Ringwood Best, Wadworths 6X and a guest ale; roomy carpeted beamed bar with big open fire; children welcome, pleasant garden, three bedrooms in adjacent former fire station (Phyl and Jack Street)

SWAY [SZ2898]

Hare & Hounds SO41 6AL [Durns Town, just off B3055 SW of Brockenhurst]: Bright, airy and comfortable New Forest family dining pub; good generous fresh food, Greene King and Ringwood ales, good coffee, friendly staff, low beams, central log fire; piped music; dogs welcome, picnic-sets and play frame in neatly kept garden, open all day Sat (Michael Dandy, Ann and Colin Hunt, B R Merritt, LYM)

TANGLEY [SU3252]

☆ *Cricketers Arms* SP11 0SH [towards the Chutes]: Relaxed old-fashioned tucked-away country pub with good blackboard food, well kept Bowman ales tapped from the cask, friendly landlord and good staff; massive inglenook log fire in simple tiled-floor front bar, bar billiards, friendly black labradors (Pots and Harvey), bistro-ish back flagstoned extension into conservatory with a one-table alcove off, some good cricketing prints; dogs welcome, tables on neat terrace, good Nordic-style back bedroom block, unspoilt countryside *(Pete Baker, I A Herdman, LYM)*

THRUXTON [SU2945]

☆ *White Horse* SP11 8EE [Mullens Pond, just off A303 eastbound]: Attractive 16th-c thatched pub tucked below A303 embankment, polished and comfortable, with good if not cheap food, well kept Fullers London Pride and Greene King Abbot, nice choice of wines by the glass, nice sofas; log fire, a couple of sofas, very low beams, horse-racing décor, separate dining area; good-sized garden and terrace, four bedrooms *(J D G Isherwood, Phyl and Jack Street, Mark Flynn)*

TIMSBURY [SU3325]

☆ *Bear & Ragged Staff* SO51 0LB [A3057 towards Stockbridge; pub marked on OS Sheet 185 map ref 334254]: Reliable roadside dining pub with wide blackboard choice of popular food all day, friendly efficient service, lots of wines by the glass, Greene King IPA; log fire, good-sized beamed interior; children in eating area, tables in extended garden with play area, handy for Mottisfont, good walks *(J V Dadswell, LYM, Ann and Colin Hunt)*

Malthouse SO51 0NG [A3057 N of village]: Spacious roadside family pub, very popular in good weather for its secluded lawn and terrace and big well equipped play area; fireside leather sofas in pleasant lounge area, real ales such as Gales, Ringwood and Wadworths from central bar, conservatory-style dining area, wide choice of decent food inc good value carvery, fast friendly service; nr fine Norman church, pleasant paths to Michelmersh, handy for Mottisfont Abbey (NT) *(Chris Turner)*

TITCHFIELD [SU5406]

☆ *Fishermans Rest* PO15 5RA [Mill Lane, off A27 at Titchfield Abbey]: Airy open-plan pub/restaurant with wide choice of good value fresh food, informal tables throughout, good service, well kept Greene King ales and Ringwood Best, two log fires, daily papers, trouty décor; fine riverside position opp Titchfield Abbey, tables out behind overlooking water, open all day *(Ann and Colin Hunt, Peter Meister, LYM)*

☆ *Titchfield Mill* PO15 5RF [A27, junction with Mill Lane]: Open, airy Vintage Inn family dining pub in neatly kept converted River Meon watermill, olde-worlde room off main bar, smarter dining room, upstairs gallery, stripped beams and interesting old machinery; efficient friendly staff, good value wines by the glass, real ales, freshly squeezed orange juice; piped music; sunny terrace by mill stream with two waterwheels (food not served out here), open all day *(Phyl and Jack Street, Gael Pawson)*

Wheatsheaf PO14 4AD [East St; off A27 nr Fareham]: Welcoming young licensees, good atmosphere, well kept ales such as Batemans, Flowerpots and Hydes, small choice of enjoyable food, long bow-windowed front bar, side snug, back dining room, log fires; piped music may obtrude *(Val and Alan Green)*

TURGIS GREEN [SU6959]

Cricketers RG27 0AH [Bottle Lane]: Dining pub doing well under current welcoming licensees, particularly good lunches and popular theme nights, good wine choice, local real ale; charming early 19th-c building *(George Williams, Colin and Bernardine Perry, Peter Sampson)*

TWYFORD [SU4824]

☆ *Bugle* SO21 1QT [Park Lane]: Contemporary décor keeping period features in long bar, good enterprising food, good young staff; Bowman, Flowerpots and Fullers, beech tables on flagstones, fireside leather chesterfield and armchairs one carpeted end; attractive verandah seating area (used by smokers) *(Val and Alan Green, Phyl and Jack Street, Bruce and Penny Wilkie)*

UPPER CLATFORD [SU3543]

Crook & Shears SP11 7QL [off A343 S of Andover, via Foundry Rd]: Cosy two-bar 17th-c thatched pub, several homely olde-worlde seating areas, bare boards and panelling; good changing ale range, decent food from doorstep sandwiches up, woodburner, small dining room, back skittle alley with own bar; pleasant secluded garden behind *(the Didler)*

UPTON GREY [SU6948]

Hoddington Arms RG25 2RL [signed off B3349 S of Hook; Bidden Rd]: Unpretentious open-plan beamed 18th-c local doing traditional food and Greene King ales; log fire, small games room with bar billiards and darts; well behaved children and dogs welcome, enclosed garden with terrace and play area, quiet pretty village, nice walking/cycling countryside *(BB, Julia and Richard Tredgett)*

WALHAMPTON [SZ3396]

Walhampton Arms SO41 5RE [B3054 NE of Lymington; aka Walhampton Inn]: Large comfortable Georgian-style family roadhouse with emphasis on restauranty food inc reliable carvery (not Mon) in raftered former stables and two adjoining areas; pleasant lounge, Ringwood ales, good-humoured helpful staff; attractive courtyard, good walks, open all day *(Phyl and Jack Street, Rita and Keith Pollard)*

WALTHAM CHASE [SU5616]

Chase SO32 2LL [Winchester Rd (B2177)]: Neat two-bar pub with changing ales inc a Hampshire seasonal beer, bargain generous food from baguettes to good Sun lunch, friendly helpful staff (Stephen and Jean Curtis)

WEST END [SU4714]

Southampton Arms SO30 2HG [Moorgreen Rd, off B3035]: Sizeable 1920s roadside pub with enjoyable reasonably priced food, well kept Ringwood ales, comfortable and cosy bar, attractive conservatory restaurant; sports TV; good garden (Stephen and Jean Curtis, Val and Alan Green, B M Eldridge)

White Swan SO18 3HW [Mansbridge Rd]: Pleasantly refurbished family food pub in nice spot, Wells & Youngs ales, busy carvery restaurant, conservatory; attractive terrace by River Itchen (so liable to flooding) (Phyl and Jack Street)

WEST TYTHERLEY [SU2730]

Black Horse SP5 1NF: Unspoilt village local, welcoming licensees, three real ales, reasonably priced food, nicely set dining area off traditional bar; dogs welcome (Ann and Colin Hunt)

WEST WELLOW [SU2817]

Rockingham SO51 6DE [pub signed off A36 Romsey—Ower, at Canada roundabout]: Beamed 19th-c pub down New Forest-edge dead end; furnishings and décor nicely perked up under good new landlady, good choice of reasonably priced food, well kept changing ales, good value wines by the glass, friendly atmosphere, open fire, comfortable and attractive back restaurant; children welcome, garden opening on to pretty heathland with roaming horses (Phyl and Jack Street)

WHITCHURCH [SU4648]

White Hart RG28 7DN [Newbury St]: Handsome former coaching inn, smartly refurbished, with good short but varied food choice from light dishes up, well kept Arkells, good value wines by the glass, comfortable dining areas, friendly staff; bedrooms, open all day inc breakfast (Val and Alan Green, Ann and Colin Hunt)

WICKHAM [SU5711]

Kings Head PO17 5JN [The Square]: Comfortably worn-in, with good friendly service, decent food, well kept Fullers ales, good wines and coffee; log fire, big-windowed and solidly furnished open-plan bar, restaurant nicely secluded up some steps; some customers not always as you'd wish; tables out on square and in back garden (former coach yard) with play area (Phyl and Jack Street, BB, Val and Alan Green)

WINCHESTER [SU4829]

Bakers Arms SO23 9JX [down passage off High St]: Busy old town pub with cheap, quick, usual food, real ales such as Fullers and Shepherd Neame Spitfire; TV; pretty wrought-iron and glass canopy over passageway tables (Dave Braisted, Val and Alan Green)

Bishop on the Bridge SO23 9JX [High St/Bridge St]: Neat open Fullers pub with good beer range inc a guest, varied food not

overpriced, efficient friendly staff, relaxing civilised atmosphere; leather sofas, old local prints; nice riverside back terrace (Val and Alan Green, Michael and Alison Sandy, John R Ringrose)

☆ *Eclipse* SO23 9EX [The Square, between High St and cathedral]: Chatty licensees in picturesque 14th-c local with massive beams and timbers in its two small cheerful rooms; chilled ales inc Fullers London Pride and Ringwood, decent choice of wines by the glass, usually good value lunchtime food from ciabattas to popular Sun roasts, open fire, oak settles, friendly burmese cat; children in back area, seats outside, very handy for cathedral (Michael and Alison Sandy, Ann and Colin Hunt, Mike and Mary Clark, Val and Alan Green, LYM)

Hyde Tavern SO23 7DY [Hyde St (B3047)]: Homely old-fashioned 15th-c pub with two charming simply furnished bars (with hardly a true right-angle); friendly landlady and chatty locals, well kept Ringwood Best and guests such as Bowman and Flowerpots; steps down to lovely secluded garden, opens 12.30 (Michael and Alison Sandy, Pete Baker, Phil and Sally Gorton, Bruce Bird, Val and Alan Green)

Old Gaol House SO23 8RZ [Jewry St]: Traditional Wetherspoons, good choice of real ales, knowledgeable barman, sensibly priced food all day, decent coffee, walls of books; children welcome (Ann and Colin Hunt, Val and Alan Green)

Old Market SO23 9EX [The Square]: Pleasantly refurbished, rambling corner pub, with proper pizzas and pasta among wide choice of other dishes, Fullers London Pride and Ringwood ales, welcoming landlord; on Cathedral Close (Val and Alan Green, LYM)

☆ *Old Vine* SO23 9HA [Great Minster St]: Smart, friendly and efficient service even when busy, good up-to-date food choice, Ringwood Best, Timothy Taylors Landlord and two guest ales, light and airy décor, good furniture on oak boards; opp cathedral, with sheltered terrace, partly covered and heated, charming bedrooms, open all day, (Ann and Colin Hunt, Michael and Alison Sandy, Pat and Roger Davies, Simon Rodway, Geoff Barden)

Parchments SO23 8DA [North Walls]: Previously the 'North Walls'; pub/restaurant with Bass and good selection of bottled beers (John and Annabel Hampshire)

Roebuck SO22 6RP [Stockbridge Rd (B3049)]: Smart Victorianised sitting-room-style; decent food at a price from lunchtime sandwiches and light dishes up, young helpful staff, attractive conservatory restaurant, darts, Greene King ales; piped music; terrace tables, disabled access, car park – rare in this city (Matt Cole, Michael and Alison Sandy)

Royal Oak SO23 9AU [Royal Oak Passage, off upper end of pedestrian part of High St, opp St Thomas St]: Otherwise standard pub with Greene King ales and decent food, notable for the intriguing cellar bar (not always open) whose massive 12th-c beams and Saxon wall give it some claim to be the country's oldest drinking spot; piped music, games machines; packed with young people Fri, Sat nights *(Ann and Colin Hunt, the Didler, LYM)*

Westgate Hotel SO22 5BE [Romsey Rd/Upper High St]: Big-windowed corner pub with red carpets and traditional oak fittings, ebullient landlord, light lunchtime food inc good sandwiches, fuller evening choice with steaks cut to order; smallish back panelled eating area, well kept changing ales such as Banks's Original, Brakspears Oh Be Joyful and Sharps Doom Bar, small choice of good wines, daily papers; bedrooms *(Michael and Alison Sandy, Val and Alan Green, BB)*

WOLVERTON [SU5658]

George & Dragon RG26 5ST [Towns End; just N of A339 Newbury—Basingstoke]: Low-beamed pub in remote rolling country, linked cosy areas, wide choice of enjoyable unpretentious food, long-serving licensees and attentive service, good beer range, decent wines, log fire, pleasant dining area; no piped music, skittle alley; children welcome, big garden with small terrace, separate bedroom block, good breakfast *(J V Dadswell, Miss A Hawkes)*

WOODLANDS [SU3211]

Gamekeeper SO40 7GH [Woodlands Rd, just N of A336 Totton—Cadnam]: Unspoilt traditional village local by New Forest; friendly landlord, reasonably priced food, low-priced ales inc Wadworths 6X and one brewed for the pub, good coffee, dining room with conservatory; terrace tables *(Ann and Colin Hunt)*

A very few pubs try to make you leave a credit card at the bar, as a sort of deposit if you order food. They are not entitled to do this. The credit card firms and banks which issue them warn you not to let them out of your sight. If someone behind the counter used your card fraudulently, the card company or bank could in theory hold you liable, because of your negligence in letting a stranger hang on to your card. Suggest instead that if they feel the need for security, they 'swipe' your card and give it back to you. And do name and shame the pub to us.

Herefordshire

This is the home of great ciders, particularly Weston's, and local brewers are also well represented, with most good pubs stocking Wye Valley beers, perhaps alongside Hobsons, Ludlow and Breconshire from neighbouring counties. Look out too for Spinning Dog beers, from their quirky home, the Victory in Hereford (now serving bargain food). Other pubs on top form are the Crown in Woolhope, flourishing under a newish landlord who brings it back to the *Guide* after quite a break, the Feathers in Ledbury, a thriving showpiece, the cheery Cottage of Content at Carey, and for a really timeless feel, the Carpenters Arms at Walterstone. The Bell at Yarpole does particularly good imaginative food these days, and the crisply modern Mill Race at Walford sources produce from its own farm and woodlands. It's the very civilised Stagg at Titley, with its great wine list, home-grown vegetables and home-reared pigs and hens, that is Herefordshire Dining Pub of the Year. Some notable Lucky Dip pubs are the Royal Oak at Bromyard Downs, Boot at Orleton and Chase in Upper Colwall.

AYMESTREY   SO4265   MAP 6

Riverside Inn
A4110, at N end of village, W of Leominster; HR6 9ST

Lovely spot with a terrace making the most of the view; cosy rooms and open fires

The rambling beamed bar at this half-timbered inn has several cosy areas with décor drawn from a pleasant mix of periods and styles. Fine antique oak tables and chairs mix with stripped-pine country kitchen tables, fresh flowers, hops strung from a ceiling wagon-wheel, horse tack, nice pictures and warm winter log fires; fairly quiet piped pop music. The landlord clearly enjoys chatting to his customers, and service is efficient and friendly. Wye Valley and Hobsons on handpump, two local draft ciders and bottled Brook Farm cider (pressed in the next village), and more than 20 malt whiskies. With big overflowing summer flower pots framing the entrances, the pub stands right by an ancient stone bridge over the River Lugg (residents can try fly-fishing) and there are picnic-sets in the tree-sheltered garden.

Ⓜ Using local specialist producers and growing much of their own fruit and vegetables, **enjoyable lunchtime bar food includes filled baguettes, battered cod, lasagne, confit of pork belly with apple and rhubarb compote and red wine jus, and beef and oxtail stew. There is some emphasis on the more expensive restaurant menu, which might include scallops with smoked bacon, pea salad and celeriac and apple purée, and fried venison with spicy red cabbage, caramelised walnuts, port and orange jus.** *Starters/Snacks: £4.95 to £6.25. Main Courses: £6.50 to £12.95. Puddings: £5.15*

Free house ~ Licensees Richard and Liz Gresko ~ Real ale ~ Bar food ~ Restaurant ~ (01568) 708440 ~ Children welcome ~ Dogs allowed in bar and bedrooms ~ Folk first Thurs of month ~ Open 11-3, 6-11; 12-3, 6-10.30 Sun; closed lunchtime Mon and Sun evening in winter ~ Bedrooms: £45B/£70B

Recommended by Doreen Maddock, Brian and Jacky Wilson, Brian Brooks, Jayne Richards, John Morris, Alan and Eve Harding, Jeff and Wendy Williams, David Morgan, Mr and Mrs D Moir, Stephen Bennett, Ian and Helen Stafford

BODENHAM

S05454 MAP 4

Englands Gate

On A417 at Bodenham turn-off, about 6 miles S of Leominster; HR1 3HU

Some fine original features in this comfortable 16th-c inn; pleasant garden

The ancient interior of this 1540s building is historically atmospheric with a vast central stone chimneypiece, heavy brown beams and joists in low ochre ceilings, well worn flagstones, sturdy timber props, one or two steps, and lantern-style lighting. One corner has a high-backed settle with scatter cushions, a cosy partly stripped-stone room has a long stripped table (just right for a party of eight) and a lighter upper area with flowers on its tables has winged settles painted a soft eau de nil. Wye Valley Butty Bach and a couple of guests from brewers such as Spinning Dog are on handpump, and the pub holds a beer and sausage festival in July; piped pop music, board games and TV. There are tables with sun umbrellas out in the garden and on the terrace.

Ⅲ **Bar food might include filled baguettes, a platter of cured meats, ploughman's, meatballs in spicy tomato sauce with linguine, battered fish, gammon, egg and chips, pork steak with caramelised apples and cider sauce and steak and ale pie.** *Starters/Snacks: £3.95 to £5.75. Main Courses: £7.95 to £16.95. Puddings: £4.50*

Free house ~ Licensee Evelyn McNeil ~ Real ale ~ Bar food (12-2.30, 6-9.30; 12-3 Sun) ~ (01568) 797286 ~ Children welcome ~ Dogs allowed in bar ~ Open 12-11(midnight Sat, 10 Sun)

Recommended by Roger and Anne Newbury, Clive Watkin, Reg Fowle, Helen Rickwood, Dr A J and Mrs Tompsett, Ann and Colin Hunt

BRIMFIELD

S05267 MAP 4

Roebuck Inn 🛏

Village signposted just off A49 Shrewsbury—Leominster; SY8 4NE

Smart dining pub with bistro-style food and updated bedrooms

The contemporary-feeling interior at this neatly kept place has dark brown and red club chairs, sofas, logs stylishly stacked to the ceiling in one alcove and an open fire in the impressive inglenook fireplace in the front lounge bar. There's also an open fire and a more pubby feel in the middle bar area, and the bistro dining room has chunky cord seating in brown and apricot around contemporary wooden tables and modern art on deep-coloured walls; piped music. Banks's is on handpump alongside farm cider and several wines by the glass; terrace.

Ⅲ **Food here can be very good. As well as lunchtime sandwiches and filled baguettes, croque monsieur, carrot and pistachio strudel, terrine of piglet and foie gras, fish of the day, caramelised fennel and goats cheese tartlet, ravioli of lobster with mussel and basil cream, coq au vin, beef wellington, and puddings such as poached pear in sweet red wine and white chocolate and raspberry trifle.** *Starters/Snacks: £4.50 to £12.50. Main Courses: £10.50 to £22.50. Puddings: £3.50 to £5.95*

Marstons ~ Tenant Oliver Bossut ~ Real ale ~ Bar food (12-2.30, 6.30-9.30) ~ Restaurant ~ (01584) 711230 ~ Children welcome ~ Dogs allowed in bar ~ Open 11.30-3, 6-11(1am Sat); 11.30-4 Sun; closed Sun evening ~ Bedrooms: £65B/£85S(£75B)

Recommended by Geoffrey Wordsworth, J E Shackleton, Ian Phillips, R T and J C Moggridge, Denys Gueroult, Jeff and Wendy Williams, Mike and Mary Carter, Michael and Joan Johnstone

---

Bedroom prices normally include full english breakfast, VAT and any inclusive service charge that we know of. Prices before the '/' are for single rooms, after for two people in double or twin (B includes a private bath, S a private shower). If there is no '/', the prices are only for twin or double rooms (as far as we know there are no singles). If there is no B or S, as far as we know no rooms have private facilities.

BRINGSTY COMMON   SO6954   MAP 4

Live & Let Live 🍺

Off A44 Knightwick—Bromyard 1.5 miles W of Whitbourne turn; take track southwards at black cat inn sign, bearing right at fork; WR6 5UW

Restored country tavern surrounded by rolling partly wooded common

Reopened in 2007 following a long closure and extensive restoration, this 17th-c pub has a remarkably rustic feel. The sort of place to enjoy after a long walk, the cosy bar has non-matching scrubbed or polished old tables on its flagstones, a very high-backed traditional winged settle by the log fire in the cavernous stone fireplace, and a variety of seats from comfortably cushioned little chairs to a long stripped pew. Earthenware jugs hang from the low stripped beams, with more bygones on the mantelshelf. The landlady is usually behind the hop-hung bar counter (with old casks built into its facing) serving the well kept Wye Valley Butty Bach and a couple of local guests from brewers such as Hobsons and Ludlow from handpump, and Robertson's cider and Oliver's perry. A pair of cottagey dining rooms are tucked in upstairs under the steep rafters. Outside the timbered cottage with its massive stone chimney, a glass-topped well and big wooden hogshead have been pressed into service as tables for the flagstoned terrace. Picnic-sets giving long peaceful views from the grassy former orchard, which blends into the partly scrubby and partly wooded slopes of this high ancient-feeling common. You really do feel miles from anywhere here.

🍴 **Traditional food includes sandwiches (choice of breads), onion and three-cheese tart, steak pie, sausage and mash, beer-battered fish and chips, gammon, steaks and slow-cooked lamb or ham hock; Sunday roast** *Starters/Snacks: £4.50 to £7.75. Main Courses: £9.50 to £9.95*

Free house ~ Licensee Sue Dovey ~ Real ale ~ Bar food (12-2(3 Sun) 6-9, not Sun evening or Mon) ~ Restaurant ~ No credit cards ~ (01886) 821462 ~ Children welcome ~ Dogs welcome ~ Open 12-2.30, 5.30-11, 12-11(10.30 Sun) Sat; closed Mon lunchtime (except bank hols)

Recommended by Reg Fowle, Helen Rickwood, Chris Flynn, Wendy Jones, Chris Evans, Noel Grundy

CAREY   SO5631   MAP 4

Cottage of Content

Village signposted from good back road betweeen Ross-on-Wye and Hereford E of A49, through Hoarwithy; HR2 6NG

Country furnishings in rustic cottage and seats on terraces

The friendly owners, new at this 15th-c building when the last edition of this *Guide* came out, have settled in well and are very much at the heart of the cheery atmosphere. The building originated as three labourers' cottages with its own integral cider and ale parlour. It has kept much of its old character, with a multitude of beams and country furnishings such as stripped-pine kitchen chairs, long pews by one big table and various old-fashioned tables on flagstones or bare boards. Hobsons Best and Wye Valley Butty Bach are on handpump, and they serve a local cider during the summer months and mulled wine in winter; piped music. There are picnic-sets on the flower-filled front terrace, more on a back terrace and a couple up in the steep rural-feeling garden at the back.

🍴 **Tasty bar food includes starters such as twice baked goats cheese soufflé with basil cream, bacon-wrapped banana with spices and chutney, grilled pork medallions with creamy sage and cider sauce, roast cod on fennel and risotto with gremolata crust, fish pie, and rib-eye steak with wild mushroom and madeira jus; Sunday roast.** *Starters/Snacks: £5.25 to £6.50. Main Courses: £6.50 to £8.95. Puddings: £5.50 to £6.95*

Free house ~ Licensees Richard and Helen Moore ~ Real ale ~ Bar food ~ Restaurant ~ (01432) 840242 ~ Children welcome ~ Dogs allowed in bar ~ Open 12-2(2.30 Sat, Sun), 6-11; closed Sun evening and Mon (except bank hols) ~ Bedrooms: £50(£60B)/£60(£70B)

Recommended by Dr and Mrs Michael Smith, Mike and Mary Carter, Nick Lawless, Reg Fowle, Helen Rickwood, the Didler, Neil and Anita Christopher, John Saville, Phil Bryant, Denys Gueroult

DORSTONE

S03141 MAP 6

Pandy

Pub signed off B4348 E of Hay-on-Wye; HR3 6AN

Ancient timbered inn by village green, with flagstones, vast open fireplace, decent food and play area

With parts of the building dating back to 1185, some say this is Herefordshire's oldest inn. Its neatly kept homely rooms are comfortably traditional with low heavy hop-strung beams in the ochre ceilings, stout timbers, upright chairs on broad worn flagstones and in various alcoves, upholstered stools ranged along the counter (and locals to occupy them) and a vast open fireplace stacked with logs. They keep Wye Valley Butty Bach and Hancocks HB on handpump alongside decent wines, just under two dozen malt and irish whiskies, and a summer farm cider; board games, quoits and piped music. The handsome red setter is called Apache, and the neat side garden has picnic-sets and a play area. More reports please.

🍴 Bar food includes filled baguettes, scampi, fish pie, pizza, goats cheese salad, **fried bass with chive, cream and Martini sauce, fillet of beef on red cabbage and mixed peppers, lamb shank with redcurrant and red wine sauce, thai-style butternut squash curry,** and puddings such as caribbean bread and butter pudding and chocolate pot. *Starters/Snacks: £4.50 to £7.50. Main Courses: £8.95 to £13.95. Puddings: £4.75*

Free house ~ Licensees Bill and Magdalena Gannon ~ Real ale ~ Bar food (not Mon lunchtime) ~ Restaurant ~ (01981) 550273 ~ Children welcome ~ Dogs allowed in bar ~ Open 12-3, 6-11; 12-11 Sat; 12-3, 6.30-10.30 Sun; closed Mon lunchtime (except summer and bank hols)

Recommended by the Didler, Richard

HEREFORD

S05139 MAP 6

Victory 🍺 £

St Owen Street, opposite fire station; HR1 2QD

Home of Spinning Dog beers; humorous nautical décor

An entertaining nautical surprise awaits you inside this unassuming-looking city pub. The counter re-creates a miniature galleon complete with cannon poking out of its top, and down a companionway the long back room is amusingly decked out as the inside of a man o' war with dark wood, rigging and netting everywhere, benches along sides that curve towards a front fo'c'sle, stanchions and ropes forming an upper crow's nest, and appropriate lamps. Service is friendly and informal, and if they're not too busy they'll show you around the Spinning Dog brewery. They keep a good choice of drinks here, including six of their own beers, several farm ciders and a perry; juke box, piped music, darts, games machine, TV, skittle alley, table skittles, board games and a back pool table. The garden has a pagoda, climbing plants and some seats. This is such a great pub, we'd love to get more reports on it.

🍴 **Friday night is curry night; on Saturday afternoons they serve pubby dishes such as casseroles, steak and ale pie, battered fish, and oatmeal stout bread and butter pudding; they also do Sunday roasts.** *Starters/Snacks: £2.50 to £3.75. Main Courses: £5.25 to £10.25. Puddings: £2.50 to £3.75*

Own brew ~ Licensee James Kenyon ~ Real ale ~ Bar food (5-9.30 Fri, 12-5 Sat, 12-4.30 Sun) ~ Restaurant (Sun only) ~ No credit cards ~ (01432) 342125 ~ Children welcome ~ Dogs welcome ~ Live band Sat ~ Open 3(1 Fri, 11 Sat, 12 Sun)-12

Recommended by Ann and Colin Hunt, Reg Fowle, Helen Rickwood

> Post Office address codings confusingly give the impression that a few pubs are in
> Herefordshire when they're really in Gloucestershire or even Wales
> (which is where we list them).

LEDBURY   SO7137   MAP 4

Feathers 🍴 ⧠ ⇌

High Street (A417); HR8 1DS

Handsome timbered hotel with chatty relaxed bar, more decorous lounges, good food, friendly staff and comfortable bedrooms

Very much at the heart of the town, this comfortable and welcoming half-timbered hotel attracts a convivial mix of chatty drinkers in the Top Bar and informal diners. It's a well run place, with polite friendly staff. The beamed interior has restored brickwork, seats around oak tables on oak flooring, hop bines, some country antiques, 19th-c caricatures and fancy fowl prints on the stripped brick chimneybreast (lovely winter fire), copper jam pots and fresh flowers on the tables – some very snug and cosy, in side bays. The lounge is a civilised place for afternoon teas, with high-sided armchairs and sofas in front of a big log fire and newspapers to read. Fullers London Pride and a guest such as Timothy Taylors Landlord are on handpump, with several wines by the glass and 30 malt whiskies. In summer, the sheltered back terrace has abundant pots and hanging baskets.

🍽 The menu might include chicken caesar salad, pigeon and duck leg terrine with red onion marmalade, bass with braised fennel, shallot and caper butter, provençale vegetable risotto, confit of pork belly with caramelised onion potatoes, and puddings such as apple mousse with ginger shortbread, steamed rum and raisin pudding and local cheeseboard. *Starters/Snacks: £4.25 to £9.50. Main Courses: £9.50 to £19.50. Puddings: £4.75 to £6.00*

Free house ~ Licensee David Elliston ~ Real ale ~ Bar food ~ Restaurant ~ (01531) 635266 ~ Children welcome ~ Dogs allowed in bar ~ Open 10-11; 12-10.30 Sun ~ Bedrooms: £89.50B/£130B

Recommended by J E Shackleton, T A R Curran, Dave Braisted, Reg Fowle, Helen Rickwood, Phil Bryant, Hansjoerg Landherr, Tracey and Stephen Groves, Jenny and Dave Hughes, Ann and Colin Hunt, George and Maureen Roby, David Howe

LITTLE COWARNE   SO6050   MAP 4

Three Horseshoes ⧠

Pub signposted off A465 SW of Bromyard; towards Ullingswick; HR7 4RQ

Long-serving licensees and welcoming staff in a bustling country pub with well liked food and home-grown summer salad

Having run this carefully kept place for 20 years now, a good many of their customers are well known to the friendly licensees, but you can be sure of an equally kindly welcome as a newcomer. Unusually for a country pub, this is a fairly modern brick-built building. The quarry tiled L-shaped middle bar has leather-seated bar stools, upholstered settles and dark brown kitchen chairs around sturdy old tables, old local photographs above the corner log fire, and hop-draped black beams in the dark peach ceiling. Opening off one side is a skylit sun room with wicker armchairs around more old tables and at the other end there's a games room with darts, pool, juke box, games machine and cribbage. Greene King Old Speckled Hen, Ruddles Best and Wye Valley Bitter are on handpump, with farm ciders and perry, and a dozen wines by the glass; obliging service and disabled access. A popular Sunday lunchtime carvery is offered in the roomy and attractive stripped-stone raftered restaurant extension. The delightful rural position here makes the terrace or lawn in the particularly lovely garden a distinct lure at warmer times of the year.

🍽 Using their own-grown produce and carefully sought out suppliers, enjoyable food might include tomato and basil soup, devilled lambs kidneys, salmon and lime fishcake, steak and ale pie, fried venison with sloe gin sauce, lasagne, portuguese fish stew, and rump steak. Arrive early for a table on Thursday as their pensioners' lunch is very popular. *Starters/Snacks: £4.00 to £5.50. Main Courses: £7.50 to £14.95. Puddings: £3.95 to £4.25*

Free house ~ Licensees Norman and Janet Whittall ~ Real ale ~ Bar food ~ Restaurant ~ (01885) 400276 ~ Children welcome ~ Dogs allowed in bar ~ Open 11-3(3.30 Sat), 6.30-11; 12-4, 7-10.30 Sun; closed Sun evening in winter ~ Bedrooms: £35S/£60S

Recommended by Tim and Joan Wright, MLR, Denys Gueroult, Theocsbrian, J E Shackleton, Ann and Colin Hunt, Noel Grundy, Alan and Eve Harding, Reg Fowle, Helen Rickwood, Ian and Jane Irving, Anthony Barnes, Stuart Turner

SELLACK   SO5526   MAP 4

Lough Pool ★ ♀
Back road Hoarwithy—Ross-on-Wye; HR9 6LX

Black and white cottage with individual furnishings in beamed bars, a good choice of food and drinks, and lots of seats outside in the pretty garden

This characterful, cottagey place is full of thoughtful touches, from books and newspapers left out for customers, to crayons and paper for children, and dogs get a friendly welcome too. Its beamed central room has rustic chairs and cushioned window seats around wooden tables on the mainly flagstoned floor, sporting prints, bunches of dried flowers and fresh hop bines, and a log fire at one end with a woodburner at the other. Leading off are other rooms, gently brightened up with attractive individual furnishings and antique bottles, and nice touches such as the dresser of patterned plates. Wye Valley Bitter and Butty Bach and a guest such as Butcombe Bitter are on handpump, with around 20 malt whiskies, local farm ciders, perries and apple juices, and several wines by the glass from a thoughtful wine list. Outside are picnic-sets on an inviting front lawned area.

🍴 We're delighted to see that they're now offering a pubby bar menu as well as their more elaborate restaurant-style menu. Using home-grown herbs and rare-breed meat from nearby farms, food (from both menus) might include lunchtime open sandwiches, bouillabaisse, liver and bacon with onion gravy, steak and ale pie, crab linguine, wild mushroom and artichoke risotto, fried duck breast with cherry jus, pork tenderloin stuffed with apple, sage and mascarpone and wrapped in pancetta with brandy jus, puddings such as apple crumble and crème anglaise, and pistachio cheesecake with stewed apple crème fraîche, and a british and local cheeseboard. *Starters/Snacks: £4.95 to £8.50. Main Courses: £8.95 to £17.95. Puddings: £5.95*

Free house ~ Licensees David and Janice Birch ~ Real ale ~ Bar food ~ Restaurant ~ (01989) 730236 ~ Children welcome ~ Dogs allowed in bar ~ Open 11.30(12 Sun)-3, 6.30-11; closed Sun evening and Mon (except bank hols)

Recommended by Nick Lawless, Duncan Cloud, Matt Anderson, Reg Fowle, Helen Rickwood, Mrs B Barker, Mike and Mary Carter

ST OWEN'S CROSS   SO5424   MAP 4

New Inn
Junction A4137 and B4521, W of Ross-on-Wye; HR2 8LQ

Beams and timbers, food all day, fine choice of drinks, and a big garden with views

The lounge bar and restaurant at this half-timbered 16th-c dining pub have huge inglenook fireplaces, dark beams and timbers, various nooks and crannies, old pews and a mix of tables and chairs, and lots of watercolours on warm red walls. Marstons Burton Bitter, Wychwood Hobgoblin and a guest on handpump, farm cider and perry, several malt whiskies and ten wines by the glass; piped music, table and outdoor games. Views extend to the Black Mountains, and in decent weather the spacious enclosed garden is particularly inviting.

🍴 Served all day, bar food includes smoked mackerel mousse, pear, stilton and walnut pancake, poached duck egg with black pudding and toasted brioche, steak, mushroom and ale pie, honey roasted duck breast with redcurrant sauce, sweet and sour mixed bean hot pot, rib-eye steak with stout sauce, and puddings such as bakewell tart and warm chocolate fudge brownie. *Starters/Snacks: £4.25 to £6.50. Main Courses: £6.25 to £14.95. Puddings: £4.95*

Marstons ~ Lease Nigel and Tee Maud ~ Real ale ~ Bar food (12-9) ~ Restaurant ~ (01989) 730274 ~ Children welcome ~ Dogs allowed in bar ~ Open 11(12 Sun)-11 ~ Bedrooms: £45B/£65S(£70B)

Recommended by Rodney and Norma Stubington, Lucien Perring, Reg Fowle, Helen Rickwood, Dr and Mrs Michael Smith, Canon Michael Bourdeaux, Robert Turnham

STOCKTON CROSS   SO5161   MAP 4

Stockton Cross Inn

Kimbolton; A4112, off A49 just N of Leominster; HR6 0HD

Half-timbered pub with local ales and tasty food, huge log fire, and seats in pretty garden

With something of a timeless atmosphere, this pleasant old coaching inn is cosy with delightful nooks and crannies, and logs burning in a large stone fireplace in the character-laden, heavily beamed long bar. It's attractively furnished with a handsome antique settle and old leather chairs and brocaded stools, and at the far end is a woodburning stove with heavy cast-iron-framed tables and sturdy dining chairs, and up a step, a small area has more tables. Old-time prints, a couple of épées on one beam and lots of copper and brass complete the traditional picture; piped music. Served by efficient staff are Wye Valley Butty Bach and Herefordshire Pale Ale and a guest on handpump, local cider and several wines by the glass. There are tables out in the pretty garden. More reports please.

⦿ **Reasonably priced bar food typically includes sandwiches, sausage and mash, sirloin steak, roast black pudding with cider rarebit, poached haddock in smoked prawn sauce, fried lambs liver and bacon with onion gravy, goats cheese and pepper filo parcels, and puddings such as dark chocolate and orange tart.** *Starters/Snacks: £3.95 to £5.95. Main Courses: £8.95 to £13.95. Puddings: £4.50 to £5.50*

Free house ~ Licensee Mike Betley ~ Real ale ~ Bar food ~ (01568) 612509 ~ Children welcome ~ Open mike night second Weds of month ~ Open 12-3, 7-11; 12-3 Sun; closed Sun evening and Mon (except bank hols)

Recommended by Alan and Eve Harding, Reg Fowle, Helen Rickwood, Matthew Shackle, Mrs B Barker

SYMONDS YAT   SO5616   MAP 4

Saracens Head 🛏

Symonds Yat E, by ferry, ie over on the Gloucestershire bank; HR9 6JL

Lovely riverside spot, with contemporary food and a fine range of drinks in a friendly inn; waterside terraces, comfortable bedrooms and plenty to do nearby

It's well worth approaching this popular inn (far beneath the Symonds Yat viewpoint in the Wye gorge) on foot. It's an amusing river walk that crosses the Wye a little downstream by an entertainingly bouncy wire bridge at the Biblins and recrosses at the pub by the long-extant hand-hauled chain ferry that one of the pub staff operates. Picnic-sets out on the waterside terrace make the most of the river view. Inside, it is warm and relaxed with cheerful staff who make you feel at home. The busy, basic flagstoned public bar has Theakstons Old Peculier, Wye Valley Butty Bach and Herefordshire Pale Ale plus a couple of guests such as Butcombe Bitter and Greene King Old Speckled Hen on handpump, and several wines by the glass; pool. There's also a cosy lounge and a modernised bare-boards dining room. As well as bedrooms in the main building (no under-7s), there are two contemporary ones in the boathouse annex.

⦿ **As well as lunchtime sandwiches, ciabatta bruschettas and ploughman's, interesting modern food might include moules marinière, smoked haddock and salmon fishcake with tomato and chive butter, beef burger, gnocchi with sun-dried tomato and pesto cream, roast lamb with cider, honey and mint sauce, fried bream fillet with fennel and orange salad, and roast tomato salad and rib-eye steak.** *Starters/Snacks: £4.50 to £6.95. Main Courses: £9.50 to £14.95. Puddings: £4.50 to £5.50*

Free house ~ Licensees P K and C J Rollinson ~ Real ale ~ Bar food (12-2.30, 6.30-9) ~ Restaurant ~ (01600) 890435 ~ Children welcome ~ Dogs allowed in bar ~ Open 11-11 ~ Bedrooms: £55B/£79B

Recommended by Dr D J and Mrs S C Walker, Malcolm and Pauline Pellatt, Keith and Chris O'Neill, Reg Fowle, Helen Rickwood, Michael Mellers, David and Sue Atkinson, Sue and Dave Harris

TITLEY   SO3359 MAP 6

Stagg

B4355 N of Kington; HR5 3RL

HEREFORDSHIRE DINING PUB OF THE YEAR

Terrific food using tip-top ingredients served in extensive dining rooms, a fine choice of drinks, two-acre garden, comfortable bedrooms

Commendable thought and effort goes into maintaining the high standards at this top-notch dining pub – they even rear their own pigs. The little bar is comfortably hospitable with a civilised atmosphere and a great collection of 200 jugs attached to the ceiling. Hobsons and a guest such as Ludlow are on handpump, and they've several wines by the glass including champagne and pudding wines from a carefully chosen 100-bin wine list, home-made sloe gin, local ciders, perry, apple juice and pressés. Readers also enjoy staying here, in bedrooms above the pub or in the additional rooms within a Georgian vicarage four minutes away, and the breakfasts are wonderful too. The two-acre garden has seats on the terrace and a croquet lawn.

🍴 **Particularly good food, prepared using their own-grown vegetables, pigs and free-range chickens, includes a bar snack menu (not Saturday evenings or Sunday lunch) that might have open sandwiches, devilled kidneys, sausage and mash, and a steak sandwich. A more elaborate menu might have baked pressed pig's head with onion purée, butternut and hazelnut risotto, pasta with squid, chorizo, tomato and chilli, pork belly with haricot beans and apple, monkfish with spinach and beurre blanc and beef fillet with watercress purée, and puddings such as treacle tart with lemon yoghurt ice-cream, bread and butter pudding and rhubarb jelly with rhubarb compote. The british cheeseboard is stupendous, with 23 different ones, mostly from Herefordshire and Wales.** *Starters/Snacks: £3.90 to £7.90. Main Courses: £9.90 to £17.90. Puddings: £5.50 to £7.50*

Free house ~ Licensees Steve and Nicola Reynolds ~ Real ale ~ Bar food ~ Restaurant ~ (01544) 230221 ~ Children welcome ~ Dogs allowed in bar and bedrooms ~ Open 12-3, 6.30-11; closed Sun evening, Mon and first two weeks Nov ~ Bedrooms: £70B/£85B

Recommended by Dennis and Gill Keen, Chris Flynn, Wendy Jones, Alan and Jill Bull, Reg Fowle, Helen Rickwood, Theo, Anne and Jane Gaskin, Norman and Sarah Keeping, Andy Witcomb, Di and Mike Gillam, D and M T Ayres-Regan, Peter and Jean Hoare, Dr and Mrs Michael Smith, P J and R D Greaves, Mr and Mrs W W Burke, David Heath

ULLINGSWICK   SO5949 MAP 4

Three Crowns 🍴 ♀

Village off A465 S of Bromyard (and just S of Stoke Lacy) and signposted off A417 N of A465 roundabout – keep straight on through village and past turn-off to church; pub at Bleak Acre, towards Little Cowarne; HR1 3JQ

Well presented food in busy candlelit dining pub with nice terrace views

With its bustling but civilised atmosphere and rather good food, this attractive dining pub is a jolly nice place for a special meal. Attractive old timbered rooms have open fires, hops strung along the low beams of its smallish bar, traditional settles, old wooden tables, and more usual seats. Gently sophisticated touches such as candles on tables and proper napkins make it all feel that bit more special. Wye Valley and a guest such as Hobsons Best are on handpump, with several wines by the glass or half-bottle, and local apple juice. Tables out on the attractively planted lawn have pleasant views, and a walk down the lane reveals splendid south-easterly views across the county.

🍴 **The interesting food might include fish soup with aioli, chicken liver parfait, grilled rump of beef with grain mustard butter, good steak and kidney pudding, fish casserole, lamb heart with marsala wine gravy, gougère of asparagus with broccoli and blue cheese, and puddings such as rhubarb crème brûlée and chocolate marquise with poached cherries, and a british cheeseboard. Every dish in each course is priced at the same amount.** *Starters/Snacks: £6.50. Main Courses: £14.95. Puddings: £5.00*

Free house ~ Licensee Brent Castle ~ Real ale ~ Bar food (12-2.30, 7-9.30) ~ Restaurant ~
(01432) 820279 ~ Children welcome ~ Dogs allowed in bar and bedrooms ~
Open 12-3, 7-11(10 Sun) ~ Bedrooms: /£95B

Recommended by Alan and Eve Harding, Alan and Jill Bull, Dr and Mrs Michael Smith, Ann and Colin Hunt,
Bernard Stradling, J A Ellis, Noel Grundy, J E Shackleton, Chris Flynn, Wendy Jones

WALFORD
SO5820 MAP 4

Mill Race ♀
B4234 Ross-on-Wye—Lydney; HR9 5QS

**Contemporary furnishings in uncluttered rooms, an emphasis on good quality food
ingredients, attentive staff, terrace tables, nearby walks**

The décor at this spacious dining pub is fresh and contemporary, with a row of strikingly
tall arched windows giving an airy feel to the main area. It's relaxed modern feel and
determination to hit all the right notes makes it a stylish place for a meal. There are
comfortable leather armchairs and sofas on flagstones, as well as smaller chairs around
broad pedestal tables. The granite-topped modern bar counter has Wye Valley ale and a
guest on handpump, and reasonably priced wines by the glass; opposite are a couple of
tall nicely clean-cut tables with matching chairs. The walls are mainly cream or dark pink,
with photographs of the local countryside and good unobtrusive lighting. One wall
stripped back to the stonework has a woodburning stove, also open to the comfortable
and compact dining area on the other side; piped music. There are tables out on the
terrace and a leaflet available at the pub details a pleasant round walk of an hour or so.
More reports please.

🍽 **The pub owns a 1,000-acre farm and woodland which supplies them with game, rabbits,
poultry, beef, fruit and vegetables – other ingredients come from rigorously sourced local
(where possible) suppliers. The menu is not over elaborate, relying instead on the quality
of the produce. Maybe sandwiches, air-dried ham and mozzarella salad, pork sausages and
mash, beef, onion and mushroom pie, and leek and cheddar gratin at lunchtime, with crab
and jerusalem artichoke salad, basil and pea tagliatelle, fish and chips, confit of pork
belly with apple mash and lentil gravy, and steaks in the evening. Puddings might include
baked vanilla cheesecake with strawberry ice-cream and orange and ginger pudding.**
Starters/Snacks: £4.50 to £6.50. Main Courses: £7.00 to £16.00. Puddings: £3.95 to £5.00

Free house ~ Licensee Jane Thompson ~ Real ale ~ Bar food (12-2(2.30 Sat, 3 Sun),
6-9.30(9 Sun)) ~ (01989) 562891 ~ Children welcome ~ Open 11-3, 5-11.30; 10-11.30 Sat;
12-10 Sun

Recommended by Paul Boot, Neil Kellett, Reg Fowle, Helen Rickwood, Bernard Stradling, Nick Lawless

WALTERSTONE
SO3424 MAP 6

Carpenters Arms
*Village signposted off A465 E of Abergavenny, beside Old Pandy Inn; follow village signs,
and keep eyes skinned for sign to pub, off to right, by lane-side barn; HR2 0DX*

Unchanging country tavern in the same family for many years

Vera, the delightful landlady, born at this unchanging cottage tavern some seventy years
ago, took over the business from her mother. For her it's a labour of love and every
customer is welcomed as special. Thankfully, little has changed over the years, its
traditional rooms, with Breconshire Golden Valley and Wadworths 6X tapped from the
cask, have ancient settles against stripped-stone walls, some pieces of carpet on broad
polished flagstones, a roaring log fire in a gleaming black range (complete with pot-iron,
hot-water tap, bread oven and salt cupboard), and pewter mugs hanging from beams. The
snug main dining room has mahogany tables and oak corner cupboards and maybe a big
vase of flowers on the dresser. Another little dining area has old oak tables and church
pews on flagstones. The refurbished outside lavatories are cold but in character. More
reports please.

🍴 Straightforward food such as sandwiches and rolls, soup, chicken suprême, steaks, lamb cutlet with redcurrant and rosemary sauce, a vegetarian choice, daily specials, Sunday roasts, and puddings (made by the landlady's daughter) such as treacle tart and bread and butter pudding. *Starters/Snacks: £4.00 to £4.75. Main Courses: £8.50 to £16.50. Puddings: £4.00*

Free house ~ Licensee Vera Watkins ~ Real ale ~ Bar food ~ Restaurant ~ No credit cards ~ (01873) 890353 ~ Open 12-11

Recommended by MLR, Reg Fowle, Helen Rickwood

WELLINGTON   SO4948   MAP 6

Wellington ◀

Village signposted off A49 N of Hereford; pub at far end; HR4 8AT

Welcoming pub with good food, good beer and a warm log fire

A good all-round approach seems to draw the crowds at this welcoming red-brick establishment, that has good bar and restaurant-style food, well kept beer and friendly efficient service. The interior has been imaginatively reworked to generate a comfortably civilised atmosphere. The bar has big high-backed dark wooden settles, an open brick fireplace with a log fire in winter and fresh flowers in summer, historical photographs of the village, and antique farm and garden tools around the walls; the charming candlelit restaurant is in the former stables and includes a conservatory. Hobsons Best and Wye Valley Butty Bach and HPA are on handpump, and they hold a beer festival in July. Good attentive service; board games and piped music. A pleasant back garden has tables, and they may hold summer barbecues out here.

🍴 Good bar food includes sandwiches, ham, egg and chips, beer-battered fish, and sausage and mash. The restaurant menu (not cheap) might have parma ham and ricotta ravioli with warm basil and sun-dried tomato dressing, fried ducks' hearts on brioche, venison fillet with beetroot and cheese gratin and red wine sauce, fried halibut with celeriac dauphinoise, roast butternut and goats cheese tortellini with creamy pesto dressing, and puddings such as rhubarb crème brûlée and baked vanilla and white chocolate cheesecake with a red berry coulis. *Main Courses: £6.50 to £9.50. Puddings: £5.25*

Free house ~ Licensees Ross and Philippa Williams ~ Real ale ~ Bar food ~ Restaurant ~ (01432) 830367 ~ Children welcome ~ Dogs allowed in bar ~ Open 12-3, 6-11; closed Sun evening, Mon lunchtime

Recommended by Chris Flynn, Wendy Jones, Alan and Eve Harding, Rosemary Richards, Reg Fowle, Helen Rickwood, Dr A J and Mrs Tompsett, H G Dyke, Denys Gueroult

WOOLHOPE   SO6135   MAP 4

Crown

Village signposted off B4224 in Fownhope; HR1 4QP

Cheery local with quickly rotating guest beer and tasty food

In the most sympathetic of arrangements, this genuinely enthusiastic landlord takes great pride in keeping his bustling old pub at the heart of the local community, and in his very quickly rotating guest ale – Willoughby Trust Gold, as we went to press. Wye Valley Bitter is the house beer and there's usually a guest cider too. The bar is straightforwardly traditional, with cream walls, some standing timbers, patterned carpets, dark wood pubby furniture, blush built-in banquettes, cottagey curtained windows and a couple of woodburners; piped music, darts and TV for sports events. There are terrific views from the lovely big garden, which also has darts and cushions in the particularly comfortable smoking shelter; disabled access.

🍴 Well liked food includes mini spiced pork burger with tomato salsa, twice baked hop soufflé with cream and mushroom soup, trout pâté with walnut toast, chilli, beef, ale and mushroom pie, cider-braised ham, egg and chips, summer vegetable risotto and lamb fillet with lemon and mint dressing, and puddings such as eton mess, apple and

blackberry crumble and lavender crème brûlée. *Starters/Snacks: £3.95 to £5.75. Main Courses: £7.95 to £14.95. Puddings: £4.25*

Free house ~ Licensees Matt and Annalisa Slocombe ~ Real ale ~ Bar food (12-2(3 Sun), 6.30-9) ~ (01432) 860468 ~ Children welcome ~ Open 12-2.30, 6.30-11; 12-midnight Fri, Sat; 12-11 Sun

Recommended by Noel Grundy, Reg Fowle, Helen Rickwood, R T and J C Moggridge, Richard Wyld

YARPOLE
SO4664 MAP 6

Bell ⑰

Just off B4361 N of Leominster; HR6 0BD

Modern cooking in a black and white pub, particularly good service, real ales and extensive gardens

Doing really quite well at the moment, this family-run ancient timbered building is a most enjoyable place to visit, with its cheerful welcome, good service and great food. Years ago it was extended into a former cider mill and now comprises a basic tap room, a comfortable beamed lounge bar with a log fire and a large, strikingly high-raftered restaurant featuring a cider press and mill wheel. A mix of traditional furniture, some modern art on the walls and even brass taps embedded into the stone counter, keep it all comfortably relaxed; piped music. Hook Norton Old Hooky, Timothy Taylors Landlord and Wye Valley HPA are on handpump and they've a short but interesting wine list. The golden labrador is called Marcus. There are picnic-sets under green parasols in the lovely flower-filled garden and the pub is very handy for Croft Castle.

🍴 **A good balance of innovative restaurant-style food and cheaper pubbier dishes might include sandwiches, fricassée of snails, fish pie, sausage and mash, confit of lamb belly with garlic salad and chicken, liver and home-made black pudding, home-cured salmon, and local sirloin and rib-eye steaks.** *Starters/Snacks: £4.55 to £6.50. Main Courses: £9.95 to £16.00. Puddings: £5.25*

Enterprise ~ Lease Claude Bosi ~ Real ale ~ Bar food (12-2.30, 6.30-9.30) ~ Restaurant ~ (01568) 780359 ~ Children welcome ~ Dogs allowed in bar ~ Open 12-3, 6.30-11(10.30 Sun); closed Sun evening in winter; closed Mon (except bank hols)

Recommended by Alan and Eve Harding, Reg Fowle, Helen Rickwood, Dennis and Gill Keen, J E Shackleton, Doreen Maddock

LUCKY DIP

Besides the fully inspected pubs, you might like to try these Lucky Dips recommended to us and described by readers (if you do, please send us reports: feedback@goodguides.com).

ALLENSMORE [SO4533]
Three Horseshoes HR2 9AS: 17th-c timbered dining pub with attractive flowers and a good deal of character, well kept Black Sheep in cosy drinking area, enjoyable pub food, warmly friendly licensees; good walking country *(Reg Fowle, Helen Rickwood)*
ALMELEY [SO3351]
Bell HR3 6LF [off A480, A4111 or A4112 S of Kington]: Welcoming family-owned beamed country local with original jug-and-bottle entry lobby, well kept Wye Valley and a guest ale; small lounge with room for just a dozen or so people eating, american chef doing enjoyable food from good value sandwiches to Sun roasts and nice key lime pie; bar with traditional games, no piped music; children and dogs welcome, pleasant garden with decked area and boules *(MLR)*

ASTON CREWS [SO6723]
☆ ***Penny Farthing*** HR9 7LW: Roomy and civilised partly 15th-c pub, well kept Black Sheep, good choice of reasonably priced food and wines, good service; log fires, easy chairs, lots of beams and country bric-a-brac, feature well in bar with skeleton; newspapers, two restaurant areas, one with pretty valley and Forest of Dean views; tables in charming garden, bedrooms *(Julian Cox, Reg Fowle, Helen Rickwood, BB)*
BROMYARD DOWNS [SO6755]
☆ ***Royal Oak*** HR7 4QP [just NE of Bromyard; pub signed off A44]: Beautifully placed open-plan low-beamed 17th-c pub with wide views, carpeted bar with interesting bric-a-brac, dining room with huge bay window; enjoyable bargain food inc some interesting dishes, well kept Spinning Dog ales,

Weston's farm cider, friendly service; flagstoned bar with woodburner, pool, darts, juke box and TV; piped music; walkers welcome, picnic-sets on colourful front terrace, orchard, swings; open all day *(Ann and Colin Hunt, Dave Braisted, BB)*

COLWALL [SO7542]

Colwall Park WR13 6QG [Walwyn Rd (B4218 W of Malvern)]: Unpretentiously comfortable hotel bar with nice pubby atmosphere, good choice of real ales inc Wye Valley, local cider, nice wines by the glass, good food from shortish menu inc generous sandwiches (home-baked bread), friendly staff; dogs allowed, terrace tables, bedrooms *(Roger and Diana Morgan)*

☆ *Wellington* WR13 6HW [A449 Malvern—Ledbury]: Welcoming enthusiastic landlord, wide choice of food from good reasonably priced standards to more imaginative dishes, special set price lunch wkdys; well kept ales such as Goffs, good wines by the glass, neat two-level bar and bright dining area; children welcome *(Chris Evans, M G Hughes, Dave Braisted, Bob Adey, Karen Waller, Patricia Battelley)*

CRASWALL [SO2736]

Bulls Head HR2 0PN [Hay-on-Wye—Llanfihangel Crucorney Golden Valley rd]: Remote stone-built country pub purposefully keeping original low-beamed flagstoned bar with its peeling wallpaper and crumbling plaster; log fire in old cast-iron stove, hatch servery for Hobsons and Wye Valley ales and for farm ciders tapped from the cask; contrasting smart spacious dining area up steps; good-sized enclosed garden with play area, peaceful walking country; cl Mon, Tues except July and Aug *(MLR, LYM)*

EARDISLAND [SO4158]

White Swan HR6 9BD [just off A44]: Interesting old traditional pub in lovely black and white village, well kept Black Sheep and a local guest, enjoyable generous home-made pubby food at reasonable prices; pleasant bar and L-shaped dining area, two good fires, some live music; children and dogs welcome, picnic-sets in back garden, cl Mon lunchtime *(BB, Martin and Pauline Jennings)*

EARDISLEY [SO3149]

Tram HR3 6PG: Old beamed community-active village local with enjoyable home cooking from chef/landlord, two beers such as Wye Valley Butty Bach and Timothy Taylors Landlord; one bar with woodburner, another served by hatch, with log fire and pool, resident cats; dogs welcome, smokers' annex, garden with boules *(H Paulinski, Reg Fowle, Helen Rickwood, MLR, C E Clarke)*

EWYAS HAROLD [SO3828]

Dog HR2 0EX: Three well kept changing ales inc unusual and seasonal ones, pubby food, chatty locals, wknd live music; open all day *(Reg Fowle, Helen Rickwood)*

GORSLEY [SO6726]

Roadmaker HR9 7SW [B4221, just off M50 junction 3]: 19th-c village pub now run by group of retired Gurkha soldiers; tasty pub food from baguettes up, also good nepalese curries (wkdy takeaways), well kept Brains Rev James and Butcombe, large carpeted lounge bar with central log fire, evening restaurant (also Sun lunch), courteous service; no dogs; terrace with water feature, open all day *(Neil and Anita Christopher, Alastair Stevenson, Reg Fowle, Helen Rickwood)*

HAREWOOD END [SO5227]

Harewood End Inn HR2 8JT [A49 Hereford—Ross-on-Wye]: Attractive and comfortable panelled dining lounge with wide choice of reliable food, even Mon night, inc good vegetarian options; efficient staff, well kept ales such as Brains Rev James and Wye Valley, sensibly priced wines, magazines; nice garden and walks, good bedrooms *(Dr and Mrs Michael Smith)*

HEREFORD [SO5139]

Barrels HR1 2JQ [St Owen St]: Two-bar local with excellent low-priced Wye Valley ales from barrel-built counter, several farm ciders, no food, friendly efficient staff; side pool room with games, juke box and big-screen sports TV, lots of modern stained-glass; piped blues and rock, some live jazz, beer festival end Aug; picnic-sets out on partly decked and covered area behind, open all day *(MLR, Reg Fowle, Helen Rickwood, Dr and Mrs Michael Smith, the Didler, BB)*

Bay Horse HR4 0SD [Kings Acre Rd]: Large, freshly refurbished two-level main room and smaller side room, conservatory extension, friendly staff, decent food, and real ales such as Wye Valley, local farm cider; bedrooms *(Reg Fowle, Helen Rickwood, Dr and Mrs Michael Smith)*

Belmont Lodge & Golf Club HR2 9SA [Ruckhall Lane; S of A465]: Non-members welcome, good value Sun carvery with local meats, well kept Wye Valley ale, modern stripped-stone bar, relaxed dining area; terrace views *(Jestyn Phillips, Reg Fowle, Helen Rickwood)*

Black Lion HR4 9DG [Bridge St]: Wye Valley ales, daytime food bargains, plenty of seating, wknd live music (small dance floor); courtyard tables *(Reg Fowle, Helen Rickwood)*

Grapes HR1 2LW [East St]: Substantial old building, good atmosphere with pleasantly broad range of ages, efficient staff, pool; keg beer *(Reg Fowle, Helen Rickwood)*

Herdsman HR4 9HG [Widemarsh St]: Old-fashioned local, busy evenings but quiet during daytime, friendly staff, food inc Sun roasts, wknd live music; open all day *(Reg Fowle, Helen Rickwood)*

Kings Fee HR1 2BP [Commercial Rd]: Big Wetherspoons with good value well kept ales inc one specially brewed for it, good coffee, their usual food, cheerful service; open all day from breakfast time on *(Dave Braisted, Ann and Colin Hunt)*

Lichfield Vaults HR1 2LR [Church St]: Comfortable and roomy half-timbered traditional pub in picturesque pedestrianised street nr cathedral; charming new greek landlord and friendly staff, refurbished front and back bars with chunky olde-worlde décor, beams and dark panelling, wood and quarry-tiled floors, some exposed brickwork, inglenook fireplace; Bass and Theakstons Black Bull and XB from long bar, good value food from sandwiches to greek platters; picnic-sets in pleasant back courtyard, open all day *(Reg Fowle, Helen Rickwood, Phil Bryant)*

Seven Stars HR2 9SL [B4349]: Handy for walks (though often cl lunchtimes and does not do food), with Flowers IPA and two entertaining small dogs; large boules pitch *(Reg Fowle, Helen Rickwood)*

Spread Eagle HR4 9BW [King St]: Busy beamed pub in side alley opp cathedral's west front; several comfortable modern linked areas with chunky wood furniture, generous bar food from pub staples to imaginative dishes, well kept ales such as Wychwood Hobgoblin, efficient staff, upstairs restaurant; children welcome, tables in back courtyard *(Reg Fowle, Helen Rickwood, Keith and Chris O'Neill)*

Stagecoach HR4 0BX [West St]: 16th-c black and white building, comfortable unpretentious lounge with dark oak panelling, Wye Valley ales, friendly service; good value food, low-beamed upstairs restaurant; TV in bar; open all day *(Reg Fowle, Helen Rickwood, Jestyn Phillips)*

HOARWITHY [SO5429]

☆ *New Harp* HR2 6QH [off A49 Hereford—Ross-on-Wye]: Contemporary décor in cosy open-plan country dining pub under newish owners; locally sourced food, friendly service, three changing ales often inc Malvern Hills, 40 bottled beers, local ciders, several wines by the glass, woodburner, flagstones, some stripped masonry and modern artwork; piped music; children and dogs welcome, pretty tree-sheltered garden with stream, picnic-sets and decked area, unusual italianate Victorian church; open all day wknds *(LYM, Reg Fowle, Helen Rickwood)*

HOLMER [SO5042]

Rose Gardens HR1 1LH [Coldwells Rd]: Recently comfortably refurbished, with modern artwork, enjoyable food using local produce, popular bargain OAP wknd roasts, John Smiths or Tetleys; nice countryside *(Reg Fowle, Helen Rickwood)*

KINGSLAND [SO4461]

Angel HR6 9QS: Open-plan 17th-c traditional beamed and timbered dining pub smartened up by new friendly licensees; locally sourced home-made food inc early-bird bargains, well kept Hobsons, Wye Valley Butty Bach and local guest beers, decent wines; comfortable bar with big hot stove, pool, neat restaurant extension, live music Fri; picnic-sets on front grass, back garden *(Jayne Richards, MLR, BB)*

Corner HR6 9RY [B4360 NW of Leominster]: New chef doing good low-priced food at this welcoming 16th-c black and white inn; well kept Hobsons and a guest beer, good wine

choice, friendly service, timbered bar, restaurant in converted hay loft; good value bedrooms *(Alan and Eve Harding, Jayne Richards, Reg Fowle, Helen Rickwood)*

KINGTON [SO2956]

Burton HR5 3BQ [Mill St]: Friendly old coaching inn, two bars, Wye Valley ale, thriving morning coffee trade, good range of bar and restaurant food inc inviting puddings; garden tables, bedrooms, fairly handy for Hergest Croft and good walks *(Dave Braisted)*

☆ *Olde Tavern* HR5 3BX [Victoria Rd, just off A44 opp B4355 – follow sign to Town Centre, Hospital, Cattle Market; pub on right opp Elizabeth Rd, no inn sign but Estd 1767 notice]: Like stepping into an old sepia photograph of a pub (except for the strip lights – it's not at all twee), mainly local ales, back bistro using fresh produce (Fri-Sat evening and Sun lunch), hatch-served side room opening off small plain parlour and public bar; plenty of dark brown woodwork, big windows, old settles and other antique furniture on bare floors, gas fire, china, pewter and curios, welcoming locals; no music or games machines; children welcome, though not a family pub; cl wkdy lunchtimes, outside gents'; licence has been taken over recently and they no longer brew Dunn Plowman ales *(the Didler, BB, Reg Fowle, Helen Rickwood, Pete Baker)*

Oxford Arms HR5 3DR [Duke St]: Recently reopened, with woodburners in main bar on left and dining area on right, smaller lounge with sofas and armchairs, two well kept Spinning Dog ales, good value food *(MLR)*

Royal Oak HR5 3BE [Church Rd]: Cheerful two-bar pub with good value generous pubby food, well kept Hook Norton and Wye Valley, friendly efficient service, restaurant; garden with terrace, neat simple bedrooms, cl Mon lunchtime *(Alan and Eve Harding, MLR)*

LEA [SO6621]

Crown HR9 7JZ [A40 Ross-on-Wye—Gloucester]: Old rambling roadside pub with several well kept changing ales such as Brains Rev James, Ludlow and Wells & Youngs, good coffee; hard-working landlady cooking decent reasonably priced food inc takeaway fish and chips, friendly dog, original features, traditional dining area; plenty of regulars around bar, window seats, open all day *(Guy Vowles, Reg Fowle, Helen Rickwood)*

LEDBURY [SO7137]

☆ *Prince of Wales* HR8 8DL [Church Lane; narrow passage from Town Hall]: Friendly local, charmingly old-fashioned, tucked nicely down narrow cobbled alley; well kept ales such as Hobsons, Sharps Doom Bar and Wye Valley, Weston's cider, foreign bottled beers, bargain simple home-made food from sandwiches up, attentive staff, low-beamed front bars, long back room; a couple of tables in flower-filled yard *(TB, Brian and Jacky Wilson, Reg Fowle, Helen Rickwood, Phil Bryant, Malcolm and Pauline Pellatt)*

LEOMINSTER [SO4958]

Black Horse HR6 8JF [South St]: Two-bar pub smartened up by new owners, three well kept Hobsons ales and guests, interesting bargain lunchtime food in bar, lounge and dining area; woodburner *(MLR, BB)*

Chequers HR6 8AE [Etnam St]: Attractive 15th-c beamed and timbered two-bar pub under new management; well kept ales such as Box Steam Tunnel Vision and Wye Valley Butty Bach, good value food from sandwiches up, cosy window seats, log fires (not always lit), back two-level dining room; children and dogs welcome, courtyard, open all day *(Chris Glasson, David M Smith)*

LETTON [SO3346]

Swan HR3 6DH [A438 NW of Hereford]: Doing well under newish family ownership, friendly atmosphere and accommodating service; good value home-made food inc bargain Sun lunch, two well kept local ales, large opened-up beamed bar; well appointed bedrooms, good garden *(MLR, Reg Fowle, Helen Rickwood)*

LINTON [SO6525]

Alma HR9 7RY: Cheerful unspoilt local in small village, well kept and reasonably priced ales such as Butcombe, Oakham and Three Tuns, no food; good fire, games room with pool, friendly collie and cats, summer music festival; piped music; children very welcome, good-sized garden behind, cl wkdy lunchtimes *(Reg Fowle, Helen Rickwood, TB)*

LITTLE BIRCH [SO5031]

Castle HR2 8BB: Small, friendly and olde-worlde, doing well under newish licensees, with great choice of bargain food inc popular Sun carvery in comfortably homely dining area; Otter, Thwaites and a guest such as Spinning Dog Owd Bull, good young staff, woodburner; lovely garden in quiet country setting *(Victoria Poolman, Reg Fowle, Helen Rickwood)*

LUGWARDINE [SO5441]

☆ *Crown & Anchor* HR1 4AB [just off A438 E of Hereford; Cotts Lane]: Cheerful attractively cottagey timbered pub with good food inc plenty of lunchtime sandwiches and splendid smoked ham and eggs, well kept Butcombe, Timothy Taylors Landlord and guest beers, several wines by the glass; various smallish rooms, some interesting furnishings, fresh flowers, big log fires, daily papers; no piped music or machines; children welcome, pretty garden, open all day *(Dr A J and Mrs Tompsett, Denys Gueroult, Paul Goldman, Martin and Jane Wright, LYM)*

LYONSHALL [SO3355]

Royal George HR5 3JN [A480 S]: Unpretentious beamed and timbered village inn, friendly and well run, with good fresh food inc some lunchtime bargains, Black Sheep, Shepherd Neame Spitfire and good value wines by the glass; log fire in small lounge bar, two pleasant dining areas, old photographs and *Royal George* ship prints; comfortable bedrooms, picnic-sets on back terrace and in flower-filled garden *(Dr A J and Mrs Tompsett, BB)*

MADLEY [SO4138]

Red Lion HR2 9PH: Under new management and kitchen's being refurbished as we went to press; well kept real ale, log fire in comfortable dining area, flagstoned public bar, beams and interesting bric-a-brac, back pool table, friendly labrador called Charlie *(Reg Fowle, Helen Rickwood)*

MORTIMERS CROSS [SO4263]

Mortimers Cross Inn HR6 9PD [A4110/B4362 NW of Leominster]: Sympathetically renovated, with good open fires and high beams giving hunting-lodge look; Black Sheep, Greene King IPA and Wychwood from long counter, comfortable chairs; big-screen sports TV *(Mike and Eleanor Anderson)*

MUCH BIRCH [SO4931]

Pilgrim HR2 8HJ: Substantially extended hotel; lounge bar with comfortable sofas and armchairs leading to dining room and conservatory, well kept Wye Valley ales, good value simple lunches inc Fri OAP bargains and wider restaurant menu; beautiful grounds, terrace tables with sweeping Black Mountains' view, 20 bedrooms *(MLR)*

MUCH DEWCHURCH [SO4831]

Black Swan HR2 8DJ [B4348 Ross-on-Wye—Hay]: Roomy and attractive beamed and timbered pub, partly 14th-c, with warm local atmosphere and log fires in cosy well worn bar and lounge with eating area; well kept Hook Norton ales, decent wines, basic food; pool room with darts, TV, juke box; no credit cards; dogs welcome *(Reg Fowle, Helen Rickwood, Anne Helne)*

MUCH MARCLE [SO6533]

☆ *Slip Tavern* HR8 2NG [off A449 SW of Ledbury]: Unpretentious country pub with splendidly colourful gardens overlooking cider orchards (Weston's Cider Centre is close by); welcoming landlady and friendly informal service, good enterprising food, reasonable prices, Wye Valley ale and local farm cider, attractive conservatory restaurant *(Denys Gueroult, LYM)*

ORLETON [SO4967]

☆ *Boot* SY8 4HN [off B4362 W of Woofferton]: Very popular, but changing hands as we went to press; small, with beams, timbering, even some 16th-c wattle and daub, inglenook fireplace in charming cosy traditional bar, steps up to further bar area, good-sized two-room dining part; has had Hobsons and a guest beer like Ludlow; seats in garden under huge ash tree, barbecue, fenced-in play area *(LYM)*

PEMBRIDGE [SO3958]

Kings House HR6 9HB [East St]: Comfortable and tidy timber-framed former merchant's house, more restaurant than pub; popular with older people, enjoyable food, attentive staff, Wye Valley ale (a bit pricey), log fire, interesting old cameras, framed ephemera and memorabilia, good book collection *(Reg Fowle, Helen Rickwood, Mrs P Sumner)*

New Inn HR6 9DZ [Market Sq (A44)]: Timeless ancient inn overlooking small black and white town's church; unpretentious three-room bar with antique settles, beams, worn flagstones and substantial log fire, one room with sofas, pine furniture and books; Black Sheep and Fullers London Pride, farm cider, generous plain food, friendly service, traditional games, quiet little family dining room; simple bedrooms *(Ann and Colin Hunt, MLR, David Heath, LYM)*

Red Lion HR6 9DS [High St]: Friendly local well placed for walkers, particularly well kept changing ales such as Brains Rev James and Ring o' Bells, hot pies etc; daily papers, darts, dominoes and cribbage; unobtrusive sports TV *(Reg Fowle, Helen Rickwood)*

PETERSTOW [SO5524]

Red Lion HR9 6LH [A49 W of Ross-on-Wye]: Country pub doing well under new family management, good food, well kept real ales, farm cider, friendly staff; open-plan bar with large dining area and modern conservatory, log fires; children welcome, back play area *(Reg Fowle, Helen Rickwood, Ralph Mears)*

PRESTON [SO3841]

Yew Tree HR2 9JT: Small tucked-away pub handy for River Wye, simple and welcoming, with two quickly changing real ales tapped from the cask, no menu but food can be arranged in advance; children welcome, cl lunchtime except Sun *(MLR)*

PRIORS FROME [SO5739]

☆ **Yew Tree** HR1 4EH [aka Len Gees; off A438 at Dormington, then second left and right at T; or off B4224 at Mordiford E of Hereford; OS Sheet 149 map ref 575390]: Friendly country pub with good imaginative food at bargain prices inc carvery, rather more ambitious downstairs restaurant, changing real ales, summer farm cider; terrace, fine views to Black Mountains; cl Mon lunchtime and Tues *(BB, Reg Fowle, Helen Rickwood)*

ROSS-ON-WYE [SO5924]

Kings Head HR9 5HL [High St]: Comfortable, warm and friendly hotel bar with beams and panelling, log-effect fire, lots of old pictures and some cosy armchairs; good generous sensibly priced lunchtime food from sandwiches and baked potatoes up, swift friendly service, two Wye Valley beers perhaps with a guest beer, airy dining extension; dogs welcome, bedrooms, good breakfast, open all day *(Sally and Tom Matson, Mr and Mrs D J Nash, B M Eldridge)*

Vine Tree HR9 5RS [Walford Rd (B4234), Tudorville]: Three real ales, good reasonably priced home cooking in small restaurant; popular with walkers *(Lucien Perring)*

SHOBDON [SO4061]

☆ **Bateman Arms** HR6 9LX: Striking 18th-c inn with enjoyable, generous, bargain food freshly made from local supplies (so can take a while; not Mon), Sun roasts, well kept Wye Valley Butty Bach and guest beers, good wines by the glass; cheerful service, log fire in comfortable beamed bar with relaxed local feel, a couple of shih-tzus, well decorated restaurant; nine bedrooms, good walks, open all day *(Ann and Colin Hunt, Alan and Eve Harding, Reg Fowle, Helen Rickwood)*

STAUNTON-ON-WYE [SO3645]

New Inn HR4 7LR: Compact 16th-c two-bar village pub, pleasantly relaxed and old-fashioned, with well kept Wye Valley ale, good value home-made food lunchtimes and Fri, Sat evenings, friendly landlord and regulars, cosy alcoves; nice garden with quoits and boules, cl Mon *(MLR)*

Portway HR4 7NH [A438 Hereford—Hay-on-Wye, by Monnington turn]: Popular roomy 16th-c pub doing well under newish management, elegant oak-beamed lounge, bargain lunches, wider evening choice, well kept Brains and Thwaites, restaurant; pool league (Tues), entertainment (Fri), busy wknds; bedrooms *(Reg Fowle, Helen Rickwood)*

TARRINGTON [SO6140]

Tarrington Arms HR1 4HX [A438 E of Hereford]: New licensees and some australian influences on the menu such as crocodile steaks, Wye Valley ales; bellringers may be in at 9pm after Fri practice *(Neasa Braham)*

TILLINGTON [SO4645]

☆ **Bell** HR4 8LE: Family-run pub with warmly welcoming landlord, good proper home cooking (so can be a wait) in bar and compact restaurant from good baguettes and other lunchtime snacks up, good value Sun carvery (must book); Wye Valley and a guest beer, neat attentive service, daily papers, comfortable pine furniture with banquettes in lounge extension; children and dogs welcome, steps up to good big garden with play area *(Reg Fowle, Helen Rickwood, Neasa Braham, A Wintour)*

UPPER COLWALL [SO7643]

☆ **Chase** WR13 6DJ [Chase Rd, off B4218 Malvern—Colwall, 1st left after hilltop on bend going W]: Friendly staff in welcoming buoyant two-bar pub, plenty of tables for enjoyable good value generous food from sandwiches to good Sun lunch, good range of real ales and wines by the glass; dogs and walkers welcome, small neat garden, sweeping views; open all day *(Mark Sykes, Dr and Mrs Jackson, Ian and Denise Foster)*

UPTON BISHOP [SO6326]

☆ **Moody Cow** HR9 7TT [B4221 E of Ross-on-Wye]: Recent licensee changes at this smart dining pub; current chef/landlord doing some interesting food (not Sun evening), local real ales and cider; snug areas in L-shaped bar with sandstone walls, slate floor and open fire, cow-related ornaments and pictures, biggish raftered restaurant and second more intimate eating area *(LYM)*

WESTON-UNDER-PENYARD [SO6323]

Weston Cross Inn HR9 7NU [A40 E of Ross-on-Wye]: Substantial creeper-covered stone-built pub overlooking picturesque village; wide range of good value generous food cooked by friendly landlord's wife, special diets covered, Bass, Boddingtons and Brains Rev James, Stowford Press cider, efficient service; comfortably worn-in beamed dining lounge, separate public bar; walkers welcome (they have a walks' map), good-sized garden with plenty of picnic-sets and play area *(BB, Reg Fowle, Helen Rickwood, Sally and Tom Matson)*

WHITBOURNE [SO7156]

Live & Let Live WR6 5SP [off A44 Bromyard—Worcester at Wheatsheaf]: Two-bar pub under newish owners, well kept Wye Valley, enjoyable good value pubby food, good choice of wines by the glass; beams and big log fire, red plush seats and a couple of settees, darts, nice relaxed atmosphere in big-windowed restaurant, attentive service; children welcome, garden with terrace and views *(Chris Evans, BB)*

WHITNEY-ON-WYE [SO2447]

☆ *Rhydspence* HR3 6EU [A438 Hereford—Brecon]: Splendid half-timbered inn on the border with Wales, rambling rooms with heavy beams and timbers, attractive old-fashioned furnishings, log fire in fine big stone fireplace in central bar; Bass and Robinsons, tasty bar food and grills, enjoyable Sun lunch, restaurant; children welcome, but no dogs inside, garden with Wye valley views, comfortable bedrooms *(Dr and Mrs Michael Smith, LYM, Guy Vowles, Rodney and Norma Stubington)*

WIGMORE [SO4168]

Olde Oak HR6 9UJ: Welcoming with olde-worlde front bar and elegant back lounge, well kept Hobsons ales, enjoyable good value generous food, cheerful service; tables in garden behind *(Alan and Eve Harding)*

WINFORTON [SO2946]

Sun HR3 6EA [A438]: Friendly unpretentious pub with enjoyable home-made food all sourced locally; Wye Valley Butty Bach, country-style beamed areas either side of central servery, stripped stone and woodburners; garden tables *(Mr and Mrs J P Syner, MLR, LYM)*

WOOLHOPE [SO6135]

☆ *Butchers Arms* HR1 4RF [off B4224 in Fownhope]: This tucked-away 14th-century inn, a popular previous Main Entry, was closed as we went to press; we expect it to reopen under new management – news, please *(LYM)*

WOONTON [SO3552]

☆ *Lion* HR3 6QN [A480 SE of Kington]: Congenial 17th-c country pub on busy road; warmly welcoming affable landlord and informal atmosphere, landlady using prime local produce for good plain cooking inc gluten-free and dishes suitable for vegans, sandwiches too, Wye Valley ales; inglenook beamed bar with plush banquettes, family restaurant, good views; monthly vintage sports car meeting second Tues of the month; picnic-sets out at front and in back garden with games *(Reg Fowle, Helen Rickwood, Richard and Gillian Fothergill, Denys Gueroult)*

WORMELOW TUMP [SO4930]

Tump HR2 8EJ: Ancient timbered low-ceilinged pub with more modern bar area, Brains Dark and Flowers IPA, well presented food inc good value Sun lunch; interesting locals *(Reg Fowle, Helen Rickwood)*

Several well known guide books make establishments pay for entry, either directly or as a fee for inspection. These fees can run to many hundreds of pounds. We do not. Unlike other guides, we never take payment for entries. We never accept a free meal, free drink, or any other freebie from a pub. We do not accept any sponsorship – let alone from commercial schemes linked to the pub trade. All our entries depend solely on merit. And we are the only guide in which virtually all the Main Entries have been gained by a unique two-stage sifting process: first, a build-up of favourable reports from our thousands of reader-reporters; then anonymous vetting by one of our senior editorial staff.

Hertfordshire

On top form here this year are the White Horse in Hertford, setting a standard for town-centre pubs, and, another good value all-rounder, the family-run Holly Bush out in Potters Crouch. The county's best pub food is to be found at the calmly collected Fox at Willian, and at our Hertfordshire Dining Pub of the Year, the stylishly bustling but still pubby Alford Arms at Frithsden, with its imaginative seasonal cooking. The White Horse in Harpenden, a new entry this year, puts an interesting modern slant on pubbing, and strong Lucky Dip entries are the Bull in Cottered, Crown & Sceptre outside Hemel Hempstead, Catherine Wheel at Gravesend and Wicked Lady near Wheathampstead. The newish Buntingford brewery is quickly making a real mark, and other quite widely available local beers are Tring and the much longer-established McMullens, which owns over 100 pubs.

ALDBURY   SP9612   MAP 4

Greyhound

Stocks Road; village signposted from A4251 Tring—Berkhamsted, and from B4506; HP23 5RT

Spacious yet cosy old dining pub with traditional furnishings, popular food and courtyard

Benches at the front of this handsome virginia creeper-covered inn face a picturesque village green complete with whipping post and stocks and a duck pond lively with wildfowl. The beamed interior shows some signs of considerable age (around the copper-hooded inglenook, for example) towards the front, and is fairly traditionally furnished. The interior becomes more contemporary as you work your way through to leather chairs, a sofa and coffee table, then wicker chairs at big new tables in the airy oak-floored restaurant at the back which overlooks a suntrap gravel courtyard. In winter the lovely warm fire and subtle lighting make it all feel really cosy. Three beers on handpump are usually Badger Best, King & Barnes and Tanglefoot.

🍴 **The tasty food here does draw a crowd, but the friendly staff cope well and meals are served promptly. As well as toasted panini, the short but sensible menu might include thai spiced crab cakes, potted ham hock with piccalilli and toast, scallop and king prawn risotto with parmesan wafers, fried calves liver with crispy bacon and thyme gravy, gnocchi with creamy blue cheese and baby spinach sauce, roast cinnamon-coated fillet of pork with apple mash and black pudding and rib-eye steak.** *Starters/Snacks: £3.75 to £7.50. Main Courses: £9.00 to £16.50. Puddings: £4.55 to £5.55*

Badger ~ Tenant Tim O'Gorman ~ Real ale ~ Bar food (12-2.30, 6.30-9.30; 12-9.30(8 Sun) Sat) ~ Restaurant ~ (01442) 851228 ~ Children welcome ~ Dogs allowed in bar ~ Open 11-11; 11-10.30 Sun ~ Bedrooms: £65S/£75B

Recommended by Roy Hoing, Cathy Robinson, Ed Coombe, Mrs P Sumner, Dennis Jones

---

Post Office address codings confusingly give the impression that some pubs are in Hertfordshire, when they're really in Bedfordshire, Buckinghamshire or Cambridgeshire (which is where we list them).

Valiant Trooper ◀

Trooper Road (towards Aldbury Common); off B4506 N of Berkhamsted; HP23 5RW

Cheery traditional all-rounder with appealing interior, six real ales, generous helpings of pubby food and garden

They keep a jolly decent range of half a dozen well kept beers on handpump at this very pleasant old country pub: Fullers London Pride, local Tring Blonde and Trooper Ale and three guests such as Brakspears Bitter, Everards Tiger and Wadworths 6X, alongside local Millwhite's cider and around a dozen wines by the glass. The first of a series of lovely unspoilt old rooms is beamed and tiled in red and black, with built-in wall benches, a pew and small dining chairs around attractive country tables, and an inglenook fireplace. Further in, the middle bar has spindleback chairs around tables on a wooden floor and some exposed brickwork. The far room has nice country kitchen chairs around individually chosen tables and a woodburning stove, and the back barn has been converted to house a restaurant; dominoes, cribbage and bridge on Monday nights. The enclosed garden has a play house for children and the pub is well placed for walks through the glorious beech woods of the National Trust's Ashridge estate.

⏴ **Quickly served bar food includes home-made pasties and pork pies, sandwiches, well filled baked potatoes, battered fish, mushroom and tarragon tagliatelle, calves liver with bacon and roast chicken and chips. The specials board might have venison sausages, chicken curry and steak, with home-made puddings such as cheesecake and chocolate brownie; popular Sunday lunch.** *Starters/Snacks: £3.50 to £7.50. Main Courses: £9.50 to £13.50. Puddings: £3.00 to £3.50*

Free house ~ Licensee Beth Parmar ~ Real ale ~ Bar food (12-3, 7-9; 12-9(6 Sun) Sat) ~ (01442) 851203 ~ Children welcome ~ Dogs welcome ~ Open 11.30-11; 12-10.30 Sun

Recommended by Peter and Giff Bennett, Gordon Neighbour, Peter Martin, Michael Butler, D J and P M Taylor, N R White, Pam Adsley, Dave Braisted, Tim Maddison

ASHWELL   TL2739   MAP 5

Three Tuns ♀

Off A505 NE of Baldock; High Street; SG7 5NL

Comfortable gently old-fashioned hotel bars, generous helpings of tasty food, and a substantial garden

This well run hotel and pub offers plenty to keep its customers happy – everything from breakfasts to boules in the shaded garden. Wood panelling, relaxing chairs, big family tables, lots of pictures, stuffed pheasants and fish, piped light classical music and antiques lend an air of Victorian opulence to the cosy lounge. The public bar is more modern, with leather sofas on reclaimed oak flooring, and pool, cribbage, dominoes, games machine and TV. They stock a good choice of wines (with 16 by the glass), as well as Greene King IPA, Abbot and a guest on handpump. A big terrace has metal tables and chairs, while a large garden has picnic-sets under apple trees. The charming village is full of pleasant corners and is popular with walkers as the landscape around rolls enough to be rewarding.

⏴ **Nicely presented food might include filled baguettes, chicken liver pâté, herring fillets in a sweet cure marinade, devilled whitebait, melon with raspberry coulis, lamb brochette with mint couscous, mixed vegetable and mushroom curry, chicken and coconut curry, spanish pork casserole and grilled salmon fillet; Sunday roast.** *Starters/Snacks: £4.95 to £6.95. Main Courses: £8.95 to £17.95. Puddings: £5.00*

Greene King ~ Tenants Claire and Darrell Stanley ~ Real ale ~ Bar food (12-2.30, 6.30-9.30; 12-9.30 Sat, Sun) ~ Restaurant ~ (01462) 742107 ~ Children welcome ~ Dogs allowed in bar and bedrooms ~ Open 11-11.30(12.30 Sat); 12-11.30 Sun ~ Bedrooms: £39(£53B)/£59(£69S)(£79B)

Recommended by Colin McKerrow, Grahame Brooks, Gordon Neighbour, Mrs Margo Finlay, Jörg Kasprowski, R T and J C Moggridge, Conor McGaughey, Eithne Dandy

BARKWAY   TL3834   MAP 5

Tally Ho ♀ 🍺

London Road (B1368, which parallels A10 S of Royston); SG8 8EX

Quirky little local with great range of drinks

At the last count, the extraordinary range of drinks in the cottagey little bar here
included 48 wines by the glass, 63 malt whiskies, over 170 different spirits, Aspall's farm
cider and Buntingford Highwayman and a couple of guests, which look as if they are
tapped from big casks behind the bar, but in fact are gently pumped. Everything else
here couldn't be more genuine: the inviting old sofa and cosy armchairs in the big end
bow window, the horsebrasses, the warm log fire and the friendly professional service.
There's another fire through in the dining area angling back on the left – very old-world,
with fresh flowers and silver candelabra, old-fashioned prints on brown ply panelling. At
the end here is a little terrace and beyond the car park is a proper garden with well
spaced picnic-sets, a weeping willow and fruit trees.

🍽 **Bar food might include** potato and celery soup, smoked salmon with rocket and citrus
dressing, chicken caesar salad, steak and mushroom pudding, chicken breast with wild
mushroom sauce, home-made haggis and sirloin steak, and puddings such as apple and
cinnamon crumble, crème brûlée and baked chocolate fondant with banana ice-cream.
Starters/Snacks: £4.95 to £6.95. Main Courses: £8.95 to £17.95. Puddings: £3.95 to £6.95

Free house ~ Licensees Paul and Ros Danter ~ Real ale ~ Bar food (12-2, 6-9) ~ Restaurant ~
(01763) 848389 ~ Children welcome ~ Dogs allowed in bar ~ Open 11.30-11; 12-4 Sun;
closed Sun evening

Recommended by Conor McGaughey, Simon Watkins, R T and J C Moggridge

BATFORD   TL1415   MAP 5

Gibraltar Castle

Lower Luton Road; B653, S of B652 junction; AL5 5AH

**Pleasantly traditional pub with interesting militaria displays, some emphasis on food
(booking advised); pretty terrace**

Tables on a front terrace overlooking a nature reserve, on a pretty little decked area at
the back with lots of flowers and in a tree-lined garden to one side of this neatly kept
welcoming pub are all appealing places to while away a pleasant summer's day. Inside,
you'll find an impressive collection of military paraphernalia, including rifles, swords,
medals, uniforms and bullets (with plenty of captions to read). The long carpeted bar has
a pleasant old fireplace, comfortably cushioned wall benches, and a couple of snugly
intimate window alcoves, one with a fine old clock. Pictures depict its namesake and
various moments in the Rock's history. In one area the low beams give way to soaring
rafters. Several board games are piled on top of the piano, and they've piped music. They
stock a thoughtful choice of wines by the glass, a good range of malt whiskies, and serve
three Fullers beers on handpump; more reports please.

🍽 **Bar food includes** a good range of lunchtime sandwiches, ploughman's, smoked salmon
and rocket fishcake with sweet chilli dressing, risotto of the day, fish and chips, sausage
of the day, steak and kidney pudding, spinach and ricotta with tomato, goats cheese and
mushroom, chicken stuffed with boursin with tarragon sauce and lamb shank with
rosemary gravy; booking is advised for Sunday lunch. *Starters/Snacks: £2.50 to £6.95. Main
Courses: £8.95 to £16.95. Puddings: £3.95 to £4.95*

Fullers ~ Lease Hamish Miller ~ Real ale ~ Bar food (12-2.30(4 Sun), 6-9; not Sun evening) ~
Restaurant ~ (01582) 460005 ~ Children if eating ~ Dogs allowed in bar ~
Open 11.30-11(12 Fri, Sat); 12-10.30 Sun

Recommended by Michael Dandy, David Jackson, Pat and Roger Davies, Adrian Johnson, David and Ruth Shillitoe

---

If you know a pub's ever open all day, please tell us.

EPPING GREEN

TL2906   MAP 5

Beehive

Off B158 SW of Hertford, via Little Berkhamsted; back road towards Newgate Street and Cheshunt; SG13 8NB

Cheerful bustling country pub, popular for its good value food

During the winter months, a warm woodburning stove in a brown-painted panelled corner forms the heart of this well run pub. The pleasantly traditional bar is cosily chatty with a low shiny ceiling, wheelback chairs and brocaded benches around dark tables on a patterned green carpet. Adnams, Greene King IPA and Old Speckled Hen are on handpump alongside a good range of wines by the glass; service is prompt and pleasant; piped music. Picnic-sets are out on a neat lawn between the low tiled weatherboarded building and the quiet country road; good woodland walks nearby.

As well as good sandwiches, bar food might include crab and mango salad, smoked haddock and spring onion fishcakes, battered fish, steak, mushroom and ale pudding, penne with roast vegetables in pesto cream sauce, baked cod with bacon, mushroom and thyme sauce, and puddings such as vanilla and rosemary crème brûlée and white chocolate and blueberry sponge pudding. *Starters/Snacks: £3.95 to £8.95. Main Courses: £8.95 to £15.95. Puddings: £4.25*

Punch ~ Lease Martin Squirrell ~ Real ale ~ Bar food (12-2.30, 6-9.30; 12-8(4 in winter) Sun) ~ (01707) 875959 ~ Children welcome ~ Open 11.30-3, 5.30-11; 11.30-11 Sat; 12-10.30 Sun; closed Sun evening, Sat afternoon in winter

Recommended by David Jackson, Professors Alan and Ann Clarke, J Marques, Gordon Neighbour

FLAUNDEN

TL0101   MAP 5

Bricklayers Arms ♀

Off A41; Hogpits Bottom; HP3 0PH

Cosy country restaurant with an emphasis on fairly elaborate food (not cheap) and a very good wine list

Most people at this low brick and tiled virginia creeper-covered dining pub are here for the calmly civilised dining atmosphere. The well refurbished low-beamed bar is snug and comfortable, with roaring winter log fires and dark brown wooden wall seats with pink plush cushions. Stubs of knocked-through oak-timbered walls keep some feeling of intimacy in three areas that were originally separate rooms. The extensive wine list includes about 20 by the glass, and they've Fullers London Pride, Greene King IPA and Abbot and a guest or two from brewers such as Tring and Rebellion on handpump. This is a lovely peaceful spot in summer, when the beautifully kept old-fashioned garden with its foxgloves against sheltering hedges comes into its own. Just up the Belsize road there's a path on the left which goes through delightful woods to a forested area around Hollow Hedge.

Some of the herbs and vegetables come from the pub's garden, and they smoke their own meats and fish. Food, which can be very good, might include brochette of tiger prawns with a light curry sauce, a plate of their own smoked fish with lemon coriander butter and tomato chutney, puff pastry top with mushrooms in a calvados cream, fried bass with smoked paprika and scallop cream sauce, battered cod with home-made tartare sauce, confit leg of duck with sweet and sour orange jus, beef fillet with green peppercorn and brandy cream sauce, and puddings such as crêpe filled with Cointreau mascarpone cream with citrus jus and apple, rhubarb bread and butter pudding. *Starters/Snacks: £5.00 to £12.00. Main Courses: £13.00 to £19.50. Puddings: £4.50 to £7.00*

Free house ~ Licensee Alvin Michaels ~ Real ale ~ Bar food (12-2.30(3.30 Sun); 6-9.30(8.30 Sun)) ~ Restaurant ~ (01442) 833322 ~ Dogs allowed in bar ~ Open 12-11.30(12.30 Sat, 10.30 Sun)

Recommended by Sue Griffiths, Martin Terry, Bruce and Penny Wilkie, Alex Gifford, G K Smale, Peter and Giff Bennett, Peter and Jan Humphreys

FRITHSDEN   TL0109   MAP 5

Alford Arms 🍽 🍷

From Berkhamsted take unmarked road towards Potten End, pass Potten End turn on right,
then take next left towards Ashridge College; HP1 3DD

HERTFORDSHIRE DINING PUB OF THE YEAR

Thriving dining pub with chic interior, good food from an imaginative menu and a
thoughtful wine list

Still going very strong, this on-the-ball place is one of the county's most popular dining
pubs. That said, they remain determined to keep a pubby feel, at least in one area, so
you might find a few locals (and perhaps a jack russell perched on a stool) chatting at
the bar. Usually, though, it's full to the brim with cheerful diners so service can slow
down just a little, and you do need to book. The fashionably elegant but understated
interior has simple prints on pale cream walls, with blocks picked out in rich Victorian
green or dark red, and an appealing mix of good antique furniture (from Georgian chairs
to old commode stands) on bare boards and patterned quarry tiles. It's all pulled
together by luxurious opulently patterned curtains; darts and piped jazz. All the wines
on their list are european, with most of them available by the glass, and they've
Brakspears, Flowers Original, Marstons Pedigree and Rebellion IPA on handpump. The pub
stands by a village green and is surrounded by lovely National Trust woodland. There are
plenty of tables outside.

🍽 The seasonally changing menu might include starters such as pepper squid with red
pepper sauce, cornish crab, spring onion and chilli vol-au-vent, orange, pea shoot and
sultana salad, pork belly on calamari and chorizo stew with osso bucco sauce, spaghetti
with tiger prawns, bacon, dried tomatoes and chilli oil, lamb suet pudding with crispy
sweetbreads and parsley sauce, grilled halloumi, aubergine and courgette pastry stack and
rib-eye steak with café de paris butter, and puddings such as vanilla and gingerbread
cheesecake, lemon curd crème brûlée and warm fig chocolate brownie with crème fraîche
ice-cream; Sunday roast. *Starters/Snacks: £3.75 to £7.25. Main Courses: £11.25 to £16.75.*
Puddings: £4.25 to £6.75

Salisbury Pubs ~ Lease Richard Coletta ~ Real ale ~ Bar food (12-2.30(3 Sat, 4 Sun),
6.30(7 Sun)-9.30(10 Sat)) ~ Restaurant ~ (01442) 864480 ~ Children welcome ~
Dogs allowed in bar ~ Open 11-11; 12-10.30 Sun

Recommended by Gordon Davico, Michael Dandy, Peter and Giff Bennett, Michael J Boniface, J Marques,
Susan and Nigel Brookes, John Faircloth, Tim Maddison, John and Joyce Snell, Howard Dell, Cathy Robinson,
Ed Coombe, Giles Barr, Eleanor Dandy, David Restarick

HARPENDEN   TL1312   MAP 5

White Horse

Redbourn Lane, Hatching Green (B487 just W of A1081 roundabout); AL5 2JP

Smart up-to-date dining pub with civilised bar side

We inspected this a few weeks following the collapse, in spring 2009, of its parent
company, linked to the restaurateur Jean-Christophe Novelli. Though there had to be a
question mark over the pub's future as it was in the hands of administrators, we were
impressed by its style – and, given the circumstances, by the fact that it had plenty of
cheerful customers and a good confident atmosphere. So fingers crossed that it ends up
in good hands. The smallish front bar has Adnams on handpump as well as a good range
of wines by the glass and an imposing row of keg beer founts; modern brown leather
seating contrasts with traditional white-painted plank panelling. On the right, a cosy
roomful of dark red leather armchairs has an odd lighting unit masquerading as a wall of
old books (rather droll unless you view stripping leather-bound books of their spines as
mutilation). It looks past a rack of wine bottles into the main back dining area: long,
pale grey button-back banquettes and matching chairs, maroon walls, pale floorboards.
There are modern decorative touches throughout, the piped music is fairly unobtrusive,
service by neat staff is prompt and helpful, and they do good coffee and have the daily
papers. An extensive newish stone terrace has plenty of teak tables.

🍴 The very wide food choice runs from inventive lunchtime sandwiches served with chips to tapas boards priced by how many you order and sharing plates, to nicely tweaked staples such as sausage and mash, fish and chips with mint pea purée and seafood bolognese. There's also a more elaborate restaurant menu. *Starters/Snacks: £4.50 to £10.00*

Free House ~ Licensee Harwood Warrington ~ Real ale ~ Bar food (12-3, 6-9.30(9 Sun); sandwiches all day) ~ Restaurant ~ (01582) 469290 ~ Children welcome ~ Dogs welcome ~ Open 12-11(midnight Sat, 10.30 Sun)

Recommended by Judi Lambeth, Michael Dandy

HERTFORD
TL3212 MAP 5

White Horse 🍺 £

Castle Street; SG14 1HH

Nine real ales at traditional town-centre local

The chatty landlord at this unpretentious tucked-away little pub keeps a terrific range of about eight Fullers beers and possibly a guest such as Adnams, with more during their May and August bank holiday beer festivals; also a dozen country wines. Parts of the timber-framed building date from the 14th c and you can still see Tudor brickwork in the three quietly cosy upstairs family rooms. Its two downstairs rooms are small and homely, the one on the left being more basic, with bare boards, some brewery memorabilia and a few rather well worn tables, stools and chairs. A warming open fire separates it from the more comfortable beamed right-hand bar, which has a winged leather armchair, some old local photographs and a red-tiled floor; bar billiards and TV for some sports events. Two simple benches out on the pavement face the castle, and there are tables and chairs on a back terrace with hanging baskets and window boxes.

🍴 Very inexpensive pubby food includes sandwiches, baguettes, ploughman's, chilli, lasagne, sausages, Sunday roast and, on summer Thursday evenings, maybe sirloin steak and chicken. *Starters/Snacks: £3.25 to £4.95. Main Courses: £6.95 to £11.95. Puddings: £4.00 to £4.95*

Fullers ~ Lease John Ash ~ Real ale ~ Bar food (12-2(1-3 Sun)) ~ No credit cards ~ (01992) 501950 ~ Children till 9pm ~ Dogs welcome ~ Jazz first Sun of month ~ Open 12-3, 5-11; 12-(10.30 Sun)midnight Fri, Sat

Recommended by Pat and Tony Martin, LM, Gordon Tong, N R White

POTTERS CROUCH
TL1105 MAP 5

Holly Bush 🍺 £

2.25 miles from M25 junction 21A: A405 towards St Albans, then first left, then after a mile turn left (ie away from Chiswell Green), then at T-junction turn right into Blunts Lane; can also be reached fairly quickly, with a good map, from M1 exits 6 and 8 (and even M10); AL2 3NN

Lovingly kept cottage with gleaming furniture, fresh flowers and china, well kept Fullers beers, good value food and an attractive garden

Everything at this pretty wisteria-swamped white building is immaculately kept. Thoughtfully positioned fixtures create the illusion that there are lots of different rooms – some of which have the feel of a smart country house. In the evening, neatly placed candles cast glimmering light over darkly varnished tables, all sporting fresh flowers. There are quite a few antique dressers (several filled with plates), a number of comfortably cushioned settles, a fox's mask, some antlers, a fine old clock, daily papers, and, on the left as you go in, a big fireplace. The long, stepped bar has particularly well kept Fullers Chiswick, ESB, London Pride and a Fullers seasonal beer on handpump. Service is calm, friendly and sincere, even when they're busy. Behind the pub, the fenced-off garden has a nice lawn, handsome trees and sturdy picnic-sets – it's a very pleasant place to sit in summer. Though the pub seems to stand alone on a quiet little road, it's only a few minutes' drive from the centre of St Albans (or a pleasant 45-minute walk).

⑪ Food here offers impressive value for money, so no wonder it's so popular. The lunchtime menu is still very pubby – sandwiches, baked potatoes, ploughman's, burgers and platters, with heartier evening dishes (still good value) such as mushroom stroganoff, pork loin steak with cheese and parsley crust, roast chicken breast with tarragon and mustard sauce and bass with prawns and parsley butter. *Starters/Snacks: £3.50 to £8.50. Main Courses: £8.50 to £14.00. Puddings: £3.90*

Fullers ~ Tenants Ray and Karen Taylor ~ Real ale ~ Bar food (12-2(2.30 Sun), 6-9 (not Sun-Tues)) ~ (01727) 851792 ~ Open 12-2.30, 6-11(7-10.30 Sun)

Recommended by Michael Butler, Peter and Giff Bennett, J Marques, Amy Farnham, John and Joyce Snell, Paul Goldman, Paul Humphreys, Julie Oakes

PRESTON   TL1824   MAP 5

Red Lion 🍺

Village signposted off B656 S of Hitchin; The Green; SG4 7UD

Homely village local with changing beers and neatly kept colourful garden

As the result of a Whitbread threat back in 1982 to close this nice old village pub, it became the first in the country to be acquired by a village and to this day it extends a cheery, inviting welcome to locals and visitors alike. The main room on the left is pubbily simple with sturdy well varnished pub furnishings including padded kitchen-kitchen chairs and cast-iron-framed tables on a patterned carpet, a log fire in a brick fireplace, and foxhunting prints. The somewhat smaller room on the right has steeplechasing prints, some varnished plank panelling, and brocaded bar stools on flagstones around the servery; dominoes. They keep very good beer, with Fullers London Pride and Wells & Youngs alongside three regularly changing guests from brewers such as Adnams, Crouch Vale and Harviestoun. They also tap farm cider from the cask, have several wines by the glass (including an english house wine), a perry and mulled wine in winter. A few picnic-sets out on the front grass face across to lime trees on a peaceful village green. At the back, a pergola-covered terrace gives way to many more picnic-sets (with some shade from a tall ash tree) and a neatly kept colourful herbaceous border in a good-sized sheltered garden beyond.

⑪ Reasonably priced changing bar food might include sandwiches and ploughman's, fish pie, chicken curry, ham, egg and chips, grilled plaice with caper butter, steaks, and chocolate fudge cake. *Starters/Snacks: £3.75 to £4.75. Main Courses: £6.75 to £8.95. Puddings: £3.75*

Free house ~ Licensee Raymond Lamb ~ Real ale ~ Bar food (12-2, 7-8.30; not Sun evenings and Tues) ~ (01462) 459585 ~ Dogs welcome ~ Open 12-3(4 Sat), 5.30-11; 12-4, 7-10.30 Sun

Recommended by Ben Williams, Ross Balaam, Martin Wilson, John and Joyce Snell

SARRATT   TQ0498   MAP 5

Cock

Church End: a very pretty approach is via North Hill, a lane N off A404, just under a mile W of A405; WD3 6HH

Plush pub popular with older dining set at lunchtime and families outside during summer weekends; Badger beers

A play area and summer bouncy castle will keep children happily entertained, leaving parents to take in open country views from picnic-sets on the pretty, sheltered lawn and terrace. Picnic-sets in front look out across a quiet lane towards the churchyard. A latched front door opens into the homely carpeted snug with a vaulted ceiling, original bread oven and a cluster of bar stools where you're likely to find an older set making the most of the good value OAP lunchtime meals (also Tuesday evening). Through an archway, the partly oak-panelled cream-walled lounge has a lovely log fire in an inglenook, pretty Liberty-style curtains, pink plush chairs at dark oak tables, lots of interesting artefacts, and several namesake pictures of cockerels; Badger Best, Sussex,

Tanglefoot and a Badger guest on handpump; piped music. The restaurant is in a nicely converted barn.

🍴 **Bar food includes sandwiches, ploughman's, whitebait, cheese and broccoli tagliatelle, chicken caesar salad, battered cod, steak and ale pie and sirloin steak.** *Starters/Snacks: £4.95 to £6.25. Main Courses: £9.95 to £15.95. Puddings: £4.95*

Badger ~ Tenants Brian and Marion Eccles ~ Real ale ~ Bar food (12-2.30(4 Sun), 6-9; not Sun, Mon evenings) ~ Restaurant ~ (01923) 282908 ~ Children welcome if eating ~ Dogs allowed in bar ~ Jazz Sun afternoon and alternate Mon evenings ~ Open 12-11(9 Sun)

Recommended by C Galloway, Howard Dell, D J and P M Taylor, Peter and Judy Frost, David Jackson, Susan and John Douglas, Roy Hoing, N R White, Peter and Giff Bennett

TRING

SP9211   MAP 5

Robin Hood
Brook Street (B486); HP23 5ED

Really welcoming pub with good beer and good pubby food

The several immaculately kept smallish linked areas at this carefully run pub have quite a homely feel. The main bar is pleasingly traditional with banquettes, cast-iron stools and standard pub chairs on spotless bare boards or carpets. Early in the evening, regulars pop in to occupy the stools lined along the counter, then later on, couples arrive for the tasty food. Beers include five very well kept Fullers brews and a guest such as Brakspears. Towards the back, you'll find a conservatory with a vaulted ceiling and woodburner. The licensees' two little yorkshire terriers are called Buddy and Sugar; piped music. There are tables out on the small pleasant back terrace.

🍴 **Enjoyably pubby food includes filled baguettes, mini lamb koftas with mint raita, thai spiced fishcakes, ham, egg and chips, steak and kidney or chicken and leek pudding, scampi, steak and fish specials, puddings such as crème brûlée and chocolate fudge cake; Tuesday and Thursday nights are sausage night.** *Starters/Snacks: £3.65 to £5.95. Main Courses: £7.95 to £19.95. Puddings: £4.00*

Fullers ~ Tenants Terry Johnson and Stewart Canham ~ Real ale ~ Bar food (12-2.15, 6-9.15; not Sun evening) ~ (01442) 824912 ~ Children welcome ~ Dogs welcome ~ Open 11.30-3, 5.30-11; 12-4, 6-11 Sat; 12-4, 7-11 Sun

Recommended by Tracey and Stephen Groves, John Branston, Ross Balaam

WILLIAN

TL2230   MAP 5

Fox
A mile from A1(M) junction 9; A6141 W towards Letchworth then first left; SG6 2AE

Civilised dining pub with good food from pubby favourites to more imaginative dishes, nice range of drinks

The contemporary styling at this well run dining pub is fresh and clean-cut. There are comfortable light wood chairs and tables on stripped boards or big ceramic tiles, with modern pictures on white or pastel walls. Carefully lit, with boxy contemporary bar stools running along its pale blue frontage, the modern counter serves Adnams, Fullers London Pride, Woodfordes Wherry, and a guest from a brewer such as Brancaster, from handpumps, a good wine list with just over a dozen by the glass, and a nice range of spirits; well reproduced piped music, relatively unobtrusive TV. Pleasantly attentive young staff seem to really enjoy their work. A side terrace has smart tables under cocktail parasols, and there are picnic-sets in the good-sized garden behind, below the handsome tower of the 14th-c All Saints church.

🍴 **As well as sandwiches, the well executed changing menu might include starters such as cumin spiced butternut soup with coriander crème fraîche, moroccan spiced chickpea, carrot and coriander cake with apricot relish, oysters, black pepper tempura squid with chorizo and tomato salad, main courses such as jerusalem artichoke and pea risotto, battered cod with pea purée, sausage and mash, tiger prawns in linguine with sweet**

chilli, lime and basil dressing and sirloin steak, and puddings such as lemon and cinnamon crème brûlée with orange shortbread and warm rhubarb and custard tart with crumble topping, and a british cheese platter; they add service automatically.
Starters/Snacks: £4.90 to £9.95. Main Courses: £8.95 to £13.95. Puddings: £5.25 to £5.50

Free house ~ Licensee Cliff Nye ~ Real ale ~ Bar food (12-2(2.45 Sun), 6.45-9.15; not Sun evening) ~ Restaurant ~ (01462) 480233 ~ Children welcome ~ Dogs welcome ~ Open 12-11(midnight Fri, Sat, 10.30 Sun)

Recommended by Ross Balaam, Julian and Jill Tasker, Allan Finlay, Gordon Neighbour, J Marques, David and Ruth Shillitoe

LUCKY DIP

Besides the fully inspected pubs, you might like to try these Lucky Dips recommended to us and described by readers (if you do, please send us reports: feedback@goodguides.com).

ASHWELL [TL2639]
Rose & Crown SG7 5NP [High St]: Friendly traditional local with enjoyable food inc good baguettes and fish and chips, Greene King ales; 16th-c beams, lovely log fire, candlelit restaurant, games in plainer end of L-shaped bar; big pretty country garden (*Andrew Marrison*)
AYOT GREEN [TL2213]
Waggoners AL6 9AA [off B197 S of Welwyn]: Refurbished former 17th-c coaching inn doing well under new french owners; food in cosy low-beamed bar, more upmarket french cooking in comfortable good-sized restaurant extension, friendly attentive staff, good wine list, real ales; attractive and spacious suntrap back garden with sheltered terrace (some A1(M) noise), wooded walks nearby (*Leon Warner, Ben Williams, BB, Alex Gifford, J Marques*)
BELSIZE [TL0300]
Plough WD3 4NP: Small friendly local doing well under new owners, central bar and barn-like beamed lounge with open fire, Tring beers, enjoyable good value home-made food; picnic-sets in nice garden, good walks (*Andrew Scarr, Roy Hoing*)
BERKHAMSTED [SP9808]
Lamb HP4 1AJ [High St]: Two-bar pub, not over-modernised, in an old building; prompt good-humoured service, decent food from sandwiches and pubby staples to more elaborate blackboard dishes, Adnams, Fullers London Pride, Greene King IPA and Tring Ridgeway (*John Saul*)
Old Mill HP4 2NB [A4251, Hemel end]: Huge rambling dining pub, attractive layout, three well kept ales such as Black Sheep, very wide choice of enjoyable food (usually something available all day), friendly efficient staff, two good fires; tables outside, some overlooking unspectacular stretch of Grand Union Canal (*BB, Ross Balaam*)
BOURNE END [TL0206]
☆ ***Three Horseshoes*** HP1 2RZ [Winkwell; just off A4251 Hemel—Berkhamsted]: Friendly recently renovated 16th-c family pub in charming setting by unusual swing bridge over Grand Union Canal; low-beamed three-room core with inglenooks, well kept

Adnams Broadside, Black Sheep and Shepherd Neame Spitfire, reasonably priced food all day, efficient uniformed staff; bay-windowed extension overlooking canal; children welcome, tables out by water, open all day (*LYM, John Branston, John Faircloth*)
BOXMOOR []
Swan HP1 2RA [London Rd; A4251]: Tastefully refurbished with well thought-out eating and sitting areas, enjoyable reasonably priced food, decent wine list, good choice of beer, good service (*Geoff Goddard*)
BRAUGHING [TL3925]
Axe & Compass SG11 2QR [just off B1368; The Street]: Pleasant country local in pretty village with ford, enjoyable straightforward food inc good steaks, real ales, friendly service; modern décor and mix of furnishings in two roomy bars (one an unusual corner-shape) and restaurant; well behaved dogs and children welcome (*Eleanor Dandy, Giles Barr, Maureen and Keith Gimson*)
BURNHAM GREEN [TL2516]
White Horse AL6 0HA [off B1000 N of Welwyn; Whitehorse Lane]: Well run village-green dining pub restored after 2001 fire, a mix of modern and traditional rustic décor inc attractive 17th-c beamed core; enjoyable popular food, friendly young staff, McMullens ales; good-sized pretty garden behind (*N R White, LYM*)
CHANDLERS CROSS [TQ0698]
☆ ***Clarendon*** WD3 4LU [Redhall Lane]: Reopened after major refurbishment with emphasis now on dining; busy ultra-modern bar (walkers welcome), lounge with fire, two restaurants, food from bar snacks to pricey upmarket british cooking, Fullers London Pride and Greene King, smart competent staff; children welcome, small attractive garden, woodland and canal walks (*Peter and Giff Bennett*)
CHAPMORE END [TL3216]
☆ ***Woodman*** SG12 0HF [off B158 Wadesmill—Bengeo; pub signed 300 yards W of A602 roundabout; OS Sheet 166 map reference 328164]: Peaceful early Victorian country local with newish landlord, plain seats around stripped pub tables, floor tiles or

broad bare boards, working period fireplaces; well kept Greene King beers tapped from the cask, minimal lunchtime food (also a winter Sun roast and summer barbecues), backgammon, shove-ha'penny and cribbage; dogs welcome, children till 8pm, picnic-sets out in front under a couple of walnut trees, bigger back garden with fenced play area and boules, open all day Sat, cl Mon lunchtime (LYM)

CHIPPERFIELD [SP0401]

Royal Oak WD4 9BH [The Street]: Two immaculate small bars, enjoyable food from lunchtime snacks and sandwiches up, Adnams Broadside and Wells & Youngs Special, friendly relaxed atmosphere, log fire, vintage car photographs (Peter and Judy Frost)

Two Brewers WD4 9BS [The Common]: Recent refurbishment at this attractive 18th-c country hotel housing popular bay-windowed Chef & Brewer, roomy linked areas, two log fires, pretty décor; good food all day from sandwiches up inc set price offers, good choice of wines by the glass, well kept Adnams, Fullers and Wells & Youngs, pleasant staff; provision for children, disabled facilities, terrace seating, 20 comfortably redone bedrooms, nice spot on common and handy for M25, open all day (Peter and Judy Frost, LYM)

CHISWELL GREEN [TL1304]

Three Hammers AL2 3EA [just S of St Albans; Watford Rd]: Good Ember Inn with enjoyable well priced food, up to six ales, decent wines, friendly competent staff; several areas on different levels around central bar, lots of beams (some quite low), comfortable sofas and armchairs by fireplace, abstracts and photographs of old St Albans; no children inside; garden tables (Val and Alan Green, KC, Jack and Sandra Clarfelt)

CHORLEYWOOD [TQ0395]

☆ *Black Horse* WD3 5EG [Dog Kennel Lane, the Common]: Very welcoming to all, inc children, walkers and dogs (biscuit basket on mantelpiece), good value food (not Mon) from good sandwiches up, OAP lunch some days, well kept Adnams, Shepherd Neame Spitfire, Wadworths 6X and Wells & Youngs Bitter and Bombardier, decent wines (and tea and coffee), quick helpful service; plenty of good-sized tables under low dark beams in attractively divided traditional room with thick carpet, daily papers, coal-effect fire; no music; family area, separate bar with SkyTV; pretty setting, picnic-sets overlooking common (Tom Evans, Roy Hoing, Peter and Giff Bennett, Peter and Judy Frost)

☆ *Gate* WD3 5SQ [Rickmansworth Rd]: Open-plan family dining pub with clean-cut and attractive contemporary décor, wide range of enjoyable up-to-date food inc sharing plates; Bass and Timothy Taylors Landlord, Aspall's cider, good choice of wines by the glass, genial and helpful largely antipodean staff; piped music; plenty of garden tables

(Michael Dandy, John Branston, Tom Evans, LYM)

Land of Liberty Peace & Plenty WD3 5BS [Long Lane, Heronsgate; just off M25 junction 17]: Welcoming unpretentious open-plan pub with relaxed chatty atmosphere, Red Squirrel, Tring and other interesting ales, Weston's cider and perry, belgian bottled beers, good soft drinks' choice, enjoyable bar lunches; brewery memorabilia, cosy corner banquette, bare boards and warm fire; no music or mobiles; skittles; no children inside; dogs welcome, garden behind, open all day (LM, N R White)

Rose & Crown WD3 5LW [Common Rd, off A404 W of M25 junction 18]: Cheerful unpretentious pub, pretty setting facing common; well kept Fullers London Pride, sofa and oak settles in compact bar with homely old-fashioned atmosphere and log fire, enjoyable fresh food (not Sun evening or Mon), pleasant staff, small dining room; picnic-sets outside, two-bed cottage adjacent (Peter and Judy Frost)

COLE GREEN [TL2811]

Cowper Arms SG14 2NL [Cole Green Lane]: Friendly and tastefully reworked M&B beamed dining pub, popular for varied food from sandwiches and bar snacks to restaurant meals, helpful staff; roaring fire, good choice of wines by the glass, Adnams, Timothy Taylors Landlord and Wells & Youngs Bombardier, pleasant setting (Peter and Margaret Glenister, Mr and Mrs Robin Marson)

COTTERED [TL3229]

☆ *Bull* SG9 9QP [A507 W of Buntingford]: Good well run dining pub with airy low-beamed front lounge, good furniture on stripped wood, log fire; good if not cheap food from sandwiches up (may add 10% service charge), Greene King IPA and Abbot, decent wines; unobtrusive piped music; no prams, no under-7s Mon-Sat, big garden with tables under majestic old trees, open all day Sun (Lois Dyer, J Marques, Charles Gysin, Gordon Neighbour, R T and J C Moggridge, Pam and Wally Taylor, LYM, Jack and Sandra Clarfelt)

DATCHWORTH [TL2717]

☆ *Horns* SG3 6RZ [Bramfield Rd]: Pretty flower-decked Tudor pub facing small green, low beams and big inglenook one end, high rafters and rugs on patterned bricks the other, attractive décor; wide choice of good reasonably priced food from proper sandwiches to splendid paella (best to book Sun), quick friendly service, real ales inc one brewed for the pub; picnic-sets on front lawn (LYM, Gordon Neighbour)

Tilbury SG3 6TB [Watton Rd; off A602 SE of Stevenage]: Civilised and attractively timbered two-room dining pub with imaginative seasonal food and good value Sun lunch, good choice of wines; big garden (J Marques)

ESSENDON [TL2608]

Candlestick AL9 6BA [West End Lane]: Busy McMullens country pub with their ales, good service and bargain food under new landlord, comfortable two-room mock-Tudor lounge, log fires, bright public bar; plenty of seats outside *(BB, Gordon Neighbour)*

Rose & Crown AL9 6HW [High Rd (B158)]: Recently refurbished family-run pub with good choice of enjoyable local food (but veg extra), pleasant attentive staff, Greene King beer; terrace and garden with picnic-sets *(Peter and Margaret Glenister, Gordon Neighbour)*

GRAVELEY [TL2327]

Waggon & Horses SG4 7LE [High St (B197), a mile from A1(M) junction 8]: Attractive former coaching inn with enjoyable generous fair-priced food from sandwiches up, well kept Adnams, Flowers and Fullers London Pride, good wine choice, friendly staff; comfortable beamed and timbered lounge, big open fire; secluded streamside back garden with terrace, duck pond over road *(Jerry Brown)*

GRAVESEND [TL4325]

☆ *Catherine Wheel* SG11 2LW [off A120 at Little Hadham]: Dining pub rebuilt in sympathetic style after 15th-c original burnt down; luxurious interior, good reasonably priced food from pubby favourites to more unusual options like rabbit and oxtail, friendly efficient staff even at busy times, well kept Black Sheep and Wells & Youngs ales, nice choice of wines by the glass inc champagne; plenty of outside seating *(Ross Balaam, Peter and Margaret Glenister, DM, Charles Gysin)*

GREAT HORMEAD [TL4030]

Three Tuns SG9 0NT: Proper, old, timbered country pub with warm welcome, good home cooking (just roasts on Sun), Greene King ales, small linked areas, huge inglenook with another great hearth behind, big back conservatory extension; lovely surroundings *(J D C Smellie)*

HARPENDEN [TL1413]

Engineer AL5 1DJ [St Johns Rd]: Two-bar pub in residential area; Adnams, Black Sheep, Fullers London Pride and Shepherd Neame Spitfire, good choice of wines by the glass, good value bar food from sandwiches up, welcoming helpful staff, conservatory restaurant with different menu inc Sun roasts; piped music, games, TV; pleasant garden with terrace and small fish pond *(Michael Dandy, Giles Barr, Eleanor Dandy)*

Fox AL5 3QE [Luton Rd, Kinsbourne Green; 2.2 miles from M1 junction 10; A1081 towards town]: Contemporary dining pub, tiled floor, usual leather armchairs and sofas, lots of modern dining tables in alcoves; enjoyably up-to-date pubby food, friendly helpful service, interesting wines by the glass, Adnams and Timothy Taylors Landlord, open fire; piped music; terrace tables *(Giles Barr, Eleanor Dandy, Eithne Dandy, Michael Dandy)*

Old Bell AL5 3BN [Luton Rd (A1081)]: Compact Chef & Brewer with decent food, good choice of wines by the glass, Adnams

and Wells & Youngs Bombardier, friendly helpful service, daily papers, pub games; large back tree-shaded garden *(Michael Dandy)*

☆ *Silver Cup* AL5 2JF [just off St Albans Rd (A1081)]: Well kept Wells & Youngs ales, good choice of wines by the glass, wide-ranging food inc sandwiches and pubby favourites, quick service; neat traditional public bar and rather plusher carpeted lounge leading into extensive dark-tabled dining area; terrace picnic-sets with heated canopy, four comfortable bedrooms, ample breakfast (even for non-residents), open all day from 7.30am *(Dr David Cockburn, Michael Dandy, BB)*

HEMEL HEMPSTEAD [TL0411]

☆ *Crown & Sceptre* HP2 6EY [Bridens Camp; leaving on A4146, right at Flamstead/Markyate sign opp Red Lion]: New welcoming licensees at this relaxed neatly refurbished rambling pub, well kept ales from Black Sheep, Greene King and St Austell, good pubby food at low prices, friendly efficient staff, log fires; children and dogs welcome, garden and heated front picnic-sets, good walks, open all day summer wknds *(Mr and Mrs Graham Wood, LYM, Ross Balaam, Dennis Jones)*

HIGH WYCH [TL4614]

Rising Sun CM21 0HZ: Cosy old-fashioned local, serving hatch to carpeted lounge with log fire, central area with well kept Courage Best and a guest tapped from the cask; friendly landlord and locals, bar food (not Sun evening or Mon), bare-boards games room (children allowed) with darts and woodburner; no mobile phones; small garden *(the Didler, Pete Baker)*

HUNSDON [TL4114]

☆ *Fox & Hounds* SG12 8NJ [High St]: Welcoming family-run dining pub with chef/landlord doing good enterprising seasonal food – some quite pricey; friendly efficient service, Adnams, Meantime and a local guest ale, wide choice of wines by the glass, organic fruit juices, beams, panelling and fireside leather sofas, more formal restaurant with chandelier and period furniture, bookcase door to lavatories; no piped music; heated covered terrace, children and dogs welcome, cl Sun evening, Mon *(LYM, J Marques)*

HUNTON BRIDGE [TL0800]

Kings Lodge WD4 8RF [just off A41 nr M25 junctions 19/20; Bridge Rd]: 17th-c, recently well restored as attractive pub/restaurant, traditional food inc all-day bar snacks and popular Sun lunch, Fullers London Pride and weekly guest beer; cheerful landlord, log fire; four bedrooms, open all day *(Peter and Giff Bennett)*

KNEBWORTH [TL2320]

Lytton Arms SG3 6QB [Park Lane, Old Knebworth]: Lutyens-designed pub with spotless big-windowed rooms around large central servery, good selection of changing ales and ciders, beer festivals, good choice of wines inc champagne by the glass, food from sandwiches and baked potatoes up; good log fire, daily papers, conservatory; children and dogs welcome, picnic-sets on front terrace, back garden with covered terrace and summer barbecue, nice surroundings, open all day *(Pat and Tony Martin, Mike and Jennifer Marsh, LYM)*

LEMSFORD [TL2212]

Sun AL8 7TN: Rather smart low-beamed and timbered pub nr River Lea, friendly enthusiastic licensees, half a dozen well kept changing ales, enjoyable generous food up to giant steaks; Victorian prints *(Anthony and Marie Lewis, Jerry Brown, LYM)*

LITTLE BERKHAMSTED [TL2908]

Five Horseshoes SG13 8LY [Church Rd]: 16th-c Chef & Brewer nr church; beams, dark wood and stripped brickwork, two log fires, well kept Courage Directors, Wells & Youngs Bombardier and up to four changing guests, decent wines, good food inc fixed price deals; low lighting, comfortable restaurant, cosy little upper dining room; children welcome, disabled facilities, garden with picnic-sets (busy in summer), heated smokers' shelter, attractive countryside, open all day *(Gordon Neighbour)*

LITTLE GADDESDEN [SP9913]

Bridgewater Arms HP4 1PD [Nettleden Rd, off B4506]: Pleasant well cared for 19th-c stone dining pub, reasonably priced food inc enjoyable set lunches, Greene King IPA and Abbot, good wine choice inc rosé by the glass, good coffee, friendly attentive service; daily papers, carpeted bar with log fire, smart high-ceilinged restaurant, games in small bare-boards public area; garden tables, good walks from the door *(John and Penelope Massey Stewart, LYM)*

LITTLE HADHAM [TL4322]

Nags Head SG11 2AX [Hadham Ford, towards Much Hadham]: Popular 16th-c country dining pub with small linked heavily black-beamed rooms, reasonably priced food from snacks up, small bar with three Greene King beers and decent wines, restaurant down a couple of steps; children in eating areas, tables in pleasant garden *(Gordon Neighbour, LYM)*

MARSWORTH [SP9114]

Anglers Retreat HP23 4LJ [Startops End]: Homely unpretentious pub nr Grand Union Canal; smallish L-shaped angler-theme bar with stuffed fish, well kept Fullers London Pride, Tring and two guest beers, reasonably priced tasty food from fresh baguettes to generous piping hot dishes, good friendly service even when busy; outside gents'; children and dogs welcome, handy for Tring Reservoirs – special for waterfowl *(Tony Hobden)*

MUCH HADHAM [TL4219]

☆ *Bull* SG10 6BU [High St]: Neatly kept dining pub with good home-made food changing daily, good choice of wines by the glass inc champagne, well kept Hancocks HB, cheerful efficient service even when busy; inglenook log fire in an unspoilt bar, attractive pastel

décor in roomy and civilised dining lounge and back dining room; children welcome, good-sized garden *(Ross Balaam, LYM, Sally Gagen)*

NORTHAW [TL2802]

Two Brewers EN6 4NW [Northaw Rd W (B156)]: Several traditional snug areas, nice light dining room and garden with view of ancient parish church; well kept Adnams, enjoyable food, friendly efficient staff *(Ross Balaam)*

NUTHAMPSTEAD [TL4134]

☆ *Woodman* SG8 8NB [off B1368 S of Barkway]: Tucked-away thatched and weatherboarded village pub, welcoming and well run; sofa and other furnishings in comfortable unspoilt core with worn tiled floor, nice inglenook log fire, another fire opposite and 17th-c low beams and timbers, plainer extension; enjoyable home-made food (not Sun evening) inc good home-baked bread, efficient friendly service, interesting USAF memorabilia (nearby World War II airfield), inc a memorial outside; benches out overlooking tranquil lane, comfortable bedrooms, open all day Sat *(Mike and Lynn Robinson, BB, Ms Alexander, Marion and Bill Cross)*

PERRY GREEN [TL4317]

Hoops SG10 6EF [off B1004 Widford—Much Hadham]: Village pub opp Henry Moore Foundation (guided tours in summer by appointment); stripped brick, beams, standing timbers and inglenook, enjoyable reasonably priced food, friendly service, Fullers, Greene King and a guest, cosy dining area (children allowed); garden with large covered terrace, open all day Sun *(LYM, Mrs Margo Finlay, Jörg Kasprowski)*

POTTEN END [TL0108]

Martins Pond HP4 2QQ [The Green]: Welcoming traditional pub with enjoyable food, helpful service, real ales such as Adnams and Fullers London Pride; small garden with picnic-sets, opp pretty green and pond, good walks *(Jane Lawrence)*

RADLETT [TL1699]

Red Lion WD7 7NP [Watling St]: Pleasant Victorian hotel with lots of prints in neatly modernised carpeted bar, Wells & Youngs ales, bar food inc all-day sandwiches, large restaurant; front terrace, 13 bedrooms *(Mike and Lynn Robinson)*

REDBOURN [TL1111]

Chequers AL3 7AD [St Albans Rd (A5183), nr M1 junction 9]: Small rebuilt Chef & Brewer family dining pub with thatch, flagstones and dark wood, usual good value food, Adnams, Stonehenge and Wells & Youngs ales, good choice of wines by the glass; piped music, games; large back terrace and small pleasant garden *(Michael Dandy, Giles Barr, Eleanor Dandy, David M Smith)*

Cricketers AL3 7ND [East Common]: Well refurbished under new management; well kept ales such as Greene King, Hadrian & Border and Tring, good interesting bar food, alcoved back dining area; upper restaurant overlooking cricket pitch and common *(David M Smith, John Picken)*

Hollybush AL3 7DU [Church End]: Picturesque 17th-c pub popular for its reasonably priced generous home-made food, good friendly service, well kept Brakspears and Wychwood; black-beamed lounge with big brick fireplace and heavy wooden doors, larger area with some built-in settles; no children in bar, sunny garden (distant M1 noise), pretty spot nr medieval church *(Andy Lickfold, Conor McGaughey, David M Smith, Ross Balaam)*

ROYSTON [TL3540]

☆ **Old Bull** SG8 9AW [High St]: Chatty and relaxed bow-fronted Georgian coaching inn with roomy high-beamed bar, exposed timbers, handsome fireplaces, big pictures, fine flooring, easy chairs and a leather sofa, papers and magazines; dining area with cheerfully served good value food, Greene King ales, several decent wines by the glass; unobtrusive piped music; children welcome, dogs in bar, suntrap courtyard with heaters and modern furniture, bedrooms, open all day *(Alistair and Kay Butler, R T and J C Moggridge, John Wooll, LYM, Ross Balaam, Lois Dyer)*

SARRATT [TQ0499]

Boot WD3 6BL [The Green]: Early 18th-c tiled pub under newish ownership; popular for enjoyable home-made pubby food at reasonable prices from interesting sandwiches up, well kept Greene King ales, good service; rambling bar with unusual inglenook, more modern dining room; good-sized garden, pleasant spot facing green, handy for Chess valley walks *(Jack and Sandra Clarfelt, LYM, John Branston, John and Joyce Snell, Julia Keeley, Brian and Rosalie Laverick, Sue Harris, Tom Evans)*

ST ALBANS [TL1307]

Blue Anchor AL3 4RY [Fishpool St]: Good value sandwiches and other more ambitious food (not Sun evening), McMullens ales, attractive prices; welcoming landlord, daily papers, flagstoned bar, real fire, modern restaurant extension; sizeable garden, handy for Roman remains *(Andy and Jill Kassube, the Didler, Michael Dandy)*

Boot AL3 5DG [Market Pl]: Old-fashioned city-centre pub opp clock tower, open-plan, with real ales such as Adnams, Jennings and Wells & Youngs, decent wines by the glass, generous pub food inc good sandwich range and tasty help-yourself soup; friendly attentive staff, low beams and timbers, open fire *(Neil Hardwick)*

Farmers Boy AL1 1PQ [London Rd]: Tastefully refurbished bay-windowed pub with its own Alehouse brews, continental bottled beers, log fire, back open kitchen doing bar lunches, helpful staff; SkyTV; suntrap back terrace, open all day *(the Didler)*

Farriers Arms AL3 4PT [Lower Dagnall St]: Plain, friendly two-bar local in no-frills old part, McMullens inc Mild and guest beers, bar food wkdys, lots of old pictures of the pub (Campaign for Real Ale started here in the early 1970s) *(the Didler)*

Garibaldi AL1 1RT [Albert St; left turn down Holywell Hill past White Hart – car park left at end]: Busy friendly Fullers local with their ales and guest beers, good wines by the glass, lunchtime food (not Sun, Mon) inc some unusual dishes; children welcome, open all day *(the Didler, LYM)*

Hare & Hounds AL1 1RL [Sopwell Lane]: Traditonal pub with real ales such as Timothy Taylors Landlord, Sharps Doom Bar and Woodfordes Wherry, enjoyable food using local ingredients inc Sun lunch, open fire; sports TV; seats outside *(Nick Rowe)*

Lower Red Lion AL3 4RX [Fishpool St]: Hospitable beamed local dating from the 17th c (right-hand bar has the most character); up to eight or so well kept changing ales inc local Alehouse (regular beer festivals), imported beers, inexpensive enjoyable lunchtime food inc sandwiches, speciality sausages and popular Sun roast; red plush seats and carpet, board games; no nearby parking; tables in good-sized back garden, bedrooms (some sharing bath), open all day Fri-Sun *(Pete Baker, the Didler, Phil Bryant, Andy and Jill Kassube)*

Peahen AL1 1NQ [London Rd]: Much modernised, with woody contemporary furniture and décor, good range of wines by the glass and of lagers, alongside McMullens and a guest ale, reasonably priced up-to-date bar food from sandwiches up; piped music; heated courtyard tables *(Michael Dandy)*

☆ **Plough** AL4 0RW [Tyttenhanger Green, off A414 E]: Village pub with well kept Fullers and a half-dozen changing guest beers, friendly efficient staff, bargain straightforward lunchtime food; good log fire, interesting old beer bottles and mats, longcase clock, back conservatory; big garden with play area *(LYM, the Didler, John and Joyce Snell)*

Portland Arms AL3 4RA [Portland St/Verulam Rd]: Relaxed local with good value home-made food (not Sun evening, Mon lunchtime) from new french chef, Fullers full beer range kept well; friendly licensees, big open fire; takeaway fish and chips Tues-Sat, open all day Fri-Sun *(Andy and Jill Kassube)*

Rose & Crown AL3 4SG [St Michaels St]: 16th-c, with low beams, timbers and panelling, good speciality lunchtime sandwiches and a few hot dishes, Adnams, Fullers London Pride and Shepherd Neame Spitfire, welcoming service, big log fire, small snug; piped music; children and dogs welcome, lots of tables and benches outside, pretty floral and ivy-hung back yard; handy for Verulamium Musem *(LYM, Michael Dandy, Mike and Jennifer Marsh, Pat and Roger Davies)*

☆ **Six Bells** AL3 4SH [St Michaels St]: Well kept rambling pub popular for its good fresh generous food from lunchtime ciabattas to interesting specials, nice relaxed atmosphere, cheerful attentive service even when busy, several well kept ales from Fullers, Greene King and Timothy Taylors; low beams and timbers, log fire, quieter panelled dining room; children welcome, occasional barbecues in small back garden, handy for Verulamium Museum, open all day *(Michael Dandy, P M Newsome, LYM, Gordon Prince, Mike and Jennifer Marsh, Ross Balaam, John Silverman)*

STANDON [TL3922]

Star SG11 1LB [High St]: Friendly pub with enjoyable pubby food, good service, well kept Greene King ales; garden tables *(Ross Balaam)*

STAPLEFORD [TL3017]

Woodhall Arms SG14 3NW [High Rd]: Well kept Greene King, Wells & Youngs and guest ales, good bar food (not Sat evening), Sun roasts, separate spacious restaurant; ten bedrooms, good breakfast *(Mike and Lynn Robinson)*

TEWIN [TL2715]

Plume of Feathers AL6 0LX [signed off B1000 NE of Welwyn; Upper Green Rd, N end of village]: Nicely laid out country pub with well kept Greene King ales, good coffee, decent wines, good food inc pubby favourites, friendly efficient staff; garden tables *(Ross Balaam, LYM)*

THORLEY STREET [TL4818]

Coach & Horses CM23 4AS [A1184 Sawbridgeworth—Bishop's Stortford]: Vintage Inn dining pub with good value food choice changing daily, prompt service, good range of wines by the glass; piped music turned down on request *(Charles Gysin)*

WADESMILL [TL3517]

Sow & Pigs SG12 0ST [Cambridge Rd, Thundridge (A10 N of Ware)]: Cheerful recently refurbished dining pub, enjoyable generous food from sandwiches up, friendly staff, changing real ales, good house wines, nice coffee with home-made shortbread; spacious beamed dining room off central bar with pig ornaments, log fire; no dogs, children in eating areas, tables outside, open all day *(LYM, J Marques)*

WALKERN [TL2826]

White Lion SG2 7PA [B1037]: Comfortably cottagey open-plan 17th-c pub, low beams, bare boards, good inglenook log fire; well kept Greene King and a guest beer, enjoyable home-made bar food from sandwiches and baguettes up, Sun roasts, small restaurant, friendly staff; piped music; children in eating areas, good play areas, open all day *(LYM, Aimee Brame)*

WARE [TL1435]

Vine SG12 9BY [High St]: Friendly well run town pub with changing choice of ales and a strong wine list (runs off-licence across road); fresh food in bar and dining room all day inc wknd breakfast, daily papers; children welcome *(Richard Salthouse)*

WARESIDE [TL3915]

Chequers SG12 7QY: Well kept ales inc Timothy Taylors Landlord, good straightforward home-made food, friendly staff *(Ross Balaam, Gordon Neighbour)*

White Horse SG12 7QX: Good honest food inc cheaper dishes and plenty of game in an attractive old pub, Greene King ales; tables outside, play area *(Gordon Neighbour)*

WATER END [TL2204]

Old Maypole AL9 7TT [Warrengate Rd, off Swanland Rd N of M25 junction 23 (back rd to North Mymms/Welham Green from South Mymms service area)]: Attractive 16th-c split-level pub, low ceilings, big inglenook log fire, lots of brasses, miniatures and bric-a-brac; well kept Greene King IPA and Abbot, bar meals, friendly service, family room; outside tables *(Colin Moore)*

WATFORD HEATH [TQ1194]

Royal Oak WD19 4EU [Watford Green, off Pinner Rd]: Smartly refurbished and welcoming, with bare boards and plush furniture, a step or two between two main areas, plenty of dining tables, well kept Fullers London Pride, good choice of wines by the glass *(Tracey and Stephen Groves)*

WATTON-AT-STONE [TL3019]

☆ *George & Dragon* SG14 3TA [High St (B1001)]: Friendly and appealing country dining pub with good imaginative food from sandwiches up, menu changes monthly and uses local produce (gluten-free diets catered for), warmly welcoming attentive staff; well kept Greene King IPA and Abbot and guest beers, well chosen reasonably priced wines, interesting mix of antique and modern prints on partly timbered walls, big inglenook fireplace, daily papers; children in eating areas, pretty shrub-screened garden with heaters, boules, open all day wknds *(LYM, Rod Sharp, Cedric Robertshaw)*

WELLPOND GREEN [TL4122]

Kick & Dicky SG11 1NL: Early 18th-c former Nags Head, now completely reworked with stripped pine and comfortable modern furnishings; pleasantly relaxed bistro atmosphere (drinkers welcome too), good if not cheap local food, well kept Adnams Broadside, friendly service; neat bedrooms *(N R White)*

WHEATHAMPSTEAD [TL1714]

Bull AL4 8BS [High St]: Big Miller & Carter chain dining pub, refurbished while keeping original features, generous pubby food at reasonable prices, helpful service, good choice of wines by the glass, Fullers London Pride *(Michael Dandy, Giles Barr, Eleanor Dandy)*

Cross Keys AL4 8LA [off B651 at Gustard Wood 1.5 miles N]: 17th-c pub attractively placed in rolling wooded countryside, enjoyable food in bar and beamed restaurant, inglenook woodburner, model car collection; good garden, three comfortable bedrooms, good breakfast *(Mike and Lynn Robinson, LYM)*

☆ *Wicked Lady* AL4 8EL [Nomansland Common; B651 0.5 mile S]: Unpretentious chain dining pub with clean contemporary décor, wide range of good well presented food inc some unusual dishes, well kept Timothy Taylors Landlord, good choice of wines by the glass, reasonable prices, friendly attentive young staff; various rooms and alcoves, plenty of tables, low beams, log fires, lots of stainless steel, conservatory; large garden with terrace *(Michael Dandy, Giles Barr, Eleanor Dandy, LYM, John and Joyce Snell)*

WIGGINTON [SP9310]
Greyhound HP23 6EH [just S of Tring]: Fairly new landlord at friendly Rothschild estate pub in quiet village; reasonably priced standard pub food, real ales; garden, good Ridgeway walks *(Roy Hoing)*

If a pub tries to make you leave a credit card behind the bar, be on your guard. The credit card firms and banks which issue them condemn this practice. After all, the publican who asks you to do this is in effect saying: 'I don't trust you'. Have you any more reason to trust his staff? If your card is used fraudulently while you have let it be kept out of your sight, the card company could say you've been negligent yourself – and refuse to make good your losses. So say that they can 'swipe' your card instead, but must hand it back to you. Please let us know if a pub does try to keep your card.

Isle of Wight

Most of the island's pubs suit a family holiday really well, with a great holiday atmosphere in places like the buoyantly cheerful Folly in Cowes, the Spyglass in Ventnor (seaview terrace) and the Buddle at Niton with its clifftop garden – and new licensees bringing the menu up a notch or two. New licensees are also injecting fresh energy into the Crab & Lobster at Bembridge. Their own fishermen catch the good seafood they serve here, and it is our Isle of Wight Dining Pub of the Year. A couple of favourite Lucky Dips, both inspected and approved by us, are the Blacksmiths Arms at Carisbrooke and Fishermans Cottage on Shanklin beach. The island has no fewer than three breweries, the most popular being Goddards.

ARRETON   SZ5386   MAP 2
White Lion
A3056 Newport—Sandown; PO30 3AA

Pleasantly pubby local with basic food and three real ales

Little changes from year to year at this welcoming white-painted village house – indeed the friendly conscientious licensees have been here many years now. The neatly kept beamed lounge is traditional, with dark pink walls or stripped brick above stained pine dado, gleaming brass and horse tack and lots of cushioned wheelback chairs on the patterned red carpet. The piped music tends to be very quiet, and the public bar has a games machine, darts and board games; Bass, Timothy Taylors Landlord and a guest such as Ringwood Fortyniner on handpump. There's also a restaurant, family room and stable room. The pleasant garden has a small play area. More reports please.

🍴 Straightforward but very tasty food is served in generous helpings and includes sandwiches, baguettes, ploughman's, whitebait, feta and black olive salad, chilli, vegetable or chicken curry, haddock and chips, pie of the day, steaks, and maybe duck breast with orange and brandy sauce and lamb stew. *Starters/Snacks: £3.95 to £6.25. Main Courses: £7.25 to £15.95. Puddings: £3.95*

Enterprise ~ Lease Chris and Kate Cole ~ Real ale ~ Bar food (12-9) ~ (01983) 528479 ~ Children in family room ~ Dogs allowed in bar ~ Open 11-11; 12-10.30 Sun

Recommended by Neil Ingoe, Neil and Anita Christopher, Andy and Yvonne Cunningham, Penny and Peter Keevil

---

BEMBRIDGE   SZ6587   MAP 2
Crab & Lobster 🛏
Foreland Fields Road, off Howgate Road (which is off B3395 via Hillway Road); PO35 5TR
ISLE OF WIGHT DINING PUB OF THE YEAR

Seafood speciality and prime location; pleasant bedrooms

Given its lovely position and good seafood, it's not surprising that this well placed inn draws the summer crowds. It's perched on low cliffs within yards of the shore, with great views over the Solent from the terrace, dining area and some of the bedrooms. Inside it's roomier than you might expect and is done out in an almost parlourish style, with lots of yachting memorabilia, old local photographs and a blazing winter fire; darts, dominoes and cribbage. Courage, Goddards Fuggle-Dee-Dum and Greene King IPA are on handpump, with decent house wines, about 20 malt whiskies and good coffee; piped music.

🍽 **Lobster and crab are the things to go for here as they are brought straight to the door by the pub's own fishermen and prepared in most ways you can imagine – anything from sandwiches to crab cakes and seafood tagliatelle, to crab salad, mixed seafood grill or whole lobster. Other meals (all in generous helpings) include sandwiches, steak sandwich, ploughman's, chicken caesar salad, curries, lasagne and steaks; beware, they may try to keep your credit card while you eat.** *Starters/Snacks: £4.25 to £7.50. Main Courses: £8.50 to £15.95. Puddings: £4.25 to £6.95*

Enterprise ~ Lease Caroline and Ian Quekett ~ Real ale ~ Bar food (12-2.30, 6-9(9.30 Fri, Sat) with limited menu 2.30-5.30 weekends and holidays) ~ (01983) 872244 ~ Children welcome ~ Dogs allowed in bar ~ Open 11(12 Sun)-11; 12-10.30 Sun; 11-3, 6-11 in winter ~ Bedrooms: £50S(£55B)/£85S(£90B)

Recommended by Mrs Maricar Jagger, Philip Vernon, Kim Maidment, Evelyn and Derek Walter, Felicity Davies, Mr and Mrs H J Langley

BONCHURCH
SZ5778   MAP 2

Bonchurch Inn

Bonchurch Shute; from A3055 E of Ventnor turn down to Old Bonchurch opposite Leconfield Hotel; PO38 1NU

Unusual italian-owned establishment rambling around central courtyard; italian influence in menu and wines

A delightful paved and cobbled courtyard (feeling slightly continental with its tables, fountain and pergola) awaits when you round the corner at this distinctively run place. The bar, restaurant, family room and kitchens are spread around this sheltered little square, and the entire set-up is snuggled below a steep, rocky slope. The unusual layout derives from its Victorian origins as the stables for the nearby manor house. The furniture-packed bar has a good chatty local atmosphere and conjures up sea voyages, with its floor of narrow-planked ship's decking and old-fashioned steamer-style seats. A separate entrance leads to the fairly basic family room, which can feel a little cut off from the congenial atmosphere of the public bar. As well as Courage Directors and Best tapped from the cask, there are a couple of italian wines by the glass and a few french ones; piped music, darts, shove-ha'penny, dominoes and cribbage. The pub owns a holiday flat for up to six people.

🍽 **Tasty bar food includes italian dishes such as lasagne, tagliatelle carbonara, seafood risotto or spaghetti, as well as traditional dishes such as sandwiches, a good crab cocktail, grilled plaice, battered squid, chicken chasseur and steak.** *Starters/Snacks: £4.50 to £7.50. Main Courses: £5.50 to £17.50. Puddings: £3.50 to £6.00*

Free house ~ Licensees Ulisse and Gillian Besozzi ~ Real ale ~ Bar food (12-2, 6.30-8.45) ~ Restaurant ~ (01983) 852611 ~ Children in family room ~ Open 12-3, 6.30(7-10.30 Sun)-11 ~ Bedrooms: /£70B

Recommended by David Jackson, Dr D and Mrs B Woods

COWES
SZ5092   MAP 2

Folly

Folly Lane – which is signposted off A3021 just S of Whippingham; PO32 6NB

Glorious water views from popular place with cheery family holiday atmosphere, moorings and good range of food served from breakfast on

Sailors, locals and families gather at this happiest of pubs (late night dancing on the tables is not unheard of here). Rumour has it that the splendidly positioned building originated from a french sea-going barge that beached here during a smuggling run in the early 1700s. The laid-back timbered interior certainly gives the sense of a ship's below decks. Straightforward but atmospheric furnishings include simple wooden tables and chairs, and stools at the bar. Greene King IPA and Old Speckled Hen and Goddards on handpump; pool, TV, games machine and piped music. Big windows in the bar and seats on a waterside terrace enjoy entertaining views of all the nautical activity on the wide Medina estuary. If you're using the river, they have moorings, a water taxi, showers and long-term parking on a field, and they keep an eye on weather forecasts and warnings. All in all this is a cheery lighthearted place, with happy hands-on staff. Watch out for the sleeping policemen along the lane if you come by car.

🍴 **Breakfast is served first thing, followed by the lunchtime and (more substantial) evening menus. Dishes are generously served and sensibly priced and include sandwiches, duck and hoisin salad, sharing boards, pork steak with roast red pepper and chilli sauce, fish and chips, beef and ale pie, sirloin steak and daily specials such as roast duck in blueberry and port sauce, and puddings such as lemon tart and apple pie and custard.** *Starters/Snacks: £2.95 to £7.45. Main Courses: £7.45 to £10.45. Puddings: £3.75 to £5.25*

Greene King ~ Managers Andy and Cheryl Greenwood ~ Real ale ~ Bar food (9-11 then 12-9.30) ~ (01983) 297171 ~ Children welcome ~ Dogs welcome ~ Live music Sat evening ~ Open 11-11(11.30 Sat, 10.30 Sun)

Recommended by Mrs Romey Heaton, B and M Kendall

FRESHWATER   SZ3487   MAP 2

Red Lion ♀

Church Place; from A3055 at E end of village by Freshwater Garage mini-roundabout follow Yarmouth signpost, then take first real right turn signed to Parish Church; PO40 9BP

Good mix of locals and visiting diners, decent food and composed atmosphere

The not over-done but comfortably furnished open-plan bar at this firmly run place has fires, low grey sofas and sturdy country-kitchen style furnishings on mainly flagstoned floors, and bare board flooring, too. The well executed paintings (between photographs and china platters) are by the licensee's brother and are worth a look. Though food is quite a draw, chatting locals, occupying stools along the counter, keep up a pubby atmosphere. Flowers Original, Shepherd Neame Spitfire, Wadworths 6X and a guest such as Goddards are kept under light blanket pressure, and the good choice of wines includes 16 by the glass. Be careful as they fine for mobile phones (money to the RNLI). There are tables on a carefully tended grass and gravel area at the back (some under cover), beside the kitchen's herb garden, and a couple of picnic-sets in a quiet square at the front have pleasant views of the church. The pub is virtually on the Freshwater Way footpath that connects Yarmouth with the southern coast at Freshwater Bay.

🍴 **Food is listed on blackboards behind the bar and includes a sensible cross-section of dishes. As well as lunchtime filled baguettes and ploughman's, it might include herring roes on toast, crispy duck salad, whitebait, steak and ale pie, battered cod and mushy peas, crab risotto, braised lamb shank with mint gravy, fried skate, mushroom stroganoff, with puddings such as apple and blackberry crumble and banana split; Sunday roast.** *Starters/Snacks: £4.75 to £7.00. Main Courses: £9.75 to £16.00. Puddings: £4.50 to £7.00*

Enterprise ~ Lease Michael Mence ~ Real ale ~ Bar food (12-2, 6.30(7 Sun)-9) ~ (01983) 754925 ~ Children must be over 10 ~ Dogs welcome ~ Open 11.30-3, 5.30-11; 11.30-4, 6-11 Sat; 12-3, 7-10.30 Sun

Recommended by Chris Sale, Mr and Mrs A Garforth, Mrs Mary Woods, B and M Kendall, Dr D and Mrs B Woods

HULVERSTONE   SZ3984   MAP 2

Sun 🍺

B3399; PO30 4EH

Lovely thatched building with terrific coastal views, down-to-earth old-world appeal and four quickly changing real ales

Feeling cheerily pubby, the unpretentiously traditional and low-ceilinged bar at this thatched whitewashed country pub is full of friendly chatter, has a blazing fire at one end (with horsebrasses and ironwork hung around the fireplace), a nice mix of old furniture on flagstones and floorboards, and brick stone and walls; piped music, darts and board games. Leading off from one end is the traditionally decorated more recently constructed dining area, with large windows making the most of the view. Friendly helpful staff serve four quickly changing real ales that might be from brewers such as Charles Wells, Goddards, Ringwood and Sharps. Staff are helpful and friendly. The building is in a captivating setting, with views from its charmingly secluded split level cottagey garden (which has a terrace and several picnic-sets) down to a wild stretch of coast. It's very well positioned for some splendid walks along the cliffs, and up Mottistone Down to the prehistoric Long Stone.

🍴 **The new licensees source all their pork, lamb and beef from the adjacent farm for bar food which includes sandwiches, ploughman's, moules marinière, shortcrust pie of the day, cod and chips with mushy peas, chilli, smoked haddock and spring onion fishcakes, chicken and bacon tagliatelle and bass with mussels.** *Starters/Snacks: £4.25 to £5.95. Main Courses: £7.25 to £13.95. Puddings: £4.25*

Enterprise ~ Lease Mark and Leslie Blanchard ~ Real ale ~ Bar food (12-9) ~ (01983) 741124 ~ Children welcome ~ Dogs welcome ~ Live music Sat evening ~ Open 11-11; 12-10.30 Sun

Recommended by Guy and Caroline Howard, Mrs Mary Woods, B and M Kendall, Liz and Brian Barnard

NINGWOOD
SZ3989 MAP

Horse & Groom

A3054 Newport—Yarmouth, a mile W of Shalfleet; PO30 4NW

Spacious family dining pub with enjoyable all-day food, excellent play area and crazy golf

There's a relaxed pubby feel and staff are friendly and helpful at this welcoming pub. The roomy interior is thoughtfully arranged, with comfortable leather sofas grouped around low tables and a nice mix of sturdy tables and chairs, well spaced for a relaxing meal. Walls are pale pink, which works nicely with the old flagstone flooring. Greene King IPA, Goddards Special and Ringwood Best are kept under light blanket pressure; staff are friendly and helpful; piped music, games machine. There are plenty of tables in the garden, which has a terrific children's play area and other entertainments.

🍴 **Good value food includes sandwiches, burgers, ploughman's, whitebait, duck spring rolls with chilli dip, curry, grilled fish of the day and steaks. They've a thoughtful children's menu, offer free baby food and do a very good value Sunday carvery.** *Starters/Snacks: £3.95 to £5.95. Main Courses: £7.95 to £18.95. Puddings: £3.00 to £4.75*

Enterprise ~ Lease Pete Tigwell ~ Real ale ~ Bar food (12-9) ~ (01983) 760672 ~ Children welcome ~ Dogs allowed in bar ~ Open 11-11; 12-10.30 Sun

Recommended by E Brooks

NITON
SZ5075 MAP

Buddle 🍺

St Catherines Road, Undercliff; off A3055 just S of village, towards St Catherines Point; PO38 2NE

Distinctive stone pub with imaginative menu and six real ales; nice clifftop garden

Though new licensees have injected some fresh energy here, there's still a fabulously timeless feel in the heavily black-beamed bar. Big flagstones, a broad stone fireplace, massive black oak mantelbeam, old-fashioned captain's chairs arranged around solid wooden tables, and walls hung with pewter mugs and the like conjure up the time when this rambling old pub was the haunt of notorious local smugglers. Six real ales will probably include Adnams Best, Fullers HSB, Goddards Fuggle-Dee-Dum, Ringwood Fortyniner, Sharps Doom Bar and Yates; piped music. Along one side of the lawn, and helping to shelter it, the old family room has just been converted into a cocktail lounge and restaurant. You can look out over the cliffs from the well cared-for garden, with its tables spread over the sloping lawn and stone terraces, and there is a good walk to the nearby lighthouse – the pub is handy for the coast path.

🍴 The menu has moved up a notch or two and the new people like to source ingredients locally. Tasty dishes include chicken breast in beer batter, spinach, ricotta and red onion quiche, scallops and smoked bacon salad with lemon grass, pork loin in creamy wholegrain mustard and honey sauce and sirloin steak. *Starters/Snacks: £4.25 to £5.95. Main Courses: £7.95 to £14.95. Puddings: £4.25*

Enterprise ~ Lease John and Fiona Page ~ Real ale ~ Bar food (12-2.45, 6-9) ~ (01983) 730243 ~ Children welcome ~ Dogs welcome ~ Open 11-11(12 Fri, Sat); 12-10.30 Sun

Recommended by Glenn and Gillian Miller

SEAVIEW   SZ6291   MAP 2

Seaview Hotel ♀ 🛏

High Street; off B3330 Ryde—Bembridge; PO34 5EX

Small relaxed hotel with informal bar, good wine list and lovely bedrooms

You'll need to make your way through to the back of this gently civilised 200-year-old hotel to reach the simple pubby bar. Here you'll find a relaxing down-to-earth atmosphere, traditional wood furnishings on bare boards, lots of seafaring paraphernalia around softly lit ochre walls and a log fire. The comfortable front bar, with good soft furnishings, is modelled on a naval wardroom and is home to one of the most extensive private collections of naval pictures, photographs and artefacts to be found on the island. Drinks include Goddards, Yates Undercliff Experience and a guest on handpump, a good selection of malt whiskies, a farm cider (in summer) and a good wine list (including a couple from local vineyards); TV, darts and board games. Tables on little terraces on either side of the path to the front door take in glimpses of the sea and coast, and some of the comfortable bedrooms also have a sea view. If you run a tab, they may ask to keep your credit card behind the bar.

🍴 Very good, well presented and generously served bar food (not cheap) includes hot crab ramekin, sandwiches and baguettes, fried herring on toast with caper and herb cream sauce, mussels in white wine and cream, fish pie, scampi, venison and wild boar sausages and mash, sirloin steak, battered haddock and mushy peas, and puddings such as bakewell tart and lemon cheesecake with strawberry ice-cream; Sunday roast. There is a much more elaborate restaurant menu. *Starters/Snacks: £5.75 to £7.50. Main Courses: £7.95 to £16.95. Puddings: £5.75 to £6.75*

Free house ~ Licensee Andrew Morgan ~ Real ale ~ Bar food (12-2.30(3 Sun), 6.30-9.30) ~ Restaurant ~ (01983) 612711 ~ Children welcome ~ Dogs allowed in bar ~ Open 10-11; 11-10.30 Sun ~ Bedrooms: £155B/£155B

Recommended by David Glynne-Jones, Franklyn Roberts, B and M Kendall

SHALFLEET   SZ4089   MAP 2

New Inn ♀

A3054 Newport—Yarmouth; PO30 4NS

Cheerful pub with seafood specialities, good beers and wines too

The cheery welcome, great seafood and well kept beer are a winning combination at this rambling 18th-c former fisherman's haunt. As it's popular you will need to book, and there may be double sittings in summer. The partly panelled flagstoned public bar has yachting photographs and pictures, a boarded ceiling, scrubbed pine tables and a log fire in the big stone hearth. The carpeted beamed lounge bar has boating pictures and a coal fire, and the snug and gallery have slate floors, bric-a-brac and more scrubbed pine tables. Goddards, Ringwood and a guest such as Greene King IPA are kept under a light blanket pressure, and they stock around 60 wines; piped music. More reports please.

⊞ Their famous crab sandwich, seafood platter and crab and lobster salads are served alongside a good choice of fish dishes, such as pollack fillets with rocket, pesto, tomato and chorizo, thai marinated sole filled with pak choi, and pubbier options such as sandwiches, baguettes, ploughman's, sausage and mash, steak and ale pie, spinach and ricotta cannelloni and various steaks. *Starters/Snacks: £4.95 to £8.95. Main Courses: £6.95 to £9.95. Puddings: £3.95 to £5.95*

Enterprise ~ Lease Mr Bullock and Mr McDonald ~ Real ale ~ Bar food (12-2.30, 6-9) ~ (01983) 531314 ~ Children welcome ~ Dogs welcome ~ Open 12-11(10.30 Sun)

Recommended by Terry and Nickie Williams, Philip Vernon, Kim Maidment

SHORWELL
SZ4582   MAP 2

Crown

B3323 SW of Newport; PO30 3JZ

Popular pub with good choice of food and pretty stream-side garden with play area

In a tranquil village, just a few miles from the sea, this country pub consists of four pleasant opened-up rooms, all spread around a central bar, with either carpet, tiles or flagstones. Chatty regulars lend some local character. The beamed knocked-through lounge has blue and white china in an attractive carved dresser, old country prints on stripped stone walls and a winter log fire with a fancy tile-work surround. Black pews form bays around tables in a stripped-stone room off to the left with another log fire; piped music and board games. Four real ales will probably be Goddards Special, Ringwood Best and Fortyniner and Sharps Doom Bar, all on handpump. A pretty tree-sheltered garden has closely spaced picnic-sets and white garden chairs and tables set out by a sweet little stream, which broadens out into a small trout-filled pool, and a decent children's play area within easy view. Needless to say such a lovely spot can draw the summer crowds.

⊞ Bar food includes sandwiches, ploughman's, filled baked potatoes, pâté of the day, crab cocktail, mushroom stroganoff, pizzas, cottage or fisherman's pie, burgers, steaks, and daily specials such as dover sole with lemon, caper and prawn butter and cod and chorizo fishcakes with sweet chilli and chive mayonnaise, and puddings made by a local farmer's wife. *Starters/Snacks: £4.25 to £6.25. Main Courses: £7.25 to £16.25. Puddings: £3.50 to £4.95*

Enterprise ~ Lease Nigel and Pam Wynn ~ Real ale ~ Bar food (12-9) ~ (01983) 740293 ~ Children welcome ~ Dogs welcome ~ Open 10.30(11.30 Sun)-11

Recommended by Mr and Mrs H J Langley, Stephen Moss, Chris Bell, Terry and Nickie Williams

VENTNOR
SZ5677   MAP 2

Spyglass ◀

Esplanade, SW end; road down very steep and twisty, and parking nearby can be difficult – best to use the pay-and-display (free in winter) about 100 yards up the road; PO38 1JX

Interesting waterside pub with appealing seafaring bric-a-brac, five well kept beers and enjoyable food

A fascinating jumble of seafaring memorabilia (anything from ships' wheels to stuffed seagulls) fills the snug quarry-tiled old interior of this cheery bubbling place – no matter what the season, it seems to brim with customers enjoying themselves. Ringwood Best and Fortyniner are well kept alongside three guests such as Fullers London Pride, Goddards Fuggle-Dee-Dum and Marstons Pedigree; games machine and piped music. In a super position, perched on the wall just above the beach, tables outside on a terrace have lovely views over the sea. There are strolls westwards from here along the coast towards the Botanic Garden, as well as heftier hikes up on to St Boniface Down and towards the eerie shell of Appuldurcombe House.

🍴 Generous helpings of tasty bar food might include seafood chowder, crab and chive pâté, beef bourguignon, sausage, mushroom and bacon casserole, lamb braised in red wine and rib-eye steak; they may ask to hold your credit card. *Starters/Snacks: £4.50 to £6.50. Main Courses: £6.95 to £21.95. Puddings: £4.25 to £5.50*

Free house ~ Licensees Neil and Stephanie Gibbs ~ Real ale ~ Bar food (12-9.30) ~ (01983) 855338 ~ Children welcome but not in bedrooms ~ Dogs allowed in bar ~ Sea shanties most nights ~ Open 10.30am-11pm ~ Bedrooms: /£75B

Recommended by Penny and Peter Keevil, Neil and Anita Christopher, Glenn and Gillian Miller, Stephen Moss

LUCKY DIP

Besides the fully inspected pubs, you might like to try these Lucky Dips recommended to us and described by readers (if you do, please send us reports: feedback@goodguides.com).

BEMBRIDGE [SZ6488]
Pilot Boat PO35 5NN [Station Rd/Kings Rd]: Harbourside pub reworked in style of a ship, enjoyable food from good sandwiches up, well kept Ventnor Golden; tables out overlooking water in pleasant courtyard behind, well placed for coast walks, open all day *(Mrs Maricar Jagger, Andy and Yvonne Cunningham, Quentin and Carol Williamson)*

CARISBROOKE [SZ4687]
☆ *Blacksmiths Arms* PO30 5SS [B3401 1.5 miles W]: Quiet hillside pub with friendly landlord and staff, great choice of good fresh specials, decent wines and cider, scrubbed tables in neat beamed and flagstoned front bars, good Solent views from airy bare-boards family dining extension; children, dogs and walkers welcome, terrace tables and smallish back garden with play area, open all day *(LYM, Penny and Peter Keevil)*

CULVER DOWN [SZ6385]
Culver Haven PO36 8QT [seaward end, nr Yarborough Monument]: Isolated clifftop pub with superb Channel views, modern, clean and very friendly, with popular fair-priced home cooking, quick service, well kept Fullers London Pride, good coffee, big restaurant; children welcome, small terrace, good walks *(Mrs Maricar Jagger)*

FRESHWATER [SZ3285]
Highdown PO39 0HY [Highdown Lane, SW off Moons Hill]: Welcoming roadside inn with log-fire in stripped-wood floor bar, refurbished restaurant, popular food inc local fish, seasonal game and plenty of vegetarian options; children welcome, garden with terrace and play area, four updated bedrooms *(B and M Kendall, Chris Sale)*

Prince of Wales PO40 9ED [Princes Rd]: One for fans of the decidedly plain and unsmart local which has all but vanished now, up to six well kept ales, summer farm cider, down-to-earth regulars and long-serving licensees, pickled eggs, pub games inc pool, juke box; outside lavatories; garden tables, open all day *(Chris Sale)*

GODSHILL [SZ5381]
Griffin PO38 3JD [High St]: Substantial and carefully restored stone-built pub in pretty honeypot village, beams and low ceilings, good for families yet with plenty of quiet places, generous well presented standard food from good hot rolls up, friendly helpful staff, several well kept beers inc Goddards, good wine choice; darts, pool and machines; good-sized garden with play area, mini football pitch, and griffin-shaped maze *(Colin Gooch, Glenn and Gillian Miller)*

NEWCHURCH [SZ5685]
☆ *Pointer* PO36 0NN [High St]: Good value generous fresh food (not Sun evening) using local produce from sandwiches up, well kept Fullers ales, proper bar with flame-effect fire, comfortable dining room, fortnightly live music Fri; pleasant back garden, open all day Sat *(Franklyn Roberts, BB)*

SANDOWN [SZ6084]
Driftwood PO36 8AT [Culver Parade]: Laid-back modern beach bar with friendly service, lots of lagers and ciders, sizeable menu; plenty of tables outside *(Colin Gooch)*
Ocean Deck PO36 8JS [Esplanade]: Wide choice of tasty food from plenty of sandwiches and snacks to seafood from their own boat, brisk friendly service, good beer range, nautical décor inc figurehead and photographs; big seaview terrace *(Colin Gooch)*

SHANKLIN [SZ5880]
Crab PO37 6NS [High St (A3055 towards Ventnor)]: Famously photogenic thatched village pub with tables out in front and above the Chine behind, spreading and modernised inside with well kept Goddards ales and wide choice of food from sandwiches up, rows of tables in dining area; walled garden, open all day *(LYM, Colin Gooch)*
☆ *Fishermans Cottage* PO37 6BN [bottom of Shanklin Chine]: Thatched shoreside cottage in terrific setting surrounded by beached boats, tucked into the cliffs, steep walk down beautiful chine, lovely seaside walk to Luccombe; flagstones and some stripped stone, repro furniture, nets slung from low beams, old local pictures and bric-a-brac, simple good value bar lunches from sandwiches and baked potatoes up, more enterprising evening choice (till 8pm),

convivial atmosphere, helpful staff, well kept ales inc Goddards, frequent entertainment; piped music; wheelchair access, children welcome, terrace tables, open all day in summer when fine (closed winter) *(David Jackson, Martin Gough, BB, Colin Gooch)*

TOTLAND [SZ3285]

High Down PO39 0HY [Highdown Lane]: Out-of-the-way pub in great spot at foot of NT Tennyson Down, well kept real ales, cheerful service, straightforward good value food in bar and small dining room inc popular Sun lunch; piped music; dogs and walkers welcome, picnic-sets out in raised paddock area, good value bedrooms *(Liz and Brian Barnard)*

VENTNOR [SZ5677]

Mill Bay PO38 1JR [Esplanade]: Seafront pub with cosy bar and light airy conservatory, good value generous food inc special deals, Goddards, Greene King and Ventnor Golden, friendly staff, darts and cribbage; quiz nights, good live music; big beachside terrace with play area *(Liz and John Soden, BB)*

YARMOUTH [SZ3589]

Kings Head PO41 0PB [Quay St]: Cosy low-ceilinged traditional pub opp car ferry, rather dark and quaint, with real ales, good food till quite late in evening inc well prepared local fish; plush seats, open fires, friendly staff, children's eating area; unobtrusive piped music; dogs welcome, bedrooms *(Franklyn Roberts)*

Please tell us if any Lucky Dips deserve to be upgraded to a Main Entry – and why: feedback@goodguides.com, or (no stamp needed) The Good Pub Guide, FREEPOST TN1569, Wadhurst, E Sussex TN5 7BR.

Kent

Many of the pubs doing particularly well here this year offer extremely good food. These include the Three Chimneys just outside Biddenden, Timber Batts near Bodsham, Harrow on Ightham Common, Hare in Langton Green, Rose & Crown at Selling, Chaser at Shipbourne, Red Lion at Stodmarsh and Sankeys in Tunbridge Wells. For the second year running, our award of Kent Dining Pub of the Year goes to the Three Chimneys near Biddenden. New to the *Guide* this year are the Bull in Benenden (enthusiastic licensees, super food), White Horse in Chilham (in a lovely village square, with an emphasis on organic produce), Duke William in Ickham (family-owned village pub with a friendly relaxed atmosphere), Woodcock at Iden Green (hard-working and keen young landlord in unspoilt country tavern), Plough at Ivy Hatch (now attractively refurbished) and Bottle House near Penshurst (original features and contemporary décor combined with good food and drink). Particularly promising Lucky Dip entries are the Parrot in Canterbury, Kentish Rifleman at Dunks Green, George & Dragon in Ightham, Sportsman in Seasalter and White Rock at Under River. Kent's leading brewery is the long-established Shepherd Neame; Larkins, Goachers, Westerham, Hopdaemon and Whitstable stand out among a good number of smaller, newer ones.

BEKESBOURNE

TR1856   MAP 3

Unicorn

Coming from Patrixbourne on A2, turn left up Bekesbourne Hill after passing railway line (and station); coming from Littlebourne on A257, pass Howletts Zoo – Bekesbourne Hill is then first turning on right; turning into pub car park is at bottom end of the little terrace of houses on the left (the pub is the far end of this terrace); CT4 5ED

Small, friendly pub, simply furnished bars and pubby food

Under new licensees since our last edition, this is a cosy little pub with simply furnished bars. There are just a few scrubbed old pine tables and wooden pubby chairs on worn floorboards, a nice old leather sofa beside the open fire, a canary ceiling and walls above a dark green dado, minimal décor and a handful of bar stools against the neat counter. Harveys Best, Ramsgate Gadds No. 5 and Shepherd Neame Master Brew on handpump, several wines by the glass and Biddenden cider; piped music and board games. A side terrace is prettily planted and there's a garden with benches and boules. Parking in front is tricky but there is a large car park at the back reached from the small track at the end of the adjacent terrace of cottages. More reports please.

🍽 **Bar food includes lunchtime ciabattas and ploughman's, soup, ham hock and apple terrine, curried cauliflower fritters with minted yoghurt dip, chicken with barbecue sauce, cheese and bacon, ham and eggs, beer-battered cod, minted couscous with roasted vegetables, a changing pie, and puddings like lemon tart and chocolate tiramisu.**
Starters/Snacks: £3.95 to £4.25. Main Courses: £6.95 to £9.95. Puddings: £3.95

Free house ~ Licensee Martin Short ~ Real ale ~ Bar food (12-2, 7-9; 12-5 Sun;
not Sun evening and limited menu Mon) ~ (01227) 830210 ~ Children welcome ~
Open 12-3, 6-11; 12-10.30 Sun

Recommended by Rob and Catherine Dunster, R J Anderson, Kevin Thorpe, Laurence John, N R White

BENENDEN

TQ8032   MAP 3

Bull 🍴 🍺

The Street; by village green; TN17 4DE

**Attractive and friendly old inn with relaxed and informal atmosphere, enjoyable home-
made food, four local real ales, cheerful hands-on landlord; bedrooms**

Next to the sizeable village green, this is an attractive and extended 17th-c inn with
unusual leaded bay windows. The main part of the bar has a roaring winter log fire in the
brick inglenook, cushioned seats built into the bay window, a mix of spindleback, rush-
seated dining chairs and brocaded stools around a few tables on the stripped wooden
floor, a small unobtrusive flat-screen TV, big church candles on pewter dishes on each
table, light ceiling joists and historic local photographs. Dark Star Hophead and Over The
Moon, Harveys Best and Larkins Traditional on handpump from the carved wooden bar
counter topped by a mass of hops; you can also take beer and cider away with you in
two-pint hoppers. Good coffees. There's also a little two-sided woodburning stove and
piped jazz. Through an open doorway, and down a couple of steps is a bigger room with
similar dining chairs and a mix of cushioned settles on dark terracotta tiles, hops on the
white-painted beams, old photographs of the pub on the green wallpapered walls, a
cupboard of darts trophies (and a darts board) and a tucked-away fruit machine. The
atmosphere is relaxed and informal and the friendly, hands-on landlord and his chatty
staff give quick, efficient service. To the right of the entrance is the dining room with
burgundy patterned and brocaded dining chairs, built-in cushioned seats, a mix of tables,
another woodburning stove and a cream corner cupboard with decorative plates. In front
of the pub by the road are some picnic-sets. The bedrooms are newly refurbished and
comfortable.

🍴 With daily delivered fresh fish and meat bought only from a local farmer and butcher,
the good, enjoyable food includes sandwiches and filled baguettes, ploughman's, soup,
baked french brie with a berry coulis, burgers with cheese or bacon toppings, home-
cooked ham and eggs, a chilli, a proper fish pie, and daily specials like aubergine filled
with courgettes, mushrooms, tomatoes, feta cheese and with a cheddar cheese topping,
wild rabbit casserole, fresh salmon and dill fishcakes with home-made tartare sauce,
lambs liver with smoked bacon and rich onion gravy and slow-cooked pork belly with
apple chutney; Thursday curry night and popular Sunday roasts. *Starters/Snacks: £4.25 to
£7.95. Main Courses: £7.95 to £10.50. Puddings: £4.25*

Free house ~ Licensees Mark Reid and Lucy Bligh ~ Real ale ~ Bar food (12-2.15(4 Sun),
7-9.15; not Sun evening, not Mon lunchtime) ~ Restaurant ~ (01580) 240054 ~
Children welcome ~ Dogs allowed in bar ~ Monthly Thursday music club, live music most Sun
afternoons ~ Open 12-11.30(midnight Sat, 11pm Sun); 4-11.30 Mon; closed Mon lunchtime

Recommended by Mrs J Ekins-Daukes

BIDDENDEN

TQ8238   MAP 3

Three Chimneys 🍴 🍷

A262, 1 mile W of village; TN27 8LW

KENT DINING PUB OF THE YEAR

**Pubby beamed rooms of considerable individuality, log fires, imaginative food and pretty
garden**

A conservatory has been built on to this pretty, old-fashioned cottage which has provided
much-needed dining space without upsetting the very distinctive character of the place.
It remains a fine all-rounder with particularly efficient, friendly staff and a civilised and

relaxed atmosphere. There's a series of low-beamed, very traditional little rooms with plain wooden furniture and old settles on flagstones and coir matting, some harness and sporting prints on the stripped brick walls and good log fires. Adnams Best, Greene King Old Speckled Hen and Youngs Bitter tapped straight from casks racked behind the counter, several wines by the glass, local cider and apple juice and ten malt whiskies. The simple public bar has darts, dominoes and cribbage. French windows in the candlelit bare-boards restaurant open on to the garden where there are seats. Sissinghurst Gardens are nearby.

🍽 **Excellent – if not cheap – bar food includes soup, ploughman's, deep-fried breadcrumbed brie with fruity cumberland sauce, baked field mushroom topped with caramelised onions and goats cheese, a changing tart like warm thai crab or broccoli, stilton and bacon, potted brown shrimps, local pork and sage sausages with a port and red onion gravy, sunblush tomato couscous with balsamic roasted vegetables, goats cheese and a tomato sauce, local lamb rump with roast sweet potatoes, butternut squash, aubergine purée and a tomato and pancetta ragoût, guinea fowl with braised spring greens and parmesan new potatoes, smoked haddock, bacon and spring onion hash cake with a chive velouté, duck leg confit with dauphinoise potatoes and braised red cabbage, and puddings like dark chocolate and brandy parfait and sticky toffee pudding.** *Starters/Snacks: £3.95 to £8.95. Main Courses: £11.95 to £19.95. Puddings: £4.50 to £6.50*

Free house ~ Licensee Craig Smith ~ Real ale ~ Bar food (12-2.30, 6-9(9.30 Fri-Sun)) ~ Restaurant ~ (01580) 291472 ~ Children welcome ~ Dogs allowed in bar ~ Open 11.30-3.30(4 Sat and Sun), 6-11.30(11 Sun)

Recommended by Peter Meister, Tracey and Stephen Groves, Cathryn and Richard Hicks, Anthony Longden, B Forster, Steve and Nina Bullen, Oliver and Sue Rowell, Pat and Tony Martin, the Didler, Tina and David Woods-Taylor, Liz Hryniewicz, Robin and Glenna Etheridge, Louise English, Jeff and Wendy Williams, Kevin Thorpe, Dr Kevan Tucker, Michael Doswell

BODSHAM   TR1045   MAP 3

Timber Batts 🍽 ♀

Following Bodsham, Wye sign off B2068 keep right at unsigned fork after about 1.5 miles; TN25 5JQ

Lovely french food (bar snacks too) and charming french owner in cottagey old country pub, good real ales, enjoyable wines and fine views

---

Despite the strong emphasis on the extremely good french food in this popular old country farmhouse, the charming french landlord likes to keep the public bar for those wanting a drink and a chat (and maybe a lunchtime snack) with Adnams Bitter and Woodfordes Wherry on handpump; very good french wines by the glass (some from Mr Gross's cousin's vineyard). The little heavy-beamed cottagey area to the right of the door has a couple of comfortable armchairs and two wicker chairs each with a small table, an open fire in the brick fireplace with photographs of the pub above it, some hunting horns and a few high bar chairs; down a little step is more of a drinking part with a mix of cushioned dining chairs, a wall settle, two long tables and several bar stools. There are various froggy cushions and knick-knacks on the window sills (the pub is known locally as Froggies at the Timber Batts). To the left of the entrance is the large but informally rustic beamed restaurant with a happy mix of attractive stripped pine tables and pews and all sorts of dark tables and dining chairs on the carpet, wine labels in a glass frame and wine box tops on the walls, a nice stripped pine cupboard in one corner and a brick fireplace. From straightforward seats and tables in the back hilltop garden there are lovely views over the wide-spreading valley.

🍽 **As well as pubby choices such as filled baguettes, croque monsieur, omelettes, ham and egg, moules marinière and frites, and sausage and mash, the delicious french food using top local produce (cooked by the landlord's son) might include interesting soup, calamari with garlic butter, goats cheese salad, duck foie gras terrine, roasted rack of local lamb with herbs, fillet of beef with roquefort sauce, whitstable rock oysters, duck leg confit, pheasant poached in cider, wild halibut in cider cream sauce, and puddings such as crème brûlée and lemon posset; lovely french cheeses. They list their suppliers on their menu and offer a three-course lunch menu (not Sunday).** *Starters/Snacks: £5.50 to £9.00. Main Courses: £8.00 to £23.00. Puddings: £6.50*

Free house ~ Licensee Joel Gross ~ Real ale ~ Bar food ~ Restaurant ~ (01233) 750237 ~
Children welcome ~ Dogs welcome ~ Open 12-3(4 Sat and Sun), 6.30(7 Sun)-11;
closed 23 Dec-4 Jan

*Recommended by Derek Thomas, Hunter and Christine Wright, Dr Kevan Tucker, Bruce Eccles, N R White,
Virginia Williams, Alan Cowell*

BOUGH BEECH

TQ4846   MAP 3

Wheatsheaf ♀ ☖

B2027, S of reservoir; TN8 7NU

**Ex-hunting lodge with lots to look at, fine range of local drinks, popular food and plenty
of seats in appealing garden**

This ivy-clad old pub is an enjoyable place for either a drink or a meal. There's a lot of
history and masses of interesting things to look at and the neat central bar and long
front bar (which has an attractive old settle carved with wheatsheaves) have unusually
high ceilings with lofty oak timbers, a screen of standing timbers and a revealed king
post; dominoes and board games. Divided from the central bar by two more rows of
standing timbers – one formerly an outside wall to the building – are the snug and
another bar. Other similarly aged features include a piece of 1607 graffiti, 'Foxy
Holamby', thought to have been a whimsical local squire. On the walls and above the
massive stone fireplaces there are quite a few horns and heads as well as african masks,
a sword from Fiji, crocodiles, stuffed birds, swordfish spears and a matapee. Thoughtful
touches include piles of smart magazines, tasty nibbles and winter chestnuts to roast.
Harveys Best, Wells & Youngs Bombardier, and from a village just three miles away,
Westerham Brewery British Bulldog and Grasshopper Kentish Bitter on handpump, three
farm ciders (one from nearby Biddenden), a decent wine list, several malt whiskies,
summer Pimms and winter mulled wine. Outside is appealing too, with plenty of seats,
flowerbeds and fruit trees in the sheltered side and back gardens and there's a heated
smokers' gazebo. Shrubs help divide the garden into various areas, so it doesn't feel too
crowded even when it's full.

🍴 **Enjoyable – if not cheap – bar food includes ciabatta with garlic field mushrooms or
grilled goats cheese with caramelised red onion and pesto, local pork sausages, leek and
cheese macaroni, lambs liver, bacon and black pudding, grilled gammon with cheesy
mash, spiced pork casserole, various curries, poached smoked haddock with citrus cream
sauce, crispy duck with plum sauce, and puddings such as blueberry and lemon
cheesecake and apple and caramelised bread and butter pudding.** *Starters/Snacks: £4.95 to
£8.95. Main Courses: £5.95 to £8.95. Puddings: £4.25 to £4.75*

Enterprise ~ Lease Liz and David Currie ~ Real ale ~ Bar food (12-10) ~ (01732) 700254 ~
Children welcome if seated and in one part of bar only ~ Dogs welcome ~
Open 11am-11.30pm(11pm Sun)

*Recommended by Bob and Margaret Holder, John Branston, Pat and Tony Martin, Mike and Sue Loseby,
Louise English, Jeremy and Jane Morrison, Oliver and Sue Rowell, DFL, Mrs J Ekins-Daukes, Michael and
Maggie Betton, B J Harding, Tina and David Woods-Taylor, Peter and Heather Elliott, Tom and Jill Jones*

BOYDEN GATE

TR2265   MAP 3

Gate Inn ☖ £

*Off A299 Herne Bay—Ramsgate – follow Chislet, Upstreet signpost opposite Roman Gallery;
Chislet also signposted off A28 Canterbury—Margate at Upstreet – after turning right into
Chislet main street keep right on to Boyden; the pub gives its address as Marshside, though
Boyden Gate seems more usual on maps; CT3 4EB*

**Long-serving landlord in unchanging pub, well kept beers, simple food, and tame ducks
and geese to feed**

This is a lovely spot right on the edge of the marshes with lots of water fowl and this
unspoilt local has seats in its sheltered garden, bounded by two streams, with tame
ducks and geese; they sell bags of duck food for 10p. The comfortably worn and

traditional interior is properly pubby with an inglenook log fire serving both the well worn quarry-tiled rooms, flowery-cushioned pews around tables of considerable character, hop bines hanging from the beams and attractively etched windows. Shepherd Neame Master Brew, Spitfire and a seasonal ale are tapped from the cask and you can also get interesting bottled beers and several wines by the glass; board games.

🍴 **Bar food includes lots of different sandwiches, winter soup, a big choice of baked potatoes and burgers, ploughman's, home-made vegetable flan, spicy hotpots and gammon and egg.** *Starters/Snacks: £3.40 to £4.55. Main Courses: £6.75 to £9.95. Puddings: £2.50 to £3.00*

Shepherd Neame ~ Tenant Chris Smith ~ Real ale ~ Bar food (12-2, 6(7 Sun)-9) ~ No credit cards ~ (01227) 860498 ~ Well behaved children in eating area of bar and family room ~ Dogs welcome ~ Open 11-2.30(3 Sat), 6-11; 12-4, 7-10.30 Sun

Recommended by Kevin Thorpe, John Wooll, E D Bailey, Bruce Eccles

BROOKLAND   TQ9825   MAP 3

Royal Oak 🍽️
Just off A259 Rye—New Romney; High Street; TN29 9QR

Lovely old building with carefully modernised rooms, comfortable atmosphere, good bar food and seats in garden; bedrooms

Although this is a 17th-c inn with plenty of ancient features, the inside has been cleverly and tastefully modernised with warm terracotta paintwork, knocked-through walls, standing timbers and lovely big windows. The bar is light and airy with leather upholstered chairs around oak tables and one nice old pew spread over a floor surface that runs from flagstones into oak boards then bricks; piped music and a woodburning stove. Locals pop in to sit on the high bar chairs by the granite-topped counter for a chat and a pint of Adnams Best and Harveys Best on handpump, and the informative and friendly landlord knows a lot about the local area – so do ask him if you get a chance. His equestrian interests are manifest in a lovely set of racing watercolours and a couple of signed photographs on the lime white wall panelling in the bar, and in a rather special set of Cecil Aldin prints displayed in the beamed restaurant (with its well spaced tables and big inglenook fireplace). French windows from here open on to a terrace with metal chairs and there are picnic-sets in the narrow garden which is laid out around a terrace; quaint views of the ancient church and graveyard next door.

🍴 **Using local suppliers and producers which they list on their menu, the well presented and very good bar food might include filled baguettes, ploughman's, soup, twice-baked goats cheese and thyme soufflé with beetroot chutney, home-cooked honey-roast ham with free-range eggs, beer-battered fish, chargrilled barbecue spare ribs, halloumi with cherry tomatoes and red onion on couscous with a mint dressing, wild bass fillet on salsa verde, chump of local lamb with rosemary pesto and wild garlic mash, daily specials such as potted crab, seared pigeon breasts marinated in juniper and thyme, rabbit in a cider, mustard and cream sauce, dover sole with brown shrimps and lemon butter, and puddings like panna cotta with roasted rhubarb and chocolate nemesis.** *Starters/Snacks: £4.95 to £6.25. Main Courses: £8.95 to £15.50. Puddings: £5.95*

Enterprise ~ Lease David Rhys Jones ~ Real ale ~ Bar food (not Sun evening) ~ Restaurant ~ (01797) 344215 ~ Children must be over 10 in evening restaurant and leave pub by 9pm ~ Dogs allowed in bar and bedrooms ~ Open 12-3, 6-11; closed Sun evening ~ Bedrooms: /£75(£95B)

Recommended by B and M Kendall, Louise English, Peter Meister, V Brogden, E D Bailey

Woolpack

On A259 from Rye, about 1 mile before Brookland, take the first right turn signposted Midley where the main road bends sharp left, just after the expanse of Walland Marsh; OS Sheet 189 map reference 977244; TN29 9TJ

15th-c pub with simple furnishings, massive inglenook fireplace, big helpings of tasty food and large garden

This pretty white pub is a popular place at any time of the year, though in the winter you may have to vie for a place in front of the log fire with the two pub cats, Liquorice and Charlie Girl. In summer, the award-winning hanging baskets are really quite a sight and there are plenty of picnic-sets under parasols in the attractive garden with its barbecue area; it's all nicely lit up in the evenings. Inside, there's plenty of marshland character and a good, friendly bustling atmosphere. The ancient entrance lobby has an uneven brick floor and black-painted pine-panelled walls, and to the right, the simple quarry-tiled main bar has basic cushioned plank seats in the massive inglenook fireplace, a painted wood-effect bar counter hung with lots of water jugs and some very early ships' timbers (maybe 12th century) in the low-beamed ceiling; a long elm table has shove-ha'penny carved into one end and there are other old and newer wall benches, chairs at mixed tables with flowers and candles and photographs of locals on the walls. To the left of the lobby is a sparsely furnished little room and an open-plan family room; piped music. Shepherd Neame Master Brew, Spitfire and a seasonal brew on handpump.

🍴 **Reasonably priced, the good pubby food includes sandwiches, filled baked potatoes, ploughman's, soup, garlic mushrooms, sausages, steak pie, stilton and vegetable bake, lasagne, bacon and mushroom quiche, battered cod, generous moules marinière, lamb shank, mixed grill, and puddings like honey and cinnamon pudding and lattice cherry pie.** *Starters/Snacks: £4.00 to £7.95. Main Courses: £5.50 to £17.95. Puddings: £4.50*

Shepherd Neame ~ Tenant Barry Morgan ~ Real ale ~ Bar food (12-2.30, 6-9; all day weekends and during school holidays) ~ (01797) 344321 ~ Children in family room ~ Dogs welcome ~ Open 11-3, 6-11 (all day during school holidays); 11-11 Sat; 12-10.30 Sun

Recommended by Kevin Thorpe, Tim and Claire Woodward, Peter Meister, Conrad Freezer, Louise English, Pat and Tony Martin, V Brogden, Adrian Johnson, Dave Braisted

CHILHAM   TR0653   MAP 3

White Horse

The Square; CT4 8BY

Popular old pub on lovely village square with fresh modern décor in several areas, local beers and good organic bar food

Standing on the edge of one of the prettiest village squares in Kent, this neatly kept, white-painted pub offers a friendly welcome to both locals and visitors. The building proudly declares on the front that it's 15th century, and the handsomely carved ceiling beams bear witness to this, as does a massive fireplace with the Lancastrian rose carved at the end of its mantelbeam – a relic of the Wars of the Roses, uncovered only in 1966 during refurbishments. There's a central bar and three separate but connected seating areas: white paintwork, bright modern paintings, chunky light oak seating and tables on pale wooden flooring and more traditional pubby furniture on quarry tiles, a log fire, horsebrasses, a couple of stained-glass panels, Harveys Best and Shepherd Neame Master Brew on handpump and several wines by the glass. The grand park of nearby Chilham Castle makes a good outing.

🍴 **Using organic local produce, the good, popular bar food includes sandwiches using their home-made bread, ploughman's, soup, pâté with fig relish, smoked mackerel and couscous salad, meatballs in local wine and tomato sauce, ham and egg, local sausages with onion gravy, tasty fish pie, free-range chicken in truffle cream sauce, a changing vegetarian dish, pork belly with apple sauce, and puddings like lemon fool or chocolate pot; good Sunday roast and they may serve home-made cakes and coffee all day.** *Starters/Snacks: £3.95 to £6.95. Main Courses: £7.95 to £12.95. Puddings: £4.95*

Enterprise ~ Lease Lisa Smart ~ Real ale ~ Bar food (12-2.30, 6.30-9.30; 12-4 Sun;
not Sun evening) ~ (01227) 730355 ~ Children welcome ~ Dogs allowed in bar ~
Live music first Sun of month ~ Open 12-11(10.30 Sun)

Recommended by Alan Cowell

GROOMBRIDGE
TQ5337   MAP 3

Crown
B2110; TN3 9QH

**Charming village pub with quite a bit of bric-a-brac in snug, low-beamed rooms, local
beers and well liked bar food**

Appreciated by both locals and visitors, this pretty tile-hung cottage is a cosy place with
a relaxed atmosphere. The snug left-hand room has old tables on worn flagstones and a
sizeable brick inglenook with a big winter log fire. The other low-beamed rooms have
roughly plastered walls, some squared panelling and timbering and a quite a bit of bric-a-
brac, from old teapots and pewter tankards to antique bottles. Walls are decorated with
small topographical, game and sporting prints and there's a circular large-scale map with
the pub at its centre. The end dining room has fairly close-spaced tables with a variety of
good solid chairs, and a log-effect gas fire in a big fireplace. Harveys Best, Hepworth
Sussex Bitter and Larkins Best on handpump and several wines by the glass. There's a
back car park, pub garden and picnic-sets out in front on a wonky but sunny brick terrace
that overlooks the steep village green. A public footpath across the road beside the small
chapel leads through a field to Groombridge Place Gardens.

🍴 **Well liked bar food at lunchtime includes filled baguettes and baked potatoes,
ploughman's, soup, cumberland sausage with onion gravy, beer-battered haddock, home-
cooked ham and eggs, popular home-made steak burgers with applewood cheese and
bacon, steak in ale pie, chicken on pasta with bacon, avocado and tomato and grilled
smoked haddock with mediterranean vegetables.** *Starters/Snacks: £3.95 to £6.50.
Main Courses: £6.50 to £16.90. Puddings: £4.50*

Free house ~ Licensee Peter Kilshaw ~ Real ale ~ Bar food (12-2.30(3 Sun),
7-9(6.30-9.30 Fri and Sat); not Sun evening) ~ Restaurant ~ (01892) 864742 ~
Children welcome ~ Dogs allowed in bar ~ Open 11-3, 6-11; 11-11 summer Fri and Sat;
12-10.30 Sun; 12-5 Sun in winter; closed winter Sun evening ~ Bedrooms: £40/£45(£60S)

Recommended by B J Harding, Nigel and Jean Eames, N R White, R and S Bentley

HAWKHURST
TQ7531   MAP 3

Great House ♀
Gills Green; pub signed just off A229 N; TN18 5EJ

**Emphasis on good bistro-style food, drinkers' area too, several wines by the glass,
attractive furnishings and plenty of space**

Although much extended, this attractive white-weatherboarded pub was once two
thatched farm cottages from which the wife of the hop grower living there was granted a
licence in 1615 to sell ales and ciders. That tradition continues today with locals still
popping in for a pint and a chat, though most customers are here to enjoy the
interesting food. Just inside the main door are a couple of heavy-beamed small drinking
areas with sofas, armchairs and bright scatter cushions, and there are high-backed bar
chairs by the counter where they serve Harveys Best and Shepherd Neame Master Brew on
handpump; good wines by the glass. There are some dark wooden slatted dining tables
and smart clothed chairs on the slate floor, gilt-framed pictures on the red or
green walls and a small brick fireplace. Stairs lead down to a light and airy dining room
with big picture windows, carved built-in seating with more colourful cushions and high-
backed leather dining chairs around various wooden tables; Farrow & Ball paintwork and
plenty of modern art. The atmosphere throughout is relaxed and chatty and the french
staff are friendly. Outside on the terrace are some turquoise seats and tables.

🍴 Good bistro-style food includes sandwiches and toasted panini, soup, a fish or meat platter, ham hock terrine with spiced pear chutney, seared scallops with pea purée, pancetta crisps and lemon grass sauce, guinea fowl with rhubarb chutney and pomegranate jus, home-made seasonal vegetable spring rolls with egg noodles and sweet chilli, local sausages with onion gravy, beer-battered fresh haddock, confit pork belly with carrot purée and cider jus, chicken supreme with bubble and squeak, fricassée of mushroom and chorizo and red wine jus, and puddings like dark chocolate tart with white chocolate ice-cream and apple and rhubarb crumble with honeycomb ice-cream. *Starters/Snacks: £3.95 to £8.95. Main Courses: £6.95 to £17.95. Puddings: £4.95 to £5.50*

Free house ~ Licensees Martial and Natasha Chaussy ~ Real ale ~ Bar food (12-3, 6-9.30; all day weekends) ~ Restaurant ~ (01580) 753119 ~ Children welcome ~ Dogs allowed in bar ~ Open 11.30-11; closed Mon during Jan and Feb

Recommended by Elizabeth Stowe, Colin and Stephanie McFie, BOB

HODSOLL STREET   TQ6263   MAP 3
Green Man
Hodsoll Street and pub signed off A227 S of Meopham; turn right in village; TN15 7LE

Bustling pub by village green, friendly atmosphere, lots of food specials, real ales and seats in garden

In summer, the pretty hanging baskets at the front of this little pub are very pretty, and there are seats on the well tended lawn and a children's climbing frame. Inside, the friendly licensees are sure to make you welcome, and the big airy carpeted rooms work their way around a central bar with Greene King Old Speckled Hen, Harveys Best, Timothy Taylors Landlord and changing guest such as Black Sheep on handpump; decent wines. There are traditional neat tables and chairs spaced tidily around the walls, interesting old local photographs and antique plates on the walls and a warm winter log fire; piped music. There may be summer morris dancers; the nearby North Downs have plenty of walks.

🍴 As well as a popular two-course weekday lunch, the well liked bar food includes sandwiches, soup, deep-fried breaded brie with cranberry sauce, mushroom provençale on toasted brioche, beer-battered cod, cherry tomato and stilton risotto, steak and kidney wrapped in filo pastry, trout stuffed with thai prawns, lamb shank with red wine jus, pork fillet stuffed with black pudding and wrapped in bacon, a mixed grill, and puddings; they also have a steak and rib night on Tuesdays and a fish evening on Wednesdays. *Starters/Snacks: £4.50 to £6.00. Main Courses: £8.50 to £16.00. Puddings: £4.50*

Enterprise ~ Lease John, Jean and David Haywood ~ Real ale ~ Bar food (12-2(3 weekends), 6.30-9.30(9 Sun)) ~ (01732) 823575 ~ Children welcome ~ Dogs welcome ~ Live music every second Thurs of month ~ Open 11-2.30, 6-11; 11-11 Fri and Sat; 12-10.30 Sun

Recommended by Pat and Barbara Stancliffe, E D Bailey, Annette Tress, Gary Smith, Jan and Rod Poulter, Arthur S Maxted, Jan and Alan Summers

HOLLINGBOURNE   TQ8354   MAP 3
Windmill
A mile from M20 junction 8: A20 towards Ashford (away from Maidstone), then left into B2163 – Eyhorne Street village; ME17 1TR

Small pubby core with several real ales but mainly set for dining; sunny little garden

Handy for the M20 this attractive pub is usefully open all day. There are several small or smallish mainly carpeted areas with heavy low black beams that link together around the central island serving bar – sometimes partly separated by glazed or stained-glass panels. There's a pleasantly old-world feel, a good log fire in the huge inglenook fireplace, solid pub tables with padded country or library chairs, soft lighting, black timbers in ochre walls and shelves of books. The pubbiest part can be found tucked away up steps towards the back with bar stools and Harveys Best, Shepherd Neame Master Brew and Wychwood Hobgoblin on handpump and several wines by the glass; piped music. A neatly kept sunny little garden has picnic-sets under cocktail parasols and a play area.

⑪ At lunchtime, bar food includes sandwiches, filled baked potatoes and baguettes, ploughman's, ham and egg, liver and bacon with onion gravy, citrus-battered fish and tagliatelle carbonara, as well as garlic king prawns, whitebait with horseradish mayonnaise, chicken liver pâté with red onion marmalade, wok-tossed vegetables with pasta, various home-made burgers, a pie of the day, and daily specials such as tempura king prawns with sweet chilli sauce, rib-eye steak with tomato and pepper jam and dover sole; they also offer a good value two-course set menu on Monday and Tuesday. *Starters/Snacks: £4.75 to £6.95. Main Courses: £7.25 to £18.25. Puddings: £3.50 to £5.95*

Enterprise ~ Lease Lee and Jan Atkinson ~ Real ale ~ Bar food (12-2.30, 6-10; 12-10 Sat(till 9.30 Sun) ~ Restaurant ~ (01622) 880280 ~ Children must remain seated in bar ~ Dogs welcome ~ Open 12-11(11.30 Sat, 10.30 Sun)

Recommended by Dr Kevan Tucker, Stephen Moss, B and M Kendall, Tim and Claire Woodward

ICKHAM   TR2258   MAP 3
Duke William
Off A257 E of Canterbury; The Street; CT3 1QP

Friendly, relaxed family-owned village pub with light, airy spreading bar and back dining conservatory, real ales and decent wines, newspapers to read and WIFI internet access, enjoyable modern bar food; plenty of seats outside; bedrooms

In a pretty village, this family-owned pub is a welcoming place with a friendly, informal atmosphere. The big spreading bar has huge new oak beams and stripped joists, a fine mix of seats from settles to high-backed cushioned dining chairs, dark wheelback and bentwood chairs around all sorts of wooden tables on the stripped wooden floor, a log fire with a couple of settles and a low barrel table in front of it, a central bar counter with high stools and brass coat books, and a snug little area with one long table, black leather high-backed dining chairs, a flat-screen TV and computer monitor; daily papers, quiet piped music, cheerful modern paintings and large hop bines. Fullers London Pride, Harveys Sussex and Shepherd Neame Master Brew on handpump and decent wines; Happy Hour is from 4-6pm. Staff are chatty and attentive. A low-ceilinged dining room leads off to the left with dark wood chairs, tables and more cushioned settles, with paintings and mirrors on the walls. At the back of the pub, there's a light dining conservatory with all manner of interesting paintings, prints and heraldry on the walls and similar furniture on the slate floor; doors from here lead to a big terrace with a covered area to one side, plenty of wooden and metal tables and chairs and a lawn with picnic-table sets and some swings and a slide; there's also a designated smokers' area, too. Although we have not heard from readers, this would be very pleasant place to stay.

⑪ Enjoyable bar food includes filled baguettes, soup, chicken liver pâté, whitebait, field mushroom topped with goats cheese, seared scallops with chorizo, steak in ale pie, calves liver and bacon, slow-roasted belly of pork with cider and apple sauce, chicken stuffed with sunblush tomatoes with a green pepper sauce, bass with lemon butter, and puddings like chocolate brownie and banoffi pie; there's also a good value two-course lunch menu and Sunday roasts. *Starters/Snacks: £4.95 to £6.95. Main Courses: £6.95 to £16.95. Puddings: £4.75*

Free house ~ Licensee Louise White ~ Real ale ~ Bar food (12-3, 6-9) ~ Restaurant ~ (01227) 721308 ~ Well behaved children welcome ~ Dogs allowed in bar ~ Live music Sun 4-7pm ~ Open 11-11(midnight Sat, 10.30 Sun); 12-10.30 Sun ~ Bedrooms: /£65S

Recommended by Prof and Mrs J Fletcher

Bedroom prices are for high summer. Even then you may get reductions for more than one night, or (outside tourist areas) weekends. Winter special rates are common, and many inns cut bedroom prices if you have a full evening meal.

IDEN GREEN
TQ8031 MAP 3

Woodcock

From village centre follow Standen Street signpost, then fork left down Woodcock Lane (this is not the Iden Green near Goudhurst); TN17 4HT

Simple country local with friendly staff, chatty regulars, an informal atmosphere, well liked food and pretty garden

This is an unpretentious little country local tucked away down lanes on the edge of Standen Wood with a friendly young licensee. The low-ceilinged bar has an open woodburning stove in a fine old inglenook fireplace with a comfortable squishy sofa and low table in front of it, stripped brick walls hung with horse tackle, horsebrasses and various copper and brass items, a couple of big standing timbers, a second sofa and cushioned settle to one side of the bar and some high bar chairs. The chatty regulars tend to congregate around the high bar stools enjoying the Greene King Abbot and Morlands Mild on handpump served by friendly staff. A couple of steps lead up to the two rooms of the panelled dining area with some old photographs and hunting prints on the walls and pine tables and chairs. There are seats in the pretty back garden and a car park just along the lane from the pub.

🍽 **Well liked bar food includes lunchtime filled baguettes, ploughman's, soup, salmon fishcakes with tartare sauce, game terrine, home-made burgers, sausages with bubble and squeak, ham and egg, butternut squash and goats cheese risotto, popular steak and kidney pudding, a medley of seafood, guinea fowl with mushroom and brandy gravy, and puddings like chocolate and orange cheesecake and sticky toffee pudding with toffee sauce and caramel ice-cream.** *Starters/Snacks: £4.95 to £6.95. Main Courses: £8.95 to £18.50. Puddings: £5.50*

Greene King ~ Lease Andrew Hemmings ~ Real ale ~ Bar food (12.30-2.30(3 Sun), 6.30-9.30; not Sun evening) ~ Restaurant ~ (01580) 240009 ~ Children in eating area of bar ~ Dogs allowed in bar ~ Open 12-11; closed all day Mon except bank holidays

Recommended by BOB

IGHTHAM COMMON
TQ5855 MAP 3

Harrow

Signposted off A25 just W of Ightham; pub sign may be hard to spot; TN15 9EB

Emphasis on good food in friendly, smart dining pub, fresh flowers and candles; pretty back terrace

Our readers have very much enjoyed their visits to this civilised and friendly dining pub over the last year – especially on Sunday lunchtimes. And while most customers are here to enjoy the particularly good food, there is a tiny bar inside the door and a larger bar area to the right. Both these two rooms are attractively decorated with fresh flowers and candles on tables, smart dining chairs on the herringbone-patterned wood floor with a winter fire. The bigger room is painted a cheerful sunny yellow above the wood-panelled dado, there's a charming little antiquated conservatory and a more formal dining room. Greene King IPA and Abbot on handpump, several wines by the glass and a warm welcome from the amiable landlord and his attentive staff. There are tables and chairs out on a pretty little pergola-enclosed back terrace; the pub is handy for Ightham Mote.

🍽 **Good, popular food includes bar dishes like pork sausages with onion gravy, home-baked ham and eggs, risotto verde, thai-style prawn curry, beef in Guinness and cajun chicken, as well as more elaborate dishes such as duck liver pâté with redcurrant jelly, salmon and chive fishcake with citrus cream sauce, goats cheese and caramelised red onion tart with grape salad, supreme of chicken with tagliatelle, tomato, mushroom and cream, duck suprême with dauphinoise potatoes and morello cherry sauce, king scallops wrapped in pancetta with a garlic and herb dressing and seasonal game like venison wellington; Sunday roasts.** *Starters/Snacks: £4.50 to £7.50. Main Courses: £8.95 to £18.95. Puddings: £5.75*

Free house ~ Licensees John Elton and Claire Butler ~ Real ale ~ Bar food (12-2(2.30 Sun), 6-9; not Sun evening or Mon) ~ Restaurant ~ (01732) 885912 ~ Children welcome but not in dining room on Sat evening ~ Open 12-3, 6-11; 12-3 Sun; closed Sun evening and all day Mon

Recommended by Derek Thomas, Dave Braisted, Martin and Karen Wake, David and Sharon Collison, Andrea Rampley, B and M Kendall, Susan Wilson, Peter and Jan Humphreys

IVY HATCH   TQ5854   MAP 3

Plough ♀

Village signposted off A227 N of Tonbridge; High Cross Road; TN15 0NL

New licensees for refurbished old pub, real ales and wines by the glass, interesting bar food cooked by the landlord and seats in newly landscaped garden

Enthusiastic licensees have taken over this tile-hung country pub and completely refurbished it. There's a light wooden floor throughout, leather chesterfields grouped around an open fire, quite a mix of cushioned dining chairs around wooden tables, some large plants dotted about and high bar chairs by the wooden-topped bar counter where they keep Harveys Best and a seasonal ale plus a seasonal guest from Westerham Brewery on handpump and quite a few wines by the glass, some local. There's also a conservatory. Seats in the landscaped garden surrounded by cob trees. Ightham Mote is close by.

⑪ Using seasonal local produce and maybe home-grown herbs, the good bar food cooked by the landlord includes sandwiches, ploughman's, chicken liver parfait with chutney, sweet-cured salmon with cucumber jelly and lemon cream, crab with lemon mayonnaise, ham and egg, home-made steak burger, roasted courgettes, broad beans, pea and parmesan risotto, beer-battered haddock, roast rump of lamb with dauphinoise potatoes, confit of duck leg with citrus jus, lancashire hotpot, and puddings like dark chocolate tart with mascarpone and sticky toffee pudding; Sunday roasts. *Starters/Snacks: £5.95 to £8.95. Main Courses: £8.95 to £16.95. Puddings: £4.00 to £6.00*

Free house ~ Licensee Miles Medes ~ Real ale ~ Bar food (12-2.45, 6-9; all day Sat; 12-5.30 Sun) ~ Restaurant ~ (01732) 810100 ~ Children welcome ~ Open 12-3, 6-11; 10am-11pm(10pm summer Sun) Sat; may close earlier Sun evening in winter

Recommended by Bob and Margaret Holder

LANGTON GREEN   TQ5439   MAP 3

Hare ⑪ ♀

A264 W of Tunbridge Wells; TN3 0JA

Interestingly decorated Edwardian pub with a fine choice of drinks and popular food

This Edwardian roadside pub is well run and relaxed with a friendly welcome from the helpful young landlord and his efficient staff. The front bar tends to be where drinkers gather and the knocked-through interior has big windows and high ceilings that give a spacious feel. Décor, more or less in period with the building, runs from dark-painted dados below light walls, 1930s oak furniture and turkish-style carpets on stained wooden floors to old romantic pastels and a huge collection of chamber-pots hanging from beams. Interesting old books, pictures and two huge mahogany mirror-backed display cabinets crowd the walls of the big room at the back, which has lots of large tables (one big enough for at least a dozen) on a light brown carpet. Greene King IPA, Abbot and Old Speckled Hen and guests such as Bath Ales Gem Bitter, Holdens Golden Glow, and St Austell Tribute on handpump, over 100 whiskies, up to 30 wines by the glass and a fine choice of vodkas and other spirits. French windows open on to a big terrace with picnic-sets and pleasant views of the tree-ringed village green. Parking is limited.

⑪ Good, popular bar food includes sandwiches, ploughman's, tasty moules marinière, ham hock, cider and apple terrine with fruit chutney, crab and ginger wonton with teriyaki dipping sauce, beetroot and mascarpone risotto with crumbled wensleydale, home-cooked ham and eggs, venison burger with pepper sauce, salmon, smoked haddock and dill fishcakes, local sausages and mash, chicken and bacon pie topped with horseradish mash, pork belly with caramel sauce, glazed pear and mustard mash, and puddings like chocolate

hazelnut meringue roulade and pear and almond tart. *Starters/Snacks: £4.70 to £7.50. Main Courses: £6.50 to £14.00. Puddings: £4.75 to £5.50*

Brunning & Price ~ Lease Christopher Little ~ Real ale ~ Bar food (all day) ~ (01892) 862419 ~ Children welcome ~ Dogs allowed in bar ~ Open 11-11(midnight Fri and Sat); 12-10.30 Sun

Recommended by B and M Kendall, Revd R P Tickle, Gerry and Rosemary Dobson, Dr and Mrs A K Clarke, John Branston

LOWER HARDRES
TR1453 MAP 3

Granville ♀

B2068 S of Canterbury; Faussett Hill, Street End; CT4 7AL

Surprisingly modern décor in several connected rooms, a fine choice of wines, good service and popular food; cosy little shady garden

Most customers come to this light and airy pub to enjoy the interesting food but you must book in advance to be sure of a table – especially on weekend lunchtimes. There are several linked areas with attractive contemporary furnishings such as comfortable squashy sofas, a mix of pale and dark tables with cushioned dining chairs, and – through shelves of large coloured church candles – a glimpse of the chefs hard at work in the kitchen. The appealing décor includes interesting modern photographs and animal lino cuts on pale yellow walls above a dark red dado, a couple of large modern candelabra-type ceiling lights, one area with the floor attractively patterned in wood and tiles and an unusual central fire with a large conical hood; daily papers and board games. The proper public bar has settles, farmhouse chairs, a woodburning stove, Shepherd Neame Master Brew and a seasonal beer on handpump and good wines from a long blackboard list. French windows lead to the garden with rustic-style picnic-sets under a large spreading tree and there are some more traditional picnic-sets on a small sunny terraced area. More reports please.

🍽 **Well liked bar food includes soup, smoked local wigeon with remoulade, pea and mint risotto, pear, walnut and roquefort salad, seared ray with shrimp and parsley butter, crispy duck with smoked chilli salsa and sour cream, whole roast bream with garlic and rosemary, braised pork belly with crackling and apple sauce, and puddings like rhubarb sorbet with burnt cream and tiramisu with marinated cherries.** *Starters/Snacks: £4.95 to £7.95. Main Courses: £9.95 to £18.95. Puddings: £5.50 to £7.50*

Shepherd Neame ~ Tenant Gabrielle Harris ~ Real ale ~ Bar food (not Sun evening or Mon) ~ (01227) 700402 ~ Children welcome ~ Dogs welcome ~ Open 12-3, 5.30-11; 12-10.30 Sun; closed 25 and 26 Dec

Recommended by Dr Kevan Tucker, Rob and Catherine Dunster, R Goodenough

NEWNHAM
TQ9557 MAP 3

George

The Street; village signposted from A2 just W of Ospringe, outside Faversham; ME9 0LL

Old-world village pub with open-plan rooms, a fair choice of drinks and food, and seats in spacious garden; pleasant walks nearby

Happily, not much changes in this friendly local. There's a series of spreading open-plan rooms with stripped, polished floorboards, stripped brickwork, gas-type chandeliers, candles and lamps on handsome tables and attractively upholstered mahogany settles. Blazing fires, hop-strung beams and Shepherd Neame Master Brew and a seasonal beer on handpump and several wines by the glass; piped music. The spacious sheltered garden has some picnic-sets and there are pleasant nearby walks. More reports please.

🍽 **Bar food includes lunchtime sandwiches, filled baguettes and baked potatoes, ploughman's, ham and eggs, bangers and mash, vegetable curry, steak and kidney pudding, daily specials, and puddings such as banoffi pie.** *Starters/Snacks: £5.00 to £8.00. Main Courses: £10.00 to £17.00. Puddings: £4.25 to £5.25*

Shepherd Neame ~ Tenants Chris and Marie Annand ~ Real ale ~ Bar food (12-2.30, 7-9.30) ~
Restaurant ~ (01795) 890237 ~ Children welcome ~ Open 11-3, 6.30-11; 12-4, 7-10.30 Sun
Recommended by Chris Bell, Keith and Chris O'Neill

OARE   TR0163   MAP 3

Shipwrights Arms

*S shore of Oare Creek, E of village; coming from Faversham on the Oare road, turn right into
Ham Road opposite Davington School; or off A2 on B2045, go into Oare village, then turn
right towards Faversham, and then left into Ham Road opposite Davington School; OS Sheet
178 map reference 016635; ME13 7TU*

**Remote pub in marshland with lots of surrounding bird life and up to five real ales in
simple little bars**

Well off the beaten track, this unspoilt old tavern has plenty of character and is popular
with locals and walkers (often with a dog in tow). The three simple little bars are dark
and separated by standing timbers and wood partitions or narrow door arches. A medley
of seats runs from tapestry-cushioned stools and chairs to black wood-panelled built-in
settles forming little booths, and there are pewter tankards over the bar counter, boating
jumble and pictures, pottery boating figures, flags or boating pennants on the ceilings,
several brick fireplaces and a good woodburning stove. Look out for the electronic wind
gauge above the main door which takes its reading from the chimney. A beer from
Goachers, Hopdaemon and Whitstable breweries and maybe a couple of guests tapped
from the cask; piped local radio. There are seats in the large garden and nearby walks.

🍴 **Traditional bar food such as sandwiches, ploughman's, sausage and mash, liver and
bacon and fish pie.** *Starters/Snacks: £3.95 to £6.95. Main Courses: £7.25 to £14.95.
Puddings: £3.95 to £4.50*

Free house ~ Licensees Derek and Ruth Cole ~ Real ale ~ Bar food (12-2.30, 7-9;
not Sun evening or Mon) ~ Restaurant ~ (01795) 590088 ~ Children welcome away from bar
area ~ Dogs allowed in bar ~ Open 11-3(4 Sat), 6-11; 12-4, 6-10.30 Sun; closed Mon

*Recommended by N R White, the Didler, Colin Moore, Kevin Flack, Rob and Kirstin, Andrea Rampley,
Louise English, Pete Baker, Bruce Eccles*

PENSHURST   TQ5142   MAP 3

Bottle House

*Coldharbour Lane; leaving Penshurst SW on B2188 turn right at Smarts Hill signpost, then
bear right towards Chiddingstone and Cowden; keep straight on B2188; TN11 8ET*

**Low beamed, connected bars in country pub, friendly, chatty atmosphere, real ales and
decent wines, popular bar food and sunny terrace; nearby walks**

Although the open-plan rooms in this tile-hung old country pub are all connected, there
are plenty of nooks and crannies (perfect for a more cosy drink or meal) and standing
timbers that give a sense of being separate and yet part of the chatty, bustling
atmosphere. There are beams and joists (one or two of the especially low ones are leather
padded), an attractive mix of old wheelback and other dining chairs around all sorts of
wooden tables, photographs of the pub and local scenes on the walls (some of which are
stripped stone), an old brick floor by the carved wooden bar counter with dark wooden
boarding elsewhere and some Farrow & Ball-type paintwork; the fireplace houses a
woodburning stove and most of the tables are set with fresh flowers. Harveys Best and
Larkins Traditional on handpump and a good choice of wines; friendly, helpful young
service and piped music. The sunny, brick-paved terrace has green-painted picnic-sets
under parasols and some olive trees in white pots. Good surrounding walks.

🍴 **The popular bar food includes soup, ploughman's, duck liver and orange parfait, a
charcuterie board, seared scallops with pea purée and crispy pancetta, linguine carbonara,
chargrilled steak burger topped with swiss cheese, a trio of local sausages with
caramelised red onion gravy, home-baked honey and mustard ham with free-range eggs,**

beer-battered cod, wild mushroom stroganoff, corn-fed chicken stuffed with cream cheese and pesto, wrapped in parma ham and rump of local lamb wellington with a port and redcurrant sauce; Sunday roasts. *Starters/Snacks: £2.50 to £8.95. Main Courses: £9.95 to £17.95. Puddings: £4.95 to £5.50*

Free house ~ Licensee Paul Hammond ~ Real ale ~ Bar food (12-10(9 Sun)) ~ Restaurant ~ (01892) 870306 ~ Children welcome ~ Dogs allowed in bar ~ Open 11-11(10.30 Sun)

Recommended by Tina and David Woods-Taylor, Jamie May, N R White

Rock 🍺

Hoath Corner, Chiddingstone Hoath, on back road Chiddingstone—Cowden; OS Sheet 188 map reference 497431; TN8 7BS

Tiny rural cottage, simple furnishings, local beer and pubby food

There are usually several chatty locals and their dogs in this very small and unspoilt tile-hung cottage. It's all quite unpretentious, with beams, a lovely, uneven and very old brick floor, a woodburning stove in a fine old brick inglenook and pretty basic furniture – a few red plush or brocaded stools, a couple of barrel tables, a well worn armchair and a large stuffed bull's head for ring the bull (well used by regulars). Up a step to the right is a smaller room with a long wooden settle by an equally long and rather nice table and a couple of other tables with wheelback chairs. Larkins Best and Traditional on handpump brewed on the Dockertys' nearby farm. In front of the building are a couple of picnic-sets, with more on the back lawn.

🍴 As well as blackboard specials using local venison and game and organic veal, bar food includes sandwiches, soup, pâté, ham and eggs, bangers and mash, cod and peas, a curry and lamb shank. *Starters/Snacks: £2.75 to £6.25. Main Courses: £6.95 to £12.95. Puddings: £4.00*

Own brew ~ Licensee Robert Dockerty ~ Real ale ~ Bar food (not Sun evening or Mon) ~ (01892) 870296 ~ Dogs welcome ~ Open 11.30-3, 6-11; 12-3.30 Sun; closed Sun evening and Monday (except bank hols)

Recommended by Andrea Rampley, Heather and Dick Martin, Tina and David Woods-Taylor, Bob and Margaret Holder

PLUCKLEY   TQ9243   MAP 3

Dering Arms 🍷 🛏

Pluckley Station, which is signposted from B2077; or follow Station Road (left turn off Smarden Road in centre of Pluckley) for about 1.3 miles S, through Pluckley Thorne; TN27 0RR

Fine fish dishes plus other good food in handsome building, stylish main bar, carefully chosen wines and roaring log fire; comfortable bedrooms

Our readers very much enjoy staying overnight in this striking old building – and the breakfasts are smashing. And while much emphasis is also placed on the fish and seafood, the bar is characterful and comfortable and they do keep a beer named for the pub from Goachers on handpump, a good wine list, 30 malt whiskies and occasional local cider. High-ceilinged and stylishly plain, this main bar has a solid country feel with a variety of wooden furniture on the flagstone floors, a roaring log fire in the great fireplace, country prints and some fishing rods. The smaller half-panelled back bar has similar dark wood furnishings, and an extension to this area has a woodburning stove, comfortable armchairs, sofas and a grand piano; board games. Classic car meetings (the long-serving landlord has a couple of classics) are held here on the second Sunday of the month.

🍴 In the bar, pubby dishes include filled baguettes, ploughman's, soft herring roes with crispy bacon, sautéed chicken livers with onions, bacon and mushrooms in a creamy brandy sauce, garlic king prawns, a pie of the day, and puddings like lemon posset and chestnut, chocolate and brandy cake with apricot compote. Many people, though, are here to eat the very good (if not cheap) fish: salmon fillet with Pernod and lemon butter sauce, tuna steak with garlic and lemon, skate wing with capers and brown butter, seafood platter (24 hours' notice), and daily specials. *Starters/Snacks: £4.95 to £7.95. Main Courses: £9.95 to £25.00. Puddings: £4.95 to £6.95*

Free house ~ Licensee James Buss ~ Real ale ~ Bar food (not Sun evening, not Mon) ~ Restaurant ~ (01233) 840371 ~ Children welcome ~ Dogs allowed in bar ~ Open 11.30-3.30, 6-11; 12-4 Sun; closed Sun evening, all Mon, 25-28 Dec, 1 Jan ~ Bedrooms: £40(£65S)/£50(£75S)

Recommended by Sara Fulton, Roger Baker, Michael Doswell, Peter Meister, Louise English, Derek Thomas, Joan and Alec Lawrence, Bruce Eccles

SELLING   TR0455   MAP 3

Rose & Crown

Signposted from exit roundabout of M2 junction 7: keep right on through village and follow Perry Wood signposts; or from A252 just W of junction with A28 at Chilham follow Shottenden signpost, then right turn signposted Selling, then right signposted Perry Wood; ME13 9RY

Nice summer garden, winter log fires, hop-covered beams and several real ales

Much enjoyed by our readers and with a good mix of chatty locals and visitors, this tucked-away country pub is run by friendly licensees. The bustling bars have comfortably cushioned seats, winter log fires in two inglenook fireplaces, hop bines strung from the beams and fresh flowers; steps lead down to another timbered area. Adnams Broadside and Southwold, Goachers Mild and Harveys Best on handpump, quite a few whiskies and several ciders; piped music and board games. The flowering tubs and hanging baskets in front of the pub are very pretty in summer and the cottagey back garden is lovely then, too; children's play area. There are good walks in the ancient surrounding woodland, particularly lovely when the bluebells are out.

Ⅲ Bar food includes sandwiches, ploughman's, soup, rabbit terrine with chutney, stilton and mushroom bake, home-baked ham or sausage with egg, vegetarian risotto, steak in ale or fish pie, winter irish stew, chicken and bacon in barbecue sauce, and puddings like fruit crumble or popular chocolate fudge cake. *Starters/Snacks: £3.95 to £5.95. Main Courses: £7.45 to £10.45. Puddings: £3.95 to £4.25*

Free house ~ Licensees Tim Robinson and Vanessa Grove ~ Real ale ~ Bar food (not Mon evening) ~ Restaurant ~ (01227) 752214 ~ Children welcome ~ Dogs welcome ~ Quiz night first Weds of month ~ Open 11.30-3(3.30 summer Sat), 6.30-11; 12-4, 7-10.30 Sun; closed Mon evening and evenings 25 and 26 Dec and 1 Jan

Recommended by R and M Thomas, Louise English, the Didier, Andrew Clarke, Stephen Corfield, Tom and Jill Jones

SHIPBOURNE   TQ5952   MAP 3

Chaser ⑪ ♀

Stumble Hill (A227 N of Tonbridge); TN11 9PE

Comfortable, civilised country pub, log fires, good, popular food, quite a few wines by the glass; covered and heated outside terrace

Extremely popular – you need to book in advance to be sure of a table – this well run pub is civilised and rather smart but with a friendly atmosphere and efficient, helpful staff. Most customers are here to enjoy the good food but they do keep Greene King IPA and Abbot and a couple of guest beers like Brains Rev James and H&H Olde Trip on handpump, a huge number of wines by the glass, 40 malt whiskies and a fair choice of brandies and liqueurs; piped music and board games. There are several open-plan areas that meander into each other, all converging on a large central island bar counter: stripped wooden floors, frame-to-frame pictures on deepest red and cream walls, stripped pine wainscoting, an eclectic mix of solid old wood tables (with candles) and chairs, shelves of books and open fires. A striking school chapel-like restaurant right at the back has dark wood panelling and a high timber-vaulted ceiling. French windows open on to a covered and heated central courtyard with teak furniture and big green parasols, and a side garden, with the pretty church rising behind (well worth a visit), is nicely enclosed by hedges and shrubs. There's a small car park at the back or you can park in the lane opposite by a delightful green; farmer's market on Thursday morning.

🍴 Using carefully chosen local produce, the enjoyable food includes sandwiches, ploughman's, soup, home-made duck spring roll on chinese vegetables with a plum dressing, potted crab and crayfish set with lobster butter, mixed mushroom omelette with free-range eggs, steak burger with bacon and emmenthal cheese, beer-battered haddock, fillet of beef and wild mushroom stroganoff, half a shoulder of lamb with dijon mustard and herb crust and a rosemary and redcurrant sauce, daily specials like whole plaice with a citrus and herb crust and lamb kofta with hummus and tzatziki, and puddings such as chocolate brownie with white chocolate sauce and passion fruit and raspberry crème brûlée; they serve breakfast on Thursday, Friday and Saturday. *Starters/Snacks: £3.95 to £9.95. Main Courses: £6.95 to £15.95. Puddings: £4.95 to £6.25*

Whiting & Hammond ~ Lease Darren Somerton ~ Real ale ~ Bar food (all day) ~ Restaurant ~ (01732) 810360 ~ Children welcome but must be well behaved ~ Dogs allowed in bar ~ Open 11-11(midnight Sat); 12-10 Sun

Recommended by B J Harding, Tina and David Woods-Taylor, Tom and Jill Jones, Derek Thomas, N R White, Bob and Margaret Holder, Martin and Pauline Jennings, Mrs G R Sharman, Neil Hardwick, Gordon and Margaret Ormondroyd, Gene and Kitty Rankin

SNARGATE   TQ9928   MAP 3

Red Lion ★ 🍺

B2080 Appledore—Brenzett; TN29 9UQ

Unchanging, simple pub, good chatty atmosphere and straightforward furnishings; no food

For 99 years the same family have run this quite unspoilt and unchanging village tavern. The three little rooms have a timeless, old-fashioned charm as well as their original cream tongue and groove wall panelling, heavy beams in a sagging ceiling, dark pine Victorian farmhouse chairs on bare boards, lots of old photographs and other memorabilia and there's a coal fire; outdoor lavatories, of course. Lighting is dim but candles are lit at night. One small room, with a frosted glass wall through to the bar and a sash window looking out to a cottage garden, has only two dark pine pews beside two long tables, a couple more farmhouse chairs and an old piano stacked with books. Toad in the hole, darts, shove-ha'penny, cribbage, dominoes, nine men's morris and table skittles. Four ales from Goachers and a guest like Northumberland Northumbrian Fayre are tapped straight from casks on a low rack behind an unusual shop-like marble-topped counter (little marks it out as a bar other than a few glasses on two small shelves, some crisps and half a dozen spirits bottles); you can also get Double Vision cider from nearby Staplehurst and country wines.

🍴 **No food.**

Free house ~ Licensee Mrs Jemison ~ Real ale ~ No credit cards ~ (01797) 344648 ~ Children in family room only ~ Dogs allowed in bar ~ Open 12-3, 7-11(10.30 Sun)

Recommended by the Didler, N R White, Adrian Johnson, Simon Rodway, Louise English, Kevin Thorpe, Phil and Sally Gorton, Peter Meister, Pete Baker

SPELDHURST   TQ5541   MAP 3

George & Dragon 🍷

Village signposted from A264 W of Tunbridge Wells; TN3 0NN

Fine old pub, beams, flagstones and huge fireplaces, local beers, good food and attractive outside seating areas

This fine half-timbered building has massive, ancient beams, some beautiful old flagstones and, in the main room, a huge sandstone fireplace with a winter log fire. The entrance hall (where there is a water bowl for thirsty dogs) is rather splendid – though we're still not sure about the chandelier. On the right, the half-panelled room is set for dining with a mix of old wheelback and other dining chairs and a cushioned wall pew around several tables, a few little pictures on the walls, horsebrasses on one huge beam and a sizeable bar counter with Harveys Best, Larkins Traditional Ale and a changing guest from Harveys on handpump and 16 wines by the glass; friendly, efficient staff. A doorway leads through to another dining room with similar furnishings and another big inglenook. To the left of the main door is a room more used for those wanting a drink and a chat (though people do eat in here, too) with a woodburning stove in a small fireplace, high-winged cushioned settles and various wooden tables and dining chairs on the wooden-strip floor; piped music. There's also an upstairs restaurant. In front of the pub are teak tables, chairs and benches on a nicely planted gravel terrace, while at the back there's a covered area with big church candles on more wooden tables and a lower terrace with seats around a 300-year-old olive tree; more attractive planting here and some modern sculpturing.

🍴 Enjoyable – if not cheap – bar food at lunchtime includes sandwiches, ploughman's, soup, hop sausages with onion marmalade, beer-battered cod and roast chicken legs with lemon and rosemary, as well as smoked mackerel and salmon pâté, artichoke ravioli with basil and chilli butter, seared pigeon breasts with smoked bacon and lentils, fillet of hake with mussel and saffron broth, venison rump with dauphinoise potatoes, slow-roast pork belly with apple compote, and puddings such as white chocolate and mascarpone cheesecake and elderflower, berry and rhubarb trifle. They may add a 12.5% service charge to all bills. *Starters/Snacks: £5.50 to £10.00. Main Courses: £10.50 to £18.50. Puddings: £5.00 to £5.50*

Free house ~ Licensee Julian Leefe-Griffiths ~ Real ale ~ Bar food ~ Restaurant ~ (01892) 863125 ~ Children welcome ~ Dogs allowed in bar ~ Open 12-11(10.30 Sun)
Recommended by Derek Thomas, Andrea Rampley, N R White

ST MARGARET'S BAY   TR3744   MAP 3

Coastguard ♀ 🍺

Off A256 NE of Dover; keep on down through the village towards the bay, pub off on right; CT15 6DY

Terrific views, some nautical décor, fine range of drinks and well liked food

The setting here is rather special and you must arrive early in good weather to bag one of the tables out on the prettily planted balcony from where you can look across the Straits of Dover; there are more seats down by the beach below the National Trust cliffs. Inside, the warm, carpeted, wood-clad bar has some shipping memorabilia, three quickly changing real ales like Hogs Back Light Spring Ale, Hopdaemon Incubus and Westerham WGV on handpump, interesting continental beers, 40 malt whiskies, Weston's cider and a carefully chosen wine list including those from local vineyards; good service even when busy. The restaurant has wooden dining chairs and tables on a wood-strip floor and more fine views; piped music. More reports please.

🍴 Well presented bar food includes sandwiches, soup, pork, liver and bacon terrine, scallops seared with garlic butter, moroccan-spiced roast vegetable frittata with slow-roast tomatoes, free-range chicken with bacon and caesar salad, beer-battered cod, local sirloin steak, and puddings such as dark chocolate, coffee and walnut torte and plum and rosewater flapjack crumble. *Starters/Snacks: £4.50 to £7.50. Main Courses: £8.50 to £14.00. Puddings: £4.50*

Free house ~ Licensee Nigel Wydymus ~ Real ale ~ Bar food (12.30-2.45, 6.30-8.45) ~ Restaurant ~ (01304) 853176 ~ Children allowed away from bar ~ Dogs allowed in bar ~ Open 10.30am-11pm(10.30 Sun)
Recommended by Adrian Johnson, Andrew York, Dr Kevan Tucker

Real ale may be served from handpumps, electric pumps (not just the on-off switches used for keg beer) or – common in Scotland – tall taps called founts (pronounced 'fonts') where a separate pump pushes the beer up under air pressure.

TQ7846 MAP 3

Lord Raglan

About 1.5 miles from town centre towards Maidstone, turn right off A229 into Chart Hill Road opposite Chart Cars; OS Sheet 188 map reference 785472; TN12 0DE

Simple pub with chatty locals, beams and hops, well liked bar food and nice little terrace

There's a friendly, relaxed atmosphere in this well run country pub and the interior is cosy but compact. You walk in almost on top of the narrow bar counter and chatting locals and it then widens slightly at one end to a small area with a big winter log fire. In the other direction it works its way round to an intimate area at the back, with lots of wine bottles lined up on a low shelf. Low beams are covered with masses of hops, and the mixed collection of comfortably worn dark wood furniture on quite well used dark brown carpet tiles and nice old parquet flooring is mostly 1930s. Goachers Light, Harveys Best and a guest like Surrey Hills Shere Drop on handpump, a good wine list, local Double Vision farm cider and Weston's perry. Small french windows lead out to an enticing little high-hedged terraced area with green plastic tables and chairs, and there are wooden picnic-sets in the side orchard; reasonable wheelchair access. More reports please.

🍴 **Well liked bar food includes sandwiches, filled baguettes, ploughman's, garlic mushrooms, smoked venison and pickled quince, ham or sausage and egg, macaroni cheese, steak burger with mozzarella and bacon, poached salmon with a herby lemon sauce, stir-fried beef with peppers, guinea fowl breast with red wine sauce, grilled lamb chops, and puddings.** *Starters/Snacks: £3.95 to £5.95. Main Courses: £7.95 to £14.95. Puddings: £4.50*

Free house ~ Licensees Andrew and Annie Hutchison ~ Real ale ~ Bar food (12-2.30, 7-9.30; not Sun) ~ (01622) 843747 ~ Children welcome ~ Dogs welcome ~ Open 12-3, 6.30-11.30; closed Sun

Recommended by Alec and Joan Laurence, Richard Abnett

TR2160 MAP 3

Red Lion 🛏

High Street; off A257 just E of Canterbury; CT3 4BA

Super country pub with very cheerful landlord, lots to look at, super choice of food and drink and pretty garden with roaming ducks and chickens

Full of character and run by a warmly friendly if slightly eccentric landlord who also has a lot of character, this is a smashing country pub hidden away down a network of country lanes. The idiosyncratic bar rooms wrap themselves around the big island bar and have lots of interesting things to look at: hops, wine bottles (some empty and some full) crammed along mantelpieces and along one side of the bar, all manner of paintings and pictures, copper kettles and old cooking implements, well used cookery books, big stone bottles and milk churns, trugs and baskets, old tennis racquets and straw hats; one part has a collection of brass instruments, sheet music all over the walls, some jazz records and a couple of little stall areas have hop sacks draped over the partitioning. There are green-painted, cushioned mate's chairs around a mix of nice pine tables, lit candles in unusual metal candleholders, a big log fire and fresh flowers; piped jazz and bat and trap. The conservatory adds welcome dining space. Greene King IPA and maybe a guest are tapped straight from the cask, and they've a good wine list with several by the glass, excellent summer Pimms, winter mulled wine and cider. There are picnic-sets under umbrellas in the back garden, with pretty flowerbeds and roaming ducks and chickens. Please note that the bedrooms don't have their own bathrooms.

🍴 **Extremely good, interesting food using top quality local meat and seasonal produce includes lunchtime filled cottage rolls, smoked belly of pork and apricot terrine with chutney, warm salad of black pudding and pancetta with a poached egg, scallops with chives and cracked white pepper, moules marinière, free-range chicken stuffed with asparagus and home-grown herbs and wrapped in parma ham, pork shoulder with thyme, cinnamon and apples, loin of lamb stuffed with wild shi-itake mushrooms with rosemary** jus, wild duck breast on root vegetable stir fry with a light sweet chilli sauce, and puddings like raspberry and vanilla cheesecake and chocolate roulade. *Starters/Snacks: £5.00 to £7.00. Main Courses: £12.95 to £19.95. Puddings: £4.95*

Free house ~ Licensee Robert Whigham ~ Real ale ~ Bar food (12.30-2.30, 7-9.30) ~ Restaurant ~ (01227) 721339 ~ Children welcome ~ Dogs allowed in bar ~ Open 11-11 ~ Bedrooms: £45/£70

Recommended by David Dyson, N R White, David and Ruth Shillitoe, Kevin Thorpe, Dr Kevan Tucker, Tom and Ruth Rees

STOWTING   TR1241   MAP 3

Tiger ◀

3.7 miles from M20 junction 11; B2068 N, then left at Stowting signpost, straight across crossroads, then fork left after 0.25 miles and pub is on right; coming from N, follow Brabourne, Wye, Ashford signpost to right at fork, then turn left towards Posting and Lyminge at T junction; TN25 6BA

Peaceful pub with friendly staff, interesting traditional furnishings, well liked food, several real ales and open fires; good walking country

Run by friendly licensees, this is a fine country pub with a lovely quaint interior. It's traditionally furnished with a happy mix of wooden tables and chairs and built-in cushioned wall seats on wooden floorboards and has woodburning stoves at each end of the bar. There's an array of books meant to be read rather than left for decoration, candles in bottles, brewery memorabilia and paintings, lots of hops and some faded rugs on the stone floor towards the back of the pub. Fullers London Pride, Greene King IPA and Shepherd Neame Master Brew and a couple of guests like Harveys Best and Woodfordes Wherry on handpump, lots of malt whiskies, several wines by the glass and local cider. There are seats out on the front terrace and an outside smokers' shelter with an environmentally friendly heater and stools made from tractor seats. Plenty of nearby walks along the Wye Downs or North Downs Way. More reports please.

🍴 Good bar food includes sandwiches, soup, chicken liver pâté with cranberry and red onion chutney, caramelised goats cheese with sweet and sour strawberries, oak-smoked local duck with a carpaccio of plums and oranges, home-made chunky burger with mozzarella and tomato, steak and mushroom in ale pie, local pork, honey and mustard sausages with red onion gravy, cannelloni stuffed with baby spinach, cream cheese and pine nuts with a toasted red pepper sauce, free-range chicken with pesto cream and dauphinoise potatoes, pork belly with creamed leeks and bacon and apple purée, and puddings like rhubarb and ginger crumble and cranberry and Baileys bread and butter pudding. *Starters/Snacks: £4.95 to £8.95. Main Courses: £9.95 to £20.00. Puddings: £5.50 to £7.50.*

Free house ~ Licensees Emma Oliver and Benn Jarvis ~ Real ale ~ Bar food (all day; not Sun evening, Mon lunchtime, Tues) ~ Restaurant ~ (01303) 862130 ~ Children welcome ~ Dogs allowed in bar ~ Jazz every second Mon evening ~ Open 12-midnight (4-midnight Mon); closed Mon lunchtime, Tuesday

Recommended by John Silverman, Dr Kevan Tucker

TOYS HILL   TQ4752   MAP 3

Fox & Hounds

Off A25 in Brasted, via Brasted Chart and The Chart; TN16 1QG

Country pub in fine surroundings with well liked food and nice garden

Handy for Chartwell and Emmetts Garden, this traditional country pub is surrounded by good walks. The bars have a relaxed atmosphere, the small first room has a few plain tables and chairs on dark boards, and under the shiny pinkish ceiling (which looks as old as the building itself) there's a leather sofa and easy chair by an open log fire. Also, a mix of other tables and chairs, hunting prints, illustrated plates, old photographs, pewter mugs, copper jugs and another log fire. In a brick and stone extension is a carpeted dining room with big windows overlooking the garden. Greene King IPA, Abbot and Morlands Original on handpump and several wines by the glass; piped music, dominoes, cribbage and board games; no mobile phones. As you approach the pub from the pretty village you will glimpse one of the most magnificent views in Kent. The appealing tree-sheltered garden has seats, with more in a covered and heated area.

Ⓜ **Well liked bar food includes lunchtime filled baguettes that come with coleslaw, salad and crisps, ploughman's, soup, chicken liver pâté with chutney, home-made burger with cheese and bacon, steak in ale pie, pork sausages with rich onion gravy, pasta with roasted tomatoes, spinach, olives and parmesan, lambs liver and bacon, daily specials like venison casserole with dumplings, fish pie with cheesy top, pork stroganoff, various curries, bass on red pepper risotto with pesto, and puddings such as bakewell tart or sticky toffee pudding with toffee sauce; they also offer a winter weekday two-course set menu and Sunday roast.** *Starters/Snacks: £3.95 to £7.95. Main Courses: £8.95 to £18.00. Puddings: £4.95 to £5.25*

Greene King ~ Tenants Tony and Shirley Hickmott ~ Real ale ~ Bar food (12-2(2.30 Sat, 3 Sun), 6-9(9.30 Sat); not Sun or Mon evenings) ~ Restaurant ~ (01732) 750328 ~ Children welcome away from bar ~ Dogs allowed in bar ~ Summer live music last Fri of month ~ Open 10am-11pm; 10-3, 6-11(8 Sun) in winter; closed Mon evening

Recommended by Alan Cowell, Robert Gomme, Glen and Nola Armstrong, Sheila Topham, Cathryn and Richard Hicks, Andrea Rampley

TUNBRIDGE WELLS

TQ5839   MAP 3

Sankeys

Mount Ephraim (A26 just N of junction with A267); TN4 8AA

Pubby street-level bar, informal downstairs brasserie, real ales and good wines, chatty atmosphere and super fish dishes

The most pubby part in this bustling place is the street-level bar, which is light and airy and interestingly decorated with a unique collection of rare enamel signs, antique brewery mirrors and old prints, framed cigarette cards and lots of old wine bottles and soda siphons. It's comfortably laid out with leather sofas and pews around all sorts of tables on bare wooden boards, and they keep a couple of beers from Goachers and Westerham on handpump, fruit beers and exotic brews and several wines by the glass from a good list; big flat screen TV for sports (not football) and piped music. Downstairs is quite different. It's a brasserie with big mirrors on the stripped brick walls, pews or chairs around sturdy tables, a chatty, informal atmosphere and there's an oyster bar and fresh fish display. French windows open on to an inviting sun-trap decked garden with wicker and chrome chairs and wooden tables.

Ⓜ **Very good value pubby food at lunchtime in the upstairs bar includes filled baguettes, filled baked potatoes, bangers and mash, steak pie, home-made burgers and fishcakes, chilli and a sharing seafood plate, with evening choices like moules frites or fish and chips with a free drink (6-8pm). Downstairs, the emphasis is on fish: oysters, pickled cockles, fresh anchovies, potted shrimps, local lemon sole, plaice, john dory, black bream, lobster and huge cornish cock crabs. Sunday roasts and summer barbecues.** *Starters/Snacks: £4.00 to £5.50. Main Courses: £4.50 to £13.50. Puddings: £4.50*

Free house ~ Licensee Guy Sankey ~ Real ale ~ Bar food (12-3(4 Sun), 6-10; not Sun or Mon evenings) ~ Restaurant ~ (01892) 511422 ~ Children welcome only lunchtime in bar but any time in restaurant ~ Dogs welcome ~ Live bands second Sun of month and bank hols ~ Open 12-12(2am Fri and Sat); 12-11 Sun

Recommended by Bob and Margaret Holder, BOB, Pat and Tony Martin

---

People named as recommenders after the Main Entries have told us that the pub should be included. But they have not written the report – we have, after anonymous on-the-spot inspection.

ULCOMBE
TQ8550   MAP 3

Pepper Box 🍺

Fairbourne Heath; signposted from A20 in Harrietsham, or follow Ulcombe signpost from A20, then turn left at crossroads with sign to pub, then right at next minor crossroads; ME17 1LP

Friendly country pub with homely bar, lovely log fire, well liked food, fair choice of drinks and seats in pretty garden

Traditional and charming, this popular country pub is nicely placed on high ground above the Weald, looking out over a plateau of rolling arable farmland. The homely bar has standing timbers and a few low beams (some hung with hops), copper kettles and pans on window sills, some very low-seated windsor chairs and two leather sofas by the splendid inglenook fireplace (nice horsebrasses on the bressumer beam) with its lovely log fire. A side area, more functionally furnished for eating, extends into the opened-up beamed dining room with a range in another inglenook and more horsebrasses. Shepherd Neame Master Brew, Spitfire and a seasonal beer on handpump, local apple juice and several wines by the glass; piped music. The two cats are called Murphy and Jim. There's a hop-covered terrace and a garden with shrubs, flowerbeds and a small pond. The name of the pub refers to the pepperbox pistol – an early type of revolver with numerous barrels; the village church is worth a look. The Greensand Way footpath is nearby.

🍴 As well as lunchtime sandwiches and filled baguettes and ploughman's, the well liked bar food includes soup, goats cheese and roasted tomato tartlet, salt and pepper squid with sesame and soy dressing on a sweet pepper salad, local ham and egg, sausages with onion gravy, chicken curry, beer-battered haddock, chinese-style pork belly, chargrilled lamb fillet with beetroot, crème fraîche and mint dressing, and steaks with a choice of sauces. *Starters/Snacks: £4.50 to £7.00. Main Courses: £6.50 to £9.50. Puddings: £5.00*

Shepherd Neame ~ Tenants Geoff and Sarah Pemble ~ Real ale ~ Bar food (12-2.15, 7-9.45; 12-3.30 Sun; not Sun evening) ~ Restaurant ~ (01622) 842558 ~ Well behaved children allowed lunchtime only and must be over 8 ~ Dogs allowed in bar ~ Open 11-3, 6.30-11; 12-4 Sun; closed Sun evening

Recommended by N R White, Michael Doswell, Donna and Roger, Tina and David Woods-Taylor

---

LUCKY DIP

Besides the fully inspected pubs, you might like to try these Lucky Dips recommended to us and described by readers (if you do, please send us reports: feedback@goodguides.com).

ADDINGTON [TQ6559]
Angel ME19 5BB [just off M20 junction 4; Addington Green]: 14th-c pub in classic village-green setting, olde-worlde décor with candles in bottles on scrubbed deal tables and big fireplaces, enjoyable fairly priced up-to-date food, fair choice of beers, lots of wines by the glass, good friendly service, stables restaurant *(A N Bance)*
APPLEDORE [TQ9529]
Black Lion TN26 2BU [The Street]: Compact 1930s village pub with bustling atmosphere, very welcoming helpful staff, good generous food all day from simple cheese sandwiches to imaginative dishes, lamb from Romney Marsh and local fish, three or four well kept changing ales, Biddenden farm cider, log fire, partitioned back eating area; tables out on green, attractive village, good Military Canal walks *(Alec and Joan Laurence)*
BARFRESTONE [TR2650]
Yew Tree CT15 7JH [off A256 N of Dover; or off A2 at Barham]: Stripped boards and pastel décor in dining area, log-effect gas fire, hops

around white-joisted ceiling, lit candles, pine tables and cushioned dining chairs, a few bar stools, great wine choice (opera-singer landlord has a local vineyard), Gadds 80/-, Hopdaemon Incubus and Whitstable Winkle Picker, daily papers, modern pub food, smaller bar and second dining room with nice botanical paintings, country views and small woodburner, live jazz (last Sun of month); children welcome, back decking overlooking car park, wonderful Norman carvings in next-door church, open all day (winter open all day wknds) *(Kevin Thorpe, Rob and Catherine Dunster, LYM)*
BOUGHTON [TR0559]
Queens Head ME13 9BH [The Street]: Village pub (named in 1703 for Queen Anne) rejuvenated under friendly new landlady, enjoyable and imaginative reasonably priced food, Shepherd Neame ales, short good value wine list, civilised dining room; newly reworked garden *(Will and Anne Watson)*
BRENCHLEY [TQ6841]
Halfway House TN12 7AX [Horsmonden Rd]:

Attractive olde-worlde mix of rustic and traditional furnishings on bare boards, two log fires, particularly friendly landlord and efficient staff, enjoyable home-made pub food and very popular Sun carvery, good changing ale choice tapped from the cask, two tranquil eating areas; dogs welcome, picnic-sets and play area in big garden, bedrooms *(Jamie May)*

BROADSTAIRS [TR3866]

Brown Jug CT10 2EW [Ramsgate Rd]: Long-serving landlady in basic and unchanging old-style two-bar local, well kept Greene King and guest beers, some tapped from the cask, board and quiz games; lunchtime opening hours may vary, open all day wknds *(the Didler)*

BURMARSH [TR1032]

Shepherd & Crook TN29 0JJ [Shear Way]: Friendly two-bar traditional marshside local, well kept Adnams and a guest beer, Weston's cider, good straightforward home-made food at low prices, prompt service, interesting photographs and blow lamp collection *(Kevin Thorpe, Pete Baker)*

CANTERBURY [TR1558]

Bell & Crown CT1 2DZ [Palace St]: Three real ales, local wines and ciders in convivial relaxed pub, bar lunches, good-humoured service and atmosphere even on busy Fri and Sat nights *(Andrew York)*

Millers Arms CT1 2AA [St Radigunds St/Mill Lane]: Shepherd Neame pub in quiet street near river with friendly helpful staff, good value generous pub food inc good Sun lunch, changing guest beers, good wine choice, flagstoned front bar, bare-boards back area, traditional solid furniture, small conservatory, unobtrusive piped music; good seating in attractive part-covered courtyard, handy for Marlow Theatre and cathedral, 11 comfortable bedrooms, ample breakfast, open all day *(Dr and Mrs Michael Smith, Phil Bryant)*

Old Brewery Tavern CT1 2RX [Stour St, back of Abode Hotel]: Attractive and comfortable contemporary beamed bistro bar, good if not cheap food from sandwiches up, well kept ales such as Hopdaemon, Otter and Shepherd Neame, pine flooring, modern prints on pastel walls, flame-effect fires, soft settees and more dining tables in adjoining high-ceilinged former warehouse, also good hotel restaurant; TVs; children welcome, good bedrooms, open all day *(Kevin Thorpe, Keith and Chris O'Neill, Bruce M Drew)*

Old Gate CT1 3EL [New Dover Rd (A2050 S)]: Big reliable Vintage Inn, stripped brick and beams, two large open fires, bookshelves, big prints, old wooden furniture, reasonably priced food all day, wide range of wines by the glass, real ale choice, well organised staff, daily papers; some piped music; easy disabled access, bedrooms in adjacent Innkeeper's Lodge, small back garden *(Kevin Thorpe, Norman Fox)*

☆ *Parrot* CT1 2AG [Church Lane – the one off St Radigunds St, 100 yds E of St Radigunds

car park]: Former Simple Simons, reopened by Youngs after sympathetic update, heavy beams, wood and flagstone floors, stripped masonry, dark panelling, big open fire, good value bar food with more extensive traditional menu in upstairs vaulted restaurant, Wells & Youngs and guest ales, decent wine choice, friendly efficient staff; nicely laid out courtyard with central wood-burning barbecue, open all day *(Pete Coxon, Duncan Smart, Bruce M Drew, Norman Fox)*

Phoenix CT1 3DB [Old Dover Rd]: Two friendly linked rooms in olde-worlde beamed tavern with lots of prints and central woodburner, up to eight changing ales inc Wells & Youngs Bombardier, cheap hearty all-day pub food; piped music, TV; disabled access, picnic-sets on back terrace, smokers' shelter, open all day *(Tony Hobden, Kevin Thorpe)*

West Gate Inn CT2 7EB [North Lane]: Well worn-in Wetherspoons with good choice of well priced ales *(Bruce M Drew)*

CHARTHAM HATCH [TR1056]

☆ *Chapter Arms* CT4 7LT [New Town St]: Sizeable 18th-c dining pub overlooking orchards, enjoyable generous meals, Adnams and Woodfordes Wherry, decent wine, friendly efficient staff, flowers and candles, heavily hop-hung ceiling with brass instruments and fairy lights, attractive restaurant; quiet piped music; charming garden with good furniture and water features *(Keith and Chris O'Neill, Lady Dobson, Ron and Sheila Corbett, BB)*

CHIDDINGSTONE CAUSEWAY [TQ5247]

Greyhound TN11 8LG [Charcott, off back rd to Weald]: Unpretentious traditional local with enjoyable bar lunches, log fire, real ale, friendly staff; dogs welcome, tables out in front, good for walkers *(Heather and Dick Martin)*

Little Brown Jug TN11 8JJ [B2027]: Open-plan Whiting & Hammond pub with comfortable bar and big dining extension, good food from sandwiches to full meals, well kept Greene King ales, good wine list, friendly efficient service; attractive garden with play area, beer and music festivals, open all day wknds *(R and S Bentley, Oliver and Sue Rowell, Gerry and Rosemary Dobson, Martin Stafford, Robert Gomme, John Branston)*

CHIPSTEAD [TQ4956]

Bricklayers Arms TN13 2RZ [Chevening Rd]: Attractive pub overlooking lake and green, good value food (not Sun evening), full range of Harveys beers kept well and tapped from casks behind long counter, good atmosphere, heavily beamed bar with open fire and fine racehorse painting, unpretentious larger back restaurant *(B J Harding)*

COWDEN [TQ4642]

☆ *Queens Arms* TN8 5NP [Cowden Pound; junction B2026 with Markbeech rd]: Friendly two-room country pub like something from the 1930s, with splendid landlady, well kept

Adnams, coal fire, darts; dogs welcome, occasional folk music or morris dancers; may be cl wkdy lunchtimes but normally opens 10am (the Didler, Pete Baker)

CROCKHAM HILL [TQ4450]

Royal Oak TN8 6RD [Main Rd]: Cosy two-bar village pub with friendly service, good value home-made pub lunches from sandwiches up, well kept Westerham ales, daily papers, comfortable high-backed seats, cartoons by local artist, no music or machines; dogs welcome, small garden, handy for walks and Chartwell (Godfrey Hurst, N R White, C and R Bromage)

DEAL [TR3752]

☆ *Bohemian* CT14 6HY [Beach St]: Airy and chatty modern-fronted café-bar opp pier, four or more ales such as Adnams, Shepherd Neame, Skinners and Woodfordes, continental beers, perry and good choice of wines by the glass, friendly helpful staff, L-shaped bar with chunky pine furniture and big squishy brown built-in leather sofa, decorative fireplace, a few photographs and contemporary paintings, magazines to read, decent food lunch wknd brunch, good seafront views from upstairs restaurant with well presented modern food; TV in area off, piped jazz; wheelchair access, heated back decking, open all day Fri-Sun and summer, cl Mon in winter (BB, Guy Vowles, N R White, Kevin Thorpe, Dr Kevan Tucker, Mr and Mrs P R Thomas, John and Annabel Hampshire)

Green Berry CT14 7EQ [Canada Rd]: Small no frills local opp old Royal Marine barracks, welcoming enthusiastic couple, L-shaped bar, four well kept ales (tasting notes on slates), farm cider and perry, no food, quiz and darts teams, pool; small vine-covered terrace, open all day wknds (Dr Kevan Tucker)

☆ *Kings Head* CT14 7AH [Beach St]: Handsome three-storey Georgian inn just across from promenade and sea, good landlord and atmosphere, interesting maritime décor and cricket memorabilia in comfortable areas around central servery, flame-effect gas fires, Shepherd Neame ales, usual food from cheap sandwiches up, darts; piped music, TV, popular with young locals wknd evenings; good front terrace area, good value bedrooms, open all day (LYM, N R White, John and Annabel Hampshire, David Gregory, Rob and Catherine Dunster)

Prince Albert CT14 6LW [Middle St]: One-room corner pub in conservation area, ornate interior with old agricultural bric-a-brac, three changing real ales, food (not Mon or Tues) inc popular Sun carvery, live folk music (Dr Kevan Tucker)

Ship CT14 6JZ [Middle St]: Dim-lit local in historic maritime quarter, five well kept changing ales inc Gadds, friendly landlord, lots of dark woodwork, stripped brick and local ship and wreck pictures, piano and woodburner in side bar; dogs welcome (pub has own), small pretty walled garden, open all day (N R White, Dr Kevan Tucker, Mr and Mrs P R Thomas)

DENTON [TR2147]

Jackdaw CT4 6QZ [A260 Canterbury—Folkestone]: Imposing old open-plan brick and flint pub, recently reopened, welcoming service, enjoyable family food all day, half a dozen real ales, friendly young staff, RAF memorabilia in front area, large back restaurant; quiet piped music; children welcome, good-sized charming garden, picturesque village, open all day (Andrew York, Arthur Pickering)

DOVER [TR3042]

Three Cups CT17 0RX [Crabble Hill (A256)]: Bistro-style open-plan pub, friendly staff, good value food from open kitchen, Marstons Pedigree, blackboard wines, daily papers, comfortable settees, some high stools and bar tables, modern sunken fireplace, local panoramas, back pool table; piped music, TV; tables out on decking, open all day (Darren Croucher, Kevin Thorpe)

DUNGENESS [TR0916]

Pilot TN29 9NJ [Battery Rd]: Bustling unaffected single-storey mid-20th-c seaside café-bar by shingle beach, Adnams, Courage and Greene King ales, simple food inc good value fresh fish and chips, two bars and barn family extension, dark plank panelling inc the slightly curved ceiling, prints and local memorabilia, books for sale (proceeds to Lifeboats), quick friendly service (even when packed); piped music; picnic-sets in side garden (Peter Meister)

DUNKS GREEN [TQ6152]

☆ *Kentish Rifleman* TN11 9RU [Dunks Green Rd]: Tudor pub restored in modern rustic style, friendly helpful staff, well kept real ales such as Greene King and Westerham, reasonably priced enjoyable pubby food, cosy log fire, rifles on low beams, enlarged dining room, small public bar; service charge levied; children and dogs welcome, tables in pretty garden behind, good walks (Mr and Mrs C Prentis, Bob and Margaret Holder, BB, N R White, Simon and Sally Small, Robert Gomme, Tina and David Woods-Taylor, B and M Kendall)

DUNTON GREEN [TQ5156]

Bullfinch TN13 2DR [London Rd, Riverhead]: Open-plan modern décor with mix of sofas, armchairs and banquettes, snacks and slightly upmarket traditional food, pleasant efficient staff, real ales such as Adnams, Sharps and Westerham, good wine choice, daily papers; nice garden, open all day wknds (Mike Buckingham, Derek Thomas)

EAST FARLEIGH [TQ7453]

Walnut Tree ME15 0HJ [Forge Lane]: Extended 16th-c beamed pub with log fires, decent pub food, well kept Shepherd Neame ales, restaurant, live music Thurs evenings; children welcome until 9pm, dogs on leads (pub has two), lovely garden with terrace and barbecue, open all day (Gene and Kitty Rankin)

EASTLING [TQ9656]

☆ *Carpenters Arms* ME13 0AZ [off A251 S of M2 junction 6, via Painters Forstal; The

Street]: Pretty, cosy and cottagey 14th-c oak-beamed pub doing well under new management, good imaginative food (not Sun evening), well kept Shepherd Neame, big log fires front and back, nice mix of old furniture inc pews on bare boards, old local photographs, piano, live music inc jazz; children welcome in small candlelit restaurant, dogs allowed in bar, small garden with picnic-sets *(LYM, Prof and Mrs J Fletcher, Mrs J A Stubblefield)*

ELHAM [TR1743]

Kings Arms CT4 6TJ [St Marys Rd]: Attractive traditional pub with welcoming lounge bar, good open fire, good value standard food inc two-for-one deals, well kept Harveys and Flowers Original, good wine list, friendly attentive service, steps down to dining area, public bar with games; opp church in pretty village square, attractive sheltered garden *(B and E Palmer, Dudley and Moira Cockroft, D F Clarke)*

Rose & Crown CT4 6TD [High St]: Comfortable partly 16th-c inn in charming village in Kent's prettiest valley, low beams, uneven floors, inglenook and woodburner, enjoyable pub food, Shepherd Neame ales, several wines by the glass, restaurant; children welcome, flagstoned back terrace, bedrooms, open all day wknds *(Jerry Brown, Richard Tingle, LYM, John and Annabel Hampshire)*

ETCHINGHILL [TR1639]

New Inn CT18 8DE [Canterbury Rd (former B2065)]: Neatly kept bright and airy pub with wide range of enjoyable food (good with special diets), friendly efficient staff, real ales such as Fullers London Pride, Hydes Jekylls Gold and Shepherd Neame, good value wines by the glass, beams and flagstones, spacious dining room; children welcome, handy for Channel Tunnel *(Paul)*

FARNINGHAM [TQ5466]

Pied Bull DA4 0DG [High St]: Pub/restaurant with interesting choice of enjoyable food inc fresh seafood and home-made puddings, popular restaurant, good friendly service; pleasant small garden, handy for Brands Hatch *(Steve Short)*

FAVERSHAM [TR0161]

Albion ME13 7DH [Front Brents]: Light and airy beamed waterside mexican bar with simple furnishings, modern pictures on terracotta walls, some traditional bar food but emphasis is on the enjoyable mexican/latino dishes, well kept Shepherd Neame ales inc seasonal from the nearby brewery, friendly staff, flowers and candles on tables; children welcome, disabled lavatories, picnic-sets out by riverside walkway (Saxon Shore long-distance path), open all day summer *(the Didler, Pat and Tony Martin, LYM)*

Anchor ME13 7BP [Abbey St]: Friendly two-bar pub with good food from baguettes up, well kept Shepherd Neame ales, simple bare-boards bar with log fire, ancient beams, dark panelling, low lighting, frosted windows,

boat pictures and models, small side room with pub games and books, restaurant; piped radio; dogs welcome, tables in pretty enclosed garden with bat and trap, attractive 17th-c street nr historic quay, open all day *(Peter Meister, Conor McGaughey, M and GR, Mrs M S Forbes, the Didler)*

Elephant ME13 8JN [The Mall]: Well run dim-lit traditional town pub, friendly and chatty, with five changing local ales, belgian beers, Weston's cider, central log fire; juke box, games machine; children welcome, suntrap back terrace with fishpond, open from 3 wkdys, all day wknds *(N R White, the Didler, Kevin Thorpe, Kevin Flack, BB)*

Sun ME13 7JE [West St]: Popular rambling old-world 15th-c pub with good unpretentious atmosphere in small low-ceilinged partly panelled rooms, big inglenook, Shepherd Neame beers inc seasonal one from nearby brewery, OAP deals, smart restaurant; unobtrusive piped music; wheelchair access possible (small step), pleasant back courtyard, eight bedrooms, open all day *(Anthony Barnes, the Didler, Bob and Val Collman, Tony and Wendy Hobden)*

FAWKHAM GREEN [TQ5865]

Rising Sun DA3 8NL: Pleasant pub overlooking green, local beers inc Harveys and Westerham, also Courage and Fullers London Pride, courteous service, enjoyable food *(Geoffrey Hughes)*

FINGLESHAM [TR3353]

☆ *Crown* CT14 0NA [just off A258 Sandwich—Deal; The Street]: Popular neatly kept low-beamed 16th-c country pub, good value generous home-made food from usual pub dishes to interesting specials, warmly friendly helpful service, well kept ales inc Gadds, Biddenden cider, daily papers, softly lit carpeted split-level bar with stripped stone and inglenook log fire, two other attractive dining rooms; lovely big garden with play area, bat and trap, field for caravans, open all day wknds *(N R White, Dr Kevan Tucker, Mrs S Etheridge, Kevin Thorpe, Sue Rowland)*

FOLKESTONE [TR2235]

Chambers CT20 2BE [Sandgate Rd]: Relaxed friendly basement bar and adjoining coffee bar, good range of real ales and bottled imports, tex/mex food, frequent live music; tables outside *(Andrew York)*

FORDWICH [TR1859]

Fordwich Arms CT2 0DB [off A28 in Sturry]: Handsome 1930s pub with smart green settees and attractive log fire, enjoyable food inc two-course lunches, real ales such as Flowers Original, Shepherd Neame and two from Wadworths; spacious terrace and garden by River Stour, ancient town hall opposite is worth visiting *(LYM, Tony Hobden)*

George & Dragon CT2 0BX [off A28 at Sturry]: Friendly place doubling as good value dining pub and local, good choice of wines by the glass; pleasant garden down to River Stour *(Andrew York)*

GOUDHURST [TQ7237]

☆ **Star & Eagle** TN17 1AL [High St]: Striking medieval building, now small hotel, with settles and Jacobean-style seats in heavily beamed open-plan areas, intriguing smuggling-days history, log fires, good choice of enjoyable well presented food, well kept Adnams, Harveys and Westerham (bar itself fairly modern), lovely views from restaurant, friendly staff; children welcome, tables out with same views, attractive village, ten up-to-date character bedrooms, good breakfast, open all day *(LYM, Sara Fulton, Roger Baker, Grahame Brooks, D C O'Neill, Kevin Thorpe)*

GRAVESEND [TQ6473]

Crown & Thistle DA12 2BJ [The Terrace]: Chatty old-fashioned local with interesting changing beers, bar nibbles, brewery pictures, may be filled rolls (can bring in food); no children, occasional live music; handy for historic riverside, open all day *(the Didler)*

HALSTEAD [TQ4861]

Rose & Crown TN14 7EA [Otford Lane]: Friendly 19th-c flint village local, comfortable and not over-modernised, well kept Larkins, Whitstable and three guest beers, food inc popular Sun lunch, welcoming staff, log fire, two bars with lots of village photographs; garden behind *(N R White)*

HARBLEDOWN [TR1358]

Old Coach & Horses CT2 9AB [Church Hill]: Airy yet cosy modern two-room split-level bistro/bar with interesting enjoyable food, helpful friendly service, real ales inc Greene King, good wines by the glass; great views from garden, peaceful setting *(Kevin Thorpe, Tudor Rowe, Charlotte, Jennifer Hurst)*

HEADCORN [TQ8344]

George & Dragon TN27 9NL [High St]: Good atmosphere and service, welcoming landlady, wide range of enjoyable home-made food using mostly local ingredients, good drinks, open fires, separate dining room *(Jan and Alan Summers)*

HERNE [TR1865]

☆ **Butchers Arms** CT6 7HL [Herne St (A291)]: Tiny pub with well kept changing ales tapped from the cask inc Dark Star, Fullers and Harveys, interesting bottled beers and Biddenden farm cider, chatty former motorcycle-racing landlord, just a couple of benches and butcher's-block tables, some wines too but no food (you can bring your own) beyond fierce pickles and other nibbles, chess, no music or TV; dogs welcome, tables out under awning, cl Sun, Mon, short lunchtime opening *(Paul Narramore, Kevin Thorpe)*

HERNHILL [TR0660]

☆ **Red Lion** ME13 9JR [off A299 via Dargate, or A2 via Boughton Street and Staplestreet]: Pretty Tudor inn by church and attractive village green, densely beamed and flagstoned, log fires, pine tables, friendly helpful staff, enjoyable food, well kept

Fullers, Shepherd Neame and a guest beer, decent house wines, upstairs restaurant, reasonable prices; children welcome, big garden with good play area, bedrooms *(LYM, B and E Palmer)*

HUCKING [TQ8458]

Hook & Hatchet ME17 1QT [village signed off A249; Church Rd]: Isolated country pub in enviable spot by Woodland Trust's Hucking Estate, plenty of nearby interesting walks, enterprising food inc lunch deals, three Shepherd Neame ales, friendly service, modern rustic refurbishment with bare boards and open fire; piped music; children welcome, tables out on heated verandah, picnic-sets in pretty sloping garden with play area, open all day *(Alan Gull, N R White, LYM)*

IDEN GREEN [TQ7437]

Peacock TN17 2PB [A262 E of Goudhurst]: Tudor, with blazing inglenook log fire in low-beamed main bar, quarry tiles and old sepia photographs, pubby food (all day Sat, not Sun evening) from sandwiches up, very helpful service, Harveys and Shepherd Neame ales, pastel dining room with cork-studded walls, public bar; well behaved dogs welcome, good-sized garden *(BB, Nigel and Jean Eames)*

IGHTHAM [TQ5956]

☆ **George & Dragon** TN15 9HH [A227]: Picturesque and very popular timbered dining pub, early 16th-c but much modernised, good food from generous snacks (all day till 6.30, not Sun) up, plenty of smartly dressed staff, Shepherd Neame ales, decent wines, sofas among other furnishings in long sociable main bar, heavy-beamed end room, woodburner and open fires, restaurant; children and dogs welcome, back terrace, handy for Ightham Mote (NT), good walks, open all day *(Bob and Margaret Holder, LYM, Steve and Nina Bullen, Derek Thomas, Brian Goodson, Colin and Janet Roe)*

IGHTHAM COMMON [TQ5955]

Old House TN15 9EE [Redwell, S of village; OS Sheet 188 map ref 591559]: Basic two-room country local tucked down narrow lane, no inn sign, bare bricks and beams, huge inglenook, interesting ales tapped from the cask, retired cash register and small TV in side room, darts; no food, cl wkdy lunchtimes, opens 7pm (even later Tues) *(N R White, Pete Baker, the Didler, BB)*

KILNDOWN [TQ7035]

☆ **Globe & Rainbow** TN17 2SG [signed off A21 S of Lamberhurst]: Welcoming well cared-for pub with small cheerful bar, good Harveys and Fullers London Pride, decent wines, simple bare-boards dining room with good sensibly priced fresh local food; piped music; country views from decking out by cricket pitch *(Alec and Joan Laurence, H E Waters, BB)*

KINGSDOWN [TR3748]

Kings Head CT14 8BJ [Upper St]: Chatty tucked-away local with Fullers London Pride,

Greene King IPA and a guest beer, wknd bar lunches, four small split-level rooms, black timbers, faded cream walls, pubby decorations and open fires, darts; piped music, games machine; garden with skittle alley, open all day Sun, cl wkdy lunchtimes (*N R White*)

LADDINGFORD [TQ6848]

Chequers ME18 6BP: Friendly old beamed village pub with good sensibly priced food, well kept ales such as Adnams, plenty for children; children and dogs welcome, big garden, Medway walks nearby (*Clare Bramham*)

LAMBERHURST [TQ6535]

☆ *Elephants Head* TN3 8LJ [Furnace Lane, Hook Green; B2169 towards T Wells]: Rambling 15th-c timber-framed pub, mullioned windows, heavy beams, brick or oak flooring, big inglenook, plush-cushioned pews etc, Harveys, good service, good value food inc very busy Sun carvery; darts and games machine in small side area; children welcome, picnic-sets by front green and in big back garden with peaceful view, terrace and good play area, nr Bayham Abbey and Owl House (*Peter Meister, Nigel and Jean Eames, N R White, LYM*)

LEIGH [TQ5446]

Fleur de Lis TN11 8RL [High St]: Bright clean décor in former cottage row, helpful staff, pubby food from well filled baguettes up, Greene King ales, bare-boarded saloon, separate public bar, third room with welcoming old-fashioned traditional feel (*Alan Cowell*)

LEYSDOWN-ON-SEA [TR0266]

Ferry House ME12 4BQ [Harty Ferry Rd, Sheerness]: At seaside end of long bumpy single-track road through salt marshes full of birds, friendly staff, sensibly short choice of enjoyable food inc fish and game, decent wines by the glass (keg beers), bare boards, panelled dado, cask stools, games room with pool, TV and machines, attractive newish barn-style high-raftered restaurant; they may try to keep your credit card while you eat; children welcome, disabled access, picnic-sets in large garden looking across to Kent mainland, play area, open all day Sat, cl Sun evening and Mon (*Colin Moore*)

LUDDESDOWN [TQ6667]

☆ *Cock* DA13 0XB [Henley St, N of village – OS Sheet 177 map reference 664672; off A227 in Meopham, or A228 in Cuxton]: Early 18th-c country pub, friendly long-serving landlord, several ales inc Adnams, Goachers Mild, Shepherd Neame and Whitstable, all-day pubby food (not Sun evening) from wide choice of sandwiches up, rugs on polished boards in pleasant bay-windowed lounge bar, quarry-tiled locals' bar, two woodburners, pews and other miscellaneous furnishings, aircraft pictures, masses of beer mats and bric-a-brac inc stuffed animals, model cars and beer can collections, traditional games inc bar billiards and three types of darts board, back dining conservatory; no children

in bar or part-covered heated back terrace; dogs welcome, big secure garden, good walks, open all day (*LYM, N R White, Kevin Thorpe*)

MAIDSTONE [TQ7655]

Pilot ME15 6EU [Upper Stone St (A229)]: Cosy old roadside pub, enjoyable simple home-made bar lunches (not wknds), Harveys and lots of guest beers, friendly landlord, hanging whisky-water jugs, darts and pool; back terrace (*the Didler*)

Rifle Volunteers ME14 1EU [Wyatt St/Church St]: Relaxed backstreet pub tied to local Goachers, three of their ales inc Mild, good value simple home-made food, friendly long-serving landlord, two gas fires, darts, no machines; tables outside (*the Didler*)

MARSH GREEN [TQ4344]

Wheatsheaf TN8 5QL [Marsh Green Rd (B2028 SW of Edenbridge)]: Harveys and other well kept changing ales, Biddenden cider, good value fresh food from lunchtime sandwiches up, friendly helpful staff, simple linked bare-boards areas with old photographs and wooden partitions, roomy conservatory; TV; garden and small terrace, open all day (*Gavin Robinson, R and S Bentley, N R White, Kevin Thorpe*)

MINSTER [TR9474]

Playa ME12 2NL [The Leas]: Big smart clifftop pub with wide Thames estuary views, Shepherd Neame ales, enjoyable sensibly priced pub food in bar and restaurant; tables outside (*Colin Moore*)

NORTHBOURNE [TR3352]

Hare & Hounds CT14 0LG [off A256 or A258 nr Dover; The Street]: Chatty village pub with good choice of ales inc well kept Harveys, popular generous food (lamb from nearby farm), friendly efficient service, modernised brick and wood interior with log fires each end of carpeted room; terrace tables (*N R White*)

OARE [TR0063]

Three Mariners ME13 0QA [Church Rd]: Good food inc good value wkdy lunch deals, well kept Shepherd Neame ales, good choice of wines by the glass, charming staff; attractive garden overlooking Faversham Creek, open all day wknds, cl Mon (operates then as mid-morning post office) (*Hilary Jones*)

OTFORD [TQ5259]

Bull TN14 5PG [High St]: Attractively laid out 15th-c Chef & Brewer, wide food choice from sandwiches up all day, good Sun lunch, friendly attentive staff, four well kept ales, decent wines, several quite spacious rooms, two huge log fires, panelling, soft lighting and candles; nice garden, good walks nearby (*Robert Gomme, B J Harding, N R White*)

Crown TN14 5PQ [High St, pond end]: 16th-c two-bar local opp village pond, pleasantly chatty lounge with sofas, well kept Harveys Best, Westerham and guest ales, cheerful friendly staff, locally sourced food inc good Sun roasts, darts, frequent interesting events; walkers and dogs welcome (*N R White, Conor McGaughey*)

PLAXTOL [TQ6054]

☆ *Golding Hop* TN15 0PT [Sheet Hill (0.5 miles S of Ightham, between A25 and A227)]: Secluded traditional country local, simple dim-lit two-level bar with hands-on landlord who can be very welcoming, Adnams, Wells & Youngs and guest beers, local farm ciders (sometimes their own), basic good value fresh bar snacks (not Mon, Tues evenings), woodburner, bar billiards; portable TV for big sports events, games machine; suntrap streamside lawn and well fenced play area over lane, good walks, open all day Sat *(Bob and Margaret Holder, the Didler, B and M Kendall, LYM)*

PLUCKLEY [TQ9144]

☆ *Mundy Bois* TN27 0ST [Mundy Bois – spelt Monday Boys on some maps – off Smarden Road SW of village centre]: Creeper-clad and tile-hung local, informal main bar, massive inglenook, Shepherd Neame and a beer from Hopdaemon, pubby food plus restaurant choices, sensible prices, small snug bar with sofas by log fire, board games, darts, pool; piped music, juke box, TV, games machine; children and dogs welcome, pretty garden and terrace with views, play area, cl Sun evening, Mon, Tues *(LYM)*

ROCHESTER [TQ7468]

Coopers Arms ME1 1TL [St Margarets St]: Jettied Tudor building behind cathedral, cosily unpretentious and quaint inside, bustling local atmosphere, friendly staff, two comfortable bars, generous cheap wkdy bar lunches, well kept Courage Best and Directors; tables in attractive courtyard *(B J Harding)*

ROLVENDEN [TQ8431]

Bull TN17 4PB [Regent St]: Good sensibly priced food inc popular Sun lunch, Harveys ale and friendly licensees, recently refurbished split-level bar with dark leather chairs, pictures on pale walls and grey panelling, restaurant on right, labrador called Milo; sports TV; big garden behind *(BB)*

ROUGH COMMON [TR1259]

Dog CT2 9DE [Rough Common Rd]: Small friendly local under new landlord, well kept Adnams Broadside and Fullers London Pride, generous lunches inc good value Sun roast *(Keith and Chris O'Neill)*

RYARSH [TQ6759]

Duke of Wellington ME19 5LS [Birling Rd; not far from M20 junction 4, via Leybourne and Birling]: Appealing Tudor bar and bar/restaurant, good food choice, big helpings *(Gordon Stevenson)*

SANDGATE [TR2035]

Ship CT20 3AH [High St]: Friendly traditional two-room pub with lots of changing ales tapped from the cask inc Hopdaemon and Hop Back Summer Lightning, local cider, decent fairly priced wine, usual pub food and local fish, affable long-serving landlord, unpretentious décor, barrel seats and tables, lots of nautical prints and posters; sea views from tables out behind, bedrooms *(Bruce Bird, David and Ruth Hollands, BB)*

SANDWICH [TR3358]

George & Dragon CT13 9EJ [Fisher St]: Civilised open-plan 15th-c beamed pub keeping feel of small original rooms, enjoyable good value food from open-view kitchen inc popular Sun lunch, friendly staff, well kept ales such as Adnams, Harveys and Shepherd Neame, good choice of wines by the glass; children and dogs welcome, pretty back terrace *(N R White, Barry and Sue Pladdys)*

SEAL [TQ5755]

Crown Point TN15 0HB [A25]: Well modernised roomy old building, quiet and peaceful, set back from road among trees in attractive hollow, friendly staff, enjoyable food, good drinks range; handy for Ightham Mote (NT) *(DFL)*

SEASALTER [TR0864]

☆ *Sportsman* CT5 4BP [Faversham Rd, off B2040]: Restauranty dining pub just inside sea wall, good imaginative contemporary cooking with plenty of seafood (not Sun evening or Mon, best to book and not cheap), two plain linked rooms and long conservatory, wooden floor, pine tables, big film star photographs, wheelback and basket-weave dining chairs, good wine choice (inc english), Shepherd Neame ales; children welcome, open all day Sun *(Prof and Mrs J Fletcher, LYM, Colin and Stephanie McFie, Kevin Thorpe)*

SELLING [TR0356]

☆ *White Lion* ME13 9RQ [off A251 S of Faversham (or exit roundabout, M2 junction 7); The Street]: 17th-c pub with well kept Shepherd Neame ales from unusual semicircular bar counter, decent wines, friendly helpful staff, wide blackboard food choice, log fire in hop-hung main bar with paintings for sale, another fire in small lower lounge with comfortable settees, back restaurant; quiz nights; children welcome, picnic-sets in attractive garden, colourful hanging baskets *(LYM, C and R Bromage)*

SEVENOAKS [TQ5555]

☆ *Bucks Head* TN15 0JJ [Godden Green, just E]: Relaxed flower-decked pub with welcoming thoughtful service, some good value blackboard food from sandwiches up, roast on Sun, well kept Shepherd Neame and a guest beer, log fires in splendid inglenooks, neatly kept bar and restaurant area, no piped music; children and dogs welcome, front terrace overlooking informal green and duck pond, back lawn with mature trees, bird fountain, pergola and views over quiet country behind Knole *(Neil Powell, Simon and Sally Small, Robert Gomme, Tina and David Woods-Taylor)*

SHEERNESS [TQ9374]

Ship on Shore ME12 2BX [Marine Parade, towards Minster]: Civilised pub with good value food, Courage Directors and summer guest beers, games area with pool well separated from quieter bar/dining area; apparently built partly with solidified concrete from 19th-c shipwreck *(Colin Moore)*

SMARDEN [TQ8642]

☆ **Bell** TN27 8PW [from Smarden follow lane between church and Chequers, then left at T junction; or from A274 take unsignposted turn E a mile N of B2077 to Smarden]: Pretty 17th-c inn with welcoming landlady, enjoyable pub food, Shepherd Neame ales, local cider, country wines, inglenook fire, rambling low-beamed little rooms, dim-lit and snug, nicely creaky old furnishings on ancient brick and flagstones or quarry tiles, end games area; picnic-sets in attractive mature garden (Peter Meister, the Didler, LYM, J H Bell, Colin McKerrow)

Chequers TN27 8QA [The Street]: Refurbished low-beamed 14th-c inn in pretty village, Fullers London Pride, Greene King IPA and Harveys, food from good baguettes up, good atmosphere; attractive garden and terrace, bedrooms, open all day (Tom and Jill Jones, LYM)

SOLE STREET [TR0949]

Compasses CT4 7ES [note – this is the Sole Street near Wye]: Unspoilt 15th-c country pub, enjoyable food, relaxed low-ceilinged rambling bars with bare boards or flagstones, massive brick bread oven, well kept real ales such as Fullers, extended family garden room; big neatly kept garden with play area, good walks (LYM, Ron and Sheila Corbett)

ST MARGARET'S AT CLIFFE [TR3544]

Smugglers CT15 6AU [High St]: Friendly spanish landlord and wife doing wide choice of food from good value baguettes up inc good tapas, home-made pizzas, mexican dishes and some more standard items, well kept Bass, Greene King and a guest ale, cosy bar with unusual curved counter, octagonal dining room; covered back terrace (Dr Kevan Tucker)

STALISFIELD GREEN [TQ9552]

Plough ME13 0HY [off A252 in Charing]: 15th-c hall house on village green high on N Downs, good local ales such as Hopdaemon, bottled belgian beers, enjoyable country cooking using local produce, friendly licensees (and cats), beams and log fires, large old-fashioned tables and chairs in dining areas each side of bar; unobtrusive piped music, some live; big pleasant garden, good view and walks (Annette Tress, Gary Smith)

STAPLEHURST []

Bell TN12 0AY [High St]: Attractively refurbished, with welcoming young licensees and staff, enjoyable fairly priced food inc Sun carvery, well kept Westerham ales, good wines by the glass, local farm cider, log fire; open all day (Tony and Vivien Smith)

STONE IN OXNEY [TQ9428]

☆ **Ferry** TN30 7JY: Attractive 17th-c smugglers' haunt, small choice of enterprising local food (scallops the hot tip) from belgian chef, attentive landlady, a beer brewed for them by Westerham, small friendly bar with woodburner and inglenook, bare boards, steps to pleasant dining area, games room;

suntrap front courtyard, big back garden, lovely setting by marshes (Louise English)

STONE STREET [TQ5754]

☆ **Snail** TN15 0LT: Smart well run pub-styled restaurant, good food at big oak farmhouse tables, plenty of fish, good wines, Harveys and a guest beer, ad lib coffee, friendly relaxed brasserie layout with beams, oak panelling and some stripped stone; attractive rambling garden, handy for Ightham Mote (NT) Alan Cowell, BB, Derek Thomas, Oliver and Sue Rowell, Mrs P Sumner)

TENTERDEN [TQ8833]

☆ **White Lion** TN30 6BD [High St]: 16th-c behind Georgian façade, beams and timbers, masses of pictures, china and books, cheerful helpful young staff, wide choice of generous popular food, Marstons and related beers, sensibly priced wines, big log fire, relaxed and friendly even when crowded with young people at night, cosy area off bar, softly lit back panelled restaurant; piped music, games machines; dogs welcome, heated terrace overlooking street, 15 charming beamed bedrooms, good breakfast, open all day (Kevin Thorpe, Donna and Roger, Louise English)

☆ **William Caxton** TN30 6JR [West Cross; top of High St]: Hospitable 15th-c local, heavy beams and bare boards, huge inglenook, woodburner in smaller back bar, enjoyable reasonably priced food from moules frites to venison casserole, well kept Marstons Pedigree and Shepherd Neame Spitfire, darts, daily papers, pleasant small dining room; piped music; children and dogs welcome, tables in attractive front area, back courtyard (Peter Meister, B J Harding, Donna and Roger, the Didler)

TEYNHAM [TQ9661]

Plough ME9 9JJ [Lewson St]: Picturesque 13th-c weatherboarded pub in quiet village, well worn with low beams and inglenook fires in two split-level carpeted bars with comfortable furnishings, friendly staff and atmosphere, full Shepherd Neame range inc seasonal ales, good wines, wide choice of generous food from bar lunches to restaurant meals and Sun roasts; piped music (live on Weds); children and dogs welcome, front terrace with cast-iron tables, large well kept back garden with play area overlooking meadow (Mr and Mrs P R Thomas)

THURNHAM [TQ8057]

☆ **Black Horse** ME14 3LD [not far from M20 junction 7; off A249 at Detling]: Olde-worlde dining pub with enjoyable food all day, children's menu, well kept changing ales such as Adnams, Sharps Doom Bar and Westerham Grasshopper, farm ciders and country wines, efficient service, bare boards, hop bines and log fires; dogs welcome, pleasant garden with partly covered back terrace, water features and nice views, by Pilgrims Way, comfortable modern bedroom block, good breakfast (Tom and Jill Jones, Phil Bryant, Peter Meister)

TUNBRIDGE WELLS [TQ5638]

☆ *Beacon* TN3 9JH [Tea Garden Lane, Rusthall Common]: Cheery and airy Victorian pub with Harveys Best, Larkins and Timothy Taylors Landlord, lots of wines by the glass, good coffee, fireside sofas, stripped panelling, bare boards and ornate wall units, linked dining area; good-natured service can struggle at peak times; children welcome, decking tables with fine view, paths between lakes and springs, three bedrooms, open all day *(Dr Ron Cox, Ron and Sheila Corbett, Peter Meister, Gerry and Rosemary Dobson, LYM, Kevin Thorpe, Lorry Spooner)*

Compasses TN1 1YP [Little Mount Sion, off High St]: Several separate timbered areas, well kept Greene King and guest ales, good coffee, friendly efficient young staff, speciality sausage menu, open fires; forecourt tables, open all day *(LYM, LM)*

TYLER HILL [TR1461]

Ivy House CT2 9NE [Hackington Rd]: Very good food under current licensees (formerly at Dove, Dargate), well kept real ale, two magnificent weimaraners, some live music *(Prof and Mrs J Fletcher)*

UNDER RIVER [TQ5552]

☆ *White Rock* TN15 0SB [SE of Sevenoaks, off B245]: Friendly village pub, attractive and relaxed, with good pubby food (all day Sun), coffee and cakes between times, Fullers London Pride, Harveys and usually a Westerham ale, beams, bare boards and stripped brickwork in cosy original part with adjacent dining area, public bar with pool in modern extension; quiet piped music; children welcome, nice front garden, back terrace and large lawn, pretty churchyard and walks nearby, open all day *(Tina and David Woods-Taylor, B J Harding, DFL, Mrs P Sumner, Robert Gomme, E D Bailey)*

WAREHORNE [TQ9832]

Woolpack TN26 2LL [off B2067 nr Hamstreet]: Popular neatly kept 16th-c dining pub in lovely spot, good generous food in rambling bar and big candlelit restaurant, popular carvery Weds evening (booking essential), elaborate puddings, well kept local ales, decent wines, efficient service, huge inglenook, heavy beams, plain games room; picnic-sets out overlooking quiet lane and meadow with lovely big beech trees, lots of flower tubs and little fountain *(Nick Hawksley, BB)*

WEALD [TQ5350]

Edwards TN14 6QR [Morleys Rd]: Light and spacious modern bistro-style layout with small comfortable sitting area on right of central bar, large eating area extended into new conservatory, good choice of enjoyable up-to-date food, three well kept ales inc Harveys Best, efficient friendly service *(Gerry and Rosemary Dobson)*

WEST FARLEIGH [TQ7152]

Tickled Trout ME15 0PE [B2010 SW of Maidstone]: Popular dining pub with OAP specials (Tues-Thurs), Fullers London Pride, Greene King Old Speckled Hen and Shepherd

Neame Spitfire, several wines by the glass, staff cheerful even when rushed; Medway views esp from big garden with play area, path down to river, good walks *(N R White, LYM, Glenwys and Alan Lawrence)*

WEST PECKHAM [TQ6452]

Swan on the Green ME18 5JW [off A26/B2016 W of Maidstone]: Main draw here is the good range of beers brewed by the pub – and the charming village green is great for a summer drink (the church is partly Saxon); relaxed unpretentious open-plan beamed bar with modern artwork and some stripped brickwork, mixed furnishings, Biddenden farm cider, some ambitious food (not Sun, Mon evenings, may close other times out of season); piped classical music; children and dogs welcome, open all day summer wknds *(N R White, Tina and David Woods-Taylor, Sue Demont, Tim Barrow, Kevin Thorpe, LYM, Mrs J Ekins-Daukes)*

WESTERHAM [TQ4454]

Grasshopper TN16 1AS [The Green]: Old village pub overlooking green, three linked bar areas with good log fire at back, low ceilings, lots of bric-a-brac and royal pictures, friendly efficient staff, food from good value sandwiches up, Wells & Youngs ales, upstairs restaurant; children welcome, seating out at front and in back garden, open all day *(Ian and Nita Cooper, N R White)*

WHITSTABLE [TR1066]

Duke of Cumberland CT5 1AP [High St]: Large open-plan Shepherd Neame pub with four of their ales, good choice of generous food; courtyard with stage for bands *(Gwyn and Anne Wake)*

Old Neptune CT5 1EJ [Marine Terr]: Great view over Swale estuary from picturesque seafront pub, unpretentious olde-worlde feel inside, enjoyable lunchtime food, real ales, wknd live music; dogs and children welcome, picnic-sets on beach (plastic glasses out here) *(Keith and Chris O'Neill, N R White)*

Pearsons CT5 1BT [Sea Wall]: Smartly refurbished 18th-c food pub under welcoming newish management, bright and airy with lots of stripped pine, popular well presented fresh fish and seafood, Gadds beers, good service, upstairs restaurant with sea view, downstairs bar with limited seating; children welcome in eating areas, open all day wknds, just above shingle beach *(LYM, Roger Thornington, N R White)*

Royal Naval Reserve CT5 1BQ [High St]: Friendly, comfortable and cosy, roomier than it looks from outside, with well kept Shepherd Neame ales, nice house wines, good value home cooking inc fresh local fish and great steak and kidney pudding, attractive upstairs dining room; some tables under back awning *(Norman Fox)*

Ship Centurion CT5 1AY [High St]: Friendly and chatty unpretentious pub, well kept Adnams and changing guest beers from small breweries, local cider, modest range of bargain food inc german dishes, old local photographs, conservatory; TV lounge, live music Thurs *(Pete Baker, Gwyn and Anne Wake)*

Whitstable Brewery Bar CT5 2BP [East Quay]: Friendly beach bar with real ales and various lagers and fruit beers from the associated Whitstable brewery (over nr Maidstone), light, airy and simple, with sea-view picture windows, functional span ceiling, flagstone floor with mainly standing room (some seats), big log fire, lunchtime food, Fri music night; July beer festival; picnic-sets out on the shingle (plastic glasses here), cl winter Mon-Weds, open all day *(Keith and Chris O'Neill, N R White)*

WITTERSHAM [TQ8927]

Swan TN30 7PH [Swan St]: Large village local dating from 17th c, well kept Harveys Best, Goachers Light and Mild and four changing microbrews, beer festivals, bargain food from sandwiches up, back lounge bar with open fire, china and pictures, public with darts and pool; TV; garden with picnic-sets, open all day *(Peter Meister)*

WORTH [TR3356]

☆ **St Crispin** CT14 0DF [signed off A258 S of Sandwich]: Dating from 16th c, stripped brickwork, bare boards and low beams, generous popular home-made food here and in restaurant and back conservatory from good baguettes to some imaginative dishes, welcoming attentive staff, changing real ales, belgian beers, local farm cider, well chosen wines, central log fire; good bedrooms (inc motel-style extension), charming big garden behind with terrace and barbecue, lovely village position *(Dr Kevan Tucker, N R White)*

WROTHAM [TQ6258]

Moat TN15 7RR [London Rd]: Well refurbished Badger family dining pub in Tudor-style building with flagstones and stripped beams and masonry, good value food, their usual ales, friendly staff; children welcome, garden tables, great playground, open all day *(Gordon and Margaret Ormondroyd)*

'Children welcome' means the pub says it lets children inside without any special restriction. If it allows them in, but to restricted areas such as an eating area or family room, we specify this. Places with separate restaurants often let children use them, hotels usually let them into public areas such as lounges. Some pubs impose an evening time limit – let us know if you find one earlier than 9pm.

Lancashire
(with Greater Manchester and Merseyside)

We found more than 30 local breweries competing here – great for keeping prices down, with quite a few pints well under £2.50. The main local brewers are Thwaites, Robinsons and Hydes (who also brew Boddingtons) and the most successful among the many smaller ones are Moorhouses, Bowland, Lancaster and Phoenix; Holts is a low-price champion. A notable number of good pubs either brew their own or keep a remarkable range of beers. The Sun in Lancaster, appealing on all levels, offers eight real ales plus a tremendous range of bottled beers and the cheery landlord at the Taps in Lytham also stocks eight and hosts meet-the-brewer evenings. They've eight at the Stalybridge Station Buffet, ten at the sumptuous Victorian Philharmonic Dining Rooms in Liverpool, four interesting guests and six of their own brews at the striking Marble Arch in Manchester and loads of their own Saddleworth beers at the quirky Church Inn at Uppermill. That old gem the Britons Protection in Manchester deserves mention for its good value pubby food, but for a special meal head to the civilised Bay Horse in Bay Horse, the stylish Highwayman at Nether Burrow (with its emphasis on genuinely locally sourced ingredients, it's our Lancashire Dining Pub of the Year) or the Three Fishes at Great Mitton (same owners, similar style). Three newcomers to the *Guide* are also really strong on food: the Eagle at Barrow, Clog & Billycock at Pleasington and (back after a break) Spread Eagle at Sawley. The Borough in Lancaster, a splendid all-rounder, and remote-seeming Fishermans Retreat in Ramsbottom (an amazing choice of whiskies) are two further distinctive new entries. With nearly 200 good pubs in the Lucky Dip section, you're spoilt for choice here: top picks include the Red Pump at Bashall Eaves, Assheton Arms at Downham, Arden Arms in Stockport and Calfs Head at Worston.

BARNSTON   SJ2783 MAP 7
Fox & Hounds ◗■ £
3 miles from M53 junction 3: A552 towards Woodchurch, then left on A551; CH61 1BW

Tidy pub with unusual collections, reasonably priced lunchtime food and good range of drinks including interesting guest beers

The immaculately kept rooms at this popular friendly place, well lit by big windows and painted a fresh cream, have a 1960s feel to their fixtures and fittings. The main part of the roomy carpeted bay-windowed lounge bar has blue plush pleated built-in banquettes and plush-cushioned captain's chairs around solid tables, and plenty of old local prints below a delft shelf of china, with a collection of police and other headgear. Tucked away opposite the serving counter is a charming old quarry-tiled corner with an antique kitchen range, copper kettles, built-in pine kitchen cupboards and lots of earthenware or enamelled food bins. With its own entrance at the other end of the pub, a small locals' bar is worth a peek for its highly traditional layout and collection of hundreds of horsebrasses and metal ashtrays up on its delft shelf; darts, TV and board games. Next to it is a snug where children are allowed. They serve six real ales, with Websters Yorkshire and Theakstons Best and Old Peculier alongside interesting guests from brewers such as Betwixt, Brimstage and Storm on handpump; in addition are more than 60 whiskies and a dozen wines by the glass. There are some picnic-sets under cocktail parasols out in the yard behind, with a profusion of colourful baskets and tubs.

🍴 Good value traditional food includes toasted ciabattas, open sandwiches, soup, filled baked potatoes, quiche and various platters. Main courses include lamb shank, hot pie of the day, fish of the day, sausage and mash and Sunday roasts. *Starters/Snacks: £2.75 to £5.50. Main Courses: £5.50 to £10.00. Puddings: £3.25 to £4.50*

Free house ~ Licensee Ralph Leech ~ Real ale ~ Bar food (12-2(2.30 Sun); not evenings) ~ (0151) 648 1323 ~ Children in snug ~ Dogs allowed in bar ~ Open 11-11; 12-10.30 Sun

Recommended by Paul Boot, Alan and Eve Harding, Derek and Sylvia Stephenson

BARROW

SD7337 MAP 7

Eagle

Village signposted off A59; Clitheroe Road (A671 N of Whalley); BB7 9AQ

Stylishly redesigned pub with splendid food, relying on fresh local ingredients; appealing modern furnishings and good buzzy atmosphere

---

With emphasis on really excellent food, this stylish place serves arguably the best sausages you'll ever taste. Open for only a few months, it's already established itself as a favourite with all sorts of people and ages; on our midweek evening visit much of the lively chatter came from smartly turned-out young couples, but there were plenty of older groups in the mix too. The building has been transformed, and you'd be forgiven for thinking it new; there's a carved wooden eagle as you walk in, past glass cases showing off champagne bottles and some of the landlord's awards, then on the right is the bar, its light leather chairs and sofas and big low tables giving a nice blend of the individual and comfortably modern. To the left is the brasserie-style dining room, with a busy open kitchen and a glass cabinet displaying their 35-day dry-aged steaks; an area at the back has chandeliers and big mirrors. Blackboards on the walls stress the provenance of fresh, local ingredients – the day we went, the new potatoes had all been dug at dawn that morning on a nearby farm. At the back is a clubby and elegantly panelled piano bar, with its own bar counter and a pianist three evenings a week. Polite, uniformed young staff serve five real ales including Caledonian Deuchars IPA, Courage Directors, Theakstons Best and guests from the Barrow, Moorhouses or Skipton Brewery; good, changing wine list. A few tables outside overlook the enormous car park.

🍴 Very good, promptly served food includes exceptional sausages made on the premises using organic local pork or beef (try the Connoisseur: pork with apple poached in calvados and cider, and a hint of honey, thyme and blueberries), as well as soup, lobster linguine in tomato and cream sauce, grilled scallops with black pudding beignets, braised local lamb shank with port and rosemary jus, fish pie, beef, mushroom and oxtail pie, steaks, daily specials, local cheeses, and puddings like chocolate orange fondant. *Starters/Snacks: £4.75 to £8.75. Main Courses: £9.95 to £27.95. Puddings: £5.50*

Free house ~ Licensee Kevin Berkins ~ Bar food (12-2.30, 6-9.30 (10 Fri, Sat); 12-8 Sun) ~ Restaurant ~ (01254) 825285 ~ Children welcome ~ Pianist Weds, Fri and Sat ~ Open 11-11; 11-1am Sat

Recommended by Steve Whalley

'Children welcome' means the pub says it lets children inside without any special restriction; some may impose an evening time limit earlier than 9pm – please tell us if you find this.

BAY HORSE   SD4952   MAP 7

Bay Horse ⊕ ♀

1.2 miles from M6 junction 33: A6 southwards, then off on left; LA2 0HR

Comfortably stylish pub with emphasis on innovative food; good range of drinks, garden

---

The series of small rambling linked areas at this comfortable dining pub has the feel of a civilised country restaurant, with red décor, a log fire, candle-flame-effect lights and nice tables, including one or two good-sized ones in intimate self-contained corners. A beamed red-walled bar is cosily pubby, attractively decorated as it is with cushioned wall banquettes in bays, gentle lighting, including table lamps on window sills and fresh flowers on the counter, with a good log fire. As well as a decent, fairly priced wine list (15 wines by the glass), 15 malt whiskies, freshly squeezed orange juice and pressed apple juices, helpful efficient staff serve Black Sheep, Moorhouses Pendle Witches Brew and a guest such as Lancaster Bomber from handpumps; quiet piped music. The pub is in a peaceful location (though the railway is not far off) and there are tables out in the garden behind. Note they don't accept lunchtime bookings for parties of fewer than eight people.

🍴 **A good deal of effort goes into the food here, with innovative use of carefully sourced ingredients and lovely presentation. Though not cheap, helpings are generous. As well as imaginative lunchtime sandwiches, lunch and evening menus might include starters such as ox tongue, beetroot and horseradish, smoked chicken caesar salad with anchovies and roast scallops with parsnip purée, main courses such as pork and leek sausages with caramelised onion gravy, roast pork fillet with mustard mash and black pudding, poached chicken breast with truffle mash, port and wild mushrooms, halibut fillet with tomato, shallot and tarragon dressing, and puddings such as bread and butter pudding with marmalade ice-cream and chocolate and pecan tart with peanut butter ice ceam; they also have a lancashire cheeseboard.** *Starters/Snacks: £4.25 to £7.95. Main Courses: £11.95 to £21.95. Puddings: £4.95 to £6.95*

Mitchells ~ Tenant Craig Wilkinson ~ Real ale ~ Bar food ~ Restaurant ~ (01524) 791204 ~ Children welcome ~ Open 12-3, 6.30-11(midnight Sat); 12-4 Sun; closed Sun evening and Mon (except bank hols), Tues after bank hols ~ Bedrooms: /£89B

Recommended by Maurice and Gill McMahon, Mr and Mrs B Watt, Jo Lilley, Simon Calvert, Karen Eliot, Revd D Glover, Martin Stafford, Chris Stevenson, Rory and Jackie Hudson, Rob and Catherine Dunster, Dr and Mrs A K Clarke, Dr Kevan Tucker

BISPHAM GREEN   SD4813   MAP 7

Eagle & Child ⊕ ♀ ◀

Maltkiln Lane (Parbold—Croston road, off B5246); L40 3SG

Well liked pub with antiques in stylishly simple interior, interesting range of beers, appealing rustic garden

---

Understated but spot on the mark, the largely open-plan bustling bar at this country feeling pub is discerningly furnished with a lovely mix of small old oak chairs, an attractive oak coffer, several handsomely carved antique oak settles (the finest apparently made partly from a 16th-c wedding bed-head), old hunting prints and engravings and low hop-draped beams. There are red walls and coir matting up a step and oriental rugs on ancient flagstones in front of the fine old stone fireplace and counter. Friendly young staff serve an interesting range of five changing beers which might typically be from brewers such as Bowland, Greene King IPA, Southport and Thwaites Original. They also keep Saxon farm cider, decent wines and around 25 malt whiskies. They hold a popular beer festival over the first May bank holiday weekend. Around the back you'll find a spacious slightly rustic garden a well tended but unconventional bowling green, and beyond, a wild area that is home to crested newts and moorhens. A handsome side barn houses a deli; the pub's dogs are called Betty and Doris.

🍴 **There's quite an emphasis on the well cooked food (you need to book) which includes several imaginative sandwiches, steamed mussels with white wine and garlic, steak and** ale pie, crayfish and lemon risotto, grilled sweet cure gammon with pineapple, egg or cheese, chick and bacon carbonara, and specials such as scallops with parma ham and lemon and caper salad and fried duck with orange and sherry vinegar reduction. *Starters/Snacks: £5.00 to £7.50. Main Courses: £8.75 to £13.50. Puddings: £4.50*

Free house ~ Licensee David Anderson ~ Real ale ~ Bar food (12-2, 5.30-8.30(9 Fri, Sat); 12-8.30 Sun) ~ (01257) 462297 ~ Children welcome ~ Dogs welcome ~ Jazz last Sun of month ~ Open 12-3, 5.30-11; 12-11 Sat; 12-10.30 Sun

Recommended by Margaret Dickinson, Jeremy King, Deirdre Holding, Ann and Tony Bennett-Hughes, Ian and Nita Cooper, Michael Butler, Yvonne and Mike Meadley, W K Wood, Revd D Glover, Karen Eliot

BROUGHTON

SD4838 MAP 7

Plough at Eaves

A6 N through Broughton, first left into Station Lane just under a mile after traffic lights, then bear left after another 1.5 miles; PR4 0BJ

Cosy old place in peaceful spot; good value traditional food

The two homely low-beamed lattice-windowed bars at this pleasant old tavern are traditionally furnished with a mix of wooden chairs, tables and upholstered seats. There are three aged guns over a log-burning stove, and a row of Royal Doulton figurines above an open log fire in the restaurant bar, which extends into a conservatory. Thwaites Original and Lancaster Bomber on handpump, quiet piped music and games machine. This is a lovely backwater spot by a quiet country lane, with metal and wood-slat seats on the front terrace from which to watch the world go by and a well equipped children's play area at the back. More reports please.

🍴 Bar food includes sandwiches, potted shrimps, steak and kidney pie, fish, steaks, and home-made puddings including fresh fruit pavlova and chocolate fudge cake. *Starters/Snacks: £3.95 to £8.00. Main Courses: £5.75 to £16.00. Puddings: £4.25*

Thwaites ~ Tenants Doreen and Mike Dawson ~ Real ale ~ Bar food (12-2.15(3.15 Sat), 6-9(9.15 Sat); 12-8 Sun) ~ Restaurant ~ (01772) 690233 ~ Children welcome ~ Open 12-3, 5.30-11.30; 12-1 Sat; 12-10.30 Sun; closed Mon (except bank hols)

Recommended by Keith and Rowena Ward

CHIPPING

SD6141 MAP 7

Dog & Partridge

Hesketh Lane; crossroads Chipping—Longridge with Inglewhite—Clitheroe; PR3 2TH

Comfortable old-fashioned dining pub in grand countryside, with traditional food

---

A recent traditionally furnished extension at this nicely old-fashioned feeling yet much modernised pub has pleasing views across fields to the Fells. Dating back nearly 500 years, the main lounge has small armchairs around fairly close-set low tables on a blue patterned carpet, brown-painted beams, a good winter log fire and multicoloured lanterns; piped music. Friendly helpful staff serve Tetleys Bitter and Mild and a weekly changing guest such as Black Sheep Bitter on handpump. Smart casual dress is preferred in the stable restaurant. More reports please.

🍴 Enjoyable bar food includes sandwiches, prawn cocktail, broccoli and stilton pancakes, steak and kidney pie, roast duckling with apple sauce and stuffing, pork chops and grilled sirloin steak with home-made puddings such as sticky toffee pudding and sherry trifle. Do take special note of the food service times. *Starters/Snacks: £3.30 to £5.50. Main Courses: £9.00 to £14.75. Puddings: £4.00 to £4.30*

Free house ~ Licensee Peter Barr ~ Real ale ~ Bar food (12-1.30; 7(6.30 Sat)-9; 12-8.30 Sun) ~ Restaurant (7(6.30 Sat)-9 Mon-Sat; 12-8.30 Sun) ~ (01995) 61201 ~ Children welcome ~ Open 11.45-3, 6.45(6.15 Sat)-11; 11.45-10.30 Sun; closed Mon

Recommended by Mr and Mrs J L Blakey, Tim and Rosemary Wells, Bob Broadhurst, Jane Anne Ingleson

DENSHAW

SD9711   MAP 7

Rams Head

2 miles from M62 junction 2; A672 towards Oldham, pub N of village; OL3 5UN

Roaring fires and tasty food in inviting old-world moorland pub with farm shop

Though emphasis at this snug old place tends to be on the attractively presented food it does still have the appealing atmosphere of a moorland haven. Placed 1,200 feet high, with terrific views, it's a useful objective for walkers. The cosily traditional interior has beam-and-plank ceilings and good log fires, and is furnished with oak settles and benches built into the panelling of its four thick-walled little rooms. Black Sheep, Copper Dragon and Timothy Taylors are on handpump; piped music. You can buy locally sourced meat and other produce and have a coffee in their rather nice little adjacent deli.

🍴 Tasty bar food features seasonal game and plenty of seafood: game terrine with celery and sultana compote and cumberland sauce, thai fish balls, seared king scallops with pear purée and garlic lardons, baked haddock fillet on spring onion mash with cheddar sauce, roast suckling pig stuffed with garlic and herbs on stir-fried noodles, roast wild mallard with port and juniper jus, fish pie and passion fruit, and puddings such as treacle sponge; good value three-course set menus. *Starters/Snacks: £4.95 to £7.95. Main Courses: £8.95 to £15.95. Puddings: £3.95 to £4.95*

Free house ~ Licensee Geoff Haigh ~ Real ale ~ Bar food (12-2, 6-10; 12-8.30 Sun) ~ Restaurant ~ (01457) 874802 ~ Children welcome till 8pm, not Sat evening ~ Open 12-2.30, 6-11; 12-10.30 Sun; closed Mon evening

Recommended by Andy and Jill Kassube, Mrs P J Carroll, Julian and Jill Tasker

GREAT MITTON

SD7139   MAP 7

Three Fishes

Mitton Road (B6246, off A59 NW of Whalley); BB7 9PQ

Stylish modern conversion, tremendous attention to detail, excellent regional food with a contemporary twist, interesting drinks

Stretching back much further than you'd initially expect, the cleverly appealing layout of this stylishly revamped dining pub keeps it feeling snug and intimate, despite its size. It's a popular bustling place, but does things very well even at the busiest of times (which are often), with friendly staff serving well considered regional cuisine. The areas closest to the bar are elegantly traditional with a couple of big stone fireplaces, rugs on polished floors, newly upholstered stools and a good chatty feel. Then there's a series of individually furnished and painted rooms with exposed stone walls, careful spotlighting and wooden slatted blinds, ending with another impressive fireplace; facilities for the disabled. The long bar counter (with elaborate floral displays) serves Thwaites Original, Lancaster Bomber and Wainwright and a guest from Bowland, cocktails, a dozen wines by the glass and unusual soft drinks such as locally made sarsaparilla and dandelion and burdock. Overlooking the Ribble Valley, the garden and terrace have tables and perhaps their own summer menu. They don't take bookings at the weekend (except for groups of eight or more), but write your name on a blackboard when you arrive and find you when a table becomes free – the system works surprisingly well. This pub is under the same ownership as the Highwayman at Nether Burrow and Clog & Billy Cock at Pleasington, just outside Blackburn.

🍴 You order your meal at various food points dotted around, and the emphasis is on traditional lancastrian dishes with a modern twist. Products are carefully sourced from small local suppliers, many of whom are immortalised in black and white photographs on the walls, and located on a map on the back of the menu. Most dish descriptions indicate the origins of the main ingredient – the beef particularly is exclusive to here. As well as imaginative lunchtime sandwiches, there might be starters such as seared tuna salad and morecambe bay shrimps, treacle-baked cumbrian ribs, main courses such as toad in the hole, shin of beef braised in red wine, sirloin steak, curd cheese and onion pie with short-crust pastry, and puddings such as apple crumble with vanilla custard, rice pudding with mead-soaked yellow raisins, or bread and butter pudding with apricot glaze;

children's menu. You may need to order side dishes with some main courses. They take a brief half an hour break between serving sessions and serve a limited snack menu in the afternoon. *Starters/Snacks: £3.50 to £7.50. Main Courses: £9.50 to £19.60. Puddings: £5.00 to £5.50*

Free house ~ Licensees Nigel Haworth, Andy Morris ~ Real ale ~ Bar food (12-9(8.30 Sun)) ~ (01254) 826888 ~ Children welcome ~ Dogs welcome ~ Open 12-11(10.30 Sun)

Recommended by Gerry and Rosemary Dobson, GLD, Steve Whalley, Dr Kevan Tucker, W K Wood, Richard Pitcher, Cedric Robertshaw, J F M and M West, Margaret Dickinson, Jo Lilley, Simon Calvert, Ken Richards, Peter and Josie Fawcett, Paul Boot, Pauline and Derek Hodgkiss, Ray and Winifred Halliday, Sally Anne and Peter Goodale

LANCASTER SD4761 MAP 7

Borough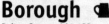
Dalton Square; LA1 1PP

Enterprising city-centre pub with chattily civilised atmosphere, excellent range of beers and drinks and good locally sourced food

Much bigger than it looks from the outside, this handsome stone pub is full of surprises – not just its wide range of meticulously sourced drinks and food, but also unexpected bonuses like the deli counter that will whip up tasty local snacks all day, and the lovely little garden at the back. Relaxed and civilised, the front areas with their chandeliers and dark leather sofas and armchairs have something of the look of the private members club this once was; there are carefully chosen antique tables and lamps, as well as panelled stained glass, old prints and photographs, chunky candles, high stools and elbow tables. Behind here is the bar, where friendly staff serve eight well kept local ales such as Bowland Hen Harrier, Coniston Old Man and Special Oatmeal Stout, a beer brewed for them by Hawkshead, Lancaster Amber and Thwaites Original and Wainwrights; also a wider than usual range of bottled beers, a good choice of wines and malt whiskies and a pile of fresh oranges ready for juicing. Beyond this area is a big dining room with tables in the middle and booths along one side; on the other side is the deli counter and a little shop selling jams and other local produce. The tree-sheltered garden, with wooden tables, opens off. The statue of Queen Victoria in the square outside is among several notable gifts to the city by one of its most famous sons, Lord Ashton.

🍴 With a real emphasis on independent local suppliers, the menu includes soup, sandwiches, black pudding with sliced new potatoes, herb salad, poached egg and pancetta crisp, home-made chicken liver pâté with organic oatcakes, morecambe bay potted shrimps, hotpot with spiced red cabbage, beer-battered haddock in newspaper, steak and ale pie, herb-marinated ostrich steak with sweet potato purée, and various steaks and salads. The deli counter has various local cheeses and snacks like smoked mackerel available all day and there's a home-made crêpe menu too. *Starters/Snacks: £1.95 to £5.95. Main Courses: £8.95 to £15.95. Puddings: £3.50*

Free house ~ Licensee Hannah and Martin Horner ~ Real ale ~ Bar food (12-2.30, 5.30-9 (9.30 Fri); Sat 12-9.30, Sun 12-9) ~ (01524) 64170 ~ Children welcome ~ Dogs allowed in bar ~ Monthly Sun evening comedy club ~ Open 12-11.30 (12 Fri, Sat)

Recommended by Jo Lilley, Simon Calvert, Maria S

Sun
Church Street; LA1 1ET

Great updated town pub with fantastic range of drinks including eight real ales, food served from breakfast on and comfortably modern bedrooms

Exactly what a town-centre pub should be (says one reader), this thriving place is both warmly traditional and comfortably contemporary, attracting a bustling range of customers, some popping in to sample the impressive range of drinks, with others staying to make the most of the tasty food. Thoughtfully restored several years ago, the designers successfully blended new styling with the old existing structure. The beamed bar is atmospheric and characterful, with plenty of panelling, chunky modern tables on the part flagged and part wooden floors, a 300-year-old oak door (discovered during renovations), several fireplaces (the biggest filled with a huge oak cask) and subtly effective spotlighting. The little bar counter belies the range of drinks available: you'll generally find four real ales from the Lancaster Brewery (set up in 2005 by the company behind the pub's transformation), four changing guests from brewers such as Moles, Thwaites and Ufford, 50 belgian and bottled beers, over 20 well chosen wines by the glass, 50 whiskies and some unique teas and coffees from a local wholesaler. There's a discreet TV in a corner and piped music. A passageway leads to a long narrow room that's altogether cooler, still with exposed stone walls, but this time covered with changing art exhibitions; the furnishings in here are mostly soft and low, with lots of dark brown sofas and stools. An area with some more substantial wooden tables and high-backed chairs leads into a conservatory.

🍽 **Bar food kicks off with very traditional breakfasts (featuring devilled kidneys, smoked kippers and eggs benedict). Lunchtime and evening food includes good helpings of traditional dishes such as hotpot, steak and ale pie and generous cheese, cold meat and pâté boards.** *Starters/Snacks: £3.50 to £6.00. Main Courses: £5.00 to £10.00. Puddings: £3.50 to £4.50*

Free house ~ Licensee Dominic Kiziuk ~ Real ale ~ Bar food (12-3, 4-9(7 Fri, Sat); 12.30-3.30, 4.30-9 Sun) ~ (01524) 66006 ~ Children welcome away from bar ~ Open 10am-midnight(1am Fri, Sat)11.30 Sun) ~ Bedrooms: £65B/£65S(£75B)

Recommended by Les Baldwin, John Ashford, Ray and Winifred Halliday, Paul Boot, Jo Lilley, Simon Calvert, Karen Eliot, Mike Horgan, David Kirkcaldy

LIVERPOOL   SJ3589   MAP 7
Philharmonic Dining Rooms ★ 🍺 £
36 Hope Street; corner of Hardman Street; L1 9BX

Beautifully preserved Victorian pub with superb period interior, ten real ales and sensibly priced food

This stunningly preserved sumptuous Victorian building originated as a gentlemen's club. Its centrepiece is a mosaic-faced serving counter, from which heavily carved and polished mahogany partitions radiate under the intricate plasterwork high ceiling. The echoing main hall boasts stained-glass including contemporary portraits of Boer War heroes Baden-Powell and Lord Roberts, rich panelling, a huge mosaic floor and copper panels of musicians in an alcove above the fireplace. More stained-glass in one of the little lounges declares 'Music is the universal language of mankind' and backs this up with illustrations of musical instruments. Two side rooms are called Brahms and Liszt, and there are two plushly comfortable sitting rooms. This is no museum piece, however, and it can be very busy here, with ten handpumps as testament to a high turnover. As well as Caledonian Deuchars IPA, Youngs & Wells Bombardier, up to eight changing guest ales might be from brewers such as Everards, Jennings and St Austell with usually an array of seasonal brews, as well as several malt whiskies; quiz machine, fruit machine and piped music. Don't miss the original 1890s Adamant gents' lavatory (all pink marble and mosaics); ladies are allowed a look if they ask first.

🍽 **Reasonably priced food (available in the bar or in the table-service grand lounge dining room) includes soup, baked potatoes, sandwiches, ploughman's, steak pie, fish and chips, and puddings; in the evenings they do nachos, spicy prawns and a sharing platter, sausage and mash, and pies.** *Starters/Snacks: £2.95 to £8.95. Main Courses: £4.95 to £9.95*

Mitchells & Butlers ~ Manager Marie-Louise Wong ~ Real ale ~ Bar food (10-10) ~ Restaurant ~ (0151) 707 2837 ~ Open 10am-midnight

Recommended by Karen Eliot, the Didler, Darren Le Poidevin, Jeremy King, John and Helen Rushton

Post Office address codings confusingly give the impression that some pubs are in Lancashire when they're really in Cumbria or Yorkshire (which is where we list them).

LONGRIDGE   SD6038   MAP 7

Derby Arms ♀

Chipping Road, Thornley; 1.5 miles N of Longridge on back road to Chipping; PR3 2NB

Convivial traditional country pub with hunting and fishing paraphernalia (and menu to match) and very decent wine list

Welcoming licensees put tremendous effort and enthusiasm into running this nice old place. They put on lots of themed evenings – anything from an oyster festival on St Patrick's day to a stand up comedian. Among hunting and fishing bric a brac in its main bar, old photographs commemorate notable catches and there's some nicely mounted bait above the comfortable red plush seats, together with a stuffed pheasant that seems to be flying in through the wall. To the right a smaller room has sporting trophies, mementoes and a regimental tie collection; piped music and darts. The gents' has dozens of riddles on the wall – you can buy a sheet of them in the bar and the money goes to charity. Along with a good range of wines, including several by the glass and half bottles (they're particularly strong on south african), you'll find Black Sheep and Marstons Pedigree on handpump. A few tables out in front, and another two behind the car park, have fine views across to the Forest of Bowland.

🍴 **You order your meal at the bar and will be shown to your table when it's ready. They do lots of seasonal game such as pheasant, hare, rabbit, partridge, woodcock, rabbit and mallard and offer several fresh fish dishes such as potted shrimps, mussels, fresh dressed crab, oysters and monkfish. Other enjoyable food might include sandwiches, ploughman's, duck spring rolls, ham, egg and chips, vegetarian hotpot, steak and kidney pudding, venison platter and aberdeen angus fillet steak rossini; good chips and generous vegetables; the two or three-course table d'hôte menu is good value; puddings such as home-baked fruit pies, sherry trifle and bread and butter pudding.** *Starters/Snacks: £3.95 to £5.95. Main Courses: £7.95 to £10.95. Puddings: £3.95 to £4.95*

Punch ~ Lease Will and Carole Walne ~ Real ale ~ Bar food (12-2.15, 6-9.15(10 Fri, Sat); 12-9.15 Sun) ~ Restaurant ~ (01772) 782623 ~ Children welcome ~ Open 12-3, 6(5.30 Sat)-12; 12-11.30 Sun

Recommended by Roger Thornington, Margaret Dickinson, Dr and Mrs T E Hothersall, Steve Whalley

LYDGATE   SD9704   MAP 7

White Hart 🍴 ♀ 🛏

Stockport Road; Lydgate not marked on some maps so not to be confused with the one near Todmorden; take A669 Oldham—Saddleworth, and after almost 2.5 miles turn right at brow of hill to A6050, Stockport Road; OL4 4JJ

Smart up-to-date dining pub (drinkers welcome too) with excellent food (not cheap), five beers, good wine list, garden and comfortable bedrooms

The modern refurbishment of this stylish place is a successful blend of new and old, with the new marking out some of the remaining older features, though the overall impression is fairly contemporary. Beams and exposed stonework are blended skilfully with deep red or purple walls, punctuated with a mix of modern paintings, black and white photos and stylised local scenes; most rooms have a fireplace and fresh flowers. The warmly elegant brasserie is the biggest of the main rooms and service from the smartly dressed staff is good. Many come here to dine, but there are often a good few locals clustered round the bar, or in the two simpler rooms at the end. The very extensive wine list includes around 16 by the glass, and beers are Lees Bitter, Timothy Taylors Golden Best and Landlord with a couple of changing guests from a brewers such as Phoenix and Pictish on handpump; piped music; TV in front lounge. The pub is located just outside the eastern fringes of Oldham, on the moors of the Pennines and a few miles from the border of the Peak District National Park – picnic-sets on the lawn behind make the most of the postion. More reports please.

🍴 **The thoughtfully prepared meals are pricier than in most pubs around here, but the quality is consistently high. The bar food menu typically includes sandwiches, potted shrimps, oysters, fried scallops with grilled chorizo, pea purée and fried leeks, battered** haddock with marrowfat peas, braised beef cheek with haggis mash, fried bass with smoked bacon and king prawn risotto, roast pork fillet with black pudding and apple and tarragon hash brown, parsnip and blue cheese risotto, and puddings such as bakewell tart or glazed lemon tart with honey ice-cream and red wine sauce; there is also a separate restaurant menu. *Starters/Snacks: £4.50 to £7.50. Main Courses: £12.50 to £17.00. Puddings: £4.50 to £5.50*

Free house ~ Licensee Charles Brierley ~ Real ale ~ Bar food (12-2.30, 6-9.30; 1-7.30 Sun) ~ Restaurant ~ (01457) 872566 ~ Children welcome ~ Dogs allowed in bar ~ Open 12-midnight ~ Bedrooms: £95B/£127.50B

Recommended by Revd D Glover, Paul Bailey, Marcus Mann

LYTHAM   SD3627   MAP 7

Taps 🍺 £

A584 S of Blackpool; Henry Street – in centre, one street in from West Beach; FY8 5LE

Thriving seaside pub with down-to-earth atmosphere, spirited landlord, eight real ales and straightforward lunchtime snacks; open all day

The landlord at this cheery town pub is a tremendous character – he's been known to lay turf through the pub during the golf Open Championship and at Christmas he sets his tree up horizontally. He's a rugby fan, with an expanding collection of rugby memorabilia and old photographs and portraits of rugby stars on the walls so it rather goes without saying that beer is important here (and perhaps explains why there are seat belts on the bar and headrests in the gents'). An impressive choice of six ever-changing guests are kept alongside Greene King IPA and Taps Best which is brewed for the pub by Titanic on handpump (you can see them all in the view-in cellar), and the landlord hosts meet the brewer evenings; also country wines and a farm cider. With a good mix of customers, the Victorian-style bare-boarded bar has a sociable unassuming feel, plenty of stained-glass decoration in the windows, depictions of fish and gulls reflecting the pub's proximity to the beach (it's a couple of minutes' walk away), captain's chairs in bays around the sides, open fires and a coal-effect gas fire between two built-in bookcases at one end; shove-ha'penny, dominoes, quiz machine and fruit machine. There are a few seats and a heated canopied area outside. Parking is difficult near the pub so it's probably best to park at the West Beach car park on the seafront (free on Sunday) and walk. One reader felt the ladies' lavatories could do with a good freshening up.

🍽 **A handful of cheap bar snacks includes sandwiches, soup, hot roast sandwich, filled baked potatoes, burgers, chilli and curry.** *Starters/Snacks: £2.25 to £4.45. Puddings: £1.95 to £2.75*

Greene King ~ Manager Ian Rigg ~ Real ale ~ Bar food (12-2, not Sun) ~ No credit cards ~ (01253) 736226 ~ Children welcome away from bar till 7pm ~ Open 11-11(midnight Fri, Sat)

Recommended by Pam and John Smith, Ken Richards, Steve Whalley, J F M and M West, John Fiander, the Didler

MANCHESTER   SJ8397   MAP 7

Britons Protection 🍺 £

Great Bridgewater Street, corner of Lower Mosley Street; M1 5LE

Lively city pub with maze of unspoilt rooms, huge range of whiskies, five real ales and inexpensive lunchtime snacks; garden

From a historical point of view alone this centrally located Grade II listed pub is rather special, though in fact, it's far too dynamic to be just a museum piece. Although busy at lunchtime, it's usually quiet and relaxed in the evenings when they host poetry readings, storytelling, silent film shows and acoustic gigs. As well as a terrific range of around 235 malt whiskies and bourbons, they have Jennings Cumberland, Robinsons Unicorn, Tetleys and a couple of interesting changing guests such as Coach House Honeypot and good wines. One of the most notable features here are the tiled battle murals depicting the Peterloo Massacre of 1819, which took place a few hundred yards away. The first of a series of unspoilt little rooms, the plush little front bar has a fine chequered tile floor, some glossy brown and russet wall tiles, solid woodwork and elaborate plastering. There are two cosy inner lounges, both served by hatch, with attractive brass and etched glass wall lamps, a mirror above the coal-effect gas fire in the simple art nouveau fireplace and again, good solidly comfortable furnishings. As something of a tribute to Manchester's notorious climate, the massive bar counter has a pair of heating pipes as its footrail. There are tables out on the garden behind. They may close early on match days.

🍴 Straightforward bar food includes soup, various pies and home-made daily specials such as steak with mushroom sauce, hotpot, lasagne or minted lamb chop. *Main Courses: £4.50 to £6.50*

Punch ~ Lease Peter Barnett ~ Real ale ~ Bar food (11-2) ~ (0161) 236 5895 ~ Quiz night first Mon of month ~ Open 11.30-midnight; 12-midnight Sun

Recommended by John Fiander, Ian and Nita Cooper, Revd D Glover, the Didler, Neil Whitehead, Victoria Anderson, GLD, Pam and John Smith, Mrs Hazel Rainer, Dr Kevan Tucker, DC, Darren Le Poidevin

Dukes 92

Castle Street, below the bottom end of Deansgate; M3 4LZ

Waterside conversion with spacious interior, great range of cheeses and pizzas all day

Minimalist but comfortable, this big converted stable block is now even bigger with a stylish new gallery bar, accessed by an elegant spiral staircase and overlooking the canal. Old and modern furnishings, including comfortable chaises-longues and deep armchairs, throughout the ground floor are well spaced and contrast with boldly bare whitewashed walls. The handsome granite-topped counter serves three real ales, two usually from Moorhouses, as well as decent wines and a wide choice of spirits; piped music. The building is in the basin and bottom lock of the Rochdale Canal among other restored Victorian warehouses, and tables outside on a big terrace enjoy good waterside views.

🍴 The menu is short but includes an excellent range of over three dozen cheeses and pâtés with generous helpings of granary bread; also sandwiches and salads. From mid-afternnon onwards they serve pizzas only. Puddings include chocolate fudge cake and sticky toffee pudding; the restaurant has a grill menu with burgers and steaks. *Starters/Snacks: £3.95 to £7.95. Main Courses: £6.95 to £19.95. Puddings: £5.95*

Free house ~ Licensee James Ramsbottom ~ Real ale ~ Bar food (12-10.30(11 weekends)) ~ Restaurant ~ (0161) 839 8646 ~ Children welcome till 8.30pm ~ Open 11.30-11(midnight Thurs, 1 Fri, Sat); 12-11 Sun

Recommended by Howard and Sue Gascoyne, Ben Williams, Mrs Hazel Rainer, Darren Le Poidevin

Marble Arch 🍺

Rochdale Road (A664), Ancoats; corner of Gould Street, just E of Victoria Station; M4 4HY

Cheery town pub with noteworthy Victorian interior, ten real ales including own brews, very reasonably priced food and small garden

This splendidly preserved Victorian alehouse is well worth a special trip. The interior has a magnificently restored lightly barrel-vaulted high ceiling and extensive marble and tiling. A frieze advertising various spirits, the chimney breast above the carved wooden mantelpiece and sloping mosaic floor particularly stand out. Furniture is a cheerful mix of rustic tables and chairs, including a long communal table and a display cabinet with pump clips. From windows at the back, you can look out over the brewery (tours by arrangement) where they produce their distinctive Ginger Marble, J P Best, Lagonda IPA, Manchester Bitter, Marble Best and seasonal brews. They also have four guest ales from brewers such as Abbeydale, Phoenix and Pictish and a farm cider; games machine, piped music, juke box and the Laurel and Hardy Preservation Society meet here on the third Wednesday of the month and show old films; small garden.

🍴 Freshly cooked food, from a weekly changing menu, might include aubergine and mozzarella sandwich, oxtail ravioli, scallops with black pudding and celeriac, pies, lamb loin with rosemary potatoes and grilled rib-eye steak. *Starters/Snacks: £3.95 to £7.50. Main Courses: £7.50 to £13.50. Puddings: £4.50*

Own brew ~ Licensee Jan Rogers ~ Real ale ~ Bar food (12-9(8 Sun)) ~ (0161) 832 5914 ~
Children welcome ~ Dogs welcome ~ Open 12-11.30(midnight Sat)

*Recommended by the Didler, Chris Johnson, Neil Whitehead, Victoria Anderson, Jeremy King, Joe Green,
Revd D Glover, Darren Le Poidevin, John and Helen Rushton*

MELLOR   SJ9888   MAP 7

Devonshire Arms

*This is the Mellor near Marple, S of Manchester; heading out of Marple on the A626 towards
Glossop, Mellor is the next road after the B6102, signposted off on the right at Marple
Bridge; Longhurst Lane; SK6 5PP*

Charming little pub with wide choice of food, attractive gardens and play area

Just the sort of haven you'd wish for on a wintery day, this snugly unpretentious little
place, just off the Moors, is warm, welcoming and cosy. Locals gather in the cheerful
little front bar with its heartening winter fire in a sizeable Victorian fireplace with a
deep-chiming clock above it, an unusual curved bar (with Robinsons Best and Mild and a
Robinsons guest and sangria in summer), and a couple of old leather-seated settles,
among other seats. Both of the two small back rooms have Victorian fireplaces – the one
on the right has an unusual lion couchant in place of a mantelpiece. Through french
windows you'll find a delightful garden, with plenty of tables, and a waterfall tumbling
into a well stocked fish pond, over which a japanese bridge leads to a covered terrace.
There's a children's play area tucked away in the small tree-sheltered lawn, a boules piste
and more picnic-sets out in front.

🍴 **The wide choice of good generously served pubby food includes pea and ham soup,
mussel chowder, sandwiches, baked potatoes, ploughman's, spicy lamb and bean casserole,
beef rogan josh, battered haddock, mixed grill, steaks and pies such as steak and kidney
or chicken and ham; children's menu.** *Starters/Snacks: £3.75 to £6.25. Main Courses: £6.25 to
£15.95. Puddings: £3.95 to £4.50*

Robinsons ~ Tenants John and Liz Longworth ~ Real ale ~ Bar food (11.45-2, 6-9; 12-9 Sat,
Sun) ~ Restaurant ~ (0161) 4272563 ~ Children welcome ~ Jazz second Tues of month ~ Open
11.45-3, 6-11; 11.45-11 Sat; 12-11 Sun

Recommended by David Hoult, Dr and Mrs A K Clarke

NETHER BURROW   SD6175   MAP 7

Highwayman 🍴 ♇

A683 S of Kirkby Lonsdale; LA6 2RJ

LANCASHIRE DINING PUB OF THE YEAR

**Substantial old stone house with country interior serving carefully sourced and prepared
food; lovely gardens**

This upmarket dining pub is a really special place, beautifully refurbished a few years ago
by the owners of the Three Fishes at Great Mitton, and loved by readers. Although large,
its stylishly simple flagstoned 17th-c interior is nicely divided into intimate corners, with
a couple of big log fires and informal wooden furnishings. The owners are keen to
actively promote local suppliers, hence the black and white wall prints (and placemats)
showing the characterful local farmers and producers from whom the pub gets its
ingredients. Local Thwaites Lancaster Bomber, Double Century and Wainwright and a
guest such as Bowland Sawley Tempted are served on handpump, alongside good wines
by the glass, just over a dozen whiskies and a particularly good range of soft drinks.
Service is busy, welcoming and efficient. French windows open to a big terrace and lovely
gardens. They don't take bookings at the weekend (except for groups of eight or more),
but write your name on a blackboard when you arrive, and they will find you when a
table becomes free.

⑪ Traditional lancastrian recipes are tweaked to bring them up to date and prepared using carefully sourced products (marked on a map on the back of the menu). As well as bar nibbles and imaginative sandwiches, ploughman's and platters of local seafood and cured meats, starters might include slow-cooked pork belly with crumbed black pudding and deep-fried apple purée, crab cake with tomato and caper sauce, twice-baked mushroom soufflé omelette and seared tuna salad, with main courses such as battered haddock with marrowfat peas, mutton pudding, cheese and onion pie, lamb hotpot with pickled red cabbage, dry cured gammon steak with poached egg, and puddings such as lancashire curd tart and bread and butter pudding. They take a brief half an hour break between serving sessions and do just snacks in the afternoon. *Starters/Snacks: £3.50 to £7.50. Main Courses: £9.50 to £19.60. Puddings: £5.00 to £5.50*

Thwaites ~ Licensees Andy Morris and Craig Bancroft ~ Real ale ~ Bar food (12-9(8.30 Sun)) ~ (01254) 826888 ~ Children welcome ~ Dogs allowed in bar ~ Open 12-11(10.30 Sun)

Recommended by Jane Taylor, David Dutton, Dr Kevan Tucker, Jo Lilley, Simon Calvert, Ray and Winifred Halliday, Steve Whalley, GLD, Michael Doswell, Karen Eliot, Margaret Dickinson, Dr Peter Andrews, G Jennings

PLEASINGTON

SD6528   MAP 7

Clog & Billycock ⑭ ♟

Village signposted off A677 Preston New Road on W edge of Blackburn; Billinge End Road; BB2 6QB

Excellent, well sourced local food in appealingly modernised stone-built village pub; very busy, but service is efficient and unhurried

The third in Nigel Haworth's burgeoning group of Ribble Valley Inns, this big, briskly efficient village pub sticks to the same successful formula, with the main attraction being the very good, locally sourced food. What's not made on the premises won't have travelled far, and the menu identifies most of their suppliers, some of whom can also be seen in photographs. Named after the preferred attire of a former landlord, the building has been extended on both sides and completely redesigned; light and airy, with flagstoned floors and pale grey walls, in places it has the feel of an upmarket barn conversion, though there's a cosier room opening off, with high-backed settles and a fireplace at the end. The whole pub is packed with light wooden tables, all of them full when we arrived, but such is the size of the place, we didn't have to wait long in the little bar area for one to become free. Nor was there any delay with our order – indeed a delightful ploughman's appeared no more than a minute or two after it had been requested. Staff are polite and helpful, and the sheer volume of satisfied customers ensures a very good, chatty atmosphere. Well kept Thwaites Original and Bomber, a very good choice of wines and a wide range of other drinks too. There are some tables outside, beside a small garden.

⑪ Making good use of local ingredients, but adding a few surprises too, particularly good food includes well filled sandwiches, deep-fried cauliflower fritters with curried mayonnaise, warm morecambe bay shrimps with butter and a toasted muffin, crab cake with tomato and caper sauce, lamb sweetbreads with fresh broad beans, peas and caper and parsley mash, an excellent hotpot with pickled red cabbage, steak and kidney pudding, slow-cooked crispy duck legs with spiced lentils, mint yoghurt and deep-fried courgette, very good steaks, seasonal specials, local cheeses and organic ice-creams, and puddings such as gooseberry and elderflower meringue pie. There's a snack menu during the afternoon. *Starters/Snacks: £3.50 to £7.50. Main Courses: £8.95 to £17.95. Puddings: £5.00*

Thwaites ~ Licensees Andy Morris and Craig Bancroft ~ (01254) 201163 ~ Children welcome ~ Dogs allowed in bar ~ Open 12-11; 12-10.30 Sun

Recommended by GLD, W K Wood, Steve Whalley, Ray and Winifred Halliday, Margaret Dickinson, Jim and Maggie Cowell

RABY   SJ3179   MAP 7

Wheatsheaf

Off A540 S of Heswall; Raby Mere Road; CH63 4JH

Cottagey village pub, decent lunchtime bar food; eight real ales

New licensees are unlikely to change the delightfully timeless feel of this popular
timbered and whitewashed country cottage, known locally as The Thatch. Its nicely
chatty rambling rooms are simply furnished, with an old wall clock and homely black
kitchen shelves in the cosy central bar, and a nice snug formed by antique settles built in
around its fine old fireplace. A second, more spacious room, has upholstered wall seats,
small hunting prints on cream walls and a smaller coal fire. The spacious restaurant
(Tuesdays to Saturday evening) is in a converted cowshed that leads into a larger
conservatory; piped music is played in these areas only. Eight changing real ales are
thoughtfully sourced and might be from brewers such as local Brimstage, Greene King,
St Austell, Tetleys, Thwaites, Wells and Youngs. There are picnic-sets on the terrace and
in the pleasant garden behind, with more seats out front.

🍴 **Reasonably priced pubby lunchtime food is home made and as well as a wide range of
sandwiches and toasties includes baked potatoes, ploughman's, omelettes, steak and ale
pie, fish and chips, braised knuckle of lamb; three-course Sunday lunch; more expensive à
la carte restaurant food.** *Starters/Snacks: £2.05 to £4.25. Main Courses: £4.25 to £12.95.
Puddings: £3.95*

Free house ~ Licensee Alan Philip Davies ~ Real ale ~ Bar food (12-2(3 Sun)) ~ Restaurant
(evenings 6-9.30, Tues-Sat; not Sun and Mon) ~ (0151) 336 3416 ~ Children welcome ~
Dogs allowed in bar ~ Open 11.30-11(midnight Fri, Sat); 12-10.30 Sun

Recommended by Paul Boot, Alan and Eve Harding, MLR

RAMSBOTTOM   SD8017   MAP 7

Fishermans Retreat 🍴

Twine Valley Park/Fishery signposted off A56 N of Bury at Shuttleworth; Bye Road; BL0 0HH

**Good views from friendly remote-feeling pub with hundreds of whiskies, all for sale by the
bottle in new shop; trout and some meats on menu come from their own land**

Feeling much more remote than it really is – mainly because of the final single-track drive
– this stone-built pub has fine views of the surrounding farmland and trout lakes, from
which the family that run it get the fish, beef and venison used in their food. But what
really makes it stand out is the incredible range of malt whiskies, currently numbering
around 500. Almost half are ranked on shelves above the bar counter, each new one added
as the collection grew, but all are available in the new whisky shop in a corner of the
main room; this also sells wines and half the fun is looking at the price stickers on some
of the rarer or vintage bottles. They do occasional tutored whisky tastings. The bar has
something of the feel of a mountain lodge, with its bare stone walls and beamed ceilings,
though the wallpaper around the fireplace adds a more civilised touch. A similar dining
room opens off. Five well kept beers such as Black Sheep, Timothy Taylors Landlord and
changing beers from Moorhouse, Phoenix and Skipton, plus a good wine list, with the
emphasis on new world ones; particularly friendly staff. There are a few picnic-sets
outside. Over the next year they plan a few changes, adding a new dining room so the
main room can become a lounge for drinkers. You can arrange coarse fishing on the lakes.

🍴 **Home-made food includes soup, field mushrooms filled with sautéed sweet balsamic
leeks, crushed hazelnuts and blacksticks blue cheese, black pudding and queen scallops in
a smoked bacon and lancashire cheese sauce, fish pie, steak pudding, chicken breast
stuffed with black pudding and brie, burgers, fresh fish, and daily specials like roast pork
belly on celery mash with sweet red onion and celery jus. They don't take bookings
(though with notice can arrange a suckling pig for groups).** *Starters/Snacks: £5.00 to £7.50*

Free house ~ Licensee Hervey Magnall ~ Real ale ~ Restaurant ~ (01706) 825314 ~
Children in eating area of bar ~ Open 12-11; closed Mon, 25 Dec

Recommended by Steve Whalley, Mark and Diane Grist

SAWLEY

SD7746 MAP 7

Spread Eagle

Off A59 NE of Clitheroe; BB7 4NH

Nicely refurbished pub with imaginative food and riverside restaurant

New owners have done a beautiful job refurbishing this riverside pub – if you've been before you'll be amazed to see that they've removed all the dull white render from the front, thus exposing some nice old stonework. The fresh clean interior has a pleasing mix of nice old and quirky modern furniture – anything from an old settle and pine tables to new low chairs upholstered in animal print fabric, all set off well by the grey rustic stone tiled floor. Low ceilings, cosy sectioning, a warming fire and cottagey windows keep it all feeling intimate. The dining areas are more formal, with modern stripes, and, as a bit of a quip on the decorative trend for walls of unread books, a bookshelf mural – much easier to keep dust free; piped music. Real ales include Theakstons, Thwaites Wainwright, Timothy Taylors Landlord and a guest such as Hawkshead on handpump. The pub is in a lovely location by the River Ribble and the ruins of a 12th-c cistercian abbey, and is handy for the Forest of Bowland – an upland with terrific scope for exhilarating walks; there are two smoking porches.

🍴 **Good food includes nibbles such as battered black pudding fritter with mayonnaise, tempting sandwiches, starters such as fried scallops with pancetta, corned beef hash cake with a poached egg, meat, fish and spanish sharing platters for two, main courses such as battered haddock with mushy peas, seared bass with roast basil and cherry tomatoes with parsley and parmesan crust, gnocchi with mushroom and broad bean pesto cream, baked eggs and ratatouille with garlic croûtes, and puddings such as white chocolate brûlée with marinated berries and cassis sorbet in a tuile basket and carrot cake with cream cheese and coconut sorbet and warm orange syrup.** *Starters/Snacks: £5.00 to £8.00. Main Courses: £9.00 to £17.00. Puddings: £5.00*

Free house ~ Licensee Kate Peill ~ Real ale ~ Bar food (12-2, 6-9.30; 12-7.30 Sun) ~ Restaurant ~ (01200) 441202 ~ Children welcome ~ Open 11-11; 12-10.30 Sun

Recommended by G Dobson, Mrs Sheila Stothard, Steve Whalley, Christopher Mobbs

STALYBRIDGE

SJ9598 MAP 7

Station Buffet 🍺 £

The Station, Rassbottom Street; SK15 1RF

Classic Victorian station buffet bar with eight quickly changing beers and a few cheap basic meals

If only waiting for a train could always be as splendidly diverting and well refreshed as this. Here you can happily linger a good while away in this atmospheric Victorian refreshment room or at picnic-sets out on sunny Platform One by the Manchester to Huddersfield line. Busy with happy customers, the bar has a welcoming fire below an etched-glass mirror, period advertisements and photographs of the station and other railway memorabilia on cosy wood panelled and red walls, and there's a cute little conservatory with coloured glass (possibly subject to renovation work). An extension along the platform leads into what was the ladies' waiting room and part of the station-master's quarters featuring original ornate ceilings and Victorian-style wallpaper. The tremendous range of beers here rotates quickly but usually includes Boddingtons, Flowers, an alternating beer from Greenfield and Millstone and four quickly rotating guests from brewers such as All Gates, Coach House and Phoenix, alongside belgian and other foreign bottled beers and a farm cider; board games, cards, newspapers and magazines.

🍴 **They do cheap old-fashioned snacks such as tasty black peas and sandwiches, and three or four daily specials such as home-made meat and potato pie and mushy peas, bacon casserole and all day breakfast; freshly made coffee and tea by the pot.** *Starters/Snacks: £2.50. Main Courses: £3.50. Puddings: £1.50*

Free house ~ Licensees John Hesketh and Sylvia Wood ~ Real ale ~ Bar food (12-7.30) ~
No credit cards ~ (0161) 303 0007 ~ Children till 7.30pm ~ Dogs welcome ~ Open 11-11;
12-10.30 Sun

Recommended by Brian and Anna Marsden, John Fiander, Dennis Jones, Mike Horgan, Bob Broadhurst, Tony and Maggie Harwood, the Didler

TUNSTALL   SD6073   MAP 7

Lunesdale Arms ⦿ ♀

A683 S of Kirkby Lonsdale; LA6 2QN

Light and airy civilised pub with emphasis on good imaginative food; separate area with traditional games

Bright, fresh and airy yet still feeling homely, this well run cheerful country pub places
some emphasis on its thoughtfully prepared food. A white-walled area, with bare boards
creating a lively acoustic, has a good mix of stripped solid dining tables and blue sofas
facing each other across a low table (with daily papers) by a woodburning stove in a
solid stone fireplace. Another area has pews and armchairs (some of the big unframed oil
paintings are for sale) and to one end, an airy games section with pool, table football,
board games and TV. A snugger little flagstoned back part has another woodburning
stove. Besides Black Sheep and a local guest on handpump, they have several wines by
the glass and 20 malts; piped music. The church in this Lune Valley village has Brontë
associations.

⦿ **Food is prepared with admirable attention to detail – readers particularly praise the
home-made bread and chips. The constantly changing menu might include lunchtime
sandwiches, beetroot and dill soup, sharing platter with prosciutto and dips, Guinness and
mushroom pie, fried hake fillet with chorizo and butterbean sauce, battered haddock and
chips with mushy peas, rib-eye steak with béarnaise sauce, and puddings such as lemon
soufflé with gingerbread biscuit, chocolate tart and rhubarb crumble cake; smaller
helpings of some main courses, good value two- and three-course menus Tuesday to
Thursday evenings; Sunday lunch.** *Starters/Snacks: £4.95 to £5.50. Main Courses: £8.95 to
£15.95. Puddings: £4.95*

Free house ~ Licensee Emma Gillibrand ~ Real ale ~ Bar food ~ (01524) 274203 ~
Children welcome ~ Dogs allowed in bar ~ Open 11-3, 6-midnight; 11-3.30, 6-1am Sat;
12-3.30, 6-11 Sun; closed Mon (except bank hols)

*Recommended by Mrs B Hemingway, Chris and Meredith Owen, Jo Lilley, Simon Calvert, Ken and Jenny Simmonds,
Ann and Tony Bennett-Hughes, Dr Kevan Tucker, Michael Doswell*

UPPERMILL   SD0006   MAP 7

Church Inn ◖ £

*From the main street (A607), look out for the sign for Saddleworth Church, and turn off up
this steep narrow lane – keep on up! OL3 6LW*

**Lively good value community pub with own brews from big range, lots of pets and good
food; children very welcome**

One reader described this appealingly unconventional place as 'an absolute joy'. He was
particularly delighted with the fabulous range of own-brew beers and the very good value
straightforward pubby food. High up in an elevated position on the moors, the big
unspoilt L-shaped main bar at this quirky place has high beams and some stripped stone.
One window at the end of the bar counter looks down over the valley and there's a valley
view from the quieter dining room; the conservatory opens on to a new terrace.
Comfortable furnishings include settles and pews as well as a good individual mix of
chairs, lots of attractive prints and staffordshire and other china on a high delft shelf,
jugs, brasses and so forth; TV (only when there's sport on) and unobtrusive piped music.
The horse-collar on the wall is worn by the winner of their annual gurning (face-pulling)
championship which is held during the lively traditional Rush Cart Festival which is
usually over the August bank holiday. Local bellringers arrive on Wednesdays to practise

with a set of handbells that are kept here, while anyone is invited to join the morris dancers who meet here on Thursdays. When the spring water levels aren't high enough for brewing, they bring in guest beers such as Black Sheep and Hydes Jekylls Gold. At other times you might find up to 11 of their own-brew Saddleworth beers, starting at just £1.50 a pint. Some of the seasonal ones (look out for Rubens, Ayrtons, Robins and Indya) are named after the licensee's children, only appearing around their birthdays; continental wheat beer and dark lager on tap too. There's a delightful assortment of pets roaming around in the garden: rabbits, chickens, dogs, ducks, geese, horses, a couple of peacocks in the adjacent field and an army of rescued cats resident in an adjacent barn. Children and dogs are made to feel very welcome.

🍴 **Reasonably priced bar food includes soup, sandwiches, steak and ale pudding, a range of pies, lasagne, jumbo cod, and puddings such as jam roly poly or hot chocolate fudge cake and ice-creams.** *Starters/Snacks: £2.20 to £5.25. Main Courses: £5.85 to £12.00. Puddings: £2.75*

Own brew ~ Licensee Julian Taylor ~ Real ale ~ Bar food (12-2.30, 5.30-9; 12-9 Sat, Sun) ~ (01457) 820902 ~ Children welcome ~ Dogs welcome ~ Open 12-12(11 Sun)

Recommended by John Fiander, Dr Kevan Tucker, the Didler

WADDINGTON
SD7243   MAP 7

Lower Buck
Edisford Road; BB7 3HU

Popular village pub with reasonably priced, tasty food; five real ales

Tucked away behind the church, this sweet little stone building is a proper chatty local, nicely old-fashioned and welcoming, with several little cream-painted rooms, each with welcoming coal fires; darts, pool and dominoes; two dining rooms. The friendly landlord keeps a range of five ales, usually from local Bowland and Moorhouses, and Timothy Taylor, over a dozen malts and several wines by the glass. There is seating at the back in a sunny garden and a few tables out in front and it's handily placed for walks in the Ribble Valley.

🍴 **Using meat reared at a farm in nearby Longridge, and vegetables grown in Longridge too, the reasonably priced tasty food includes lunchtime sandwiches and ploughman's, morecambe bay shrimps, short-crust pastry pies, fish pie, hotpot, sirloin steak, specials such as cream of cauliflower and cheese soup, scallops with cheddar sauce, steak and kidney pudding and seared tuna steak marinated in coriander, lime and chilli, and puddings such as apple and cinnamon pie.** *Starters/Snacks: £3.95 to £5.50. Main Courses: £8.50 to £15.00. Puddings: £3.95 to £4.95*

Free house ~ Licensee Andrew Warburton ~ Real ale ~ Bar food (12-2.30, 6-9; 12-9 Sat, Sun and bank hols) ~ Restaurant ~ (01200) 423342 ~ Children welcome ~ Dogs welcome ~ Open 11(12 Sun)-11(midnight Sat)

Recommended by Noel Grundy, Len Beattie, John and Eleanor Holdsworth, Steve Whalley

WHEATLEY LANE
SD8338   MAP 7

Old Sparrow Hawk
Wheatley Lane Road; towards E end of village road which runs N of and parallel to A6068; one way of reaching it is to follow Fence, Newchurch 1¼ signpost, then turn off at Barrowford ¾ signpost; BB12 9QG

Comfortably civilised pub, with well prepared food and five real ales

Though there is some emphasis on the food here, locals do pop in to enjoy the early evening buoyantly chatty but relaxing atmosphere. Attractively laid out in several distinct areas, some with carpet and some with red tiles, it's nicely characterful with dark oak panelling and timbers, stripped stonework, lots of snug corners including a nice area with a fire, interesting furnishings including a sofa under a domed stained-glass skylight; daily papers. The cushioned leatherette bar counter (cheerful with fresh flowers) carries

Bass, Black Sheep, Thwaites, a couple of guests such as Dent Aviator and Moorhouses Blonde Witch on handpump, draught Fransizkaner wheat beer and good wines by the glass. TV, piped music (one reader found it intrusive) and board games. Heavy wood tables out on a spacious and attractive front terrace (pretty flower beds and a water feature) have good views to the moors beyond Nelson and Colne.

🍴 Good fresh bar food includes interesting sandwiches, wraps and ciabattas, pressed ham and black pudding terrine with beetroot salad, caesar or crispy duck salad, sausage and mash, fish and chips, rib-eye steak, specials such as goosnargh duck breast on bacon and lentil stew, and puddings such as rum and raisin cheesecake, eton mess and home-made ice-creams. *Starters/Snacks: £5.00 to £7.00. Main Courses: £9.00 to £14.00. Puddings: £4.00 to £5.00*

Mitchells & Butlers ~ Lease Stephen Turner ~ Real ale ~ Bar food (12-2.30, 5-9; 12-9.30 Sat; 12-8.30 Sun) ~ Restaurant ~ (01282) 603034 ~ Children welcome ~ Dogs welcome ~ Open 12-11(midnight Sat, 10.30 Sun)

Recommended by Dr Kevan Tucker, Pauline and Derek Hodgkiss, Dr and Mrs T E Hothersall, Steve Whalley, Margaret Dickinson

WHEELTON   SD6021   MAP 7

Dressers Arms 🍺

2.1 miles from M61 junction 8; Briers Brow, off A674 Blackburn road from Wheelton bypass (towards Brinscall); 3.6 miles from M65 junction 3, also via A674; PR6 8HD

Good choice of beer at traditional pub

It's worth looking in at this converted cottage row for the range of eight real ales, including their own Milk of Amnesia and Mild (now brewed off the site), Black Sheep and Tetleys and four or five guests from brewers such as Copper Dragon and George; also 16 malt whiskies and some well chosen wines, with several by the glass. The series of snug low-beamed rooms here is traditionally furnished with dark wood benches and red plush furnishings on patterned carpets, with a handsome old woodburning stove in the flagstoned main bar; newspapers, magazines, piped music, juke box, pool table, games machine and TV. There are lots of picnic-sets under a large umbrella with lighting and heaters on a terrace in front of the pub.

🍴 Pubby bar food includes breaded mushrooms, sandwiches, steak pudding, liver and onions, fish and chips and 14oz sirloin steak; Sunday carvery. We've had rather mixed feedback on the food in recent months so do wonder if the chef has changed. *Starters/Snacks: £3.95 to £5.95. Main Courses: £6.95 to £10.50. Puddings: £4.50*

Own brew ~ Licensees Steve and Trudie Turner ~ Real ale ~ Bar food (12-2.30, 5-9; 12-9 Sun and bank hols) ~ Restaurant ~ (01254) 830041 ~ Children welcome ~ Dogs allowed in bar ~ Open 10am-12.30am(1am Sat)

Recommended by W K Wood, Charles and Pauline Stride, Norma and Noel Thomas, Pam and John Smith, Michael Butler, Mr and Mrs Barrie, Donna and Roger, Jo Lilley, Simon Calvert, Dr Kevan Tucker

WHITEWELL   SD6546   MAP 7

Inn at Whitewell ★ 🍷 🛏

Most easily reached by B6246 from Whalley; road through Dunsop Bridge from B6478 is also good; BB7 3AT

Very civilised hotel with smartly pubby atmosphere, good bar food and luxury bedrooms

Surely one of the most beautifully decorated places in the *Guide*, the interior of this elegant manor house hotel has been simply designed with great sensitivity to the history of the building. Handsome old wood furnishings including antique settles, oak gateleg tables and sonorous clocks stand out well against powder blue walls that are neatly hung with big attractive prints. The pubby main bar has roaring log fires in attractive stone fireplaces and heavy curtains on sturdy wooden rails; one area has a selection of newspapers and magazines, local maps and guide books, there's a piano for anyone who wants to play and even an art gallery; board games. Early evening sees a cheerful bustle which later settles to a more tranquil and relaxing atmosphere. Drinks include a good wine list of around 230 wines with 18 by the glass (there is a good wine shop in the reception area), organic ginger beer, lemonade and fruit juices and three real ales on handpump that might be from Bowland, Copper Dragon and Timothy Taylor. Staff are courteous and friendly. The building is nicely positioned with delightful views from the riverside bar and adjacent terrace and is well placed if you want to spend a day or two walking on the nearby moors of the Forest of Bowland. They own several miles of trout, salmon and sea trout fishing on the Hodder, and can arrange shooting and make up a picnic hamper.

⑪ Besides lunchtime sandwiches, well presented bar food might include grilled baby squid filled with chorizo with carrot salad, fish and chips, sausage and mash, cheese and onion pie, sirloin steak and daily specials such as grilled goats cheese on pepper and red onion salad and roast breast of duck with red onion marmalade and celeriac purée; more reports on the food please. *Starters/Snacks: £4.10 to £7.50. Main Courses: £7.50 to £16.70. Puddings: £4.90*

Free house ~ Licensee Charles Bowman ~ Real ale ~ Bar food (12-2, 7.30-9.30) ~ Restaurant ~ (01200) 448222 ~ Children welcome ~ Dogs welcome ~ Open 10-midnight ~ Bedrooms: £77B/£105B

Recommended by Jo Lilley, Simon Calvert, Steve Whalley, Noel Grundy, GLD, N R White, Fiona Salvesen, Ross Murrell, Karen Eliot, John and Jackie Chalcraft, Revd R P Tickle, J F M and M West, John and Helen Rushton, Steve and Sarah Eardley, John and Sylvia Harrop, Steve Kirby, Revd D Glover, Michael Doswell

WRAY   SD6067   MAP 7

Inn at Wray

2 miles E of Hornby off A683 Kirkby Lonsdale—Lancaster; LA2 8QN

Comfortable and civilised family-run dining pub with good interesting food

Refurbished just a couple of years ago, this dining pub was thoughtfully updated, in a restrained way, keeping its original small-room layout. It's fresh and airy with cream walls and some light exposed stone. As you go in, a snug room, feeling just like a little sitting room, has comfortable soft leather sofas and easy chairs and a low table (with magazines) in front of a coal fire. A short corridor opens into further rooms, with oriental rugs on polished boards or flagstones, logs stacked by a big fire in one, a big woodburning stove in another and quite a few carefully placed pictures – one lot more a collection of grand frames, really. A larger end room has rather more imposing tables and a cabinet of home-made preserves, cordials and country wines. Two elegant upstairs carpeted dining rooms have comfortably upholstered chairs around smart tables and a wall of books; welcoming and obliging service; piped music. They have Thwaites Wainwrights and a beer brewed for them by Tirril on handpump, and do good coffee.

⑪ As well as a couple of particularly good value meal deals, enjoyable food includes sandwiches, salmon and dill parfait, breaded brie with berry compote, fish pie, scampi, spinach and feta parcels with tomato and garlic sauce, fried duck breast with garlic and thyme sauce, and puddings such as syrup sponge with vanilla custard and white chocolate and Malteser cake with chocolate sauce. *Starters/Snacks: £4.50 to £10.50. Main Courses: £10.95 to £16.25. Puddings: £4.25 to £6.25*

Free house ~ Licensee Phillip Montgomery ~ Real ale ~ Bar food (12-2, 6-9 (12-9 Sat, Sun)) ~ Restaurant ~ (01524) 221722 ~ Children welcome ~ Dogs allowed in bar ~ Open 12-3, 6-11; 12-11 Sat; 12-10.30 Sun; closed Mon (except bank hols) ~ Bedrooms: £45B/£65B

Recommended by Michael Doswell, Karen Eliot, Paul Boot

Stars after the name of a pub show exceptional quality. One star means most people (after reading the report to see just why the star has been won) would think a special trip worth while. Two stars mean that the pub is really outstanding – for its particular qualities it could hardly be bettered.

YEALAND CONYERS

SD5074   MAP 7

New Inn

3 miles from M6 junction 35; village signposted off A6; LA5 9SJ

Good generous food all day and a warm welcome at village pub near M6

Handy if you're in the area, this old village pub stays open all day and is the sort of traditional place where locals gather along the little counter. The small beamed bar is traditionally furnished with sets of plush upholstered stools grouped around closely set round tables on patterned carpet, and there's a log fire in the big stone fireplace. On the right, two communicating blue themed dining rooms have closely set tables with dark wood pub chairs on navy carpet, navy table cloths and blue spriggy wallpaper. Robinsons Hartleys XB and another of their beers are served on handpump alongside around 30 malt whiskies; piped music and very friendly service. A sheltered lawn at the side has picnic-sets among colourful roses and flowering shrubs and this is a useful place if you're walking in the area or visiting Leighton Moss RSPB reserve.

🍴 Hearty helpings of bar food include sandwiches, baguettes and baked potatoes (all with interesting fillings), goat's cheese salad, new zealand green lipped mussels with creamy garlic sauce, cumberland sausage with bacon and apricot stuffing and spinach mash, spicy bean tortilla, scampi, pie of the day, battered haddock and chips (Fridays), beef in beer, fillet steak, and a good choice of puddings such as trifle and lemon soufflé with orange sauce. *Starters/Snacks: £4.25 to £6.50. Main Courses: £9.50 to £11.50. Puddings: £4.35 to £4.85*

Robinsons ~ Tenants Bill Tully and Charlotte Pinder ~ Real ale ~ Bar food (11.30(12 Sun)-9.30) ~ Restaurant ~ (01524) 732938 ~ Children welcome ~ Dogs allowed in bar ~ Open 11.30-11; 12-10.30 Sun

Recommended by Ray and Winifred Halliday, Jane and Martin Bailey, Don Bryan, Tony and Maggie Harwood, Canon George Farran, Dr D J and Mrs S C Walker, Paul and Margaret Baker, Jo Lilley, Simon Calvert, John and Hilary Penny

LUCKY DIP

Besides the fully inspected pubs, you might like to try these Lucky Dips recommended to us and described by readers (if you do, please send us reports: feedback@goodguides.com).

ALTHAM [SD7732]
Walton Arms BB5 5UL [Burnley Rd (A678)]: Attractive and relaxed with wide range of good reasonably priced food, well kept Jennings, very good value wines, friendly efficient service, oak furniture in flagstoned dining room *(Bob Broadhurst)*
ALTRINCHAM [SJ7689]
Railway Inn WA14 5NT [153 Manchester Rd (A56), Broadheath]: Early Victorian, with lounge, bar, games room (darts and dominoes), snug and dining room, church pews, bargain Holts Bitter and Mild, friendly landlady and locals; back terrace, open all day *(the Didler)*
ARKHOLME [SD5872]
Bay Horse LA6 1AS [B6254 Carnforth—Kirkby Lonsdale]: Neatly kept and homely old three-room country pub with one or two well kept changing ales such as Black Sheep and Moorhouses, friendly landlord and prompt service, basic food inc children's menu, lovely inglenook, pictures of long-lost London pubs; bowling green, handy for Lune Valley walks, cl Mon *(MLR, Jane Taylor, David Dutton)*

ASHTON-UNDER-LYNE [SD9400]
Oddfellows Arms OL6 9LJ [Alderley St, just off Kings Road]: This small friendly unpretentious pub has been in the same family for 100 years; several areas around single bar, log fires, well kept Robinsons, no food, traditional games; garden pond with huge koi carp *(Dennis Jones)*
BALDERSTONE [SD6131]
Myerscough Hotel BB2 7LE [Whalley Rd, Samlesbury; A59 Preston—Skipton, just over 2 miles from M6 junction 31]: Solid traditional furnishings in cosy and relaxed softly lit dark-beamed bar, four well kept Robinsons ales, good soft drinks choice, traditional games, good basic home-made food from sandwiches up, darts, quiz night; no dogs; children allowed in eating area, disabled access, garden picnic-sets, bedrooms *(Abi Benson, LYM)*
BARTON [SD5137]
Sparling PR3 5AA [A6 N of Broughton]: Popular contemporary gastropub with some imaginative food inc set deals, roomy bar with comfortable settees and other seats, plenty of tables in linked areas off, wood and flagstones floors, real ales, good choice

of wines by the glass, bright young staff; children welcome, handy for M6 *(Margaret Dickinson)*

BASHALL EAVES [SD6943]

☆ **Red Pump** BB7 3DA [NW of Clitheroe, off B6478 or B6243]: Peacefully tucked-away 18th-c country pub with good local food (usually all day wknds) inc game and good value Sun lunch, well kept northern ales such as Lancaster Blonde and Tirril Old Faithful, good wine choice, two pleasantly up-to-date dining rooms, cosy more traditional central bar with bookshelves, cushioned settles and log fire (perhaps even in summer), coach-house café (cl winter) and deli, pub ghost; children welcome (good menu), terrace tables, own River Hodder fishing, three nice bedrooms, good views and breakfast, cl Mon and winter Tues, open all day wknds *(BB, Rob Bowran, Roger Thornington)*

BELMONT [SD6715]

☆ **Black Dog** BL7 8AB [Church St (A675)]: Nicely set Holts pub with their usual sensibly priced food (not Tues evening, all day Fri-Sun) and bargain beers, cheery small-roomed traditional core, coal fires, friendly attentive staff, picture-window extension; children welcome, seats outside with moorland views above village, attractive part-covered smokers' area, good walks, decent good value bedrooms, open all day *(Len Beattie, the Didler, Steve Whalley, Norma and Noel Thomas, Peter Dearing, Ben Williams, LYM, Pam and John Smith, Peter Heaton)*

BIRKENHEAD [SJ3288]

Crown CH41 6JE [Conway St]: Friendly old three-room pub popular for interesting changing ales inc Cains, Weston's farm cider, good value generous food all day till 6pm, nice tilework; terrace tables, open all day *(the Didler)*

Stork CH41 6JN [Price St]: Early Victorian, four well restored civilised rooms around island bar, polished mosaic floor, old photographs, several changing ales, bargain basic food wkdy lunchtime and early evening, tiled façade; open all day *(the Didler, Pete Baker)*

BLACKO [SD8542]

Moorcock BB9 6NG [A682 towards Gisburn]: Beautifully placed moorland dining pub, roomy and comfortably old fashioned, with big picture windows for breathtaking views, tables set close for the huge range of popular and often enterprising food inc lamb from their own flock and excellent beef, very friendly helpful staff, decent wine, Thwaites Bitter and Mild under top pressure; tables in hillside garden with various animals, open all day for food Sun, children and dogs welcome, bedrooms *(Norma and Noel Thomas, LYM)*

Rising Sun BB9 6LS [A682 towards Gisburn]: Welcoming traditional village pub now tied to Moorhouses, with their ales kept well; enjoyable well priced food, tiled entry, open

fires in three rooms off main bar; tables out on front terrace, open all day wknds *(Len Beattie)*

BLACKSTONE EDGE [SD9617]

☆ **White House** OL15 0LG [A58 Ripponden—Littleborough, just W of B6138]: Beautifully placed moorland dining pub with remote views, emphasis on good value hearty food from sandwiches up (all day Sun), prompt friendly service, Theakstons Best and changing regional guests, belgian bottled beers, cheerful atmosphere, carpeted main bar with hot fire, other areas off, most tables used for food; children welcome *(Andy and Jill Kassube, K C and B Forman, LYM)*

BOLTON [SD7107]

Brooklyn BL3 2EF [Green Lane]: Large pleasantly appointed ale Holts pub, low-priced Bitter and seasonal ale, good value baguettes etc; spacious tree-sheltered grounds *(Ben Williams)*

Howcroft BL1 2JU [Pool St]: Friendly local serving as tap for good Bank Top ales, also guest beers, enjoyable good value pubby lunches, lots of small screened-off rooms around central servery with fine glass and woodwork inc cosy snug with coal fire, bright and airy front room, conservatory, plenty of pub games, popular monthly poetry nights; crown bowling green, open all day *(the Didler)*

Southfields Brewers Fayre BL3 2EE [Green Lane]: Large recently refurbished pub worth knowing for bargain food, real ales *(Ben Williams)*

Watermillock BL1 8TJ [Crompton Way (A58 ring rd)]: Useful for reasonably priced food inc bargain carvery, real ales, friendly staff *(Ben Williams)*

Wilton Arms BL1 7BT [Belmont Rd, Horrocks Fold]: Friendly low-beamed roadside pub improved under new management, enjoyable fresh food, well kept real ales, open fires; garden overlooking valley, Pennine walks, open all day *(W K Wood, Dave Davies)*

BOLTON BY BOWLAND [SD7849]

Coach & Horses BB7 4NW [Main St]: Big beamed and stone-built pub reopened 2008 after refurbishment, enjoyable food, friendly staff, log fires; open all day wknds, lovely streamside village with interesting church *(BB, Mr and Mrs P Eastwood)*

BRINDLE [SD5924]

☆ **Cavendish Arms** PR6 8NG [3 miles from M6 junction 29, by A6 and B5256 (Sandy Lane)]: Enthusiastic new management at refurbished traditional village pub dating from 15th c, inexpensive home-made food from sandwiches up inc all-day Sun roasts, Banks's and three changing guest ales, beams, cosy snugs with open fires, stained-glass windows, carpets throughout; children welcome, dogs in tap room, heated canopied terrace with water feature, more tables in side garden, good walks, open all day *(Dr D J and Mrs S C Walker, LYM, David and Sue Smith)*

BURNLEY [SD8432]

Bridge BB11 1UH [Bank Parade]: Neatly updated open-plan pub with well kept Hydes Original, several other changing ales (hundreds each year), continental beers on tap and many dozen by the bottle, farm ciders, bargain lunchtime food, friendly atmosphere, good young staff, simple chairs and tables on left, small snug and leather sofas on right; open all day, cl Mon, Tues *(Len Beattie, Dr Kevan Tucker)*

Inn on the Wharf BB11 1JG [Manchester Rd (B6240)]: Well converted wharfside buildings by Leeds—Liverpool Canal, handy for centre, clean and spacious, with smart décor of beams, stripped stone and flagstones, friendly efficient staff, good choice from sandwiches up at all-day food bar (busy lunchtime), well kept Greene King ales, sensible prices; children welcome, waterside terrace, next to little Toll House Museum *(Len Beattie)*

Royal Butterfly BB11 3QH [Hufling Lane]: Recently refurbished local well worth knowing for its bargain beers; no dogs *(Len Beattie)*

Sparrow Hawk BB11 2DN [Church St/ Ormerod Rd]: Imposing stone-faced hotel with comfortable beamed bar, good food in lounge, welcoming cheerful staff, several well kept ales inc Moorhouses, wknd entertainment, fine views; 35 bedrooms, open all day *(Noel Grundy)*

Stanley BB11 3HB [Oxford Rd]: Local worth knowing for its particularly well kept Moorhouses *(Len Beattie)*

Thornton Arms BB10 3JS [Brownside Rd]: Converted from old barn a few decades ago by the man whose name it bears, friendly and popular with families, decent low-priced pubby food all day, well kept Thwaites; pleasant short walk down to Rowley Fishing Lodge, open all day *(Len Beattie)*

BURY [SD7912]

Brown Cow BL8 1DA [Woodhill Rd, Burrs Country Park]: Roomy open-plan bar, quiet, simple and very out of the way, with reasonably priced pubby food and two real ales; steam East Lancs Light Railway runs by garden *(TB)*

☆ *Lord Raglan* BL9 6SP [Mount Pleasant, Nangreaves, via Walmersley Old Rd off A56, N edge of Bury]: Moorland pub with phenomenal views and eight of its own good Leydens beers (June beer festival), interesting foreign bottled beers and 25 malt whiskies, food from sandwiches up (all-day wknds), assorted bric-a-brac in snug beamed front bar with mix of spindleback chairs and old settles, back room with big open fire (not always lit), plainer blond-panelled dining room; piped music; children welcome, dogs in bar, open all day wknds *(Mr and Mrs John Taylor, Dr Kevan Tucker, LYM, Pauline Jepson)*

Swan & Cemetery BL9 9NS [Manchester Rd]: Enjoyable straightforward mainstays and interesting specials, well kept Thwaites, reasonable prices *(Peter Johnston)*

Trackside BL9 0EY [East Lancs railway station, Bolton St]: Welcoming busy station bar by East Lancs steam railway, bright, airy and clean with great range of changing ales and bottled imports, farm cider, good choice of bargain wkdy lunches (from breakfast time till 5pm wknds), fine display of beer labels on ceiling; platform tables, open all day *(the Didler, Mrs Hazel Rainer, TB)*

CARNFORTH [SD5173]

Longlands LA6 1JH [Tewitfield, about 2 miles N; A6070, off A6]: Bustling family-run village inn with good local beer range, friendly helpful staff, good interesting food in bar and restaurant (worth booking), live music Mon; bedrooms, self-catering cottages *(MLR, Tony and Maggie Harwood, Alan and Eve Harding)*

Shovel LA5 9NA [North Rd]: Friendly traditional local with well kept changing ales such as Coniston and Jennings *(anon)*

CHEADLE HULME [SJ8785]

Church Inn SK8 7EG [Ravenoak Rd (A5149 SE)]: Bustling friendly local, smart and genuinely old, with good fresh food (all day Sun) in restaurant and (ordered from small hatch) in bar, pleasant waitresses, well kept Robinsons, coal fire; open all day *(G D K Fraser)*

March Hare SK8 5PG [Mill Lane (narrow, with speed bumps)]: Streamside mill-look Vintage Inn, high roof, rustic timber, stonework, flagstones, log fires and old photographs, good value fresh food inc wkdy deals, ales such as Black Sheep and Thwaites, happy staff; garden with play area *(Terry Buckland)*

CHORLEY [SD5817]

Yew Tree PR6 9HA [Dill Hall Brow, Heath Charnock – out past Limbrick towards the reservoirs]: Attractive tucked-away restauranty pub with good value enjoyable food (all day Sun) from open kitchen, lunchtime sandwiches too, helpful friendly staff; children welcome, picnic-sets in sheltered garden, cl Mon *(Norma and Noel Thomas)*

CLITHEROE [SD7241]

Edisford Bridge Hotel BB7 3LJ [B6243 W]: Lovely spot above River Ribble, enjoyable food inc bargain lunch, friendly staff, well kept Jennings ales, several quiet rooms with separate dining area; pleasantly shady garden behind *(KC)*

COLNE [SD8939]

Admiral Lord Rodney BB8 0TA [Mill Green]: Welcoming chatty three-room local, well kept changing ales inc some from small breweries, bargain pubby food (not Mon), open fire, upside-down table and chairs on bar ceiling, football ties collection; children and dogs welcome *(Len Beattie)*

Black Lane Ends BB8 7EP [Skipton Old Rd, Foulridge]: Neatly kept country inn with good food inc some unusual dishes and popular Sun lunch, welcoming relaxed atmosphere, well kept Copper Dragon ales and guest, small restaurant; children welcome, garden with play area, good

Pennine views, handy for canal and reservoir walks – there's a walkers clean up area *(John and Helen Rushton, Len Beattie, Richard and Karen Holt)*

COMPSTALL [SJ9690]

Andrew Arms SK6 5JD [George St (B6104)]: Enjoyable good value food inc special deals, well kept Robinsons ales, enterprising choice of wines by the glass, friendly efficient staff, busy back dining room, bric-a-brac on walls; garden, handy for Etherow Country Park *(Dennis Jones)*

CONDER GREEN [SD4655]

Thurnham Mill Hotel LA2 0BD [signed off A588 just S]: Converted early 19th-c stone-built mill, comfortable beamed and flagstoned bar with good reasonably priced food, Everards and other ales, lots of whiskies, friendly staff and log fires, restaurant overlooking Lancaster Canal lock; tables out on terrace, comfortable bedrooms, good breakfast, open all day *(Ray and Winifred Halliday)*

COWAN BRIDGE [SD6277]

☆ **Whoop Hall** LA6 2HP [off A65 towards Kirkby Lonsdale]: Spacious and comfortable linked areas, wide choice of interesting quick food (all day from 8am) from popular buttery, pleasant neat staff, Black Sheep and Greene King, decent wines, log fire, pool; piped music; children welcome, garden well off road with back terrace views, play area, comfortable bedrooms *(Chris and Meredith Owen, Margaret Dickinson, LYM)*

CROSBY [SJ3100]

Crows Nest L23 7XY [Victoria Rd, Gt Crosby]: Unspoilt and interesting roadside local with cosy bar, snug and Victorian-style lounge, chatty friendly landlady, well kept Cains, Theakstons and two guests; tables outside, open all day *(the Didler)*

DENTON [SJ9395]

Lowes Arms M34 3FF [Hyde Rd (A57)]: Smart pub brewing its own cheap LAB ales, other guest beers inc local Hornbeam, good bargain food inc vegetarian and tapas, jovial landlord and efficient staff, separate large games room; tables outside, open all day wknds *(Dennis Jones)*

DOLPHINHOLME [SD5153]

Fleece LA2 9AQ [back rds, a couple of miles from M6 junction 33]: Friendly hotel with good food inc imaginative specials, helpful staff, well kept ales (beer festivals), dining area off comfortable beamed lounge, bar with darts and table skittles, log fire; garden, bedrooms *(Chris Stevenson)*

DOWNHAM [SD7844]

☆ **Assheton Arms** BB7 4BJ [off A59 NE of Clitheroe, via Chatburn]: Neatly kept 18th-c pub in lovely village location with Pendle Hill view, good range of food (all day Sun) inc good seafood menu, quick service, lots of wines by the glass, two real ales, cosy low-beamed L-shaped bar with pews, big oak tables and massive stone fireplace; piped music; children and dogs welcome, picnic-sets outside, open all day wknds

(Michael Lamm, K C and B Forman, Ian and Suzy Masser, Maurice and Gill McMahon, Norma and Noel Thomas, LYM)

DUKINFIELD [SJ9497]

Astley Arms SK16 4BT [Chapel Hill]: Robinsons pub with their real ales inc Old Stockport, three roomy areas off bar, short choice of bargain food all day inc carvery, friendly helpful staff *(Dennis Jones)*

ECCLES [SJ7798]

Albert Edward M30 0LS [Church St]: Cheery roadside local with three rooms, flagstones and old tiles, fire, bargain Sam Smiths; small back terrace, open all day *(the Didler)*

Grapes M30 7HD [Liverpool Rd, Peel Green; A57 0.5 miles from M63 junction 2]: Handsome brawny Edwardian local with superb etched glass, wall tiling and mosaic floor, lots of mahogany, eye-catching staircase, well kept bargain Holts and a good guest beer, fairly quiet roomy lounge areas (children welcome till 7pm), pool in classic billiards room, vault with Manchester darts, drinking corridor; tables outside, open all day *(the Didler, Pete Baker)*

Lamb M30 0BP [Regent St (A57)]: Full-blooded Edwardian three-room local, splendid etched windows, fine woodwork and furnishings, extravagantly tiled stairway, trophies in display case, bargain Holts and lunchtime sandwiches, full-size snooker table in original billiards room; open all day *(the Didler)*

Royal Oak M30 0EN [Barton Lane]: Large old-fashioned Edwardian corner pub, several busy rooms off corridor, handsome tilework, mosaic floors and fittings, cheap Holts, good licensees, pool; children allowed daytime in back lounge (may be organ singalongs), open all day *(the Didler)*

Stanley Arms M30 0QN [Eliza Ann St/Liverpool Rd (A57), Patricroft]: Lively unspoilt mid-Victorian corner local with bargain Holts, popular front bar, hatch serving lobby and corridor to small back rooms, one with cast-iron range, lunchtime filled rolls, friendly licensees; open all day *(the Didler)*

White Lion M30 0ND [Liverpool Rd, Patricroft, a mile from M63 junction 2]: Welcoming Edwardian traditional local, clean, tidy and popular with older people, great value Holts, games in lively public bar, other rooms off tiled side drinking corridor inc one with piano *(the Didler, Pete Baker)*

EDENFIELD [SD7919]

Coach & Horses BL0 0HJ [Market St]: Locally popular for freshly made pubby food (all day) from ploughman's and plenty of other salads to steaks, nicely priced dishes for smaller appetites, helpful friendly staff, three real ales, decent wines, tasteful extension; good new disabled facilities *(John and Helen Rushton)*

EDGWORTH [SD7416]

White Horse BL7 0AY [Bury Rd/Blackheath Rd]: Big stone-built pub with friendly efficient staff, good choice of well kept ales, open-plan bar with open fire, carved dark oak panelling and beams, old local photographs, end dining room; piped music, big-screen TV; children welcome, tables outside, open all day at least in summer (LYM, Norma and Noel Thomas)

EUXTON [SD5520]

Railway PR7 6LA [The Ordnance, Wigan Rd]: Civilised pub with enjoyable local food (all day Sun) from sandwiches and light dishes up, children's menu, leather sofas in comfortable lounge, open-plan dining areas, real ale; heated partly enclosed terrace (Wendy Rogers, Megan Rogers)

FENCE [SD8237]

☆ *Fence Gate* BB12 9EE [2.6 miles from M65 junction 13; Wheatley Lane Road, just off A6068 W]: Imposing 17th-c building refurbished into smart pub/brasserie, Caledonian Deuchars IPA, Courage Directors, Theakstons Best and two changing guests, plenty of wines by the glass, teas and coffees, bar food and more expensive brasserie menu, carpeted bar divided into distinct areas with polished panelling, timbers, big fire, mix of wooden tables and chairs, sofas, sporting prints, contemporary brasserie with topiary; piped music, TV; children welcome, open all day (till 1am Fri and Sat) (Mike Horgan, LYM, Pauline and Derek Hodgkiss, Pat and Tony Martin, K C and B Forman)

FORTON [SD4950]

New Holly PR3 0BL [Lancaster Rd (A6)]: Smart spotless family-friendly pub, wide choice of good sensibly priced fresh food using local supplies, Thwaites ales, brisk friendly service; tables out under cover, play area, sumptuous hanging baskets, bedrooms (Margaret Dickinson, Mrs Nikki Mellor)

GARSTANG [SD4945]

☆ *Th'Owd Tithebarn* PR3 1PA [off Church St]: Large barn with flagstoned terrace overlooking Lancaster Canal marina, Victorian country life theme with very long refectory table, old kitchen range, masses of farm tools, stuffed animals and birds, flagstones and high rafters, simple food all day from filled baguettes up, Flowers and Tetleys, good value wine by the glass, quieter parlour welcoming children; piped music; open all day summer (Bruce and Sharon Eden, LYM, Abi Benson)

GOOSNARGH [SD5738]

☆ *Horns* PR3 2FJ [pub signed off B5269, towards Chipping]: Plush early 18th-c inn with relaxed atmosphere, neatly kept rooms with patterned carpets and log fires, food from pubby standards up inc signature roast duck and some interesting specials, Bowland Hen Harrier and a guest such as Black Sheep, a dozen wines by the glass, good choice of malts; piped music; children welcome, chintzy bedrooms, not far from M6 (Susan and Nigel Brookes, LYM, W K Wood, K C and B Forman, Piotr Chodzko-Zajko)

GREAT HARWOOD [SD7332]

Royal BB6 7BA [Station Rd]: Substantial Victorian pub with good changing range of beers from small breweries, tap for nearby Red Rose brewery, good soft drinks choice (own sarsaparilla), great selection of bottled beers, enjoyable wholesome food, simple traditional fittings, friendly atmosphere, pub games inc pool and darts; big-screen TV, live music Fri; partly covered terrace, three bedrooms, cl lunchtime Mon-Thurs, open all day Fri-Sun (the Didler)

Victoria BB6 7EP [St Johns St]: Splendid beer range with Bowland Gold and eight changing guests, friendly landlady and regulars, unspoilt traditional Edwardian layout with five rooms off central bar, one with darts, one with pool, two quiet snugs, some handsome tiling; tables out behind, opens 4.30 (3 Fri, all day wknds), cl wkdy lunchtimes (Pam and John Smith, the Didler, Richard Pitcher, Pete Baker)

GREAT MITTON [SD7138]

☆ *Mitton Hall* BB7 9PQ [B6246 NW of Whalley]: Bowland and Thwaites ale, good bar food, nice staff and comfortable sofas and armchairs in handsomely refurbished main bar of lovely Tudor mansion, magnificent panelling in Gothic great hall, fantastic staircase from lounge/reception; balustraded terrace over wooded grounds by River Ribble, stylish and comfortable bedrooms (Margaret Dickinson)

GRINDLETON [SD7545]

Duke of York BB7 4QR [off A59 via Chatburn; Brow Top]: Smartly refurbished dining pub in attractive Ribble Valley countryside, enjoyable food and wine, Black Sheep and Thwaites, good service, heavy well set tables in various areas inc one with open fire; tables out in front, garden behind (John and Sylvia Harrop, John and Helen Rushton, John and Eleanor Holdsworth)

HALSALL [SD3709]

Saracens Head L39 8RH [Summerwood Lane; over bridge, just off A567]: Canalside pub reopened in 2008 after careful refurbishment, short choice of enjoyable food, well kept Adnams and Greene King Old Speckled Hen; plenty of tables outside, simple play area (Peter Dowd)

HASLINGDEN [SD7823]

Griffin BB4 5AF [Hud Rake, off A680 at N end]: Friendly basic local brewing its own cheap Pennine ales in the cellar, farm cider, L-shaped bar with good valley views from comfortable lounge end, darts in public end; open all day (Pete Baker, Len Beattie)

HAWK GREEN [SJ9687]

Crown SK6 7HU [just S of Marple]: New landlord doing wide choice of good value food in lively and spacious bar and well laid out barn restaurant, well kept Robinsons, good friendly service; handy for canal (BOB)

HAWKSHAW [SD7515]

☆ *Red Lion* BL8 4JS [Ramsbottom Rd]: Roomy, comfortable and attractive pub/hotel, friendly welcome and efficient cheerful service, good generous fresh local food in cosy bar and separate well run restaurant, good changing ales; comfortable if rather creaky bedrooms, quiet spot by River Irwell, open for food all day wknds *(K C and B Forman, W K Wood)*

Waggon & Horses BL8 4JL [Bolton Rd]: Short choice of good home-made food using fresh local ingredients (worth booking Fri and Sat evenings) in bar and small restaurant *(Norma and Noel Thomas)*

HEYSHAM [SD4161]

Royal LA3 2RN [Main St]: Four changing ales, well priced wines and decent food inc early evening bargains in charming 16th-c low-beamed two-bar pub; no dogs at meal times; tables out in front, good-sized sheltered garden, pretty fishing village with great views from interesting church *(Abi Benson, Tony and Maggie Harwood, Margaret Dickinson)*

HOGHTON [SD6225]

Boatyard PR5 0SP [A675 Preston—Bolton, NW of A674 junction]: Neat modern pub/motel by Leeds & Liverpool Canal, plenty of boats to watch, friendly staff, good value all-day food from imaginative sandwiches up, carvery, Thwaites ales, coffee shop, live music last Sat in month; children welcome, tables outside, own narrowboat, six bedrooms, handy for M65, open all day *(Peter Hacker, Ben Williams)*

Old Oak PR5 0JE [Hoghton Lane]: Pleasant roadside pub with charming staff and pubby food; lovely area *(Margaret Dickinson)*

HOLDEN [SD7749]

☆ *Copy Nook* BB7 4NL [Bolton by Bowland Rd]: Roomy and attractive dining pub, friendly relaxing atmosphere, pleasant helpful staff, generous popular food from sandwiches up in bar's two dining areas and restaurant, reasonable prices, well kept Black Sheep, Timothy Taylors Landlord and Tetleys, good wine choice, log fire; piped music; children welcome, good walking area, six comfortable bedrooms *(BB, Norma and Noel Thomas)*

HORWICH [SD6509]

Beehive BL6 4BA [Chorley New Rd, Lostock]: Two-for-one bargains, good value wines; big-screen sports TV, keg beer *(J D O Carter)*

HYDE [SJ9495]

Cheshire Ring SK14 2BJ [Manchester Rd (A57, between M67 junctions 2 and 3)]: Welcoming pub tied to Beartown brewery, their ales well priced, guest beers and imports on tap, beer festivals, farm ciders and perries, good house wines, bargain home-made curries Thurs; piped music; open all day wknds, from 4pm Mon, Tues, 1pm Weds-Fri, *(Dennis Jones, the Didler)*

Sportsman SK14 2NN [Mottram Rd]: Bright and cheerful revamp for Victorian local popular for its eight real ales, welcoming licensees, bargain bar food, cuban restaurant, open fires, pub games, full-size snooker table upstairs; children and dogs welcome *(Dennis Jones, the Didler)*

KNOWLE GREEN [SD6439]

Newdrop PR3 2YX [N off B6243, 2nd left at crossroads]: Popular and well run with good food, wine and beer inc Black Sheep and Bowland, beams and log fires, modern restaurant extension; children welcome, magnificent setting on Longridge Fell, cl Mon *(John and Helen Rushton)*

LANCASTER [SD4761]

Golden Lion LA1 1QD [Moor Lane]: Old-fashioned town pub with several small bars and long history, good changing ale choice, frequent live music; open all day *(Chris Stevenson)*

John o' Gaunt LA1 1JG [Market St]: Small unspoilt city local with great array of malt whiskies, up to half a dozen well kept ales such as Caledonian Deuchars IPA, Greene King Abbot and Otter, good choice of enjoyable cheap lunchtime food from sausage specialities to kangaroo burger, friendly staff, music memorabilia; piped jazz, live many evenings; small back terrace, open all day *(Martin Grosberg)*

Ring o' Bells LA1 1RE [King St]: Newish management doing well, enjoyable home-made food, well kept beer, good friendly staff; big garden *(Natalie Hughes, Tony and Maggie Harwood)*

☆ *Water Witch* LA1 1SU [parking in Aldcliffe Rd behind Royal Lancaster Infirmary, off A6]: Attractive conversion of 18th-c canalside barge-horse stabling under new management; flagstones, stripped stone, rafters and pitch-pine panelling, changing ales and good choice of wines from mirrored bar, enjoyable food, upstairs restaurant; children in eating areas, tables outside, open all day *(Paul Boot, Chris Stevenson, LYM)*

Yorkshire House LA1 1DB [Parliament St]: Unusual (for what's primarily a cool live music place) in having a good range of well kept ales; courtyard tables, cl lunchtime *(Chris Stevenson)*

LATHOM [SD4511]

Ship L40 4BX [off A5209 E of Burscough; Wheat Lane]: Under new management, big pub tucked below embankment at junction of Leeds & Liverpool and Rufford Branch canals, several beamed rooms, some interesting canal and naval memorabilia, up to six changing real ales (beer festivals), good value standard pubby food, games room with pool, darts and machines, Mon quiz night, folk evenings first Weds of month; TV in bar; children and dogs welcome, lots of tables outside, open all day *(BB, Jeremy King)*

LEIGH [SJ6799]

Bowling Green WN7 2LD [Manchester Rd]: Busy largely open-plan local, good value food ordered from kitchen door, bargain Holts; sports TV; open all day *(Tony and Wendy Hobden)*

Waterside WN7 4DB [Twist Lane]: Civilised pub in tall converted 19th-c warehouses by Bridgewater Canal, handy for indoor and outdoor markets, wide choice of enjoyable bargain food all day inc OAP and other deals, Greene King ales, good friendly service, chatty lunchtime atmosphere; live music or disco Thurs-Sat; children welcome, disabled access and facilities, plenty of waterside tables, ducks and swans, open all day *(Ben Williams)*

LITTLE ECCLESTON [SD4240]

Cartford PR3 0YP [Cartford Lane, off A586 Garstang—Blackpool, by toll bridge]: Refurbished 17th-c coaching inn in scenic countryside by River Wyre toll bridge; rambling interior on four levels with beams, log fire, oak boards and flagstones, pine wall seats, pews, burgundy paintwork and pink/white patterned wallpaper, good food inc notable fish pie; welcoming french licensees, friendly staff, well kept Harts ales (brewery adjoins the pub) and guest beers, well priced wines; tables in landscaped garden overlooking river, good bedrooms *(Peter and Josie Fawcett, Alison Playfoot, Donna and Roger)*

LITTLE LEVER [SD7407]

Jolly Carter BL3 1BW [Church St]: Bright and comfortable, with good value home-made food, Bank Top, Greene King Old Speckled Hen and Timothy Taylors Landlord, modern décor, friendly helpful long-serving licensees; handy for Bolton Branch of Manchester, Bolton & Bury Canal *(Ben Williams)*

LIVERPOOL [SJ3489]

☆ *Baltic Fleet* L1 8DQ [Wapping, nr Albert Dock]: Triangular pub with own good Wapping brews and interesting guest ales, vibrant mix of customers, good value straightforward food (not Sat lunchtime), nautical paraphernalia, bare boards, big arched windows, unpretentious mix of furnishings, newspapers, upstairs lounge; piped music, TV; children welcome in eating areas, dogs in bar, back terrace, open all day *(LYM, Pete Baker, the Didler, Paul Boot, Darren Le Poidevin)*

Belvedere L7 7EB [Sugnall St]: Unspoilt Victorian pub with friendly chatty small bar, original fittings inc etched glass, coal fire, well kept beers such as Copper Dragon and Spitting Feathers, good pizzas, darts and other games; open all day *(Pete Baker, the Didler)*

☆ *Brewery Tap* L8 5XJ [Stanhope St]: Victorian pub with full Cains range at reasonable prices, guest beers, friendly efficient staff, good value food wkdy lunchtimes, nicely understated décor, wooden floors, plush raised side snug, interesting old prints and breweriana, handsome bar, gas fire, daily papers; sports TV, no dogs; children till 8pm, disabled access, brewery tours, open all day *(the Didler)*

Crown L1 1JQ [Lime St]: Well preserved art nouveau showpiece with fine tiled fireplace and copper bar front, dark leather banquettes, splendid ceiling in airy corner bar, smaller back room with another good fireplace, impressive staircase sweeping up

under splendid cupola to handsome area with ornate windows; generous bargain food till early evening, well priced Cains and guest beers *(the Didler, John and Helen Rushton, Brian and Janet Ainscough)*

☆ *Dispensary* L1 2SP [Renshaw St]: Small chatty central pub with Cains ales and two guests, bottled imports, friendly staff, good value wkdy food 12-7, polished panelling, marvellous etched windows, bare boards, comfortable raised back bar, Victorian medical artefacts; open all day *(the Didler, Darren Le Poidevin, Jeremy King, John and Helen Rushton)*

☆ *Doctor Duncan* L1 1HF [St Johns Lane]: Friendly Victorian pub with several rooms inc impressive back area with pillared and vaulted tiled ceiling, full Cains range and guest beers well kept, belgians on tap, enjoyable good value food, pleasant helpful service, daily papers; may be piped music, can get lively evenings, busy wknds; family room, open all day *(Giles and Annie Francis, the Didler)*

Everyman Bistro L1 9BH [Hope St, below Everyman Theatre]: Popular low-ceilinged tile-floor clattery basement with long wooden tables, four well kept ales such as Brimstage and George Wrights, side room with good value fresh food; open all day, cl Sun *(the Didler)*

Fly in the Loaf L1 9AS [Hardman St]: Former bakery with smart gleaming bar serving Okells (from Isle of Man) and up to six ales from smaller brewers, foreign beers too, popular home-made food, one long room, small raised front area with sofas and high stools; sports TV, upstairs lavatories, open all day, till 12pm wknds *(Martin Grosberg)*

Globe L1 1HW [Cases St, opp station]: Chatty traditional little local in busy shopping area (can get packed), pleasant staff, well kept ales such as Black Sheep, Cains and Caledonian Deuchars IPA, lunchtime filled cobs, sloping floor, quieter cosy back room, prints of old Liverpool; 60s piped music; open all day *(the Didler)*

Grapes L2 6RE [Mathew St]: Friendly open-plan local with well kept Cains ales, good value bar food till 6.30, cottagey décor with flagstones, old range, wall settles, mixed furnishings, unusual old photographs, plans and documents; piped music, karaoke, SkyTV, may be evening dress code; open all day *(the Didler, Jeremy King)*

Hole In Ye Wall L2 2AW [off Dale St]: Well restored 18th-c pub, thriving local atmosphere in high-beamed panelled bar, Cains ale unusually fed by gravity via oak pillars from upstairs cellar, plenty of woodwork, plate glass and old Liverpool photographs *(Jeremy King)*

Lion L2 2BP [Moorfields, off Tithebarn St]: Ornate Victorian tavern with great changing choice of real ales, friendly atmosphere and landlord interested in pub's history; lunchtime food inc splendid cheese and pie

specialities, sparkling etched glass and serving hatches in central bar, unusual wallpaper and matching curtains, big mirrors, panelling and tilework, two small back lounges one with fine glass dome, coal fire; silent fruit machine; open all day *(the Didler, Jeremy King, Pete Baker)*
Peter Kavanaghs L8 7LY [Egerton St, off Catherine St]: Shuttered Victorian pub with interesting décor in several small rooms inc old-world murals, stained-glass and lots of bric-a-brac (bicycle hanging from ceiling), piano, wooden settles and real fires; Cains, Greene King, Wychwood and guests, friendly licensees happy to show you around inc cellars, popular with locals and students; open all day *(the Didler, Pete Baker)*
Poste House L1 6BU [Cumberland St]: Small comfortably refurbished early 19th-c chatty backstreet local surrounded by huge redevelopment, Fullers London Pride and a guest, good wkdy lunches, football memorabilia, daily papers, room upstairs (may be loud music); open all day *(the Didler, Jeremy King)*
Roscoe Head L1 2SX [Roscoe St]: Unassuming old local with cosy bar and two other spotless unspoilt little rooms, friendly long-serving landlady, well kept Jennings, Marstons, Tetleys and guests from smaller brewers, inexpensive home-made lunches, interesting memorabilia, traditional games inc cribbage; open all day *(the Didler, Pete Baker)*
Ship & Mitre L2 2JH [Dale St]: Friendly gaslit local popular with university people, up to 12 changing unusual ales (many beer festivals), imported beers, farm ciders, friendly staff, good value basic food lunchtime and (not Mon-Weds) early evening; pool, weekly themed beer nights; piped music; open all day, cl Sun lunchtime *(the Didler, Martin Grosberg)*
Swan L1 4DQ [Wood St]: Neon sign for this busy unsmart three-floor pub, bare boards, deep red lighting, Hydes, Phoenix and six changing guests, Weston's farm cider, good value cobs and wkdy lunches, friendly staff; rock juke box draws younger crowd, open all day *(the Didler, Jeremy King)*
☆ **Thomas Rigbys** L2 2EZ [Dale St]: Spacious beamed and panelled Victorian pub with mosaic flooring, old tiles and etched glass, great range of beers inc Okells and imports, impressively long bar, steps up to main area, table service, reasonably priced hearty home-made food all day till 7pm; disabled access, outside seating, open all day *(the Didler, John and Helen Rushton)*
White Star L2 6PT [Rainford Gdns, off Matthew St]: Lively traditional Victorian local with lots of woodwork, boxing photographs, White Star shipping line and Beatles memorabilia (they used to rehearse in back room), Bowland and changing guest beers, basic lunchtime food, friendly staff; sports TVs; open all day *(Pete Baker, the Didler)*

LYDIATE [SD3604]
Scotch Piper L31 4HD [Southport Rd; A4157]: Medieval thatched pub, well worn-in, with heavy low beams, flagstones, thick stone walls and fires sprawled in front of roaring fires, well kept Banks's and guest ale from tiny counter in main room, corridor to middle room with darts and back snug, no food; bikers' night Weds, outside lavatories; big garden with aviary, chickens and donkey, open all day wknds *(the Didler, Pete Baker)*
LYTHAM ST ANNES [SD3427]
Fairhaven FY8 1AU [Marine Drive]: Neat modern pub with wide choice of generous fresh food from sandwiches and baguettes up, mainstream real ales, helpful staff; handy for beach and Fairhaven Lake *(Ken Richards)*
MANCHESTER [SJ8498]
Angel M4 4BR [Angel St, off Rochdale Rd]: Formerly the Beer House, rescued from demolition and restored by local chef, good value food from pub standards to upscale dishes inc game and fish, monthly gourmet evenings, good wine choice, Facers Angel (brewed for the pub) and three changing guests, bottled beers, farm ciders, smaller upstairs dining room, exhibitions of local artists; children welcome till 9pm, dogs allowed, disabled facilities, tables out in small area behind, open all day *(Chris Johnson, Jeremy King)*
☆ **Ape & Apple** M2 6HQ [John Dalton St]: Big friendly open-plan pub with bargain Holts and hearty bar food, comfortable seats in bare-boards bar with lots of old prints and posters, armchairs in upstairs lounge; piped music, TV area, games machines, Thurs quiz night; unusual brick cube garden, bedrooms, open all day, cl Sun *(the Didler, Darren Le Poidevin)*
Bar Fringe M4 5JN [Swan St]: Long bare-boards bar specialising in continental beers, also five changing ales from small local breweries and farm cider, friendly staff, basic snacks till 4pm (no food wknds), daily papers, shelves of empty beer bottles, cartoons, posters, motorcycle hung above door, rock juke box; no children or dogs; tables out behind, open all day, till 12.30am Sat and Sun *(the Didler, Jeremy King)*
☆ **Bridge** M3 3BW [Bridge St]: Dining pub with enjoyable food in bar and back restaurant, two good changing real ales, long narrow panelled room with two fine tiled and ironwork fireplaces, leather sofas, upstairs room with small roof terrace; piped music; children welcome till 7pm, back terrace (dogs allowed here), open all day *(Jeremy King)*
Castle M4 1LE [Oldham St, about 200 yards from Piccadilly, on right]: Refurbished 17th-c pub reopened under former *Coronation Street* actor, simple traditional front bar, small snug, full Robinsons range from fine bank of handpumps, games in back room, nice tilework outside, live music; open all day *(the Didler)*

Circus M1 4GX [Portland St]: Compact traditional two-room pub with particularly well kept Tetleys from minute corridor bar (or may be table service), friendly landlord, celebrity photographs, leatherette banquettes in panelled back room; often looks closed but normally open all day (you may have to knock); can get very busy *(the Didler, Neil Whitehead, Victoria Anderson)*

City Arms M2 4BQ [Kennedy St, off St Peters Sq]: Tetleys and five quickly changing guests (guess the mystery ale competition on Fri), belgian bottled beers, occasional beer festivals, busy for bargain bar lunches, quick friendly service, coal fires, bare boards and banquettes, prints, panelling and masses of pump clips, handsome tiled façade and corridor; piped music, TV, games machine; wheelchair access but steps down to back lounge, open all day *(the Didler, Dennis Jones)*

Coach & Horses M45 6TB [Old Bury Rd, Whitefield; A665 nr Besses o' the Barn station]: Early 19th-c, several separate rooms, popular and chatty, bargain Holts beers, table service, darts, cards; open all day *(the Didler)*

Crescent M5 4PF [Crescent (A6) – opp Salford Uni]: Three areas off central servery with eight changing ales (regular beer festivals), many continental bottled beers and real cider, friendly licensees and young staff, buoyant local atmosphere (popular with uni), low-priced home-made food inc good breakfast and Weds curry night, bare boards and open fire, plenty of character, pool room, juke box; small enclosed terrace, open all day *(the Didler, Ben Williams, Jeremy King, Martin Grosberg)*

Crown & Kettle M4 5EE [Oldham Rd/Gt Ancoats St]: Busy three-room refurbished Victorian pub, Greenfield and changing guest ales (beer festivals), belgian beers, several farm ciders, good choice of malts, popular bar food inc good value Sun roasts, bare boards and carpet, some panelling and exposed brick, decorative windows, ornate high ceilings with remarkably intricate plasterwork, area with bookcases, coal fire; sports TV; open all day *(the Didler, BB, Jeremy King)*

Dutton M3 1EU [Park St, Strangeways]: Welcoming old-fashioned corner local nr prison, three unusually shaped cosy rooms, Hydes from central servery, lots of bric-a-brac; open all day *(the Didler)*

Egerton Arms M3 5FP [Gore St, Salford; A6 by station]: Well cared-for character local with chandeliers, art nouveau lamps, attractive prints and dark varnished tables, well kept low-priced Holts and guest beers, friendly service, small room with pool and TV; piped music, silent fruit machines; open all day *(the Didler, Ben Williams, Jeremy King)*

Fletcher Moss M20 6RQ [William St]: Well kept Hydes and guest beers inc Mild, lunchtime hot pies *(Noel Grundy)*

Font M1 5NP [New Wakefield St]: Modern open-plan café-style bar by railway viaduct, good home-cooked food, well kept changing ales (usually have Bazens), lots of foreign bottled beers, reasonable prices, downstairs bar; loud music evenings when popular with students, monthly live bands; open all day *(the Didler)*

Grey Horse M1 4QX [Portland St, nr Piccadilly]: Small traditional one-bar Hydes local, their Bitter and Mild kept well, some unusual malt whiskies, panelled servery with colourful gantry, lots of prints, photographs and plates, friendly atmosphere; piped 60s/70s music, small TV, net curtains; can bring good sandwiches from next door, open all day *(the Didler, Dr and Mrs A K Clarke)*

Hare & Hounds M4 4AA [Shudehill, behind Arndale]: Unpretentious 18th-c local, long narrow bar linking front snug and comfortable back lounge (with TV), notable tilework, panelling and stained-glass, good Holts and Tetleys, friendly staff; games machine, karaoke nights; open all day *(Pete Baker, Joe Green, the Didler)*

Jolly Angler M1 2JW [Ducie St]: Plain backstreet local, long a favourite, small and friendly, well kept Hydes ales, coal or peat fire, informal folk nights Thurs and Sat; darts, pool and sports TV; open all day Sat *(the Didler, BB, Pete Baker)*

Kings Arms M3 6AN [Bloom St, Salford]: Plain tables, bare boards and flagstones contrasting with opulent maroon and purple décor and stained-glass, Bazens, Moorhouses and other changing ales, good value lunchtime food (till 6.30pm, not Sat); juke box, music, poetry or theatre nights upstairs; open all day (cl Sun evening) *(the Didler)*

Knott Fringe M3 4LY [Deansgate]: Friendly modern glass-fronted café-bar with Marble organic ales and guest beers, good range of continental imports, good value all-day food with emphasis on greek dishes, upstairs smokers' balcony overlooking Rochdale Canal; under railway arch, by Castlefield heritage site, open all day *(Dennis Jones, the Didler)*

Lass o' Gowrie M1 7DB [36 Charles St; off Oxford St at BBC]: Lively tiled Victorian sidestreet local, big-windowed long bar with cosy room off, stripped brickwork, hop pockets draped from the ceiling, good range of real ales inc Black Sheep, Greene King and house beer brewed by Titanic, good bargain food inc home-made pies, friendly service; new terrace overlooking river, open all day *(the Didler, LYM)*

☆ **Mr Thomas Chop House** M2 7AR [Cross St]: Good home-made traditional lunchtime food inc some unusual choices like pigeon and beetroot salad with candied walnuts; friendly well informed staff who cope quickly however busy, beer from Black Sheep, Boddingtons and Lees, good wines by the glass; attractive Victorian décor, basic front bar with bare boards, panelling, original gas lamp fittings and stools at wall and window shelves, back tiled eating area with two rows of tables, period features inc wrought-iron gates for wine racks; open all day *(Darren Le Poidevin, the Didler, Jeremy King, GLD, Dennis Jones)*

New Oxford M3 6DB [Bexley Sq, Salford]: Up to 15 well kept changing beers and a house ale brewed by Northern (regular beer festivals), good range of imported beers, farm ciders, friendly staff; light and airy café-style feel in small front bar and back room, coal fire, good value basic food till 6pm; nice terrace, open all day *(the Didler, Ben Williams)*

Paramount M1 4BH [Oxford St]: Well run Wetherspoons with their usual good prices and good value food, particularly friendly service, bargain beer festivals *(Ben Williams)*

☆ **Peveril of the Peak** M1 5JQ [Gt Bridgewater St]: Vivid art nouveau green external tilework, interesting pictures, lots of mahogany, mirrors and stained or frosted glass, log fire, very welcoming family service; changing mainstream ales from central servery, cheap basic lunchtime food (not Sun), three sturdily furnished bare-boards rooms, busy lunchtime but friendly and homely evenings; TV; children welcome, pavement tables, cl wknd lunchtimes, open all day Fri *(Jeremy King, the Didler, Dr Kevan Tucker, Neil Whitehead, Victoria Anderson, GLD, LYM)*

Plough M18 7FB [Hyde Rd (A57), Gorton]: Classic tiling, windows and gantry in unspoilt old Robinsons local, wooden benches in large public bar, two quieter back lounges, small pool room, lots of pub games; TV; open all day *(the Didler)*

☆ **Rain Bar** M1 5JG [Gt Bridgewater St]: Lots of woodwork and flagstones in former umbrella works, well kept Lees beers, masses of wines by the glass, good value pubby food all day inc 9am wknd breakfast; welcoming efficient staff, relaxed atmosphere, daily papers, coal fire in small snug, large upstairs café-bar too; piped music may be loud, can be busy with young people evenings; good back terrace overlooking spruced-up Rochdale Canal, handy for Bridgwater Hall, open all day *(the Didler)*

Rising Sun M2 5HX [Queen St, off Deansgate]: Long pleasantly traditional 18th-c pub with well kept Black Sheep and Wells & Youngs Bombardier, bargain food inc curry choice, old pictures *(Jeremy King)*

☆ **Sinclairs** M3 1SW [Cathedral Gates, off Exchange Sq]: Charming low-beamed and timbered 18th-c pub (rebuilt here in redevelopment), bargain Sam Smiths, good all-day menu inc fresh oysters, brisk friendly service, bustling atmosphere, quieter upstairs bar with snugs and Jacobean fireplace; tables out in Shambles Sq (plastic glasses), open all day *(the Didler, Ben Williams, John and Helen Rushton, Pam and John Smith, LYM)*

MARPLE [SJ9588]

Ring o' Bells SK6 7AY [Church Lane; by Macclesfield Canal, Bridge 2]: Robinsons local with canal and other local memorabilia in four linked rooms, enjoyable mainly straightforward food, reasonable prices *(David Hoult)*

MARPLE BRIDGE [SJ9889]

Hare & Hounds SK6 5LW [Mill Brow]: Classic comfortable stone-built country pub in lovely spot, smallish and can get crowded, new downstairs kitchen doing enjoyable interesting food (not Mon or Tues) using local produce, well kept Robinsons, log fires; garden behind *(David Hoult, E A McClelland)*

MELLOR [SD6530]

☆ **Millstone** BB2 7JR [the one up nr Blackburn; Mellor Lane]: Restaurantly stone-built village dining pub, smart and well run, panelled bar with comfortable lounge one side, modern dining extension the other, good food from all-day bar meals to enterprising cooking and popular substantial Sun lunch, obliging friendly staff; well kept Thwaites, good choice of wines by the glass, big log fire, mementos of former landlord and England cricketer Big Jim Smith; good bedrooms, open all day *(Pam and John Smith, GLD, BB, Ashley Dinsdale)*

MERECLOUGH [SD8730]

Kettledrum BB10 4RG [off A646 Burnley—Halifax]: Friendly and cosy country local with wide choice of good value genuine home cooking (so may take a while), well kept Theakstons, good service, fine views, gaslit upstairs dining room; children welcome, tables outside *(Len Beattie, LYM)*

MORECAMBE [SD4264]

Midland Grand Plaza LA4 4BZ [Marine Rd W]: Classic art deco hotel in splendid seafront position, brought bang up to date with comfortable if unorthodox contemporary furnishings in spacious seaview Rotunda Bar; rather pricey food from tapas to restaurant meals, helpful staff; children welcome, 44 comfortably redone bedrooms, open all day *(Margaret Dickinson, BB)*

Palatine LA4 5BZ [The Crescent]: Recently refurbished by owners of Sun in Lancaster, friendly knowledgeable staff *(Tony and Maggie Harwood)*

NEWTON [SD6950]

Parkers Arms BB7 3DY [B6478 7 miles N of Clitheroe]: Refurbishment by welcoming newish licensees, locally sourced food (suppliers listed) in bar and restaurant (which has lovely views), beers from Bowland and Copper Dragon, good range of wines, log fires; children welcome, garden, bedrooms, lovely spot *(LYM, Len Beattie, Norma and Noel Thomas)*

OSWALDTWISTLE [SD7226]

☆ **Britannia** BB5 3RJ [A677/B6231]: Convivial traditional core with log-burning ranges, cosy button-back banquettes, attractive décor, well kept Thwaites ales, friendly bar service and character locals, dining area extended into adjoining barn, enjoyable food (all day Sun), good quiz Fri night; children in family restaurant, sun-trap back terrace with moorland views and play area, open all day *(BB, Steve Whalley)*

PAYTHORNE [SD8351]

Buck BB7 4JD: Friendly country pub, busy in season (nr big caravan park), generous good value food largely local (not Tues, all day wknds), two local ales, reasonably priced wines, fire; outside seating *(Dudley and Moira Cockroft)*

PRESTON [SD5329]

Black Horse PR1 2EJ [Friargate]: Friendly unspoilt pub in pedestrian street, good Robinsons ales, inexpensive lunchtime food, unusual ornate curved and mosaic-tiled Victorian main bar, panelling, stained-glass and old local photographs, two quiet cosy snugs, mirrored back area, upstairs 1920s-style bar, good juke box; no children, open all day from 10.30pm, cl Sun evening *(the Didler, Pete Baker, Dr and Mrs A K Clarke)*

RIBCHESTER [SD6535]

☆ *White Bull* PR3 3XP [Church St]: New management for this 18th-c inn, which has been very popular for its food – reports please; carpets and bare boards, traditional-looking spacious main bar, good range of real ales, friendly service; may be piped music, TV, games machine and pool; big garden adjacent to ruins of Roman bathhouse (look out for the Tuscan porch pillars), three comfortable bedrooms *(LYM, Cedric Robertshaw)*

RILEY GREEN [SD6225]

☆ *Royal Oak* PR5 0SL [A675/A6061]: Cosy low-beamed three-room former coaching inn, good generous home cooking inc notable steaks, four well kept Thwaites ales from long back bar, friendly efficient service, ancient stripped stone, open fires, seats from high-backed settles to red plush armchairs, lots of nooks and crannies, turkey carpet, soft lighting, impressive woodwork, fresh flowers, interesting model steam engines and plenty of bric-a-brac, two comfortable dining rooms; can be packed Fri night and wknds; tables outside, short walk from Leeds & Liverpool Canal, footpath to Hoghton Tower, open all day Sun *(Norma and Noel Thomas, John and Eleanor Holdsworth, Charles and Pauline Stride, BB)*

RIMINGTON [SD8045]

Black Bull BB7 4DS: This rather unusual pub with its huge collection of transport models was closed as we went to press – news please *(LYM)*

ROCHDALE [SD8913]

Baum OL12 0NU [Toad Lane]: Old-fashioned charm, food from tapas and good sandwiches to home-made casseroles etc, good changing beer range such as local Boggart Hole Clough and Pictish, good bottled choice, lots of old advertisements, conservatory; garden tables, handy for Co-op Museum, open all day *(Andy and Jill Kassube)*

SCARISBRICK [SD4011]

Heatons Bridge Inn L40 8JG [Heatons Bridge Rd]: Pretty pub by bridge over Leeds & Liverpool Canal (popular with boaters), pleasant staff, bargain home-made food inc Sun roast, Black Sheep and Tetleys, four cosy room areas and dining room; lovely hanging baskets *(Margaret Dickinson)*

SLAIDBURN [SD7152]

☆ *Hark to Bounty* BB7 3EP [B6478 N of Clitheroe]: Attractive old stone-built pub with linked rooms, wide choice of fresh food (lots of tables) inc light dishes and old-fashioned puddings, friendly service, four real ales, decent wines and whiskies, comfortable chairs by open fire, games room one end, restaurant the other; pleasant garden behind, good walks, bedrooms, charming Forest of Bowland village, open all day *(Neil Whitehead, Victoria Anderson, LYM, John and Sylvia Harrop, Julian and Janet Dearden, Norma and Noel Thomas, Mr and Mrs Barrie)*

SLYNE [SD4765]

Keys LA2 6AU [A6 N of Lancaster]: Cross Keys recently given contemporary refurbishment (and abbreviated name), good drinks choice, interesting menu, amusing pictures *(Tony and Maggie Harwood)*

STANDISH [SD5711]

☆ *Crown* WN1 2XF [not far from M6 junction 27; Platt Lane]: Refurbished traditional country pub with open fire in comfortable panelled bar, wide range of well kept ales (even a daily beers list) inc local Mayflower and Prospect, several bottled continentals, good food inc grills priced and chosen by weight from chiller, early-eater deals and Sun roasts, airy dining extension and pleasant conservatory; children allowed away from bar, bedrooms *(Stuart Parkinson, LYM, Peter Johnston)*

White Crow WN1 2XL [Chorley Rd (A5106)]: Enjoyable food all day inc wkdy bargain offers in former coaching inn dating from 16th c, well kept changing ales; ask why the stuffed bird on the mantelpiece is turned to the wall; open all day *(Peter Johnston)*

STOCKPORT [SJ8990]

☆ *Arden Arms* SK1 2LX [Millgate St, behind Asda]: Welcoming Victorian pub with good reasonably priced lunchtime food, well kept Robinsons, cheerful service, well preserved traditional horseshoe bar, old-fashioned tiny snug through servery, two coal fires, longcase clocks, well restored tiling and panelling; tables in sheltered courtyard, open all day *(Dennis Jones, the Didler, G D K Fraser, Pete Baker)*

Armoury SK3 8BD [Shaw Heath]: Friendly traditional local with small bar and comfortable old-fashioned lounge, well kept Robinsons ales, perhaps Old Tom tapped from cask in winter, family room upstairs; big-screen TV; open all day *(the Didler, G D K Fraser)*

Crown SK4 1AR [Heaton Lane, Heaton Norris]: Partly open-plan Victorian pub popular for its 16 well kept changing ales, also bottled beers and real cider, three cosy lounge areas off gaslit bar, spotless stylish décor, wholesome bargain lunches, pool, darts; frequent live music; tables in cobbled courtyard, huge viaduct above *(G D K Fraser, Ben Williams, Dennis Jones, the Didler)*

Navigation SK4 1TY [Manchester Rd (B6167, former A626)]: Friendly traditional pub with six Beartown ales and a guest beer, farm ciders tapped from cellar casks, continental bottled beers; open all day *(the Didler)*

Nursery SK4 2NA [on narrow cobbled lane at E end of N part of Green Lane, Heaton Norris; off A6]: Very popular for enjoyable straightforward lunchtime food from kitchen servery on right inc good value Sun lunch, friendly efficient service, well kept Hydes, big bays of banquettes in panelled front lounge, brocaded wall banquettes in back one; children welcome if eating, immaculate bowling green behind, open all day wknds *(Pete Baker, the Didler, BB)*

Olde Woolpack SK3 0BY [Brinksway, just off M60 junction 1 – junction A560/A5145]: Well run busy three-room pub with Thwaites and changing guests, good value home-made food, traditional layout with drinking corridor; open all day *(the Didler)*

Railway SK1 2BZ [Avenue St (just off M63 junction 13, via A560)]: Bright and airy L-shaped bar with full Pennine range and changing guest ales, lots of foreign beers, farm cider, home-made pub lunches (not Sun), bargain prices, friendly staff, old Stockport prints and memorabilia, two billiards, tables out behind; open all day *(the Didler)*

☆ *Red Bull* SK1 3AY [Middle Hillgate]: Steps up to friendly well run local, impressive beamed and flagstoned bar with dark panelling, substantial settles and seats, open fires, lots of pictures, mirrors and brassware, traditional island servery with well kept Robinsons ales, good value home-cooked bar lunches (not Sun); has recently expanded into adjoining building, open all day exc Sun afternoon *(the Didler, LYM)*

Swan With Two Necks SK1 1RY [Princes St]: Traditional local reopened under new licensees, comfortable panelled bar, back skylit lounge and drinking corridor, bargain pub lunches from sandwiches up, teas with home-made scones, Robinsons ales; open all day *(the Didler)*

STRINES [SJ9686]

Sportsmans Arms SK6 7GE [B6101Marple–New Mills]: Pleasant roadside pub with panoramic Goyt Valley view from picture-window lounge bar, good changing ale range, generous good value food, small separate bar; tables out on side decking, heated smokers' shelter, open all day wknds *(David Hoult)*

THORNTON HOUGH [SJ3080]

Seven Stars CH63 1JW [Church Rd]: Comfortable two-room pub with good local atmosphere and particularly good service,

well kept ales such as Shepherd Neame Spitfire and Wells & Youngs Bombardier, usual food *(Tom and Jill Jones, LYM)*

TYLDESLEY [SD6902]

Mort Arms M29 8DG [Elliott St]: Bargain Holts ales in two-room 1930s pub, etched glass and polished panelling, comfortable lounge with old local photographs, friendly landlord and regulars, darts and dominoes, TV horseracing Sat; open all day *(the Didler)*

WADDINGTON [SD7243]

Waddington Arms BB7 3HP [Clitheroe Rd]: Tall stone coaching inn with reasonably priced food (all day wknds) using fresh local produce from sandwiches up, cheerful staff, five well kept ales, decent wines, stripped-pine tables on flagstones and bare boards, woodburner in big 17th-c inglenook, small dining room with motor-racing prints, modern décor; children welcome, pleasant back garden, six good value bedrooms (church bells) *(Noel Grundy, Steve Whalley, Dr and Mrs T E Hothersall, Ashley Dinsdale, J A Snell)*

WEETON [SD3834]

Eagle & Child PR4 3NB [Singleton Rd (B5260)]: Rustic dining pub doing well under present owners, enjoyable home-made food using good produce, good choice of well kept ales, log fires, low brick walls with old curved standing timbers *(anon)*

WEST BRADFORD [SD7444]

Three Millstones BB7 4SX [Waddington Rd]: Attractive old dining pub with good reasonably priced food in four comfortable linked areas, compact bar with Black Sheep and Moorhouses, good coffee, friendly efficient service, open fire *(John and Helen Rushton, John and Eleanor Holdsworth)*

WEST KIRBY [SJ2186]

White Lion CH48 4EE [Grange Rd (A540)]: Interesting 17th-c sandstone building, friendly proper pub with several small beamed areas on different levels, four mainstream beers, good value simple bar lunches inc lots of sandwiches, coal stove; no children even in attractive secluded back garden up steep stone steps, open all day *(MLR, Clive Watkin)*

WHALLEY [SD7336]

Swan BB7 9SN [King St]: 17th-c coaching inn in great countryside, nicely refurbished under current owners, long light-wood bar, local Bowland and other beers, enjoyable food, good service; disabled access, bedrooms *(GLD)*

WORSLEY [SD7500]

Barton Arms M28 2ED [Stablefold; just off Barton Rd (B5211), handy for M60 junction 13)]: Bright clean Ember Inn, popular and friendly, with good value food, Black Sheep, Caledonian Deuchars IPA and Timothy Taylors Landlord; children welcome *(Tony and Wendy Hobden, Ben Williams)*

John Gilbert M28 2YA [Worsley Brow, just off M60 junction 13]: Big recently reworked Greene King family dining pub, small linked areas on several levels, wide choice of reasonably priced food from sandwiches up, guest beers such as Black Sheep *(Gerry and Rosemary Dobson)*

Old Hall M28 2QT [Walkden Rd]: Imposing old place, sensitively modernised, with good value Brewers Fayre food inc two-for-one bargains *(Peter Johnston)*

Woodside M28 1ES [Ellenbrook Rd, just off A580]: Vintage Inn with several eating areas around central bar, good value food all day, good choice of wines by the glass, Thwaites Original and Lancaster Bomber, open fires; children welcome *(Gerry and Rosemary Dobson)*

WORSTON [SD7642]

☆ *Calfs Head* BB7 1QA: Large old stone-built coaching inn, well run and friendly, very busy with mostly older people eating wide choice of moderately priced food inc popular Sun carvery in bar and spacious conservatory looking towards Pendle Hill, soup and sandwiches all day too, well kept ales such as Black Sheep and Jennings, snug with coal fire; lovely big garden with summer house and stream, 11 comfortable bedrooms, open all day *(Steve Whalley, Margaret Dickinson,*

BB, Alan and Eve Harding, Len Beattie, John and Helen Rushton, Bob Broadhurst)

WREA GREEN [SD3931]

Villa PR4 2PE [Moss Side Lane (B5259)]: Lots of small seating areas in smart hotel's welcoming panelled bar, well kept Copper Dragon, Jennings and guests, enjoyable food, log fire, daily papers, Fri jazz; disabled facilities, good-sized garden, bedrooms, open all day *(the Didler, Ken Richards)*

WRIGHTINGTON [SD5011]

Rigbye Arms WN6 9QB [3 miles from M6 junction 27; off A5209 via Robin Hood Lane and left into High Moor Lane]: 17th-c inn in attractive moorland setting, welcoming and relaxed, with good value generous food (all day Sun) inc some interesting specials, good fresh veg, friendly prompt service even when busy, well kept real ales such as Black Sheep and Timothy Taylors Landlord, decent wines, several carpeted rooms, open fires; garden, bowling green, open all day Sun *(John and Sylvia Harrop, Mrs Dorothy King, Margaret Dickinson)*

If a service charge is mentioned prominently on a menu or accommodation terms, you must pay it if service was satisfactory. If service is really bad, you are legally entitled to refuse to pay some or all of the service charge as compensation for not getting the service you might reasonably have expected.

Leicestershire
and Rutland

Though the cream of this area's best food pubs has in the past tended to be concentrated around Rutland, standards are now definitely on the up in wider Leicestershire, too. Both our new Main Entries are here, the Queens Head in Belton and Joiners Arms in Bruntingthorpe – both places with rewarding food, very up-to-date. Other Leicestershire pubs on fine form include the Wheatsheaf at Woodhouse Eaves, nice little Staff of Life at Mowsley (imaginative food and still feeling like a proper pub), very foody Red Lion up in Stathern, and enterprising Cow & Plough at Oadby, with its noteworthy collection of breweriana and seven real ales. Current Rutland favourites include the good-natured Jackson Stops in Stretton, Kings Arms in Wing (impressive local sourcing for its imaginative food) and the superb Olive Branch at Clipsham, which again takes the title of Leicestershire and Rutland Dining Pub of the Year. The area's main brewer is the long-established Everards; Grainstore (brewed at the good pub of that name, on the edge of Oakham) is much the most successful of the smaller, newer breweries, with Belvoir and Bees both gaining ground in the better pubs. Three hot picks from the Lucky Dip section: Wheel at Branston, Fox & Hounds at Knossington and Noel Arms at Langham.

BARROWDEN
SK9400 MAP 4
Exeter Arms 🍺
Main Street, just off A47 Uppingham—Peterborough; LE15 8EQ

Own-brew beers and decent food in a quietly set old pub; plenty of seats outside

The hard-working licensee at this peaceful 17th-c coaching inn keeps the pub nicely in touch with the local community – it's genuinely a social centre for the village. The long cheery yellow open-plan bar stretches away either side of a long central counter, and is quite straightforwardly furnished with wheelback chairs at tables at either end, on bare boards or a blue patterned carpet. There's quite a collection of pump clips, beer mats and brewery posters; darts, board games, cribbage, dominoes, piped music and boules. An old free-standing barn houses the pub's brewery where they produce the Beach, B, Bee, C, Black Five Hope Gear and Own Gear, a combination of which are served on handpump alongside a couple of guests. Picnic-sets on a narrow front terrace overlook the pretty village green and ducks on the pond, with broader views stretching away beyond; more well spaced picnic-sets in a big informal grassy garden at the back. There are red kites in the nearby Fineshades woods – nice walks here too.

🍽 **As well as lunchtime sandwiches and ploughman's, bar food includes soup, a changing pâté, mushrooms stuffed with stilton and walnuts, ham and egg, sausages with red wine gravy, steak in ale pie, chicken wrapped in bacon with boursin cheese sauce, baked salmon with cream and white wine sauce, and puddings such as chocolate sponge with hot chocolate sauce or treacle tart.** *Starters/Snacks: £4.50 to £5.25. Main Courses: £8.95 to £11.50. Puddings: £4.50*

Own brew ~ Licensee Martin Allsopp ~ Real ale ~ Bar food (12-2, 6.30-9; not Mon) ~
(01572) 747247 ~ Children welcome ~ Dogs allowed in bar ~ Open 12-2.30(3.30 Sat),
6(6.30 in winter)-11; 12-5 Sun; closed Sun evening, Mon lunchtime ~ Bedrooms: £45S/£79S

*Recommended by the Didler, T R and B C Jenkins, Jim Farmer, Michael Doswell, O K Smyth, Barry and Sue Pladdys,
Mike and Sue Loseby, Noel Grundy*

BELTON   SK4420 MAP 7

Queens Head

*4.4 miles from M1 junction 23: after about 2.6 miles turn right off A512 Ashby Road; Long
Street/B5324; can return to M1 junction 23A via A42; LE12 9TP*

Relaxing and very up-to-date all round, with comfortable modern bedrooms

Once inside, there's little to suggest that this relaxed place was once a coaching inn. It's
had a complete makeover, and the bar – a former alehouse – has modern brown leather
bucket seats and cushioned sofas on bare boards, minimalist décor, an unusual
contemporary gas fire, a few chunky brown leather bar stools by the cushioned bar
counter, and a flat-screen TV. Marstons Pedigree and a beer named after the pub are on
handpump, with good wines by the glass, and proper coffee; helpful and efficient young
bar staff. To the left of the main door is the two-roomed dining room with similar seats
and sofas in front of the fire, and smart high-backed brown suede dining chairs around
neatly set tables on more bare boards. It's all very different and unusual, but appealing
and relaxing. There's a covered verandah outside the restaurant with teak tables and
chairs, and picnic-sets under umbrellas on a side lawn.

🍽 **Interesting, up-to-date food includes scallops with sweet corn purée, ham hock terrine
with pineapple and chilli jam, goats cheese ravioli with onion marmalade, fish and chips,
mushroom risotto, confit pork belly with black pudding purée, fried black bream with
tomato and chorizo risotto and sweet potato curry, and puddings such as raspberry tart
with raspberry and white chocolate milkshake, chocolate parfait with orange mascarpone
and ginger snaps, and a cheese platter.** *Starters/Snacks: £5.50 to £7.50.
Main Courses: £9.00 to £21.00. Puddings: £5.00 to £7.00*

Free house ~ Licensee Liam Paul Mahoney ~ Real ale ~ Bar food (12-2.30(4 Sun), 7-10;
12-10 Sat; not Sun evening) ~ Restaurant ~ (01530) 222359 ~ Dogs welcome ~
Open 7am(9am Sun)-1am ~ Bedrooms: £65B/£85(£90S)(£100B)

Recommended by Michael Doswell

BREEDON ON THE HILL   SK4022 MAP 7

Three Horse Shoes 🍽

Main Street (A453); DE73 1AN

Comfortable pub with friendly licensees and tasty, not cheap, food

This 18th-c dining pub has been restored to reveal the attractive structure of the
building. Heavy, worn flagstones, a log fire, pubby tables, a dark wood counter and
green walls and ceilings give a stylishly simple and timeless feel to the clean-cut central
bar: Marstons Pedigree on handpump, 30 malt whiskies and decent house wines. Beyond
here, a further eating room has maroon walls, dark pews and cherry-stained tables. The
two-room dining area on the right has a comfortably civilised chatty feel with big quite
close-set antique tables on seagrass matting and colourful modern country prints and
antique engravings on canary walls. Even at lunchtime there are lighted candles in
elegant modern holders.

🍽 **Very good, if pricey food, includes sandwiches, ploughman's, grilled goats cheese with
piccalilli, beefburger, sausage and mash with onion gravy, beef stroganoff, leek and
potato bake, halibut with garlic butter, beef and mushroom suet pudding, sticky toffee
pudding and lemon cheesecake.** *Starters/Snacks: £4.95 to £7.95. Main Courses: £8.95 to
£25.50. Puddings: £4.99*

Free house ~ Licensees Ian Davison, Jennie Ison, Stuart Marson ~ Real ale ~ Bar food (12-2(3 Sun), 5.30-9.15) ~ Restaurant ~ (01332) 695129 ~ Dogs allowed in bar ~ Open 11.30-2.30, 5.30-11; 12-3 Sun; closed Sun evening

Recommended by H Paulinski, Dr and Mrs A K Clarke, Michael Doswell, Derek and Sylvia Stephenson, Michael and Maggie Betton, Mrs Terry Dodd, Comus and Sarah Elliott, Gilly Middleburgh

BRUNTINGTHORPE   SP6089   MAP 4

Joiners Arms ♀

Off A5199 S of Leicester: Church Walk/Cross Street; LE17 5QH

Good contemporary cooking in civilised and attractive dining pub – which has kept a proper bar too

Although this is rather more bistro/restaurant than pub, there is an area to the left by the small, light oak bar counter that is set aside for drinkers: Greene King IPA on handpump and good wines, including nearly two dozen by the glass, too. There's a long black-cushioned pew with a linenfold centre, and various dining chairs around five tables on the wood-effect floor, and a coal and wood fire. The rest of the two beamed rooms are set for eating with a mix of elegant dining chairs (antique, cushioned and farmhouse ones), candles on the tables, terracotta tiles, and a big bowl of lilies. It's all very civilised but relaxed with sparkling glass and gleaming cutlery, and service is friendly and efficient; piped middle-of-the-road music. In front of the pub are a couple of picnic-sets.

🍴 **Good, imaginative up-to-date food includes pubby lunchtime dishes such as fish and chips and sausage and mash, as well as more elaborate dishes such as scallops with black pudding and garlic mash, crab spring rolls with chilli jam, bass with chinese vegetables and crab ravioli, blade of beef with red wine jus, and puddings such as blueberry soufflé, lemon tart with raspberry sorbet and sticky toffee pudding.** *Starters/Snacks: £4.50 to £7.50. Main Courses: £11.00 to £18.50. Puddings: £5.00 to £6.00*

Free house ~ Licensee Stephen Fitzpatrick ~ Real ale ~ Bar food ~ (0116) 247 8258 ~ Children welcome ~ Open 12-2, 6-11; closed Sun evening and all day Mon

Recommended by Jeff and Wendy Williams

CLIPSHAM   SK9716   MAP 8

Olive Branch ★

Take B668/Stretton exit off A1 N of Stamford; Clipsham signposted E from exit roundabout; LE15 7SH

LEICESTERSHIRE AND RUTLAND DINING PUB OF THE YEAR

A special place for an exceptional meal in comfortable surroundings, fine choice of drinks and luxury bedrooms

Never failing to please, this civilised place is beautifully run, with tremendous attention to detail, and the genuine aspiration that every customer should have an enjoyable time. Its various small but charmingly attractive rooms have a relaxed country cottage atmosphere, with dark joists and beams, rustic furniture, an interesting mix of pictures (some by local artists), candles on tables, and a cosy log fire in the stone inglenook fireplace. Many of the books were bought at antiques fairs by one of the partners, so it's worth asking if you see something you like, as much is for sale; piped music. A carefully chosen range of drinks includes Grainstore Olive Oil and a guest beer on handpump, an enticing wine list (with a dozen by the glass), a fine choice of malt whiskies, armagnacs and cognacs, and quite a few different british and continental bottled beers. Outside, there are tables, chairs and big plant pots on a pretty little terrace, with more on the neat lawn, sheltered in the L of its two low buildings. The bedrooms (in Beech House just opposite) are lovely and the breakfasts are wonderful too.

🍴 **Excellent food (not cheap) might include dressed crab with lemon mayonnaise, venison bresaola with beetroot rémoulade, fish and chips with minted peas, pork and stilton pie, steak and kidney suet pudding, rib-eye steak, roast john dory with crab ravioli and** shellfish bisque, and puddings such as croissant and butter pudding with marmalade ice-cream, blackcurrant treacle tart with yoghurt ice-cream, and a cheeseboard. *Starters/Snacks: £4.50 to £12.50. Main Courses: £8.50 to £21.50. Puddings: £6.75 to £9.50*

Free house ~ Licensees Sean Hope and Ben Jones ~ Real ale ~ Bar food (12-2(3 Sun), 7-9.30(9 Sun)) ~ Restaurant ~ (01780) 410355 ~ Children welcome ~ Dogs allowed in bar and bedrooms ~ Open 12-3, 6-11; 12-11(10.30 Sun) Sat ~ Bedrooms: £85S(£95B)/£100S(£110B)

Recommended by Noel Grundy, Dr and Mrs J Temporal, Michael Doswell, Derek and Sylvia Stephenson, Jeff and Wendy Williams, Ian and Helen Stafford, Howard and Margaret Buchanan, Pat and Stewart Gordon, Michael Sargent, W N F Boughey, DFL, Mike and Sue Loseby, Roy Bromell, Miss J F Reay, M S Catling, Mrs Brenda Calver, Glenwys and Alan Lawrence, Bruce and Sharon Eden, Gordon and Margaret Ormonroyd, B and F A Hannam, Barry and Sue Pladdys

EXTON   SK9211   MAP 7

Fox & Hounds 🍴

Signposted off A606 Stamford—Oakham; LE15 8AP

Bustling and well run with popular food including pizzas, log fire in the comfortable lounge and a quiet garden

Facing a delightful village green, this handsome old coaching inn, with its well managed and carefully attentive service, is an enjoyably relaxing place to visit. The comfortable high-ceilinged lounge bar is traditionally civilised with some dark red plush easy chairs, and wheelback seats around lots of pine tables, with maps and hunting prints on the walls, fresh flowers, and a winter log fire in a large stone fireplace. Grainstore Ten Fifty, Greene King IPA and a Greene King guest ale on handpump, with a good range of wines by the glass; TV, piped music. The lovely sheltered walled garden has seats among large rose beds overlooking pretty paddocks. The inn is a handy stopping place for Rutland Water and the gardens at Barnsdale.

🍴 **Bar food includes filled panini (lunchtime only), butternut squash soup, bruschetta, seabass and leek risotto, sausage and mash, duck breast with mushrooms and red wine sauce, scampi, a full pizza list (the landlord is italian), and puddings such as pecan pie and apple and raisin crumble.** *Starters/Snacks: £4.50 to £6.95. Main Courses: £9.25 to £17.25. Puddings: £4.75*

Free house ~ Licensees Valter and Sandra Floris ~ Real ale ~ Bar food (not Sun evening) ~ Restaurant ~ (01572) 812403 ~ Children welcome ~ Dogs allowed in bar and bedrooms ~ Open 11-3, 6-11; 11-11 summer Sat; 11-4 Sun ~ Bedrooms: £40(£45B)/£60(£70B)

Recommended by Richard and Jean Green, Mr and Mrs Staples, Leslie and Barbara Owen, Paul Humphreys, S Holder, Barry Collett, Roy Bromell, Jim Farmer, Trevor and Sylvia Millum, P A Rowe, Ian and Helen Stafford, Colin McKerrow, Mrs Hazel Rainer

LYDDINGTON   SP8796   MAP 4

Old White Hart 🍴 🛏️

Village signposted off A6003 N of Corby; LE15 9LR

Well run, popular inn with welcoming staff, roaring fires and very good food; pretty garden

The very friendly couple that run this fine old place have been here over ten years now and it's clearly their pride and joy. They are consistently friendly and attentive and nothing is too much trouble for them. The softly lit front bar has a glass-shielded log fire, low ceilings and heavy bowed beams, a relaxed local atmosphere and just four close-set tables. This room opens into an attractive restaurant, and on the other side is another tiled-floor room with rugs, lots of fine hunting prints, cushioned wall seats and mate's chairs and a woodburning stove. Three real ales might be Fullers London Pride, Greene King Abbot and Timothy Taylors Golden Best on handpump, alongside several wines by the glass; shove-ha'penny, cribbage, dominoes and petanque. The pretty walled garden (with eight floodlit boules pitches) is very pleasant with seats under outdoor heaters; if you sit out here on Thursday evening you may hear the church bell-ringers. The pub is handy for Bede House and there are good nearby walks.

🍴 The menu changes monthly but has included goose liver parfait with brioche and plum compote, home-cured gravadlax, home-made sausages, chicken, mushroom and thyme pie, rolled stuffed saddle of pork with apple sauce, seared duck breast with beetroot sauce, rib-eye steak, and puddings such as apple and custard pie or white chocolate crème brûlée. *Starters/Snacks: £3.50 to £6.50. Main Courses: £11.95 to £15.95. Puddings: £5.95 to £6.50*

Free house ~ Licensees Stuart and Holly East ~ Real ale ~ Bar food (12-2(2.30 Sun), 6.30(7 Sun)-9; not winter Sun evening) ~ Restaurant ~ (01572) 821703 ~ Children welcome ~ Open 12-3, 6-11; 12-3.30, 7-10.30 Sun ~ Bedrooms: £65B/£85B

Recommended by Jeff and Wendy Williams, Susan and Neil McLean, Brian and Janet Ainscough, Dr Brian and Mrs Anne Hamilton, R L Borthwick, Mike and Sue Loseby, John Wooll, P A Rowe

MOWSLEY
SP6488   MAP 4

Staff of Life 🍽 🍷

Village signposted off A5199 S of Leicester; Main Street; LE17 6NT

Neat, high-gabled pub popular for a good meal out; seats in back garden

---

Tucked behind this well run little pub is a delightful little deck, shaded by leafy foliage and clearly someone's pride and joy. The roomy bar is spotlessly kept and quite traditional with a panelled ceiling, high-backed settles on flagstones, warming fire, wicker chairs on shiny wood floors and stools lined up along the unusual circular counter. Banks's Bitter and possibly Jennings Cumberland on handpump and up to 20 wines (and champagne) are served by friendly helpful staff; piped music.

🍴 As well as a pubby lunchtime bar menu with sandwiches, ham, egg and chips and pork and leek sausages with wholegrain mustard mash, specials might include peking duck pancakes, seared scallops on chorizo with lemon and Cointreau butter, roast pork belly with raisin mash, black pudding and red wine jus, grilled bass with blackberry shallots, watercress and fennel salad and hollandaise sauce, mushroom, stilton and roast vegetable wellington with hazelnut pesto, and puddings such as white chocolate and raspberry cheesecake and lemon meringue pie with burnt orange sauce. *Starters/Snacks: £4.25 to £10.00. Main Courses: £8.50 to £22.00. Puddings: £5.00 to £6.75*

Free house ~ Licensee Spencer Farrell ~ Real ale ~ Bar food (12-2.30(3.30 Sun), 6.30-9.30(6-8.30 Mon); not Sun evening or Mon lunchtime) ~ Restaurant ~ (0116) 240 2359 ~ Children welcome but on back terrace ~ Open 12-3, 6-11; 12-10.30 Sun; closed Mon lunchtime (except bank hols)

Recommended by John Coatsworth, Veronica Brown, P Tailyour, Michael Sargent, George Atkinson, P M Newsome, Rob and Catherine Dunster, Leslie and Barbara Owen, Duncan Cloud

OADBY
SK6202   MAP 4

Cow & Plough 🍺

Gartree Road (B667 N of centre); LE2 2FB

Fantastic collection of brewery memorabilia, real ales and good, interesting food

---

If you have the feeling that you're heading on to an agricultural property when you arrive here, it's because this is a fairly recent conversion of a farm yard. The pub opened about 20 years ago and so quickly did the place become popular that the few original cosily individual rooms were soon supplemented by an extensive long, light, flagstoned front extension. It wasn't just the customers that needed more space, by now the landlord had amassed a noteworthy collection of breweriana. Two of the original dark back rooms, known as the Vaults, contain an extraordinary collection – almost every piece has a story behind it: enamel signs and mirrors advertising long-forgotten brews, an aged brass cash register, and furnishings and fittings salvaged from pubs and even churches (there's some splendid stained-glass behind the counter). One section has descriptions of all Leicester's pubs. The long front extension has plenty of plants and fresh flowers, a piano, beams liberally covered with hops, and a real mix of traditionally pubby tables and chairs, with lots of green leatherette sofas, and small round cast-iron tables. The conservatory too has a fine collection of brewery and pub signs and the like, and a very eclectic mix of chairs and tables. As you might expect, the collector of such fine breweriana keeps jolly good beer too. Seven real ales include four from the local Steamin' Billy brewery, alongside guests such as Dark Star Hophead, Ossett Silver King and Sharps Atlantic IPA on handpump; also a dozen country wines, several wines by the glass and up to six ciders; TV, darts, board games and shove-ha'penny. There are picnic-sets outside in the old yard.

🍴 Food includes lunchtime sandwiches, moules marinière, parma ham, asparagus and goats cheese tart, fried tiger prawns, pie of the day, battered fish with mushy peas, fried red snapper with five-spice vegetables, chicken suprême stuffed with chorizo with garlic and spinach rösti, and steak; Sunday carvery. *Starters/Snacks: £4.50 to £9.50. Main Courses: £7.90 to £9.50. Puddings: £3.90 to £5.90*

Free house ~ Licensee Barry Lount ~ Real ale ~ Bar food (12-3(5 Sun), 6-9) ~ Restaurant ~ (0116) 272 0852 ~ Children welcome ~ Dogs welcome ~ Open 11(midday Sun)-11; 11-3, 5-11 Mon-Thurs in winter

Recommended by Jim Farmer, the Didler, Rona Murdoch, Duncan Cloud, David Field, John Fiander, Dr and Mrs A K Clarke

OAKHAM

SK8509 MAP 4

Grainstore 🍺 £

Station Road, off A606; LE15 6RE

Super own-brewed beers in a converted railway grain warehouse, friendly staff, cheerful customers and pubby food

Friendly staff will happily let you sample some of the own-brewed Grainstore beers that are brewed above the down-to-earth bar here. They use the traditional tower method, and during work hours you'll hear noises of the brewery workings filtering down from the floors above. There are seven beers, and they are served traditionally at the left end of the bar counter and through swan necks with sparklers on the right. Laid-back or lively, depending on the time of day, the interior of this converted three-storey Victorian grain warehouse is plain and functional with wide, well worn bare floorboards, bare ceiling boards above massive joists supported by red metal pillars, a long brick-built bar counter with cast-iron bar stools, tall cask tables and simple elm chairs; games machine, darts, board games, shove-ha'penny, giant Jenga and bottle-walking. In summer they pull back the huge glass doors which open the bar on to a terrace with picnic-sets, often stacked with barrels. You can tour the brewery by arrangement, they do takeaways, and hold a real ale festival with over 65 real ales and lots of live music during the August bank holiday weekend; disabled access.

🍴 Wholesome unfussy food includes panini, baked potatoes, mussels prepared in three ways, good sharing platters, burgers, sausage and mash, and chicken curry. *Starters/Snacks: £2.95 to £3.95. Main Courses: £4.95 to £8.95*

Own brew ~ Licensee Peter Atkinson ~ Real ale ~ Bar food (11-3; not Sun) ~ (01572) 770065 ~ Children welcome till 8pm ~ Dogs welcome ~ Jazz Weds, blues first Sun of month, rock and pop third Thurs of month ~ Open 11-11(midnight Fri, Sat)

Recommended by John Fiander, Jim Farmer, the Didler, Barry Collett, Mike and Sue Loseby, Dr and Mrs T E Hothersall, Alan and Eve Harding, Michael Dandy, Derek and Sylvia Stephenson

---

Several well known guide books make establishments pay for entry, either directly or as a fee for inspection. These fees can run to many hundreds of pounds. We do not. Unlike other guides, we never take payment for entries. We never accept a free meal, free drink, or any other freebie from a pub. We do not accept any sponsorship – let alone from commercial schemes linked to the pub trade. All our entries depend solely on merit.

PEGGS GREEN   SK4117   MAP 7

New Inn £

Signposted off A512 Ashby—Shepshed at roundabout, then turn immediately left down
Zion Hill towards Newbold; pub is 100 yards down on the right, with car park on opposite
side of road; LE67 8JE

Intriguing bric-a-brac in an unspoilt pub, a friendly welcome, good value food and drinks;
cottagey garden

There is something quite unique about this unspoilt little pub. Its two cosy tiled front
rooms, popular with chatty locals, radiate a genuinely warm irish welcome and
quirkiness. Each is filled with a diverting collection of old bric-a-brac which covers
almost every inch of the walls and ceilings. The little room on the left, a bit like an old
kitchen parlour (they call it the Cabin), has china on the mantelpiece, lots of prints and
photographs, and little collections of this and that, three old cast-iron tables, wooden
stools and a small stripped kitchen table. The room to the right has nice stripped
panelling and more appealing bric-a-brac. The small back Best room, with a stripped
wooden floor, has a touching display of old local photographs, including some colliery
ones. Bass, Caledonian Deuchars IPA and Marstons Pedigree on handpump; board games.
Plenty of seats in front of the pub, with more in the peaceful back garden. During the
summer they may open Tuesday to Thursday lunchtimes.

🍴 Unbelievably cheap food includes ham, egg and chips, corned beef hash, steak in ale
pie, faggots and peas, sausages with onion gravy and smoked haddock. When they're not
serving food you are welcome to order local takeaways and they will provide you with
crockery. *Starters/Snacks: £1.50 to £4.95. Puddings: £1.95 to £2.50*

Enterprise ~ Lease Maria Christina Kell ~ Real ale ~ Bar food (12-2, Mon, Fri-Sat; 6-8 Mon) ~
No credit cards ~ (01530) 222293 ~ Children welcome ~ Dogs welcome ~ Open 12-2.30,
5.30-11; 12-3, 6.30-11 Sat; 12-3, 7-10.30 Sun; closed Tues-Thurs lunchtime
Recommended by JJW, CMW, the Didler, Paul J Robinshaw, Philip Bishop, Duncan Cloud

SOMERBY   SK7710   MAP 7

Stilton Cheese 🍺

High Street; off A606 Oakham—Melton Mowbray, via Cold Overton, or Leesthorpe and
Pickwell; can also be reached direct from Oakham via Knossington; LE14 2QB

Established place with chatty staff, local real ales and seats on a heated terrace

Neatly kept and traditional, this solidly built ironstone pub extends a cheery village
welcome. The comfortable hop-strung beamed bar/lounge has dark red patterned carpets,
upholstered banquettes, dark wood pubby tables and chairs, country prints on its
stripped-stone walls, copper pots hung from beams and, quite rare these days, a stuffed
badger; shove-ha'penny, cribbage and dominoes. A decent range of real ales includes
Grainstore Ten Fifty, Marstons Pedigree and Tetleys, alongside a couple of guests from
brewers such as Belvoir and Newby Wyke; over a dozen wines by the glass, over 30 malt
whiskies and a proper cider. There are seats and outdoor heaters on the terrace; more
reports please.

🍴 Bar food includes sandwiches, ploughman's, mushrooms stuffed with stilton, crab
salad, stilton and mushroom lasagne, salmon and spinach en croûte, chicken and bacon
burger topped with stilton, and pork fillet with sage and cider sauce; puddings such as
ginger and walnut treacle tart and sherry trifle. *Starters/Snacks: £3.50 to £5.50.*
Main Courses: £8.50 to £13.95. Puddings: £3.95

Free house ~ Licensees Carol and Jeff Evans ~ Real ale ~ Bar food (12-2, 6(7 Sun)-9) ~
Restaurant ~ (01664) 454394 ~ Children welcome ~ Dogs allowed in bedrooms ~
Open 12-3, 6(7 Sun)-11 ~ Bedrooms: £30/£40
Recommended by Philip and Susan Philcox, Mike and Margaret Banks, Richard Tingle, Jim Farmer, JJW, CMW

STATHERN
SK7731   MAP 7

Red Lion 🍴 ♟ 🍺

Off A52 W of Grantham via the brown-signed Belvoir road (keep on towards Harby and Stathern signposted on left); or off A606 Nottingham—Melton Mowbray via Long Clawson and Harby; LE14 4HS

Splendid range of drinks and imaginative food in civilised dining pub with open fires and good garden with a play area; own shop, too

Decorated in a charming rustic style, the interior of this well run place (under the same ownership as the Olive Branch in Clipsham) is filled with appealing vintage furniture and kitchen paraphernalia, all picked up by one of the licensees at Newark Antiques Fair. The yellow room on the right, with its delightful collection of wooden spoons and lambing chairs, has a simple country pub feel. The lounge bar has sofas, an open fire, a big table with books, newspapers and magazines, and leads off the smaller, more traditional flagstoned bar with terracotta walls, another fireplace with a pile of logs beside it, and lots of beams and hops. A little room with tables set for eating leads to the long, narrow main dining room, and out to a nicely arranged suntrap with good hardwood furnishings spread over its lawn and terrace. The atmosphere throughout is relaxed and informal and service is very good indeed; piped music. Red Lion Ale (from Grainstore) and a couple of guests such as Brewsters Hophead and Greene King Abbot are well kept alongside draught belgian and continental bottled beers, several ciders, a varied wine list (several by the glass), winter mulled wine and summer home-made lemonade. There's an unusually big play area behind the car park, with swings, climbing frames and so on.

🍴 As well as lunchtime ploughman's and sandwiches, the excellent bar food (not cheap, but good value) might include starters such as pigeon breast with madeira sauce, moules marinière, cauliflower fritters with stilton sauce, fried calamari with sweet chilli mayonnaise, main courses such as tomato tart with glazed goats cheese, venison burger, slow-roast pork belly with sage gratin and black pudding, salmon with sorrel sauce, mediterranean vegetable lasagne, rabbit pie with creamed chicory, and puddings such as apple and prune crumble with warm crème anglaise and carrot cake with orange crème fraîche. *Starters/Snacks: £4.25 to £6.50. Main Courses: £6.50 to £13.50. Puddings: £4.95 to £6.50*

Free house ~ Licensees Sean Hope and Ben Jones ~ Real ale ~ Bar food (12-2(3 Sun), 6-9) ~ Restaurant ~ (01949) 860868 ~ Children welcome ~ Dogs allowed in bar ~ Open 12-3, 6-11; 12-11 Sat; 12-6.30 Sun; closed Sun evening

Recommended by Leslie and Barbara Owen, Jeff and Wendy Williams, Dr and Mrs J Temporal, W K Wood, David Glynne-Jones, Roy Bromell

STRETTON
SK9415   MAP 8

Jackson Stops

Rookery Lane; a mile or less off A1, at B668 (Oakham) exit; follow village sign, turning off Clipsham road into Manor Road, pub on left; LE15 7RA

Happy former farmhouse with decent drinks and jolly good food

The very competitive world nurdling championship takes place at this cheery old thatched place every year on Whit Sunday. A bit like pitch and toss, it's apparently unique to this pub and to one in Norfolk. It excites great passion amongst the locals and if you want to have a go we're sure the bright and breezy landlady or one of the chatty staff members will help you out. The homely black-beamed country bar down on the left has some timbering in its ochre walls, a couple of bar stools, a cushioned stripped wall pew and an elderly settle on the worn tile and brick floor, with a coal fire in the corner. The smarter main room on the right is light and airy with linen napkins and lit candles in brass sticks on the nice mix of ancient and modern tables, dark blue carpeting, a couple of striking modern oils alongside a few tastefully disposed farm tools on the mainly canary-coloured stone walls, and another coal fire in a stone corner fireplace. Right, along past the bar, is a second dining room, older in style, with stripped-stone walls, a tiled floor and an old open cooking range. The unobtrusive piped classical music doesn't disturb the chatty relaxed atmosphere. Oakham JHB and a guest such as Black Sheep are on handpump.

⚑ At lunchtime you can invent your own baguette or panini from the huge range of fillings here. Other generous helpings of very enjoyable food from the changing menu might include mushrooms topped with bacon, brie with red onion marmalade, asparagus wrapped in smoked salmon en croûte with hollandaise sauce, braised pork belly stuffed with sausage and apple with honey and mustard gravy, braised lamb shank with red wine gravy, roast mullet with creamy mint sauce, and puddings such as raspberry torte, eton mess and white chocolate tart. *Starters/Snacks: £4.25 to £5.85. Main Courses: £7.95 to £13.25. Puddings: £4.85*

Free house ~ Licensees Simon and Catherine Davy ~ Real ale ~ Bar food (12-2.15, 6.30-9.15) ~ Restaurant ~ (01780) 410237 ~ Children welcome ~ Dogs allowed in bar ~ Open 12-3, 6-11; 12-6 Sun; closed Sun evening and Mon

Recommended by Gordon and Margaret Ormondroyd, Leslie and Barbara Owen, Arthur Pickering, W M Paton, Michael Doswell

SWITHLAND
SK5512   MAP 7

Griffin ⚑

Main Street; between A6 and B5330, between Loughborough and Leicester; LE12 8TJ

A good mix of cheerful customers, well liked food and half a dozen real ales in a bustling atmosphere

This attractively converted and well run stone-built pub is a popular place, but even at its busiest things stay well under control. The beamed communicating rooms have some panelling, a nice mix of wooden tables and chairs and bar stools. Everards Beacon, Original and Tiger plus guests such as Adnams Bitter, Fullers London Pride, Greene King Abbot and Marstons Pedigree on handpump, several malt whiskies and several wines by the glass from a good list; piped music and skittle alley. The tidy streamside garden, overlooking open fields, has been reworked this year. The pub is handy for Bradgate Country Park and there are walks in Swithland Woods.

⚑ Enjoyable bar food might include ploughman's, sardine and chive pâté, smoked salmon with dill and lime dressing, mushroom risotto, venison casserole with dumplings, cottage pie and monkfish, tiger prawns and scallops in white wine cream. *Starters/Snacks: £3.45 to £7.95. Main Courses: £7.95 to £17.95. Puddings: £4.00 to £5.00*

Everards ~ Tenant John Cooledge ~ Real ale ~ Bar food (12-2, 6-9; 12-9(8 Sun) Weds-Sat; not Mon evening) ~ Restaurant ~ (01509) 890535 ~ Children welcome ~ Open 11-11(10.30 Sun)

Recommended by David Jackson, Duncan Cloud, John and Fiona Merritt, Pam and John Smith, Pete Baker, Michael Butler, JJW, CMW

WING
SK8902   MAP 4

Kings Arms 🍽 ♟ 🛏

Village signposted off A6003 S of Oakham; Top Street; LE15 8SE

Nicely kept old pub, big log fires, super choice of wines by the glass and good modern cooking

This neatly kept 17th-c inn is a civilised understated place for an enjoyable drink or a meal. Though the emphasis is on dining, readers have popped in for just a drink. The attractive low-beamed bar is pubbily neat, with various nooks and crannies, nice old beams and stripped stone, two large log fires (one in a copper-canopied central hearth), and flagstoned or wood-strip floors. Friendly, helpful staff serve over two dozen wines by the glass, as well as Bass, Grainstore Cooking and Shepherd Neame Spitfire on handpump and Sheppey's cider; board games. There are seats out in front, and more in the sunny yew-sheltered garden; the new car park has plenty of space. There's a medieval turf maze just up the road, and we are told that the pub is just a couple of miles away from one of England's two osprey hot-spots.

⚑ They put tremendous effort into sourcing genuine local produce here, so bread and biscuits are baked daily from flour milled not ten miles from where the grain grew. They have their own smoke house, producing everything from charcuterie to smoked nuts, and even make their own tomato ketchup. As to be expected, such attention to quality does incur a small premium on prices. The imaginative menu changes about twice a week and, depending on available produce, has included french onion soup with chorizo, moules marinière with cream, rabbit, mushroom, cognac and prune risotto, battered cod with beef-dripping chips, brill with saffron and spring onion crab cake and tomato fondue, pork cooked four ways: suckling, cheek, black pudding and pancetta crisp with red cabbage marmalade and roast apple, and puddings such as chocolate brownie, cognac flambé crêpes with orange and toasted almond syrup, and local cheeses. *Starters/Snacks: £3.50 to £8.75. Main Courses: £8.75 to £20.00. Puddings: £5.75 to £15.00*

Free house ~ Licensee David Goss ~ Real ale ~ Bar food (12-2(2.30 Sat), 6.30-9(9.30 Fri, Sat)) ~ Restaurant ~ (01572) 737634 ~ No children in restaurant after 7pm Sat, Sun ~ Open 12-3, 6.30-11(midnight Sat); 12-4 Sun; closed Sun evening, Mon lunchtime and all day Mon Nov-Apr ~ Bedrooms: £65S/£75S

Recommended by Mike and Sue Loseby, Gary Kelly, Phil and Jane Hodson, Derek and Sylvia Stephenson

WOODHOUSE EAVES   SK5313   MAP 7

Wheatsheaf 🛏

Brand Hill; turn right into Main Street, off B591 S of Loughborough; LE12 8SS

Bustling and friendly country pub with charming licensees, interesting things to look at, good bistro-type food and a fair choice of drinks; well equipped bedrooms

This rather smart country pub is both the home of several local clubs and a reflection of the licensees' many interests – everything from hunting to sailing. Its open-plan interior is full of interesting motor-racing, family RAF and flying memorabilia, and a cosy dining area called The Mess even has an RAF Hurricane propeller. The beamed bar areas are traditionally furnished, with log fires and wood pews, and daily papers. Even when busy, service remains welcoming and helpful and the atmosphere cheerily chatty. Adnams Broadside, Greene King IPA, Timothy Taylors Landlord and a guest such as Caledonian Deuchars IPA are on handpump (one or two readers have been a little irked by the price of a pint) alongside several wines, including champagne, by the glass from a thoughtfully compiled list. The floodlit, heated terrace has plenty of seating.

🍴 As well as sandwiches, ciabattas, filled baguettes and ploughman's, the enjoyable bistro-style menu might include chicken liver pâté, haddock smokies with wine, cream, tomatoes and cheese, chargrilled burger, roast vegetable nut loaf, sausage and mash, fish and chips, prawn and salmon linguine, and puddings such as fruit crumble and meringues. *Starters/Snacks: £4.50 to £5.75. Main Courses: £10.95 to £20.00. Puddings: £5.25*

Free house ~ Licensees Richard and Bridget Dimblebee ~ Real ale ~ Bar food (12-2(2.30 Sat), 6.30-9.15; 12-3.30 only Sun) ~ Restaurant ~ (01509) 890320 ~ Children welcome ~ Dogs allowed in bar ~ Open 12-3, 6-11; 12-5, 7-10.30 Sun; closed Sun evening in winter ~ Bedrooms: £60S/£80B

Recommended by the Didler, C J Pratt, George Ozols, Gordon and Margaret Ormonroyd, John and Helen Rushton, John Saville, Gillian Grist, Adrian Johnson

LUCKY DIP

Besides the fully inspected pubs, you might like to try these Lucky Dips recommended to us and described by readers (if you do, please send us reports: feedback@goodguides.com).

AB KETTLEBY [SK7519]
☆ *Sugar Loaf* LE14 3JB [Nottingham Rd (A606 NW of Melton)]: Well run friendly pub with comfortably modernised open-plan carpeted bar, country prints and big photographs of Shipstones brewery dray horses, bare-boards end with coal-effect gas fire; reasonably priced all-day food, well kept Bass, Grainstore, Marstons Pedigree and guests, friendly staff, dining

conservatory; quiet juke box, games machine; children welcome if eating, picnic-sets out by the road and car park, open all day *(John and Sylvia Harrop, Robert F Smith, LYM)*

BITTESWELL [SP5385]
Man at Arms LE17 4SB [The Green]: Popular for quickly served, cheap generous food inc lunchtime bargains; pleasant staff, decent beers, L-shaped bar with long front bar,

small snug and big eating area *(Dave Irving, Jenny Huggins)*

BOTTESFORD [SK8038]

Red Lion NG13 0DF: Friendly traditional low-beamed village pub with well kept Greene King and related ales, enjoyable bargain pubby food; disabled access, gardens with play area and smokers' den *(M J Winterton)*

BRANSTON [SK8129]

☆ ***Wheel*** NG32 1RU [Main St]: Refurbished, beamed 18th-c village pub with stylishly simple décor, friendly attentive landlady and staff, chef/landlord doing proper country food, some quite out of the ordinary, changing ales such as Adnams and Batemans from central servery, log fires; attractive garden, next to church, splendid countryside nr Belvoir Castle, cl Mon *(BB, Kate Davies, Mike and Jan Beckett, David Russell, B R Wood)*

BRAUNSTON [SK8306]

☆ ***Old Plough*** LE15 8QT [off A606 in Oakham; Church St]: Welcoming black-beamed village local, comfortably opened up, with log fire, well kept Grainstore and interesting guest ales, generous enjoyable pubby food inc beer-based dishes; friendly staff, appealing back dining conservatory (children allowed); tables in small sheltered garden, open all day *(Duncan Cloud, Geoff and Teresa Salt, Jim Farmer, LYM)*

CASTLE DONINGTON [SK4427]

Jolly Potters DE74 2NH [Hillside]: Genuine unspoilt town local, basic and friendly, with pews on flagstones, good coal fire, hanging mugs and jugs, well kept Bass, Fullers, Marstons Pedigree and guest beers; open all day *(the Didler)*

COLEORTON [SK4117]

George LE67 8HF [Loughborough Rd (A512 E)]: Attractive bar with lots of bric-a-brac, beams, stripped brick and timber; good reasonably priced pubby food inc light dishes, friendly landlord and staff, well kept changing ales such as Adnams; unobtrusive piped music; large garden behind with play area *(Ian and Jane Irving, Comus and Sarah Elliott, Phil and Jane Hodson)*

COPT OAK [SK4812]

Copt Oak LE67 9QB [Whitwick Rd, handy for M1 junction 22]: Comfortable family dining pub with good views over Charnwood Forest; wide choice of food (all day Sun), quick friendly service, Marstons Pedigree, and a woodburner; piped music; can be very busy wknds *(Duncan Cloud, Adrian Johnson)*

COTTESMORE [SK9013]

☆ ***Sun*** LE15 7DH [B668 NE of Oakham]: 17th-c thatched stone-built village pub with good atmosphere and pleasant staff, good choice of wines by the glass, Adnams Best, Everards Tiger and a guest, good coffee, wide choice of reasonably priced enjoyable bar food from lunchtime sandwiches up; stripped pine on flagstones, inglenook fire, lots of pictures and ornaments, carpeted back restaurant; piped music; dogs and children welcome, terrace tables, open all day wknds

(Jeremy Hancock, Barry Collett, LYM, Michael and Maggie Betton)

CROXTON KERRIAL [SK8329]

☆ ***Peacock*** NG32 1QR [A607 SW of Grantham]: Much modernised 17th-c former coaching inn with enjoyable good value straightforward food, real ales such as Black Sheep, Greene King IPA and Wells & Youngs, decent wines; log fire in big open-plan bare-boards beamed bar with chunky stripped tables, small simple dining room and garden room; said to be haunted by former landlord (never does anything that might upset customers); well behaved children welcome, picnic-sets in inner courtyard and pleasant sloping garden with views, good bedroom block *(Phil and Jane Hodson, BB)*

DADLINGTON [SP4097]

Dog & Hedgehog CV13 6JB [The Green]: We were on the point of making this popular dining pub a new Main Entry, after inspection had impressed us with its remarkable food value, when it closed at the end of 2008 – news, please *(BB)*

DESFORD [SK4902]

White Horse LE9 9JJ [B582 SE, nr A47 junction]: Pleasantly refurbished with good generous food inc reasonably priced lunches (best to book Sun), Marstons and related guest beers, good value wines; pleasant staff, comfortable bar with leather sofas, stylishly old-fashioned dining room; cl Sun, Mon evenings *(C J Pratt)*

EAST LANGTON [SP7292]

Bell LE16 7TW [off B6047; Main St]: Appealing country pub buzzing with locals and families, Brewsters, Greene King and local Langton ale kept well, nice wine, good if rather pricey food, popular Sun lunch (should book), good service; long low-ceilinged stripped-stone beamed bar, woodburner, modern pine tables and chairs; tables on sloping front lawn *(Joan and Tony Walker, Rona Murdoch, LYM, Duncan Cloud)*

EMPINGHAM [SK9908]

☆ ***White Horse*** LE15 8PS [Main St; A606 Stamford—Oakham]: Sizeable old stone pub handy for Rutland Water; bustling open-plan carpeted lounge bar, big log fire, Adnams, Oakham and Timothy Taylors Landlord, good choice of wines by the glass, pubby food with more elaborate specials; TV, piped music; children welcome, rustic tables out among flower tubs, bedrooms, open all day *(Leslie and Barbara Owen, Duncan Cloud, Glenwys and Alan Lawrence, Dave and Jenny Hughes, LYM, Phil and Jane Hodson)*

FLECKNEY [SP6493]

Golden Shield LE8 8AN [Main St]: Spotless music-free pub popular for good value lunches, Greene King and other ales; successful evening restaurant *(P Tailyour)*

FOXTON [SP6989]

☆ ***Foxton Locks*** LE16 7RA [Foxton Locks, off A6 3 miles NW of Market Harborough (park by bridge 60/62 and walk)]: Large busy comfortably reworked L-shaped bar, good choice of food inc set menu, converted boathouse now does snacks, quick friendly service, half a dozen well kept ales such as Caledonian Deuchars IPA, Fullers London Pride and Theakstons; large raised terrace and covered decking, steps down to fenced waterside lawn – nice setting at foot of long flight of canal locks, good walks *(Jeff and Wendy Williams, John Wooll, Gerry and Rosemary Dobson, Martin Smith, Jim Farmer)*

GLASTON [SK8900]

Old Pheasant LE15 9BP [A47 Leicester—Peterborough, E of Uppingham]: Attractive family-run stone-built pub, good food, good choice of wines by the glass, Greene King and a guest beer, fast friendly service; spacious bar with central servery, alcoves, big woodburner in inglenook and some comfortable leather armchairs, restaurant; children welcome, picnic-sets on sheltered terrace, nine comfortable modern bedrooms *(Colin McKerrow, LYM, Revd John E Cooper)*

GREETHAM [SK9314]

Wheatsheaf LE15 7NP [B668 Stretton—Cottesmore]: Linked L-shaped rooms, popular well prepared food from interesting soups up, inc good open sandwiches using home-baked bread, friendly welcoming service; three well kept ales such as Greene King IPA, Marstons Pedigree and Wells & Youngs Best, good choice of wines, blazing open stove, soft piped music, games room with darts, pool and big-screen sports TV; wheelchair access, front lawn and back terrace by pretty stream, annex bedrooms, open all day Sat *(Michael and Jenny Back, BB)*

GUMLEY [SP6890]

☆ *Bell* LE16 7RU [NW of Market Harborough; Main St]: Although still for sale as we went to press, there were no changes at this cheerful, neatly kept, beamed village pub; has had good value food (not Mon evening) inc bargain OAP lunches, friendly helpful staff and ales such as Black Sheep, Greene King and Timothy Taylors; traditional country décor, darts, cribbage and dominoes, separate dining room, friendly jack russell called Suzie; pretty terrace garden (not for children or dogs) with aviary; has been cl Sun evening *(Gerry and Rosemary Dobson, LYM, David Field, George Atkinson, P Tailyour, Ken and Barbara Turner, Jim Farmer, Veronica Brown)*

HALLATON [SP7896]

Bewicke Arms LE16 8UB [off B6047 or B664]: New licensees for this attractive thatched pub dating from the 16th c; Greene King IPA, local Langton and Timothy Taylors Landlord, two bar dining areas, restaurant of small linked areas, two log fires, scrubbed pine tables, memorabilia of ancient local Easter Monday inter-village bottle-kicking match, darts; piped music; children in eating areas, dogs allowed on leads, disabled facilities, stables tearoom/gift shop, big terrace overlooking paddock and lake with play area, three bedrooms in yard, open all day Sun *(Duncan Cloud, Geoff and Lesley Kipling, Mark Farrington, Jim Farmer, LYM)*

HATHERN [SK5021]

Dew Drop LE12 5HY [Loughborough Rd (A6)]: Traditional two-room beamed local with welcoming landlord, Greene King ales, plenty of malt whiskies, coal fire, good lunchtime cobs, darts and dominoes; tables outside *(the Didler)*

HEMINGTON [SK4527]

☆ *Jolly Sailor* DE74 2RB [Main St]: Cheerful and welcoming, picturesque three-room village pub under newish management; generous fresh food inc popular Sun lunch (best to book), six well kept ales, Weston's Old Rosie cider, decent wines by the glass, good range of soft drinks; warm log fire, big country pictures, bric-a-brac on heavy beams and shelves, table skittles, daily papers, restaurant; piped classical music; children welcome, picnic-sets out in front, open all day wknds *(MP, JJW, CMW, Rona Murdoch, Richard and Jean Green, the Didler)*

HOBY [SK6717]

☆ *Blue Bell* LE14 3DT [Main St]: Attractive rebuilt thatched pub doing well under new licensee, good range of enjoyable realistically priced food inc some unusual things like kangaroo steaks (all day wknds – best to book), Sun roasts, good uniformed service; four well kept ales, good choice of wines by the glass and of teas and coffees, open-plan and airy with beams, comfortable traditional furniture, old local photographs, skittle alley, darts; piped music; children and dogs welcome, garden with picnic-sets and boules, open all day *(Phil and Jane Hodson, R L Borthwick)*

HOSE [SK7329]

Black Horse LE14 4JE [Bolton Lane]: Down-to-earth beamed and quarry-tiled Tynemill pub with amiable landlord, interesting quickly served local food (not Sun, Mon evenings), well kept Castle Rock and changing ales; coal fire, darts, panelled restaurant; pretty village, nice countryside, cl Mon-Thurs lunchtimes *(the Didler)*

HOUGHTON ON THE HILL [SK6703]

Old Black Horse LE7 9GD [Main St (just off A47 Leicester—Uppingham)]: Lively and comfortable, with above-average home-made food (no hot food Mon lunchtime), welcoming helpful staff, Everards ales, guest beer, good wines by the glass, reasonable prices; bare-boards dining area with lots of panelling; piped music; big attractive garden *(R L Borthwick)*

ILLSTON ON THE HILL [SP7099]

☆ *Fox & Goose* LE7 9EG [Main St, off B6047 Market Harborough—Melton]: Individualistic two-bar local, plain, comfortable and convivial, with interesting pictures and assorted oddments, well kept Everards and guest ales, quick service, good coal fire; no food; cl Mon lunchtime *(Jim Farmer, LYM, the Didler, Rona Murdoch)*

KEGWORTH [SK4826]

☆ *Cap & Stocking* DE74 2FF [handy for M1 junction 24, via A6; Borough St]: Unchanging nicely old-fashioned three-room pub, brown paint, etched glass, coal fires, big cases of stuffed birds and locally caught fish; Bass (from the jug) and well kept guest beers such as Jennings and Wells & Youngs Bombardier, home-made food (not Weds evening) from fresh sandwiches to bargain Sun lunch; dominoes, back room opening to secluded garden with decking; piped music; no credit cards; children welcome *(the Didler, LYM, Pete Baker)*

Red Lion DE74 2DA [a mile from M1 junction 24, via A6 towards Loughborough; High St]: Half a dozen or more good changing real ales and good range of whiskies and vodkas in four brightly lit traditional rooms around a small servery; limited choice of good wholesome food (not Sun), assorted furnishings, coal and flame-effect fires, delft shelf of beer bottles, daily papers, darts and cards, family room; small back yard, garden with play area, well equipped bedrooms, open all day *(the Didler, Pete Baker, BB)*

KIBWORTH BEAUCHAMP [SP6894]

Coach & Horses LE8 0NN [A6 S of Leicester]: New landlord at snug 16th-c carpeted local with mugs on beams and a candlelit restaurant; wide choice of home-made food inc good value OAP lunches and all-day Sun roasts, well kept Bass, Fullers London Pride, Greene King IPA and Wadworths 6X, regular events; piped music, TVs; children welcome, dogs in bar, disabled access, some outside seating at front and on side terrace; open all day wknds, cl Mon lunchtime *(Mike and Margaret Banks, BB)*

KILBY [SP6295]

Dog & Gun LE18 3TD [Main St, off A5199 S of Leicester]: Welcoming, much-extended, cleanly kept pub, locally popular for wide choice of good straightforward food from baguettes up inc bargain set lunches, helpful service, Bass, Fullers London Pride and Greene King IPA, good wine choice, coal fire, attractive side restaurant with grandfather clock; disabled access, colourful back garden with terrace and pergola *(Veronica Brown, Duncan Cloud, Michael and Jenny Back)*

KIRBY MUXLOE [SK5104]

Royal Oak LE9 2AN [Main St]: Comfortable modernish pub with wide range of baguettes, good value bar dishes, fish specialities and Sun lunch; good friendly service, well kept Adnams and Everards, good wine choice, sizeable restaurant; nearby 15th-c castle ruins *(Gerry and Rosemary Dobson, Mr and Mrs J D Garner)*

KNOSSINGTON [SK8008]

Fox & Hounds LE15 8LY [off A606 W of Oakham; Somerby Rd]: Handsome 18th-c ivy-covered building under new licensees, simply modernised knocked-through beamed bar with log fire, comfortable end dining area, good range of food from pubby favourites up using local produce, Sun roasts; Fullers, Greene King and a guest such as Adnams, good choice of wines; piped music; children and dogs welcome, big back

garden, open all day wknds, cl Mon (but open evening in summer) *(LYM)*

LANGHAM [SK8411]

☆ **Noel Arms** LE15 7HU [Bridge St]: Well refurbished country pub with low beams, flagstones, central log fire and new conservatory; enjoyable food from bar or restaurant inc good value Sun lunch, well kept Caledonian, Greene King and Marstons ales, nice wines; children welcome *(J V Dadswell, LYM, Derek and Sylvia Stephenson)*

LEICESTER [SK5804]

Ale Wagon LE1 1RE [Rutland St/Charles St]: Basic 1930s two-room local with great beer choice inc own Hoskins ales, Weston's cider and perry, coal fire, events such as comedy nights; juke box and sports TV; handy for station, open all day (Sun afternoon break) *(the Didler)*

Criterion LE1 5JN [Millstone Lane]: Great choice of changing real ales and continental beers in modern building with dark wood and burgundy décor in carpeted main room, decent wines by the glass, good value pizzas and more traditional pub food (not Sun evening, Mon); relaxed room on left with games, some live music; reasonable wheelchair access (small front step), picnic-sets outside, open all day *(the Didler, Jim Farmer)*

☆ **Globe** LE1 5EU [Silver St]: Lots of woodwork in cheerfully well worn partitioned areas off central bar, mirrors and wrought-iron gas lamps, charming more peaceful upstairs dining room; five Everards ales and four guest beers, friendly staff, bargain food (12-7) from snacks up inc a good vegetarian choice; piped pop music (not in snug); very popular with young people wknd evenings; children welcome, open all day *(the Didler, Val and Alan Green, Valerie Baker, LYM)*

☆ **Out of the Vaults** LE1 6RL [King St/New Walk]: Remarkable changing range of real ales inc Oakham, in long high-ceilinged bar, regular beer festivals, friendly chatty landlady, enthusiastic landlord; enjoyable wkdy lunchtime cobs, baguettes and curries, decent reasonably priced wines by the glass, farm cider, simple seating and stripped tables on bare boards; open all day *(the Didler, Jim Farmer)*

Pump & Tap LE3 5LX [Duns Gate (nr Polytechnic)]: Popular roadside pub with two long narrow rooms, panelling, old wicker chairs, large log fire and stove, old photographs, well kept ales; sports TV *(the Didler)*

Shakespeares Head LE1 5SH [Southgates]: Welcoming local with low-priced Oakwell Barnsley and Old Tom Mild, well filled rolls and simple hot dishes inc Sun roasts, basic bar and chatty lounge popular with older regulars; open all day *(the Didler)*

☆ **Swan & Rushes** LE1 5WR [Oxford St/Infirmary Sq]: Well kept Oakham and fine range of guest and bottled beers, farm cider, thriving atmosphere in two rooms with big oak tables, enjoyable bar food lunchtime and Weds, Fri evening; live music Sat; open all day Fri-Sun *(the Didler, Jim Farmer)*

LOUGHBOROUGH [SK5320]

Albion LE11 1QA [canal bank, about 0.2 mile from Loughborough Wharf]: Cheerful chatty local by Grand Union Canal, four unusual ales inc local Wicked Hathern, friendly owners, cheap straightforward home-made food, coal fire, darts; children welcome, big courtyard, occasional barbecues *(the Didler, Clive and Fran Dutson)*

☆ *Swan in the Rushes* LE11 5BE [The Rushes (A6)]: Bare-boards town local with good value Castle Rock and interesting changing ales, foreign bottled beers, farm cider, good value chip-free food (not Sat, Sun evenings); good service, daily papers, traditional games, open fire, three smallish high-ceilinged rooms; good juke box, music nights; children in eating areas, tables outside, four bedrooms, open all day *(the Didler, Rona Murdoch, Comus and Sarah Elliott, Andrew Seymour, Sue Demont, Tim Barrow, LYM, Pete Baker)*

Tap & Mallet LE11 1EU [Nottingham Rd]: Basic friendly pub with well kept Jennings, Marstons and five changing microbrews, foreign beers, farm cider and perry; nice cobs, coal fire, pool, juke box; walled back garden with play area and pets corner, open all day wknds *(the Didler)*

MANTON [SK8704]

Horse & Jockey LE15 8SU [St Marys Rd]: Welcoming stripped-down early 19th-c pub with minimalist décor, well kept Grainstore and Timothy Taylors Landlord, promptly served food from baguettes up all day (at least wknds), big coal fire; picnic-sets outside, on Rutland Water cycle route; four bedrooms *(R L Borthwick)*

MARKET HARBOROUGH [SP7387]

Angel LE16 7AF [High St]: Popular former coaching inn with bargain food from sandwiches and other pubby lunchtime bar food to restaurant meals, friendly and efficient uniformed staff; Marstons and guest ales, good coffee, daily papers; 24 bedrooms *(P Tailyour, Michael Dandy, Gerry and Rosemary Dobson)*

Oat Hill LE16 8AN [Kettering Rd]: Contemporary bar with mixed furnishings inc sofas; Hook Norton, Oakham, Timothy Taylors and a beer brewed for the pub by Langton, farm ciders and perry, good choice of wines and lagers; enjoyable up-to-date food from sandwiches up, attentive staff, back restaurant; piped music; nice garden, open all day (till 1am Fri, Sat) *(R L Borthwick, Michael Dandy)*

Sugar Loaf LE16 7NJ [High St]: Popular Wetherspoons, smaller than many, with half a dozen sensibly priced real ales, good value food all day; children allowed, frequent beer festivals, open all day *(Michael Dandy, Gerry and Rosemary Dobson, George Atkinson)*

☆ *Three Swans* LE16 7NJ [High St]: Comfortable banquettes and plush-cushioned

library chairs in traditional bay-windowed front bar of Best Western conference hotel; Langton and Wells & Youngs Bombardier, good spread of pubby food from sandwiches up, decent wines, flame-effect fires (one in grand coaching-era inglenook), flagstoned back area; corridor to popular coffee lounge/bistro, more formal upstairs restaurant; piped music; attractive suntrap courtyard, useful parking, good bedrooms *(George Atkinson, Gerry and Rosemary Dobson, John Wooll, Michael Dandy, BB)*

MEDBOURNE [SP7992]

☆ *Nevill Arms* LE16 8EE [B664 Market Harborough—Uppingham]: Handsome Victorian stone-built streamside inn smartened up by newish owners, wide range of enjoyable bar and restaurant food inc Sun roasts, well kept ales such as Fullers London Pride and Greene King IPA; beams and mullion windows, log fires, modern artwork, stylish back restaurant; no dogs; back terrace, garden overlooking stream and village green, 11 nicely refurbished bedrooms, good breakfast, open all day *(R L Borthwick, John Wooll, Ian and Helen Stafford, Mike and Sue Loseby, John Saville, Rona Murdoch, LYM, George Atkinson, Mark Farrington)*

NAILSTONE [SK4107]

Nut & Squirrel CV13 0QE [Main St]: Enjoyable food under current newish couple *(Simon, Kelly, Jack)*

NETHER BROUGHTON [SK6925]

☆ *Red House* LE14 3HB [A606 N of Melton Mowbray]: Substantial and elegant extended Georgian roadside inn, with emphasis on good popular restaurant (best to book), also good more reasonably priced bar food (all day Mon-Thurs, till 7pm Fri, Sat) from sandwiches and local cheeses to steaks, good service; comfortable lounge bar with red leather fireside settees and armchairs, bar on right with TV, changing real ales, fine range of spirits; children welcome in restaurant (50% discount), dogs in bar; courtyard and garden with picnic-sets, eight well equipped stylish bedrooms *(BB, Phil and Jane Hodson)*

NEWTON BURGOLAND [SK3709]

☆ *Belper Arms* LE67 2SE [off B4116 S of Ashby]: Ancient rambling pub said to date from the 13th c, roomy lounge with low-beamed areas off, changing floor levels, stripped brick, open fire, some good antique furniture and plenty to look at inc framed story of the pub ghost; five mainstream ales, farm cider, many wines by the glass, several malt whiskies, reasonably priced food, restaurant; children and dogs welcome, big garden with terrace, open all day *(Mark Toussaint, Dr and Mrs A K Clarke, the Didler, Lee Fraser, Robert F Smith, Ian and Jane Irving, LYM)*

OADBY [SP6399]

Grange Farm LE2 4RH [Glen Rd (A6)]: Roomy Vintage Inn based on early 19th-c farmhouse, friendly young staff, bargain food, good wine choice, Batemans, Black Sheep and Everards, log fires, old local photographs, daily papers, good mix of customers; children welcome, tables out in front, open all day *(Duncan Cloud, R L Borthwick, P Tailyour, Dr and Mrs A K Clarke)*

OAKHAM [SK8508]

Admiral Hornblower LE15 6AS [High St]: Several differently decorated areas from panelling and traditional to fresher informality; warm and inviting with three log fires, good variety of food from snacks to interesting dishes using own herbs, well organised service, well kept ales, conservatory; country-feel garden, comfortable bedrooms *(P Dawn, Michael and Maggie Betton)*

☆ **OLD DALBY** [SK6723]

Crown LE14 3LF [Debdale Hill]: Three or four intimate little farmhouse rooms up and down steps, black beams, one or two antique oak settles among other seats, rustic prints, open fires, several ales inc Belvoir and Castle Rock from recently expanded bar area, plenty of wines by the glass; good up-to-date fresh local food (not Sun evening or Mon) from bar menu or more expensive evening menu, good service, newly extended dining room opening on to terrace; children and dogs welcome, disabled facilities, attractive garden with boules, cl Mon lunchtime *(Phil and Jane Hodson, MP, Dominic Markham, LYM, the Didler)*

PEATLING PARVA [SP5889]

Shires LE17 5PU [Main St]: Large comfortable restaurant rather than pub, wide choice from pubby staples to wknd carvery, three real ales from small bar, conservatory; big garden *(Dennis Jones)*

QUORNDON [SK5516]

Manor House LE12 8AL [Woodhouse Rd]: Newish dining pub with enjoyable if not cheap lunchtime food; handy for station *(John and Helen Rushton)*

REARSBY [SK6414]

Horse & Groom LE7 4YR [Melton Rd (A607)]: Popular village pub with realistically priced food running up to monster steaks, up to four real ales such as Banks's, small dining area upstairs; some live music *(Phil and Jane Hodson)*

SIBSON [SK3500]

Cock CV13 6LB [A444 N of Nuneaton; Twycross Rd]: Ancient, picturesque, black and white timbered and thatched building, Bass and Hook Norton, a dozen wines by the glass; low doorways, heavy black beams and genuine latticed windows, immense inglenook; piped music, games machine; children welcome, tables in courtyard and small garden; handy for Bosworth Field *(Ian and Jane Irving, LYM, Martin Smith)*

SILEBY [SK6014]

Free Trade LE12 7RW [Cossington Rd]: Ancient thatched pub with twisted beams in its two bar areas, friendly staff *(Phil and Jane Hodson)*

SMISBY [SK3418]

Tap House LE65 2TA [Annwell Lane]: Enjoyable food largely from local farms inc good Sun carvery, helpful family service, real ales; terrace tables, play area and covered pool table *(Mr and Mrs Cowan)*

STRETTON [SK9415]

☆ *Ram Jam Inn* LE15 7QX [just off A1 by B668 Oakham turn-off]: Handy for the A1, this bustling dining place serves buffet food and snacks from 7am to 7pm; big open-plan bar/dining area with bucket chairs, sofas and mix of tables, two back rooms, one with fire; daily papers, changing beers such as Wells & Youngs Bombardier, good house wines and coffee; children welcome away from bar, garden tables, comfortable bedrooms, open all day *(LYM, DC, Paul and Ursula Randall, Ryta Lyndley, John Branston, J F M and M West, Dr Kevan Tucker)*

SYSTON [SK6111]

Gate Hangs Well LE7 1NH [Lewin Bridge, Fosse Way (A46)]: Large pub doing well under current licensees, traditional bar and several snug areas, wide range of enjoyable realistically priced food (all day wknds), speedy friendly service; Everards ales and a guest, open fires and lots of photographs, conservatory overlooking terrace; big riverside garden looking over Wreake Valley, pétanque, children's play area; open all day *(Phil and Jane Hodson)*

THORPE LANGTON [SP7492]

☆ *Bakers Arms* LE16 7TS [off B6047 N of Market Harborough]: Civilised restaurant with bar rather than a pub, good regularly changing imaginative food in cottagey beamed linked areas (must book), stylishly simple country décor, well kept local Langton ale, good choice of wines by the glass, friendly attentive staff; no under-12s; garden picnic-sets, cl wkdy lunchtimes, Sun evening and Mon *(LYM, Gerry and Rosemary Dobson, Duncan Cloud, Jeff and Wendy Williams, Mike and Sue Loseby)*

THRUSSINGTON [SK6415]

Star LE7 4UH [The Green]: 18th-c beamed pub reopened in 2008 after refurbishment, enjoyable fairly priced food with some enterprising cooking, good beers and wines; more modern back area; children welcome *(Dian Fear)*

TUGBY [SK7600]

Fox & Hounds LE7 9WB [A47 6 miles W of Uppingham]: Attractively refurbished village-green pub, family-run with friendly landlord, enjoyable food inc mid-week OAP bargains, fine range of well kept ales, Weston's Old Rosie cider; two-level layout with pleasant décor and relaxed atmosphere, real fires; walled terrace *(Michael and Jenny Back, O K Smyth, Allan Westbury)*

TUR LANGTON [SP7194]

Crown LE8 0PJ [off B6047; Main St (follow Kibworth signpost from centre)]: Attractive pub improved under current management, well cooked competitively priced food, prompt friendly service, well kept ales inc

Timothy Taylors Landlord; flagstoned bar with central log fire, side room, back restaurant with own bar; terrace tables *(Gerry and Rosemary Dobson, LYM)*

UPPER HAMBLETON [SK8907]

☆ *Finchs Arms* LE15 8TL [off A606; Oakham Rd]: Stone-built 17th-c inn with outstanding views over Rutland Water, three log fires, bustling beamed and flagstoned bar with nice old wooden furniture inc settles, elegant water-view restaurant with decorative bay trees and wicker/chrome chairs on stripped wood floor; Greene King Abbot, Tetleys, Timothy Taylors Landlord and perhaps a guest, several wines by the glass, food (all day Sun) from panini up inc cheaper set menus, breakfast from 8am; piped music; children welcome, suntrap back hillside terrace, comfortable bedrooms, open all day *(LYM, Bruce and Sharon Eden, Patrick Frew, R L Borthwick, Michael Dandy)*

WALTHAM ON THE WOLDS [SK8024]

Marquis of Granby LE14 4AH [High St]: Friendly stone-built country local with generous bargain pubby food inc lunchtime carvery, quick service, well kept ales, decent wines by the glass, upper games area with pool, skittle alley; children welcome, tables out on decking, cl Mon *(Phil and Jane Hodson)*

WESTON BY WELLAND [SP7791]

Wheel & Compass LE16 8HZ [Valley Rd]: Old stone-built pub with wide choice of enjoyable generous food at attractive prices, Bass, Marstons Pedigree and three changing guests, friendly staff, good wine and soft drinks' choice; comfortable bar, good-sized back dining area and restaurant; children welcome, open all day *(Jim Farmer, Guy and Caroline Howard, JJW, CMW)*

WHITWELL [SK9208]

Noel at Whitwell LE15 8BW [Main Rd (A606)]: Smart spacious pub-restaurant handy for Rutland Water, wide choice of enjoyable well presented food inc good value two-course lunches, friendly service, real ales, decent wines by the glass, good coffee; children welcome, suntrap tables outside, play area, bedrooms *(Roy Bromell, LYM)*

WHITWICK [SK4316]

Three Horseshoes LE67 5GN [Leicester Rd]: Utterly unpretentious unchanging local, friendly long bar and tiny snug, well kept Bass and Marstons Pedigree, log fires, darts, dominoes and cards, newspapers; no food; outdoor lavatories; no proper pub sign so easy to miss *(the Didler, Pete Baker)*

WOODHOUSE EAVES [SK5214]

Old Bulls Head LE12 8RZ [Main St]: Large open-plan dining pub on two levels with enjoyable food inc some interesting dishes, well kept Marstons Pedigree and Timothy Taylors Landlord, reasonable prices, friendly staff; beamery, books and bric-a-brac, games area *(Hunter and Christine Wright)*

WYMESWOLD [SK6023]

☆ *Hammer & Pincers* LE12 6ST [East Rd (A6006)]: Busy restaurant rather than pub with good food, early-bird deals and good value Sat brunch, more expensive evening meals; small smart entrance bar with black leather sofas and armchairs, shallow steps up to linked eating areas with chunky pine furniture, contemporary lighting and big cheery artworks, decent wines, friendly helpful staff; piped music; no real ale; picnic-sets on sheltered well landscaped back terrace, sturdy play area behind *(BB, R L Borthwick, Ron Anderson)*

Three Crowns LE12 6TZ [Far St (A6006)]: Snug chatty 18th-c village local with good friendly staff, good value food inc lots of specials, four or five real ales such as Adnams, Belvoir and Marstons, good soft drinks' choice; pleasant character furnishings in beamed bar and lounge, darts; picnic-sets out on decking *(the Didler, Comus and Sarah Elliott, P Dawn)*

Windmill LE12 6TT [Brook St]: Side street village pub with good food from compact menu using local ingredients, charming quick service, well kept ales; central servery separating bar and smallish (but not cramped) dining area, minimalist décor – a few abstracts on pastel walls; children welcome *(Phil and Jane Hodson, Comus and Sarah Elliott)*

WYMONDHAM [SK8518]

Berkeley Arms LE14 2AG [Main St]: Welcoming new licensees at this attractive 16th-c stone pub, contemporary refurbishment but keeping rustic character in main bar, dining lounge and oak-floor restaurant; enjoyable home-made pubby food (not Sun evening) with more imaginative dishes Thurs-Sat, traditional Sun lunch, Greene King IPA, Marstons Pedigree and guests; piped music, games machine; children welcome (and dogs – not evening), tables out at front and in large garden with decked smokers' shelter, nice village, cl Mon lunchtime *(Ken Marshall, George and Beverley Tucker)*

Post Office address codings confusingly give the impression that some pubs are in Leicestershire, when they're really in Cambridgeshire (which is where we list them).

Lincolnshire

A surprisingly high proportion of the good pubs here have qualified for a Food Award this year. So there's a fine choice for a special meal out: the Blue Bell at Belchford, Brownlow Arms at Hough-on-the-Hill, Inn on the Green at Ingham, Wig & Mitre in Lincoln, George of Stamford, and Chequers at Woolsthorpe. With the Wig & Mitre close on its heels, the civilised George of Stamford, with its well balanced variety of dining options, retains its title of Lincolnshire Dining Pub of the Year. Other pubs giving special enjoyment these days are the Welby Arms in Allington and the Ship at Barnoldby le Beck. This is Batemans country; the archetypal family-owned brewery (with a splendid visitor centre) has quite a few charming traditional tied pubs. Among several smaller, newer local brewers, the top ones to try are Oldershaws, Newby Wyke, Tom Woods and Brewsters.

ALLINGTON   SK8540   MAP 7

Welby Arms 🍷 🍺 🛏

The Green; off A1 at N end of Grantham bypass; NG32 2EA

Friendly inn near A1, with popular food, six real ales and seats outside; pleasant bedrooms

A welcoming oasis from the nearby A1, this is a well run pub with helpful, friendly staff and a bustling atmosphere. The large traditionally furnished bar is divided by a stone archway and has black beams and joists, log fires (one in an attractive arched brick fireplace), red velvet curtains and comfortable burgundy button-back wall banquettes and stools. They keep a fine choice of six real ales on handpump: Adnams Broadside, Badger Tanglefoot, Bass, Jennings Cumberland, John Smiths and Timothy Taylors Landlord. Also, 20 malt whiskies and 22 wines by the glass; piped music. The civilised back dining lounge (where they prefer you to eat) looks out on to tables in a sheltered walled courtyard with pretty summer hanging baskets, and there are more picnic-sets out on the front lawn.

🍽 Popular bar food might include hot and cold filled baguettes, filled baked potatoes, ploughman's, soup, deep-fried whitebait with paprika dusting, home-cooked ham and eggs, home-made burger topped with bacon and cheese, mediterranean vegetable and wild mushroom lasagne, steak and mushroom ale pie, mixed grill and daily specials like black pudding with smoked bacon and a poached free-range egg, lamb and apricot tagine with couscous and pepper-crusted monkfish with a sweet pepper. *Starters/Snacks: £3.95 to £7.95. Main Courses: £6.95 to £7.95. Puddings: £3.95*

Enterprise ~ Lease Matt Rose ~ Real ale ~ Bar food (12-2, 6-9; all day Sun) ~ Restaurant ~ (01400) 281361 ~ No children after 7pm ~ Open 12-3, 6-11; 12-10.30 Sun ~ Bedrooms: £48S/£70S

Recommended by Michael and Jenny Back, Gordon and Margaret Ormondroyd, JJW, CMW, Mrs Brenda Calver, Julian and Jill Tasker, Trevor Gaston, Bruce M Drew, Blaise Vyner, John Robertson, W M Paton, Maurice Ricketts, Leslie and Barbara Owen, Mr and Mrs W D Borthwick

BARNOLDBY LE BECK

TA2303   MAP 8

Ship ♀

Village signposted off A18 Louth—Grimsby; DN37 0BG

Very good fish menu (and other choices) at this tranquil plush dining pub

Of course, many customers are here to enjoy the first-class fish dishes, but drinkers do pop in too, and they have Black Sheep and Timothy Taylors Landlord on handpump, a good wine list, and up to a dozen malt whiskies. It's a neatly kept pub with a friendly welcome and the fine collection of Edwardian and Victorian bric-a-brac is well worth looking at: stand-up telephones, violins, a horn gramophone, bowler and top hats, old racquets, crops, hockey sticks and a lace dress. Heavy dark-ringed drapes swathe the windows, with plants in ornate china bowls on the sills. Furnishings include comfortable dark green plush wall benches with lots of pretty propped-up cushions and heavily stuffed green plush Victorian-looking chairs on a green fleur de lys carpet; piped music. A fenced-off sunny area behind has hanging baskets and a few picnic-sets under pink parasols.

🍴 Using top-quality fish (some of which comes from their own boats), the good food includes scallops with garlic and ginger, cod cheeks with lime and lemon, crispy battered haddock, skate wing with lemon and caper butter, red fish wrapped in parma ham with a button mushroom, bacon and shallot reduction, and salmon and prawn lattice with a creamy leek sauce; non-fishy dishes include sandwiches, chicken liver and Cointreau pâté with redcurrant and mint jelly, thai green vegetable curry, beef in ale pie, duck breast with a honey, chilli and coriander dressing, and chicken breast stuffed with leek and stilton with a smoky bacon sauce. *Starters/Snacks: £5.00 to £6.95. Main Courses: £8.95 to £17.00. Puddings: £4.95 to £5.50*

Inn Business ~ Manager Michele Hancock ~ Real ale ~ Bar food ~ Restaurant ~ (01472) 822308 ~ Children welcome ~ Open 12-3, 6-11(12 Sat)

Recommended by Alistair and Kay Butler, Dr and Mrs J Temporal, Michael and Maggie Betton

BELCHFORD

TF2975   MAP 8

Blue Bell ⊕

Village signposted off A153 Horncastle—Louth (and can be reached by the good Bluestone Heath Road off A16, just under 1.5 miles N of the A1104 roundabout); Main Road; LN9 6LQ

Emphasis on imaginative modern food at a cottagey 18th-c dining pub

They do keep a couple of real ales on handpump in this smart restaurany place, but most customers have booked up to enjoy the first-class food. The cosy comfortable bar has a relaxing pastel décor, some armchairs and settees, as well as more upright chairs around good solid tables, several wines by the glass, and beers like Black Sheep and Riverside Dixons Major. Service is pleasant and attentive. The neat terraced garden behind has picnic-sets, and this is a good base for Wolds walks and the Viking Way; hikers must remove their boots.

🍴 They do have some good value pubby lunchtime dishes like filled ciabatta rolls, beef, mushroom and Guinness pie, sausage and mash with shallot red wine jus, gammon and egg, and breaded scampi, but most emphasis is on the more inventive (and pricey) choices such as crispy black pudding on chive mash topped with onion marmalade and pancetta in a red wine sauce, sliced warm smoked duck breast on stir-fried julienne of vegetables with a balsamic ice-cream, twice-baked cheese soufflé, local ostrich fillet with butternut squash and sage risotto with smoked bacon sauce, and pollack fillet with a fresh herb crust on parmesan and dried tomato mash with a vermouth cream sauce, and puddings like dark chocolate truffle torte and iced bramley apple parfait with a warm cinnamon muffin. *Starters/Snacks: £4.25 to £5.95. Main Courses: £9.50 to £17.95. Puddings: £4.95*

Free house ~ Licensees Darren and Shona Jackson ~ Real ale ~ Bar food ~ Restaurant ~ (01507) 533602 ~ Children welcome ~ Open 11.30-2.30, 6.30-11; 12-4 Sun; closed Sun evening, Mon and second and third weeks in Jan

Recommended by D F Clarke, Derek and Sylvia Stephenson, Chris Brooks, Malcolm Brown, Mrs Brenda Calver

BILLINGBOROUGH   TF1134 MAP 8

Fortescue Arms

B1177, off A52 Grantham—Boston; NG34 0QB

Low-beamed country pub with bric-a-brac, several real ales, traditional food and pretty gardens

The décor and bric-a-brac here are what you'd expect in a traditional rural pub – everything from Victorian prints to fresh flowers and pot plants, brass and copper, a stuffed badger and pheasant, and various quiz books. The several turkey-carpeted rooms have lots of ancient stonework, exposed brickwork, wood panelling and beams, bay-window seats and a big see-through fireplace. Attractive dining rooms at each end have flagstones and another open fire. Unusually, a long red and black tiled corridor runs right the way along behind the serving bar, making it an island. Here you'll find Fullers London Pride, Greene King Abbot, and Swaton Dozy Bull and Happy Jack on handpump; piped music. There are picnic-sets on a lawn under apple trees on one side, and on the other a sheltered courtyard with flowers planted in tubs and a manger. More reports please.

🍴 **Bar food includes sandwiches and filled baguettes, ploughman's, soup, crispy whitebait, several pies, chicken breast in white wine and mushroom sauce, battered cod, a vegetarian dish, roast duck in orange sauce, and steaks; Sunday roasts.** *Starters/Snacks: £4.95 to £6.95. Main Courses: £7.95 to £18.95. Puddings: £3.95 to £5.95*

Charnwood Pub Company ~ Managers Terry and Nicola Williams ~ Real ale ~ Bar food (12-2, 6-9; 12-9 Sun) ~ Restaurant ~ (01529) 240228 ~ Well behaved children in restaurant (in bar until 7pm) ~ Open 12-3, 5.30-11; 12-11 Sat and Sun

Recommended by Brian and Jean Hepworth

CONINGSBY   TF2458 MAP 8

Lea Gate Inn

Leagate Road (B1192 southwards, off A153 E); LN4 4RS

Cosy old-fashioned interior, attractive garden, play area

The three cosy areas in this traditional 16th-c inn are dimly lit and linked together around the corner bar counter, with heavy black beams supporting ochre ceiling boards. They are attractively furnished with a variety of tables and chairs including antique oak settles with hunting-print cushions, and two great high-backed settles forming a snug around the biggest of the fireplaces. In the main lounge, above the fireplace, look out for the engraving titled the 'Last Supper'. It is believed that the last rites were given to condemned criminals here. Adnams, Batemans, Wells & Youngs Bombardier on handpump. The appealing garden has tables and an enclosed play area. At the front of the inn is an enclosure known as Gibbet Nook Close, the site of the gibbet or gallows used for public executions (the bodies were left hanging).

🍴 **Bar food includes lunchtime sandwiches, soup, mushroom stroganoff, cottage pie, chilli con carne, steak and kidney pie, seasonal game dishes, and puddings.** *Starters/Snacks: £3.95 to £6.95. Main Courses: £7.95 to £13.95. Puddings: £1.95 to £3.50*

Free house ~ Licensee Mark Dennison ~ Real ale ~ Bar food (all day Sun) ~ Restaurant ~ (01526) 342370 ~ Children welcome ~ Dogs allowed in bar ~ Open 11.30-3, 6-11; 12-11 Sun ~ Bedrooms: £65B/£85B

Recommended by Anthony Barnes, Janet and Peter Race, John Robertson, Mrs P Bishop, the Didler

---

If a service charge is mentioned prominently on a menu or accommodation terms, you must pay it if service was satisfactory. If service is really bad you are legally entitled to refuse to pay some or all of the service charge as compensation for not getting the service you might reasonably have expected.

DRY DODDINGTON
SK8546   MAP 8

Wheatsheaf

1.5 miles off A1 N of Grantham; Main Street; NG23 5HU

Happy bustling pub with good food cooked by chef/patron; handy for A1

This 16th-c colourwashed village pub is well run by a young enthusiastic couple (Mr Bland is also the chef) and you can be sure of a genuinely warm and friendly welcome. The front bar is basically two rooms – with a woodburning stove, a variety of settles and chairs, and tables in the windows facing across to the green and the lovely 14th-c church with its crooked tower. The serving bar on the right has Greene King Abbot, Timothy Taylors Landlord, Tom Woods Best and a guest ale on handpump, and a nice choice of 11 wines by the glass. A slight slope takes you down to the comfortable thickly carpeted and extended dining room with its relaxing red and cream décor. Once a cow byre, this part is even more ancient than the rest of the building, perhaps dating from the 13th c. The front terrace has neat dark green tables under cocktail parasols, among tubs of flowers; disabled access at the side.

🍴 Using their own-grown vegetables and herbs and supporting small local rare-breed producers, the good food includes filled ciabattas, ploughman's, soup, smoked salmon and scrambled egg, omelettes, black pudding and poached egg salad, chicken with brie and bacon sauce, roast aubergine pasta, loin of gloucester old spot pork with cider gravy, whole plaice with capers and nut-brown butter, and puddings like vanilla panna cotta with home-grown rhubarb and strawberry compote and chocolate torte with toffee ice-cream. *Starters/Snacks: £3.45 to £9.95. Main Courses: £9.95 to £13.95. Puddings: £1.95 to £4.95*

Free house ~ Licensees Dan Bland and Kate Feetham ~ Real ale ~ Bar food (12-2(3 Sun), 6-9(6.30-9.30 Sat; 5-7 Sun); not Mon) ~ Restaurant ~ (01400) 281458 ~ Children welcome ~ Dogs allowed in bar ~ Open 12-2.30, 5-11; 12-11(10.30 Sun) Sat; closed Mon

Recommended by Michael and Jenny Back, Alan Bowker, Beryl and Bill Farmer, A Wadkin

HOUGH-ON-THE-HILL
SK9246   MAP 8

Brownlow Arms 🍴 ♀

High Road; NG32 2AZ

Refined country house with beamed bar, real ales, imaginative food, and a graceful terrace; bedrooms

They do keep Marstons Bitter and Pedigree and Timothy Taylors Landlord on handpump in this terribly smart upmarket old stone inn, though, in practice, most people are here for the sophisticated dining experience (you will probably need to book). The beamed bar is comfortable with plenty of panelling, some exposed brickwork, local prints and scenes, a large mirror and a pile of logs beside the big fireplace. Seating is on elegant stylishly mismatched upholstered armchairs, and the carefully arranged furnishings give the impression of several separate and surprisingly cosy areas; piped easy listening, several wines by the glass and a good choice of malt whiskies served by friendly, impeccably polite staff. The well equipped bedrooms are attractive and breakfasts are hearty.

🍴 First-class (though not cheap) food might include soup, chicken liver parfait with spiced fruit chutney, cheese soufflé with natural smoked haddock, leeks and cream, breast of chicken with black pudding, bacon and creamed cabbage, portobello mushroom, plum tomato, sweet and sour red onions and melting goats cheese, rib-eye of lamb with dauphinoise potatoes and rosemary jus, lemon sole fillets with lemon beurre blanc, and puddings such as chocolate marquise with mandarin sorbet and orange jelly and caramel mousse with apple terrine and almond ice-cream. *Starters/Snacks: £4.95 to £6.95. Main Courses: £14.95 to £18.95. Puddings: £5.95*

Free house ~ Licensee Paul L Willoughby ~ Real ale ~ Bar food (6.30-9.30; 12-2.30 Sun; not lunchtimes Mon) ~ Restaurant ~ (01400) 250234 ~ Children allowed if over 12 ~ Open 6-11; 12-3.30 Sun; closed Mon; two weeks Jan, two weeks Sept, 25 and 26 Dec ~ Bedrooms: £65B/£96B

Recommended by Ruby and Andrew Jones, Michael Holdsworth, D F Clarke, Mr and Mrs B Watt

INGHAM   SK9483   MAP 8

Inn on the Green ⓎⓎ
The Green; LN1 2XT

Nicely modernised place popular for good, thoughtfully prepared food; chatty atmosphere

With a friendly welcome and a warm log fire, this modernised dining pub has a good, chatty atmosphere. And it does still feel like a proper pub – particularly in the locals' bar – despite the emphasis on the popular food. It's quite likely that most tables (apart from the bar) will be occupied by diners – no mean feat given that the beamed and timbered dining room is spread over two floors. There's lots of exposed brickwork, and a mix of brass and copper, local prints and bric-a-brac. The brick bar counter has home-made jams, marmalade and chutney for sale alongside Black Sheep, a couple of guests such as Adnams Explorer and Exmoor Gold, and half a dozen or so wines by the glass. Opposite is a comfortably laid-back area with two red leather sofas; piped music; good service.

🍴 Using some home-grown produce, the good food includes sandwiches, soup, potted pheasant with sweet pickled apple, a mini tapas plate, home-made fishcakes with sweet chilli jam, lightly spiced chestnut and chickpea filo parcel with rocket pesto, chicken breast with mushroom stuffing baked in pastry, halibut fillet with chive and butter sauce, roasted duck breast with coarse grain mustard sauce, escalope of free-range pork with wild mushroom sauce, and puddings like double chocolate mousse and baked lemon cheesecake with orange sorbet. *Starters/Snacks: £3.75 to £5.50. Main Courses: £5.95 to £14.95. Puddings: £3.60 to £4.95*

Free house ~ Licensees Andrew Cafferkey and Sarah Sharpe ~ Real ale ~ Bar food (12-2, 6.30-9(9.30 Fri and Sat); 12-5.30 Sun; not Mon, not Tues lunchtime) ~ Restaurant ~ (01522) 730354 ~ Children only allowed if eating ~ Open 11.30-3, 6-11; 12-11 Sun; closed Mon, 26 Dec, one week Feb, one week Sept

Recommended by Mr and Mrs J L Blakey, G Dobson, Alistair and Kay Butler

LINCOLN   SK9771   MAP 8

Victoria 🍺 £
Union Road; LN1 3BJ

Simple and popular real ale pub with up to nine beers and very good value lunchtime food; new bedrooms

Just the place for a chat and a pint, this is a good old-fashioned back-street local with friendly staff. They keep up to eight real ales on handpump, which might include Batemans XB, Castle Rock Harvest Pale and Timothy Taylors Landlord, and five guests such as Batemans Eggs-B, Derby Dashingly Dark, Grafton Lady Catherine, Oldershaws Caskade and Riverside Dixons Dynamite; also, foreign draught and bottled beers, farm cider and good value soft drinks. They hold beer festivals at the end of June, August bank holiday and at Halloween. The simply furnished little tiled front lounge has a coal fire and pictures of Queen Victoria, and attracts a nicely mixed clientele. Being a proper town pub, it gets especially busy at lunchtime and later on in the evening. There's a small conservatory and heated terraced area with lots of tables and chairs, which has good views of the castle. They now offer bedrooms.

🍴 Basic lunchtime food, from a short menu, includes filled cobs, toasties, baked potatoes, pies, sausage and mash; Sunday roast. *Starters/Snacks: £1.50 to £3.75. Main Courses: £5.95 to £6.95. Puddings: £1.95 to £2.95*

Batemans ~ Tenant Neil Renshaw ~ Real ale ~ Bar food (12-2.30(2 Sun); not evenings) ~ (01522) 541000 ~ Children welcome ~ Dogs allowed in bar ~ Open 11am(12 Sun)-midnight(1am Fri and Sat) ~ Bedrooms: /£69S(£59B)

Recommended by Chris Johnson, John Honnor, the Didler, Ryta Lyndley, John Fiander, John and Helen Rushton

> Post Office address codings confusingly give the impression that a few pubs are in Lincolnshire, when they're really in Cambridgeshire (which is where we list them).

Wig & Mitre ★ ⊕ ♀

Steep Hill; just below cathedral; LN2 1LU

Very popular multi-faceted town bar with imaginative (though not cheap) food all day and a chatty, bustling atmosphere

Full of character and with plenty of attractive period architectural features, this civilised and relaxed café-style dining pub spreads over a couple of floors. The big-windowed beamed downstairs bar has exposed stone walls, pews and gothic furniture on oak floorboards, and comfortable sofas in a carpeted back area. Upstairs, the somewhat calmer dining room is light and airy, with views of the castle walls and cathedral, shelves of old books and an open fire. Walls are hung with antique prints and caricatures of lawyers and clerics, and there are plenty of newspapers and periodicals lying about – even templates to tempt you to a game of noughts and crosses. They have nearly three dozen wines by the glass (from a good list), lots of liqueurs and spirits and well kept Batemans XB and Black Sheep on handpump. It can get busy at peak times, so it's useful to know that you can pop in and get something to eat at almost any time of day.

⊞ **As well as a full breakfast and a sandwich menu, the enjoyable bar food might include soup, chicken thigh and bacon terrine with tomato fondue, black pudding with poached egg and crispy bacon, haddock risotto with leeks, peas and curried butter, lamb scrumpets with garlic, parsley and mint mayonnaise, broccoli vignette and pine nut pastry, chicken with creamed spring greens, blade of beef with caper vierge, confit of duck leg with sour cherries, spring onion tempura and parmentier potatoes, and puddings like dark chocolate steamed sponge with white chocolate sauce and star anise and orange crème brûlée with milk chocolate shortbread.** *Starters/Snacks: £4.50 to £7.95. Main Courses: £10.95 to £24.95. Puddings: £4.95 to £5.25*

Free house ~ Licensee Toby Hope ~ Real ale ~ Bar food (8am-midnight) ~ Restaurant ~ (01522) 535190 ~ Children welcome ~ Dogs allowed in bar ~ Open 8am-midnight

Recommended by Revd R P Tickle, Adrian Johnson, Phil and Jane Hodson, Keith and Chris O'Neill, Mr and Mrs A H Young, Chris Flynn, Wendy Jones, Ryta Lyndley, Richard, Pete Coxon

STAMFORD   TF0306   MAP 8

George of Stamford ★ ⊕ ♀ ⇌

High Street, St Martins (B1081 S of centre, not the quite different central pedestrianised High Street); PE9 2LB

LINCOLNSHIRE DINING PUB OF THE YEAR

Handsome coaching inn, beautifully relaxed and civilised, with very good food and wines, and a lovely courtyard and garden; bedrooms

All very civilised but not in the least bit stuffy, this is an exceptional place on all counts. It's a carefully preserved and rather grand old coaching inn with various lovely reception areas furnished with all manner of seats from leather, cane and antique wicker to soft settees and easy chairs. The central lounge has sturdy timbers, broad flagstones, heavy beams and massive stonework, and the York Bar is surprisingly pubby with a relaxed, local feel. There's an oak-panelled restaurant (jacket or tie required) and a less formal Garden Restaurant which has well spaced furniture on herringbone glazed bricks around a central tropical grove. The staff are professional and friendly, with waiter drinks service in the charming cobbled courtyard at the back: comfortable chairs and tables among attractive plant tubs and colourful hanging baskets on the ancient stone buildings. A fine range of drinks includes Adnams Broadside, Grainstore Triple B and Greene King Ruddles County on handpump, an excellent choice of wines (many of which are italian, with about 17 by the glass), freshly squeezed orange juice and malt whiskies. The immaculately kept walled garden is beautifully planted and there's a sunken lawn where croquet is often played.

⊞ **Quality as high as this does come at a price. York Bar snacks include sandwiches and toasties, ploughman's, soup, chicken liver pâté with cumberland sauce, and sausages and mash. In the restaurants there might be moules marinière, caesar salads with chargrilled chicken or cajun salmon, eggs benedict, home-ground beefburger with cheese, smoked** bacon, garlic mayonnaise and chilli, pasta with tomato and basil sauce finished with cream, rump of lamb in a garlic and herb crust with redcurrant and rosemary jus, seared calves liver with crispy pancetta and sage fritters, fillet of brill with girolle mushrooms and chervil, and puddings. Their morning coffee and full afternoon teas are popular. *Starters/Snacks: £5.50 to £10.70. Main Courses: £7.35 to £19.35. Puddings: £6.45*

Free house ~ Licensees Chris Pitman and Ivo Vannocci ~ Real ale ~ Bar food (12-11) ~ Restaurant ~ (01780) 750750 ~ Children over 10 in restaurant ~ Dogs allowed in bar and bedrooms ~ Open 11(12 Sun)-11 ~ Bedrooms: £93B/£132B

Recommended by Louise English, Ryta Lyndley, Gerry and Rosemary Dobson, Paul Humphreys, Roy Hoing, John Wooll, J F M and M West, John Honnor, Michael Dandy, Michael Sargent, W N F Boughey, Mike and Sue Loseby, Rosemary K Germaine, the Didler, Eithne Dandy, Roy Bromell, Pete Coxon, D F Clarke, Mrs P Bishop, Edward Mirzoeff

STOW

SK8881   MAP 8

Cross Keys

Stow Park Road; B1241 NW of Lincoln; LN1 2DD

Reliable dining pub with traditional décor

Mr and Mrs Davies have been running this reliable, extended dining pub for over 20 years now. Many customers are here to enjoy the good food and most tend to head for the cosy, popular bar. This is carpeted and fairly traditional with a big woodburner, dark wheelback chairs and tables, dark wood panelling, country prints on cream walls and decorative china on a delft shelf; piped music. Further in, you'll find a couple of neatly laid dining areas. Fairly priced drinks include Batemans XB, Greene King Old Speckled Hen, and Theakstons Best and Old Peculier on handpump. Well worth a visit, nearby Stow Minster is notable for its fantastic Saxon arches and, among other things, its Viking ship graffiti.

🏮 **Bar food includes sandwiches, twiced-baked cheese soufflé with red onion marmalade, duck and port pâté with plum and apple chutney, dill pancakes filled with crab and asparagus, sausages on parsley mash with gravy, pasta with mediterranean vegetables in a tomato sauce, lambs liver with bacon and onion sauce, lamb cutlets with a redcurrant and rosemary gravy, breast of gressingham duck with an orange and grand marnier sauce, and puddings like vanilla panna cotta with caramelised oranges and steamed treacle sponge with custard.** *Starters/Snacks: £3.95 to £8.00. Main Courses: £8.95 to £17.00. Puddings: £4.75*

Free house ~ Licensees Richard and Helen Davies ~ Real ale ~ Bar food (12-2, 6-10; all day Sun; not Mon) ~ Restaurant ~ (01427) 788314 ~ Children welcome ~ Open 12-3, 6-11; 12-8 Sun; closed Mon (except bank hols)

Recommended by Dr and Mrs J Temporal, Mrs Jennifer Marris

WOOLSTHORPE

SK8334   MAP 8

Chequers 🍴 🍷

The one near Belvoir, signposted off A52 or A607 W of Grantham; NG32 1LU

Interesting food at comfortably relaxed inn with good drinks; appealing castle views from outside tables

This is the sort of enjoyable pub that our readers return to again and again. It's a 17th-c coaching inn run with great care by the friendly licensees, and the heavy-beamed main bar has two big tables (one a massive oak construction), a comfortable mix of seating including some handsome leather chairs and leather banquettes, and a huge boar's head above a good log fire in the big brick fireplace. Among cartoons on the wall are some of the illustrated claret bottle labels from the series commissioned from famous artists, initiated by the late Baron Philippe de Rothschild. The lounge on the right has a deep red colour scheme, leather sofas and a big plasma TV, and on the left there are more leather seats in a dining area in what was once the village bakery. A corridor leads off to the light and airy main restaurant, with contemporary pictures, and another bar; piped music. Everards Tiger and Wadworths 6X on handpump, over 30 wines by the glass,

50 malt whiskies, and local fruit pressés. There are good quality teak tables, chairs and benches outside and, beyond these, some picnic-sets on the edge of the pub's cricket field, with views of Belvoir Castle.

🍽 Good, often interesting bar food includes sandwiches, soup, terrine of confit duck with orange and port syrup, risotto of wild mushrooms and truffles, beer-battered haddock, home-made pie or burger with melted cheese, moules marinière, wild mushroom and lentil gratin, breast of chicken with tomato and tarragon sauce, cassoulet of pork belly with chorizo and white beans, and puddings like lemon panna cotta with raspberry sorbet and sticky toffee pudding with butterscotch sauce; they have an early-bird deal and a three-course set option. *Starters/Snacks: £4.95 to £6.50. Main Courses: £10.00 to £10.50. Puddings: £5.50 to £6.50*

Free house ~ Licensee Justin Chad ~ Real ale ~ Bar food (12-2.30, 6-9.30; 12-4, 6-8.30 Sun) ~ Restaurant ~ (01476) 870701 ~ Children welcome ~ Dogs allowed in bar and bedrooms ~ Open 12-3, 5.30-11; 12-11(10.30 Sun) Sat ~ Bedrooms: £49B/£59B

Recommended by Alan and Jill Bull, J B Young, Felicity Davies, Bob and Angela Brooks, M Mossman, Gordon and Margaret Ormondroyd, John Honnor, Michael and Maggie Betton, Trevor Gaston

LUCKY DIP

Besides the fully inspected pubs, you might like to try these Lucky Dips recommended to us and described by readers (if you do, please send us reports: feedback@goodguides.com).

BRANDY WHARF [TF0196]
☆ *Cider Centre* DN21 4RU [B1205 SE of Scunthorpe (off A15 about 16 miles N of Lincoln)]: Up to 15 draught ciders, many more in bottles etc, also country wines and meads; plain take-us-as-you-find-us bright main bar and dimmer lounge with lots of cider memorabilia and jokey bric-a-brac, reasonably priced straightforward food (all day Sun); piped music; children in eating area, simple glazed verandah, tables and play area in meadows or by river with moorings and slipway, open all day wknds, may be cl Mon *(the Didler, LYM, Rosemary K Germaine)*

CASTLE BYTHAM [SK9818]
☆ *Castle Inn* NG33 4RZ [off A1 Stamford—Grantham, or B1176]: Comfortable black-beamed 17th-c village pub with landlady cooking enjoyable food from good value snacks up; friendly staff, Adnams Bitter, Newby Wyke Bear Island, Wells & Youngs Bombardier and two changing guests, occasional beer festivals, good cider, good hot drinks; mixed wooden furniture, huge blazing fire; children and dogs welcome, disabled access, tables on back terrace, cl wkdy lunchtimes but may open for advance group bookings *(Michael and Jenny Back, LYM)*

CLAYPOLE [SK8449]
Five Bells NG23 5BJ [Main St]: Well kept village pub with lots of bric-a-brac in long beamed bar, popular all-day dining area beyond servery, three real ales, good choice of other drinks, reasonable prices, good friendly service, back pool room and darts; open all day wknds, grassy back garden with play area *(Phil and Jane Hodson)*

CLEETHORPES [TA3009]
No 2 Refreshment Room DN35 8AX [Station Approach]: Half a dozen well kept ales in comfortably refurbished, carpeted platform bar, friendly staff; no food; tables out under heaters, open all day from 9am *(the Didler)*

☆ *Willys* DN35 8RQ [Highcliff Rd; south promenade]: Open-plan bistro-style seafront pub with panoramic Humber views, café tables, tiled floor and painted brick walls; visibly brews its own good beers, also Batemans and other changing ales, belgian beers, good value home-made lunches; friendly staff, nice mix of customers from young and trendy to weather-beaten fishermen; quiet juke box; a few tables out on the prom, open all day *(the Didler)*

EPWORTH [SE7803]
Red Lion DN9 1EU [Market Pl]: Welcoming hotel bar with several separate beamed areas, roaring fire, decorative leaded glass, some stripped brick; decent food inc Sun roast, children's menu, two or three real ales, restaurant, armchairs in conservatory; piped music or juke box, games machine; dogs allowed in courtyard, bedrooms; handy for Old Rectory – John Wesley's birthplace *(JJW, CMW)*

GAINSBOROUGH [SK8189]
Eight Jolly Brewers DN21 2DW [Ship Court, Silver St]: Small comfortable real ale pub with up to eight from small breweries (one at a bargain price), farm cider, country wines, simple lunchtime food (not Sun); friendly staff and locals, beams, bare bricks and brewery posters, quieter areas upstairs, folk club; terrace, open all day *(the Didler)*

GEDNEY [TF4024]
Old Black Lion PE12 0BJ [Main Rd]: Cosy country pub with hospitable landlord, good choice of enjoyable reasonably priced traditional food, children's helpings, good service, Greene King Abbot and Wells & Youngs Bombardier, decent house wines;

beer garden, bedrooms *(John Wooll, S Holder)*

GRANTHAM [SK9136]

☆ *Blue Pig* NG31 6RQ [Vine St]: Small three-bar Tudor pub with good value basic pub lunches, home-baked bread, OAP bargains, half a dozen interesting changing ales, quick cheerful service; low beams, panelling, stripped stone and flagstones, open fire, daily papers, lots of pig ornaments, prints and bric-a-brac; piped music, juke box, games machines; no children or dogs; tables out behind, open all day *(the Didler, Alan and Eve Harding, Trevor Gaston, BB)*

Chequers NG31 6LR [Market Pl]: Basic, friendly, open-plan local, popular for its good range of well kept changing ales, often unusual; beer-related magazines, juke box, games machine; open all day *(the Didler)*

Lord Harrowby NG31 9AB [Dudley Rd, S of centre]: Friendly 60s-feel local, lots of RAF pictures and memorabilia in pleasant lounge, well kept Wells & Youngs Bombardier, Tom Woods Best and guest beers; games-oriented public bar; cl wkdy lunchtimes, open all day wknds *(the Didler)*

Nobody Inn NG31 6NU [North St]: Friendly; basic, bare-boards open-plan local with five or six good mainly local ales inc Newby Wyke; back games room with pool, table football; sports TV; open all day *(the Didler)*

GREAT CASTERTON [SK9909]

Plough PE9 4AA [Main St]: Unassuming pub with newish licensees doing enjoyable and interesting food (not Sun evening or Mon), using carefully sourced supplies, real ales and good choice of wines by the glass; comfortable bow-windowed bar and neatly refurbished dining room; picnic-sets out on sheltered lawn with weeping willow *(BB)*

GREATFORD [TF0811]

Hare & Hounds PE9 4QA: Appealing dining pub doing well under new owners; wide choice of good fresh food inc very popular bargain lunch (worth booking), pleasant staff, well kept ales such as Adnams Broadside, Oakham and Charles Wells Bombardier, large beamed bar, smaller dining room; picnic-sets in small back garden; attractive village *(LYM, Steve Spooner)*

HAXEY [SK7699]

Loco DN9 2HY [Church St (B1396)]: Flagstoned shop conversion, friendly and chatty, with front of a steam loco' in the comfortable lounge; two real ales, good wine choice, blackboard bar food inc Sun roasts, also indian restaurant/evening takeaways (not Mon); pool room; TV, games machine; disabled access, bedrooms *(JJW, CMW)*

IRNHAM [TF0226]

Griffin NG33 4JG [Bulby Rd]: Small old stone-built pub taken in hand by enthusiastic new licensees, enjoyable generous home-made food, new bar furniture, refurbished dining room, log fires; nice village setting *(Tim Miller-Dewing)*

KIRKBY ON BAIN [TF2462]

Ebrington Arms LN10 6YT [Main St]:

Enjoyable, generous, good value food inc cheap Sun lunch, five or more well kept changing ales such as Black Sheep, prompt welcoming service, daily papers; low 16th-c beams, two open fires, nicely set out dining areas each side, copper-topped tables, wall banquettes, jet fighter and racing car pictures; games area with darts, back restaurant; beer festivals Easter and Aug bank hols; may be piped music; wheelchair access, tables out in front, swings on side lawn, camp site behind, open all day *(Alistair and Kay Butler, W M Lien)*

KIRMINGTON [TA1011]

Marrowbone & Cleaver DN39 6YZ [High St]: Popular and friendly with wide choice of good value unpretentious food, well kept ales inc Timothy Taylors Landlord *(Trevor and Sylvia Millum, C A Hall)*

LEADENHAM [SK9452]

Willoughby Arms LN5 0PP [High St; A17 Newark—Sleaford]: Stripped stone and beams, good reasonably priced food, well kept beer; handy for Viking Way walks; bedrooms *(Tully)*

LINCOLN [SK9871]

Dog & Bone LN2 5BH [John St]: Comfortable and neatly kept, with light bar lunches, well kept ales inc Batemans, open fires, exchange-library of recent fiction; picnic-sets on gravel terrace *(Michael and Maggie Betton)*

Morning Star LN2 4AW [Greetwell Gate]: Friendly traditional local, handy for cathedral; enjoyable good value lunches, reasonably priced Bass, Greene King, Tetleys, Wells & Youngs Bombardier and guest beers, helpful service; coal fire, aircraft paintings, two bar areas and comfortable snug, some live music; nice covered outside area, open all day *(Pete Baker, the Didler)*

Pyewipe LN1 2BG [Saxilby Rd; off A57 just S of bypass]: Much extended and well worn-in 18th-c waterside pub, particularly popular for Sun lunch, wide range of other decent food inc good fish choice, friendly attentive staff, well kept Boddingtons, Greene King Abbot, Timothy Taylors Landlord and Wells & Youngs Bombardier; great position by Roman Fossdyke Canal (nice two-mile walk out from centre); pleasant tables outside, comfortable reasonably priced bedroom block *(Stephen Colling)*

☆ *Strugglers* LN1 3BG [Westgate]: Smartly simple characterful local with thriving atmosphere, six well kept mainstream ales with a guest like Rudgate Ruby, above-average low-priced food (from 10.30am-2.45pm, not Sun) inc fresh Grimsby fish; coal-effect fire in back snug, interesting pictures, live music; no children inside; dogs welcome on leads after 3pm, heaters and canopy for terrace tables, open all day (till 1am Thurs-Sat) *(John and Helen Rushton, the Didler, Julian Saunders, Pete Coxon)*

Treaty of Commerce LN5 7AF [High St]: Warmly welcoming, lively and simple pub in beamed Tudor building, fine stained glass, panelling, etchings; good value bar lunches from generous baguettes up, well kept Batemans and guest beers, darts; open all day *(the Didler, John and Helen Rushton)*

LITTLE BYTHAM [TF0117]

Willoughby Arms NG33 4RA [Station Rd, S of village]: Former 19th-c private railway station, well kept Batemans XB, Ufford White Hart and four interesting guests inc a porter (beer festivals), Weston's farm cider, reasonably priced substantial food from baguettes up, friendly helpful staff; daily papers, leather sofa and armchairs on bare boards, coal fire, cellar bar, some live music inc an annual festival; piped music; children and dogs welcome, good disabled access, picnic-sets in pleasant good-sized back garden with country views, three bedrooms, good breakfast, open all day *(the Didler, Mike Markwick, BB)*

LITTLE LONDON [TF2421]

Golden Ball PE11 3AA [River Bank]: Well run traditional pub with good atmosphere, enjoyable restaurant-standard food at pub prices *(Robert Darnell)*

LONG BENNINGTON [SK8344]

☆ *Reindeer* NG23 5DJ [just off A1 N of Grantham]: Thriving atmosphere in old inn with popular long-serving landlady; enjoyable home-made food from good sandwiches up in bar and more formal dining lounge, cut-price small helpings, good choice of well kept ales, good wines *(D F Clarke, Maurice and Janet Thorpe)*

LOUTH [TF3190]

Brackenborough Hotel LN11 0SZ [Brackenborough, off A16 N]: Sensibly priced generous food inc fish specialities, refreshing modern furnishings in two welcoming bars with well kept real ale and good choice of bottled beers; 24 comfortable bedrooms *(RS, ES)*

Wheatsheaf LN11 9YD [Westgate]: Cheerful 17th-c low-beamed pub nr interesting church; coal fires in all three bars, changing ales, inexpensive food from breakfast on, inc bargain OAP lunches, nice staff, old photographs; can get busy; tables outside, open all day Sat *(Val and Alan Green, Roy Bromell, the Didler)*

NETTLEHAM [TF0075]

Plough LN2 2NR [just off A46/A15; 1 The Green]: Spotless old stone-built village local with lovely hanging baskets, good choice of enjoyable reasonably priced food inc bargain OAP lunches (Mon-Sat), four well kept ales inc Batemans, obliging landlady; darts; quiz night; quiet piped music; under-18s discouraged, no dogs, parking can be tricky *(JJW, CMW)*

NEWTON [TF0436]

Red Lion NG34 0EE [off A52 E of Grantham]: Country pub of some character, beams and partly stripped-stone walls with old farm tools and stuffed animals, open fire and woodburner; well kept Oldershaws Newton's Drop, Thatcher's cider, enjoyable home-made food (not Sun, Mon evenings) from

sandwiches up inc carvery (Weds, Sun lunch), restaurant; piped music; children and dogs welcome, disabled access, tables in sheltered back garden with terrace and barbecue *(LYM, Mr and Mrs Staples)*

ROTHWELL [TF1499]

☆ *Blacksmiths Arms* LN7 6AZ [off B1225 S of Caistor]: Pleasant low-beamed bar divided by arches and a warm coal fire, spacious dining area; Black Sheep, Tom Woods Shepherds Delight and three guests, several malt whiskies, enjoyable pubby food, pool; piped music, games machine; children welcome, plenty of tables outside, walks on nearby Viking Way and Lincolnshire Wolds; open all day wknds *(Tim and Claire Woodward, LYM, Alistair and Kay Butler)*

SANDILANDS [TF5280]

Grange & Links LN12 2RA [Sea Lane, off A52 nr Sutton on Sea]: Attractive hotel popular with older people for good value generous food (and the golf), Batemans and Wadworths 6X and wide choice of other drinks in neat bars; fine gardens with play areas (and tennis courts), some 200 yards from good beach, comfortable bedrooms *(RS, ES)*

SCOTTER [SE8800]

☆ *White Swan* DN21 3UD [The Green]: Comfortable well kept dining pub, enjoyable well prepared generous food inc bargain set lunches and early evening deals (Mon-Sat), welcoming cheerful staff, Black Sheep, John Smiths, Websters and interesting changing guest beers; several levels inc snug panelled area by fireplace, big-windowed raftered restaurant looking over lawn with picnic-sets to duck-filled River Eau (best to book wknds); piped music, steps up to entrance; children welcome, 14 comfortable bedrooms in modern extension, open all day Fri-Sun *(BB, Alistair and Kay Butler)*

SKEGNESS [TF5661]

☆ *Vine* PE25 3DB [Vine Rd, off Drummond Rd, Seacroft]: Best Western hotel based on late 18th-c country house; well kept Batemans ales, good generous bar food using local produce, welcoming fire, imposing antique seats and grandfather clock in turkey-carpeted hall, inner oak-panelled room, restaurant; big back sheltered lawn with swings, comfortable bedrooms, peaceful suburban setting not far from beach and bird-watching; open all day *(the Didler, Barry Collett, BB)*

SLEAFORD [TF0645]

Barge & Bottle NG34 7TR [Carre St]: Large busy open-plan pub handsomely done by local furniture-making family; impressive range of nine well kept changing ales, wide range of usual food from baguettes to full meals and good value Sun carvery, also children's dishes, teas, bargain early breakfasts and plenty of special offers; back restaurant/conservatory, friendly efficient staff; piped music; riverside terrace, children welcome, handy for arts centre, open all day *(Brian and Anna Marsden)*

SOUTH ORMSBY [TF3675]
☆ *Massingberd Arms* LN11 8QS [off A16 S of Louth]: Small brick-built village local, friendly and relaxed, with unusual arched windows; obliging landlord, good range of changing ales, short choice of good fresh food inc game and good Sun lunch, restaurant; no credit cards; pleasant garden, good Wolds walks; open all day Weds-Sun, cl Mon lunchtime *(the Didler)*

SOUTH RAUCEBY [TF0245]
Bustard NG34 8QG [Main St]: Much modernised, beamed, stone-built pub with good bar food inc unusual dishes, well kept ales, welcoming staff; comfortable plush seating, log fire, pictures of bustards and other birds, small dining area; children welcome, attractive sheltered garden *(BB, Sarah Flynn)*

SOUTH WITHAM [SK9219]
Blue Cow NG33 5QB [just off A1 Stamford—Grantham]: Unpretentious two-bar pub serving its own-brew beers from big central counter, dark low beams and standing timbers, stripped stone, old fireplace, cottagey windows, flowery carpets and flagstones; food all day from sandwiches up inc popular Weds OAP lunch and Sun carvery, smallish restaurant, pool, darts; piped music, TVs; children and dogs welcome, attractive garden with terrace tables, bedrooms, open all day *(the Didler, LYM, Gordon and Margaret Ormondroyd, Pete Coxon)*

STAMFORD [TF0207]
☆ *Crown* PE9 2AG [All Saints Pl]: Substantial modernised stone-built hotel with emphasis on good seasonal country cooking, using local produce, from good sandwiches up; friendly helpful staff, well kept Adnams, Fullers and Ufford ales, decent wines, whiskies and coffee; spacious main bar, long leather-cushioned bar counter, substantial pillars, step up to more traditional flagstoned area with stripped stone and lots of leather sofas and armchairs, civilised dining room; back courtyard, 26 comfortable bedrooms, good breakfast, open all day *(Gerry and Rosemary Dobson, BB, Michael Dandy, Eithne Dandy, Paul Humphreys)*

Kings Head PE9 2AZ [Maiden Lane]: Carefully refurbished beamed pub with friendly accommodating landlord, well kept Fullers London Pride, Greene King Abbot, Timothy Taylors Landlord, Woodfordes Wherry and a guest beer, good choice of wines by the glass; simple lunchtime bar food, woodburner; two levels *(Clare Jackson)*

Tobie Norris PE9 2BE [St Pauls St]: Great period atmosphere in carefully run flagstoned pub with well kept Adnams, Ufford White Hart and three guest beers; good pizzas especially the one with duck (no food Fri-Sun evenings); open all day *(Sarah Flynn, David Carr)*

SURFLEET [TF2528]
☆ *Mermaid* PE11 4AB [B1356 (Gosberton Rd), just off A16 N of Spalding]: Traditional pub

with two high-ceilinged carpeted rooms, huge netted sash windows, navigation lanterns, banquettes and stools; small central glass-backed counter with Babycham décor, Adnams Broadside and Greene King IPA and Abbot, good choice of straightforward food, friendly staff, restaurant with similar décor; piped music; pretty terraced garden with bar and seats under thatched parasols, children's play area walled from River Glen, open all day summer *(Michael and Jenny Back, M J Winterton, Beryl and Bill Farmer, LYM)*

SUSWORTH [SE8302]
☆ *Jenny Wren* DN17 3AS [East Ferry Rd]: Neatly kept, in nice setting overlooking the River Trent, long partly divided bar/dining area, good enterprising reasonably priced food inc lots of fish and local produce, pleasant relaxed service, real ales such as John Smiths and Tom Woods, good wines by the glass; two open fires, panelling, stripped brickwork, low beams and brasses, busy décor; terrace picnic-sets, more across quiet road by water *(BB, Derek and Sylvia Stephenson)*

TATTERSHALL THORPE [TF2159]
Blue Bell LN4 4PE [Thorpe Rd; B1192 Coningsby—Woodhall Spa]: Attractive very low-beamed pub said to date from the 13th c and used by the Dambusters; RAF memorabilia and appropriate real ales such as Tom Woods Bomber County, well priced pubby bar food, log fires, small dining room; garden tables, bedrooms *(Andy and Jill Kassube, the Didler)*

THEDDLETHORPE ALL SAINTS [TF4787]
Kings Head LN12 1PB [off A1031 N of Maplethorpe; Mill Rd]: Remote 15th-c thatched and low-beamed pub doing well under current good licensees; food in carpeted bar and dining room well above average, using fresh local produce with plenty of fish, lunchtime deals; open fires, Batemans XB and two guest beers – often from the North-East; open all day wknds, cl Mon *(Robert Vevers)*

WAINFLEET [TF5058]
☆ *Batemans Brewery* PE24 4JE [Mill Lane, off A52 via B1195]: Circular bar in brewery's ivy-covered windmill tower, with Batemans ales in top condition, czech and belgian beers on tap; ground-floor dining area with unpretentious lunchtime food such as local sausages and pork pies, plenty of old pub games (more outside), lots of brewery memorabilia and plenty for families to enjoy; entertaining brewery tours at 2.30pm, brewery shop (helpful service), tables out on terrace and grass, opens 11.30-3.30pm *(the Didler, John Honnor)*

WESTON [TF2925]
☆ *Chequers* PE12 6RA [High Rd]: Good inventive food (not Sun evening) using local produce – best to book evenings and wknds; nice wines, cool uncluttered contemporary décor, bare boards, leather sofas and armchairs, comfortable dining areas; disabled

access, garden with heated covered terrace and play area, open all day Sun, cl Mon *(Sally Anne and Peter Goodale, Ken Marshall)*

WOODHALL SPA [TF1962]

☆ *Abbey Lodge* LN10 6UH [B1192 towards Coningsby]: Family-run roadside inn with enjoyable reasonably priced food from sandwiches up, affable staff, nice pubby feel mixing eating and drinking sides well; bustling discreetly decorated bar with good choice of beers and wines, Victorian and older furnishings, World War II RAF pictures, Marstons Pedigree; children over 10 in restaurant, may be piped music; cl Sun *(John Robertson, John Branston, LYM, Mr and Mrs J Brown)*

Village Limits LN10 6UJ [Stixwould Rd]: Landlord/chef doing good choice of reasonably priced local food inc enjoyable Sun lunch, well kept ales such as Batemans, Poachers and Tom Woods, friendly service; smallish bar with plush banquettes and aeroplane prints; nine courtyard bedrooms *(Mr and Mrs J Brown, RS, ES, Mrs Brenda Calver)*

WRAGBY [TF1378]

Turnor Arms LN8 5QU [Market Pl (A158 Lincoln—Skegness)]: Comfortable, recently refurbished and friendly, with enjoyable generous locally sourced blackboard food cooked by landlord; well kept Tom Woods ales *(Malcolm Brown)*

A very few pubs try to make you leave a credit card at the bar, as a sort of deposit if you order food. They are not entitled to do this. The credit card firms and banks which issue them warn you not to let them out of your sight. If someone behind the counter used your card fraudulently, the card company or bank could in theory hold you liable, because of your negligence in letting a stranger hang on to your card. Suggest instead that if they feel the need for security, they 'swipe' your card and give it back to you. And do name and shame the pub to us.

Norfolk

This is now one of the UK's best areas for good pubs. We've a fine choice of new entries here, each quite different, with real individual character: the Crown in Burston (really friendly and relaxed), George in Cley next the Sea (smashing for a drink or meal after a walk out on the nearby bird marshes), Crown in East Rudham (contemporary, stylish and very friendly, with excellent food and drink), Dabbling Duck at Great Massingham (civilised, cosy and welcoming), Hunny Bell at Hunworth (newly refurbished, good all round), Kings Head at Letheringsett (same small group as Crown in East Rudham, similar virtues), Jolly Farmers at North Creake (easy-going village pub), Eagle in Norwich (another fine all-rounder), and Ship at Weybourne (six real ales in this cheerful village pub). Other pubs well worth mentioning are the Kings Head at Bawburgh, White Horse at Brancaster Staithe, Hoste Arms in Burnham Market, Pigs at Edgefield, Walpole Arms at Itteringham, Fat Cat in Norwich, Gin Trap at Ringstead, Rose & Crown in Snettisham, Three Horseshoes at Warham, Crown and Globe both in Wells-next-the-Sea, and Fur & Feather at Woodbastwick. Many of the pubs listed above offer exceptional food, but it's a new entry, the Crown in East Rudham, which takes the top title of Norfolk Dining Pub of the Year. Notable Dips are the Buckinghamshire Arms at Blickling, Kings Head at Coltishall, Rose & Crown at Harpley, Buck at Honingham and King William IV at Sedgeford. Woodfordes is the county's outstanding brewer. There is a host of other worthwhile small local breweries, led by Wolf, Yetmans, Brancaster, Beeston, Humpty Dumpty and Grain.

AYLSHAM

Black Boys 🍷 🍴 🛏

Market Place, just off B1145; NR11 6EH

Good value food with lots of fresh fish in this nicely updated traditional market-place inn with a warm-hearted bar

'A cracking pub' is how one of our readers describes this bustling place. The quite imposing Georgian façade fronts a building which dates back to 1650 but it's been appealingly brought up to date inside: high dark beams in the ochre ceiling, some walls stripped back to the warm red brickwork with a dark-panelled dado, neat wood flooring, and comfortably old-fashioned chairs or built-in wall seats around good well spaced solid tables. Friendly helpful young staff jolly along the cheery thriving atmosphere in the bar and the adjoining dining area. Adnams Best and Woodfordes Wherry and couple of guests such as Adnams Broadside and Batemans XB on handpump, and a large choice of decent wines by the glass. Neat modern tables and chairs out in front face the market place. The four bedrooms (there's a £5 charge for dogs if they stay) are attractively refurbished.

🍴 With some fair priced snacks and light meals, the generous helpings of well liked bar food includes sandwiches, filled baguettes and baked potatoes, ploughman's, soup, deep-fried devilled local sprats, ham and egg, home-made vegetable quiche, giant bowl of moules marinière, sausage and mash with onion gravy, and red thai chicken curry, with more elaborate choices such as baked mini camembert with tomato compote, kiln roast salmon with watercress salad, halibut with brown shrimp butter, five-spice roasted duck with stir-fried noodles, monkfish and scallops with smoked bacon lardons, white wine and cream, and roast chicken with wholegrain mustard sauce and dauphinoise potatoes. *Starters/Snacks: £4.75 to £6.95. Main Courses: £9.95 to £19.95. Puddings: £4.75*

Unique (Enterprise) ~ Lease Matthew Miller ~ Real ale ~ Bar food (11-2, 6-9.30; all day Sun) ~ Restaurant ~ (01263) 732122 ~ Children welcome ~ Dogs welcome ~ Open 11-11; 12-10.30 Sun ~ Bedrooms: £51.50B/£57.50B

Recommended by John Wooll, Mrs Hilarie Taylor, William Mack, Ian and Nita Cooper

BAWBURGH
TG1508   MAP 5

Kings Head ⊕ ♀

Pub signposted down Harts Lane off B1108, which leads off A47 just W of Norwich; NR9 3LS

Bustling old pub, small rooms with plenty of atmosphere, cheerful service, wide choice of interesting bar food and several real ales

With pleasant, helpful service and long-serving owners (the same family have been here for 25 years now), this 17th-pub is a popular place with a good mix of customers; to be sure of a table at peak times, it's best to book in advance. There are leather sofas and seats, a variety of nice old wooden tables and wooden or leather dining chairs on stripped wooden floors, low beams and some standing timbers, a warming log fire in a large knocked-through canopied fireplace, and a couple of woodburning stoves in the restaurant areas. Adnams Bitter and Broadside, Woodfordes Wherry and a guest such as Fullers London Pride on handpump,16 wines by the glass and several malt whiskies; piped music. There are seats outside in the garden and a little green opposite.

📖 They list their suppliers on the monthly changing menu which might include sandwiches, nibbles like home-made pork scratchings, beef dripping on toast and home-made pork pie, soup, jellied ham hock and parsley with piccalilli and kettle crisps, fishcakes with green sauce and lemon oil, free-range ham with free-range egg, beef and ale sausages with slow-roasted treacle onions and rich beef bone gravy, beetroot, caraway and vodka risotto with blue cheese fritters and wild garlic and nettle pesto, beer-battered locally caught cod, free-range chicken breast with pancetta and wild mushroom and tarragon sauce, and puddings like coconut parfait, mango curd and a cookie, and a trio of puddings (bakewell tart, sherry trifle and bread pudding). *Starters/Snacks: £4.50 to £5.95. Main Courses: £10.50 to £20.50. Puddings: £5.50 to £6.50*

Free house ~ Licensee Anton Wimmer ~ Real ale ~ Bar food (12-2, 5.30-9; 12-6 Sun) ~ Restaurant ~ (01603) 744977 ~ Children welcome ~ Open 11-11; 12-10.30 Sun; closed evenings 25 and 26 Dec and 1 Jan

Recommended by John Robertson, Derek and Maggie Washington, Sally Anne and Peter Goodale, Ian and Nita Cooper, John Millwood, John Cook, David and Cathrine Whiting

BINHAM
TF9839   MAP 8

Chequers ◖

B1388 SW of Blakeney; NR21 0AL

Friendly, hard-working licensees, own-brewed beers and generous helpings of pubby food

This is a very rewarding pub and a favourite with many of its customers. Run by hard-working, extremely friendly licensees, there's a cheerful, happy atmosphere, hearty, generous bar food and own-brewed real ales. From their brewery, these Front Street ales include Binham Cheer, Callum's Ale, Ebony Stout and Unity Strong. They also keep around 30 belgian bottled beers and decent house wines. The long low-beamed building has splendid coal fires at each end, sturdy plush seats and some nice old local prints. There are picnic-sets out in front and on the grass behind the building. This is an interesting village with a huge priory church.

🍴 Tasty, well liked bar food includes lunchtime sandwiches, filled baguettes and baked potatoes, soup, deep-fried crumbed brie with home-made chutney, ham and egg, sausages and mash, chicken breast with a creamy mushroom sauce, steak in ale pie, lasagne, 8oz rump steak, and puddings such as white chocolate and brioche pudding and apple crumble. *Starters/Snacks: £3.25 to £5.75. Main Courses: £7.25 to £12.50. Puddings: £3.25 to £4.95*

Free house ~ Licensees Mr and Mrs Chroscicki ~ Real ale ~ Bar food (12-2, 6(7 Sun)-9) ~ (01328) 830297 ~ Children welcome ~ Open 11.30-2.30, 6-11; 12-2.30, 7-11 Sun

Recommended by Martin Conybeare, Pete Baker, David Rule, Mike Proctor, Derek and Sylvia Stephenson, Tracey and Stephen Groves, Derek Field

BLAKENEY
TG0243 MAP 8

White Horse
Off A149 W of Sheringham; High Street; NR25 7AL

Cheerful small hotel with popular dining conservatory, enjoyable food and drinks and helpful staff; bedrooms

Just a stroll from the small tidal harbour, this is a former coaching inn popular with customers hoping to enjoy the very good food. Those just wanting a drink and a chat do pop in and they keep Adnams Bitter and Broadside, Woodfordes Wherry and Yetmans on handpump and a fine choice of 30 wines by the glass. But the emphasis is on dining in either the bar, the airy conservatory (liked by families) or the smarter restaurant; best to book a table in advance. The informal long main bar is predominantly green with a venetian red ceiling and restrained but attractive décor, including watercolours by a local artist. There are tables in a suntrap courtyard and a pleasant paved garden. This area is a haven for bird-watchers and sailors.

🍴 Good food at lunchtime includes sandwiches or filled ciabattas, deep-fried soft herring roes on toast, ploughman's, ham and free-range eggs, and smoked haddock and crayfish kedgeree with a soft boiled egg, as well as soup, pork rillettes with spiced chutney, seared scallops with butternut squash purée, crab apple aioli and crisp parma ham, moules marinière, warm tart of beetroot, blue cheese and chives, beer-battered haddock, confit of duck leg with chestnuts, bacon and lyonnaise potatoes, rib-eye steak with their own black pudding, and puddings like cinnamon panna cotta with roast plum coulis and cardamon ice-cream and warm chocolate and almond brownie with crème chantilly and chocolate sauce. *Starters/Snacks: £5.00 to £9.00. Main Courses: £11.00 to £20.00. Puddings: £5.00 to £6.50*

Free house ~ Licensee Dan Goff ~ Real ale ~ Bar food (12-2.15, 6-9.30) ~ Restaurant ~ (01263) 740574 ~ Children in conservatory ~ Open 11-11 ~ Bedrooms: /£100S(£70B)

Recommended by Michael Dandy, Mark Farrington, Malcolm and Jane Levitt, Brian and Anna Marsden, MDN, David Field, Ken and Jenny Simmonds

BRANCASTER STAITHE
TF7944 MAP 8

Jolly Sailors 🍺
Main Road (A149); PE31 8BJ

Refurbished rooms, own-brewed beers, pubby food, and plenty of seats in sizeable garden; great for bird-watching nearby

Now run by Mr Nye's son, this little village pub has been newly refurbished and they have re-opened the brewery – though it is sited nearby now rather than in the pub itself. The smartened-up main bar still has its country charm, log fire and Brancaster Best Bitter plus Adnams Broadside and Woodfordes Wherry on handpump and a dozen wines by the glass; there's now a serving hatch to the outside terraced seating area. There are two further snug areas with darts, TV and board games, and a spacious, rustic back dining room with traditional tables and chairs, local artwork and another log fire. Plenty of seats outside in the enclosed garden. This is prime bird-watching territory and the pub is set on the edge of thousands of acres of National Trust dunes and salt flats; walkers are welcome.

🍴 As well as takeaway pizzas, bar food now includes filled baguettes, ploughman's, soup, salt and chilli pork ribs, whitebait with home-made tartare sauce, baked camembert, gammon and eggs, leek and mushroom bread pudding, fish and chips, a home-made pie of the day, lambs liver and bacon, a curry of the day, and daily specials. *Starters/Snacks: £2.95 to £4.50. Main Courses: £7.95 to £10.50. Puddings: £4.95 to £6.95*

Free house ~ Licensees Cliff and James Nye ~ Real ale ~ Bar food (12-9; pizza takeaway Fri and Sat until 10.45pm) ~ Restaurant ~ (01485) 210314 ~ Children welcome ~ Dogs allowed in bar ~ Open 12-11(10.30 Sun)

Recommended by Tracey and Stephen Groves, Mrs Carolyn Dixon, JJW, CMW, Len Clark, PHB, Pete Baker, Mr and Mrs John Taylor, Gwyn and Anne Wake

White Horse 🍴 ☐ 🛏

A149 E of Hunstanton; PE31 8BY

Bustling, popular bar, big airy dining conservatory looking over tidal bird marshes, real ales and lovely food; comfortable bedrooms

Of course, this is a smashing place to visit in good weather when you can sit on the sun deck with a pint of beer and look out to Scolt Head, but our readers very much enjoy their visits in cold weather, too, when the light conservatory restaurant is warm and lively and you can look across the wide tidal marshes. This room joins on to the dining area and both have well spaced furnishings in unvarnished country-style wood and some light-hearted seasidey decorations. At the front of the building there's an informal bar with plenty of locals dropping in, good photographs on the walls, bar billiards, occasional piped music, TV, and Adnams Bitter, Fullers London Pride, Woodfordes Wherry, and a guest like Brancaster Best Bitter on handpump, several malt whiskies and about a dozen wines by the glass from an extensive and thoughtful wine list; good, brisk, friendly service. On the right is a quieter group of cushioned wicker armchairs and sofas by a table with daily papers and local landscapes for sale. There are plenty of seats outside in front, some under cover and with heaters, for casual dining. The coast path runs along the bottom of the garden. This is an especially nice place to stay for a few days.

🍴 The food, using delicious local fish, is very good indeed. From the fair value little bar menu, there might be sandwiches, toasties and ciabattas, ploughman's, local oysters and mussels, pork and leek sausages with onion gravy, a proper caesar salad, smoked haddock with a poached egg and herb butter sauce, and slow-roasted pork belly with caramelised root vegetables and apple compote; dining room choices such as dressed local crab with lime mayonnaise, confit of duck with agen prune sauce and spring onion croquette, sea trout suprême with citrus dressing and local asparagus, and suprême of salmon with wild mushrooms and chive butter sauce, with puddings like orange and stem ginger sponge with sauce and cardamom ice-cream, and milk chocolate mousse with white chocolate ice-cream. *Starters/Snacks: £3.95 to £5.00. Main Courses: £7.50 to £16.95. Puddings: £3.95 to £4.95*

Free house ~ Licensees Cliff Nye and Kevin Nobes ~ Real ale ~ Bar food (all day in bar and on outside terrace; 12-2, 6.30-9 restaurant) ~ Restaurant ~ (01485) 210262 ~ Children welcome ~ Dogs allowed in bar and bedrooms ~ Open 12-11(10.30 Sun) ~ Bedrooms: £78B/£136B

Recommended by Michael Dandy, Brian and Anna Marsden, Len Beattie, George and Beverley Tucker, John Honnor, Dennis and Gill Keen, Mike and Sue Loseby, Mrs J Andrews, M E and J R Hart, JJW, CMW, P Waterman, PHB, Brian and Janet Ainscough, Tracey and Stephen Groves, Mrs Brenda Calver, Brian and Pamela Everett, John Wooll, Roger and Kath, Glenwys and Alan Lawrence, Neil Ingoe, Derek and Sylvia Stephenson, Mr and Mrs A H Young

---

Bedroom prices normally include full english breakfast, VAT and any inclusive service charge that we know of. Prices before the '/' are for single rooms, after for two people in double or twin (B includes a private bath, S a private shower). If there is no '/', the prices are only for twin or double rooms (as far as we know there are no singles). If there is no B or S, as far as we know no rooms have private facilities.

BURNHAM MARKET

Hoste Arms ⊕ ⏛ ⌂

TF8342 MAP 8

The Green (B1155); PE31 8HD

Civilised and stylish with first-class food and drinks, a proper bar plus lounge, conservatory and dining rooms, and a lovely garden; super bedrooms

---

Of course this is not a pub, it's a very civilised and smart old coaching inn but it does have a proper bar at the front with all the atmosphere of a village pub. This room is panelled, with a log fire, a series of watercolours showing scenes from local walks, a nice mix of chatty customers, and Greene King Abbot and Woodfordes Nelsons Revenge and Wherry on handpump; quite a few wines by the glass and several malt whiskies. There's a conservatory with leather armchairs and sofas, a lounge for afternoon tea, and several restaurants (for which it's best to book to be sure of a table). The lovely walled garden has plenty of seats, and a big awning covers the moroccan-style dining area.

▥ The imaginative food includes lunchtime sandwiches, ploughman's, and sausages with bubble and squeak and onion gravy, as well as chicken liver parfait with caramelised figs, roasted breast of local pigeon with rhubarb compote and black pepper ice-cream, salads like bang bang chicken with a chilli and ginger dressing, open lasagne of wild mushrooms and leeks, poached egg and a mushroom and madeira cream sauce, steak and kidney pudding, corn-fed chicken breast with sweetcorn purée, potato fritter and a cider and grain mustard sauce, and fillet of bass with thai spiced potatoes, pak choi and cashew nuts and a sesame and coriander dressing, with puddings such as rice pudding with candied lemon zest and a raspberry and chilli sorbet and warm dark chocolate fondant with chocolate sauce. *Starters/Snacks: £4.85 to £8.10. Main Courses: £9.65 to £18.15. Puddings: £6.15 to £6.80*

Free house ~ Licensees Paul Whittome and Emma Tagg ~ Real ale ~ Bar food (12-2.15, 6-9.15) ~ Restaurant ~ (01328) 738777 ~ Children welcome ~ Dogs allowed in bar and bedrooms ~ Summer jazz concerts in garden ~ Open 11-11(10.30 Sun) ~ Bedrooms: £90S/£122B

Recommended by Alan and Jill Bull, Philip Vernon, Kim Maidment, Dan and Holly Pitcher, Sally Anne and Peter Goodale, Ken and Jenny Simmonds, Mike and Sue Loseby, Peter and Giff Bennett, Alistair and Kay Butler, Fred and Lorraine Gill, Malcolm and Jane Levitt, Tracey and Stephen Groves, Simon Rodway, Roy Hoing, Pete Coxon, Derek and Sylvia Stephenson, Mike Proctor, Roger Wain-Heapy, Neil and Angela Huxter, Keith and Sue Ward, George Atkinson, David Cosham

BURSTON

Crown ◀

TM1383 MAP 8

Village signposted off A140 N of Scole; Mill Road; IP22 5TW

Friendly, relaxed village pub, usefully open all day, warm welcome, several real ales and a warm winter fire

---

As soon as you walk through the main door into this village pub you'll be welcomed by the friendly staff and immediately feel at home. It's usefully open all day, with a nice flow of customers dropping in for a chat and a drink. There are several rooms, though locals like to gather by the standing area next to the bar with its high bar chairs and well kept Adnams Bitter, Elmtree Golden Pale Ale, Greene King Abbot and Wolf Romulus on handpump. In cold weather, the best places to sit in this heavy-beamed, quarry-tiled room are on the comfortably cushioned sofas in front of the big log fire in its huge brick fireplace; there are some stools as well by the low chunky wooden table, newspapers and magazines to read, and some ornate wall lamps. The public bar on the left has a nice long table and panelled settle on an old brick floor in one alcove, another sofa, straightforward seating on the carpet by the pool table, darts and juke box, and up a step, more tables and chairs. Both of these cream-painted rooms are hung with cheerful naive local character paintings. There's also a simple beamed dining room off the bar with pine tables and chairs on the big modern quarry tiles, and logs piled up in another big brick fireplace. Outside, there's a smokers' shelter, a couple of picnic-sets in front of the old brick building, and more seats in a hedged-off area with a barbecue. They hold all sorts of events: beer and music festivals, quiz and live music evenings, specialist food events, and so forth.

🍴 Well liked bar food, using local suppliers, includes sandwiches, filled baguettes, soup, home-made beefburgers, linguine with mushrooms, red onions, capers and olives, ham and egg, and beef, mushroom and Guinness pie as well as chicken caesar salad, a tapas plate, moules marinière, red onion and asparagus tart, vietnamese chicken balls, beer-battered haddock and a mixed grill. *Starters/Snacks: £5.00 to £6.50. Main Courses: £9.00 to £15.00. Puddings: £4.50 to £5.00*

Free house ~ Licensees Bev and Steve Kembery and Jonathan Piers-Hall ~ Real ale ~ Bar food (12-2(4 Sun), 6.30-9) ~ Restaurant ~ (01379) 741257 ~ Children welcome ~ Dogs allowed in bar ~ Live music Thurs evening and every other Sun at 5pm ~ Open 12-11(10.30 Sun)

Recommended by Richard and Ruth Dean, Sue Austin

CLEY NEXT THE SEA   TG0443   MAP 8

George ♀ 🛏

Off A149 W of Sheringham; High Street; NR25 7RN

Well liked inn with pubby bar, real ales, super choice of wines, bar food and more restauranty choices; bedrooms

In a quiet brick and flint village overlooking the salt marshes – a fantastic place for bird-watchers – this sizeable inn appeals to a wide mix of customers. If it's just a drink you want, head for the little public bar with its green-painted, wood-topped bar counter lined with high bar chairs, where they serve Adnams Broadside and Woodfordes Wherry on handpump; 30 wines by the glass from a good list. There's also a long leather settle and sturdy dark wooden chairs by a couple of green-topped tables on the carpet, cream walls above a green-painted planked high dado, photographs of Norfolk wherries and other local scenes, a huge candle in a big glass jar on one window sill, a table of newspapers, and big windows, one with stained-glass showing St George and the dragon. The two dining rooms are both similarly furnished with pale wooden cushioned dining chairs around a mix of wooden tables; the end room has prints of Leonardo drawings on the fleur-de-lys wallpaper, brown blinds on the windows, an ornamental woodburning stove in the end room with nightlights along the mantelbeam, and some rather nice old-fashioned glass wall lamps. There are seats in the garden across the quiet road, and nearby walks. Some of the bedrooms overlook the salt flats, and three are in a back annex.

🍴 Tasty bar food includes sandwiches and filled ciabattas, ploughman's, soup, confit of duck rillettes with spiced apple chutney, local smoked prawn and herring rollmop platter, lasagne, beer-battered haddock, courgette bake with walnut and pickled quince salad, plaice with herb couscous and rocket pesto, line-caught bass fillets with mascerated fennel, and puddings like carrot cake with coffee ice-cream and thai-style fruit salad with green tea ice-cream. *Starters/Snacks: £5.00 to £8.00. Main Courses: £9.00 to £18.00. Puddings: £5.00 to £6.00*

Free house ~ Licensee Daniel Goff ~ Real ale ~ Bar food ~ (01263) 740652 ~ Children welcome ~ Dogs allowed in bar and bedrooms ~ Open 11-11 ~ Bedrooms: /£80S(£60B)

Recommended by Nigel Long

COLKIRK   TF9226   MAP 8

Crown ♀

Village signposted off B1146 S of Fakenham, and off A1065; Crown Road; NR21 7AA

Neatly kept, bustling local with cheerful landlord, splendid wines, popular tasty food and a pleasant garden

There's a welcome for everyone at this cottagey local, with regulars enjoying a pint in the bar to the right and those lunching in the room on the left. Both rooms are comfortable and cosy and kept spotless with solid country furniture on the rugs and flooring tiles, interesting things to look at and open fires. Greene King IPA and Abbot and a guest beer on handpump and a splendid range of wines, many by the glass; quick service even when busy. There's also a dining room. Outside, there's a suntrap terrace, a pleasant garden and plenty of picnic-sets.

🍴 **Popular bar food includes lunchtime sandwiches and filled baguettes, soup, a changing pâté, anchovy and bacon salad, leek and stilton flan, chicken in a creamy mushroom and brandy sauce, haddock and chips, salmon and halibut in a white wine sauce, pork fillet in a creamy madeira sauce, steak in ale pie, and puddings like lemon and lime cheesecake and bread and butter pudding.** *Starters/Snacks: £4.25 to £5.25. Main Courses: £8.95 to £17.95. Puddings: £4.95*

Greene King ~ Tenant Roger Savell ~ Real ale ~ Bar food (12-1.45, 7-9) ~ Restaurant ~ (01328) 862172 ~ Children welcome ~ Dogs allowed in bar ~ Open 11-2.30, 6-11; 12-3, 7-10.30 Sun

Recommended by Jim Farmer, Tracey and Stephen Groves, Mark, Amanda, Luke and Jake Sheard, Dan and Holly Pitcher, Sally Anne and Peter Goodale

EAST RUDHAM

TF8228   MAP 8

Crown 🍴 ♟ 🛏

A148 W of Fakenham; The Green; PE31 8RD

NORFOLK DINING PUB OF THE YEAR

Beautifully refurbished in contemporary style with open-plan seating areas, cosy back sitting room and further dining room, civilised and friendly atmosphere, real ales and fine wines by the glass, and super modern food; bedrooms

This beamed pub, standing at the head of the village green, has been extensively renovated recently. It's been beautifully done in contemporary fashion with Farrow & Ball paintwork, lots of wood, and plenty of light from the big windows. The open-plan bar has several distinct seating areas, the atmosphere is civilised but informal, and the welcome from the enthusiastic young staff is genuinely friendly. At one end, there's a log fire in the modern brick fireplace, with a grandfather clock to one side and bookshelves on the other, brown leather and wood dining chairs around a mix of tables (including a huge round one), and rugs on the stripped boards. High bar chairs beside the handsomely slate-topped counter are popular, and they keep Adnams Bitter, Ufford Golden Drop and Woodfordes Wherry on handpump, and a good choice of wines by the glass. The other end of the room is slightly more informal with a mix of leather-seated dining chairs around all sorts of tables, a couple of built-in wall seats, another bookshelf beside a second fireplace, and 1950s and 1960s actor prints in Shakespearean costume on the walls. There's also more of a pubby part with planked and cushioned white-painted built-in seats, and pink walls hung with all sorts of nice photographs. Newspapers on hangers and drinks' prices neatly written on a blackboard. A cosy lower area at the back of the pub on the left has leather sofas and armchairs and wicker chairs on tiles, a low table of magazines, a big flat-screen TV, and various swords and antlers on the walls; and up some carpeted stairs from here is another dining room with a high-pitched ceiling, cane-backed dining chairs on bare boards, lots more books on bookshelves and another TV. Outside are neat picnic-sets under parasols on the front gravel. The gents' has piped sports highlights and the ladies' music – we've never come across this before, and it was quite fun. The new bedrooms are attractive, light and airy. This pub is in the same little group as the newly refurbished Kings Head at Letheringsett and the Crown, Wells-next-the-Sea.

🍴 **Attractively set out and very good, the modern bar food includes sandwiches with crisps, soup, ham hock, apricot and smoked chicken terrine with piccalilli, trout mousse and smoked salmon parcel with lemon and chive cream, butternut and sage fettucine, burger with gruyère cheese and red pepper chutney, breast and confit leg of guinea fowl with parsley mash and sautéed wild mushrooms, roast rack of lamb with parmesan risotto and olive jus, seared sea bream with couscous and a beetroot and orange salad, and puddings like white chocolate iced parfait with passion fruit coulis and spiced apple cake with maple syrup ice-cream; they also offer breakfasts and morning coffee.** *Starters/Snacks: £4.95 to £9.00. Main Courses: £11.50 to £16.95. Puddings: £5.50 to £7.50*

Free house ~ Licensee Chris Coubrough ~ Real ale ~ Bar food (12-2.30, 6-9.30; breakfast from 8.30am-10am) ~ (01485) 528530 ~ Children welcome ~ Dogs allowed in bar and bedrooms Open 10am-11pm(10.30 Sun) ~ Bedrooms: /£80B

Recommended by R C Vincent, Tracey and Stephen Groves

EDGEFIELD

TG0934   MAP 8

Pigs ♀ ◖

Norwich Road; B1149 S of Holt; NR24 2RL

Enthusiastically run pub, half a dozen real ales and good wine list, plenty of room, and popular food

As we went to press, they were hoping to open a new shop here selling produce made in the kitchen and grown in the garden, and offering a second-hand cookbook swap. It's a friendly place with helpful staff and enthusiastic licensees and there's a fair balance between drinkers and diners. The carpeted central bar greets you with the reassuring sight of a good row of handpumps, with Adnams Bitter and Broadside, Greene King Abbot, Woodfordes Wherry and a couple of changing guests. They have continental beers on tap and a good range of wines by the glass, in two glass sizes; they do coffee in two sizes, too. No crisps – instead they do their own pork scratchings and interesting seed, bean and nut snacks. A games area has darts, bar billiards and board games and there's a proper children's playroom, too. On the left, arches open through to a simply refurbished area with a mix of random dining chairs and built-in pews around the plain tables on broad stripped-pine boards. On the right, a light and airy dining extension is similar in style, with some tables in stalls formed by low brick stub walls and single standing timbers; the kitchen gives an open view. Outside, a big covered terrace has sturdy rustic tables and benches on flagstones, and there is an adventure play area; pétanque. Wheelchair access is easy.

🍴 **Carefully sourced local produce from an honest menu includes dishes like soup, tapas, omelette arnold bennett, sardines with lemon and capers, a plate of piggy pieces (pig's cheek, black pudding, ear, and so forth), steamed mushroom pudding, pork sausages with mustard mash, mutton burger with cucumber and mint chutney, beer-battered haddock, slow-cooked pork belly with beans, black pudding, apple chutney and crackling, and puddings such as fruit crumble and baked alaska.** *Starters/Snacks: £4.50 to £5.95. Main Courses: £10.25 to £14.95. Puddings: £5.00*

Free house ~ Licensee Cloe Wasey ~ Real ale ~ Bar food (12-2.30(3 Sun), 6-9; not Sun evening or Mon (except bank hols)) ~ Restaurant ~ (01263) 587634 ~ Children welcome ~ Dogs allowed in bar ~ Open 11-3, 6-11; 12-4, 7-10.30 Sun; closed Mon (except bank hols when they open 12-4)

Recommended by William Mack, Derek Field, Tracey and Stephen Groves, Charles Gysin, Ian and Nita Cooper, Roger and Lesley Everett, Sheila Topham, Bill and Marian de Bass, Philip and Susan Philcox, KN-R

ERPINGHAM

TG1732   MAP 8

Saracens Head 🍽 ♀ 🛏

At Wolterton – not shown on many maps; Erpingham signed off A140 N of Aylsham; keep on through Calthorpe, then where road bends right, take the straight-ahead turn-off signposted Wolterton; NR11 7LZ

Charming long-serving landlord in a simply furnished dining pub, gently civilised atmosphere and good interesting food; bedrooms

This rather civilised place 'continues to offer charm and character unlike any other' says one of our readers, and many others agree with him. The two-room bar is simple and stylish with high ceilings, terracotta walls, and red and white striped curtains at its tall windows – all lending a feeling of space, though it's not actually large. There's a mix of seats from built-in leather wall settles to wicker fireside chairs as well as log fires and flowers, and the windows look out on to a charming old-fashioned gravel stableyard with picnic-sets. A pretty six-table parlour on the right has another big log fire. Adnams Bitter and Woodfordes Wherry on handpump, an interesting wine list, local apple juice and cider, and decent malt whiskies; the atmosphere is enjoyably informal. The Shed next door (run by Mr Dawson-Smith's daughter Rachel) is a workshop and showcase for furniture and interior pieces. Lovely, comfortable bedrooms that our readers like very much.

🍴 **Good, enjoyable food includes game and cranberry terrine, deep-fried brie with apricot sauce, mussels with cider and cream, red onion and goats cheese tart, baked cromer crab**

THE GOOD PUB GUIDE

The Good Pub Guide
FREEPOST TN1569
WADHURST
E. SUSSEX
TN5 7BR

2

Please use this card to tell us which pubs *you* think should or should not be included in the next edition of *The Good Pub Guide*. Just fill it in and return it to us – no stamp or envelope needed. Don't forget you can also use the report forms at the end of the *Guide*

ALISDAIR AIRD

In returning this form I confirm my agreement that the information I provide may be used by The Random House Group Ltd, its assignees and/or licensees in any media or medium whatsoever.

YOUR NAME AND ADDRESS (BLOCK CAPITALS PLEASE)

☐ *Please tick this box if you would like extra report forms*

REPORT ON *(pub's name)*

Pub's address

☐ **YES Main Entry**   ☐ **YES Lucky Dip**   ☐ **NO don't include**
Please tick one of these boxes to show your verdict, and give reasons and descriptive comments, prices etc

☐ Deserves FOOD award   ☐ Deserves PLACE-TO-STAY award

REPORT ON *(pub's name)*

Pub's address

☐ **YES Main Entry**   ☐ **YES Lucky Dip**   ☐ **NO don't include**
Please tick one of these boxes to show your verdict, and give reasons and descriptive comments, prices etc

☐ Deserves FOOD award   ☐ Deserves PLACE-TO-STAY award

By returning this form, you consent to the collection, recording and use of the information you submit, by The Random House Group Ltd. Any personal details which you provide from which we can identify you are held and processed in accordance with the Data Protection Act 1998 and will not be passed on to any third parties. The Random House Group Ltd may wish to send you further information on their associated products. Please tick box if you do not wish to receive any such information. ☐

with apple and sherry, roast pheasant with calvados and cream, venison medallions with a red fruit jus, leg of lamb with red and white beans, wok-sizzled strips of sirloin with anchovy and tomato, and puddings like Baileys dark chocolate pot with orange jus and treacle tart; they also offer a two- and three-course weekday lunch option. *Starters/Snacks: £3.95 to £7.95. Main Courses: £12.25 to £15.95. Puddings: £5.25 to £5.50*

Free house ~ Licensee Robert Dawson-Smith ~ Real ale ~ Bar food (12-2-ish, 7.30-9-ish; not Mon (except bank hols) or Tues lunchtime) ~ (01263) 768909 ~ Children welcome but must be well behaved ~ Dogs allowed in bedrooms ~ Open 11.30-3, 6-11.30; 12-3, 7-10.30 Sun; closed Mon (except bank hols) and Tues lunchtime ~ Bedrooms: £45B/£90B

Recommended by Dan and Holly Pitcher, Sally Anne and Peter Goodale, Dr and Mrs P Truelove, John Robertson, Pete Devonish, Ian McIntyre, Mike and Shelley Woodroffe, MDN, Philip and Susan Philcox

GREAT MASSINGHAM   TF7922   MAP 8

Dabbling Duck 🍺

Off A148 King's Lynn—Fakenham; Abbey Road; PE32 2HN

Unassuming from outside, civilised and friendly within, with traditional furnishings, warm coal fires, several real ales, and enjoyable food

Owned by a small local consortium, this is an unassuming-looking pub by the sizeable village green with its big duck ponds; there are tables and chairs on a terrace out in front. Inside, it's a good combination of civilised atmosphere with traditional furnishings. The bar to the right of the door is nicely informal, with a very high-backed settle, and some comfortable armchairs and a leather and brass-button settle facing each other across a pine table in front of a coal fire in the huge raised fireplace. There are some beams and standing timbers, an attractive mix of wooden dining chairs and tables (set with candles), reproduction prints of 18th- and 19th-c cartoons on pale grey walls, rugs on the stripped wooden floor, and another fireplace with shelves of books to one side. At the back of the pub is a room just right for a party of people, with a very long wooden table, a big rug on old floor tiles, and a mix of *Vanity Fair* cartoons and old local photographs on the dark red walls. On the left is more of a drinking bar with library chairs and leather easy chairs on bare boards, darts, another coal fire, and country prints above a tall grey dado. Well kept Adnams, Beestons Worth the Wait, Greene King IPA and Woodfordes Wherry on handpump from a bar counter made of great slabs of polished tree trunk; there are daily papers on a rod.

🍴 Enjoyable bar food includes sandwiches, ploughman's, soup, crab and samphire pot wrapped in smoked salmon, home-made beefburger, moules frites, baked gnocchi and sautéed mushrooms with spinach, peas and basil pesto, sausages and mash, gammon and egg, lamb shank with couscous, halibut with brown shrimp risotto, and puddings like rhubarb crumble and rich dark minted chocolate mousse with coconut ice-cream. *Starters/Snacks: £4.00 to £6.50. Main Courses: £8.50 to £14.95. Puddings: £5.75 to £6.50*

Free house ~ Licensees Mark and Jess Lapping, Dominic Symington and Steve Kilham ~ Real ale ~ Bar food (12-2.30(3 Sun), 6.30-9; not Sun evening) ~ Restaurant ~ (01485) 520827 ~ Children welcome ~ Dogs welcome ~ Open 12-11(10.30 Sun) ~ Bedrooms: /£80B

Recommended by Tracey and Stephen Groves, Hansjoerg Landherr, Pete Devonish, Ian McIntyre, Derek and Sylvia Stephenson, Sally Anne and Peter Goodale, David Baines

HUNWORTH   TG0735   MAP 8

Hunny Bell

Signed off B roads S of Holt; NR24 2AA

Refurbished village pub with seats overlooking the green, neat bar and airy dining room, four real ales and popular food

This carefully refurbished 18th-c pub has a new terrace with picnic-sets that look across the lane to the village green; there are more seats amongst fruit trees in the garden, too. The neatly kept bar has ceiling joists, a nice mix of cushioned dining chairs around wooden tables on the stone-tiled floor, a woodburning stove, and high bar stools by the oak bar counter; there's also a cosy snug with homely armchairs, pouffes and housekeeper's chairs on old floor tiles, and throughout there are some original stripped-brick walls. The high-raftered dining room has a red colour theme and another woodburning stove. Adnams Bitter, Greene King Abbot, Woodfordes Wherry and a guest beer like Burton Bridge Stairway to Heaven on handpump; friendly staff, and piped music.

⑪ **Popular bar food includes lunchtime sandwiches, soup, smoked mackerel and kipper salad with preserved lemon piccalilli, mussels with white wine and cream, omelette arnold bennett, roast butternut squash and blue cheese risotto with candied walnuts, lasagne, and beer-battered cod; also, more elaborate choices such as shrimp and avocado tian with celeriac rémoulade, basil roast free-range chicken with streaky bacon, lemon infused mash and red pepper oil, and 21-day-aged beef tenderloin with port jus and horseradish crème fraîche. Puddings like white chocolate crème brûlée with blood orange sorbet and orange salad and apple and almond tart with clotted cream ice-cream.** *Starters/Snacks: £4.95 to £6.95. Main Courses: £8.95 to £17.95. Puddings: £5.00 to £5.95*

Animal Inns ~ Manager Henry Watt ~ Real ale ~ Bar food (12-2.15, 6-9.30) ~ Restaurant ~ (01263) 712300 ~ Children welcome ~ Dogs allowed in bar ~ Open 11.30-3, 5.30-11; 11.30-11 Sat; 12-10.30 Sun

Recommended by Derek Field, Bill and Marian de Bass, Pete Devonish, Ian McIntyre, Charles Gysin, Keith and Jenny Grant

ITTERINGHAM   TG1430   MAP 8

Walpole Arms ⑪ ♀ ◀

Village signposted off B1354 NW of Aylsham; first right to Itteringham 1 mile after Blickling Hall; NR11 7AR

Ambitious food in popular dining pub, quietly chatty open-plan bar, decent drinks and a good garden

Close to Blickling Hall, this attractive 18th-c brick pub has a fine two-acre landscaped garden with seats and tables on a vine-covered terrace. Inside, the sizeable open-plan bar is rather civilised and has exposed beams, stripped-brick walls, little windows, lit candles on a mix of dining tables and a quietly chatty atmosphere. Adnams Bitter and Broadside, Woodfordes Wherry and a guest beer on handpump, and a dozen wines by the glass; friendly young manager supported by helpful staff. The dining room is light and airy with beamery and pale high-backed dining chairs around white-clothed tables on the pale pink carpet.

⑪ **Well presented, interesting bar food includes ploughman's, soup, escabeche of red mullet with pine nuts, sultanas and butter beans, crayfish tails with spicy vietnamese cabbage, mango purée and prawn crackers, mussels in cider, thyme and onions with frites, warm tart of sweet potato, mushroom, spinach, red onion and gruyère, corned beef hash cake with a fried egg, chicken and ham pie, catalonian pork sausage with black-eyed beans, paella of chicken, rabbit, chorizo and prawns, bass with saffron mash, baked tomato and gazpacho salsa, and puddings like saffron poached pear with orange flower rice pudding and toasted seeds, and baked white chocolate cheesecake with raspberry purée.** *Starters/Snacks: £5.50 to £6.95. Main Courses: £7.95 to £18.95. Puddings: £5.50 to £6.50*

Free house ~ Licensees Mr and Mrs Sayers ~ Real ale ~ Bar food (12(12.30 Sun)-2(2.30 Sun), 7-9; not Sun evening) ~ Restaurant ~ (01263) 587258 ~ Children welcome ~ Dogs allowed in bar ~ Open 12-3, 6-11; 12-5 Sun; closed Sun evening

Recommended by Barry and Patricia Wooding, John Cook, Martin Wilson, Pete Devonish, Ian McIntyre, Mrs B Barwick, MDN, Philip and Susan Philcox, Charles and Pauline Stride, Joyce and Maurice Cottrell, Mike and Shelley Woodroffe, Sheila Topham, Virginia Williams

---

The letters and figures after the name of each town are its Ordnance Survey map reference. 'Using the *Guide*' at the beginning of the book explains how it helps you find a pub, in road atlases or large-scale maps as well as in our own maps.

LARLING

TL9889   MAP 5

Angel 🍺 🛏

From A11 Thetford—Attleborough, take B1111 turn-off and follow pub signs; NR16 2QU

In same family since 1913, with good-natured chatty atmosphere, real ales and popular food; bedrooms

Handy for the A11, this is a genuinely friendly pub with a chatty, relaxed atmosphere and a good mix of both locals and visitors. It's been in the same family since 1913 and they still have the original visitors' books with guests from 1897 to 1909. The comfortable 1930s-style lounge on the right has cushioned wheelback chairs, a nice long cushioned and panelled corner settle, some good solid tables for eating, and squared panelling; also, a collection of whisky-water jugs on the delft shelf over the big brick fireplace, a woodburning stove, a couple of copper kettles and some hunting prints. Adnams Bitter and four guests from breweries like Brewsters, Old Cannon, Tydd Steam and Wissey Valley on handpump, 100 malt whiskies, and ten wines by the glass. They hold an August beer festival with over 70 real ales and ciders, live music and barbecues. The quarry-tiled black-beamed public bar has a good local feel with darts, games machine, juke box (a rarity nowadays), board games and piped music. A neat grassy area behind the car park has picnic-sets around a big fairy-lit apple tree, and there's a safely fenced play area. They also have a four-acre meadow and offer caravan and camping sites from March to October. Peter Beale's old-fashioned rose nursery is nearby as is St George's, England's only whisky distillery.

🍴 **Fair value, popular bar food includes sandwiches, filled baked potatoes, ploughman's, soup, home-made pâté, ham or sausages and egg, omelettes, stilton and mushroom bake, chicken korma, smoked haddock mornay, steak and kidney pie, pork slices in a red wine, wild mushroom and tomato sauce, steaks with green peppercorn or stilton, whisky and cream sauces, and puddings like apricot and cinnamon sponge pudding and chocolate fudge cake.** *Starters/Snacks: £3.95 to £6.25. Main Courses: £8.25 to £17.50. Puddings: £4.75*

Free house ~ Licensee Andrew Stammers ~ Real ale ~ Bar food (all day) ~ Restaurant ~ (01953) 717963 ~ Children welcome ~ Open 10am-midnight ~ Bedrooms: £45B/£80S

Recommended by Stuart and Alison Ballantyne, Roy Hoing, R T and J C Moggridge, Peter and Anne Hollindale, Kevin Thomas, Nina Randall, Dr and Mrs A K Clarke, Andy and Claire Barker

LETHERINGSETT

TG0638   MAP 8

Kings Head ♀

A148 (Holt Road) W of Holt; NR25 7AR

Newly refurbished, with several comfortably contemporary areas, friendly chatty young staff, real ales and good wines by the glass, bistro-type food and plenty of outside seating; bedrooms opening shortly

In the same small group as the Crowns in East Rudham and Wells-next-the-Sea, this handsome old pub had just reopened on our inspection visit, after extensive refurbishment. It's all very civilised and contemporary – but done with plenty of interest and character. To the right of the main door, a small room has dining chairs around scrubbed wooden tables, bookshelves beside a black fireplace, a flatscreen TV, and apple-green paintwork. The main bar, to the left, has some high wooden bar chairs by the counter, Adnams, Woodfordes Wherry and maybe a couple of guest beers on handpump, quite a choice of wines by the glass, and good coffee; it's comfortable, with daily papers, big black leather armchairs and sofas and various stools and dining chairs, reproduction hunting and coaching prints on the mushroom paintwork, rugs on the quarry-tiled floor, and an open fire in an ornate black fireplace. Lighting from the chunky sculptured lamps, and from the small lit oil lamps on each table, is soft. Further in is the partly skylit dining room with built-in white-painted planked wall seating with maroon cushions and a mix of dining chairs around wooden tables, rugs on stripped wood, a few farm tools and cabinets of taps and spiles on the cream-painted flint and cob walls. A back area under a partly pitched ceiling with painted rafters has more comfortable leather sofas and armchairs in front of another big flatscreen TV; Scrabble. Outside are lots of picnic-sets under parasols on the front gravel, with many more on a grass side lawn, where there's also a play fort under tenting. The bedrooms should be up and running by the time this *Guide* is published.

⑪ Good bistro-style food includes sandwiches at lunchtime, soup, tempura king prawns with sweet chilli sauce, chicken liver parfait with red onion chutney, chicken breast stuffed with sunblush tomato, mozzarella and basil, butternut squash and gorgonzola risotto with a parmesan crisp, bass with olives, red onions, garlic and pesto, breast and confit leg of guinea fowl on parsley, lemon and garlic mash, and puddings like lemon tart with clotted cream and vanilla pod crème brûlée with shortbread. *Starters/Snacks: £4.95 to £7.95. Main Courses: £9.95 to £16.95. Puddings: £5.95 to £7.25*

Free house ~ Licensee Chris Coubrough ~ Real ale ~ Bar food (12-2.30, 6.30-9.30; they serve high teas 4-6.30) ~ (01263) 712691 ~ Children welcome ~ Dogs welcome ~ Open 11-11

Recommended by Pete Devonish, Ian McIntyre, Charles Gysin

MORSTON
TG0043 MAP 8

Anchor
A149 Salthouse—Stiffkey; The Street; NR25 7AA

Quite a choice of rooms filled with bric-a-brac and prints, real ales and well liked food

New licensees have taken over this bustling pub and our readers are enjoying their visits. On the right, there are three traditional rooms with pubby seating and tables on original wooden floors, coal fires, local 1950s beach photographs and lots of prints and bric-a-brac. Greene King IPA, Old Speckled Hen and local Winters Golden on handpump, nine wines by the glass, and daily papers. The contemporary airy extension on the left has groups of deep leather sofas around low tables, grey-painted country dining furniture, fresh flowers and fish pictures. There are tables and benches out in front of the building. You can book seal-spotting trips from here and the surrounding area is wonderful for bird-watching and walking.

⑪ Using local suppliers (and organic or free-range produce where possible), the good bar food includes lunchtime sandwiches, home-cooked honey and mustard ham and fried egg, bangers with red wine gravy and a smokehouse platter, as well as soup, chicken liver and smoked bacon pâté with home-made chutney, cod and sea trout fishcakes with hollandaise, beer-battered haddock, mushroom wellington, braised shank of lamb on butternut squash mash with red wine and rosemary, and puddings like sticky toffee pudding with toffee sauce and glazed lemon tart. *Starters/Snacks: £4.50 to £8.95. Main Courses: £8.95 to £16.95. Puddings: £4.95 to £5.25*

Free house ~ Licensee Nick Handley ~ Real ale ~ Bar food (12-2.30, 6-9(9.30 Fri and Sat); 12-8 Sun) ~ Restaurant ~ (01263) 741392 ~ Children welcome ~ Dogs allowed in bar ~ Open 11-11(10.30 Sun)

Recommended by John Honnor, George Atkinson, Derek and Sylvia Stephenson, Fred and Lorraine Gill, Charles Gysin, Tracey and Stephen Groves, Derek Field, Brian and Anna Marsden, Colin McKerrow, Philip and Susan Philcox

NORTH CREAKE
TF8538 MAP 8

Jolly Farmers
Burnham Road; NR21 9JW

Friendly village local with three cosy rooms, open fires and woodburners, popular food and local beers

This yellow-painted pub, in a charming flintstone village, is doing particularly well at the moment under its present licensees, and the three cosy rooms have a friendly, relaxed atmosphere and a good mix of both locals and visitors. The main bar has a large open fire in a brick fireplace, a mix of pine farmhouse and high-backed leather dining chairs around scrubbed pine tables on the quarry-tiled floor, pale yellow walls, and some high bar chairs by the wooden bar counter where they keep Woodfordes Nelson's Revenge and Wherry on handpump and several wines by the glass; there's a cabinet of model cars, piped music, dominoes, cards and shut the box. A smaller bar has pews and a woodburning stove, and the red-walled dining room has similar furniture to the bar and another woodburning stove. There are seats outside on the terrace and in the garden.

🍴 Using produce from local fishermen and farmers, the well liked bar food includes sandwiches, soup, brie and apple chutney tart, game and redcurrant pâté, field mushrooms topped with spicy, fruity couscous, thai green chicken curry, lasagne, salmon and prawn pie, liver and bacon, slow-roasted pheasant with honey and almonds, roasted black bream with sesame and soy, steaks, and puddings; they also offer a good value two-course lunch (Wednesday-Saturday). *Starters/Snacks: £4.00 to £7.00. Main Courses: £8.00 to £13.50. Puddings: £4.00*

Free house ~ Licensees Adrian and Heather Sanders ~ Real ale ~ Bar food (not Mon or Tues) ~ Restaurant ~ (01328) 738188 ~ Children welcome ~ Dogs allowed in bar ~ Open 12-2.30, 7(5 Fri)-11; 12-3, 7-10.30 Sun; closed Mon and Tues

Recommended by Charles A Hey, John Wooll

NORWICH
TG2309　MAP 5

Adam & Eve £
Bishopgate; follow Palace Street from Tombland, N of cathedral; NR3 1RZ

Ancient place with a good mix of customers, real ales and fair value food, and seats by a fantastic array of hanging baskets and tubs

There's a lot of history in this busy old pub. It's thought to date back to at least 1249 (when it was used by workmen building the cathedral) and even has a Saxon well beneath the lower bar floor, though the striking dutch gables were added in the 14th and 15th centuries. The little old-fashioned bars have antique high-backed settles, cushioned benches built into partly panelled walls, and tiled or parquet floors. Adnams Bitter, Mauldons Moletrap Bitter, Theakstons Old Peculier and Wells & Youngs Bombardier on handpump, over 50 malt whiskies, quite a few wines by the glass and Aspall's cider; piped music and board games. The award-winning colourful tubs and hanging baskets here are quite a sight in summer and it's nice to admire them from one of the many picnic-sets. Comedy Horrid History of Norwich walks start and end here on Friday and Saturday evenings in summer, as do the Ghost Walks from May-October (the pub offers a 'spooky meal' plus the walk for £10).

🍴 Decent, good value pubby food includes sandwiches and filled baguettes, filled baked potatoes, ploughman's, soup, steak and mushroom pie, chicken or beef curry, sausages with bacon, onion and red wine gravy, lasagne, beer-battered cod, and specials like a rack of pork ribs and vegetarian cannelloni. *Starters/Snacks: £3.95 to £5.95. Main Courses: £5.95 to £8.95. Puddings: £4.45 to £4.95*

Unique (Enterprise) ~ Lease Rita McCluskey ~ Real ale ~ Bar food (12-7; 12-5 Sun; not evenings) ~ (01603) 667423 ~ Children in snug until 7pm ~ Open 11-11; 12-10.30 Sun

Recommended by John and Helen Rushton, Andy and Claire Barker, Revd R P Tickle, the Didler, Dr and Mrs A K Clarke

Eagle
Newmarket Road (A11, between A140 and A147 ring roads); NR2 2HN

Well run, plenty of differing seating areas for both drinking and dining, several real ales, lots of coffees, wines by the glass, and quite a choice of fairly priced food

Very well run by an experienced landlord, this sizeable Georgian pub is handy for anyone driving round Norwich, or coming in from the south or west. It spreads around both downstairs and upstairs, giving plenty of different seating areas. In front of the dark wooden counter – where they keep Fullers London Pride, Greene King IPA and Abbot, and a house beer from Bass called Eagles Nest on handpump – are dark wooden dining chairs and tables, and a couple of cushioned settles on the grey floor tiles, pink paintwork above a green dado, a little green woodburning stove in the ornate wooden fireplace, and some fine giltwork in the ornate plastered ceiling. There's an area with high chairs around high tables and a comfortable sofa, and a cosy end room with four dark leather sofas around some low chunky tables; newspapers in a rack. The simply furnished, low-ceilinged dining room has plenty of pale wood, and up some spiral stairs from the bar is another, very nice, contemporary dining room. Lots of coffees and decent wines; piped pop music and a couple of games machines. A 'conservatory' with chrome and bentwood chairs and wooden tables leads on to a sunny terrace with picnic-sets and a smart barbecue, and there are more seats on grass and a children's play area.

🍴 As well as a sensibly priced pubby menu, there's quite a range of fairly priced daily specials: sandwiches, soup, various platters, marinated king prawn kebabs with chilli and coriander, ham and egg, beefburger with courgette pickles, coq au vin, smoked haddock au gratin, risotto of lemon, pine nuts, feta and sunblush tomatoes, wild boar and apple sausage with dijon mash and red wine gravy, gressingham duck breast with roast sweet potato and plum sauce, and puddings like chocolate orange tart with vanilla ice-cream and apricot and apple crumble. *Starters/Snacks: £5.00 to £6.50. Main Courses: £7.95 to £15.00. Puddings: £4.95 to £5.50*

Free house ~ Licensee Nigel Booty ~ Real ale ~ Bar food ~ Restaurant ~ (01603) 624173 ~ Children welcome ~ Dogs allowed in bar ~ Open 11-11(11.30 Sat); 12-11 Sun
Recommended by Anthony Barnes

Fat Cat 🍺
West End Street; NR2 4NA

A place of pilgrimage for beer lovers, and open all day

As well as keeping an extraordinary range of interesting real ales, you can be sure of a friendly welcome in this well run and very popular little pub. As well as their own beers (brewed at their sister pub, The Cidershed) Fat Cat Bitter, Honey, Marmalade, Stout and Top Cat, the fantastic choice (on handpump or tapped from the cask in a stillroom behind the bar – big windows reveal all) might include Adnams Best, Broadside and Regatta, Dark Star Espresso Stout, Dunham Massey Light, Elgoods Black Dog Mild, Everards Old Original, Exmoor Gold, Green Jack Mahseer IPA, Greene King Abbot, Harviestoun Bitter & Twisted, Hop Back GFB, Humpty Dumpty Porter, Kelham Island Pale Rider, Orkney Red MacGregor, Timothy Taylors Landlord and Woodfordes Wherry. You'll also find ten draught beers from Belgium and Germany, up to 80 bottled beers from around the world, and ciders and perries. There's a lively bustling atmosphere at busy times, with maybe tranquil lulls in the middle of the afternoon, and a good mix of cheerful customers. The no-nonsense furnishings include plain scrubbed pine tables and simple solid seats, lots of brewery memorabilia, bric-a-brac and stained-glass. There are tables outside.

🍴 Bar food consists of rolls and good pies at lunchtime (not Sunday).

Free house ~ Licensee Colin Keatley ~ Real ale ~ Bar food (available until sold out; not Sun) ~ No credit cards ~ (01603) 624364 ~ Dogs allowed in bar ~ Open 12(11 Sat)-11(midnight Fri and Sat); 12-10.30 Sun
Recommended by the Didler, Mick Hitchman, William Mack, Dr and Mrs A K Clarke

OLD BUCKENHAM   TM0691 MAP 5
Gamekeeper
B1077 S of Attleborough; The Green; NR17 1RE

Pretty pub with nicely refurbished bars, friendly service, interesting food and seats on the terrace

With a good mix of both drinking and dining customers, this pretty 16th-c pub is a civilised and friendly place. The beamed bar, with two main areas, has leather armchairs and a sofa in front of the big open woodburning stove in the capacious inglenook fireplace, a pleasant variety of nice old wooden seats and tables on the fine old flagstones or wooden flooring, and local watercolours on the walls; there are two unusual interior bow windows. Adnams Bitter, Timothy Taylors Landlord and Woodfordes Wherry on handpump, quite a few wines by the glass, and several malt whiskies. Besides the comfortable main back dining area which includes some stripped high-backed settles and a grand piano, there's a small separate room used for private dining. The back terrace has seats and tables and there are picnic-sets on the grass beyond.

🍽 **Popular bar food includes sandwiches, soup, smoked haddock and gruyère tart, chicken liver, wild mushroom and bacon linguine, battered hake with minted mushy peas, beefburger with cheese and bacon, puy lentil and courgette shepherd's pie with goats cheese mash and parsnips, ginger tiger prawns, chicken and udon noodles with cashews, chilli and coriander, pork steak with caramelised apple and swiss cheese mash, and monkfish with chargrilled mediterranean vegetables, parsley gremolata and baby lemons.** *Starters/Snacks: £4.95 to £5.95. Main Courses: £9.95 to £17.50. Puddings: £4.75 to £6.00*

Enterprise ~ Lease David Francis ~ Real ale ~ Bar food (not Sun evening) ~ Restaurant ~ (01953) 860397 ~ Children allowed away from bar ~ Dogs allowed in bar ~ Open 11.30-3, 6-11; 12-5 Sun; closed Sun evening

Recommended by David and Cathrine Whiting, Sheila Topham, John Cook, John Wooll

RINGSTEAD   TF7040   MAP 8

Gin Trap 🍽 ♀

Village signposted off A149 near Hunstanton; OS Sheet 132 map reference 707403; PE36 5JU

Attractive coaching inn, caring, friendly licensees, good interesting food and wines; bedrooms

Our readers very much enjoy their visits to this spotlessly kept pub. It's an attractive white-painted 17th-c coaching inn and you can be sure of a genuinely warm and friendly welcome from the hard-working, hands-on licensees. The neat bar has beams, a woodburning stove, captain's chairs and cast-iron-framed tables, and Adnams Bitter, Woodfordes Wherry and a guest like Woodfordes Nelsons Revenge on handpump; piped music and board games. The light and airy dining conservatory overlooks the garden where there are seats and tables. In front of the building, a handsome spreading chestnut tree shelters the car park. The Peddar's Way is close by.

🍽 **Enjoyably good, well presented bar food includes sandwiches, soup, pressed ham hock terrine with home-made piccalilli and home-baked bread, home-cured mackerel fillet with a potato and chive salad, bacon and lemon oil, beer-battered fresh haddock with home-made tartare sauce, leek and blue cheese quiche with wild mushrooms, asparagus and chive butter sauce, organic beefburger with home-made relish and monterey jack cheese, saddleback pork belly with apple and sage tart, shallot purée and cider jus, pollack with chorizo and bean cassoulet with scallop fritters and salsa verde, and puddings like roasted spiced plums with madeira zabaglione and warm treacle tart with clotted cream ice-cream and vanilla sea salt.** *Starters/Snacks: £5.00 to £8.50. Main Courses: £9.00 to £13.00. Puddings: £5.75 to £7.50*

Free house ~ Licensees Cindy Cook and Steve Knowles ~ Real ale ~ Bar food (12-2(2.30 Sat and Sun), 6-9(9.30 Fri and Sat)) ~ Restaurant ~ (01485) 525264 ~ Children welcome (not in bedrooms) ~ Dogs allowed in bar and bedrooms ~ Open 11.30-11(midnight Sat); 11.30-2.30, 6-11 in winter ~ Bedrooms: £60S(£70B)/£100S(£120B)

Recommended by John Wooll, Brian and Anna Marsden, Tracey and Stephen Groves, KN-R, Roy Hoing, R C Vincent, Pete Devonish, Ian McIntyre, JJW, CMW, Ryta Lyndley, Andy and Claire Barker, Mrs Carolyn Dixon, Mrs V Middlebrook

'Children welcome' means the pub says it lets children inside without any special restriction. If it allows them in, but to restricted areas such as an eating area or family room, we specify this. Places with separate restaurants often let children use them; hotels usually let them into public areas such as lounges. Some pubs impose an evening time limit – let us know if you find one earlier than 9pm.

SNETTISHAM

TF6834 MAP 8

Rose & Crown ❢ ♀ ⌑

Village signposted from A149 King's Lynn—Hunstanton just N of Sandringham; coming in on the B1440 from the roundabout just N of village, take first left turn into Old Church Road; PE31 7LX

Constantly improving old pub, log fires and interesting furnishings, thoughtful food, fine range of drinks, and stylish seating on heated terrace; well equipped, popular bedrooms

It's not easy to appeal to a really wide mix of customers, but this pretty white cottage seems to do just that – helped, of course, by a warm welcome from the friendly staff, no matter how busy they are. Locals pop in and out for a chat and a pint; it's an extremely popular place for an enjoyable meal out; and our readers regularly stay overnight in the attractive bedrooms. The smallest of the three bars is a mocha coffee-colour with coir flooring and old prints of King's Lynn and Sandringham. Each of the other two bars has a separate character: an old-fashioned beamed front bar with black settles on its tiled floor and a big log fire, and a back bar with another large log fire and the landlord's sporting trophies and old sports equipment (which are being slowly edged out to make way for the pub cricket team photos). There's also the Garden Room with inviting wicker-based wooden chairs, careful lighting and a quote by Dr Johnson in old-fashioned rolling script on a huge wall board, and a residents' lounge (liked by non-residents, too) with squashy armchairs and sofas, rugs on the floor, newspapers, magazines, jigsaws and board games. Adnams Bitter and Broadside, Fullers London Pride and Greene King IPA on handpump, a dozen wines by the glass, organic fruit juices and farm cider. In the garden there are stylish café-style blue chairs and tables under cream parasols on the terrace, outdoor heaters and colourful herbaceous borders. Two of the comfortable bedrooms are downstairs and there are disabled lavatories and wheelchair ramps.

❢ Enjoyable food includes lunchtime sandwiches, soup, chorizo and black pudding with sautéed potatoes and a poached egg, smoked salmon sushi, tempura red mullet, soy sauce and sweet chilli mayonnaise, local bangers and mash with onion gravy, prime steak burger with bacon, cheese and real tomato ketchup, pasta with seafood ragoût, free-range chicken with porcini ravioli and cep velouté, daily specials such as fishcakes with citrus mayonnaise and pancetta and sun-dried tomato risotto, and puddings like orange sponge pudding with crème anglaise and chocolate and zabaglione parfait with smashed honeycomb. *Starters/Snacks: £5.50 to £7.50. Main Courses: £8.50 to £16.50. Puddings: £5.50 to £6.50*

Free house ~ Licensee Anthony Goodrich ~ Real ale ~ Bar food (12-2(2.30 weekends and school holidays), 6-9(9.30 Fri and Sat)) ~ Restaurant ~ (01485) 541382 ~ Children welcome ~ Dogs welcome ~ Open 11-11; 12-10.30 Sun ~ Bedrooms: £70B/£90B

Recommended by Alan Sutton, John Wooll, Philip Vernon, Kim Maidment, DF, NF, Conrad Freezer, Eithne Dandy, Charlie and Chris Barker, John Robertson, Peter Cole, Sally Anne and Peter Goodale, Barry and Patricia Wooding, Pete Coxon, John Saville, Tracey and Stephen Groves, Les and Sandra Brown, Michael Dandy, David Rule

STIFFKEY

TF9643 MAP 8

Red Lion

A149 Wells—Blakeney; NR23 1AJ

Traditional pub with bustling atmosphere, attractive layout, tasty food and real ales; bedrooms

Traditional and with an unpretentious feel, this bustling pub is run by a friendly landlord. The oldest parts of the simple bars have a few beams, aged flooring tiles or bare floorboards and big open fires. There's also a mix of pews, small settles and a couple of stripped high-backed settles, a nice old long deal table among quite a few others, Woodfordes Nelsons Revenge and Wherry, and a guest like Greene King Abbot on handpump, and several wines by the glass; a good mix of customers; board games. A back gravel terrace has proper tables and seats, with more on the grass further up; there are some pleasant walks nearby.

🍴 Tasty bar food includes sandwiches, ploughman's, soup, soft herring roes on toast, honey and mustard ham and eggs, apple, leek and blue cheese risotto, lasagne, lamb stew and dumplings, salmon with curried chickpeas and mint yoghurt, and puddings; Sunday roasts. *Starters/Snacks: £4.25 to £6.50. Main Courses: £7.50 to £18.00. Puddings: £4.95 to £6.95*

Free house ~ Licensee Stephen Franklin ~ Real ale ~ Bar food (11-2.30, 6-9; all day weekends) ~ (01328) 830552 ~ Children welcome ~ Dogs welcome ~ Live music monthly Fri evening ~ Open 8am-11pm ~ Bedrooms: £80B/£100B

Recommended by Mrs Carolyn Dixon, William Mack, the Didler, Derek Field, Ken and Jenny Simmonds, Mike and Shelley Woodroffe, Pete Devonish, Ian McIntyre, Mike Proctor, Tracey and Stephen Groves, Trevor and Sheila Sharman, David Field, Dr D J and Mrs S C Walker, Gwyn and Anne Wake

STOW BARDOLPH
TF6205   MAP 5

Hare Arms ♀
Just off A10 N of Downham Market; PE34 3HT

Long-serving licensees in this bustling village pub, real ales, good mix of customers, tasty bar food and a big back garden

For 33 years, this neatly kept village pub has been run by the same friendly licensees. There's always a cheerful, bustling atmosphere in the bar as well as some interesting bric-a-brac like old advertising signs and golf clubs suspended from the ceiling, as well as fresh flowers, dark pubby furniture and comfortable built-in wall seats, a good log fire, and a central servery. This bar opens into a well planted conservatory where families are allowed. Greene King IPA, Abbot, Old Speckled Hen, Ruddles County, and a guest beer on handpump, quite a few wines by the glass and several malt whiskies. There are plenty of seats in the large garden behind with more in the pretty front garden, and chickens and peacocks roam freely. Church Farm Rare Breeds Centre is a five-minute walk away and is open April-October.

🍴 As well as lunchtime sandwiches, filled baked potatoes and ploughman's, bar food includes lots of salads such as vietnamese chicken or tuna niçoise, a curry of the day, chilli con carne, steak and peppercorn pie, and gammon with pineapple, with daily specials such as sausages on spring onion mash with red onion gravy, a puff pastry parcel filled with aubergine, tomatoes and red peppers, gressingham duck leg with an apricot and orange stuffing with orange-flavoured gravy, and seared tuna on coriander and ginger noodles topped with pineapple chutney. *Starters/Snacks: £4.00 to £8.25. Main Courses: £8.50 to £18.00. Puddings: £5.50*

Greene King ~ Lease David and Trish McManus ~ Real ale ~ Bar food (12-2, 6.30-10; all day Sun) ~ Restaurant ~ (01366) 382229 ~ Children in small conservatory ~ Open 11-2.30, 6-11; 12-10.30 Sun; closed 25 and 26 Dec

Recommended by George Atkinson, Tracey and Stephen Groves, John Wooll, Mark, Amanda, Luke and Jake Sheard, John Saville, Mike Proctor, R C Vincent, Alan and Jill Bull

SWANTON MORLEY
TG0217   MAP 8

Darbys
B1147 NE of Dereham; NR20 4NY

Unspoilt country local, several real ales, plenty of farming knick-knacks, popular bar food, and children's play area

With lots to look at and several real ales, this friendly local does get busy. The long bare-boarded country-style bar has a comfortable lived-in feel, with big stripped-pine tables and chairs, lots of gin traps and farming memorabilia, a good log fire (with the original bread oven alongside) and tractor seats with folded sacks lining the long, attractive serving counter. Adnams Bitter and Broadside, Beeston Afternoon Delight, Woodfordes Wherry and two guests such as Grain Blonde Ash and Wolf Straw Dog on handpump. A step up through a little doorway by the fireplace takes you through to the attractive dining room with neat, dark tables and chairs on the wooden floor; the children's room has a toy box and a glassed-over well, floodlit from inside. Piped music and board games. There are picnic-sets and a children's play area in the back garden. Plenty to do locally (B&B is available in carefully converted farm buildings a few minutes away) as the family also own the adjoining 720-acre estate.

🍴 **Popular bar food includes filled rolls, soup, garlic and stilton mushrooms, omelettes, various salad bowls, burgers, vegetable bake, ham and egg, steak and kidney pudding, chicken with a sweet, spicy topping, steaks (from their own herd of rare breed cattle), and puddings.** *Starters/Snacks: £3.95 to £6.75. Main Courses: £5.25 to £19.95. Puddings: £4.75*

Free house ~ Licensees John Carrick and Louise Battle ~ Real ale ~ Bar food (12-2.15, 6.30-9.45; all day weekends) ~ Restaurant ~ (01362) 637647 ~ Children welcome ~ Dogs allowed in bar ~ Open 11.30-3, 6-11; 11.30-11 (summer Fri) Sat; 12-10.30 Sun ~ Bedrooms: £35S(£40B)/£60(£70S)(£75B)

Recommended by R C Vincent, John Cook, Tony Middis, Mr and Mrs Staples

THORNHAM   TF7343   MAP 8

Lifeboat 🛏

Turn off A149 by Kings Head, then take first left turn; PE36 6LT

Good mix of customers and lots of character in traditional inn, five open fires, real ales and super surrounding walks

A new licensee has taken over this popular inn but, thankfully, little has changed. The main bar has low settles, window seats, pews, carved oak tables and rugs on the tiles, and masses of guns, swords, black metal mattocks, reed-slashers and other antique farm tools; lighting is by antique paraffin lamps suspended among an array of traps and yokes on the great oak-beamed ceiling. A couple of little rooms lead off here, and all in all there are five open fires. No games machines or piped music, though they still play the ancient game of 'pennies' which was outlawed in the late 1700s, and dominoes. Up some steps from the conservatory is a sunny terrace with picnic-sets, and further back is a children's playground with a fort and slide. Adnams Bitter, Greene King IPA and Abbot, Woodfordes Wherry and a changing guest on handpump, and several wines by the glass. The inn faces half a mile of coastal sea flats and there are lots of surrounding walks.

🍴 **Good bar food includes sandwiches, ploughman's, soup, chicken and duck liver pâté with redcurrant sauce, goats cheese filo parcel with plum sauce, oriental vegetable stir fry, moules marinière, beefburger with bacon and cheese and onion marmalade, sausages on horseradish mash with onion gravy, salmon and dill fishcakes with a red pepper coulis, chicken breast stuffed with oyster mushrooms and mozzarella with a sun-dried tomato sauce, and daily specials like seared lambs liver with sweet onion gravy, and beef fillet strips in a stilton and port wine sauce.** *Starters/Snacks: £5.95 to £8.95. Main Courses: £9.95 to £19.00. Puddings: £4.50*

Maypole Group ~ Manager Tristan McEwen ~ Real ale ~ Bar food (12-2.30, 6.30-9.30) ~ Restaurant ~ (01485) 512236 ~ Children welcome ~ Dogs welcome ~ Open 10am-11pm(10.30 Sun) ~ Bedrooms: £75B/£112B

Recommended by the Didler, Rev David Maher, Mr and Mrs A H Young, Mike and Sue Loseby, Tracey and Stephen Groves, Derek and Sylvia Stephenson, David and Ruth Hollands, Bruce and Sharon Eden, Alan Sutton, Sally Anne and Peter Goodale, Michael Dandy, George Atkinson, Len Clark, Gwyn and Anne Wake, M E and J R Hart, John Saville, Mike Proctor, JJW, CMW, Malcolm and Pauline Pellatt, J K Parry, Derek Field, Allan Westbury, Roger and Kath, Brian and Anna Marsden, Alistair and Kay Butler

---

A very few pubs try to make you leave a credit card at the bar, as a sort of deposit if you order food. They are not entitled to do this. The credit card firms and banks which issue them warn you not to let them out of your sight. If someone behind the counter used your card fraudulently, the card company or bank could in theory hold you liable, because of your negligence in letting a stranger hang on to your card. Suggest instead that if they feel the need for security, they 'swipe' your card and give it back to you. And do name and shame the pub to us.

WARHAM
TF9441   MAP 8

Three Horseshoes ★ 🍺 🛏

Warham All Saints; village signposted from A149 Wells-next-the-Sea—Blakeney, and from B1105 S of Wells; NR23 1NL

Old-fashioned pub with gas lighting in simple rooms, interesting furnishings and pubby food; gramophone museum

'Worth travelling miles to see this gem' says one reader who was delighted to find such an unspoilt and old-fashioned pub. The simple interior with its gas lighting looks little changed since the 1920s and parts of the building date back to the 1720s. There are stripped deal or mahogany tables (one marked for shove-ha'penny) on a stone floor, red leatherette settles built around the partly panelled walls of the public bar, royalist photographs and open fires in Victorian fireplaces. An antique American Mills one-arm bandit is still in working order (it takes 5p pieces but might not pay out!), there's a big longcase clock with a clear piping strike and a twister on the ceiling to point out who gets the next round; darts and board games. Greene King IPA, Woodfordes Wherry and maybe a guest like Blackfriars Yarmouth Bitter on handpump, local cider and home-made lemonade; friendly service. One of the outbuildings houses a wind-up gramophone museum – opened on request. There's a courtyard with flower tubs and a well, and a garden.

🍽 **Large helpings of proper pub food such as tasty game soup, beans on toast, filled baked potatoes, home-cooked gammon, suet-topped pies, rabbit, pigeon or pheasant casseroles, and puddings like spotted dick or syrup sponge.** *Starters/Snacks: £3.80 to £5.50. Main Courses: £7.80 to £9.90. Puddings: £3.90*

Free house ~ Licensee Iain Salmon ~ Real ale ~ Bar food (12-1.45, 6-8.30) ~ No credit cards ~ (01328) 710547 ~ Children welcome away from bar area ~ Dogs welcome ~ Open 12-2.30, 6-11 ~ Bedrooms: £28/£56(£60S)

Recommended by the Didler, Dan and Holly Pitcher, Julia Mann, Tracey and Stephen Groves, Jim Farmer, John Wooll, Pete Baker, Brian and Anna Marsden, Mrs B Barwick, Neil Ingoe, John Honnor, Anthony Longden, John Beeken, Mrs M B Gregg

WELLS-NEXT-THE-SEA
TF9143   MAP 8

Crown 🍽 ♀ 🛏
The Buttlands; NR23 1EX

Smart coaching inn, friendly informal bar, local ales, good modern food, and stylish orangery; bedrooms

The friendly, relaxed bar in this rather smart 16th-c coaching inn has a good mix of both drinkers and diners and there's a bustling, cheerful atmosphere. There are beams and the odd standing timbers; and the contemporary décor includes burnt-orange walls hung with local photographs and souvenirs from the film *Hot Fuzz* (the crew and cast stayed here), grey-painted planked walls seats with orange cushions and high-backed dark brown leather dining chairs around wooden-topped tables on the stripped-wood floor, and newspapers to read in front of the open fire. Adnams Bitter, Woodfordes Wherry and a guest like Woodfordes Sundew on handpump, quite a few wines by the glass and several whiskies and brandies; helpful staff, piped music and board games. The conservatory is a stylish orangery and there's a more formal, rather smart, restaurant, too. This inn is in the same small group as the Crown at East Rudham and the Kings Head at Letheringsett (both new Main Entries this year).

🍽 **Attractively presented and very good, the bar food includes lunchtime sandwiches, soup, ham hock and duck-leg terrine with chilli ham, devilled lambs kidneys with sour cream, moules marinière, battered haddock, twice-baked goats cheese soufflé with pepper coulis, fish in thai watermelon curry, slow-roast pork belly with apple sauce and crackling, chicken stuffed with sunblush tomato, mozzarella and basil, rack of lamb with tapenade jus, and puddings; Sunday roast and good breakfasts.** *Starters/Snacks: £3.95 to £11.00. Main Courses: £10.95 to £20.95. Puddings: £6.00*

Free house ~ Licensees Chris and Jo Coubrough ~ Real ale ~ Bar food (12-2.30, 6.30-9.30) ~ Restaurant ~ (01328) 710209 ~ Children welcome ~ Dogs allowed in bar and bedrooms ~ Open 11-11 ~ Bedrooms: £110B/£130B

Recommended by John Wooll, Simon Cottrell, Len Beattie, M and GR, Mrs J C Pank, David Carr, N R White, Rod Stoneman, Bruce and Sharon Eden, Steve and Liz Tilley, Tracey and Stephen Groves, John Cook, John and Gloria Isaacs, Joyce and Maurice Cottrell, DF, NF, R C Vincent, Mrs Romey Heaton, Robert Ager, Michael Dandy, David Field

Globe
The Buttlands; NR23 1EU

Attractive contemporary layout, good food and drink, and nice back courtyard; bedrooms

Friendly and busy, this handsome Georgian inn is just a short walk from the quay, and the opened-up rooms (redecorated this year) have a relaxed contemporary feel and spread spaciously back from the front bar. Three big bow windows look over to a green lined by tall lime trees, there are well spaced tables on oak boards, walls in grey, cream or mulberry with moody local landscape photoprints, and well judged modern lighting. Adnams Bitter and Broadside, and Woodfordes Wherry and Nelsons Revenge on handpump, a thoughtful choice of wines, and nice coffee; piped music and TV. An attractive heated back courtyard has dark green cast-iron furniture on pale flagstones among trellis tubs with lavender, roses and jasmine.

⑪ Enjoyable bar food includes lunchtime sandwiches, terrine with chutney, crispy whitebait and garlic aioli, caesar salad, minted lamb burger, ham and free-range eggs, liver and bacon with red onion gravy, vegetarian chilli with saffron rice and sour cream, beer-battered fish with mushy peas and tartare sauce, and sirloin steak with mustard butter. *Starters/Snacks: £4.95 to £7.95. Main Courses: £7.95 to £12.95. Puddings: £4.95 to £5.50*

Free house ~ Licensees Viscount Coke and Ian Brereton ~ Real ale ~ Bar food (12-2.30, 7(6 in summer)-9) ~ Restaurant ~ (01328) 710206 ~ Children welcome ~ Dogs allowed in bar ~ Jazz summer Sun evenings in courtyard ~ Open 11-11; 12-10.30 Sun ~ Bedrooms: /£120B

Recommended by Tracey and Stephen Groves, Bruce and Sharon Eden, Derek Field, George Atkinson, Michael Dandy, David Carr, Brian and Anna Marsden, DF, NF, Dan and Holly Pitcher, Amanda Goodrich, Mike and Shelley Woodroffe, Gwyn and Anne Wake

WEST BECKHAM   TG1439   MAP 8

Wheatsheaf ◀
Off A148 Holt—Cromer; Church Road; NR25 6NX

Fine real ales and home-made food in nice, traditional pub, seats and children's play area in the front garden

With friendly, helpful staff and a bustling atmosphere, this brick-built pub is a popular place for a drink or a meal. There are several bars, mostly set for dining, with beams, standing timbers, cottagey doors and a couple of roaring winter log fires, and the furnishings are pleasantly traditional with plenty of dark wooden wheelback chairs, settles and comfortably cushioned wall seats around pubby tables. Greene King IPA and Abbot, and Woodfordes Admirals Reserve, Nelsons Revenge and Wherry on handpump, and quite a few wines by the glass. The charming, ramshackle garden has a covered terrace and seats both here and on the grass; there's an enclosed children's play area and some elusive rabbits.

⑪ As well as lunchtime sandwiches, the well liked bar food includes soup, mackerel pâté with lemon croûtons, avocado with crab and crayfish, mediterranean vegetable risotto with goats cheese and pesto, lamb burger with tomato and chilli relish, beef in ale pie, sardines on ratatouille and fresh tagliatelle, chicken breast in a herby crust topped with garlic butter, gammon steak strips with pineapple and coriander salsa, and puddings such as marmalade bread and butter pudding and chocolate and Baileys torte. *Starters/Snacks: £4.50 to £5.95. Main Courses: £9.50 to £13.95. Puddings: £4.95*

Free house ~ Licensees Clare and Daniel Mercer ~ Real ale ~ Bar food (12-2(4 Sun), 7-9; not Sun evening or Mon (except bank hols)) ~ Restaurant ~ (01263) 822110 ~ Children welcome ~ Dogs allowed in bar ~ Open 12-3, 6.30-11; 12-5 Sun; closed Sun evening and Mon (except bank hols)

Recommended by George Atkinson, Virginia Williams, Tracey and Stephen Groves, Sally Anne and Peter Goodale, Derek Field, Jim Farmer, D and M T Ayres-Regan, Allan Westbury, Terry Mizen, Trevor and Sheila Sharman, Mr and Mrs John Taylor

WEYBOURNE

TG1143   MAP 8

Ship 🍺

A149 W of Sheringham; The Street; NR25 7SZ

Up to six real ales in a cheerful village pub, well liked food and seats outside

With a good choice of up to six real ales on handpump and plenty of chatty locals, this well run village pub has a cheerful atmosphere. Changing regularly, the beers might include Buffys Norwich Terrier, Grain Oak, Humpty Dumpty Ale, Woodfordes Wherry and Yetmans Red; decent wines by the glass. The big comfortably straightforward bar has pubby furniture, a woodburning stove and friendly service, and there are also two dining rooms; unobtrusive piped music. There are seats in the garden and pretty hanging baskets. The Muckleburgh Military Vehicle Museum is nearby.

🍴 Using local meat which they butcher themselves and catching fish from their own boat, the well liked bar food might include sandwiches and filled baguettes, filled baked potatoes, soup, lamb terrine with minted pear chutney, wild mushroom risotto, chicken breast with home-made tagliatelle and mushroom sauce, beer-battered haddock, gammon and egg, ravioli in fresh tomato sauce, and salmon with a hot marmalade sauce. *Starters/Snacks: £4.50 to £5.75. Main Courses: £9.75 to £19.00. Puddings: £4.75*

Free house ~ Licensee Terry Rayner ~ Real ale ~ Bar food (12-2(2.30 weekends), 6.30-9(6.30-9.30 weekends)) ~ (01263) 588721 ~ Well behaved children welcome ~ Dogs allowed in bar ~ Open 11-11; 11-3, 5-11 in winter

Recommended by Derek Field

WIVETON

TG0442   MAP 8

Bell 🍽️ 🛏️

Blakeney Road; NR25 7TL

Busy, open-plan dining pub, drinkers welcomed too, local beers, fine food, and seats outside; bedrooms

Open-plan and friendly, this popular pub does keep some tables free for those just wanting a drink (and the bar stools are well used) but the emphasis is very much on the good modern food. There are some fine old beams, an attractive mix of dining chairs around wooden tables on the stripped wooden floor, a log fire and prints on the yellow walls. The sizeable conservatory has smart beige dining chairs around wooden tables on the coir flooring and, throughout, the atmosphere is chatty and relaxed. Friendly and helpful young staff serve Adnams Broadside, Woodfordes Wherry and a changing beer from Yetmans (the brewery is only a mile away) on handpump, and there are several good wines by the glass. Outside, there are picnic-sets on grass in front of the building looking across to the church, and at the back, stylish wicker tables and chairs on several decked areas are set amongst decorative box hedging. The bedrooms are comfortable and they also have a self-catering cottage to let.

🍴 Using local game and fish, the enjoyable food includes sandwiches and various bruschettas, soup, game and foie gras terrine with quince chutney, mussels with cream, garlic and white wine, warm pigeon breast with green beans, roast shallots, watercress and toasted walnuts, thai spiced salmon fishcakes with chilli dipping sauce, local field and wild mushroom risotto, beefburger with smoked cheese and relishes, beer-battered haddock with home-made tartare sauce, lamb rump with garlic confit and rosemary jus, halibut with white beans, cucumber and salsify, and puddings such as chocolate pot and

sticky toffee pudding. *Starters/Snacks: £5.25 to £7.95. Main Courses: £5.25 to £17.95. Puddings: £4.95 to £5.95*

Free house ~ Licensee Berni Morritt ~ Real ale ~ Bar food (not winter Sun evening) ~ (01263) 740101 ~ Children welcome ~ Dogs allowed in bar ~ Open 12-3, 5.30-11; 12-10.30 Sun; closed winter Sun evening ~ Bedrooms: /£95S

Recommended by Robert Watt, Mrs B Barwick, Pete Devonish, Ian McIntyre, Simon Rodway, Mark, Amanda, Luke and Jake Sheard

WOODBASTWICK   TG3214   MAP 8

Fur & Feather 🍺

Off B1140 E of Norwich; NR13 6HQ

Full range of first-class beers from next-door Woodfordes brewery, friendly service and popular bar food

In a lovely estate village, this is a row of thatched cottage buildings that have been carefully converted into a comfortably, roomy pub. The Woodfordes brewery is right next door, so the full range of their beers are in tip-top condition. Tapped from the cask and served by friendly, efficient staff, these include Admirals Reserve, Headcracker, Mardlers, Nelsons Revenge, Norfolk Nip, Norfolk Nog, Sundew and Wherry. You can also visit the brewery shop. Eleven wines by the glass and quite a few malt whiskies. The style and atmosphere are not what you'd expect of a brewery tap as it's set out more like a dining pub; piped music. There are seats and tables out in a pleasant garden.

🍴 Good bar food includes filled rolls and baked potatoes, soup, pork, chicken and ham terrine with apple and ale chutney, goats cheese tart, home-baked ham and egg, steak and kidney pudding, moroccan-style lamb, herby roast chicken with a spicy devilled sauce, pork belly with mustard mash, crackling and red wine gravy, seafood medley, and puddings like chocolate brownie with warm chocolate sauce and vanilla pod ice-cream, and crème brûlée; they also serve cream teas. *Starters/Snacks: £4.50 to £6.50. Main Courses: £9.50 to £11.25. Puddings: £5.25*

Woodfordes ~ Tenant Tim Ridley ~ Real ale ~ Bar food (12-2, 6-9; all day weekends) ~ Restaurant ~ (01603) 720003 ~ Children welcome but must be well behaved ~ Open 11.30-11; 12-10.30 Sun; 11.30-3, 6-10(11 Fri) Mon-Thurs in winter

Recommended by the Didler, Roy Hoing, R C Vincent, Mayur Shah, Robert Ager, Anthony Barnes, Mrs M B Gregg, Malcolm and Kate Dowty, Mike Proctor, Andy and Claire Barker, John Cook, David and Cathrine Whiting, Mrs Romey Heaton, Revd R P Tickle

LUCKY DIP

Besides the fully inspected pubs, you might like to try these Lucky Dips recommended to us and described by readers (if you do, please send us reports: feedback@goodguides.com).

ACLE [TG4111]
Bridge Inn NR13 3AS [N on A1064]: Big riverside pub geared to holiday traffic, two rooms off central bar, good log fire, Adnams and Woodfordes Wherry, Aspall's cider; enjoyable reasonably priced food from doorstep sandwiches inc good vegetarian choice and nice puddings such as toffee lumpy bumpy; good-sized vaulted-ceiling restaurant, several interconnecting rooms comfortably furnished with a variety of settles, chairs and tables; large garden *(John Branston)*
BLAKENEY [TG0244]
Blakeney Hotel NR25 7ND [The Quay]: Pleasant family-owned flint hotel popular with older visitors, nicely set nr bird marshes, elegant harbour-view bar with good

sensibly priced home-made food, friendly attentive staff; well kept Adnams and Woodfordes Wherry, games room, restaurant; dogs welcome, comfortable bedrooms mainly in courtyard *(Paul and Ursula Randall, Roy Bromell)*
☆ *Kings Arms* NR25 7NQ [West Gate St]: A stroll from the harbour, friendly and chatty, with popular home cooking all day, Adnams and Woodfordes; three simple linked low-ceilinged rooms and airy garden room, some mementoes of the licensees' theatrical careers, darts, board games; games machine; big garden, children and dogs welcome, bedrooms, open all day *(LYM, Len Clark, Mrs B Barwick, David Eberlin, Len Beattie, Brian and Anna Marsden, Mayur Shah, Simon Cottrell,*

C and R Bromage, Jim Farmer, William Mack, Gwyn and Anne Wake, Mr and Mrs R Thurston)

BLICKLING [TG1728]

☆ *Buckinghamshire Arms* NR11 6NF [B1354 NW of Aylsham]: Handsome Jacobean inn much visited for its enviable spot by gates to Blickling Hall (NT), small and appealing proper unpretentious bar, lounge set for eating with woodburner, smarter more formal dining room with another woodburner; Adnams, Fullers London Pride and Woodfordes Wherry, good choice of wines by the glass; lots of lawn tables, children welcome, bedrooms *(Miss L Ward, Joan York, R C Vincent, Dr and Mrs R G J Telfer, Sandra Brame, LYM, Mike Proctor, Gaye Caulkett, Terry Mizen)*

BRANCASTER [TF7743]

Ship PE31 8AR [A149]: Reworked 18th-c country inn with good value food, Greene King IPA, big coal fires, extended dining room, attractive local paintings; four comfortable bedrooms, garden picnic-sets *(JJW, CMW)*

BURNHAM OVERY STAITHE [TF8444]

Hero PE31 8JE [A149]: Modernised spacious pub welcoming locals and walkers alike, wide choice of interesting up-to-date food inc vegetarian, well priced wines by the glass, Adnams, good coffee; comfortable contemporary pastel décor, woodburner, two dining areas; tables in garden *(Roger and Lesley Everett, Bruce and Sharon Eden)*

BURNHAM THORPE [TF8541]

☆ *Lord Nelson* PE31 8HL [off B1155 or B1355, nr Burnham Market]: 17th-c pub with interesting Nelson memorabilia, little bar with antique high-backed settles and snug leading off, Greene King Abbot, Woodfordes Wherry and three guests tapped from the cask, lots of wines by the glass, rum-based recipes called Nelson's Blood and Lady Hamilton's Nip; flagstoned eating room with open fire, separate dining room (newish licensees doing italian-leaning food); children and dogs welcome, good-sized play area in big garden, open all day summer, cl Mon pm (except school, bank hols) *(David Gunn, the Didler, LYM, Mike Proctor, Allan Westbury)*

CASTLE ACRE [TF8115]

Albert Victor PE32 2AE [Stocks Green]: Welcoming dining pub with good interesting choice of tasty food from local meats to enterprising vegetarian dishes, well kept Greene King, good range of wines by the glass; large attractive back garden and pergola *(Pete Devonish, Ian McIntyre, Anthony Barnes, Tim and Mark Allen)*

CASTLE RISING [TF6624]

Black Horse PE31 6AG: All-day dining pub with plenty of tables in two front areas and back dining room, quick friendly service, real ales such as Adnams, Greene King and Woodfordes, decent choice of wines by the glass; piped music, no dogs; children particularly welcome, close-set tables out under parasols; by church and almshouses in a pleasant unspoilt village *(R C Vincent, John Wooll, JDM, KM, Tracey and Stephen Groves)*

CATFIELD [TG3821]

Crown NR29 5AA [The Street]: Archetypal village inn, immaculate and tasteful, with good choice of real ales and ciders, warmly welcoming landlady, enjoyable food from italian chef/landlord; bedrooms; not far from Hickling Broad *(Heather Weaver)*

CAWSTON [TG1422]

☆ *Ratcatchers* NR10 4HA [off B1145; Eastgate, S of village]: Beamed dining pub with old chairs and fine mix of walnut, beech, elm and oak tables, quieter candlelit dining room on right, Adnams Bitter and Broadside and a beer from Woodfordes, quite a few malt whiskies, conservatory; piped music, no dogs; children welcome, heated terrace, open all day Sun *(Philip and Susan Philcox, Dr and Mrs R G J Telfer, Roy Hoing, Jim Farmer)*

CLEY NEXT THE SEA [TG0443]

☆ *Three Swallows* NR25 7TT [off A149; Newgate Green]: Unpretentious old-fashioned local with banquettes, pine tables and log fire, steps up to small family eating area, second log fire in stripped-pine dining room on left; good choice of enjoyable reasonably priced food (all day wknds) from sandwiches up, well kept Adnams and Greene King from unusual richly carved bar, decent wines, old photographs, dominoes, cribbage; children and dogs welcome, disabled access, picnic-sets out at front facing the green, big garden with surprisingly grandiose fountain, budgerigars and friendly goat called Sadie; handy for the salt marshes, four simple annex bedrooms, open all day *(Barry Collett, Trevor and Sheila Sharman, C and R Bromage, Derek Field, Roy Hoing, Michael Tack, Jim Farmer, LYM, Mr and Mrs A H Young, Mrs M B Gregg)*

COLTISHALL [TG2719]

☆ *Kings Head* NR12 7EA [Wroxham Rd (B1354)]: Welcoming dining pub close to river, and after inspection by us a likely prospect for this edition's Main Entries, but they failed to respond to our fact-checking enquiries: good imaginative food especially fish, generous bar snacks and good value lunch deals, friendly helpful service, well kept Adnams, nice wines by the glass; open fire, fishing nets and stuffed fish inc monster pike (personable chef/landlord a keen fisherman); piped music; reasonably priced bedrooms, decent breakfast, moorings nearby *(Alun Jones, BB, David and Ruth Shillitoe, Derek and Maggie Washington)*

CROMER [TG2242]

Red Lion NR27 9HD [off A149; Tucker St/Brook St]: Pubby carpeted bar in substantial Victorian hotel with elevated sea views, stripped flint and William Morris wallpaper, old bottles and chamber-pots, lifeboat pictures; well kept Adnams, Woodfordes Wherry and two guests, friendly efficient staff, pleasant old-fashioned atmosphere, enjoyable standard food (all day Sun), restaurant, conservatory; children welcome, no dogs, disabled facilities, back courtyard tables, 12 comfortable bedrooms, open all day *(B R and M F Arnold, Denys Gueroult, JDM, KM)*

DEREHAM [TF9813]

George NR19 2AZ [Swaffham Rd]: Welcoming panelled bar with alcove seating, friendly attentive service, well kept ales such as Adnams and Woodfordes, good bar food choice; good bedrooms *(J A Ellis)*

DERSINGHAM [TF6930]

Feathers PE31 6LN [B1440 towards Sandringham; Manor Rd]: Solid Jacobean sandstone inn freshened up under new local owners, relaxed modernised dark-panelled bar, Adnams, Bass and a guest, pubby food; friendly service, log fires, back eating room, more contemporary restaurant, separate games room in converted barn with pool, darts and machines, live music here too Sat fortnightly; piped music; children and dogs welcome, large family garden with play area, attractive secluded adults' garden with pond, six comfortable well furnished bedrooms, open all day *(LYM, Tracey and Stephen Groves, John Wooll, Philip and Susan Philcox)*

DRAYTON [TG1813]

Cock NR8 6AE [Drayton High Rd]: Recently reopened after pleasant refurbishment, quick welcoming service, good choice of Marstons-related ales, good value food inc popular Sun lunch *(R C Vincent)*

EAST RUSTON [TG3428]

Butchers Arms NR12 9JG [back rd Honing—Happisburgh, N of Stalham]: Comfortable village local, friendly and well run, generous food inc bargain lunchtime dish of the day, real ales, two dining rooms; attractive garden, handy for Old Vicarage garden *(Roy Hoing)*

GAYTON [TF7219]

Crown PE32 1PA [Lynn Rd (B1145/B1153)]: Low-beamed country pub with plenty of character, unusual old features and charming snug as well as three main areas; good choice of sensibly priced food inc good value sandwiches, light dishes and lunchtime hot buffet, friendly service, Greene King ales, limited but good wine choice; good log fire, games room; tables in attractive sheltered garden *(Tracey and Stephen Groves, LYM)*

GELDESTON [TM3990]

☆ *Locks* NR34 0HW [off A143/A146 NW of Beccles; off Station Rd S of village, obscurely signed down long rough track]: Remote candlelit pub at navigable head of River Waveney, ancient tiled-floor core with beams and big log fire, Green Jack and guest ales tapped from casks, enjoyable food; large extension for summer crowds, wknd music nights; riverside garden; open all day wknds and summer; in winter cl Mon, Tues and Weds-Fri lunchtimes *(LYM, the Didler, P Dawn)*

GREAT BIRCHAM [TF7632]

☆ *Kings Head* PE31 6RJ [B1155, S end of village (called and signed Bircham locally)]:

More hotel/restaurant than pub, yet with plenty of regulars and four real ales in small attractively contemporary bar with log fire and comfortable sofas; good innovative food inc good value deals in light and airy modern restaurant, attentive friendly staff; TV in bar; tables and chairs out front and back with rustic view, comfortable bedrooms, good breakfast *(LYM, R C Vincent, Tracey and Stephen Groves)*

GREAT YARMOUTH [TG5206]

Red Herring NR30 3HQ [Havelock Rd]: Friendly open-plan alehouse with changing ales inc local Blackfriars, farm cider, rock collection, old local photographs; games area with pool; open all day wknds *(the Didler)*

St Johns Head NR30 1JB [North Quay]: Traditional pub with friendly staff, real ales inc bargain Elgoods, pool, juke box *(P Dawn, the Didler)*

HARLESTON [TM2483]

Swan IP20 9AS [The Thoroughfare (narrow main st on one-way circuit, look out for narrow coach entry)]: Newly refurbished 16th-c coaching inn, friendly chatty locals and cheerful staff, well kept Adnams, reasonably priced wine, decent good value food; two linked lounge rooms, ancient timbers, log fire in big inglenook, separate public bar; bedrooms *(KC)*

HARPLEY [TF7825]

☆ *Rose & Crown* PE31 6TW [off A148 Fakenham—King's Lynn; Nethergate St]: Refreshing contemporary décor with local artwork and old wooden tables, good value food, interesting dishes as well as usual pubby things inc popular Sun roast; welcoming young staff, good choice of wines by the glass, well kept ales inc Greene King, big log fire, dining room on left; attractive garden, cl Mon, Tues lunchtime *(Mrs Brenda Calver, Sally Anne and Peter Goodale, R C Vincent, John Wooll, Pete Devonish, Ian McIntyre, Anthony Barnes, BB)*

HEYDON [TG1127]

Earle Arms NR11 6AD [off B1149]: Well kept Adnams and Woodfordes Wherry and enjoyable food using local fish and meat; racing prints and log fire in old-fashioned bar, more formal dining room; children welcome, picnic-sets in small prettily cottagey back garden, delightfully unspoilt village *(Andrew Rudalevige, LYM)*

HICKLING [TG4123]

Greyhound NR12 0YA [The Green]: Small busy pub with enjoyable food inc good Sun roasts in bar and neat restaurant, well kept ales, friendly long-serving landlord; well behaved children welcome, pretty garden with terrace tables, bedroom annex *(Robert Ager, Roy Hoing)*

HOLKHAM [TF8943]

☆ *Victoria* NR23 1RG [A149 nr Holkham Hall]: Upmarket but informal small hotel (owned by Holkham estate), usually most enjoyable, with eclectic mix of furnishings inc deep low sofas, big log fire, fat lighted candles in heavy sticks; well kept Adnams Bitter, Woodfordes Wherry and a guest beer, nice wines, decent coffees, generally attentive service, good if not cheap local seasonal food, anglo-indian décor in linked dining rooms (best to book); piped music; children welcome, dogs in bar, sheltered courtyard with retractable awning, walks to nature-reserve salt marshes and sea; ten stylish bedrooms, open all day *(Fred and Lorraine Gill, Tracey and Stephen Groves, Michael Dandy, Mike and Sue Loseby, Kevin Thomas, Nina Randall, LYM, Dan and Holly Pitcher, John Honnor)*

HOLT [TG0738]

☆ *Kings Head* NR25 6BN [High St/Bull St]: Cheerful recently reworked two-bar pub (same owners as nearby Pigs at Edgefield – see Main Entries), reasonably priced fresh food all day from baguettes up, prompt friendly service, Adnams, Buffys, Elgoods and Woodfordes ales, fair choice of wines; open fires, some leather easy chairs, pleasant dining conservatory; children welcome, back terrace with heated smokers' shelter, good-sized garden, bedrooms planned *(John Wooll, Derek Field, David Carr, Charles Gysin, Michael Tack, BB)*

HONINGHAM [TG1011]

☆ *Buck* NR9 5BL [just off A47 W of Norwich; The Street]: Picturesque 16th-c pub, popular little dining place, all very simple and unpretentious; straightforward dark wood tables with scented nightlights, red-seated dining chairs on patterned carpet, heavily varnished beams and timbers, cream or red walls; Adnams Bitter and Broadside, a few bar stools, former inglenook at one end converted into bygones' showcase; seats on sheltered lawn, rope hanging from big sycamore and netted goal for children *(BB, Gillian Grist)*

HORSTEAD [TG2619]

☆ *Recruiting Sergeant* NR12 7EE [B1150 just S of Coltishall]: Large, friendly and pleasantly refurbished, with good value generous food from fresh baguettes up inc good fish choice, splendid service even when busy; real ales inc one brewed for the pub, impressive choice of reasonably priced wines by the glass, big open fire, brasses and muskets, music-free smaller room; children welcome *(Alun Jones)*

HUNSTANTON [TF6740]

Waterside PE36 5BQ [Beach Terrace Rd]: Former station buffet just above promenade, now bar/restaurant with great sea views from conservatory (children welcome here); Adnams and Greene King Abbot, good value wines, inexpensive straightforward food all day from sandwiches up, quick service by pleasant uniformed staff *(John Wooll)*

KELLING [TG0942]

Pheasant NR25 7EG [A149 Sheringham—Blakeney]: Beautifully placed hotel popular particularly with older people for good value bar meals and bargain lunches; Adnams

Bitter and Broadside, enthusiastic helpful staff, large comfortable lounge/bar, pleasant dining room; woodland grounds, picnic-sets on sheltered lawn, 30 bedrooms *(Paul and Ursula Randall)*

KING'S LYNN [TF6119]

☆ *Bank House* PE30 1RD [Kings Staithe Sq]: Attractive and civilised new big-windowed bar/brasserie under same management as Rose & Crown at Snettisham (see Main Entries); contemporary conversion of handsome Georgian building in splendid quiet quayside spot, Fullers London Pride and Greene King Abbot, decent food from sandwiches to steaks inc light dishes all day; daily papers, sofas, armchairs and pastel colours; 11 good bedrooms, open all day *(BB, John Wooll)*

Bradleys PE30 5DT [South Quay]: Stylishly simple bar/restaurant with good sensibly priced food, good choice of wines by the glass, Adnams beer; beautiful curtains, ornate mirrors, plenty of flowers, more expensive upstairs restaurant with lunch deals; quayside tables and small courtyard garden, open all day *(Mrs Hazel Rainer)*

Crown & Mitre PE30 1LJ [Ferry St]: Old-fashioned pub full of naval and nautical memorabilia, three or four well kept changing ales, planning their own brews too; sandwiches and a freshly made hot special, river views from back conservatory *(John Wooll)*

Dukes Head PE30 1JS [Tuesday Market Pl]: Imposing early 18th-c hotel with small cosy bar on left, popular dining room on right; good value food from baguettes to tender daily roast, chatty jolly staff, local pictures; bedrooms *(Glenwys and Alan Lawrence, John Wooll, Pete Coxon)*

Lloyds No 1 PE30 1EZ [King St/Tuesday Market Pl]: Neatly kept Wetherspoons popular in daytime for bargain food, good beer and wine choice, efficient friendly service; children welcome till 7pm, attractive back garden down to river, pleasant bedrooms, good value breakfast *(John Wooll)*

LITCHAM [TF8817]

Bull PE32 2NS [Church St; B1145]: Two-bar village pub reopened under new landlord, décor mixing old and new, good value usual food, local Beeston ales, decent wine by the glass *(Mark, Amanda, Luke and Jake Sheard)*

MARLINGFORD [TG1309]

Bell NR9 5HX [Bawburgh Rd off Mill Rd]: Friendly and neatly kept country dining pub with enjoyable food inc quickly served daily lunchtime carvery; real ales such as Adnams and Woodfordes, nicely furnished tiled-floor bar, carpeted lounge/dining extension; piped music; children and dogs welcome, terrace picnic-sets *(BB, Eugene Charlier)*

MARSHAM [TG1924]

Plough NR10 5PS [Old Norwich Rd]: Well renovated 18th-c pub with split-level open-plan bar, enjoyable cooking using local produce, real ales such as Adnams, friendly

helpful staff; comfortable clean bedrooms
(Richard Hughes)

NEEDHAM [TM2281]

Red Lion IP20 9LG [High Rd]: Popular neatly
kept dining pub with wide choice of
reasonably priced food, welcoming landlord,
real ales; large back garden with caravan
park *(Mrs Carolyn Dixon)*

NORWICH [TG2108]

Alexandra NR2 3BB [Stafford St]: Friendly
two-bar local with well kept Chalk Hill and
guest ales, cheap home-made food, open
fire, pool, classic juke box; open all day
(the Didler)

Cidershed NR3 4LF [Lawson Rd]: Brewpub
under same ownership as Fat Cat (see Main
Entries), producing its good ales, many guest
beers, interesting layout, second-hand
books, live music inc Sun jazz; open all day
(the Didler)

Coach & Horses NR1 1BA [Thorpe Rd]: Light
and airy tap for Chalk Hill brewery, friendly
staff, generous home-made food 12-9pm
(8pm Sun), also breakfast; bare-boards
L-shaped bar with open fire, dark wood,
posters and prints, pleasant back dining
area; sports TV; disabled access possible
(not to lavatories), front terrace, open all
day *(Dr and Mrs A K Clarke, the Didler)*

Duke of Wellington NR3 1EG [Waterloo Rd]:
Several changing well kept ales and foreign
bottled beers in friendly rambling local; real
fire, traditional games; nice back terrace,
Aug beer festival, open all day *(the Didler)*

☆ *Kings Arms* NR1 3HQ [Hall Rd]: Woody
Batemans local with several changing guest
beers, good whisky and wine choice, friendly
atmosphere; may be lunchtime food (or bring
your own or order out – plates, cutlery
provided), airy garden room; unobtrusive
sports TV; vines in courtyard, open all day
(the Didler)

Kings Head NR3 1JE [Magdalen St]: Lots of
well kept changing regional ales and a local
farm cider, good choice of imported beers,
handsome Victorian-style décor; open all day
(the Didler)

Ribs of Beef NR3 1HY [Wensum St, S side of
Fye Bridge]: Well used old pub, good range
of real ales inc local brews, farm cider, good
wine choice; deep leather sofas and
small tables upstairs, attractive smaller
downstairs room with river view and some
local river paintings; generous cheap food
(till 5pm Sat, Sun), quick friendly service;
tables out on narrow riverside walkway
(John Wooll, the Didler)

Wig & Pen NR3 1RN [St Martins Palace
Plain]: Friendly beamed bar opp the
cathedral close, lawyer and judge prints,
roaring stove, prompt generous food,
Adnams, Buffys and guests, good value
wines; piped music; terrace tables, open all
day, cl Sun evening *(the Didler)*

OLD HUNSTANTON [TF6842]

☆ *Ancient Mariner* PE36 6JJ [part of L'Estrange
Arms Hotel, Golf Course Rd]: Converted barns
and stables of adjacent Victorian hotel,

popular with locals and holidaymakers, low
beams, timbers, bare bricks, flagstones and
maritime bric-a-brac, several areas inc
conservatory and upstairs family gallery;
extensive menu from good sandwiches to
fish, well kept Adnams, Woodfordes and a
guest ale, good coffee and wines by the
glass, courteous and efficient young staff;
open fires, newspapers and magazines; piped
music, big-screen sports TV; terrace and long
sea-view garden down to dunes, play area,
36 bedrooms in hotel, open all day Fri-Sun
and summer *(JJW, CMW, Tracey and
Stephen Groves, BB)*

OVERSTRAND [TG2440]

White Horse NR27 0AB [High St]: Smart art
deco refurbishment, comfortable and stylish,
with well kept Greene King IPA and
Woodfordes Wherry, enjoyable up-to-date
food in bar and restaurant, friendly staff;
terrace and garden tables, newly done
bedrooms *(Trevor and Sheila Sharman)*

REEPHAM [TG0922]

☆ *Old Brewery House* NR10 4JJ [Market Sq]:
Georgian hotel with big log fire in high-
ceilinged panelled bar overlooking old-
fashioned town square, farming and fishing
bric-a-brac, changing ales inc Adnams,
decent wines by the glass; attentive friendly
staff, reasonably priced enjoyable food from
well filled sandwiches up, side lounge,
dining area, public bar and restaurant;
piped music; children and dogs welcome,
tables in attractive courtyard with covered
well and garden with pond and fountain,
bedrooms, open all day *(John Wooll,
the Didler, LYM)*

SALTHOUSE [TG0743]

☆ *Dun Cow* NR25 7XA [A149 Blakeney—
Sheringham; Purdy St]: Airy pub overlooking
salt marshes, generous unpretentious food
all day from good fresh crab sandwiches to
local fish, fast friendly service even when
busy, well kept Adnams and Woodfordes
Wherry, decent wines; open fires, high
18th-c rafters and cob walls in big main bar,
family bar and games room with pool; piped
radio, blues nights; coast views from
attractive walled front garden, sheltered
courtyard with figs and apples, separate
family garden with play area, good walks and
bird-watching; bedrooms and self-catering;
nice smokery next door *(Derek Field,
Tracey and Stephen Groves, Roy Hoing,
John Saville, John Millwood, Jim Farmer,
David Rule, BB, Derek and Sylvia Stephenson,
William Mack)*

SCULTHORPE [TF8930]

Hourglass NR21 9QD [The Street]: Former
Horse & Groom, extensively refurbished
combining light modern open style with
beams and bare boards; enjoyable good
value food, Theakstons Lightfoot and
Woodfordes Wherry, attentive service
(George Atkinson)

Sculthorpe Mill NR21 9QG [inn signed off
A148 W of Fakenham, opp village]:
Welcoming dining pub in rebuilt 18th-c mill,

appealing riverside setting, seats out under weeping willows and in attractive garden behind; light, airy and relaxed with leather sofas and sturdy tables in bar/dining area, good reasonably priced generous food from sandwiches up, well kept Greene King ales, decent house wines, upstairs restaurant; piped music; six comfortable bedrooms, good breakfast, open all day wknds and summer *(Roy Hoing, Mark, Amanda, Luke and Jake Sheard, LYM)*

SEDGEFORD [TF7036]

☆ *King William IV* PE36 5LU [B1454, off A149 King's Lynn—Hunstanton]: Friendly and roomy, with hard-working helpful staff, good value mainly traditional home-made food from baguettes up inc children's menu and Sun roasts, well kept Adnams, Woodfordes and guest ales, well chosen wines at reasonable prices; neatly refurbished bar opening through to comfortable new back dining room, warm woodburner, seaside pictures for sale; fine garden with attractive covered eating area, four nice bedrooms (more planned), good breakfast *(George Atkinson, BB, Tracey and Stephen Groves, Carolyn Browse, Len Beattie)*

SHERINGHAM [TG1543]

Lobster NR26 8JP [High St]: Almost on seafront, seafaring décor in panelled bar with old sewing-machine treadle tables and a warm fire; up to ten well kept changing ales in the summer (many more during bank hol beer festivals), farm ciders, bottled belgian beers; good value quickly served generous bar meals (helpful with special diet needs), restaurant with seafood, public bar with games inc pool; dogs on leads allowed, two courtyards, heated marquee, open all day *(Len Beattie, Jerry Brown, Brian and Anna Marsden, Fred and Lorraine Gill, M J Winterton, Dr and Mrs P Truelove)*

Windham Arms NR26 8BA [Wyndham St]: Well kept Woodfordes and other ales such as Greene King, Humpty Dumpty and Wolf in cheerful local with friendly landlady; woodburner in carpeted beamed lounge, separate recently redone public bar with pool (and TV and games machine), sensibly priced food with greek influences; picnic-sets outside, sizeable car park (useful here), open all day *(Len Beattie, BB)*

SMALLBURGH [TG3324]

☆ *Crown* NR12 9AD: 15th-c thatched and beamed village inn with friendly proper landlord, old-fashioned pub atmosphere, well kept Adnams and Black Sheep, good choice of wines by the glass; straightforward home-made food in bar and upstairs dining room, prompt service, daily papers, darts; no dogs or children inside; picnic-sets in sheltered and pretty back garden, bedrooms, cl Mon lunchtime, Sun evening *(Philip and Susan Philcox, Dr and Mrs P Truelove, BB)*

SOUTH CREAKE [TF8635]

☆ *Ostrich* NR21 9PB [B1355 Burnham Market—Fakenham]: Well kept ales inc Adnams and Woodfordes Wherry in airily redecorated

village pub with polished boards, local paintings and shelves of books; plenty of tables for the popular food from sandwiches to ostrich fillet, helpful young staff, woodburner; children and dogs welcome, stylish back terrace, bedrooms, open all day wknds *(Tracey and Stephen Groves, Tony Middis, John Wooll, Mike Proctor, Anthony Barnes, LYM)*

SOUTH WOOTTON [TF6622]

☆ *Farmers Arms* PE30 3HQ [part of Knights Hill Hotel, Grimston Rd (off A148/A149)]: Hotel complex's olde-worlde barn and stables conversion, speedily served food all day inc bargain wkdy lunchtime carvery, Adnams, Fullers and guest ales, good wines, abundant coffee; friendly polite service, stripped brick and timbers, quiet snugs and corners, hayloft restaurant; piped music; tables and play area outside, 79 comfortable bedrooms, open all day *(John Wooll, N R White, R C Vincent)*

SOUTHREPPS [TG2536]

Vernon Arms NR11 8NP [Church St]: Old-fashioned village pub with welcoming service, enjoyable food running up to steaks and well priced crab and lobster specials, real ales such as Adnams, Black Sheep, Timothy Taylors and Wells & Youngs, good choice of malt whiskies; children, dogs and muddy walkers welcome *(Trevor and Sheila Sharman)*

STOKE HOLY CROSS [TG2302]

☆ *Wildebeest Arms* NR14 8QJ [Norwich Rd]: Reopened after careful refurbishment, with emphasis on good interesting bistro-style food, cheerful relaxed atmosphere, good beer and wines by the glass, efficient friendly service; unusual decorations inc hanging rugs and african masks, stylish wicker-look chairs around chunky metal-framed tables on stripped boards; delightful garden, well lit heated terrace with huge parasols *(J F M and M West, Roger and Lesley Everett, R Goodenough)*

TERRINGTON ST JOHN [TF5314]

Woolpack PE14 7RR [off A47 W of King's Lynn]: Cheery local atmosphere, red plush banquettes, wheelback chairs, dark pub tables, large back dining room; Greene King IPA and a couple of guest beers, good value home-made pubby food; games machine, piped music; children allowed if eating, picnic-sets on neat grass, good disabled access *(Bruce and Sharon Eden, Michael and Jenny Back, LYM)*

TITCHWELL [TF7543]

☆ *Titchwell Manor* PE31 8BB [A149 E of Hunstanton]: Comfortable upmarket restaurant with rooms rather than a pub, good food inc local fish and seafood, all-day wknd menu, helpful young staff, Greene King IPA, good choice of wines by the glass; good log fire in comfortable lobby lounge, small drinks bar, airy restaurant, nice afternoon teas; children welcome, charming walled garden, lovely bedrooms, some overlooking RSPB bird marshes towards the sea, good breakfast *(Louise, LYM)*

TIVETSHALL ST MARY [TM1785]
Old Ram NR15 2DE [A140, outside village]:
Much extended dining pub, spacious main
room with stripped beams, standing
timbers, rosy brick floors, lots of tools and
huge log fire; several smaller side areas,
woodburner in dining room, second dining
room and gallery; good value food,
Adnams, Woodfordes Wherry and guest
beers, quite a few wines by glass; piped
music, games machine, TV; children
welcome, no dogs, sheltered heated
terrace, comfortable bedrooms, open all
day *(LYM, John Saville)*

WALSINGHAM [TF9336]
Bull NR22 6BP [Common Place/Shire Hall
Plain]: Cheery unpretentious pub in
pilgrimage village, darkly ancient bar's walls
covered with clerical visiting cards; well kept
Adnams, Greene King and guest ales,
welcoming landlord and good-humoured
staff, nice lunchtime sandwiches and
generous, interesting fresh hot dishes, log
fire, pool room; picnic-sets out in courtyard
and on attractive flowery terrace by busy
village square *(John and Gloria Isaacs)*

WEASENHAM ST PETER [TF8522]
Fox & Hounds PE32 2TD [A1065 Fakenham—
Swaffham; The Green]: Welcoming 18th-c
beamed local with bar and two dining areas;
cheery chatty landlord, three Tom Woods
ales, good honest food at reasonable prices,
lots of military prints; children welcome,
nice garden and terrace *(Derek Field,
George Atkinson)*

WELLS-NEXT-THE-SEA [TF9143]
Bowling Green NR23 1JB [Church St]:
Welcoming 17th-c pub, L-shaped bar with
flagstoned and brick floor, good friendly
staff, Greene King and Woodfordes ales;
generous reasonably priced traditional food,
corner settles, two woodburners, raised
dining end; back terrace, quiet spot on
outskirts *(John Wooll, Mike and
Shelley Woodroffe, Len Beattie,
John Beeken)*
Edinburgh NR23 1AE [Station Rd/Church St]:
Traditional pub nr main shopping area, doing
good affordable home-made pubby food, well
kept Bass, Woodfordes and a guest ale; open
fire, local photographs for sale, sizeable

restaurant (check winter opening times);
piped and occasional music, live sports TV,
no credit cards (bank next door); children
and dogs welcome, disabled access,
courtyard with heated smokers' shelter, three
bedrooms, open all day *(Len Beattie,
Mike and Shelley Woodroffe, John Beeken)*

WEST RUNTON [TG1842]
Village Inn NR27 9QP [Water Lane]: Roomy,
comfortable flint pub with enjoyable fresh
food, decent wines, Adnams, Greene King
and Woodfordes, helpful staff, pleasant
restaurant; large attractive garden, pleasant
village with good beach and nice circular
walk to East Runton *(Nigel Tate)*

WIGHTON [TF9439]
☆ *Carpenters Arms* NR23 1PF [High St – off
main rd, past church]: Unusual décor with
mix of brightly painted tables and chairs,
bric-a-brac on shelves, vintage Holkham
pottery, assorted artwork, leather sofas, and
a mulberry dining room; warm welcome,
good local food (not Mon lunchtime in
winter) from pub favourites to more
individual dishes, charming service, well kept
Adnams, Woodfordes and a local beer bottled
for them; picnic-sets in informal back
garden, open all day wknds and bank hols
*(BB, Tracey and Stephen Groves, MDN,
Mike and Shelley Woodroffe)*

WINTERTON-ON-SEA [TG4919]
☆ *Fishermans Return* NR29 4BN [off B1159;
The Lane]: Bustling unpretentious two-bar
local with well kept Adnams and Woodfordes
ales, roaring log fire, pubby food and long-
serving licensees; family room and dining
room, darts and pool; piped music/juke box;
children and dogs welcome, pretty front
terrace, nearby sandy beach, bedrooms, open
all day wknds *(Mayur Shah, Steve Kirby, LYM,
Sandra Brame, Mike Proctor)*

WYMONDHAM [TG1001]
☆ *Green Dragon* NR18 0PH [Church St]:
Picturesque heavily timbered 14th-c inn,
simple beamed and timbered back bar, log
fire under Tudor mantelpiece, interesting
pictures; bigger dining area (children
allowed), friendly helpful staff, Adnams and
a guest beer; children and dogs welcome,
modest bedrooms, nr glorious 12th-c abbey
church *(LYM, the Didler)*

Post Office address codings confusingly give the impression that a few pubs are in
Norfolk, when they're really in Cambridgeshire or Suffolk (which is where we list them).

Northamptonshire

Two new entries here, both with enjoyable food, exemplify the area's contrasting pub styles, from easy-going informality in the Red Lion at Sibbertoft to smartly up-to-date urbanity in the Cartwright at Aynho. Other good newcomers, both back in the *Guide* after a break, are the well reworked Olde Coach House at Ashby St Ledgers and the White Swan at Harringworth. The best food this year has been at the civilised Falcon in Fotheringhay and the Queens Head at Bulwick, a pubby-feeling place with loads to offer from great beers to a good robust country menu – it's our Northamptonshire Dining Pub of the Year. There's real value to be found on the food front, notably at the Red Lion at Crick and George at Kilsby, with its warm-hearted landlady. The thatched Windmill at Badby is another pub owing its really welcoming feel to rather special licensees. The ancient Althorp Coaching Inn at Great Brington stands out for its impressive range of up to a dozen, often locally sourced, real ales and the Samuel Pepys at Slipton puts on a good show with five local beers. The two most successful small local breweries are Potbelly and Digfield, followed by Great Oakley. Some Lucky Dips to note: the Kings Head at Apethorpe, Red Lion at Brafield-on-the-Green, Admiral Nelson at Braunston, New Inn at Buckby Wharf, Stags Head at Maidwell and Malt Shovel in Northampton.

ASHBY ST LEDGERS

SP5768   MAP 4

Olde Coach House 🛏

4 miles from M1 junction 18; A5 S to Kilsby, then A361 S towards Daventry; village also signed off A5 N of Weedon; Main Street; CV23 8UN

Carefully modernised former farmhouse with lots of different seating areas, real ales and good wines, friendly staff, popular food and plenty of outside seating; bedrooms

This handsome creeper-clad stone inn has been extensively brought up to date without losing a good deal of original charm. It's well run by a friendly young landlady and her personable staff, and is a popular place for both a drink and a meal. The right-hand front bar has been opened up and there are several dining areas too: all manner of pale wooden tables surrounded by a mix of church chairs, smart high-backed leather dining chairs and armchairs, comfortable squashy leather sofas and stools in front of the log fire, paintwork that ranges from white and light beige to purple, and flooring that includes stripped wooden boards, original red-and-white tiles and beige carpeting. There are hunting pictures, large mirrors, an old stove and oven, champagne bottles along a gantry and fresh flowers. It's all very relaxed. Wells & Youngs Bitter and Bombardier and a changing guest on handpump and good wines by the glass; piped music. There are picnic-sets in the back garden among shrubs and trees, modern tables and chairs out in front under the pretty hanging baskets, and a dining courtyard. The church nearby is interesting.

🍴 Well liked bar food includes sandwiches, soup, chicken liver parfait with onion marmalade, chinese-style crispy duck with black pudding and hoisin sauce, grazing boards (meaty, vegetarian, fishy and so forth), stone-fired pizzas, beer-battered fish, steak and coriander burger with home-made chips, wild mushroom risotto, a pie of the day, salmon fishcakes with lemon and dill mayonnaise, chicken breast with smoked bacon, goats cheese and mediterranean vegetables, steaks, and puddings like chocolate cheesecake and fruit coulis and lemon tart with raspberry sorbet; Monday evening is curry night and there are good value lunchtime deals. *Starters/Snacks: £3.95 to £6.50. Main Courses: £8.50 to £19.95. Puddings: £5.50*

Mercury Inns ~ Manager Anni Kitz ~ Real ale ~ Bar food (12-2.30, 6-9.30; all day Sun) ~ Restaurant ~ (01788) 890349 ~ Children welcome ~ Dogs allowed in bar ~ Open 12-3, 5.30-11; 12-11(10.30 Sun) Sat ~ Bedrooms: /£65S

Recommended by Rob and Catherine Dunster, Michael and Jenny Back

AYNHO
SP5133   MAP 4

Cartwright 🛏
Croughton Road (B4100); OX17 3BE

Well run modernised inn with tasty food and civilised bar

The winds of change have swept warmly though this 16th-c coaching inn leaving in their wake a beautifully refurbished stone building. Its spacious neatly modernised linked areas have well chosen artwork on cream and maroon painted or exposed stone walls, smartly contemporary furniture on wood or tiled floors, and leather sofas by a big log fire in the bar. Attentive uniformed staff greet you on arrival, and they have daily papers and a nice shortlist of wines by the glass as well as Adnams and Black Sheep from handpumps on the corner counter. Outside, there are a few tables in a pretty corner of the former coachyard. In the village, look out for the apricot trees planted against the front of the pub and against some other older houses in this pleasant village.

🍴 As well as sandwiches, bar food might include broccoli and roasted almond soup, smoked salmon with fried capers and goats cheese salad, main courses such as cod and chips, crispy duck leg with five spice jus, lamb rump with pea and mint risotto and red wine sauce, caesar salad, pancakes stuffed with mushrooms and gruyère with creamy kirsch sauce, burger topped with cheese and onions, and puddings such as strawberry mousse with chantilly cream and sticky toffee pudding and iced praline parfait with strawberry coulis and chocolate tuile; some of these dishes are from their very good value two- and three-course menu. *Starters/Snacks: £4.50 to £9.95. Main Courses: £8.95 to £18.00. Puddings: £4.95 to £7.50*

Free house ~ Licensee Caroline Parkes ~ Real ale ~ Bar food ~ Restaurant ~ (01869) 811885 ~ Children welcome ~ Open 11(12 Sun)-midnight ~ Bedrooms: £90B/£99B

Recommended by Michael Dandy, Stuart Turner, Eithne Dandy, George Atkinson, E A and D C T Frewer

Great Western Arms
Just off B4031 W, towards Deddington; Aynho Wharf, Station Road; OX17 3BP

Civilised old pub with interesting railway memorabilia, well liked food and moorings

Though sandwiched rather unceremoneously between a railway and the Oxford Canal, the interior of this much enjoyed place is cosily inviting enough. Its series of linked rooms is rambling enough to give an intimate feel. The golden stripped stone walling blends attractively with with warm cream and deep red plasterwork and works well with the fine furnishings that include good solid country tables and regional chairs on broad flagstones and a homely log fire warms cosy seats in two of the areas. There are candles and fresh flowers throughout as well as daily papers and glossy magazines and readers enjoy the extensive GWR collection which includes lots of steam locomotive photographs; the dining area on the right is rather elegant. They have well kept Hook Norton Hooky and possibly a guest on handpump, and good wines by the glass; service is welcoming and attentive; piped music. Opening out of the main bar, the former stable courtyard behind has white cast-iron tables and chairs and there are moorings and a marina nearby. They leave a continental breakfast in the comfortable bedrooms.

🍴 Under the enthusiastic new licensee, bar food might now include sandwiches, ploughman's, home smoked salmon, baked mussels and prawns with lobster sauce, chicken liver pâté, rump steak with brandy and peppercorn sauce, venison puff pastry pie, roast pork loin, grilled garlic prawns, and summer and bread and butter puddings. *Starters/Snacks: £4.50 to £5.95. Main Courses: £8.00 to £16.00. Puddings: £4.40*

Hook Norton ~ Lease René Klein and Ali Saul ~ Real ale ~ Bar food (12-2, 6-9.30; 12-9.30 Sat, Sun) ~ Restaurant ~ (01869) 338288 ~ Children welcome ~ Dogs allowed in bar ~ Open 12-3, 6-11; 12-11 Sat, Sun ~ Bedrooms: £65B/£75B

Recommended by George Atkinson, Sir Nigel Foulkes, Gerry and Rosemary Dobson, Martin and Karen Wake, Stuart Turner, Susan Crabbe, Charles and Pauline Stride, N R White, Jean and Douglas Troup, David and Lin Short, Michael Sargent

BADBY
SP5558   MAP 4

Windmill

Village signposted off A361 Daventry—Banbury; NN11 3AN

Homely thatched country dining pub with popular food and friendly service

Now getting on for 20 years or so at this welcoming 300-year-old pub, the very approachable licensees clearly enjoy their work here and their infectious good humour spreads to the cheery staff and customers alike. Two beamed and flagstoned bars have a nice relaxed country feel, though are lively enough, and are furnished with an unusual woodburning stove in an enormous tiled inglenook fireplace, simple but good solid wood country furnishings and cricketing and rugby pictures. There's also a comfortably cosy lounge. A sensible range of beers includes Flowers Original, Fullers London Pride, Timothy Taylors Landlord and a guest such as Bass on handpumps and they've good fairly priced wines by the bottle. The brightly lit carpeted restaurant has a more modern feel; quiet piped music and TV. There's a pleasant terrace out by the attractive village green, and a nice path leads south through Badby Wood (carpeted with bluebells in spring) to a landscaped lake near Fawsley Hall.

🍴 Bar food is pubby but popular and as it can get full here it's worth booking: sandwiches, smoked duck breast, steak and kidney pie, venison burgers with creamy peppercorn sauce, grilled brill with sundried tomatoes and coriander, spinach and ricotta tortellini, and puddings such as chocolate and caramel tart and lime meringue pie. *Starters/Snacks: £4.95 to £8.95. Main Courses: £9.95 to £18.95. Puddings: £4.25 to £5.50*

Free house ~ Licensees John Freestone and Carol Sutton ~ Real ale ~ Bar food (12-2(2.30 Sun), 7-9.30(6.30-9 Sun)) ~ Restaurant ~ (01327) 702363 ~ Children welcome ~ Dogs allowed in bar and bedrooms ~ Open 12-3, 5.30-11.30; 12-11.30 Sat, Sun ~ Bedrooms: £55S/£72.50S

Recommended by George Atkinson, George Cowie, Frances Gosnell, Michael Butler, Dennis and Gill Keen, Sara Fulton, Roger Baker, Dennis Haward, John and Joyce Snell, Dave Braisted, Nigel and Sue Foster

BULWICK
SP9694   MAP 4

Queens Head

Just off A43 Kettering—Duddington; NN17 3DY

NORTHAMPTONSHIRE DINING PUB OF THE YEAR

Ancient pub with cheery involved licensees, interesting beers and first-rate heartily flavoured food including game

Once again, readers are delighted with all aspects of this lovely 600-year-old stone cottage row. Whilst its unaltered appearance and character remain those of a delightfully traditional village local (bellringers pop in after their Wednesday practice and the darts and dominoes teams are very active), there's something extra here too, and it's very much down to the inspired landlord. Thoughtfully sourced beers – well kept and served from a stone bar counter – include Shepherd Neame Spitfire and three interesting guests from brewers such as Leeds, RCH and very local Rockingham. The good wine list includes interesting bin ends (nine by the glass) and they've over 25 malt whiskies. The timeless beamed bar has stone floors and a fire in a stone hearth at one end; darts, shove-ha'penny, dominoes and piped music. We're delighted to hear that several readers have spotted red kites soaring above the pub, but even if you're not so lucky there can be few more pleasant experiences than a summer evening on the garden terrace (with its own well) listening to swallows and martins, sheep in the adjacent field and bells ringing in the nearby church of this attractive bypassed village.

The licensee is passionate about field sports and this is reflected in the menu. He shoots and butchers much of the game served and catches and cures some of the fish. Mainly using traditional recipes and robustly flavoured ingredients, the changing menu might include lunchtime sandwiches, toasted marinated goats cheese bruschetta, duck and chicken liver terrine with piccalilli, seared calves liver with cassoulet of puy lentils and smoked pancetta, leek, courgette and spinach risotto, wood pigeon wrapped in prosciutto, roast saddle of lamb with lamb sweetbreads and caramelised onion and thyme sauce, and puddings such as warm lemon and almond polenta cake with lemon and vanilla syrup and dark chocolate terrine with caramel sauce. *Starters/Snacks: £4.95 to £8.95. Main Courses: £9.95 to £19.95. Puddings: £4.95 to £5.95*

Free house ~ Licensee Geoff Smith ~ Real ale ~ Bar food (12-2.30, 6-9.30; not Sun evening) ~ Restaurant ~ (01780) 450272 ~ Children welcome ~ Dogs allowed in bar ~ Open 12-3(5 Sun), 6-11(7-10.30 Sun); closed Mon

Recommended by Michael and Jenny Back, Peter Martin, Noel Grundy, Howard and Margaret Buchanan, Fred and Lorraine Gill, Val and Alan Green, Jeff and Wendy Williams, Mike and Sue Loseby, Anthony Barnes, J C M Troughton, Tracey and Stephen Groves

CRICK   SP5872   MAP 4

Red Lion 🍺 £

1 mile from M1 junction 18; in centre of village off A428; NN6 7TX

Nicely worn-in friendly coaching inn off M1 with good value straightforward lunchtime food and pricier more detailed evening menu

In the same family for 30 years now, the cosy low-ceilinged bar at this old stone thatched pub is nice and traditional with lots of comfortable seating, some rare old horsebrasses, pictures of the pub in the days before it was surrounded by industrial estates, a tiny log stove in a big inglenook and a welcoming atmosphere. Four well kept beers on handpump include Wells & Youngs Bombardier, Greene King Old Speckled Hen, Theakstons Best and a guest from a brewer such as Thwaites. There are a few picnic-sets under parasols on a terrace by the car park, and in summer you can eat out in the old coachyard which is sheltered by a perspex roof and decorated with lots of pretty hanging baskets.

Homely bar food includes sandwiches and ploughman's, chicken and mushroom or steak pie, leek and smoky bacon bake and plaice and vegetable pancake rolls. Prices go up a little in the evening when they offer a wider range of dishes that might include stuffed salmon fillet, lamb shank, half a roast duck and sirloin steak; puddings such as lemon meringue pie; bargain-price Sunday roast. *Starters/Snacks: £2.20 to £3.60. Main Courses: £4.75 to £14.00. Puddings: £2.10 to £3.00*

Wellington ~ Lease Tom and Paul Marks ~ Real ale ~ Bar food (12-2, 6.30-9; not Sun evening) ~ (01788) 822342 ~ Children lunchtimes only ~ Dogs allowed in bar ~ Open 11-2.30, 6.15-11; 12-3, 7-10.30 Sun

Recommended by George Atkinson, Dr and Mrs A K Clarke, Paul Humphreys, Mrs Margaret Ball, Ian and Denise Foster, Michael Dandy, J K Parry, Gerry and Rosemary Dobson, Dr D J and Mrs S C Walker, Ted George, I J and S A Bufton, Michael Butler, A R Mascall, Simon and Mandy King

---

Real ale to us means beer which has matured naturally in its cask – not pressurised or filtered. We name all real ales stocked. We usually name ales preserved under a light blanket of carbon dioxide too, though purists – pointing out that this stops the natural yeasts developing – would disagree (most people, including us, can't tell the difference!)

EAST HADDON

SP6668 MAP 4

Red Lion

High Street; village signposted off A428 (turn right in village) and off A50 N of Northampton; NN6 8BU

Appealing old hotel with pleasant grounds and good food

Recent alterations to this substantially-built golden stone inn were carried out with the deliberate intention of putting some pubbiness back into the heart of the building. By relaxing the feel of the dining area (and adding french windows that open to the garden) people feel more encouraged to eat in here, thus leaving the bar feeling more like a traditional village pub, with its reclaimed wood and stone floor, warm colours and antique bric-a-brac, Wells & Youngs Bombardier and Eagle and a guest such as Potbelly Pigs Do Fly. The walled side garden is pretty with lilac, fruit trees, roses and neat flowerbeds and leads back to the bigger lawn, which has well spaced picnic-sets. A small side terrace has more tables under parasols, and a big copper beech shades the gravel car park.

🍴 Bar food includes stilton mushrooms with basil pesto, spiced lamb samosa with raita and mango chutney, fish and chips, braised lamb shank with red wine sauce, seared tuna with squid in noodles, fried duck breast, baked mushroom and spinach-filled choux pastry bun with hollandaise sauce and poached egg, lobster thermidor, and puddings such as chocolate brownie and lemon bakewell tart. *Starters/Snacks: £3.95 to £6.95. Main Courses: £4.95 to £9.95. Puddings: £4.95 to £6.95*

Charles Wells ~ Lease Nick Bonner ~ Real ale ~ Bar food (12-2.30, 6-10; 12-7 Sun) ~ Restaurant ~ (01604) 770223 ~ Children welcome ~ Open 12-2.30, 5.30-11; 12-7.30 Sun; closed Sun evening ~ Bedrooms: £60S/£75S

Recommended by R W Allen, George Atkinson, Ron and Sheila Corbett, JJW, CMW, Gerry and Rosemary Dobson, J K and S M Miln, Mrs B Barwick, Michael Dandy

EYDON

SP5450 MAP 7

Royal Oak

Lime Avenue; village signed off A361 Daventry—Banbury and from B4525; NN11 3PG

Enjoyable low-beamed place with good lunchtime snacks and imaginative evening menu

Retaining plenty of its original features, including fine flagstone floors and leaded windows, this attractive 300-year-old ironstone inn is a fascinating building with an interesting layout. The cosy room on the right has cushioned wooden benches built into alcoves, seats in a bow window, some cottagey pictures and an open fire in an inglenook fireplace. The bar counter (with stools) runs down a long central flagstoned corridor room and links several other small charcterful rooms. An attractive covered terrace with hardwood furniture is a lovely place for a meal outside. Friendy staff serve well kept Fullers London Pride, Greene King IPA, Timothy Taylors Landlord and a guest, usually from Archers, by handpump; piped music and table skittles in an old stable.

🍴 The lunchtime menu is fairly pubby, with maybe ciabattas, burgers, fish and chips, fish cakes and steak. More elaborate evening food might include starters such as parsnip, apple and coriander soup, hash brown filled with black pudding and cheese with a poached egg and glazed goats cheese salad with beetroot dressing, main courses such as roast rump of lamb with redcurrant sauce, grilled bass on lemon and saffron mash with salsa verde, and puddings such as milk chocolate marquise and vanilla crème brûlée with raspberries. *Starters/Snacks: £6.50. Main Courses: £10.00 to £15.50. Puddings: £4.50 to £5.50*

Free house ~ Licensee Justin Lefevre ~ Real ale ~ Bar food (12-2, 7-9; not Mon) ~ (01327) 263167 ~ Children welcome ~ Dogs allowed in bar ~ Open 12-2.30, 6-11(7-10 Sun); closed Mon lunchtime

Recommended by Dave Braisted, Steve Piggott, George Atkinson, Kevin Thomas, Nina Randall, J V Dadswell, Malcolm and Pauline Pellatt, RJH

FARTHINGSTONE   SP6155   MAP 4

Kings Arms 🍺

Off A5 SE of Daventry; village signposted from Litchborough on former B4525 (now declassified); NN12 8EZ

Individual place with cosy traditional interior and lovely gardens

The tranquil terrace at this quirky gargoyle-embellished 18th-c stone country pub is charmingly decorated with hanging baskets, flower and herb pots and plant-filled painted tractor tyres. They grow their own salad vegetables and there's a cosy little terrace by the herb garden. The timelessly intimate flagstoned bar has a huge log fire, comfortable homely sofas and armchairs near the entrance, whisky-water jugs hanging from oak beams, and lots of pictures and decorative plates on the walls. A games room at the far end has darts, dominoes, cribbage, table skittles and board games. Drinks include Thwaites Original, a couple of guests such as Everards Beacon and St Austell Tribute, a short but decent wine list and quite a few country wines. Look out for the interesting newspaper-influenced décor in the outside gents'. This is a picturesque village and there are good walks near here including the Knightley Way. It's worth ringing ahead to check the opening and food serving times as the licensees are sometimes away unexpectedly; more reports please.

🍽 **As well as sandwiches and baguettes, bar food might include smoked duck and black pudding salad, cheese platter, salmon fishcakes with dill and mustard sauce, pork in a ginger, tomato and garlic sauce, sticky chicken thighs, and yorkshire pudding filled with spicy sausage and bean casserole. They have a short list of carefully sourced produce on sale.** *Starters/Snacks: £3.95 to £5.95. Main Courses: £5.95 to £9.95. Puddings: £3.50 to £4.25*

Free house ~ Licensees Paul and Denise Egerton ~ Real ale ~ Bar food (12-2.15 Sat, Sun only) ~ No credit cards ~ (01327) 361604 ~ Children welcome ~ Dogs welcome ~ Open 7(6 Fri)-11.30; 12-4, 7-midnight Sat; 12-4, 9-11 Sun; closed Mon, weekday lunchtimes and Weds evenings

Recommended by Pete Baker

FOTHERINGHAY   TL0593   MAP 5

Falcon 🍽 🍷

Village signposted off A605 on Peterborough side of Oundle; PE8 5HZ

Upmarket dining pub, good range of drinks and food from snacks up; attractive garden

Though the inventive food is the main draw at this civilised pub, there is a thriving little locals' tap bar (and darts team) if you do just want a drink. It's neatly kept and is sedately furnished with cushioned slatback arm and bucket chairs, good winter log fires in a stone fireplace and fresh flower arrangements. The very good range of drinks includes three changing beers from brewers such as Digfield and Greene King on handpump, good wines (20 by the glass), Weston's organic cider, organic cordials and fresh orange juice. There's a pretty conservatory restaurant and if the weather is nice the attractively planted garden is particularly enjoyable. The vast church behind is worth a visit and the ruins of Fotheringhay Castle, where Mary Queen of Scots was executed, are not far away.

🍽 **As well as imaginative sandwiches, thoughtful (if not cheap) bar food might include roast red pepper soup, moules marinière, salmon, crab and dill fishcakes with tartare sauce, red onion, red pepper and goats cheese tart, chicken breast with rösti potatoes, creamed leeks and baby onions, fillet steak with polenta and thyme jus, and puddings such as caramelised lemon tart with raspberry sorbet, italian chocolate cake with malted ice-cream and a good cheese selection.** *Starters/Snacks: £4.50 to £8.95. Main Courses: £10.50 to £22.50. Puddings: £4.50 to £5.95*

Free house ~ Licensees Sally Facer and Jim Jeffries ~ Real ale ~ Bar food (12-2.15, 6.15-9.15; 12-3, 6.15-8.30 Sun) ~ Restaurant ~ (01832) 226254 ~ Children welcome ~ Dogs allowed in bar ~ Open 12-11(10.30 Sun)

Recommended by Mike and Sue Loseby, Jim Farmer, Keith and Sue Campbell, Ian and Nita Cooper, Noel Grundy, M L and B S Rantzen, Howard and Margaret Buchanan, Oliver and Sue Rowell, O K Smyth, Bruce and Sharon Eden, Jan and Alan Summers

GREAT BRINGTON

SP6664 MAP 4

Althorp Coaching Inn ◀

Off A428 NW of Northampton, near Althorp Hall; until recently known as the Fox & Hounds; NN7 4JA

Friendly thatched pub with great choice of real ales, tasty food and sheltered garden

The ancient bar at this lovely golden-stone old coaching inn has all the traditional features you'd wish for, from a dog or two sprawled out by the fire, to old beams, saggy joists and an attractive mix of country chairs and tables (maybe with fresh flowers) on its broad flagstones and bare boards. Also plenty of snug alcoves, nooks and crannies, some stripped pine shutters and panelling, two fine log fires and an eclectic medley of bric-a-brac from farming implements to an old clocking-in machine and country pictures. The extended dining area has been altered to allow views of the 30 or so casks racked in the cellar, one of the old coaching bars is now used for pub games, and an old garden cottage, adjoining the lovely little paved courtyard (also accessible by the old coaching entry) with sheltered tables and tubs of flowers, has been improved for dining; more seating in the side garden. Cheery staff serve the splendid range of over ten real ales which include Fullers London Pride, Greene King IPA and Abbot and Old Speckled Hen with thoughtfully sourced, often local, guests from brewers such as Church End, Hoggleys and Potbelly; piped music.

🍴 Food here is popular so it's advisable to book: sandwiches and baguettes, cray fish tails with lemon mayonnaise, sweet cured bresaola, moules marinière, pork tenderloin with cream, apple and stilton sauce, vegetable lasagne, beef and Guinness casserole, lamb tagine, pigeon pie, and puddings such as cinnamon and apple strudel and walnut and almond sponge. *Starters/Snacks: £4.50 to £8.50. Main Courses: £5.00 to £18.50. Puddings: £2.50 to £5.50*

Free house ~ Licensee Michael Krempels ~ Real ale ~ Bar food (12-2.30(3 Sat, Sun), 6.30-9.30(9 Sun)) ~ Restaurant ~ (01604) 770651 ~ Dogs allowed in bar ~ Quiz night Mon, live music Tues evening ~ Open 11.30-11.30(12.30 Sat); 12-11 Sun

Recommended by Gerry and Rosemary Dobson, Tim and Ann Newell, Michael Dandy, George Atkinson, Chris and Jeanne Downing, J K and S M Miln, JJW, CMW, Alan Sutton

GREAT OXENDON

SP7383 MAP 4

George 🍷 🛏

A508 S of Market Harborough; LE16 8NA

Elegant 16th-c pub with emphasis on dining (you may need to book); garden and comfortable bedrooms

The tried and trusted format at this well run inn continues to please. The bar, with its dark walls, dark brown panelled dado, green leatherette bucket chairs around little tables and big log fire, has the intimate feel of a cosy gentleman's club – and the very helpful staff wouldn't be amiss in such an environment. The entrance lobby has easy chairs and a former inn-sign, and the turkey-carpeted conservatory overlooks a big well tended shrub-sheltered garden; piped easy-listening music. The gents' lavatories are entertainingly decked out with rather stylish naughty pictures. Well kept Black Sheep and Timothy Taylors Landlord on handpump, a dozen or so wines by the glass and around ten malts.

🍴 As well as filled baguettes, good bar food might include gruyère fritters with cranberry sauce, italian platter, steak and ale pie, lamb shank with onion gravy, duck breast with marmalade and Cointreau sauce, steaks, and puddings such as sticky toffee pudding with lemon and butterscotch sauce and chocolate fondant with coffee ice-cream. They do a good value curry on Monday evening and a very fairly priced weekday set menu; two- and three-course Sunday lunch. *Starters/Snacks: £4.50 to £7.25. Main Courses: £9.95 to £19.95. Puddings: £5.25 to £5.95*

Free house ~ Licensee David Dudley ~ Real ale ~ Bar food (12-2, 6-9) ~ Restaurant ~ (01858) 465205 ~ Children welcome ~ Dogs allowed in bedrooms ~ Open 11.30-3, 5.30-11.30; 12-3 Sun; closed Sun and bank hol evenings ~ Bedrooms: £57.50B/£65.50B

Recommended by Gerry and Rosemary Dobson, David Kirkcaldy, Michael Dandy, Dave Braisted, Jeff and Wendy Williams, Dennis Jones, Adele Summers, Alan Black, Tom and Jill Jones, O K Smyth, Sally Anne and Peter Goodale, Rob and Catherine Dunster, Julian Saunders

HARRINGWORTH   SP9197   MAP 4

White Swan

Seaton Road; village SE of Uppingham, signposted from A6003, A47 and A43; NN17 3AF

Handsome country pub with good food and local real ales; bedrooms

Not far from the majestic 82-arch Victorian railway viaduct spanning the River Welland, this eye-catching 16th-c former coaching inn has a Cotswoldy look with its pretty hanging baskets on limestone walls and an imposing central gable. With plenty of exposed stone, the welcoming bar has pictures of World War II aircraft at nearby Spanhoe Airfield, old village photographs and, behind the hand-crafted oak counter with a mirror base and an attractive swan carving, an enticing row of sweets in old-fashioned jars, along with scales and paper bags. Friendly staff serve Fullers London Pride and a couple of guests such as local Great Oakley Wot's Occurring and Potbelly Best from handpump, and they have a summer cocktail board. An open fire divides the bar and two cosy dining areas which have solid country pine tables, attractive window seats and high cushioned settles; piped music, darts and board games. There are tables out on a partly covered terrace.

🍴 **Attractively presented well prepared bar food might include ploughman's, potted shrimps, fish of the day, chicken breast stuffed with camembert and tarragon wrapped in parma ham, loin of lamb with rosemary jus, scampi, warm guinea fowl salad, and puddings such as lemon and raspberry brûlée and sticky ginger pudding with poached rhubarb. Lamb served here is grazed in the village and butchered at the pub.** *Starters/Snacks: £3.95 to £5.95. Main Courses: £7.50 to £14.95. Puddings: £5.25 to £5.50*

Free house ~ Licensees Adam and Gina Longden ~ Real ale ~ Bar food (till 3 Sun) ~ Restaurant ~ (01572) 747543 ~ Children welcome ~ Open 12-2.30(3 Sat, 3.30 Sun), 6-11; closed Sun evening, Mon lunchtime ~ Bedrooms: £45S/£70S

Recommended by John Wooll, Mrs K Hooker

KILSBY   SP5671   MAP 4

George

2.5 miles from M1 junction 18: A428 towards Daventry, left on to A5 – look out for pub off on right at roundabout; CV23 8YE

Handy for M1; warm welcome, good local atmosphere, proper public bar, old-fashioned décor and tasty wholesome food

Readers are eager to point out that the very friendly hardworking landlady at this relaxing pub is exceptionally good at her job – visitors are really made to feel like locals and she keeps a good balance between the popular dining aspect and the traditional public bar. The high-ceilinged wood panelled lounge on the right, with plush banquettes, a coal-effect gas stove and a big bay window, opens on the left into a smarter but relaxed attractive area with solidly comfortable furnishings. The long brightly decorated back public bar has a juke box, darts, TV and that rarity these days, a play pool table. Adnams, Fullers London Pride, Greene King Abbot and a guest such as Thwaites Lancaster Bomber are well kept on handpump, and they've a splendid range of malt whiskies, served in generous measures. There are picnic-sets out in the back garden.

🍴 **The pubby lunch menu includes sandwiches, filled baguettes, faggots with spring onion mash and mushy peas, sausage, egg and chips and daily specials, while the evening menu typically features sweet and sour rack of pork ribs, lamb shank braised in red wine, beef and ale shortcrust pie, chicken breast stuffed with olives and wrapped in parma ham with sweet pepper and paprika sauce, pancakes filled with spinach and feta and steaks (up to 16oz should you be so inclined).** *Starters/Snacks: £3.90 to £5.90. Main Courses: £4.90 to £10.90. Puddings: £4.90*

Punch ~ Lease Maggie Chandler ~ Real ale ~ Bar food (12-2(4 Sun), 6-9) ~ Restaurant ~ (01788) 822229 ~ Children welcome ~ Dogs allowed in bar ~ Open 11.30-3, 5.30(6 Sat)-11; 12-5, 7.30-10.30 Sun ~ Bedrooms: £38/£56

Recommended by Ted George, Rob and Catherine Dunster, Keith and Sue Ward, Bruce and Sharon Eden, Michael Butler, Michael Dandy

NETHER HEYFORD   SP6658   MAP 4

Olde Sun 🍺 £

1.75 miles from M1 junction 16: village signposted left off A45 westbound – Middle Street; NN7 3LL

Unpretentious place with diverting bric-a-brac, reasonably priced food and garden with play area

---

Rather like a dusty old emporium, all nature of bric-a-brac is packed into nooks and crannies in the several small linked rooms at this tucked-away 18th-c golden-stone pub. There's brassware (one fireplace is a grotto of large brass animals), colourful relief plates, 1930s cigarette cards, railway memorabilia and advertising signs, World War II posters and rope fancywork. The nice old cash till on one of the two counters where they serve the well kept Banks's, Greene King Ruddles, Marstons Pedigree and a guest such as Fullers, is wishfully stuck at one and a ha'penny. Furnishings are mostly properly pubby, with the odd easy chair. There are beams and low ceilings (one painted with a fine sunburst), partly glazed dividing panels, steps between some areas, rugs on parquet, red tiles or flagstones, a big inglenook log fire – and up on the left a room with full-sized hood skittles, a games machine, darts, Sky TV, cribbage, dominoes and sports TV; piped music. The enjoyable collections continue into the garden, where there are blue-painted grain kibblers and other antiquated hand-operated farm machines, some with plants in their hoppers, beside a fairy-lit front terrace with picnic-sets.

🍽 **A short choice of snacky meals includes tasty sandwiches, scampi and chips, potato baked with bacon, onions and cream cheese, cottage pie, chilli, curry, coq au vin and steak.** *Starters/Snacks: £3.75 to £5.45. Main Courses: £5.95 to £14.50. Puddings: £3.25 to £4.35*

Free house ~ Licensees P Yates and A Ford ~ Real ale ~ Bar food (not Sun evenings) ~ Restaurant ~ (01327) 340164 ~ Children welcome ~ Dogs welcome ~ Open 12-2.30, 5-11; 12-11 Sat, Sun

Recommended by George Atkinson, Ian and Helen Stafford, Michael Butler, A R Mascall, Dr D J and Mrs S C Walker, R T and J C Moggridge, Gordon and Margaret Ormondroyd, Dennis Haward

OUNDLE   TL0388   MAP 5

Ship 🍺

West Street; PE8 4EF

Bustling down-to-earth town pub with interesting beers and good value pubby food

---

Sounds of hearty companionable chatter in the well worn rooms here authenticate it as a proper enjoyable local. None of the bustle seems to disturb Midnight, the sleepy black and white pub cat, though we suspect he might disappear on the odd occasion that there's a live band or salsa here. The heavily beamed lounge bar (watch your head if you are tall) is made up of three cosy areas that lead off the central corridor. Up by the street there's a mix of leather and other seats, with sturdy tables and a warming log fire in a stone inglenook, and down one end a charming little panelled snug has button-back leather seats built in around it. The wood-floored public side has a TV, games machine and board games and you can play poker here on Wednesdays; piped music. Friendly staff serve Brewsters Hophead, Digfield March Hare, Elgoods Black Dog and Oakham Bishops Farewell, and they've a good range of malt whiskies. The wooden tables and chairs out on the series of small sunny sheltered terraces are lit at night.

🍽 **Enjoyable bar food served in generous helpings might include soup, vegetarian or beef lasagne, haddock, chicken breast with mushroom sauce, pork curry and rib-eye steak;**

Sunday roast. *Starters/Snacks: £3.95 to £5.50. Main Courses: £7.50 to £10.50. Puddings: £3.95 to £4.50*

Free house ~ Licensees Andrew and Robert Langridge ~ Real ale ~ Bar food (12-3, 6-9; 12-9 Sat, Sun) ~ (01832) 273918 ~ Children welcome ~ Dogs welcome ~ Open 11-11.30(11.45 Sat); 12-11.30 Sun ~ Bedrooms: £30(£35S)/£60(£60S)(£70B)

Recommended by the Didler, George Atkinson, Ryta Lyndley

SIBBERTOFT   SP6782   MAP 4

Red Lion ♀ ◖

Village signposted off A4303 or A508 SW of Market Harborough; Welland Rise; LE16 9UD

Relaxed village inn with fine choice of drinks including good wines and quickly changing real ales, simple furnishings and good food; self-catering studio flats

Run by friendly, hard-working licensees, this simple little village inn had a good bustling atmosphere on our pre-Christmas visit, with plenty of customers enjoying the good food. The unpretentious bar has brown suede dining chairs around modern pine tables, some brown leatherette cushioned wall banquettes, pastel-painted, half-panelled walls (some wine box tops on one), a big gilt-edged mirror over the fireplace and a little corner area with red-cushioned bar stools around a very high table. As well as Black Sheep, Fullers London Pride and Timothy Taylors Landlord on handpump, a blackboard lists several 'beers of the world' and they keep a splendid choice of over 200 wines, with nearly two dozen by the glass, and hold wine tastings. The back dining room has contemporary high-backed brown leather dining chairs around nice light wooden tables and there's a little woodburning stove (you might spot Noodles the pub cat hanging around here). There are seats on a covered terrace and in a sizeable garden (where they grow some of their own vegetables) and they have two straightforward studio flats.

⏱ **The seasonally changing menu might include grilled sardine fillets with chorizo and tomatoes, duck and orange pâté with apple and ale chutney, beef stroganoff, bass with spinach and prawn sauce, cajun spiced chicken with mango and coconut sauce, pork steak with stilton sauce, and puddings such as orange and marmalade bread and butter pudding and Cointreau crème brûlée: good value curries Monday evening.** *Starters/Snacks: £2.50 to £6.50. Main Courses: £6.00 to £15.00. Puddings: £3.25 to £4.50*

Free house ~ Licensees Andrew and Sarah Banks ~ Real ale ~ Bar food (12-2(3 Sun), 6.30-9.30) ~ Restaurant ~ (01858) 880011 ~ Children welcome ~ Dogs allowed in bedrooms ~ Open 12-3, 6.30-12; 12-6 Sun; closed Sun evening, Mon, Tues lunchtime ~ Bedrooms: £40B/£60B

Recommended by Gerry and Rosemary Dobson, George Atkinson, John Wooll

SLIPTON   SP9579   MAP 4

Samuel Pepys ♀ ◖

Off A6116 at first roundabout N of A14 junction, towards Twywell and Slipton, bearing right to Slipton; the pub (in Slipton Lane) is well signed locally; NN14 3AR

Exemplary dining pub with friendly service, good beers, nice surroundings and garden

The long back bar, full of activity and chatter, is the cheerful hub of this smartly reworked old stone pub. It's gently modern and airy with good lighting, very heavy low beams, a log fire in a stone fireplace (with plenty of logs stacked around) and chapel chairs on a simple mauve carpet. At one side, beyond a great central pillar that looks as if it was once part of a ship's mast, is an area with squashy leather seats around low tables. Beyond, the main dining room (with comfortably modern chairs around neatly set tables) extends into a roomy conservatory, with pleasant country views; piped music. The white-painted bar counter stocks a good range of five real ales on handpump or tapped straight from the cask, often from local brewers, that might include Digfield, Elgoods, Hop Back and Potbelly. They have an interesting choice of reasonably priced wines by the glass and bottle. Service is prompt, friendly and helpful, and there is wheelchair access throughout. The sheltered garden is spacious and well laid out, with picnic-sets under cocktail parasols and a terrace with heaters.

🍴 Good value well presented tasty bar food includes sandwiches, sausage with black pudding mash, cod and chips, steak and ale pie, green thai fish curry, mushroom risotto, duck breast with plum and caraway sauce, rib-eye steak, and puddings such as lemon and brandy syllabub. *Starters/Snacks: £8.95 to £9.70. Main Courses: £7.70 to £11.70. Puddings: £3.60 to £5.20*

Mercury Inns ~ Manager Frazer Williams ~ Real ale ~ Bar food (12-2.30, 6.30-9.30) ~ Restaurant ~ (01832) 731739 ~ Children welcome ~ Dogs allowed in bar ~ Open 12-3, 6-11; 12-11 Sat, Sun

Recommended by Michael and Jenny Back, Mike and Sue Loseby, Tracey and Stephen Groves, Andy and Claire Barker, Ryta Lyndley, Dr and Mrs Michael Smith, Oliver and Sue Rowell, Rob and Catherine Dunster, Mrs Margo Finlay, Jörg Kasprowski, Mrs K Hooker

SULGRAVE

SP5545   MAP 4

Star

E of Banbury, signposted off B4525; Manor Road; OX17 2SA

Pleasant country pub with decent food and nice gardens

A restful calm gently permeates the little bar at this lovely old creeper-covered farmhouse. It's quietly furnished with small pews, cushioned window seats and wall benches, kitchen chairs and cast-iron tables. Framed newspaper front pages record historic events such as Kennedy's assassination and the death of Churchill, and a stuffed fox appears to leap through the wall. There are polished flagstones in an area by the big inglenook fireplace, with red carpet elsewhere. Hook Norton Hooky, Old Hooky and a guest such as Wells & Youngs Special are served from handpumps on the tiny counter. In summer you can eat outside under a vine-covered trellis and there are benches at the front and in the back garden. The building dates from the 17th c, is just a short walk from Sulgrave Manor, the ancestral home of George Washington and is handy for Silverstone.

🍴 Bar food includes sandwiches, chicken liver and brandy pâté, burger, hot chicken salad, sausage and mash, thai chicken curry, fish risotto, fillet steak, and puddings such as rum and raisin chocolate trifle and sticky toffee pudding *Starters/Snacks: £4.95 to £7.45. Main Courses: £8.75 to £19.50. Puddings: £4.00 to £7.00*

Hook Norton ~ Tenant Andron Ingle ~ Real ale ~ Bar food (12-2, 6-9; 11.30-2.15, 6.15-9.30 Sat; 11.30-2.30 Sun) ~ Restaurant ~ (01295) 760389 ~ Children welcome ~ Dogs allowed in bar ~ Open 12(11.30 Sat)-3, 6-11; 11.30-3.30 Sun; closed Sun evening, Mon ~ Bedrooms: £50S/£80B

Recommended by Malcolm and Pauline Pellatt, Howard and Margaret Buchanan, David and Diane Young, Roger Noyes, P M Newsome

WADENHOE

TL0183   MAP 5

Kings Head

Church Street; village signposted (in small print) off A605 S of Oundle; PE8 5ST

Country pub in idyllic riverside spot; decent range of beers, pubby food

---

This cheery stone-built 16th-c inn is in a wonderful spot with picnic-sets among willows and aspens on grass leading down to the River Nene – you can even arrive by boat and moor here. Inside, there's an uncluttered simplicity (maybe too much so for some) to the very welcoming partly stripped-stone main bar, which has pleasant old worn quarry-tiles, solid pale pine furniture with a couple of cushioned wall seats and a leather-upholstered chair by the woodburning stove in the fine inglenook. The bare-boarded public bar has similar furnishings and another fire; steps lead up to a games room with darts, dominoes and table skittles, and there's more of the pale pine furniture in an attractive little beamed dining room. As well as either Digfield Barnwell or Digfield Kings Head, they keep a guest or two, maybe from Grainstore or Ruddles, and a dozen wines by the glass.

⚑ As well as lunchtime sandwiches and panini, pubby bar food might include mediterranean soup, garlic mushrooms on toasted brioche, greek salad, lasagne, battered haddock, sausage and mash, rump steak, bread and butter pudding and eton mess. *Starters/Snacks: £3.95 to £4.95. Main Courses: £7.95 to £11.95. Puddings: £1.50 to £4.95*

Free house ~ Licensee Peter Hall ~ Real ale ~ Bar food (12-2.30, 6.30-9.30; not Sun evening) ~ Restaurant ~ (01832) 720024 ~ Children welcome ~ Dogs allowed in bar ~ Open 11-3, 6-11; 11-11 Sat; 11-8 Sun

Recommended by Barry and Sue Pladdys, Michael Tack, Ryta Lyndley, Mike and Mary Carter, Barry Rolfe, Tom and Ruth Rees, Sally Anne and Peter Goodale

LUCKY DIP

Besides the fully inspected pubs, you might like to try these Lucky Dips recommended to us and described by readers (if you do, please send us reports: feedback@goodguides.com).

APETHORPE [TL0295]

☆ **Kings Head** PE8 5DG [Kings Cliffe Rd]: Roomy and attractive stone-built pub in conservation village, comfortable and welcoming lounge with log fire, cosy bar, well kept Fullers, Timothy Taylors and a guest ale, good coffee, friendly obliging service, arch to big dining area with wide choice of good fairly priced fresh food inc fish, separate bar food menu (not Mon), theme nights and live music; children welcome, picnic-sets in charming sheltered courtyard (*Colin Dean, Mrs M G Uglow, M B Manser, Keith and Sue Campbell*)

ASHTON [TL0588]

Chequered Skipper PE8 5LD [the one NE of Oundle, signed from A427/A605 island]: Handsomely rebuilt thatched pub on chestnut-tree green of elegant estate village, helpful and friendly young staff; changing ales such as Crouch Vale, Newby Wyke, Oakham and Rockingham, enjoyable reasonably priced food (not Mon) from baked potatoes and ciabattas to restaurantry main courses, light and airy open-plan layout with dining areas either side (*George Atkinson*)

BOUGHTON [SP7565]

Whyte-Melville NN2 8SF [off A508 N of Northampton; Church St]: Very popular for reasonably priced bar lunches, Greene King ales, beams, bare boards and carpeting, blazing coal fire, lots of brasses and Victorian pictures; piped music; tables out behind (*George Atkinson*)

BRACKLEY HATCH [SP6441]

☆ **Green Man** NN13 5TX [A43 NE of Brackley (tricky exit)]: Big Chef & Brewer dining pub on busy dual carriageway nr Silverstone, comfortable old-look beamed lounge area, conservatory overlooking road, big family restaurant, wide range of all-day food, relaxed atmosphere, quick, friendly and helpful service, Adnams and other ales, good wines and coffee, daily papers, log fire; pervasive piped music, games; tables on lawn, bedrooms in Premier Lodge behind, open all day (*Meg and Colin Hamilton, BB, Michael Dandy*)

BRAFIELD-ON-THE-GREEN [SP8258]

☆ **Red Lion** NN7 1BP [A428 5 miles from Northampton towards Bedford]: Smart comfortably modern bistro-style McManus dining pub with good traditional and upscale food in two main rooms, small drinking area with a couple of settees, good choice of wines by the glass, beers such as Adnams and Great Oakley, friendly attentive staff; picnic-sets front and back, open all day (*Eithne Dandy, Michael Dandy, Jeremy King*)

BRAUNSTON [SP5465]

☆ **Admiral Nelson** NN11 7HJ [Dark Lane, Little Braunston, overlooking Lock 3 just N of Grand Union Canal tunnel]: 18th-c ex-farmhouse in peaceful setting by Grand Union Canal and hump bridge, new management doing good value food (all day Fri and Sat in summer, not Sun evening), Adnams, Sharps Doom Bar and Shepherd Neame Spitfire, cheery attentive service, canal pictures, tiled-floor part by bar with log fire, longer dining end and back restaurant, games area with hood skittles and darts; no dogs; well behaved children welcome, disabled access, lots of waterside picnic-sets, play area across bridge, open all day (*George Atkinson, BB*)

BRAYBROOKE [SP7684]

Swan LE16 8LH [Griffin Rd]: Nicely kept thatched pub with good drinks choice inc Everards ales, good value food (all day Sat), friendly service, fireside sofas, soft lighting, exposed brickwork, stone-ceilinged alcoves, restaurant; quiet piped music, silent fruit machine; children very welcome, dogs too; disabled facilities, attractive hedged garden with covered terrace, open all day wknds (*Jeremy King, JJW, CMW*)

BUCKBY WHARF [SP6066]

☆ **New Inn** NN6 7PW [A5 N of Weedon]: Good range of tasty quickly served pubby food from good baguettes to popular 'Desperate Dan Pie', friendly staff, well kept Frog Island, Hook Norton and guest ales, good short choice of wines; several rooms radiating from central servery inc small dining room with nice fire, games area with table skittles; two TVs, games machine; children welcome, dogs outside only, pleasant terrace with heated smokers' area, by busy Grand Union Canal lock, open all day *(Alison and Graham Hooper, LYM, G Robinson, Brian and Anna Marsden, John Saville, George Atkinson, Rob and Catherine Dunster)*

BUGBROOKE [SP6756]

Wharf Inn NN7 3QB [The Wharf; off A5 S of Weedon]: Super spot by Grand Union Canal, plenty of tables on big lawn with moorings; refurbished by new licensees with emphasis on big water-view restaurant, also bar/lounge with small informal raised eating area either side, lots of stripped brickwork; good food using local organic produce inc Sun roasts, well kept local Frog Island and other beers, lots of wines by the glass, woodburner; piped music; children welcome, dogs in garden only, disabled facilities, heated smokers' shelter, open all day *(Mary McSweeney, Gerry and Rosemary Dobson, George Atkinson, BB)*

CHAPEL BRAMPTON [SP7366]

☆ *Brampton Halt* NN6 8BA [Pitsford Rd, off A5199 N of Northampton]: Well laid out pub on Northampton & Lamport Railway (which is open wknds), large restaurant, railway memorabilia and train theme throughout (some furnishings like railway carriages), wide choice of enjoyable generous food (smaller helpings available) from sandwiches up inc Sun roasts, ales such as Everards Tiger, Sharps Doom Bar and Wells & Youngs Bombardier, cheerful efficient service even when busy, games and TV in bar; piped music; children welcome, lots of tables in garden with awnings and heaters, summer barbecues, pretty views over small lake, Nene Valley Way walks *(Michael Dandy, LYM, Eithne Dandy, Revd R P Tickle, George Atkinson, Gerry and Rosemary Dobson)*

CHARLTON [SP5235]

Rose & Crown OX17 3DP [Main St]: Thatched pub with friendly prompt service, enjoyable food from bar snacks up inc lunchtime bargains (Tues-Sat), three Greene King ales, beams, stripped stone and inglenook fireplaces, well spaced pale wood tables and chairs; picnic-sets outside, wisteria arbour, nice village *(Sir Nigel Foulkes, E A and D C T Frewer, LYM, George Atkinson)*

CLIPSTON [SP7181]

Bulls Head LE16 9RT [B4036 S of Market Harboro]: Village pub with friendly landlord, enjoyable good value food, Everards and guest ales, over 200 malt whiskies inc some old rarities, log fire and heavy beams – coins in the cracks put there by World War II airmen who never made it back for their next drink; unobtrusive piped music, games machine, Thurs night quiz, CCTV in lounge; children and dogs welcome, terrace tables, comfortable bedrooms *(LYM, Phil and Jane Hodson)*

COLLYWESTON [SK9902]

☆ *Collyweston Slater* PE9 3PU [A43; The Drove]: Stone-built stepped former cottage row refurbished as comfortable modern restaurant pub, sensibly short fresh menu inc

lunchtime tapas, three well kept ales inc Everards, good choice of wines by the glass, friendly young staff, slate-mining memorabilia; children welcome, picnic-sets outside, five good bedrooms (double-glazed – traffic all night) *(Roy Bromell, Jan and Alan Summers, Jan Murton)*

CRANFORD ST JOHN [SP9276]

Red Lion NN14 4AA [handy for A14 junction 11; High St]: Mellow two-bar stone-built pub with hard-working new licensee, good value food from sandwiches up using local produce, real ales, conservatory dining room; pleasant small garden, quiet village, nearby walks *(M and GR)*

DUDDINGTON [SK9800]

Royal Oak PE9 3QE [A43 just S of A47]: Attractive stone-built refurbished hotel; modern bar area with leather sofas and chairs on stone floor, log fire, wood panelling, flowers on top of brick bar, three changing real ales; dining room with stone walls, oak floor and oak furniture, enjoyable home-made food inc OAP bargain lunches (Mon-Fri) and two-course evening deals (Mon-Thurs), roasts all day Sun; piped music, no dogs; children welcome, disabled facilities, picnic-sets out at front, five good bedrooms, pleasant village, open all day wknds *(Carolyn Browse)*

GAYTON [SP7054]

Queen Victoria NN7 3HD [High St]: Four comfortable neat areas off central bar, Wells & Youngs and occasional guests, good wine choice, enjoyable food (not Sun evening) from snacks to blackboard specials inc good value Sun lunch, light panelling, beams, lots of pictures, books and shelves of china, inglenook woodburner, pool; piped music, games machines, Tues quiz night; bedrooms, cl Mon *(LYM, George Atkinson, Gerry and Rosemary Dobson)*

GRAFTON REGIS [SP7546]

☆ *White Hart* NN12 7SR [A508 S of Northampton]: Good pubby food (not Sun evening) inc lots of splendid winter soups, fine range of baguettes and popular Sun roasts in thatched dining pub with several linked rooms, Greene King ales, good wines by the glass, friendly hard-working helpful staff, african grey parrot (can be very vocal), small restaurant with open fire and separate menu; piped music; good-sized garden (food not usually served there) with terrace tables, cl Mon *(George Atkinson, BB)*

GREAT BILLING [SP8162]

Elwes Arms NN3 9DT [High St]: Thatched stone-built 16th-c village pub, two bars (steps between rooms), wide choice of good value tasty food (all day Fri-Sun), three real ales, good choice of other drinks, pleasant dining room (children allowed), darts; piped music, TV, no dogs; garden tables, covered decked terrace, play area *(JJW, CMW)*

GREAT HOUGHTON [SP7959]

Old Cherry Tree NN4 7AT [Cherry Tree Lane; No Through Road off A428 just before

White Hart]: Thatched village pub with low beams, open fires, stripped stone and panelling, enjoyable fresh food from lunchtime baguettes up, wider evening choice, prompt friendly service, well kept Wells & Youngs and occasional guest ales, good wine choice, steps up to restaurant; quiet piped music; garden tables *(Gerry and Rosemary Dobson)*

White Hart NN4 7AF [off A428 Northampton—Bedford; High St]: Unpretentious thatched pub with steps between linked areas, good value blackboard food (not Mon evening) from sandwiches up, Sun roast, well kept Adnams, Everards and Greene King, good choice of wines; piped music, TV, games machine, they may try to keep your card while you eat; attractive small garden with terrace *(Gerry and Rosemary Dobson, Eithne Dandy)*

GREENS NORTON [SP6649]

Butchers Arms NN12 8BA [High St]: Comfortably refurbished village pub, four well kept changing ales, enjoyable food from sandwiches up, friendly staff, separate bar and games room with darts and pool; piped music, some live; children and dogs allowed, disabled access, picnic-sets and play area, pretty village nr Grafton Way walks *(JJW, CMW, David Smith)*

HACKLETON [SP8054]

White Hart NN7 2AD [B526 SE of Northampton]: Comfortably traditional 18th-c country pub with wide choice of generous food from sandwiches and baked potatoes up inc early evening bargains, Fullers London Pride, Greene King IPA and a guest beer, decent choice of other drinks, good coffee, dining area up steps with flame-effect fire, stripped stone, beamery and brickwork, illuminated well, brasses and artefacts, split-level flagstoned bar with log fire, pool and hood skittles, curry and quiz night Tues; quiet piped music; children (not in bar after 5pm) and dogs welcome, disabled access, garden with picnic-sets and goal posts,
open all day *(JJW, CMW)*

HARLESTONE [SP7064]

Fox & Hounds NN7 4EW [A428, Lower Harlestone]: Contemporary M&B dining pub with pale wood furnishings and flooring, light and airy décor, enjoyable food inc popular Sun lunch, prompt helpful waiter service throughout, Timothy Taylors Landlord, good choice of wines by the glass; children welcome, tables in nice garden, handy for Althorp and Harlestone Firs walks, open all day *(Tim and Ann Newell, JJW, CMW, Michael Dandy)*

HARRINGTON [SP7780]

Tollemache Arms NN6 9NU [High St; off A508 S of Mkt Harboro]: Pretty thatched Tudor pub in lovely quiet ironstone village, very low ceilings in compact bar with log fire and in pleasant partly stripped stone dining room; good food choice from sandwiches up, well kept ales such as

Potbelly and Wells & Youngs, neat, friendly and attentive young staff; children welcome, nice back garden with country views *(George Atkinson, BB)*

HELLIDON [SP5158]

☆ *Red Lion* NN11 6LG [Stockwell Lane, off A425 W of Daventry]: Small wisteria-covered inn under new licensees, enjoyable food inc bargain OAP lunches and other deals, Greene King Abbot, softly lit low-ceilinged stripped-stone dining area with lots of hunting prints, cosy lounge, bar with woodburner, hood skittles and pool in back games room; picnic-sets in front, beautiful setting by unspoilt village's green, windmill vineyard and pleasant walks nearby, good bedrooms *(George Atkinson)*

KETTERING [SP8778]

Alexandra Arms NN16 0BU [Victoria St]: Friendly real ale pub, with up to ten changing quickly, hundreds each year, also their own Nobbys ale, may be sandwiches, back games bar with hood skittles; back terrace, open all day (from 2pm wkdys) *(the Didler, P Dawn)*

KISLINGBURY [SP6959]

Cromwell Cottage NN7 4AG [High St]: Sizeable low-ceilinged M&B dining pub recently upgraded, informal lounge seating, large bistro dining area, well kept Adnams, Timothy Taylors Landlord and Wells & Youngs Bombardier *(Gerry and Rosemary Dobson)*

Olde Red Lion NN7 4AQ [High St, off A45 W of Northampton]: Roomy renovated 19th-c stone-fronted pub, enjoyable freshly cooked bar and restaurant food, well kept Timothy Taylors and a guest ale; beams, woodburners and open fire, bar, dining room and restaurant, events inc summer beer festival; piped music and some live, no dogs; children welcome, disabled access, suntrap back terrace with marquee, barbecues, two bedrooms, cl Sun to Tues lunchtime, *(Robin M Corlett, Tracey Lamb)*

LITTLE ADDINGTON [SP9573]

Bell NN14 4BD [signed off A6 NW of Rushden; High St]: Much-extended stone-built village pub with popular restaurant (especially for its midweek bargains), sofas in solidly furnished bar, Greene King IPA, Marstons Pedigree and a guest such as local Potbelly, pool; tables out under sturdy arbour on front terrace by big orderly car park *(Gerry and Rosemary Dobson, BB)*

LITTLE BRINGTON [SP6663]

☆ *Saracens Head* NN7 4HS [4.5 miles from M1 junction 16, first right off A45 to Daventry; also signed off A428; Main St]: Friendly old pub with enjoyable reasonably priced food from interesting baguettes and wraps up, well kept real ales such as Adnams Broadside, Greene King IPA, Shepherd Neame Spitfire and Timothy Taylors Landlord, roomy U-shaped lounge with good log fire, flagstones, chesterfields and lots of old prints, book-lined dining room; plenty of tables in neat back garden, handy for Althorp House and Holdenby House

(Gerry and Rosemary Dobson, Geoffrey Hughes, Mrs S Hall, BB, Tim and Ann Newell)

LITTLE HARROWDEN [SP8671]

Lamb NN9 5BH [Orlingbury Rd/Kings Lane – off A509 or A43 S of Kettering]: Two-level lounge with log fire and brasses on 17th-c beams, dining area, good bargain food, Wells & Youngs Bombardier and a guest beer, good coffee, games bar with darts and machines; piped music; children welcome, small raised terrace and garden, delightful village (Howard and Margaret Buchanan)

LODDINGTON [SP8178]

Hare NN14 1LA [Main St]: Welcoming 17th-c stone-built dining pub, carpeted throughout, with wide choice of good reasonably priced food (not Sun evening or Mon) from good sandwiches to restaurant dishes, good-sized helpings, tablecloths and fresh flowers, Adnams Broadside and Timothy Taylors Landlord in small bar, good wine and soft drinks choice, good coffee, pleasant helpful service; piped music; picnic-sets on front lawn (Mike and Margaret Banks, Michael Dandy)

LOWICK [SP9780]

☆ *Snooty Fox* NN14 3BH [off A6116 Corby—Raunds]: Attractively reworked and spacious 16th-c stone-built pub, welcoming and immaculately kept, with leather sofas and chairs, beams and stripped stonework, log fire in huge fireplace, open kitchen doing bar food from sandwiches up inc steak counter, bargain set lunch and other deals, Greene King IPA and two guests, good wine choice, board games; piped music, games machine; dogs and children welcome, picnic-sets on front grass, play area, open all day (Mike and Sue Loseby, Mike and Margaret Banks, J C M Troughton, Mike Buckingham, LYM)

MAIDWELL [SP7477]

☆ *Stags Head* NN6 9JA [Harborough Rd (A508 N of Northampton)]: Light and spacious with comfortable carpeted areas off neatly kept beamed front bar with log fire, good pubby food very popular at lunchtime with older people, efficient friendly staff and cheery locals; Black Sheep, Tetleys and maybe a couple of guests, good choice of wines and soft drinks; quiet piped music; disabled facilities, terrace (dogs on leads allowed here) by neat back lawn with paddock beyond; bedrooms; not far from splendid Palladian Kelmarsh Hall in its parkland (Gerry and Rosemary Dobson, Mr and Mrs D J Nash, R L Borthwick, George Atkinson, Michael Dandy)

MEARS ASHBY [SP8466]

Griffins Head NN6 0DX [Wilby Rd]: Good choice of changing ales and of food from sandwiches to much more ambitious dishes, substantial OAP bargain wkdy lunches, attentive friendly staff, front lounge with pleasant outlook, hunting prints and log fire in huge fireplace, small dining room, basic back bar with juke box; children welcome,

neat flower-filled garden, open all day (George Atkinson, Gerry and Rosemary Dobson)

NEWNHAM [SP5759]

Romer Arms NN11 3HB [The Green]: Pine panelling, mix of flagstones, quarry tiles and carpet, log fire, light and airy back dining conservatory; cheerful obliging licensees, good generous home cooking (not Sun evening) inc bargain deals, Adnams, Wells & Youngs and the occasional guest, good soft drinks choice, public bar with darts and pool; piped music; enclosed back garden looking over fields, small attractive village (George Atkinson)

NORTHAMPTON [SP7261]

Hopping Hare NN5 6DF [Harlestone Rd (A428), New Duston]: Stylish contemporary refurbishment, with sofas etc around big servery, real ales such as Adnams, Marstons Pedigree and Wells & Youngs Bombardier, good choice of wines by the glass inc champagne, enjoyable good value up-to-date food, good friendly service, comfortable modern restaurant; nine modern bedrooms (Michael Dandy, G Jennings)

☆ *Malt Shovel* NN1 1QF [Bridge St (approach rd from M1 junction 15); best parking in Morrisons opp back entrance]: Up to 14 ales inc full Great Oakley range kept well (beer festivals), Rich's farm cider, belgian bottled beers, good choice of other drinks, friendly landlord and staff, cheap generous pubby lunchtime food (not Sun), daily papers, breweriana inc some from Carlsberg Brewery opposite, open fire, darts; piped music, live blues Weds, folk club 1st and 3rd Tues of month; children and dogs welcome, disabled facilities, picnic-sets on small back terrace (G Jennings, JJW, CMW, the Didler, George Atkinson, Bruce Bird, P Dawn)

RAVENSTHORPE [SP6670]

☆ *Chequers* NN6 8ER [Chequers Lane]: Warmly welcoming extended local with good choice of generous sensibly priced food from baguettes to popular Sun lunch, well kept ales such as Elgoods, Greene King and Jennings, attentive staff, open fire, lots of bric-a-brac hung from beams and stripped stone walls, mix of bench seating, high tables with stools and booths, back dining room, games room; quiet piped music, games machine; children welcome, small secluded back terrace and play area, open all day Sat (Richard and Audrey Chase, Rob and Catherine Dunster, George Atkinson, JJW, CMW)

RINGSTEAD [SP9875]

Axe & Compass NN14 4DW [Carlow Rd]: Extended stone-built village pub with flagstones and lots of bric-a-brac, enjoyable home-made food (even the chocolates) inc two-for-one midweek bargains, cheerful service, Banks's and Marstons Pedigree, good wines and coffee; piped music; garden and play area (Ryta Lyndley)

RUSHDEN [SP9566]

Station Bar NN10 0AW [Station Approach]: Not a pub, part of station HQ of Rushden

Historical Transport Society (non-members can sign in), restored in 1940s/60s style, with Fullers, Oakham and guests, tea and coffee, friendly staff, filled rolls (perhaps some hot dishes), gas lighting, enamelled advertisements, old-fangled furnishings; authentic waiting room with piano, also museum and summer steam-ups; open all day Sat, cl wkdy lunchtimes *(the Didler)*

RUSHTON [SP8483]

Thornhill Arms NN14 1RL [Station Rd]: Popular pleasantly furnished rambling dining pub opp attractive village's cricket green, wide choice of good value food from hot baguettes up in several neatly laid out dining areas inc smart high-beamed back restaurant, friendly helpful service, well kept Adnams, open fire; garden tables, bedrooms *(Philip and Susan Philcox, R T and J C Moggridge)*

STAVERTON [SP5461]

☆ *Countryman* NN11 6JH [Daventry Rd (A425)]: Beamed and carpeted with front bar leading to back and side dining areas, wide choice of reasonably priced food from sandwiches and baguettes to lots of fish (best to book Fri and Sat nights and Sun lunch), Fullers London Pride and two changing guests, good choice of wines by the glass, friendly attentive staff; piped music, no dogs inside; children welcome, disabled access, some tables outside and in small garden *(George Atkinson)*

STOKE ALBANY [SP8087]

White Horse LE16 8PY [Harborough Rd]: Civilised place for wide choice of enjoyable pubby food from sandwiches up, Fullers London Pride, Greene King IPA and St Austell Tribute, good choice of wines by the glass, games room, restaurant; comfortable terrace tables, five bedrooms *(Mike and Margaret Banks)*

STOKE BRUERNE [SP7449]

Boat NN12 7SB [3.5 miles from M1 junction 15 – A508 towards Stony Stratford then signed on right; Bridge Rd]: Old-world flagstoned bar in picturesque canalside spot by beautifully restored lock (plus more modern central-pillared back bar and bistro without the views); Marstons and related ales, usual food from baguettes up, extension with all-day tearooms and comfortable upstairs restaurant; piped music, can get very busy in summer; children and dogs welcome, disabled facilities, tables out by towpath opp British Waterways Museum and shop, canal boat trips, bar open all day summer Sats *(George Atkinson, Brian and Anna Marsden, LYM, Gerry and Rosemary Dobson)*

Navigation NN12 7SD: Large canalside Marstons pub, several levels and cosy corners, sturdy wood furniture, good Jennings Sneck Lifter and Timothy Taylors Landlord, quite a few wines by the glass, wide choice of pubby food, busy young staff, separate family room, pub games; piped music; plenty of tables out overlooking water, big play area, open all day *(Brian and Anna Marsden, John Cook, Charles and Pauline Stride, Rob and Catherine Dunster)*

STOKE DOYLE [TL0286]

Shuckburgh Arms PE8 5TG [S of Oundle]: 17th-c stone-built pub nicely refurbished in pale wood and pastels under new licensees, chef/landlord doing enjoyable food using very local supplies, real ales inc local Digfield, friendly service, woodburner in original inglenook; garden with play area, bedrooms *(anon)*

THORPE MANDEVILLE [SP5344]

☆ *Three Conies* OX17 2EX [off B4525 E of Banbury]: Attractive welcoming 17th-c pub with wide choice of food from good value sandwiches up, Weds curry night, well kept Hook Norton ales inc a bargain beer brewed for the pub (even cheaper Fri afternoon), beamed bare-boards bar with some stripped stone, mix of old dining tables, three good log fires, large dining room; piped music; children and dogs welcome, disabled facilities, tables out in front and behind on decking and lawn, open all day *(LYM, Richard and Audrey Chase)*

THORPE WATERVILLE [TL0281]

Fox NN14 3ED [A605 Thrapston—Oundle]: Extended stone-built pub under newish chef/landlord, enjoyable food inc Sun roasts, well kept Wells & Youngs ales from central bar, several wines by the glass, nice fire, light and airy modern dining area; piped music; children welcome, small garden with play area, open all day *(Grahame Sherwin)*

TOWCESTER [SP6948]

Brave Old Oak NN12 6BT [Watling St E]: Attractive furnishings and panelling, decent pub food inc bargains, well kept Marstons, friendly efficient service; bedrooms *(Alan and Eve Harding)*

Red Lion NN12 8LB [Foster's Booth (A5 3m N)]: Attractive 16th-c former posting inn with new licensees, Shepherd Neame Spitfire, good soft drinks choice, good value food from sandwiches and bargain light dishes up, daily papers, dark wood furniture in carpeted lounge bar/dining area with big inglenook, beams, bric-a-brac, copper and brass, another fire in quarry-tiled public bar with hood skittles and darts in carpeted games room; quiet piped music; children welcome, garden picnic-sets *(JJW, CMW)*

Saracens Head NN12 6BX [Watling St W]: Substantially modernised coaching inn with interesting *Pickwick Papers* connections (especially in the kitchen Dickens described, now a meeting room), open fire in long comfortable three-level lounge with dining area, Greene King ales, good value pub food inc bargain OAP set lunch, neat staff, games bar; piped music, TV; children welcome, small back courtyard with smokers' shelter, well equipped bedrooms, good breakfast *(LYM, Dr and Mrs Michael Smith, Michael Dandy, Alan and Eve Harding)*

WALGRAVE [SP8072]
Royal Oak NN6 9PN [Zion Hill, off A43
Northampton—Kettering]: Welcoming old
stone-built local, up to five well kept
changing real ales, decent wines, wide
choice of enjoyable good value food (not
Sun evening) inc some unusual dishes, quick
pleasant service, long three-part carpeted
beamed bar, small lounge, restaurant
extension behind; children welcome, small
garden, play area, open all day Sun
*(Gerry and Rosemary Dobson, J V Dadswell,
Barry Collett)*

WEEDON [SP6359]
Crossroads NN7 4PX [3 miles from M1
junction 16; A45 towards Daventry; High St,
on A5 junction]: Plush and spacious Chef &
Brewer with beamed bar and dining area,
dimly lit with lots of nooks and crannies, log
fires, friendly attentive staff, beers such as
Beartown and Wells & Youngs, decent all-day
food inc set deals, good coffee; piped jazz or
classical music; children welcome, disabled
facilities, tables on terrace and in attractive
gardens down to river, comfortable Premier
Lodge bedroom block, open all day
(George Atkinson, LYM)

Heart of England NN7 4QD [A45, handy for
M1 junction 16; High St]: Much refurbished
and enlarged around 18th-c beamed core,
popular with families and canal users, wide
choice of decent reasonably priced food inc
two-for-one deals, Banks's Bitter, Marstons
Pedigree and an occasional guest, friendly
hard-working staff, busy lounge bar with

small areas off, large airy panelled restaurant
and conservatory; unobtrusive piped music;
big garden leading down to Grand Union
Canal moorings, good value pine-furnished
bedrooms *(George Atkinson)*

WELLINGBOROUGH [SP9069]
Locomotive NN8 4AL [Finedon Rd (A5128)]:
Traditional two-bar local with up to six
interesting changing real ales, nice
lunchtime baguettes, friendly landlord, lots
of train memorabilia inc toy locomotive
running above bar, log fire, daily papers,
games room with pool, pin table and hood
skittles; may be quiet piped music; dogs
welcome, picnic-sets in small front garden,
open all day (Sun afternoon break)
(the Didler)

YARDLEY HASTINGS [SP8656]
☆ *Red Lion* NN7 1ER [High St, just off A428
Bedford—Northampton]: Pretty thatched
pub, friendly and relaxed, with enjoyable
good value seasonal food, wider evening
choice (not Sun, Mon), well kept Wells &
Youngs and one or two guest beers, good
range of soft drinks, prompt cheerful service,
linked rooms with beams and stripped stone,
lots of pictures, old photographs, plates and
interesting brass/copper, small annexe with
hood skittles; quiet piped music, games
machine, TV; children and dogs welcome,
nicely planted sloping garden, open all day
wknds *(Bruce and Sharon Eden,
Michael Dandy, Jeremy King, Gerry and
Rosemary Dobson, JJW, CMW, BB,
George Atkinson)*

Please tell us if the décor, atmosphere, food or drink at a pub is different from our
description. We rely on readers' reports to keep us up to date:
feedback@goodguides.com, or (no stamp needed) The Good Pub Guide,
FREEPOST TN1569, Wadhurst, E Sussex TN5 7BR.

Northumbria
(County Durham, Northumberland and Tyneside)

Quite a few good places to stay make the most of this lovely countryside for a weekend break. The Lord Crewe Arms at Blanchland, Morritt Arms at Greta Bridge and Rose & Crown at Romaldkirk are perhaps the most comfortable. The bustling Olde Ship in little Seahouses has been a harbourside inn for many years, the Fox & Hounds at Cotherstone is traditionally homely, the Pheasant at Stannersburn is ideal for England's largest forest and the newly refurbished rooms at the cheerful Victoria in Durham look inviting. New entries, both with enjoyable food, are the neatly modernised old Angel in Corbridge (six real ales too) and the clean-cut Mill Race at Wolsingham. Other pubs doing well include the Cook & Barker Arms at Newton on the Moor, liked for its generous pubby food, and the nicely informal Feathers at Hedley on the Hill, its careful use of good local produce winning for it the title of Northumbria Dining Pub of the Year – for the second year running. The North East has a good range of enterprising small breweries. The most popular are Hadrian & Border, Wylam, Mordue and Northumberland, and other favourites are Allendale, Durham, High House, Camerons and Jarrow. Serious sampling of the Big Lamp beers brewed at the pubby Keelman in Newburn suggests an overnight stay in one of their spacious rooms. Two other good own-brew pubs here are the nicely rural Dipton Mill Inn at Diptonmill with its five Hexhamshire beers (like Big Lamp quite widely available elsewhere) and the beautifully placed Ship at Newton-by-the-Sea.

ANICK

Rat 🍺

Village signposted NE of A69/A695 Hexham junction; NE46 4LN

Views over North Tyne Valley from terrace and garden, lots of interesting knick-knacks and half a dozen mainly local real ales

A coal fire blazes invitingly in the blackened kitchen range at this pleasantly relaxed country pub. The cosily traditional bar has old-fashioned pub tables and is full of cottagey knick-knacks, from antique floral chamber-pots hanging from the beams to china and glassware on a delft shelf. Little curtained windows allow a soft and gentle light; piped music, daily papers and magazines. The conservatory has pleasant valley views. Half a dozen changing real ales on handpump always include Bass and Caledonian Deuchars together with guests, usually from local breweries, such as Allendale, Geltsdale, Hadrian & Border and Wylam; also several wines by the glass from a reasonable list. Parking is limited, but you can also park around the village green. From tables out on the terrace you look over the North Tyne Valley; the charming garden has a dovecote, statues and attractive flowers.

❑ **Meat here comes from local named farms and the interesting and enjoyable bar food changes daily. Along with sandwiches there might be starters such as celeriac with apple cream soup, rabbit and black pudding terrine with onion marmalade, braised pork with cider and leeks, leek and thyme risotto with pigeon, baked mushrooms with goats cheese, fried cod with parsley sauce, beef and baby onions braised in Bitter and roast rib of beef for two, and puddings such as apple and blueberry crème brûlée and white chocolate and coconut bread and butter pudding and a local cheeseboard.** *Starters/Snacks: £3.50 to £5.95. Main Courses: £8.95 to £19.50. Puddings: £4.50*

Free house ~ Licensees Phil Mason and Karen Errington ~ Real ale ~ Bar food (12-2(3 Sun), 6-9; not Sun evening, Mon (except bank hols)) ~ Restaurant ~ (01434) 602814 ~ Children welcome ~ Open 12-3, 6-11; 12-11 Sat; 12-10.30 Sun

Recommended by Chris Clark, Shea Brookes Johnson, W K Wood, Comus and Sarah Elliott, K R Greenhalgh, Pat and Stewart Gordon, Dr Peter D Smart, Michael Doswell, Dr and Mrs R G J Telfer

BARRASFORD   NY9173   MAP 10

Barrasford Arms
Village signposted off A6079 N of Hexham; NE48 4AA

Friendly proper pub with good country cooking, plenty of nearby walks; bedrooms

Though you can have a fine dining experience at this sandstone inn, the compact traditional bar has a genuinely local atmosphere – a quoits league, darts club, ladies luncheon club and local vegetable shows have all evolved here. There's a good log fire, old local photographs and some country bric-a-brac, from horsebrasses to antlers, with Hadrian & Border Gladiator and a couple of guests from brewers such as Wylam on handpump, and good value wines by the glass. One nice dining room, carefully decorated in greys and creams and dominated by a great stone chimneybreast hung with guns and copper pans, has wheelback chairs around half a dozen neat tables; a second, perhaps rather more restrained, has more comfortably upholstered dining chairs; piped music, TV. They have well equipped bunkhouse accommodation as well as 11 bedrooms. The pub is on the edge of a small North Tyne village quite close to Hadrian's Wall, with lovely valley views and looks across to impressive medieval Haughton Castle (not open to the public); there may be sheep in the pasture just behind.

❑ **The cooking here is good, using carefully sourced local meats, game and fish to produce unpretentious and thoroughly rewarding dishes, full of flavour. The choice, changing daily, is usually kept sensibly short but might include purée of cauliflower and chive soup, twice-baked cheddar soufflé, seared organic salmon with sauce vierge, roast butternut squash and sage risotto, roast pork shoulder with black pudding, apple compote, calvados and sage jus, and puddings such as sticky pistachio meringue with vanilla mascarpone and poached rhubarb and raspberries. The local cheeses are carefully chosen, the puddings are a high point worth saving space for and the roast potatoes on Sunday are said to be outstanding.** *Starters/Snacks: £4.00 to £6.00. Main Courses: £9.00 to £16.50. Puddings: £5.00 to £6.00*

Free house ~ Licensee Tony Binks ~ Real ale ~ Bar food (12-2(3 Sun), 7-9) ~ Restaurant ~ (01434) 681237 ~ Children welcome ~ Open 12-2.30, 6-midnight; 12-1am Sat; 12-11.30 Sun; closed Mon lunchtime ~ Bedrooms: £65B/£85B

Recommended by Peter Logan, R L Borthwick

Bedroom prices normally include full english breakfast, VAT and any inclusive service charge that we know of. Prices before the '/' are for single rooms, after for two people in double or twin (B includes a private bath, S a private shower). If there is no '/', the prices are only for twin or double rooms (as far as we know there are no singles).

BLANCHLAND

NY9650 MAP 10

Lord Crewe Arms 🛏

B6306 S of Hexham; DH8 9SP

Ancient, historic building with some unusual features and straightforward bar food

The ancient-feeling bar below this comfortable hotel is housed in an unusual long and narrow stone barrel-vaulted crypt, its curving walls being up to eight feet thick in some places. Plush stools are lined along the bar counter on ancient flagstones and next to a narrow drinks shelf down the opposite wall; TV. Upstairs, the Derwent Room has low beams, old settles and sepia photographs on its walls, and the Hilyard Room has a massive 13th-c fireplace once used as a hiding place by the Jacobite Tom Forster (part of the family who had owned the building before it was sold in 1704 to the formidable Lord Crewe, Bishop of Durham). Black Sheep Best Bitter and Ale on handpump, and a good selection of wines. High up on the moors, and built by the Premonstratensians around 1235 as the abbot's lodging for their adjacent monastery, the building is immersed in history, with a lovely walled garden that was formerly the cloisters, and this is a most appealing place to stay.

🍴 **Straightforward bar food includes soup, filled rolls, generous ploughman's, cumberland sausage with black pudding and daily specials, as well as more elaborate restaurant food (available in the evening).** *Starters/Snacks: £3.00 to £3.95. Main Courses: £6.25 to £11.50. Puddings: £3.75*

Free house ~ Licensees A Todd and Peter Gingell ~ Real ale ~ Bar food ~ Restaurant ~ (01434) 675251 ~ Children welcome ~ Dogs welcome ~ Open 11-11; 12-10.30 Sun ~ Bedrooms: £50B/£100B

Recommended by Pat and Stewart Gordon, Comus and Sarah Elliott, Mr and Mrs P L Spencer

CARTERWAY HEADS

NZ0452 MAP 10

Manor House Inn 🍺

A68 just N of B6278, near Derwent Reservoir; DH8 9LX

Popular inn with local beers, food all day, nice views and bedrooms

Simple but heartwarming, the locals' bar at this country inn is a relaxing place to try a local pint if you've worked up a thirst enjoying the nearby Derwent Valley and reservoir. It's gently pubby, with an original boarded ceiling, pine tables, chairs and stools, old oak pews and a mahogany counter. The comfortable lounge bar, warmed by a woodburning stove, and restaurant both have picture windows that make the most of the lovely setting. Five changing real ales on handpump might be from brewers such as Hadrian and Border, Hexhamshire, High House and Northumberland, alongside around 70 malt whiskies; darts, TV and dominoes. There are rustic tables in the garden.

🍴 **Bar food includes sandwiches, garlic and chilli king prawn, bruschetta, chicken caesar salad, fish pie, roast pork belly filled with leeks, oxtail on black pudding mash with Guinness gravy, vegetable pancake topped with cheese sauce and sirloin steak. You can buy local produce, as well as chutneys, puddings and ice-cream made in the kitchens from their own little deli.** *Starters/Snacks: £3.95 to £6.95. Main Courses: £9.95 to £18.95. Puddings: £3.95*

Free house ~ Licensees Neil and Emma Oxley ~ Real ale ~ Bar food (12-9.30(9 Sun)) ~ Restaurant ~ (01207) 255268 ~ Children welcome ~ Dogs allowed in bar and bedrooms ~ Open 11-11; 12-10.30 Sun ~ Bedrooms: £45S/£65S

Recommended by R Hayworth, Pat and Stewart Gordon, Brian Brooks, Comus and Sarah Elliott, Fiona Salvesen, Ross Murrell, Mrs Carolyn Dixon, Sheena W Makin

---

Real ale may be served from handpumps, electric pumps (not just the on-off switches used for keg beer) or – common in Scotland – tall taps called founts (pronounced 'fonts') where a separate pump pushes the beer up under air pressure.

CORBRIDGE NY9964 MAP 10

Angel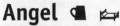

Main Street; NE45 5LA

Enterprising food and fine drinks range in modernised inn; comfortable bedrooms

The sizeable main bar of this imposing white coaching inn is functional in a briskly modern style – light and airy, with just a few prints on its pastel walls, plain light wood tables and chairs, overhead spotlighting, even a big-screen TV. The carpeted lounge bar has quite a modern feel, too, with its strongly patterned wallpaper and some tall metal-framed café-bar seats as well as its more homely leather bucket armchairs. The best sense of the building's age is in a separate lounge, with button-back wing armchairs, a sofa, oak panelling and a big stone fireplace; and look out for the fine 17th-c arched doorway in the left-hand porch. A smart raftered restaurant has local artwork and some stripped masonry; piped music. They keep up to half a dozen real ales from brewers such as Black Sheep, Hadrian & Border, Mordue, Timothy Taylor and Wylam on handpump, and do good wines by the glass and coffees; daily papers. You can sit out in front, on the cobbles below a wall sundial; the building is nicely set at the end of a broad street, facing the handsome bridge over the River Tyne.

⚓ **As well as a good range of sandwiches, bar food might include starters such as chicken, leek and mushroom soup, seared scallops on black pudding and chorizo, seared pigeon breast on rocket and raspberry salad with raspberry coulis and pepper dressing, main courses such as fried lambs liver with bacon and champ, battered cod, hand-cut chips and mushy peas, venison burger, honey and five spice roast duck breast on asian salad with tempura battered potatoes and mushroom and pea risotto, and puddings such as warm gooseberry cake and vanilla ice-cream and white chocolate and ginger cheesecake with chantilly cream.** *Starters/Snacks: £4.50 to £8.95. Main Courses: £8.95 to £16.95. Puddings: £5.00*

Free house ~ Licensee John Gibson ~ Real ale ~ (01434) 632119 ~ Children welcome away from cocktail bar ~ Open 11-11(midnight Sat); 12-10.30 Sun ~ Bedrooms: £70S(£85B)/£105B

Recommended by Andy and Jill Kassube, Michael Doswell, Carole Hall, Sue Milliken, Dr Peter D Smart

Errington Arms

About 3 miles N of town; B6318, on A68 roundabout; NE45 5QB

Relaxed and friendly 18th-c stone-built inn with enjoyable food and local beer

Good value lunches and its location right beside Hadrian's Wall attract a dining set to this 18th-c roadside inn – indeed most of the tables are laid for dining and staff are uniformed for efficient service. Following a fire in 2006, it was stylishly refurbished by a father and son team, with exposed oak beams, a nice mix of candlelit tables on the light wooden floor, some pine planking and stripped stonework, burgundy paintwork, ornamental plaques, a large heavy mirror and a log fire; there is still a modicum of bric-a-brac, on window sills and so forth. Jennings Cumberland and Mordue Workie Ticket on handpump; piped music. Out on the front terrace are some sturdy metal and teak tables under canvas parasols.

⚓ **As well as sandwiches, ploughman's and salads, the enjoyable food includes fried calamari, lambs liver, bacon, sausage and cranberry terrine, fried king prawns with tomato rocket salad, chicken schnitzel with bacon in a bap, spanish omelette, steak and kidney pie with puff pastry, thai-style vegetables, cod with chorizo salad and crispy pork loin with black pudding, pork sausage and cider and rosemary jus.** *Starters/Snacks: £4.95 to £7.95. Main Courses: £7.95 to £13.95. Puddings: £2.95 to £4.00*

Punch ~ Lease Nicholas Shotton ~ Real ale ~ Bar food (12-2.30(3 Sun), 6.30-9) ~ Restaurant ~ (01434) 672250 ~ Children welcome ~ Open 11-3, 6-11; 12-3 Sun; closed Sun evening, Mon (exc bank hols)

Recommended by Alan Thwaite, Mrs Marion Matthewman, Mike Goddard, GSB, David and Sue Smith, Mike and Lynn Robinson

COTHERSTONE   NZ0119 MAP 10

Fox & Hounds 🛏️

B6277 – incidentally a good quiet route to Scotland, through interesting scenery; DL12 9PF

Redecorated 18th-c inn with cheerful beamed bar, homely bar food and quite a few wines by the glass

Readers enjoy the genuine Northumbrian hospitality at this bustling country inn. The simple but cheery beamed bar has a partly wooden floor (elsewhere it's carpeted), a good winter log fire, thickly cushioned wall seats and local photographs and country pictures on the walls in its various alcoves and recesses. Black Sheep Best and a guest such as York Yorkshire Terrier are on handpump alongside several malt whiskies from smaller distilleries; efficient service from the friendly staff. Don't be surprised by the unusual lavatory attendant – an african grey parrot called Reva. Seats outside on a terrace and quoits. More reports please.

🍽️ **As well as Tuesday night fish and chips, bar food typically includes lunchtime sandwiches, wensleydale cheese and hazelnut pâté, smoked salmon platter, roast halibut with prawn and pesto dressing, steak, black pudding and ale pie, ratatouille filled pancake baked with wensleydale cheese crust, fried pork tenderloin with sage, apple and onion cream sauce, and puddings such as dark chocolate and almond brownie and raspberry and apple crêpe.** *Starters/Snacks: £4.30 to £6.45. Main Courses: £7.95 to £16.50. Puddings: £4.50*

Free house ~ Licensees Nichola and Ian Swinburn ~ Real ale ~ Bar food (12-2, 7-9(8.30 Sun)) ~ Restaurant ~ (01833) 650241 ~ Children welcome if dining ~ Dogs welcome ~ Open 12-3, 6.30(6 Sat)-11(10.30) ~ Bedrooms: £47.50B/£75B

Recommended by Mike Wignall, Vicky Sherwood, Maurice and Janet Thorpe, Brian and Rosalie Laverick, R Hayworth, John Urquhart, M J Winterton

DIPTONMILL   NY9261 MAP 10

Dipton Mill Inn ♀ 🍺 £

Just S of Hexham; off B6306 at Slaley, Blanchland and Dye House, Whitley Chapel signposts (and HGV route sign); not to be confused with the Dipton in Durham; NE46 1YA

Own-brew beers, good value bar food and garden with terrace and aviary

The cheery landlord at this ivy-covered rural pub is a brewer in the family-owned Hexhamshire Brewery and all five of their brews are well kept here on handpump: Devils Water, Devils Elbow, Old Humbug, Shire Bitter and Whapweasel; also a dozen wines by the glass, over 20 malt whiskies, and Weston's Old Rosie cider. The neatly kept snug bar has dark ply panelling, low ceilings, red furnishings, a dark red carpet and newspapers to read by two welcoming open fires. In fine weather it's pleasant to sit out on the sunken crazy-paved terrace by the restored mill stream, or in the attractively planted garden with its aviary. There's a nice walk through the woods along the little valley and Hexham race course is not far away.

🍽️ **As well as a fine range of northumbrian cheeses, the inexpensive food includes sandwiches, ploughman's, leek and potato soup, mince and dumplings, duck breast with orange and cranberry, tagliatelle with creamy basil sauce and parmesan, lamb steak in wine and mustard sauce, and puddings such as rhubarb crumble and chocolate rum truffle torte.** *Starters/Snacks: £2.50 to £3.75. Main Courses: £6.00 to £8.00. Puddings: £2.25 to £3.00*

Own brew ~ Licensee Geoff Brooker ~ Real ale ~ Bar food (12-2, 6.30-8.30; not Sun evening) ~ No credit cards ~ (01434) 606577 ~ Children welcome ~ Open 12-2.30, 6-11; 12-3 Sun; closed Sun evening

Recommended by Alex and Claire Pearse, the Didler, Mr and Mrs T Stone, Mike and Lynn Robinson

DURHAM   NZ2742   MAP 10

Victoria 🍺 🛏

Hallgarth Street (A177, near Dunelm House); DH1 3AS

Unchanging and neatly kept Victorian pub with royal memorabilia, cheerful locals and well kept regional ales; good value bedrooms

Brimming with friendliness and the cheery character of the landlord, Angie the barmaid and their sociable locals, the unsullied traditional layout of this absolutely timeless-feeling late Victorian tavern has three little rooms leading off a central bar with typically Victorian décor: mahogany, etched and cut glass and mirrors, colourful William Morris wallpaper over a high panelled dado, some maroon plush seats in little booths, leatherette wall seats, long narrow drinkers' tables, handsome iron and tile fireplaces for the coal fires, a piano and some photographs and articles showing a very proper pride in the pub; there are also lots of period prints and engravings of Queen Victoria and staffordshire figurines of her and the Prince Consort. Big Lamp and Hexhamshire Devils Water and four guests from brewers such as Durham, Hambleton, Hadrian & Border Gladiator and Wylam on handpump; also cheap house wines, around 40 malts and a great collection of 40 irish whiskeys. Dominoes. If you're staying, a hearty breakfast (good vegetarian one, too) is served in the upstairs dining room – do let us know what you think of the recently refurbished bedrooms if you stay here.

🍴 **Lunchtime toasties only.**

Free house ~ Licensee Michael Webster ~ Real ale ~ (0191) 386 5269 ~ Children welcome ~ Dogs welcome ~ Open 11.45-3, 6-11; 12-2, 7-10.30 Sun ~ Bedrooms: £48B/£65B

Recommended by Jeff Edwards, Mark Walker, the Didler, Pete Baker, Eric Larkham, Pam and John Smith, Stephen Locke, Chris Sale, J A Ellis, Mike and Lynn Robinson

GREAT WHITTINGTON   NZ0070   MAP 10

Queens Head 🍺

Village signposted off A68 and B6018 just N of Corbridge; NE19 2HP

Relaxed and civilised inn with log fires and outside seating

There's a rather nice hunting mural above the old fireplace in the long narrow bar at this calming old golden-stone place. High stools on bare boards are arranged along the counter – with three real ales from brewers such as High House, Timothy Taylor and Wylam on handpump, and quite a few malt whiskies as well as several wines by the glass – with more stools opposite along a wall counter. Emphasis tends to be on the laid-up dining areas with their modern furnishings on bright tartan carpeting. There are seats on the small front lawn.

🍴 **As well as lunchtime sandwiches, bar food includes cold ham and duck eggs, battered cod with mushy peas and handcut chips, smoked haddock and leek fishcakes with lemon and dill tartare sauce and seared lambs liver with red wine sauce, roast boneless quail with apricot stuffing and red onion marmalade, mixed vegetable tikka in wholemeal pitta bread, and puddings such as chocolate fudge brownie sundae and banoffi pie.** *Starters/Snacks: £4.25 to £6.00. Main Courses: £6.00 to £15.50. Puddings: £4.95*

Free house ~ Licensee Claire Murray ~ Real ale ~ Bar food (12-2.30, 6-9; 12-9.30 Fri, Sat; 12-6 Sun) ~ Restaurant ~ (01434) 672267 ~ Children welcome ~ Open 12-3, 5.30-11; 12-midnight(11 Sun) Sat

Recommended by GSB, Jenny and Dave Hughes

'Children welcome' means the pub says it lets children inside without any special restriction. If it allows them in, but to restricted areas such as an eating area or family room, we specify this. Some pubs may impose an evening time limit. We do not mention limits after 9pm as we assume children are home by then.

GRETA BRIDGE

NZ0813 MAP 10

Morritt Arms ♀ ⇌

Hotel signposted off A66 W of Scotch Corner; DL12 9SE

Country house hotel with nice pubby bar, extraordinary mural, interesting food, attractive garden with play area, nice bedrooms

Around the nicely pubby bar at the heart of this striking 17th-c former coaching inn runs a remarkable mural of Dickensian characters painted in 1946 by J T Y Gilroy – better known for his old Guinness advertisements. (In 1839 Charles Dickens visited one of the three inns at Greta Bridge whilst researching Nicholas Nickleby.) Big windsor armchairs and sturdy oak settles cluster around traditional cast-iron-framed tables, large windows look out on the extensive lawn, and there are nice open fires. Black Sheep and Timothy Taylors Landlord and Theakstons XB are on handpump alongside an extensive wine list with over a dozen wines by the glass. The attractively laid-out garden has some seats with teak tables in a pretty side area looking along to the graceful old bridge by the stately gates to Rokeby Park; there's also a play area for children.

🍴 **Good modern bar food includes sandwiches, mushrooms on toast, battered cod fillet, steaks, warm chocolate brownie and apple charlotte.** *Starters/Snacks: £4.50 to £8.00. Main Courses: £9.00 to £22.00. Puddings: £6.00 to £7.00*

Free house ~ Licensees Peter Phillips and Barbara Johnson ~ Real ale ~ Bar food (12-3, 6-9.30 (soup and sandwiches 3-6)) ~ Restaurant ~ (01833) 627232 ~ Children welcome ~ Dogs allowed in bar and bedrooms ~ Open 11-11; 12-10.30 Sun ~ Bedrooms: £80S(£85B)/£110B

Recommended by Pat and Stewart Gordon, Richard Cole, S G N Bennett

HALTWHISTLE

NY7166 MAP 10

Milecastle Inn

Military Road; B6318 NE – OS Sheet 86 map reference 715660; NE49 9NN

Close to Hadrian's Wall and some wild scenery, with cosy little rooms warmed by winter log fires; fine views and walled garden

Just the sort of place to warm up in after a blowy walk, this solitary 17th-c pub is close to some of the most celebrated sites of Hadrian's Wall, and the straight moorland road it stands on was the military road that was contemporary with the Wall itself. The snug little rooms of the beamed bar are decorated with brasses, horsey and local landscape prints and attractive fresh flowers, and have two winter log fires; at lunchtime the small comfortable restaurant is used as an overflow. Friendly hard-working staff serve Big Lamp Prince Bishop and a couple of guests from Camerons Nimmo from handpumps and they have a fair collection of malt whiskies and a good wine list. The tables and benches out in a pleasantly sheltered big walled garden with a dovecote and rather stunning views are popular in summer, and there are two self-catering cottages and a large car park.

🍴 **Sensible straightforward bar food includes sandwiches, game pâté, filo duck rolls, scampi, cheese and broccoli pasta bake, all sorts of pies (even wild boar and duck), battered haddock, steaks and daily specials such as chicken breast in tomato and onion gravy.** *Starters/Snacks: £1.95 to £6.95. Main Courses: £8.25 to £14.75. Puddings: £4.25*

Free house ~ Licensees Clare and Kevin Hind ~ Real ale ~ Bar food (12-8.45(8.30 Sun); 12-2.30, 6-8.30 in winter) ~ Restaurant ~ (01434) 321372 ~ Children welcome if eating ~ Open 12-10.30(11 Sat); 12-3, 6-10 in winter

Recommended by Neil Whitehead, Victoria Anderson, Dr Kevan Tucker, Sylvia and Tony Birbeck

---

Anyone claiming to arrange or prevent inclusion of a pub in the *Guide* is a fraud. Pubs are included only if recommended by genuine readers and if our own anonymous inspection confirms that they are suitable.

HAYDON BRIDGE
NY8364 MAP 10

General Havelock
A69 Corbridge—Haltwhistle; NE47 6ER

Civilised, chatty riverside dining pub with local beers and interesting food

The terrace and stripped-stone barn dining room at this quiet little house make the most of the fine South Tyne river views from here. The attractively lit L-shaped bar is imaginatively decorated in shades of green, and is at its best in the back part with stripped pine chest-of-drawers topped with bric-a-brac, colourful cushions on long pine benches and a sturdy stripped settle, interestingly shaped mahogany-topped tables and good wildlife photographs. They stock a couple of local beers such as Allendale or High House alongside a guest such as Durham Definitive on handpump, good wines and a choice of apple juices; board games and boules. Haydon Bridge itself is a short and very pretty stroll downstream.

🍽 **The food is well above average and freshly prepared, with home-made bread, local game and meat; the menu might include lunchtime baguettes and panini, bacon-wrapped chicken breast stuffed with cheddar and leeks, sirloin steak and beef, Guinness and mushroom stew, a fish of the day, cumberland sausage with mash and game pie, with puddings like warm walnut tart and bread and butter pudding; set evening meals and Sunday lunches.** *Starters/Snacks: £4.00. Main Courses: £6.00 to £13.00. Puddings: £4.00 to £5.75*

Free house ~ Licensees Gary and Joanna Thompson ~ Real ale ~ Bar food (12-4, 7-9) ~ Restaurant ~ (01434) 684376 ~ Children welcome ~ Dogs allowed in bar ~ Open 12-4, 7-midnight; closed Sun evening, Mon
Recommended by Bob Richardson, Chris Clark, Comus and Sarah Elliott, Michael Doswell

HEDLEY ON THE HILL
NZ0759 MAP 10

Feathers
Village signposted from New Ridley, which is signposted from B6309 N of Consett; OS Sheet 88 map reference 078592; NE43 7SW
NORTHUMBRIA DINING PUB OF THE YEAR

Interesting beers, imaginative food and a friendly welcome in quaint tavern

This comfortable hilltop tavern is very much at the heart of the local community, attracting a good mix of customers, from local farmers and fisherman bartering their wares for a pint, to visitors here for the very good food. All are warmly welcomed and made to feel part of the pubby atmosphere. Its three neat beamed bars are warmly traditional, with open fires, stripped stonework, solid furniture, including settles, and old black and white photographs of local places and farm and country workers; a selection of traditional pub games, with dominoes, darts, bar skittles and shove-ha'penny. Small-scale breweries are well represented with four real ales (usually mainly local) from brewers such as Hadrian & Border, Mordue, Wylam and Orkney on handpump; about three dozen wines by the glass, over 40 bourbons and malt whiskies, and local soft drinks. They hold a beer and food festival at Easter with over two dozen real ales (and a barrel race on Easter Monday). Picnic-sets in front are a nice place to sit and watch the world drift by.

🍽 **Details of their carefully chosen suppliers are listed on the daily changing menu, and the appealing choice of food features several regional dishes, using wild salmon from the South Tyne, home butchered game from local shoots and beef from rare breeds and home-baked bread. Dishes run from straightforward to more imaginative and might include carrot and parsnip soup, charcuterie, ploughman's, hot smoked eel with northumbrian bacon and horseradish, cheese and leek pie with mushroom gravy, battered fish, cumberland sausage and mash, roast duck with apple and sage, jugged hare with tarragon and fried bread, and puddings such as quince, pear and almond tart and dark chocolate and chestnut mousse.** *Starters/Snacks: £4.00 to £6.00. Main Courses: £7.00 to £15.00. Puddings: £4.00 to £5.00*

Free house ~ Licensees Rhian Cradock and Helen Greer ~ Real ale ~ Bar food (12-2(2.30 Sun), 6-8 not Sun evening, Mon) ~ (01661) 843607 ~ Children welcome ~ Open 6-11 Mon; 12-11(10.30 Sun)

Recommended by M and GR, Jenny and Dave Hughes, M A Borthwick, Michael Doswell, Miss J Smith,
Denis Newton, Andy and Jill Kassube, Mike and Lynn Robinson, Bruce and Sharon Eden, Alex and Claire Pearse,
Alan Thwaite, Mike Goddard, Rachel Greer, W K Wood, Christine and Phil Young

NEW YORK   NZ3269   MAP 10

Shiremoor Farm

Middle Engine Lane/Norham Road, off A191 bypass; NE29 8DZ

Large dining pub with interesting furnishings and décor, popular food all day, decent drinks and covered, heated terrace

Hidden away in somewhat unpromising suburban surroundings, this large dining pub has a huge clientele and serves an astonishing number of meals a week. The building is a spacious transformation of derelict agricultural buildings, with the conical rafters of the former gin-gan showing in one area. Gentle lighting in several well divided spacious areas cleverly picks up the surface modelling of the pale stone and beam ends. It's furnished with a mix of interesting and comfortable furniture, a big kelim on broad flagstones, warmly colourful farmhouse paintwork on the bar counter and several other tables, a few farm tools and evocative country pictures. Black Sheep Ale, Mordue Workie Ticket, Timothy Taylors Landlord and possibly a guest are on handpump, together with decent wines by the glass. There are seats outside on the covered, heated terrace.

▥ The blackboard menus change constantly and, as well as sandwiches, might include starters such as honey-roast pork fillet and cajun king prawns, main courses such as vegetarian quiches and pasta dishes, spicy sausage, steak and ale casserole, chicken breast stuffed with mushrooms and bacon with stilton sauce and szechuan and ginger marinated beef with king prawn kebab, and puddings such as double chocolate and waffle cheesecake and warm dutch apple pie. *Starters/Snacks: £2.95 to £5.95. Main Courses: £7.45 to £12.95. Puddings: £4.45*

Free house ~ Licensee C W Kerridge ~ Real ale ~ Bar food (12-10) ~ (0191) 2576302 ~ Children welcome ~ Open 11-11

Recommended by Mike and Lynn Robinson, Michael Doswell, Comus and Sarah Elliott

NEWBURN   NZ1665   MAP 10

Keelman ▉ £ ⇌

Grange Road: follow Riverside Country Park brown signs off A6085 (the riverside road off A1 on Newcastle's west fringes); NE15 8ND

Impressive range of own-brewed beers in converted pumping station, easy-going atmosphere, excellent service, straightforward food, bedroom block

The hands-on landlord at this big popular pub is quick to help out when needed and the entire establishment is kept spick and span. Perhaps the most striking feature is the splendid array of beers from their own Big Lamp Brewery. The impressive array of eight handpumps usually dispenses the full range, obviously kept in tip-top condition and very reasonably priced. If you're confused about which one to go for, the neatly dressed staff will happily let you sample a couple first: Big Lamp Bitter, Blackout, Double M, Embers, Premium, Prince Bishop Ale, Summerhill Stout and Sunny Daze. There's a relaxed atmosphere and a good mix of customers, from families to beer lovers, in the high-ceilinged bar, which is light and airy with lofty arched windows and well spaced tables and chairs. There are more tables in an upper gallery and the modern all-glass conservatory dining area (pleasant at sunset) contrasts stylishly with the original old building; piped music. You'll find plenty of picnic-sets, tables and benches out on the spacious terraces, among flower tubs and beds of shrubs, and there's a good play area. Bedroom prices are for room only.

▥ Reasonably priced and served in generous helpings, the straightforward food includes sandwiches, soup, filled baked potatoes, beef in ale pie, fish and chips, grilled trout and chicken, bacon and leek dumpling in white wine sauce; early evening weekday special

offer from 5 till 7pm. *Starters/Snacks: £2.95 to £5.45. Main Courses: £5.95 to £8.95. Puddings: £3.40*

Own brew ~ Licensee George Story ~ Real ale ~ Bar food (12-9) ~ Restaurant ~ (0191) 267 0772 ~ Children welcome ~ Dogs welcome ~ Open 11-11; 12-10.30 Sun ~ Bedrooms: £42.50S/£57S

Recommended by GSB, M J Winterton, Paul and Ursula Randall, Mike and Lynn Robinson, Mr and Mrs Maurice Thompson, Gerry and Rosemary Dobson, Joe Green, David and Sue Smith, Alan Thwaite, Lawrence Pearse, Brian and Rosalie Laverick, George Cowie, Frances Gosnell

NEWCASTLE UPON TYNE

NZ2563   MAP 10

Crown Posada 🍺

The Side; off Dean Street, between and below the two high central bridges (A6125 and A6127); NE1 3JE

Busy city-centre pub with grand architecture, lots of locals in long narrow bar, tip-top beers and a warm welcome

A golden crown and magnificent pre-Raphaelite stained-glass windows add grandeur to the imposing carved stone façade of this marvellously unchanged pub. Inside, architectural highlights include the elaborate coffered ceiling, stained-glass in the counter screens and a line of gilt mirrors each with a tulip lamp on a curly brass mount matching the great ceiling candelabra. It's a long narrow room, making quite a bottleneck by the serving counter; beyond that, a long soft green built-in leather wall seat is flanked by narrow tables. Fat low-level heating pipes make a popular footrest when the east wind brings the rain off the North Sea and an old record player in a wooden cabinet provides mellow background music when the place is quiet. During the week, regulars sit reading papers in the front snug, but at weekends it is often packed. From half a dozen handpumps and kept in fine condition, the real ales include Hadrian & Border Gladiator, Jarrow Bitter and Timothy Taylors Landlord with three guests from brewers such as Bathams, Mordue and Wylam. It's only a few minutes' stroll to the castle.

🍴 **Lunchtime sandwiches only.**

Sir John Fitzgerald ~ Licensee Derek Raisbeck ~ Real ale ~ (0191) 232 1269 ~ Open 11(12 Sat)-11; 7-10.30 Sun; closed Sun lunchtime

Recommended by Pete Baker, John and Gloria Isaacs, Dr and Mrs A K Clarke, Chris Sale, Joe Green, the Didler, Eric Larkham, Mike and Lynn Robinson, Andy and Jill Kassube, Mrs Hazel Rainer

NEWTON ON THE MOOR

NU1705   MAP 10

Cook & Barker Arms 🛏

Village signposted from A1 Alnwick-Felton; NE65 9JY

Emphasis on food but with a nicely traditional country-pub feel in the bar, and quite a range of drinks; comfortable bedrooms

Most customers at this friendly stone-built inn are here to enjoy the fairly priced tasty food, with efficient staff coping really well even when things get busy. The relaxed and unfussy long beamed bar feels distinctly pubby, with stripped stone and partly panelled walls, brocade-seated settles around oak-topped tables, brasses, a highly polished oak servery and lovely coal fires. The restaurant has oak-topped tables with comfortable leather chairs and french windows opening on to the terrace; TV. Drinks include Black Sheep, Jennings Cumberland and a guest or two such as Hadrian & Border Secret Kingdom on handpump, an extensive wine list and quite a few malt whiskies. Surprisingly quiet given its proximity to the A1, it has an inviting garden and the bedrooms are very comfortable.

🍴 **The licensees own a farm which supplies their beef, lamb and pork.** Served in generous helpings the menu might include sandwiches, starters such as crab and prawn risotto, warm muffin with smoked salmon, poached egg and butter sauce, grilled sardines, thai shredded beef, main courses such as beef and onion pie, roast pigeon with bacon and mushrooms, fish and chips, squid, mussels and king prawns in garlic chilli sauce and roast bass with smoked salmon, dill and linguine. *Starters/Snacks: £3.95 to £7.00. Main Courses: £8.00 to £15.00. Puddings: £4.95*

Free house ~ Licensee Phil Farmer ~ Real ale ~ Bar food (12-2, 6-9; limited menu all day) ~ Restaurant (12-2, 7-9) ~ (01665) 575234 ~ Children welcome ~ Open 11-11(10.30 Sun) ~ Bedrooms: £60B/£80B

Recommended by Louise English, Michael Doswell, R N and M I Bailey, Alex and Claire Pearse, Joyce and Maurice Cottrell, Comus and Sarah Elliott, Tony Baldwin, Rory and Jackie Hudson, Roy and Jean Russell, Julian and Jill Tasker, Sue Milliken, Brian Brooks, Tina and David Woods-Taylor, MJVK

NEWTON-BY-THE-SEA NU2424 MAP 10

Ship

Village signposted off B1339 N of Alnwick; Low Newton – paid parking 200 metres up road on right, just before village (none in village); NE66 3EL

In charming square of fishermen's cottages by green sloping to sandy beach, good simple food, fine spread of drinks; best to check winter opening times

The coastal setting of this row of converted fishermen's cottages, looking across a sloping village green to a sandy beach just beyond, is quite enchanting – not surprisingly it does draw the lunchtime crowds with walkers sheltering from the blustery beach or summer sun. It's quieter in the evening but it's still advisable to book. The plainly furnished but cosy bare-boards bar on the right has nautical charts on its dark pink walls. Another simple room on the left has beams and hop bines and some bright modern pictures on stripped-stone walls, and a woodburning stove in its stone fireplace; darts, dominoes. They started brewing here a couple of years ago: Dolly Daydream, Sandcastles at Dawn, Sea Wheat and Ship Hop are on handpump, with a local guest at busier times. Out in the corner of the square are some tables among pots of flowers, with picnic-sets over on the grass. There's no nearby parking, but there's a car park up the hill.

⑪ The snacky lunchtime menu, which includes soup, kipper pâté and toast, crab stottie, ploughman's and toasted ciabattas, gives way to a more extensive evening menu with dishes such as grilled goats cheese with tomato and basil, sausages cooked with onions and red wine, tagliatelle with pesto, baked tomatoes and local cheese, sirloin steak, lobster, and puddings such as apple crumble and chocolate brownies. *Starters/Snacks: £3.50 to £5.95. Main Courses: £8.00 to £22.50. Puddings: £3.00 to £4.95*

Free house ~ Licensee Christine Forsyth ~ Real ale ~ Bar food (12-2.30, 7-8 (check in winter)) ~ No credit cards ~ (01665) 576262 ~ Children welcome ~ Dogs welcome ~ Live folk, blues and jazz – phone for details ~ Open 11(12 Sun)-11; 11(12 Sun)-3; 7.30-11(cl Sun-Weds evening) winter

Recommended by Lawrence Pearse, Comus and Sarah Elliott, Danny and Gillian O'Sullivan, Tony and Jill Radnor, Roger Fox, Mike and Sue Loseby, the Didler, Graham Oddey, Reg Fowle, Helen Rickwood, Michael Doswell, Peter and Eleanor Kenyon, GSB, Paul Newberry

ROMALDKIRK NY9922 MAP 10

Rose & Crown ★ ⑪ ♀ ⇔

Just off B6277; DL12 9EB

Civilised base for the area, with accomplished cooking, attentive service and lovely bedrooms

This comfortable country inn is enjoyed by readers for its excellent food and very helpful staff. The cosily traditional beamed bar has old-fashioned seats facing a warming log fire, a Jacobean oak settle, lots of brass and copper, a grandfather clock, gin traps, old farm tools and black and white pictures of Romaldkirk on the walls. Black Sheep Best Bitter and Theakstons Best are on handpump alongside 14 wines by the glass, organic fruit juices and pressed vegetable juices. The smart brasserie-style Crown Room (bar food is served in here) has large cartoons of french waiters on dark red walls, a grey carpet and smart high-back chairs. The hall has farm tools, wine maps and other interesting prints, along with a photograph (taken by a customer) of the Hale Bopp comet over the interesting old church. There's also an oak-panelled restaurant. Tables outside look over the village green, with its original stocks and water pump. Romaldkirk is close to the extraordinary Bowes Museum and High Force waterfall. The owners also provide their own in-house guide to days out and about in the area and a *Walking in Teesdale* book.

🍴 **Everything on the seasonally changing menu is home made, apart from the frites and ice-cream. As well as sandwiches and ploughman's, well presented imaginative food might include baked smoked salmon soufflé with chive cream, leek, bacon and black pudding risotto with poached egg, yorkshire blue, roast walnut and chicory salad with sweet pear dressing, sausage with mustard mash and shallot gravy, steak, kidney and mushroom pie, grilled venison with green peppercorn cream, grilled bass with roast fennel and tomato broth, and puddings such as orange panna cotta and lime, chocolate cheesecake and sticky toffee pudding. You do need to book to be sure of a table.** *Starters/Snacks: £4.50 to £6.75. Main Courses: £10.50 to £15.95. Puddings: £5.25*

Free house ~ Licensees Christopher and Alison Davy ~ Real ale ~ Bar food (12-1.45, 6.30-9.30) ~ Restaurant ~ (01833) 650213 ~ Children welcome but must be over 6 in restaurant ~ Dogs allowed in bar and bedrooms ~ Open 11(12 Sun)-11; closed 24-26 Dec ~ Bedrooms: £89B/£140S(£160B)

Recommended by Rodney and Norma Stubington, Mike and Sue Loseby, Malcolm Wood, Brian Brooks, Julian and Jill Tasker, Pat and Stewart Gordon, Hunter and Christine Wright

SEAHOUSES   NU2232   MAP 10

Olde Ship ★ 🍺 🛏

Just off B1340, towards harbour; NE68 7RD

Lots of atmosphere, fine choice of ales and maritime memorabilia in bustling little hotel; views across harbour to Farne Islands

A rich assemblage of nautical bits and pieces fills this genuine little hotel, first licensed in 1812 to serve visiting herring fishermen and in the same family for over a century. Often busy with friendly locals, the bar is gently lit by stained-glass sea picture windows, lantern lights and a winter open fire, and remains a tribute to the sea and seafarers. Even the floor is scrubbed ship's decking and, if it's working, an anemometer takes wind speed readings from the top of the chimney. Besides lots of other shiny brass fittings, ship's instruments and equipment, and a knotted anchor made by local fishermen, there are sea pictures and model ships, including fine ones of the North Sunderland lifeboat, and Seahouses' lifeboat the *Grace Darling*. There's also a model of the *Forfarshire*, the paddle steamer that local heroine Grace Darling went to rescue in 1838 (you can read more of the story in the pub), and even the ship's nameboard. The battlemented side terrace (you'll find fishing memorabilia out here too) and one window in the sun lounge look out across the harbour to the Farne Islands, and as dusk falls you can watch the Longstones lighthouse shine across the fading evening sky. Their fine choice of beers features Bass, Black Sheep Best Bitter, Courage Directors, Greene King Old Speckled Hen, Hadrian & Border Farne Island Pale and a guest; good wine list and quite a few malt whiskies; piped music and TV. It's not really suitable for children though there is a little family room and, along with walkers, they are welcome on the terrace. You can book boat trips to the Farne Islands Bird Sanctuary at the harbour, and there are bracing coastal walks, particularly to Bamburgh, Grace Darling's birthplace.

🍴 **Bar food might include sandwiches, ploughman's, prawn and pineapple mayonnaise, game casserole, scampi, sirloin steak and fried onions, lamb shank with root vegetable mash, and puddings such as apricot crumble and white and dark chocolate sponge with chocolate sauce.** *Starters/Snacks: £3.75 to £5.00. Main Courses: £7.50 to £12.75. Puddings: £4.50 to £5.75*

Free house ~ Licensees Judith Glen and David Swan ~ Real ale ~ Bar food (no evening food mid-Dec to mid-Jan) ~ Restaurant ~ (01665) 720200 ~ Children in family room ~ Dogs allowed in bar and bedrooms ~ Open 11(12 Sun)-11 ~ Bedrooms: £56S/£112B

Recommended by Comus and Sarah Elliott, Mr and Mrs A Hetherington, Dave Irving, Jenny Huggins, Reg Fowle, Helen Rickwood, Derek and Sylvia Stephenson, Mike and Sue Loseby, Mrs Marion Matthewman, M J Winterton, Mike and Lynn Robinson, R Hayworth, Mrs Brenda Calver, Louise English, the Didler, George Cowie, Frances Gosnell, Malcolm Wood, Tracey and Stephen Groves, Mike and Shelley Woodroffe

STANNERSBURN

NY7286   MAP 10

Pheasant 🏠

Kielder Water road signposted off B6320 in Bellingham; NE48 1DD

Warmly friendly village local close to Kielder Water with quite a mix of customers and homely bar food; streamside garden

The low-beamed comfortably traditional lounge at this inviting village haven has ranks of old local photographs on stripped stone and panelling, red patterned carpets and upholstered stools ranged along the counter. A separate public bar is similar but simpler and opens into a further cosy seating area with beams and panelling; piped music. Timothy Taylors Landlord and a guest, probably from Wylam, are on handpump (only one real ale during the winter), alongside over 40 malt whiskies and a decent reasonably priced wine list; courteous staff. The pub is in a restful valley amid quiet forests, not far from Kielder Water, with picnic-sets in its streamside garden and a pony paddock behind.

🍴 **Very good bar food typically includes lunchtime sandwiches, caramelised onion and goats cheese tart, sweet marinated herring, poached bass, game and mushroom pie, roast lamb with redcurrant and rosemary jus, and puddings such as rhubarb and apple crumble and bread and butter marmalade pudding; northumbrian cheeseboard.** *Starters/Snacks: £3.95 to £8.75. Main Courses: £8.50 to £14.00. Puddings: £3.90 to £4.75*

Free house ~ Licensees Walter and Robin Kershaw ~ Real ale ~ Bar food (12-2.30, 6.30-8.30) ~ Restaurant ~ (01434) 240382 ~ Children welcome ~ Dogs allowed in bedrooms ~ Open 11-3, 6.30-12; 12-3, 6.30-11 Sun; 12-2.30, 7-11 in winter ~ Bedrooms: £55S/£90S

Recommended by Dr Peter D Smart, Pauline Shaw, Sylvia and Tony Birbeck, Mr and Mrs D J Nash

STANNINGTON

NZ2179   MAP 10

Ridley Arms

Village signposted just off A1 S of Morpeth; NE61 6EL

Comfortably airy, with several differing linked rooms; good choice of real ales

This attractive 18th-c stone building has been arranged into several separate areas, each with a slightly different mood and style from the next. The front is a proper bar area with darts, a fruit machine and stools along the counter. The beamed dining areas lead back from here, with a second bar counter, comfortable bucket armchairs around shiny dark wood tables on polished boards or carpet, portraits and cartoons on cream, panelled or stripped stone walls, careful lighting and some horsey statuettes. Black Sheep and Timothy Taylors Landlord are well kept alongside four guests from brewers such as Big Lamp, Derwent, Fyne Ales and Ossett; good choice of wines by the glass; piped music. There are picnic-sets in front by the road and tables on a terrace behind; good disabled access.

🍴 **Bar food includes sandwiches, garlic prawn crostini with tomato salad, grilled chicken, avocado and blue cheese salad, fish and chips, pie of the day with mushy peas, prosciutto-wrapped chicken breast with herb risotto, lamb, pearl barley and vegetable pie, leek, cheese and potato hotpot, and puddings such as apple tart with vanilla pod ice-cream.** *Starters/Snacks: £4.25 to £6.50. Main Courses: £8.95 to £12.00. Puddings: £4.50 to £4.95*

Sir John Fitzgerald ~ Manager Craig Fortune ~ Real ale ~ Bar food (12-9.30(9 Sun)) ~ (01670) 789216 ~ Children welcome ~ Open 11.30-11; 12-10.30 Sun

Recommended by Jan Moore, Derek and Sylvia Stephenson, Comus and Sarah Elliott, Sheena W Makin, Dr Peter D Smart, Mike and Lynn Robinson

---

Bedroom prices are for high summer. Even then you may get reductions for more than one night, or (outside tourist areas) weekends. Winter special rates are common, and many inns cut bedroom prices if you have a full evening meal.

WARK

Battlesteads ◀

B6320 N of Hexham; NE48 3LS

Good local ales, fair value tasty food and relaxed atmosphere; comfortable bedrooms

This friendly stone hotel originated as an 18th-c farmstead and served for a period as a temperance hotel. To this day exhibiting a genuine conscience, they've recently won an award for green tourism initiatives – for example, using forest wood chippings to fuel the heating and hot water system. The nicely restored carpeted bar has a wood-burning stove with traditional oak surround, low beams, comfortable seats including some low leather sofas and old *Punch* country life cartoons on the terracotta walls above its dark dado. This leads through to the restaurant and spacious conservatory. There's a relaxed unhurried atmosphere and five good changing local ales from brewers such as Black Sheep, Durham, Hadrian & Border Gladiator and Wylam from handpumps on the heavily carved dark oak bar counter; good coffee, cheerful service and piped music. Disabled access to some of the ground floor bedrooms. There are tables on a terrace in the walled garden. More reports please.

🍴 **They grow some of their own vegetables and make an effort with sourcing their produce. Good value food includes lunchtime sandwiches, baked figs wrapped in ham with cheese, a smoked platter, pheasant terrine, gammon steak, cajun chicken, cod and chips, mushroom and halloumi stack with roast tomato, chargrilled rib-eye steak, and puddings such as berry trifle and whisky and marmalade bread and butter pudding.** *Starters/Snacks: £3.25 to £5.75. Main Courses: £8.50 to £22.50. Puddings: £4.75 to £5.75*

Free house ~ Licensees Richard and Dee Slade ~ Real ale ~ Bar food (12-3, 6.30-9.30) ~ Restaurant ~ (01434) 230209 ~ Children welcome ~ Dogs allowed in bar and bedrooms ~ Open 11-11 ~ Bedrooms: £60S/£95B

Recommended by Dr A McCormick, R L Borthwick, Matt and Vicky Wharton

WELDON BRIDGE

Anglers Arms 🛏

B6344, just off A697; village signposted with Rothbury off A1 N of Morpeth; NE65 8AX

Large helpings of straightforward food in appealing bar or converted railway dining car; comfortable bedrooms, fishing on River Coquet and good play area

Comfortable and nicely lit, the traditional turkey-carpeted bar tucked into the heart of this sizeable hotel is divided into two parts: cream walls on the right and oak panelling and some shiny black beams hung with copper pans on the left, with a grandfather clock and sofa by the coal fire, staffordshire cats and other antique ornaments on its mantelpiece, old fishing and other country prints, some in heavy gilt frames, a profusion of other fishing memorabilia, and some taxidermy. Some of the tables are lower than you'd expect for eating, but their chairs have short legs to match – different and rather engaging. Timothy Taylors Landlord and three guests such as Greene King Old Speckled Hen are on handpump, with around 30 malt whiskies and decent wines; piped music. The restaurant is in a former railway dining car with crisp white linen and a pink carpet. There are tables in the attractive garden with a good play area that includes an assault course. The pub is beside a bridge over the River Coquet and they have rights to fishing along a mile of the river bank.

🍴 **Generous helpings of bar food include sandwiches, home-made chicken liver pâté, prawn and smoked salmon salad, cod and chips, steak in ale pie, steaks and oriental platter.** *Starters/Snacks: £6.25 to £14.95. Main Courses: £8.95 to £19.50. Puddings: £4.75 to £4.95*

Enterprise ~ Lease John Young ~ Real ale ~ Bar food (12-9.30(9 Sun)) ~ Restaurant ~ (01665) 570271 ~ Dogs allowed in bedrooms ~ Open 11-11; 12-10.30 Sun ~ Bedrooms: £42.50S/£80S

Recommended by Pat and Stewart Gordon, Michael Butler, Dr Peter D Smart, Sheena W Makin

WOLSINGHAM

NZ0737 MAP 10

Mill Race ♀

A689; West End; DL13 3AP

Comfortable modern furnishings in several bar and dining areas, friendly welcome, beer and wine tasting events, and quite a choice of good food

This enterprising dining pub has an airy high-ceilinged bar with understated contemporary furnishings and a friendly welcome from the young bar staff. There's a big black leather sofa, leather and fabric armchairs, a sizeable L-shaped dark fabric wall banquette with toning scatter cushions, several bar stools, a low pale wooden table and other little tables on the attractively stripped wooden floor, quite a few bar chairs and a little brick fireplace. Drinks include Black Sheep Bitter and several good wines by the glass; well chosen piped rock/pop music. Just off the bar is a small, informal dining room with high-backed pine dining chairs around white-clothed tables and a more formal back restaurant has lots of modern art on the walls. Up some stairs is an art gallery.

⑪ Using locally sourced produce, the good upscale food includes leek and gruyère soufflé, meze, prawn cocktail, fishcake with fish cream, fried cod with mussels, garlic and parsley broth, venison, bacon and mushroom pie, sirloin steak, and puddings like frozen peanut parfait with melted Snickers and crème brûlée. They also offer two- and three-course choices and various themed evenings. *Starters/Snacks: £4.00 to £6.00. Main Courses: £10.50 to £16.50. Puddings: £4.00 to £6.00*

Free house ~ Licensee Martyn Hunter ~ Real ale ~ Restaurant ~ (01388) 526551 ~ Children welcome ~ Open 12-11

Recommended by Roger Shipperley, John Bruder, Joan Kureczka

LUCKY DIP

Besides the fully inspected pubs, you might like to try these Lucky Dips recommended to us and described by readers (if you do, please send us reports: feedback@goodguides.com).

ALLENDALE [NY8355]
Golden Lion NE47 9BD [Market Place]: 18th-c two-room village inn with fairly priced enjoyable food, several mainly local well kept ales, good choice of other drinks inc reasonably priced wines, chatty Yorkshire landlord, games area with pool and darts, upstairs restaurant, occasional live music; children and dogs welcome (two pub dogs), bedrooms *(JJW, CMW, Comus and Sarah Elliott)*
Kings Head NE47 9BD [Market Place (B6295)]: Early 18th-c former coaching inn with several Marstons-related ales inc Jennings, wide choice of pubby food, dozens of malt whiskies, good log fire, pews and cane-back chairs in carpeted bar/lounge, interesting bric-a-brac, darts; children welcome, open all day *(Comus and Sarah Elliott)*
ALNMOUTH [NU2410]
☆ *Red Lion* NE66 2RJ [Northumberland St]: Former 18th-c coaching inn, relaxed and unpretentious, with good food from baguettes to local fish, cheerful staff, well kept Black Sheep and local guest ales, mainly new world wines by the glass, attractive bistro-style dining room, log fire in cosy panelled locals' bar; dogs welcome, neat garden by alley with raised deck looking over Aln estuary, comfortable bedrooms, open all

day (Sun till 8pm) *(Pete Devonish, Ian McIntyre, Mr and Mrs D J Nash)*
Sun NE66 2RA [Northumberland St]: Recently redone, with comfortable banquettes in low-beamed carpeted bar, friendly chatty staff, good value food inc interesting sandwiches, Black Sheep and Wells & Youngs Bombardier, good coffee, small contemporary dining area; attractive seaside village *(Michael Doswell)*
ALNWICK [NU1813]
☆ *Blackmores* NE66 1PN [Bondgate Without]: Light and airy reworking of stone building into contemporary pub/boutique hotel; Black Sheep and Caledonian ales in lively front bar, good choice of wines by the glass, above-average food; bedrooms *(Comus and Sarah Elliott, GSB)*
AYCLIFFE [NZ2822]
☆ *County* DL5 6LX [off A1(M) junction 59, by A167]: Popular village-green dining pub under newish ownership, light minimalist décor in extended bar and bistro, early supper deals, three ales inc well kept Mordue, good choice of wines by the glass; children welcome, handy for A1, cl Sun evening *(Tom and Jill Jones, Michael Butler, Mary Goodfellow, MJVK, LYM, Mike and Lynn Robinson, Mrs Hazel Rainer)*
BACKWORTH [NZ3072]
Pavilion NE27 0FG [Hotspur North]: Brightly modern new Fitzgeralds pub, nice food

choice, good range of real ales *(Mike and Lynn Robinson)*

BAMBURGH [NU1834]

☆ *Victoria* NE69 7BP [Front St]: Substantial Victorian hotel with sofas, squashy leather chairs and high stools in mildly contemporary partly divided bar, chunky tables and chairs in dining room, friendly young staff, good quickly served food all day from sandwiches up, two real ales from Black Sheep and/or Mordue, good wines by the glass, young children's playroom; comfortable bedrooms, lovely setting, open all day *(Louise English, Tina and David Woods-Taylor, Comus and Sarah Elliott, Sylvia and Tony Birbeck)*

BARDON MILL [NY7566]

Twice Brewed NE47 7AN [Military Rd (B6318 NE of Hexham)]: Large busy pub well placed for fell-walkers and major Wall sites, five local real ales, malt whiskies, reasonably priced wines, good value hearty pub food from baguettes up, quick friendly staff, nice photographs; quiet piped music; children allowed in restaurant, tables outside, warm bedrooms, open all day *(Michael Doswell, Dave Irving, Jenny Huggins)*

BARNARD CASTLE [NZ0416]

White Swan DL12 9BE [Bowes rd, signposted to A67]: Enjoyable home-made food, friendly staff and relaxed atmosphere in linked panelled rooms, dramatic setting on rocks above River Tees, opp castle ruins *(Joyce Barnett, LYM)*

BEADNELL [NU2229]

Beadnell Towers NE67 5AU: Large welcoming off-season haven with above-average food, Black Sheep, Hadrian & Border and Mordue ales, reasonably priced wines by the glass, good service; can get more touristy in summer; good bedrooms *(Reg Fowle, Helen Rickwood, Comus and Sarah Elliott)*

Craster Arms NE67 5AX [The Wynding]: Popular pubby food, Black Sheep, friendly efficient service, roomy old building with modern fittings; children welcome, nice front garden, open all day *(Reg Fowle, Helen Rickwood, Danny Savage)*

BELFORD [NU1033]

Blue Bell NE70 7NE [off A1 S of Berwick; Market Place]: Substantial old coaching inn (hotel rather than pub) with decent food from sandwiches up in pubby bar, Black Sheep, good choice of wines and whiskies, sensible prices, friendly service, two restaurant areas; piped music; children welcome, big garden, pleasant bedrooms *(Comus and Sarah Elliott, LYM)*

BOULMER [NU2614]

Fishing Boat NE66 3BP: Worth knowing for its position, with decking overlooking sea; light and airy inside, with usual food, real ales (not cheap), interesting pictures, dogs welcome *(Reg Fowle, Helen Rickwood, Comus and Sarah Elliott, Peter and Eleanor Kenyon)*

BOURNMOOR [NZ3051]

Dun Cow DH4 6DY [Primrose Hill (A1052)]: Traditional country pub with comfortable bar

and restaurant, friendly landlord, efficient young staff, food all day, two changing ales; piped music, TV; children welcome, garden with smokers' marquee *(Mark Walker)*

Floaters Mill DH4 6BQ [A1052]: Comfortable country pub with big lounge bar and conservatory, friendly service, enjoyable food inc popular Sun carvery, Marstons-related ales; children welcome, tables outside, play area, open all day *(Mark Walker)*

CATTON [NY8358]

Crown NE47 9QS: Cosy traditional local reopened by local Allendale brewery, their full beer range kept well, farm cider, reasonably priced malt whiskies, fresh local food; log fire, warmly friendly atmosphere, dominoes and board games, stripped stone and local art, dining extension; children and dogs welcome, small garden, lovely walks *(Marcus Byron)*

CAUSEY PARK BRIDGE [NZ1894]

Oak NE61 3EL [off A1 5 miles N of Morpeth]: Friendly open-plan country pub with good food inc bargain Sun lunch and cut-price small evening helpings, friendly attentive staff, conservatory; children welcome, garden with play area *(Guy and Caroline Howard, Michael Doswell)*

CHATTON [NU0528]

Percy Arms NE66 5PS [B6348 E of Wooler]: Comfortable stone-built country inn with cheerful efficient staff, pubby food in bar and attractive panelled dining room from lunchtime sandwiches up, lounge bar extending through arch, public bar with games, plenty of malt whiskies, changing ales; piped music; children in good family area and dining room, small front lawn, bedrooms (12 miles of private fishing) *(Comus and Sarah Elliott, Tony Baldwin, LYM)*

CONSETT [NZ1050]

Company Row DH8 5AB [Front St]: Large Wetherspoons with their usual low-priced food and drink – a useful find for lunch (may get more lively evenings); sunny tables outside *(Dave Irving, Jenny Huggins)*

Grey Horse DH8 6NE [Sherburn Terr]: Well run two-bar beamed 19th-c pub brewing its own Consett ales such as Red Dust and Steel Town in former back stables, dozens of malt whiskies, occasional beer festivals, very friendly licensees, two coal fires, pool; pavement tables, open all day *(Mike and Lynn Robinson)*

CORBRIDGE [NY9864]

☆ *Black Bull* NE45 5AT [Middle St]: Rambling linked rooms, reasonably priced food all day from sandwiches and light lunches up, good friendly service, Greene King ales, good attractively priced wine choice, roaring fire, neat comfortable seating inc traditional settles on flagstones in softly lit low-ceilinged core; open all day *(Pam and John Smith, Andy and Jill Kassube, Gerry and Rosemary Dobson)*

CORNHILL-ON-TWEED [NT8639]

Collingwood Arms TD12 4UH: Well kept ales such as Caledonian, enjoyable food all day, willing friendly service, pleasant décor *(Comus and Sarah Elliott)*

CRAMLINGTON [NZ2373]

☆ **Snowy Owl** NE23 8AU [just off A1/A19 junction via A1068; Blagdon Lane]: Large Vintage Inn, relaxed and comfortable, with reasonable prices, good choice of wines, reliable all-day food inc popular Sun lunch, friendly efficient young staff, beers such as Black Sheep, Jennings Cumberland and Timothy Taylors Landlord, beams, flagstones, stripped stone and terracotta paintwork, soft lighting and an interesting mix of furnishings and decorations, daily papers; may be piped music; disabled access, bedrooms in adjoining Innkeepers Lodge, open all day *(Dr Peter D Smart, Comus and Sarah Elliott, Louise English, Guy and Caroline Howard)*

CRASTER [NU2519]

☆ **Jolly Fisherman** NE66 3TR [off B1339, NE of Alnwick]: Simple local in great spot, long a favourite for its lovely sea and coast views from picture window and grass behind, and for its good value crab sandwiches, crab soup and locally smoked seafood (good chips, too); this makes up for the take-us-as-you-find-us style, which can verge on scruffiness; well kept ales such as Black Sheep or Mordue, games area with pool; children and dogs welcome, open all day in summer *(Paul Newberry, the Didler, Reg Fowle, Helen Rickwood, John and Sylvia Harrop, C A Hall, LYM, Michael Doswell, Phil Bryant)*

DURHAM [NZ2742]

Court Inn DH1 3AW [Court Lane]: Comfortable town pub with good hearty home-made food all day from sandwiches to steaks and late-evening lunches, real ales such as Bass, Marstons Pedigree and Mordue, extensive stripped brick eating area, no mobile phones; bustling in term-time with students and teachers, piped pop music; seats outside, open all day *(BB, David and Laraine Webster, Mark Walker, Pete Baker)*

☆ **Dun Cow** DH1 3HN [Old Elvet]: Unchanging backstreet pub in pretty 16th-c black and white timbered cottage, cheerful licensees, tiny chatty front bar with wall benches, corridor to long narrow back lounge with banquettes, machines etc (can be packed with students), particularly well kept Camerons and other ales such as Black Sheep and Caledonian Deuchars IPA, good value basic lunchtime snacks, decent coffee; piped music; children welcome, open all day Mon-Sat, Sun too in summer *(Pete Baker, LYM, Chris Sale, Mark Walker, the Didler, Pam and John Smith, Dave Irving, Jenny Huggins, Danny and Gillian O'Sullivan)*

Half Moon DH1 3AQ [New Elvet]: Well preserved Victorian pub handy for castle and cathedral, Bass, Durham White Amarillo, Fullers London Pride and Timothy Taylors Landlord, good wine choice, lunchtime toasties and rolls, low prices, good service from bare-boards top bar, leather banquettes and period pictures, daily papers, step down to second room; machines, sports TV *(Danny and Gillian O'Sullivan, Chris Sale)*

Market Tavern DH1 3NJ [Market Place]: Lively old-fashioned bare-boards pub with two or three well kept ales and good value fresh bar lunches *(Mike and Lynn Robinson, Comus and Sarah Elliott)*

Swan & Three Cygnets DH1 3AG [Elvet Bridge]: Refurbished Victorian pub in good bridge-end spot high above river, city views from big windows and picnic-sets out on terrace, bargain lunchtime food and Sam Smiths OB; open all day *(Mike and Lynn Robinson, the Didler, Mark Walker, BB)*

EBCHESTER [NZ1054]

☆ **Derwent Walk** DH8 0SX [Ebchester Hill (B6309 outside)]: Interesting pub by Gateshead—Consett walk of same name, reliable good value home-made food from unusual hot sandwiches up, great choice of wines by the glass at reasonable prices, good friendly staff, full Jennings range kept well, good log fire and appealing old photographs, conservatory with fine Derwent Valley views; walkers welcome, pleasant heated terrace *(Andy and Jill Kassube, Bruce and Sharon Eden, Mike and Lynn Robinson)*

EGLINGHAM [NU1019]

Tankerville Arms NE66 2TX [B6346 Alnwick—Wooler]: Traditional pub with some nice contemporary touches, open fire each end, plush banquettes, some stripped stone, decent pubby food inc evening restaurant and afternoon tea, Black Sheep and Mordue, good choice of wines by the glass, friendly service; quiet piped music; children welcome, nice views from garden, attractive village *(Michael Doswell, Louise English, Peter and Eleanor Kenyon, Mary Goodfellow, LYM, Reg Fowle, Helen Rickwood)*

ELLINGHAM [NU1625]

Pack Horse NE67 5HA [signed off A1 N of Alnwick]: Compact stone-built country local with light and airy dining room, feature fireplace in beamed bar, small comfortable lounge; enclosed garden, good value bedrooms, peaceful village *(Comus and Sarah Elliott)*

EMBLETON [NU2322]

Dunstanburgh Castle Hotel NE66 3UN: Comfortable hotel in attractive spot near magnificent coastline, bar and restaurant food inc game and fresh fish, pleasant young staff, beers such as Black Sheep and Theakstons, well priced wines; bedrooms *(Mr and Mrs D J Nash)*

FELTON [NU1800]

☆ **Northumberland Arms** NE65 9EE [West Thirston; B6345, off A1 N of Morpeth]: Attractive old inn with beams, stripped stone and good coal fires in roomy and comfortable open-plan bar, nice mix of furnishings inc big settees, elegant small restaurant, good well priced food, well kept Bass and Black Sheep, good coffee and wines, friendly service and atmosphere; well reproduced piped music, especially in conservatory pool room; dogs welcome, steps down to bench by River Coquet, five bedrooms, open all day *(Peter Jones, Comus and Sarah Elliott, Mr and Mrs D J Nash, BB)*

FRAMWELLGATE MOOR [NZ2644]

Tap & Spile DH1 5EE [Front St; B6532 just N of Durham]: Thriving two-bar pub with fine range of changing local ales, farm ciders, good staff, warm and comfortable atmosphere, pub and board games; children welcome *(Chris Sale)*

FROSTERLEY [NZ0236]

☆ *Black Bull* DL13 2SL [just off A689 W of centre]: Great atmosphere in three interesting traditional beamed and flagstoned rooms with two coal fires, landlord's own fine photographs, four well kept northern ales, farm cider and perry, carefully chosen wines and malt whiskies, good food using local and organic ingredients, short and interesting evening menu (not Sun, Mon), popular Sun lunch, live music Tues, occasional art shows; attractive no smoking terrace with wood-fired bread oven and old railway furnishings (opp steam station), open all day, cl Mon lunchtime *(Arthur Pickering, M J Winterton, JHBS, Mr and Mrs Maurice Thompson)*

GATESHEAD [NZ2559]

Aletaster NE9 6JA [Durham Rd (A167), Low Fell]: Great range of real ales and friendly helpful staff, traditional pub, Newcastle United memorabilia; TV *(Dr and Mrs A K Clarke, Rachel McGraffin)*

Green NE10 8YB [White Mare Pool, Wardley; W of roundabout at end of A194(M)]: Large refurbished pub, light and airy, half a dozen or more reasonably priced ales inc local Mordue, good range of wines, good value bar/bistro food, friendly helpful staff, picture-window outlook on golf course; light piped music, very busy wknds *(Gerry and Rosemary Dobson)*

HALTWHISTLE [NY6860]

Wallace Arms NE49 0JF [Rowfoot, Featherstone Park, about 3 miles SW]: Friendly linked rooms of remote rambling former farmhouse handy for South Tyne Trail, beams, dark wood, some stripped stone, good log fire, well kept ales such as Greene King Old Speckled Hen, Jarrow Rivet Catcher and Timothy Taylors Landlord, decent basic food from sandwiches to Sun roast, lots of malt whiskies, games room with another fire; children in eating areas and family room, disabled access, picnic-sets with lovely fell views, play area, open all day wknds *(Dr Kevan Tucker, LYM)*

HIGH HESLEDEN [NZ4538]

Ship TS27 4QD [off A19 via B1281]: Half a dozen good value changing ales from the region, log fire, sailing ship models inc big one hanging with lanterns from boarded ceiling, landlady cooks enjoyable bar food and some interesting restaurant dishes; yacht and shipping views from car park, six bedrooms in new block, cl Mon *(JHBS)*

HOLY ISLAND [NU1241]

Crown & Anchor TD15 2RX [causeway passable only at low tide, check times (01289) 330733]: Comfortably unpretentious pub/restaurant with generous food, Wells & Youngs Bombardier and Caledonian Deuchars IPA, friendly staff, compact bar, roomy modern back dining room; enclosed garden with picnic-sets, bedrooms *(John and Sylvia Harrop, Dave Irving, Jenny Huggins)*

HORNCLIFFE [NT9249]

Fishers Arms TD15 2XW [off A698]: Nicely old-fashioned village local high above River Tweed, obliging staff, well kept Caledonian Deuchars IPA and John Smiths, good value wines by the glass, simple home-made food inc well priced Sun lunch; monthly folk night first Sun, cl Tues *(Comus and Sarah Elliott, Mrs Marion Matthewman)*

HUTTON MAGNA [NZ1212]

Oak Tree DL11 7HH [off A66 SE of Greta Bridge]: Low building, now more cosy candlelit evening restaurant than pub under welcoming new chef/landlord – enterprising contemporary cooking (not Mon) inc their own garden produce *(Peter and Eleanor Kenyon, Michael Doswell)*

JARROW [NZ3363]

Robin Hood NE32 5UB [Primrose Hill]: Popular and friendly local, Jarrow beers from adjoining brewery and a guest ale, several rooms, restaurant *(Mr and Mrs Maurice Thompson)*

KNITSLEY [NZ1148]

Knitsley Mill DH8 9EL: Enjoyable food changing weekly inc bargain lunches, real ale, good wine list; five comfortable bedrooms, lovely lakeside surroundings *(Jenny and Dave Hughes)*

LANGDON BECK [NY8531]

Langdon Beck Hotel DL12 0XP [B6277 Middleton—Alston]: Unpretentious isolated inn with two cosy bars and spacious lounge, well placed for walks and Pennine Way, Black Sheep, Jarrow and a guest ale, good choice of generous food inc local teesdale beef, helpful friendly staff; garden, wonderful views, bedrooms, open all day, cl Mon winter *(Mr and Mrs Maurice Thompson)*

LANGLEY ON TYNE [NY8160]

Carts Bog Inn NE47 5NW [A686 S, junction B6305]: This appealing isolated moorside pub was closed as we went to press; news please *(LYM)*

LESBURY [NU2311]

☆ *Coach* NE66 3PP: Candlelit stone-built pub with carpeted low-beamed bar, armchairs and sofas, pretty dining room, welcoming efficient staff, wide choice of enjoyable food from good crab sandwiches to full meals using local ingredients, well kept Black Sheep, good choice of wines; children welcome till 7.30pm, rustic tables outside with thatched umbrellas, lots of hanging baskets and tubs *(GSB, Comus and Sarah Elliott, Michael Doswell, Dr Peter D Smart)*

LONGFRAMLINGTON [NU1301]
Granby NE65 8DP: Attractive and comfortably modernised two-room bar, wide choice of enjoyable food inc good value set meals, good range of malt whiskies, decent wines, small restaurant; bedrooms *(Mr and Mrs D J Nash, LYM)*

LONGHORSLEY [NZ1494]
Shoulder of Mutton NE65 8SY [East Rd; A697 N of Morpeth]: Comfortable bar and restaurant, wide food choice, good-sized helpings, two real ales, good choice of other drinks, Tues quiz night; piped music may obtrude; children welcome, tables outside *(JJW, CMW)*

LOWICK [NU0139]
☆ *Black Bull* TD15 2UA [Main St (B6353, off A1 S of Berwick-upon-Tweed)]: Welcoming village pub, bright and cheerful, with good modestly priced food using local produce, takeaways too, Belhaven 60/- and 70/- and Theakstons (just one real ale at quiet seasons), quick friendly service even when busy, comfortable main bar, small back bar, spotless big back dining room; children welcome, three attractive bedrooms, on edge of small pretty village *(Alan and Gill Bridgman, W H Stalker)*

LUCKER [NU1530]
☆ *Apple* NE70 7JH [off A1 N of Morpeth]: Reopened after refurbishment under new landlord, sensibly priced pubby dishes and more adventurous specials, Allendale and Hadrian & Border ales, good value wines, woodburner in comfortable bar's big fireplace, roomy big-windowed side dining area *(Comus and Sarah Elliott, LYM)*

MICKLEY [NZ0761]
Blue Bell NE43 7LP [Mount Pleasant, off A695 Prudhoe—Stocksfield]: Well run local, Fullers London Pride, Greene King Old Speckled Hen and Hadrian & Border ales, good value food cooked to order inc popular Sun roasts, relaxed rural feel (though on edge of built-up area) *(Malcolm and Pauline Pellatt)*

MILBOURNE [NZ1275]
Waggon NE20 0DH [Higham Dykes; A696 NW of Ponteland]: Popular comfortably traditional open-plan bar with soft lighting, beams, stripped stone and panelling, huge fire each end, wide choice of good value food from lunchtime sandwiches to restaurant dishes, friendly staff, two local ales *(Gerry and Rosemary Dobson)*

MILFIELD [NT9333]
Red Lion NE71 6JD [Main Rd (A697 Wooler—Cornhill)]: Welcoming chef/landlord doing good sensibly priced food at this newly decorated 17th-c former coaching inn, organic wine, good service *(John and Liz Stillard)*

MITFORD [NZ1785]
Plough NE61 3PR [just off A1 Morpeth bypass]: Roomy and welcoming open-plan family-friendly pub in small village, enjoyable food largely locally sourced, Sun roasts, well kept Theakstons Best and a

guest, cafetière coffee with home-made shortbread, comfortable bay-window banquettes, horsebrasses *(Dr Peter D Smart)*

NETHERTON [NT9807]
Star NE65 7HD [off B6341 at Thropton, or A697 via Whittingham]: Simple local in remote countryside, many original features, Castle Eden tapped from cellar casks and served from hatch in small entrance lobby, large high-ceilinged room with panelled wall benches, charming service and welcoming regulars; no food, music or children; cl lunchtime *(the Didler)*

NEWBIGGIN-BY-THE-SEA [NZ3188]
Queens Head NE64 6AT [High St]: Friendly talkative landlord, lots of guest beers besides bargain-price John Smiths, several high-ceilinged rooms, thriving atmosphere, dominoes; dogs welcome (not in sitting room), open all day from 10am *(the Didler)*

NEWCASTLE UPON TYNE [NZ2464]
☆ *Bacchus* NE1 6BX [High Bridge E, between Pilgrim St and Grey St]: Smart and comfortable, with ocean liner look, ship and shipbuilding photographs, good modern lunchtime food from interesting doorstep sandwiches and ciabattas through unusual light dishes to more substantial things, keen prices, half a dozen changing ales, plenty of bottled imports, perhaps farm cider, relaxed atmosphere; open all day (usually just evening Sun) *(Mike and Lynn Robinson, Eric Larkham)*

☆ *Bridge Hotel* NE1 1RQ [Castle Sq, next to high level bridge]: Big cheery high-ceilinged well divided bar around servery with replica slatted snob screens, well kept changing ales such as Black Sheep, Keelburn, Lees and Mordue, farm cider, friendly staff, bargain generous lunchtime food (not Sat), Sun afternoon teas, magnificent fireplace, great river and bridge views from raised back area; sports TV, piped music, games machines, live music upstairs inc long-standing Mon folk club; flagstoned back terrace overlooking part of old town wall, open all day *(Eric Larkham, Andy and Jill Kassube, Dr and Mrs A K Clarke, the Didler, LYM)*

Centurion NE1 5HL [Central Station, Neville St]: Glorious high-ceilinged Victorian décor with tilework and columns in former 1st-class waiting room well restored, comfortable leather seating, landlord proud of his local ales such as Allendale and Jarrow, farm cider, useful deli next door *(Chris Sale, Andy and Jill Kassube)*

☆ *Cluny* NE1 2PQ [Lime St]: Trendy bar/café in interesting 19th-c mill/warehouse, striking setting below Metro bridge, reasonably priced food all day (home made so may be a wait), well kept Banks's Best, Big Lamp Prince Bishop and guests like Jarrow and Wylam, exotic beers and rums, cheerful staff, settees in comfortable raised area with daily papers and local art magazines, back gallery with artwork from studios in same complex; piped music, good live music nightly; children welcome till 7pm, open all day (cl Mon afternoon) *(Mike and Lynn Robinson, LYM, Andy and Jill Kassube, Mrs Hazel Rainer, Eric Larkham)*

Cooperage NE1 3RF [The Close, Quayside]: Ancient building under new management, four real ales, great whisky choice, stripped stone bar and beamed lounge, good waterfront setting; disabled facilities *(LYM, Dr and Mrs A K Clarke, the Didler)*

Cumberland Arms NE6 1LD [Byker Buildings]: Friendly traditional local with four particularly well kept changing local ales (straight from the cask if you wish), farm cider, organic beer festivals, good value toasties, obliging staff; live music or other events most nights (pub has its own ukelele band), tables out overlooking Ouseburn Valley, cl winter wkdy lunchtimes, open all day wknds *(Mike and Lynn Robinson, Eric Larkham)*

Eye on the Tyne NE1 3DQ [Broad Chare]: Stylishly converted warehouse, lots of stripped brick and flagstones or bare boards (as well as plusher carpeted parts) in warren of separate areas, good value pubby food, Greene King ales *(Andy and Jill Kassube)*

Falcons Nest NE3 5EH [Rotary Way, Gosforth – handy for racecourse]: Roomy Vintage Inn with comfortably olde-worlde linked rooms, good value food, pleasant staff, good choice of wines by the glass, well kept Black Sheep and Timothy Taylors Landlord; open all day, bedrooms in adjacent Innkeepers Lodge *(J McKenna, Dr Peter D Smart)*

Free Trade NE6 1AP [St Lawrence Rd, off Walker Rd (A186)]: Splendidly basic proper pub with outstanding views up river from big windows, terrace tables and seats on grass, real ales such as High House, Jarrow and Mordue, good sandwiches, warmly friendly atmosphere, real fire, original Formica tables; steps down to back room and lavatories; open all day *(Andy and Jill Kassube, Eric Larkham)*

Quayside NE1 3RN [The Close]: Lloyds No 1 (Wetherspoons) in floodlit Tyneside warehouse, linked rooms with small areas up and down stairs, food all day till 10pm, reasonably priced drinks; children welcome, disabled facilities with baby-changing, tables out in central courtyard, open all day *(D J and P M Taylor)*

Waterline NE1 3DH [Quayside, by New Law Courts]: Stylish Tyne warehouse conversion by Millennium Bridge, lots of beams and pillars, nooks and crannies, maritime bric-a-brac, welcoming staff, full Theakstons range kept well, good value food inc good pizzas all day from open kitchen, open fires, games room; children welcome *(Dave Irving, Jenny Huggins)*

PONTELAND [NZ1771]

☆ *Badger* NE20 9BT [Street Houses; A696 SE, by garden centre]: Well done Vintage Inn, enjoyable food all day, real ales, good range of wines by the glass and good hot drinks, prompt friendly service, good log fire, relaxing rooms and alcoves, old furnishings and olde-worlde décor; children welcome, open all day *(Peter and Eleanor Kenyon, Gerry and Rosemary Dobson, Dr Peter D Smart, BB)*

RENNINGTON [NU2118]

☆ *Horseshoes* NE66 3RS [B1340]: Comfortable flagstoned pub with friendly efficient service, well kept ales such as Hadrian & Border and John Smiths, good value generous food inc two-course lunch deals, good meat and smoked fish, decent wines by the glass, good local feel (may be horses in car park), simple neat bar with woodburner, spotless compact restaurant with blue and white china; children welcome, tables outside, attractive quiet village near coast, cl Mon *(Grahame Sherwin, Comus and Sarah Elliott, Guy and Caroline Howard)*

☆ *Masons Arms* NE66 3RX [Stamford Cott; B1340 N]: Comfortably carpeted beamed bar with neat pubby furniture, well kept Hadrian & Border and Northumberland ales, good value straightforward bar food, smiling relaxed service; children welcome, sturdy rustic tables on front lavender-edged terrace, more picnic-sets behind, comfortable bedrooms in former stables block, open all day summer Mon-Sat *(Christine and Malcolm Ingram, LYM, Comus and Sarah Elliott, Guy and Caroline Howard, Roy and Jean Russell, George Cowie, Frances Gosnell, J M Renshaw, Mr and Mrs P L Spencer)*

ROTHBURY [NU0501]

☆ *Newcastle Hotel* NE65 7UT: Small solid Victorian pub/hotel at end of green, comfortable lounge with dining area, second bar, friendly service, good reasonably priced food inc seasonal game (extra credit card charge), high teas Apr-Oct, Caledonian Deuchars IPA and Greene King Abbot and Old Speckled Hen, upstairs dining room; good value bedrooms, pretty village with river walks, handy for Cragside (NT), open all day *(Dave Irving, Jenny Huggins)*

Turks Head NE65 7TE [High St]: Chatty and friendly, with two real ales, good soft drinks choice, bar and restaurant food; picnic-sets in good-sized garden with play area and smokers' terrace *(JJW, CMW)*

SEATON DELAVAL [NZ2975]

Hastings Arms NE25 0QH [Wheatridge Row]: Friendly and comfortably worn-in, with good value traditional food, a guest ale such as Camerons Nimmos XXXX, interesting local photographs and mementoes; unobtrusive piped music *(Paul and Ursula Randall)*

SHINCLIFFE [NZ2940]

☆ *Seven Stars* DH1 2NU [High St N (A177 S of Durham)]: 18th-c village pub with good choice of gently upmarket food at sensible prices, well kept ales inc Black Sheep, good service, coal fire and plenty of atmosphere in lounge bar, candlelit dining room; children in eating areas, some picnic-sets outside, eight bedrooms, open all day *(LYM, Danny and Gillian O'Sullivan, Arthur Pickering)*

SOUTH SHIELDS [NZ3668]

Beacon NE33 2AQ [Greens Place]: Open-plan local overlooking river mouth, well kept ales from central bar, good value lunchtime food, obliging service, stove in back room, two raised eating areas, sepia photographs and bric-a-brac, darts, dominoes; games machine, quiet piped music *(the Didler)*

Sand Dancer NE33 2LD [Sea Rd]: Right on beach, with decent food at good prices, friendly staff and good atmosphere *(John Coatsworth)*

ST JOHN'S CHAPEL [NY8838]

Blue Bell DL13 1QJ [Hood St]: Attractive cosy village local with real fires, friendly atmosphere, well kept ales such as Allendale and Greene King, darts, dominoes, Sun quiz night; no food *(Joan Kureczka)*

STOCKTON-ON-TEES [NZ4419]

Sun TS18 1SU [Knowles St]: Popular town local noted for its Bass, good prices, quick service; open all day *(the Didler)*

SUNDERLAND [NZ3956]

Fitzgeralds SR1 3PZ [Green Terrace]: Bustling two-bar city pub popular with locals and students (especially on match days), up to nine real ales inc several from local Darwin, helpful staff, friendly atmosphere, generous cheap bar lunches; children welcome lunchtime *(Mr and Mrs Maurice Thompson, Mike and Lynn Robinson, Mark Walker)*

Rosedene SR2 9BT [Queen Alexandra Rd]: Former Georgian mansion, large main room and central bar area, restaurant, conservatory, four Greene King beers *(Mr and Mrs Maurice Thompson)*

THROPTON [NU0302]

Cross Keys NE65 7HX [B6341]: Attractive little village pub, enjoyable reasonably priced food with emphasis on fish, Black Sheep, good wine and soft drinks choice, open fires in small cosy beamed bar with rooms off inc snug with high-backed settles, games room with darts and pool, back dining area; games machine, sports TV; dogs welcome, steeply terraced garden looking over village to hills, open all day at least in summer *(Paul and Sue Merrick, LYM, JJW, CMW, Phil Bryant)*

☆ *Three Wheat Heads* NE65 7LR [B6341]: 300-year-old village inn with welcoming licensees, good generous food inc daily roasts, well kept Black Sheep and Theakstons, good coal fires (one in a fine tall stone fireplace), newly renovated public bar with darts and pool, dining room with lovely views; quiet piped music; children and dogs welcome, garden with play area, chickens and ducks, good value comfortable bedrooms, good breakfast, handy for Cragside, open all day wknds *(LYM, David Hassall, Christine and Malcolm Ingram, JJW, CMW, Dr Peter D Smart, Dave Irving, Jenny Huggins)*

WARDEN [NY9166]

☆ *Boatside* NE46 4SQ [0.5 miles N of A69]: Cheerful attractively modernised old stone-built pub with good service, enjoyable fresh pubby food inc good sandwiches, well kept Black Sheep, Tetleys and Wylam, pine dining room; children and muddy walkers welcome, small neat enclosed garden, active quoits, attractive spot by Tyne bridge, bedrooms in adjoining cottages *(Bruce and Sharon Eden, Comus and Sarah Elliott, R Macfarlane)*

WARKWORTH [NU2406]

Hermitage NE65 0UL [Castle St]: Down to earth rambling local with friendly staff, Jennings ales, good value food cooked to order all day inc fresh local fish, interesting quaint décor, old range for heating, dining area and small plush upstairs restaurant; TV or piped music; bedrooms, tables out in front, attractive setting *(Matt and Gayle Wiles, BB)*

Masons Arms NE65 0UR [Dial Place]: Welcoming village pub in shadow of castle, good value generous home-made food inc local fish and bargain lunch, attentive young staff, Caledonian Deuchars IPA, Theakstons XB and a guest such as Wells & Youngs, good coffee and wine choice, local memorabilia; dogs welcome, disabled access and facilities, attractive back flagstoned courtyard, appealing village not far from sea *(Guy and Caroline Howard, Clive Flynn)*

WASHINGTON [NZ3054]

Courtyard NE38 8AB [Arts Centre, Biddick Lane, Fatfield]: Popular with locals, walkers and cyclists, modernish open-plan stone and beamed bar with up to six changing ales, Black Rat cider and Hereford perry, bottled belgian beers, good value food inc bargain Sun lunch, beer festivals (Easter and August bank hol), live folk music Mon; benches in large courtyard, open all day *(Mr and Mrs Maurice Thompson, Kevin Thorpe)*

WHITLEY BAY [NZ3473]

Briardene NE26 1UE [The Links]: Smart brightly decorated two-room pub, fine seaview spot, up to eight interesting changing ales, good value pubby food from sandwiches up, friendly efficient staff; seats outside, open all day *(Mike and Lynn Robinson)*

WYLAM [NZ1164]

☆ *Boathouse* NE41 8HR [Station Rd, handy for Newcastle—Carlisle rail line; across Tyne from village (and Stephenson's birthplace)]: Thriving convivial riverside pub with splendid ale range inc local Wylam, keen prices, good choice of malt whiskies, bargain wknd lunches, polite helpful young staff, open stove in bright low-beamed bar, dining room; loud band nights; children and dogs welcome, seats outside, open all day *(Comus and Sarah Elliott, the Didler, Lawrence Pearse)*

Nottinghamshire

Nottingham itself has almost a surfeit of good pubs, often selling bargain food – moreover, all five Main Entries there stock an extraordinary range of beers. The city's top pub these days is the cheery Lincolnshire Poacher. Elsewhere, the bustling Victoria in Beeston is good value for food (with a great beer range, too), as is the homely Black Horse at Caythorpe (brewing its own beer, which you can find in a few other good pubs). Other pubs where good food is the main strength are the smart Martins Arms at Colston Bassett, Caunton Beck at Caunton and caringly refurbished Full Moon at Morton. Nottinghamshire Dining Pub of the Year is the Caunton Beck at Caunton. Two Lucky Dips to pick out are the Robin Hood at Elkesley and Stratford Haven in West Bridgford. Castle Rock is the area's most successful brewery, with the newer Nottingham popular too, and several other good small breweries such as Springhead and Mallards. Former local champion Hardys & Hansons now comes from Greene King down in Suffolk, and Mansfield is brewed over in Wolverhampton by Marstons.

BEESTON

SK5336   MAP 7

Victoria 🍷 ◖

Dovecote Lane, backing on to railway station; NG9 1JG

Genuine down-to-earth all-rounder with an impressive choice of drinks (including up to 15 real ales) and enjoyable, fairly priced food

Getting through as many as 500 widely sourced beers a year, up to a dozen guest ales at this welcoming converted railway inn could be from brewers such as Acorn, Caythorpe, Bradfield, Full Mash, Lancaster, Oldershaws and Ossett, all very well kept alongside Batemans XB, Castle Rock Harvest Pale and Everards Tiger. The quite extraordinary range of drinks continues with continental draught beers, two farm ciders, over 120 malt whiskies, 20 irish whiskeys, about 30 wines by the glass and a very good range of soft drinks including Belvoir fruit pressés. With a genuinely pubby feel, the three fairly simple rooms here have kept their original long narrow layout and are nicely unpretentious, with unfussy décor and simple solid traditional furnishings, stripped woodwork and floorboards (woodblock in some rooms), fires and stained-glass windows; newspapers, dominoes, cribbage and board games. The chatty lounge and bar back on to the railway station and a covered heated area outside has tables overlooking the platform, with trains passing just a few feet away. A nice varied crowd gathers here, but even at busy times service is helpful and efficient. A great time to visit is during their two-week beer and music festival at the end of July; no mobile phones; limited parking.

⊞ The good value menu, of which about half is vegetarian, might include chicken liver pâté with tequila and cranberry, smoked trout fillets with dill mayonnaise, beef bourguignon, grilled tuna loin on niçoise salad, goan vegetable curry, roast peppers stuffed with mediterranean vegetable couscous, lemon and herb crêpe with butternut, courgettes and brie, and puddings such as apple and cinnamon crumble. *Starters/Snacks: £3.90 to £6.95. Main Courses: £7.95 to £14.95. Puddings: £3.50 to £4.50*

Free house ~ Licensees Neil Kelso and Graham Smith ~ Real ale ~ Bar food (12-9.30(8.45 Sun-Tues)) ~ (0115) 925 4049 ~ Children welcome till 8pm ~ Dogs welcome ~ Live folk Sun evening, jazz Mon evening ~ Open 10.30(12 Sun)-11

CAUNTON   SK7459   MAP 7

Caunton Beck 🍴 🍷

Newark Road; NG23 6AE

NOTTINGHAMSHIRE DINING PUB OF THE YEAR

Civilised dining pub with very good (if not cheap) food all day from breakfasts first thing, good wine list, nice terrace

A determination to offer kind, accommodating service is a fundamental goal here, and the proof is in the pudding, as the warm flexible hospitality does indeed contribute to making this lovely inn a memorable place. Surprisingly, given its aged appearance, the building is almost new, but as it was reconstructed using original timbers and reclaimed oak, around the skeleton of the old Hole Arms, it seems old. Scrubbed pine tables, clever lighting, an open fire, country-kitchen chairs, low beams and rag-finished paintwork in its spacious interior create a comfortably relaxed atmosphere. Over two dozen of the wines on the very good wine list are available by the glass, and they've well kept Batemans Valiant, Marstons Pedigree and a guest such as Castle Rock Harvest Pale on handpump; espresso coffee, daily papers and magazines. With lots of summer flowers and plants, the terrace is very pleasant.

ⓘ Food service begins first thing with hearty english breakfasts (served until midday; 11.30 weekends and bank holidays) and continues with delicious sandwiches and a fairly elaborate seasonally changing menu and specials list later on: twice-baked leek and cheese soufflé, tuna carpaccio, toulouse sausage and duck leg cassoulet, fried monkfish with garlic and parsley butter, beef fillet with mustard and tarragon crème fraîche, and puddings such as lemon and elderflower posset and baked panettone pudding with rum ice-cream, and a good cheeseboard. *Starters/Snacks: £4.75 to £7.95. Main Courses: £12.50 to £24.95. Puddings: £4.95*

Free house ~ Licensee Julie Allwood ~ Real ale ~ Bar food (8am-11pm) ~ Restaurant ~ (01636) 636793 ~ Children welcome ~ Dogs allowed in bar ~ Open 8am-midnight

CAYTHORPE   SK6845   MAP 7

Black Horse ◧

Turn off A6097 0.25 miles SE of roundabout junction with A612, NE of Nottingham; into Gunthorpe Road, then right into Caythorpe Road and keep on; NG14 7ED

Quaintly old-fashioned little pub brewing its own beer, simple interior and homely enjoyable food; no children or credit cards

You can be sure of a good value meal at this timeless 300-year-old country local (booking essential), and the two tasty Caythorpe beers brewed in outbuildings here are well worth a taste. These are well kept alongside a couple of changing guests such as Adnams and Greene King Abbot. Little has changed in the near-on 40 years that the current licensee family has been here. The uncluttered carpeted bar has just five tables, brocaded wall banquettes and settles, a few bar stools (for the cheerful evening regulars), a warm woodburning stove, decorative plates on a delft shelf and a few horsebrasses on the ceiling joists. Off the front corridor is a partly panelled inner room with a wall bench running right the way around three unusual long copper-topped tables, and quite a few old local photographs; darts and dominoes. Down on the left, an end room has just one huge round table. There are some plastic tables outside, and the River Trent is fairly close for waterside walks.

⏹ Simple freshly cooked traditional food from a shortish menu includes parsnip soup, ploughman's, prawn cocktail, rollmops, good fried cod, haddock or plaice with parsley sauce, beef in mushroom sauce, fillet steak, baked plums with baked egg custard or golden sponge with custard. *Starters/Snacks: £3.00 to £5.50. Main Courses: £6.00 to £16.00. Puddings: £2.50 to £4.75*

Own brew ~ Licensee Sharron Andrews ~ Real ale ~ Bar food (12-1.45, 7-8.30; not Sat evening, Sun) ~ No credit cards ~ (0115) 966 3520 ~ Dogs allowed in bar ~ Open 12-2.30, 6-11; 12-5, 8-11 Sun; closed Mon (except bank hols)

Recommended by P Dawn, the Didler, Rob and Chris Warner, Pam and Wally Taylor

COLSTON BASSETT
SK6933   MAP 7

Martins Arms ♀ ▥

Village signposted off A46 E of Nottingham; School Lane, near market cross in village centre; NG12 3FD

Smart dining pub with imaginative food (if pricey), good range of drinks including seven real ales, and lovely grounds

Neatly uniformed staff, antique furnishings, hunting prints and warm log fires in Jacobean fireplaces are the backdrop for the comfortably civilised atmosphere at this lovely country pub. Though the emphasis is on the fine food, they do carry half a dozen or so well kept real ales on handpump, including Bass, Greene King IPA, Marstons Pedigree, Timothy Taylors Landlord, Woodfordes Wherry, and a guest or two from brewers such as Jennings and Brakspears. Also Belvoir organic ginger beer, a good range of malt whiskies and cognacs, and an interesting wine list. The little tap room even has its own corner bar; cribbage and dominoes. If you choose to eat in the elegant restaurant (smartly decorated with period fabrics and colourings) you are getting into serious dining. The sizeable lawned garden (summer croquet here) backs on to estate parkland. You might be asked to leave your credit card behind the bar if you want to eat out here. They've converted the stables into an antiques shop, and readers recommend visiting the church opposite and Colston Bassett Dairy, which sells its own stilton cheese and is just outside the village.

⏹ Not cheap but very good food includes imaginatively filled sandwiches and ciabattas, ploughman's, starters such as whipped colston bassett stilton with roast figs, watercress salad and redcurrant dressing, smoked duck breast with mozzarella and marmalade dressing, antipasti platter, main courses such as fish and chips with pea purée, mushroom, onion and goats cheese tart with tomato and basil salsa, roast rump of lamb with couscous and port wine jus, grilled salmon with roast pine nuts and grapes, sour cream and dill, and puddings such as caramel poached pears with crème fraîche mousse and chocolate sauce and bakewell tart with cinnamon anglais and condensed milk ice-cream. *Starters/Snacks: £4.95 to £7.50. Main Courses: £9.95 to £15.95. Puddings: £5.95*

Free house ~ Licensees Lynne Strafford Bryan and Salvatore Inguanta ~ Real ale ~ Bar food (12-2(2.30 Sun), 6-10; not Sun evenings) ~ Restaurant ~ (01949) 81361 ~ Children welcome ~ Open 12-3.30(4 Sat, Sun), 6-11(10.30 Sun)

Recommended by the Didler, D F Clarke, John Honnor, Richard, Harry Whinney, Maurice and Janet Thorpe

HALAM
SK6754   MAP 7

Waggon & Horses ⏍

Off A612 in Southwell centre, via Halam Road; NG22 8AE

Civilised dining pub with inventive seasonally changing menu

The neatly kept open-plan interior of this old low-ceilinged but much altered place has a congenial dining atmosphere, and is nicely divided into intimate sections naturally formed by the layout of the original 17th-c building. Various floral pictures (some painted by the staff) hang on calming pale green walls, and sturdy high-back pine dining chairs are set around a mix of solid mainly stripped tables on wood and tiled floors. Two

Thwaites beers are well kept on handpump; piped music. Out past a grandfather clock in the lobby are a few roadside picnic-sets by pretty window boxes.

Imaginative food might include fish terrine, scallop and pancetta salad, ham, egg and chips, pork fillet with fennel and mustard, roast sea trout with tomato and rosemary sauce and rib-eye steak with stilton; good value two-course menu (lunchtime and 6pm to 7pm Tuesday-Friday). *Starters/Snacks: £4.00 to £10.00. Main Courses: £10.00 to £24.00. Puddings: £5.00 to £6.50*

Thwaites ~ Tenant Roy Wood ~ Real ale ~ Bar food (11.30-2, 5.45-8(8.30 Sat)) ~ (01636) 813109 ~ Children welcome till 7pm ~ Open 11.30-3, 5.45-10(10.30 Sat); 11.30-3.30 Sun; closed Sun evening, Mon (except bank hols)

Recommended by R and M Tait, Derek and Sylvia Stephenson, Richard, Michael and Maggie Betton, Colin Fisher, Patrick Stevens

MORTON   SK7251   MAP 7

Full Moon

Pub and village signposted off Bleasby—Fiskerton back road, SE of Southwell; NG25 0UT

Five real ales and good food at a stylish village local with play area in the nice garden

The enthusiastic new licensees at this attractive old pub talked us through the concept behind the redecorations they've done here in the last year – do let us know if you feel their ideas have worked. Earthy colours and materials are intended to bring the feel of the countryside into the building, at the same time giving a contemporary twist to the traditional notion of a cosy local. So, for example, you'll still find comfy carpets here, but now think of the green, brown and cream stripes as reminiscent of a ploughed field. There's an eclectic mix of reclaimed furnishings, restful pale green curtains, and the cream and mushroom walls are simple and clean without pictures. Smart grey slate runs the length of the long counter, which was constructed from good quality reclaimed pitch pine: Bass and Abbeydale Moonshine are on handpump alongside three guests from brewers such as Blue Monkey, Nottingham and Oldershaws; TV, piped music and board games. Lots of effort has gone into the garden which comprises a peaceful shady back terrace with picnic-sets, a sizeable lawn and some sturdy play equipment.

The menu is fairly short and pubby but thought goes into the ingredients and readers enjoy it. As well as lunchtime sandwiches and omelettes, there might be whitebait, a nibbling platter, burgers, battered haddock, linguine with king prawns or meat balls, beef and ale pie and rib-eye steak. *Starters/Snacks: £5.00 to £7.50. Main Courses: £5.00 to £19.50. Puddings: £4.50 to £6.00*

Free house ~ Licensees Will and Rebecca White ~ Real ale ~ Bar food (12-2.30, 6-9.30; 12-3, 6-9 Sun) ~ Restaurant ~ (01636) 830251 ~ Children welcome ~ Dogs welcome ~ Open 10-3, 5.30-11.30; 10-11.30 Sat, Sun

Recommended by M Mossman, the Didler, Derek and Sylvia Stephenson, David Glynne-Jones, R and M Tait, Phil and Jane Hodson, Pete Yearsley, Prof Kenneth Surin, M Smith

NOTTINGHAM   SK5739   MAP 7

Bell ♣ £

Angel Row, off Market Square; NG1 6HL

Up to a dozen real ales from remarkable cellars in historic yet thriving place with regular live music and simple food

Its venerable age is clearly evident throughout the interior of the two 500-year-old timber-framed buildings that form this pub, though from the exterior they are masked by a late Georgian frontage. With quite a café feel in summer, the front Tudor bar is perhaps the brightest with french windows opening to tables on the pavement and bright blue walls with glass panels protecting patches of 300-year-old wallpaper. The room with the most aged feel is the very pubby low-beamed Elizabethan Bar, with its half-panelled walls, maple parquet floor and comfortable high-backed armchairs. Upstairs, at the back of the heavily panelled Belfry (usually open only at lunchtime), you can see the rafters of the 15th-c crown post roof and look down on the busy street below; TV, fruit machine and piped music. The labyrinthine cellars (tours by appointment) are dug about ten metres into the sandstone rock – the efforts of the hard-working Carmelite monks from the attached friary who are said to have made them are still much appreciated as they now house the well kept beers that are served here – usually Greene King Abbot, IPA and Old Speckled Hen and guests from carefully sourced brewers such as Milton, Nottingham and Saffron. The friendly welcoming staff and landlord also serve ten wines by the glass, quite a few malt whiskies and a farm cider.

🍴 **Reasonably priced straightforward bar food includes soup, burgers, ploughman's, beef pie, battered cod, vegetable risotto and cider apple pie.** *Starters/Snacks: £2.85 to £4.95. Main Courses: £4.00 to £8.95. Puddings: £1.95 to £2.95*

Greene King ~ Manager Craig A Sharp-Weir ~ Real ale ~ Bar food (10am-9pm) ~ Restaurant ~ (0115) 947 5241 ~ Children welcome till 6pm if dining ~ Live jazz Sun lunchtime and Mon, Tues evenings ~ Open 10am-11.30pm(1am Sat)

Recommended by Jeremy King, the Didler

Keans Head 🍷 🍺 £

St Marys Gate; NG1 1QA

Bustling central pub, usefully serving good value food all day, wide choice of drinks, smiling service and informal chatty atmosphere

Looking quite like a café, this cheery unpretentious Tynemill pub is in the attractive Lace Market area. Its single room has some exposed brickwork and red tiling, simple wooden furnishings on the wood-boarded floor, a low sofa by a big window overlooking the street, various pieces of artwork and beer advertisements on the walls, and a small fireplace. Friendly staff serve Batemans XB, Castle Rock Harvest Pale and Screech Owl alongside three well kept guests from brewers such as Beartown, Springhead and Thwaites from handpumps, draught belgian beers, interesting bottled beers and soft drinks, over a dozen wines by the glass and lots of teas and coffees; daily newspapers and piped music. St Mary's church next door is worth a look.

🍴 **An interesting mix of traditional english and italian food includes home-made focaccia, antipasti, whitebait, pork pie, sandwiches, pizzas, pie of the day, sausage of the day and mash and ploughman's.** *Starters/Snacks: £3.95 to £5.95. Main Courses: £6.50 to £10.95. Puddings: £3.25 to £4.95*

Tynemill ~ Manager Charlotte Blomeley ~ Real ale ~ Bar food (12-9(5 Sun, Mon); not Sun, Mon evenings) ~ (0115) 947 4052 ~ Children allowed until 5pm (7pm weekends) ~ Open 11.30am-11pm(12.30 Fri, Sat); 12-10.30 Sun

Recommended by David Carr, the Didler, Richard, P Dawn

Lincolnshire Poacher 🍺 £

Mansfield Road; up hill from Victoria Centre; NG1 3FR

Chatty down-to-earth pub with great range of drinks (including a dozen real ales), good value food and outdoor seating

There can be no doubt that this relaxing place will keep a real ale lover happy. The impressive range of drinks includes Batemans XB, Castle Rock Harvest Pale and Screech Owl, alongside well kept guests from a good variety of brewers such as Fullers, Kelham, Newby Wyke, Oldershaws and Salopian. Other drinks include seven continental draught beers, around 20 continental bottled beers, good farm cider, around 85 malt whiskies and ten irish ones, and very good value soft drinks. The traditional big wood-floored front bar has a cheerful atmosphere, wall settles, plain wooden tables and breweriana. It opens on to a plain but lively room on the left with a corridor that takes you down to the chatty panelled back snug, with newspapers, cribbage, dominoes, cards and backgammon. A conservatory overlooks tables on a large heated area behind. It can get very busy in the evening with a younger crowd.

🍴 **Very good value tasty bar food from a changing blackboard menu might include sweet potato and roast pepper soup, full english breakfast, sausages and champ, meatballs with tomato sauce and penne, butternut squash and sweet potato thai curry.** *Starters/Snacks: £2.50 to £5.00. Main Courses: £5.00 to £7.50. Puddings: £2.00 to £3.50*

Tynemill ~ Manager Karen Williams ~ Real ale ~ Bar food (12-8(6 Sun);10-5 Sat) ~ (0115) 941 1584 ~ Children welcome till 8pm, please ask ~ Dogs welcome ~ Live music Sun evening ~ Open 11am(10am Sat)-11pm(midnight Fri, Sat); 12am-11pm Sun

Recommended by Rona Murdoch, the Didler, John Robertson, Bruce Bird, David Carr, Jeremy King, Derek and Sylvia Stephenson, Geoff and Kaye Newton, David Hunt, MP

Olde Trip to Jerusalem ★ 🍺 £

Brewhouse Yard; from inner ring road follow The North, A6005 Long Eaton signpost until you are in Castle Boulevard, then almost at once turn right into Castle Road; pub is up on the left; NG1 6AD

Unusual pub partly built into sandstone caves, good range of real ales, reasonably priced pubby food

Probably unlike any other pub you will ever visit, some of the rambling rooms at this famous place are burrowed into the sandstone rock below the castle. The siting of the current building (largely 17th c) is attributed to the days when a brewhouse was established here to supply the needs of the castle above. Carved into the rock, the downstairs bar has leatherette-cushioned settles built into dark panelling, tables on flagstones and snug banquettes built into low-ceilinged rocky alcoves. The pub's name refers to the 12th-c crusaders who used to meet nearby on their way to the Holy Land – pub collectors of today still make their own crusades here, and no doubt enjoy the pub's little tourist shop with its panelled walls soaring up into a dark rock cleft. Staff cope efficiently with the busy mix of tourists, conversational locals and students; piped music. As well as half a dozen beers from the Greene King stable (kept in top condition on handpump), you'll find a changing guest, probably from Nottingham. They've ring the bull, a rather out of place games machine, and seats in a snug courtyard, and they host medieval food nights, beer festivals and book launches. You need to book if you want to do their cellar tour.

🍴 **Straightforward bar food includes breakfasts, sandwiches, burgers, fish and chips, roast beef in a giant yorkshire pudding, beef and ale pie, sausage and mash, and steaks.** *Starters/Snacks: £2.95 to £5.45. Main Courses: £5.55 to £11.45. Puddings: £2.15 to £3.95*

Greene King ~ Manager Rosie St John-Lowther ~ Real ale ~ Bar food (10-8) ~ (0115) 947 3171 ~ Children welcome till 7pm ~ Storyteller last Thurs of month ~ Open 10-11(midnight Fri, Sat)

Recommended by the Didler, Derek and Sylvia Stephenson, Colin Gooch, Barry Collett, David and Felicity Fox, Rona Murdoch, Ross Balaam, John Fiander, Jeremy King, John Honnor, Steve Kirby, P Dawn

Vat & Fiddle 🍺 £

Queens Bridge Road, alongside Sheriffs Way (near multi-storey car park); NG2 1NB

Eleven real ales at a very welcoming down-to-earth pub next to the Castle Rock brewery

Steady and unchanging, it's the personalised, chatty relaxed atmosphere at this plain little brick pub that makes it stand out from other Nottingham entries (not to mention its fabulous range of beers). The fairly functional but well loved open-plan interior has a strong unspoilt 1930s feel, with cream and navy walls and ceiling, varnished pine tables and bentwood stools and chairs on parquet and terrazzo flooring, patterned blue curtains and some brewery memorabilia, and Kipper the landlady's cat. An interesting display of photographs depicts nearby demolished pubs and there are magazines and newspapers, piped music some of the time and a quiz machine. As well as six Castle Rock beers (the pub is next door to the brewery – you'll probably see some comings and goings), they serve five or so interesting guests from brewers such as Burton Bridge, Crouch Vale, Hop Back, Magpie, Newby Wyke and Oakham. They also have around 60 malt whiskies, a changing farm cider, a good range of continental bottled beers, several polish vodkas and good value soft drinks; they host occasional beer festivals. There are picnic-sets in front by the road.

⊞ **Two or three specials, such as chilli or curry are served at lunchtime, and rolls are available until they run out of stock.** *Starters/Snacks: £1.80 to £2.50. Main Courses: £2.95 to £5.95*

Tynemill ~ Manager Sarah Houghton ~ Real ale ~ Bar food (12-2.30 Mon-Fri; cobs all day) ~ (0115) 985 0611 ~ Children welcome ~ Dogs welcome ~ Open 11-11(midnight Fri, Sat); 12-11 Sun

Recommended by the Didler, Bruce Bird, Rona Murdoch

LUCKY DIP

Besides the fully inspected pubs, you might like to try these Lucky Dips recommended to us and described by readers (if you do, please send us reports: feedback@goodguides.com).

ASKHAM [SK7375]
Duke William NG22 0RS [Town St]: Pleasant 18th-c brick-built beamed village pub, Greene King Ruddles County, Wells & Youngs Bombardier and perhaps a guest ale, good choice of other drinks; wide choice of reasonably priced food, old farm tools in dining room and back bar/lounge with woodburner; hanging baskets and a couple of picnic-sets outside *(Phil and Jane Hodson)*
AWSWORTH [SK4844]
Gate NG16 2RN [Main St, via A6096 off A610 Nuthall—Eastwood bypass]: Friendly old traditional local nr site of once-famous railway viaduct (photographs in passage); well kept Greene King ales, coal fire in quiet comfortable lounge, cosy bar with TV, small pool room, skittle alley; tables out in front, open all day *(the Didler)*
BAGTHORPE [SK4751]
Dixies Arms NG16 5HF [2 miles from M1 junction 27; A608 towards Eastwood, then first right on to B600 via Sandhill Rd, then first left into School Rd; Lower Bagthorpe]: Reliably well kept ales such as Greene King Abbot and Theakstons Best in unspoilt 18th-c beamed and tiled-floor local, good fire in small part-panelled parlour's fine fireplace, entrance bar with tiny snug, longer narrow room with toby jugs, darts and dominoes; busy wknds with live music and Sun quiz; good big garden with play area and football pitch, own pigeon, gun and morris dancing clubs, open all day *(the Didler)*
Shepherds Rest NG16 5HF [2 miles from M1 junction 27, via A608 towards Eastwood, then off B600; Lower Bagthorpe]: Extensively refurbished old pub with pleasant staff, four changing ales, sensibly priced food (not Sun evening) inc good fish and Thurs steak night, children's helpings; piped music; dogs welcome, garden with play area, pretty surroundings, open all day *(JJW, CMW, Derek and Sylvia Stephenson)*
BATHLEY [SK7758]
Crown NG23 6DA [Main St]: Cheerful and chatty family-run village local with three well kept Marstons-related beers, good soft drinks' choice, wide choice of enjoyable low-priced food inc Sun roasts; log fire, newspapers, piano and pub games; small

garden with barbecue, open all day Fri-Sun *(JJW, CMW)*
BEESTON [SK5236]
Crown NG9 1FY [Church St]: Welcoming, beamed traditional corner local with Greene King ales, small bar with high-backed settles, darts in larger panelled room, comfortable lounge; terrace tables, open all day *(Dr and Mrs A K Clarke, the Didler)*
BILSTHORPE [SK6560]
Copper Beech NG22 8SS [Kirklington Rd]: Pleasant pub with well kept Marstons-related beers, good staff, lots of mining memorabilia; dogs welcome, nice garden *(Geoff and Kaye Newton)*
BINGHAM [SK7039]
☆ *Horse & Plough* NG13 8AF [off A52; Long Acre]: Low beams, flagstones and stripped brick, prints and old brewery memorabilia, comfortable open-plan seating inc pews; well kept Caledonian Deuchars IPA, Fullers London Pride, Wells & Youngs Bombardier and three guest beers (may offer tasters), good wine choice, good value home-made wkdy bar food; popular upstairs evening grill room (Tues-Sat, and Sun lunch) with polished boards, hand-painted murals and open kitchen; piped music; children and dogs welcome, disabled facilities, open all day *(P Dawn, MP, the Didler, Richard, BB)*
BLEASBY [SK7149]
Waggon & Horses NG14 7GG [Gypsy Lane]: Banquettes in carpeted lounge, coal fire in character bar with pub games, pleasant chatty landlord, wife makes good value fresh lunchtime food from snacks up, well kept Marstons ales; comfortable back lobby with play area; piped music; tables outside, small camping area *(the Didler)*
BUNNY [SK5829]
☆ *Rancliffe Arms* NG11 6QT [Loughborough Rd (A60 S of Nottingham)]: Substantial early 18th-c former coaching inn reworked with emphasis on extensive bistro-style dining area, upscale food inc adventurous dishes, popular Sun carvery, friendly efficient service; sofas and armchairs in comfortable bar with interesting well kept changing ales and a log fire; children welcome *(Gerry and Rosemary Dobson, John and Sylvia Harrop, Phil and Jane Hodson, Patricia Sharp, Malcolm and Pauline Pellatt)*

CAR COLSTON [SK7242]
Royal Oak NG13 8JE [The Green, off Tenman Lane (off A46 not far from A6097 junction)]: Helpful licensees doing reliably good home-made food in biggish 18th-c pub opp one of England's largest village greens; Adnams, Jennings and other well kept ales, decent choice of wines by the glass, woodburner in lounge bar with tables set for eating, public bar with unusual barrel-vaulted brick ceiling; children welcome, picnic-sets on spacious back lawn, open all day wknds, cl Mon lunchtime *(Richard and Jean Green, MP, David Glynne-Jones)*

COLLINGHAM [SK8361]
Kings Head NG23 7LA [High St]: Gently upscale modern pub/restaurant behind an unpretentious Georgian façade, two changing ales from long steel bar, courteous staff, food from baguettes to good restaurant dishes with unusual touches; pine furniture, abstracts on light and airy dining area's colourwashed walls; children welcome, no dogs, disabled access, garden tables, open all day Sun *(David and Ruth Hollands)*

COTGRAVE [SK6435]
Rose & Crown NG12 3HQ [Main Rd, off A46 SE of Nottingham]: Friendly and comfortable village pub, good value generous food all day inc mid-week and early evening bargains, more elaborate evening/wknd dishes, young helpful staff; four changing ales such as Caledonian Deuchars IPA, good soft drinks' choice, log fires, back eating area with fresh flowers and candles; children welcome, garden picnic-sets *(Piotr Chodzko-Zajko, John and Sylvia Harrop, Richard Butler, Marie Kroon)*

DUNHAM [SK8174]
White Swan NG22 0TY [Main St (A57 Retford—Lincoln)]: Two comfortable, light and airy lounge areas, pleasant staff, good beer range inc Tom Woods, good value usual food, nice eating area; large grass area, caravan site, sizeable fishing pond *(M Mossman)*

EASTWOOD [SK4846]
Foresters Arms NG16 2DN [Main St, Newthorpe]: Friendly cosy local with Greene King ales, darts, dominoes and table skittles; open fire, old local photographs, lounge with wknd organ sing-along; TV; nice garden *(the Didler)*

EDINGLEY [SK6655]
Old Reindeer NG22 8BE [off A617 Newark—Mansfield at Kirklington; Main St]: Dating from the 18th c, with well kept Marstons-related ales, good food (all day wknds) inc bargain carvery; comfortably refurbished bar, pool in games area, upstairs restaurant; piped music, machines, TV; children and dogs welcome, attractive garden, four bedrooms, open all day *(Derek and Sylvia Stephenson, JJW, CMW)*

EDWINSTOWE [SK6266]
Forest Lodge NG21 9QA [Church St]: Family-run 17th-c inn with smiling efficient service, good range of enjoyable reasonably priced home-made food in welcoming pubby bar or restaurant, good beer range inc Cottage, Milton and Wells & Youngs, log fire; children welcome, 13 comfortable bedrooms, handy for Sherwood Forest, open all day *(Malcolm and Pauline Pellatt)*

ELKESLEY [SK6875]
☆ *Robin Hood* DN22 8AJ [just off A1 Newark—Blyth; High St]: Neat dining pub with good food inc mid-week deals, friendly staff, Black Sheep, Marstons Pedigree and Theakstons; dark furnishings on patterned carpets, yellow walls, pool and board games; piped music, TV; children and dogs welcome, picnic-sets and play area, cl Sun evening, Mon lunchtime *(Richard Cole, Patrick Stevens, Virginia Williams, Simon Collett-Jones, MJVK, Rita and Keith Pollard)*

FARNDON [SK7652]
Boat House NG24 3SX [North End]: Attractively placed by River Trent, with good food and atmosphere, friendly efficient staff, real ale, open fires, appealing understated contemporary décor; open all day wknds *(G Musson)*

FISKERTON [SK7351]
Bromley Arms NG25 0UL [Main St]: Unpretentious, popular Trent-side pub with friendly helpful service, four Greene King ales, good soft drinks' range, wide choice of reasonably priced generous food; piped music, can get very busy in summer; children welcome *(JJW, CMW, Alan Bulley)*

GAMSTON [SK6037]
Bridge NG2 6NP [Radcliffe Rd]: Marstons pub with good service, reasonably priced standard food inc two for one deals *(R C Vincent)*

GRANBY [SK7436]
☆ *Marquis of Granby* NG13 9PN [off A52 E of Nottingham; Dragon St]: Stylish and friendly 18th-c pub in attractive Vale of Belvoir village, tap for Brewsters with their ales and interesting guests from chunky yew bar counter, decent local food (Fri evening to Sun lunchtime); two small comfortable rooms with broad flagstones, some low beams and striking wallpaper, open fire; children and dogs welcome, open from 4pm Mon-Fri, all day wknds *(the Didler, David Glynne-Jones, Richard, BB)*

HOVERINGHAM [SK6946]
☆ *Reindeer* NG14 7GR [Main St]: Unpretentious low-beamed pub with friendly staff, four or five good changing ales such as Black Sheep, Castle Rock and Caythorpe, good wines by the glass, good short choice of enjoyable food from pubby things to enterprising dishes; coal fires in bar and back dining lounge, daily papers; children welcome, picnic-sets outside, cl Sun evening, Tues lunchtime and Mon, open all day Sat and Sun till 5pm *(Richard, the Didler, Derek and Sylvia Stephenson)*

KIMBERLEY [SK4944]
☆ *Nelson & Railway* NG16 2NR [Station Rd; handy for M1 junction 26 via A610]: Beamed Victorian pub with well kept Greene King

ales and guests, mix of Edwardian-looking furniture, brewery prints (was tap for defunct H&H brewery) and railway signs; dining extension, traditional games inc alley and table skittles; piped music, games machine; children and dogs allowed, tables and swings in sizeable front cottagey garden, good value bedrooms, open all day *(the Didler, LYM, Barry Rolfe, Pete Baker)*

Stag NG16 2NB [Nottingham Rd]: Friendly 16th-c traditional local kept spotless by devoted landlady, two cosy rooms, small central counter and corridor, low beams, dark panelling and settles, good range of ales (May beer festival); no food; vintage working penny slot machines and Shipstones brewery photographs; attractive back garden with play area, opens 5pm (1.30 Sat, 12 Sun) *(the Didler)*

LAXTON [SK7266]

☆ **Dovecote** NG22 0NU [off A6075 E of Ollerton]: Village pub with three traditionally furnished dining areas, enjoyable food, well kept changing beers such as Black Sheep, Fullers London Pride and Springhead Roaring Meg, farm cider; pool room with darts and dominoes; piped music – live last Fri of month; children welcome, dogs in bar, small front terrace and sloping garden with church views, orchard and field camping, bedrooms, open all day Sun *(M Mossman, Keith and Chris O'Neill, LYM, Noel Thomas, Derek and Sylvia Stephenson, DC)*

LINBY [SK5351]

Horse & Groom NG15 8AE [Main St]: Picturesque three-room village pub with welcoming enthusiastic landlord, Theakstons, Wells & Youngs and changing guest ales, friendly staff, enjoyable well presented food (not Sun-Thurs evenings) from shortish menu, inglenook log fire, conservatory; no mobile phones; quiet piped music, big-screen TV, games machine in lobby; tables outside, big play area, attractive village nr Newstead Abbey, open all day *(M Mossman, the Didler, P Dawn)*

LOWDHAM [SK6646]

Worlds End NG14 7AT [Plough Lane]: Small village pub with reasonably priced food most of the day (not Sun evening) inc popular OAP wkdy lunches and other deals; friendly attentive staff, three real ales, log fire in pubby beamed bar, restaurant; piped music; children welcome, garden with picnic-sets (some covered), lots of flower tubs, open all day *(Richard, M Mossman, JJW, CMW)*

MANSFIELD [SK5260]

Nell Gwynne NG18 5EX [Sutton Rd (A38 W of centre)]: Former gentlemen's club, chatty and welcoming with locals of all ages, Greene King Abbot and a guest beer, log-effect gas fire, old colliery plates and mementoes of old Mansfield pubs; games room; sports TV, piped music; has been cl Mon-Thurs lunchtimes *(the Didler)*

Railway Inn NG18 1EF [Station St; best approached by viaduct from nr Market Place]:

Friendly traditional local with long-serving landlady, well priced Batemans XB and two guest ales, good bottled beer choice, bargain home-made lunches; bright front bar and cosier back room; small courtyard garden, handy for Robin Hood Line station, cl Sun evening and Tues till 8pm, otherwise open all day *(the Didler, Pete Baker)*

MANSFIELD WOODHOUSE [SK5463]

Greyhound NG19 8BD [High St]: Friendly 17th-c village local with Greene King Abbot, Theakstons Mild and two guest ales, cosy lounge, darts, dominoes and pool in busy bar; regular beer festivals, open all day *(the Didler)*

MAPLEBECK [SK7160]

☆ **Beehive** NG22 0BS [signed down pretty country lanes from A616 Newark—Ollerton and from A617 Newark—Mansfield]: Relaxing, beamed country tavern in a nice spot, chatty landlady, tiny front bar, slightly bigger side room, traditional furnishings and antiques, coal or log fire; changing ales such as Maypole; no food; tables on small terrace with flower tubs and grassy bank running down to little stream, summer barbecues, play area with swings, may be cl winter wkdy lunchtimes, very busy wknds and bank hols *(LYM, the Didler, Richard)*

NETHER LANGWITH [SK5370]

Jug & Glass NG20 9EW [just off A632]: Friendly 15th-c pub in lovely spot, dark-beamed lounge with lots of brass, copper, plates and pictures; bargain food, good service, Greene King ales; picnic-sets out facing village stream and paddling pool *(Keith and Chris O'Neill)*

NEWARK [SK7953]

Castle & Falcon NG24 1TW [London Rd]: John Smiths and two interesting guest beers, friendly landlord, comfortable back lounge and family conservatory; lively games bar with darts, dominoes, pool and TV; skittle alley; small terrace, evening opening 7pm, cl lunchtime Mon-Thurs *(the Didler)*

☆ **Fox & Crown** NG24 1JY [Appleton Gate]: Convivial bare-boards open-plan Castle Rock pub with their ales and several interesting guests from a central servery, Stowford Press cider, dozens of whiskies, vodkas and other spirits, good tea, coffee and decent wines by the glass; friendly obliging staff, bargain simple food from filled rolls and baked potatoes up, several side areas; piped pop music; children welcome, good wheelchair access, open all day *(Stuart Paulley, Mrs Hazel Rainer, Phil and Jane Hodson, the Didler, N R White, BB)*

Mail Coach NG24 1TN [London Rd, nr Beaumond Cross]: Friendly open-plan former Georgian coaching inn, three candlelit separate areas with old-world décor, lots of chicken pictures, hot coal fires and comfortable chairs; Flowers IPA and Original and local guest ales, pleasant staff, good value lunchtime food (not Mon), pub games; upstairs ladies'; tables on back terrace *(the Didler)*

Navigation NG24 4TS [Mill Gate]: Lively open-plan bar in converted warehouse, big windows on to River Trent, flagstones, bare boards, iron pillars and nautical decorations; Everards Tiger and Marstons Pedigree, inexpensive home-made food inc salad bar; weekly live music *(Keith and Chris O'Neill)*

NEWSTEAD [SK5252]

Station Hotel NG15 0BZ [Station Rd]: Basic, down-to-earth red-brick village local opp Robin Hood Line station, several unmodernised character rooms off central bar, well kept bargain Oakwell ales; no food; chatty welcoming landlady, fine railway photographs, pub games; juke box, TV *(the Didler, Pete Baker, P Dawn)*

NORMANTON ON SOAR [SK5123]

Plough LE12 5HB [village signed from A6006; Main St]: Large pleasantly refurbished pub by canalised River Soar, Banks's-related ales, nice choice of good well priced food in spacious dining room, efficient friendly service; tables in sizeable waterside garden, own moorings *(Derek and Sylvia Stephenson)*

NORTH MUSKHAM [SK7958]

Muskham Ferry NG23 6HB [Ferry Lane, handy for A1 (which has small sign to pub)]: Traditional well furnished panelled pub in splendid location on River Trent, relaxing views from bar/restaurant, fairly priced food inc children's meals and Sun roast, three real ales, good wine and soft drinks' choice; piped radio, games machine, pool; dogs welcome, waterside terrace, moorings, open all day *(JJW, CMW, LYM, David and Ruth Hollands)*

NOTTINGHAM [SK5739]

Approach NG1 6DQ [Friar Lane]: Big open-plan pub attracting younger crowd, wood floor with raised carpeted areas, purple walls and lighting, large modern art prints, leather sofas and mixed tables; Batemans, Mallards and Nottingham ales, good wine range, enjoyable food, comedy and music nights; piped music, silent fruit machine and sports TV; open all day *(P Dawn, Jeremy King)*

Boat NG7 2NX [Priory St]: Well kept ales such as Sharps Doom Bar in opened-up town local, a couple of snug areas; unobtrusive sports TV; dogs welcome, children till 5.30pm, small, well fenced garden *(MP)*

Bread & Bitter NG3 5JL [Woodthorpe Drive]: Tynemill pub in former suburban bakery still showing ovens, three bright airy rooms, Castle Rock and great choice of other beers, farm cider, decent wine choice, good value home-made food all day; defunct brewery memorabilia; open all day from 9am *(Richard, the Didler)*

☆ *Canal House* NG1 7EH [Canal St]: Converted wharf building, bridge over indoors canal spur complete with narrowboat, lots of bare brick and varnished wood, huge joists on steel beams; long bar with good choice of house wines, Castle Rock and changing guest beers, lively efficient staff, sensibly priced pubby food, lots of standing room; good

upstairs restaurant and second bar, masses of tables out on attractive waterside terrace; piped music (live Sun), busy with young people at night; open all day *(David Carr, Derek and Sylvia Stephenson, the Didler, BB, Mrs Hazel Rainer)*

Cast Bar NG1 5AL [Wellington Circus, nr Playhouse Theatre]: Adjoining theatre, more cool wine bar/restaurant than pub and recently taken over by a small restaurant chain; lots of chrome and glass, decent range of wines by the glass, real ale such as Castle Rock or Nottingham (handpumps hidden below counter), good value light menu, more adventurous restaurant meals, good integral all-day deli; children welcome, plenty of tables out on notable courtyard terrace by huge Anish Kapoor *Sky Mirror* sculpture, open all day *(Richard)*

Cock & Hoop NG1 1HF [High Pavement]: Tiny front bar and flagstoned cellar bar attached to decent hotel under newish management, characterful décor, interesting food (all day Sun) inc fresh fish, well kept Fullers London Pride, Nottingham Cock & Hoop and Timothy Taylors Landlord; piped music; children and dogs welcome, disabled facilities, smart bedrooms (ones by the street can be noisy wknds), open all day *(the Didler, Simon J Barber, LYM)*

Falcon NG7 3JE [Canning Circus/Alfreton Rd]: Refurbished and doing well under newish owners, Adnams, Black Sheep, Caledonian Deuchars IPA and Greene King in spotless bare-boards bar with flame-effect fire, and black and white décor; all-day food in bar or compact carpeted upstairs restaurant with jazz photographs; terrace tables, open all day *(P Dawn)*

☆ *Fellows Morton & Clayton* NG1 7EH [Canal St (part of inner ring road)]: Former canal warehouse under new management; own good beers (finished by Nottingham) plus Black Sheep, Fullers, Mallard and Timothy Taylors, good value all-day pubby food (not Sun evening); softly lit bustling downstairs bar with red plush alcove seats, shiny wood floors and lots of exposed brickwork, two raised areas, daily papers, restaurant; piped music – live Fri, games machines, several big TVs, no dogs; well behaved children in eating areas, large canal-view deck, open all day, till late Fri, Sat *(the Didler, R T and J C Moggridge, Martin Grosberg, LYM)*

Fox & Crown NG6 0GA [Church St/Lincoln St, Old Basford]: Good range of Alcazar beers brewed behind refurbished open-plan pub (window shows the brewery, tours Sat, next-door beer shop), also guest ales, continentals and good choice of wines; enjoyable fresh food inc thai and wide choice of early evening home-made pizzas; good piped music, games machines, big-screen sports TV; disabled access, terrace tables behind, open all day *(the Didler)*

Gladstone NG5 2AW [Loscoe Rd, Carrington]: Welcoming back-street local with well kept

Caledonian Deuchars IPA, Fullers London
Pride, Greene King Abbot, Nottingham
Legend and Timothy Taylors Landlord, good
range of malt whiskies; comfortable lounge
with reading matter, basic bar with old
sports equipment and darts; piped music,
big-screen sports TV; upstairs folk club Weds,
quiz Thurs; tables in yard with lots of
hanging baskets, cl wkdy lunchtimes, open
all day wknds (from 3pm Fri) *(the Didler,
Richard, David and Sue Atkinson)*
Globe NG2 3BQ [London Rd]: Light and airy
roadside pub with six well kept ales inc
Mallard and Nottingham, good value food,
coal fire; sports TV; handy for cricket or
football matches, open all day *(the Didler,
P Dawn)*
Horse & Groom NG7 7EA [Radford Rd, New
Basford]: Eight good changing ales in well
run, unpretentious open-plan local by former
Shipstones brewery, still with their name and
other memorabilia; good value fresh
straightforward food from sandwiches to Sun
lunch, daily papers, nice snug; live music,
nostalgic discos and regular beer festivals in
stable block behind, open all day
(the Didler)
King William IV NG2 4PB [Manvers St/Eyre
St, Sneinton]: Two-room refurbished
Victorian corner pub with Kelham Island,
Newby Wyke, Oakham and several other well
kept changing ales from circular bar,
Weston's Old Rosie cider, bargain cobs,
friendly staff; fine tankard collection, pool
upstairs, irish music Thurs; silenced sports
TV; heated smokers' shelter, handy for
cricket, football and rugby grounds, open all
day *(the Didler, P Dawn)*
Larwood & Voce NG2 6AJ [Fox Rd, West
Bridgford]: Well run open-plan dining pub
mixing modern and traditional, good locally
sourced home-made food all day from
lunchtime bar meals to more extensive and
imaginative evening menu, good choice of
wines by the glass inc champagne, nice
cocktails, three real ales; Sky Sports TV; on
the edge of the cricket ground and handy for
Nottingham Forest FC, open all day, from
9am wknds for breakfast *(Kate Davies,
P Dawn)*
☆ *Lion* NG7 7FQ [Lower Mosley St, New
Basford]: Ten changing ales such as
Abbeydale, Batemans and Mallard from one
of city's deepest cellars (glass viewing panel
– can be visited at quiet times), farm ciders,
ten wines by the glass; good value home-
made food all day inc doorstep sandwiches,
children's helpings and summer barbecues;
well fabricated feel of separate areas, bare
bricks and polished dark oak boards, coal or
log fires, daily papers; wknd live music inc
Sun lunchtime jazz; terrace and smokers'
shelter, open all day *(the Didler, David and
Sue Atkinson)*
Moot NG3 2DG [Carlton Rd, Sneinton – aka
Old Moot Hall]: Bright refurbishment with
comfortable banquettes and bare boards,
wide choice of well kept ales inc Oakham,

friendly staff, enjoyable simple food;
upstairs games room, Sun quiz night; piped
music, TV; open all day *(the Didler,
David and Sue Atkinson)*
News House NG1 7HB [Canal St]: Friendly
two-room Tynemill pub with half a dozen or
more well kept changing ales inc bargain
Castle Rock, belgian and czech imports on
tap, farm cider, good wine and hot drinks'
choice; decent fresh lunchtime food inc good
value Sun lunch, mix of bare boards and
carpet, local newspaper/radio memorabilia,
bar billiards, darts; big-screen sports TV;
tables out at front, attractive blue exterior
tiling, open all day *(the Didler)*
Pit & Pendulum NG1 2EW [Victoria St]:
Entertaining, dark, gothick-theme bar on
two levels with ghoulish carving and
creeping ivy lit by heavy chandeliers and
(electronically) flaring torches, all sorts of
other more or less cinematic horror allusions
in the décor; standard fairly priced all-day
bar food, well reproduced piped music (can
be loud), lavatories through false bookcase;
keg beers; good wheelchair access, open all
day *(David Carr, Jeremy King, LYM,
Rona Murdoch)*
☆ *Plough* NG7 3EN [St Peters St, Radford]:
Enthusiastic young landlord for friendly
19th-c local brewing its own good value
Nottingham ales, also a guest beer and farm
cider; two coal fires, bar billiards and other
traditional games, cheap food inc fresh cobs,
Thurs quiz; prominent games machine and
sports TV; open all day Fri-Sun *(the Didler)*
Rope Walk NG1 5BB [Derby Rd]: Appealing
and civilised, with enjoyable good value
food served quickly, decent beer choice;
nicely divided open-plan layout, comfortable
chairs around low tables *(Dave Irving,
Jenny Huggins)*
Salutation NG1 7AA [Hounds Gate/Maid
Marion Way]: Proper pub, low beams,
flagstones, ochre walls and cosy corners inc
two small quiet rooms in ancient lower back
part, plusher modern front lounge; half a
dozen real ales, quickly served food till 7pm,
helpful staff; piped music; open all day
(P Dawn, Barry Collett, BB)
Sir John Borlase Warren NG7 3GD [Ilkeston
Rd/Canning Circus (A52 towards Derby)]:
Roadside pub with four comfortable linked
rooms, interesting Victorian decorations,
enjoyable good value limited food, friendly
staff, several real ales inc Everards; artwork
for sale; children welcome (not Fri, Sat
evenings), tables in nicely lit back garden
(the Didler, BB, P Dawn)
Vale NG5 3GG [Mansfield Rd]: Half a dozen
changing ales in 1930s local with original
layout, panelling and woodwork, low-priced
food, Sun quiz night; open all day
(the Didler)
OLLERTON [SK6464]
Rose Cottage NG22 9DD [Old Rufford Rd
(A614) S]: Attractive pub handy for Rufford
Country Park; Marstons ales *(John and
Helen Rushton)*

ORSTON [SK7741]

Durham Ox NG13 9NS [Church St]:
Comfortable split-level open-plan village pub
opp church, good range of mainstream beers
and changing guests, lunchtime
sandwiches/baps (may be other food); hot
coal fire, interesting RAF/USAF memorabilia;
terrace tables, nice garden, pleasant
countryside, open all day Sat *(the Didler,
David and Sue Atkinson)*

PAPPLEWICK [SK5450]

Griffins Head NG15 8EN [Moor Rd
(B683/B6011)]: Refurbished pub with log
fire and attractive raftered dining area, food
from pubby favourites up, well kept Black
Sheep, Brakspears and Timothy Taylors
Landlord, friendly efficient staff; picnic-sets
outside, handy for Newstead Abbey
(David Glynne-Jones)

RADCLIFFE ON TRENT [SK6439]

Horse Chestnut NG12 2BE [Main Rd]: Smart
pub with eight well priced changing ales,
good wine and soft drinks' choice, enjoyable
food from new extended menu, Sun roasts
(12-5), friendly efficient staff; two-level
main bar, plenty of Victorian features inc
panelling, parquet, polished brass and
woodwork and impressive lamps, handsome
leather seating and fine autobiography
collection in lounge; Thurs quiz; piped
music, may keep your credit card if running
tab; disabled access, attractive terrace with
hanging baskets, open all day *(M Mossman,
P Dawn, MP, David Glynne-Jones, JJW, CMW,
the Didler)*

RUDDINGTON [SK5733]

Three Crowns NG11 6LB [Easthorpe St]:
Popular open-plan village local with well
kept Adnams, Fullers, Nottingham and guest
ales, popular back thai restaurant (evenings,
not Sun, Mon); open all day wknds
(the Didler, P Dawn)

White Horse NG11 6HD [Church St]: Cheerful
two-room 1930s village local with half a
dozen real ales, old photographs, games inc
pool; TV; heated back terrace, nice garden,
open all day wknds *(P Dawn, the Didler)*

SELSTON [SK4553]

Horse & Jockey NG16 6FB [handy for
M1 junctions 27/28; Church Lane]: Dating
from the 17th c, intelligently renovated with
interesting 18th/19th-c survivals and good
carving, different levels, low beams,
flagstones and a good log fire in cast-iron
range; friendly staff, cask-tapped Greene
King, Timothy Taylors and six guest ales,
real cider, bargain cobs wkdys; games area
with darts and pool; dogs welcome,
top-end smokers' shelter *(Roger Noyes,
the Didler)*

SOUTH LEVERTON [SK7881]

Plough DN22 0BT [Town St]: Tiny village
local doubling as morning post office, basic
trestle tables, benches and pews, log fire;
helpful welcoming staff, Greene King and a
guest beer, traditional games; nice garden,
open all day (from early afternoon wkdys)
(the Didler, Paul J Robinshaw)

SOUTHWELL [SK7053]

Hearty Goodfellow NG25 0HQ [Church St
(A612)]: Refurbished traditional pub with
friendly newish licensees doing good value
food from sandwiches up, real ales such as
Abbeydale Moonshine, Milton Pegasus and
Wells & Youngs Special, good range of
house wines; garden, handy for Southwell
Workhouse (NT) and Minster
*(Paul J Robinshaw, Malcolm and
Pauline Pellatt)*

TEVERSAL [SK4761]

Carnarvon Arms NG17 3JA [Fackley Rd
(B6014)]: Reopened after spacious reworking
under new owners, enjoyable good value
food, well kept Greene King ales, friendly
well trained staff, separate dining room;
handy for Hardwick Hall *(Malcolm Wood,
Derek and Sylvia Stephenson)*

THURGARTON [SK6949]

☆ ***Red Lion*** NG14 7GP [Southwell Rd (A612)]:
Cheery 16th-c pub with sensibly priced food
(all day wknds and bank hols) in brightly
decorated split-level beamed bars and
restaurant; Black Sheep, Marstons and
Springhead, comfortable banquettes and
other seating, fire, lots of nooks and
crannies, big windows to attractive sizeable
two-level back garden with well spaced
tables (dogs on leads allowed here);
steepish walk back up to car park; children
welcome *(Maurice and Janet Thorpe,
David Glynne-Jones, Derek and
Sylvia Stephenson, BB)*

UNDERWOOD [SK4751]

☆ ***Red Lion*** NG16 5HD [off A608/B600, nr M1
junction 27; Church Lane]: Reliable, sensibly
priced family food inc set-lunch deals (Mon-
Fri), other bargains and good fresh fish (best
to book) in welcoming 17th-c split-level
beamed village pub; Caledonian Deuchars
IPA, Marstons Pedigree and interesting guest
beers, good soft drinks' choice, pleasant
service, open-plan quarry-tiled bar with
slightly enlarged dining area, open fire,
some cushioned settles, pictures and plates
on dressers; piped music, games machine in
lobby; no children or dogs in bar, picnic-sets
and large adventure playground in big
garden with terrace and barbecues,
attractive setting with nearby walks, open
all day Fri-Sun *(Derek and Sylvia Stephenson,
David Chapman, JJW, CMW)*

WATNALL CHAWORTH [SK5046]

☆ ***Queens Head*** NG16 1HT [3 miles from
M1 junction 26: A610 towards Nottingham,
left on B600, then keep right; Main Rd]:
Good value pubby food (all day summer) inc
good fish and chips in tastefully extended
17th-c roadside pub; well kept ales such as
Adnams, Everards, Greene King and Wells &
Youngs Bombardier, efficient staff, beams
and stripped pine, coal fire, intimate snug,
dining area; piped music; picnic-sets on
attractive back lawn with big play area,
open all day *(the Didler, Derek and
Sylvia Stephenson, Glen and Nola Armstrong)*

Royal Oak NG16 1HS [Main Rd; B600 N of

Kimberley]: Friendly beamed village local with interesting plates and pictures, Greene King and guest ales, good fresh cobs, woodburner, back games and pool rooms, upstairs lounge open Fri-Sun; some live music and beer festivals; sports TV; tables outside, open all day *(the Didler)*

WEST BRIDGFORD [SK5837]

☆ *Stratford Haven* NG2 6BA [Stratford Rd, Trent Bridge]: One of Tynemill's best pubs, bare-boards front bar leading to linked areas inc airy skylit back part with relaxed local atmosphere, well kept Castle Rock and interesting changing guests (monthly brewery nights), exotic bottled beers, farm ciders, ample whiskies and wines; good value home-made food all day, good service, daily papers, some live music (nothing too noisy); dogs welcome, handy for cricket ground and Nottingham Forest FC, tables outside, open all day *(the Didler, Derek and Sylvia Stephenson, MP, Rona Murdoch, Richard, BB)*

WINTHORPE [SK8156]

☆ *Lord Nelson* NG24 2NN [Handy for A1 Newark bypass, via A46 and A1133; Gainsborough Rd]: Former watermill with characterful old interior, but closed as we went to press *(Mrs Carolyn Dixon, Mr and Mrs W W Burke, David and Ruth Hollands, LYM)*

Post Office address codings confusingly give the impression that a few pubs are in Nottinghamshire, when they're really in Derbyshire (which is where we list them).

Oxfordshire

There's every kind of pub you could wish for here: unpretentious town ones, tucked-away country taverns, stylish dining pubs with delicious modern cooking, and comfortable hotels with relaxed bars. The county's top performers this year include the Chequers in Chipping Norton, Crown at Church Enstone, Chequers at Churchill, Eyston Arms in East Hendred, White Hart in Fyfield, Falkland Arms in Great Tew, King William IV at Hailey, Bell at Langford, Olde Leathern Bottel in Lewknor, Nut Tree at Murcott, Eagle & Child and Turf Tavern in Oxford, and Kings Arms in Woodstock. This edition also has quite an influx of good new entries: the Highway in Burford (an interesting variation on the dining pub theme), the Lamb there (proper pubby bar in a civilised hotel), Clanfield Tavern (marvellous food cooked by the young landlord using rare breeds, organic produce, own-grown veg and so forth), Plough at Finstock (super – the hub of the village), Plough in Kingham (imaginative food and a nice bar), Lamb at Satwell (cosy beamed country pub with big gardens), and Plough in West Hanney (a friendly village pub with good beers). With young talented chef/landlords and several places growing their own good produce and even rearing their own livestock, there is hot competition for the top title of Oxfordshire Dining Pub of the Year: it goes to the Half Moon in Cuxham. The Lucky Dip section is bulging with strong entries, perhaps most notably the Lord Nelson in Brightwell Baldwin, Angel in Burford, Crown & Tuns and Deddington Arms in Deddington, Catherine Wheel in Goring, Dog & Duck at Highmoor, Bell in Shenington, Lamb in Shipton-under-Wychwood and Duck on the Pond in South Newington. The dominant local breweries are the long-established independent Hook Norton, and Brakspears/Wychwood (part of the Marstons combine). Loddon and White Horse are the pick of the smaller breweries.

ALVESCOT   SP2704   MAP 4
Plough
B4020 Carterton—Clanfield, SW of Witney; OX18 2PU

Useful for wide choice of popular food all day, bric-a-brac and aircraft prints in neat pubby bar, colourful hanging baskets

There's always a bustling, cheerful atmosphere in this popular pub and the genial landlord and his staff are sure to make you welcome. As well as a collection of keys in the entrance hall, the neatly kept bar has aircraft prints and a large poster of Concorde's last flight, as well as plenty of cottagey pictures, china ornaments and house plants, a big antique case of stuffed birds of prey, sundry bric-a-brac, and a log fire. Comfortable seating includes cream, red and green cushioned dark wooden chairs around dark wooden tables, some cushioned settles, and of course the bar stools bagged by chatty regulars in the early evening. Wadworths IPA, 6X and Horizon on handpump. There's a proper public bar with TV, games machine, darts and piped music; skittle alley. The back terrace has some picnic-sets and the hanging baskets are particularly colourful; aunt sally, a children's play area, chickens and a pair of japanese quail. The pub cats are called Dino, Bo and Patch.

🍴 **The wide choice of well liked bar food includes smoked haddock and spring onion fishcakes, sausages and gravy in a giant yorkshire pudding, mozzarella and sun-dried tomato quiche, lasagne, liver and bacon casserole, chicken and mushroom or minted lamb and leek pie, steak and kidney suet pudding, chicken kiev, a daily roast, and puddings; they offer good value deals if two people are eating.** *Starters/Snacks: £4.50 to £5.95. Main Courses: £8.95 to £17.95. Puddings: £3.95 to £4.95*

Wadworths ~ Tenant Kevin Robert Keeling ~ Real ale ~ Bar food (all day) ~ (01993) 842281 ~ Children welcome ~ Open 11.30-11(midnight Sat); 12-10.30 Sun

Recommended by Keith and Sue Ward, David Lamb, KN-R, Peter and Audrey Dowsett, Paul Humphreys

ASTON TIRROLD   SU5586   MAP 2

Chequers 🍴 🍷
Village signposted off A417 Streatley—Wantage; Fullers Road; OX11 9EN

Atmosphere and food of a rustic french restaurant in pubby surroundings, nice french wines, restrained décor and stylish service; charming cottagey garden

'A little bit of France in Oxfordshire' is how one reader describes this charming place. It formally calls itself the Sweet Olive at the Chequers and is almost more of a rustic french restaurant than a village pub, but it does have a relaxed pubby feel, and Brakspears Bitter and Fullers London Pride on handpump. The chatty main room has a proper bar counter, complete with sturdy bar stools (and people using them), grass matting over its quarry tiles, six or seven sturdy stripped tables with mate's chairs and cushioned high-backed settles against the walls, a small fireplace and plain white walls. There are two or three wine cartoons, and wine box-ends, mainly claret and sauternes, panelling the back of the servery, a nice range of french wines by the glass, including a pudding wine, and good coffees; attentive service. A second rather smaller room, set more formally as a restaurant, has a similarly restrained décor of pale grey dado, white-panelled ceiling and red and black flooring tiles; piped music. A small cottagey garden, well sheltered by flowering shrubs, angles around the pub, with picnic-sets under cocktail parasols and a play tree; aunt sally.

🍴 **First-class food includes filled baguettes, soup, warm goats cheese salad with roasted peppers, tempura tiger prawns with a spicy soy dressing, good onglet of beef with shallots and white wine sauce, slow-cooked moroccan lamb, escalope of venison with port wine sauce, panaché of fish with a champagne and saffron sauce, oxtail in puff pastry with red burgundy sauce, scallops with lime butter sauce and mushroom risotto, and puddings like dark chocolate mousse with espresso ice-cream and vanilla sauce, and crème brûlée.** *Starters/Snacks: £4.50 to £8.95. Main Courses: £12.95 to £19.95. Puddings: £5.95*

Enterprise ~ Lease Olivier Bouet and Stephane Brun ~ Real ale ~ Bar food (not Sun evening, all day Weds, all Feb, one week July) ~ Restaurant ~ (01235) 851272 ~ Children welcome ~ Dogs allowed in bar ~ Open 12-3, 6-midnight; closed Weds, Sun evening, all Feb and one week July

Recommended by Rob Winstanley, J V Dadswell, Gordon Davico, Malcolm Rand, Dr and Mrs P Reid

BANBURY   SP4540   MAP 4

Olde Reindeer 🍺 £
Parsons Street, off Market Place; OX16 5NA

Plenty of shoppers and regulars in this interesting town pub, fine real ales, simple food and roaring log fires; no under-21s

There's always a good mix of customers enjoying this unpretentious and very well run town pub. The warmly welcoming front bar has a chatty, friendly atmosphere, heavy 16th-c beams, very broad polished oak floorboards, magnificent carved overmantel for one of the two roaring log fires, and traditional solid furnishings. It's worth looking at the handsomely proportioned Globe Room used by Cromwell as his base during the Civil War. Quite a sight, it still has some wonderfully carved 17th-c dark oak panelling. Six real ales such as Hook Norton Best Bitter, Old Hooky, Hooky Mild and three changing guests on handpump, country wines, several whiskies, and winter mulled wine; piped music. The little back courtyard has tables and benches under parasols, aunt sally and pretty flowering baskets. No under-21s (but see below).

🍴 **Served only at lunchtime, straightforward bar food in generous helpings might include sandwiches, soup, omelettes, good filled baked potatoes, all day breakfast, popular bubble and squeak, and daily specials.** *Starters/Snacks: £3.50 to £7.00. Main Courses: £4.90 to £7.50. Puddings: £3.15 to £4.00*

Hook Norton ~ Tenants Tony and Dot Puddifoot ~ Real ale ~ Bar food (11-2.30; not evenings) ~ Restaurant ~ (01295) 264031 ~ Children allowed in own area with parents ~ Dogs allowed in bar ~ Open 11-11; 12-3 Sun; closed Sun evening

Recommended by Ann and Colin Hunt, Chris Bell, David and Felicity Fox, the Didler, Stuart Doughty, Sally and Tom Matson, George Atkinson, Ted George

BLOXHAM   SP4235   MAP 4

Joiners Arms
Off A361; Old Bridge Road; OX15 4LY

Interestingly furnished rooms on several levels, a good mix of customers, and attractive seating areas outside

You'll feel just as at home having a pint and reading the paper as those who've come to enjoy the well liked food in this attractively modernised pub. Several rambling, appealing rooms have careful spotlighting and some light furnishings that give them a nice airy feel and the atmosphere is relaxed and friendly. The main bar has a big stone fireplace, traditional wooden chairs and tables, half-panelled walls, and Courage Best and a changing guest beer on handpump. A big room just off the bar has rafters in the high ceiling and an exposed well in the floor. Outside, there are plenty of seats on the various levels – the most popular is down some steps by a stream, with picnic-sets and heater. More reports please.

🍴 **Bar food includes lunchtime filled baguettes, deep-fried brie wedges with cranberry sauce, devilled whitebait, mushroom stroganoff, cumberland sausages with onion gravy, home-cooked ham and eggs, beer-battered fresh haddock, pork loin steaks in an orange and sage sauce, fish pie, chicken tikka, steaks, and puddings.** *Starters/Snacks: £3.95 to £5.25. Main Courses: £6.95 to £11.95. Puddings: £4.00 to £4.95*

Free house ~ Licensee Matthew Hanson ~ Real ale ~ Bar food (12-2.30, 6.30-9; all day Sun) ~ Restaurant ~ (01295) 720223 ~ Children welcome ~ Dogs allowed in bar ~ Open 11.30-11(11.30 Sat)

Recommended by BOB

BROUGHTON   SP4238   MAP 4

Saye & Sele Arms ◀▮
B4035 SW of Banbury; OX15 5ED

Smartly refurbished 16th-c house with four real ales, attentive service and seats on the terrace and lawn

Handy for Broughton Castle, this attractive old stone house was first licensed in 1782. Though essentially one long room, the refurbished bar has three distinct areas – a dining room at one end with over 200 colourful water jugs hanging from the beams and neatly folded napkins on the tables, then a tiled area beside the bar counter with cushioned window seats, a few brasses and dark wooden furnishings, and finally a carpeted room with red walls and a mirror above the big fireplace. Adnams Best and guests such as Goffs Tournament, Slaters Top Totty and Vale Tramway on handpump; friendly service. There are pretty hanging baskets around the pleasant terrace with picnic-sets and new hardwood tables and seats on the lawn; aunt sally.

🍴 Cooked by the landlord, the bar food includes lunchtime sandwiches and ploughman's, soup, chicken liver pâté, jumbo sausages, ham and eggs, specials such as seafood thermidor ramekin, a pie of the day, and salmon fillet with creamy mushroom sauce; and puddings like chocolate cheesecake with dark chocolate ice-cream and meringue stack with vanilla ice-cream and red berry compote; Sunday roasts and regular themed food evenings. *Starters/Snacks: £4.95 to £7.95. Main Courses: £6.25 to £19.25. Puddings: £4.95 to £6.25*

Free house ~ Licensees Danny and Liz McGeehan ~ Real ale ~ Bar food (not Sun evening) ~ Restaurant ~ (01295) 263348 ~ Children allowed if dining with an adult ~ Open 11-2.30(3 Sat), 7-11; 12-5 Sun; closed Sun evenings, 25 Dec and evenings 26 Dec and 1 Jan

Recommended by Ann and Colin Hunt, Carolyn Drew, George Atkinson, John and Sharon Hancock

BURFORD
SP2512   MAP 4

Highway 🛏
High Street (A361); OX18 4RG

Comfortable and welcoming old inn overlooking this honeypot village's main street; good all round

Dating from the 15th c and an inn for most of that time, this recently had a 15-year break (as a B&B, with a sewing shop on the ground floor) but has now reopened, under a landlord who comes from a local farming family and his australian wife, who has retired early from a career in fashion – a good thing, reckons one reader, who says that she's clearly born to be a landlady. Her sense of style comes through in the main bar, in touches like the stag candlesticks for the rather close-set tables on the well worn floorboards, the neat modern dark leather chairs, the Cecil Aldin hunting prints, the careful balance of ancient stripped stone with filigree black and pale blue wallpaper, even the nice old station clock above the big log fire in the attractively simple stone fireplace. The room's main feature is the pair of big windows each made up of several dozen panes of old float glass, and a long cushioned window seat. A small corner counter has well kept Hook Norton Hooky and Wye Valley Butty Bach on handpump and 13 wines (including champagne) by the glass. Welcoming efficient service; piped music and board games. On the right a second bar room, with another big window seat, is carpeted but otherwise similar in style; there is a cellar restaurant. A few front picnic-sets stand above the pavement. The pub springer spaniels are called Cassie and Oscar.

🍴 Using only top-quality local produce and baking their own bread, the enjoyable bar food includes sandwiches, soup, tempura king prawns with dipping sauce, potted ham hock and caper rillettes with apricot and tomato chutney, beer-battered fish, sausages with mustard mash and caramelised onion sauce, pork and apple burger, chicken with a wild mushroom and bacon sauce, steak and mushroom pie, daily specials, and puddings like banana tarte tatin and vanilla pod crème brûlée. *Starters/Snacks: £3.50 to £7.95. Main Courses: £9.50 to £19.95. Puddings: £5.50 to £7.50*

Free house ~ Licensees Scott and Tally Nelson ~ Real ale ~ Bar food (12-2.30(3 Sun), 6.30-9(9.30 Fri and Sat)) ~ (01993) 823661 ~ Children welcome ~ Dogs allowed in bar and bedrooms ~ Open 10am-11pm(10.30 Sun) ~ Bedrooms: £75B/£85B

Recommended by Ben and Laurie Braddick, Steve and Liz Tilley, Graham Oddey

Lamb 🍷 🍴 🛏
Sheep Street (B4425); OX18 4LR

Proper pubby bar in civilised inn, real ales and an extensive wine list, traditional bar food and more elaborate restaurant menu, and pretty gardens; bedrooms

Although this is a civilised 15th-c inn with quite an emphasis on the lovely bedrooms and modern food, the cosy bar is just the place for a pint and a chat. There's a good mix of both hotel guests and locals, an informal, friendly atmosphere, high-backed settles and old chairs on flagstones in front of the log fire, Brakspears Bitter and Hook Norton Best on handpump, and an extensive wine list with a dozen by the glass. The roomy beamed main lounge is charmingly traditional, with distinguished old seats including a chintzy high-winged settle, ancient cushioned wooden armchairs, and seats built into its stone-mullioned windows, bunches of flowers on polished oak and elm tables, rugs on the wide flagstones and polished oak floorboards, and a winter log fire under its fine mantelpiece; plenty of antiques and other decorations including a grandfather clock. A pretty terrace with teak furniture leads down to small neatly kept lawns surrounded by flowers, flowering shrubs and small trees, and the garden itself is a real suntrap, enclosed as it is by the warm stone of the surrounding buildings.

🍴 **Bar food includes sandwiches, deli boards (charcuterie, fish or antipasti), potted shrimps with toasted home-made bread, chicken livers with apple and pickled walnut salad, smoked haddock risotto with poached egg, bangers and mash with thyme jus, leek and mature cheddar tart with home-made pickle, gammon and eggs, confit pork belly with champ mash and cider jus, and puddings such as bakewell tart and chocolate fondant; good breakfasts.** *Starters/Snacks: £5.95 to £6.95. Main Courses: £9.95 to £15.95. Puddings: £5.95 to £7.50*

Free house ~ Licensee Paul Heaver ~ Real ale ~ Bar food (12-2.30, 6.30-9.30; sandwiches all day until 6.30) ~ Restaurant ~ (01993) 823155 ~ Children welcome ~ Dogs allowed in bar and bedrooms ~ Open 11-11 ~ Bedrooms: £115B/£145B

Recommended by Malcolm Ward, the Didler, Steve and Liz Tilley, Julie and Bill Ryan

CAULCOTT   SP5024   MAP 4

Horse & Groom

Lower Heyford Road (B4030); OX25 4ND

Bustling and friendly with obliging licensees, particularly good food, and changing beers

Run by a friendly french chef/patron, this is a lovely, traditional cottage. It's not a huge place: an L-shaped red-carpeted room angles around the servery, with plush-cushioned settles, chairs and stools around a few dark tables at the low-ceilinged bar end and a blazing fire in the big inglenook, with brasswater under its long bressumer beam; shove-ha'penny and board games. The far end, up a shallow step, is set for dining with lots of decorative jugs hanging on black joists and some decorative plates; also, attractive watercolours and original drawings. The friendly staffordshire bull terrier is called Minnie. Hook Norton Bitter and three changing guests on handpump, and decent house wines. There is a small side sun lounge and picnic-sets under cocktail parasols on a neat lawn.

🍴 **Very good bar food includes lunchtime sandwiches, soup (the clam chowder is well liked), pâté de campagne, croque monsieur, king prawns in garlic butter, moules marinière, speciality sausages (12 different types), wild mushroom or asparagus and pea risotto, chicken and mushroom pie, fish and chips, popular jugged hare, fillet of beef with a green peppercorn sauce, and puddings like sticky toffee pudding and pineapple and coconut cheesecake.** *Starters/Snacks: £4.75 to £9.95. Main Courses: £9.50 to £11.75. Puddings: £4.75 to £5.25*

Free house ~ Licensees Anne Gallacher and Jerome Prigent ~ Real ale ~ Bar food (not Sun evening or Mon) ~ Restaurant ~ (01869) 343257 ~ Children over 7 and only in dining room ~ Dogs welcome ~ Open 12-3, 6-11; 12-3, 7-10.30 Sun

Recommended by Mr and Mrs W W Burke, Karen Eliot, Stephen Moss, Dennis Haward, David Lamb, Ken and Barbara Turner

CHECKENDON   SU6684   MAP 2

Black Horse

Village signposted off A4074 Reading—Wallingford; coming from that direction, go straight through village towards Stoke Row, then turn left (the second turn left after the village church); OS Sheet 175 map reference 666841; RG8 0TE

Simple place liked by walkers and cyclists for a pint and snack

This is a real boon for walkers. It's a delightfully old-fashioned country local tucked into woodland well away from the main village, and has now been run by the same family for

104 years. The back still room where Hook Norton Hooky Bitter and three changing West Berkshire beers are tapped from the cask has a relaxed, unchanging feel and the room with the bar counter has some tent pegs ranged above the fireplace, a reminder that they used to be made here. A homely side room has some splendidly unfashionable 1950s-look armchairs and there's another room beyond that. There are seats out on a verandah and in the garden.

🍴 They offer only filled rolls and pickled eggs.

Free house ~ Licensees Margaret and Martin Morgan ~ Real ale ~ No credit cards ~ (01491) 680418 ~ Children allowed but must be very well behaved ~ Open 12-2(2.30 Sat), 7-11; 12-3, 7-10.30 Sun

Recommended by Pete Baker, the Didler, Torrens Lyster, Richard Greaves, Phil and Sally Gorton

CHIPPING NORTON   SP3127   MAP 4

Chequers ★ ♀ 🍺
Goddards Lane; OX7 5NP

Busy, friendly town pub open all day, with several real ales, popular bar food, cheerful mix of customers and simple bars

With five well kept real ales on handpump and a relaxed, cheerful atmosphere, this bustling town pub is popular with loyal regulars and visitors alike. The three softly lit beamed rooms have no frills, but are clean and comfortable with low ochre ceilings, lots of character, and a blazing log fire. Efficient staff serve Fullers Chiswick, London Pride, ESB, Gales HSB and Hydes Original Bitter on handpump, and they have good house wines, many available by the glass. The conservatory restaurant is light and airy and used for more formal dining. The town's theatre is next door.

🍴 As well as sandwiches, the well liked bar food might include greek sausages, pasta with chilli prawns, beer-battered fish and chips with home-made tartare sauce and minty pea purée, a pie of the day, slow-braised lamb shoulder with red wine jus, crab and salmon fishcakes, and good sirloin steak with home-made mushroom ketchup. *Starters/Snacks: £4.00 to £8.95. Main Courses: £7.50 to £16.50. Puddings: £4.00 to £4.75*

Fullers ~ Lease John Cooper ~ Real ale ~ Bar food (12-2.30, 6-9.30; 12-4 Sun; not Sun evening) ~ Restaurant ~ (01608) 644717 ~ Children allowed in public bar ~ Dogs allowed in bar ~ Open 11-11(11.30 Sat); 12-10.30 Sun

Recommended by Brian and Rosalie Laverick, Chris Glasson, Richard Greaves, George Atkinson, the Didler, Richard Tilbrook, Helene Grygar, Stuart Turner, Robert Gomme, R C Vincent, Bruce M Drew, Ann and Colin Hunt, Michael Butler, Guy Vowles

CHURCH ENSTONE   SP3725   MAP 4

Crown
Mill Lane; from A44 take B4030 turn-off at Enstone; OX7 4NN

Friendly country pub with helpful licensees, enjoyable food cooked by the landlord, and well kept real ales

'It's always a pleasure to come here' says one of our readers – and many others agree with him. It's an attractive old pub run by friendly hands-on licensees and the atmosphere is cheerful and relaxed. The smart and uncluttered congenial bar has beams, wheelback chairs and built-in cushioned wall seats around heavy wooden tables, country pictures on the stone walls, and a good log fire in the large stone fireplace with horsebrasses along its bressumer beam. Hook Norton Hooky Bitter, Marston Moor Brewers Droop and Timothy Taylors Landlord on handpump and several decent wines by the glass. There's also a beamed, red-walled, carpeted dining room and an airy slate-floored conservatory, both with farmhouse chairs and tables. On the front terrace are some white metal tables and chairs overlooking the quiet lane, with picnic-sets in the sheltered back garden.

🍴 Cooked by Mr Warburton, the good enjoyable bar food includes lunchtime filled baguettes, soup, pigeon breast with bubble and squeak and peppercorn sauce, fishcakes with coriander and chilli mayonnaise, steak in ale pie, pasta with wild mushrooms, pesto and cream, pork loin steak with black pudding and cider sauce, daily specials like squid with garlic and chilli, and calves liver with horseradish mash, bacon and balsamic gravy; and puddings such as rich chocolate pot and lemon panna cotta with raspberry compote. *Starters/Snacks: £4.75 to £9.50. Main Courses: £7.95 to £14.95. Puddings: £4.75*

Free house ~ Licensees Tony and Caroline Warburton ~ Real ale ~ Bar food (not Sun evening) ~ Restaurant ~ (01608) 677262 ~ Children welcome ~ Dogs allowed in bar ~ Open 12-3, 6-11; 12-4 Sun; closed Sun evening, 26 Dec, 1 Jan

Recommended by Richard Marjoram, Keith and Sue Ward, M E and J R Hart, Stuart Turner, Helene Grygar, Richard Greaves, Chris Glasson

CHURCHILL   SP2824   MAP 4

Chequers

B4450 Chipping Norton—Stow-on-the-Wold (and village signposted off A361 Chipping Norton—Burford); Church Road; OX7 6NJ

Exceptionally welcoming licensees in a busy village pub with plenty of space and popular food

A first-class landlady and an object lesson in hospitality, Mrs Golding's remarkable memory continues to amaze her customers; even after a seven-month gap and not a regular visitor, one of our contributors was remembered by name. Furnished in a country house style with a relaxed, friendly atmosphere, the front bar has a light flagstoned floor, a couple of old timbers, modern oak furnishings, some exposed stone walls around a big inglenook (with a good winter log fire) and country prints on the walls; newspapers are laid out on a table. At the back there's a big extension that's a bit like a church with soaring rafters and upstairs is a cosy but easily missed area mainly laid out for eating. Hook Norton Hooky Bitter and a changing guest such as Fullers London Pride or Greene King Old Speckled Hen on handpump, and a good wine list. The pub's exterior is Cotswold stone at its most golden, and the village church opposite is impressive.

🍴 Popular bar food includes sandwiches, soup, black pudding and poached egg florentine, steak and kidney or fish pie, broad bean, parmesan and sun-dried tomato risotto, pork tenderloin with a bacon and port wine sauce, grilled salmon with a tomato and spring onion white wine sauce, daily specials like avocado and chicken salad and baked ham with cider and apple sauce, and puddings such as a red berry and white chocolate cheesecake with dark chocolate sauce and lemon and lime bavarois with lemon syrup; Sunday roasts. *Starters/Snacks: £5.00 to £6.50. Main Courses: £10.00 to £16.00. Puddings: £5.00 to £6.00*

Free house ~ Licensees Peter and Assumpta Golding ~ Real ale ~ Bar food (12-2(3 Sun), 7-9.30(9 Sun) ~ Restaurant ~ (01608) 659393 ~ Children welcome ~ Open 11-11(10.30 Sun)

Recommended by J Crosby, Stuart Turner, Caroline and Michael Abbey, Sir Nigel Foulkes, Jean and Douglas Troup, Ann and Colin Hunt, Bernard Stradling, P and J Shapley, Di and Mike Gillam, Tom Evans, Dennis Haward, Graham Oddey, Tracey and Stephen Groves, Richard Greaves

CLANFIELD   SP2802   MAP 4

Clanfield Tavern 🍽 ♟

Bampton Road (A4095 S of Witney); OX18 2RG

Newish owners concentrating on fresh seasonal food, in a pleasantly extended ancient pub with a good choice of drinks

Tiny windows peep from this 17th-c pub's heavy stone-slabbed roof, and picnic-sets on a flower-bordered small lawn look across to the village green and a stream. Inside, it's been largely opened up but keeps the feel of several separate areas, rambling below heavy beams around a central stairwell enclosed in very broad old bare boards. Mainly carpeted, it's not over-cluttered with furniture: a built-in high-backed settle by the log fire in one big fireplace under a heavy black mantelbeam, some other nice old cushioned settles, mixed more or less pubby chairs, a table of newspapers and magazines, one snug flagstoned area behind the bar with a couple of sofas by a big glass-fronted woodburning stove. The smallish serving bar has changing ales on handpump such as Banks's, a Brakspears seasonal ale and Ringwood Porter (they offer a tasting board with three third-of-a-pint tasters), with a good choice of wines by the glass and of soft drinks. On the left, this part has ancient pale polished flagstones, an attractive bow-window seat and darts. For a meal, perhaps the best place is the attractive conservatory through on the right, with neat comfortably modern furnishings and good blinds.

🍴 **Using local ingredients including their own herbs and vegetables, free-range eggs and rare breed meat, they do enjoyable bar food such as sandwiches, soup with home-made bread, cornish crab cake with tomato and fennel salad and chilli oil, sea trout ballotine, rock oyster fritter and cucumber dressing, pea and wild garlic risotto, gloucester old spot pork belly with caramelised apples and roast celeriac, poached fillet of lemon sole with smoked haddock mash and sorrel velouté, home-made sausages with onion gravy, chargrilled charolais rib-eye steak, fondant potato and béarnaise sauce, and puddings like organic coffee brûlée with home-made crunchie and chocolate mousse with glazed banana and white chocolate jelly; they offer a good value weekday two-course lunch, Monday evening takeaway fish and chips, and popular Sunday roasts.** *Starters/Snacks: £4.50 to £8.50. Main Courses: £8.50 to £12.50. Puddings: £4.50 to £5.50*

Real Food Pub Company ~ Lease Tom Gee ~ Real ale ~ Bar food (12-2.30(3 Sat and Sun), 6.30-9(9.30 Fri and Sat); not Sun evening or Mon lunchtime) ~ Restaurant ~ (01367) 810223 ~ Children welcome ~ Dogs allowed in bar ~ Open 12-3, 5.30-11; 12-12 Sat; closed Mon lunchtime

Recommended by Graham Oddey, Ian Phillips

CUXHAM   SU6695   MAP 4

Half Moon 🍴

4 miles from M40 junction 6; S on B4009, then right on to B480 at Watlington; OX49 5NF

OXFORDSHIRE DINING PUB OF THE YEAR

Lovely 17th-c country pub with relaxed atmosphere and delicious food cooked by the friendly landlord

This is a lovely 17th-c country pub where there's no doubt that most customers are here to enjoy the first-class food cooked by the young chef/patron. But there is a small red and black tiled bar with a brick fireplace and Brakspears Bitter on handpump, and the atmosphere is friendly and informal. The two main eating areas have old beams, an attractive mix of Edwardian tables, dining chairs and cushioned settles, a modicum of antique lamps, pewter tankards, stone bottles, mirrors and wall prints, several wines by the glass and home-made ginger beer and lemonade. There are wooden slatted chairs and tables in the good-sized garden and pretty window boxes. This is a sleepy village surrounded by fine countryside.

🍴 **Using home-grown vegetables, home-reared gloucester old spot pigs, their own free-range eggs, locally shot game and other local and organic produce, the excellent food might include sandwiches, soup, potted crab, pigeon pâté with apple chutney, mussels in cream, wine and garlic, butternut squash risotto, mutton burger with chilli and mint and cumin chips, home-made sausages with onion gravy, muntjac three ways, venison 'scotch pie' and baked beans, a proper fish stew with rouille, pork belly with scallops, lentils and green sauce, and puddings like dark chocolate brownie with cherry compote and lemon curd cheesecake with raspberry sorbet; good Sunday roasts.** *Starters/Snacks: £4.75 to £8.50. Main Courses: £10.50 to £17.50. Puddings: £5.50*

Brakspears ~ Tenants Andrew Hill and Eilidh Ferguson ~ Real ale ~ Bar food (12-2(3 Sun), 6-9; not Sun evening or Mon) ~ (01491) 614151 ~ Children welcome ~ Dogs welcome ~ Open 12-3, 5.30-11; 12-11 Sat; 12-5 Sun; closed Sun evening and all Mon

Recommended by LM, David Lamb, Karen Eliot, Malcolm and Barbara Lewis

---

Post Office address codings confusingly give the impression that some pubs are in Oxfordshire, when they're really in Berkshire, Buckinghamshire, Gloucestershire or Warwickshire (which is where we list them).

EAST HENDRED   SU4588   MAP 2

Eyston Arms ⊗

Village signposted off A417 E of Wantage; High Street; OX12 8JY

Attractive bar areas with low beams, flagstones, log fires and candles, imaginative food and helpful service

Locals do pop in here for a drink and a chat, they often have bar nibbles, and they do keep Fullers London Pride and Wadworths 6X on handpump, but many of this attractive pub's customers are here to eat the good, interesting food. There's a friendly welcome from the cheerful staff and several separate-seeming areas with contemporary paintwork and modern country-style furnishings: low ceilings and beams, stripped timbers, the odd standing timber, an inglenook fireplace, nice tables and chairs on the flagstones and carpet, some cushioned wall seats, a piano, and a pleasant atmosphere. Even on a sunny day the candles may be lit; good wines and piped pop music (which some readers think unnecessary). Picnic-sets outside overlook the pretty village lane and there are seats in the back courtyard garden.

⊞ **Inventive bar food includes lunchtime sandwiches, king prawns with persillade and garlic crostini, carpaccio with chilli, ginger, soy and sesame oil, lamb burger with tzatziki and melted cheese, chicken satay salad with crushed peanuts, mint and coriander, gloucester old spot sausages with onion gravy, chilli king prawn and smoked salmon linguine, chargrilled canon of lamb on a feta, basil and roast red pepper couscous with sauce vierge, good steaks with café de paris butter or béarnaise sauce, daily fresh fish, and puddings like chocolate and pistachio brownie with crème fraîche and summer berry and vanilla crème brûlée with raspberries and shortbread; they also offer Sunday brunch (11am-12.30pm) as well as Sunday roasts.** *Starters/Snacks: £5.00 to £11.00. Main Courses: £11.00 to £23.50. Puddings: £5.50*

Free house ~ Licensees George Dailey and Daisy Barton ~ Real ale ~ Bar food (12-2.30, 7-10) ~ Restaurant ~ (01235) 833320 ~ Children must be well behaved – no babies ~ Dogs allowed in bar ~ Open 11-11

Recommended by Alan and Audrey Moulds, Susan and John Douglas, Tony Winckworth, Henry Midwinter, Michael Doswell, Roger Thornington, JJW, CMW, Ken and Margaret Grinstead, Guy Vowles, Bruce and Sharon Eden, Terry Miller

FERNHAM   SU2991   MAP 4

Woodman

A420 SW of Oxford, then left into B4508 after about 11 miles; village a further 6 miles on; SN7 7NX

Good choice of real ales and generous food in a charming old-world country pub

Usefully open all day and with a decent choice of beers, this country pub is popular locally and with visiting customers, too. The heavily beamed rooms are full of an amazing assortment of old objects like clay pipes, milkmaids' yokes, leather tack, coach horns, an old screw press, some original oil paintings and good black and white photographs of horses. Comfortable seating includes cushioned benches, pews and windsor chairs, and the candlelit tables are simply made from old casks; big wood fire. Tapped from the cask, the real ales change regularly: Brakspears Bitter, Greene King Abbot, Hop Back Crop Circle, Millstone Tiger Rut and Timothy Taylors Landlord. Several wines by the glass and winter mulled wine; piped music and TV. There are seats outside on the terrace. Disabled lavatories.

⊞ **Quite a choice of bar food includes lunchtime filled baguettes and panini, ploughman's, soup, whitebait with chive mayonnaise, chicken caesar salad, rump burger with monterey jack cheese, local sausages with red wine gravy, curry of the day, pasta with peas, sunblush tomatoes and mint pesto, steak and mushroom in ale pie, salmon with prawns, crayfish and lemon mayonnaise, and slow-roast lamb shank with rosemary mash and redcurrant gravy; Sunday roasts.** *Starters/Snacks: £4.95 to £7.95. Main Courses: £8.95 to £17.95. Puddings: £2.95 to £5.50*

Free house ~ Licensee Steven Whiting ~ Real ale ~ Bar food ~ Restaurant ~ (01367) 820643 ~ Children welcome ~ Dogs allowed in bar ~ Folk music first Weds of month ~ Open 11(12 Sun)-11

Recommended by Phyl and Jack Street, Tony and Tracy Constance, Peter and Audrey Dowsett

FINSTOCK
SP3616   MAP 4

Plough 🍴 🍷 🍺
Just off B4022 N of Witney; High Street; OX7 3BY

Friendly and thoroughly nice village pub with smashing food cooked by licensee, good choice of drinks, open fire and seats outside

Very much the hub of the village, this thatched pub appeals to a wide mix of customers and is run with care by the friendly licensees. Nicely split up by partitions and alcoves, the long low-beamed rambling bar is comfortable and relaxed, with leather sofas by the massive stone inglenook fireplace, and some unusual horsebrasses and historical documents to do with the pub on the walls. The roomy, low-beamed dining room has candles and fresh flowers on the stripped-pine tables. Adnams Broadside and Butts Organic Jester and West Berkshire Good Old Boy on handpump, several wines by the glass, 25 malt whiskies, and Old Rosie and Sheppy's ciders; bar billiards, cribbage, dominoes and scrabble. The pub cats are called Rufus and Pushka, and visiting dogs are often spoilt with a home-cooked pig's ear or slice of beef. Outside, the neatly kept garden has tables and chairs, and aunt sally. Popular local walks amongst woodland and along the River Evenlode.

🍴 **Particularly good bar food, cooked by one of the landlords, includes lunchtime sandwiches with crisps and garnish, soup, crab mayonnaise, terrine of partridge and pheasant with chutney, sautéed chicken livers in port and thyme on a crouton, dry-cure ham and free-range eggs, steak in ale pie, beer-battered fish, thai green coconut curry with toasted cashews, gressingham duck breast with black cherries and port, venison with red wine and juniper sauce, and puddings such as warm chocolate puddle cake and lemon and blueberry posset with shortbread.** *Starters/Snacks: £4.75 to £7.00. Main Courses: £8.75 to £16.00. Puddings: £5.25 to £5.75*

Free house ~ Licensees Joe McCorry and Martin Range ~ Real ale ~ Bar food (not Sun evening or Mon) ~ Restaurant ~ (01993) 868333 ~ Children welcome if over 5 and well behaved ~ Dogs allowed in bar ~ Occasional bands ~ Open 12-2.30, 6-11; 12-11 Sat; 12-6(4 in winter) Sun; closed Sun evening, Mon (except bank hols), maybe two weeks Feb

Recommended by Guy Vowles, D R Ellis

FYFIELD
SU4298   MAP 4

White Hart 🍴 🍷 🍺
In village, off A420 8 miles SW of Oxford; OX13 5LW

Impressive place with grand main hall, minstrel's gallery and interesting side rooms, imaginative modern food, fine choice of drinks and seats outside

This was originally built for Sir John Golafre in about 1450 to house priests who would pray for his soul for ever; the atmosphere may be less pious these days but it's still impressive. The bustling main restaurant is a grand hall with soaring eaves, beams, huge stone-flanked window embrasures and flagstoned floors; it's overlooked by a minstrel's gallery on one side and several other charming and characterful side rooms on the other. In contrast, the side bar is cosy with a large inglenook fireplace at its centre and a low-beamed ceiling; there are flowers all around and evening candles. Hook Norton Hooky Bitter, Loddon Life of Riley, Sharps Doom Bar, White Horse Village Idiot and Vale Black Swan on handpump, around 16 wines by the glass including champagne and pudding wines, Thatcher's cider, and several malt whiskies; they hold beer festivals on May and August bank holiday weekends. Piped music and board games. There are elegant metal seats around tables under smart umbrellas on the spacious heated terrace, and lovely gardens that include their own kitchen garden. Plenty to see nearby and the Thames-side walks are well worth taking.

⊞ Using their own herbs, vegetables and fruit, and cooked by the licensees, the excellent – if not cheap – food includes soup, hare and chicken rillette with pickled plums, pigeon breast, caramelised red onion tart and wild garlic dressing, sharing boards (meze, fish or antipasti), calves liver, bacon, mustard mash and madeira and onion gravy, crispy gilt-head bream with coconut rice and mango and pawpaw salsa, slow-roasted pork belly with celeriac purée, crackling and cider jus, 28-day aged rib-eye steak with dijon and tarragon butter, and puddings like hot chocolate fondant with marmalade ice-cream and peach and almond frangipane tart with chantilly cream; they also offer a two- and three-course set lunch and Sunday roasts. *Starters/Snacks: £5.50 to £7.50. Main Courses: £13.00 to £18.00. Puddings: £5.50 to £6.50*

Free house ~ Licensee Mark Chandler ~ Real ale ~ Bar food (12-2.30, 7(bar snacks from 6)-9.30; 12-4 Sun; not Sun evening and Mon) ~ Restaurant ~ (01865) 390585 ~ Children welcome but must be well behaved ~ Open 12-3, 5.30-11; 12-11(10.30 Sun) Sat; closed Mon (except bank hols)

Recommended by Bruce and Sharon Eden, Andy and Claire Barker, Dr and Mrs A K Clarke, Helene Grygar, David and Jill Wyatt, I J and S A Bufton, GSB, Tony and Tracy Constance, Andrea and Guy Bradley, Henry Midwinter, Yvonne and Mike Meadley, J Crosby

GREAT TEW   SP3929   MAP 4

Falkland Arms ◖

Off B4022 about 5 miles E of Chipping Norton; The Green; OX7 4DB

Idyllic golden-stone cottage in lovely village, with plenty of character in the unspoilt bar and a fine choice of ales

Now usefully open all day at weekends and serving food all day then, too, this lovely thatched pub remains as untouched as ever and is just one of the fine golden-stone buildings in this idyllic village. The unspoilt and partly panelled bar has high-backed settles and a diversity of stools around plain stripped tables on flagstones and bare boards, one-, two- and three-handled mugs hanging from the beam-and-board ceiling, dim converted oil lamps, shutters for the stone-mullioned latticed windows, and an open fire in the fine inglenook fireplace. Wadworths IPA, 6X and a seasonal ale, plus guests from breweries such as Jennings, Ramsbury, St Austell and Vale on handpump. The counter is decorated with tobacco jars and different varieties of snuff which you can buy, and you'll also find 30 malt whiskies, country wines and Weston's farm cider; darts and board games. You have to go out into the lane and then back in again to use the lavatories. There are tables out in front of the pub and picnic-sets under cocktail parasols in the garden behind. Dogs must be on a lead. Small good value bedrooms (no under-16s).

No mobile phones.

⊞ Lunchtime bar food includes filled baguettes, ploughman's, soup, pork and herb sausages with cider gravy, stilton, broccoli and potato bake, cod fillet with herb crust and a lemon butter sauce, and chicken casserole, with evening choices like spinach and mushroom risotto, smoked haddock with cream, thyme and a poached egg, and slow-cooked lamb shank with rosemary and garlic; Sunday roasts. *Starters/Snacks: £4.50 to £5.95. Main Courses: £7.95 to £9.95. Puddings: £4.95*

Wadworths ~ Managers Paula and James Meredith ~ Real ale ~ Bar food (12-2.30, 6-9; all day weekends) ~ Restaurant ~ (01608) 683653 ~ Children allowed in restaurant at lunchtimes only ~ Dogs allowed in bar ~ Live folk music Sun evening ~ Open 11.30-3, 6-11; 11.30am-midnight Sat; 12-10.30 Sun ~ Bedrooms: £50S/£85S(£115B)

Recommended by Richard Greaves, Guy Vowles, Paul Boot, Stuart Turner, MDN, Dr and Mrs Michael Smith, the Didler, Stephen Moss, Ann and Colin Hunt

---

Please keep sending us reports. We rely on readers for news of new discoveries, and particularly for news of changes – however slight – at the fully described pubs: feedback@goodguides.com, or (no stamp needed) The Good Pub Guide, FREEPOST TN1569, Wadhurst, E Sussex TN5 7BR.

HAILEY   SU6485   MAP 2

King William IV

The Hailey near Ipsden, off A4074 or A4130 SE of Wallingford; OX10 6AD

Attractive old pub, wonderful views from seats in the garden, friendly staff, well liked food and several real ales

Despite being off the beaten track, this 400-year-old pub has a good thriving atmosphere and plenty of customers. It's a delightful place where you get a real sense of peace and the wide-ranging views across peaceful rolling pastures – with maybe red kites patrolling overhead – are outstanding. Inside, the beamed bar has some good, sturdy furniture on the tiles in front of the big winter log fire, and there are three other cosy seating areas that open off here. Brakspears Bitter and a seasonal guest are tapped from the cask, there's an interesting wine list, and farm cider; good, friendly service. The terrace and large garden have plenty of seats and tables, and the pub is popular with walkers and horse riders (you can tether your horse in the car park); the Ridgeway National Trail is nearby.

🍴 Enjoyable bar food includes lunchtime filled baguettes (not Sunday), soup, chicken liver pâté, goats cheese salad, local sausages with chips, spaghetti carbonara, steak in ale pie, liver and bacon, pork medallions in a mushroom, white wine and cream sauce, a daily special, and puddings such as sticky toffee pudding with butterscotch sauce and various cheesecakes. Sunday roasts and summer barbecues. *Starters/Snacks: £4.75 to £6.25. Main Courses: £8.95 to £13.00. Puddings: £4.75*

Brakspears ~ Tenant Neal Frankel ~ Real ale ~ Bar food ~ (01491) 681845 ~ Childen allowed in two rooms off bar area ~ Dogs welcome ~ Open 11.30-2.30, 6-11; 12-3, 6.30-10.30 Sun; closed 25-26 Dec and evening 1 Jan

Recommended by Mr and Mrs C Prentis, Colin and Bernardine Perry, Malcolm and Barbara Lewis, Richard and Sissel Harris, the Didler, Steve and Linda Langdon, Mr Ray J Carter, Jane and Martin Bailey

HIGHMOOR   SU6984   MAP 2

Rising Sun

Witheridge Hill, signposted off B481; OS Sheet 175 map reference 697841; RG9 5PF

Thoughtfully run and pretty pub with a mix of diners and drinkers

You can be sure of a warm welcome from the friendly, chatty licensees and their pleasant staff in this pretty black and cream pub. The two front rooms are for those just wanting a drink – the rest of the place is laid out for dining. On the right by the bar, there are wooden tables and chairs and a sofa on the stripped wooden floors, cream and terracotta walls and an open fire in the big brick inglenook fireplace. The main area spreading back from here has shiny bare boards and a swathe of carpeting with well spaced tables and attractive pictures on the walls. Brakspears Bitter and Oxford Gold and a guest beer on handpump, and Weston's cider; piped music and board games. Seats and tables in the back garden; boules.

🍴 Using home-grown herbs (which they also sell), the bar food includes sandwiches, wraps and rarebits, ploughman's, soup, various nachos, all sorts of tapas, deep-fried breaded camembert with cranberry sauce, toad in the hole with onion gravy, spaghetti with stilton and watercress sauce, tiger prawn, pollack and saffron stew, slow-roasted duck leg in a juniper and red wine sauce, and guinea fowl suprême in a sticky orange sauce. *Starters/Snacks: £4.50 to £7.00. Main Courses: £8.95 to £14.00. Puddings: £4.80 to £7.00*

Brakspears ~ Tenant Judith Bishop ~ Real ale ~ Bar food (12-2(2.30 Fri and Sat), 6.30-9(7-9.30 Fri and Sat); 12-3 Sun (not Sun evening) ~ Restaurant ~ (01491) 640856 ~ Children allowed if eating and must be strictly supervised by parents ~ Dogs allowed in bar ~ Open 12-3, 5.30-11; 12-11 Sat; 12-10 Sun; closed Sun evening in winter

Recommended by Torrens Lyster, Anthony and Marie Lewis, Paul Humphreys, Martin and Karen Wake, David and Sue Smith

KINGHAM

SP2624 MAP 4

Plough ♀ 🛏

Village signposted off B4450 E of Bledington; or turn S off A436 at staggered crossroads a mile SW of A44 junction – or take signed Daylesford turn off A436 and keep on; The Green; OX7 6YD

Friendly restaurant-with-rooms combining an informal pub atmosphere with upmarket food

The properly pubby bar, perhaps with a lively knot of young locals at the counter, has some nice old high-backed settles as well as brightly cushioned chapel chairs on its broad dark boards, candles on its stripped tables, a big log fire at one end, a woodburning stove at the other (by an unusual cricket table), and cheerful farmyard animal and country prints. There's a piano in one corner, and a snug separate one-table area opposite the servery, which has well kept Hook Norton Hooky on handpump and good wines by the glass; they do mulled wine in winter and an invigorating bloody mary, and have an interesting range of wines by the bottle. As well as the blackboard bar food, you can eat from the full menu in here, but might prefer the relative quiet of the fairly spacious carpeted and raftered two-part dining room, up a few steps. If you stay, the breakfast is good. There is a heated smokers' shelter at the back.

🍴 **As well as bar snacks like warm scotch quail eggs, home-made sausage roll, and snails and mushrooms on toast, the inventive food might include pressed ham hock terrine with cox apple salad, cornish lemon sole and crispy courgette flower salad, burger made from aged beef with home-made ketchup, twice-baked pea and st wulfstan cheese soufflé with pea shoot tempura, devilled lambs liver with home-cured crispy bacon and shallots, turbot with seashore vegetables (samphire and sea purslane) with potato pancake and herb butter, fillet of hereford beef, and puddings like elderflower and raspberry eton mess and hot chocolate fondant with cookie dough ice-cream.** *Starters/Snacks: £6.00 to £9.00. Main Courses: £10.00 to £22.00. Puddings: £6.00*

Free house ~ Licensees Emily Watkins and Miles Lampson ~ Real ale ~ Bar food (all day) ~ Restaurant ~ (01608) 658327 ~ Children welcome ~ Dogs allowed in bar and bedrooms ~ Open 12-10.45(11.30 Sat, 10.15 Sun) ~ Bedrooms: /£85S(£110B)

Recommended by Myra Joyce, Graham Oddey, Richard Greaves, Fred Beckett, A G Marx, J Harvey, Bernard Stradling, Keith and Sue Ward, Guy Vowles, Mr and Mrs W W Burke, Anthony and Pam Stamer

LANGFORD

SP2402 MAP 4

Bell ♀

Village signposted off A361 N of Lechlade, then pub signed; GL7 3LF

Civilised pub with beams, flagstones, a good log fire, well chosen wines and beer, and enjoyable bar food

Consistently enjoyable, this is a popular little dining pub where nothing is too much trouble for the friendly licensees. The simple low-key furnishings and décor add to the appeal here: the main bar has just six sanded and sealed mixed tables on grass matting, a variety of chairs, three nice cushioned window seats, an attractive carved oak settle, polished broad flagstones by a big stone inglenook fireplace with a good log fire, low beams, and butter-coloured walls with two or three antique engravings. A second even smaller room on the right is similar in character; daily papers on a little corner table. Hook Norton Hooky Bitter, Sharps Doom Bar and Timothy Taylors Landlord on handpump, farm cider and several wines by the glass. The bearded collie is called Madison. There are two or three picnic-sets out in the small garden with a play house; aunt sally. This is a quiet and charming village.

🍴 **As well as smashing fish dishes such as seared king scallops with bacon and a basil and balsamic dressing, fillet of smoked haddock with wholegrain mustard and leek mash and a white wine cream sauce, and fillet of hake, crab and leek risotto with lobster sauce, the changing food might include sandwiches, soup, chicken liver pâté with caramelised onion chutney, warm salad of black pudding, pancetta and quail eggs with a sun-dried tomato, fennel and tarragon dressing, pork and apple burger, thai green chicken curry, steak and**

mushroom pie, breast of duck with red cabbage and apple, herby roast potatoes and a red wine jus, and puddings like hot chocolate fondant with coffee ice-cream and crêpe suzette with mandarin and Cointreau ice-cream. *Starters/Snacks: £4.50 to £8.95. Main Courses: £8.95 to £15.95. Puddings: £4.75*

Free house ~ Licensees Paul and Jackie Wynne ~ Real ale ~ Bar food (not Sun evening or Mon) ~ Restaurant ~ (01367) 860249 ~ Children welcome but no under-5s after 7pm ~ Dogs allowed in bar ~ Open 12-3, 7-11(11.30 Sat); 12-3.30 Sun; closed Sun evening, all day Mon

Recommended by Grahame and Myra Williams, KN-R, Guy Charrison, Graham Oddey, George Atkinson, Thomas Holman, Henry Midwinter

---

LEWKNOR
SU7197   MAP 4

Olde Leathern Bottel
Under a mile from M40 junction 6; just off B4009 towards Watlington; OX49 5TH

Unchanging bustling country local with decent food and beer, and seats in sizeable garden

Particularly at weekends, this well run, warmly friendly pub is popular with a wide mix of customers – including horse riders who can tether their horses. The attractive sizeable garden is splendid (and you can forget how close you are to the M40) and there are plenty of picnic-sets under parasols and a children's play area; boules and an outside dartboard, too. Inside, there are heavy beams and low ceilings in the two bar rooms as well as rustic furnishings, open fires and an understated décor of old beer taps and the like; best to arrive early to be sure of a table. The family room is separated only by standing timbers, so you won't feel segregated from the rest of the pub. Brakspears Bitter and Hook Norton Hooky Dark on handpump, and all their wines are available by the glass.

🍴 **Good, honest bar food includes lunchtime sandwiches, soup, chicken liver parfait, barbecue ribs, whitebait with tartare sauce, roasted red pepper and spinach lasagne, ham and free-range eggs, poached smoked haddock with cheese sauce and a poached egg, and puddings.** *Starters/Snacks: £4.95 to £6.95. Main Courses: £6.95 to £15.95. Puddings: £4.50 to £6.95*

Brakspears ~ Tenant L S Gordon ~ Real ale ~ Bar food (12-2(2.30 weekends), 7(6 Fri and Sat)-9.30) ~ (01844) 351482 ~ Children welcome ~ Dogs welcome ~ Open 11-2.30(3.30 Sat), 6-11; 12-3.30, 7-10.30 Sun

Recommended by P Tailyour, Ross Balaam, Tracey and Stephen Groves, Chris Glasson, N R White, Torrens Lyster, David and Lexi Young, Andy and Jill Kassube

---

MURCOTT
SP5815   MAP 4

Nut Tree 🍴 ☆
Off B4027 NE of Oxford; OX5 2RE

Imaginative food (using own produce), good wines and real ales in friendly village pub

Although there's quite an emphasis on the imaginative food in this neatly thatched and pretty pub, the friendly licensees are keen that this remains the heartbeat of the village. And to encourage that, the bar counter is at one end of the main room where there's a comfortable seating area for those just popping in for a chat and a pint. The dining area is split into three areas – the main room, the conservatory and a room behind the bar which is popular for private parties; there are a couple of woodburning stoves. Hook Norton Hooky Bitter and a couple of guests such as Vale Spring Gold and West Berkshire Good Old Boy on handpump and several wines (including champagne) by the glass from a carefully chosen list. There are seats outside in the garden and pretty hanging baskets and tubs; aunt sally. On a wall in front of the pub is an unusual collection of gargoyles, each loosely modelled on local characters. There are ducks on the village pond.

🍴 **Using their own gloucester old spot pigs and growing their own salads and vegetables, the interesting – if not cheap – bar food includes filled baguettes, soup, ploughman's, ballottine of foie gras with rhubarb, diver-caught scallops with fennel salad, lemon curd** and olive dressing, pavé of home-smoked orkney salmon with whipped horseradish cream, risotto of wild mushrooms with white truffle oil, roast chump of lamb with ratatouille, hake fillet with asparagus and lemon broth, confit of pork belly with celeriac purée and apple gravy, and puddings such as hot lime and coconut soufflé with milk chocolate ice-cream and bitter chocolate tart with golden raisin and rum ice-cream; they also offer a two- and three-course set menu (not weekends). *Starters/Snacks: £5.50 to £10.00. Main Courses: £15.00 to £19.00. Puddings: £6.00 to £7.50*

Free house ~ Licensees Mike and Imogen North ~ Real ale ~ Bar food ~ Restaurant ~ (01865) 331253 ~ Children welcome ~ Dogs welcome ~ Open 12-11(10.30 Sun); closed winter Sun evenings

Recommended by Mike Buckingham, George and Beverley Tucker, Peter Sampson, Jenny and Peter Lowater

OXFORD

SP5106 MAP 4

Eagle & Child
St Giles; OX1 3LU

Lots of genuine atmosphere in this bustling town pub, well kept real ales, wide choice of well liked pubby food and a friendly welcome

There's plenty of atmosphere in the two charmingly old-fashioned panelled front rooms here – plus a friendly welcome from the staff and a fine choice of drinks. Brakspears Bitter and Hook Norton Old Hooky and guests such as Caledonian Deuchars IPA and Jennings Cumberland on handpump, 15 wines by the glass and several malt whiskies and ciders; piped music, games machine and board games. There's a stripped-brick back extension with a conservatory. J R R Tolkien and C S Lewis used to meet here for discussions and a pint and there's a memorial plaque, a couple of portraits and a framed paper with their signatures (along with others of their group, the Inklings) saying they had drunk to the landlord's health.

🍴 **Good value bar food includes sandwiches, a cooked breakfast (until noon), soup, little starters you can share like chicken and chorizo skewers, mini nachos with sour cream, guacamole and cheese, mushroom and cheese wedges, and baked baby camembert with real ale chutney, various platters, gammon and eggs, ravioli with ricotta and red peppers, sausage and mash, chicken, veggie or aberdeen angus burger, and puddings like crumble or chocolate pot; they often have special offers.** *Starters/Snacks: £2.95 to £5.75. Main Courses: £6.95 to £9.95. Puddings: £2.65 to £3.65*

Mitchells & Butlers ~ Manager Darren Amena ~ Real ale ~ Bar food (all day) ~ (01865) 302925 ~ Children in back room before 8pm ~ Open 10am-11pm(12.30 Fri and Sat)

Recommended by Phil and Sally Gorton, Chris Glasson, Roger Shipperley, Dennis Jones, Michael Dandy, Michael Sargent, the Didler, Dick and Madeleine Brown

Rose & Crown
North Parade Avenue; very narrow, so best to park in a nearby street; OX2 6LX

Long-serving licensees in this lively friendly local, a good mix of customers, fine choice of drinks and proper home cooking

This traditional and rather straightforward local has been run by the same licensees for over 25 years. Sharp-witted Mr Hall and his wife make all well behaved customers welcome (not children or dogs) and the front door opens into little more than a passage by the bar counter. The panelled back room, with traditional pub furnishings, is slightly bigger, and you'll find reference books for crossword buffs; no mobile phones, piped music or noisy games machines, but they do have board games. Adnams Bitter and Broadside, Hook Norton Old Hooky and Timothy Taylors Landlord on handpump, around 30 malt whiskies and a large choice of wines. The pleasant walled and heated back yard can be completely covered with a huge awning; at the far end is a 12-seater dining/meeting room. The lavatories are pretty basic.

🍴 **Traditional but enjoyable food at honest prices includes a good choice of interesting sandwiches and baguettes, filled baked potatotes, ploughman's, omelettes, sausage or** ham with egg, chips and beans, a hot dish of the day such as gammon, apple and cider pie, beef stew with herb dumplings or chicken breast with a honey glaze, and puddings like apple pie or cheesecake; popular Sunday roast. *Starters/Snacks: £4.95 to £5.95. Main Courses: £5.95 to £11.95. Puddings: £3.95*

Punch ~ Tenants Andrew and Debbie Hall ~ Real ale ~ Bar food (12-2.15(3.15 Sun), 6-9) ~ No credit cards ~ (01865) 510551 ~ Open 10-midnight(1am Sat)

Recommended by Chris Glasson, Jane Taylor, David Dutton, the Didler, Torrens Lyster

Turf Tavern ☕

Tavern Bath Place; via St Helen's Passage, between Holywell Street and New College Lane; OX1 3SU

Interesting pub hidden away behind high walls, with a dozen ales, regular beer festivals, nice food, and knowledgeable staff

---

Hidden behind the high stone walls of some of the city's oldest buildings, this is arguably Oxford's most characterful pub, and there's always a really good mix of customers of all ages. The two dark-beamed and low-ceilinged small bars fill up quickly, though many prefer (whatever the time of year) to sit outside in the three attractive walled-in, flagstoned or gravelled courtyards (one has its own bar); in winter, they have coal braziers so you can roast chestnuts or toast marshmallows and there are canopies with lights and heaters. Up to a dozen real ales on handpump: Greene King IPA, Abbot, Morlands Old Speckled Hen and Ruddles Best, Hop Back Challenger, Salopian Hop Twister, Titanic Captain Smith's Strong Ale and Steerage, Tom Woods Father's Pride, and three from the White Horse Brewery including one named for the pub. Regular beer festivals, Weston's Old Rosie cider and winter mulled wine; bright, knowledgeable service.

🍽 Reasonably priced bar food includes sandwiches, filled baked potatoes, soup, three-bean chilli, chicken caesar salad, sausages and mash, lasagne, a pie and a curry of the day, beer-battered fish, and puddings like chocolate cheesecake and lemon and blueberry burst. *Starters/Snacks: £3.25 to £6.45. Main Courses: £5.45 to £7.95. Puddings: £3.75 to £3.95*

Greene King ~ Manager Chuck Berry ~ Real ale ~ Bar food (12-7.30(6 Sun)) ~ (01865) 243235 ~ Dogs welcome ~ Live music Thurs evening ~ Open 11-11; 12-10.30 Sun

Recommended by Gordon Davico, LM, Michael Dandy, Rob and Catherine Dunster, Tim and Ann Newell, Lawrence Pearse, Andy and Claire Barker, Peter Dandy, Roger Shipperley, the Didler, Martin Grosberg, Ann and Colin Hunt, Alan Thwaite, Philip and June Caunt, Phil and Sally Gorton, Dick and Madeleine Brown, David Heath, Michael Butler

RAMSDEN   SP3515   MAP 4

Royal Oak ♀ ☕

Village signposted off B4022 Witney—Charlbury; OX7 3AU

Chatty, unpretentious pub with friendly licensees, 30 wines by the glass, good food and a heated back terrace

---

This is a friendly and unpretentious village inn where it's easy to while away an hour or so. The basic furnishings are comfortable, with fresh flowers, bookcases with old and new copies of *Country Life* and, when the weather gets cold, a cheerful log fire; no piped music or games machines – just a relaxed and chatty atmosphere. Butts Barbus Barbus, Hook Norton Hooky Bitter, White Horse Village Idiot and Wye Valley Mappa Mundi on handpump, a fine choice of 30 wines by the glass from a carefully chosen list, Weston's Old Rosie cider and several armagnacs. There are tables and chairs out in front and on the heated terrace behind the restaurant (folding back doors give easy access). The bedrooms are in separate cottages.

🍽 Using as much local produce as possible, the popular – if not particularly cheap – bar food includes lunchtime sandwiches, soup, devilled lambs kidneys, moules marinière, home-made burgers with cheese or bacon, a pie of the week, fresh pasta with a wild mushroom truffle sauce, crab and salmon fishcakes with a tomato and sweet pepper sauce, beef curry, half a shoulder of saltmarsh lamb with rosemary and garlic jus, confit

duck in a red berry and quince sauce, daily specials, and puddings. *Starters/Snacks: £3.95 to £5.50. Main Courses: £6.95 to £21.00. Puddings: £5.50*

Free house ~ Licensee Jon Oldham ~ Real ale ~ Bar food (12-2(2.30 Sun), 7-10) ~ Restaurant ~ (01993) 868213 ~ Children in restaurant with parents ~ Dogs allowed in bar ~ Open 11.30-3, 6.30-11; 12-3.30, 7-10.30 Sun ~ Bedrooms: £45S/£65S

Recommended by Simon Cottrell, Tracey and Stephen Groves, Sue Demont, Tim Barrow, Michael Doswell, Nigel Epsley, Mr and Mrs John Taylor, JJW, CMW, Dennis Haward, Howard and Margaret Buchanan, J Crosby, Chris Glasson, Richard Marjoram

SATWELL   SU7083   MAP 2

Lamb

2 miles S of Nettlebed; follow Shepherds Green signpost; RG9 4QZ

16th-c country pub with sizeable gardens, cosy bar and dining room, real ales, wines by the glass and good bar food

On the edge of the Chilterns, this 16th-c pub is under new owners. It was originally two cottages and at its heart is the low-beamed bar with a log fire in the original inglenook fireplace, nice pubby furniture on the floor tiles, lots of old photographs of nearby Henley-on-Thames, and various agricultural and other antique knick-knacks on the walls. Four real ales on handpump: Fullers London Pride, Loddon Hoppit, Marlow Rebellion IPA and a changing guest. There are several wines by the glass, and piped music. The dining room next to the bar is a cosy place for a meal. Outside, there's a large garden with a woodland area, seats on a sizeable lawn, and chickens; boules and summer barbecues. Plenty of surrounding walks.

🍴 **Good bar food includes lunchtime sandwiches, crispy lamb goujons with gribiche sauce, chicken and mushroom pie, spinach and mushroom tart, beer-battered fish, pork and herb sausages with onion gravy, fish pie, chicken kiev, wiener schnitzel with poached egg, and puddings such as lemon tart with mascarpone cream and melting chocolate pudding with cinnamon ice-cream; Sunday roasts.** *Starters/Snacks: £4.95 to £10.95. Main Courses: £8.95 to £14.95. Puddings: £4.95 to £5.95*

Free house ~ Licensees Chris and Emma Smith ~ Real ale ~ Bar food (12-3, 6-9.30; all day Sat; 12-6 Sun) ~ Restaurant ~ (01491) 628482 ~ Children welcome ~ Dogs welcome ~ Open 12-3, 6-11; 12-11 Sat; 12-9 Sun

Recommended by BOB

SHILTON   SP2608   MAP 4

Rose & Crown

Just off B4020 SE of Burford; OX18 4AB

Simple and appealing little village pub, with a relaxed civilised atmosphere, real ales and a fair choice of bar food

Our readers continue to enjoy their visits to this 17th-c stone-built village pub, and it remains as simple and as unspoilt (in a subtly upmarket way) as ever. The small front bar has proper wooden beams and timbers, exposed stone walls, and a log fire in a big fireplace, with half a dozen or so tables on the red tiled floor, and a few locals at the planked counter. This opens into a similar, bigger room used mainly for eating, with flowers on the tables, and another fireplace. Hook Norton Old Hooky and Hooky Dark, and Wells & Youngs Bitter on handpump and several wines by the glass. At the side, an attractive garden has picnic-sets.

🍴 **Using local game and meat, bar food includes lunchtime ciabattas, interesting soups, gravadlax, venison terrine with plum chutney, ham and egg, sausages with onion gravy, aubergine parmigiana baked with mozzarella, steak and mushroom in ale pie, harissa chicken with couscous, sultanas and pine nuts, salmon fillet with spinach and dill sauce, and puddings such as bread and butter pudding and chocolate pear tarte tatin.** *Starters/Snacks: £4.50 to £6.00. Main Courses: £7.50 to £15.50. Puddings: £4.50 to £5.00*

Free house ~ Licensee Martin Coldicott ~ Bar food (12-2.45, 7-9; not winter Sun evening) ~
Restaurant ~ (01993) 842280 ~ Well behaved children welcome ~ Dogs allowed in bar ~
Open 12-3, 6-11; 12-12 Fri and Sat; 12-10 Sun

Recommended by Helene Grygar, Ian and Nita Cooper, J L Wedel, David Lamb

SHIPLAKE   SU7779   MAP 2

Baskerville ♀

Station Road, Lower Shiplake (off A4155 just S of Henley); RG9 3NY

**Emphasis on imaginative food though a proper public bar too; real ales, several wines by
the glass, interesting sporting memorabilia and a pretty garden**

The licensees of this neat brick pub are keen that despite the emphasis on the good
interesting food, it remains a village pub where locals drop in for a pint and a chat.
There are some bar chairs around the light, modern bar counter, a few beams, pale
wooden dining chairs and tables on the light wood floors, plush red banquettes around
the windows, and a brick fireplace with plenty of logs next to it. A fair amount of
sporting memorabilia and pictures, especially old rowing photos (the pub is very close to
Henley) and signed rugby shirts and photographs (the pub runs its own rugby club), plus
some maps of the Thames are hung on the red walls, and there are flowers and large
house plants dotted about. It all feels quite homely, but in a smart way, with some
chintzy touches such as a shelf of china cow jugs. Fullers London Pride, Loddon Hoppit
and Timothy Taylors Landlord on handpump, 30 malt whiskies and eight wines by the
glass. The dining room has been extended this year to include a small room for private
family or business groups. The pretty garden has a proper covered barbecue area and
smart teak furniture under huge parasols.

🍽 **As well as lunchtime sandwiches and wraps, ploughman's, omelettes, herby sausages
and beer-battered haddock, the good, interesting food also includes an antipasti plate,
crispy aromatic lamb and vegetable spring rolls with sweet chilli and soy dip, tagliatelle
with roasted mediterranean vegetables, olives and pesto, beef bourguignon, free-range
pork with stilton mash and baked apple and calvados jus, marinated and chargrilled
swordfish steak with roast pepper couscous and lime and saffron mayonnaise; and
puddings such as raspberry and white chocolate brûlée with vanilla shortbread and sticky
toffee pudding with butterscotch sauce and vanilla ice-cream; they have a seafood night
every Tuesday and a good value winter two-course menu.** *Starters/Snacks: £5.00 to £7.50.
Main Courses: £7.95 to £10.95. Puddings: £5.25 to £6.50*

Free house ~ Licensee Allan Hannah ~ Real ale ~ Bar food (12-2, 7-9.30(10 Fri and Sat);
12-4 Sun; not Sun evening) ~ Restaurant ~ (0118) 940 3332 ~ Children welcome but not in
restaurant after 8pm Fri and Sat ~ Dogs allowed in bar and bedrooms ~ Open 11.30-2.30, 6-11;
12-4, 7-10.30 Sun; closed 26 Dec, 1 Jan ~ Bedrooms: £75S/£85S

*Recommended by Rob Winstanley, Joe Green, Graham and Toni Sanders, MP, G Fry, Michael Dandy, David Heath,
Paul Humphreys*

STANTON ST JOHN   SP5709   MAP 4

Star

*Pub signposted off B4027, in Middle Lane; village is signposted off A40 heading E of Oxford
(heading W, you have to go to the Oxford ring-road roundabout and take the unclassified
road signposted to Stanton St John, Forest Hill, etc); OX33 1EX*

**Nice old village pub with interesting rooms, friendly landlord, Wadworths beers and
generously served bar food**

Especially cosy on a chilly winter evening, this chatty and relaxed old place is
appealingly arranged over two levels. The oldest parts are two characterful little low-
beamed rooms, one with ancient brick flooring tiles and the other with quite close-set
tables. Up some stairs is an attractive extension on a level with the car park with old-
fashioned dining chairs, an interesting mix of dark oak and elm tables, rugs on
flagstones, bookshelves on each side of an attractive inglenook fireplace (a fine fire in

winter), shelves of good pewter, terracotta-coloured walls with a portrait in oils, and a stuffed ermine. Wadworths IPA, 6X and a guest beer on handpump, several wines by the glass, and country wines. There's a family room and conservatory, too; piped music, darts and board games. The walled garden has seats among the flowerbeds, and there's some children's play equipment.

🍴 Bar food includes sandwiches, deep-fried whitebait, steak in ale pie, moussaka, lasagne, spinach and mushroom strudel, battered haddock, red thai chicken curry, lamb in redcurrant and rosemary, daily specials, and puddings such as spotted dick and banoffi pie. *Starters/Snacks: £4.95 to £7.95. Main Courses: £9.95 to £14.75. Puddings: £4.75*

Wadworths ~ Tenant Michael Urwin ~ Real ale ~ Bar food (12-2.3-, 7-9.30) ~ (01865) 351277 ~ Children welcome ~ Dogs welcome ~ Open 12-3, 6.30-11; 12-3, 7-10.30 Sun

Recommended by Brian and Rosalie Laverick, Tracey and Stephen Groves, W N Murphy, Roy Hoing, Peter Sampson, Tina and David Woods-Taylor, M Greening

STEEPLE ASTON   SP4725   MAP 4
Red Lion
Off A4260 12 miles N of Oxford; OX25 4RY

Friendly village pub with beamed bar, nice straightforward food, local beers, and a suntrap terrace

This is a nice little pub in a rambling village, and you can be sure of a friendly welcome from the hard-working licensees. The comfortable partly panelled bar is welcoming and relaxed with beams, an antique settle and other good furnishings. Hook Norton Hooky Bitter and Hooky Gold and a guest beer on handpump, and several wines by the glass; good service. There's a back conservatory-style dining extension, too. The suntrap front terrace has lovely flowers and shrubs.

🍴 As well as lunchtime sandwiches and ploughman's, the well liked bar food includes soup, chicken and pork pâté with red onion chutney, scallops with black pudding and smoked bacon, beefburger with cheese and bacon, chicken caesar salad, local pork sausages with onion gravy, chicken, ham and leek pie, king prawns and mussels with pasta in a tomato and chilli sauce, and rack of lamb with rosemary and red wine; Sunday roasts and a good value two-course weekday menu. *Starters/Snacks: £4.00 to £7.50. Main Courses: £6.50 to £15.00. Puddings: £3.45 to £3.95*

Hook Norton ~ Tenants Melvin and Sarah Phipps ~ Real ale ~ Bar food (12-2.30, 6-9; 12-4 Sun (not Sun evening)) ~ Restaurant ~ (01869) 340225 ~ Well behaved children welcome ~ Dogs allowed in bar ~ Open 12-3, 5.30-11; 12-11(5 Sun) Sat; closed Sun evening
Recommended by Gill and Keith Croxton, Dr S J Shepherd, Chris Bell, George and Beverley Tucker, Dale Mason

SWERFORD   SP3830   MAP 4
Masons Arms 🍴 ♀
A361 Banbury—Chipping Norton; OX7 4AP

Attractive dining pub with modern cooking by chef/landlord, airy dining extension, civilised and relaxed atmosphere, country views from outside tables

There's no doubt that most customers come to this attractive dining pub to enjoy the interesting food cooked by the chef/patron. But the atmosphere is friendly and relaxed which prevents it becoming an out-and-out restaurant. The dining extension is light and airy and the bar has pale wooden floors with rugs, a carefully illuminated stone fireplace, thoughtful spotlighting, and beige and red armchairs around big round tables in light wood. Doors open on to a small terrace with a couple of stylish tables, while steps lead down into a cream-painted room with chunky tables and contemporary pictures. Round the other side of the bar is another roomy dining room with great views by day, candles at night, and a civilised feel. Hook Norton Best and a guest beer on handpump, a dozen wines by the glass and ten malt whiskies. Behind is a neat square lawn with picnic-sets and views over the Oxfordshire countryside.

🍴 Good, interesting food at lunchtime includes sandwiches, nachos with tomato salsa, guacamole and sour cream, ploughman's, home-baked ham and free-range eggs, chicken caesar salad, vegetarian pasta of the day and chicken korma; in the evening (when they also offer two- and three-course choices), there might be crab with lemon grass, coconut and ginger, roasted william pear with blue cheese, walnuts, balsamic onions and cress, aubergine, mushroom and ricotta bake, fillets of mackerel with lentils, chicory and gooseberry relish, chicken suprême with sage and parma ham, roasted courgettes and balsamic and red wine dressing, and lamb tagine with apricots, figs and chickpeas. Also, daily specials, puddings like dark chocolate profiteroles with white chocolate sauce and tiramisu with almond biscuit; also Sunday roasts. *Starters/Snacks: £5.65 to £7.50. Main Courses: £6.50 to £10.95. Puddings: £5.50*

Free house ~ Licensee Bill Leadbeater ~ Real ale ~ Bar food (12-2, 7-9; 12-4 Sun; not Sun evening) ~ Restaurant ~ (01608) 683212 ~ Children welcome ~ Open 10-3, 6-11; 12-6 Sun; closed Sun evening; 25 and 26 Dec

Recommended by Helene Grygar, K H Frostick, P Brown, Phil and Jane Hodson, E A and D C T Frewer, Martin and Pauline Jennings, Sir Nigel Foulkes, Michael Dandy, Paul and Suzanne Martin, Carole Hall

SWINBROOK

SP2812 MAP 4

Swan 🍴 ♀ 🛏

Back road a mile N of A40, 2 miles E of Burford; OX18 4DY

Civilised 17th-c pub with handsome oak garden room, nice, smart bars, local beers and contemporary food; new bedrooms

Six charming bedrooms have now been opened in a smartly converted stone barn beside this civilised 17th-c pub. This is an interesting place, owned by the Duchess of Devonshire – the last of the Mitford sisters who grew up in the village – and there are lots of old Mitford family photographs blown up on the walls. There's a little bar with simple antique furnishings, settles and benches, an open fire, and (in an alcove) a stuffed swan; locals do still drop in here for a pint and a chat. The small dining room to the right of the entrance opens into this room, and there's a green oak garden room with high-backed beige and green dining chairs around pale wood tables and views over the garden and orchard. Hook Norton Hooky Bitter, Sharps Doom Bar and Wadworths 6X on handpump, several wines by the glass, Weston's organic cider, a proper bloody mary and local apple juice; piped music. This is a lovely spot by a bridge over the River Windrush and seats by the fuchsia hedge make the best of the view.

🍴 Good modern bar food includes lunchtime sandwiches, soup, warm smoked duck breast with crispy pancetta, sweet and sour onion salad and walnut dressing, a charcuterie plate, battered fish and chips with minted peas, crispy belly of gloucestershire old spot pork with fennel, amalfi lemon and baby capers, fish and shellfish cassoulet with haricot beans and a cheddar herb crust, fillet of bass with crayfish salsa, chargrilled steak with tarragon sauce, and puddings like hot dark chocolate brownie with chocolate ice-cream and custard and strawberry shortbread with lime crème fraîche and basil syrup. *Starters/Snacks: £5.00 to £8.00. Main Courses: £9.00 to £14.00. Puddings: £5.00 to £7.00*

Free house ~ Licensees Archie and Nicola Orr-Ewing ~ Real ale ~ Bar food (12-2(3 Sun), 7-9(9.30 weekends)) ~ (01993) 823339 ~ Children welcome ~ Dogs welcome ~ Live music monthly Sun ~ Open 11-3, 6-11.30; 11(12 Sun)-11.30 Sat ~ Bedrooms: £60B/£100B

Recommended by Guy Vowles, Gill and Keith Croxton, Mrs Margaret Weir, J L Wedel, Derek Thomas, Graham Oddey, Mr and Mrs John Taylor, Dennis Haward, Anthony and Pam Stamer, Susan and John Douglas, Di and Mike Gillam, David Glynne-Jones, Richard Greaves, Ann and Colin Hunt, Keith and Sue Ward, Andy and Claire Barker, Henry Midwinter, Richard Marjoram

---

Bedroom prices normally include full english breakfast, VAT and any inclusive service charge that we know of. Prices before the '/' are for single rooms, after for two people in a double or twin (B includes a private bath, S a private shower). If there is no '/', the prices are only for twin or double rooms (as far as we know there are no singles). If there is no B or S, as far as we know no rooms have private facilities.

TADPOLE BRIDGE

SP3200   MAP 4

Trout ♀ 🛏

Back road Bampton—Buckland, 4 miles NE of Faringdon; SN7 8RF

Busy country inn with River Thames moorings, fine choice of drinks, popular modern food, and a lovely summer garden; bedrooms

In a peaceful spot by the Thames, this is a civilised and comfortable pub. The L-shaped bar has attractive pink and cream checked chairs around a mix of nice wooden tables, some rugs on the flagstones, a modern wooden bar counter with terracotta paintwork behind, fresh flowers, a woodburning stove, and a large stuffed trout. The airy restaurant is appealingly candlelit in the evenings. Ramsbury Bitter, Wells & Youngs Bitter and guests like Fullers London Pride and White Horse Village Idiot on handpump, a dozen wines by the glass from a wide-ranging and carefully chosen list, some fine sherries and several malt whiskies. There are good quality teak chairs and tables under blue parasols in the lovely garden and six moorings for visiting boats; you can also hire punts with champagne hampers.

🍽 **As well as lunchtime filled baguettes (not Sunday), the popular bar food includes salad of smoked eel, Noilly Prat jelly, shallot purée and lemon vinaigrette, port-marinated pigeon breast with pear and cranberry chutney, slow-roasted belly of pork with pearl barley and clams, free-range chicken breast with chorizo and tomato salsa, saddle of rabbit with beetroot purée and lardons with cabbage, and daily specials like mussels with tomato and basil sauce, blue brie and sunblush tomato strudel with creamed leeks, steamed beef and ale pudding, and crayfish risotto.** *Starters/Snacks: £4.95 to £8.25. Main Courses: £10.50 to £19.95. Puddings: £5.95 to £6.95*

Free house ~ Licensees Gareth and Helen Pugh ~ Real ale ~ Bar food (not winter Sun evening) ~ Restaurant ~ (01367) 870382 ~ Children welcome ~ Dogs welcome ~ Open 11.30-3, 6-11; 12-3.30, 6.30-10.30 Sun; closed winter Sun evening; 25-26 Dec ~ Bedrooms: £75B/£110B

Recommended by Jenny Clarke, Andy and Claire Barker, Sally Anne and Peter Goodale, Jim and Nancy Forbes, Mary Rayner, J Crosby, William Goodhart, Julia and Richard Tredgett, Fred Beckett, Bob and Margaret Holder, Terry Miller, Graham Oddey, Henry Midwinter, Paul Humphreys

WEST HANNEY

SU4092   MAP 2

Plough

Just off A338 N of Wantage; Church Street; OX12 0LN

Thatched village pub with good choice of drinks, decent food and plenty of seats outside

This pretty and neatly thatched village pub has a loyal local following, and often quite a family atmosphere. The comfortable simply furnished bar has horsebrasses on beams, some bar stools and large beer barrels by the wooden bar counter, wheelback chairs around wooden tables, a log fire in the stone fireplace, and lots of photographs of the pub on the walls. Three pub cats and some house plants add to the friendly, informal feel. Brakspears Bitter, Ferrymans Gold, Timothy Taylors Landlord and Titanic Iceberg on handpump, several wines by the glass and six ciders. There are seats and tables on the back terrace and plenty of picnic-sets on the grass; aunt sally. Good walks start with a village path right by the pub.

🍽 **Well liked bar food includes sandwiches, chicken caesar salad, toad in the hole, broccoli and cream cheese bake, aberdeen angus burgers with different toppings, scampi, chicken tikka masala, lamb shank in red wine and rosemary, and steaks topped with herb butter or pepper sauce.** *Starters/Snacks: £3.50 to £5.95. Main Courses: £6.50 to £12.95. Puddings: £4.50*

Punch ~ Licensee Trevor Cooper ~ Real ale ~ Bar food (12-2(3 Sun), 6-9) ~ Restaurant ~ (01235) 868674 ~ Children welcome ~ Dogs welcome ~ Open 12-3, 6-11; 12-11 Sat and Sun

Recommended by David Lamb, D R Williams, Alan and Carolin Tidbury

---

If we know a pub does summer barbecues, we say so.

WOODSTOCK

SP4416   MAP 4

Kings Arms 🛏

Market Street/Park Lane (A44); OX20 1SU

Stylish hotel in centre of attractive town, good creative food, enjoyable atmosphere and a fine choice of drinks; comfortable bedrooms

Our readers really enjoy their visits to this stylish town-centre hotel and feel it's just the place for a drink, a meal or even afternoon tea. It's got an informal, relaxed atmosphere and the neat, uniformed staff are genuinely welcoming and helpful. The simple and unfussy bar has a good mix of customers, brown leather furnishings on the stripped wooden floor, smart blinds and black and white photos throughout, and at the front an old wooden settle and interesting little woodburner. There's a marble bar counter, and, in the room leading to the brasserie-style dining room, an unusual stained-glass structure used for newspapers and magazines. The restaurant is attractive, with its hanging lights and fine old fireplace. Marstons Pedigree and Theakstons Best on handpump, good coffees, freshly squeezed orange juice, ten wines by the glass and 20 malt whiskies; piped music. Comfortable bedrooms and good breakfasts (available from 7.30-noon for non-residents too). There are a couple of tables on the street outside.

🍴 As well as filled rolls, the lunchtime menu includes soup, ham hock and rabbit terrine with spiced rhubarb compote, baked nut loaf with chestnut mushroom and braised celery cream sauce, honey roast ham with a free-range egg, kedgeree with a soft boiled egg and chive oil, and cumberland sausage with roast parsnip mash and shallot and ale gravy; also inventive evening choices such as scallops in a crab and tomato cream sauce with crispy potato cake, slow-roast shoulder of pork with pear and cracked black pepper and elderflower dressing, calves liver with watercress and thyme sauce, and lemon sole with crayfish mousse, white wine sauce and olive potato cake. Puddings like chocolate quartet (four different puddings on one plate) and poached apple and vanilla brûlée with stem ginger ice-cream. *Starters/Snacks: £4.75 to £8.50. Main Courses: £8.75 to £19.75. Puddings: £5.50 to £7.75*

Free house ~ Licensees David and Sara Sykes ~ Real ale ~ Bar food (all day Sun) ~ Restaurant ~ (01993) 813636 ~ Children welcome in bar and restaurant but no under-12s in bedrooms ~ Dogs allowed in bar ~ Open 11-11 ~ Bedrooms: £75S/£140S

Recommended by Rob and Catherine Dunster, Mr and Mrs John Taylor, Paul Goldman, Michael and Maggie Betton

LUCKY DIP

Besides the fully inspected pubs, you might like to try these Lucky Dips recommended to us and described by readers (if you do, please send us reports: feedback@goodguides.com).

ADDERBURY [SP4735]
Bell OX17 3LS [High St; just off A4260, turn opp Red Lion]: Unpretentious ancient beamed village local with nice relaxed atmosphere, good generous fresh food, very well kept Hook Norton ales and a guest; homely front room with sofas by huge log fire, lounge area, smaller back music room with piano, old settles and folk nights (1st and 3rd Mon of month), morris dancers; children and dogs welcome, disabled access, back terrace with decking and aunt sally, two bedrooms *(BB, Andy and Jill Kassube, Giles and Annie Francis)*
APPLETON [SP4401]
Plough OX13 5JR [Eaton Rd]: Greene King pub cosily refurbished under new welcoming chatty landlord, good sensibly priced home-made food, six real ales; no dogs; children welcome, big back garden with play things, cl Weds lunchtime *(Helene Grygar)*

ARDINGTON [SU4388]
☆ *Boars Head* OX12 8QA [signed off A417 Didcot—Wantage]: Enjoyable restauranty food at one end of civilised low-beamed pub with attractively simple country décor; good wines, real ales, locals' end with traditional games, warmly welcoming licensees; TV, piped music; children welcome, cl Sun evening, peaceful attractive village *(Rob and Chris Warner, LYM)*
ASCOTT UNDER WYCHWOOD [SP2918]
☆ *Swan* OX7 6AY [Shipton Rd]: Fresh contemporary refurbishment, with good reasonably priced food from ciabattas to more adventurous things in bar and restaurant; Brakspears, Hook Norton and Wadworths 6X, friendly helpful staff, beams and some stripped stone, woodburner; disabled access, terrace tables, good bedrooms *(Caroline and Michael Abbey, Helene Grygar, Miss Sue Callard, J C Burgis, Richard Greaves)*

ASTHALL [SP2811]

Maytime OX18 4HW [off A40 at W end of Witney bypass, then 1st left]: Comfortably refurbished dining pub with good reasonably priced food from sandwiches and snacks up (just set lunch Sun), welcoming helpful service, good wine range inc champagne by the glass, Timothy Taylors Landlord and a guest ale, real cider; flagstones and log fire, Beryl Cook prints, slightly raised neat dining lounge, airy conservatory restaurant; piped music in bar; children and dogs welcome, nice views of Asthall Manor and watermeadows from garden, attractive walks; six quiet redone bedrooms around pretty courtyard garden, good breakfast *(BB, Mrs Margaret Weir, Martin and Pauline Jennings, Theocsbrian)*

BECKLEY [SP5611]

☆ *Abingdon Arms* OX3 9UU [signed off B4027; High St]: Welcoming old pub in unspoilt village, comfortably modernised simple lounge, smaller public bar with antique carved settles and board games, open fires; well kept Brakspears, fair range of wines, enjoyable food from reasonably priced snacks up; children welcome, big garden dropping away from floodlit terrace to trees, summer house, superb views over RSPB Otmoor reserve – good walks *(Peter and Anne Hollindale, George and Beverley Tucker, Martin and Pauline Jennings, Peter and Audrey Dowsett, LYM, Colin McKerrow)*

BINFIELD HEATH [SU7479]

☆ *Bottle & Glass* RG9 4JT [off A4155 at Shiplake; between village and Harpsden]: Chocolate-box, thatched, black and white timbered Tudor cottage, with emphasis on good value interesting food from sandwiches up; bleached pine tables, low beams and flagstones, fine fireplace, black squared panelling, pastel shades; Brakspears and Wychwood, good choice of wines by the glass, friendly service, shove-ha'penny, dominoes; no children or dogs inside; lovely big garden with tables under little thatched roofs *(Susan and John Douglas, LYM, the Didler)*

BRIGHTWELL [SU5890]

Red Lion OX10 0RT [signed off A4130 2 miles W of Wallingford]: Locally popular for its well kept changing ales; friendly new management, good value unpretentious food, snug seating by log fire, two-part bar with games in simple public end, unobtrusive dining extension; dogs welcome, tables outside, peaceful village *(Stephen Rudge)*

BRIGHTWELL BALDWIN [SU6594]

☆ *Lord Nelson* OX49 5NP [off B480 Chalgrove—Watlington, or B4009 Benson—Watlington]: Civilised popular dining pub with wide range of good if not cheap food especially game (two-course set lunch is good value); stylish décor, dining chairs around big candlelit tables, efficient welcoming staff, well kept ales inc Black Sheep, decent house wines; good log fires, snug armchair area, plenty of Nelson memorabilia; children and dogs welcome, front verandah, charming back garden *(Roy Hoing, Peter and Giff Bennett, LYM, Hunter and Christine Wright, Torrens Lyster)*

BUCKLAND [SU3497]

Lamb SN7 8QN [off A420 NE of Faringdon]: Smart 18th-c stone-built dining pub with popular food (not Mon) from lunchtime special deals to grander and more expensive evening menus; Hook Norton Best, good choice of wines by the glass, lamb motif everywhere, formal restaurant; piped music; children welcome, pleasant tree-shaded garden, good walks nearby, comfortable bedrooms, cl Sun evening and over Christmas, New Year *(the Didler, Mr and Mrs John Taylor, Henry Midwinter, Helene Grygar, Tony Winckworth, LYM)*

BUCKNELL [SP5525]

☆ *Trigger Pond* OX27 7NE [handy for M40 junction 10; Bicester Rd]: Neatly kept and welcoming stone-built pub opp the pond; wide choice of good sensibly priced food from baguettes up (must book Sun lunch), helpful staff and friendly obliging young licensee, full Wadworths beer range, good value wines, restaurant; colourful terrace and garden *(Bruce Braithwaite, David Lamb, Guy Vowles)*

BURCOT [SU5695]

Chequers OX14 3DP [A415 Dorchester—Abingdon]: Friendly thatched dining pub with newish chef/landlord doing enjoyable food using good local supplies from lunchtime sandwiches and other pubby dishes up; real ales such as Adnams, Hook Norton and Ridgeway, good wine range, leather sofas around big log fire, neat contemporary black and white décor; children welcome, wheelchair access, floodlit terrace and lawn with flowers and fruit trees *(Roy Hoing, LYM)*

BURFORD [SP2512]

☆ *Angel* OX18 4SN [Witney St]: Long heavy-beamed dining pub in attractive ancient building, warmly welcoming with good reasonably priced brasserie food, good range of drinks; big secluded garden, three comfortable bedrooms *(KN-R, David Glynne-Jones, LYM)*

Bay Tree OX18 4LW [Sheep St]: Attractive old village inn with smart yet informal and comfortable beamed bar, big log fires, cosy armchairs and leaded lights in small front room, second room with tartan seating, polished boards and sets of antlers; Brakspears, good choice of bar food from sandwiches up, friendly helpful staff, more formal restaurant; charming small walled terraced garden, bedrooms *(Michael Dandy)*

Cotswold Arms OX18 4QF [High St]: Enjoyable good value pubby food from sandwiches to steaks, in cosy bar and larger back dining area; good selection of real ales, welcoming staff, beautiful stonework, two flame-effect stoves; children welcome, tables out in front and in back garden *(Michael Dandy, Jason Reynolds)*

Cotswold Gateway OX18 4HX [The Hill]: Hook Norton and Wadworths 6X in hotel's welcoming and relaxed traditional bar with good locally sourced bar food, friendly efficient staff, more formal restaurant; comfortable bedrooms (Keith and Sue Ward)

Golden Pheasant OX18 4QA [High St]: Small early 18th-c hotel's flagstoned split-level bar, civilised yet relaxed and pubby, settees, armchairs, well spaced tables and a woodburner; enjoyable food from sandwiches to steaks, well kept Greene King ales, good house wines, back dining room down steps; children welcome, pleasant back terrace, open all day (Michael Dandy, Peter Dandy, Michael Butler, David Spurgeon, BB)

☆ **Royal Oak** OX18 4SN [Witney St]: Relaxed, homely, 17th-c stripped-stone local, an oasis in this smart village, long-serving friendly landlord, Wadworths ales and an occasional guest from central servery, sensible choice of generous good value food using local produce from filled rolls up, good service; over a thousand beer mugs, steins and jugs hanging from beams, antlers over big log fire (underfloor heating too), light wood tables, chairs and benches on flagstones, more in carpeted back room with bar billiards; well behaved children and dogs welcome, terrace tables, sensibly priced bedrooms by garden behind, good breakfast, open all day Sat, cl Tues lunchtime (Pete Baker, Michael Dandy, Mr and Mrs C Prentis, Mrs S Sturgis)

CHADLINGTON [SP3222]

☆ **Tite** OX7 3NY [off A361 S of Chipping Norton; Mill End]: Friendly 17th-c country pub with inviting choice of reasonably priced good food, well kept beers; big log fire in huge fireplace, settles, wooden chairs, prints, rack of guide books, daily papers, small vine-covered back restaurant; dogs welcome, big terrace and attractive shrub-filled garden with stream (runs under pub), good walks nearby (Helene Grygar, BB, Chris Glasson, Martin and Pauline Jennings)

CHALGROVE [SU6397]

☆ **Red Lion** OX44 7SS [High St (B480 Watlington—Stadhampton)]: Friendly new licensees doing good interesting home-made food in attractive and nicely placed beamed village pub; owned by local church trust since 1640 and kept spotless (LYM, Judith Curthoys)

CHESTERTON [SP5521]

Red Cow OX26 1UU [The Green]: Comfortably updated traditional stone local with a nice welcome, beams, brasses, old photographs, two log fires; enjoyable simple food from baguettes to good value hot dishes, well kept Greene King ales, decent wines, good coffee, small dining area; dogs welcome, picnic-sets out under parasols (Chris Glasson)

CHIPPING NORTON [SP3127]

Fox OX7 5DD [Market Pl]: Well placed unpretentious pub with lots of pictures and open fire in the quiet lounge, well kept Hook Norton, good coffee, simple inexpensive bar

food, welcoming landlord; upstairs dining room; children and dogs welcome, good value bedrooms (Chris Glasson, LYM)

CHISLEHAMPTON [SU5998]

☆ **Coach & Horses** OX44 7UX [B480 Oxford—Watlington, opp B4015 to Abingdon]: Extended former 16th-c coaching inn with two beamed bars, homely and civilised, and sizeable restaurant (polished oak tables and wall banquettes); good value well prepared food from baguettes and good ploughman's to game specials, friendly attentive service, well kept Fullers London Pride and Hook Norton, big log fire; piped music; neat terraced gardens overlooking fields by River Thame, some tables out in front, good bedrooms in back courtyard block (Anne and Jeff Peel, Roy Hoing, BB)

CHRISTMAS COMMON [SU7193]

Fox & Hounds OX49 5HL [off B480/B481]: Upmarket Chilterns pub in lovely countryside, with emphasis on airy and spacious front barn restaurant and conservatory with interesting food from open kitchen; Brakspears and Hook Norton, proper coffee; two compact beamed rooms simply but comfortably furnished, bow windows, red and black tiles and a big inglenook, snug little back room; children and dogs welcome (there's a friendly pub dog), rustic benches and tables outside, open all day wknds (the Didler, Susan and John Douglas, LYM, Fred and Kate Portnell)

CHURCH HANBOROUGH [SP4212]

Hand & Shears OX29 8AB [opp church; signed off A4095 at Long Hanborough, or off A40 at Eynsham roundabout]: Open-feeling bistro-style pub with enjoyable fresh food, Wells & Youngs ales, long gleaming bar, open fires; steps down into roomy back dining extension (E A and D C T Frewer, Edward Leetham, BB)

CLIFTON [SP4931]

☆ **Duke of Cumberlands Head** OX15 0PE [B4031 Deddington—Aynho]: Warmly welcoming thatch and stone pub with big low-beamed lounge, good log fire in vast fireplace and simple furnishings; well kept Hook Norton and guest beers, good wine and whisky choice, friendly service, food from good reasonably priced bar snacks up, cosy stripped-stone dining room; live music (classical/jazz) Sat night; children and dogs welcome, garden with barbecue, ten minutes' walk from canal, six bedrooms (Chris Glasson, Mandy and Simon King, Roy Hoing, Mr and Mrs A Woolstone, Sir Nigel Foulkes, LYM, Stephen Moss, Andy and Jill Kassube, JJW, CMW, K H Frostick)

COLESHILL [SU2393]

☆ **Radnor Arms** SN6 7PR [B4019 Faringdon—Highworth; village signposted off A417 in Faringdon and A361 in Highworth]: Pub and village owned by NT, bar with cushioned settles, plush carver chairs and woodburner, back alcove with more tables, steps down to main dining area, once a blacksmith's forge with lofty beamed ceiling, log fire, dozens of tools and smith's gear on walls; Brakspears and Loddon Hoppit tapped from cask, summer home-made lemonade, relaxed atmosphere, quite a choice of bar food; children and dogs welcome, cl Sun evening, Mon *(Tony and Tracy Constance, Evelyn and Derek Walter, Helene Grygar, Graham Oddey, Edward Mirzoeff, Andy and Claire Barker, LYM)*

CRAYS POND [SU6380]

☆ *White Lion* RG8 7SH [Goring Rd (B471 nr junction with B4526, about 3 miles E of Goring)]: Low-ceilinged pub with good food from bar lunches to full meals, friendly efficient service, well kept beer, good wine choice; nice relaxed atmosphere with proper front bar, open fire, attractive conservatory; big garden with play area, lovely countryside *(I H G Busby, I A Herdman)*

CROPREDY [SP4646]

Brasenose OX17 1PW [Station Rd]: Welcoming family-run village inn nr Oxford Canal, good choice of enjoyable pub food at pine tables in attractive dining room, well kept Adnams and Hook Norton beers, long bar with woodburner; comfortable bedrooms, decent breakfast, self-service laundry useful for boaters, has been open all day Fri-Sun *(BB, John Buckeridge)*

Red Lion OX17 1PB [off A423 N of Banbury]: Popular, rambling, old thatched stone-built pub charmingly placed opp pretty village's churchyard; welcoming helpful landlady, enjoyable good value food from sandwiches to steaks, on a hot stone and Sun lunch, several changing ales; low beams, inglenook log fire, high-backed settles, brass, plates and pictures, unusual dining room mural, games room; piped music, limited parking; children allowed in dining part, picnic-sets under cocktail parasols on back terrace *(Chris Bell, Dennis Haward, LYM, Charles and Pauline Stride)*

CROWELL [SU7499]

Shepherds Crook OX39 4RR [B4009, 2 miles from M40 junction 6]: Traditional local under new ownership but little changed; unpretentious beamed bar with stripped brick and flagstones, open fire, high-raftered dining area, enjoyable food with emphasis on fish (particularly good value Weds evening), interesting well kept real ales, board games; children and dogs welcome, tables out on the green, decent walks *(Torrens Lyster, Tracey and Stephen Groves, LYM)*

CUMNOR [SP4503]

☆ *Bear & Ragged Staff* OX2 9QH [signed from A420; Appleton Rd]: Extensive restaurant/pub dating from 16th c, clean contemporary décor in linked rooms with wood floors, leather-backed dining chairs and mix of tables, enjoyable food with emphasis on local and organic ingredients from charcuterie and meze plates to pub standards and more upmarket dishes inc game; flagstoned bar with log fire, changing beers and good wine choice, leather sofas and armchairs in airy garden room; children

welcome, decked terrace, fenced play area, open all day *(LYM, Bruce and Sharon Eden)*

DEDDINGTON [SP4631]

☆ *Crown & Tuns* OX15 0SP [New St]: Bistro-style conversion of 16th-c coaching inn, speciality home-made pies in big earthenware dishes and other good food inc Sun roast, helpful friendly service, well kept Hook Norton and Ringwood ales, log fires; well behaved children welcome, walled garden, open all day Sun, cl Mon lunchtime *(Andy and Jill Kassube, Richard Hodges, Mr and Mrs A Woolstone)*

☆ *Deddington Arms* OX15 0SH [off A4260 (B4031) Banbury—Oxford; Horse Fair]: Beamed and timbered hotel with emphasis on sizeable contemporary back dining room with tiled floor; comfortable bar with mullioned windows and log fire, good bar food, ales such as Adnams, Black Sheep and Greene King, good choice of wines by the glass, attentive friendly service; unobtrusive piped music; attractive village with lots of antiques shops and good farmers' market 4th Sat of the month, nice walks; comfortable chalet bedrooms around courtyard, good breakfast, open all day *(R C Vincent, LYM, Michael Dandy, George Atkinson, Paul Humphreys, Les and Sandra Brown)*

☆ *Unicorn* OX15 0SE [Market Pl]: Cheerful 17th-c inn run by helpful mother and daughter, good sensibly priced generous food (not Sun evening) inc plenty of fish in L-shaped bar and beamed dining areas off; Hook Norton and Wells & Youngs, good choice of wines by the glass, proper coffee, daily papers, inglenook fireplace, pub games; piped music; dogs welcome in bar, cobbled courtyard leading to long walled back garden, open all day (from 9am for good 4th Sat of the month farmers' market); good bedrooms and breakfast *(Paul Wilson, BB, Michael Dandy, George Atkinson, Andy and Jill Kassube)*

DENCHWORTH [SU3891]

Fox OX12 0DX [off A338 or A417 N of Wantage; Hyde Rd]: Picturesque thatched village pub with good choice of reasonably priced food inc good Sun carvery, friendly efficient staff, Greene King ales, good house wines; two good log fires and plush seats in low-ceilinged connecting areas, old prints and paintings, airy dining extension; children welcome, tables in pleasant sheltered garden, peaceful village *(Dick and Madeleine Brown, David Lamb, BB)*

DORCHESTER [SU5794]

Fleur de Lys OX10 7HH [High St]: New licensees at this former 16th-c coaching inn opp abbey; traditional two-level interior, good creative cooking from enthusiastic chef/landlord, efficient service, Greene King ales, interesting old photographs of pub; parking can be tricky – public car park nearby; children welcome, picnic-sets on front terrace and in back garden *(Philip Kingsbury, David Lamb, Torrens Lyster)*

FIFIELD [SP2318]

Merrymouth OX7 6HR [A424 Burford—Stow]: Simple but comfortable 13th-c inn, L-shaped bar, bay-window seats, flagstones, low beams, some walls stripped back to old masonry, warm stove, quite dark in some areas; Hook Norton Old Hooky and West Berkshire Good Old Boy, large helpings of quickly served food, friendly informal staff; piped music; children and dogs welcome, tables on terrace and in back garden, nine stable-block bedrooms (*Chris and Jeanne Downing, LYM, Neil and Anita Christopher, Stuart Turner, Gavin, Canon Michael Bourdeaux*)

FILKINS [SP2304]

Five Alls GL7 3JQ [signed off A361 Lechlade—Burford]: Big 18th-c Cotswold-stone pub much improved under new landlord, good sensibly priced home-made food, good service, well kept Brakspears; beams, flagstones, stripped stone and a log fire, sofas, armchairs and rugs on polished boards, good-sized eating areas; quiz night 2nd Sun of the month, piped music, TV; well behaved, children and dogs welcome, tables on front and back terraces, neat lawns, five refurbished bedrooms, nice village, cl Mon lunch, open all day wknds (*BB, Graham Oddey, Mr and Mrs O P Davies, Peter and Marion Gray*)

FINSTOCK [SP3616]

Crown OX7 3DJ [School Rd]: Welcoming old-fashioned family pub with bar and dining area, three real ales, reasonably priced enjoyable food, traditional games inc aunt sally (*Keith Puddefoot*)

FOREST HILL [SP5807]

White Horse OX33 1EH [Wheatley Rd (B4027)]: Small friendly beamed village pub with good thai food (must book evenings), central log fire in restaurant; handy for Oxfordshire Way (*BB, Tim Venn*)

FRINGFORD [SP6028]

Butchers Arms OX27 8EB [off A421 N of Bicester; Main St]: Welcoming partly thatched Victorian local in Flora Thompson's 'Candleford' village; wide choice of pubby food from sandwiches and ciabattas up, Adnams Broadside, Caledonian Deuchars IPA and Marstons Pedigree, nice fires, darts in L-shaped bar, separate smaller dining room; piped music, TV; dogs welcome, tables out under parasols facing cricket green (*JJW, CMW, Conor McGaughey, Iain Helstrip, Guy Vowles*)

FULBROOK [SP2512]

Carpenters Arms OX18 4BH [Fulbrook Hill]: 17th-c Cotswold-stone pub under new management – reports please; daily changing menu inc some quite pricey upscale dishes, Greene King Abbot from long bar serving beamed rooms with neat country furnishings; good-sized dining room and conservatory; children welcome, disabled access and facilities, attractive terrace tables in garden behind, play area, cl Sun evening and Mon (*anon*)

Masons Arms OX18 4BU [Shipton Rd]: Spotless village pub, very friendly, with enjoyable fresh food cooked by landlady, well kept real ale; nice log fire open to both rooms off bar, stripped stone and tiled floor, lots of plants, pleasant window seats, small dining room; children and dogs welcome, open wknds only (*Caroline and Michael Abbey*)

GALLOWSTREE COMMON [SU7081]

☆ *Greyhound* RG9 5HT [off B481 at N end of Sonning Common; Gallowstree Rd]: This attractive restauranty country pub, a Main Entry last year under Antony Worrall Thompson, was closed as we went to press – news please (*LYM*)

GODSTOW [SP4809]

☆ *Trout* OX2 8PN [off A40/A44 roundabout via Wolvercote]: Pretty medieval pub in lovely riverside location (gets packed in fine weather); an M&B dining pub with often very good bistro-style food all day, four beamed linked rooms with contemporary furnishings, flagstones and bare boards, log fires in three huge hearths, Adnams and Timothy Taylors Landlord, several wines by the glass, friendly young staff; piped music; children welcome till 7pm, plenty of terrace seats under big parasols (dogs allowed here), footbridge to island (may be cl), abbey ruins opposite; open all day (*LYM, Peter Sampson, Glenn and Evette Booth, John and Elisabeth Cox, Martin and Pauline Jennings, Michael and Maggie Betton, Susan and John Douglas, Mrs M E Mills, John Silverman, Mrs P Lang, Geoff and Teresa Salt, Phil and Jane Hodson, Dr and Mrs Michael Smith*)

GORING [SU5980]

☆ *Catherine Wheel* RG8 9HB [Station Rd]: Smart and well run with nice informal atmosphere in two neat and cosily traditional bar areas, especially the more individual lower room with its low beams and big inglenook log fireplace; enjoyable home-made food inc game and some unusual choices, Brakspears, Hook Norton and Wychwood ales, Stowford Press cider, good value wine, good coffee; back restaurant (children welcome here), notable doors to lavatories; nice courtyard and garden behind, handy for Thames Path, attractive village, open all day (*Paul Humphreys, Rob Winstanley, Paul Humphreys, Iwan and Sion Roberts, Michael and Deborah Ethier, the Didler, BB, Phil Bryant*)

☆ *Miller of Mansfield* RG8 9AW [High St]: Contemporary very dark green décor, lots of easy chairs, log fires and modern art in three linked areas of large bow-windowed bar; good if not cheap bar food all day, Marlow Rebellion and West Berkshire Good Old Boy, friendly young staff, up-to-date meals in large, smart and airy back restaurant; well reproduced piped music; children welcome, good tables under big canopy on heated terrace, open all day (*Michael and Deborah Ethier, Rob Winstanley, BB*)

GOZZARD'S FORD [SU4698]

☆ *Black Horse* OX13 6JH [off B4017 NW of Abingdon; N of A415 by Marcham—Cothill rd]: Ancient traditional pub in tiny hamlet, four well kept Greene King ales, sensibly short choice of good generous food (all day Sun) especially fish and seafood, decent wines; cheerful family service, carpeted beamed main bar partly divided by stout timbers and low steps, end woodburner, separate plainer public bar with darts and pool; nice garden, open all day *(BB, Helene Grygar, William Goodhart)*

GREAT BOURTON [SP4545]

Bell OX17 1QP [just off A423, 3 miles N of Banbury; Manor Rd, opp church]: Friendly pub by church doing well under expert new licensees, good reasonably priced food, appealing little dining area, well kept Hook Norton; nice view from small garden *(Dennis Haward)*

HAILEY [SP3414]

Bird in Hand OX29 9XP [Whiteoak Green; B4022 Witney—Charlbury]: Extended beamed dining pub, real ales, quick friendly service; comfortable armchairs on polished boards, large open fire, some stripped stone, cosy corners in attractive carpeted restaurant, nice views; garden tables, good value bedrooms *(Helene Grygar, BB)*

HARWELL [SU4988]

☆ *Kingswell* OX11 0LZ [A417; Reading Rd]: Substantial hotel with dependably good imaginative bar food as well as restaurant meals, helpful staff; comfortable bedrooms *(Henry Midwinter)*

HEADINGTON [SP5407]

☆ *Black Boy* OX3 9HT [Old High St]: Stylish refurbishment with two bars, dining area and restaurant, good food, inventive without being pretentious, well kept ales inc a weekly guest beer, good coffee and tea; charming landlady, Thurs jazz nights; children welcome (kids' cooking class Sun morning), cl Sun evening and Mon *(Tim Venn)*

Masons Arms OX3 8LH [Quarry School Pl]: Open-plan local with beers such as Brains, Caledonian Deuchars IPA, West Berkshire and its own Old Bog brews; darts, Sat quiz night; children welcome, heated outside seating, aunt sally; cl wkdy lunchtimes, open all day Sat *(Roger Shipperley)*

HENLEY [SU7682]

☆ *Anchor* RG9 1AH [Friday St]: Old-fashioned, homely and individualistic, two nicely lived-in front rooms, hearty food (not Sun, Mon evenings) from lunchtime open sandwiches up, proper traditional puddings, well kept Brakspears, good range of malt whiskies and New World wines by the glass; friendly chocolate labrador called Ruger, straight-talking landlady, simple back dining room; well behaved children welcome, charming back terrace, open all day *(Ian Phillips, Mrs M S Forbes, the Didler, Clive Watkin, David Heath, LYM)*

Argyll RG9 2AA [Market Pl]: Smartly comfortable and well run, with pleasant efficient service; sensibly priced pub food all day from sandwiches up, Greene King ales, good choice of wines by the glass, soft lighting, dark panelling; unobtrusive piped music; large covered back terrace, useful parking *(Ian Phillips, Phil Bryant, LYM)*

HIGHMOOR [SU7084]

☆ *Dog & Duck* RG9 5DL [B481]: Appealing unspoilt 17th-c country pub with good home-made food such as venison casserole, also good vegetarian options, well kept Brakspears ales, nice choice of wines by the glass, helpful friendly staff; cheery log fires in small cosily furnished beamed bar and not much larger flagstoned dining room with old prints and pictures, family room off; children and dogs welcome, attractive long garden with some play equipment and small sheep paddock, surrounding walks *(H P Hampton, the Didler, Howard Dell, Roy Hoing, Emma Pearson, Robert Watt, J Donavon, LYM)*

HOOK NORTON [SP3534]

☆ *Gate Hangs High* OX15 5DF [N towards Sibford, at Banbury—Rollright crossroads]: Snug tucked-away pub, low-ceilinged bar with traditional furniture and attractive inglenook, good reasonably priced home-made food from bar snacks up, well kept Hook Norton ales and a guest, decent wines; slightly chintzy side dining extension (booking advised Sat evening and Sun); piped music; pretty courtyard and country garden, four good value bedrooms, good breakfast, quite nr Rollright Stones *(Stuart Turner, LYM, Mark Farrington, Mike and Sue Shirley, Ann and Colin Hunt)*

Pear Tree OX15 5NU [Scotland End]: Take-us-as-you-find-us village pub with engaging landlord and characterful locals, full Hook Norton beer range kept well from nearby brewery, country wines, bar food (not Sun evening) from doorstep sandwiches to enjoyable bargain Sun roast; knocked-together bar area with country-kitchen furniture, good log fire, daily papers, locally made walking sticks for sale; occasional live music Tues, TV; children and dogs welcome, attractive flower-filled garden with play area, bedrooms, open all day *(K H Frostick, LYM, Ann and Colin Hunt, Barry Collett, Giles and Annie Francis)*

☆ *Sun* OX15 5NH [High St]: Beamed bar with good atmosphere, friendly staff, huge log fire and flagstones, cosy carpeted back room leading into attractive dining room; enjoyable entirely local food from bar snacks to restaurant meals, well kept Hook Norton ales, several wines by the glass, darts and dominoes; children and dogs welcome, disabled facilities, tables out in front and on back terrace, well equipped bedrooms, good breakfast *(Robert Gomme, Pete Baker, Chris Brooks, Sir Nigel Foulkes, LYM)*

KIDLINGTON [SP4914]

Kings Arms OX5 2AJ [The Moors, off High St (not the Harvester out on the Bicester rd)]:

Small friendly local with good affordable wkdy lunchtime food from sandwiches up, Greene King IPA and a couple of other changing ales, homely lounge, games in the proper public bar; children welcome, courtyard tables with occasional barbecues, open all day wknds *(Pete Baker, J A Ellis)*

KINGHAM [SP2523]

☆ *Tollgate* OX7 6YA [Church St]: Neat, modern, leather bucket chairs, easy chairs and dining tables in friendly and civilised flagstoned and bare-boards bar divided by big stone fireplace with woodburner, back dining room; good choice of well cooked food (not Sun evening or Mon) from lunchtime baguettes and light dishes to restaurant meals inc good if not cheap Sun lunch, Hook Norton and unusual local Cotswold Lager, good wines by the glass, prompt polite service; dogs welcome (elderly terrier called Guinness), outside seating, nine comfortable bedrooms *(BB, Hunter and Christine Wright)*

KINGSTON BLOUNT [SU7399]

☆ *Cherry Tree* OX39 4SL [Park Lane (B4009, handy for M40)]: Reopened under friendly new licensees after a short closure; interesting food from sandwiches up inc special deals, may be bargain summer hog roast, Brakspears ales, long contemporary bar with stripped-wood floor and small brick fireplace, spacious back dining room; may be piped music; children welcome *(LYM, Susan and John Douglas)*

KINGSTON LISLE [SU3287]

Blowing Stone OX12 9QL [signed off B4507 W of Wantage]: Being taken over by ex landlord and chef from the good White Horse at Woolstone as we went to press – reports please; log fire, comfortable lounge, modernised bar and dining conservatory; tables out in lovely garden, handy for Uffington Castle hill fort and the downs *(LYM)*

KIRTLINGTON [SP4919]

☆ *Oxford Arms* OX5 3HA [Troy Lane]: Oak-beamed 19th-c pub popular for generous food from proper sandwiches up, imaginative starters up, using good local produce, genial hands-on landlord/chef and charming young staff; good reasonably priced wines by the large glass, Hook Norton Best and two other ales from congenial central bar with small standing area, leather settees and log fire one end, separate dining room; well behaved children and dogs on leads welcome, disabled access, small sunny back garden with big heated umbrellas, cl Sun evening *(Briege Gormley, Oxana Mismina, Phillip and Margaret-Ann Minty, Guy Vowles)*

LONG HANBOROUGH [SP4214]

Bell OX29 8JX [A4095 Witney—Woodstock]: Recently refurbished with some emphasis on the enjoyable food (Sun evenings too); good service under newish landlord, Greene King ales, comfortable bar with armchairs and sofas; games machine, some quiet live music nights; back terrace *(Alan Thwaite)*

☆ *George & Dragon* OX29 8JX [Main Rd (A4095 Bladon—Witney)]: Comfortable and clean single-storey L-shaped thatched pub, good generous food (best to book wknds) from extensive menu inc vegetarian and gluten-free choices, friendly efficient staff; well kept Brakspears, Fullers London Pride and Wells & Youngs Bombardier, Weston's cider, good range of wines; modern dining extension to 18th-c or older core (originally a low-beamed farm building), wood floors and stone walls; soft piped music; children welcome *(Alan Thwaite, Peter and Audrey Dowsett, Helene Grygar)*

LONG WITTENHAM [SU5493]

Plough OX14 4QH [High St]: Friendly chatty local with low beams, inglenook fires and lots of brass; Greene King ales and usually a guest, good wines by the glass, wide choice of generous good value food (all day wknds), good service, dining room, games in public bar; dogs welcome, Thames moorings at bottom of nice spacious garden with aunt sally; bedrooms *(David Lamb, Canon Michael Bourdeaux, Chris Glasson)*

LONGWORTH [SU3899]

☆ *Blue Boar* OX13 5ET [Tucks Lane]: 17th-c thatched stone pub with three small low-beamed rooms, well worn in, two log fires, one by fine old settle, brasses, hops and assorted knick-knacks, main eating area plus restaurant extension; Brakspears, Fullers London Pride and Ringwood Fortyniner, good choice of other drinks, standard bar food; piped music; children and dogs welcome, tables in front and on back terrace, short walk from the Thames, open all day *(Peter and Audrey Dowsett, LYM)*

MARSH BALDON [SU5699]

Seven Stars OX44 9LP [the Baldons signed off A4074 N of Dorchester]: Small beamed village-green pub with new welcoming landlord, two bar areas and snug dining room; good choice of enjoyable food inc two-course set menu, efficient service, well kept Brakspears and Timothy Taylors Landlord *(Philip and June Caunt)*

MIDDLE ASSENDON [SU7385]

Rainbow RG9 6AU [B480]: Well run friendly country pub, pretty and cottagey, with unspoilt low-beamed cosy bar and simple L-shaped carpeted dining room; tasty food home-made by landlady, well kept Brakspears, good choice of wines by the glass, pleasant attentive landlord and assistant, friendly dog; picnic-sets on front lawn, peaceful setting, may be red kites overhead *(Susan and John Douglas, Ross Balaam, Phil Bryant)*

MIDDLE BARTON [SP4425]

Carpenters Arms OX7 7DA [North St]: Thatched village local, landlady doing good value generous food, nice beer range inc St Austell Tribute; warm-hearted open-plan bar, restaurant; bedrooms *(J Harvey)*

MILTON [SP4535]

☆ *Black Boy* OX15 4HH [off Bloxham Rd; the one nr Adderbury]: Neatly refurbished dining pub with good comfortable furnishings, but still plenty of oak beams, exposed stonework, flagstones and a lovely big inglenook; most tables set for the enjoyable and affordable home-made food, friendly licensees, good service, Greene King and White Horse; daily papers, some cricket memorabilia, candlelit restaurant; piped music; dogs welcome in bar, tables across road in spacious garden beyond car park, heaters and aunt sally *(George Atkinson, BB)*

NETTLEBED [SU6986]

White Hart RG9 5DD [High St (A4130)]: Enjoyable food and friendly staff in civilised rambling two-level beamed bar, discreet rather hotelish atmosphere, good log fires, spacious restaurant; children welcome, bedrooms *(LYM, Roy Hoing)*

NORTH HINKSEY [SP4905]

Fishes OX2 0NA [off A420 just E of A34 ring rd; North Hinksey Lane, then pass church into cul-de-sac signed to rugby club]: Brick and tile Victorian pub set in three acres of wooded grounds, open-plan lounge and pleasant conservatory; good choice of food inc some imaginative dishes and innovative summer picnic baskets, friendly staff, well kept Greene King, decent house wines, traditional games; piped music; children welcome, tables out at front and on back decking, streamside garden with good play area and two aunt sally pitches, open all day *(LM)*

NORTH MORETON [SU5689]

Bear at Home OX11 9AT [off A4130 Didcot—Wallingford; High St]: Dating from the 15th c with traditional beamed bar, cosy fireside areas and dining part with stripped-pine furniture; enjoyable reasonably priced food from baguettes up, Timothy Taylors, a guest ale and a beer brewed for the pub, Weston's cider, several wines by the glass; attractive garden overlooking cricket pitch *(Tim Hayworth)*

NUFFIELD [SU6787]

☆ *Crown* RG9 5SJ [A4130/B481]: Another change of management at this attractive small country pub; enjoyable generous home-made food, good service, well kept Brakspears, good house wines, simple country furniture and inglenook log fire in beamed lounge bar; children and dogs in small garden room, disabled access, walkers welcome (good walks nearby), pleasant garden with tables front and back; cl Sun evening, Mon *(Roy Hoing, Howard Dell, LYM, Kate McMahon)*

OXFORD [SP5007]

Anchor OX2 6TT [Hayfield Rd]: Chef/landlord at this 1930s pub continues to produce good quality interesting food using local supplies, friendly efficient service, good value house wine, well kept beers such as Vale Pale and Wadworths 6X; period furnishings, log fire, separate dining area; nr Bridge 240 (Aristotle) on Oxford Canal *(Clive and Fran Dutson)*

☆ *Bear* OX1 4EH [Alfred St/Wheatsheaf Alley]:

Two charming little low-ceilinged and partly panelled ancient rooms, not over-smart and often packed with students; thousands of vintage ties on walls and beams, some reasonably priced lunchtime food most days inc sandwiches with big chunky chips, and pie of the day, four well kept changing ales from centenarian handpumps on pewter bar counter; upstairs ladies'; tables outside, open all day summer *(LYM, Paul Humphreys, the Didler, Michael Dandy, Michael Sargent)*

Harcourt Arms OX2 6DG [Cranham Terrace]: Friendly local with proper landlord and some character, pillars dividing it; good value snacks, Fullers ales inc London Porter, two log fires, modern art, good choice of board games, well reproduced jazz *(Andrew Barron)*

Head of the River OX1 4LB [Folly Bridge; between St Aldates and Christchurch Meadow]: Civilised well renovated pub by river, boats for hire and nearby walks; spacious split-level downstairs bar with dividing brick arches, flagstones and bare boards, Fullers range inc Gales HSB, good choice of wines by the glass, popular pubby food from sandwiches up inc some contemporary dishes, good service, daily papers; piped music, games machines; tables on stepped heated waterside terrace, bedrooms *(LM, Michael Dandy)*

Isis Farmhouse OX4 4EL [off Donnington Bridge Rd; no car access]: Charming waterside spot for an early 19th-c former farmhouse, relaxed and informal under newish private owners (was brewery-owned); short choice of hearty food, local Appleford ales, lots of mainly nautical bric-a-brac hanging from high ceiling and covering the walls, traditional games; bowling alley, picnic-sets out on heated terrace and in garden, aunt sally by arrangement; short walk to Iffley Lock and nearby lavishly decorated early Norman church; open all day *(LYM, Tim and Ann Newell)*

☆ *Kings Arms* OX1 3SP [Holywell St]: Dating from the early 17th c, convivial, relaxed and popular with students, quick helpful service, Wells & Youngs ales and four guests such as Bath Gem and Oxfordshire Triple B, fine choice of wines by the glass; eating area with counter servery doing enjoyable good value food (all day wknds, children allowed) from sandwiches and baked potatoes up, cosy comfortably worn-in partly panelled side and back rooms, interesting pictures and posters, daily papers; a few tables outside, open all day from 10.30 *(LYM, Roger Shipperley, Alan Thwaite, Paul Humphreys, the Didler, Michael Dandy, J C Burgis, Lawrence Pearse)*

Lamb & Flag OX1 3JS [St Giles/Banbury Rd]: Old pub owned by nearby college, modern airy front room with big windows over street, more atmosphere in back rooms with stripped stonework and low-boarded ceilings; a beer brewed by Palmers for the pub (L&F Gold), Shepherd Neame Spitfire and Skinners Betty Stogs, some lunchtime food inc baguettes, cheerful service *(Roger Shipperley, Michael Dandy)*

Perch OX2 0NG [narrow lane on right just before MFI, leaving city on A420]: Beautifully set thatched pub in tiny riverside hamlet, refurbished after fire and flood; much emphasis on good french cooking from shortish menu using local produce, prompt friendly service, Hook Norton and other beers, sofas by winter log fire; garden running down to Thames Path and moorings, outside summer bar and barbecue, river cruises *(LYM, William Goodhart)*

Royal Oak OX2 6HT [Woodstock Rd, opp Radcliffe Infirmary]: Maze of little rooms meandering around central bar, low beams, simple furnishings; wide and interesting range of beers on tap and in bottles inc belgian imports, lunchtime food bar, daily papers, open fire, prints and bric-a-brac; games room with darts, pool etc; piped music; small back terrace, open all day *(Michael Sargent)*

Victoria OX2 6EB [Walton St]: Recent thorough-going refurbishment inc modern touches such as a biplane suspended from oval upper balcony, Marstons-related ales, low-priced food inc speciality pies; stunning new back terrace *(Edward Leetham)*

☆ *White Horse* OX1 3BB [Broad St]: Bustling and studenty, squeezed between bits of Blackwells bookshop; small narrow bar with snug one-table raised back alcove, low beams and timbers, ochre ceiling, beautiful view of the Clarendon building and Sheldonian; Brakspears, St Austell and Timothy Taylors Landlord, friendly staff, good value simple lunchtime food (the few tables reserved for this) *(Roger Shipperley, Michael Dandy, the Didler, Ann and Colin Hunt, Phil and Sally Gorton, BB)*

PISHILL [SU7190]

☆ *Crown* RG9 6HH [B480 Nettlebed—Watlington]: Ancient wisteria-covered dining pub under new hard-working licensees; black beams and timbers, good log fires and candlelight; picnic-sets on attractive side lawn, pleasant cottage bedroom, pretty country setting, walks; reports please *(Susan and John Douglas, Peter Dandy, the Didler, LYM, E Seymour)*

RADLEY [SU5298]

Bowyer Arms OX14 3AE [Foxborough Rd]: Well kept Greene King IPA and Abbot, enjoyable inexpensive food; nice garden, good Thames towpath walks *(Roger Wain-Heapy)*

ROTHERFIELD GREYS [SU7282]

☆ *Maltsters Arms* RG9 4QD: Quietly set country local with friendly helpful young staff, well kept Brakspears ales, good reasonably priced home-made food from panini to steak and kidney pudding and Sun lunch (best to book wknds); good wines by the glass, cafetière coffee, lots of cricket memorabilia, dining room with open fire; soft piped music; terrace with heated smokers' area, garden picnic-sets, not far from Greys Court (NT),

lovely country views and walks *(Howard Dell, Roy Hoing, R K Phillips, Paul Humphreys, DHV, Ross Balaam, Fred and Kate Portnell, Malcolm and Barbara Lewis)*

SHENINGTON [SP3742]

☆ *Bell* OX15 6NQ [off A422 NW of Banbury]: Good hearty wholesome home cooking in hospitable 17th-c two-room pub, good sandwiches too; well kept Hook Norton Best, good wine choice, fair prices, friendly informal service and long-serving licensees, relaxed atmosphere, heavy beams, some flagstones, stripped stone and pine panelling, coal fire; amiable dogs, cribbage, dominoes; children in eating areas, nice tables out in front, small attractive back garden, charming quiet village, good walks; simple comfortable bedrooms, generous breakfast, cl Mon (and perhaps other wkdy) lunchtimes *(Susan and Peter Ferris-Williams, Graham and Nicky Westwood, LYM, Sir Nigel Foulkes, Ed Tyley, Roy Davenport)*

SHIPLAKE [SU7476]

Flowing Spring RG4 9RB [A4155 towards Play Hatch and Reading]: New licensees in pleasantly countrified pub, open fires in small two-room bar, good value food inc speciality pies, friendly staff; bright modern sun room with floor-to-ceiling windows overlooking the water meadows; picnic-sets out on heated deck and on lawn *(Paul Humphreys, LYM)*

Plowden Arms RG9 4BX [Reading Rd (A4155)]: Three neatly kept linked rooms and side dining room, log fire, good range of home-made food from well filled baguettes up, Brakspears, good coffee (only with a meal); handy for Thames walk (no muddy boots) *(Roy Hoing, Roy and Jean Russell)*

SHIPTON-UNDER-WYCHWOOD [SP2717]

☆ *Lamb* OX7 6DQ [off A361 to Burford; High St]: A welcome for all (not just diners) under newish family management; racing-theme bar with wood floor, stripped-stone walls and log fire, good if not cheap home-made food (not Sun evening), Weds pie night, Greene King ales and guests, good wines by the glass; restaurant area in Elizabethan core with open fire; children and dogs welcome, tables on heated paved terrace, five attractive themed bedrooms (some over bar), open all day *(Guy Vowles, LYM, Richard Greaves)*

☆ *Shaven Crown* OX7 6BA [High St (A361)]: Ancient building with magnificent lofty medieval rafters and imposing double stairway in hotel part's hall, separate more down-to-earth back bar with booth seating, lovely log fires; enjoyable good value food from sandwiches up, Archers, Hook Norton and Wychwood Hobgoblin, several wines by the glass, restaurant; piped music; children and dogs welcome, peaceful courtyard with outside heaters, bowling green *(Chris Glasson, Keith and Sue Ward, LYM)*

SHRIVENHAM [SU2488]

☆ *Prince of Wales* SN6 8AF [High St; off A420 or B4000 NE of Swindon]: Warmly friendly

17th-c stone-built local with thriving atmosphere, hearty food (not Sun evening) from enterprising sandwiches to Sun roasts, well kept Wadworths, good soft drinks' choice; spotless low-beamed lounge, pictures, lots of brasses, log fire and candles, small dining area, side bar with darts, board games and machines; may be quiet piped music, no dogs; children welcome, picnic-sets and heaters in secluded back garden *(Helene Grygar)*

SOULDERN [SP5231]

Fox OX27 7JW [off B4100; Fox Lane]: Pretty village pub under new management, enjoyable home-made food, well kept ales (beer festivals) and good choice of wines by the glass; comfortable open-plan beamed layout, big log fire, settles and chairs around oak tables, quiz nights; delightful village, garden and terrace tables, aunt sally; four bedrooms *(Marc Ballmann, Ali)*

SOUTH MORETON [SU5688]

Crown OX11 9AG [off A4130 or A417 E of Didcot; High St]: Rambling open-plan 17th-c village pub brightened up by newish licensees; bare-boards bar with centre brick fireplace, chef/landlord doing good range of inexpensive generous food with some upmarket twists in dining area with woodburner, traditional Sun lunch, well kept Wadworths, decent well priced wines, good service; bar billiards, Mon quiz night; children welcome, steps up to front terrace, more tables in small garden *(Stephen Rudge)*

SOUTH NEWINGTON [SP4033]

☆ *Duck on the Pond* OX15 4JE: Thriving dining pub with tidy modern-rustic décor in small flagstoned bar and linked carpeted eating areas up a step, with fresh flowers and candles, good generous food from wraps, melts and other light dishes to steaks and family Sun lunch; changing ales such as Archers and Wye Valley, attentive landlord and neat friendly young staff, woodburner; piped music; spacious grounds with tables on deck and lawn, aunt sally, pond with waterfowl, walk to River Swere; open all day Sat, Sun *(BB, George Atkinson, Jay Bohmrich)*

SPARSHOLT [SU3487]

Star OX12 9PL [Watery Lane]: Friendly 16th-c country pub, comfortable and compact, with blackboard choice of good freshly made straightforward food at sensible prices, two well kept real ales; daily papers, log fire, attractive pictures; may be soft piped music; back garden, pretty village – snowdrops fill churchyard in spring *(David Lamb)*

STANFORD IN THE VALE [SU3393]

Horse & Jockey SN7 8NN [Faringdon Rd]: Homely welcoming old local in racehorse country, low ceilings, flagstones and woodburner in big fireplace, good drawings and paintings of horses and jockeys; Batemans XXB and Greene King ales, decent wine choice, enjoyable good value food, charming restaurant; dogs welcome, play area *(R K Phillips)*

STANTON HARCOURT [SP4105]

Harcourt Arms OX29 5RJ [Main Rd]: Roomy and cheerfully informal country dining pub, efficient friendly licensees, Adnams, Black Sheep and a guest, decent beers, good sensibly priced food; huge fireplaces in attractive simply furnished linked dining areas, beams, flagstones and stripped stone; children welcome *(LYM, André and Jack Anker)*

STANTON ST JOHN [SP5709]

☆ *Talk House* OX33 1EX [Middle Rd/Wheatley Rd (B4027 just outside)]: Well refurbished part-thatched 17th-c inn, good restaurant-style food and pub favourites, Hook Norton Best, Wadworths 6X and a guest beer, nice wines by the glass, good helpful service; partly stripped-stone walls, lots of oak beams, flagstones and tiles, simple and solid rustic furnishings, pleasant area by log fire, raftered restaurant; children welcome, tables in sheltered courtyard, four revamped bedrooms, has been open all day in summer *(Miss A G Drake, LYM)*

STEVENTON [SU4691]

North Star OX13 6SG [Stocks Lane, The Causeway, central westward turn off B4017]: Carefully restored old-fangled village pub with tiled entrance corridor, main area with ancient high-backed settles around central table, Greene King ales from pump set tucked away in side tap room, hatch service to another room with plain seating, a couple of tables and good coal fire; simple lunchtime food, young friendly staff; piped music, sports TV, games machine; tables on side grass, front gateway through living yew tree *(Pete Baker, Helene Grygar, Phil and Sally Gorton, the Didler, LYM)*

STOKE LYNE [SP5628]

Peyton Arms OX27 8SD [from minor rd off B4110 N of Bicester, fork left into village]: Beautifully situated and largely unspoilt stone-built pub, Hook Norton from casks behind small corner bar in front snug, filled rolls, tiled floor, inglenook fire, memorabilia; games room with darts and pool; no children or dogs in bar; pleasant garden with aunt sally, open all day Sat, cl Sun evening and Mon *(Roger Shipperley, Pete Baker, the Didler, Torrens Lyster)*

STOKE ROW [SU6884]

☆ *Cherry Tree* RG9 5QA [off B481 at Highmoor]: Contemporary upscale pub restaurant with particularly good food, Sun lunch till 5pm, attentive staff, Brakspears ales, good choice of wines by the glass; minimalist décor and solid country furniture in four linked rooms with stripped wood, heavy low beams and some flagstones; TV in bar; good seating in attractive garden, nearby walks, five good bedrooms in converted barn, open all day except Sun evening *(Roy and Jean Russell, Bob and Margaret Holder, BB, Penny and Peter Keevil)*

☆ *Crooked Billet* RG9 5PU [Nottwood Lane, off B491 N of Reading – OS Sheet 175 map ref

684844]: Very nice place, but restaurant not pub (you can't have just a drink); charming rustic pub layout though, with heavy beams, flagstones, antique pubby furnishings and great inglenook log fire as well as crimsonly Victorian dining room; wide choice of well cooked interesting food using local produce (you can have just a starter), cheaper set lunches Mon-Sat, helpful friendly staff, Brakspears tapped from the cask (no bar counter), good wines, relaxed homely atmosphere – like a french country restaurant; children truly welcome, occasional live music, big garden by Chilterns beechwoods, open all day Sat, Sun *(Bob and Margaret Holder, LYM, Bruce and Sharon Eden)*

SWINFORD [SP4308]

Talbot OX29 4BT [B4044 just S of Eynsham]: Roomy and comfortable 17th-c beamed pub, wide changing choice of generous fresh food, up to five well kept ales direct from the cask, good choice of wines and soft drinks; friendly landlord and staff, long attractive bar with some stripped stone, cheerful log-effect gas fire, newspapers, games room; may be piped music; children and dogs welcome, tables in garden (some traffic noise), pleasant walk along lovely stretch of the Thames towpath, eight bedrooms *(JJW, CMW, Anthony Double)*

TACKLEY [SP4720]

Gardiner Arms OX5 3AH [Medcroft Rd, off A4260]: Comfortable 17th-c beamed village local, enjoyable generous home-made pub food, three well kept Greene King ales, coal-effect gas fire in inglenook, prints, brasses, old photographs and cigarette cards; separate public bar with darts, TV and fruit machine; piped music; bookable skittle alley; picnic-sets on sunny front terrace, handy for Rousham House *(Michael Tack)*

THAME [SP7105]

Cross Keys OX9 3HP [Park St/East St]: Single bar, reopened under new landlord with Vale ales and guests from other small breweries *(Roger Shipperley)*

Falcon OX9 3JA [Thame Park Rd]: Open-plan local with well kept Hook Norton ales, friendly service, decent food (not Sat lunchtime); open all day *(Roger Shipperley, Tim and Ann Newell)*

THRUPP [SP4815]

☆ *Boat* OX5 1JY [off A4260 just N of Kidlington]: Stone-built pub in good spot very nr Oxford Canal; bar snacks and good upscale food in restaurant, friendly landlord and efficient service, Greene King ales and decent wine; coal fire, old canal pictures and artefacts, bare boards and stripped pine; gets busy in summer; children welcome, fenced garden behind with plenty of tables, nearby moorings *(Pete Baker, Clive and Fran Dutson, Mark, Amanda, Luke and Jake Sheard, Sue Demont, Tim Barrow)*

TIDDINGTON [SP6405]

Fox OX9 2LH [Oxford Rd]: Indian food in

neat 17th-c pub's restaurant, large bar with big log fire, low beams and stripped stone; tables outside *(Tim and Ann Newell)*

WALLINGFORD [SU6089]

Partridge OX10 0ET [St Marys St]: Contemporary airy décor and comfortably modern furnishings, enjoyable food (not Sun evening) using carefully sourced fish and meat, good wine choice, attentive service *(Rachel Nkepe-Vwem)*

WANTAGE [SU3987]

King Alfreds Head OX12 8AH [Market Pl]: Pub/bistro reopened under new management, interestingly refurbished linked areas, enjoyable food, real ale, helpful friendly staff; unusual garden and barn area *(R K Phillips)*

Lamb OX12 9AB [Mill St, past square and Bell; down hill then bend to left]: Low beams, log fire and cosy corners, well kept Greene King ales, wide choice of generous good value food, quick smiling service; children welcome, disabled facilities, garden tables *(LYM)*

WARBOROUGH [SU6093]

Six Bells OX10 7DN [The Green S; just E of A329, 4 miles N of Wallingford]: Attentive and welcoming licensees doing good reasonably priced food in thatched 16th-c pub facing the cricket green; Brakspears ales, attractive country furnishings in linked small areas off bar, low beams, stripped stone, big log fire; tables in pleasant orchard garden *(LYM, Barry Collett, Roy Hoing)*

WATLINGTON [SU6994]

Carriers Arms OX49 5AD [Hill Rd]: Popular no-frills local with well kept Adnams, Black Sheep and Wells & Youngs Bombardier, wide range of cheap food from filled rolls to Sun roast, genial landlord; garden tables looking up to Chilterns, high kite-feeding table (plenty circling), good walks *(BB, Chris Buckle)*

WESTON-ON-THE-GREEN [SP5318]

Ben Jonson OX25 3RA [B430 nr M40 junction 9]: Ancient thatched and stone-built country pub, smart beamed bar with oak furniture, pastel décor and interesting sculpture, woodburner; enjoyable if not cheap food (helpings can be small) from baguettes up, well kept Hook Norton and Wadworths 6X, decent wines; newish dining room *(Tom McLean, Mr and Mrs W W Burke, Val and Alan Green)*

Chequers OX25 3QH [handy for M40 junction 9, via A34; Northampton Rd (B430)]: Extended thatched pub with three smart areas off large semicircular raftered bar; Fullers ales, good wines by the glass, welcoming service, enjoyable food all day from thick beef sandwiches up; tables under parasols in attractive garden *(Val and Alan Green, Paul Goldman, Conor McGaughey)*

WHITCHURCH [SU6377]

Ferry Boat RG8 7DB [High St]: Comfortable welcoming two-room pub, smart décor with pastel shades and contemporary furnishings; enjoyable home-made food from baguettes up at reasonable prices, friendly young staff, real ale such as Adnams, Black Sheep and Timothy Taylors Landlord, decent wine choice by the glass; TV; bedrooms, cl Sun evening, Mon *(Phil Bryant)*

Greyhound RG8 7EL [High St, just over toll bridge from Pangbourne]: Pretty 16th-c cottage with neat, relaxed, low-beamed L-shaped bar, good value fresh food (not Sun evening), Black Sheep and Wells & Youngs Bombardier and Special, friendly staff; flame-effect fire, no music or machines; pleasant garden, attractive village on Thames Path *(Phil Bryant)*

WITNEY [SP3509]

Fleece OX28 4AZ [Church Green]: Smart and civilised town pub on the green, popular for its wide choice of good food inc early bird deals; prompt friendly service, Greene King ales, leather armchairs on wood floors, daily papers; piped music; children welcome, tables outside *(David and Sue Smith, Richard Atherton)*

WOODSTOCK [SP4416]

Woodstock Arms OX20 1SX [Market St]: 16th-c heavy-beamed stripped-stone pub, lively and stylishly modernised, with prompt welcoming service by helpful young staff; Greene King IPA and Old Speckled Hen, good wine choice, daily papers, log-effect gas fire in splendid stone fireplace, long narrow bar, end eating area; piped music; dogs welcome, tables out in attractive yard, bedrooms, open all day *(Chris Glasson)*

WOOLSTONE [SU2987]

White Horse SN7 7QL [off B4507]: Appealing, old, partly thatched pub with Victorian gables, plush furnishings, spacious beamed and part-panelled bar, two big open fires, Arkells beers, restaurant; plenty of seats in front and back gardens, secluded interesting village handy for White Horse and Ridgeway; charming bedrooms, has been open all day; new management early summer 2009 – too soon for us to form a firm view, so news please *(LYM)*

WOOTTON [SP4320]

Killingworth Castle OX20 1EJ [Glympton Rd; B4027 N of Woodstock]: Striking three-storey 17th-c coaching inn with newish licensees doing enjoyable food, Greene King ales, long narrow main bar with pine furnishings, parquet floor, brasses and log fire; bar billiards, darts and shove-ha'penny in smaller games end; garden, bedrooms *(Pete Baker, Helene Grygar, BB)*

WYTHAM [SP4708]

White Hart OX2 8QA [off A34 Oxford ring rd]: 16th-c country dining pub, several eating areas with log fires, some settles, handsome panelling and flagstones; good if pricey food from french chef inc Sun roasts, cosy bar area with well kept Hook Norton and Timothy Taylors Landlord, good value house wines; conservatory (dogs allowed here); children welcome, pretty garden with big tables, unspoilt preserved village, open all day wknds *(William Goodhart, LYM)*

Shropshire

Some of Shropshire's pubs stand out as particularly special. New this year is the Pound at Leebotwood, a minimalist-style dining pub within a fine old thatched building, much liked for its food. In Ludlow, the Church Inn has a terrific selection of eight real ales and its position right at the hub of this historic, prosperous hilltop town makes it a very useful place to know. Two Brunning & Price pubs in this county are both excellent all-rounders: the Armoury in Shrewsbury, with eight real ales and tasty food, is an outstanding town pub in an imaginatively converted warehouse; the Fox at Chetwynd Aston has a great drinks range and its caring staff serve excellent food – it's our Shropshire Dining Pub of the Year. At Bromfield, the Clive is a sophisticated dining place with the accent firmly on the food; for those seeking simpler pubs in lovely rural surroundings, the Royal Oak at Cardington, the Sun at Norbury and the Stiperstones Inn (another new entry) stand out. The unspoilt Marches town of Bishop's Castle has the distinction of having two thoroughly likeable, no-gimmicks own-brew pubs, the Six Bells and the Three Tuns, their beers (particularly the Three Tuns') turning up in other good pubs, too. The top local ale is Hobsons, followed by Salopian, with Woods heading quite a clutch of other good small breweries. Three fine Lucky Dip pubs are the Mytton & Mermaid at Atcham, Hundred House at Norton and Willey Moor Lock near Whitchurch.

BISHOP'S CASTLE

SO3288   MAP 6

Six Bells 🍺
Church Street; SY9 5AA

Deservedly popular own-brew pub

The friendly atmosphere, good-value fresh food and superb beers make a compelling case for seeking out this town pub; you can arrange a tour of the brewery, and they have a beer festival on the second full weekend in July. The excellent beers brewed by the landlord include Big Nevs (most people's favourite), Cloud Nine, Goldings Best and a seasonal brew; there is also a wide range of country wines and farm cider in summer. The no-frills bar is really quite small, with an assortment of well worn furniture and old local photographs and prints. The second, bigger room has bare boards, some stripped stone, a roaring woodburner in the inglenook, plenty of sociable locals on the benches around plain tables, and lots of board games (you may find people absorbed in Scrabble or darts). The service is very friendly and it can be packed here at the weekend.

🍴 Good value tasty bar food includes lunchtime soup, sandwiches, ploughman's and quiche, and in the evening there's sausages and mash, a fish dish and a couple of vegetarian options such as cheese and leek sausage and pork tenderloin with mustard and cider sauce; indulgent puddings such as sherry trifle. Booking is strongly advised for Friday and Saturday evenings. *Starters/Snacks: £3.50 to £6.00. Main Courses: £8.00 to £10.00. Puddings: £4.00*

Own brew ~ Licensee Neville Richards ~ Real ale ~ Bar food (12-1.45, 6.30-8.45; not Sun evening or Mon except bank hols) ~ No credit cards ~ (01588) 630144 ~ Children welcome if supervised ~ Dogs allowed in bar ~ Open 12-2.30, 5-11; 12-11 Sat; 12-3.30, 7-10.30 Sun; closed Mon lunchtime

Recommended by Alan and Eve Harding, the Didler, David M Smith, William Goodhart, David Field, Steven and Victoria James

Three Tuns

Salop Street; SY9 5BW

Unpretentious own-brew pub scoring well for food as well as beer from its unique four-storey Victorian brewhouse

This is pleasantly airy place to sit and enjoy a meal or sample one of the four excellent beers that are brewed in the Victorian John Roberts brewhouse (which is a separate business) across the yard. These are served from old-fashioned handpumps; also several wines by the glass, carry-out kegs and the brewery sells beer by the barrel. Although there's a smartly modernised oak and glass dining room, the front bar remains as characterfully ungimmicky as it's always been. It's genuinely part of the local community – you might chance upon the film club, live jazz, morris dancers, a brass band playing in the garden or the local rugby club enjoying a drink, and in July they hold a popular annual beer festival. There are newspapers to read and a good range of board games.

Tasty, and in generous portions, bar food includes soup and sandwiches, starters such as spiced cajun chicken salad, breaded calamari and organic smoked salmon pâté, and main courses like the popular braised beef and wild mushrooms in beer with potato cake, rumpsteak burger with bacon, oriental stir fry and chargrilled tuna and king prawn kebabs; puddings such as chocolate brownie and strawberry kebab, and hot pear and chocolate pudding. *Starters/Snacks: £3.95 to £5.25. Main Courses: £8.95 to £12.95. Puddings: £4.25*

Scottish Courage ~ Lease Tim Curtis-Evans ~ Real ale ~ Bar food (12-3, 7-9; not Sun evening) ~ (01588) 638797 ~ Children welcome ~ Dogs allowed in bar ~ Live music Fri or Sat evening ~ Open 12-11(10.30 Sun)

Recommended by Leigh and Gillian Mellor, Robert Turnham, David and Doreen Beattie, MLR, David Field, the Didler, Denise Dowd, Marek Theis

BROMFIELD   SO4877   MAP 6

Clive

A49 2 miles NW of Ludlow; SY8 2JR

Sophisticated minimalist dining pub with similarly stylish bedrooms

Liked for its friendly service as well as for its interesting food, this elegant dining pub takes its name from Clive of India, who once lived here. Its crisp Georgian brick exterior contrasts with a refreshing minimalist look inside. The focus is on the dining room, with its modern light wood tables. A door leads through into the bar, sparse but neat and welcoming, with round glass tables and metal chairs running down to a sleek bar counter with fresh flowers, newspapers and spotlights. Then it's down a step to the Clive Arms Bar, where traditional features like the huge brick fireplace (with woodburning stove), exposed stonework, soaring beams and rafters are appealingly juxtaposed with well worn sofas and new glass tables; piped jazz. The good wine list includes several by the glass, and Hobsons Best and a guest such as Ludlow Gold are on handpump; they also have a range of coffees and teas. An attractive secluded terrace has tables under cocktail parasols and a fish pond. They have 15 stylishly modern, good-sized bedrooms and breakfast is excellent.

Besides interestingly filled baguettes and sandwiches, good bar food includes, soup, battered cod, shropshire ham with poached egg and handcut chips, and sirloin steak. There's a longer more elaborate restaurant menu that might include fillet of beef with dauphinoise potatoes, a daily-changing fish dish or braised leek and jerusalem artichoke gratin with saffron fettuccine; puddings such as lime mousse with coconut jelly and ginger bread or orange tart with chocolate sorbet. *Starters/Snacks: £3.95 to £6.95. Main Courses: £8.95 to £13.95. Puddings: £4.50 to £5.95*

Free house ~ Licensees Paul and Barbara Brooks ~ Real ale ~ Bar food (12-3, 6.30-10; 12-10 Sat; 12-9.30 Sun) ~ Restaurant ~ (01584) 856565 ~ Children welcome ~ Open 11-11; 12-10.30 Sun ~ Bedrooms: £60B/£85B

Recommended by Alan and Eve Harding, David Heath, Mike and Mary Carter, Guy Vowles, Ian Phillips, Mr and Mrs W W Burke, Michael Sargent

CARDINGTON

SO5095 MAP 4

Royal Oak

Village signposted off B4371 Church Stretton—Much Wenlock, pub behind church; also reached via narrow lanes from A49; SY6 7JZ

Wonderful rural position, heaps of character inside too

Reputedly Shropshire's oldest continually licensed pub, this beautifully sited rural place dates back to the 15th century and inside little has changed over the years. Its rambling low-beamed bar has a roaring winter log fire, cauldron, black kettle and pewter jugs in its vast inglenook fireplace, the old standing timbers of a knocked-through wall and red and green tapestry seats solidly capped in elm; shove ha'penny and dominoes. A comfortable dining area has exposed old beams and studwork. Bass, Hobsons Best and a couple of guests such as Three Tuns XXX and Wye Valley Butty Bach are on handpump. This is glorious country for walks, like the one to the summit of Caer Caradoc a couple of miles to the west (ask for directions at the pub), and the front courtyard makes the most of the setting. Dogs are only allowed in the bar when food isn't being served.

🍴 **Bar food includes lunchtime baguettes, ploughman's and light bites such as burgers and lasagne, and there are seasonal specials. Starters might include celery and stilton soup or garlic mushrooms crostini, with main courses like sausage and chilli casserole, their signature dish of fidget pie made with gammon and apples, moroccan lamb stew, rabbit, bacon and cider casserole, and fisherman's pie; puddings such as apple crumble, velvet chocolate torte and tiramisu.** *Starters/Snacks: £3.95 to £9.50. Main Courses: £7.95 to £18.95. Puddings: £2.95 to £4.25*

Free house ~ Licensees Steve Oldham and Eira Williams ~ Real ale ~ Bar food (12-2 (2.30 Sun), 7-9) ~ Restaurant ~ (01694) 771266 ~ Children welcome ~ Dogs allowed in bar ~ Open 12-2.30(3.30 Sun), 7-midnight(1am Fri, Sat); closed Mon (except bank hol lunchtimes)

Recommended by Brian Brooks, TOH, Edward Leetham, John Dwane, David Heath, Graeme Moisey

CHETWYND ASTON

SJ7517 MAP 7

Fox

Village signposted off A41 and A518 just S of Newport; TF10 9LQ
SHROPSHIRE DINING PUB OF THE YEAR

Civilised dining pub with generous food and a fine array of drinks served by ever-attentive staff

The young staff continue to keep well on top of things even at peak times in this thriving and cheerfully run place. The 1920s building was handsomely done up by Brunning & Price a few years ago – its style will be familiar to anyone who has tried their other pubs. A series of linked semi-separate areas, one with a broad arched ceiling, has plenty of tables in all shapes and sizes, some quite elegant, and a vaguely matching diversity of comfortable chairs, all laid out in a way that's fine for eating but serves equally well for just drinking and chatting. There are masses of attractive prints, three open fires, a few oriental rugs on polished parquet or boards, some attractive floor tiling; big windows and careful lighting help towards the relaxed and effortless atmosphere. The handsome bar counter, with a decent complement of bar stools, serves an excellent changing range of about 23 wines by the glass, 50 malt whiskies and

Hobsons Best, Salopian Oracle, Woods Shropshire Lad and three guests from brewers such as Everards, Weetwood and Worfield are well kept on handpump. Disabled access and facilities are good (no push chairs or baby buggies, though); there is a selection of board games. The spreading garden is quite lovely, with a sunny terrace, picnic-sets tucked into the shade of mature trees and extensive views across quiet country fields.

🍴 Served in generous helpings, well liked food from a changing menu could include sandwiches, ploughman's with local cheeses, tomato and bean soup, starters and light bites like potted salt beef, asparagus and pea frittata, courgette and leek risotto and crispy duck hash, and main courses such as smoked salmon and haddock fishcakes, steak burger, braised shoulder of lamb or sweet potato, gorgonzola and spinach lasagne; puddings might feature passion-fruit cheesecake, bread and butter pudding and lemon and chocolate tart; a cheeseboard for sharing comes with grapes and fruit cake. *Starters/Snacks: £4.50 to £6.50. Main Courses: £8.95 to £17.95. Puddings: £4.95 to £5.25*

Brunning & Price ~ Manager Samantha Malloy ~ Real ale ~ Bar food (12-10(9.30 Sun)) ~ (01952) 815940 ~ Children welcome till 7pm ~ Dogs allowed in bar ~ Open 12-11(10.30 Sun)

Recommended by Gary Rollings, Debbie Porter, Michael Beale, R T and J C Moggridge, Leslie and Barbara Owen, Dr Phil Putwain, J S Burn, Suzy Miller, Henry Pursehouse-Tranter, Mark Blackburn, Paul and Margaret Baker, Bruce and Sharon Eden, Dennis Jenkin, Chris Smith

LEEBOTWOOD
SO4798   MAP 6

Pound
A49 Church Stretton—Shrewsbury; SY6 6ND

Upmarket dining pub in ancient cruck-framed building, with interesting modern cuisine

Thought to be the oldest building in the village, this thatched pub dates from 1458 and at one time served as a hostelry for drovers on their way to market. Inside it's stylishly modern and minimalist, with well chosen wooden furnishings. Pleasant staff serve Fullers London Pride and a guest such as Salopian Shropshire Gold on handpump, plus several wines by the glass; background music. More tables are on a flagstoned terrace outside. The pub changed hands as we were going to press; news, please.

🍴 Cooked by the new landlord, the interesting food includes lunchtime sandwiches, soup, crayfish and orange cocktail with capers and crispy parsley, salad of watermelon, feta, olives, fine beans and cherry tomatoes, sausages with spring onion and cheddar mash and caramelised onion gravy, home-made burger with apricots, fennel relish and apple chutney, beer-battered fillet of haddock, slow-cooked local belly pork with honey and spices and thyme and garlic roast potatoes, confit of local lamb with mustard mash and madeira sauce, 28-day dry-aged rare breed sirloin of beef with herb butter, and puddings such as a trifle of ginger cake with raspberries, whipped mascarpone and espresso syrup and chocolate pudding with home-made malted and minted white chocolate ice-cream. *Starters/Snacks: £3.95 to £7.50. Main Courses: £9.95 to £16.95. Puddings: £4.95 to £5.75*

Enterprise ~ Licensees John and Debbie Williams ~ Real ale ~ Bar food (12-2.30, 6.30-9; 12-9 Sat, Sun) ~ Restaurant ~ (01694) 751477 ~ Children welcome ~ Open 11-11; 12-10.30 Sun

Recommended by David Heath, Alan and Eve Harding, DHV, Neil and Anita Christopher

LUDLOW
SO5174   MAP 4

Church Inn 🍺
Church Street, behind Butter Cross; SY8 1AW

Characterful town-centre inn with impressive range of real ales

Eight real ales are served on handpump at this bustling pub at the very centre of this enchanting hilltop town, with Hobsons Mild and Town Crier, Ludlow Boiling Well and Gold, Weetwood Eastgate and Wye Valley, as well as a couple of guest from brewers such as Box Steam and Goffs; they also serve several malt whiskies and mulled cider. Appealingly decorated, with comfortable banquettes in cosy alcoves off the island bar, and pews and stripped stonework from the church (part of the bar is a pulpit), the interior is divided into three areas; hops hang from the heavy beams; daily papers and piped music. There are displays of old photographic equipment, plants on windowsills and church prints in the side room; a long central area with a fine stone fireplace (good winter fires) leads to lavatories. The more basic side bar has old black and white photos of the town. The civilised upstairs lounge has vaulted ceilings and long windows overlooking the church, display cases of glass, china and old bottles, and musical instruments on the walls, along with a mix of new and old pictures. The bedrooms are simple but comfortable; good breakfasts. Car parking is some way off. The landlord (a former mayor of Ludlow) is also the owner of the Charlton Arms, down the hill on Ludford Bridge.

⊞ **Tasty straightforward pubby food includes sandwiches, ludlow sausage baguette, soup, scampi and chips, sausage and mash, cod in beer batter, sirloin steak, shropshire pork pies and a changing choice of vegetarian dishes such as quiche.** *Starters/Snacks: £3.95 to £6.95. Main Courses: £6.95 to £14.95. Puddings: £3.95 to £4.95*

Free house ~ Licensee Graham Willson-Lloyd ~ Real ale ~ Bar food (12-2.30, 6.30-9) ~ (01584) 872174 ~ Children welcome away from bar ~ Dogs welcome ~ Open 10am-midnight(1am Fri-Sun) ~ Bedrooms: £40B/£70B

Recommended by Ian and Helen Stafford, Malcolm and Pauline Pellatt, Pam and John Smith, Paul J Robinshaw, Mr and Mrs W W Burke, Joe Green, MLR, Theo, Anne and Jane Gaskin, Dave Braisted, Mike and Lynn Robinson, Andy Lickfold, Peter Martin

MUCH WENLOCK   SO6299   MAP 4

George & Dragon 🍺 £
High Street (A458); TF13 6AA

Bustling, snugly atmospheric, plenty to look at, reasonably priced food, good beer selection and usefully open all day

---

There's a thoroughly engaging collection of all sorts of pub paraphernalia at this cosy old place in the centre of this delightful town. You'll find old brewery and cigarette advertisements, bottle labels, beer trays and George-and-the-Dragon pictures, as well as around 500 jugs hanging from the beams. Furnishings such as antique settles are among more conventional seats and there are a couple of attractive Victorian fireplaces (with coal-effect gas fires). At the back is the restaurant. Five real ales on handpump feature Greene King Abbot and either St Austell Tribute or Wadworths 6X, and with three guests such as Caledonian IPA, Morrissey Fox Blonde or Wadsworth Strong in the Arm; and they also have a very wide selection of wines by the glass; piped music, dominoes, cards board games. More reports on the newish licensees please.

⊞ **Available in the restaurant or bar, food includes lunchtime sandwiches, soup, fish and chips, faggots and peas and evening dishes such as lamb shank or butternut squash and cashew nut roast.** *Starters/Snacks: £3.95 to £4.50. Main Courses: £5.95 to £9.95. Puddings: £3.95*

Punch ~ Lease James Scott ~ Real ale ~ Bar food (12-2.30, 6-9 (not Weds or Sun evenings)) ~ Restaurant ~ (01952) 727312 ~ Children welcome until 9pm ~ Dogs allowed in bar ~ Open 11(12 Sun)-11(am Fri, Sat)

Recommended by Chris Glasson, Jenny and Peter Lowater, Pete Baker, Les and Sandra Brown

Talbot 🛏
High Street (A458); TF13 6AA

Ancient building with friendly welcome, tasty food, pretty courtyard and bedrooms

---

A thoroughly welcoming place to stay in a characterful street in the centre of this little town, this unspoilt medieval inn was described by one reader as 'the kind of local I dream of living near'. Its several neatly kept traditional areas (good for both drinkers or diners) have low ceilings and comfortable red tapestry button-back wall banquettes around their tables. The walls are decorated with local pictures and cottagey plates, and there are art deco-style lamps and gleaming brasses. Bass and a guest such as Wye Valley

Dorothy Goodbody are served on handpump and they've several malt whiskies and nine wines by the glass; quiet piped music. It also has a little courtyard with green metal and wood garden furniture and pretty flower tubs. There's a cheap car park close by. More up-to-date reports please.

🍴 **The lunchtime menu has soup, sandwiches and baked potatoes, starters like stilton and walnut pâté, coquilles st jacques, liver and onions, lamb and leek pie, lasagne, steaks, good Sunday roasts, giant yorkshire pudding, smoked haddock and pasta bake, and pheasant wrapped in bacon with a creamy whisky sauce. There are daily specials and a more elaborate evening menu.** *Starters/Snacks: £4.00 to £5.50. Main Courses: £8.95 to £14.95. Puddings: £4.25*

Free house ~ Licensees Mark and Maggie Tennant ~ Real ale ~ Bar food (12-2.30, 6-9 (8.30 Sun)) ~ Restaurant ~ (01952) 727077 ~ Children welcome ~ Open 11am-midnight ~ Bedrooms: £40B/£80B

Recommended by Adrian Johnson, David and Jill Head, John Oates, Denise Walton, R J Herd, Mr and Mrs W W Burke, Pete Yearsley

MUNSLOW   SO5287   MAP 4

Crown

B4368 Much Wenlock—Craven Arms; SY7 9ET

Cosy, ancient village inn with local ales, cider, good wines and imaginative food

Full of nooks and crannies, this comfortable inn was once a Tudor court house and very busy at peak times (when you may have a wait for your meal). The split-level lounge bar has a pleasantly old-fashioned mix of furnishings on its broad flagstones, a collection of old bottles, country pictures and a bread oven by its good log fire. There are more seats in a traditional snug with its own fire and the eating area has tables around a central oven chimney, stripped stone walls and more beams and flagstones; piped music. Three beers on handpump are Holdens Black Country and Golden Glow and Three Tuns XXX, alongside a local farm cider, several malt whiskies and a good wine list. Look out for Jenna, the boxer who usually makes her rounds at the end of the evening.

🍴 **The imaginative food is produced with thought – they display a list of their local suppliers up on the bar wall. As well as lunchtime sandwiches, the changing menu might include butternut squash risotto, own-smoked haddock and crayfish fishcake with sweet chilli sauce, rump steak, confit of gressingham duck leg with cassoulet sauce, king scallops with cauliflower puree and salsa, and roast belly pork with chilli and basil cornmeal fritter; regional cheeseboard.** *Starters/Snacks: £4.75 to £6.50. Main Courses: £9.50 to £12.50. Puddings: £4.95*

Free house ~ Licensees Richard and Jane Arnold ~ Real ale ~ Bar food ~ Restaurant ~ (01584) 841205 ~ Children in eating area of bar and restaurant ~ Open 12-3, 6.30-11; closed Sun evening, Mon ~ Bedrooms: £55B/£85S(£90B)

Recommended by Denise Dowd, Marek Theis, James and Lucinda Woodcock, Alan and Eve Harding, Julia and Richard Tredgett, Michael and Margaret Slater, Les and Sandra Brown, Sue Demont, Tim Barrow, Patricia Walker

NORBURY   SO3692   MAP 6

Sun 🛏

Off A488 or A489 NE of Bishop's Castle; OS Sheet 137 map reference 363928; SY9 5DX

Civilised dining pub with lovely bar and bedrooms, in prime hill-walking country not far from the Stiperstones

A romantic place to stay, with excellent breakfasts too, this is in a bucolic setting, in a sleepy village beneath the southern flank of Norbury Hill and with a particularly pretty little rustic garden and pond. Its proper tiled-floor bar has sofas and Victorian tables and chairs, cushioned stone seats along the wall by the woodburning stove, and a few mysterious farming implements (the kind that it's fun to guess about) on its neat white walls. The restaurant side has a charming lounge with button-back leather wing chairs, easy chairs and a chesterfield on its deep-pile green carpet, as well as a welcoming log fire, nice lighting, willow-pattern china on a good dark oak dresser, fresh flowers, candles and magazines; service is friendly. Wye Valley Bitter and a guest such as Woods Shrosphire Lad are on handpump under a light blanket pressure, and they have several malts and decent house wines; piped music. Note the unusual opening times; more reports please.

🍴 **The bar menu is fairly short but food is carefully sourced, with baguettes, ploughman's, cumberland sausage and chips, shropshire rump steak, smoked trout and scampi. The elegantly furnished dining room has an unpretentious evening menu that might include starters like smoked trout salad and main courses such as local free-range chicken provençale with wild mushrooms or fillet steak au poivre; puddings might include lemon syllabub. They also do a traditional Sunday roast lunch (booking required) with local beef or pork cooked to order.** *Starters/Snacks: £4.95. Main Courses: £8.75. Puddings: £4.50*

Free house ~ Licensee Carol Cahan ~ Real ale ~ Bar food (7-9 Weds-Fri; 12-2, 7-9 Sat; 12-2 Sun) ~ Restaurant ~ (01588) 650680 ~ Children welcome lunchtime only ~ Dogs allowed in bar ~ Open 7-11; 12-3, 7-11 Sat; 12-3 Sun; closed weekday lunchtimes, Sun evening and all day Mon (except bank holidays) and Tues ~ Bedrooms: £75S/£90S

Recommended by S J and C C Davidson, Richard Belcher, M J Daly

SHREWSBURY
SJ4812 MAP 6

Armoury
Victoria Quay, Victoria Avenue; SY1 1HH

Vibrant atmosphere in interestingly converted riverside warehouse, run by enthusiastic young staff, good food all day, excellent drinks selection

'A rare thing: a town pub that has the laid-back atmosphere of a country pub, yet has that buzz of being in the town' commented one reader of this very well run place in a former warehouse. With an initial wow factor and lit by long runs of big arched windows with views across the broad river, the spacious open-plan interior is light and fresh, but the eclectic décor, furniture layout and lively bustle give a personal feel. Mixed wood tables and chairs are grouped on expanses of stripped wood floors, a display of floor-to-ceiling books dominates two huge walls, there's a grand stone fireplace at one end and masses of old prints mounted edge to edge on the stripped brick walls. Colonial-style fans whirr away on the ceilings, which are supported by occasional green-painted standing timbers and small wall-mounted glass cabinets displaying smoking pipes. The long bar counter has a terrific choice of drinks with up to eight real ales from brewers such as Adnams, Cottage, Hobsons, Slaters, Thwaites, Three Tuns, Weetwood and Worfield well kept on handpump, a great wine list (with 20 by the glass), around 50 malt whiskies, a dozen different gins, lots of rums and vodkas, a variety of brandies and some unusual liqueurs. The massive uniform red brick exteriors are interspersed with hanging baskets and smart coach lights at the front; there may be queues at the weekend. The pub doesn't have its own parking, but there are plenty of places nearby.

🍴 **Superbly cooked bar food, from an interesting daily changing menu, could include sandwiches, ploughman's, leek and potato soup, warm duck salad, grilled mackerel, welsh rarebit with poached egg, and main courses like like smoked haddock and salmon fishcakes, rump steak or potato gnocchi with wild mushrooms.** *Starters/Snacks: £4.35 to £6.35. Main Courses: £8.95 to £16.60. Puddings: £5.15*

Brunning & Price ~ Manager John Astle-Rowe ~ Real ale ~ Bar food (12-10) ~ (01743) 340525 ~ Children welcome ~ Dogs allowed in bar ~ Open 12-11(10.30 Sun)

Recommended by Ian and Helen Stafford, Michael Beale, Kerry Law, Denise Dowd, Marek Theis, Tony and Wendy Hobden, Henry Pursehouse-Tranter, Jacquie Jones, Owen Davies, Steve and Liz Tilley

> Post Office address codings confusingly give the impression that some pubs are in Shropshire, when they're really in Cheshire (which is where we list them).

STIPERSTONES   SJ3600   MAP 6

Stiperstones Inn

Signed off A488 S of Minsterley; OS Sheet 126 map reference 364005; SY5 0LZ

Welcoming, simple country inn run by caring owners, in fine walking country

Open fires warm this walkers' haunt out in one of the most scenic corners of Shropshire. Inside, the pub's tortoiseshell cat, Skittles, usually presides over the small modernised lounge, which has comfortable leatherette wall banquettes and lots of brassware on ply-panelled walls. The plainer public bar has darts, board games, TV, games machine and mancala. Reasonably priced Stonehouse Station Bitter and Woods Parish are on handpump. The landlady, Lara, is always happy to advise about local walks, on the Long Mynd or up the dramatic quartzite ridge of the Stiperstones; the industrial archaeology of the abandoned lead mines at nearby Snailbeach is also fascinating. They have two inexpensive bedrooms; we would welcome reports from readers who stay here.

🍴 **Served all day, the good value bar menu features traditional pubby food, with sandwiches, ploughman's and baked potatoes, starters such as garlic mushrooms and breaded brie wedges and main courses such as steak and ale pie, gammon, battered haddock, steaks, curries and lasagne. Very hungry diners are invited to request larger portions at no extra cost. The changing pudding menu specialises in using local fruit, including whinberries gathered from the surrounding hills and made into pies and crumbles.** *Starters/Snacks: £2.95 to £5.50. Main Courses: £3.95 to £13.50. Puddings: £2.00 to £3.25*

Free house ~ Licensee Lara Sproson ~ Real ale ~ Bar food (12-9) ~ Restaurant ~ (01743) 791327 ~ Children welcome until 9pm in bar ~ Dogs allowed in bar and bedrooms ~ Open 11.30am-midnight(2am Sat) ~ Bedrooms: £35S/£60S

Recommended by Bruce and Sharon Eden, Tracy Collins

LUCKY DIP

Besides the fully inspected pubs, you might like to try these Lucky Dips recommended to us and described by readers (if you do, please send us reports: feedback@goodguides.com).

ALL STRETTON [SO4595]
Yew Tree SY6 6HG [Shrewsbury Rd (B4370)]: Appealing old pub with enjoyable food (not Mon evening), small helpings available, Bass, Hobsons Best and a changing guest such as Wye Valley, pleasant service, good log fire, houseplants and lots of interesting watercolours, lounge bar and lively nicely worn-in public bar with darts, two big dogs, four cats; no credit cards; well behaved children and dogs welcome, small village handy for Long Mynd *(A N Bance)*
ALVELEY [SO7584]
Three Horseshoes WV15 6NB: Ancient pub with good welcoming service, good value food, well kept ales such as Brakspears Pride of the River *(Alan and Eve Harding)*
ATCHAM [SJ5409]
☆ ***Mytton & Mermaid*** SY5 6QG: Comfortable 18th-c hotel rather than pub, but with really nice friendly atmosphere, big log fire and sofas in relaxed bar, good interesting food here (all day Sun) or in large bustling restaurant, efficient young staff, well kept real ales such as Salopian Shropshire Gold, good wine choice; limited parking; pleasant Severn-view bedrooms – more in courtyard, nice setting opp entrance to Attingham Park (NT) *(Tony and Wendy Hobden,*

Clifford Blakemore, Brian Brooks, Canon George Farran, Pete Yearsley)
BASCHURCH [SJ4221]
New Inn SY4 2EF [Church Rd]: Attractively refurbished, real ales such as Banks's and Greene King Abbot, good choice of wines by the glass, enjoyable fresh home-made food in bar and restaurant; terrace *(Noel Grundy)*
BISHOP'S CASTLE [SO3288]
☆ ***Castle Hotel*** SY9 5BN [Market Sq, just off B4385]: Imposing 18th-c panelled coaching inn with three neatly kept bar areas, fire in each, enjoyable food inc more extensive evening choice, well kept Big Nevs, Hobsons and Six Bells Goldrings, decent wines and malt whiskies, bar billiards and other games; dogs welcome, disabled access, tables in front and in back garden with nice views, seven bedrooms, good breakfast, cl bank hol Mon *(the Didler, LYM, Leigh and Gillian Mellor, Mike and Lynn Robinson, Di and Mike Gillam, Denise Dowd, Marek Theis, Steven and Victoria James)*
BRATTON [SJ6314]
Gate TF5 0BX: Reopened under friendly new landlady, enjoyable food, four real ales *(anon)*
BRIDGNORTH [SO7193]
Kings Head WV16 4QN [Whitburn St]: Well restored 17th-c timbered coaching inn with

high-raftered back stable bar tap for their good Bridgnorth ales, changing guest beers, lots of wines by the glass, enjoyable good value food from lunchtime sandwiches to chargrills, three log fires, beams and flagstones, pretty leaded windows; courtyard picnic-sets, open all day (John Oates, Denise Walton, the Didler)

Old Castle WV16 4AB [West Castle St]: Lovely old-fashioned pub dating from 14th c, generous good value food, Adnams and Greene King ales, two good ciders, friendly efficient service; good-sized garden overlooking town, may be bouncy castle in summer (Mike and Mary Clark, Robert W Buckle, Karl Becker)

☆ **Railwaymans Arms** WV16 5DT [Severn Valley station, Hollybush Rd (off A458 towards Stourbridge)]: Bathams, Hobsons and other good value local ales kept well in chatty old-fashioned converted waiting-room at Severn Valley steam railway terminus, bustling on summer days, with coal fire, old station signs and train nameplates, superb mirror over fireplace, may be simple summer snacks, annual beer festival; awkward disabled access; children welcome, tables out on platform – the train to Kidderminster (another bar there) has an all-day bar and bookable Sun lunches, pub open all day wknds (Colin Moore, the Didler, Henry Pursehouse-Tranter, Kerry Law, LYM)

BROCKTON [SO5793]

☆ **Feathers** TF13 6JR [B4378]: Stylish restaur/country dining pub with good interesting food inc lunchtime and early evening deals, home-baked bread, good friendly service even when busy, well kept Woods, comfortable seats in attractively decorated beamed rooms and delightful conservatory; children allowed, has been cl wkdy lunchtimes and Mon (Alan and Eve Harding, LYM)

BUCKNELL [SO3574]

Baron of Beef SY7 0AH [Chapel Lawn Rd; just off B4367 Knighton Rd]: Rather smart dining pub (may have good value food deals), friendly efficient staff, well kept ales inc Hobsons and Wye Valley, farm cider, decent house wines, big log fire in front bar, back dining lounge/garden room, interesting prints, rustic memorabilia inc grindstone and cider press, largish upstairs restaurant with own bar and popular wknd carvery; wknd live music; well behaved children and dogs welcome, lovely views, big garden with skittles and play area, camping field (Alan and Eve Harding, MLR)

BURLTON [SJ4526]

☆ **Burlton Inn** SY4 5TB [A528 Shrewsbury—Ellesmere, nr B4397 junction]: Attractively refurbished old pub with friendly landlord, wide food choice at well spaced tables, Robinsons ales, sporting prints, log fires, comfortable snug, restaurant with garden dining room; children welcome, disabled facilities, garden with pleasant terrace, bedrooms, good breakfast (LYM, Noel Grundy,

J S Burn, Mrs Jane Kingsbury, Alan and Eve Harding, Bruce and Sharon Eden)

CLEE HILL [SO5975]

Kremlin SY8 3NB [track up hill off A4117 Bewdley—Cleobury, by Victoria Inn]: Newish owners for Shropshire's highest pub, enjoyable good value straightforward food inc Sun roasts, friendly service, real ales and farm cider; splendid view south from garden and terrace, play area, bedrooms, cl Mon till 4.30 otherwise open all day (David Elliott)

CLEEHILL [SO5875]

Royal Oak SY8 3PE [Ludlow Rd (A4117)]: Friendly unassuming pub dating from 17th c, wide range of daily-changing food, all freshly made (they are helpful with special requests), seasonal game and fish, OAP discounts Thurs, charming staff, well kept local ales; good view from front (David Elliott)

CLUN [SO3080]

☆ **White Horse** SY7 8JA [The Square]: Refurbished pub dating from 18th c, helpful cheerful staff and buoyant atmosphere, generous good value home-made food in bar and separate dining room, half a dozen well kept changing ales such as Hobsons, Salopian, Three Tuns, Woods and Wye Valley, perhaps a home-brewed beer, Weston's farm cider and perry, good coffee, daily papers, low beams, inglenook and woodburner, occasional entertainment and quiz nights; children welcome, small back garden, four comfortable bedrooms, open all day (Alan and Eve Harding, A N Bance, MLR, Peter and Sheila Longland)

CLUNTON [SO3381]

Crown SY7 0HU: Cosy old country local with welcoming landlady and good-humoured service, good changing ales such as Hobsons and Six Bells, good value wines by the glass, log fire in small flagstoned bar, dining room with good choice of popular food inc Sun lunch, small games room (A N Bance, Alan and Eve Harding)

COALBROOKDALE [SJ6604]

☆ **Coalbrookdale Inn** TF8 7DX [Wellington Rd, opp Museum of Iron]: Handsome dark brick 18th-c pub with half a dozen quickly changing ales from square counter in simple convivial tiled-floor bar, good sensibly priced food cooked to order using local produce here or in quieter dining room, farm ciders, country wines, good log fire, local pictures, piano, naughty beach murals in lavatories; long flight of steps to entrance; dogs welcome, a few tables outside, good bedrooms (Ann Harrison, the Didler, BB, DC)

COCKSHUTT [SJ4329]

☆ **Leaking Tap** SY12 0JQ [A528 Ellesmere—Shrewsbury]: Comfortable and attractive, with good varied food (Sun lunch very popular), reasonable prices, good friendly service, well kept Everards Tiger, decent wines by the glass (Alan and Eve Harding)

CORFTON [SO4985]

☆ **Sun** SY7 9DF [B4368 Much Wenlock—Craven Arms]: Welcoming and chatty long-serving landlord (if he's not busy in the back brewery) in unchanging three-room country local with its own good Corvedale ales (inc an unfinned beer) and guest, lots of breweriana, quarry-tiled public bar with darts and pool, good value pubby food from generous baguettes to bargain Sun lunch, quieter carpeted lounge, dining room with covered well, tourist information; piped music; children and dogs (in bar) welcome, particularly good wheelchair access throughout and disabled lavatories, tables on terrace and in large garden with good play area *(BB, MLR)*

CRAVEN ARMS [SO4382]

Craven Arms SY7 9QJ [Shrewsbury Rd]: Cheerful efficient service, good value food inc bargain OAP carvery lunch, well kept Salopian Shropshire Gold *(A N Bance, Alan and Eve Harding)*

DORRINGTON [SJ4703]

Bridge Inn SY5 7ED [A49 N]: Attractively refurbished streamside pub with bargain lunches Mon-Sat inc choice of roasts, Sun carvery, settees and armchairs as well as plenty of tables and chairs in roomy lounge bar, well spaced tables in conservatory restaurant; tables outside, caravan spaces in paddock behind *(TOH)*

FORD [SJ4113]

Pavement Gates SY5 9LE [Welshpool Rd (A458 W of Shrewsbury)]: Warmly welcoming dining pub with appealing contemporary refurbishment, comfortable lounge with leather sofas and daily papers, smart airy restaurant, enjoyable food all day from enterprising light dishes up, good bargain Sun carvery, friendly prompt service, up to four real ales, sensibly priced wines; fruit machine in back bar; children welcome, disabled facilities, open all day *(Pete Yearsley)*

GRINSHILL [SJ5223]

☆ *Inn at Grinshill* SY4 3BL [off A49]: Upmarket early Georgian country dining inn, Greene King Ruddles, Rowton, Theakstons XB and a guest, good wine with several by the glass, malt whiskies, smartly comfortable 19th-c bar with open log fire, spacious contemporary main restaurant; piped music, TV; children welcome, dogs in bar, disabled facilities, back garden with views, seven good bedrooms, cl Sun and perhaps Mon, Tues (best to check) *(Alan and Eve Harding, Ken Marshall, Noel Grundy, Martin Stafford, J S Burn, LYM, Brian and Diane Mugford, David Field)*

HAMPTON LOADE [SO7486]

River & Rail WV16 6BN [off A442 Kidderminster—Bridgenorth]: Spacious tucked-away modern pub handy for River Severn and steam railway, enjoyable good value food all day from sandwiches to specials (may be evening two-for-one deals), friendly efficient service; big attractive garden with plenty of under-cover seating, adjacent passenger ferry (Apr-Sept), self-catering cottages *(Colin Moore, Dave Braisted)*

HINDFORD [SJ3333]

Jack Mytton SY11 4NL: Enjoyable food from bar snacks up, good choice of changing ales inc favourites such as Sharps Doom Bar, pleasant rustic bar with log fire, airy raftered dining room; picnic-sets in attractive garden by Llangollen Canal, good-sized courtyard with summer bar and carved bear (pub named after eccentric squire who rode a bear), moorings *(Meg and Colin Hamilton, Bob and Laura Brock)*

HODNET [SJ6128]

☆ *Bear* TF9 3NH [Drayton Rd (A53)]: Friendly efficient service, good fairly priced food inc bargain set menu (Mon-Sat), four well kept ales inc Woods Shropshire Lad, good wines by the glass, rambling open-plan carpeted main area with blond seats and tables, snug end alcoves with heavy 16th-c beams and timbers, small beamed quarry-tiled bar with log fire; children welcome, six good value bedrooms, opp Hodnet Hall gardens and handy for Hawkstone Park, open all day *(BB, Alan and Eve Harding, J S Burn)*

HOPTON WAFERS [SO6376]

☆ *Crown* DY14 0NB [A4117]: Attractive 16th-c beamed and creeper-covered inn with relaxed atmosphere and cheerful efficient staff, enjoyable food (all day Sun) from home-baked bread up, big inglenook, light and comfortable décor and furnishings, well kept ales inc Hobsons and Ludlow, good choice of wines; children and dogs welcome, inviting garden with duck pond, stream and terraces, bedrooms, open all day *(Roger and Linda Norman, Alan and Eve Harding, LYM)*

IRONBRIDGE [SJ6603]

☆ *Malthouse* TF8 7NH [The Wharfage (bottom road alongside Severn)]: Converted 18th-c malthouse wonderfully located in historic gorge, some refurbishment by new owners, spacious bar with iron pillars supporting heavy pine beams, lounge/dining area, good choice of food all day, friendly staff, three changing beers, live music Fri/Sat; children and dogs welcome, terrace tables, 12 bedrooms inc separate cottage, open all day; reports on new regime please *(LYM)*

Robin Hood TF8 7HQ [Waterloo St]: Friendly Severn-side pub with five comfortable linked rooms, various alcoves inc barrel-vaulted dining room, well kept Holdens, freshly made pub food, lots of brass, old photographs and clocks; dogs welcome, attractive seating area out in front, nice setting handy for museums, bedrooms, good breakfast *(Dr and Mrs P Truelove, Adrian Johnson)*

Swan TF8 7NH [Wharfage]: Ex-warehouse with dark woodwork and lots of alcoves, good range of decent food from baguettes to some interesting dishes, friendly service, local real ales and a continental beer on tap, separate candlelit red-décor dining area; tables outside *(Adrian Johnson, Alan and Eve Harding)*

White Hart TF8 7AW [Wharfage]: 18th-c inn with fresh and airy contemporary décor, enjoyable sensibly priced bistro-style food (all day Sun summer), upstairs dining room with Severn views; children and dogs welcome, picnic-sets out facing river over road, five comfortable bedrooms, open all day *(Michael and Margaret Slater)*

KNOWBURY [SO5874]

Penny Black SY8 3LL: Attractive and comfortable, with good value fresh food cooked by landlord inc good Sun carvery with remarkable choice of veg; well kept real ales, farm cider, decent wines, enthusiastic staff, small restaurant; big garden, view of 18th-c aqueduct; no credit cards, cl Sun evening *(Ian Gaskin)*

LEINTWARDINE [SO4175]

☆ *Jolly Frog* SY7 0LX [Toddings; A4113 out towards Ludlow]: Restauranty pub/bistro with welcoming cheerful atmosphere, frequently changing menus with emphasis on good fresh fish, not cheap but lunchtime and early evening better value set meals, imaginative cooking without being fussy or pretentious, also pizza oven and home-baked bread, good wine list and coffees, well kept Ludlow Gold, mix of tables sizes (high chairs for small children), log fire; good views from tables out on decking *(Alan and Eve Harding)*

LITTLE STRETTON [SO4492]

☆ *Ragleth* SY6 6RB [off A49; Ludlow Rd]: Nicely opened up and refurbished 17th-c dining pub, light wood old tables and chairs in airy bay-windowed front bar, heavily beamed brick-and-tile-floored public bar with huge inglenook, enjoyable home-made food from bar snacks to full meals, Sun roasts, real ales, darts, board games; piped music; tulip tree by lawn looking across to thatched and timbered church, good play area, open all day summer weekends *(Michael and Margaret Slater, Dan Bones, LYM)*

LLANFAIR WATERDINE [SO2376]

Waterdine LD7 1TU [signed from B4355; turn left after bridge]: Spotless old inn nicely set near good stretch of Offa's Dyke path, emphasis on good if not cheap food (must book) inc inventive recipes in rambling series of heavy-beamed rooms with cosy alcoves, woodburner and some flagstones, small back conservatory looking down to River Teme (the Wales border); picnic-sets in lovely garden *(LYM, Rodney and Norma Stubington)*

LONGVILLE [SO5393]

☆ *Longville Arms* TF13 6DT [B4371 Church Stretton—Much Wenlock]: Two neat and spacious bars with beams, stripped stone and some oak panelling, good service, real ales inc Woods, good food in bar and large comfortable restaurant, games room with darts and pool; piped music; children welcome and dogs (may get a biscuit), disabled facilities, terraced side garden with good play area, lovely countryside, bedrooms, open all day wknds *(TOH, LYM, David and Doreen Beattie)*

LOPPINGTON [SJ4729]

Dickin Arms SY4 5SR [B4397]: Cheerful two-bar country local, comfortably plush banquettes, open fire, shallow steps to neat back dining room with good value generous food inc landlady's speciality curries, lunchtime deals, well kept Bass and an interesting guest beer; pool; play area, pretty village *(Alan and Eve Harding, BB)*

LUDLOW [SO5174]

Blue Boar SY8 1BB [Mill St]: Big rambling pub, lots of linked areas, old-world décor with woodwork, old prints and notices, country bygones and boar memorabilia, friendly efficient service, bargain generous food, well kept Black Sheep; piped music, TVs; lovely back suntrap courtyard with tables under parasols, big bedrooms, open all day *(Alan and Eve Harding)*

Charlton Arms SY8 1PJ [Ludford Bridge]: Recently refurbished former coaching inn in great spot overlooking River Teme and the town, two bars, lounge and restaurant, good food, cheerful efficient service, well kept ales inc local Ludlow Gold; waterside garden and terrace, ten bedrooms (may be traffic noise), open all day *(Andy Lickfold, Alan and Eve Harding, Joe Green)*

Horse & Jockey SY8 1NU [Old St]: Recently refurbished, with cheerful efficient service, bargain pubby food, enjoyable Sun lunch; Marstons-related keg beer; tables out on decking *(Alan and Eve Harding)*

Queens SY8 1RU [Lower Galdeford]: Family-run pub with enjoyable food concentrating heavily on fresh local produce, long bar, pine tables in dining area, friendly pub dog *(anon)*

Squirrel SY8 1LS [Foldgate Lane; off Sheet Rd off A49]: Cheerful efficient service even when busy, wide choice of good value generous food from light dishes up, well kept Marstons-related ales, proper dining room *(Alan and Eve Harding)*

Wheatsheaf SY8 1PQ [Lower Broad St]: Traditional 17th-c beamed pub spectacularly built into medieval town gate, good value generous pubby food, Sun carvery, efficient cheerful staff, well kept Marstons and related ales; attractive comfortable bedrooms *(Alan and Eve Harding, Dr and Mrs Jackson, Joe Green)*

MARTON [SJ2903]

Lowfield SY21 8JX [B4386 Chirbury—Westbury]: Comfortably rebuilt in traditional style, local real ales, enjoyable fresh food, friendly staff, relaxed atmosphere, woodburner; peaceful country views from teak terrace tables and garden picnic-sets, three bedrooms *(Alex Jagger)*

☆ *Sun* SY21 8JP [B4386 NE of Chirbury]: Family-run village pub with welcoming efficient service, father and son team doing good bar food and more adventurous dishes in contemporary restaurant, good Sun lunch, well kept Marstons and Hobsons, nice choice of wines; cl Sun evening to Tues lunchtime *(Alan and Eve Harding)*

MUCH WENLOCK [SO6299]
Gaskell Arms TF13 6AQ [High St (A458)]:
Two comfortable areas divided by brass-canopied log fire, friendly attentive service, enjoyable straightforward bar food at sensible prices, well kept Stonehouse Station, brasses, prints and banknotes, civilised old-fashioned restaurant; subdued piped music, games machine in lobby; roomy neat garden, bedrooms *(Alan and Eve Harding)*

NEWCASTLE [SO2482]
☆ *Crown* SY7 8QL [B4368 Clun—Newtown]:
Pretty village pub, warm and friendly, with good choice of reasonably priced well kept beers such as Hobsons and Timothy Taylors Landlord, sofas and woodburner in smart stripped stone lounge with well spaced tables in two dining areas, good coffee, attractively priced standard food from sandwiches to steak, rustic locals' bar and games room; piped music; tables outside, charming well equipped bedrooms above bar, attractive views and walks, open all day Sat *(A N Bance, LYM)*

NORTON [SJ7200]
☆ *Hundred House* TF11 9EE [A442 Telford—Bridgnorth]: Neatly kept bar with appealing gothic décor, Highgate and a Bitter and Mild brewed to the pub's recipes, good wine choice, very good food in bar and two tucked-away dining areas inc two-course lunch deals, log fires in handsome old fireplaces or working coalbrookdale ranges; prompt pleasant service, spotless quirky ladies'; piped music; lovely garden (they sell seeds for charity), comfortable and individual bedrooms *(Jill Sparrow, Jenny Jackson, LYM, John Silverman)*

NORTON IN HALES [SJ7038]
Hinds Head TF9 4AT [Main Rd]: Welcoming comfortably extended three-room country pub, good food choice from bar snacks to restaurant meals, friendly attentive service, four real ales inc Timothy Taylors Landlord, open fire, conservatory; disabled access, beautiful village setting by church *(John and Helen Rushton)*

PICKLESCOTT [SO4399]
Bottle & Glass SY6 6NR [off A49 N of Church Stretton]: This remote unspoilt 16th-c country pub is under new management – reports please; quarry-tiled bar and lounge/dining areas, log fires, well kept real ales, picnic-sets out in front *(LYM, Mr and Mrs D Hammond)*

PONTESBURY [SJ3906]
Horseshoe SY5 0QJ [Minsterley Rd (A488)]: Good welcoming service, good value pubby food, well kept ales inc Salopian Matrix and Wye Valley Butty Bach *(Alan and Eve Harding)*

SELATTYN [SJ2633]
Cross Keys SY10 7DN [B4579 NW of Oswestry]: Unspoilt traditional 17th-c village local in glorious remote countryside, Banks's/Marstons ales and low-priced soft drinks, may be home-made pickled eggs, two

small rooms, games room with pool and large screened-in porch (children allowed here), no music or machines – just chat, led by friendly landlord; attractive split-level garden, cl lunchtimes except Sun and Mon, Tues evenings *(Alan Poole)*

SHIFNAL [SJ74508]
White Hart TF11 8BH [High St]: Half a dozen or more interesting changing ales inc local ones in friendly 17th-c timbered roadside pub, quaint and old-fashioned, separate bar and lounge, comfortable without pretension, wide range of sandwiches and promptly served good value home-made hot dishes (not Sun), good choice of wines by the glass, welcoming staff; couple of steep steps at front door, open all day Fri-Sun *(the Didler)*

SHREWSBURY [SO4912]
Coach & Horses SY1 1NF [Swan Hill/Cross Hill]: Friendly old-fashioned Victorian local, panelled throughout, with main bar, cosy little side room and back dining room, enjoyable fresh food inc daily roast and some imaginative dishes, Salopian Shropshire Gold, Wye Valley and three guest ales, real cider, relaxed atmosphere, prompt helpful service even when busy, interesting Guinness prints, quiz night first Mon of month; piped music – live music on Sun; children allowed in dining room, dogs in bar, disabled facilities, smokers' roof terrace, open all day *(the Didler, Alan and Eve Harding, Joe Green, Tony and Wendy Hobden, Pete Baker)*

Golden Cross SY1 1LP [Princess St]: Attractive partly Tudor hotel with restaurant and quiet bar, welcoming attentive service, short choice of good interesting food inc home-baked bread and midweek lunch deals, good range of wines by the glass, well kept ales such as Hobsons and Salopian; four good value bedrooms *(Alan and Eve Harding, Clifford Blakemore)*

Loggerheads SY1 1UG [Church St]: Chatty old-fashioned local, panelled back room with flagstones, scrubbed-top tables, high-backed settles and coal fire, three other rooms with lots of prints, flagstones and bare boards, quaint linking corridor and hatch service of Banks's Bitter and Mild and other Marstons-related ales, exemplary bar staff, bargain lunchtime food (not Sun); darts, dominoes, poetry society, occasional live music; open all day *(Joe Green, the Didler, Pete Baker)*

Old Bucks Head SY3 8JR [Frankwell]: Quietly placed old inn with traditional bar and restaurant, cheerful staff, enjoyable pubby food inc bargain Sun lunch, well kept local Salopian; pleasant raised terrace garden, ten good value bedrooms, open all day Sat *(Alan and Eve Harding, Robert W Buckle)*

☆ *Three Fishes* SY1 1UR [Fish St]: Well run timbered and heavily beamed 16th-c pub in quiet cobbled street, small tables around three sides of central bar, flagstones, old pictures, well kept changing beers from mainstream and smaller breweries like Thornbridge, good value wines, good friendly service even when busy, no mobiles; normally have good value hearty bar food (not Sun evening) ordered from separate servery; open all day Fri, Sat *(LYM, John and Helen Rushton, Martin Grosberg, the Didler, Tony and Wendy Hobden)*

UPTON MAGNA [SJ5512]

Corbet Arms SY4 4TZ: Welcoming new licensees, landlord/chef doing above-average food inc good reasonably priced Sun lunch, well kept Marstons-related ales and guests, big L-shaped panelled dining lounge, fireside sofas, interesting old signage, darts in smaller public bar; great view to the Wrekin from attractive garden, handy for Haughmond Hill walks and Attingham Park (NT), neat bedrooms *(Alan and Eve Harding, Robert W Buckle)*

WALL UNDER HEYWOOD [SO5092]

Plough SY6 7DS [B4371]: Country pub under new management, comfortable spotless bars and conservatory restaurant, generous food (not Sun evening) from baguettes to pub favourites and specials, Sun roasts; up to four well kept ales inc Fullers London Pride and Theakstons; children welcome, tables in back garden (dogs allowed here), good walks, cl Mon till 6pm *(Roger Brown)*

WELLINGTON [SJ6410]

Old Orleton TF1 2HA [Holyhead Road (B5061, off M54 Junction 7)]: Sympathetically modernised old coaching inn with restaurant and bar, good upmarket food, well kept Hobsons beers, Weston's farm cider, good service; bedrooms *(Paul J Robinshaw)*

Swan TF1 2NH [Watling St]: Enjoyable bargain lunches, well kept Salopian

Shropshire Gold, friendly efficient service *(Alan and Eve Harding)*

WENLOCK EDGE [SO5696]

Wenlock Edge Inn TF13 6DJ [B4371 Much Wenlock—Church Stretton]: Newly renovated stone-built country pub in lovely spot, public bar, lounge and more modern dining extension, enjoyable home-made traditional food all day, Adnams, Greene King and Hobsons ales, open fire and inglenook woodburner; children welcome in eating areas, dogs in bar, terrace tables front and back, lots of walks, five bedrooms, open all day *(TOH, LYM)*

WHITCHURCH [SJ5345]

☆ *Willey Moor Lock* SY13 4HF [Tarporley Rd; signed off A49 just under 2 miles N]: Large opened-up family-run pub in picturesque spot by Llangollen Canal, low beams, countless teapots, two log fires, cheerful chatty atmosphere, half a dozen changing ales from small breweries, around 30 malt whiskies, enjoyable good value quickly served pub food from sandwiches up; piped music, games machine, several dogs and cats, various 'rule' notices; children welcome away from bar, terrace tables, secure garden with big play area *(Donna Davies, LYM, MLR)*

YORTON [SJ5023]

Railway SY4 3EP: Run by same family for over 70 years, friendly and chatty mother and daughter, unchanging atmosphere, plain tiled bar with hot coal fire, old settles and a modicum of railway memorabilia, big back lounge (not always open) with fishing trophies, Woods and other mainly local real ales, farm ciders, may be sandwiches on request, darts and dominoes – no piped music or machines; seats out in yard *(the Didler)*

Somerset

An engaging lack of pretension particularly endears this county's best pubs to our readers. And this doesn't only apply to the simple taverns but to the civilised dining pubs as well. The welcome is as warm if you just pop in for a drink as it is if you stay overnight after an excellent meal. It's very refreshing. Pubs doing especially well this year include the Red Lion at Babcary, Three Horseshoes at Batcombe, Old Green Tree in Bath, Cat Head at Chiselborough, Black Horse at Clapton-in-Gordano, George in Croscombe, Woods in Dulverton, Tuckers Grave at Faulkland, Pilgrims at Lovington, Royal Oak at Luxborough, Notley Arms at Monksilver, Montague Inn at Shepton Montague, and Blue Ball at Triscombe. Prime new entries are the Highbury Vaults in Bristol (eight real ales and good value bar food), Rose & Crown at Hinton Charterhouse (doing well under its current friendly young couple), Pack Horse at South Stoke (lots of history and atmosphere in this former priory), Rose & Crown at Stoke St Gregory (reopened after a devastating fire) and Fountain in Wells (thoroughly enjoyable little city pub with good food and drink). Many of these also offer delicious food using carefully chosen local (or even home-grown) produce; Somerset Dining Pub of the Year is Woods in Dulverton. The Lucky Dip section is particularly strong in this county – among its nearly 200 good pubs, too many stand out (mostly already inspected and approved by us) to list individually here. It's almost the same with the area's considerable number of flourishing small breweries. Top of the tree is Butcombe, with the most successful of its competitors being Exmoor, Bath, Cotleigh and Cottage.

APPLEY   ST0721   MAP 1

Globe

Hamlet signposted from the network of back roads between A361 and A38, W of B3187 and W of Milverton and Wellington; OS Sheet 181 map reference 072215; TA21 0HJ

Friendly licensee in bustling country pub, tasty food, real ales and seats in garden

There's lots to look at in this 15th-c pub – and a good mix of customers, too. The simple beamed front room has a built-in settle and bare wood tables on the brick floor, and another room has a GWR bench and 1930s railway posters; there's a further room with easy chairs and other more traditional ones, open fires, a growing collection of musical posters and instruments, art deco items and Titanic pictures; skittle alley. A brick entry corridor leads to a serving hatch with Cotleigh Harriers and Otter Ale on handpump. There are seats outside in the garden; the path opposite leads eventually to the River Tone.

🍴 Bar food includes lunchtime filled baguettes, soup, fried calamari with garlic mayonnaise, a choice of burgers, chilli with rice, four cheese and roast vegetable pasta bake, sausages braised in red wine with mustard mash, pork chop with a creamy Pernod and onion sauce, spicy chicken curry, pollack with a parmesan crust and lemon and white wine sauce, and puddings like chocolate pot with white chocolate honeycomb ice-cream

and a cheesecake of the day. *Starters/Snacks: £3.95 to £7.95. Main Courses: £7.95 to £14.25. Puddings: £4.95*

Free house ~ Licensee LeBurn Maddox ~ Real ale ~ Bar food (not Mon except bank hols) ~ Restaurant ~ (01823) 672327 ~ Children welcome ~ Open 12-3, 6.30-11.30; 12-3, 7-10 Sun; closed Mon except bank hols

Recommended by Bob and Margaret Holder, John and Fiona McIlwain, MB, the Didler, Dr and Mrs C W Thomas, Peter John West, Sara Fulton, Roger Baker

ASHILL   ST3116   MAP 1

Square & Compass

Windmill Hill; off A358 between Ilminster and Taunton; up Wood Road for 1 mile behind Stewley Cross service station; OS Sheet 193 map reference 310166; TA19 9NX

Friendly simple pub with local ales, tasty food and good regular live music in separate sound-proofed barn

---

As we went to press the friendly licensees here told us that by January 2010 they hoped to have bedrooms up and running in a new stable block. This is a traditional pub with sweeping views over the rolling pastures around Neroche Forest and a nice mix of chatty customers. The little bar has upholstered window seats that take in the fine view, heavy hand-made furniture, beams, an open winter fire – and perhaps the pub cat, Lilly. Exmoor Ale and St Austell Tinners and Tribute on handpump and good house wines by the glass. The piped music is often classical. There's a garden with picnic-sets, a large glass-covered walled terrace and good regular live music in their sound-proofed barn.

🍴 Cooked by the landlady, the generously served bar food includes sandwiches, filled baguettes and baked potatoes, ploughman's, soup, hot garlic king prawns, local sausages with onion gravy, ham and egg, mushroom stroganoff, sweet and sour pork, chicken with bacon and stilton, lambs kidneys braised with sherry and dijon mustard, mixed grill, and puddings such as banoffi pie or chocolate fudge cake; Sunday roasts. *Starters/Snacks: £4.00 to £6.50. Main Courses: £6.50 to £15.00. Puddings: £4.00 to £6.00*

Free house ~ Licensees Chris, Janet and Beth Slow ~ Real ale ~ Bar food ~ Restaurant ~ (01823) 480467 ~ Children welcome ~ Dogs welcome ~ Monthly live music in separate barn ~ Open 12-3, 6.30(7 Sat and Sun)-11

Recommended by Kieran Charles-Neale, Dr A McCormick, Nick Hawksley, Alain and Rose Foote, John and Fiona McIlwain

BABCARY   ST5628   MAP 2

Red Lion 🍴 ⚲

Off A37 south of Shepton Mallett; 2 miles or so N of roundabout where A37 meets A303 and A372; TA11 7ED

Relaxed, friendly thatched pub with interesting food, local beers and comfortable rambling rooms

---

A cheerful mix of customers (often with their happy dogs) and a friendly welcome from the chatty staff help create a particularly relaxed and informal atmosphere in this well run thatched pub. Several distinct areas work their way around the carefully refurbished bar. To the left of the entrance is a longish room with dark pink walls, a squashy leather sofa and two housekeeper's chairs around a low table by the woodburning stove and a few well spaced tables and captain's chairs (including a big one in a bay window with built-in seats). There are elegant rustic wall lights, some clay pipes in a cabinet and local papers to read; board games and gardening magazines too. Leading off here, with lovely dark flagstones, is a more dimly lit public bar area with a panelled dado, a high-backed old settle and other more straightforward chairs; darts, board games and bar billiards. The good-sized smart dining room has a large stone lion's head on a plinth above the open fire (with a huge stack of logs to one side), a big rug on polished boards and properly set tables. Otter Bright and Teignworthy Reel Ale on handpump, around ten wines by the glass and a few malt whiskies. There's a long informal garden with picnic-sets and a play area with a slide for children. The pub is handy for the A303 and for shopping at Clark's Village at Street.

🍴 Good bar food includes sandwiches, soup, pigeon breast with puy lentil salad, double baked cheese soufflé, butternut squash and sage risotto, honey-glazed ham with eggs, beef in ale pie, battered haddock with tartare sauce, chicken kiev, slow-roasted pork belly with celeriac purée, caramelised apples and cider sauce, free-range duck breast with wild mushroom cream sauce, and puddings like light and dark chocolate torte with espresso ice-cream and poached plum crumble with custard; popular Sunday roasts (it does get pretty busy then). *Starters/Snacks: £4.75 to £6.75. Main Courses: £7.75 to £10.50. Puddings: £4.75*

Free house ~ Licensee Charles Garrard ~ Real ale ~ Bar food ~ Restaurant ~ (01458) 223230 ~ Children welcome ~ Dogs allowed in bar ~ Open 12-3, 6-midnight; 12-4 Sun; closed Sun evening

Recommended by D P and M A Miles, M G Hart, Martin Hatcher, Bob and Margaret Holder, Guy Consterdine, Paul and Annette Hallett, Dr and Mrs C W Thomas, Steve Whalley, Terry Buckland, Chris and Angela Buckell, Tony Winckworth

BATCOMBE   ST6839   MAP 2

Three Horseshoes

Village signposted off A359 Bruton—Frome; BA4 6HE

Well run, attractive dining pub with smart rooms, friendly staff, elaborate food and quite a choice of drinks; bedrooms

As well as being an enjoyable place to stay (the bedrooms are comfortable and the breakfasts are good), this 17th-c honey-coloured stone building is popular for its interesting food, too. There's a warm welcome from the friendly staff and the long, rather narrow main room is smartly traditional: beams, local pictures on the lightly ragged dark pink walls, built-in cushioned window seats, solid chairs around a nice mix of old tables, and a woodburning stove at one end with a big open fire at the other. At the back on the left, the Gallery Bar has light panelled walls, tiled floors and modern pictures for sale and there's also a pretty stripped stone dining room (no mobile phones); best to book to be sure of a table, especially at weekends. Butcombe Bitter, Wadworths 6X and a guest beer on handpump, eight wines by the glass and farm cider. There are picnic-sets on the heated back terrace with more on the grass and a pond with koi carp. The pub is on a quiet village lane by the church which has a striking tower.

🍴 Using their own free-range eggs, home-grown vegetables and home-cured bacon and ham, the very good bar food at lunchtime includes filled ciabattas, soup, chicken liver pâté, goujons of fresh lager-battered fish served in paper with tartare sauce, bangers and mash with onion gravy, lambs liver with crispy home-cured bacon and sage, and thai salmon fishcake with cucumber, red radish and baby shoots in a lime yoghurt dressing, with evening choices such as scallops with tarragon and garlic butter, seared pigeon breast with a green pea vinaigrette and crispy prosciutto, free-range chicken suprême on steamed leeks, tian of chargrilled aubergine, cassoulet of vegetables, wilted spinach and parmentier potatoes topped with welsh rarebit, and slow-braised organic lamb shoulder with roast beetroot, confit garlic and shallots and a red wine gravy. Puddings might be rich dark chocolate mousse with black cherries in kirsch and sticky toffee pudding with butterscotch sauce and vanilla ice-cream. *Starters/Snacks: £6.75 to £8.75. Main Courses: £9.25 to £14.75. Puddings: £5.50*

Free house ~ Licensees Bob Wood and Shirley Greaves ~ Real ale ~ Bar food (not Sun evening or Mon) ~ Restaurant ~ (01749) 850359 ~ Children in eating area of bar and restaurant ~ Dogs allowed in bar and bedrooms ~ Live music some Thurs evenings ~ Open 12-3, 6.30-11; 12-3, 7.30-10.30 Sun; closed Mon (except bank holidays) ~ Bedrooms: /£75B

Recommended by Lt Col and Mrs Patrick Kaye, Caroline Battersby, Keith Bayliss, Mr and Mrs M Charge

BATH   ST7564   MAP 2

Old Green Tree 🍺
Green Street; BA1 2JZ

Super little pub with fine choice of real ales, enjoyable traditional food, lots of cheerful customers and friendly service

As ever, this particularly well run town pub is a delightful place with a wide mix of customers and excellent licensees; it can get packed, so to get a table you must arrive before midday. Green Tree Bitter (brewed for them by Blindmans Brewery), plus Butcombe Bitter and RCH Pitchfork, with guests such as Stonehenge Old Smokey and Wickwar Cotswold Way on handpump, a dozen wines by the glass from a nice little list with helpful notes, 35 malt whiskies, winter hot toddies and a proper Pimms. It's laid-back and cosy rather than particularly smart, and the three small oak-panelled and low wood-and-plaster ceilinged rooms include a comfortable lounge on the left as you go in, its walls decorated with wartime aircraft pictures in winter and local artists' work during spring and summer, and a back bar; the big skylight lightens things up attractively. No music or machines; chess, cribbage, dominoes, backgammon, shut the box, Jenga. The gents' is down steep steps. No children.

🍽 **Generous helpings of popular lunchtime bar food includes soup and sandwiches, ploughman's, a changing pâté, bangers and mash with beer and onion sauce, summer salads such as smoked duck and poached apple and smoked trout with asparagus, and winter beef in ale pie and pork and cider casserole; no starters or puddings.** *Main Courses: £6.50 to £10.00*

Free house ~ Licensees Nick Luke and Tim Bethune ~ Real ale ~ Bar food (12-3; not evenings, not Sun) ~ No credit cards ~ Open 11-11; 12-10.30 Sun; closed Sun lunch during May-July, 25 and 26 Dec

Recommended by Pete Coxon, Colin and Peggy Wilshire, Malcolm Ward, the Didler, Terry and Nickie Williams, Roger Wain-Heapy, Dr and Mrs A K Clarke, Martin and Marion Vincent, Michael Dandy, John Saville, Comus and Sarah Elliott, Donna and Roger, Pete Baker, Tom andRuth Rees, JJW, CMW, Barry Collett, Dr and Mrs M E Wilson

Star 🍺
Vineyards; The Paragon (A4), junction with Guinea Lane; BA1 5NA

Quietly chatty and unchanging old town local, brewery tap for Abbey Ales; filled rolls only

With friendly staff and customers, this honest old town pub does get particularly busy at weekends. It's the brewery tap for Abbey Ales and keeps Bellringer plus Bass, Hook Norton Hooky Gold, Marstons Pedigree and Smiles Heritage on handpump; 25 malt whiskies. The interior is unchanging and there's a quiet, chatty atmosphere not spoilt by noisy fruit machines or music; shove-ha'penny. The four (well, more like three and a half) small linked rooms are served from a single bar, separated by panelling with glass inserts. They are furnished with traditional leatherette wall benches and the like – even one hard bench that the regulars call Death Row – and the lighting's dim and not rudely interrupted by too much daylight.

🍽 **Filled rolls only, though they may have bar nibbles on Thursday evenings.**

Punch ~ Lease Paul Waters and Alan Morgan ~ Real ale ~ Bar food (see text) ~ (01225) 425072 ~ Children allowed but must be well behaved ~ Dogs welcome ~ Open 12-2.30, 5.30-midnight; noon-1am Sat; 12-midnight Sun

Recommended by the Didler, Roger Wain-Heapy, Catherine Pitt, Michael Cooper, Dr and Mrs A K Clarke, Phil and Sally Gorton, Pete Coxon, Pete Baker

---

> Real ale may be served from handpumps, electric pumps (not just the on-off switches used for keg beer) or – common in Scotland – tall taps called founts (pronounced 'fonts') where a separate pump pushes the beer up under air pressure.

BLAGDON
ST5058 MAP 2

New Inn
Off A368; Park Lane; BS40 7SB

**Lovely view over Blagdon Lake from nicely set pub; comfortable old furnishings in
bustling bar, real ales and traditional food**

This is a lovely spot with a fine view from the outside tables down over fields to the
wood-fringed Blagdon Lake and to the low hills beyond. Inside, there are two log fires in
inglenook fireplaces, heavy beams hung with horsebrasses and a few tankards, some
comfortable antique settles and mate's chairs among more modern furnishings, old prints
and photographs, and Wadworths IPA, 6X and JCB and a guest beer on handpump;
several wines by the glass. There's a plainer side bar, too; cheerful, helpful service.
Wheelchair access (best from the front) but no disabled facilities.

**Tasty bar food includes sandwiches and toasties, filled baked potatoes, ploughman's,
garlic mushrooms, ham and free-range eggs, vegetable risotto, beef in ale, cajun chicken,
a mixed grill, and puddings like hot chocolate fudge pudding and bakewell tart.**
Starters/Snacks: £4.25 to £5.50. Main Courses: £6.95 to £12.75. Puddings: £3.50

Wadworths ~ Tenant Roger Owen ~ Real ale ~ Bar food ~ (01761) 462475 ~ Children allowed if
over 10 ~ Dogs welcome ~ Open 11-3, 6-11; 12-3, 6.30-11 Sun
Recommended by John and Gloria Isaacs, Steve and Liz Tilley, Stuart Paulley, Chris and Angela Buckell

BRISTOL
ST5773 MAP 2

Albion
Boyce's Avenue, Clifton; BS8 4AA

Chatty local close to boutiquey shops with modern food and a good choice of drinks

In the heart of Clifton village, this is a busy and friendly little 18th-c pub with quite a
mix of customers. By the main door there's a flagstoned area with a big old pine table
and a couple of candlesticks, a dresser filled with jars of pickles, and an open kitchen.
Further in, the L-shaped bar has high chairs by the counter with its extravagant flower
arrangement, chapel chairs around good oak tables on the stripped wooden floor, brown
leather armchairs in front of the coal-effect gas fire with its neat log stacks on either
side of the brick fireplace and some cushioned wall seats; up a step is an end room with
a rather fine and very long high-backed new settle right the way across one wall, similar
tables and chairs and unusual silvery peony-type wallpaper (elswhere, the sage green
half-panelled walls are hung with modern photographs of the village). Arbor Brigstow,
Butcombe Bitter, Otter Bright and Sharps Doom Bar on handpump, good wines by the
glass, a couple of farm ciders, 25 malt whiskies and winter hot cider; piped music. The
covered and heated front terrace has plenty of picnic-sets and other seats under fairy
lights and there are church candles in hurricane lanterns.

**Interesting – though not cheap – modern cooking might include soup, rabbit terrine,
duck hearts and foie gras, smoked haddock rarebit with tomatoes, a plate of charcuterie,
gnocchi with beetroot and goats curd, whole crab and turbot with mayonnaise, sole with
tartare sauce, dry-aged forerib of aberdeen angus, ox cheek and chips (for two), and
puddings like chocolate fondant, milk sorbet and salt butter caramel and fig and pine nut
tart with brown butter ice-cream.** *Starters/Snacks: £5.00 to £7.50. Main Courses: £8.00 to
£14.00. Puddings: £5.00 to £7.00*

Enterprise ~ Lease James Phillips ~ Real ale ~ Bar food (12-3, 7-9.30; not Sun evening or Mon)
~ Restaurant ~ (0117) 973 3522 ~ Children welcome until 9pm ~ Dogs allowed in bar ~
Open 12-midnight(11 Sun); 5-midnight Mon; closed Mon lunchtime, 25 and 26 Dec
Recommended by Bob and Margaret Holder, Jeremy King, Donna and Roger

---

You can send reports directly to us at feedback@goodguides.com

Highbury Vaults ♨ £

St Michael's Hill, Cotham; BS2 8DE

Unpretentious and cheerful town pub with eight real ales, good value tasty bar food and friendly atmosphere

As this thriving if slightly scruffy town pub is so close to Bristol University, it can get pretty packed with students and teachers but there's a genuine welcome for visitors as well and the atmosphere is relaxed and cheerful. The little front bar, with the corridor beside it, leads through to a long series of small rooms – wooden floors, green and cream paintwork and old-fashioned furniture and prints, including lots of period royal family engravings and lithographs in the front room. There's now a model railway running on a shelf the full length of the pub, including tunnels through the walls. Bath Ales Gem Bitter, Brains SA, St Austell Tribute, Wells & Youngs Bitter and Special, and three guests on handpump and several malt whiskies. The attractive back terrace has tables built into a partly covered flowery arbour. In early Georgian days, this was used as the gaol where condemned men ate their last meal – the bars can still be seen on some windows.

🍴 **Good value, popular bar food includes filled rolls, ploughman's, soup, sausage or a pie and mash, various curries, chilli con carne and winter casseroles.** *Starters/Snacks: £1.75 to £5.50. Main Courses: £5.75 to £6.50. Puddings: £3.25*

Youngs ~ Manager Bradd Francis ~ Real ale ~ Bar food (12-2(2.30 Sat, 3 Sun), 5.30-8.30; not Sat or Sun evenings) ~ No credit cards ~ (0117) 973 3203 ~ Children welcome ~ Dogs allowed in bar ~ Open 12-12(11 Sun); closed evening 25 Dec, lunchtimes 26 Dec and 1 Jan

Recommended by Chris and Angela Buckell, the Didler, Donna and Roger

CHISELBOROUGH

ST4614 MAP 1

Cat Head

Leave A303 on A356 towards Crewkerne; take the third left turn (at 1.4 miles), signposted Chiselborough, then after another 0.2 miles turn left; Cat Street; TA14 6TT

Handy for the A303, with a consistently warm welcome, neat attractive bars, enjoyable food and thoughtful choice of drinks; pretty garden

You can be sure of a friendly welcome from the hard-working hands-on licensees in this bustling old sandstone pub and as it has a degree of sophistication with the atmosphere of a village local, it's much enjoyed by our readers. The spotless, traditional flagstoned rooms have light wooden tables and chairs, some high-backed cushioned settles, flowers and plants, a woodburning stove in a fine fireplace and curtains around the small mullioned windows. Butcombe Bitter, Otter Bitter and Sharps Doom Bar on handpump, a good wine list and Thatcher's cider; piped music, darts, skittle alley, shove-ha'penny and board games. There are seats on the terrace and in the attractive garden where there are plenty of colourful plants; nice views over the peaceful village, too.

🍴 **As well as lunchtime filled baguettes, ploughman's, soup, whitebait with aioli and salmon and prawn tart, the very good, well presented food includes lambs kidneys in madeira sauce, baked crab and scallops mornay, spinach and ricotta tortellini with tomato and basil sauce, chicken breast stuffed with blue cheese, half a crispy duck with scrumpy sauce, braised haunch of venison with juniper and red wine, and daily specials like mussels in white wine and cream, braised oxtail in Guinness, wild rabbit with mustard and thyme and grilled bass fillets with tarragon butter.** *Starters/Snacks: £4.80 to £6.20. Main Courses: £5.60 to £8.90. Puddings: £4.30*

Enterprise ~ Lease Duncan and Avril Gordon ~ Real ale ~ Bar food ~ (01935) 881231 ~ Children welcome ~ Open 12-3, 6.30-11; closed Sun evening

Recommended by Bob and Margaret Holder, Ray Edwards, Frank Willy, Sheila Topham, Mr and Mrs P D Titcomb, R T and J C Moggridge, Dr and Mrs M E Wilson, Richard O'Neill, Kate and Ian Hodge, Guy Consterdine, George and Gill Rowley, Douglas Allen, I D Barnett

CHURCHILL

ST4459   MAP 1

Crown 🍺 £

The Batch; in village, turn off A368 into Skinners Lane at Nelson Arms, then bear right;
BS25 5PP

Unspoilt and unchanging small cottage with friendly customers and staff, super range of
real ales and homely lunchtime food

The rambling L-shaped bar in this civilised place does still attract customers dropping
in for a pint but of course there's quite an emphasis on the hotel and restaurant side,
too. This friendly bar has Copper Dragon Golden Pippin and Theakstons Best on
handpump and quite a few wines by the glass as well as an interesting jumble of
seats from antique high-backed and other settles through settees and wing armchairs
heaped with cushions to tall and rather theatrical corner seats; the tables are almost as
much of a mix, and the walls and available surfaces are quite a jungle of bric-a-brac
including lots of race tickets, with standard and table lamps and candles keeping even
the lighting pleasantly informal. There's also a cosy main restaurant and a dining
pavilion with big tropical plants, nautical bits and pieces, and Edwardian sofas; piped
music. The gardens have bamboo and palm trees lining the paths, there's a gazebo at
the end of the walkways and seats on a mediterranean-style terrace. The opulent
bedrooms (based on famous hotels around the world) are in the surrounding house
which has seven acres of mature gardens and a 180-metre golf hole with full practice
facilities.

🍴 **Using beef from the field next door, the straightforward lunchtime bar food includes**
sandwiches (the rare roast beef is popular), good soup, filled baked potatoes,
ploughman's, cauliflower cheese, chilli con carne, beef casserole, and puddings like
treacle pudding and apple crumble. *Starters/Snacks: £4.25 to £4.95. Main Courses: £5.45*
to £8.25. Puddings: £3.90

Free house ~ Licensee Tim Rogers ~ Real ale ~ Bar food (12-2.30; not evenings) ~
No credit cards ~ (01934) 852995 ~ Children welcome away from bar ~ Dogs welcome ~
Open 11-11(midnight Fri and Sat); 12-10.30 Sun

Recommended by Tom Evans, Roger Wain-Heapy, the Didler, Bob and Margaret Holder, Barry and Anne, Ellie Weld,
Lt Col and Mrs Patrick Kaye, Michael Beale

CLAPTON-IN-GORDANO

ST4773   MAP 1

Black Horse 🍺

4 miles from M5 junction 19; A369 towards Portishead, then B3124 towards Clevedon; in
N Weston opposite school turn left signposted Clapton, then in village take second right,
maybe signed Clevedon, Clapton Wick; BS20 7RH

Ancient pub with lots of cheerful customers, friendly service, real ales and cider and
straightforward bar food; pretty garden

If you like old-fashioned, unspoilt pubs with a good range of real ales and
straightforward pub grub, then this friendly place will fit the bill. The partly flagstoned
and partly red-tiled main room has winged settles and built-in wall benches around
narrow, dark wooden tables, window seats, a big log fire with stirrups and bits on the
mantelbeam, and amusing cartoons and photographs of the pub. A window in an inner
snug is still barred from the days when this room was the petty-sessions gaol; high-
backed settles – one a marvellous carved and canopied creature, another with an art
nouveau copper insert reading East, West, Hame's Best – lots of mugs hanging from its
black beams, and plenty of little prints and photographs. There's also a simply furnished
room which is the only place families are allowed; darts and TV. Butcombe Bitter,
Courage Best, Shepherd Neame Spitfire, Skinners Cornish Knocker and Wadworths 6X on
handpump or tapped from the cask, several wines by the glass, farm ciders and efficient
service. There are some old rustic tables and benches in the garden, with more to one
side of the car park, and the summer flowers are really quite a sight. Paths from the pub
lead up Naish Hill or along to Cadbury Camp.

🍴 Straightforward lunchtime bar food includes filled baguettes, ploughman's and a few hot dishes like soup, shepherd's pie, cauliflower and broccoli bake, chicken and chorizo in spicy tomato sauce, slow-cooked pork in scrumpy and beef stew with dumplings. *Starters/Snacks: £3.50 to £4.95. Main Courses: £6.25 to £7.95*

Enterprise ~ Licensee Nicholas Evans ~ Real ale ~ Bar food (not evenings, not Sun) ~ No credit cards ~ (01275) 842105 ~ Children in very plain family room only ~ Live music Mon evening ~ Open 11-11; 12-10.30 Sun

Recommended by Rona Murdoch, the Didler, Dave Braisted, Dr D J and Mrs S C Walker, Donna and Roger, Roy Hoing, Bob and Margaret Holder, R T and J C Moggridge, Chris and Angela Buckell, Dr and Mrs A K Clarke, Tom Evans

CORTON DENHAM
ST6322 MAP 2

Queens Arms 🛏

Village signposted off B3145 N of Sherborne; DT9 4LR

Informally smart inn, super choice of drinks, interesting food and sunny garden

Tucked away in a very quiet village near Cadbury Castle hill fort, this Georgian honey-coloured stone inn is a civilised place. The plain high-beamed bar has a woodburning stove in the inglenook at one end with rugs on flagstones in front of the raised fireplace at the other end, some old pews, barrel seats and a sofa, church candles and maybe a big bowl of flowers; a little room off here has just one big table – nice for a party of eight or so. On the left, the comfortable dining room (dark pink with crisp white paintwork) has good oak tables and a log fire. Butcombe Bitter and Moor Revival with guests such as Abbeydale Riot, Harveys Best and Mathews Brassknocker on handpump, local ciders and apple juice, quite a few malt whiskies, several wines by the glass and lots of bottled beers from around the world. A south-facing back terrace has teak tables and chairs under parasols (or heaters if it's cool), with colourful flower tubs. The village lane has some parking nearby, though not a great deal.

🍴 Using their own pigs and chickens, the good food at lunchtime might include sandwiches, ploughman's, soup, cider-glazed pigs kidneys on granary toast, sausage and mash with red onion marmalade, honey-roast ham and eggs, stinging nettle risotto with parmesan crisp, home-made beefburger and beer-battered whiting with tartare sauce, with often inventive evening choices like local rabbit rillettes with spicy tomato chutney, baby squid stuffed with black pudding with vine tomato sauce, bass with sage risotto, roasted crayfish and a lemon and watercress purée, lamb loin with asparagus, goats cheese and honey vinaigrette, and duck with lavender mash. *Starters/Snacks: £4.25 to £6.50. Main Courses: £7.20 to £15.50. Puddings: £5.25 to £6.00*

Free house ~ Licensees Rupert and Victoria Reeves ~ Real ale ~ Bar food (12-3, 6-10) ~ Restaurant ~ (01963) 220317 ~ Children welcome ~ Dogs allowed in bar ~ Open 11-11(10.30); 11-3, 6-11 winter ~ Bedrooms: £60S(£70B)/£85S(£100B)

Recommended by Colin and Janet Roe, Mrs Angela Graham, Barry Steele-Perkins, Mike and Heather Watson, Samantha McGahan, Mark Flynn, Charles Gysin, Graham and Toni Sanders

CRANMORE
ST6643 MAP 2

Strode Arms 🍴 ☻

West Cranmore; signposted with pub off A361 Frome—Shepton Mallet; BA4 4QJ

Interesting food and wide choice of drinks in pretty country pub with attractive, comfortable bars; seats on front terrace and in back garden

Pretty views through the stone-mullioned windows in this early 15th-c former farmhouse look down to the village duck pond. The rooms have charming country furnishings, fresh flowers and pot plants, a grandfather clock on the flagstones, remarkable old locomotive engineering drawings and big black and white steam train murals in a central lobby; there are newspapers to read and lovely log fires in handsome fireplaces. Wadworths 6X, IPA and a seasonal beer on handpump, around eight wines by the glass from an interesting list, several malt whiskies and quite a few liqueurs and ports. In summer, the building is an attractive sight with its neat stonework, cartwheels on the walls, pretty tubs and hanging baskets, and seats under umbrellas on the front terrace; there are more seats in the back garden. The East Somerset Light Railway is nearby and there may be a vintage sports car meeting on the first Tuesday of each month.

🍴 **Well liked food at fair prices includes filled baguettes, ploughman's, soup, puy lentil, bacon and watercress salad topped with a free-range poached egg, warm goats cheese and red onion confit tart with home-made chutney, butternut squash and saffron risotto, steak and kidney pie, mussel and prawn linguine with basil pesto, salt beef hash with honey and rosemary carrots and cider sauce, chicken breast filled with garlic butter wrapped in parma ham with a chicken velouté sauce, and puddings like pecan nut praline bombe with raspberry compote and banana, rum and muscavado bread pudding with vanilla crème anglaise.** *Starters/Snacks: £3.95 to £5.95. Main Courses: £7.50 to £13.95. Puddings: £4.50*

Wadworths ~ Tenants Tim and Ann-Marie Gould ~ Real ale ~ Bar food ~ Restaurant ~ (01749) 880450 ~ Children welcome ~ Dogs welcome ~ Open 11.30-3, 6-11; 12-3, 7-10.30 Sun

Recommended by Frank Willy, Meg and Colin Hamilton, Tony and Rosemary Warren, Lt Col and Mrs Patrick Kaye, Bob and Margaret Holder, Richard Wyld, Cathryn and Richard Hicks, Sylvia and Tony Birbeck

CROSCOMBE   ST5844   MAP 2

George 🍺

Long Street (A371 Wells—Shepton Mallet); BA5 3QH

Carefully renovated old coaching inn, cheerful canadian landlord, bar food cooked by landlady, good local beers, attractive garden; bedrooms

You can be sure of a genuinely warm welcome from the chatty, informative and enthusiastic landlord in this 17th-c coaching inn with its homely atmosphere and interesting mementoes and pictures. A snug has been renovated this year using canadian timber reclaimed from the local church and a fireplace opened up. The main bar has some stripped stone, dark wooden tables and chairs and more comfortable seats, a winter log fire in the inglenook fireplace, and the family grandfather clock. The attractive dining room has more stripped stone, local artwork and photographs on the dark orange walls, and high-backed cushioned dining chairs around a mix of tables. King George the Thirst is brewed exclusively for them by Blindmans as is Georgeous George by Cheddar Ales, and they also keep Butcombe Bitter and St Austell HSD on handpump, three local ciders and have ten wines by the glass. Darts, board games, a skittle alley, shut the box, and a canadian wooden table game called crokinole; occasional piped music. The friendly pub dog is called Tessa. The attractive, sizeable garden has seats on the heated and covered terrace; children's area and boules.

🍴 **Cooked by the landlady, the popular bar food includes sandwiches, filled baked potatoes, ploughman's, soup, chicken liver pâté, crab au gratin, goats cheese and aubergine stack, chicken with bacon and stilton, various curries, steak in ale pie, lemon sole with sapphire, gressingham duck breast with port and cherry, local organic or aberdeen angus steaks, and puddings like apple and blackberry crumble and chocolate and brandy cheesecake.** *Starters/Snacks: £2.65 to £6.85. Main Courses: £5.95 to £14.75. Puddings: £4.65 to £5.85*

Free house ~ Licensees Peter and Veryan Graham ~ Real ale ~ Bar food (12-2, 6-9) ~ Restaurant ~ (01749) 342306 ~ Children welcome ~ Dogs allowed in bar ~ Live jazz monthly ~ Open 12-2.30, 6-11 ~ Bedrooms: £35S/£70S

Recommended by Richard and Mary Bailey, Sylvia and Tony Birbeck, M G Hart, R E Spain, Terry Buckland, Bruce Eccles, Richard and Judy Winn

---

Stars after the name of a pub show exceptional quality. One star means most people (after reading the report to see just why the star has been won) would think a special trip worth while. Two stars mean that the pub is really outstanding – for its particular qualities it could hardly be bettered.

DULVERTON

SS9127 MAP 1

Woods ★ ⑪ ♀ ◀

Bank Square; TA22 9BU

SOMERSET DINING PUB OF THE YEAR

Smartly informal place with exceptional wines and enjoyable food

The wine list in this gently upmarket place is quite fantastic. You can order any of the 400 or so that they keep on this list by the glass and the landlord also has an unlisted collection of about 500 well aged new world wines which he will happily chat about. It's comfortably relaxed with a good mix of drinkers and diners and very Exmoor – plenty of good sporting prints on the salmon pink walls, some antlers, other hunting trophies and stuffed birds and a couple of salmon rods. There are bare boards on the left by the bar counter, which has well kept Bays Best, Devon Dumpling and Gold, and St Austell Dartmoor Best, HSD and Proper Job tapped from the cask, a farm cider, many sherries and some unusual spirits; attentive, helpful staff and daily papers to read. Its tables partly separated by stable-style timbering and masonry dividers, the bit on the right is carpeted and has a woodburning stove in the big fireplace set into its end wall, which has varnished plank panelling; may be unobjectionable piped music. Big windows keep you in touch with what's going on out in the quiet town centre (or you can sit out on the pavement at a couple of metal tables). A small suntrap back courtyard has a few picnic-sets.

⑪ Using their own-bred pigs, the excellent bar food includes filled baguettes, ploughman's, soup, venison pâté with red onion jam, port wine syrup and pickled mushrooms, a plate of cured meats with pork rillettes and home-made piccalilli and beer mustard dressing, linguine with wild mushroom cream sauce and truffle oil, slow-roast pork belly, fine slices of tenderloin and fried liver on smoked black pudding with apple compote and port wine juices, confit leg of organic chicken with jerusalem artichoke purée, peas and pancetta and poultry sauce, grilled fillet of cornish gilthead sea bream on saffron couscous with ratatouille and shellfish bisque, and puddings such as iced strawberry and white chocolate parfait with white chocolate mousse and confit pineapple with rum and raisin ice-cream. *Starters/Snacks: £5.00 to £8.50. Main Courses: £7.50 to £16.50. Puddings: £5.50 to £6.50*

Free house ~ Licensee Patrick Groves ~ Real ale ~ Bar food ~ Restaurant ~ (01398) 324007 ~ Well behaved children welcome ~ Dogs welcome ~ Open 11-3, 6-11.30; 12-3, 7-11 Sun

Recommended by Tony and Tracy Constance, Annette Tress, Gary Smith, Sheila Topham, Millie and Mick Dunk, Dennis and Gill Keen, Richard and Anne Ansell, Lynda and Trevor Smith, Mr and Mrs P D Titcomb, Bob and Margaret Holder, Len Clark

EAST COKER

ST5412 MAP 2

Helyar Arms ♀ ⛏

Village signposted off A37 or A30 SW of Yeovil; Moor Lane; BA22 9JR

Neat village pub, comfortable big bar, well liked bar food and a fair range of drinks; attractive bedrooms

In a charming village, this partly 15th-c pub is a handsome and neatly kept place enjoyed by our readers. There's a heavy beamed, spacious and comfortable turkey-carpeted bar carefully laid out to give a degree of intimacy to its various candlelit tables, soft lighting, a couple of high-backed settles and squashy leather sofas in front of a warm log fire. Also, lots of hunting and other country pictures, brass and copper ware and daily papers to read. Steps lead up to a good-sized back high-raftered dining room with well spaced tables. Black Sheep, Butcombe Bitter and Wychwood Hobgoblin on handpump and several wines by the glass; piped music, board games, TV and skittle alley. There are a few picnic-sets out on a neat lawn.

⑪ Popular bar food cooked by the landlord includes sandwiches, ploughman's, soup, game terrine with sweet and sour red onions, home-smoked duck breast with beetroot and lentil salad, honey-glazed ham and free-range egg, beer-battered cod with home-made tartare sauce, smoked haddock and prawns with tagliatelle, belly of pork with sweet potato bubble and squeak and apple reduction, partridge with garlic potatoes, crispy bacon and cranberry bread sauce, daily specials, 28-day aged steaks, and puddings like vanilla panna cotta with rhubarb and warm lemon and ginger tart with clotted cream. *Starters/Snacks: £5.00 to £8.00. Main Courses: £8.00 to £18.00. Puddings: £4.00 to £8.00*

Punch ~ Lease Mathieu Eke ~ Real ale ~ Bar food (12-2.30, 6.30-9.30(9 Sun)) ~ Restaurant ~ (01935) 862332 ~ Children welcome ~ Dogs welcome ~ Open 11-3, 6-11; 11am-midnight Sat; 12-11 Sun ~ Bedrooms: £65S/£89S

Recommended by Paul and Gail Betteley, Theo, Anne and Jane Gaskin, Mr and Mrs P R Thomas, S G N Bennett, Mike and Heather Watson, Ian Malone

FAULKLAND   ST7555   MAP 2

Tuckers Grave ★ £

A366 E of village; BA3 5XF

Unspoilt and unchanging little cider house with friendly locals and charming licensees

Quite unchanging, this little pub is very special and at its best when you can chat to the friendly locals and charming licensees. Little is certainly the operative word – it's one of the two tiniest pubs in the *Guide*. The flagstoned entrance opens into a teeny unspoilt room with casks of Bass and Butcombe Bitter on tap and Thatcher's Cheddar Valley cider in an alcove on the left. Two old cream-painted high-backed settles face each other across a single table on the right and a side room has shove-ha'penny. There are winter fires and maybe newspapers to read; also a skittle alley and lots of tables and chairs on an attractive back lawn with good views.

🍴 **There may be lunchtime sandwiches.**

Free house ~ Licensees Ivan and Glenda Swift ~ Real ale ~ No credit cards ~ (01373) 834230 ~ Children in separate little room ~ Open 11.30-3, 6-11; 12-3, 7-10.30 Sun

Recommended by Donna and Roger, Ian Phillips, the Didler, E McCall, T McLean, D Irving, Pete Baker

HINTON CHARTERHOUSE   ST7758   MAP 2

Rose & Crown

B3110 about 4 miles S of Bath; BA2 7SN

18th-c village pub with friendly young licensees, well kept ales and traditional bar food

You'll get a warm welcome from the friendly young licensees here – and probably from Guinness the pub cat as well as he likes to wait and greet customers by the front door. It's a neatly kept, traditionally furnished pub with a partly divided bar, some lovely panelling, blue plush cushioned wall seats and bar stools, a mix of wooden chairs and tables on the spreading carpet, candles in bottles and an ornate carved stone fireplace; there's a second small brick fireplace on the other side, Butcombe Bitter and guests like Black Sheep and Fullers London Pride on handpump and Orchard Pig ciders; piped music. The long dining room, with steps down to a lower area, has an unusual beamed ceiling. There are picnic-sets under parasols in the terraced garden and some pretty window boxes.

🍴 **Tasty, straightforward bar food includes sandwiches, soup, pâté with apple and tomato chutney, whitebait with garlic mayonnaise, ham and free-range eggs, home-made burger, cauliflower, broccoli and stilton bake, liver and bacon with onion gravy, steak in ale pie, barbecue chicken, and steaks.** *Starters/Snacks: £4.00 to £6.00. Main Courses: £6.00 to £14.00. Puddings: £4.25 to £5.25*

Butcombe ~ Manager Tom Watson ~ Real ale ~ Bar food (12-2, 6-9.30(9 Mon); 12-2.30, 6-8.30 Sun) ~ Restaurant ~ (01225) 722153 ~ Children welcome away from bar ~ Dogs allowed in bar ~ Open 11-3, 5-midnight; 11am-midnight(11 Sun) Sat ~ Bedrooms: £50S/£70B

Recommended by Dr and Mrs M E Wilson, Meg and Colin Hamilton

HINTON ST GEORGE

ST4212 MAP 1

Lord Poulett Arms ⊕ ♀ ⇋

Off A30 W of Crewkerne and off Merriott road (declassified – former A356, off B3165) N of Crewkerne; TA17 8SE

Attractive old stone inn with charming antiques-filled rooms, well presented food, good choice of drinks and pretty garden; bedrooms

To be sure of a table here, it's best to book in advance as this substantial 17th-c thatched pub is usually pretty busy. There are several extremely attractive and cosy linked areas: rugs on bare boards or flagstones, open fires (one in an inglenook and one in a raised fireplace that separates two rooms), walls of honey-coloured stone or painted in bold Farrow & Ball colours, hops on beams, antique brass candelabra, fresh flowers and candles, and some lovely old farmhouse, windsor and ladderback chairs around fine oak or elm tables. The atmosphere is civilised and relaxed with plenty of locals dropping in for a drink. Branscombe Branoc and Otter Ale on handpump, 11 wines by the glass, jugs of Pimms, cider and home-made sloe gin. The cat is called Honey. Outside, under a wisteria-clad pergola, there are white metalwork tables and chairs in a mediterranean-style lavender-edged gravelled area and picnic-sets in a wild flower meadow; boules. The bedrooms have baths and you may have to ask for a shower attachment. This is a charming and peaceful golden hamstone village; nearby walks.

⊞ Using home-grown vegetables and local organic produce, the well presented bar food includes lunchtime filled baguettes and duck and pork burger with orange, chilli and cashew marmalade, as well as soup, wild and exotic mushrooms with cheddar and apple brandy cream and crusty bread for dipping, pigeon with black pudding, caramelised apple and maple and berry dressing, vegetable tagine, beer-battered fish, pork tenderloin with a tomato and honey dijon dressing, lamb casserole with goats cheese, extra mature steaks, and puddings like banoffi eton mess and champagne rhubarb, stem ginger and treacle tart with blood orange and rhubarb curd. *Starters/Snacks: £4.50 to £6.00. Main Courses: £9.00 to £16.00. Puddings: £4.50 to £5.50*

Free house ~ Licensees Steve Hill and Michelle Paynton ~ Real ale ~ Bar food (12-9.15) ~ (01460) 73149 ~ Children welcome ~ Dogs allowed in bar ~ Open 12-3, 6.30-11; closed 26 Dec, 1 Jan ~ Bedrooms: /£88B

Recommended by Cathryn and Richard Hicks, Dr and Mrs M E Wilson, Michael Doswell, George and Gill Rowley, Martin and Karen Wake, Jonathon Bunt, Theo, Anne and Jane Gaskin, Guy Consterdine, Bob and Margaret Holder, Pamela and Alan Neale, Fred Beckett, John and Fiona McIlwain, Heidi Montgomery

HUISH EPISCOPI

ST4326 MAP 1

Rose & Crown £

Off A372 E of Langport; TA10 9QT

In the same family for over 140 years and a real throwback; local ciders and beers, simple food and friendly welcome

Shut for five months due to extreme flooding, this unpretentious and unspoilt thatched tavern has been freshly painted and has a new kitchen. There's no bar as such – to get a drink, you just walk into the central flagstoned still room and choose from the casks of Teignworthy Reel Ale and guests such as Butcombe Bitter, Exmoor Gold and Hop Back Crop Circle; Borrowhill farm cider, too. This servery is the only thoroughfare between the casual little front parlours, with their unusual pointed-arch windows and genuinely friendly locals; good helpful service. Shove-ha'penny, dominoes and cribbage, and a much more orthodox big back extension family room has pool, darts, games machine and juke box; skittle alley and popular quiz nights. There are tables in a garden and a second enclosed garden has a children's play area; you can camp (free to pub customers) on the adjoining paddock. Summer morris men, fine nearby walks and the site of the Battle of Langport (1645) is close by.

⊞ Using some home-grown fruit and vegetables, the simple, cheap food includes generously filled sandwiches, filled baked potatoes, ploughman's, pork, apple and cider cobbler, steak in ale pie, stilton and broccoli tart, chicken breast in tarragon sauce and

puddings such as chocolate torte with chocolate sauce and lemon sponge pudding with lemon cream. *Starters/Snacks: £3.50 to £4.50. Main Courses: £6.75 to £7.25. Puddings: £3.75*

Free house ~ Licensee Stephen Pittard ~ Real ale ~ Bar food (12-2, 5.30-7.30; not Sun or Mon evenings) ~ No credit cards ~ (01458) 250494 ~ Children welcome ~ Dogs welcome ~ Folk singing third Sat of month (not summer); irish music last Thurs of month ~ Open 11.30-2.30, 5.30-11; 11.30-11 Fri and Sat; 12-10.30 Sun

Recommended by Meg and Colin Hamilton, Rona Murdoch, the Didler, Andrea Rampley, Pete Baker, Phil and Sally Gorton

LOVINGTON   ST5831   MAP 2

Pilgrims 🍴 �

B3153 Castle Cary—Keinton Mandeville; BA7 7PT

Rather smart but relaxed dining pub with particularly good food cooked by landlord, local beer and cider; decked terrace; bedrooms

Most customers come to this civilised and rather upmarket dining pub to enjoy the particularly good food cooked by the landlord, but the bar is chatty and relaxed and there are a few stools by a corner counter used regularly by locals. Cottage Champflower on handpump from the nearby brewery, 16 wines by the glass, Orchard Pig cider and apple juice, cider brandy and a rack of daily papers. A cosy little dark green inner area has sunny modern country and city prints, a couple of shelves of books and china, a cushioned pew and some settees by the big fireplace. With flagstones throughout, this runs into the compact eating area, with candles on tables and some stripped stone. There's also a separate, more formal carpeted dining room. The landlady's service is efficient and friendly. The enclosed garden has tables, chairs and umbrellas on a decked terrace. The car park exit has its own traffic lights – on your way out line your car up carefully or you may wait for ever for them to change.

🍴 **Growing much of their own vegetables and naming their local suppliers, the rewarding bar food includes light lunches or starters such as sandwiches, soup, mussels in cider, leeks and garlic, duck and pork rillettes, tiger prawns in tempura batter with a soy and lime dipping sauce, and hot potted haddock in cheese sauce on piquant tomato salsa; also, monkfish and scallops with smoked bacon, wild mushrooms and black rice, tagliatelle with mushrooms, garlic and mascarpone, beer-battered cod, breast of free-range chicken stuffed with goats cheese with bacon lardons and a cider cream sauce, rack of lamb roasted pink, a duo of beef (slow-braised blade and quickly seared fillet), and puddings like chocolate mousse and lemon tart; good local cheeses.** *Starters/Snacks: £4.00 to £10.00. Main Courses: £10.00 to £23.00. Puddings: £5.00 to £8.00*

Free house ~ Licensees Sally and Jools Mitchison ~ Real ale ~ Bar food (not Sun evening, Mon, Tues lunchtime) ~ Restaurant ~ (01963) 240597 ~ Children welcome ~ Dogs allowed in bar ~ Open 12-3, 7-11; closed Sun evening, Mon, Tues lunchtime ~ Bedrooms: /£80B

Recommended by Edward Mirzoeff, Paul and Annette Hallett

LUXBOROUGH   SS9837   MAP 1

Royal Oak 🍴 🛏

Kingsbridge; S of Dunster on minor roads into Brendon Hills – OS Sheet 181 map reference 983378; TA23 0SH

Smashing place in wonderful countryside, interesting bar food, local beers and ciders, and attentive, friendly staff; bedrooms

Our readers are very fond of this well run Exmoor inn and it's an extremely popular place to stay for a few days (they often have special winter deals, too). There's always a friendly welcome from the licensees and their staff and a really good mix of visitors and chatty locals (often with their dogs). The compact bar, which has the most character and a relaxed, cheerful atmosphere, has lovely old flagstones, several rather fine settles (one with a very high back and one still with its book rest), scrubbed kitchen tables, lots of beer mats on beams, a cart horse saddle and a huge brick fireplace with a warm log fire; a simpler back room has an ancient cobbled floor, some quarry tiles and a stone fireplace. One room just off the bar is set for dining, with attractive old pine furniture and horse and hunting prints, and there are two dining rooms as well. One is green painted and a larger end one has stuffed fish in glass cabinets, fish paintings and fishing rods on the dark red walls, leather and brass-tack dining chairs and more formal ones around quite a mix of old tables, with turkey rugs on the black slate floor. Cotleigh Tawny, Exmoor Ale and Gold and Quantock White Hind on handpump; darts and board games. There are some seats out in the charming back courtyard, and memorable nearby walks in the wonderful surrounding countryside; the Coleridge Way is popular.

🍴 **Using lamb from 50 metres away and Exmoor beef, the enjoyable bar food includes mussels with garlic, shallots and white wine, smoked salmon terrine with minted cucumber and crème fraîche, butternut squash and leek risotto with cep mushroom dressing, chicken breast with pak choi, ginger and soy, calves liver with spring onion mash, grilled bacon and red wine jus, roast salmon fillet with olives, red pepper and basil, slow-roast pork belly with white beans, toulouse sausage and herbs, daily specials, and puddings; during the summer holidays they serve filled baguettes throughout the afternoon and cream teas.** *Starters/Snacks: £3.95 to £7.95. Main Courses: £5.95 to £15.95. Puddings: £3.95 to £4.95*

Free house ~ Licensees James and Sian Waller ~ Real ale ~ Bar food ~ Restaurant ~ (01984) 640319 ~ Children must be over 10 in evening and in bedrooms ~ Dogs allowed in bar and bedrooms ~ Open 12-2.30, 6-11 (all day during summer school hols); 12-11 Sun and Sat ~ Bedrooms: £55B/£65B

Recommended by Dennis and Gill Keen, Mike and Eleanor Anderson, Roy and Jean Russell, Helene Grygar, S G N Bennett, Richard Cole, the Didler, Henry Beltran, Barry and Anne, Bob and Margaret Holder, R O'Connell, Dr and Mrs Michael Smith, Chris and Meredith Owen, Lynda and Trevor Smith

MONKSILVER
ST0737   MAP 1

Notley Arms
B3188; TA4 4JB

Friendly, busy pub in lovely village with beamed rooms, a fair choice of drinks and well liked food; neat streamside garden

On the edge of Exmoor National Park, this is a friendly pub in a lovely village. The beamed and L-shaped bar has small settles and kitchen chairs around the plain country wooden and candlelit tables, original paintings on the ochre-coloured walls, fresh flowers, and a couple of woodburning stoves. The Tack Room is decorated with saddles, bridles and so forth and used by families. Bath Ales Gem, Exmoor Ale and Wadworths 6X on handpump, five farm ciders (and a perry) and several wines by the glass; good service from the welcoming licensees. In fine weather, there are plenty of picnic-sets under parasols in the immaculate garden which has a swift clear stream at the bottom; riders can tether their horses while they enjoy a drink.

🍴 **Enjoyable bar food includes soup, whitebait with home-made tartare sauce, pâté with red onion and date marmalade, beer-battered cod, thai butternut, cherry tomato, pineapple and green bean laksa with egg noodles, lamb shank in red wine and rosemary, venison pie, lambs liver with crispy bacon and black pudding with a redcurrant and red wine gravy, beef in Guinness casserole with cheese suet dumplings, and puddings like treacle tart with clotted cream and triple chocolate brownies with hot chocolate sauce.** *Starters/Snacks: £4.95 to £7.95. Main Courses: £7.95 to £12.95. Puddings: £3.95 to £4.95*

Unique (Enterprise) ~ Lease Russell and Jane Deary ~ Real ale ~ Bar food (not Mon lunchtime or winter Mon) ~ (01984) 656217 ~ Children in family room ~ Dogs welcome ~ Open 12-2.30, 6.30-10.30(11 Sat, 10 Sun); closed Mon lunchtime (all day Mon in winter)

Recommended by David A Hammond, the Didler, Terry Miller, Martin Hatcher

---

We mention bottled beers and spirits only if there is something unusual about them – imported belgian real ales, say, or dozens of malt whiskies; so do please let us know about them in your reports.

NORTH CURRY   ST3125   MAP 1

Bird in Hand

Queens Square; off A378 (or A358) E of Taunton; TA3 6LT

Village pub with beams and timbers, cricketing memorabilia, friendly staff and west country beers

There's a friendly atmosphere in this bustling village pub and a good welcome from the obliging staff. The cosy main bar has nice old pews, settles, benches and old yew tables on the flagstones, some original beams and timbers, locally woven willow work, cricketing memorabilia and a log fire in the inglenook fireplace. Otter Bitter and guest beers like Cotleigh Barn Owl, Exmoor Fox and Teignworthy Old Moggie on handpump, Parson's farm cider and ten wines by the glass; piped music.

🍴 **Bar food includes a lunchtime deli board, beer-battered fish, steak in ale pie, a trio of sausages, a couple of vegetarian options, chargrilled steaks, plenty of seasonal game such as rabbit, venison and pheasant, and puddings like lemon and ginger crunch.** *Starters/Snacks: £5.00 to £6.95. Main Courses: £7.50 to £15.00. Puddings: £5.00*

Free house ~ Licensee James Mogg ~ Real ale ~ Bar food (12-2, 6.30(7 Fri and Sat)-9(9.30 Fri and Sat)) ~ Restaurant ~ (01823) 490248 ~ Children welcome ~ Dogs allowed in bar ~ Open 12-3(3.30 Sat), 6-11; 12-10.30 Sun

Recommended by Alan and Pam Atkinson, Steve and Liz Tilley, Richard Benthall, Michelle and Graeme Voss, Bob and Margaret Holder, R T and J C Moggridge, Gary Rollings, Debbie Porter, K Turner, John Day

NORTON ST PHILIP   ST7755   MAP 2

George 🛏

A366; BA2 7LH

Wonderful ancient building full of history and interest with well liked food, real ales, wines by the glass and characterful bedrooms

This is one of Britain's most interesting pub buildings, well worth a good look around – and it has a real sense of history. It was built about 700 years ago to house merchants buying wool and cloth from the rich sheep-farming Hinton Priory at the great August cloth market. The central Norton Room, which was the original bar, has really heavy beams, an oak panelled settle and solid dining chairs on the narrow strip wooden floor, a variety of 18th-c pictures, an open fire in the handsome stone fireplace, and a low wooden bar counter. Wadworths IPA, 6X, Bishops Tipple and a guest beer on handpump and several wines by the glass. As you enter the building, there's a room on the right with high dark beams, squared dark half-panelling, a broad carved stone fireplace with an old iron fireback and pewter plates on the mantelpiece, a big mullioned window with leaded lights and a round oak 17th-c table reputed to have been used by the Duke of Monmouth. He stayed here before the Battle of Sedgemoor – after their defeat, his men were imprisoned in what is now the Monmouth Bar. The Charterhouse Bar is mostly used by those enjoying a drink before a meal: a wonderful pitched ceiling with trusses and timbering, heraldic shields and standards, jousting lances and swords on the walls, a fine old stone fireplace, high-backed cushioned heraldic-fabric dining chairs on the big rug over the wood plank floor and an oak dresser with some pewter. The dining room (a restored barn with original oak ceiling beams, a pleasant if haphazard mix of early 19th-c portraits and hunting prints, and the same mix of vaguely old-looking furnishings) has a good relaxing, chatty atmosphere. The bedrooms are very atmospheric and comfortable – some reached by an external Norman stone stair-turret and some across the cobbled and flagstoned courtyard and up into a fine half-timbered upper gallery (where there's a lovely 18th-c carved oak settle). A stroll over the meadow behind the pub (past the picnic-sets on the narrow grass pub garden) leads you to an attractive churchyard around the medieval church whose bells struck Pepys (here on 12 June 1668) as 'mighty tuneable'.

🍴 **Well liked bar food includes sandwiches or wraps, soup, stilton and port pâté, goats cheese and red onion tartlet, sausages with mustard mash and gravy, liver and bacon,** home-made burgers, beef in ale or fish pie, and puddings such as a crumble of the day and Baileys and sultana bread and butter pudding; the more elaborate restaurant menu (though you can eat the bar food in the restaurant, too) might have king prawns and crayfish with lemon, chilli and garlic, free-range chicken breast with brie wrapped in smoked bacon with a creamy leek and mushroom sauce, local venison with plum and madeira sauce, and fillet of grey mullet with a clam, caper and pink peppercorn sauce. *Starters/Snacks: £4.95 to £6.25. Main Courses: £8.50 to £10.50. Puddings: £5.50*

Wadworths ~ Manager Mark Jenkinson ~ Real ale ~ Bar food (12-2.30, 6-9(9.30 Fri); all day weekends) ~ Restaurant ~ (01373) 834224 ~ Well behaved children welcome ~ Dogs allowed in bar and bedrooms ~ Open 11.30(12 Sat)-11; 12-10.30 Sun ~ Bedrooms: £70B/£90B

Recommended by Roger Wain-Heapy, David Field, the Didler, Mr and Mrs W W Burke, Donna and Roger, Dr and Mrs M E Wilson, Mr and Mrs A H Young, Ian Phillips, Paul Humphreys, Pete Coxon

PITNEY
ST4527   MAP 1

Halfway House 🍺

Just off B3153 W of Somerton; TA10 9AB

Up to ten real ales, local ciders and continental bottled beers in bustling friendly local; good simple food

As well as a fine range of ten real ales, the friendly licensees here also keep three local ciders and around 20 or so continental bottled beers; several wines by the glass and 15 malt whiskies, too. Tapped from the cask and changing regularly, the beers might include Adnams Broadside, Bath Ales SPA, Branscombe Vale Branoc, Butcombe Bitter, Exmoor Fox, Hop Back Crop Circle and Summer Lightning, Otter Ale, RCH Pitchfork and Teignworthy Reel Ale. It's a traditional village local with a good mix of people chatting at communal tables in the three old-fashioned rooms, all with roaring log fires and there's a homely feel underlined by a profusion of books, maps and newspapers; cribbage, dominoes and board games. There are tables outside.

🍴 As well as lunchtime sandwiches, the simple generous food includes filled baked potatoes, soup, ploughman's, sausage and mash, ham and egg, curries with all the trimmings, casseroles, and specials like greek salad, cheese and courgette bake, and pork in cider; they also have their own garden smokery. *Starters/Snacks: £3.50 to £5.95. Main Courses: £7.00 to £10.50. Puddings: £3.50 to £4.95*

Free house ~ Licensees Julian Lichfield and Caroline Lacy ~ Real ale ~ Bar food (12-2.30, 7.30-9; not Sun) ~ (01458) 252513 ~ Children welcome ~ Dogs allowed in bar ~ Open 11.30-3, 5.30-11(midnight Fri and Sat); 12-3, 7-11 Sun

Recommended by the Didler, R T and J C Moggridge, Andrea Rampley, Theo, Anne and Jane Gaskin, Evelyn and Derek Walter

PORTISHEAD
ST4576   MAP 1

Windmill 🍺

3.7 miles from M5 junction 19; A369 into town, then follow Sea Front sign off left and into Nore Road; BS20 6JZ

Lovely views from large and efficient family dining pub with quite a few real ales and decent food; big changes happening

There are huge changes afoot here. It has been a well run family dining pub but a double-storey extension is to be added on to the front of the building and the whole of the top floor will have a curved wall of glass to take in the fantastic views over the Bristol Channel to Newport and Cardiff (with the bridges on the right). The inside is to be completely re-styled with new kitchens and new furnishings to give a more contemporary feel to the place. But the plan, as we went to press, is to keep the bottom floor as a family area and the middle floor as the bar. They will keep their six real ales on handpump such as Bass, Butcombe Bitter and Gold, Courage Best and two quickly changing guests from local breweries, and 13 wines by the glass. Out on the seaward side are picnic-sets on three tiers of lantern-lit terrace, but they may add substantial decking areas, too; disabled access.

🍴 At the moment to eat (though this is likely to change), you find a numbered table, present yourself at the order desk, pay for your order and return to the table with a tray of cutlery, condiments and sauce packets. It works well: sandwiches, filled baked potatoes, soup, beer-battered tiger prawns with hoisin sauce, aubergine and chickpea curry, sausage and mash, shepherd's pie, smoked fish lasagne, chargrilled chicken strips in barbecue sauce, pork loin with cider and apple chutney, and puddings like a cheesecake of the day and banoffi pie. *Starters/Snacks: £1.75 to £6.95. Main Courses: £7.25 to £13.95. Puddings: £1.95 to £4.50*

Free house ~ Licensee J S Churchill ~ Real ale ~ Bar food (all day) ~ (01275) 843677 ~ Children in family area ~ Dogs allowed in bar ~ Open 11-11; 12-10.30 Sun

Recommended by Tom Evans, Jim and Frances Gowers, Chris and Angela Buckell, R T and J C Moggridge, John and Fiona McIlwain

SHEPTON MONTAGUE   ST6731 MAP 2

Montague Inn 🍽 ♀

Village signposted just off A359 Bruton—Castle Cary; BA9 8JW

Popular new restaurant extension in busy country pub, friendly licensees

The new restaurant extension here is very successful and makes the most of the view. It's bright and spacious with french windows opening on to the terrace where there are smart teak seats and tables; steps lead down to the garden. Inside, there's a good welcome from the friendly, knowledgeable landlord and a warm atmosphere, and the rooms are simply but tastefully furnished with stripped wooden tables and kitchen chairs; there's a log fire in the attractive inglenook fireplace. Bath Ales Gem, Wadworths IPA and a guest from Cottage tapped from the cask, local apple brandy, ten wines by the glass and home-made lemonade.

🍴 Using carefully sourced, very local and seasonal produce, the good, enjoyable bar food includes lots of fish and game specials, lunchtime choices such as open sandwiches, ploughman's, soup, home-made terrine and chutney, dill and whisky home-cured salmon with a potato and spring onion cake and poached egg, risotto of smoked haddock, leeks and red cheddar, and confit of free-range duckling with butter beans, lardons and gnocchi, with evening dishes like an antipasti plate, parfait of duck livers and cognac with pear and vanilla relish, twice-baked cheddar and leek soufflé with roast vegetables, chicken breast with a parmesan and herb glaze, garlic mash and thyme sauce and slow-baked pork with sage and apple jus. Puddings might be tarte tatin with cinnamon syrup and vanilla ice-cream, and milk chocolate and cherry mousse with mango sorbet. They do good value midweek special deals. *Starters/Snacks: £4.50 to £8.50. Main Courses: £7.00 to £18.50. Puddings: £5.50*

Free house ~ Licensee Sean O'Callaghan ~ Real ale ~ Bar food (12-2(3 Sun), 7-9; not Sun evening) ~ Restaurant ~ (01749) 813213 ~ Well behaved children welcome ~ Dogs allowed in bar ~ Live jazz summer weekend lunchtimes ~ Open 12-3, 6-11; 12-4 Sun; closed Sun evening

Recommended by Edward Mirzoeff, G Vyse, J L and C J Hamilton

SIMONSBATH   SS7739 MAP 1

Exmoor Forest Inn 🛏

B3223/B3358; TA24 7SH

In lovely surroundings with plenty of fine walks, comfortable inn with enjoyable food, a good range of drinks and friendly licensees; bedrooms

This friendly inn is an enjoyable place to stay as it's in lovely surroundings with fine walks all round and they have 1¼ miles of wild brown trout and salmon fishing on the River Barle; dogs are most welcome and they provide dog beds, bowls and towels. The bar has a few red plush stools around little circular tables by the bar counter and steps up to a larger area with joists in the ceiling, cushioned settles, upholstered stools and mate's chairs around a mix of dark tables, a woodburning stove with two shelves of stone flagons to one side and hunting prints, trophies and antlers on the walls. The walls of the Tack Room are covered with saddles, bridles, stirrups, horseshoes and so forth and there are similar tables and chairs as well as one nice long table for a bigger party. Cotleigh Harrier, Cottage Somerset and Dorset Ale, Exmoor Hound Dog and St Austell Proper Job on handpump, ten wines by the glass, local cider and 30 malt whiskies. There's a cosy little residents' lounge and an airy dining room. Piped music, board games, shove-ha'penny, dominoes and bar skittles. Picnic-sets and benches around tables under parasols in the front garden. The collie is called Noddy and the jack russell, Pip.

🍴 Using home-grown vegetables and local suppliers when they can, the reliable bar food includes lunchtime filled rolls and filled baked potatoes, soup, free-range pork terrine with crab apple and chilli jelly, local smoked trout, sausages with onion gravy, spring rolls with mixed oriental mushrooms and a sweet chilli sauce, chicken suprême with a tarragon crust and a white wine and tarragon sauce, confit duck on home-made onion marmalade, fillets of john dory with olives, rosemary, capers and sun-dried tomatoes, and puddings like apple and pecan tart and dark chocolate, coffee and caramel set cream with hazelnut praline. Starters/Snacks: £3.95 to £6.95. Main Courses: £8.50 to £14.95. Puddings: £4.50 to £5.50

Free house ~ Licensees Chris and Barry Kift ~ Real ale ~ Bar food ~ Restaurant ~ (01643) 831341 ~ Children welcome ~ Dogs allowed in bar and bedrooms ~ Open 12-3, 6(6.30 Sun)-11(10.30 Sun); closed Sun evening in winter and Mon (except bank hols) ~ Bedrooms: £45S/£85S

Recommended by George Atkinson, Laurence Smith, John Urquhart, Dave Braisted, Lynda and Trevor Smith, John and Jackie Walsh

SOUTH STOKE

ST7461   MAP 2

Pack Horse

Off B3110, S edge of Bath; BA2 7DU

Fine old pub with plenty of history, friendly, helpful staff, a pubby local feel, lots of farm ciders and enjoyable food

In a lovely village, this former priory is into its sixth century and has a central alleyway that runs right through the middle – it used to be the route along which the dead were carried to the church cemetery; it stops along the way at a central space by the serving bar with its Butcombe Bitter, Sharps Doom Bar and guest ale on handpump and fine choice of eight farm ciders. Service is friendly and helpful. The ancient main room has a good local atmosphere and plenty of regulars dropping in, a log fire in the handsome stone inglenook, antique oak settles (two well carved) and cushioned captain's chairs on the quarry-tiled floor, some royalty pictures, a chiming wall-clock, a heavy black beam-and-plank ceiling, and rough black shutters for the stone-mullioned windows (put up in World War I). There's another bar down to the left which also has an open fireplace; a couple of shove-ha'penny slates are set into two tables, dominoes, piped music and winter quiz evenings. The spacious back garden has seats and pretty roses; boules. Dogs must be kept on a lead.

🍴 Enjoyable bar food includes sandwiches, soup, stilton, bacon and walnut cheesecake, halloumi and mango salad with a mint dressing, pork and chorizo burger, home-cooked ham on bubble and squeak topped with an egg, beer-battered fresh haddock, courgettes stuffed with ricotta, roasted almonds and pine kernels with a roasted red pepper couscous, pork chops in cider with mustard mash, brixham crab cakes with watercress mayonnaise, rabbit in a dijon mustard sauce, and puddings like chocolate and raspberry terrine and eton mess. Starters/Snacks: £5.00 to £8.00. Main Courses: £10.00 to £14.00. Puddings: £4.50 to £6.00

Innspired Inns ~ Lease Stephen Peart ~ Real ale ~ Bar food (12-2(3 Sun), 6.30-9; not Mon) ~ Restaurant ~ (01225) 832060 ~ Children welcome ~ Dogs allowed in bar ~ Open 12-3, 6(5 Sat)-11; 12-10 Sun; closed Mon lunchtime

Recommended by Guy Vowles

STANTON WICK
ST6162   MAP 2

Carpenters Arms ⊕ ♀ ⇔
Village signposted off A368, just W of junction with A37 S of Bristol; BS39 4BX

Bustling warm-hearted dining pub in nice country setting with interesting bar food, friendly staff and good drinks

Once a row of miners' cottages, this is now a neatly kept dining pub well run by a friendly licensee and his attentive staff. There are plenty of chatty customers, blazing log fires, and a civilised and relaxed atmosphere. The Coopers Parlour on the right has one or two beams, seats around heavy tables and attractive curtains and plants in the windows; on the angle between here and the bar area, there's a fat woodburning stove in an opened-through corner fireplace. The bar has wood-backed built-in wall seats and some leather fabric-cushioned stools, stripped stone walls and a big log fire. There's also a snug inner room (lightened by mirrors in arched 'windows') and a restaurant with leather sofas and easy chairs in a comfortable lounge area. Bath Ales Gem Bitter, Butcombe Bitter and Sharps Doom Bar on handpump, ten wines by the glass and several malt whiskies; games machine and TV. This is a lovely rural setting and there are picnic-sets on the front terrace, pretty flowerbeds and attractive hanging baskets and tubs. This is only ten minutes' drive to the Chew Valley – the perfect place to walk off lunch. The bedrooms are comfortable and attractive and we'd love to have feedback from readers.

⊞ Enjoyable bar food includes sandwiches and light lunchtime classics such as chicken caesar salad, sausages and mash with onion gravy and linguine with bacon, mushrooms, garlic and cream, as well as soup, salmon fishcake with tomato and chilli salsa, baked field mushrooms filled with garlic and stilton crumb, chicken filled with boursin cheese wrapped in parma ham with mushroom sauce, roast pork belly with sage and dijon mustard sauce and braised savoy cabbage and black pudding, fillet of bass on crispy vegetable stir fry with egg noodles and thai dressing, and puddings like banoffi cheesecake and strawberry tart with clotted cream. *Starters/Snacks: £4.95 to £6.95. Main Courses: £7.95 to £15.95. Puddings: £4.95 to £6.95*

Free house ~ Licensee Simon Pledge ~ Real ale ~ Bar food (12-2, 6-9.30(10 Fri and Sat); all day Sun) ~ Restaurant ~ (01761) 490202 ~ Children welcome ~ Dogs allowed in bar ~ Open 11-11; 12-10.30 Sun; closed evenings 25 and 26 Dec ~ Bedrooms: £72.50B/£105B

Recommended by JCW

STOKE ST GREGORY
ST3527   MAP 1

Rose & Crown ⊕ ♀ ⇔
Off A378/A358; Woodhill; TA3 6EW

Re-opened and carefully rebuilt after a dreadful fire, same friendly family in charge, good choice of drinks and very good food; new bedrooms

'Like a phoenix rising from the ashes' is how several of our readers have described the changes to this lovely pub. Rebuilt after a devastating fire, it's been beautifully thought out and is still run by the same exceptionally friendly and professional family who have been here for 30 years. More or less open-plan, there's a bar area with wooden stools by a curved brick and pale wood-topped counter and this leads into a large, airy dining room with all manner of light and dark wooden dining chairs and pews around a mix of tables under a high-raftered ceiling. There are two other beamed dining rooms with similar furnishings, photographs on the walls of the fire damage, the village and so forth, and one room has a woodburning stove and another has an 18th-c glass-covered well in one corner. Throughout, there are flagstoned or wooden floors. Exmoor Ale, Otter Ale and Taunton Ale on handpump and several wines by the glass. There are seats outside on the sheltered front terrace.

⊞ Particularly good bar food at lunchtime includes sandwiches, ploughman's, soup, mussels in creamy perry (pear cider) sauce with home-made chips, smoked duck breast and poached egg salad, pasta with fresh tomato and basil sauce, lambs liver with bacon and onion gravy, steak and kidney pie, and gammon steak marinated in cider with fresh pineapple, mushrooms and egg, with evening choices such as king scallops with cardamon and garlic butter, goats cheese, strawberry and hazelnut salad with honey, mustard and balsamic dressing, lamb shank braised in red wine, tandoori chicken with onions and sweet bell peppers, and crispy duck with spicy madeira and blood orange sauce; puddings like chocolate panna cotta with clotted cream and apple and berry crumble. *Starters/Snacks: £3.75 to £6.75. Main Courses: £8.95 to £16.50. Puddings: £4.25 to £4.75*

Free house ~ Licensees Stephen, Sally, Richard and Leonie Browning ~ Real ale ~ Bar food ~ Restaurant ~ (01823) 490296 ~ Children welcome ~ Dogs allowed in bar ~ Open 11-3, 6-11; 12-10.30 Sun; 11-3, 6.30-10.30 Sun in winter ~ Bedrooms: £55B/£85B

Recommended by Peter Cusworth, Bill Rees, Bob and Margaret Holder

TARR   SS8632   MAP 1

Tarr Farm 🛏️

Tarr Steps – rather narrow road off B3223 N of Dulverton, very little nearby parking (paying car park quarter-mile up road); OS Sheet 181 map reference 868322 – as the inn is on the E bank, don't be tempted to approach by car from the W unless you can cope with a deep ford; TA22 9PY

Lovely Exmoor setting looking over Tarr Steps and lots to do nearby, decent range of drinks, well liked food and seats outside; bedrooms

From the slate-topped stone tables outside this remote but busy inn you can look down on Tarr Steps just below – that much-photographed clapper bridge of massive granite slabs for medieval packhorses crossing the River Barle as it winds through this lightly wooded combe. The pub part consists of a line of compact and unpretentious rooms, also with good views, slabby rustic tables, stall seating, wall seats and pub chairs, a woodburning stove at one end, salmon pink walls, nice game bird pictures and a pair of stuffed pheasants. The serving bar up a step or two has Exmoor Ale and Gold on handpump, eight wines by the glass and a good choice of other drinks. The residents' end has a smart little evening restaurant (you can eat from this menu in the bar), and a pleasant log-fire lounge with dark leather armchairs and sofas.

🍴 Bar food includes lunchtime sandwiches, soup, pork pâté with armagnac-soaked prunes wrapped in parma ham, honey-roast ham and free-range eggs, cod fishfingers with aioli, chicken roulade with morel and riesling sauce, calves liver and bacon with sage mash and shallot sauce, twice-baked goats cheese soufflé with candied walnuts and date and walnut chutney, devon ruby rib-eye steak with béarnaise sauce, and puddings like lemon tart with lemon sorbet and a cassis and blueberry sauce and chocolate fondant with passion fruit ice-cream and hazelnut ice-cream. *Starters/Snacks: £3.95 to £7.00. Main Courses: £7.00 to £13.00. Puddings: £4.00 to £5.00*

Free house ~ Licensees Richard Benn and Judy Carless ~ Real ale ~ Bar food (12-3, 7-9) ~ Restaurant ~ (01643) 851507 ~ Children must be over 10 in evening ~ Dogs allowed in bar and bedrooms ~ Open 11-11; closed 1-13 Feb ~ Bedrooms: £90B/£150B

Recommended by George and Gill Rowley, John and Jackie Chalcraft, Helene Grygar, Richard Cole, Dr A McCormick, Lynda and Trevor Smith, Glenwys and Alan Lawrence, Sheila Topham, Mr and Mrs P D Titcomb

TRISCOMBE   ST1535   MAP 1

Blue Ball 🍽️ 🍷

Village signposted off A358 Crowcombe—Bagborough; turn off opposite sign to youth hostel; OS Sheet 181 map reference 155355; TA4 3HE

Fine old building, enjoyable food and drink, and seats on decking making the most of the views; bedrooms

A friendly new licensee has taken over this 15th-c thatched stone-built inn and is very keen that drinkers should be made just as welcome as those coming for a meal. On the first floor of the original stables, it's a smart place, sloping down gently on three levels, each with its own fire, and cleverly divided into seating by hand-cut beech partitions. Cotleigh Tawny, Cottage Thames Tunnel and Taunton Mayor on handpump, a dozen wines by the glass and local farm cider; piped music. The decking at the top of the woodside, terraced garden makes the most of the views. There's a chair lift to the bar/restaurant area for the disabled.

⑪ **Good, interesting bar food includes lunchtime filled rolls and ploughman's, soup, an antipasti plate, a shellfish bowl with razor clams, clams, cockles and mussels with white wine and cream, pear poached in red wine with gorgonzola and walnuts, ham and eggs, home-made burgers with bacon and cheese, slow-roast pork belly on a butter bean cassoulet, mixed meat stew with roast potatoes, king prawns with lemon grass, chilli and kaffir lime sauce, and puddings like a trio of chocolate (white chocolate and Baileys crème brûlée, milk chocolate marquise and dark chocolate fondant) and winter berry tart with champagne sabayon.** *Starters/Snacks: £5.00 to £7.00. Main Courses: £10.00 to £18.00. Puddings: £5.00 to £5.50*

Punch ~ Lease Alex Finch ~ Real ale ~ Bar food (12-2.30, 6.30-9; 12-6, 7-9.30 Sat; 12-6 Sun; not Sun evening) ~ Restaurant ~ (01984) 618242 ~ Well behaved children welcome ~ Dogs allowed in bar ~ Open 12-4, 6-11(9 Sun) ~ Bedrooms: £50B/£55B

Recommended by Mr and Mrs P D Titcomb, A J Bowen, Peter Meister, Dr and Mrs A K Clarke, Helene Grygar, Terry Miller

WATERROW   ST0525   MAP 1

Rock ♀ 🛏

A361 Wiveliscombe—Bampton; TA4 2AX

Friendly, family-run half-timbered inn, local ales, good food and a nice mix of customers; bedrooms

Although there's quite an emphasis on the imaginative food and attractive bedrooms in this striking timbered inn, locals do drop in regularly for a pint and a chat. It's a friendly, civilised place run by a mother and son partnership and is on the edge of Exmoor National Park. The bar area has a dark brown leather sofa and low table with newspapers and books in front of the stone fireplace with its log fire and big blackboard menus. There's a mix of dining chairs and wooden tables on the partly wood and partly red carpeted floor, a few high-backed bar chairs, hunting paintings and photographs, a couple of built-in cushioned window seats, Cotleigh Tawny, Exmoor Ale and Otter Ale on handpump, Sheppy's cider and 15 wines by the glass. A back room has a popular pool table; darts and piped music. Up some steps from the bar is the heavily beamed restaurant. The welsh collie is called Meg. There are a few seats under umbrellas by the road.

⑪ **Using local produce and beef from their own farm, the good bar food includes sandwiches, soup, whitebait with smoked paprika mayo, thai crab cakes with bean sprout and pak choi salad and a sweet chilli dressing, local sausages and mash with onion gravy, beer-battered fresh haddock, steak and kidney pie, spinach, ricotta and pine nut pancakes, venison steak with red wine and port sauce, barbary duck breast with a honey and soy reduction, and puddings like panna cotta with gin-poached plums and warm chocolate brownie.** *Starters/Snacks: £4.50 to £6.75. Main Courses: £9.95 to £16.95. Puddings: £4.50 to £7.95*

Free house ~ Licensees Matt Harvey and Joanna Oldman ~ Real ale ~ Bar food (12-2.30, 6-9.30) ~ Restaurant ~ (01984) 623293 ~ Children welcome ~ Dogs allowed in bar and bedrooms ~ Open 12-3, 6-11 ~ Bedrooms: £50S/£75S

Recommended by Bob and Margaret Holder, Heather Coulson, Neil Cross, Nigel Cant

---

'Children welcome' means the pub says it lets children inside without any special restriction. If it allows them in, but to restricted areas such as an eating area or family room, we specify this. Places with separate restaurants often let children use them, hotels usually let them into public areas such as lounges. Some pubs impose an evening time limit – let us know if you find one earlier than 9pm.

WELLS

City Arms ◧
High Street; BA5 2AG

Busy town centre pub with seven real ales, fine choice of whiskies and wines, and food served all day from 9am

As well as keeping a fine range of up to seven real ales, this busy town pub also usefully serves breakfast from 9am. There are always customers dropping in and out and the main bar has leather sofas around low tables, leather chairs around large, heavy tables with carved legs, a gas-effect log fire and plenty of prints and paintings on the cream walls. The upstairs restaurant has a vaulted ceiling, red walls and chandeliers, and there's also a first floor terrace in the cobbled courtyard. Board games and piped music. On handpump, the real ales might include Butcombe Bitter and Gold, Cheddar Ales Gorge Best Bitter and Potholer, Glastonbury Hedgemonkey and Sharps Doom Bar; 35 malt whiskies and up to 20 wines by the glass. The building was originally a jail and you can still see a couple of small, barred windows, a solitary cell and chains and locks in the courtyard.

🍴 As well as the breakfasts, bar food includes sandwiches, soup, salmon goujons with herb mayonnaise, chicken salad with onion confit, olives and crispy croûtons, smoked haddock and spinach bake with a cheesy mash topping, home-cooked honey and mustard-glazed ham with free-range eggs, tagliatelle with pesto and roasted peppers, beer-battered cod, chicken stuffed with sausage meat and herbs wrapped in bacon with red wine gravy, steaks, and puddings like warm chocolate brownies with fudge sauce and strawberry fool. *Starters/Snacks: £2.75 to £5.25. Main Courses: £5.75 to £8.50. Puddings: £3.95 to £5.25*

Free house ~ Licensee Penelope Lee ~ Real ale ~ Bar food (all day till 9.30(10 Sat); breakfast from 9am) ~ Restaurant ~ (01749) 673916 ~ Children welcome ~ Dogs allowed in bar ~ Open 9am(10am Sun)-11.30pm (midnight Sat); 10am opening winter weekdays
Recommended by Terry Buckland, Mr and Mrs Sandhurst, Joe Green, David Lamb, Sylvia and Tony Birbeck, Steve and Liz Tilley, Dr and Mrs A K Clarke

Fountain
St Thomas Street; BA5 2UU

Friendly and attractive small pub behind cathedral with plenty of room, bustling atmosphere, and good drinks and food

This is an attractive little pub, yellow painted with blue shutters and pretty window boxes, built in the 18th-c to house builders working on the nearby cathedral; some parts are said to be even older and there is talk of it having been a Tudor jail. It's run by friendly people and you can be sure of warm welcome despite the many customers popping in and out. There's a big, comfortable L-shaped rambling bar with a bustling atmosphere, some interesting bric-a-brac, Butcombe Bitter and Sharps Doom Bar on handpump and several wines by the glass; piped music and board games. There's a popular upstairs restaurant, too. The cobbled courtyard is most attractive with well planted flower tubs.

🍴 Well liked bar food includes lunchtime sandwiches, soup, chicken liver pâté with balsamic onion marmalade, hot prawn and chilli patties with sweet chilli sauce, ham and eggs, mediterranean roasted vegetable strudel, sausages with mash and onion gravy, chicken breast with lentils, bacon and herbs, moroccan-style lamb with couscous, roast belly of pork with caramelised parsnips and apples, popular 10oz rib-eye steak, and puddings like lemon cheesecake and Guinness spice cake with custard. *Starters/Snacks: £4.50 to £6.95. Main Courses: £8.95 to £14.50. Puddings: £4.50 to £4.95*

Punch ~ Tenants Adrian and Sarah Lawrence ~ Real ale ~ Bar food ~ Restaurant ~ (01749) 672317 ~ Children welcome ~ Open 12-2.30, 6(7 Sun)-11
Recommended by R K Phillips, Terry Buckland, Dr and Mrs A K Clarke, Nick Patton, Sylvia and Tony Birbeck

WOOKEY

ST5245 MAP 2

Burcott 🍺

B3139 W of Wells; BA5 1NJ

Unspoilt, friendly roadside pub with neat bars, real ales and reliable food; bedrooms

If you're staying in the converted stable bedrooms here, you'll find plenty to do nearby. Wells and Wookey Hole are close as are the bird reserves on the Somerset Levels and moors. The two simply furnished and old-fashioned small front bar rooms have exposed flagstoned floors, lantern-style lights on the walls and a woodburning stove. The lounge has a square corner bar counter, a tiny stone fireplace, Parker-Knollish brocaded chairs around a couple of tables and high bar stools; the other bar has beams (some willow pattern plates on one), a solid settle by the window and a high-backed old pine settle by one wall, cushioned mate's chairs around nice old pine tables and a hunting horn on the bressumer above the fireplace. Darts, shove-ha'penny, cribbage and board games, and built-in wall seats and little framed advertisements in a small right-hand room; piped music. Hop Back Summer Lightning, Otter Ale and RCH Pitchfork on handpump, and several wines by the glass. The window boxes and tubs in front of the building are pretty in summer and a sizeable garden has picnic-sets, plenty of small trees, shrubs and Mendip Hill views.

🍽 Fairly priced bar food includes sandwiches, garlic mushrooms, salmon and dill fishcake with a lemon and chive dip, vegetable and cashew nut bake, honey-roast ham and eggs, egg and prawn salad, chicken goujons in an apricot and stilton cream sauce, steak in ale pie, baked salmon steak in an orange and red wine reduction, steaks with various sauces, and puddings. *Starters/Snacks: £4.50 to £6.95. Main Courses: £8.25 to £11.95. Puddings: £4.50*

Free house ~ Licensees Ian and Anne Stead ~ Real ale ~ Bar food (not Sun or Mon evenings) ~ Restaurant ~ (01749) 673874 ~ Children in restaurant but must be well behaved ~ Open 11.30(12 Sat)-2.30, 6-11.30; 12-3, 7-10.30 Sun; closed 25 and 26 Dec, 1 Jan ~ Bedrooms: /£60S

Recommended by Phil and Sally Gorton, Sylvia and Tony Birbeck, Jenny and Brian Seller, Tom Evans, M G Hart

---

LUCKY DIP

Besides the fully inspected pubs, you might like to try these Lucky Dips recommended to us and described by readers (if you do, please send us reports: feedback@goodguides.com).

ASHCOTT [ST4337]
☆ *Ring o' Bells* TA7 9PZ [High St; pub well signed off A39 W of Street]: Friendly neatly kept local with wide choice of good value fresh food from sandwiches and pubby things to imaginative specials, three quickly changing mainly local ales, Wilkins's farm cider, steps up and down making snug comfortably modernised areas, decent wines, helpful service, inglenook woodburner, skittle alley; piped and some live music, games machines; attractive back garden with play area and shaded terrace *(Joe Green, Chris and Angela Buckell, Frank Willy, BB)*

AXBRIDGE [ST4354]
☆ *Lamb* BS26 2AP [The Square; off A371 Cheddar—Winscombe]: Big rambling carpeted pub with heavy 15th-c beams and timbers, stone and roughcast walls, large stone fireplaces, old settles, unusual bar front with old bottles set in plaster, Butcombe and guest ales, well chosen wines, wide choice of good food inc vegetarian, children's and OAP deals (Tues, Thurs), friendly service, board games, table skittles,

skittle alley; they may try to keep your credit card while you eat; children and dogs allowed, pretty and sheltered small back garden, medieval King John's Hunting Lodge opposite (NT), open all day wknds *(Mel de Wit, Chris and Angela Buckell, LYM)*

BACKWELL [ST4767]
New Inn BS48 3BE [West Town Rd (A370 W of Bristol)]: Cottagey dining pub slowly being refurbished by cheerful and helpful newish licensees, enjoyable food inc fresh fish, good choice of wines by the glass, Courage Best, St Austell Tribute and Websters Green Label; stripped stone and ochre paintwork in carpeted dining area, partly stripped brick bar, horsey prints; disabled access with help, big back garden *(Chris and Angela Buckell)*

BARROW GURNEY [ST5367]
Princes Motto BS48 3RY [B3130, just off A370/A38]: Cosy and well run, with unpretentious local feel in traditional tap room, long refurbished lounge/dining area up behind, real ales such as Butcombe and Wadworths, good value wkdy lunchtime food,

log fire, some panelling, cricket team photographs, jugs and china; pleasant garden with terrace, open all day *(LYM, Steve and Liz Tilley)*

BATH [ST7564]

Ale House BA1 1NG [York St]: Quiet and unassuming city-centre local with big windows to street, helpful friendly landlord, Courage Best, Fullers London Pride and a guest such as Bath Gem, flame-effect fire, Bath RFC memorabilia, bargain lunchtime food from baked potatoes up in rambling cellar bar, more seating upstairs; unobtrusive corner TV *(Colin and Peggy Wilshire, Michael Dandy)*

Bell BA1 5BW [Walcot St]: Eight regular real ales, interesting guest beers and farm cider in long narrow split-level dark-ceilinged pub with lots of pump clips and gig notices, good value baguettes, bar billiards; packed and lively evenings with loud music; canopied garden, open all day *(the Didler, Dr and Mrs A K Clarke, Pete Baker)*

Boathouse BA1 3NB [Newbridge Rd]: Large, light and airy family-friendly pub in nice riverside spot nr Kennet & Avon marina, good value food, efficient courteous service, well kept Brains ales, decent house wines, rugs on wooden floor, conservatory on lower level; children very welcome, picnic-sets out in neat garden with steps up to boat-view balcony *(Dr and Mrs A K Clarke)*

☆ *Coeur de Lion* BA1 5AR [Northumberland Place; off High St by W H Smith]: Tiny stained-glass fronted single-room pub, perhaps Bath's prettiest; simple, cosy and jolly, with candles and log-effect gas fire, well kept Abbey ales and local guests, good food from huge baps to roasts (vegetarian options too), good mulled wine at Christmas; may be piped music, stairs to lavatories; tables out in charming flower-filled flagstoned pedestrian alley, open all day *(Dr and Mrs A K Clarke, LYM, Barry Collett, Pete Coxon, Roger Wain-Heapy, Michael Dandy, the Didler, Michael and Alison Sandy, Dr and Mrs M E Wilson)*

Crystal Palace BA1 1NW [Abbey Green]: Cheerfully busy two-room pub with something of a wine-bar feel, dark panelling and tiled floors, freshly prepared straightforward food (not Sun evening) inc lunchtime snacks, speedy friendly service, well kept ales such as Abbey Bellringer, Jennings and Marstons Pedigree, log fire, family room and conservatory; piped music; sheltered heated courtyard with lovely hanging baskets *(Dr and Mrs A K Clarke, LYM, Ian Phillips, Donna and Roger)*

Forester & Flower BA2 5BZ [Bradford Rd, Combe Down]: Interesting friendly place with good caribbean-influenced food, jolly landlady, well kept ales, L-shaped bar with comfortable sofas and large unusual wooden table, big raised dining area beyond, another room with sofas, books, magazines and a few small dining tables, affable cat *(Dr and Mrs M E Wilson)*

☆ *Garricks Head* BA1 1ET [Theatre Royal, St Johns Place]: Relaxed and attractive food pub, good snacks in bare-boards bar with armchairs, sofa, wooden tables and open fire, separate dining room doing very good meals (not Sun evening) served quickly if not cheaply (and 10% service on all food bills), good blackboard choice of wines, notably friendly helpful staff, Otter and guest ales such as Cottage and Stonehenge, daily papers; piped music, steep steps down to gents'; pavement tables, handy for theatre next door (they do pre-show meals), open all day *(Dr and Mrs M E Wilson, Jeremy King, Dr and Mrs A K Clarke, Mr and Mrs W W Burke, Edward Mirzoeff)*

☆ *George* BA2 6TR [Bathampton, E of Bath centre, off A36 or (via toll bridge) off A4; Mill Lane]: Beautifully placed canalside Chef & Brewer, wide blackboard food options all day, five real ales, good choice of wines by the glass, well organised young uniformed staff, good-sized bar opening through arches into rambling beamed rooms with three log fires, candles on nice mix of tables, rugs on polished boards, dark panelling, period portraits and plates; children welcome, enclosed suntrap terrace and waterside tables (may be drinks only out here) *(Dr and Mrs A K Clarke, Pete Coxon, Donna and Roger, Richard Fendick)*

Hare & Hounds BA1 5TJ [Lansdown Rd, Lansdown Hill]: Elegant popular stone pub with superb views from big garden and terrace, attractive and comfortably furnished long well divided bar, Abbey Bellringer and Courage, simple substantial food inc special deals, friendly staff, leaded lights in mullioned windows, lots of woodwork, hanging bird cages and shelves of bric-a-brac, roomy eating area and conservatory; children welcome, open all day *(Dr and Mrs A K Clarke, Meg and Colin Hamilton, MRSM, Mr and Mrs A H Young, Dave Irving, Jenny Huggins)*

☆ *Hop Pole* BA1 3AR [Albion Buildings, Upper Bristol Rd]: Bustling family-friendly Bath Ales pub with guest beers, decent wines by the glass, enjoyable food (not Sun evening, Mon lunchtime) from sandwiches to full meals in bar and former skittle alley restaurant, traditional settles and other pub furniture on bare boards in four tastefully reworked linked areas, lots of black woodwork and ochre walls, some bric-a-brac, board games, daily papers; Mon quiz night, piped music, discreet sports TV; wheelchair accessible, attractive two-level back courtyard with boules, fairy-lit vine arbour and summer houses with heaters, opp Victoria Park with its great play area, open all day *(Jeremy King, Roger Wain-Heapy, Dr and Mrs A K Clarke, Chris and Angela Buckell, the Didler, GSB, BB, Colin and Peggy Wilshire)*

☆ *King William* BA1 5NN [Thomas St/A4 London Rd]: Small unpretentious two-bar corner pub, chunky old tables on dark bare boards, a few lit church candles and perhaps a big bunch of flowers on counter, Bristol Beer Factory Sunrise, Newmans Red Stag Bitter and Palmers Dorset Gold, good choice of wines by the glass, good imaginative food (not Sun evening) from short menu, daily papers, steep stairs up to simple attractive dining room (set menu, used mainly Weds-Sat evenings); piped music; children and dogs welcome, open all day wknds (LYM, Roger Wain-Heapy, Dr and Mrs A K Clarke, Paul Goldman)

Pig & Fiddle BA1 5BR [Saracen St]: Lively, not smart, with good sensibly priced ales such as Abbey, Bath and Butcombe, pleasant staff, two big open fires, clocks on different time zones, bare boards and bright paintwork, steps up to darker bustling servery and little dining part, games area and several TVs; lots of students at night, good piped trendy pop music then; picnic-sets on big heated front terrace, open all day (Dr and Mrs M E Wilson, Dr and Mrs A K Clarke, the Didler, BB)

Raven BA1 1HE [Queen St]: Small pub with well kept Blindmans and guest ales, a changing farm cider, particularly good lunchtime pies, sausages and savoury mash, quick service, open fire, charity bookshelves, some stripped stone, upstairs dining room, live acoustic music; open all day (Pete Coxon, John Robertson, Dr and Mrs A K Clarke, the Didler, Andy Lickfold, Michael Dandy, Catherine Pitt)

Salamander BA1 2JL [John St]: Busy city local tied to Bath Ales, their full range and guest beers, bare boards, black woodwork and dark ochre walls, bargain basic bar lunches (get there early for a table), two rooms downstairs, open-kitchen upstairs restaurant, decent wines, daily papers, live irish music Tues; open all day (Dr and Mrs M E Wilson, BB, the Didler, Dr and Mrs A K Clarke, Pete Coxon, LM, Ian Phillips, Michael Dandy)

Wagon & Horses BA1 7DD [London Rd W]: Roomy pub popular for good bargain OAP lunch, helpful staff, pleasant roomy décor, Avon Valley views (Meg and Colin Hamilton)

BATHFORD [ST7866]

Crown BA1 7SL [Bathford Hill, towards Bradford-on-Avon, by Batheaston roundabout and bridge]: Popular family pub, roomy with several linked areas, attractive central fireplace, wood floors and cheerful décor, two dining areas (one overlooking garden), generous reasonably priced food, friendly service, three well kept beers, decent wines, public bar with pool; piped music; terrace tables (LYM, Meg and Colin Hamilton, Dr and Mrs M E Wilson)

BATHPOOL [ST2525]

Bathpool Inn TA2 8BE [Bridgwater Rd (A38, between M5 junctions 24 and 25)]: Welcoming neatly kept family pub under friendly helpful new landlord, several linked rooms each in a different style, decent fresh

food, real ales such as Wadworths 6X, big glasses of wine; safe garden with play park (Bob and Margaret Holder)

BECKINGTON [ST8051]

☆ *Woolpack* BA11 6SP [Warminster Rd, off A36 bypass]: Well refurbished and civilised old inn with charming helpful staff, unusual and well prepared if not cheap food from well filled ciabattas up, well kept Greene King, decent wines, farm cider, big log fire and chunky candlelit tables in flagstoned bar, attractive smarter oak-panelled dining room and conservatory; can get very busy Sat night and service may slow; children welcome, appealing period bedrooms, open all day (Simon and Sally Small, Norman and Sarah Keeping, LYM)

BINEGAR [ST6149]

Horse & Jockey BA3 4UH: Welcoming pub with three long rooms, friendly staff, substantial bar food especially pizzas, real ales inc Wadworths, local Thatcher's farm cider, skittle alley (Anne Morris)

BLEADON [ST3457]

☆ *Queens Arms* BS24 0NF [just off A370 S of Weston; Celtic Way]: 16th-c village pub with informal chatty atmosphere in carefully divided areas, candles on sturdy tables flanked by winged settles, solid fuel stove, old hunting prints, bar food (not Sun evening) from lunchtime baguettes to steaks, Butcombe and guests tapped from the cask, several wines by the glass, flagstoned and terracotta-walled restaurant and stripped-stone back bar with woodburner, darts; games machine; children (away from bar) and dogs welcome, picnic-sets on pretty heated terrace, open all day (LYM, Comus and Sarah Elliott, Dr and Mrs A K Clarke, KC)

BLUE ANCHOR [ST0243]

Smugglers TA24 6JS [end of B3191, off A39 E of Minehead]: Mellow building in spectacular clifftop setting, well run hotel bars inc airy flagstoned dining room, civilised upper restaurant, small beamed and flagstoned cellar, good range of enjoyable food, real ales inc Otter, pleasant staff, comforting log fires; piped music; children welcome (dogs, too, if bar not busy), big sheltered garden, comfortable pretty bedrooms, site for touring caravans (Mr and Mrs D J Nash)

BRADLEY GREEN [ST2438]

Malt Shovel TA5 2NE [off A39 W of Bridgwater, nr Cannington]: Recently reopened low-beamed pub with interconnecting rooms, mix of old and new furniture on quarry-tiles and carpet, some stripped stone, old hunting prints, woodburner, well kept Butcombe ales, real cider, decent wines by the glass, enjoyable food from snacks up inc good value lunchtime carvery, wknd breakfast till 10.30am, helpful staff, sizeable skittle alley; piped music; children in eating areas, disabled parking and access (highish door sills into restaurant), picnic-sets on paved laneside area, bedrooms *(Chris and Angela Buckell, LYM)*

BRENDON HILLS [ST0334]

Raleghs Cross TA23 0LN [junction B3190/B3224]: Busy family-friendly upland inn with helpful friendly staff, Cotleigh, Exmoor and a guest beer, good local cider, wide choice of food, rows of plush banquettes in big bar, back restaurant/carvery; children in restaurant and family room, no dogs; plenty of tables outside with play area, views to Wales on clear days, good walking country, 17 comfortable bedrooms, open all day in summer *(John and Bryony Coles, Paul Thompson, Roy and Jean Russell, John Saville, LYM)*

BRENT KNOLL [ST3251]

Red Cow TA9 4BE [2 miles from M5 junction 22; right on to A38, then first left into Brent St]: Well run pub with enjoyable unpretentious home-made food in dining lounge (children allowed), well kept Butcombe, considerate friendly service, family room, skittle alley; no dogs inside; pretty gardens front and back *(MP, BB, John and Elisabeth Cox)*

BRISTOL [ST5672]

☆ *Adam & Eve* BS8 4ND [Hope Chapel Hill, Hotwells]: Quietly tucked-away pub, refurbished under newish management, dark bare boards and clean cheerful décor, several real ales inc well kept Bath Gem, cider and perry, belgian beers, good organic wines and juices, good inexpensive creative food changing daily, interesting recipes and organic ingredients, friendly staff, relaxed country-pub atmosphere, log fire, pleasant nooks and corners, café chairs and wall settles, interesting photographs and pictures; not much parking nearby *(Mark O'Sullivan, Lil Sheeley, BB)*

Apple BS1 4SB [Welsh Back]: Barge specialising in ciders, cheap comfort food – popular with students; quayside seating under huge umbrella *(Mrs Jane Kingsbury, Kerry Law)*

☆ *Bag o' Nails* BS1 5UW [St Georges Rd, by B4466/A4 Hotwells roundabout]: No-frills place popular for its half a dozen or more changing ales and bottled beers, friendly staff and locals, good cobs; piped music; beer festivals, open all day Fri-Sun *(the Didler, WW, Simon and Amanda Southwell)*

Colston Yard BS1 5BD [Upper Maudlin St/Colston St]: Former Smiles Brewery Tap reopened as a Butcombe pub, very popular, with their full range kept well, interesting bottled beers, good choice of wines and spirits, enjoyable food from lunchtime sandwiches to grills and evening restaurant menu, two floors in minimalist pastel style; wheelchair access *(Chris and Angela Buckell)*

☆ *Commercial Rooms* BS1 1HT [Corn St]: Spacious Wetherspoons with lofty domed ceiling, gas lighting, comfortable quieter back room with ornate balcony; wide changing choice of good real ales inc local ones, usual food all day, cheap prices, friendly chatty bustle (busiest wknd evenings), surprising ladies' with chesterfields and open fire; no dogs; children welcome, good location, side wheelchair access and disabled facilities, open all day from 9am and till late Fri-Sun *(Simon and Amanda Southwell, the Didler, Dr and Mrs A K Clarke)*

Cornubia BS1 6EN [Temple St]: 18th-c backstreet real ale pub with good Hidden ales and several recherché guest beers, interesting bottled beers, farm cider and perry, wkdy pubby food till 7.30pm (Sun till 6) inc substantial ploughman's, friendly service, small woody seating areas; can be crowded evenings, not for wheelchairs; picnic-sets on cobbles outside, open all day *(Luke Daniels, Susan and Nigel Brookes, the Didler, John and Gloria Isaacs)*

Cross Hands BS16 5AA [Staple Hill Rd, Fishponds (A432/B4465)]: Comfortable carpeted open-plan bar with up to a dozen well kept ales, good choice of bar food, cheerful chatty staff, flower prints on pastel walls and flowers on tables, lots of nibbles inc nuts and sweets; good disabled access and facilities, picnic-sets on cobbled terrace *(Chris and Angela Buckell)*

Eldon House BS8 1BT [Lower Clifton Hill]: Very popular under current management, three friendly and individual rooms, decent food inc some interesting evening dishes, all-day Sat breakfast, Bath ales and a guest, good value wines, refurbished cellar; piped music from jazz to classical, Tues quiz night; wheelchair access, metal tables and chairs out by pavement *(Chris and Angela Buckell)*

Famous Royal Naval Volunteer BS1 4EF [King St]: Well done re-creation of traditional city pub in genuinely ancient building, locals' front snug, long bar, nice dark wood décor with small well furnished rooms and relaxed civilised atmosphere (more lively wknd evenings), several well kept mostly local ales, lunchtime bar food (Tues-Fri), prompt friendly service, live music Tues night; wheelchair access, cobbled streets, handy for Theatre Royal *(Chris and Angela Buckell)*

Grain Barge BS8 4RU [Hotwell Rd]: Floating 100-ft barge tied to Bristol Beer Factory, their full range, good well priced freshly made food inc ale sausages/pies and beer-battered fish, picnic-sets on top deck, sofas and tables with metal chairs on wood floor below; live music Fri night, open all day *(the Didler, WW, Donna and Roger, Kerry Law)*

Green Man BS2 8HD [aka Bell; Alfred Place, Kingsdown]: Small cosy local, candlelit at night, with four well kept organic ales, Luscombe and Weston's farm cider, organic spirits and wines by the glass, limited organic bar lunches (not Mon, Tues), bare boards and dark woodwork; wheelchair access just about possible with help *(Chris and Angela Buckell)*

Hatchet BS1 5NA [Frogmore St]: Old pub with plenty of character, well priced simple bar lunches, well kept Butcombe, good young staff *(Stan Edwards, Dr and Mrs A K Clarke)*

☆ *Hope & Anchor* BS8 1DR [Jacobs Wells Rd, Clifton]: Friendly 18th-c pub with half a dozen changing ales such as Cotleigh, Otter and Wickwar from central bar, tables of various sizes on bare boards, darker back area, good range of sensibly priced food all day inc good ploughman's choice and some interesting dishes – very popular lunchtime, pleasant staff; soft piped and occasional live music, can get crowded late evening; children welcome, disabled access, summer evening barbecues in good-sized tiered back garden with interesting niches *(Jeremy King, the Didler, Simon and Amanda Southwell)*

Inn on the Green BS7 0PA [Filton Rd, Horfield]: Civilised real ale pub with changing choice of up to a dozen or more, four farm ciders, tasters offered, sensibly priced baguettes and a few hot dishes, friendly service, wood and quarry-tile floors, some half-panelling, pubby furniture inc pews and settles, more seating in former skittle alley, occasional live music *(Chris and Angela Buckell)*

☆ *Kensington Arms* BS6 6NP [Stanley Rd]: Smart dining pub in discreet shades of grey and cream, cheerful helpful young staff, enjoyable food from light pub lunches to bigger pricier evening dishes, well kept Greene King ales, good if not cheap wine choice, interesting rums etc, flowers and lit candles; may be piped music; wheelchair facilities and access (not to dining room/upstairs dining room), well behaved children and dogs welcome, heated terrace *(Chris and Angela Buckell, Susan and Nigel Brookes, John and Gloria Isaacs)*

☆ *Kings Head* BS1 6DE [Victoria St]: Friendly relaxed 17th-c pub with big front window and splendid mirrored back bar, corridor to cosy panelled back snug with serving hatch, Bath Gem, Wadworths 6X and Sharps Doom Bar, toby jugs on joists, old-fashioned local prints and photographs, interesting gas pressure gauge, generous reasonably priced food wkdy lunchtimes (get there early if you want a seat); 1960s piped music, no credit cards; pavement tables, cl Sat lunchtime, open all day Weds-Fri *(Pete Baker, Jeremy King, G Russell, Susan and Nigel Brookes, the Didler, WW, Dr and Mrs A K Clarke, BB)*

Lamplighters BS11 9XA [Station Rd, Shirehampton]: Welcoming riverside pub with decent sensibly priced straightforward food, Butcombe, Sharps Doom Bar and guests, efficient friendly service, log fire, old shipping prints on rough plastered walls, daily papers, upstairs balcony, downstairs children's room; piped and some live music, games machines; good-sized garden with play area *(Chris and Angela Buckell)*

Lion BS8 4TX [Church Lane, Clifton]: Good value generous bistro-type food and good beer in two well refurbished bare-boards bars, friendly welcome; some live music; cl lunchtimes Mon-Thurs, open all day Fri-Sun *(Anne Helne)*

Llandoger Trow BS1 4ER [off King St/Welsh Back]: By docks, interesting as the last timber-framed building built here, impressive flower-decked façade, reasonably priced bar food inc daytime bargains (not Sun), upstairs restaurant, well kept Greene King and Shepherd Neame, friendly staff, some small alcoves and rooms with original fireplaces and carvings around central servery, wood and stone floors, exposed brickwork, wide mix from students to tourists; piped music; children welcome, picnic-sets out by cobbled pedestrianised street, bedrooms in adjacent Premier Lodge *(John Saville, Jeremy King, Sue and Mike Todd)*

Nova Scotia BS1 6XJ [Baltic Wharf, Cumberland Basin]: Unreconstructed old local on S side of Floating Harbour, views to Clifton and Avon Gorge, Bass, Courage Best and guest beers, Thatcher's farm cider, bargain hearty food from good doorstep sandwiches to Sun roasts, pubby seats in four linked areas, snob screen, mahogany and mirrors, nautical charts as wallpaper; wheelchair access (two steps), plenty of tables out by water, bedrooms sharing bathroom *(Chris and Angela Buckell, LM, Stan Edwards)*

Old Duke BS1 4ER [King St]: Duke Ellington, that is – inside festooned with jazz posters, besides one or two instruments, good bands most nights and Sun lunchtime, usual pub furnishings, simple food; in attractive cobbled area between docks and Bristol Old Vic, gets packed in evenings *(David A Hammond, BB)*

Old Fish Market BS1 1QZ [Baldwin St]: Imposing building well converted, good mural showing it in 1790s, lots of dark wood inc handsome counter, parquet floor, relaxed friendly atmosphere, good value mainly thai food all day, well kept Fullers ales and Butcombe as guest, good coffee, daily papers; quiet piped music, big-screen sports TVs, games machines; open all day *(Simon and Amanda Southwell, Dr and Mrs A K Clarke, Donna and Roger, Jeremy King)*

Ostrich BS1 6TJ [Lower Guinea St, Bathurst Basin – follow General Hospital sign from inner ring road]: Unassuming three-room pub in good dockside position, well kept Brains, Marstons Pedigree and St Austell, decent good value food, small dining area down a few steps; plenty of waterside seating across cobbled street *(LM)*

Portcullis BS8 4LE [Wellington Terrace]: Compact two-storey pub with spectacular views, well kept local Cheddar Potholer and Matthews Brassknocker and several changing guest beers, farm ciders, fine range of wines by the glass and spirits, friendly service, basic cheap bar food (not Mon) inc well filled rolls, flame-effect gas fire, dark wood and usual pubby furniture, jack russell called Daisy, cards, Thurs quiz night; wheelchair access with difficulty and help *(Chris and Angela Buckell, Donna and Roger)*

☆ *Pump House* BS8 4PZ [Merchants Rd]: Spacious and attractively converted dockside building, charcoal-grey brickwork, tiled floors, high ceilings, well kept Bath ales, decent wine by the glass, enjoyable bar food, friendly staff, cheerful atmosphere, good smart candlelit mezzanine restaurant; waterside tables *(LYM, Rhona Macpherson)*

☆ *Royal Oak* BS8 4JG [The Mall, Clifton]: Simple traditional open-plan pub with well kept Bath Gem, Butcombe, Courage Best, Otter and Sharps Doom Bar, real ciders and perry, short choice of bargain lunchtime food from soup and sandwiches to roasts, friendly welcoming service, beams and bare boards, stripped stone and painted brick walls, Aga in front bar, open fire and settles in upper back part, rugby memorabilia, darts; quiet piped music and occasional live, TV; smokers' area out at back, cl Sun evening otherwise open all day *(Georgina Chambers, Jeremy King, Georgina Wolfe, Chris and Angela Buckell, B and K Hypher)*

Seven Stars BS1 6JG [Thomas Lane]: Unpretentious one-room real ale pub near harbour (and associated with Thomas Clarkson and slave trade abolition), much enjoyed by students and local office workers, up to eight real ales inc Absolution brewed for them by Sharps, occasional farm cider and perry festivals, dark wood, bare boards, old local prints and photographs, can bring in take-aways; juke box, pool, games machines; disabled access, if you can manage the narrow alley's uneven cobbles and cast-iron kerbs *(Chris and Angela Buckell)*

Severn Shed BS1 4RB [The Grove]: Clever contemporary conversion of historic Brunel boat shed on Floating Harbour, striking lightweight roof truss design, intriguing mobile hover bar, decent fairly priced food inc good value two-course menu 12-7pm, Weston's farm cider, interesting bottled beers, a variety of malt whiskies and rums, good reasonably priced wines, welcoming attentive staff, children welcome in the restaurant, wheelchair access throughout, splendid disabled facilities, good views from terrace tables with awnings *(Chris and Angela Buckell)*

☆ *Star & Dove* BS3 4RY [St Lukes Rd]: Simple but imaginative food at sensible prices, strong on light and italian dishes, good choice of wines by the glass, real ales such as Bath and Butcombe, unpretentious up-to-date décor with some sofas and easy chairs on parquet floor; tables and chairs out on partly covered flagstoned back terrace, cl til 4 wkdys, open all day Fri-Sun *(John Urquhart)*

Van Dyck Forum BS16 3UA [Fishponds Rd]: Wetherspoons cinema conversion, imaginative if less ornate than some, usual value, dark panelling, big hanging fish models; big-screen TV, machines; disabled facilities and access by stairlift, open all day *(Chris and Angela Buckell)*

Victoria BS8 2BH [Southleigh Rd]: Modest two-room pub with half a dozen or more changing ales, interesting lagers and belgian beers, dozens of malt whiskies, good wines by the glass inc organic, open fire, cards and board games, big mirrors; disabled access (more or less – poor pavements and people park on them), opens mid-afternoon (all day wknds) *(Chris and Angela Buckell)*

Wellington BS7 8UR [Gloucester Rd, Horfield (A38)]: Lively and roomy 1920s pub refitted in traditional style by Bath Ales, their beers served by friendly knowledgeable staff, enjoyable fresh traditional food inc generous Sun roasts, large horseshoe bar, sofas and low tables in newly extended lounge with dining area overlooking sunny terrace; very busy on home match days for Bristol RFC or Bristol Rovers; children welcome, dogs outside only, disabled facilities, open all day *(Chris and Angela Buckell)*

Windmill BS3 4LU [Windmill Hill, Bedminster]: Good relaxed atmosphere, sofas and bare boards, pleasant décor, enjoyable food inc good pies, Bath, Bristol Beer Factory and guest ales, farm ciders, pub games; 1970s juke box, TV; small deck *(Mrs Jane Kingsbury)*

BRUTON [ST6834]

Sun BA10 0AH [High St]: Unpretentious old local, small bar with nice conical woodburner, larger room beyond with dark tables and chairs, farming plaques and tools, Black Sheep and Yeovil ales, simple cheapish food; TV *(Dr and Mrs M E Wilson)*

BURROW BRIDGE [ST3530]

King Alfred TA7 0RB: Proper old-fashioned pub doing well under new licensees, enjoyable fresh food (meat all from Somerset) inc popular Sun lunch, reasonable prices, friendly atmosphere, four well kept ales and local farm cider, some live music *(Alison Clewes, Bob and Margaret Holder, Jim Winkworth)*

CASTLE CARY [ST6432]

George BA7 7AH [just off A371 Shepton Mallet—Wincanton; Market Place]: Civilised thatched country-town hotel, busy small front bar with big inglenook, inner lounge off main central reception area, enjoyable straightforward food from sandwiches up, Greene King ales, decent house wines; children welcome, 16 bedrooms, open all day *(Norman and Sarah Keeping, LYM, Derek and Sylvia Stephenson)*

CATCOTT [ST3939]

☆ *Crown* TA7 9HQ [off A39 W of Street; Nidon Lane, via Brook Lane]: Roomy country pub under new welcoming owners, wide choice of generous home-made pub food inc good Sun carvery, real ales such as Butcombe and

Fullers London Pride, farm cider, decent wines by the glass, cosy area by log fire, skittle alley; children welcome, picnic-sets and play area out behind, bedrooms *(LYM, Frank Willy, KC, R Lewis, Mr and Mrs H J Stephens)*

King William TA7 9HU [signed off A39 Street—Bridgwater]: Rugs on flagstones, big stone fireplaces, traditional furnishings, old prints, good value food, well kept Palmers, pub games, big back extension with skittle alley and glass-topped well; piped music; children welcome *(LYM, Joe Green)*

CHARLTON HORETHORNE [ST6623]

☆ **Kings Arms** DT9 4NL: Formerly closed village pub reopened spring 2009 after extensive reworking by licensees who have made a great success of their previous pubs, now an upmarket bar and restaurant with good interesting food from open-view kitchen, well kept Butcombe and Wadworths IPA and 6X, impressive range of wines by the glass, local artwork, no piped music; children welcome, big garden, ten attractive and comfortable bedrooms, good breakfast *(Edward Mirzoeff, the Gravelles, Charles Gysin, Mark Flynn, Neville and Anne Morley)*

CHEDDAR [ST4553]

Bath Arms BS27 3AA [Bath St]: Roomy pub with good value home-made food all day from breakfast on (quite a few dishes using cheddar cheese), Bass, Courage Best and Greene King Old Speckled Hen, decent wines, friendly atmosphere, public bar, some live music and quiz nights; children and dogs welcome, garden (may have bouncy castle), comfortable bedrooms, open all day *(Walter)*

☆ **Gardeners Arms** BS27 3LE [Silver St]: Relaxed and cheerful, tucked away in the old part, with good generous food (service can suffer when busy) from familiar pub lunches to beautifully presented exotic dishes, well kept Adnams, Butcombe and Courage Best, cheery log fires, attractive two-room beamed dining area, interesting old local photographs; children and dogs welcome, play things and wendy house in quiet back garden, open all day *(K Botten, S Longman, JCW, John Marsh, LYM, John and Gloria Isaacs)*

CHEW MAGNA [ST5763]

☆ **Bear & Swan** BS40 8SL [B3130 (South Parade)]: Now a Fullers pub, open-plan, with new landlord, their ales and a guest, good choice of wines, enjoyable food, mix of pine tables, pews and big log fire, L-shaped dining room with stripped stone, bare boards and woodburner; TV, small car park (street parking not easy); children and dogs welcome, old-fashioned bedrooms – make your own breakfast *(Chris and Angela Buckell, Comus and Sarah Elliott, Andrea Rampley, LYM)*

☆ **Pony & Trap** BS40 8TQ [Knowle Hill, New Town; back road to Bishop Sutton]: Good local food in small gently refurbished tucked-away pub with comfortable layout, flagstones, antiques and lit candles, well

kept Butcombe and other ales, good wines by the glass and coffee, downstairs conservatory restaurant – great views from here and garden picnic-sets; wheelchair access to bar, good nearby walks (ask to find them), delightfully rural hillside setting nr Chew Valley Lake *(Chris and Angela Buckell, John Urquhart, Stephen and Jean Curtis, John and Gloria Isaacs, Martin Hatcher)*

CHEWTON MENDIP [ST5953]

Waldegrave Arms BA3 4LL [High St (A39)]: Friendly pub with hearty snacks and well kept Butcombe and Cottage ales *(Dave Braisted)*

CLEVEDON [ST3971]

Little Harp BS21 7RH [Elton Rd (seafront)]: High-throughput promenade pub, views towards Exmoor and the Welsh hills from terrace and two dining conservatories, pleasant family area with mezzanine floor, Greene King ales, all-day food *(Tony Brace)*

Moon & Sixpence BS21 7QU [The Beach]: Substantial seafront Victorian family dining pub, large bar area, balconied mezzanine floor with good view of pier and over to Brecon Beacons, reasonably priced food, helpful friendly staff, well kept Greene King ales; may be piped music *(Clive and Jenny Roberts)*

☆ **Old Inn** BS21 6AE [Walton Rd (B3124 on outskirts)]: Friendly mix of regulars and visitors in neatly extended beamed pub, good solid furniture on carpets, good value generous food all day, well kept Otter Head, Theakstons Old Peculier and regularly changing guests; bedrooms *(Tom Evans, Robin and Tricia Walker)*

COMBE FLOREY [ST1531]

☆ **Farmers Arms** TA4 3HZ [off A358 Taunton—Williton, just N of main village turn-off]: Neatly kept thatched and beamed dining pub, popular and can get packed lunchtime, good reasonably priced food using prime local produce, real ales such as Exmoor and Otter, local farm cider, comfortable drinking area with log fire; children welcome, plenty of tables in attractive garden, by summer steam line *(Bob and Margaret Holder, Christine and Neil Townend, BB)*

COMBE HAY [ST7359]

☆ **Wheatsheaf** BA2 7EG [off A367 or B3110 S of Bath]: Upscale food from sandwiches and tasty home-baked breads through short changing choice of up-to-date starters and main dishes to tempting puddings, Butcombe beers, local farm cider, good wine choice, quick friendly service, plush fireside sofas, big fresh and airy dining area with trendy light modern furnishings (a radical change for this 1576 pub); tables in attractive terraced garden overlooking church and steep valley, dovecotes built into the walls, plenty of good nearby walks, comfortable bedrooms in outbuildings, cl Mon *(Donna and Roger, LYM, Dr and Mrs A K Clarke, Mr and Mrs A H Young)*

COMPTON DUNDON [ST4832]
Castlebrook Inn TA11 6PR [Castlebrook]:
Cheerful flagstoned village pub, blazing log
fire, Greene King IPA, Sharps Doom Bar and
Wadworths 6X, quickly served pubby food
from open-view kitchen, big back simple
family restaurant with Sun carvery, daily
papers; big lawn behind with play area
(*Edward Mirzoeff, Ian Phillips*)

COMPTON MARTIN [ST5457]
Ring o' Bells BS40 6JE [A368 Bath—
Weston]: Country pub in attractive spot,
traditional front part with rugs on
flagstones, inglenook seats by log fire,
up step to spacious carpeted back part,
stripped stone, Butcombe ales and guests,
reasonably priced wine, pubby food with
some south african influences (licensees
are from there), friendly helpful service,
newspapers; well behaved children and
dogs welcome, big garden with play area,
open all day wknds (*LYM, George and
Gill Rowley, Chris and Angela Buckell,
James Morrell*)

CONGRESBURY [ST4363]
Old Inn BS49 5DH [Pauls Causeway,
down Broad St opp The Cross]: Friendly
low-beamed and flagstoned 16th-c local,
pleasant décor with pretty curtains in
deep-set windows, huge fireplaces, one
with ancient stove opening to both bar
and dining area, mix of old furniture inc
pews and upholstered benches, leather
ceiling straps, reasonably priced pubby
food (may be just bar snacks lunchtime),
well kept Wells & Youngs ales and a guest
tapped from the cask, Thatcher's cider,
decent wines, tea and coffee; tables in
back garden, open all day (*Chris and
Angela Buckell*)
Plough BS49 5JA [High St (B3133)]: Old-
fashioned flagstoned local full of life, well
kept changing ales inc Butcombe and RCH,
quick smiling service, decent simple bar
lunches, three cosy areas off main bar, two
log fires, old prints, farm tools and sporting
memorabilia, darts, table skittles, shove
ha'penny and cards; small garden with
boules and aviary, occasional barbecues,
open all day Sat (*Jim and Frances Gowers*)
Ship & Castle BS49 5JA [High St (just off
A370 from lights at W end of bypass)]:
Extensively reworked family dining pub with
pleasant series of linked rooms, open fire
and soft seats as well as eating area, food
inc some original light dishes, Greene King
ales (*M G Hart*)
☆ *White Hart* BS49 5AR [Wrington Rd, off
A370 Bristol—Weston]: Welcoming country
pub, L-shaped main bar with heavy black
beams in bowed ceiling, big stone
inglenooks each end, country kitchen
furniture, two areas off, big conservatory,
Badger beers, specialist gins, decent pub
food, board games; piped music; picnic-sets
on back terrace and in big garden, nice
walks (*LYM, Tom Evans, Richard Fendick,
Bob and Margaret Holder*)

CROWCOMBE [ST1336]
☆ *Carew Arms* TA4 4AD [just off A358
Taunton—Minehead]: New french manager
for interesting well worn-in 17th-c beamed
inn; hunting trophies and inglenook
woodburner in old-fashioned front public
bar, well kept Exe Valley, Exmoor and Otter
ales, farm cider and good choice of wines by
the glass, pubby food from new chef inc Fri
take-away fish and chips and Sun roast,
friendly efficient service, traditional games
and skittle alley, dining room allowing
children; dogs welcome, informal garden
with good play things, six bedrooms, open
all day summer wknds (*the Didler, LYM,
Tony Winckworth, Mr and Mrs Sandhurst,
Terry Miller, Mike and Sue Losebey, Jane and
Alan Bush, Peter Meister*)

DINNINGTON [ST4013]
Dinnington Docks TA17 8SX [aka Rose &
Crown; Fosse Way]: Good cheery atmosphere
in large old-fashioned country local, unspoilt
and welcoming, with good choice of
inexpensive genuine home cooking,
Butcombe and guest beers such as Archers,
Burrow Hill farm cider, log fire, friendly
attentive staff, lots of memorabilia to
bolster the myth that there was once a
railway line and dock here, sofas in family
room, skittle alley; large garden behind
(*Roger Hardisty, Dr and Mrs M E Wilson*)

DOULTING [ST6444]
Poachers Pocket BA4 4PY [Chelynch Rd, off
A361]: Popular modernised local doing well
under new landlord, flagstones with some
carpet, good hearty food, well kept
Butcombe and Wadworths, local farm cider,
log fire in stripped-stone end wall, dining
conservatory; children in eating area and
large family room/skittle alley, back garden
with country views (*Susan and Nigel Wilson,
LYM*)
Waggon & Horses BA4 4LA [Doulting
Beacon, 2 miles N]: Nicely set rambling pub,
old-fashioned feel with stonework, wrought
iron, some stained-glass and a homely mix
of tables, beamed gallery, friendly
atmosphere, well kept ales inc Wadworths
6X, quite a few wines by the glass, food
from baked potatoes up; quiet children and
dogs allowed, big walled garden with wildlife
pond and climber (*LYM, Geoff Bichard*)

DOWLISH WAKE [ST3712]
New Inn TA19 0NZ [off A3037 S of Ilminster,
via Kingstone]: Dark-beamed comfortable
village pub doing well under friendly hard-
working couple, popular food using fresh
local produce, well kept Butcombe and Otter,
local farm cider, woodburners in stone
inglenooks, pleasant dining room; attractive
garden and village, four bedrooms (*LYM,
David and Sue Smith, Douglas Allen*)

DULVERTON [SS9127]
Lion TA22 9BU [Bank Sq]: Old-fashioned
two-bar country-town hotel, big log fire,
cheerful staff, Exmoor real ale, decent wines
and coffee, sensibly priced pub food; dogs
welcome and children away from main

serving bar, 14 bedrooms, pleasant setting
(George Atkinson)
DUNSTER [SS9943]
Dunster Castle Hotel TA24 6SF [High St]:
Airy modern hotel bar with light oak
furnishings, steps down to traditional back
bar, good value food here or in dining room,
St Austell Proper Job and Tribute, attentive
friendly service; bedrooms, useful car park
(George Atkinson)
☆ *Luttrell Arms* TA24 6SG [High St; A396]: Small
hotel in 15th-c timber-framed abbey building,
well used high-beamed back bar hung with
bottles, clogs and horseshoes, stag's head and
rifles on walls above old settles and more
modern furniture, big log fires, enjoyable bar
food inc substantial sandwiches with home-
baked bread, small helpings available, friendly
attentive staff, well kept ales inc Exmoor,
good wines in three glass sizes; dogs welcome
in bar, ancient glazed partition dividing off
small galleried and flagstoned courtyard,
upstairs access to quiet attractive garden with
Civil War cannon emplacements and great
views, comfortable if pricey bedrooms (may
have to stay two nights at wknds) (Mr and
Mrs P D Titcomb, Glenwys and Alan Lawrence,
BB, Dr and Mrs A K Clarke, Paul Humphreys)
EAST LAMBROOK [ST4218]
☆ *Rose & Crown* TA13 5HF: Neatly kept stone-
built dining pub spreading extensively from
compact 17th-c core with inglenook log fire,
efficient friendly staff and relaxed
atmosphere, good generous inexpensive food
freshly made using local supplies inc very
popular wkdy OAP lunches, full Palmers real
ale range, farm cider, decent wines by the
glass, restaurant extension with old glass-
covered well; picnic-sets on neat lawn, opp
East Lambrook Manor Garden (Nick Hawksley,
JDM, KM, BB, Guy Consterdine)
EAST WOODLANDS [ST7944]
☆ *Horse & Groom* BA11 5LY [off A361/B3092
junction]: Small pretty pub tucked away
down country lanes, thoughtful choice of
enjoyable well priced fresh food worth
waiting for (not Sun evening), friendly
service, Butcombe, Palmers and Timothy
Taylors Landlord tapped from the cask,
choice of wine glass sizes, pews and settles
in flagstoned bar, woodburner in comfortable
lounge, big dining conservatory, traditional
games; dogs welcome away from restaurant,
children in eating areas, disabled access,
picnic-sets in nice front garden with more
seats behind, handy for Longleat
(Ian Phillips, LYM)
EVERCREECH [ST6336]
Natterjack BA4 6NA [A371 Shepton Mallet—
Castle Cary]: Wide choice of generous good
value food, three local ales inc one for the
pub from Box Steam, good wine choice,
pleasant helpful staff, long bar with eating
areas off (Michael and Jenny Back, B Read)
EXFORD [SS8538]
☆ *White Horse* TA24 7PY [B3224]: Popular and
welcoming three-storey creeper-covered inn,
more or less open-plan bar, high-backed

antique settle among more conventional
seats, scrubbed deal tables, hunting prints
and local photographs, good log fire, three
Exmoor ales and Sharps Doom Bar, over
100 malt whiskies, Thatcher's cider, hearty
food from sandwiches to good value Sun
carvery, daily Land Rover Exmoor safaris;
children and dogs welcome, play area and
outside tables, comfortable bedrooms, pretty
village, open all day from 8am (LYM,
Lynda and Trevor Smith, Paul Humphreys,
George Atkinson)
FAILAND [ST5171]
Failand Inn BS8 3TU [B3128 Bristol—
Clevedon]: Refurbished welcoming old
coaching inn with wide choice of popular
family food, Butcombe and Courage, good
wines by the glass, comfortable dining
extension; may be piped music; dogs and
children welcome, garden with play area
(Tom Evans, Comus and Sarah Elliott, Mr and
Mrs A Curry)
FARMBOROUGH [ST6660]
Butchers Arms BA2 0AE [Timsbury Rd]:
Comfortable two-bar village local with
friendly staff and atmosphere, three real
ales, good value food inc Sun roasts;
children and dogs welcome (Noel and
Barbara Chatfield)
New Inn BA2 0BY [Bath Rd (A39)]: Popular
roomy roadside Greene King pub, friendly
staff, good generous traditional food
(Stuart Paulley, Dr and Mrs A K Clarke)
FELTON [ST5265]
George & Dragon BS40 9UL [Stanshalls
Lane]: Welcoming helpful service in
unpretentious pub with bargain food and
well kept ales inc one labelled for the pub
(Tom Evans)
FRESHFORD [ST7960]
Inn at Freshford BA2 7WG [off A36 or
B3108]: Roomy beamed stone-built dining
pub tied to Box Steam with their ales and a
guest, good choice of wines by the glass,
cocktails, comfortable traditional layout inc
area with leather sofas and chairs by fire,
enjoyable food, live jazz and quiz nights;
piped music; children and dogs welcome,
pretty hillside garden, attractive spot near
river (Roger Wain-Heapy, Meg and
Colin Hamilton, LYM, MRSM, Chris and
Angela Buckell, Dr and Mrs A K Clarke)
GLASTONBURY [ST4938]
George & Pilgrims BA6 9DP [High St]:
Comfortable 15th-c inn with magnificent
carved stone façade and some interesting
features – handsome stone fireplace (flame-
effect gas fire), oak panelling and traceried
stained-glass bay window (rest of pub more
ordinary); well kept Butcombe Gold,
St Austell Tribute and a house beer, local
country wine, decent food; children in buffet
and upstairs restaurant, bedrooms (LYM,
Joe Green)
Hawthorns BA6 9JJ [Northload St]: Neat and
welcoming, well kept Wadworths, decent
wines, daily good value curry buffet, local
art for sale (Joe Green)

King Arthur BA6 9NB [Benedict St]: Great
atmosphere in friendly pub with fine range
of real ales at good prices, farm ciders, good
live music Fri – can get packed; nice outside
area *(Joe Green)*

☆ *Who'd A Thought It* BA6 9JJ [Northload St]:
High-backed curved settle, coal fire, pine
panelling, stripped brick, beams and
flagstones, nicely quirky oddments, well kept
Palmers ales, good choice of wines by the
glass, good value food from toasties to good
steaks, daily papers; children and dogs
welcome, pleasant garden, comfortable
bedrooms, open all day *(LYM, Joe Green)*

HALLATROW [ST6357]

☆ *Old Station* BS39 6EN [A39 S of Bristol]:
Good food and well kept ales such as Bass
and Butcombe in idiosyncratic bar packed
with cluttered railway, musical and other
bric-a-brac, also italian evening dishes in
Flying Scotsman railcar restaurant (can look
inside during daytime); piped music; children
in eating areas, garden with well equipped
play area, bedrooms *(Richard Fendick,
Stuart Paulley, John and Fiona McIlwain,
LYM)*

HARDWAY [ST7234]

☆ *Bull* BA10 0LN [off B3081 Bruton—
Wincanton at brown sign for Stourhead and
King Alfred's Tower]: Charming beamed
country dining pub popular locally,
especially with older people wkdy
lunchtimes, for fine choice of reliably good
and generous if not cheap food in
comfortable bar and character dining rooms,
pleasant long-serving licensees, quick
friendly obliging service, well kept
Butcombe, good wines by the glass, farm
cider, log fire; unobtrusive piped music;
tables and barbecues in new garden behind,
more in rose garden over road, bedrooms
(Colin and Janet Roe)

HINTON BLEWETT [ST5956]

☆ *Ring o' Bells* BS39 5AN [signed off A37 in
Clutton]: Charming low-beamed stone-built
country local opp village green, old-
fashioned bar with solid tables and chairs,
log fire, good value wholesome food (not
Sun evening) from sandwiches up, obliging
service, Butcombe and guest beers, good
wines by the glass and cafetière coffee,
refurbished dining room; children welcome,
pleasant view from tables in sheltered front
yard *(Tom Evans, LYM)*

HINTON CHARTERHOUSE [ST7758]

Stag BA2 7SW [B3110 S of Bath; High St]:
Attractively furnished ancient pub with good
generous sensibly priced food from
sandwiches up in cosy bar and pleasant
stripped-stone dining areas, real ales such as
Butcombe, coal-effect gas fire; provision for
children, tables outside, has been open all
day *(Pat Crabb, Meg and Colin Hamilton,
LYM)*

HOLCOMBE [ST6649]

☆ *Holcombe Inn* BA3 5EB [off A367; Stratton
Rd]: Extensively modernised quietly placed
country pub, good food, Otter and a guest

ale, local cider, several wines by the glass,
pleasant layout with several linked areas inc
pubby tables on flagstones, sofas, easy
chairs, panelling and carpet elsewhere,
woodburners, good-sized dining area;
piped music; children, dogs and walkers
welcome, picnic-sets outside, peaceful
farmland views, bedrooms, cl Sun evening
*(LYM, S G N Bennett, Stephen Bennett,
Terry Buckland, Ian Phillips)*

HOLTON [ST6826]

Old Inn BA9 8AR [off A303 W of Wincanton]:
Charming rustic 16th-c pub, unaffectedly
comfortable, with beams, ancient flagstones,
woodburner, hundreds of key fobs, nice bric-
a-brac, big open woodburner, long-serving
landlord, well kept Butcombe and Wadworths
6X, good interesting attractively priced food
in bar and restaurant (must book Sun lunch);
tables outside, sheltered garden up steps
(BB, Mark Flynn)

HUNTWORTH [ST3134]

Boat & Anchor TA7 0AQ [just off M5
junction 24, signed off exit roundabout,
then turn right towards narrow swing
bridge]: Good choice of enjoyable pub food
from baguettes to good steaks, Sun carvery,
roomy eating areas inc conservatory (not
always open), young friendly staff, well kept
Butcombe and Otter, nice house wines,
inscrutable parrot called Drew; children
welcome, lovely garden by Bridgwater &
Taunton Canal, eight bedrooms *(Bob and
Margaret Holder, Richard Fendick)*

ILCHESTER [ST5222]

Ilchester Arms BA22 8LN [Church St]:
Friendly hotel with three real ales in small
peaceful pine-panelled bar on right,
restaurant on two levels with good
reasonably priced mediterranean-leaning
food inc light lunches, efficient smiling
service; comfortable bedrooms *(Ian Malone)*

KELSTON [ST7067]

Old Crown BA1 9AQ [Bitton Rd; A431 W of
Bath]: Four small traditional rooms with
beams and polished flagstones, carved
settles and cask tables, logs burning in
ancient open range, two more coal-effect
fires, Bath, Butcombe, Fullers and Wadworths
(some tapped from the cask), Thatcher's
cider, good choice of wines by the glass and
whiskies, friendly helpful staff, cheap
wholesome bar food (not Sun or Mon
evenings) inc good salads, small restaurant
(not Sun) with some imaginative dishes, no
machines or music; dogs welcome on leads,
children in eating areas, wheelchair
accessible with help, picnic-sets under apple
trees in sunny sheltered back garden,
bedrooms in converted outbuildings, open
all day wknds *(LYM, Chris and Angela Buckell,
Donna and Roger)*

KEYNSHAM [ST6669]

☆ *Lock-Keeper* BS31 2DD [Keynsham Rd
(A4175)]: Bustling and popular, in lovely
spot on Avon island with lots of picnic-sets
out under glazed canopy, big heated deck
and steps down to shady garden by lock,

marina and weir; well kept Wells & Youngs ales, good choice of wines by the glass, enjoyable good value food from sandwiches to good old-fashioned puddings, friendly prompt service, small room by bar, arches to unpretentious main divided room with black beams and bare boards, barrel-vaulted lower area; wheelchair access; pipe music; boules *(Dr and Mrs A K Clarke, Chris and Angela Buckell)*

KILMERSDON [ST6952]

Jolliffe Arms BA3 5TD: Large attractive stone-built Georgian local overlooking pretty churchyard, Butcombe and Fullers London Pride, good wines by the glass, reasonably priced home-made pub food, friendly service, four linked areas (three mainly for dining) reminiscent of unpretentious farmhouse parlour, some huge black flagstones, fresh flowers on tables, skittle alley; piped music; front picnic-sets *(Terry Buckland, Dr and Mrs M E Wilson, Ian Phillips)*

KILVE [ST1442]

Hood Arms TA5 1EA [A39 E of Williton]: Neatly kept beamed 18th-c country pub under new ownership, good food from bar snacks up, Otter, Palmers and guest ales, cosy plush lounge, warm woodburner in bar, restaurant, skittle alley; dogs welcome, nice back garden with tables on sheltered terrace, 12 bedrooms – two in back lodge *(LYM)*

KINGSDON [ST5126]

Kingsdon Inn TA11 7LG [off B3151]: New owners for pretty thatched dining pub, three attractively decorated linked rooms, coal fire, some panelling and low beams, Butcombe, Cheddar and Otter ales; children welcome, picnic-sets on front grass, bedrooms, handy for Lytes Cary (NT) and Fleet Air Arm Museum *(Theo, Anne and Jane Gaskin, LYM, JCW)*

KINGSTON ST MARY [ST2229]

Swan TA2 8HW: Cosy and welcoming 17th-c pub with good reasonably priced home-made food, Otter and two changing guest ales, traditional cider, good choice of wines, big log fires, daily papers; children and dogs welcome *(W N Murphy, Phil Storor, Debbie Hutcheson-Davey, Bob and Margaret Holder)*

LANGFORD BUDVILLE [ST1122]

☆ *Martlet* TA21 0QZ [off B3187 NW of Wellington]: Cosy comfortable pub under new ownership, enjoyable food, good range of ales, friendly staff, inglenook, beams and flagstones, central woodburner, steps up to carpeted lounge with another woodburner; skittle alley *(John Gould, John Hopkins)*

LANSDOWN [ST7268]

Blathwayt Arms BA1 9BT: Interesting old building with helpful service, enjoyable food inc some unusual dishes and good Sun roast, well kept ales, decent wines; children welcome, racecourse view from garden, open all day *(Dr and Mrs A K Clarke, Tom and Ruth Rees)*

LITTON [ST5954]

☆ *Kings Arms* BA3 4PW [B3114, NW of Chewton Mendip]: Partly 15th-c Greene King

pub of considerable character, closed for some months 2008/9 but expected to reopen under new management – news please *(LYM)*

LONG ASHTON [ST5570]

Angel BS41 9LT [Long Ashton Rd]: Ancient local with several rooms inc two-level beamed lounge bar, log fire and local memorabilia, real ales, good value food, friendly service; dogs welcome, tables in quiet courtyard with nesting swallows, bedrooms *(Simon and Amanda Southwell)*

Dovecote BS41 9LX: Roomy Vintage Inn with their usual food and reasonably priced drinks inc good choice of wines by the glass, cheerful attentive young staff; upstairs gents'; pleasant garden, open all day *(Jim and Frances Gowers, MB)*

Miners Rest BS41 9DJ [Providence Lane]: Welcoming chatty pub, comfortable and unpretentious, with good farm ciders, well kept Bass and Fullers London Pride, reasonably priced wines, bargain pub lunches, cheerful staff (help with wheelchair access), local mining memorabilia; no credit cards; vine-covered verandah and suntrap terrace picnic-sets *(Chris and Angela Buckell)*

LONG SUTTON [ST4625]

☆ *Devonshire Arms* TA10 9LP [B3165 Somerton—Martock, just off A372 E of Langport]: Tall gabled stone inn (former hunting lodge), stylish décor, squashy leather sofas by log fire, roomy restaurant area on left, sporting and country prints, good young staff, interesting blackboard food from enterprising sandwiches up and good set lunch menu, well kept real ale, local farm cider, quite a few wines by the glass, homely flagstoned back bar with darts and TV; may be piped music; children in eating areas, disabled access, terrace and large walled garden, nine bedrooms, open all day *(LYM, Steve and Hilary Nelson, Roderick Braithwaite, Clare West, G K Smale)*

MARK [ST3747]

Pack Horse TA9 4NF [B3139 Wedmore—Highbridge; Church St]: Attractive 16th-c village pub run by welcoming greek cypriot family, very popular wknds for its wide food choice inc good Sun roast, fresh Brixham fish and delicious puddings, Butcombe and Fullers London Pride, good friendly service; next to church *(MP)*

White Horse TA9 4LT [B3139 Wedmore—Highbridge]: Spacious 17th-c pub doing well under new management, enjoyable food; dogs welcome, pleasant garden *(Mr and Mrs D J Nash)*

MARTOCK [ST4619]

Nags Head TA12 6NF [East St]: Stone-built local with great staff, good choice of food inc bargain OAP Fri lunch and Sun roasts, well kept local ales, banquettes and pubby furniture on carpet, log-effect gas fire, lots of prints, large aquarium, games room; piped music; wheelchair access *(Chris and Angela Buckell)*

MELLS [ST7249]

☆ **Talbot** BA11 3PN [W of Frome, off A362 or A361]: Interesting old inn, austere public bar in carefully restored tithe barn, farm tools on stone walls, big mural dining counter, attractive dining room in main building, sporting and riding pictures, solid dining tables and chairs, Butcombe tapped from cask, helpful pleasant staff, darts; piped music, TV; children and dogs welcome, nice cobbled courtyard, comfortable bedrooms *(Roger Wain-Heapy, Colin Watt, Dr and Mrs M E Wilson, LYM, Pete Coxon)*

MIDDLEZOY [ST3732]

George TA7 0NN [off A372 E of Bridgwater]: Friendly 17th-c country pub, well kept ales inc Butcombe, enjoyable home cooking, attentive welcoming staff, low ceilings, flagstones and traditional seating; good outside tables *(Shirley and Bob Gibbs, Liz and Jeremy Baker)*

MIDFORD [ST7660]

☆ **Hope & Anchor** BA2 7DD [Bath Rd (B3110)]: Open-plan roadside pub, wide choice of good generous home-made food from traditional to more imaginative dishes like local venison with sloe gin and blueberries, nice puddings too, civilised bar, heavy-beamed and flagstoned restaurant end, and new back conservatory, six well kept changing ales such as Butcombe Gold, Hidden Ace and Wadworths 6X, good house wines, proper coffee, relaxed atmosphere, log fire; children welcome, tables on sheltered back terrace with upper tier beyond, pleasant walks on disused Somerset & Dorset railway track, open all day *(M G Hart, Roger Wain-Heapy, John and Gloria Isaacs, Geoffrey Kemp, Dr and Mrs M E Wilson, BB)*

MIDSOMER NORTON [ST6654]

White Hart BA3 2HQ [The Island]: Well worn chatty Victorian local with several rooms, Bass, Butcombe and a guest tapped from the cask, two farm ciders, local coal-mining memorabilia, bargain simple lunchtime food, cheerful helpful staff; no credit cards; dogs welcome, open all day *(the Didler)*

MILBORNE PORT [ST6718]

Queens Head DT9 5DQ [A30 E of Sherborne]: Enjoyable generous low-priced food inc plenty of sandwiches, well kept Butcombe, good wines by the glass, good coffee, quick friendly service, neat beamed lounge, restaurant and conservatory, games in public bar, skittle alley; provision for children and quiet dogs, reasonable disabled access, tables in sheltered courtyard and garden with play area, three cosy good value bedrooms *(LYM, Ron and Sheila Corbett, Dennis Jenkin)*

MILVERTON [ST1225]

Globe TA4 1JX [Fore St]: Smartly reworked as dining pub, enjoyable food, well kept Exmoor ale *(Bob and Margaret Holder, Giles and Annie Francis)*

MONTACUTE [ST4917]

Kings Arms TA15 6UU [Bishopston]: Extended partly 16th-c inn, simple modern tables and chairs in small stripped stone carpeted bar, log fire between it and restaurant, Greene King ales, good wines by the glass and coffee, bargain food from baguettes and baked potatoes up, magazines and daily papers; children and dogs welcome, pleasant garden behind, bedrooms, handy for Montacute House (NT) *(Michael Dandy, LYM)*

MOORLINCH [ST3936]

Ring o' Bells TA7 9BT [signed off A39]: Fine old building, log fire in attractive lounge, keen chef/landlord doing good value hearty food inc good Sun roasts, well kept changing ales such as Bath and Cotleigh; sports TV in public bar *(Joe Green)*

NAILSEA [ST4469]

Blue Flame BS48 4DE [West End]: Small well worn 19th-c farmers' local, two rooms with mixed furnishings, Butcombe and RCH ales from casks behind bar, Thatcher's farm cider, good filled rolls, coal fire, pub games; plain-speaking landlord, outside lavatories inc roofless gents', limited parking (may be filled with Land Rovers and tractors); children's room, sizeable informal garden, open all day summer *(the Didler)*

NETHER STOWEY [ST2139]

☆ **Cottage** TA5 1HZ [Keenthorne, A39 E of village; not to be confused with Apple Tree Cottage]: Warm, friendly and roomy partly 16th-c local with good unpretentious home-made food from baguettes up (they also sell home-made chutneys), real ales such as Butcombe and Exmoor, farm cider, reasonable prices, good service, carpeted front dining area, back bar and lounge with woodburner; piped music; garden up steps from car park *(George Atkinson, Julian Jefferson, LYM)*

NEWTON ST LOE [ST7065]

☆ **Globe** BA2 9BB [A4/A36 roundabout]: Popular 17th-c Vintage Inn, large and rambling, with pleasant décor and dark wood partitions, pillars and timbers giving secluded feel, enjoyable food all day, well kept Butcombe, Fullers London Pride and St Austell Tribute, prompt friendly uniformed staff, good atmosphere; pleasant back terrace, open all day *(Dr and Mrs A K Clarke, Donna and Roger, Roger Wain-Heapy, Meg and Colin Hamilton, Lady Heath)*

NORTON ST PHILIP [ST7755]

☆ **Fleur de Lys** BA2 7LG [High St]: Chatty local in 13th-c thatched stone cottages, friendly landlord and helpful staff, well kept Wadworths beers, sensibly priced wine, good value home-made food from baguettes up, log fire in huge fireplace, steps and pillars giving cosy feel of separate rooms in beamed and flagstoned areas around central servery; children welcome, skittle alley *(Paul Humphreys, the Didler, Dr and Mrs M E Wilson, R K Phillips, BB)*

NUNNEY [ST7345]

George BA11 4LW [Church St; signed off A361 Shepton Mallet—Frome]: New licensees and refurbishment at this 17th-c coaching inn, open-plan lounge with beams and stripped stone, nice log fire, good bar and restaurant food inc Sun roasts, Wadworths ales, good choice of wines by the glass, separate restaurant; no children under 14, dogs welcome, walled garden, rare gallows inn-sign spanning road, in quaint village with ruined castle, nine bedrooms *(Adrie Van der Luijt, Jennifer Banks, Geoffrey Kemp, BB)*

OAKE [ST1526]

☆ **Royal Oak** TA4 1DS [Hillcommon, N; B3227]: Neat village pub with several separate-seeming areas around central servery, little tiled fireplace and big woodburner, brasses on beams and walls, well kept ales such as Cotleigh, Exe Valley, Exmoor and Sharps, some tapped from the cask, good food and service, long dining areas, skittle alley; piped music; children welcome, pleasant sheltered garden, open all day wknds (food all day then) *(Theo, Anne and Jane Gaskin, LYM, FJS and DS)*

OAKHILL [ST6347]

Oakhill Inn BA3 5HU [A367 Shepton Mallet—Radstock]: Dining pub redecorated in current dark colours, sofas and easy chairs among candlelit tables around bar, friendly atmosphere and welcoming staff, decent if not cheap food with good fresh veg, dining extension in former skittle alley *(Michael Doswell)*

ODCOMBE [ST5015]

Masons Arms BA22 8TX [41 Lower Odcombe]: Popular generous food from pubby things to some interesting dishes, good range of reasonably priced beers such as Odcombe, helpful efficient service even on busy Sat night; good bedrooms and breakfast *(Joyce and Maurice Cottrell)*

OVER STRATTON [ST4315]

Royal Oak TA13 5LQ [off A303 via Ilminster turn at S Petherton roundabout]: Relaxed thatched family dining pub, friendly enthusiastic licensees, well priced enjoyable food, well kept Badger, attractive line of linked rooms, flagstones and thick stone walls, prettily stencilled beams, scrubbed kitchen tables, pews, settles etc, log fires and rustic décor, charity library; tables outside *(LYM, Bob and Margaret Holder, Kate and Ian Hodge)*

PITMINSTER [ST2219]

Queens Arms TA3 7AZ [off B3170 S of Taunton (or reached direct); near church]: Friendly village pub with enjoyable local food inc good fish choice and some interesting dishes, good Sun roast too, well kept Cotleigh and Otter, several wines by the glass, log fires, simple wooden bar furniture, pleasant dining room, occasional live music *(Patrick and Daphne Darley, Mike Gorton, John and Fiona Merritt, Geoff and Carol Thorp)*

PORLOCK WEIR [SS8846]

☆ **Ship** TA24 8QD [separate from but run in tandem with neighbouring Anchor Hotel]: Unpretentious thatched bar in wonderful spot by peaceful harbour (so can get packed – although no sea views), long and narrow with dark low beams signed by customers, flagstones and stripped stone, big log fire, simple pub furniture, four well priced ales inc Cotleigh, Exmoor and Otter, Inch's cider, good whisky and soft drinks choice, friendly prompt staff, bargain food from thick sandwiches up, plainer overflow rooms across small back yard; piped music, big-screen TV, little free parking but pay & display opposite; children and dogs welcome, sturdy picnic-sets on side terraces, good coast walks, decent bedrooms *(Mr and Mrs D J Nash, Paul Humphreys, Dr and Mrs M E Wilson, John Saville, Barry and Anne, BB)*

PORTBURY [ST4975]

☆ **Priory** BS20 7TN [Station Rd, 0.5 miles from A369 (just S of M5 junction 19)]: Consistently good well extended Vintage Inn dining pub/hotel, several beamed rooms with appealing mix of comfortable furnishings in alcoves, log fire, friendly prompt staff, well kept ales, good range of wines by the glass, interesting fresh fruit juices, wide choice of enjoyable well priced food all day till 10pm inc good fish specials; piped music; front and back garden tables, bedrooms, open all day *(Roger Braithwaite, George and Gill Rowley, JCW)*

PORTISHEAD [ST4676]

Poacher BS20 6AJ [High St]: Large pub popular with older lunchers for wide range of freshly made low-priced food, well kept Butcombe Blond, Courage Best and two other ales (a proper part for village beer-drinkers, with a big fireplace), friendly staff; quiz nights, cl Sun evening *(Tom Evans)*

Royal BS20 7HG [Pier Rd (NE end of town, near sea)]: 1830s former hotel popular in summer for superb location overlooking Severn estuary and bridges, light and spacious with linked Victorian parlours, well kept Butcombe and Sharps Doom Bar, good food inc children's helpings and wider evening choice, friendly staff; piped music; large terrace, open all day, cl Sun evening *(Richard Fendick, George and Gill Rowley, Mr and Mrs P R Thomas)*

PRIDDY [ST5450]

☆ **Hunters Lodge** BA5 3AR [from Wells on A39 pass hill with TV mast on left, then next left]: Welcoming and unchanging farmers', walkers' and potholers' pub above Ice Age cavern, in same family for generations, well kept beers such as Bath, Blindmans, Butcombe, Cheddar Ales and Exmoor tapped from casks behind the bar, Wilkins's farm cider, simple cheap food, log fires in huge fireplaces, low beams, flagstones and panelling, old lead mining photographs; no mobiles or credit cards; children and dogs in family room, wheelchair access, garden picnic-sets, bedrooms *(Phil and Sally Gorton, the Didler, Chris and Angela Buckell, LYM)*

☆ **Queen Victoria** BA5 3BA [village signed off B3135; Pelting Drove]: Relaxed character country local in lovely position, friendly staff and regulars, three good log fires (one open on two sides), well kept Butcombe ales tapped from the cask, three local ciders, good coffee, wholesome food inc good steaks and fish, stripped stone and flagstones, interesting bric-a-brac, collected furnishings inc miscellaneous tables and pews, some live folk music; children and dogs welcome, garden over road, great walks, open all day Fri-Sun (M Mossman, Terry Buckland)

RICKFORD [ST4859]

Plume of Feathers BS40 7AH [very sharp turn off A368]: Unspoilt cottagey and partly flagstoned local with limited choice of simple reasonably priced home-made food, relaxed atmosphere, well kept Butcombe and Sharps Doom Bar, country ciders, friendly family service, ochre walls and pale green panelling, mix of furniture inc cast-iron tables and settles, log fires, table skittles, pool; well behaved children and dogs welcome, rustic tables on narrow front terrace, pretty streamside hamlet, bedrooms (Chris and Angela Buckell, Daniel Jackson, BB)

RODE [ST8053]

☆ *Cross Keys* BA11 6NZ [High St]: Spotless and cheerful, with good fresh local food, well kept beer, good new licensees and top-notch service; in former brewery, with front bar, side eating area and old well (Ted George)

Mill BA11 6AG: Popular family pub in beautifully set former watermill, smart restaurary layout and up-to-date décor and artwork, good quality food, children's room with impressive games; live music Fri (may be loud); garden and decks overlooking River Frome, big play area (Mr and Mrs A Curry)

RODNEY STOKE [ST4850]

Rodney Stoke Inn BS27 3XB [A371 Wells—Weston]: Comfortable pub with good imaginative food, Butcombe and Cheddar ale, cheerful efficient service, airy high-beamed restaurant extension; children welcome, roadside terrace and back lawn (Hugh Roberts, BB)

ROWBERROW [ST4458]

☆ *Swan* BS25 1QL [off A38 S of A368 junction]: Neat and spacious dining pub opp pond, olde-worlde beamery and so forth, good log fires, friendly atmosphere especially in nicely unsophisticated old bar part, good food from baguettes up, well kept Butcombe ales, decent choice of wines by the glass, Thatcher's cider, perry; good-sized garden over road (LYM, George and Gill Rowley, M G Hart, Steve and Liz Tilley, John and Fiona McIlwain, Tom Evans, Mrs Sheila Clarke)

RUMWELL [ST1923]

Rumwell Inn TA4 1EL [A38 Taunton—Wellington, just past Stonegallows]: Good comfortable atmosphere, old beams and cosy corners, lots of tables in several areas, wide range of enjoyable food from lunchtime snacks up inc good home-made puddings and

Sun roasts, changing real ales, good coffee, roaring log fire, family room; tables in nice garden, handy for Sheppy's Cider (Peter Salmon)

SALTFORD [ST6867]

Bird in Hand BS31 3EJ [High St]: Comfortable and friendly, with lively front bar, good range of beers such as Abbey and Butcombe, farm cider, attractive back conservatory dining area popular locally for good value fresh food from mini-ploughman's to daily roast, huge omelettes and Whitby fish, quick service even when quite a queue for food, lots of bird pictures, small family area; live entertainment; picnic-sets down towards river, handy for Bristol—Bath railway path (Dr and Mrs M E Wilson, Dr and Mrs A K Clarke)

☆ *Jolly Sailor* BS31 3ER [off A4 Bath—Keynsham; Mead Lane]: Great spot by lock and weir on River Avon, with dozens of picnic-sets, garden heaters and own island between lock and pub; enjoyable standard food from well filled lunchtime baguettes to several fish dishes, cheerful efficient service, well kept changing ales such as Butcombe, Theakstons Old Peculier and Wells & Youngs Bombardier, good value wines by the glass, flagstones, low beams, log fires, daily papers, conservatory restaurant; children allowed if eating, disabled facilities, open all day (Chris and Angela Buckell, John and Gloria Isaacs)

STAPLE FITZPAINE [ST2618]

☆ *Greyhound* TA3 5SP [off A358 or B3170 S of Taunton]: Light rambling country pub with wide range of good food (best to book evenings), changing ales, good wines by the glass, welcoming atmosphere and attentive staff, flagstones, inglenooks, pleasant mix of settles and chairs, log fires throughout, olde-worlde pictures, farm tools and so forth; children welcome, comfortable bedrooms, good breakfast (Roy and Jean Russell, LYM)

STAR [ST4358]

Star BS25 1QE [A38 NE of Winscombe]: Reopened after extensive reworking as rambling dining pub, busy at peak times, good value pubby food inc carvery, Butcombe and Marstons Pedigree, inglenook log fire in old bar area; heated terrace, picnic-sets behind, open all day (Tom Evans, George and Gill Rowley)

STOGUMBER [ST0937]

White Horse TA4 3TA [off A358 at Crowcombe]: Friendly old village pub with well kept Cotleigh, Greene King and Marstons, enjoyable food from sandwiches to Sun roasts, long neat bar, old village photographs with more recent ones for comparison, good log fires, games room and skittle alley; children welcome, nice quiet back terrace, bedrooms, open all day wknds and summer (LYM, Jennifer Banks, Terry Miller, John Marsh)

STOKE GIFFORD [ST6178]

Fox Den BS34 8TJ [New Rd]: Old-look pub, inside and out, recently built as part of

Holiday Inn Express, useful for reasonably priced standard food, with friendly efficient service and well kept real ale *(Jim and Frances Gowers)*

TAUNTON [ST2525]

☆ *Hankridge Arms* TA1 2LR [Hankridge Way, Deane Gate (nr Sainsbury); just off M5 junction 25 – A358 towards city, then right at roundabout, right at next roundabout]: Well appointed Badger dining pub based on 16th-c former farm, splendid contrast to the modern shopping complex around it, different-sized linked areas, well kept ales, generous enjoyable food from interesting soups and sandwiches through sensibly priced pubby things to restaurant dishes, quick friendly young staff, decent wines, big log fire; piped music; dogs welcome, plenty of tables in pleasant outside area *(Gill and Keith Croxton, Dr and Mrs A K Clarke, Chris Glasson)*

Vivary Arms TA1 3JR [Wilton St; across Vivary Park from centre]: Pretty low-beamed 18th-c local (Taunton's oldest), good value distinctive fresh food in snug plush lounge and small dining room, enthusiastic helpful young staff, relaxed atmosphere, well kept ales inc Butcombe, decent wines, interesting collection of drink-related items; bedrooms in Georgian house next door *(Richard Fendick, Bob and Margaret Holder, John Marsh, Robert W Buckle)*

TYTHERINGTON [ST7645]

Fox & Hounds BA11 5BN: 17th-c, with roomy and tidy L-shaped stripped-stone bar, food from meze to pub standards and Sun carvery, changing ales such as Cheddar and Jennings, farm ciders, sleepy chocolate labrador (likes the side lounge's best sofa), function room extension; piped music; children and dogs welcome, garden and terrace tables, cl Sun evening *(MRSM, Edward Mirzoeff)*

UPHILL [ST3158]

Ship BS23 4TN [Uphill Way]: Village pub with well kept beer, short choice of decent pub food, friendly staff, comfortable carpeted bar with open fire and stripped stone, upstairs restaurant; games area with darts and pool; dogs welcome, short walk from beach *(Jean and David Lewis)*

UPTON [ST0129]

☆ *Lowtrow Cross Inn* TA4 2DB: Well run by cheery landlord and staff, good fresh home-made food, nice relaxed mix of locals and diners, character low-beamed bar with log fire, bare boards and flagstones, two carpeted country-kitchen dining areas, one with enormous inglenook, plenty of atmosphere, well kept ales such as Cotleigh Tawny and Exmoor Fox; no dogs; children welcome, attractive surroundings, bedrooms *(BB, Mrs Joyce Ansell, John Hopkins, Richard and Anne Ansell)*

VOBSTER [ST7049]

☆ *Vobster Inn* BA3 5RJ [Lower Vobster]: Roomy old stone-built dining pub, good reasonably priced food from spanish chef/landlord inc good local cheese plate,

some spanish dishes and fish fresh daily from Cornwall, good service, Butcombe and a Blindmans seasonal ale, good wines by the glass, three comfortable open-plan areas with antique furniture inc plenty of room for just a drink; side lawn with colourful bantams, peaceful views, boules, adventure playground behind *(Donna and Roger, M G Hart, Ian Phillips, BB, Edward Mirzoeff, Sylvia and Tony Birbeck)*

WAMBROOK [ST2907]

Cotley Inn TA20 3EN [off A30 W of Chard; don't follow the small signs to Cotley itself]: Smartly unpretentious stone-built pub with new licensees; Otter ales, traditional food, simple flagstoned entrance bar opening on one side into small plush bar, several open fires, two-room dining area, skittle alley; piped music; children and dogs welcome, lovely view from terrace tables, nice garden below, quiet spot with plenty of surrounding walks, two good bedrooms, cl Mon lunchtime *(LYM)*

WATCHET [ST0743]

Bell TA23 0AN [Market St]: Popular family-run local with cosy carpeted lounge on right, usual food (not Tues), well kept Exmoor, St Austell Tribute and Sharps Doom Bar, public bar on left; good disabled access, handy for West Country Steam Railway *(D S Fawcett)*

Star TA23 0BZ [Mill Lane (B3191)]: Old cottagey pub nr seafront with new welcoming young landlady, low beams, good log fire, wooden furniture and bric-a-brac, straightforward reasonably priced food, five good changing ales and a local cider; dogs welcome, picnic-sets out in front and in garden *(M R Phillips, Ross Nuttycombe)*

WELLOW [ST7358]

☆ *Fox & Badger* BA2 8QG [signed off A367 SW of Bath]: Recently opened up, flagstones one end, bare boards the other, some snug corners, woodburner in massive hearth, real ales such as Fullers London Pride and Sharps Doom Bar, Thatcher's Farm cider, wide range of generous bar food from doorstep sandwiches up; children and dogs welcome, picnic-sets in covered courtyard, open all day Fri-Sun *(Dr and Mrs M E Wilson, Donna and Roger, LYM, S G N Bennett, Paul Humphreys)*

WELLS [ST5445]

Crown BA5 2RF [Market Pl]: Brightly modernised former coaching inn overlooked by cathedral, various bustling bar areas with white or blue walls, light wooden flooring, plenty of matching chairs and cushioned wall benches, up step to comfortable area with newspapers, well kept ales such as Butcombe, Moor and Sharps Doom Bar, usual food, back room for families with stone fireplace, GWR prints, TV and games machine; children until 8pm, small courtyard, bedrooms, open all day *(Dr and Mrs A K Clarke, Steve and Liz Tilley, LYM, Brian and Anna Marsden)*

Globe BA5 2PY [Priest Row]: Popular unassuming local with welcoming lived-in rooms either side of ancient flagstoned corridor, open fire, well kept ales such as Butcombe and Shepherd Neame Spitfire, food from good sandwiches up, friendly service; big-screen TV, games area *(Pete Devonish, Ian McIntyre, BB, Sue and Mike Todd)*

WEST BAGBOROUGH [ST1733]

Rising Sun TA4 3EF: Welcoming pub with new landlord in tiny village below Quantocks, attractively rebuilt after 2002 fire, appealing décor, relaxed bar and more formal dining area, decent food, real ales *(Michael Cleeve, Bob and Margaret Holder)*

WEST HATCH [ST2719]

☆ *Farmers* TA3 5RS [Slough Green, W of village]: New owners for this spreading pub, four civilised linked rooms with pale paintwork, some stripped stone and stripped boards, a mix of wooden furniture, sofas by woodburner, Exmoor and Otter ale, decent food; children welcome, picnic-sets on terrace and small lawn, bedrooms *(LYM)*

WEST MONKTON [ST2628]

☆ *Monkton* TA2 8NP: Comfortable firmly run dining pub very popular for its good low-priced fresh food inc set deals and summer tapas, always crowded and best to book, linked areas inc smallish bar serving local beers; lots of tables in streamside meadow, peaceful spot, cl Sun evening, Mon *(Sue Daly, Brian Monaghan, Bob and Margaret Holder, Heather Pitch, Patrick and Daphne Darley, Chris and Angela Buckell)*

WESTON-IN-GORDANO [ST4474]

White Hart BS20 8PU [B3124 Portishead—Clevedon, between M5 junctions 19 and 20]: Friendly neatly kept roadside pub with lots of old photographs and bric-a-brac in lower room, large pleasant dining area, good reasonably priced straightforward food cooked to order, good service, well kept real ales; Gordano valley views from fine back lawn with play area, open all day *(Shirley and Bob Gibbs)*

WESTON-SUPER-MARE [ST3762]

Woolpack BS22 7XE [St Georges, just off M5 junction 21]: Opened-up and extended 17th-c coaching inn with full Butcombe range and a guest ale kept well, decent wines, low-priced pubby food inc carvery, friendly atmosphere, pleasant window seats and library-theme area, small attractive restaurant, conservatory, skittle alley; no dogs; children welcome, disabled access, terrace areas with rustic furniture *(Chris and Angela Buckell, Comus and Sarah Elliott)*

WHEDDON CROSS [SS9238]

Rest & Be Thankful TA24 7DR [A396/B3224, S of Minehead]: Friendly new owners doing good choice of reasonably priced uncomplicated food from sandwiches up inc Sun carvery, Butcombe, Exmoor and guest ales, three real ciders, comfortably refurbished modern twin-room bar with back-to-back log fires, wooden tables and chairs, leather sofas and huge jug collection

hanging from beams, restaurant, flagstoned games area with darts and pool, skittle alley; juke box or piped music; children and clean dogs welcome, tables out in back courtyard adjoining Exmoor public car park (with disabled lavatory), five comfortable bedrooms, nice breakfast, good walking country *(LYM, Sheila Topham)*

WINSCOMBE [ST4257]

☆ *Woodborough* BS25 1HD [Sandford Rd]: Big beamed 1930s village dining pub, smart, comfortable and busy, with wide choice of good generous local food, helpful friendly staff, good wine choice, large public bar, skittle alley; disabled access, bedrooms *(George and Gill Rowley, Jim and Frances Gowers)*

WINSFORD [SS9034]

☆ *Royal Oak* TA24 7JE [off A396 about 10 miles S of Dunster]: Prettily placed thatched and beamed refurbished Exmoor inn, wide choice of good locally sourced food, friendly staff, well kept Exmoor ales, Thatcher's cider, good wines by the glass, lounge bar with big stone fireplace and large bay-window seat looking across towards village green and foot and packhorse bridges over River Winn, more eating space in second bar, several comfortable bedrooms; children and dogs welcome, good bedrooms *(LYM, Rod and Chris Pring, John Saville, Mrs P Bishop)*

WITHAM FRIARY [ST7440]

☆ *Seymour Arms* BA11 5HF [signed from B3092 S of Frome]: Well worn-in unchanging flagstoned country tavern, same friendly licensees since 1952, two simple rooms off 19th-c hatch-service lobby, one with darts, the other with central table skittles, well kept Butcombe and Rich's local cider tapped from backroom casks, low prices, open fires, panelled benches, cards and dominoes, no food; good-sized attractive garden by main rail line, open all day wknds *(Pete Baker, the Didler, Phil and Sally Gorton, Edward Mirzoeff)*

WITHYPOOL [SS8435]

☆ *Royal Oak* TA24 7QP [off B3233]: Refurbished but keeping its proper Exmoor character, two beamed bars (steps between) with some nice settles and oak tables, lovely log fire, sporting prints and trophies, well kept Exmoor ales and a guest, Thatcher's cider, several wines by the glass, generous food from good sandwiches up, friendly welcoming service, pretty dining room; children and dogs welcome, terrace seating, attractive riverside village tucked below some of Exmoor's finest parts, pleasant bedrooms, good breakfast, open all day *(Simon Daws, John and Jackie Walsh, Bob and Margaret Holder, LYM, Sheila Topham, Ian and Angela Redley, John and Fiona McIlwain, Mr and Mrs P D Titcomb, Martin Hatcher)*

WIVELISCOMBE [ST0827]

Bear TA4 2JY [North St]: Good range of well priced home-made food from burgers and good sandwiches up, well kept local Cotleigh and other west country ales, farm ciders, attentive friendly landlord, games area; garden with play area, good value bedrooms, open all day *(Jean and David Lewis)*

WOOKEY HOLE [ST5347]

Wookey Hole Inn BA5 1BP: Usefully placed family pub with unusual trendy décor, welcoming and relaxed, with three eating areas and bar, four changing real ales, several belgian beers, ciders and perry, enjoyable innovative food (10% service charge added), efficient staff, may be jazz Sun lunchtime; pleasant garden, comfortable bedrooms *(Terry Buckland)*

WOOLVERTON [ST7954]

Red Lion BA2 7QS [set back from A36 N of village]: Roomy refurbished pub, beams, panelling and lots of stripped wood, candles and log-effect fire, well kept Wadworths, decent wines by the glass, enjoyable good value food from popular filled baked potatoes and children's meals to more upmarket dishes, friendly staff, locals' bar with darts; piped music; open all day, plenty of tables outside *(LYM, Dr and Mrs M E Wilson)*

WORTH [ST5145]

☆ *Pheasant* BA5 1LQ [B3139 Wells—Wedmore]: Cheerful pub with popular italian restaurant (italian owners), good home-made food from own breads and pasta to tasty slow-cooked tuscan stew and nice puddings, also traditional things like Sun roasts; ebullient caring landlord, simple bar with well kept Butcombe and Greene King Old Speckled

Hen, Thatcher's cider, decent house wines, beams and stone fireplaces; piped music; children welcome, skittle alley, back garden, cl Mon *(Sylvia and Tony Birbeck, Jenny and Brian Seller, Terry Buckland)*

WRAXALL [ST4971]

☆ *Old Barn* BS48 1LQ [just off Bristol Rd (B3130)]: Idiosyncratic gabled barn conversion doing well under new licensees, scrubbed tables, school benches and soft sofas under oak rafters, stripped boards and flagstones, welcoming atmosphere and friendly service, Butcombe, Fullers London Pride, St Austell Tribute, Sharps Doom Bar and a guest tapped from the cask (plans for their own brews too), farm ciders, good wines by the glass, currently no food, unusual board games; occasional piped music and sports TV; children and dogs welcome, nice garden with terrace barbecue (can bring your own meat), smokers' shelter, open all day *(Steve and Liz Tilley, the Didler)*

WRINGTON [ST4762]

Plough BS40 5QA [2.5 miles off A370 Bristol—Weston, from bottom of Rhodiate Hill]: Large pub rambling around central servery with Wells & Youngs and a guest ale, good value food inc sandwiches and bargain light lunches, beams and stripped stone, step up to long dining area, two coal or log fires; children and dogs welcome, wheelchair access, lots of picnic-sets out on sloping grass, more under cover on heated terrace, open all day *(Bob and Margaret Holder, BB, Chris and Angela Buckell)*

If a pub tries to make you leave a credit card behind the bar, be on your guard. The credit card firms and banks which issue them condemn this practice. After all, the publican who asks you to do this is in effect saying: 'I don't trust you'. Have you any more reason to trust his staff? If your card is used fraudulently while you have let it be kept out of your sight, the card company could say you've been negligent yourself – and refuse to make good your losses. So say that they can 'swipe' your card instead, but must hand it back to you. Please let us know if a pub does try to keep your card.

Staffordshire

Both nicely traditional and in good walking country, the George at Alstonefield and Olde Royal Oak at Wetton stand out as beacons of hospitality, with warm welcomes and good fairly priced food – just what's called for after a long hike. The Boat near Lichfield offers a particularly good meal off the M6, and for real Burton ale in Burton upon Trent itself, the simple Burton Bridge Inn brews no less than seven. The stylishly refurbished Hand & Trumpet at Wrinehill also has a good range of beers (and other drinks), but its forte is good imaginative food: it's Staffordshire Dining Pub of the Year. The Lucky Dip section here is also full of interest. We have starred over a dozen as firm recommendations, almost all of these already inspected and approved by us. Marstons is the dominant regional brewer. Among several good small brewers, Titanic and Burton Bridge stand out as the most successful, with Slaters well worth looking out for, too.

ABBOTS BROMLEY
SK0824   MAP 7
Goats Head
Market Place; WS15 3BP

Well run old-world pub with good food; attractive location

In the centre of an unspoilt village (famous for its annual horn dance), this charming old black and white timbered pub is well liked for its good hospitable atmosphere and fairly priced tasty food. The opened-up cream-painted interior is unpretentious but comfortable, with attractive oak floors, a warming coal fire in a big inglenook, and furnishings that take in the odd traditional oak settle. Served by attentive staff, the Black Sheep, Greene King Abbot, Marstons Pedigree and a guest such as Wells & Youngs Bombardier are well kept on handpump, and you can have any of the wines on their good wine list by the glass; piped music, TV. Picnic-sets and teak tables out on a neat sheltered lawn look up to the church tower behind.

⊞ Generously served enjoyable bar food is all home-made, and the chips here are good: sandwiches, fish pie, salmon fillet with hollandaise, daily specials such as calves liver in red wine jus, local trout with citrus butter, bass with mediterranean vegetables, spaghetti with mussels, scallops and tiger prawns in tomato sauce, and traditional puddings such as spotted dick and custard and plum crumble. *Starters/Snacks: £3.75 to £5.95. Main Courses: £6.95 to £14.95. Puddings: £4.50 to £4.95*

Punch ~ Lease Dawn Skelton ~ Real ale ~ Bar food (12-2.30, 6-9; 12-2, 6-9.30 Sat; 12-4.30 Sun) ~ Restaurant ~ (01283) 840254 ~ Children welcome ~ Dogs allowed in bar ~ Open 12-midnight ~ Bedrooms: /£40

Recommended by Gwyn and Anne Wake, Dr and Mrs J Temporal, S J and C C Davidson, Neil and Brenda Skidmore, David J Austin, Susan and Nigel Brookes, Helene Grygar, Richard and Jean Green, Lawrence Bacon, Jean Scott, Henry Pursehouse-Tranter

ALSTONEFIELD SK1355 MAP 7

George ♀

Village signposted from A515 Ashbourne—Buxton; DE6 2FX

Nice old pub with decent food; a Peak District classic

Readers thoroughly enjoy the welcoming Peak District atmosphere at this stone-built pub. It's run by a very friendly landlady, who clearly puts her customers first. Set in a peaceful farming hamlet, you can sit out by the green, beneath the old inn-sign, and watch the world go by, or out in the big sheltered stableyard behind the pub. A good variety of customers, including plenty of walkers, enjoy soaking up the charming atmosphere in the unchanging straightforward low-beamed bar with its collection of old Peak District photographs and pictures, warming coal fire, and a copper-topped counter with well kept Marstons Burton Bitter and Pedigree and a guest such as Jennings Golden Hop on handpump, and a dozen wines by the glass; dominoes. The neatened-up dining room has a woodburning stove.

🍴 **The menu is fairly short but well balanced and fairly priced. As well as lunchtime sandwiches there might be ham hock and parsley terrine, whole baked camembert with oven-roast tomatoes, fried mackerel with beetroot and chutney, pea and mint risotto, sausage and mash, shepherd's pie, roast duck breast with lentils and chicory, and puddings such as trifle and sticky toffee pudding. They grow some of their own vegetables and have a little farm shop.** *Starters/Snacks: £4.00 to £9.00. Main Courses: £8.00 to £19.00. Puddings: £5.00 to £6.00*

Marstons ~ Lease Emily Hammond ~ Real ale ~ Bar food (12-2.30, 7-9; 12-3, 6.30-8 Sun) ~ Restaurant ~ (01335) 310205 ~ Children welcome ~ Dogs allowed in bar ~ Open 11.30-3, 6-11; 11.30-11 Sat; 12-10.30 Sun

Recommended by R T and J C Moggridge, the Didler, Michelle Sullivan, Paul J Robinshaw, Mike Proctor, Henry Pursehouse-Tranter, Peter J and Avril Hanson, Verity Kemp, Richard Mills, Hector and Sheila Blackhurst, Mr and Mrs John Taylor, Richard, B and M Kendall, Eileen Tierney, Annette Tress, Gary Smith, Peter F Marshall

BURTON UPON TRENT SK2523 MAP 7

Burton Bridge Inn ◀■ £

Bridge Street (A50); DE14 1SY

Straightforward cheery tap for the Burton Bridge Brewery; lunchtime snacks only

This genuinely friendly down-to-earth old brick local is the showcase for the superbly kept beers (Bitter, Festival, Golden Delicious, Gold Medal, Porter, Sovereign Gold and XL) that are brewed by Burton Bridge Brewery, housed across the long old-fashioned blue-brick yard at the back. They are served on handpump alongside a guest such as Castle Rock Harvest Pale, around 20 whiskies and over a dozen country wines. The simple little front area leads into an adjacent bar with wooden pews, and plain walls hung with notices, awards and brewery memorabilia. Separated from the bar by the serving counter, the little oak beamed lounge is snugly oak-panelled and has a flame-effect fire and a mix of furnishings; skittle alley. The panelled upstairs dining room is open only at lunchtime.

🍴 **Simple but hearty bar snacks take in filled baguettes, ploughman's, chilli, faggots and ham, egg and chips.** *Starters/Snacks: £2.20 to £5.20*

Own brew ~ Licensee Carl Stout ~ Real ale ~ Bar food (lunchtime only, not Sun) ~ No credit cards ~ (01283) 536596 ~ Children welcome ~ Dogs allowed in bar ~ Open 11.30-2.15, 5-11; 11.30-11 Sat; 12-3, 7-10.30 Sun

Recommended by Paul J Robinshaw, the Didler, Theo, Anne and Jane Gaskin, C J Fletcher, R T and J C Moggridge

---

The letters and figures after the name of each town are its Ordnance Survey map reference. 'Using the *Guide*' at the beginning of the book explains how it helps you find a pub, in road atlases or large-scale maps as well as in our own maps.

CAULDON

SK0749   MAP 7

Yew Tree ★★ £

Village signposted from A523 and A52 about 8 miles W of Ashbourne; ST10 3EJ

Treasure-trove of fascinating antiques and dusty bric-a-brac, very eccentric

Definitely not for those who like a spic and span pub, this uniquely idiosyncratic place (you'll either love or hate it) has been affectionately described as a junk shop with a bar – the housekeeping is certainly reminiscent of a junk shop. Over the years, the charming landlord has amassed a museum's worth of curiosities. The most impressive pieces are perhaps the working polyphons and symphonions – 19th-c developments of the musical box, often taller than a person, each with quite a repertoire of tunes and elaborate sound effects. But there are also two pairs of Queen Victoria's stockings, ancient guns and pistols, several penny-farthings, an old sit-and-stride boneshaker, a rocking horse, swordfish blades, a little 800 BC greek vase, and even a fine marquetry cabinet crammed with notable early staffordshire pottery. Soggily sprung sofas mingle with 18th-c settles, plenty of little wooden tables and a four-person oak church choir seat with carved heads which came from St Mary's church in Stafford; above the bar is an odd iron dog-carrier. As well as all this there's an expanding choir of fine tuneful longcase clocks in the gallery just above the entrance, a collection of six pianolas (one of which is played most nights) with an excellent repertoire of piano rolls, a working vintage valve radio set, a crank-handle telephone, a sinuous medieval wind instrument made of leather, and a Jacobean four-poster which was once owned by Josiah Wedgwood and still has his original wig hook on the headboard. Clearly, it would be almost an overwhelming task to keep all that sprucely clean. The drinks here are very reasonably priced (so no wonder it's popular with locals), and you'll find well kept Bass, Burton Bridge and Grays Dark Mild on handpump or tapped from the cask, along with about a dozen interesting malt whiskies; piped music (probably Radio 2), darts, shove-ha'penny, table skittles, dominoes and cribbage. When you arrive don't be put off by the plain exterior, or the fact that the pub is tucked unpromisingly between enormous cement works and quarries and almost hidden by a towering yew tree.

⊞ **Simple, good value tasty snacks include pork, meat and potato, chicken and mushroom and steak pies, hot big filled baps and sandwiches, quiche, smoked mackerel or ham salad, and home-made puddings.** *Starters/Snacks: £0.80 to £1.90. Puddings: £1.60 to £1.80*

Free house ~ Licensee Alan East ~ Real ale ~ Bar food ~ No credit cards ~ (01538) 308348 ~ Children in polyphon room ~ Dogs welcome ~ Folk music first Tues of month ~ Open 11-2.30(3 Sat), 6-midnight; 12-3, 7-midnight Sun

Recommended by Helene Grygar, D and J Ashdown, Mike Horgan, the Didler, Susan and John Douglas, Mike Proctor, Thomas Lane, R W Allen, Richard

KIDSGROVE

SJ8354   MAP 7

Blue Bell 🍺

25 Hardings Wood; off A50 NW edge of town; ST7 1EG

Astonishing tally of thoughtfully sourced real ales on six constantly changing pumps at this little beer pub

They take pride in keeping a tally of the number of beers that have passed through the pumps at this simple place. In the last 11 years they've achieved the grand sum of over 2,700 brews – that's about four new beers a week. The constantly changing range of six beers is carefully selected from smaller, often unusual brewers, such as Acorn, Castle Rock, Crouch Vale, Nelson, Plassey and Tring. These are topped off with around 30 belgian, czech and german bottled beers and up to three draught farm ciders. You need to keep your eyes skinned to spot this understated whitewashed place as it can look a little like a house. Its four small, carpeted rooms are unfussy and straightforward, with blue upholstered benches, basic pub furniture, a gas-effect coal fire, and maybe soft piped music. There are tables in front and more on a little back lawn. Note the limited opening hours.

⊞ **Food is limited to weekend filled rolls.**

Free house ~ Licensees Dave and Kay Washbrook ~ Real ale ~ No credit cards ~ (01782) 774052
~ Dogs welcome ~ Open 7.30-11; 1-4, 7.30-11 Sat; 12-10.30 Sun; closed lunchtimes and
Mon (except bank hols)

*Recommended by the Didler, Dave Webster, Sue Holland, Mike Proctor, R T and J C Moggridge, Martin Grosberg,
John R Ringrose*

LICHFIELD

SK0705   MAP 4

Boat

*3.8 miles from M6 Toll junction T6 (pay again when you rejoin it); head E on A5, turning
right at first roundabout on to B4155, keeping straight ahead into Barrack Lane at first
cross-roads, then left on to A461 Walsall Road; leaving pub, keep straight on to rejoin A5
at Muckley Corner roundabout; WS14 0BU*

Efficiently run dining pub, handy break for imaginative meal off the M6

The huge floor-to-ceiling food blackboards and views straight into the kitchen, as you
enter this neatly kept place, are indicative of the emphasis on the carefully prepared food
here. Well lit from above by a big skylight, this first section has a cheery café atmosphere
with bright plastic flooring, striking photoprints, leather club chairs and sofas around
coffee tables and potted palms. The comfortable dining areas are more conventional and
calmly relaxing, with sturdy modern pale pine furniture on russet pink carpets and prints
on white walls. Windows to the left have views on to the canal (currently undergoing
restoration). The solid light wood bar counter has three thoughtfully sourced changing
real ales from brewers such as Backyard Brewhouse, Salopian and Tom Woods on
handpump, and around ten wines by the glass. Service is friendly and obliging; faint
piped music. A landscaped area outside is paved with a central raised decking area; good
wheelchair access throughout.

🍴 As well as lunchtime sandwiches, attractively presented good bar food from a fairly
extensive menu might include king prawns in garlic and white wine, fried pigeon breast
with bubble and squeak potato cake, seared scallops with crispy parma ham, grilled
sardines with provençale sauce, fried duck breast with five-spice vegetables, wild
mushroom risotto, baked bream with lemon and black pepper, crispy pork belly with sage
mash and calvados sauce, fish and chips, and puddings such as chocolate mousse with
shortbread biscuits, plum and almond tart and toffee and banana crumble. *Starters/Snacks:
£3.95 to £7.95. Main Courses: £5.95 to £11.75. Puddings: £4.25*

Free house ~ Licensee Ann Holden ~ Real ale ~ Bar food (12-2, 6-9.30; 12-8.30 Sun) ~
(01543) 361692 ~ Dogs allowed in bar ~ Open 12-3, 6-11(12 Sat); 12-11 Sun

*Recommended by John and Helen Rushton, Colin Fisher, David Green, Karen Eliot, Pat and Tony Martin,
Oliver Richardson, Louise Gibbons, Glenwys and Alan Lawrence, David Wright, Bren and Val Speed,
Paul J Robinshaw, John Balfour, Peter and Heather Elliott, Julia and Richard Tredgett, Michael Beale*

Queens Head 🍺 £

*Queen Street; public car park just round corner in Swan Road, off A51 roundabout;
WS13 6QD*

**Great cheese counter, bargain lunchtime hot dishes and a good range of real ales at this
friendly place**

Done up inside like an old-fashioned alehouse, the single long room in this handsome
Victorian brick building has a mix of comfortable aged furniture on bare boards, some
stripped brick, Lichfield and other pictures on ochre walls above a panelled dado, and big
sash windows. The atmosphere is comfortably relaxed and grown-up, and staff are
friendly and helpful; terrestrial TV for sports events. As well as a couple of interesting
guests, usually from smaller brewers such as Blythe and Burton Bridge, beers include
Marstons Pedigree and Timothy Taylors Landlord; small garden. They may allow children in
on request, but don't count on it.

🍴 A highlight here is the cold cabinet of cheeses on the left of the bar, including some
interesting local ones such as dovedale blue. Throughout the day (unless it gets too busy)
you can make up your own very generous ploughman's, perhaps with some pâté too, with

a basket of their good crusty granary bread, home-made pickles, onions and gherkins. At lunchtime (not Sunday) they also have a good range of over two dozen enjoyable pubby hot dishes at amazingly low prices, such as their steak and ale pie. *Starters/Snacks: £2.50. Main Courses: £3.50 to £4.95*

Marstons ~ Lease Denise Harvey ~ Real ale ~ Bar food (12-2.15 (2 Sat; cheese all day and only cheese Sun)) ~ No credit cards ~ (01543) 410932 ~ Dogs welcome ~ Open 12-11(11.30 Fri, Sat); 12-3, 7-11 Sun

Recommended by R T and J C Moggridge, Alan and Eve Harding, Paul J Robinshaw

SALT   SJ9527   MAP 7

Holly Bush

Off A51 S of Stone; ST18 0BX

Delightful medieval pub popular for generous, mainly traditional, all-day food

The charming deep-thatched, flower-bedecked exterior of this white-painted 14th-c house makes for a picture-book pub. The interior is just as lovely with several cosy areas spreading off from the standing-room serving section, with high-backed cushioned pews, old tables and more conventional seats. The oldest part has a heavy-beamed and planked ceiling (some of the beams are attractively carved), a woodburning stove and salt cupboard built into the big inglenook, with other nice old-fashioned touches such as an ancient pair of riding boots on the mantelpiece. A modern back extension, with beams, stripped brickwork and a small coal fire, blends in well. Adnams, Marstons Pedigree and a guest are on handpump, alongside a fairly priced house wine and a dozen by the glass. The back of the pub is beautifully tended, with rustic picnic-sets on a big lawn. They operate a type of locker system for credit cards, which they will ask to keep if you are running a tab.

🍴 As well as lunchtime sandwiches, bar food might include pears stuffed with blue cheese, oatcake stuffed with black pudding in tomato sauce, fried brie with redcurrant sauce, cod and chips, steak and kidney pudding, breaded scampi, venison casserole, and steaks. *Starters/Snacks: £2.95 to £5.25. Main Courses: £7.25 to £15.95. Puddings: £3.25 to £4.25*

Admiral Taverns ~ Licensees Geoffrey and Joseph Holland ~ Real ale ~ Bar food (12-9.30(9 Sun)) ~ (01889) 508234 ~ Children welcome ~ Open 12-11

Recommended by Henry Pursehouse-Tranter, Glen and Nola Armstrong, Roger and Anne Newbury, Susan and Nigel Brookes, Mayur Shah, S J and C C Davidson, Ian and Nita Cooper, Michael and Jenny Back

STOURTON   SO8485   MAP 4

Fox

1.25 miles W along A458 from junction with A449; DY7 5BL

Cosy series of rooms at welcoming country pub, with nice bar food and garden

The neatly kept unassuming exterior of this roadside pub rather understates the inviting atmosphere within. It's been run by the same welcoming family with loving care for over 30 years, but don't get the impression that time has stood still. Where appropriate, they've kept things perky and neatly up to date. Several cosily small areas ramble back from the small serving bar by the entrance (well kept Bathams Best and a guest such as Enville Ale on handpump). Tables are mostly sturdy and varnished, with pews, settles and comfortable library or dining chairs on the green or dark blue carpet and bare boards. A good positive colour scheme is picked up nicely by the curtains, some framed exotic menus and well chosen prints (jazz and golf both feature). The woodburning stoves may be opened to give a cheery blaze on cold days, they put out big bunches of flowers, and the lighting (mainly low-voltage spots) has been done very carefully, giving an intimate bistro feel in the areas round on the right. Dining areas include a smart conservatory which has neat bentwood furniture and proper tablecloths; piped music. There are well spaced picnic-sets on a terrace and a big stretch of sloping grass, and the pub is well placed for Kinver Country Park walks and the Staffordshire Way.

🍴 Bar food includes lunchtime sandwiches, cajun mushrooms and black pudding topped with bacon, prawn cocktail, tandoori chicken with mint yoghurt, fish and chips with mushy peas, thai green curry, pie of the day, fried duck and spicy mushroom salad, mushroom and stilton pasta, salmon and prawn pasta with cream wine sauce, sausage and mash, and rib-eye steak with stilton sauce *Starters/Snacks: £3.50 to £4.50. Main Courses: £6.95 to £9.95. Puddings: £3.00 to £3.95*

Free house ~ Licensee Stefan Caron ~ Real ale ~ Bar food (12-2.30, 7-9.30; 12-5.15 Sun; not Mon evening) ~ Restaurant ~ (01384) 872614 ~ Children welcome ~ Open 11-3, 4.30-11; 11-11 Sat; 12-10.30 Sun

Recommended by Theo, Anne and Jane Gaskin, Chris Glasson, M G Hart, George and Maureen Roby, John Robertson

WETTON
SK1055   MAP 7

Olde Royal Oak

Village signposted off Hulme End—Alstonefield road, between B5054 and A515; DE6 2AF

Friendly traditional pub in lovely location; good value straightforward food

Much loved by walkers, this aged white-painted and shuttered stone-built village pub leaves covers for muddy boots at both doors and there's a croft for caravans and tents behind. Warm and cosy with open fires and beams, it's just the sort of traditionally welcoming low-key place you'd hope to find tucked in at the heart of this lovely National Trust countryside, with Wetton Mill and the Manifold valley nearby. The traditional bar has white ceiling boards above its black beams, small dining chairs around rustic tables, an oak corner cupboard, and a coal fire in the stone fireplace. It extends into a more modern-feeling area, which in turn leads to a carpeted sun lounge that looks over the small garden; piped music, darts, TV, shove-ha'penny, cribbage and dominoes. You can choose from more than 30 whiskies, and they've well kept Greene King Abbot and a guest from a brewer such as Belvoir on handpump. There is a chance that this may change hands over the next few months.

🍴 Reasonably priced pubby food includes filled baps, leek and potato soup, breaded mushrooms, spicy chicken dippers, battered cod, parsnip, sweet potato and chestnut bake, gammon with pineapple and egg, chicken tikka and steaks, and puddings such as treacle sponge or home-made bread and butter pudding. *Starters/Snacks: £3.50 to £4.95. Main Courses: £5.95 to £12.95. Puddings: £3.75*

Free house ~ Licensees Brian and Janet Morley ~ Real ale ~ Bar food ~ (01335) 310287 ~ Children welcome ~ Dogs welcome ~ Open 12-2.30(3 Sat, Sun), 7-11; 12-11 Sat high summer; closed Mon, Tues ~ Bedrooms: /£40S

Recommended by Malcolm and Pauline Pellatt, Peter F Marshall, Paul J Robinshaw, B M Eldridge, Mike Proctor, the Didler, Rob and Catherine Dunster

WRINEHILL
SJ7547   MAP 7

Hand & Trumpet 🍴 🍷 🍺

A531 Newcastle—Nantwich; CW3 9BJ

STAFFORDSHIRE DINING PUB OF THE YEAR

Big attractive dining pub with good food all day, professional service, nice range of real ales and wines; pleasant garden

Very much out of the Brunning & Price mould, this sturdy building was handsomely converted a few years ago with top-quality fixtures and fittings. Cleverly open-plan and stylish yet still intimate feeling, at its heart is a solidly built counter with half a dozen handpumps dispensing well kept Caledonian Deuchars IPA, Phoenix B&P Original, Salopian Oracle and guests from brewers such as Boggart Hole Clough, Sharps and Wood. They also keep a fine range of about 22 wines by the glass and about 85 whiskies. Linked open-plan areas working around the counter have a good mix of dining chairs and sturdy tables on polished tiles or stripped-oak boards, and several big oriental rugs that soften the acoustics and appearance. There are lots of nicely lit prints on cream walls above the mainly dark dado and below the deep-red ceilings. It's all brightened up with good natural light from bow windows and in one area a big skylight. Service is relaxed and friendly; good disabled access and facilities; board games. French windows open on to a stylish balustraded deck with teak tables and chairs looking down to ducks swimming on a big pond in the sizeable garden, which has plenty of trees.

📶 Food is well prepared, and the menu ranges from good takes on traditional dishes to more imaginative ones. As well as interesting sandwiches, the menu might include starters such as onion and thyme soup, roast sardines on toast with tomato and garlic chutney, potted rabbit and ham with apple and pear chutney, charcuterie for two, light bites such as roast butternut squash with potato gnocchi, peppers and pesto, steak sandwich, chicken and chorizo salad, ploughman's; main courses such as cumberland sausages and mash, battered haddock with mushy peas and hand-cut chips, steak burger, steamed hake fillet with lobster sauce, crispy beef salad with sweet chilli and coconut, rump steak; and puddings such as gooseberry and apple upside-down cake and warm dark chocolate tart with orange cream. *Starters/Snacks: £6.85 to £8.95. Main Courses: £9.55 to £16.75. Puddings: £4.75 to £5.25*

Brunning & Price ~ Manager John Unsworth ~ Real ale ~ Bar food (12-10) ~ (01270) 820048 ~ Children welcome ~ Dogs allowed in bar ~ Open 11.30-11(10.30 Sun)

Recommended by R T and J C Moggridge, Sue Leighton, Dr Peter Crawshaw, Liese Collier-Jones, John R Ringrose, David S Allen, Dave Webster, Sue Holland, Paul and Gail Betteley, Henry Pursehouse-Tranter, Paul Boot, Karen Eliot, Alistair and Kay Butler, J Metcalfe, Gary Rollings, Debbie Porter

---

LUCKY DIP

Besides the fully inspected pubs, you might like to try these Lucky Dips recommended to us and described by readers (if you do, please send us reports: feedback@goodguides.com).

ALREWAS [SK1715]
☆ *George & Dragon* DE13 7AE [off A38; Main St]: Three friendly low-beamed linked rooms with good value generous honest food, Marstons-related ales, efficient attentive staff, attractive paintings; piped music; children welcome in eating area, pleasant partly covered garden with good play area, opens 5pm wkdys *(Mrs Hazel Rainer, LYM)*
ALSTONEFIELD [SK1255]
☆ *Watts Russell Arms* DE6 2GD [Hopedale]: Cheerful, nicely placed light and airy 18th-c beamed pub, chef/landlord producing good food from shortish menu inc wraps, fresh fish and vegetarian options, well kept Black Sheep, Timothy Taylors Landlord and an occasional guest beer, decent range of soft drinks; traditional games; can get busy wknds; children and dogs welcome, picnic-sets on sheltered tiered terrace and in garden, open all day wknds, cl Mon *(Mike Markwick, LYM, the Didler)*
ALTON [SK0742]
Bulls Head ST10 4AQ [High St]: Good value bar lunches and pleasant restaurant, Greene King Abbot, friendly staff and locals; piped music; children welcome, good walks *(Paul J Robinshaw, D and J Ashdown)*
Ramblers Retreat ST10 4BU [Red Rd]: Dining pub with draught beers in bar, enjoyable sensibly priced pubby food, conservatory; plenty of garden tables *(John Faircloth)*
BARTON-UNDER-NEEDWOOD []
Waterfront DE13 8DZ [Barton Marina, Barton Turns]: Huge pub, new but cleverly done so

that it looks long-established, part of marina complex; wide choice of enjoyable food inc pubby favourites (light dishes all day), five real ales, thriving atmosphere; children welcome until early evening, open all day *(anon)*
BIDDULPH [SJ8959]
Talbot ST8 7RY [Grange Rd (N, right off A527)]: Well laid out Vintage Inn family dining pub with eating areas at each end, drinkers' bar and some secluded parts, enjoyable fresh food, well kept Bass and Timothy Taylors Landlord; some wood floors, open fire, newspapers; soft piped pop; handy for Biddulph Grange Garden *(Jeremy King, Oliver Richardson)*
BLACKBROOK [SJ7638]
Swan With Two Necks ST5 5EH [Nantwich Rd (A51)]: Recently well refurbished, with good food all day, good value if not cheap, civilised open-plan dining areas; friendly service, good value wines by the glass, smart contemporary décor; comfortable tables out on decking, open all day *(Susan and Nigel Brookes, John and Eleanor Holdsworth)*
BLITHBURY [SK0819]
Bull & Spectacles WS15 3HY [Uttoxeter Rd (B5014 S of Abbots Bromley)]: 17th-c pub with obliging friendly service, wide choice of homely food inc popular bargain lunchtime Hot Table – half a dozen or so generous main dishes with help-yourself veg, and some puddings *(David Green)*
BLYTHE BRIDGE [SJ9640]
Black Cock ST11 9NT [Uttoxeter Rd (A521)]: Roadside local with good staff, tables set for

the enjoyable home-made food, several real ales, good wine choice; 1950s and Beatles' memorabilia *(the Didler)*

BRANSTON [SK2221]

Bridge Inn DE14 3EZ [off A5121 just SW of Burton; Tatenhill Lane, by Trent & Mersey Canal Bridge 34]: Cosy low-beamed canalside pub very popular at wknds for italian landlord's good reasonably priced pizzas, pastas and special tiramisu (may be a wait for a table); particularly well kept Marstons Pedigree, friendly helpful staff, warm log fire; tables in waterside garden, good moorings, basic supplies for boaters and caravanners *(C J Fletcher, Paul J Robinshaw)*

BURSTON [SJ9330]

Greyhound ST18 0DR [just off A51 Sandon—Stone]: Busy dining pub extended from 17th-c core, wide choice of good value food (all day wknds), three sensibly priced real ales, quick friendly service, spacious dining areas behind rambling traditional bar *(John and Helen Rushton)*

BURTON UPON TRENT [SK2423]

☆ *Coopers Tavern* DE14 1EG [Cross St]: Appealing traditional pub, friendly and well run; well kept changing ales from casks in back room with cask tables, lunchtime food, coal fire in homely front parlour; open all day Fri, Sat *(the Didler, LYM, C J Fletcher, Pete Baker)*

Derby Inn DE14 1RU [Derby Rd]: Well worn-in idiosyncratic local with particularly good Marstons Pedigree, friendly long-serving landlord (talking of retirement – go while you can); brewery glasses' collection in cosy panelled lounge, lots of steam railway memorabilia in long narrow bar, local produce for sale; outside lavatories, sports TV; dogs welcome, open all day Fri, Sat *(the Didler, C J Fletcher)*

Elms DE15 9AE [Stapenhill Rd (A444)]: Bass, Tower and changing guest beers in compact bar with wall benches, larger lounge; open all day Fri-Sun *(the Didler)*

BUTTERTON [SK0756]

Black Lion ST13 7SP [off B5053]: Nicely placed traditional 18th-c low-beamed stone-built inn, logs blazing in inner room's kitchen range, good-humoured efficient service, enjoyable food from filled rolls up; several real ales, reasonable prices, traditional games and pool room; piped music; children in eating areas, terrace tables, tidy bedrooms, cl Mon and Tues lunchtimes *(LYM, the Didler)*

CANNOCK [SJ9710]

Linford Arms WS11 1BN [High Green]: Wetherspoons in attractive 18th-c building, eight well kept ales and their usual keenly priced food, good house wine; friendly fast service and hands-on manager, quiet family area upstairs; tables outside, open all day *(R T and J C Moggridge, Stuart Paulley)*

CANNOCK WOOD [SK0412]

Park Gate WS15 4RN [Park Gate Rd, S side of Cannock Chase]: Large family-friendly pub

with enjoyable food from sandwiches and bargain lunchtime hot dishes to wide restaurant choice, friendly efficient service, Adnams and a regularly changing guest; cushioned chairs and pews, lots of woodwork and bric-a-brac, woodburners, extensive dining area and conservatory; music Fri nights; dogs allowed in bar, plenty of picnic-sets and play area outside; by Castle Ring Iron Age fort, good Cannock Chase walks *(Paul J Robinshaw)*

CHEDDLETON [SJ9751]

☆ *Boat* ST13 7EQ [Basford Bridge Lane, off A520]: Cheerful canalside local handy for Churnet Valley steam railway, flint mill and country park; neat long bar, low plank ceilings, well kept Marstons-related and other ales, friendly staff and locals, good value generous simple food from sandwiches and filled oatcakes up; interesting pictures, attractive dining room with polished floor, black-leaded range and brass fittings; children welcome, dogs allowed in part of bar, marquee and fairy-lit heated terrace out overlooking Cauldon Canal *(Dr D J and Mrs S C Walker, Helene Grygar, Susan and Nigel Brookes, John and Helen Rushton, LYM)*

CHORLEY [SK0711]

Malt Shovel WS13 8DD [off A51 N of Lichfield via Farewell]: Friendly village pub popular for well priced food inc lots of fish; central partly stripped-brick bar, comfortable lounge, proper bare-boards public bar, real fires and real ales *(Brian and Jacky Wilson)*

CONSALL [SK0049]

☆ *Black Lion* ST9 0AJ [Consall Forge, OS Sheet 118 map ref 000491; best approach from Nature Park, off A522, using car park 0.5 miles past Nature Centre]: Traditional take-us-as-you-find-us tavern tucked away in rustic old-fashioned canalside settlement by restored steam railway station; enjoyable generous unpretentious food made by landlord (may be only sandwiches mid-week), well kept Black Sheep and Moorhouses, good coal fire; piped music, no muddy boots, busy wknd lunchtimes; good walking area *(Gwyn and Anne Wake, the Didler, Bob and Laura Brock, Clive and Fran Dutson, S J and C C Davidson, LYM)*

CRESSWELL [SJ9739]

☆ *Izaak Walton* ST11 9RE [off A50 Stoke—Uttoxeter via Draycott in the Moors; Cresswell Lane]: Well refurbished country dining pub, wide choice of enjoyable, good value, traditional home-made food (all day wknds) inc Sun roasts, friendly efficient staff, well kept ales such as Bass, Black Sheep, Titanic Iceberg and Wychwood Hobgoblin, good wines by the glass; low beams, panelling and open fires, several small rooms and larger upstairs area; well behaved children welcome (no pushchairs), disabled facilities (but some steps), attractive terrace and back garden, cl Mon, otherwise open all day *(Paul and Margaret Baker, LYM)*

DENSTONE [SK0940]
Tavern ST14 5HR [College Rd]: Comfortable lounge with antiques, Marstons ales, enjoyable food, pleasant service, dining conservatory *(John Dwane)*

ECCLESHALL [SJ8328]
Badger ST21 6BA [Green Lane]: Neat and comfortable local, good generous food, quick pleasant service, well kept sensibly priced ales with a guest such as Brakspears, conservatory dining room; tables outside, good bedrooms, quite handy for M6 *(R T and J C Moggridge)*

ENVILLE [SO8286]
☆ *Cat* DY7 5HA [A458 W of Stourbridge (Bridgnorth Rd)]: Ancient beamed pub on Staffordshire Way, two appealingly old-fashioned log-fire rooms on one side of servery, plush banquettes on the other; four local Enville ales and three or four interesting guests, well priced bar food inc sandwiches and mix-and-match range of sausage, mash and gravies, restaurant; children in family room and main lounge, dogs in bar, pretty courtyard sheltered by massive estate wall, cl Sun evening, Mon *(the Didler, Lynda and Trevor Smith, LYM, Henry Pursehouse-Tranter, John Robertson)*

FRADLEY [SK1414]
☆ *White Swan* DE13 7DN [Fradley Junction]: Perfect canalside location at Trent & Mersey and Coventry junction, bargain food from baguettes to Sun carvery, well kept Black Sheep, Greene King Abbot, Marstons Pedigree and a guest; cheery traditional public bar with woodburner, quieter plusher lounge and lower vaulted back bar (where children allowed), cribbage, dominoes; waterside tables, open all day *(LYM, Mrs Hazel Rainer, John Hopkins)*

GAILEY [SJ8810]
Bell ST19 9LN [A5 a mile S]: Former coaching inn with well kept ales inc local brews, popular reasonably priced food, good service; nice garden by ornamental pond *(anon)*

Spread Eagle ST19 5PN [A5/A449]: Spacious recently refurbished Marstons pub with nice variety of separate areas inc relaxing sofas and family part with toys, good service, lunchtime and afternoon bargains inc carvery; good disabled facilities (and for pushchairs), big terrace and lawn with play area *(Henry Pursehouse-Tranter, Pat Crabb, Neil and Brenda Skidmore)*

HANLEY [SJ8847]
Coachmakers Arms ST1 3EA [Lichfield St]: Chatty traditional town local, currently petitioning against demolition; four small rooms and drinking corridor, half a dozen or more changing ales, farm cider, darts, cards and dominoes, original seating and local tilework, open fire; live jazz and country music some Weds; children welcome, open all day, till 1am Fri, Sat *(the Didler)*

HIGH OFFLEY [SJ7725]
Anchor ST20 0NG [off A519 Eccleshall—Newport; towards High Lea, by Shropshire Union Canal, Bridge 42; Peggs Lane]: Real boaters' pub on Shropshire Union Canal, little changed in the century or more this family have run it; two small simple front rooms, Marstons Pedigree and Wadworths 6X in jugs from cellar, Weston's farm cider, may be lunchtime toasties, owners' sitting room behind bar, occasional wknd sing-alongs; outbuilding with small shop and semi-open lavatories, lovely garden with great hanging baskets and notable topiary anchor, caravan/campsite, cl Mon-Thurs winter *(the Didler)*

HILDERSTONE [SJ9437]
Spotgate ST15 8RP [Spot Acre; B5066 N]: Friendly efficient service, wide choice of good food (not Sun evening) inc lunchtime bargains in bar or in two opulent 1928 Pullman dining coaches behind; Greene King Old Speckled Hen and Marstons Pedigree, reasonably priced wines; cl Mon *(John and Helen Rushton)*

HILL CHORLTON [SJ7939]
Slaters ST5 5ED [A51]: Comfortable olde-worlde beamed bar, enjoyable food inc good value dishes for two, helpful friendly staff, decent wines, upstairs restaurant; attractive garden, adjacent crafts centre, 18 bedrooms *(LYM, Susan and Nigel Brookes)*

HIMLEY [SO8990]
☆ *Crooked House* DY3 4DA [signed down rather grim lane from B4176 Gornalwood—Himley, OS Sheet 139 map ref 896908]: Extraordinary sight, building thrown wildly out of kilter (mining subsidence), slopes so weird things look as if they roll up not down them; otherwise a basic well worn low-priced pub with Marstons-related ales, farm cider, cheery staff, straightforward food (all day in summer); some local antiques in level more modern extension, conservatory; children in eating areas, big outside terrace, open all day wknds and summer *(Dave Braisted, the Didler, LYM)*

HOAR CROSS [SK1323]
☆ *Meynell Ingram Arms* DE13 8RB [Abbots Bromley Road, off A515 Yoxall—Sudbury]: Good interesting well priced food (not Sun evening) from sandwiches to restaurant meals in comfortably extended country dining pub; well kept Blythe and Marstons Pedigree, several neat redecorated little rooms rambling around central counter, log fire, some beams and brasses, hunting pictures and bespectacled fox's head, dining room with coal-effect fire; children and dogs welcome, tables on front grass and in courtyard behind, open all day *(R J Herd, Michelle and Graeme Voss, LYM, R T and J C Moggridge, Pete Baker, Susan and Nigel Brookes)*

HOPWAS [SK1704]
☆ *Tame Otter* B78 3AT [Hints Rd (A51 Tamworth—Lichfield)]: Welcoming 19th-c Vintage Inn by Birmingham & Fazeley Canal (moorings), beams and cosy corners, three fires, nice mixed furnishings, old photographs and canalia; enjoyable fairly

priced food all day, efficient staff, well kept Banks's, Bass and Marstons Pedigree, good choice of wines; large garden *(Martin Smith, E Clark, Colin Gooch, David Green, Paul J Robinshaw)*

HUDDLESFORD [SK1509]

Plough WS13 8PY [off A38 2 miles E of Lichfield, by Coventry Canal]: Waterside dining pub extended from 17th-c cottage, good food from well priced lunchtime dishes to more expensive evening choice, children's helpings; four neat areas, log fires (not always lit), cheerful attentive staff, well kept ales such as Greene King and Marstons Pedigree, good range of wines; attractive hanging baskets, canalside tables, hitching posts *(Deb and John Arthur, Paul J Robinshaw)*

KINVER [SO8483]

Vine DY7 6LJ [Dunsley Rd]: By Staffordshire & Worcestershire Canal, with good value bar food, well kept low-priced changing ales such as Kinver, Sadlers and Wye Valley; big garden *(Dave Braisted)*

LEEK [SJ9856]

Den Engel ST13 5HG [Stanley St]: Belgian-style bar in high-ceilinged former bank, over 100 belgian beers inc lots on tap, three dozen genevers, three or four changing real ales; piped classical music; dogs welcome, tables on back terrace, open all day Weds-Sun, cl Mon, Tues lunchtimes *(the Didler)*

☆ *Wilkes Head* ST13 5DS [St Edward St]: Convivial three-room local dating from the 18th c (still has back coaching stables), tied to Whim with their ales and interesting guest beers; good choice of whiskies, farm cider, friendly chatty landlord, welcoming regulars and dogs, filled rolls, pub games, gas fire, lots of pump clips; juke box in back room, Mon music night; children allowed in one room (but not really a family pub), fair disabled access, tables outside, open all day except Mon lunchtime *(Pete Baker, the Didler)*

LICHFIELD [SK1010]

Hedgehog WS13 8JB [Stafford Rd (A51)]: Family-friendly Vintage Inn in sizeable 17th-c building, lots of well spaced tables and plenty of nooks and corners, enjoyable good value food all day inc lunchtime deals and Sun roasts; friendly staff, well kept Banks's, Bass and Marstons Pedigree; picnic-sets in big garden, bedrooms, open all day *(Martin Smith, S J and C C Davidson, Roger and Linda Norman)*

LITTLE BRIDGEFORD [SJ8727]

Worston Mill ST18 9QA [Worston Lane; nr M6 junction 14; turn right off A5013 at Little Bridgeford]: Useful sensibly priced dining pub in attractive 1814 watermill, Wells & Youngs Bombardier, conservatory; children welcome, attractive grounds with adventure playground and nature trail (lakes, islands, etc); open all day *(LYM, J D O Carter)*

LONGNOR [SK0965]

Old Cheshire Cheese SK17 0NS: 14th-c, a pub for 250 years; well kept Robinsons, good

landlord and friendly service, tasty food inc Sun carvery, open fire; plenty of bric-a-brac and pictures in traditional main bar and two attractive dining rooms; children, hikers and dogs welcome; four bedrooms, cl Mon *(David Abbot, Helene Grygar)*

MILWICH [SJ9533]

Red Lion ST15 8RU [Dayhills; B5027 towards Stone]: Unpretentious bar at end of working farmhouse, old settles, tiled floor, inglenook log or coal fire, Bass and one or two guest beers tapped from the cask, friendly welcome, darts, dominoes and cribbage; cl lunchtimes except Sun, cl Sun evening *(the Didler)*

ONECOTE [SK0455]

Jervis Arms ST13 7RU [B5053]: Black-beamed main bar with inglenook woodburner, real ales such as Butcombe, Wadworths 6X and Wychwood, good value food; separate dining and family rooms; attractive streamside garden *(Helene Grygar, LYM)*

PENKRIDGE [SJ9214]

Littleton Arms ST19 5AL [St Michaels Sq/A449 – M6 detour between junctions 12 and 13]: Busy M&B dining pub/hotel with contemporary layout, low leather stools and sofa, up-to-date enjoyable brasserie food inc pizzas, good choice of wines by the glass; Bass and Slaters Queen Bee, friendly young staff; piped music; children welcome, ten bedrooms, open all day *(John and Helen Rushton, Jeremy King, Colin Gooch)*

☆ *Star* ST19 5DJ [Market Pl]: Charming busy open-plan local with big helpings of bargain food, well kept Marstons-related ales, efficient cheery service; lots of low black beams and button-back red plush, open fires; no credit cards, piped music, sports TV; open all day, terrace tables *(Dave Irving, Jenny Huggins, Colin Gooch, R T and J C Moggridge, BB)*

RANTON [SJ8422]

☆ *Hand & Cleaver* ST18 9JZ [Butt Lane, Ranton Green]: Tastefully extended country pub with landlord doing good enterprising well priced food, friendly attentive service, good wines by the glass, four changing well kept ales; log fires, lots of exposed beams and timber, piano, darts, restaurant; children and dogs welcome, cl Mon *(Henry Pursehouse-Tranter)*

ROLLESTON ON DOVE [SK2427]

Jinnie DE13 9AB [Station Rd]: Comfortable and friendly two-room pub with generous inexpensive food (not Mon), four Marstons-related ales, coal-effect gas fires, pale blue décor; picnic-sets on small lawn by pony paddock *(Dennis Jones)*

Spread Eagle DE13 9BE [Church Rd]: Old Vintage Inn family dining pub by Rolleston Brook, sensibly priced standard food all day, great choice of wines by the glass, Bass and Marstons Pedigree, three linked areas and separate dining room; disabled access and facilities, attractive shrubby garden, bedrooms *(Dennis Jones, B M Eldridge)*

RUSHTON SPENCER [SJ9362]
Rushton Inn SK11 0SE [A523]: Low-beamed 18th-c sandstone country inn with nooks and well stoked fires, welcoming landlord; enjoyable good value fresh food, Greene King Old Speckled Hen and a guest; two bedrooms, handy for Rudyard Lake and the Roaches, cl wkdy lunchtime *(Simon Le Fort)*

SHENSTONE [SK1004]
Fox & Hounds WS14 0NB [Main St]: Family-run 18th-c pub, traditional snug bar with woodburner, revamped lounge with leather sofas and armchairs, extended modern dining room; good value local food (not Sun evening, Mon) from bar snacks up inc traditional Sun lunch, good service even when busy, Adnams, Marstons Pedigree, Timothy Taylors Landlord and guests; open all day *(John and Helen Rushton)*

SLITTING MILL [SK0217]
Horns WS15 2UW [Slitting Mill Rd]: Under new licensees, two large comfortably furnished rooms, one with bar and pool, the other set for dining; good choice of food (not Mon) inc bargain bar menu, Adnams, Greene King and John Smiths; garden *(David Green)*

STAFFORD [SJ9222]
Picture House ST16 2HL [Bridge St/Lichfield St]: Art deco cinema converted by Wetherspoons keeping ornate ceiling plasterwork and stained-glass name sign; bar on stage with up to five real ales at competitive prices, farm cider, seating in stalls, circle and upper circle, popular food all day, lively atmosphere, film posters, Peter Cushing mannequin in preserved ticket box; good disabled facilities, spacious terrace overlooking river, open all day *(Alan and Eve Harding, Dave Braisted)*
Radford Bank ST17 4PG [Radford Bank (A34)]: Very child-friendly Innkeepers Fayre with bargain all-day carvery in large downstairs lounge – easy wheelchair access; nice outdoor seating area and play area *(Henry Pursehouse-Tranter)*
Shire Horse ST16 1GZ [1 mile from M6 junction 14, via A34 – junction A34/A513]: New Chef & Brewer built to look old, small secluded areas and open fires, bric-a-brac, welcoming staff and good atmosphere; attractive wide-ranging choice of all-day food served quickly even when very busy, lunchtime set deals, three changing ales; children welcome, disabled facilities, outside tables by road, bedrooms in next-door Premier Inn, open all day *(Martin Grosberg)*
Vine ST16 2JU [Salter St]: Large traditional hotel with comfortable well divided bar, wide all-day food choice inc restaurant bargains for two, well kept low-priced Banks's, good service; children welcome, 27 bedrooms *(Henry Pursehouse-Tranter, John Tav)*

STOWE [SK0027]
Cock ST18 0LF [off A518 Stafford—Uttoxeter]: Nicely laid out bistro-style conversion of old village pub, good food inc

bargain set lunches, friendly efficient service *(Leslie and Barbara Owen, Susan and Nigel Brookes)*

SWINSCOE [SK1348]
Dog & Partridge DE6 2HS [A52 3 miles W of Ashbourne; Town End Lane]: 17th-c stone-built beamed coaching inn set down from road, superb views from dining room's conservatory extension; reasonably priced food from sandwiches and several soups up, good service, Greene King ales, lots of bric-a-brac; children and dogs welcome, garden with play area *(Dennis Jones)*

SWYNNERTON [SJ8535]
Fitzherbert Arms ST15 0RA [off A51 Stone—Nantwich]: Olde-worlde beamed country pub reopened under new landlady; above-average food at good prices in bar and new restaurant, well kept real ale, friendly helpful staff, log fires; comfortable bedrooms, lovely village setting *(R T and J C Moggridge, Susan and Nigel Brookes)*

TAMWORTH [SK2004]
Bolebridge B79 7PA [Bolebridge St]: Comfortable Wetherspoons, well kept beers and wines by the glass, and their usual food, friendly service; games machines; small terrace *(Colin Gooch)*
Moat House B79 7QQ [Lichfield St]: Impressive Tudor former manor house, much refurbished inside while keeping beams and panelling; friendly staff, wide food choice; big garden overlooking river, big play area *(Colin Gooch)*

TATENHILL [SK2021]
Horseshoe DE13 9SD [off A38 W of Burton; Main St]: Bargain food all day (can take a while) inc good children's meals, Marstons ales, good wine range; tiled-floor bar, cosy side snug with woodburner, two-level restaurant and back family area; pleasant garden, good play area with pets corner *(C J Fletcher, Paul J Robinshaw, David and Felicity Fox, John and Helen Rushton, LYM)*

UTTOXETER [SK0832]
Plough ST14 8DW [Stafford Rd]: Friendly efficient service, good value food, well kept ales such as Bass and Marstons Pedigree *(Alan and Eve Harding)*

WHEATON ASTON [SJ8512]
Hartley Arms ST19 9NF [Long St (canalside, Tavern Bridge)]: Roomy and restful, eclectic choice of decent food, well kept Marstons-related ales, attractive prices, quick friendly service; tables outside, pleasant spot just above Shropshire Union Canal, nice long view to next village's church tower *(Ben Williams)*

WHITTINGTON [SK1608]
Bell WS14 9JR [Main St]: Two smallish rooms with open fires, friendly landlord and locals; good value food from lunchtime sandwiches up (Thurs fish and chips night), three well kept real ales, friendly staff; terrace picnic-sets, big well planted garden with play area; pleasant village; open all day wknds *(Paul J Robinshaw, David M Smith)*

YOXALL [SK1420]
Foresters DE13 8PH [Wood Lane]: Three-room dining pub refurbished under newish licensees; good freshly cooked food from lunchtime panini up, with more elaborate pricey evening dishes, decent sensibly priced wine list, friendly proficient service, small bar area; children welcome, outside seating, cl Sun evening, Mon *(Leo and Barbara Lionet)*

Golden Cup DE13 8NQ [Main St (A515)]: Well furnished friendly village inn dating from early 18th c, attentive staff, reasonably priced home-made food from sandwiches up, well kept Marstons and Timothy Taylors Landlord; lounge bar, games in public bar; waterside garden, good reasonably priced bedrooms, open all day wknds *(Paul and June Holmes)*

Post Office address codings confusingly give the impression that some pubs are in Staffordshire, when they're really in Cheshire or Derbyshire (which is where we list them).

Suffolk

Along with Norfolk, this county is enjoying a surge of real progress on the pub front – reflected in the fact that we have no less than nine new entries here, spanning a diverse range from the properly pubby own-brew White Horse at Edwardstone (the first pub we've met with its own wind turbine) to the civilised Swan in Monks Eleigh, with its good food. Enjoyable food is at least part of the headline appeal of all nine newcomers. It's also a major factor at the Anchor at Nayland (supplied by its own farm), Crown at Stoke-by-Nayland (terrific wine list), Anchor in Walberswick and Crown at Westleton (both with modern menus), and at what are now the county's two top food pubs, the impressive old Crown in Southwold (another place with excellent wines by the glass) and cottagey Golden Key in Snape. The unelaborated menu at the Golden Key, relying on delicious ingredients from their own farm for flavour, makes it Suffolk Dining Pub of the Year. Some other pubs worth a special trip include the charming old Kings Head at Laxfield (seven real ales tapped straight from casks), medieval St Peters Brewery at South Elmham, Crown at Great Glemham and Plough & Sail in Snape (both rewarding all-rounders), Fat Cat in Ipswich (for its 18 or so real ales) and Old Cannon in Bury St Edmunds (interesting views of the brewing process). Some top Lucky Dip pubs are the Plough at Brockley Green, Ship at Dunwich, Kings Head at East Bergholt and Greyhound at Pettistree. Greene King, based here, is now a major national brewer. By far the most successful local brewer is Adnams, though the county has several good much smaller brewers too.

ALDEBURGH

TM4656   MAP 5

Cross Keys ◀

Crabbe Street; IP15 5BN

Seats outside near beach, chatty atmosphere, friendly licensee and local beer

One of the few places in Suffolk where you can eat out by the beach, the terrace behind this nestling 16th-c pub is sheltered by two walls and has views across the promenade and shingle to the sea. Inside, there's a cheery bustling atmosphere helped along by the obliging licensee and his staff. The low-ceilinged interconnecting bars have two inglenook fireplaces, antique and other pubby furniture, the landlord's collection of oils and Victorian watercolours, and paintings by local artists on the walls. Adnams Bitter, Broadside and Explorer on handpump, decent wines by the glass and Aspall's cider; piped music and games machine. The bedrooms are elegant.

📶 Simple bar food includes sandwiches, ploughman's, cod and chips, moules frites, trout stuffed with prawns, steak and kidney pie, cromer crab, lobster, daily specials such as braised oxtail and coq au vin, and puddings such as treacle sponge and summer pudding.
Starters/Snacks: £3.95 to £6.00. Main Courses: £7.95 to £10.95. Puddings: £3.25

Adnams ~ Tenants Mike and Janet Clement ~ Real ale ~ Bar food (12-2(2.30 Sat, Sun), 7-9; not Sun evening) ~ No credit cards ~ (01728) 452637 ~ Children welcome ~ Dogs welcome ~ Open 11(12 Sun)-midnight ~ Bedrooms: £55B/£85S(£79.50B)

Recommended by Tracey and Stephen Groves, Hilary Edwards, Michael Dandy, Simon Rodway, Charles and Pauline Stride, P Dawn, MDN

BURY ST EDMUNDS

TL8564 MAP 5

Nutshell

The Traverse, central pedestrian link off Abbeygate Street; IP33 1BJ

Tiny, simple local with lots of interest on the walls and a couple of real ales

If it's not the smallest pub in the country, this quaint little 17th-c bare-boards local haunt must be a close runner-up. The timeless interior contains a short wooden bench along its shop-front corner windows, one cut-down sewing-machine table, an elbow rest running along its rather battered counter, and Greene King IPA and Abbot on handpump. A mummified cat, found walled up here, hangs from the dark brown ceiling (and also seems to have a companion rat), along with stacks of other bric-a-brac, from bits of a skeleton through vintage bank notes, cigarette packets and military and other badges to spears and a great metal halberd; piped music, chess and dominoes. The stairs up to the lavatories are very steep and narrow; more reports please.

⊞ **No food.**

Greene King ~ Lease Jack Burton ~ Real ale ~ No credit cards ~ (01284) 764867 ~ Children welcome till 7pm ~ Dogs welcome ~ Open 11-11; 12-10.30 Sun
Recommended by the Didler

Old Cannon 🍺 🛏

Cannon Street, just off A134/A1101 roundabout at N end of town; IP33 1JR

Busy own-brew town pub with local drinks and good bar food

The bar at this spacious bustling place is dominated by two huge gleaming stainless-steel brewing vessels, and has views up to a steel balustraded open-plan malt floor above the counter which serves the pub's own Black Pig, Blonde Bombshell, Bow Chaser, Gunner's Daughter and Old Cannon Best. A row of chunky old bar stools line the ochre-painted counter (which also serves a guest or two such as Bank Top Pavilion on handpump, suffolk cider and apple juice, a local lager, continental beers and a dozen wines by the glass) with its steel handrail, and into the room, a mix of old and new chairs and tables and upholstered banquettes stand on a well worn bare-boards floor. Walls are pale green and ochre, and contemporary looking; piped music. Behind, through the old side coach arch, is a good-sized cobbled courtyard neatly set with rather stylish metal tables and chairs, and planters and hanging baskets. The recently refurbished bedrooms are in what was the old brewhouse across the courtyard. Dogs allowed on Sunday and Monday evenings only; August bank holiday beer festival.

⊞ **Uncomplicated but particularly tasty bar food includes lunchtime baguettes, cromer crab with lime mayonnaise, thai vegetable spring rolls with sweet chilli dipping sauce, pigeon breast and black pudding salad, ploughman's, beer-battered haddock, sausages, colcannon and yorkshire pudding (made with Bitter), roast chicken breast on leek and mustard mash with watercress and lager cream sauce; thai banquet first Tuesday of the month.** *Starters/Snacks: £4.50 to £6.00. Main Courses: £7.95 to £14.95. Puddings: £4.25 to £5.50*

Free house ~ Licensees Mike and Judith Shallow ~ Real ale ~ Bar food (12-2(3 Sun), 6-9.15; not Sun, Mon evenings) ~ (01284) 768769 ~ Folk club third Mon of month ~ Open 12-3, 5-11; 12-11 Sat; 12-10.30 Sun; 12-3, 5-11 Sat and 12-4, 7-10.30 in winter ~ Bedrooms: £65S/£79S

Recommended by M and GR, Mike and Shelley Woodroffe

CHELMONDISTON   TM2037   MAP 5

Butt & Oyster

Pin Mill – signposted from B1456 SE of Ipswich; IP9 1JW

Chatty old pub above River Orwell with nice views, decent food and drink, and seats on the terrace

The suntrap terrace outside this simple old bargeman's pub has fine views of ships coming down the river from Ipswich and across to long lines of moored black sailing barges. Window seats inside share the same pleasing view. The half-panelled timeless little smoke room is pleasantly worn and unfussy, and has model sailing ships around the walls and high-backed and other old-fashioned settles on the tiled floor. Adnams Best, Broadside and Explorer are on handpump or tapped from the cask; several wines by the glass and local cider; board games and dominoes. The annual Thames Barge Race (end June/beginning July) is fun. The pub is named for the flounders and oysters which used to be caught here.

🍴 Well liked bar food includes sandwiches, mussels done several different ways, chicken liver parfait with real ale chutney, whitebait, beer-battered cod, home-cooked ham and eggs, honey-glazed goats cheese with toasted pine nut and olive salad, burgers with various toppings, salmon and prawn fishcakes, smoked paprika chicken breast with a tomato and herb dressing, steaks and sharing platters. *Starters/Snacks: £3.00 to £5.95. Main Courses: £4.95 to £16.95. Puddings: £3.95 to £5.95*

Adnams ~ Lease Steve Lomas ~ Real ale ~ Bar food (12-9.30) ~ Restaurant ~ (01473) 780764 ~ Children welcome ~ Dogs allowed in bar ~ Folk Sun evenings monthly ~ Open 11-11

Recommended by the Didler, Pat and Tony Martin, JDM, KM, Sue Demont, Tim Barrow, Simon Rodway, Bob and Margaret Holder, Peter Meister

EARL SOHAM   TM2263   MAP 5

Victoria 🍺 £

A1120 Yoxford—Stowmarket; IP13 7RL

Nice beers from brewery across the road, in this friendly informal local

The three beers on handpump at this friendly unpretentious pub are brewed across the road in the Earl Soham brewery. They also keep a local cider. Fairly basic and definitely well worn, the bar has an easy-going local atmosphere and is sparsely furnished with kitchen chairs and pews, plank-topped trestle sewing-machine tables and other simple scrubbed-pine country tables, and there's stripped panelling, tiled or board floors, an interesting range of pictures of Queen Victoria and her reign, and open fires. There are seats on a raised back lawn, with more out in front. The pub is quite close to a wild fritillary meadow at Framlingham, and a working windmill at Saxtead.

🍴 Straightforward bar food includes sandwiches, ploughman's, soup, corned beef hash, vegetarian pasta dishes, an enjoyable changing curry, and puddings. *Starters/Snacks: £4.00 to £5.50. Main Courses: £7.50 to £9.50. Puddings: £4.50*

Own brew ~ Licensee Paul Hooper ~ Real ale ~ Bar food (12-2, 7-10) ~ (01728) 685758 ~ Children welcome ~ Dogs allowed in bar ~ Open 11.30-3, 6-11; 12-3, 7-10.30 Sun

Recommended by Pete Baker, Charles and Pauline Stride, Ian and Nita Cooper, Mike and Sue Loseby, Tim Maddison, Julia Mann

---

Several well known guide books make establishments pay for entry, either directly or as a fee for inspection. These fees can run to many hundreds of pounds. We do not. Unlike other guides, we never take payment for entries. We never accept a free meal, free drink, or any other freebie from a pub. We do not accept any sponsorship – let alone from commercial schemes linked to the pub trade. All our entries depend solely on merit.

EASTBRIDGE

Eels Foot 🛏

Off B1122 N of Leiston; IP16 4SN

Handy for Minsmere bird reserve, friendly welcome, fair value food, and Thursday evening folk sessions; bedrooms

With a proper pubby hospitable atmosphere, the upper and lower parts of the bar at this cheerful little beamed country local have light modern furnishings on stripped-wood floors, a warming fire, and Adnams Bitter, Broadside, Old Ale and seasonal beers on handpump, several wines by the glass, and Aspall's cider; darts in a side area, board games, and a neat back dining room. There are seats on the terrace and benches out in the lovely big back garden. This is a popular spot with bird-watchers, cyclists and walkers and the fresh water marshes bordering the inn offer plenty of opportunity for watching the abundance of birds and butterflies; a footpath leads you directly to the sea. The bedrooms (one with wheelchair access) in the newish building are comfortable and attractive.

🍴 **Good value popular bar food includes baguettes, whitebait, wild boar terrine, warm goats cheese salad with caramelised onion chutney, beer-battered cod, steak in ale pie, smoked haddock and spring onion fishcakes, three-cheese cannelloni, and puddings such as treacle tart and white chocolate and berry pudding.** *Starters/Snacks: £4.50 to £6.95. Main Courses: £7.25 to £12.95. Puddings: £4.50*

Adnams ~ Tenants Simon and Corinne Webber ~ Real ale ~ Bar food (12-2.30, 7-9 (6.30-8 Thurs)) ~ Restaurant ~ (01728) 830154 ~ Children welcome ~ Dogs allowed in bar ~ Live music Thurs evening and last Sun of month ~ Open 12-11; 11-11 Sat; 12-10.30 Sun ~ Bedrooms: £65B/£80B

Recommended by Mrs M S Forbes, Mrs Carolyn Dixon, Danny Savage, RS, ES, Charles and Pauline Stride, Julia Mann

EASTON

White Horse 🍷

N of Wickham Market on back road to Earl Soham and Framlingham; IP13 0ED

Lovely old pub with sensibly short choice of jolly good food, good wines and local beers.

A nice new landlord took over this delightfully quirky-looking pub about two years ago. With just a gentle tidy-up, he's kept the two neat and smartly simple rooms unspoilt and traditional, with country kitchen chairs, good small settles, cushioned stripped pews and stools, and open fires. You can have any wine, from the carefully chosen list of about 30, by the glass, and they've two Adnams beers and a local guest such as Woodfordes Wherry on handpump. There are darts in the separate games room, and tables in the rustic garden.

🍴 **Using thoughtfully sourced local products and with a high standard set in the kitchen, the seasonally changing menu tends to be imaginative takes on traditional dishes: maybe filled baguettes, seared scallops with rocket salad, lime and chilli dressing, jellied ham hock and parsley terrine with piccalilli, sausages and mash, wild rabbit shortcrust pie, cod fillet with samphire and lemon butter sauce, venison ragoût with pappardelle and pomegranate seeds, and puddings such as crumble of the day, sherry trifle and chocolate brownies.** *Starters/Snacks: £3.95 to £5.50. Main Courses: £7.95 to £14.95. Puddings: £4.95*

Punch ~ Lease Tim Wood ~ Real ale ~ Bar food ~ (01728) 746456 ~ Children welcome ~ Dogs welcome ~ Open 12-3, 6-11.30

Recommended by Ian Phillips, Pamela Goodwyn, David Blackburn, Simon Cottrell

---

We say if we know a pub allows dogs.

EDWARDSTONE   TL9542   MAP 5

White Horse ◖

Village signposted off A1071 in Boxford; pub at Mill Green, just E; CO10 5PX

Chatty own-brew pub, traditional furnishings in simple rooms, hearty food, self-catering and a campsite

This is a fairly remote and interesting pub with a good village atmosphere, and it's eco-friendly, too. As well as installing a wind turbine, the friendly landlord uses sustainable methods as much as possible in the brewing of their own Mill Green ales in the neat new back brewery. There are several varying-sized bar rooms as well as a tiny little room with just one table and lots of beer mats on the walls. The floors are bare boards throughout, the cream walls above a pink dado are hung with rustic prints and photographs, there's a mix of second-hand tables and chairs including an old steamer bench and panelled settle, a piano, and woodburning stove as well as a fireplace. Adnams and Crouch Vale Brewers Gold are well kept alongside their own Bulls Gold, Lovelys Fair and Mawkin Mild, and guests such as Adnams Extra, Harviestoun Bitter & Twisted and two more of their own brews such as Good Ship Arabella and Marathon Gold; also strong local farm cider. Piped music, darts, bar billiards, dominoes, cards and board games. There are some sturdy teak tables and seats on an end terrace, an attractive smokers' shelter with green panelled seating, and some makeshift picnic-sets on a grassy area. The self-catering 'cottages' are rather scandinavian in style, and there's a campsite with a shower block.

⫴ **Hearty pub food such as swede and fennel soup, goats cheese and onion tart, ploughman's, salads, venison pie, salmon on spinach with cheddar cheese, sausage and mash, apple and almond sponge and dark chocolate pots. Salads and vegetables are grown for the pub at nearby organic farms.** *Starters/Snacks: £1.50 to £4.95. Main Courses: £4.95 to £10.95. Puddings: £3.95 to £4.95*

Own brew ~ Licensee Amy Mitchell ~ Real ale ~ Bar food (12-3, 5-9; not Sun evening and Mon except bank hols) ~ (01787) 211211 ~ Children welcome ~ Dogs welcome ~ Folk jam second Weds of month, blues jam fourth Thurs of month ~ Open 12-3(not Mon), 5-11; 12-11 Fri-Sun; cl Mon-Thurs lunchtime (and 3-5 Fri) in winter ~ Bedrooms: /£80B

Recommended by Giles and Annie Francis, John Prescott

GREAT GLEMHAM   TM3461   MAP 5

Crown ◖

Between A12 Wickham Market—Saxmundham and B1119 Saxmundham—Framlingham; IP17 2DA

Pleasant friendly pub in pretty village, log fires and fresh flowers, real ales and tasty food

Beautifully maintained, this comfortable pub has a big entrance hall with sofas on rush matting, and an open-plan beamed lounge with wooden pews and captain's chairs around stripped and waxed kitchen tables, and local photographs and interesting paintings on cream walls; fresh flowers, some brass ornaments and log fires in two big fireplaces. The good-natured landlord serves changing real ales such as Adnams Bitter, Earl Soham Gannet Mild and Victoria, and Woodfordes Nelsons Revenge from old brass handpumps, and they've eight wines (including sparkling) by the glass, Aspall's cider and several malt whiskies. A tidy flower-ringed lawn, raised above the corner of the quiet village lane by a retaining wall, has some seats and tables under cocktail parasols; there's a smokers' shelter and disabled access.

⫴ **As well as sandwiches, the most enjoyable bar food, from a seasonally changing menu, might include smoked duck with roast figs and home-made plum sauce, tempura of king prawns with sweet chilli and ginger sauce, roast pepper, rocket, halloumi and tomato quiche, wild boar sausages with onion gravy, pork medallions with apple and cider jus, seared tuna niçoise, and puddings such as apple and cinnamon crumble, white chocolate panna cotta with pineapple and mango syrup and bread and butter pudding; Sunday roast.** *Starters/Snacks: £3.95 to £6.25. Main Courses: £6.95 to £14.95. Puddings: £4.50*

Free house ~ Licensee Dave Cottle ~ Real ale ~ Bar food (12-2.30, 7-9) ~ (01728) 663693 ~ Children welcome ~ Dogs welcome ~ Open 11.30-3, 6.30-11.30; 12-3, 7-10.30 Sun; closed Mon (except bank hols) ~ Bedrooms: /£80B

Recommended by Simon Cottrell, Ian and Margaret Wade, Mrs Margo Finlay, Jörg Kasprowski, Simon Rodway, Tracey and Stephen Groves, Chris and Vannessa O'Neill, Neil Powell, Julia and Richard Tredgett, Brenda Crossley, Charles and Pauline Stride

GRUNDISBURGH   TM2250   MAP 5

Dog 🍴 ♀

Off A12 via B1079 from Woodbridge bypass; The Green – village signposted; IP13 6TA

Civilised, friendly pub run by two brothers; enjoyable food, nice choice of drinks and a log fire; garden with play area

You can enjoy a jolly good meal in a welcoming pubby atmosphere at this lovingly run pink-washed pub. Nicely villagey, the public bar on the left has oak settles and dark wooden carvers around a mix of tables on the tiles, and an open log fire. The softly lit and relaxing carpeted lounge bar has comfortable seating around dark oak tables, antique engravings on raspberry walls and unusual flowers in the windows; it links with a similar bare-boards dining room, with some attractive antique oak settles; TV and darts. Adnams, Caledonian Deuchars IPA and a guest from a brewer like Jennings on handpump, half a dozen wines by the glass, ciders, and good espresso coffee. There are quite a few picnic-sets out in front by flowering tubs and the fenced back garden has a play area. The jack russell is called Poppy.

🍴 They cure a lot of their own produce and the seasonal ingredients they use are carefully sourced, with game coming from local estates and meat from local farms. The particularly good bar food includes lunchtime sandwiches, ham hock terrine and pâté with apple jelly, fried tiger prawns, fried lambs liver with bacon and sage butter, roast duck confit with orange sauce, home-made sausages, well hung rump steak, specials such as fried pigeon with damsons, cod with pea and mint purée, spinach and blue cheese cannelloni and roast bacon-wrapped rabbit with red wine gravy, and puddings such as spotted dick and custard, treacle pudding and lemon tart with chantilly cream; good value set lunch menu. *Starters/Snacks: £3.50 to £7.95. Main Courses: £6.00 to £7.95. Puddings: £3.00 to £4.50*

Punch ~ Lease Charles and James Rogers ~ Real ale ~ Bar food (12-2(2.30 Sat, Sun), 5.30-9) ~ Restaurant ~ (01473) 735267 ~ Children welcome away from bar ~ Dogs allowed in bar ~ Open 12-3, 5.30-11; 12-11 Fri and Sat; 12-10.30 Sun; closed Mon

Recommended by Richard and Margaret McPhee, MDN, Mrs J Ekins-Daukes, Charles and Pauline Stride, Christopher Sims, Tom Gondris, J F M and M West

HOXNE   TM1877   MAP 5

Swan ♀

Off B1118, signed off A140 S of Diss; Low Street; IP21 5AS

Friendly, relaxed, old pub with good choice of drinks, bar food and seats in large garden

With its lovely time-warped exterior timbering and ancient interior beams and mortar, this striking pub has an appealingly historic atmosphere (it was built for the Bishop of Norwich back in 1480). The relaxed pubby bar has two solid oak counters, broad oak floorboards and a deep-set inglenook fireplace. Adnams Best and Broadside, Woodfordes Wherry and a guest such as Timothy Taylors Landlord are on handpump or tapped from the cask, alongside nine wines by the glass and Aspall's cider; they hold an annual beer festival. There are seats under parasols on two sheltered terraces and in a lovely extensive garden by a small stream. They hold outdoor theatre performances, a monthly quiz night, and have regular live music; piped music. Nearby, the tree to which King Edmund was tied to at his execution is said to form part of a screen in the neighbouring church.

🍴 Bar food includes filled sandwiches and baguettes, prawn cocktail, cold honey-roast duck on cucumber and spring onions with plum sauce and pomegranate, fish and chips with mushy peas, chilli, pork tenderloin stuffed with apricots, thyme, shallots and garlic with sherry cream sauce, steak and kidney pie, spinach and mushroom ravioli, fried venison with berry sauce and rib-eye steak, and specials such as gammon steak with caramelised pineapple slices. *Starters/Snacks: £4.95 to £6.95. Main Courses: £9.95 to £15.95. Puddings: £5.00*

Enterprise ~ Lease Jo-Anne and David Rye ~ Real ale ~ Bar food ~ Restaurant ~ (01379) 668275 ~ Children welcome ~ Dogs allowed in bar ~ Open 12-3, 6-11; 12-10.30 Sun

Recommended by Conrad Freezer, Evelyn and Derek Walter, John Saville

ICKLINGHAM
TL7872   MAP 5

Red Lion

A1101 Mildenhall—Bury St Edmunds; IP28 6PS

Characterful old pub with civilised but relaxed atmosphere, good food and four usually local beers

Back in the *Guide* with new licensees, this fine old 16th-c thatched pub is very handy for West Stow Country Park or the Anglo-Saxon Village. From behind the counter Fudge, the pub dog, offers a cheery meet-and-greet service while the helpful landlord serves well kept Woodfordes Wherry and three guests from brewers such as Brandon, Humpty Dumpty and Woodfordes on handpump, several wines by the glass and lots of country wines. With a pleasant chatty atmosphere and plenty of historic character throughout, the best part is the beamed bar with its cavernous inglenook fireplace, attractive furnishings including a nice mixture of wooden chairs, big candlelit tables and turkey rugs on the polished wood floor. The dining area, behind a knocked-through fireplace, has old oak tables on carpets. There are picnic-sets with colourful parasols on a lawn in front (the pub is well set back from the road).

🍴 Bar food might include sweet potato, apple and ginger soup, toasted goats cheese and black pudding salad with sweet chilli dressing, ploughman's, battered haddock with minted mushy peas and chunky chips, slow-cooked pressed pork belly with crackling, black pudding slice and creamy wholegrain mustard sauce, local pork and ale sausages with cheese, mushroom and chive risotto, goan chicken curry, beef in ale with gnocchi, and puddings such as almond tart with crème anglaise and plum apricot ice-cream and sticky toffee pudding with rum and raisin ice-cream. *Starters/Snacks: £3.75 to £5.00. Main Courses: £5.75 to £11.95. Puddings: £4.50 to £5.00*

Free house ~ Licensees Ed Lockwood and Aileen Towns ~ Real ale ~ Bar food (12-3(4 Sun), 6.30-9; not Sun evening) ~ Restaurant ~ (01638) 711698 ~ Children welcome ~ Dogs allowed in bar ~ Open 12-3, 6-11.30; 12-4, 7.30-10.30 Sun; closed Mon, Tues

Recommended by Russell Sawyer, Mrs D M Bailey, N R White, M and GR, Stephen Read, George Cowie, Frances Gosnell, Sheila Topham, Nick and Ginny Law, D M Picton

IPSWICH
TM1844   MAP 5

Fat Cat 🍺

Spring Road, opposite junction with Nelson Road (best bet for parking up there); IP4 5NL

Fantastic range of changing real ales in a well run town pub; garden

Saturday night might see 18 real ales at this very busy and extremely friendly town pub. With just Adnams on handpump, the rest are tapped straight from the cask in the tap room. Coming from far and wide they might be from brewers such as Crouch Vale, Dark Star, Elgoods, Fat Cat, Fullers, Green Jack, Hop Back, Moles, Oakham, St Peters, RCH and Woodfordes – the list is pretty much endless. They also stock quite a few belgian bottled beers, farm cider and fruit wines. The bare-boarded bars have a mix of café and bar stools, unpadded wall benches and cushioned seats around cast-iron and wooden pub tables, and lots of enamel brewery signs and posters on canary-yellow walls. Often to be seen perched on a pub stool, the pub cat is called Dave, and the sausage dog is called Stanley. There's also a spacious back conservatory, and several picnic-sets on the terrace and lawn. Very little nearby parking.

🍴 **They don't have a kitchen but keep a supply of scotch eggs, pasties, pies and sometimes filled baguettes in the fridge and are quite happy for you to bring in takeaways (not Fri, Sat).** *Starters/Snacks: £2.40 to £2.60.*

Free house ~ Licensees John and Ann Keatley ~ Real ale ~ Bar food ~ (01473) 726524 ~ Open 12-11; 11am-midnight Sat

Recommended by Ian and Nita Cooper, Danny Savage, the Didler, Mrs Hazel Rainer

LAVENHAM

TL9149   MAP 5

Angel ♀ 🍺 🛏

Market Place; CO10 9QZ

Handsome Tudor inn with good range of drinks, sizeable back garden and comfortable bedrooms

Making a good base for a weekend break in this prettiest of towns, this attractive Tudor inn is now in its second year under its new managers and as part of the Maypole pub group. The light and airy long bar area has plenty of polished dark tables, a big inglenook log fire under a heavy mantelbeam, and some attractive 16th-c ceiling plasterwork (even more elaborate pargeting in the residents' sitting room upstairs). Round towards the back, on the right of the central servery, is a further dining area with heavy stripped-pine country furnishings. They have shelves of books, dominoes and lots of board games. Adnams Bitter, Greene King IPA and Nethergate Suffolk County and Woodfordes Wherry on handpump, Aspall's cider, and nine wines by the glass. Picnic-sets out in front overlook the former market square and there are tables under parasols in a sizeable sheltered back garden; it's worth asking if they've time to show you the interesting Tudor cellar.

🍴 **Ambitious bar food includes twice-baked cheese and chive soufflé, grilled tuna niçoise salad, salmon, shrimp and salmon terrine with tartare sauce, poached haddock fillet with spinach, poached egg and tarragon cream sauce, red mullet fillets with creamy cannellini beans, lemon and dill, orange and rosemary stuffed loin of lamb with apricot compote, and puddings such as rhubarb syllabub, vanilla terrine and chocolate marquise with raspberry coulis and lemon and lime cheesecake; roasts only on Sunday.** *Starters/Snacks: £4.50 to £6.25. Main Courses: £7.95 to £14.95. Puddings: £4.50 to £5.75*

Maypole Group ~ Managers Katherine Thompson and James Haggar ~ Real ale ~ Bar food (12-2.15, 6.45-9.15) ~ Restaurant ~ (01787) 247388 ~ Children welcome ~ Dogs welcome ~ Open 11-11; 12-10.30 Sun ~ Bedrooms: £80B/£95B

Recommended by John Saville, the Didler, MDN, Michael Doswell, Mrs M B Gregg, P A Rowe, Michael and Maggie Betton, Mrs Carolyn Dixon, C Galloway, DFL, Simon and Mandy King, Tom and Jill Jones, Peter Meister, Stuart Orton, Anne Walton, John and Patricia White, Stephen and Jean Curtis, Mrs Margo Finlay, Jörg Kasprowski, N R White, B R and M F Arnold

LAXFIELD

TM2972   MAP 5

Kings Head ★ 🍺

Gorams Mill Lane, behind church; IP13 8DW

Unspoilt old pub of real character, helpful staff, well liked bar food and several real ales; bedrooms and self-contained flat

The charming rooms at this unspoilt 15th-c pub have solid old-fashioned character and a tremendously informal atmosphere – though it's by no means in a time warp. People are intrigued by the chequer-tiled front room, with its striking high-backed square settle that works its way right round the room and is accessed by one corner and takes in an open fire and accommodates one substantial table. It's all dimly lit by a single overhead bulb. Two other equally unspoilt rooms – the card and tap rooms – have pews, old seats, scrubbed deal tables and some interesting wall prints. There's no bar – instead, the helpful staff potter in and out of a cellar tap room (don't be shy to wander in here too) to pour pints of Adnams Bitter, Broadside, Explorer and two seasonal beers, and guests such as Woodfordes Wherry and Timothy Taylors Landlord straight from the cask; several wines by the glass, piped music, cards and board games. Outside, the garden has an immaculately mown lawn, colourful herbaceous borders, an arbour covered by a grape and hop vine, a small pavilion for cooler evenings and plenty of benches and tables.

🍴 Bar food includes sandwiches, chicken and smoked mackerel pâté, dublin bay prawns, bananas baked in stilton cream, ploughman's, lasagne, a fine choice of local sausages such as chilli or apricot and ginger, steak and ale pie, lamb shank in mint gravy, fish pie, and puddings such as sherry trifle and sticky toffee pudding. *Starters/Snacks: £4.50 to £5.95. Main Courses: £6.50 to £9.50. Puddings: £4.50*

Adnams ~ Tenant Bob Wilson ~ Real ale ~ Bar food (not Mon evening) ~ Restaurant ~ (01986) 798395 ~ Children welcome ~ Dogs welcome ~ Open 12-3, 6-11; 12-10.30 Sun ~ Bedrooms: /£60S

Recommended by Ian and Nita Cooper, John M Murphy, Tim Maddison, Richard Armstrong, Jeremy and Jane Morrison, Charles and Pauline Stride, the Didler, Simon and Mandy King, Pete Baker, Philip and Susan Philcox, Stephen and Jean Curtis

LEVINGTON
TM2339   MAP 5

Ship

Gun Hill; from A14/A12 Bucklesham roundabout take A1156 exit, then first sharp left into Felixstowe road, then after nearly a mile turn right into Bridge Road at Levington signpost, bearing left into Church Lane; IP10 0LQ

Delightful place with a good welcome, tasty food and beer tapped from the cask

Now owned by Adnams, this charming old pub has quite a nautical theme, with lots of ship prints and photographs of sailing barges, a marine compass under the serving counter in the middle room, and a fishing net slung overhead. Along with benches built into the walls, there are comfortably upholstered small settles (some of them grouped round tables as booths) and a big black round stove. The flagstoned dining room has more nautical bric-a-brac and beams taken from an old barn. Tapped straight from the barrel or under light blanket pressure, Adnams Bitter and Broadside and a guest such as Woodfordes Wherry are served alongside several wines by the glass and Aspall's cider. Surrounded by lovely countryside (with good nearby walks), the pub is attractively placed by a little lime-washed church and has views (if a little obscured) over the River Orwell estuary.

🍴 You must arrive early if you want to eat as the food is very popular and there can be quite a wait for tables. May be dressed crab, liver and bacon with madeira sauce, quite a few fresh fish dishes such as griddled skate and seared scallops with wild mushroom risotto, and puddings such as white chocolate and summer berry mousse or pear and cinnamon strudel with vanilla sauce. Main courses can be a couple of pounds dearer in the evening. *Starters/Snacks: £4.75 to £8.95. Main Courses: £8.95 to £15.95. Puddings: £5.40*

Adnams ~ Tenants Stella and Mark Johnson ~ Real ale ~ Bar food (12-2(3 Sun), 7-9; light meals 2-5.30 in summer) ~ (01473) 659573 ~ Open 11.30-11 Sat; 12-10.30 Sun; 11.30-2.30, 6-11 weekdays

Recommended by J F M and M West, Allison and Graham Thackery, Tony and Shirley Albert, Ian and Nita Cooper, Mrs Carolyn Dixon, Charles and Pauline Stride, Rosemary Smith

---

Bedroom prices normally include full english breakfast, VAT and any inclusive service charge that we know of. Prices before the '/' are for single rooms, after for two people in a double or twin (B includes a private bath, S a private shower). If there is no '/', the prices are only for twin or double rooms (as far as we know there are no singles).

LIDGATE
TL7257 MAP 5

Star ♀
B1063 SE of Newmarket; CB8 9PP

Attentive service, spanish and english food, a warm welcome, and seats out in front and in the back garden

Delightful to arrive at, this charmingly snug-looking old pub is prettily painted in traditional pink Suffolk wash. Nicely pubby, the main room has handsomely moulded heavy beams, a good big log fire, candles in iron candelabra on polished oak or stripped-pine tables, and some antique catalan plates over the bar; darts, ring the bull and piped music. Besides a second similar room on the right, there's a cosy little dining room on the left. Greene King IPA, Abbot and Ruddles County on handpump and decent house wines. There are some tables out on the raised lawn in front and in a pretty little rustic back garden. Dogs may be allowed with permission from the landlady.

🍴 Most customers come to enjoy the wide choice of spanish and english dishes on the characterful spanish landlady's menu, and whilst the food is good and interesting, the main course prices are pretty high for a pub (though there is a cheaper set lunch): soup including gazpacho, boquerones (fresh anchovies floured and fried), catalan salad, carpaccio of salmon, grilled squid, spanish meatballs, lasagne, lamb steaks in blackcurrant, pig cheeks, daube of beef, venison steaks in port, paella valenciana, seafood casserole and magret of duck. *Starters/Snacks: £5.55 to £7.95. Main Courses: £16.95 to £19.95. Puddings: £6.00*

Greene King ~ Lease Maria Teresa Axon ~ Real ale ~ Bar food (12-2.30, 7-10; not Sun evening) ~ (01638) 500275 ~ Children welcome ~ Open 12-3, 6-11

Recommended by M and GR, Brian and Elizabeth Tora, Tony and Shirley Albert, P and D Carpenter, John Saville

LINDSEY TYE
TL9846 MAP 5

Red Rose
Village signposted off A1141 NW of Hadleigh; IP7 6PP

Friendly and bustling, with a couple of neat bars, enjoyable food, real ales and plenty of outside seating

Now calling itself the Lindsey Rose, this is a carefully kept 15th-c pub with a neat gravelled car park, flowering tubs and a few picnic-sets in front, and more picnic-sets at the back – where there's also a children's play area and a football pitch. Inside the ancient building, the main room on our visit was full of happy, chatty diners, though if it is just a drink you want, you'll be made just as welcome. There are low beams and some standing timbers, a mix of wooden tables and chairs, red-painted walls, a few pieces of corn dolly work, and dried teasels in glass jugs on the window sills. In front of a splendid log fire in its old brick fireplace are a couple of comfortable red leather squishy sofas, a low table, and some brass measuring jugs. A second room is furnished exactly the same and has a second big brick fireplace, but is much simpler in feel, and perhaps quieter. Adnams Bitter and a couple of Mauldons guests on handpump, a dozen wines by the glass, and friendly, hard-working staff.

🍴 As well as filled baguettes and nibbles like venison salami and oysters, the popular home-made food includes goats cheese in filo pastry with chutney, fish of the day, fried pork loin steak with parsnip and sage purée and black pudding, fish and chips, twice-baked goats cheese soufflé, walnut and beetroot salad, and choose-your-own steak. *Starters/Snacks: £4.50 to £6.95. Main Courses: £8.50 to £18.00. Puddings: £4.95 to £7.00*

Free house ~ Licensee Peter Miller ~ Real ale ~ Bar food (12-2.30, 6.30(7 Fri, Sat)-9.30; 12-3, 6.30-9 Sun) ~ (01449) 741424 ~ Children welcome ~ Dogs welcome ~ Live jazz second Sun lunchtime of month ~ Open 11-3, 5.30-11; 11-10.30 Sun

Recommended by Mrs Carolyn Dixon, MDN

Tipping is not normal for bar meals, and not usually expected.

LONG MELFORD   TL8646   MAP 5

Black Lion ⑪ ⚲ 🛏

Church Walk; CO10 9DN

Civilised hotel with relaxed and comfortable bar, modern bar food, attentive uniformed staff and lovely bedrooms

---

Not really a straightforward pub, this is a most civilised and comfortable hotel, but customers do continue to drop in for just a drink, and they do keep Adnams Bitter and Broadside on handpump alongside several wines by the glass. One side of the oak serving counter is decorated in ochre and has bar stools, deeply cushioned sofas, leather wing armchairs and antique fireside settles, while the other side, decorated in shades of terracotta, has leather dining chairs around handsome tables set for the good modern food; open fires in both rooms. Big windows with swagged-back curtains have a pleasant outlook over the village green and there are large portraits including some of racehorses. Service by neatly uniformed staff is friendly and efficient; piped music and board games. There are seats and tables under terracotta parasols on the terrace and more in the appealing Victorian walled garden; more reports please.

🍽 **Eclectic, attractively presented – if not cheap – food might include smoked haddock and leek soup, crispy calamari, king prawns and whitebait, warm smoked pigeon rocket salad with blackcurrant dressing, red onion and goats cheese tart, fish pie, sausage and mash with onion gravy, japanese seaweed wrapped salmon with wasabi mash, fried bass with lime butter, sirloin steak with béarnaise sauce, and puddings such as white chocolate crème brûlée and banana fritter with maple syrup and vanilla ice-cream, and british cheeses; afternoon cream teas.** *Starters/Snacks: £5.25 to £7.50. Main Courses: £9.95 to £18.50. Puddings: £5.50*

Ravenwood Group ~ Manager Craig Jarvis ~ Real ale ~ Bar food (12-2, 7-9.30) ~ Restaurant ~ (01787) 312356 ~ Children welcome ~ Dogs allowed in bar and bedrooms ~ Open 11-11(10.30 Sun) ~ Bedrooms: £99.50B/£153B

Recommended by John Saville, Mrs Margo Finlay, Jörg Kasprowski

MONKS ELEIGH   TL9647   MAP 5

Swan ⑪ ⚲

B1115 Sudbury—Stowmarket; IP7 7AU

Delicious restauranty food in well run, civilised dining pub, real ales, good wines and friendly efficient service

---

Although there's no doubt that the excellent, rather restauranty food is the main draw to this civilised timber-framed thatched village pub, you will be made just as welcome if all you want is a drink – and the atmosphere is relaxed and friendly. The long pleasantly bright room has modern high-backed leather-seated wooden dining chairs around light wooden tables on the pale oak flooring, and red walls hung with Jack Vetriano prints and framed UK special edition stamps; there's an open fire in a little brick fireplace in the high-ceilinged end room. There are fresh flowers on top of the cream-painted, wooden-topped bar counter, some narrow ceiling beams, Adnams Bitter and Broadside on handpump, and a good choice of wines by the glass; quietly efficient service. The little village post office is in the pub car park.

🍽 **As well as a good value set lunch, the imaginative food includes starters such as pea and asparagus soup, crispy duck salad with hoi sin sauce, dressed cromer crab, breaded scallops and tuna carpaccio, main courses such as plum tomato tart, parma ham wrapped monkfish on samphire, roast bass with ginger and coriander butter, spicy rump burger on bruschetta with rocket and parmesan salad, moroccan-style chicken, and lobster, with puddings such as baked chocolate and Amaretto cheesecake, caramelised fig tart and ice whisky parfait.** *Starters/Snacks: £4.50 to £7.50. Main Courses: £8.75 to £17.00. Puddings: £5.50 to £7.00*

Free house ~ Licensee Carol Robson ~ Real ale ~ Bar food ~ Restaurant ~ (01449) 741391 ~ Children welcome ~ Open 12-3, 7-11; closed Sun evening, Mon

Recommended by Mrs Carolyn Dixon

NAYLAND

TL9734 MAP 5

Anchor ⊛ ♀

Court Street; just off A134 – turn off S of signposted B1087 main village turn; CO6 4JL

Friendly well run pub with interesting food using home farm and smokehouse produce, wines from own vineyard, and a riverside terrace

Keeping lots of traditional character, this well run pub is light and sunny, with an enjoyable mix of customers, from regulars gathering for a pint and a chat, to diners here for the very good food. The bare-boards bar has interesting old photographs of pipe-smoking customers and village characters on its pale yellow walls, farmhouse chairs around a mix of tables, and coal and log fires at each end. Another room behind has similar furniture and an open fire, and leads into a small carpeted sun room. Up some quite steep stairs is the stylish restaurant. Adnams Bitter, Greene King IPA and an interesting guest or two from brewers such as Harwich Town and Mill Green are on handpump alongside several wines by the glass, some from their own vineyard; piped music. This is a lovely spot in summer, when you can sit out on the back terrace and look across to the peaceful River Stour and its quacking ducks. Next door, their farmland is worked by suffolk punch horses – visitors are welcome to watch these magnificent animals or try their hands at the reins.

🍴 From their Heritage Farm next door they produce the free-range eggs, vegetables, lamb, pork and beef used here, and they have their own smokehouse. Dishes tend to be simple, relying on the good produce for flavour. As well as lunchtime home-baked bread sandwiches, the imaginative food might include starters such as herb soup with cheese and croûtons, rabbit and lentil terrine with dates and apricots, fried squid and chorizo with spinach tagliatelle, main courses such as cottage pie, smoked platter, tomato, courgette and pepper frittata, ploughman's, lamb fillet with marjoram sauce, and steak; also puddings such as lemon cheesecake and sticky toffee pudding. To be sure of a table, you must book. *Starters/Snacks: £4.50 to £6.00. Main Courses: £8.50 to £16.00. Puddings: £4.50 to £5.50*

Free house ~ Licensee Daniel Bunting ~ Real ale ~ Bar food (12-2(2.30 Sat), 6.30-9(9.30 Sat); 12-3, 5-8.30 Sun) ~ (01206) 262313 ~ Children welcome ~ Open 11-11(10.30 Sun); 11-3, 5-11 weekdays in winter

Recommended by Christopher Sims, Mr Ray J Carter, Mrs P Lang, Jane and Alan Bush, Mrs Carolyn Dixon

NEWBOURNE

TM2743 MAP 5

Fox

Off A12 at roundabout 1.7 miles N of A14 junction; The Street; IP12 4NY

Friendly, relaxed pub with good generous food in attractive rooms; seats by lovely hanging baskets and in the nice garden

Although the tasty food at this popular, well run pub is one of the main reasons for coming here, this pink-washed 16th-c pub does have a relaxed and pubby atmosphere. As you come in, there's an eye-catching array of some two or three dozen little hanging blackboards showing what food's on offer, one dish to each. The characterful bar has a few shiny black beams in the low rather bowed ceiling, slabby elm and other dark tables on the tiled floor, a stuffed fox sitting among other decorations in an inglenook, and a warm décor in crushed raspberry. A comfortable carpeted dining room, with a large modern artwork and several antique mirrors on its warm yellow walls, opens off on the left and overlooks the courtyard. Adnams Bitter and Greene King IPA with a couple of guests such as Adnams Broadside and Woodfordes Wherry on handpump, decent wines by the glass, and prompt, friendly service; piped music. This is a delightfully peaceful spot and there are picnic-sets out in front by the lovely flowering baskets, with more seats in the attractive grounds with its secluded rose garden and well stocked pond; more reports please.

🍴 As well as daily specials and lunchtime sandwiches, the quickly served food might include chicken liver and port pâté with real ale chutney, fishcakes, beer-battered cod with home-made tartare sauce, steak in ale pie, stilton and vegetable crumble, fish pie,

trio of lamb cutlets, sausage and mash, and steak and kidney pudding. *Starters/Snacks: £3.95 to £7.95. Main Courses: £7.95 to £14.95. Puddings: £4.95 to £5.95*

Deben Inns ~ Lease Steve and Louise Lomas ~ Real ale ~ Bar food (12-2.30, 6.30-9.30; 12-9.30 weekends) ~ Restaurant ~ (01473) 736307 ~ Children welcome ~ Dogs allowed in bar ~ Open 11-11

Recommended by Charles and Pauline Stride, M and GR, P Clark, Peter Meister

ORFORD
TM4249   MAP 5

Jolly Sailor
Quay Street; IP12 2NU

New licensees at a lovely old pub with interesting daily specials, views from the garden, camping and bedrooms

Filling rather special shoes, the new licensees at this 17th-c brick pub have imprinted their own cheerful character on its traditional rooms – it's now filled with boating pictures and shipping charts, and the new Thames room (it was the old landlord's sitting room) celebrates that river. Built mainly from wrecked ships' timbers, the several snug rooms have lots of exposed brickwork, and are served from counters and hatches in an old-fashioned central cubicle. There's an unusual spiral staircase in the corner of the flagstoned main bar – which also has horsebrasses, local photographs, two cushioned pews and a long antique stripped-deal table, and an open woodburning stove in the big brick fireplace (with nice horsebrasses above it). Four Adnams beers are well kept on handpump. Several picnic-sets on grass at the back have views over the marshes; there's a play tower and camping in the orchard. The refurbished bedrooms look rather nice: do let us know what you think if you stay here.

🍴 **The bar menu includes pâtés and potted fish, welsh rarebit, ploughman's, steak burger, ham, egg and pineapple, lemon, basil and parmesan linguine with crab or chicken, fried skate and steak with red wine shallot reduction, with daily specials such as herrings in oatmeal with home-smoked bacon, tobago kidneys, bouillabaisse, venison medallions with port and cranberries, and puddings such as crêpe suzette with Grand Marnier.** *Starters/Snacks: £4.50 to £11.95. Main Courses: £5.75 to £12.95. Puddings: £4.50 to £4.75*

Adnams ~ Tenant Gordon Williams ~ Real ale ~ Bar food (12-3, 6-9.30; 12-9.30 Sat, Sun) ~ (01394) 450243 ~ Children welcome ~ Dogs welcome ~ Open 12-12; 12-3, 6-12 weekdays in winter ~ Bedrooms: /£85B

Recommended by RS, ES, Simon Rodway, Neil Powell, Tony Middis, Hilary Morris

Kings Head
Front Street; IP12 2LW

Traditional village pub with sensibly priced bar food and Adnams beers

With new licensees since the last edition, this pubby place is still comfortably busy with locals who pop in for the three well kept Adnams beers, and visitors who come for the sensibly priced food. The main bar is fairly straightforward but snug, with heavy low beams and traditional furniture on red carpets. There are nice old stripped-brick walls, and rugs on the ancient bare boards in the candlelit dining room; piped music.

🍴 **Bar food might include half a pint of prawns, duck liver and apricot terrine, charcuterie, halloumi and aubergine salad, caesar salad, sausage and mash, battered cod and chips, game and fish pies, vegetable and goats cheese quiche, and puddings such as white chocolate panna cotta and american cheesecake with apricot sauce.** *Starters/Snacks: £3.50 to £6.50. Main Courses: £7.50 to £16.50. Puddings: £4.50*

Adnams ~ Lease Mr and Mrs Searing ~ Real ale ~ Bar food (12-2.30(3 Sun), 6.30(6 Sat)-9; not Sun evening except during school hols) ~ Restaurant ~ (01394) 450271 ~ Children welcome ~ Dogs welcome ~ Open 11.30-3, 6-11; 11.30-11.30 Sat; 12-10.30 Sun; close 10pm Sun in winter ~ Bedrooms: £65S/£75S

Recommended by RS, ES, Edward Mirzoeff, Neil Powell, Conrad Freezer, Michael Dandy, Martin and Alison Stainsby, Malcolm and Pauline Pellatt

RATTLESDEN
TL9758 MAP 5

Brewers Arms ⑪

Off B1115 or A45 W of Stowmarket; Lower Road; IP30 0RJ

Friendly welcome and interesting food at a 16th-c village pub

Recently refurbished, this solidly built village local does well for its knowledgeably helpful service and well prepared food. There's a mix of pubby seating and more comfortable chairs, and a beamed lounge bar on the left winds back through standing timbers to the main eating area – a partly flint-walled room with a magnificent old bread oven. French windows open on to the garden. Greene King IPA and Old Speckled Hen and a changing guest beer are on handpump. They hold regular themed evenings; more reports please.

⑪ **Good, interesting bar food includes some inventive sandwiches and filled baguettes (like fish fingers and minted pea mayonnaise), starters such as stilton and port rarebit and toasted muffin topped with roast goats cheese and red peppers with pesto; main courses such battered haddock, chilli, green thai tiger prawn curry, vegetable steamed pudding with herb cream sauce, steak and Guinness puff pastry pie, roast ham hock with cider and mustard gravy and herb-crusted sole fillet with red onion and tomato salsa; and puddings including crunchy chocolate honeycomb slice and syrup sponge pudding.** *Starters/Snacks: £2.95 to £6.95. Main Courses: £8.95 to £9.95. Puddings: £4.95 to £5.95*

Greene King ~ Tenants Jeff and Nina Chamberlain ~ Real ale ~ Bar food (not Sun evening or Mon) ~ Restaurant ~ (01449) 736377 ~ Children welcome ~ Dogs welcome ~ Open 12-3, 6.30-midnight; 12-3.30, 9-11.30 Sun; closed Mon

Recommended by J F M and M West, I A Herdman, Charles and Pauline Stride

REDE
TL8055 MAP 5

Plough ⑨

Village signposted off A143 Bury St Edmunds—Haverhill; IP29 4BE

Promptly served, well liked food in a 16th-c pub, several wines by the glass and friendly service

With its lovely nestled-into-the-ground appearance, this cream-painted thatched old pub is a popular place for a meal, especially at weekends (it's best to book ahead to be sure of a table). Its pretty bar is traditional with low beams, comfortable seating and a solid-fuel stove in its brick fireplace. Adnams Bitter, Greene King IPA and a guest such as Fullers London Pride are on handpump, with quite a few wines by the glass; piped music. There are picnic-sets in front and a sheltered cottagey garden at the back.

⑪ **Big blackboards list a quickly changing range of food that is served in generous helpings. May be grilled scallops, shrimps with aioli, wild boar sausages with mash, braised local rabbit with tarragon and spring onion sauce, wild boar with red beans and sour plums, pork belly and apples braised in cider, monkfish with walnuts and capers, crispy belly of pork with bacon and sage butter, hock of local venison in red wine and port, and puddings such as bread and butter pudding and Amaretti chocolate crunch.** *Starters/Snacks: £3.95 to £6.95. Main Courses: £9.95 to £16.95. Puddings: £4.50*

Admiral Taverns ~ Tenant Brian Desborough ~ Real ale ~ Bar food (not Sun evening) ~ Restaurant ~ (01284) 789208 ~ Children welcome ~ Open 11-3, 6.30-midnight; 12-3, 7-11 Sun

Recommended by Marianne and Peter Stevens, Bettye Reynolds, John Saville, Philip and Susan Philcox, Adele Summers, Alan Black

---

'Children welcome' means the pub says it lets children inside without any special restriction. If it allows them in, but to restricted areas such as an eating area or family room, we specify this. Some pubs may impose an evening time limit. We do not mention limits after 9pm as we assume children are home by then.

REYDON

TM4977   MAP 5

Randolph 🛏

Wangford Road (B1126 just NW of Southwold); IP18 6PZ

Contemporary furnishings in chatty, relaxed bar, friendly service, Adnams beers, good wines and enjoyable food; bedrooms

The light and airy bar in this relaxed inn is popular with a good mix of customers, and there's a happy, chatty atmosphere, with those enjoying a pint of Adnams Bitter, Broadside, Extra or maybe a guest or local cider, sitting at high bar stools by the cream-painted bar counter. The rest of the room tends to be a mixture of drinkers and diners, with contemporary high-backed black leather dining chairs on parquet flooring around a mix of pale chunky wooden tables (each set with a nightlight in a little red glass holder), a few photographs of Southwold beach on the purple and white paintwork, and blinds for the big windows; there's also a couple of comfortable armchairs, and a high-backed settle by one table, just inside the door. Staff are friendly and efficient. The dining room, just across the way, has rush-seated, high-backed dining chairs around similar tables to those in the bar, red carpeting and a pretty little Victorian fireplace (filled with candles rather than logs); piped music, TV, games machine, darts and board games. Dogs are allowed in the little back bar only. There are picnic-sets on a decked area and on grass, and wheelchair access. The bedrooms are good value, with good breakfasts.

🍽 The nicely varied menu includes enoyable food such as chilli beef wrap, smoked chicken caesar salad, mussels with tomato and basil linguine, chinese braised pork belly with vegetable and noodle stir fry and hoi sin sauce, battered cod and hand-cut chips, fried bass with lemon aioli and fennel and radish salad, roast chump of lamb with rosemary jus, rib-eye steak, and puddings such as dark chocolate and marmalade tart with mascarpone and crème brûlée with rhubarab compote and ginger biscuits. *Starters/Snacks: £4.50 to £6.25. Main Courses: £9.95 to £13.95. Puddings: £4.50 to £5.95*

Adnams ~ Lease David and Donna Smith ~ Real ale ~ Bar food (12-2, 6.30-9) ~ Restaurant ~ (01502) 723603 ~ Children welcome ~ Dogs allowed in bar ~ Open 11-11 ~ Bedrooms: £65B/£100B

Recommended by Derek and Sylvia Stephenson, Tracey and Stephen Groves, Guy Vowles

ROUGHAM

TL9063   MAP 5

Ravenwood Hall 🍽 ♟ 🛏

Just off A14 E of Bury St Edmunds; IP30 9JA

Welcoming and civilised all-day bar in comfortable country house hotel with lovely grounds, fine wines, imaginative food and good service; peaceful A14 break

Of course, this very civilised place is a well run country house hotel (and very much the place for weddings), but its thoroughly welcoming all-day bar does warrant it a place in this book. Basically two fairly compact rooms, there are tall ceilings, gently patterned wallpaper and heavily draped curtains for big windows overlooking a sweeping lawn with a stately cedar. The part by the back serving counter is set for food, its nice furnishings including well upholstered settles and dining chairs, sporting prints and a log fire. Adnams Bitter and Broadside on handpump, good wines by the glass, mulled wine around Christmas, and freshly squeezed orange juice; neat unobtrusive staff give good service. The other end of the bar, the lounge area, has horse pictures, several sofas and armchairs with lots of plump cushions, one or two attractively moulded beams, and a good-sized fragment of early Tudor wall decoration above its big inglenook log fire; piped music and TV. They have a more formal quite separate restaurant. Outside, teak tables and chairs (some under a summer house) stand around a swimming pool; big enclosures by the car park hold geese and pygmy goats; croquet.

🍽 Unfailingly good and often imaginative, the attractively presented bar food uses their own smoked meats and fish and home-made preserves: sandwiches, grilled sardines with garlic and lemon, crab and risotto cake with stir-fried bean sprouts and pak choi, tagliatelle with watercress purée, seared scallops with pickled pink ginger and cauliflower purée, grilled calves kidneys with pearl barley risotto, tarragon and vermouth, fried pork escalope with capers, parsley and nut-brown butter and swiss chard and goats cheese tart and salad, sausage and mash, and well hung rib-eye steak; also puddings such as brioche pain perdu with roast pears and praline ice-cream and incredibly tempting ice-creams such as hazelnut and chocolate truffle and stem ginger. *Starters/Snacks: £5.50 to £9.75. Main Courses: £11.95 to £22.95. Puddings: £5.50 to £6.75*

Free house ~ Licensee Craig Jarvis ~ Real ale ~ Bar food (12-2.30, 7-9.30(10 Fri and Sat)) ~ Restaurant ~ (01359) 270345 ~ Children welcome ~ Dogs welcome ~ Open 9am-midnight ~ Bedrooms: £99.50B/£153B

Recommended by J F M and M West, Derek Field

SIBTON   TM3570   MAP 5
White Horse
Halesworth Road; IP17 2JJ

Friendly, nicely old-fashioned bar, good mix of customers, real ales and enjoyable food; bedrooms

Carefully run by well organised friendly licensees, this nicely laid-out 16th-c inn is decorated in a genuinely old-fashioned style. The comfortable bar has horsebrasses and tack on the walls, old settles and pews and a large inglenook fireplace with a roaring log fire. Adnams Bitter, Greene King Abbot and a guest such as Woodfordes Wherry on handpump, several wines by the glass and a local cider are served from the old oak-panelled counter, and there's a viewing panel showing the working cellar and its Roman floor. Steps take you up past an ancient partly knocked-through timbered wall into a carpeted gallery, and there's a smart dining room too. The big garden has plenty of seats, and the comfortable bedrooms are in a converted outbuilding.

[T] They put thought into sourcing ingredients for the enjoyable bar food and at lunchtime the menu sensibly includes pubby dishes such as sandwiches and rolls with warm fillings, ploughman's, ham and free-range eggs and lamb and mint sausages with redcurrant jus. In the evening there might be curried parsnip soup, confit duck leg with poached pear and hoi sin sauce, monk fish medallions in a thai coconut sauce with prawn and spring onion risotto, mushrooms in blue cheese sauce, sirloin steak with hand-cut chips, mushroom tagliatelle with chicken breast, pancetta and white wine sauce, and puddings such as treacle tart, almond and walnut dark chocolate torte, and east anglian cheeses. *Starters/Snacks: £4.25 to £6.00. Main Courses: £7.50 to £16.50. Puddings: £5.00*

Free house ~ Licensees Neil and Gill Mason ~ Real ale ~ Bar food (till 2.30 Sun) ~ Restaurant ~ (01728) 660337 ~ Children welcome ~ Dogs allowed in bar ~ Open 12-2.30(3.30 Sun), 6.30-11(10.30 Sun); closed Mon lunchtime ~ Bedrooms: £65S/£90B

Recommended by Mr and Mrs B Watt, Keith and Susan Moore, R Chessells, Neil Powell, Brent and Gillian Payne, Stephen Sheldrake, Philip Bishop, Stuart and Joan Bloomer, S Norton, Lorraine Brennan, Robin Jackson, K G Moore

SNAPE   TM4058   MAP 5
Golden Key 🍴 ♀
Priory Lane; IP17 1SA
SUFFOLK DINING PUB OF THE YEAR

Friendly landlord, cottagey rooms, and genuinely good quality food prepared from home-grown and reared produce

The friendly young landlord at this 17th-c pub brims with enthusiasm and is always aiming to offer his customers that little bit extra. He's recently put in a boules pitch, ordered a paella ring, pizza oven and barbecues for the terrace, and he puts on evenings where you can meet the wine-maker and the brewer or the like. His garden has a herb bed and greenhouse, and beyond are his sheep and pigs. He's moved his chickens to his new pub (the Oyster at Butley), and keeps his bees out of harm's way up the road from the pub. You can buy the honey in his little shop, which also sells sheepskins, cook books, local art and so forth. The traditional low-beamed lounge bar has an old-fashioned settle curving around a couple of venerable stripped tables on the chequer-board tiled floor, a winter open fire, a mix of pubby tables and chairs, fresh flowers, and local art and horsebrasses on the walls. This leads through to a cottagey little carpeted dining room with older-style stripped-pine furniture, and more local art including some embroidery and sheepskins on light yellow walls. The low-ceilinged larger dining room is similarly furnished and has small oil paintings of the landlord's animals and so forth on its walls. Adnams Bitter, Broadside and Explorer are on handpump, with a dozen wines by the glass, Aspall's cider and good coffee. Outside are two terraces (one for the morning and a suntrap evening one) both with contemporary wood and steel tables and chairs under large green parasols, and plenty of hanging baskets.

🍴 Using their own chickens, rare-breed sheep and pigs, home-butchered and hung beef, their own honey and herbs and other local produce, the rewarding bar food is not over elaborate, but instead places emphasis on these good ingredients (nor is the menu riddled with elaborate terms): sandwiches, ploughman's, chicken liver pâté with fig relish, whitebait with tartare sauce, potted shrimps, shredded sticky pork belly with apples and raisins on granary toast, main courses such as polenta-coated white bean sausages with tomato and coriander concasse, steak and kidney pudding, battered cod, roast chicken with courgette and lettuce sauce, steak with peppercorn sauce, and puddings such as chocolate and walnut brownie with butterscotch sauce and ice-cream, pistachio crème brûlée with shortbread and bread and butter pudding. *Starters/Snacks: £4.50 to £8.50. Main Courses: £8.50 to £15.00. Puddings: £5.50*

Adnams ~ Tenant Nick Attfield ~ Real ale ~ Bar food (12-2(2.30 Sun), 6.30(7 Sun)-9) ~ (01728) 688510 ~ Children welcome ~ Dogs allowed in bar ~ Open 12-3.30, 6(7 Sun)-11

Recommended by Tom Gondris, Peter and Pat Frogley, Charles and Pauline Stride, Simon Cottrell, Simon Rodway, David Rule, Terry and Jackie Devine, Ron and Betty Broom, Michael Dandy, Tony Middis, Neil Powell

Plough & Sail

The Maltings, Snape Bridge (B1069 S); IP17 1SR

Nicely placed dining pub extended airily around an older bar, real ales, food all day weekends, handy for the Maltings, seats outside

Deceptively large inside, this pink-washed roadside cottage has a light café feel to most of its partly open-plan interior – perhaps it's the wicker and café-style furnishings. Its older heart has a woodburning stove, some high bar chairs by the serving counter and rustic pine dining chairs and tables on terracotta tiling. Another cosy little room has comfortable blue sofas and low coffee tables. Most diners head for the simply furnished bar hall and spacious airy dining room with blue-cushioned dining chairs around straightforward tables on the light, woodstrip flooring and high ceilings with A-frame beams; motifs illustrating the history of the Maltings decorate the walls. Another restaurant upstairs has similar furnishings; piped music and darts. Adnams Best and Broadside and Explorer on handpump, and several wines by the glass. The flower-filled terrace has plenty of teak chairs and tables, and there are some picnic-sets in front of the building. The shops and other buildings in the attractive complex are interesting to wander through.

🍴 Much liked bar food includes sandwiches, filled baguettes and baked potatoes, ploughman's, garlic mushrooms in herb cream on garlic ciabatta, smoked fish platter, vegetable lasagne, steak and ale suet pudding, pork belly with cider apple chutney, grilled lamb steak with garlic and rosemary, and puddings such as apple and cinnamon crumble and dark chocolate pot with gingerbread. *Starters/Snacks: £3.95 to £6.25. Main Courses: £4.95 to £14.95. Puddings: £3.95 to £5.95*

Deben Inns ~ Licensees Steve and Louise Lomas ~ Real ale ~ Bar food (12-2.30, 6-9.30; 12-9.30 weekends) ~ Restaurant ~ (01728) 688413 ~ Children welcome ~ Dogs allowed in bar ~ Open 11-11

Recommended by Oliver and Sue Rowell, Tony Middis, Simon Cottrell, Louise Gibbons, Michael Dandy, Mr and Mrs A Curry

---

Every entry includes a postcode for use in Sat-Nav devices.

SOUTH ELMHAM

TM3385   MAP 5

St Peters Brewery

St Peter South Elmham; off B1062 SW of Bungay; NR35 1NQ

Lovely manor dating back to the 13th c with some fine original features, own-brew beers and inventive food

St Peter's Hall, a medieval manor house, is a stunning building. It dates back to the late 13th c but was much extended in 1539 using materials from the then recently dissolved Flixton Priory. It's simply but beautifully furnished with antique tapestries and furnishings that are completely in keeping with the building. As well as the bar there's a particularly dramatic high-ceilinged dining hall with elaborate woodwork, a big flagstoned floor, an imposing chandelier, and candles and fresh flowers on crisp white-clothed dining tables with smart dining chairs. A couple more appealing old rooms are reached up some steepish stairs. The brewery buildings are laid out around a courtyard and the three beers on handpump here are made using water from a 100-metre (300-ft) bore hole. Others are available from the shop. Outside, tables overlook the original moat where there are friendly black swans.

🍴 The pubby lunchtime menu includes, chicken liver pâté with cumberland port sauce, battered calamari with sweet chilli sauce, smoked salmon, ham, egg and chips, wild boar sausages, chicken curry, chicken chasseur, game pie and steak and ale puff pastry pie. The evening menu is a little more elaborate with pork medallions topped with stilton with masala and sage jus, bass fillet with lemon hollandaise sauce, duck breast with fruit sauce, and puddings such as eton mess and treacle sponge; Sunday roast. *Starters/Snacks: £5.00 to £7.00. Main Courses: £7.00 to £20.00. Puddings: £4.00 to £5.50*

Own brew ~ Licensee Sam Goodbourn ~ Real ale ~ Bar food (12-2(4 Sun), 7-9) ~ Restaurant ~ (01986) 782288 ~ Children over 11 evenings ~ Open 12-3, 6-10; 12-4 Sun; closed Sun evening, Mon (except bank hols)

Recommended by Mike and Shelley Woodroffe, Mrs Jane Kingsbury, Mrs M B Gregg, Peter and Pat Frogley, P Dawn, Mayur Shah, John Saville, Mike and Sue Loseby, the Didler, Simon Cottrell, Adrian Johnson, Tony Middis, Philip and Susan Philcox, Sue Demont, Tim Barrow

SOUTHWOLD

TM5076   MAP 5

Crown

High Street; IP18 6DP

Civilised and smart old hotel with relaxed bars, a fine choice of drinks, papers to read, lovely food and seats outside; bedrooms

Tables at this smart old hotel are available on a first-come first-served basis so you do need to arrive early for the extremely good, imaginative food. Thankfully, however, the cosy smaller back oak-panelled locals' bar, with its pubby atmosphere and red leatherette wall benches on the red carpet, is reserved for drinkers. Three or four Adnams beers are on handpump alongside a splendid wine list, with a monthly-changing choice of 20 interesting varieties by the glass or bottle, quite a few malt whiskies and local cider. The elegant beamed front bar has a relaxed, informal atmosphere, with courteous knowledgeable service, a stripped curved high-backed settle and other dark varnished settles, kitchen chairs and some bar stools, and a carefully restored and rather fine carved wooden fireplace; maybe newspapers to read. The tables out in a sunny sheltered corner are very pleasant, and the bedrooms are comfortable, light and airy.

🍴 Using local, organic produce, the interesting bar food (not cheap) includes smoked cod and butter bean soup, grilled sardines, seafood and vegetarian sharing platters, half a pint of shell-on prawns, mushroom and herb linguine, roast chicken with pea and leek risotto and morel mushroom sauce, lamb neck and liver with pease pudding and pea and mint dressing, confit duck leg with roast garlic mash and chorizo and lentil sauce, and puddings such as rhubarb and champagne jelly, warm pistachio and olive oil cake, and local cheeses. *Starters/Snacks: £4.95 to £7.00. Main Courses: £12.95 to £19.95. Puddings: £6.00 to £7.95*

Adnams ~ Manager Francis Guildea ~ Real ale ~ Bar food (12-2, 6.30-9) ~ (01502) 722275 ~
Children welcome ~ Dogs allowed in bar ~ Open 11(12 Sun)-3, 6-11(10.30 Sun) ~
Bedrooms: £90B/£140B

*Recommended by Tina and David Woods-Taylor, Mike and Sue Loseby, Sheila Topham, Tony and Shirley Albert,
David Rule, MJVK, P Dawn, Julia Mann, Michael Dandy, Guy Vowles, Sue Demont, Tim Barrow*

Harbour Inn 🍺

*Blackshore, by the boats; from A1095, turn right at the Kings Head, and keep on past the
golf course and water tower; IP18 6TA*

Bustling waterside pub with lots of outside seats, interesting nautical décor and real ales

This busy pub, well placed by the Blyth estuary, has a genuine nautical character (the
friendly licensee is even a lifeboatman) and serves terrific fish and chips. Tables outside
take in views of all the waterside activity and across the marshy fields towards the town
and lighthouse. Filled with seafaring bric-a-brac, the back bar has a wind speed indicator,
model ships, a lot of local ship and boat photographs, smoked fish hanging from a line
on a beam, a lifeboat line launcher and brass shellcases on the mantelpiece over a stove;
also, rustic stools and cushioned wooden benches built into its stripped panelling. The
tiny, low-beamed, tiled and panelled front bar has antique settles, and Adnams Bitter,
Broadside, Explorer and maybe a seasonal guest on handpump, a dozen wines by the
glass and local cider.

🍴 **Popular bar food includes lunchtime filled baguettes, grilled sardines, fried herring
roes, tasty sprats, scampi, fish pie, shepherd's pie, linguine with mushroom basil pesto,
daily specials such as pork and leek sausages, chicken with wine, tarragon and cream
sauce, stir-fried chilli beef and battered smoked haddock, and puddings such as lemon
and ginger sponge pudding and spicy oat apple crumble.** *Starters/Snacks: £4.50 to £7.95.
Main Courses: £8.95 to £11.95. Puddings: £4.95*

Adnams ~ Tenant Colin Fraser ~ Real ale ~ Bar food (12-2.30, 6-9) ~ Restaurant ~
(01502) 722381 ~ Children welcome ~ Dogs allowed in bar ~ Shindig first and third Sun of
month ~ Open 11-11; 12-10.30 Sun

*Recommended by Michael Dandy, Hilary Edwards, Dr Peter Crawshaw, Simon Rodway, Charles and Pauline Stride,
Mike and Sue Loseby, the Didler, Pete Baker, Tim Maddison*

Lord Nelson 🍺

East Street, off High Street (A1095); IP18 6EJ

**Cheerful town pub with lots of locals and visitors, excellent service, home-made pubby
food and good choice of drinks; seats outside**

This charmingly bow-windowed old pub is a just stone's throw up from the seafront and
has been in the same family for nearly 20 years now. It's very popular with lots of locals
and visitors coming and going, but even at its liveliest the good-natured service remains
friendly, quick and attentive. The partly panelled traditional bar and its two small side
rooms are kept spotless, with good lighting, a small but extremely hot coal fire, light
wood furniture on the tiled floor, lamps in nice nooks and corners and some interesting
Nelson memorabilia, including attractive nautical prints and a fine model of HMS *Victory*.
They serve a terrific range of well kept Adnams beers alongside Aspall's cider, and several
good wines by the glass; daily papers and board games. There are seats out in front with
a sidelong view down to the sea and more in a sheltered (and heated) back garden, with
the brewery in sight (and often the appetising fragrance of brewing in progress).
Disabled access is not perfect but is possible.

🍴 **Well liked bar food includes sandwiches, ploughman's, soup, ham with pineapple, half
a roast chicken with chips, vegetable or chicken curry, chilli con carne, popular beer-
battered cod, and daily specials.** *Starters/Snacks: £4.25 to £7.50. Main Courses: £6.75 to
£15.00. Puddings: £4.50*

Adnams ~ Tenant David Sanchez ~ Real ale ~ Bar food (12-7 bank hol Mons) ~ (01502) 722079
~ Children welcome in side rooms ~ Dogs welcome ~ Open 10.30-11; 12-10.30 Sun

Recommended by Mrs M B Gregg, Malcolm and Pauline Pellatt, Derek Field, Derek and Sylvia Stephenson, P Dawn, Michael Dandy, Terry Mizen, Pete Baker, Richard Armstrong, Mike and Sue Loseby, Simon Rodway, Ian and Nita Cooper, Bob and Margaret Holder, Charles and Pauline Stride, Mr and Mrs B Watt, the Didler, Sheila Topham, Tim Maddison, Sue Demont, Tim Barrow

STOKE-BY-NAYLAND   TL9836   MAP 5

Crown ★

Park Street (B1068); CO6 4SE

Smart dining pub with attractive modern furnishings, bistro-style food, fantastic wine choice and comfortable bedrooms

Of course, the emphasis at this busy, smart and friendly dining pub is on the interesting, bistro-style food, but those popping in for a drink and a chat are just as welcome. Most of the place is open to the three-sided bar servery, but there are two or three cosy tucked-away areas too. The main part, with a big woodburning stove, has quite a few closely spaced tables in a variety of shapes, styles and sizes; elsewhere, several smaller areas have just three or four tables each. Seating varies from deep armchairs and sofas to elegant dining chairs and comfortable high-backed woven rush seats – and there are plenty of bar stools.There are cheerful wildlife and landscape paintings on the pale walls, quite a few attractive table lamps, low ceilings (some with a good deal of stripped old beams), and floors varying from old tiles through broad boards or dark new flagstones to beige carpet; daily papers. Three real ales are from brewers such as Downton and Woodfordes on handpump and they offer a fantastic choice of 37 wines by the glass from a list of around 200 kept in an unusual glass-walled wine 'cellar' in one corner. A sheltered back terrace, with cushioned teak chairs and tables under big canvas parasols, looks out over a neat lawn to a landscaped shrubbery and there are many more picnic-sets out on the front terrace. Disabled access is good and the car park is big.

Imaginative modern food, using carefully sourced local produce, might include steak tartare with fried quail eggs and game chips, smoked sprats with mustard sauce, smoked haddock fishcake with buttered mussels and samphire, pappardelle with spring vegetables in lemon oil and basil, squid, chorizo, feta and broad bean salad, haddock and chips, southern fried rabbit with coleslaw, roast quails with pomegranate and goats cheese salad and rosemary and garlic parmentier potatoes, and puddings such as chocolate tart with peanut butter and jelly ice-cream, gooseberry, elderflower and vanilla fool with almond, and cheese platter with quince jelly. *Starters/Snacks: £4.25 to £7.25. Main Courses: £8.50 to £17.95. Puddings: £4.25 to £5.95*

Free house ~ Licensee Richard Sunderland ~ Real ale ~ Bar food (12-2.30, 6-9.30 (10 Fri, Sat); 12-9 Sun) ~ (01206) 262001 ~ Children welcome ~ Dogs allowed in bar ~ Open 11-11; 12-10.30 Sun ~ Bedrooms: £80S(£90B)/£110S(£135B)

Recommended by Mrs P Lang, MDN, Mark Farrington, Mrs Carolyn Dixon, Mrs M B Gregg, John Prescott, Ken Millar, Marion and Bill Cross

THORPENESS   TM4759   MAP 5

Dolphin

Just off B1353; village signposted from Aldeburgh; IP16 4NB

Neatly kept light and airy extended pub in interesting village, with enjoyable food and plenty of outside seating; bedrooms

At the heart of this quaint seaside holiday village with its boating lake (all purpose-built in the early 1900s) stands this neatly refurbished and extended pub. The main bar is a light airy room with an almost scandinavian feel: little candles in glass vases on each of the well spaced, pale wooden tables and a nice mix of old chairs on broad modern quarry tiles, a built-in cushioned seat in the sizeable bay window, a winter log fire in its brick fireplace, and fresh flowers on the wooden bar counter where they keep Adnams Bitter and Broadside and Brandon Rusty Bucket on handpump; piped local radio and TV. The public bar to the left of the door is more traditional with a mix of pubby furniture on the stripped wooden floor, some built-in cushioned wall seats with open 'windows' to the bar, and some fine old photographs of long-ago sporting teams, villagers and local scenes on the bottle-green planked walls; there's also a small area with a few high bar stools. The sizeable dining room has lots of windows hung with cheerful curtains, wide strips of coir matting on light wooden flooring, similar wooden furniture, and seaside prints. French windows lead on to a terrace with teak tables and chairs and, beyond that, there are picnic-sets on an extensive stretch of grass; you can hire electric bikes from here. The little village stores (where the pub is hoping to sell some of their meals) was just about to reopen on our visit in early spring.

🍴 As well as sandwiches, bar food might include roast pumpkin soup with sage croutons, confit guinea fowl terrine with grape and apple chutney, home-smoked trio of salmon, mackerel and prawns, grilled lamb chops with niçoise salad and poached egg, chicken caesar salad, linguine with chilli seafood sauce, grilled salmon with avocado salsa, and puddings such as baked lemon cheesecake with fig compote, pear and almond tart and chocolate pot with crème fraîche. *Starters/Snacks: £4.50 to £7.00. Main Courses: £7.95 to £15.00. Puddings: £3.25 to £6.25*

Free house ~ Licensee David Jones ~ Real ale ~ Bar food (12-2.30(3 Sun), 6-9.30; not Sun evening) ~ Restaurant ~ (01728) 454994 ~ Children welcome ~ Dogs welcome ~ Open 11-11(10.30 Sun); 11-3, 6-11, cl Mon in winter ~ Bedrooms: £55B/£85B

Recommended by Adrian Johnson, Charles and Pauline Stride

TUDDENHAM

TM1948   MAP 5

Fountain ♀

Village signposted off B1077 N of Ipswich; The Street; IP6 9BT

17th-c village dining pub with well thought-of contemporary cooking and plenty of outside seating

Though there is a nod to drinkers with space in the bar and Adnams Bitter on handpump, most people visit this neatly renovated 17th-c dining pub to enjoy the good cooking. Its several linked almost café-style rooms have heavy beams and timbering, stripped wooden floors, a mix of wooden dining chairs around a medley of light wood tables, an open fire and a few prints (including some Giles' ones; he spent some time here after World War II) on the white walls – décor is minimal. Several wines by the glass and piped music. Outside on the covered and heated terrace are wicker and metal chairs and wooden tables, and there tables under huge parasols out on a sizeable lawn.

🍴 As well as a two- and three-course set menu, bar food might include smoked chicken, apple and walnut salad, duck and spring onion samosas with sweet chilli ginger dip, salmon and crab sweet potato cake with pineapple and red pepper salsa, grilled gilt-head bream fillet with tomato and tarragon dressing, lemon and thyme marinated chicken breast, pork loin chop with cider and mustard cream sauce, grilled cod loin with broad bean and rocket salad, and puddings such as eton mess, apple, rhubarb and ginger crumble and chocolate brownie and pecan pie. *Starters/Snacks: £4.95 to £5.95. Main Courses: £8.00 to £14.95. Puddings: £4.75*

Punch ~ Lease Charles Lewis and Scott Davidson ~ Real ale ~ Bar food (12-2(3 Sun), 6-9(9.30 Sat); not Sun evening) ~ Restaurant ~ (01473) 785377 ~ Children welcome ~ Open 12-2.30, 6-11; 12-4 Sun; closed Sun evening, first week Jan

Recommended by Tom Gondris, J F M and M West, Mrs Carolyn Dixon, MDN, Christopher Sims

---

If a pub tries to make you leave a credit card behind the bar, be on your guard. The credit card firms and banks which issue them condemn this practice. After all, the publican who asks you to do this is in effect saying: 'I don't trust you'. Have you any more reason to trust his staff? If your card is used fraudulently while you have let it be kept out of your sight, the card company could say you've been negligent yourself – and refuse to make good your losses. So say that they can 'swipe' your card instead, but must hand it back to you. Please let us know if a pub does try to keep your card.

WALBERSWICK

Anchor ⓘⓘ ♀ ◧

Village signposted off A12; The Street (B1387); IP18 6UA

Good mix of locals and visitors in well run, attractively furnished inn, fine range of drinks, appetising modern cooking, and friendly, helpful service

The emphasis at this 1920s pub is very much on the relaxed informal dining, indeed they take your order and you pay at the table. Having said that, there can be a fairly lively atmosphere here by closing time. Light and airy with big windows, the bar is simply furnished with heavy stripped tables on original oak flooring, sturdy built-in wall seats cushioned in green leather and nicely framed black and white photographs of local fishermen and their boats on the colourwashed panelling. Log fires in the chimneybreast divide this room into two snug halves. They have loads of bottled beers from all over the world, 23 interesting wines by the glass including champagne and a pudding one, Adnams Bitter, Broadside and a guest such as Woodfordes Nelsons Revenge on handpump, and good coffee; particularly good service, daily papers and board games. Quite an extensive dining area, stretching back from a more modern-feeling small lounge on the left, is furnished much like the bar – though perhaps a bit more minimalist – and looks out on a good-sized sheltered and nicely planted garden. A garden bar serves the flagstoned terrace that overlooks the beach and village allotments, and the pub is right by the coast path. There's a pleasant walk across to Southwold and in summer there may be a pedestrian ferry. We're sure this will be a jolly nice place to stay once the bedrooms are refurbished.

🍴 Using local producers (and vegetables from their allotment), the extremely good food might include oysters, squid tempura with ginger soy sauce, salt cod galette with horseradish dressing, skate filled with brown shrimps and baked with tomatoes, garlic and capers, mutton and cannellini bean stew, stuffed rabbit with cider, prunes and pork with buttered polenta and roast butternut, rib-eye steak on potato, celeriac and parsnip dauphinoise with red wine sauce, and puddings such as hot chocolate pudding, lavender panna cotta and apple tarte tartin with crème fraîche. *Starters/Snacks: £4.75 to £9.75. Main Courses: £10.75 to £19.75. Puddings: £4.75*

Adnams ~ Lease Mark and Sophie Dorber ~ Real ale ~ Bar food (12-3, 6-9; 12-9 Aug) ~ (01502) 722112 ~ Children welcome ~ Dogs allowed in bar ~ Open 11-11 ~ Bedrooms: £75B/£90B

Recommended by Ryta Lyndley, Pete and Sue Robbins, Mr and Mrs B Watt, P Dawn, Simon Rodway, David Rule, Mike and Sue Loseby, Simon and Mandy King, Tom and Ruth Rees, Mrs M S Forbes, Adrian Johnson, Tracey and Stephen Groves, Jeff and Wendy Williams, Mrs Brenda Calver, P A Rowe, Rob and Catherine Dunster

Bell 🛏

Just off B1387; IP18 6TN

Close to beach, nice original features, fine choice of drinks and well liked food; bedrooms

The 400-year-old brick floors, well worn uneven flagstones and wonky steps and oak beams at this busy but characterful old pub were here when this sleepy little village was a flourishing port. The rambling traditional main bar has curved high-backed settles, tankards hanging from oars above the counter, a woodburning stove in the big fireplace, and between three and seven Adnams beers on handpump; a second bar has a very large open fire; darts and board games. The pub is in a fine setting close to the beach and most of the well appointed bedrooms look over the sea or river, while tables on the sizeable lawn are sheltered from the worst of the winds by a well placed hedge. The pub has a little shop selling craft and hand-made items.

🍴 Under the new licensee, bar food includes lunchtime sandwiches, potted shrimps, scotch eggs, chicken, bacon and blue cheese salad, chowder, fish and chips, fish pie, grilled chicken breast with linguine and rocket pesto, pork and leek sausages with red wine jus, and puddings such as chocolate and walnut brownie and banoffi tart *Starters/Snacks: £4.50 to £6.75. Main Courses: £8.50 to £13.95. Puddings: £5.25*

Adnams ~ Tenant Toby Dillaway ~ Real ale ~ Bar food (12-2.30, 6-9) ~ (01502) 723109 ~ Children in eating area of bar ~ Dogs allowed in bar and bedrooms ~ Open 11-11; 11-3, 6-11 weekdays in winter ~ Bedrooms: £70S/£80S(£120B)

WALDRINGFIELD

TM2844   MAP 5

Maybush

Off A12 S of Martlesham; The Quay, Cliff Road; IP12 4QL

Busy pub with tables outside making the most of a lovely riverside position; nautical décor and fair choice of drinks and bar food

You will need to get here early if you are after a table on the popular big waterside terrace (with steps right down to the water itself) on the banks of the River Deben. The knocked-through spacious bar is divided into separate areas by fireplaces or steps. There's a hint at a nautical theme, with an elaborate ship's model in a glass case, and a few more in a light, high-ceilinged extension, as well as lots of old lanterns, pistols and aerial photographs on buttermilk walls; piped music, cards, dominoes and an original Twister board. Three Adnams beers are on handpump with a fair choice of wines by the glass. There are river cruises available nearby but you have to pre-book.

🍴 **Popular uncomplicated food includes sandwiches, pâté of the day, deep-fried garlic mushrooms with mayonnaise, smoked salmon, burgers with various toppings, much enjoyed, fresh large fillets of cod and haddock, spinach and ricotta cannelloni, chicken curry, steak and kidney pudding, lamb shank with redcurrant and rosemary jus and a mixed grill.** *Starters/Snacks: £3.95 to £7.95. Main Courses: £7.95 to £16.95. Puddings: £4.95*

Adnams ~ Lease Steve and Louise Lomas ~ Real ale ~ Bar food (12-9.30) ~ Restaurant ~ (01473) 736215 ~ Children welcome ~ Dogs allowed in bar ~ Open 11-11

Recommended by Mrs Carolyn Dixon, David Blackburn, Bob and Margaret Holder, Howard and Sue Gascoyne

WESTLETON

TM4469   MAP 5

Crown

B1125 Blythburgh—Leiston; IP17 3AD

Lovely old coaching inn with a cosy chatty bar, plenty of dining areas, carefully chosen drinks and particularly good food; comfortable and stylish bedrooms

At the heart of this comfortably stylish old coaching inn is an attractive little bar with a lovely log fire and plenty of original features. Although the emphasis here is on the carefully cooked food, locals do pop in for the Adnams Bitter and three guests such as Brandon Rusty Bucket, Green Jack Lurcher and Nethergate Suffolk County on handpump; also local cider and a thoughtfully chosen wine list; piped music and board games. There's also a parlour, a dining room and conservatory. The charming terraced gardens have plenty of well spaced tables.

🍴 **With quite a modern twist, using only fresh local produce, their own bread, chutneys and ice-creams, the imaginative food (and sandwiches) might include cod on squid ink linguine with mussel broth, home-cured gravadlax with celeriac rémoulade, stout and ham hock welsh rarebit with fruit chutney and pine nut salad, mushroom tart with creamed leeks and crisp vegetables, main courses such as battered haddock and chips, roast duck breast with confit tomatoes and sherry vinegar jus, fried pollack with smoked eel tortellini, salsify purée and caper butter sauce, herb gnocchi, steak and kidney pudding, and puddings such as steamed orange pudding with vanilla custard and mascarpone panna cotta with star anise poached rhubarb.** *Starters/Snacks: £4.95 to £11.50. Main Courses: £10.50 to £25.00. Puddings: £4.50 to £6.50*

Free house ~ Licensee Matthew Goodwin ~ Real ale ~ Bar food (12-9.30) ~ Restaurant ~ (01728) 648777 ~ Children welcome ~ Dogs allowed in bar and bedrooms ~ Open 11-11; 12-10.30 Sun ~ Bedrooms: £115B/£140B

Recommended by Tony Middis, Michael and Ann Cole, Simon and Mandy King, Brian and Elizabeth Torr, Michael Dandy, K Almond, Lorraine Brennan, Edward Mirzoeff, Richard and Margaret McPhee

LUCKY DIP

Besides the fully inspected pubs, you might like to try these Lucky Dips recommended to us and described by readers (if you do, please send us reports: feedback@goodguides.com).

ALDEBURGH [TM4656]

☆ *Mill* IP15 5BJ [Market Cross Pl, opp Moot Hall]: Cheery 1920s seaside pub, good value food (not Sun evening) from sandwiches and baguettes to very local fish and crabs, well kept Adnams, decent coffee; three smallish rooms inc back dining room, log-effect gas fire, RNLI and RN Air Corps memorabilia, cushioned wall seats and padded stools, cosy beamed dining room; games machine, piped pop music may be loud; dogs welcome, bedrooms, open all day *(BB, Michael Dandy, the Didler, P Dawn)*

Wentworth IP15 5BB [Wentworth Rd]: Old-fashioned hotel not pub, popular with older people for good value above average bar food (not Sun evening), well kept Adnams and a good choice of wines by the glass, pleasant long-serving staff; conservatory, colourful seafront flagstoned terrace and suntrap sunken garden, bedrooms *(Michael Dandy, Terry Mizen)*

ASHLEY [TL6961]

Old Plough CB8 9DX [High St]: Enjoyable food in popular dining pub's bar and more expensive restaurant, good service; cl lunchtimes except Sun *(Adele Summers, Alan Black)*

BARNBY [TM4789]

Swan NR34 7QF [off A146 Beccles—Lowestoft; Swan Lane]: Plush beamed dining pub with Lowestoft connections, offering excellent choice of good fresh fish, Adnams and Greene King, good house wines; large bar with raised eating area, pleasant good-sized dining room, fishing décor *(Roger and Lesley Everett)*

BARTON MILLS [TL72173]

Olde Bull IP28 6AA [just S of Mildenhall; The Street]: Attractive rambling bars and restaurant, wide choice of home-made food all day from sandwiches and baguettes up, Sun roasts, big log fire, Adnams, Greene King and a local guest such as Brandon or Wolf, decent wine list and coffee; some live music; well behaved children welcome, 14 bedrooms, open all day *(BB)*

BECCLES [TM4290]

Kings Head NR34 9HA [New Market]: Hospitable hotel, Tudor behind handsome 18th-c red brick front and refitted in uncluttered unfussy style, with cheerful small bar, Adnams and guest beers; helpful staff, good range of enjoyable reasonably priced pub food, comfortable restaurant; in central pedestrian area, 12 bedrooms *(Jenny and Brian Seller, Peter and Eleanor Kenyon)*

BECK ROW [TL6877]

Bird in Hand IP28 8ES [The Street]: Bargain generous food, good beer range, lively atmosphere, friendly staff *(John and Elisabeth Cox)*

BILDESTON [TL9949]

☆ *Crown* IP7 7EB [B1115 SW of Stowmarket]: Good upmarket food in picturesque and impressively refurbished 15th-c timbered country inn, smart beamed main bar with leather armchairs and inglenook log fire, Adnams ales, good choice of wines by the glass, farm cider, good service, dining room; children welcome, disabled access and parking, nice tables out in attractive central courtyard, more in large attractive garden with decking, quiet comfortable bedrooms *(G Warboys, J F M and M West, Simon and Mandy King, LYM)*

BLYTHBURGH [TM4575]

White Hart IP19 9LQ [A12]: Open-plan family dining pub with fine ancient beams, woodwork and staircase; full Adnams ale range kept well, Aspall's cider and good choice of wines, good coffee, friendly efficient service; children in eating areas, spacious lawns looking down on tidal bird marshes, magnificent church over road, four bedrooms, open all day *(Edward Mirzoeff, Charles and Pauline Stride, LYM, Derek and Sylvia Stephenson)*

BOXFORD [TL9640]

White Hart CO10 5DX [Broad St]: Contemporary dining pub with light modern furniture and décor in an old building, enjoyable well priced generous food (can take a while), friendly helpful service, Greene King and a guest ale *(MDN, Mrs P Lang)*

BRAMFIELD [TM3973]

☆ *Queens Head* IP19 9HT [The Street; A144 S of Halesworth]: High-raftered redecorated lounge with scrubbed pine tables, impressive fireplace and some old farm tools, side room with comfortable fireside seats; well kept Adnams, Aspall's cider, several wines by the glass, seasonal home-made elderflower cordial, reasonably priced food with an emphasis on local organic, home-made bread and ice-creams; monthly live music (Fri); children (away from bar) and dogs welcome, cheerful blue-painted picnic-sets in pretty garden with dome-shaped willow bower, nice church next door *(Robert F Smith, Neil Powell, LYM, Tina and David Woods-Taylor, Anne Morris, Roger and Lesley Everett, J F M and M West, Simon Rodway, Gerry and Rosemary Dobson, Derek and Sylvia Stephenson, Richard and Margaret McPhee, Mike and Shelley Woodroffe)*

BRENT ELEIGH [TL9348]

☆ *Cock* CO10 9PB [A1141 SE of Lavenham]: Timeless thatched country local now serving food; Adnams, Greene King Abbot and a guest, organic farm cider, cosy ochre-walled snug and second small room, antique flooring tiles, lovely coal fire, old photographs of village (church well worth a look); darts and toad in the hole; well behaved children and dogs welcome, picnic-sets up on side grass with summer hatch service, attractive inn-sign, one bedroom, open all day Fri-Sun *(Mrs Carolyn Dixon, the Didler, Mrs M B Gregg, BB)*

BROCKLEY GREEN [TL7247]

☆ *Plough* CO10 8DT: Friendly neatly kept knocked-through bar, beams, timbers and stripped brick, scrubbed tables and an open fire; enjoyable food from lunchtime sandwiches to some enterprising dishes and good puddings, cheerful staff, Greene King IPA, Woodfordes Wherry and a guest beer, good choice of wines by the glass and malt whiskies, restaurant; children and dogs welcome, extensive attractive grounds with good tables and terrace, newly refurbished bedrooms, lovely situation *(Dave Braisted, Marianne and Peter Stevens, LYM)*

BURY ST EDMUNDS [TL8563]

☆ *Rose & Crown* IP33 1NP [Whiting St]: Cheerful black-beamed town local with affable helpful landlord, bargain simple lunchtime home cooking (not Sun), particularly well kept Greene King ales inc Mild, pleasant lounge with lots of piggy pictures and bric-a-brac; good games-oriented public bar, rare separate off-sales counter; pretty back courtyard, open all day wkdys *(Julia Mann, Pete Baker, Tom and Jill Jones)*

BUTLEY [TM3650]

Oyster IP12 3NZ [B1084 E of Woodbridge]: Friendly country local, well kept Adnams, good value fresh food (not Sun evening), good wine by the glass, helpful staff; stripped-pine tables and pews, high-backed settles and more conventional seats on bare boards, good coal fire; darts, dominoes; children and dogs welcome *(LYM, Jeremy and Jane Morrison)*

CAVENDISH [TL8046]

☆ *George* CO10 8BA [The Green]: Attractively laid out as more restaurant than pub, good food from interesting lunchtime sandwiches and light dishes to a nice slant on pubby favourites; good atmosphere and charming efficient service, beamed and bow-windowed front part, further good-sized eating area, good value wines, good coffees and teas; tables out in garden behind, lovely village *(Hunter and Christine Wright, BB)*

CLARE [TL7645]

Bell CO10 8NN [Market Hill]: Large timbered inn with comfortably rambling lounge, log fires, splendidly carved black beams, old panelling and woodwork; good friendly service, well kept Greene King ales and decent wines, enjoyable food from sandwiches up inc afternoon teas; dining room, conservatory opening on to terrace, darts and pool in public bar; games machine, TV; nice bedrooms off back courtyard (special village, lovely church), open all day Sun *(Mrs Margo Finlay, Jörg Kasprowski, Clive Flynn, Tom and Jill Jones, LYM)*

COCKFIELD [TL9152]

Three Horseshoes IP30 0JB [Stows Hill (A1141 towards Lavenham)]: New licensees for two-bar thatched village local dating from the 14th c; raftered main area with notable crown post, log fire, well kept Adnams, Greene King and Woodfordes, good food in dining lounge and conservatory; piped music; children welcome, picnic-sets in front and back gardens *(Dr and Mrs Michael Smith)*

COTTON [TM0667]

☆ *Trowel & Hammer* IP14 4QL [off B1113 N of Stowmarket; Mill Rd]: Spreading linked areas, lots of beamery and timber baulks, plenty of wheelbacks and one or two older chairs and settles around a mix of tables, big log fire; Adnams and Greene King, some food available all day; may be live music Sat; piped music, pool, games machine, juke box; well behaved children welcome, colourful back garden great for them, swimming pool; open all day *(LYM, Ian and Nita Cooper, M Walker, Andrew Gardner)*

DENNINGTON [TM2867]

Queens Head IP13 8AB [A1120; The Square]: Nicely refurbished beamed and timbered Tudor pub prettily placed by the church, L-shaped main bar, Adnams and may be a guest, local cider, good food (can take a while) inc creative children's menu; piped music; children in family room, side lawn by noble lime trees, pond at back with ducks and carp, backs on to Dennington Park with swings and so forth *(LYM, Eamonn and Natasha Skyrme)*

DUNWICH [TM4770]

☆ *Ship* IP17 3DT [St James St]: Appealing traditional tiled bar with good fish and chips, Adnams and Mauldons from antique handpumps, woodburner, and lots of sea prints and nauticalia, simple conservatory; children and dogs welcome, large sheltered garden, bedrooms, open all day *(Julia Mann, Mrs S Bezant, LYM, Tracey and Stephen Groves, Mike and Sue Loseby, Tim Maddison, M and GR, Giles and Annie Francis, Tony Middis, P Dawn, Michael Dandy)*

EAST BERGHOLT [TM0734]

☆ *Kings Head* CO7 6TL [Burnt Oak, towards Flatford Mill]: Enjoyable food inc unusual dishes in popular well laid out dining pub, friendly obliging staff, well kept Adnams and Greene King, decent wines and coffee; beamed lounge with comfortable sofas in softly lit part by servery, Constable prints and book, two-room restaurant; quiet piped music; garden and small terrace *(Mike and Mary Carter, MDN, N R White, Mrs Carolyn Dixon, BB)*

ERWARTON [TM2134]

☆ *Queens Head* IP9 1LN [off B1456 Ipswich—Shotley Gate]: 16th-c pub newly refurbished for more emphasis on dining side, bowed oak beams, wooden flooring, sea paintings and photographs, coal fire; Adnams, Greene King and Shepherd Neame, conservatory; piped music; children allowed lunchtimes in some areas, front picnic-sets under summer hanging baskets may have view to Stour estuary (if foliage trimmed enough), cl Sun evening *(LYM, Christopher Sims, Mrs Carolyn Dixon)*

FELIXSTOWE FERRY [TM3237]

Ferry Boat IP11 9RZ: Much modernised 17th-c pub tucked between golf links and dunes nr harbour, Martello tower and summer rowing-boat ferry; good value food from snacks to fresh fish and tasty curries (lunch stops 2pm on the dot), Adnams and Greene King, good log fire; piped music, busy summer wknds, and they may try to keep your credit card while you eat; dogs welcome, tables out in front, on the green opposite and in fenced garden, good coast walks *(Mrs Hazel Rainer, David Blackburn, LYM)*

FELSHAM [TL9457]

Six Bells IP30 0PJ [Church Rd]: Friendly open-plan beamed country local with nice décor, Greene King and guests in good lively bar with darts and cribbage, fresh flowers in quiet cosy restaurant, good pubby food from landlord/chef inc home-baked bread; children and dogs welcome *(Ben and Chris Francis, J F M and M West, Clive Flynn)*

FORWARD GREEN [TM0959]

☆ *Shepherd & Dog* IP14 5HN [A1120 E of Stowmarket]: Smart modern dining-pub refurbishment with attractive pastel décor, comfortable dining tables and some sofas; good interesting food in contemporary bar (inc tempting nibbles) and restaurant, well kept Greene King IPA and Fullers London Pride, good wines by the glass and coffee; disabled access, terrace tables, cl Sun evening and Mon *(BB, Ian and Nita Cooper, Tom Gondris, Charles and Pauline Stride)*

FRAMLINGHAM [TM2863]

Castle Inn IP13 9BP [Castle St]: Small and smartly decorated next to the castle (which has no food); decent food (not evenings) from interesting snacks to specials, cream teas too, three Adnams beers, Aspall's cider, good service even when busy; juke box; children and dogs welcome, front picnic-sets overlooking duck pond, more in pretty back courtyard, open all day *(Ian Phillips)*

Crown IP13 9AP [Market Hill]: Traditional heavy-beamed front bar, log-fire lounge and eating area; Greene King ales, several wines by the glass, contemporary back extension restaurant (evenings, Sun carvery); courtyard tables, 14 comfortable period bedrooms *(LYM, Ian and Nita Cooper, Michael Dandy)*

HADLEIGH [TM0143]

Donkey IP7 6DN [Stone St (A1141 N)]: Recently renovated and enlarged as a restaurant with bar, good food, pleasant ambience, Adnams *(Mrs Carolyn Dixon)*

HALESWORTH [TM3877]

☆ *Angel* IP19 8AH [thoroughfare (now pedestrianised)]: Civilised, comfortable and substantial, with lounge bar looking out on pedestrianised street from tall windows,

more tables in roofed-in galleried coachyard with Act of Parliament clock; three well priced Adnams ales, nice wines, busy espresso machine, good log fire, friendly efficient staff; sandwiches and baps all day, cheap traditional bar dishes and pizzas, sizeable italian restaurant; piped music, small inner bar with machines; children welcome (but no babies/toddlers after 7pm), seven well equipped bedrooms, car park – useful here, open all day *(Keith and Susan Moore, BB)*

HARTEST [TL8352]

☆ *Crown* IP29 4DH [B1066 S of Bury St Edmunds]: Pink-washed old pub by the church behind a pretty village green; friendly staff, enjoyable food inc good value mid-week lunches, well kept Greene King, smart minimalist décor with quality tables and chairs on tiled floor, good log fire in impressive fireplace, two dining rooms and conservatory; piped music; children and dogs welcome, tables on big back lawn and in sheltered side courtyard, good play area *(John Saville, LYM)*

HAWKEDON [TL7953]

Queens Head IP29 4NN [between A143 and B1066]: Charming unpretentious 17th-c village pub, good choice of well kept changing regional ales, friendly helpful staff; log fire, good sensibly priced food, pretty dining room; tables outside front and back in a big garden, cl wkdy lunchtimes, open all day wknds *(Marianne and Peter Stevens)*

HORRINGER [TL8261]

☆ *Beehive* IP29 5SN [A143]: This rambling series of cottagey rooms has been a very popular Main Entry in previous editions under its long-serving licensees – but they plan to leave as this new edition reaches the shops, so we have no way of knowing how things will turn out; we hope the new people will prove just as popular – news, please *(LYM)*

HUNTINGFIELD [TM3473]

Huntingfield Arms IP19 0PU [The Street]: Handsome late 18th-c building by the green, friendly licensees, enjoyable inexpensive food inc home-smoked fish, well kept Adnams and a guest beer; light wood tables and chairs, beams and stripped brickwork, blazing woodburner in front room; pleasant back games area with pool, restaurant; tables outside, cl Sun evening *(Charman family, John M Murphy)*

IPSWICH [TM1743]

Brewery Tap IP3 0AZ [Cliff Rd]: Cottagey early 19th-c building nestling under former Tolly brewery, looking over road to docks, brewing their own Cliff Quay Tolly Roger, with guests such as Crouch Vale and Earl Soham; decent food (not Sun evening), friendly staff; piped music; wheelchair access *(LYM, Allison and Graham Thackery)*

IXWORTH [TL9370]

Pykkerel IP31 2HH [High St; just off A143 Bury—Diss]: Friendly and attractive Elizabethan pub with several rooms off central servery, big fireplaces, antique tables and comfortable old settles, oriental rugs on polished boards, beams, stripped brickwork, panelling and paintings; sensibly priced food (not Sun evening) from sandwiches to a dozen or more local fish dishes, well kept Greene King ales, restaurant; children and dogs welcome, comfortable bedrooms *(Ryta Lyndley, LYM)*

KENTFORD [TL7066]

Cock CB8 7PR [Bury Rd, just off A14]: Comfortable and attractive, with inglenook log fire and beautiful carved beams, good interesting range of food, friendly service, Greene King real ales; airy restaurant; neat garden *(M and GR)*

KESGRAVE [TM2346]

Kesgrave Hall IP5 2PU [Hall Rd]: Recently refurbished country hotel with Greene King ales in comfortably contemporary bare-boards bar, enjoyable all-day bistro food; attractive heated terrace with huge retractable awning, 15 stylish bedrooms *(J F M and M West)*

LAVENHAM [TL9149]

Swan CO10 9QA [High St]: Smart, well equipped and by no means cheap hotel incorporating handsome medieval buildings, well worth a look for its appealing network of beamed and timbered alcoves and more open areas, inc a peaceful little tiled-floor inner bar with leather chairs and memorabilia of its days as the local for US 48th Bomber Group; well kept Adnams and a guest beer, wide choice of food from good sandwiches up, good young staff, informal eating area as well as lavishly timbered restaurant; children welcome, sheltered courtyard garden *(Mrs Carolyn Dixon, LYM, Tom and Jill Jones)*

LONG MELFORD [TL8645]

☆ *Bull* CO10 9JG [Hall St (B1064)]: Medieval small hotel, beautifully carved beams in old-fashioned timbered front lounge, antique furnishings, log fire in huge fireplace, more spacious back bar with sporting prints; well kept Greene King ales, good reasonably priced food, cheerful helpful staff, daily papers, restaurant; children welcome, courtyard garden, open all day Sat, Sun *(I A Herdman, LYM)*

Crown CO10 9JL [Hall St]: Partly 17th-c, doing well under newish young landlord and chef, fresh traditional and more contemporary food using local ingredients, real ales such as Adnams and Nethergate from central servery with unusual bar chairs; big log fire, some stripped brickwork and nicely placed furnishings, restaurant; attractive terrace with big awnings, 11 well equipped bedrooms *(LYM, Angela Cole)*

MARKET WESTON [TL9777]

☆ *Mill* IP22 2PD [Bury Rd (B1111)]: Opened-up pub with attractively priced lunches using local produce, OAP discounts, thoughtful evening menu, Adnams, Greene King IPA, Woodfordes Wherry and an Old Chimneys beer from the village brewery; local farm

cider, enthusiastic effective service, two log fires, dominoes; children welcome, small well kept garden *(Derek Field)*

MARTLESHAM [TM2446]

☆ *Black Tiles* IP12 4SP [off A12 Woodbridge—Ipswich; Black Tiles Lane]: Spotless and spacious family dining pub, comfortable contemporary bistro-style restaurant with garden room (children allowed here), big woodburner in appealing bar, wide choice of good generous home-made food using local produce, served quickly by smart helpful staff, daily roast; Adnams and a guest beer, good choice of wines by the glass; attractive garden with heated terrace tables, play area, open all day *(Danny Savage, LYM)*

MELTON [TM2850]

Wilford Bridge IP12 2PA [Wilford Bridge Rd]: Light, roomy and well organised, with reliable good value food all day inc local fish in two spacious carpeted bars and restaurant; Adnams and smaller brewery ales such as Brandons, good wines by the glass, prompt friendly service; terrace picnic-sets, nearby river walks, handy for Sutton Hoo, open all day *(P Clark, Gordon Neighbour)*

ORFORD [TM4249]

Crown & Castle IP12 2LJ: Restaurant with rooms rather than pub (new head chef expected to continue good food reputation – reports, please); small smartly minimalist bar (used largely for pre-meal drinks – well kept Greene King and good wines by the glass), tables outside, residents' garden; 18 good chalet bedrooms *(Conrad Freezer, Don More, M and GR, Michael Dandy)*

PAKENHAM [TL9267]

Fox IP31 2JU [signed off A1088 and A143 S of Norwich]: Neatly kept beamed village pub under new licensees, enjoyable good value pub food inc popular Sun lunch (booking advised), Adnams and changing guest ales, good choice of wines by the glass; log fire, compact dining room (old reading room); children and dogs welcome, disabled access, tables in big streamside garden with barbecue, boules and summer bar, open all day Sun *(anon)*

PETTISTREE [TM2954]

☆ *Greyhound* IP13 0HP [off A12 just S of Wickham Market]: Old beamed village pub reopened after long closure by charming new owners, good imaginative home-made food (not Mon), Earl Soham, Greene King and Woodfordes Wherry, bottled organic and fruit beers, unusual soft drinks; plenty of neat tables in carpeted bar and pleasant dining room, open fires; folk evenings 2nd Mon of the month; garden picnic-sets *(Mrs Hilarie Taylor, Justin and Emma King)*

Three Tuns IP13 0HW [off B1438 (old A12) just S of Wickham Market; Main Rd]: Dining pub/hotel with comfortably chintzy armchairs and sofas in linked rooms with old-fashioned lamps, decorative china, old master reproductions, carpet or highly polished boards; reasonably priced food, well kept Greene King, good coffee, pleasant service, log fire, conservatory; may be piped music, piano one end; bedrooms *(Gordon Neighbour, BB)*

POLSTEAD [TL9840]

Brewers Arms C06 5BZ [A1071 Ipswich—Sudbury, away from village]: Good value tasty pub food, good fire in old two-way fireplace, Greene King beers *(Giles and Annie Francis)*

Cock C06 5AL [signed off B1068 and A1071 E of Sudbury, then pub signed; Polstead Green]: Beamed and timbered local with unassuming pink-walled bar, woodburner and open fire; well kept Adnams, Greene King IPA and a guest, good choice of wines and malt whiskies, good coffee, welcoming landlord and friendly young staff, bar food from lunchtime baguettes up; smarter light and airy barn restaurant; piped music; good disabled access and facilities, children and dogs welcome, picnic-sets out overlooking the quiet green, side play area, cl Mon *(BB, Martin and Alison Stainsby, Tom and Jill Jones, John Prescott, Hazel Morgan, Bernard Patrick, N R White)*

RAMSHOLT [TM3041]

☆ *Ramsholt Arms* IP12 3AB [signed off B1083; Dock Rd]: Lovely isolated spot overlooking River Deben, easy-going open-plan nautical bar busy on summer wknds and handy for bird walks and Sutton Hoo; wide choice of quickly served food inc good value seafood and game, you can just have a pudding, two sittings for Sun lunch, Adnams and a guest beer, decent wines by the glass, winter mulled wine, good log fire; children welcome and very happy here, plenty of tables outside with summer afternoon terrace bar (not Sun), roomy bedrooms with stunning view, open all day *(LYM, J F M and M West, John Coatsworth, Mr and Mrs M J Girdler)*

REDGRAVE [TM0477]

Cross Keys IP22 1RW [The Street]: Friendly village local with comfortable lounge bar, Adnams, Greene King and a guest beer, decent wines, pubby food *(A Black)*

SAXTEAD GREEN [TM2564]

Old Mill House IP13 9QE [B1119; The Green]: Roomy dining pub across the green from the windmill, beamed carpeted bar, neat country-look flagstoned restaurant extension, wooden tables and chairs, wide choice of generous good value fresh food inc daily carvery, good friendly service, well kept Adnams, decent wines; discreet piped music; children very welcome, attractive and sizeable garden with terrace and good play area *(LYM, Eamonn and Natasha Skyrme)*

SHIMPLING STREET [TL8753]

Bush IP29 4HU [off A134 Sudbury—Bury; The Street]: Friendly pub with enjoyable good value food inc bargain lunches Tues-Thurs, neat dining room; good-sized garden *(Mrs Carolyn Dixon)*

SHOTTISHAM [TM3244]

Sorrel Horse IP12 3HD [Hollesley Rd]: Charming two-bar thatched Tudor local, attentive helpful landlord, Greene King and

guest ales tapped from the cask, limited home-made food from cobs up; good log fire in tiled-floor bar with games area, attractive dining room, game prints; tables out on the green, open all day wknds *(J F M and M West, the Didler)*

SNAPE [TM3958]

Crown IP17 1SL [Bridge Rd (B1069)]: Small beamed pub revamped under newish tenants, inglenook log fire, Adnams ales, enjoyable fresh food; children and dogs welcome, newly landscaped garden, three bedrooms up steep stairs *(Simon Rodway, Tom and Ruth Rees, Christopher Sims, Jean and Douglas Troup, LYM, Brian and Elizabeth Torr, George Cowie, Frances Gosnell)*

SOUTH COVE [TM4982]

Five Bells NR34 7JF [B1127 Southwold—Wrentham]: Friendly, well run and spacious creeper-covered pub with stripped pine; three Adnams ales, local Aspall farm cider, generous good value pubby meals in bar and airy restaurant inc Sun lunch, good service; tables out in front, play area, caravan site in back paddock, bedrooms *(RS, ES)*

SOUTHWOLD [TM5076]

☆ *Red Lion* IP18 6ET [South Green]: Good atmosphere, warm friendly service, reasonably priced pubby food from sandwiches up, well kept Adnams; big windows looking over the green towards the sea, pale panelling, ship pictures, lots of brassware and copper, pub games, separate dining room; children and dogs welcome, lots of tables outside, right by the Adnams retail shop *(BB, Roger and Lesley Everett, Sue Demont, Tim Barrow, Ian and Nita Cooper, Michael Dandy, P Dawn, Janet Whittaker)*

STANSFIELD [TL7851]

Compasses C010 8LN [High St]: Italian licensees doing good italian food inc pasta night (Weds), fish night (Fri) and lovely puddings – best to book as they serve 20 max; charming rustic atmosphere and décor *(Wendy Dye)*

STOKE-BY-NAYLAND [TL9836]

☆ *Angel* C06 4SA [B1068 Sudbury—East Bergholt]: Handsomely beamed dining pub recently taken over and refurbished by small group, helpful manageress; stripped brickwork and timbers, a mix of pubby furnishings, big log fire, well kept Adnams and guests, good choice of wines by the glass, friendly efficient service; enjoyable food from shortish menu inc good value all-day Sun roasts, takeaway fish and chips, high-ceilinged restaurant with gilt clocks and mirrors; quiz nights, some live music; children welcome, sheltered terrace, comfortable bedrooms, good breakfast, open all day *(Tom and Jill Jones, Brian and Elizabeth Tora, Hazel Morgan, Bernard Patrick, N R White, LYM)*

SUDBURY [TL8741]

☆ *Waggon & Horses* C010 1HJ [Church Walk]: Appealing bar, interesting and comfortable, with good choice of reasonably priced fresh food inc good sandwiches, proper pies and good value OAP deals, well kept Greene King ales, decent house wines; friendly helpful staff, log fire, boothed dining room, games area; very busy wkdy lunchtimes, get there early or book; pleasant walled garden with picnic-sets, handy for Gainsborough House *(MLR)*

UFFORD [TM2952]

White Lion IP13 6DW [Lower St (off B1438, towards Eyke)]: 16th-c village pub tucked away nr quiet stretch of River Deben; well kept Adnams, Earl Soham Victoria and Woodfordes Wherry tapped from the cask (August beer festival), enjoyable home-made food inc Sun roasts; good central log fire, flagstone floors, rustic furniture, knick-knacks; nice views from outside tables, barbecue *(Keith Sale)*

WANGFORD [TM4679]

☆ *Angel* NR34 8RL [signed just off A12 by B1126 junction; High St]: Handsome 17th-c village inn with well spaced tables in light and airy bar, Adnams, Fullers London Pride, Greene King Abbot and Shepherd Neame Spitfire, decent wines, good value plentiful food from sandwiches up; friendly efficient service, family dining room; comfortable bedrooms (the church clock sounds on the quarter), good breakfast *(Brett Massey, Charles and Pauline Stride, Marcus Mann, LYM)*

WESTLETON [TM4469]

☆ *White Horse* IP17 3AH [Darsham Rd, off B1125 Blythburgh—Leiston]: Homely comfort and friendly staff in traditional pub with generous straightforward food inc good sandwiches, OAP bargain lunch, well kept Adnams; unassuming high-ceilinged bar with bric-a-brac and central fire, steps down to attractive Victorian back dining room; children in eating area, picnic-sets in cottagey back garden with climbing frame, more out by village duck pond, bedrooms, good breakfast *(Michael Dandy, Stephen and Jean Curtis, Robert F Smith)*

WHEPSTEAD [TL8258]

White Horse IP29 4SS [off B1066 S of Bury; Rede Rd]: As we went to press, this was being extensively refurbished by the landlord of the Beehive at Horringer (good dining

pub – see above), with plans to open in summer 2009 *(anon)*

WISSETT [TM3679]

Plough IP19 0JE [The Street]: Newish licensees boosting their real ale quality in this refurbished open-plan pub dating from the 17th c; late July beer festival, good value pub food; teak tables and chairs outside *(anon)*

WOODBRIDGE [TM2648]

Cherry Tree IP12 4AG [opp Notcutts Nursery, off A12; Cumberland St]: Comfortably worn-in open-plan pub, well kept Adnams and guest ales helpfully described (beer festival), good wines by the glass, welcoming helpful staff, pubby food inc breakfast; beams and two log fires, pine furniture, old local photographs and aircraft prints; children welcome, garden with play area, three good bedrooms in adjoining barn conversion, open all day wknds *(Tony and Shirley Albert)*

Olde Bell & Steelyard IP12 1DZ [New St, off Market Sq]: Ancient and unpretentious with friendly helpful new licensees, two smallish bars and compact dining section, Greene King IPA and Abbot, food from enjoyable baguettes up, darts; steelyard still overhanging street; back terrace *(Rob and Catherine Dunster, Jeremy and Jane Morrison)*

Seckford Hall IP13 6NU [signed off A12 bypass, N of town; Seckford Hall Rd, Great Bealings]: Civilised Tudor country-house hotel not pub, but its dark and friendly comfortable bar makes a good coffee break, and it has good bar snacks and reasonably priced set lunches, helpful staff, Adnams, good wines inc lots of half bottles; also good value if not cheap restaurant meals, sunny conservatory; terrace tables, extensive grounds with lake, leisure centre and swimming pool, good bedrooms *(R and S Bentley, Mrs Ann Faulkner, J F M and M West)*

YAXLEY [TM1173]

Auberge IP23 8BZ [Ipswich Rd (A140 Ipswich—Norwich)]: Recently extended pub with good food using local supplies, good service; big fireplace in pretty dining area, beams and timbers; bedrooms *(Patrick Harrington, Sarah Flynn)*

Post Office address codings confusingly give the impression that some pubs are in Suffolk, when they're really in Cambridgeshire, Essex or Norfolk (which is where we list them).

Surrey

Surrey, so often thought of as commuter belt, is actually England's most wooded county, with a lot of attractive walking country, and some lovely old pubs. Most serve good food, as do our two interesting new entries, the Red Barn at Blindley Heath and, particularly, Jolly Farmers at Buckland. The two hottest contenders for Surrey Dining Pub of the Year are the Parrot at Forest Green (with its own farm) and the charmingly run Inn at West End. By a narrow margin the Inn at West End takes the title. Keen pricing is rare in Surrey pubs, so all the more praise to Marneys in Esher, Surrey's first Bargain Award winner in several years. For a good range of fair-priced beers, head for the Jolly Farmer in Bramley or Surrey Oaks at Newdigate; the Plough at Coldharbour brews its own Leith Hill beers. Strong Lucky Dip pubs are the Prince of Wales in Esher, Red Lion at Horsell, Castle in Ottershaw and Royal Oak in Pirbright; there are currently good special deals at the Chef & Brewer and Vintage Inns chains, both of which have some prime examples here. Hogs Back is the pre-eminent small local brewery, with Surrey Hills leading several other good microbreweries.

BLINDLEY HEATH   TQ3645   MAP 3

Red Barn ♀
Tandridge Lane, just off B2029, which is off A22; RH7 6LL

Splendidly converted farmhouse and barn, food all day starting with breakfast, lots of space and character

---

The unusual granite tables outside are the first hint that this pretty 300-year-old farmhouse isn't quite as traditional as it appears. Inside are plenty of appealing modern twists around the scrubbed beams and timbers, but the chief glory of the place is the huge barn at the far end, dramatically converted into a comfortably upscale dining room that feels like the grand hall of a slightly mad country house. Funky round modern lights (and a large model plane) hang from the soaring rafters, while one wall is dominated by shelves of books stretching high above the window; another wall has antlers, and there's a distinctive woodburning stove among the central tables. There are cosier areas on either side, each with its own character, and an eclectic mix of modern furnishings includes everything from leather or wicker chairs to cow-print pouffes. Efficient, smartly dressed staff take your order at the table, but this is very much a pub, with bar billiards and a pile of board games in the adjacent bar, along with sofas by another sizeable fireplace. A lighter farmhouse-style room they call the pantry has big wooden tables and a red cooking range; it's where they serve breakfast. Two real ales like Sharps Doom Bar or Westerham British Bulldog, and a good wine list. As we went to press they'd been having a big farmers' market the first Saturday morning of each month; they may also have summer barbecues, and various food promotions and events.

The details at the end of each Main Entry start by saying whether the pub is a free house, or if it belongs to a brewery or pub group (which we name).

🍴 Not cheap, but worth it, the well presented bar food relies on fresh local ingredients, and from a daily changing menu might include sandwiches, soup, asparagus, pea and mint risotto, smoked haddock fishcakes, pork, apple and cider pie with mash topping and buttered carrots and beans, fish and chips, rib-eye steak, various salads like confit duck with lambs lettuce and pickled cherries, and puddings such as eton mess. *Starters/Snacks: £5.50 to £6.00. Main Courses: £9.00 to £18.50. Puddings: £4.50 to £5.00*

Geronimo Inns ~ Manager Stuart Kemp ~ Real ale ~ Bar food (9-10(8 Sun)) ~ Restaurant ~ (01342) 830820 ~ Children welcome ~ Dogs allowed in bar ~ Open 9-11

Recommended by Grahame Brooks, Derek Thomas, Louise English

BRAMLEY
TQ0044 MAP 3

Jolly Farmer 🍺
High Street; GU5 0HB

Relaxed village inn near the Surrey hills with a wide selection of beers, pleasant staff and daily specials

---

This welcoming village inn is a jolly good all-rounder, with readers enjoying the tasty food and impressive range of real ales. Its attractive interior is a mixture of brick and timbering, with an open fireplace and timbered semi-partitions, and furnished with a homely miscellany of wooden tables and chairs; various assemblages of plates, enamel advertising signs, antique bottles, prints and old tools hang from the walls; the back restaurant area is inviting; piped music, dominoes and board games. Friendly staff serve up to 20 different local real ales each week, typically eight at a time including Hogs Back HBB and Sharps Eden Pure alongside unusual guests from brewers such as Cottage, Dark Star, Idle, Redscar and Thomas Guest, also three changing belgian draught beers and 18 wines by the glass. The village is handy for Winkworth Arboretum and walks up St Martha's Hill.

🍴 As well as lunchtime sandwiches, bar food includes prawn and smoked salmon salad, ham, egg and chips, pie of the day, burgers and steaks, and daily specials such as chicken liver piri-piri, seafood tagliatelle, vegan risotto, venison and red wine sausages with red wine jus, confit pork belly with apple mash, and roast chicken breast with mushroom and tarragon cream sauce; Sunday roast. *Starters/Snacks: £4.75 to £7.00. Main Courses: £10.00 to £18.00. Puddings: £4.50 to £5.00*

Free house ~ Licensees Steve and Chris Hardstone ~ Real ale ~ Bar food (12-2.30, 6(6.30 Sun)-9.30) ~ Restaurant ~ (01483) 893355 ~ Children welcome ~ Dogs allowed in bar and bedrooms ~ Live music some Tues ~ Open 11-11(11.30 Sat); 12-11 Sun ~ Bedrooms: £60S(£75B)/£70S(£80B)

Recommended by Phil Bryant, M and GR, Guy Wightman, Phil and Sally Gorton, Dr and Mrs A K Clarke, Mr and Mrs Gordon Turner

BUCKLAND
TQ2250 MAP 3

Jolly Farmers 🍽️
Reigate Road (A25 W of Reigate); RH3 7BG

Wide range of local produce in part-pub, part-restaurant and part-deli; a good place to eat or shop, but atmospheric too

---

There aren't many pubs where the first things you might spot are a basket of farm-fresh broad beans for sale, or a showcase of home-made cupcakes, but both sum up what this unusual place is all about: good, meticulously sourced local produce, both on the menu, and in the well stocked farm shop at the back. Most people are here to eat (or to buy), but the flagstoned bar with its smart, brown leather sofas and armchairs has a comfortably relaxed feel, and though there weren't many people doing it when we visited, we got the feeling you'd be made equally welcome if you just dropped in for a drink. On the wall is a big regional map with drawing pins marking their suppliers, and hops, beams and timbers keep things traditional. A small brick fireplace separates the bar from the small wooden-floored dining room. Friendly young staff serve a couple of local beers such as Harveys Sussex and whatever's in season from the local Kings brewery (a wider range is available in the shop); a few local wines pop up on the wine list, and they make various fruit juices. The shop stretches across three little rooms, with plenty of fresh vegetables, deli meats, cheeses, cakes, chocolates, and their own range of produce; they do a weekly food market with stalls outside (Saturdays, 9-3), and organise several food festivals and events throughout the year. There are tables out on a back terrace overlooking the car park. The owners run the Wise Old Owl at Kingsfold in Sussex along similar lines.

🍴 **You can get something to eat pretty much all day – pastries and coffees from 9am (full breakfast at weekends), then things like stuffed roasted aubergine with portabello mushroom, fresh chervil, wilted spinach and grain mustard cream sauce, goats cheese mousse with pumpkin seeds and spiced wine, poached pear, celery and walnut salad, a good ploughman's with a hefty chunk of cheese, roast lamb rump with black pudding, savoy cabbage bubble and squeak and rosemary sauce, devilled seared calves liver on red onion mash with winter herb gravy and smoked back bacon, and slow-roasted pork belly on parsnip mash with cabbage and apple jus. They do afternoon teas, and the children's menu is above average.** *Starters/Snacks: £3.95 to £6.95. Main Courses: £7.95 to £17.95. Puddings: £5.00*

Mitchells & Butlers ~ Lease John and Paula Briscoe ~ Real ale ~ Bar food (12-3, 5.30-9.30) ~ Restaurant ~ (01737) 221355 ~ Children welcome ~ Open 9-11

Recommended by Dan and Holly Pitcher, Cathryn and Richard Hicks, John Branston, C and R Bromage

COBHAM   TQ1058   MAP 3

Cricketers

Downside Common, S of town past Cobham Park; KT11 3NX

In relaxing village green location; lots of character, low beams, good bar food (all day Sunday) and a pretty garden

You step from idyllic terrace views across the village green into a lovely traditional interior when you visit this unchanging old place. Crooked standing timbers give structure to the comfortable open-plan layout with very low heavy oak beams (some have crash-pads on them) and a blazing log fire. In places you can see the wide oak ceiling boards and ancient plastering laths. Furnishings are quite simple, and there are horsebrasses and big brass platters on the walls. Fullers London Pride and Greene King IPA and Old Speckled Hen are on handpump alongside a guest such as Surrey Hills Shere Drop and a good choice of wines including several by the glass; piped music. It's worth arriving early (particularly on Sunday) to be sure of a table. You may have to queue for food and service can slow down when they get busy; they may retain your credit card. The delightful neatly kept garden is well stocked with standard roses, magnolias, dahlias, bedding plants, urns and hanging baskets.

🍴 **Bar food (not cheap but well above average) includes sandwiches (weekdays only), duck pâté with cranberry sauce and toast, smoked haddock and spring onion fishcakes with crème fraîche, battered haddock and chips, steak and ale or chicken, mushroom and leek pie, pork and apple sausages with mash, rib-eye steak and daily specials; there's also a separate, more elaborate restaurant menu; popular Sunday roast.** *Starters/Snacks: £6.15 to £8.45. Main Courses: £8.95 to £14.95. Puddings: £4.75*

Enterprise ~ Tenant Mustafa Ozcan ~ Real ale ~ Bar food (12-3, 6.30-9.30; 12-8 Sun) ~ Restaurant ~ (01932) 862105 ~ Children welcome ~ Dogs allowed in bar ~ Open 11-11; 12-10.30 Sun

Recommended by K F Winknorth, Phil Bryant, Ian Phillips, LM, Conor McGaughey, DGH, Mr and Mrs Mike Pearson, Geoffrey Kemp, Stephen Funnell, Susan and John Douglas

---

If you stay overnight in an inn or hotel, they are allowed to serve you an alcoholic drink at any hour of the day or night.

Plough

3.2 miles from M25 junction 10; A3, then right on A245 at roundabout; in Cobham, right at Downside signpost into Downside Bridge Road; Plough Lane; KT11 3LT

Civilised and welcoming country local with generous bar food

Now under new licensees, this cheery pub has a buoyant local atmosphere in its attractive low-beamed bar; Courage Best, Hogs Back TEA and St Austell Tribute. Round to the right, a cosy parquet-floored snug has cushioned seats built into nice stripped-pine panelling and horseracing prints. The main part is carpeted, with a mix of pubby furnishings, and past some standing timbers a few softly padded banquettes around good-sized tables by a log fire in an ancient stone fireplace. The restaurant (with pews, bare boards and white table linen) rambles around behind this. A terrace has picnic-sets sheltering beside a very high garden wall; disabled facilities.

🍴 **Besides sandwiches and baguettes, generously served bar food might include sausage and mash, fish and chips, chicken caesar salad, braised oxtail with madeira jus, and puddings such as chocolate fondant, sticky toffee pudding and raspberry and white chocolate crème brûlée.** *Starters/Snacks: £5.00 to £8.00. Main Courses: £8.00 to £17.00. Puddings: £5.00 to £8.00*

S&N ~ Lease Neil Mason ~ Real ale ~ Bar food (12-3, 7-9.30; 12-4 Sun) ~ Restaurant ~ (01932) 862514 ~ Children welcome ~ Dogs allowed in bar ~ Open 11-11; 12-10.30 Sun

Recommended by Rita and Keith Pollard, David M Smith, Ian Phillips, Geoffrey Kemp, Dr and Mrs A K Clarke, Tom and Ruth Rees

COLDHARBOUR   TQ1544   MAP 3

Plough 🍺

Village signposted in the network of small roads around Leith Hill; RH5 6HD

Straightforward place in good walking country, with own-brew beers

Properly pubby, this little place has its own brewery (Leith Hill) which produces the excellent Crooked Furrow and Tallywhacker served here on handpump, alongside a couple of guests such as Ringwood Best and Timothy Taylors Landlord; also Biddenden farm cider and several wines by the glass. Its two bars (each with a lovely open fire) have stripped light beams and timbering in warm-coloured dark ochre walls, with quite unusual little chairs around the tables in the snug red-carpeted games room on the left (darts, board games and cards), and little decorative plates on the walls; the room on the right leads through to the candlelit restaurant; piped music, TV. This is a very handy place to stop for a meal or drink if you're walking or cycling in some of the best scenery in the Surrey hills – around Leith Hill or Friday Street, for instance. If you stay here, it may be advisable to ask for a quieter room not over the bar. The quiet back garden has views across neighbouring fields and there are picnic-sets on the front terrace; more reports please.

🍴 **Bar food (some readers feel it's a little over-priced) includes chicken liver and brandy pâté, tomato and mozzarella salad, ham, egg and chips, chicken caesar salad, mushroom risotto, baked trout with herb butter, pork and leek sausages, steaks, and fruit crumble of the day or trifle. In summer they may open earlier and do good value breakfasts for cyclists and walkers.** *Starters/Snacks: £5.25 to £6.95. Main Courses: £10.00 to £16.50. Puddings: £5.25*

Own brew ~ Licensees Richard and Anna Abrehart ~ Real ale ~ Bar food (12-2.30(3 Sat, Sun), 6-9.30(9 Sun)) ~ Restaurant ~ (01306) 711793 ~ Children welcome if dining; not in accommodation ~ Dogs allowed in bar ~ Open 11.30-11.30; 12-10.30 Sun ~ Bedrooms: /£99.50B

Recommended by Anthony Barnes, John Branston, Kevin Thorpe, Sara Fulton, Roger Baker, Tony Hobden, Pete Baker, Franklyn Roberts, Derek and Heather Manning

COMPTON

SU9646 MAP 2

Withies

Withies Lane; pub signposted from B3000; GU3 1JA

Smartly civilised, with attractive pubby bar, upmarket restaurant and a pretty garden

The cosy low-beamed bar at this sympathetically altered 16th-c tavern is civilised, but a lively chatty atmosphere saves it from being too sedate. Pleasing interior features include some fine 17th-c carved panels between the windows and a splendid art nouveau settle among old sewing-machine tables, and even on cool summer days logs burn in its massive inglenook. Even when it's busy, the pleasant uniformed staff are helpful and efficient, serving Adnams, Badger K&B and Hogs Back TEA from handpump. The nicely old-fashioned beamed restaurant is a favourite of the well heeled local set. A mass of flowers border the neat front lawn, and weeping willows shade the immaculate garden behind, which has plenty of dining tables under an arbour of creeper-hung trellises, with more on a crazy-paved terrace and others under old apple trees. The pub is situated on the edge of Loseley Park and close to the extraordinary Watts Gallery of works by the Victorian artist GF Watts.

🍴 **Quickly served tasty bar food includes good sandwiches (even hot salt beef), filled baked potatoes, ploughman's, cumberland sausage and mash, greek or hawaiian salad and a seafood platter.** *Starters/Snacks: £4.00 to £7.50. Main Courses: £9.50 to £11.50. Puddings: £5.75*

Free house ~ Licensees Brian and Hugh Thomas ~ Real ale ~ Bar food (12-2.30(3 Sat, Sun), 7-10) ~ Restaurant ~ (01483) 421158 ~ Open 11-3, 6-11; 12-4 Sun; closed Sun evening

Recommended by Marianne and Peter Stevens, Jeremy and Jane Morrison, Ian Phillips, Gerry and Rosemary Dobson, Helen and Brian Edgeley, Michael Sargent, Andrea Rampley, Norma and Noel Thomas

ELSTEAD

SU9044 MAP 2

Mill at Elstead ♀ ◖

Farnham Road (B3001 just W of village, which is itself between Farnham and Milford); GU8 6LE

Fascinating building, big attractive waterside garden, Fullers beers, bar food

Rising through four storeys, this sensitively converted largely 18th-c watermill is in a special location above the prettily banked River Wey. With good floodlighting at night, there are plenty of picnic-sets dotted around by the water, with its millpond, swans and weeping willows. Inside, you'll see the great internal waterwheel, and the hear the gentle rush of the stream turning below your feet, and big windows throughout the building make the most of the charming surroundings. A series of rambling linked bar areas on the spacious ground floor, and a restaurant upstairs, change in mood from one part to the next: brown leather armchairs and antique engravings by a longcase clock; neat modern tables and dining chairs on pale woodstrip flooring; big country tables and rustic prints on broad ceramic tiles; dark boards and beams, iron pillars and stripped masonry; a log fire in a huge inglenook. Service is commendably helpful, friendly and personal. They have Fullers London Pride, ESB, HSB and perhaps a seasonal beer on handpump, and a good range of wines by the glass; piped music; dogs allowed in certain areas only.

🍴 **Under new licensees, bar food has improved a little: mixed bread and dips, greek salad, mushroom risotto, organic salmon, battered cod and chips, steakburger, and tuna steak salad, with a carvery on winter Sundays. Do let us know what you think.** *Starters/Snacks: £4.50 to £6.00. Main Courses: £7.95 to £14.95. Puddings: £4.25 to £4.75*

Fullers ~ Managers Kate and Richard Williamson ~ Real ale ~ Bar food (12-10(8 Sun) ~ Restaurant ~ (01252) 703333 ~ Children welcome ~ Dogs welcome ~ Open 11.30-11(10.30 Sun)

Recommended by Peter Dandy, Ian Phillips, Phil Bryant, Susan and Nigel Brookes, Martin and Karen Wake, Simon and Sally Small, N R White

ENGLEFIELD GREEN

Fox & Hounds

Bishopsgate Road, off A328 N of Egham; TW20 0XU

Neat friendly tavern, useful for Windsor Park; log fires and tasty bar food

A variety of customers from office workers to visitors to nearby Windsor Park and Savile Garden head for this spotlessly kept old pub. It's fairly extensive inside, with pubby tables and chairs on bare floorboards in the bar area, opening to a pair of leather sofas and the J-shaped dining area with some exposed brick and café chairs on carpets. This, in turn, extends out into the conservatory. It's all cosy and nicely warmed by three log fires. Brakspears, Hogs Back Brewery TEA and a guest such Sharps Doom Bar are on handpump, with an extensive wine list with ten wines by the glass and several malt whiskies; piped music. There are picnic-sets on the terrace, on decking and on the front lawn.

🍴 **Enjoyable bar food includes an interesting choice of lunchtime sandwiches, starters such as duck liver pâté with cranberry, port and ginger compote, smoked fish, citrus cream cheese and fennel terrine and fried pigeon breast with pickled walnuts, pears and stilton; main courses such as lasagne, gammon, egg and chips, risotto of the day, roast aubergine moussaka, battered fish with minted mushy peas and hand-cut chips, well hung sirloin steak, and puddings such as crème brûlée and apple crumble.** *Starters/Snacks: £4.90 to £7.15. Main Courses: £9.95 to £16.50. Puddings: £4.90 to £7.15*

Free house ~ Licensee Andy Eaton-Carr ~ Real ale ~ Bar food (12-2.30, 6.30-9.30; 12-9.30 (4 Sun) Sat; not Sun evening) ~ Restaurant ~ (01784) 433098 ~ Children welcome ~ Dogs allowed in bar ~ Live jazz last Sun evening and Mon of month ~ Open 11-11; 12-10.30 Sun

Recommended by Martin and Karen Wake, Ian Phillips, Jack and Sandra Clarfelt, Chris Glasson, Evelyn and Derek Walter

ESHER

Marneys ♀ £

Alma Road (one-way only), Weston Green; heading N on A309 from A307 roundabout, after Lamb & Star pub turn left into Lime Tree Avenue (signposted to All Saints Parish Church), then left at T junction into Chestnut Avenue; KT10 8JN

Cottagey little pub with good value food and an attractive garden

A good local following enjoy the chatty low-beamed black and white plank-panelled bar, the convivial company of the cheery landlord and perhaps the horseracing on the unobtrusive corner TV at this cottagey pub. Hens, ducks and other ornaments fill its shelves, there are small blue-curtained windows. On the left, past a little cast-iron woodburning stove, a dining area (somewhat roomier but still small) has big pine tables, pews and pale country kitchen chairs, and attractive goose pictures. Courage Best, Fullers London Pride and Wells & Youngs Bombardier are on handpump. The front terrace has dark blue cast-iron tables and chairs under matching parasols, with some more black tables too, with table lighting and views over the rural-feeling wooded common and duck pond; and the pleasantly planted sheltered garden has a decked area, bar, black picnic-sets and tables under green and blue canvas parasols; more reports please.

🍴 **Very reasonably priced changing bar food might include courgette and pasta bake, baked camembert and redcurrant jelly, moules marinière, warm chicken and bacon salad, steak pie, salmon salad, liver and bacon, and steaks.** *Starters/Snacks: £4.95 to £6.00. Main Courses: £4.95 to £9.00. Puddings: £4.95*

Free house ~ Licensee Harry Muller ~ Real ale ~ Bar food (12-2.30(3 Sun), 6-9) ~ (020) 8398 4444 ~ Children welcome ~ Dogs welcome ~ Open 11-11; 12-10.30 Sun

Recommended by John Sleigh, Shirley Mackenzie, LM, David and Ruth Shillitoe, Michael Dandy, Ian Wilson, Norma and Noel Thomas

---

We say if we know a pub allows dogs.

FOREST GREEN   TQ1241   MAP 3

Parrot ★ ⑪ ♀ ◀

B2127 just W of junction with B2126, SW of Dorking; RH5 5RZ

Beamed pub with produce from the owners' farm on the menu and in the attached shop, good range of drinks, and a lovely garden

It's not just the splendid position with views over fields and the village cricket pitch that is so appealing about this old place. Inside, the building retains all the charm of a genuinely aged village pub, with its fine profusion of heavy beams, timbers, flagstones, and nooks and crannies hidden away behind the inglenook fireplace. Ringwood Best and Wells & Youngs are served alongside three guests such as Dorking Number One, Hogs Back TEA and Ringwood Old Thumper on handpump, as well as freshly squeezed orange juice, local farm apple juice and over a dozen wines by the glass; newspapers. There are tables out in several attractive gardens, one with apple trees and rose beds. The owners have their own farm not far away at Coldharbour and you can buy the meat, as well as cheese, cured and smoked hams, pies, bread and preserves in the farm shop at the pub.

⑪ With the pork, beef and lamb on the frequently changing menu coming from their own farm, the changing menu might include griddled scallops with minted pea purée and crispy bacon, pork and pistachio terrine with fruit chutney, home-cured white pudding with bacon and caramelised pears, grilled pollack with shrimp and parsley potatoes, baked spinach, mushroom and feta filo with cream and tarragon sauce, paprika and lemon roast chicken with rocket, white wine and sour cream pappardelle, mutton, red wine and juniper pie, and puddings such as poached pear on brioche with hot cinnamon sauce and hot cross bun and butter pudding; they may ask to keep your credit card. *Starters/Snacks: £4.50 to £10.00. Main Courses: £8.00 to £13.00. Puddings: £4.00 to £7.00*

Free house ~ Licensee Charles Gotto ~ Real ale ~ Bar food (12-3(5 Sun), 6-10; not Sun evening) ~ Restaurant ~ (01306) 621339 ~ Children welcome ~ Dogs allowed in bar ~ Open 10-midnight; 12-10 Sun

Recommended by Sheila Topham, Derek Thomas, Mike Gorton, Ian and Barbara Rankin, Simon and Mandy King, Tim and Alice Wright, Tom and Ruth Rees, Norma and Noel Thomas, C and R Bromage, Louise English, Richard and Sissel Harris, N R White, Christopher and Elise Way, Bernard Stradling, Derek and Maggie Washington, John and Joan Nash, Gordon Stevenson, Conor McGaughey, John Branston, Tim Crook, Hunter and Christine Wright

LEIGH   TQ2147   MAP 3

Seven Stars ♀

Dawes Green, S of A25 Dorking—Reigate; RH2 8NP

Popular welcoming dining pub with enjoyable food and good wines

There's a particularly grown-up atmosphere at this welcoming tile-hung 17th-c tavern, with just the murmur of contented chatter to greet you as you are offered a table. The comfortable saloon bar has a 1633 inglenook fireback showing a royal coat of arms, and there's a plainer public bar. The sympathetically done restaurant extension at the side incorporates 17th-c floor timbers imported from a granary. Greene King Old Speckled Hen, Fullers London Pride and Wells & Youngs Bitter are served from handpump, alongside decent wines with about a dozen by the glass. Outside, there's plenty of room in the beer garden at the front, on the terrace and in the side garden.

⑪ The nicely varied menu includes lunchtime ciabattas and baked potatoes, risotto of the day, whitebait with caper and lemon mayonnaise, curry and rice, cumberland sausage and mash, fried calves liver and bacon with dijon mustard mash, haddock with mustard cream sauce and poached egg, mushroom and goats cheese lasagne, and puddings such as crumble of the day and chocolate mousse with orange syrup. They do two sittings for Sunday lunch and it's advisable to book at all times. *Starters/Snacks: £5.50 to £6.95. Main Courses: £8.95 to £16.50. Puddings: £4.95 to £5.25*

Punch ~ Lease David and Rebecca Pellen ~ Real ale ~ Bar food (12-2.30(4 Sun), 6-9(6.30-9.30 Fri, Sat); not Sun evening) ~ Restaurant ~ (01306) 611254 ~ Dogs allowed in bar ~ Open 12-11(8 Sun)

Recommended by Ian Macro, Norma and Noel Thomas, C and R Bromage, Donna and Roger, Ron and Sheila Corbett, Mike and Sue Shirley, Terry Buckland, Neil Powell, Grahame Brooks

LINGFIELD   TQ3844   MAP 3

Hare & Hounds

Turn off B2029 N at the Crowhurst/Edenbridge signpost, into Lingfield Common Road (coming from the A22 towards Lingfield on B2029, this is the second road on your left); RH7 6BZ

Interesting bar food at easy-going pub, interestingly decorated and more sophisticated than it looks; garden

Don't be deterred by the slightly unkempt blue exterior – inside, this dining pub is agreeably individual and informal in style and full of the chatter of happy customers, some drinking, some eating. The smallish open-plan bar is light and airy by day, with soft lighting and nightlights burning on a good mix of different-sized tables in the evening. Partly bare boards and partly flagstones, it has a trendily eclectic mix of well worn scatter-cushioned dining chairs and other seats from cushion-laden pews to a button-back leather chesterfield and a pair of old cinema seats, with black and white pictures of jazz musicians on brown tongue-and-groove panelling. The bar opens into a quieter dining area with big abstract-expressionist paintings. Well kept Greene King IPA and a guest such as Fullers London Pride are on handpump, and eight of their decent wines are available by the glass. Tables are set out in a pleasant split-level garden, with some on decking. This is good walking country near Haxted Mill – walkers can leave their boots in the porch.

🍴 Under new licensees, the daily changing bar food (booking advised) might include curried parsnip soup, duck terrine with tarragon, smoked magret and cress salad, confit rabbit shoulder with mayonnaise and black radish, confit pork belly with roast apples and celery, macaroni gratin, caramelised swede ravioli with thyme and goats chese on toast and swede linguine, poached haddock fillet with sweet wine, jerusalem artichoke and black olive cake, and hot chocolate fondant with crunchy peanut butter ice-cream and caramelised apple tarte tatin with cinnamon ice-cream. *Starters/Snacks: £6.00 to £12.00. Main Courses: £10.00 to £16.00. Puddings: £5.00 to £6.50*

Punch ~ Lease Eric and Tracy Payet ~ Real ale ~ Bar food ~ Restaurant ~ (01342) 832351 ~ Children welcome ~ Dogs welcome ~ Open 12-11; 12-8 Sun

Recommended by Annette Tress, Gary Smith, R J Anderson, Kevin Thorpe, N R White, Cathryn and Richard Hicks, Derek Thomas, Evelyn and Derek Walter, Alan Cowell, Louise English

MICKLEHAM   TQ1753   MAP 3

Running Horses

Old London Road (B2209); RH5 6DU

Upmarket pub with elegant restaurant and comfortable bar, and sandwiches through to very imaginative dishes

Smart with an easy-going atmosphere, this rather nice place is an accomplished all-rounder, liked equally as a local drinking haunt, walkers' stop and dining destination. The calming bar is neatly kept and spaciously open-plan, with hunting pictures, racing cartoons and Hogarth prints, lots of race tickets hanging from a beam, fresh flowers or a fire in an inglenook at one end and some cushioned wall settles and other dining chairs around straightforward pubby tables and bar stools. Adnams, Fullers London Pride, Shepherd Neame Spitfire and Wells & Youngs Bitter are on handpump alongside good wines by the glass, from a serious wine list; piped music. The extensive restaurant is open to the bar and although set out quite formally with crisp white cloths and candles on each table, it shares the relaxing atmosphere of the bar. There are picnic-sets on a terrace in front by lovely flowering tubs and hanging baskets, with a peaceful view of the old church with its strange stubby steeple. You may be asked to leave your credit card and it's best to get here early, both to secure parking in the narrow lane and for a table.

🍴 There is a tempting choice of food running from traditional pubby meals to a more elaborate restaurant menu (available in the bar): well filled lunchtime chunky sandwiches, moules marinière, shellfish bisque with chive crème fraîche, game and mushroom rillette with red onion marmalade, thai fishcakes with scallops, crispy fennel and vanilla aioli, shepherd's pie, steak, mushroom and Guinness pudding, globe artichoke filled with saffron and pumpkin risotto, sausage and mash, venison and beef burger, chicken breast wrapped in parma ham filled with crayfish tails on a bed of leeks with orange cream sauce, and tournedos rossini; also puddings such as Grand Marnier summer pudding, date and sultana pudding with butterscotch sauce and toffee ice-cream and coconut panna cotta with mango and pawpaw soup and sugar-frosted strawberries. *Starters/Snacks: £5.75 to £11.50. Main Courses: £11.50 to £25.75. Puddings: £6.25*

Punch ~ Lease Steve and Josie Slayford ~ Real ale ~ Bar food (12-2.30, 7-9; 12-9.30(9 Sun) Sat) ~ Restaurant ~ (01372) 372279 ~ Dogs allowed in bar ~ Open 11.30-11; 12-10.30 Sun ~ Bedrooms: £95S(£105B)/£110S(£135B)

Recommended by Sheila Topham, Ian Phillips, Fiona Smith, John and Joyce Snell, Mike Gorton, Mr Ray J Carter, Conor McGaughey, N R White, Gordon Stevenson, Paul Humphreys

NEWDIGATE
TQ2043   MAP 3

Surrey Oaks 🍺
Off A24 S of Dorking, via Beare Green; Parkgate Road; RH5 5DZ

Interesting real ales at this traditional village pub with straightforward bar food and an enjoyable garden for children

On good form himself, the friendly landlord at this former wheelwright's cottage has a passionate interest in real ale, and keeps three quickly rotating guests from smaller brewers such as Bowman, Houston and Westerham alongside well kept Harveys Best and Surrey Hills Ranmore. He holds beer festivals over the May Spring and August bank holiday weekends, and meet the brewer evenings; also belgian bottled beers, several wines by the glass, a farm cider like Mole's Black Rat and a farm perry such as Weston's Country. The pubby interior is interestingly divided into four areas. In the older part locals gather by an open fire in a snug little beamed room. A standing area with unusually large flagstones has a woodburning stove in an inglenook fireplace, and rustic tables are dotted around the light and airy main lounge to the left, and there's a pool table in the separate games room; fruit machine and piped classical music. The garden is pleasingly complicated, with a terrace, and a rockery with pools and a waterfall, and a diverting play area.

🍴 Reasonably priced bar food includes filled baguettes, ploughman's, ham, eggs and chips, battered fish, with specials such as sausage and mash, fish pie, steak and ale pie and lambs liver, bacon and onion gravy; three Sunday roasts; they may retain your credit card if you eat outside. *Starters/Snacks: £4.00 to £5.00. Main Courses: £7.00 to £8.50. Puddings: £3.75*

Admiral Taverns ~ Lease Ken Proctor ~ Real ale ~ Bar food (12-2, 6.30-9; not Sun, Mon evening) ~ Restaurant ~ (01306) 631200 ~ Children welcome ~ Dogs allowed in bar ~ Open 11.30-2.30, 5.30-11; 11.30-3, 6-11 Sat; 12-10.30 Sun

Recommended by Ian Phillips, C and R Bromage, Sara Fulton, Roger Baker, the Didler, Bruce Bird, Norma and Noel Thomas, Malcolm and Pauline Pellatt

THURSLEY
SU9039   MAP 2

Three Horseshoes
Dye House Road, just off A3 SW of Godalming; GU8 6QD

Civilised country village pub with good restaurant food as well as bar snacks

Owned by a consortium of villagers who rescued it from closure, this pretty tile-hung village pub is an appealing combination of gently upmarket country local and attractive restaurant. The convivial beamed front bar has Fullers HSB, Hogs Back TEA and a guest such as Surrey Hills Shere Drop on handpump, farm ciders, a winter log fire, and warmly welcoming service; piped music. There's some emphasis on the attractive restaurant area behind, with beamery and paintings of local scenes. The attractive two-acre garden has picnic-sets and a big play fort, and smart comfortable chairs around terrace tables; pleasant views over the green.

🍴 As well as the burger and pizza menus, a more elaborate menu includes minestrone soup with pecorino, caesar salad, cornish crab, duck, rabbit, pigeon and mushroom terrine with piccalilli, scallops and parma ham with mini rösti, pea purée and mint vinaigrette, cottage pie, rib-eye steak with garlic butter, fried skate with caper berry vinaigrette, smoked haddock and salmon fishcakes with endive salad and dill mayonnaise, and puddings such as cappuccino crème brûlée and treacle tart with jersey untreated cream. Some of the vegetables are grown in gardens in the village, and game and fish are caught locally. *Starters/Snacks: £4.50 to £12.00. Main Courses: £9.00 to £15.00. Puddings: £4.50 to £5.00*

Free house ~ Licensees David Alders and Sandra Proni ~ Real ale ~ Bar food (12.30-2.15, 7-9.15; 12-3 Sun; not Sun evening) ~ Restaurant ~ (01252) 703268 ~ Children welcome ~ Dogs allowed in bar ~ Open 12-3, 5.30-11; 12-11 Sat; 12-10.30 Sun

Recommended by Hunter and Christine Wright, DGH, Michael Sargent, LM, Michael B Griffith, Simon and Sally Small, Dan and Holly Pitcher, Bernard Stradling

WEST END   SU9461   MAP 2

Inn at West End 🍴 �

Just under 2.5 miles from M3 junction 3; A322 S, on right; GU24 9PW

SURREY DINING PUB OF THE YEAR

Enjoyable fresh-feeling dining pub, with prompt friendly service; excellent food, good wines, and terrace

This is a beautifully run pub, polished and well organised, but with an enjoyably relaxed feel throughout. The charming licensee is a wine merchant, so the thoughtfully created food is well complemented by the knowledgeably chosen wines (with around a dozen by the glass), several sherries and dessert wines that lean particularly towards Spain and Portugal. He holds wine tastings and can supply by the case. The pub is open-plan, with bare boards, attractive modern prints on canary-yellow walls above a red dado, and a line of dining tables with crisp white linen over pale yellow tablecloths on the left. The bar counter (Fullers London Pride and a guest such as Black Sheep on handpump), straight ahead as you come in, is quite a focus, with chatting regulars perched on the comfortable bar stools. The area on the right has a pleasant relaxed atmosphere, with blue-cushioned wall benches and dining chairs around solid pale wood tables, broadsheet daily papers, magazines and a row of reference books on the brick chimneybreast above a woodburning stove. This opens into a garden room, which in turn leads to a grape and clematis pergola-covered terrace and very pleasant garden; boules.

🍴 Skilfully prepared using carefully sourced ingredients (some of the herbs and vegetables are grown here, they pluck their own game and use organic meat), not cheap but very good bar food might include smoked fish platter, fried chicken livers with black pudding and croutons, chicken caesar salad, kedgeree, cumberland sausage and mash, vegetable cottage pie, well hung sirloin steak, roast chicken breast with garlic and herb sauce, and puddings such as crème brûlée with cranberry shortbread, south african vinegar pudding and toffee, banana, apple and pecan crumble pie with toffee sauce. *Starters/Snacks: £5.50 to £9.95. Main Courses: £5.25 to £19.75. Puddings: £6.25 to £6.75*

Enterprise ~ Lease Gerry and Ann Price ~ Real ale ~ Bar food (12-2.30, 6-9.30; 12-3, 6-9 Sun) ~ Restaurant ~ (01276) 858652 ~ Children over 5 welcome if seated and dining ~ Dogs allowed in bar ~ Open 12-3, 5-11; 12-11 Sat; 12-10.30 Sun

Recommended by Mr and Mrs G M Pearson, Guy Vowles, Bernard Stradling, Ian Herdman, Robin Paterson, Guy Charrison, Bruce M Drew, Ian Phillips, Guy Consterdine, Sylvia and Tony Birbeck, Edward Mirzoeff

---

Virtually all the pubs in this book sell wine by the glass.
We mention wines if they are a cut above the average.

WORPLESDON

SU9854   MAP 3

Jolly Farmer

Burdenshott Road, off A320 Guildford—Woking, not in village – heading N from Guildford on the A320, turn left after Jacobs Well roundabout towards Worplesdon Station; OS Sheet 186 map reference 987542; GU3 3RN

Traditional place with pubby food, good service and an attractive sheltered garden

The new licensee clearly takes pride in managing this traditional village pub, with reader reports already indicating that it is well run, with attention to detail. The bar retains a pubby feel, with dark beams and pub furniture; Fullers Discovery, London Pride and HSB and a guest such as Fullers IPA on handpump, and there's a large wine list with around a dozen by the glass, as well as several malt whiskies. You can eat here, or in a dining extension with stripped brickwork, rugs on bare boards and well spaced tables; piped music. With a very pleasant woodland setting, the garden with grape vines and fruit trees has tables under cocktail parasols. The car park is shared with Whitmore Common.

🍴 Bar food (not cheap) includes smoked mackerel pâté, balsamic roast figs with parma ham and black olive tapenade, smoked duck salad with raspberry vinaigrette, battered haddock and chips, seared tuna niçoise, burger and chips, tomato and basil tart, sirloin steak with a choice of sauces, and puddings such as eton mess and double chocolate tart with chocolate ice-cream and sticky toffee pudding. *Starters/Snacks: £4.95 to £6.95. Main Courses: £9.95 to £17.95. Puddings: £4.95 to £5.50*

Fullers ~ Manager Jason Woodger ~ Real ale ~ Bar food (12-3, 6-9.30; 12-8 Sun) ~ (01483) 234658 ~ Children welcome ~ Dogs welcome ~ Open 10-11(10.30 Sun)

Recommended by LM, Ian Phillips, John and Rosemary Haynes, Liz and Brian Barnard, Guy Consterdine

LUCKY DIP

Besides the fully inspected pubs, you might like to try these Lucky Dips recommended to us and described by readers (if you do, please send us reports: feedback@goodguides.com).

ABINGER COMMON [TQ1146]
Abinger Hatch RH5 6HZ [off A25 W of Dorking, towards Abinger Hammer]: Modernised dining pub in beautiful woodland spot, popular food (not Sun evening) from light dishes up, Fullers London Pride and Ringwood Best and Fortyniner, sociable landlord and good service; heavy beams and flagstones, log fires, pews forming booths around oak tables in carpeted side area, plenty of space (very busy wknds); piped music, plain family extension; dogs welcome, tables and friendly ducks in nice garden, nr pretty church and pond, summer barbecues, open all day *(Conor McGaughey, C and R Bromage, Franklyn Roberts, Richard and Sissel Harris, LYM, Ian Phillips)*

ADDLESTONE [TQ0464]
Waggon & Horses KT15 1QH [Simplemarsh Rd]: Pretty and very welcoming suburban mock-Tudor local kept spotless; with genial licensees, Fullers London Pride and guests such as Batemans and Thwaites, bargain food, cups and trophies, daily papers; flowers and picnic-sets on small front terrace, back terrace and garden *(Ian Phillips)*
White Hart KT15 2DS [New Haw Rd (corner A318/B385)]: Smartly reworked in grey and white, bare boards and dark leather, light

dining area, food inc full thai menu; Adnams, Fullers London Pride, Sharps Eden and Skinners Betty Stogs; play area in attractive garden by Wey Navigation canal lock side stream *(Ian Phillips, LYM)*

ALDERSHOT [SU8749]
White Lion GU12 4EA [Lower Farnham]: Friendly pub tied to fff with their full ale range, pizzas, pews and stripped tables *(Andy and Jill Kassube)*

ASH VALE [SU8952]
Swan GU12 5HA [Hutton Rd, off Ash Vale Rd (B3411) via Heathvale Bridge Rd]: Popular three-room Chef & Brewer on the workaday Basingstoke Canal; huge choice of decent food all day (can take a while when very busy), good sandwiches, Courage, Fullers London Pride, Wadworths 6X and a guest beer, good value wines by the glass, cheerful staff, large log fire; piped classical music; children welcome, attractive garden, neat heated terraces and window boxes, open all day *(E Stein, Phil Bryant)*

BANSTEAD [TQ2659]
Mint SM7 3DS [Park Rd, off High St towards Kingswood]: Rambling Vintage Inn, beams and flagstones, friendly helpful staff, good value food inc lunch deals, real ales and good choice of wines by the glass *(Jenny and Brian Seller, Mrs G R Sharman)*

BATTS CORNER [SU8140]
Blue Bell GU10 4EX: Light fresh décor in friendly country pub with enjoyable fresh food from good choice of lunchtime sandwiches and salads up, well kept fff Moondance, a beer brewed by them for the pub and Hogs Back TEA, half a dozen wines by the glass, roaring log fire, restaurant; children, dogs and muddy boots welcome; big garden with rolling views and play area, handy for Alice Holt Forest, open all day, cl Sun evening (N R White, BB)

BETCHWORTH [TQ2150]
☆ **Red Lion** RH3 7DS [Old Rd, Buckland]: Light and comfortable dining pub under enthusiastic newish management; long flagstoned room and candlelit dining room, good home-made sensibly priced food, friendly unobtrusive service, Adnams and guest beers; children welcome, picnic-sets on lawn with cricket ground beyond, dining terrace, bedroom block, open all day (Mrs G R Sharman, Jenny and Brian Seller, LYM, Dr Ron Cox)

BLETCHINGLEY [TQ3250]
Prince Albert RH1 4LR [Outwood Lane]: Fullers ales, good wines by the glass, linked beamed rooms, panelling and simple furnishings; terrace tables, pretty garden (LYM, Conor McGaughey)
William IV RH1 4QF [3 miles from M25 junction 6; Little Common Lane, off A25 on Redhill side of village]: Tile-hung and weatherboarded country local under cheerful new management; Wells & Youngs ales, reasonably priced generous simple food, two-level garden (C and R Bromage, John Branston, LYM)

BROCKHAM [TQ1949]
Dukes Head RH3 7JS: Huge helpings of enjoyable pubby food from sandwiches up and more unusual specials, Adnams, Fullers London Pride and Greene King Old Speckled Hen, friendly attentive staff; relaxed traditional bare-boards bar overlooking the pretty village green, log fire, informal stripped-brick dining area, sofas in more modern raised carpeted area; piped music, TV in games vestibule; children welcome away from bar, garden behind (Phil Bryant)

BURROWHILL [SU9763]
Four Horseshoes GU24 8QP [B383 N of Chobham]: Unpretentious local with beams and log fires, three well kept changing ales such as Batemans, Hydes and St Austell, good sensibly priced pubby food from sandwiches up, modern dining extension; piped music, games machine, sports TV; picnic-sets out overlooking the green (some under an ancient yew) (Phil Bryant, Ian Phillips)

BYFLEET [TQ0661]
Plough KT14 7QT [High Rd]: Outstanding ale range such as 3 Rivers, Church End, fff, Goffs and Storm, relaxed atmosphere, simple food from sandwiches to three or four bargain hot dishes lunchtime and Weds evening, friendly service; two log fires, rustic furnishings,

farm tools, brass and copper, dominoes; terrace and small shady back garden (Ian Phillips, B and K Hypher, Phil Bryant)

CHARLESHILL [SU8844]
☆ **Donkey** GU10 2AU [B3001 Milford—Farnham nr Tilford; coming from Elstead, turn left as soon as you see pub sign]: Old-fashioned beamed dining pub with friendly service, enterprising home-made food from good lunchtime sandwiches to quite a lot of fish, great choice of wines by the glass, real ales such as Fullers London Pride, Greene King or Harveys; traditional games, conservatory restaurant; children and dogs welcome, attractive garden with wendy house, two much-loved donkeys, good walks, open all day Sun (LYM, Michael Sargent, John and Joyce Snell, J and E Dakin, Richard and Sissel Harris, Dominic Barrington, PHB, Peter Sampson)

CHERTSEY [TQ0566]
Boathouse KT16 8JZ [Bridge Rd]: Roomy, modern family pub in good Thames-side spot, reasonably priced food from sandwiches up, Courage Best, Fullers London Pride and Wells & Youngs Special; attractive waterside terrace, moorings, good value bedrooms in adjoining Bridge Lodge (Ian Phillips)
Coach & Horses KT16 9DG [St Anns Rd]: Fullers local with particularly well kept London Pride, good home-made wkdy food, cheerful barman; bedrooms (Hunter and Christine Wright)
Crown KT16 8AP [London St (B375)]: Extended Youngs pub/hotel, mixed furnishings in spreading high-ceilinged bar, decent wines by the glass, Wells & Youngs ales and Hogs Back TEA, food all day from sandwiches up, Sun roasts, restaurant; big-screen sports TV each end, games machines; children and dogs welcome, garden bar with conservatory, tables in courtyard and garden with pond, wknd barbecues, 49 bedrooms (Gerry and Rosemary Dobson, Ian Phillips)
Kingfisher KT16 8LF [Chertsey Bridge Rd (Shepperton side of river)]: Big Vintage Inn particularly liked by older people for its delightful spot nr Thames lock; repro period décor and furnishings in spreading series of small intimate areas; Adnams and Fullers London Pride, good wine choice, reasonably priced food, friendly attentive staff, good log fires, daily papers, large-scale map for walkers, interesting old pictures; soft piped music; families welcome if eating (no other under-21s), roadside garden, open all day (Ian Phillips, Mike Longman)
Olde Swan KT16 8AY [Windsor St]: Recently renovated, up-to-date main bar with back eating area, good value bar lunches, good service, Fullers London Pride and Wells & Youngs Bitter; cosy lower seating area with sofas, quiet lunchtimes, can be busy evenings; lots of new covered areas outside, bedrooms, open all day (Shirley Mackenzie, Ian Phillips)

CHIDDINGFOLD [SU9635]

Crown GU8 4TX [The Green (A283)]: Recently refurbished picturesque medieval inn with fine carving, Elizabethan plaster ceilings, massive beams, lovely inglenook log fire and panelled restaurant; friendly new management, enjoyable traditional food, good choice of well kept ales inc Butcombe; verandah tables, attractive village-green surroundings, comfortable bedrooms *(LYM, Phil and Sally Gorton)*

Swan GU8 4TY [Petworth Rd (A283 S)]: Attractive hotel/dining pub, comfortably up to date, with good choice of enjoyable if not cheap food in light and airy dining bar and restaurant, several well kept ales, thoughtful wine choice, friendly relaxed service; pleasant back terrace with big sunshades, 11 good bedrooms *(Hunter and Christine Wright, LYM, Gerry and Rosemary Dobson, C and R Bromage, J V Dadswell)*

CHIPSTEAD [TQ2757]

Ramblers Rest CR5 3NP [Outwood Lane (B2032)]: Rambling M&B country dining pub with contemporary furnishings and cocktail bar décor in a partly 14th-c building, with panelling, flagstones, low beams and log fires; young friendly staff, good value wines by the glass, up-to-date food inc popular Sun lunch, daily papers; children welcome, big pleasant garden with terrace, attractive views, good walks, open all day *(BB, N R White, Maureen and Keith Gimson)*

Well House CR5 3SQ [Chipstead signed with Mugswell off A217, N of M25 junction 8]: Partly 14th-c, cottagey, comfortable and friendly, with log fires in all three rooms, Adnams, Fullers London Pride and a seasonal guest, huge helpings of plainly served food (not Sun evening) from hefty sandwiches up, conservatory; dogs allowed (they have cats); large attractive hillside garden with a well reputed to be mentioned in Domesday Book, delightful setting *(LYM, Conor McGaughey, LM)*

CHOBHAM [SU9761]

Sun GU24 8AF [High St, off A319]: Congenial low-beamed timbered pub with Courage Best, Fullers London Pride and Hogs Back TEA; pizzas etc, friendly staff, daily papers, woodburner, shining brasses *(LYM, Ian Phillips)*

CHURT [SU8538]

Crossways GU10 2JE: Two distinct down-to-earth bar areas, busy evenings for great changing beer range at reasonable prices; good value home-made pub lunches (not Sun) from good sandwiches up, simple suppers Weds, cheerful young staff; garden, open all day Fri, Sat *(R B Gardiner, Tony and Jill Radnor)*

CLAYGATE [TQ1663]

Griffin KT10 0HW [Common Rd]: Properly old-fashioned Victorian village local with well kept Fullers London Pride, some interesting dishes as well as usual pub food (new chef studied in Mexico) *(Gordon Stevenson)*

Hare & Hounds KT10 0JL [The Green]: Renovated flower-decked Victorian/ Edwardian village pub with small restaurant, good sensibly priced french food, good wine choice, fine service; outside seating at front and in small back garden *(Geoffrey Kemp, Franklyn Roberts)*

COBHAM [TQ1159]

Running Mare KT11 3EZ [Tilt Rd]: Attractive old pub overlooking the green, popular for its good food (very busy Sun lunchtime); good service, Fullers, Hogs Back and Wells & Youngs ales, two timbered bars and restaurant; children very welcome, a few tables out at front and on back rose-covered terrace *(C and R Bromage, Ian Phillips)*

DORKING [TQ1649]

☆ *Kings Arms* RH4 1BU [West St]: Rambling 16th-c pub in antiques area, timbers and low beams, nice lived-in furniture in olde-worlde part-panelled lounge; bargain home-made food from sandwiches to roasts and a good pie of the day, interesting guest ales, friendly efficient service, warm relaxed atmosphere; attractive old-fashioned back dining area; piped music; open all day *(Conor McGaughey)*

DORMANSLAND [TQ4042]

Old House At Home RH7 6QP [West St]: Warmly, friendly, comfortable country local with well kept Shepherd Neame ales, wide choice of good generous food using fresh produce (booking recommended for Sun lunch); good-natured proper landlord; children and dogs welcome *(John Branston)*

EASHING [SU9543]

☆ *Stag* GU7 2QG [Lower Eashing, just off A3 southbound]: Attractive beamed pub dating partly from the 15th c; comfortable rambling areas with log fires, enjoyable food inc some interesting dishes, Hogs Back TEA and guests such as Fullers London Pride and Shepherd Neame Spitfire, friendly helpful young staff, daily papers; piped music; dogs welcome, pleasant streamside garden with terrace, bedrooms, open all day wknds *(Conor McGaughey, LM, Simon and Sally Small, LYM)*

EFFINGHAM [TQ1153]

☆ *Plough* KT24 5SW [Orestan Lane]: Popular Youngs pub with consistently well kept ales from traditional bar, good choice of enjoyable if a little pricey food inc Sun roasts, plenty of wines by the glass, nice staff; two coal-effect gas fires, beamery, panelling, old plates and brassware in long lounge; plenty of tables on forecourt and in attractive garden, handy for Polesden Lacey (NT) *(Mr and Mrs A Sawder)*

ELLENS GREEN [TQ0936]

Wheatsheaf RH12 3AS [B2128 N of Rudgwick]: Dining pub doing well under current management; good food from ciabattas or doorstep sandwiches up, nice relaxed service, Harveys and a guest beer, good choice of wines by the glass; no piped music; pleasant garden *(Shirley Mackenzie)*

ELSTEAD [SU9043]

Woolpack GU8 6HD [B3001 Milford—Farnham]: Welcoming pub with enjoyable generous food, well kept Brakspears and Greene King ales tapped from the cask, good choice of wines by the glass, friendly efficient staff; high-backed settles in long airy main bar, open fires each end, country décor, darts in back room; children allowed, garden with picnic-sets, open all day wknds *(Joan and Tony Walker, Mrs P Sumner, LYM)*

ENGLEFIELD GREEN [SU9971]

Barley Mow TW20 0NX [Northcroft Rd]: Friendly pub doing popular food from snacks up, good choice of real ales, quick pleasant service; refurbished pastel interior with tiled floors and modern furniture, back dining area; piped music, TV; tables overlooking cricket green, nice garden behind; summer steam fairs *(Martin Wilson, Phil Bryant)*

Happy Man TW20 0QS [Harvest Rd]: Friendly and unpretentious two-bar late Victorian backstreet local with good value pubby food, well kept changing ales such as Hogs Back and Scattor Rock, farm cider, good service; darts area; open all day *(Pete Baker, Chris Pluthero, Andy and Jill Kassube)*

EPSOM [TQ2158]

Rubbing House KT18 5LJ [Epsom Downs]: Restaurany dining pub with attractive modern décor, good value food promptly served even when busy, Fullers London Pride and Greene King IPA, serious wine list; racecourse views, upper balcony; tables outside *(Mrs G R Sharman, Maureen and Keith Gimson, Sue and Mike Todd, Conor McGaughey)*

ESHER [TQ1264]

☆ *Prince of Wales* KT10 8LA [West End Lane; off A244 towards Hersham, by Princess Alice Hospice]: Particularly well run rambling Chef & Brewer dining pub, wide choice of reasonably priced food from warm baguettes up, well kept Fullers London Pride and Wells & Youngs Bombardier, good wine choice, friendly efficient staff; quiet corners, turkey carpets, old furniture, prints and photographs, daily papers; children welcome, disabled access, big shady garden with good decking, lovely village setting by the green and duck pond *(Ron and Sheila Corbett, LM, Ian Phillips, Richard and Sheila Fitton, Tom and Ruth Rees, Phil Bryant)*

FARNHAM [SU8346]

Hop Blossom GU9 7HX [Long Garden Walk]: Cosy and convivial, with well kept Fullers, friendly chatty atmosphere *(Phil and Sally Gorton)*

Shepherd & Flock GU9 9JB [Moor Park Lane, on A31/A324/A325 roundabout]: Flower-decked pub on Europe's largest inhabited roundabout; welcoming landlord, eight interesting changing well kept ales, enjoyable food from baguettes up, simple up-to-date décor; they may try to keep your credit card while you eat; picnic-sets out in front and in pleasant enclosed back garden

with barbecue, open all day wknds *(David M Smith, E Ling)*

FICKLESHOLE [TQ3960]

White Bear CR6 9PH [Featherbed Lane/Fairchildes Lane; off A2022 Purley Rd just S of A212 roundabout]: Rambling, interestingly furnished partly 15th-c country dining pub, popular with families even at mid-week lunchtimes for good value food; lots of small rooms, beams and flagstones, friendly staff, well kept ales, good coffee, restaurant; games machines, piped music; children welcome, play area in pleasant sizeable garden, lots of picnic-sets on front terrace, open all day Sat *(LYM, Conor McGaughey)*

FRIDAY STREET [TQ1245]

Stephan Langton RH5 6JR [off B2126]: Prettily placed pub with good nearby walks; well kept Dorking, Fullers and Surrey Hills, farm cider, good choice of other drinks inc dozens of whiskies, sensible if not cheap home-made food (not Sat, Sun evening or Mon), welcoming log fire in bar, woodburner in dining area; children and dogs welcome, tables outside, open all day *(LYM, Ian Phillips, Tad Brown, Gordon and Margaret Ormondroyd, Phil Bryant, Gerald and Gabrielle Culliford, JMM, Stephen Funnell)*

GODALMING [SU9643]

Star GU7 1EL [Church St]: Friendly 17th-c local in cobbled pedestrian street, cosy low-beamed and panelled carpeted bar with nice mix of furnishings; impressive range of changing real ales and farm ciders, limited choice of bar food (not Sun-Weds), more modern back extension; juke box, small TV; tables under trees in yard behind, open all day *(Phil Bryant)*

GODSTONE [TQ3551]

Bell RH9 8DX [under a mile from M25 junction 6, via B2236]: Good choice of up-to-date and more traditional food in open-plan M&B family dining pub; comfortably modern furnishings and lighting in handsome old building, separate bar with Timothy Taylors Landlord and nice fireplace; pretty garden *(LYM, Grahame Brooks, N R White, A Flynn)*

GUILDFORD [SU9949]

Keep GU1 3UW [Castle St]: Attractive refurbishment, relaxed upmarket feel, good value all-day bar food (not Fri-Sun evenings), Surrey Hills Shere Drop and a guest such as fff; subdued lighting and candles, stripped brick, bare boards and panelling, medley of furnishings inc assorted tables and chairs, a pew, settle and settees; new covered outdoor area, open all day *(Phil Bryant)*

Kings Head GU1 3XQ [Quarry St]: 17th-c, lots of beams and stripped brickwork, inglenook fire, cosy corners with armchairs, stylish oval tables; well kept Courage, Hogs Back and Wychwood, decent wines, reasonably priced standard food (not wknd evenings), polite young staff; quiz nights, piped music, games machines, big-screen sports TV; no dogs; picnic-sets in pleasant back courtyard with roof terrace giving castle views, open all day *(Phil Bryant)*

Kings Head GU1 4JW [Kings Rd]: Sizeable Fullers pub with their ales, good value food all day (not Sun evening), several areas; children welcome, flower-filled back terrace with barbecues, open all day *(Ian Phillips)*

Rodboro Buildings GU1 4RY [Bridge St]: Wetherspoons in converted Dennis automotive factory and later Rodboro Print Works; wide range of well priced ales, good value food and coffee *(Ian Phillips)*

HASCOMBE [TQ0039]

White Horse GU8 4JA [B2130 S of Godalming]: Picturesque old rose-draped pub under newish management, real ales such as Harveys, Hook Norton and Ringwood, enjoyable food, interesting wines by the glass, friendly young staff; beamed bar with cushioned pews and woodburner, quiet small-windowed alcoves and further dining areas; small front terrace, spacious sloping back lawn, pretty village with good walks, handy for Winkworth Arboretum (NT); has been open all day wknds *(Martin and Karen Wake, Terry Buckland, Mr and Mrs A H Young, LYM)*

HOLMBURY ST MARY [TQ1144]

☆ *Kings Head* RH5 6NP: Friendly bare-boards pub in walking country, good fresh food using local supplies, helpful young licensees, well kept ales such as Kings and Surrey Hills, good wines by the glass; two-way log fire (not always lit mid-week), small traditional back restaurant (fish recommended), public bar with darts, TV and games machine; pretty spot with seats out facing the green, more in big sloping back garden, open all day at least wknds and summer *(Barry Steele-Perkins)*

Royal Oak RH5 6PF: Low-beamed 17th-c coaching inn, enjoyable food from baguettes to some interesting dishes, helpful staff, well kept ales, decent wine by the glass, fresh flowers, log fire; tables on front lawn, pleasant spot by the green and church, good walks, bedrooms *(Conor McGaughey, Tom and Ruth Rees, Tom and Rosemary Hall)*

HORLEY [TQ2844]

Farmhouse RH6 9LJ [Langshott]: 17th-c former farmhouse, a pub since 1985, with linked beamed rooms, pubby food all day inc late-night pizzas, well kept Courage Best, Fullers London Pride, Shepherd Neame Spitfire and a guest beer; big child-friendly back garden, front smokers' shelter *(Tony Hobden)*

HORSELL [SU9859]

Cricketers GU21 4XB [Horsell Birch]: Warm friendly country local, good sensibly priced food (all day Sun and bank hols), Courage Best, Fullers London Pride and Greene King Old Speckled Hen, cheerful service; log fire, quietly comfortable end sections, extended back eating area, carpet and shiny boards, children well catered for; picnic-sets out in front and in big well kept garden, wide views over Horsell Common *(Ian Phillips, Guy Consterdine)*

☆ *Red Lion* GU21 4SS [High St]: Large casually smart pub with good generous pubby and more sophisticated good all-day snacks like chicken satay skewers or hand-cut chips with peppercorn sauce; Courage Best, Fullers London Pride and Wells & Youngs Bombardier, good wines and other drinks, friendly attentive service even when busy; split-level bar with contemporary décor, bare boards and fire, picture-filled barn restaurant (children allowed), daily papers; ivy-clad passage to garden and comfortable tree-sheltered terrace, good walks, open all day *(Ian Phillips, Phil Bryant, Frances Naldrett, BB, Gill and Keith Croxton, Michael Hasslacher)*

HORSELL COMMON [TQ0160]

☆ *Bleak House* GU21 5NL [Chertsey Rd, The Anthonys; A320 Woking—Ottershaw]: Smart restauranty pub aka Sands at Bleak House, grey split sandstone for floor and face of bar counter, cool décor with black tables, sofas and stools; good if not cheap food, Hogs Back TEA and Surrey Hills Shere Drop, fresh juices, friendly attentive uniformed staff; lively acoustics; smokers' marquee in pleasant back garden merging into woods, with good shortish walks to sandpits which inspired H G Wells's *War of the Worlds*; bedrooms *(Phil Bryant, Ian Phillips)*

IRONS BOTTOM [TQ2546]

Three Horseshoes RH2 8PT [Sidlow Bridge, off A217]: Down-to-earth country local with newish friendly manager, good value carefully made food, good attentive service, Fullers London Pride, Surrey Hills Ranmore and a guest; darts; tables outside, summer barbecues *(C and R Bromage)*

KNAPHILL [SU9557]

Hunters Lodge GU21 2RP [Bagshot Rd]: Vintage Inn with comfortable linked beamed rooms, good log fires, assorted tables and chairs; reasonably priced standard food and some more upmarket dishes, good choice of wines by the glass, Fullers London Pride and Timothy Taylors Landlord, daily papers; disabled facilities, tables in pleasant well established garden *(Phil Bryant)*

LIGHTWATER [SU9262]

Red Lion GU18 5RP [Guildford Rd]: Pleasant brightly modern décor in mock-Tudor pub, cheerful and friendly, with decent food, real ales such as Hogs Back HBB and TEA, several wines by the glass; sofas and low tables at front of L-shaped carpeted bar, farmhouse tables behind; piped music may obtrude, two big-screen sports TVs; tables outside *(Phil Bryant)*

MARTYRS GREEN [TQ0857]

Black Swan KT11 1NG [handy for M25 junction 10; off A3 south-bound, but return N of junction]: Chunky seating and spacious contemporary restauranty décor (utterly changed from its days as the 'Slaughtered Lamb' in *An American Werewolf in London*); grand choice of wines and champagnes, several real ales inc Sharps Doom Bar and

Surrey Hills Shere Drop, pub food (not cheap, veg extra), log fire and under-floor heating; service can be slow when busy; children welcome, stylish black slate furniture out on extensively landscaped terrace, open all day *(John and Verna Aspinall, G Pincus, Susan and John Douglas, Harry Hersom)*

MERSTHAM [TQ3051]

Inn on the Pond RH1 4EU [Nutfield Marsh Rd, off A25 W of Godstone]: Recently well reworked as a dining pub, good value food, children's menu; beamed proper front bar area rambling around central fireplace, good service, Greene King and Sharps ales, Weston's cider, good choice of wines by the glass inc champagne, comfortable casually contemporary dining room, back conservatory; sheltered back terrace, views over small pond and nearby cricket ground to North Downs *(BB, Richard Abnett)*

MOGADOR [TQ2453]

Sportsman KT20 7ES [from M25 up A217 past 2nd roundabout, then Mogador signed; edge of Banstead Heath]: Nicely refurbished and extended low-ceilinged pub on Walton Heath (originally 16th-c royal hunting lodge); emphasis on good if not cheap plentiful food, welcoming traditional landlord, Badger, Courage, Sharps and Wells & Youngs, log fire, flagstoned bar with carpeted raised area, restaurant; soft piped music; picnic-sets out on common and on back lawn, more seats on front verandah, popular with walkers and riders *(Conor McGaughey, N R White, Phil Bryant, Graham Hill)*

NEWCHAPEL [TQ3641]

☆ *Wiremill* RH7 6HJ [Wire Mill Lane; off A22 just S of B2028 by Mormon Temple]: Spacious big-windowed two-storey pub, weatherboarded mill said to have been built with 16th-c ship's timbers; low beams and olde-worlde décor, relaxed atmosphere, good range of well kept ales, up-to-date locally sourced home-made food, friendly efficient service; lots of tables out on terrace by watersports lake (can be noisy speedboats), bedrooms, open all day *(Pam Adsley, Poppy Jones)*

OCKHAM [TQ0756]

Hautboy GU23 6NP: This remarkable red stone gothick folly, with its high-vaulted upstairs brasserie bar, nice outside area and bedrooms, closed summer 2008 amid objectionable plans to turn it into offices or have housing built around it; boarded-up and partly vandalised *(LYM)*

OCKLEY [TQ1440]

Inn on the Green RH5 5TD [Billingshurst Rd (A29)]: Welcoming former 17th-c coaching inn on the green of attractive village; good choice of enjoyable reasonably priced fresh food, well kept ales inc Adnams and Greene King, friendly attentive service; steps up to quiet eating area and dining conservatory; tables in secluded garden, six comfortable bedrooms, good breakfast *(BB, Pam Adsley, Derek and Heather Manning)*

☆ *Kings Arms* RH5 5TS [Stane St (A29)]: Attractive 17th-c country inn reworked as more restaurant than pub though keeping a proper bar; well kept mainstream ales, good choice of wines by the glass, good service, starched napkins and pretty tablecloths, comfortable olde-worlde décor inc lots of antique prints; good inglenook log fire, heavy beams and timbers, low lighting; children welcome, immaculate big back garden, good bedrooms *(LYM, David Dyson, Shirley Mackenzie)*

☆ *Punchbowl* RH5 5PU [Oakwood Hill, signed off A29 S]: Smart old-fashioned country pub, cheerful relaxed atmosphere, pleasant service, wide food choice (all day wknds) from good sandwiches to some imaginative dishes, Badger ales; daily papers, huge inglenook, polished flagstones, low beams, side restaurant, public bar with darts and pool; children allowed in dining area, picnic-sets in pretty garden, smokers' awning, quiet spot with good walks inc Sussex Border Path *(C and R Bromage, Conor McGaughey, LYM, Marianne and Peter Stevens)*

OTTERSHAW [TQ0261]

☆ *Castle* KT16 0LW [Brox Rd, off A320 not far from M25 junction 11]: Friendly two-bar early Victorian local with log fires, country paraphernalia on black ceiling joists and walls, six well kept ales inc Adnams, Greene King, Harveys and Timothy Taylors, Addlestone's cider, lunchtime and evening bar food (not Sun evening); TV, piped music; children welcome in conservatory till 7pm, dogs in bar, tables on terrace and grass, open all day wknds *(JMM, Ian Phillips, Guy Charrison, Dr and Mrs A K Clarke, Phil Bryant, LYM, S J and C C Davidson)*

OUTWOOD [TQ3246]

☆ *Bell* RH1 5PN [Outwood Common, just E of village; off A23 S of Redhill]: Attractive extended 17th-c country pub/restaurant, friendly prompt service, enjoyable generous food inc plenty of fish in softly lit smartly rustic beamed bar and restaurant area; Fullers and a guest such as Harveys, good wines by the glass, log fires; children and dogs welcome, piped music (turned down on request); summer barbecues and cream teas, pretty garden with play area and country views, handy for windmill *(LYM, Terry Buckland, C and R Bromage)*

Castle RH1 5QB [Millers Lane]: Welcoming panelled and carpeted country pub with well kept ales such as Adnams, Fullers and Harveys, short interesting choice of food from ciabattas up; log fire and old wooden tables, no piped music or machines; garden with heated decking and play area *(Chris Mills)*

OXSHOTT [TQ1460]

Victoria KT22 0JR [High St]: Low-ceilinged pubby bar with good range of real ales, good thai food in restaurant *(Gordon Stevenson)*

OXTED [TQ4048]

Royal Oak RH8 0RR [Caterfield Lane, Staffhurst Wood, S of town]: Cheerful and comfortable traditional bar, good value house wines, good ale range, enjoyable mainly local food inc imaginative dishes; country-view back dining room *(William Ruxton)*

PIRBRIGHT [SU9454]

☆ *Royal Oak* GU24 0DQ [Aldershot Rd; A324S of village]: Comfortable currently well run old Tudor pub, well kept Greene King, Hogs Back TEA and perhaps guest ales, good range of wines by the glass, sensibly priced pubby food; three log fires, heavily beamed and timbered rambling side areas, ancient stripped brickwork, family room; soft piped music; disabled facilities, extensive colourful gardens, good walks, open all day *(KC, Ian Phillips, LYM)*

White Hart GU24 0LP [The Green]: Dining pub with smart modern décor, sturdy pale wood furniture on black and white tartan carpet, some original flagstones, sofas by log fires in restored fireplaces; well kept Hogs Back TEA and Timothy Taylors Landlord, daily papers; area up steps popular with ladies who lunch; soft piped music; good tables and chairs in pleasant fenced front garden, play area behind *(Michael Dandy, David and Sue Smith)*

PUTTENHAM [SU9347]

☆ *Good Intent* GU3 1AR [signed off B3000 just S of A31 junction; The Street/Seale Lane]: Well worn-in beamed village local with up to half a dozen well kept changing ales, lively and convivial with friendly enthusiastic licensees, good value generous pubby food (not Sun, Mon evenings) from sandwiches up, popular Weds fish night; pre-ordering for muddy walkers available, farm cider, decent wine choice, log fire in cosy front bar with alcove seating, old photographs of the pub, simple dining area; children and dogs welcome, small sunny garden, good walks, free-range eggs for sale, open all day wknds *(Phil Bryant, Phil and Sally Gorton, E Ling, BB)*

PYRFORD LOCK [TQ0559]

☆ *Anchor* GU23 6QW [3 miles from M25 junction 10 – S on A3, then take Wisley slip rd and go on past RHS Garden]: Light and airy Badger family dining pub, pubby food all day (small helpings available), lunchtime sandwiches too; good value wines, cheerful service, daily papers, simple tables on bare boards, quieter more comfortable panelled back area, narrow-boat memorabilia, conservatory; shame there's no 'drinks only' queue; children welcome, dogs allowed in part, splendid terrace in lovely spot by bridge and locks on River Wey Navigation (very handy for RHS Wisley), fenced-off play area, open all day *(Mr and Mrs W W Burke, Phil Bryant, Ian Phillips, Mrs G R Sharman, Susan and Erik Falck-Therkelsen, C and R Bromage, LYM, Kevin Flack, David and Sue Smith, Gordon Stevenson, Sue and Mike Todd, Susan and John Douglas, Shirley Mackenzie)*

REDHILL [TQ2750]

Garland RH1 6PP [Brighton Rd]: Friendly smartly kept 19th-c Harveys local, their full

range kept well, bargain wkdy bar lunches; dim lighting, darts *(N R White, Tony Hobden)*

REIGATE HEATH [TQ2349]

Skimmington Castle RH2 8RL [off A25 Reigate—Dorking via Flanchford Rd and Bonny's Rd]: Small country pub revamped under attentive new management with emphasis on dining; panelled beamed rooms with big log fireplace *(Ian and Nita Cooper, Conor McGaughey, LYM)*

RIPLEY [TQ0556]

Anchor GU23 6AE [High St]: Friendly and comfortable former 16th-c almshouse with interesting low-beamed linked areas, Fullers London Pride, Greene King IPA and Hogs Back TEA; nautical memorabilia and photographs of Ripley's cycling heyday; log fires, newspapers, pubby food emphasising thai dishes; piped music; disabled facilities, tables in sunny coachyard *(Ian Phillips, BB)*

Seven Stars GU23 6DL [Newark Lane (B367)]: Neatly run traditional 1930s pub, popular lunchtimes for good generous food from sandwiches to plenty of seafood, lots of blackboards, good Sun lunches; well kept Fullers London Pride, Greene King and Shepherd Neame Spitfire, good wines and coffee, open fire; quiet piped music; picnic-sets in large tidy garden *(Ian Phillips, N R White, Phil Bryant, Shirley Mackenzie, Kevin Flack)*

SEND [TQ0156]

New Inn GU23 7EN [Send Rd, Cartbridge]: Well placed old pub by Wey Navigation canal, long bar decorated to suit, Adnams, Fullers London Pride, Greene King Abbot, Kings and Ringwood Best; friendly landlord, good value food from toasted sandwiches up, log-effect gas fires; large waterside garden with moorings and smokers' shelter *(Ian Phillips, Phil Bryant)*

SENDMARSH [TQ0455]

☆ *Saddlers Arms* GU23 6JQ [Send Marsh Rd]: Genial and attentive licensees in unpretentious low-beamed local, homely and warm, with Courage Best, Fullers London Pride, Greene King Old Speckled Hen and Shepherd Neame Spitfire; good value generous home-made food (all day Sun) from sandwiches to pizzas and pubby favourites, open fire, toby jugs, brassware etc; no music or TV; picnic-sets out front and back *(Phil Bryant, DWAJ, Shirley Mackenzie, Ian Phillips)*

SHACKLEFORD [SU9345]

Cyder House GU8 6AN [Peper Harow Lane]: Smart comfortably refurbished pub doing well under friendly helpful new licensees; Badger ales, decent house wines, good if pricey generous food (all day Tues-Sat, till 4pm Sun, Mon) from sandwiches and bar snacks up inc Sun roasts, children's helpings, morning coffee and afternoon tea; mix of furniture inc leather sofas in light and airy linked areas around central servery, log fire, signed celebrity photographs; well behaved dogs welcome, terrace seating and lawn, play area, nice leafy village setting, good

walks, open all day, till 7pm Sun
(Mr N McGill, Martin and Karen Wake, BB)

SHALFORD [SU9946]

Parrot GU4 8DW [Broadford]: Big warmly welcoming pub with wide range of fairly priced food from good snacks up, Fullers London Pride, Hogs Back TEA and Surrey Hills Shere Drop, quick friendly staff; rows of neat pine dining tables, some easy chairs around low tables, pleasant conservatory; attractive garden *(Mrs P J Pearce, C and R Bromage, Kevin Flack, John and Heather Wright)*

☆ ***Seahorse*** GU4 8BU [A281 S of Guildford; The Street]: Former Vintage Inn reopened 2008 as one of about 40 gently upmarket M&B dining pubs, mainly in the Midlands; enjoyable food inc popular reasonably priced lunch menu, substantial snacks through the afternoon, friendly well trained young staff, Hogs Back TEA and good choice of other drinks (bargain mojitos or Martinis 5-8); good contemporary furniture and artwork, smart dining room, comfortable part nr entrance with sofas and huge window; big lawned garden with picnic-sets, covered terrace *(Martin and Karen Wake, BB)*

SHEPPERTON [TQ0765]

Thames Court TW17 9LJ [Shepperton Lock, Ferry Lane; turn left off B375 towards Chertsey, 100yds from square]: Huge Vintage Inn dining pub well placed by the Thames, good choice of wines by the glass, ales inc Fullers London Pride, Hogs Back TEA and Timothy Taylors Landlord, usual food from sandwiches up all day; galleried central atrium with attractive panelled areas up and down stairs, two good log fires, daily papers; can get very busy summer wknds but copes well; children welcome, large attractive tree-shaded terrace with heaters, open all day *(Mayur Shah, Phil Bryant, Ian Phillips)*

SHERE [TQ0747]

☆ ***White Horse*** GU5 9HF [signed off A25 3 miles E of Guildford; Middle St]: Splendid Chef & Brewer, popular with families and a lovely place to take foreign visitors – uneven floors, massive beams and timbers, Tudor stonework, olde-worlde décor with oak wall seats and two log fires, one in a huge inglenook, several rooms off small busy bar; good value food all day from sandwiches up, friendly efficient staff and warm atmosphere, real ales such as Courage, Hogs Back TEA and Greene King, lots of sensibly priced wines by the glass; dogs welcome, big back garden, beautiful film-set village; open all day *(Ian Phillips, LYM, Mrs G R Sharman)*

SOUTH GODSTONE [TQ3549]

Fox & Hounds RH9 8LY [Tilburstow Hill Rd/Harts Lane, off A22]: Pleasant old country pub with woodburner in low-beamed bar, welcoming staff, enjoyable food from pubby staples to good seafood, nice puddings; well kept Greene King and a guest such as Brains Rev James from tiny bar counter, restaurant with inglenook; open all day *(John Branston, LYM)*

STAINES [TQ0471]

Old Red Lion TW18 4PB [Leacroft]: Pleasant local with well kept Courage Best, Fullers London Pride and Wells & Youngs Bitter, decent pub food; terrace tables opp the small green *(Chris Sale)*

SUNBURY [TQ1068]

Flower Pot TW16 6AA [Thames St, handy for M3 junction 1, via Green St off exit roundabout]: Friendly busy 18th-c inn across road from the Thames; trendy décor and nice artwork; good home-made food with emphasis on fish, snacks too, well kept Brakspears, Fullers London Pride and Greene King, good choice of wines by the glass; helpful cheerful young staff, newspapers, live music nights; six bedrooms *(Gerry and Rosemary Dobson, Arthur S Maxted, Ian Phillips, Neil and Anita Christopher, Edward Mirzoeff)*

SUTTON GREEN [TQ0054]

Olive Tree GU4 7QD [Sutton Green Rd]: Modern dining pub with good honest food (not Sun, Mon evenings) inc fish and seafood, cheaper bar menu inc sandwiches; well kept Fullers London Pride, Harveys and Timothy Taylors Landlord, good choice of wines by the glass, attentive staff; relaxing back dining room with minimalist décor *(JMM, C and R Bromage, Ian Phillips)*

TADWORTH [TQ2355]

Dukes Head KT20 5SL [Dorking Rd (B2032 opp common and woods)]: Roomy and comfortable, with good range of enjoyable food from good sandwiches up, well kept Adnams, good choice of wines by the glass, friendly service; two big inglenook log fires; plenty of garden tables, open all day *(Jenny and Brian Seller)*

THAMES DITTON [TQ1567]

Albany KT7 0QY [Queens Rd, signed off Summer Rd]: M&B bar-with-restaurant in lovely Thames-side position, upscale food, choice of wines by the glass; beers inc Fullers London Pride and Timothy Taylors Landlord, log fire, daily papers, river pictures; nice balconies, river-view terrace and lawn, moorings, open all day *(Ian Phillips, Gordon Stevenson, Tom and Ruth Rees)*

TILFORD [SU8743]

☆ ***Barley Mow*** GU10 2BU [The Green, off B3001 SE of Farnham; also signed off A287]: Opposite pretty cricket green, with woodburner in snug little low-ceilinged traditional bar, nice scrubbed tables in two small rooms set for food on the left, interesting cricketing prints and old photographs; pubby food inc popular late Sun lunch (bar snacks earlier till 2pm that day), wknd afternoon teas, charming friendly service, well kept Adnams, Courage Best and Fullers London Pride, imaginative wine list; darts and table skittles; no children except in back coach house; narrow front terrace, picnic-sets and barbecue in back garden fenced off from small stream *(LM, BB)*

UPPER HALE [SU8349]
Alfreds GU9 0JA [Bishops Rd, Upper Hale]:
Prince Alfred given humbler name by
welcoming new licensees, good home-made
food in restaurant, reasonable prices, top-
notch service, comfortable bar
(Philippa Heelis)
VIRGINIA WATER [TQ9768]
Wheatsheaf GU25 4QF [London Rd; A30]:
Several linked areas in large Chef & Brewer
with reasonably priced food, Fullers London
Pride, Hogs Back TEA and Wells & Youngs
Bombardier; garden tables (traffic noise), by
wooded entry to lake area *(Phil Bryant)*
WALLISWOOD [TQ1138]
Scarlett Arms RH5 5RD [signed from
Ewhurst—Rowhook back rd, or off A29 S of
Ockley]: Smartly unpretentious country pub,
friendly helpful staff, enjoyable home-made
food inc bargain deals, Badger ales; low
black oak beams, flagstones, simple
furniture, two log fires (huge inglenook),
back dining room; peaceful benches in front,
garden tables under cocktail parasols, good
walks *(LYM, Richard and Sissel Harris)*
WALTON ON THE HILL [TQ2255]
Blue Ball KT20 7UE [not far from M25
junction 8; Deans Lane, off B2220 by pond]:
Facing common nr duck pond, cosily
refurbished, with good choice of home-made
food, good atmosphere, friendly uniformed
staff, several real ales, decent wines;
restaurant (open all day Sun) overlooking
big garden; good walking area *(Pam Adsley)*
Chequers KT20 7SF [Chequers Lane]: Mock-
Tudor Youngs pub with several rooms
rambling around central servery, quick
friendly service, well kept ales, enjoyable bar
food and more expensive restaurant; terrace,
neat sheltered garden *(C and R Bromage,
LYM, Sarah Howes)*
WALTON-ON-THAMES [TQ1065]
Ashley Park KT12 1JP [Station
Approach/Ashley Park Rd]: Comfortable and
well run Ember Inn with good atmosphere,
reasonably priced food, well kept real ales;
open all day, bedrooms in adjoining
Innkeepers Lodge *(Ron and Sheila Corbett)*
WARLINGHAM [TQ3955]
☆ *Botley Hill Farmhouse* CR6 9QH [S on
Limpsfield Rd (B269)]: Busy pub dating back
to 16th c, with standard food inc popular
Sun roasts, well kept Greene King and Kings
ales, good choice of wines by the glass,
hard-working friendly staff; low-ceilinged
linked rooms up and down steps, soft
lighting, quite close-set tables, big log
fireplace in one attractive flagstoned room;
wknd entertainment in marquee inc loud live
music; children and dogs welcome, disabled
access, side and back terraces with plastic
furniture, neat garden with play area, ducks
and aviary *(LM, N R White, BB,
Conor McGaughey)*
White Lion CR6 9EG [Farleigh Rd (B269)]:
Extended from low-beamed dark-panelled
Tudor core, with fireplace snugged in by
high-backed settles; sensibly priced food

(not Sun evening), well kept real ales,
friendly atmosphere; neat back garden
(Conor McGaughey, LYM)
WEST CLANDON [TQ0451]
☆ *Bulls Head* GU4 7ST [A247 SE of Woking]:
Comfortable and spotless, based on 1540s
timbered hall house, popular especially with
older people lunchtime for good value hearty
food from sandwiches up inc home-made
proper pies (no food Sun evening); small
lantern-lit beamed front bar with open fire
and some stripped brick, old local prints and
bric-a-brac, simple raised back inglenook
dining area, friendly helpful staff, Courage
Best, Greene King and Surrey Hills, good
coffee; no piped music, games room with
darts and pool; no credit cards; children
and dogs on leads welcome, disabled
access, good play area in neat garden,
handy for Clandon Park, good walks *(DWAJ,
Ian Phillips)*
WEST HORSLEY [TQ0853]
Barley Mow KT24 6HR [off A246
Leatherhead—Guildford at Bell & Colvill
garage roundabout; The Street]: Tree-shaded
traditional pub with low beams, flagstones
and carpets, leather settees on bare boards,
big log fire, cottagey lighting; real ales such
as Fullers London Pride, Greene King IPA,
Shepherd Neame Spitfire and Wells & Youngs,
decent wines and spirits, good value food
(not Sun evening); daily papers, vintage and
classic car pictures (may be an AC Cobra or
Jaguar XK outside too), comfortable barn-
like softly lit dining room; unobtrusive piped
music, wide-screen TV; dogs and children
welcome, picnic-sets in good-sized garden,
open all day *(David and Sue Smith, John and
Joan Nash, Michael Dandy, Dr and
Mrs A K Clarke, LYM, Ian Phillips,
David Jackman, John Branston, Mr and
Mrs A Sawder, BOB, William Ruxton)*
King William IV KT24 6BG [The Street]:
Comfortable and welcoming early 19th-c pub
with very low-beamed open-plan rambling
bar, good food from sandwiches up here and
in conservatory restaurant; decent choice of
wines by the glass, well kept Courage Best
and Directors and Surrey Hills Shere Drop,
good coffee, log fire, board games; children
and dogs very welcome, good disabled
access, small garden with decking and lovely
hanging baskets *(Ian Phillips, Michael Dandy,
Dr and Mrs A K Clarke, Shirley Mackenzie,
Gillian and Tory Moorby)*
WESTHUMBLE [TQ1751]
Stepping Stones RH5 6BS [just off A24
below Box Hill]: Comfortable dining pub
with good sensibly priced lunchtime food inc
Sun roasts, more elaborate evening menu,
good friendly service even when busy;
circular bar with Fullers London Pride,
Greene King Abbot and a guest beer (drinks
brought to table), clean uncluttered décor,
open fire, no music; children and walkers
welcome, terrace and garden with summer
barbecue and play area *(DWAJ, Norma and
Noel Thomas, Conor McGaughey)*

WEYBRIDGE [TQ0764]

British Volunteer KT13 8TH [Heath Rd/Waverley Rd]: Friendly local with roomy bar around central servery, Fullers London Pride, St Austell Tribute, Timothy Taylors Landlord and Wells & Youngs Bombardier, good value pubby food, quick cheerful service; pool, quieter back lounge; piped music, big-screen sports TV, machines; children and dogs welcome, small terrace *(Phil Bryant, Tony and Wendy Hobden)*

Hand & Spear KT13 8TX [Old Heath Rd/Station Rd]: Big Youngs pub well refurbished with several different areas, enjoyable generous food, large informal tables and more formal dining room, their ales and a guest, friendly staff; good seating outside *(Ian Phillips, Minda and Stanley Alexander)*

Jolly Farmer KT13 9BN [Princes Rd]: Attractive and civilised small low-beamed local opp picturesque cricket ground; friendly efficient service, good value pubby food from sandwiches up, several Marstons-related ales, good choice of wines by the glass, daily papers, toby jugs and interesting old photographs; no music or TV; smart front terrace, nice back garden *(Ian Phillips, Phil Bryant)*

Minnow KT13 8NG [Thames St/Walton Lane]: Attractive M&B dining pub with contemporary pastel décor and unusual decorative panels, chunky tables and chairs, some sofas and armchairs; helpful staff, enjoyable fresh food inc pizzas, pasta and traditional dishes, good range of real ales such as Timothy Taylors Landlord, good wines by the glass; open fire in raised hearth; big front garden with heaters and awning *(Phil Bryant)*

Oatlands Chaser KT13 9RW [Oatlands Chase]: Very big attractively modernised building in quiet residential road, large rambling bar with stylish modern décor, pastels and glazed panels, flagstones and painted boards, feature central fireplace; carefully mismatched furnishings mainly laid out for the wide range of good food (all day) inc bargain set menu, Sun roasts and proper children's meals; Timothy Taylors Landlord, good wine choice, newspapers; disabled access, lots of tables on alluringly lit front terrace, some under trees, 19 immaculate bedrooms, open all day *(Phil Bryant, Minda and Stanley Alexander, Ian Phillips, BB)*

☆ **Old Crown** KT13 8LP [Thames St]: Comfortably old-fashioned three-bar pub dating from the 16th c, very popular for good value traditional food (not Sun-Tues evenings) from sandwiches to fresh grimsby fish, well kept Courage Directors and Wells & Youngs, good choice of wines by the glass, service good even when busy; family lounge and conservatory, coal-effect gas fire; may be sports TV in back bar with Lions RFC photographs; children welcome, suntrap streamside garden *(Minda and*

Stanley Alexander, Ian Phillips, DWAJ, JMM, Phil Bryant)*

☆ **Prince of Wales** KT13 9NX [Cross Rd/Anderson Rd off Oatlands Drive]: Civilised and attractively restored, good value generous pubby food inc Sun roasts, real ales such as Adnams, Fullers ESB and London Pride, Wells & Youngs and one brewed for the pub, ten wines by the glass; relaxed lunchtime atmosphere, friendly service, daily papers, log-effect fire, tribal mask collection, stripped-pine dining room down a couple of steps; big-screen TVs for major sports events; well behaved children welcome *(Ian Phillips, Phil Bryant, Minda and Stanley Alexander)*

Queens Head KT13 8XS [Bridge Rd]: Real ales such as Courage Best, Fullers London Pride and Sharps Doom Bar, friendly french staff, interesting reasonably priced bar food, good value french bistro; piped music may be loud; picnic-sets out by pavement and in back yard *(Hunter and Christine Wright)*

WINDLESHAM [SU9264]

Bee GU20 6PD [School Rd]: Stylishly refurbished under new owners with emphasis on eating; enjoyable if pricey upscale food, Sun roasts, morning coffee and pastries, good choice of wines by the glass, four well kept real ales; picnic-sets on small front terrace and in nice back garden with play area *(Dr Martin Owton)*

☆ **Half Moon** GU20 6BN [Church Rd]: Enjoyable if not cheap much-extended pub mainly laid for pubby food from sandwiches up, well kept ales such as Fullers London Pride, Hogs Back TEA, Ringwood Fortyniner, Timothy Taylors Landlord and Theakstons Old Peculier; Weston's farm cider, decent wines, plenty of children's drinks, cheerful young staff; log fires, World War II pictures, modern furnishings, attractive barn restaurant out along covered flagstoned walkway; piped music, silenced games machine; huge tidy garden with two terraces and play area *(Gordon Stevenson, Guy Consterdine, Martin Wilson, Phil Bryant)*

WOKING [TQ9958]

Bridge Barn GU21 6NL [Bridge Barn Lane; right off Goldsworth Rd towards St Johns]: Pleasant extended Beefeater by Basingstoke Canal (lots of waterside tables), interesting layout – restaurant up in barn rafters, nooks and crannies in flagstoned bars below; their usual food inc bargains, Greene King IPA and Shepherd Neame Spitfire, log fire; disabled facilities, well fenced play area, comfortable Premier Inn bedroom block *(Ian Phillips)*

Inn at Maybury GU22 8AB [Maybury Hill/Old Woking Rd (B382)]: Recently reopened refurbished Victorian dining pub, wide food range, pizza oven and rotisserie, good wine choice, Bass and Timothy Taylors Landlord; log fire, conservatory; piped music, no dogs; children welcome, disabled facilities, plenty of outside tables, open all day *(Ian Phillips)*

Rowbarge GU21 7SA [St Johns Rd]: Recently quite smartly modernised cottage-style pub backing on to Basingstoke Canal; Courage Best and Shepherd Neame Spitfire, pubby food, log fires; neat hardwood deck, picnic-sets on lawn with big play area *(Ian Phillips)*

Wetherspoons GU21 5AJ [Chertsey Rd]: Large and busy with shoppers yet with lots of cosy areas and side snugs, good range of food all day, half a dozen or more interesting well kept real ales, good choice of coffees; bargain prices, friendly helpful staff, daily papers, old local pictures; no music; open all day from 9am *(Tony Hobden, Ian Phillips, Tony and Wendy Hobden)*

Wheatsheaf GU21 4AL [Chobham Rd]: Ember Inn with enthusiastic and capable young staff, good choice of ales such as Batemans, Thwaites Nutty Black and Wadworths 6X, quickly served tasty bargain food; lots of alcoves and smaller areas; open all day *(David M Smith, Ian Phillips)*

WRECCLESHAM [SU8344]

☆ **Bat & Ball** GU10 4SA [Bat & Ball Lane, South Farnham; approach from Sandrock Hill and Upper Bourne Lane, then narrow steep lane to pub]: Neatly refurbished welcoming pub tucked away in hidden valley; wide range of above-average pubby and more upmarket food (small helpings available) inc good puddings display, Wells & Youngs, Harveys and four guest ales (Jun beer festival); good choice of wines by the glass, friendly efficient staff, live music (last Sun of month); TV; children and dogs welcome, disabled facilities, tables out on attractive heated terrace with vine arbour and in garden with substantial play fort, open all day *(BB, J and H Turner)*

Sandrock GU10 4NS [Sandrock Hill Road]: Popular recently reworked real ale pub, two minimalist front bars with chunky furniture on bare boards; helpfully described ales from Arundel, Bowman, Exmoor, fff, Hop Back, Otter and Timothy Taylors; friendly staff, good pubby food (not Sun evening), open fires; children and dogs welcome, pleasant heated terrace, open all day *(Janet Whittaker, Simon Fletcher, Phil Bryant)*

Post Office address codings confusingly give the impression that some pubs are in Surrey when they're really in Hampshire or London (which is where we list them). And there's further confusion from the way the Post Office still talks about Middlesex – which disappeared in local government reorganisation nearly 50 years ago.

Sussex

Many of the best pubs here pre-date the Pilgrim Fathers, so there's bags of genuine character and some conspicuously old-fashioned country taverns – the George & Dragon near Coolham and Royal Oak at Wineham particularly stand out. And there's often now a delicious slant towards food. Notable dining pubs are the nicely unchanging Three Horseshoes at Elsted, Half Moon at Warninglid, Jolly Sportsman at East Chiltington, Star & Garter at East Dean and Griffin in Fletching. The Jolly Sportsman at East Chiltington is our Sussex Dining Pub of the Year. Perhaps less easily, sheer value can be found here, too, with real food bargains at the Basketmakers Arms in Brighton, Six Bells at Chiddingly and Lewes Arms in Lewes (one of eight new Sussex Main Entries – all interestingly varied and all properly pubby rather than just would-be restaurants). Among numerous rewarding all-rounders, the Rose Cottage at Alciston, Cricketers Arms at Berwick, Fox Goes Free at Charlton and Giants Rest at Wilmington make a nice group beneath the South Downs. We have three contrasting Main Entries in Rye, with the Ship now joining the Mermaid and Ypres Castle. Other current favourites include the Stag at Balls Cross, Blackboys Inn (now doing accommodation), Anchor Bleu in Bosham, Black Horse at Byworth and Huntsman at Eridge Station. There are too many really good Lucky Dip entries to pick out individually here, with nearly four dozen earning a star – most already inspected and approved by us. The area has a lot of good small breweries, too. Harveys is very widely available and Dark Star is becoming a favourite, with Kings, Ballards, Arundel, Langham and Hepworths well worth looking out for.

ALCISTON   TQ5005   MAP 3

Rose Cottage
Village signposted off A27 Polegate—Lewes; BN26 6UW

Old-fashioned cottage with fresh local food, cosy fires and country bric-a-brac, a good little wine list and local beers; bedrooms

Snuggled in beneath the downs in a tranquil one-street village and in super territory for walks and mountain bike rides, this informal, traditional little pub scores consistently for food. There are cosy winter log fires, half a dozen tables with cushioned pews under quite a forest of harness, traps, a thatcher's blade and lots of other black ironware, and more bric-a-brac on the shelves above the stripped pine dado or in the etched-glass windows; in the mornings you may also find Jasper the parrot (he gets too noisy in the evenings and is moved upstairs). There's a lunchtime overflow into the restaurant area as they don't take bookings in the bar then. Dark Star Hophead and Harveys Best on handpump, and a good little wine list with fair value house wines and a few nice bin ends; the landlord is quite a plain-speaking character. Piped music, darts and board games. There are heaters outside for cooler evenings and the small paddock in the garden has ducks and chickens; boules. Nearby fishing and shooting. The charming small village (and local church) are certainly worth a look. They take self-catering bedroom bookings for a minimum of two nights.

⚟ **Using fresh local and often organic produce, the well liked food includes ploughman's, soup, starters like smoked salmon cornet, home-made pâté or guacamole with pitta bread, salads, sausages, steaks from locally reared beef and blackboard specials which might feature potted brown shrimps, pancakes with cream cheese and spinach, steak and ale pie with shortcrust pastry, cheesy topped grilled mussels, a daily fish dish and their popular 'jolly posh fish pie' with salmon and tiger prawns. They add a 10% service charge for meals served in the restaurant.** Starters/Snacks: £3.25 to £6.50. Main Courses: £8.50 to £17.95. Puddings: £3.50 to £4.95

Free house ~ Licensee Ian Lewis ~ Real ale ~ Bar food ~ (01323) 870377 ~ Children allowed if over 10 ~ Dogs allowed in bar ~ Open 11.30-3, 6.30-11 ~ Bedrooms: /£60S

Recommended by Ian and Barbara Rankin, Mark Farrington, Jenny and Peter Lowater, Paul Boot, Alan Cowell, Andrea Rampley, Paul Lucas, the Didler, Paul Lloyd, David Cosham, Bruce Bird, MP, Mrs L M Beard, Peter and Giff Bennett

ALFRISTON
TQ5203   MAP 3

George
High Street; BN26 5SY

Venerable inn in lovely village with comfortable, heavily beamed bars, good wines, several real ales and bedrooms; fine nearby walks

---

In the centre of this much-visited showcase village, this well-heeled, ancient inn has a spacious, peaceful flint-walled garden. The long bar has massive low beams hung with hops, appropriately soft lighting and a log fire (or summer flower arrangement) in a huge stone inglenook fireplace that dominates the room, with lots of copper and brass around it. There are settles and chairs around sturdy stripped tables, Greene King IPA and Abbot, and a guest like Hardys & Hansons Old Trip on handpump, decent wines including champagne by the glass, board games and piped music; the lounge has comfortable sofas, standing timbers and rugs on the wooden floor. The restaurant is cosy and candlelit. Two long-distance paths, the South Downs Way and Vanguard Way, cross here and Cuckmere Haven is close by.

⚟ **Bar food at lunchtime includes sandwiches served with soup or chips, a rustic sharing board, mussels in garlic and cream with chips and mayonnaise, flat mushrooms sautéed in garlic and topped with smoked bacon and goats cheese, pork and leek sausages, and steak, mushroom and Guinness suet pudding; evening choices such as grilled bass fillet on curried mussel broth, sirloin steak with red onion compote, vegetarian risotto and lamb rump with redcurrant and mint sauce.** Starters/Snacks: £4.00 to £6.50. Main Courses: £10.00 to £16.95. Puddings: £5.50

Greene King ~ Lease Roland and Cate Couch ~ Real ale ~ Bar food (12-2.30, 7-9(10 Fri and Sat)) ~ Restaurant ~ (01323) 870319 ~ Children welcome ~ Dogs allowed in bar and bedrooms ~ Open 11-11(midnight Fri and Sat) ~ Bedrooms: £60S/£90B

Recommended by Paul Humphreys, Peter and Giff Bennett, Trevor and Sylvia Millum, C and R Bromage, Mrs L M Beard, Tina and David Woods-Taylor, Eddie Edwards, Jean and Douglas Troup, J A Snell, Mark Farrington, Ann and Colin Hunt, Mrs Hazel Rainer

ARLINGTON
TQ5507   MAP 3

Old Oak
Caneheath, off A22 or A27 NW of Polegate; BN26 6SJ

Comfortable rooms in pleasant country pub, tasty pubby food, real ales and quiet garden

---

Usefully open all day, this former almshouse stands on a quiet country lane close to Abbots Wood nature reserve. The L-shaped bar is open-plan with heavy beams, well spaced tables and comfortable seating, log fires and Badger K&B, Harveys Best and a changing guest such as Sharps Doom Bar Bitter tapped from the cask; several malt whiskies, piped music and toad in the hole (a Sussex pub game involving tossing a coin into a hole). There are seats in the peaceful garden. More up-to-date reports please.

⏢ **Decent bar food includes filled baguettes and baked potatoes, soup, ploughman's, duck and orange pâté, tiger prawns in garlic oil with a sweet chilli dip, home-baked honey and mustard ham with eggs, spinach and mascarpone lasagne, steak in ale pie, curry with mango chutney, a roast of the day, bass with mediterranean vegetables, and puddings.** *Starters/Snacks: £2.95 to £5.95. Main Courses: £5.95 to £8.95. Puddings: £2.95 to £3.95*

Free house ~ Licensees Mr J Boots and Mr B Slattery ~ Real ale ~ Bar food (12-2.30, 6.30-9.30; all day weekends) ~ Restaurant ~ (01323) 482072 ~ Children welcome ~ Dogs allowed in bar ~ Open 11-11

Recommended by Jenny and Peter Lowater, David and Candy Owens, Tina and David Woods-Taylor, Stuart and Diana Hughes

BALLS CROSS
SU9826 MAP 2

Stag ◨

Village signposted off A283 at N edge of Petworth, brown sign to pub there too; GU28 9JP

Popular little local with a friendly landlord, well kept beer, nice traditional food and seats in sizeable garden

Run by genial staff, this convivial 17th-c country pub has a good-sized garden behind, divided by a shrubbery, with teak or cast-iron tables and chairs, picnic-sets and, in summer, a couple of canvas awnings. The tiny flagstoned bar has a winter log fire in a huge inglenook fireplace, just a couple of tables, a window seat and a few chairs and leather-seated bar stools. On the right, a second room with a rug on its bare boards has space for just a single table. Beyond is an appealing old-fashioned dining room with quite a few horsey pictures. There are yellowing cream walls and low shiny ochre ceilings throughout, with soft lighting from little fringed wall lamps, and fishing rods and country knick-knacks hanging from the ceilings. On the left, a separate carpeted room with a couple of big Victorian prints has bar skittles, darts and board games. Badger K&B, First Gold and Hopping Hare on handpump, decent wines by the glass, summer cider and some nice malt whiskies. There are more picnic-sets out under green canvas parasols in front and the hitching rail does get used. The veteran gents' (and ladies') are outside.

⏢ **Bar food features locally reared game, beef and pork and includes lunchtime filled baguettes and baked potatoes, soup, home-made pies and pâté.** *Starters/Snacks: £5.50 to £9.50. Main Courses: £7.50 to £16.00. Puddings: £4.50 to £5.50*

Badger ~ Tenant Hamish Barrie Hiddleston ~ Real ale ~ Bar food (not Sun evening) ~ Restaurant ~ (01403) 820241 ~ Well behaved children welcome ~ Dogs welcome ~ Open 11-3, 6-11; 12-3.30, 7-10.30 Sun ~ Bedrooms: £35/£60

Recommended by Tony and Wendy Hobden, Gerry and Rosemary Dobson, Michael B Griffith, the Didler, R B Gardiner

BERWICK
TQ5105 MAP 3

Cricketers Arms

Lower Road, S of A27; BN26 6SP

Cottagey and unchanging in a quiet setting with welcoming little bars, nice staff, traditional food (all day weekends and summer weekdays); charming garden

A thoroughly likeable country pub with no pretensions, this is valued by readers for its warm welcome, good food and abundant character. The three small cottagey rooms are all similarly furnished with simple benches against the half-panelled walls, a pleasant mix of old country tables and chairs, a few bar stools and some country prints; quarry tiles on the floors (nice worn ones in the middle room), two log fires in little brick fireplaces, a huge black supporting beam in each of the low ochre ceilings, and (in the end room) some attractive cricketing pastels; some of the beams are hung with cricket bats. Harveys Best and three seasonal ales tapped from the cask and decent wines with a dozen by the glass; cribbage, dominoes and an old Sussex coin game called toad in the hole. In fine weather, the garden in front of the pub is delightful, with seats amidst small brick paths and mature flowering shrubs and plants; there are more seats behind the building. The wall paintings in the nearby church done by the Bloomsbury Group during World War II are worth a look, and the pub is very well placed for walks on and beneath the South Downs.

🍴 **Popular bar food includes starters like chicken liver and mushroom terrine, crayfish cocktail or crispy whitebait, various platters (the spanish one is much liked), and main courses like warm herb couscous salad with feta cheese, local pork and herb sausages with free-range egg, warm chicken salad, summer dressed crab salad, daily specials, and puddings.** *Starters/Snacks: £5.75 to £6.75. Main Courses: £8.50 to £13.95. Puddings: £4.95*

Harveys ~ Lease Peter Brown ~ Real ale ~ Bar food (12-2.15, 6.15-9; all day weekends and summer weekdays) ~ (01323) 870469 ~ Children in family room only ~ Dogs welcome ~ Open 11-11; 12-10.30 Sun; 11-3, 6-10.30 weekdays in winter; closed 25 Dec

Recommended by Pierre Richterich, Alan Cowell, Richard Endacott, C and R Bromage, M G Hart, the Didler, Andrea Rampley, Peter and Giff Bennett, Jenny and Peter Lowater

BLACKBOYS   TQ5220   MAP 3

Blackboys Inn
B2192, S edge of village; TN22 5LG

Pretty 14th-c pub, bustling locals' bar, nice old dining rooms, good choice of drinks, often interesting food and plenty of seats in attractive garden

In the lush, folded landscape of the Weald, this nicely unchanged medieval pub is set back from a country road, with a large, informal lawn laid out with tables partly shaded by chestnut trees and overlooking a pond. Inside, the bustling locals' bar to the left has a good, chatty atmosphere, there's a bar area to the right with bar stools and a couple of tables, and the other rooms – used for dining – have dark oak beams, bare boards or parquet, antique prints and, usually, a good log fire in the inglenook fireplace. Harveys Best, Hadlow and a couple of seasonal guests on handpump and ten wines by the glass; piped music. They now also have accommodation; we would welcome reports from readers who stay here. The Vanguard Way passes the pub, the Wealdway goes close by and there's the Woodland Trust opposite.

🍴 **The bar food includes soup, sandwiches, burgers, chilli con carne, beer-battered cod and specials such as smoked duck breast salad or seafood risotto; the restaurant menu – often interesting, though there may be quite a wait – has more elaborate items like chorizo and bacon salad, chicken escalope with parma ham on saffron risotto, pork medallions with cannellini beans, and bass fillet with mussel and saffron broth. Daily specials and Sunday roasts might feature local game, and they use vegetables and herbs from their own garden; puddings like triple chocolate brownie, banoffi pie and apple crumble.** *Starters/Snacks: £4.95 to £9.95. Main Courses: £6.50 to £12.50. Puddings: £5.50*

Harveys ~ Tenant Paul James ~ Real ale ~ Bar food (12-3, 6-10; 12-10 Sat; 12-9 Sun) ~ Restaurant ~ (01825) 890283 ~ Children welcome ~ Dogs allowed in bar ~ Open 12-12 ~ Bedrooms: /£85B

Recommended by Alec and Joan Laurence, the Didler, Michael and Ann Cole, B J Harding

BOSHAM   SU8003   MAP 2

Anchor Bleu
High Street; PO18 8LS

Waterside inn overlooking Chichester Harbour and usefully open all day in summer, several real ales in snug old bars, and decent food (lots of summer fish dishes)

On a summer's day the seats on the back terrace here make an idyllic spot to spend the afternoon, as it's placed right up against a tidal inlet of the vast complex of creeks and marshes that make up Chichester Harbour. A massive wheel-operated bulkhead door wards off high tides (cars parked on the seaward side are often submerged). Inside, two nicely simple bars have low shiny ochre ceilings, some beams, worn flagstones and exposed timbered brickwork, lots of nautical bric-a-brac, and robust, simple furniture. Hogs Back TEA, Hop Back Summer Lightning (in summer) or Ringwood Fortyniner (in winter) are on handpump alongside a couple of guests such as Otter Ale or Sharps Cornish Coaster; friendly, helpful staff. As King Canute had a palace here, this may be the spot where he showed his courtiers that however much they flattered him as all-powerful, he couldn't turn the tide back. The church a few yards up the lane figures in the Bayeux tapestry, and the village and shore are worth exploring.

🍴 Lunchtime bar food includes filled baguettes, ploughman's, fisherman's lunch with smoked fish, soup, crayfish with lime mayonnaise, poached salmon, battered haddock, moussaka and shepherd's pie, with evening dishes such as whole plaice with caper butter, sea bream with herbs and lemon, leg of lamb steak with bacon and onion gravy, vegetable and sweet chilli stir fry with pumpkin seeds, chicken with parma ham, brie and leek sauce, and puddings such as pear and Amaretto crumble and pecan pie; afternoon tea and cakes. *Starters/Snacks: £4.75 to £6.50. Main Courses: £8.95 to £14.00. Puddings: £4.25*

Enterprise ~ Lease Kate Walford ~ Real ale ~ Bar food (12-3(2.30 winter), 7-9) ~ Restaurant ~ (01243) 573956 ~ Children welcome ~ Dogs allowed in bar ~ Open 11-11; 12-3, 5.30-11 Mon-Thurs and 11-11 Fri-Sun in winter

Recommended by Neil Hardwick, Nick Lawless, Mr and Mrs P D Titcomb, Ann and Colin Hunt, Terry and Nickie Williams, Francis Vernon, Chris Glasson, David H T Dimock

BRIGHTON
TQ3104   MAP 3

Basketmakers Arms £

Gloucester Road – the E end, near Cheltenham Place; off Marlborough Place (A23) via Gloucester Street; BN1 4AD

Bustling backstreet pub with friendly landlord, plenty of chatty customers, great drinks range and enjoyable food

Only a short stroll from the Royal Pavilion, this street-corner local has a good choice of drinks with eight real ales on offer: in addition to Fullers London Pride, Butser, Discovery, ESB, HSB, London Porter and Seafarers, they have two guests like Butcombe Bitter and Castle Rock Preservation Ale on handpump, alongside good wines by the glass, at least 100 malt whiskies and quite a range of vodkas, gins and rums. The two small low-ceilinged rooms have brocaded wall benches and stools on the stripped wood floor, lots of interesting old tins all over the walls, cigarette cards on one beam with whisky labels on another, beermats and some old advertisements, photographs and posters; piped music; staff are helpful and cheerful. There are three metal tables out on the pavement. Dogs must be on a lead.

🍴 Good value enjoyable bar food using south downs lamb, beef from Ditchling and locally caught fish includes lots of sandwiches, filled baguettes and baked potatoes, ploughman's, soup, particularly good home-made meaty and vegetarian burgers, mexican beef or vegetarian chillis and fish of the day; daily and seasonal specials such as chicken and leek pie or cauliflower and chickpea salad; popular Sunday roasts, and puddings like brownies or sticky toffee pudding; good range of coffees. *Starters/Snacks: £3.95 to £7.95. Main Courses: £3.95 to £4.95*

Gales (Fullers) ~ Lease Peter Dowd ~ Real ale ~ Bar food (12-8.30(7 Fri, 6 Sat, 5 Sun)) ~ (01273) 689006 ~ Children welcome until 8pm ~ Dogs allowed in bar ~ Open 11-11(midnight Fri and Sat); 12-11 Sun

Recommended by Alec Lewery, Michael Dandy, the Didler, Mark Sykes, N R White, Ian Phillips

---

Please tell us if the décor, atmosphere, food or drink at a pub is different from our description. We rely on readers' reports to keep us up to date: feedback@goodguides.com, or (no stamp needed) The Good Pub Guide, FREEPOST TN1569, Wadhurst, E Sussex TN5 7BR.

Greys ⚑🍴 ♀

Southover Street, off A270 Lewes Road opposite The Level (public park); BN2 9UA

A good mix of drinkers and diners in friendly, bustling and interesting local, thoughtful choice of drinks, popular food; live music Monday evenings

You'll often find a cheerful local crowd in here during the evenings, and they have live music on Mondays (tickets needed for entry). Basic furnishings like simple wall seats and stools are placed around mixed pub tables on bare boards and flagstones, magnolia walls and some wood panelling around a flame-effect stove below a big metal canopy; piped music is at a reasonable level. The serving bar is on the right, with Harveys Best and Timothy Taylors Landlord on handpump, a carefully chosen wine list and several bottled belgian beers and a local crowd on the bar stools and at the nearby tables. The five or six tables on the left, each with a little vase of flowers and lighted tea lamp, are the food bit – one corner table is snuggled in by a high-backed settle and another at the back is tucked into a quiet corner. The stair wall is papered with posters and flyers from bands, singers and poets who have performed here. The house wines, from Burgundy, are excellent value. There is not much daytime parking on this steep lane or the nearby streets. No children inside. Do note the opening hours. More reports please.

🍴 **The menu, changing monthly and with daily specials, has good food with some unusual accompaniments. Roz, the chef (formerly a pastry chef at Claridges in London), produces an 'any questions' sheet explaining some of the less well known items. Snacks and starters might include Leffe beer-battered mushrooms, pigs ear goujons with sweet chilli sauce, gypsy quail eggs, smoked trout or grilled sardines with preserved lemons, with main courses such as fried fillet of bream with pink fir apple potatoes, rib-eye steak with garlic and thyme tomatoes and portabella mushrooms, and sweet potato gnocchi with roasted pepper; puddings like 70% cocoa chocolate truffles and yorkshire parkin with poached rhubarb.** *Starters/Snacks: £2.50 to £4.50. Main Courses: £9.50 to £13.00. Puddings: £4.00 to £5.00*

Enterprise ~ Lease Chris Taylor and Gill Perkins ~ Real ale ~ Bar food (6-9; not Sun evening, Tues-Thurs lunch or Mon, Fri) ~ Restaurant ~ (01273) 680734 ~ Dogs welcome ~ Live music Mon evening (tickets only) ~ Open 4-11.30; 12pm-12.30am Fri and Sat; 12am-11pm Sun

Recommended by N R White, Sue Demont, Tim Barrow, Ian Phillips, Francis Vernon, Ann and Colin Hunt

BYWORTH   SU9821   MAP 2

Black Horse ⚑

Off A283; GU28 0HL

Enjoyable country pub with open fires, newspapers to read, several real ales, tasty food and nice garden

At weekends there can be quite a crowd here, when people spread out and enjoy the lovely garden. This has tables on a steep series of grassy terraces sheltered by banks of flowering shrubs that look across a drowsy valley to swelling woodland. Inside there's a good mix of customers, a quietly chatty atmosphere, and large open fires, and the simply furnished though smart bar has pews and scrubbed wooden tables on its bare floorboards, pictures and old photographs on the walls and newspapers to read. The back dining room has lots of nooks and crannies, there's a spiral staircase to a heavily beamed function room, and stairs up to a games room with pool, darts, two games machines and board games; lovely views of the downs. Flowerpots Bitter, Fullers London Pride and two guests like Dark Star Hophead and Sharps Doom Bar are on handpump.

🍴 **As well as good-value lunchtime filled baguettes, baked potatoes and ploughman's with cheese, ham or sausage, the changing menu might include soup, starters such as guinea fowl, leek and wild mushroom terrine or brioche crusted cornish sardines, and main courses like a duo of shepherd's pie and lamb cutlet, baked smoked haddock, beer-battered fish of the day, or asparagus and pea risotto; daily specials and Sunday roasts, and puddings like Pimm's jelly or spotted dick with golden syrup and custard; children's menu.** *Starters/Snacks: £4.50 to £6.95. Main Courses: £5.95 to £16.50. Puddings: £5.00*

Free house ~ Licensee Jeff Paddock ~ Real ale ~ Bar food (12-3, 6-9(9.30 Fri and Sat, 8.30 Sun)) ~ Restaurant ~ (01924) 342424 ~ Children welcome away from bar and until 9pm ~ Dogs allowed in bar ~ Open 11.30-11; 12-11 Sun

Recommended by Nick Lawless, Tracey and Stephen Groves, Mr Ray J Carter, Martin and Karen Wake, the Didler, Bruce Bird, Jonathan Neil-Smith, John and Annabel Hampshire, Kevin Flack, M G Hart

CHARLTON
SU8812   MAP 2

Fox Goes Free
Village signposted off A286 Chichester—Midhurst in Singleton, also from Chichester—Petworth via East Dean; PO18 0HU

Comfortable old pub with well organised staff, popular food and drink; nice surrounding walks; bedrooms and big garden

Popular with walkers as well as race-goers from nearby Goodwood, this friendly old pub is in a delightfully unspoilt village street. Its bustling bar has an informal and relaxed atmosphere and is the first of the dark and cosy series of separate rooms: old irish settles, tables and chapel chairs, and an open fire. Standing timbers divide a larger beamed bar which has a huge brick fireplace with a woodburning stove and old local photographs on the walls. A dining area with hunting prints looks over the garden. The family extension is a clever conversion from horse boxes and the stables where the 1926 Goodwood winner was housed; darts, games machine, board games and piped music. Ballards Best and a beer named for the pub on handpump along with a guest from a brewer such as Harveys, and several wines by the glass as well as home-made lemonade and malt whiskies; friendly, helpful staff. You can sit at one of the picnic-sets under the apple trees in the attractive back garden with the downs as a backdrop; there are rustic benches and tables on the gravelled front terrace, too. It's handy for the Weald and Downland Open Air Museum and West Dean gardens; good surrounding walks include up to the prehistoric earthworks on the Trundle.

🍽 **Well presented bar food (not cheap) includes lunchtime filled baguettes and ploughman's (not Sun), chilli con carne, honey-roast ham and eggs, lasagne and chips, and steak and kidney pie, as well as changing menu dishes such as roast fillet of bass with sun-dried tomatoes, olives and rocket, chicken breast in parma ham with creamed leeks, and roast shoulder of lamb with braised red cabbage, with puddings like raspberry crème brûlée or vanilla rice pudding.** *Starters/Snacks: £6.50 to £7.95. Main Courses: £9.50 to £10.95. Puddings: £5.50*

Free house ~ Licensee David Coxon ~ Real ale ~ Bar food (12-2.30, 6.30-10; all day weekends) ~ Restaurant ~ (01243) 811461 ~ Children welcome ~ Dogs allowed in bar ~ Live music Weds evenings ~ Open 11-11(11.30 Sat); 12-10.30 Sun ~ Bedrooms: £60S/£85S

Recommended by Ann and Colin Hunt, Peter Meister, Alec and Joan Laurence, LM, J Stickland, Francis Vernon, Roger and Lesley Everett, Tony Brace

CHIDDINGLY
TQ5414   MAP 3

Six Bells ★ £
Village signed off A22 Uckfield—Hailsham; BN8 6HE

Lively, unpretentious village local with good weekend live music, extremely good value bar food and friendly long-serving landlord

A perennial favourite for live music at weekends, this cheery place manages to keep its food prices at a bargain level. The bars have a shabby charm, lots of fusty artefacts and interesting bric-a-brac collected over the years by the landlord, solid old wood pews and antique seats, plenty of local pictures and posters, and log fires. A sensitive extension provides some much-needed family space; cribbage and dominoes. Courage Directors, Harveys Best and a guest beer on handpump. Outside at the back, there are some tables beyond a big raised goldfish pond and a boules pitch; the church opposite has an interesting Jefferay monument. Vintage and Kit car meetings outside the pub every month. This is a pleasant area for walks. Note that dogs are allowed in one bar only.

▯▯ The tasty but traditional bar food is exceptionally good value: sandwiches, french onion soup, filled baked potatoes, ploughman's, stilton and walnut pie, lasagne, shepherd's or steak and kidney pies, chicken curry, barbecue spare ribs, ham hock, and puddings such as banana split and steamed puddings. *Starters/Snacks: £2.50. Main Courses: £4.20 to £7.95. Puddings: £3.60*

Free house ~ Licensees Paul Newman and Emma Bannister ~ Real ale ~ Bar food (11.30-2.30, 6-9; all day Fri-Sun) ~ (01825) 872227 ~ Children welcome away from main bar ~ Dogs allowed in bar ~ Live music Fri-Sun evenings and Sun lunchtime ~ Open 10-3, 6-11; 10am-midnight (Fri and Sat); 12-11 Sun

Recommended by Miriam Warner, Ann and Colin Hunt, John Roots, Mrs Mary Woods, Jenny and Peter Lowater, C Shaw

CHILGROVE
SU8116   MAP 2

Royal Oak
Off B2141 Petersfield—Chichester, signed Hooksway down steep single track; PO18 9JZ

Unchanging and peaceful country pub with welcoming landlord and big pretty garden

Run for many years by the same licensees and in a lovely rural position down a wooded track, this simple two-room place is popular with walkers. It's simply furnished with plain country-kitchen tables and chairs and there are huge log fires in the two cosy rooms of the partly brick-floored beamed bar. There's also a cottagey dining room with a woodburning stove and a plainer family room. Exmoor Beast, Gales HSB and Sharps Doom Bar and Weston's Bounds Brand Scrumpy cider are on handpump; piped music, cribbage, cards and shut the box. There are plenty of picnic-sets under parasols on the grass of the big, pretty garden. More reports please.

▯▯ Basic bar food includes filled rolls, ploughman's, filled baked potatoes, chicken curry, meat or vegetarian pies, and rump steak. *Starters/Snacks: £4.95. Main Courses: £8.95 to £13.45. Puddings: £4.50*

Free house ~ Licensee Dave Jeffery ~ Real ale ~ Bar food ~ Restaurant ~ (01243) 535257 ~ Children in family room until 9pm ~ Dogs allowed in bar ~ Live music second and last Fri evening of month ~ Open 11.30-2.30, 6-11; 12-3 Sun; closed Sun evening and Mon

Recommended by R C Vincent, John Beeken, N R White, J A Snell, LM, R B Gardiner

COOLHAM
TQ1423   MAP 3

George & Dragon
Dragons Green, Dragons Lane; pub signed just off A272, about 1.5 miles E of village; RH13 8GE

Pleasant little country cottage with beamed bars: decent food and drink

Stretching behind this unchanging old tile-hung cottage is a lovely orchard garden, which is neatly kept with pretty flowers and shrubs and has quite a few picnic-sets; the little front garden has a sad 19th-c memorial to the son of a previous innkeeper. The chatty, cosy bar has heavily timbered walls, a partly woodblock and partly polished-tile floor, unusually low and massive black beams (see if you can decide whether the date cut into one is 1677 or 1577), simple chairs and rustic stools, some brass, fresh flowers on tables and a big inglenook fireplace with an early 17th-c grate. There's also a smaller back bar and restaurant. Badger K&B, Tanglefoot and a seasonal ale are served on handpump by helpful, friendly staff, and all the wines are sold by the glass; cribbage, bar skittles, shove ha'penny, dominoes and darts.

▯▯ Bar food includes lunchtime filled baguettes, ploughman's, soup, garlic mushrooms, baked brie with cranberry sauce, cod and chips, bacon and onion suet pudding, spicy burger, mushroom and asparagus risotto, giant yorkshire pudding filled with sausage and mash, steak and ale pie, lamb pie, and puddings such as chocolate brownie and a fruit pie. *Starters/Snacks: £3.50 to £6.00. Main Courses: £8.00 to £12.00. Puddings: £4.00*

Badger ~ Tenants Peter and Anne Snelling ~ Real ale ~ Bar food (12-2, 6.30-9; not Sun evening) ~ Restaurant ~ (01403) 741320 ~ Children welcome ~ Dogs allowed in bar ~ Live music last Sun of month ~ Open 12-3, 6-11; 12-midnight(11 Sun) Sat

Recommended by John Beeken, Francis Vernon, Philip and Cheryl Hill, David Cosham, Ian Phillips, Louise English

EAST CHILTINGTON
TQ3715   MAP 3

Jolly Sportsman 🍴 ☿

2 miles N of B2116; Chapel Lane – follow sign to 13th-c church; BN7 3BA

SUSSEX DINING PUB OF THE YEAR

Excellent modern food in civilised, rather smart place, small bar for drinkers, contemporary furnishings, fine wine list and huge range of malt whiskies; nice garden

With attentive service and accomplished cooking, this civilised country dining pub – on a no-through lane beneath the South Downs – is well worth seeking out for a special meal. There's a roaring winter fire, a mix of furniture on the stripped wood floors, Dark Star Hophead and a guest like Triple fff Altons Pride or Dark Star Old tapped from the cask, a remarkably good wine list with 12 by the glass, Black Rat farm cider, fresh lime and mint soda, home-made lemonade, over 100 malt whiskies and an extensive list of cognacs, armagnacs and grappa. The larger restaurant is smart but informal with contemporary light wood furniture and modern landscapes on coffee-coloured walls. There are rustic tables and benches under gnarled trees in a pretty cottagey front garden with more on the terrace and the front bricked area, and the large back lawn with a children's play area looks out towards the downs; good walks and cycle rides nearby. More reports please.

🍴 **Carefully sourced, imaginative and seasonal – though not cheap – food might include ploughman's, starters like fennel soup, slow-cooked beef ribs bourguigon or crab and courgette mousse with tomato and piquillo pepper sauce, and main courses like grilled gurnard fillet with saffron dressing, slow-cooked ditchling lamb, whole lemon sole with vanilla and lime butter or 28-day aged rib-eye steak, with puddings such as chocolate and hazelnut parfait or jellied alfonso mango and yoghurt terrine; they also offer good value, interesting two- and three-course menus (not Sunday).** *Starters/Snacks: £6.50 to £9.50. Main Courses: £8.75 to £15.00. Puddings: £5.75 to £9.85*

Free house ~ Licensee Bruce Wass ~ Real ale ~ Bar food (12.30-2.30(3.15 Sun), 6.45-9.30(10 Fri and Sat); not Sun evening) ~ Restaurant ~ (01273) 890400 ~ Children welcome ~ Dogs welcome ~ Open 12-11(10 Sun); closed 3-6 Mon-Thurs

Recommended by Laurence Smith, Susan and John Douglas, Jane and Alan Bush, John Redfern

EAST DEAN
SU9012   MAP 2

Star & Garter 🍴 ☿

Village signposted with Charlton off A286 in Singleton; also signposted off A285; note that there are two East Deans in Sussex (this one is N of Chichester) – OS Sheet 197 map reference 904129; PO18 0JG

Attractively furnished bar and restaurant in light and airy well run pub, relaxed atmosphere and enjoyable food and drink; bedrooms

This roomy and carefully remodelled brick and flint dining pub puts the emphasis on the very enjoyable food. With stripped wooden panelling, exposed brickwork and solid oak floors, the squarish interior has sturdy, individual, mainly stripped and scrubbed tables in various sizes and an interesting mix of seats from country kitchen chairs through chunky modern dining chairs to cushioned pews and some 17th-c and 18th-c carved oak settles. The high ceilings, big sash windows and uncluttered walls give a light and airy feel. The bar counter, with a few bar stools, is on the left, with Arundel Best and a couple of guests such as Arundel ASB and Ballards Best tapped from the cask, ten wines by the glass, a couple of farm ciders and a few malt whiskies; tables in this area are usually left unlaid while those to the right of the front door and further on are set for diners. Newspapers to read, board games and piped music; dogs must be on a lead. The sheltered terrace behind has teak tables and chairs with big canvas parasols and heaters, and a gazebo for smokers; steps go up to a walled lawn with picnic-sets. A gate provides level access from the road to the terrace and into the pub for those who might not manage the front steps. The South Downs Way is close by.

🍴 The popular fresh seafood is listed on a board over the fireplace and might include selsey crab and lobster, line-caught bass, local mackerel, cod, mussels, scallops and there's a seafood platter featuring lobster, several prawn dishes, crab and smoked salmon. There are non-fishy choices, too, such as lunchtime filled baguettes (not cheap) and ploughman's, tapas, dishes such as salad of pigeon breast and pancetta available as starter or larger portions, and main courses such as lamb noisettes in thyme and port sauce, cottage pie, or wild mushroom and butternut squash risotto. Puddings might feature white chocolate panna cotta with summer berries, or lemon and ginger cheesecake with lemon sorbet. *Starters/Snacks: £4.50 to £11.50. Main Courses: £10.50 to £18.50. Puddings: £5.50 to £6.00*

Free house ~ Licensee Oliver Ligertwood ~ Real ale ~ Bar food (12-2.30, 6.30-10; all day weekends) ~ Restaurant ~ (01243) 811318 ~ Children welcome ~ Dogs allowed in bar ~ Open 11-3, 6-11; 11am-midnight Sat; 12-10.30 Sun ~ Bedrooms: £70S(£90B)/£90S(£110B)

Recommended by Martin and Karen Wake, Mrs Mary Woods, Sue Ruffhead, Ann and Colin Hunt, M G Hart, Paul and Annette Hallett, Mrs Romey Heaton

ELSTED   SU8119   MAP 2

Three Horseshoes 🍴 🍺

Village signposted from B2141 Chichester—Petersfield; also reached easily from A272 about 2 miles W of Midhurst, turning left heading W; GU29 0JY

Bustling, friendly and well run country pub, congenial little beamed rooms, enjoyable food and good drinks; wonderful views from flower-filled garden

Under a sweep of the South Downs, this former drovers' rest is a smashing all-rounder, where the friendly staff cope admirably even at the busiest times. There are ancient beams and flooring, antique furnishings, log fires and candlelight, fresh flowers on the tables, and attractive prints and photographs; it's best to book to be sure of a table. Racked on a stillage behind the bar counter, the four real ales include Ballards Best, Bowman Wallops Wood, Youngs Bitter and a guest such as Hop Back Spring Zing or Wadworths 6X; summer cider; dominoes. The flower-filled garden in summer is lovely with plenty of tables and super views of the downs, which have abundant scope for walks.

🍴 Generous helpings of good, popular food include ploughman's with a good choice of cheeses, and options such as potted shrimps on toast, prawn mayonnaise wrapped in smoked salmon, smoked duck, roasted pepper and bacon salad, pork and herb sausages, venison either as a fillet with a port and redcurrant sauce or in a winter stew, steak and kidney in Guinness pie, lamb with apples and apricots, seasonal crab and lobster, and puddings like lemon posset or panna cotta with blueberries. *Starters/Snacks: £4.50 to £10.00. Main Courses: £9.00 to £14.00. Puddings: £5.50*

Free house ~ Licensee Sue Beavis ~ Real ale ~ Bar food ~ (01730) 825746 ~ Well behaved children allowed ~ Dogs allowed in bar ~ Open 11-2.30, 6-11; 12-3, 7-10.30 Sun

Recommended by Tony and Jill Radnor, Paul and Annette Hallett, Mrs Mary Woods, M G Hart, Mrs K Hooker, R B Gardiner, Patrick Spence, Jennifer Hurst, Michael B Griffith, John Beeken, Mrs M Grimwood, J A Snell, N B Vernon, Mrs Romey Heaton, DGH

ERIDGE STATION   TQ5434   MAP 3

Huntsman ♀

Signposted off A26 S of Eridge Green; Eridge Road; TN3 9LE

No-gimmicks country local with friendly landlord, interesting bar food (lots of seasonal game), excellent wines and seats in sizeable garden

With a refreshing absence of piped music and machines, this homely, pubby place is spotlessly kept by caring staff. The quietly friendly landlord has considerable wine expertise (they offer a fantastic choice of over two dozen wines by the glass) and they keep Badger K&B and First Gold and a seasonal guest such as Badger Hopping Hare on handpump under a light blanket pressure and farm cider, as well as organic fruit juice and several malt whiskies. The two opened-up rooms have dark wooden dining chairs and a nice mix of matching tables on the wooden floorboards, and plenty of amusing pictures of hunting scenes on the walls. There are picnic-sets and outdoor heaters on the decking, an outside bar and more seating on the lawn among weeping willows and other trees. The pub is virtually alone here apart from the station itself – which on weekdays is responsible for filling the hamlet's roadside verges with commuters' cars (plenty of space at weekends, though); as we went to press the pub was negotiating with a farmer for the use of a field for overflow parking.

🍴 As well as sandwiches, the interesting bar food from a daily changing menu might include crayfish and lobster spaghetti or rare beef salad starters, and main courses like local venison fillet, flounder with herb and caper butter, chicken breast filled with tarragon and sussex camembert, and the popular bavette of beef with dauphinoise potatoes; puddings such as apple crumble, stem ginger cheesecake and chocolate sponge pudding. Many ingredients come from local farms, and some vegetables are from customers' allotments. *Starters/Snacks: £4.50 to £8.00. Main Courses: £8.00 to £21.00. Puddings: £4.50 to £6.00*

Badger ~ Tenants Simon Wood and Nicola Tester ~ Real ale ~ Bar food (12-2(2.30 Sat), 6-9; not Sun evening or Mon (except bank hols)) ~ (01892) 864258 ~ Children welcome ~ Dogs welcome ~ Open 11.30-2.30, 5.30-11; 11.30-11.30 Sat; 12-10.30 Sun; closed Mon (except bank hols) and first full week in Jan

Recommended by BOB, Simon and Sally Small, Heather and Dick Martin, G Stapely, Mr Clifton, Miss A L Tester, Derek Thomas

EWHURST GREEN

TQ7924   MAP 3

White Dog

Turn off A21 to Bodiam at S end of Hurst Green, cross B2244, pass Bodiam Castle, cross river then bear left uphill at Ewhurst Green sign; TN32 5TD

Comfortable pub handy for Bodiam Castle and Great Dixter, nice little bar, popular food

As we went to press, the owners of this attractive partly 17th-c dining pub were planning to increase the outdoor seating by building a terrace at the back to make the most of the terrific views across to Bodiam Castle. The bar on the left has a proper pubby feel with a fine inglenook fireplace, hop-draped beams, wood-panelled walls, farm implements and horsebrasses, just a few tables with high-backed, rush-seated dining chairs and quite a few red plush-topped bar stools by the curved wooden counter on the old brick or flagstoned floor; there's also a high-backed cushioned settle by the counter; Fullers London Pride, Harveys Best and a guest beer on handpump and an extensive wine list with several wines by the glass. To the right of the door is the busy but fairly plain dining room with more big flagstones, the same tables and chairs as the bar, fresh flowers, black joists and hops, paintings by local artists for sale, and again, one high-backed settle by the bar; piped music. There's also a games room with darts, pool and a games machine. More reports on the newish owners please.

🍴 There's a garden menu (available in the garden or bar) of baguettes, ploughman's and chips, and a main menu (not cheap, with vegetables mostly from nearby farms) featuring dishes like a savoury suet pudding of the day, pot-roasted belly of pork, luxury fish pie, rib-eye steak and fillets of lemon sole. Puddings like raspberry and white chocolate cheesecake, sticky toffee pudding and apple crumble; children's menu. Sunday roasts (booking advisable) are served in two sittings. *Starters/Snacks: £5.25 to £6.95. Main Courses: £8.95 to £13.95. Puddings: £5.50*

Free house ~ Licensees Bill and Jacqui Tipples ~ Real ale ~ Bar food (two sittings for Sun lunch, at 12.30 and 3) ~ Restaurant ~ (01580) 830264 ~ Children welcome ~ Dogs allowed in bar ~ Open 12-3, 6-11(11.30 Sat); 12-6 Sun; closed Sun evening and Mon in winter ~ Bedrooms: /£75B

Recommended by R and S Bentley, Philip and Cheryl Hill, V Brogden, Leslie and Barbara Owen

FLETCHING

Griffin ⊗🍴 ♀

Village signposted off A272 W of Uckfield; TN22 3SS

Busy, gently upmarket inn with a fine wine list, bistro-style bar food, real ales and big garden with far-reaching views; bedrooms

In a handsome village street not far from Sheffield Park and the terminus of the Bluebell Railway, this bustling inn has a very spacious two-acre garden, with choice views of rolling countryside; there are plenty of seats here and on the sandstone terrace with its woodburning oven. There are beamed and quaintly panelled bar rooms with blazing log fires, old photographs and hunting prints, straightforward close-set furniture including some captain's chairs and china on a delft shelf. There's a small bare-boarded serving area off to one side and a snug separate bar with sofas and TV. Harveys Best, Kings Horsham Best and a couple of guests on handpump and a fine wine list with 20 (including champagne and sweet wine) by the glass. They may try to keep your credit card while you eat.

🍴 As well as a more elaborate restaurant menu, the often interesting – if not cheap – food in the bar might include starters such as mediterranean fish soup, chicken liver and foie gras parfait, or bruschetta with roast courgettes, and classic main courses like beer-battered rye bay cod, fried skate wing with crushed new potatoes, slow-roast belly of pork, moules marinière and braised wild boar sausages; puddings could feature lemon polenta cake, chocolate and pecan tart or rosewater panna cotta with rhubarb and ginger compote. Salads and vegetables are from a Fletching market garden and venison, game and beef from local farmers. Sunday barbecues in the garden in summer. *Starters/Snacks: £6.00 to £9.50. Main Courses: £12.00 to £15.00. Puddings: £6.00 to £8.00*

Free house ~ Licensees J Pullan and M W Wright ~ Real ale ~ Bar food (12-2.30(3 weekends), 7-9.30(9 Sun)) ~ Restaurant ~ (01825) 722890 ~ Children welcome if supervised ~ Dogs allowed in bar ~ Live jazz Fri evening and Sun lunchtime ~ Open 12-11(midnight Sat) ~ Bedrooms: £80B/£85S(£95B)

Recommended by Henny Davison, Peter Meister, Phil Bryant, Harriet Kininmonth, Andy and Claire Barker, Mr and Mrs M Stratton, J A Snell, Kevin Malia, Tina and David Woods-Taylor, C A Turner, Lucilla Lunn, Hugh Roberts, Alan Cowell, Mrs Mary Woods, Laurence Smith

HORSHAM

Black Jug ♀

North Street; RH12 1RJ

Bustling town pub with wide choice of drinks, efficient staff, well liked food

A very wide range of drinks at this well run Brunning & Price town pub features an impressive array of wines (with 35 by the glass), half a dozen real ales on handpump – Harveys Best and five guests such as Caledonian Deuchars, Greene King Ruddles, Scottish & Newcastle Courage Directors and Wickwar Porter – and around 100 malt whiskies, lots of gins, vodkas and rums, and farm cider. The one large open-plan, turn-of-the-century bar room has a large central bar, a nice collection of sizeable dark wood tables and comfortable chairs on a stripped wood floor, board games, and interesting old prints and photographs above a dark wood panelled dado on the cream walls. A spacious conservatory has similar furniture and lots of hanging baskets. The pretty flower-filled back terrace has plenty of garden furniture. The small car park is for staff and deliveries only but you can park next door in the council car park.

🍴 Interesting bar food includes sandwiches, pork pie ploughman's, crispy parma ham and mozzarella salad, a charcuterie plate for two, smoked duck breast, grilled minute steak, spiced lamb couscous, chorizo and black pudding salad, grilled lamb rump, honey-roast duck breast, and mushroom and walnut stuffed pancakes; puddings like marmalade and treacle tart, chocolate cake and italian lemon trifle; cheeseboard served with quince jelly. *Starters/Snacks: £4.50 to £6.25. Main Courses: £8.95 to £16.25. Puddings: £4.95 to £5.75*

Brunning & Price ~ Manager Alastair Craig ~ Real ale ~ Bar food (12-10(9.30 Sun)) ~
(01403) 253526 ~ No children under 6, or under 12 after 6pm ~ Dogs welcome ~
Open 11.30-11(10.30 Sun)

Recommended by Francis Vernon, Dr and Mrs A K Clarke

ICKLESHAM
TQ8716   MAP 3

Queens Head ♀ ◑

Just off A259 Rye—Hastings; TN36 4BL

**Friendly, well run country pub, extremely popular with locals and visitors, with a good
range of beers, proper home cooking and seats in garden with fine views**

Tucked away from the main village this welcoming pub has a peaceful garden with
boules, a children's play area and picnic-sets that make the most of the sweeping view of
the Brede valley. Inside, the open-plan areas work round a very big serving counter which
stands under a vaulted beamed roof, the high beamed walls and ceiling of the easy-going
bar are lined with shelves of bottles and covered with farming implements and animal
traps, and there are well used pub tables and old pews on the brown patterned carpet.
Other areas have big inglenook fireplaces, and the back room has some old bikes hanging
from the ceiling and is decorated with old bicycle and motorbike prints; piped jazz or
blues and darts. Greene King IPA and Abbot, Harveys Best, Ringwood Fortyniner and a
couple of guests like Dark Star Hophead and Whitstable IPA are on handpump, along with
Biddenden cider, and there are several wines by the glass. This is well placed for walks to
Winchelsea.

🍴 Straightforward, reasonably priced bar food includes sandwiches, filled baked potatoes,
ploughman's, soup, starters like chicken liver pâté, prawn cocktail and deep-fried brie
with cranberry sauce, a range of pies, large steak and kidney pudding, soft herring roes
on toast, all day breakfasts, leek, brie and bacon pasta, ham and eggs, a curry of the day,
steaks and a mixed grill. They do smaller portions of main courses at a reduced price;
short children's menu. *Starters/Snacks: £5.25 to £6.95. Main Courses: £8.75 to £13.95.
Puddings: £3.75 to £4.25*

Free house ~ Licensee Ian Mitchell ~ Real ale ~ Bar food (12-2.30, 6-9.30; all day weekends) ~
(01424) 814552 ~ Well behaved children away from bar until 2.30pm ~ Dogs allowed in bar ~
Live music Sun 4-6pm ~ Open 11-11; 12-10.30 Sun

*Recommended by Tony Brace, Tom and Jill Jones, V Brogden, Peter Meister, Simon Rodway, Conrad Freezer,
Lorry Spooner, Dr A J and Mrs Tompsett, Bruce Bird*

LEWES
TQ4110   MAP 3

Lewes Arms ◑ £

Castle Ditch Lane/Mount Place – tucked behind castle ruins; BN7 1YH

Cheerful little local, several real ales, enjoyable, homely bar food and friendly staff

Run by the same people as another of our Sussex Main Entries, the Basketmakers in
Brighton, this is an unpretentious little back street local with a friendly welcome for all.
There's a tiny front bar on the right with stools along the nicely curved counter and
bench window seats, and two other simple rooms with half-panelled walls in cream,
brown or pink hung with information and photographs to do with the famously noisy
Lewes bonfire night, and straightforward tables and chairs ranging from high-backed
settles to cushioned wheelbacks and other dining seats; stripped wooden floors
throughout, a couple of Victorian fireplaces (with a decorative woodburner in one), beer
mats pinned over doorways and a cheerful, chatty atmosphere. Fullers ESB and London
Pride, Gales HSB and Seafarers, and Harveys Best on handpump. At the top of some
stairs, a door leads to an attractive small back terrace on two levels with picnic-sets
under umbrellas, outdoor heaters and a barbecue.

⚑ Generous helpings of good value bar food using organic produce include lunchtime sandwiches, soup, country pork pâté, a plate of meze, home-made burgers, vegetable curry, beer-battered haddock, jerk chicken, moussaka, sirloin steak, and puddings like treacle or chocolate puddings. *Starters/Snacks: £3.75 to £4.95. Main Courses: £5.95 to £7.95. Puddings: £3.95 to £4.25*

Fullers ~ Tenants Abigail Mawer and Peter Dowd ~ Real ale ~ Bar food (12-3, 5.30-8.30; 12-5 Sat and Sun (not weekend evenings)) ~ (01273) 473152 ~ Children welcome but not in front bar ~ Dogs allowed in bar ~ Open 11-11(midnight Fri and Sat); 12-11 Sun

Recommended by Conor McGaughey

LODSWORTH   SU9321   MAP 2

Halfway Bridge Inn ♀ ⇌
Just before village, on A272 Midhurst—Petworth; GU28 9BP

Restauranty coaching inn, with contemporary décor in several dining areas, log fires, local real ales, modern food; lovely bedrooms

Standing by itself and well set back from the main road, this smartly refurbished country dining inn has an abundance of intimate little corners. The three or four bar rooms are carefully furnished with good oak chairs and an individual mix of tables, and one of the log fires is contained in a well polished kitchen range. The inter-connecting restaurant rooms have beams, wooden floors and a cosy atmosphere. Langham Halfway to Heaven, Skinners Betty Stogs and a guest like Sharps Doom Bar on handpump and 14 wines by the glass; piped music (which one reader found intrusive). At the back there are seats on a small terrace. The bedrooms in the former stable yard are extremely stylish and comfortable.

⚑ The well conceived, restauranty food (not cheap) includes lunchtime sandwiches, soup, starters like partridge and pheasant terrine, whitebait or poached scallops, and main courses such as game suet pudding with creamed potatoes, char-grilled vegetable millefeuilles, slow-cooked belly of pork and seafood risotto; puddings might include dark chocolate and pistachio tart or upside-down treacle and apple sponge. *Starters/Snacks: £5.95 to £9.95. Main Courses: £9.95 to £14.95. Puddings: £5.50 to £5.95*

Free house ~ Licensee Paul Carter ~ Real ale ~ Bar food (12-2.30, 6.30-9.15(8.30 Sun)) ~ Restaurant ~ (01798) 861281 ~ Children welcome ~ Dogs allowed in bar ~ Open 11-11; 12-10.30 Sun ~ Bedrooms: £85B/£120B

Recommended by Hunter and Christine Wright, Ralph and Jean Whitehouse, M G Hart, Colin and Janet Roe

Hollist Arms
Off A272 Midhurst—Petworth; GU28 9BZ

Friendly village pub, civilised and relaxed, with local beers, good choice of wines; seats outside in pretty garden

A pub for some 200 years, this is in a lovely spot by a little village green, and the friendly landlord and his chatty staff are sure to make you welcome. Inside, a small room to the right of the main door has a couple of tables by an open fire, with a row of pewter mugs along its mantelpiece – just the place for a cosy drink or meal; the pub's two golden retrievers are often at large. The public bar area on the left has bar stools against the pale wooden counter, Kings Horsham Best, Timothy Taylors Landlord and a guest from local Langham on handpump, a good choice of wines, local champagne-style cider, wooden stools around a few tables and a comfortable built-in window seat; shove ha'penny. Beyond, the L-shaped dining room has a couple of big squidgy sofas facing each other across a low table covered with books and magazines in front of a huge woodburning stove, and plenty of elegant spoked dining chairs and wheelbacks around tables set for dining on the wood-strip floor; the red walls are completely covered with genuinely interesting prints and paintings, and there are pretty paper flowers on each table and big vases of fresh flowers on window sills. Up some steps, the pretty and cottagey back garden has picnic-sets on a covered terrace, or you can sit on a seat beneath the huge horse chestnut tree on the green. Good nearby walks.

🍴 The food includes lunchtime warm ciabattas, coronation chicken, prawn or garlic mushrooms on toast, macaroni cheese, scampi and home-made beefburger, and a more elaborate main menu (not cheap) with dishes such as smoked haddock, spinach and egg pie, gressingham duck breast in hoisin sauce, boeuf bourguignon and morrocan-style lamb shank. *Starters/Snacks: £5.00 to £9.00. Main Courses: £6.00 to £15.00. Puddings: £4.00 to £5.00*

Free house ~ Licensees George and Juliet Bristow ~ Real ale ~ Bar food (12-3, 6.30-8.30) ~ Restaurant ~ (01798) 861310 ~ Children welcome ~ Dogs welcome ~ Open 11-11(midnight Sat)12; 12-10.30 Sun

Recommended by M G Hart, Michael B Griffith, Mrs Romey Heaton, Martin and Karen Wake, Mike and Eleanor Anderson, Glen and Nola Armstrong

MAYFIELD   TQ5927   MAP 3
Rose & Crown
Fletching Street; TN20 6TE

Pretty weatherboarded cottage with unspoilt bars, relaxed atmosphere, local beers and simple pubby food

New licensees (two sisters) have taken over this pretty 16th-c weatherboarded pub and there's a genuinely relaxed and friendly atmosphere. Several bars wander round the little central servery but the two cosy small front rooms have the most character: low ceiling boards with coins embedded in the glossy paintwork, bench seats built into the partly panelled walls, pewter tankards hanging above the bar and along a beam, and a mix of simple dining chairs around wooden tables on the stripped floorboards. There are candles in the first brick fireplace, a big log fire in the inglenook, Harveys Best and Olympia on handpump and decent wines by the glass. Down some steps to the left is a larger carpeted room with a couple of big comfortable cushioned sofas, similar tables and chairs, a woodburning stove, several mirrors and steps at the other end of the room that lead up to a less-used back room. There are picnic-sets under parasols on the front terrace.

🍴 Simple bar food includes sandwiches and filled ciabattas, ploughman's, mackerel pâté, welsh rarebit with red onion relish, warm goats cheese salad with apple and walnut vinaigrette, spring vegetable risotto, honey-glazed ham and eggs, local sausages and mash topped with parsnip crisps, home-made burger topped with mushroom and stilton or cheese, and puddings like treacle sponge and chunky apple flan; on Thursdays they have a tapas evening. *Starters/Snacks: £4.25 to £6.90. Main Courses: £6.90 to £10.50. Puddings: £4.50*

Free house ~ Licensees Christine Currer and Elizabeth Maltman ~ Real ale ~ Bar food (12-9) ~ (01435) 872200 ~ Children welcome ~ Dogs allowed in bar ~ Open 11-11; 12-10.30 Sun
Recommended by N R White

OVING   SU9005   MAP 2
Gribble Inn 🍺
Between A27 and A259 just E of Chichester, then should be signposted just off village road; OS Sheet 197 map reference 900050; PO20 2BP

Own-brewed beers in bustling 16th-c thatched pub with beamed and timbered linked rooms, traditional bar food and pretty garden

Much enjoyed for its fine range of beers, this pleasant thatched pub also holds a four-day beer festival over long weekends in April and summer. The eight real ales on handpump feature their own-brewed Gribble Ale, CHI.P.A., Fuzzy Duck, Plucking Pheasant and Reg's Tipple, plus Badger Best, First Gold and Hopping Hare; several wines by the glass. The chatty bar has lots of heavy beams and timbering, old country-kitchen furnishings and pews and the several linked rooms have a cottagey feel, huge winter log fires and occasional piped music; the basset hound is called Puzzle. Board games and skittle alley with its own bar. There are seats outside under a covered area and more chairs in the pretty garden with apple and pear trees; at the end of the garden are some rabbits. More reports on the food please.

⑪ Bar food at lunchtime includes doorstep sandwiches, filled baked potatoes, ploughman's, soup, mushrooms in garlic, steak and kidney pudding, beery sausages with gravy, steaks, a daily vegetarian pasta dish, lambs liver and bacon, and home-cooked ham and egg; in the evening, there are quite a few daily specials and fresh fish dishes. *Starters/Snacks: £3.25 to £6.25. Main Courses: £7.95 to £15.95. Puddings: £3.95 to £4.95*

Badger ~ Licensees Dave and Linda Stone ~ Real ale ~ Bar food (12-2.30, 6.30-9.30(8.30 Sun)) ~ Restaurant ~ (01243) 786893 ~ Children in family room ~ Dogs allowed in bar ~ Jazz first Tues of month, live bands last Fri of month ~ Open 11-3, 5.30-11; 11-11 Sat; 12-10.30 Sun

Recommended by Sue and Mike Todd, Paul Rampton, Julie Harding, David H T Dimock, Val and Alan Green, the Didler, Stephen Moss, Rob and Penny Wakefield, Phil and Jane Villiers, Mr and Mrs P D Titcomb, John Beeken

RINGMER   TQ4313   MAP 3

Cock

Uckfield Road – blocked-off section of road off A26 N of village turn-off; BN8 5RX

Popular food in 16th-c pub, log fire in heavily beamed bar, a fine choice of drinks, garden with wide views – nice sunsets

Run by convivial staff, this secluded weatherboarded pub is well screened from the A26 and has a good-sized garden. The unspoilt, heavily beamed bar has traditional pubby furniture on flagstones, a log fire in the inglenook fireplace (lit from October to May), and Harveys Best and Fullers London Pride together with a Darkstar Hophead in summer or Harveys Old in winter and a guest like Adnams Broadside are on handpump; nine wines by the glass, mulled wine in winter, Weston's cider and a dozen malt whiskies; piped music. There are three dining areas. Outside on the terrace and in the garden, there are lots of picnic-sets with views across open fields to the South Downs; visiting dogs are offered a bowl of water and a chew, and their own dogs are called Fred and Tally. More up-to-date reports please.

⑪ The extensive choice of popular bar food is set out on a blackboard and includes lunchtime sandwiches and ploughman's (not Sunday), soup, starters like chicken liver pâté, egg and prawn mayonnaise and spicy cajun chicken strips, several vegetarian choices such as mixed nut roast with red wine sauce, or chickpea, courgette and coconut curry, pork and herb sausages, honey-roast ham with free-range eggs, steak and kidney pudding, sussex lamb chops in garlic and rosemary, liver and bacon with onion gravy or bass fillets. House specials such as venison sausages and stilton-stuffed sirloin steak stuffed with creamy mushroom sauce; puddings like treacle tart, stem ginger sponge or rhubarb crumble; Sunday roasts. *Starters/Snacks: £4.50 to £5.95. Main Courses: £6.95 to £17.25. Puddings: £3.95 to £4.85*

Free house ~ Licensees Ian and Matt Ridley ~ Real ale ~ Bar food (12-2.15(2.30 Sat), 6-9.30; all day Sun) ~ Restaurant ~ (01273) 812040 ~ Children welcome away from bar ~ Dogs allowed in bar ~ Open 11-3, 6-11.30; 11am-11.30pm Sun

Recommended by Dominic Lucas, M G Hart, Tracey and Stephen Groves, Tony and Wendy Hobden, Conor McGaughey, Tina and David Woods-Taylor

RYE   TQ9220   MAP 3

Mermaid ♀ ⇐

Mermaid Street; TN31 7EY

Lovely old timbered inn on famous cobbled street with civilised, antiques-filled bar, good wine list and short choice of decent bar food; smart restaurant and bedrooms

One of the most photographed buildings in Rye, this striking half-timbered inn dates back well over 500 years. This is an extremely civilised place to stay, eat or drink, with prices to match, and the little bar is where those in search of a light lunch and a drink tend to head: quite a mix of quaint, closely set furnishings such as Victorian gothic carved oak chairs, older but plainer oak seats and a massive deeply polished bressumer beam across one wall for the huge inglenook fireplace. Three antique but not ancient wall paintings show old english scenes. Courage Best, Fullers London Pride and Greene King Old Speckled Hen on handpump, several malt whiskies and a good wine list; piped music in the bar only, playing cards and board games on request. Seats on a small back terrace overlook the car park where – at bank holiday weekends – there may be morris dancers.

🍴 **The short bar menu includes sandwiches and tasty dishes with a fishy theme such as smoked fish chowder, moules marinière, fish pie, seafood platter and smoked haddock and salmon fishcake, as well as free-range chicken goujons caramelised with lemon and black pepper, steak and kidney pudding, and minute steak with blue cheese salad; puddings such as crème brûlée with fresh berries and strawberry pavlova with chantilly cream. The smart restaurant offers fixed-price lunches and dinners from a richly traditional menu.** *Starters/Snacks: £8.75 to £9.75. Main Courses: £11.25 to £16.50. Puddings: £6.50*

Free house ~ Licensees Robert Pinwill and Mrs J Blincow ~ Real ale ~ Bar food (12-2.30, 7-9.30) ~ Restaurant ~ (01797) 223065 ~ Children welcome ~ Open 12-11 ~ Bedrooms: £90B/£180B

Recommended by Lorry Spooner, B and M Kendall, Mr and Mrs W W Burke, Louise English, Adrian Johnson, DFL, the Didler

Ship
The Strand, foot of Mermaid Street; TN31 7DB

New team doing good food in prettily set old inn, relaxed and informal

By no means smart, this easy-going place is well worth knowing for its food and is good on the drinks side, too: Harveys Best and guests like Dark Star Espresso and Rother Valley Copper Ale on handpump, local farm cider and perry, 16 wines by the glass and some really inventive house cocktails. It's an old building, with 16th-c stripped beams and timbers; its mixed bag of rather secondhand-feeling furnishings – a cosy group of overstuffed leather armchairs and sofa, random stripped or Formica-topped tables and various café chairs – suit it nicely, as do the utilitarian bulkhead wall lamps. The ground floor is all opened up, from the sunny big-windowed front part to a snugger part at the back, with a log fire in the stripped brick fireplace below a stuffed boar's head and a feeling of separate areas is enhanced by the varied flooring: composition, stripped boards, flagstones, a bit of carpet in the armchair corner. The young staff are good-natured and helpful; darts, board games and unobtrusive piped pop music, and the young black german shepherd is called Star. Out by the quiet lane are picnic-sets and one or two cheerful oilcloth-covered tables. We have not yet heard from readers who have stayed the night here, and would welcome reports.

🍴 **The food uses good fresh ingredients from named local sources, often organic, and is cooked with flair – not fussy, but full of flavour. The choice for our early summer inspection lunch included a generous rare roast beef sandwich, smoked prawns with saffron mayonnaise, caramelised red onion and gruyère tart, devilled kidneys on toasted brioche, grilled chorizo hash with black pudding and egg, plaice and chips, slow-roasted lamb shoulder with an unusual pearl barley and couscous salad, and a delicious seared sea trout served with poached egg and local asparagus. They take care over details such as bread and the neat Peugeot pepper and salt grinders, and do breakfasts for non-residents at weekends and in summer.** *Starters/Snacks: £5.00 to £8.00. Main Courses: £9.00 to £17.00. Puddings: £5.25*

Enterprise ~ Licensee Karen Northcote ~ Real ale ~ Bar food (12-3.30(5.30 weekends), 6.30-10; breakfast from 9am) ~ Restaurant ~ (01797) 222233 ~ Children welcome ~ Dogs welcome ~ Open 10am-11pm; 12-10.30 Sun; 11.30 opening in winter ~ Bedrooms: /£90B

Recommended by Conrad Freezer

Ypres Castle 🍺
Gun Garden; steps up from A259, or down past Ypres Tower; TN31 7HH

Traditional pub in quiet corner of historic town centre, enjoyable bar food, lots of fish, several real ales and friendly service; seats in sheltered garden

Somewhat hidden away behind the 13th-c castle usually known as Ypres Tower and perched above the River Rother, this lively place has a nice mix of locals and visitors. The bars have various old tables and chairs, and somehow, the informal almost scruffy feel adds to its character. There are comfortable seats by the winter log fire, local artwork and a restaurant area; piped music (can be obtrusive). Fullers ESB and London Pride, Harveys Best and Timothy Taylors Landlord on handpump and friendly, helpful service. The sheltered garden is a pleasant place to sit; boules.

🍴 Good bar food includes soup, lunchtime ciabattas, ploughman's and sandwiches, platters with antipasti, hummus or smoked fish, beefburgers, romney marsh lamb cutlets and lots of fish based on the catch of the day from Rye Bay, such as beer-battered cod or bass with basil mash and white wine sauce, with interesting puddings like sussex pond pudding or triple chocolate cake; Sunday roasts (booking recommended) feature winchelsea beef, romney marsh saddle of lamb and nut roast. *Starters/Snacks: £4.90 to £6.75. Main Courses: £8.50 to £14.00. Puddings: £5.75*

Free house ~ Licensee Ian Fenn ~ Real ale ~ Bar food ~ Restaurant ~ (01797) 223248 ~ Children welcome at lunchtime ~ Dogs allowed in bar ~ Live music Fri evening ~ Open 11-11(dusk Sun)

Recommended by Richard Endacott, Peter Meister, Sue and Mike Todd, Mike and Eleanor Anderson, Louise English, Tom and Jill Jones

SALEHURST   TQ7424 MAP 3

Salehurst Halt

Village signposted from Robertsbridge bypass on A21 Tunbridge Wells—Battle; Church Lane; TN32 5PH

Relaxed little local in quiet hamlet, chatty atmosphere and real ales; nice back garden

This pleasantly unpretentious place is next to an attractive 14th-c church and looks out over the Rother valley. It's at its busiest in the evening when there's quite a mix of customers of all ages. To the right of the door there's a small stone-floored area with a couple of tables, a piano, settle, TV and an open fire. To the left there's a nice long scrubbed pine table with a couple of sofas, a mix of more ordinary pubby tables and wheelback and mates' chairs on the wood-strip floor, and maybe piped music; board games. Dark Star American Pale Ale or Hop Head and Harveys Best and on handpump along with a guest such as a Harveys seasonal beer, several malt whiskies and decent wines by the glass. There's a back terrace with metal chairs and tiled tables with more seats in the landscaped garden, which has table tennis. More reports please.

🍴 Lunchtime bar food usually includes filled baguettes, soup, ploughman's, greek salad, a large, popular fishcake with tartare sauce, pork pie (with pork from the neighbouring farm) and proper burgers; Sunday roasts in winter. The evening menu changes monthly and might include hastings cod in beer batter, ham and eggs, a curry, pizza and steaks. *Starters/Snacks: £4.00 to £5.00. Main Courses: £7.00 to £13.00. Puddings: £4.00*

Free house ~ Licensee Andrew Augarde ~ Real ale ~ Bar food (not Mon or Sun and Tues evenings) ~ (01580) 880620 ~ Children welcome ~ Dogs welcome ~ Live music second Sun of month 4-7pm ~ Open 12-3, 6-11; 12-11 Fri, Sat; 12-10.30 Sun; closed Mon

Recommended by Nigel and Jean Eames, N R White

SIDLESHAM   SZ8697 MAP 2

Crab & Lobster 🍴 ☐ 🛏

Mill Lane; off B2145 S of Chichester; PO20 7NB

RestaurANTy pub with new bedrooms, plenty of fresh fish dishes, real ales and a good choice of wines, stylish furnishings and seats on terrace overlooking bird reserve

In a most romantic spot beside the tranquil marshy expanse of Pagham Harbour, this upmarket dining venue mostly focuses on food and accommodation but is still welcoming to walkers and bird-watchers just calling in for a drink. Inside, there's a flagstoned bar with comfortable bucket seats around a mix of wooden tables, some bar stools by the light wooden-topped bar counter, a log fire, Harveys Best and Timothy

Taylors Landlord on handpump and 21 wines by the glass. But the main emphasis here is on the stylish, upmarket restaurant side with fabric dining chairs around tables set for eating, and walls painted in pale pastel colours. Good lighting, piped music (which one reader found intrusive) and friendly, helpful staff. The bedrooms are stylish, and there's also a self-catering cottage. On the back terrace, seats and tables overlook Pagham Harbour bird reserve.

🍴 Specialising in fresh fish, the imaginative, if rather pricy, food includes lunchtime open sandwiches (not Sundays), soup, starters like calamari with chorizo, crab parcel or scottish scallops with beetroot, and main courses such as selsey white crabmeat risotto with sea trout fillet, fish stew with saffron potatoes, slow-roasted pork belly and marinated courgette in garlic and rosemary; daily specials, and puddings like rhubarb and custard tart, deep-fried ice-cream with butterscotch sauce and poached pear in spiced red wine soup. Starters/Snacks: £4.95 to £12.50. Main Courses: £13.50 to £21.00. Puddings: £6.25 to £7.80

Free house ~ Licensee Sam Bakose ~ Real ale ~ Bar food (12-2.30, 6-9.30) ~ (01243) 641233 ~ Children welcome ~ Open 11-11 ~ Bedrooms: £80B/£130B

Recommended by J A Snell, DHV, Mr and Mrs P D Titcomb, Tim Gray

SUTTON
SU9715   MAP 2

White Horse
The Street; RH20 1PS

Opened-up country inn, contemporary creamy décor and attractive furniture, real ales and good wines by the glass, modern food; smart bedrooms

In a quiet little hamlet not far from Bignor Roman villa, this refurbished country inn is doing well under its newish owners. Our most recent visit found several locals enjoying a pint on the cushioned high bar chairs, and plenty of diners enjoying the good, interesting modern bar food. The bar has a couple of little open brick fireplaces each end, nightlight candles on mantelpieces, Harveys Best, Sharps Doom Bar and a guest like Adnams on handpump, good wines by the glass and friendly service. The wooden-topped island servery separates the bar from the two-room barrel-vaulted dining areas (coir carpeting here) and throughout the minimalist décor is a contemporary clotted cream colour, with modern hardwood chairs and tables on stripped wood and a few small photographs; there's another little log fire, church candles and fresh flowers. Stairs from the back go up to a couple of big wooden tables by the sizeable air vent and more steps up to a lawned area with plenty of picnic-sets; there are more seats out in front. Good nearby walks (packed lunches on request); we haven't yet heard from readers using the smart comfortable bedrooms but would expect them to deserve our Stay Award.

🍴 Popular modern bar food includes lunchtime sandwiches, soup and simpler dishes such as a half pint or pint of prawns, pork and sage sausages and mash, platters of italian meats or english cheeses, and substantial salads; main courses from the full menu such as halibut with duchesse potatoes, rib-eye steak, confit of duck or sunblush tomato and goats cheese soufflé; puddings such as triple chocolate brownie or sticky toffee pudding. Unusual home-made ice-creams might include chocolate cookie or liquorice with sambucca syrup. Starters/Snacks: £5.00 to £7.00. Main Courses: £8.00 to £15.00. Puddings: £5.00

Enterprise ~ Lease Nick Georgiou ~ Real ale ~ Bar food ~ Restaurant ~ (01798) 869221 ~ Children welcome ~ Dogs allowed in bar ~ Open 11-3, 6-11; 12-4, 7-10.30 Sun ~ Bedrooms: £65S/£85B

Recommended by LM, Guy Vowles, Cathy Robinson, Ed Coombe

If a service charge is mentioned prominently on a menu or accommodation terms, you must pay it if service was satisfactory. If service is really bad you are legally entitled to refuse to pay some or all of the service charge as compensation for not getting the service you might reasonably have expected.

TROTTON

SU8322 MAP 2

Keepers Arms 🍴 🍷

A272 Midhurst—Petersfield; pub tucked up above road, on S side; GU31 5ER

Low ceilings, comfortable furnishings on polished wooden boards, open fires, real ales, contemporary food and seats on sunny terrace

This pretty tile-hung cottage has tables and seats on its south-facing terrace. The beamed L-shaped bar has timbered walls and some standing timbers, comfortable sofas and winged-back old leather armchairs around the big log fire, and simple rustic tables on the oak flooring. Elsewhere, there are a couple of unusual adult high chairs at an oak refectory table, two huge Georgian leather high-backed chairs around another table and, in the dining room, elegant oak tables, comfortable dining chairs and a woodburning stove; there's another cosy little dining room with bench seating around all four walls and a large central table. Ballards Best, Dark Star Hophead and Ringwood Fortyniner on handpump, and several wines from a comprehensive list. More reports please.

🍽 There's a choice of some pubby bar food such as ciabattas, ploughman's, cod in beer batter, sirloin steak, bass lunchtime soup, as well as a short à la carte menu (not cheap) offering the likes of carpaccio of yellow-fin tuna or slow-roasted pork belly with seared scallops. *Starters/Snacks: £3.95 to £9.75. Main Courses: £10.00 to £19.00. Puddings: £4.25 to £6.25*

Free house ~ Licensee Nick Troth ~ Real ale ~ Bar food ~ Restaurant ~ (01730) 813724 ~ Children welcome ~ Dogs allowed in bar ~ Open 12-3.30, 6-11; 12-4, 7-10.30 Sun
Recommended by Paul Humphreys, Martin and Karen Wake, Jennifer Hurst, Janet Whittaker, Bruce Young

TURNERS HILL

TQ3435 MAP 3

Red Lion 🍺

Lion Lane, just off B2028; RH10 4NU

Happy country local, warmly welcoming, with good value home cooking

This pretty tiled cottage is nicely old fashioned and unpretentious inside, with plenty of bar stools for the regulars in the snugly curtained parquet-floored bar, which has plush-cushioned wall benches, quite high black beams, a small fire and lots of homely memorabilia – one reader was surprised to find a photograph of himself in a world marbles championship held here in 1973, and another was delighted that the landlord and landlady both remembered him from some years back. A few steps lead up to a carpeted area with a roaring log fire in its big brick inglenook, cushioned pews and built-in settles forming booths. They have a good choice of wines by the glass, Harveys Best and a couple of seasonal ales on handpump, and daily papers; cheerful service, with a good landlord and very long-serving lunchtime barmaid; piped music, games machine and darts. The pub is quietly set on a slope overlooking the village and has picnic-sets up on the side grass.

🍽 The lunchtime food is proper country sustenance: sandwiches, soup, ploughman's, and baked potatoes, sausages and specials like steak and ale pie, cod, pheasant casserole or haddock and prawn in creamy cheese sauce. *Starters/Snacks: £3.75 to £7.25. Main Courses: £7.50 to £9.95*

Harveys ~ Tenant Ashley Whitby ~ Real ale ~ Bar food (12-2.30) ~ (01342) 715416 ~ Children welcome ~ Dogs welcome ~ Open 11-3, 5-11; 11-11.30 Fri; 11-11 Sat; 12-10(8 in winter) Sun
Recommended by N R White, Louise English, Terry Buckland, Mike Gorton, William Ruxton

---

Real ale may be served from handpumps, electric pumps (not just the on-off switches used for keg beer) or – common in Scotland – tall taps called founts (pronounced 'fonts') where a separate pump pushes the beer up under air pressure.

VINES CROSS

TQ5917   MAP 3

Brewers Arms

Vines Cross Road of B2203 then left at T junction; 1 mile E of Horam; TN21 9EN

Busy little pub run by chef/patron with good popular food, real ales, decent wines and monthly comedy club

Run by a friendly chef/patron, this is a popular little pub in a quiet hamlet. There's a genuine mix of both drinkers and diners and a friendly welcome for all. The sizeable public bar has some stools by the bar counter, quite a mix of dining chairs, benches and settles around wooden tables on the stripped floorboards and an informal atmosphere; Greene King Old Speckled Hen, St Austell Tribute and a guest beer on handpump; decent wines by the glass. The three other connecting rooms are similarly furnished; one has an open fire, another with red walls has one large table (just right for a large group of friends) and an end room has a woodburning stove in a brick fireplace. Church candles, lots of wall prints and helpful staff. There are a few picnic-sets in front of the pub and pretty flower tubs. They hold a monthly Monday comedy club.

🍴 Good, popular food includes sandwiches, soup, warm quail salad with pine nuts, spinach and a honey and mustard dressing, chicken liver pâté with pumpkin chutney, beefburger with bacon and cheese (good chips), ham and egg, home-made pork and hop sausages with champ potatoes and red wine gravy, breast of guinea fowl with confit leg and a lentil compote, loin of organic veal with rösti potatoes, wild sea trout with crayfish risotto, and puddings like orange rice pudding with caramelised banana and praline ice-cream and almond and treacle tart with clotted cream. *Starters/Snacks: £5.50 to £8.00. Main Courses: £8.00 to £16.00. Puddings: £5.50*

Greene King ~ Lease Tim Early ~ Real ale ~ Bar food (12-2.30, 6.30-9.30(10 Fri and Sat); 12-3, 6.30-9) ~ (01435) 812288 ~ Children welcome ~ Dogs allowed in bar ~ Comedy evening last Mon of month ~ Open 12-3, 6(5.30 Fri)-11(midnight Fri); 12-12 Sat; 12-11 Sun

Recommended by Mrs J Ekins-Daukes

WARNINGLID

TQ2425   MAP 3

Half Moon 🍴

B2115 off A23 S of Handcross, or off B2110 Handcross—Lower Beeding – village is signposted; The Street; RH17 5TR

Good modern cooking in simply furnished, newly extended village pub, informal chatty atmosphere, friendly service, real ales, decent wines, and seats in sizeable garden

Since the last edition of the *Guide* the friendly owners of this well run, friendly and very popular pub have opened up the former kitchen as an extension to the bar area, with oak beams and flagstones. This leads off from the lively little locals' bar, which has straightforward pubby furniture on the bare boards and a small victorian fireplace. A couple of steps lead from here down to the main bar which again, is pretty unpretentious, with an informal chatty feel, plank panelling and bare brick, old photographs of the village, built-in cushioned wall settles and a mix of tables (all with candles and fresh flowers) on bare boards; another step down to a smaller carpeted area with big paintings. There's also a recently created dining area. It's all spotless. Harveys Best and changing guests like Greene King Old Speckled Hen and Ringwood Best and Fortyniner on handpump, several decent wines by the glass, and some malt whiskies; they press their own cider to sell on behalf of a children's hospice on certain charity days in summer. There are quite a few picnic-sets outside on the lawn in the sheltered, sizeable garden, which has a most spectacular avenue of trees, with uplighters that glow at night. No children inside.

🍴 Very popular and extremely good (booking strongly advised), the food is all made on the premises, apart from the chips and ice-cream, with whole animals brought in from farms in Sussex and butchered here, and includes lunchtime filled ciabattas and ploughman's as well as starters like smoked chicken chowder or seared scallops with red pepper jam, and main courses such as fish and chips, wild mushroom risotto, corn-fed chicken breast with mustard sauce, calves liver and pies, with puddings like vanilla panna cotta with rhubarb compote or hazelnut chocolate brownie with orange sauce. *Starters/Snacks: £5.00 to £9.00. Main Courses: £6.50 to £19.00. Puddings: £5.50*

Free house ~ Licensees John Lea and James Amico ~ Real ale ~ Bar food (12-2, 6-9.30; 12-3; not Sun evening) ~ Restaurant ~ (01444) 461227 ~ Dogs allowed in bar ~ Open 11.30-2.30, 5.30-11; 12-10.30 Sun

Recommended by Terry Buckland, Mr and Mrs R Green, Susan and Neil McLean, C and R Bromage, N R White, David Cosham, Karen Eliot, Andy and Claire Barker, Martin and Karen Wake, Derek and Maggie Washington

WARTLING   TQ6509   MAP 3

Lamb ♀

Village signposted with Herstmonceux Castle off A271 Herstmonceux—Battle; BN27 1RY

Friendly country pub, comfortable seating areas, cosy little bar, changing real ales, popular bar food and seats on pretty back terrace

On a gentle rise in the tranquil low-lying expanse of the Pevensey Levels this amiable family-owned pub is often busy with customers, and it's best to get there early to be sure of a table or to book in advance. There's a little entrance bar with a couple of tables and this leads through to the beamed and timbered snug (mind your head on the low entrance beam) with comfortable leather sofas and some wooden chairs and tables; the separate restaurant is off here. Log fires, Harveys Best, Kings Horsham Best and Wells & Youngs Bombardier on handpump and ten wines by the glass. Up some steps at the back of the building there are seats on a pretty, flower-filled terrace. More reports please.

🍴 The changing menu of well liked bar food includes filled home-made baps, ploughman's, soup, starters or lighter meals such as grilled king scallops with pesto and parmesan breadcrumbs or chicken, mushroom and port pâté, with main courses (using meat from named local farms), such as rib-eye steak, fish pie, stuffed free-range chicken breast with bacon and vegetarian risotto; puddings like steamed plum and blackberry sponge or kirsch-soaked cherry eton mess. *Starters/Snacks: £4.25 to £8.95. Main Courses: £7.95 to £13.95. Puddings: £2.95 to £4.95*

Free house ~ Licensees Robert and Alison Farncombe ~ Real ale ~ Bar food (12-2.15, 7-9; 12-2.30 Sun; not Sun evening) ~ Restaurant ~ (01323) 832116 ~ Children in eating areas ~ Dogs allowed in bar ~ Open 11-3, 6-11; 12-3 Sun; closed Sun evening

Recommended by Conrad Freezer, Christopher Turner, M G Hart, Mr and Mrs R A Saunders, Mrs Mary Woods, V Brogden, C and R Bromage

WEST HOATHLY   TQ3632   MAP 3

Cat

Signed from A22 and B2028 S of East Grinstead; North Lane; RH19 4PP

Sensitively refurbished gimmick-free medieval inn, with enjoyable food, Sussex ales and roaring open fires

Run by a father and son team, this pleasant 16th-c tile-hung place next to the church is a satisfying blend of old and new, and there's nothing in the way of piped music or games machines. Its characterful old core features polished tables with candles, lots of beams and two log fires in the bar areas; look out for a glass cover over the 75-foot deep well. Dark Star Hophead, Harveys Best and a guest such as Dark Star Sussex Stout are on handpump, and there are nine wines by the glass. From the contemporary-style garden room, glass doors open on to a terrace and herb garden. There are four en-suite double bedrooms: we would welcome reports from readers who stay here.

🍴 The well prepared bar food includes sandwiches, ploughman's and a lunchtime menu with simple dishes like Harveys beer-battered fish, grilled goats cheese salad, tiger prawn kebabs, steak and ale pie and sirloin steak with a more extensive evening menu, and daily changing and seasonal blackboard specials such as local game terrine, pan-fried loin of venison with blackberry jus, fresh sole or bream from Newhaven, and vegetarian

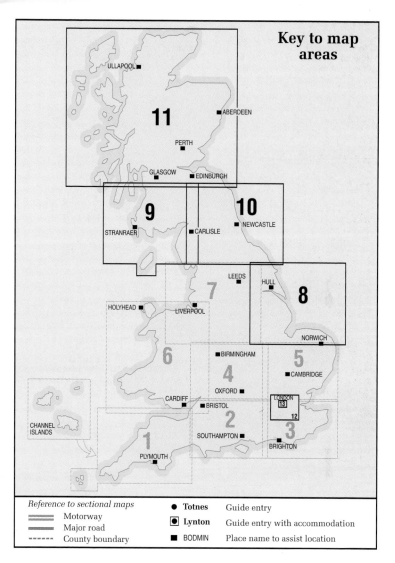

Key to map areas

ULLAPOOL

11

ABERDEEN

PERTH

GLASGOW EDINBURGH

9

STRANRAER

CARLISLE

10

NEWCASTLE

LEEDS

HULL

7

8

HOLYHEAD

LIVERPOOL

NORWICH

6

BIRMINGHAM

5

4

CAMBRIDGE

OXFORD

CARDIFF

BRISTOL

LONDON 13

12

2

CHANNEL ISLANDS

1

SOUTHAMPTON

3

PLYMOUTH

BRIGHTON

Reference to sectional maps

▤ Motorway
▤ Major road
----- County boundary

● **Totnes** Guide entry
◉ **Lynton** Guide entry with accommodation
■ **BODMIN** Place name to assist location

MAPS IN THIS SECTION

For Maps 1 – 7 see earlier colour section

8

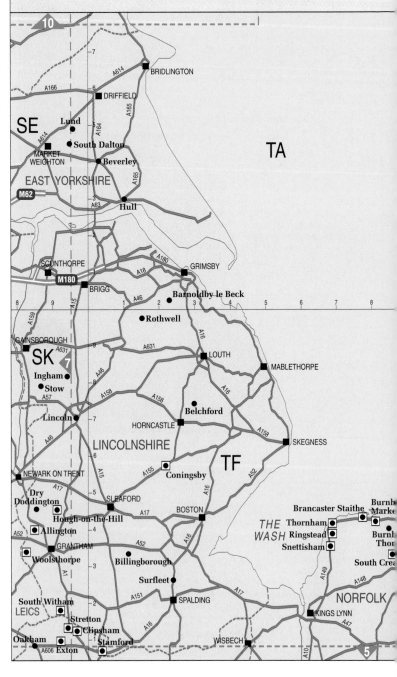

10

A614
BRIDLINGTON

A166
■ DRIFFIELD

A165

SE
● Lund
A164
A614
● **South Dalton**
■
MARKET
WEIGHTON
● **Beverley**

TA

EAST YORKSHIRE

A165

M62
A63
● Hull

SCUNTHORPE
A180
M180
A18
● GRIMSBY
■ BRIGG
A46
● **Barnoldby le Beck**

A159

8   9   1   2   3   4   5   7   8

● Rothwell

GAINSBOROUGH
A631
SK
A631
A46
A631
● LOUTH
■ MABLETHORPE
● Ingham
● Stow
A46
A57
A158
A158
A16
● **Belchford**
● Lincoln
HORNCASTLE
A158

A46   **LINCOLNSHIRE**   ■ SKEGNESS

NEWARK ON TRENT
A15
A155
● Coningsby
TF
A52

● Dry
Doddington
A17
● SLEAFORD
A16
Brancaster Staithe
Burnh
Marke
● **Hough-on-the-Hill**
A17
■ BOSTON
THE
● **Thornham**
A52
● Allington
A52
WASH
● **Ringstead**
Burnh
Thor
● **Snettisham**
GRANTHAM
A16
● **Billingborough**
South Crea
Woolsthorpe
A1
● **Surfleet**
A149
A148
South Witham
A151
■ SPALDING
A17
NORFOLK
LEICS
● **Stretton**
A16
KINGS LYNN
A47
Oakham ● **Chipsham**
A606 Exton ● **Stamford**
WISBECH
A10
5

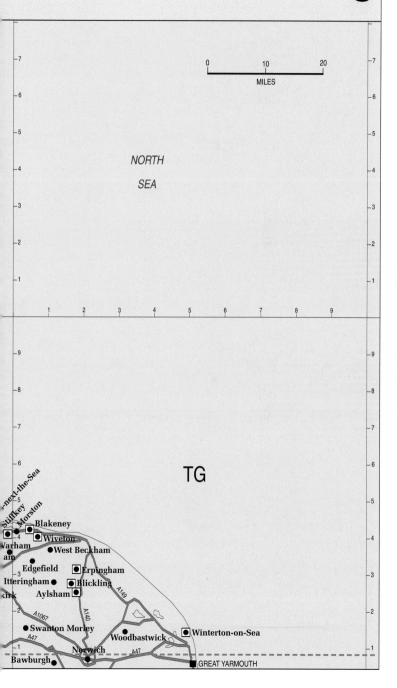

NORTH

SEA

MILES

TG

-next-the-Sea
Stiffkey
Morston
Blakeney
Wiveton
Warham
am
West Beckham
Edgefield
Erpingham
Itteringham
Blickling
kirk
Aylsham
A149
Swanton Morley
A1067
A140
Woodbastwick
Winterton-on-Sea
Bawburgh
A47
Norwich
A47
GREAT YARMOUTH

9

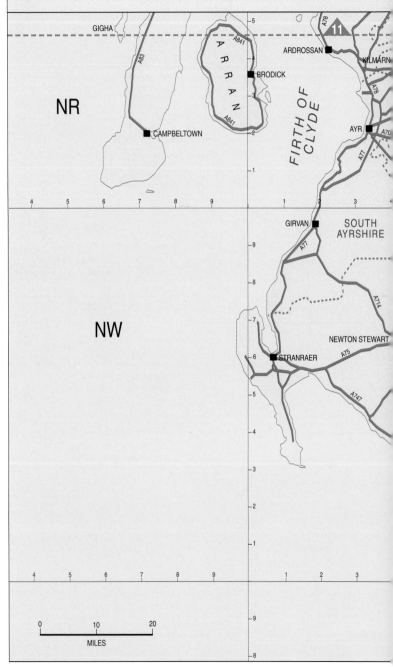

GIGHA

A83

A R R A N

A841

NR

BRODICK

A841

CAMPBELTOWN

FIRTH OF CLYDE

A78

11

ARDROSSAN

KILMARN

A78

A70

AYR

A77

GIRVAN

A77

SOUTH AYRSHIRE

A714

NW

NEWTON STEWART

A75

STRANRAER

A747

0   10   20
MILES

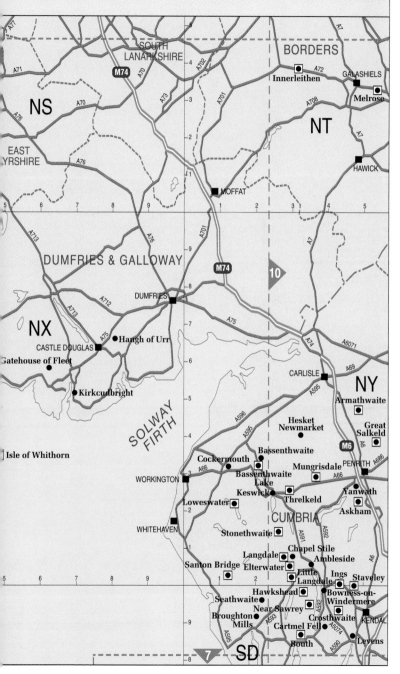

A77
A71
A76

SOUTH LANARKSHIRE

M74

A70

A70

A73

A702

A701

BORDERS

Innerleithen
A72

GALASHIELS

Melrose

NS

NT

EAST AYRSHIRE

A76

A7

A708

HAWICK

A701

MOFFAT

5   6   7   8   1   2   3   4   5

A713

A76

A701

DUMFRIES & GALLOWAY

M74

10

A712

DUMFRIES

M74

A74

A6071

NX

A713

A75

A7

A69

A75

CASTLE DOUGLAS

Hangh of Urr

CARLISLE

NY

Gatehouse of Fleet

A595

Armathwaite

Kirkcudbright

A596

Hesket Newmarket

Great Salkeld

A6

A686

SOLWAY FIRTH

A595

Bassenthwaite

M6

PENRITH

Isle of Whithorn

Cockermouth

Mungrisdale

A66

A66

WORKINGTON

A66

Bassenthwaite Lake

Yanwath

Keswick

Threlkeld

Askham

Loweswater

CUMBRIA

WHITEHAVEN

Stonethwaite

A591

A592

A6

Chapel Stile

Langdale

Ambleside

Santon Bridge

Elterwater

Little Langdale

Ings

Staveley

Hawkshead

Bowness-on-Windermere

Seathwaite

Near Sawrey

A592

Broughton Mills

Crosthwaite

KENDAL

A593

Cartmel Fell

A5074

Bouth

Levens

A595

A590

7   SD

5   6   7   8   9   1

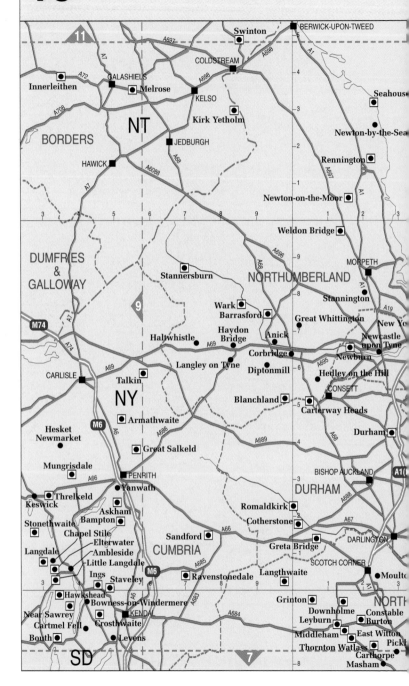

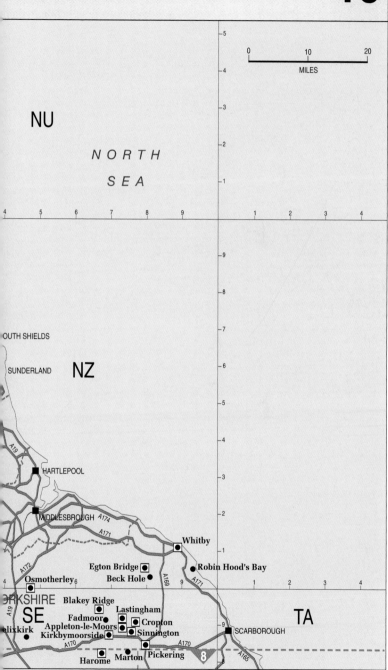

NU

NORTH

SEA

NZ

OUTH SHIELDS

SUNDERLAND

HARTLEPOOL

MIDDLESBROUGH *A174*

A171

Whitby

Egton Bridge

Robin Hood's Bay

Beck Hole

Osmotherley

Blakey Ridge

Lastingham

Fadmoor

Cropton

Appleton-le-Moors

Sinnington

Kirkbymoorside

ЭRKSHIRE

SE

TA

SCARBOROUGH

Harome Marton Pickering

8

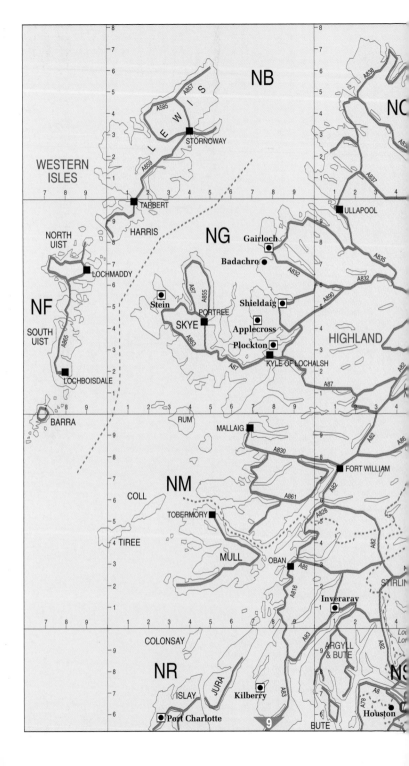

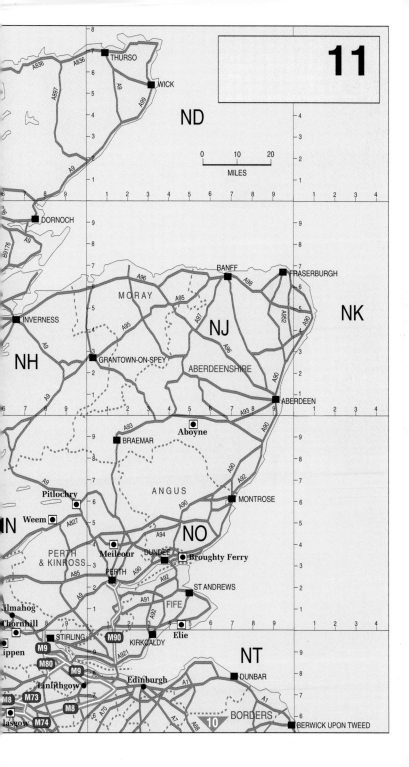

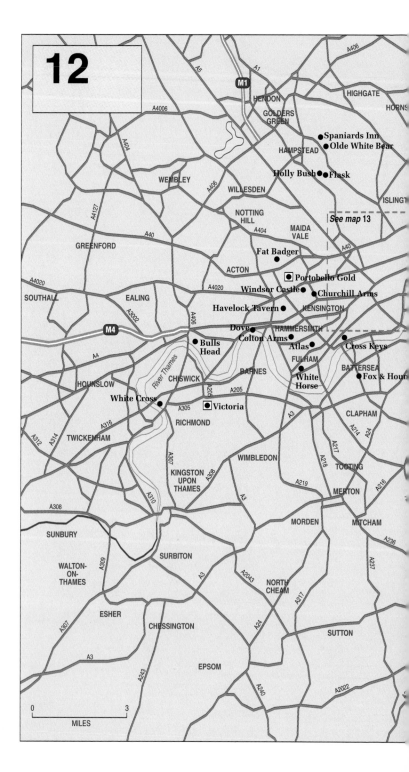

12

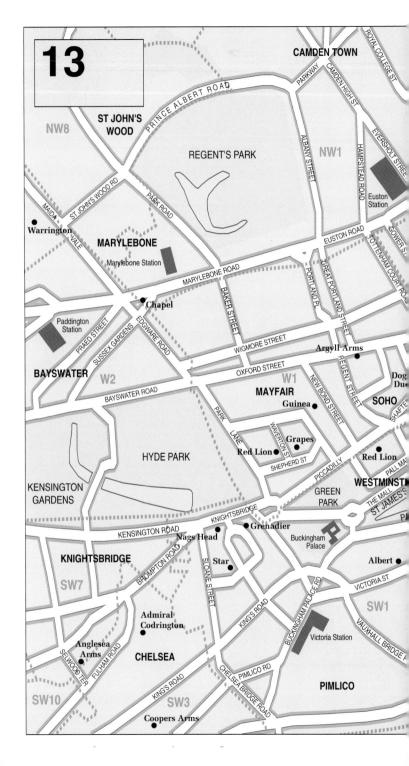

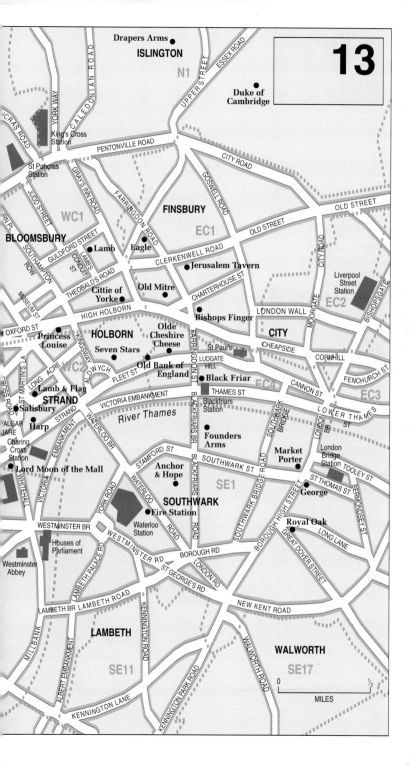

SEARCH *THE GOOD PUB GUIDE* ONLINE WITH OUR NEW, UPDATED SITE

The recently improved *Good Pub Guide* website, **www.thegoodpubguide.co.uk**, provides the opportunity to search through not only all of the 5,000 pubs listed in the *Guide,* but also some 50,000 other pubs around the country.

Search by town, county, postcode or even pub name to find pubs listed by distance and *Good Pub Guide* recommendation.

All pub and food reviews in the *Guide* are on the site – as well as important details like opening times, pub facilities and licensee names. However, the site offers more – for the first time licensees can add extra details about their pubs, and readers can add comments for all to see, so please get involved. Help your fellow *Guide* readers find that perfect pub!

In addition to the pub reviews, you'll also find articles, news and blogs on the site. We track the latest Daily Pub News and the *Good Pub Guide* editorial team will write articles throughout the year. Additionally, we'll be

having regular blogs posted by people from all aspects of the pub world – licensees, breweries and *Guide* readers.

Help us to build the best Pub database we can at
www.thegoodpubguide.co.uk

Search
Find pubs by name or location, or use the drop-down menu

Add your comments
We want to hear what you think – your comments are added beneath the *Good Pub Guide* review

Directory information
Full pub address, telephone number and opening and closing times

Map
Moveable map with the pub's precise location

Reviews
We display the full *Good Pub Guide* review for both the pub and its food to give you in-depth coverage

Awards
Shows how many *Good Pub Guide* awards have been won by the pub and in which categories

HOW YOU CAN GET INVOLVED IN *THE GOOD PUB GUIDE* WEBSITE

www.thegoodpubguide.co.uk

All pub and food reviews in this *Guide* appear on the site. However, we also want you to have your say. Register to tell us what you think about your favourite pubs – and your comments will help readers decide which pubs might suit them. Tell us if a pub is good for beer, food, accommodation, local walks or just has a cracking atmosphere. If other visitors to the website agree, it might be enough for the pub to become a *Good Pub Guide* recommendation next year!

We want licensees to get involved too – and the site allows them to add details about their own pubs for FREE, including recent photos, latest updates on facilities, guest ales, quiz nights, BBQs, beer festivals and any other pub events. So if you're a licensee, please sign up and add your pub details!

You can also register to receive our regular newsletter to get pub news and access to special offers, competitions and more.

LINK WITH US

As well as leaving comments on the website, look for us on Twitter (**twitter.com/goodpubguide**), Facebook and on your mobile phone as we open up more ways for you to be involved with *The Good Pub Guide*.

THE GOOD PUB GUIDE SAT NAV EDITION

In conjunction with Garmin, *The Good Pub Guide* is now available for your Sat Nav. Available as an SD card or download, it integrates quickly and easily into your Garmin Sat Nav and gives you access to all 5,000 recommended pubs from the 2010 *Guide*.

Search for Main Entry or Lucky Dip pubs (or both!) and have the Sat Nav direct you straight to the pub door. The perfect solution for finding your way to those hidden gems across the country.

For more details on this, and how you can buy it, go to
www.garmin.co.uk

options such as roasted butternut squash, beetroot, red onion and blue cheese ta
Sunday roasts. Puddings might include treacle and walnut tart, lemon and lime
cheesecake or chocolate truffle torte with raspberries. *Starters/Snacks: £6.00 to £8.50. Main
Courses: £9.00 to £18.00. Puddings: £5.50*

Free house ~ Licensees Nick and Mark White ~ Real ale ~ Bar food (12-2(2.30 Sat), 6-9.30) ~
Restaurant ~ (01342) 810369 ~ Children over 8 welcome ~ Dogs allowed in bar ~
Open 12-2.30(3 Sat), 6-11; 12-3 Sun; closed Sun evening, Mon ~ Bedrooms: /£80B

Recommended by JMM, Terry Buckland, John Branston, Roger and Diana Morgan

WILMINGTON
TQ5404   MAP 3

Giants Rest
Just off A27; BN26 5SQ

**Busy country pub with friendly welcome from cheerful landlord, informal atmosphere,
popular bar food and real ales; bedrooms**

In a high-ceilinged Victorian building, this pub has paintings by the highly individual
Beryl Cook all over its walls, and its tables have wooden puzzles you can attempt while
waiting for a meal or enjoying a drink. It's a popular place and the long wood-floored bar
and adjacent open areas have simple chairs, candles on tables, an open fire and a nice
informal atmosphere; you must book to be sure of a table, especially on Sunday
lunchtimes. Harveys Best, Hop Back Summer Lightning and Timothy Taylors Landlord on
handpump; piped music. Plenty of seats in the front garden. From here you can walk up
the village street and the huge chalk-carved figure of the Long Man of Wilmington, and
then up on to the South Downs.

🍴 Reasonably priced and well liked, the bar food includes ploughman's, soup and starters
like garlic king prawns with lemon mayonnaise, with main courses such as warm salads of
smoked duck and bacon or halloumi cheese, free-range sausages or home-cooked ham
with bubble and squeak and home-made chutney, grilled lemon sole and their popular
rabbit and bacon pie, with puddings such as sticky date and walnut pudding or warm
chocolate fudge brownie. Booking is particularly recommended at weekends; on Sunday
lunchtimes there may not be much space left for people wanting just a drink.
Starters/Snacks: £4.00 to £6.00. Main Courses: £7.50 to £14.50. Puddings: £3.50 to £5.00

Free house ~ Licensees Adrian and Rebecca Hillman ~ Real ale ~ Bar food (12-2, 6.30-9;
all day Sat, Sun) ~ (01323) 870207 ~ Children welcome ~ Dogs welcome ~ Open 11-3, 6-11;
11-11 Sat; 12-10.30 Sun ~ Bedrooms: /£60

*Recommended by Jean and Douglas Troup, Paul Boot, Bob and Val Collman, Laurence Smith, Ian and
Barbara Rankin, Jenny and Peter Lowater*

WINEHAM
TQ2320   MAP 3

Royal Oak
Village signposted from A272 and B2116; BN5 9AY

**Splendidly old-fashioned local with interesting bric-a-brac in simple rooms, attentive
staff, real ales and well liked food**

Very few pubs in Sussex are as enjoyably unchanged as this delightful local, where you
might find customers' dogs snoozing by the log fire that blazes in an enormous inglenook
fireplace, with its cast-iron Royal Oak fireback. There's a collection of cigarette boxes, a
stuffed stoat and crocodile, some jugs and ancient corkscrews on the very low beams
above the serving counter and other bits of bric-a-brac; views of quiet countryside from
the back parlour, and the bearded collie is called Bella. Harveys Best and a couple of
guests such as Greene King Ruddles or Dark Star Hophead tapped from the cask in a still
room and several wines by the glass. There are some picnic-sets outside – picturesque if
you are facing the pub.

🍴 Using local suppliers named in the pub's weekly notices, the bar food is simple, good
value and includes sandwiches, rarebit on toast, soup, ploughman's (attractively set out

on big boards), fishcakes, sausage and mash, various pies, game from local shoots, and puddings such as apple crumble and lemon posset with shortbread; on Mondays they do home-cooked ham with bubble and squeak and parsley sauce and their Sunday roasts are popular. *Starters/Snacks: £4.25 to £5.95. Main Courses: £6.95 to £12.00. Puddings: £4.95 to £5.25*

Punch ~ Tenants Sharon and Michael Bailey ~ Real ale ~ Bar food (12-2.30(3.30 Sun), 7-9.30; no food Sun evening) ~ Restaurant ~ (01444) 881252 ~ Children welcome ~ Dogs welcome ~ Open 11-2.30(3.30 Sat), 5.30(6 Sat)-11; 12-4, 7-10.30 Sun

Recommended by Terry Buckland, Neil Hardwick, B and M Kendall, N R White, the Didler, Donna and Roger, Ian Phillips, Phil and Sally Gorton

LUCKY DIP

Besides the fully inspected pubs, you might like to try these Lucky Dips recommended to us and described by readers (if you do, please send us reports: feedback@goodguides.com).

ALFRISTON [TQ5203]

☆ *Olde Smugglers* BN26 5UE [Waterloo Sq]: Charming 14th-c pub, low beams and panelling, huge inglenook in white-panelled bar, masses of bric-a-brac and smuggling mementoes, welcoming licensees, good value generous bar food from sandwiches to steaks, Dark Star, Harveys and Timothy Taylors, real cider, good choice of wines by the glass; can get crowded – lovely village draws many visitors; children in eating area and conservatory, dogs welcome, tables on well planted back suntrap terrace *(LYM, N R White, Pam Adsley, Eddie Edwards, Bruce Bird, John Beeken, Ann and Colin Hunt)*

Star BN26 5TA [High St]: Fascinating fine painted medieval carvings outside, heavy-beamed old-fashioned bar (busy lunchtime, quiet evenings) with some interesting features inc medieval sanctuary post, antique furnishings and big log fire in Tudor fireplace, easy chairs in comfortable lounge, more space behind for eating; some 35 good modern bedrooms in up-to-date part behind, open all day summer *(the Didler, Tina and David Woods-Taylor, LYM)*

AMBERLEY [TQ0313]

☆ *Sportsmans* BN18 9NR [Crossgates; Rackham Rd, off B2139]: Warmly welcoming licensees, well kept Dark Star, Harveys and guests, good food, three bars inc brick-floored games room, great views over Amberley Wild Brooks from pretty back conservatory restaurant and tables outside, good walks; dogs welcome, neat up-to-date bedrooms *(LYM, Bruce Bird, N R White)*

ANGMERING [TQ0704]

☆ *Spotted Cow* BN16 4AW [High St]: Good interesting sensibly priced food (very popular wkdy lunchtimes with older people) from sandwiches up, friendly and enthusiastic chef/landlord, good service, well kept ales such as Black Sheep, Fullers, Greene King and Harveys, good choice of wines by the glass, smallish bar on left, long dining extension with large conservatory on right, two log fires, smuggling history, sporting caricatures, no piped music;

children welcome, big garden with boules and play area, lovely walk to Highdown hill fort, open all day Sun (afternoon jazz sometimes then) *(Tony and Wendy Hobden, Pam Adsley, Mike and Sue Shirley)*

ANSTY [TQ2923]

Ansty Cross Inn RH17 5AG [Cuckfield Rd (A272)]: Extended pub with young friendly staff, local ales such as Dark Star, Harveys and Kings, good choice of lagers and wines by the glass, enjoyable food (not Sun evening), inglenook log fire *(Neil Hardwick)*

ARDINGLY [TQ3430]

☆ *Gardeners Arms* RH17 6TJ [B2028 2 miles N]: Reliable reasonably priced pub food in olde-worlde linked rooms, Badger beers, pleasant efficient service, daily papers, standing timbers and inglenooks, scrubbed pine on flagstones and broad boards, old local photographs, mural in back part; children and dogs welcome, disabled facilities, attractive wooden furniture on pretty terrace, lots of picnic-sets in side garden, opp S of England show ground and handy for Borde Hill and Wakehurst Place, open all day *(Susan and John Douglas, LM, Louise English, BB)*

ARUNDEL [TQ0208]

☆ *Black Rabbit* BN18 9PB [Mill Rd, Offham; keep on and don't give up!]: Nicely refurbished busy riverside pub well organised for families, lovely spot near wildfowl reserve with timeless views of water meadows and castle; long bar with eating areas either end, enjoyable range of all-day pub food inc good ploughman's, Badger ales, good choice of decent wines by the glass, friendly young staff, log fires; piped music; doubles as summer tea shop, lots of tables outside, pretty hanging baskets, play area, boat trips, good walks, open all day *(John Beeken, M Greening, LM, Mr and Mrs P D Titcomb, Gene and Kitty Rankin, LYM)*

☆ *Swan* BN18 9AG [High St]: Smart but comfortably relaxed open-plan L-shaped bar with attractive woodwork and matching fittings, friendly efficient young staff, well kept Fullers ales, good tea and coffee, good value enjoyable food from baguettes and baked potatoes to restaurant meals, sporting bric-a-brac and old photographs, beaten brass former inn-sign on wall, fire, restaurant; good bedrooms, open all day *(LYM, B and M Kendall, Jude Wright)*

ASHURST [TQ1816]

☆ *Fountain* BN44 3AP [B2135 S of Partridge Green]: Attractive and well run 16th-c country local with fine old flagstones, friendly rustic tap room on right with some antique polished trestle tables and housekeeper's chairs by inglenook log fire, second inglenook in opened-up heavy-beamed snug, cheery attentive staff, good interesting blackboard food as well as pub staples, Fullers, Harveys and Kings ales; no under-10s; dogs welcome, pretty garden with duck pond (pay ahead if you eat out here) *(Mike and Sue Shirley, Karen Eliot, LYM, PL)*

ASHURSTWOOD [TQ4136]

Three Crowns RH19 3TJ [Hammerwood Rd]: Roomy well decorated family pub with separate dining area, good value food using local meat and fish, friendly service, good beer and wine choice; sizeable garden *(Glenn and Gillian Miller, Neil Hardwick)*

BALCOMBE [TQ3033]

Cowdray Arms RH17 6QD [London Rd (B2036/B2110 N of village)]: Bright and airy main-road pub with good choice of blackboard bar food using local supplies, well kept Greene King and a guest such as St Austell Tribute, good value wines by the glass, chatty attentive staff, comfortable sofas in L-shaped bar, darts, conservatory restaurant; children and dogs welcome, large garden *(Matthew Simmonds, Terry Buckland)*

BARNS GREEN [TQ1227]

Queens Head RH13 0PS [Chapel Rd]: Traditional village pub doing well under welcoming new landlord, pubby food from good baguettes up, real ales such as Langham, reasonable prices *(Bob Hinton)*

BATTLE [TQ7515]

Chequers TN33 0AT [Lower Lake (A2100 SE)]: Attractive partly-medieval stone-built pub, roomy with several linked beamed areas, open fires, enjoyable pubby food from sandwiches up, well kept Fullers London Pride, Harveys and a guest beer, friendly staff, pool; back terrace tables, bedrooms (one said to be haunted by a dog), open all day *(Arthur Pickering)*

BEPTON [SU8620]

Country Inn GU29 0LR [Severals Rd]: Old-fashioned friendly local with well kept ales such as Bowmans Swift One, Sharps Doom Bar and Wells & Youngs Bitter, good value pubby food, log fire, heavy beams and stripped brickwork, darts-playing regulars; picnic-sets and play area in big garden, quiet spot *(Tony and Wendy Hobden)*

BEXHILL [TQ7208]

Denbigh TN39 4JE [Little Common Rd (A259 towards Polegate)]: Friendly local with enjoyable freshly prepared food, well kept Harveys Best, decent wine, cheery service; enclosed side garden *(MP)*

BILLINGSHURST [TQ0830]

☆ *Blue Ship* RH14 9BS [The Haven; hamlet signposted off A29 just N of junction with A264, then follow signpost left towards Garlands and Okehurst]: Unspoilt pub in quiet country spot, good friendly landlord, beamed and brick-floored front bar with blazing inglenook log fire, scrubbed tables and wall benches, Badger ales served from hatch, good value home-made traditional food (not Sun or Mon evenings), two small carpeted back rooms, darts, bar billiards, shove-ha'penny, cribbage, dominoes, no mobile phones; children and dogs welcome, seats by trees or tangle of clematis around front door, local produce for sale *(C and R Bromage, LYM)*

BOGNOR REGIS [SZ9298]

Navigator PO21 2QA [Marine Drive W]: Good value pubby food in picture-window seafront dining area, Greene King, good staff, lively local atmosphere in carpeted bar; comfortable bedrooms, some with sea view *(Terry and Nickie Williams, David H T Dimock)*

BOLNEY [TQ2623]

Bolney Stage RH17 5RL [London Rd, off old A23 just N of A272]: Child-friendly timbered dining pub, neat and comfortably olde-worlde, with good varied food inc good children's choice, prompt welcoming service even though busy, big log fire; handy for Sheffield Park and Bluebell Railway, open all day *(Mrs Pat Tribe)*

Eight Bells RH17 5QW [The Street]: Wide food choice from ciabattas and light dishes up, three real ales inc one brewed for the pub, good log fire, exemplary lavatories; newly furnished outside decking with neatly lit steps *(Michael and Mabs Cross)*

BRIGHTON [TQ3104]

Colonnade BN1 1UF [New Rd, off North St; by Theatre Royal]: Small richly restored Edwardian bar, with red plush banquettes, velvet swags, shining brass and mahogany, gleaming mirrors, interesting pre-war playbills and lots of signed theatrical photographs. Fullers London Pride, Harveys, lots of lagers, bar snacks, daily papers; tiny front terrace overlooking Pavilion gardens *(Ian Phillips, BB)*

☆ *Cricketers* BN1 1ND [Black Lion St]: Cheerful and genuine town pub, friendly bustle at busy times, good relaxed atmosphere when quieter, cosy and darkly Victorian with lots of interesting bric-a-brac – even a stuffed bear; attentive quick service, Fullers, Greene King, Harveys and Sharps tapped from the cask, good coffee, well priced pubby lunchtime food from sandwiches up in covered ex-stables courtyard and upstairs bar, restaurant (where children allowed); piped music; tall tables out in front, open all day *(LYM, Sue Demont, Tim Barrow, Keith and Chris O'Neill, Ian Phillips, Michael Dandy)*

☆ *Evening Star* BN1 3PB [Surrey St]: Chatty pub with several good Dark Star ales (originally brewed here), lots of changing guest and bottled belgian beers, friendly staff (may let you sample before you buy), farm ciders and perries, country wines, good lunchtime baguettes (rolls Sun), simple pale wood furniture on bare boards, nice mix of customers; unobtrusive piped music, some live music; pavement tables, open all day *(N R White, the Didler, Ian Phillips, Michael Dandy, BB)*

Master Mariner BN2 5WD [Inner Lagoon, Village Sq, Marina]: Nicely done in old-fashioned style with beamery etc, enjoyable changing food choice using local supplies, wknd carvery upstairs, well kept Fullers London Pride and Harveys; rustic tables out by marina *(Alec and Marie Lewery)*

☆ *Pub du Vin* BN1 1AD [Ship St]: Next to Hotel du Vin, long and narrow, comfortable wall seating one end, soft lighting, local photographs, stripped boards, Dark Star and Harveys from ornate pewter bar counter, good choice of wines by the glass, friendly helpful staff, enjoyable pubby food, modern grey leather-seated bar chairs and light oak tables, flame-effect fire, small cosy coir-carpeted room opposite with squishy black armchairs and sofas; marvellous original marble urinals worth a look; 11 comfortable new bedrooms *(BB)*

BURPHAM [TQ0308]

☆ *George & Dragon* BN18 9RR [off A27 nr Warningcamp]: Popular dining pub in great setting with fine views, wide range of food, small area for drinkers, well kept ales such as Arundel, Harveys and Wadworths; children welcome, dogs in bar, a few tables outside, good walks nearby, open all day *(Fiona Wynn, Pete Stroud, Cathryn and Richard Hicks, Bruce Bird, LYM, Karen Eliot, M G Hart, Sue Demont, Tim Barrow, Martin and Karen Wake)*

BURWASH [TQ6724]

Bell TN19 7EH [High St (A265)]: Pretty tile-hung pub with friendly local atmosphere, interesting farming bric-a-brac and good log fire, Harveys and a guest, decent house wines, good choice of sensibly priced blackboard food inc fish, cosy dining room, traditional pub games; piped music, TV; children and dogs welcome, disabled access, roadside picnic-sets facing Norman church, charming village, open all day *(Richard Mason, LYM, Hugh Bower)*

BURY [TQ0013]

☆ *Squire & Horse* RH20 1NS [Bury Common; A29 Fontwell—Pulborough]: Smartly kept beamed roadside pub, wide range of good well presented fresh food inc fish and nice puddings (worth booking as it can get very busy), friendly efficient service, well kept Fullers and Harveys, good choice of wines, several attractive partly divided areas, pink plush wall seats, hunting prints and ornaments, log fire, fresh flowers; pleasant garden and pretty terrace (some road noise) with a few chrome tables and chairs *(Ann and Colin Hunt, BB, Terry and Nickie Williams, Mrs Pat Tribe, LM, J Bryant)*

CHAILEY [TQ3919]

☆ *Five Bells* BN8 4DA [A275 9 miles N of Lewes]: Attractive rambling roadside pub, spacious and interesting, with enjoyable food putting unusual touches to good local and organic ingredients, well kept Harveys and Wells & Youngs, decent wine choice, young helpful staff, lots of different rooms and alcoves leading from low-beamed central bar with fine old brick floor, brick walls, inglenook, leather sofas and settles, live jazz Fri; quiet piped music; pretty front and side garden with picnic-sets, cl Mon *(Anne Clarke, Paul Humphreys, BB, John Beeken)*

CHICHESTER [SU8605]

Bell PO19 6AT [Broyle Rd]: Friendly and comfortable country-pub feel, good interesting changing real ales and wines, generous reasonably priced food from separate counter inc good vegetarian choices, efficient service even when busy, bric-a-brac on high beams, theatre posters, daily papers, darts and cribbage; Sun quiz night, piped music in bar, games machines; children and dogs welcome, disabled access, pleasant partly covered heated back terrace, opp Festival Theatre, cl Sun till 7pm *(Val and Alan Green, N R White, Tony and Wendy Hobden)*

Nags Head PO19 7SJ [St Pancras]: Bustling panelled bar and big eating area, locally popular Sun carvery, cheerful young staff, real ales, log fires; bedrooms *(Terry and Nickie Williams)*

CHIDHAM [SU7804]

☆ *Old House At Home* PO18 8SU [off A259 at Barleycorn pub in Nutbourne; Cot Lane]: Gently updated cottagey pub, particularly good friendly service, good food esp local fish, four real ales, decent wines, log fire, low beams and timbering, restaurant area; children in eating areas, tables outside, remote unspoilt farm-hamlet location, nearby walks by Chichester Harbour, open all day wknds *(Tony and Wendy Hobden, LYM, J A Snell, Joan and Tony Walker)*

CHILGROVE [SU8214]

Fish House PO18 9HX [B2141 Petersfield—Chichester]: Former White Horse turned into an upmarket fish restaurant/hotel but welcoming drinkers; light and airy beamed bar with old irish marble-topped counter, antique french fireplace and chunky teak furniture on oak boards, Black Sheep, Harveys and Timothy Taylors Landlord, expensive bar and restaurant food; piped music; children and dogs welcome, disabled facilities, terrace tables and garden, 15 luxury bedrooms, open all day *(LYM)*

CLAYTON [TQ2914]

☆ *Jack & Jill* BN6 9PD [Brighton Rd (A273)]: Friendly unsmart country pub with wide range of consistently good food, well kept mainly local beers, good wine, open fires, corner settles, lots of memorabilia on walls and ceilings, small restaurant area; children and dogs welcome, big back garden with play area, landmark twin windmills nearby, bedrooms (Tony and Wendy Hobden, Fr Robert Marsh, John Beeken, Mary M Grimshaw, Terry and Nickie Williams, Martin Gillard)

CLIMPING [SU9902]

Oystercatcher BN17 5RU [A259/B2233]: Roomy part-thatched popular Vintage Inn dining pub, olde-worlde décor, friendly young well trained staff, wide choice of reasonably priced traditional food all day from sandwiches and starters doubling as light dishes up, well kept Harveys Best, Shepherd Neame Spitfire and Timothy Taylors Landlord, good wines by the glass, nicely served coffee, log fires; disabled lavatories, picnic-sets in pleasant front garden (some traffic noise) (David H T Dimock)

COLDWALTHAM [TQ0216]

Labouring Man RH20 1LF [pub signed down lane off A29 about 2 miles S of Pulborough]: Recently refurbished but retaining village pub atmosphere, welcoming landlord and staff, enjoyable food, well kept Ringwood Best and two changing beers, log fires; children and dogs welcome, five comfortable new downs-view bedrooms, cl Mon lunchtimes (Tony and Wendy Hobden, Sian Morris, Bruce Bird)

COLEMANS HATCH [TQ4533]

☆ *Hatch* TN7 4EJ [signed off B2026, or off B2110 opp church]: Quaint and attractive little weatherboarded Ashdown Forest pub dating from 1430, big log fire in quickly filling beamed bar, small back dining room with another fire, very wide choice of good generous home-made food, well kept Harveys, Larkins and one or two guest beers, friendly quick young staff, good mix of customers inc families and dogs; not much parking so get there early; picnic-sets on front terrace and in beautifully kept big garden, open all day Sun and summer Sat (the Didler, LYM, Terry Buckland)

COLGATE [TQ2232]

Dragon RH12 4SY [Forest Rd]: Small two-bar Victorian pub with friendly helpful staff, good low-priced home-made food from tasty baguettes up, lovely log fire, well kept Badger ales, dining area, afternoon tea; picnic-sets in big secluded garden – good for children, dogs welcome, open all day wknds (Francis Vernon, Ian Phillips)

COWBEECH [TQ6114]

Merrie Harriers BN27 4JQ [off A271]: White clapboarded village local under new ownership, beamed public bar with inglenook log fire, high-backed settle and mixed tables and chairs, old local photographs, Harveys Best and a guest, carpeted lounge, brick-walled back restaurant; a few picnic-sets out in front, rustic seats in terraced garden with country views (LYM)

COWFOLD [TQ2122]

Coach House RH13 8BT [Horsham Rd]: Smart, comfortable and welcoming, with enjoyable food inc OAP bargains, Fullers

London Pride, good coffee and service, attractive traditional main bar, sofas by log fire, roomy neatly laid restaurant area, locals' bar (no children in this bit) with darts and pool; dogs welcome, large garden with corner play area, open all day (David H T Dimock)

CROWBOROUGH [TQ5329]

Wheatsheaf TN6 2NF [off Mount Pleasant]: Friendly three-room Harveys pub with their full range, reasonably priced pubby food (not Fri-Sun evenings or Mon), log fire, occasional live music; bedrooms in adjacent cottage, open all day (Tony Hobden)

CUCKFIELD [TQ3024]

Talbot RH17 5JX [High St]: Unassuming pub with hearty home-made food, three Harveys ales; separate upstairs sports bar; pleasant cobbled side mews (Terry Buckland)

DALLINGTON [TQ6619]

☆ *Swan* TN21 9LB [Woods Corner, B2096 E]: Bustling local with friendly staff and regulars, cheerful chatty atmosphere, well kept Harveys, decent wines by the glass, well liked pubby food inc good value two-course options and take-away fish and chips (Tues), bare-boards bar divided by standing timbers, woodburner, mixed furniture inc cushioned settle and high-backed pew, candles in bottles and fresh flowers, simple back restaurant with far-reaching views to the coast; piped music; steps down to smallish back garden (BB)

DANEHILL [TQ4128]

☆ *Coach & Horses* RH17 7JF [off A275, via School Lane towards Chelwood Common]: Well run dining pub in attractive countryside, good restauranty food (not Sun evening) served with style, well kept Harveys, good wines by the glass, little hatch-served public bar with small woodburner and simple furniture on polished boards, main bar with big Victorian prints, attractive old tables and fine brick floor, dining extension, darts, home-made chutneys and jams for sale; may try to keep your credit card while you eat outside; children and dogs welcome (nice pub dog), lovely views from big attractive garden with terrace under huge maple (Oliver and Sue Rowell, Susan and John Douglas, Michael Hasslacher, Alan Cowell, LYM)

DELL QUAY [SU8302]

☆ *Crown & Anchor* PO20 7EE [off A286 S of Chichester – look out for small sign]: Modernised 19th/20th-c beamed pub in splendid spot overlooking Chichester Harbour – best at high tide and quiet times, can be packed on sunny days; comfortable bow-windowed lounge bar, panelled public bar (dogs welcome), two log fires, lots of wines by the glass, four Wells & Youngs ales, cheerful staff, popular food all day inc great burgers and plenty of seafood; terrace, nice walks (Dick and Madeleine Brown, Kevin Flack, Mr and Mrs W W Burke, J Stickland, Terry and Nickie Williams, John Beeken, Nigel and Kath Thompson,

R and M Thomas, BB, Mr and Mrs P D Titcomb)

DENTON [TQ4502]

☆ **Flying Fish** BN9 0QB [Denton Rd]: Attractive 17th-c flint village pub by South Downs Way, floor tiles throughout, simple main bar, tiny end room with sofas facing each other over low table, nice middle room with little log fire by built-in wall seats, long cushioned pews and mixed dining chairs, cheerful modern paintings, white or pastel green walls, and high-ceilinged end dining room, Shepherd Neame ales, decent wines by the glass, friendly service, fish and game and more pubby food cooked by french chef/landlord; picnic-sets in front and on long back decking looking up to sloping garden, good bedrooms *(BB, John Beeken, the Didler)*

DIAL POST [TQ1519]

☆ **Crown** RH13 8NH [Worthing Rd (off A24 S of Horsham)]: Former staging inn with chef/landlord doing some imaginative cooking using local produce (not Sun evening), well kept Harveys, Kings and a local guest, good wines, log fires, lots of beams, carpets throughout, good service, front dining conservatory with pine tables, back dining room with extension down steps; some picnic-sets out at front, more on strip of lawn by back car park, two stable-block bedrooms *(Jennifer Hurst, Martin Stafford, Bruce Bird, A D Lealan)*

DITCHLING [TQ3215]

☆ **Bull** BN6 8TA [High St (B2112)]: Handsome rambling old building, old wooden furniture, beams, floorboards and fire, well kept Harveys, Timothy Taylors Landlord and two guests, home-made food from sandwiches up inc good Sun roasts, nicely furnished dining rooms with mellow décor and candles, snug area with chesterfields; piped music – live folk last Sun; children welcome, dogs in bar, disabled access, good-sized pretty garden and suntrap terrace, barbecue, bedrooms, open all day *(Alec and Joan Laurence, Tracey and Stephen Groves, John Silverman, Martin and Karen Wake, LYM, Nick Lawless, Tina and David Woods-Taylor, Andy and Claire Barker)*

White Horse BN6 8TS [West St]: Village pub under new management; neat and tidy with nice chatty local atmosphere, well kept ales inc Dark Star and Harveys, enjoyable food, quick friendly service, log fire and chunky tables in L-shaped panelled bar; pretty courtyard *(N R White)*

DONNINGTON [SU8501]

☆ **Blacksmiths Arms** PO20 7PR [B2201 S of Chichester]: Small white roadside cottage, low ceilings, Victorian prints, solid comfortable furnishings, relaxed atmosphere, back restaurant, Fullers London Pride and a guest beer, enjoyable but pricey food, friendly service; piped music, TV; children and dogs welcome, picnic-sets on grass at front and in big back garden with good play area, open all day wknds in summer *(Nigel and Kath Thompson, Val and Alan Green, J A Snell, LYM, Alan Cowell)*

DUNCTON [SU9517]

☆ **Cricketers** GU28 0LB [set back from A285]: Doing well under current licensees, well kept Kings, Skinners Betty Stogs and a local guest such as Arundel or Langham, decent wines by the glass, good home-made food using local ingredients, friendly service, inglenook fireplace, cricketing memorabilia, traditional games; children and dogs welcome, disabled facilities, garden behind with terrace, open all day *(Bruce Bird, LYM, David Cosham, Sally and Tom Matson, J A Snell)*

DURRINGTON [TQ1004]

Trout BN13 3RT [Titnore Way]: Former farmhouse, generous bargain lunches (even cheaper for OAPs), more elaborate evening menu, Hammerpot Red Hunter and Shepherd Neame Spitfire, helpful staff, conservatory link to barn-style dining room; tables out on decking *(Tony and Wendy Hobden)*

EAST ASHLING [SU8207]

☆ **Horse & Groom** PO18 9AX [B2178]: Busy country pub with well kept Harveys, Hop Back Summer Lightning and Wells & Youngs Bitter, good wines, bar food from sandwiches up, unchanging front drinkers' bar with old pale flagstones and inglenook woodburner, carpeted area with scrubbed trestle tables, fresh and airy extension with solid pale country-kitchen furniture on neat bare boards; children and dogs in some parts, garden with picnic-sets under umbrellas, bedrooms, cl Sun evening *(J A Snell, Ann and Colin Hunt, R and M Thomas, LYM, Tracey and Stephen Groves, Nick Lawless)*

EAST DEAN [TV5597]

☆ **Tiger** BN20 0DA [off A259 Eastbourne—Seaford]: Another change of management at this pretty pub overlooking delightful cottage-lined sloping green; own-brewed Beachy Head ales, Harveys and a guest, Stowford Press farm cider, good choice of wines by the glass, enjoyable food, friendly young staff; two smallish rooms, low beams, polished rustic tables and distinctive antique settles, old prints and portraits, inglenook woodburner; children and dogs welcome, picnic-sets out in front and in side garden, open all day *(Andrea Rampley, LM, LYM)*

EAST GRINSTEAD [TQ3936]

☆ **Old Mill** RH19 4AT [Dunnings Rd, S towards Saint Hill]: Interesting low-ceilinged 16th-c former mill cottage built over stream, attractively reworked as good informal Whiting & Hammond dining pub with lots of wood panelling, old photographs and pictures, carpeted dining area with mix of old tables, bare-boards bar, roaring winter fires, enjoyable hearty fresh food (all day), good choice of wines by the glass, four Harveys ales, friendly efficient service; children welcome, picnic-sets in front garden, covered decking next to working waterwheel, handy for Standen (NT) *(LYM, Phil Bryant)*

EAST HOATHLY [TQ5216]

☆ **Kings Head** BN8 6DR [High St/Mill Lane]: 1648 ales brewed here inc Original and a seasonal beer, also Harveys Best, in long friendly and comfortably worn-in open-plan log-fire bar with some dark panelling, stripped brick, old local photographs and upholstered settles, wide choice of enjoyable sensibly priced hearty food, friendly helpful service, daily papers, restaurant; TV; tables in garden up steps behind *(John Beeken)*

EAST LAVANT [SU8608]

☆ *Royal Oak* PO18 0AX [Pook Lane, off A286]: Good restauranty dining pub in pretty Georgian house, low beams, stripped brickwork, crooked timbers, log fires, church candles, small drinking area with wall seats and sofas, Sharps Doom Bar and Skinners Betty Stogs tapped from cask, good wine list, friendly attentive staff, leather dining chairs around scrubbed pine tables; no children or dogs; tables on flagstoned front terrace with far views, comfortable bedrooms, self-catering cottages, open all day *(Tony Brace, Paul and Annette Hallett, Michael B Griffith, LYM, Bernard Stradling, Miss A E Dare, MDN)*

EAST PRESTON [TQ0701]

Sea View BN16 1PD [Sea Rd]: Hidden-away comfortable seaside pub with neat, friendly and efficient staff, well kept ales inc Arundel Castle, enjoyable good value home-made food (not Sun and Mon evenings), OAP lunches Mon, Tues; children's menu, smart lavatories; nice garden, limited parking, bedrooms *(Bruce Bird, Tony and Wendy Hobden)*

EASTBOURNE [TV6098]

Dolphin BN21 4XF [South St]: Sensitively refurbished keeping its panelling and open fires, with leather sofas alongside traditional pub furnishings, consistently enjoyable food using good local ingredients from ciabattas up, three ales inc Harveys Best *(Val and Alan Green, Marcus and Lienna Gomm)*

☆ *Lamb* BN21 1HH [High St]: Ancient pub freshened up by new landlord; two main heavily beamed traditional bars off central servery, antique furnishings (but not too smart), good inglenook log fire, well kept Harveys ales, enjoyable home-made food, upstairs dining room (Sun lunch), events such as live opera; by ornate church away from seafront, open all day *(Marcus and Lienna Gomm, the Didler)*

ELSTED [SU8320]

☆ *Elsted Inn* GU29 0JT [Elsted Marsh]: Refurbished country pub under new ownership, attractive and quietly civilised with enjoyable food, good choice of wines by the glass, real ales such as Ballards, welcoming helpful staff, log fires, nice country furniture, dining area at back; dogs welcome, plenty of seating in lovely enclosed downs-view garden with big terrace, four comfortable bedrooms, good breakfast, cl Sun evening *(LYM, R Goodenough, Mrs Mary Woods)*

FAIRWARP [TQ4626]

Foresters Arms TN22 3BP [B2026]: Chatty Ashdown Forest local handy for Vanguard

Way and Weald Way, comfortable lounge bar, wide choice of enjoyable well priced food, friendly staff, Badger and Harveys ales, farm cider, woodburner; piped music; children and dogs welcome, tables out on terrace and in garden, play area on small village green opposite, has been open all day summer *(Nigel and Jean Eames, LYM)*

FELPHAM [SZ9599]

Fox PO22 7EH [Waterloo Rd]: Roomy traditional flint pub with four well kept ales inc Harveys Best, Timothy Taylors Landlord and Wells & Youngs Bitter, enjoyable generous home-made food from sandwiches up, comfortable seats, dark panelling, associations with William Blake and George Morland; garden seating, smokers' shelter *(Tony and Wendy Hobden)*

FERNHURST [SU9028]

Red Lion GU27 3HY [The Green, off A286 via Church Lane]: Wisteria-covered 16th-c pub tucked quietly away by green and cricket pitch near church, heavy beams and timbers, attractive furnishings, food from interesting sandwiches and snacks up, well kept Fullers, good wines, friendly efficient service, restaurant; children welcome, pretty gardens front and back *(John Beeken, Tim Loryman, N R White, BB)*

FERRING [TQ0903]

Henty Arms BN12 6QY [Ferring Lane]: Well kept changing ales, generous attractively priced food even Sun evening, neat friendly staff, log fire, opened-up lounge/dining area, separate bar with games and TV; garden tables *(Bruce Bird, Tony and Wendy Hobden)*

FINDON [TQ1208]

Village House BN14 0TE [High St; off A24 N of Worthing]: Attractive converted 16th-c coach house, panelling, pictures and big open fire in large L-shaped bar, restaurant beyond, enjoyable fresh pubby food inc bargains for two, Fullers London Pride, Harveys Best and a guest such as Skinners Cornish Knocker; small attractive walled garden, six comfortable bedrooms, handy for Cissbury Ring and downland walks *(Tony and Wendy Hobden)*

FIRLE [TQ4607]

☆ *Ram* BN8 6NS [village signed off A27 Lewes—Polegate]: 17th-c village pub geared for dining but welcoming drinkers, popular food – can get busy, and well kept reasonably priced Dark Star and Harveys, real cider, friendly staff, traditional décor, dim lighting, log fires, toad in the hole; children and dogs welcome, big walled garden behind, open all day *(Huw and Sarah, BB, N R White, J H Bell)*

FISHBOURNE [SU8304]

☆ *Bulls Head* PO19 3JP [Fishbourne Rd (A259 Chichester—Emsworth)]: Comfortable beamed village pub with popular good value food (not Sun evening), Fullers ales, neat attentive staff, good log fire, daily papers, fair-sized main bar, children's area, restaurant area, prize-winning lavatories; terrace picnic-sets and pretty window boxes, four bedrooms *(David H T Dimock, Terry and Nickie Williams, J A Snell, Mrs K Hooker)*

FITTLEWORTH [TQ0118]

☆ **Swan** RH20 1EL [Lower St (B2138, off A283 W of Pulborough)]: Pretty tile-hung inn with comfortable beamed main bar, windsor armchairs and bar stools on wood and carpeted floor, big inglenook log fire, Fullers, Wells & Youngs and a guest ale, food in bar and separate panelled dining room; piped music; children and dogs welcome, big back lawn with plenty of tables (they ask to keep a credit card if you eat here), good nearby walks, 15 refurbished bedrooms *(LYM, Bruce Bird, R and M Thomas, Patrick Spence, Conor McGaughey, Glen and Nola Armstrong, Ian Phillips, MDN, Barry Collett)*

FLETCHING [TQ4223]

Rose & Crown TN22 3ST [High St]: Well run 16th-c beamed village pub refurbished by new owners, inglenook log fire and comfortable wall banquettes in carpeted bar, wide range of home-made food from baguettes up, small restaurant, good attentive service, Harveys and guest ales; dogs welcome, tables in pretty garden, three bedrooms, open all day *(Michael and Ann Cole, Linda Parker, Paul Humphreys)*

GLYNDE [TQ4508]

☆ **Trevor Arms** BN8 6SS: New management summer 2009, impressive dining room with interesting mix of high-backed settles, pews and cushioned dining chairs around mixed tables, lots of pewter tankards hanging from joists, carpeted middle room leading to nice little traditional pubby bar with small fireplace and fine downland views; wholesome reasonably priced food, good service, well kept Harveys ales, basic locals' bar with parquet flooring, panelled dado, sporting prints, darts and toad in the hole; big garden with rows of picnic-sets and downland backdrop, popular with walkers, railway station next door *(Alec and Marie Lewery, John Beeken, Alec and Joan Laurence, BB)*

GOLDEN CROSS [TQ5312]

Golden Cross Inn BN27 4AW [A22 NW of Hailsham]: Under new family management, welcoming and friendly with well kept Harveys and hearty enjoyable food, separate public bar; big garden with vegetables and chickens *(Niki)*

GORING-BY-SEA [TQ1002]

Bulls Head BN12 5AR [Goring St]: Reopened under new management; several linked beamed areas inc barn-style dining room, good choice of decent pubby food all day inc deals, friendly efficient staff, Harveys, Sharps Doom Bar and Wells & Youngs Bombardier; large walled garden *(B and M Kendall, Tony and Wendy Hobden)*

Toby Carvery BN12 4AS [Goring Rd]: Proper pub with Harveys, Tetleys and Wells & Youngs Bombardier, carvery and other low-priced food inc good puddings, reasonably priced wines, friendly service – good value for families *(Ian Phillips)*

GRAFFHAM [SU9218]

☆ **Foresters Arms** GU28 0QA [off A285]: 16th-c pub under new licensees, heavy beams, big contemporary hunting photographs, log fire in huge brick fireplace, pews and pale windsor chairs around light modern tables, two other areas with nice mix of tables, one with long pew and table on sisal flooring, Ballards, Sharps, Skinners and Wells & Youngs, enjoyable food; piped music turned off on request; children and dogs welcome, garden tables, bedrooms, open all day *(LYM, Tony and Wendy Hobden)*

GUN HILL [TQ5614]

☆ **Gun** TN21 0JU [off A22 NW of Hailsham, or off A267]: Big welcoming country dining pub thriving under current licensees, several interesting rambling areas either side of large central bar, beams and log fires, enjoyable fresh food using local supplies, two real ales, good wines, efficient friendly service, locals' shop in former coach house; children welcome, hay for visiting horses, lovely garden with play area, right on Wealden Way *(LYM, Hunter and Christine Wright, Mike and Eleanor Anderson)*

HAILSHAM [TQ5809]

Grenadier BN27 1AS [High St (N end)]: Striking early 19th-c pub with warm welcome, traditional games in nice panelled locals' bar, comfortable lounge bar, well kept Harveys, Shepherd Neame and Wells & Youngs, simple lunchtime meals; children welcome in lounge, dogs in public bar *(Pete Baker, LM)*

HALNAKER [SU9008]

☆ **Anglesey Arms** PO18 0NQ [A285 Chichester—Petworth]: Bare boards, settles and log fire, Adnams Best, Wells & Youngs and local guest beers, decent wines, good varied if not cheap food inc local organic produce and Selsey fish, friendly accommodating licensees, simple but smart L-shaped dining room with woodburners, stripped pine and some flagstones (children allowed), traditional games; tables in big tree-lined garden *(Leslie and Barbara Owen, John Beeken, DHV, Val and Alan Green, Bruce Bird, LYM, David H T Dimock, M G Hart)*

HAMMERPOT [TQ0605]

☆ **Woodmans Arms** BN16 4EU: Pretty thatched pub comfortably rebuilt after 2004 fire, beams and timbers, enjoyable pubby food from sandwiches and baked potatoes up, Fullers and a guest beer, Sun bar nibbles, neat polite staff, log fire in big fireplace; piped music; tables outside with summer marquee, open all day Fri, Sat and summer Sun, may be cl Sun evening *(Tony and Wendy Hobden, LYM)*

HARTFIELD [TQ4735]

Anchor TN7 4AG [Church St]: Popular 15th-c local, heavy beams and flagstones, two woodburners (one in inglenook), little country pictures and houseplants, comfortable dining area, well kept Harveys, Kings and Larkins, generous food inc vegetarian choices, own pickled eggs and onions, darts and shove-ha'penny in lower room; piped music; children and dogs welcome, disabled facilities, front verandah, big garden, two bedrooms, open all day (Adele Summers, Alan Black, LYM, the Didler, Colin McKerrow)

HASTINGS [TQ8209]

First In Last Out TN34 3EY [High St, Old Town]: Congenial and chatty beer-drinkers' local brewing its own good value FILO beers, a guest ale too, monthly beer and music festivals, farm cider, central raised log fire, good simple bar lunches (not Sun, Mon), open-plan bar with dark wood booths, posts and character cat presiding in central armchair, no machines or piped music; gents' down a few steps, parking nearby difficult; small covered back terrace, open all day (MP, Arthur Pickering)

Pissarros TN34 1SA: An oasis for the area, good fresh brasserie food, good service, real ales such as Bass, wknd jazz (Jo Hill)

HEATHFIELD [TQ5920]

Star TN21 9AH [Old Heathfield, off A265/B2096 E; Church St]: Lovely ancient pub with magnificent country views from pretty garden, L-shaped beamed bar with inglenook log fire, built-in wall settles and window seats, a few old wooden tables, further room off, well kept 1648, Dark Star and Harveys ales, food from pricey sandwiches up; has had a series of recent management changes (Mike and Eleanor Anderson, LYM)

HENFIELD [TQ2115]

George BN5 9DB [High St]: Roomy beamed former coaching inn, good value food inc OAP lunches, Harveys and Shepherd Neame, friendly young staff, open fires, panelled restaurant; children welcome (Terry Buckland, Tony and Wendy Hobden)

HENLEY [SU8925]

☆ *Duke of Cumberland Arms* GU27 3HQ [off A286 S of Fernhurst]: Rather special wisteria-covered 15th-c stone-built pub with big scrubbed pine or oak tables in two small rooms each with a bright log fire, low ceilings, white-painted wall boards and rustic decorations, Harveys, Langham and guests tapped from the cask (beer prices reduced early evening), farm cider, good wine choice, popular food; children welcome, beautiful hill views from gnarled seats in charming big sloping garden criss-crossed by stream and trout ponds, open all day (LYM, Terry and Nickie Williams, Michael B Griffith, the Didler, Christopher and Elise Way, Phil and Sally Gorton)

HERMITAGE [SU7505]

☆ *Sussex Brewery* PO10 8AU [A259 just W of Emsworth]: Bustling, welcoming and interesting, with small boards-and-sawdust bar, good fire in huge brick fireplace, simple furniture, little flagstoned snug, well kept Wells & Youngs and a guest beer, several wines by the glass, good value hearty food inc wide choice of speciality sausages, small upstairs restaurant; children and dogs welcome, picnic-sets in small back courtyard,

open all day (LYM, Ann and Colin Hunt, Gael Pawson, Harriette Scowen, Mr and Mrs P D Titcomb)

HEYSHOTT [SU8918]

☆ *Unicorn* GU29 0DL [well signed off A286 S of Midhurst]: Welcoming village-green pub, well kept Fullers and Kings, good if not cheap food from lunchtime sandwiches and baguettes up, cheerful service even when busy, thriving atmosphere, comfortable L-shaped bar with beams, exposed brick and open fire, attractive dining area; children allowed, reasonable disabled access, big garden with barbecue, charming downland setting handy for South Downs Way (John Beeken)

HOOE [TQ6708]

Lamb TN33 9HH [A259 E of Pevensey]: Quick friendly young staff in prettily placed olde-worlde Vintage Inn with lots of stripped brick and flintwork, one snug area around huge log fire and lots of other seats, big tables, good choice of wines by the glass and a couple of real ales, streamlined but enjoyable food range; children welcome (Simon and Philippa Hughes, John and Jill Perkins)

HORAM [TQ5717]

Horam Inn TN21 0EL [High St]: 1920s railway hotel tidied up under current welcoming and obliging landlord, enjoyable food, well kept ales, cosy atmosphere; bedrooms (Phil and Sally Gorton)

HUNSTON [SU8601]

Spotted Cow PO20 1PD [B2145 S of Chichester]: Flagstoned pub with friendly staff, locals and dog, wide choice of enjoyable food, chilled Fullers/Gales ales, big fires, up-to-date décor, small front bar, roomier side lounge with armchairs, sofas and low tables as anteroom for airy high-ceilinged restaurant; may be piped music; good disabled access, children welcome to eat, big pretty garden, handy for towpath walkers (Nigel and Kath Thompson, David H T Dimock, Ann and Colin Hunt)

HURSTPIERPOINT [TQ2816]

Poacher BN6 9PU [High St]: Small friendly local, wkdy bar lunches, well kept Harveys, Sharps Doom Bar and a guest; heated terrace, garden (Gary and Karen Turner)

ISFIELD [TQ4516]

Halfway House TN22 5UG [Rose Hill (A26)]: Welcoming roadside pub under new management, low-beamed timbered bar with intimate drinking alcoves, long dining area, well kept Harveys inc seasonal beers, good choice of pubby food, spotless lavatories; children and dogs welcome, terrace seating, play area in back field (John Beeken, BB)

Laughing Fish TN22 5XB: Victorian local opened-up by enterprising landlord, good value home-made pubby food (not Sun evening), Greene King and guest ales, friendly staff, open fire, traditional games, events inc entertaining beer race Easter bank hol Mon; children and dogs welcome, disabled access, small pleasantly shaded walled garden with enclosed play area, right by Lavender Line, open all day *(BB, Tony and Wendy Hobden, John Beeken)*

JEVINGTON [TQ5601]

Eight Bells BN26 5QB: Village pub with simple furnishings, heavy beams, panelling, parquet floor and inglenook flame-effect fire, good choice of home-made bar food (all day Sun) from sandwiches up, nice puddings, Adnams Broadside, Flowers Original and Harveys Best; piped music; dogs welcome, front terrace, secluded downs-view garden with some sturdy tables under cover, adjacent cricket field, good walking country, open all day *(John Beeken, Eddie Edwards, BB, Mike and Carol Williams)*

KINGSTON [TQ3908]

☆ *Juggs* BN7 3NT [village signed off A27 by roundabout W of Lewes]: Ancient rose-covered pub with heavy 15th-c beams and very low front door, lots of neatly stripped masonry, sturdy wooden furniture on bare boards and stone slabs, smaller eating areas inc family room, enjoyable straightforward good value food, well kept Shepherd Neame ales, good coffee and wine list, log fires; piped music; children and dogs welcome, disabled lavatory, nice seating areas outside, lots of hanging baskets, good walks, open all day *(Tina and David Woods-Taylor, Tom and Rosemary Hall, PL, LYM, R and M Thomas)*

LAMBS GREEN [TQ2136]

☆ *Lamb* RH12 4RG: Comfortable old beamed pub with well kept Kings and guest ales, farm cider, decent wines, good generous blackboard food, takeaway fish and chips Fri, home-made jams and chutneys, friendly helpful staff, flagstones and nice two-sided log fire in main bar, some horse tack and so forth, conservatory restaurant; piped music, Tues poker night; terrace tables, pleasant walks *(DGH, Douglas and Ann Hare, BB, Kevin Thorpe, Tony and Wendy Hobden)*

LAUGHTON [TQ5013]

Roebuck BN8 6BG [Lewes Rd; B2124]: Simple and welcoming, with short choice of tasty food inc local game and good beef and venison pie, well kept Harveys ales, chatty regulars; neat good value bedrooms, good breakfast *(Simon Le Fort)*

LEWES [TQ4210]

Dorset BN7 2RD [Malling St]: Comfortably refurbished, light and airy, with large mellow area around central bar, smaller snug, lots of bare wood, neat welcoming staff, decent value food from panini to lots of fish, well kept Harveys, smart restaurant; large terrace, six bedrooms *(Tony Hobden, Ann and Colin Hunt, Tony and Wendy Hobden, BB)*

Elephant & Castle BN7 2DJ [White Hill]: Friendly bare-boards local popular for its big-screen sports TV, enthusiastic chatty landlord, well kept Harveys Best and guest ales, farm cider, food (not Fri to Mon evenings) inc burgers made from organic sussex beef, interesting mix of bric-a-brac, large main room and side room with pool, table football and some settles, Sun quiz

night, home to the Commercial Square Bonfire Society; terrace *(BB, Gene and Kitty Rankin)*

Gardeners Arms BN7 2AN [Cliffe High St]: Warmly welcoming unpretentious small local opp brewery, light and airy with well kept Harveys and interesting changing ales, farm ciders, limited lunchtime food inc pies, plain scrubbed tables on bare boards around three narrow sides of bar, daily papers and magazines, Sun bar nibbles, toad in the hole played here; open all day *(Pete Baker, BB, the Didler, Guy Vowles, Mike and Eleanor Anderson)*

John Harvey BN7 2AN [Bear Yard, just off Cliffe High St]: No-nonsense tap for nearby Harveys brewery, all their beers inc seasonal ones kept perfectly, some tapped from the cask, decent value food from huge lunchtime sandwiches, baked potatoes and ciabattas up, friendly efficient young staff, basic dark flagstoned bar with one great vat halved to make two towering 'snugs' for several people, lighter room on left; piped music and machines; a few tables outside, open all day, breakfast from 10am *(Ian Thurman, Ann and Colin Hunt, N R White, the Didler, Gene and Kitty Rankin, Phil Bryant, BB, Tony and Wendy Hobden)*

Pelham Arms BN7 1XL [High St]: Rambling pub with three Badger ales, enjoyable food; small courtyard *(BB)*

LITLINGTON [TQ5201]

Plough & Harrow BN26 5RE [between A27 Lewes—Polegate and A259 E of Seaford]: Attractive neatly extended beamed flint pub, large bar with smaller rooms off, well kept ales inc Dark Star, Harveys and Kings, decent wines by the glass, enjoyable home-made food from pub staples to more enterprising dishes using local ingredients, friendly attentive service, carpeted dining area with banquettes; piped music; children and dogs welcome, little suntrap front terrace, attractive back garden, barbecue, on South Downs Way, open all day wknds *(Paul Gilliland, LYM)*

LOXWOOD [TQ0331]

Onslow Arms RH14 0RD [B2133 NW of Billingshurst]: Comfortable, relaxing and popular, with enjoyable food inc light dishes and smaller helpings, friendly informal service, Badger ales, good house wines, plenty of coffees and teas, lovely old log fireplaces, daily papers; dogs welcome, picnic-sets in good-sized garden sloping to river and nearby restored Wey & Arun canal, secluded smokers' shelter, good walks and boat trips *(Ian Phillips)*

LURGASHALL [SU9327]

Noahs Ark GU28 9ET [off A283 N of Petworth]: 16th-c beamed country pub perfectly placed overlooking churchyard and cricket green, open bar with two fireplaces, small dining room with inglenook log fire and assorted scrubbed tables and chairs, larger barn-like dining area with hops and fireside sofas, good interesting seasonal home-made food, children's menu, good wines by the glass, Greene King ales and a guest, summer plays; children welcome, some picnic-sets out on the green, more in big side garden, cl Sun evening *(Martin and Karen Wake, LYM)*

LYMINSTER [TQ0204]

Six Bells BN17 7PS [Lyminster Rd, Wick]: Small well kept former 18th-c flint coaching inn, friendly welcoming service, enjoyable elegantly presented food from sandwiches and baguettes up, traditional Sun lunch, good house wine, Fullers London Pride and Greene King Abbot in small central part between bar dining area and restaurant with inglenook; terrace and garden seating *(Allison and Graham Thackery)*

MAPLEHURST [TQ1924]

White Horse RH13 6LL [Park Lane]: Friendly long-serving licensees in peaceful beamed country local, four seating areas inc homely cosy corners and sun lounge with church furniture and plants, log fire, well kept Harveys, Hogs Back, Weltons and interesting guests, local farm cider, decent wines, bargain coffee, good value snacks and one or two simple hot dishes, good service, lots of traditional games, no music or machines; children welcome, pleasant outlook from back garden with play area, beautiful wisteria in front, car enthusiasts' evenings *(Bruce Bird)*

MARESFIELD [TQ4623]

Chequers TN22 2EH [High St]: Imposing three-storey Georgian coaching inn with two smallish front bars and a larger one at the back, enjoyable fresh food here and in more contemporary panelled restaurant, well kept Harveys and guest beers, good coffee, decent house wine, friendly staff, daily papers; picnic-sets under cocktail parasols in neat garden, 16 bedrooms *(Anne Clarke, Mike and Eleanor Anderson)*

MARK CROSS [TQ5831]

☆ *Mark Cross Inn* TN6 3NP [A267 N of Mayfield]: Big Whiting & Hammond pub, linked areas on varying levels, good friendly service, well kept ales inc Harveys Best and Timothy Taylors Landlord, good wines by the glass, nice coffee, huge helpings of hearty food (all day), real mix of dark wood tables and cushioned dining chairs, walls crowded with prints, old photographs and postcards, books, church candles, houseplants, working Victorian fireplace; children welcome, decking with nice teak furniture, picnic-sets out on grass, broad Weald views, open all day *(Conor McGaughey, Gerry and Rosemary Dobson, BB)*

MID LAVANT [SU8508]

Earl of March PO18 0BQ [A286]: Refurbished and extended with emphasis on eating but a few seats for drinkers in flagstoned log-fire bar serving Harveys, Hop Back and other ales; good if pricey food, much sourced locally, in plush dining area and conservatory with seafood bar, polite efficient staff; nice view up to Goodwood

from neatly kept garden with good furniture, local walks *(J A Snell, Tony Brace, Tracey and Stephen Groves, Kathryn Gill, Terry and Nickie Williams)*

MIDDLETON-ON-SEA [SU9800]

Elmer PO22 6HD [Elmer Rd]: Friendly and comfortable, with attractively priced food from baguettes up, Fullers ales, games room, back restaurant; bedrooms *(Meg and Colin Hamilton, Tony and Wendy Hobden)*

MIDHURST [SU8821]

Wheatsheaf GU29 9BX [Wool Lane/A272]: Dating from 16th c and under new ownership; cosy low-beamed and timbered bars, enjoyable reasonably priced food, good range of well kept ales *(Michael B Griffith)*

MILTON STREET [TQ5304]

☆ *Sussex Ox* BN26 5RL [off A27 just E of Alfriston – brown sign to pub]: Attractive and friendly country pub with magnificent downs views, smallish beamed and brick-floored bar with roaring woodburner, enjoyable straightforward home-made food, well kept Dark Star, Harveys and an interesting guest beer, enthusiastic young licensees and quick service even when busy, good family dining area (book well ahead in summer) with nice prints, piped music; big lawn and decked terrace, lots of good walks *(Peter Meister, Julian Thomas, LYM, Laurence Smith)*

NORTH CHAILEY [TQ3921]

Kings Head BN8 4DH [A275/A272]: Good value wholesome pub food, attentive landlord, well kept Greene King ales, long light bar and eating area with log fire, darts and pool in games end; garden behind *(John Beeken, Alec and Joan Laurence)*

NUTBOURNE [SU7805]

Barleycorn PO18 8RS [A259 W of Chichester]: Refurbished open-plan local with welcoming staff, reasonably priced all-day food inc bargain Sun roast, Ringwood Best and other beers; tables outside *(Tony and Jill Radnor, Ann and Colin Hunt)*

NYETIMBER [SZ8998]

Lamb PO21 4NJ [Pagham Rd]: Welcoming licensees, newish chef doing interesting changing restaurant dishes as well as the locally popular bar food, good choice of real ales, decent wines *(Terry and Nickie Williams)*

OFFHAM [TQ3912]

☆ *Blacksmiths Arms* BN7 3QD [A275 N of Lewes]: Civilised and comfortable open-plan dining pub with chef/owner doing wide choice of good food inc bargain two-course specials, Harveys Best and a seasonal beer, good friendly uniformed staff, huge end inglenook fireplace; french windows to terrace with picnic-sets, four bedrooms *(Mrs Pat Tribe, LYM)*

Chalk Pit BN7 3QF [Offham Rd (A275 N of Lewes)]: Former late 18th-c chalk pit office building on three levels, well kept Harveys and a guest ale, decent wines by the glass, good choice of generous home-made food inc OAP bargains, attentive friendly staff, neat restaurant extension, skittle alley, toad in the hole played Mon nights; children welcome, garden with terrace seating, smokers' shelter with pool table, three bedrooms, open all day Fri-Sun (food all day then too) *(John Beeken, Ann and Colin Hunt, Phil Bryant)*

PARTRIDGE GREEN [TQ1819]

Partridge RH13 8JS [Church Rd]: Spacious recently renovated village pub, warm welcome, well kept Fullers London Pride, fresh pubby food from sandwiches up, darts and pool; games machine; terrace, dog-free garden and play area *(Colin Gooch)*

PATCHING [TQ0705]

Fox BN13 3UJ [Arundel Rd; signed off A27 eastbound just W of Worthing]: Generous good value home-made food inc good puddings and vegetarian options, popular Sun roasts (best to book), good prompt service, well kept Harveys Best and two guests, good wine choice, large dining area off roomy panelled bar, hunting pictures; quiet piped music; children and dogs welcome, disabled access, nice tree-shaded garden with play area *(Tony and Wendy Hobden, Jude Wright, Mrs Pat Tribe)*

PETT [TQ8613]

Two Sawyers TN35 4HB [Pett Rd; off A259]: Reopened under new family ownership after long closure and quickly gaining local support; meandering low-beamed rooms inc bare-boards bar with stripped tables, tiny snug, passage sloping down to restaurant allowing children, friendly staff; well kept ales such as Dark Star, Harveys, Ringwood and Sharps, local farm cider, wide range of wines, enjoyable food freshly made so can take a while, early-bird bargains; piped music; dogs allowed in bar, suntrap front brick courtyard, back garden with shady trees and well spaced picnic-sets, three bedrooms, open all day *(Peter Meister, LYM, David Nicholls, Paul Bantock)*

PETWORTH [SU9719]

☆ *Badgers* GU28 0JF [Station Rd (A285 1.5 miles S)]: Smart restauranty dining pub with up-to-date rather upmarket food served generously at well spaced tables mixing old mahogany and waxed stripped pine, charming wrought-iron lamps, log fires, friendly staff, Badger Best and K&B (there is a fireside drinking area with sofas), good range of wines; children in eating area of bar if over 5, stylish tables and seats out on terrace by water lily pool, bedrooms, cl winter Sun evenings *(LYM, Kevin Flack)*

☆ *Welldiggers Arms* GU28 0HG [Low Heath; A283 E]: Unassuming L-shaped bar, low beams, pictures on shiny ochre walls, long rustic settles with tables to match, some stripped tables laid for eating, side room, no music or machines, enjoyable if not cheap food, Wells & Youngs, decent wines; children (in family area) and dogs welcome, plenty of tables on attractive lawns and terrace, nice views, cl Mon, also evenings Tues, Weds, Sun *(Christopher and Elise Way, Peter Sampson, LYM, Gerry and Rosemary Dobson)*

PLUMPTON [TQ3613]

Half Moon BN7 3AF [Ditchling Rd (B2116)]: Refurbished by new owners, beamed and timbered bar, good log fire with unusual flint chimney-breast, back dining area, enjoyable home-made food using local produce, children's menu, Sun roasts, local ales and wines (even an organic sussex lager); juke box; tables in wisteria-clad front courtyard and on new terrace in big downs-view garden, picnic area, campsite, good walks *(Richard Prout)*

PLUMPTON GREEN [TQ3617]

☆ *Plough* BN7 3DF: Whiting & Hammond pub with enjoyable sensibly priced food from filled bagels up (they list many of their suppliers), friendly attentive service, well kept Harveys ales inc seasonal, good value wines, log fires in both bars, striking Spitfire and Hurricane pictures (there's a pilots' memorial outside), books and bric-a-brac; covered terrace and large attractive downs-view garden with play area, hanging baskets, open all day *(John Beeken)*

POYNINGS [TQ2611]

☆ *Royal Oak* BN45 7AQ [The Street]: Large darkly beamed bar with wide choice of good food (best to book Sun lunch), good service even when very busy, real ales from three-sided servery, woodburner, traditional rustic furnishing, no piped music; dogs welcome, big attractive garden with barbecue, climbing frame and country/downs views *(J Graveling, Tim Loryman, N R White, Adele Summers, Alan Black)*

PUNNETTS TOWN [TQ6320]

☆ *Three Cups* TN21 9LR [B2096 towards Battle]: Bustling little country pub with U-shaped bar, lots of pewter tankards hanging from beams, inglenook fire, a few dark shiny pubby tables with wheelback chairs on parquet flooring, some built-in cushioned pews and window seats, local photographs, friendly helpful staff, enjoyable food (often fully booked in evenings), Harveys ales, decent wines, separate dining room; piped music; back garden, small front smokers' shelter, play area *(J H Bell, Conor McGaughey, Mike Gorton, LYM)*

ROBERTSBRIDGE [TQ7323]

☆ *George* TN32 5AW [High St]: Attractive contemporary dining pub, armchairs and sofa by inglenook log fire on right, friendly helpful licensees, Adnams, Harveys, Hop Back Crop Circle and Timothy Taylors Landlord, good wines by the glass, enterprising and enjoyable reasonably priced food, bustling, chatty atmosphere; piped music, live lunchtime last Sun of month; children and dogs welcome, back courtyard *(Simon Tayler, BB, Alan Covall)*

ROGATE [SU8023]

☆ *White Horse* GU31 5EA [East St; A272 Midhurst—Petersfield]: Rambling heavy-beamed local in front of village cricket field, civilised and friendly, with Harveys full range kept particularly well, relaxed atmosphere, flagstones, stripped stone, timbers and big log fire, attractive candlelit sunken dining area, good generous reasonably priced food (not Sun evening), friendly helpful staff, traditional games (and quite a collection of trophy cups), no music or machines; quiz and folk nights; some tables on back terrace, open all day Sun *(LYM, Bruce Bird, Michael B Griffith, Gary and Karen Turner)*

ROWHOOK [TQ1234]

Chequers RH12 3PY [off A29 NW of Horsham]: Attractive welcoming 16th-c pub, relaxing beamed and flagstoned front bar with portraits and inglenook fire, step up to low-beamed lounge, well kept Harveys, Wells & Youngs and guests, decent wines by the glass, good coffee, enjoyable food, separate restaurant; piped music; children and dogs welcome, tables out on terraces and in pretty garden with good play area, attractive surroundings *(LYM, Barry Steele-Perkins)*

RUNCTON [SU8802]

Walnut Tree PO20 1QB [Vinnetrow Rd, towards N Mundham]: Attractive building with friendly efficient staff, good food choice especially puddings, good wine list, local beers, big open fires and flagstones, character touches, two steps up to spacious raftered dining room; big garden with play area *(R and M Thomas)*

RUSHLAKE GREEN [TQ6218]

☆ *Horse & Groom* TN21 9QE [off B2096 Heathfield—Battle]: Cheerful village-green local, little L-shaped low-beamed bar with small brick fireplace and local pictures, small room down a step with horsey décor, simple beamed restaurant, friendly landlady and sister, enjoyable food inc local fish and game, Shepherd Neame ales, decent wines by the glass; children and dogs welcome, cottagey garden with pretty country views, nice walks *(John and Jill Perkins, R L Borthwick, Conor McGaughey, David and Cathrine Whiting, J H Bell, E D Bailey, LYM)*

RUSPER [TQ2037]

Plough RH12 4PX [signed from A24 and A264 N and NE of Horsham]: Country local dating from 16th c doing well under new licensees, very low beams, panelling and enormous inglenook, good food, well kept ales, good wine list, dining area; pretty front terrace, back garden *(Martin Stafford, LYM)*

☆ *Royal Oak* RH12 4QA [Friday St, towards Warnham; back road N of Horsham, E of A24]: Cosy traditional tile-hung pub in very rural spot on Sussex Border Path; narrow bar with small rooms each end, one set for dining with big log fire, interesting bric-a-brac, prints and panelling, friendly staff and locals, seven changing well kept ales such as Dark Star, Goddards, Oakleaf and Surrey Hills, farm ciders, limited but good generous fresh food at reasonable prices inc traditional Sun lunch, local farm produce for sale; open all day Fri, Sat, till 9pm Sun *(Kevin Thorpe, Martin Stafford, the Didler, Bruce Bird, Tony and Wendy Hobden)*

RYE [TQ9220]

George TN31 7JT [High St]: Sizeable hotel with lively up-to-date feel in bar and adjoining dining area, beams, bare boards, log fire, leather sofa and armchairs, Adnams, Harveys Best and Greene King Old Speckled Hen, a couple of continental beers on tap, enjoyable interesting food, some french staff; good bedrooms *(Louise English)*

Hope Anchor TN31 7HA [Watchbell St]: Fine views from family-run 18th-c hotel, well kept Harveys and other ales, friendly helpful staff, good reasonably priced food inc sandwiches and fresh fish in attractive bar, log-fire lounge and roomy and tasteful dining room; 14 bedrooms *(Mike and Sue Shirley, V Brogden)*

SELHAM [SU9320]

☆ *Three Moles* GU28 0PN [village signed off A272 Petworth—Midhurst]: Small, quiet and relaxing pub smartened up by new landlady, steep steps up to bar with ales such as Bowmans Swift One, Sharps Doom Bar and Skinners Betty Stogs, farm cider, limited snacky food, blazing coal fires, church furniture; garden tables, tucked away in woodland village with tiny late Saxon church, nice walks *(Tony and Wendy Hobden)*

SHIPLEY [TQ1321]

☆ *Countryman* RH13 8PZ [SW of village, off A272 E of Coolham]: Friendly neatly kept country pub, small bar with cushioned pews either side of inglenook woodburner, red leather bucket armchairs and high-backed leather chairs around small tables, well kept Dark Star, Fullers and Harveys, good choice of wines by the glass, good food using local produce inc own veg, spreading dining areas with warm coal fire, heavy beams and joists, linen napkins and tablecloths, musical instruments, Dixieland prints; piped jazz, no children; dogs welcome, tables, pergolas, and small marquees in country garden, open all day Sat and summer Sun *(Terry Buckland)*

SHOREHAM-BY-SEA [TQ2105]

Red Lion BN43 5TE [Upper Shoreham Rd]: Modest dim-lit low-beamed and timbered 16th-c pub with settles in snug alcoves, wide choice of good value pubby food, half a dozen well kept changing ales such as Arundel and Hepworths (Easter beer festival), farm cider, decent wines, friendly efficient staff, log fire in unusual fireplace, another open fire in dining room, further bar with covered terrace; pretty sheltered garden behind, old bridge and lovely Norman church opposite, good downs views and walks *(Bruce Bird, Jestyn Phillips, Tracey and Stephen Groves, Val and Alan Green)*

SHORTBRIDGE [TQ4521]

☆ *Peacock* TN22 3XA [Piltdown; OS Sheet 198 map ref 450215]: Civilised and comfortable traditional dining pub with beams, timbers and big inglenook, good generous food inc nice fish, well kept Fullers London Pride, Harveys Best and Wadworths 6X, wide range of wines by the glass, friendly attentive staff, restaurant; loud piped music; children welcome, good-sized garden *(BB, Dr Ron Cox, Phil Bryant, David and Doreen Beattie)*

SLAUGHAM [TQ2528]

Chequers RH17 6AQ [off A23 S of Handcross]: Leather sofas, polished boards and soft lighting, rustic wooden furniture around chatty bar, wide choice of home-made food from simple bar lunches to smart evening meals, real ales such as Kings, good wines by the glass, young staff, open fire, modern back extension; dogs welcome, pleasant sloping garden with country views, lakeside walks *(Terry Buckland, C and R Bromage, N R White)*

SLINDON [SU9708]

Spur BN18 0NE [Slindon Common; A29 towards Bognor]: Civilised, roomy and attractive 17th-c pub, good choice of upmarket but good value food changing daily, well kept Courage Directors and Greene King Ruddles, cheerful efficient staff, welcoming atmosphere, two big log fires, pine tables, large elegant restaurant, games room with darts and pool (for over-18s), friendly dogs; children welcome, pretty garden (traffic noise) *(Terry and Nickie Williams)*

SLINFOLD [TQ1131]

Red Lyon RH13 0RR [The Street]: Attractive country pub with enjoyable fresh food a cut above the pub norm; big garden with large heated umbrellas on terrace, play area, regular summer events *(Ian Phillips, Helen Markham)*

SOUTHWATER [TQ1528]

Bax Castle RH13 0LA [Two Mile Ash, about 1 mile NW]: Popular early 19th-c flagstoned country pub pleasantly extended with ex-barn restaurant, big log fire in back room, Ringwood and Wychwood ales, good value generous bar food inc good Sun lunch (best to book), no music or machines; dogs welcome, picnic-sets on two pleasant lawns, play area, near Downs Link Way on former rail track *(Ian Phillips)*

STEDHAM [SU8522]

Hamilton Arms GU29 0NZ [School Lane (off A272)]: Proper english local but decorated with thai artefacts and run by friendly thai family, basic pub food but also good interesting thai bar snacks and restaurant dishes (cl Mon), well kept Ballards and Gales; pretty hanging baskets, tables out by village green and quiet lane, village shop in car park, good walks nearby *(John Beeken, J A Snell)*

STEYNING [TQ1711]

White Horse BN44 3YE [High St]: Rambling creeper-covered inn refurbished to a high standard, enjoyable interesting food, Greene King ales, good courteous uniformed service; tables on spacious terrace *(John Redfern)*

STOPHAM [TQ0318]

☆ *White Hart* RH20 1DS [off A283 E of village, W of Pulborough]: Fine old pub by medieval River Arun bridge, gently smartened up under friendly newish management, heavy beams, timbers and panelling, log fire and

sofas in one of its three snug rooms, well kept Arundel Gold, Hogs Back TEA and Weltons, good generous home-made food (unusual pictorial puddings menu), some interesting bric-a-brac; children welcome, waterside tables, some under cover *(Bruce Bird, N R White, LYM, Colin McKerrow)*

TELSCOMBE CLIFFS [TQ3901]

Badgers Watch BN10 7BE [South Coast Rd (A259)]: Spacious and popular two-bar Vintage Inn overlooking the sea, wide food choice, well kept Greene King Old Speckled Hen, Harveys Best, Shepherd Neame Spitfire and Timothy Taylors Landlord, helpful cheerful staff; piped music may obtrude; lots of tables outside *(John Beeken)*

THAKEHAM [TQ1017]

☆ *White Lion* RH20 3EP [off B2139 N of Storrington; The Street]: Two-bar 16th-c pub still smoking hams in inglenook, chatty locals, good robust home-made food (not Sun-Weds evenings) from open kitchen, friendly informal service, real ales such as Caledonian, Fullers and Harveys, good choice of wines by the glass, heavy beams, panelling, bare boards and traditional furnishings inc corner settles, pleasant dining room with woodburner, fresh flowers; dogs welcome, sunny terrace tables, more on small lawn, wendy house and rabbits, small pretty village, open all day *(Terry Buckland, Tony and Wendy Hobden, Bruce Bird)*

TICEHURST [TQ6831]

Bull TN5 7HH [Three Legged Cross; off B2099 towards Wadhurst]: Attractive 14th-c pub with friendly newish landlady, well kept Harveys, two big log fires in very heavy-beamed old-fashioned simple two-room bar, contemporary furnishings and flooring in light and airy dining extension; charming front garden (busy in summer), bigger back one with play area *(BB)*

TILLINGTON [SU9621]

Horse Guards GU28 9AF [off A272 Midhurst—Petworth]: Prettily set dining pub converted from three cottages, friendly newish licensees, some traditional dishes as well as fancier pricier things, home-baked bread, changing ales such as Harveys, good choice of wines by the glass, log fire and country furniture in neat low-beamed front bar, lovely views from bow window, simple pine tables in dining room with fire; children welcome, terrace tables and sheltered garden behind, attractive ancient church opposite, three neat bedrooms, good breakfast *(LYM, Sally and Tom Matson, M G Hart)*

WALDRON [TQ5419]

Star TN21 0RA [Blackboys—Horam side road]: Big inglenook log fire in candlelit beamed and panelled bar, padded window seat and nice mix of furniture inc small settle on bare boards and quarry tiles, old prints and photographs, snug off to left, Harveys ales and a guest such as 1648 or Bass, reliable food from good lunchtime sandwiches up, friendly prompt service, separate back dining room; picnic-sets in pleasant garden, a couple more at front overlooking pretty village *(Mike and Eleanor Anderson, Phil and Sally Gorton, PL, BB)*

WASHINGTON [TQ1213]

Frankland Arms RH20 4AL [just off A24 Horsham—Worthing]: Below Chanctonbury Ring, wide choice of unpretentious food all day, helpful welcoming service, two or three real ales, good value wines, log fires, sizeable restaurant, public bar with pool and TV in games area; disabled facilities, neat garden *(Tony and Wendy Hobden, Alec and Joan Laurence, John Redfern)*

WEST CHILTINGTON [TQ0917]

Five Bells RH20 2QX [Smock Alley, off B2139 SE]: Large open-plan beamed and panelled bar with old photographs, unusual brass bric-a-brac, five changing ales inc a Mild kept carefully by friendly landlord, farm cider, shortish choice of generous pubby food (not Sun evening or Mon) inc good pies, log fire, daily papers, big pleasant conservatory dining room; peaceful garden with terrace, bedrooms *(Bruce Bird, Tony and Wendy Hobden)*

WEST WITTERING [SZ8099]

Lamb PO20 8QA [Chichester Rd; B2179/A286 towards Birdham]: Warmly friendly staff in spotless 18th-c country pub, decent choice of reasonably priced home-made food from separate servery inc OAP bargains, Badger ales, decent wines, rugs on tiles, blazing fire; dogs on leads allowed, lots of tables out in front and in small sheltered back garden – good for children; busy in summer when handy for beach *(R and M Thomas, BB, Terry and Nickie Williams)*

WHATLINGTON [TQ7619]

Royal Oak TN33 0NJ [A21 N of village]: White weatherboarded beamed pub dating from 14th c, good choice of enjoyable reasonably priced food, friendly quick service, well kept Shepherd Neame ales, big log fire, internal well, end dining area with stripped pine tables and chairs, separate restaurant; garden behind *(BB, Peter Meister)*

WISBOROUGH GREEN [TQ0526]

Cricketers Arms RH14 0DG [Loxwood Rd, just off A272 Billingshurst—Petworth]: Attractive

old pub, well kept Fullers and Harveys, cheerful staff, open-plan with two big woodburners, pleasant mix of country furniture, stripped brick dining area on left; live music nights; tables out on terrace and across lane from green *(Tom and Jill Jones, LYM)*

WITHYHAM [TQ4935]

☆ *Dorset Arms* TN7 4BD [B2110]: Pleasantly unpretentious 16th-c pub handy for Forest Way walks, friendly service, well kept Harveys, decent wines inc local ones, good fresh food from filled rolls to seasonal game, reasonable prices, good log fire in Tudor fireplace, sturdy tables and simple country seats on wide oak boards, darts, dominoes, shove-ha'penny, cribbage, pretty restaurant; piped music; dogs welcome, white tables on brick terrace by small green, cl Mon *(LYM, the Didler, Angus and Carol Johnson)*

WORTHING [TQ1204]

North Star BN13 1QY [Littlehampton Rd (A259)]: Comfortable Ember Inn, sensibly priced food inc speciality burgers noon till 8pm, Fullers London Pride, Harveys and unusual guest ales such as Daleside Pride of England and Grainstore Phipps, good choice of wines by the glass, friendly service *(Tony and Wendy Hobden)*

Selden Arms BN11 2DB [Lyndhurst Rd, between Waitrose and hospital]: Friendly chatty local with welcoming lancashire landlady, Dark Star Hophead and several changing guests, belgian beers and farm cider, bargain lunchtime food (not Sun) inc chilli made to taste, log fire, lots of old pub photographs, no piped music; dogs welcome, open all day *(Tony and Wendy Hobden, Bruce Bird, N R White)*

YAPTON [SU9704]

Maypole BN18 0DP [signed off B2132 Arundel rd; Maypole Lane]: Chatty landlord and regulars in old-fashioned quiet 19th-c local with simple bargain bar food inc Sun roasts, well kept Arundel Mild, Bowmans Swift One, Skinners Betty Stogs and several changing guests, log fire in cosy lounge, skittle alley, spring and autumn beer festivals, occasional live music; seats outside, smokers' shelter, open all day *(Tony and Wendy Hobden)*

'Children welcome' means the pub says it lets children inside without any special restriction. If it allows them in, but to restricted areas such as an eating area or family room, we specify this. Places with separate restaurants often let children use them, hotels usually let them into public areas such as lounges. Some pubs impose an evening time limit – let us know if you find one earlier than 9pm.

Warwickshire
(with Birmingham and West Midlands)

With the great West Midlands conurbations as well as the small towns and villages of the Warwickshire and North Cotswolds countryside, this chapter has a remarkable cross section of pubs, from time-warp simplicity (Turf in Bloxwich and Case is Altered at Five Ways), a down-to-earth Black Country welcome (Vine in Brierley Hill) and own-brew beers (Griffin at Shustoke), all the way up to contemporary cooking (Crabmill at Preston Bagot) and civilised accommodation (Howard Arms in Ilmington). A good batch of five new entries is similarly varied, from the splendidly pubby Holly Bush in Alcester to smarter dining places like the Granville at Barford or Red Lion at Hunningham. The Howard Arms in Ilmington takes the title of Warwickshire Dining Pub of the Year, just triumphing over the Crabmill, and the Bell at Welford-on-Avon. Some hot picks from the Lucky Dip section: Golden Cross at Ardens Grafton, Bulls Head at Barston, Wellington in Birmingham, Golden Lion at Easenhall, Boot at Lapworth and Blue Boar at Temple Grafton. Banks's, part of the Marstons combine, is the region's main brewer. Among quite a number of good smaller brewers, Bathams and Holdens have long been good value, while the younger Purity is rapidly becoming a favourite, and Church End, North Cotswold, Warwickshire and Highgate are also popular.

ALCESTER
SP0957   MAP 0

Holly Bush ◧

Henley Street (continuation of High Street towards B4089; not much nearby parking); B49 5QX

Classic traditional tavern, neatly smartened up without losing its timeless appeal; up to eight unusual real ales and imaginative food

---

This relaxed 17th-c pub has lots of small or smallish rooms to choose from, with a variety of unpretentious pub furniture on bare boards or flagstones, an abundance of coal or log fires, some stripped masonry, dark board panelling and antique prints, mainly black and white. The chatty heart of the place is at the back on the left, with a few big Victorian lithographs, a warm woodburning stove in a capacious fireplace, and two long wall pews, each with a couple of plain tables, facing each other across age-pocked broad bare boards. Here, the serving counter has a splendid changing array of about eight well kept ales: on our visit, Black Sheep Best, Marstons Ugly Sisters (yes, it was pantomime time), Purity Pure Gold, Sharps Doom Bar and Wye Valley Dorothy Goodbodys Christmas Stocking. They have farm cider and dozens of whiskies, and the hard-working landlady is helped by friendly staff. This main room has a window on to the central corridor, which broadens to include a couple of soft pale leather sofas before exiting to a pretty little garden with a sheltered side terrace. There is good disabled access.

🍴 Enjoyable food runs from pubby dishes such as sandwiches, wraps, ploughman's and a tapas menu to a more imaginative restaurant menu (you can eat from this in the bar), with dishes such as duck and Cointreau pâté, fried chicken livers in cognac and cream, fried tiger prawns with lemon and lime risotto, fried bass with cherry tomato and olive sauce and caper-crushed new potatoes, honey glazed gressingham duck breast with orange and port sauce, pork belly with apple mash, fillet steak with mushroom compote and pepper sauce, baked mushroom, spinach, hazelnut and blue cheese wellington, and puddings such as apple and cinnamon crumble with custard and chocolate, brandy and cherry terrine. *Starters/Snacks: £3.95 to £5.95. Main Courses: £4.50 to £18.50. Puddings: £3.00 to £4.75*

Free house ~ Licensee Teej Deffley ~ Real ale ~ Bar food (12-2.30(4 Sun), 6.30-9.30; not Sun evening) ~ Restaurant ~ (01789) 762482 ~ Children welcome ~ Dogs welcome ~ Open 12-12

Recommended by Pete Baker, Di and Mike Gillam, Alan and Eve Harding, Derek and Sylvia Stephenson, Andrew McKeand

ASTON CANTLOW   SP1360   MAP 4

Kings Head ♀
Village signposted just off A3400 NW of Stratford; B95 6HY

Gently civilised Tudor pub with nice old interior, pubby and imaginative food, and a pleasant garden

This creeper-swathed pub, in the middle of a very pretty village, is on good form at the moment. The beautifully kept bar on the right is charmingly old, with flagstones, low beams and old-fashioned settles around its massive inglenook log fireplace. A chatty quarry-tiled main room has attractive window seats and big country oak tables – it's all the perfect setting for a civilised meal out. A good range of drinks includes Greene King Abbot, M&B Brew XI and a guest such as Purity Pure Gold on handpump, several wines by the glass from a very decent list and local cider; piped jazz in the restaurant. A big chestnut tree graces the lovely garden, and the pub looks really pretty in summer with its colourful hanging baskets and wisteria.

🍴 As well as a pubby bar menu with dishes such as battered fish of the day, sausage and mash, lamb curry, pie of the week, burger and ploughman's, an elaborate menu might include king scallops, baked camembert with red onion chutney, duck, pear and rocket salad with star anise glaze, cod loin with crab linguine, parsley and chilli, mushroom and parmesan risotto and seared bass with chorizo and tapenade dressing, duck breast on thyme-crushed potato with butternut purée, and puddings such as bakewell tart with raspberry coulis and chocolate truffle cake. *Starters/Snacks: £3.95 to £7.95. Main Courses: £10.00 to £16.50. Puddings: £5.50*

Enterprise ~ Lease Peter and Louise Sadler ~ Real ale ~ Bar food (12-2.30, 6.30-9.30; 12.30-3 Sun, not Sun evening) ~ Restaurant ~ (01789) 488242 ~ Children welcome ~ Dogs allowed in bar ~ Open 12-3, 6-11; 12-11 Sat; 12-8.30(7.30 in winter) Sun

Recommended by Gordon Davico, Dr and Mrs S G Barber, Martin and Pauline Jennings, Michael and Maggie Betton, Di and Mike Gillam, Dennis and Gill Keen, Howard and Margaret Buchanan, Mike and Mary Carter, Graham Findlay, Pete Coxon, Keith and Sue Ward, David Spurgeon

BARFORD   SP2660   MAP 4

Granville
1.7 miles from M40 junction 15; A429 S (Wellesbourne Road); CV35 8DS

Civilised and attractive respite from the motorway, for fireside comfort or a good meal

Soft leather deco sofas nestle by the fire in the angle of the L-shaped main bar, which has an up-to-date feel, with its sage-green paintwork, berber-pattern hangings on the end walls and contemporary lighting. You can eat here, at newish pale wood tables and chairs on pale boards or simple more mixed tables and chairs in a carpeted section, or you can head through to a more formally laid raftered and stripped-brick restaurant. They have Hook Norton Hooky and Purity Pure Gold and UBU on handpump, and decent wines by the glass; service is efficient. A floodlit back terrace has teak tables and chairs under huge retractable awnings, and the grass beyond rises artfully to a hedge of pampas grass and the like, which neatly closes the view.

🍽 **The current team (who took over in 2007) do good food from doorstep sandwiches, moules marinière and delicious whitebait to dishes such as crispy pork with tomato, orange and cumin, lightly battered haddock, pie of the day, braised lamb shank or chicken breast stuffed with peppers and spinach, butternut, spinach and stilton lasagne, lamb shank with rosemary jus, sirloin steak, and puddings such as lemon posset.** *Starters/Snacks: £4.95 to £8.75. Main Courses: £9.95 to £16.95. Puddings: £4.95 to £5.95*

Enterprise ~ Lease Val Kersey ~ Real ale ~ Bar food (12-2.30, 6-9; 12-10.30 Fri, Sat; 12-5, 6.30-9 Sun) ~ Restaurant ~ (01926) 624236 ~ Children welcome ~ Dogs welcome ~ Live band last Sun of month ~ Open 12-3.30, 5.30-11; 12-11.30(11 Sun) Fri-Sat

Recommended by Philippa Wilsom, Dr and Mrs A K Clarke, David S Allen, Keith and Sue Ward, Clive and Fran Dutson

BIRMINGHAM

SP0686   MAP 4

Old Joint Stock 🍺

Temple Row West; B2 5NY

Big bustling Fullers pie-and-ale pub with impressive Victorian façade and interior, and a small back terrace

As far as we know, this impressive establishment is the northernmost venue to be owned by London-based brewer Fullers, who recently spent a considerable sum on a smart purpose-built little theatre on the first floor. Housed in what used to be the City Library, this well run city centre pub (opposite the cathedral) has a surprisingly impressive interior. Chandeliers hang from the soaring pink and gilt ceiling, gently illuminated busts line the top of the ornately plastered walls, and there's a splendid, if well worn, cupola above the centre of the room. Big portraits and smart long curtains create an air of unexpected elegance. Around the walls are plenty of tables and chairs, some in cosy corners, with more on a big dining balcony overlooking the bar and reached by a grand staircase. A separate room, with panelling and a fireplace, has a more intimate, clubby feel. Half a dozen well kept Fullers beers and a local guest on handpump, a dozen wines by the glass and a decent range of malt whiskies are served from a handsome dark wood island bar counter. It does get busy, particularly with local office workers, but effortlessly absorbs what seems like huge numbers of people; helpful friendly service, daily papers, games machine and piped music. A small back terrace has some cast-iron tables and chairs and wall-mounted heaters.

🍽 **The very reasonably priced pubby menu includes sandwiches, lots of pies, fish and chips, chickpea, artichoke and tomato salad, fried salmon fillet with white wine and wholegrain mustard sauce, smoked chicken, tomato and spinach quiche, puddings such as rhubarb crumble, and a few daily specials.** *Starters/Snacks: £4.25 to £10.00. Main Courses: £7.95 to £10.00. Puddings: £3.25 to £5.50*

Fullers ~ Manager Paul Bancroft ~ Real ale ~ Bar food (12-8) ~ Restaurant ~ (0121) 200 1892 ~ Children welcome away from main bar ~ Theatre; jazz in the bar monthly ~ Open 11-11; closed Sun and bank hols

Recommended by the Didler, Dr and Mrs A K Clarke, Colin Gooch, D J and P M Taylor, Ian and Nita Cooper, Ian and Jane Irving, Ian and Helen Stafford, Michael Dandy, R T and J C Moggridge

BLOXWICH

SJ9902   MAP 4

Turf 🍺

Wolverhampton Road, off A34 just S of A4124, N fringes of Walsall; WS3 2EZ

Simple eccentric family-run pub, utterly uncontrived, with five good beers

Tucked away in a side street and blending in with the other Victorian terraced houses, this basic but very special place (aka Tinky's) has been in the same family for about 140 years, remaining virtually unchanged in all that time. Once through the front door it still doesn't immediately look like a pub, but more like the hall of a 1930s home. The public bar is through a door on the right, and, reminiscent of a waiting room, it has wooden slatted benches running around the walls, with a big heating pipe clearly visible underneath; there's a tiled floor, three small tables, William Morris curtains and wallpaper, and a simple fireplace. What's particularly nice is that even though the unspoilt rooms are Grade II listed, it's far more than just a museum piece but is alive and chatty with friendly locals happy to tell you the history of the place. The friendly landladies serve Titanic Mild and a particularly impressive changing range of four beers, always very well kept. There's hatch service out to the hall, on the other side of the old smoking room, which is slightly more comfortable, with unusual padded wall settles with armrests. There's also a tiny back parlour with chairs around a tiled fireplace. The pub's basic charms won't appeal to those who like their creature comforts: the no-frills lavatories are outside, at the end of a simple but pleasant garden. The landladies are not keen on filling in our paperwork, so do please check opening times before you visit.

🍽 **No food.**

Free house ~ Licensees Doris and Zena Hiscott-Wilkes ~ Real ale ~ No credit cards ~ (01922) 407745 ~ Open 12-2.30, 7-11(10.30 Sun)
Recommended by the Didler, John Dwane, Mike Begley, Pete Baker

BRIERLEY HILL   SO9286   MAP 4

Vine 🍺 £

B4172 between A461 and (nearer) A4100; straight after the turn into Delph Road; DY5 2TN

Incredibly good value, friendly classic down-to-earth Bathams tap; tables in back yard and lunchtime snacks

This Black Country pub offers a true taste of the West Midlands, with its traditional food, good beer and down-to-earth no-nonsense welcome. Often bustling with chatty locals, the interior meanders through a series of rooms, each different in character. The traditional little front bar has wall benches and simple leatherette-topped oak stools, the comfortable extended snug on the left has solidly built red plush seats, and the tartan decorated larger back bar has brass chandeliers, darts, dominoes and a big-screen TV. A couple of tables and games machines stand in a corridor. Some of the memorabilia you'll see, including one huge pair of horns over a mantelpiece, relates to the Royal Ancient Order of Buffalos, who meet in a room here. The very cheap Bitter and Mild (with perhaps Delph Strong in winter) are kept in top condition and come from the next-door Bathams brewery. There are tables in a back yard, and the car park is opposite. The good stained-glass bulls' heads and the very rough representation of bunches of grapes in the front bow windows are a reference to the pub's nickname, the Bull & Bladder – this name harks back to its previous life as a butcher's shop.

🍽 **A couple of simple but wholesome fresh lunchtime snacks (sandwiches, baguettes, cottage or steak and mushroom pie, and faggots, chips and peas) are tremendously good value.** *Starters/Snacks: £2.50 to £3.00*

Bathams ~ Manager Melvyn Wood ~ Real ale ~ Bar food (12-1.30 Mon-Fri) ~ No credit cards ~ (01384) 78293 ~ Children welcome ~ Dogs welcome ~ Open 12-11(10.30 Sun)
Recommended by Theo, Anne and Jane Gaskin, the Didler, Andy and Jill Kassube, MLR

A very few pubs try to make you leave a credit card at the bar, as a sort of deposit if you order food. They are not entitled to do this. The credit card firms and banks which issue them warn you not to let them out of your sight. If someone behind the counter used your card fraudulently, the card company or bank could in theory hold you liable, because of your negligence in letting a stranger hang on to your card. Suggest instead that if they feel the need for security, they 'swipe' your card and give it back to you. And do name and shame the pub to us.

FIVE WAYS

SP2270   MAP 4

Case is Altered 🍺

Follow Rowington signposts at junction roundabout off A4177/A4141 N of Warwick, then right into Case Lane; CV35 7JD

Unspoilt convivial local serving well kept beers, including a couple of interesting guests

The servery at this tiled white-painted brick cottage has been licensed to sell real ale for over three centuries – these days the friendly landlady keeps four changing beers that might include Goffs Jouster, Greene King IPA, Sharps Doom Bar and Slaughterhouse Saddleback, all served by a rare type of handpump mounted on the casks that are stilled behind the counter. A door at the back of the building leads into a modest old-fashioned little room with a tiled floor, and an antique bar billiards table protected by an ancient leather cover (it takes pre-decimal sixpences). From here, the simple little main bar has a fine old poster showing the old Lucas Blackwell & Arkwright brewery (now flats) and a clock with its hours spelling out Thornleys Ale – another defunct brewery; there are just a few sturdy old-fashioned tables, with a couple of stout leather-covered settles facing each other over the spotless tiles. Behind a wrought-iron gate is a little brick-paved courtyard with a stone table. Full disabled access.

🍴 **No food.**

Free house ~ Licensee Jackie Willacy ~ Real ale ~ No credit cards ~ (01926) 484206 ~ Open 12-2.30, 6-11; 12-2, 7-10.30 Sun
Recommended by Pete Baker, Martin Smith, Dr and Mrs A K Clarke, the Didler

GAYDON

SP3654   MAP 4

Malt Shovel 🍺

M40 junction 12; Church Road; CV35 OET

In a quiet village just off the M40; nice mix of pubby bar and smarter restaurant, tasty food and five real ales

Mahogany-varnished boards through to bright carpeting link the entrance, the bar counter on the right and the blazing log fire on the left at this bustling pub. The central area has a high-pitched ceiling, milk churns and earthenware containers in a loft above the bar. A few stools are lined up along the counter where they serve five real ales that might be from brewers like Adnams, Courage, Greene, Fullers, Hook Norton and Wadworths, and most of their dozen or so wines are available by the glass. Three steps take you up to a snug little space with some comfortable sofas overlooked by a big stained-glass window and reproductions of classic posters. At the other end is a busy dining area with flowers on the mix of kitchen, pub and dining tables. Service is friendly and efficient; piped music, darts and games machine; they may try to keep your credit card while you eat. The springer spaniel is called Rosie, and the jack russell is Mollie.

🍴 **Enjoyable food, cooked by the chef/landlord, includes good lunchtime sandwiches and panini, ploughman's, tempura prawns, salads, moroccan lamb shank, duck with orange, lemon and honey, gammon, egg and chips, battered fish, sticky toffee pudding and lemon cheesecake.** *Starters/Snacks: £3.95 to £6.95. Main Courses: £5.95 to £15.95. Puddings: £3.50 to £3.95*

Enterprise ~ Lease Richard and Debi Morisot ~ Real ale ~ Bar food (12-2, 6.30-9) ~ Restaurant ~ (01926) 641221 ~ Children welcome ~ Dogs allowed in bar ~ Open 11-3, 5-11; 11-11 Fri, Sat; 12-10.30 Sun

Recommended by Nigel and Sue Foster, Dennis Jones, Ian Herdman, John and Elisabeth Cox, Paul Humphreys, George Atkinson, Catherine Dyer, John and Helen Rushton, Dennis Jenkin, Phil and Jane Hodson, Karen Eliot, Susan and John Douglas, Rory and Jackie Hudson, D J and P M Taylor, Clive Watkin, Mary McSweeney

---

We say if we know a pub has piped music.

GREAT WOLFORD

SP2434 MAP 4

Fox & Hounds

Village signposted on right on A3400 3 miles S of Shipston-on-Stour; CV36 5NQ

Thoughtfully prepared food at a lovely old country inn

The unpretentious aged bar at this unspoilt 16th-c stone inn has a timeless atmosphere, with a roaring log fire in the inglenook fireplace (with fine old bread oven), hops strung from low beams, and an appealing collection of tall pews, old chairs and candlelit tables on spotless flagstones, and antique hunting prints. An old-fashioned little tap room serves Hook Norton Hooky, Purity Pure UBU and a guest such as Purity Mad Goose on handpump; piped music. A terrace has solid wood furniture and a well.

📖 **The chef here is careful about sourcing ingredients, and cooks virtually everything from fresh (including the breads): roast garlic and potato soup, cornish crab and spring onion salad with crab and coriander fritter, wild turbot fillet with broad beans, pancetta and chive cream, venison burger with home-cured blue cheese, fillet steak with oxtail risotto and mushroom cream, and puddings such as treacle tart with ice-cream and orange and olive oil cake with clotted cream.** *Starters/Snacks: £4.50 to £12.00. Main Courses: £12.00 to £23.00. Puddings: £5.95 to £8.00*

Free house ~ Licensee Gillian Tarbox ~ Real ale ~ Bar food (not Sun evening, Mon) ~ (01608) 674220 ~ Children welcome ~ Dogs welcome ~ Open 12-2.30, 6-11(11.30 Sat); 12-10.30 Sun; closed Mon ~ Bedrooms: £50B/£80B

Recommended by M Mossman, J C Burgis, David Gunn, Dennis and Gill Keen

HAMPTON IN ARDEN

SP2080 MAP 4

White Lion

High Street; handy for M42 junction 6; B92 0AA

Useful village local; bedrooms

This old former farmhouse is fairly traditional, with a mix of pubby furniture trimly laid out in the carpeted bar, neatly curtained little windows, low-beamed ceilings and some local memorabilia on the fresh cream walls. Adnams, Black Sheep, Everards M&B Brew XI and a guest such as Dartmoor Bitter are served on handpump from the timber-planked bar; piped music, TV and board games. It's in an attractive village, oppposite a church mentioned in Domesday Book, and is handy for the NEC.

📖 **Pubby bar food includes sandwiches, chicken caesar salad, fish and chips, sausage and mash, vegetable risotto, sirloin steak, summer pudding and lemon tart.** *Starters/Snacks: £4.25 to £9.95. Main Courses: £9.95 to £15.95. Puddings: £4.95*

Punch ~ Tenant John Thorne ~ Real ale ~ Bar food (12-2.30(3.30 Sun), 6.30-9.30; not Sun evening) ~ Restaurant ~ (01675) 442833 ~ Children if eating after 7pm ~ Open 12-11(12.30 Sat, 10.30 Sun) ~ Bedrooms: £54S/£64S

Recommended by Malcolm and Kate Dowty

HENLEY-IN-ARDEN

SP1566 MAP

Blue Bell

High Street (A3400, 3.3 miles from M40 junction 16 – exit south-bound only, joining north-bound only); B95 5AT

Friendly and attractive contemporary update of impressive beamed and timbered building

It's good that the individuality of this ancient building, its handsome coach entry tilted drunkenly over the ages, has now been echoed in the personal way that newish owners have brought it into the 21st century. Inside, the rambling layout keeps low beams, some wall timbers, dark slate flagstones and a big fireplace, featuring a dark red leather sofa and armchair here, a couple of dark mulberry-coloured tables there, lots of scatter cushions along one bow-window seat, dark basket-weave high-backed chairs by further mixed dining tables elsewhere – it all adds up to a stylish yet relaxed place. They have well kept changing ales such as Black Sheep, Purity UBU and Warwickshire Shakespeare's County on handpump, over a dozen good wines by the glass, home-made lemonade in summer and mulled wine in winter; service is interested, friendly and efficient; daily papers such as the *Guardian*; there may be cheery piped music. There are tables out on decking behind.

⚑ **Virtually everything on the nicely varied menu is prepared here, from bread to ice-cream. As well as a good range of sandwiches and a ploughman's there might be jerusalem artichoke soup with parmesan croûte, air-dried ham with pea mousse, dressed peas, pea shoots and mint dressing, meat and potato pie, local cheese and caramelised onion pie, roast bass with mushroom risotto, fishcake with poached egg and sorrel sauce, roast pork cutlet with braised pig's trotter, and puddings such as irish spiced cake with lemon curd and berry syrup and white chocolate panna cotta with orange caramel and fresh raspberries.** *Starters/Snacks: £4.50 to £7.95. Main Courses: £9.95 to £14.25. Puddings: £5.50 to £6.60*

Free house ~ Licensees Duncan and Leigh Taylor ~ Real ale ~ Bar food (12-9.30(4.30 Sun)) ~ (01564) 793049 ~ Children welcome ~ Dogs welcome ~ Open 11(4 Mon)-11; 12-10.30 Sun

Recommended by Sophie Leatharvey

HUNNINGHAM

SP3768   MAP 4

Red Lion ♀

Village signposted off B4453 Leamington—Rugby just E of Weston, and off B4455 Fosse Way 2.5 miles SW of A423 junction; CV33 9DY

Informal, airy and civilised, with good individual food; fine riverside spot

The chef/landlord here is an avid collector of vintage comic books and there are 320 bright and colourful covers framed and crammed on the white walls at this spacious place. You'd swear this was a Brunning & Price pub, given the general atmosphere and open yet partly divided layout, the mix of seating from varnished chapel chairs to a variety of dining chairs, various mainly stripped tables from simple to elaborate, the rugs on bare boards or even the chunkily old-fashioned radiators. Born near here, and the son of a local vicar, the landlord did indeed work for B&P, and has brought many of that group's virtues here, including staff attitudes (cheerful and helpful), pleasing lighting, an enterprising changing choice of about three dozen wines by the glass, and a good range of spirits including 35 single malts. Beers though are more restricted, with well kept Greene King IPA, Abbot and Old Speckled Hen on handpump; they have good coal fires and the day's *Times*. Big windows look out past a terrace with teak tables to picnic-sets on the lawn by a charming 14th-c bridge over the River Leam; no prams or pushchairs inside.

⚑ **The food is good, fresh, generous, and individual, with soup and plenty of light dishes such as potted pheasant and hazelnut, home-cured gravadlax on toasted sourdough, shepherd's pie, devilled kidneys, smoked salmon and crab linguine or pork belly with bubble and squeak. Main dishes might include beef and chorizo pie, smoked haddock and cod fishcakes, ham and eggs with sturdy chips, pork chop with blue cheese and apple risotto and venison casserole.** *Starters/Snacks: £4.50 to £8.95. Main Courses: £8.95 to £15.95. Puddings: £4.95 to £8.50*

Greene King ~ Lease Sam Cornwall-Jones ~ Real ale ~ (01926) 632715 ~ Children welcome ~ Dogs welcome ~ Open 12-11(10.30 Sun)

Recommended by Geoffrey Hughes, Martin Stafford, Myles Abell, Terry Buckland

---

People named as recommenders after the Main Entries have told us that the pub should be included. But they have not written the report – we have, after anonymous on-the-spot inspection.

ILMINGTON   SP2143   MAP 4

Howard Arms ⊗ ⟁ ⇔

Village signposted with Wimpstone off A3400 S of Stratford; CV36 4LT

WARWICKSHIRE DINING PUB OF THE YEAR

Emphasis on imaginative food and good wine list in a lovely mellow-toned interior; attractive bedrooms

A lovely place for a delicious and civilised meal, or weekend away, this top-notch golden-stone inn is doing well in new hands since the last edition of this *Guide*. The stylishly simple interior is light, airy and gently traditional, with a cosy log fire in a huge stone inglenook, a few good prints on warm golden walls, broad polished flagstones, and a nice mix of furniture from hardwood pews to old church seats; piped music. Drinks include Hook Norton Old Hooky, Purity Pure Gold and a guest from a local brewer such as North Cotswold on handpump, organic soft drinks and over two dozen wines by the glass. The garden is charming with fruit trees sheltering the lawn, a colourful herbaceous border, and a handful of tables on a neat york-stone terrace. Readers very much enjoy staying in the comfortable bedrooms – the breakfasts are particularly good. The pub is nicely set beside the village green, and there are lovely walks on the nearby hills and pleasant strolls around the village outskirts.

▥ **The seasonally changing menu is thoughtfully varied, ranging from traditional pubby to more elaborate dishes, prepared using local produce where possible: may be duck liver and sage pâté with red onion chutney, jellied ham hock and parsley terrine with mustard piccalilli and soda bread, warm mozzarella, tomato and spinach tart, pork belly, chorizo and white bean cassoulet, fried lemon sole with caper, lemon and parsley butter, steak, mushroom and ale pie, fish and chips, ham, egg and chips, and puddings such as warm strawberry jam bakewell tart and dark chocolate mousse with shortbread biscuit.** *Starters/Snacks: £4.50 to £6.50. Main Courses: £9.75 to £17.50. Puddings: £4.50 to £6.50*

Free house ~ Licensee Quentin Creese ~ Real ale ~ Bar food (12-2.30, 6.30-9.30) ~ Restaurant ~ (01608) 682226 ~ Children welcome ~ Dogs allowed in bar ~ Open 11-11; 12-10.30 Sun ~ Bedrooms: £85B/£115B

Recommended by Noel Grundy, Keith and Sue Ward, Robin and Glenna Etheridge, Eithne Dandy, Robert and Elaine Smyth, Theo, Anne and Jane Gaskin, Hugh Bower, K H Frostick, David Gunn, Michael Dandy, Stuart Doughty, Leslie and Barbara Owen, Andrew and Judith Hudson, Bernard Stradling, Andrea Rampley, Mike and Mary Carter, Graham Findlay, Julian Saunders, David S Allen, K Turner, Nina Sohal, Chris Glasson

NETHERTON   SO9488   MAP 4

Old Swan ⊲ £

Halesowen Road (A459 just S of centre); DY2 9PY

Traditional, unspoilt, friendly local serving own-brew beers and bar food

The four beers they brew at this characterful local (known locally as Ma Pardow's) are Bumblehole, Dark Swan, Entire and Olde Swan Original, and they do a couple of seasonal ones. The unchanged multi-roomed layout here should appeal to readers who are keen on original interiors. The front public bar is a delightful piece of unspoilt pub history, with a lovely patterned enamel ceiling with a big swan centrepiece, mirrors behind the bar engraved with a swan design, an old-fashioned cylinder stove with its chimney angling away to the wall, and traditional furnishings. The cosy back snug is fitted out very much in keeping with the rest of the building, using recycled bricks and woodwork, and even matching etched window panels; back car park.

▥ **Lunchtime bar food includes soup of the day, baked potatoes, ploughman's and fish and chips. The longer evening menu includes lamb kebabs, goats cheese salad, mediterranean lamb and chicken curry. Traditional home-made puddings include cheesecake, profiteroles and crème brûlée; pork sandwiches only on Sunday evening.** *Starters/Snacks: £2.50 to £4.50. Main Courses: £6.00 to £14.00. Puddings: £2.50 to £4.50*

Punch ~ Tenant Tim Newey ~ Real ale ~ Bar food (12-2, 6.30-9(not Sun evening)) ~ Restaurant ~ (01384) 253075 ~ Dogs allowed in bar ~ Open 11-11; 12-4, 7-11 Sun

Recommended by the Didler, Pete Baker

PRESTON BAGOT

SP1765 MAP 4

Crabmill ⑪ ♀

A4189 Henley-in-Arden—Warwick; B95 5EE

Mill conversion with comfortable modern décor, relaxed atmosphere and smart bar food

The contemporary interior of this rambling old cider mill is strikingly decorated in unusual colour combinations. With its nicely chatty atmosphere, the smart two-level lounge area has comfortable settees and easy chairs, low tables, big table lamps and one or two rugs on bare boards. The elegant and roomy low-beamed dining area has candles and fresh flowers, and a beamed and flagstoned bar area has some stripped-pine country tables and chairs, snug corners and a gleaming metal bar serving Greene King Abbot, Tetleys and a guest such as Purity Pure Ubu on handpump, with several wines by the glass from a mostly new world list. Piped music is well chosen and well reproduced. There are lots of tables (some of them under cover) out in a large attractive decked garden. Booking is advised, especially Sunday lunchtime when it's popular with families.

⑪ **Well prepared, modern imaginative cooking might include potted rabbit and pheasant with spiced redcurrant jelly and crostini, lamb kebab with pine nut and herb couscous, goats cheese, caramelised onion and thyme tart, meze, haddock and spring onion fishcake with poached egg and hollandaise, toulouse sausages with chilli and fennel-roasted sweet potato and jus, seared duck breast with fried asian vegetables, egg noodles and sweet chilli sauce, seared tuna with bean, shallot and tomato salad, and rib-eye steak; good value set menu Monday to Friday lunchtimes and Monday to Thursday evenings.** *Starters/Snacks: £3.50 to £8.25. Main Courses: £9.95 to £16.95. Puddings: £5.25 to £6.95*

Enterprise ~ Lease Sally Coll ~ Real ale ~ Bar food (12-2.30(5 Sun), 6.30-9.30) ~ Restaurant ~ (01926) 843342 ~ Children welcome ~ Dogs allowed in bar ~ Open 11-11; 12-6 Sun; closed Sun evening

Recommended by Karen Eliot, Paul Boot, Roger and Anne Newbury, Rod Stoneman, Dr A B Clayton, Peter and Heather Elliott, Andy and Claire Barker, Dr and Mrs D Scott, Hansjoerg Landherr, R L Borthwick, Dick Vardy, Keith and Sue Ward, Gordon Davico, Dr and Mrs A K Clarke, Tim and Sue Jolley, John and Helen Rushton, Martin Smith

SEDGLEY

SO9293 MAP 4

Beacon ★ ◀

Bilston Street (no pub sign on our visit, but by Beacon Lane); A463, off A4123 Wolverhampton—Dudley; DY3 1JE

Good unusual own-brew beers and interesting guests at a beautifully preserved down-to-earth Victorian pub

The front door of this plain-looking old brick pub (it's worth walking round from the car park) opens into a simple quarry-tiled drinking corridor where you may find a couple of cheery locals leaning up the stair wall, chatting to the waistcoated barman propped in the doorway of his little central serving booth. Go through the door into the little snug on your left and you can easily imagine a 19th-c traveller tucked up on one of the wall settles, next to the imposing green-tiled marble fireplace with its big misty mirror, the door closed for privacy and warmth, and a drink handed through the glazed hatch. The dark woodwork, turkey carpet, velvet and net curtains, heavy mahogany tables, old piano and little landscape prints all seem unchanged since those times. A timelessly sparse snug on the right has a black kettle and embroidered mantel over a blackened range, and little more than a nice old stripped wooden wall bench. The corridor then runs round the serving booth, past the stairs and into a big well proportioned dark-panelled old smoking room with impressively sturdy red leather wall settles down the length of each side, gilt-based cast-iron tables, a big blue carpet on the lino, and dramatic old sea prints. Round a corner (where you would have come in from the car park) the conservatory is densely filled with plants and has no seats. Named after a former landlady, the well kept Sarah Hughes beers brewed and served here include Dark Ruby, Pale Amber and Surprise Bitter. You can arrange to look round the traditional Victorian tower brewery at the back. They also keep a couple of unusual guests. A children's play area in the garden has a slide, climbing frame and roundabout.

🍴 **They may serve cheese and onion and ham cobs.**

Own brew ~ Licensee John Hughes ~ Real ale ~ No credit cards ~ (01902) 883380 ~ Children allowed in family room ~ Dogs welcome ~ Open 12-2.30, 5.30-11; 12-3, 6-11 Sat; 12-3, 7-10.30 Sun

Recommended by Pete Baker, the Didler, R T and J C Moggridge

SHUSTOKE   SP2290   MAP 4

Griffin 🍺 £

5 miles from M6 junction 4; A446 towards Tamworth, then right on to B4114 and go straight through Coleshill; pub is at Church End, a mile E of village; B46 2LB

Ten real ales including own-brew beers, and simple good value lunchtime snacks at this unpretentious country local; garden and play area

Despite the Birmingham views from the garden, this notably friendly place is a genuine country local. Usually busy with a cheery crowd, the low-beamed L-shaped bar has log fires in two stone fireplaces (one's a big inglenook), fairly simple décor from cushioned café seats (some quite closely spaced) and sturdily elm-topped sewing trestles, to one nice old-fashioned settle, lots of old jugs on the beams, beer mats on the ceiling, and a games machine. Griffin 'Ere It Is, Black Magic Women and Firkin Slurcher are now being brewed by the chatty landlord in the barn next door and are served alongside a smashing choice of changing guests from brewers such as Holdens, Hook Norton, Jennings, Marstons, Moorhouses, RCH and Thornbridge; also lots of english wines, farm cider, and mulled wine in winter. Outside, there are old-fashioned seats and tables on the back grass, a play area and a large terrace with plants in raised beds.

🍴 **Straightforward but tasty bar food in substantial helpings includes sandwiches, ploughman's, cheese and broccoli bake, scampi, steak and ale pie, mixed grill and 10oz sirloin steak.** *Starters/Snacks: £3.25 to £5.95. Main Courses: £5.50 to £10.50*

Own brew ~ Licensee Michael Pugh ~ Real ale ~ Bar food (12-2; not Sun or evenings) ~ No credit cards ~ (01675) 481205 ~ Children in conservatory ~ Dogs welcome ~ Open 12-2.30, 7-11(10.30 Sun)

Recommended by Michael Beale, Rob and Catherine Dunster, Peter Cole, John Dwane

WELFORD-ON-AVON   SP1452   MAP 4

Bell 🍽 🍷 🍺

Off B439 W of Stratford; High Street; CV37 8EB

Enjoyably civilised pub with appealing ancient interior, good food and a great range of drinks including five real ales; terrace

Still on tremendous form, this delightful 17th-c place offers the sort of service where the customer really does come first – staff are knowledgeable, organised and kind. As most people are here to dine, booking is advised. The attractive interior (full of signs of the building's great age) is divided into five comfortable areas, each with its own character, from the cosy terracotta-painted bar to a light and airy gallery room with its antique wood panelling, solid oak floor and contemporary Lloyd Loom chairs. Flagstone floors, stripped or well polished antique or period-style furniture, and three good fires (one in an inglenook) add warmth and cosiness. Flowers Original, Hook Norton Old Hooky, Purity Pure Gold and Pure UBU, and a guest such as Hobsons, are well kept on handpump, and they've a dozen or so wines including champagne and local wines by the glass; piped music and board games. In summer the creeper-covered exterior is hung with lots of colourful baskets, and there are tables and chairs on a vine-covered dining terrace. This riverside village has an appealing church and pretty thatched black and white cottages.

🍴 **The menu and daily specials take in a varied range of dishes including a good choice of** sandwiches, chicken goujons with spiced crème fraîche, ploughman's, beer-battered cod, minty lamb curry, bass fillet on lemon grass and fennel rice with salsa verde, lentil and aubergine moussaka, chicken and prawn paella, steak and horseradish pie, chicken breast stuffed with crayfish on creamy coconut curry sauce, fried partridge on thyme-roasted vegetables with mushroom and bacon jus, and puddings such as creme brûlée and sticky toffee pudding. *Starters/Snacks: £4.95 to £6.95. Main Courses: £8.50 to £17.95. Puddings: £5.50 to £6.95*

Laurel (Enterprise) ~ Lease Colin and Teresa Ombler ~ Real ale ~ Bar food (11.45-2.30(3 Sat), 6.30-9.30(6-10 Fri, Sat); 12-9.30 Sun) ~ Restaurant ~ (01789) 750353 ~ Children welcome ~ Open 11.30-3, 6-11; 11.30-11.30 Sat; 12-10.30 Sun

Recommended by Keith and Sue Ward, Jean and Richard Phillips, George Bell, Rod Stoneman, Leslie and Barbara Owen, Denys Gueroult, R T and J C Moggridge, Martin and Pauline Jennings, John Saville, Mrs L Mills, David Heath, Graham Findlay, Mr and Mrs A Curry, Mike and Mary Carter, Lyn Ellwood

LUCKY DIP

Besides the fully inspected pubs, you might like to try these Lucky Dips recommended to us and described by readers (if you do, please send us reports: feedback@goodguides.com).

ALDERMINSTER [SP2348]
☆ *Bell* CV37 8NY [A3400 Oxford—Stratford]: Neatly kept open-plan Georgian dining pub under newish ownership; good imaginative food, flagstones or polished wood floors, inglenook stove, small proper bar with well kept Greene King ales, good range of wines by the glass; conservatory with Stour valley views; children and dogs welcome, terrace and garden *(Graham Findlay, Denys Gueroult, Robert Ager, Keith and Sue Ward, LYM, Gordon Davico)*
ANSLEY [SP3091]
Lord Nelson CV10 9PQ [Birmingham Rd]: Enjoyable reasonably priced food in ample space inc unusual galleon-style restaurant; good beers from neighbouring Tunnel microbrewery (tours available), great staff; terrace tables, open all day wknds *(Martin Smith, Chris Evans)*
ARDENS GRAFTON [SP1153]
☆ *Golden Cross* B50 4LG [off A46 or B439 W of Stratford, OS Sheet 150 map ref 114538; Wixford Rd]: Attractive open-plan 18th-c stone-built dining pub, wide choice of good affordable generous food from lunchtime sandwiches to game, alert attentive staff, well kept Wells & Youngs and a guest such as local Purity, decent wines; comfortable light wood furniture on flagstones, log fire, nice décor and good lighting; piped music; wheelchair access, attractive garden with newly built terrace (big heated umbrellas), nice views *(George Atkinson, Keith and Sue Ward, Stanley and Annie Matthews)*
ARMSCOTE [SP2444]
☆ *Fox & Goose* CV37 8DD [off A3400 Stratford—Shipston]: Former blacksmith's forge with locals' bar and woodburner in dining area, Black Sheep, Butcombe, Hook Norton Old Hooky and a guest such as Warwickshire, food all day Fri-Sun; piped music, TV; children and dogs welcome, vine-covered deck overlooking lawn, brightly painted bedrooms named after characters in *Cluedo*; open from 9am, all day Fri-Sun

(Keith and Sue Ward, George Atkinson, LYM, Stuart Doughty, Noel Grundy)
BAGINTON [SP3375]
☆ *Old Mill* CV8 3AH [Mill Hill]: Popular olde-worlde Chef & Brewer conversion of watermill nr airport, Midland Air Museum and Lunt Roman fort; heavy beams, timbers and candlelight, slate and wood floors, warm rustic-theme bar, leather seating by open fire, linked dining areas; good wine selection, well kept Courage, Greene King and Wells & Youngs Bombardier, good choice of food all day inc fixed-price menu (Mon-Thurs), friendly uniformed staff; children welcome, lovely terraced gardens down to River Sowe, disabled facilities, 26 newly refurbished bedrooms *(Martin and Alison Stainsby, LYM, Duncan Cloud, Susan and John Douglas, Nigel and Sue Foster)*
BALSALL COMMON [SP2476]
White Horse CV7 7DT [Kenilworth Rd]: Comfortably refurbished, with relaxed atrmosphere, friendly helpful staff, enjoyable changing food; open all day *(Will Barnes)*
BARNT GREEN [SP0074]
☆ *Barnt Green Inn* B45 8PZ [Kendal End Rd]: Large civilised Elizabethan dining pub with friendly young staff, good innovative food from breads with dipping oils through shared tapas and wood-fired pizzas to rotisserie; real ales such as Black Sheep and Greene King Old Speckled Hen, log fire, relaxed atmosphere, comfortable contemporary décor, clubby seating in panelled front bar, large brasserie area; can get very busy; tables outside, handy for Lickey Hills walks *(Paul J Robinshaw, Mike and Mary Carter)*
BARSTON [SP2078]
☆ *Bulls Head* B92 0JU [from M42 junction 5, A4141 towards Warwick, first left, then signed down Barston Lane]: Unassuming and unspoilt partly Tudor village pub, friendly landlord and efficient service, well kept Adnams, Hook Norton and two guests, enjoyable traditional food from sandwiches

to good fresh fish and Sun lunch; log fires, comfortable lounge with pictures and plates, oak-beamed bar with some Buddy Holly memorabilia, separate dining room; children and dogs allowed, good-sized secluded garden alongside, hay barn, open all day Fri-Sun *(R T and J C Moggridge, Martin Smith, Pete Baker, Geoffrey Hughes)*

BILSTON [SO9496]

Trumpet WV14 0EP [High St]: Well kept Holdens and perhaps a guest ale, good free nightly jazz bands (quiet early evening before they start); trumpets and other instruments hang from the ceiling, lots of musical memorabilia and photographs, back conservatory *(the Didler)*

BINLEY WOODS [SP3977]

Roseycombe CV3 2AY [Rugby Rd]: Warm and friendly 1930s pub with wide choice of bargain home-made food, Bass and Theakstons; Weds quiz night, some live music; children welcome, big garden *(Alan Johnson)*

BIRMINGHAM [SP0788]

☆ *Bartons Arms* B6 4UP [High St, Aston (A34)]: Magnificent Edwardian landmark, a trouble-free oasis in rather a daunting area; impressive linked richly decorated rooms from the palatial to the snug, original tilework murals, stained-glass and mahogany, decorative fireplaces, sweeping stairs to handsome rooms upstairs; well kept Oakham and guests from ornate island bar with snob screens in one section, interesting imported bottled beers and frequent mini beer festivals, good choice of well priced thai food (not Mon), nice young staff; open all day *(BB, the Didler)*

Bennetts B2 5RS [Bennetts Hill]: Bank conversion with egyptian/french theme, big mural, high carved domed ceiling, snugger side areas with lots of old pictures, ironwork and wood; relaxed atmosphere, comfortably worn seating, well kept Marstons-related ales, good choice of wines by the glass, good coffee, friendly staff, low-priced food; piped music; good wheelchair access, but parking restrictions *(Mrs Hazel Rainer, Michael Dandy)*

Black Eagle B18 5JU [Factory Rd, Hockley]: Welcoming late 19th-c pub with half a dozen well kept ales, generous popular home-made food inc bargain specials, friendly traditional landlord and efficient service; small bare-boards bar, three-part lounge inc one area with banquettes, bay window and old pictures, some original Minton tilework, compact back dining room; summer beer festival with live music; shaded tables in nice small garden, open all day Fri, cl Sun evening *(Roger Shipperley, Stephen Corfield, John Dwane)*

Briar Rose B2 5RE [Bennetts Hill]: Civilised open-plan Wetherspoons with deep pink décor, well kept changing guest beers, their usual food offers from breakfast on, friendly staff, separate back family dining room; lavatories downstairs; can get busy;

reasonably priced bedrooms, open all day *(Michael Dandy, the Didler, Henry Pursehouse-Tranter, Roger Shipperley)*

Lord Clifden B18 6AA [Great Hampton St]: Clean, fresh refurbishment and nice bustling atmosphere, good value food from sandwiches to steaks and generous Sun roasts, Bathams, Wye Valley and two guests, prompt friendly service; contemporary artwork, dominoes in locals' front bar; nostalgic juke box, Thurs quiz night and wknd DJs; plenty of tables on attractive back terrace *(Stephen Corfield)*

Old Fox B5 4TD [Hurst St (follow Hippodrome signs)]: Traditional two-room pub with splendid early 19th-c façade, changing ales such as Greene King Old Speckled Hen, St Austell and Tetleys from island bar, bargain simple lunchtime food; friendly staff, interesting old photographs and posters; pavement tables *(Joe Green, G Jennings)*

Prince of Wales B1 2NP [Cambridge St]: Traditional pub surviving behind the rep theatre and symphony hall amidst the concrete newcomers; L-shaped bar with friendly mix of customers, half a dozen or more well kept beers such as Everards, Timothy Taylors and Wells & Youngs, bargain straightforward lunchtime food, fast friendly service; may be piped music; popular with Grand Union Canal users in summer *(Chris Evans, Pete Baker)*

Red Lion B18 6NG [Warstone Lane]: Recently refurbished combining Victorian and modern; real ales from beautiful wooden bar, lunchtime food, leather armchairs, interesting pictures *(Stephen Corfield)*

Ropewalk B3 1RB [St Pauls Sq]: Friendly pub, comfortable and roomy, opp attractive churchyard; appealing up-to-date décor, good staff, Marstons ales *(Liz and John Soden)*

☆ *Wellington* B2 5SN [Bennetts Hill]: Superb range of changing beers mostly from small breweries (always one from Black Country Ales), also farm ciders, in roomy old-fashioned high-ceilinged pub; experienced landlord and friendly staff, can get very busy; no food, but plates and cutlery if you bring your own – on cheese nights people bring different ones that are pooled; tables out behind, open all day *(Roger Shipperley, John Dwane, Dr and Mrs A K Clarke, Richard Tingle, the Didler, Martin Grosberg, Michael Dandy, John Rushton)*

BROWNHILLS [SK0504]

Royal Oak WS8 6DU [Chester Rd]: Good village-local atmosphere, well kept ales such as Caledonian Deuchars IPA and Greene King, pleasant staff, bask eating area with bargain food from sandwiches up from an open kitchen; comfortable art deco lounge with Clarice Cliff pottery etc, 1930s-feel public bar; reasonable disabled access, pleasant garden *(John and Helen Rushton, R T and J C Moggridge)*

CHERINGTON [SP2836]
☆ **Cherington Arms** CV36 5HS [off A3400]: Old-fashioned creeper-covered stone house with enjoyable food (not Mon evening) inc interesting dishes, well kept Hook Norton ales, farm cider, good value wines, cafetière coffee, efficient friendly service; nice beamed bar with piano and blazing log fire, separate dining room; monthly local live music; children and dogs welcome, tables on terrace and in big garden with trees, aunt sally, good nearby walks, open till 1am Sat, Sun *(BB, JHBS)*

CHURCHOVER [SP5180]
Haywaggon CV23 0EP [handy for M6 junction 1, off A426; The Green]: Neapolitan landlord does some italian dishes as well as pubbier staples (must book Sun lunch), changing ales such as Fullers London Pride and Shepherd Neame Spitfire, good coffee and wines by the glass; relaxed atmosphere and friendly young staff, two snug eating areas, lots of beams, standing timbers, brasses, nooks and crannies; may be piped music; tables outside with play area, on edge of quiet village, beautiful views over Swift valley *(R L Borthwick, BB, John Wooll)*

CLAVERDON [SP2064]
☆ **Red Lion** CV35 8PE [Station Rd; B4095 towards Warwick]: Beamed Tudor dining pub, new management doing good imaginative food (all day Sun), not cheap but worth it, friendly knowledgeable staff, decent wines and well kept local ales; log fire, linked rooms inc back dining area with country views over sheltered back heated deck and gardens; open all day *(Roger Braithwaite, BB)*

COVENTRY [SP3279]
Old Windmill CV1 3BA [Spon St]: Well worn timber-framed 15th-c pub with lots of tiny old rooms, exposed beams in uneven ceilings, carved oak seats on flagstones, inglenook woodburner; half a dozen real ales, farm cider, basic lunchtime bar food (not Mon) served from the kitchen door, restaurant; popular with students and busy at wknds; games machine and juke box; no credit cards; open all day *(the Didler, LYM)*
Town Wall CV1 4AH [Bond St, among car parks behind Belgrade Theatre]: Busy Victorian town local with real ales inc Adnams, farm cider, nice hot drinks' choice, good generous lunchtime doorstep sandwiches, filled rolls and cheap hot dishes; unspoilt basic front bar and tiny snug, engraved windows and open fires, bigger back lounge with actor and playwright photographs; big-screen sports TV; open all day *(Alan Johnson, BB)*
☆ **Whitefriars** CV1 5DL [Gosford St]: Pair of well preserved medieval town houses, three old-fashioned rooms on both floors, lots of ancient beams, timbers and furniture, flagstones, cobbles and coal fire; up to nine well kept changing ales (more during beer festivals), daily papers, bar lunches; some live music; no children; smokers' shelter on

good-sized terrace behind, open all day *(Alan Johnson, BB)*

DEPPERS BRIDGE [SP3959]
Great Western CV47 2ST [4 miles N of M40 junction 12; B4451]: Welcoming, roomy and airy pub with model train often clattering round overhead in dining room, short lunchtime menu, more sumptuous evening choice; friendly helpful staff, several real ales; terrace tables, good value bedrooms, hearty breakfast *(Simon Le Fort, George Atkinson)*

DUDLEY [SO9487]
Park DY2 9PN [George St/Chapel St]: Tap for adjacent Holdens brewery, their beers kept well, decent simple lunchtime food, low prices, friendly service; conservatory, small games room; sports TV; open all day *(the Didler, Colin Fisher)*

DUNCHURCH [SP4871]
Dun Cow CV22 6NJ [a mile from M45 junction 1: A45/A426]: Handsomely beamed Vintage Inn with massive log fires and other traditional features; friendly staff, wide and reasonably priced food choice all day, good range of wines by the glass, well kept Bass, Everards, Marstons and guests from small counter; piped music; children welcome, tables in attractive former coachyard and on sheltered side lawn, bedrooms in adjacent Innkeepers Lodge, open all day *(Revd R P Tickle, LYM, Martin and Pauline Jennings)*

EARLSWOOD [SP1174]
Red Lion B94 6AQ [Lady Lane (past the lakes)]: Imposing twin-gabled black and white Georgian pub, good value traditional food all day (busy wknds) inc good Sun roast, prompt friendly service; several small but high-ceilinged rooms each with its own character, sturdy tables and chairs, some wall settles, back room with open fire, chandeliers and bigger tables; disabled access, skittle alley, Stratford Canal moorings *(Tim Venn)*

EASENHALL [SP4679]
☆ **Golden Lion** CV23 0JA [Main St]: Spotless bar in 16th-c part of a busy comfortable hotel, low beams, dark panelling, settles and an inglenook log fire; Greene King ales, enjoyable food inc Sun carvery; piped music; children welcome, disabled access, tables out at side and on spacious lawn, 20 well equipped bedrooms, attractive village; open all day *(Rob and Catherine Dunster, Alan Johnson, Simon Cottrell, WW, LYM, R T and J C Moggridge, Dr and Mrs C W Thomas)*

EATHORPE [SP3968]
☆ **Plough** CV33 9DQ [village signed just off B4455 NW of Leamington Spa; The Fosse]: Exceptional value, generous pub food cooked by landlord, speedy jolly service under hands-on landlady, good wine choice and coffee, Shepherd Neame Spitfire and Wychwood Hobgoblin; beams, flagstones, step up to long neat dining room, simple back bar with leather sofa by open fire;

piped music; garden picnic-sets *(Carol and David Havard, C A Hall, David Green, Michael and Jenny Back, BB)*

EDGE HILL [SP3747]

☆ *Castle* OX15 6DJ [off A422]: Curious crenellated octagonal tower perched on a steep hill with good views, built 1749 as a gothic folly, arched doorways, Civil War memorabilia and armoury; splendid log fire, new landlord serving at least four Hook Norton beers, Stowford Press cider, standard well priced pubby food, board games; sports TV; children and dogs welcome, big attractive garden with aunt sally, four bedrooms, open all day (check winter) *(JHBS, Ian Herdman, Roger and Anne Newbury, George Atkinson, LYM, John Branston, Susan and John Douglas)*

ETTINGTON [SP2748]

Chequers CV37 7SR [Banbury Rd (A422)]: Reopened after careful refitting under experienced new management, increasingly popular locally for its enterprising yet unpretentious home-made food, friendly service; back garden with raised area *(LYM)*

FENNY COMPTON [SP4352]

Wharf Inn CV47 2FE [A423 Banbury— Southam, nr Fenny Compton]: Open-plan pub by Bridge 136 on South Oxford Canal, own moorings; good contemporary layout and furnishings, small central flagstoned bar, Brakspears, Hook Norton and Shepherd Neame, limited menu; piped music, games machine; children welcome, disabled facilities, waterside garden, open all day *(JHBS, LYM)*

FLECKNOE [SP5163]

Old Olive Bush CV23 8AT [off A425 W of Daventry]: Characterful unspoilt Edwardian pub in quiet photogenic village, friendly atmosphere, limited choice of nice food inc Sun lunch, good beer and wine; attractive garden behind *(Geoff and Teresa Salt)*

FRANKTON [SP4270]

Friendly CV23 9NY [just over a mile S of B4453 Leamington Spa—Rugby; Main St]: Two friendly and efficient new landladies doing good reasonably priced food in old low-ceilinged village dining pub; two neat well furnished rooms, open fire *(Ted George)*

HALESOWEN [SO9683]

Waggon & Horses B63 3TU [Stourbridge Rd]: Regular beers inc Bathams and up to seven or so changing ales from small brewers in a chatty bare-boards bar and more spacious lounge; country wines and belgian brews, good snacks, low prices, brewery memorabilia, lots of character; TV; Tues music night; open all day *(the Didler)*

HAMPTON LUCY [SP2557]

Boars Head CV35 8BE [Church St, E of Stratford]: Refurbished roomy low-beamed two-bar local next to lovely church; changing real ales, good value pubby food inc lunchtime baguettes, log fire; discreet piped music; secluded back garden, pretty village nr Charlcote House *(Joan and Tony Walker, Keith and Sue Ward)*

HATTON [SP2367]

☆ *Falcon* CV35 7HA [Birmingham Rd, Haseley (A4177, not far from M40 junction 15)]: Smartly refurbished dining pub with relaxing rooms around island bar, lots of stripped brickwork and low beams, tiled and oak-planked floors; good moderately priced food (not Sun evening) from pub favourites up inc Sun roasts, good choice of wines by the glass, well kept Marstons-related beers, friendly service; barn-style back restaurant; children welcome, disabled facilities, garden (dogs allowed here) with new heated terrace, eight bedrooms in converted barn, open all day *(Miss A E Dare, R J Herd, LYM, Cedric Robertshaw)*

Waterman CV35 7JJ [A4177, by Grand Union Canal]: Above Hatton flight of 21 locks 'Stairway to Heaven'; refurbished former 18th-c coaching inn with far views from sunny balcony and huge garden, linked rooms, log fire; good range of food all day from sandwiches to pub classics and some unusual dishes, Sun roasts, local ales, great choice of wines by the glass, friendly efficient staff; children welcome, barbecues, good walks nearby, moorings *(Martin Smith)*

KENILWORTH [SP2872]

Milsoms CV8 1LZ [High St]: Former Clarendon House reopened by boutique hotel group after major refurbishment inc new fish restaurant; good sensibly priced all-day food from light meals to impressive shellfish platters, friendly helpful staff, more traditional bare-boards bar (food here too from sandwiches up) with leather armchairs and settees, Greene King ales, decent wines; no dogs; children welcome, split-level back terrace, 31 good bedrooms, open all day *(LYM, Joan and Tony Walker)*

Virgin & Castle CV8 1LY [High St]: Maze of intimate rooms off inner servery, small snugs by entrance corridor, flagstones, heavy beams, lots of woodwork inc booth seating, coal fire, quick friendly service; Everards ales and guests, good coffee, bar food from generous sandwiches and baked potatoes up; upstairs games bar, restaurant; children in eating area, disabled facilities, tables in sheltered garden, open all day *(LYM, Donna and Roger)*

LADBROKE [SP4158]

Bell CV47 2BY [signed off A423 S of Southam]: Rambling, beamed and comfortable, front bar with light and airy side and back areas; wide choice of enjoyable food inc popular Tues and Sun carvery, useful meal deals, Adnams Broadside and Wells & Youngs Eagle and Bombardier, coal fire; garden tables, pleasant surroundings *(George Atkinson)*

LAPWORTH [SP1871]

☆ *Boot* B94 6JU [Old Warwick Rd (B4439, by Grand Union Canal)]: Popular upmarket dining pub good contemporary brasserie menu from panini and interesting light dishes up, efficient friendly service by smart young staff, upscale wines (big glasses),

Wadworths 6X; cosy fires, charming raftered upstairs dining room; children and good-natured dogs welcome, beautifully done waterside garden, pleasant walks, open all day *(Martin Smith, R L Borthwick, Patti Mickelson)*

Navigation B94 6NA [Old Warwick Rd (B4439 S)]: Busy two-bar beamed and flagstoned local by Grand Union Canal; warm coal fire and some bright canal ware, modern back dining room, wide range of generous food from sandwiches up, real ales such as Holdens, Timothy Taylors Landlord and Warwickshire; children welcome, hatch service to waterside terrace, open all day *(Martin Smith, Michael and Alison Sandy, LYM)*

LEAMINGTON SPA [SP3165]

Somerville Arms CV32 4SX [Campion Terrace]: Neat timeless local with cosy unspoilt Victorian back lounge, well kept Adnams Broadside, Fullers London Pride and Greene King IPA, friendly staff, darts; quiz and live folk nights; tables on pavement and in small courtyard, cl lunchtime *(Bob Clucas, Antony Townsend, Katie Carter)*

LITTLE COMPTON [SP2530]

☆ **Red Lion** GL56 0RT [off A44 Moreton-in-Marsh—Chipping Norton]: The cheerful licensees who made this pleasant low-beamed 16th-c Cotswold stone inn so popular with readers are emigrating (Oct 2009); snug alcoves, log fire, nice bedrooms and pretty garden, but we know nothing yet of the new regime – news, please *(LYM)*

LONG COMPTON [SP2832]

☆ **Red Lion** CV36 5JS [A3400 S of Shipston-on-Stour]: Nice local atmosphere with old-fashioned built-in settles among other pleasantly assorted seats and tables, beams, panelling, flagstones, stripped stone, old prints; some innovative food inc good set-price lunch in bar and restaurant areas, children's helpings, good service, well kept real ales such as Adnams Broadside and Hook Norton, good wines by the glass; log fires and woodburners, simple public bar with pool; dogs and children welcome, big back garden with terrace, picnic-sets and climber, comfortable bedrooms *(John Wooll, LYM, Chris Glasson, S M Livingstone, Helene Grygar)*

LONG ITCHINGTON [SP4165]

Blue Lias CV47 8LD [Stockton Rd, off A423]: Pretty flower-decked pub by Grand Union Canal, unpretentious with good honest food, well kept Adnams, Greene King, Wychwood and a local guest, quick pleasant service, snug booth seating in eating area; children welcome, new disabled facilities, plenty of tables in waterside grounds (dogs allowed here), marquee for functions; may open all day if busy *(Adrian Johnson, Geoff and Teresa Salt)*

Buck & Bell CV47 9PH [The Green]: Handsome country dining pub, warm, light and cosy with linked rooms on two levels, lots of stripped brick, woodburners; good up-to-date food with separate menus for light and

full meals (some quite pricey), well kept real ales such as Church End and Jennings Sneck Lifter, ample wine choice, charming uniformed staff; piped music *(Nigel and Sue Foster, Rob and Catherine Dunster)*

☆ **Duck on the Pond** CV47 9QJ [just off A423 Coventry—Southam; The Green]: Bistro-style village dining pub doing good interesting food and some two-for-one-deals (booking advised); interesting and individual décor, Wells & Youngs Bombardier and a couple of guests from wicker-fronted counter, good choice of wines by the glass, coal fire; well reproduced piped music; no children after 7pm Fri, Sat, tables out at front overlooking pond, open all day wknds, cl Mon *(LYM, George Atkinson, Dennis and Gill Keen, Dr and Mrs C W Thomas, Dr Kevan Tucker, Peter Sampson)*

LOWER GORNAL [SO9191]

Fountain DY3 2PE [Temple St]: Lively two-room local with helpful friendly landlord and staff, eight changing ales (beer festivals), two farm ciders, country wines and imported beers; enjoyable inexpensive food all day (not Sun evening), back dining area; pigs-and-pen skittles; piped music; open all day *(the Didler)*

Old Bulls Head DY3 2NU [Redhall Rd]: Busy Victorian local with own Black Country ales from back microbrewery and two guest beers, may be good filled cobs; open fire, back games room, some live music; open all day wknds (from 4pm wkdys) *(the Didler)*

LOXLEY [SP2552]

☆ **Fox** CV35 9JS [signed off A422 Stratford—Banbury]: Neatly refurbished and welcoming, very popular even mid-week lunchtimes for good value inventive generous food from sandwiches to fish specialities, real ales inc Hook Norton, prompt service and cheerful local landlord; panelling and a few pictures, pleasant dining area; piped music; tables in good-sized garden behind, sleepy village handy for Stratford *(R J Herd, K H Frostick)*

MERIDEN [SP2482]

Bulls Head CV7 7NN [Main Rd]: All-day M&B dining pub dating from the 15th c, log fires, beams, bare boards and flagstones, lots of nooks and crannies with plenty of interest; well kept ales such as Black Sheep and Timothy Taylors Landlord, good choice of wines by the glass; disabled facilities, garden tables, 13 Innkeepers Lodge bedrooms *(anon)*

MONKS KIRBY [SP4682]

☆ **Bell** CV23 0QY [just off B4027 W of Pailton]: Hospitable long-serving spanish landlord and his sweet dogs enliven this dimly lit pub; dark beams, timber dividers, flagstones and cobbles; very wide choice of largely good spanish food inc starters doubling as tapas and notable zarzuela fish stew, fine range of spanish wines and of brandies and malt whiskies; relaxed informal service, well kept Greene King ales; appropriate piped music; children and dogs welcome, streamside back terrace with country view, may be cl Mon

*(Susan and John Douglas,
Rob and Catherine Dunster, LYM, Jill and
Julian Tasker, Michael Doswell)*

NAPTON [SP4661]

Napton Bridge Inn CV47 8NQ [Southam Rd
(A425), Oxford Canal Napton Bottom Lock]:
Big family-run canalside pub with pine
panelling, open fires and simple furnishings
in three smallish rooms; enjoyable good
value food (lots of offers) inc some unusual
things like local water buffalo burgers,
changing real ales, friendly hard-working
staff; restaurant overlooking water; piped
music, no dogs; children welcome, back
garden, moorings *(George Atkinson, E Clark)*

NETHER WHITACRE [SP2192]

Railway B46 2EH [Station Rd]: Well kept
beer, good value food inc bargains for two,
lovely service from mother and daughter
team (mother is the chef); real fire in
lounge, pool in bar (dogs welcome here)
(Jan Everton)

NORTHEND [SP3952]

Red Lion CV47 2TJ [off B4100 Warwick—
Banbury; Bottom St]: Bright and neat open-
plan pub with good range of beers inc
Marstons and Timothy Taylors Landlord, good
coffee and choice of wines by the glass,
enjoyable blackboard food, reasonable
prices, friendly service; restaurant area;
quite handy for National Herb Centre *(BB,
Paul Whitehead)*

NUNEATON [SP3790]

Attleborough Arms CV11 4PL [Highfield Rd,
Attleborough]: Large fairly recently rebuilt
pub, attractively open, modern and
comfortable, with wide choice of enjoyable
cheap food, good range of beers and wines,
helpful staff; exemplary lavatories; good
disabled access *(David Green)*

OLD HILL [SO9686]

Waterfall B64 6RG [Waterfall Lane]: Good
value unpretentious two-room local, friendly
staff, well kept Holdens, Bathams and
guests, good value plain home-made food
from hot filled baguettes with chips to Sun
lunch; tankards and jugs hanging from
boarded ceiling; piped music; children
welcome, back garden with play area, open
all day Fri-Sun *(the Didler)*

OLDBURY [SO9989]

Waggon & Horses B69 3AD [Church St,
nr Savacentre]: Copper ceiling, original
etched windows, open fire and Black Country
memorabilia in busy town pub with Enville
and two or three guest beers; wide choice of
generous lunchtime food (not wknds) from
sandwiches up inc lots of puddings, decent
wines, friendly efficient service even when
busy; ornate Victorian tiles in corridor to
lively comfortable back lounge with tie
collection, side room with high-backed
settles and big old tables; bookable upstairs
bistro Weds-Fri night; open all day
(the Didler, Pete Baker)

OXHILL [SP3149]

☆ *Peacock* CV35 0QU [off A422 Stratford—
Banbury]: Popular pleasantly upgraded

stone-built pub with daily changing food
from traditional dishes to stir fries and fresh
fish inc wkdy two-course deals; Timothy
Taylors Landlord and more local ales, good
selection of wines by the glass, cosy bar and
dining room; garden seating, pretty village;
open all day Fri-Sun, cl Mon lunchtime
*(K H Frostick, Roger M Hancock,
Prof H G Allen)*

PRIORS HARDWICK [SP4756]

☆ *Butchers Arms* CV47 7SN [off A423 via
Wormleighton or A361 via Boddington, N of
Banbury; Church End]: Upmarket old-
fashioned restaurant in pleasantly reworked
14th-c building, oak beams, flagstones,
panelling, antiques and soft lighting; huge
choice of good if pricey food inc fixed-price
set lunch menu, friendly portuguese
landlord, punctilious formal service,
distinguished wine list (the beer is keg);
small bar with inglenook used mainly by
people waiting for tables, also simple public
bar, conservatory; country garden with
terrace, lovely setting, cl Sat lunchtime,
Sun evening *(K H Frostick, BB)*

RATLEY [SP3847]

☆ *Rose & Crown* OX15 6DS [off A422 NW of
Banbury]: Ancient golden-stone beamed
village pub, cosy and charming, with five
well kept ales, enjoyable good value
straightforward food from sandwiches up,
friendly welcoming staff; daily papers,
woodburners in flagstoned area on left and
in right carpeted part with wall seats, small
back restaurant; dogs and children welcome,
tables in gravel garden, nr lovely church in
sleepy village *(E A and D C T Frewer,
George Atkinson, BB)*

REDHILL [SP1356]

Stag B49 6NQ [Alcester Rd (A46 Alcester—
Stratford)]: Under same ownership as Golden
Cross at Ardens Grafton; airy, linked, beamed
and timbered rooms around central bar, some
with pine tables, others with leather sofas,
open fires; Greene King ales, good range of
wines by the glass, wide choice of well
presented interesting food, special offers,
newspapers; children welcome, large terrace
(traffic noise out here), ten bedrooms
*(Carol and Colin Broadbent, Keith and
Sue Ward)*

RUGBY [SP5075]

Merchants CV21 3AN [Little Church St]: Up
to eight real ales and lots of foreign beers in
busy open-plan bare-boards pub, bar food,
brewery memorabilia; live music Tues
(Adrian Johnson)

Raglan Arms CV22 6AD [Dunchurch Rd]:
Two-bar pub reopened not long ago, with
notable choice of well kept ales, food
gaining popularity too *(Ted George)*

RUSHALL [SK03001]

Manor Arms WS4 1LG [Park Rd, off A461]:
Low-beamed 18th-c pub on much older
foundations) by Rushall Canal; several rooms
in contrasting styles, big inglenook fireplace,
good value generous simple pubby food,
friendly staff, well kept Banks's ales from

pumps fixed to the wall, shelves of bottles around them; waterside garden, by Park Lime Pits nature reserve; open all day *(Chris Evans)*

SHIPSTON-ON-STOUR [SP2540]

☆ *Black Horse* CV36 4BT [Station Rd (off A3400)]: Cheerful newish family enlivening 16th-c thatched pub with low-beamed bars off central entrance passage, good honest english cooking (not Sun evening), Adnams and Greene King; good inglenook log fire, darts, dominoes and cribbage, small dining room; back garden with terrace and aunt sally, open all day Sun *(K H Frostick, JHBS)*

☆ *Horseshoe* CV36 4AP [Church St]: Pretty timbered inn with new landlord, refurbished open-plan carpeted bar with big fireplace, separate restaurant; three changing ales such as Bass, Sharps Doom Bar and local Wizard, enjoyable reasonably priced food, friendly atmosphere; children welcome, small back terrace, bedrooms, open all day *(BB, David Gunn, K H Frostick, JHBS)*

SOLIHULL [SP1780]

Boat B91 2TJ [Hampton Lane, Catherine de Barnes (B4102, handy for M42 junctions 5 and 6)]: Chef & Brewer by Grand Union Canal, enjoyable all-day food, good friendly service, three changing ales; children welcome (good pushchair access), garden (dogs allowed here), open all day *(Henry Pursehouse-Tranter)*

STONNALL [SK0603]

Old Swann WS9 9DX [off A452; Main St]: Good value home-made pub lunches in big dining extension, real ales such as local Backyard, Greene King IPA, St Austell Tribute and Timothy Taylors Landlord *(Colin Fisher)*

Royal Oak WS9 9DY [just off A452 N of Brownhills; Main St]: Popular welcoming pub with well kept Hook Norton, Charles Wells Bombardier and good range of changing guest beers, farm cider, jovial attentive landlord and helpful staff; enjoyable evening food in beamed bar and small restaurant, also Sun lunch; no music *(Colin Fisher)*

STRATFORD-UPON-AVON [SP2054]

☆ *Garrick* CV37 6AU [High St]: Bustling ancient pub with heavy beams and timbers, odd-shaped rooms and simple furnishings on bare boards; good-natured efficient staff, enjoyable food from sandwiches and light dishes up all day, well kept Greene King ales, decent wines by the glass; small air-conditioned back restaurant; piped music, TV, games machine; children welcome, open all day *(Rob and Catherine Dunster, LYM, John Millwood, Roger Thornington)*

Old Thatch CV37 6LE [Rother St/Greenhill St]: Cosy and welcoming, with well kept ales, enjoyable food inc Sun carvery, log fire, rustic décor, slate or wooden floors, country-kitchen furniture; covered tables outside *(Ted George)*

☆ *West End* CV37 6DT [Bull St]: Attractively modernised and neatly kept old pub, a rare exception to Greene King's domination here, with well kept changing ales such as Adnams

Broadside, Fullers London Pride, Hook Norton, Timothy Taylors Landlord and Uley Pig's Ear; friendly young staff, thriving atmosphere in nice lounge and several eating areas, shortish choice of good value seasonal food, good wine choice and interesting soft drinks' range and plenty of coffees; film star photographs; piped music; appealing terrace *(Val and Alan Green)*

Windmill CV37 6HB [Church St]: Ancient pub beyond the attractive Guild Chapel, with town's oldest licence, very low black beams and big log fire; typical old-fashioned town local, complete with piped music, sports TV and games machines, given visitor appeal by its friendly efficient staff; wide choice of attractively priced food (till 7pm wkdys) from sandwiches to substantial Sun lunch and some unusual main dishes, Flowers Original, nice wine; tables outside, open all day from noon *(Val and Alan Green, Roger Thornington)*

STRETTON-ON-FOSSE [SP2238]

☆ *Plough* GL56 9QX [just off A429]: Popular unpretentious olde-worlde 17th-c village pub; enjoyable food from baguettes to spit roasts, inglenook log fire, happy local atmosphere, Hook Norton and interesting guest beers; small bar and larger lounge, stripped stone and some flagstones, jugs and mugs on oak beams, small attractive candlelit dining room on right; darts, dominoes and cribbage; dogs welcome, a few tables outside, has been cl Mon lunchtime *(Keith and Sue Ward, K H Frostick, BB)*

TANWORTH-IN-ARDEN [SP1170]

☆ *Bell* B94 5AL [The Green]: Smartly comfortable contemporary bar-style décor, good food from light lunchtime dishes to full meals, good choice of wines by the glass, well kept ales such as Banks's, Black Sheep and Timothy Taylors Landlord, friendly staff; also houses deli and back post office; children in eating areas, outlook on pretty village's green and lovely 14th-c church, back terrace with alloy planters, stylish modern bedrooms – good base for walks *(LYM, Cedric Robertshaw, Hansjoerg Landherr)*

TEMPLE GRAFTON [SP1355]

☆ *Blue Boar* B49 6NR [a mile E, towards Binton; off A422 W of Stratford]: Welcoming refurbished stone-built dining pub with good food from imaginative sandwiches up, four well kept Marstons ales, good coffee and wine choice, friendly efficient young staff; beams, stripped stonework and log fires, glass-covered well with goldfish, dining room with attractive farmhouse-kitchen mural; big-screen TVs; children and dogs welcome, good disabled access, picnic-sets outside, pretty flower plantings, comfortable well equipped bedrooms, open all day summer wknds *(Reg Fowle, Helen Rickwood, Mike and Mary Carter, Martin and Pauline Jennings, Carol and Colin Broadbent, LYM)*

TIPTON [SO9792]

Rising Sun DY4 7NH [Horseley Rd (B4517, off A461)]: Friendly Victorian pub with well kept Banks's, Oakham and six guests, farm ciders, enjoyable lunchtime food; back lounge with coal fires, alcoves and original bare boards and tiles; tables outside, open all day *(the Didler)*

UPPER BRAILES [SP3039]

Gate OX15 5AX: Attractively old-fashioned low-beamed village pub, welcoming landlord, wife cooks good generous well priced country food (not lunchtime Tues) inc good fresh fish Tues, Weds; well kept Hook Norton and guest beers, big log fire, sizeable part-panelled bar, smaller stripped-stone lounge, alsatian called Shade; piped music in stripped-stone restaurant; dogs and well behaved children welcome, tables in extensive back garden with wendy house, pretty hillside spot, lovely walks, cl Sun evening, Mon lunchtime *(JHBS, Martin and Pauline Jennings, R J Herd)*

UPPER GORNAL [SO9292]

☆ *Britannia* DY3 1UX [Kent St (A459)]: 19th-c chatty old-fashioned local with particularly well kept Bathams Best and Mild (bargain prices); tiled floors, coal fires in front bar and time-trapped back room down corridor, some bar snacks inc cobs; sports TV; nice flower-filled back yard, open all day *(the Didler)*

Jolly Crispin DY3 1UL [Clarence St (A459)]: Friendly well run 18th-c local with up to nine interesting quickly changing ales (beer festivals), two farm ciders or perry; compact front bar, wall seats and mixed tables and chairs on tiled floor, aircraft pictures in larger back room; dogs welcome, beer garden, open all day Fri-Sun, cl lunchtime Mon-Thurs *(the Didler)*

WALSALL [SP0198]

Arbor Lights WS1 1SY [Lichfield St]: May be new licensees as we go to press; relaxed, modern, open-plan brasserie-style bar and restaurant, wide choice of wines, Fullers London Pride and Wadworths 6X, has had enjoyable fresh food all day from sandwiches and unusual starter/light dishes to good fish choice *(Stephen Corfield, Tony and Wendy Hobden)*

Fountain WS1 1XB [Lower Forster St]: Appealing backstreet pub with friendly atmosphere, some real ales, small dining section *(Stephen Corfield)*

Oak WS2 8HH [Green Lane]: Recently reopened after major refurbishment, friendly and lively evenings, with real ales inc Wychwood Hobgoblin; karaoke nights *(Stephen Corfield)*

Victoria WS1 2AA [Lower Rushall St]: Unassuming pub with quickly changing well kept ales inc interesting ones *(Stephen Corfield)*

Wheatsheaf WS1 2NA [Birmingham Rd]: Run with flair and individuality, cheerful landladies, wide food choice from good sandwiches up, well kept Wells & Youngs Bombardier and two or three quickly changing guest beers, good choice of malt whiskies; children and dogs welcome *(John and Helen Rushton)*

White Lion WS1 3EQ [Sandwell St]: Hillside local (so its two rooms are known as Deep End and Shallow End), good range of well kept ales usually inc Highgate Dark Mild and Sharps Doom Bar, well priced lunchtime food, friendly staff; games room, open all day *(Stephen Corfield)*

WARMINGTON [SP4147]

☆ *Plough* OX17 1BX [just off B4100 N of Banbury]: Attractive old country pub, unspoilt and well cared for by new friendly landlord; low heavy beams, log fire in big fireplace, ancient settle, nice chairs, Victorian prints; four ales inc Bass and Greene King IPA, good well priced pubby food, extended dining room; tables on back terrace, delightful village with interesting church *(Keith and Sue Ward, LYM)*

WARWICK [SP2766]

Cape of Good Hope CV34 5DP [Lower Cape]: Traditional unsmart two-room pub on Grand Union Canal by Warwick Top Lock; friendly atmosphere, half a dozen well kept changing real ales, enjoyable basic food, darts; hatch service for waterside seats *(Pete Baker, Martin Smith)*

Old Fourpenny Shop CV34 6HJ [Crompton St, nr racecourse]: Cosy and comfortable split-level pub with up to five well kept changing beers, welcoming licensees, good value food in bar and heavily beamed restaurant, cheerful service; no piped music; pleasant reasonably priced bedrooms *(Pam and John Smith)*

☆ *Rose & Crown* CV34 4SH [Market Pl]: Up-to-date uncluttered refurbishment, bustling and friendly, with big leather sofas and low tables by open fire, red-walled dining area with large modern photographs; good choice of sensibly priced interesting food all day, well kept real ales and plenty of fancy keg dispensers, good wines and coffee, cheerful efficient service; tables out under parasols, comfortable good-sized bedrooms *(Alan Johnson, Revd R P Tickle, Ian and Nita Cooper, LYM)*

☆ *Tudor House* CV34 6AW [West St]: Heavily timbered Tudor inn opp the castle car park; lots of black wood, tiles and parquet floor, leaded lights, lofty pitched ceiling, massive stone fireplace, galleried landing, solid furnishings and Tudoresque décor inc armour; real ales such as Greene King, decent wine, pubby food; tables in front and on back terrace, bedrooms *(Colin Moore, BB)*

☆ *Zetland Arms* CV34 4AB [Church St]: Cosy town pub with good sensibly priced traditional food (not wknd evenings) inc good sandwich choice, friendly quick service even when busy, Marstons Pedigree and Tetleys, decent wines in generous glasses; neat but relaxing small panelled front bar with toby jug collection, comfortable larger L-shaped back eating area with small conservatory; sports TV; children welcome, interestingly planted sheltered garden, bedrooms sharing bathroom *(Graham Findlay, LYM, Alan Johnson)*

WEST BROMWICH [SO0190]
Vine B70 6RD [Roebuck St, just off
M5 junction 1]: Changing ale such as
Bathams, enjoyable indian food from kitchen
and barbecue; nr West Bromwich Albion so
packed on match days *(Dave Statham)*
WHATCOTE [SP2944]
☆ *Royal Oak* CV36 5EF: Dating from the 12th c,
quaint and unpretentious low-beamed small
room with Civil War connections and lots of
knick-knacks and curios, good log fire in
huge inglenook, cheery helpful landlord; well
kept Hook Norton ales, good choice of
reasonably priced generous fresh food from
baguettes up, decent wines, quiet dining
room; children welcome, picnic-sets in
informal garden, muddy walkers welcome
*(LYM, Michael and Jenny Back, Prof H G Allen,
Martin and Pauline Jennings)*
WILLOUGHBY [SP5267]
Rose CV23 8BH [just off A45 E of Dunchurch;
Main St]: Old beamed pub re-thatched and
refitted after fire; new licensee doing home-
made pubby food, Black Sheep and Timothy
Taylors Landlord; children welcome, disabled
facilities, seating in side garden (dogs
allowed here) with gate to park and play
area, open all day Fri-Sun *(anon)*
WITHYBROOK [SP4384]
Pheasant CV7 9LT [B4112 NE of Coventry,
not far from M6 junction 2]: Comfortable
dining pub with very wide choice of usual
food from sandwiches up, mainstream real
ales, good coffee; big log fires, lots of dark
tables with plush-cushioned chairs; piped
music; children welcome, tables under
lanterns on brookside terrace, open all day
Sun *(Alan Johnson, LYM, Martin Smith)*
WOLVERHAMPTON [SO9298]
☆ *Great Western* WV10 0DG [Corn Hill/Sun St,
behind railway station]: Smartened up under
newish licensee, this cheerful pub is hidden
away by a cobbled lane down from the main
line station to the GWR low-level one; well
kept Bathams, Holdens and guest ales, real
cider, bargain home-made food, interesting
railway memorabilia, traditional front bar,
other rooms inc neat dining conservatory;
SkyTV; yard with barbecues, open all day
(may be Sun afternoon break) *(Pete Baker,
Tony and Wendy Hobden, BB, the Didler,
Andrew Bosi, Martin Grosberg, Robert Garner)*
Royal Tiger WV11 1ST [High St]: Modern
Wetherspoons with good atmosphere,
friendly locals, good service, wide choice of
beers inc some local brews such as Hobsons;
children welcome in good spacious back
family area with comfortable high-backed
settles; good disabled facilities, terrace out
by canal *(Henry Pursehouse-Tranter)*

Real ale to us means beer which has matured naturally in its cask – not pressurised
or filtered. We name all real ales stocked. We usually name ales preserved under a
light blanket of carbon dioxide too, though purists – pointing out that this
stops the natural yeasts developing – would disagree (most people, including us,
can't tell the difference!)

Wiltshire

Three good new entries here, with rewarding food and genuine pubby warmth, are the Potting Shed at Crudwell, Rattlebone at Sherston (back in the *Guide*, and much improved, after a break) and Outside Chance at Manton. Outstanding among other foody places are the Compasses at Chicksgrove, Bridge Inn at West Lavington, Malet Arms at Newton Tony, Linnet at Great Hinton and – more restauranty in mood – Three Crowns at Brinkworth and Bath Arms at Crockerton. The ancient thatched Compasses is Wiltshire Dining Pub of the Year. Food bargains are to be found at the Red Lion at Kilmington and Dumb Post at Bremhill. Some rural favourites, often with decent walks nearby: the Forester at Donhead St Andrew, Fox & Hounds at East Knoyle, Horseshoe at Ebbesbourne Wake, George in Lacock, Hatchet at Lower Chute and White Horse at Winterbourne Bassett. The Spread Eagle at Stourton (by the NT Stourhead estate), Pear Tree at Whitley and Cross Keys at Upper Chute all have very pleasant bedrooms. For charming idiosyncrasy, the Two Pigs in Corsham takes some beating, while in Salisbury the Haunch of Venison is one of the city's most memorable historic buildings. Top Lucky Dips include the Boot at Berwick St James, Horse & Groom at Charlton, Bell in Ramsbury and Seven Stars at Winsley. Wadworths is the county's great brewer (and sells good wines, too); Arkells and Archers are its other major suppliers. Hop Back is much the most successful of Wiltshire's many good smaller breweries, with Hidden, Stonehenge, Moles, Box Steam and Ramsbury also prominent.

ALDBOURNE

SU2675   MAP 2

Blue Boar
The Green (off B4192 in centre); SN8 2EN

Bags of character in chatty, low-beamed, traditional pub

'A lovely setting: it's a delight and the beer is good too' commented one regular of this unspoilt, cheery place by the village green. The left-hand bar is homely, with partly bare boards, partly flagstones, pubby seats around heavily rustic tables, lots of low black beams in the ochre ceiling, a boar's head above the bigger of the two fireplaces, a stuffed pine marten over one table, darts, board games and a corner cupboard of village trophies. Lots of unusual bottled beers line the rail above the dark pine dado. Wadworths IPA and 6X and a guest such as Theakstons on handpump and beer festivals twice a year during April and October, and they have 20 malt whiskies. A separate bare-boards dining bar on the right, stretching back further, has more table space, and is rather more modern in style, with its country pictures on cream or dark pink walls, but has a similar nicely pubby atmosphere. Picnic-sets and a couple of tall hogshead tables under big green canvas parasols out in front face the green (and its parked cars). More-up-to-date reports please.

🍴 **Very generous helpings of food from a shortish menu include lunchtime ploughman's, baked potatoes, and well filled baguettes and sandwiches, along with pubby food like chilli, deep-fried haddock, scampi, or ham, egg and chips. Daily specials might feature** starters like apple and black pudding, or garlic mushrooms, with main courses such as minted lamb shank, wild boar with apple, cream and horseradish, steak and kidney pie, or tuna steak with chilli and ginger oil; puddings like apple pie, rice pudding or chocolate fudge cake; popular Sunday roasts (booking recommended). *Starters/Snacks: £3.50 to £13.50. Main Courses: £7.50 to £14.95. Puddings: £4.15*

Wadworths ~ Tenants Jez and Mandy Hill ~ Real ale ~ Bar food (12-2, 6.30-9.30) ~ Restaurant ~ (01672) 540237 ~ Children welcome ~ Dogs allowed in bar ~ Open 11.30-3, 5.30-11; 11.30am-midnight Sat; 12-11 Sun

Recommended by Mary Rayner, Dr and Mrs M E Wilson, Richard Tilbrook, Paul A Moore

BERWICK ST JOHN   ST9422   MAP 2
Talbot
Village signposted from A30 E of Shaftesbury; SP7 0HA

Unspoilt and friendly pub in attractive village, with simple furnishings and tasty, reasonably priced food

This unpretentious village local is well placed for choice walks southwards through the deep countryside of Cranborne Chase and towards Tollard Royal. The heavily beamed bar has plenty of character and is simply furnished with solid wall and window seats, spindleback chairs, a high-backed built-in settle at one end, and a huge inglenook fireplace with a good iron fireback and bread ovens; darts. Ringwood Best, Wadworths 6X and a couple of guests such as Ringwood Fortyniner and Wadworths St George and the Dragon on handpump; darts and cribbage. There are seats outside.

⅋ Good, reasonably priced bar food at lunchtime includes sandwiches, hot filled baguettes, ploughman's, and lighter dishes such as soup or nachos. The main menu has starters like garlic mushrooms, whitebait or deep-fried brie, and main courses such as steak, mixed grill, ham, egg and chips, cajun chicken, salmon and broccoli mornay, and sausage and mash with onion gravy; daily specials, puddings and Sunday roasts. *Starters/Snacks: £4.50 to £7.00. Main Courses: £8.00 to £16.00. Puddings: £3.50 to £4.00*

Free house ~ Licensees Pete and Marilyn Hawkins ~ Real ale ~ Bar food ~ Restaurant ~ (01747) 828222 ~ Children welcome ~ Dogs welcome ~ Open 12-2.30, 6.30-11; 12-4 Sun; closed Sun evening, all day Mon

Recommended by D and J Ashdown, Colin and Janet Roe, Mr and Mrs P D Titcomb, Bruce and Sharon Eden

BOX   ST8369   MAP 2
Quarrymans Arms
Box Hill; coming from Bath on A4 turn right into Bargates 50 yards before railway bridge, then at T junction turn left up Quarry Hill, turning left again near the top at grassy triangle; from Corsham, turn left after Rudloe Park Hotel into Beech Road, then third left on to Barnetts Hill, and finally right at the top of the hill; OS Sheet 173 map reference 834694; SN13 8HN

Cheerful and unpretentious, with great views, real ales and good value food

Tucked away down winding country lanes, this isolated place has an interesting selection of drinks. In addition to 50 malt whiskies and 11 wines by the glass, they serve Butcombe Best, Moles Best, Wadworths 6X and a couple of changing guests such as Mole Slayer and Wadworths St George and the Dragon on handpump. It's atmospheric and comfortable rather than overly smart (some parts have an air of mild untidiness) and one modernised room with an open fire is entirely set aside for drinking. There's plenty of mining-related photographs and memorabilia dotted around – this was once the local of the Bath-stone miners and the welcoming licensees run interesting guided trips down the mine itself. There are lovely sweeping views from the big windows of the dining room; piped music, games machine, TV and board games, and there's free wi-fi in the bar and bedrooms. An attractive outside terrace has picnic-sets. The pub is ideally placed for cavers, potholers and walkers. More reports please.

⚏ **Bar food includes sandwiches, baked potatoes, soup, all-day breakfast, macaroni cheese, ham, egg and chips, calves liver, sausages and mash, their own pies, local venison bourguignon in season, and a range of vegetarian choices such as thai curry, stir fry or vegetable carbonara, with puddings such as bread and butter pudding. You can book tables outside the times shown; breakfasts available.** *Starters/Snacks: £3.95 to £6.50. Main Courses: £6.50 to £16.95. Puddings: £4.95 to £5.50*

Free house ~ Licensees John and Ginny Arundel ~ Real ale ~ Bar food (12-3, 6-9) ~ Restaurant ~ (01225) 743569 ~ Children welcome ~ Dogs allowed in bar ~ Open 11-3, 6-11; 11-midnight Fri, Sat; 11-11 Sun ~ Bedrooms: £35B/£65B

Recommended by Ian Herdman, Dr and Mrs A K Clarke, Mr Reader

BREMHILL
ST9772   MAP 2

Dumb Post £

Off A4/A3102 just NW of Calne; Hazeland, just SW of village itself, OS Sheet 173 map reference 976727; SN11 9LJ

With something of the character of a faded hunting lodge; a proper country local with no frills and very inexpensive food

Perhaps not for those with fussier tastes, this quirky, unspoilt place has absolutely no pretensions but heaps of character. The main lounge is a glorious mix of mismatched, faded furnishings, vivid patterned wallpaper and stuffed animal heads, its two big windows boasting an unexpectedly fine view down over the surrounding countryside. There are half a dozen or so tables, a big woodburner in a brick fireplace (not always lit), a log fire on the opposite side of the room, comfortably worn armchairs and plush banquettes, a standard lamp, mugs, bread and a sombrero hanging from the beams, and a scaled-down model house between the windows; in a cage is an occasionally vocal parrot, Oscar. The narrow bar leading to the lounge is more dimly lit, but has a few more tables, exposed stonework, and quite a collection of toby jugs around the counter; there's a plainer third room with pool, darts and piped music. Wadworths 6X and a changing beer from the local brewery Three Castles on handpump; an amiable landlord. There are a couple of picnic-sets outside and some wooden play equipment. Note the limited lunchtime opening times. More reports please.

⚏ **Bar food (served lunchtimes only) is simple, hearty and well liked by locals: toasted sandwiches, ploughman's, winter hotpot or curry, ham with egg and chips, steak and kidney pudding, and fish and chips; Sunday roasts.** *Starters/Snacks: £2.00 to £2.90. Main Courses: £3.90 to £6.30. Puddings: £3.50*

Free house ~ Licensee Bryan Pitt ~ Real ale ~ Bar food (lunchtimes Fri-Sun only) ~ No credit cards ~ (01249) 813192 ~ Children welcome ~ Dogs allowed in bar ~ Open 12-2.30, 7-11(midnight Sat); closed Mon-Thurs lunchtimes

Recommended by JJW, CMW

BRINKWORTH
SU0184   MAP 2

Three Crowns 🍴 🍷

The Street; B4042 Wootton Bassett—Malmesbury; SN15 5AF

Excellent food deservedly takes centre stage here, but this is still a pub, with five good beers and a carefully chosen wine list

With a very interesting range of food from the mainstream to the exotic, this dining pub has kept some pubby elements. The bar part of the building is the most traditional, with big landscape prints and other pictures, some horsebrasses on dark beams, a log fire, a dresser with a collection of old bottles, big tapestry-upholstered pews, a stripped-deal table, and a couple more made from gigantic forge bellows. Sensibly placed darts, shove-ha'penny, dominoes, cribbage, board games, games machine and piped music. Abbey Ales Bellringer, Bass, Fullers London Pride, Greene King IPA and Wadworths 6X on handpump; a carefully chosen, extensive wine list with 25 by the glass, and around 20 malt whiskies.

Most people choose to eat in the conservatory or the light and airy garden room. There's a terrace with outdoor heating to the side of the conservatory; smoking shelter. The garden stretches around the side and back, with well spaced tables and a climbing frame, and looks over a side lane to the church, and out over rolling prosperous farmland.

🍴 **The extensive menu covers an entire wall; at lunchtimes, as well as filled rolls, they might have a range of curries, fresh mussels or faggots with basil mash. From a more elaborate (and more expensive) menu, there might also be dover sole, asparagus with garlic cream cheese in filo pastry, vegetarian kataifi tartlet, crispy duck with strawberry sauce, slices of kangaroo, venison and ostrich marinated in a secret recipe, and puddings such as raspberry and white chocolate bread and butter pudding or a duo of crème brûlée.** *Starters/Snacks: £5.95 to £12.95. Main Courses: £10.95 to £21.95. Puddings: £5.75 to £6.95*

Enterprise ~ Lease Anthony Windle ~ Real ale ~ Bar food (12-2, 6-9.30; 12-9 Sun) ~ Restaurant ~ (01666) 510366 ~ Well behaved children welcome ~ Dogs allowed in bar ~ Open 10am-11.30pm; 10-4, 6-midnight Sat; 12-10.30 Sun

Recommended by Andrew Shore, Maria Williams, Dr and Mrs J Temporal, Nigel and Sue Foster, Ian Herdman, Mr and Mrs P R Thomas, John Saville, Tom and Ruth Rees, Robyn Selley

CASTLE COMBE
ST8477 MAP 2

Castle Inn ♀ 🛏
Off A420; SN14 7HN

Good food and drinks in the friendly pubby bar of a well run small hotel, in a remarkably preserved Cotswold village

Tables out in front of this welcoming hotel look down the idyllic main street and on to the market place of this improbably perfect-looking village. The bustling beamed bar has a big inglenook log fire, comfortably padded bar stools as well as a handsome old oak settle and other good seats around the sturdy tables, and hunting and vintage motor-racing pictures on the walls. Butcombe Bitter and a guest like Wells & Youngs Bombardier are on handpump, good wines by the glass, a fine choice of malt whiskies and brandies, and well liked morning coffee and afternoon cream teas; efficient, obliging service. On either side of the bar are two snug old-world sitting rooms with comfortable settees and easy chairs, and besides the smart and attractive high-ceilinged formal dining room there is a big light-hearted upstairs eating room with a very effective sunblind system for its conservatory-style roof. This opens on to a charming small roof terrace with good cast-iron furniture. The medieval church clock is fascinating. Very limited parking (if you're staying and have mobility problems they do try to help). As we went to press we heard the hotel was up for sale; more up-to-date reports please.

🍴 **Enjoyable bar food includes filled baguettes, ploughman's, soup, smoked haddock fishcake on baby spinach with a herb and cream sauce, interesting summer salads like pear, apple and glazed walnut with stilton dressing, a pie of the day, tagliatelle with mushrooms, garlic and cream sauce, chicken curry, fillet of salmon with stir-fried vegetables and coriander pesto, and puddings such as dark chocolate and kirsch crème brûlée or treacle tart with clotted cream; there's also a more elaborate dining menu.** *Starters/Snacks: £5.25 to £9.50. Main Courses: £7.25 to £13.75. Puddings: £5.75 to £8.25*

Free house ~ Licensees Ann and Bill Cross ~ Real ale ~ Bar food (11.30-3, 6-9.15) ~ Restaurant ~ (01249) 783030 ~ Children welcome ~ Open 9.30am-11pm(10pm Sun) ~ Bedrooms: £69.50S(£85B)/£110B

Recommended by Guy Vowles, John and Enid Morris, Martin and Pauline Jennings, John Saville, Peter and Audrey Dowsett

---

Anyone claiming to arrange or prevent inclusion of a pub in the *Guide* is a fraud. Pubs are included only if recommended by genuine readers and if our own anonymous inspection confirms that they are suitable.

CHICKSGROVE

ST9729 MAP 2

Compasses ★ ⊛ ♀ 🛏

From A30 5.5 miles W of B3089 junction, take lane on N side signposted Sutton Mandeville, Sutton Row, then first left fork (small signs point the way to the pub, in Lower Chicksgrove; look out for the car park); can also be reached off B3089 W of Dinton, passing the glorious spire of Teffont Evias church; SP3 6NB

WILTSHIRE DINING PUB OF THE YEAR

Ancient thatched house with enjoyable food, a genuine welcome and splendid bedrooms – an excellent all-rounder

A lovely place to stay or enjoy a meal, this splendid 14th-c place has no piped music, just the buzz of conversation. The bar has old bottles and jugs hanging from beams above the roughly timbered counter, farm tools and traps on the partly stripped-stone walls, and high-backed wooden settles forming snug booths around tables on the mainly flagstoned floor. Bass, Hidden Quest and Keystone Large One and Solar Brew are kept under a light blanket pressure on handpump, eight wines by the glass and several malt whiskies. The quiet garden, terraces and flagstoned farm courtyard are very pleasant places to sit. Lovely surrounding walks and plenty to do in the area.

🍴 **Carefully sourced food includes lunchtime filled onion loaves, ploughman's and interesting salads, rib-eye steak, salmon steak or ham, egg and chips, and a frequently changing blackboard menu featuring seasonal and locally available ingredients. This might include starters such as beetroot cured gravadlax, mussels or scallops from Brixham market, or local game terrine, and main courses such as slow-roasted lamb shoulder, bass fillet on braised fennel, spinach and wild mushroom roulade or beef and Guinness pie; puddings like pear tarte tatin with home-made cinnamon ice-cream or chocolate mousse with orange sorbet.** *Starters/Snacks: £5.00 to £8.50. Main Courses: £9.00 to £21.00. Puddings: £5.50*

Free house ~ Licensee Alan Stoneham ~ Real ale ~ Bar food ~ (01722) 714318 ~ Children welcome ~ Dogs welcome ~ Open 12-3, 6-11; 12-3, 7-10.30 Sun ~ Bedrooms: £65B/£85S(£90B)

Recommended by Edward Mirzoeff, Andrew Hollingshead, Bruce and Sharon Eden, Helen and Brian Edgeley, Russell Sunderland, Colin and Janet Roe, Dr and Mrs Michael Smith, Geoffrey Kemp, Mark Coppin, S G N Bennett, Simon Lindsey, Rosemary Rogers, John and Jane Hayter

CORSHAM

ST8670 MAP 2

Two Pigs 🍺

A4, Pickwick; SN13 0HY

Wonderfully eccentric pub for fans of beer and music, open evenings only (except Sun) and at its best on Monday nights

This thoroughly idiosyncratic place will appeal to those in search of all things quirky. The cheerfully eccentric feel owes much to the individualistic landlord, and there's a zany collection of bric-a-brac in the narrow and dimly lit flagstoned bar, including enamel advertising signs on the wood-clad walls, pig-theme ornaments and old radios. There's usually a good mix of customers around the long dark wood tables and benches, and friendly staff; piped blues. Stonehenge Pigswill and three guests like Cotswold Spring Codger, Hop Back Summer Lightning or Moles Best are on handpump. Monday evenings is great fun, with a big crowd enjoying the live music. A covered yard outside is called the Sty. Do note their opening times – the pub is closed every lunchtime, except on Sunday. No under-21s.

🍴 **No food.**

Free house ~ Licensees Dickie and Ann Doyle ~ Real ale ~ No credit cards ~ (01249) 712515 ~ Live blues/rock Mon evening ~ Open 7-11; 12-2.30, 7-10.30 Sun; closed lunchtimes Mon-Sat

Recommended by Catherine Pitt, Mr and Mrs P R Thomas, Dr and Mrs A K Clarke

CROCKERTON

ST8642 MAP 2

Bath Arms

Just off A350 Warminster—Blandford; BA12 8AJ

Attractively modernised dining pub, with pretty gardens, relaxed atmosphere and two very stylish bedrooms

Often very busy with customers enjoying a meal, this is very appealing both inside and out. Inside, it's warmly welcoming with a thriving informal atmosphere, lots of well spaced tables on the parquet floor in the long, stylishly modernised two-roomed bar, beams in the whitewashed ceiling, and brasses. There's a restaurant at one end and a log fire in a stone fireplace at the other. Courage Best, Potters Ale, Wessex Crockerton Classic and a guest on handpump, and quite a few wines by the glass; piped music. There are plenty of inviting places to sit outside too, with various garden areas featuring plenty of picnic-sets. We've yet to hear from readers who've stayed in the two splendidly stylish bedrooms, but imagine they would merit one of our Stay Awards – they're what you might expect to find in a chic boutique hotel rather than a country pub. Longleat is very close by.

🍴 **Cooked by the landlord using local produce, the enjoyable food might include filled baguettes, nice soups, pressed tomato terrine with cornish crab mayonnaise, smoked duck breast and lambs sweetbreads with apple and watercress, sausages and champ, roast fennel with artichokes and parmesan, belly of pork with spiced aubergine and merguez sausage, sticky beef with braised red cabbage, poached duck in a scallop and vegetable broth, and puddings such as rhubarb trifle with vanilla cream and hot chocolate fondant with caramel ice-cream.** *Starters/Snacks: £4.50 to £7.50. Main Courses: £10.95 to £14.95. Puddings: £4.25*

Wellington ~ Licensee Dean Carr ~ Real ale ~ Bar food (12-2, 6.30-9) ~ Restaurant ~ (01985) 212262 ~ Children welcome ~ Dogs allowed in bar ~ Open 11-3, 6-11; 11-11 Sat, Sun; closed 3-6 Sat and Sun in winter ~ Bedrooms: /£80S

Recommended by Edward Mirzoeff, Colin and Janet Roe, Dr and Mrs J Temporal, John Redfern, Andy and Claire Barker, Paul Goldman, R J Herd, Richard and Sally Beardsley, Douglas and Ann Hare, I H Curtis, J Stickland, Mr and Mrs P R Thomas, Bruce and Sharon Eden, Wyndham Hamilton, Jill Bickerton

CRUDWELL

ST9592 MAP 4

Potting Shed ★ 🍴 ♀ 🍺

A429 N of Malmesbury; The Street; SN16 9EW

Appealing new variation on the 'traditional country tavern' theme, good beers, wines and country cooking

Opened at the end of 2007 after complete reworking by the owners of the nearby Rectory Hotel, this friendly place comes straight into the *Guide* with a star; one of the nicest places we've come across recently. It is very much a proper country pub rather than just another pub/restaurant, with cheerful and interested young staff, well kept Butcombe, Timothy Taylors Landlord and Bath Gem or Theakstons Best on handpump as well as an excellent range of over two dozen wines by the glass, interesting drinks of the day such as wild damson brandy bubbly, good coffees, log fires – one in a big worn stone fireplace – and very mixed plain tables and chairs on pale flagstones in the low-beamed rooms that ramble around the bar; visiting dogs may meet Barney and Rubbles (the owners') and be offered biscuits. There are well worn easy chairs in one corner, and a couple of black-top daily papers. Four steps take you up into a high-raftered further area, with coir carpeting, and there's one separate smaller room ideal for a lunch or dinner party. The rustic decorations are not overdone, and quite fun: a garden-fork door handle, garden-tool beer pumps, rather witty big black and white photographs. And if you must have piped music (here it masks traffic noise that might otherwise intrude at quiet times), at least let it be well chosen, like theirs; board games. They have summer barbecues on fine Saturdays; there are sturdy teak seats around cask tables as well as picnic-sets out on the side grass among weeping willows.

🍴 Growing some of their own fruit and veg in workmanlike plots beyond the car park, and getting other supplies as freshly and locally as possible (and they hope from the villagers to whom they've loaned allotments), they punctuate their shortish lunchtime menu with good old country dishes such as oxtail terrine, ploughman's, fish and chips, chip butty, sweetbreads or bubble and squeak. The evening menu includes seasonally changing dishes such as citrus-marinated salmon with shaved fennel and melba toast, mussels in cider and smoked bacon sauce, roasted cod loin with orange and mint, roast chicken breast with fennel and chorizo risotto with lemon and thyme dressing, rump steak, and puddings such as lemon posset and dark chocolate cheesecake and raspberry milkshake. *Starters/Snacks: £4.95 to £6.25. Main Courses: £7.95 to £15.50. Puddings: £5.00*

Enterprise ~ Lease Jonathan Barry, Julian Muggridge and Laura Sheffield ~ Real ale ~ Bar food (12-2.30(3.30 Sun), 7-9.30; not Sun evening) ~ (01666) 577833 ~ Children welcome ~ Dogs welcome ~ Open 11-12

Recommended by Guy Vowles, E McCall, T McLean, D Irving, Jules Vaux, Michael Doswell

DEVIZES

SU0061   MAP 2

Bear ⚲ £
Market Place; SN10 1HS

Comfortable coaching inn with plenty of history, beers fresh from the local brewery, pleasant terrace, and unpretentious, reasonably priced food

This coaching inn dates back some 450 years and is just 150 yards away from Wadworths brewery (you can buy beer in splendid old-fashioned half-gallon earthenware jars); Wadworths Horizon, IPA and 6X are on handpump, and they do a good choice of wines (including 15 by the glass), with quite a few malt whiskies. The big main carpeted bar has log fires, black winged wall settles and muted cloth-upholstered bucket armchairs around oak tripod tables; the classic bar counter has shiny black woodwork and small panes of glass. Separated from here by some steps, a room named after the portrait painter Thomas Lawrence (his father ran the establishment in the 1770s) has dark oak-panelled walls, a parquet floor, a big open fireplace, shining copper pans, and plates around the walls. A mediterranean-style courtyard with olive trees, hibiscus and bougainvillea has some outside tables. They will keep your credit card behind the bar if you wish to run a food tab. More up-to-date reports please, especially on the food.

🍴 Inexpensive bar food at lunchtime includes a sizeable choice of sandwiches and filled panini and baguettes, filled baked potatoes, soup, ploughman's, omelettes, full breakfast, gammon and egg, chicken breast with mexican salad, and beer-battered fish; with evening dishes such as chargrilled steaks, mushroom stroganoff, and fish and chips; puddings like tiramisu or apple pie; children's menu. *Starters/Snacks: £3.50 to £5.25. Main Courses: £4.65 to £8.25. Puddings: £3.25 to £3.95*

Wadworths ~ Tenants Andrew and Angela Maclachlan ~ Real ale ~ Bar food (11.30-2.30, 7-9.30 Mon-Sat; 12-2, 7.45-9.30 Sun) ~ Restaurant ~ (01380) 722444 ~ Children welcome ~ Dogs allowed in bar ~ Open 10am-11.30pm; 10.30am-11pm Sun ~ Bedrooms: £80S/£105B

Recommended by Steven and Victoria James, Mary Rayner, the Didler, Blaise Vyner, Barry Collett, Mr and Mrs P D Titcomb, Dr and Mrs A K Clarke

DONHEAD ST ANDREW

ST9124   MAP 2

Forester 🍽 ⚲
Village signposted off A30 E of Shaftesbury, just E of Ludwell; Lower Street; SP7 9EE

Attractive old thatched pub in charming village, good food – especially west country fish – and fine views from the very pleasant, big terrace

You can build up an appetite for a meal at this well run dining pub by taking in a walk up White Sheet Hill and past the old and 'new' Wardour castles. The appealing bar has a welcoming atmosphere, stripped tables on wooden floors, a log fire in its big inglenook fireplace, and usually a few locals chatting around the servery: Butcombe Bitter,

Ringwood Best and a guest from a brewery like Adnams on handpump, and 15 wines (including champagne) by the glass. Off here is an alcove with a sofa and table and magazines to read. The comfortable main dining room has country-kitchen tables in varying sizes and there's also a second smaller and cosier dining room. Outside, seats on a good-sized terrace have fine country views. The neighbouring cottage used to be the pub's coach house.

As well as lunchtime sandwiches, the changing menu of carefully sourced and enjoyable food (not cheap) might include starters like moules marinière, butternut squash and sage soup, or oxtail ravioli with pickled red cabbage, and main courses such as pot-roasted pheasant with turnips, pancetta, lemon and pearl barley, seared wing of skate with black beans and pak choi, bouillabaisse of cornish fish, or sirloin steak; puddings such as dark chocolate risotto with caramelised pear and pistachios and elderberry and basil jelly with almond beignet and raspberry sorbet; good cheeseboard. From Tuesday to Friday they do fixed-price two- and three-course seafood lunches (£15.50 for two courses).
Starters/Snacks: £4.50 to £10.00. Main Courses: £10.00 to £17.50. Puddings: £4.95 to £7.00

Free house ~ Licensee Chris Matthew ~ Real ale ~ Bar food ~ Restaurant ~ (01747) 828038 ~ Children welcome ~ Dogs welcome ~ Open 12-3, 6.30-11; 12-4 Sun; closed Sun evenings

Recommended by Roger Wain-Heapy, Colin and Janet Roe, Mr and Mrs W W Burke, Robert Watt, Samantha McGahan, G Vyse, Russell Sunderland, John Robertson

EAST KNOYLE
ST8731 MAP 2

Fox & Hounds ♀

Village signposted off A350 S of A303; The Green (named on some road atlases), a mile NW at OS Sheet 183 map reference 872313; or follow signpost off B3089, about 0.5 miles E of A303 junction near Little Chef; SP3 6BN

Beautiful thatched village pub with splendid views, welcoming service, good beers and popular food

There's a good mix of customers at this pleasantly rambling country pub, and its fine views and location by the green make it well worth the effort of seeking out. Inside, there's the warmly welcoming feel of a proper long-established pub (rather than a more formal pub/restaurant), and service is prompt and cheerful. Around the central horseshoe-shaped servery are three linked areas on different levels, with big log fires, plentiful oak woodwork and flagstones, comfortably padded dining chairs around big scrubbed tables with vases of flowers, and a couple of leather settees; the furnishings are all very individual and uncluttered. There's a small light-painted conservatory restaurant. Butcombe Bitter, Hidden Potential, Palmers Copper and a guest like Hop Back Summer Lightning on handpump, 20 wines by the glass and farm cider. Piped music, board games and skittle alley. The nearby woods are good for a stroll, and the Wiltshire Cycle Way passes through the village.

At lunchtime, the well liked food listed on the regularly changing blackboard menu includes ploughman's, starters like crab pâté, chowder soup, tempura squid or deep-fried brie, stone-baked pizzas, beer-battered fish and chips, thai green chicken curry, calves liver and bacon, and aubergine stuffed with pine nuts, spinach and pecorino cheese; evening extras such as bacon-wrapped chicken breast with a wild mushroom sauce, pork tenderloin with a calvados and prune sauce, or lemon sole; puddings like pavlova, apple and caramel pancake stack, or bread and butter pudding with Baileys liqueur; children's menu. *Starters/Snacks: £4.00 to £6.95. Main Courses: £7.95 to £18.00. Puddings: £4.50*

Free house ~ Licensee Murray Seator ~ Real ale ~ Bar food (12-2.30, 6.15-9.30) ~ (01747) 830573 ~ Children welcome ~ Dogs welcome ~ Open 11.30-3, 5.30-11(10.30 Sun)

Recommended by Hugh Stafford, Paul Goldman, G Vyse, Martin and Karen Wake, Bruce and Sharon Eden, Edward Mirzoeff, Roger Wain-Heapy, Chris and Meredith Owen

We checked prices with the pubs as we went to press in summer 2009.
They should hold until around spring 2010.

EBBESBOURNE WAKE

ST9924 MAP 2

Horseshoe ★ 🍺 🛏

On A354 S of Salisbury, right at signpost at Coombe Bissett; village is around 8 miles further on; SP5 5JF

Restful, unspoilt country pub with a good welcome, beers tapped from the cask, and views from the pretty garden

As well as farm cider, there's a good selection of five regional beers tapped from the cask at this warmly welcoming rural pub, with Bowman Swift One, Otter Best, Palmers Copper and two guests like Bowman Wallops Wood or Yeovil Spring Forward. The neatly kept, comfortably furnished bar has fresh home-grown flowers on the tables, lanterns, a large collection of farm tools and other bric-a-brac crowded along its beams, and an open fire; a conservatory extension seats ten people. Booking is advisable for the small restaurant, especially at weekends when it can fill quite quickly. There are pleasant views over the steep sleepy valley of the River Ebble from seats in the pretty little garden, a goat and a chicken in a paddock; good nearby walks. Morris dancers may call some evenings in summer.

🍽 **Traditional bar food includes lunchtime sausages, ploughman's, ham and eggs, vegetarian lasagne, a popular range of pies, half a roast duck with a choice of sauces, and puddings like treacle tart.** *Starters/Snacks: £4.75 to £6.95. Main Courses: £6.95 to £17.00. Puddings: £1.95 to £4.75*

Free house ~ Licensees Tony and Pat Bath ~ Real ale ~ Bar food (not Sun evening or Mon) ~ Restaurant ~ (01722) 780474 ~ Children welcome but not in main bar ~ Open 12-3, 6.30-11; 12-4 Sun; closed Sun evening and Mon lunchtime; 26 Dec ~ Bedrooms: /£75B

Recommended by John Robertson, Mr and Mrs P D Titcomb, David Kirkcaldy, the Didler, G Vyse, Robert Watt, Dr and Mrs M E Wilson

GREAT BEDWYN

SU2764 MAP 2

Three Tuns

Village signposted off A338 S of Hungerford, or off A4 W of Hungerford via Little Bedwyn; High Street; SN8 3NU

Thriving village pub with good food, local real ales, helpful staff and eclectic décor

As we went to press, this pleasantly traditional pub was about to become a free house, and they were planning to make the beer selection feature three or four local real ales on handpump (the cellar was once the village morgue); helpful service. The atmosphere remains thoroughly pubby despite the emphasis on food, and you won't feel out of place if you just want a pint. The traditional décor in the beamed, bare-boards front bar is lifted out of the ordinary by some quirky touches and almost every inch of the walls and ceiling is covered by either the usual brasses, jugs, hops and agricultural implements, or more unusual collections such as ribbons from sailors' hats, showbiz photos and yellowing cuttings about the royal family; occasional piped music. There's an inglenook fireplace, and lighted candles in the evenings. In front of the whitewashed building are quite a few plants, while behind is a raised garden with a heated smoking area. It does get pretty packed at weekends.

🍽 **Food was about to change as we went to press, but includes an eclectic mix of pubby dishes like fish and chips as well as more restauranty items such as game from local shoots.** *Starters/Snacks: £3.95 to £6.95. Main Courses: £8.95 to £15.95. Puddings: £4.95*

Free house ~ Licensees Amanda and Jason Gard ~ Real ale ~ Bar food ~ Restaurant ~ (01672) 870280 ~ Children welcome ~ Dogs allowed in bar ~ Open 12-3, 6-11; 12-6 Sun; closed Sun evening

Recommended by Mr and Mrs Ian Campbell, Alvin and Yvonne Andrews, Paul Boot, Mary Rayner, Evelyn and Derek Walter

GREAT HINTON

ST9059 MAP 2

Linnet 🍴

3.5 miles E of Trowbridge, village signposted off A361 opposite Lamb at Semington; BA14 6BU

Attractive dining pub, very much a place to come for a good meal rather than just a drink

The imaginative food at this brick dining pub is undoubtedly the main draw. The comfortable bar to the right of the door has Wadworths 6X on electric pump, several wines by the glass and around two dozen malt whiskies; there are bookshelves in a snug end part of the room. The restaurant is candlelit at night; piped music. In summer, the window boxes and flowering tubs, with seats dotted among them, are quite a sight.

🍴 **Served by efficient staff, the popular lunchtime food includes sandwiches, soup, substantial salads, steaks, a £5 lunch dish of the day and a short list of favourites which might feature beer-battered salmon fillet, spring lamb stew or rabbit, pork and cider paté. The evening menu (not cheap) has soup, starters like home-smoked haddock and leek rarebit tart, and main courses such as baked tenderloin of pork or salmon en croûte; puddings like rhubarb and vanilla mascarpone cheesecake and stem ginger pudding with toffee sauce.** *Starters/Snacks: £4.95 to £8.95. Main Courses: £7.50 to £19.95. Puddings: £5.50 to £7.95*

Wadworths ~ Tenant Jonathan Furby ~ Real ale ~ Bar food ~ Restaurant ~ (01380) 870354 ~ Children welcome ~ Dogs welcome ~ Open 11-3, 6-11; 12-4, 7-10.30 Sun; closed Mon

Recommended by Dr and Mrs J Temporal, Dennis and Gill Keen, Martin Clifton, Michael Doswell, Lise Chace, Stan and Dot Garner

GRITTLETON

ST8680 MAP 2

Neeld Arms 🍷 🍺 🛏

Off A350 NW of Chippenham; The Street; SN14 6AP

Bustling village pub with popular food and beer, friendly staff and comfortable bedrooms

Readers have enjoyed the neat bedrooms as well as the beer and wine at this likeable black-beamed pub. Wadworths IPA and 6X and guests like Butcombe Bitter and Wickwar Bankers Draft on handpump from the substantial central bar counter, and a good choice of reasonably priced wines by the glass. It's largely open-plan, with stripped stone and some black beams, a log fire in the big inglenook on the right and a smaller coal-effect fire on the left, flowers on tables, and a pleasant mix of seating from windsor chairs through scatter-cushioned window seats to some nice arts and crafts chairs and a traditional settle; board games. The back dining area has yet another inglenook, with a big woodburning stove – even back here, you still feel thoroughly part of the action. There's an outdoor terrace, with pergola. The golden retriever is called Soaky.

🍴 **Straightforward, reasonably priced bar food at lunchtime includes filled ciabattas, soup, ploughman's, sausage or pie of the week, ham, egg and chips, salmon and dill fishcakes or beefburger. The changing evening menu might feature starters such as tomato, mozzarella and basil salad, smoked salmon cornet filled with trout mousse, or parma ham and brie tartlet, and main courses like fish pie, local venison sausages with mash, slow-roasted pork belly stuffed with apple, or roast vegetable pancakes; puddings like treacle tart, cherry cheesecake and profiteroles; Sunday roasts and Monday curry nights; children's menu.** *Starters/Snacks: £4.50 to £6.25. Main Courses: £8.95 to £13.95. Puddings: £4.25*

Free house ~ Licensees Charlie and Boo West ~ Real ale ~ Bar food ~ Restaurant ~ (01249) 782470 ~ Children welcome ~ Dogs welcome ~ Open 12-3(3.30 Sat), 5.30-midnight; 12-4, 7-11 Sun ~ Bedrooms: £60B/£80B

Recommended by Sara Fulton, Roger Baker, Dr and Mrs A K Clarke, Peter and Audrey Dowsett, John and Enid Morris, Richard Stancomb, Paul A Moore, Matthew Shackle, Carol and Phil Byng, Henry Snell, Alistair Forsyth

Unlike other guides, entry in this *Guide* is free. All our entries depend solely on merit.

HORTON   SU0363   MAP 2

Bridge Inn

Signposted off A361 Beckhampton road just inside the Devizes limit; Horton Road; SN10 2JS

Well run and distinctive canalside pub, with good traditional pub food, and a pleasant garden with aviary

Right beside the Kennet & Avon Canal, this convivial place served some 200 years ago as a flour mill and bakery, and one of the original grinding wheels is set in the terrace. Inside, on the red walls above a high-panelled dado are black and white photos of bargee families and their barges among other old photographs and country pictures. In the carpeted area on the left all the sturdy pale pine tables may be set for food, and there's a log fire at the front; to the right of the bar is a pubbier part with similar country-kitchen furniture on reconstituted flagstones and some stripped brickwork. Wadworths IPA and 6X tapped from the cask and several decent wines by the glass. Disabled lavatories, piped music, TV, board games, table skittles and shove-ha'penny. There are moorings for boats by the safely fenced garden, which features an aviary and fantail doves as well as picnic-sets. It's handy for walks on the downs and along the canal tow path.

🍴 As well as filled baguettes, crusty rolls and ploughman's, bar food includes soup, pâté with toast, ham or sausage and eggs, and home-made specials such steak and ale pie or mixed fish pie. *Starters/Snacks: £3.50 to £7.50. Main Courses: £6.95 to £9.95. Puddings: £4.50*

Wadworths ~ Tenant Adrian Softley ~ Real ale ~ Bar food (12-2, 6-8.30) ~ Restaurant ~ (01380) 860273 ~ Well behaved children welcome ~ Dogs allowed in bar ~ Open 11-3, 6-11; 12-3, 7-10.30 Sun

Recommended by M R Phillips, Sheila and Robert Robinson, Dr and Mrs M E Wilson, Mr and Mrs A H Young, Andrew Gardner

KILMINGTON   ST7835   MAP 2

Red Lion £

B3092 Mere—Frome, 2.5 miles S of Maiden Bradley; 3 miles from A303 Mere turn-off; BA12 6RP

Atmospheric, no-nonsense country inn owned by the National Trust, with good value traditional lunches and an attractive garden

'Unchangingly delightful: a real pub'; 'Could not have been more welcoming to our family' enthused two readers about this ancient former drovers' inn. Its snug, low-ceilinged bar has a good convivial atmosphere, pleasant furnishings such as a curved high-backed settle and red leatherette wall and window seats on the flagstones, photographs of locals pinned up on the black beams, and a couple of big fireplaces (one with a fine old iron fireback) with log fires in winter. A newer big-windowed eating area is decorated with brasses, a large leather horse collar and hanging plates. Darts, shove-ha'penny and board games. Butcombe Bitter, Butts Jester and a guest like Hidden Quest on handpump, elderflower pressé and several wines by the glass; helpful service. There are picnic-sets in the big attractive garden (look out for Kim the labrador). A gate gives on to the lane which leads to White Sheet Hill, where there are riding, hang-gliding and radio-controlled gliders, and Stourhead Gardens are only a mile away. Though dogs are generally welcome, they're not allowed at lunchtime. There's a smokers' shelter in a corner of the car park.

🍴 Served only at lunchtime, the well liked, unpretentious bar menu includes soup, sandwiches, toasties, filled baked potatoes, ploughman's, pasties, steak and kidney, lamb, fish or game pies, meat or vegetable lasagne, daily specials like cottage pie or chicken casserole, and one pudding such as apple strudel. *Starters/Snacks: £1.95 to £3.45. Main Courses: £5.75 to £8.85. Puddings: £4.60*

Free house ~ Licensee Chris Gibbs ~ Real ale ~ Bar food (12-1.50; not evenings) ~ No credit cards ~ (01985) 844263 ~ Children welcome till 8.30pm ~ Dogs allowed in bar in evenings ~ Open 11.30-2.30, 6.30-11; 12-3, 7-11 Sun

Recommended by Edward Mirzoeff, Andrea Rampley, Michael Doswell, Mr and Mrs P D Titcomb, Joan and Michel Hooper-Immins, Steve Jackson

LACOCK

ST9168   MAP 2

George

West Street; village signposted off A350 S of Chippenham; SN15 2LH

Unspoilt and homely, with plenty of character and an attractive back garden in summer

Full of little, informal areas and run by pleasantly chatty staff, this delightfully rambling inn stands in the centre of a showpiece village owned by the National Trust. It's just the place for a drink and the low-beamed bar has upright timbers in the place of knocked-through walls making cosy corners, armchairs and windsor chairs around close-set tables, seats in the stone-mullioned windows, and flagstones just by the counter; quiet piped music. The treadwheel set into the outer breast of the original great central fireplace is a talking point – worked by a dog, it was used to turn a spit for roasting. The walls are covered with things to look at, including a little exhibition on William Henry Fox Talbot together with a collection of vintage cameras, pictures for sale, a copy of an 1840 photo of Lacock by Fox Talbot, souvenirs from the filming in the village of the TV series *Cranford* and for a Harry Potter film, and even a framed cover of the 2008 edition of this *Guide* which depicted the George itself. Wadworths IPA, JCB and 6X on handpump. Outside, there are picnic-sets with umbrellas in the attractive courtyard, which has a pillory and a well; extensive lawn beyond with children's play area.

🍴 **Straightforward bar food includes sandwiches and snacks, main courses such as steak, stilton and potato pie, faggots and chips, bass fillets, and goats cheese, mushroom and sweet potato tart; puddings such as bread and butter pudding and chocolate torte.** *Starters/Snacks: £3.25 to £6.95. Main Courses: £8.50 to £12.50. Puddings: £4.75*

Wadworths ~ Manager John Glass ~ Real ale ~ Bar food (12-2.30, 5.30-9.30; all day Sun) ~ Restaurant ~ (01249) 730263 ~ Children in eating area of bar ~ Dogs allowed in bar ~ Open 9am-11pm(10.30 Sun); 9am-3, 5-11 Mon-Weds in winter

Recommended by Blaise Vyner, David Field, Andrew Shore, Maria Williams, Ian Herdman, Dr and Mrs M E Wilson, Richard and Sheila Fitton, Bryan and Mary Blaxall, Dr and Mrs J Temporal, J Stickland, Dr and Mrs A K Clarke, Adrian Johnson

Rising Sun 🍺

Bewley Common, Bowden Hill – out towards Sandy Lane, up hill past abbey; OS Sheet 173 map reference 935679; SN15 2PP

Unassuming stone pub with welcoming atmosphere and great views from the garden

This nicely unpretentious pub is an enjoyable spot to sample local Moles ales: on handpump are Moles Best Bitter, Tap, Rucking Mole, Capture and a seasonal guest, as well as Black Rat cider and several wines by the glass. There are three welcoming little rooms knocked together to form one simply furnished area, with a mix of old chairs and basic kitchen tables on stone floors, country pictures and open fires. The conservatory shares the same fantastic views as the big two-level terrace (where there are plenty of seats) – on a clear day you can see up to 25 miles over the Avon valley; the sunsets can be stunning. More up-to-date reports on the newish licensees, please.

🍴 **The menu is served throughout the pub and includes ploughman's, ham, egg and chips, and more elaborate items like chicken wrapped in bacon with cider and stilton sauce.** *Starters/Snacks: £4.50 to £6.50. Main Courses: £8.50 to £14.50. Puddings: £3.50 to £4.50*

Moles ~ Manager Louise Hall ~ Real ale ~ Bar food (12-2(5 Sun), 6-9; all day Sat and Sun in July and Aug; no food Sun evening in winter) ~ Restaurant ~ (01249) 730363 ~ Children welcome ~ Dogs welcome ~ Live entertainment every Weds evening ~ Open 12-3, 6-11; 12-11 Sat, Sun; closed 3-6 Sat and Sun in winter

Recommended by Michael Doswell, P Waterman, Ian Herdman, Mrs Sheila Pearley, David A Hammond, George Atkinson

LOWER CHUTE   SU3153   MAP 2

Hatchet
The Chutes well signposted via Appleshaw off A342, 2.5 miles W of Andover; SP11 9DX

Unchanged, neatly kept, 16th-c thatched country pub, with a restful atmosphere

Few other pubs in Wiltshire approach this cottagey place for sheer rural charm. The very low-beamed bar has a splendid 17th-c fireback in the huge fireplace (and a roaring winter log fire), a mix of captain's chairs and cushioned wheelbacks around oak tables, and a peaceful local feel. Timothy Taylors Landlord and two guests such as Otter Amber Triple and fff Altons Pride on handpump, and several wines by the glass; piped music, board games. There are seats out on a terrace by the front car park or on the side grass, as well as a smokers' hut and a children's sandpit.

⊞ **Thursday night is curry night and other bar food includes lunchtime filled baguettes, ploughman's, liver and bacon, steak and ale pie, spinach and red pepper lasagne, and daily specials such as fishcakes and calves liver with mash.** *Starters/Snacks: £5.50 to £5.95. Main Courses: £8.75 to £11.95. Puddings: £3.95*

Free house ~ Licensee Jeremy McKay ~ Real ale ~ Bar food (12-2.15, 6.30-9.45; 12-2.15, 7-9.30 Sun) ~ Restaurant ~ (01264) 730229 ~ Children in restaurant and side bar only, and in bedrooms by arrangement ~ Dogs allowed in bar and bedrooms ~ Open 11.30-3, 6-11; 12-3, 7-11 Sun ~ Bedrooms: £60S/£70S

Recommended by N B Vernon, Steven and Victoria James, J Stickland, Mr and Mrs H J Langley, Phyl and Jack Street, Ian Herdman, Henry Midwinter

LUCKINGTON   ST8384   MAP 2

Old Royal Ship
Off B4040 SW of Malmesbury; SN14 6PA

Friendly pub by the village green, with a fair choice of drinks and decent bar food

You get a warm welcome at this pub, which has a good mix of locals and visitors (including the Beaufort Hunt). It's been pleasantly opened up, making in effect one long bar divided into three areas, and the central servery has Bass, Wadworths 6X, Wells & Youngs Bitter and a guest such as Cotswold Way served under a light blanket pressure, and a dozen wines by the glass. On the right are neat tables, spindleback chairs and small cushioned settles on dark bare boards, with a small open fireplace and some stripped masonry. Skittle alley, games machine, TV and piped music. The garden beyond the car park has boules, a play area with a big wooden climbing frame, and plenty of seats on the terrace or grass. More reports please.

⊞ **Bar food includes sandwiches, deep-fried chicken goujons with chilli dip, steak and ale pie, ham and eggs, chicken caesar salad, and specials like spinach and brie tart or braised lamb shank in a red wine, rosemary and garlic sauce.** *Starters/Snacks: £3.25 to £8.95. Main Courses: £6.50 to £18.95. Puddings: £2.50 to £4.50*

Free house ~ Licensee Helen Johnson-Greening ~ Real ale ~ Bar food (12-2.15, 6(7 Sun)-9.15) ~ Restaurant ~ (01666) 840222 ~ Children allowed away from bar area ~ Jazz second Weds of month ~ Open 11.30-3, 6-11; 11.30-11 Sat; 12-4, 7-10.30 Sun

Recommended by Richard Stancomb, Michael Doswell, Chris and Angela Buckell

---

'Children welcome' means the pub says it lets children inside without any special restriction. If it allows them in, but to restricted areas such as an eating area or family room, we specify this. Some pubs may impose an evening time limit. We do not mention limits after 9pm as we assume children are home by then.

MANTON   SU1768   MAP 2

Outside Chance ♀

Village (and pub) signposted off A4 just W of Marlborough; High Street; SN8 4HW

Good new dining pub, civilised and traditional, nicely reworked with interesting sporting theme

The former Oddfellows, this was reopened under its new name towards the end of 2008. The décor celebrates unlikely winners, such as 100-1 Grand National winners like Coughoo or Fuinavon, Mr Spooner's Only Dreams (a 100-1 winner at Leicester in 2007), or the odd-gaited little Seabiscuit who cheered many thousands of Americans with his dogged pursuit of victory during the Depression years. It has three small linked rooms, with a thriving loudly chatty atmosphere, flagstones or bare boards, hops on beams, and mainly plain pub furnishings such as chapel chairs and a long, cushioned pew; one room has a more cosseted feel, with panelling and a comfortable banquette. The lighting is soft (nightlights on tables), the pub is usually full of fresh flowers, there's a splendid log fire in the big main fireplace; piped music and board games. They have well kept Wadworths IPA and 6X and a guest such as Wells & Youngs Waggle Dance on handpump, quite a few good wines by the glass, and nicely served coffees, and the neatly dressed young staff are friendly and helpful. A suntrap side terrace has contemporary metal-framed granite-topped tables, and the good-sized garden has sturdy rustic tables and benches under ash trees. The garden opens into the local playing fields, with a children's play area.

▥ **Bar food includes goats cheese and red onion tart, smoked salmon, ham, egg and chips, eggs benedict, seafood tagliatelle, mushroom risotto, beef burger, pie of the day, plaice fillet with brown shrimp and caper sauce, and puddings such as poached pear with dark chocolate sauce, meringues filled with seasonal fruit and cream, and chocolate brownie with white chocolate sauce.** *Starters/Snacks: £3.50 to £6.95. Main Courses: £7.95 to £12.95. Puddings: £2.95 to £4.50*

Wadworths ~ Lease Sarah Emmott and Hannah Lampard ~ Real ale ~ Bar food (12-2.30, 7-9(9.30 Fri, Sat)) ~ (01672) 512352 ~ Children welcome ~ Dogs welcome ~ Bridge Mon evening ~ Open 12-3, 5.30-11; 12-11.30 Sat; 12-10.30 Sun

Recommended by Suzy Miller, Sheila and Robert Robinson, Mr and Mrs A Curry

NEWTON TONY   SU2140   MAP 2

Malet Arms

Village signposted off A338 Swindon—Salisbury; SP4 0HF

Smashing village pub with no pretensions, a good choice of local beers and tasty home-made food

With much-liked food, well kept beer and a very friendly landlord, this character-laden village pub is a strong all-rounder, and there's nothing in the way of games machines or piped music. The two low-beamed interconnecting rooms have nice furnishings including a mix of different-sized tables with high-winged wall settles, carved pews, chapel and carver chairs, and lots of pictures, mainly from imperial days. The main front windows are said to have come from the stern of a ship, and there's a log and coal fire in a huge fireplace. At the back is a homely dining room. As well as beers on handpump from breweries such as Fullers, Hop Back, Palmers and Stonehenge are Old Rosie Scrumpy, several malt whiskies and wines by the glass. The small front terrace has old-fashioned garden seats and some picnic-sets on the grass, and there are more tables in the back garden, along with a wendy house. There's also a little aviary, and a horse paddock behind. Getting to the pub takes you through a ford and it may be best to use an alternative route in winter, as it can be quite deep.

▥ **Chalked up on a blackboard, the very good, changing range of carefully sourced food (their beef is all from Somerset cattle) might include soup, olives and antipasti with hot ciabatta, duck confit salad, pasta with gorgonzola and walnuts in pesto sauce, thai salmon fishcakes with sweet chilli, popular burgers with blue cheese and bacon, gammon with free-range eggs, chicken curry, and game dishes such as wood pigeon wrapped in smoked** bacon, or haunch of venison (the landlord runs the deer management on a local estate); puddings such as walnut tart, treacle tart and chocolate brownies. *Starters/Snacks: £5.95 to £6.95. Main Courses: £8.75 to £14.00. Puddings: £4.50*

Free house ~ Licensee Noel Cardew ~ Real ale ~ Bar food (12-2.30, 6.30-10 (7-9.30 Sun)) ~ Restaurant ~ (01980) 629279 ~ Children allowed but not in bar area ~ Dogs allowed in bar ~ Open 11-3, 6-11; 12-3, 7-10.30 Sun; closed 25 and 26 Dec, 1 Jan

Recommended by Nigel and Sue Foster, J Stickland, Pat and Tony Martin, Mark Flynn, Dr and Mrs M E Wilson, N R White, P Waterman, John Robertson, Bren and Val Speed, Mr and Mrs P D Titcomb

NORTON

ST8884   MAP 2

Vine Tree 🍴 🍷

4 miles from M4 junction 17; A429 towards Malmesbury, then left at Hullavington, Sherston signpost, then follow Norton signposts; in village turn right at Foxley signpost, which takes you into Honey Lane; SN16 0JP

Civilised, friendly dining pub, beams and candlelight, seasonal food using local produce, fine choice of drinks and a big garden

The accent at this welcoming dining pub – which feels pleasantly remote despite its proximity to the M4 – is firmly on food, served by efficient staff. They've made considerable efforts with wine, with around 40 wines by the glass from an impressive list (they do monthly tutored tastings and have their own wine shop), and quite a choice of malt whiskies and armagnacs. Butcombe Bitter and St Austell Tinners, with a guest beer like Bath Ales Gem, are on handpump. Three neatly kept little rooms open into each other, with aged beams, some old settles and unvarnished wooden tables on the flagstone floors, big cream church altar candles, a woodburning stove at one end of the restaurant and a large open fireplace in the central bar, and limited edition and sporting prints; look out for Clementine, the friendly and docile black labrador. It's best to book if you want to eat here, especially at weekends. There are picnic-sets and a children's play area in a two-acre garden plus a pretty suntrap terrace with teak furniture under big cream umbrellas, a lion fountain, lots of lavender and box hedging; there's an attractive smoking shelter, too. They have a busy calendar of events, with outdoor music in summer, vintage car rallies and lots going on during the Badminton horse trials.

🍽 **The usually enjoyable food includes sandwiches, interesting soups, light bites such as scampi, filled ciabattas, and honey and mustard gammon with egg and chips, and a frequently changing menu with a wide range of dishes using local seasonal produce such as game, oysters, mussels and asparagus. Starters and snacks might include mussel and saffron soup or warm salad of pigeon breast and black pudding; main courses such as venison and juniper suet crust pie, roast saddle and leg of wild rabbit with prune and armagnac compote, freshly minced beefburger served with a bloody mary, coq au vin, lobster thermidor, shetland mussel, clam and seafood risotto, or pumpkin ravioli with walnut sauce; puddings like eton mess, belgian double chocolate roulade, lemon tart or pink champagne and wild strawberry jelly; good cheeseboard. New seafood and champagne area serves seafood from traditional french tiered stands; Sunday roasts include beef sirloin from the neighbouring farm; children's portions.** *Starters/Snacks: £4.95 to £9.95. Main Courses: £11.70 to £17.50. Puddings: £5.25 to £7.50*

Free house ~ Licensees Charles Walker and Tiggi Wood ~ Real ale ~ Bar food (12-2(2.30 Sat, 3.30 Sun), 7-9.30(9.45 Fri, 10 Sat)) ~ Restaurant ~ (01666) 837654 ~ Well behaved children welcome ~ Dogs allowed in bar ~ Live jazz and blues on terrrace some days in summer ~ Open 12-3-ish, 6-midnight

Recommended by Chris and Libby Allen, Evelyn and Derek Walter, J Crosby, Richard and Sheila Fitton, Di and Mike Gillam, Michael Doswell, Nina Randall, Kevin Thomas, Rod Stoneman, M Fitzpatrick, Richard Stancomb, the Brewers, Rob Holt, Guy Vowles, Dr and Mrs J Temporal

---

If a service charge is mentioned prominently on a menu or accommodation terms, you must pay it if service was satisfactory. If service is really bad, you are legally entitled to refuse to pay some or all of the service charge as compensation for not getting the service you might reasonably have expected.

PITTON

SU2131 MAP 2

Silver Plough ♀

Village signposted from A30 E of Salisbury (follow brown tourist signs); SP5 1DU

Bustling country dining pub that feels instantly welcoming, good drinks and nearby walks

This village dining pub is well placed for walks, served as it is by a good network of woodland and downland paths, including the Clarendon Way. The comfortable front bar has plenty to look at, as the black beams are strung with hundreds of antique boot-warmers and stretchers, pewter and china tankards, copper kettles, toby jugs, earthenware and glass rolling pins, painted clogs, glass net-floats, coach horns and so forth. Seats include half a dozen cushioned antique oak settles (one elaborately carved, beside a very fine reproduction of an Elizabethan oak table), and the timbered white walls are hung with Thorburn and other game bird prints, and a big naval battle glass-painting. The back bar is simpler, but still has a big winged high-backed settle, cased antique guns, substantial pictures and – like the front room – flowers on its tables. There's a skittle alley next to the snug bar; piped music. Badger Gold, K&B, Tanglefoot and a seasonal guest on handpump, 12 wines by the glass and quite a few country wines. A quiet lawn has picnic-sets and other tables under cocktail parasols, and on the terrace is a heated area for smokers. More up-to-date reports on the food, please.

🍴 **Straightforward bar food includes lunchtime filled baguettes, baked potatoes, various salads, and pubby dishes like scampi, lasagne and steak and kidney pie; evening menu (not Sunday) with quite a few dishes like salads or scallops available as a starter or in larger portions; mostly meaty main courses such as chicken suprême, rib-eye steak and roast lamb shank; children's menu; Sunday roasts.** *Starters/Snacks: £4.50 to £7.95. Main Courses: £5.95 to £10.95. Puddings: £2.95 to £5.95*

Badger ~ Tenants Hughen and Joyce Riley ~ Real ale ~ Bar food (12-2, 6-9; 12-2.15, 6.30-8.30 Sun) ~ Restaurant ~ (01722) 712266 ~ Children allowed but not in bedrooms ~ Dogs allowed in bar ~ Open 11-3, 6-11.30(midnight Sat); 12-3, 6.30-11 Sun ~ Bedrooms: /£50S

Recommended by Ian Herdman, Virginia Williams, Chris Glasson, Phyl and Jack Street, Helen and Brian Edgeley, John Robertson, Edward Mirzoeff, Howard and Margaret Buchanan, Stan Edwards

ROWDE

ST9762 MAP 2

George & Dragon 🍴 ♀

A342 Devizes—Chippenham; SN10 2PN

Gently upmarket coaching inn with good, varied food and a nice atmosphere

Not far from the Kennet & Avon Canal, this convivial place has a pretty back garden with tables and chairs, and occasional summer barbecues. Although there's quite an emphasis on the interesting food, they do keep Butcombe Bitter and Sharps Doom Bar, and a guest like Wadworths Horizon, on handpump; several wines by the glass. The two low-ceilinged rooms have plenty of wood, beams and open fireplaces, and there are large wooden tables, antique rugs and walls covered with old pictures and portraits; the atmosphere is pleasantly chatty. Board games and piped music. Smart contemporary bedrooms. More up-to-date reports, please.

🍴 **Good, if not cheap, bar food includes soup, starters (some also available in main course sizes) like potted crab, carpaccio of beef, or wild mushroom and parmesan risotto, and main courses such as grilled lemon sole, lamb and cider stew, or roast monkfish; vegetarian and children's menus; puddings like strawberry eton mess or chocolate and orange bread and butter pudding; three-course set menus; Sunday roasts.** *Starters/Snacks: £6.50 to £10.50. Main Courses: £13.50 to £22.50. Puddings: £6.00*

Free house ~ Licensees Philip and Michelle Hale, Christopher Day ~ Real ale ~ Bar food (12-3, 7-10.30; 12-4, 6.30-10.30 Sat; 12-4 Sun) ~ Restaurant ~ (01380) 723053 ~ Children welcome ~ Dogs allowed in bar ~ Open 12-3, 7-11; 12-4, 6.30-11 Sat; 12-4 Sun; closed Sun evening ~ Bedrooms: £55/£65(£85S)(£75B)

Recommended by Suzy Miller, Betsy and Peter Little, Chris and Meredith Owen, Mary Rayner, Andrew Shore, Maria Williams

SALISBURY   SU1429   MAP 2

Haunch of Venison
Minster Street, opposite Market Cross; SP1 1TB

Ancient pub oozing history, with tiny beamed rooms, unique fittings, and a famous mummified hand; lovely atmosphere and well kept beers

A must if you're in the city, this marvellously atmospheric old building (which originates from 1320) tends to lure visitors into a long and lingering visit. The two tiny downstairs rooms are quite spit-and-sawdust in spirit, with massive beams in the white ceiling, stout oak benches built into the timbered walls, black and white floor tiles, and an open fire. A tiny snug (popular with locals, but historically said to be where the ladies drank) opens off the entrance lobby. Courage Best, Greene King IPA, Hop Back Summer Lightning and a guest such as Buntingford Challenger on handpump from a unique pewter bar counter, and there's a rare set of antique taps for gravity-fed spirits and liqueurs. They've also 100 malt whiskies, decent wines (ten by the glass), herbal teas, and a range of brandies. Halfway up the stairs is a panelled room they call the House of Lords, which has a small-paned window looking down on to the main bar, and a splendid fireplace that dates back to the building's early years; behind glass in a small wall slit is the smoke-preserved mummified hand of an 18th-c card sharp still clutching his cards.

🍽 **The reasonably priced lunchtime menu has filled panini and baguettes, soup, snacks and starters like potato wedges and prawn cocktail, and fixed-price main courses (discount for two) like home-made cheeseburger, sausages and mash, beer-battered fish and chips, and stuffed aubergine; daily specials. The more elaborate evening menu includes roasted quail stuffed with foie gras, wild boar, haunch of venison, sea bass and stuffed beefsteak tomato; puddings such as chocolate brownie with hot chocolate sauce and fresh fruit salad.** *Starters/Snacks: £2.50 to £7.50. Main Courses: £7.50 to £16.95. Puddings: £3.90 to £6.50*

Scottish Courage ~ Lease Anthony Leroy and Justyna Miller ~ Real ale ~ Bar food (12-2.30, 6-9.30(10 Thurs-Sat)) ~ Restaurant ~ (01722) 411313 ~ Children welcome ~ Dogs allowed in bar ~ Open 11am-11.30pm; 12-10.30 Sun

Recommended by Andrea Rampley, Ann and Colin Hunt, Dr S J Shepherd, the Didler, Pete Coxon, M Wood, Stuart Doughty, Mike Parkes, John Saville, Philip and June Caunt, Phil and Sally Gorton

SEEND   ST9361   MAP 2

Barge
Seend Cleeve; signposted off A361 Devizes—Trowbridge, between Seend village and signpost to Seend Head; SN12 6QB

Popular canalside pub with a nice garden to watch the boats; decent beer, good choice of wines by the glass and tasty food

This delightfully positioned waterside pub beside the Kennet & Avon Canal gets very busy on warm days, particularly its garden – ideal for watching the boating scene – while in winter the inside makes a cosy retreat. The bar has a medley of eye-catching seats which includes milk churns, unusual high-backed chairs (made from old boat parts), a seat made from an upturned canoe, and the occasional small oak settle among the rugs on the parquet floor; there's a well stocked aquarium and a pretty Victorian fireplace; piped music. Wadworths IPA, Horizon, 6X and a seasonal beer under air pressure, and 40 wines by the glass; friendly, helpful staff.

🍽 **Well liked bar food includes filled baguettes, duck liver and pistachio pâté with cumberland sauce, thai-style crab cakes with sweet chilli sauce, fish, cheese and meat boards with crusty bread for sharing, and main courses like slow-roasted belly pork with mustard mash, lamb and rosemary sausages with caramelised onion gravy, free-range chicken on roasted pepper and rocket linguine, beer-battered hake, daily specials such as fish pie and confit of duck with spiced grape sauce; puddings such as sticky chocolate and almond sponge pudding and mixed berry pavlova; Sunday roasts.** *Starters/Snacks: £3.75 to £8.75. Main Courses: £8.25 to £13.50. Puddings: £4.25 to £4.95*

Wadworths ~ Managers Paul and Sarah Haynes ~ Real ale ~ Bar food (12-3, 6-10 (cold food between 3 and 5)) ~ Restaurant ~ (01380) 828230 ~ Children welcome ~ Dogs allowed in bar ~ Open 11-11

Recommended by Dr and Mrs M E Wilson, John Saville, Meg and Colin Hamilton, Barry Collett, Mr and Mrs A Curry, Mr and Mrs P D Titcomb, Michael Doswell

SEMINGTON   ST9259   MAP 2

Lamb 🍴 ♀

The Strand; A361 Devizes—Trowbridge; BA14 6LL

Very good food in busy, ivy-covered dining pub, with wide range of wines and spirits, reliable service and an attractive garden

As we went to press we heard that a new licensee was about to take on the running of this popular dining pub, though we understood that the chef would be staying on. A series of corridors and attractively decorated separate rooms radiates from the serving counter, with antique settles, a woodburning stove and a log fire. Tables in the bar are kept on a first-come, first-serve basis and tend to be snapped up rather quickly (particularly on Saturday evening or Sunday lunchtime) but you can reserve a table in advance in the dining areas. The emphasis is very much on dining, but there is a small area if you just want a drink: Butcombe, Ringwood Best and a guest like Sharps Doom Bar on handpump, a good wine list with 15 by the glass, and an interesting range of armagnacs, cognacs and rums. There is a pleasant colourfully planted walled garden with seats and tables, and views towards the Bowood estate. Reports on the new regime, please.

🍴 **Good seasonal food includes baguettes, soup, smoked mackerel pâté with red onion marmalade, warm salad of scallops and crispy bacon, sausages of the day with mash and onion gravy, ham, egg and chips, cheesy pudding soufflé, pork belly, fillet of salmon with chive hollandaise, pie of the day, and puddings; the fresh fish is delivered daily.** *Starters/Snacks: £4.50 to £6.00. Main Courses: £8.50 to £14.95. Puddings: £5.50*

Free house ~ Real ale ~ Bar food (not Sun evening) ~ Restaurant ~ (01380) 870263 ~ Children welcome ~ Dogs allowed in bar ~ Open 12-3, 6.30-11; 12-3 Sun; closed Sun evening

Recommended by Dr and Mrs M E Wilson, Andrew Shore, Maria Williams, Paul Goldman, Adrian Johnson, David and Diane Young, Michael Doswell, Mark Flynn

SHERSTON   ST8585   MAP 2

Rattlebone ♀

Church Street (B4040 Malmesbury—Chipping Sodbury); SN16 0LR

Enjoyably pubby, atmospheric village local with good food

Since this was last a Main Entry in the *Guide*, this village pub has been nicely revamped and become more food-oriented, but it is still very much a place just to pop in for a drink and perhaps try one of their large selection of board games. The public bar is a bustling place with a mixture of locals and visitors, and you can find relative quiet elsewhere in one of several rambling rooms, with pews, settles and country-kitchen chairs around a mix of tables. Wells & Youngs Bitter and two guests like St Austell Tribute and Wells & Youngs Bombardier served on handpump under a light blanket pressure, 14 wines by the glass, elderflower pressé and home-made sloe gin. Outside are a skittle alley and two boules pitches, often in use by one of the many pub teams, and a boules festival takes place on the second Saturday of July. The two pretty gardens include a newly extended terrace; outdoor food events include barbecues and spit roasts.

🍴 **The bar menu includes lunchtime 'doorstep' sandwiches, ploughman's and salads, hot lunchtime and early evening snacks like creamy smoked salmon, fennel and parmesan lasagne, chicken curry, home-made beefburger or spicy italian meatballs; and changing short fixed-price and longer main menus feature starters like local wild boar salami, spinach and mushroom pancake, or camembert fondue, with main courses such as beef,** medallions of pork tenderloin, chargrilled steaks, seared yellow-fin tuna steak, and tomato and red onion risotto; puddings like lemon tart and rich chocolate and cappuccino parfait. *Starters/Snacks: £4.00 to £10.00. Main Courses: £6.00 to £18.00. Puddings: £4.00 to £6.00*

Youngs ~ Tenant Jason Read ~ Real ale ~ Bar food (12-2.30(3 Sun), 6-9.30; not Sun evening) ~ Restaurant ~ (01666) 840781 ~ Children welcome (in bar until 8pm) ~ Dogs allowed in bar ~ Open 12-3, 5-11; 12-midnight Sat; 12-11 Sun

Recommended by D Nightingale, Tom and Ruth Rees, Chris and Angela Buckell

STOURTON   ST7733 MAP 2

Spread Eagle 🛏

Church Lawn; follow Stourhead brown signs off B3092, N of junction with A303 just W of Mere; BA12 6QE

Comfortable country inn next to famous gardens; some food all day in summer; busy at lunchtimes, quieter later on

At the entrance to the magnificent Stourhead estate, this fine Georgian brick inn is a thoroughly civilised place to stay; a bonus is that overnight guests can wander freely around the famous National Trust gardens outside their normal opening times. The interior has an old-fashioned, rather civilised feel with antique panel-back settles, a mix of new and old solid tables and chairs, handsome fireplaces with good winter log fires, smoky old sporting prints, prints of Stourhead, and standard lamps or brass swan's-neck wall lamps; piped music. One room by the entrance has armchairs, a longcase clock and a corner china cupboard. Butcombe Bitter, Wessex Kilmington Best and a couple of guests such as Keystone Bedrock and Otter Amber on handpump, and several wines by the glass. There are benches in the courtyard behind.

🍴 Bar food includes lunchtime sandwiches, soup, ploughman's, fish pie, game casserole, and puddings like chocolate brownie and lemon posset; ploughman's, sandwiches and cake available all afternoon in summer; evening dishes with starters such as baked camembert with cranberry coulis or smoked salmon and home-cured gravadlax with sour cream and chives, and main courses like bass fillets on creamed leeks, free-range chicken suprême, rib-eye steak, and wild mushroom and asparagus pie. *Starters/Snacks: £4.95 to £7.95. Main Courses: £9.95 to £15.95. Puddings: £4.95 to £7.95*

Free house ~ Licensee Andrew Wilson ~ Real ale ~ Bar food (12-2.30(3 Sat, Sun), 7-9) ~ Restaurant (evening) ~ (01747) 840587 ~ Children welcome ~ Open 11-11; 12-10.30 Sun ~ Bedrooms: £80B/£110B

Recommended by Andrea Rampley, Edward Mirzoeff, Dr and Mrs J Temporal, Michael Doswell, Colin and Janet Roe, Laurence Milligan, Martin and Karen Wake, Sheila Topham

UPPER CHUTE   SU2953 MAP 2

Cross Keys ♀ 🍺 🛏

Tucked-away village N of Andover, best reached off A343 via Tangley, or off A342 in Weyhill via Clanville; SP11 9ER

Peacefully set, proper country pub, welcoming and relaxed, with enjoyable food and good beer and wines

In a lovely spot and run by welcoming staff, this country inn has far-ranging rural views over wooded hills from picnic-sets placed under flowering cherries on its south-facing terrace; recently a children's fort has been installed. Inside, it's open-plan and well run with a relaxed, unstuffy atmosphere, early 18th-c beams, some sofas, a cushioned pew built around the window, and a good log fire in the big hearth on the left; pubby tables and a couple of leather armchairs by the woodburning stove on the right, darts sensibly placed in an alcove, and shut the box, board games, TV for special events and piped music. Fullers London Pride, Discovery and a seasonal Hop Back Ale alongside a changing guest beer such as Goddards on handpump, and 11 good wines by the glass; service is helpful, and the charming staffordshire bull terriers are called Pepper, Pudding and Mouse. The bedrooms are very clean and peaceful, and if you're exploring the area on horseback you can use one of the two stables at the back of the pub.

🍴 **Deliberately unpretentious and very good food using seasonal ingredients includes filled baguettes, various pies such as seafood or steak in ale, rib-eye steak, lamb cutlets, whole mackerel, and vegetarian dishes such as aubergine casserole; puddings might be ginger steamed pudding or fruit trifle.** *Starters/Snacks: £3.95 to £6.00. Main Courses: £7.95 to £15.95. Puddings: £3.95*

Free house ~ Licensees George and Sonia Humphrey ~ Real ale ~ Bar food (12-2(2.30 Sat, Sun), 6-9(9.30 Fri, Sat)) ~ Restaurant ~ (01264) 730295 ~ Children allowed until 9pm ~ Dogs allowed in bar and bedrooms ~ Open 11-2.30, 5-11; 11am-midnight Sat; 12-11 Sun ~ Bedrooms: £60S/£70S

Recommended by Dave Braisted, Paul A Moore, Kelly Newton, Martin Hatcher, George Atkinson

WEST LAVINGTON
SU0052 MAP 2

Bridge Inn 🍴
A360 S of Devizes; Church Street; SN10 4LD

Friendly village pub with good, french-influenced food and a light, comfortable bar

At the back of this extremely welcoming and deservedly popular place, the raised lawn makes a pleasant place to spend a summer's afternoon, with several tables under a big tree, and there's a boules pitch too. Inside it's comfortable and quietly civilised, and the light, spacious bar mixes contemporary features such as spotlights in the ceiling with firmly traditional fixtures like the enormous brick inglenook that may be filled with big logs and candles; at the opposite end is a smaller modern fireplace, in an area set mostly for eating. Pictures on the cream-painted or exposed brick walls are for sale, as are local jams, and there are plenty of fresh flowers on the tables and bar; timbers and the occasional step divide the various areas. Wadworths IPA and two guests like Brakspears Oxford Gold or Plain Ales Innspiration on handpump, 11 wines by the glass and several malt whiskies; piped music in the evenings.

🍴 **Extremely good food with a french leaning includes lunchtime filled baguettes, ploughman's, starters like fish soup, warm smoked duck breast salad, charcuterie sharing platter, or escargots, and main courses such as cheese soufflé, seared bass fillet with hollandaise dill sauce, pheasant in season, provençale chicken, or courgette risotto with sun-dried tomatoes; Sunday roasts. Puddings like tarte tatin, brown sugar meringue or raspberry pavlova ice-cream in a brandy snap basket, or a miniatures plate with a small sample of each to try. It's best to book for meals: they can get packed.** *Starters/Snacks: £4.50 to £6.25. Main Courses: £8.45 to £18.95. Puddings: £5.20 to £6.20*

Enterprise ~ Lease Cyrille and Paula Portier ~ Real ale ~ Bar food ~ Restaurant ~ (01380) 813213 ~ Children welcome ~ Open 12-3, 6.30-11; 12-3 Sun; closed Sun evening and all day Mon; two weeks Feb

Recommended by Mr and Mrs A Curry, Michael Doswell, George Atkinson, Dr and Mrs A K Clarke, Mr and Mrs P R Thomas, Ken and Margaret Grinstead

WHITLEY
ST8866 MAP 2

Pear Tree 🍷 🛏
Off B3353 S of Corsham, at Atworth 1.5, Purlpit 1 signpost; or from A350 Chippenham—Melksham in Beanacre turn off on Westlands Lane at Whitley 1 signpost, then left and right at B3353; SN12 8QX

Attractive, upmarket old stone-built farmhouse, a good choice of drinks and comfortable bedrooms; plenty of seats in neat gardens

As inviting outside as inside, this lovely old former farmhouse has plenty of seating in the carefully maintained gardens, which are prettily lit at night to show features like the ruined pigsty. The charming front bar has quite a pubby feel, with cushioned window seats, some stripped shutters, a mix of dining chairs around good solid tables, a variety of country pictures, a little fireplace on the left, and a lovely old stripped stone one on the right. Candlelit at night, the popular big back restaurant (best to book) has dark wood cushioned dining chairs, quite a mix of tables, and a pitched ceiling at one end with a quirky farmyard theme – wrought-iron cockerels and white scythe sculpture. Fullers London Pride, Sharps Doom Bar and a guest like Shepherd Neame Spitfire on handpump, and 20 wines by the glass. A bright spacious garden room opens on to a terrace with good teak furniture and views over the gardens; boules. More reports on the newish licensee please.

🍴 **The bar food includes lunchtime filled baguettes and ploughmans, starters such as deep-fried cornish mussels or smoked chicken and avocado salad, and main courses like the popular black treacle and whisky-baked ham, free-range eggs and triple-cooked chips, beer-battered fish, or smoked haddock, saffron and pea risotto; the more elaborate restaurant menu (not cheap) includes roast loin of lamb, chargrilled rib-eye steak, fillet of wild black bream, and ricotta and spinach tortellini, all served with imaginative accompanying vegetables; puddings like orange panna cotta, warm raspberry torte, and crème caramel; british cheeseboard.** *Starters/Snacks: £4.95 to £7.95. Main Courses: £8.50 to £17.95. Puddings: £3.00 to £5.95*

Maypole Group ~ Lease Lisa Penny ~ Real ale ~ Bar food (12-2.30, 6.30-9.30(9 Sun)) ~ Restaurant ~ (01225) 709131 ~ Children welcome ~ Dogs allowed in bar and bedrooms ~ Open 11-11; 12-10.30 Sun ~ Bedrooms: £95B/£125B

Recommended by Joyce and Maurice Cottrell, Ian Malone, Ian and Jane Irving, Ray and Winifred Halliday, Richard and Mary Bailey, Helene Grygar, P Waterman, Michael Doswell, Mike and Mary Carter, Roger Wain-Heapy, Dr and Mrs M E Wilson

WINTERBOURNE BASSETT

SU1075 MAP 2

White Horse

Off A4361 S of Swindon; SN4 9QB

Neat dining pub, wide choice of enjoyable food, thoughtful choice of drinks; garden

'As enjoyable as ever' and 'One of our favourite food pubs' are comments from readers who regularly drop in for a meal or a drink at this well run dining pub. The licensees are helpful and friendly, and the neat big-windowed bar is attractively extended with traditional tables and chairs on the waxed wooden floors, old prints and paintings on the walls, plants dotted about and a little brick fireplace. There's a comfortable dining room and warm conservatory, too. Wadworths IPA, JCB and 6X on handpump, a dozen wines by the glass, and maybe winter mulled wine and summer Pimms by the jug; piped music, darts and board games. There are tables outside on a good-sized lawn and lovely hanging baskets.

🍴 **Making their own bread and ice-creams, they offer a wide choice of well liked bar food including lunchtime filled baguettes, ploughman's, soup, starters such as thai spiced beef patties or cajun mushrooms, main courses like braised beef casserole, chicken curry, baked salmon or almond and nut roast; daily specials; puddings such as sponge and custard, pancake suzette or fruit crumble; children's menu; Sunday roasts.** *Starters/Snacks: £4.25 to £6.25. Main Courses: £9.65 to £17.85. Puddings: £4.95 to £5.65*

Wadworths ~ Tenants Chris and Kathy Stone ~ Real ale ~ Bar food ~ Restaurant ~ (01793) 731257 ~ Children welcome ~ Open 11.30-3, 6-11; 12-3, 7-11 Sun

Recommended by Sheila and Robert Robinson, Jan and Roger Ferris, Eric and Mary Barrett, Tony Baldwin, Michael Doswell, Anne Morris, Tim and Rosemary Wells

---

Bedroom prices normally include full english breakfast, VAT and any inclusive service charge that we know of. Prices before the '/' are for single rooms, after for two people in a double or twin (B includes a private bath, S a private shower). If there is no '/', the prices are only for twin or double rooms (as far as we know there are no singles). If there is no B or S, as far as we know no rooms have private facilities.

LUCKY DIP

Besides the fully inspected pubs, you might like to try these Lucky Dips recommended to us and described by readers (if you do, please send us reports: feedback@goodguides.com).

ALDBOURNE [SU2675]

Crown SN8 2DU [The Square]: Prettily facing the green with pond and Early English church; good value straightforward food, real ales such as Shepherd Neame Spitfire, friendly staff, comfortable two-part beamed lounge with sofas by log fire in huge inglenook linking to public bar, old tables and bare boards, small nicely laid out dining room; tables under cocktail parasols in neat courtyard *(Dr and Mrs M E Wilson)*

AXFORD [SU2470]

☆ *Red Lion* SN8 2HA [off A4 E of Marlborough]: Pretty beamed and panelled pub with big inglenook, comfortable sofas, cask seats and other solid chairs; popular food from pub staples to pricier fish etc, friendly staff, real ales such as Cottage, Ramsbury and West Berkshire, good choice of wines by the glass, picture-window restaurant; valley views from nice terrace, children welcome, cl Sun evening *(Mr and Mrs A Curry, Ian Herdman, Bernard Stradling, LYM, Mrs Mary Woods)*

BADBURY [SU1980]

☆ *Bakers Arms* SN4 0EU [a mile from M4 junction 15, off A346 S]: Proper unassuming village local, a relaxing motorway escape, friendly licensees, good value pubby food (not Sun evening) inc speciality sandwiches, Arkells ales, generous coffee; warm fire, three small old-fashioned rooms, pool and darts area; TV, silenced games machine, piped music; no under-10s; picnic-sets in pretty tended garden with heated smokers' area *(JJW, CMW, Ellie Weld, Neil Kellett, Dr and Mrs A K Clarke, Bill and Sally Leckey, Edward Mirzoeff, LYM, Paul Humphreys)*

☆ *Plough* SN4 0EP [A346 (Marlborough Rd) just S of M4 junction 15]: Good food all day at attractive prices inc Sun roasts in light and airy dining room (children allowed), coffee from 10am, friendly helpful staff; well kept Arkells, decent wines, large rambling bar area (dogs welcome), daily papers; play area in sunny garden above, open all day *(Richard and Judy Winn, Pat Crabb, Nigel and Sue Foster, Mary Rayner, Keith and Sue Ward)*

BECKHAMPTON [SU0868]

☆ *Waggon & Horses* SN8 1QJ [A4 Marlborough—Calne]: Handsome old stone-and-thatch pub handy for Avebury, old-fashioned settles and comfortably cushioned wall benches in open-plan beamed bar with what some might call the patina of ages; dining area, sensible food (not Sun evening), well kept Wadworths and a guest, pool and pub games; children in restaurant, pleasant raised garden with good play area, open all day, bedrooms *(Sheila and Robert Robinson, LYM)*

BERWICK ST JAMES [SU0739]

☆ *Boot* SP3 4TN [High St (B3083)]: Welcoming flint and stone pub not far from Stonehenge,

with unfussy proper country cooking changing daily inc good light lunches; friendly efficient staff, well kept Wadworths, huge log fire in inglenook one end, sporting prints over small brick fireplace at other, small back dining room with collection of celebrity boots; children welcome, sheltered side lawn *(Gerry and Rosemary Dobson, Mark Davies, Howard and Margaret Buchanan, Bryan Reed, Jerry Brown, Terry and Nickie Williams, LYM, K H Frostick, Malcolm and Jane Levitt)*

BIDDESTONE [ST8673]

Biddestone Arms SN14 7DG [off A420 W of Chippenham; The Green]: Spacious village pub mostly set out for eating, straightforward food and some blackboard specials, Wadworths 6X and Wychwood Hobgoblin; games in compact public bar; pretty garden with well spaced tables, attractive village with lovely pond *(Michael Doswell, BB)*

BISHOPSTONE [SU2483]

☆ *Royal Oak* SN6 8PP [the one nr Swindon; Cue's Lane]: Old two-bar pub taken over by local organic farmers and sympathetically opened up in light and airy refurbishment; emphasis on seasonal organic supplies such as properly hung home-reared steaks, veg from the school allotment, game and local crayfish, even home-made elderflower cordial and pork scratchings, alongside well kept Arkells; beams, oak panelling and wood floors, good landlord; sizeable garden, bedrooms in outbuildings, beautiful village below Ridgeway and White Horse, open all day Sun *(Tony and Tracy Constance, Guy Taylor, Michael Snelgrove)*

BOX [ST8168]

Northey Arms SN13 8AE [A4, Bath side]: Stone-built dining pub with simple contemporary décor, chunky modern furniture on pale hardwood floor, food from tapas and satisfying bar lunches to more ambitious evening menu, Wadworths ales, decent wines by the glass; children welcome, garden tables *(Dr and Mrs A K Clarke)*

BRADFORD LEIGH [ST8362]

Plough BA15 2RW [B2109 N of Bradford]: Welcoming landlord, Wadworths 6X, enjoyable meals in extended dining area, cheery public bar with fire, darts and pool; children welcome, big garden with play area *(Dr and Mrs A K Clarke, Dr and Mrs M E Wilson, MRSM)*

BRADFORD-ON-AVON [ST8260]

Barge BA15 2EA [Frome Rd]: Reopened after refurbishment and return of a former popular landlord, real ales such as Fullers London Pride, stripped stone and flagstones, two dining areas with solid modern furniture; children welcome, attractive canalside tables *(Dr and Mrs M E Wilson)*

Bunch of Grapes BA15 1JY [Silver St]: Dim-lit wine-bar style décor, good value food inc bargain lunches, good real ales, range of wines and malt whiskies; cask seats and rugs on bare boards in small front room, bigger tables on composition floor of roomier main bar, more room upstairs; back terrace *(D Miles, BB, Susan and Nigel Wilson)*

☆ *Castle* BA15 1SJ [Mount Pleasant/Masons Lane]: Imposing 18th-c stone building well reworked in relaxed contemporary style, enjoyable up-to-date food (all day), well kept ales inc Three Castles (called Flatcappers here), good wine choice; friendly young staff, big log fire, largish low-ceilinged flagstoned bar with long farmhouse tables and fireside armchairs, sofas in cosy snug, lighter dining room; children welcome, nice garden, good bedrooms, open all day *(Dr and Mrs M E Wilson, Susan and Nigel Wilson, Michael Doswell, Dr and Mrs A K Clarke)*

Cross Guns BA15 2HB [Avoncliff, 2 miles W; OS Sheet 173 map ref 805600]: A festive bustle on busy summer days, friendly staff generally coping pretty well with swarms of people in floodlit partly concreted areas steeply terraced above the bridges, aqueducts and river; appealingly quaint at quieter times, with stripped-stone low-beamed bar, well kept ales such as Butcombe, Box Steam and Theakstons Old Peculier, lots of malt whiskies and country wines, 16th-c inglenook, upstairs river-view restaurant; children welcome, open all day *(Dr and Mrs M E Wilson, LYM, Jim and Frances Gowers, Roger Wain-Heapy)*

Dandy Lion BA15 1LL [Market St]: More continental café/bar than typical local, stripped-wood floor and panelling, steps to snug bare-boarded back room, restaurant upstairs; Wadworths and guest beer, several wines by the glass, friendly service (can be slow); they may try to keep your credit card while you eat; children away from bar area *(Dr and Mrs M E Wilson, John Robertson, Guy Vowles, LYM)*

BROAD HINTON [SU1176]

Bell SN4 9PF [A4361 Swindon—Devizes]: Enjoyable reasonably priced pubby food, well kept Greene King and Wadworths, decent wines by the glass, pleasant contemporary open-plan décor, friendly informal service; children welcome, pleasant garden *(Tony Baldwin, Mary Rayner)*

BROUGHTON GIFFORD [ST8764]

Bell on the Common SN12 8LX [The Common]: Imposing rose-draped stone-built local on village common, friendly long-serving licensees; lounge with Wadworths from handpumps on back wall, big coal fire, enjoyable homely food, dining room full of copper and country prints, rustic bar with local photographs, small pool room with darts; live irish music last Sun of the month; children welcome, dogs in public bar, charming flower-filled crazy-paved garden, boules, bowls club next door; open all day Fri-Sun *(MRSM, Dr and Mrs M E Wilson, Dr and Mrs A K Clarke)*

☆ *Fox* SN12 8PN [The Street]: Friendly chef/landlord doing good fresh food from lunchtime standbys to more inventive evening dishes; well kept Greene King, helpful service, fresh décor alongside traditional timbers, armchairs and sofa by entrance; big well kept garden behind *(Dr and Mrs M E Wilson, Catherine Pitt, Philip and Jan Medcalf)*

CASTLE COMBE [ST8379]

Salutation SN14 7LH [The Gibb; B4039 Acton Turville—Chippenham, nr Nettleton]: Roomy old pub with plenty of beamery, choice of seating areas inc comfortable lounge and locals' bar, huge handsome fireplace, prompt welcoming service, friendly staff; well kept ales such as Greene King IPA, Wickwar Cotswold Way and Wychwood Hobgoblin, good choice of wines; enjoyable food from big baguettes up, separate raftered thatched and timbered barn restaurant; no piped music; children welcome, pretty garden with pergola, open all day *(Nigel and Sue Foster, MRSM)*

CHAPMANSLADE [ST8247]

Three Horseshoes BA13 4AN [A3098 Westbury—Frome; High St]: 16th-c beamed country inn with well kept beer, enjoyable modestly priced food, good service, big fires at each end of neatly furnished carpeted bar, lots of brass and pewter; extra dining room up steps; no piped music; pleasant garden, fine views *(Alan Punchard)*

CHARLTON [ST9688]

☆ *Horse & Groom* SN16 9DL [B4040 towards Cricklade]: Smartly refurbished stone-built pub, appealing and relaxing, with flagstones and log fire in proper bar (dogs welcome), and interlinked dining areas with stylish understated décor; good reasonably priced fresh pub food as well as interesting modern dishes, polished friendly service, well kept Greene King ales, good choice of wines by the glass; tables out under trees, five good bedrooms *(Eric and Mary Barrett, Michael Doswell, John Monks, LYM)*

CHIRTON [SU0757]

Wiltshire Yeoman SN10 3QN [Andover Rd (A342)]: Current chef/landlord doing some imaginative cooking inc good fish and bargain two-course lunches without losing the local atmosphere; enthusiastic cheerful service, well kept Wadworths, Stowford Press cider, good value wines; pool in back bar area; cl Mon *(Alan and Audrey Moulds, Eric and Mary Barrett, Philip and Christine Kenny, Roger Edward-Jones, Mr and Mrs A Curry)*

CHITTERNE [ST9843]

Kings Head BA12 0LJ [B390 Heytesbury—Shrewton]: This appealing traditional pub, in a pretty village and handy for Salisbury Plain walks, was changing hands in early 2009 – news please *(BB)*

CHOLDERTON [SU2242]

Crown SP4 0DW [A338 Tidworth—Salisbury roundabout, just off A303]: Thatched low-beamed cottage with nicely informal eating areas in L-shaped bar; friendly staff, three real ales, good food, log fire, restaurant; terrace tables (Dr and Mrs M E Wilson, Alec and Susan Hamilton)

CHRISTIAN MALFORD [ST9679]

Mermaid SN15 4BE [B4069 Lyneham—Chippenham, 3.5 miles from M4 junction 17]: Long cheerful bar divided into areas, simple enjoyable food using local produce, well kept Wadworths 6X, decent wines by the glass, friendly service; garden tables, open all day (BB, James Bender)

CLYFFE PYPARD [SU0776]

Goddard Arms SN4 7PY: Cheery 16th-c local with log fire and raised dining area in split-level main bar, small sitting room with another fire and two old armchairs, down-to-earth chatty and welcoming licensees; Wadworths 6X and guest beers like Great Western, farm cider, good value basic food, artwork for sale, pool room with darts, cribbage etc; sports TV, no credit cards; picnic-sets in back courtyard, bedrooms, also Youth Hostel accommodation in former skittle alley; tiny pretty thatched village in lovely countryside; open all day wknds (Dave Braisted, BB, Pete Baker)

COMPTON BASSETT [SU0372]

White Horse SN11 8RG: Enjoyable food in bar and popular restaurant, cheerful attentive service, Wadworths and guest beers; children welcome (Alvin and Yvonne Andrews, Mr and Mrs Ian Campbell)

CORSHAM [ST8770]

☆ *Flemish Weaver* SN13 0EZ [High St]: Smart relaxed town pub in attractive 17th-c building, three main areas mostly set for good value food inc more elaborate evening choices, Bath Gem, Sharps Doom Bar and a guest, friendly staff; blue banquettes and matching chairs on slate floors, fresh flowers, board games; piped classics or jazz; children and dogs welcome, tables in back courtyard, cl Sun evening (Dr and Mrs A K Clarke, Michael Doswell, Dr and Mrs M E Wilson, LYM, John Robertson, BB, Paul A Moore, Mark O'Sullivan)

CORSLEY HEATH [ST8145]

Royal Oak BA12 7PR [A362 Frome—Warminster]: Proper pub, very popular lunchtime for good modestly priced pubby food, friendly landlady and attentive staff; well kept Wadworths and a guest beer, roomy beamed and panelled bar (no dogs), good fire, pleasant big back family extension with pool, restaurant; dogs welcome in small side bar, disabled facilities, attractive terrace and big garden, valley views, handy for Longleat (Richard Fendick, Terry Buckland, Alan Punchard)

CRICKLADE [SU1093]

Red Lion SN6 6DD [off A419 Swindon—Cirencester; High St]: 16th-c former coaching inn with lots of changing well kept ales, two farm ciders, good choice of malt whiskies, friendly landlord and helpful staff; pubby food (not Mon, Tues), log fire, interesting signs and bric-a-brac in large bar,

less cluttered front lounge, no music or mobile phones; good garden, bedrooms, open all day (E McCall, T McLean, D Irving, Pete Baker, Paul Boot)

DERRY HILL [ST9570]

☆ *Lansdowne Arms* SN11 9NS [A342 Chippenham—Calne]: Stately stone-built pub opp one of Bowood's grand gatehouses; roomy, airy and civilised, with good pub food (can take a while), Wadworths ales, good value wines by the glass, cheerful service, relaxed period flavour, hearty log fire; children welcome, fine views, neat side garden, good play area (David Crook, Dr and Mrs A K Clarke, Dr and Mrs M E Wilson, David and Sheila Pearcey, BB)

DEVIZES [SU0262]

Hourglass SN10 2RH [Horton Ave]: Opened 2007 under good landlord (ex Barge at Seend), with an emphasis on enjoyable enterprising food; well kept Marstons-related ales, good wine list, well trained staff, appealing separate bar area – cookies and chocolate here too (Dave Pritchard, Mr and Mrs A Curry)

DOWNTON [SU1821]

Kings Arms SP5 3PG [High St (A3080)]: Dating from the 14th c and well updated, with charming newish landlady, enjoyable food, Ringwood and guest ales, log fires; tables outside, open all day (Jennifer Banks)

EAST CHISENBURY [SU1352]

☆ *Red Lion* SN9 6AQ: Welcoming new licensees (both trained chefs) doing enterprising food (all home-made, even the bread and chocolates), children's helpings; good wine choice, bare boards and flagstones, mixed tables and chairs, large fireplace with woodburner, area with black leather sofa and armchairs, daily papers, dining room; soft piped music; dogs welcome, play area on lawn, open all day wknds, cl Mon (LYM, Alan and Audrey Moulds)

EAST KNOYLE [ST8830]

☆ *Seymour Arms* SP3 6AJ [The Street; just off A350 S of Warminster]: New licensees for attractive rambling pub, nice seating areas inc high-backed settle by log fire, Wadworths and a guest ale, decent wines by the glass; has had enjoyable pubby food inc more elaborate evening meals; children welcome, garden tables, bedrooms – reports on new regime please (LYM)

EASTERTON [SU0255]

Royal Oak SN10 4PE [B3098]: Attractive comfortably renovated 16th-c thatched pub, with low beams, flagstones, alcoves and soft lighting; two dining areas and separate simpler locals' bar, enjoyable traditional food, well kept Wadworths, good choice of wines by the glass, log fires; small front garden (anon)

FONTHILL GIFFORD [ST9231]

Beckford Arms SP3 6PX [off B3089 W at Fonthill Bishop]: This smartly informal 18th-c country inn beside a parkland estate closed suddenly in early 2009; we hope for its reopening – news, please (LYM)

FORD [ST8474]
White Hart SN14 8RP [off A420 Chippenham—Bristol]: Attractive 16th-c stone-built Marstons country inn, their ales and a guest such as Wadworths 6X, good food (especially puddings) all day; quietly friendly landlord, heavy black beams and good log fire in ancient fireplace; dogs welcome, attractive stream-side grounds, comfortable bedrooms (some in annex) *(Dr and Mrs A K Clarke, Phil and Jane Hodson, Mary Rayner, Michael Doswell, Andrew Parry, LYM)*

FOXHAM [ST9777]
Foxham Inn SN15 4NQ [NE of Chippenham]: Small country dining pub with appealingly simple traditional décor, enterprising food strong on local produce, their own smokehouse and daily fresh fish from Cornwall, home-baked bread; Bath Gem, Wadworths 6X and a guest beer, good choice of wines by the glass, good coffee; woodburner, compact more contemporary back restaurant; children and dogs welcome, terrace tables with pergola, extensive views from front, peaceful village; cl Mon *(Stephanie Pudsey)*

GREAT BEDWYN [SU2764]
Cross Keys SN8 3NU [High St]: Interesting food, Wadworths ales, decent wines, comfortable chairs and settles; garden with terrace, bedrooms *(Robert Watt)*

GREAT DURNFORD [SU1337]
☆ *Black Horse* SP4 6AY [follow Woodfords sign from A345 High Post traffic lights]: Cheery and homely, with some nice alcoves, one room with ship pictures, models and huge ensigns, another with a large inglenook woodburner, masses of bric-a-brac; well kept Fullers London Pride and Marstons ales, genial staff, food from baguettes and panini up, traditional pub games; piped blues and jazz, jokey notices, even talking lavatories; children and dogs welcome, big outdoor garden with play area and barbecues, decent bedrooms, cl Sun evening and Mon in winter *(Dr and Mrs M E Wilson, LYM, Alan Wright)*

GREAT WISHFORD [SU0735]
Royal Oak SP2 0PD [off A36 NW of Salisbury]: New management at this two-bar pub with big family dining area, enjoyable food, well kept Butcombe, Otter and Ringwood; beams, dark panelling, pastel walls, bare boards and log fires, step up to carpeted restaurant (cl Tues); piped music; dogs allowed, disabled access; pretty village *(Chris and Angela Buckell, LYM)*

HEDDINGTON [ST9966]
☆ *Ivy* SN11 0PL [off A3102 S of Calne]: Picturesque thatched 15th-c village local, good inglenook log fire in old-fashioned L-shaped bar, heavy low beams, timbered walls, assorted furnishings on parquet floor, brass and copper; Wadworths ales tapped from the cask, good plain fresh home-made food (not Sun-Weds evenings, may take a time if many locals in), back family eating room; sensibly placed darts, piano, dog and

cat; may be piped music; disabled access, front garden, open all day wknds *(LYM, Pete Baker, the Didler)*

HIGHWORTH [SU2092]
☆ *Saracens Head* SN6 7AG [High St]: Civilised pub/hotel with relaxed rambling bar, several real ales inc Arkells 2B and 3B tapped from casks, wide choice of reasonably priced blackboard food, good soft drinks' selection; comfortably cushioned pews in several interesting areas around great four-way central log fireplace, timbers and panelling, no mobile phones; quiet piped music; children in eating area, tables in smart partly covered courtyard with heaters, comfortable bedrooms, open all day wkdys *(LYM, Peter and Audrey Dowsett, Dr and Mrs M E Wilson)*

HINDON [ST9032]
Angel SP3 6DJ [B3089 Wilton—Mere]: Dining pub with new landlord, good staff, usual food, good choice of wines, Bass, Ringwood and Sharps Doom Bar; big log fire, flagstones and other coaching-inn survivals; children welcome, dogs allowed in bar, courtyard tables, seven comfortable bedrooms, good breakfast, open all day in summer *(Bruce and Sharon Eden, LYM)*

Lamb SP3 6DP [B3089 Wilton—Mere]: Newish management for this attractive old hotel; long roomy bar with log fire, two flagstoned lower sections with very long polished table, high-backed pews and settles, up steps a third, bigger area; well kept Wells & Youngs ales and a guest beer, good choice of wines by the glass and whiskies, enjoyable good value home-made bar food; children and dogs welcome, picnic-sets over the road, bedrooms, open all day *(Louise Gibbons, Bruce and Sharon Eden, Edward Mirzoeff, LYM, Mike Gorton)*

HODSON [SU1780]
Calley Arms SN4 0QG [not far from M4 junction 15, via Chiseldon; off B4005 S of Swindon]: Open-plan pub with simple choice of enjoyable generous fresh food, reasonable prices, well kept Wadworths, open fire in main area, woodburner in bare-boards part; piped music may obtrude; picnic-sets on sheltered back grass, pleasant walks *(Sheila and Robert Robinson, Nigel and Sue Foster, BB)*

HOLT [ST8561]
Toll Gate BA14 6PX [Ham Green; B3107 W of Melksham]: Appealing individual décor and furnishings and thriving atmosphere in comfortable bar, friendly service; five good interesting changing ales, farm cider, daily papers; log fire, another in more sedate high-raftered ex-chapel restaurant up steps; piped music; dogs welcome, no under-12s, back terrace, compact bedrooms, cl Sun evening, Mon *(Mr and Mrs A H Young, Dr and Mrs A K Clarke, Dr and Mrs M E Wilson, LYM)*

HONEYSTREET [SU1061]
Barge SN9 5PS [off A345 W of Pewsey]: Early 19th-c open-plan pub by Kennet & Avon Canal, not overmodernised, with original

carpentry and fittings still in downstairs lavatories; log fires, well kept ales such as Butcombe, Flowers and Wychwood, farm ciders, crop circle photographs in back room, friendly cats and dogs; pool; may be quiet piped music, live Sat; waterside picnic-sets, bedrooms, camping field – nice setting, good walks *(Dr and Mrs M E Wilson)*

KINGSDOWN [ST8067]

Swan SN13 8BP: Perched on a steep hillside with great views, welcoming landlord and well kept beer such as Sharps Doom Bar, food inc good steaks; three small rooms, flagstones and stripped stone; small side garden, bedrooms, cl Tues lunchtime, Mon *(Dr and Mrs M E Wilson)*

KINGTON LANGLEY [ST9277]

☆ *Hit or Miss* SN15 5NS [off A350 S; Days Lane]: Cottagey pub useful for M4; welcoming licensees, log fire in restaurant, cosily plush middle bar with low beams, cricket memorabilia, northern ales such as Hydes, Robinsons and Timothy Taylors Landlord, bar food, darts; children and dogs welcome, tables out in front *(Dr and Mrs A K Clarke, LYM, John and Gloria Isaacs)*

KINGTON ST MICHAEL [ST9077]

Jolly Huntsman SN14 6JB [handy for M4 junction 17]: Roomy stone-built pub with charming service, well kept Greene King and guests, popular home-made food from baguettes up inc Sun roasts; scrubbed tables, comfortable settees, good log fire, pleasant décor; seven well equipped bedrooms in separate block *(Deb Thomas, Mr and Mrs Graham Prevost, Mrs E Appleby)*

LACOCK [ST9268]

Bell SN15 2PJ [back rd, bottom of Bowden Hill]: Friendly and cheerful, wide food choice, changing ales such as Bath, Keystone and Palmers, decent wines by the glass, lots of malt whiskies; linked rooms off bar inc a pretty restaurant; children welcome, disabled access, well kept sizeable garden *(BB, Chris and Angela Buckell)*

Carpenters Arms SN15 2LB [Church St]: Good value home-made food, well kept Wadworths 6X and a guest beer, decent wines by the glass, warmly friendly staff; cottagey-style rambling bar with log fire and woodburner, country prints, back restaurant; children in eating area, bedrooms *(Mr and Mrs A Curry, Alan Wright, LYM)*

☆ *Red Lion* SN15 2LQ [High St]: NT-owned Georgian inn, sizeable bar with log fire, heavy tables and oriental rugs on flagstones, cosy snug with leather armchairs; Wadworths ales, good choice of bar food (all day wknds) including home-made casseroles and pies; piped music; children and dogs welcome, seats outside, bedrooms, open all day *(Keith and Sue Ward, Donna and Roger, LYM, Jim and Frances Gowers, Susan and Nigel Brookes)*

LANDFORD [SU2419]

☆ *Cuckoo* SP5 2DU [village signed down B3079 off A36, then right towards Redlynch]: Chatty thatched local on edge of New Forest;

four simple rooms (three with fires), several well kept ales tapped from the cask, farm cider, pasties and baguettes, traditional games; dogs and muddy walkers welcome, nice gardens front and back, play area, open all day wknds *(the Didler, Christopher Owen, LYM)*

LIDDINGTON [SU2081]

Village Inn SN4 0HE [handy for M4 junction 15, via A419 and B4192; Bell Lane]: Comfortable, warm and welcoming, good value food inc wkdy OAP bargains, linked bar areas and stripped stone and raftered back dining extension, well kept Arkells ales, log fire, conservatory; no under-8s; disabled facilities, terrace tables *(KC)*

LIMPLEY STOKE [ST7861]

☆ *Hop Pole* BA2 7FS [off A36 and B3108 S of Bath]: Largely panelled 16th-c stone-built pub, warmly welcoming, with well kept Butcombe; wide choice of fairly priced good food inc OAP specials Mon and Weds, prompt cheerful service, log fire, traditional games; TV; children in eating areas, disabled access with help, though not to nice enclosed garden behind *(LYM, Dr and Mrs M E Wilson, Chris and Angela Buckell, Barry Collett)*

LOWER WOODFORD [SU1235]

☆ *Wheatsheaf* SP4 6NQ [signed off A360 just N of Salisbury]: Well run and comfortable 18th-c Badger dining pub, large, warm and friendly, with fairly priced traditional food using local seasonal ingredients (some small helpings available), good service, well kept ales, good wines, log fire; piped music; children welcome, baby-changing, good disabled access, pleasant big tree-lined garden with play area, pretty setting *(Rudolph, J Stickland, Keith and Sue Ward, B and F A Hannam, LYM, David Barnes)*

MAIDEN BRADLEY [ST8038]

☆ *Somerset Arms* BA12 7HW [Church St]: Georgian pub elegantly refurbished under new licensees, bare boards and grey/green panelling, bar with log fire and traditional cast-iron tables, adjoining lounge with sofas, magazines and unusual bookshelf wallpaper; interesting seasonal food with spanish influences, Wadworths ales, good unusual wine choice, restaurant; great dane called Henry; Tues folk night, local market first Sat of the month; nice garden, five boutique-style bedrooms *(Lucia Golding, Edward Mirzoeff)*

MALMESBURY [ST9287]

Smoking Dog SN16 9AT [High St]: Twin-fronted local with two cosy flagstoned front bars, good choice of wines by the glass, well kept ales inc Brains, log fire, cheerful staff; children and dogs welcome, small quiet colourful garden up steep steps, bedrooms, open all day *(LYM, Les and Judith Haines)*

Whole Hog SN16 9AS [Market Cross]: Basic bare-boards pub with market cross view from bar stools at window counter; piggy theme, quick friendly service, real ales such as Archers, Cotleigh, Wadworths 6X and Wells & Youngs, enjoyable reasonably priced pub food using good ingredients, daily papers, peaceful dining room (not Sun evening); open all day *(Peter and Audrey Dowsett)*

MARDEN [SU0857]

☆ *Millstream* SN10 3RH [off A342]: Comfortably upmarket open-plan bar/restaurant with good food from home-baked bread to imaginative dishes using fresh local organic ingredients, well kept Wadworths and a great wine choice; beams, flagstones, log fires and woodburners, charming service; maps, guides and daily papers; children and well behaved dogs welcome, pleasant garden and neat terrace, cl Mon *(Mr and Mrs A H Young, Michael Doswell)*

MARKET LAVINGTON [SU0154]

Green Dragon SN10 4AG [High St]: Rambling early 17th-c pub with enjoyable food inc good deli platters, well kept Wadworths and guest beers, good value wines, efficient service; wheelchair access, garden with play area and aunt sally *(John and Lesley Bennett, Guy Vowles, LYM)*

MARLBOROUGH [SU1869]

Castle & Ball SN8 1LZ [High St]: Georgian coaching inn with nicely worn-in lounge bar, unusually wide choice of decent food inc good speciality pie, quieter and slightly simpler eating area, Greene King ales, good range of well listed wines by the glass, young enthusiastic staff; seats out under projecting colonnade, good value bedrooms *(Michael Sargent, Pete Coxon, Jennifer Banks)*

Lamb SN8 1NE [The Parade]: Well worn-in old-fashioned 17th-c coaching inn with further stable-block eating area; good value up-to-date food, well kept Wadworths, good choice of wines; pretty courtyard, six attractive bedrooms *(Tony Baldwin)*

MARSTON MEYSEY [SU1297]

Old Spotted Cow SN6 6LQ [off A419 Swindon—Cirencester]: Civilised country pub with enjoyable fresh food from compact menu, wide choice of real ales from proper bar, good value wines, welcoming staff; two open fires, light wood furniture and cosy sofas, rugs on bare boards and parquet, plants and cow pictures on stripped-stone walls; children and dogs welcome, spacious garden with play area, open all day wknds, cl Mon *(Richard and Sheila Fitton)*

MERE [ST8132]

Old Ship BA12 6JE [Castle St]: Recently reopened coaching inn famous for 17th-c carved fireplace with Charles I portrait, some refurbishment in cosy panelled hotel bar and more spacious bar across coach entry; well presented inexpensive food, carvery Sun lunch (under-12s eat free), OAP helpings; local Wessex ales, farm ciders, timbered and raftered upstairs restaurant; children and dogs welcome, big good value bedrooms, picturesque village *(Chris Buckle, LYM)*

Walnut Tree BA12 6BH [Shaftesbury Rd]: Good value home-made food all day inc Sun, Weds carvery *(Yana Pocklington, Patricia Owlett)*

MINETY [SU0390]

White Horse SN16 9QY [Station Rd (B4040)]: Friendly two-bar pub with good value food inc wkdy bargains, small helpings available, prompt service; several real ales such as Goffs, good range of wines by the glass, attractive décor, some stripped brick and stone; children welcome, heated balcony tables overlooking pond below, bedrooms *(Guy Vowles)*

MONKTON FARLEIGH [ST8065]

Kings Arms BA15 2QH [signed off A363 Bradford—Bath]: Imposing 17th-c building with sofas, open fire and dining tables in one bar, huge inglenook and more dining tables in L-shaped beamed lounge; changing real ales, good wine and whisky choice, good if not cheap food (all day wknds) using local supplies; piped music, unobtrusive big-screen TV; front partly flagstoned courtyard, well tended two-level back garden, lovely village *(Mr and Mrs A H Young, John and Gloria Isaacs, Dr and Mrs M E Wilson)*

NETHERAVON [SU1448]

Dog & Gun SP4 9RQ [Salisbury Rd]: Recently taken well in hand, with sensibly limited choice of enjoyable food, local beer, cane chairs around good solid tables in carpeted lounge, plus other improvements *(K H Frostick)*

NOMANSLAND [SU2517]

Lamb SP5 2BP [signed off B3078 and B3079]: Lovely New Forest village-green setting, unpretentious local feel, good value food inc lots of pasta and fish, popular Sun roasts; Gales HSB, Ringwood Fortyniner, Skinners and Timothy Taylors Landlord, short sensible wine list, fast friendly service; log fire, pool, small dining room; TV; children and dogs welcome, tables on terrace, green and garden behind, open all day *(Dr S J Shepherd, Ann and Colin Hunt, Peter Meister, BB)*

OAKSEY [ST9993]

☆ *Wheatsheaf* SN16 9TB [off A429 SW of Cirencester; Wheatsheaf Lane]: Imaginative food (not Sun evening) and comfortably modern back dining area alongside the relaxed unpretentious atmosphere of a proper village pub, with Bath Gem, Hook Norton and a guest beer, good choice of wines by the glass; log fires, stripped stone, low beams, darts and pool; piped music; children and dogs welcome, quiet front terrace and garden, open all day Sun, cl Mon *(Richard and Sheila Fitton, Paul A Moore, Dr and Mrs A K Clarke, M G Hart, Michael Doswell, J Crosby, LYM, KC)*

PEWSEY [SU1561]

French Horn SN9 5NT [A345 towards Marlborough; Pewsey Wharf]: Two-part back bar with steps down to pleasant rather smarter front dining area (children allowed here), flagstones and log fires; good choice of enjoyable home-made food if a bit pricey, well kept Wadworths, good choice of wines by the glass, cheery attentive australian staff even when busy; piped music; one or two picnic-sets out behind, walks by Kennet & Avon Canal below, cl Tues (BB, Bob and Laura Brock, M G Hart, Alan and Audrey Moulds)

POULSHOT [ST9760]

☆ **Raven** SN10 1RW [off A361]: Friendly pub across from village green, well kept Wadworths tapped from cask, wide range of bar food; two cosy black-beamed rooms traditionally furnished with sturdy tables and chairs and comfortable banquettes, obliging service; children and dogs welcome, cl Mon (Dr and Mrs A K Clarke, LYM, Myra Joyce)

RAMSBURY [SU2771]

☆ **Bell** SN8 2PE [off B4192 NW of Hungerford, or A4 W]: Neat dining pub with cheerful service, good mildly upmarket food (can take a while), well kept Ramsbury Gold (brewed for the pub) and a guest, Black Rat cider, several malt whiskies, good choice of wines by the glass; log fires in small beamed bar, sunny bay windows, restaurant; children and dogs welcome, disabled access, picnic-sets on raised lawn, cl Sun evening (Roger Wain-Heapy, Chris and Angela Buckell, Mary Rayner, LYM, Nina Randall, Kevin Thomas, Dr and Mrs J Temporal)

SALISBURY [SU1429]

☆ **New Inn** SP1 2PH [New St]: Good value generous food from sandwiches to grills, Badger ales, decent house wines and good cheerful service; inglenook log fire, massive beams and timbers, quiet cosy alcoves; children's area; walled garden with striking view of nearby cathedral spire, open all day summer wknds (Edward Mirzoeff, Alan and Eve Harding, LYM)

☆ **Old Mill** SP2 8EU [Town Path, West Harnham]: Charming 17th-c pub/hotel in tranquil setting, unpretentious beamed bars with prized window tables, good value food from sandwiches up, helpful staff, real ales, good wines and malt whiskies; attractive restaurant showing mill race; children welcome, small floodlit garden by duck-filled millpond, delightful stroll across water-meadows from cathedral (classic view of it from bridge beyond garden), bedrooms (Pete Coxon, LYM, Charles Gysin)

Rai d'Or SP1 2AS [Brown St]: 16th-c, with real ales such as Dark Star and Downton, authentic thai food, chatty landlord; relaxed and friendly pub atmosphere, reasonably priced wines; cl lunchtimes and Sun (Joan and Michel Hooper-Immins, Gavin Robinson)

Wyndham Arms SP1 3AS [Estcourt Rd]: Friendly modern corner local with full Hop Back beer range, country wines, simple bar food; small front room, longer main bar, board games; children welcome in front room, open all day wknds, cl lunchtime other days (Andy and Jill Kassube, N R White, the Didler)

SEMLEY [ST8926]

☆ **Benett Arms** SP7 9AS [off A350 N of Shaftesbury]: Doing well under newish owners, good reasonably priced food,

Butcombe and Ringwood Best, decent wines; log fire, bright cheery dining rooms; children and well behaved dogs allowed, pleasant tables outside (Steve Jackson, LYM, Graham Jones, Colin and Janet Roe, Robert Watt)

SHALBOURNE [SU3162]

Plough SN8 3QF [off A338]: Low-beamed village pub on the green, good food choice, Butcombe and Wadworths, friendly helpful landlady; neat tiled-floor bar with sofa and armchairs in snug; disabled access, small garden with play area (Bruce and Jo Shawyer, Michael and Jenny Back)

SHERSTON [ST8586]

Carpenters Arms SN16 0LS [Easton (B4040)]: Small interconnecting rooms with low beams and stripped-stone walls, log fire; well kept Bath and Otter ales, decent good value wines, reasonably priced food, fish specials (Thurs, Fri); settles and leather sofas, modern conservatory dining area with flowers on tables; disabled access, tables in pleasant garden with boules (Chris and Angela Buckell)

SOUTH WRAXALL [ST8364]

☆ **Long Arms** BA15 2SB [Upper South Wraxall, off B3109 N of Bradford-on-Avon]: Partly 17th-c small open-plan country pub with good value fresh food inc bargain daily roast, fish and homely puddings; Wadworths, good range of wines by the glass, friendly efficient staff, cheerful atmosphere; character dark décor with beams, flagstones and some stripped stone, log fire; pretty garden (Mark Flynn, Mr and Mrs P R Thomas, Michael Doswell, Dr and Mrs A K Clarke)

STAVERTON [ST8560]

☆ **Old Bear** BA14 6PB [B3105 Trowbridge—Bradford-on-Avon]: Friendly obliging staff, good value food inc bargain steak nights, well kept ales such as Bass, Sharps Doom Bar and Wadworths 6X; neatly kept long divided bar, nice mix of seats inc some high-backed settles, stone fireplaces (biggest in end dining area) (Norman and Sarah Keeping, D Miles, Mrs P Bishop, Barry Collett, BB)

SWINDON [SU1583]

Victoria SN1 3BD [Victoria Rd]: Small split-level character pub with slight hippie feel (appeals to all ages); three well kept ales inc Shepherd Neame Spitfire and Wadworths 6X, decent freshly made bargain food, art for sale, gig posters (frequent live music); low-volume piped rock (Jeremy King)

TILSHEAD [SU0348]

Rose & Crown SP3 4RZ [A360 Salisbury—Devizes]: Well cared for pub with welcoming service, well kept beer and decent food (Mr and Mrs Draper)

TOLLARD ROYAL [ST9317]

King John SP5 5PS [B3081 Shaftesbury—Sixpenny Handley]: Recently reopened after refurbishment, Ringwood and two changing guest beers, good value wines by the glass, careful food choice inc some interesting cooking and plenty of light dishes;

welcoming landlady, assorted tables on flagstones, end woodburner, black and white prints; dogs welcome, tables out in front, eight comfortable bedrooms, good walks *(Samantha McGahan, Colin and Janet Roe)*

UPAVON [SU1355]

Ship SN9 6EA [High St]: Good choice of enjoyable food, friendly helpful staff, welcoming locals, good range of real ales and whiskies; interesting nautical memorabilia, some gentle live music *(Martin Gough)*

UPTON LOVELL [ST9441]

Prince Leopold BA12 0JP: Prettily tucked-away modernised Victorian village inn, cheerful staff, good well priced food from interesting ciabattas up, Ringwood and John Smiths, good value wines; airy newish dining extension with river views from end tables; tables in small attractive garden beside the clear Wylye trout stream, comfortable quiet bedrooms *(Nigel Lander)*

UPTON SCUDAMORE [ST8647]

Angel BA12 0AG [off A350 N of Warminster]: Stylish contemporary dining pub with airy bustling upper part, a few steps down to sofas and armchairs by more traditionall lower dining area; well kept Butcombe, Wadworths 6X and a guest beer, good value house wines; artwork for sale, daily papers, pub games; piped music, TV; sheltered flagstoned back terrace with big barbecue, bedrooms in house across car park *(LYM, Ken and Sylvia Jones)*

WANBOROUGH [SU2083]

Cross Keys SN4 0AP [Burycroft, Lower Wanborough]: New management doing enjoyable food in bar and attractive conservatory restaurant, well kept Wadworths ales; pleasantly extended traditional village pub, individual décor inc lots of bric-a-brac *(Tim and Rosemary Wells)*

WILTON [SU2661]

Swan SN8 3SS [the village S of Great Bedwyn]: Light and airy 1930s pub under newish ownership, enjoyable food inc fresh fish (not Sun evening), good service, reasonably priced wines, two Ramsbury ales and a local guest, farm ciders; stripped-pine

tables, high-backed settles, pews and a woodburner; children and dogs welcome, disabled access, front garden with picnic-sets, picturesque village with windmill, open all day wknds *(James and Hilary Arnold-Baker, Chris Gooch, David Whiteley)*

WINGFIELD [ST8256]

☆ *Poplars* BA14 9LN [B3109 S of Bradford-on-Avon (Shop Lane)]: Attractive country pub with beams and log fires, very popular for good sensibly priced interesting food, especially with older people at lunchtime; Wadworths ales, friendly fast service even when busy, warm atmosphere, light and airy family dining extension; nice garden, own cricket pitch *(MRSM, Dr and Mrs M E Wilson, LYM)*

WINSLEY [ST7960]

☆ *Seven Stars* BA15 2LQ [off B3108 bypass W of Bradford-on-Avon (pub just over Wiltshire border)]: Roomy low-beamed linked areas refurbished as a dining pub, good food all home-made from the bread to the ice-cream, Sharps Doom Bar and Bath Ales Gem, cheerful young staff; cool light pastel décor, stripped stone, flagstones and carpet; piped music; picnic-sets out on neat terrace, an adjacent bowling green, attractive village *(Jane Fuller, BB, Dr and Mrs M E Wilson)*

WOOTTON RIVERS [SU1963]

☆ *Royal Oak* SN8 4NQ [off A346, A345 or B3087]: 16th-c beamed and thatched pub, good food from lunchtime sandwiches up, well kept ales, some tapped from the cask, inc Fullers London Pride and Wadworths 6X, good choice of wines by the glass, cheerful attentive service; comfortable L-shaped dining lounge with woodburner, timbered bar with small games area; children and dogs welcome, tables out in yard, pleasant village, bedrooms in adjoining house *(Mr and Mrs P D Titcomb, LYM, Ian Herdman, John and Hazel Sarkanen)*

ZEALS [ST7831]

Bell & Crown BA12 6NJ [A303]: Reworked as a pleasant dining pub, warm and friendly, with nicely served good value generous meals; big log fire in bar, restaurant *(Edward Mirzoeff)*

Worcestershire

The best pubs here have plenty of character and individuality – not even counting that great eccentric the Monkey House near Defford. The Three Kings at Hanley Castle, back in the *Guide* after a break, is a good strong antidote to the blandness that infects so many pubs these days. The Fleece at Bretforton is a must for anyone who relishes really interesting pub buildings, and the Nags Head in Malvern has a similar sort of appeal, as well as being a top-notch pub. Two happy favourites are the Farmers Arms at Birtsmorton and the Bell at Pensax. The Butchers Arms at Eldersfield, with its own cows grazing next door, is right on the crest of the trend for thoughtfully prepared food in a simple unspoilt environment. The charming Bell & Cross at Holy Cross, spot on in all respects, wins our award of Worcestershire Dining Pub of the Year. In the Lucky Dip section, we like the Admiral Rodney at Berrow Green, the Bear & Ragged Staff at Bransford, the Crown & Trumpet in Broadway, the Childswickham Inn, the Royal Oak at Leigh Sinton, the Bellmans Cross at Shatterford and the Brewers Arms at West Malvern. The county has ten or so good, even though very small-scale, brewers.

BAUGHTON

SO8742 MAP 4

Jockey ♀

4 miles from M50 junction 1; A38 northwards, then right on to A4104 Upton—Pershore; WR8 9DQ

Thoughtfully run dining pub with an appealing layout

Readers love the friendly home-from-home atmosphere at this steady dining pub – the cheery licensees here certainly extend a warm welcome. The open-plan layout is nicely divided by stripped brick half walls, some with open timbering to the ceiling, and there's a mix of good-sized tables, a few horse-racing pictures on butter-coloured walls and a cream Rayburn in one brick inglenook; piped music. Drinks include Courage Directors, Butcombe, Wye Valley and a changing guest from a brewer such as Wickwar, and they've farm cider and a rewarding choice of wines, with ten by the glass. There are picnic-sets out in front, with an array of flowers.

🍴 As well as lunchtime sandwiches, baguettes and baked potatoes (not Sundays), bar food includes starters such as whitebait or king prawns in garlic butter, main courses such as poached salmon fillet with oyster mushroom white wine sauce, steak and kidney pie, sirloin or fillet steak, and specials that could include mushroom stroganoff, poached salmon in tarragon sauce and venison steak in port and cranberry sauce. *Starters/Snacks: £4.25 to £7.95. Main Courses: £8.95 to £18.95. Puddings: £3.95 to £4.95*

Free house ~ Licensee Colin Clarke ~ Real ale ~ Bar food (12-2(2.30 Sun), 6(7 Sun)-9) ~ (01684) 592153 ~ Children welcome ~ Open 11.30-3, 6-11; 11.30-11 Sat; 12-10.30 Sun; 11.30-3, 6-11 Sat, 12-4 Sun in mid-winter ~ Bedrooms: £45B/£70B

Recommended by R T and J C Moggridge, Mike and Mary Carter, Chris Evans, Andy and Claire Barker

BEWDLEY   SO7875   MAP 4

Little Pack Horse

High Street; no nearby parking – best to park in main car park, cross A4117 Cleobury road,
and keep walking on down narrowing High Street; DY12 2DH

Friendly town pub full of interesting paraphernalia; decent food

There's no parking (see directions above) and not much pavement outside this old pub
which looks very much like the other houses in this tucked-away historic street.
Cheerfully chatty and warmed by a woodburning stove, the interior is cosily traditional
with reclaimed oak panelling and floorboards, and an eye-catching array of old
advertisements, photos and other memorabilia. Alongside Black Sheep, they keep a
couple of guests from brewers such as Brains and Highgate, a selection of bottled ciders,
perry and just under two dozen wines; piped music and TV. An area outside has heaters.

🍴 Some of the sensibly priced pubby dishes are very usefully offered in two sizes:
sandwiches, seafood tempura, nachos, tiger prawn, crab and avocado lime cocktail,
lasagne, vegetarian moussaka, pies, pork fillet stuffed with creamed leeks, apples and
sage and wrapped in bacon with apple brandy cream sauce, and steaks. *Starters/Snacks:*
£3.25 to £8.20. Main Courses: £7.45 to £18.00. Puddings: £3.85 to £5.50

Punch ~ Lease Mark Payne ~ Real ale ~ Bar food (12-2.15, 6-9.15(9.30 Fri); 12-4,
5.30-9.30(8.30 Sun) weekends) ~ Restaurant ~ (01299) 403762 ~ Children welcome away
from bar ~ Dogs allowed in bar ~ Blues last Sun of month ~ Open 12-3, 6-11; 12-midnight Sat;
12-10.30 Sun

Recommended by Alan and Eve Harding

BIRTSMORTON   SO7936   MAP 4

Farmers Arms 🍴 £

Birts Street, off B4208 W; WR13 6AP

Unspoilt, unrushed half-timbered village local with plenty of character

This lovely old half-timbered pubby place is quietly free of piped music or games
machines, but is home to the local cribbage and darts teams – you can also play shove-
ha'penny or dominoes. Chatty locals gather at the bar for Hook Norton Hooky and Old
Hooky, which are on handpump alongside a changing guest or two from brewers such as
Slaters and Timothy Taylor. The big flagstoned room on the right rambles away under very
low dark beams, with some standing timbers, a big inglenook and flowery-panelled
cushioned settles as well as spindleback chairs. A lower-beamed room on the left seems
even cosier, and in both, white walls are broken up by black timbering. You'll find seats
and swings out on the lovely big lawn with view over the Malvern Hills – the pub is
surrounded by plenty of walks.

🍴 Very inexpensive simple bar food typically includes sandwiches, soup, ploughman's,
cauliflower cheese, steak and kidney pie and burgers. *Starters/Snacks: £2.55 to £4.95.*
Main Courses: £4.65 to £7.55. Puddings: £3.10 to £3.45

Free house ~ Licensees Jill and Julie Moore ~ Real ale ~ Bar food ~ (01684) 833308 ~
Children welcome ~ Dogs welcome ~ Open 11-4, 6-midnight; 12-4, 7-midnight Sun

Recommended by Dave Braisted, the Didler, Mike and Mary Carter, Ian and Nita Cooper, R T and J C Moggridge,
Dr A J and Mrs Tompsett, Sue and Dave Harris

> Post Office address codings confusingly give the impression that some pubs are in
> Worcestershire, when they're really in Gloucestershire, Herefordshire, Shropshire,
> or Warwickshire (which is where we list them).

BREDON

SO9236 MAP 4

Fox & Hounds

4.5 miles from M5 junction 9; A438 to Northway, left at B4079, then in Bredon follow signpost to church and river on right; GL20 7LA

Appealingly old-fashioned 15th-c pub not far off the motorway

The open-plan carpeted bar at this pleasantly welcoming pub is a relaxing M5 break. A cottagey-looking timber and stone thatched building, it has low beams, stone pillars, stripped timbers and a central woodburning stove. Traditional furnishings take in upholstered settles, a variety of wheelback, tub and kitchen chairs around handsome mahogany and cast-iron-framed tables, dried grasses and flowers and elegant wall lamps. There's a smaller side bar. Friendly efficient staff serve Banks's Bitter and Greene King Old Speckled Hen along with a guest such as Butcombe on handpump, and eight wines by the glass; piped music. Some of the picnic-sets outside are sheltered under Perspex.

Ⅲ Decent bar food includes lunchtime sandwiches, salads and ploughman's, as well as chicken liver pâté, duck pancake, pork and leek sausages, red onion tart with goats cheese, smoked haddock on spring onion mash, battered cod, steak and kidney pudding, half a crispy duck with orange and Grand Marnier sauce, hog roast and steaks, and puddings such as plum and marzipan tart with Amaretto cream. *Starters/Snacks: £3.95 to £6.25. Main Courses: £9.95 to £18.95. Puddings: £4.50*

Enterprise ~ Lease Cilla and Christopher Lamb ~ Real ale ~ Bar food (12-2(2.30 Sun), 7-9(6.30-7.30 Sun)) ~ Restaurant ~ (01684) 772377 ~ Children welcome ~ Dogs allowed in bar ~ Open 12-3, 6.30-11(midnight Sat)

Recommended by GSB, Dennis and Doreen Haward, Richard and Maria Gillespie, Jo Rees, Gerry and Rosemary Dobson, Tom and Jill Jones, M Mossman

BRETFORTON

SP0943 MAP 4

Fleece

B4035 E of Evesham: turn S off this road into village; pub is in centre square by church; there's a sizeable car park at one side of the church; WR11 7JE

Marvellously unspoilt medieval pub owned by the National Trust

Best visited mid-week, this museum-like old farmhouse and its contents are pretty famous these days and can draw a weekend crowd. Before becoming a pub in 1848 the building was owned by the same family for nearly 500 years and many of the furnishings, such as the great oak dresser that holds a priceless 48-piece set of Stuart pewter, are heirlooms passed down generations of that family, now back in place. Its little dark rooms have massive beams, exposed timbers and marks scored on the worn and crazed flagstones to keep out demons. There are two fine grandfather clocks, ancient kitchen chairs, curved high-backed settles, a rocking chair and a rack of heavy pointed iron shafts, probably for spit roasting, in one of the huge inglenook fireplaces, and two more log fires. Plenty of oddities include a great cheese-press and set of cheese moulds, and a rare dough-proving table; a leaflet details the more bizarre items and photographs report the terrible fire that struck this place several years ago. Four or five real ales are from brewers such as Hook Norton Best, Cannon Royall, Enville and Purity, and the landlord has been known to brew his own Dog in a Fog and No.1. Also farm cider, local apple juices, german wheat beer and fruit wines, and ten wines by the glass; darts and various board games. As part of the Vale of Evesham Asparagus Festival they hold an asparagus auction at the end of May and host the village fête on August bank holiday Monday; there's sometimes morris dancing and the village silver band plays here regularly too. The lawn (with its fruit trees) around the beautifully restored thatched and timbered barn is a lovely place to sit, and there are more picnic-sets and a stone pump-trough in the front courtyard.

Ⅲ Bar food includes sandwiches, baked camembert with cranberry jelly, chicken liver and bacon pâté, sausages or faggots and mash, chicken curry, pork, cider and winter vegetable casserole, fish dish of the day, beefburger, cheesecake and chocolate torte; they may ask to take an imprint of your card if you run a tab. *Starters/Snacks: £3.75 to £6.50. Main Courses: £7.50 to £8.95. Puddings: £4.75 to £5.25*

Free house ~ Licensee Nigel Smith ~ Real ale ~ Bar food (12-2.30 (4 Sun), 6.30-9(8.30 Sun)) ~
(01386) 831173 ~ Children welcome ~ Morris dancing and folk session Thurs evening ~
Open 11(12 Sun)-11; 11-3, 6-11 Mon-Fri in winter ~ Bedrooms: /£85S

Recommended by Jean and Douglas Troup, Mr and Mrs W W Burke, Mike and Mary Carter

CLENT
SO9279   MAP 4

Fountain ♀

*Off A491 at Holy Cross/Clent exit roundabout, via Violet Lane, then turn right at T junction;
Adams Hill/Odnall Lane; DY9 9PU*

Restauranty pub often packed to overflowing

This hugely popular, upmarket dining pub (booking is advised) has a buoyant
atmosphere, efficient uniformed staff and possibly space for drinkers to stand at the
counter. The long carpeted dining bar (three knocked-together areas) has teak chairs and
pedestal tables, with some comfortably cushioned brocaded wall seats. There are nicely
framed local photographs on the ragged pinkish walls above a dark panelled dado, pretty
wall lights and candles on the tables (flowers in summer). Keen to please uniformed staff
are friendly and efficient. Three changing real ales might be from brewers such as
Brakspear, Marstons and Wychwood, and most of their 40 wines are served by the glass;
also a choice of speciality teas and good coffees, and freshly squeezed orange juice; alley
skittles. There are tables out on a deck.

🍽 **As well as a tremendous range of lunchtime butties (anything from chicken and garlic
mayonnaise to chips and cheese), the daily changing menu might include tomato soup,
battered tiger prawns with chilli dip, butternut and ginger bake, chicken breast on
cassoulet, braised lamb, and puddings such as chocolate bread and butter pudding;
Sunday roast** *Starters/Snacks: £5.25 to £6.95. Main Courses: £8.50 to £15.95. Puddings: £3.95
to £5.50*

Marstons ~ Lease Richard and Jacque Macey ~ Real ale ~ (01562) 883286 ~ Children welcome
till 7.30pm ~ Open 11-11; 12-8 Sun

*Recommended by Theo, Anne and Jane Gaskin, Dr and Mrs A K Clarke, Gill and Keith Croxton, Dave Braisted,
Lynda and Trevor Smith, Neil and Brenda Skidmore*

DEFFORD
SO9042   MAP 4

Monkey House

*A4104 towards Upton – immediately after passing Oak public house on right, there's a
small group of cottages, of which this is the last; WR8 9BW*

Astonishingly unspoilt time-warp survival with farm cider and a menagerie of animals

This adorable little black and white cider house, its thatch slung low and ponderous, has
been in the same family for some 150 years. Drinks are limited to Weston's Medium or
Special Dry cider tapped from barrels, poured by jug into pottery mugs (some locals have
their own) and then served from a hatch beside the door. In the summer you could find
yourself sharing the garden with the hens and cockerels that wander in from an adjacent
collection of caravans and sheds; there's also a pony called Mandy, and Marie and Jana
the rottweilers. A small spartan side outbuilding has a couple of plain tables, a settle and
an open fire. The pub's name is said to come from a story about a drunken customer, who
some years ago, fell into brambles and swore that he was attacked by monkeys. Please
note the limited opening times below.

🍽 **No food but you can bring your own.**

Free house ~ Licensee Graham Collins ~ No credit cards ~ (01386) 750234 ~ Open 11-2 Fri
(3 Sun), 6-10 Weds, Thurs and Sat; closed all day Mon, lunchtime on Tues, Weds, Thurs and Sat,
evening on Fri and Sun

Recommended by Pete Baker, the Didler

ELDERSFIELD   SO8131   MAP 4

Butchers Arms 🍴 🍺

Village signposted from B4211; Lime Street (coming from A417, go past the Eldersfield turn and take the next one), OS Sheet 150 map reference 815314; also signposted from B4208 N of Staunton; GL19 4NX

Booking required for good interesting cooking of prime ingredients in unspoilt country local's compact dining room

The young chef/landlord and his wife have rather brilliantly kept the interior of this pretty little cottage completely simple and unspoilt. With farm cider and well kept changing ales such as St Austell Tribute and Wye Valley Bitter, Dorothy Goodbody and Butty Bach tapped from the cask (and a short but well chosen choice of wines), the little locals bar has one or two high bar chairs, plain but individual wooden chairs and tables on bare oak boards, a big woodburner in quite a cavernous fireplace, black beams, cream paintwork and a traditional quoits board. Picnic-sets in the good-sized sheltered tree-shaded garden look out on pasture grazed by their own steers.

🍴 **The little dining room, also simple, has just three tables, and at lunchtime James Winter cooks only for those who have booked. Using first-class ingredients from named local farms, including rare-breed meats, line-caught fresh fish and all sorts of freshly gathered wild mushrooms (something of a speciality here), he keeps the choice short and seasonal, and changes it day by day. The results are full of flavour and interest. Starters might include slow-roast pig's cheek with crackling, scallops with chorizo and rocket, braised squid with fennel, chilli and couscous, roast pigeon breasts with parsnip purée and red cabbage, roast duck breast with lentils and bacon, and puddings such as orange marmalade pudding with custard and rhubarb and ginger sorbet.** *Starters/Snacks: £6.25 to £9.25. Main Courses: £14.50 to £19.00. Puddings: £4.50 to £7.50*

Free house ~ Licensees James and Elizabeth Winter ~ Real ale ~ Bar food (12-1, 7-8.45; not Tues lunchtime, Sun evening) ~ Restaurant ~ (01452) 840381 ~ Children over 10 welcome ~ Open 12-2.30, 7-12(12.30 Fri, Sat, 10.30 Sun); closed Mon; one week early Jan, one week end Sept

Recommended by John Holroyd, Dr A J and Mrs Tompsett, Catherine Myers

HANLEY CASTLE   SO8342   MAP 4

Three Kings 🍺 £

Church End, off B4211 N of Upton upon Severn; WR8 0BL

Timeless hospitable gem with five real ales and simple snacks

It's a cheerful welcome, rather than the housekeeping, that counts in the eyes of the characterful family that have run this genuinely unspoilt friendly country local since 1911. Readers have had a great time here so we've certainly no quibbles with their happy relaxed approach. A homely little tiled-floor tap room on the right is separated from the entrance corridor by the monumental built-in settle which faces its equally vast inglenook fireplace. A hatch here serves very well kept Butcombe Bitter, Hobsons and three guests on handpump from smaller breweries such as Beowulf, Scatter Rock and Tring, around 50 malt whiskies and farm cider. On the left, another room has darts, dominoes and cribbage. A separate entrance leads to the timbered lounge with another inglenook fireplace and a neatly blacked kitchen range, little leatherette armchairs and spindleback chairs around its tables, and another antique winged and high-backed settle. Bow windows in the three main rooms and old-fashioned wood-and-iron seats on the front terrace look across to the great cedar which shades the tiny green.

🍴 **Food is limited to sandwiches, toasties and ploughman's.**

Free house ~ Licensee Sue Roberts ~ Real ale ~ Bar food (12-2; not Sun and evenings) ~ No credit cards ~ (01684) 592686 ~ Children welcome ~ Dogs allowed in bar ~ Jam sessions Fri lunchtime, Sun evening and alternate Sat evenings ~ Open 12-3, 7-11

Recommended by Chris Evans, the Didler, Michael Beale, Pete Baker

HOLY CROSS
SO9278   MAP 4

Bell & Cross ★ ⓦ ♟

4 miles from M5 junction 4: A491 towards Stourbridge, then follow Clent signpost off on left; DY9 9QL

WORCESTERSHIRE DINING PUB OF THE YEAR

Super food, staff with a can-do attitude, delightful old interior and pretty garden

Everything at this charming place is geared to ensure that you have a most enjoyable visit. Successful as a dining pub, yet still extremely welcoming if you're just popping in for a drink, it's arranged in a classic unspoilt early 19th-c layout with five quaint little rooms and a kitchen opening off a central corridor with a black and white tiled floor. Rooms give a choice of carpet, bare boards, lino or nice old quarry tiles, a variety of moods from snug and chatty to bright and airy, and an individual décor in each – theatrical engravings on red walls here, nice sporting prints on pale green walls there, racing and gundog pictures above the black panelled dado in another room. Two of the rooms have small serving bars, with Kinver Edge, Enville, Wye Valley HPA and a guest such as Timothy Taylors Landlord on hand or electric pump, around 50 wines (with about a dozen by the glass) and a variety of coffees; daily papers, coal fires in most rooms, perhaps regulars playing cards in one of the two front rooms, and piped music. You get pleasant views from the garden terrace.

🍴 As well as lunchtime sandwiches, panini and ploughman's, delicious dishes from a **changing seasonal menu might include prosciutto with fig, mozzarella and toasted pine nut salad, pork rillette with apple chutney, smoked haddock with risotto of asparagus, sweet pea and saffron with dried tomato and chervil cream, grilled calves liver with smoked bacon and tomato and caper butter, fish and chips, steak pie, spaghetti with spicy meatballs, puddings such as lemon curd cheesecake with honeycomb crisp and gooey chocolate and Grand Marnier oranges with crushed meringue and toasted almonds.** *Starters/Snacks: £4.75 to £7.00. Main Courses: £7.75 to £15.75. Puddings: £5.00 to £5.75*

Enterprise ~ Lease Roger and Jo Narbett ~ Real ale ~ Bar food (12-2, 7-9; 12-7 Sat) ~ (01562) 730319 ~ Children welcome ~ Dogs allowed in bar ~ Open 12-3(3.30 Sat), 6-11; 12-10.30 Sun

Recommended by Pete Baker, Heather McQuillan, David and Doreen Beattie, Paul Boot, John and Hilary Penny, Susan and John Douglas, Clifford Blakemore, Dr D J and Mrs S C Walker, Mrs E Thomas, Peter Martin, Tom and Jill Jones, Dr Kevan Tucker, Joan E Hilditch, Dr and Mrs A K Clarke, Gordon and Margaret Ormondroyd

KEMPSEY
SO8548   MAP 4

Walter de Cantelupe ♟

3.7 miles from M5 junction 7: A44 towards Worcester, left on to A4440, then left on A38 at roundabout; Main Road; WR5 3NA

Useful roadside inn with interesting beers and decent food

Making a handy M5 break, this informal pub is comfortably relaxed with a pleasant mix of well worn furniture. The traditional carpeted bar has an inglenook fireplace, with Cannon Royall Kings Shilling, Timothy Taylors Landlord and a guest or two from brewers such as local Blue Bear on handpump alongside locally pressed apple juices, a farm cider in summer and wines from a local vineyard. Decorated in neutral colours, the dining area has various plush or yellow leather dining chairs, an old settle and candles and flowers on the tables; piped music in the evenings, TV for sports events, board games, cribbage, dominoes and table skittles. There's a pretty suntrap walled garden at the back.

🍴 Bar food, which can be good, might include **leek and potato soup, chicken liver pâté, devilled mushrooms, steak and ale pie, sausages and mash, pork tenderloin with dijon mustard, roast duck breast with orange and Cointreau sauce, and puddings such as hot banana and toffee pancake with crème fraîche and steamed jam sponge pudding; Sunday roast and maybe Sunday evening tapas.** *Starters/Snacks: £3.75 to £6.50. Main Courses: £7.50 to £13.50. Puddings: £3.75 to £5.00*

Free house ~ Licensee Martin Lloyd Morris ~ Real ale ~ Bar food (12-2(2.30 Sat,
7.30 (3 in winter), Sun), 6-9(10 Fri, Sat)) ~ (01905) 820572 ~ Children in dining area until
8.15pm ~ Dogs allowed in bar ~ Open 12-2, 6-11; 11-3, 5.30-11 Sat; 12-10.30 Sun; 12-3,
6-10.30 Sun in winter; closed Mon (except bank hols) ~ Bedrooms: £45S(£50B)/£65S(£80B)

Recommended by Richard and Judy Winn, Phil and Jane Hodson, Peter and Jean Hoare, Comus and Sarah Elliott,
Brian and Janet Ainscough, Andy and Jill Kassube, Ian and Nita Cooper, R T and J C Moggridge, Mike and
Mary Carter

KIDDERMINSTER   SO8376   MAP 4
King & Castle 🍺 £
Railway Station, Comberton Hill; DY10 1QX

**Railway refreshment room within earshot of steam locos, and with one of the cheapest
pints around**

This neatly re-created Edwardian refreshment room, owned and run by the Severn Valley
Railway, opens on to the station platform, so you can take your drink outside and while
away time watching steam trains shunt in and out and passionate enthusiasts as they
lovingly go about their work. Inside, the atmosphere is lively and sometimes noisily
good-humoured, with a good mix of customers. Furnishings are solid and in character,
and there's the railway memorabilia and photographs that you'd expect. Bathams,
Hobsons Mile, Wyre Piddle Royal Piddle (just £1.80 a pint) are well kept alongside a
changing guest or two from brewers such as Cotswold Spring on handpump, and they've
several malt whiskies. The cheerful landlady and friendly staff cope well with the bank
holiday and railway gala day crowds, though you'll be lucky to find a seat then. You can
use a Rover ticket to shuttle between here and the Railwaymans Arms in Bridgnorth (see
Shropshire Lucky Dips) and there's a little museum just a few metres away.

🍽 **You order the reasonably priced straightforward food in the new adjacent dining room
and you can either eat it there or in the pub: toasted sandwiches, soup, ploughman's, a
proper breakfast, hamburger and chips, vegetable or chicken kiev, cottage pie, chicken
tikka masala and battered cod; they also do children's meals, and sometimes Sunday
lunch.** *Starters/Snacks: £2.25 to £2.95. Main Courses: £4.25 to £5.95. Puddings: £2.25 to £2.95*

Free house ~ Licensee Rosemary Hyde ~ Real ale ~ Bar food (9-3; not weekends) ~
No credit cards ~ (01562) 747505 ~ Children welcome if seated ~ Dogs welcome ~ Open 9-11;
9-10.30 Sun

Recommended by Colin Moore, Andrew Bosi, R T and J C Moggridge

KNIGHTWICK   SO7355   MAP 4
Talbot 🍷 🍺 🛏
Knightsford Bridge; B4197 just off A44 Worcester—Bromyard; WR6 5PH

Interesting old coaching inn with good beer from its own brewery and riverside garden

The heavily beamed and extended traditional lounge bar at this rambling 15th-c country
hotel can be lively with locals warming up by the good log fire and drinking the This,
That, T'other and the seasonal ale that are brewed in their own Teme Valley microbrewery
using locally grown hops. These are served alongside Hobsons Bitter, over two dozen
wines by the glass and a number of malt whiskies. A variety of traditional seats runs from
small carved or leatherette armchairs to the winged settles by the windows, and a vast
stove squats in the big central stone hearth. The bar opens on to a terrace and arbour
with summer roses and clematis. The well furnished back public bar has pool on a raised
side area, a games machine and juke box; cribbage. In contrast, the dining room is a
sedate place for a quiet (if not cheap) meal. Across the lane, a lovely lawn has tables by
the River Teme (they serve out here too), or you can sit out in front on old-fashioned
seats. A farmers' market takes place here on the second Sunday in the month; dogs may
be allowed to stay in the bedrooms by prior arrangement.

🍴 Bar food (not cheap) might include ploughman's, moules marinière, ham hock terrine and chutney, chicken caesar salad, rabbit casserole with ginger and cider, roast butternut squash and turnip risotto, chicken and leek pie, fish and chips, sirloin steak, and puddings such as treacle tart and custard. There is a more elaborate restaurant menu. *Starters/Snacks: £6.50 to £9.50. Main Courses: £10.00 to £14.00. Puddings: £8.00*

Own brew ~ Licensee Annie Clift ~ Real ale ~ Bar food (12-2, 6.30(7 Sun)-9) ~ Restaurant ~ (01886) 821235 ~ Children welcome ~ Dogs allowed in bar ~ Open 10-11; 12-10 Sun ~ Bedrooms: £55S/£90B

Recommended by John Holroyd, Colin and Peggy Wilshire, David Dyson, Simon Rodway, Ann and Colin Hunt

MALVERN

S07845   MAP 4

Nags Head 🍺

Bottom end of Bank Street, steep turn down off A449; WR14 2JG

Warmly welcoming with a remarkable range of real ales, appealing layout and décor

If you feel confused by the astonishing range of 16 beers at this terrifically enjoyable little pub, they will happily help you with a taster. House beers are Banks's, Bathams, St Georges Charger, Dragon Blood, Sharps Doom Bar and Woods Shropshire Lad and their nine changing guests (last year they got through over 1,000) from brewers spread far and wide. They also keep a fine range of malt whiskies, belgian beers, Barbourne farm cider and decent wines by the glass. The superb range of well kept beer and tasty bar food attracts a good mix of customers, including plenty of locals, and readers love the splendid individuality and easy-going chatty mood here. A series of snug individually decorated rooms, with one or two steps between, give plenty of options on where to sit. Each is characterfully filled with all sorts of chairs including leather armchairs, pews sometimes arranged as booths, a mix of tables with sturdy ones stained different colours, bare boards here, flagstones there, carpet elsewhere, and plenty of interesting pictures and homely touches such as house plants, shelves of well thumbed books and broadsheet newspapers and there's a coal fire opposite the central servery; shove-ha'penny, cribbage and dominoes. Outside are picnic-sets and rustic tables and benches on the front terrace (with heaters and umbrellas) and in the garden.

🍴 Tasty lunchtime bar food includes good sandwiches, ploughman's, soup, ham, egg and chips and fish and chips. In the evenings meals are served in the barn extension dining room only. *Starters/Snacks: £4.50 to £8.70. Main Courses: £3.50 to £8.70. Puddings: £4.00*

Free house ~ Licensee Clare Willets ~ Real ale ~ Bar food (12-2, 6.30-8.30) ~ Restaurant ~ (01684) 574373 ~ Children welcome ~ Dogs allowed in bar ~ Open 11-11.15(11.30 Fri, Sat); 12-11 Sun

Recommended by Michael Beale, C Galloway, Beryl and David Sowter, Dr and Mrs Jackson, Chris Evans, Mike and Mary Carter, Nigel and Sue Foster, Chris Glasson, Steve Whalley, Mrs B Barker, Arthur S Maxted, Chris Flynn, Wendy Jones, Giles and Annie Francis, Ray and Winifred Halliday

OMBERSLEY

S08463   MAP 4

Kings Arms

Main Road (A4133); WR9 0EW

Inviting Tudor building with tasty food and attractive courtyard

Said to date from about the 1400s, the charming aged interior at this rambling black and white timbered inn is cosy with various wood-floored nooks and crannies, three splendid fireplaces with good log fires, fresh flowers throughout and lots of rustic bric-a-brac. King Charles is said to have stopped here after fleeing the Battle of Worcester in 1651 and one room has his coat of arms moulded into its decorated plaster ceiling as a trophy of the visit. Marstons Best and a couple of guests from brewers such as Jennings and Titanic are on handpump and they've darts and board games. A tree-sheltered courtyard has tables under cocktail parasols, and colourful hanging baskets and tubs in summer, and there's another terrace.

🍴 As well as lunchtime sandwiches, fairly priced food might include antipasti, crayfish and avocado tian, mussels with tomato, garlic and basil sauce, beef madras, mustard and beer-battered fish, sausage and red wine jus, confit duck leg with red current jus, seared tuna salad and well hung rib-eye steak. *Starters/Snacks: £3.95 to £4.95. Main Courses: £6.95 to £16.95. Puddings: £4.95 to £5.95*

Banks's (Marstons) ~ Lease Caroline Cassell ~ Real ale ~ Bar food (12-2.30(3 Sun), 6-9.30; not Sun evening) ~ (01905) 620142 ~ Children welcome ~ Dogs welcome ~ Open 12-11.30(midnight Fri, Sat, 10.30 Sun)

Recommended by Paul and Sue Merrick, Robert W Buckle, Arthur S Maxted

PENSAX   SO7368   MAP 4

Bell 🍺 £

B4202 Abberley—Clows Top, SE of the Snead Common part of the village; WR6 6AE

Admirably welcoming all-rounder, good fire and reasonably priced tasty food

Enjoyably down-to-earth, this mock-Tudor place has a proper country pub atmosphere and extends a genuinely friendly welcome. Beer is an important feature here with the landlord turning over a good range of (often local) guests. Alongside Hobsons bitter, they might be from brewers such as Cannon Royall, Timothy Taylors, Woods and Wye Valley. He also keeps three local ciders, a local perry and organic fruit juices and hosts a beer festival over the last weekend in June. The L-shaped main bar has a restrained traditional décor with hanging hops, long cushioned pews on its bare boards, good solid pub tables and a woodburning stove. Beyond a small area on the left, with a couple more tables, is a more airy dining room, with french windows opening on to a wooden deck. Picnic-sets in the back garden look out over rolling fields and copses to the Wyre Forest.

🍴 Besides sandwiches, a short choice of good value tasty lunchtime weekday specials might include game or steak and ale pie, vegetable stir fry, sausage and mash and pasta bake, with hearty enjoyable evening specials such as steaks, faggots and pork chop with black pudding; Sunday roast and children's menu. *Starters/Snacks: £4.95 to £5.50. Main Courses: £8.50 to £14.95. Puddings: £2.50 to £3.95*

Free house ~ Licensees John and Trudy Greaves ~ Real ale ~ Bar food (12-2(3 Sun), 7(6 Sat)-9; not Sun evening) ~ (01299) 896677 ~ Children welcome away from the bar ~ Dogs allowed in bar ~ Open 12-2.30, 5-11; 12-10.30 Sun; closed Mon lunchtime except bank hols

Recommended by Ian and Helen Stafford, Dr A J and Mrs Tompsett, M G Hart, Dave Braisted, Lynda and Trevor Smith, Dennis and Gill Keen

LUCKY DIP

Besides the fully inspected pubs, you might like to try these Lucky Dips recommended to us and described by readers (if you do, please send us reports: feedback@goodguides.com).

ALVECHURCH [SP0272]
Red Lion B48 7LG [in village, handy for M42 junction 2]: Beamed Vintage Inn with side snugs that nicely conceal its size, big log fires, soft lighting, wide choice of enjoyable food all day inc bargain lunch deals, good service, good choice of wines by the glass and hot drinks, ales such as Bass and Marstons Pedigree, special summer soft drinks; quiet piped music; back garden, open all day *(Frank Blanchard)*
Weighbridge B48 7SQ [Scarfield Wharf]: Converted house by Worcester & Birmingham Canal marina, several neat linked rooms, well kept ales such as Blue Bear, Weatheroak and Windsor Castle, bargain unpretentious food with home-

grown veg; tables outside *(Dave Braisted)*
ASHTON UNDER HILL [SO9938]
Star WR11 7SN [Elmley Rd]: Small comfortably carpeted pub in quiet village below Bredon Hill, decent quickly served pubby food from fresh baguettes up, real ales inc Greene King IPA, friendly staff; good garden *(Pat Crabb, Alain and Rose Foote, Martin and Pauline Jennings)*
BARNARDS GREEN [SO7945]
Blue Bell WR14 3QP [junction B4211 to Rhydd Green with B4208 to Malvern Show Ground]: Comfortable panelled dining pub in pleasant setting, wide choice of reasonably priced standard food inc bargains, Marstons-related ales; disabled facilities, nice garden *(LYM, Chris Evans)*

BELBROUGHTON [SO9277]

Olde Horse Shoe DY9 9ST [High St]: Clean black and white beamed interior, smallish slate-floor bar with open fire, wide choice of good fresh food inc reasonably priced set lunches in separate restaurant, friendly service, real ales, good value wines; big garden, bedrooms *(Ian Jones, Colin Moore)*

☆ *Queens* DY9 0DU [Queens Hill (B4188 E of Kidderminster)]: 18th-c pub by Belne Brook, several linked areas with nice mix of comfortable seating, 19th-c oak and other tables in varying sizes, popular food inc interesting puddings, Burton Bridge, Marstons Pedigree and a guest, good choice of wines by the glass, friendly efficient staff, fresh flowers; children welcome, picnic-sets on small roadside terrace, pleasant village *(Clifford Blakemore)*

BERROW [SO7835]

Duke of York WR13 6JQ [junction A438/ B4208]: Friendly country pub with two linked rooms, 15th-c beams, nooks and crannies, good log fire, reasonably priced pub food, real ales and farm cider, dominoes, cribbage, back restaurant; piped music; children welcome, picnic-sets in big back garden, handy for Malvern Hills *(Chris Evans, BB)*

BERROW GREEN [SO7458]

☆ *Admiral Rodney* WR6 6PL [B4197, off A44 W of Worcester]: Light and roomy high-beamed dining pub, big stripped kitchen tables and two woodburners, Wye Valley and two guest ales, good coffee and choice of wines by the glass, enjoyable food inc good value OAP lunches, charming end restaurant in rebuilt barn; well behaved children and dogs welcome, disabled facilities, tables outside with pretty view and heated covered terrace, good walks, three good bedrooms (more planned), cl Mon lunchtime, open all day wknds *(Robert Roxburgh, Denys Gueroult, Antony Townsend, Katie Carter, Noel Grundy, LYM)*

BEWDLEY [SO7875]

Mug House DY12 2EE [Severn Side N]: Pleasantly renovated 18th-c pub in charming spot by River Severn, friendly helpful service, enjoyable traditional food, good local ales inc Wye Valley, log fire, restaurant; disabled access, terrace tables, bedrooms, open all day *(Henry Pursehouse-Tranter)*

BIRLINGHAM [SO9343]

Swan WR10 3AQ [off A4104 and B4080 S of Pershore; Church St]: Thatched and timbered country pub in quiet village backwater, good reasonably priced straightforward food (great faggots), friendly efficient service, well kept and interesting quickly changing ales, friendly well fed dog; nice garden (and snowdrops in village churchyard well worth seeing in season) *(Caroline and Michael Abbey, Jo Rees, Phyllis McCombie, Chris Evans)*

BRANSFORD [SO8052]

☆ *Bear & Ragged Staff* WR6 5JH [off A4103 SW of Worcester; Station Rd]: Popular dining pub with good choice of bar and restaurant food, friendly licensees and staff, several wines by the glass, lots of malt whiskies, well kept Fullers London Pride, open fire, country views from relaxed linked rooms, exemplary lavatories; piped music; children welcome, good disabled access and facilities, pleasant secluded garden *(Mike and Mary Carter, LYM, Chris Evans, Ray and Winifred Halliday, John Saville, Jeff and Wendy Williams)*

BROADWAY [SP0937]

☆ *Crown & Trumpet* WR12 7AE [Church St]: Small 17th-c golden-stone beamed local just behind green, friendly welcoming staff, changing ales such as Flowers, Stroud and Timothy Taylors, Weston's cider, decent home-made food from baguettes and panini up, even own pork scratchings, log fires, traditional games; may try to keep your credit card while you eat, piped music, live music on Sat, games machines; children welcome, front terrace, bedrooms, open all day wknds and summer *(Robert Ager, Bruce Braithwaite, Tracey and Stephen Groves, Guy Vowles, Ted George, LYM, Michael Dandy)*

BROMSGROVE [SO9570]

Golden Cross B61 8HH [High St]: Wetherspoons, their usual well priced food all day from 9am, good beer choice; pay and display behind *(Dave Braisted, Tony and Wendy Hobden)*

Guild B61 0BA [Birmingham Rd]: Large well managed Brewers Fayre, very child-friendly *(Peter and Eleanor Kenyon)*

CALLOW HILL [SP0164]

Brook Inn B97 5UD [Elcocks Brook, off B4504]: Rambling country inn, well kept Marstons-related ales, quite adventurous food choice, welcoming fire, occasional live music; tables outside *(Dave Braisted)*

CASTLEMORTON [SO7838]

Plume of Feathers WR13 6JB [B4208]: Small friendly 16th-c country local with new licensees, well kept Greene King and guests, heavy black beams, big log fire snugged in by built-in settles, side room with piano (Weds night music), generous home-made bargain food (all day wknds, not Mon), neat dining room; children and dogs welcome, disabled access, picnic-sets out at front, play area on side lawn, good views, open all day *(Dr and Mrs Jackson, Chris Evans, BB)*

CHADDESLEY CORBETT [SO8973]

Talbot DY10 4SA [off A448 Bromsgrove— Kidderminster]: Comfortably refurbished and neatly kept late medieval timbered pub in quiet village street, friendly staff, changing ales, enjoyable generous food; comfortable outside area, attractive village and church *(Chris Evans)*

CHARLTON [SP0145]

Gardeners Arms WR10 3LJ [the one near Pershore; Strand]: Friendly basic local on green of pretty thatched village, enjoyable standard food inc lunchtime bargains (not Sun, Mon) especially for OAPs, helpful service, well kept Marstons Pedigree, Tetleys and Wadworths 6X, limited wines, roomy dining area inc raised parlour-like part, inglenook woodburner, plain public bar with darts and pool room; children welcome, tables outside (John Hancox)

CHILDSWICKHAM [SP0738]

☆ **Childswickham Inn** WR12 7HP [off A44 NW of Broadway]: Good restauranty dining pub with big rugs on boards or terracotta tiles, contemporary artwork on part timbered walls, woodburner, good food from pubby things to more pricey brasserie food, friendly attentive staff, locals' lounge bar with leather sofas and armchairs, good choice of wines, may have Hook Norton and Greene King ales; piped music; children and dogs welcome, disabled facilities, good-sized garden with decked area, barbecue, cl Sun evening, Mon (Chris Glasson, Michael Dandy, Dr and Mrs A K Clarke, Alan and Eve Harding, Dr A J and Mrs Tompsett, LYM)

CLEEVE PRIOR [SP0849]

Kings Arms WR11 8LQ [Bidford Rd (B4085)]: Tucked-away 16th-c beamed village local, well run and comfortable, with good local seasonal food at reasonable prices, friendly helpful staff, well kept Wadworths 6X and a guest beer, family dining room; children welcome, tables outside (Joanne Robinson)

CROPTHORNE [SO9944]

New Inn WR10 3NE [Main Rd (B4084 former A44 Evesham—Pershore)]: Comfortable village pub with good home-made food (all day wknds) using local produce, friendly service, well kept ales such as Adnams and Black Sheep; piped music; children welcome, large garden, open all day wknds (Amanda Smith, Norman Lewis, Matt)

CROWLE [SO9256]

Old Chequers WR7 4AA [Crowle Green, not far from M5 junction 6]: Civilised dining pub mixing traditional and contemporary decor; oak beams and log fires, leather sofas, modern tables and chairs in bar and restaurant, friendly prompt service, enjoyable home-made food (not Sun evening) inc fresh fish and bargain two-course lunches, baby grand, occasional live jazz on Sun; children welcome, disabled access, picnic-sets in garden behind, open all day (LYM, Mike and Mary Carter, Pat and Tony Martin, P G Wooler)

CUTNALL GREEN [SO8868]

Chequers WR9 0PJ [Kidderminster Rd]: Comfortable and stylish beamed country dining pub with good food from pubby lunchtime snacks and sandwiches to some imaginative dishes, good wine choice, real ales, good service; dogs welcome in bar (Mrs E Thomas, David and Doreen Beattie)

DODFORD [SO9371]

Park Gate Inn B61 9AJ [A448 Bromsgrove—Kidderminster]: Sympathetically extended and modernised, usually around three real ales, lovely views towards Chaddesley Woods and Clent Hills; garden tables (Dave Braisted)

DOVERDALE [SO8666]

Honey Bee WR9 0QB [pub signed off A449 Kidderminster—Worcester at Texaco garage]: Country pub full of bee-related and more random bric-a-brac, red leather sofas and easy chairs, pleasant extension dining room with quiet country views and glass-panelled viewing hive, bargain pubby food, friendly service, Greene King Abbot, a beer brewed for the pub and farm cider, honey for sale; children welcome, back terrace with giant play hive, picnic-sets in garden with lots of disused beehives (and some working ones at a safe distance), good disabled access and facilities (Robert Turnham, BB)

DROITWICH [SO8963]

Gardeners Arms WR9 8LU [Vines Lane]: Friendly traditional pub with limited bargain food inc Sun carvery, Banks's beer; bikers welcome (Dave Braisted)

Hop Pole WR9 8ED [Friar St]: Heavy-beamed 16th-c local with friendly staff, well kept ales such as Malvern Hills and Wye Valley, Enville Ginger Beer, bargain home-made lunchtime food inc popular Sun roasts, dominoes, darts, pool; may be loud music Thurs-Sat evenings; partly canopied back garden, open all day (Andy and Jill Kassube, Chris Evans, Pete Baker, R T and J C Moggridge)

Old Cock WR9 8EQ [Friar St]: Reliable local with sensibly short choice of good reasonably priced fresh food, friendly staff, well kept real ales, several distinctive rooms, beams and stained glass; garden courtyard with pool and fountain (Michael and Lynne Gittins)

Railway WR9 9AY [Kidderminster Rd]: Small traditional local with friendly licensees, good railway memorabilia in two-room lounge bar, well kept Marstons and Wychbold, good value straightforward lunches (not early week), cribbage, dominoes and darts; big balcony with views of restored canal basin, open all day (Dave Braisted)

EVESHAM [SP0344]

Evesham Hotel WR11 6DA [Coopers Lane]: Large hotel's busy bar with amazing range of malt whiskies and spirits, good if quirky wine list, interesting menu inc good value lunchtime buffet (no tips or service charge), remarkable lavatories; children welcome, indoor swimming pool, 40 bedrooms (Denys Gueroult)

FERNHILL HEATH [SO8658]

White Hart WR3 8RP [Droitwich Rd (A38)]: Enjoyable generous pubby food inc lots of puddings, well kept Fullers London Pride (Chris Evans)

FORHILL [SP0575]

☆ **Peacock** B38 0EH [handy for M42 junctions 2 and 3; pub at junction Lea End Lane and Icknield St]: Attractive, quietly placed and well run Chef & Brewer with wide range of generous enjoyable food all day inc fixed price menu, plenty of tables in comfortably fitted knocked-through beamed rooms, woodburner in big inglenook, Greene King, Highgates, Hobsons, Wells & Youngs and guest ales, friendly prompt helpful service; piped music; children and dogs welcome, disabled facilities, picnic-sets on back terrace and front grass, other heated covered areas, open all day *(Dennis and Gill Keen, LYM)*

GREAT WITLEY [SO7566]

☆ *Hundred House* WR6 6HS [Worcester Rd]: Handsome much-modernised hotel (former Georgian coaching inn and magistrates' court), friendly fast service, well kept Banks's and a guest like Malvern Hills, good house wines, wide choice of enjoyable generous food inc good value Sun lunch, pleasant restaurant; no dogs; 27 bedrooms, handy for ruined Witley Court and remarkable church *(Tony and Wendy Hobden, Chris Evans, Alan and Eve Harding)*

GRIMLEY [SO8359]

Camp House WR2 6LX [A443 5 miles N from Worcester, right to Grimley, right at village T junction]: Unspoilt old character pub in pleasant Severn-side setting with own landing stage, generous bargain food from huge cobs to good seafood, well kept Bathams, local farm cider as well as Thatcher's, friendly staff; children and well behaved dogs welcome, nice lawns *(Chris Evans, Kerry Law)*

Wagon Wheel WR2 6LU: Attractive and pleasantly extended timbered country pub with enjoyable food in bar and restaurant inc good value Sun lunch, friendly staff *(Chris Evans)*

GUARLFORD [SO8245]

Plough & Harrow WR13 6NY [B4211 W of Malvern]: Charmingly updated timbered country pub, friendly helpful licensees, good if not cheap food inc their own produce, well kept Wadworths, good choice of wines by the glass, comfortable cottage bar and beamed barn-like restaurant; attractive good-sized garden, nice spot on village common, cl Sun evening, Mon *(Peter Wickens, Chris Flynn, Wendy Jones, P Dawn)*

HALLOW [SO8258]

Royal Oak WR2 6LD [Main Rd (A443 N of Worcester)]: Smartly refurbished traditional local with ales such as Wye Valley, low-priced pubby food, cheerful helpful service, old local photographs; good-sized garden *(Alan and Eve Harding)*

HANLEY SWAN [SO8142]

Swan WR8 0EA [B4209 Malvern—Upton]: Attractive contemporary rustic décor and furnishings blending well with old low beams, bare boards and log fire, extended back part set for dining, enjoyable food inc Sun carvery, friendly service, well kept Adnams, Wells & Youngs Bombardier and Shepherd Neame Spitfire; piped music; children and dogs welcome, disabled facilities, good-sized side lawn with play area, nice spot facing green and big duck pond, five bedrooms *(Mark Clare, LYM, P Dawn, Chris Evans)*

HIMBLETON [SO9458]

Galton Arms WR9 7LQ [Harrow Lane]: Friendly old-fashioned country pub, log fires, oak beams, enjoyable food in bar and restaurant inc lunchtime bargains, well kept

Banks's, Bathams and a house ale brewed by Wye Valley; garden with play area *(Chris Evans, Dave Braisted)*

KINGTON [SO9855]

Red Hart WR7 4DD [Cockshot Lane]: Old pub with good value food, Marstons ales, friendly attentive young staff, smart contemporary décor, attractive restaurant *(Mike and Mary Carter)*

KINNERSLEY [SO8743]

☆ *Royal Oak* WR8 9JR [off A38 S of Worcester]: Welcoming well run 18th-c pub with chef/landlord doing interesting reasonably priced fresh food, friendly staff, good atmosphere and log fire in comfortable carpeted bar, well kept ales such as Fullers London Pride, Hook Norton and Timothy Taylors Landlord, good choice of wines by the glass, conservatory restaurant; disabled access, a few outside tables, three bedrooms in refurbished back block *(Chris Evans, Mr and Mrs M J Girdler, Mr and Mrs J Berrisford, Moira Terrett, Dr A J and Mrs Tompsett, J Graveling, C D Watson, Mrs Helen Thomson, Ann Carver)*

LEIGH SINTON [SO7850]

Royal Oak WR13 5DZ [Malvern Rd, junction with A4103 SW of Worcester]: Dining pub under new management doing low-priced pubby food, good Marstons-related ales, short choice of reasonably priced wines, log fire, cheerful cartoons and polished bric-a-brac in carpeted beamed bar, attractive smallish restaurant; flower-filled garden behind with seats in sheltered alcoves *(Chris Evans, Denys Gueroult)*

LONG BANK [SO7674]

Running Horse DY12 2QP [A456 W of Bewdley]: Large well run Chef & Brewer family dining pub, well kept changing ales, enjoyable food, beams and log fires, pleasant atmosphere; disabled facilities, large garden and terrace, big fenced play area *(Mark Clare)*

LONGDON [SO8434]

☆ *Hunters Inn* GL20 6AR [B4211 S, towards Tewkesbury]: Beams, flagstones, timbers, some stripped brick and log fires, owned and run by local farming family, big helpings of locally sourced food (all day wknds) inc fresh fish and popular Sun lunch, real ales such as Malvern Hills, Wells & Youngs Bombardier and one brewed for the pub, good choice of wines by the glass, raftered dining area, good views; extensive well tended garden, bedrooms, open all day wknds till 1am *(Dr A J and Mrs Tompsett, LYM)*

LOWER MOOR [SO9847]

Chestnut Tree WR10 2NZ [Manor Rd]: Friendly welcome, good service, good value pub food; keg beer *(Alan and Eve Harding)*

LULSLEY [SO7354]

Fox & Hounds WR6 5QT [signed 1 mile off A44 Worcester—Bromyard]: Pleasant tucked-away country pub with generous reasonably priced food, well kept Hook Norton, nice wines, smallish parquet-floored bar stepping down into neat dining lounge, open fire, pretty little restaurant on left, attractive conservatory, Tues jazz night; dogs welcome, quiet and colourful side rose garden, nice walks *(Chris Evans, Lynda and Trevor Smith, BB)*

MALVERN [SO7746]

Red Lion WR14 4RG [St Anns Rd]: Enjoyable food (all day wknds) from substantial sandwiches up inc some interesting dishes, well kept Marstons-related ales, contemporary décor, chunky pine, bare boards, flagstones and pastel colours; attractive partly covered front courtyard, well placed for walks *(Phil Bryant)*

Three Horseshoes WR14 3JW [Poolbrook Rd]: Enjoyable sensibly priced pubby food in small neatly kept pub *(Chris Evans)*

Unicorn WR14 4PZ [Belle Vue Terrace]: Welcoming cottage pub dating from 17th c, three real ales inc Greene King IPA and Ringwood, bargain simple food, pleasant efficient young staff *(D W Stokes)*

MARTLEY [SO7759]

Masons Arms WR6 6YA [B4204 E]: Unusually good thai food as well as standard dishes, bargain lunch deals, charming attentive service, four real ales, good coffee, decent wines, comfortable bar and dining lounge, separate raftered restaurant (lively acoustics), live music Weds; garden with country views and play area *(Denys Gueroult, Chris Evans)*

NEWLAND [SO7948]

Swan WR13 5AY [Worcester Rd (A449)]: Well run and attractive old former coaching inn in estate village, well kept St Georges ales, enjoyable food inc good Sun lunch; pleasant garden *(Chris Evans)*

NORTON [SO8850]

Retreat WR5 2PT [Woodbury Lane]: Pleasant Marstons pub, good value meals inc light dishes *(Dave Braisted)*

OMBERSLEY [SO8463]

☆ *Cross Keys* WR9 0DS [just off A449; Main Rd (A4133, Kidderminster end)]: Nicely decorated beamed front bar with cosy areas inc armchairs and sofa, well kept Banks's and Timothy Taylors, good value wines by the glass, good food inc enterprising dishes, friendly efficient service, smart conservatory restaurant *(Dave Braisted)*

PERSHORE [SO9545]

☆ *Brandy Cask* WR10 1AJ [Bridge St]: Plain high-ceilinged bow-windowed bar, own good ales from courtyard brewery, guest beers too, Aug beer festival, quick friendly helpful service, coal fire, food from sandwiches to steaks, quaintly decorated dining room; well behaved children allowed, long attractive garden down to river (keep a careful eye on the kids), with terrace, vine arbour and koi pond *(BB, Kerry Law, the Didler)*

POWICK [SO8151]

Three Nuns WR2 4SB [Colletts Green Rd]: Quietly placed pub with pubby food running up to huge mixed grill, good beer *(Chris Evans)*

REDDITCH [SP0367]

Golden Cross B97 4RA [Unicorn Hill]: Well

kept Banks's and guest beers such as Black Sheep and Freeminer, good value Arthurian-theme carvery *(J K Knight, Roger Fletcher)*

RYALL [SO8640]

Blue Bell WR8 0PP [Grove Cres]: Popular main-road pub with generous food (breadcrumbed potato cubes a nice change from chips), well kept beer *(Chris Evans)*

SEVERN STOKE [SO8544]

Rose & Crown WR8 9JQ [A38 S of Worcester]: Attractive 15th-c black and white pub, oldest in the area, low beams, knick-knacks and good fire in character front bar, well kept Marstons-related ales, decent choice of wines by the glass, good value home-made food inc vegetarian and children's, friendly staff, extended restaurant and snug dining room; picnic-sets in nice big garden, play area, Malvern Hills views, open all day wknds *(Chris Evans)*

SHATTERFORD [SO7981]

☆ *Bellmans Cross* DY12 1RN [Bridgnorth Rd (A442)]: Welcoming french-mood dining pub with good well presented interesting food from sandwiches up inc good Sun lunch, smart tasteful restaurant with kitchen view, french chefs and bar staff, pleasant deft service, neat timber-effect bar with Bass, Greene King Old Speckled Hen and a guest beer, good choice of wines by the glass inc champagne, teas and coffees; picnic-sets outside, handy for Severn Woods walks, open all day wknds *(BB, Theo, Anne and Jane Gaskin, Robert Roxburgh)*

SHRAWLEY [SO7966]

New Inn WR6 6TE [B4196 Holt Heath—Stourport]: Attractive pub in quiet village, enjoyable generous food nicely served, well kept ales such as Theakstons Paradise; good garden *(Chris Evans)*

SINTON GREEN [SO8160]

Hunters Lodge WR2 6NT: Attractive welcoming country pub with owner cooking enjoyable reasonably priced food, cosy bar, log fire *(Peter Travis)*

STOCK GREEN [SO9959]

Bird in Hand B96 6SX: Proper old-fashioned rural pub with Banks's, Hobsons and Wye Valley, good cheap lunchtime cobs, tapas on Tues *(Dave Braisted)*

STOKE PRIOR [SO9565]

Country Girl B60 4AY [B4091 S towards Hanbury; Sharpway Gate]: Attractive country pub with good value food, friendly staff, well kept ales, inglenook log fire in beamed lounge, informal rustic eating area with some stripped brick and pitched rafters, separate more formal dining room; nice terrace tables, walks on Dodderhill Common *(BB, Dave Braisted)*

STOKE WHARF [SO9468]

Navigation B60 4LB [Hanbury Rd (B4091), by Worcester & Birmingham Canal]: Friendly and comfortable, popular for good value food and well kept changing ales *(Phyllis McCombie, Dave Braisted)*

STOKE WORKS [SO9365]

Bowling Green B60 4BH [1 mile from M5

Junction 5, via Stoke Lane; handy for Worcester & Birmingham Canal]: Attractive and comfortable, with bargain traditional food, Banks's Bitter and Mild, friendly atmosphere, polished fireplace; big garden with neat bowling green *(Dave Braisted)*

TENBURY WELLS [SO5968]

☆ ***Pembroke House*** WR15 8EQ [Cross St]: Striking timbered building, oldest in town, combining bustling pub side (lots to look at in well divided open-plan beamed bars) with upmarket dining side, popular with older people at lunchtime (not Mon) for good fair-priced food, more elaborate evening meals (not Sun, Mon), friendly staff, Hobsons and a guest ale such as Bathams, woodburner; open all day wknds *(David Elliott, Denys Gueroult)*

UPTON SNODSBURY [SO9454]

Oak WR7 4NW [A422 Worcester—Stratford]: Civilised modern refurbishment inc leather seats in flagstoned bar with ceiling wine bottle feature, good value lunches, friendly attentive staff; sturdy terrace tables, lawn picnic-sets, handy for Spetchley Park gardens *(Mike and Mary Carter)*

UPTON UPON SEVERN [SO8540]

Kings Head WR8 0HF [High St]: Lovely riverside setting, four real ales inc Butcombe and Fullers, popular food, extended well furnished lounge bar, separate eating area; fine Severn-side terrace with plenty of seating *(Dave Braisted)*

WEST MALVERN [SO7645]

☆ ***Brewers Arms*** WR14 4BQ [The Dingle]: Attractive little two-bar beamed country local down steep path, friendly landlord, eight well kept ales inc Malvern Hills, Marstons and Timothy Taylors (Oct beer festival), good value food (all day wknds, breakfast from 9am then) from fresh sandwiches to good fish, bargain OAP wkdy lunches, neat and airy dining room, Sun night cheese club, amiable pub cat; walkers and dogs welcome, glorious view from small garden, smokers' folly *(Chris Evans, Paul Kloss, Alan Bowker, Ian and Denise Foster,*

Roger and Diana Morgan, Dave Braisted)

WILLERSEY [SP1039]

New Inn WR12 7PJ [Main St]: Friendly and attractive old stone-built local, generous good value pub food all day from sandwiches up, well kept Donnington ales, ancient flagstones, darts and raised end area in traditional main bar, pool in separate public bar, skittle alley; tables outside, good local walks *(Martin and Pauline Jennings, Roger Fox, Neil and Anita Christopher)*

WORCESTER [SO8456]

Alma WR3 7HT [Droitwich Rd (A38)]: Good value hearty food inc generous mixed grill with tender local meats, well kept Batemans *(Chris Evans)*

Bridges WR3 8SB [Hindlip Lane]: Good value carvery, enjoyable entertainment most nights and wknd lunchtimes; smokers' shelter *(Chris Evans)*

Dragon WR1 1JT [The Tything]: Lively simply furnished open-plan alehouse with six well described and well kept unusual changing microbrews inc a Mild and Porter, belgian beers, local farm cider, friendly staff, bargain wkdy lunchtime food; piped pop, folksy live bands; partly covered back terrace, open all day Sat *(Andy and Jill Kassube, Alan and Eve Harding)*

Eagle Vaults WR1 2LZ [Friar St]: Open-plan Victorian pub with panelling, etched windows and other original features, cheery new licensees, enjoyable bargain food from good deli rolls up, Marstons-related ales; piped music may obtrude; pavement tables *(Phil Bryant)*

Farriers Arms WR1 2HN [Fish St]: Relaxed and welcoming, rambling through pleasant lounge and basic public bar, inexpensive unpretentious food, good cheerful service, well kept ales, good house wines; very handy for cathedral *(LYM, Robert Ager)*

Postal Order WR1 1DN [Foregate St]: Popular Wetherspoons with good range of well kept beer, Weston's cider and their usual food at good prices *(the Didler, Chris Evans)*

Please tell us if the décor, atmosphere, food or drink at a pub is different from our description. We rely on readers' reports to keep us up to date: feedback@goodguides.com, or (no stamp needed) The Good Pub Guide, FREEPOST TN1569, Wadhurst, E Sussex TN5 7BR.

Yorkshire

With more Main Entries than any other county in this *Guide*, it comes as no surprise to find such a diverse choice of pubs. But whether it's a simple walkers' tavern, a fine dining pub or even a cheery bar in a civilised and smart hotel, what continues to shine throughout Yorkshire is the genuine and open friendliness of the landlords and landladies. Food, too, plays a major part in pubs here, with nearly half our Main Entries holding a Food Award. And it doesn't seem to matter whether it's just a simple snack or an imaginative evening meal, the produce is just as local, just as carefully chosen – and sometimes even home grown. It's never any easy task choosing a dining pub from so many strong contenders: the title of Yorkshire Dining Pub of the Year goes to the Star at Harome. We're pleased with our new entries this year: the Bay Horse at Burythorpe (a charming and civilised dining pub), the Kings Arms in Sandhutton (a cheerful, busy village pub with a father and son cooking team), the Triton at Sledmere (a charmingly placed traditional country pub with friendly owners), the Castle Arms in Snape (immaculately kept and with popular food, in a pretty village), and the Blackwell Ox in Sutton-on-the-Forest (several real ales and appetising food). Among older favourites, the Birch Hall at Beck Hole, Blue Lion at East Witton, Tempest Arms at Elslack, Gray Ox at Hartshead, Angel at Hetton, Sandpiper in Leyburn, Fountaine at Linton in Craven, Crown at Roecliffe and Fox & Hounds at Sinnington have been setting a cracking pace in the last few months, working really hard to keep us all happy. And among the nearly 300 pubs we recommend in the Lucky Dip section here, no fewer than 85 have now achieved a star rating. Yorkshire has dozens of breweries, large and small; this year we found beers from nearly 50 different Yorkshire breweries in at least some of our pubs. Much the most successful are Timothy Taylors and Black Sheep, with Theakstons also very popular (and now bringing the brewing of Theakstons Best back to the family brewery in Masham – it had been brewed elsewhere for many years) and John Smiths, Tetleys and Copper Dragon are also widely available.

AMPLEFORTH   SE5878   MAP 10
White Swan
Off A170 W of Helmsley; East End; YO62 4DA

Quite a choice of seating areas in attractive pub, attentive service, enjoyable food and real ales; seats on back terrace

This year, the lounge bar in this neat golden-stone pub with its pretty window boxes has been extended but they've kept the beams, cream-coloured décor, sporting prints and mix of tables and chairs on the slate flooring. It's a civilised place that also has a more conventional beamed front bar liked by locals, with a blazing log fire, red-patterned wall seating and plenty of stools, some standing timbers and a comfortable end seating area with big soft red cushions. Black Sheep Best and John Smiths Bitter on handpump, and good wines by the glass. The restaurant area is more formal with plush furnishings and crisp, white linen-covered tables; piped music, TV, darts and dominoes. There are seats and tables on the large, attractive back terrace and the pub is just a couple of miles from Ampleforth Abbey.

🍽 **At lunchtime, the popular bar food includes sandwiches and toasties, soup, smoked chicken caesar salad, steak in ale pie, burger with mozzarella and bacon, lasagne, linguine with mixed mushrooms in a cream and brandy sauce and salmon suprême with creamed lobster sauce; evening dishes such as a plate of fresh and marinated seafood, battered black pudding and sausage meat fritter with grain mustard dressing, chicken breast on chorizo risotto with basil dressing, pork fillet with cider brandy sauce and half a gressingham duck with orange sauce, with puddings like raspberry and passion fruit crème brûlée and treacle sponge and custard.** *Starters/Snacks: £4.75 to £7.25. Main Courses: £7.25 to £17.25. Puddings: £4.95 to £6.25*

Free house ~ Licensees Mr and Mrs R Thompson ~ Real ale ~ Bar food (12-2, 6-9) ~ Restaurant ~ (01439) 788239 ~ Children welcome ~ Open 12-3, 6-11; 12-11 Sun and Sat

Recommended by Dr and Mrs Jackson, R L Borthwick, WW, Dr and Mrs R G J Telfer, Janet and Peter Race, R Pearce

APPLETON-LE-MOORS   SE7388   MAP 10

Moors 🛏

Village N of A170 just under 1.5 miles E of Kirkby Moorside; YO62 6TF

Neat and unfussy pub with a good choice of drinks, proper country cooking using own-grown produce and plenty of nearby walks; comfortable bedrooms

Most customers come to this little stone-built pub to enjoy the good evening food but the friendly landlady does keep Black Sheep and Courage Best on handpump, over 50 malt whiskies and a reasonably priced wine list. It's all strikingly neat and surprisingly bare of the usual bric-a-brac; sparse decorations include just a few copper pans and earthenware mugs in a little alcove, a couple of plates, one or two pieces of country ironwork and a delft shelf with miniature whiskies. The whiteness of the walls and ceiling is underlined by the black beams and joists, and the bristly grey carpet. Perfect for a cold winter evening, there's a nice built-in high-backed stripped settle next to an old kitchen fireplace and other seating includes an unusual rustic seat for two cleverly made out of stripped cartwheels; plenty of standing space. Darts and board games. There are tables in the lovely walled garden with quiet country views and walks straight from here to Rosedale Abbey or Hartoft End, as well as paths to Hutton-le-Hole, Cropton and Sinnington. More reports please.

🍽 **Cooked by the landlady using own-grown vegetables and salads and local organic produce, the enjoyable food might include soup, chicken stuffed with cheese, wrapped in bacon with a leek sauce, pork in cider with apple sauce, celeriac and blue cheese or fish pie, lamb shoulder with apricot stuffing, baked gammon in pear and ginger, pheasant casserole, half a roast duck with orange sauce, and puddings like Baileys chocolate fondue with fresh fruit and sticky toffee pudding.** *Starters/Snacks: £4.00 to £8.00. Main Courses: £8.95 to £16.00. Puddings: £4.25 to £4.50*

Free house ~ Licensee Janet Frank ~ Real ale ~ Bar food (see opening hours; not Mon (except for residents)) ~ Restaurant ~ No credit cards ~ (01751) 417435 ~ Children welcome ~ Dogs allowed in bar and bedrooms ~ Open 7-11; 12-3, 7-10.30 Sun; closed Mon; closed Tues-Sat lunchtimes ~ Bedrooms: £45B/£70B

Recommended by BOB, Blaise Vyner, I D Barnett

Bedroom prices are for high summer. Even then you may get reductions for more than one night, or (outside tourist areas) weekends. Winter special rates are common, and many inns cut bedroom prices if you have a full evening meal.

ASENBY

SE3975   MAP 7

Crab & Lobster ⍟ ⍩ ⌂

Village signposted off A168 – handy for A1; YO7 3QL

Interesting furnishings and décor in rambling bar, ambitious and enjoyable restauranty food, good drinks choice, attractive terrace; smart bedrooms

---

The rambling L-shaped bar in this civilised place does still attract customers dropping in for a pint but of course there's quite an emphasis on the hotel and restaurant side, too. This friendly bar has Copper Dragon Golden Pippin and Theakstons Best on handpump and quite a few wines by the glass, as well as an interesting jumble of seats from antique high-backed and other settles through sofas and wing armchairs heaped with cushions, to tall and rather theatrical corner seats; the tables are almost as much of a mix, and the walls and available surfaces are quite a jungle of bric-a-brac including lots of race tickets, with standard and table lamps and candles keeping even the lighting pleasantly informal. There's also a cosy main restaurant and a dining pavilion with big tropical plants, nautical bits and pieces and Edwardian sofas; piped music. The gardens have bamboo and palm trees lining the paths, there's a gazebo at the end of the walkways, and seats on a mediterranean-style terrace. The opulent bedrooms (based on famous hotels around the world) are in the surrounding house which has seven acres of mature gardens and a 180-metre golf hole with full practice facilities.

⍟ **Imaginative – if not cheap – food includes a lunchtime fish club sandwich (not Sunday), baked queenie scallops with caramelised shallots, gruyère, cheddar and garlic, terrine of duck confit, ham hock and foie gras with peppered apricot and cranberry chutney, cod and pot-roast pork belly with five spice sauce and duck fat roasties, pasta with roast italian vegetables, pesto and garlic and mozzarella toasts, beer-battered fresh local haddock, herb-crusted lamb loin with cumin-roasted carrots and lamb and pea shepherd's pie, roast fillet of prime aged fillet steak with oxtail and shallot ravioli, wild mushrooms and smoked bacon, and puddings such as white chocolate torte with warm belgian chocolate sauce and raspberries and pear almond tart with calvados poached pear.** *Starters/Snacks: £5.95 to £10.00. Main Courses: £12.00 to £30.00. Puddings: £7.00*

Vimac Leisure ~ Licensee Mark Spenceley ~ Real ale ~ Bar food (12-2.30, 7(6.30 Sat)-9) ~ Restaurant ~ (01845) 577286 ~ Well behaved children allowed ~ Live jazz Sun lunchtime ~ Open 11.30am–midnight ~ Bedrooms: £90B/£150B

Recommended by Mike and Lynn Robinson, Gordon and Margaret Ormondroyd, Sally Anne and Peter Goodale, Jennifer Hurst, Dr and Mrs R G J Telfer, Pete Coxon, Janet and Peter Race, Tim and Liz Sherbourne, Paul Humphreys

BECK HOLE

NZ8202   MAP 10

Birch Hall

Signed off A169 SW of Whitby, from top of Sleights Moor; YO22 5LE

Extraordinary pub-cum-village-shop in lovely valley with friendly landlady, real ales and simple snacks, seats outside and wonderful surrounding walks

---

Resolutely walker and dog friendly, this tiny idiosyncratic pub-cum-village-shop is a delightful place in beautiful surroundings. It's quite unchanging and there are two rooms, with the shop selling postcards, sweeties and ice-creams in between, and a hatch service to both sides. Furnishings are simple – built-in cushioned wall seats and wooden tables (spot the one with 136 pennies, all heads up, embedded in the top) and chairs on the flagstones or composition flooring, and there are some strange items such as french breakfast cereal boxes, a tube of Macleans toothpaste priced 1/3d and a model railway train running around a shelf just above head height. Well kept Captain Cook Endeavour, Durham Spring Goddess and a beer from North Yorkshire named for the pub (called Beckwater) on handpump; several malt whiskies. Service could not be more friendly and helpful; dominoes and quoits. Outside, an ancient oil painting of the view up the steeply wooded river valley hangs on the pub wall, there are benches out in front and steps up to a little steeply terraced side garden. They have a self-catering cottage attached to the pub. It's in a lovely steep valley and surrounded by marvellous walks; you can go along the disused railway line from Goathland – part of the path from Beck Hole to Grosmont is surfaced with mussel shells.

🍴 **Bar snacks such as locally made pies, butties and home-made scones and cakes that include their lovely beer cake.** *Starters/Snacks: £1.80 to £2.60*

Free house ~ Licensee Glenys Crampton ~ Real ale ~ Bar food (available during all opening hours) ~ No credit cards ~ (01947) 896245 ~ Children in small family room ~ Dogs allowed in bar ~ Open 11-11; 1 Sun; 11-3, 7.30-11 Weds-Sun in winter; closed winter Mon evening, all day Tues Nov-March

Recommended by Pete Baker, Fred and Lorraine Gill, Paul Newberry, the Didler, Stephen Corfield, Phil Bryant, Rona Murdoch, Maurice and Gill McMahon, Alison and Pete, Dr and Mrs Jackson

BLAKEY RIDGE
SE6799   MAP 10

Lion 🍺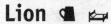

From A171 Guisborough—Whitby follow Castleton, Hutton le Hole signposts; from A170 Kirkby Moorside—Pickering follow Keldholm, Hutton le Hole, Castleton signposts; OS Sheet 100 map reference 679996; YO62 7LQ

Extended pub in fine scenery and open all day; bedrooms

Although this extended pub is in the middle of nowhere, it's always busy and one of our readers was very happy to get snowed in here. In kinder weather it's a popular place with walkers on the nearby Coast to Coast Footpath and there are plenty of other surrounding hikes, too. This is the highest point of the North York Moors National Park and the views are stunning. The beamed and rambling bars have warm open fires, a few big high-backed rustic settles around cast-iron-framed tables, lots of small dining chairs, a nice leather sofa, and stone walls hung with some old engravings and photographs of the pub under snow (it can easily get cut off in winter). A fine choice of real ales on handpump might include Copper Dragon Golden Pippin, Greene King Morlands Original and Old Speckled Hen and Theakstons Best, Old Peculier, Black Bull and XB; piped music and games machine. If you are thinking of staying, you must book well in advance. This is a regular stop-off for coach parties.

🍴 **Usefully served all day, the generous helpings of basic bar food include lunchtime sandwiches and filled baked potatoes as well as soup, giant yorkshire pudding with gravy, pâté with toast, pizza and chips, home-cooked ham and egg, roasted vegetable lasagne, well liked steak and mushroom pie, battered cod, chicken curry, steaks, and puddings such as jam roly poly with custard and strawberry cheesecake.** *Starters/Snacks: £3.95 to £4.95. Main Courses: £9.95 to £15.75. Puddings: £3.95*

Free house ~ Licensee Barry Crossland ~ Real ale ~ Bar food (12-10) ~ Restaurant ~ (01751) 417320 ~ Children welcome ~ Dogs allowed in bar ~ Open 10am-11pm(midnight Sat) ~ Bedrooms: £20(£41.50B)/£58(£72B)

Recommended by DC, Dr J Barrie Jones, WW, Joan York, Pete Coxon, Maurice and Gill McMahon

BOROUGHBRIDGE
SE3966   MAP 7

Black Bull 🍷

St James Square; B6265, just off A1(M); YO51 9AR

Bustling and friendly old town pub with a good mix of customers, real ales, several wines by the glass and generously served bar food; bedrooms

---

Even though this attractive old town pub is popular with travellers from the A1, plenty of cheerful locals drop in regularly for a pint and a chat. It's run by a friendly landlord and there are lots of separate drinking and eating areas. The main bar area has a big stone fireplace and comfortable seats and is served through an old-fashioned hatch; there's also a cosy snug with traditional wall settles, a tap room, lounge bar and restaurant. John Smiths, Theakstons Best and Timothy Taylors Landlord on handpump, ten wines by the glass and 20 malt whiskies; dominoes. The two borzoi dogs are called Spot and Sadie, and the two cats Kia and Mershka; the local mummers perform here on the first Sunday of every month. The hanging baskets are lovely.

🍽 As well as lots of hot and cold sandwiches, the bar food includes soup, chicken liver pâté, deep-fried prawns with sweet chilli sauce, pork and chive sausages with onion gravy, a pie of the day, smoked salmon and scrambled eggs, beef curry, gammon and egg, mexican spiced vegetables with a hot, sweet salsa sauce, crispy duck with hoisin and plum sauce, chargrilled chicken, tuna and steaks, and puddings such as chocolate fudge cake and lemon tart. *Starters/Snacks: £3.75 to £5.95. Main Courses: £5.95 to £16.95. Puddings: £3.75 to £3.95*

Free house ~ Licensees Anthony and Jillian Burgess ~ Real ale ~ Bar food (12-2, 6-9) ~ Restaurant ~ (01423) 322413 ~ Children welcome ~ Dogs allowed in bar and bedrooms ~ Folk music first Sun of month, 12-5 ~ Open 11-11(midnight Fri and Sat); 12-11 Sun ~ Bedrooms: £42S/£65S

Recommended by the Didler, Michael Doswell, Comus and Sarah Elliott, Janet and Peter Race, Pete Baker, Mike and Lynn Robinson

BRADFIELD

SK2290   MAP 7

Strines Inn 🛏

From A57 heading E of junction with A6013 (Ladybower Reservoir) take first left turn (signposted with Bradfield) then bear left; with a map can also be reached more circuitously from Strines signpost on A616 at head of Underbank Reservoir, W of Stocksbridge; S6 6JE

Friendly, bustling inn with fine surrounding scenery, good mix of customers, well liked food and changing real ales; four-poster bedrooms

In an area known as Little Switzerland, this isolated moorland inn was originally built as a manor house in 1275, although most of the building dates from the 16th c. It's surrounded by superb scenery on the edge of the High Peak National Park and there are fine views, plenty of picnic-sets and peacocks, geese and chickens. Inside, it's well run and enjoyable, and the main bar has a welcoming atmosphere, a good mix of customers, black beams liberally decked with copper kettles and so forth, quite a menagerie of stuffed animals, homely red-plush-cushioned traditional wooden wall benches and small chairs and a coal fire in the rather grand stone fireplace. A room off on the right has another coal fire, hunting photographs and prints, and lots of brass and china, and on the left is another similarly furnished room. Copper Dragon Golden Pippin, Jennings Cocker Hoop and Marstons Pedigree on handpump and several wines by the glass; piped music. The bedrooms have four-poster beds and a dining table as the good breakfasts are served in your room – the front room overlooks the reservoir.

🍽 Good value, tasty bar food includes sandwiches and panini, filled baked potatoes, soup, game and port pâté, giant yorkshire pudding filled with sausages and gravy, burgers, cheese and mushroom pasta, a pie of the day, gammon and egg, a huge mixed grill, daily specials like hunters chicken, lamb chops with mint sauce and T-bone steak with garlic or pepper sauce, and puddings such as apple and blackberry crumble and bread and butter pudding. *Starters/Snacks: £3.10 to £4.50. Main Courses: £5.10 to £12.75. Puddings: £3.50 to £3.70*

Free house ~ Licensee Bruce Howarth ~ Real ale ~ Bar food (12-2.30, 5.30-8.30 winter weekdays; all day summer and winter weekends) ~ (0114) 285 1247 ~ Children welcome ~ Dogs welcome ~ Open 10.30am-11pm; 10.30-3, 5.30-11 weekdays in winter ~ Bedrooms: £60B/£80B

Recommended by the Didler, Giles and Annie Francis, Neil Whitehead, Victoria Anderson, Brian and Anna Marsden

BURN

SE5928   MAP 7

Wheatsheaf 🍺 £

A19 Selby—Doncaster; Main Road; YO8 8LJ

Plenty to look at and a friendly welcome, half a dozen real ales and good value straightforward food

With good value bar food, a fine range of real ales and some amazing memorabilia to look at, it's not surprising that this friendly mock-Tudor roadside pub is so well liked. There really is masses to see: gleaming copper kettles, black dagging shears, polished buffalo horns and the like around its good log and coal fire (and a drying rack with bunches of herbs above it), decorative mugs above one bow-window seat and cases of model vans and lorries on the cream walls. The highly polished pub tables in the partly divided, open-plan bar have comfortable seats around them and John Smiths and Timothy Taylors Best and guests such as Copper Dragon Golden Pippin, Great Heck Staggering Genius, Saltaire Titus Black and York Constantine on handpump at reasonable prices and 20 malt whiskies. A pool table is out of the way on the left; cribbage, dominoes, games machine, TV and maybe unobtrusive piped music. A small garden behind has picnic-sets on a heated terrace.

🍴 **Straightforward bar food at very fair prices includes sandwiches, filled baked potatoes, ploughman's, burgers, chicken curry, cumberland sausage, haddock and chips, steak in ale pie, daily specials such as moussaka and lamb shank, and puddings like apple crumble and zesty lime cheesecake; Sunday roasts.** *Starters/Snacks: £1.25 to £3.25. Main Courses: £5.95 to £7.95. Puddings: £2.95*

Free house ~ Licensee Andrew Howdall ~ Real ale ~ Bar food (12-2 daily, 6.30-8.30 Thurs, Fri and Sat; no food Sun-Weds evenings) ~ (01757) 270614 ~ Children welcome ~ Dogs welcome ~ Open 12-midnight

Recommended by Tim and Claire Woodward, Matt Waite, Roger and Anne Newbury, Hugh Stafford, Mrs Margaret Ball, Pat and Tony Martin, R T and J C Moggridge, G Dobson

BURYTHORPE

SE7964 MAP 7

Bay Horse ♀

Off A64 8.5 miles NE of York ring road, via Kirkham and Westow; 5 miles S of Malton, by Welham Road; YO17 9LJ

Civilised dining pub with warm welcome for both locals and visitors, contemporary décor in comfortable stylish rooms, real ales, good wines by the glass, and enjoyable cooking

In a pretty Wolds-edge village, this is a charming dining pub with a warm welcome from the genuinely friendly staff for both locals and visitors. The linked rooms are cosy, relaxed and civilised, with up-to-date paintwork, stripped floorboards, a mix of chunky pine tables and elegant high-backed black or wooden dining chairs and shelves of books. The end dining room has several attractive and amusing farmyard animal paintings, the main bar has a couple of nice old carved antique pews with interesting cushions and some ancient hunting prints, and there's a tiny end room with a sofa and open log fire; there's also a separate red-walled room with rugs on flagstones. Black Sheep and Tetleys on handpump and good wines by the glass. On the outside terrace are some good contemporary tables and seats under parasols. The nearby Burythorpe House hotel, a former gentleman's residence, is under the same ownership.

🍴 **Enjoyable modern cooking includes sandwiches, soup, deep-fried goats cheese with beetroot and green bean salad and apple chutney, mussels with home-made chips, ham and egg, toad in the hole with champ and ale gravy, home-made tagliatelle with wild mushrooms and herbs, fish or corn-fed chicken, ham and tarragon pies, slow-braised venison with thyme mash and parsnip crisps, and puddings like chocolate and walnut brownie with home-made vanilla ice-cream and apple crumble with crème anglaise.** *Starters/Snacks: £3.95 to £4.25. Main Courses: £6.25 to £8.95. Puddings: £4.50*

Free house ~ Licensee Dawn Pickering ~ Real ale ~ Bar food (12-2.30(3 Sun), 6-9.30(7.30 Tues); no food Sun evening, Mon or Tues lunchtime) ~ Restaurant ~ (01653) 658302 ~ Children welcome ~ Dogs allowed in bar ~ Open 12-3, 6-11.30(midnight Sat); 12-11.30 Sun; closed Mon, Tues lunchtime

Recommended by Pat and Graham Williamson, Andy and Jill Kassube, Dr Ian S Morley, Christopher Turner, Marlene and Jim Godfrey

---

The letters and figures after the name of each town are its Ordnance Survey map reference. 'Using the *Guide*' at the beginning of the book explains how it helps you find a pub, in road atlases or large-scale maps as well as in our own maps.

CARTHORPE

SE3083   MAP 10

Fox & Hounds ⊕ ♀

Village signposted from A1 N of Ripon, via B6285; DL8 2LG

Emphasis on ambitious food in friendly dining pub but drinkers welcome too; real ales and extensive wine list

You can be sure of a genuinely friendly yorkshire welcome from the very long-serving licensees in this neatly kept and friendly dining pub – and it's a popular and relaxing lunchtime stopping point from the A1. The cosy L-shaped bar has quite a few mistily evocative Victorian photographs of Whitby, a couple of nice seats by the larger of its two log fires, plush button-back built-in wall banquettes and chairs, plates on stripped beams and some limed panelling; piped light classical music. There's some theatrical memorabilia in the corridors and an attractive high-raftered restaurant with lots of neatly black-painted farm and smithy tools. Black Sheep Best and Worthingtons on handpump and an extensive wine list; helpful service.

🍴 Generously served and very good, the popular restaurant-style food includes lunchtime sandwiches and ploughman's, soup, honey-roast ham hock terrine with home-made piccalilli, smoked chicken and mango salad with toasted pine nuts, caramelised onion and goats cheese tart, chicken breast filled with coverdale cheese in a creamy sauce, rack of lamb on a blackcurrant croûton with redcurrant gravy, whole bass with a thai stuffing, half a roasted gressingham duckling with parsley and thyme stuffing and orange sauce, and puddings like sticky ginger pudding with home-made honeycomb ice-cream and vanilla panna cotta with cinnamon shortbread; a good cheese list, a Tuesday-Thursday two- and three-course set menu and Sunday roasts. *Starters/Snacks: £3.55 to £6.95. Main Courses: £9.95 to £15.95. Puddings: £3.95 to £5.25*

Free house ~ Licensees Vince and Helen Taylor ~ Real ale ~ Bar food (not Mon) ~ Restaurant ~ (01845) 567433 ~ Children welcome ~ Open 12-3, 7-11(10.30 Sun); closed Mon and first week Jan

Recommended by David Carr, P A Rowe, Michael Doswell, Dennis and Amanda Parkyn, Gerry and Rosemary Dobson, Alan Thwaite, Walter and Susan Rinaldi-Butcher, Dr Ian S Morley, Jill and Julian Tasker, Brian Brooks, Blaise Vyner, Mr and Mrs Ian King, R N and M I Bailey

CHAPEL LE DALE

SD7477   MAP 7

Hill Inn ☕

B5655 Ingleton—Hawes, 3 miles N of Ingleton; LA6 3AR

Friendly inn with fine surrounding walks, appealing food cooked by the licensees and a fair choice of real ales; comfortable bedrooms

With wonderful remote walks all round and fantastic views to Ingleborough and Whernside from the bedrooms, many of the customers in this bustling former farmhouse, are walkers who help create a relaxed and chatty atmosphere. There are beams and log fires, straightforward seats and tables on the stripped wooden floors, nice pictures on the walls, stripped-stone recesses and a friendly welcome from the licensees. Black Sheep Best, Dent Aviator, Golden Fleece and Porter and Theakstons Best on handpump; several wines by the glass. There's a dining room and a well worn-in sun lounge.

🍴 Cooked by the licensees, the enjoyable food might include lunchtime sandwiches, sausages with red wine and onion gravy and hot home-cooked ham with a creamy parsley sauce, as well as soup, beetroot and marcarpone risotto, aubergine and polenta stack with blue cheese and roasted plum tomatoes, beef in ale casserole, chicken breast with Noilly Prat, cream, lemon and herb sauce, lamb shank with rich lamb gravy, mint sauce and redcurrant jelly, salmon with chive mash and a light thai curry sauce, and puddings such as chocolate indulgence with raspberry sauce, chocolate shavings and home-made vanilla ice-cream and apple, almond and honey tart with sauce anglaise. *Starters/Snacks: £4.25 to £9.50. Main Courses: £9.50 to £15.50. Puddings: £5.95*

Free house ~ Licensee Sabena Martin ~ Real ale ~ Bar food (12-2.30(3 Sun), 6.30(6 Sat)-8.45; not Mon) ~ Restaurant ~ (015242) 41256 ~ Children welcome ~ Dogs allowed in bar ~ Open 12-3.30, 6.30-11; 12-11 Sat; 12-4, 6.30-11 Sun; closed Mon ~ Bedrooms: /£75S

Recommended by S Gainsley, Karen Eliot, John and Sylvia Harrop, Gordon and Margaret Ormondroyd

CONSTABLE BURTON

SE1690   MAP 10

Wyvill Arms ⊕ ⊻ ◧
A684 E of Leyburn; DL8 5LH

Well run and friendly dining pub with imaginative food, a dozen wines by the glass, real ales and efficient helpful service; bedrooms

Although there's much emphasis on the good restauranty food in this very efficiently run and spotlessly kept dining pub, there's a small bar area where those just wanting a drink are most welcome. This has a mix of seating, a finely worked plaster ceiling with the Wyvill family's coat of arms and an elaborate stone fireplace. The second bar has been refurbished this year and now has a lower ceiling with ceiling fans, leather seating, old oak tables and various alcoves; the reception area of this room includes a huge leather sofa which can seat up to eight people, another carved stone fireplace and an old leaded church stained-glass window partition. Both rooms are hung with pictures of local scenes. Black Sheep Bitter and John Smiths on handpump, a dozen wines by the glass and some rare malt whiskies; darts. There are several large wooden benches under large white parasols for outdoor dining and picnic-sets by the well. Constable Burton Gardens are opposite and worth a visit. More reports please.

🍴 Using home-grown herbs and vegetables and game (including wild boar and pigeon) from the estate across the road, the first-class food includes lunchtime sandwiches, soup, terrine of smoked ham, wensleydale cheese and duck mousse with pear and apple chutney, suckling pig stir fry with fajita wraps, wild mushroom risotto, steak and onion pie, confit duck leg salad with bacon and croûtons, breaded chicken suprême stuffed with mozzarella and smoked bacon on creamed leeks with stilton sauce, local lamb fillet with a herb crust on parsnip and mint dauphinoise with lamb jus, fresh fish dishes, steaks, and daily specials like breast of pigeon and smoked duck with beetroot and orange sauce, fish and chips with tartare sauce and fillet of venison on spiced red cabbage with a berry and venison jus. *Starters/Snacks: £4.50 to £6.95. Main Courses: £9.75 to £24.50. Puddings: £5.95*

Free house ~ Licensee Nigel Stevens ~ Real ale ~ Bar food ~ Restaurant ~ (01677) 450581 ~ Children welcome ~ Dogs allowed in bar and bedrooms ~ Open 11-3, 5.30-11; closed Mon (Nov-April) ~ Bedrooms: £60B/£80B

Recommended by Mrs Brenda Calver, David and Cathrine Whiting, Mr and Mrs Ian King, Michael Tack, Anna Cooper, John and Eleanor Holdsworth, Jane and Alan Bush

COXWOLD

SE5377   MAP 7

Fauconberg Arms ⊕ ⊻ ⊨
Off A170 Thirsk—Helmsley, via Kilburn or Wass; easily found off A19, too; YO61 4AD

Friendly family run and nicely updated 17th-c inn, enjoyable generous food, a good range of drinks and overhauled garden; comfortable bedrooms

The garden behind this friendly family-run pub has now been overhauled and there's a new terrace with seats, tables and views across the fields to Byland Abbey; picnic-sets and teak benches out on the front cobbles look along the village's broad tree-lined verges, bright with flower tubs. The heavily beamed and flagstoned bar has log fires in both linked areas, one in an unusual arched fireplace in a broad low inglenook, muted Farrow & Ball colours, some attractive oak chairs by local craftsmen alongside more usual pub furnishings and nicely chosen old local photographs and other pictures, copper implements and china give a stylish feel without being at all pretentious. Theakstons Best, Thwaites Wainwright and John Smiths on handpump, a thoughtful choice of wines by the glass and 28 malt whiskies. The pub dogs Peggy, Bramble and Phoebe welcome other four-legged friends, if well behaved. The candlelit dining room is quietly elegant with a gently upmarket yet relaxed atmosphere. The charming village is quite unchanging.

🍴 Using seasonal local game and other local produce, the excellent bar food includes lunchtime sandwiches, soup, ploughman's, salads and their own burgers with home-made chips, as well as goats cheese tart with onion marmalade, garlicky portobella mushrooms, lager-battered fish, aubergine shell stuffed with tomato and mushroom with a parmesan crust, lamb rump with a rosemary and red wine reduction, duck with a honey, orange and Cointreau glaze and slow-roasted pork belly with ginger, apple and cider gravy; Sunday roasts. *Starters/Snacks: £4.95 to £7.50. Main Courses: £7.95 to £14.50. Puddings: £4.95*

Free house ~ Licensee Simon Rheinberg ~ Real ale ~ Bar food (12-3, 6.30-10) ~ Restaurant ~ (01347) 868214 ~ Children welcome ~ Dogs allowed in bar ~ Open 11-3, 6-11(midnight Fri); 11-midnight(11 Sun) Sat; closed Tues ~ Bedrooms: £55S/£65S

Recommended by R Pearce, Dr and Mrs R G J Telfer, Earl and Chris Pick, Phil and Susan Turner, E M Mason

CRAYKE
SE5670 MAP 7

Durham Ox 🍽 ⭐ 🛏
Off B1363 at Brandsby, towards Easingwold; West Way; YO61 4TE

Friendly, well run inn, interesting décor in old-fashioned, relaxing rooms, fine drinks and excellent food; lovely views and comfortable bedrooms

This is a bustling, friendly place and although many customers are here to have a meal or stay overnight, it remains properly pubby with locals popping in for a chat and a pint of Black Sheep, Theakstons Best and Timothy Taylors Landlord on handpump. The old-fashioned lounge bar has an enormous inglenook fireplace, pictures and photographs on the dark red walls, interesting satirical carvings in the panelling (Victorian copies of medieval pew ends), polished copper and brass, and venerable tables, antique seats and settles on the flagstones. In the bottom bar is a framed illustrated account of the local history (some of it gruesome) dating back to the 12th c, and a large framed print of the original famous Durham Ox which weighed 171 stone; several wines by the glass, a dozen malt whiskies and organic juices, all served by knowledgeable, welcoming staff; piped music. There are seats outside on a terrace and in the covered courtyard and fantastic views over the Vale of York on three sides; on the fourth side there's a charming view up the hill to the medieval church. The comfortable bedrooms are in converted farm buildings and the breakfasts are good. The tale is that this is the hill up which the Grand Old Duke of York marched his men.

🍴 Particularly good – if not cheap – food includes sandwiches and toasties, pressed ham hock terrine with pineapple chutney, baked queen scallops with garlic and parsley butter and a gruyère and mature cheddar crust, gammon and eggs, burger with bacon and cheese, poached smoked haddock with spinach, a poached egg and grain mustard sauce, wild mushroom, spinach and ricotta roulade with butternut squash velouté, corn-fed chicken with piri-piri and aioli, braised lamb shoulder with red wine sauce and minted pesto, daily specials, and puddings like sticky ginger pudding with toffee sauce and vanilla ice-cream and rhubarb fool with rhubarb sorbet. *Starters/Snacks: £4.95 to £8.95. Main Courses: £8.95 to £16.95. Puddings: £4.95 to £6.95*

Free house ~ Licensee Michael Ibbotson ~ Real ale ~ Bar food (12-2.30(3 Sun), 6-9.30) ~ Restaurant ~ (01347) 821506 ~ Children welcome but must be well behaved ~ Dogs allowed in bedrooms ~ Open 12-3, 6-midnight; 12-midnight Sat; 12-11 Sun ~ Bedrooms: £70B/£80B

Recommended by G Dobson, David S Allen, John and Eleanor Holdsworth, Peter and Anne Hollindale, Richard and Mary Bailey, John and Sylvia Harrop, Dr and Mrs Jackson, Ian Malone, Pat and Graham Williamson, Joan York, Keith and Margaret Kettell, Mrs Sheila Stothard

CROPTON
SE7588 MAP 10

New Inn 🍺
Village signposted off A170 W of Pickering; YO18 8HH

Genuinely warm welcome in modernised village pub with own-brew beers, traditional furnishings and brewery tours; bedrooms

Both the licensees and the cheerful locals in this comfortable modernised village inn are exceptionally friendly and if you stay overnight, you'll be made to feel like one of the family. The own-brewed beers on handpump remain quite a draw (and you can take some home with you, too): Cropton Blonde Ale, Endeavour, Honey Gold, Monkmans Slaughter,

Morrissey Fox, Two Pints and Yorkshire Warrior. They also keep several malt whiskies and half a dozen wines by the glass. The traditional village bar has wooden panelling, plush seating, lots of brass and a small fire. A local artist has designed historical posters all around the downstairs conservatory that doubles as a visitor centre during busy times. The elegant restaurant has locally made furniture and paintings by local artists. Piped music, TV, games machine, darts, pool and a juke box. There's a neat terrace, a garden with a pond and a brewery shop. Brewery Tours (not Sunday or Monday), 11am and 2pm, cost £4.95 per person.

🍴 **Generous helpings of bar food include lunchtime sandwiches and filled ciabatta rolls, ploughman's, soup, vegetable spring rolls with hoisin sauce, steak in ale pie, chicken curry, beer-battered cod, basil and sun-dried tomato tart, sausage with yorkshire pudding and onion gravy, steaks, and puddings like eton mess and rhubarb and apple crumble.** *Starters/Snacks: £3.95 to £5.95. Main Courses: £8.95 to £16.95. Puddings: £3.95 to £5.95*

Own brew ~ Licensee Philip Lee ~ Real ale ~ Bar food (12-2, 6-9) ~ Restaurant ~ (01751) 417330 ~ Children welcome ~ Dogs allowed in bar and bedrooms ~ Open 11(11.30 Sun)-11(midnight Sat) ~ Bedrooms: £45B/£80B

Recommended by Maurice and Gill McMahon, Michael Butler, Mrs Angela Graham, P Dawn, Rona Murdoch, Pat and Graham Williamson, Rosemary K Germaine, Anne and Paul Horscraft, Roger Shipperley, Brian and Anna Marsden, Pete Coxon, Christopher Turner, J F M and M West

DOWNHOLME
SE1197 MAP 10

Bolton Arms
Village signposted just off A6108 Leyburn—Richmond; DL11 6AE

Enjoyable food in unusual village's cosy country pub, lovely views; bedrooms

The Ministry of Defence own this little stone-built pub (like the village itself) which makes it one of the last pubs in Britain owned by the state. It's surrounded by MoD land – a largely unspoilt swathe of Swaledale and there are super views over it from the red-walled back conservatory dining room. This is simple, quiet and attractive, up a few steps from the bar. If you eat, they take your order down there, then call you through when it's ready. The black-beamed and carpeted bar, warm, friendly and softly lit, has two smallish linked areas off the servery, with Black Sheep Best and Theakstons Best on handpump from a small stone counter and good wines by the glass at fair prices. There are comfortable plush wall banquettes, a log fire in one neat fireplace and quite a lot of gleaming brass, a few small country pictures and drinks advertisements on pinkish rough-plastered walls. Service is friendly and efficient; piped music, dominoes and quoits. The neat garden, on the same level as the dining room (and up steps from the front), shares its view; there are also some lower picnic-sets and benches. The two bedrooms, sharing a bathroom, are good value. More reports please.

🍴 **Good bar food cooked by the landlord includes sandwiches, soup, smoked chicken caesar salad, fresh seafood pancake, garlic king prawns, steak and mushroom pie, pasta with button mushrooms in a creamy garlic sauce, keftiko (a cypriot lamb dish) with mint and redcurrant gravy, lambs liver and bacon, duck breast with honey, orange and ginger sauce, a spicy thai chicken stir fry, fillet of salmon with a creamy prawn sauce, and puddings.** *Starters/Snacks: £3.95 to £7.50. Main Courses: £8.95 to £20.50. Puddings: £4.50 to £5.50*

Free house ~ Licensees Steve and Nicola Ross ~ Real ale ~ Bar food (not Tuesday lunchtime) ~ Restaurant ~ (01748) 823716 ~ Children welcome ~ Open 11-3, 6-11(midnight Thurs-Sun); closed Tues lunchtime ~ Bedrooms: /£60S

Recommended by John and Sylvia Harrop, Anna Cooper

Real ale to us means beer which has matured naturally in its cask – not pressurised or filtered. We name all real ales stocked. We usually name ales preserved under a light blanket of carbon dioxide too, though purists – pointing out that this stops the natural yeasts developing – would disagree (most people, including us, can't tell the difference!)

EAST WITTON

SE1486   MAP 10

Blue Lion 🍴 ⚐ 🛏

A6108 Leyburn—Ripon; DL8 4SN

Civilised dining pub with interesting rooms, daily papers and real ales, inventive food and courteous service; comfortable bedrooms

'Everything about this place oozes quality' is just one of the comments from our many readers who enjoy this smart and civilised dining pub so much. Of course, the first class food and very comfortable bedrooms draw much praise, but so, too, does the fact that the proper bar welcomes drinkers and dogs as well, creating a relaxed and unstuffy atmosphere. This big squarish room has high-backed antique settles and old windsor chairs on the turkey rugs and flagstones, ham-hooks in the high ceiling decorated with dried wheat, teazles and so forth, a delft shelf filled with appropriate bric-a-brac, several prints, sporting caricatures and other pictures on the walls, a log fire and daily papers. Black Sheep Best and Riggwelter, and Theakstons Best on handpump and an impressive wine list with quite a few (plus champagne) by the glass; courteous, attentive service. Picnic-sets on the gravel outside look beyond the stone houses on the far side of the village green to Witton Fell and there's a big, pretty back garden.

🍴 Excellent, if not cheap, the delicious food includes soup, soft shell crab deep fried with chilli and ginger with a fennel salad, home-made pork pie with pickled onions and piccalilli, sautéed king scallops with lemon and sage risotto and crispy bacon, beef and onion suet pudding, slow-braised masala mutton with cumin sweet potato, poached fillet of smoked haddock topped with a poached egg, leek and mushroom sauce and gruyère, crispy pork belly, gloucester old spot sausage and fried black pudding with honey and apple sauce, roast roe deer with thyme, pancetta and red wine, and puddings like dark chocolate terrine with rum and raisin ice-cream and iced liquorice terrine with caramel sauce. *Starters/Snacks: £5.25 to £10.25. Main Courses: £10.95 to £26.50. Puddings: £5.25 to £6.95*

Free house ~ Licensee Paul Klein ~ Real ale ~ Bar food ~ Restaurant ~ (01969) 624273 ~ Children welcome ~ Dogs allowed in bar and bedrooms ~ Open 11-11 ~ Bedrooms: £67.50S/£89S(£99B)

Recommended by Dr Kevan Tucker, Jane Taylor, David Dutton, Michael and Maggie Betton, Mrs Sheila Stothard, Kay and Alistair Butler, Dr Ian S Morley, Neil and Angela Huxter, Peter and Giff Bennett, Peter Hacker, Lynda and Trevor Smith, the Didler, Edward Mirzoeff, Terry Mizen, Comus and Sarah Elliott

EGTON BRIDGE

NZ8005   MAP 10

Horseshoe

Village signposted from A171 W of Whitby; via Grosmont from A169 S of Whitby; YO21 1XE

Ongoing refurbishment in attractively positioned inn, several real ales and seats in pretty garden; bedrooms

As well as refurbishing the bedrooms, the licensees in this charmingly placed inn now plan to redecorate the bar and dining room. As we went to press, the bar had old oak tables, high-backed built-in winged settles, wall seats and spindleback chairs, a big stuffed trout (caught near here in 1913) and a warm log fire. Black Sheep Best, John Smiths and three guests like Adnams Broadside, Durham Definitive and Theakstons Paradise on handpump; piped music, darts and board games. This is a peaceful spot and the attractive gardens have flowering shrubs, pretty roses and mature redwoods. There are seats on a quiet terrace and lawn. A different way to reach the pub is to park by the Roman Catholic church, walk through the village and cross the River Esk by stepping stones. Not to be confused with a similarly named pub up at Egton. Reports on the changes, please.

🍴 Bar food includes lunchtime sandwiches, filled baguettes, baked potatoes and ploughman's, as well as soup, chicken liver pâté, mushrooms in creamy stilton sauce, deep-fried breaded brie wedges with cranberry dip, ham and eggs, lasagne, fish pie and daily specials; hearty breakfasts. *Starters/Snacks: £4.50 to £6.50. Main Courses: £6.75 to £15.00. Puddings: £2.75 to £4.00*

Free house ~ Licensee Alison Underwood ~ Real ale ~ Bar food ~ Restaurant ~ (01947) 895245 ~ Children welcome ~ Dogs allowed in bar ~ Open 11.30-3, 6.30-11; 11.30-11 Sat; 12-10.30 Sun ~ Bedrooms: /£55(£70S)

Recommended by Pete Baker, Paul Vates, Matt and Vicky Wharton, Chris and Jeanne Downing, Dave Braisted, P Dawn, Rona Murdoch, Brian Brooks, Alex and Claire Pearse, Neil Ingoe

ELSLACK
SD9249   MAP 7

Tempest Arms ⓘ ♀ ◧ ⇌

Just off A56 Earby—Skipton; BD23 3AY

Friendly inn with three log fires in stylish rooms, several real ales, good food and tables outside; bedrooms

With plenty of pubby character and really friendly, cheerful staff, this bustling inn has a good mix of both locals and visitors. It's stylish but understated with cushioned armchairs, built-in wall seats with comfortable cushions, stools and lots of tables and three log fires – one greets you at the entrance and divides the bar and restaurant. There's quite a bit of exposed stonework, amusing prints on the cream walls and maybe Molly the friendly back labrador. Hawkshead Bitter, Hetton Dark Horse, Moorhouses Premier Bitter, Theakstons Best, Thwaites Wainwright, Timothy Taylors Landlord, and a changing guest beer on handpump, ten wines by the glass and several malt whiskies. There are tables outside largely screened from the road by a raised bank, and a smokers' shelter. The bedrooms in the newish purpose built extension are comfortable.

🅄 **Generous helpings of good, enjoyable food – using the same menu in the bar and restaurant – include lunchtime sandwiches, soup, tiger prawn and crab spring rolls with a lemon grass, cucumber and lime dip, smoked chicken with sweet and sour noodles and shreds of stir-fried vegetables, huge pork pie with piccalilli and minted gravy, beer-battered haddock, lambs liver with black pudding, crispy bacon and red wine sauce, gammon and eggs, confit duck leg on bubble and squeak with madeira jus, marinated lamb with mint and redcurrant gravy, a generous mixed grill, daily specials, and puddings; Sunday roast.** *Starters/Snacks: £3.95 to £6.50. Main Courses: £8.95 to £13.50. Puddings: £1.99 to £4.80*

Free house ~ Licensees Martin and Veronica Clarkson ~ Real ale ~ Bar food (12-2.30, 6-9(9.30 Fri and Sat); 12-7.30 Sun) ~ Restaurant ~ (01282) 842450 ~ Children welcome ~ Dogs allowed in bedrooms ~ Open 11-11; 12-10.30 Sun ~ Bedrooms: £62.50B/£79.95B

Recommended by Pat and Graham Williamson, Christopher Mobbs, Neil Kellett, Richard, David Heath, Margaret Dickinson, Andy Witcomb, Dr Kevan Tucker, Ian and Helen Stafford, Karen Eliot, Mrs R A Cartwright, Brian and Janet Ainscough, Steve Whalley

FADMOOR
SE6789   MAP 10

Plough ⓘ ♀

Village signposted off A170 in or just W of Kirkbymoorside; YO62 7HY

Well run and enjoyable dining pub with a friendly welcome, civilised little rooms, particularly good food and fine wines

'A dependable favourite' is how one reader describes this popular and well run dining pub – and it's clear that many others agree with him. The elegantly simple little rooms have cushioned settles and a range of armed wheelbacks and other wooden dining chairs on seagrass floors (some fine rugs too), horse tack attached to beams, all sorts of prints and pictures on the yellow walls, and lots of wine bottles on display. Black Sheep Best and Great Newsome Sleck Dust on handpump, and an extensive wine list; piped music. There are seats on the terrace. They also have a quiet little caravan site for Caravan Club registered members.

🅄 **Interesting, enjoyable bar food includes sandwiches, soup, baked figs stuffed with brie and wrapped in parma ham with a chilled cumberland and port sauce, button mushrooms in a wensleydale cheese sauce topped with toasted breadcrumbs, crispy battered haddock with home-made tartare sauce, mediterranean vegetable lasagne, steak and mushroom** suet pudding, boneless half a gressingham duckling with an orange, mandarin and brandy sauce, medallions of monkfish with a thai green curry sauce, and puddings like chilled white and dark chocolate terrine with a mandarin and cranberry ice-cream and vanilla scented crème brûlée; they also offer a good value two-course menu (not Saturday evening or Sunday lunchtime). *Starters/Snacks: £4.95 to £7.95. Main Courses: £7.95 to £15.95. Puddings: £5.50*

Holf Leisure Ltd ~ Licensee Neil Nicholson ~ Real ale ~ Bar food (12-2(3.30 Sun), 6.30-9) ~ Restaurant ~ (01751) 431515 ~ Children welcome ~ Open 12-3, 6.30-11; 12-5 Sun; closed Sun evening, Mon and Tues, 25 Dec, 1 Jan

Recommended by WW, Joyce and Maurice Cottrell, Maurice and Gill McMahon, Dennis and Gill Keen, Christopher Turner

FELIXKIRK   SE4684   MAP 10

Carpenters Arms ⊕ ♀
Village signposted off A170 E of Thirsk; YO7 2DP

Busy family-run dining pub with pubby choices and more interesting dishes, good wine list and several real ales

Run by a friendly mother and daughter team, this is a busy dining pub in a picturesque small moors-edge village. Of course, many people are here to enjoy the good food but they do keep a table free for those just wanting a drink and the locals tend to gather every evening around the high bar stools by the counter for a pint of beer and a chat: Black Sheep,Theakstons Best and a guest from both Copper Dragon and Moorhouses on handpump. Ten wines by the glass and lots of coffees, too. The bistro bar has carpenters' tools and miniature hot air balloons hanging from beams in the yellow ceiling, oil lamps, red and blue gingham tablecloths with matching cushions on the built-in wall seats and various knick-knacks dotted about; piped music and board games. The restaurant is more formal with locally made furniture, crystal glasses and white linen napery. More reports please.

⊞ **Good, often inventive food includes sandwiches, chicken liver and foie gras parfait with spiced apple and plum chutney, moules marinière, pea and parmesan risotto with griddled asparagus and parmesan crisp, beer-battered haddock, honey-glazed wensleydale gammon with egg and pineapple, pork chop with chorizo, herb and garlic potatoes and a herb dressing, chargrilled rib-eye steak with caesar salad and shoestring chips, daily specials like crayfish cocktail with bourbon marie rose sauce, grilled swordfish steak with sautéed queen scallops and garlic and corn-fed chicken with mushroom and bacon linguine, and puddings such as Pimms jelly with green apple sorbet, mint syrup and Pimms shot and sticky toffee and date pudding with butterscotch sauce and home-made vanilla pod ice-cream.** *Starters/Snacks: £5.25 to £7.95. Main Courses: £9.95 to £19.95. Puddings: £5.50*

Free house ~ Licensee Karen Bumby ~ Real ale ~ Bar food (not Sun evening or Mon) ~ Restaurant ~ (01845) 537369 ~ Children welcome ~ Open 11.30-3, 6.30-11(midnight Sat); 12-3 Sun; closed Sun evening, Mon, 25 Dec, 1 week Feb

Recommended by H Bramwell, M and GR, WW, R Pearce, Peter Burton, Sally Anne and Peter Goodale

FERRENSBY   SE3660   MAP 7

General Tarleton ⊕ ♀ ⇔
A655 N of Knaresborough; HG5 0PZ

Civilised coaching inn with interesting food, lots of wines by the glass, friendly service and relaxed atmosphere; comfortable bedrooms

More of a bar/brasserie than a traditional pub, this is a smart and civilised old coaching inn with a clean, contemporary feel. There's no doubt that most customers are here to enjoy the very good, interesting food but they do keep Black Sheep and Timothy Taylors Landlord on handpump, lots of wines by the glass from a fine list and quite a few coffees; efficient service. The beamed bar area has brick pillars dividing up the several different areas to create the occasional cosy alcove, some exposed stonework and neatly framed pictures of staff on the cream walls. Dark brown leather chairs are grouped around wooden tables, there's a big open fire, a friendly, relaxed atmosphere and a door that leads out to a pleasant tree-lined garden – seats here as well as in a covered courtyard. The bedrooms are comfortable and the breakfasts excellent.

🍴 **First rate – if not cheap – food includes soup, little moneybags (seafood in a crisp pastry bag with lobster sauce), parfait of chicken livers with marrow chutney and toasted brioche, queen scallops with garlic and lemon butter topped with gruyère and cheddar, vegetable cannelloni, sausages with red wine onion marmalade sauce, steak in ale pudding, slowly braised and rolled pork cheek, crisp braised belly, black pudding and mock goose pie, haunch of venison with roast shallots, bacon lardons and mushrooms in a rich red wine sauce, bass fillet on a crispy vine tomato tart with rocket and basil pesto, and puddings such as custard tart with armagnac-soaked prunes and Valrhona chocolate fondant with white chocolate ice-cream; they also have a two- and three-course set menu (not Friday evening, Saturday or Sunday).** *Starters/Snacks: £4.95 to £7.95. Main Courses: £9.95 to £18.95. Puddings: £4.50 to £6.00*

Free house ~ Licensee John Topham ~ Real ale ~ Bar food (12-2, 6-9.15) ~ Restaurant ~ (01423) 340284 ~ Children welcome ~ Open 12-3, 6-11 ~ Bedrooms: £85B/£129B

Recommended by Keith and Margaret Kettell, Dr and Mrs J Temporal, Janet and Peter Race, Ian and Jane Haslock, Tony and Tracy Constance, Keith and Sue Ward, Alison and Pete, Blaise Vyner, Roy and Jean Russell, Michael Doswell, Roger Noyes, Hunter and Christine Wright

GRINTON   SE0498   MAP 10

Bridge Inn 🍺 🛏

B6270 W of Richmond; DL11 6HH

Bustling pub with welcoming landlord, comfortable bars, log fires, a fine choice of drinks and good food; neat bedrooms

On the banks of the River Swale, this former coaching inn is a popular place for a drink or a meal after enjoying one of the good surrounding walks. There are picnic-sets outside and the inn is right opposite a lovely church known as the Cathedral of the Dales. Inside, the pub's cheerful, gently lit and red-carpeted, with bow window seats and a pair of stripped traditional settles among more usual pub seats, all cushioned, a good log fire, Jennings Cumberland and Cocker Hoop, and guests such as Caledonian Deuchars IPA and Hop Back Crop Circle on handpump, nice wines by the glass and 25 malt whiskies. On the right, a few steps take you down into a dark red room with darts, board games, a well lit pool table, ring the bull, and piped music. Friendly, helpful service. On the left, past leather armchairs and a sofa by a second log fire (and a glass chess set), is an extensive two-part dining room. The décor is in mint green and shades of brown, with a modicum of fishing memorabilia. The bedrooms are neat and simple, and breakfasts are good.

🍴 **As well as growing their own herbs and rearing their own pigs, the popular bar food includes lunchtime filled baguettes and baked potatoes, soup, grilled goats cheese with a honey, thyme and walnut dressing, smoked mackerel pâté, cod in cider and dill batter, butternut squash risotto, steak in ale pie, cumberland sausage with onion gravy, garlic and sage pork belly on a stew of lentils, smoked bacon and tomatoes, lamb casserole with minted dumplings, chinese five-spice breast of duck on crispy noodles with plum sauce, and puddings such as dark, milk and white chocolate tart and lemon and lime cheesecake.** *Starters/Snacks: £4.95 to £5.49. Main Courses: £7.95 to £19.95. Puddings: £4.50*

Jennings (Marstons) ~ Lease Andrew Atkin ~ Real ale ~ Bar food (all day) ~ Restaurant ~ (01748) 884224 ~ Children welcome ~ Dogs allowed in bar and bedrooms ~ Informal live music Thurs evenings ~ Open 12-midnight(1am Sat) ~ Bedrooms: £48B/£76B

Recommended by Lynda and Trevor Smith, Jo Lilley, Simon Calvert, Chris and Jeanne Downing, Mr and Mrs Ian King, Ann and Tony Bennett-Hughes, Blaise Vyner, Peter Dearing, Ken and Barbara Turner, Dr and Mrs P Truelove, Dr A McCormick

---

Food details, prices, timing etc refer to bar food (if that's separate and different from any restaurant there).

HALIFAX   SE1027   MAP 7

Shibden Mill ⓘ ♀ 🍺

Off A58 into Kell Lane at Stump Cross Inn, near A6036 junction; keep on, pub signposted from Kell Lane on left; HX3 7UL

Tucked-away restored mill with cosy rambling bar, five real ales and inventive bar food

At the bottom of a peaceful wooded valley, this warmly friendly 17th-c restored mill comes as a nice surprise. The rambling bar has cosy side areas with banquettes heaped with cushions and rugs, there are well spaced nice old tables and chairs, and the candles in elegant iron holders give a feeling of real intimacy; also, old hunting prints, country landscapes and so forth and a couple of big log fireplaces. Theakstons XB, a beer named after the pub and brewed for them by Moorhouses, and a couple of guests like Copper Dragon Golden Pippin, Saltaire Blonde and Titanic English Glory on handpump, and a dozen wines by the glass (and two champagnes as well). There's an upstairs restaurant; piped music. There are plenty of seats and tables on an attractive heated terrace and the building is prettily floodlit at night.

🍴 Using carefully chosen local suppliers and produce, the imaginative bar food includes **sandwiches, soup, mussels in parsley, garlic and ale, seared scallops with bacon, crème caramel, peas and girolles, sausages of the day, braised spring lamb with suet pudding, parmesan gnocchi with wild mushrooms and baby spinach, cod with egg yolk ravioli, truffle mash, parmesan and parsley oil, honey-roast bacon joint with parsley sauce, pot-roasted chicken with goose liver and morel cream, daily specials, and puddings like banana tarte tatin and chocolate crunchy; good breakfasts.** *Starters/Snacks: £4.50 to £9.50. Main Courses: £9.50 to £18.95. Puddings: £4.50 to £6.75*

Free house ~ Licensee Glen Pearson ~ Real ale ~ Bar food (12-2, 6-9.30; 12-7.30 Sun) ~ Restaurant ~ (01422) 365840 ~ Children welcome ~ Dogs allowed in bar and bedrooms ~ Open 12-2.30, 5.30-11; 12-11 Sat; 12-10.30 Sun ~ Bedrooms: £75B/£90B

Recommended by Cathy Robinson, Ed Coombe, Gordon and Margaret Ormondroyd, Clive Flynn, Jo Lilley, Simon Calvert, Brian and Ruth Young, Richard Marjoram, John Honnor, Pat and Tony Martin, Hunter and Christine Wright

HAROME   SE6482   MAP 10

Star ★ ⓘ ♀ 🍺 🛏

Village signposted S of A170, E of Helmsley; YO62 5JE
YORKSHIRE DINING PUB OF THE YEAR

Ambitious modern cooking by young landlord in pretty thatched pub, proper bar with real ales and fine wines, smart restaurant and cocktail bar, and seats on terrace and in garden; stylish bedrooms

The exceptional food cooked by the affable young chef/patron in this pretty, thatched 14th-c inn continues to win enthusiastic praise from our many readers. But the bar still has a proper pubby atmosphere, a dark bowed beam-and-plank ceiling, plenty of bric-a-brac, interesting furniture (this was the first pub that 'Mousey Thompson' ever populated with his famous dark wood furniture), a fine log fire, a well polished tiled kitchen range and daily papers and magazines; as they don't take reservations, you must arrive early to be sure of a seat. There's also a popular coffee loft in the eaves. This year, the restaurant has been extended and there's also a new cocktail bar (where bar snacks are available). A couple of changing real ales from breweries like Hambleton, Leeds and Timothy Taylors on handpump, 17 wines by the glass, home-made fruit liqueurs and all manner of coffees and teas with home-made chocolates; piped music. There are some seats and tables on a sheltered front terrace with more in the garden. You may have to book the stylish bedrooms and suites a long way ahead. They now own the nearby, freshly refurbished Pheasant Hotel. The Corner Shop opposite the inn and Pern's delicatessen in Helmsley sell home-made delicacies from the Star's kitchen and other local gifts.

🍴 Using their own herbs and vegetables and first rate local produce, the inventive and meticulously presented, if expensive, food includes lunchtime sandwiches and salads, soup, dressed white crab meat with plum tomato and basil salad, green herb mayonnaise and bloody mary dressing, terrine of ham knuckle with spiced pineapple, pickle, fried quail egg and grain mustard vinaigrette, risotto of sorrel with blue wensleydale cheese and roast hazelnut pesto, pork belly with a warm black pudding and apple salad, fried duck egg and devilled sauce, haunch of roe deer with venison cottage pie, girolle mushroom and tarragon juices, fillet of bass with garlic roast snails, burgundy-style sauce and shavings of truffle, and puddings like baked ginger parkin with rhubarb ripple ice-cream and spiced syrup and chocolate and stout pudding with black treacle ice-cream. *Starters/Snacks: £5.00 to £12.00. Main Courses: £16.00 to £24.00. Puddings: £5.00 to £11.00*

Free house ~ Licensees Andrew and Jacquie Pern ~ Real ale ~ Bar food (12-2, 7-9; 12-6 Sun; not Mon) ~ Restaurant ~ (01439) 770397 ~ Children welcome ~ Open 11.30-3, 6.15-11; 12-11 Sun; closed Mon lunchtime ~ Bedrooms: /£140S(£150B)

Recommended by Ian and Jane Haslock, Sally Anne and Peter Goodale, P R Stevens, Andy and Jill Kassube, Richard Cole, Mr and Mrs P L Spencer, David Robertson, Maurice and Gill McMahon, Michael and Lynne Gittins, Derek Thomas, David Thornton, Peter and Josie Fawcett

HARTSHEAD
SE1822   MAP 7

Gray Ox 🍴 🍷

3.5 miles from M62 junction 25; A644 towards Dewsbury, left on to A62, next left on to B6119, then first left on to Fall Lane; pub on right; WF15 8AL

Appealing modern cooking in attractive dining pub, cosy beamed bars, real ales, several wines by the glass and fine views

Handy for the M6, this extremely popular and attractive stone-built dining pub is at its most pubby at lunchtime. The bars have beams and flagstones, a cosy décor, bentwood chairs and stripped pine tables, roaring log fires and a buoyant atmosphere; comfortable carpeted dining areas with bold paintwork and leather dining chairs around polished tables lead off. Jennings Cumberland and Cocker Hoop with a guest like Sneck Lifter on handpump, and several wines by the glass; piped music. There are picnic-sets outside, and fine views through the latticed pub windows across the Calder Valley to the distant outskirts of Huddersfield – the lights are pretty at night.

🍴 First class, imaginative food includes lunchtime sandwiches, soup, feta with red onion marmalade and home-dried tomato, oak-smoked salmon and crab mousse, cockles and bloody mary dressing, seared pigeon breast with a warm salad of chorizo and black pudding, beer-battered haddock, steak in ale pie, baked beef tomato with mozzarella, tomato and basil pesto risotto, their popular pig on a plate dish (pork tenderloin wrapped in pancetta with crispy pork belly, pig's cheek, black pudding, apple sauce and red wine jus), sea trout with moules marinière sauce and crispy bacon, and puddings such as rhubarb crème brûlée and pear crumble with caramel custard; they also offer a good value early-bird two- and three-course set menu (not weekends). *Starters/Snacks: £3.95 to £8.95. Main Courses: £8.95 to £18.95. Puddings: £4.95 to £5.25*

Banks's (Marstons) ~ Lease Bernadette McCarron ~ Real ale ~ Bar food (12-2, 6-9(9.30 Sat); 12-7 Sun) ~ Restaurant ~ (01274) 872845 ~ Children welcome ~ Open 12-3, 6-midnight; 12-midnight Sat; 12-11 Sun

Recommended by Gordon and Margaret Ormondroyd, Andy and Jill Kassube, Bernie, John Saville, Marcus Mann, Dr Kevan Tucker, Pat and Tony Martin, R T and J C Moggridge, Roger Newton

HEATH
SE3520   MAP 7

Kings Arms 🍺

Village signposted from A655 Wakefield—Normanton – or, more directly, turn off to the left opposite Horse & Groom; WF1 5SL

Old-fashioned gaslit pub in interesting location with dark-panelled original bar, up to seven real ales and standard bar food; seats outside

Unchanging and enjoyable, this is a traditional, old-fashioned pub still with gas lighting, which adds a lot to the atmosphere. The original bar has a fire burning in the old black range (with a long row of smoothing irons on the mantelpiece), plain elm stools, oak settles built into the walls and dark panelling. A more comfortable extension has carefully preserved the original style, down to good wood-pegged oak panelling (two embossed with royal arms) and a high shelf of plates; there are also two other small flagstoned rooms and the conservatory opens on to the garden. Clarks Classic Blonde, Tetleys, Timothy Taylors Landlord and guest beers such as Black Sheep Riggwelter, Wadworths 6X and Wychwood Hobgoblin on handpump. Sunny benches outside face the village green which is surrounded by 19th-c stone merchants' houses; there are picnic-sets on a side lawn and a nice walled garden.

🍴 Straightforward bar food includes sandwiches, soup, yorkshire pudding and onion gravy, steak in ale pie, beer-battered haddock, daily specials, and puddings like lemon cheesecake and chocolate fudge cake. *Starters/Snacks: £3.95 to £6.95. Main Courses: £7.95 to £14.95. Puddings: £3.95*

Clarks ~ Manager Andrew Shepherd ~ Real ale ~ Bar food (12-2(2.30 Sat), 6-9.30; 12-5 Sun) ~ Restaurant ~ (01924) 377527 ~ Children allowed away from main lounge ~ Dogs allowed in bar ~ Open 12-11(midnight Sat); 12-3, 5-11 weekdays in winter

Recommended by the Didler, Rosemary K Germaine, R T and J C Moggridge, Dr and Mrs A K Clarke, Helen Beaumont, John Saville, Michael Butler

HETTON
SD9658 MAP 7

Angel 🍴 ♀ 🛏
Just off B6265 Skipton—Grassington; BD23 6LT

Dining pub with rambling timbered rooms, lots of wines by the glass, real ales, imaginative food and seats on the heated terrace; smart bedrooms

Surrounded by glorious countryside, this is a creeper-clad, neatly kept and very popular dining pub. The three timbered and panelled rooms ramble around, though perhaps the one with the most pubby atmosphere (and where you can feel comfortable just popping in for a drink) is the main bar with its Victorian farmhouse range in the big stone fireplace. There are lots of cosy nooks and alcoves, comfortable country-kitchen and smart dining chairs, button-back plush seats window seats, all manner of wooden or tableclothed tables, Ronald Searle wine-snob cartoons plus older engravings and photographs, and log fires. Black Sheep, Dark Horse Hetton Pale Ale and Timothy Taylors Landlord on handpump, around 20 wines by the glass including champagne from a carefully chosen list and quite a few malt whiskies. Outside in front of the building, there are smart wooden tables and chairs on two covered terraces.

🍴 Imaginative bar food using top quality local produce includes soup, crab, goats cheese and avocado tian with tomato salsa and curry dressing, duck and orange sausage with cranberry purée and red wine reduction, seafood lasagne, almond galette of wensleydale ewes cheese with spinach, crushed potato, tomato and cardamon relish, chicken breast with baked pea parcel and thyme and red wine sauce, rare breed suckling pig with black pudding and brawn sausage, cider and apple purée and five spice sauce, daily specials like baked queen scallops with garlic butter and gruyère, duo of halibut and sea trout with cockles and mussels in a mussel cider foam and bass with chive mash, carrot purée and lemon butter sauce, and puddings such as dark chocolate fondant with a sage and apricot centre and a mini cherry crème brûlée and rhubarb three ways (a parfait, jelly and clafoutis); there's also a good value two-course set lunch. *Starters/Snacks: £6.25 to £7.50. Main Courses: £11.25 to £18.75. Puddings: £5.50 to £7.25*

Free house ~ Licensee Bruce Elsworth ~ Real ale ~ Bar food (12-2.15(2.30 Sun), 6-9(10 Sat)) ~ Restaurant ~ (01756) 730263 ~ Children welcome ~ Dogs allowed in bedrooms ~ Open 12-3, 6-11(10 Sun); closed 25 Dec, one week Jan ~ Bedrooms: £115B/£130B

Recommended by Michael Doswell, Richard and Mary Bailey, Dr Kevan Tucker, Richard, Karen Eliot, George Ozols, Margaret and Jeff Graham, Revd D Glover, Ray and Winifred Halliday, Jeremy King, Dr and Mrs Michael Smith, Hunter and Christine Wright, Peter and Giff Bennett, Pierre Richterich

---

For those of you who use Sat-Nav devices, we include a postcode for every entry in the *Guide*.

KETTLESING

SE2257 MAP 7

Queens Head 🍺

Village signposted off A59 W of Harrogate; HG3 2LB

Lots to look at in friendly stone pub with open fires, chatty atmosphere, real ales and decent food; bedrooms

With good value food and a warm, welcoming atmosphere, it's not surprising that this quietly placed and pleasant stone pub is so popular – particularly with older people at lunchtime. The L-shaped, carpeted main bar is decorated with Victorian song sheet covers, lithographs of Queen Victoria, little heraldic shields and a delft shelf of blue and white china. There are also lots of quite close-set elm and other tables around its walls, with cushioned country seats, coal or log fires at each end and maybe unobtrusive piped radio. A smaller bar on the left, with built-in red banquettes, has cricketing prints and cigarette cards, coins and banknotes, and in the lobby there's a life-size portrait of Elizabeth I. Black Sheep, Roosters Hooligan and Theakstons Old Peculier on handpump; good service. There are seats in the neatly kept suntrap back garden and benches in front by the lane.

🍽 **Popular bar food includes sandwiches, soup, filled yorkshire puddings, home-made burger, salads, omelettes, battered haddock, gammon and egg, well liked daily specials, and homely puddings; they also do a good value three-course meal.** *Starters/Snacks: £3.00 to £6.00. Main Courses: £6.95 to £12.95. Puddings: £3.95*

Free house ~ Licensees Louise and Glen Garbutt ~ Real ale ~ Bar food (11.30-2, 6-9; 12-9) ~ (01423) 770263 ~ Children welcome ~ Open 11-3, 6-11; 12-10.30 Sun ~ Bedrooms: £74.75S/£86.25S

Recommended by Mr and Mrs Staples, Peter Hacker, Tim and Claire Woodward, Yana Pocklington, Patricia Owlett

KIRKBYMOORSIDE

SE6986 MAP 10

George & Dragon 🛏

Market Place; YO62 6AA

17th-c coaching inn with convivial front bar, snug and bistro, good wines, real ales and decent bar food; comfortable bedrooms

This handsome old coaching inn is in the market square of a pretty little town which is at its liveliest on Wednesdays (market day). The convivial front bar has beams and panelling, smart tub seats around a mix of wooden tables on the part-carpet and part-solid-oak flooring and a roaring log fire in a rather fine fireplace. Black Sheep, Copper Dragon Challenger IPA, Greene King Abbot, Roosters Special and Tetleys on handpump from the hand-made ash counter and ten wines by the glass; piped music. There's also a snug, a bistro and a smart separate restaurant. Outside on both the front and back terraces, there are plenty of seats, a giant parasol and outdoor heater.

🍽 **As well as lunchtime filled baguettes and baked potatoes, bar food includes soup, duck liver pâté and chutney, mushroom and courgette risotto, sausages with mustard mash and onion gravy, battered haddock, gammon and free-range egg, chicken stuffed with oven-dried tomatoes and brie, wrapped in bacon and served with dauphinoise potatoes, braised lamb shoulder with a port and redcurrant glaze, duck with honey, sage and an orange sauce, and puddings such as fruit crumble and profiteroles with hot chocolate sauce.** *Starters/Snacks: £4.50 to £6.50. Main Courses: £7.50 to £15.50. Puddings: £4.50 to £6.25*

Free house ~ Licensees David and Alison Nicholas ~ Real ale ~ Bar food (12-2(3 Sun), 6.30-9) ~ Restaurant ~ (01751) 433334 ~ Children welcome ~ Dogs allowed in bedrooms ~ Open 10.30am(11 Sun)-11pm ~ Bedrooms: £60B/£90B

Recommended by D and M T Ayres-Regan

LANGTHWAITE

NY0002 MAP 10

Charles Bathurst

Arkengarthdale, 1 mile N towards Tan Hill; DL11 6EN

Friendly country inn with bustling atmosphere, good mix of customers, thoughtful wine list, decent real ales, and interesting bar food; comfortable bedrooms, lots of walks

If staying overnight here (which many of our readers do), it's quite a bonus to be able to enjoy one of the lovely surrounding walks straight from the front door; there are fine views over Langthwaite village and Arkengarthdale. It's a well run inn with a friendly, bustling atmosphere and plenty of customers – both local and visiting. And while there's a strong emphasis on the good food, the long bar does still have a pubby feel and light pine scrubbed tables, country chairs and benches on stripped floors, plenty of snug alcoves and a roaring fire. The island bar counter has bar stools, Black Sheep Best and Riggwelter, Theakstons Best and Timothy Taylors Landlord on handpump and ten wines by the glass from a sensibly laid-out list with helpful notes. Piped music, darts, pool, TV, dominoes, board games and quoits. There's also a wooden floored dining room with views of Scar House (a shooting lodge owned by the Duke of Norfolk), Robert 'the Mouseman' Thompson tables and chairs, and an open truss ceiling; there are other dining areas as well. The bedrooms are pretty and comfortable (the ones not above the dining area are the quietest). The pub is generally known as the CB Inn.

[|] Using the best local seasonal produce, the imaginative food includes filled baguettes, soup, blue cheese and caramelised white onion tartlet, suprême of pigeon in breadcrumbs with mushroom duxelles and veal jus, steamed steak and red wine suet pudding with parsnip mash, corn-fed chicken with shallots and a pea and chicken consommé, halibut steak with squid, prawns and cherry tomato linguine, rump of lamb with ratatouille and red wine sauce, duck breast with apple and marjoram rösti and beurre blanc, and puddings like orange and cardamon crème brûlée and plum crumble with crème anglaise; the second Tuesday of the month is fish night with a two- and-three course set menu.
Starters/Snacks: £4.25 to £6.50. Main Courses: £9.99 to £19.95. Puddings: £4.95 to £5.75

Free house ~ Licensees Charles and Stacy Cody ~ Real ale ~ Bar food ~ Restaurant ~ (01748) 884567 ~ Children welcome ~ Open 11am-midnight ~ Bedrooms: /£97.50B

Recommended by Mike and Lynn Robinson, Brian and Janet Ainscough, Jane and Alan Bush, Bruce and Sharon Eden, Richard and Sissel Harris, Professors Alan and Ann Clarke, Alison and Pete, Helen Clarke, Mary Goodfellow

LEDSHAM

SE4529 MAP 7

Chequers

1.5 miles from A1(M) junction 42: follow Leeds signs, then Ledsham signposted; also some 4 miles N of junction M62; Claypit Lane; LS25 5LP

Enjoyable bar food and more elaborate choices in friendly village pub, handy for the A1, log fires in several beamed rooms and real ales; pretty back terrace

With a lovely warm welcome, five real ales and particularly good food, it's not surprising that this 16th-c stone-built inn is so popular. There are several small, individually decorated rooms with low beams, lots of cosy alcoves, toby jugs and all sorts of knick-knacks on the walls and ceilings, and log fires. From the old-fashioned little central panelled-in servery they keep Brown Cow Bitter, John Smiths, Theakstons Best, Timothy Taylors Landlord and a changing guest on handpump; good, attentive service. A sheltered two-level terrace behind the house has tables among roses and the hanging baskets and flowers are very pretty. RSPB Fairburn Ings reserve is close by.

[|] As well as bar food like sandwiches, smoked salmon and scrambled eggs, sausage and mash and steak and mushroom pie, there are more elaborate choices such as lambs kidneys in madeira, crab meat and marinated sardines on herb blinis drizzled with gazpacho sauce, corn-fed chicken breast on wild mushrooms and roast onions, vegetable and stilton bake, and slow-roast venison with smoked bacon, black pudding and game jus, daily specials that include chicken liver parfait, wild boar loin with paprika and sweet chilli sauce on sweet potato and saddle of rabbit with sage and apple stuffing, sautéed kidney and cider sauce, and puddings like eton mess and chocolate and Baileys

cheesecake. *Starters/Snacks: £4.80 to £9.65. Main Courses: £10.55 to £18.85. Puddings: £5.35 to £5.85*

Free house ~ Licensee Chris Wraith ~ Real ale ~ Bar food (12-9.15 Mon-Sat; not Sun) ~ Restaurant ~ (01977) 683135 ~ Well behaved children allowed ~ Dogs allowed in bar ~ Open 11-11; closed Sun

Recommended by Dr and Mrs A K Clarke, Louise English, Pat and Stewart Gordon, Stephen Shepherd, the Didler, Dr and Mrs J Temporal

LEYBURN   SE1190   MAP 10

Sandpiper ⊕ ♀
Just off Market Place; DL8 5AT

Emphasis on appealing food though cosy bar for drinkers in 17th-c cottage, real ales and an amazing choice of whiskies; bedrooms

There's a good balance in this attractive 17th-c stone cottage between those dropping in for a drink and a chat and diners here to enjoy the good, interesting food. The small cosy bar – liked by locals – has a couple of black beams in the low ceiling, wooden or cushioned built-in wall seats around a few tables, and the back room up three steps has attractive Dales photographs; get here early to be sure of a seat. Down by the nice linenfold panelled bar counter there are stuffed sandpipers, more photographs and a woodburning stove in the stone fireplace; to the left is the attractive restaurant with dark wooden tables and chairs on floorboards, and fresh flowers. Black Sheep Best and Special and Copper Dragon Scotts 1816 on handpump, over 100 malt whiskies and a decent wine list with several by the glass; piped music. In good weather, you can enjoy a drink on the front terrace among the lovely hanging baskets and flowering climbers.

⊞ Cooked by the chef/patron, the very popular food includes lunchtime choices such as sandwiches, beer-battered fish, local gammon and eggs, sausage and mash with onion gravy, and a pie of the day, as well as soup, organic smoked salmon and crab salad with mango salsa, caramelised belly pork with black pudding, crispy duck leg with plum and orange sauce, asparagus and mushoom risotto, moroccan-spiced chicken on lemon and coriander couscous, pressed slow-cooked local lamb, and puddings like warm raspberry and almond tart with cinnamon cream and creamed rice pudding with glazed oranges; Sunday roasts. *Starters/Snacks: £5.00 to £7.50. Main Courses: £7.50 to £10.50. Puddings: £5.50 to £7.50*

Free house ~ Licensee Jonathan Harrison ~ Real ale ~ Bar food (12-2.30(2 Sun), 6.30-9(9.30 Fri and Sat); not Mon or winter Tues) ~ Restaurant ~ (01969) 622206 ~ Children welcome ~ Dogs allowed in bar ~ Open 11.30-3, 6.30-11; 12-3, 6.30-10.30 Sun; closed Mon, winter Tues, three days over Christmas ~ Bedrooms: £65S(£70B)/£75S(£80B)

Recommended by Stuart Pauley, Alun Jones, John and Sharon Hancock, David and Cathrine Whiting, John Robertson, Jane and Alan Bush, Dr Ian S Morley, David S Allen, Richard and Sissel Harris, Blaise Vyner

LINTON IN CRAVEN   SD9962   MAP 7

Fountaine
Just off B6265 Skipton—Grassington; BD23 5HJ

Neatly kept pub in charming village, attractive furnishings, open fires, five real ales, decent wines and well liked bar food; seats on terrace

At any time of the year, this neatly kept pub is deservedly busy and the staff are friendly and helpful; it's best to arrive early as parking can be difficult. There's a relaxed atmosphere, beams and white-painted joists in the low ceilings, log fires (one in a beautifully carved heavy wooden fireplace), attractive built-in cushioned wall benches and stools around a mix of copper-topped tables, little wall lamps and quite a few prints on the pale walls. Dark Horse Hetton Pale Ale, John Smiths, Tetleys and Thwaites Original and Wainwright on handpump; several wines by the glass; piped music, darts, and board games. Outside on the terrace there are teak benches and tables under green parasols and pretty hanging baskets; this is a delightful hamlet and there are fine surrounding walks in the lovely Dales countryside.

⏹ **Well liked bar food includes sandwiches and wraps, ploughman's, soup, black pudding and apricots in puff pastry with a mustard seed drizzle, thai fishcakes with sweet chilli sauce, a beefburger, beer-battered haddock, gammon and eggs, local pork sausages with red onion marmalade and gravy, slow-cooked lamb shoulder in mint and redcurrant sauce, fish stew, braised beef rump with root vegetables and a yorkshire pudding, and puddings; they also offer morning coffee and nibbles.** *Starters/Snacks: £3.95 to £5.95. Main Courses: £8.95 to £16.95. Puddings: £3.25 to £4.95*

Individual Inns ~ Manager Christopher Gregson ~ Real ale ~ Bar food (12-9) ~ Restaurant ~ (01756) 752210 ~ Children welcome ~ Dogs allowed in bar ~ Open 11-11; 12-10.30 Sun

Recommended by Lynda and Trevor Smith, Hunter and Christine Wright, WW, Richard, Pat and Graham Williamson, Gordon and Margaret Ormondroyd, John and Helen Rushton, Jon Sudlow

LONG PRESTON   SD8358   MAP 7

Maypole ⏹ ⏤

A65 Settle—Skipton; BD23 4PH

A good base for walkers with friendly staff, a bustling atmosphere, well liked pubby food and a fair choice of real ales

Handy for this busy road (and a good base for walking in the Dales), this pleasant inn is run by attentive and helpful licensees. The carpeted two-room bar has sporting prints and local photographs and a list of landlords dating back to 1695 on its butter-coloured walls, with good solid pub furnishings – heavy carved wall settles and the like, and cast-iron-framed pub tables with unusual inset leather tops. There's a separate dining room. Moorhouses Premier Bitter, Timothy Taylors Landlord and a couple of guests like Adnams Bitter and Moorhouses Blond Witch on handpump, ten wines by the glass, Weston's cider (in summer) and several malt whiskies. The left-hand tap room has been redecorated this year: darts, board games, dominoes and TV for important sporting events. On a back terrace there are a couple of picnic-sets under an ornamental cherry tree, with more tables under umbrellas on another terrace (which has outdoor heaters).

⏹ **Reasonably priced bar food includes sandwiches and filled baguettes, ploughman's, soup, chicken liver pâté with plum chutney, salmon and tuna fishcakes with lemon and chilli mayonnaise, ham and eggs, battered haddock, chestnut and root vegetable pie, steak in ale pie, local trout with tarragon and lemon butter, braised shank of lamb with mint, and daily specials; they also offer a good value two- and three-course menu on weekday lunchtimes.** *Starters/Snacks: £3.95 to £6.95. Main Courses: £8.50 to £13.50. Puddings: £3.75 to £5.25*

Enterprise ~ Lease Robert Palmer ~ Real ale ~ Bar food (12-2, 6.30(6 Fri)-9(9.30 Fri); all day weekends) ~ Restaurant ~ (01729) 840219 ~ Children welcome ~ Dogs allowed in bar and bedrooms ~ Open 12-3, 6-midnight(12.30 Fri); midday-12.30(midnight Sun) Sat; 11-3, 5-12.30 winter Fri ~ Bedrooms: £35S/£60B

Recommended by Richard Blackwell, Mr and Mrs Ian King, Steve Whalley, Mike and Linda Hudson, Dudley and Moira Cockroft, Michael Butler

LOW CATTON   SE7053   MAP 7

Gold Cup

Village signposted with High Catton off A166 in Stamford Bridge or A1079 at Kexby Bridge; YO41 1EA

Friendly, pleasant pub with refurbished bars, real ales, decent food, seats in garden and ponies in paddock

This year, the bars in this spacious white-rendered house have been refurbished and there's more of a country feel: coach lights on the rustic-looking walls, new beams, smarter furniture on the stripped wooden floors, an open fire at one end opposite the woodburning stove, new pictures and new curtains hanging from poles. The restaurant has solid wooden pews and tables (said to be made from a single oak tree) and pleasant views of the surrounding fields. John Smiths and Theakstons Best on handpump; piped music and pool. The garden has a grassed area for children and the back paddock houses Candy the horse and Polly the shetland pony. They also own Boris the retired greyhound and have fishing rights on the adjoining River Derwent. More reports please.

🍴 **Reasonably priced bar food includes sandwiches, soup, three-egg omelettes, breaded brie wedges with a port and orange dip, cheese and mushroom pasta bake, gammon and pineapple with melted cheese, chicken breast wrapped in bacon with a red wine and mushroom sauce, salmon fillet with lemon and dill hollandaise, braised venison steak on creamy mash, steaks, and puddings; Sunday roast served all day.** *Starters/Snacks: £4.00 to £5.75. Main Courses: £6.50 to £13.75. Puddings: £4.25*

Free house ~ Licensees Pat and Ray Hales ~ Real ale ~ Bar food (12-2, 6-9; all day weekends; not Mon lunchtime) ~ Restaurant ~ (01759) 371354 ~ Children welcome ~ Dogs allowed in bar ~ Open 12-2.30, 6-11; 12-11(10.30 Sun) Sat; closed Mon lunchtime, evenings 25 and 26 Dec

Recommended by Gordon and Margaret Ormondroyd, Pat and Graham Williamson, Pat and Tony Martin, Roger A Bellingham

LUND   SE9748   MAP 8

Wellington 🍴 ☲

Off B1248 SW of Driffield; YO25 9TE

Busy, smart pub with plenty of space in several rooms, real ales, helpfully noted wine list and interesting changing food

---

With reliably good food and real ales, this smart pub is liked by both drinkers and diners. The cosy Farmers Bar has beams, a quirky fireplace, well polished wooden banquettes and square tables, and gold-framed pictures and corner lamps on the walls. Off to one side is a plainer, no less smart, flagstoned room with a wine theme. At the other end of the bar a york-stoned walkway leads to a room with a display of the village's Britain in Bloom awards. There's also a restaurant and a bistro dining area with another open log fire. The main bar in the evening is a haven for drinkers only: John Smiths and Timothy Taylors Landlord and guests such as Summer Wine Elbow Grease and Wold Top Gold on handpump, a good wine list with a helpfully labelled choice by the glass and 30 malt whiskies. Piped music and TV. There are some benches in a small, pretty back courtyard. More reports please.

🍴 **Good bar food includes sandwiches, soup, chicken liver parfait with redcurrant and orange sauce, smoked haddock fishcakes with a mild curried apple sauce, honey-roast ham hock terrine, calves liver with bacon, rocket mash and shallot dressing, bass on a goats cheese and sunblush tomato filo tart, confit duck leg with honey and red wine reduction, grilled rib-eye steak with blue cheese and horseradish, and puddings like chocolate brownie with chocolate sauce and plum bakewell tart with custard.** *Starters/Snacks: £4.25 to £8.95. Main Courses: £10.95 to £15.95. Puddings: £5.95 to £6.95*

Free house ~ Licensees Russell Jeffery and Sarah Jeffery ~ Real ale ~ Bar food (not Sun evening or Mon) ~ Restaurant (Tues-Sat evenings) ~ (01377) 217294 ~ Children welcome ~ Open 12-3, 6.30-11; 12-11 Sun; closed Mon lunch

Recommended by Pat and Graham Williamson, Dr Ian S Morley, Marcus Mann

MASHAM   SE2281   MAP 10

Black Sheep Brewery ◀

Crosshills; HG4 4EN

Lively place with friendly staff, quite a mix of customers, unusual décor in big warehouse room, well kept beers (brewery tours and shop) and well liked food

---

Extremely popular, this is a lively place and a mix between a bar and a bistro – but it works well. A huge upper warehouse room has a bar serving well kept Black Sheep Best, Ale, Golden Sheep and Riggwelter on handpump, several wines by the glass and a fair choice of soft drinks. Most of the good-sized tables have cheery american-cloth patterned tablecloths and brightly cushioned green café chairs but there are some modern pubbier tables near the bar. There's a good deal of bare woodwork, with some rough stonework painted cream and green-painted steel girders and pillars. This big area is partly divided by free-standing partitions and some big plants; piped music and friendly service. Interesting brewery tours and a shop selling beers and more or less beer-related items from pub games and T-shirts to pottery and fudge. A glass wall lets you see into the brewing exhibition centre. Picnic-sets out on the grass.

🍽 **Enjoyable bar food includes sandwiches, filled baguettes and baked potatoes, ploughman's, soup, chicken liver pâté with sweet onion marmalade, dry-cured gammon and egg, liver and bacon with black pudding with onion sauce, roasted beer-battered haddock, pork and beer sausages with mustard mash and spicy beans, mediterranean vegetable lasagne, steak in ale pie with root vegetables, salmon steak niçoise, daily specials like barbecued spare ribs, lasagne and chicken stuffed with wensleydale cheese wrapped in bacon with a tomato and sage sauce, and puddings like crème brûlée and lemon meringue pie; Sunday roasts.** *Starters/Snacks: £4.50 to £5.95. Main Courses: £6.50 to £10.95. Puddings: £4.95*

Free house ~ Licensee Paul Theakston ~ Real ale ~ Bar food (12-2.30(3 Sun), 7(6.30 Thurs-Sat)-9) ~ (01765) 680100 ~ Children welcome ~ Open 11-4.30 Mon-Weds; 11-11 Thurs, Fri and Sat; 12-4.30 Sun; closed two weeks Jan

Recommended by Adrian Johnson, Paul and Ursula Randall, M and GR, Mr and Mrs Maurice Thompson, WW, Janet and Peter Race, Mark Walker, Mr and Mrs John Taylor

MIDDLEHAM   SE1287   MAP 10

White Swan 🍷 🛏

Market Place; DL8 4PE

Smartly extended inn with proper pubby bar, well liked food and real ales; individually decorated bedrooms

This is a pleasant, extended coaching inn in a charming small market town and set opposite the cobbled square; there are some seats and tables on the pavement. Inside, there's a beamed and flagstoned entrance bar with a proper pubby atmosphere, a long dark pew built into a big window, a mix of chairs around a handful of biggish tables, some high wooden bar chairs by the counter and an open woodburning stove. Black Sheep Best, John Smiths and Theakstons Best on handpump from the curved counter, 12 wines by the glass, 20 malt whiskies and quite a few teas and coffees. The dining room is light, spacious and modern with dark wooden tables and chairs on the pale oak flooring, a large fireplace and, in an area opposite the bar, some contemporary leather chairs and a sofa; quite a few big house plants dotted about. The back room offers more dining space; piped music. The bedrooms are comfortable and well appointed.

🍽 **Popular bar food includes filled baguettes, ploughman's, soup, ham hock terrine with parsley and a yellow split pea purée, gloucester old spot sausage with bubble and squeak and onion gravy, home-made beefburgers topped with cheddar and bacon or blue cheese and red onion, various pizzas, tagliatelle with wild mushrooms, thyme and parmesan, steak in ale pie, crisp belly pork with apple sauce and gravy, chicken breast wrapped in parma ham, lemon and sage with a lemon butter sauce, and puddings like iced liquorice terrine with caramel sauce and white chocolate crème brûlée; they offer a dish of the day and a two- and three-course early-bird menu (6-7.30 Sunday-Friday).** *Starters/Snacks: £4.25 to £7.95. Main Courses: £8.25 to £15.95. Puddings: £5.50*

Free house ~ Licensee Kim Woodcock ~ Real ale ~ Bar food (all day including breakfast from 8am) ~ Restaurant ~ (01969) 622093 ~ Children welcome ~ Dogs allowed in bar and bedrooms ~ Open 11-11(midnight Sat); 12-11 Sun ~ Bedrooms: £55B/£85S(£95B)

Recommended by John Robertson, Anthony Barnes, Bruce and Sharon Eden, Michael Tack

---

The knife-and-fork award distinguishes pubs where the food is of exceptional quality.

MILL BANK

SE0321   MAP 7

Millbank 🍴 🍷

Mill Bank Road, off A58 SW of Sowerby Bridge; HX6 3DY

Imaginative food in cottagey-looking dining pub, real ales, fine wines and specialist gin list, friendly staff and interesting garden sculptures; walks nearby and good views

A new oak-floored conservatory with colourful blinds has been built on top of what was the terrace of this impressive dining pub. It's a cottagey, traditional-looking building but once you get inside, the rooms have a clean-cut minimalist modern décor and there are local photographs for sale. It's divided into the tap room, bar and restaurant, with Tetleys, Timothy Taylors Landlord and a guest like Goose Eye Chinook on handpump, 20 wines by the glass including champagne, port and pudding wines and a specialised gin list; friendly staff. This is a glorious setting overlooking an old textile mill and the Calderdale Way is easily accessible from the pub.

🍴 Cooked by the licensee, the food remains good and contemporary: sandwiches, soup, potted shrimps with toasted brioche, little fritters of blue cheese with beetroot salad, fishcake of oak roast salmon and crayfish with orange hollandaise, smoked chicken risotto with tarragon, almonds and roast jerusalem artichoke, mushroom and leek shepherd's pie, steak and onion pudding with mustard mash, fricassée of rabbit with smoked bacon, bass fillet with crab tortellini, asparagus and lemon grass, and puddings like chocolate brownie with white chocolate sauce and peanut butter ice-cream and eton mess with apple jelly. *Starters/Snacks: £3.95 to £6.95. Main Courses: £9.95 to £14.50. Puddings: £1.95 to £6.25*

Free house ~ Licensee Glenn Futter ~ Real ale ~ Bar food (12-2.30, 6-9.30(10 Fri and Sat); 12.30-4.30, 6-8 Sun; not Mon) ~ Restaurant ~ (01422) 825588 ~ Children welcome ~ Dogs allowed in bar ~ Jazz bank hol Sun evenings; quiz first Thurs of month ~ Open 12-2.30, 5.30-11(midnight Sat); 12-10.30 Sun; closed Mon (except bank hols)

Recommended by Stuart Doughty, Dr Kevan Tucker, GLD, Jean and Douglas Troup, Gordon and Margaret Ormondroyd

MOULTON

NZ2303   MAP 10

Black Bull 🍴 🍷

Just off A1 near Scotch Corner; DL10 6QJ

Civilised, enjoyable dining pub, characterful bar with interesting furnishings, very good bar food, more elaborate restaurant menu and smart dining areas (one is a Pullman dining car)

Handy for the A1, this is an enjoyable and civilised dining pub. The bar has a lot of character, as well as an antique panelled oak settle and an old elm housekeeper's chair, built-in red cushioned black settles and pews around cast-iron tables, silver-plated turkish coffee pots and copper cooking utensils hanging from black beams, fresh flowers and a huge winter log fire. In the evening you can also eat in the polished brick-tiled conservatory with bentwood cane chairs or in the Brighton Belle dining car. Eight wines, including champagne by the glass and 50 malt whiskies. There are some seats outside in the central court.

🍴 The food is extremely good, and at lunchtime the bar food includes sandwiches and toasties, soup, feuilleté of smoked haddock with white wine and prawn sauce, ham hock and parsley terrine with piccalilli, caesar salad with anchovy and garlic toast, seafood pancake thermidor, risotto of peas with mint and lemon balsamic, and bangers and mash with onion gravy; also, mackerel pâté with sweet pickled cucumber salad, mature cheddar and spinach soufflé, hot and crunchy rock oysters with crab and lemon mayonnaise, calves liver on a tarte tatin with shallots and aged sherry dressing, free-range coq au vin, paupiette of lemon sole and smoked salmon with Noilly Prat and herb beurre blanc, and puddings like sherry trifle with apricot and toasted almonds and burnt lemon custard pot with lemon and lime biscotti. *Starters/Snacks: £4.95 to £7.25. Main Courses: £6.50 to £8.50. Puddings: £4.75 to £5.95*

Free house ~ Licensee Mr Barker ~ Bar food (12-2.30(2 Sat), 6.30-9.30(10 Fri and Sat);
12-4 Sun) ~ Restaurant (evening) ~ (01325) 377289 ~ Children welcome ~ Open 12-2.30,
6-10.30(11 Sat); 12-4 Sun; closed Sun evening

*Recommended by Jill and Julian Tasker, John and Eleanor Holdsworth, Patrick and Barbara Knights,
Rebecca Sutton*

NUNNINGTON
SE6679 MAP 7

Royal Oak

Church Street; at back of village, which is signposted from A170 and B1257; YO62 5US

**Friendly staff and good food in reliable, neat pub, lots to look at in beamed bar, winter
open fires and real ales**

This is an enjoyable and attractive little pub with a warmly friendly landlady. The neatly
kept bar has high black beams strung with earthenware flagons, copper jugs and lots of
antique keys, one of the walls is stripped back to the bare stone to display a fine
collection of antique farm tools and there are open fires; carefully chosen furniture such
as kitchen and country dining chairs and a long pew around the sturdy tables on the
turkey carpet. Black Sheep Best, Theakstons XB and Wold Top Wolds Way on handpump
and several wines by the glass; friendly, efficient staff and piped music. The terraced
garden has been landscaped. Nunnington Hall (National Trust) is nearby.

**🍴 Enjoyable bar food includes chicken liver pâté with red onion marmalade, egg
mayonnaise with prawns, toasted goats cheese with crispy bacon and apple and tomato
chutney, hog and hop sausages with wholegrain mustard mash, local haddock in batter,
fresh pasta vegetable bake, steak and kidney casserole with herb dumplings, salmon and
asparagus tartlets, lamb shank in port and mint gravy, and puddings like triple chocolate
mousse and port-poached rhubarb pavlova.** *Starters/Snacks: £5.50 to £7.00. Main Courses:
£9.95 to £19.95. Puddings: £5.50*

Free house ~ Licensee Anita Hilton ~ Real ale ~ Bar food (not Mon) ~ Restaurant ~
(01439) 748271 ~ Children welcome ~ Dogs welcome ~ Open 11.45(12 Sun)-2.30, 6.30(7 Sun)-
11; closed Mon (except bank hols)

*Recommended by Mary Goodfellow, Maggie Horton, Pat and Graham Williamson, Roger A Bellingham, Andy and
Jill Kassube*

OSMOTHERLEY
SE4597 MAP 10

Golden Lion 🍴 🍺

The Green, West End; off A19 N of Thirsk; DL6 3AA

**Welcoming, busy pub with simply furnished rooms, lots of malt whiskies, real ales,
interesting bar food and fine surrounding walks**

With a friendly welcome from the attentive staff, good food and real ales, it's not
surprising that this attractive old stone pub is so popular; you'll need to book ahead to
be sure of a table. There's an enjoyably bustling atmosphere and the roomy beamed bar
on the left is simply furnished with old pews with just a few decorations on its white
walls, candles on tables, John Smiths, Timothy Taylors Landlord and a guest such as York
Guzzler on handpump and 46 malt whiskies. On the right, there's a similarly
unpretentious and well worn-in eating area as well as a separate dining room, mainly
open at weekends, and a covered courtyard; piped music. Benches out in front look
across the village green to the market cross, and there are seats on the terrace. As the
inn is the start of the 44-mile Lyke Wakes Walk on the Cleveland Way and quite handy for
the Coast to Coast Walk, it's naturally popular with walkers.

**🍴 Reliably good and interesting, the bar food includes soup, rough pâté with onion and
apricot relish, sticky barbecue spare ribs, home-made lamb burger with mint jelly and
balsamic vinegar dip, spinach, ricotta and pine nut lasagne, smoked haddock and spring
onion fishcake with chive and beurre blanc sauce, charcoal-grilled poussin with rosemary
and garlic, steak and kidney pudding, daily specials like halibut with samphire,
hollandaise and red pepper purée, gressingham duck with bean cassoulet and venison**

fillet with red wine jus, and puddings such as middle eastern orange cake with marmalade cream and poached pear in wine with hot chocolate sauce. *Starters/Snacks: £4.95 to £7.95. Main Courses: £7.95 to £18.95. Puddings: £4.95*

Free house ~ Licensee Christie Connelly ~ Real ale ~ Bar food (12-2.30, 6-9) ~ (01609) 883526 ~ Children welcome ~ Dogs allowed in bar ~ Open 12-2.30, 6-11; 12-11 Sat; closed Mon (except bank hols) and Tues lunchtimes ~ Bedrooms: £60S/£90S

Recommended by Mr and Mrs Maurice Thompson, Louise Gibbons, David and Sue Smith, Janet and Peter Race, Blaise Vyner, Pat Bradbury, Tony and Rosemary Swainson

PICKERING   SE7984   MAP 10

White Swan ⓨ 🍷 🛏️

Market Place, just off A170; YO18 7AA

Relaxed little bar in civilised coaching inn, several smart lounges, attractive restaurant, real ales, an excellent wine list and first-class food; luxurious bedrooms

Staying overnight here is a real treat as the bedrooms are lovely and the breakfasts excellent. It's a smart old coaching inn with quite an emphasis on the first-class restaurant but there's a small bar with real ales and a friendly welcome. This room has a relaxed atmosphere, wood panelling, sofas and just four tables, a log fire and Black Sheep Best and Timothy Taylors Landlord on handpump, 11 wines by the glass from an extensive list that includes super old st emilions and pudding wines, and 20 malt whiskies. Opposite, a bare-boards room with a few more tables has another fire in a handsome art nouveau iron fireplace, a big bow window and pear prints on its plum-coloured walls. The restaurant has flagstones, a fine open fire, rich tweed soft furnishings, comfortable settles and gothic screens, and the residents' lounge is in a converted beamed barn. The old coach entry to the car park is very narrow.

🍴 **At lunchtime, you can enjoy the excellent food in both the bar and restaurant but in the evening you may eat only in the restaurant. There might be lunchtime bar choices such as filled baguettes, ploughman's, soup, ham hock terrine with parsley and yellow split pea purée, fishcakes with tartare sauce, pizzas, home-made burgers with various toppings, steak in ale pie, and gloucester old spot sausages with onion gravy, as well as more elaborate brasserie dishes such as marinated king prawns with sesame and ginger, tagliatelle with wild mushrooms, thyme and parmesan, red snapper with chorizo risotto and lemon parsley butter, and crisp pork belly with apple sauce and gravy, and puddings like iced liquorice terrine with caramel sauce and white chocolate crème brûlée; there's also a two- and three-course early-bird menu (6-7pm not Saturday).** *Starters/Snacks: £4.95 to £10.95. Main Courses: £9.95 to £21.00. Puddings: £6.95*

Free house ~ Licensees Marion and Victor Buchanan ~ Real ale ~ Bar food ~ Restaurant ~ (01751) 472288 ~ Children welcome ~ Dogs allowed in bar and bedrooms ~ Open 10am-11pm; 11am-10.30pm Sun ~ Bedrooms: £110B/£145B

Recommended by Derek Thomas, Dr Ian S Morley, Peter Burton, P Dawn, Marian and Andrew Ruston, Janet and Peter Race, G D Affleck, Phil Bryant, Pat and Graham Williamson, John and Barbara Hirst, Margaret Walker

PICKHILL   SE3483   MAP 10

Nags Head ⓨ 🍷 🛏️

Take the Masham turn-off from A1 both N and S, and village signposted off B6267 in Ainderby Quernhow; YO7 4JG

Busy dining pub with excellent food, a fine choice of carefully chosen drinks, a tap room, smarter lounge and friendly service

This is a popular dining pub with friendly staff and enjoyable bar food – just the place to take a break from the A1. Most of the tables are laid for eating so if it's just a drink you're after, head for the bustling tap room on the left: beams hung with jugs, coach horns, ale-yards and so forth, and masses of ties hanging as a frieze from a rail around the red ceiling. The smarter lounge bar has deep green plush banquettes on the matching carpet, pictures for sale on its neat cream walls and an open fire. There's also a library-themed restaurant. Black Sheep Best, Theakstons Black Bull and a guest like York Guzzler on handpump, a good choice of malt whiskies, vintage armagnacs and a carefully chosen wine list with several by the glass. One table is inset with a chessboard; darts and piped music. There's a front verandah, a boules and quoits pitch and a nine-hole putting green.

🍴 **Extremely good bar food includes sandwiches, soup, duck liver parfait with rhubarb compote, whitby crab with avocado purée and lemon emulsion, beef and lamb burger with cheddar cheese glaze and tomato jam, smashing scampi, tortellini of blue cheese and spinach with a tomato and herb sauce, smoked haddock on lightly curried risotto with a free-range poached egg, steak and kidney suet pudding, belly of pork with black pudding and cider reduction, crispy duckling with honey apples and duck gravy, and puddings like roasted white peach with sweetened mascarpone and marzipan dust and treacle tart with raspberry sorbet.** *Starters/Snacks: £3.95 to £8.95. Main Courses: £8.95 to £16.95. Puddings: £3.95 to £5.95*

Free house ~ Licensee Edward Boynton ~ Real ale ~ Bar food (12-2, 6-9.30; 12-2.30, 6-9 Sun) ~ Restaurant ~ (01845) 567391 ~ Well behaved children welcome until 7.30pm ~ Dogs allowed in bedrooms ~ Open 11-11(10.30 Sun) ~ Bedrooms: £55B/£80B

Recommended by Melvyn Dyson, Janet and Peter Race, J K Parry, Gordon and Margaret Ormondroyd, Jill and Julian Tasker, Mrs Brenda Calver, Roger and Lesley Everett

RIPLEY
SE2860   MAP 7

Boars Head ♀ 🍺 🛏
Off A61 Harrogate—Ripon; HG3 3AY

Friendly bar/bistro in smart hotel, several real ales, excellent wine list and malt whiskies, good food and helpful service; comfortable bedrooms

Of course this isn't a pub, it's a comfortable hotel with a bistro/bar but this long flagstoned room does have a relaxed and informal atmosphere and they do keep Black Sheep Best and Golden Sheep, Daleside Crackshot Ale, Hambleton White Boar and Theakstons Old Peculier on handpump, an excellent wine list (with ten or so by the glass), around 20 malt whiskies, and lots of teas and coffees. There are green checked tablecloths (most of the tables are arranged to form individual booths), warm yellow walls with jolly little drawings of cricketers or huntsmen running along the bottom, a boar's head (part of the family coat of arms), an interesting religious carving and a couple of cricket bats; efficient staff even when very busy. Some of the furnishings in the hotel came from the attic of next door Ripley Castle, where the Ingilbys have lived for over 650 years. A pleasant little garden has plenty of tables.

🍴 **Using some home-grown produce, the good food includes sandwiches, soup, prawn and lovage mousse, mushroom stroganoff, pork and leek sausages with caramelised onion mash, lambs liver with smoked bacon, herb-crusted haddock fillet with butter beans and tomato, haunch of venison with spicy red cabbage, lamb rump with cumin, chickpeas and tomatoes, and puddings like sticky toffee pudding and iced tiramisu with coffee cream.** *Starters/Snacks: £3.75 to £6.00. Main Courses: £10.95 to £15.95. Puddings: £4.50 to £6.00*

Free house ~ Licensee Sir Thomas Ingilby ~ Real ale ~ Bar food (12-2.30, 6.30-9.30) ~ Restaurant ~ (01423) 771888 ~ Children welcome ~ Dogs allowed in bedrooms ~ Open 11-11; 12-10.30 Sun; 11-2.30, 5-11 in winter ~ Bedrooms: £105B/£125B

Recommended by Janet and Peter Race, Dr and Mrs J Temporal, John Saul, Christopher Turner, Tim and Ann Newell, J F M and M West, the Didler, Ian and Joan Blackwell, Mr and Mrs Maurice Thompson

---

Please keep sending us reports. We rely on readers for news of new discoveries, and particularly for news of changes – however slight – at the fully described pubs: feedback@goodguides.com, or (no stamp needed) The Good Pub Guide, FREEPOST TN1569, Wadhurst, E Sussex TN5 7BR.

RIPPONDEN   SE0419   MAP 7

Old Bridge ♀ ◖

From A58, best approach is Elland Road (opposite Golden Lion), park opposite the church in pub's car park and walk back over ancient hump-back bridge; HX6 4DF

Pleasant old pub by medieval bridge with relaxed communicating rooms, half a dozen real ales, quite a few wines by the glass, lots of whiskies and well liked food

By the medieval pack-horse bridge over the little River Ryburn, this 14th-c pub has a garden overlooking the water. Inside, there are three communicating rooms, each on a slightly different level and all with a relaxed, friendly atmosphere. Oak settles are built into the window recesses of the thick stone walls, and there are antique oak tables, rush-seated chairs, a few well chosen pictures and prints and a big woodburning stove. There's a fine range of beers on handpump such as Timothy Taylors Best, Golden Best and Landlord and three changing guests like Brass Monkey Bitter, Burton Bridge Bitter and East Coast Bonhomme Richard on handpump, quite a few foreign bottled beers, a dozen wines by the glass and 30 malt whiskies. More reports please.

🍴 On weekday lunchtimes, bar food only includes sandwiches and soup or the popular help-yourself carvery and salad buffet; at weekends and in the evening (but not Saturday or Sunday evening), there might be whitby crab and avocado tian with bloody mary dressing, king scallops with chorizo and celeriac purée, meat and potato pie with mushy peas, greek-style mediterranean vegetable and bean wraps topped with cheese and sour cream, corn-fed chicken on creamed mustard leeks with black pudding and potato rösti, soy and chilli duck breast with pak choi, and puddings. *Starters/Snacks: £3.50 to £5.75. Main Courses: £4.95 to £13.50. Puddings: £3.50*

Free house ~ Licensees Tim and Lindsay Eaton Walker ~ Real ale ~ Bar food (12-2, 6.30-9.30; not Sat or Sun evenings) ~ (01422) 822595 ~ Children in eating area of bar until 8pm but must be well behaved ~ Open 12-3, 5.30-11; 12-11(10.30 Sun) Sat

Recommended by G Dobson

ROBIN HOOD'S BAY   NZ9505   MAP 10

Laurel

Village signposted off A171 S of Whitby; YO22 4SE

Charming little pub in unspoilt fishing village, neat friendly bar and real ales

Especially popular with walkers, this is an unspoilt little local with a charming landlord. It's at the heart of one of the prettiest fishing villages on the north-east coast, and the beamed and welcoming main bar is neatly kept and decorated with old local photographs, Victorian prints and brasses, and lager bottles from all over the world. There's an open fire and Caledonian Deuchars IPA and maybe Theakstons Best or Old Peculier on handpump; darts, board games and piped music. In summer, the hanging baskets and window boxes are lovely. They have a self-contained apartment for two people.

🍴 You can buy sandwiches from the Old Bakery Tearooms and eat them in the pub.

Free house ~ Licensee Brian Catling ~ Real ale ~ No credit cards ~ (01947) 880400 ~ Children in snug bar only ~ Dogs welcome ~ Open 12-11(10.30 Sun); opening time 2pm Mon-Thurs in winter (best to phone beforehand)

Recommended by Brian and Anna Marsden, P Dawn, the Didler, Alison and Pete

ROECLIFFE

SE3765 MAP 7

Crown 🍽 🍷

Off A168 just W of Boroughbridge; handy for A1(M) junction 48; YO51 9LY

Smartly updated and attractively placed pub with a civilised bar, good enterprising food and fine choice of drinks

The Maineys run this thriving pub with considerable enthusiasm and not a little humour. Each week they dress the mannequins sitting outside in different clothes and they've papered the gents' in vintage *Playboy* covers. You can be sure of a friendly welcome, some first-class food, four real ales, and a fine choice of wines, and reports from our many readers are full of warm praise. The bar has a contemporary colour scheme of dark reds and near-whites, with attractive prints carefully grouped and lit; one area has chunky pine tables on flagstones, another part, with a log fire, has dark tables on plaid carpet. John Smiths, Theakstons Best and changing guests like Caledonian Deuchars IPA and Sharps Doom Bar on handpump, and 20 wines by the glass; neat, helpful staff. For meals, you have a choice between a small candlelit olive-green bistro, with nice tables, a longcase clock and one or two paintings, and a more formal restaurant; at weekends, it's always wise to book ahead. The pub faces the village green; the bedrooms they're refurbishing should be open by the end of 2009.

🍴 **Smoking their own fish and baking fresh daily bread, the excellent contemporary bar food includes lunchtime sandwiches, soup, smoked salmon with lemon-infused frozen vodka and chopped dill, home-made winter fruit black pudding and crisp parma ham over apple and vanilla compote, home-made beefburger, steak in ale en croûte with chive mash, gloucester old spot hotpot with organic red cabbage and crispy crackling, fish pie with sole, pollack and scarborough woof, lamb shoulder roasted with parma ham over bubble and squeak with minted jus, and puddings like a home-made fresh doughnut filled with organic apple, calvados crème brûlée and cinnamon ice-cream and irish whiskey bread and butter pudding with crème fraîche ice-cream and poached kumquats; they also offer an evening two-course early-bird menu (before 7.30pm).** *Starters/Snacks: £4.25 to £6.95. Main Courses: £9.95 to £12.95. Puddings: £5.95 to £6.50*

Free house ~ Licensee Karl Mainey ~ Real ale ~ Bar food (12-2.30, 6-9.30; 12-7 Sun; not Sun evening) ~ Restaurant ~ (01423) 322300 ~ Children welcome ~ Dogs allowed in bar ~ Open 12-3.30, 5-12; 12-11 Sun
Recommended by WW, Keith and Sue Ward, Les and Sandra Brown, Peter and Josie Fawcett, Michael Doswell, Hunter and Christine Wright

SANDHUTTON

SE3882 MAP 10

Kings Arms 🍺

A167, 1 mile N of A61 Thirsk—Ripon; YO7 4RW

Good chef/landlord in cheerful and appealing pub with friendly service and comfortable furnishings

On our early December visit, this charmingly refurbished village-edge pub was packed with chatty, cheerful diners. The bustling bar has an unusual circular woodburner in one corner, a high central table with four equally high stools, high-backed brown leather seated dining chairs around light pine tables, a couple of cushioned wicker armchairs, some attractive modern bar stools, and photographs of the pub in years gone by. A shelf has some odd knick-knacks such as fish jaws and a bubble-gum machine, there are various pub games and a flatscreen TV. Black Sheep Best, Grainstore BBB, John Smiths and Theakstons Black Bull on handpump, and efficient, friendly service. The two connecting dining rooms have similar furnishings to the bar (though there's also a nice big table with smart high-backed dining chairs), arty flower photographs on the cream walls and a shelf above the small woodburning stove with more knick-knacks and some candles. We have not yet heard from readers who have stayed in one of the two bedrooms here, but would expect them to be good value. Parking is slightly haphazard.

🍴 **Good food cooked by the chef/landlord and his son includes sandwiches, ploughman's, local bangers with mustard mash and onion gravy, a pie of the day, and whitby scampi** with tartare sauce, as well as more elaborate choices such as black pudding, dry-cured bacon, apple and madeira sauce, field mushroom filled with a wild mushroom duxelles glazed with blue cheese, roasted mediterranean vegetable lasagne, fillet of salmon with chive beurre blanc, suprême of chicken filled with feta cheese and olives, and puddings like gooseberry crème brûlée with brandysnap biscuit and lemon and passion-fruit parfait with elderflower syrup. *Starters/Snacks: £3.50 to £6.50. Main Courses: £6.75 to £11.95. Puddings: £4.25 to £4.75*

Free house ~ Licensee Raymond and Alexander Boynton ~ Real ale ~ Bar food (12-2.30, 5.30-9; 12-5 Sun; not Sun evening) ~ Restaurant ~ (01845) 587887 ~ Children welcome ~ Open 12-midnight ~ Bedrooms: £35S/£60S

Recommended by Richard Cole, Mr and Mrs J Culf, Dr J Garside, Dennis and Amanda Parkyn

SAWLEY   SE2467   MAP 7

Sawley Arms ♀
Village signposted off B6265 W of Ripon; HG4 3EQ

Old-fashioned dining pub with good restauranty food, decent house wines and comfortable furnishings in small carpeted rooms; pretty garden

This is a spotlessly kept dining pub with meticulous attention. It's ultra-civilised in an old-fashioned, decorous sort of way and particularly popular with older customers. The small turkey-carpeted rooms have log fires and comfortable furniture ranging from small softly cushioned armed dining chairs and sofas, to the wing armchairs down a couple of steps in a side snug; maybe daily papers and magazines to read; piped music. There's also a conservatory; good house wines. In fine weather you can sit in the pretty garden where the flowering tubs and baskets are lovely; there are two stone cottages in the grounds for rent. Fountains Abbey (the most extensive of the great monastic remains – floodlit on late summer Friday and Saturday evenings, with a live choir on the Saturday) – is not far away.

🍴 As well as lunchtime sandwiches, the good food includes soup with croûtons, salmon mousse with cucumber pickle, deep-fried brie with pear, apple and ginger chutney, steak or chicken, leek and mushroom pie, pork, sage and apricot cassoulet, slow-roasted boned duckling with mandarin and cardamon crust, plaice mornay, lamb shank with rosemary and madeira gravy, and puddings such as steamed butterscotch pudding with mascarpone vanilla custard and butterscotch sauce and baked lemon and ginger cheesecake with a compote of bilberries. *Starters/Snacks: £4.25 to £6.95. Main Courses: £9.95 to £17.75. Puddings: £5.75*

Free house ~ Licensee Mrs June Hawes ~ Bar food (not Mon evening) ~ Restaurant ~ (01765) 620642 ~ Well behaved children in conservatory ~ Open 11.30-3, 6.30-10.30; Mon evenings in winter

Recommended by Ian and Joan Blackwell, P and J Shapley, Janet and Peter Race

SHEFFIELD   SK3687   MAP 7

Fat Cat 🍺 £
23 Alma Street; S3 8SA

Super own-brewed beers and guests in this friendly, bustling town local; plenty of bottled beers too and remarkably cheap tasty food; brewery visits

It's the smashing choice of up to ten real ales that draws customers to this busy and friendly town local. As well as their own-brewed Kelham Island Bitter, Pale Rider and Easy Rider, there's Timothy Taylors Landlord and guests from breweries such as Milk Street, Millstone, Rudgate, Saltaire, Spire and Tigertops, all well kept on handpump. Also, draught and bottled belgian beers, Weston's cider and country wines. The two small downstairs rooms have brewery-related prints on the walls, coal fires, simple wooden tables and cushioned seats around the walls and jugs, bottles and some advertising mirrors; cards and dominoes and maybe the pub cat wandering around. The upstairs room has a TV for sport. The Brewery Visitor Centre (you can book brewery trips by phoning (0114) 249 4804) has framed beer mats, pump clips and prints on the walls. There are picnic-sets in a fairylit back courtyard.

🍴 **Extremely cheap bar food includes sandwiches, soup, ploughman's, leek and sweet potato, pork or chicken casseroles, popular steak pie, chickpea and pepper stew, mushroom and tomato pasta with melted mozzarella, and puddings like jam roly-poly and apple crumble; Monday evening curries and Sunday roast.** *Main Courses: £4.40. Puddings: £1.75*

Own brew ~ Licensee Duncan Shaw ~ Real ale ~ Bar food (12-3, 6-8; all day Sat; not Sun evening) ~ (0114) 249 4801 ~ Children welcome away from main bar ~ Dogs welcome ~ Open 12-11(midnight Fri and Sat)

Recommended by Pete Baker, Giles and Annie Francis, P Dawn, the Didler, Marian and Andrew Ruston, Ian and Debs, John Honnor, David Carr

New Barrack 🍺 £

601 Penistone Road, Hillsborough; S6 2GA

Lively and friendly, with 11 real ales and a fine range of other drinks, good value food and lots going on

As well as their own-brew beers, this lively pub is popular for its evening activities. At the weekend, there's live music and comedy acts, and every weekday evening there's a different theme from chess club to games night to general knowledge quiz competitions; it's even busier on match days. The comfortable front lounge has upholstered seats, old pine floors and a log fire, the tap room has another log fire and darts, and the back room can be used for small functions. TV, dominoes, cards, cribbage and daily papers to read. As well as regular beers such as Acorn Barnsley Bitter, Batemans XXXB, Bradfield Farmers Bitter, Castle Rock Harvest Pale and Screech Owl, there are six constantly changing guests; also, real cider, a range of bottled belgian beers and 28 malt whiskies. The small walled back garden has won awards. Local parking is not easy.

🍴 **Tasty bar food includes sandwiches and filled baguettes, all day breakfast, pie and peas, pizzas, sausage and mash, mixed grill, and their very popular beer-battered cod.** *Starters/Snacks: £2.00 to £4.95. Main Courses: £4.35 to £10.95. Puddings: £1.50 to £4.50*

Tynemill ~ Managers Kevin and Stephanie Woods ~ Real ale ~ Bar food (11-3, 5-9 (Fri and Sat light suppers till midnight); 12-4, 7-9 Sun) ~ (0114) 234 9148 ~ Children welcome until 9pm ~ Dogs welcome ~ Live music Fri, Sat and Sun evenings ~ Open 11-11(midnight Fri and Sat); 12-11 Sun

Recommended by the Didler, David Carr, Don and Shirley Parrish

SHELLEY
SE2112   MAP 7

Three Acres 🍴 🍷 🍺 🛏️

Roydhouse (not signposted); from B6116 heading for Skelmanthorpe, turn left in Shelley (signposted Flockton, Elmley, Elmley Moor) and go up lane for 2 miles towards radio mast; HD8 8LR

Delicious food and friendly service in busy, smart dining pub, several real ales, fine choice of other drinks and relaxed atmosphere; good bedrooms and lovely views

A yorkshire institution, this is a civilised former coaching inn offering excellent food and comfortable bedrooms. But despite the emphasis on the stylish cooking, they do keep Black Sheep Best, Tetleys and Timothy Taylors Landlord on handpump, over 40 whiskies and a fantastic (if not cheap) choice of wines with at least 17 by the glass; attentive staff. The roomy lounge bar has a relaxed, informal atmosphere, tankards hanging from the main beam, high bar chairs and stools, button-back leather sofas, old prints and so forth. To be sure of a table you must book quite a way ahead – try to get a place with a view across to Emley Moor; piped music. There are also more formal dining rooms.

🍴 **From a sizeable – if pricey – menu, the food might include sandwiches, ploughman's, soup, toulouse sausage and black pudding with crispy bacon, onion and chilli relish, apple** tempura and grain mustard dressing, mussels with lemon grass, ginger, chilli coconut milk and coriander, potted shrimps, salad of warm, crispy venison with sesame and sweet chilli leaves, risotto of baked aubergine, slow-roasted plum tomato, breaded goats cheese and aged honey and balsamic vinegar, beer-battered whitby haddock, free-range chicken with ham hock and leek pasty and tarragon and mustard jus, steak, kidney and mushroom pie cooked in beer, creamy fish pie, duck with confit of belly pork and rhubarb and onion tatin, and puddings like mixed red berry sherry trifle and chocolate mocha pot with home-made biscotti; Sunday roasts. *Starters/Snacks: £5.95 to £10.95. Main Courses: £13.95 to £26.95. Puddings: £7.95*

Free house ~ Licensees Neil Truelove and Brian Orme ~ Real ale ~ Bar food (12-2, 6.30-9.30) ~ Restaurant ~ (01484) 602606 ~ Children welcome ~ Open 12-3, 6-11(10.30 Sun); closed 25 and 26 Dec, 1 Jan ~ Bedrooms: £80B/£120B

Recommended by Colin McKerrow, Pat and Stewart Gordon, Revd D Glover, Richard Cole, John and Barbara Hirst, Richard Marjoram, Andy and Jill Kassube, Cedric Robertshaw

SINNINGTON   SE7485   MAP 10

Fox & Hounds 🍴 🍷 🛏️

Just off A170 W of Pickering; YO62 6SQ

Carefully run coaching inn with welcoming staff, fine choice of drinks, imaginative food and comfortable beamed bar; bedrooms

The friendly licensees continue to run this neatly kept coaching inn with much care and attention and our readers enjoy their visits here very much. The beamed bar has various pictures and old artefacts, a woodburning stove and comfortable wall seats and carver chairs around the tables on its carpet. The curved corner bar counter has Black Sheep and Copper Dragon Best Bitter on handpump, several wines by the glass and some rare malt whiskies. There's a lounge and separate restaurant, too. The cartoons in the gents' are worth a peek; piped music. In front of the building are some picnic-sets, with more in the garden. The bedrooms are comfortable and quiet and the charming village is well worth strolling around.

🍴 Growing some of their own produce and sourcing everything else very locally, the excellent food might include lunchtime sandwiches, soup, coriander crab cakes, spiced vegetable and cashew salad with a sweet chilli dipping sauce, Old Peculier cheese soufflé, with sweet onion marmalade, fish pie topped with cheddar and parsley mash, beer-battered fresh haddock with home-made tartare sauce, a trio of chicken (crispy medallions with onion, herbed roast bread with scallop potatoes and little kiev with crushed peas), slow-cooked shoulder of lamb with gratin dauphinoise, a vegetarian dish of the day, chargrilled rump steak with a choice of sauces, and puddings like crème brûlée and bread and butter pudding. *Starters/Snacks: £4.95 to £8.25. Main Courses: £9.95 to £22.95. Puddings: £4.75 to £5.25*

Free house ~ Licensees Andrew and Catherine Stephens ~ Real ale ~ Bar food ~ Restaurant (evening) ~ (01751) 431577 ~ Children must be well behaved and must leave by 7.45pm ~ Dogs allowed in bar and bedrooms ~ Open 12-2, 6-11.30(11 Sun); 6.30 evening opening in winter; closed 25 and 26 Dec ~ Bedrooms: £59S(£69B)/£90S(£100B)

Recommended by Catherine Hyde, Mr and Mrs D Hammond, Janet and Peter Race, Alison and Pete, Julie Preddy, Maurice and Gill McMahon, I H M Milne, Pat and Stewart Gordon, Martin Cawley, Mrs Romey Heaton, Marian and Andrew Ruston, M S Catling

SKIPTON   SD9851   MAP 7

Narrow Boat 🍺 £

Victoria Street; pub signed down alley off Coach Street; BD23 1JE

Extended pub near canal with eight real ales, proper home cooking and a good mix of customers

With a friendly welcome and up to eight real ales on handpump, this extended pub does get pretty busy at peak times: Black Sheep, Copper Dragon Best Bitter and Golden Pippin,

Timothy Taylors Landlord and four guests such as Great Heck YPA, Leeds Ascension, Phoenix Wobbly Bob and Riverhead Sparth Mild. Several continental beers and decent wines, too. The bar has a good mix of both locals and visitors, old brewery posters and nice mirrors decorated with framed beer advertisements on the walls, church pews, dining chairs and stools around wooden tables, and an upstairs gallery area with an interesting canal mural. The pub is down a cobbled alley, with picnic-sets under a front colonnade, and the Leeds & Liverpool Canal is nearby.

🍴 **Reasonably priced and well liked, the bar food includes lunchtime sandwiches and ploughman's, soup, wild mushrooms in brandy cream on toast, cumberland sausages with sweet red onion gravy, omelettes, wild mushroom and spinach risotto, beef in ale pie, roast belly pork with braised red cabbage and local leg of lamb steak with rosemary and red wine jus; they offer a very good value weekday lunchtime dish, and sausage and pie nights are every Monday and Tuesday.** *Starters/Snacks: £3.50 to £4.95. Main Courses: £8.25 to £13.95. Puddings: £3.95 to £4.25*

Market Town Taverns ~ Manager Tim Hughes ~ Real ale ~ Bar food (12-2.30, 5.30-9; 12-4 Sun; not Sun evening) ~ (01756) 797922 ~ Children welcome if dining ~ Dogs welcome ~ Folk club Mon evenings ~ Open 12-11

Recommended by Dr Kevan Tucker, Jo Lilley, Simon Calvert, Michael and Lynne Gittins, Richard, Alan and Eve Harding, Mrs Hazel Rainer, the Didler, Charles and Pauline Stride

SLEDMERE   SE9364   MAP 8

Triton

B1252/B1253 junction, NW of Great Driffield; YO25 3XQ

Handsome inn in fine countryside with an open-plan interior, traditional furnishings and values, fine range of drinks (50 gins) and enjoyable food; bedrooms

On an old posting road that strides over fine open rolling country and by the walls of Sledmere House, this is a neatly kept 18th-c inn with a genuinely friendly landlord and attentive staff. It's open-plan with a determinedly old-fashioned atmosphere, dark wooden farmhouse furniture and some bar stools by the counter on the red patterned carpet, 15 clocks ranging from a grandfather to a cuckoo, lots of willow pattern plates, all manner of paintings and pictures of the area, and an open fire. They don't take bookings except in the restaurant area and there's a happy mix of drinkers and diners. Copper Dragon Orange Pippin, John Smiths, Tetleys and Timothy Taylors Landlord on handpump, a dozen wines by the glass and over 50 different gins.

🍴 **Honest bar food includes sandwiches, filled baked potatoes, ploughman's, soup, chicken liver pâté with plum and apple chutney, ham or sausage and egg, steak in ale pie, mushroom stroganoff, smoked haddock on spinach topped with cheese sauce, marinated and slow-cooked pork belly with onion mash, chicken in a creamy dijon mustard and tarragon sauce, braised lamb shank with port, rosemary and redcurrant gravy, and puddings like lemon tart and kumquat cheesecake; popular Sunday roasts.** *Starters/Snacks: £3.99 to £8.99. Main Courses: £8.99 to £14.99. Puddings: £4.50*

Free house ~ Licensee Lance Moxon ~ Real ale ~ Bar food (12-2, 6-9; 12-7.30 Sun) ~ Restaurant ~ (01377) 236078 ~ Children welcome until 8pm ~ Open 12-3, 6-11.30; 12-9.30 Sun; closed winter Mon lunchtime ~ Bedrooms: £45S/£70S

Recommended by C A Hall, Roger A Bellingham, David S Allen, Mrs R Mehlman

SNAPE   SE2684   MAP 10

Castle Arms

Off B6268 Masham—Bedale; DL8 2TB

Hospitable, neat pub, handy for the A1, with friendly service, flagstoned rooms, open fires, a fair choice of drinks and food (smashing puddings) and seats outside; bedrooms

This immaculately kept, homely pub is in a very pretty village surrounded by fine walks on the Yorkshire Dales and the North York Moors. The partly flagstoned and partly carpeted bar has an open fire, straightforward pubby tables and chairs, a few bar stools, lots of horsebrasses along beams and a relaxed, happy atmosphere. The flagstoned dining room has candlesticks along the mantelpiece above another open fire, plenty of dark tables and chairs, and a glass-fronted cabinet of china. Banks's Bitter, Jennings Bitter and Marstons Pedigree on handpump and several malt whiskies; friendly, welcoming service. There are picnic-sets at the front with more in the courtyard. The pub is handy for Thorp Perrow.

🍴 Popular bar food includes sandwiches, soup, parfait of chicken livers with onion chutney, smoked duck breast with an orange and walnut salad, tartlet of mediterranean vegetables with gruyère topping, sausages on coarse grain mustard mash with caramelised onion sauce, beef, venison and Guinness pie, beer-battered haddock, chicken strips in a mild curried cream, apricot and almond sauce, best end of lamb with chickpeas and sage and a red wine sauce, and puddings (the chef's passion) such as white chocolate and chestnut mousse with dark chocolate-coated honeycomb pieces and tangy lemon and gingernut biscuit cheesecake. *Starters/Snacks: £4.00 to £6.50. Main Courses: £8.95 to £14.50. Puddings: £4.25*

Marstons ~ Lease Sandra Haxby ~ Real ale ~ Bar food ~ Restaurant ~ (01677) 470270 ~ Children welcome ~ Dogs allowed in bar and bedrooms ~ Open 12-3, 6-11; 12-3m 7-10.30 Sun ~ Bedrooms: £55S/£75S

Recommended by Comus and Sarah Elliott, Michael Doswell, Janet and Peter Race, WW

SOUTH DALTON
SE9645   MAP 8

Pipe & Glass 🍴 🍷
West End; brown sign to pub off B1248 NW of Beverley; HU17 7PN

Attractive dining pub with a proper bar area, real ales, interesting modern cooking, good service; garden and front terrace

There is a proper bar area in this attractive whitewashed dining pub with four real ales but there's no doubt that most customers are here to enjoy the first-class food cooked by the young landlord. This bar area – where they don't take bookings – is beamed and bow-windowed, with a log fire, some old prints, plush stools and traditional pubby chairs around a mix of tables, and even high-backed settles. Beyond that, all is airy and comfortably contemporary, angling around past some soft modern dark leather chesterfields into a light restaurant area overlooking Dalton Park, with high-backed stylish dining chairs around well spaced country tables on bare boards. The decorations – a row of serious cookery books and framed big-name restaurant menus – show how high the licensee aims. Black Sheep Best, guest beers from breweries like Copper Dragon, Cropton and Wold Top on handpump, ten wines by the glass and Old Rosie cider. Service is friendly and prompt by bright and attentive young staff; disabled access, piped music. There are tables out on the garden's peaceful lawn beside the park and picnic-sets on the front terrace; people say the yew tree is some 500 years old. The village is charming and its elegant Victorian church spire, 62 metres (204 ft) tall, is visible for miles around. More reports please.

🍴 Imaginative and very good – if not cheap – food cooked by the young chef/patron includes lunchtime sandwiches and ploughman's, crispy rabbit rissoles with cockles, capers and sorrel, a little jar of potted gloucester old spot pork with sticky apple, crackling salad and toasted spelt bread, baked goats cheese tart with honey-roast beetroot, red chard and hazelnut pesto, pork sausages with bubble and squeak and onion gravy, crispy lamb with a mutton and kidney faggot, wild garlic mash and pearl barley, free-range herby chicken breast with morel mushrooms and crispy air-dried ham, and puddings like warm treacle tart with honey-roast plums and egg nog ice-cream and hot dark chocolate and cherry pudding with seville orange marmalade sorbet. *Starters/Snacks: £3.95 to £8.95. Main Courses: £9.95 to £19.95. Puddings: £4.95 to £8.95*

Free house ~ Licensees Kate and James Mackenzie ~ Real ale ~ Bar food (12-2, 6.30-9.30; 12-4 Sun; not Sun evening or Mon (except bank hols)) ~ Restaurant ~ (01430) 810246 ~ Children welcome ~ Open 12-3, 6.30-11; 12-11(10.30 Sun) Sat; closed Mon (except bank hols), two weeks Jan

Recommended by Marlene and Jim Godfrey, David and Cathrine Whiting

SUTTON UPON DERWENT

SE7047   MAP 7

St Vincent Arms 🍴 ♀ ◢

B1228 SE of York; YO41 4BN

Consistently cheerful, with nine real ales plus other drinks, well liked bar food and more elaborate evening choices, and friendly service

Even on cold and wet mid-week winter lunchtimes, this welcoming and cheerful pub is always busy. It's best to book to be sure of a table in the bustling bar where they keep up to nine real ales on handpump: Fullers London Pride and ESB, Gales HSB, Old Mill Bitter, Theakstons XB, Timothy Taylors Landlord and Golden Best, York Yorkshire Terrier and Wells & Youngs Bombardier. Also, 14 wines and two champagnes by the glass and several malt whiskies. This parlour-style, panelled front room has traditional high-backed settles, a cushioned bow-window seat, windsor chairs and a gas-effect coal fire; another lounge and separate dining room open off. There are seats in the garden. The pub is named after the admiral who was granted the village and lands by the nation as thanks for his successful commands – and for coping with Nelson's infatuation with Lady Hamilton. Handy for the Yorkshire Air Museum.

🍴 Appetising lunchtime bar food includes sandwiches and filled hot ciabattas, soup, salads like griddled chicken caesar or prawn and egg, steak and mushroom in ale pie, lasagne and especially good haddock and chips with mushy peas, with more elaborate evening dishes such as rabbit terrine with tomato chutney, queenie scallops with garlic butter and cheese, smoked haddock fishcakes with a grain mustard dressing, beef stroganoff, chicken and ginger or vegetable stir fries, roast pork belly with apple chutney and sage jus and steak au poivre. *Starters/Snacks: £3.50 to £7.00. Main Courses: £8.50 to £16.00. Puddings: £4.00 to £5.00*

Free house ~ Licensee Simon Hopwood ~ Real ale ~ Bar food ~ Restaurant ~ (01904) 608349 ~ Children welcome ~ Open 11.30-3, 6-11; 12-3, 6.30-10.30 Sun

Recommended by Dr and Mrs J Temporal, Derek and Sylvia Stephenson, Andy and Jill Kassube, Tim and Liz Sherbourne, Susan and Nigel Brookes, Pierre Richterich

SUTTON-ON-THE-FOREST

SE5864   MAP 7

Blackwell Ox 🛏

Just off B1363, 5.7 miles N of York ring road; Huby Road; YO61 1DT

Enjoyable food in back bar, some emphasis on the good front restaurant, comfortable bedrooms and a warm welcome

You can be sure of a warm welcome from the friendly landlady in this neatly kept, extended roadside inn, even when they might be – as they were on our visit – busy with a conference. The L-shaped bar has a winter coal and wood fire in the little stone fireplace, cushioned farmhouse and dining chairs around dark shiny tables on the polished floorboards, high bar chairs under the beamed and boarded ceiling by the bar counter, a long table and settle against one wall, and on the part yellow-painted and part green-wallpapered walls, horse pictures and photographs, and a nice little sampler. Black Sheep Best, Copper Dragon IPA, John Smiths and Timothy Taylors Landlord on handpump and interesting, well described wines by the glass; piped music and a small flat-screen TV. The two-roomed front dining room has sofas by the door, dusky pink walls and neat modern dining chairs around smartly set tables on pale floorboards. There are some circular picnic-sets on the outside terrace.

🍴 Good bar food at lunchtime includes sandwiches, ploughman's, soup, blue goats cheese and pear tart with hazelnuts and local heather honey, duck liver parfait with green fig and walnut chutney, smoked haddock with leek and herb risotto and mustard cream, pork and leek sausages with sweet onion jus, fresh cep tagliatelle with toasted pine nuts, rocket and pesto, and mutton chops with lambs kidney and pan juices, with evening choices like a plate of spanish charcuterie and cheese, vegetable tagine with spicy couscous, bass with sherry lentil and green bean salad, peppered loin of venison with armagnac prunes and rack of lamb with carrot and swede purée, and puddings like apple and elderflower jelly with calvados panna cotta and chocolate and Amaretto mousse; they also offer a good

value two- and three-course set menu. *Starters/Snacks: £5.75 to £7.95. Main Courses: £6.95 to £17.95. Puddings: £3.95 to £5.95*

Free house ~ Real ale ~ Bar food (12-2, 6-9.30; 12-4 Sun; not Sun evening) ~ Restaurant ~ (01347) 810328 ~ Children welcome ~ Open 12-11(10.30 Sun) ~ Bedrooms: £65B/£95B

Recommended by C A Hall, Walter and Susan Rinaldi-Butcher

THORNTON WATLASS   SE2385   MAP 10

Buck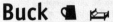

Village signposted off B6268 Bedale—Masham; HG4 4AH

Friendly village pub with five real ales, traditional bars, well liked food and popular Sunday jazz

The five real ales, brunch menu and lunchtime jazz make Sundays at this honest village pub – run by the same licensees for 23 years now – a very popular time to visit. Our readers tend to head for the pleasantly traditional bar on the right which has upholstered old-fashioned wall settles on the carpet, a fine mahogany bar counter, a high shelf packed with ancient bottles, several mounted fox masks and brushes, and a brick fireplace. The Long Room (which overlooks the cricket green) has large prints of old Thornton Watlass cricket teams, signed bats, cricket balls and so forth. Black Sheep, Theakstons Best and Black Bull and guests like Great Newsome Stoney Binks and Harviestoun Bitter & Twisted on handpump, over 40 interesting malt whiskies and seven wines by the glass; darts, cribbage and dominoes. The sheltered garden has an equipped children's play area and summer barbecues, and they have their own cricket team; quoits. More reports please.

⊞ Traditional bar food includes sandwiches, soup, chicken liver parfait with red onion marmalade, rarebit with home-made pear chutney, a charcuterie board, omelettes, lasagne, gammon with egg or pineapple, steak in ale pie, pasta with spinach and ricotta, beer-battered fish, lamb cutlets with rosemary and redcurrant sauce, daily specials like scallops with garlic butter and gruyère and venison sausages with lyonnaise potatoes, and puddings. *Starters/Snacks: £4.00 to £8.00. Main Courses: £7.50 to £15.00. Puddings: £3.75 to £4.25*

Free house ~ Licensees Michael and Margaret Fox ~ Real ale ~ Bar food (12-2(3 Sun), 6.30-9.30) ~ Restaurant ~ (01677) 422461 ~ Dogs allowed in bedrooms ~ Jazz Sun lunchtimes ~ Open 11-11 ~ Bedrooms: £65S/£80(£90B)

Recommended by David Hoult, Michael Doswell, Mr and Mrs Barrie, Terry Mizen, Michael Butler

WASS   SE5579   MAP 7

Wombwell Arms

Back road W of Ampleforth; or follow brown tourist-attraction sign for Byland Abbey off A170 Thirsk—Helmsley; YO61 4BE

Consistently enjoyable village pub, friendly, bustling atmosphere, good mix of locals and visitors, well liked bar food and real ales; bedrooms

Since taking over this bustling village pub, Mr and Mrs Walker have made some careful changes and refurbishments and have plans to build a microbrewery in one of the outbuildings; some of the bedrooms have been updated and the walls of the Poacher's Bar are now hung with brewery memorabilia. The two bars are cosy and neatly kept with plenty of simple character, log fires, Theakstons Old Peculier and Black Bull (served from wooden casks) and Timothy Taylors Landlord on handpump, a new wine list (quite a few from Mrs Walker's South Africa) and several malt whiskies; darts. The two restaurants are incorporated into a 17th-c former granary and the outside seating area has been extended.

⊞ Popular bar food includes sandwiches and filled ciabattas, ploughman's, soup, smoked salmon and scrambled eggs, black pudding and pancetta salad, twice-baked cheese soufflé, with red onion marmalade, haddock and chips with mushy peas, chickpea curry, sausages of the week with creamy mash and gravy, steak, mushroom and Guinness pie, popular rabbit, venison and pheasant in ale casserole with a horseradish dumpling, chicken breast with a creamy leek and stilton sauce, king prawn risotto, and puddings; they offer winter food deals. *Starters/Snacks: £3.95 to £9.45. Main Courses: £8.95 to £18.95. Puddings: £4.25 to £6.95*

Free house ~ Licensees Ian and Eunice Walker ~ Real ale ~ Bar food (12-2(2.30 Sat, 3 Sun), 6.30-9(9.30 Fri and Sat); 12-3; not Sun evening (except bank hol weekends)) ~ Restaurant ~ (01347) 868280 ~ Children welcome ~ Dogs allowed in bar ~ Open 12-3, 6-11; 12-11 Sat; 12-4 Sun; closed Sun evening ~ Bedrooms: £50S/£70S

Recommended by WW, Pat and Graham Williamson, Hansjoerg Landherr, R Pearce, Pat and Tony Martin

WATH IN NIDDERDALE

SE1467   MAP 7

Sportsmans Arms

Nidderdale road off B6265 in Pateley Bridge; village and pub signposted over hump-back bridge on right after a couple of miles; HG3 5PP

Beautifully placed restaurant with welcoming bar, real ales, super choice of other drinks and imaginative food; comfortable bedrooms

Of course, this is not a traditional inn – it's a charming and civilised restaurant-with-rooms with a friendly, long-serving owner. But our readers have enjoyed their visits consistently over many years and there is a welcoming bar with an open fire, Black Sheep and Timothy Taylors Landlord on handpump, and locals who do still pop in – though most customers are here to enjoy the particularly good food. There's a very sensible and extensive wine list with 15 by the glass (including champagne), over 30 malt whiskies and several russian vodkas; maybe quiet piped music. Benches and tables outside and seats in the pretty garden; croquet. As well as their own fishing on the River Nidd, this is an ideal spot for walkers, hikers and ornithologists, and there are plenty of country houses, gardens and cities to explore.

Ⓜ Using the best local produce, the excellent food includes lunchtime filled rolls and sandwiches, pear, roquefort and walnut salad, terrine of local game with pistachios and home-made chutney, seared scallops with garlic butter and an emmental glaze, sausages with red wine and haricot bean gravy, pheasant with bacon and wild mushrooms, best end of lamb with provençale tomatoes and natural jus bass on spinach mash with a red pepper sauce, and rib-eye steak with fries and aioli. *Starters/Snacks: £4.80 to £12.00. Main Courses: £9.50 to £20.00. Puddings: £3.95 to £6.50*

Free house ~ Licensee Ray Carter ~ Real ale ~ Bar food ~ Restaurant ~ (01423) 711306 ~ Children welcome ~ Dogs allowed in bar ~ Open 12-2.30, 6.30-11 ~ Bedrooms: £70B/£120B

Recommended by Stephen Woad, Lynda and Trevor Smith, Richard Cole, Hunter and Christine Wright, Peter and Josie Fawcett, Janet and Peter Race, Hugh Stafford

WHITBY

NZ9011   MAP 10

Duke of York

124 Church Street, Harbour East Side; YO22 4DE

Fine harbourside position, window seats and bedrooms with a view, several real ales and standard bar food

It's certainly worth trying to get to this busy pub early so you can bag a table by the window and enjoy the view over the harbour entrance and the western cliff. The comfortable beamed lounge bar has fishing memorabilia (including the pennant numbers of local trawlers chalked on the beams) and Caledonian Deuchars IPA, Courage Directors, Shepherd Neame Spitfire and Wells & Youngs Bombardier on handpump; decent wines by the glass and quite a few malt whiskies, piped music, TV and games machine. All the bedrooms (apart from one) overlook the water. The pub is close to the famous 199 Steps that lead up to the abbey. There is no nearby parking.

🍴 **Straightforward bar food includes sandwiches, chilli con carne, steak in ale or fish pie, large local cod or haddock in batter and seasonal crab salad.** *Starters/Snacks: £2.00 to £5.00. Main Courses: £5.50 to £8.95. Puddings: £3.50*

Enterprise ~ Lease Lawrence Bradley ~ Real ale ~ Bar food (all day) ~ (01947) 600324 ~ Children welcome ~ Live music Mon evening ~ Open 11-11(midnight Sat); 12-11 Sun ~ Bedrooms: /£60B

Recommended by the Didler, Chris and Jeanne Downing, P Dawn, David Carr, Pete Coxon, Gwyn and Anne Wake, Tim and Claire Woodward

WIDDOP
SD9531   MAP 7

Pack Horse 🍺 £

The Ridge; from A646 on W side of Hebden Bridge, turn off at Heptonstall signpost (as it's a sharp turn, coming out of Hebden Bridge road signs direct you around a turning circle), then follow Slack and Widdop signposts; can also be reached from Nelson and Colne, on high, pretty road; OS Sheet 103 map reference 952317; HX7 7AT

Friendly pub high up on the moors and liked by walkers for generous, tasty food, five real ales and lots of malt whiskies; bedrooms

As well as comfortable bedrooms and hearty breakfasts, this isolated, traditional inn also offers a smart self-catering apartment; it's a popular spot with walkers on the Pennine Way and Pennine Bridleway. You can be sure of a welcome from the friendly staff and the bar has warm winter fires, window seats cut into the partly panelled stripped stone walls that take in the moorland view, sturdy furnishings, horsey mementoes, and Black Sheep, Copper Dragon Challenger IPA and Copper Dragon and Thwaites Bitter and Lancaster Bomber on handpump, around 130 single malt whiskies and some irish ones as well, and eight wines by the glass. The friendly golden retrievers are called Padge and Purdey, and there's another dog called Holly. Seats outside and pretty summer hanging baskets. Leave your boots and backpacks in the porch.

🍴 **Decent bar food at fair prices includes sandwiches, ploughman's, soup, pâté, garlic mushrooms, large burgers, steak and kidney pie, lasagne, vegetable bake, gammon and eggs, and daily specials like pork fillet with an orange and ginger sauce and pheasant with sausage and bacon; they also offer cream teas on Sundays and bank holidays. They do stop food service promptly.** *Starters/Snacks: £3.50 to £4.50. Main Courses: £4.50 to £15.95. Puddings: £4.50*

Free house ~ Licensee Andrew Hollinrake ~ Real ale ~ Bar food (not Mon or weekday lunchtimes Oct-Easter) ~ (01422) 842803 ~ Children in eating area of bar until 8pm ~ Dogs allowed in bar ~ Open 12-3, 7-11; 12-11 Sun; closed Mon ~ Bedrooms: £43S/£48B

Recommended by Simon Le Fort, Ian and Nita Cooper

YORK
SE5951   MAP 7

Maltings 🍺 £

Tanners Moat/Wellington Row, below Lendal Bridge; YO1 6HU

Bustling, friendly city pub with cheerful landlord, interesting real ales and other drinks, plus good value standard food

Popular locally and with those who enjoy well kept real ales, this is a lively city pub tucked away by the riverside. The tricksy décor is entirely contrived and strong on salvaged, somewhat quirky junk: old doors for the bar front and much of the ceiling, a marvellous collection of railway signs and amusing notices, an old chocolate dispensing machine, cigarette and tobacco advertisements alongside cough and chest remedies, what looks like a suburban front door for the entrance to the ladies', partly stripped orange brick walls and even a lavatory pan in one corner. As well as Black Sheep Bitter, the jovial landlord keeps six guest ales on handpump including one each from Roosters and York, and four that change daily. He also has four or five continental beers on tap, lots of bottled beers, up to four farm ciders, a dozen or so country wines and more irish whiskeys than you normally see. Get there early to be sure of a seat; games machine. The day's papers are framed in the gents'. Nearby parking is difficult; the pub is very handy for the Rail Museum and the Yorkshire Eye.

🍽 **Straightforward bar food in generous helpings might include sandwiches, good chips with cheese, chilli or curry, filled baked potatoes, burger, battered haddock and beef in ale pie.** *Starters/Snacks: £2.95 to £3.95. Main Courses: £5.25 to £5.50*

Free house ~ Licensee Shaun Collinge ~ Real ale ~ Bar food (12-2 weekdays, 12-4 weekends; not evenings) ~ No credit cards ~ (01904) 655387 ~ Children allowed only during meal times ~ Open 11-11.30; 12-10.30 Sun

Recommended by Michael Butler, the Didler, Bruce Bird, Pat and Graham Williamson, Mark Walker, WW, Donna and Roger, Martin Grosberg, Pete Coxon, Andy Lickfold, Peter F Marshall, Alison and Pete, David Carr

LUCKY DIP

Besides the fully inspected pubs, you might like to try these Lucky Dips recommended to us and described by readers (if you do, please send us reports: feedback@goodguides.com).

ABERFORD [SE4337]
Swan LS25 3AA [best to use A642 junction to leave A1; Main St N]: Busy dining pub (may have to wait for a table), vast choice of good generous food from sandwiches to bargain carvery, lots of black timber, prints, pistols, cutlasses and stuffed animals, well kept Black Sheep and Tetleys, generous glasses of wine, good friendly uniformed service, upstairs evening restaurant; children welcome, tables outside *(G Dobson, Michael Butler, Marlene and Jim Godfrey, Gordon and Margaret Ormondroyd)*
ACKLAM [SE7861]
Half Moon YO17 9RG: Old pub with straightforward décor, good range of honest value home-made food, well kept local beers, friendly local staff, tiny Wolds village, good views from the front *(Andrew and Deborah Cullen)*
ADDINGHAM [SE0749]
☆ *Fleece* LS29 0LY [Main St]: Nice farmhouse-style eating area on right with good value home-made food from hearty sandwiches (home-baked bread) to sophisticated blackboard meals using good local ingredients, popular all-day Sun roasts, quick friendly service, well kept Yorkshire ales, good choice of wines by the glass, low ceilings, flagstones and log fire, plain tap room with darts and dominoes, quiz nights Tues, trad jazz Weds; very busy wknds; children and dogs welcome, lots of picnic-sets on front terrace, open all day *(Michael and Lynne Gittins, Michael Doswell, John and Sylvia Harrop, Tina and David Woods-Taylor, Gordon and Margaret Ormondroyd, Stuart Doughty)*
Sailor LS29 0PD [Main St]: Well run local, smart and comfortable, with well kept ales inc Timothy Taylors Landlord and Best, enjoyable pub cooking inc highly recommended barnsley chop *(Gordon and Margaret Ormondroyd)*
AINDERBY QUERNHOW [SE3480]
Black Horse YO7 4HX [B6267, just off A1]: Relaxed, friendly and well refurbished, hearty

tasty food, Black Sheep and John Smiths, coal fire *(John Robertson, Rory and Jackie Hudson)*
APPLETREEWICK [SE0560]
☆ *Craven Arms* BD23 6DA [off B6160 Burnsall—Bolton Abbey]: Creeper-covered 17th-c beamed pub with comfortably down-to-earth settles and rugs on flagstones, oak panelling, coal fire in old range, good friendly service, up to eight well kept ales, good choice of wines by the glass, home-made food from baguettes and baked potatoes up, small dining room and splendid thatched and raftered barn extension with gallery; dogs and walking boots welcome (plenty of surrounding walks), nice views from front picnic-sets, more seats in back garden *(LYM, Colin McIlwain, WW, Pat and Tony Martin, Pat and Graham Williamson)*
ARNCLIFFE [SD9371]
☆ *Falcon* BD23 5QE [off B6160 N of Grassington]: Basic no frills country tavern in same family for generations, lovely setting on moorland village green, coal fire in small bar with elderly furnishings, well kept Timothy Taylors Landlord tapped from cask to stoneware jugs in central hatch-style servery, low-priced simple lunchtime and early evening food from old family kitchen, attractive watercolours, sepia photographs and humorous sporting prints, back sunroom (children allowed lunchtime) overlooking pleasant garden; no credit cards, cl winter Thurs evenings; miles of trout fishing, two plain bedrooms (not all year), good breakfast and evening meal *(Michael B Griffith, the Didler, WW, LYM, B and M Kendall, Neil and Angela Huxter)*
ASKRIGG [SD9491]
☆ *Crown* DL8 3HQ [Main St]: Friendly open-plan local in James Herriot village, three areas off main bar, blazing fires inc old-fashioned range, relaxed atmosphere, simple home-made food inc cut-price small helpings, cheerful staff, Black Sheep, Theakstons XB and guest beers; children,

dogs and walkers welcome, tables outside *(Dr and Mrs D Scott, Derek Allpass, Ewan and Moira McCall, Robin and Ann Taylor, Mrs Margo Finlay, Jörg Kasprowski)*

Kings Arms DL8 3HQ [signed from A684 Leyburn—Sedbergh in Bainbridge]: Great log fire in former coaching inn's flagstoned high-ceilinged main bar, traditional furnishings and décor, well kept ales such as Black Sheep, John Smiths and Theakstons, decent wines by the glass, good choice of malts, upscale enjoyable bar food, friendly staff, restaurant with fire, barrel-vaulted former beer cellar; piped music; dogs welcome, pleasant courtyard, bedrooms run separately as part of Holiday Property Bond complex behind *(Robin and Ann Taylor, LYM, Lynda and Trevor Smith, Mrs Margo Finlay, Jörg Kasprowski, Stuart Brown)*

White Rose DL8 3HG [Main St]: Good food from lunchtime sandwiches up in neat carpeted bar or dining room with conservatory, friendly efficient staff, local real ales, pool; suntrap back terrace, 12 comfortable bedrooms *(Mr and Mrs Maurice Thompson, Mrs Margo Finlay, Jörg Kasprowski, Caroline and Michael Abbey, Derek Allpass)*

AUSTWICK [SD7668]

Game Cock LA2 8BB [just off A65 Settle—Kirkby Lonsdale]: Quaint civilised place in pretty spot below Three Peaks, good log fire in old-fashioned beamed bare-boards back bar, friendly staff and locals, Thwaites ales, mulled wine, nice coffee, most space devoted to the food side, with good fairly priced choice from french chef/landlord, two dining rooms and modern front conservatory-type extension; walkers and dogs welcome, tables out in front with play area, three neat bedrooms, good walks, open all day Sun *(Karen Eliot, BB, Tony and Maggie Harwood, MDN)*

BAILDON [SE1538]

Junction BD17 6AB [Baildon Rd]: Wedge-shaped traditional alehouse with linked rooms, good range of beers inc Fullers and locals like Saltaire, brewery memorabilia, basic food served till 7pm, popular Tues curry night, live music and singalongs Sun evening, pool *(Jeremy King, Ros Lawler)*

BARDSEY [SE3642]

☆ *Bingley Arms* LS17 9DR [Church Lane]: Recently redecorated ancient pub with good value fresh food inc some bargains, welcoming efficient service, well kept Black Sheep, John Smiths and Tetleys, good wines by the glass, spacious lounge divided into separate areas, huge fireplace, smaller public bar, picturesque upstairs brasserie; children welcome, attractive terraced garden, lovely Saxon church nearby *(Danny Savage, LYM)*

BEVERLEY [TA0339]

Dog & Duck HU17 8BH [Ladygate]: Cheerful popular two-bar local handy for playhouse and Sat market, good home-made lunchtime food using local produce from sandwiches to bargain Sun lunch, OAP deals too; well kept

Caledonian Deuchars IPA, Copper Dragon, John Smiths and guests, good value wines, several malts, helpful friendly staff, coal fires; piped music, games machine; cheap basic courtyard bedrooms up iron stairs *(David Carr, the Didler, Mark Walker)*

Rose & Crown HU17 7AB [North Bar Without]: Imposing black and white pub with spotless 1930s interior, wide range of good value food inc indian and eastern european dishes from polish landlady, bargain deals too, John Smiths and a guest beer, prompt cheerful service even when busy *(Marlene and Jim Godfrey, Clive Gibson)*

Tiger HU17 8JG [Lairgate]: Simple interesting local with four small rooms, enjoyable bargain food (not Sun evening, Mon) inc good curries, well kept Adnams and Black Sheep, folk nights, darts; comfortable terrace, smokers' shelter, open all day, till late Fri, Sat *(the Didler, D W Stokes, Marlene and Jim Godfrey)*

☆ *White Horse* HU17 8BN [Hengate, off North Bar]: Long-serving landlady has now left this no-frills pub, and food's standard issue, but its carefully preserved Victorian feel (and bargain Sam Smiths) survive, with basic little rooms huddled around central bar, brown leatherette seats (high-backed settles in one little snug) and plain chairs and benches on bare boards, antique cartoons, sentimental engravings, gaslit chandelier, open fires, games room, upstairs family room; children till 7pm, open all day *(the Didler, John Fiander, LYM)*

BILTON [SE4750]

☆ *Chequers* YO26 7NN [pub signed just off B1224]: Well kept Black Sheep and two guests such as Brains Rev James and Wells & Youngs Bitter, interesting wines, lots of whiskies, sensibly priced fresh food, pleasant staff, nicely refurbished linked bar areas, leather sofa and armchairs by warm woodburner, part-panelled dining room; piped music may obtrude; outside heated seating shelter, small garden, three bedrooms *(Malcolm and Pauline Pellatt, John and Eleanor Holdsworth, Grahame Sherwin, Rita and Keith Pollard, BB)*

BIRSTALL [SE2126]

Black Bull WF17 9HE [Kirkgate, off A652; head down hill towards church]: Medieval stone-built pub opp part-Saxon church, dark panelling and low beams in long row of five small linked rooms, traditional décor complete with stag's head and old local photographs, low-priced home-made food, real ales such as Boddingtons and Worthington, upstairs former courtroom (now a function room, but they may give you a guided tour); children welcome *(BB, Michael Butler)*

BIRSTWITH [SE2459]

Station Hotel HG3 3AG [off B6165 W of Ripley]: Welcoming stone-built Dales local with public bar and pleasantly modernised lounge/dining room, good well priced home-made pubby food (small helpings available),

Thurs curry night, well kept Caledonian Deuchars IPA, John Smiths and Tetleys, good choice of wines by the glass, Mon quiz; tables outside, picturesque valley, cl Sun evening, Mon lunchtime *(Ian and Joan Blackwell)*

BISHOPTHORPE [SE5947]

☆ *Woodman* YO23 2RB [village signed just off A64 York S bypass; Main St]: Cheerful chatty local atmosphere, appealing open layout, plainly and nicely furnished, quick pleasant service, good reasonably priced pubby food, John Smiths and Timothy Taylors Landlord, good choice of wines by the glass, log fire; piped music; small heated terrace *(BB, Ian and Joan Blackwell)*

BRADFIELD [SK2692]

Old Horns S6 6LG [High Bradfield]: Friendly old stone-built pub with comfortable divided L-shaped bar, lots of pictures, good value home-made pub food, efficient service, real ales inc Thwaites and continental beers on tap; children welcome, picnic-sets and play area outside, hill village with stunning views, interesting church, good walks *(Giles and Annie Francis)*

BRADFORD [SE1528]

Chapel House BD12 0HP [Chapel House Buildings, Low Moor]: Busy pub in pretty setting opp church, plenty of atmosphere in L-shaped bar, well kept Greene King, usual food *(Clive Flynn)*

Fighting Cock BD7 1JE [Preston St (off B6145)]: Busy bare-boards alehouse by industrial estate, 12 well kept changing ales, foreign bottled beers, farm ciders, lively atmosphere, all-day doorstep sandwiches and good simple lunchtime hot dishes (not Sun), low prices, coal fires; open all day *(the Didler, Martin Grosberg)*

Kings Head BD6 1JQ [Halifax Rd]: Newish licensees keeping pub traditional, with affordable pub food all home made; open all day Sat, cl Mon, Tues *(anon)*

New Beehive BD1 3AA [Westgate]: Robustly old-fashioned Edwardian inn with several rooms inc good pool room, wide range of changing ales, gas lighting, candles and coal fires; basement music nights; nice back courtyard, bedrooms, open all day (till 2am Fri, Sat) *(the Didler)*

Stansfield Arms BD10 0NP [Apperley Lane, Apperley Bridge; off A658 NE]: Smartly refurbished roomy pub with enjoyable food, well kept Black Sheep, Timothy Taylors Landlord and Tetleys, cheerful attentive staff, beams, stripped stone and dark panelling, restaurant; can get very busy; tables out on front decking, pleasant setting *(Gordon and Margaret Ormondroyd)*

BRAMHAM [SE4242]

Swan LS23 6QA [just off A1 2 miles N of A64]: Civilised three-room country local with engaging long-serving landlady and good mix of customers, well kept Black Sheep, Caledonian Deuchars IPA and John Smiths, no food, machines or music *(Les and Sandra Brown)*

BRAMHOPE [SE2444]

Dyneley Arms LS21 1ET [A660/A658; Pool Bank New Rd]: Upmarket Sam Smiths dining pub rebuilt after fire, good value food inc light dishes, modest-sized rooms each with own décor, one with log fire *(John and Eleanor Holdsworth, Ray and Winifred Halliday)*

BRANTINGHAM [SE9329]

Triton HU15 1QE [Ellerker Rd]: Spacious and comfortably refurbished, with welcoming licensees, good choice of enjoyable home-made local food in conservatory bar and restaurant with french windows to terrace; sheltered garden, play area *(B Woodford, BB)*

BREARTON [SE3260]

☆ *Malt Shovel* HG3 3BX [Village signposted off A61 N of Harrogate]: 16th-c beamed and candlelit dining pub, wood or slate floors, modern conservatory with lemon trees and piano, imaginative food (not Sun evening) from swiss chef/landlord inc own-smoked fish and meats, also cheaper bistro menu and new thai menu, regular opera/dinner evenings (two licensees are trained singers), well kept Black Sheep and guest ales, several good wines by the glass; no dogs; children welcome, garden tables, cl Sun evening from 9pm, Mon, Tues *(Les and Sandra Brown, David S Allen, Jeremy King, Gordon and Margaret Ormondroyd, Tim and Claire Woodward, LYM, Michael Doswell, Brian and Janet Ainscough)*

BRIGHOUSE [SE1421]

Globe HD6 3EL [Rastrick Common]: Civilised local with thriving atmosphere, good value home cooking inc good Sun lunch, well kept Camerons Strongarm, friendly staff, pleasant restaurant *(Gordon and Margaret Ormondroyd)*

Sun HX3 8TH [N, on A649; Wakefield Rd, Lightcliffe]: Comfortably updated and extended 18th-c stone building, real ales inc Timothy Taylors, farm cider, wide choice of sensibly priced enjoyable food, carvery (Thurs, Fri, Sat evenings, all day Sun) *(Gordon and Margaret Ormondroyd)*

BROUGHTON [SD9450]

Bull BD23 3AE: Recently taken over and extensively refurbished by Ribble Valley Inns (the small lancashire pub group that runs the good Three Fishes at Great Mitton), emphasis on traditional regional dishes with a modern twist, real ales such as Copper Dragon, Dark Horse and Timothy Taylors Landlord, cheerful staff, flagstones and open fires, open all day *(LYM)*

BUCKDEN [SD9477]

Buck BD23 5JA [B6160]: Large creeper-covered stone-built pub/hotel with Black Sheep ales and guests in modernised and extended open-plan bar, log fire and flagstones in original core, good range of bar meals, restaurant; very busy summer and wknds; terrace with good surrounding moorland views, popular walking spot, 14 bedrooms, open all day *(Mr and Mrs Maurice Thompson, Dudley and Moira Cockroft, LYM)*

BURLEY IN WHARFEDALE [SE1646]
Malt LS29 7DN [Main St]: Former Malt Shovel renamed, imposing Victorian building overlooking village green, welcoming attentive service, enjoyable food all day from sandwiches and enterprising light dishes up, two bar areas, smart evening restaurant (Sun lunch too), small conservatory; terrace tables, open all day *(Michael Sargent)*
Queens Head LS29 7BU [Main St]: Victorian pub that has gained local popularity since 2006 refurbishment *(Vicky Hurley)*

BURNISTON [TA0192]
Oak Wheel YO13 0HR [A171 N of Scarborough]: Thriving under current licensees, quick friendly service, lively atmosphere, enjoyable pubby food inc fresh local fish, well kept ales; five bedrooms, cl lunchtime, opens 4pm *(Neil and Brenda Skidmore, Joan York)*

BURTON LEONARD [SE3263]
☆ *Hare & Hounds* HG3 3SG [off A61 Ripon—Harrogate, handy for A1(M) exit 48]: Civilised country dining pub, good reasonably priced food, well kept Black Sheep, Timothy Taylors and Tetleys from long counter, good coffee, large carpeted main area divided by log fire, traditional furnishings, bright little side room; children in eating areas, pretty back garden *(Justin and Emma King, B and M Kendall, Brian and Janet Ainscough, LYM)*

BYLAND ABBEY [SE5478]
☆ *Abbey Inn* YO61 4BD [off A170 Thirsk—Helmsley]: By the beautiful abbey ruins and now too owned by English Heritage, prettily refurbished to include Thompsons of Kilburn sturdy oak furniture, polished boards and flagstones, big fireplaces, some discreet stripping back of plaster to show signs of venerable past, former piggery nicely converted to sitting area with octagonal skylight, good interesting food using local produce, Black Sheep Best and a guest beer, several wines by the glass; may close for private functions; children allowed if eating, terrace tables and pretty garden, three comfortable bedrooms, cl Sun evening, Mon lunchtime *(LYM, Peter Burton, H Bramwell, Andy and Jill Kassube)*

CADEBY [SE5100]
Cadeby Inn DN5 7SW [Main St]: 17th-c pub under new management, enjoyable locally sourced food inc good value set menu, Black sheep, stripped stone, polished beams and open fire, several linked areas, separate public bar; tables out in sunny garden *(A J Dobson, LYM)*

CARLTON [SE0684]
☆ *Foresters Arms* DL8 4BB [off A684 W of Leyburn]: Friendly landlord, good food inc local game and venison, own-brewed Wensleydale and guest ales, decent wines by the glass, log fire, low beams and flagstones; children welcome, picnic-sets out among tubs of flowers, pretty village in heart of Yorkshire Dales National Park,

comfortable bedrooms, lovely views *(Terry Mizen, the Didler, LYM, Ken and Barbara Turner, Mr and Mrs Maurice Thompson)*

CAWOOD [SE5737]
Castle Inn YO8 3SH [Wistowgate]: Comfortable pub with friendly efficient service, wide range of good home-made pubby food inc smaller-appetite helpings, sandwiches too, Black Sheep, John Smiths and a weekly guest, good choice of sensibly priced wines by the glass, log fire, air-conditioned dining areas; back caravan standing *(Michael Butler)*

CAWTHORNE [SE2808]
Spencer Arms S75 4HL [off A635 W of Barnsley]: Low-beamed welcoming stone-built pub in attractive village by Cannon Hall, good standard food, lots of cosy alcoves, contemporary restaurant, good choice of real ales, friendly helpful staff *(Marcus Mann, Derek and Sylvia Stephenson, Michael Butler)*

CLIFTON [SE1622]
☆ *Black Horse* HD6 4HJ [Westgate/Coalpit Lane; signed off Brighouse rd from M62 junction 25]: 17th-c pub/hotel with pleasant décor, front dining rooms with good generous food from lunchtime snacks up, can be pricey but good value set meals, back bar area with beam and plank ceiling and open fire, well kept Black Sheep and Timothy Taylors Landlord, decent wines, english setter called Arthur; nice courtyard area, 21 comfortable bedrooms, pleasant village *(Michael Butler, BB, Marcus Mann)*

COLEY [SE1226]
Brown Horse HX3 7SD [Lane Ends, Denholme Gate Rd (A644 Brighouse—Keighley, 1 mile N of Hipperholme)]: Attractive and comfortable, with tables set close for good value traditional food from sandwiches up, Greene King Ruddles, Timothy Taylors Landlord and Golden Best and Tetleys, decent house wines, open fires in three bustling rooms, lots of bric-a-brac on ceilings and walls, restaurant, small light back conservatory overlooking garden; open all day *(Gordon and Margaret Ormondroyd)*

COLTON [SE5444]
☆ *Olde Sun* LS24 8EP [off A64 York—Tadcaster]: Immaculate 17th-c beamed dining pub with wide choice of good upscale food using prime local produce (must book Sun lunch), good welcoming service, well kept ales such as Black Sheep and Greene King, good choice of wines by the glass, several linked low-ceilinged rooms, antique settle and nice old chairs around good solid tables, log fires, back delicatessen; front terrace and decking, bedrooms next door, cl Mon *(BB, Pete Coxon, Tim and Sue Halstead, Robert Wivell, G Dobson, P G Wooler, Kelly McCarthy)*

CONEYTHORPE [SE3958]
☆ *Tiger* HG5 0RY [E of Knaresborough]: Pretty dining pub on green of charming village, friendly efficient staff, enjoyable wholesome home-made food sensibly priced inc Sun

carvery, well kept local ales, straightforward open-plan décor in linked areas around bar and adjoining dining room *(WW, Mrs Sheila Stothard, Michael Doswell)*

CONONLEY [SD9846]

New Inn BD20 8NR [Main St/Station Rd]: Compact busy village pub with good value generous home-made food, five well kept Timothy Taylors ales, good service, pig pictures, games room *(Dudley and Moira Cockroft)*

CRACOE [SD9760]

Devonshire Arms BD23 6LA [B6265 Skipton—Grassington]: Sympathetically updated low-beamed pub with some exposed stonework, wood and carpet floors, bar with two woodburners, adjoining snug with open log fire and leather sofas, oak-panelled restaurant, good value standard food, Marstons related ales; garden with terrace, five comfortable bedrooms *(Dudley and Moira Cockroft, LYM)*

CRATHORNE [NZ4407]

Crathorne Arms TS15 0BA: Large dining pub with good range of enjoyable fresh food inc meal deals and popular Sun lunch, good Yorkshire beers, friendly obliging staff, thriving atmosphere; pleasant village *(Andy and Jill Kassube)*

CRAY [SD9479]

☆ *White Lion* BD23 5JB [B6160 N of Kettlewell]: New welcoming owners for highest Wharfedale pub, in lovely countryside, popular with walkers; simple bar, open fire, flagstones, back room, enjoyable food, Copper Dragon, John Smiths and Timothy Taylors Landlord, board games; children and dogs welcome, picnic-sets above quiet steep lane or can sit on flat limestone slabs in shallow stream opposite, has been open all day *(the Didler, David Jackson, LYM, Terry Mizen, Richard Blackwell)*

CRIGGLESTONE [SE3217]

Red Kite WF4 3BB [Denby Dale Rd, Durkar (A636, by M1 junction 39)]: Vintage Inn dining pub done like a Georgian house adjoining a cottage row, good service, their usual good value food and wide range of wines by the glass, well kept ales such as Black Sheep, Marstons Pedigree and Timothy Taylors Landlord, log fire, pleasant décor, newspapers; lots of tables outside, bedrooms in adjacent Holiday Inn Express *(Derek and Sylvia Stephenson, Michael Butler)*

DEWSBURY [SE2622]

Huntsman WF12 7SW [Walker Cottages, Chidswell Lane, Shaw Cross – pub signed]: Cosy low-beamed converted cottages alongside urban-fringe farm, lots of agricultural bric-a-brac, hot log fire, small front extension, friendly locals, well kept Black Sheep, Chidswell (brewed for them) and Timothy Taylors Landlord, decent home-made food (not evenings or Sun, Mon) *(Michael Butler, the Didler)*

Spinners WF12 8PX [Wakefield Rd (A638 towards Ossett)]: Well renovated old pub

with good atmosphere, two lounges and new dining extension, enjoyable if not cheap food *(Marcus Mann)*

☆ *West Riding Licensed Refreshment Rooms* WF13 1HF [Station, Wellington Rd]: Convivial three-room early Victorian station bar, particularly well kept Timothy Taylors and several interesting changing ales, farm ciders, bargain generous lunchtime food on scrubbed tables, popular pie night Tues, curry night Weds and steak night Thurs, friendly staff, daily papers, coal fire, lots of steam memorabilia inc paintings by local artists, impressive juke box, jazz nights; children in two end rooms, disabled access, open all day *(Andrew York, the Didler, Joe Green, Andy Lickfold, Pat and Tony Martin, Tony and Maggie Harwood)*

DONCASTER [SK6299]

Hare & Tortoise DN4 7PB [Parrots Corner, Bawtry Rd, Bessacarr (A638)]: Civilised Vintage Inn all-day dining pub, varying-sized antique tables in several small rooms off bar, log fire, friendly attentive young staff, good choice of well priced food, beers and wines by the glass *(Stephen Woad)*

DRIGHLINGTON [SE2228]

Railway BD11 1JJ [Birstall Lane]: Bargain home-made food, friendly efficient staff, small bar, large dining area *(John and Eleanor Holdsworth)*

DUNGWORTH [SK2889]

Royal S6 6HF [Main Rd (B6076 W of Sheffield)]: 19th-c village local on edge of Peak District (lovely views), chatty landlord, well priced food (not wkdy lunchtimes nor Sun evening), good soft drinks choice, a real ale; children and dogs welcome, three bedrooms *(JJW, CMW)*

EASINGWOLD [SE5270]

☆ *George* YO61 3AD [Market Place]: Neat, bright and airy market town hotel popular with older people, pleasant bustle though quiet corners even when busy, helpful cheerful service, Black Sheep, Daleside and Moorhouses, food in bar and restaurant, warm log fires, interesting bric-a-brac; good value pleasant bedrooms, good breakfast *(Derek and Sylvia Stephenson, Pete Coxon, Kay and Alistair Butler)*

EAST MARTON [SD9050]

Cross Keys BD23 3LP [A59 Gisburn—Skipton]: Behind small green nr Leeds & Liverpool Canal (and Pennine Way), abstract prints on pastel walls contrasting with heavy beams, antique oak furniture and big log or coal fire, reasonably priced food from good fresh sandwiches up, well kept Copper Dragon ales with a guest such as Black Sheep, decent wines, quick friendly helpful service, more restauranty dining room; quiet piped music; tables outside *(LYM, Charles and Pauline Stride, Steve Whalley, D W Stokes)*

EAST WITTON [SE1487]

☆ *Coverbridge Inn* DL8 4SQ [A6108 out towards Middleham]: Homely 16th-c flagstoned country local with eight well kept

Yorkshire ales, good generous home-made food inc prime local steak and their renowned ham and eggs, sensible prices, helpful knowledgeable landlord and welcoming staff, small character bar and larger eating areas off, roaring fires; children and dogs welcome, riverside garden, three bedrooms, open all day (Mr and Mrs Ian King, WW, the Didler, Dr Ian S Morley, Comus and Sarah Elliott, Mr and Mrs Maurice Thompson, LYM)

EGTON BRIDGE [NZ8005]

Postgate YO21 1UX [signed off A171 W of Whitby]: Moorland village pub, wide choice of enjoyable good value food, friendly staff, Black Sheep and a guest, traditional quarry-tiled panelled bar with beams, panelled dado and coal fire in antique range, elegant restaurant; children and dogs welcome, garden picnic-sets, three nice bedrooms (LYM, P Dawn, Jane and Alan Bush, Dr and Mrs R G J Telfer)

ELLAND [SE1021]

Barge & Barrel HX5 9HP [quite handy for M62 junction 24; Park Rd (A6025, via A629 and B6114)]: Large rambling pub with several changing ales inc local Eastwood/Elland, farm cider, limited but generous low-priced tasty lunchtime food (not Mon), special supper evenings, real fire, family room, some live music; piped radio; seats by Calder & Hebble Canal, limited parking, open all day (the Didler, John R Ringrose)

ELLERBY [NZ7914]

Ellerby Hotel TS13 5LP [just off A174 Whitby rd; Ryeland Lane]: Small friendly well looked-after hotel with good pub atmosphere, enjoyable good value traditional food from lunchtime sandwiches up, well kept ales inc Courage Directors, log fire, restaurant; comfortable reasonably priced bedrooms, good breakfast (Peter Thompson)

FEARBY [SE1980]

Black Swan HG4 4NF: Long low two-bar beamed pub with massive collection of chamber-pots, Black Sheep and other regional ales, wide food choice, helpful service, valley view (Hugh Stafford)

FINGHALL [SE1889]

☆ *Queens Head* DL8 5ND [off A684 E of Leyburn]: Welcoming new licensees at this comfortable pub; log fires either end of tidy low-beamed bar, settles making stalls around big tables, Black Sheep, Greene King, John Smiths and Theakstons, good choice of traditional food and vegetarian options, much extended back Wensleydale-view dining room; children and dogs welcome, disabled facilities, back garden with decking sharing view, three bedrooms (Mr and Mrs Williams, Sandra Taylor, BB, Blaise Vyner)

FLAMBOROUGH [TA2270]

☆ *Seabirds* YO15 1PD [Tower St (B1255/B1229)]: Friendly early 19th-c pub with shipping-theme bar, woodburner and local pictures in comfortable lounge, smart light and airy dining extension,

enjoyable low-priced food from sandwiches to fresh fish and Sun roasts, good cheerful service, well kept John Smiths and guests, decent wine list; children and dogs welcome, disabled access, tables in sizeable garden, plenty of hanging baskets and tubs (DC, Robert Wivell, Pat and Graham Williamson, Danny Savage, Pat and Tony Martin, Mr and Mrs Staples, LYM, Michael Butler)

GARSDALE HEAD [SD7992]

☆ *Moorcock* LA10 5PU [junction A684/B6259; marked on many maps, nr Garsdale station on Settle—Carlisle line]: Isolated stone-built inn with Black Sheep and own Moorcock ale brewed in Hawes, good value enjoyable food all day from overstuffed sandwiches up, good choice of wines by the glass, good coffee, welcoming landlord and helpful staff, informal eclectic décor, log fire in small flagstoned bar, cosy corners in lounge bar, occasional live music; muddy walkers welcome, tables outside with views of viaduct and Settle—Carlisle railway, bedrooms, open all day (Bruce and Sharon Eden, Peter Salmon)

GIGGLESWICK [SD8164]

☆ *Black Horse* BD24 0BE [Church St]: Very hospitable father-and-son landlords in prettily set 17th-c village pub, spotless cosy bar with horsey bric-a-brac and gleaming brasses, coal-effect fire, good choice of reasonably priced hearty food inc sandwiches and nice home-made puddings, John Smiths, Timothy Taylors and Tetleys, intimate dining room, good service; heated back terrace, smokers' shelter, three good value comfortable bedrooms, good breakfast, self-catering cottage (Michael Butler, D W Stokes)

Harts Head BD24 0BA [Belle Hill]: Cheerful family-run village inn, real ales such as Black Sheep, a bargain malt whisky, good choice of wines by the glass, public bar (dogs welcome) with dominoes, good choice of enjoyable reasonably priced food in restaurant, folk night first Fri; new outside smokers' area, bedrooms (Ros Lawler, Michael Butler)

GILLING EAST [SE6176]

☆ *Fairfax Arms* YO62 4JH [Main St (B1363)]: Attractive stone-built country inn now under same management as the good White Swan at Ampleforth – reports please; traditional food with some upmarket twists, Black Sheep and Tetleys, good wine choice, beams and log fire, restaurant; piped music; children welcome, dogs outside only, disabled access, streamside front lawn, pleasant village with castle and miniature steam railway, 11 good bedrooms, open all day wknds (WW)

GLUSBURN [SD9944]

Dog & Gun BD20 8DS [Colne Rd (A6068 W) opp Malsis School]: Comfortably refurbished traditional pub very popular for wide choice of enjoyable bargain food (evening booking advised), good friendly service, four well kept Timothy Taylors ales (Dudley and Moira Cockroft, Rob Bowran)

GOATHLAND [NZ8200]

Mallyan Spout Hotel YO22 5AN [opp church]: More hotel than pub, popular from its use by TV's *Heartbeat* cast, three spacious lounges, friendly traditional bar, good open fires, fine views, enjoyable bar lunches, well kept Theakstons, good malt whiskies and wines; children in eating area, handy for namesake waterfall, comfortable bedrooms, usually open all day *(LYM, Pete Coxon, Roger A Bellingham)*

GOLDSBOROUGH [NZ8314]

☆ *Fox & Hounds* YO21 3RX [off A174 NW of Whitby]: Snug, homely and spotlessly kept with simple furnishings, welcoming landlady, short choice of very good unfussy food changing daily from chef/landlord, prices reflect quality, well kept beers *(Mrs Sheila Stothard, David Robertson)*

GOOSE EYE [SE0240]

☆ *Turkey* BD22 0PD [between Oakworth and Laycock, W of Keighley]: Another new landlord for this pleasant old pub, own brewery now closed but well kept Adnams, Fullers London Pride, Greene King Abbot and Timothy Taylors Landlord, lots of malt whiskies, standard bar food, various nooks and alcoves, beams, pubby furniture, local photographs, two log fires, games room with pool, darts and games machine; children welcome, dogs in bar, open all day *(LYM)*

GRANGE MOOR [SE2215]

Kaye Arms WF4 4BG [A642 Huddersfield—Wakefield]: Civilised dining pub, good food with plenty of fish, well kept Black Sheep and Theakstons, log fire; children welcome, handy for Mining Museum *(Michael Butler, Dr Rob Watson, LYM)*

GRASSINGTON [SE0064]

Foresters Arms BD23 5AA [Main St]: Cheerful opened-up old coaching inn with friendly efficient staff, good well priced food, good choice of ales, log fires, dining room off on right; pool and sports TV on left; children welcome, 14 affordable bedrooms, open all day *(Dudley and Moira Cockroft, Dave Braisted, the Didler, Michael Butler)*

GREAT AYTON [NZ5610]

Royal Oak TS9 6BW [off A173 – follow village signs; High Green]: Wide range of generous good traditional food inc early-bird bargains, children's menu, afternoon tea, well kept Courage, John Smiths and Theakstons, unpretentious convivial bar with good log fire, beam-and-plank ceiling, bulgy old partly panelled stone walls, traditional furnishings inc antique settles, pleasant views of elegant village green from bay windows, long dining lounge, separate appealingly old-fashioned restaurant catering for tour groups; comfortable bedrooms, handy for Cleveland Way *(LYM, David and Sue Smith)*

GREAT BROUGHTON [NZ5405]

Bay Horse TS9 7HA [High St]: Big thoughtfully planned dining pub in attractive village, good value straightforward food inc appealing puddings, attentive

service, real ales *(Janet and Peter Race)*

GREAT HABTON [SE7576]

☆ *Grapes* YO17 6TU: Homely and cosy, traditionally refurbished beamed dining pub in small village, good cooking inc fresh local fish and game, Marstons-related ales, open fire, friendly and hard-working young couple; piped pop music may obtrude, small public bar with darts and TV; a few roadside picnic-sets (water for dogs – nice walks), open all day Sun, cl Tues lunchtime and Mon *(BB, David S Allen)*

GREEN HAMMERTON [SE4656]

Bay Horse YO26 8BN [just off A59 York—Harrogate]: Village pub with several nicely decorated snug areas, good range of reasonably priced food, Black Sheep and Timothy Taylors Landlord, good value wines; children in eating areas, garden tables, bedrooms in separate block behind, open all day Sun and summer Sats *(Michael Butler, LYM)*

GUNNERSIDE [SD9598]

Kings Head DL11 6LD [B6270 Swaledale rd]: Small recently refurbished two-room local in pretty riverside Dales village, enjoyable food inc vegetarian choices, four local ales, log fire, flagstones and carpet, old village photographs; children, dogs and muddy boots welcome, some tables out by bridge, good walks nearby, open all day wknds *(Peter Dearing, Mr and Mrs Maurice Thompson)*

HALIFAX [SE1026]

Stump Cross Inn HX3 7AY [Kell Lane, Stump Cross]: Smart dining pub, airy and modern, with enjoyable reasonably priced food, pleasant helpful staff, good coffee; attractive terrace *(Gordon and Margaret Ormondroyd)*

HAMPSTHWAITE [SE2558]

Joiners Arms HG3 2EU [about 5 miles W of Harrogate; High St]: Yorkshire ales, decent wines and popular food inc Sun roast, good service, big fireplace, decorative plates on lounge beams, public bar and barrel-vaulted snug, spacious and airy back dining extension with dozens of sauceboats on beams and corner chest of joiner's tools; unobtrusive piped music; tables out in front and pleasant back garden, attractive village *(Mr and Mrs Maurice Thompson, Pierre Richterich)*

HARDROW [SD8691]

☆ *Green Dragon* DL8 3LZ: Friendly traditional Dales pub full of character, stripped stone, antique settles on flagstones, lots of bric-a-brac, low-beamed snug with log fire in old iron range, another in big main bar, well kept ales inc one brewed for the pub by Yorkshire Dales, enjoyable generous food, small neat restaurant, annual brass band competition, access (for a small fee) to Britain's highest single-drop waterfall; children and dogs welcome, bedrooms *(LYM, Tony and Maggie Harwood, Tom and Ruth Rees, Danny Savage, Ewan and Moira McCall, Jane and Alan Bush)*

HARROGATE [SE3155]

Coach & Horses HG1 1BJ [West Park]: Very friendly bustling pub (can be almost too busy) with speciality pies and other reasonably priced food, several good Yorkshire ales; open all day *(the Didler, Ian Phillips)*

Empress HG1 4SP [Church Sq]: Comfortably worn-in panelled pub on the Stray, welcoming local atmosphere, several well kept ales inc local Daleside, good choice of wines by the glass, enjoyable food inc popular Sun lunch, pool, bar billiards, darts and dominoes; dogs welcome, open all day *(anon)*

Gardeners Arms HG1 4DH [Bilton Lane (off A59 either in Bilton itself or on outskirts towards Harrogate – via Bilton Hall Drive)]: Stone-built house converted into friendly down-to-earth local, tiny bar and three small rooms, flagstone floors, panelling, old prints and little else; very cheap Sam Smiths OB, decent bar lunches (not Weds), big fire in stone fireplace, dominoes; children welcome, surrounding streamside garden with play area, lovely peaceful setting nr Nidd Gorge *(the Didler, Pam and John Smith, Hunter and Christine Wright)*

☆ *Old Bell* HG1 2SZ [Royal Parade]: Thriving Market Town Taverns pub with eight mainly Yorkshire beers from handsome counter, lots of bottled continentals, impressive choice of wines by the glass, friendly helpful staff, good lunchtime snacks inc sandwiches (interesting choice of breads), more elaborate evening meals upstairs, newspapers, panelling, old sweet shop ads and breweriana, no music or machines; no children; open all day *(Canon Michael Bourdeaux, Martin and Pamela Clark, the Didler, Jo Lilley, Simon Calvert, Pat and Tony Martin, Pam and John Smith, Bruce Bird, Ian Phillips)*

HARTHILL [SK4980]

Beehive S26 7YH [Union St]: Smart two-bar village pub opp attractive church, welcoming service, chef/landlord doing wide range of enjoyable well priced generous food (not Mon) inc proper pies and Sun lunch, well kept Kelham Island Easy Rider, Timothy Taylors Landlord and Tetleys, good wine and soft drinks choice, fresh flowers, games room with pool; piped music; children welcome if eating, picnic-sets in attractive garden, walks nearby, cl Mon lunchtime *(JJW, CMW, Mrs Hazel Rainer, Peter Hacker)*

HAWORTH [SE0337]

Fleece BD22 8DA [Main St]: Well run open bar and small lounge, some panelling and flagstones, coal fires, full Timothy Taylors range kept well, good bottled beers, popular food inc wknd breakfasts, *Railway Children* film stills, restaurant *(Andy and Jill Kassube, John and Helen Rushton)*

Haworth Old Hall BD22 8BP [Sun St]: New landord at this open-plan 17th-c beamed and panelled pub with valley views, long bar, log fire, stripped stonework, appropriately

plain furnishings, Jennings ales, quick cheerful young staff, enjoyable food; piped music; plenty of tables out in front, bedrooms, open all day *(Greta and Christopher Wells, C A Hall, Gordon and Margaret Ormondroyd, Dudley and Moira Cockroft, the Didler, Richard Tosswill)*

HEBDEN BRIDGE [SD9927]

☆ *White Lion* HX7 8EX [Bridge Gate]: Solid stone-built inn with welcoming comfortable bar and country-furnished bare-boards back area with coal fire, sound reasonably priced home cooking all day (just lunchtime Sun), fish specialities, well kept Timothy Taylors Landlord and a guest beer, good service; disabled facilities, attractive secluded riverside garden, ten comfortable bedrooms *(John Fiander, Roy and Lindsey Fentiman, Derek and Sylvia Stephenson, Mrs Hazel Rainer, Ian and Nita Cooper)*

HECKMONDWIKE [SE2123]

New Charnwood WF16 0EH [Westgate]: Cheerful town pub with enjoyable food from great sandwiches to stews and pies, well kept local ales such as Anglo Dutch and Ossett *(Andy and Jill Kassube)*

HEPTONSTALL [SD9828]

White Lion HX7 7NB [Towngate]: Quietly friendly old inn with bargain fresh food, Thwaites ales, delightful Pennine village *(LYM, Jean and Douglas Troup)*

HEPWORTH [SE1606]

Butchers Arms HD9 1TE [off A616 SE of Holmfirth; Towngate]: Dark-beamed country dining pub under new ownership and refurbished to a high standard, very good food from Le Manoir trained chef, panelling, stonework and large log fire; outside seating, open all day *(Tracy Barlow, John and Eleanor Holdsworth)*

HESSLE [TA0326]

Weir Bar & Grill HU13 0SB [The Weir]: Very modern, with huge range of drinks and enjoyable food inc Sun roast *(Matthew James)*

HOLMFIRTH [SD1408]

Nook HD9 2DN [Victoria Sq; aka Rose & Crown]: Now brewing its own ales alongside Timothy Taylors and guest microbrews, home-made pubby food all day and adjoining tapas bar, low beams, flagstones and big open fire, some live music; heated streamside terrace, open all day *(anon)*

HOLYWELL GREEN [SE0919]

Rock HX4 9BS [handy for M62 junction 24]: Smart and comfortable, with good atmosphere and open fire in cosy bar areas, chatty staff, great choice of good food (all day Sun) inc lunchtime bargains, Timothy Taylors Landlord, conservatory, popular restaurant; nicely decorated bedrooms *(Gordon and Margaret Ormondroyd)*

HORBURY [SE2918]

Boons WF4 6LP [Queen St]: Lively, chatty and comfortably unpretentious flagstoned local, Clarks, John Smiths, Timothy Taylors Landlord and up to four quickly changing guests, no food, bare walls, Rugby League memorabilia, back tap room with pool; TV, no children; courtyard tables *(Michael Butler, the Didler)*

Bulls Head WF4 5AR [Southfield Lane]: Large well divided pub deservedly popular for food, smart attentive staff, Black Sheep and Tetleys, lots of wines by the glass, panelling and wood floors, relaxing linked rooms inc library, snug and more formal restaurant; front picnic-sets *(Malcolm and Wendy Butler, Michael Butler)*

Ship WF4 5PR [Bridge Rd]: Cheerful local with well kept beer, bargain food from sandwiches to full meals, friendly family service, pool; children welcome *(Dave Warren)*

HORSEHOUSE [SE0481]

Thwaite Arms DL8 4TS [Coverdale rd Middleham—Kettlewell]: Early 19th-c former farm building in wonderful village setting nr beautiful little church, lots of paths to nearby villages and moors, great drive along dale; bargain simple food inc fine Sun roast (only a few tables in pretty homely dining room, so worth booking), well kept Theakstons Best, farm cider, genial landlord, good coal fire in cosy snug, bigger plainer locals' bar; children welcome, fell views from charming garden, two bedrooms *(Hunter and Christine Wright)*

HORSFORTH [SE2438]

Town Street Tavern LS18 4RJ [Town St]: A Market Town Taverns pub with eight well kept ales inc Black Sheep, Copper Dragon, Leeds Pale and Timothy Taylors Best, lots of continental bottled beers, good food in small bare-boards bar and (Tues-Sat) in upstairs evening bistro, good service; small terrace, open all day *(Andy and Jill Kassube, Brian and Janet Ainscough)*

HOVINGHAM [SE6675]

Malt Shovel YO62 4LF [Main St (B1257 NW of Castle Howard)]: Attractive and comfortably unpretentious, with friendly staff, enjoyable sensibly priced home-made food using own veg, well kept Black Sheep and Tetleys, good coffee, cosy dining room; children welcome, appealing village setting *(Andy and Jill Kassube)*

☆ **Worsley Arms** YO62 4LA [High St]: Smart inn in pretty village handy for Castle Howard, good food in friendly and welcoming back bar and separate restaurant (different menu), Hambleton ales, several malts, good wines and coffee, friendly attentive staff, lots of Yorkshire cricketer photographs especially from 1930/40s; nice tables by stream, pleasant bedrooms, some in cottages across green *(Andy and Jill Kassube, BB)*

HUBBERHOLME [SD9278]

☆ **George** BD23 5JE: Small beautifully placed ancient Dales inn with River Wharfe fishing rights, heavy beams, flagstones and stripped stone, quick simple food, well kept Black Sheep and Copper Dragon, friendly landlord, good log fire, perpetual candle on bar; may charge for water, no dogs, outside lavatories; children allowed in dining area, terrace,

seven bedrooms, cl Mon *(LYM, Michael and Maggie Betton, Michael Tack, Robin M Corlett, Richard, Matt Waite, Peter Dearing, W M Lien, Ann and Tony Bennett-Hughes)*

HUDDERSFIELD [SE1416]

Albert HD1 2QF [Victoria Lane]: Well preserved high Victorian pub with good choice of changing ales, handsome mahogany, marble, mirrors, etched glass and chandeliers, traditional red leather wall seats, steps up to compact lounge and dining room; bedrooms *(the Didler)*

Cherry Tree HD1 1BA [John William St]: Open-plan split-level Wetherspoons with good choice of mainly Yorkshire beers, farm cider, decent food in back dining room, good views, more seating downstairs *(the Didler)*

Green Cross HD5 8AG [Wakefield Rd]: Comfortable and welcoming, with lots of mainly local real ales *(the Didler)*

Grove HD1 4BP [Spring Grove St]: Lots of exotic bottled beers, well kept Timothy Taylors Landlord and fine range of interesting changing guest ales at sensible prices (own microbrewery planned), huge vodka choice, snacks from latvian crisps to dried anchovies, occasional Sun afternoon entertainment, art gallery; back terrace, open all day *(John R Ringrose, the Didler, Martin Grosberg)*

☆ **Head of Steam** HD1 1JF [Station, St Georges Sq]: Railway memorabilia, model trains, cars, buses and planes for sale, friendly staff, long bar with up to eight changing ales, lots of bottled beers, farm ciders and perry, fruit wines, black leather easy chairs and sofas, hot coal fire, good value enjoyable back buffet, some live jazz and blues nights; unobtrusive piped music, can be very busy; open all day *(Tony and Maggie Harwood, Andrew York, David Hoult, Brian and Anna Marsden, the Didler, Pat and Tony Martin)*

High Park HD2 1PX [Bradley Rd, Bradley]: Neatly kept dining pub, attractively done and keeping plenty of room for drinking and chatting, Hardys & Hansons beers (unusual around here), good value pub food inc OAP and other deals, quick friendly service; children welcome, open all day *(Gordon and Margaret Ormondroyd)*

Kings Head HD1 1JF [St Georges Sq]: Handsome victorian station building housing friendly well run pub, large open-plan room with original tiled floor, two smaller rooms off, eight regularly changing ales, bargain cobs, live afternoon/evening music (Sun, Thurs); disabled access via platform 1, open all day *(the Didler)*

Star HD1 3PJ [Albert St, Lockwood]: Unpretentious friendly local with seven competitively priced changing ales particularly well kept by enthusiastic landlady, continental beers, farm cider, beer festivals in back marquee, bric-a-brac and customers' paintings; no food; cl Mon and lunchtime Tues-Thurs, open all day wknds *(the Didler, John R Ringrose)*

HULL [TA0929]

Hop & Vine HU1 3TG [Albion St]: Small pub with three real ales, bottled belgian beers, farm ciders and perry, friendly licensees, good sandwiches and bargain basic specials all day; open all day, cl Sun lunchtime, Mon *(the Didler)*

☆ *Olde White Harte* HU1 1JG [passage off Silver St]: Ancient pub with Civil War history under new management, attractive stained-glass, carved heavy beams, two big inglenooks with frieze of delft tiles, Caledonian Deuchars IPA, McEwans 80/-, Theakstons Old Peculier and a guest from copper-topped counter, 80 malt whiskies, decent standard food; children welcome in upstairs restaurant, dogs in bar, heated courtyard, open all day *(the Didler, LYM)*

Wellington HU2 9AB [Russell St]: Smartly kept 19th-c bar with Tetleys and half a dozen or so well kept guest beers, impressive cabinets of bottled imports, Weston's and guest ciders, friendly staff, interesting memorabilia; back terrace, open all day Fri-Sun, cl lunchtime Mon-Thurs *(the Didler)*

Whalebone HU2 0PA [Wincolmlee]: Friendly local brewing its own ales, good guest beers and farm ciders, bar food, old-fashioned décor; open all day *(the Didler)*

HUTTON-LE-HOLE [SE7089]

Crown YO62 6UA [The Green]: Spotless pub overlooking pretty village green with wandering sheep in classic coach-trip country, good sandwiches and huge helpings of no-fuss food (all day Sun), well kept Black Sheep, cheerful efficient service, opened-up bar with varnished woodwork and whisky-water jugs, dining area; children and dogs welcome, near Folk Museum, handy for Farndale walks *(Dr and Mrs R G J Telfer, Mrs Romey Heaton, Paul Humphreys, Simon Collett-Jones)*

ILKLEY [SE1147]

Bar t'at LS29 9DZ [Cunliffe Rd]: Market Towns Tavern pub with eight mainly Yorkshire ales, good wine and bottled beer choice, lively lunchtime bistro atmosphere with good sandwiches and bargain hot dishes, more elaborate evening food (candlelit cellar dining area may open then), quick polite service, daily papers, front conservatory; dogs welcome, heated back terrace, open all day *(WW, N R White, Pat and Tony Martin)*

INGBIRCHWORTH [SE2106]

Fountain S36 7GJ [off A629 Shepley—Penistone; Welthorne Lane]: Relaxed beamed dining pub, good food at low prices, friendly efficient service, well kept ales such as Black Sheep, nice coffee, log fires, roomy red plush lounge, cosy front bar and family room; well reproduced piped music; garden tables overlooking reservoir with pretty walks, good bedrooms, hearty breakfast *(Michael Butler, BB, Roger A Bellingham)*

KEIGHLEY [SE0541]

Brown Cow BD21 2LQ [Cross Leeds St]: Popular and friendly extensively refurbished

local, good licensee keeping Timothy Taylors ales and guest beers in top condition; open all day wknds *(the Didler)*

Globe BD21 4QR [Parkwood St]: New friendly landlord at this comfortable local by Worth Valley steam railway track, Timothy Taylors ales, new kitchen doing pubby food Fri-Sun lunchtimes, coal fire, darts, games room with pool and SkyTV; karaoke, Sun quiz; tables out behind, cl till 4pm Mon-Thurs, open all day Fri-Sun *(the Didler)*

KELD [NY8900]

Keld Lodge DL11 6LL: Remote former youth hostel now pub/restaurant, four well kept ales such as Greene King IPA, Hambleton, Thwaites and Timothy Taylors Landlord, good service, popular blackboard food, small rooms (can get packed) *(Arthur Pickering)*

KETTLEWELL [SD9672]

☆ *Blue Bell* BD23 5QX [Middle Lane]: Roomy knocked-through 17th-c coaching inn, Copper Dragon ales kept well, good wine choice, friendly obliging service, home-made food using local ingredients, snug simple furnishings, log fire, low beams and flagstones, old country photographs, attractive restaurant, daily papers; children welcome, picnic-sets on cobbles facing Wharfe bridge, six newly refurbished annex bedrooms, good breakfast *(Comus and Sarah Elliott, Stephen Corfield, LYM, Jeremy King, WW, B and M Kendall)*

☆ *Racehorses* BD23 5QZ [B6160 N of Skipton]: Comfortable, civilised and friendly two-bar pub with dining area, generous good value food from substantial lunchtime rolls and baguettes to local game, popular early evening bargains Sun-Thurs, well kept Timothy Taylors and Tetleys, good choice of wines by the glass, good log fire; children welcome (dogs in bars), front and back terrace seating, well placed for Wharfedale walks, 13 good bedrooms, open all day *(BB, Brian and Janet Ainscough, Stephen Corfield)*

KILBURN [SE5179]

☆ *Forresters Arms* YO61 4AH [between A170 and A19 SW of Thirsk]: Welcoming inn next to Robert Thompson furniture workshops (early examples of his work in both bars), roaring fires, real ales such as Hambleton, John Smiths and Tetleys, good choice of home-made food using local produce, lounge and restaurant; TV, games machine, piped music; children and dogs (in some areas) welcome, suntrap seats out in front, smokers' shelter at back, ten refurbished bedrooms, open all day *(LYM, Roger and Lesley Everett)*

KILNSEA [TA4016]

Crown & Anchor HU12 0UB [Kilnsea Rd]: Unpretentious building typical of the area, in great remote location overlooking eroding Spurn Point bird reserve and Humber estuary, single bar opening into two beamed lounges and linen-set restaurant, prints and bric-a-brac, good range of well kept ales, low-priced wines, variety of enjoyable reasonably priced food inc good fresh fish, friendly staff and locals; piped music; picnic-sets in back garden and out in front facing estuary, four bedrooms, open all day *(Mr and Mrs Staples)*

KIRK DEIGHTON [SE3950]

Bay Horse LS22 4DZ [B6164 N of Wetherby; Main St]: Cosy beamed dining lounge under new management, comfortable banquettes and other seats, rugs on dark flagstones, simpler public bar by entrance, has served Black Sheep, Copper Dragon, John Smiths and Timothy Taylors; piped music; may cl Mon lunchtime *(LYM)*

KIRKBYMOORSIDE [SE6986]

Kings Head YO62 6AT [High Market Place]: 16th-c inn with enjoyable home-made food using local produce, good value wkdy early evening set menu, friendly service, Jennings ales, carpeted bar with stone walls, steps down to lounge/dining area with wood floor and open fire, beamed restaurant with dark wood furniture on rugs, conservatory; children welcome, terrace and walled garden, barbecue, comfortable good value bedrooms *(Andy and Jill Kassube)*

KIRKHAM [SE7365]

☆ *Stone Trough* YO60 7JS [Kirkham Abbey]: Bustling beamed country pub under new management, several cosy log-fire rooms, well kept Timothy Taylors Landlord and Theakstons Old Peculier, wide food choice, good service, restaurant; seats outside, lovely valley views, good walks, Kirkham Abbey and Castle Howard nearby, has been open all day Sun, cl Mon *(LYM, Jan Everton, D W Stokes)*

KNAPTON [SE5652]

Red Lion YO26 6QG [Main St]: Small village pub doing well under new management, enjoyable sensibly priced food inc small blackboard specials choice *(John and Eleanor Holdsworth)*

KNARESBOROUGH [SE3556]

☆ *Blind Jacks* HG5 8AL [Market Place]: Friendly individualistic multi-floor tavern in 18th-c building, low beams, simple attractive furnishings, brewery posters etc, particularly well kept Black Sheep, Timothy Taylors (inc their great Dark Mild) and other changing ales, foreign bottled beers, farm cider, friendly helpful staff, limited food, bubbly atmosphere downstairs, quieter up; well behaved children allowed away from bar, open all day wknds, cl Mon till 5.30pm; Beer Ritz two doors away sells all sorts of rare bottled beers *(the Didler, Paul Smurthwaite, Pam and John Smith, Joe Green, Ros Lawler, LYM)*

LANGSETT [SE2100]

Waggon & Horses S36 4GY [A616 Stocksbridge—Huddersfield]: Welcoming and comfortable main-road moors pub, blazing log fire, stripped stone and woodwork, good sensibly priced food inc speciality pies and nice Sun lunch, well kept ales such as Bradfield, Timothy Taylors Landlord and Theakstons; children welcome, three bedrooms, holiday cottage, cl Sun evening, Mon *(Pat and Tony Martin, James A Waller)*

LASTINGHAM [SE7290]

☆ *Blacksmiths Arms* YO62 6TL [off A170 W of Pickering]: Old-fashioned beamed pub opp beautiful Saxon church in attractive village, log fire in open range, traditional furnishings, Theakstons and other regional ales, several wines by the glass, popular food, darts, board games; piped music – live music second Sun of month; children and walkers welcome, seats in back garden, nice bedrooms, open all day summer *(Maurice and Gill McMahon, P Dawn, Blaise Vyner, Paul Humphreys, LYM, Brian and Anna Marsden)*

LEALHOLM [NZ7607]

Board YO21 2AJ [off A171 W of Whitby]: In wonderful moorland village spot by wide pool of River Esk, unpretentious locals' bars, stripped stone, big log fire, welcoming licensees and chatty friendly staff, changing ales such as Black Sheep, Camerons Ruby Red and Wychwood Dirty Tackle, bar snacks (own pickled eggs) and good seasonal food in restaurant, games room/lounge with darts and pool; TV; children and dogs welcome, secluded riverside garden with decking, five bedrooms, open all day Sat, cl wkdy winter lunchtimes *(James Goodwill, Ian and Anne Read)*

LEEDS [SE3033]

Adelphi LS10 1JQ [Hunslet Rd]: Thoroughly refurbished (but they've kept the handsome Edwardian mahogany screens, panelling, tiling, cut and etched glass and impressive stairway), Tetleys and guest ales, decent lunchtime food inc good vegetarian option, prompt friendly service, board games; live jazz Sat *(Mishal Islam)*

Brewery Tap LS1 5DL [New Station St]: Tied to Leeds Brewery, their ales and guest beers kept well, good value food, neat friendly efficient staff; unobtrusive piped music *(Bruce Bird)*

Cross Keys LS11 5WD [Water Lane]: Designer bar with flagstone floors, stripped brick, original tiling, metal and timbers, good choice of Yorkshire ales and imported bottled beers, enjoyable good value interesting food, upstairs room; children welcome, tables under big canvas parasols in sheltered courtyard, barbecues, open all day *(the Didler)*

☆ *Grove* LS11 5PL [Back Row, Holbeck]: Unspoilt 1930s-feel local overshadowed by towering office blocks, friendly long-serving landlord, tables and stools in main bar with marble floor, panelling and original fireplace, large back room (some live music here) and snug off drinking corridor, good choice of well kept ales inc Caledonian Deuchars IPA, Weston's cider, good live music; open all day *(Mike and Eleanor Anderson, the Didler, Barrie Pepper)*

Midnight Bell LS11 5QN [Water Lane]: Friendly tap for Leeds Brewery, four of their ales, enjoyable food, flagstones and light contemporary décor; waterside tables outside *(the Didler)*

Mr Foleys LS1 5RG [159 The Headrow]: In former insurance firm's HQ and named for its founder, four York ales and several others from local brewers, usual pub food all day from sandwiches up, mixed furnishings on several levels inc some leather sofas; TV may obtrude; balcony tables (Tony and Wendy Hobden)

Mustard Pot LS7 3QY [Stainbeck Lane, Chapel Allerton]: Friendly new management in relaxed easy-going dining pub with above-average up-to-date food (all day Sat, till 8pm Sun), a changing real ale such as Marstons or Wychwood, decent wines by the glass, comfortable banquettes and leather chesterfields, pastel paintwork; unobtrusive piped music; pleasant front garden, summer barbecues, open all day (anon)

Palace LS2 7DJ [Kirkgate]: Pleasantly uncityfied, with stripped boards and polished panelling, unusual lighting from electric candelabra to mock street lamps, lots of old prints, friendly helpful staff, good value lunchtime food till 7pm from sandwiches up inc popular Sun roasts in dining area, fine changing choice of ales, may be bargain wine offers; games end with pool, TV, good piped music; tables out in front and in small heated back courtyard, open all day
(Joe Green, the Didler)

Pin LS11 9RU [Sydenham Rd]: Modern bar tied to newish Leeds Brewery, their full ale range, enjoyable home-made bar lunches from sandwiches to pies, fishcakes, etc; handy for Clarence Dock (Andy and Jill Kassube)

☆ *Victoria* LS1 3DL [Gt George St]: Opulent early Victorian pub with grand cut and etched mirrors, impressive globe lamps extending from majestic bar, carved beams, leather-seat booths with working snob-screens, smaller rooms off, changing ales such as Cottage, Leeds, Timothy Taylors and Tetleys, friendly efficient service even when busy, reasonably priced food 12-6 from sandwiches and light dishes up in separate room with serving hatch; open all day
(Joe Green, the Didler, Neil Whitehead, Victoria Anderson, Jeremy King)

☆ *Whitelocks* LS1 6HB [Turks Head Yard, off Briggate]: Nicely restored classic Victorian pub, long narrow old-fashioned bar, tiled counter, grand mirrors, mahogany and glass screens, heavy copper-topped tables and green leather, well kept Caledonian Deuchars IPA, John Smiths, Theakstons Best and Old Peculier and fine range of guests, good all-day food (not Sun evening), hard-working young staff; crowded at lunchtime; children in restaurant and top bar, tables in narrow courtyard, open all day (Neil Whitehead, Victoria Anderson, Andy Lickfold, Joe Green, the Didler, LYM, Janet and Peter Race, N R White)

LELLEY [TA2032]

Stags Head HU12 8SN [Main St; NE of Preston]: Stylishly refurbished pub well run by long-serving landlady, good enterprising fresh food (small helpings available),

Marstons Pedigree and John Smiths, decent wines by the glass, helpful cheerful staff, sofas and a couple of high-stool tables, dining area one side, comfortable restaurant the other; TV (Rob and Penny Wakefield)

LEVISHAM [SE8390]

☆ *Horseshoe* YO18 7NL [off A169 N of Pickering]: Attractive welcoming inn doing well under new regime, old beams, simple attractive furnishings on broad boards, handsome log fire, enjoyable generous food from sandwiches up, free coffee refills, real ale such as Black Sheep; picnic-sets on pretty green, delightful unspoilt village, good walks, simple nicely refurbished bedrooms, cl Sun evening, Tues
(Paul Humphreys, Helen Royds, LYM)

LEYBURN [SE1190]

Black Swan DL8 5AS [Market Place]: Attractive old creeper-clad hotel with chatty locals in cheerful open-plan bar, entertaining landlord, good service, decent range of food inc popular Sun carvery, well kept Black Sheep and other ales, good wines by the glass; no credit cards; children and dogs welcome, good disabled access, tables on cobbled terrace, seven bedrooms, open all day (Dorothy and Brian Rutter, the Didler, Andy Lickfold, Michael Tack, A and B D Craig, Colin Smith)

Bolton Arms DL8 5BW [Market Place]: Substantial stone-built inn at top of market place, popular with locals, well kept ales inc Black Sheep, varied choice of good value home-made food; bedrooms (Michael Tack)

Golden Lion DL8 5AS [Market Place]: Comfortable panelled and bay-windowed hotel bar, two light and airy rooms with log-effect gas fire in eating area, varied good value generous food, well kept Black Sheep, decent coffee, friendly efficient service, paintings for sale, evening restaurant; very busy on Fri market day; dogs allowed, tables out in front, good value bedrooms, open all day (BB, Michael Tack)

LINTHWAITE [SE1014]

☆ *Sair* HD7 5SG [Lane Top, Hoyle Ing, off A62]: Old-fashioned four-room pub about to resume brewing its eight good value beers as we went to press, pews and chairs on rough flagstones or wood floors, log-burning ranges, dominoes, cribbage and shove-ha'penny, vintage rock juke box; no food or credit cards; dogs welcome, children till 8pm, plenty of tables out in front with fine Colne Valley views, restored Huddersfield Narrow Canal nearby, open all day wknds, from 5pm wkdys (John R Ringrose, the Didler, LYM)

LINTON [SE3846]

☆ *Windmill* LS22 4HT [off A661 W of Wetherby]: Upmarket pub, beams, stripped stone, antique settles around copper-topped tables, log fires, lunchtime bargains, more expensive evening restaurant, John Smiths, Theakstons Best and guests, several wines by the glass; piped music; children and dogs welcome, sunny back terrace and sheltered garden with pear tree raised from seed brought back from Napoleonic Wars, open all day wknds *(Ray and Winifred Halliday, Maurice and Janet Thorpe, LYM, Dr and Mrs A K Clarke)*

LITTON [SD9074]

☆ **Queens Arms** BD23 5QJ [off B6160 N of Grassington]: Beautifully placed pub under friendly new local licensees, main bar with coal fire, rough stone walls, brown beam-and-plank ceiling, stools around cast-iron-framed tables on stone floor, dining room with old Dale photographs, own-brewed ales and guests, fresh food from sandwiches up; children and dogs welcome, two-level garden, plenty of good surrounding walks, bedrooms *(LYM)*

LOW BRADFIELD [SK2691]

☆ **Plough** S6 6HW [New Rd]: Attractively refurbished popular pub, very good value home-made food (not Mon or Tues evenings), well kept local Bradfield and guest beers, cheery efficient service, inglenook log fire, restaurant; children welcome, picnic-sets in attractive garden, lovely scenery *(JJW, CMW, Peter F Marshall)*

LOW BRADLEY [SE0048]

Slaters Arms BD20 9DE [Crag Lane, off A629 S of Skipton]: Well kept ales such as Black Sheep, Timothy Taylors and Wells & Youngs, belgian beers, generous fresh home cooking inc good value Sun lunch, real fires *(Sandra Brame)*

LOW ROW [SD9898]

☆ **Punch Bowl** DL11 6PF [B6270 Reeth—Muker]: Under same ownership as Charles Bathurst at Langthwaite, fresh, light and almost scandinavian in style, with friendly helpful staff, good interesting food (menu on huge mirror), popular Sun carvery (best to book), several good wines by the glass, well kept Black Sheep, log fire, leather armchairs, sturdy tables and chairs; children welcome, great Swaledale views from terrace, 11 comfortable bedrooms, good breakfast, open all day summer *(Bruce and Sharon Eden, Alison and Pete, John and Verna Aspinall, Richard, Mrs Ruth Lewis, Mrs Sheila Stothard, Mike and Lynn Robinson, Professors Alan and Ann Clarke)*

LUDDENDEN [SE0426]

Lord Nelson HX2 6PX [High St]: Cheerful modernised 18th-c local with interesting features, where Branwell Brontë borrowed books, Timothy Taylors, generous fresh food; attractive very steep streamside village *(Jean and Douglas Troup, LYM)*

MALHAM [SD9062]

Lister Arms BD23 4DB [off A65 NW of Skipton]: Friendly creeper-covered stone-built inn tied to Thwaites, their ales kept well, lots of bottled imports, good value food inc lunchtime sandwiches, roaring fire; pool and games machines; children and dogs welcome, seats out overlooking small green, more in back garden, lovely spot by river, good walking country, comfortable clean bedrooms *(Karen Eliot, David Field,*

Lynda and Trevor Smith, Arthur Pickering)

MANFIELD [NZ2213]

Crown DL2 2RF [Vicars Lane]: Old-fashioned welcoming village local with enjoyable simple food such as baguettes and a few hot dishes, Village Premium and a guest beer such as Mordue Workie Ticket, traditional clean décor, pool *(Dan Connolly)*

MARSDEN [SE0412]

Tunnel End HD7 6NF [Reddisher Rd (off A62 via Peel St)]: Pleasant setting overlooking mouth of restored Standedge Canal Tunnel – at three miles under the Pennines, the UK's longest; very warm welcome, well kept ales such as Black Sheep and Timothy Taylors Landlord, simple generous well made food from sandwiches to Sun roasts, reasonable prices, four good-sized but homely rooms, hot log fire in back room, pub cat, quiz nights; children welcome *(anon)*

MARTON [SE7383]

Appletree YO62 6RD [off A170 W of Pickering]: Welcoming licensees who put this dining pub right in the top class have left, and we know nothing yet of their replacements; beamed lounge, comfortable settees around low tables, open fire in stone fireplace, small bar, dining room and little bay leading off with more tables; sheltered flagstoned back courtyard *(LYM)*

MARTON CUM GRAFTON [SE4263]

Olde Punch Bowl YO51 9QY [signed off A1 3 miles N of A59]: Recently reopened and now home to the Morrissey Fox microbrewery, their beers plus Cropton and John Smiths, some interesting home-made food using local produce, roomy heavy-beamed open-plan bar, open fires, contemporary art, restaurant; children and dogs welcome, disabled facilities, picnic-sets in pleasant garden, early evening Sun barbecues with live acoustic music, open all day *(Marian and Andrew Ruston, LYM)*

MASHAM [SE2281]

☆ **White Bear** HG4 4EN [Wellgarth, Crosshills; signed off A6108 opp turn into town]: Cheerful comfortably refurbished stone-built beamed pub, small public bar with well kept local ales and darts, comfortable larger lounge with coal fire, good fairly priced food (not Sun evening) from sandwiches up, decent wines by the glass, efficient staff; piped music; children and dogs welcome, terrace tables, 14 bedrooms, open all day *(BB, the Didler, Julian and Jill Tasker, WW, Janet and Peter Race, Clive Gibson)*

MIDDLESMOOR [SE0974]

Crown HG3 5ST [top of Nidderdale rd from Pateley Bridge]: Remote inn with beautiful view over stone-built hamlet high in upper Nidderdale, warmly welcoming former gamekeeper landlord, well kept Black Sheep, rich local atmosphere, blazing log fires in cosy spotless rooms full of photographs, bric-a-brac and awards, usual food, homely dining room; small garden, good value simple bedrooms, good breakfast *(Simon Le Fort)*

MIRFIELD [SE2017]

Hare & Hounds WF14 8EE [Liley Lane (B6118 2m S)]: Popular smartly refurbished Vintage Inn dining pub, decent good value food all day, Black Sheep, Marstons Pedigree and Timothy Taylors Landlord, cheerful helpful staff; tables outside with good Pennine views, open all day (Michael Butler, Gordon and Margaret Ormondroyd)

MOORSHOLM [NZ6912]

Jolly Sailor TS12 3LN [A171 nearly 1 mile E]: Good food all day, good service, well kept Black Sheep, cosy little booths in long beamed and stripped-stone bar; children welcome, tables looking out to the surrounding moors, open all day (LYM, Cheryl Wright)

MORLEY [SK2529]

Woodlands LS27 7LY [Gelderd Rd]: Enjoyable food in hotel's Bentley Room – nice setting, trendy and upmarket; bedrooms (Matthew James)

MUKER [SD9097]

☆ **Farmers Arms** DL11 6QG [B6270 W of Reeth]: Small unpretentious walkers' pub in beautiful valley village, warm fire, friendly staff and locals, well kept Black Sheep, John Smiths and Theakstons, wines, teas and coffees, enjoyable straightforward good value food inc lunchtime baps, simple modern pine furniture, flagstones and panelling, darts and dominoes; children welcome, hill views from terrace tables, River Swale across road, self-catering flat (Edward Mirzoeff, LYM, the Didler, Dr and Mrs D Scott, Bruce and Sharon Eden, Mr and Mrs Maurice Thompson)

MYTHOLMROYD [SE0125]

Shoulder of Mutton HX7 5DZ [New Rd, just across river bridge (B6138)]: Comfortable friendly local, emphasis on popular low-priced home cooking (not Tues) inc carvery, fish, good range of puddings, OAP lunches and children's helpings, efficient service, family dining areas and cosy child- and food-free areas, well kept ales inc Marstons Pedigree, toby jugs and other china; streamside terrace (John and Helen Rushton, Pete Baker)

NEWTON UNDER ROSEBERRY [NZ5613]

Kings Head TS9 6QR: Nicely converted cottage row in attractive village below Roseberry Topping, emphasis on wide choice of enjoyable well priced food in large restaurant area, good service, real ales inc Theakstons; stylish modern bedrooms, good breakfast (Peter F Marshall)

NORLAND [SE0521]

Moorcock HX6 3RP: L-shaped bar and restaurant reopened after refurbishment, wide choice of enjoyable food inc children's helpings, Timothy Taylors and Thwaites (Pat and Tony Martin)

NORTH GRIMSTON [SE8467]

Middleton Arms YO17 8AX: Comfortable, with enjoyable good value simple food from sandwiches up, well kept Wold Top ales, homely dining area; garden tables, nice

Wolds-edge spot (WW)

NORTHALLERTON [SE3794]

Tithe Bar DL6 1DP [Friarage St]: Market Town Tavern with five quickly changing ales such as Durham and Timothy Taylors, plenty of continental beers, friendly staff, tasty food lunchtime and early evening, three traditional bar areas with tables and chairs, settle and armchairs, upstairs evening brasserie; open all day (Pete Coxon, Mr and Mrs Maurice Thompson)

NORWOOD GREEN [SE1326]

☆ **Old White Beare** HX3 8QG [signed off A641 in Wyke, or off A58 Halifax—Leeds just W of Wyke; Village St]: Doing well under new owners; well renovated and extended old pub named after ship whose timbers it incorporates, well kept Copper Dragon and Timothy Taylors, traditional good value home-made food all day, good friendly service, bar with steps up to dining area, small character snug, imposing galleried flagstoned barn restaurant; children and dogs welcome, front terrace, back garden, Calderdale Way and Brontë Way pass the door, open all day (Gordon and Margaret Ormondroyd, Michael Butler)

OLDSTEAD [SE5380]

☆ **Black Swan** YO61 4BL [Main St]: Enjoyable traditional food in comfortable and attractive back dining areas (good disabled access here) with antique furnishings, simpler beamed and flagstoned bar with pretty valley views from two big bay windows, log fire, well kept Black Sheep and Copper Dragon, nice staff; children welcome, picnic-sets outside, bedroom extension, beautiful surroundings (Walter and Susan Rinaldi-Butcher, John and Eleanor Holdsworth, Hansjoerg Landherr, BB)

OSMOTHERLEY [SE4597]

Queen Catherine DL6 3AG [West End]: Unpretentious pub in attractive village, simple modern décor with old local prints, Tetleys and a guest such as Hanbys, hearty helpings of popular good value food all day, log fire, separate dining area; children welcome, simple comfortable bedrooms, good breakfast (R C Vincent)

OSSETT [SE2719]

☆ **Brewers Pride** WF5 8ND [Low Mill Rd/Healey Lane (long cul-de-sac by railway sidings, off B6128)]: Friendly basic local with Bobs Brewing Co's White Lion (brewed at the back of the pub), Rudgate Ruby Mild and several guests such as Ossett, cosy front room and bar both with open fires, brewery memorabilia, good well priced food (not Sun), new dining extension, small games room, live music third Sun of the month; big back garden, nr Calder & Hebble Canal, open all day (the Didler, Michael Butler)

OSWALDKIRK [SE6278]

Malt Shovel YO62 5XT [signed off B1363/B1257 S of Helmsley]: Attractive former small 17th-c manor house, enjoyable good value food, well kept Sam Smiths OB, friendly service, huge log fires, heavy beams and flagstones, fine staircase, simple traditional furnishings, two cosy bars, interestingly decorated dining room; views from good unusual garden (Andy and Jill Kassube, LYM)

OVERTON [SE2516]

Black Swan WF4 4RF [off A642 Wakefield—Huddersfield; Green Lane]: Traditional local, two cosy knocked-together low-beamed rooms full of brasses and bric-a-brac, well kept John Smiths, popular Thurs quiz night (Michael Butler)

OXENHOPE [SE0434]

☆ **Dog & Gun** BD22 9SN [off B6141 towards Denholme]: Beautifully placed roomy 17th-c moorland pub, smartly extended and comfortable, with good varied generous food from sandwiches to lots of fish and Sun roasts (worth booking then), thriving atmosphere, cheerful landlord and attentive staff, full Timothy Taylors range kept well, beamery, copper, brasses, plates and jugs, big log fire each end, padded settles and stools, wonderful views; five bedrooms in adjoining hotel (Gordon and Margaret Ormondroyd, John and Eleanor Holdsworth, Andy and Jill Kassube)

PICKERING [SE7983]

Black Swan YO18 7AL [Birdgate]: Hotel dating from 16th c, good sensibly priced food inc familiar favourites, efficient friendly staff, two real ales, broad low-beamed bar, comfortably relaxed dining room on left; bedrooms (Gwyn and Anne Wake, Michael and Lynne Gittins)

POOL [SE2445]

White Hart LS21 1LH [just off A658 S of Harrogate, A659 E of Otley]: M&B dining pub with enjoyable food all day, efficient service, good choice of wines by the glass, well kept Greene King and Timothy Taylors, stylishly simple bistro eating areas, armchairs and sofas on bar's flagstones and bare boards; tables outside (Michael Butler, Ros Lawler, Pat and Graham Williamson, Gordon and Margaret Ormondroyd, LYM)

PUDSEY [SE2131]

Bankhouse LS28 8DY [Scholebroke Lane]: Welcoming modernised Tudor-style pub, enjoyable food, Black Sheep and guest beers, several nooks and alcoves, warm lighting and comfortable chairs; dogs welcome, front terrace picnic-sets, good walking base (Jeremy Akeroyd)

RAMSGILL [SE1171]

☆ **Yorke Arms** HG3 5RL [Nidderdale]: Upmarket small hotel (not a pub), small smart bar with some heavy Jacobean furniture and log fires, Black Sheep Special, a fine wine list, good choice of spirits and fresh juices, good restaurant; piped music, no under-12s even in restaurant; comfortable bedrooms, good quiet moorland and reservoir walks (Hunter and Christine Wright, LYM, Peter and Giff Bennett)

RASTRICK [SE1421]

Globe HD6 3EL [Rastrick Common]: High above Brighouse, with bright smart

décor, bargain home-made food, friendly young staff, well kept Black Sheep, Greene King and Tetleys, large attractive back dining conservatory (Gordon and Margaret Ormondroyd)

REDMIRE [SE0491]

Bolton Arms DL8 4EA: Nicely refurbished village inn with good food cooked by landlady, well kept ales inc Black Sheep, convivial landlord, comfortable carpeted bar, attractive dining room, darts, exemplary lavatories; small garden with quoits, handy for Wensleydale Railway and Bolton Castle, three courtyard bedrooms (Lynda and Trevor Smith, Michael Tack, Mr and Mrs Maurice Thompson)

RICHMOND [NZ1700]

Kings Head DL10 4HS [Market Place]: Civilised and chatty lounge bar in friendly Best Western hotel overlooking square, good value food inc all-day snacks, Theakstons Best, decent wines by the glass, friendly service, comfortable bistro; 30 bedrooms (Bruce and Sharon Eden, BB)

ROBIN HOOD'S BAY [NZ9504]

Bay Hotel YO22 4SJ [The Dock, Bay Town]: Friendly old village inn at end of the 191-mile coast-to-coast walk, fine sea views from cosy picture-window upstairs bar (Wainwright bar downstairs open too if busy), three real ales, log fires, good value home-made food in bar and separate dining area; tables outside, cosy bedrooms, open all day (P Dawn, Mrs Romey Heaton, the Didler, David and Sue Smith)

ROSEDALE ABBEY [SE7295]

Coach & Horses YO18 8SD: Good value hearty pubby food, friendly landlord and staff, Black Sheep and two Wold Top ales, modern dining room off central bar, family games room with pool on right (Gerry and Rosemary Dobson)

White Horse YO18 8SE [300 yds up Rosedale Chimney Bank – entering village, first left after Coach House Inn]: Roomy rambling bar with dining room on left, good value generous straightforward food, Copper Dragon ales, reasonably priced wines by the glass, good choice of malt whiskies, great views from terrace (and from restaurant and bedrooms); good walks (LYM, Gerry and Rosemary Dobson,)

ROTHERHAM [SK4292]

Blue Coat S60 2DJ [The Crofts]: Civilised Wetherspoons with friendly staff, good well kept ales, upstairs seating; open all day (Mrs Hazel Rainer)

SALTBURN-BY-THE-SEA [NZ6621]

☆ **Ship** TS12 1HF [A174 towards Whitby]: Beautiful setting among beached fishing boats, sea views from smart nautical-style black-beamed bars and big summer dining lounge with handsome ship model, wide range of inexpensive generous food inc fresh fish, well kept Tetleys, good choice of wines by the glass, friendly helpful service, evening restaurant (not Sun), children's room; busy at holiday times; tables outside, smuggling exhibition next door (LYM, David and Sue Smith)

SAXTON [SE4736]

☆ **Greyhound** LS24 9PY [by church in village, 2.5 miles from A1 via B1217]: Quaint unchanging medieval stone-built local by church in attractive quiet village, well kept cheap Sam Smiths OB tapped from the cask, three small unspoilt rooms on linking corridor, old prints, open fires and settles, masses of china plates; TV in room on right; a couple of picnic-sets in attractive side yard, open all day wknds (LYM, Robert Wivell)

SCARBOROUGH [TA0588]

Golden Ball YO11 1PG [Sandside, opp harbour]: Seafront pub with good harbour and bay views (busy in summer), panelled bar with nautical memorabilia, lunchtime food (not Sun), well kept low-priced Sam Smiths; basic family lounge upstairs, tables outside (David Carr)

Highlander YO11 2AF [Esplanade]: Clean, bright and comfortable, with magnificent collection of whiskies in wall-top cabinets, tartan décor, well kept Tetleys and changing ales, good value pub food from generous sandwiches and toasties up, friendly obliging service, civilised atmosphere, sea views from front bar; front courtyard tables, bedrooms, handy for South Bay beach (David and Sue Smith)

Leeds Arms YO11 1QW [St Marys St]: Proper traditional pub, interesting and friendly, with lots of fishing and RNLI memorabilia, great atmosphere, no food or music (David Carr)

Lord Rosebery YO11 1JW [Westborough]: Wetherspoons in former local Liberal HQ (and Co-op), galleried upper bar, good beer range, enjoyable quickly served food inc Sun roast, obliging staff, local prints; busy and lively evenings; disabled facilities, open all day (Mrs Hazel Rainer, David Carr)

Old Scalby Mills YO12 6RP [seafront, Scalby Mills]: Seafront pub (once a 15th-c watermill, though scarcely evident now) with Copper Dragon, Derwent and other ales, good value simple food all day in large eating area (children welcome here), friendly service; handy for Sea Life Centre (D W Stokes)

Valley YO11 2LX [Valley Rd]: L-shaped bar with banquettes, friendly helpful service, good value simple food using local produce inc popular speciality nights (authentic sri lankan curries Weds), seven farm ciders, up to eight changing ales, beer festivals, open all day (Dave and Shirley Shaw, Bruce Bird)

SCORTON [NZ2400]

White Heifer DL10 6DH [B1263; High Row]: Two-bar beamed pub with contemporary wine-bar-style layout and restaurant extension, enjoyable food inc traditional favourites, relaxed atmosphere, friendly service, Black Sheep and John Smiths, sensibly priced wines; opp large green of pretty village (Richard Cole)

SETTLE [SD8163]

☆ **Golden Lion** BD24 9DU [B6480 (main rd through town), off A65 bypass]: Warm friendly old-fashioned atmosphere in market-town inn with grand staircase sweeping down into baronial-style high-beamed hall bar, lovely log fire, comfortably worn settles, plush seats, brass, prints and plates on dark panelling; enjoyable good value food (all day wknds) inc interesting specials, well kept Thwaites, decent wines by the glass, splendid dining room; public bar with darts, pool, games machines and TV; children in eating area, 12 good-sized comfortable bedrooms, hearty breakfast, open all day (C and G Mangham, Martin Smith, Michael and Maggie Betton, John and Helen Rushton, LYM, Phil Bryant, Arthur Pickering)

SHEFFIELD [SK3688]

Corner Pin S4 7QN [Carlisle St East]: Restored 19th-c pub with good range of ales, bar food changing daily, basic locals' bar, quiet lounge; open all day (the Didler)

☆ **Devonshire Cat** S1 4HG [Wellington St (some local parking)]: Plain roomy contemporary bar with polished light wood and big modern prints, friendly staff knowledgeable about the dozen mainly Yorkshire ales inc Abbeydale and Kelham Island, some tapped from the cask, eight foreign beers on tap, masses of bottled beers in glass-walled cool room, two farm ciders, tea and coffee, cheap food more interesting than usual from end servery, board games, Weds folk night; well reproduced piped music, TV, silenced games machine, ATM; good disabled access and facilities, open all day (Don and Shirley Parrish, BB, Valerie Baker, the Didler, James Tringham)

Harlequin S3 8GG [Nursery St]: Comfortable and welcoming open-plan pub, well kept Bradfield, John Smiths and eight regularly changing guests (beer festivals), also imports and two farm ciders, cobs and other bargain food (free buffet Fri evening), good staff, live music Sat night; dogs welcome, children till 7pm, outside seating on back and roof terraces, open all day (Valerie Baker, the Didler)

☆ **Hillsborough** S6 2UB [Langsett Rd/Wood St; by Primrose View tram stop]: Chatty and friendly pub-in-hotel, eight beers inc own microbrews and quickly changing guests, good wine and soft drinks choice, bargain food inc Sun roasts, daily papers, open fire, bare-boards bar, lounge, views to ski slope from attractive back conservatory and terrace tables; silent TV; children and dogs welcome, six good value simple bedrooms, covered parking, open all day (the Didler, JJW, CMW, Don and Shirley Parrish, David Carr)

☆ **Kelham Island Tavern** S3 8RY [Kelham Island]: Busy backstreet local, friendly and comfortable, with well organised staff, well kept Acorn, Pictish and lots of interesting guest ales, continental imports, farm cider, filled cobs and other bar lunches (not Sun), low prices, nice artwork, Sun folk night; disabled facilities, unusual sheltered flower-filled back terrace, open all day (Sun afternoon break) (the Didler, P Dawn, Bruce Bird)

Ranmoor S10 3GD [Fulwood Rd]: Open-plan Victorian local with good value home cooking (not Sun, Mon), well kept Abbeydale and guest ales; pleasant garden, open all day (the Didler)

Rawson Spring S6 2LN [Langsett Rd]: Popular airy Wetherspoons in former swimming baths, their usual value, well kept changing ales, impressive décor with unusual skylights, inviting atmosphere (the Didler, JJW, CMW)

Rising Sun S10 3QA [Fulwood Rd]: Friendly drinkers' pub with full Abbeydale range and guests kept well (summer beer festival), bottled beers, decent food, large lounge with games and reference books; nice back garden, open all day (the Didler, James A Waller)

Stag S11 8YL [Psalter Lane]: Big busy pub with friendly staff, four real ales, good soft drinks choice, home-made food (all day wknds) from sandwiches up inc sharing platters, two dining areas and conservatory; Sun quiz, games machine; children welcome, garden picnic-sets, play area, open all day (JJW, CMW)

Three Merry Lads S10 4LJ [W on Redmires Rd]: Enjoyable good value food inc children's meals and all-day Sun carvery, also some unusual things, four ales inc Kelham Island, good wine and soft drinks choice, good service, chatty bar and dining extension with uninterrupted views; terrace picnic-sets, open all day wknds (Derek Stapley, JJW, CMW)

Union S11 9EF [Union Rd, Netheredge]: Well run and spotless with good value home-made lunchtime food, well kept ales, lots of bric-a-brac (Peter F Marshall)

Walkley Cottage S6 5DD [Bole Hill Rd]: Warm-hearted 1930s pub with seven ales, farm cider, good coffee and other drinks choice, decent home-made food (not Sun evening) inc bargain OAP lunch and Sun roasts, some takeaways, daily papers; piped music, TV; children and dogs welcome, disabled access, views from picnic-sets in small back garden, play area, lovely hanging baskets, open all day (JJW, CMW, Valerie Baker)

☆ *Wellington* S3 7EQ [Henry St; Shalesmoor tram stop right outside]: Unpretentious relaxed pub with up to ten changing beers inc own bargain Little Ale Cart brews, bottled imports, farm cider, coal fire in lounge, photographs of old Sheffield, daily papers, pub games, friendly staff; tables out behind, open all day with afternoon break Sun (the Didler, Martin Grosberg, David Carr, Pete Baker)

SHEPLEY [SE1809]
☆ *Farmers Boy* HD8 8AP [links A629 and A635,

from village centre by Black Bull]: Good if pricey food in comfortably modern barn restaurant, good friendly service, well kept Black Sheep and Tetleys in welcoming cottage-conversion beamed bar (Gordon and Margaret Ormondroyd, Michael Butler)

SHERBURN IN ELMET [SE4933]
Oddfellows Arms LS25 6BA [Low Street]: Traditional village pub with new landlord, enjoyable low-priced fresh pubby food, friendly service, John Smiths, good house wine (Ian and Anne Read)

SHERIFF HUTTON [SE6566]
Highwayman YO60 6QZ [The Square]: Friendly old coaching inn nr Castle Howard, welcoming landlord, good value food from good sandwiches to delicious puddings and popular Sun lunch, well kept Timothy Taylors and Tetleys, decent house wines, log fires, oak beams in lounge and dining room, homely snug bar; good wheelchair access, big garden, attractive village with castle ruins and 12th-c church (Andy and Jill Kassube)

SHIPLEY [SE1437]
Fannys Ale & Cider House BD18 3JN [Saltaire Rd]: Interesting gaslit two-room roadside local, up to nine well kept changing ales inc Timothy Taylors, foreign beers, farm cider; open all day Fri, Sat, cl Mon lunchtime (the Didler)

SKELTON [SE3668]
Black Lion HG4 5AJ [off B6265]: Enjoyable lunches in pleasant dining room, more elaborate evening menu, good service; tables outside, caravan site behind (Stephen James)

SKIPTON [SD9951]
Red Lion BD23 1DT [High St/Market Sq]: Recently refurbished, with good choice of well kept ales, wide food range using local produce, good cheerful service even on bustling market days (Mon, Weds, Fri, Sat) (Dudley and Moira Cockroft)

☆ *Royal Shepherd* BD23 1LB [Canal St; from Water St (A65) turn into Coach St, then left after bridge over Leeds & Liverpool Canal]: Convivial old-fashioned local with big bustling bar, snug and dining room, open fires, Copper Dragon ales, decent wine, interesting whiskies, cheery landlord and brisk service, low-priced standard food from sandwiches up, photographs of Yorks CCC in its golden days; games and piped music; children welcome in side room, tables out in pretty spot by canal (Chris and Jeanne Downing, the Didler, Mrs Hazel Rainer)

Woolly Sheep BD23 1HY [Sheep St]: Big bustling pub with full range of Timothy Taylors ales, prompt friendly enthusiastic service, daily papers, two beamed bars off flagstoned passage, exposed brickwork, stone fireplace, lots of sheep prints and bric-a-brac, attractive and comfortable raised lunchtime dining area, good value food (plenty for children); unobtrusive piped music; spacious pretty garden, six good value bedrooms, good breakfast (David and

Ruth Hollands, Mrs Hazel Rainer)

SLINGSBY [SE6975]

Grapes YO62 4AL [off B1257 Malton—Hovingham; Railway St]: Stone-built village local, popular food, real ales such as Black Sheep, cheerful staff, dining room, games area; tables in garden behind *(Pat and Graham Williamson, BB)*

SNAINTON [TA9182]

Coachman YO13 9PL [Pickering Rd W (A170)]: New owners doing enjoyable food; more reports please *(Peter Burton)*

SOUTH CAVE [SE9231]

☆ *Fox & Coney* HU15 2AT [Market Place (A1034)]: Pleasant village pub with good mix of customers, enjoyable generous food from baguettes though steaks to imaginative specials, friendly efficient staff, real ales such as Caledonian Deuchars IPA and Timothy Taylors Landlord from central servery, coal fire, bright and comfortable Victorian open-plan main bar and dining areas; bedrooms in adjoining hotel *(Marlene and Jim Godfrey)*

SOWERBY [SE0423]

Travellers Rest HX6 1PE [Steep Lane, above Sowerby Bridge]: Much extended, yet keeping cosy and comfortable little rooms, with beams, stripped stone, flagstones and open fires, enjoyable fresh local food, Timothy Taylors ales, separate restaurant; gents' up steps; fine country setting, good view over Halifax and Calder Valley from garden (lovely at night) *(Roy and Lindsey Fentiman)*

SOWERBY BRIDGE [SE0623]

Shepherds Rest HX6 2BD [On A58 Halifax to Sowerby Bridge]: Friendly two-room Ossett pub, their full range and guest ales; no food; suntrap terrace, open from 3pm (all day wknds) *(Pat and Tony Martin)*

Works HX6 2QG [Hollins Mill Lane, off A58]: Big airy two-room bareboards pub in converted joinery workshop, seating from pews to comfortable sofas, nine real ales, good bargain food from sandwiches to spicy sausage cassoulet, Weds curry night, Sun brunch, poetry readings and live music in back yard (covered in poor weather); open all day *(Pat and Tony Martin, Andy and Jill Kassube)*

STAITHES [NZ7818]

Royal George TS13 5BH [High St]: Nicely worn-in old inn nr harbour, lively locals' bar, three plusher linked rooms, quickly served hearty pub food, well kept Tetleys Imperial, decent wines by the glass, low prices; children welcome *(David and Sue Smith)*

STAMFORD BRIDGE [SE7055]

☆ *Three Cups* YO41 1AX [A166 W of town]: Clean and spacious Vintage Inn family dining pub in cosy timbered country style, reliable food all day, plenty of wines by the glass, real ales, good staff, two blazing fires, glass-topped well; children welcome, disabled access, play area behind, bedrooms, open all day *(Joan York, LYM, David Carr, Pat and Graham Williamson)*

STAXTON [TA0179]

Hare & Hounds YO12 4TA [Main St]: Five real ales inc Black Sheep, Theakstons and Wold Top, home-made food inc good mixed grill, may be fresh lobster and crab *(C A Hall)*

STOKESLEY [NZ5208]

☆ *White Swan* TS9 5BL [West End]: Good Captain Cook ales brewed in neat attractive flower-clad pub, friendly young staff, three relaxing seating areas in L-shaped bar, log fire, lots of brass on elegant dark panelling, lovely bar counter carving, hat display, unusual clock, no food, music or machines; cl Tues lunchtime, open all day Fri, Sat *(the Didler, Pete Baker, Don and Shirley Parrish, Blaise Vyner)*

SUTTON-UNDER-WHITESTONECLIFFE [SE4983]

Whitestonecliffe Inn YO7 2PR [A170 E of Thirsk]: Beamed roadside pub with wide choice of good value food from sandwiches up in bar and restaurant, good condition Caledonian Deuchars IPA and Tetleys, interesting 17th-c stone bar, log fire, friendly staff, games room; children welcome, six self-catering cottages *(Mike and Shelley Woodroffe, David and Sue Smith, Don and Shirley Parrish)*

SWINTON [SE7673]

Blacksmiths Arms YO17 6SQ [the one nr Malton]: Village pub with good value home cooking inc bargains for two, attentive service *(Pat and Graham Williamson)*

TAN HILL [NY8906]

Tan Hill Inn DL11 6ED [Arkengarthdale rd Reeth—Brough, at junction Keld/W Stonesdale rd]: Basic old pub in wonderful bleak setting on Pennine Way – Britain's highest, full of bric-a-brac and interesting photographs, simple sturdy furniture, flagstones, ever-burning big log fire (with prized stone side seats), chatty atmosphere, five real ales inc one for the pub by Dent, good cheap pubby food, family room, live music wknds, swaledale sheep show here last Thurs in May; can get overcrowded, often snowbound; children, dogs and even the pub's ducks welcome, seven bedrooms, bunk rooms and camping, open all day; for sale as we went to press but still operating as usual *(LYM, Ewan and Moira McCall)*

TERRINGTON [SE6770]

☆ *Bay Horse* YO60 6PP [W of Malton]: Friendly new landlord at 17th-c pub with cosy log-fire lounge bar, own Storyteller ales and guest like Wylam, several wines by the glass, over 30 whiskies, enjoyable home-made seasonal food inc good set Sun lunch (best to book), refurbished dining area, conservatory with old farm tools, traditional games in public bar; children and dogs welcome, garden tables, unspoilt village, may be cl lunchtimes Mon-Weds winter, open all day Thurs-Sun *(Pat and Tony Martin, Alex and Claire Pearse, LYM, J F M and M West)*

THIRSK [SE4282]

Darrowby YO7 1HA [Market Pl]: Open-plan but plenty of character, well kept John

Smiths and Wells & Youngs Bombardier, enjoyable bargain food; tables outside, open all day *(Cheryl Wright)*

THOLTHORPE [SE4766]

New Inn YO61 1SL: Traditional village-green local with beamed bar and candlelit dining room, friendly staff, good local food (not Sun evening) inc early evening deals and Sun roasts, allergies catered for, real ales; children welcome, bedrooms, cl Mon *(Rosemary Kind, Dionne Felten)*

THORALBY [SE9986]

George DL8 3SU: Prettily set Dales village pub, two smallish cosy linked areas with four well kept ales inc Black Sheep, sensibly priced bar food from sandwiches to steaks, interesting bric-a-brac, coal fire and woodburner, some banquettes, darts and dominoes; walkers welcome, terrace tables, two bedrooms, cl Mon lunchtime *(Ewan and Moira McCall)*

THORNTON [SE0933]

☆ *Ring o' Bells* BD13 3QL [Hill Top Rd, off B6145 W of Bradford]: 19th-c moortop dining pub very popular for wide choice of reliably good home-made food inc bargain early suppers, separate sittings Sat night and Sun lunch (best to book), real ales such as Black Sheep, efficient service, large spotless bar, elegant restaurant with linen tablecloths, pleasant conservatory lounge; wide views towards Shipley and Bingley *(Margaret White, Steve Narey, John and Eleanor Holdsworth)*

White Horse BD13 3SJ [Well Heads]: Reopened after refurbishment in current style, popular for good value food especially wknd evenings *(John and Eleanor Holdsworth)*

THORNTON-LE-CLAY [SE6865]

☆ *White Swan* YO60 7TG [off A64 York—Malton; Low St]: Comfortable welcoming early 19th-c family-run dining pub, good generous food such as local sausages with different types of mash, Sun roasts, John Smiths and a guest, decent wines, reasonable prices, beams and brasses, board games and toys; children welcome, disabled access, neat grounds with terrace tables, duck pond, herb and vegetable gardens, orchard, two summerhouses, donkey paddock, attractive countryside nr Castle Howard, cl all day Mon *(Michael Page, Kate Dobson, Rev Giles Galley, Ian Maclaren)*

THRESHFIELD [SD9863]

Old Hall Inn BD23 5HB [B6160/B6265 just outside Grassington]: Three old-world linked rooms inc smart candlelit dining room, well kept John Smiths, Timothy Taylors and Theakstons, helpful friendly staff, enjoyable food, log fires, high beam-and-plank ceiling, cushioned wall pews, tall well blacked kitchen range; children in eating area, neat garden *(Mr and Mrs D Moir, Gordon and Margaret Ormondroyd, LYM)*

THUNDER BRIDGE [SE1811]

Woodman HD8 0PX [off A629 Huddersfield—Sheffield]: Two roomy spotless bars with fresh décor and light woodwork, welcoming service, enjoyable good value food, well kept Timothy Taylors and Tetleys, upstairs restaurant; 12 good bedrooms in adjoining cottages *(Gordon and Margaret Ormondroyd)*

TOCKWITH [SE4652]

Spotted Ox YO26 7PY [Westfield Rd, off B1224]: Welcoming traditional beamed village local, three areas off central bar, well kept ales inc Tetleys carefully served the old-fashioned way, good choice of enjoyable sensibly priced home-made food, attentive staff, relaxed atmosphere, interesting local history; open all day Fri-Sun *(Les and Sandra Brown)*

TODMORDEN [SD9324]

Golden Lion OL14 7LA [Rochdale Rd]: Comfortable pub by Rochdale Canal, bargain food, real ales inc Copper Dragon, friendly staff *(Ben Williams)*

Masons Arms OL14 7PN [A681/A6033, S of centre]: Welcoming traditional local, well kept Copper Dragon ales and local guest beers, enthusiastic landlord, generous good value food till 6pm, Sun roasts, pump clips on beams and interesting local photographs and cuttings in two knocked-together rooms, darts, cards and pool in popular games end, open all day *(Bruce Bird)*

TONG [SE2230]

Greyhound BD4 0RR [Tong Lane]: Traditional stone-built, low-beamed and flagstoned local by village cricket field, distinctive areas inc small dining room, good value food, Black Sheep, Greene King Abbot and Tetleys, many wines by the glass, good service; tables outside *(Dudley and Moira Cockroft, Michael Butler)*

TOTLEY [SK3080]

Cricket S17 3AZ [signed from A621; Penny Lane]: Dining pub style with pews, mixed chairs and pine tables on bare boards and flagstones, good quality blackboard food (all day wknds) from sandwiches and pubby staples to some interesting dishes, friendly service, Thornbridge ales, log fires, bay-window views of rustic cricket field; children and dogs welcome, terrace tables, open all day *(James A Waller)*

WAKEFIELD [SE3320]

Fernandes Brewery Tap WF1 1UA [Avison Yard, Kirkgate]: Owned by Ossett but still brewing Fernandes ales in cellar, interesting guest beers, bottled imports, farm ciders, new ground-floor bar with flagstones, bare brick and panelling, original raftered top-floor bar with unusual breweriana; cl Mon-Thurs lunchtime, open all day Fri-Sun with some lunchtime food *(the Didler)*

Harrys Bar WF1 1EL [Westgate]: Cheery local with Bobs, Ossett, Timothy Taylors and guest beers, log fire, stripped masonry; cl lunchtime exc Sun *(the Didler)*

Henry Boons WF2 9SR [Westgate]: Two-room bare-boards tap for Clarks brewery, also several guests beers and bottled imports, friendly staff, barrel tables and breweriana, side pool area; gets busy late on with young people, juke box, machines, live bands; open all day *(the Didler)*

WALTON [SE4447]

Fox & Hounds LS23 7DQ [Hall Park Rd, off back rd Wetherby—Tadcaster]: Popular dining pub with enjoyable food (should book Sun lunch), thriving atmosphere, well kept John Smiths and guest such as Black Sheep or Caledonian Deuchars IPA *(Robert Wivell, Ian and Jane Haslock)*

WEAVERTHORPE [SE9670]

☆ *Blue Bell* YO17 8EX: Upscale country dining pub with beautifully presented good food, fine choice of wines, well kept Black Sheep and Timothy Taylors Landlord, pre-meal home-made crisps and dips, cosy and cheerful bar with unusual collection of bottles and packaging, intimate back restaurant, charming efficient waitresses; 12 bedrooms, good breakfast, interesting village *(Pat and Graham Williamson, Marlene and Jim Godfrey, Colin McKerrow)*

WELBURN [SE7168]

Crown & Cushion YO60 7DZ [off A64]: Welcoming 18th-c village pub with two cosy rooms separated by central bar, log fires, well kept changing ales such as Brains, Clarks, Holdens and Tetleys, generous home-made food (not Sun or Mon evenings) from sandwiches to local game and Sun roasts; piped music; children welcome, picnic-sets out at front and in attractive small back garden with terrace, handy for Castle Howard, open all day wknds *(Robert Wivell, Dr and Mrs Jackson, LYM, Andy and Jill Kassube)*

WELL [SE2682]

Milbank Arms DL8 2PX [Bedale Rd]: Well restored cosy beamed pub with interesting layout, cheery welcoming landlord, enjoyable food inc light lunchtime dishes, well kept Black Sheep, good coffee, log fire, immaculate lavatories; piped music – turned off on request; picnic-sets out in front *(Peter Hacker, Janet and Peter Race)*

WENTBRIDGE [SE4817]

Blue Bell WF8 3JP [B6474, just off A1]: Wide choice of good value quick generous food inc OAP bargain lunches and Tues, Fri thai nights, well kept ales inc Tetleys and Timothy Taylors Landlord, good choice of wines by the glass, several linked rooms, beams, stripped stone, farm tools and other bric-a-brac, solid wooden furnishings, family room; good view from garden, bedrooms *(Dave and Jenny Hughes)*

WENTWORTH [SK3898]

☆ *George & Dragon* S62 7TN [3 miles from M1 junction 36; Main St]: Friendly rambling split-level bar, good range of real ales and of generous good value food cooked to order (worth the wait), flagstones and assorted old-fashioned furnishings, ornate stove in lounge, small back games room; tables out on big back lawn, crafts and antiques shop, pleasant village *(Jo Lilley, Simon Calvert, LYM, Mrs Hazel Rainer, John and Eleanor Holdsworth)*

WEST TANFIELD [SE2678]

Bruce Arms HG4 5JJ [Main St (A6108 N of Ripon)]: Landlord doing good food like beef fillet with crispy shallots and maple-glazed guinea fowl, friendly landlady, well kept Black Sheep, flagstones and log fires; two bedrooms, cl Sun evening and Mon *(Janet and Peter Race, Andy and Jill Kassube, LYM)*

WEST WITTON [SE0588]

☆ *Wensleydale Heifer* DL8 4LS [A684 W of Leyburn]: Stylish restaurant-with-rooms rather than pub, good fresh fish/seafood and some local meat, cosy informal upmarket food bar and extensive main formal restaurant; nice bedrooms (back ones quietest), good big breakfast *(Mr and Mrs P L Spencer, BB, David and Cathrine Whiting)*

WESTOW [SE7565]

Blacksmiths YO60 7NE [off A64 York—Malton; Main St]: Closed as we went to press in summer 2009 – we hope the talk of its reopening turns out to be true; attractive beamed bar with traditional furnishings, woodburner in inglenook, two small linked rooms making up main dining area, has had Jennings and Thwaites beers on handpump; picnic-sets on side terrace, separate bedroom block *(LYM)*

WETHERBY [SE4048]

Muse Café LS22 6NQ [Bank St]: Very popular bistro-bar with good brasserie food inc early-bird deals, good range of well kept ales, continental lagers, nice coffee, young friendly helpful staff; seats outside, open all day *(WW, Danny Savage, Stuart Paulley, Andy and Jill Kassube)*

Royal Oak LS22 6NR [North St]: Spacious beamed pub kept spotless under new management, local real ales, good choice of bar food *(Simon Le Fort)*

WHISTON [SK4490]

Chequers S60 4HB [under 2 miles from M1 junction 33, via A630, A631, A618: Pleasley Rd/Chaff Lane]: Much modernised 1930s pub with lounge and large dining area, four real ales, enjoyable food (not Mon, Tues lunch, Sun evening), bargain Sun roast, pool area; piped pop music, games machine; children welcome, limited parking *(JJW, CMW)*

WHITBY [NZ9011]

Black Horse YO22 4BH [Church St]: Tastefully refurbished to reflect its age (gas lamps, stained-glass), well kept changing ales such as Adnams, Black Dog Rhatas, Timothy Taylors Landlord and Tetleys Imperial, enterprising Yorkshire-flavoured tapas, friendly staff, seafaring memorabilia *(Stephen Corfield)*

Board YO22 4DE [Church St]: Nice spot opp fish quay, big windows for old town view, well kept Theakstons, good value food, good friendly staff *(Cheryl Wright)*

Elsinore YO21 3BB [Flowergate]: Comfortable, well kept and friendly, lifeboat and Whitby fishing boat photographs on dark panelling, changing beers such as

Camerons Strongarm and John Smiths, lunchtime food; may be piped music *(Stephen Corfield)*

Little Angel YO21 3BA [Flowergate]: Friendly old-fashioned local with real ales such as Tetleys Imperial, boating theme, good value generous lunchtime food, service quick even if busy; well behaved children allowed *(Stephen Corfield)*

Station Inn YO21 1DH [New Quay Rd]: Friendly three-room bare-boards pub with good choice of well kept changing ales, farm cider, good wines by the glass, lunchtime snacks, thriving atmosphere, traditional games; piped music – live music, plastic seat covers; open all day *(P Dawn, David and Sue Smith, the Didler, Sara Fulton, Roger Baker, Stephen Corfield, David Carr)*

YORK [SE5951]

☆ **Ackhorne** YO1 6LN [St Martins Lane, Micklegate]: Proper unspoilt relaxed pub with several changing mainly Yorkshire ales, up to four farm ciders, perry, country wines, foreign bottled beers, bargain basic food (not Sun) from good choice of sandwiches up, friendly helpful family service, beams, panelling, stained-glass, leather wall seats, open fire, Civil War prints, bottles and jugs, carpeted snug, daily papers, traditional games; silenced games machine; suntrap back terrace, smokers' shelter, open all day *(Mrs Hazel Rainer, David Carr, Bruce Bird, Michael Butler, Mark Walker, the Didler, Pete Coxon, WW)*

☆ **Black Swan** YO1 7PR [Peaseholme Green (inner ring road)]: Striking timbered and jettied Tudor building reopened after brief closure, compact panelled front bar, crooked-floored central hall with fine period staircase, black-beamed back bar with vast inglenook, good choice of real ales, basic low-priced food, decent wines, jazz and folk nights; piped music; useful car park, open all day *(Pete Baker, the Didler, Pete Coxon, WW, Marlene and Jim Godfrey, Peter Dandy, LYM)*

☆ **Blue Bell** YO1 9TF [Fossgate]: Delightfully old-fashioned Edwardian pub, very friendly and chatty, with well kept ales such as Adnams Bitter, Black Sheep, Caledonian Deuchars IPA and Timothy Taylors Landlord, good value sandwiches till 5pm (not Sun), daily papers, tiny tiled-floor front bar with roaring fire, panelled ceiling, stained-glass, bar pots and decanters, corridor to small back room, hatch service, lamps and candles, pub games; may be piped music; open all day *(Mark Walker, Eric Larkham, Pete Baker, WW, Pete Coxon, the Didler, Bruce Bird)*

☆ **Brigantes** YO1 6JX [Micklegate]: Comfortably traditional Market Town Taverns bar/bistro, eight mainly Yorkshire ales, good range of bottled beers, good wines and coffee, enjoyable unpretentious brasserie food all day, friendly helpful staff, simple pleasant décor, upstairs dining room; open all day *(WW, Bruce Bird, Pat and Tony Martin, the Didler, Pete Coxon, Sue Demont, Tim Barrow)*

Golden Ball YO1 6DU [Cromwell Rd/Bishophill]: Unspoilt and buoyant 1950s local feel in friendly and well preserved four-room Edwardian pub, enjoyable straightforward wkdy lunchtime food, well kept changing ales such as Caledonian Deuchars IPA, Marstons Pedigree and John Smiths, Sept beer festival, bar billiards, cards and dominoes; TV, can be lively evenings, live music Thurs; lovely small walled garden, open all day Thurs-Sun *(the Didler, Pete Baker)*

Golden Fleece YO1 9UP [Pavement]: Allegedly York's most haunted pub; good value usual food from sandwiches up all afternoon, good beer range inc local ales, long corridor from bar to comfortable back lounge (beware the sloping floors – it dates from 1503), interesting décor with quite a library, lots of pictures and ghost stories, pub games; piped music; children welcome, bedrooms *(Pete Coxon, Pat and Tony Martin)*

Golden Lion YO1 8BG [Church St]: Big, comfortable and popular open-plan pub done up in bare-boards Edwardian style (in fact first licensed 1771), beams, plenty of lamps, old photographs and brewery signs, good changing real ale choice, sensible food all day from good sandwiches up, good range of wines by the glass, pleasant young staff; piped music; open all day *(Mark Walker, David Carr, Pete Coxon, WW)*

Golden Slipper YO1 7LG [Goodramgate]: Dating from 15th c, unpretentious bar and three comfortably old-fashioned small rooms, one lined with books, cheerful efficient staff, good cheap plain lunchtime food from sandwiches up inc an OAP special, John Smiths and up to three other beers; TV; tables in back courtyard *(Mark Walker, Pat and Graham Williamson, David Carr, Jeremy King, Pete Coxon, Alan Thwaite)*

Lamb & Lion YO1 7EH [High Petergate]: New pub in 18th-c house (former small hotel), sparse furnishings and low lighting inc candles giving a spartan Georgian feel, friendly helpful service, up to four well kept changing regional ales, simple food (not Fri-Sun evenings, all day summer Mon-Thurs), pews and long tables in bar, compact rooms off dark corridors; steep steps up to small attractive garden below city wall and looking up to Minster (barbecues), 12 bedrooms (related Guy Fawkes in same street used for anything more than a light continental breakfast) *(David Carr, Alan Thwaite)*

☆ **Last Drop** YO1 8BN [Colliergate]: Basic traditional York Brewery pub, their own beers and one or two well kept guests, decent wines and country wines, friendly helpful young staff, big windows, bare boards, barrel tables and comfortable seats (some up a few steps), nice simple fresh food 12-4 inc sandwiches and good salads; piped music, no children, can get very busy lunchtime, attic lavatories; tables out behind, open all day *(Ian and Jane Haslock, Phil and*

Jane Hodson, WW, Susan and Nigel Brookes, the Didler, Mark Walker, Bruce Bird)

Lendal Cellars YO1 8AA [Lendal]: Bustling rather studenty split-level ale house in broad-vaulted 17th-c cellars, stripped brickwork, stone floor, linked rooms and alcoves, good choice of fairly priced changing ales and wines by the glass, farm cider, decent coffee, foreign bottled beers, good plain food 11.30-7 (5 Fri, Sat), daily papers, well reproduced piped music; can get packed, service can slow, no dogs; children allowed if eating, open all day (the Didler, Peter Dandy, LYM)

Old White Swan YO1 7LF [Goodramgate]: Bustling pub with Victorian, Georgian and Tudor themed bars, popular lunchtime food inc nine types of sausage, Black Sheep and several other well kept ales, pleasant young staff, big L-shaped dining area, central covered courtyard good for families; piped and frequent live music, big-screen sports TV, games machines; open all day (WW, Lawrence Miller, Mark Walker, David Carr)

Punch Bowl YO1 8AN [Stonegate]: Bustling family-run 17th-c local, friendly helpful service, wide range of generous bargain food all day, small panelled rooms off corridor, TV in interesting beamed one on left of food servery, well kept Greene King, Leeds and John Smiths, good wine choice; unobtrusive piped music, games machines, regular quiz nights (Jeremy King, David Carr, Phil and Jane Hodson)

Rook & Gaskill YO10 3WP [Lawrence St]: Traditional Tynemill pub, up to a dozen ales inc local York, enjoyable food (not Sun), dark wood tables, banquettes, chairs and high stools, conservatory; open all day (the Didler, David Carr, WW, Eric Larkham, Pete Coxon)

☆ **Royal Oak** YO1 7LG [Goodramgate]: Comfortably worn-in three-room black-beamed 16th-c pub simply remodelled in Tudor style 1934, blazing log fire in front room, prints, swords, busts and old guns, bargain generous pubby dishes (limited Sun evening) 11.30-8, sandwiches with home-baked bread after 3pm, cheerful bustling young staff, Caledonian Deuchars IPA and Greene King Abbot, decent wines, good coffee, family room, games; piped music, can get crowded, outside gents'; handy for Minster, open all day (Pete Coxon, Ian and Joan Blackwell, BB)

Swan YO23 1JH [Bishopgate St, Clementhorpe]: Unspoilt 1930s interior, friendly and chatty, hatch service to lobby for two small rooms off main bar, great staff, several changing ales and ciders; busy with young people wknds; small pleasant walled garden, nr city walls, cl wkdy lunchtime, open all day wknds (the Didler, Pete Baker, Alison and Pete, David Carr)

☆ **Tap & Spile** YO31 7PB [Monkgate]: Friendly open-plan late Victorian pub with Roosters and other mainly northern ales, farm cider and country wines, decent wines by the glass, bookshelves, games in raised back area, cheap straightforward lunchtime bar food (not Mon); children in eating area, garden and heated terrace, open all day (Pete Coxon, LYM, David Carr, the Didler, WW)

☆ **Three Legged Mare** YO1 7EN [High Petergate]: Bustling light and airy modern café-bar with York Brewery's full range kept well, plenty of belgian beers, quick friendly young staff, interesting sandwiches and some basic lunchtime hot food, low prices, back conservatory; no children; disabled facilities (other lavatories down spiral stairs), back garden with replica of local gallows (hence pub's name), open all day (WW, Bruce Bird, David Carr, Phil and Jane Hodson, Donna and Roger)

☆ **York Brewery Tap** YO1 6JT [Toft Green, Micklegate]: Members only for York Brewery's upstairs lounge (annual fee £3 unless you live in Yorkshire or go on brewery tour), their own full cask range in top condition at bargain price, also bottled beers, nice clubby atmosphere with friendly staff happy to talk about the beers, lots of breweriana and view of brewing plant, comfortable sofas and armchairs, magazines and daily papers, brewery shop; no food; children allowed, open all day except Sun evening (Sue Demont, Tim Barrow, the Didler)

Yorkshire Terrier YO1 8AS [Stonegate]: York Brewery shop, behind this a smallish well worn-in bar with their full beer range and guests, tasting trays of four one-third pints, interesting bottled beers, winter mulled wine, dining room upstairs (where the lavatories are – there's a stair lift) allowing children, limited range of food inc bargain curry and pint Weds evening, small conservatory; handy for Minster, open all day (Derek and Sylvia Stephenson, Pete Coxon, David Carr, Pat and Tony Martin)

Please tell us if the décor, atmosphere, food or drink at a pub is different from our description. We rely on readers' reports to keep us up to date: feedback@goodguides.com, or (no stamp needed) The Good Pub Guide, FREEPOST TN1569, Wadhurst, E Sussex TN5 7BR.

London

London

Mention the words 'city pubs' and you could be forgiven for immediately conjuring up thoughts of Happy Hours, under-age drinking, loud, noisy bars and backstreet boozers. And of course London, like any other city, has its fair share of places just like these. But this vast metropolis also has some real gems, full of history and individual character with some astonishing architecture and décor, and atmosphere more akin to a country local than a city-centre pub. These places, almost without exception, get incredibly busy at peak times – especially just after work. Though many of our readers very much enjoy the hustle and bustle, to take them in fully it's best to try and see them just as they open before lunch, or during the afternoon when they will be at their quietest. Pubs doing particularly well in Central London this year are the Guinea, Harp, Jerusalem Tavern, Lamb, Nags Head, Old Bank of England, Olde Cheshire Cheese, Olde Mitre, Red Lion (Duke of York Street), Salisbury and Seven Stars. East London favourites are the Grapes, Narrow and Prospect of Whitby. In North London we'd highlight the Compton Arms, Drapers Arms, Duke of Cambridge and Marquess Tavern. South London's top places are the Cutty Sark, Greenwich Union and Market Porter; and in the West, the Windsor Castle takes the honours. We're pleased with our new entries this year: the Gun in East London (a top-notch gastropub with a riverside terrace), Bull & Last in North London (a bustling Highgate local with distinctive food and drink), Telegraph in South London (a really good summer pub with a very un-London feel) and Duke of Sussex in West London (interesting spanish food, unusual beers and a lovely big garden). Prices in London are oddly mixed. On one hand, the beer is extremely expensive, but on the other, the food is often very good value – and, indeed, may well be cheaper than many places elsewhere. The meals are very often simple home-made dishes like lunchtime sandwiches, soup, fish and chips, a pie of the day and sausages. There are also plenty of more or less informal dining pubs with restaurant-style cooking at reasonable prices. Up to very recently, our favourite has been the Duke of Cambridge in North London. After this year's inspections, though, we award the title of London Dining Pub of the Year to the new entry, the Gun in East London. Some notable Lucky Dip pubs, all inspected by us: in Central London, the Lamb (EC3), Buckingham Arms (SW1) and Chandos (WC2); in North, the Doric Arch (NW1); South, the Anchor & Hope (SE1); and West, the Princess Victoria (W12). Fullers is the great London brewer. Two much younger local breweries gaining favour are Sambrooks and Twickenham, and Meantime is interesting, producing less traditional styles of beer.

CENTRAL LONDON   MAP 13

Argyll Arms 🍺 £

Argyll Street; ⊖ Oxford Circus, opposite tube side exit; W1F 7TP

Unexpectedly individual pub just off Oxford Street, with interesting little front rooms, appealing range of beers and good value food all day

Handy for Oxford Circus, this busy Victorian pub has a surprising amount of genuine character. Particularly unusual are the three atmospheric and secluded little cubicle rooms at the front, essentially unchanged since they were built in the 1860s. All oddly angular, they're made by wooden partitions with remarkable frosted and engraved glass, with hops trailing above. A long mirrored corridor leads to the spacious back room; newspapers to read, two fruit machines, piped music. Fullers London Pride, Greene King IPA, Timothy Taylors Landlord and up to four changing guest beers on handpump, and quite a few malt whiskies. The quieter upstairs bar, with theatrical photographs, overlooks the pedestrianised street – and the Palladium theatre, if you can see through the impressive foliage outside the window.

🍴 **Under the new licensee, the popular bar food includes sandwiches, ploughman's, breakfast (until noon), soup, baby baked camembert with ale chutney, various platters, sausage and mash with red onion gravy, aberdeen angus burger with a choice of toppings, goats cheese and red pepper risotto, corn-fed barbecue chicken, gammon and free-range eggs, steak in ale pie, and puddings like chocolate pot and banoffi pie.** *Starters/Snacks: £2.95 to £3.50. Main Courses: £5.95 to £9.95. Puddings: £3.50*

Mitchells & Butlers ~ Manager Barry Smith ~ Real ale ~ Bar food (10am-10pm) ~ Restaurant ~ (020) 7734 6117 ~ Children in upstairs bar till 9pm ~ Open 10am-11pm(11.30 Sat; 10.30 Sun); closed 24 Dec

Recommended by Joe Green, the Didler, Derek Thomas, Mike Gorton, Michael Dandy, Ros Lawler, Barry Collett, Mrs Hazel Rainer, Andrea Rampley, Mike and Sue Loseby, Peter Dandy, DC, Dr and Mrs M E Wilson, Tim Maddison

Bishops Finger 🍷

West Smithfield – opposite Bart's Hospital; ⊖ ⇄ Farringdon; EC1A 9JR

Nicely civilised little pub with particularly welcoming atmosphere and good beers

Close to Smithfield Market, this is a neatly kept and smartly civilised little pub. The well laid-out bar room has cream walls, big windows, fresh flowers on elegant tables, polished bare floorboards, a few pillars, and cushioned chairs under one wall lined with framed prints of the market. It can be busy after work, but rather relaxed and peaceful during the day; the atmosphere is friendly and welcoming. Shepherd Neame Bitter, Spitfire, Bishops Finger and seasonal brews on handpump, six wines by the glass, half a dozen malt whiskies, and several ports and champagnes; prompt, efficient service. There are a few tables outside.

🍴 **Most people go for one of the ten or so varieties of sausage, all served with mash, but they also do sandwiches, burgers, steaks, and specials like gammon, or beer-battered cod.** *Starters/Snacks: £4.50 to £4.95. Main Courses: £6.95 to £7.95. Puddings: £4.95*

Shepherd Neame ~ Manager Paul Potts ~ Real ale ~ Bar food (12-3, 6-9 (not Fri evening or weekends)) ~ (020) 7248 2341 ~ Children welcome ~ Open 11-11; closed weekends and bank hols

Recommended by N R White, Dr and Mrs M E Wilson, Donna and Roger, John and Gloria Isaacs, Steve Kirby, Peter Dandy, Michael Dandy

---

The 🍺 symbol shows pubs which keep their beer unusually well, have a particularly good range or brew their own.

Black Friar

Queen Victoria Street; ⊖ *Mansion House, Temple (not Sundays)* ⇌ *Blackfriars; EC4V 4EG*

Remarkable art nouveau décor, a good choice of beers, friendly atmosphere and decent food all day

Mid-afternoon or mid-evening is the best time to visit this pub – that way you avoid the worst of the crowds and get a chance to look at the unique and quite extraordinary décor. This includes some of the best Edwardian bronze and marble art nouveau work to be found anywhere. The inner back room (known as the Grotto) has big bas-relief friezes of jolly monks set into richly coloured florentine marble walls, an opulent marble-pillared inglenook fireplace, a low vaulted mosaic ceiling, gleaming mirrors, seats built into rich golden marble recesses, and tongue-in-cheek verbal embellishments such as Silence is Golden and Finery is Foolish. See if you can spot the opium-smoking hints modelled into the fireplace of the front room. The other large room has a fireplace and plenty of seats and tables. Fullers London Pride, Greene King IPA and Timothy Taylors Landlord, and guests like Adnams Broadside, St Austell Tribute and Sharps Doom Bar on handpump, over a dozen wines by the glass, and several malt whiskies; piped music; and attentive, friendly service. In the evenings, lots of people spill out on to the wide forecourt, near the approach to Blackfriars Bridge; there's some smart furniture out here. Please note that Blackfriars tube station is closed until late 2011, so we've suggested alternatives.

🍴 **They specialise in pies such as fish, steak and kidney, and game; other traditional meals, served all day, include sausages and mash, steak in ale pie, a vegetarian dish of the day, and fish and chips, some in a choice of sizes.** *Starters/Snacks: £2.50 to £3.95. Main Courses: £6.95 to £9.95. Puddings: £2.65 to £3.65*

Mitchells & Butlers ~ Manager Cecilia Soderholm ~ Real ale ~ Bar food (10-10; 12-9 Sun) ~ (020) 7236 5474 ~ Children welcome if quiet ~ Open 10am-11pm(11.30 Thurs and Fri); 10-11 Sat; 12-10 Sun

Recommended by Barry Collett, the Didler, Dr and Mrs A K Clarke, N R White, Lawrence Pearse, John Saville, Russell and Alison Hunt, John Wooll, Mrs Hazel Rainer, Eithne Dandy, Ian Phillips, Anthony Longden

Cittie of Yorke 🍺

High Holborn – find it by looking out for its big black and gold clock; ⊖ *Chancery Lane (not Sundays), Holborn; WC1V 6BN*

Bustling old pub where the splendid back bar with its old-fashioned cubicles rarely fails to impress – and the beer is refreshingly low priced

The impressive back bar here is the place to head for as it's rather like a baronial hall, with an extraordinarily extended bar counter stretching off into the distance. There are thousand-gallon wine vats resting above the gantry, big, bulbous lights hanging from the soaring high-raftered roof, and a nice glow from the fire. It can get busy in the evenings, with a fine mix of customers from students to lawyers and City types, but there's plenty of space to absorb the crowds – and indeed it's at the busiest times that the pub is at its most magnificent (it never feels quite right when it's quiet). Most people tend to congregate in the middle, so you should still be able to bag one of the intimate, old-fashioned and ornately carved booths that run along both sides. Cheap Sam Smiths OB on handpump. The triangular Waterloo fireplace, with grates on all three sides and a figure of Peace among laurels, used to stand in the Hall of Gray's Inn Common Room until less obtrusive heating was introduced. A smaller, comfortable panelled room has lots of little prints of York and attractive brass lights, while the ceiling of the entrance hall has medieval-style painted panels and plaster York roses. Fruit machine. A pub has stood on this site since 1430, though the current building owes more to the 1695 coffee house erected here behind a garden; it was reconstructed in Victorian times, using 17th-c materials and parts.

🍴 **Served from buffet counters in the main hall and cellar bar, bar food (not perhaps the pub's finest feature) includes sandwiches, soup, and half a dozen daily-changing hot dishes.** *Starters/Snacks: £4.25 to £4.95. Main Courses: £5.95 to £7.50. Puddings: £2.95*

Sam Smiths ~ Manager Stuart Browning ~ Real ale ~ Bar food (12-3, 5-9.30; not Sun) ~ Restaurant ~ (020) 7242 7670 ~ Children welcome ~ Open 11.30-11; closed Sun

Recommended by Jeremy King, P Dawn, N R White, Neil Whitehead, Victoria Anderson, Chris Sale, Di and Mike Gillam, the Didler, Anthony Longden, Dr and Mrs Jackson, Barry Collett, Michael Dandy, Simon Collett-Jones

Coopers Arms

Flood Street; ✚ Sloane Square, but quite a walk; SW3 5TB

Well positioned pub with real ales and decent food, and a useful bolthole for Kings Road shoppers

If you want a rest from shopping in the Kings Road, head for this relaxed and spacious place. It's properly pubby (especially in the evenings), and the open-plan bar has interesting furnishings such as kitchen chairs and some dark brown plush chairs on the floorboards, a mix of nice old good-sized tables, and a pre-war sideboard and dresser; also, LNER posters and maps of Chelsea and the Thames on the walls, an enormous railway clock, a fireplace with dried flowers, and tea-shop chandeliers – all watched over by the heads of a moose and a tusky boar. Wells & Youngs Bitter and Special on handpump, and quite a few wines by the glass. There are seats in the courtyard garden.

🍴 Under the new licensee, bar food might include sandwiches, soup, various platters, smoked haddock rarebit, beer-battered fish, beefburger, sausages with red onion gravy, all-day breakfast, ham and eggs, vegetarian cannelloni, free-range chicken breast with lemon and thyme and butternut squash, steaks, and puddings like sticky toffee pudding and vanilla crème brûlée with marinated berries; Sunday roasts. *Starters/Snacks: £3.95 to £6.95. Main Courses: £8.95 to £14.95. Puddings: £3.95 to £6.95*

Youngs ~ Manager Sarah Bludger ~ Real ale ~ Bar food (all day) ~ (020) 7376 3120 ~ Well behaved children allowed until 7pm ~ Dogs allowed in bar ~ Open 11-11(10.30 Sun)
Recommended by Tracey and Stephen Groves, Peter, Ian Phillips

Cross Keys

Lawrence Street; ✚ Sloane Square, but some distance away; SW3 5NB

New licensee for bustling Chelsea landmark, friendly bar, airy back restaurant, attentive staff and a fair choice of food and drink

The new licensee is planning to upgrade this bustling 18th-c pub. It's a warmly convivial and civilised place with a roomy, high-ceilinged bar, painted wheelback chairs and settles on the flagstones, two open fires and a good range of customers. The light and airy conservatory-style back restaurant has a fully retractable roof. Courage Directors and Theakstons XB on handpump, and a good choice of wines by the glass from an extensive list; attentive young staff; piped music. Like most pubs in the area, this can be busy and lively on Friday and Saturday evenings.

🍴 From the updated kitchen (which now has a live charcoal grill), bar food includes sandwiches, soup, a plate of charcuterie, mexican nachos, beefburger with a choice of toppings, sausages with red onion gravy, spaghetti bolognese, fish and chips, steak pie, pasta of the day, and puddings like chocolate mousse and tiramisu. *Starters/Snacks: £4.00 to £7.00. Main Courses: £5.00 to £8.00. Puddings: £3.00 to £6.00*

Free house ~ Licensee John Bond ~ Bar food (12-3, 6-10.45) ~ Restaurant ~ (020) 7349 9111 ~ Children welcome ~ Dogs welcome ~ Open 11am-midnight(11pm Sun); closed bank hols
Recommended by Peter

Dog & Duck ◼ £

Bateman Street, on corner with Frith Street; ✚ Tottenham Court Road, Leicester Square; W1D 3AJ

Tiny Soho pub squeezing in bags of character, with unusual old tiles and mosaics, good beers and a warmly welcoming atmosphere

Not a lot has changed in the last 40 years at this small Soho landmark (apart from the staff who seem to change rather frequently). Afternoons are probably the best time to fully appreciate the décor, which has some interesting detail and individual touches; it does get very busy indeed in the evenings. On the floor near the door is an engaging mosaic showing a dog with its tongue out in hot pursuit of a duck; the same theme is embossed on some of the shiny tiles that frame the heavy old advertising mirrors. There are some high stools by the ledge along the back wall, further seats in a slightly roomier area at one end, and a fire in winter; the piped music is usually drowned out by the good-natured chatter. There's also a rather cosy upstairs bar where there's often some free space. Fullers London Pride, Greene King IPA and a couple of guest beers on handpump from the unusual little bar counter, maybe Addlestone's cider, and quite a few wines by the glass. In good weather, most people tend to spill out on to the bustling street.

Served all day, the good value bar food includes sandwiches, soup, beer-battered fish and chips, aberdeen angus beefburger with various toppings, platters of sausage or fish and vegetables, gammon and eggs, chicken, ham and leek pie, barbecue chicken, steaks, roast duck with marmalade gravy, and puddings like apple crumble and chocolate brownie sundae. *Starters/Snacks: £2.50 to £3.50. Main Courses: £6.50 to £9.95. Puddings: £2.65*

Mitchells & Butlers ~ Manager Natalie Hubbard ~ Real ale ~ Bar food (all day) ~ (020) 7494 0697 ~ Children allowed in dining room ~ Dogs allowed in bar ~ Open 11-11(11.30 Sat; 10 Sun)

Recommended by Dr and Mrs M E Wilson, P Dawn, Mike Gorton, LM, the Didler, Mel Smith

Eagle 🍴 ☏

Farringdon Road; opposite Bowling Green Lane car park; ⊖ ⇄ Farringdon, Old Street; EC1R 3AL

London's original gastropub is busy and noisy, with gutsy mediterranean cooking, a couple of real ales and quite a few wines by the glass

To enjoy the rustic, mediterranean-style of cooking in what was London's first gastropub, you must get there before serving time starts to be sure of a table, and on weekday lunchtimes especially. Dishes from the blackboard menu can run out or change fairly quickly. The open-plan room is dominated by a giant open range and it's all pretty busy, noisy and slightly scruffy for some tastes. Furnishings are basic and well worn – school chairs, a random assortment of tables, a couple of sofas on bare boards and modern paintings on the walls (there's an art gallery upstairs, with direct access from the bar). Wells & Youngs Eagle and Bombardier on handpump, good wines including around 14 by the glass, and decent coffee; piped music (sometimes loud). Not the ideal choice for a quiet dinner, or a smart night out, the pub is generally quieter at weekends. More reports please.

Changing constantly, the short choice of gutsy food might include hearty soups, popular steak sandwich, tapas, risottos, grilled mackerel with tabbouleh and chilli tomato jam, chicken breast with lemon zest, paprika and potato salad with olives and spring onions, spanish-style roast vegetable salad, napoli sausages with onions and polenta, cod with lentils and aioli, and puddings like lemon and almond cake with crème fraîche and berry compote and portuguese custard tart. *Main Courses: £5.00 to £15.00. Puddings: £4.50*

Free house ~ Licensee Michael Belben ~ Real ale ~ Bar food (12.30-3(3.30 weekends), 6.30-10.30; not Sun evening) ~ (020) 7837 1353 ~ Children welcome ~ Dogs welcome ~ Open 12-11(5 Sun); closed Sun evening, bank hols and a week at Christmas

Recommended by Barry Collett

Grapes 🍴 £

Shepherd Market; ⊖ Green Park, Hyde Park Corner; W1J 7QQ

Genuinely old-fashioned and individual, and always packed in the evenings for the six real ales and thai food

At the heart of Shepherd Market, this engagingly old-fashioned pub continues to draw in the crowds keen to sample the fine choice of six real ales and thai food. On handpump, the beers might include Fullers London Pride, Sharps Doom Bar and Wells & Youngs

Bombardier, with three changing guests like Cottage Champflower Ale, Everards Sunchaser Blonde and Sambrooks Wandle Ale. Genuinely atmospheric, it's an enjoyable place at lunchtime when you can more easily take in its traditional charms, but is perhaps best when it's so very busy in the evenings, and the cheery bustle rather adds to the allure. The dimly lit bar has plenty of well worn plush red furnishings, stuffed birds and fish in glass display cases, wooden floors and panelling, a welcoming coal fire, and a snug little alcove at the back; readers like the seats on the raised platform by the window. You'll generally see smart-suited drinkers spilling on to the square outside.

🍴 There's a huge choice of thai dishes cooked by a thai chef and set meals for two or more people, as well as some traditional english dishes like sausage and mash, a pie, and battered cod and chips. *Starters/Snacks: £2.00 to £4.95. Main Courses: £5.95 to £6.95*

Free house ~ Licensees John Shannon, Leigh Kelly ~ Real ale ~ Bar food (12-3.30, 5-9.30; 12-9 Sat; 12-5 Sun) ~ Restaurant ~ (020) 7493 4216 ~ Children allowed until 5pm ~ Open 11.30-11; 12-10.30 Sun

Recommended by N R White, Darren Le Poidevin, the Didler, Peter Dandy, Michael Dandy, Ian Phillips

Grenadier

Wilton Row; the turning off Wilton Crescent looks prohibitive, but the barrier and watchman are there to keep out cars; walk straight past – the pub is just around the corner; ⊖ Knightsbridge, Hyde Park Corner; SW1X 7NR

Atmospheric old pub with lots of character and military history – though not much space; famous for its ghost and its bloody marys

To enjoy this characterful and cosy little pub at its best try to avoid peak times – especially between 5-7pm. It was originally built in 1720 as the officers' mess for the First Royal Regiment of Foot Guards and a portrait of the Duke of Wellington hangs above the fireplace, alongside neat prints of guardsmen through the ages; there's even a sentry box out in front. Away from the busiest of times you should generally be able to plonk yourself on one of the stools or wooden benches in the simple, unfussy bar. Fullers London Pride, Timothy Taylors Landlord and maybe a guest beer like Batemans XXXB on handpump at the rare pewter-topped bar counter, though on Sundays, especially, you'll find several of the customers here to sample their famous bloody marys, made to a unique recipe. At the back is an intimate (and extremely popular) restaurant and you absolutely must book to be sure of a table. There's a single table outside in the attractive mews – surprisingly peaceful given the proximity to Knightsbridge and Hyde Park Corner. They may be closed to all but ticket holders on events such as the anniversary of the Battle of Waterloo or Wellington's birthday. No children under eight, no mobiles and no photography.

🍴 Well liked, traditional bar food includes sandwiches, a pie of the day, ham and eggs, sausage and mash, whitby scampi, and fish and chips, and there's a formal à la carte menu in the tiny restaurant. *Main Courses: £5.95 to £7.95*

Punch ~ Manager Cynthia Weston ~ Real ale ~ Bar food (12-3, 6-9.30) ~ Restaurant ~ (020) 7235 3074 ~ Children welcome if over 8 ~ Dogs welcome ~ Open 12-11(10.30 Sun)

Recommended by LM, Chris Glasson, Simon and Sally Small, N R White, Peter, Mike and Sue Loseby, Brian and Rosalie Laverick, Franki McCabe, Ian Phillips, Darren Le Poidevin

Guinea

Bruton Place; ⊖ Bond Street, Green Park, Piccadilly Circus, Oxford Circus; W1J 6NL

Prize-winning steak and kidney pie in a tiny old-fashioned pub with friendly staff, and bustling atmosphere after work – when customers spill on to the street

Inside this old-fashioned little place it's almost standing room only, so at peak times the mix of suited workers, tourists and diners for the upmarket restaurant spill out on to the little mews in front with its pretty flowering tubs. The look of the place is appealingly simple: bare boards, yellow walls, old-fashioned prints, and a red-planked ceiling with raj fans. Three cushioned wooden seats and tables are tucked to the left of the entrance to the bar, with a couple more in a snug area at the back, underneath a big old clock; most people tend to prop themselves against a little shelf running along the side of the small room. Friendly, cheery staff serve Wells & Youngs Bitter, Special and seasonal brews from the striking bar counter, which has some nice wrought-iron work above it. Take care to pick the right entrance – it's all too easy to walk into the upscale Guinea Grill which takes up much of the same building; uniformed doormen will politely redirect you if you've picked the door to that by mistake. No children.

🍴 **The main draw is the lunchtime steak and kidney pie though the summer barbecues are popular, too; the adjacent restaurant serves the famous pie too, albeit more expensively.** *Main Courses: £3.50 to £8.50*

Youngs ~ Manager Carl Smith ~ Real ale ~ Bar food (12.30-9; not weekends) ~ Restaurant ~ (020) 7409 1728 ~ Open 11.30-11; 6-11 Sat; closed Sat lunchtime, all day Sun and bank hols

Recommended by N R White, Michael Dandy, Peter Dandy, the Didler, Michael and Alison Sandy, Mike Gorton

Harp 🍺 £

47 Chandos Place; ⊖ ⇌ Charing Cross, Leicester Square; WC2N 4HS

Quietly civilised little pub with seven real ales, friendly service and nice sausages

This is a smashing little pub, much enjoyed by our readers, and it's run by a warmly friendly, long-serving landlady who keep her seven real ales very well. There's an unpretentious, relaxed atmosphere in the long, narrow bar, a mix of quietly chatty customers, lots of high bar stools along the wall counter and around elbow tables, big mirrors on the red walls, some lovely front stained-glass, and lots of interesting if not always well executed star portraits. If it's not too busy, you may be able to get one of the prized seats looking out through the front windows. Black Sheep, Harveys Best, Timothy Taylors Landlord and four quickly changing guest beers on handpump, decent wines by the glass, farm cider, and 27 malt whiskies. Upstairs, there's a little room with comfortable furniture and a window looking over the road below; if the bar gets too crowded, customers spill out into the back alley.

🍴 **Bar food consists of good changing sausages such as kangaroo, venison, wild boar, pork in ale, and so forth, served in baps with lots of fried onions.** *Starters/Snacks: £2.50 to £3.50*

Punch ~ Lease Bridget Walsh ~ Real ale ~ Bar food (11-7) ~ (020) 7836 0291 ~ Open 10.30am-11pm; 12-10.30 Sun

Recommended by Matt and Vicky Wharton, Tim Maddison, Joe Green, Mike Gorton, Michael and Alison Sandy, Dr and Mrs M E Wilson, N R White, Michael Dandy, Tracey and Stephen Groves

Jerusalem Tavern ★

Britton Street; ⊖ ⇌ Farringdon; EC1M 5UQ

A London favourite, delightfully atmospheric, even at its busiest, with the full range of splendid St Peters beers, good lunchtime food and helpful staff

This first-class pub is the only place to stock the whole range of brews from the Suffolk-based St Peters other than the brewery itself, with half a dozen tapped from casks behind the little bar counter, and the rest available in their elegant, distinctively shaped bottles. Depending on the season you'll find St Peters Best, Golden Ale, Grapefruit, Organic Best, and two other changing guests from their range, and you can buy them to take away too. Particularly inviting when it's candlelit and the coal fires are burning on a cold winter's evening, the pub is a vivid re-creation of a dark 18th-c tavern, seeming so genuinely old that you'd hardly guess the work was done only a few years ago. The current building was developed around 1720, originally as a merchant's house, then becoming a clock and watchmaker's. It still has the shopfront added in 1810, immediately behind which is a light little room with a couple of wooden tables and benches and some remarkable old tiles on the walls at either side. This leads to the tiny dimly lit bar, which has a couple of unpretentious tables on the bare boards, and another up some stairs on a discreetly precarious-feeling though perfectly secure balcony – a prized vantage point. A plainer back room has a few more tables, a fireplace and a stuffed fox in a case. Staff are always friendly and attentive, even at peak times when it can get horribly crowded. There are some green metal tables and chairs outside on the pavement. The brewery's headquarters in South Elmham is a Main Entry in our Suffolk chapter. No children.

🍴 **Blackboards list the well liked weekly-changing lunchtime bar food: ploughman's, wild mushrooms on sourdough toast, full english breakfast, very good home-made minted lamb burger with chilli aioli, a choice of sausages with gravy, ham and organic eggs, steak in ale stew with dumplings, and rib-eye steak.** *Starters/Snacks: £6.00 to £8.00. Main Courses: £7.00 to £10.00. Puddings: £3.00 to £5.00*

St Peters ~ Manager David Hart ~ Real ale ~ Bar food (12-3, and 6-9 Tues-Thurs evenings only) ~ (020) 7490 4281 ~ Dogs welcome ~ Open 11-11; closed weekends, bank hols, 24 Dec-1 Jan

Recommended by Anthony Longden, the Didler, Stephen and Jean Curtis, Revd R P Tickle, Michael Dandy, Donna and Roger, Giles and Annie Francis, Sue Demont, Tim Barrow, P Dawn, Mike Gorton, N R White, Peter Dandy

Lamb ★ 🍺

Lamb's Conduit Street; ⊖ Holborn, Russell Square; WC1N 3LZ

Famously unspoilt Victorian pub, full of character, with unique fittings and atmosphere

A splendid place to unwind in the afternoon (it does get very busy in the evening), this characterful pub remains, thankfully, quite unchanging and the staff are friendly and efficient. It stands out for its unique Victorian fittings and atmosphere, with the highlight being the bank of cut-glass swivelling snob-screens all the way round the U-shaped bar counter. Sepia photographs of 1890s actresses on the ochre panelled walls and traditional cast-iron-framed tables with neat brass rails around the rim add to the overall effect. Six real ales on handpump like Wells & Youngs Bitter, Bombardier, Special and Waggle Dance plus a couple of guests, and a good choice of malt whiskies. No machines or music. There's a snug little room at the back, slatted wooden seats out in front, and more in a little courtyard beyond. Like the street, the pub is named for the kentish clothmaker William Lamb who brought fresh water to Holborn in 1577. No children.

🍴 **Standard bar food includes sandwiches, soup, ploughman's, vegetable curry, chicken or lamb burgers, and steak pie.** *Starters/Snacks: £3.50 to £5.50. Main Courses: £8.50 to £10.00. Puddings: £3.50*

Youngs ~ Manager John Quinlin ~ Real ale ~ Bar food (12-9) ~ (020) 7405 0713 ~ Children allowed until 5pm ~ Open 12-midnight(10.30 Sun)

Recommended by Derek and Sylvia Stephenson, James A Waller, Donna and Roger, John and Gloria Isaacs, Ros Lawler, P Dawn, Dr and Mrs A K Clarke, Roy Hoing, the Didler, Brian and Anna Marsden

Lamb & Flag 🍺 £

Rose Street, off Garrick Street; ⊖ Leicester Square, Covent Garden; WC2E 9EB

Historic yet unpretentious, full of character and atmosphere, and with six real ales; especially busy in the evening

There's always an overflow of customers chatting in the little alleyways outside this tucked-away old pub, even in winter, as it does get packed – especially in the early evening with after-work drinkers. It's an unspoilt and in places rather basic old tavern, and the more spartan front room leads into a snugly atmospheric low-ceilinged back bar with high-backed black settles and an open fire; in Regency times this was known as the Bucket of Blood thanks to the bare-knuckle prize-fights held here. Half a dozen well kept real ales typically include Adnams Best, Courage Directors, Greene King Old Speckled Hen, and Wells & Youngs Bitter, Bombardier and Special on handpump, and there are a good few malt whiskies. The upstairs Dryden Room is often less crowded and has more seats (though fewer beers). The pub has a lively and well documented history: Dryden was nearly beaten to death by hired thugs outside, and Dickens made fun of the Middle Temple lawyers who frequented it when he was working in nearby Catherine Street.

🍴 **A short choice of simple food is served upstairs, lunchtimes only: soup, baked potatoes, and a few daily changing specials like cottage pie, cauliflower cheese and fish and chips.** *Starters/Snacks: £2.00 to £4.00. Main Courses: £5.75 to £7.75. Puddings: £3.50*

Free house ~ Licensees Terry Archer and Adrian and Sandra Zimmerman ~ Real ale ~
Bar food (11-3 Mon-Fri; 11(12 Sun)-4.30 weekends) ~ (020) 7497 9504 ~ Children in upstairs
dining room lunchtime only ~ Open 11-11; 12-10.30 Sun; closed 25-26 Dec, 1 Jan

*Recommended by Dr Kevan Tucker, Michael Dandy, Dr and Mrs Jackson, N R White, the Didler, Mike and
Sue Loseby, Ian Phillips, Rosemary K Germaine, Barry and Anne, John and Sharon Hancock*

Lord Moon of the Mall ◖ £
Whitehall; ⊖ ⇌ Charing Cross; SW1A 2DY

**Superior Wetherspoons pub with excellent value food and drink in a perfect location close
to all the sights**

At its best during the day (the evenings are just so busy), this nicely converted former
bank offers incredible value for both food and drink. The impressive main room has a
splendid high ceiling and quite an elegant feel, with old prints, big arched windows
looking out over Whitehall, and a huge painting that seems to show a well-to-do 18th-c
gentleman; in fact it's Tim Martin, founder of the Wetherspoons chain. Once through an
arch the style is more recognisably Wetherspoons, with a couple of neatly tiled areas and
bookshelves opposite the long bar; silenced fruit machines, trivia, and a cash machine.
There's a fine range of real ales, including rapidly changing guests: Greene King Abbot
and Ruddles Best and up to seven quickly changing guest beers on handpump, and
Weston's cider. The back doors (now only an emergency exit) were apparently built as a
secret entrance for the bank's account holders living in Buckingham Palace (Edward VII
had an account here from the age of three). As you come out, Nelson's Column is
immediately to the left, and Big Ben a walk of ten minutes or so to the right.

🍴 **Good value bar food from the standard Wetherspoons menu includes sandwiches, filled
baked potatoes, caesar salad, spicy battered prawns with sweet chilli dip, sharer plates of
nachos, all sorts of meaty or vegetable burgers, ham and egg, sausage, chips and beans,
meatballs in a red wine and tomato sauce with pasta, chicken tikka masala, beef in ale
pie, mixed grill, and puddings like sticky toffee pudding and apple and raspberry crumble.**
Starters/Snacks: £2.59. Main Courses: £6.00 to £8.20. Puddings: £1.79 to £3.99

Wetherspoons ~ Manager Jay Blower ~ Real ale ~ Bar food (9am-11pm) ~ (020) 7839 7701 ~
Children welcome ~ Dogs welcome ~ Open 9am-11.30pm(midnight Fri and Sat; 11pm Sun)

*Recommended by Ian Phillips, Dave Irving, Jenny Huggins, Richard, E McCall, T McLean, D Irving, Meg and
Colin Hamilton, Phil Bryant, Dr and Mrs A K Clarke, Alan Thwaite, Dr and Mrs M E Wilson*

Nags Head ◖
Kinnerton Street; ⊖ Knightsbridge, Hyde Park Corner; SW1X 8ED

Genuinely unspoilt; distinctive bar filled with theatrical mementoes and friendly locals

Although just a few minutes from Harrods, this is more like a country local than a
London pub. It's hidden away in a peaceful and attractive mews and remains quite
unspoilt and full of character. There's a cosy and relaxed feel in the small, panelled and
low-ceilinged front room, where friendly regulars sit chatting around the unusual sunken
bar counter. The seats by the log-effect gas fire in an old cooking range are snapped up
pretty quickly, and a narrow passage leads down steps to an even smaller back bar with
stools and a mix of comfortable seats. Adnams Best, Broadside and Regatta are pulled on
attractive 19th-c china, pewter and brass handpumps, while other interesting old
features include a 1930s what-the-butler-saw machine and a one-armed bandit that takes
old pennies. The piped music is rather individual: often jazz, folk or 1920s-40s show
tunes, and around the walls are drawings of actors and fading programmes from variety
performances. There are a few seats and sometimes a couple of tables outside.

🍴 **Bar food (which often sells out) includes sandwiches, ploughman's, salads, sausage,
mash and beans, chilli con carne, daily specials, and a choice of roasts; there's usually a
£1.50 surcharge added to all dishes in the evenings and at weekends.** *Main Courses: £4.50
to £7.00*

Free house ~ Licensee Kevin Moran ~ Real ale ~ Bar food (11-9.30; 12-9.30 Sun) ~
(020) 7235 1135 ~ Children welcome ~ Dogs allowed in bar ~ Open 11-11; 12-10.30 Sun

*Recommended by Pete Baker, John and Gloria Isaacs, Darren Le Poidevin, Dr and Mrs A K Clarke, the Didler,
N R White, LM, Ian Phillips*

Old Bank of England ♀

Fleet Street; ⊖ *Chancery Lane (not Sundays), Temple (not Sundays)* ⇌ *Blackfriars;
EC4A 2LT*

**Dramatically converted former bank building, with gleaming chandeliers in impressive,
soaring bar, well kept Fullers beers, and good pies**

This rather austere italianate building still looks very much like the subsidiary branch of
the Bank of England it once was and it rarely fails to impress first- or even second-time
visitors – though it's best appreciated in the daytime when things are quieter. The
soaring, spacious bar has three gleaming chandeliers hanging from the exquisitely
plastered ceiling, high above an unusually tall island bar counter, crowned with a clock.
The end wall has big paintings and murals that look like 18th-c depictions of Justice, but
in fact feature members of the Fuller, Smith and Turner families, who run the brewery the
pub belongs to. There are well polished dark wooden furnishings, plenty of framed prints,
and, despite the grandeur, some surprisingly cosy corners, with screens between some of
the tables creating an unexpectedly intimate feel which readers really enjoy. Tables in a
quieter galleried section upstairs offer a bird's-eye view of the action, and some smaller
rooms (used mainly for functions) open off. Fullers Chiswick, Discovery, ESB, London
Pride and seasonal brews on handpump, a good choice of malt whiskies, and a dozen
wines by the glass. At lunchtimes the piped music is generally classical or easy listening;
it's louder and livelier in the evenings. There's also a garden with seats (one of the few
pubs in the area to have one). Pies have a long if rather dubious pedigree in this area; it
was in the vaults and tunnels below the Old Bank and the surrounding buildings that
Sweeney Todd butchered the clients destined to provide the fillings in his mistress
Mrs Lovett's nearby pie shop.

🍽 **Available all day, the good bar food has an emphasis on well liked home-made pies
such as sweet potato and goats cheese, chicken, broccoli or gammon, leek and whole
grain mustard, but also includes sandwiches, soup, sausages and mash, proper burgers,
fish and chips, puddings like banoffi pie, and popular afternoon teas.** *Starters/Snacks:
£4.25 to £5.50. Main Courses: £7.50 to £10.00. Puddings: £4.50 to £5.50*

Fullers ~ Manager Jo Farquhar ~ Real ale ~ Bar food (12-9) ~ (020) 7430 2255 ~
Children allowed before 5pm ~ Open 11-11; closed weekends, bank hols

*Recommended by Neil Whitehead, Victoria Anderson, Peter Dandy, P Dawn, the Didler, Dr and Mrs A K Clarke,
Peter, Michael Dandy, Anthony Longden, David and Sue Smith, Barry Collett, N R White, Michael and Alison Sandy,
Donna and Roger*

Olde Cheshire Cheese

Wine Office Court, off 145 Fleet Street; ⊖ *Chancery Lane (not Sundays), Temple
(not Sundays)* ⇌ *Blackfriars; EC4A 2BU*

**Much bigger than it looks, soaked in history, with lots of warmly old-fashioned rooms,
cheap Sam Smiths beer and a convivial atmosphere**

The warren of dark, historic rooms in this 17th-c former chop house have hardly changed
at all and although it can get busy with office workers, legal types and tourists, there are
plenty of hidden corners to absorb the crowds. The unpretentious rooms have bare
wooden benches built in to the walls, bare boards and, on the ground floor, high beams,
crackly old black varnish, Victorian paintings on the dark brown walls, and big open fires
in winter. A particularly snug room is the tiny one on the right as you enter, but the
most rewarding bit is the Cellar Bar, down steep narrow stone steps that look as if they're
only going to lead to the loo, but in fact take you to an unexpected series of cosy areas
with stone walls and ceilings, and some secluded alcoves. The back bar is noisy and
usually crowded and a bit like a drinking barn. Sam Smiths OB on handpump, as usual for
this brewery, extraordinarily well priced (over £1 less than the beer in some of our other
London Main Entries). Service from smartly dressed staff is helpful, though sometimes
less quick for food than it is for drinks. In the early 20th c the pub was well known for

its famous parrot that for over 40 years entertained princes, ambassadors and other distinguished guests; she's still around today, stuffed and silent, in the restaurant on the ground floor.

🍴 Bar food includes macaroni cheese, fish and chips, lamb shank, pheasant, and puddings such as sticky toffee pudding; the cellar serves a lunchtime pie and mash buffet. *Starters/Snacks: £3.50 to £4.25. Main Courses: £4.95 to £7.95. Puddings: £3.95*

Sam Smiths ~ Manager Gordon Garrity ~ Real ale ~ Bar food (12-10; not Sun) ~ Restaurant ~ (020) 7353 6170 ~ Children allowed in eating area lunchtime only ~ Open 11.30(12 Sat)-11; 12-4 Sun; closed Sun evening

Recommended by Tracey and Stephen Groves, Neil Whitehead, Victoria Anderson, Anthony Longden, N R White, the Didler, Barry Collett, Dr and Mrs M E Wilson, Bruce Bird, B and M Kendall, LM, P Dawn, Sue Demont, Tim Barrow

Olde Mitre 🍺 £

Ely Place; the easiest way to find it is from the narrow passageway beside 8 Hatton Garden; ⊖ *Chancery Lane (not Sundays); EC1N 6SJ*

Hard to find but well worth it – an unspoilt old pub with lovely atmosphere, unusual guest beers and bargain toasted sandwiches

Tucked away and unspoilt, this is a lovely little pub and a refuge from the modern city nearby. The cosy small rooms have lots of dark panelling as well as antique settles and – particularly in the popular back room, where there are more seats – old local pictures and so forth. It gets good-naturedly packed between 12.30 and 2.15, filling up again in the early evening, but in the early afternoons and by around 9pm becomes a good deal more tranquil. An upstairs room, mainly used for functions, may double as an overflow at peak periods. Adnams Broadside, Caledonian Deuchars IPA, Fullers London Pride and a couple of guests like Gales HSB and Orkney Dragonhead Stout on handpump; they do hold three beer festivals (phone for details). Friendly service from the convivial landlord and obliging staff; no music, TV or machines – the only games here are cribbage and dominoes. There's some space for outside drinking by the pot plants and jasmine in the narrow yard between the pub and St Ethelreda's church (which is worth a look). Note the pub doesn't open weekends. The iron gates that guard one entrance to Ely Place are a reminder of the days when the law in this district was administered by the Bishops of Ely. The best approach is from Hatton Garden, walking up the right-hand side away from Chancery Lane; an easily missed sign on a lamp post points the way down a narrow alley. No children.

🍴 Served all day, bar snacks are limited to scotch eggs, pork pies and sausage rolls, and really good value toasted sandwiches with cheese, ham, pickle or tomato. *Starters/Snacks: £1.40 to £2.25*

Fullers ~ Managers Eamon and Kathy Scott ~ Real ale ~ Bar food (11-9.30) ~ (020) 7405 4751 ~ Open 11-11; closed weekends and bank hols

Recommended by the Didler, N R White, Dr and Mrs Jackson, Mike Gorton, K Almond, Darren Le Poidevin, Donna and Roger, Joe Green, Michael Dandy, Anthony Longden, P Dawn

Princess Louise

High Holborn; ⊖ *Holborn, Chancery Lane (not Sundays); WC1V 7EP*

Beautifully refurbished Victorian gin-palace with fabulously extravagant décor

Of course, this splendid Victorian gin-palace is worth visiting for its amazing décor, but it's also a proper pub with a welcoming winter fire, pleasant staff and very well priced Sam Smiths OB on handpump. Restored to its former glory only quite recently, the gloriously opulent main bar once again has wood and glass partitions in lots of different areas, splendid etched and gilt mirrors, brightly coloured and fruity-shaped tiles, and slender portland stone columns soaring towards the lofty and deeply moulded plaster ceiling. Even the gents' has its own preservation order. It's generally quite crowded on early weekday evenings (for some, adding to the appeal), but is usually quieter later on. No children.

ⓘ **Bar food includes pies, scampi, sausage and mash, gammon and egg, and steaks.**
Starters/Snacks: £2.95 to £5.00. Main Courses: £4.95 to £7.00. Puddings: £2.95

Sam Smiths ~ Manager Campbell Mackay ~ Real ale ~ Bar food (12-2.30, 5-8.30; not Fri and not weekends) ~ (020) 7405 8816 ~ Open 11-11; 12-11(10.30 Sun) Sat
Recommended by the Didler, Roger Shipperley, David M Smith, Bruce Bird, Joe Green, Tracey and Stephen Groves, Barry Collett, Tim Maddison

Red Lion ◀

Duke of York Street; ⊖ *Piccadilly Circus; SW1Y 6JP*

Remarkably preserved Victorian pub, all gleaming mirrors and polished mahogany, though right in the heart of town, so does get busy

Consistently enjoyed by our readers over many years, this is a smart and pretty little pub that's probably best appreciated as soon as it opens; it can be very crowded at lunchtime and early evening (try inching through to the back room where there's sometimes more space), but the many customers are happy to spill out on to the pavement by the mass of foliage and flowers cascading down the wall. When it was built, its profusion of mirrors was said to enable the landlord to keep a watchful eye on local prostitutes, but the gleaming glasswork isn't the only feature of note: the series of small rooms also has a good deal of polished mahogany, as well as crystal chandeliers and cut and etched windows, and a striking ornamental plaster ceiling. Adnams Best and Fullers Chiswick plus up to four guest beers on handpump. Diners have priority on a few of the front tables. No children.

ⓘ **Under the new licensee, the simple bar food includes sandwiches, filled baked potatoes, salads, bangers and mash, pies like steak and stilton and cottage, and fish and chips.** *Starters/Snacks: £3.25 to £5.25. Main Courses: £6.50 to £8.50*

Fullers ~ Manager Sarah Bird ~ Real ale ~ Bar food (12-4(6 Thurs-Sat); not evenings) ~ (020) 7321 0782 ~ Open 11-11; closed Sun, bank hols
Recommended by Dr and Mrs M E Wilson, Ian Phillips, Dr and Mrs A K Clarke, the Didler, Tracey and Stephen Groves, Barry and Anne, Michael Dandy, N R White

Salisbury ♈ ◀

St Martins Lane; ⊖ *Leicester Square; WC2N 4AP*

Gleaming Victorian pub surviving unchanged in the heart of the West End, good atmosphere, wide choice of drinks; it does get crowded

Full of character and handy for the West End, this bustling pub has changed little over the years. There's a wealth of cut glass and mahogany, and the busily pubby main bar is perhaps best enjoyed mid-afternoon on a weekday – it can be rather packed in the evenings. A curved upholstered wall seat creates the impression of several distinct areas, framed by wonderfully ornate bronze light fittings shaped like ethereal nymphs each holding stems of flowers; there are only four of these, but mirrors all around make it seem as though there are more, and that the room extends much further than it does. A back room, popular for eating, has plenty more glasswork, and there's a separate little side room with its own entrance. On the walls are old photographs and prints, and, tucked behind the main door, a well known picture of Marianne Faithfull taken here in 1964; Richard Burton and Liz Taylor had their wedding drinks in the main bar and there's a picture in the back room of Dylan Thomas enjoying a drink here in 1941. Every inch of the walls and ceiling around the stairs down to the lavatories is coated with theatre posters (the pub is right in the heart of theatreland). Cheerful staff serve six real ales such as Caledonian Deuchars IPA, Wells & Youngs Bitter and Bombardier, and guests like Roosters Special, Sharps Doom Bar and Timothy Taylors Landlord on handpump, as well as a dozen wines by the glass, coffees, winter hot toddies and summer Pimms. There are fine details on the exterior of the building too, and tables in a pedestrianised side alley.

ⓘ **Bar food includes sandwiches, filled baked potatoes, soup, speciality pies and sausages, popular fish and chips, chicken kiev, and plenty of pasta dishes and salads.**
Starters/Snacks: £3.55 to £7.85. Main Courses: £5.35 to £9.15. Puddings: £2.95 to £3.70

Punch ~ Manager Jas Teensa ~ Bar food (12-9.30) ~ (020) 7836 5863 ~ Children allowed until 5pm ~ Open 11-11(11.30 Thurs, midnight Fri); 12-2am(10.30 Sun) Sat

Recommended by Tracey and Stephen Groves, Anthony and Marie Lewis, Joe Green, the Didler, N R White, Mike Gorton, Alan Thwaite, Michael Dandy

Seven Stars ◀

Carey Street; ⊖ Holborn (just as handy from Temple or Chancery Lane (both stations closed Sundays), but the walk through Lincoln's Inn Fields can be rather pleasant); WC2A 2JB

Quirky pub with cheerful staff, an interesting mix of customers, and good choice of drinks

You can be sure of a friendly welcome from the cheerful bar staff in this busy and characterful little pub and there's always a good mix of customers – though as it faces the back of the Law Courts, it's a favourite with lawyers and reporters covering notable trials; there are plenty of caricatures of barristers and judges on the red-painted walls of the two main rooms. There are also posters of legal-themed british films, big ceiling fans, and a relaxed, intimate atmosphere; checked tablecloths add a quirky, almost continental touch. A third area is in what was formerly a legal wig shop next door – it still retains the original frontage, with a neat display of wigs in the window. Despite the extra space, the pub can fill up very quickly, with lots of the tables snapped up by people here for the often individual food. Adnams Best and Broadside, Black Sheep Best, and a guest like Dark Star Hophead on handpump. On busy evenings there's an overflow of customers on to the quiet road in front; things generally quieten down after 8pm, and there can be a nice, sleepy atmosphere some afternoons. The Elizabethan stairs up to the lavatories are rather steep, but there's a good strong handrail. Tom Paine, the large and somewhat po-faced pub cat, still remains very much a centre of attention. The licensees have a second pub, the Bountiful Cow, on Eagle Street near Holborn, which specialises in beef. No children.

⊞ **Changing daily, the often interesting – if not cheap – food might include mozzarella, piquillo peppers and green salad, a plate of charcuterie, vegetable lasagne, game stews and roast game in season, portuguese fish pie, and veal chops.** *Main Courses: £8.00 to £10.50. Puddings: £6.00*

Free house ~ Licensee Roxy Beaujolais ~ Real ale ~ Bar food (12(1-ish Sat and Sun)-9.45(9 Sun)) ~ Restaurant ~ (020) 7242 8521 ~ Open 11-11; 12-11 Sat; 12-10.30 Sun; closed some bank hols (usually including Christmas)

Recommended by LM, Pete Coxon, David and Sue Smith, Joe Green, Edward Mirzoeff, N R White, Sue Demont, Tim Barrow, Dr and Mrs A K Clarke, Donna and Roger, the Didler, Tracey and Stephen Groves, Anthony Longden, Tim Maddison, P Dawn

Star ◀

Belgrave Mews West, behind the German Embassy, off Belgrave Square; ⊖ Knightsbridge, Hyde Park Corner; SW1X 8HT

Bustling local with restful bar, upstairs dining room, Fullers ales, well liked bar food and colourful hanging baskets

It's said that this is the pub where the Great Train Robbery was planned. It's a friendly, pleasant place with sash windows, wooden floors and an upstairs dining room, and the small bar has a restful local feel outside peak times (when it is busy), stools by the counter and tall windows. An arch leads to the main seating area with well polished tables and chairs, and good lighting. Fullers Chiswick, Discovery, ESB and London Pride, with a changing guest beer on handpump, and quite a choice of whiskies. The astonishing array of hanging baskets and flowering tubs make a lovely sight in summer.

⊞ **Bar food includes sandwiches, filled baked potatoes, various platters, honey and mustard glazed ham with free-range eggs, salmon and smoked haddock fishcakes with lemon butter sauce, liver and bacon on spring onion mash with caramelised red onion gravy, beefburger with mustard, bacon and cheese, popular beer-battered cod with tartare sauce, chargrilled rib-eye steak, and puddings like treacle tart and mixed berry eton mess.** *Starters/Snacks: £4.00 to £5.50. Main Courses: £7.90 to £12.00. Puddings: £4.00 to £4.50*

Fullers ~ Managers Jason and Karen Tinklin ~ Real ale ~ Bar food (12-4, 5-9; 12-5 Sun; no food Sat) ~ Restaurant ~ (020) 7235 3019 ~ Children welcome ~ Dogs welcome ~ Open 11(12 Sat)-11; 12-10.30 Sun

Recommended by N R White, Tracey and Stephen Groves, the Didler, Sue Demont, Tim Barrow

EAST LONDON   MAP 12

Crown ♀

Grove Road/Old Ford Road; ✈ Mile End; E3 5SN

Civilised bar in smart dining pub with interesting food and a choice of moods in the upstairs dining rooms

This stylish dining pub has a relaxed and informal bar with contemporary furnishings, Adnams Best, Fullers London Pride and Sharps Doom Bar on handpump, and a good choice of wines by the glass. There are high bar stools covered with faux animal hides by the simple bar counter, two-person stools in the same material around chunky pine tables on the polished boards, candles in coloured glass holders, a big bay window with a comfortable built-in seated area with cushions in browns, pinks and greens, a brown leather sofa beside a couple of cream easy chairs, and a scattering of books and objects on open shelves. Upstairs, the three individually decorated dining areas – again, with simple, contemporary but stylish furniture on carpeted or wooden floors – overlook Victoria Park. More reports please.

🍴 Under the new licensee the good modern food might include soup, chicken liver salad with pancetta and raspberry vinegar, tomato tart with red pepper fondue and parmesan, cheese and bacon burger, roast pork fillet with smoked black pudding and horseradish mash, bass with risotto cake, baby pak choi and sweet chilli sauce, braised ox cheek with swede and cider jus, and sirloin steak with green peppercorn sauce. *Starters/Snacks: £4.50 to £6.50. Main Courses: £8.95 to £15.95. Puddings: £5.00*

Geronimo Inns ~ Lease Finlay MacLeod ~ Real ale ~ Bar food (12-3(5 Sat), 7-10; 12-9 Sun) ~ Restaurant ~ (020) 8880 7261 ~ Children allowed until 6pm ~ Dogs allowed in bar ~ Open 12-11(10.30 Sun)

Recommended by Simon Rodway

Grapes

Narrow Street; ✈ ≷ Limehouse (or Westferry on the Docklands Light Railway); the Limehouse link has made it hard to find by car – turn off Commercial Road at signs for Rotherhithe Tunnel, then from the Tunnel Approach slip road, fork left leading into Branch Road, turn left and then left again into Narrow Street; E14 8BP

Relaxed waterside pub, unchanged since Dickens knew it, with particularly appealing cosy back room, helpful friendly staff, well liked Sunday roasts, and good upstairs fish restaurant

In summer, the small balcony at the back of this 16th-c pub is a fine place for a sheltered waterside drink and steps lead down to the foreshore. Inside, it has bags of atmosphere, a good mix of customers and friendly service. The chatty, partly panelled bar has lots of prints, mainly of actors, and old local maps, as well as some elaborately etched windows, plates along a shelf, and newspapers to read; the cosy back part has a winter open fire. The pub remains almost exactly as Charles Dickens knew it – all the more remarkable considering the ultra-modern buildings that now surround it. Adnams Best, Marstons Pedigree, Timothy Taylors Landlord, and a guest like Black Sheep on handpump, several wines by the glass, and Addlestone's cider; board games. The upstairs fish restauarant is very popular, with fine views of the river. The pub was a favourite with Rex Whistler, who used it as the viewpoint for his rather special river paintings. No children, but they do have a bowl of water for dogs.

🍴 From the new kitchen, generous helpings of bar food include sandwiches, soup, a tankard of whitebait, sausage and mash with onion gravy, very good fish and chips, home-made fishcake with caper sauce, and puddings like apple crumble and bread and butter pudding; **Sunday roast is highly regarded (no other meals then).** *Starters/Snacks: £3.85 to £7.95. Main Courses: £7.50 to £17.95. Puddings: £3.60*

Free house ~ Licensee Barbara Haigh ~ Real ale ~ Bar food (12-2.30, 7-9.30; 12-3.30 Sun; not Sun evening) ~ Restaurant ~ (020) 7987 4396 ~ Dogs allowed in bar ~ Open 12-3.30, 5.30-11; 12-11 Sat; 12-10.30 Sun; closed 25-26 Dec, 1 Jan

Recommended by Mike Gorton, LM, Michael and Deborah Ethier, Peter, Donna and Roger, N R White, Clare Graham, John and Gloria Isaacs, Derek Thomas, Steve Kirby

Gun ⑪ ♈

27 Coldharbour; ✪ Blackwall on the DLR is probably closest, although the slightly longer walk from Canary Wharf has splendid Dockland views; E14 9NS

LONDON DINING PUB OF THE YEAR

Top-notch gastropub, pricey but worth it, great views from the riverside terrace, plenty of character and history, well chosen wines

'Magical' is the word some people have used to describe this busy riverside pub, slightly off the beaten path, but worth a special trip for the exquisite food. Lovingly restored by its owners after a fire destroyed much of the building that Nelson and Lady Hamilton knew (they often had their assignations upstairs), it's by no means a cheap place to eat, but on our visit the quality and service easily outclassed almost any gastropub we can think of, and there's plenty to appeal if all you want is a drink. The terrace in particular is a delight: long and narrow, with plenty of smart wooden tables, and uninterrupted views of the Dome across a broad sweep of the Thames. Heaters and huge umbrellas make it a fine spot whatever the weather. Unusually, the dining room takes up most of the characterful front bar, with smart white tablecloths and napkins on all but a handful of the tables; there's a warmly chatty feel nonetheless, as well as a couple of big framed naval prints on the white walls, piles of logs in two arched alcoves, candles, a smart oak bar counter, and perhaps an elaborate flower display on the window sill. Towards the terrace is a busy flagstoned bar for drinkers, with antique guns on the wall, and no tables except for a large barrel in the centre of the room. It shares a fireplace with a wonderfully cosy room next door, which has a couple of leather sofas and armchairs, a stuffed boar's head, some modern prints, well stocked bookshelves and views on to the terrace. Friendly uniformed staff serve three real ales such as Adnams, Fullers London Pride and Greene King Abbot, and a good choice of wines. In summer, they open up another terrace as an alfresco portuguese barbecue restaurant. They may occasionally close the pub on Saturdays for weddings.

⑪ The bar menu has snacks like welsh rarebit or sautéed chicken livers on toast, smoked haddock and salmon fishcake with poached egg and chive butter sauce, and ox cheeks with mashed potatoes and onion jus, while the fuller menu – making good use of fresh fish from Billingsgate – might include green pea and pig's cheek soup, seared yellow-fin tuna loin with avocado mousse, red onion and dandelion, pan-seared fillet of gilt-head bream with samphire and lemon thyme butter, roast organic salmon with crab dumplings, rump of herdwick mutton with faggots and spring beans, specials like bouillabaisse, excellent puddings such as lemon cheesecake with warm blackberry beignet or a delicious cold chocolate fondant, and a monthly changing choice of cheeses. *Starters/Snacks: £5.00 to £9.00. Main Courses: £12.00 to £21.00. Puddings: £5.00*

Punch ~ Lease Ed and Tom Martin ~ Real ale ~ Bar food (12-3(4 Sat), 6-10.30(9.30 Sun)) ~ Restaurant ~ (020) 7515 5222 ~ Children welcome ~ Open 11am-midnight(11pm Sun)

Recommended by Susan and John Douglas, Jamie May, N R White

A few pubs try to make you leave a credit card at the bar, as a sort of deposit if you order food. This is a bad practice, and the banks and credit card firms warn you not to let your card go like this.

Narrow 🍴 ♀

Narrow Street; ⊖ ⇌ Limehouse; E14 8DJ

Stylish and popular with interesting contemporary food, real ales, good wines by the glass, and seats outside on the waterside terrace; you need to book well ahead for a table

Given that the owner of this stylish place is Gordon Ramsay most people, therefore, do come here to eat. And there's no doubt that it is more of a restaurant/bar than a pub, but there is a bar area with a pubby feel which is simple and smart with white-painted walls and ceilings, and dark blue doors and woodwork. There are two mosaic-tiled fireplaces, each with a mirror above, a couple of hat stands, bar stools at the counter, and some colourfully striped armchairs; piped music. Adnams Bitter and Broadside and Caledonian Deuchars IPA on handpump, a good range of bottled beers, a fine wine list, and quite a choice of spirits and cocktails. The dining room is white too, with a glass skylight and big window, the floors are polished wood, and the furnishings simple, matching and dark; on the walls are maps and prints of the area, and a couple of oars. This room opens on to the sizeable terrace where there are plenty of riverside tables with views around a breezy bend of the Thames.

🍴 **The food is modern, brasserie-style fare rather than fine restaurant dining, and although there are a few bar snacks, the main menu is served only in the small, sunny dining room (with limited tables), and you may need to book up some time in advance. Excellent quality bar snacks include a mug of soup, ploughman's, country pâté with pickled red cabbage, pea and leek tart, bangers with colcannon and onion gravy, smoked salmon and haddock fishcake with horseradish cream, and puddings like chocolate and pecan brownie and banoffi pie. From the main menu there might be morecambe bay brown shrimps, hake and chips, slow-roasted pork belly, and lamb leg steak with portabello mushroom and anchovy butter.** *Starters/Snacks: £3.50 to £6.50. Main Courses: £10.50 to £16.50. Puddings: £5.00 to £5.50*

Free house ~ Licensee Marina Anderson ~ Real ale ~ Bar food (12-5, 6-10; all day weekends) ~ Restaurant ~ (020) 7592 7950 ~ Children in restaurant only ~ Open 11(12 Sat)-11(10.30 Sun)

Recommended by Tina and David Woods-Taylor, John Saville, Mike Gorton

Prospect of Whitby

Wapping Wall; ⊖ Wapping; E1W 3SH

Waterside pub with colourful history and good river views – welcoming to visitors and families

For a while, this ancient place (it claims to be the oldest pub on the Thames, dating back to 1543) was better known as the Devil's Tavern, thanks to its popularity with smugglers and other ne'er-do-wells. Pepys and Dickens both regularly popped in, Turner came for weeks at a time to study the scene, and in the 17th c the notorious Hanging Judge Jeffreys was able to combine two of his interests by enjoying a drink at the back while looking down over the grisly goings-on in Execution Dock. It's all very cheerful and friendly and loved by tourists. There are plenty of bare beams, bare boards, panelling and flagstones in the L-shaped bar (where the long pewter counter is over 400 years old), and, from tables in the waterfront courtyard, an unbeatable river view towards Docklands. Adnams Best, Courage Directors, Fullers London Pride, Greene King IPA, and John Smiths on handpump, lots of wines by the glass, and a dozen malt whiskies; very helpful, efficient staff.

🍴 **Bar food includes sandwiches, pies like chicken and pancetta or steak and kidney, fish and chips, burgers, and puddings such as chocolate fondant and treacle sponge pudding.** *Starters/Snacks: £2.95 to £4.95. Main Courses: £6.95 to £9.95. Puddings: £3.95*

Punch ~ Manager John Towler ~ Real ale ~ Bar food (12-9.45(9 Sun)) ~ (020) 7481 1095 ~ Children allowed until 5pm but must eat after then ~ Open 12-11(10.30 Sun)

Recommended by the Didler, Ross Balaam, Donna and Roger

NORTH LONDON   MAP 12

Bull & Last ⑩ ♀ ◀

Highgate Road; ⊖ Kentish Town – then a 20-minute walk; NW5 1QS;

Really distinctive food in bustling Highgate local; good range of drinks and friendly, chatty atmosphere

Thriving on our Monday night visit – when every one of the closely packed tables was full – this nicely refurbished cornerhouse stands out for its well sourced and well prepared food. The menus, though a little pricey, are full of imaginative and unusual touches: bar snacks, for example, include pig's ears for dogs. With a bustling, chatty feel (and a real mix of customers and age groups), the single room has big windows with blinds along the side overlooking the street, then at the far end a wooden wall has a brick fireplace, a faded map of London and a collection of tankards; the wooden planked ceiling has colonial-style fans. Above the bar are three stuffed bulls' heads, as well as a blackboard listing their suppliers, and there are a couple of stuffed pheasants beside the open kitchen. Friendly staff serve well kept beers such as Bath Golden Hare, Black Sheep and Greene King IPA; the good wine list includes several carefully selected ports and dessert wines by the glass. They do takeaway tubs of their home-made ice-cream, and can prepare picnic hampers to take to Hampstead Heath; you can get various coffees to take away too. There are some rather nice plants by the door, and hanging baskets above picnic-sets on the street.

🍴 Bar snacks include pasties, scotch eggs, oysters and artisan cheeses with pickled egg and oatcakes, while the main menu might take in rabbit brawn with cornichons and apple chutney, grilled sardines and salsa verde, a distinctive home-made charcuterie board (with duck prosciutto, chicken liver parfait, pork rillettes and breaded veal head), ox heart kebabs, pea gnocchi with cow curd and mint, pig cheek ravioli with sour apple, crispy ears, dandelion and caper salad, roasted cornish hake with courgette salad and marinated tomato, roast lamb rump with violetti aubergine, sweetbreads, peas and bacon, and puddings such as gooseberry fool and elderflower ice-cream, or french toast with prune and armagnac ice-cream. *Starters/Snacks: £6.00 to £9.00. Main Courses: £12.00 to £20.00. Puddings: £5.00 to £7.00*

Free house ~ Licensees Ollie Pudney and Freddie Fleming ~ Real ale ~ Bar food (12-3, 6.30-10; 12.30-4.30, 6.30-10(7-9.30 Sun) Sat) ~ Restaurant ~ (020) 7267 8955 ~ Children welcome ~ Dogs welcome ~ Open 11-11(10.30 Sun)

Recommended by Richard Greaves

Chapel ⑩ ♀

Chapel Street ⊖ Edgware Road; NW1 5DP

Very good food in bustling modern gastropub; it does get busy and sometimes noisy – all part of the atmosphere

There's a rather cosmopolitan atmosphere at this bustling gastropub – perhaps more relaxed and civilised at lunchtime, when it's a favourite with chic local office workers, and then altogether busier and louder in the evenings. The cream-painted rooms are light and spacious and dominated by the open kitchen, and the furnishings are smart but simple, with plenty of plain wooden tables around the bar, a couple of comfortable sofas at the lounge end and a big fireplace. You may have to wait for a table during busier periods. Adnams Best and Greene King IPA on handpump, a decent choice of wines by the glass, cappuccino and espresso, fresh orange juice, and a choice of tisanes such as peppermint or strawberry and vanilla. In the evening, trade is more evenly split between diners and drinkers, and the music is more noticeable then, especially at weekends. A real bonus is the sizeable back garden with picnic-sets and other seats on wooden decking under large heated umbrellas. More reports please.

🍴 As well as lunchtime open sandwiches, the interesting food includes a choice of antipasti, soup, moules marinière, lamb kofta with tzatziki and balsamic syrup, linguine with chilli, parsley, broccoli and parmesan, home-made burger with confit shallots and tartare sauce, chicken breast with parsnip mash and honey glazed vegetables, beef and ginger stir fry with noodles and sweet chilli sauce, salmon and salt cod fishcake with

lemon mayonnaise, and puddings like warm chocolate and almond tart and Baileys crème brûlée. *Starters/Snacks: £3.00 to £6.00. Main Courses: £7.50 to £16.00. Puddings: £3.00 to £5.00*

Punch ~ Lease Lakis Hondrogiannis ~ Real ale ~ Bar food (12-2.30, 7-10) ~ (020) 7402 9220 ~ Children welcome ~ Dogs welcome ~ Open 12-11(10.30 Sun); closed 25-26 Dec, Easter

Recommended by Sue Demont, Tim Barrow

Compton Arms £

Compton Avenue, off Canonbury Road; ⊖ ⇌ *Highbury & Islington; N1 2XD*

Tiny, well run pub with particularly good value food, and a very pleasant garden

An unexpected bonus here is the very pleasant back terrace, with tables among flowers under a big sycamore tree and a glass-covered, heated area. It's a tiny little place (once George Orwell's local) tucked away in a quiet mews and feels like a village local with a proper pubby atmosphere. The unpretentious low-ceilinged rooms are simply furnished with wooden settles and assorted stools and chairs, and there are local pictures on the walls; TV for sport (which is used quite a lot) and a Sunday evening quiz (donations to the Lifeboat Station at Waterloo Bridge). Greene King Abbot and IPA and a couple of changing guests on handpump, and a choice of malt whiskies; friendly service. The pub is deep in Arsenal country, so can get busy on match days.

🍴 **Decent, very good value bar food includes baguettes, filled baked potatoes, pasta of the day, ham and eggs, fish and chips, steak in ale pie, eight different types of sausage with mashed potato and home-made red onion gravy, liver and bacon, and popular daily specials; good Sunday roasts.** *Main Courses: £5.95 to £8.95*

Greene King ~ Tenants Scott Plomer and Eileen Shelock ~ Real ale ~ Bar food (12-2.30, 6-8.30; 12-4 weekends; not Mon) ~ (020) 7359 6883 ~ Children welcome away from main bar until 7pm ~ Dogs welcome ~ Open 12-11(10.30 Sun)

Recommended by Steve Kirby, Tim Maddison, Tracey and Stephen Groves, Mike and Eleanor Anderson

Drapers Arms

Far west end of Barnsbury Street; ⊖ ⇌ *Highbury & Islington; N1 1ER*

Under new owners and refurbished throughout, a good mix of drinkers and diners, thoughtful choice of beers, wines and imaginative modern food, and seats in the attractive back garden

Newly opened and freshly refurbished, this handsome Georgian townhouse is run by enthusiastic young owners who are keen that it remains a proper pub where customers can pop in for a drink and a chat with friends and family, have an easy meal or enjoy a celebration in the smart restaurant; to this effect, they don't take bookings downstairs or in the garden. The spreading bar has a mix of elegant dark wooden tables and dining chairs on the bare boards, a little corner where there's a sofa and some comfortable chairs, bar stools against the green-painted counter, Black Sheep, Harveys Best and Shepherd Neame Spitfire on handpump, and carefully chosen wines by the glass or carafe. Upstairs, the restaurant (where you can book a table in advance) has similar tables and chairs on the big black and white tiled floor. Several fireplaces throughout. The back terrace is most attractive with white or green benches and chairs around slate-topped tables (each set with a church candle), flagstones and large parasols.

🍴 **Good modern cooking might include sandwiches, ploughman's, soup, duck liver pâté with cornichons, cured sea trout with cucumber and dill, roast chicken with garlic mash, kedgeree, braised salt marsh lamb with aioli, quail with pearl barley, red onions and mint, diver-caught plaice with tomatoes and warm butter, whole crab with mayonnaise, and puddings like lardy cake with home-made crème fraîche and gooseberry and elderflower fool.** *Starters/Snacks: £2.50 to £6.00. Main Courses: £8.00 to £15.00. Puddings: £5.00 to £6.50*

Free house ~ Licensees Ben Maschler and Nick Gibson ~ Real ale ~ Bar food (12-2.30(4 weekends), 6-10.30(10 Sun)) ~ Restaurant ~ (020) 7619 0348 ~ Children welcome, but after 6pm must be seated and eating ~ Dogs allowed in bar ~ Open 11-11

Recommended by BOB

Duke of Cambridge ⓘ ♀ ◖

St Peters Street; ⊖ Angel, though 15 minutes' walk away; N1 8JT

Trail-blazing organic pub with carefully sourced, imaginative food, excellent range of drinks, and a nice, chatty atmosphere with the feel of a comfortably upmarket local

This was London's first organic pub and as much as possible is re-used and re-cycled. Even the real ales on handpump are organic: Pitfield East Kent Goldings, Eco Warrior and SB, and St Peters Best. They also have organic draught lagers and cider, organic spirits, a wide range of organic wines (many of which are available by the glass), quite a few teas and coffees, and a spicy ginger ale. The atmosphere is warmly inviting, and it's the kind of place that somehow encourages conversation, with a steady stream of civilised chat from the varied customers. The big, busy main room is simply decorated and furnished with lots of chunky wooden tables, pews and benches on bare boards, a couple of big metal vases with colourful flowers, and daily papers. A corridor leads off past a few tables and an open kitchen to a couple of smaller candlelit rooms, more formally set for eating, and a conservatory. It's worth arriving early to eat, as they can get very busy.

🍽 **Using top quality seasonal food from small producers, the good, interesting bar food might include soup, smoked sprats and salmon with beetroot, apple, watercress and horseradish, mussels in tomato, chorizo and ale sauce with garlic toast, beer-battered pollack with mushy peas and tartare sauce, asparagus and confit summer garlic risotto with ewe's cheese, game burger with red cabbage coleslaw, pickled cucumber and chips, chicken and mushroom pie, rabbit and red wine stew with bubble and squeak, and puddings like warm chocolate and nut brownie with coffee and rum ice-cream and rhubarb fool with coconut macaroon.** *Starters/Snacks: £4.00 to £11.00. Main Courses: £9.00 to £20.00. Puddings: £6.00 to £6.50*

Free house ~ Licensee Geetie Singh ~ Real ale ~ Bar food (12.30-3(3.30 weekends), 6.30-10.30(10 Sun)) ~ Restaurant ~ (020) 7359 3066 ~ Children welcome ~ Dogs allowed in bar ~ Open 12-11(10.30 Sun)

Recommended by John M Murphy, P Dawn, Tracey and Stephen Groves, Dr and Mrs M E Wilson

Flask ♀

Flask Walk; ⊖ Hampstead; NW3 1HE

Properly old-fashioned and villagey local, real ales, a fine choice of wines by the glass and pubby food

This is a peaceful old local and the bar – a popular haunt of Hampstead artists, actors and local characters – is unassuming, properly old-fashioned and rather villagey, with a nice old wooden counter and pubby tables and chairs. A unique Victorian screen divides this from the cosy lounge at the front with smart red plush banquettes curving round the panelled walls, and an attractive fireplace. There are some more old wooden tables and dining chairs on rugs or on the dark floorboards, lots of little prints on the walls, and quite a few wine and champagne bottles dotted about. Wells & Youngs Bitter, Special and Bombardier on handpump, around 30 wines by the glass and quite a few malt whiskies; piped music and TV. Outside in the alley, there are several seats and tables. The pub's name is a reminder of the days when it distributed mineral water from Hampstead's springs.

🍽 **Well liked bar food includes sandwiches, various sharing boards, summer salads, steak in ale pie, smoked haddock and salmon fishcakes with parsley and lemon butter, ham and free-range eggs, a pie of the day, good chicken breast with lemon and thyme on roasted butternut squash, asparagus and pea shoots, nice beer-battered haddock, and puddings like vanilla crème brûlée with marinated berries and chocolate cheesecake with orange sauce.** *Starters/Snacks: £4.50 to £6.50. Main Courses: £8.00 to £14.00. Puddings: £4.50*

Youngs ~ Manager Claudia McCarthy-Malcher ~ Real ale ~ Bar food (12-3, 6-10; all day weekends) ~ (020) 7435 4580 ~ Children welcome till 8pm in dining room ~ Dogs welcome ~ Open 11-11(midnight Fri and Sat); 12-10.30 Sun

Recommended by N R White, the Didler, Donna and Roger

Holly Bush ♀ ◀

Holly Mount; ⊖ Hampstead; NW3 6SG

Unique village local, with good food and drinks, and a lovely unspoilt feel

Now a free house, this timeless old favourite was originally a stable block and is tucked away among some of Hampstead's most villagey streets. The attractively old-fashioned front bar has a dark sagging ceiling, brown and cream panelled walls (decorated with old advertisements and a few hanging plates), open fires, bare boards, and cosy bays formed by partly glazed partitions. Slightly more intimate, the back room, named after the painter George Romney, has an embossed red ceiling, panelled and etched glass alcoves, and ochre-painted brick walls covered with small prints; lots of board and card games. Adnams Broadside, Harveys Best, Hook Norton Old Hooky, and a guest beer on handpump, as well as plenty of whiskies and a good wine list. The upstairs dining room has table service at the weekend, as does the rest of the pub on a Sunday. There are benches on the pavement outside.

🍴 **Usefully served all day at weekends, the bar food includes lunchtime sandwiches and ploughman's, soup, an omelette of the day, a choice of pies like beef in ale or chicken and wild mushroom, pork sausages with mustard mash and caramelised onion gravy, tomato tart with stuffed courgette flower and girolle cream, scottish salmon fillet with spinach and herb purée and shellfish sauce, and puddings such as dark chocolate slice with orange ice-cream and honeycomb and summer berry pudding with elderflower sorbet; Sunday roasts.** *Starters/Snacks: £2.50 to £7.50. Main Courses: £9.50 to £13.90. Puddings: £4.90*

Free house ~ Licensee Nicolai Outzen ~ Real ale ~ Bar food (12-4, 6-10; all day weekends) ~ Restaurant ~ (020) 7435 2892 ~ Children welcome if with parents in dining area ~ Dogs allowed in bar ~ Open 12-11(10.30 Sun)

Recommended by N R White, Tim Maddison, Pat and Tony Martin, Sue Demont, Tim Barrow, the Didler, Mike and Mary Clark, Steve Kirby

Marquess Tavern ♀

Canonbury Street/Marquess Road; ⊖ ⇄ Highbury & Islington; N1 2TB

New licensees for popular gastropub, imaginative cooking, good range of drinks, and the feel of a proper local in the front bar

New owners have taken over this imposing Victorian place – in a nice villagey corner of Islington – and plan to keep it as a cosy local where people can drop in for a drink and a chat as well as enjoy some good, modern cooking. The bar is reassuringly traditional and fairly plain, with bare boards and a mix of candlelit wooden tables arranged around a big, horseshoe servery; there's a fireplace either side, one topped by a very tall mirror, as well as an old leather sofa and faded old pictures. You can eat either in the bar or in the slightly more formal back dining room, feeling much brighter with its white paint and skylight; it has an impressive brass chandelier. Wells & Youngs IPA, Bitter and Bombardier on handpump, quite a few bottled beers, and around 50 malt whiskies; piped music. There are some peaceful picnic-sets in front. Note they don't open weekday lunchtimes.

🍴 **Carefully sourced produce goes into the modern cooking here: sandwiches, soup, rabbit and crayfish terrine with pea purée, beef in Guinness or lentil and wild mushroom pies, pork loin chop with celeriac mash, crackling and caramelised pear, brown trout and samphire with fennel sauce, venison wellington, and puddings like chilled plum soup with star anise, strawberries and cracked black pepper and rice pudding with stewed rhubarb; they also offer a very good value two- and three-course set menu (not weekends).** *Starters/Snacks: £4.50 to £6.50. Main Courses: £9.50 to £17.00. Puddings: £4.50 to £6.00*

Youngs ~ Manager Damien Geninazza ~ Real ale ~ Bar food (6-10; 12-5, 6-10(8.30 Sun) Sat) ~ Restaurant ~ (020) 7354 2975 ~ Children welcome until 8pm ~ Dogs allowed in bar ~ Open 5-11(4-midnight Fri); 12-12(10.30 Sun) Sat; closed weekday lunchtimes

Recommended by Steven Kirby

There are report forms at the back of the book.

Spaniards Inn 🍺

Spaniards Lane; ⊖ *Hampstead (but some distance away) or from Golders Green tube station take 220 bus; NW3 7JJ*

New licensee for busy old pub with lots of character and history, delightful big garden, and a wide range of drinks and good food

In fine weather, head for the big, rather charming garden behind this historic former toll house. It's nicely arranged in a series of areas separated by careful planting of shrubs, and there's a crazy-paved terrace with slatted wooden tables and chairs and a flagstoned walk around a small raised area with roses; a side arbour has wisteria, clematis and hops. As it's popular with families and those with dogs (they even have a dog wash) you may need to move fast to bag a table. There's an outside bar, regular summer barbecues, and an area for smokers. Dating back to 1585, the pub is well known for its tales of hauntings and highwaymen (some of which are best taken with a very large pinch of salt), and the low-ceilinged oak-panelled rooms are attractive and full of character, with open fires, genuinely antique winged settles, candle-shaped lamps in shades and snug little alcoves. There's an impressive range of drinks with half a dozen ales including Adnams Best, Fullers London Pride, Timothy Taylors Landlord and three guests on handpump, a couple of ciders, quite a few continental draught lagers and wines by the glass. The car park fills up fast and other parking nearby is difficult.

🍴 **Under the new licensee and served all day, the bar food includes lunchtime sandwiches and ploughman's, soup, fish and chips, a choice of three sausages, organic pies like chicken and mushroom, beef and stilton and goats cheese with roasted red pepper, moroccan chicken, barnsley chops, rib-eye steak, and puddings like chocolate sponge and apple crumble.** *Starters/Snacks: £5.50 to £5.90. Main Courses: £6.90 to £11.00. Puddings: £4.00*

Mitchells & Butlers ~ Manager Olivier Jolly ~ Real ale ~ Bar food (12-10) ~ (020) 8731 8406 ~ Children welcome ~ Dogs welcome ~ Open 12(11 weekends)-11

Recommended by N R White, John Wooll, Jo Lilley, Simon Calvert

SOUTH LONDON   TQ4963   MAP 12

Bo-Peep

Chelsfield; 1.7 miles from M25 junction 4; Hewitts Road, which is last road off exit roundabout; BR6 7QL

Useful M25, country-feeling meal-stop

Said to date from the 16th c, the main bar at this village pub has very low old beams and an enormous inglenook. Prettily candlelit at night, two cosy little rooms for eating open off, one with smart cushions and a wooden floor, and there's a light side room looking over the country lane. Adnams, Courage Best and Harveys Sussex on handpump; efficient service from cheery, helpful staff, and look out for Milo, the licensees' miniature english bull terrier; piped easy listening. A big terrace behind has lots of picnic-sets; more reports please.

🍴 **As well as ploughman's and sandwiches, other reliable home-made dishes might include grilled sardines, sausage and mash, spinach, pea and mushroom risotto, fish and chips, steak and ale pudding, sausage and mash in giant yorkshire pudding, and rib-eye steak.** *Starters/Snacks: £4.95 to £5.95. Main Courses: £7.95 to £15.95. Puddings: £4.25*

Enterprise ~ Lease Kate Mansfield, Graham Buckley ~ Real ale ~ Bar food (12-9.30(5.30 Sun); not Sun evening) ~ Restaurant ~ (01959) 534457 ~ Children welcome ~ Open 11-11; 12-10.30 Sun

Recommended by BOB

> Half pints: by law, a pub should not charge more for half a pint than half the price of a full pint, unless it shows that half-pint price on its price list.

Crown & Greyhound ♀

Dulwich Village; ⇌ North Dulwich; SE21 7BJ

Comfortable Victorian pub with big back garden, good beers and popular Sunday carvery

Worth a look for its Victorian interior and traditional atmosphere, this lively pub is known locally as the Dog. It was built at the turn of the last century to replace two inns that had stood here previously, hence the unusual name. The spacious interior (which readers suggest could do with a good dusting) has some quite ornate plasterwork and lamps over on the right, and a variety of nicely distinct seating areas, some with traditional upholstered and panelled settles, others with stripped kitchen tables on stripped boards; there's a coal-effect gas fire and some old prints; piped music and board games. Adnams Broadside, Fullers London Pride, Harveys and a guest such as Sambrooks Wandle are on handpump alongside a good range of draught lagers and ciders, and just under two dozen wines by the glass. They hold an Easter beer festival and a summer cider, festival. Busy in the evenings, but quieter during the day. It's handy for walks through the park and Dulwich Picture Gallery and boasts a very pleasant back garden, with tables shaded by a chestnut tree; barbecues on summer weekends, and a fence has murals painted by local schoolchildren. A big back dining room and conservatory open on to here, leading from the pleasantly furnished roomy main bar at the front.

🍴 **Bar food might include sandwiches, calamari with lime mayonnaise, lamb kofta, nachos, sausage and mash, ploughman's, home-made burger, beef bourguignon pie, steaks, and puddings such as chocolate brownie with vanilla pod ice-cream and baked vanilla cheesecake with red berry compote. It's best to arrive early for the popular Sunday carvery as they don't take bookings.** *Starters/Snacks: £3.80 to £5.00. Main Courses: £5.95 to £9.95. Puddings: £3.50 to £4.95*

Mitchells & Butlers ~ Manager Mike Earp ~ Real ale ~ Bar food (12-10(11 Fri, Sat, 9.30 Sun)) ~ Restaurant (evenings only) ~ (020) 8299 4976 ~ Children in restaurant ~ Dogs allowed in bar ~ Open 11-11(12 Thurs-Sat, 10.30 Sun)

Recommended by Giles and Annie Francis, Jim and Frances Gowers

Cutty Sark

Ballast Quay, off Lassell Street; ⇌ Maze Hill, from London Bridge; or from the river front, walk past the Yacht in Crane Street and Trinity Hospital; SE10 9PD

Interesting old tavern with genuinely unspoilt bar, great Thames views, organic wines, and a wide range of fairly straightforward but popular food

Reached by a winding central staircase, the upstairs room at this enjoyable white-painted Thames-side pub feels just like a ship's deck. The prize seat in a big bow window that juts out over the pavement has splendid views of the river and O2 Arena. Alive with young people on Friday and Saturday evenings and at the weekends, but surprisingly quiet some weekday lunchtimes, the dark flagstoned bar has a genuinely old-fashioned feel, with rough brick walls, wooden settles, barrel tables, open fires, low lighting and narrow openings to tiny side snugs. Five real ales are likely to include Fullers London Pride, Adnams Broadside, Greene King Abbot and St Austell Tribute, with a good choice of malt whiskies and a range of organic wines; piped music. There's a busy riverside terrace across the narrow cobbled lane; morris dancers occasionally drop by. Parking is limited nearby – though, unusually for London, if you can bag a space it's free.

🍴 **Tasty traditional food includes sandwiches, prawn cocktail, whitebait, ploughman's, chicken caesar salad, sausage and mash, steak and ale pie, good fish and chips, vegetable wellington, scampi, knickerbocker glory and chocolate fudge cake.** *Starters/Snacks: £4.50 to £5.00. Main Courses: £8.95 to £12.95. Puddings: £4.95*

Free house ~ Licensee Stewart Turdy ~ Real ale ~ Bar food (12-9(10 Sat)) ~ (020) 8858 3146 ~ Children welcome ~ Dogs welcome ~ Open 11-11(12-10.30 Sun)

Recommended by Mrs Margo Finlay, Jörg Kasprowski, N R White, Ian Phillips, Ross Balaam, the Didler, Robert Gomme, Susan and John Douglas, Nick Patton

Fire Station ♀

Waterloo Road; ❸ Waterloo, Southwark ⇌ Waterloo East; SE1 8SB

Unusual conversion of former fire station, with lively after-work atmosphere (it does get crowded then), and good food all day

Handy for the Old Vic and Waterloo Station, this busy conversion of the former LCC central fire station always seems to be packed – some readers have found its loud acoustics overpower conversation. The bar is two huge knocked-through tiled rooms (a little like an old-fashioned public bath), with lots of wooden tables and a mix of chairs, a couple of pews and worn leather armchairs, some sizeable plants, and distinctive box-shaped floral lampshades hanging from the high ceilings; the back wall has three back-lit mirrored panels, and, as a token to its former life, some red fire buckets on a shelf. The back dining room has smarter chairs and tables. Fullers London Pride, Marstons Pedigree and a guest such as Brakspear are on handpump, they've an excellent choice of wines, and a good range of spirits and cocktails. There are tables in front and picnic-sets in a scruffy side alley.

🍴 They do breakfasts from 9am, then have a pubby all-day menu with sandwiches, **charcuterie and nachos for two, beef or falafel burger, crab, herb and chilli linguine, fish and chips with mushy peas, pie of the day, chicken caesar salad, wild boar sausages, lamb shank with pea and lemon couscous, chocolate brownie with pistachio ice-cream and baked vanilla cheesecake with lemon cream, and there's a more elaborate restaurant menu.** *Starters/Snacks: £4.00 to £10.00. Main Courses: £6.50 to £12.00. Puddings: £4.50 to £5.50*

Marstons ~ Manager Tom Alabaster ~ Real ale ~ Bar food (9-11; 11-10.30 Mon, Sun) ~ Restaurant ~ (020) 7620 2226 ~ Children welcome till 6pm ~ Open 9-midnight

Recommended by Ian Phillips, Michael and Alison Sandy, Simon Collett-Jones, Dr Ron Cox, Peter Dandy, Jane Taylor, David Dutton

Founders Arms ♀

Hopton Street (Bankside); ❸ St Paul's (and cross the Millennium Bridge), Southwark ⇌ Blackfriars, and cross Blackfriars Bridge; SE1 9JH

Superb location, with outstanding terrace views along the Thames, and handy for south bank attractions; decent efficiently served food

Not the most attractive of buildings, this big modern pub is in a prime embankment spot with views from the conservatory-feeling interior and slightly raised terrace out across the Thames. Taking in St Paul's, the Millennium Bridge, and even the Tower of London way off in the distance, it's probably the best view you'll find at any pub along the river, particularly in the City; the menu provides a useful map of the buildings you can see. It's a busy place, popular with city types, tourists, theatre and gallery goers, who in summer spill on to the nearby pavement and walls. Charles Wells Bombardier, Wells & Youngs Bitter, Special and and maybe a guest such as Caledonian Deuchars IPA are served from the modern bar counter angling along one side, and you can have most of the wines on their list by the glass. Efficient, cheerful service; piped music.

🍴 Available all day (starting at 9am for breakfast at the weekend) and served without **fuss or too much waiting around, the very useful menu might include sandwiches, ciabattas, moules and frites, charcuterie, fish and cheeseboards to share, warm goats cheese salad, beer-battered fish, slow-roast pork belly, beef, mushroom and ale pie and baked sweet potato topped with vegetable and bean chilli.** *Starters/Snacks: £4.75 to £6.25. Main Courses: £8.95 to £12.95*

Youngs ~ Manager Paul Raynor ~ Real ale ~ Bar food (12-10) ~ (020) 7928 1899 ~ Children welcome ~ Open 10(9 Sat, Sun)-11(12 Fri, Sat)

Recommended by Val and Alan Green, Meg and Colin Hamilton, Dr and Mrs M E Wilson, N R White, Dr and Mrs A K Clarke, Howard and Margaret Buchanan, Tracey and Stephen Groves, John Saville, the Didler, Mike and Sue Loseby, Ian Phillips, Michael Doswell, Chris and Angela Buckell

---

If we know a pub has an outdoor play area for children, we mention it.

Fox & Hounds 🍴 ☐

Latchmere Road; ⇌ Clapham Junction; SW11 2JU

Victorian local standing out for its excellent mediterranean cooking; mostly evenings only, but some lunchtimes too

Fairly unremarkable in appearance, this big Victorian local, serving good mediterranean food (evenings only) can fill quickly, so you may have to move fast to grab a table, though it's still very much the kind of place where locals happily come to drink. The spacious, straightforward bar has bare boards, mismatched tables and chairs, two narrow pillars supporting the dark red ceiling, photographs on the walls, and big windows overlooking the street (the view partially obscured by colourful window boxes). There are fresh flowers and daily papers on the bar, and a view of the kitchen behind. Two rooms lead off, one more cosy with its two red leatherette sofas. Fullers London Pride, Harveys and a guest such as Caledonian Deuchars IPA are on handpump and the carefully chosen wine list (which includes over a dozen by the glass) is written out on a blackboard; the varied piped music fits in rather well; TV. The garden has big parasols and heaters for winter; more reports please.

🍴 Changing every day, a typical choice might include tomato and paprika soup with goats cheese, caesar salad, bruschetta, beef ravioli with parmesan and sage butter, mushroom risotto with thyme, parmesan and spring onion salad, grilled tuna with niçoise salad, grilled italian sausages with red onion jam, grilled rib-eye with salsa verde, and puddings such as dark chocolate and almond cake with butterscotch ice-cream and apple and blackberry crumble with strawberry ice-cream. *Starters/Snacks: £5.00 to £8.00. Main Courses: £8.00 to £15.50. Puddings: £4.50 to £5.50*

Free house ~ Licensees Richard and George Manners ~ Real ale ~ Bar food (12-4 Sat, 6-10 Mon-Sat, 12-10 Sun; not Mon-Fri lunchtimes) ~ (020) 7924 5483 ~ Children welcome till 7pm ~ Dogs welcome ~ Open 12-3, 5-11; 12-11(10.30 Sun) Fri, Sat; closed Mon lunchtime

Recommended by BOB

George ★

Off 77 Borough High Street; ⊖ ⇌ Borough, London Bridge; SE1 1NH

Beautifully preserved 16th-c coaching inn, with lots of tables in bustling courtyard to take in the galleried exterior

Mentioned in *Little Dorrit* and perhaps the country's best example of a historic coaching inn, this splendidly preserved building is well known (and can attract lots of tourists) for its stunning tiers of outside open galleries. Tables in the cobbled courtyard give you plenty of time to take it all in. Owned by the National Trust, the building dates from the 16th c, but was rebuilt to the original plan after the great Southwark fire of 1676. What survives today is only a third of the original building; it was 'mercilessly reduced', as E V Lucas put it, during the period when it was owned by the Great Northern Railway Company. Unless you know where you're going you may well miss it, as apart from the great gates and sign there's little to indicate that such a gem still exists behind the less auspicious-looking buildings on the busy high street. The row of no-frills ground-floor rooms and bars all have square-latticed windows, black beams, bare floorboards, some panelling, plain oak or elm tables and old-fashioned built-in settles, along with a 1797 'Act of Parliament' clock, dimpled glass lantern-lamps, and so forth. The best seats indoors are in a snug room nearest the street, where there's an ancient beer engine that looks like a cash register. An impressive central staircase goes up to a series of dining rooms and to a gaslit balcony. In summer they open a bar with direct service into the courtyard (when it's busy it may be quicker to order your drinks inside) and though staff cope well with the crowds, for some readers it can have the same impersonal feel as other National Trust pubs. Greene King Abbot, IPA, Old Speckled Hen and a beer brewed by them are on handpump; mulled wine in winter, tea and coffee; darts, trivia games machine.

🍴 Good value lunchtime bar food includes doorstop sandwiches and wraps, filled baked potatoes, ham, egg and chips, scampi, sausage and mash, fish and chips, and puddings like black forest gateau or apple crumble; they do a Sunday carvery. In the evening you

can only eat in the balcony restaurant. *Starters/Snacks: £2.95 to £4.25. Main Courses: £5.45 to £8.95. Puddings: £3.75 to £4.50*

Greene King ~ Manager Scott Masterson ~ Real ale ~ Bar food (12-9.30; not Sun evening) ~ Restaurant (5-10 (not Sun)) ~ (020) 7407 2056 ~ Children welcome away from bar ~ Open 11-11; 12-10.30 Sun

Recommended by Dr and Mrs A K Clarke, the Didler, Darren Le Poidevin, Ian and Nita Cooper, N R White, Mike and Sue Loseby, Howard and Margaret Buchanan, Ian Phillips, Susan and John Douglas

Greenwich Union ◀
Royal Hill; ⊖ ⇌ Greenwich; SE10 8RT

Enterprising pub with distinctive beers from small local Meantime Brewery, plus other unusual drinks, and good, popular food

This nicely renovated friendly pub is the tap for the small Meantime Brewery in nearby Charlton, and is the only place with all their distinctive unpasteurised beers on draught. The range includes a traditional pale ale (served cool, under pressure) a mix of proper pilsners, lagers and wheat beers, one a deliciously refreshing raspberry flavour, and a stout. The helpful, knowledgeable staff will generally offer small tasters to help you choose. They also have Adnams on handpump, and a draught cider, as well as a helpfully annotated list of unusual bottled beers including some of their own. The rest of the drinks can be unfamiliar too, as they try to avoid the more common brands. Perhaps feeling a little more like a bar than a pub, the long, narrow stone-flagged room has several different parts: a simple area at the front with a few wooden chairs and tables, a stove and newspapers, then, past the counter with its headings recalling the branding of the brewery's first beers, several brown leather cushioned pews and armchairs under framed editions of *Picture Post* on the yellow walls; piped music, TV. Beyond here a much lighter, more modern-feeling conservatory has comfortable brown leather wall benches, a few original pictures and paintings, and white fairy lights under the glass roof; it leads out to an appealing back patio with green picnic-sets and a couple of old-fashioned lamp posts. The fence at the end is painted to resemble a poppy field, and the one at the side a wheat field. Though there are plenty of tables out here, it can get busy in summer (as can the whole pub on weekday evenings). In front are a couple of tables overlooking the street. The pub is slightly removed from Greenwich's many attractions and there's a particularly good traditional cheese shop as you walk towards the pub.

🍴 **Good popular food is on a seasonally changing menu that might include lunchtime sandwiches, a risotto, crumbed cod fillet with minted pea purée, smoked eel with salsa verde and soft boiled eggs, poached haddock, fish and chips, slow-cooked pork belly with carrot purée and braised lentils, rib-eye steak, and puddings such as vanilla panna cotta with champagne-poached rhubarb and apple sorbet and chocolate and walnut brownies with white chocolate ice-cream. They do brunch on Saturdays, and a choice of roasts on Sunday.** *Starters/Snacks: £2.90 to £6.90. Main Courses: £7.90 to £14.95. Puddings: £3.90 to £4.90*

Free house ~ Licensee Andrew Ward ~ Real ale ~ Bar food (12-4, 5.30-10; 12-10(9 Sun) Sat) ~ (020) 8692 6258 ~ Children welcome ~ Dogs welcome ~ Open 12-11; 11-11 Sat; 11.30-10.30 Sun

Recommended by the Didler, Nick Patton, Michael and Deborah Ethier, N R White

Market Porter ◀
Stoney Street; ⊖ ⇌ Borough, London Bridge; SE1 9AA

Up to ten unusual real ales in a very popular, properly pubby place opening at 6am for workers at the neighbouring market

With usually about ten on offer, they get through around 60 different guest beers a week at this no-frills down-to-earth pub. Very well kept alongside Harveys, they are sourced from all sorts of often far-flung brewers – to name but a few, Beowulf, Cotleigh, Elland, Hop Back, Oakham and RCH. During the week, workers and porters from Borough Market come here for a very early breakfast; it then tends to be quieter in the afternoons, getting crowded and noisy with good-natured chatter at the end of the working day. Service is particularly helpful and friendly at all times. The main part of the bar is pretty manly and straightforward (making one reader nostalgic for the sort of pubs he used to know in London) with rough wooden ceiling beams with beer barrels balanced on them, a heavy wooden counter with a beamed gantry, cushioned bar stools, an open fire, and 1920s-style wall lamps – it gets more old-fashioned the further you venture in; piped music.

🍴 **Usually served in the upstairs restaurant (with views of the market), well liked sensibly priced lunchtime bar food includes sandwiches, panini, burger and skin-on fries, chilli, scampi, cod and chips and sirloin steak; good Sunday roasts.** *Starters/Snacks: £3.95 to £7.95. Main Courses: £6.95 to £10.95. Puddings: £3.95*

Free house ~ Licensee Sarah Nixon ~ Real ale ~ Bar food (6am-9am, then 12-3(4 Fri-Sun)) ~ Restaurant ~ (020) 7407 2495 ~ Children Sat, Sun only ~ Dogs welcome ~ Open 6-9am weekdays, then 11-11; 12-11 Sat; 12-10.30 Sun

Recommended by John Saville, Ian Phillips, E McCall, T McLean, D Irving, N R White, Joe Green, the Didler, Mike and Sue Loseby, P Dawn, Phil Bryant, Bruce Bird, Steve Kirby, Sue Demont, Tim Barrow, Mike Gorton

Old Jail

Jail Lane, Biggin Hill (first turn E off A233 S of airport and industrial estate, towards Berry's Hill and Cudham); no station nearby; TN16 3AX

Popular country pub close to the city, with big family garden and RAF memorabilia in traditional bars

Just ten minutes or so from busy Croydon and Bromley this good all-rounder is on a narrow leafy lane and has the feel of a proper country pub. Its lovely big garden with well spaced picnic-sets on the grass, several substantial trees and nicely maintained play area means it's popular with families, especially at weekends, when it can get very busy. At these times they might limit food to the snack menu, so to be sure you get the full choice it's best to book. Several traditional beamed and low-ceilinged rooms ramble around a central servery, the nicest parts being the two cosy little areas to the right of the front entrance; divided by dark timbers, one has a very big inglenook fireplace with lots of logs and brasses, and the other has a cabinet of Battle of Britain plates – a reference perhaps to the pub's popularity with RAF pilots based at nearby Biggin Hill. Other parts have wartime prints and plates too, especially around the edge of the dining room, up a step beyond a second, smaller fireplace. There's also a plainer, flagstoned room; discreet piped music. Fullers London Pride, Harveys and Shepherd Neame Spitfire on handpump; friendly, efficient service. With nice hanging baskets in front, the attractive building wasn't itself part of any jail, but was a beef shop until becoming a pub in 1869. More reports please.

🍴 **There's a standard menu with things like good value sandwiches, baked potatoes and ploughman's, but the food to go for is the wide choice of good, blackboard specials, which might include local sausages with mash and red onion gravy, chicken tarragon with bacon and onion potato cake, slow-cooked beef with new potatoes and swede mash, pork belly with black pudding and red wine jus, rib-eye steak, and puddings such as white chocolate raspberry cheesecake and Baileys crème brûlée; they do a choice of roasts on Sundays.** *Starters/Snacks: £4.25 to £5.50. Main Courses: £7.95 to £16.95. Puddings: £1.95 to £4.95*

Punch ~ Lease Richard Hards ~ Real ale ~ Bar food (12-2.30(3 Sat), 7-9(9.30 Sat); not Sun evening or bank hols) ~ (01959) 572979 ~ Children welcome ~ Dogs welcome ~ Open 11.30-3, 6-11.30; 11.30-11 Fri; 12-11 Sat; 12-10.30 Sun

Recommended by Rob Liddiard, Chris Pluthero, LM

Royal Oak 🍺

Tabard Street/Nebraska Street; ⊖ ⇌ Borough, London Bridge; SE1 4JU

Old-fashioned Harveys corner house, with all their beers excellently kept; good, honest food too

Slightly off the beaten track, in rather unprepossessing surroundings, this very enjoyable old-fashioned corner house is the only London pub belonging to Sussex brewer Harveys – needless to say they stock the full range. The brewery transformed the pub when they took over, and painstakingly re-created the look and feel of a traditional London alehouse – you'd never imagine it wasn't like this all along. Filled with the noisy sounds of happy chat, two busy little L-shaped rooms meander around the central wooden servery, which has a fine old clock in the middle. They're done out in a cosy, traditional style with patterned rugs on the wooden floors, plates running along a delft shelf, black and white scenes or period sheet music on the red-painted walls, and an assortment of wooden tables and chairs; disabled ramp available on the Nebraska Street entrance.

🍴 **Well liked by readers, honest good value bar food includes impressive doorstep sandwiches, and generously served daily specials like fillets of sea bass, or pies such as vegetable and stilton, lamb and apricot, or game and steak and kidney pudding; Sunday roasts.** *Starters/Snacks: £4.50. Main Courses: £7.25. Puddings: £4.25*

Harveys ~ Tenants John Porteous, Frank Taylor ~ Real ale ~ Bar food (12-2.45, 5-9.15; 12-4.45 Sun) ~ (020) 7357 7173 ~ Children welcome ~ Dogs welcome ~ Open 11(12 Sat)-11; 12-6 Sun; closed Sun evening

Recommended by Brian and Rosalie Laverick, Andrew Bosi, Sue Demont, Tim Barrow, the Didler, Mike and Sue Loseby, Simon and Mandy King, N R White, Darren Le Poidevin

Telegraph 🍺

Telegraph Road; ⇌ Putney ⊖ East Putney, Southfields but quite a walk; SW15 3TU

A good summer pub, with plenty of outdoor seats and a very un-London feel; nicely reworked inside too, with an excellent choice of beers, reliable food, and good live blues on Fridays

---

They like to call this 'a country pub in London', and walking past the cricket played on the heath nearby, or sitting at one of the many tables on the grass in front, it seems no idle boast: though just a few minutes up the road, the city seems a world away. It's the outdoor space that for most visitors is the main draw, and on fine weekends it can get very busy indeed out here, with families and dogs a big part of the mix. Some tables are nicely sheltered under big trees (the pergola is slightly less effective), and there are a couple of quirky cow-print sofas under a little verandah by the entrance. The two rooms inside have been attractively modernised in recent years; both have plenty of comfortable leather armchairs and sofas, and lots of framed period prints and advertisements. The long main bar on the left also has quite a variety of wooden furnishings, including some unusually high tables and stools, and a rather grand dining table at one end; there's a TV for sport, rugs on the polished wooden floor, and an appealing little alcove rather like a private lounge, with a fireplace and a table of newspapers; piped music and board games. You'll generally find some notable guests among the six regularly changing real ales; on our visit the choice included two from the Twickenham Brewery, as well as Adnams Broadside, St Austell Tribute and Timothy Taylors Landlord. There's a good wine list too. On Friday nights they have a blues bar of some renown, featuring international artists specialising in vintage acoustic blues. The pub is named after the Admiralty telegraph station that used to stand nearby, one of a chain of ten between Chelsea and Portsmouth (on a clear day, a message could be sent between the two in 15 minutes).

🍴 **As well as a sandwich menu, sharing platter and grill menu, good quality and generously served bar food might include chicken caesar salad, cumberland sausage with cheddar mash and gravy, fish and chips, steaks, Sunday roasts, daily specials such as provençale-style rabbit stew or oven-baked mackerel with pesto, risotto and olive oil, and puddings like bakewell tart.** *Starters/Snacks: £4.25 to £6.95. Main Courses: £8.95 to £13.95. Puddings: £5.25*

Free house ~ Licensee Nick Stafford ~ Real ale ~ Bar food (12-9.30(10 Fri, Sat; 9 Sun)) ~ (020) 8788 2011 ~ Children welcome ~ Dogs welcome ~ Live blues Fri evening ~ Open 12-11; 11-12 Fri, Sat

Recommended by LM, Michael Dandy, John Styles, Shanonne Parsons, Charles and Christina McComb, Harry Hersom, Colin McKerrow, Peter Dandy

---

For those of you who use Sat-Nav devices, we include a postcode for every entry in the *Guide*.

Victoria ♀ 🛏

West Temple Sheen; ⇌ Mortlake; SW14 7RT

Contemporary styling with emphasis on conservatory restaurant; children's play area, comfortable bedrooms

Just a short stroll from Richmond Park's Sheen Gate, there is a particularly nice garden with wooden tables and benches on terracing and a sheltered play area behind this recently renovated dining pub. Not that big, the bar has wooden floors, armchairs and a fireplace, and leads into a huge dining conservatory at the back which is especially lovely in the evening. Fullers London Pride and Timothy Taylors Landlord are on handpump alongside a thoughtfully put-together wine list and a good range of whiskies; piped music, board games.

🍴 Breakfast is served first thing, then later on the menu (not cheap) might include half a pint of prawns, oysters, chicken and bacon sandwich, butternut chowder, sausage and mash with onion gravy, chicken and mushroom linguine, risotto prima vera, steamed bream with pasta, clams and braised fennel and well hung rib-eye steak; also puddings such as chocolate and peanut cookies with white chocolate sauce and peanut butter ice-cream and baked lemon ricotta cake with raspberries. Products are sourced with care.
Starters/Snacks: £5.00 to £10.50. Main Courses: £7.75 to £17.50. Puddings: £5.00 to £6.50

Enterprise ~ Lease Greg Bellamy ~ Real ale ~ Bar food (8.30am-11am, then midday-10pm Mon-Fri; 8.30am-10pm Sat; 12-8 Sun) ~ Restaurant ~ (020) 8876 4238 ~ Children welcome ~ Dogs allowed in bar ~ Live entertainment fortnightly ~ Open 8.30-11; 12-10.30 Sun ~ Bedrooms: £105S/£115S

Recommended by Noel Ferrin

White Cross ♀

Water Lane; ⊖ ⇌ Richmond; TW9 1TH

Thames-side pub with paved waterside area; busy in fine weather, but comfortable in winter too – watch out for the tides

Superbly set by the river, the very pleasant paved garden in front of this place enjoys terrific river views. It gets quite busy out here in summer, when it can even feel rather like a cosmopolitan seaside resort, and there's an outside bar to make the most of the sunshine (they may use plastic glasses for outside drinking). Boats leave from immediately outside for Kingston and Hampton Court, and it's not unknown for the water to reach right up the steps into the bar and cut off the towpath at the front – if you're leaving your car by the river, check tide times so as not to return to find it marooned in a rapidly swelling pool of water. Inside, the two chatty main rooms have something of the air of the hotel this once was, with local prints and photographs, an old-fashioned wooden island servery, and a good mix of variously aged customers. Two of the three log fires have mirrors above them – unusually, the third is below a window. A bright and airy upstairs room has lots more tables, and a pretty cast-iron balcony opening off, with a splendid view down to the water; piped music in some areas. Wells & Youngs Bitter, Special Bombardier and Waggle Dance and a guest such as Caledonian Deuchars IPA are on handpump, with a dozen or so carefully chosen wines by the glass; welcoming service.

🍴 Served all day from a food counter (thus eliminating a wait even when it's busy) bar food includes sandwiches, wraps and baked potatoes, salads, sharing plates, sausage and mash, pie of the day, rump steak, and (in summer) scones and clotted cream.
Starters/Snacks: £4.25 to £8.95. Main Courses: £7.85 to £12.95. Puddings: £4.25

Youngs ~ Manager Alex Gibson ~ Real ale ~ Bar food (12-9.30(8 Sun)) ~ (020) 8940 6844 ~ Children welcome in upstairs room till 6pm ~ Dogs welcome ~ Open 11-11; 12-10.30 Sun

Recommended by N R White, the Didler, Tracey and Stephen Groves, Bruce Bird, Peter Dandy, Michael Dandy, Michael Butler

WEST LONDON
MAP 13

Anglesea Arms ♀ 🍺
Selwood Terrace; ⊖ South Kensington; SW7 3QG

Busy Victorian pub with good range of beers, enjoyably chatty atmosphere in the evenings (when it can get packed)

At quiet times, the characterful bar at this often bustling pub can have an air of faded late-Victorian grandeur with its heavy portraits, large brass chandeliers, panelling, dark painted ceilings and big windows with swagged curtains. It has a mix of cast-iron tables on the bare wood-strip floor and at one end several booths with partly glazed screens have worn leather pews and spindleback chairs. On particularly busy days you'll need to move fast to grab a seat, but most people seem happy leaning on the central elbow tables. A good choice of half a dozen real ales takes in Adnams Bitter and Broadside, Brakspears, Fullers London Pride, Sambrooks Wandle and a guest such as Sharps Doom Bar; also a few bottled belgian beers, around 15 whiskies, and a varied wine list of about 20 wines with everything available by the glass. Down some steps, a clubby feeling dining room has a fireplace and table service – and generally a bit more space if you're eating; service is friendly and helpful. In summer the place to be is the leafy front terrace, with outside heaters for chillier evenings; TV.

🍴 **Changing every day, the menu might include ciabatta with chips, watercress soup, ham hock and parsley terrine, langoustines, linguine with crab, chilli, parsley and garlic, home-made pies, lamb apple and mint burger, battered whiting and chips, sausage and mash with onion gravy and crisp sage, oriental duck salad, sirloin steak, and puddings such as lemon tart with raspberries and warm chocolate fondant.** *Starters/Snacks: £2.95 to £14.75. Main Courses: £9.50 to £15.95. Puddings: £3.50 to £4.75*

Free house ~ Licensee Emma Whittingham ~ Real ale ~ Bar food (12-3, 6.30-10; 12-5, 6-10(9.30 Sun) Sat) ~ Restaurant ~ (020) 7373 7960 ~ Children welcome ~ Dogs allowed in bar ~ Open 11-11; 12-10.30 Sun

Recommended by Sue Demont, Tim Barrow, the Didler, N R White, Barry and Anne, John and Jill Perkins, Susan and John Douglas, Tracey and Stephen Groves, P Dawn

Atlas 🍴 ♀
Seagrave Road; ⊖ West Brompton; SW6 1RX

Highly prized evening tables for very popular, consistently excellent, mediterranean cooking; handy for Earls Court

The constantly changing choice of very good interesting food here means tables are highly prized, so do arrive early. The long, simple knocked-together bar has been well renovated without removing the original features; there's plenty of panelling and dark wooden wall benches, a couple of brick fireplaces, a mix of school chairs and well spaced tables. Well kept Caledonian Deuchars IPA, Fullers London Pride, Timothy Taylors Landlord and a guest such as Twickenham Naked Ladies are on handpump, and they've a very good, carefully chosen wine list, with plenty by the glass; big mugs of coffee; friendly service. The piped music covers a real cross section – on various visits we've come across everything from salsa and jazz to vintage TV themes; it can be loud at times, and with all the chat too, this isn't the place to come for a quiet dinner. Down at the end, by a hatch to the kitchen, is a TV (though big sports events are shown in a room upstairs); board games. Outside is an attractively planted narrow side terrace, with an overhead awning; heaters make it comfortable even in winter. Some readers have told us that they may ask to keep your credit card if you run a tab.

🍴 **The strongly mediterranean menu changes twice a day but might include things like tomato bruschetta, baked sardines with pine nuts, sultanas, breadcrumbs and rocket, beef carpaccio with caperberries, rocket and parmesan, antipasti to share, pappardelle with roast squash, ricotta and pesto, rabbit and porcini risotto, roast cod with chickpea purée, spinach and chorizo, grilled italian sausages with red onion marmalade, grilled lamb skewer with couscous, rib-eye steak with salsa verde, and puddings such as chocolate truffle torte with Amaretti and profiteroles.** *Starters/Snacks: £5.00 to £7.50. Main Courses: £9.50 to £15.50. Puddings: £4.50 to £5.00*

Enterprise ~ Lease Toby Ellis, Richard and George Manners ~ Real ale ~ Bar food (12-3(4 Sat),
6-10; 12-10 Sun) ~ (020) 7385 9129 ~ Children welcome till 7pm ~ Dogs welcome ~
Open 12-11(10.30 Sun); closed 24 Dec-1 Jan

Recommended by Evelyn and Derek Walter, Robert Lester

Bulls Head 🍺

Strand-on-the-Green; ⊖ *Gunnersbury, Chiswick Park* ⇌ *Kew Bridge; W4 3PQ*

**Cosy old Thames-side pub with tables by river with atmospheric little rooms, half a dozen
real ales and pubby food all day**

If you arrive at this cosy Chef & Brewer pub early enough (the pub can fill up fast) you
should be able to bag one of the highly prized tables by the little windows, with nice views
of the Thames beyond the attractively planted hanging baskets – a very pleasant place to
sit and read one of the newspapers they lay out for customers. In summer there are a few
tables out in front by the river. A series of beamed rooms rambles up and down steps, with
plenty of polished dark wood and beams, and old-fashioned benches built into the simple
panelling. The black-panelled alcoves make snug cubby-holes, and there are lots of empty
wine bottles dotted around. All in all the refurbishments provide a good mock-historic
pubby setting for a decent meal though, in truth, the building itself is actually very old –
it served as Cromwell's HQ several times during the Civil War. Six real ales might be from
brewers such as Robinsons and Ruddles, they do pitchers of Pimms in summer, and have
around 20 wines by the glass; good service from friendly uniformed staff.

🍽 **Served all day, food is fairly pubby and includes good sandwiches and filled baguettes
(with a good value soup and sandwich offer), sharing platters, fish and chips and beef
and ale pie, thai king prawn curry and fish pie; popular Sunday roasts.** *Starters/Snacks:
£2.95 to £7.80. Main Courses: £6.40 to £14.20. Puddings: £3.95 to £4.45*

Punch ~ Manager Julie Whittingham ~ Real ale ~ Bar food (12-10(9.30 Sun)) ~
(020) 8994 1204 ~ Children welcome ~ Open 11.30-11; 12-10.30 Sun

Recommended by Susan and John Douglas, N R White, John Saville, Sue Demont, Tim Barrow

Churchill Arms 🍷 🍺 £

Kensington Church Street; ⊖ *Notting Hill Gate, Kensington High Street; W8 7LN*

**Cheery irish landlord at bustling old friendly local, with very well kept beers and excellent
thai food; even at its most crowded, it stays relaxed and welcoming**

The amiable irish landlord at this flower-swamped pub will celebrate his 25th year at the
helm in 2010 and we're sure there will be quite a few celebrations. The wonderfully cheery
atmosphere here owes a lot to his enthusiasm and commitment. He's always very much in
evidence, delightedly mixing with customers as he threads his way through the evening
crowds, making everyone feel at home. Some years ago his buoyant enthusiasm led him to
start planting up flower pots and baskets. It quickly became something of an obsession
(indeed the façade has pretty much disappeared behind the glorious display) and a couple
of years ago his efforts were rewarded when the pub's 85 window boxes and 42 hanging
baskets won the Chelsea Flower Show's first-ever Boozers in Bloom competition. Another
of his hobbies is collecting butterflies – you'll see a variety of prints and books on the
subject dotted around the bar. He wasn't ready to stop there though – the pub is also
filled with countless lamps, miners' lights, horse tack, bedpans and brasses hanging from
the ceiling, a couple of interesting carved figures and statuettes behind the central bar
counter, prints of american presidents, and lots of Churchill memorabilia. On handpump,
the Fullers Chiswick, ESB, London Pride and Fullers seasonal beers are particularly well
kept, and he offers two dozen wines by the glass. The spacious and rather smart plant-
filled dining conservatory may be used for hatching butterflies, but is better known for its
big choice of excellent thai food. Look out for special events and decorations around
Christmas, Hallowe'en, St Patrick's Day, St George's Day, and Churchill's birthday (30
November) – along with more people than you'd ever imagine could feasibly fit inside this
place; they have their own cricket and football teams; fruit machine and TV. There can be
quite an overspill on to the street, where there are some chrome tables and chairs.

⏷ **Good quality and splendid value, the conservatory has authentic thai food with everything from a proper thai curry to various rice, noodle and stir-fried dishes. At lunchtimes they usually also have a very few traditional dishes such as fish and chips or sausage and chips, and they do a good value Sunday roast.** *Starters/Snacks: £2.50 to £4.50. Main Courses: £6.50. Puddings: £2.50*

Fullers ~ Manager Gerry O'Brien ~ Real ale ~ Bar food (12-10(9 Sun)) ~ Restaurant ~ (020) 7727 4242 ~ Children welcome ~ Dogs allowed in bar ~ Open 11-11(12 Thurs-Sat); 12-10.30 Sun

Recommended by P Dawn, LM, Derek Thomas, Peter, Brian and Anna Marsden, Tracey and Stephen Groves, the Didler

Colton Arms

Greyhound Road; ⊖ *Barons Court, West Kensington; W14 9SD*

Unspoilt little pub kept unchanged thanks to its dedicated landlord; it's peaceful and genuinely old-fashioned, with well kept beer

Don't be deterred by the inconspicuous exterior of this unspoilt little gem. Thanks to the friendly, dedicated landlord (and his son) this peaceful, unassuming place has survived intact down the years – it's been exactly the same for the last 40 years. Like an old-fashioned country pub in town, the main U-shaped front bar has a log fire blazing in winter, highly polished brasses, a fox's mask, hunting crops and plates decorated with hunting scenes on the walls, and a remarkable collection of handsomely carved antique oak furniture. That room is small enough, but the two back rooms, each with their own little serving counter with a bell to ring for service, are tiny. Well kept Fullers London Pride, Harveys, Sharps Doom Bar and, in summer, possibly Sharps Cornish Coaster on handpump. When you pay, note the old-fashioned brass-bound till. Pull the curtain aside for the door out to a charming back terrace with a neat rose arbour. The pub is next to the Queens Club tennis courts and gardens. More reports please.

⏷ **Just sandwiches, weekday lunchtimes only.** *Starters/Snacks: £3.50*

Enterprise ~ Lease N J and J A Nunn ~ Real ale ~ Bar food (weekday lunchtimes only) ~ No credit cards ~ (020) 7385 6956 ~ Children welcome till 7pm ~ Dogs allowed in bar ~ Open 12-3(4 Sun), 5.30(7 Sat, Sun)-11

Recommended by Susan and John Douglas, Sue Demont, Tim Barrow

Dove

Upper Mall; ⊖ *Ravenscourt Park; W6 9TA*

One of London's best-known pubs with a lovely riverside terrace, cosily traditional front bar and an interesting history

This quaint old place has played host to many writers, actors and artists over the years and there's a rather fascinating framed list of them all on a wall. It's said to be where *Rule Britannia* was composed, and it was a favourite with Turner, who painted the view of the Thames from the delightful back terrace, and Graham Greene. The street itself is associated with the foundation of the Arts and Crafts movement – William Morris's old residence (open certain afternoons) is nearby. By the entrance from the quiet alley, the front snug (said to be Britain's smallest and apparently listed in *The Guinness Book of Records* is cosy and traditional, with black panelling, and red leatherette cushioned built-in wall settles and stools around dimpled copper tables; it leads to a bigger, similarly furnished room, with old framed advertisements and photographs of the pub. That opens on to the terrace, where the main flagstoned area, down some steps, has a verandah and some highly prized tables looking over the low river wall to the Thames reach just above Hammersmith Bridge. There's a tiny exclusive area up a spiral staircase, a prime spot for watching the rowing crews out on the water. They stock the full range of Fullers beers, with Chiswick, Discovery, ESB, London Pride and seasonal beers on handpump; more reports please.

⏷ **Bar food typically includes lunchtime sandwiches, ardennes pâté, grilled mediterranean vegetable bruschetta, fish and chips, burgers, pork and leek sausages and mash, fish and** chips with crushed peas, steak and ale pie, grilled lamb steak with rosemary and balsamic glaze and rib-eye steak with béarnaise sauce. *Starters/Snacks: £4.50 to £7.25. Main Courses: £7.95 to £13.95. Puddings: £4.25 to £5.50*

Fullers ~ Manager Nick Kiley ~ Real ale ~ Bar food (12-3, 6-9; 12-9(7 Sun) Sat) ~ (020) 8748 9474 ~ Dogs welcome ~ Open 11-11; 12-10.30 Sun

Recommended by Pat and Tony Martin, N R White, the Didler

Duke of Sussex 🍴 🍷 📙

South Parade; ⊖ ⇄ *Chiswick Park, South Acton; W4 5LF*

Attractively restored Victorian local, now a better than average gastropub with plenty of spanish food, unusual beers and a lovely big garden

There's no shortage of top-drawer neighbourhood gastropubs in the capital these days, but what distinguishes this one is firstly the wide choice of very tasty spanish-influenced food, and secondly the most unexpected big garden behind. With plenty of tables, nicely laid out plants and carefully positioned lighting, it's a real oasis, and though that does mean it gets packed on sunny days, on the evening we visited we could have had it almost to ourselves. The smartly refurbished Victorian bar is simple and classy, with huge windows, some original etched glass, and a big horseshoe-shaped counter where a large vase of flowers adds a splash of vibrancy to the otherwise dark colours. The lighting is mostly modern, but there are a few standard lamps and table lamps which, at night, create a warm yellow glow that from the street makes the place look warmly inviting. Leading off is a carefully restored room used mainly for eating, again with plenty of simple wooden furnishings, but also a few little booths, chandeliers and a splendid skylight framed by colourfully painted cherubs. There are a couple of big mirrors, one above a small tiled fireplace, and lots of black and white local photos. The three real ales always include at least one uncommon brew alongside the regular Adnams: Hop Back lemon grass-flavoured Thaiphoon on our visit, but perhaps Kelham Island Eastern Promise or Harviestoun Bitter & Twisted. They also stock a dozen draught lagers, a great range of bottled lagers including trappist beers and Aspall's cider, and a good choice of wines includes half-bottle carafes.

🍴 With a strong spanish bent, the menu includes an extensive list of starters that many choose to have as tapas: fried cuttlefish with aioli, razor clams with chorizo and chilli, serrano ham croquettes and leek and mushroom tart, main courses such as mackerel with roast mediterranean vegetables, grilled lobster, steak pie for two, marinated skirt of angus beef with aioli, vegetable paella, and puddings such as rhubarb sherry trifle, lemon syllabub and apricot crumble. *Starters/Snacks: £4.50 to £6.50. Main Courses: £9.50 to £17.00. Puddings: £5.00*

Free house ~ Licensees Mike Buurman and Chris Payne ~ Real ale ~ Bar food (12(6 Mon)-10.30(9.30 Sun)) ~ Restaurant ~ (020) 8742 8801 ~ Children welcome ~ Dogs allowed in bar ~ Open 12(5 Mon)-11(12 Fri, Sat, 10 Sun); closed Mon lunchtime

Recommended by Simon Rodway

Havelock Tavern 🍴 🍷

Masbro Road; ⊖ ⇄ *Kensington(Olympia); W14 OLS*

Popular gastropub with friendly, often vibrant, atmosphere, very good food and well chosen wines

Light and airy, the L-shaped bar at this buoyantly chatty dining pub is welcoming, plain and unfussy with bare boards and long wooden tables that you may end up sharing at busy times. Until 1932 this blue-tiled building was two separate shops and it still has huge shop-front windows. A second little room with pews leads to a small paved terrace, with benches, a tree and wall climbers. Friendly staff serve Fullers London Pride, Sharps Doom Bar and a couple of guests from brewers such as Sambrooks and Twickenham from handpumps on the elegant modern bar counter, as well as a good range of well chosen wines, with around a dozen by the glass; mulled wine in winter, and in May and June perhaps home-made elderflower soda; backgammon, chess, Scrabble and other board games.

🍴 You may have to wait for a table in the evenings (when some dishes can run out quite quickly) for the well conceived and executed flavoursome cooking: tomato, basil and potato soup, honey roast figs stuffed with dolcelatte, grilled sardines with tapenade, leek, spinach and gruyère tart, roast pork belly with apple sauce, confit duck leg with butter beans with white wine, olives and tomato, and puddings such as sauternes and caramel custard, apple and treacle tart and chocolate torte. *Starters/Snacks: £5.00 to £8.50. Main Courses: £9.00 to £15.00. Puddings: £4.50 to £5.00*

Free house ~ Licensees Helen Watson and Andrew Cooper ~ Real ale ~ Bar food (12.30-2.30(3 Sun), 7-10(9.30 Sun)) ~ (020) 7603 5374 ~ Children welcome ~ Dogs welcome ~ Open 11-11; 12-10.30 Sun

Recommended by Martin and Karen Wake, Derek Thomas

Portobello Gold ♀

Middle of Portobello Road; ⊖ Notting Hill Gate, Ladbroke Grove; W11 2QB

Engaging combination of pub, hotel, restaurant and even Internet café, with relaxed atmosphere, wide choice of enjoyable food (especially in attractive dining conservatory), excellent range of drinks, and good value bedrooms

Lively and almost bohemian, this enterprising Notting Hill stalwart always seems to have something interesting going on, anything from live music sessions to a new art or photograph display, and it's a great place for a morning coffee, pastry and the papers. Our favourite part is the exotic-seeming dining room with its big tropical plants (they had a good crop of bananas last year), an impressive wall-to-wall mirror, comfortable wicker chairs, stained wooden tables, and a cage of vocal canaries adding to the outdoor effect – in summer they open up the sliding roof. The smaller front bar has a nice old fireplace, cushioned banquettes, and, more unusually, several Internet terminals (which disappear in the evening). It's all very relaxed, cheerful and informal, though can get a bit rushed when they're busy in the evening. The very well stocked bar has Fullers London Pride and very fairly priced Harveys, as well as several draught belgian beers, Thatcher's farm cider, a good selection of bottled beers from around the world, a wide range of interesting tequilas and other well sourced spirits, and a particularly good wine list (with just under two dozen by the glass) which can be attributed to the landlady who has written books on matching wine with food. They also have a cigar menu; piped music, TV, chess, backgammon. There are one or two tables and chairs on the pretty street outside, which, like the pub, is named in recognition of the 1769 Battle of Portobello, fought over control of the lucrative gold route to Panama. Parking nearby is restricted but you can usually find a space, though Saturday can be a problem. Some of the bedrooms are small, but they're all particularly good value for the area (you get the best price by booking on line), and there's a spacious apartment with a rooftop terrace and putting green.

🍴 As well as nibbles like their secret-recipe roasted peanuts, the carefully sourced food includes sandwiches, soup, rock oysters, good fajitas and nachos, popular thai mussels, wild boar and apple sausages, salads like greek and caesar, or a cold roast meat of the day, top quality burgers and steaks, shepherd's pie, organic salmon marinated in caribbean seasoning, cajun jumbo shrimp, muntjac prepared several ways, and puddings such as lemon cheesecake and pecan nut pie. They also offer cream teas and excellent Sunday roasts. *Starters/Snacks: £5.00 to £10.00. Main Courses: £6.70 to £16.00. Puddings: £4.50 to £5.50*

Enterprise ~ Lease Michael Bell and Linda Johnson-Bell ~ Real ale ~ Bar food (12-10.30(8 Sun)) ~ Restaurant ~ (020) 7460 4910 ~ Children welcome ~ Dogs allowed in bar ~ Live music Sun evening ~ Open 10-12; 9-12.30 Sat; 10-10.30 Sun; closed 25-31 Dec ~ Bedrooms: /£70S(£130B)

Recommended by Darren Le Poidevin, Brian and Anna Marsden

We mention bottled beers and spirits only if there is something unusual about them – imported belgian real ales, say, or dozens of malt whiskies; so do please let us know about them in your reports.

Warrington

Warrington Crescent; ⊖ Maida Vale; W9 1EH

Beautifully refurbished Victorian gin palace with extraordinary décor; short but good menu

Restored at huge expense by Gordon Ramsay, this opulent art nouveau building was reopened a couple of years ago. A splendid marble and mahogany bar counter is topped by an extraordinary structure that's rather like a cross between a carousel and a ship's hull, with cherubs thrown in for good measure. Throughout are elaborately patterned tiles, ceilings and stained-glass, and a remarkable number of big lamps and original light fittings; there's a small coal fire and two exquisitely tiled pillars. The drawings of nubile young women here and above a row of mirrors on the opposite wall are later additions, very much in keeping with the overall style, and hinting at the days when the building's trade was rather less respectable than today. Three real ales include Adnams Broadside, Fullers London Pride, Greene King IPA plus a guest such as Caledonian Deuchars IPA, and they've several unusual bottled beers as well as a dozen or so wines by the glass from a fine list.

🍴 **The short bar menu is almost resoundingly british, with potato and leek soup, whitebait, veal and pork pie with pickled cucumber, bubble and squeak with fried egg, chicken and mushroom pie, steamed bass with spring vegetables and roast pork belly with creamed leeks, and puddings such as steamed treacle pudding and banoffi pie.**
Starters/Snacks: £1.75 to £8.00. Main Courses: £5.75 to £18.00. Puddings: £5.50 to £7.00

Free house ~ Licensee Dominic Marriott ~ Real ale ~ Bar food (12-2.30 Fri, till 3 Sat, 5.30(6 Sat)-10.30; 12-9 Sun; not Mon-Thurs lunchtimes) ~ Restaurant (6-10.30) ~ (020) 7592 7960 ~ Children welcome till 7pm ~ Open 12-11(midnight Sat, 10.30 Sun)

Recommended by BOB

White Horse ♀ ◖

Parsons Green; ⊖ Parsons Green; SW6 4UL

Cheerfully relaxed local with big terrace and an excellent range of carefully sourced drinks

Overlooking the green and feeling a little removed from the traffic, the front terrace at this easy-going place has something of a continental feel on summer evenings and at weekends with a cheery crowd drinking alfresco, and they have barbecues out here most sunny evenings. The stylishly modernised U-shaped bar has plenty of sofas, wooden tables, and huge windows with slatted wooden blinds, and winter coal and log fires, one in an elegant marble fireplace. The pub is usually busy (and can feel crowded at times), but there are enough smiling, helpful staff behind the solid panelled central servery to ensure you'll rarely have to wait too long to be served. An impressive range of drinks takes in Harveys and half a dozen or so nicely varied guests on handpump from brewers such as Breconshire, Crouch Vale, Oakham, Sarah Hughes and Westerham, two dozen well chosen draught beers from overseas (usually belgian and german but occasionally from further afield), 15 trappist beers, around 120 other foreign bottled beers, a perry on handpump, ten or so malt whiskies, and a constantly expanding range of about 70 good, interesting and reasonably priced wines. They have quarterly beer festivals, often spotlighting regional breweries.

🍴 **Changing bar food might include pressed tongue with watercress and piccalilli salad, scallops, wild boar sausages, leek and mushroom pappardelle, haddock and chips, faggots with bubble and squeak, salmon steak with tarragon vinaigrette, and puddings such as vanilla rice pudding with apricot syrup and lime and orange crème caramel.**
Starters/Snacks: £5.75 to £7.25. Main Courses: £9.95 to £14.75. Puddings: £4.50 to £6.75

Mitchells & Butlers ~ Manager Dan Fox ~ Real ale ~ Bar food (9.30-10.30) ~ Restaurant ~ (020) 7736 2115 ~ Children welcome ~ Dogs welcome ~ Open 9.30-11.30(12 Thurs-Sat)

Recommended by Sue Demont, Tim Barrow, Jonathan Evans, Steve Kirby, the Didler, LM

Windsor Castle

Campden Hill Road; ⊖ Holland Park, Notting Hill Gate; W8 7AR

Genuinely unspoilt, with lots of atmosphere in the tiny, dark rooms, and a bustling summer garden; good beers and reliable food

With its wealth of dark oak furnishings, high-backed sturdy built-in elm benches, time-smoked ceilings, soft lighting and a coal-effect fire, this warmly characterful Victorian pub oozes with genuine old-fashioned charm. Three of the tiny unspoilt rooms have their own entrances from the street, but it's much more fun trying to navigate through the minuscule doors between them inside (one leads to a cosy pre-war-style dining room). Usually fairly quiet at lunchtime, it tends to be packed most evenings. Fullers London Pride and Timothy Taylors Landlord are well kept alongside a couple of guests such as Shepherd Neame Spitfire and Titanic English Glory on handpump, five draught ciders, decent house wines, various malt whiskies, jugs of Pimms in summer, and perhaps mulled wine in winter, and they have occasional beer festivals. It's especially cosy in winter, but the pub's appeal is just as strong in summer, thanks to the tree-shaped garden behind, easily one of London's best pub gardens. It's always busy out here when the sun's shining, but there's quite a secluded feel thanks to the high ivy-covered sheltering walls. They have a bar out here in summer, as well as heaters for cooler days, and lots of tables and chairs on the flagstones.

🍴 Bar food includes sandwiches, calamari, ploughman's, sausage and mash, beef bourguignon pie, burgers, scampi, chicken caesar salad, sirloin steak, chocolate brownie and baked vanilla cheesecake with red berry compote. *Starters/Snacks: £3.70 to £5.00. Main Courses: £5.95 to £12.50. Puddings: £3.80*

Mitchells & Butlers ~ Manager James Platford ~ Real ale ~ Bar food (12-3, 5-10, 12-10(9 Sun) Fri, Sat) ~ (020) 7243 8797 ~ Children welcome till 6pm ~ Dogs welcome ~ Open 12-11(10.30 Sun)

Recommended by Tracey and Stephen Groves, Brian and Anna Marsden, the Didler, N R White, Darren Le Poidevin, J V Dadswell

---

LUCKY DIP

Besides the fully inspected pubs, you might like to try these Lucky Dips recommended to us and described by readers (if you do, please send us reports: feedback@goodguides.com).

CENTRAL LONDON

EC1

Butchers Hook & Cleaver EC1A 9DY [West Smithfield]: Fullers bank conversion with their full ale range and pubby food all day especially pies, breakfast from 7.30am; friendly staff, daily papers, relaxed atmosphere, nice mix of chairs inc some button-back leather armchairs, wrought-iron spiral stairs to pleasant mezzanine with waitress service; piped music, big-screen sports TV; open all day, cl wknds *(Peter Dandy, Steve Kirby, Michael Dandy, Derek Thomas, BB, DC)*

Coach & Horses EC1R 3DJ [Ray St]: Enterprising food under newish landlord inc good Sun lunch, good wines by the glass, quick friendly service; courtyard tables *(Keith and Inga Davis-Rutter)*

Fence EC1M 6BP [Cowcross St]: Contemporary furniture on bare boards, up-to-date food, good choice of wines and lagers, daily papers; piped music, TV; tables out on sizeable back deck and terrace *(Michael Dandy)*

Fox & Anchor EC1M 6AA [Charterhouse St]: Long, slender, all-wood bar with narrow tables, small back snugs, interesting paintings, period prints and Edwardian photographs; mainstream ales in metal tankards *(Chris Sale)*

Green EC1R 0DU [Clerkenwell Green]: Welcoming pub with good lunchtime menu, evening tapas, pleasant dining bar downstairs, upstairs restaurant; two tables outside *(Michael and Maggie Betton)*

Melton Mowbray EC1N 2LE [Marlborough Court, Holborn]: Large busy pastiche of an Edwardian pub with Fullers ales, good food service (Melton Mowbray pies among other dishes); lots of woodwork, etched glass, mix of furniture inc front button-back banquettes, back booths below small mezzanine gallery; opens out in summer to pavement café tables *(Michael Dandy, Peter Dandy)*

Sekforde Arms EC1R 0HA [Sekforde St]: Small unspoilt and comfortably simple corner local with friendly landlord, Wells & Youngs ales and guest such as Caledonian Deuchars IPA, simple good value standard food; nice pictures inc Spy caricatures, upstairs restaurant (not always open); darts, cards and board games; pavement tables *(the Didler, Tim Maddison)*

Three Kings EC1R 0DY [Clerkenwell Close]: Cosy and well run, old no-frills pub with plenty of atmosphere, especially when candlelit in winter, real ales such as Wells & Youngs Bombardier, some interesting food, efficient service even when busy; rhino head above open fire, two more small rooms upstairs *(Tim Maddison)*

EC2

☆ *Dirty Dicks* EC2M 4NR [Bishopsgate]: Busy re-creation of traditional City tavern, fun for foreign visitors; booths, barrel tables, low beams, interesting old prints, Wells & Youngs ales, enjoyable food inc interesting sandwiches and sharing platters, pleasant service; calmer cellar wine bar with wine racks overhead in brick barrel-vaulted ceiling, further upstairs area too; piped music, games machines and TV; cl wknds *(LYM, Michael Dandy, the Didler, Ian Phillips)*

Globe EC2M 6SA [Moorgate]: Everards Sunchaser, Fullers London Pride, Greene King Abbot and Timothy Taylors Landlord in modest-sized bar with mixed furniture, food all day (breakfast from 8am) inc pubby staples and more unusual things; daily papers, restaurant and pool room upstairs; TV *(Michael Dandy, Peter Dandy)*

☆ *Hamilton Hall* EC2M 7PY [Bishopsgate; also entrance from Liverpool Street Station]: Showpiece Wetherspoons with flamboyant Victorian baroque décor, plaster nudes and fruit mouldings, chandeliers, mirrors, good-sized comfortable mezzanine; reliable food all day, lots of real ales inc interesting guest beers, decent wines and coffee, good prices; silenced machines, can get crowded; good disabled access, tables outside, open all day *(Valerie Baker, Tracey and Stephen Groves, Ian Phillips, LYM)*

Kings Arms EC2M 1RP [Wormwood St]: Low-ceilinged bar with reasonably priced pubby food from short menu inc afternoon snack platters, Courage Directors, Fullers London Pride and Greene King IPA; pool downstairs; piped music; back terrace *(Michael Dandy)*

Lord Aberconway EC2M 1QT [Old Broad St]: Victorian feel with dark panelling and furniture, real ales such as Fullers, Greene King and Hydes, reasonably priced food from sandwiches up; wrought-iron railed upper dining gallery *(Michael Dandy)*

Railway Tavern EC2M 7NX [Liverpool St]: Light and airy, with high ceilings and vast front windows, Greene King ales and several wines by the glass from a long bar, pubby food from sandwiches up inc sharing platters; second room upstairs; pavement tables *(Michael Dandy)*

White Hart EC2M 3TH [Bishopsgate]: Typical City pub with plenty of tables and standing shelves, appealing candlelit vaulted dining basement; Fullers London Pride, Timothy Taylors Landlord and many guests, lots of wines and whiskies, pubby food from sandwiches up *(Michael Dandy)*

EC3

Counting House EC3V 3PD [Cornhill]: Youngs pub with good choice of food in modern dining area; landscaped garden with decking *(Peter Dandy)*

East India Arms EC3M 4BR [Fenchurch St]: Standing-room Victorian pub refurbished by Shepherd Neame, good service; unobtrusive TV; cl wknds *(N R White, Ian Phillips)*

Elephant EC3M 5BA [Fenchurch St]: Small ground-floor bar, larger basement lounge, well kept Wells & Youngs ales, good sandwiches and other mainly snacky food, friendly helpful staff; intrusive piped music; cl wknds *(Tony and Wendy Hobden, Ian Phillips)*

☆ *Lamb* EC3V 1LR [Leadenhall Market]: Well run stand-up bar, staff always polite and efficient even when very busy with sharp City lads; Wells & Youngs ales, good choice of wines by the glass, engraved glass, plenty of ledges and shelves, spiral stairs up to tables and seating in small light and airy carpeted gallery overlooking market's central crossing; corner servery doing good lunchtime carvery, baguettes, sharing platters, brunches from 10am; separate stairs to nice bright dining room (not cheap), also basement bar with shiny wall tiling and own entrance; discreet TV, silenced games machine; lots of tables outside after 4pm when stalls pack up – crowds here in warmer months; cl wknds *(Derek Thomas, N R White, Dr and Mrs M E Wilson, Michael Dandy, Ian Phillips, BB, Valerie Baker)*

Simpsons Tavern EC3V 9DR [just off Cornhill]: Dating from 18th c, with Bass and Harveys in panelled bar, enjoyable simple food, upstairs restaurant *(Peter Dandy)*

EC4

Centre Page EC4V 5BH [aka the Horn; Knightrider St nr Millennium Bridge]: Modernised old pub with window booths or 'traps' in narrow entrance room, more space beyond, traditional style with panelling and subdued lighting; chatty atmosphere, mix of after-work drinkers and tourists having cappuccino; friendly efficient young staff, simple appetising bar menu (from breakfast at 9am), downstairs dining room, well kept Fullers beers, good tea, various coffees; piped music may be a bit loud; tables outside have good view of St Paul's *(BB, Dr and Mrs M E Wilson, N R White, Tim and Ann Newell)*

Old Bell EC4Y 1DH [Fleet St, nr Ludgate Circus]: 17th-c tavern backing on to St Bride's, heavy black beams, flagstones, brass-topped tables, dim lighting, stained-glass bow window; good changing choice of real ales from island servery (can try before you buy), friendly efficient young foreign staff; usual food, coal fire, cheerful atmosphere; piped music *(N R White, BB, the Didler, Michael Dandy)*

Paternoster EC4M 7DZ [Queens Head Passage]: In modern development in sight of

St Paul's, Wells & Youngs ales, good choice of food and of wines by the glass, good coffee, some sofas; TV, games *(Michael Dandy, Peter Dandy)*

SE1

Rake SE1 9AG [Winchester Walk]: Tiny discreetly modern bar with amazing bottled beer range in wall-wide cooler, as well as half a dozen continental lagers on tap and perhaps a couple of rare real ales; fair-sized terrace with decking and heated marquee *(Tracey and Stephen Groves, E McCall, T McLean, D Irving)*

SW1

Adam & Eve SW1H 9EX [Petty France]: Dark ceilings and furniture but big light windows, Adnams, Fullers London Pride and Wells & Youngs, well priced pubby food from sandwiches up, friendly service; piped music, TV and games machine *(Michael Dandy)*

☆ *Albert* SW1H 0NP [Victoria St]: Handsome contrast to the cliffs of dark glass around it, open-plan airy bar with cut and etched windows, gleaming mahogany, ornate ceiling, solid comfortable furnishings; good value food all day from sandwiches up, Fullers London Pride, Wells & Youngs Bombardier and guests, 24 wines by the glass, handsome staircase lined with portraits of prime ministers up to carvery/dining room; piped music, games machine; lavatories down steep stairs; children welcome if eating till 9pm, open all day from 8am *(Donna and Roger, Michael Dandy, Darren Le Poidevin, LYM, BB, Mike and Sue Loseby)*

☆ *Botanist* SW1W 8EE [Sloane Sq]: Stylish and modern, good wines, enjoyable interesting food, efficient friendly young staff even when really pushed; big windows overlooking Sloane Square, candles on tables, bustling bar with chrome and leather high bar seats, dark bucket chairs, cream stools and banquettes on stripped wooden floor, mirrored wall for spacious feel; busy dining room with long leather wall banquettes and contemporary cream and chrome chairs, wall of botanical illustration blow-ups *(Jamie May, BB)*

☆ *Buckingham Arms* SW1H 9EU [Petty France]: Relaxed bow-windowed 18th-c local with welcoming landlord, good value pubby food (evenings too) from back open kitchen, Wells & Youngs ales and guests from long bar, good wines by the glass; elegant mirrors and woodwork, unusual side corridor fitted out with elbow ledge for drinkers; TVs; dogs welcome, handy for Buckingham Palace, Westminster Abbey and St James's Park, open all day *(LYM, the Didler, Robert F Smith, Dr and Mrs M E Wilson, Michael Dandy, Dr and Mrs A K Clarke, N R White)*

Cask & Glass SW1E 5HN [Palace St]: Good range of Shepherd Neame ales, friendly staff and atmosphere, good value lunchtime sandwiches; old prints and shiny black panelling; quiet corner TV; handy for Queen's Gallery *(N R White)*

Clarence SW1A 2HP [Whitehall]: Civilised olde-worlde beamed pub with well spaced tables, varied seating inc tub chairs and banquettes, several real ales, decent wines by the glass, friendly chatty landlord; popular reasonably priced food all day from sandwiches up, upstairs dining area; pavement tables *(Dr and Mrs M E Wilson, Phil Bryant)*

Feathers SW1H 0BH [Broadway]: Large comfortable pub, a Scotland Yard local, with atrium and upstairs dining area; good choice of sensibly priced pubby food from sandwiches up, six well kept ales inc Fullers London Pride, Marstons Pedigree and Timothy Taylors Landlord, several wines by the glass; piped music; open all day (from 8am for breakfast) *(Michael Dandy, BB, Dr and Mrs M E Wilson)*

☆ *Fox & Hounds* SW1W 8HR [Passmore St/ Graham Terrace]: Small convivial local, Wells & Youngs ales, friendly staff and civilised customers; wall benches, warm red décor, big hunting prints, old sepia photographs of pubs and customers, some sofas and toby jugs, book-lined back room, hanging plants under attractive skylight, coal-effect gas fire; some low-priced pubby food; can be very busy Fri night *(the Didler, Jeremy King, N R White)*

Golden Lion SW1Y 6QY [King St]: Busy bow-fronted Victorian pub opp Christie's auction rooms; well kept Fullers, Greene King and Wells & Youngs from decorative servery, decent wines by the glass, good value food; friendly service, ornate 1900s Jacobean décor and dark panelling, upstairs bar; piped music *(PHB, Dr and Mrs A K Clarke, N R White)*

Jugged Hare SW1V 1DX [Vauxhall Bridge Rd/Rochester Row]: Popular Fullers Ale & Pie pub in former colonnaded bank with balustraded balcony, chandelier, dark wood, old London photographs and busts; good service, reasonably priced traditional food from sandwiches up inc jugged hare pie; piped music, silent fruit machine; open all day *(Jeremy King, N R White, the Didler, BB)*

☆ *Morpeth Arms* SW1P 4RW [Millbank]: Sparkling clean Victorian pub facing the Thames, roomy and comfortable, some etched and cut glass, old books and prints, photographs, earthenware jars and bottles; well kept Wells & Youngs, good choice of wines and of good value food all day, good welcoming service even at busy lunchtimes; upstairs dining room; games machine, may be unobtrusive sports TV; seats outside (a lot of traffic), handy for Tate Britain *(BB, PHB, Dr and Mrs A K Clarke, the Didler, Robert W Buckle, Dr Ron Cox)*

☆ *Red Lion* SW1Y 6PP [Crown Passage, behind St James's St]: Cheerful, brightly lit late 18th-c local tucked down narrow passage nr St James's Palace; red décor, dark panelling, nice prints, settles and leaded lights; well kept ales inc Adnams, friendly service, good bargain lunchtime sandwiches, room upstairs; unobtrusive corner TV; colourful hanging baskets (N R White, Tracey and Stephen Groves, Sue Demont, Tim Barrow, BB)

Red Lion SW1A 2NH [Parliament St]: Congenial pub by Houses of Parliament, used by Foreign Office staff and MPs; soft lighting, parliamentary cartoons and prints, Fullers ales and decent wines from the long bar, good range of food, efficient staff; also cellar bar and small narrow upstairs dining room, outside seating (Peter Dandy, N R White, Dr and Mrs A K Clarke, BB, Michael Dandy)

Royal Oak SW1P 4BZ [Regency St/Rutherford St]: Compact one-bar Youngs pub with good choice of wines by the glass as well as their real ales; good value home-made wkdy lunchtime bar food, friendly mainly antipodean staff (Hazel Morgan, Bernard Patrick)

Sanctuary House SW1H 9LA [Tothill St]: Pub/hotel's roomy high-ceilinged bar with Fullers ales, pubby food from sandwiches to speciality pies and good fish and chips; cheerful helpful staff, plenty of tables, nice stools and armchairs, raised and balustraded back area with monkish mural, ornate outside scrollwork; piped music; children welcome, 30 or more bedrooms, open all day (Dr and Mrs A K Clarke, Eithne Dandy, Michael Dandy)

Speaker SW1P 2HA [Great Peter St]: Pleasant chatty atmosphere in unpretentious corner pub, well kept Shepherd Neame Spitfire, Wells & Youngs and two guest beers; lots of whiskies, limited popular food inc good sandwiches, friendly helpful staff; political cartoons and prints; open all day, cl Sun evening and Sat (N R White, PHB, Mike Begley)

☆ **St Stephens Tavern** SW1A 2JR [Parliament St]: Elegantly refurbished Victorian pub opp Houses of Parliament and Big Ben, lofty ceilings with brass chandeliers, tall windows with etched glass and swagged gold curtains, gleaming mahogany, charming upper gallery bar (may be reserved for functions); four well kept Badger ales from handsome counter with pedestal lamps, friendly efficient staff, good value food from baguettes up; Division Bell for MPs; open all day (John Saville, Phil Bryant, LM, BB, N R White)

Strutton Arms SW1P 2HP [Strutton St]: Smallish panelled carpeted bar with bargain pubby food, Fullers London Pride, Greene King IPA and Hook Norton Old Hooky, lots of wines by the glass; TV (Michael Dandy)

Walkers of St James SW1Y 6DF [Duke St]: Busy basement pub, lots of dark wood and part partitions, simple bar food from sandwiches up, real ales such as Timothy Taylors Landlord (Dr and Mrs M E Wilson)

Walkers of Whitehall SW1A 2DD [Craigs Court, off Whitehall]: Pleasant pub on three floors with decent choice of freshly prepared food at reasonable prices, real ales and good selection of wines, friendly efficient service, open all day, till 8pm Sun (Charles Harvey)

Westminster Arms SW1P 3AT [Storeys Gate]: Unpretentious busy pub nr Westminster Abbey and Houses of Parliament; lots of real ales inc Adnams, Brakspears, Greene King, Thwaites and a beer named for the pub brewed by Hogs Back, several malt whiskies; straightforward all-day food (not wknd evenings), rather sparse bar with old-fashioned furnishings, panelling, wine bar downstairs (may close early); piped music; children in eating areas lunchtime, tables outside, open all day, cl Sun evening (P Dawn, Michael Dandy, Ian Phillips, Dr and Mrs A K Clarke, Edward Mirzoeff, Peter Dandy, LYM, N R White, Andrew Hollingshead)

Willow Walk SW1V 1LW [Wilton Rd]: Large open-plan Wetherspoons pub with their usual menu and solid comfortable décor, eight real ales; open all day (Ian Phillips)

SW3

☆ **Admiral Codrington** SW3 2LY [Mossop St]: Pleasing café feel with comfortable sofas, cushioned wall seats and elegant tables, polished boards, panelling, sporting prints, house plants around big bow windows; enjoyable lunchtime food, more elaborate evening menu, Sun roasts, Black Sheep Best and Shepherd Neame Spitfire (not cheap, even for round here), decent wines by the glass and coffees, friendly uniformed young staff, quieter dining room with retractable sunroof; piped music; children and dogs welcome, heated side terrace, open all day (Mark Flynn, Tracey and Stephen Groves, LYM)

Hour Glass SW3 2DY [Brompton Rd]: Small well run pub handy for the V&A and other nearby museums; well kept Black Sheep and Fullers London Pride, freshly squeezed fruit juice, good value pubby food (not Sun), friendly landlady and efficient young staff; sports TV; pavement picnic-sets (LM)

W1

Angel in the Fields W1U 2QY [Thayer St/Marylebone High St]: Well run pub with comfortable cosy bar, dark panelling and latticed windows, nice fire; more room upstairs; keg Sam Smiths (LYM, Tracey and Stephen Groves)

☆ **Audley** W1K 2RX [Mount St]: Classic Mayfair pub where Michelle Obama and her children dropped in for lunch; classy and relaxed, with opulent red plush, mahogany panelling and engraved glass, chandelier and clock hanging in lovely carved wood bracket from ornately corniced ceiling; Fullers London Pride, Greene King IPA, Wells & Youngs Bombardier from long polished bar, friendly efficient service, good standard food (reasonably priced for the area) and service, good coffee; upstairs panelled dining room; games machines; pavement tables, open all day (Tracey and Stephen Groves, LYM, Ian Phillips)

Blue Posts W1B 5PX [Kingly St/Ganton St]: Compact two-floor pub with Greene King ales, lots of wines, bargain food; nostalgic piped music; tables out on pedestrianised street (Peter Dandy, Jeremy King, Michael Dandy)

Clachan W1B 5QH [Kingly St]: Ornate plaster ceiling supported by two large fluted and decorated pillars (used to be owned by Liberty), comfortable screened leather banquettes, smaller drinking alcove up three or four steps; well kept changing ales such as Batemans, Fullers and Timothy Taylors Landlord from handsome counter, food from sandwiches up; can get busy, but very relaxed in afternoons (Sue Demont, Tim Barrow, DM, Michael Dandy, Peter Dandy, BB)

Cock W1W 8QE [Great Portland St]: Big corner local with enormous lamps over picnic-sets outside, florid Victorian/Edwardian décor with gleaming mahogany and plasterwork, some cut and etched glass, high tiled ceiling and mosaic floor, velvet curtains, coal-effect gas fires, upstairs lounge; cheap Sam Smiths OB from all four handpumps, friendly efficient service, reasonably priced food (not Fri-Sun evenings); open all day (Michael Dandy, the Didler, Tracey and Stephen Groves, BB, John and Gloria Isaacs)

Crown W1F 9TP [Brewer St]: Compact traditional L-shaped pub with dark wood, bare boards, warm lighting, Timothy Taylors Landlord, upstairs restaurant (Dr and Mrs M E Wilson)

De Hems W1D 5BW [Macclesfield St]: Typical London pub recycled as pastiche of a old dutch bar (but roomier and less intimate), old dutch engravings, mixed tables on bare boards, big continental founts and good range of interesting bottled beers; friendly service; can get very busy (DM, Jeremy King)

Duke of York W1G 9TR [New Cavendish St]: Small one-room Sam Smiths pub, smart and cosy, with tastefully adorned red walls; keg beer (Tracey and Stephen Groves)

French House W1D 5BG [Dean St]: Theatre memorabilia, good wines by the glass, plenty of bottled beers (no pint glasses), lively chatty atmosphere – mainly standing room, windows keeping good eye on passers-by; efficient staff, good food in upstairs restaurant, no mobile phones; can get very busy evenings; open all day (Ros Lawler, Peter Dandy, DM, Tim Maddison, John and Gloria Isaacs)

Goat W1S 4RP [Albemarle St]: Long narrow panelled bar, plushly carpeted and mirrored, well kept ales inc Moorhouses (Tracey and Stephen Groves)

☆ **Golden Eagle** W1U 2NY [Marylebone Lane]: Well updated, neat Victorian local with well kept Fullers and St Austell ales from elegant curving bar, relaxing perimeter seating, blue and yellow décor, striking stained-glass, fresh flowers, friendly landlord; piano sing-along Thurs and Fri; piped music (Tracey and Stephen Groves, Terry Buckland)

Jack Horner W1T 7QN [Tottenham Court Rd]: Fullers bank conversion with full range of their ales from island counter, good service, pie-based food, neat tables in quiet areas; lots of woodwork, photographs of old London (Jeremy King, Dr and Mrs M E Wilson, Peter Dandy)

King & Queen W1W 6DL [Foley St]: Small welcoming corner pub, real ales such as Adnams, St Austell Tribute and Wells & Youngs Bombardier, decent wines and an enthusiast's spirits range; enjoyable wkdy lunchtime food inc fresh sandwiches and pubby hot dishes, reasonable prices; open all day (Sue Demont, Tim Barrow, John and Gloria Isaacs)

Kings Arms W1J 7QA [Shepherd Market]: Minimalist décor in old low-ceilinged pub with good value standard bar food, Fullers London Pride, Greene King IPA and Wells & Youngs Bombardier, good choice of wines; upper dining gallery (Michael Dandy, LYM)

Kings Arms W1F 8QJ [Poland St]: Lots of character in unspoilt little backstreet local with several real ales, upstairs overflow inc a nice window seat (DM)

Newman Arms W1T 1NG [Rathbone St/Newman Passage]: In the same family for three generations, small panelled bar with particularly well kept Fullers London Pride, decent home-made food in traditionally redecorated room upstairs, pictures and prints reflecting pub's association with George Orwell and director Michael Powell; good friendly staff and old-school character landlord (Tim Maddison)

Red Lion W1J 5QN [Waverton St]: This civilised Mayfair pub, a popular Main Entry for many years, sadly closed in autumn 2008 (LYM)

Red Lion W1B 5PR [Kingly St]: Dark panelling, narrow front bar with deep leather banquettes, back bar with darts, usual food in comfortable upstairs lounge; cheap Sam Smiths keg beers (Michael Dandy, Peter Dandy, Jeremy King, BB)

Shakespeares Head W1F 7HZ [Great Marlborough St]: Panelled pub dating from the early 18th c, soft lighting, dark beams, deep red and green décor; changing ales such as Shepherd Neame Spitfire and Wells & Youngs Bombardier, standard pubby food from sandwiches up, friendly staff; upstairs dining room (Michael Dandy, Stephen Moss)

Three Tuns W1H 6HP [Portman Mews South]: Large bare-boards front bar and sizeable lounge/dining area with beams and nooks and crannies; Courage Directors and Wells & Youngs Bombardier and Special, pubby food from panini up, good staff (Jennifer Banks)

Yorkshire Grey W1W 7AX [Langham St]: Small bare-boards corner pub with well kept cheap Sam Smiths OB, lots of wood, bric-a-brac and prints, comfortable seating inc a snug little parlour, friendly staff, attractively priced bar lunches; open all day (John and Gloria Isaacs)

W2

Mad Bishop & Bear W2 1HB [Paddington Station]: Up escalators from concourse, full Fullers ale range and a guest beer, good wine choice, good value standard food inc breakfast (7.30pm on); ornate plasterwork, etched mirrors and fancy lamps, parquet, tiles and carpet, booths with leather banquettes, lots of wood and prints, train departures screen; sports TV, piped music, games machine; open all day, tables out overlooking concourse (Dr and Mrs A K Clarke, Donna and Roger, Joe Green, Jeremy King, Michael Dandy, Dave Irving, Jenny Huggins, Dr and Mrs M E Wilson, BB, Tracey and Stephen Groves)

☆ **Victoria** W2 2NH [Strathearn Pl]: Lots of Victorian pictures and memorabilia, cast-iron fireplaces, gilded mirrors and mahogany panelling, brass mock-gas lamps above an attractive horseshoe bar, bare boards and banquettes; relaxed atmosphere, good service, full Fullers ale range, good choice of wines by the glass, well priced food counter; upstairs has leather club chairs in small library/snug (and, mostly used for private functions now, a replica of the Gaiety Theatre bar, all gilt and red plush); quiet piped music, TV (off unless people ask); pavement picnic-sets, open all day (Tracey and Stephen Groves, LYM, N R White, Ian Herdman)

WC1

Bountiful Cow WC1R 4AP [Eagle St]: Distinctive sister-pub to Seven Stars in Carey St (see Central London Main Entry section) neat mildly modernist décor, large cellar restaurant strong on burgers and steaks, well kept real ales and good value wines by the glass; Sat jazz night; open all day (cl Sun evening) (Dr Martin Owton)

Calthorpe Arms WC1X 8JR [Grays Inn Rd]: Plush wall seats, Wells & Youngs ales, popular generous food upstairs lunchtime and evening, good staff; pavement tables, open all day (the Didler)

Dolphin WC1R 4PF [Red Lion St]: Small one-bar corner pub with high stools and wide shelves around the walls, old photographs, horsebrasses, hanging copper pots and pans, and so forth; simple wkdy lunchtime food, well kept Adnams and Greene King; open all day wkdys and most Sat lunchtimes (Tracey and Stephen Groves, the Didler)

Enterprise WC1R 4PN [Red Lion St]: Smartly simple, with candles on tables, bare boards, high ceiling, attractive tiled walls and big mirrors; wide range of reasonably priced food inc tapas, two or three well kept ales such as Caledonian Deuchars IPA; lighter back area (Tracey and Stephen Groves)

Friend At Hand WC1N 1HX [Herbrand St]: Panelled pub with quickly served pubby food (even bank hols), Courage, Fullers and Wells & Youngs Bombardier (Dave Braisted)

Mabels WC1H 9AZ [just off Euston Rd]: Neat open-plan pub on two levels, reasonably

priced food from sandwiches and baguettes up, with an emphasis on burgers; well kept Shepherd Neame ales, good wine choice, friendly welcoming staff, bright décor; big-screen TV; pavement tables, open all day (Martin Grosberg, Tracey and Stephen Groves)

Museum Tavern WC1B 3BA [Museum St/Great Russell St]: Traditional, high-ceilinged, ornate Victorian pub facing the British Museum; busy lunchtime and early evening, but can be quite peaceful other times, good choice of beers inc some unusual ones, several wines by the glass, good hot drinks, straightforward food from end servery; one or two tables out under gas lamps, open all day (LYM, Tracey and Stephen Groves, Dr and Mrs M E Wilson)

Penderels Oak WC1V 7HJ [High Holborn]: Vast Wetherspoons with attractive décor and woodwork, lots of books, pew seating around central tables, their usual well priced food and huge choice of good value real ales, charming staff; open all day (Dr and Mrs A K Clarke)

Rugby WC1N 3ES [Great James St]: Sizeable pub with Shepherd Neame ales from central servery, decent usual food, good service; darts, appropriate photographs; pleasant terrace (the Didler)

☆ **Skinners Arms** WC1H 9NT [Judd St]: Richly decorated, with glorious woodwork, marble pillars, high ceilings, good lighting, lots of London prints, and an interesting layout inc a comfortable back seating area; well kept Greene King ales from attractive bar, friendly staff, bar food; unobtrusive piped music, corner TV; pavement picnic-sets, interesting tiled frontage, handy for British Library; open all day, cl wknds (N R White, Tracey and Stephen Groves)

Swintons WC1X 9NT [Swinton St]: Comfortable modern dining pub, impressive choice from contemporary snacks up inc takeaways, efficient friendly service, Black Sheep and Fullers London Pride; no TVs or machines (Joe Green)

WC2

Bear & Staff WC2H 7AX [Bear St]: Fullers London Pride, St Austell Tribute, Timothy Taylors Landlord and Wells & Youngs Bombardier, standard pubby food from sandwiches and sharing platters up; upstairs dining room (Michael Dandy)

Brewmaster WC2H 7AD [Cranbourn St]: Busy with standard pubby food from sandwiches and sharing platters up, Greene King ales, good wine choice, quick friendly service; room upstairs (Michael Dandy)

☆ **Chandos** WC2N 4ER [St Martins Lane]: Busy bare-boards bar with snug cubicles, lots of theatre memorabilia on stairs up to smarter more comfortable lounge with opera photographs, low wooden tables, panelling, leather sofas, coloured windows; cheap Sam Smiths OB, prompt cheerful service, bargain food, air conditioning, darts; can get packed early evening; piped music and games machines; note the automaton on the roof (working 10-2 and 4-9); children upstairs till 6pm, open all day from 9am (for breakfast) *(Conor McGaughey, Michael Dandy, Dr and Mrs M E Wilson, Ian Phillips, Mrs Hazel Rainer, LYM, Bruce Bird, Michael and Alison Sandy)*

Coach & Horses WC2E 7BD [Wellington St]: Old-fashioned copper-topped bar, Fullers London Pride and Marstons Pedigree, lots of whiskeys, lunchtime baps; irish sports mementoes and cartoons, restaurant; can get crowded, handy for Royal Opera House *(John and Gloria Isaacs)*

Coal Hole WC2R 0DW [Strand]: Chatty and comfortable front bar, softly lit relaxed downstairs dining bar with wall reliefs, mock-baronial high ceiling and raised back gallery, basement snug; Batemans, Fullers London Pride, Sharps Doom Bar and Timothy Taylors Landlord, decent wines by the glass, pubby food *(N R White, Valerie Baker, BB, Michael Dandy, Dr and Mrs A K Clarke, Bernard Stradling, Pete Coxon)*

☆ *Cross Keys* WC2H 9EB [Endell St/Betterton St]: Relaxed and friendly, quick service even at busy times, good lunchtime sandwiches and a few bargain hot dishes, Courage Best and Wells & Youngs ales, decent wines by the glass; masses of photographs and posters inc Beatles memorabilia, brassware and tasteful bric-a-brac; games machine; gents' downstairs; sheltered picnic-sets out on cobbles, pretty flower tubs, open all day *(John and Gloria Isaacs, the Didler, LYM)*

Edgar Wallace WC2R 3JE [Essex St]: Simple spacious open-plan pub dating from 18th c despite its modern name; well kept Adnams, a beer brewed for them by Nethergate and several unusual guests, friendly efficient service, good value all-day food inc doorstep sandwiches; half-panelled walls and red ceilings, interesting old London and Edgar Wallace memorabilia; open all day, cl wknds *(LM, N R White, Michael and Alison Sandy)*

Freemasons Arms WC2E 9NG [Long Acre]: Roomy and relaxed two-level pub, scrupulously clean, with ornate dark woodwork and cupola ceiling, big windows, gas-style wall lamps, pleasing semicircular bar, nice raised back area, interesting prints (and FA inaugurated here), high backed banquettes and small tables; up to five ales inc Shepherd Neame, attentive staff, good bargain pubby food; silent big-screen TVs, fruit machine; open all day *(BB, Tracey and Stephen Groves, Dr Ron Cox, Michael and Alison Sandy)*

George WC2R 1AP [Strand]: Timbered pub nr law courts, long narrow bare-boards bar, Fullers London Pride, Sharps Doom Bar and Wells & Youngs Bitter, good choice of wines by the glass, sandwiches and limited basic hot food; upstairs bar with carvery *(Michael Dandy)*

Knights Templar WC2A 1DT [Chancery Lane]: Wetherspoons in big-windowed former bank, marble pillars, handsome fittings and plasterwork; good bustling atmosphere on

two levels, some interesting real ales at bargain prices, good wine choice, all-day food, friendly staff; remarkably handsome lavatories; open all day inc Sun *(Dr and Mrs A K Clarke)*

Lyceum WC2R 0HS [Strand]: Panelling and pleasantly simple furnishings downstairs, several small discreet booths, steps up to a bigger alcove with darts; food in much bigger upstairs panelled lounge with deep button-back leather settees and armchairs, low-priced Sam Smiths beer, civilised atmosphere *(Chris Sale)*

Marquess of Anglesey WC2E 7AU [Bow St/Russell St]: Light and airy, with Wells & Youngs and a guest beer, decent food inc interesting specials, friendly staff, a couple of big sofas; more room upstairs *(Michael Dandy)*

Moon Under Water WC2H 7LE [Leicester Sq]: Well placed Wetherspoons with reasonably priced beers and generous good value food all day; long and narrow with lots of high tables, good staff; no piped music *(Michael and Alison Sandy)*

Nags Head WC2E 8BT [James St/Neal St]: Etched brewery mirrors, red ceiling, mahogany furniture, some partitioned booths, lots of old local prints; bargain bar lunches from separate side counter, friendly staff, three McMullens ales; open all day *(Michael Dandy, Meg and Colin Hamilton)*

Nell of Old Drury WC2B 5JS [Catherine St]: Small friendly bow-windowed pub, lots of theatrical posters, soft lighting, comfortable seats, friendly service, real ales inc Badger Tanglefoot, chatty atmosphere (but can get packed); room upstairs; cl Sun, open all day Sat *(N R White)*

Opera Tavern WC2B 5JS [Catherine St, opp Theatre Royal]: Cheerful cosy bare-boards Victorian pub, not too touristy, five quickly changing real ales (over 20 a week), enjoyable bar food; some interesting fittings, lamps and windows *(Donna and Roger, Bruce Bird)*

☆ *Porterhouse* WC2E 7NA [Maiden Lane]: Good daytime pub (can be packed evenings), London outpost of Dublin's Porterhouse microbrewery, their interesting if pricey draught beers inc Porter and two Stouts (comprehensive tasting tray), also their TSB real ale and a guest, lots of bottled imports, good choice of wines by the glass; reasonably priced food from soup and open sandwiches up with some emphasis on rock oysters; shiny three-level labyrinth of stairs (lifts for disabled), galleries and copper ducting and piping, some nice design touches, sonorous openwork clock, neatly cased bottled beer displays; piped music, irish live music, big-screen sports TV (repeated in gents'); tables on front terrace, open all day *(Michael and Alison Sandy, BB, Tracey and Stephen Groves, Peter Dandy)*

Prince of Wales WC2B 5TD [Drury Lane]: Big busy neatly kept corner pub with efficient friendly staff, Adnams Broadside, Brains Rev

James, Fullers London Pride, Greene King IPA and Wells & Youngs Bombardier; good choice of reasonably priced pub food, raised dining area, half-panelled walls, some settles *(Michael and Alison Sandy)*

Ship WC2A 3HP [Gate St]: Tucked-away bare-boards pub with pews and high-backed settles forming candlelit nooks, open fire, leaded lights, painted plaster relief ceiling and upstairs overflow; well kept changing ales, decent pubby food inc superb ploughman's, friendly service; piped music *(Joe Green)*

☆ *Ship & Shovell* WC2N 5PH [Craven Passage, off Craven St]: Well kept Badger ales and a guest, good friendly staff, decent reasonably priced food inc wide range of baguettes etc; brightly lit with dark wood, etched mirrors and interesting mainly naval pictures, plenty of tables, open fire, compact back section; separate partitioned bar across *Underneath the Arches* alley; TV; open all day, cl Sun *(Ian Phillips, Michael and Alison Sandy, N R White, the Didler, Tim Maddison)*

Wellington WC2R 0HS [Strand/Wellington St]: Long narrow corner pub with room upstairs, Fullers London Pride, Greene King Abbot and Timothy Taylors Landlord; low-priced standard simple food till 5pm, friendly staff; tables outside *(Michael Dandy, Conor McGaughey)*

White Lion WC2E 8NT [James St]: Panelling, bare boards, Batemans Valiant, Fullers London Pride, Marstons Pedigree and Timothy Taylors Landlord; reasonably priced standard pubby food from sandwiches up, dining room upstairs *(Michael Dandy)*

EAST LONDON

E1

☆ *Dickens Inn* E1W 1UH [Marble Quay, St Katharines Way]: Outstanding position looking over smart docklands marina to Tower Bridge; bare boards, baulks and timbers, wide choice of enjoyable food inc good Sun roasts (pizza/pasta upstairs, smarter restaurant above that), friendly helpful staff; real ales such as Adnams, Greene King and Wells & Youngs, decent wines by the glass; piped music, machines; tables outside *(N R White, John Saville, the Didler, LYM)*

Mariners E1 0HY [Commercial Rd]: Friendly and nicely appointed, with some creative dishes from open-view kitchen, Adnams Broadside *(Michael and Deborah Ethier)*

☆ *Pride of Spitalfields* E1 5LJ [Heneage St]: Nicely worn-in little East End local with cheery regulars and friendly cat called Lenny; well kept Sharps Doom Bar and perhaps unusual guests from central servery, bargain simple food, prompt efficient service; atmospheric lighting, interesting prints, comfortable banquettes, coal fire, TV in smaller room opening off; two pavement tables *(Tracey and Stephen Groves, Derek and Sylvia Stephenson, BB, Jerry Brown, Mike and Eleanor Anderson)*

Town of Ramsgate E1W 2PN [Wapping High St]: Interesting old-London Thames-side setting, with restricted but evocative river view from small back floodlit terrace with mock gallows (hanging dock was nearby); long narrow chatty bar with squared oak panelling, real ales inc Adnams, friendly helpful service, good choice of standard food and daily specials; piped music; open all day *(N R White, Mrs M S Forbes, BB)*

E4

Royal Forest E4 7QH [Rangers Rd (A1069)]: Large timbered Brewers Fayre backing on to Epping Forest and dating partly from 17th c; friendly helpful service, Fullers London Pride, good choice of reasonably priced food; play area *(Robert Lester, N R White)*

E9

Royal Inn on the Park E9 7HJ [Lauriston Rd]: Substantial Victorian building overlooking Victoria Park, handsome dark-wood interior with solid if casual furniture on bare boards; friendly staff, restaurant-standard food in bar and small dining room, several real ales, german beers; Tues quiz night; dogs welcome (hooks on bar for leads), tables in good-sized garden and out in front *(Caroline McArthur)*

E13

Army & Navy E13 8JW [New Barn St]: Traditional East End local, great animal-lover landladies, darts, pool; big-screen sports TV, some live music *(David Albert)*

E14

Cat & Canary E14 4DH [Fishermans Walk]: Very good choice of wines by the glass, Fullers and guest ales, decent bar food inc speciality burgers, traditional décor; piped music may obtrude; heated dockside tables *(Colin Moore, N R White)*

North Pole E14 8LG [Manilla St]: Convivial sympathetically refurbished traditional pub, bargain home-made food, well kept ales inc Fullers London Pride and Timothy Taylors Landlord; darts; cl wknds *(Pete Baker)*

E15

King Edward VII E15 4BQ [Broadway]: New licensees working hard to source prime ingredients for their bar and restaurant food; four changing real ales, pews, dark woodwork and etched glass screens in traditional bar, sofas in small lounge area, pleasant back dining area with well lit prints above panelled dado; daily papers; well reproduced piped music, live music Thurs *(Karen Sloan)*

E18

Napier Arms E18 2QD [Woodford New Rd (A104), corner of Fullers Rd]: Comfortable, with good lively atmosphere, thai restaurant upstairs; big-screen sports TV *(Robert Lester)*

NORTH LONDON

N1

Camden Head N1 8DY [Camden Walk]: Comfortably preserved Victorian pub in pedestrianised street, well kept Fullers London Pride, Greene King and a guest from oval island servery, enjoyable food; comedy nights upstairs (not Tues); piped music, TV, silent games machine; downstairs ladies'; children welcome till 7pm, no dogs, front terrace, open all day *(Jeremy King)*

Charles Lamb N1 8DE [Elia St]: Well kept Fullers Chiswick, Timothy Taylors Landlord and a guest beer, some interesting imports on tap or bottled, good choice of wines by the glass; good blackboard food, delightful staff, big windows, polished boards and simple traditional furniture *(John M Murphy)*

Crown N1 OEB [Cloudesley Rd]: Good food and bustling atmosphere in nicely modernised Victorian pub, helpful friendly staff; Fullers Chiswick, London Pride and ESB from impressive island bar with snob screens, scrubbed boards, plenty of light oak panelling and cut and etched glass; tables out on small railed front terrace *(Nigel and Sue Foster, Tracey and Stephen Groves)*

George & Vulture N1 6BU [Pitfield St]: Remarkably tall pub, recently refurbished, with well kept Fullers, enjoyable food, open fire, warm relaxed atmosphere; weekly live music; barbecues *(Charlie Baker)*

☆ *Island Queen* N1 8HD [Noel Rd]: Fine high-ceilinged Victorian pub handy for Camden Passage antiques area; Fullers London Pride, a guest ale, lots of imported beers and good value wines from island bar, sensibly short choice of fresh often unusual food; pleasant staff, old-fashioned compartmentalised feel, dark wood and big decorative mirrors, intimate back area, upstairs room; children welcome *(Tracey and Stephen Groves, LYM)*

Steam Passage N1 OPN [Upper St]: Typical London pub with nice lively atmosphere, enjoyable hearty food, well kept Adnams, Fullers London Pride and Greene King Abbot; pavement tables *(Nigel and Sue Foster, Ian Phillips)*

Wenlock Arms N1 7TA [Wenlock Rd]: Well worn-in local in a bleak bit of London, friendly service, half a dozen or more well kept changing ales from central servery (always inc a Mild), farm cider and perry, foreign bottled beers, doorstep sandwiches (good salt beef); alcove seating, piano in pride of place, coal fires, darts, back pool table; Fri, Sat jazz nights, piano Sun afternoon; piped music; open all day *(Joe Green, the Didler, Bruce Bird, Roger Shipperley)*

N6

Angel N6 5JT [Highgate High St]: Neat L-shaped panelled bar with well kept ales such as Adnams and Fullers London Pride, decent wines by the glass; good value food from sandwiches up for most of the day, friendly helpful staff, leather settees, dim lighting; open all day *(John Wooll, Donna and Roger)*

N14

Cherry Tree N14 6EN [The Green]: Roomy beamed Vintage Inn with wide choice of wines by the glass, food all day from breakfast on, mix of big tables, some leather chesterfields; children welcome, tables out behind, bedrooms in adjacent Innkeepers Lodge, open all day *(Colin Moore)*

N21

Kings Head N21 1BB [The Green, nr Winchmore Hill Station]: Relaxing pub with stripped floors, sofas and gentle modern touches; log fire dividing off eating area with good food, beer choice inc belgian trappists, good wine range, friendly staff *(Ros Lawler)*

NW1

Bree Louise NW1 2HH [Cobourg St/Euston St]: Former Jolly Gardener, partly divided open-plan bar with half a dozen or more interesting real ales, food emphasising pies (Mon-Thurs bargains); basic décor with prints, UK flags, mixed used furnishings; can get very busy early evening; open all day *(Martin Grosberg, Lynda Payton, Sam Samuells, Joe Green, Bruce Bird)*

Crown & Goose NW1 7HP [corner of Arlington Rd/Delancey St]: Good food (get there early) inc Sun roasts; well kept Fullers London Pride from horseshoe bar with stools, tables set for eating at back (front tables are smaller); wood floors, shabby chic, candles at night; piped music *(Mrs Hazel Rainer, Jeremy King)*

☆ *Doric Arch* NW1 2DN [Eversholt St]: Virtually part of Euston Station, up stairs from bus terminus, with raised back part overlooking it; well kept Fullers and guests such as Kelham Island, Weston's farm cider, friendly helpful staff, good value pubby food lunchtime and from 4pm wkdys (12-5 wknds); pleasantly nostalgic atmosphere and some quiet corners, intriguing train and other transport memorabilia inc big clock at entrance, downstairs restaurant; discreet sports TV, machines; lavatories on combination lock; open all day *(BB, Ian Phillips, Dr and Mrs A K Clarke, Tracey and Stephen Groves, Joe Green, the Didler, Jeremy King, Sue Demont, Tim Barrow)*

Edinboro Castle NW1 7RU [Mornington Terrace/Delancy St]: Open-plan bare-boards pub with reasonably priced simple pubby food (all day wknds, mainly roasts Sun) from open kitchen; lots of wines by the glass, Caledonian Deuchars IPA, relaxed young atmosphere, raised skylit back area, some low tables, attractive beaded lampshades; large pleasant terrace *(Jeremy King)*

Euston Flyer NW1 2RA [Euston Rd, opp British Library]: Open-plan pub with warm welcome, full Fullers beer range, good choice of food all day, relaxed lunchtime atmosphere; plenty of light wood, tile and wood floors, mirrors, smaller more private raised areas, big doors open to street in warm weather; piped music, SkyTV, silent games machine, can get packed in evenings; open all day, cl 8.30pm Sun *(Dr and Mrs A K Clarke, Michael and Alison Sandy, the Didler, Stephen and Jean Curtis, Jeremy King)*

Metropolitan NW1 5LA [Baker Street Station, Marylebone Rd]: Wetherspoons in impressively ornate Victorian hall, large with lots of tables on one side, very long bar the other, leather sofas and some elbow tables; wide range of well priced ales inc some unusual ones, friendly efficient staff, good coffee, inexpensive food; silent fruit machine; family area, open all day *(John Branston, Jeremy King, Tony and Wendy Hobden, Michael and Alison Sandy, Robert Lester)*

☆ **Queens Head & Artichoke** NW1 4EA [Albany St]: Stylish pub/restaurant, unusual choice of good sensibly priced serious food (all day Sun) inc tapas, good choice of wines by the glass, well kept Adnams and Marstons Pedigree; smart modern furnishings inc leather settees, some panelling, conservatory, upstairs dining room; may be piped music; pavement picnic-sets *(Michael Butler, David Morgan, Sue Demont, Tim Barrow)*

NW3

☆ **Olde White Bear** NW3 1LJ [Well Rd]: Chatty and friendly unchanging Hampstead local, Victorian prints, actor and playwright photographs, elegant panelling, armchairs and sofa among other seats, open fire; good range of changing ales and other drinks, cards and chess, basic all-day bar food; TV, piped music; children and dogs welcome, pretty front terrace and back courtyard, handy for Hampstead Heath, open all day *(the Didler, N R White, Derek Wilson, LYM)*

NW5

Junction Tavern NW5 1AG [Fortess Rd]: Former corner Victorian local reworked as gastropub, good fresh food with some enterprising dishes, Caledonian Deuchars IPA and three other well kept ales; good atmosphere, well reproduced piped music; back conservatory, seats outside *(Stephen Nussey)*

NW6

Black Lion NW6 2BY [Kilburn High Rd]: Former railway hotel, amazing ornate gilded ceiling and walls in huge main bar, meals in smaller room off; decent simple bedrooms (no disabled access) *(Hazel Morgan, Bernard Patrick)*

NW7

☆ **Rising Sun** NW7 4EY [Marsh Lane/Highwood Hill, Mill Hill]: Attractive wisteria-covered local dating from 17th c, nicely worn-in cottagey bar with dark panelling, timber, prints and old local photographs, low-ceilinged candlelit snug up a step, big plainer lounge with beams and coal fire (watch your head going in); friendly helpful staff, well kept Adnams, Greene King Abbot and Wells & Youngs, good wines by the glass and malt whiskies, enjoyable quickly served generous food from fresh lunchtime sandwiches up; children welcome, picnic-sets in front and on suntrap back terrace, good walks nearby, open all day *(Tim Maddison, BB, Jestyn Phillips, Barry and Anne)*

SOUTH LONDON

SE1

Anchor SE1 9EF [Bankside]: In great spot nr Thames with river views from upper floors and roof terrace, extensively refurbished with beams, stripped brickwork and old-world corners; well kept Fullers London Pride and Greene King IPA, good choice of wines by the glass, popular fish and chip bar inc takeaways, other all-day food inc breakfast and tearoom; piped music; provision for children, disabled access, bedrooms in friendly quiet Premier Travel Inn behind, open all day *(Michael Doswell, Mike and Sue Loseby, N R White, Ian Phillips, LYM)*

☆ **Anchor & Hope** SE1 8LP [The Cut]: Informal bare-boards gastropub, almost too popular, changing food from potted shrimps to guinea fowl (pricey; can be top-notch though a test meal in Apr 2009 disappointed); well kept Wells & Youngs and guest beers, wine by tumbler or carafe; plain bar with big windows and mix of furniture inc elbow tables, curtained-off dining part with tight-packed scrubbed tables, small open kitchen area and contemporary art on purple walls; children and dogs welcome, open all day, cl Sun evening, Mon lunchtime *(Ian Phillips, Canon Michael Bourdeaux, LYM, Mike and Sue Loseby, Jeremy King, Edward Mirzoeff, M Fitzpatrick)*

Barrow Boy & Banker SE1 9QQ [Borough High St, by London Bridge Station]: Comfortable, civilised bank conversion with roomy upper gallery, full Fullers beer range kept well, decent wines, efficient young staff, no-nonsense food inc good pies; music-free; right by Southwark Cathedral *(Sue and Mike Todd, Bruce Bird, Charles Gysin)*

Bridge House SE1 2UP [Tower Bridge Rd]: Relaxed Adnams bar with upmarket modern décor and sofas, their full ale range and good wine choice, good value generous food, friendly efficient service; downstairs dining area *(N R White)*

Garrison SE1 3XB [Bermondsey St]: Interesting pub with scrubbed tables upstairs, cinema downstairs; enjoyable reasonably priced food, more emphasis on wine than beer *(Mrs Jane Kingsbury)*

☆ **Hole in the Wall** SE1 8SQ [Mepham St]:

Quirky no-frills hideaway in railway arch virtually underneath Waterloo, rumbles and shakes with the trains, fine range of well kept ales, bargain basic food all day, plush red banquettes in small quieter front bar, well worn mix of tables set well back from long bar in larger back room; big-screen sports TV; open all day, cl wknd afternoons *(LM, Stephen and Jean Curtis, Michael and Alison Sandy, Tracey and Stephen Groves, Chris Sale, Joe Green, LYM, Ian Phillips)*

☆ **Horniman** SE1 2HD [Hays Galleria, off Battlebridge Lane]: Spacious, bright and airy Thames-side drinking hall with lots of polished wood, comfortable seating inc a few sofas, upstairs seating; several real ales with unusual guests (may offer tasters), teas and coffees at good prices, lunchtime bar food from soup and big sandwiches up, snacks other times; efficient service coping with large numbers after work; unobtrusive piped music; fine river views from picnic-sets outside, open all day *(Derek Thomas, Tracey and Stephen Groves, Dr and Mrs Jackson, LYM)*

☆ **Kings Arms** SE1 8TB [Roupell St]: Proper corner local, bustling and friendly, curved servery dividing traditional bar and lounge; Adnams, Fullers London Pride, Greene King IPA and Wells & Youngs Bombardier; good friendly service, flame-effect fires, food from thai dishes to good Sun roast, big back extension with conservatory/courtyard dining area, long central table and high side tables; attractive local prints and eccentric bric-a-brac; piped music; open all day *(N R White, Sue Demont, Tim Barrow, Tracey and Stephen Groves, Phil Bryant, Ian Phillips)*

☆ **Lord Clyde** SE1 1ER [Clennam St]: Neat panelled L-shaped local in same friendly efficient family for over 50 years, well kept Adnams Best, Fullers London Pride, Greene King IPA, Shepherd Neame Spitfire and Wells & Youngs; simple food from good salt beef sandwiches up wkdy lunchtimes and early evenings, darts in small hatch-service back public bar; striking tiled façade, open all day (Sat early evening break, cl 7pm Sun) *(Pete Baker, Mike and Sue Loseby, N R White)*

Mad Hatter SE1 9NY [Stamford St, Blackfriars Rd end]: Smartly Edwardianised, with stained-glass, coaching prints, books and interesting hats; good range of food, Fullers ales, fine choice of wines by the glass, helpful staff *(Tracey and Stephen Groves)*

Mudlark SE1 9DA [Montague Close (office estate off arch under London Bridge to Tooley St)]: Comfortable multi-level pub handy for Southwark Cathedral; Fullers London Pride and Wells & Youngs, fair choice of wines, popular bar lunches; small terrace *(Valerie Baker, N R White)*

Ring SE1 8HA [Blackfriars Rd/The Cut, opp Southwark tube station]: Neat and convivial, with lots of boxing photographs and memorabilia, stripped pale boards, brown décor; thai food, good choice of wines

by the glass, Courage Best and Fullers London Pride; seats outside *(Tracey and Stephen Groves, Jeremy King)*

White Hart SE1 8TJ [Cornwall Rd/Whittlesey St]: Vibrant local in upcoming area, friendly bustle, comfortable sofas, stripped boards and so forth; Fullers London Pride, Greene King IPA, Wells & Youngs Bitter, several belgian beers, good range of ciders, sensibly priced up-to-date food; piped music *(Ian Phillips, N R White, Giles and Annie Francis)*

SE10

Ashburnham Arms SE10 8UH [Ashburnham Grove]: Friendly chatty Shepherd Neame local, good pasta and other food (not Mon), mixed décor and customers; pleasant garden with barbecues *(N R White, the Didler)*

Plume of Feathers SE10 9LZ [Park Vista]: Low-ceilinged Georgian local with good value food from sandwiches up, well kept ales such as Greene King Ruddles and Harveys, good coffee, friendly service; flame-effect fire in large fireplace, lots of pictures and plates, some nautical artefacts, back dining area; sports TV; children welcome, playroom across back yard with trees (Greenwich Park playground nearby too), handy for Maritime Museum, open all day *(Pete Baker, N R White, B J Harding, LM, Tom and Rosemary Hall)*

☆ **Richard I** SE10 8RT [Royal Hill]: Friendly recently refurbished two-bar Youngs local, with popular food inc Sun lunch; carpets and panelling; children welcome, picnic-sets out in front, lots more in pleasant paved back garden with wknd barbecues – busy summer wknds and evenings *(N R White, the Didler)*

SE12

Crown SE12 0AJ [Burnt Ash Hill]: Typical civilised suburban Youngs pub, cheerful staff and relaxed atmosphere, some seats in cosy alcoves, good range of bar food, Wells & Youngs ales; pleasant garden *(Clive Flynn)*

SE16

☆ **Angel** SE16 4NB [Bermondsey Wall East]: Appealing and civilised Thames-side pub, superb views from back lounge, upstairs area, back jetty and side garden; softly lit front bars with two public areas on either side of snug, low-backed settles, old local photographs and memorabilia, etched glass and glossy varnish; cheap Sam Smiths, kind friendly service, usual food; children and dogs welcome, interesting walks round Surrey Quays *(Valerie Baker, LYM)*

☆ **Mayflower** SE16 4NF [Rotherhithe St]: Unchanging cosy old riverside pub in unusual street with lovely Wren church; wide choice of enjoyable generous food all day, black beams, panelling, nautical bric-a-brac, high-backed settles and coal fires; good Thames views from upstairs restaurant (cl Sat lunchtime), Greene King ales, good coffee and good value wines, friendly service; piped music; children welcome, nice jetty/terrace over water, open all day *(LYM, N R White, the Didler)*

SE18
Bull SE18 3HP [Shooters Hill]: Neat and friendly two-bar local, plusher at back; well kept changing ales such as Courage Best, Fullers/Gales ESB, Harveys Best, St Austell Tribute, Sharps Doom Bar and Wells & Youngs Best; no piped music; dogs welcome, by entry to ancient Oxleas Woods *(Michael and Deborah Ethier)*

SE22
Bishop SE22 8EW [Lordship Lane]: Contemporary dining pub with good food and friendly staff; children and dogs welcome *(Jamie Ross)*

SE24
Florence SE24 0NG [Dulwich Rd]: Handsome Victorian pub visibly brewing its own Weasel ale, farm cider, enjoyable food, friendly atmosphere; glossy bar and appealing contemporary décor, comfortable booth seating, dining conservatory; children welcome, good terrace tables *(Dave W Holliday, Giles and Annie Francis, Bill Adie)*
Prince Regent SE24 0NJ [Dulwich Rd]: Good range of changing ales, belgian beers, friendly staff; books on window sills, good if not cheap changing menu, dining area downstairs *(Bill Adie)*

SW4
Bread & Roses SW4 6DZ [Clapham Manor St]: Three well kept and chosen ales, contemporary café-style; piped music *(Tracey and Stephen Groves)*
Manor Arms SW4 6ED [Clapham Manor St]: Warm comfortable beamed pub, friendly and civilised, with well kept Fullers London Pride and Timothy Taylors Landlord; striking burgundy colour scheme *(Tracey and Stephen Groves)*
Windmill SW4 9DE [Clapham Common South Side]: Big bustling pub by the common, contemporary front bar, quite a few original Victorian features mainly in the more old-fashioned panelled back area; Wells & Youngs ales, good choice of wines by the glass, food (all day wknds) from soup and baguettes up; piped music, TV; good bedrooms, open all day *(LYM, Tracey and Stephen Groves)*

SW8
Priory Arms SW8 2PB [Lansdowne Way]: Friendly country atmosphere in town, packed old corner bookshelf and committed regulars; good beer range inc Harveys Best, belgian and german beers on tap and in bottle, enjoyable food from ploughman's to good Sun roasts *(Gillian Rodgers)*

SW11
Bolingbroke SW11 6RE [Northcote Rd]: Discreetly decorated dining pub with antique panelling, lighting, furniture and paintings, up-to-date food strong on carefully chosen ingredients, enterprising choice of children's food (toys and such for them, too); Caledonian Deuchars IPA and Timothy Taylors Landlord, good choice of wines by the glass, Weston's farm cider, interesting juices; open all day *(anon)*
Eagle SW11 6HG [Chatham Rd]: Attractive and warmly welcoming old backstreet local, real ales such as Fullers London Pride, Timothy Taylors Landlord and Westerham British Bulldog, friendly prompt service; leather sofas in fireside corner of L-shaped bar; big-screen sports TV; back terrace with marquee, small front terrace too *(Sue Demont, Tim Barrow, Stephen Funnell, Dave Braisted)*
Falcon SW11 1RU [St Johns Hill]: Edwardian pub with several beers inc well kept Fullers London Pride from the remarkably long, light oak bar, bargain pub food such as pie and mash, friendly service; lively front bar, period partitions, cut glass and mirrors, quieter back dining area; daily papers; big-screen TV *(N R White, Sue Demont, Tim Barrow, Vickie Metcalfe)*

SW12
Devonshire SW12 9AN [Balham High Rd]: Duke of Devonshire shorn of its proper title in 2008 after extensive bright refurbishment of this large Victorian pub; retains some of the original features and etched glass, alongside more modern furnishings, lighting and paintings; Wells & Youngs ales, neat staff, standard bar food with more choice in back carpeted restaurant; piped music (can get loud), attracts youngish crowd in evenings; contemporary tables out on heated back decking, barbecue, open all day *(Jasmine Voos)*
☆ **Nightingale** SW12 8NX [Nightingale Lane]: Cosy and civilised early Victorian local, small woody front bar opening into larger back area and attractive family conservatory; well kept Wells & Youngs ales, enjoyable bar food, sensible prices, friendly staff; sports TV; small secluded back garden *(Sue Demont, Tim Barrow, Giles and Annie Francis, BB)*

SW13
☆ **Brown Dog** SW13 0AP [Cross St]: Impressively renovated with thriving atmosphere, enjoyable food, good choice of wines, friendly helpful staff; subtle lighting and open fires; children and dogs welcome *(Alastair Stevenson, BB)*
☆ **Idle Hour** SW13 0PQ [Railway Side (off White Hart Lane between Mortlake High St and Upper Richmond Rd)]: Chatty tucked-away organic gastropub, very good individually cooked food, good range of organic soft drinks, wines and beers; nice chunky old tables on bare boards, relaxed atmosphere,

daily papers and magazines, a profusion of wall clocks on different times, comfortable sofa by the small fireplace; chill-out piped music, no children; if driving, park at end of Railway Side and walk (road gets too narrow for cars); tables with candles and cocktail parasols out in small pretty yard behind, elaborate barbecues, cl wkdy lunchtimes *(Simon Rodway, BB)*

Sun SW13 9HE [Church Rd]: Open-plan pub popular with youngish crowd, Black Sheep and other beers from central servery, sofas and lots of tables and chairs, enjoyable varied food from chunky sandwiches up; piped music, sports TV; tables over the road overlooking the green and pond, busy on fine days *(Edward Mirzoeff)*

Tree House SW13 0PW [White Hart Lane]: Old pub nicely done up with dark wood and comfortable seats, enjoyable food inc good Sun lunch, decent wines *(Guy Vowles)*

SW14

Ship SW14 7QR [Thames Bank]: Comfortable pub with good Thames views, prompt friendly service, Fullers London Pride, Greene King IPA and Wells & Youngs Bombardier; good range of reasonably priced generous pubby food from sandwiches up, conservatory; terrace tables, not on river side *(Edward Mirzoeff, Peter Dandy)*

SW15

☆ *Bricklayers Arms* SW15 1DD [down cul-de-sac off Lower Richmond Rd nr Putney Bridge]: Tidy traditional local with well kept Timothy Taylors range and guest beers, real cider, friendly young staff; limited but enjoyable evening food, scrubbed tables, woodburner, dim lighting; sports TV; side terrace *(N R White, Peter Dandy, Susan and John Douglas, Gavin Robinson)*

Dukes Head SW15 1JN [Lower Richmond Rd, nr Putney Bridge]: Smartly modernised and expanded Victorian pub, comfortable furnishings in knocked-together front bars and trendy downstairs cocktail bar in long disused skittle alley (very popular with young people wknds); good range of well presented pubby food all day inc sharing platters and snacks, Wells & Youngs ales, lots of wines by glass, light and airy back dining room with great river views; plastic glasses for outside terrace or riverside pavement across the road; children welcome (high chairs and smaller helpings), open all day *(Peter Dandy, BB)*

Green Man SW15 3NG [Wildcroft Rd, Putney Heath]: Small friendly old local by Putney Heath, nicely redecorated rooms and alcoves; good choice of enjoyable food, well kept Wells & Youngs ales with a guest such as St Austell; TV; attractive back garden with decking, also some seats out at front nr road, open all day *(Peter Dandy, LYM, Colin McKerrow, Michael Dandy)*

Prince of Wales SW15 2SP [Upper Richmond Rd]: Neatly refurbished by young landlord,

country-pub feel, good reasonably priced, unusual food inc game and tasty rotisserie chicken, well kept Black Sheep and Fullers London Pride, good choice of wine; efficient friendly staff, bar lined with pewter mugs, good countryside photographs and interesting skylight in back restaurant *(Peter Dandy, Richard Greaves)*

SW16

Earl Ferrers SW16 6JF [Ellora Rd]: Family-friendly pub under popular new management, good choice of well kept ales such as Archers, Fullers London Pride, local Sambrooks Wandle and Timothy Taylors Landlord; good informal service, interesting bar snacks, games and books; live music every other Sun; some tables outside *(Tim Fairhurst)*

SW18

☆ *Cats Back* SW18 1NN [Point Pleasant]: Distinctive backstreet haven with well kept Downton ales, good choice of wines by the glass, reasonably priced food (till 10.30pm) from good sandwiches up in bar and popular upstairs restaurant, friendly efficient service; motley furnishings from pews and scrubbed pine tables to pensioned-off chairs and sofas, loads of bric-a-brac, pictures on red walls, dimmed chandeliers and lit candelabra; customers in keeping with the eccentric décor; blazing fire in small fireplace; interesting piped music such as East European folk; pavement tables and diverse chairs, open all day *(BB, LM, Peter Dandy)*

County Arms SW18 3SH [Trinity Rd]: Good Victorian décor in big Youngs pub, busy wknds, relaxed wkdy lunchtimes, with enjoyable food in pleasant candlelit eating area; good service, well kept ales, big open fires, comfortable sofas; jazz nights *(Mrs G R Sharman, BB)*

Earl Spencer SW18 5JL [Merton Rd]: Nicely stripped-down, with bare boards, mixed old furnishings, log fire, relaxed atmosphere; some emphasis on the food side (reasonable prices), real ales such as Fullers London Pride, Hook Norton, Sharps Doom Bar and Theakstons Old Peculier, good choice of wines by the glass; dogs welcome *(Susan and John Douglas)*

Ship SW18 1TB [Jews Row]: Popular riverside pub by Wandsworth Bridge, with light and airy conservatory-style décor, pleasant mix of furnishings on bare boards, basic public bar; well kept Wells & Youngs ales and Caledonian Deuchars IPA, freshly cooked interesting bistro food in recently extended restaurant with own garden, attractive good-sized terrace with barbecue and outside bar; dogs and children welcome, open all day *(LYM, Peter Dandy)*

SW19

Alexandra SW19 7NE [Wimbledon Hill Rd]: Large busy Youngs pub with Wells & Youngs ales and good choice of wines by the glass from central bar, enjoyable food from sandwiches to good Sun roasts, friendly helpful service; comfortably up-to-date décor in linked rooms inc bare-boards dining areas; TVs; attractive roof terrace, tables also out in mews (Peter Dandy, Michael Dandy)

Dog & Fox SW19 5EA [Wimbledon High St]: Striking large pub, smartly modernised with contemporary furniture, Wells & Youngs ales and a guest such as St Austell Tribute, good choice of wines, nice coffee; enjoyable interesting food from sandwiches up, friendly helpful staff, sizeable dining area (Peter Dandy, Michael Dandy)

Fox & Grapes SW19 4UN [Camp Rd]: 18th-c pub by the common with slightly old-fashioned lived-in feel, enjoyable interesting food, ales such as Greene King, Harveys and Sharps, good wine choice, friendly service; big-screen sports TV in larger raftered bar, piped music; can get busy wknds; children welcome till 7pm, open all day (Michael Dandy, Peter Dandy, BB)

☆ **Rose & Crown** SW19 5BA [Wimbledon High St]: Comfortably refurbished 17th-c Youngs pub, alcove seating in roomy bar, old prints inc interesting religious texts and drawings; friendly attentive staff, pubby food inc enjoyable Sun lunch, back dining conservatory; partly covered former coach yard, bedrooms (LYM, Peter Dandy, Colin McKerrow, Michael Dandy)

WEST LONDON

SW6

Sands End SW6 2PR [Stephendale Rd]: Irish chef doing enterprising fresh food with new twists to old traditions from home-baked bread up, real ales such as Black Sheep, Greene King Old Speckled Hen and Hook Norton, simple country furnishings and open fire (anon)

Waterside SW6 2SU [The Boulevard, Imperial Wharf, Imperial Rd]: Modern light and airy three-level Youngs pub in new riverside development, relaxed yet vibrant; with popular food and friendly service, interesting mix of modern and traditional décor, back sofas and chaises longues, high ceilings and picture windows; wide Thames views to heliport; lots of tables out on waterside terrace by Thames Path (N R White)

SW7

Prince Regent SW7 4PL [Gloucester Rd]: Modernised open-plan dining pub, mixed furnishings on bare wood; good choice of wines by the glass, Adnams Regatta and Wells & Youngs Bombardier, up-to-date pub food (Michael Dandy)

Queens Arms SW7 5QL [Queens Gate Mews]: Victorian pub with enjoyable home cooking, good wines by the glass, real ales inc Fullers London Pride; period furniture, heavy plush seating, massive mahogany bookcases,

lithographs inc two of nearby Albert Hall (Pat and Roger Davies, N R White)

W4

Bell & Crown W4 3PF [Strand on the Green]: Well run, panelled Fullers local, friendly staff, sensibly priced food, log fire, great Thames views from back bar and conservatory; may be piped music; dogs welcome, back terrace and towpath area, good walks, open all day (N R White)

Devonshire House W4 2JJ [Devonshire Rd]: Spacious Gordon Ramsay gastropub, not cheap; comfortable dining chairs and banquettes, bare boards, panelling and coal-effect fire; friendly atmosphere, attentive service, Caledonian Deuchars IPA and Fullers London Pride; open all day, cl Mon (Ian Phillips)

Mawson Arms W4 2QA [Chiswick Lane South, by Great West Rd at Fullers Brewery; aka Fox & Hounds]: Virtual tap for Fullers brewery, their beers particularly well kept, some good home-made food inc proper sandwiches (Chris Evans)

Roebuck W4 1PU [Chiswick High Rd]: Friendly and relaxing dining pub with comfortable leather seats in front bar, roomy and attractive back dining area opening into sheltered paved garden with hanging baskets; enjoyable reasonably priced food all day from open kitchen, good choice of wines by the glass, real ales such as Wells & Youngs; dogs welcome, open all day (Simon Rodway)

Swan W4 5HH [Evershed Walk, Acton Lane]: Enjoyable food with some interesting dishes, informal style, friendly staff; good range of wines by the glass, three real ales; they may try to keep your credit card while you eat (Simon Rodway)

W6

☆ **Anglesea Arms** W6 0UR [Wingate Rd; nr Ravenscourt Park tube station]: Good interesting food inc wkdy set lunches in homely bustling gastropub, most enjoyable, with good choice of wines by the glass and of real ales; close-set tables in dining room facing kitchen, roaring fire in simply decorated panelled bar; children welcome, tables out by quiet street, open all day (John and Annabel Hampshire, Nigel and Sue Foster, the Didler, LYM)

☆ **Black Lion** W6 9TJ [South Black Lion Lane]: Welcoming and civilised cottagey pub kept spotless; helpful landlord and friendly staff, well kept ales such as Caledonian Deuchars IPA and Fullers London Pride, good choice of wines by the glass, modest choice of decent generous food from baguettes and baked potatoes up; comfortable mix of furnishings inc some high-backed settles, nicely varnished woodwork, candles at night, dining area behind big log-effect gas fire; no TV or music but Mon film night; large pleasant heated terrace on quiet corner (BB, Simon Rodway)

Blue Anchor W6 9DJ [Lower Mall]: Recently refurbished pub right on the Thames (first licensed 1722); two traditional linked areas with oak floors and panelling, good value generous bar lunches, real ales, pleasant river-view room upstairs; disabled facilities, riverside tables, busy wknds (BB)

Queens Arms W6 8NL [Greyhound Rd]: Contemporary updating of Victorian corner pub, well kept Fullers London Pride, good range of other drinks, tasty pub food inc sharing platters; mixed tables and chairs, easy chairs and sofas on dark bare boards, high stools along long, narrow, free-standing counter, colourful artworks on off-white walls; glazed and steel-framed staircase to upstairs dining area; sports TVs (LM)

Stonemasons Arms W6 0LA [Cambridge Grove]: Good changing food from open kitchen in relaxed Hammersmith gastropub; fair prices, good service, plain décor, basic furnishings, lots of modern art, ceiling fans; mostly young customers in evenings; piped music (BB, Simon Rodway)

W8

Britannia W8 6UX [Allen St, off Kensington High St]: Well designed uncluttered L-shaped dining pub, a bit off the beaten track so a Sun lunchtime oasis of peace and calm; enjoyable interesting food, Wells & Youngs ales (Jill Bickerton)

☆ **Uxbridge Arms** W8 7TQ [Uxbridge St]: Friendly and cottagey backstreet local with three brightly furnished linked areas, well kept Fullers and a guest, good choice of bottled beers; china, prints and photographs; sports TV; open all day (the Didler, Tracey and Stephen Groves)

W9

Waterway W9 2JU [Formosa St]: Bookable picnic-sets out on terrace by Grand Union Canal, enjoyable food inc fish and chargrills from open kitchen, well kept beer, good wines by the glass, cocktails, happy staff; scandinavian feel, settees in bar area, restaurant (Jeremy King)

W11

Ladbroke Arms W11 3NW [Ladbroke Rd]: Busy dining pub with good food, four real ales, friendly staff and pleasant warm atmosphere; daily papers; tables on front terrace with nice hanging baskets (Dr and Mrs M E Wilson, LYM, Dr Martin Owton)

W12

☆ **Princess Victoria** W12 9DH [Uxbridge Rd]: Impressively restored grand Victorian bar and dining room, original features especially around skylights; emphasis on carefully sourced good food (interesting menu, unusual bar snacks inc distinctive pork board), wide choice of wines, attentive friendly staff, four real ales inc Harveys and Hop Back Summer Lightning; interesting collection of old tables and chairs; small

back terrace, adjoining wine and cigar shop, Sat morning food market in front (not Jan or Feb), wine tastings then too (Richard Greaves, BB)

W14

Radnor Arms W14 8PX [Warwick Rd]: Convivial and pubby, Everards and guest ales, friendly staff who are real ale enthusiasts, good choice of whiskies; plenty of small tables in both rooms, pub games; open all day (the Didler)

OUTER LONDON

BARKING [TQ4484]
Britannia IG11 8PR [Tanner St/Church Rd]: Large softly lit yet airy Youngs pub with their real ales and a guest beer, good value food from sandwiches and baked potatoes up inc bargain wkdy lunches and very popular Sun lunch; friendly family service, events, pool; tables outside (Stuart Hall)
Spotted Dog IG11 8TN [Longbridge Rd (A124)]: Friendly and appealing old-style panelled Davys local, separate bars, easy chairs at the back, good wines by the glass inc ports, Shepherd Neame Spitfire (labelled Wallop here); restaurant (John Taylor)
BECKENHAM [TQ3769]
Jolly Woodman BR3 6NR [Chancery Lane]: Small friendly old-fashioned local in conservation area, five or so good changing real ales, welcoming friendly service, good value lunchtime sandwiches or a hot home-made special; flower-filled back yard and pavement tables, open all day, cl Mon lunchtime (N R White, B J Harding)
BEXLEY [TQ4973]
Kings Head DA5 1AA [High St]: Dating from the 14th c, linked rooms, low beams and brasses, open fires, Greene King ales (Michael and Deborah Ethier)
BROMLEY [TQ4070]
Prince Frederick BR1 4DE [Nichol Lane]: Quiet old-fashioned end-of-terrace local, Greene King Abbot and guest beers, darts, quiz night; TV cricket (Greg Tassell)
Red Lion BR1 3LG [North Rd]: Chatty backstreet local, shelves of books, green velvet drapes; well kept Greene King, Harveys and guest beers, good service; front terrace, open all day (N R White)
Two Doves BR2 8HD [Oakley Rd (A233)]: Popular and comfortable unpretentious pub notable for its lovely garden with terrace tables; friendly staff and locals, well kept Courage Directors, St Austell Tribute and Wells & Youngs Special, no hot food but ploughman's and snacks; modern back conservatory (N R White, B and M Kendall, Mr and Mrs Rob W Miles)
CHISLEHURST [TQ4369]
Ramblers Rest BR7 5ND [Mill Pl, just off Bickley Park Rd and Old Hill, by Summer Hill (A222)]: White weatherboarded local in picturesque hillside setting on edge of

Chislehurst Common; well kept Adnams
Broadside, Brakspears, Courage Best, Fullers
London Pride and Wells & Youngs
Bombardier, good value basic food; friendly
staff, pleasant unpretentious atmosphere,
upper and lower bars; neat terrace behind,
grassy slope out in front (plastic glasses for
there), handy for Chislehurst Caves
(N R White, Tony and Glenys Dyer)
Sydney Arms BR7 6PL [Old Perry St]:
Friendly atmosphere, quick service even
when busy, good range of inexpensive basic
food, well kept real ales, big conservatory;
pleasant garden good for children, almost
opp entrance to Scadbury Park, country
walks *(B J Harding, N R White)*
Tigers Head BR7 5PJ [Watts Lane/Manor
Park Rd (B264 S of common, opp St Nicholas
church)]: Airy Chef & Brewer overlooking
church and common, cosy low-beamed areas,
wide food choice inc a variety of fish and
Sun lunch, good wine list, Adnams, Fullers
and guest ales; quiet piped music, parking
can be difficult; children welcome till 6pm,
side terrace tables (dogs allowed here only),
open all day *(Dr Ron Cox)*
COULSDON [TQ3157]
Tudor Rose CR5 1EB [Old Coulsdon]:
Spacious Ember Inn, smart modern
refurbishment, good range of real ales and of
wines by the glass, bargain food all day,
quick friendly service; piped music, small TV,
games machine; garden behind *(Phil Bryant,
BB)*
CROYDON [TQ3564]
Sandrock CR0 5HA [Upper Shirley Rd]: Good
value enterprising food, good service,
pleasantly informal atmosphere; real ales
such as Black Sheep and Timothy Taylors
Landlord, good choice of wines by the glass
(Alan Gull)
ENFIELD [TQ3599]
Pied Bull EN3 6TE [Bullsmoor Lane (A1055);
handy for M25 junction 25, by A10]: Rustic
red-tiled 17th-c pub, spotless with local
prints on bared walls, low beam-and-plank
ceilings, lots of comfortable little rooms and
extensions, rugs on bare boards; friendly
staff, well kept Adnams, Fullers London Pride
and Greene King Old Speckled Hen, wide
choice of sensibly priced food; conservatory,
pleasant garden *(Robert Lester)*
HAMPTON COURT [TQ1668]
☆ *Kings Arms* KT8 9DD [Hampton Court Rd, by
Lion Gate]: Civilised pub by Hampton Court
itself (so popular with tourists), comfortable
furnishings inc sofas in back area, attractive
Farrow & Ball colours, good open fires, lots
of oak panelling, beams and some stained-
glass; well kept Badger beers, good choice of
wines by the glass, friendly service, sensibly
priced pubby food from sandwiches up,
restaurant too; piped music; children and
dogs welcome, picnic-sets on roadside front
terrace, charming new bedrooms, open all
day *(Susan and John Douglas, Michael Butler,
LYM, N R White, David and Ruth Shillitoe)*

ISLEWORTH [TQ1675]
London Apprentice TW7 6BG [Church St]:
Large Thames-side pub furnished with
character, reasonably priced food inc good
value sandwiches, well kept ales inc Adnams
and Fullers, good wine choice; log fire,
pleasant friendly service, brown décor,
upstairs river-view restaurant (open all Sun
afternoon); may be piped music; children
welcome, attractive waterside terrace, small
riverside lawn, open all day *(LM, LYM)*
KEW [TQ1977]
Coach & Horses TW9 3BH [Kew Green]:
Modernised open-plan pub overlooking the
green, decent Wells & Youngs ales and good
coffees, standard bar food from sandwiches
up; young friendly staff, relaxed atmosphere,
armchairs and sofas, restaurant; sports TV;
teak tables on front terrace, nice setting
handy for Kew Gardens and National Archive
(Pat and Tony Martin, Michael Butler)
Inn at Kew Gardens TW9 3NG [Sandycombe
Rd, close to tube station]: Roomy pub/hotel
with comfortably refurbished Victorian bar,
friendly and relaxed; well kept ales, helpful
staff, enjoyable fresh food inc good
sandwich choice, nice dining room; tables
outside, 19 good bedrooms *(Chris Smith,
John Wooll)*
Railway TW9 3PZ [Station Parade]:
Appealing former station buffet, Adnams
Broadside, Shepherd Neame Spitfire and
Wells & Youngs Bombardier, three draught
ciders, decent choice of wines by the glass;
reasonably priced food, mix of comfortable
sofas, tall and more regular tables,
newspapers; TVs; large covered and heated
area outside *(Ian Phillips)*
KINGSTON [TQ1869]
Canbury Arms KT2 6LQ [Canbury Park Rd]:
Big-windowed open-plan local with good
value enterprising food inc up-to-date food
inc breakfast from 9am (not Sun), well kept ales
such as Harveys, Sharps and Timothy Taylors,
very good wine choice (bargains Mon night);
young friendly staff, simple fresh
contemporary décor, cosy easy chairs as well
as neat tables and chairs, large side
conservatory; frequent events; children and
dogs welcome, heated terrace with
retractable awning *(LM)*
MALDEN RUSHETT [TQ1763]
☆ *Star* KT22 0DP [Kingston Rd (A243 just N of
M25 junction 9)]: Substantial dining pub on
Surrey border, reliable and well run with
three traditionally refurbished areas, well
kept Fullers and Greene King ales, decent all-
day pubby food from ciabattas up inc
popular Sun roasts; friendly welcoming
service and atmosphere, wood and carpeted
floors, two large log fires, newspapers; quiet
piped music and occasional live; children
welcome (high chairs and baby changing
facilities), tables with umbrellas on heated
front terrace with awning, walks on Ashstead
Common *(the Didler, Ron Neale, Sue and
Mike Todd, LM, DWAJ)*

NEW MALDEN [TQ2168]
Glasshouse KT3 4QE [Coombe Rd]:
Modernised pub with contemporary feel,
good choice of food, real ales such as
Adnams, Sharps Doom Bar and Wells &
Youngs Bombardier; lots of evening events
(Peter Dandy)
OSTERLEY [TQ1578]
☆ *Hare & Hounds* TW7 5PR [Windmill Lane
(B454, off A4 – called Syon Lane at that
point)]: Roomy suburban Fullers dining pub,
wide choice of enjoyable food from
sandwiches to hearty reasonably priced main
dishes, prompt friendly service, pleasant
dining extension; spacious terrace and big
floodlit mature garden, nice setting opp
beautiful Osterley Park *(Tom and Ruth Rees,
Mrs M S Forbes, C and R Bromage)*
PETERSHAM [TQ1873]
Café Dysart TW10 7AA [Petersham Rd]: Opp
Richmond Park gate, former Dysart Arms
done up rather like a bistro/wine bar, chunky
furniture and clever modern lighting, relaxed
atmosphere (may be a classical guitarist);
decent food, Adnams and Twickenham ale;
seats out in front *(LM)*
RICHMOND [TQ1774]
Princes Head TW9 1LX [The Green]: Large
open-plan pub overlooking cricket green nr
theatre; low-ceilinged panelled areas off big
island bar, full Fullers range, fresh bar food
from sandwiches to steak, relaxed mature
atmosphere, open fire; seats outside – fine
spot *(N R White, Michael Dandy)*
Watermans Arms TW9 1TJ [Water Lane]:
Friendly old-fashioned Youngs local, well
kept beer, open fire, traditional layout; pub
games, enjoyable thai food; handy for
Thames *(Chris Sale)*
White Swan TW9 1PG [Old Palace Lane]:
Civilised and relaxed, with smart yet rustic
dark-beamed open-plan bar, friendly service,
real ales such as Fullers London Pride and
Wells & Youngs Bombardier, fresh wholesome
bar lunches; coal-effect fires, popular
upstairs restaurant; piped music; children
allowed in back conservatory, pretty little
walled terrace below railway *(Meg and
Colin Hamilton, N R White, LYM)*

Roebuck TW10 6RN [Richmond Hill]:
Comfortable and attractive 18th-c bay-
windowed pub with helpful young staff, well
kept changing ales, usual food; stripped-
brick alcoves, some substantial bygones, old
Thames photographs and prints; children and
dogs welcome, terrace over road with fine
views of meadows and Thames, open all day
(Bruce Bird, N R White)
ROMFORD [TQ5188]
Golden Lion RM1 1HR [High St]: Warm and
cosy local in listed building with quite a
history, Greene King and guest beers,
sensible food, good mix of ages, friendly
staff; Weds folk night *(anon)*
TEDDINGTON [TQ1671]
Tide End Cottage TW11 9NN [Broom
Rd/Ferry Rd, nr bridge at Teddington Lock]:
Friendly low-ceilinged pub in Victorian
cottage terrace next to Teddington Studios;
two rooms united by big log-effect gas fire,
well kept Greene King ales and a guest such
as Clarks Westgate Flankers Tackle, decent
low-priced bar food to numbered tables from
sandwiches up; lots of river, fishing and
rowing memorabilia and photographs,
interesting Dunkirk evacuation link, back
dining extension; sports TV in front bar;
minimal parking; children welcome till
7.30pm, small back terrace *(Chris Evans,
Ian Phillips)*
WANSTEAD [TQ4088]
George E11 2RL [opp Underground; High St]:
Big popular Wetherspoons, good friendly
atmosphere, good value food; big-screen
sports TVs *(Robert Lester)*
WOODFORD GREEN [TQ4092]
Cocked Hat IG8 8LG [Southend Rd (A1400),
just off M11 terminal roundabout]: Popular
main-road Toby Carvery with good value
food, friendly service; Bass, separate proper
bar area, interesting photographs
(Robert Lester)
Cricketers IG8 9HQ [High Rd]: Two-bar pub
with Winston Churchill memorabilia,
enjoyable reasonably priced food (get there
early to be sure of the specials), good
friendly management; Sun quiz night (no
food then) *(Robert Lester)*

Please tell us if any Lucky Dips deserve to be upgraded to a Main Entry –
and why: feedback@goodguides.com, or (no stamp needed)
The Good Pub Guide, FREEPOST TN1569, Wadhurst, E Sussex TN5 7BR.

Scotland

Scotland

Here, naturally, you'll find some of the world's finest ranges of whisky, but this year even we were surprised by the number that some pubs are stocking, with the tallies reading rather like cricket scores: a spectacularly set new entry, the Sligachan Hotel on Skye, keeps 260 (and brews its own beer), the Bon Accord in Glasgow 230, Edinburgh's Bow Bar 160, the Port Charlotte Hotel on Islay 140 malts just from that island, and the Stein Inn on Skye has 125. Real ale, let alone local real ale, used to be quite hard to find in pubs here, but this year in our listed pubs we found beers from no fewer than 30 scottish brewers, the main one being Caledonian (part of the Heineken empire), with the most popular independents being Harviestoun, Isle of Skye, Fyne, Orkney, Cairngorm and Inveralmond. Glasgow and particularly Edinburgh have some great pubs to try them in, and pubs brewing their own good beers are the Fox & Hounds in Houston and cheery Lade at Kilmahog. Scottish pub food has come on in leaps and bounds recently. We used to complain that even seaside places here relied too much on the freezer pack, but now places like the Applecross Inn, Badachro Inn, Kilberry Inn, Plockton Hotel, Port Charlotte Hotel and Tigh an Eilean Hotel at Shieldaig, all within sight of the sea, do good seafood. Top inland places for food are the smart Burts Hotel in Melrose and the civilised Wheatsheaf at Swinton. For a special occasion, though, we'd recommend the long drive to Kilberry and an overnight stay at the Kilberry Inn, our Scotland Dining Pub of the Year.

ABOYNE NO5298   MAP 11

Boat

Charlestown Road (B968, just off A93); AB34 5EL

Welcoming pub by the River Dee, open all day, and with bedrooms

This convivial place takes its name from the ferry across the Dee that once operated here, before the bridge was built, and the tables outside make the most of the position. Inside, you are now greeted by the presence of a model train chugging its way around at just below ceiling height. The partly carpeted bar – with a counter running along through the narrower linking section – also has scottish pictures and brasses, a woodburning stove in a stone fireplace and games in the public-bar end; piped music and games machine. Spiral stairs take you up to a roomy additional dining area. They have three guests such as Deeside, Inveralmond and Timothy Taylors Landlord on handpump, as well as some 30 malt whiskies. There are six bedrooms; we would welcome reports from readers who stay here.

🍴 Bar food includes a lunchtime menu with soup, sandwiches, ploughman's and straightforward dishes like battered haddock or lasagne, as well as several vegetarian dishes; the more elaborate evening menu typically includes mussels and bacon on toast, smoked chicken with couscous salad, rack of lamb with redcurrant glaze, steaks, and puddings like rhubarb and ginger cheesecake or treacle tart; children's menu.
Starters/Snacks: £2.95 to £5.95. Main Courses: £7.95 to £17.90. Puddings: £4.25 to £5.50

Free house ~ Licensees Wilson and Jacqui Clark ~ Real ale ~ Bar food (12-2(2.30 Sat, Sun), 5.30-9(9.30 Fri, Sat)) ~ Restaurant ~ (01339) 886137 ~ Children welcome ~ Dogs allowed in bar ~ Open 11-11(12 Fri, Sat) ~ Bedrooms: £59.95B/£119.90B

Recommended by David and Betty Gittins, Christine and Neil Townend, J F M and M West

APPLECROSS   NG7144   MAP 11

Applecross Inn ★ ⇌

Off A896 S of Shieldaig; IV54 8LR

Wonderfully remote pub reached by extraordinarily scenic drive; particularly friendly welcome and good seafood

The editors of this *Guide* will never forget the stunning long drive to get to this splendidly remote waterside pub. Not somewhere you're likely to stumble across unexpectedly, it's reached by what's undoubtedly one of Britain's greatest scenic drives (providing there's no low cloud), over the hair-raising Pass of the Cattle (Beallach na Ba). The alternative route, along the single-track lane winding round the coast from just south of Shieldaig, has equally glorious sea loch and then sea views nearly all the way. Tables in the nice shoreside garden enjoy magnificent views across to the Cuillin Hills on Skye. With a friendly mix of locals and visitors, the no-nonsense but welcoming bar has a woodburning stove, exposed stone walls and upholstered pine furnishings on the stone floor; Isle of Skye Blaven and Red Cuillin, and over 50 malt whiskies; pool (winter only), board games and juke box (musicians may take over instead); some disabled facilities.

🍽 Your best bet here is the fresh seafood which usually includes rollmop herrings, lobster cocktail, prawns in garlic butter, scallops with crispy bacon and garlic butter, battered haddock, dressed crab, oysters and squid. As well as good sandwiches and ploughman's, other dishes might be green thai curry, gammon and egg, venison casserole, and puddings such as hot chocolate fudge cake. *Starters/Snacks: £2.75 to £7.95. Main Courses: £7.95 to £16.25. Puddings: £4.25*

Free house ~ Licensee Judith Fish ~ Real ale ~ Bar food (12-9) ~ (01520) 744262 ~ Children welcome ~ Dogs welcome ~ Live music some Thurs evenings ~ Open 12-11(midnight Sat) ~ Bedrooms: /£100B

Recommended by Richard and Emily Whitworth, Martin Stafford, Brian Abbott, Revd D Glover, Peter Black, Peter Meister, the Dutchman, Comus and Sarah Elliott

BADACHRO   NG7873   MAP 11

Badachro Inn 🍴

2.5 miles S of Gairloch village turn off A832 on to B8056, then after another 3.25 miles turn right in Badachro to the quay and inn; IV21 2AA

Convivial waterside pub with chatty local atmosphere, great views and excellent fresh fish

Nautically styled decking, with even sails and rigging, runs right down to the water's edge, making the most of the lovely views over Loch Gairloch at this very friendly white-painted house. It's in a tiny village on a quiet road that comes to a dead end a few miles further on at the lovely Redpoint beach. The bay is very sheltered, virtually landlocked by Eilean Horrisdale just opposite; you may see seals in the water and occasionally even otters. They have three pub moorings (free for visitors) and showers are available at a small charge. Sailing visitors and chatty locals mix happily in the welcoming bar (some interesting photographs and collages on the walls, and Sunday newspapers) which can get quite busy in summer. Friendly staff serve a couple of beers from the An Teallach or Caledonian breweries and a farm cider on handpump, and they've over 50 malt whiskies and a good changing wine list, with several by the glass; piped music. The quieter dining area on the left has big tables by a huge log fire and there's a dining conservatory overlooking the bay. Look out for the sociable pub spaniel Kenzie.

🍽 Featuring locally smoked produce and caught seafood, with the good fresh fish earning the place its Food Award, enjoyable dishes might include snacks such as sandwiches, hot panini with interesting fillings, beef and onion baguette, smoked salmon, smoked mussels and local venison terrine, creel-caught prawns, haggis, neeps and tatties, beef and spring onion burger, chicken breast on crushed haggis, neeps and tatties, smoked haddock topped with welsh rarebit, and langoustines and bass en papillote, with home-made puddings such as chocolate marquise and sticky toffee pudding. *Starters/Snacks: £3.25 to £6.50. Main Courses: £9.95 to £14.50. Puddings: £5.25*

Free house ~ Licensee Martyn Pearson ~ Real ale ~ Bar food (12-3, 6-9) ~ (01445) 741255 ~ Children welcome ~ Dogs allowed in bar and bedrooms ~ Open 12-12; 12.30-11 Sun; 4.30-10 Mon-Fri, 12.30-6 Sun winter ~ Bedrooms: /£70B

Recommended by Comus and Sarah Elliott, Peter Meister, Revd D Glover

BROUGHTY FERRY   NO4630   MAP 11

Fishermans Tavern ♀ ◖

Fort Street; turning off shore road; DD5 2AD

Welcoming pub with good choice of beers and enjoyable food

Quite charming from the outside, you can still clearly see the three fishermen's cottages that this friendly place was converted from. On the right, a secluded lounge area with an open coal fire runs into a little carpeted snug with nautical tables, light pink soft fabric seating, basket-weave wall panels and beige lamps. The carpeted back bar (popular with diners) has a Victorian fireplace, dominoes, TV, fruit machine and a coal fire. The good range of drinks includes Caledonian Deuchars IPA, five guests on handpump, typically from brewers such as Atlas, Bass, Cairngorm and Inveralmond, draught wheat beer, a dozen wines by the glass and a good range of malt whiskies, and they have about 40 beers at their May festival. On summer evenings there are tables on the front pavement or you can sit out in the secluded walled garden. They have disabled lavatories and baby changing facilities. More reports please.

🍴 Reasonably priced pubby bar food includes sandwiches, smoked fish pie, lasagne, steak pie, macaroni cheese, scampi, bread and butter pudding and sticky toffee pudding. *Starters/Snacks: £2.79 to £5.99. Main Courses: £5.99 to £10.99. Puddings: £3.00 to £3.29*

Free house ~ Licensee Tracey Cooper ~ Real ale ~ Bar food (12-8) ~ Restaurant ~ (01382) 775941 ~ Children welcome if eating ~ Dogs allowed in bar ~ Scots fiddle music Thurs night from 10, Mon quiz night ~ Open 11-midnight Mon-Weds; 11-1am Thurs-Sat; 12.30-midnight Sun ~ Bedrooms: £39B/£64B

Recommended by Kay and Alistair Butler, Derek Thomas, BOB

EDINBURGH   NT2574   MAP 11

Abbotsford

Rose Street; E end, beside South St David Street; EH2 2PR

Bustling well preserved Victorian pub with changing beers and good value food

Purpose built in 1902 and virtually unaltered since its construction, this traditional city-centre pub has a rather handsome green and gold plaster-moulded high ceiling and, perched at its centre on a sea of red carpet, a hefty highly polished Victorian island bar ornately carved from dark spanish mahogany. Stools around the bar and long wooden tables and leatherette benches running the lengths of the dark wooden high-panelled walls keep it feeling pubby. Up to five changing real ales, usually scottish and served from a set of air pressure tall founts might be from Atlas, Cairngorm, Highland, Strathaven and Orkney along with around 50 malt whiskies. Low level or silent large screen sports TV. The smarter upstairs restaurant, with its white tableclothes, black walls and high ornate white ceilings looks impressive.

🍴 Bar food includes soup, sandwiches, haggis, neeps and tatties, battered haddock, meat pie, burger, leek and parmesan risotto cakes with baked portabella mushrooms, rump steak, and good home-made puddings. *Starters/Snacks: £3.50 to £5.50. Main Courses: £7.95 to £12.95. Puddings: £3.95 to £6.50*

Free house ~ Licensee Daniel Jackson ~ Real ale ~ Bar food (12-3, 5.30-9.30(10 Fri, Sat)) ~
Restaurant (12-2.15, 5.30-9.30) ~ (0131) 225 5276 ~ Children in restaurant ~
Open 11-11(12 Fri, Sat)

Recommended by the Didler, Michael Dandy, Andy and Claire Barker, Joe Green, Simon Daws, Mark Walker, Jeremy King, Dave Webster, Sue Holland

Bow Bar ★ ◧

West Bow; EH1 2HH

**Eight splendidly kept beers – and lots of malts – in well run and friendly alehouse of
considerable character**

Usefully tucked away near the castle, this wonderful old place continues to be treasured
by readers for its atmosphere and outstanding range of drinks served by knowledgeable
staff. The neatly kept rectangular bar stars an impressive carved mahogany gantry, and
the tall 1920s founts on the bar counter dispense eight superbly kept beers with
Caledonian Deuchars IPA, Stewarts 80/-, Timothy Taylors Landlord alongside various
changing guests such as Cairngorm Trade Winds, Fyne Avalanche, Highland Orkney Blast,
Skinners Betty Stoggs and Vale Best. Also on offer are some 160 malts, including six
'malts of the moment' and a good choice of rums, international bottled beers and gins.
A fine collection of enamel advertising signs and handsome antique brewery mirrors
festoons the walls, with sturdy leatherette wall seats and heavy narrow tables on its
wooden floor, and café-style bar seats.

⊞ **Lunchtime snacks are limited to tasty pies.** *Starters/Snacks: £1.75*

Free house ~ Licensee Helen McLoughlin ~ Real ale ~ Bar food (12-2; not Sun) ~
(0131) 226 7667 ~ Dogs welcome ~ Open 12-11.30; 12.30-11 Sun

*Recommended by Dave Webster, Sue Holland, Pam and John Smith, Joe Green, the Didler, Simon Daws,
Mark Walker, Andy and Claire Barker*

Café Royal

West Register Street; EH2 2AA

Stunning listed interior, bustling atmosphere and rewarding food

Readers hugely appreciate this grandiose Victorian gem. It was constructed in 1863 with
no expense spared – with state-of-the art plumbing and gas fittings that were probably
the pride and joy of its owner, Robert Hume, who was a local plumber. Its floors and
stairway are laid with marble, chandeliers hang from the magnificent plasterwork ceilings,
and the substantial island bar is graced by a carefully re-created gantry. The high-
ceilinged vienna café-style rooms have a particularly impressive series of highly detailed
Doulton tilework portraits of historical innovators Watt, Faraday, Stephenson, Caxton,
Benjamin Franklin and Robert Peel (forget police – his importance here is as the
introducer of calico printing), and the stained-glass well in the restaurant is well worth a
look. Alongside a decent choice of wines, with several by the glass, they've 15 malt
whiskies, and Caledonian Deuchars IPA and three guests from breweries such as
Harviestoun, Inveralmond, Kelburn and Orkney on handpump; piped music and TV when
there's rugby on. It can get very busy at lunchtimes (when the acoustics lend themselves
to a lively lunch rather than intimate chat), so if you're keen to fully take in the look of
the place, try to visit on a quieter afternoon.

⊞ **Bar food includes some seafood: mussels (half a kilo or a kilo – that's a lot of
mussels), fine oysters with lovely bread, cullen skink and fish pie, as well as sandwiches,
neeps and haggis with whisky cream pie and steak, with puddings such as raspberry
cranachan with heather honey and oats, and a local cheese plate.** *Starters/Snacks: £3.95 to
£7.95. Main Courses: £7.95 to £9.95. Puddings: £4.25 to £9.50*

Punch ~ Manager Valerie Graham ~ Real ale ~ Bar food (11-10) ~ Restaurant ~ (0131) 556 1884 ~
Children welcome in restaurant until 10pm ~ Open 11am-11.30pm; 11am-1am Sat; 12.30-11 Sun

*Recommended by Eithne Dandy, Janet and Peter Race, Andy and Claire Barker, Mark Walker, Michael Dandy,
the Didler, Pam and John Smith, Dr Kevan Tucker, Christine and Neil Townend, Joe Green, Simon Daws,
Peter Dandy, Jeremy King, Michael and Alison Sandy, Pat and Stewart Gordon, Dave Webster, Sue Holland,
David M Smith*

Guildford Arms 🍺

West Register Street; EH2 2AA

Busy and friendly, with spectacular Victorian décor and an extraordinary range of real ales

This bustling, sumptuously fitted bar is a memorable place for a drink. Beyond its elaborate façade, the interior is opulently excessive with ornate painted plasterwork, dark mahogany fittings, heavy swagged velvet curtains at the huge arched windows and a busy patterned carpet. The snug little upstairs gallery restaurant, with strongly contrasting modern décor, gives a fine dress-circle view of the main bar (notice the lovely old mirror decorated with two tigers on the way up). Another key part of the appeal is the extraordinary range of ten very well kept beers – typically Caledonian Deuchars IPA, Fyne Avalanche, Harviestoun Bitter & Twisted and Orkney Dark Island, with quickly changing guests from brewers such as Butcombe, Cotleigh, Hop Back, St Austell and Stewart, and farm cider; the helpful, friendly staff may offer a taste before you buy. Also, they do a good range of wines by the glass and two dozen or so malt whiskies; board games, TV, fruit machine, piped music. They may have occasional mini beer festivals. Service can be slow at times.

🍽 **Straightforward bar food includes sandwiches, soup, steak and ale pie, breaded haddock, various steaks, and specials; in the evenings, food from the same menu is served only in the gallery restaurant.** *Starters/Snacks: £3.50 to £6.00. Main Courses: £8.00 to £17.00. Puddings: £4.20*

Stewart ~ Lease Scott Wilkinson ~ Real ale ~ Bar food ~ Restaurant (12(12.30 Sun)-2.30, 6-9.30(10 Fri, Sat)) ~ (0131) 556 4312 ~ Live music during Festival ~ Open 11-11(12 Fri, Sat); 12.30-11 Sun

Recommended by Mark Walker, Dr Kevan Tucker, Pam and John Smith, Janet and Peter Race, Joe Green, Jeremy King, the Didler, Simon Daws, Michael Dandy, Andy and Claire Barker

Kays Bar 🍺 £

Jamaica Street W; off India Street; EH3 6HF

Cosy, enjoyably traditional back-street pub with excellent choice of well kept beers

Appealingly straightforward, this nicely unpretentious tavern has all the qualities of a classic chatty local. They stock a great range of beers and whiskies, including more than 70 malts between eight and 50 years old and ten blended whiskies, and superbly well kept on handpump, Caledonian Deuchars IPA and Theakstons Best alongside five or six guests from brewers such as Fyne and Stewarts. The interior is decked out with various casks and vats, old wine and spirits merchant notices, gas-type lamps, well worn red plush wall banquettes and stools around cast-iron tables, and red pillars supporting a red ceiling. A quiet panelled back room (a bit like a library) leads off, with a narrow plank-panelled pitched ceiling and a collection of books ranging from dictionaries to ancient steam-train books for boys; lovely warming coal fire in winter. In days past, the pub was owned by John Kay, a whisky and wine merchant; wine barrels were hoisted up to the first floor and dispensed through pipes attached to nipples which can still be seen around the light rose. Service is friendly, obliging and occasionally idiosyncratic; TV (which one reader found rather obtrusive), dominoes and cribbage, Scrabble and backgammon.

🍽 **Straightforward but good value lunchtime bar food includes soup, sandwiches, haggis and neeps, mince and tatties, steak pie, beefburger and chips, and chicken balti.** *Starters/Snacks: £2.50 to £6.50*

Free house ~ Licensee David Mackenzie ~ Real ale ~ Bar food (12(12.30 Sun)-2.30) ~ (0131) 225 1858 ~ Children allowed in back room until 6pm ~ Dogs allowed in bar ~ Open 11am-midnight(1am Fri, Sat); 12.30-11 Sun

Recommended by the Didler, Peter F Marshall, John and Annabel Hampshire, Pam and John Smith

Starbank ♀ ◀ £

Laverockbank Road, off Starbank Road, just off A901 Granton—Leith; EH5 3BZ

Half a dozen real ales, good value food and great views over Firth of Forth at cheery, well run pub

It's hard to believe that the city centre is just a couple of miles away from this characterful place, with its impressive views over the Firth of Forth. The long light and airy bare-boarded bar is uncluttered, comfortably elegant and friendly, with Belhaven 80/, Caledonian Deuchars IPA, Timothy Taylors Landlord on handpump alongside two or three guests from brewers such as Atlas, Broughton, Cairngorm and Isle of Skye, about a dozen wines by the glass and a good selection of malt whiskies. You can eat in the conservatory restaurant, and there's a sheltered back terrace; TV. Dogs must be on a lead. Parking is on the adjacent hilly street.

🍴 **Good-value bar food includes soup, herring rollmop salad, a daily vegetarian dish, ploughman's, steak and ale pie, chicken stuffed with haggis, cottage pie, roast lamb with mint sauce, smoked haddock with poached egg, poached salmon, and minute steak.** *Starters/Snacks: £2.50 to £3.75. Main Courses: £5.25 to £9.00. Puddings: £3.50 to £3.75*

Free house ~ Licensee Valerie West ~ Real ale ~ Bar food (12-2.30, 6-9; 12-9 Sat, 12.30-9 Sun) ~ Restaurant ~ (0131) 552 4141 ~ Children welcome till 8.30pm ~ Dogs allowed in bar ~ Live music alternate Suns ~ Open 10-11; 11-12 Sat; 12.30-11 Sun

Recommended by Jeremy King, Ken Richards, John and Annabel Hampshire

ELIE
NO4999   MAP 11

Ship 🛏

The Toft, off A917 (High Street) towards harbour; KY9 1DT

Friendly seaside inn with views over broad sandy bay, unspoilt bar and good seafood

The position is really special here – by an expansive bay between jutting headlands, with oystercatchers and gulls much in evidence and games of cricket played by the pub's own team on the beach. The unspoilt, villagey beamed bar has a buoyantly nautical feel, with friendly locals and staff, warming winter coal fires, partly panelled walls studded with old prints and maps, Caledonian Deuchars IPA, several wines by the glass and half a dozen malt whiskies. There's also a simple carpeted back room; cards, dominoes and shut the box. The very positive licensees here are hands-on and interested, and the pub is very much a cheery part of the local community; they've recently bought the Golf Tavern at Earlsferry, at the other end of the village. The comfortable bedrooms are in a guesthouse next door. More reports please.

🍴 **Bar food typically includes lunchtime open sandwiches, soup, haddock crêpe, seafood platter, steak and Guinness pie, and specials like fruit steamed honey ham; children's menu.** *Starters/Snacks: £4.95 to £5.50. Main Courses: £8.50 to £16.00. Puddings: £4.50*

Free house ~ Licensees Richard and Jill Philip ~ Real ale ~ Bar food (12-2.30(11-3 Sun), 6-9(9.30 Fri, Sat)) ~ Restaurant ~ (01333) 330246 ~ Children welcome ~ Open 11am-midnight(1am Fri, Sat); 12.30-midnight Sun ~ Bedrooms: £55B/£80B

Recommended by Ken Richards

Bedroom prices normally include full english breakfast, VAT and any inclusive service charge that we know of. Prices before the '/' are for single rooms, after for two people in a double or twin (B includes a private bath, S a private shower). If there is no '/', the prices are only for twin or double rooms (as far as we know there are no singles). If there is no B or S, as far as we know no rooms have private facilities.

GAIRLOCH

NG8075   MAP 11

Old Inn ♀ ◧

Just off A832/B8021; IV21 2BD

Quietly positioned old inn with local fish and seafood; good beers too

You might spot eagles over the crags of the nearby Flowerdale valley, within strolling distance of this 18th-c inn, quietly positioned away from the main shoreside road. The relaxed public bar is popular with chatty locals, and drinks include An Teallach Crofters and Isle of Skye Blind Piper (a blend of Isle of Skye ales made for the pub and named after a famed 17th-c local piper), two guests from breweries such as Everards and Cairngorm, quite a few fairly priced wines by the glass, around 20 malt whiskies and speciality coffees. It's quite traditional, with paintings and murals on exposed stone walls and stools lined up along the counter; board games, TV, fruit machine and juke box. There are picnic-sets prettily placed by the trees that line a stream that flows past under the old stone bridge. Credit (but not debit) cards incur a surcharge of £1.75. More up-to-date reports please.

🍴 As well as fresh local fish, the menu usually includes dishes such as soup, cullen skink, haggis flan, whole home-smoked chicken, fish and chips, wild mushroom or lamb burger, steak and ale pie, and puddings such as clootie dumpling, cheesecake and sticky date pudding. *Starters/Snacks: £3.95 to £5.50. Main Courses: £7.50 to £16.95. Puddings: £3.95 to £5.95*

Free house ~ Licensees Alastair and Ute Pearson ~ Real ale ~ Bar food (12-9.30; not 2.30-5 in winter) ~ Restaurant ~ (01445) 712006 ~ Children welcome ~ Dogs allowed in bar and bedrooms ~ Live music Fri evening ~ Open 11am-11.45pm; 12-11.15 Sun ~ Bedrooms: £55B/£95B

Recommended by WAH, Martin Stafford, J K Parry, Peter Meister

GATEHOUSE OF FLEET

NX6056   MAP 9

Masonic Arms 🍴 ♀

Ann Street, off B727; DG7 2HU

Nicely transformed pub with good, very popular food and relaxed, traditional bar

The bar and restaurant at this welcoming flower-bedecked white-painted pub are quite contrasting in mood and style. The comfortable two-room bar still feels quite pubby, with well kept Caledonian Deuchars IPA and a beer brewed for them by Sulwath on handpump, a good choice of whiskies, wines by the glass, traditional seating, pictures on its lightly timbered walls and blue and white plates on a delft shelf; piped music, TV and pool. It opens into an airily attractive conservatory, with comfortable cane bucket chairs around good tables on terracotta tiles, pot plants and colourful pictures on one wall, which in turn opens through into a contemporary restaurant, with high-backed dark leather chairs around modern tables on bare boards. There are picnic-sets under cocktail parasols out in the neatly kept sheltered garden and seats out in front. This is an appealing small town, between the Solway Firth and the Galloway Forest Park.

🍴 Food is quite a draw here so it's worth booking. As well as lunchtime baguettes, there might be haggis and tattie scone tower with Drambuie sauce, wild mushroom and ratatouille tart, medallions of teriyaki beef fillet with cucumber noodles, fish and chips, chicken or vegetable stir fry with cardamon rice, roast duck breast with blackcurrant jus, seared bass, pork loin with apple purée and caramelised apple, steaks, and puddings such as vanilla crème brûlée with cinnamon shortbread and belgian white chocolate cheesecake with raspberry compote. *Starters/Snacks: £3.95 to £7.25. Main Courses: £9.55 to £15.50. Puddings: £4.95*

Challenger Inns ~ Lease Daniel Cipa ~ Real ale ~ Bar food (12-2, 6-9) ~ Restaurant ~ (01557) 814335 ~ Children welcome ~ Dogs allowed in bar ~ Open 11.30-2, 5-11; 11.30-11 Sat, Sun

Recommended by Pat Crabb, Ken and Jenny Simmonds, GSB, Richard J Holloway

GLASGOW

Babbity Bowster ⓘ ♀

Blackfriars Street; G1 1PE

A Glasgow institution: friendly, comfortable and sometimes a lively mix of traditional and modern, with almost a continental feel; good food

We're rather surprised at the lack of reports for this highly distinctive city-centre pub, and would love to hear from readers how it is faring. It's a blend of both scottish and continental, traditional and modern, with a big ceramic of a kilted dancer and piper in the bar illustrating the mildly cheeky 18th-c lowland wedding pipe tune (Bab at the Bowster) from which the pub takes its name – the friendly landlord or his staff will be happy to explain further. The simply decorated light interior has fine tall windows, well lit photographs and big pen-and-wash drawings of the city, its people and musicians, dark grey stools and wall seats around dark grey tables on the stripped wooden boards, and a peat fire. The bar opens on to a pleasant terrace with tables under cocktail parasols, trellised vines and shrubs; they may have barbecues out here in summer. You'll find Caledonian Deuchars IPA, Kelburn Misty Law and a guest such as Harviestoun on air pressure tall fount, and a remarkably sound collection of wines, malt whiskies and farm cider; good tea and coffee, too. On Saturday evenings they have live traditional scottish music, while at other times you may find games of boules in progress outside. Note the bedroom price is for the room only.

🍴 A short but interesting bar menu includes scottish and french items such as hearty home-made soup, cullen skink, potted rabbit, croques monsieur, haggis, neeps and tatties (they also do a vegetarian version), stovies, mussels, a pie of the day, platter of scottish smoked salmon, roast leg of duck on a bed of haricot beans and sautéed potatoes, and a daily special. The airy upstairs restaurant has more elaborate meals. *Starters/Snacks: £3.95 to £7.95. Main Courses: £5.25 to £11.75. Puddings: £3.75 to £3.95*

Free house ~ Licensee Fraser Laurie ~ Real ale ~ Bar food (12-10; 10-10 Sun) ~ Restaurant ~ (0141) 552 5055 ~ Children welcome ~ Live traditional music on Sat ~ Open 11am(11.30 Sun)-midnight ~ Bedrooms: £45S/£60S
Recommended by BOB

Bon Accord 🍺 £

North Street; G3 7DA

Fabulous choice of drinks, with an impressive choice of whiskies, ten real ales, a good welcome and bargain food

The number of malt whiskies on offer at this splendid drinkers' haunt seems to increase yearly, with some 230 currently available, as well as lots of gins, vodkas and rums. Additionally there's an impressive choice of ten real ales on handpump, with Caledonian Deuchars IPA and Marstons Pedigree as house beers, and daily changing guest beers sourced from breweries around Britain – maybe Arran, Fullers, Fyne, Harviestoun, Kelburn, Timothy Taylors and Wells & Youngs, and they keep a farm cider. With a good mix of customers, the interior is neatly kept; partly polished bare-boards and partly carpeted, with a mix of tables and chairs, terracotta walls and pot plants throughout; TV, fruit machine, board games and piped music. More reports please.

🍴 Very reasonably priced bar food includes baguettes, baked potatoes, lasagne, scampi and steak; they do a bargain two-course lunch. *Starters/Snacks: £2.10 to £3.20. Main Courses: £3.60 to £7.95. Puddings: £1.50 to £1.95*

Scottish Courage ~ Tenant Paul McDonagh ~ Real ale ~ Bar food (12(12.30 Sun)-8) ~ (0141) 248 4427 ~ Children welcome ~ Live band Sat ~ Open 11am-midnight; 12.30-11 Sun
Recommended by BOB

Virtually all pubs in this book sell wine by the glass.
We mention wines if they are a cut above the average.

Counting House ◨ £
St Vincent Place/George Square; G1 2DH

Impressive Wetherspoons conversion of former bank with impressive range of mostly scottish beers and good value food all day

It's worth a look into this former bank just to see the striking conversion that has been done here. The imposing interior rises into a lofty, richly decorated coffered ceiling which culminates in a great central dome, with well lit nubile caryatids doing a fine supporting job in the corners. You'll also find the sort of decorative glasswork that nowadays seems more appropriate to a landmark pub than to a bank, as well as wall-safes, plenty of prints and local history, and big windows overlooking George Square. Away from the bar, several areas have solidly comfortable seating, while a series of smaller rooms – once the managers' offices – lead around the perimeter of the building. Some of these are surprisingly cosy, one is like a well stocked library, and a few are themed with pictures and prints of historical characters such as Walter Scott or Mary, Queen of Scots. The very reasonable prices surely contribute to drawing in the crowd here, but even when really busy the atmosphere remains civilised, and staff are friendly and efficient. The central island servery has a splendid choice of up to nine real ales on handpump with Caledonian Deuchars IPA and 80/- and Greene King IPA, alongside half a dozen guests from all sorts of far flung little brewers such as Arundel, Batemans, Brains, Coach House, Harviestoun and Oakham. They also do a good choice of bottled beers, 22 malt whiskies, a farmhouse cider and seven wines by the glass; games machines.

🍴 Served all day, by friendly staff, the usual wide choice of straightforward bargain Wetherspoons food includes baguettes and wraps, haggis, neeps and tatties, chilli con carne, liver and bacon casserole, breaded scampi, pasta, sausages and mash, Sunday roasts, and children's meals. Steak night is Tuesday, with curry club on Thursday. *Starters/Snacks: £2.59. Main Courses: £3.09 to £9.39. Puddings: £1.99 to £3.99*

Wetherspoons ~ Manager Rhoda Thompson ~ Real ale ~ Bar food (9am-10pm) ~ (0141) 225 0160 ~ Children welcome till 8pm ~ Open 9am-midnight
Recommended by Dave Braisted

HOUSTON
NS4066 MAP 11

Fox & Hounds ♀ ◨
South Street at junction with Main Street (B789, off B790 at Langbank signpost E of Bridge of Weir); PA6 7EN

Welcoming village pub with award-winning beers from their own brewery as well as interesting food

This 18th-century pub is home to the Houston Brewery, and the five own-brew beers are constantly changing. There might be Jock Frost, Killellan, Peters Well, Texas or Warlock Stout – you can look through a window in the bar to the little brewery where they are produced. The welcoming family who have run this place for many years also stock a guest such as Caledonian Deuchars IPA, 12 wines by the glass and more than 100 malt whiskies. The clean plush hunting-theme lounge has comfortable seats by a fire and polished brass and copper; piped music. Popular with a younger crowd, the lively downstairs bar has a large-screen TV, pool, juke box and fruit machines; board games, piped music. At the back is a covered and heated area with decking.

🍴 Served upstairs (downstairs they only do substantial sandwiches), a good choice of enjoyable bar food might include soup, cod and chips, fillets of bass with citrus and herb butter, charred crayfish and scallop skewer, scampi tails dipped in Houston ale batter, game casserole, baked mushroom with herb stuffing and camembert, steaks, and puddings such as apple crumble or warm chocolate fudge cake. They have regular lobster nights in summer. *Starters/Snacks: £3.75 to £7.00. Main Courses: £8.00 to £24.00. Puddings: £3.50 to £5.00*

Own brew ~ Licensee Jonathan Wengel ~ Real ale ~ Bar food (12-10(9 Sun)) ~ Restaurant ~ (01505) 612448 ~ Children in lounge and restaurant till 8pm ~ Dogs allowed in bar ~ Quiz Tues ~ Open 11am-midnight; 11am-1am Sat; 12-midnight Sun
Recommended by Richard J Holloway, Ken Richards, Ailsa Russell

INNERLEITHEN   NT3336   MAP 9

Traquair Arms 🛏

B709, just off A72 Peebles—Galashiels; follow signs for Traquair House; EH44 6PD

Comfortably refurbished inn, popular with families, with friendly welcome and nice food

Very handy if you're exploring the Borders and warmed by a log fire, this welcoming village inn is one of only three places where you can taste draught Traquair ale, which is produced using original oak vessels in the 18th-c brewhouse at nearby Traquair House. They also stock Caledonian Deuchars IPA, Timothy Taylors Landlord and several malt whiskies; piped music, TV. There's a relaxed light and airy bistro-style restaurant with high chairs. The garden at the back has picnic-sets and a big tree on a neatly kept lawn. Bedrooms are comfortable, clean and fresh. More reports please.

🍽 **Well-liked bar food includes sandwiches, ciabattas, steak and ale pie, local venison, chilli, rack of lamb, pasta dishes and traditional puddings.** *Starters/Snacks: £3.90 to £4.25. Main Courses: £8.25 to £14.25. Puddings: £4.25*

Free house ~ Licensee Dave Rogers ~ Real ale ~ Bar food (12-2, 7-9; 12-9 Sat, Sun) ~ Restaurant ~ (01896) 830229 ~ Children welcome ~ Dogs allowed in bar and bedrooms ~ Open 11(12 Sun)-11 ~ Bedrooms: £50S/£80B

Recommended by Joe Green

INVERARAY   NN0908   MAP 11

George £ 🛏

Main Street E; PA32 8TT

Well placed and attractive, with atmospheric old bar, enjoyable food and pleasant garden; comfortable bedrooms

Ideally placed for Loch Fyne and its glorious woodland gardens, and with Inveraray Castle a range of good walks nearby, this civilised Georgian inn makes a comfortable place to stay. Oozing a sense of the past, the dark bustling pubby bar has bare stone walls and shows plenty of age in its exposed joists, old tiles and big flagstones. It has antique settles, cushioned stone slabs along the walls, carved wooden benches, nicely grained wooden-topped cast-iron tables and four cosy log fires. The bar carries over 100 malt whiskies and a couple of beers from Fyne on handpump; darts. A smarter flagstoned restaurant has french windows that open to tables tucked into nice private corners on a series of well laid-out terraces. The bedrooms are individually decorated, have jacuzzis or four-poster beds and are reached by a grand wooden staircase.

🍽 **Generously served enjoyable bar food (you order at the table) typically includes soup, ploughman's, starters like oat-crumbed brie fritters with gooseberry jelly or a medley of prawns and crayfish tails, main courses like battered haddock, mussels with chips, haggis, neeps and tatties, shoulder of lamb marinated in tandoori spices or grilled goats cheese with red onion marmalade, with home-made puddings.** *Starters/Snacks: £2.95 to £6.25. Main Courses: £6.25 to £8.25. Puddings: £2.95 to £4.75*

Free house ~ Licensee Donald Clark ~ Real ale ~ Bar food (12-9) ~ (01499) 302111 ~ Children welcome ~ Dogs allowed in bar and bedrooms ~ Live entertainment Fri, Sat ~ Open 11am-1am ~ Bedrooms: £35B/£70B

Recommended by David Heath, Peter Black, Brian Abbott, Kay and Alistair Butler, Dave Braisted, David and Sue Atkinson, Dr A McCormick

---

Several well known guide books make establishments pay for entry, either directly or as a fee for inspection. These fees can run to many hundreds of pounds. We do not. Unlike other guides, we never take payment for entries. We never accept a free meal, free drink, or any other freebie from a pub. We do not accept any sponsorship – let alone from commercial schemes linked to the pub trade. All our entries depend solely on merit.

ISLE OF WHITHORN

NX4736   MAP 9

Steam Packet ♀ ⇌

Harbour Row; DG8 8LL

Unfussy family-run inn with splendid views of working harbour from bar and some bedrooms; good food

This is an enchantingly peaceful spot near the end of the Machars peninsula at the most southerly point of Scotland, right by a harbour, with picture windows making the most of the view. Run by the same family for over 27 years, it's an unfussy but welcoming place. The comfortable low-ceilinged bar is split into two: on the right, plush button-back banquettes and boat pictures, and on the left, green leatherette stools around cast-iron-framed tables on big stone tiles, and a woodburning stove in the bare stone wall. Bar food can be served in the lower-beamed dining room, which has excellent colour wildlife photographs, rugs on its wooden floor, and a solid fuel stove, and there's also a small eating area off the lounge bar, as well as a conservatory. Three guests from brewers such as Houston, Kelburn and Orkney are kept alongside the Timothy Taylors Landlord on handpump, and they've quite a few malt whiskies and a good wine list; pool table. There are white tables and chairs in the garden. You can walk from here up to the remains of St Ninian's Kirk, on a headland behind the village.

🍴 Bar food includes lunchtime baguettes and sandwiches, starters like haggis-stuffed mushroom deep fried in yeast batter or warm chorizo salad, main courses like fish and chips, steak pie, baked salmon with white wine and prawn sauce, and braised lamb shank; Sunday lunch features a three-course buffet for £10. *Starters/Snacks: £2.75 to £7.95. Main Courses: £7.95 to £18.95. Puddings: £2.50 to £5.50*

Free house ~ Licensee Alastair Scoular ~ Real ale ~ Bar food (12-2, 6.30-9) ~ Restaurant ~ (01988) 500334 ~ Children welcome ~ Dogs allowed in bar and bedrooms ~ Open 11(12 Sun)-11; closed 2.30-6 Tues-Thurs in winter ~ Bedrooms: £30B/£60B

Recommended by Pat Crabb, Christine and Neil Townend

KILBERRY

NR7164   MAP 11

Kilberry Inn 🍴 ⇌

B8024; PA29 6YD

SCOTLAND DINING PUB OF THE YEAR

A stylish place to stay in wonderfully remote setting; no real ale but pubby feel to bar and excellent, locally sourced food

'Lovely country, warm welcome, gorgeous food... we specially liked the bedrooms' enthused one reader of this upmarket, restauranty small inn on the Knapdale peninsula. Topped by its trademark pinky red corrugated iron roof, it's a simple low-slung whitewashed building, ready to batten down the hatches in winter but lovely when they put tables outside in summer. The small beamed dining bar, tastefully and simply furnished, is relaxed and warmly sociable, with a good log fire; piped music. There's no real ale, but they do Fyne bottled beers, have a selection of malt whiskies (with quite a few local ones) and a good wine list.

🍴 Thoughtfully prepared food from the delicious lunchtime or evening menus might include starters like butternut and lemon soup, Loch Fyne queenie scallops or potted crab, and main courses like monkfish fired with chorizo and cannellini beans, rib-eye steak with bloody mary butter and roasted red peppers, fresh-caught fish or fish pie, with puddings like chocolate crème brûlée, sticky toffee pudding or pear and frangipane tart, and a local cheese platter. *Starters/Snacks: £4.50 to £8.00. Main Courses: £12.75 to £17.00. Puddings: £5.00 to £6.95*

Free house ~ Licensees Clare Johnson and David Wilson ~ Bar food (12.15-2.15, 6.15-9) ~ Restaurant ~ (01880) 770223 ~ Children welcome in smaller dining room, and in bedrooms if over 12 ~ Open 12.15-2.15, 6.30-11; closed Mon, plus weekdays in Nov and Dec, and also closed all Jan and Feb ~ Bedrooms: /£175S

Recommended by J K Parry, Peter Logan, Elizabeth Powell

KILMAHOG
NN6008 MAP 11

Lade ♀ ◀

A84 just NW of Callander, by A821 junction; FK17 8HD

Lively and pubby, with own-brew beers and shop specialising in scottish brews; traditional scottish music at weekends and good home-made food

In the heart of the Trossachs and close to the Falls of Leny, this family-run inn is splendidly placed for walks. One of the licensees is passionate about real ale, which explains not just their own excellent beers, but also the scottish real ale shop with over 100 bottled brews from microbreweries around Scotland. In the bar they always have their own WayLade, LadeBack and LadeOut on handpump, along with nine wines by the glass and about 40 malts; beer festival in late August to early September. There's plenty of character in the several small beamed areas – cosy with red walls, panelling, stripped stone and decorated with highland prints and works by local artists; piped music, cards and board games. A big windowed restaurant (with a more ambitious menu) opens on to a terrace and a pleasant garden with three fish ponds and a bird-feeding station.

🍴 **Using local ingredients, food includes soup, sandwiches, battered haggis balls, fresh battered haddock, steak and ale pie, mediterranean bean and lentil casserole on pilau rice, whole fried local trout, and puddings like raspberry cranachan and chocolate fudge cake. They do smaller portions of many dishes for children.** *Starters/Snacks: £4.00 to £7.00. Main Courses: £7.00 to £11.00. Puddings: £3.00 to £6.00*

Own brew ~ Licensees Frank and Rita Park ~ Real ale ~ Bar food (12(12.30 Sun)-9; 12-3, 5-9 Mon-Fri in winter) ~ Restaurant ~ (01877) 330152 ~ Children welcome ~ Dogs allowed in bar ~ Live music Fri and Sat evenings ~ Open 12-11(1am Fri, Sat); 12-10.30 Sun

Recommended by Paul and Margaret Baker, Simon Rodway, Alan Sutton, Michael Butler

KIPPEN
NS6594 MAP 11

Cross Keys 🛏

Main Street; village signposted off A811 W of Stirling; FK8 3DN

Cosy village inn, popular with locals and visitors

Run by obliging staff, this 18th-c inn is a comfortable yet unpretentious place for a meal or a drink. The cosy bar is timelessly stylish with lovely dark panelling and subdued lighting. A straightforward lounge has a good log fire, and there's a coal fire in the attractive family dining room. Harviestoun Bitter & Twisted and a guest such as Harviestoun Schiehallion are on handpump, and they've over 30 malt whiskies; cards, dominoes, TV in the separate public bar; piped music. Tables in the garden have good views towards the Trossachs.

🍴 **Bar food might include lunchtime sandwiches, soup, asparagus, home-smoked duck breast with berry dressing, sirloin steak, guinea fowl and pearl barley risotto, roasted rack of lamb, fish of the day, chilli crab linguine with roasted tomato basil sauce, fish and chips, and puddings such as dark chocolate pudding or lemon and lime tart with mixed berry coulis, and a scottish cheeseboard.** *Starters/Snacks: £4.00 to £6.00. Main Courses: £6.00 to £17.00. Puddings: £4.00 to £8.00*

Free house ~ Licensees Debby McGregor and Brian Horsburgh ~ Real ale ~ Bar food (12-9(8 Sat)) ~ Restaurant ~ (01786) 870293 ~ Children welcome ~ Dogs welcome ~ Open 12-3, 5-11; all day Fri-Sun; closed Mon ~ Bedrooms: £50S/£60S

Recommended by Michael Butler, Lucien Perring, Neil and Anita Christopher, Simon Rodway

---

Please keep sending us reports. We rely on readers for news of new discoveries, and particularly for news of changes – however slight – at the fully described pubs: feedback@goodguides.com, or (no stamp needed) The Good Pub Guide, FREEPOST TN1569, Wadhurst, E Sussex TN5 7BR.

KIRK YETHOLM

NT8328   MAP 10

Border 🛏

Village signposted off B6352/B6401 crossroads, SE of Kelso; The Green; TD5 8PQ

Welcoming and comfortable hotel with good inventive food and a famous beer story

Run by thoughtful staff and serving carefully sourced local food, this hospitable inn in the Cheviot Hills is a welcoming sight for walkers, placed as it is at the very northern end of the 256-mile Pennine Way National Trail. The author of the classic guide to the Pennine Way, Alfred Wainwright, determined anyone who walked the entire length of the trail would get a free drink. He left some money here to cover the bill, but it has long since run out, and the pub now generously foots the bill. They have a couple of beers on handpump – usually from Broughton brewery plus another Scottish beer such as Cairngorm Trade Winds, decent wines by the glass, organic scrumpy and a good range of malt whiskies and bottled beers. The cheerfully unpretentious bar has beams and flagstones, a log fire, a signed photograph of Wainwright and other souvenirs of the Pennine Way, and appropriate borders scenery etchings and murals; snug side rooms lead off. There's a roomy dining room, a comfortable lounge with a second log fire, and a neat conservatory; piped music, TV, darts, board games, children's games and books, and there's a water bowl for dogs. A sheltered back terrace has picnic-sets and a play area, and the colourful window boxes and floral tubs make a very attractive display outside. The bedrooms are comfortable.

🍴 **Using carefully sourced ingredients (including local fish, game, organic pork and organic free-range eggs), food from the seasonal menu is inventive without being at all pretentious: soup, terrine of smoked salmon, cullen skink, marinated border lamb, cock a leekie pie, venison burger, steaks and game casserole.** *Starters/Snacks: £3.25 to £5.75. Main Courses: £8.95 to £12.95. Puddings: £3.25 to £4.55*

Free house ~ Licensees Philip and Margaret Blackburn ~ Real ale ~ Bar food (12-2, 6-9) ~ Restaurant ~ (01573) 420237 ~ Children welcome ~ Dogs allowed in bar and bedrooms ~ Open 11.30-11(midnight Sat); 12-11 Sun; may close earlier in winter ~ Bedrooms: £45B/£90B

Recommended by Tina and David Woods-Taylor, Dave Braisted, Comus and Sarah Elliott, Brian McCaucs

KIRKCUDBRIGHT

NX6850   MAP 11

Selkirk Arms

High Street; DG6 4JG

Well run hotel with good service, enjoyable imaginative food and local sports bar

A civilised place in a notably attractive town, this thoughtfully updated 18th-c hotel stands right by the mouth of the Dee, within sight of fishing boats and the quay. Burns was a regular visitor, and there's a strong tradition that Burns composed the Selkirk Grace here (though a rival school of thought is that he did so while staying at St Mary's Isle with Lord Daer, Selkirk's son). Either way, the staff serve a beer called The Grace, which is brewed especially for them by Sulwath, alongside a guest beer such as Black Sheep. The bars here range from the very simple locals' front bar which has its own street entrance to a welcoming partitioned high-ceilinged lounge bar at the heart of the hotel, with comfortable upholstered armchairs and wall banquettes and original paintings which are for sale; piped music. There's also a bistro and restaurant. Service is thoughtful and efficient and there's a nice friendly atmosphere. A neatly set out garden has smart wooden furniture with contrasting blue umbrellas and a 15th-c font.

🍴 **Food in the locals bar is limited to items like sandwiches, burgers and fish and chips, but the enjoyable food served in the bistro might include starters like breaded haggis with cheddar and beetroot chutney or seared local scallops, main courses such as lamb and mint sausages and sweet red onion mash or halibut with basil crust, and puddings like white chocolate crème brûlée or cherry bakewell tart.** *Starters/Snacks: £3.95 to £7.95. Main Courses: £8.95 to £16.95. Puddings: £4.25 to £4.50*

Free house ~ Licensees Douglas McDavid and Chris Walker ~ Real ale ~ Bar food (12-2, 6-9) ~ Restaurant ~ (01557) 330402 ~ Children welcome but not after 9pm at public bar ~ Dogs welcome ~ Open 11(11.30 Sun)-11(midnight Sat) ~ Bedrooms: £75B/£102B

Recommended by Janet and Peter Race, Malcolm M Stewart, Pat Crabb

LINLITHGOW

NS0077   MAP 11

Four Marys 🍺 £

High Street; 2 miles from M9 junction 3 (and little further from junction 4) – town signposted; EH49 7ED

Very popular old pub with Mary, Queen of Scots memorabilia, excellent range of beers, and good food and service

This character-laden and nicely cared for old place should be on the itinerary of anyone making a tour of historic Scotland. The building dates from the 16th c and takes its name from the four ladies-in-waiting of Mary, Queen of Scots, born at nearby Linlithgow Palace in 1542. Accordingly the pub is stashed with mementoes of the ill-fated queen, such as pictures and written records, a piece of bed curtain said to be hers, part of a 16th-c cloth and swansdown vest of the type she's likely to have worn, and a facsimile of her death-mask. Spotlessly kept, the L-shaped bar has mahogany dining chairs around stripped period and antique tables, a couple of attractive antique corner cupboards, and an elaborate Victorian dresser serving as a bar gantry. The walls are mainly stripped stone, including some remarkable masonry in the inner area; piped music. Six or seven real ales are kept on handpump, with changing guests such as Aviemore Latitude, Greene King Old Speckled Hen, Isle of Skye Red Cuillin and Timothy Taylors Best joining the regular Belhaven 80/- and St Andrews and Caledonian Deuchars IPA; they also have a good range of malt whiskies (including a bargain malt of the month) and several wines by the glass. During their May and October beer festivals they have 20 real ale pumps and live entertainment. There's an outdoor smoking area with heaters, tables and chairs. Parking can be difficult, but the pub is handy for the station. More up-to-date reports please.

🍽 Generously served good value bar food (with around half a dozen qualifying for our Bargain Award) typically includes sandwiches, baked potatoes, ploughman's, good cullen skink, haddock and chips, steak and ale pie, curry, tasty haggis, neeps and tatties, scampi, pork fillet medallions in creamy peppercorn sauce, burgers, steaks, and puddings such as banoffi pie and baked apple pie. *Starters/Snacks: £3.95 to £4.95. Main Courses: £5.95 to £12.95. Puddings: £3.95*

Belhaven (Greene King) ~ Managers Eve and Ian Forrest ~ Real ale ~ Bar food (12-3, 5-9; 12-9 Sat; 12.30-8.30 Sun) ~ Restaurant ~ (01506) 842171 ~ Children in dining area ~ Open 12(12.30 Sun)-11(midnight Sat)

Recommended by Christine and Malcolm Ingram, Richard J Holloway, Peter F Marshall, Tony and Wendy Hobden

MEIKLEOUR

NO1539   MAP 11

Meikleour Hotel 🛏

A984 W of Coupar Angus; PH2 6EB

Friendly, civilised and well run, with good bar food and real ales, comfortable bedrooms

You can look out to distant hills by sitting outside this creeper-covered early 19th-c inn on Victorian-style seats out in a small colonnaded verandah, or at tables and picnic-sets under tall conifers on the gently sloping lawn of a garden sheltered by clipped box. The main lounge bar is a friendly place, basically two rooms, both with oil-burning fires. One is carpeted and decorated in gentle toning colours, with comfortable seating and an elegant white-painted fireplace, the other is broadly similar, again with well padded seats, but with a stone floor. There is a modicum of fishing equipment (the River Tay is nearby) and pictures of fishing and shooting scenes. Service is welcoming and efficient, and they have local bottled water as well as two or three beers from Inveralmond and other breweries, one of which, Lure of Meikleour, is brewed especially for them. The elegant fully panelled restaurant specialises in local game and fish; piped music. If you stay, the breakfast is good. Don't miss the spectacular nearby beech hedge, planted over 250 years ago and said to be the grandest in the world. More up-to-date reports please.

🍴 **Local suppliers are listed on the menus, which feature fish from Aberdeen quayside, soft fruit berries from Blairgowrie in summer and game from local shoots. Lighter lunchtime bar options include sandwiches, baked potatoes and a children's menu; the main menu features soup, smoked haddock rarebit, goats cheese with pear and toasted pine nut salad, fried haddock, fillet of bass, steaks, and specials such as grilled sardines or braised lamb shank; puddings like flourless chocolate cake or nougatine parfait.** *Starters/Snacks: £4.25 to £6.50. Main Courses: £8.50 to £16.50. Puddings: £4.50*

Free house ~ Licensee Kia Mathieson ~ Real ale ~ Bar food (12.15-2.30, 6.30-9) ~ Restaurant ~ (01250) 883206 ~ Children welcome if eating but not in bar ~ Dogs allowed in bedrooms ~ Open 11-3, 6-10; 11-10.45 Sat; 12-10 Sun; closed 25-30 Dec ~ Bedrooms: £75B/£120B

Recommended by Christine and Neil Townend, Dr A McCormick

MELROSE   NT5433   MAP 9

Burts Hotel 🍴 🛏

B6374, Market Square; TD6 9PL

Comfortably civilised hotel with tasty food and lots of malt whiskies

Right at the heart of an attractive border town, this smart 200-year-old hotel is just a few steps away from the abbey ruins and makes a lovely base for exploring the area. It's very well run with comfortable rooms and emphasis on mainly fairly unpubby food that is served by polite smartly uniformed staff. Pleasantly informal and inviting, the lounge bar has lots of cushioned wall seats and windsor armchairs, and scottish prints on the walls; piped music. There are 90 malt whiskies to choose from, Caledonian Deuchars IPA and 80/- and a guest on handpump, ten wines by the glass from a good wine list and a farm cider. In summer you can sit out in the well tended garden.

🍴 **Gently imaginative (not cheap) bar food might include confit chicken and bacon terrine, tian of crab and baby squid rings with lemon crème fraîche, red pepper and basil mousse with parmesan tuile, basil pine nut salad and tomato brioche, chicken caesar salad, almond and gruyère trout fillets on prawn chowder, thai green vegetable curry, battered haddock, roast duck with honey-roast vegetable and sesame jus, lamb shank with garlic jus, sirloin steak, and puddings such as pear frangipane tart with raspberry sauce and sticky toffee pudding with butterscotch ice-cream.** *Starters/Snacks: £3.75 to £9.95. Main Courses: £9.95 to £20.00. Puddings: £5.00 to £5.90*

Free house ~ Licensees Graham and Anne Henderson ~ Real ale ~ Bar food (12-2, 6-9.30(10 Fri, Sat)) ~ Restaurant ~ (01896) 822285 ~ Children over 10 in restaurant ~ Dogs allowed in bar and bedrooms ~ Open 11-2.30, 5-11; 12-2.30, 6-11 Sun ~ Bedrooms: £70B/£130B

Recommended by J K Parry, Comus and Sarah Elliott, Mike and Lynn Robinson, Di and Mike Gillam, Malcolm Wood, Ken Richards

PLOCKTON   NG8033   MAP 11

Plockton Hotel ★ 🍴 🛏

Village signposted from A87 near Kyle of Lochalsh; IV52 8TN

Welcoming loch-side hotel with wonderful views, excellent food and particularly friendly staff – a real favourite with many readers

This warmly welcoming and lively hotel continues to delight readers. Forming part of a long, low terrace of stone-built houses, it's set in a charming waterfront National Trust for Scotland village. Tables in the front garden look out past the village's trademark palm trees and colourfully flowering shrub-lined shore, across the sheltered anchorage to the rugged mountainous surrounds of Loch Carron; a stream runs down the hill into a pond in the attractive back garden. With a buoyant, bustling atmosphere, the comfortably furnished lounge bar has window seats looking out to the boats on the water, as well as antiqued dark red leather seating around neat Regency-style tables on a tartan carpet, three model ships set into the woodwork, and partly panelled stone walls. The separate public bar has darts, pool, board games, TV and piped music. Drinks include Isle of Skye Hebridean Gold and local Plockton Crags on handpump, bottled beers from the Isle of Skye brewery, a good collection of malt whiskies and a short wine list. Most of the comfortable bedrooms (it's worth booking well ahead) are in the adjacent building – one has a balcony and woodburning stove and half of them have extraordinary views over the loch, and you can expect good breakfasts. A hotel nearby changed its name a few years ago to the Plockton Inn, so don't get the two confused.

🍴 **Especially strong on fresh local seafood, bar food includes panini, cream of smoked fish soup, lobster tails, whisky pâté, baked smoked mackerel layered with cream, cheese and tomato, fish and chips, scampi, wild boar burger, pork medallions with brandy cream apricot sauce, haggis, neeps and tatties, seafood platter and steaks.** *Starters/Snacks: £2.95 to £9.75. Main Courses: £7.95 to £25.00. Puddings: £2.50 to £4.50*

Free house ~ Licensee Tom Pearson ~ Real ale ~ Bar food (12(12.30 Sun)-2.15, 6-9) ~ Restaurant ~ (01599) 544274 ~ Children welcome ~ Traditional folk music Weds evenings in summer ~ Open 11-midnight; 12.30-11 Sun ~ Bedrooms: £55B/£120B

Recommended by Richard and Emily Whitworth, Joan and Tony Walker, Martin Stafford, Peter Black, Comus and Sarah Elliott, Mr R Croker, Ms C Crew, Mike and Sue Loseby, Richard Tosswill, Christine and Phil Young, Revd D Glover

PORT CHARLOTTE   NR2558   MAP 11

Port Charlotte Hotel 🛏

Main Street, Isle of Islay; PA48 7TU

Welcoming hotel with exceptional collection of local malts, cheery bar, lots of seafood, lovely views and comfortable bedrooms

Port Charlotte was built originally as a distillery village (its own Lochindaal distillery closed in 1929, though the island still has another eight), and pride of place in the rounded central bar at this friendly hotel goes to an exceptional collection of about 140 Islay and rare Islay malts. If you decide you want one, the friendly staff will give you a menu to help you choose; also Black Sheep and local Islay Angus Og and Saligo, and good wines by the glass. Light and airy with big windows, the bar is fairly pubby, with a good log and peat fire, well padded wall seats, the usual chairs on bare boards and attractive charcoal prints. The comfortable and relaxed back lounge has a case of books about the area, and there is a good restaurant. The roomy conservatory, with well upholstered seats around its tables, opens on to a garden with more seats. With lovely views over Loch Indaal (a sea inlet) and across to the mountains of Jura and just a short stroll from a sandy beach, this is is a prime spot in the most beautiful of Islay's carefully planned Georgian villages.

🍴 **The island has good local lamb and beef, so even the straightforward dishes are full of flavour. There is often local seafood, too – maybe scallops, oysters, langoustines, sea bass on minted pea mash with caper sauce and a seafood platter – and game in season. Other dishes might include lunchtime sandwiches and salads, as well as red thai curry, couscous and stir-fried vegetables, chilli and mushroom stroganoff.** *Starters/Snacks: £3.75 to £8.95. Main Courses: £7.95 to £13.95. Puddings: £5.25 to £5.50*

Free house ~ Licensee Graham Allison ~ Real ale ~ Bar food (12-2, 5.30-8.30) ~ Restaurant ~ (01496) 850360 ~ Children welcome ~ Dogs allowed in bedrooms ~ Traditional live music weekly ~ Open 12-1 ~ Bedrooms: £95B/£150B

Recommended by Chris Evans, Kay and Alistair Butler, Richard J Holloway, D S and J M Jackson

---

We accept no free drinks, meals or payment for inclusion. We take no advertising, and are not sponsored by the brewing industry – or by anyone else. So all reports are independent.

SHIELDAIG   NG8153   MAP 11

Tigh an Eilean Hotel 🛏
Village signposted just off A896 Lochcarron—Gairloch; IV54 8XN

Particularly fine views, good beers and well liked food, especially seafood, in new bar

Separate from the civilised little hotel itself, the brand new bar here (completed later last year than anticipated) is on two storeys with an open staircase, dining on the first floor and a decked balcony with a magnificent loch and village view. It's gently contemporary and nicely relaxed with timbered floors, timber boarded walls, shiny bolts through exposed timber roof beams and an open kitchen. A couple of beers from Black Isle and Isle of Skye Black Cuillin and Red Cuillin are on handpump, alongside up to ten wines by the glass and several malt whiskies; winter darts and pool. Tables outside in a sheltered little courtyard are well placed to enjoy the gorgeous position at the head of Loch Shieldaig (which merges into Loch Torridon), beneath some of the most dramatic of all the highland peaks, and looking out to Shieldaig Island – a sanctuary for a stand of ancient caledonian pines. Next door, the bedrooms are comfortable and peaceful.

🍴 **Bar food might include sandwiches, steak and onion baguette, marinated herring salad with oakcakes, garlic and chilli seared scallops, croque monsieur, caesar salad, crab cakes, fisherman's pie, bream with lemon and garlic butter, grilled loin chop with cider syrup and caramelised apples, rib-eye steak, pizzas from a pizza oven, and puddings such as apricot tart and cloutie dumpling with whisky custard.** *Starters/Snacks: £4.00 to £6.75. Main Courses: £8.25 to £12.50. Puddings: £4.00 to £4.95*

Free house ~ Licensee Cathryn Field ~ Real ale ~ Bar food (12-9 (winter 12-2.30, 6-9)) ~ Restaurant ~ (01520) 755251 ~ Children welcome ~ Dogs welcome ~ Traditional live folk music some weekends and holidays ~ Open 11-11; 12-10 Sun ~ Bedrooms: £75B/£160B

Recommended by Comus and Sarah Elliott, Martin Stafford, Will Stevens

SLIGACHAN   NG4930   MAP 11

Sligachan Hotel 🛏
A87 Broadford—Portree, junction with A863; IV47 8SW

Uniquely set summer-opening hotel in the Cuillins with walkers' bar and plusher side, food all day, impressive range of whiskies and useful children's play area

This place, with plenty on offer, couldn't be a better bet for the Cuillins, with the Black Cuillin looming nearby. The huge modern pine-clad main bar, falling somewhere between an original basic climbers' bar and the plusher more sedate hotel side, is spaciously open to its ceiling rafters and has geometrically laid out dark tables and chairs on neat carpets; pool and darts. The splendid range of 260 malt whiskies makes a most impressive display behind the bar counter at one end, where they also serve their own Cuillin Pinnacle, Skye ales and scottish guest beers. It can get quite lively in here some nights, but there is a more sedate lounge bar with leather bucket armchairs on plush carpets and a coal fire; piped highland and islands music. A feature here is the little museum charting the history of the island, and children should be delighted with the big play area which can be watched from the bar. There are tables out in a pretty garden, and they've a campsite with caravan hook-ups across the road.

🍴 **Just the sort of pubby food you might want after a good walk, the short bar menu includes sandwiches (during the day only), fish and chips, venison burger, lamb and ale pie, penne with tomato sauce, a couple of daily specials, and home-made cakes with tea or coffee; more elaborate meals in hotel restaurant.** *Starters/Snacks: £5.00 to £8.00. Main Courses: £9.00 to £17.00. Puddings: £4.00*

Own Brew ~ Licensee Sandy Coghill ~ Real ale ~ Bar food (9.30-9.30) ~ Restaurant ~ (01478) 650204 ~ Children welcome ~ Dogs allowed in bar ~ Live music some nights ~ Open 9.30-11; closed Nov-Mar ~ Bedrooms: £49B/£98B

Recommended by Dave Braisted, Michael Garner, Tracey and Stephen Groves

STEIN NG2656 MAP 11

Stein Inn 🛏

End of B886 N of Dunvegan in Waternish, off A850 Dunvegan—Portree; OS Sheet 23 map reference 263564; IV55 8GA

Lovely setting on northern corner of Skye, especially welcoming inn with good, simple food and lots of whiskies; rewarding place to stay

Tables outside this welcoming 18th-c inn, just a stone's throw from the water's edge in a far-flung northern corner of Skye, are an ideal place to sit with one (or more) of their 125 whiskies and watch the sunset. Inside, the unpretentious original public bar has great character, with its sturdy country furnishings, flagstone floor, beam and plank ceiling, partly panelled stripped-stone walls and coal fire in a grate between the two rooms. There's a games area with pool table, darts, board games, dominoes and cribbage, and maybe piped music. Caledonian Deuchars IPA and a couple of local guests from brewers such as Black Isle and Isle of Skye are kept on handpump, and in summer they have several wines by the glass. The atmosphere can be surprisingly lively, and there's a good welcome from the owners and the evening crowd of local regulars (where do they all appear from?). Good service from smartly uniformed staff. There's a lively children's inside play area and showers for yachtsmen. All the bedrooms have sea views and breakfasts are good – it's well worth pre-ordering the tasty smoked kippers if you stay.

🍴 **Using local fish and highland meat, the short choice of good, simple and very sensibly priced food includes sandwiches, a tasty haggis and beer toastie, mussels, scallops, fish of the day, lamb shank with mint gravy, steak in ale pie, venison and chocolate casserole, battered haddock, stuffed aubergine, langoustines, steak, and puddings such as seasonal fruit crumble, raspberry cranachan meringues and sticky toffee pudding.** *Starters/Snacks: £4.50 to £9.50. Main Courses: £4.95 to £16.00. Puddings: £4.75 to £6.00*

Free house ~ Licensees Angus and Teresa Mcghie ~ Real ale ~ Bar food (12(12.30 Sun)-4, 6-9.30(9 Sun)) ~ Restaurant ~ (01470) 592362 ~ Children welcome ~ Dogs welcome ~ Open 11-midnight(12.30 Sat); 11.30-11 Sun; 12-12 Mon-Sat in winter ~ Bedrooms: £37.50S/£65S(£98B)

Recommended by Joan and Tony Walker, Comus and Sarah Elliott, Dave Braisted, Mike and Sue Loseby

SWINTON NT8347 MAP 10

Wheatsheaf 🍴 🍷 🛏

A6112 N of Coldstream; TD11 3JJ

Civilised, upmarket restaurant with imaginative, elaborate food – not cheap, but rewarding; good range of drinks, well chosen wines and comfortable bedrooms

If it's just a drink you're after, it's probably best to ring this restaurant-with-rooms before turning up as they may stop drinks service if it's too busy. That said, they keep a decent range, from Stewart Pentland IPA on handpump to around 40 malt whiskies, and a fine choice of 150 wines (with a dozen by the glass). The carefully thought-out main lounge area has an attractive long oak settle and comfortable armchairs, with sporting prints and plates on the bottle-green wall covering; a small lower-ceilinged part by the counter has pubbier furnishings and small agricultural prints on the walls, especially sheep. A further lounge area has a fishing-theme décor (with a detailed fishing map of the River Tweed). The front conservatory has a vaulted pine ceiling and walls of local stone; piped music. Breakfasts are good, with freshly squeezed orange juice.

🍴 **Skilfully prepared with fresh local ingredients, bar food might include starters such as toasted goats cheese on marinated peppers, smoked haddock risotto with tempura spring onions, pigeon breast and black pudding with celeriac, orange and redcurrant sauce, main courses such as mushroom, parmesan and basil omelette, battered haddock, pork and leek meatballs with cider gravy, roast duck on roast sweet potato with plum and port sauce, sirloin steak with peppercorn and brandy sauce, and puddings such as white chocolate cheesecake with strawberry sorbet and ginger and pear pudding with warm fudge sauce and vanilla ice-cream.** *Starters/Snacks: £4.25 to £6.95. Main Courses: £8.95 to £19.95. Puddings: £5.45 to £7.95*

Free house ~ Licensees Chris and Jan Winson ~ Real ale ~ Bar food (12-2, 6-9(8.30 Sun)) ~ Restaurant ~ (01890) 860257 ~ No children under 6 after 7pm ~ Open 11(12 Sun)-11 ~ Bedrooms: £75B/£112B

Recommended by Dr Peter D Smart, Christine and Malcolm Ingram, James A Waller, Mrs Marion Matthewman, John and Annabel Hampshire

THORNHILL   NS6699   MAP 11

Lion & Unicorn
A873; FK8 3PJ

Busy, interesting pub with emphasis on its good home-made food, well liked locally

What more could you ask for than the cheery blazing log fires, especially good natured service and enjoyable food at this warmly run family owned inn? The bar at the back is nicely pubby with some exposed stone walls, wood floor and stools lined along the counter. It opens to a games room with a pool table, juke box, fruit machine, darts, TV and board games. The more restauranty feeling carpeted front room has pub furniture, usually set for dining, a beamed ceiling and – as evidence of the building's 17th-c origins – an original massive fireplace with a log fire in a high brazier, almost big enough to drive a car into. One or two real ales such as Caledonian Deuchars IPA and Harviestoun Bitter & Twisted are on handpump (it's cheaper in the public bar than it is in the lounge), and they've a good choice of malt whiskies; play area in the garden, quiz nights and piped music.

🍴 Served all day, enjoyable bar food includes baked potatoes, prawn cocktail, tempura prawns, red thai skewers with spicy dip, steak pie, battered haddock, scampi, vegetable lasagne, lamb rump steak with sweet mint sauce and rosemary and garlic potatoes, chicken and haggis wrapped with bacon with a whisky sauce, duck with teriyaki sauce, baked bass with tomato salsa, steaks, and puddings such as profiteroles, apple and toffee brioche and cheesecake. *Starters/Snacks: £2.95 to £5.95. Main Courses: £7.50 to £8.95. Puddings: £3.95 to £5.95*

Free house ~ Licensees Fiona and Bobby Stevenson ~ Real ale ~ Bar food (12-9) ~ Restaurant ~ (01786) 850204 ~ Children welcome ~ Open 11(12 Sun)-midnight (1 Sat) ~ Bedrooms: £55B/£75B

Recommended by the Dutchman, Tom and Rosemary Hall, Karen Eliot

WEEM   NN8449   MAP 11

Ailean Chraggan 🍴 ♀
B846; PH15 2LD

Changing range of well sourced creative food in friendly family-run hotel

Small and friendly, this unchanging old hotel is homely and welcoming with lovely views from its two flower-filled terraces to the mountains beyond the Tay, and up to Ben Lawers – the highest peak in this part of Scotland, and the owners can arrange fishing nearby. Chatty locals gather in the simple bar which carries around 100 malt whiskies, a couple of beers from the local Inveralmond Brewery on handpump, and a very good wine list with several by the glass, or you can dine in the neatly laid old-fashioned dining room; winter darts and board games; good breakfasts.

🍴 As well as sandwiches, the changing menu, served in either the comfortably carpeted modern lounge or the dining room, might include starters such as cullen skink, gravadlax, oysters, pistachio, chestnut and game terrine with plum chutney, moules marinière, breaded scampi, chicken stuffed with haggis, lasagne, venison sausages, pork fillet roulade stuffed with chorizo with potato rösti and tomato and black eye bean sauce, sirloin steak, and puddings such as chocolate and almond meringue, ice chocolate praline torte with Drambuie sauce and blueberry cheesecake with blackcurrant sorbet and raspberry coulis. *Starters/Snacks: £3.25 to £5.95. Main Courses: £8.95 to £14.95. Puddings: £4.95*

Free house ~ Licensee Alastair Gillespie ~ Real ale ~ Bar food ~ Restaurant ~ (01887) 820346 ~ Children welcome ~ Dogs allowed in bar and bedrooms ~ Open 11-11 ~ Bedrooms: £57.50B/£95B

Recommended by Mrs Hazel Rainer, Comus and Sarah Elliott, Peter Martin, Brian Abbott, Andy and Claire Barker, Ian and Helen Stafford, J R Holt

LUCKY DIP

Besides the fully inspected pubs, you might like to try these Lucky Dips recommended to us and described by readers (if you do, please send us reports: feedback@goodguides.com).

ABERDEENSHIRE

ABERDEEN [NJ9406]

Archibald Simpson AB11 5BQ [Castle St]: Good bank-conversion Wetherspoons, well kept beers at low prices, good value food *(Dr and Mrs A K Clarke)*

Carriages AB11 6HH [Brentford Hotel, Crown St]: Hotel's welcoming and comfortable basement lounge bar, excellent range of well kept ales, popular good value food (in restaurant too); bedrooms *(Dr and Mrs A K Clarke)*

Grill AB11 6BA [Union St]: Old-fashioned traditional local with enormous range of whiskies, well kept Caledonian 80/- and guest beers, polished dark panelling, basic snacks; open all day *(the Didler, Joe Green, Dr and Mrs A K Clarke)*

☆ *Prince of Wales* AB10 1HF [St Nicholas Lane]: Eight changing ales from individual and convivial old tavern's very long bar counter, bargain hearty food, flagstones, pews and screened booths, smarter lounge; children welcome in eating area, open all day from 10am *(LYM, Joe Green, Dr and Mrs A K Clarke, Gwyn and Anne Wake, the Didler)*

BALLATER [NO3795]

Alexandra AB35 5QJ [Bridge Sq]: Same simple style under new young couple, enjoyable pub food and well kept Belhaven *(J F M and M West)*

CRATHIE [NO2293]

Inver AB35 5XN [A93 Balmoral—Braemar]: Friendly chatty family-run 18th-c inn by River Dee, sensitively and comfortably refurbished bar areas with log fires, some stripped stone and good solid furnishings inc leather sofas, sensible choice of enjoyable fresh home-made food especially in restaurant, decent wine by the glass, lots of whiskies, may be a real ale in summer; comfortable bedrooms *(Peter Cobb, J F M and M West, Ken and Jenny Simmonds)*

GLENKINDIE [NJ4413]

Glenkindie Arms AB33 8SX [A97]: Small 17th pub with new hospitable chef/landlord doing good locally sourced wholesome food, two local beers and often an own-brewed ale, 40 whiskies, reasonably priced wines, open fire, restaurant; no dogs; children welcome, side terrace, three bedrooms, open all day *(David and Betty Gittins)*

MILLTOWN OF ROTHIEMAY [NJ5448]

Forbes Arms AB54 7LT: Two neatly renovated bars in riverside hotel, two well kept ales, honest pub food (not Mon, Tues lunchtimes), cheerful owners, restaurant; children welcome, garden picnic-sets, six bedrooms *(Anthony Sharp)*

ANGUS

ARBROATH [NO6440]

Corn Exchange DD11 1HR [Market Place]: Well run Wetherspoons with good staff and their usual good value pricing *(Mike and Lynn Robinson)*

MEMUS [NO4259]

Drovers DD8 3TY: Quaint bar nicely updated by new owner, cosy lounge, real ales and good choice of whiskies, good food, two-room restaurant divided by woodburner, large dining conservatory; children welcome, charming garden with peaceful country views, adventure play area, open all day *(Brian Knight, Rory and Jackie Hudson)*

ARGYLL

ARDRISHAIG [NM8585]

Argyll Arms PA30 8DX [Chalmers St; A83 S of Lochgilphead]: Well placed snug pub favoured by locals, friendly new owners doing good low-priced food, decent beer; dogs welcome in basic public bar *(Dave Braisted, Dr D J and Mrs S C Walker, Chris Glasson)*

BELLOCHANTUY [NR6632]

Argyll PA28 6QE [A83]: Friendly staff and locals, well kept Caledonian Deuchars IPA, enjoyable simple bar food, stunning sea view from restaurant; dogs welcome in comfortably basic public bar *(Dr D J and Mrs S C Walker)*

CONNEL [NM9034]

☆ *Oyster* PA37 1PJ: Cosy 18th-c inn opp former ferry slipway, lovely view across the water (especially at sunset), attractive bar and restaurant, good thriving Highland atmosphere, enjoyable well prepared standard food, helpful friendly service even when busy, keg beers but good range of wines by the glass and of malt whiskies; comfortable bedrooms *(J K Parry)*

CRINAN [NR7894]

Crinan Hotel PA31 8SR [B841, off A816]: Elegant hotel by Crinan Canal's entrance basin, picture-window views of fishing boats and yachts wandering out towards the Hebrides, smart nautical cocktail bar, simple snug public bar opening on to side terrace, coffee shop with sandwiches etc, good if pricey restaurant, good wines, whiskies and soft drinks (keg beer), efficient helpful staff; children and dogs welcome, 20 comfortable bedrooms, good breakfast, open all day *(Dr D J and Mrs S C Walker, LYM)*

GLENCOE [NN1058]

☆ *Clachaig* PH49 4HX [old Glencoe rd, behind NTS Visitor Centre]: Lively extended inn doubling as mountain rescue post, cheerfully crowded in season with outdoors people, mountain photographs in basic flagstoned walkers' bar (two woodburners and pool), quieter pine-panelled snug, big modern-feel dining lounge, hearty all-day bar food, wider evening choice, great selection of scottish ales inc An Teallach, Glenfinnan and Williams, unusual bottled beers, Weston's Old Rosie cider, over 120 malts, live music Sat – great atmosphere; children in dining area, good warm simple bedrooms, spectacular setting surrounded by soaring mountains *(Andy and Jill Kassube, LYM, Peter Black, Gwyn and Anne Wake)*

KILMARTIN [NR8399]
Kilmartin Hotel PA31 8RQ [A816 N of Lochgilphead]: Enjoyable food in traditional bar and restaurant inc fresh local seafood, friendly family service, good choice of whiskies, real ales such as Caledonian Deuchars IPA and 80/- and Fyne Highlander, pool; dogs welcome in bar (friendly resident spaniel), six bedrooms (two sharing bath), cl lunchtime winter wkdys, open all day wknds and summer *(LYM, Dr D J and Mrs S C Walker)*

KINLOCHLEVEN [NN1862]
Tailrace PH50 4QH [Riverside Rd]: Friendly and neatly kept with Atlas seasonal ales from nearby brewery, decent wines by the glass and several malts, good value enjoyable food all day, pleasantly decorated partly carpeted bar, separate newly refurbished restaurant, traditional music (instruments provided); SkyTV, juke box, pool, fruit machine; wet dogs and walkers welcome, picnic-sets outside, six bedrooms, open all day *(Pete, Andy and Jill Kassube)*

TIGHNABRUAICH [NR9772]
Tighnabruaich Hotel PA21 2DT [Main St]: Small hotel with friendly family staff, great views over Kyles of Bute, neat modern bar with comfortable bar chairs; bedrooms *(Dave Braisted)*

AYRSHIRE

LARGS [NS2059]
Charlie Smiths KA30 8LX [Gallowgate St]: Seafront pub handy for ferry, Theakstons Old Peculier and usual scottish beers *(Dave Braisted)*

BANFFSHIRE

PORTSOY [NJ5866]
Shore AB45 2QR [Church St]: Small harbourside pub, bare-boards L-shaped bar with dark bentwood seats, masses of nautical and other bric-a-brac, prints and pictures, good value straightforward food cooked with flair, real ale such as Caledonian Deuchars IPA, cheerful chatty regulars, darts; subdued piped music, small TV *(Mike and Lynn Robinson)*

BERKWICKSHIRE

ALLANTON [NT8654]
☆ *Allanton Inn* TD11 3JZ [B6347 S of Chirnside]: Pretty stone-built village inn, light and airy, with friendly chef/landlord doing short choice of good food inc fresh fish (not Mon, Tues lunch), helpful kind service, changing ales such as Harviestoun, farm cider, good choice of wines by the glass, log fire in small attractive side dining room; sheltered garden behind, five comfortable bedrooms, open all day wknds *(BB, Comus and Sarah Elliott)*

EYEMOUTH [NT9464]
Ship TD14 5HT [Harbour Road]: Old inn comfortably refurbished keeping some original features, friendly bar well liked by locals, enjoyable food inc scottish dishes and lots of fresh seafood, good service, local real ales, restaurant; six well equipped bedrooms, good breakfast, nice spot on quay of pretty fishing village *(John and Sylvia Harrop)*

LAUDER [NT5347]
Black Bull TD2 6SR [Market Place]: Comfortably refurbished 17th-c inn under new management, good choice of beer and wine, cosy atmosphere, food served in three linked areas; children welcome, bedrooms, open all day *(Malcolm Wood, Comus and Sarah Elliott, LYM)*

CLACKMANNANSHIRE

GLENDEVON [NN9804]
An Lochan Tormaukin FK14 7JY [A823]: Plenty of atmosphere in pleasant softly lit bar with stripped stone, panelling and log fires, large bistro extension with enjoyable fresh food (all day Sun) inc interesting dishes, three scottish ales such as Inveralmond, decent wines; children and dogs welcome, comfortable bedrooms, good walks nearby *(LYM, Andy and Jill Kassube)*

POOL OF MUCKHART [NO0001]
Inn at Muckhart FK14 7JN [A91 NE of Dollar]: Unpretentious low building with lovely open fires, good Devon beers from own local brewery, good value wholesome substantial food, welcoming efficient service; picturesque village *(Christopher Tait)*

DUMFRIESSHIRE

DUMFRIES [NX9776]
☆ *Cavens Arms* DG1 2AH [Buccleuch St]: Good food (all day Sat, not Mon) from pubby standards to enterprising dishes using prime ingredients, well kept interesting ales with up to six changing guests, Stowford Press cider and perhaps a perry, fine choice of malts, friendly landlord and staff, civilised front part with lots of wood, bar stools and a few comfortable tables for drinkers at back; can get very busy (efficient table-queuing system), discreet TV, no children or dogs; open all day *(Joe Green)*

Globe DG1 2JA [High St]: Proper town pub with strong Burns connections, especially in old-fashioned dark-panelled 17th-century snug and little museum of a room beyond; main part more modern in feel, good value bar and restaurant food, good choice of local ales and whiskies, friendly service; children in eating areas, side terrace seating, open all day *(M J Winterton, LYM)*

ECCLEFECHAN [NY1974]
Cressfield DG11 3DR [Townfoot]: Country-house hotel with enjoyable and interesting food in bar with handsome fireplace (even more imposing one in bedroom); bedrooms *(Dave Braisted)*

GRETNA [NY3367]
Gretna Chase DG16 5JB [B7076, just off M6/A74(M)]: Hotel just yards from the border, with good range of food and drink in modernised bar, pleasant staff, interesting copperware; lovely garden, bedrooms *(Pat and Stewart Gordon)*

KINGHOLM QUAY [NX9773]
☆ *Swan* DG1 4SU [B726 just S of Dumfries]: Small dining pub in quiet spot overlooking old fishing jetty on River Nith, handy for Caerlaverock nature reserve, coal fire in well ordered dining lounge, neat nicely furnished public bar, Timothy Taylors Landlord, standard pub food; quiet piped music, TV; children welcome, pleasant garden, open all day Thurs-Sun *(Joe Green, M J Winterton, Richard J Holloway, LYM)*

MOFFAT [NT0805]
Black Bull DG10 9EG [Churchgate]: Attractive small hotel, plush dimly lit bar with Burns memorabilia, willing helpful staff, good value pubby food all day, well kept ales, several dozen malts, good value wine by the glass, friendly public bar across courtyard with railway memorabilia and good open fire, simply furnished tiled-floor dining room; piped music, side games bar, big-screen TV for golf; children and dogs welcome, tables in courtyard, well worn-in bedroom annex (come back quietly from late night revels), hearty breakfast, open all day *(Dr D J and Mrs S C Walker, Julian Knights, LYM, M J Winterton, John Urquhart, Joe Green, Patricia Walker)*

DUNBARTONSHIRE

ARROCHAR [NN2903]
Village Inn G83 7AX [A814, just off A83 W of Loch Lomond]: Friendly, cosy and interesting with well kept local Fyne and changing ales inc english guests, home-made hearty food in simple all-day dining area with heavy beams, bare boards, some panelling and big open fire, steps down to unpretentious bar, several dozen malts, good coffee, fine sea and hill views; piped music, juke box, can be loud busy summer Sats; children welcome in eating areas till 8pm, tables out on deck and lawn, comfortable bedrooms inc spacious ones in former back

barn, good breakfast, open all day *(Tracey and Stephen Groves, LYM)*

EAST LOTHIAN

GIFFORD [NT5368]
Goblin Ha' EH41 4QH [Main St]: Contemporary décor and colour scheme in roomy comfortable front dining lounge, sensibly priced pubby food (all day at least wknds), quick friendly service, four real ales, airy back conservatory, lively stripped-stone public bar with games area; children welcome in lounge and conservatory, tables and chairs in good big garden with small play area, bedrooms, open all day at least Fri-Sun *(Ken Richards, Comus and Sarah Elliott)*
Tweeddale Arms EH41 4QU [S of Haddington; High St (B6355)]: Old refurbished hotel in peaceful setting overlooking attractive village green and doing well under new family management, comfortably chintzy lounge bar with several malt whiskies, good restaurant meals, public bar with fire and darts; children welcome, 13 bedrooms, open all day *(LYM, Russel and Liz Stewart, Christine and Phil Young)*

GULLANE [NT4882]
☆ *Old Clubhouse* EH31 2AF [East Links Rd]: Two spotless bars with Victorian pictures and cartoons, pre-war sheet music and other memorabilia, stuffed birds, open fires, wide range of enjoyable generous bar food, fast friendly service, McEwans 80/- and guests, views over golf links to Lammermuirs; children welcome, open all day *(Ken Richards)*

FIFE

ABERDOUR [NT1985]
Cedar KY3 0TR [Shore Rd]: Two-bar pub with friendly service, thai as well as scottish food, some interesting whiskies; short pretty walk to the shore, bedrooms *(Ruth Johnson)*

ANSTRUTHER [NO5603]
Dreel KY10 3DL [High St W]: Cosy low 16th-c building in attractive spot with garden overlooking Dreel Burn, lots of gleaming brass, low beams and timbers, small two-room bar with pleasant conservatory eating area, good value generous varied bar food inc fresh fish, ales such as Caledonian, Harviestoun and Thwaites, welcoming efficient staff, open fire in stripped-stone dining room, back pool room; dogs welcome, open all day *(anon)*

CERES [NO3911]
Meldrums KY15 5NA [Main St]: 19th-c coaching inn popular for good choice of enjoyable reasonably priced bar lunches in roomy clean and attractive beamed dining lounge, well kept Caledonian Deuchars IPA, good friendly service even when busy (best to book Sun lunch), cottagey parlour bar; seven well appointed bedrooms, charming village nr Wemyss Pottery *(Lucien Perring)*

CULROSS [NS9885]
Red Lion KY12 8HN [Low Causeway]: Popular locals' pub with amazing painted ceilings, well kept Inveralmond Independence, good value food and efficient friendly staff; seats outside *(David M Smith)*

LOWER LARGO [NO4102]
Crusoe KY8 6BT [Harbour]: Popular harbourside hotel with beams, stripped stonework and open fire, lounge bar with Crusoe/Alexander Selkirk mementoes, good fish-based menu (fresh daily – supplies may be limited if busy), nice home-made puddings, well kept beers, cheerful staff; large TV; roomy bedrooms with good sea views *(Chris Clark)*

PITLESSIE [NO3309]
Village Inn KY15 7SU [Cupar Rd]: Popular and warmly welcoming family-run inn with tartan-carpeted bar, good range of fresh food inc local produce and game, good service, Caledonian Deuchars IPA and Jennings Cumberland, attractive candlelit restaurant, neat games room with darts and pool *(Lucien Perring)*

ST MONANCE [NO5201]
Mayview KY10 2BN [Station Rd]: Hotel with good mix of locals and visitors in big public bar, welcoming helpful staff, enjoyable food especially seafood, well kept Inveralmond ales, good wine choice; tables outside, children welcome, comfortable bedrooms, good breakfast *(John and Hilary Penny)*

INVERNESS-SHIRE

AVIEMORE [NH8612]
Cairngorm PH22 1PE [Grampian Rd (A9)]: Large flagstoned bar in traditional hotel, lively and friendly, with prompt helpful service, good value bar food using local produce, Cairngorm Gold and Stag, good choice of other drinks, informal dining lounge/conservatory; sports TV; children welcome, comfortable bedrooms *(George Atkinson, Gwyn and Anne Wake)*
☆ *Old Bridge* PH22 1PU [Dalfaber Rd, southern outskirts off B970]: Bustling and well run inn with cosy log-fire bar, good value home-made food inc some imaginative choices, friendly staff, two or three scottish ales such as Isle of Skye Red Cuillin, good choice of wines by the glass, large airy restaurant extension; may be piped music; children welcome, bunkhouse, open all day *(Mary Goodfellow, Tracey and Stephen Groves, Jim Sargent, Christine and Phil Young)*

CARRBRIDGE [NH9022]
Cairn PH23 3AS [Main Rd]: Friendly tartan-carpeted bar with welcoming landlady, bargain all-day snacks, lunches and suppers, well kept Black Isle Yellowhammer and Highland Scapa Special, log fire, old local pictures; children and dogs welcome, seven comfortable bedrooms, open all day *(George Atkinson)*

FORT WILLIAM [NN1073]
Ben Nevis Bar PH33 6DG [High St]: Stylish pub with several real ales, good value food, harbour views from upstairs restaurant *(Mike Proctor, Andy and Jill Kassube)*
Ben Nevis Inn PH33 6TE [N off A82: Achintee]: Roomy well converted raftered barn by path up to Ben Nevis, good value mainly straightforward food, Isle of Skye Hebridean Gold, prompt cheery service, some wknd bands; bunkhouse below *(Mike Proctor, Sarah and Peter Gooderham)*
Grog & Gruel PH33 6AD [High St]: Busy alehouse-style pub in pedestrian part, barrel tables, dark woodwork and bygones, friendly helpful staff, half a dozen well kept changing ales, good value food all day from baguettes, pasta and pizzas to upstairs tex-mex restaurant; piped and live music, machines; dogs and children welcome, open all day *(Andy and Jill Kassube, Mike Proctor)*

GLEN SHIEL [NH0711]
☆ *Cluanie Inn* IV63 7YW [A87 Invergarry—Kyle of Lochalsh, on Loch Cluanie]: Welcoming inn in lovely isolated setting by Loch Cluanie, stunning views, friendly table service for drinks inc well kept local ale, fine malt range, big helpings of enjoyable bar food in three knocked-together rooms with dining chairs around polished tables, overspill into restaurant, warm log fire, parrot in lobby; children and dogs welcome, big comfortable pine-furnished modern bedrooms, new bunkhouse, great breakfasts inc non-residents *(Brian Abbott, Peter Black, Revd D Glover)*

INVERIE [NG7500]
☆ *Old Forge* PH41 4PL: Utterly remote waterside stone pub with fabulous views, comfortable mix of old furnishings, lots of charts and sailing prints, open fire, buoyant atmosphere, good reasonably priced bar food inc fresh seafood and unusual dishes like haggis lasagne, two well kept changing ales in season, lots of whiskies, good wine choice, restaurant extension, occasional live music and ceilidhs (instruments provided); the snag's getting there – boat (jetty moorings and new pier), Mallaig foot ferry three days a week, or 15-mile walk through Knoydart from nearest road; open all day, late wknds *(Dave Braisted, Peter Meister, David Hoult)*

INVERMORISTON [NH4216]
Glenmoriston Arms IV63 7YA: Small village hotel with comfortable lounge, cheery bar and restaurant, good selection of snacks and full meals, McEwans 80/-, lots of malt whiskies; handy for Loch Ness, bedrooms, open all year *(LYM, J A Snell)*

INVERNESS [NH6644]
Castle Tavern IV2 4SA [1-2 View Place, top of Castle St]: Welcoming bare-boards bar with four well kept ales inc one brewed for them by Isle of Skye, fine whisky choice, knowledgeable friendly staff, good value pubby food from local produce, informal upstairs restaurant; castle-view terrace *(Mike Proctor, Joe Green, Gwyn and Anne Wake, E Michael Holdsworth)*

☆ *Clachnaharry Inn* IV3 8RB [High St, Clachnaharry (A862 NW of city)]: Congenial and pleasantly updated beamed real ale bar with lots of well kept interesting beers, warm chatty atmosphere, bargain freshly made food all day, good staff, great log fire as well as gas stove, bottom lounge with picture windows looking over Beauly Firth; children welcome, heated terrace overlooking railway, lovely walks by big flight of Caledonian Canal locks, open all day *(Mrs Hazel Rainer, Joe Green)*

Snow Goose IV2 7PA [Stoneyfield, about 0.25 miles E of A9/A96 roundabout]: Useful Vintage Inn dining pub, the most northerly of this chain, recently extended and well laid out with beams, flagstones and log fires, soft lighting, interesting décor, their standard all-day food (inc huge sandwiches till 5pm), decent wines by the glass, Caledonian and Timothy Taylors; lots of tables outside, comfortable bedrooms in adjacent Travelodge *(J F M and M West)*

KINCARDINESHIRE

BANCHORY [NO6995]
Ravenswood AB31 5TS [Ramsay Rd]: Royal British Legion Scotland's country club rather than pub, but welcomes non-member visitors, with enjoyable food, well kept ales, two bars and restaurant, entertainment (well used dance floor); good-sized garden and grounds, 12 bedrooms *(Mike and Lynn Robinson)*

CATTERLINE [NO8678]
☆ *Creel* AB39 2UL: Good generous imaginative food (all day Sun) esp soups and local fish/seafood in big plain but comfortable lounge with woodburner, plenty of tables, several real ales and many unusual bottled beers, welcoming service, small second bar, compact sea-view restaurant (same menu, booking advised); bedrooms, nice clifftop position in old fishing village, open all day Sun *(Mike and Lynn Robinson)*

FETTERCAIRN [NO6573]
Ramsay Arms AB30 1XX: Hotel with wholesome reasonably priced bar and restaurant food, friendly service, well kept real ale; children welcome, garden tables, attractive village (liked by Queen Victoria who stayed at the hotel) *(Mike and Lynn Robinson)*

STONEHAVEN [NO8785]
Marine Hotel AB39 2JY [Shore Head]: Busy harbourside pub with up to five well kept ales, good choice of whiskies, good value food esp local fish, large lively stripped stone bar with log fire in cosy side room, upstairs lounge bar and seaview restaurant; children welcome, pavement tables, open all day *(Mike and Lynn Robinson, Mark Walker)*

KIRKCUDBRIGHTSHIRE

HAUGH OF URR [NX8066]
☆ *Laurie Arms* DG7 3YA [B794 N of Dalbeattie; Main St]: Neatly kept and attractively decorated 19th-c pub, a few tables in log-fire bar with steps up to similar area, food from bar snacks to steaks, changing real ales, decent wines by the glass, welcoming attentive service, restaurant, games room with darts, pool and juke box, splendid Bamforth comic postcards in the gents'; tables out at front and on sheltered terrace behind, open all day wknds *(Joe Green, LYM)*

KIPPFORD [NX8355]
☆ *Anchor* DG5 4LN [off A710 S of Dalbeattie]: Popular waterfront inn overlooking yachting estuary and peaceful hills, nautical theme décor with panelling and slight 1960s feel, good fire in small traditional back bar (dogs welcome here), more tables in area off, simple bright roomy dining room, nice seafood (great crab sandwiches), quick friendly service, two or three ales inc Sulwath, lots of malts, lounge bar (cl out of season); piped music, TV and machines; children welcome, front terrace tables, good walks and birdwatching, open all day in summer *(LYM, Mr and Mrs Staples)*

NEWTON STEWART [NX4165]
Galloway Arms DG8 6DB [Victoria St]: Family-run hotel with good range of enjoyable food, modern lounge with exposed brick, leather chairs, banquettes and assorted tables on wood floor, Caledonian Deuchars IPA, Belhaven 60/- and 70/- from cask-fronted bar, 125 or so whiskies, second transport-theme bar with sports TVs, restaurant; dogs welcome, garden, bedrooms *(Alan Timbrell, M Rowley)*

PALNACKIE [NX8256]
Glenisle DG7 1PG [Port Rd]: Good village atmosphere in busy neatly refurbished bar, pleasant service in carpeted dining room, enjoyable food *(Mr and Mrs Staples)*

LANARKSHIRE

GLASGOW [NS5865]
☆ *Horseshoe* G2 5AE [Drury St, nr Central Stn]: Classic high-ceilinged standing-room pub with enormous island bar, gleaming mahogany and mirrors, snob screens, other high Victorian features and interesting music-hall era memorabilia and musical instruments; friendly staff and atmosphere, well kept and priced ales inc Caledonian Deuchars IPA and 80/-, lots of malt whiskies, bargain simple food served speedily in plainer upstairs bar and restaurant (children allowed here), inc long-served McGhees hot pies; sports TVs, silent fruit machine, piped music; open all day (breakfast from 9) *(Gwyn and Anne Wake, Jeremy King, Joe Green, LYM)*

Ingram G1 3BX [Queen St]: Civilised and well run Greene King (Belhaven) pub with perhaps Orkney as a guest, several dozen malt whiskies ranked along island bar, enterprising sandwiches and bargain generous home-made hot dishes, dark panelling, interesting *Daily Herald* papers from 1953 (pub's opening) lining narrow stairs down to lavatories *(Joe Green)*

Republic Bier Halle G1 3PL [Gordon St]: Dim-lit basement with bare masonry not unlike a continental beer hall, large shared tables and big stools, over 50 beers from around the world, knowledgeable friendly staff, food inc pizzas and special deals; popular with young people, piped music can be loud at night *(Jeremy King)*

State G2 4NG [Holland St]: High-ceilinged bar with marble pillars, lots of carved wood inc handsome oak island servery, half a dozen or so well kept changing ales, bargain basic lunchtime food from sandwiches up, good atmosphere, friendly staff, armchair among other comfortable seats, coal-effect gas fire in big wooden fireplace, old prints and theatrical posters; piped music, TVs, games machine, wknd live music *(Jeremy King)*

MILNGAVIE [NS5574]

Talbot Arms G62 6BU [Main St]: Pleasantly refurbished, warm welcome, three real ales, many others on tap and frequent beer festivals, sensible prices, good value lunchtime food; TV; handy for start or finish of West Highland Way *(Andrew P)*

MIDLOTHIAN

BALERNO [NT1566]

Johnsburn House EH14 7BB [Johnsburn Rd]: Handsome old-fashioned beamed bar in former 18th-c mansion with masterpiece 1911 ceiling by Robert Lorimer; Caledonian Deuchars IPA and interesting changing ales, coal fire, panelled dining lounge with good food inc shellfish and game, more formal evening dining rooms; children and dogs welcome, open all day *(the Didler)*

CRAMOND [NT1877]

Cramond Inn EH4 6NU [Cramond Glebe Rd (off A90 W of Edinburgh)]: Charming 18th-c inn nr quayside, softly lit smallish traditional beamed rooms, open fires, old photographs on dark-brown walls, large carved settle, up to six mainly local ales inc a wheat beer, ciders, popular pubby food, good friendly service and atmosphere; picturesque village at mouth of River Almond, delightful views from tables out on grass *(Adrian Johnson, LYM)*

EDINBURGH [NT2574]

☆ **Bennets** EH3 9LG [Leven St]: Ornate Victorian bar with original glass, mirrors, arcades, fine panelling and tiles, friendly service, real ales inc Caledonian Deuchars IPA from tall founts, masses of malt whiskies, bar snacks and bargain homely lunchtime dishes (not Sun), second bar with counter salvaged from old ship; children allowed in eating area, open all day, cl Sun *(the Didler, LYM, Pam and John Smith)*

☆ **Canny Man's** EH10 4QU [Morningside Rd; aka Volunteer Arms]: Utterly individual and distinctive, saloon, lounge and snug with fascinating bric-a-brac, ceiling papered with sheet music, huge range of appetising smorgasbord, very efficient friendly service, lots of whiskies, well kept ales such as Caledonian Deuchars IPA, cheap children's drinks; courtyard tables *(Dr and Mrs R G J Telfer)*

Cloisters EH3 9JH [Brougham St]: Friendly and interesting ex-parsonage alehouse with Caledonian Deuchars IPA and 80/- and several interesting guest ales, dozens of malts, several wines by the glass, decent food till 4pm (6pm Tues-Thurs) from toasties to Sun roasts, pews and bar gantry recycled from redundant church, bare boards and lots of brewery mirrors; lavatories down spiral stairs, folk music Fri, Sat; dogs welcome, open all day *(the Didler, Pam and John Smith)*

☆ **Ensign Ewart** EH1 2PE [Lawnmarket, Royal Mile; last pub on right before Castle]: Charming dimly lit old-world pub handy for Castle (so gets busy), beams peppered with brasses, huge painting of Ewart at Waterloo capturing french banner, assorted furniture inc elbow tables, friendly efficient staff, well kept Caledonian, plenty of whiskies, simple food; piped music – traditional most nights, games machine, keypad entry to lavatories *(Christine and Neil Townend, Peter F Marshall, Jeremy King)*

☆ **Halfway House** EH1 1BX [Fleshmarket Cl (steps between Cockburn St and Market St, opp Waverley station)]: Tiny single-room pub off steep steps, under new management but little changed, a few round tables, railway memorabilia, four ales, good range of malt whiskies, good value all-day food; 1960s/70s juke box, small TV; dogs and children welcome *(Joe Green, Jeremy King)*

Milnes EH2 2PJ [Rose St/Hanover St]: Much reworked traditional city pub rambling down to several areas below street level, old-fashioned bare-boards feel, dark décor and panelling, open fire, cask tables, lots of old photographs and mementoes of poets who used the 'Little Kremlin' room here, Adnams, Caledonian, Courage and Greene King, good choice of wines by the glass, good value coffees, reasonably priced bar food and day from sandwiches up, breakfast from 10am; piped music, games; pavement seats, open all day *(Tony and Wendy Hobden, Michael Dandy, the Didler, BB)*

☆ **Old Peacock** EH6 4TZ [Lindsay Rd, Newhaven]: Good low-priced food all day inc fresh fish in massive helpings in neat plushly comfortable beamed pub, very popular so best to book evenings and Sun lunchtime, several linked areas inc bright family room and conservatory-style back room leading to garden, friendly efficient staff, good beer and wine choice; open all day *(Mike and Sue Shirley, LYM)*

Oxford EH2 4JB [Young St]: Friendly no-frills pub with two built-in wall settles and friendly locals in tiny bustling bar, steps up to quieter back room with dominoes, lino floor, well kept Caledonian Deuchars IPA and Belhaven 80/-, good whisky range, cheap filled cobs; links with scottish writers and artists *(Peter F Marshall, Joe Green, Dave Webster, Sue Holland, Pam and John Smith)*

Roseleaf EH6 6EW [Sandport Pl]: Small pub nr Leith harbour revived by newish couple, partly through their all-day food's growing popularity, enterprising choice of soft and hot drinks as well as the usuals, attractively individual furnishings and lighting *(anon)*

Royal McGregor EH1 1QS [High St]: Family-run long modern traditional-style bar with raised back area, enjoyable food all day (10am-10pm) from massive breakfasts to good value set meals, well kept ales such as Broughton Merlin and Stewarts Pentland IPA, good coffee, friendly staff, Georgian Edinburgh prints; piped music, TV; pavement tables, open all day *(Michael Dandy, Michael and Alison Sandy)*

☆ *Standing Order* EH2 2JP [George St]: Grand Wetherspoons bank conversion in three elegant Georgian houses, imposing columns, enormous main room with elaborate colourful ceiling, lots of tables, smaller side booths, other rooms inc two with floor-to-ceiling bookshelves, comfortable clubby seats, Adam fireplace and portraits; efficient young staff, good value food, real ales inc some interesting ones from long counter; sports TV, wknd live music, extremely popular Sat night; disabled facilities, open all day till 1am *(Ian and Jane Haslock, David M Smith, Michael and Alison Sandy, BB)*

White Hart EH1 2JU [Grassmarket]: One of Edinburgh's oldest pubs and popular with tourists, small, basic and relaxed with efficient friendly young staff, enjoyable good value food all day, ales such as Caledonian Deuchars IPA, decent whisky choice, various coffees; piped music, live wkdy nights and Sun afternoon, SkyTV; pavement tables popular with smokers, open all day *(Jeremy King)*

MUSSELBURGH [NT3372]

Volunteer Arms EH21 6JE [N High St; aka Staggs]: Same family since 1858, unspoilt busy bar, dark panelling, old brewery mirrors, great gantry with ancient casks, Caledonian Deuchars IPA and a guest beer, overflow lounge wknds; dogs welcome, open all day *(the Didler, Joe Green)*

MORAYSHIRE

FINDHORN [NJ0464]

☆ *Kimberley* IV36 3YG: Simple cosy seaside pub with good generous food especially the fresh seafood collected by landlord from Buckie dawn fish market, fast friendly service, two ales such as Caledonian and Timothy Taylors, many whiskies, wood floors and big log fire, cheerful busy atmosphere; children and dogs welcome, heated sea-view terrace *(Ken and Jenny Simmonds, Lee Fraser, Russel and Liz Stewart)*

NAIRNSHIRE

CAWDOR [NH8449]

☆ *Cawdor Tavern* IV12 5XP [just off B9090]: Popular pub in lovely conservation village, Atlas and Orkney beers, lots of bottled beers, proper seasonal food freshly cooked (worth the wait), great choice of malt whiskies, pleasant attentive staff, elegant panelled lounge, nice features in public bar, restaurant; children in eating areas, attractive front terrace, open all day wknds and summer *(LYM, Neil and Anita Christopher, the Dutchman)*

PERTHSHIRE

BLAIR ATHOLL [NN8765]

☆ *Atholl Arms* PH18 5SG: Sizeable hotel's stable-theme pubby bar in lovely setting nr castle, full Moulin ale range, well priced good food all day from sandwiches to interesting dishes and local wild salmon and meat, helpful friendly staff; 31 good value bedrooms, open all day *(Joe Green)*

CALLANDER [NN6207]

Waverley FK17 8BD [Main St]: Good value bar food, three scottish real ales, friendly staff, large dining area partitioned off from main bar with nice mix of traditional and modern; roughly opp Rob Roy centre *(Dennis Jones)*

DUNBLANE [NN7801]

Tappit Hen FK15 0AL [Kirk St]: Across close from cathedral, four or five changing real ales, good value toasties, friendly atmosphere *(Andy and Jill Kassube)*

DUNNING [NO0114]

Kirkstyle PH2 0RR [B9141, off A9 S of Perth; Kirkstyle Sq]: Unpretentious olde-worlde streamside pub with chatty landlady and regulars, log fire, well kept Cairngorm and good whisky choice, enjoyable generous home-made food inc interesting dishes (book in season), good service, charming flagstoned and stripped stone back restaurant *(Andy and Jill Kassube)*

GLENFARG [NO1613]

Bein PH2 9PY [A912/B996, 4 miles S of M90 junction 9]: Newly refurbished, with friendly staff, good drinks range inc Inveralmond, enjoyable food from sandwiches up; comfortable bedrooms *(Pat and Stewart Gordon)*

KENMORE [NN7745]

☆ *Kenmore Hotel* PH15 2NU [A827 W of Aberfeldy]: Civilised small hotel dating from 16th-c in pretty Loch Tay village, comfortable traditional front lounge with warm log fire and poem pencilled by Burns himself on the chimney-breast, dozens of malts helpfully arranged alphabetically, polite uniformed staff, restaurant; back bar and terrace overlooking River Tay with some enjoyable food from lunchtime soup and sandwiches up, Belhaven Best, decent wines by the glass; pool and winter darts, juke box, TV, fruit machine; entertainment Weds, Sun; children and dogs welcome, good bedrooms, open all day *(LYM, J F M and M West)*

KILLIN [NN5732]

Falls of Dochart FK21 8SL [Gray St]: Former coaching inn overlooking the falls, big log fire in attractive flagstoned bar, good choice of ales, interesting home-made food all day; dogs welcome, bedrooms *(Paul Steeples, Peter Martin)*

LOCH TUMMEL [NN8160]

☆ *Loch Tummel Inn* PH16 5RP [B8019 4 miles E of Tummel Bridge]: Beautifully placed traditional loch-side inn renovated by friendly new owners, great views over water to Schiehallion, cosy bar area with woodburner, good fresh seasonal food, Belhaven ales, converted hayloft restaurant; lots of walks and wildlife, six bedrooms, now open all year *(Guy Dixon, LYM)*

PITLOCHRY [NN9163]

☆ *Killiecrankie Hotel* PH16 5LG [Killiecrankie, off A9 N]: Comfortable and splendidly placed country hotel smartened up under friendly newish owner, attractive panelled bar, airy and relaxed conservatory, good nicely varied reasonably priced food here and in restaurant, smiling efficient service, well kept real ales, good choice of wines; children in eating area, extensive peaceful grounds and dramatic views, bedrooms *(LYM, David Hunt, Joan and Tony Walker)*

☆ *Moulin* PH16 5EH [Kirkmichael Rd, Moulin; A924 NE of Pitlochry centre]: Attractive much extended 17th-c family-run inn with comfortably traditional atmosphere, own-brewed beers, 40 malt whiskies, wide food choice, busy pubby bar with cushioned booths divided by stained-glass country scenes, big fireplace, some stripped stone, local and sporting prints, bar billiards and board games, traditional music summer Weds; children welcome, picnic-sets out on gravel looking across to village kirk, small garden, comfortable bedrooms, open all day *(Comus and Sarah Elliott, Derek Thomas, the Dutchman, Glenn and Evette Booth, Ian Wilson, Mrs Hazel Rainer, J K Parry)*

Old Mill PH16 5BH [Mill Lane]: Comfortable and very popular dining stop with enjoyable food especially steaks, friendly staff, real ales inc Timothy Taylors, draught continental beers, good wine choice, great range of malt whiskies; courtyard tables by Moulin Burn *(Dave Braisted)*

STRUAN [NN8065]

Struan Inn PH18 5UB [B847 off A9]: Nicely old-fashioned 19th-c stone-built inn with good sensibly priced food, Belhaven ale, open fire; six bedrooms, most with own bathroom *(Dave Braisted)*

ROSS-SHIRE

ALTANDHU [NB9812]

Fuaran IV26 2YR [15 miles off A835 N of Ullapool]: Splendidly remote, in gorgeous coastal scenery, enjoyable food inc good value toasties and takeaways, McEwans beer, good whiskies and wine by the glass, open fire, old local photographs, farm tools, antlers and bagpipes; beautiful Summer Isles views from decking *(J F M and M West)*

AULTGUISH INN [NH3570]

Aultguish Hotel IV23 2PQ: Isolated highland inn nr Loch Glascarnoch, new chef/landlord doing good imaginative food, reasonable prices, friendly service; children and dogs welcome, bedrooms *(David and Carole Sayliss, LYM)*

FORTROSE [NH7256]

☆ *Anderson* IV10 8TD [Union St, off A832]: Good small 19th-c hotel with appealing pub side, over 200 malts, well kept changing ales from interesting small breweries, dozens of bottled belgian beers, real cider, fine choice of wine, sofas by log fire, friendly helpful landlord, enterprising food with a scottish touch in bar and restaurant; children welcome (games for them), nine comfortable bedrooms, open all day *(anon)*

KYLE OF LOCHALSH [NG7627]

Lochalsh Hotel IV40 8AF [Ferry Rd]: Large friendly hotel's lounge bar with armchairs and sofas around low tables, plainer eating area, good simple bar food from generous inexpensive double sandwiches to dishes of the day, nice Skye Bridge views, quick friendly helpful service, good coffee; picnic-sets on spreading front lawns, bedrooms *(Joan and Tony Walker)*

SHIEL BRIDGE [NG9319]

Kintail Lodge IV40 8HL: Lots of varnished wood in large plain bar adjoining hotel, convivial bustle in season, lots of malt whiskies, Isle of Skye Black Cuillin, particularly good food from same kitchen as attractive conservatory restaurant with magnificent view down Loch Duich to Skye, local game, wild salmon and own smokings, also children's helpings, friendly efficient service, traditional music Thurs night; 12 good value bedrooms, bunkhouse, good breakfast *(Elaine Hynd)*

ULLAPOOL [NH1293]

Arch IV26 2UR [West Shore St]: Neatly kept welcoming courtyard pub, popular reasonably priced food from good soup and hearty sandwiches to fish and chips, local beer, magnificent sea loch views, local paintings for sale; seats out by quay wall, bedrooms *(J F M and M West, Dave Braisted)*

ROXBURGHSHIRE

KELSO [NT7234]

Cobbles TD5 7JH [Bowmont St]: Small comfortably refurbished 19th-c dining pub just off main square, friendly and well run with good value home-made food emphasising Borders produce inc some enterprising dishes, two ales, decent wines and malts from end bar, wall banquettes and panelling, welcoming fire, overspill dining room upstairs, folk evenings Fri till late; children welcome, disabled facilities *(Jane and David Barrie)*

STIRLINGSHIRE

STIRLING [NS7995]
Birds & the Bees FK9 5PB [Causewayhead; off A9 N of Stirling centre]: Interestingly furnished ex-byre, own-brewed beer and guest ales, enjoyable food; children welcome, two good beer gardens, open all day *(LYM, Jim McDonald)*
Nicky-Tams FK8 1BJ [Baker St]: Cheerful bar said to have almost more ghosts than its many living customers (very popular with young people early evening), good value local fresh food all day, some live music; open all day *(anon)*
☆ *Portcullis* FK8 1EG [Castle Wynd]: Attractive former 18th-c school below castle, overlooking town and surroundings, entry through high-walled courtyard, spacious and elegant high-ceilinged stripped-stone bar with central pillar, inglenooks and brocades, friendly helpful staff, nice choice of sandwiches and good generous pubby hot dishes (not Mon evening, best to book other evenings), Isle of Skye Red Cuillin and Orkney Dark Island from handsome counter, good choice of whiskies; lush sheltered terrace garden, good bedrooms and breakfast *(Jim Sargent)*

WIGTOWNSHIRE

BLADNOCH [NX4254]
Bladnoch Inn DG8 9AB: Cheerful bar, neat and bright, with eating area, enjoyable pubby food from sandwiches up using quality ingredients, friendly obliging service, well proportioned restaurant; keg beer, piped radio; children and dogs welcome, picturesque riverside setting across from Bladnoch distillery (tours), good value modernised bedrooms *(Richard J Holloway)*
DRUMMORE [NX1336]
Ship DG9 9PU [Shore St]: Modernised pub with friendly staff, good value carefully cooked pubby food inc Thurs bargain set lunch, may have real ale *(Don and Shirley Parrish, Mark O'Sullivan)*
PORT LOGAN [NX0940]
☆ *Port Logan Inn* DG9 9NG [Laigh St]: Lovely sea-view spot in pretty fishing harbour, family-run and welcoming, well kept ales such as Caledonian Deuchars IPA or Sulwath Criffel, lots of malt whiskies, enjoyable food inc local fish and game, log fire, old local photographs and electronic equipment; handy for Logan Botanic Garden, bedrooms *(Kay and Alistair Butler, Mark O'Sullivan, Derek Roughton)*

PORTPATRICK [NW9954]
Crown DG9 8SX [North Crescent]: Seafront hotel in delightful harbourside village, decent choice of food all day from good crab sandwiches up, helpful friendly staff, several dozen malts, decent wine by the glass, warm fire in rambling old-fashioned bar with cosy corners, attractively decorated early 20th-c dining room opening through quiet conservatory into sheltered back garden; TV, games machine, piped music; children and dogs welcome, tables out in front, open all day *(Kay and Alistair Butler, LYM, A and B D Craig)*

SCOTTISH ISLANDS

ARRAN

BRODICK [NS0136]
Brodick Bar KA27 8BU [Alma Rd]: Simple modern bar tucked away off seafront, wide choice of good sensibly priced food in restaurant, friendly attentive service, Caledonian ales, several malt whiskies *(Ken Richards, Will Stevens)*
KILMORY [NR9521]
Lagg KA27 8PQ: Relaxing old-fashioned streamside inn, decent bar food, good value evening meals for residents, friendly service; bedrooms, hearty breakfast, delightful view *(John Coatsworth)*
LAMLASH [NS0231]
Pier Head Tavern KA27 8JN: Wide choice of tasty generous food, reasonable prices, efficient friendly service *(E A Eaves)*
SANNOX [NS0145]
Sannox Bay KA27 8JD [aka Ingledene Hotel]: Neat bar popular with locals and visitors, good value generous food in conservatory and restaurant, pleasant staff; garden tables, seaview bedrooms, sandy beach *(Ken Richards, Will Stevens)*

BUTE

PORT BANNATYNE [NS0767]
☆ *Port Royal* PA20 0LW [Marine Rd]: Stone-built inn looking across sea to Argyll, bare boards and timbers to evoke pre-revolution russian tavern (think black and white film versions of *Boris Godunov*), all-day russian food inc good local fish, seafood and venison, choice of russian vodkas as well as real ales such as Fyne tapped from casks on the bar, russian and german beers, Weston's farm cider, good value house wine, cheerful atmosphere and landlord prepared to chat at length about Old Russia, open fire, tapestries and wild flowers; right by beach, deer on golf course behind, open 8am-midnight, five annex bedrooms (some sharing bath), substantial russian breakfasts *(Michael Greenbaum)*

COLONSAY

SCALASAIG [NR3893]

☆ *Colonsay* PA61 7YP: Haven for ramblers and birders, cool and trendy décor with log fires, interesting old islander pictures, pastel walls and polished painted boards, bar with sofas, board games, enjoyable food from soup and toasties to fresh seafood, game and venison, good local Colonsay ale, lots of malt whiskies, informal restaurant; children and dogs welcome, pleasant views from gardens, comfortable bedrooms *(Dave Braisted, David Hoult)*

GIGHA

GIGHA [NR6549]

Gigha Hotel PA41 7AA: Nicely modernised old pub/hotel, pine-décor public bar, sofas in drawing-room bar, well cooked local food in bars or restaurant, afternoon teas; garden tables, good value bedrooms, lovely spot overlooking the Sound and Kintyre *(Ian and Deborah Carrington)*

HARRIS

TARBERT [NB1500]

☆ *Harris Hotel* HS3 3DL [Scott Rd]: Large hotel with nice small panelled bar, local Hebridean ales, rare malt whiskies, enjoyable bar lunches from good range of sandwiches through some interesting light dishes to steak, good choice of evening restaurant meals; comfortable bedrooms *(Dr A McCormick, BB, Dave Braisted)*

ISLAY

BOWMORE [NR3159]

Lochside Hotel PA43 7LB [Shore St]: Neatly modernised family-run hotel, great collection of Islay malts, Islay ale (draught and bottled, Colonsay beer too), enjoyable straightforward food inc local fish and lamb, good service, two bars, bright conservatory-style back restaurant with lovely Loch Indaal views; ten bedrooms *(David Hoult, Richard J Holloway)*

PORTNAHAVEN [NN1652]

An Tighe Seinnse PA47 7SJ [Queen St]: Friendly end-of-terrace harbourside pub tucked away in remote attractive fishing village, cosy bar with room off, open fire, good food inc local seafood, good choice of malts, bottled local Islay ales *(David Hoult, T A R Curran)*

JURA

CRAIGHOUSE [NR5266]

Jura Hotel PA60 7XU: Superb setting, view over the Small Isles to the mainland, decent fairly priced home-made food in bar and restaurant; tables and seats in garden down to water's edge, bedrooms, most with sea view – great island for walkers, birdwatchers and photographers *(John Coatsworth)*

MULL

DERVAIG [NM4251]

☆ *Bellachroy* PA75 6QW: Island's oldest inn, friendly landlady cooks good pub and restaurant food inc local seafood and plenty of other fresh produce, reasonable prices, children's helpings, good choice of beers, whiskies and wine, traditional basic bar, informal dining area and lounge used more by residents, fine atmosphere, nice spot in sleepy village; children and dogs welcome, six comfortable bedrooms, open all year *(T Walker)*

RAASAY [NG5436]

Borodale House IV40 8PB [N of Clachan]: Former Isle of Raasay Hotel renamed, lovely setting on small island, enjoyable food, lounge bar and simple public bar, dining room; dogs welcome, garden seats, 12 bedrooms *(Dave Braisted, Dr A McCormick)*

SKYE

ARDVASAR [NG6303]

☆ *Ardvasar Hotel* IV45 8RS [A851 at S of island, nr Armadale pier]: Lovely sea and mountain views from comfortable white stone inn in peaceful very pretty spot, friendly staff, good home-made food inc local fish (children welcome in eating areas), lots of malt whiskies, two or three real ales inc Isle of Skye Red Cuillin, two bars and games room; TV, piped music; tables outside, bedrooms, good walks, open all day *(LYM, Ian and Helen Stafford)*

ISLE ORNSAY [NG7012]

☆ *Eilean Iarmain* IV43 8QR [off A851 Broadford—Armadale]: Small traditional bar at smart determinedly old-fashioned hotel in beautiful location, friendly locals and staff, enjoyable bar food from same kitchen as charming sea-view restaurant, an Isle of Skye real ale, good choice of vatted (blended) malt whiskies inc its own Te Bheag, banquettes, open fire; piped gaelic music; children welcome, very comfortable bedrooms *(Tracey and Stephen Groves, LYM)*

KYLEAKIN [NG7526]

Saucy Marys Lodge IV41 8PH: Enjoyable simple food such as venison stew, well kept Isle of Skye Red Cuillin, helpful staff; bedrooms and bunkhouse *(Dave Braisted)*

Wales

Wales

New Main Entries (some returning to the *Guide* after a break) are the Bryn Tyrch at Capel Curig and Grapes at Maentwrog (both in Snowdonia National Park), Nantyffin Cider Mill near Crickhowell in mid-Wales (this good dining pub earns a Food Award), and in west Wales, the Carew Inn at Carew (choice views) and nicely revamped Golden Lion in Newport (good food). The pick of the other Main Entries here includes a clutch of impressive Brunning & Price pubs – the Corn Mill in Llangollen, Glasfryn in Mold, Pant-yr-Ochain in Gresford and Pen-y-Bryn in Colwyn Bay – all with good food. Other food stars are the Queens Head near Llandudno Junction, Griffin at Felinfach, beautifully placed Harp at Old Radnor, White Swan at Llanfrynach, Bell at Skenfrith and Hardwick near Abergavenny. Some of these are not cheap, but all give genuine quality and therefore value. The Hardwick, with its superb food and most hospitable service, gives a real sense of occasion, and you leave knowing that you've had a treat; it is Wales Dining Pub of the Year. Other notable pubs here include the Ship on Red Wharf Bay (memorable coastal setting), Hand at Llanarmon Dyffryn Ceiriog (idyllic place to stay), Pen-y-Gwryd up above Llanberis (atmospheric Snowdon mountaineers' haunt), Penhelig Arms in Aberdovey (doing well under its new licensee), Blue Boar in Hay-on-Wye (just right for this town of bookshops), friendly Bear in Crickhowell, Nags Head in Usk and remote Goose & Cuckoo at Rhyd-y-Meirch. Three splendid old places in the south are the Bush at St Hilary, Blue Anchor at East Aberthaw and Plough & Harrow at Monknash, and in the west, two favourite riverside pubs are the simple Cresselly Arms at Cresswell Quay and the Nags Head at Abercych. Brains is the area's main brewer (also brewing Hancocks for the Coors beer empire). We found nearly 20 other welsh brewers' beers stocked by at least some good pubs – the most popular being Rhymney, Breconshire, Evan Evans, Conwy, Great Orme, Purple Moose, Tomos Watkins, Facers, Otley, Newmans and Felinfoel.

ABERAERON
SN4562   MAP 6

Harbourmaster
Harbour Lane; SA46 0BA

Stylish, thriving waterside dining pub/hotel, interesting food (at a price), up-to-date bedrooms

Readers enjoy the setting of this restauranty place, by a yacht-filled harbour with an array of colourwashed buildings. The hotel has been extended into a former grain warehouse, featuring a zinc-clad and blue-walled bar, with french windows; there's an assortment of leather sofas, as well as a stuffed albatross reputed to have collided with a ship belonging to the owner's great-grandfather. The former panelled bar and restaurant have been knocked through into one large dining area, where new light wood furniture looks stylishly modern on light wood floors against light and aqua-blue walls, while there's also a four-seater cwtch, or snug, within the former porch; piped music. Evan Evans Best Bitter and Purple Moose together with a guest like Penlon Cottage Best on handpump, and a good wine list, with a dozen sold by the glass. The owners are chatty and welcoming, and if you stay the breakfasts are good; disabled access.

🍴 The usually enjoyable bar food, featuring welsh recipes and seasonal ingredients, includes soup, starters like potted cardigan bay crab, welsh rarebit or a sharing platter of cured meats and local cheeses, and main courses such as sirloin steak with wild garlic butter, fish of the day, and creamed pearl barley with spring vegetables and parmesan; puddings like profiteroles, chocolate mousse or sherry trifle; children's menu; morning breakfasts too. In the restaurant there's a choice of good, fashionable food (not cheap, but there are set-price two- and three-course lunches): booking advisable. *Starters/Snacks: £4.00 to £8.50. Main Courses: £9.00 to £17.00. Puddings: £5.50*

Free house ~ Licensees Glyn and Menna Heulyn ~ Real ale ~ Bar food (12-2.30, 6-9) ~ Restaurant ~ (01545) 570755 ~ Children welcome ~ Open 10am-11.30pm ~ Bedrooms: £60S/£120B

Recommended by M J Daly, B and M Kendall, Martin Cawley, Mr and Mrs P R Thomas, Di and Mike Gillam, Mike and Mary Carter, M Fitzpatrick, Blaise Vyner

ABERCYCH   SN2539   MAP 6

Nags Head 🍺
Off B4332 Cenarth—Boncath; SA37 0HJ

Enticing riverside position, good value own-brew beer and gargantuan quantities of bar food

One thing to try in this pleasantly tucked-away riverside pub is the much-enjoyed Old Emrys beer, made in a microbrewery and named after one of the regulars; two others might include Brains Rev James and Marstons Pedigree. The dimly lit beamed and flagstoned bar has a big fireplace, clocks showing the time around the world, stripped-wood tables, a piano, photographs and postcards of locals, and hundreds of beer bottles displayed around the brick and stone walls – look out for the big stuffed rat. A plainer small room leads down to a couple of big dining areas, and there's another little room behind the bar; piped music and TV. Service is pleasant and efficient. They sometimes have barbecues out here in summer, and outside it's lit by fairy lights in the evening; there's a children's play area. Benches in the garden look over the river, where you might see a coracle being rowed – and there's one hanging from the wall inside.

🍴 Served in huge helpings (so you might struggle to get through a three-course meal), the bar food might include sandwiches, cawl (lamb stew), steak and Old Emrys ale pie, mixed grill, faggots with chips and mushy peas, lamb and leek pie, or chicken and caerphilli cheese pie, plus specials such as sewin (sea trout) caught in the Teifi by coracle. *Starters/Snacks: £4.00 to £6.00. Main Courses: £6.00 to £15.00. Puddings: £4.25*

Own brew ~ Licensee Samantha Jamieson ~ Real ale ~ Bar food (12-2, 6-9) ~ Restaurant ~ (01239) 841200 ~ Children welcome ~ Dogs allowed in bar ~ Open 11.30-3, 6-11.30; 12-10.30 Sun; closed Mon

Recommended by Colin Moore, John and Enid Morris, Brian Brooks, Gareth Lewis, B and M Kendall

ABERDOVEY   SN6196   MAP 6

Penhelig Arms
Opposite Penhelig railway station; LL35 0LT

Fine harbourside location, enjoyable food, and a nice place to stay

We've had very good feedback from readers of this waterside hotel, where the food and service have been particularly commended since Glyn Davies, the former manager, took charge. Good log fires in the small original beamed bar make it especially cosy in winter, and there's nothing in the way of fruit machines or piped music. Three ales on handpump feature Brains Bitter, Rev James and a guest from a brewery such as Adnams or Greene King; two dozen malt whiskies and a good wine selection with 22 by the glass. The bedrooms are comfortable (some have balconies overlooking the estuary) but the ones nearest the road can be noisy.

🍴 **In addition to lunchtime sandwiches, the daily lunch and dinner menus could include soup, starters such as grilled goats cheese or mullet fillets, and main courses like lambs liver and bacon, grilled monkfish, honey-roasted duck, chicken pie or spinach and ricotta cannelloni; puddings like caramelised lemon tart or summer pudding.** *Starters/Snacks: £2.00 to £10.50. Main Courses: £8.95 to £16.95. Puddings: £4.95*

Brains ~ Manager Glyn Davies ~ Real ale ~ Bar food (12-2, 6-9) ~ Restaurant ~ (01654) 767215 ~ Children welcome ~ Dogs allowed in bar and bedrooms ~ Open 11-11; 12-10.30 Sun; closed 24-26 Dec ~ Bedrooms: £60S/£100S(£120B)

Recommended by B and M Kendall, Mike and Mary Carter, Jacquie Jones, Colin Moore, David Glynne-Jones, Clive Watkin, Neil Kellett, Brian and Anna Marsden

ABERGAVENNY   SO3111   MAP 6

Hardwick 🍴 ♐

Hardwick; B4598 SE, off A40 at A465/A4042 exit – coming from E on A40, go right round the exit system, as B4598 is final road out; NP7 9AA

WALES DINING PUB OF THE YEAR

Very good interesting food in smartly simple dining pub, good beers and wines too

'We always come away feeling we have had a treat' remarked one reader of this very well run dining pub. The emphasis is clearly on the cooking, though they do have two changing ales on handpump, from Breconshire, Otley or Rhymney, as well as local bottled ciders and a splendid choice of good interesting wines by the glass, in a choice of glass sizes. The bar, with a small functional corner servery, is a simple room with spindleback chairs around pub tables, and some stripped brickwork around a disused fireplace. The better of the two dining rooms actually has rather more of a pub feel, given its dark beams, a winged high-backed settle by the end serving counter, another facing a small pew across one table tucked in by a huge fireplace, and a nice mix of other tables and chairs on bare boards with a big rug (the lack of soft furnishings here can make the acoustics rather lively). The second dining room in a carpeted extension is lighter and simpler, more modern in style, with big windows; there is some interesting artwork. Service is welcoming and helpful; there may be piped music. They have teak tables and chairs out under umbrellas by the car park, and the garden is neatly kept. They plan to open bedrooms.

🍴 **Owner-chef Stephen Terry's talent in using carefully selected largely local ingredients to create both supercharged variations on familiar dishes and more original recipes is well known to us from at least two of his previous businesses. Nothing's cheap here, but given the quality it's all good value. His crisp thrice-cooked chips add something special to the tender home-baked ham and eggs, and the grilled lunchtime sandwiches might include delicate goats cheese with tapenade and mixed vegetables as an eye-opening variant on the humble cheese toastie. The extensive lunch and dinner menus might include provençale-style fish soup, starters like confit duck hash with fried local duck egg, salad of buffalo mozzarella with polenta croûtons, anchovies and sun-dried tomato, or mussels on bruschetta, and main courses such as fried sea trout with roasted beetroot, sauté new potatoes, smoked bacon, rocket and horseradish, home-made local gloucester old spot pork meatballs in tomato sauce with penne pasta, caesar salad made with locally smoked chicken, and roast boneless wing of skate with wild garlic mash, carrots and braised fennel; puddings like sticky toffee and medjool date loaf with toffee sauce, or vanilla panna cotta with rhubarb jelly and stem ginger shortbread. Children's menu, fixed-price two- and three-course lunches; Sunday roasts.** *Starters/Snacks: £6.50 to £13.50. Main Courses: £11.95 to £21.00. Puddings: £4.95 to £8.50*

Free house ~ Licensees Stephen and Joanna Terry ~ Real ale ~ Bar food (12-3, 6.30-9.30) ~ Restaurant ~ (01873) 854220 ~ Children welcome ~ Open 12-3, 6.30-11.30; 12-3 Sun; closed Mon (except bank hols)

Recommended by Michael and Maggie Betton, Dr Kevan Tucker, Joyce and Maurice Cottrell, Duncan Cloud, Ian Herdman, Alastair Stevenson

BEAUMARIS

SH6076   MAP 6

Olde Bulls Head ♀ 🛏

Castle Street; LL58 8AP

Interesting historic pub with brasserie food, accommodation and wines

Since it was built in 1472, this cosy inn near the castle has been used by a great range of people, including Samuel Johnson and Charles Dickens, both of whom would find much of it familiar today. It's not really pubby, but its low-beamed bar is a nicely rambling place, with plenty of interesting reminders of the town's past: a rare 17th-c brass water clock, a bloodthirsty crew of cutlasses and even an oak ducking stool tucked among the snug alcoves. There are also lots of copper and china jugs, comfortable low-seated settles, leather-cushioned window seats, a good log fire, and Bass, Hancocks and a guest such as Purple Moose Snowdonia Ale on handpump. Quite a contrast, the busy brasserie behind is lively and stylishly modern, with a wine list including a dozen available by the glass; the restaurant list runs to 120 bottles. The entrance to the pretty courtyard is closed by what is listed in *The Guinness Book of Records* as the biggest simple-hinged door in Britain (11 feet wide and 13 feet high). Named after characters in Dickens's novels, the bedrooms are very well equipped; some are traditional, and others more up to date, and there are now also new bedrooms in the Townhouse, an adjacent property with disabled access. More reports on the food please.

🍴 Lunchtime snacks such as soup and sandwiches now available in the bar; the brasserie menu includes starters like filo parcel of goats cheese, and snails in garlic and parsley butter, ploughman's, and main courses such as fish and chips, salmon escalope with pink peppercorn hollandaise, rib-eye steak, and spanish omelette; puddings like crème caramel with biscotti, or rhubarb bread and butter pudding; welsh cheeseboard; children's menu. There is also a smart restaurant upstairs. *Starters/Snacks: £4.25 to £6.40. Main Courses: £6.50 to £15.75. Puddings: £4.25 to £5.80*

Free house ~ Licensee David Robertson ~ Real ale ~ Bar food (12-2(3 Sun), 6-9) ~ Restaurant ~ (01248) 810329 ~ Children welcome in brasserie but no under-7s in loft restaurant ~ Open 11-11; 12-10.30 Sun ~ Bedrooms: £80B/£105B

Recommended by Mrs Angela Graham, Gordon and Margaret Ormonroyd, Chris Brooks, Brian and Anna Marsden, Ken and Margaret Grinstead, Michael Dandy, John McDonald, Ann Bond, Di and Mike Gillam, Neil Whitehead, Victoria Anderson, Bob and Val Collman, Revd D Glover, Mike and Mary Carter

CAPEL CURIG

SH7257   MAP 6

Bryn Tyrch 🛏

A5 E; LL24 OEL

Perfectly placed for the mountains of Snowdonia, welcoming licensees, pleasant bedrooms, and interesting food (all day weekends) featuring tasty vegetarian dishes

Now run by the daughter and son-in-law of the previous licensee, this splendidly placed inn in the mountains was being refurbished as we went to press, in a style that promises to be nicely rustic and in keeping. Comfortably relaxed, the bar has several easy chairs round low tables, some by a coal fire with magazines and outdoor equipment catalogues piled to one side; they're putting in pine tables rescued from a local church that closed down, and the plainer hikers' bar is planned to have large, communal tables and natural stone walls. Great Orme IPA, Ormes and Three Feathers on handpump, with perhaps a guest, and quite a few malt whiskies, including some local ones; chess, draughts, cards and pool. You can take in the terrific views from the large picture windows that run the length of one wall – looking across the road to picnic-sets on a floodlit patch of grass by a stream running down to a couple of lakes, and the peaks of the Carneddau, Tryfan and Glyders in close range; there are also tables on a steep little garden at the side, and on a terrace off the breakfast room. Bedrooms have recently been very nicely updated in country-style, and are all ensuite; some have views; £12.50 cleaning charge for dogs (who are only allowed in some bedrooms).

🍴 Wholesome food, with an emphasis on vegetarian and vegan dishes, could include lunchtime sandwiches, vegetable broth, lamb burger and chunky chips, spicy pork sausages with mash, steak and ale pie, vegetable and bean shepherd's pie, fishcakes; children's menu. *Starters/Snacks: £4.95 to £7.95. Main Courses: £8.95 to £17.95. Puddings: £5.00*

Free house ~ Licensees Rachel and Neil Roberts ~ Real ale ~ Bar food (12-2, 6-9; 12-9 Sat, Sun) ~ (01690) 720223 ~ Children welcome ~ Dogs allowed in bar and some bedrooms ~ Open 12-3(11.30 Sat, Sun); closed first three weeks of Jan ~ Bedrooms: £47.50B/£75B

Recommended by Mrs J Skinner, DC, John and Helen Rushton, John and Bryony Coles, Trudie Hudson

CAREW
SN0403   MAP 6

Carew Inn

A4075, just off A477; SA70 8SL

Appealing cottagey atmosphere, pleasant gardens, good pubby food

The gardens here have really distinctive views – down to the river in front, where a tidal watermill is open for afternoon summer visits, and from the back to the imposing ruins of Carew Castle and a remarkable 9th-c Celtic cross. Inside, the pub is homely and unpretentious: run by the same owner-managers for over 18 years, it has open fires in winter, and the landlady is chatty and attentive. The little panelled public bar and comfortable lounge have old-fashioned settles, scrubbed pine furniture, interesting prints and decorative china hanging from the beams. The upstairs dining room has an elegant china cabinet, a mirror over the tiled fireplace and sturdy chairs around well spaced tables. Beers include Brains Rev James and Worthington and perhaps a guest beer from a brewer such as Evan Evans on handpump; several wines by the glass; piped music and outdoor pool table. The back garden has outdoor heating in summer, and it's safely enclosed for children to play, with a wendy house, climbing frame, slide and other toys.

🍽 **Served by friendly staff, the well liked bar food includes lunchtime ploughman's, sandwiches and baguettes, mussels, starters such as garlic mushrooms or smoked mackerel pâté, good value favourites like steak and ale pie or curry of the day, and main courses including minted lamb steak, ostrich strips fried with mushrooms, cream and madeira sauce, and stuffed chicken breast wrapped in puff pastry; children's menu; daily specials like queen scallops, lemon sole or mixed grill; Sunday roasts; puddings such as syrup sponge and raspberry fool.** *Starters/Snacks: £2.00 to £5.50. Main Courses: £7.95 to £17.95. Puddings: £3.95 to £4.95*

Free house ~ Licensee Mandy Scourfield ~ Real ale ~ Bar food (12-2.30(not outside school hols), 6-9) ~ Restaurant ~ (01646) 651267 ~ Children in eating area of bar and restaurant ~ Dogs allowed in bar ~ Live music Thurs and Sun evenings in summer hols ~ Open 11-11

Recommended by Colin Moore, Di and Mike Gillam, the Didler

COLWYN BAY
SH8478   MAP 6

Pen-y-Bryn 🍽 🍷 🍺

B5113 Llanwrst Road, on S outskirts; when you see the pub, turn off into Wentworth Avenue for its car park; LL29 6DD

Modern pub in great position overlooking the bay, reliable food all day, good range of drinks, obliging staff

The views alone are reason for seeking out this efficiently run place, which is much more special than its bungalow exterior suggests. Its light and airy open-plan interior has big windows looking far across the bay and to the Great Orme. Extending around the three long sides of the bar counter, the mix of seating and well spaced tables, oriental rugs on pale stripped boards, shelves of books, welcoming coal fires, profusion of pictures, big pot plants, careful lighting and dark green school radiators are all typical of the pubs in this small chain. Besides Flowers Original, Great Orme Best and Thwaites Original, you'll find three changing guests such as Black Sheep Best Bitter, Conwy Rampart and Timothy Taylors Landlord on handpump. They also have well chosen good value wines including 20 by the glass, and more than 60 malts; board games and piped music. Outside there are sturdy tables and chairs on a side terrace and a lower one by a lawn with picnic-sets. We're surprised we haven't had recent feedback from readers on what has always been a much-liked and well run pub; more reports please.

🍴 Served all day, the reliable and much-liked food from a changing menu could typically include substantial sandwiches, ploughman's with welsh cheeses, soup, starters and light dishes such sardines fried in lemon and chilli oil, roasted fennel and orange salad, or menai mussels in white wine and garlic sauce, main courses like braised half-shoulder of welsh lamb, spicy moroccan chicken and chickpea casserole, coconut crumbed salmon, and wild mushroom, spinach and leek shepherd's pie; puddings such as white chocolate and raspberry trifle. *Starters/Snacks: £4.25 to £7.95. Main Courses: £7.95 to £14.95. Puddings: £4.25 to £5.25*

Brunning & Price ~ Licensees Graham Arathoon and Graham Price ~ Real ale ~ Bar food (12–9.30(9 Sun)) ~ (01492) 533360 ~ Children under 14 welcome till 7pm ~ Open 11.30–11; 12–10.30 Sun

Recommended by Paul and Margaret Baker, R T and J C Moggridge, Keith and Sue Ward

CRESSWELL QUAY   SN0506   MAP 6

Cresselly Arms

Village signposted from A4075; SA68 0TE

Marvellously simple alehouse, with benches outside overlooking a tidal creek

---

Lovers of unchanged, down-to-earth rustic pubs should beat a path to this beautifully positioned waterside tavern. Often full of locals, the two simple and comfortably old-fashioned communicating rooms have a relaxed and jaunty air, as well as red and black floor tiles, built-in wall benches, kitchen chairs and plain tables, an open fire in one room, a working Aga in the other, and a high beam-and-plank ceiling hung with lots of pictorial china. A third red-carpeted room is more conventionally furnished, with red-cushioned mate's chairs around neat tables. Worthington BB and a winter guest beer are tapped straight from the cask into glass jugs by the landlord, whose presence is a key ingredient of the atmosphere. If you time the tides right, you can arrive by boat; seats outside make the most of the view. No children.

🍴 No food, except filled rolls on Saturday mornings.

Free house ~ Licensees Maurice and Janet Cole ~ Real ale ~ No credit cards ~ (01646) 651210 ~ Open 12–3, 5–11; 11–11 Sat; 12–10.30 Sun

Recommended by Mark Farrington, Mrs P Bishop, Richard Pitcher, Pete Baker, the Didler, Julian Distin, Blaise Vyner

CRICKHOWELL   SO2118   MAP 6

Bear ★ ♟ 🛏

Brecon Road; A40; NP8 1BW

Civilised and interesting inn with splendid old-fashioned bar area warmed by a log fire, good and sensibly priced food, and comfortable bedrooms

---

This fine old inn is consistently praised for its thoroughly convivial atmosphere and efficient staff. Its comfortably decorated, heavily beamed lounge has fresh flowers on tables, lots of little plush-seated bentwood armchairs and handsome cushioned antique settles, and a window seat looking down on the market square. Up by the great roaring log fire, a big sofa and leather easy chairs are spread among rugs on the oak parquet floor. Other good antiques include a fine oak dresser filled with pewter mugs and brass, a longcase clock and interesting prints. Bass, Brains Rev James, Thwaites and a guest such as Rhymney Bitter on handpump, as well as 34 malt whiskies, vintage and late-bottled ports, unusual wines (with several by the glass) and liqueurs; disabled lavatories. It is a welcoming place to stay – some refurbished bedrooms are in a country style, though the older rooms have antiques, and breakfast is excellent; more expensive rooms have jacuzzis and four-poster beds. Readers tell us the staff are especially welcoming to dogs.

🍴 Enjoyable bar food from a changing menu includes sandwiches and baguettes, starters and light meals such as chicken liver parfait, smoked haddock fishcake, or shredded duck salad with sweet chilli sauce, and main courses like welsh black beef steaks, fish and chips, faggots, slow-braised welsh lamb shank, and potato rösti millefeuilles with sauté wild mushrooms; daily changing specials board; puddings like strawberry pavlova. Starters/Snacks: £4.25 to £8.50. Main Courses: £8.95 to £12.95. Puddings: £5.00 to £6.50

Free house ~ Licensee Judy Hindmarsh ~ Real ale ~ Bar food (12-2, 6-10; 12-2, 7-9.30 Sun) ~ Restaurant ~ (01873) 810408 ~ Children welcome (not in restaurant if under 6) ~ Dogs allowed in bar and bedrooms ~ Open 11-3, 6-11; 12-3, 7-10.30 Sun ~ Bedrooms: £70S(£80B)/£86S(£96B)

Recommended by Tom and Ruth Rees, Mr and Mrs P J Fisk, Steven and Victoria James, Patrick and Daphne Darley, Joyce and Maurice Cottrell, Roy Hoing, Roy Charlton, David Jackman, Malcolm and Sue Scott, Guy Vowles, Gareth Lewis, Reg Fowle, Helen Rickwood, Colin Moore, Mike and Mary Carter, Mr and Mrs C Gothard, Mrs Margo Finlay, Jörg Kasprowski, David and Lin Short, Herbert and Susan Verity

Nantyffin Cider Mill 🍴 ♀
A40/A479 NW; NP8 1LP

Foody and discerning; former drovers' inn with imaginative brasserie food and interesting drinks, and meat mostly from a local farm

Looking on to the River Usk, this pink-painted 16th-c drovers' inn has been handsomely updated into a very good dining pub that also retains a traditional pubby atmosphere. You can see the old cider press that gives the pub its name in the raftered barn that has been converted into the striking restaurant; appropriately, they still serve farm cider. With warm grey stonework, the bar has good solid comfortable tables and chairs and a woodburner in a fine broad fireplace. The counter at one end of the main open-plan area has Brains Rev James and SA on handpump, as well as thoughtfully chosen new world wines (a few by the glass or half-bottle), Pimms and home-made lemonade in summer, organic farmhouse apple juice, and hot punch and mulled wine in winter. A ramp makes disabled access easy. Tables on the lawn make the most of the rural views.

🍴 Largely featuring meat and poultry from Glaisfer Uchaf Farm, a few miles away, the seasonally changing menus of carefully presented food include lunchtime ploughman's with home-made bread, sandwiches and pies, starters and light dishes like greek meze, grilled goats cheese, garlic mushroom bruschetta, or welsh cockle, bacon and leek fritters; main courses such as chargrilled rib-eye steak, confit of farm mountain lamb, grilled rack of pork, and cherry tomato, feta and olive open tart; specials board with fresh fish; puddings like spring rhubarb and oat crumble and banana and chocolate pavlova; fixed price two- and three-course Sunday lunches. Starters/Snacks: £5.25 to £6.95. Main Courses: £7.95 to £17.95. Puddings: £5.25 to £5.50

Free house ~ Lease Vic and Ann Williams ~ Real ale ~ Bar food (12-2.30(3 Sun), 6(7 Sun)-9.30) ~ Restaurant ~ (01873) 810775 ~ Children welcome ~ Dogs allowed in bar ~ Open 12-3, 6-11; 12-3, 7-10.30 Sun; closed Mon (except bank hols) and Sun evening in winter

Recommended by Simon Daws, Rodney and Norma Stubington, Gareth Lewis, Steve and Liz Tilley, Mike and Mary Carter

EAST ABERTHAW   ST0366   MAP 6

Blue Anchor 🍺
B4265; CF62 3DD

Ancient thatched pub, loaded with character and a popular place for a beer

Readers thoroughly enjoy the appealing warren of little rooms and cosy corners in this character-laden 600-year-old tavern. The building has massive walls, low-beamed rooms and tiny doorways, with open fires everywhere, including one in an inglenook with antique oak seats built into its stripped stonework. Other seats and tables are worked into a series of chatty little alcoves, and the more open front bar still has an ancient lime-ash floor. Friendly staff serve Brains Bitter, Theakstons Old Peculier, Wadworths 6X and Wye Valley Hereford Pale Ale on handpump, alongside a changing guest such as

Rhymney Bitter; games machine. Rustic seats shelter peacefully among tubs and troughs of flowers outside, with more stone tables on a newer terrace. The pub can get very full in the evenings and on summer weekends, and it's used as a base by a couple of local motorbike clubs. From here a path leads to the shingly flats of the estuary.

🍴 As well as lunchtime baguettes and filled baked potatoes, bar food includes soup, caesar salad with smoked salmon or smoked chicken, ploughman's, rib-eye steak, calves liver, thai green chicken curry, and caramelised red onion and goats cheese tartlet; daily specials such as mussels, faggots, or roasted suprême of chicken with ratatouille; puddings such as chocolate truffle torte or cherry and frangipane tart; they grow their own herbs and soft fruit. *Starters/Snacks: £3.50 to £5.50. Main Courses: £7.95 to £10.75. Puddings: £3.95*

Free house ~ Licensee Jeremy Coleman ~ Real ale ~ Bar food (12-2.15(2.30 Sun), 6-9; not Sun evening) ~ Restaurant ~ (01446) 750329 ~ Children welcome ~ Dogs allowed in bar ~ Open 11-11; 12-10.30 Sun

Recommended by H L Dennis, Prof Kenneth Surin, R T and J C Moggridge

FELINFACH   SO0933   MAP 6

Griffin 🍴 �़ 🛏

A470 NE of Brecon; LD3 0UB

A classy dining pub for enjoying good, unpretentious cooking featuring lots of home-grown vegetables; upbeat rustic décor, nice bedrooms

Open all day, this friendly, accomplished dining pub looks after its guests extremely well. The back bar is quite pubby in an up-to-date way, with three leather sofas around a low table on pitted quarry tiles, by a high slate hearth with a log fire, and behind them mixed stripped seats around scrubbed kitchen tables on bare boards, and a bright blue-and-ochre colour scheme, with some modern prints. The acoustics are pretty lively, with so much bare flooring and uncurtained windows; maybe piped radio. The two smallish front dining rooms, linking through to the back bar, are attractive: on the left, mixed dining chairs around mainly stripped tables on flagstones, and white-painted rough stone walls, with a cream-coloured Aga in a big stripped-stone embrasure; on the right, similar furniture on bare boards, with big modern prints on terracotta walls and good dark curtains. Efficient staff serve a fine array of drinks, including a thoughtful choice of wines (with 20 by the glass and carafe), welsh spirits, cocktails, local bottled ciders and apple juice, unusual continental beers, sherries and Wye Valley Butty Bach and Hereford Pale Ale, with a guest like Breconshire Red Dragon, on handpump. Wheelchair access is good, and there are tables outside. Bedrooms are comfortable and tastefully decorated, and the hearty breakfasts nicely informal: you make your own toast on the Aga (which can be a somewhat leisurely process) and help yourself to home-made marmalade and jam.

🍴 As well as two- and three-course set lunches and evening meals, the particularly good modern food might include sandwiches, ploughman's, mediterranean fish soup, foie gras with fig chutney, cherry beer jelly and toasted sourdough bread, smoked salmon tartare with watercress panna cotta and crème fraîche, pork and leek sausages, risotto with roasted girolles, peas and feta, grey mullet fillet with capers, brown butter and chips, grain-fed rib-eye of beef with onion purée and confit and béarnaise, rump of herdwick lamb, shepherd's pie, carrots and peas, and puddings like vanilla crème brûlée with rhubarb juice and bakewell tart with Chantilly cream. *Starters/Snacks: £4.90 to £12.50. Main Courses: £10.50 to £18.90. Puddings: £6.00 to £8.50*

Free house ~ Licensees Charles and Edmund Inkin ~ Real ale ~ Bar food (12.30(12 Sun)-2.30, 6.30-9.30(9 Sun)) ~ Restaurant ~ (01874) 620111 ~ Children welcome ~ Dogs welcome ~ Open 11-11; closed one week in Jan ~ Bedrooms: £75B/£115B

Recommended by M Fitzpatrick, James Paterson, Rodney and Norma Stubington, Simon Daws, MLR, Miss K Hunt, Mr M Smith, G M Benson, Derek Hills, Dr Kevan Tucker, Paul Goldman, R T and J C Moggridge

---

If you have to cancel a reservation for a bedroom or restaurant, please telephone or write to warn them. You may lose your deposit if you've paid one.

GRESFORD   SJ3453   MAP 6

Pant-yr-Ochain ⊕ ☼ ◖

Off A483 on N edge of Wrexham: at roundabout take A5156 (A534) towards Nantwich,
then first left towards the Flash; LL12 8TY

Thoughtfully run, gently refined dining pub with rooms, good food all day, very wide range
of drinks, pretty lakeside garden

As well as thoughtfully prepared food, they have a terrific range of drinks at this 16th-c
former country house. Ten well kept real ales on handpump feature Flowers Original and
Timothy Taylors Landlord alongside guests such as Derwent Pale Ale, Oakham White Dwarf
and Salopian Monarchy; they have a good range of decent wines (strong on up-front new
world ones), with 27 by the glass, and around 100 malt whiskies. It has been nicely
refurbished inside: the light and airy rooms are stylishly decorated, with a wide range of
interesting prints and bric-a-brac on walls and on shelves, and a good mix of individually
chosen country furnishings, including comfortable seats for relaxing as well as more
upright ones for eating, and there's a recently rebuilt conservatory as well as a good
open fire; one area is set out as a library, with floor-to-ceiling bookshelves; TV. Disabled
access is good. The garden overlooks a lake frequented by waterfowl and has benches,
mature trees and shrubs.

🍽 **Good food, from a well balanced daily changing menu, and using free-range eggs and**
chicken, includes sandwiches, ploughman's, soup, starters and lighter choices like seared
scallops with spiced carrot purée, welsh rarebit, or lamb kofta, and main courses such as
battered haddock, steak burger, game and steak suet pudding, spiced chickpea cakes with
bean casserole, and spinach, butternut squash and shropshire blue cheese filo pie;
puddings such as apple and berry crumble, eton mess or cherry bakewell tart; Sunday
roasts; good choice of coffee. *Starters/Snacks: £4.50 to £8.95. Main Courses: £7.25 to £19.95.*
Puddings: £4.50 to £5.50

Brunning & Price ~ Licensee Lindsey Douglas ~ Real ale ~ Bar food (12-9.30(9 Sun)) ~
(01978) 853525 ~ Children welcome (no toddlers or babies after 7pm) ~ Open 12-11.30(11 Sun)

Recommended by David Johnson, Mr and Mrs J Palmer, Peter and Josie Fawcett, Clive Watkin, Adair Cameron,
Roger and Anne Newbury, Dr Phil Putwain

HAY-ON-WYE   SO2242   MAP 6

Blue Boar

Castle Street/Oxford Road; HR3 5DF

Generous home cooking in dual-personality pub – dark cosy medieval bar, light and airy
modern dining area

They've recently opened up the secluded, tree-shaded garden here, which has tables for
diners. The irregular shape of the bar here gives cosy corners, and its candlelight or
shaded table lamps, squared dark ply panelling and handsome fireplace (with a good
winter fire) make for a relaxed atmosphere. There are pews, country chairs and stools at
the counter, which has Bass, Blue Boar (which is Hydes IPA, named for the pub), Flowers
Original, Timothy Taylors Landlord, a good choice of wines by the glass and whiskies, and
bottled Dunkerton's organic cider and perry; the service is good, under a friendly
landlady. The long open dining room is light and airy, thanks to big sash windows, fresh
cheery décor and bright tablecloths. There's a fire here too, and local artwork for sale;
good coffees and teas; piped Radio Four or occasional music.

🍽 **Enjoyable bar food typically includes sandwiches, soup, smoked trout, welsh rarebit,**
sausages with onion gravy, cod and chips, chicken and mushroom pie, tuscan bean
casserole on couscous, welsh cawl (lamb stew), and puddings like apple pie or fruit
pavlova. They also do breakfasts (9.30-11.30am). *Starters/Snacks: £3.95 to £6.95. Main*
Courses: £8.95 to £15.95. Puddings: £4.50

Free house ~ Licensees John and Lucy Golsworthy ~ Real ale ~ Bar food (12-9(9.30 Sat, Sun)) ~
Restaurant ~ (01497) 820884 ~ Children welcome if dining ~ Dogs allowed in bar ~ Open 11-11

Recommended by Reg Fowle, Helen Rickwood, Sue Demont, Tim Barrow, Michael Butler, David Howe, Brian and Jacky Wilson, Jarrod and Wendy Hopkinson

LITTLE HAVEN

SM8512   MAP 6

St Brides Inn

St Brides Road – in village itself, not St Brides hamlet further W; SA62 3UN

Cheerful seaside inn with anglo-russian owners, tasty food and a log fire

Right next to the Pembrokeshire Coast Path this likeable, well run little place has a sheltered suntrap terraced garden across the road, with troughs of colourful plants. There's a neat stripped-stone bar and linking carpeted dining area, and a good log fire. Banks's and Marstons Pedigree are kept under a light blanket pressure on handpump, and several malt whiskies are available. Because space is restricted, babies and prams are not allowed inside. A curious well in a back corner grotto is thought to be partly Roman. The two bright bedrooms, in a separate building, have pine furniture and are ensuite; we would welcome reports from readers who stay here.

🍽 **Menus change frequently and, along with lunchtime sandwiches and interesting soups such as welsh cawl, might feature beef stroganoff (made to the russian landlady Mila's family recipe), confit of duck leg with roasted vegetables, baked bass fillets with chorizo mash, and egg pasta with roasted tomato sauce; blackboard specials including pies, curries, salads, fish of the day and, in summer, st brides bay dressed crab; puddings like apple strudel; Sunday roasts and summer barbecues; theme nights such as russian, french, spanish and mediterranean.** *Starters/Snacks: £4.00 to £9.50. Main Courses: £8.50 to £16.00. Puddings: £3.00 to £5.20*

Marstons ~ Lease Graham Harrison-Jones ~ Real ale ~ Bar food (12-2, 6-9) ~ Restaurant ~ No credit cards ~ 01437 781266 ~ Children welcome (no babies or prams) ~ Dogs allowed in bar ~ Open 10am-11pm; 11.30-3, 6-11 (closed Mon) in winter; closed two weeks in early Jan ~ Bedrooms: /£60S

Recommended by R and Z Davies, Steve Godfrey, Pat Crabb

LLANARMON DYFFRYN CEIRIOG

SJ1532   MAP 6

Hand 🛏

On B4500 from Chirk; LL20 7LD

Comfortable rural hotel in a remote valley; cosy low-beamed bar area, good bedrooms

In deepest rural Wales, this peaceful inn is a delightful place to stay: 'The only thing I could hear from my bed was an owl' commented one reader. Happy and welcoming staff help towards the warm atmosphere. The black-beamed carpeted bar on the left of the broad-flagstoned entrance hall has a good log fire in its inglenook fireplace, a mixture of chairs and settles, and old prints on its cream walls, with bar stools along the modern bar counter, which has Weetwood Eastgate and a guest such as Stonehouse Station Bitter on handpump, several malt whiskies and reasonably priced wines by the glass. Round the corner is the largely stripped-stone dining room, with a woodburning stove and carpeted floor; TV, darts and pool. Bedrooms are attractive and spacious, and breakfasts are very satisfying; the residents' lounge on the right is comfortable and attractive. There are tables out on a crazy-paved front terrace, with more in the garden, which has flowerbeds around another sheltered terrace.

🍽 **Besides lunchtime sandwiches and ploughman's, items from a seasonally changing menu, using named local suppliers, includes soup, starters such as scallops, chicken liver parfait or gravadlax, pubby favourites like scampi, sausage and mash and steak and ale pie, local roast ceiriog lamb with red wine sauce, a vegetarian dish such as frittata, and grilled trout from a trout farm in the valley; puddings like tiramisu or passion fruit and mango cheesecake.** *Starters/Snacks: £4.50 to £6.00. Main Courses: £7.50 to £20.00. Puddings: £3.50 to £5.50*

Free house ~ Licensees Gaynor and Martin de Luchi ~ Bar food (12-2.20, 6.30-8.45; 12.30-2.45, 6.30-8.30 Sun) ~ Restaurant ~ (01691) 600666 ~ Well supervised children welcome ~ Dogs allowed in bar and bedrooms ~ Open 11(12 Sun)-11(12.30 Sat) ~ Bedrooms: £65B/£110B

Recommended by K and J Whitehead, James Barnes, Mike and Mary Carter, BOB, Stuart Pugh, Simon Daws

LLANBERIS   SH6655   MAP 6

Pen-y-Gwryd 🛏️

Nant Gwynant; at junction of A498 and A4086, ie across mountains from Llanberis –
OS Sheet 115 map reference 660558; LL55 4NT

In the hands of the same family for decades, an illustrious favourite with the mountain fraternity

Isolated among the high mountains of Snowdonia, this long-established climbers' haunt has a cheery and simple atmosphere. It was used as a training base for the 1953 Everest team, whose fading signatures can still be made out, scrawled on the ceiling. One snug little room in the homely slate-floored log cabin bar has built-in wall benches and sturdy country chairs to let you gaze at the surrounding mountain landscape – like precipitous Moel Siabod beyond the lake opposite. A smaller room has a worthy collection of illustrious boots from famous climbs, and a cosy panelled smoke room has more fascinating climbing mementoes and equipment; darts, pool, board games and table tennis. Purple Moose Cwrw Glaslyn and Cwrw Madogs are on handpump, and they've several malts. Staying here in the comfortable but basic bedrooms can be quite an experience, and the excellent, traditional breakfast is served at 8.30am (they're not generally flexible about this); dogs £2 a night. The inn has its own chapel (built for the millennium and dedicated by the Archbishop of Wales), sauna and outdoor natural pool. More up-to-date reports please.

🍴 **The short choice of simple, good value, home-made lunchtime bar food (you order it through a hatch) might include sandwiches, soup, chicken liver pâté, a platter of cold meats, roast lamb or welsh black beef, slow-braised pork, salmon steak or cheese and onion tart; puddings such as chocolate pudding or apple and blackberry pie. The five-course fixed-price meal in the evening restaurant, presenting a similarly hearty range of fare, is signalled by a gong at 7.30pm – if you're late, you'll miss it, and there's no evening bar food.** *Starters/Snacks: £4.25 to £6.95. Main Courses: £8.50. Puddings: £2.00 to £4.00*

Free house ~ Licensee Jane Pullee ~ Real ale ~ Bar food (lunchtime only) ~ (01286) 870211 ~ Children welcome ~ Dogs allowed in bar ~ Open 11-11; closed all Nov and Dec, and mid-week Jan-Feb ~ Bedrooms: £40/£80(£94B)

Recommended by Neil and Angela Huxter, John and Enid Morris, Alec and Joan Laurence, Julian and Janet Dearden, Steve Kirby

LLANDDAROG   SN5016   MAP 6

White Hart 🍺

Just off A48 E of Carmarthen, via B4310; aka Yr Hydd Gwyn; SA32 8NT

Popular thatched pub full of interest and antiques, unusual own-brew beers and good portions of bar food

Packed with all types of engaging bric-a-brac, this lovely ancient building deserves seeking out for the own-brew beers: named after the family in charge, the small Coles brewery produces ales such as Cwrw Blasus, Llanddarog, Swyn-y-Dail as well as a roasted barley stout, and there are usually three available on handpump. The rooms reveal fascinating details and sundry bits and pieces – 17th-c welsh oak carving, a tall grandfather clock, stained-glass, a collection of hats and riding boots, china, brass and copper on walls and dark beams, antique prints and even a suit of armour. The heavily carved fireside settles by the huge crackling log fire are the best place to sit. But the main attraction today is the range of beers they make using water from their own 300-foot borehole. There are steps down to the high-raftered dining room, also interestingly furnished. They may charge for tap water (unless you're eating). There are picnic-sets out on a terrace, a children's play area and farmyard; they can put a ramp in place for disabled access. Look out for Zac the macaw and Bendy the galah.

🍴 **Using poultry and meat from local farms and fish from Haverfordwest, generous helpings of tasty bar food from the extensive menu include sandwiches, baked potatoes, ploughman's, curries, a range of pizzas, steaks and grills with a choice of sauces (charged extra), battered cod, roast dinners, and vegetarian dishes such as cheese and broccoli bake, with specials such as welsh mutton, speciality pies, fresh fish and sometimes kangaroo or ostrich steaks; children's menu; puddings.** *Starters/Snacks: £3.95 to £6.95. Main Courses: £6.95 to £21.50. Puddings: £1.95 to £4.95*

Own brew ~ Licensees Marcus and Cain Coles ~ Real ale ~ Bar food (11.30-2, 6.30-10; 12-2, 7-9.30 Sun) ~ Restaurant ~ (01267) 275395 ~ Children welcome ~ Open 11.30-3, 6.30-11; 12-3, 7-10.30 Sun

Recommended by Robert Turnham, Michael and Alison Sandy, Dr and Mrs A K Clarke, Di and Mike Gillam, Mrs G R Sharman, B and M Kendall

LLANDUDNO JUNCTION   SH8180   MAP 6

Queens Head 🍴 🍷

Glanwydden; heading towards Llandudno on B5115 from Colwyn Bay, turn left into Llanrhos Road at roundabout as you enter the Penrhyn Bay speed limit; Glanwydden is signposted as the first left turn off this; LL31 9JP

Classy food (all day at weekends) prepared with considerable care in comfortably modern dining pub; some interesting drinks too

Much praised by readers for its excellent food, cheerful staff and fine wine selection, this gets full marks for consistency; one reader has been visiting for over 20 years and has never once found fault. Despite the accent on eating, you are equally welcome if you're just popping in for a drink, and you'll find Adnams and a guest such as Great Orme Best on handpump, as well as decent wines (including some unusual ones and 11 by the glass), several malt whiskies and good coffee. The spaciously comfortable modern lounge bar – partly divided by a white wall of broad arches – has brown plush wall banquettes and windsor chairs around neat black tables, and there's a little public bar; unobtrusive piped music. There's an outdoor seating area, available for smokers. Northern Snowdonia is in easy reach, and you can rent the pretty stone cottage (which sleeps two) across the road.

🍴 **With an emphasis on fresh produce, the well presented and efficiently served dishes include soup, lunchtime ciabattas and burgers, starters like smoked salmon and trout mousse or grilled goats cheese tart with poached pears, pasta, vegetarian choices, a good range of fishy dishes such as baked cod topped with welsh rarebit, seafood platter, or anglesey scallops, and hearty meat courses like grilled loin pork steak, roast duck, or jamaican chicken curry; puddings like lemon curd cheesecake and chocolate nut and raisin fudge pie; daily specials and all-day Sunday roasts.** *Starters/Snacks: £4.75 to £7.95. Main Courses: £9.50 to £21.95. Puddings: £4.75 to £5.95*

Free house ~ Licensees Robert and Sally Cureton ~ Real ale ~ Bar food (12-2, 6(5.30 Fri)-9; 12-9 Sat, Sun) ~ Restaurant ~ (01492) 546570 ~ Children over 7 in evening ~ Open 11-3, 6-11; 11-11 Sat; 11-10.30 Sun

Recommended by Matt Anderson, Joan E Hilditch, Margaret and Jeff Graham, Roger Noyes, Heather McQuillan, Mike Proctor, Owen Davies, M J Winterton, Revd D Glover

---

Real ale to us means beer which has matured naturally in its cask – not pressurised or filtered. We name all real ales stocked. We usually name ales preserved under a light blanket of carbon dioxide too, though purists – pointing out that this stops the natural yeasts developing – would disagree (most people, including us, can't tell the difference!)

LLANELIAN-YN-RHOS
SH8676 MAP 6

White Lion
Signed off A5830 (shown as B5383 on some maps) and B5381, S of Colwyn Bay; LL29 8YA

Pretty pub with friendly staff, pleasantly traditional bar and roomy dining area

You can sit outside at tables in an attractive courtyard (also used for parking) next to the church in front of this pretty village pub. Inside it comprises two distinct parts, each with its own personality, linked by a broad flight of steps. Up at the top is a neat and very spacious dining area, while down at the other end is a traditional old bar, with antique high-backed settles angling snugly around a big fireplace, and flagstones by the counter where they serve Marstons Burton and Pedigree and a guest such as Nant Pen Dafad; on the left, another dining area has jugs hanging from the beams and teapots above the window. Prompt service, good wine list with several by the glass, and malt whiskies; piped music. More up-to-date reports please, especially on the food.

🍴 Food includes sandwiches, ciabattas and hot baguettes, baked potatoes, soup, mussels poached in garlic, traditional roasts, fish stew, steaks, chicken suprême and stuffed roasted pepper; daily specials; puddings; children's menu. *Starters/Snacks: £3.95 to £5.95. Main Courses: £6.95 to £14.95. Puddings: £2.95 to £4.25*

Free house ~ Licensee Simon Cole ~ Real ale ~ Bar food (12-2, 6-9; 12-2.30, 6-10 Sun) ~ Restaurant ~ (01492) 515807 ~ Children welcome ~ Live jazz every Tues evening, bluegrass Weds ~ Open 11.30-3, 6-midnight; 12-4, 6-10.30 Sun; closed Mon

Recommended by Michael and Jenny Back, Mr and Mrs B Hobden

LLANFERRES
SJ1860 MAP 6

Druid
A494 Mold—Ruthin; CH7 5SN

Warmly welcoming 17th-c inn with beams, antique settles and a log fire in the bar; well liked food and wonderful views

From here you get choice views of the Alyn valley and the Clwydian Hills from tables outside at the front and from the broad bay window in the civilised, smallish plush lounge. The hills are also in sight from the bigger beamed and characterful back bar, with its two handsome antique oak settles as well as a pleasant mix of more modern furnishings. There's a quarry-tiled area by the log fire, and a three-legged cat, Chu. Marstons Burton and a guest from breweries such as Brains or Jennings are on handpump, as well as several wines by the glass and some 40 malt whiskies. A games room has darts and pool, along with board games; piped music, TV. There are superb hill walks just above here along the Offa's Dyke Path and up to the summit of Moel Famau.

🍴 Readers have commented on the wide choice of food (which you can eat in the bar or restaurant), which might feature several soups, filled baps, steak and ale pie, poached cod loin with parmesan crust, leek and mushroom pie, grilled leg of welsh lamb, sirloin steak with wild mushroom sauce, or mushrooms stuffed with stilton; daily specials; children's menu. *Starters/Snacks: £4.95 to £5.95. Main Courses: £7.50 to £17.95. Puddings: £2.95 to £4.25*

Union Pub Company ~ Lease James Dolan ~ Real ale ~ Bar food (12-2.30, 6-9; all day Fri-Sun and bank holiday Mon) ~ Restaurant ~ (01352) 810225 ~ Children welcome ~ Dogs allowed in bar and bedrooms ~ Open 12-3, 5.30-11; 12-11 Sat, Sun ~ Bedrooms: £48S/£70S

Recommended by Jacqui Atlas, KC, Anne Morgan, Gordon and Margaret Ormondroyd, Marcus Mann

---

Post Office address codings confusingly give the impression that some pubs are in Gwent or Powys, Wales when they're really in Gloucestershire or Shropshire (which is where we list them).

LLANFRYNACH

SO0725   MAP 6

White Swan ♀

Village signposted from B4558, off A40 E of Brecon – take second turn to village, which is also signed to pub; LD3 7BZ

Revamped, comfortably upmarket country dining pub with a pretty terrace

This cosily mellow place is well placed for undemanding saunters along the towpath of the Monmouthshire and Brecon Canal or for energetic hikes up the main Brecon Beacons summits. The original part of its beamed bar has stripped stone and flagstones, with sturdy oak tables and nice carver chairs in a polished country-kitchen style, a woodburning stove, and leather sofas and armchairs in groups around low tables; it opens into an apricot-walled high-ceilinged extension, light and airy, with bare boards and different sets of chairs around each table. On handpump are Brains Bitter and Rhymney Bitter; good wines and coffees; piped music. The charming secluded back terrace has stone and wood tables with a good choice of sun or shade, and is attractively divided into sections by low plantings and climbing shrubs.

⛿ **The good food is very much the centre of attention, with changing lunch menus and à la carte evening fare; at lunchtimes there is a choice of items like crispy chicken, suprême of cod with welsh rarebit or butternut squash with creamy garlic; evening food might include starters like seared scallops with cajun spices or wye valley asparagus with ham hock and boiled egg, and main courses like trio of welsh lamb, fillets of bass stuffed with asparagus spears and wrapped in pancetta, and breast of free-range guinea fowl stuffed with bacon, apple, onion and thyme, with delicious puddings like raspberry and white chocolate cheesecake or apple and blueberry crumble tart.** *Starters/Snacks: £4.95 to £6.95. Main Courses: £12.50 to £18.95. Puddings: £5.50*

Free house ~ Licensee Richard Griffiths ~ Real ale ~ Bar food (12-2(2.30 Sun), 7-9(8 Sun)) ~ Restaurant ~ (01874) 665276 ~ Children welcome (not Sat evening) ~ Open 12-3, 6.30-11(10.30 Sun); closed Mon (except bank hols), and first week of Jan

Recommended by the Brewers, Julia and Richard Tredgett, Robert Ager, John and Joan Nash, Mr and Mrs R B Berry, Dr Kevan Tucker, Mike and Mary Carter, Michael and Maggie Betton, Mrs Margo Finlay, Jörg Kasprowski, G M Benson

LLANGOLLEN

SJ2142   MAP 6

Corn Mill ♀

Dee Lane, very narrow lane off Castle Street (A539) just S of bridge; nearby parking can be tricky, may be best to use public park on Parade Street/East Street and walk; LL20 8PN

Excellent on all counts, with personable young staff, super food all day, good beers, and a fascinating riverside building

In a restored mill, this is an admirable all-rounder for which we consistently get enthusiastic reports for food, drink and service. The position is really special too – the mill juts over the River Dee which rushes over its rocky bed; you look across the river to the steam trains puffing away at the nearby station and maybe a horse-drawn barge on the Llangollen Canal. An area with decking and teak tables and chairs is perfect for taking in the view. Quite a bit of the mill machinery remains – most obviously the great waterwheel, still turning – but the place has been interestingly refitted with pale pine flooring on stout beams, a striking open stairway with gleaming timber and tensioned steel rails, and mainly stripped-stone walls. A lively bustling chatty feel greets you, with quick service from plenty of pleasant young staff, good-sized dining tables, big rugs, nicely chosen pictures (many to do with water) and lots of pot plants. One of the two serving bars, away from the water, has a much more local feel, with pews on dark slate flagstones, daily papers, and regulars on the bar stools. They have a great range of drinks, with five real ales from brewers such as Conwy, Facers, Phoenix, Plassey and Weetwood, around 50 sensibly priced malt whiskies and a decent wine choice. The pub can get busy, so it might be worth booking if you're planning to eat.

🍴 Good food – served all day – from a daily changing menu includes sandwiches, ploughman's, soup, lighter dishes like wild mushrooms on toast or smoked haddock chowder, and main courses such as braised shoulder of lamb, good fishcakes, local trout with braised fennel, or butternut squash risotto; puddings like mango and coconut cheesecake or bara brith bread and butter pudding; welsh and english cheeseboard. *Starters/Snacks: £4.50 to £6.95. Main Courses: £6.50 to £16.50. Puddings: £4.25 to £5.95*

Brunning & Price ~ Licensee Andrew Barker ~ Real ale ~ Bar food (12-9.30(9 Sun)) ~ (01978) 869555 ~ Children welcome ~ Open 12-11(10.30 Sun)

Recommended by Bruce and Sharon Eden, Earl and Chris Pick, Mr and Mrs J Palmer, Bob and Laura Brock, Neil Whitehead, Victoria Anderson, Michael Butler, John and Verna Aspinall, John McDonald, Ann Bond, A Darroch Harkness, Phil and Jane Hodson, Peter and Josie Fawcett, Alan and Eve Harding, Meg and Colin Hamilton

MAENTWROG
SH6640   MAP 6

Grapes
A496; village signed from A470; LL41 4HN

Lively inn with a good mix of customers and pleasant garden views; accommodation

This rambling old inn is often frequented by welsh-speaking locals here for the lively pubby bar (you may even be addressed in welsh when they greet you). Four beers on handpump are all from Evan Evans – Best, Cwrw, Warrior and a changing monthly ale. All three bars are partly filled with stripped pitch-pine pews, settles, pillars and carvings, mostly salvaged from chapels; elsewhere are soft furnishings. Two woodburning stoves are on the go in winter – there's one in the great hearth of the restaurant; piped music, darts; disabled lavatories. From the good-sized conservatory you can see trains on the Ffestiniog Railway puffing through the wood, beyond the pleasant back terrace and walled garden. More reports please – we've had none on the bedrooms since recent refurbishment.

🍴 Bar food includes sandwiches, soup, chicken liver pâté with a sour black cherry coulis, smoked haddock topped with welsh rarebit on a pickled tomato salad, vegetable curry, a trio of local pork sausages, home-made chicken kiev, lasagne, beef in ale stew, popular blackened (not burnt) pork spare ribs, roast rump of welsh lamb with garlic, honey, mint and rosemary, and puddings like strawberry shortcake stack and sticky toffee pudding. *Starters/Snacks: £4.00 to £6.00. Main Courses: £7.50 to £17.00. Puddings: £5.00*

Free house ~ Licensee Andrew Roberts-Evans ~ Real ale ~ Bar food (12-2.30, 6-8.45) ~ Restaurant ~ (01766) 590208 ~ Children welcome ~ Dogs allowed in bar ~ Open 12-11 ~ Bedrooms: £60B/£98B

Recommended by Martin Owen, Michelle Jones

MOLD
SJ2465   MAP 6

Glasfryn 🍽 🍷 🍺
N of the centre on Raikes Lane (parallel to the A5119), just past the well signposted Theatr Clwyd; CH7 6LR

Open-plan bistro-style pub with inventive, upmarket food available all day, nice décor, wide drinks' choice

On warm days, the large terrace in front of this excellent Brunning & Price pub makes an idyllic place to sit out by the wooden tables – you get sweeping views of the Clwydian Hills. Although the building is unassuming from outside, it is a really buzzing place run with considerable verve by enthusiastic and friendly staff. Open-plan rooms have both spaciousness and nice quiet corners, with an informal and attractive mix of country furnishings and interesting decorations. Besides 25 wines by the glass, local apple juice, farm cider and around 100 whiskies, they've eight beers on handpump, with Facers Flintshire, Flowers Original, Purple Moose Snowdonia, Thwaites Original and Timothy Taylors Landlord, alongside swiftly changing guests like Adnams Broadside, Hawkshead

Bitter and Sharps Doom Bar. Theatr Clwyd is just across the road.

🍴 From a daily changing menu, the full choice of good, well prepared food is available all day and includes sandwiches, ploughman's, soup, starters and lighter dishes like sticky pork ribs or smoked salmon and avocado salad, and main courses such as beer-battered haddock, braised shoulder of lamb, or smoked haddock and salmon fishcakes; puddings such as lemon posset or dark chocolate tart. *Starters/Snacks: £4.45 to £6.95. Main Courses: £7.95 to £15.95. Puddings: £4.75 to £5.25*

Brunning & Price ~ Licensee James Meakin ~ Real ale ~ Bar food (12-9.30(9 Sun)) ~ (01352) 750500 ~ Well behaved children welcome ~ Dogs allowed in bar ~ Open 11.30-11; 12-10.30 Sun

Recommended by R T and J C Moggridge, Tom and Jill Jones, Keith and Sue Ward, Bruce and Sharon Eden, Clive Watkin, Mr and Mrs J Palmer, Dave Braisted, Peter and Josie Fawcett, Chris Flynn, Wendy Jones, Gordon and Margaret Ormondroyd

MONKNASH   SS9170   MAP 6

Plough & Harrow 🍺

Signposted Marcross, Broughton off B4265 St Brides Major—Llantwit Major – turn left at end of Water Street; OS Sheet 170 map reference 920706; CF71 7QQ

Marvellously evocative old building full of history and character, with a good choice of real ales

---

This splendidly ancient-feeling place (part of a former monastic grange, the walls and dovecote of which are still in evidence) makes the ideal stopping point if you're visiting the spectacular stretch of coastal cliffs nearby, and you can walk from here to the lighthouse at Nash Point. Built with massively thick stone walls, the dimly lit unspoilt main bar used to be the scriptures room and mortuary. The heavily black-beamed ceiling has ancient ham hooks, an intriguing arched doorway to the back, and a comfortably informal mix of furnishings that includes three fine stripped-pine settles on the broad flagstones. There's a log fire in a huge fireplace with a side bread oven large enough to feed a village. The room on the left has lots of Wick Rugby Club memorabilia (it's their club room); daily papers, piped music and darts. It can get crowded at weekends, when it's popular with families (they do children's helpings). You can enjoy a fine choice of up to seven real ales on handpump or tapped from the cask: the choice includes Bass, Otley O1 and Wye Valley Hereford Pale Ale alongside guests such as Matthews Brassknocker, RCH Old Slug Porter, Skinners Betty Stogs or Tomos Watkins Abercwrw. They also have a good range of local farm cider, welsh and malt whiskies; helpful service from knowledgeable staff. There are picnic-sets in the front garden (with a covered area available to smokers), which has a boules pitch, and they hold barbecues out here in summer. Dogs are welcome in the bar – but not while food is being served.

🍴 Written up on blackboards, the reasonably priced daily changing lunchtime bar food includes sandwiches and dishes such as leek and stilton bake, sausages and mash, moussaka and welsh faggots; the evening menu could feature starters such as smoked duck salad or home-made onion bhajis and main courses like steaks, haddock with welsh rarebit crust, beef in Guinness, broccoli bake or game stew; children's menu. *Starters/Snacks: £4.50 to £9.50. Main Courses: £6.50 to £9.50. Puddings: £3.95*

Free house ~ Licensee Gareth Davies ~ Real ale ~ Bar food (12-2.30(5 Sat), 6-9; 12-6 Sun) ~ Restaurant ~ (01656) 890209 ~ Children welcome until 9pm (must be accompanied in bar) ~ Dogs allowed in bar ~ Live music Sat evening ~ Open 12-11(10.30 Sun)

Recommended by the Brewers, Prof Kenneth Surin

'Children welcome' means the pub says it lets children inside without any special restriction. If it allows them in, but to restricted areas such as an eating area or family room, we specify this. Places with separate restaurants often let children use them; hotels usually let them into public areas such as lounges. Some pubs impose an evening time limit – let us know if you find one earlier than 9pm.

NEWPORT

Golden Lion

East Street (A487); SA42 0SY

Nicely refurbished, friendly local, with tasty food and pleasant staff

They've made some imaginative refurbishments to this pleasant country inn, which has a revamped dining room with stylish blond wood oak furniture, whitewashed walls and potted plants. The bar area remains traditionally pubby, with a pleasant, local atmosphere in its cosy series of beamed linked rooms, some with distinctive old settles; there's also pool, darts, juke box, TV and games machine. Bass and Brains Rev James along with a guest like Tomos Watkins Cwrw Haf are on handpump. The 13 ensuite bedrooms are good value and have recently been completely remodelled; and we would like to hear from readers who stay here. There are tables outside at the front and in a side garden. Good disabled access and facilities.

⊞ **Very enjoyable, carefully presented food includes sandwiches, starters like calamari or spring rolls, welsh steaks, fish specials and classic pubby dishes like steak and ale pie and mushroom stroganoff; puddings like eton mess or double chocolate truffle with raspberry coulis.** *Starters/Snacks: £3.95 to £4.85. Main Courses: £8.25 to £20.50. Puddings: £4.75 to £5.95*

Free house ~ Licensee Daron Paish ~ Real ale ~ Bar food (12-3, 6.30-9) ~ Restaurant ~ (01239) 820321 ~ Children welcome (not unaccompanied in bar after 9pm) ~ Dogs allowed in bar ~ Live music most Fri and Sat nights in winter ~ Open 12pm-2am ~ Bedrooms: £30(£50B)/£55(£75B)

Recommended by Norman and Sarah Keeping, Ellie O'Mahoney, Brian and Jacky Wilson, M E and F J Thomasson

OLD RADNOR

Harp 🍴 🛏

Village signposted off A44 Kington—New Radnor in Walton; LD8 2RH

Delightfully placed pub with a cosy cottagey bar and comfortable bedrooms; tasty food served by caring staff

In a glorious hilltop position at the end of a lane in a tiny village, this is much enjoyed by readers and has a good mix of locals and visitors. Outside, tables on the grassy area beneath a sycamore tree look across to the high massif of Radnor Forest. In the evening and at weekends, chatty locals gather in the atmospherically unchanged public bar, which has high-backed settles, an antique reader's chair and other elderly chairs around a log fire; board games, cribbage. The snug slate-floored lounge has a handsome curved antique settle and another log fire in a fine inglenook, and there are lots of local books and guides for residents; a dining area is off to the right. They have two changing real ales, from brewers such as Shepherd Neame, Three Tuns and Wye Valley, Dunkerton's farm cider, Ralph's perry, local apple juice, and a beer and cider festival in June; several malt whiskies; friendly, helpful service. They don't allow large dogs in the bedrooms, which are generally much enjoyed by readers. The impressive church is worth a look for its interesting early organ case (Britain's oldest), fine rood screen and ancient font. Note they don't open weekday lunchtimes.

⊞ **Featuring produce from the publicans' own garden, the well liked food typically includes Saturday lunchtime baguettes, soups, starters like venison and juniper berry terrine or parma ham with rocket and mango, and main courses such as welsh black rump steak, fried haddock with puy lentils, cassoulet, gressingham duck breast, and spinach and ricotta cannelloni; puddings such as chocolate brownie or apple and pear crumble.** *Starters/Snacks: £3.95 to £5.95. Main Courses: £8.95 to £15.95. Puddings: £4.95 to £5.95*

Free house ~ Licensees David and Jenny Ellison ~ Real ale ~ Bar food ~ Restaurant ~ (01544) 350655 ~ Children welcome ~ Dogs allowed in bar ~ Open 6-11; 12-3, 6-11 Sat; 12-3, 6-10.30 Sun; closed weekday lunchtimes, all day Mon (except bank hols) ~ Bedrooms: £45B/£75B

Recommended by the Didler, MLR, Reg Fowle, Helen Rickwood, Michael Butler, Pete Yearsley, Mike and Eleanor Anderson, Steven and Victoria James

PORTH DINLLAEN   SH2741   MAP 6

Ty Coch
Beach car park signposted from Morfa Nefyn, then 15-minute walk; LL53 6DB

Idyllic location right on the beach, far from the roads; simple fresh lunches

A wonderful miscellany of nautical paraphernalia packs the inside of this bewitchingly placed pub. It is said to have been used by 17th-c smugglers and pirates, and every inch of the walls and beams are hung with pewter, riding lights, navigation lamps, lanterns, small fishing nets, old miners' and railway lamps, copper utensils, an ale-yard, and lots of RNLI photographs and memorabilia; there are ships in bottles, a working barometer, a Caernarfon grandfather clock, and simple furnishings. An open coal fire burns at one end of the bar; occasional piped music. There are tables outside. Although there's no real ale here, there's a range of bottled beers. You can arrive at low tide along a beach backed by low grassy hills and sand-cliffs, with gulls and curlews for company (otherwise you can walk across via the golf course). More reports please.

▥ From a short menu, simple lunchtime bar food includes sandwiches, soup, baked potatoes, mussels in garlic butter, pies, warm melted brie with chutney topping, ham or beef salad, and local mussels. *Starters/Snacks: £3.95. Main Courses: £6.95 to £9.95*

Free house ~ Licensee Mrs Brione Webley ~ Bar food (12-2.30) ~ (01758) 720498 ~ Children welcome ~ Dogs welcome ~ Open 11-11(11-3 daily, 6-11 Fri, Sat, Easter to spring bank hol); 11-4 Sun; open during day in Christmas week; Sat and Sun 12-4 only in winter

Recommended by Rodney and Norma Stubington

RED WHARF BAY   SH5281   MAP 6

Ship � ▤
Village signposted off B5025 N of Pentraeth; LL75 8RJ

Nicely old-fashioned inside, with good drinks, sweeping coastal views from benches outside

The enchanting location of this unchanging old coastal pub on the north coast of Anglesey makes it justly popular, so it can get very busy in season. It's cosily old-fashioned inside, with lots of nautical bric-a-brac in big rooms on each side of the busy stone-built bar counter, both with long, cushioned, varnished pews built around the walls, glossily varnished cast-iron-framed tables and roaring fires; piped Classic FM (in lounge only). Adnams, Brains, Felinfoel and a guest from a brewery like Conwy on handpump, over 50 malt whiskies, and a wider choice of wines than is usual for the area (with about ten by the glass). If you want to run a tab, they'll ask to keep your credit card behind the bar in a locked numbered box (to which you are given the key). On fine days there are plenty of takers for tables outside that get terrific views over a bay fringed by dunes and headlands, and often dotted with yachts.

▥ Using food sourced in Anglesey wherever possible, the changing bar menu includes soup, lunchtime sandwiches, starters like smoked haddock rarebit or goats cheese and field mushroom crostini, and main courses such as baked half-shoulder of welsh lamb, fish of the day and smoked trout and poached salmon salad; puddings like chocolate orange panna cotta and sticky toffee pudding; children's menu. *Starters/Snacks: £3.45 to £7.95. Main Courses: £8.95 to £14.95. Puddings: £3.50 to £4.50*

Free house ~ Licensee Neil Kenneally ~ Real ale ~ Bar food (12-2.30, 6-9(9.30 Sat); 12-9 Sun) ~ Restaurant ~ (01248) 852568 ~ Children welcome until 9.30 in family rooms ~ Open 11-11

Recommended by Gordon and Margaret Ormondroyd, John McDonald, Ann Bond, Mike and Mary Carter, Julian and Jill Tasker, John and Enid Morris, Mike Proctor, Bob and Val Collman, Neil Whitehead, Victoria Anderson

RHYD-Y-MEIRCH

SO2907   MAP 6

Goose & Cuckoo 🍺

Upper Llanover signposted up narrow track off A4042 S of Abergavenny; after 0.5 miles take first left, then keep on up (watch for handwritten Goose signs at the forks); NP7 9ER

Remote single-room pub looking over a picturesque valley just inside the Brecon Beacons National Park, good drinks' range

'Happily some things in life never change, and this is one of them' observed one reader of this simple place above the Usk valley. It is essentially one small rustically furnished room with a woodburner in an arched stone fireplace. A small picture-window extension makes the most of the view down the valley. They have Newmans Red Stag, Rhymney Bitter, and a couple of guests like Stonehenge Eye-Opener or Sign of Spring on handpump, as well as more than 80 whiskies; daily papers, cribbage, darts and board games. A variety of rather ad hoc picnic-sets is out on the gravel below. The licensees keep sheep, geese and chickens, and may have honey for sale.

🍽 **The choice of simple food, cooked in an Aga, includes filled home-made rolls, soups, pies such as chicken and ham or steak and kidney, and hot dishes like cajun chicken, and liver and bacon casserole; puddings and home-made ice-cream; Sunday roast (bookings only).** *Main Courses: £7.00 to £8.50. Puddings: £3.00*

Free house ~ Licensees Michael and Carol Langley ~ Real ale ~ Bar food (not Sun evening) ~ No credit cards ~ (01873) 880277 ~ Children welcome ~ Dogs allowed in bar ~ Open 11.30-3, 7-11; 11.30-11 Sat; 12-10.30 Sun; closed Mon (except bank hols) ~ Bedrooms: £30S/£60S

Recommended by John and Helen Rushton, Guy Vowles, Reg Fowle, Helen Rickwood

SKENFRITH

SO4520   MAP 6

Bell 🍽 🍷 🛏

Just off B4521, NE of Abergavenny and N of Monmouth; NP7 8UH

Elegant but relaxed, generally much praised for classy though pricey food and excellent accommodation

A useful objective if you are visiting the Three Castles area of the Marches, this inn is within sight of the massive ruins of Skenfrith Castle. Its big back bare-boards dining area is very neat, light and airy, with dark country-kitchen chairs and rush-seat dining chairs, church candles and flowers on the dark tables, canary walls and a cream ceiling, and brocaded curtains on sturdy big-ring rails. The flagstoned bar on the left has a rather similar décor, with old local and school photographs, a couple of pews plus tables and café chairs. From an attractive bleached oak bar counter, Kingstone Gold, Wye Valley Bitter and a guest like Timothy Taylors Landlord are on handpump, plus bottled local cider. They have good wines by the glass and half-bottle, and a good range of brandies. The lounge bar on the right, opening into the dining area, has a nice jacobean-style carved settle and a housekeeper's chair by a log fire in the big fireplace. There are good solid round picnic-sets as well as the usual rectangular ones out on the terrace, with steps up to a sloping lawn; it's a quiet spot. The bedrooms are comfortable, with thoughtful touches. Disabled access is good.

🍽 **Using named local suppliers of carefully chosen fresh ingredients and own-grown vegetables, soft fruit and herbs from their kitchen garden, now officially classed as organic (and which guests are welcome to look around), the changing menus (not cheap) include lunchtime open sandwiches, soup, starters like smoked haddock and welsh rarebit on spinach or free-range chicken terrine, and main courses such as braised pork belly, vegetable risotto, spring lamb, and bass fillet with laver bread and crispy bacon; puddings like lemon parfait and eton mess.** *Starters/Snacks: £4.00 to £7.00. Main Courses: £8.50 to £16.00. Puddings: £5.00 to £6.00*

Free house ~ Licensees William and Janet Hutchings ~ Real ale ~ Bar food (12-2.30, 7-9.30(9 Sun)) ~ (01600) 750235 ~ Children under 9 welcome in restaurant until 7pm ~ Dogs allowed in bar and bedrooms ~ Open 11-11(10 Sun); closed all day Tues in winter, and last week Jan and first week Feb ~ Bedrooms: £75B/£110B

Recommended by Michael and Jenny Back, Dr C C S Wilson, Guy Vowles, Pauline Jones, Tom and Ruth Rees, LM, Denys Gueroult

ST HILARY

ST0173   MAP 6

Bush

Village signposted from A48 E of Cowbridge; CF71 7DP

Cosily old-fashioned village pub, low beams and settles; good food served by helpful staff

From the front of this unspoilt thatched pub, tables and chairs look out to the church and pretty village in the Vale of Glamorgan. Comfortable in a quietly stylish way, it has stripped old stone walls, and farmhouse tables and chairs in the low-beamed carpeted lounge bar, while the other bar is pubbier with old settles and pews on aged flagstones, and a log fire burns in an inglenook. Bass, Greene King Abbot, Hancocks HB and a guest or two from a brewery such as Shepherd Neame or Vale of Glamorgan on handpump or tapped from the cask, and farm cider; subdued piped music. You can also sit out in the back garden; reasonable disabled access.

🍴 The well presented bar food includes lunchtime ciabattas, baguettes, ploughman's and soup; and weekly changing menus featuring starters such as thai fishcake or roasted field mushroom, and main courses like chargrilled welsh sirloin, mussels, fillet of hake wrapped in bacon, and red onion, brie and stilton tartlets; daily specials; puddings include an assortment for sharing; the popular Sunday fixed-price three-course menu with roasts is good value. *Starters/Snacks: £3.95 to £6.00. Main Courses: £7.95 to £19.00. Puddings: £4.50 to £4.95*

Punch ~ Lease Phil Thomas ~ Real ale ~ Bar food (12-2.30, 6.30-9.30) ~ (01446) 772745 ~ Children welcome ~ Dogs allowed in bar ~ Open 11-11; 12-10.30 Sun

Recommended by the Brewers, Steve Cocking, Dr and Mrs Michael Smith, Jeremy King

STACKPOLE

SR9896   MAP 6

Stackpole Inn

Off B4319 S of Pembroke; SA71 5DF

Enjoyable food, friendly service and usefully placed for exploring the Stackpole estate

This cottagey dining pub makes a perfect stopping point after a walk across the sandy beaches, through the woodland, around the lily ponds or along the craggy cliffs of the Stackpole estate. One spacious area has pine tables, chairs and a pool table, but the major part of the pub, L-shaped on four different levels, is given over to diners, with neat light oak furnishings, and ash beams and low ceilings to match; piped music. Brains Rev James and a guest like Fullers London Pride or Rhymney Export on handpump, 12 wines by the glass and several malt whiskies. There are tables out in the attractive gardens, with colourful flowerbeds and mature trees around the car park. We would welcome reports from readers who stay here.

🍴 Bar food includes lunchtime baguettes, ploughman's, home-made pâté and simpler dishes like spaghetti bolognaise, battered cod and deep-fried whitebait; the evening menu has soup, starters like mussels or chicken liver, toasted hazelnut and roast garlic parfait, and main courses such as rack of welsh lamb, king prawn and cherry tomato thermidor or braised belly pork; daily specials featuring local fish and seafood; puddings such as Baileys chocolate mousse cups or lemon and lime cheesecake; Sunday roast lunches. *Starters/Snacks: £4.90 to £5.90. Main Courses: £11.90 to £19.90. Puddings: £3.75 to £4.50*

Free house ~ Licensees Gary and Becky Evans ~ Real ale ~ Bar food (12-2(2.30 Sun), 6.30-9) ~ Restaurant ~ (01646) 672324 ~ Children welcome ~ Dogs allowed in bar ~ Open 12-3, 6-11; 12-11 Sat; 12-4, 6-11 Sun; closed Sun evening in winter and two weeks Jan ~ Bedrooms: £55S/£80S

Recommended by Angus and Rosemary Campbell, Alan Skingsley, Brian and Jacky Wilson, Pat Crabb, Simon Daws, Mrs P Bishop, Mark Farrington

TAL-Y-CAFN

Tal-y-Cafn Hotel
A470 Conway—Llanwrst; LL28 5RR

Useful for northern Snowdonia, family-friendly and with efficient staff and sensibly priced bar food

Popular with walkers and families, this roadside inn makes a handy stopping point in the Conwy valley. Off the entrance lobby are the dining area, the snug and the wood-panelled main bar, with terracotta walls and captain's chairs around the low tables on its turkey carpet, and settles round an enormous inglenook fireplace; piped music, TV. Served by air pressure by efficient staff are Boddingtons, Black Sheep and Tetleys (the latter at only £1.85 a pint). You can also sit out in the spacious hedged garden, which has rustic tables and seats by a rose border. It's very popular with families, and there's a large play area. The refurbished bedrooms have wireless internet access. Reports on the new licensees please.

🍴 Straightforward bar food includes sandwiches, ploughman's, soup, Sunday roast, steak and ale pie, steaks, and puddings like cheesecake or bread and butter pudding; children's menu. *Starters/Snacks: £3.25 to £4.95. Main Courses: £7.25 to £12.95. Puddings: £3.75*

Punch ~ Lease Richard and Anna Scott ~ Real ale ~ Bar food (12-9(8 Sun)) ~ Restaurant ~ (01492) 650203 ~ Children welcome ~ Dogs allowed in bedrooms ~ Open 12-12(11 Sun) ~ Bedrooms: £39S/£78S

Recommended by KC, Roger and Cynthia Calrow

TY'N-Y-GROES

Groes 🍴 ⛄ 🛏
B5106 N of village; LL32 8TN

Lots of antiques in welcoming hotel and bar in northern Snowdonia

Run by friendly staff, this gracious old hotel has an idyllic back garden with flower-filled hayracks; there are more seats on the flower-decked roadside. Past the hot stove in the entrance area, the rambling, low-beamed and thick-walled rooms are nicely decorated with antique settles and an old sofa, old clocks, portraits, hats and tins hanging from the walls, and fresh flowers. A fine antique fireback is built into one wall, perhaps originally from the formidable fireplace in the back bar, which houses a collection of stone cats as well as cheerful winter log fires. You might find a harpist playing here on certain days. There is also an airy and verdant conservatory. From the family's own Great Orme brewery, a couple of miles away, are Great Orme and Groes Ale (brewed for the pub), and several bottled Great Orme beers too; piped music. The spotless and well equipped bedroom suites (some have terraces or balconies) have gorgeous views. They also rent out a well appointed wooden cabin idyllically placed nearby, as well as a cottage in the historic centre of Conwy. Dogs are allowed in some bedrooms and in certain areas of the bar. More up-to-date reports on the food please.

🍴 Using local lamb, salmon and game, and herbs from the hotel garden, bar food includes soup, lunchtime sandwiches, starters like garlic king prawns, crab cakes or ham hock terrine, and main courses such as seafood pie, sausages and mash, chicken curry, asparagus and artichoke tart, and fillet steak with pepper sauce; puddings such as rhubarb crumble and orange posset; daily specials. *Starters/Snacks: £4.90 to £8.20. Main Courses: £9.95 to £23.95. Puddings: £5.60 to £6.10*

Free house ~ Licensee Dawn Humphreys ~ Real ale ~ Bar food ~ Restaurant ~ (01492) 650545 ~ Children welcome until 7.15pm in bar if dining ~ Dogs allowed in bar and some bedrooms ~ Open 12-3, 6-11; 12-11 Sat; 12-10.30 Sun; open Sat 12-3, 6-9 in winter ~ Bedrooms: £85B/£103B

Recommended by Steve and Sarah Eardley, Margaret and Jeff Graham, Mike and Mary Carter, David Glynne-Jones, Richard and Mary Bailey, Susan and Nigel Brookes, Mike Horgan, Phil and Jane Hodson, Joan E Hilditch, Carol and Phil Byng, Clive Watkin, Simon Daws, Neil and Angela Huxter

USK   SO3700   MAP 6

Nags Head 🍴 �
The Square; NP15 1BH

Spotlessly kept by the same family for many years, traditional in style, as warm a reception as could be hoped for, with good food and drinks

---

This friendly pub continues its winning ways, and brings back many readers time and time again. With a friendly chatty atmosphere, the beautifully kept traditional main bar has lots of well polished tables and chairs packed under its beams (some with farming tools), lanterns or horsebrasses and harness attached, as well as leatherette wall benches, and various sets of sporting prints and local pictures – look out for the original deeds to the pub. Tucked away at the front is an intimate little corner with some african masks, while on the other side of the room a passageway leads to a new dining area converted from the old coffee bar; piped music. There may be prints for sale, and perhaps a knot of sociable locals. They do several wines by the glass, along with Brains Bitter, Bread of Heaven, Rev James and SA on handpump. The centre of Usk is full of pretty hanging baskets and flowers in summer, and the church is well worth a look.

🍴 Popular, generously served and reasonably priced food includes soup, grilled sardines, **frogs' legs in hot provençale sauce, rabbit pie, steak pie, chicken in red wine, faggots, and vegetable pancake, with specials such as brace of boned quail with stuffing and sauce or poached salmon. You can book tables, some of which may be candlelit at night; nice proper linen napkins.** *Starters/Snacks: £4.50 to £6.75. Main Courses: £8.95 to £16.50. Puddings: £4.00 to £4.75.*

Free house ~ Licensee the Key family ~ Real ale ~ Bar food (11.30-2, 5.30-9.30) ~ Restaurant ~ (01291) 672820 ~ Children welcome ~ Dogs welcome ~ Open 10.30-2.30, 5-11; 11-3, 5.30-10 Sun

Recommended by David Howe, Dr and Mrs C W Thomas, Eryl and Keith Dykes, Reg Fowle, Helen Rickwood, Mike and Mary Carter, Sue and Ken Le Prevost, Gareth Lewis, M G Hart, Mr and Mrs C Gothard, Meg and Colin Hamilton, Dr C C S Wilson, Michael and Maggie Betton

---

LUCKY DIP

Besides the fully inspected pubs, you might like to try these Lucky Dips recommended to us and described by readers (if you do, please send us reports: feedback@goodguides.com).

ANGLESEY

BEAUMARIS [SH6076]
George & Dragon LL58 8AA [Church St]: Cheery local atmosphere, good value food, well kept real ale, friendly staff; Tudor beams and timbers, good lighting and gleaming brass, original fireplace and section of wattle and daub wall, welcoming landlord happy to show rare wall paintings and painted beams upstairs; may be live entertainment; dogs welcome *(Carol Drummond)*
MENAI BRIDGE [SH5571]
Anglesey Arms LL59 5EA [Mona Rd]: By suspension bridge, pleasant lounge with wide choice of food inc local fish, vegetarian and children's dishes, good service; well kept beers, locals' bar, conservatory restaurant; tables outside, good views, three comfortable bedrooms *(Mathew Morris)*
Gazelle LL59 5PD [Glyngarth; A545, halfway towards Beaumaris]: Hotel and restaurant rather than pub in outstanding waterside situation looking across to Snowdonia; (recent refurbishment after flooding), lively main bar, smaller rooms off, enjoyable food

inc fresh fish, Robinsons real ale; children welcome, steep and aromatic mediterranean garden behind, good bedrooms *(Mark, Amanda, Luke and Jake Sheard, LYM, David Abbot)*
RHOSCOLYN [SH2675]
White Eagle LL65 2NJ [off B4545 S of Holyhead]: Splendid remote setting with panoramic views towards Snowdonia from dining area; smartly refurbished with relaxed upmarket feel, good food (all day in summer), well kept real ales (May beer festival), friendly efficient staff; children welcome, good large garden, lane down to beach, open all day in summer *(Pat and Tony Hinkins, J D C Smellie)*

CLWYD

CARROG [SJ1143]
Grouse LL21 9AT [B5436, signed off A5 Llangollen—Corwen]: Small unpretentious pub with superb views over River Dee and beyond from bay window and balcony; Lees real ales, enjoyable food all day from

sandwiches up, reasonable prices, friendly helpful staff; local pictures, pool in games room, piped music; narrow turn into car park; children welcome, wheelchair access (side door a bit narrow), tables in pretty walled garden (covered terrace for smokers), handy for Llangollen steam railway, bedrooms *(John Francis, Michael and Jenny Back, Ann and Tony Bennett-Hughes)*

CHIRK [SJ2937]

Bridge Inn LL14 5BU [Chirk Bank, B5070 S (just over Shropshire border)]: Friendly old local, a short walk below Llangollen Canal nr aqueduct; enjoyable quickly served pub food, well kept ales, water-jugs on beams, black eating area; children welcome, picnic-sets on raised terrace *(Paul Schofield)*

CILCAIN [SJ1765]

☆ *White Horse* CH7 5NN [signed from A494 W of Mold; The Square]: Homely and welcoming country local, several unspoilt rooms, low joists, mahogany and oak settles, two blazing fires, old photographs; long-serving landlord, interesting changing ales, good choice of enjoyable home-made food inc vegetarian; quarry-tiled back bar allowing dogs and muddy boots; pub games, cat; no children inside; picnic-sets outside, delightful village *(Rosemary Kirkus, LYM)*

COLWYN BAY [SH8278]

Mountain View LL28 5AT [Mochdre, S off A55—A470 link rd]: New management and decoration in roomy big-windowed modern pub, enjoyable food and Burtonwood ales, pleasant staff, public bar; tables on front terrace *(KC, LYM)*

GWERNYMYNYDD [SJ2162]

Rainbow CH7 5LG [Ruthin Rd (A494)]: Welcoming staff, good value generous food inc some enterprising dishes; no piped music *(KC)*

HALKYN [SJ2171]

Britannia CH8 8BY [Britannia Pentre Rd, off A55 for Rhosesmor]: Great views over Dee estuary from terrace and restaurant, comfortably refurbished heavy-beamed bar, enjoyable food, well kept Lees; children in eating areas, open all day *(KC, LYM)*

HANMER [SJ4539]

Hanmer Arms SY13 3DE: Relaxed country inn with good range of reasonably priced straightforward food inc popular Sun lunch, friendly staff, well kept ales such as Stonehouse, big family dining room upstairs; attractive garden with the church as pleasant backdrop, good value bedrooms in former courtyard stable block, pretty village *(Alan and Eve Harding)*

LLANGOLLEN [SJ2044]

Abbey Grange LL20 8DD [A542 N]: More hotel than pub, but welcoming, in beautiful spot with superb views nr Valle Crucis Abbey; two bars, Banks's and Marstons, good value generous food from sandwiches up, restaurant; piped music; children welcome, picnic-sets outside, comfortable bedrooms *(Dave Braisted, Michael Butler)*

Gales LL20 8PF [Bridge St]: Warmly popular darkly panelled wine bar, friendly helpful young staff, enjoyable ample food, eclectic wines, wide choice of bottled beers; comfortable bedrooms, secure overnight parking *(Earl and Chris Pick)*

MOLD [SJ2364]

Bryn Awel CH7 1BL [A541 Denbigh Rd nr Bailey Hill]: Hillside modern hotel with picture-window country views in comfortable good-sized dining area; welcoming attentive service, good value reliable food inc thai dishes, cheerful bustling carpeted lounge bar; may be piped music; 19 neat bedrooms *(KC)*

OVERTON BRIDGE [SJ3542]

☆ *Cross Foxes* LL13 0DR [A539 W of Overton, nr Erbistock]: Appealingly modernised waterside dining pub with friendly efficient staff, good home-made food all day, linked but distinct areas with lots of pictures and variously sized tables, big candles, good log fires; Banks's, Marstons and guests, splendid range of wines by the glass and of spirits, good coffees; children welcome, dogs in bar, crazy-paved terrace above lawn to River Dee, play area, open all day *(Jenny Williams, Andrew Walker, S P Watkin, P A Taylor, Mr and Mrs J Palmer, LYM)*

PONTBLYDDYN [SJ2761]

New Inn CH7 4HR [Corwen Rd (A5104, just S of A541 3 miles SE of Mold)]: Interesting consistently good generous food in unassuming building's pleasant upstairs dining room, good service; piped music *(KC)*

PONTFADOG [SJ2338]

Swan LL20 7AR: Popular family-run old inn nr river in Ceiriog valley; obliging staff, good reasonably priced home-made bar and restaurant food, well kept ales, decent wines by the glass; children welcome, garden tables, bedrooms *(Jill Sparrow)*

RHYDYMWYN [SJ2166]

Antelope CH7 5HE [Denbigh Rd (A541)]: Popular welcoming pub with pleasant bar and attractive restaurant, good choice of generous food; piped music *(KC)*

ST GEORGE [SH9775]

Kinmel Arms LL22 9BP [off A547 or B5381 SE of Abergele]: Dining pub tucked away in attractive village, several neat and tidy refurbished rooms, nice mix of tables and chairs, rugs on stripped wood; wide range of good affordable modern food from lunchtime baguettes and dutch-style open sandwiches up, friendly prompt service, changing ales such as Cains and Facers, good choice of wines by the glass, conservatory; four good bedrooms, cl Sun, Mon *(Keith and Sue Ward, Nick Sanders)*

DYFED

ABERGORLECH [SN5833]

☆ *Black Lion* SA32 7SN [B4310]: Old coaching inn in fine rural position, traditionally furnished stripped-stone bar with flagstones, coal stove, oak furniture and high-backed black settles, copper pans on beams, old jugs on shelves, fresh flowers, local paintings; dining extension with french windows opening on to enclosed garden, one Rhymney ale and a guest, inexpensive bar food; piped music; children and dogs welcome, lovely views of Cothi valley from sloping garden, open all day wknds *(LYM, Mrs Margo Finlay, Jörg Kasprowski)*

AMROTH [SN1607]

Amroth Arms SA67 8NG: Neat bar opp beach, with good chatty atmosphere, Felinfoel Cambrian or Double Dragon, friendly staff; pool area, dining room with bargain home-made food (lunchtime only off season); sea-view pavement tables *(PRT, Reg Fowle, Helen Rickwood)*

ANGLE [SM8703]

☆ *Old Point House* SA71 5AS [signed off B4320 in village, along long rough waterside track; East Angle Bay]: Dating from the 14th c, unspoilt, comfortable and in idyllic spot overlooking Milford Haven (getting there inc drive over beach is part of the pleasure); friendly down-to-earth atmosphere, good simple food (almost all fresh local fish), Felinfoel Double Dragon, cheap soft drinks, flagstoned bar;with open fire, small lounge bar, lots of charm and character, run by local lifeboat coxswain – many photographs and charts; home-made chutneys and sauces for charity, resident labradors; plenty of tables and ancient slate seats out by the shore *(Julian Distin, Reg Fowle, Helen Rickwood, Richard Pitcher)*

BROAD HAVEN [SM8614]

☆ *Druidstone Hotel* SA62 3NE [N of village on coast rd, bear left for about 1.5 miles then follow sign left to Druidstone Haven – inn a sharp left turn after another 0.5 miles; OS Sheet 157 map ref 862168, marked as Druidston Villa]: Cheerfully informal, the family's former country house in a grand spot above the sea, individualistic and relaxed, terrific views; inventive cooking with fresh often organic ingredients, helpful efficient service, folksy cellar bar with local ale tapped from the cask, good wines, country wines and other drinks; ceilidhs and folk events; chummy dogs (dogs welcomed); all sorts of sporting activities from boules to sand-yachting, attractive high-walled garden, spacious homely bedrooms, even an eco-friendly chalet, cl Nov and Jan, restaurant cl Sun evening *(Michael Quine, Pauline and Derek Hodgkiss, Adam, Colin Moore, Blaise Vyner, LYM)*

BURTON [SM9805]

Jolly Sailor SA73 1NX: Great views of River Cleddau, toll bridge and Milford Haven beyond; riverside garden with well spaced tables and play area, good choice of plentiful pubby food, reasonable prices, friendly staff; dogs welcome in bar, can moor a small boat at jetty *(K Worsford)*

CAIO [SN6739]

Brunant Arms SA19 8RD [off A482 Llanwrda—Lampeter]: Unpretentious and

interestingly furnished friendly village pub, five changing local ales, good log fire, wide regularly changing food choice from baguettes up; stripped-stone public bar with games inc pool; juke box, TV; children and dogs welcome, small Perspex-roofed verandah and lower terrace, has been open all day wknds *(LYM, David and Lin Short)*

CARMARTHEN [SN4120]

Queens SA31 1JR [Queen St]: Two lively rooms either side of bar, good value low-priced food all day from sandwiches up, well kept ales inc Felinfoel and Newmans, efficient friendly service (long-serving tenant also has adjoining Hamiltons wine bar/restaurant); very busy wknd evenings; children welcome, tables on small back terrace, open all day *(MLR)*

CILGERRAN [SN1942]

Pendre Inn SA43 2SL [off A478 S of Cardigan; High St]: Friendly local with massive medieval stone walls and broad flagstones, enjoyable home-made pub food (more evening choice), well kept Shepherd Neame Spitfire and three guests *(Colin Moore, Andrew Gardner, LYM)*

CWM GWAUN [SN0333]

☆ *Dyffryn Arms* SA65 9SE [Cwm Gwaun and Pontfaen signed off B4313 E of Fishguard]: Classic rural time warp, virtually the social centre for this lush green valley, very relaxed, basic and idiosyncratic, with much-loved veteran landlady (her farming family have run it since 1840, and she's been in charge for well over one-third of that time); 1920s front parlour with plain deal furniture inc rocking chair and draughts boards inlaid into tables, coal fire, well kept ale such as Bass served by jug through a sliding hatch, low prices; World War I prints and posters, darts, duck eggs for sale; pretty countryside, open more or less all day (may close if no customers) *(Colin Moore, Richard Pitcher, the Didler, MLR, Herbert and Susan Verity, LYM, Giles and Annie Francis)*

DINAS [SN0139]

Old Sailors SA42 0SE [Pwllgwaelod; from A487 in Dinas Cross follow Bryn-henllan signpost]: Superb position, snugged down into the sand by isolated cove below Dinas Head with its bracing walks; specialising in fresh local seafood inc crab and lobster, also good snacks, coffee and summer cream teas, decent wine, keg beers; children and dogs welcome, garden overlooking beach, open 11-6ish and all day Fri, Sat Nov-Easter (all day Weds-Sat Easter-Oct) *(LYM)*

FELINDRE FARCHOG [SN0939]

☆ *Olde Salutation* SA41 3UY [A487 Newport—Cardigan]: Well extended pub with bar food from toasties and baguettes to local beef and seasonal sea trout, Brains Rev James, Felinfoel Double Dragon and a guest, good wines by the glass; genial landlord and friendly staff, stylish conservatory restaurant; disabled access and facilities, comfortable bedroom extension, good breakfast, fishing and good walks by nearby

River Nevern *(Colin Moore, D S and J M Jackson)*

FISHGUARD [SM9537]

☆ **Fishguard Arms** SA65 9HJ [Main St (A487)]: Tiny unspoilt pub; front bar with changing jug-served ales from unusually high counter, warmly friendly staff, open fire, rugby photographs, woodburner and traditional games in back room; no food; open all day except Weds evening *(Giles and Annie Francis, the Didler, LYM)*

Royal Oak SA65 9HA [Market Sq, Upper Town]: Dark beams, stripped stone and panelling, big picture-window dining extension, pictures and tapestry commemorating defeat here of bizarre french raid in 1797; Brains and changing guest beers from bar counter carved with welsh dragon, generous good value fresh food, woodburner, bar billiards; games machine; pleasant terrace, open all day *(the Didler, MLR, BB, Simon Watkins)*

Ship SA65 9ND [Newport Rd, Lower Town]: Cheerful atmosphere and seafaring locals in ancient dimly lit red-painted local nr old harbour; friendly staff, well kept ales such as Bass and Theakstons tapped from the cask, homely food from sandwiches and cawl up; coal fire, lots of boat pictures, model ships, piano; children welcome, toys provided *(LYM, Giles and Annie Francis)*

LAMPHEY [SN0100]

Dial SA71 5NU: Victorian inn with light and airy bar and large adjacent family dining room, homely relaxed atmosphere, good varied home-made traditional food, efficient welcoming service, real ales, good value house wine; games room with pool; piped music; small front terrace, bedrooms *(Angus and Carol Johnson)*

LITTLE HAVEN [SM8512]

☆ **Castle** SA62 3UF: Welcoming pub well placed by the green looking over sandy bay (lovely sunsets); enjoyable food inc pizzas and local fish, Marstons ales, good choice of wines by the glass, tea and cafetière coffee; bare-boards bar and carpeted dining area with big oak tables, beams, some stripped stone, castle prints; pool in back area; children welcome, front picnic-sets, open 10.30am to midnight *(Pat Crabb, Mrs Barbara Barret, Adam, Paul Goldman)*

☆ **Swan** SA62 3UL [Point Rd]: Attractive seaside pub reopened in 2007 after long closure and major refurbishment; up-to-date bar with leather settees and comfortable alcove seating on new wood-laminate floor, window tables overlooking sandy bay, fires each end; Brains and another real ale, enthusiastic young staff, upstairs dining room; sports TV *(LYM, Mrs Barbara Barret, Ewan and Moira McCall, John and Enid Morris, Chris and Angela Buckell)*

LLANDDAROG [SN5016]

☆ **Butchers Arms** SA32 8NS: Ancient heavily black-beamed local with three intimate eating areas off small central bar, welcoming with charming service, generous reasonably

priced food from sandwiches through hearty welsh dishes to nice puddings, Felinfoel ales tapped from the cask, good wines by the glass; conventional pub furniture, fairy lights and candles in bottles, open woodburner in biggish fireplace; piped music; children welcome, tables outside, nice window boxes, cl Sun *(Bill and Lynne Boon, BB, Dr and Mrs A K Clarke, Tom Evans, Michael and Alison Sandy)*

LLANDEILO [SN6222]

Castle SA19 6EN [Rhosmaen St (A483)]: Traditional pub with log-fire front bar and other rooms, changing real ales, generous good value food inc bargain Sun lunch; restaurant *(RS, ES, LYM)*

LLANDOVERY [SN7634]

Red Lion SA20 0AA [Market Sq]: One basic welcoming room with no bar, changing ales tapped from cask, jovial characterful landlord; restricted opening – may be just Sat, and Fri evening *(BB, the Didler)*

LLANEGWAD [SN5321]

☆ **Halfway** SA32 7NL [A40 Llandeilo—Carmarthen]: Smart, popular and welcoming dining pub (worth booking in season, especially wknds); imaginative elegantly presented food, good wine choice, nice décor, second upstairs dining area with views; has been cl Sun evening and Mon *(R and Z Davies, PRT)*

LLANGADOG [SN7028]

Goose & Cuckoo SA19 9EE [Queens Sq; this is the Llangadog up towards Llandovery]: Popular revamped old local with well priced generous food, Evan Evans BB *(RS, ES)*

MEIDRIM [SN2920]

New Inn SA33 5QN: Chef/landlord doing enjoyable food using local ingredients, real ale, good service under landlady; comfortable bedrooms *(Bob Butterworth)*

NEWCHAPEL [SN2239]

Fynnone Arms SA37 0EH [B4332]: Doing well under newish management, reasonably priced food using local produce, well kept real ale, friendly staff; spacious beamed bar and restaurant area *(Colin Moore)*

NEWPORT [SN0539]

☆ **Royal Oak** SA42 0TA [West St (A487)]: Bustling and well run sizeable pub with friendly helpful landlady and staff, good generous food inc lunchtime light dishes, local lamb and lots of authentic curries, Tues OAP lunch, Greene King and guest beers; children welcome in lounge with eating areas, separate stone and slate bar with pool and games, upstairs dining room; some tables outside, easy walk to beach and coast path *(Colin Moore, Blaise Vyner)*

PEMBROKE FERRY [SM9704]

Ferry Inn SA72 6UD [below A477 toll bridge]: Former sailors' haunt by the Cleddau estuary, seafaring pictures and memorabilia, open fire and sea view; Bass, Felinfoel Double Dragon and a guest beer under light blanket pressure, good well cooked simple food; games machine, unobtrusive piped music; children welcome, dogs allowed in bar, tables on terrace *(Julian Distin, Henry Paulinski, Steve and Liz Tilley, LYM)*

PENRHIWLLAN [SN3641]

Daffodil SA44 5NG: Well reworked contemporary coaching pub, good choice of enjoyable home-made food, good service, three well kept ales, good value wines; eating areas on different levels off quarry-tiled and flagstoned bar, nice furnishings old and new, welcoming and friendly; back verandah, good views *(Paul Wright, Peter Hobson, Chris Wall)*

PONTERWYD [SN7480]

George Borrow SY23 3AD [A44 about 0.25 miles W of A4120 junction]: Well kept Brains, enjoyable bar food, warm homely welcome (from cat and big sheepdog too); lounges front and back, restaurant; children welcome, nice views (fine spot by Eagle Falls and gorge, so lots of summer visitors), low-priced bedrooms *(Piotr Chodzko-Zajko)*

PONTRHYDFENDIGAID [SN7366]

Black Lion SY25 6BE [B4343 Tregaron—Devils Bridge]: Friendly informal country inn with enjoyable well priced traditional food all day, beams and log fire, real ales; picnic-sets outside, five good value bedrooms, good breakfast, handy for Strata Florida Abbey, open all day *(Mrs J Main)*

PORTHGAIN [SM8132]

Shed SA62 5BN: In what looks to be a seaside former boat shed, not a pub but does sell beer and is well worth knowing for good seafood in upstairs evening bistro (not winter Sun-Weds); daytime tearoom *(Simon Watkins, Blaise Vyner)*

☆ *Sloop* SA62 5BN [off A487 St David's—Fishguard]: Good spot between headlands on Pembrokeshire Coast Path, lots of seafaring memorabilia in bar inc relics from local wrecks, eating area with simple wooden furniture and cushioned wall seats; Brains Rev James, Felinfoel Double Dragon and Greene King IPA, bar food featuring fresh fish, games room, quick friendly service; TV, juke box, no dogs; children welcome, heated terrace overlooking harbour, self-catering cottage, open all day from breakfast time *(Steve Godfrey, Ewan and Moira McCall, Simon Watkins, Herbert and Susan Verity, Theo, Anne and Jane Gaskin, LYM, Di and Mike Gillam, Ann and Tony Bennett-Hughes, BB, Tom and Ruth Rees)*

ROSEBUSH [SN0729]

☆ *Tafarn Sinc* SA66 7QU [B4329 Haverfordwest—Cardigan]: Unpromising (a big corrugated iron shed) but really interesting inside – reconditioned railway halt, full of local history, with panelling, mix of chairs and pews, piano and woodburners; a beer brewed for the pub and a changing guest, basic food, dining room; piped music, games machine, TV; children welcome, platform with life-size dummy passengers and steam sound-effects in big garden, open all day, cl Mon *(the Didler, LYM, Paul Goldman, Herbert and Susan Verity,*

Peter and Anne Hollindale, Julian Distin, Tom Evans, Colin Moore)

TENBY [SN1300]

Hope & Anchor SA70 7AX [Julian St]: Pleasant pub nr seafront, friendly staff, generous pubby food (all day at least in summer), three or four well kept changing ales such as Otley; coal fire, upstairs family dining room, terrace tables, open all day *(Richard Pitcher, MLR)*

TRESAITH [SN2751]

☆ *Ship* SA43 2JL: Tastefully decorated spacious bistro-style pub on Cardigan Bay with magnificent views of sea, beach, famous waterfall, perhaps even dolphins and seals; enjoyable generous home-made food from ploughman's with local cheeses to local fish, speciality paella, takeaway pizzas, cheerful staff, Brains Rev James and Hancocks HB, good choice of other drinks; they may try to keep your credit card while you eat; small car park (fills quickly in summer); children welcome, tables with heaters out on decking stepped down to garden *(Gareth Lewis)*

TREVINE [SM8332]

Ship SA62 5AX [off A487 at Croes-Goch or via Penparc; Ffordd y Felin]: Well positioned just up from coast path, friendly helpful staff, reasonably priced food inc fresh local crab, ales such as Adnams and Greene King; back garden overlooking fields *(Giles and Annie Francis)*

GLAMORGAN

CARDIFF [ST1776]

Black Pig CF11 9HW [Sophia Close; aka Y Mochyn Du]: Enjoyable food, well kept Brains and guest beers, good welcoming atmosphere, interesting décor; terrace tables, open all day *(the Didler, Dr and Mrs A K Clarke)*

☆ *Cayo Arms* CF11 9LL [Cathedral Rd]: Helpful young staff, well kept Tomos Watkins ales with a guest beer, good value food all day from ciabattas to full meals inc Sun lunch; daily papers, pubby front bar with comfortable side area in Edwardian style, more modern back dining area; piped music, big-screen TV in one part, very busy wknds; tables out in front, more in yard behind (with parking), good value bedrooms, open all day *(the Didler, Dr and Mrs A K Clarke)*

Cottage CF10 1AA [St Mary St, nr Howells]: Proper down-to-earth pub with good value generous home-cooked lunches inc Sun, good cheerful service, well kept Brains ales, decent choice of wines; long bar with narrow frontage and back eating area, lots of polished wood and glass, relaxed friendly atmosphere (even Fri, Sat when it's crowded – may be impromptu singing on rugby international days); quiet other evenings); open all day *(Alan and Eve Harding)*

Goat Major CF10 1PU [High St, opp castle]: Recently smartly refurbished former Bluebell (renamed for Royal Welsh Regiment mascot, plenty of pictures), Victorian-style décor;

Brains full range kept well (knowledgeable landlord may offer tasters), pleasant helpful young staff, bargain pubby food all day; panelling and some armchairs; open all day *(Tony and Wendy Hobden, Bruce Bird, Phil and Sally Gorton)*

Monkstone CF3 4LL [Newport Rd, Rumney]: Comfortably refurbished with generous good value fresh food, four real ales, good choice of wines; Severn estuary views *(H L Dennis)*

Old Arcade CF10 1BG [Church St]: Busy city pub with rugby décor, Brains full beer range kept well, good value food all day; piped music may obtrude; tables out in front, back smokers' shelter, open all day *(Bruce Bird)*

Vulcan CF24 2FH [Adam St]: Largely untouched Victorian local surrounded by redevelopment; jovial landlord, well kept Brains, good value lunches (not Sun) in sedate lounge with some original features inc ornate fireplace; maritime pictures in lively public bar with darts, dominoes, cards and juke box; open all day, cl Sun evening *(the Didler, Dr and Mrs A K Clarke)*

Westgate CF11 9AD [Cowbridge Rd East]: Friendly and comfortable, with well kept Brains, good value food, helpful efficient staff; caricatures, old photographs and plaques showing former Cardiff pubs; open all day *(Bruce Bird)*

Yard CF10 1AD [St Mary St]: Unusual conversion of the loading bay of Brains' original brewery (the well kept ales now come from the nearby former Hancocks' brewery), good reasonably priced food especially chargrills cooked in front of you; functional décor using some original girders etc, upper gallery with Brains' family portraits in comfortable 'board room'; piped music may be loud, lighting dim; courtyard tables, open all day till late *(Prof Kenneth Surin)*

COITY [SS9281]

Six Bells CF35 6BH [Heol West Plas]: Nicely positioned, upgraded family-run pub, friendly and chatty with reasonably priced food inc good pies, puddings and popular Sun lunch; good service, well kept real ales such as Everards; several ghosts; tables out by road opp 12th-c castle *(R C Vincent, Phil and Jane Hodson)*

KENFIG [SS8081]

☆ **Prince of Wales** CF33 4PR [2.2 miles from M4 junction 37; A4229 towards Porthcawl, then right when dual carriageway narrows on bend, signed Maudlam and Kenfig]: Ancient local with plenty of individuality by historic sand dunes; welcoming landlord, well kept Bass and Worthington tapped from cask and usually two guests, good choice of malts, decent wines, enjoyable generous straightforward food at low prices; chatty panelled room off main bar, log fires, stripped stone, lots of wreck pictures; traditional games, small upstairs dining room for summer and busy wknds (should book); big-screen TV for special sports events; children and (in non-carpet areas)

dogs welcome, handy for nature reserve (orchids Jun) *(Phil and Sally Gorton, the Didler, John and Joan Nash, LYM)*

LLANCARFAN [ST0570]

Fox & Hounds CF62 3AD [signed off A4226; can also be reached from A48 from Bonvilston or B4265 via Llancadle]: Good carefully cooked food using local ingredients such as fresh fish, welsh black beef and farmhouse cheeses in neat comfortably modernised village pub; friendly open-plan bar rambling through arches, coal fire, Brains Bitter and Rev James kept well, good wine choice, traditional settles and plush banquettes, candlelit bistro, simple end family room; children welcome, unobtrusive piped music; tables out behind, pretty streamside setting by interesting church, eight comfortable bedrooms, good breakfast, open all day wknds *(Rainer Gliss, A C Powell, BB)*

LLANGYNWYD [SS8588]

Old House CF34 9SB [off A4063 S of Maesteg; pub behind church, nearly a mile W of modern village]: Pretty thatched and beamed dining pub now under son of former good landlord; enjoyable food especially fish, cheerful helpful staff, Flowers Original, decent wines by the glass, huge fireplace, attractive conservatory extension; children welcome, garden tables, nearby huge churchyard and valley views worth a look *(John and Joan Nash, LYM)*

LLANRHIDIAN [SS4992]

Dolphin SA3 1EH: 1950s-style pub with long leather banquettes, Fullers London Pride and a guest beer such as Brains Rev James; simple snacks inc local cockle and laver bread bake served 1-8pm; big garden with chicken run, open all day summer (cl till 6pm Tues, and may be much more restricted opening winter) *(Michael and Alison Sandy)*

LLANTWIT FADRE [ST0784]

Crown CF38 2HL [A473]: Friendly 19th-c roadside pub under new ownership; leather sofas and local artwork in lounge, roomy bar, all-day food (not Sun evening) with a sicilian slant (landlord/chef is from there), well kept Hancocks HB and guests such as Brains and local Otley; live music wknds; children and dogs welcome, attractive terrace, bedrooms *(anon)*

LLANTWIT MAJOR [SS9668]

Old Swan CF61 1SB [Church St]: Unusual dark medieval building with interesting nooks and crannies, lancet windows, candles even midday, good log fires in big stone fireplaces; both main rooms set for wide choice of good value well prepared pubby food from baguettes up, children's menu, a couple of changing ales; tables in back garden, open all day *(LYM, Prof Kenneth Surin)*

OGMORE [SS8876]

☆ **Pelican** CF32 0QP: Nice spot above ruined castle, attractive rambling revamp with plenty of beamery and bare boards; enjoyable food from enterprising big rolls to good freshly made pies and unusual things like pigeon, nice choice of well kept ales, good cheerful service, welcoming open fire; they may try to keep your credit card while you eat; rather grand smokers' hut; tables on side terrace, lovely views, quite handy for the beaches, open all day *(K Almond, Phil and Sally Gorton, R C Vincent, LYM)*

PEN-Y-CAE [SN8413]

☆ *Penycae Inn* SA9 1FA [Brecon Rd (A4067)]: Smartly cosy, beamed and stripped-stone bar with well kept Brains Rev James and Evan Evans Warrior, good value wines; big fireplace, soft sofas or neat tables and chairs, local paintings for sale; chef/landlord's generous fresh food inc good local mussels, steaks and cheeses in upstairs restaurant, with great views from conservatory (glass lift for the less than able), good service *(Adrian and Dawn Collinge)*

PONTSTICILL [SO0511]

Red Cow CF48 2UN [N of Merthyr Tydfil]: Longish L-shaped main bar with small room up two steps at back, well kept Shepherd Neame Spitfire, Wadworths 6X and Wye Valley, good generous pub lunches, welcoming helpful landlord; handy for local Brecon Mountain Railway and cycling/walking routes *(Dr Kevan Tucker)*

PORTHCAWL [SS8176]

Salthouse on the Square CF36 3BW [The Square]: Recently opened bar/restaurant, enjoyable good value food, good service and atmosphere, bay views; back terrace *(anon)*

REYNOLDSTON [SS4889]

King Arthur SA3 1AD [Higher Green, off A4118]: Cheerful pub/hotel with timbered main bar and hall, back family summer dining area (games room with pool in winter); popular good value food from lunchtime baguettes to Sun roasts, friendly helpful staff coping well when busy, Breconshire, Felinfoel and Tomos Watkins, country-house bric-a-brac, log fire; lively local atmosphere in evenings, piped music; tables out on green, play area, open all day, bedrooms *(Tony Lewis, Dr and Mrs A K Clarke, Ian Scott-Thompson, LYM)*

SWANSEA [SS6592]

Bank Statement SA1 1EP [Wind St]: Wetherspoons in town's oldest street; huge converted bank, very grand, with marble and stained-glass, interesting little booths, smart plusher and quieter panelled lower-ceilinged eating area behind; their usual value; large back terrace, open all day *(Dave Irving, Jenny Huggins)*

Bay View SA1 3UL [Oystermouth Rd, nr Guildhall and Patti Pavilion]: Large rambling place on seafront, light and airy with old wooden furniture and leather sofas, open fire; enjoyable thai food, good service, one changing real ale *(Michael and Alison Sandy, John and Helen Rushton)*

Pump House SA1 1TT [Pumphouse Quay, Maritime Quarter]: Civilised dining pub in converted harbourside building, real ales *(Dave Irving, Jenny Huggins)*

GWENT

ABERGAVENNY [SO2914]

Hen & Chickens NP7 5EG [Flannel St]: Relaxed traditional local, wholesome cheap lunchtime food (not Sun), friendly efficient staff, well kept Brains from bar unusually set against street windows, mugs of tea and coffee; interesting side areas with some nice stripped masonry; popular darts, cards and dominoes, Sun jazz; TV; very busy on market day; terrace tables *(Reg Fowle, Helen Rickwood, the Didler, Pete Baker)*

ABERSYCHAN [SO2604]

Globe NP4 7JH [Commercial Rd (B4246)]: Traditional two-bar pub specialising in well kept ales from small local breweries such as Breconshire and Rhymney, friendly landlord and locals; darts, pool; TV; open all day wknds, cl wkdy lunchtimes *(Pete Baker)*

BRYNGWYN [SO4007]

☆ *Cripple Creek* NP15 2AA [Abergavenny Rd; off old A40 W of Raglan]: Smartly extended and civilised old country dining pub with wide range of good reasonably priced food from simple things to more elaborate meals inc fresh fish and choice of four Sun roasts; efficient cheerful staff, real ales such as Adnams Broadside, Brains and Tetleys, decent wines, teas and coffees, pleasant restaurant; country views from small terrace, play area, open all day *(James Morrell)*

BRYNMAWR [SO1912]

Bridgend NP23 4RE [King St (A467, nr A465 junction)]: Cosy bar with generous reasonably priced sandwiches and baguettes, friendly landlord, mainstream ale *(anon)*

CAERLEON [ST3490]

☆ *Bell* NP18 1QQ [Bulmore Rd; off B4236, S of bridge]: Cottagey pub with thriving atmosphere in single bar (basic and smarter ends), good well priced food inc interesting welsh and breton dishes (not Weds-Sun evening when there is a more restauranty menu instead, nor Sun-Tues lunchtime); three or four well kept ales such as Rhymney; good Weds folk night and other events; garden tables *(Pete Baker, Roger Jones)*

GOVILON [SO2613]

Lion NP7 9PT [Merthyr Rd (B4246)]: Small cosy local with extensive all-day menu, proper old-fashioned cooking generously served and worth the wait; friendly staff; Adnams Broadside and Greene King Old Speckled Hen; garden, nr Monmouthshire & Brecon Canal, open all day *(Dr A Y Drummond, Meg and Colin Hamilton)*

GROSMONT [SO4024]

Angel NP7 8EP: Friendly 17th-c local owned by village co-operative, rustic interior with simple wooden furniture; Fullers, Tomos Watkins and Wye Valley ales, farm ciders, good value straightforward bar food; pool room with darts; no lavatories – public ones close by; a couple of garden tables and boules behind, seats out by ancient market cross on attractive steep single street in sight of castle *(BB, MLR, Reg Fowle, Helen Rickwood)*

LLANDENNY [SO4103]

☆ **Raglan Arms** NP15 1DL: Good, well priced fresh food inc some rather unusual dishes cooked to order, home-baked bread and notable Sun roasts, leisurely atmosphere, nice wines, serious coffee, Wye Valley Butty Bach, friendly young staff; big pine tables and a couple of leather sofas in linked dining rooms leading through to conservatory, big log fire in flagstoned bar's handsome stone fireplace, simple pastel paintwork giving slight scandinavian feel; neat separate public bar with food and wide-screen TV; garden tables, has been cl Tues in Jan-Mar *(James Paterson, BB, LM)*

LLANISHEN [SO4703]

Carpenters Arms NP16 6QH [B4293 N of Chepstow]: Old cottagey pub with good food inc fresh fish and home-made pies, Wadworths 6X and a guest, good service; comfortable bar/lounge, coal fire, back games room with pool; stone seats and small chrome tables and chairs on back flagstoned terrace, little table lawn up steps, a couple of front picnic-sets, cl Mon, lunchtime Tues *(Pete Baker)*

LLANTHONY [SO2827]

Half Moon NP7 7NN: Well worn-in relaxed country local with flagstoned bar and carpeted lounge, character landlord, Bullmastiff beers direct from the cask, basic food, log fire, darts; piped music; gorgeous views from nice back garden, big paddock, unspoilt valley with great walks (muddy walkers welcome), simple, comfortable and clean bedrooms, has been cl Tues lunchtime, other lunchtimes out of season (though usually open wknds then) *(MLR)*

☆ **Priory Hotel** NP7 7NN [aka Abbey Hotel, Llanthony Priory; off A465, back rd Llanvihangel Crucorney—Hay]: Magical setting for plain bar in dimly lit vaulted flagstoned crypt of gracefully ruined Norman abbey, lovely in summer, with lawns around and the peaceful border hills beyond; real ales such as Felinfoel and Newmans, summer farm cider, good coffee, simple lunchtime bar food (can be long queue on fine summer days, but number system then works well), evening restaurant; occasional live music; no dogs or children; bedrooms in restored parts of abbey walls, open all day Sat and summer Sun, cl winter Mon-Thurs and Sun evening, great walks *(MLR, the Didler, LYM, Reg Fowle, Helen Rickwood, Steve Harvey)*

LLANTRISANT FAWR [ST3997]

☆ **Greyhound** NP15 1LE [off A449 nr Usk]: Prettily set 17th-c country inn with relaxed homely feel in three linked beamed rooms, steps between two, nice mix of furnishings and rustic decorations; friendly helpful staff, consistently good home cooking at sensible prices, good sandwiches, two or more well kept ales, decent wines by the glass, log fires, colourful prints in pleasant grey-panelled dining room; attractive garden with

big fountain, hill views, adjoining pine shop, good bedrooms in small attached motel *(Colin Moore, BB)*

LLANVIHANGEL GOBION [SO3409]

Charthouse NP7 9AY [A40/B4598, E of Abergavenny]: Civilised and welcoming, with varied enjoyable food inc good welsh black meat, real ales; nautical memorabilia, distant hill views *(BB, Eryl and Keith Dykes)*

MONMOUTH [SO5012]

Robin Hood NP25 3EQ [Monnow St]: Ancient pub with low-beamed panelled bar, good home cooking, four well kept ales inc Bass and Greene King, friendly service, restaurant; tables outside, play area *(B M Eldridge, Dave Braisted)*

NEWPORT [ST3188]

Olde Murenger House NP20 1GA [High St]: Fine 16th-c building with ancient dark woodwork, bargain Sam Smiths; open all day *(Jennifer Banks, the Didler)*

PANDY [SO3322]

Pandy Inn NP7 8DR [A465 Abergavenny—Hereford]: Welcoming old slate-built family pub with emphasis on good reasonably priced bar food inc good value Sun lunch, attentive service, well kept Wye Valley ales; comfortable modern settles, 3D Brecons maps; adjacent walkers' bunkhouse *(Reg Fowle, Helen Rickwood)*

PANTYGELLI [SO3017]

Crown NP7 7HR [Old Hereford Rd, N of Abergavenny]: Pretty stone-built pub below Black Mountains, welcoming inside, with nice old furnishings and dark wood; affable family service, well kept Rhymney Best, Stowford Press farm cider, good wine choice, interesting and enjoyable lunchtime food inc good plate of welsh cheeses, more extensive evening menu, Sun roasts, plenty of local produce; attractive terrace *(Reg Fowle, Helen Rickwood, R T and J C Moggridge, David Whiter)*

RAGLAN [SO4107]

Beaufort Arms NP15 2DY [High St]: Old-fashioned pub/hotel (former coaching inn); attentive friendly staff, comfortable and roomy character beamed bars, well kept ales, good range of food inc reasonably priced bar snacks, set-price Sun lunch in brasserie, log fire; piped music; children welcome, 15 bedrooms *(Eryl and Keith Dykes)*

☆ **Clytha Arms** NP7 9BW [Clytha, off Abergavenny rd – former A40, now declassified]: On edge of Clytha Park, light and airy with good mix of old country furniture on scrubbed wood floors, window seats and warming fires; bar food (not Sun evening, Mon lunchtime) inc tapas, pricier more elaborate menu in contemporary restaurant, Evan Evans, Felinfoel, Rhymney and three quickly changing guests, farm ciders and perhaps own perry (occasional cider and beer festivals); also a good choice of wines and malts; darts, shove-ha'penny and bar billiards, unusual murals in lavatories; service not always top-notch; large-screen TV for rugby; children and dogs welcome, long, heated verandahs, bedrooms, good welsh breakfast, cl Mon lunchtime *(David and Sue Atkinson, Anne Helne, Simon Fidler, J K Parry, M J Daly, Pete Baker, Dr Kevan Tucker, the Didler, LYM, G M Benson)*

SHIRENEWTON [ST4894]

☆ **Carpenters Arms** NP16 6BU [Mynydd-bach; B4235 Chepstow—Usk, about 3.5 miles N]: Former smithy with unusual interconnecting rooms, one with old bellows still hanging from planked ceiling, flagstone floors, open fires, ancient high-backed settle, pews and sewing-machine trestle tables, chamber-pots and royal chromolithographs; straightforward food inc OAP meals, Brains, Fullers, Shepherd Neame and a seasonal guest; piped music; no credit cards; children welcome, dogs in bar, tables out at front, open all day summer wknds *(LYM, Paul Goldman, Donna and Roger, Dennis Jenkin)*

SHIRENEWTON [ST4894]

Huntsman NP16 6BU [B4235 outside village]: Cheerful welcoming landlord, wide choice of enjoyable food inc smaller lunchtime helpings from evening menu, special diets catered for, Brains Rev James and Fullers London Pride; comfortably carpeted bar and dining room; children welcome, picnic-sets outside with lovely hill views, nine bedrooms *(Richard Fendick)*

ST ARVANS [ST5196]

Piercefield NP16 6EJ: Modern décor and setting in roomy, comfortable country-style dining pub, Brains ales, good choice of generous enjoyable food at sensible prices, friendly efficient staff; handy for walkers and Chepstow races *(Mike and Mary Carter, Reg Fowle, Helen Rickwood)*

TINTERN [SO5300]

Anchor NP16 6TE: Smart pub right by the abbey; reasonably priced usual food from baguettes up, local perry and cider alongside original medieval cider press in main bar, well kept real ale such as Sharps Doom Bar; plush banquettes, lots of pictures, large restaurant and separate carvery; dogs welcome in some areas, daytime teahouse, spacious lawn with pets corner, comfortable bedrooms *(Mr and Mrs D J Nash, Dave Irving, Jenny Huggins, B M Eldridge)*

Rose & Crown NP16 6SE: Welcoming unpretentious inn opp riverside abbey; enjoyable low-priced generous pubby food all day, Greene King Abbot, nice open fire, restaurant; occasional live music wknds; dogs welcome, some riverbank tables *(Robert Turnham, Reg Fowle, Helen Rickwood)*

TREDEGAR [SO1408]

Olympia NP22 3ND [Morgan St]: Friendly Wetherspoons in former cinema with some art deco touches; pubby welsh-influenced food, real ales; TVs; back garden, open all day from 9am till late *(Dave Braisted)*

USK [SO3900]

Olway NP15 1EN: Enjoyable reasonably priced home-made food, two real ales, friendly service, smart restaurant area; garden, mountain bike hire *(Mr and Mrs Cotton)*

☆ **Royal Hotel** NP15 1AT [New Market St]: Comfortably and genuinely traditional with old pictures and old-fashioned fireplaces; wide choice of good value enjoyable home cooking (not Sun evening, worth booking wknds), three changing ales from deep cellar, friendly service; may be piped music; outside gents', upstairs ladies'; well behaved children welcome, handy for Rural Life Museum, cl Mon *(Chris Flynn, Wendy Jones, LYM)*

GWYNEDD

CAERNARFON [SH4762]

☆ **Black Buoy** LL55 1RW [Northgate St]: Busy traditional pub by castle walls, renamed losing its historical connection (properly Black Boy, from King Charles II's nickname in its King's Head days), but attractively renovated, with cheery fire, beams from ships wrecked here in the 16th c, bare floors and thick walls; lots of welsh chat, food all day from baguettes and doorstep sandwiches to interesting fish and vegetarian dishes, willing friendly service, well kept ales such as Brains, Conwy and Purple Moose; character lounge bar, restaurant, public bar with TV; a few pavement picnic-sets, bedrooms *(Walter and Susan Rinaldi-Butcher)*

CLYNNOG FAWR [SH4149]

St Beuno Caoch LL54 5PB [A499]: Well refurbished 16th-c coaching inn with two large bars and restaurant, helpful friendly service, good locally sourced food from french chef, good wine list inc welsh sparkling, Brains Rev James and guest ales; bedrooms *(John and Sylvia Harrop, Michael and Anne Thomas)*

CONWY [SH7877]

☆ **Castle Hotel** LL32 8DB [High St]: Thriving, sympathetically refurbished public bar in interesting old building; plenty of well spaced tables, good substantial food all day from sandwiches to interesting dishes in bar and in restaurant, three Conwy ales, decent wines; good informed service; own car parks (which helps here), 29 bedrooms *(David Glynne-Jones, M J Winterton, Keith and Sue Ward)*

CRICCIETH [SH5038]

Prince of Wales LL52 0HB [The Square/High St]: Open-plan with some individual decorative touches, nice pictures, panelling, open fires and cosy alcoves; friendly atmosphere, good value local food, real ales *(Reg Fowle, Helen Rickwood, LYM)*

LLANDUDNO [SH7882]

Albert LL30 2TW [Madoc St]: Friendly roomy pub comfortably furnished, good staff; standard food from sandwiches up, four well kept ales *(Dennis Jones)*

Cottage Loaf LL30 2SR [Market St]: Friendly former bakery with big log fire, flagstones, bare boards and salvaged ships' timbers, mix of individual tables and chairs; small choice of good value lunchtime food, several well kept local ales *(David Abbot)*

☆ *Kings Head* LL30 2NB [Old Rd, behind tram station]: Rambling and pretty, much extended around 16th-c flagstoned core; wide range of generous food from good steak sandwiches to restaurant meals (busy at night, so get there early), well kept Greene King and a guest beer, good range of wines by the glass, efficient service; huge log fire, brightly open-plan but with interesting corners and comfortable traditional furnishings, old local tramway photographs, smart back dining room up a few steps; children welcome, seats on front terrace overlooking quaint Victorian cable tramway's station, open all day in summer *(John and Helen Rushton, LYM, John Dwane)*

Palladium LL30 2DD [Gloddaeth St]: Spacious Wetherspoons in beautifully restored former theatre, boxes and seats intact, spectacular ceilings; quick friendly helpful service, good value food and drinks inc good choice of real ales, plenty of seating *(John Dwane)*

LLANDWROG [SH4556]

Harp LL54 5SY [0.5 miles W of A499 S of Caernarfon]: Welcoming village pub with irregular layout giving cosy corners and plenty of atmosphere; good friendly service, local and other real ales, daily papers and magazines, plenty of board games and Jenga, a parrot that's bilingual if it's feeling chatty; standard food plus welsh specialities, cheerful separate dining room; picnic-sets among fruit trees overlooking quiet village's imposing church, well equipped cottagey bedrooms, good breakfast, cl Mon *(M J Winterton, BB)*

LLANYSTUMDWY [SH4738]

Tafarn y Plu LL52 0SH: Thoroughly welsh beamed two-bar pub opp Lloyd George's boyhood home and museum; real ales such as Conwy, Evan Evans and Felinfoel, welsh lager, farm ciders, enjoyable food from sandwiches to good lamb steaks most days, warmly welcoming licensees and chatty locals; log fire, panelled partitions, traditional rustic décor, small restaurant; large peaceful garden *(David Pritchard, Gwilym Prydderch)*

PENRHYN BAY [SH8181]

Penrhyn Bay LL30 3EE [Penrhyn Old Rd]: Tucked-away 16th-c pub with friendly staff, Bass and a guest beer; no food Mon evening *(John Dwane)*

Y FELINHELI [SH5267]

Gardd Fûn LL56 4RQ [Beach Rd, off A487 SW of Bangor]: Nautical-theme local by Menai Straits; enjoyable food from good sandwiches up in bar or restaurant, good friendly service, real ales; great views from tables out on grass *(David Abbot)*

POWYS

ABERCRAVE [SN8212]

Abercrave Inn SA9 1XS [Heol Tawe (just off A4067 NE of Ystradgynlais)]: Attractive old building with two or three well kept local ales, helpful friendly staff, wide choice of good value food all day from baguettes up, plenty of tables in pleasant bar and comfortable and popular dining room; separate restaurant too; handy for Dan-yr-Ogof caves *(Michael and Alison Sandy)*

BERRIEW [SJ1800]

Lion SY21 8PQ [B4390; village signed off A483 Welshpool—Newtown]: Black and white beamed 17th-c coaching inn in attractive riverside village (with lively sculpture gallery); old-fashioned inglenook public bar and partly stripped-stone lounge bar with open fire, home-made food (not Sun evening) here or in restaurant from sandwiches to good fresh fish choice, helpful cheerful service, well kept Banks's and Marstons real ales, decent house wines, dominoes and cribbage; quiet piped music; children and dogs welcome, bedrooms, open all day *(Jeremy King, LYM, B and M Kendall)*

BLEDDFA [SO2068]

Hundred House LD7 1PA [A488 Knighton—Penybont]: Small relaxed lounge with log fire in huge stone fireplace, L-shaped main bar with attractively flagstoned lower games area, cosy dining room with another vast fireplace; good value tasty food, well kept ales, friendly service; bikers welcome, tables in peaceful back garden dropping steeply to small stream, lovely countryside *(M and D Toms, BB, Guy Vowles)*

BRECON [SO0428]

George LD3 7LD [George St]: Typical well worn-in town pub useful for its well kept ales and decent reasonably priced food all day from sandwiches up, cheerful efficient service; log-effect gas fires in long bar, dining conservatory; tables in flower-filled back courtyard, open all day *(Brian Brooks)*

CARNO [SN9696]

Aleppo Merchant SY17 5LL [A470 Newtown—Machynlleth]: Good value pub food from sandwiches up (open for breakfast too), helpful friendly staff, Boddingtons and Tetleys; plushly modernised stripped-stone bar, peaceful lounge on right with open fire, restaurant (well behaved children allowed here), back extension with big-screen TV in games room; piped music; disabled access, steps up to tables in attractively enlarged garden, bedrooms, nice countryside *(LYM, Michael and Jenny Back)*

CLYRO [SO2143]

Baskerville Arms HR3 5RZ: Unusual old-fashioned panelled bar area, long and comfortable, with assorted metalwork, small log fire one end, bigger one up stone steps the other; enjoyable reasonably priced bar food inc Sun roasts, friendly welcome, Wye Valley ales, separate restaurant; TV; picnic-sets under cocktail parasols in pleasant garden, fine walking area, good bedrooms *(Reg Fowle, Helen Rickwood)*

CRICKHOWELL [SO2143]

Dragon NP8 1BE [High St]: Recently refurbished ancient inn with good value food, welcoming staff, log fire;

15 comfortable bedrooms *(Eryl and Keith Dykes)*

GLADESTRY [SO2355]

☆ *Royal Oak* HR5 3NR [B4594]: Chatty village pub on Offa's Dyke Path, simple bar for walkers with open fire, beams hung with tankards and lanterns, stripped stone, flagstones, piano, turkey-carpeted lounge with open fire; Brains Rev James and a guest like Wye Valley, basic bar food; children welcome, dogs in bar (and in bedrooms by arrangement), sheltered back garden, camping, open all day *(Mrs P Sumner, LYM)*

HAY-ON-WYE [SO2342]

☆ *Kilverts* HR3 5AG [Bell Bank/Bear St]: High-beamed bar in friendly and flexible hotel undergoing some refurbishment, five well kept ales such as Brains, Hobsons and Wye Valley, several wines by the glass, food from good baguettes up; children welcome, small front flagstoned courtyard, pretty terraced back garden with fountain, bedrooms, good breakfast, open all day *(Mike and Mary Carter, Barry and Anne, Steve and Liz Tilley, John and Bryony Coles, David Jackman, LYM, Guy Vowles, Sue Demont, Tim Barrow)*

Old Black Lion HR3 5AD [Lion St]: Comfortable low-beamed bar with old pine tables and original fireplace, mostly laid out for dining, bar and restaurant food available throughout; Wye Valley (labelled as Old Black Lion) and a changing Rhymney ale, efficient service; no dogs; children over 5 allowed if eating, sheltered back terrace, bedrooms (some above bar), open all day *(Reg Fowle, Helen Rickwood, Steve Harvey, H G Dyke, Jarrod and Wendy Hopkinson, LYM, Neasa Braham, Richard, Sue Demont, Tim Barrow, Guy Vowles)*

☆ *Three Tuns* HR3 5DB [Broad St]: Welcoming well restored pub with good range of sensibly priced up-to-date food, lovely home-baked bread, three real ales inc Wye Valley, good choice of wines; sturdy basic furniture on slate floors, blackened beams, some stripped masonry, inglenook woodburners, ancient stairs to upper raftered restaurant served by new kitchen; tables out on good covered back terrace *(Brian and Jacky Wilson, MLR)*

HOWEY [SO0558]

Laughing Dog LD1 5PT: Two-bar pub with friendly landlady and chef/landlord doing good interesting locally sourced food (not Sun evening, Mon), well kept local ales; shelf of guide books, games room with darts and pool, carpeted restaurant; children and dogs allowed; terrace tables, open all day Fri-Sun, cl Mon lunchtime *(Pip Woolf, Mrs A Davies, Norman Jones)*

KNIGHTON [SO2872]

Horse & Jockey LD7 1AE [Wylcwm Pl]: Several cosy areas, one with log fire, enjoyable traditional and innovative food at attractive prices in bar and adjoining restaurant, prompt cheerful service, real ales such as Greene King Old Speckled Hen; pool; tables in pleasant medieval courtyard, handy

for Offa's Dyke *(Alan and Eve Harding, Stephen Locke, Pete Yearsley)*

LLANBEDR [SO2320]

Red Lion NP8 1SR [off A40 at Crickhowell]: Quaint spotlessly kept old local in pretty little village set in dell; heavy beams, antique settles in lounge and snug, log fires, welcoming service, front dining area with good value home-made food; good walking country (porch for muddy boots); cl wkdy lunchtime (except 2-5pm Weds – no food then), open all day wknds *(Guy Vowles)*

LLANFIHANGEL-NANT-MELAN [SO1958]

☆ *Red Lion* LD8 2TN [A44 10 miles W of Kington]: Stripped-stone and beamed 16th-c roadside dining pub, roomy main bar with flagstones and woodburner, carpeted restaurant, front sun porch; reasonably priced home-made food from sandwiches to Sun roasts, Brains and changing guests; back bar with woodburner, pool and darts; children and dogs welcome, pleasant back garden with nice country views, seven bedrooms (three in annex), handy for Radnor Forest walks, nr impressive waterfall, open all day Sun, cl Tues *(MLR, J A Ellis, BB)*

LLANFYLLIN [SJ1419]

Cain Valley SY22 5AQ [High St (A490)]: Welcoming beamed and dark-panelled 17th-c coaching inn with friendly helpful family service, good value fresh local food from sandwiches up in bars and good restaurant; Brains Rev James, Tetleys and Wells & Youngs Bombardier, daily papers; handsome Jacobean staircase to comfortable bedrooms *(David and Jane Hill)*

LLANGATTOCK [SO2117]

Horseshoe NP8 1PA [off B4558]: Popular local with characterful old-school landlord, well kept ales, no food *(Kay Hooper)*

Vine Tree NP8 1HG [signed from Crickhowell; Legar Rd]: Small simple pub with reliable good value generous food inc fresh fish and some unusual dishes in large horsey-theme lounge and restaurant; pleasant prompt service, Rhymney ales, good coffee, coal-effect gas fire; very busy wknds and bank hols; children welcome, tables out under cocktail parasols with lovely view of medieval Usk bridge *(LYM, Guy Vowles)*

LLANGENNY [SO2417]

Dragons Head NP8 1HD: Chatty two-room bar in pretty valley setting, friendly efficient staff, quickly changing real ales such as Rhymney Best, local farm cider, reasonably priced wines, wide choice of good value home-made food from sandwiches to welsh black beef; low beams, big woodburner, pews, housekeeper's chairs and a high-backed settle among other seats, two attractive dining areas; picnic-sets on heated terrace and over the road by a stream, nearby campsite, cl wkdy lunchtimes *(Eryl and Keith Dykes, Steve and Liz Tilley, LYM)*

LLANGORSE [SO1327]

Castle Inn LD3 7UB: Friendly smallish stone-built local with comfortable cosy flagstoned main bar, side room set out more for eating, good value pubby food to suit hungry walkers, well kept ales such as Wadworths 6X; may be cl winter wkdy lunchtimes *(John and Joan Nash)*

LLANGYNIDR [SO1519]

☆ *Coach & Horses* NP8 1LS [Cwm Crawnon Rd (B4558 W of Crickhowell)]: Tidy and roomy flower-decked dining pub with good value bar food from ciabattas up, real ales, comfortable banquettes and stripped stone, nice big log fire, large attractive restaurant; no dogs; picnic-sets across road in safely fenced pretty sloping garden by lock of Newport & Brecon Canal, lovely setting and walks, open all day *(LYM, Mike and Mary Carter, Meg and Colin Hamilton)*

Red Lion NP8 1NT [off B4558; Duffryn Rd]: Creeper-covered family-run 16th-c inn, attractively furnished bow-windowed bar with good log fire, chatty locals, well kept Breconshire ales and a guest, decent local food from lunchtime rolls up inc good venison sausages; lively games room; sheltered pretty garden, good value bedrooms *(Steve and Liz Tilley, Paul J Robinshaw)*

MALLWYD [SH8612]

Brigands SY20 9HJ: Attractive and welcoming stone-built Tudor-style hotel with big sofas and woodburner in spic and span central bar, cosy snug, dining rooms either side, friendly helpful staff; good reasonably priced food from sandwiches up inc local beef and lamb, good real ales and wine choice; neat extensive lawns with play area, nice bedrooms, lovely views, sea trout fishing on River Dovey *(Rodney and Norma Stubington, Sara Fulton, Roger Baker)*

PAINSCASTLE [SO1646]

☆ *Roast Ox* LD2 3JL [off A470 Brecon—Builth Wells; former Maesllwch Arms]: Well restored pub with beams, flagstones, stripped stone, appropriate simple furnishings and some rustic bric-a-brac; well kept ales such as Black Country and Hook Norton Old Hooky tapped from the cask, Thatcher's ciders, decent roasts as well as other enjoyable hearty food, friendly prompt service; dogs welcome, picnic-sets outside, attractive hill country, ten simple comfortable bedrooms *(Guy Vowles, Reg Fowle, Helen Rickwood, LYM)*

PENTRE BACH [SN9032]

☆ *Shoemakers Arms* LD3 8UB [off A40 in Sennybridge]: Simple pleasantly furnished remote country pub owned by local farming collective, good home-made food inc lunchtime bar snacks and small restaurant Sun lunchtime and Weds-Sun evenings; helpful cheerful staff, changing real ales such as Thwaites; children welcome, disabled access, garden picnic-sets (look out for the red kites), good walks, open all day Sun, cl Mon, Tues lunchtime *(S J C Chappell)*

PENYBONT [SO0561]

Severn Arms LD1 5UA [A44/A488, NE of Llandrindod Wells]: Welcoming hotel with good choice of well kept ales inc Brains Rev James and Wye Valley, enjoyable inexpensive food from sandwiches to steaks, friendly

helpful landlady and staff; sizeable bar with games area, secluded lounge, restaurant; plenty of tables in garden by little River Ithon, own fishing, bedrooms *(Pete Yearsley)*

PEN-Y-CAE [SN8313]

Ancient Briton SA9 1YY [Brecon Rd]: Friendly opened-up roadside pub with reasonably priced food, good range of well kept ales inc Wye Valley, good service; outside seats and play area, camping, handy for Dan-yr-Ogof caves and Carig y Nos country park, open all day *(MLR)*

PRESTEIGNE [SO3164]

Dukes Arms LD8 2AD [Broad St]: Dating from the 15th c, well kept beer, pool room off bar, piped music in lounge bar; nice garden *(Giles and Annie Francis)*

RHAYADER [SN9668]

☆ *Triangle* LD6 5AR [Cwmdauddwr; B4518 by bridge over River Wye, SW of centre]: Interesting mainly 16th-c pub, small and spotless with nice chatty atmosphere and welcoming helpful service; good value home-made pubby food lunchtime and early evening, well kept Brains Rev James and Hancocks HB, small selection of reasonably priced wines; separate dining area with view over park to Wye; darts and quiz nights; three tables on small front terrace *(Pete Yearsley)*

TALGARTH [SO1729]

Castle Inn LD3 0EP [Pengenffordd, A479 3 miles S]: Pleasant roadside inn at head of Rhiangoll valley, handy for Black Mountains walks inc nearby Castell Dinas and Waun Fach; small friendly bar with new landlord serving well kept changing ales such as Brains, Rhymney and Wye Valley, larger dining room, good choice of well priced local food, log fire; picnic-sets in sheltered garden, four bedrooms, neat bunkhouses, camping, has been cl Mon and wkdy lunchtimes *(Howard Beamish, MLR)*

TALYBONT-ON-USK [SO1122]

☆ *Star* LD3 7YX [B4558]: Fine choice of changing real ales in welcoming, relaxed and unpretentious stone-built local, hearty home-made food from good cheap filled rolls to some tasty main dishes inc curries, friendly attentive service; good log fire in fine inglenook with bread oven, farm cider, three bustling plain rooms off central servery inc brightly lit games area, lots of beer mats, bank notes and coins on beams; monthly band night; dogs and children welcome, picnic-sets in sizeable tree-ringed garden below Monmouth & Brecon Canal, bedrooms, open all day Sat and summer *(LYM, the Didler, Guy Vowles, John and Joan Nash, Dr Kevan Tucker, Jackie Givens, Pete Baker, Simon Daws)*

Usk LD3 7JE [Village outskirts towards A40]: 19th-c comfortably refurbished inn with good food inc fixed-price lunch menu, Hancocks HB and a guest beer, good choice of wines, helpful friendly staff; log fire, panelling and sporting prints, restaurant; ten good value well equipped bedrooms *(Drs J and J Parker, Gareth Lewis)*

A Little
Further Afield

A Little Further Afield

We have decided this year to have only short entries for recommended Channel Islands pubs, as for the rest of the British Isles beyond Great Britain itself. The stars signify those pubs which we and readers judge to be of full Main Entry quality. This year we are not printing Lucky Dip pubs for other overseas countries, but hope eventually to add a greatly expanded Overseas section to our website. So please keep the Overseas recommendations coming!

CHANNEL ISLANDS

GUERNSEY

GRANDE HAVRE

☆ *Houmet* [part of Houmet du Nord Hotel; rte de Picquerel]: Friendly and well run, with some recent rebuilding, good choice of reasonably priced food inc good fresh local fish and seafood; big picture windows overlooking rock and sand beach; bedrooms (*BB, Simon Taylor, Steven Kirby, Roger and Anne Newbury*)

KING'S MILLS

☆ *Fleur du Jardin* [King's Mills Road]: Lovely country hotel in attractive walled garden, relaxing low-beamed bar with good log fire, unusually good food strong on local produce and seafood, friendly efficient service; several real ales such as Batemans XXB, good choice of wines by the glass, local cider, restaurant; piped music; children and dogs welcome, comfortable bedrooms, open all day (*Steven Kirby, Simon Taylor, LYM*)

TORTEVAL

☆ *Imperial* [Pleinmont (coast rd, nr Pleinmont Point)]: Good choice of enjoyable meals inc good seafood and traditional Guernsey bean jar in dining room which, like the neat and tidy bar, has a great sea view over Rocquaine Bay; Randalls beers, local cider; suntrap garden, bedrooms in separate hotel part, handy for good beach (*Roger and Anne Newbury, Gordon Neighbour*)

JERSEY

GOREY

Seymour [rue du Puits Mahaut]: Panelled nautical-theme lounge, Bass and Jersey Sunbeam, good value food (inc breakfast 10-11.30) especially freshly landed seafood and oysters from harbour opp; pleasant helpful staff, locals' bar with two pool tables (and TV), separate dining room; terrace tables (*Neil and Anita Christopher*)

GRÈVE DE LECQ

☆ *Moulin de Lecq* [Mont de la Grève de Lecq]: Cheerful family-friendly converted mill, a favourite, with massive waterwheel dominating softly lit beamed bar, prompt friendly service, good pubby food, four real ales, Weston's farm cider; lots of board games, upstairs games room, restaurant; children and dogs welcome, great play area, lots of terrace picnic-sets, quiet streamside spot, pleasant walks, open all day (*Lynda Payton, Sam Samuells, Mike and Eleanor Anderson, LYM, Chris and Jeanne Downing*)

ST AUBIN

☆ *Old Court House Inn* [Harbour Blvd]: Pubby low-beamed downstairs bar with open fire, other rambling areas inc smarter bar partly built from schooner's gig; bar food from pubby snacks to lots of fresh fish, handsome upstairs restaurant, glorious views across harbour to St Helier; board games; piped music, TV; children welcome, comfortable bedrooms, open all day (*Chris and Jeanne Downing, Lynda Payton, Sam Samuells, LYM, Michael Butler, Michael Dandy*)

ST HELIER

☆ *Lamplighter* [Mulcaster St]: Half a dozen real ales inc local Liberation, dozens of malt whiskies, bargain simple food such as crab sandwiches; heavy timbers, rough panelling and scrubbed pine tables; sports TV; can get very busy early evening; interesting façade (with only Union Flag visible during Nazi occupation), open all day (*Michael Butler, Lynda Payton, Sam Samuells, LYM*)

ST MARY

St Marys: Locally popular for good food (Sun evening too), with good choice of beers, reasonably priced wines, great log fire; children welcome in restaurant, dogs in bar; opp attractive church (*Jenny and Brian Seller*)

ST OUENS BAY

☆ **La Pulente** [start of Five Mile Rd; OS map reference 562488]: Comfortable lounge and conservatory overlooking Jersey's longest beach (stunning sunsets); enjoyable food (not Sun evening in winter), friendly atmosphere and staff, well kept Bass, restaurant; piped music; children welcome, terrace tables, open all day *(LYM, Jo Lilley, Simon Calvert, Michael Dandy, BB)*

ISLE OF MAN

LAXEY
Shore [Old Laxey Hill]: Pubby atmosphere, friendly staff, Bosuns Bitter, good value wine; picnic-sets out by lovely stream *(Dr J Barrie Jones)*
PORT ERIN
Bay [Shore Rd]: Three rooms with bare boards and good furniture, good fresh food (not Tues), up to half a dozen reasonably priced well kept local Bushys beers (brewery owner lives above), guest beers too, good value wine, friendly service; overlooks sandy beach and across to Bradda Head; live music Fri; children welcome, flexible opening times *(Dr J Barrie Jones, Derek and Sylvia Stephenson)*
Falcons Nest [Station Rd]: Bushys and Okells ales, enjoyable food; handy for steam rail terminus; 30 good bedrooms, many with sea view, good breakfast – don't miss the local kippers *(JHBS, Derek and Sylvia Stephenson)*

IRELAND (NORTHERN)

BANGOR
Jamaica [Seacliff Rd; Co Down]: Great spot overlooking bay, good food inc lots of fish, good wine list and service, full of friendly irish families; tables outside *(Barbara Wensworth)*
BUSHMILLS
Bushmills [Co Antrim]: Hotel with 17th-c core (rather than pub), linked rooms in various styles inc cosy gaslit ochre-walled inner room with sofa, settles, windsor chairs and original cooking pots by huge peat fire, another in hallway inglenook; well kept beers, wide choice of wines and spirits, exemplary service, good restaurant; flower-filled yard, comfortable bedrooms, handy for Giant's Causeway and Bushmills Distillery *(Barbara Wensworth)*

IRELAND (REPUBLIC)

BALLYVAUGHAN
O'Loclainns [Co Clare]: Tiny unchanging whiskey bar in same family for five generations, huge choice; venerable till on counter; handy for the Burren, opens 9pm (owner farms, wife teaches) *(GLD)*
CORK
Castle [South Main St]: Unspoilt old-style bar with friendly landlady, lots of knick-knacks, real fire, basic furnishings *(Mike and Eleanor Anderson)*
ENNISTIMON
Café Vienna [Co Clare]: Hot plentiful food in tapas bar and sizeable spanish restaurant – something of a surprise for mid-Clare *(GLD)*
GALWAY
Huntsman [164 College Rd]: Contemporary two-room bar and adjacent bistro, enjoyable pubby food, good wine choice, good service; piped music; pavement tables, bedrooms *(Michael Dandy)*
Kings Head [High St]: Sizeable partly medieval pub, good food choice from grilled sandwiches up, coffee and pastries too; upstairs overflow *(Michael Dandy)*
Lohans [Upper Salthill]: Modern sea-view pub useful for good choice of food all day, friendly service; seats outside *(Michael Dandy)*
GORT
Jack B Yeats [Ennis Rd; Co Galway]: New hotel's neat front bar, wood floor, bare brickwork, usual beers, pubby food; formal restaurant; piped music, TV; bedrooms *(Michael Dandy)*

Special
Interest Lists

FOOD SERVED ALL DAY

We list here all the pubs that have told us they plan to serve food all day, even if it's only one day of the week. The individual entries for the pubs themselves show the actual details.

BEDFORDSHIRE
Northill, Crown

BERKSHIRE
Cookham Dean, Chequers
White Waltham, Beehive

BUCKINGHAMSHIRE
Dorney, Pineapple
Forty Green, Royal Standard of England
Grove, Grove Lock
Wooburn Common, Chequers

CAMBRIDGESHIRE
Elton, Black Horse
Pampisford, Chequers
Peterborough, Brewery Tap

CHESHIRE
Aldford, Grosvenor Arms
Aston, Bhurtpore
Bickley Moss, Cholmondeley Arms
Bunbury, Dysart Arms
Burleydam, Combermere Arms
Burwardsley, Pheasant
Chester, Mill, Old Harkers Arms
Cotebrook, Fox & Barrel
Lach Dennis, Duke of Portland
Macclesfield, Sutton Hall
Mobberley, Roebuck
Peover Heath, Dog
Plumley, Smoker
Prestbury, Legh Arms
Tarporley, Rising Sun
Willington, Boot

CORNWALL
Mitchell, Plume of Feathers
Morwenstow, Bush
Porthtowan, Blue
Watergate Bay, Beach Hut
Widemouth, Bay View

CUMBRIA
Askham, Punch Bowl
Bampton, Mardale
Cartmel Fell, Masons Arms
Crosthwaite, Punch Bowl
Elterwater, Britannia
Ings, Watermill
Keswick, Dog & Gun
Levens, Strickland Arms
Seathwaite, Newfield Inn

DERBYSHIRE
Alderwasley, Bear
Beeley, Devonshire Arms
Fenny Bentley, Coach & Horses
Hathersage, Plough

Hayfield, Lantern Pike, Royal
Ladybower Reservoir, Yorkshire Bridge
Litton, Red Lion
Monyash, Bulls Head

DEVON
Avonwick, Turtley Corn Mill
Cockwood, Anchor
Drewsteignton, Drewe Arms
Exeter, Imperial
Noss Mayo, Ship
Sidford, Blue Ball

DORSET
Osmington Mills, Smugglers
Tarrant Monkton, Langton Arms
Winkton, Fishermans Haunt
Worth Matravers, Square & Compass

GLOUCESTERSHIRE
Almondsbury, Bowl
Brimpsfield, Golden Heart
Broad Campden, Bakers Arms
Cheltenham, Royal Oak
Ford, Plough
Guiting Power, Hollow Bottom
Littleton-upon-Severn, White Hart
Nailsworth, Weighbridge
Sheepscombe, Butchers Arms

HAMPSHIRE
Dunbridge, Mill Arms
Southsea, Wine Vaults
St Owen's Cross, New Inn

HERTFORDSHIRE
Aldbury, Valiant Trooper
Ashwell, Three Tuns

ISLE OF WIGHT
Arreton, White Lion
Cowes, Folly
Hulverstone, Sun
Ningwood, Horse & Groom
Niton, Buddle
Shorwell, Crown

KENT
Bough Beech, Wheatsheaf
Brookland, Woolpack
Hollingbourne, Windmill
Langton Green, Hare
Penshurst, Bottle House
Shipbourne, Chaser
Stowting, Tiger

LANCASHIRE
Barrow, Eagle
Bispham Green, Eagle & Child
Broughton, Plough at Eaves
Great Mitton, Three Fishes
Lancaster, Borough
Liverpool, Philharmonic Dining Rooms
Longridge, Derby Arms
Manchester, Marble Arch
Mellor, Devonshire Arms
Pleasington, Clog & Billycock
Ramsbottom, Fishermans Retreat

Waddington, Lower Buck
Wheatley Lane, Old Sparrow Hawk
Wheelton, Dressers Arms
Yealand Conyers, New Inn
Woodhouse Eaves, Wheatsheaf

LINCOLNSHIRE
Stamford, George of Stamford

NORFOLK
Brancaster Staithe, Jolly Sailors
Larling, Angel
Morston, Anchor
Woodbastwick, Fur & Feather

NORTHAMPTONSHIRE
Ashby St Ledgers, Olde Coach House
Aynho, Great Western Arms
Oundle, Ship

NORTHUMBRIA
Carterway Heads, Manor House Inn
Corbridge, Angel
Great Whittington, Queens Head
Greta Bridge, Morritt Arms
New York, Shiremoor Farm
Newburn, Keelman
Stannington, Ridley Arms
Weldon Bridge, Anglers Arms

NOTTINGHAMSHIRE
Nottingham, Bell, Olde Trip to Jerusalem

OXFORDSHIRE
Bloxham, Joiners Arms
Great Tew, Falkland Arms
Kingham, Plough
Oxford, Eagle & Child, Turf Tavern
Satwell, Lamb
Woodstock, Kings Arms

SHROPSHIRE
Bromfield, Clive
Chetwynd Aston, Fox
Leebotwood, Pound
Shrewsbury, Armoury
Stiperstones, Stiperstones Inn

SOMERSET
Hinton St George, Lord Poulett Arms
Stanton Wick, Carpenters Arms
Wells, City Arms

STAFFORDSHIRE
Lichfield, Boat

SUFFOLK
Chelmondiston, Butt & Oyster
Newbourne, Fox
Snape, Plough & Sail
Stoke-by-Nayland, Crown
Waldringfield, Maybush

SURREY
Cobham, Cricketers
Worplesdon, Jolly Farmer

SUSSEX
Arlington, Old Oak
Berwick, Cricketers Arms
Blackboys, Blackboys Inn
Charlton, Fox Goes Free
East Dean, Star & Garter
Horsham, Black Jug
Icklesham, Queens Head
Ringmer, Cock
Rye, Ship, Ypres Castle
Wilmington, Giants Rest

WARWICKSHIRE
Birmingham, Old Joint Stock
Henley-in-Arden, Blue Bell

WILTSHIRE
Brinkworth, Three Crowns
Lacock, George
Seend, Barge
Stourton, Spread Eagle

YORKSHIRE
Beck Hole, Birch Hall
Blakey Ridge, Lion
Elslack, Tempest Arms
Grinton, Bridge Inn
Halifax, Shibden Mill
Ledsham, Chequers
Linton in Craven, Fountaine
Long Preston, Maypole

LONDON
Central London, Argyll Arms, Black Friar,
   Coopers Arms, Dog & Duck, Harp,
   Olde Mitre
East London, Crown
South London, Bo-Peep, Crown & Greyhound,
   Cutty Sark, Fire Station, Founders Arms,
   Fox & Hounds, Greenwich Union,
   Telegraph, Victoria, White Cross
West London, Atlas, Bulls Head,
   Churchill Arms, Dove, Duke of Sussex,
   Portobello Gold, Warrington, White Horse,
   Windsor Castle

SCOTLAND
Broughty Ferry, Fishermans Tavern
Edinburgh, Café Royal, Starbank
Gairloch, Old Inn
Glasgow, Babbity Bowster, Counting House
Houston, Fox & Hounds
Inveraray, George
Kilmahog, Lade
Kippen, Cross Keys
Linlithgow, Four Marys
Shieldaig, Tigh an Eilean Hotel
Sligachan, Sligachan Hotel
Thornhill, Lion & Unicorn

WALES
Gresford, Pant-yr-Ochain
Hay-on-Wye, Blue Boar
Llandudno Junction, Queens Head
Llanferres, Druid
Red Wharf Bay, Ship
Tal-y-Cafn, Tal-y-Cafn Hotel

PUBS CLOSE TO MOTORWAY JUNCTIONS

The number at the start of each line is the number of the junction. The county tells you where you will find the pub in the Guide. Detailed directions are given in the Main Entry for each pub.

M1
13: Woburn, Birch (Beds) 3.5 miles
16: Nether Heyford, Olde Sun (Northants) 1.8 miles
18: Crick, Red Lion (Northants) 1 mile; Kilsby, George (Northants) 2.6 miles; Ashby St Ledgers, Olde Coach House (Northants) 4 miles
23: Belton, Queens Head (Leics) 4.4 miles

M3
3: West End, Inn at West End (Surrey) 2.4 miles
9: Winchester, Willow Tree (Hants) 1 mile; Easton, Chestnut Horse (Hants) 3.6 miles
10: Winchester, Black Boy (Hants) 1 mile

M4
7: Dorney, Pineapple (Bucks) 2.4 miles
9: Holyport, Belgian Arms (Berks) 1.5 miles; Bray, Hinds Head (Berks) 1.75 miles; Bray, Crown (Berks) 1.75 miles
11: Shinfield, Magpie & Parrot (Berks) 2.6 miles
13: Winterbourne, Winterbourne Arms (Berks) 3.7 miles
14: East Garston, Queens Arms (Berks) 3.5 miles
17: Norton, Vine Tree (Wilts) 4 miles
18: Hinton Dyrham, Bull (Gloucs) 2.4 miles

M5
4: Holy Cross, Bell & Cross (Worcs) 4 miles
7: Kempsey, Walter de Cantelupe (Worcs) 3.7 miles
9: Bredon, Fox & Hounds (Worcs) 4.5 miles
16: Almondsbury, Bowl (Gloucs) 1.25 miles
19: Portishead, Windmill (Somerset) 3.7 miles; Clapton-in-Gordano, Black Horse (Somerset) 4 miles
26: Clayhidon, Merry Harriers (Devon) 3.1 miles
30: Topsham, Bridge Inn (Devon) 2.25 miles; Woodbury Salterton, Diggers Rest (Devon) 3.5 miles

M6
T6: Lichfield, Boat (Staffs) 3.8 miles
4: Shustoke, Griffin (Warks) 5 miles
16: Barthomley, White Lion (Cheshire) 1 mile
19: Plumley, Smoker (Cheshire) 2.5 miles
33: Bay Horse, Bay Horse (Lancs) 1.2 miles
35: Yealand Conyers, New Inn (Lancs) 3 miles
36: Levens, Strickland Arms (Cumbria) 4 miles
40: Yanwath, Gate Inn (Cumbria) 2.25 miles; Askham, Punch Bowl (Cumbria) 4.5 miles

M9
3: Linlithgow, Four Marys (Scotland) 2 miles

M11
7: Hastingwood, Rainbow & Dove (Essex) 0.25 miles
8: Birchanger, Three Willows (Essex) 0.8 miles
9: Hinxton, Red Lion (Cambs) 2 miles
10: Pampisford, Chequers (Cambs) 2.6 miles; Thriplow, Green Man (Cambs) 3 miles

M20
8: Hollingbourne, Windmill (Kent) 1 mile
11: Stowting, Tiger (Kent) 3.7 miles

M25
4: South London, Bo-Peep (London) 1.7 miles
10: Cobham, Plough (Surrey) 3.2 miles; Cobham, Cricketers (Surrey) 3.75 miles
18: Chenies, Red Lion (Bucks) 2 miles; Flaunden, Bricklayers Arms (Herts) 4 miles
21A: Potters Crouch, Holly Bush (Herts) 2.3 miles

M27
1: Fritham, Royal Oak (Hants) 4 miles

M40
2: Hedgerley, White Horse (Bucks) 2.4 miles; Forty Green, Royal Standard of England (Bucks) 3.5 miles
6: Lewknor, Olde Leathern Bottel (Oxon) 0.5 miles; Cuxham, Half Moon (Oxon) 4 miles
12: Gaydon, Malt Shovel (Warks) 0.9 miles
15: Barford, Granville (Warks) 1.7 miles
16: Henley-in-Arden, Blue Bell (Warks) 3.3 miles

M42
6: Hampton in Arden, White Lion (Warks) 1.25 miles

M48
1: Littleton-upon-Severn, White Hart (Gloucs) 3.5 miles

M50
1: Baughton, Jockey (Worcs) 4 miles

M53
3: Barnston, Fox & Hounds (Lancs) 3 miles

M55
1: Broughton, Plough at Eaves (Lancs) 3.25 miles

M61
8: Wheelton, Dressers Arms (Lancs) 2.1 miles

M62
22: Denshaw, Rams Head (Lancs) 2 miles
25: Hartshead, Gray Ox (Yorks) 3.5 miles

Report Forms

We need to know about pubs in this edition, pubs worthy of inclusion and ones that should not be included. Sometimes pubs are dropped simply because very few readers have written to us about them. You can use the cut-out forms on the following pages, the card in the middle of the book, email us at **feedback@goodguides.com** or write to us and we'll gladly send you more forms:

The Good Pub Guide
FREEPOST TN1569
WADHURST
East Sussex TN5 7BR

Though we try to answer all letters, please understand if there's a delay (particularly in summer, our busiest period). We'll assume we can print your name or initials as a recommender unless you tell us otherwise.

MAIN ENTRY OR LUCKY DIP?

Please try to gauge whether a pub should be a Main Entry or Lucky Dip (and tick the relevant box). Main entries need qualities that would make it worth other readers' while to travel some distance to them. If a pub is an entirely new recommendation, the Lucky Dip may be the best place for it to start its career in the *Guide* – to encourage other readers to report on it.

The more detail you can put into your description of a pub, the better. Any information on how good the landlord or landlady is, what it looks like inside, what you like about the atmosphere and character, the quality and type of food, whether the real ale is well kept and which real ales are available, whether bedrooms are available, and how big/attractive the garden is. Other things that help (if possible) include prices for food and bedrooms, food service and opening hours, and if children or dogs are welcome.

If the food or accommodation are outstanding, tick the **FOOD AWARD** or the **STAY AWARD** box.

If you're in a position to gauge a pub's suitability or otherwise for **disabled people**, do please tell us about that.

If you can, give the full address or directions for any pub not yet in the Guide – best of all please give us its postcode. If we can't find a pub's postcode, we don't include it in the *Guide*.

I have been to the following pubs in *The Good Pub Guide 2010* in the last few months, found them as described, and confirm that they deserve continued inclusion:

Continued overleaf

PLEASE GIVE YOUR NAME AND ADDRESS ON THE BACK OF THIS FORM

Pubs visited continued...

Your own name and address *(block capitals please)*

Postcode

Please return to
The Good Pub Guide,
FREEPOST TN1569,
WADHURST,
East Sussex
TN5 7BR

IF YOU PREFER, YOU CAN SEND US REPORTS
BY EMAIL:
feedback@goodguides.com

I have been to the following pubs in *The Good Pub Guide 2010* in the last few months, found them as described, and confirm that they deserve continued inclusion:

Continued overleaf
PLEASE GIVE YOUR NAME AND ADDRESS ON THE BACK OF THIS FORM

Pubs visited continued...

Your own name and address *(block capitals please)*

Postcode

Please return to
The Good Pub Guide,
FREEPOST TN1569,
WADHURST,
East Sussex
TN5 7BR

IF YOU PREFER, YOU CAN SEND US REPORTS
BY EMAIL:
feedback@goodguides.com

REPORT ON
(PUB'S NAME)

Pub's address

☐ **YES** MAIN ENTRY   ☐ **YES** LUCKY DIP   ☐ **NO** DON'T INCLUDE

Please tick one of these boxes to show your verdict, and give reasons and descriptive comments, prices etc

☐ DESERVES **FOOD** award   ☐ DESERVES **PLACE-TO-STAY** award   2010:1

PLEASE GIVE YOUR NAME AND ADDRESS ON THE BACK OF THIS FORM

REPORT ON
(PUB'S NAME)

Pub's address

☐ **YES** MAIN ENTRY   ☐ **YES** LUCKY DIP   ☐ **NO** DON'T INCLUDE

Please tick one of these boxes to show your verdict, and give reasons and descriptive comments, prices etc

☐ DESERVES **FOOD** award   ☐ DESERVES **PLACE-TO-STAY** award   2010:2

PLEASE GIVE YOUR NAME AND ADDRESS ON THE BACK OF THIS FORM

Your own name and address *(block capitals please)*

In returning this form I confirm my agreement that the information I provide may be used by
The Random House Group Ltd, its assignees and/or licensees in any media or medium whatsoever.

DO NOT USE THIS SIDE OF THE PAGE FOR WRITING ABOUT PUBS

Your own name and address *(block capitals please)*

In returning this form I confirm my agreement that the information I provide may be used by
The Random House Group Ltd, its assignees and/or licensees in any media or medium whatsoever.

DO NOT USE THIS SIDE OF THE PAGE FOR WRITING ABOUT PUBS

IF YOU PREFER, YOU CAN SEND US REPORTS BY EMAIL:
feedback@goodguides.com

REPORT ON   (PUB'S NAME)

Pub's address

☐ **YES** MAIN ENTRY   ☐ **YES** LUCKY DIP   ☐ **NO** DON'T INCLUDE
Please tick one of these boxes to show your verdict, and give reasons and descriptive comments, prices etc

☐ DESERVES **FOOD** award   ☐ DESERVES **PLACE-TO-STAY** award   2010:3

PLEASE GIVE YOUR NAME AND ADDRESS ON THE BACK OF THIS FORM

✂ -

REPORT ON   (PUB'S NAME)

Pub's address

☐ **YES** MAIN ENTRY   ☐ **YES** LUCKY DIP   ☐ **NO** DON'T INCLUDE
Please tick one of these boxes to show your verdict, and give reasons and descriptive comments, prices etc

☐ DESERVES **FOOD** award   ☐ DESERVES **PLACE-TO-STAY** award   2010:4

PLEASE GIVE YOUR NAME AND ADDRESS ON THE BACK OF THIS FORM

Your own name and address *(block capitals please)*

In returning this form I confirm my agreement that the information I provide may be used by
The Random House Group Ltd, its assignees and/or licensees in any media or medium whatsoever.

DO NOT USE THIS SIDE OF THE PAGE FOR WRITING ABOUT PUBS

Your own name and address *(block capitals please)*

In returning this form I confirm my agreement that the information I provide may be used by
The Random House Group Ltd, its assignees and/or licensees in any media or medium whatsoever.

DO NOT USE THIS SIDE OF THE PAGE FOR WRITING ABOUT PUBS

IF YOU PREFER, YOU CAN SEND US REPORTS BY EMAIL:

feedback@goodguides.com

REPORT ON (PUB'S NAME)

Pub's address

☐ **YES** MAIN ENTRY ☐ **YES** LUCKY DIP ☐ **NO** DON'T INCLUDE
Please tick one of these boxes to show your verdict, and give reasons and descriptive comments, prices etc

☐ DESERVES **FOOD** award ☐ DESERVES **PLACE-TO-STAY** award 2010:5

PLEASE GIVE YOUR NAME AND ADDRESS ON THE BACK OF THIS FORM

✂

REPORT ON (PUB'S NAME)

Pub's address

☐ **YES** MAIN ENTRY ☐ **YES** LUCKY DIP ☐ **NO** DON'T INCLUDE
Please tick one of these boxes to show your verdict, and give reasons and descriptive comments, prices etc

☐ DESERVES **FOOD** award ☐ DESERVES **PLACE-TO-STAY** award 2010:6

PLEASE GIVE YOUR NAME AND ADDRESS ON THE BACK OF THIS FORM

Your own name and address *(block capitals please)*

In returning this form I confirm my agreement that the information I provide may be used by
The Random House Group Ltd, its assignees and/or licensees in any media or medium whatsoever.

DO NOT USE THIS SIDE OF THE PAGE FOR WRITING ABOUT PUBS

✂ ....

Your own name and address *(block capitals please)*

In returning this form I confirm my agreement that the information I provide may be used by
The Random House Group Ltd, its assignees and/or licensees in any media or medium whatsoever.

DO NOT USE THIS SIDE OF THE PAGE FOR WRITING ABOUT PUBS

IF YOU PREFER, YOU CAN SEND US REPORTS BY EMAIL:
feedback@goodguides.com

REPORT ON (PUB'S NAME)

Pub's address

☐ **YES** MAIN ENTRY ☐ **YES** LUCKY DIP ☐ **NO** DON'T INCLUDE
Please tick one of these boxes to show your verdict, and give reasons and descriptive comments, prices etc

☐ DESERVES **FOOD** award ☐ DESERVES **PLACE-TO-STAY** award 2010:7

PLEASE GIVE YOUR NAME AND ADDRESS ON THE BACK OF THIS FORM

REPORT ON (PUB'S NAME)

Pub's address

☐ **YES** MAIN ENTRY ☐ **YES** LUCKY DIP ☐ **NO** DON'T INCLUDE
Please tick one of these boxes to show your verdict, and give reasons and descriptive comments, prices etc

☐ DESERVES **FOOD** award ☐ DESERVES **PLACE-TO-STAY** award 2010:8

PLEASE GIVE YOUR NAME AND ADDRESS ON THE BACK OF THIS FORM

Your own name and address *(block capitals please)*

In returning this form I confirm my agreement that the information I provide may be used by
The Random House Group Ltd, its assignees and/or licensees in any media or medium whatsoever.

DO NOT USE THIS SIDE OF THE PAGE FOR WRITING ABOUT PUBS

✂ ···

Your own name and address *(block capitals please)*

In returning this form I confirm my agreement that the information I provide may be used by
The Random House Group Ltd, its assignees and/or licensees in any media or medium whatsoever.

DO NOT USE THIS SIDE OF THE PAGE FOR WRITING ABOUT PUBS

IF YOU PREFER, YOU CAN SEND US REPORTS BY EMAIL:
feedback@goodguides.com

REPORT ON (PUB'S NAME)

Pub's address

☐ **YES** MAIN ENTRY ☐ **YES** LUCKY DIP ☐ **NO** DON'T INCLUDE
Please tick one of these boxes to show your verdict, and give reasons and descriptive comments, prices etc

☐ DESERVES **FOOD** award ☐ DESERVES **PLACE-TO-STAY** award 2010:9

PLEASE GIVE YOUR NAME AND ADDRESS ON THE BACK OF THIS FORM

✂ --

REPORT ON (PUB'S NAME)

Pub's address

☐ **YES** MAIN ENTRY ☐ **YES** LUCKY DIP ☐ **NO** DON'T INCLUDE
Please tick one of these boxes to show your verdict, and give reasons and descriptive comments, prices etc

☐ DESERVES **FOOD** award ☐ DESERVES **PLACE-TO-STAY** award 2010:10

PLEASE GIVE YOUR NAME AND ADDRESS ON THE BACK OF THIS FORM

Your own name and address *(block capitals please)*

In returning this form I confirm my agreement that the information I provide may be used by The Random House Group Ltd, its assignees and/or licensees in any media or medium whatsoever.

DO NOT USE THIS SIDE OF THE PAGE FOR WRITING ABOUT PUBS

Your own name and address *(block capitals please)*

In returning this form I confirm my agreement that the information I provide may be used by The Random House Group Ltd, its assignees and/or licensees in any media or medium whatsoever.

DO NOT USE THIS SIDE OF THE PAGE FOR WRITING ABOUT PUBS

IF YOU PREFER, YOU CAN SEND US REPORTS BY EMAIL:
feedback@goodguides.com

REPORT ON (PUB'S NAME)

Pub's address

☐ **YES** MAIN ENTRY ☐ **YES** LUCKY DIP ☐ **NO** DON'T INCLUDE

Please tick one of these boxes to show your verdict, and give reasons and descriptive comments, prices etc

☐ DESERVES **FOOD** award ☐ DESERVES **PLACE-TO-STAY** award 2010:11

PLEASE GIVE YOUR NAME AND ADDRESS ON THE BACK OF THIS FORM

--- ✂ ---

REPORT ON (PUB'S NAME)

Pub's address

☐ **YES** MAIN ENTRY ☐ **YES** LUCKY DIP ☐ **NO** DON'T INCLUDE

Please tick one of these boxes to show your verdict, and give reasons and descriptive comments, prices etc

☐ DESERVES **FOOD** award ☐ DESERVES **PLACE-TO-STAY** award 2010:12

PLEASE GIVE YOUR NAME AND ADDRESS ON THE BACK OF THIS FORM

Your own name and address *(block capitals please)*

In returning this form I confirm my agreement that the information I provide may be used by
The Random House Group Ltd, its assignees and/or licensees in any media or medium whatsoever.

DO NOT USE THIS SIDE OF THE PAGE FOR WRITING ABOUT PUBS

✂ ....

Your own name and address *(block capitals please)*

In returning this form I confirm my agreement that the information I provide may be used by
The Random House Group Ltd, its assignees and/or licensees in any media or medium whatsoever.

DO NOT USE THIS SIDE OF THE PAGE FOR WRITING ABOUT PUBS

IF YOU PREFER, YOU CAN SEND US REPORTS BY EMAIL:
feedback@goodguides.com

REPORT ON (PUB'S NAME)

Pub's address

☐ **YES** MAIN ENTRY ☐ **YES** LUCKY DIP ☐ **NO** DON'T INCLUDE
Please tick one of these boxes to show your verdict, and give reasons and descriptive
comments, prices etc

☐ DESERVES **FOOD** award ☐ DESERVES **PLACE-TO-STAY** award 2010:13

PLEASE GIVE YOUR NAME AND ADDRESS ON THE BACK OF THIS FORM

✂

REPORT ON (PUB'S NAME)

Pub's address

☐ **YES** MAIN ENTRY ☐ **YES** LUCKY DIP ☐ **NO** DON'T INCLUDE
Please tick one of these boxes to show your verdict, and give reasons and descriptive
comments, prices etc

☐ DESERVES **FOOD** award ☐ DESERVES **PLACE-TO-STAY** award 2010:14

PLEASE GIVE YOUR NAME AND ADDRESS ON THE BACK OF THIS FORM

Your own name and address *(block capitals please)*

In returning this form I confirm my agreement that the information I provide may be used by
The Random House Group Ltd, its assignees and/or licensees in any media or medium whatsoever.

DO NOT USE THIS SIDE OF THE PAGE FOR WRITING ABOUT PUBS

Your own name and address *(block capitals please)*

In returning this form I confirm my agreement that the information I provide may be used by
The Random House Group Ltd, its assignees and/or licensees in any media or medium whatsoever.

DO NOT USE THIS SIDE OF THE PAGE FOR WRITING ABOUT PUBS

IF YOU PREFER, YOU CAN SEND US REPORTS BY EMAIL:
feedback@goodguides.com

REPORT ON (PUB'S NAME)

Pub's address

☐ **YES** MAIN ENTRY ☐ **YES** LUCKY DIP ☐ **NO** DON'T INCLUDE
Please tick one of these boxes to show your verdict, and give reasons and descriptive
comments, prices etc

☐ DESERVES **FOOD** award ☐ DESERVES **PLACE-TO-STAY** award 2010:15

PLEASE GIVE YOUR NAME AND ADDRESS ON THE BACK OF THIS FORM

--- ✂ ---

REPORT ON (PUB'S NAME)

Pub's address

☐ **YES** MAIN ENTRY ☐ **YES** LUCKY DIP ☐ **NO** DON'T INCLUDE
Please tick one of these boxes to show your verdict, and give reasons and descriptive
comments, prices etc

☐ DESERVES **FOOD** award ☐ DESERVES **PLACE-TO-STAY** award 2010:16

PLEASE GIVE YOUR NAME AND ADDRESS ON THE BACK OF THIS FORM

Your own name and address *(block capitals please)*

In returning this form I confirm my agreement that the information I provide may be used by
The Random House Group Ltd, its assignees and/or licensees in any media or medium whatsoever.

DO NOT USE THIS SIDE OF THE PAGE FOR WRITING ABOUT PUBS

Your own name and address *(block capitals please)*

In returning this form I confirm my agreement that the information I provide may be used by
The Random House Group Ltd, its assignees and/or licensees in any media or medium whatsoever.

DO NOT USE THIS SIDE OF THE PAGE FOR WRITING ABOUT PUBS

IF YOU PREFER, YOU CAN SEND US REPORTS BY EMAIL:
feedback@goodguides.com

REPORT ON (PUB'S NAME)

Pub's address

☐ **YES** MAIN ENTRY ☐ **YES** LUCKY DIP ☐ **NO** DON'T INCLUDE
Please tick one of these boxes to show your verdict, and give reasons and descriptive comments, prices etc

☐ DESERVES **FOOD** award ☐ DESERVES **PLACE-TO-STAY** award 2010:17

PLEASE GIVE YOUR NAME AND ADDRESS ON THE BACK OF THIS FORM

--------------------------------✂--------------------------------

REPORT ON (PUB'S NAME)

Pub's address

☐ **YES** MAIN ENTRY ☐ **YES** LUCKY DIP ☐ **NO** DON'T INCLUDE
Please tick one of these boxes to show your verdict, and give reasons and descriptive comments, prices etc

☐ DESERVES **FOOD** award ☐ DESERVES **PLACE-TO-STAY** award 2010:18

PLEASE GIVE YOUR NAME AND ADDRESS ON THE BACK OF THIS FORM

Your own name and address *(block capitals please)*

In returning this form I confirm my agreement that the information I provide may be used by
The Random House Group Ltd, its assignees and/or licensees in any media or medium whatsoever.

DO NOT USE THIS SIDE OF THE PAGE FOR WRITING ABOUT PUBS

✂ ....

Your own name and address *(block capitals please)*

In returning this form I confirm my agreement that the information I provide may be used by
The Random House Group Ltd, its assignees and/or licensees in any media or medium whatsoever.

DO NOT USE THIS SIDE OF THE PAGE FOR WRITING ABOUT PUBS

IF YOU PREFER, YOU CAN SEND US REPORTS BY EMAIL:
feedback@goodguides.com

REPORT ON (PUB'S NAME)

Pub's address

☐ **YES** MAIN ENTRY ☐ **YES** LUCKY DIP ☐ **NO** DON'T INCLUDE
Please tick one of these boxes to show your verdict, and give reasons and descriptive comments, prices etc

☐ DESERVES **FOOD** award ☐ DESERVES **PLACE-TO-STAY** award 2010:19

PLEASE GIVE YOUR NAME AND ADDRESS ON THE BACK OF THIS FORM

REPORT ON (PUB'S NAME)

Pub's address

☐ **YES** MAIN ENTRY ☐ **YES** LUCKY DIP ☐ **NO** DON'T INCLUDE
Please tick one of these boxes to show your verdict, and give reasons and descriptive comments, prices etc

☐ DESERVES **FOOD** award ☐ DESERVES **PLACE-TO-STAY** award 2010:20

PLEASE GIVE YOUR NAME AND ADDRESS ON THE BACK OF THIS FORM

Your own name and address *(block capitals please)*

In returning this form I confirm my agreement that the information I provide may be used by
The Random House Group Ltd, its assignees and/or licensees in any media or medium whatsoever.

DO NOT USE THIS SIDE OF THE PAGE FOR WRITING ABOUT PUBS

Your own name and address *(block capitals please)*

In returning this form I confirm my agreement that the information I provide may be used by
The Random House Group Ltd, its assignees and/or licensees in any media or medium whatsoever.

DO NOT USE THIS SIDE OF THE PAGE FOR WRITING ABOUT PUBS

IF YOU PREFER, YOU CAN SEND US REPORTS BY EMAIL:
feedback@goodguides.com